Encyclopedia
of China

Encyclopedia of China

The Essential Reference to China,
Its History and Culture

DOROTHY PERKINS

A ROUNDTABLE PRESS BOOK

Facts On File, Inc.

Encyclopedia of China: The Essential Reference to China, Its History and Culture
Copyright © 1999 by Dorothy Perkins and Roundtable Press, Inc.

A Roundtable Press Book
Directors: Susan E. Meyer, Marsha Melnick, Julie Merberg
Editorial: Alexis Wilson, Beth Russell Connelly, Ellen Wertheim, John Glenn
Consultant: Arthur H. Tafero

Facts On File, Inc.
11 Penn Plaza
New York NY 10001

Library of Congress Cataloging-in-Publication Data

Perkins, Dorothy.
Encyclopedia of China : the essential reference to China, its history and culture /
Dorothy Perkins.
p.   cm.
"A Roundtable Press book."
Includes bibliographical references and index.
ISBN 0-8160-2693-9
1. China—Encyclopedias. I. Title.
DS705.P47 1998
951'.003—dc21
97-52622

Facts On File books are available at special discounts when purchased in bulk quantities for
businesses, associations, institutions, or sales promotions. Please call our Special Sales
Department in New York at (212) 967-8800 or (800) 322-8755.

You can find Facts On File on the World Wide Web at http://www.factsonfile.com

Text design by Cathy Rincon
Cover design by Dorothy Wachtenheim

Printed in the United States of America

VB Hermitage 10 9 8 7 6 5 4 3 2 1

This book is printed on acid-free paper.

For
Herman
and
Stephen

CONTENTS

INTRODUCTION

This book provides a representative cross section of entries on all aspects of the history and culture of China. The entries, presented in alphabetical order, cover the following categories: major cities and provinces; geography and climate; animals, birds, vegetation; historical eras and figures, from ancient to contemporary; government and politics; business and economics; religion—sects, leaders, temples, festivals; language and writing system; literature; fine arts; crafts and architecture; family structure; food and customs; daily life and popular culture; sports and martial arts; important Chinese figures outside of mainland China; and important Westerners in China.

Compiling an introductory one-volume reference work on China is a daunting task. China is the third-largest country in the world and has the oldest continuous history and culture, dating back more than 4,000 years. It also has the largest population, more than 1.2 billion. The Chinese people have always thought of their country as the center of the world, the "Middle Kingdom" (Zhongguo or Chung-kuo), and regard their culture as the "true civilization." More than 44 million Chinese also live outside the People's Republic of China (PRC; mainland China) and the Republic of China (ROC; Taiwan Island), mainly in Macao (which will revert to the PRC in 1999), Southeast Asia, and North and South America. (Hong Kong reverted to the PRC on July 1, 1997.) These overseas Chinese, whose close business connections are known as the Bamboo Network, have invested enormous amounts of money in the PRC and play a major role in the world's economy.

In this volume, all Chinese personal names are given in the customary East Asian order, with family name first, followed by the given name (for example, Sun Yat-sen), except for overseas Chinese, whose names are given in the Western manner (e.g., Tan, Amy; Pei, I.M.). The romanization of Chinese words has created numerous and often confusing variations in spelling; this book attempts to follow common usage. Two romanization systems are used to write Chinese names and terms. The Wade-Giles system has been em-

ployed for more than a century and remains the primary one used outside of mainland China, in the ROC and overseas Chinese communities, and by many scholars of Chinese history and culture. The Chinese Communists who founded the PRC in 1949 developed the pinyin system, which is now also used by many people outside the PRC. The choice of which system to use is often a political issue: whether to use the Chinese Communist pinyin system or the Wade-Giles system preferred by the Nationalists on Taiwan. This book places emphasis on pinyin, but Wade-Giles equivalents are noted and cross-referenced. Regardless of political preference, anyone interested in China must be familiar with both systems. In some cases, this volume uses the Wade-Giles version of a name or term because it is well-known to Western readers (e.g., Chiang Kai-shek).

Some familiar Chinese words, such as "wok," have not been italicized. Such terms, as well as entries for which there is no ready English equivalent, are listed under their Chinese names (e.g., *sheng,* a type of reed mouth organ). Most entries, however, are listed under their English names. Copious cross-references lead the reader to related terms, and a bibliography is included for readers who wish to pursue a particular subject.

During the past two decades, China has been undergoing immense changes: rapid economic development and foreign trade and investment; the replacement of old leaders, veterans of the legendary Long March (1934–35), by younger men; new technology, such as satellite communications and the Internet; the influence of wealthy overseas Chinese on their ancestral villages; and even a change in the patriarchal Confucian family structure by the government-enforced policy of only one child per family, at least in Chinese cities. The information in this book was current as of press date. In consideration of the rapid rate of change in China—and the world—particularly in the economic and political spheres, we will make every effort to revise the text in subsequent editions.

ABACUS (*suan ban* or *suan pan*)   A device for making arithmetic calculations, based on the decimal system; still commonly used in Asian countries. The word "abacus" comes from the ancient Semitic language group. The abacus was in widespread use in the Mediterranean world by the sixth century A.D. and was probably used as early as the second century. During the Mongol Yuan dynasty (1279–1368) the abacus was brought to China from Central Asia.

An abacus is a rectangular wooden frame with vertical rods on which wooden beads are strung. The first rod represents units, the second rod 10s, the third rod 100s, the fourth rod 1,000s, and so forth. Each bead on the unit rod represents 1, each bead on the 10s rod represents 10, each bead on the 100s rod represents 100, and so forth. The Chinese form of the abacus has a horizontal bar across the frame that divides the rods into an upper section, where there are two beads on each rod, and a lower section with five beads on each rod. Each bead on the upper section represents five of the lower bead units. Addition, subtraction, multiplication and division are performed by moving up the beads on the rods. For example, to add the numbers 15 and 22 on a Chinese abacus the number 15 is first set up by moving one bead down on the upper unit rod and one bead up the lower 10s rod. Then 22 would be added by moving two more beads on the unit rod to join the five beads already there and two beads would be moved on the 10s rod to join the one already there. This provides the correct answer, 37, with three beads on the 10s rod and seven beads on the unit wire. Subtraction is performed by moving beads away. Multiplication requires repeated addition and division by repeated subtraction. Advanced calculations such as square and cubic roots can also be calculated. People who are very adept at using the abacus can even perform calculations by visualizing an abacus in their minds, and some can find their answers more quickly with an abacus than with an electronic calculator.

ABAHAI (Abukai; 1592–1643)   Also known as Raizong; a leader of the Jurchen people, a tribe from northern Manchuria (later called the Manchus), who became the second emperor of the Later Jin dynasty (1616–36) and established the Qing dynasty (1644–1911). Abahai was the eighth son of Nurhachi (1559–1626), a tribal chieftain who unified the Jurchen, founded the Later Jin dynasty and conquered much of Manchuria (modern northeastern China). Nurhachi had developed the Jurchen into a disciplined military and political force by organizing them into units under the banner system (*gusai* in the Manchu language). After he died, Abahai won the power struggle for leadership. By 1631 he controlled the entire Jin government, which had incorporated many features of the Chinese imperial bureaucratic system. In 1635 Abahai replaced the name Jurchen, under which the tribe had been paying tribute to the Ming dynasty (1368–1644), with "Manchu," the origin of which is uncertain. In 1636 Abahai changed the name of the Later Jin dynasty to Qing (Ch'ing, "Pure"), indicating the Manchu intent to overthrow the Ming, and proclaimed himself emperor. He was a brilliant military commander who led successful campaigns against the Chinese, Koreans and Mongols. By the early 1640s Abahai controlled much of the territory north of the Great Wall, which had been built by the Chinese to protect themselves against invasions by nomadic tribes from the north, including the Jurchen. One reason for Abahai's success was his ability to attract many defectors from the Chinese side, including Chinese government officials and military generals. This also helped him develop the bureaucracy that would be able to govern the enormous country of China. With the bureaucracy in place, the Manchus began their final conquest of Ming China the year after Abahai died in 1643. He was succeeded as emperor by his ninth son, Fulin (1638–61), whom historians count as the first emperor of the Qing dynasty and who is known by his reign title as Emperor Shunzhi (Shunchih). See also BANNER SYSTEM; GREAT WALL; JURCHEN; MANCHU; NURHACHI; QING DYNASTY.

ABUKAI See ABAHAI.

ACADEMIA SINICA (Academy of Science; Zhongyang yen-jiuyuan or Chung-yang yen-chiu yuan, "Central Research Institute")   The highest research organization in China. The Academia Sinica was founded in 1928 after the Chinese Nationalist Party (Kuomintang; KMT) established the capital of the Republic of China (ROC) in Nanjing in 1927 and had funded several research and training institutions. The Academia Sinica comprised twelve institutes whose members performed research and advised the government on scientific matters. Cai Yuanpei (Ts'ai Yuan-p'ei), who had been chancellor of Beijing University, China's most prestigious university, from 1916 to 1926, helped found the Academia Sinica and became its first president. One of the academy's first achievements was the excavation by its Archaeology Section of the capital of the Shang dynasty (1750–1040 B.C.) at Anyang in Henan province.

The Science Society of China had already established an important biological research laboratory in Nanjing in 1922. This society had been founded by Chinese students at Cornell University in the United States in 1949, and its members included most of China's best scientists and engineers who became members of the Academia Sinica. In 1915 the Science Society of China had begun publishing a journal, *Kexue* (*K'e-hsueh; Science*), modeled on the journal of the American Association for the Advancement of Science. The society's goals were to popularize science in China by publishing many research works, improving science education and participating in international scientific meetings. During the late 1920s and early 1930s, many more research institutes were established in China, such as the Beijing Research Laboratory, which later formed departments in a number of fields including biology, pharmacology and physics. Many Chinese scientists were trained abroad and performed high-level research at Chinese universities, government-funded research institutes and foreign organizations such as the Rockefeller Institute. Most were located in Beijing, Nanjing and Shanghai.

Chinese scientists suffered greatly and were prevented from doing significant research after Japanese troops invaded China in 1937 and China began fighting its War of Resistance against Japan (1937–45; World War II). The excavation at Anyang had to be closed down. After Japan was defeated in 1945, the Chinese Communist Party (CCP) and the Nationalist Party resumed their civil war. In 1949 the CCP defeated the KMT and established the People's Republic of China, and KMT members fled to the island of Taiwan, where they established the provisional government of the Republic of China (ROC). Some members of the Academia Sinica remained in China and others moved to Taiwan. This resulted in a split in the academy, with one organization based in Beijing, the capital of the PRC on the Chinese mainland, and the other in Taipei, the capital of the ROC on Taiwan. The Chinese Academy of Sciences (CAS) was formed in the PRC in 1949 by combining research institutes under the former Academia Sinica and the Beijing Research Academy (the former Beijing Research Laboratory). Its members include the PRC's most senior and best-known scientists. The Academia Sinica continues to function under that name on Taiwan. See also ANYANG; BEIJING UNIVERSITY; CHINESE ACADEMY OF SCIENCES; CIVIL WAR BETWEEN COMMUNISTS AND NATIONALISTS; REPUBLIC OF CHINA; WAR OF RESISTANCE AGAINST JAPAN.

ACADEMY OF SCIENCE See ACADEMIA SINICA; CHINESE ACADEMY OF SCIENCES.

ACROBATICS AND VARIETY THEATER (*zaji* or *tsa-chi*) Popular forms of entertainment in China that include many types of acts, such as dancing, juggling and balancing people and objects (bowls, large pottery jars, ladders and tables), contortionists, pole climbing, tumbling, tightrope walking, bicycle stunts, clowns, martial arts and magic acts. The performers wear colorful costumes and are accompanied by orchestras playing traditional instruments such as the gong, *sheng* (a wind instrument), *pipa* (similar to a lute) and *zheng* (*cheng;* a type of zither). Acrobatics began in China about four thousand years ago from methods for taming horses, which were staged as entertainment during the Western Zhou dynasty (1100–771 B.C.). By the Han dynasty (206 B.C.–A.D. 220), variety shows included acrobatics, music, singing and dancing, magic acts, comic performances and martial arts, and were held for many occasions, even funerals. These shows incorporated music, dance and acrobatics from regions to the west inhabited by various nomadic

Members of a Chinese acrobatic troupe perform a balancing act.
S.E. MEYER

tribes. The arts—music, dance and acrobatics—were brought into the Chinese Empire by Emperor Wudi (r. 141–87 B.C.) and other Han emperors. Spectacular variety shows were performed at banquets to honor foreign missions visiting the Han imperial court.

Acrobatics and variety shows remained within the imperial court until the Song dynasty (960–1279), when the common people were allowed to enjoy these performing arts that were quickly becoming extremely popular all over China. Since the founding of the Communist People's Republic of China (PRC) in 1949, the government has supported acrobatics and variety performers, and there are organized acrobatic troupes in many Chinese provinces and cities. The largest is the China Acrobatic Troupe, founded in 1950, which has more than 400 performers and administrators. The troupe has performed in more than 60 countries and has won many international awards. The Shanghai Circus Troupe, founded in 1958, has also performed in many countries the world over. It specializes in acts with trained animals, such as tigers, pandas, monkeys and dogs. It also includes aerial acrobatic acts. Since 1949, the exciting Lion Dance, which originated one thousand years ago, is usually the first act in a performance by a Chinese acrobatic troupe.

Many Chinese acrobats come from Wuqiao county, an agricultural region known as China's "acrobatic county," in Hebei province in northern China. The farmers there were very poor, and beginning in 1840, every spring and winter they would supplement their income as traveling street performers. By the end of the 19th century, some Wuqiao acrobatic troupes had traveled through Asia, Europe, America and Africa, being some of the first Chinese to go abroad and have contact with people in other countries. Since 1949, Wuqiao has sent 200 acrobats to the more than 50 troupes throughout China, and acrobats from Wuqiao usually become the chief performers or leaders of the troupes. All of the children in Wuqiao are taught acrobatics from a very young age. The town now has an acrobatic school and more than 100 amateur groups as well as professional troupes.

Acrobatics is an important aspect in performances by the traditional opera companies in many regions of China, such as Beijing Opera and a southern form of opera known as *kunqu.* Chinese operas combine acting, singing, dancing and acrobatic movements influenced by the martial arts. Other popular performing arts related to acrobatics include stilt walking and *yangko,* a type of folk dance, which are especially popular in northern China at the New Year of Spring Festival. See also HAN DYNASTY; HORSE; KUNQU; LION; MARTIAL ARTS; PIPA; SHENG; STILT WALKING.

ACUPUNCTURE (*zhenci* or *chen-tz'u*) A traditional technique for healing based on the concept of the flow of energy, or *qi* (*ch'i*), through channels or meridians in the body. Acupuncture was used in ancient times, as described in *The Yellow Emperor's Inner Classic.* By the third century B.C., the theory of acupuncture was further developed. The theory of acupuncture is very complex; it is based on ancient Chinese beliefs concerning balance among the principles that underly everything in the universe: *yin* and *yang* and the five material agents. Acupuncture theory maintains that disease is due to blockage of the flow of *qi* and aims to cure the body by getting rid of these blocks and opening up chan-

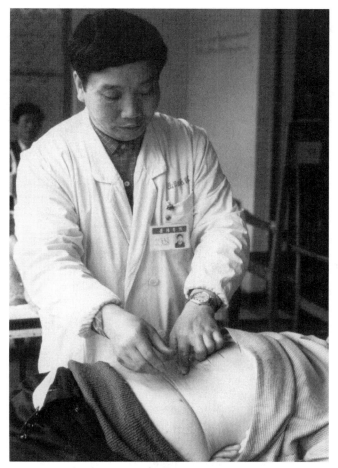

Acupuncture has been scientifically proven to stimulate natural painkillers produced by the body. DENNIS COX

nels. According to Chinese theory, each person has 14 meridians (*jing luo* or *ching-lo*) that run through the body's vital organs and limbs. An acupuncturist finds the blockages in the meridians of the patient's body and inserts tiny metal needles into specific points where they will open up the meridians. Standard charts illustrate the numerous meridians and indicate the points where the needles should be inserted. The needles are commonly made of silver, gold or stainless steel. The technique can also be performed by the use of fingertips pressing on the blocked meridian points; this is known as acupressure.

Acupuncture frequently helps alleviate the symptoms of chronic ailments, such as asthma, that cannot be completely cured by Western drugs, or that would produce an overdependence on those drugs. Acupuncture is also used to control pain. Some doctors even use it in place of anesthesia for patients who undergo surgery. It has been scientifically proven that acupuncture stimulates the production of endorphins: natural painkilling opiates produced by the body as a response to pain. Acupuncture has been an important medical treatment in Japan, since it was introduced there in the sixth and seventh centuries A.D. It is also practiced in other Asian countries and is now widely practiced in Western countries as well. Acupuncture in China is often practiced in conjunction with traditional herbal medicine and moxibustion, the burning of small cones of herbs placed on the skin. See also FIVE MATERIAL AGENTS; MEDICINE, HERBAL; MOXIBUSTION; QI; YELLOW EMPEROR; YIN AND YANG.

AGE OF GRAND HARMONY   See BOOK OF RITES.

AGRARIAN REFORM LAW   See LAND REFORM BY COMMUNISTS.

AGRICULTURE   The growing and harvesting of crops to provide food and other necessary goods, such as fibers for textiles. The Chinese still farm the land, using many of the same methods that were developed thousands of years ago, including the construction and irrigation of terraced fields, iron-tipped plows and iron spades, and a knowledge of plant breeding to develop different varieties. By the middle of the Han dynasty (206 B.C.–A.D. 220), 60 million Chinese people were registered with the government, and about 90 percent of them lived in the countryside, most practicing agriculture. Pottery models of farmhouses with tile roofs that were buried in Han tombs show that Chinese farmers have lived the same way for millenia. The most densely populated regions included the fertile valleys of the Yellow and Huai rivers and modern Sichuan province, which is irrigated by four tributaries of the Yangzi River. Terraced paddy fields for cultivating rice developed in this region. Rice was the staple crop south of the Yangzi and millet was the staple crop to the north; this remains true today, although wheat has become the most important northern crop. The Chinese call a meal *fan*, meaning "cooked rice (or any cooked grain such as millet or wheat)," and consume large quantities of grain accompanied by smaller quantities of *cai* (ts'ai), "vegetables," which includes dishes of cooked vegetables, meat, seafood and soybean curd. Growing grain and other crops and living in settled villages where the main occupation is agriculture were two of the main ways by which the Han Chinese people defined themselves as an ethnic group. They considered other peoples, especially the nomadic groups to the north and west, such as the Xiongnu and Mongols who raised herds of horses, sheep, goats and other animals, "barbarians" and tried to keep them from invading China by building the Great Wall.

Traditional Chinese society was divided into four classes, with the educated ruling class at the top and the farmers, who produced food and paid taxes in grain, in the second class. Next came the artisans, who produced goods other than food, and at the bottom were the merchants, who themselves produced nothing but only distributed the goods produced by others, although they often became very wealthy. The Chinese have always felt that the owning of land for agriculture is the basis of wealth and social prestige, and even wealthy merchants invested in land. Chinese emperors issued an annual calendar that regulated the agricultural cycle and legitimized their reigns. Even today Chinese all over the world consult the almanacs that are published annually to provide information about the weather, astrology and auspicious days for the upcoming year. (The front page of an almanac has a picture of a farmer and his ox with details that forecast information for agriculture such as the predicted amount of rain in different seasons.)

The Chinese transported grain and other products on the many rivers that cross the country, and they built canals to link the rivers. During the Sui dynasty (581–618), Emperor Wendi (Wen-ti) began constructing the Grand Canal that connects southern and northern China. In northern China there are vast plateaus of loess, a loose yellow soil that blows there from the deserts. Neolithic Chinese farmers 7,000 years ago discovered that the steep loess cliffs along the Yellow and other rivers are very fertile, and cut them into terraces on which they cultivated millet and other crops. Even today many Chinese farm the loess terraced fields and live in houses cut into the cliffs. The Yellow River (Huanghe) is so named because of the large quantities of loess that it carries. The river floods frequently, and each time it deposits a layer of loess mud over thousands of square miles on the North China Plain. For thousands of years the Chinese have built dikes along rivers to help prevent flooding.

After the Chinese Communist Party (CCP) founded the People's Republic of China (PRC) in 1949, it began organizing farm villages into collectives, based on the Soviet model, and then into larger administrative units called people's communes. Communes were divided in turn into production brigades and production teams. The central government told the communes what crops to plant and how much they were expected to produce. At the end of the year, the commune's profits were distributed to its members based on the work points they had accumulated during the year. In 1981 the PRC government introduced the "responsibility system" in agriculture, under which local managers are held responsible for the profits and losses of the enterprise. This replaced the egalitarian commune system under which the government assumed all profits and losses. In the early 1980s the communes were disbanded and replaced by townships, and most brigades and teams were replaced by townships and villages.

Today more than half of the Chinese labor force is still engaged in agriculture and in a country that has the world's largest agricultural economy. China is the world's largest producer of rice, millet, sorghum, barley, potatoes, peanuts, tea, tobacco, cotton and pork. However, only about 10 percent of the land is suitable for cultivating crops, which must feed a population of more than one billion. Hence nearly all arable land, most of it in the eastern half of the country, is used for crops. In southern China, vegetables, fruits and tea are also important crops, and mulberry trees are planted around rice paddies to provide the green leaves that are fed to silkworms. Major nonfood crops, especially cotton, other fibers such as ramie and hemp, and oil seeds comprise a large percentage of China's foreign trade revenue. China exports grain and other agricultural products, such as vegetables, fruit, and meat and meat products to Hong Kong.

Chinese farmers use farming methods that provide high yields, and the semitropical climate and abundant rainfall in the south enable farmers to produce two or more harvests a year. Jiangsu and Zhejiang provinces are known as the "rice bowl of China." However, China has to import grain owing to low government-set prices for agricultural products, a lack of sufficient facilities to distribute and store grain, and the rapidly growing Chinese population. The economy is also growing rapidly, creating a greater demand for meat, which causes farmers to use more of their land to raise livestock rather than to grow grain. Modern chemical fertilizers,

Today agriculture occupies more than half of the Chinese labor force.   S.E. MEYER

pesticides and herbicides are also used, making their work a little lighter and increasing their yields, but also causing damage to the environment. Some farmers also use small tractors known as "iron oxen," although many (in the north) still rely on oxen and water buffaloes (in the south) to cultivate their crops, for the animals actually work better than machines. See also ALMANAC; CALENDAR; CLIMATE; COOKING, CHINESE; COTTON; FAMILY STRUCTURE; GEOGRAPHY; GRAIN; GRAND CANAL; LOESS; MAOTAI; NATURAL DISASTERS; NEOLITHIC PERIOD; NOMADS AND ANIMAL HUSBANDRY; NORTH CHINA PLAIN; OX; PEOPLE'S COMMUNE; RAMIE; RICE; SILK; YANGZI RIVER; YELLOW RIVER.

AGUDA See JIN DYNASTY; JURCHEN.

AH Q See LU XUN.

AIDING, LAKE See TURPAN; TURPAN DEPRESSION.

AILAO, MOUNTAIN RANGE See YUNNAN PROVINCE.

AIRLINES AND AIRPORTS In 1930, the Chinese National Air Service began air service between Shanghai and Hankoa. After the Chinese Communists founded the People's Republic of China (PRC) in 1949, the government-run civil aviation system was operated by the General Administration of Civil Aviation of China, known as CAAC, an agency under the State Council. The Chinese Communist government had begun developing its own aircraft, known as the Yun, or Y series, in the late 1950s. Following the Cultural Revolution (1966–76), CAAC began building up its fleet with local and foreign-made airplanes and constructing new airports to welcome foreign tourism, as part of its effort to rebuild the country. Between 1981 and 1985, China built 135 civil aircraft in its own factories, and the seventh Five-Year Plan (1986–90) scheduled the building of hundreds more. Beijing International Airport, through which many tourists and diplomats enter the country, was completed in 1980. New airports were also constructed in Xi'an, Luoyang and the Shenzhen Special Economic Zone, and airports in many cities were expanded. By 1986 China had more than 90 civilian airports. By 1987 CAAC had about 150,000 miles of domestic routes and about 61,000 miles of international air routes, including flights to 28 cities in 23 countries. It also had bilateral air-service agreements with more than 40 countries and working relations with about 3,866 foreign airline companies. The CAAC also established regional airlines in the mid-1980s to provide needed links to cities in remote regions that are difficult to reach by ground transportation. Wuhan Airlines, operated by the Wuhan municipal government in Zhejiang Province, began scheduled passenger flights to nearby provinces in May 1986. The CAAC operates colleges to train airline personnel and provides air service for scientific research, communications,

To meet the needs of its rapidly expanding economy, the Chinese government has expanded such government-run carriers as Air China and now allows private airlines as well.   S.E. MEYER

agriculture, forestry control, and aerial surveying and photography.

The Chinese economy is growing rapidly; airlines and airports are expanding to keep up, and traffic control and navigation equipment are being improved. The Chinese government has recently broken up the CAAC and allowed private carriers to begin operating in the country to handle this rapidly expanding Chinese economy. The CAAC, which has computerized its services, now serves as an umbrella organization for its many subsidiaries. Its seven major divisions are Air China, China Eastern, China Southern, China Northern, China Southwest, China Northwest, and Xinjiang Airlines. There are a great number of private carriers as well. Every April and November the CAAC publishes a combined international and domestic timetable in Chinese and English. CAAC divisions and private airlines also publish their own timetables. See also SPECIAL ECONOMIC ZONES.

AKSAI CHIN AREA   See HIMALAYA MOUNTAIN RANGE; SINO-INDIAN BORDER DISPUTE; TIBET.

A-KU-TA   See JIN DYNASTY; JURCHEN.

ALCHEMY   The search for a chemical substance known as either the elixir or pill of immortality that brings immortal life when ingested. Chinese alchemy developed with the tra-

dition of Daoism (Taoism), which emphasizes harmony with nature. Traditional Chinese herbal medicine, which dates back thousands of years and is related to Daoist alchemy, still plays a major role in treating medical conditions in China and is now being used by many Western doctors. Some historians maintain that ancient Daoist alchemical experimentation with natural substances, which also attempted to transform base metal into gold, was actually the origin of scientific method. The alchemists developed a great variety of scientific equipment such as stoves and ovens for temperatures to be controlled, bamboo tubing for connecting pieces of equipment, balances for weighing ingredients and sundials and water-clocks to time chemical processes.

Because of Chinese interest in scientific experimentation, many things were invented that were not adapted by other cultures until hundreds or even thousands of years later. During the Shang dynasty (1750–1040 B.C.) the Chinese developed techniques to produce magnificent bronze containers, which have never been surpassed by another culture. The Chinese also became very skilled at producing ceramics by baking clay dishes and other objects at high temperatures in wood-fired kilns. They invented porcelain, a beautiful, thin and lustrous type of ceramic made with a special white clay called kaolin that is fired at very high temperatures. Along with pharmacology, there were two other significant results of the experiments by Daoist alchemists: the compass and gunpowder. Their knowledge of the physical properties of magnetism enabled the Chinese to invent the magnetic compass by the third century B.C. Daoists also experimented with heating sulphur and saltpeter, which caused many fires that taught them about the physical properties of explosions. By the eighth century A.D. they created an explosive mixture by mixing charcoal with sulphur and saltpeter, which they called "fire medicine" (huoyao), the term the Chinese still use for gunpowder. At first gunpowder was used to make fireworks, but by the 10th century they were also using it for military purposes.

Two of the main materials, or "medicines," that the Daoist alchemists used in their potions were jade and cinnabar or mercuric sulfide, which is actually a poison. Cinnabar has a red color and was also used as a pigment in China. Alchemists heated cinnabar to separate and purify its two elements, mercury (quicksilver) and sulfur, which they viewed in terms of the yin-yang duality which they believed underlies everything in the universe. They highly valued "returned cinnabar," the substance formed by mixing the purified mercury and purified silver. Many objects buried in Chinese tombs were covered with cinnabar, which the Chinese believed helps the deceased make the journey to the Western Paradise. Alchemists also developed many respiratory techniques and physical exercises that aimed to preserve the body's qi (ch'i; energy or vital force) and were incorporated into the Chinese martial arts (wushu), such as qigong (ch'i-kung), kung fu (gongfu) and taijiquan (t'ai-chi ch'uan).

The first emperor, Qin Shihuangdi, who unified China under the Qin dynasty (221–206 B.C.), was obsessed with finding the elixir of immortality. He brought Daoist magicians, or shamans, known as wu, into his court, and he was attracted to the school of thought which maintained that everything in the universe is composed of the Five Material Agents, associated with the five elements: water, fire, wood, metal and earth. Qin Shihuangdi became increasingly unbalanced, due perhaps to the poisonous alchemical potions he ingested, and he died on the last of several journeys to the Chinese coast in his quest for eternal life and the Islands of the Blessed or Immortals. Many later emperors, such as Emperor Wudi (Wu-ti; r. 141–87 B.C.) of the Han dynasty, also patronized Daoist alchemists and consumed many chemical substances that they believed would bring them immortality. Between 389 and 404, the emperor of the Northern Wei dynasty (386–534) established at his capital a professorship of Daoism and a Daoist laboratory for preparing medical concoctions, which were tested by prisoners who had been convicted of crimes punishable by death.

Some Daoist alchemists operated outside the imperial court and kept their knowledge a secret, and some even became political subversives. An alchemist and healer named Zhang Jiao (Chang Chiao) led the Yellow Turbans Rebellion against the Han dynasty in A.D. 184, which greatly weakened the dynasty. Many Daoist secret societies arose throughout Chinese history and threatened later dynasties, as recently as the Eight Trigrams Rebellion against the Manchu Qing dynasty (1644–1911). This secret society based its ideology on the ancient Chinese theory of the Eight Trigrams (bagua or pa kua) that symbolize heaven, earth, thunder, wind, water, fire, mountains and water. The trigrams are themselves based on the yin-yang theory.

The classical Chinese text, the Book of Changes (Yijing or I-ching), contains a complex system of divination using the trigrams. This book became one of the five classical texts of Confucianism, the other native Chinese tradition, which was accepted as orthodox by the Han and subsequent imperial dynasties. But Daoists also claimed the Book of Changes and wrote commentaries on it which reflect the attempt to develop a general scientific theory. The first such commentary was the Kinship of the Three (Cantonggi or Tsan-t'ung-ch'i), published in A.D. 142 by Wei Boyang (Wei Po-yang). Alchemists used the complex system recorded in this book to set the times for performing steps in their experiments, such as heating ingredients. Ge Hong (Ko Hung; A.D. 283–343) is considered the greatest Chinese alchemical writer. The first several chapters of his text, The Master Who Embraces Simplicity (Baopuzi or Phao Phu Tzu), contain high-level scientific reflections about natural phenomena. It should be understood that alchemy was not practiced by millions of Chinese who followed Daoism, but was an esoteric practice. See also BOOK OF CHANGES; BRONZEWARE; CINNABAR; COMPASS; DAOISM; DAOIST CLASSICAL TEXTS; EIGHT TRIGRAMS; EIGHT TRIGRAMS REBELLION; ELIXIR OF IMMORTALITY; FIREWORKS AND GUNPOWDER; FIVE MATERIAL AGENTS; GE HONG; ISLANDS OF THE BLESSED; JADE; KUNG FU; MARTIAL ARTS; MEDICINE, HERBAL; PORCELAIN; QI; QIGONG; QIN SHI HUANGDI, EMPEROR; TAIJIQUAN; YELLOW TURBANS REBELLION; YIN AND YANG.

ALCOHOLIC BEVERAGES (jiu or chiu) The Chinese use the word jiu to mean wine, beer and all other alcoholic beverages. Containers and cups excavated at the Neolithic site at Longshan in Shandong Province indicate that rice wine and beer were being produced in China as early as the third millennium B.C. Most traditional Chinese alcoholic beverages are distilled from rice, sorghum (gaoliang or kao-liang) and other grains. Grape vines were introduced from Iran before the first century A.D., and wine made from grapes was very popular during the Tang dynasty (618–907). The Chinese alcoholic drink known as maotai has become well known in the West since Mao Zedong toasted U.S. President Richard Nixon with it when Nixon visited China in 1972. maotai, named for the town in Guizhou Province where it is produced, is a clear, strong alcoholic beverage, similar to vodka, that is distiled from sorghum grown in northern China.

Another potent Chinese drink is fen jiu, produced in Apricot Blossom Village near the town of Fen Yang in Shanxi Province in northern China. Water from the Fen River, a tributary of the Yellow River, gives this drink its unique quality. Fen jiu is the base for a distilled liqueur called zhu ye xing ("bambooleaf green") which is blended with a dozen herbs, including bamboo leaves, and is a popular after-dinner digestif in Japan and Southeast Asia. Fen jiu is the finest of the type of colorless "white wine" preferred by the northern Chinese. This type of drink is called gaoliang, meaning sorghum, the grain from which it is distilled. Another famous drink of this type is xifeng ("west phoenix"). It is produced in Fengxiang, north of the Wei River in Shaanxi Province in western China. Chinese wine is always served warm in small porcelain, brass or pewter pots.

The southern Chinese prefer a milder alcoholic beverage called "yellow wine" (huangjiu) for its color, which is made from a blend of glutinous rice, millet and ordinary rice. It resembles dry sherry, and it is commonly used in Chinese cooking. The finest yellow wine in China is produced in Shaoxing (Shao Hsing) in Zhejiang Province and is not only drunk but also for use in herbal medicines. The best known brand is *hua tiao* ("carved flower"), for the floral pattern carved on the jars in which the wine is stored underground during the fermenting process. *Hua tiao* is also called "daughter's wine" because people in the region would store a few jars when a daughter was born so they could drink the wine at her wedding, usually about 19 years later. Excellent yellow wine, nearly as famous as Shaoxing wine, is produced at Longyan ("Dragon Cliffs") in southern Fujian Province. The wine is called *chen gang* for its storage jars. Chinese women often drink this wine as a tonic during pregnancy and after giving birth. *Ng ga pei* ("five-layer skin") is a famous drink produced in Guangzhou (Canton). This is a strong distilled beverage flavored with herbs and sold in a dark brown porcelain jar. Medicinal wines produced in Guangzhou are also popular in China, such as snake wine and tiger-bone wine. These are sold with the snakes and bones in the bottles. Wine containing ginseng, a root considered to have many healthful qualities, is made in northern China and is also very popular.

Red and white grape wines, similar to tawny port and medium sherry, are produced in northern Chinese areas such as the Beijing area and at Tonghua just north of the Korean border. Grape wines are made for export at Yantai and Qingdao in Shandong Province. China's most famous beer is also produced in Qingdao, using the famous mineral water from springs on Laoshan. It is marketed all over the world as Tsingtao Beer. The brewery was founded by Germans, who were given the city as a treaty port in 1895. Beer is produced in Beijing and Manchuria (northeastern China) as well. Only during the past few decades has beer drinking become popular throughout China.

The Chinese have always enjoyed drinking wine, and poets often wrote about the pleasures of getting drunk. There are many customs for drinking which, according to legends, were decreed by an emperor so that his courtiers would not get too drunk. For example, a Chinese wine cup is very small, holding the equivalent of about two thimbles. Custom also dictates that one should eat food while drinking to help absorb the wine. A category of foods similar to hors d'oeuvres, called *lenghun,* is traditionally served with wine. Since the emperor also decreed that guests should exercise their minds to keep alert while drinking, the Chinese enjoy playing finger games (*huachuan*) similar to "scissors, paper, stone" while drinking. See also BANQUETS; COOKING, CHINESE; FINGER GUESSING GAMES; MAOTAI; MEDICINE, HERBAL; QINGDAO; RICE.

ALL-CHINA FEDERATION OF TRADE UNIONS   A mass organization established by the government of the People's Republic of China to benefit members of the working class. A chapter of the federation is in every enterprise owned and operated by the Chinese government. The federation was dissolved during the Cultural Revolution (1966–76) but was reinstated on April 14, 1971, when new union councils met in Shanghai and Beijing. The federation's activities are represented by the Chinese People's Political Consultative Confer-

ence (CPPCC) but are actually directed by the United Front Work Department of the Central Committee of the Chinese Communist Party (CCP). This committee determines government policies regarding the wages, welfare and political education of industrial workers in China. It administers their health and insurance programs and even provides facilities for their vacations and retirement. During the 1970s, the government issued reforms to the All-China Federation of Trade Unions that were intended to improve workers' morale and productivity. Workers gained the right to examine and discuss the principles, management plans, reform programs, budgets and accounts of their factory directors, and also the right to vote and to supervise and appraise leaders at every level. These rights were to be exercised by the workers' congress, held twice yearly. Intellectuals were included as members of the working class. The federation was also ordered to help members gain modern scientific knowledge and technological skills. See also CENTRAL COMMITTEE OF THE CHINESE COMMUNIST PARTY; CHINESE PEOPLE'S POLITICAL CONSULTATIVE CONFERENCE.

ALL-CHINA WOMEN'S FEDERATION   A mass organization established by the Chinese Communist Party (CCP) after it founded the People's Republic of China in 1949. The federation's goal is to promote the welfare and protect the rights of women and raise their educational and technical levels. The Federation also provides assistance in family planning. The activities of the All-China Women's Federation are represented by the Chinese People's Political Consultative Conference (CPPCC) but are actually directed by the United Work Front Department of the Central Committee of the Chinese Communist Party (CCP). The Central Committee also includes the Committee on Women's Work which directs all policies having to do with women in China and has a close working relationship with the All-China Women's Federation. The Federation publishes its own journal which promotes and interprets Communist Party policies having to do with women. Activities of the All-China Women's Federation are conducted primarily at the local rather than at the national level. See also CENTRAL COMMITTEE OF THE CHINESE COMMUNIST PARTY; CHINESE PEOPLE'S POLITICAL CONSULTATIVE CONFERENCE.

ALL-CHINA YOUTH FEDERATION   A mass organization that was created to bring together Chinese young people in patriotic unity and to provide a means for communicating their concerns to government leaders who set the policy of the Chinese Communist Party (CCP). The Communist Youth League, the main organization for members of the CCP from 15 to 25 years of age, forms the core group of the All-China Youth Federation. The league is represented by the Chinese People's Political Consultative Conference (CPPCC) but is actually directed by the United Front Work Department of the CCP's Central Committee. An affiliated youth organization is the All-China Students' Federation for university and college students. The All-China Youth Federation was dissolved at the start of the Cultural Revolution (1966–76) when masses of young people were sent to work in the countryside while Red Guard groups took over many functions of the Communist Youth League, but it was revived in 1973. The All-China Youth Federation includes the China Youth

Travel Service (CYTS), which now performs many of the same functions as the larger China International Travel Service (CITS) and the China Travel Service (CTS). CYTS mainly handles travel arrangements for tour groups, although individuals may also purchase airline and train tickets through the service. See also CENTRAL COMMITTEE OF THE CHINESE COMMUNIST PARTY; CHINA INTERNATIONAL TRAVEL SERVICE; CHINESE PEOPLE'S POLITICAL CONSULTATIVE CONFERENCE; COMMUNIST YOUTH LEAGUE; RED GUARDS.

ALL MEN ARE BROTHERS See OUTLAWS OF THE MARSH.

ALL UNDER HEAVEN (*tianxia* or *t'ien-hsia*) The belief held by early Chinese kings and the emperors who succeeded them that China is the center of human civilization. This is related to the traditional name for China, Zhongguo (Chung-kuo), the "Middle Kingdom" or "Central Kingdom." A Chinese emperor was called the "Son of Heaven" (*tianzi* or *t'ien tzu*), and his reign was legitimized by the "Mandate of Heaven" (*tianming* or *t'ien-ming*) as long as he remained virtuous and cared for his subjects. Heaven (*tian* or *t'ien*) was believed to be the power that governs all created things, and the emperor was Heaven's representative on earth. Every new Chinese dynasty claimed that the previous dynasty deserved to be overthrown because it had lost the Mandate of Heaven, which Heaven transferred to the new dynasty. Since the emperor ruled "all under Heaven," those living outside his realm were considered "barbarians" who must recognize the superiority of the Middle Kingdom. The Chinese extended their suzerainty over foreign nations by permitting them to send tribute-bearing missions to kowtow, or prostrate themselves, before the emperor, for which they were granted the privilege of conducting a restricted amount of trade with China. When emperors were able to expand the borders of China and incorporate "barbarian" territories, the people who lived in those territories were allowed to adopt Chinese civilization through learning the Chinese language and practicing Confucian-based customs, a process known as "Sinicization." When the European powers tried to force China to treat them as equals in the 19th century, the meaning of "all under Heaven" changed from the concept of superiority to that of a modern nation-state within strictly-drawn borders. The Europeans forced the leaders of the Qing dynasty (1644–1911) to realize that China was not the only civilized place in the world and was only one nation-state among many. Such Western influence led to the Revolution of 1911, overthrowing the Qing and establishing the modern Republic of China. See also EMPEROR; HEAVEN; KOWTOW; MANDATE OF HEAVEN; QING DYNASTY; SINICIZATION.

ALLEYS (*hutong* or *hu-t'ung*) Narrow streets in Chinese cities, lined with traditional-style homes, where the residents spend much of their free time. Alleys or *hutongs* are especially associated with the capital city of Beijing, although they still exist in other cities such as Shanghai. The *hutongs* are slowly disappearing as old neighborhoods are torn down and replaced by modern high-rise apartment buildings. Beijing has about 4,000 *hutongs* that resemble country lanes and connect neighborhood courtyards to the city's wide main streets. (There were about 6,000 *hutongs* prior to 1949.)

The word *hutong* first appeared in the Chinese Han language seven centuries ago. It came from the language of the Mongols who ruled China under the Yuan dynasty (1279–1368) and may mean "well" or may sound like "hot," a Mongol word originally meaning "village." Many of Beijing's *hutongs* were built when the Ming dynasty (1368–1644), which overthrew the Yuan, moved its capital from Nanjing to Beijing and the population of Beijing tripled. Residents usually named a *hutong* for its features, surroundings, or a famous resident, such as a craftsman. Some examples are Yinliang ("shady and cool"), Doufuchen ("bean-curd maker Chen") and Chaoshou ("labyrinth"). Zhuanta ("brick pagoda") Hutong, named for a pagoda in the neighborhood originally built during the Yuan dynasty, is one of the oldest in Beijing. Yichi Dajie ("one-foot street"), the shortest *hutong* in Beijing, has only five houses lining it. The famous modern Chinese writer Lao She (1899–1966) was born in Beijing in Xiaoyangjuan ("small sheep pen") Hutong, now known as Xiaoyangjia ("small Yang family") Hutong, and spent his childhood there. He often mentioned this small *hutong* in his novels, such as *Rickshaw Boy*. In many cases two or more *hutongs* had the same names, so the Beijing municipal government made a survey of the *hutongs*, studying their names and histories, and changed some names so that no two *hutongs* now have the same name.

The majority of Beijing's citizens live along the winding mazelike *hutong*, where it is easy for a stranger to get lost. *Hutongs* are fairly quiet during the day, except for people who sell goods and services to the neighborhood, such as produce vendors and knife sharpeners. People whose homes border a common *hutong* develop close relationships. Children play games in the *hutong* after school, and in the evening, old people sit and talk and young people play chess. Older women look after their grandchildren and keep a careful watch on the people living in their *hutong*. Each *hutong* is supervised by a neighborhood committee elected from cadres (Communist Party members) who reside in the *hutong*. In China, a neighborhood is the term generally used for the urban administrative unit immediately below the district level. A neighborhood includes 2,000 to 10,000 families. Within a neighborhood, families are grouped into smaller units of 100 to 600 families, and these, in turn, are subdivided into residents' small groups of 15 to 40 families. See also ARCHITECTURE, TRADITIONAL; BEIJING; YUAN DYNASTY.

ALMANAC (*tongshu* or *t'ung shu*) An annual publication containing information on a wide variety of topics that interest the Chinese, such as weather predictions, solar and lunar calendars, lucky days, horoscopes, rules of etiquette, guidelines for managing a business, and *feng shui*, or the art of geomancy or placing buildings and furniture in positions that will bring good luck. Certain types of information in the almanac remain the same each year, while other types change annually, such as the dates in the traditional lunar calendar, which depend upon the phases of the moon. This form of almanac dates back more than 4,000 years in China and is still consulted by Chinese who live around the world. Legends claim that in 2254 B.C., Emperor Yao commanded his astrologers to establish the annual cycle of changing seasons so the farmers would know when to plant their crops. A government minister led a board of mathematicians in preparing the almanac each year.

Agriculture has traditionally been the most important economic activity for the majority of Chinese, and crops, especially rice and other staple grains such as sorghum, millet and wheat, can be severely affected by bad weather conditions. Disastrous flooding and drought have frequently brought tragedies of immense proportions to the Chinese people, and they are eager to gain all possible information that will help them plan for the future.

The first page of the almanac contains an illustration known as the *chunniutua,* showing a farmer (*niulang;* also called the Spirit Driver, or Mengshen) leading his spring ox (*chunniu*), a symbol of the Li Chun Festival (held in early February in the Western calendar) which marks the start of the farming year. In ancient times an ox was slaughtered as a ritual sacrifice for this festival, but was later replaced by a clay, straw and finally a paper model of an ox that was burned. In the picture, every detail provides information about the predicted weather for the upcoming year. For example, a hat on the farmer indicates a cold spring, and a yellow head on the ox predicts a very hot summer. See also AGRICULTURE; CALENDAR; FENG SHUI; OX; YAO, EMPEROR; ZODIAC, ANIMAL.

ALTAI MOUNTAIN RANGE (Altai Shan)   A great mountain range that forms the border with The People's Republic of Mongolia (Outer Mongolia) of Xinjiang-Uighur Autonomous Region in northwestern China. The Altai Mountains also lie along the northern and northwestern rim of the Dzungaria Basin. The western end of the range lies in former Soviet republics and the eastern end in the People's Republic of Mongolia. The word *altai* means gold in Mongolian, referring to gold deposits in the mountains. The peaks generally reach 9,000 to 10,000 feet and some rise above 13,000 feet, decreasing in height as they run southeast toward Inner Mongolian Autonomous Region. The highest peak is Youyi Feng (Friendship Peak), which reaches 14,350 feet. The Altai Mountains, which are very beautiful, enjoy abundant rainfall, and are covered with trees or rich pasturelands. Nomadic Kazakh and Oirat Mongol herders form the bulk of the population. See also DZUNGARIA BASIN; KAZAKH; MONGOL; XINJIANG-UIGHUR AUTONOMOUS REGION.

ALTAIC-SPEAKING TRIBES   See FIVE DYNASTIES PERIOD; LIAO DYNASTY; MINORITIES, NATIONAL; XIONGNU.

ALTAR OF HEAVEN   See TEMPLE OF HEAVEN.

AMITABHA (Omitofo or A-mi-t'o-fo)   "Immeasurable Light"; the Buddha of Boundless Light and Lord of the Western Paradise or the "Pure Land." Also known as Amitayus and Amita, Amitabha is one of the most important deities in the Buddhist religion, which was introduced into China from India about two thousand years ago. According to the *Pure Land Scripture* (*Sukhavativyuha* in Indian Sanskrit; *Wuliangshoujing* in Chinese), eons ago, Amitabha made an "Original Vow"—anyone who called on his name with single-minded devotion would be saved from suffering and death by being reborn into bliss in the Western Paradise, or Pure Land. The worship of Amitabha, already practiced in China by the end

of the fourth century A.D., grew into a very popular movement known as the Pure Land (Jingtu or Ching-t'u; Sukhavati in Sanskrit) Sect of Buddhism. Members of other Chinese Buddhist sects have also included the deity Amitabha in their meditation practices.

Chinese Buddhist teachers, such as Daochuo (562–645), originated popular devotional practices, for example, using beans to count the number of times a worshiper invoked the name of Amitabha (which led to the use of a Buddhist rosary that enabled worshipers to count beads in the same way). Shandao (613–681), Daochuo's disciple, helped to make Pure Land the most widespread Buddhist sect in China.

Amitabha is depicted in religious painting and sculpture as seated on a lotus throne in the Western Paradise with his attendants at his side—the lotus being a symbol of purity in Buddhism. One of Amitabha's attendants, Guanyin, was worshiped in India as the male deity Avalokiteshvara ("The Lord Who Looks Down"), a powerful and compassionate deity, but in China became transformed into the Goddess of Mercy. Amitabha is also associated with Gautama Buddha, the Buddha who lived on earth. See also BUDDHISM; GUANYIN; LOTUS; PURE LAND SECT OF BUDDHISM.

A-MI-T'O-FO   See AMITABHA.

AMOY   See XIAMEN.

AMUR RIVER (Heilongjiang)   A river in China's northeastern Heilongjiang Province that for more than half of its 1,800-mile length forms the border, along with the Wusuli River (Wusulijiang), between the Manchurian region of China and Russia. The Amur River is formed by the union of the Shilka River from Russia and the Argun in Manchuria. It flows southeast, then northeast, and empties into the straits that separate Sakhalin Island from the mainland of Siberia. Its main tributaries are the Sungari and Wusuli Rivers. The Amur River is frozen over about 180 days of the year, but between May and November it is completely navigable as a major shipping artery.

The Amur River valley was the home of the Jurchen, a tribal people who conquered the Liao dynasty (947–1125), proclaimed their own Jin dynasty (1115–1234), and nearly conquered the Song dynasty (960–1279), forcing the Chinese emperor to flee and establish the Southern Song dynasty in 1127. The Jurchen were ancestors of the Manchus, who conquered China in the 17th century and established the Qing dynasty (1644–1911), thus joining Manchuria with the rest of China. The Treaty of Nerchinsk (1689) between the Manchus and the Russians, was China's first bilateral agreement with a European power. It established a border between Manchuria and Siberia (eastern Russia) along the Amur River. In 1858 Russia annexed the north bank of the Amur River from China by the Treaty of Argun, and in 1860 Russia took control of all of Manchuria north of the Amur River and east of the Wusuli River. In 1954 China claimed substantial Russian territory along the Amur, Wusuli and Argun Rivers, and both countries massed troops along the border, resulting in many clashes. In 1987 the two countries finally resumed negotiations about their border dispute, but the matter has not been resolved. See also HEILONGJIANG PROVINCE; JURCHEN; MANCHURIA; WUSULI RIVER.

AN LUSHAN REBELLION   A rebellion led by An Lushan (703–57) against Emperor Xuanzong (Hsuan-tsung; r. 712–56) that nearly overthrew the Tang dynasty (618–907). During Xuanzong's reign, the Tang capital at Chang'an (modern Xi'an) was the largest and perhaps most cosmopolitan city in the world. Traders from many nations had settled in the city, and the emperor had brought artists, poets, musicians, singers and dancers to his court. The first three decades of Xuanzong's reign were a time of prosperity and good government for China. But he eventually handed over the affairs of state to his advisers and spent his time writing poetry, drinking and enjoying the entertainers with his favorite concubine, Yang Guifei (Yang Kuei-fei; d. 757), one of the most beautiful women in Chinese history.

An Lushan had fled to China with his family when he was a boy. He was born in modern Manchuria (northeastern China), where his father was a Sogdian officer in the army of a Turkish tribe to the north of China. His mother belonged to the nobility of a Turkish clan. An Lushan joined the Chinese army, fought various northern tribes that threatened China and by age 33 rose to the rank of general. In 744 he was made military governor of modern Hebei Province in northern China with his base at modern Beijing, and in 750 he was honored with the title of prince.

An Lushan became a favorite of Emperor Xuanzong and Yang Guifei; the ruler adopted him as a son in 751. Li Linfu, Xuanzong's chief minister, also favored An Lushan, who was then awarded the position of military governor of Hotung. This gave him control of the entire eastern half of China's northern frontier and put him in command of about 40 percent of China's military troops. When Li Linfu died in 752, he was succeeded by Yang Guozhong (Yang Kuo-chung), Yang Guifei's cousin, who disliked An Lushan and actively opposed him, thus contributing to his later rebellion. When An Lushan personally led a major campaign against the Khitan tribe, his army was thoroughly routed. China suffered several other military setbacks around the same time, including the defeat of Chinese troops by Arabs at the Battle of Talas and by a chieftain in modern Yunnan Province in southern China who established the independent kingdom of Nanzhao (Nan-chao) that lasted for five centuries. The Chinese also suffered from natural disasters around this time, including drought, floods and severe storms, which they interpreted as Heaven's displeasure with the reigning emperor. Xuanzong's luxurious court was insulated from the terrible suffering of the Chinese people.

In 755, An Lushan led a rebellion that took control of the wealthy northeastern Chinese provinces of Hebei and Henan. He captured Luoyang, the second Tang capital, and proclaimed a new dynasty in 756. Six months later his troops captured Chang'an. Members of the imperial court escaped shortly before the city fell to An Lushan, but the accompanying soldiers blamed Yang Guozhong and Yang Guifei for the rebellion. They killed Yang Guozhong and demanded the death of Yang Guifei. Emperor Xuanzong had no choice but to order her suicide, and she hanged herself on a tree. The soldiers then swore their allegiance to the Tang dynasty. Xuanzong was so heartbroken that he abdicated the throne to the crown prince, who ruled as the Emperor Suzong (Sutsung), and spent the rest of his life mourning his beloved concubine. Their story was immortalized by Chinese painters and poets, notably the famous poet Bai Juyi (Po Chu-yi; 772–846) in *Song of Unending Regret* (*Changhenge* or *Ch'ang-hen ko*).

An Qingshu (An Ch'ing-hsu), An Lushan's second son, assassinated him in January 757 and Tang troops suppressed the rebellion, finally defeating the rebels in 763. The Tang dynasty continued until 907 but never recovered from the effects of An Lushan's rebellion. When the Tang fell, the northeastern region that had been his base was ruled by the Khitan Liao dynasty (947–1125). See also CHANG'AN; LIAO DYNASTY; LUOYANG; TALAS, BATTLE OF; TANG DYNASTY; XUANZONG, EMPEROR; YANG GUIFEI.

ANALECTS, CONFUCIAN   (*Lunyu*)   A book that contains wise sayings as well as dialogues with students, attributed to Confucius (551–479 B.C.), whose school of thought became accepted as orthodox by the Chinese imperial government during the Han dynasty (206 B.C.–A.D. 220). The book contains 497 verses in 20 chapters. The *Analects* were compiled by disciplines of Confucius after his death and are considered the most reliable source of his ideas and methodology by which he taught them. In the *Analects*, he emphasized personal virtue and moral behavior as the way to maintain harmony in the family and society. Confucius also stressed the importance of the *Book of Songs* and the *Book of Rites*, which became canonized as two of the Five Classics (*wujing*) of Confucianism.

In the 12th century, the Confucian thinker ZhuXi (Chu Hsi; 1130–1200) canonized the *Analects*, one of the Four Books (*Sishu*) of Confucianism; they are the *Great Learning* (*Daxue*), the *Doctrine of the Mean* (*Zhongyong*), and the *Book of Mencius* (*Mengzi*; Mencius or Mengzi was a Confucian scholar who lived c. 372–289 B.C.). Chinese children were traditionally educated in the Confucian texts, beginning with the Four Books, and one of their first assignments was to memorize the *Analects*. Knowledge of the Four Books was the foundation for the examinations administered to select officials for the imperial bureaucracy. See also CONFUCIANISM; CONFUCIUS; DOCTRINE OF THE MEAN; FIVE CLASSICS OF CONFUCIANISM; FOUR BOOKS OF CONFUCIANISM; GREAT LEARNING; IMPERIAL EXAMINATION SYSTEM.

ANCESTOR WORSHIP   The practice in which a Chinese family or clan (*zu* or *tsu*) makes offerings and pays respect to its ancestors, whose spirits are believed to reside in wooden ancestral tablets (*lingwei*) kept on the altar of the family shrine. Ancestor worship remains the foundation of popular religion in China and among overseas Chinese around the world. Offerings include food, wine, incense, candles and flowers. The ancient Chinese believed that if they did not offer sacrifices of live oxen, sheep and pigs to their deceased ancestors, they would become homeless ghosts wandering the night, haunting people. These beliefs continued within the Confucian tradition, which emphasizes filial piety (*xiao* or *hsiao*) or respect for one's parents and ancestors, as the greatest virtue.

The Chinese family structure is patriarchal; that is, it requires a male heir to carry on the family line, inherit property and offer the necessary sacrifices to the ancestors. Traditionally, if a family did not have a male heir, it would pay a man to become the husband of their daughter and take her family name. Their children would also use their mother's surname. Men who agreed to join another family in this way were usually very poor and had little social status. Another alternative was the adoption of a male heir into the family, preferably one with the same surname who was a blood relation, so that the ancestors would accept his sacrifices.

When a death occurs, a Chinese family conducts a proper funeral, mourns for a prescribed period and maintains the grave site. The eldest son of every Chinese family has to give his parents a proper funeral, and the family has to maintain the shrine and ancestral tablets. Formerly, the death of a parent required a mourning period of three years, but the modern lifestyle has abbreviated such mourning rituals. Families sweep the graves of their ancestors and make offerings to them every spring at the Qing Ming Festival. They hold services for deceased ancestors in the seventh lunar month of the traditional calendar, known as the Hungry Ghosts Festival. The male head of each family places offerings on the family shrine on religious festivals and makes formal announcements of important events in the family, such as births, weddings and deaths, in front of the shrine. The women may make the daily offerings of incense and the offerings of food and incense at the beginning and middle of each month. At the New Year Festival, the whole family enjoys a banquet together and sets out cups, bowls and chopsticks for the ancestors to join in the feast. Family members kneel before the family shrine in order to their status and perform a ritual bow, known as *kowtow*, to their ancestors.

Large Chinese clans have their own ancestral cemeteries and temples for their numerous ancestors and keep documents that record their genealogies for many generations, some going back hundreds, or even thousands, of years. The most prominent Chinese family, that of the great teacher Confucius (551–479 B.C.), has maintained its family shrine in Qufu in Shandong Province. Mr. K'ung Teh-ch'eng, the 77th-generation descendant of Confucius, moved from China to Taiwan when the Communists established the People's Republic of China in 1949. Large Chinese families that have long been established in Hong Kong, Singapore and other Asian countries maintain their own temples as well.

The Chinese believe that a person has two souls: the *po*, the animal or life soul, and the *hun*, the spiritual or personality soul. At death, both souls are believed to separate from the body and are kept alive from sacrificial feedings. The *po* remains in the grave and gradually decays as the body does; the *hun* survives as long as the family remembers it and gives it offerings. The *hun* may become a powerful deity that can answer the questions of its descendants, fulfill their desires and postpone their deaths. If a family neglects a deceased ancestor, the *hun* will become a pathetic but malevolent ghost, and the *po* will become a demon (*gui* or *kuei*) that haunts the living. Ancestral spirits that are properly cared for become kindly spirits (*shen*) that send the blessings of good luck, health, wealth, success, happiness, sons, long life and peaceful death to their descendants. This concept of the interdependence of living and dead family members serves to unify and strengthen the family.

The Chinese also adopted the theory of karma from the Buddhist religion, which maintains that the soul after death must undergo trial and punishment in a series of purgato-

ries, and that it would eventually be reborn in a higher or lower status, depending on the actions it performed in its previous life. Buddhism became associated with the rituals of death in China, and a family may arrange for as many as seven weeks of memorial services in a Buddhist temple after a person dies. See also ANCESTRAL TABLETS; BUDDHISM; CONFUCIANISM; FAMILY STRUCTURE; FILIAL PIETY; FUNERALS; HUNGRY GHOSTS FESTIVAL; INCENSE; KARMA; KOWTOW; QING MING FESTIVAL.

ANCESTRAL TABLETS (*lingwei*)   Wooden tablets that are inscribed with the name and dates of birth and death of family members who have died. An ancestral tablet is made from fragrant sandalwood and is about 10 to 20 inches long and 6 inches wide. Traditionally, every Chinese family displayed its ancestral tablets on an altar in the family ancestral temple, although families may display the tablets on a living-room altar. The tablets stand in rows based on the ancestors' closeness of relationship and the generations to which they belong. Family members make daily offerings before the tablets, including three small cups of tea, burning candles and joss-sticks (incense). The smoke from the joss-sticks represents communication between living family members and their ancestors, who are believed to keep a constant watch over the family. On special feast days, the entire family gathers to offer the ancestors wine, meat and fruit. These ritual offerings are commonly called ancestor worship, but they are actually performed to request ancestors to intercede with the gods in Heaven so that the family will be blessed and gain divine protection. See also ANCESTOR WORSHIP; FAMILY STRUCTURE; FUNERALS; INCENSE; SANDALWOOD.

ANCIENT PAINTERS' CLASSIFIED RECORD See SIX CANONS OF PAINTING.

ANDERSON, JOHAN GUNNAR See ARCHAEOLOGY; XIA NAI.

ANGEL ISLAND, SAN FRANCISCO See SIX COMPANIES.

ANHUI PROVINCE   An east-central Chinese province that covers 54,000 square miles and has a population of about 54 million. The capital city, Hefei, has a population of about 1 million. Other major cities include Huaibe, Huainan, Bengbu and Wuhu. The province is divided into three regions by two of China's largest rivers, the Huai River (Huaihe) in the northwest and the Yangzi River (Changjiang) in the southeast. The northern part of Anhui belongs to the great plain of eastern China, north of the Huai River, which has been heavily settled as far back as the Han dynasty (206 B.C.–A.D. 220). The mountainous region of southern Anhui contains Mount Huang (Huangshan, Yellow Mountain; 7,251 feet high), a group of peaks considered together as one of the "five sacred mountains" of China. These mountain ranges comprise a granite massif that has been the subject of many Chinese poems and paintings over the centuries. Hot and rainy in summer and cold and dry in winter, Anhui suffers frequent droughts in the northern region.

The province has the largest freshwater fish-farming area in China and is also a major producer of wheat, soybeans, sesame, oil-bearing crops, tea, pine resin, fruit, shellfish, freshwater seafoods, silkworm cocoons, bamboo, ink, paper and hemp, a plant used to make fibers. Rice is the major crop in the Yangzi River valley. Before 1949, Anhui was the most underdeveloped province in eastern China, but it has since been greatly developed and is now a major center for the iron and steel industry. The province contains important mineral resources, including coal, and has China's largest iron reserves and second-largest copper reserves. The Cihuai Canal, opened to navigation in northern Anhui in 1984, links the Ying River, a major tributary of the Huai, with the Huai's main course, facilitating the transportation of goods between Anhui and neighboring provinces.

During the Warring States Period (403–221 B.C.), Anhui belonged to the Kingdom of Chu. After the unification of the Chinese empire under the Qin dynasty (221–206 B.C.), Anhui became the first part of South China to be settled by Han (ethnic Chinese), a process known as Sinicization. The southward migration of the Han increased after the fall of the Han dynasty in A.D. 220 and Anhui held a strategic geographic and military position as the link between north and central China. Later, in southern Anhui, a group of highly successful and wealthy merchants known as the Huizhou, or Xinan merchants, played a crucial role in trade within China during the Ming (1368–1644) and early Qing (1644–1911) dynasties.

Anhui often suffered from the power struggles connected with the rise and fall of dynasties. Beginning in 1344, a peasant rebellion was initiated by the Red Turbans (Hongjin), led by Zhu Yuanzhang (1328–98), who succeeded in overthrowing the hated Mongol Yuan dynasty (1279–1368) and establishing the Ming dynasty with himself as emperor. During the Qing dynasty, rebellions occurred once again when the Yellow River changed its course in the early 1850s and the Huai River Basin decreased, bringing disaster to farmers in northern Anhui. In 1938 the Nationalist Government (Kuomintang; KMT) led by Chiang Kai-shek attempted to stop invading Japanese troops by diverting the Yellow River south of Shandong Province, breaking the dikes in Henan Province and causing severe flooding that spread as far as Anhui and killing more than 1 million people. The Japanese occupied most of Anhui during the War of Resistance against Japan (1937–45; World War II). Nationalist troops controlled the province from 1946 until 1949, when they fled the country as the Chinese Communist Party established the People's Republic of China.

Once a small trading town, Hefei, after 1949, became modernized and industrialized and was named the capital of Anhui. The prestigious Chinese University of Science and Technology is located there. Ancient Hefei, which was located farther north than today's city, was a military stronghold of the Wei empire during the Three Kingdoms Period (220–265). During a famous battle at Hefei, troops led by the skilled general Cao Cao (155–220) defeated the much larger army of Sun Quan. During the Southern Song dynasty (1127–1279), Hefei served as the center of defense against invading Jin tribes.

The city of Wuhu is located where the Qingyi River flows into the Yangzi River. Wuhu's history goes back more than 2,000 years. It was known as Jiujiang during the Zhou dynasty (1100–256 B.C.). The city is noted for its beautiful scenery and its arts and crafts, including carved lacquerware,

pictures made from feathers, and silhouettes made from wrought iron. See also CAO CAO; HEFEI; HUAI RIVER; NATIONALIST PARTY; RED TURBANS REBELLION; SINICIZATION; WAR OF RESISTANCE AGAINST JAPAN; YANGZI RIVER.

ANHWEI PROVINCE   See ANHUI PROVINCE.

ANIMALS   See CAMEL CARAVANS; DEER; DRAGON; HORSE; LION; MONKEY; NOMADS AND ANIMAL HUSBANDRY; OX; PANDA; PHOENIX, PIG; QILIN; RABBIT; RIVER DOLPHIN, CHINESE; SABLE; SNOW LEOPARD; TAKIN; TIGER; TORTOISE; YAK.

ANNAM   See HAN DYNASTY; TRIBUTE SYSTEM; VIETNAM WAR.

ANTHEM, NATIONAL   The official song of the People's Republic of China (PRC), which was founded by the Chinese Communist Party under Mao Zedong (Mao Tse-tung) in 1949. Entitled "March of the Volunteers," the anthem is the theme song of the Chinese film *Sons and Daughters of the Storm*. This song became popular during China's War of Resistance against Japan (World War II; 1937–45) and the civil war between the Communists and Nationalists, also known as the War of Liberation. Tian Han wrote the lyrics and Nie Er (Nieh Erh) the music:

> Arise, all ye who refuse to be slaves!
> With our flesh and blood,
> Let us build our new Great Wall.
> The Chinese nation faces its greatest danger,
> From each one the urgent call for action comes forth:
> Arise! Arise! Arise!
> Millions with but one heart,
> Braving the enemy's fire, march on!
> Braving the enemy's fire, march on!
> March on! March on! March on!

See also CIVIL WAR BETWEEN COMMUNISTS AND NATIONALISTS; PEOPLE'S REPUBLIC OF CHINA; WAR OF RESISTANCE AGAINST JAPAN.

ANTI-IMPERIALIST LEAGUE   See SOONG CHING LING.

ANTI-JAPANESE WAR   See WAR OF RESISTANCE AGAINST JAPAN.

ANTIQUARIANISM   See ARCHAEOLOGY.

ANTI-RIGHTIST CAMPAIGN   A campaign by the government of the People's Republic of China (PRC) to denounce and punish the intellectual and cultural figures who had criticized the policies and programs of the Chinese Communist Party (CCP) during the Hundred Flowers Campaign, also called the Double Hundred Campaign. In 1956 Communist leader Mao Zedong (Mao Tse-tung) had encouraged the Chinese people to speak out against the party with the slogan, "Let a hundred flowers bloom and a hundred schools of thought contend." The Chinese were cautious at first, but prodded by the government, a large number of them made public criticisms. The Communists had not expected such a strong response. Early in 1957, Mao published the essay "On the Correct Handling of Contradictions among the People," which differentiated between "constructive criticisms among the people" and "hateful and destructive criticism between the enemy and ourselves." In August 1957, Communist leaders abruptly ended the Hundred Flowers Campaign by declaring the Anti-Rightist Campaign. Critics of the party, after initially being encouraged to speak their minds, were condemned as "bourgeois rightists" and "class enemies." The government sent tens of thousands of intellectuals, writers and scientists to labor camps or placed them under surveillance. Almost 10 percent of the students at Beijing University, China's most prestigious university, were sent to the countryside to work for years at manual labor to "correct" their opinions. The well-known woman writer Ding Ling (Ting Ling) was sent to the northern countryside for 20 years. Many marriages broke up when a husband or wife was accused of being a Rightist. The Anti-Rightist Campaign aimed to suppress all criticism of the Communists and to reestablish Communist ideology among the Chinese. With the campaign, party leaders declared that they had absolute authority in all legal issues. The following year the government launched the Great Leap Forward to spark the revolutionary spirit among the Chinese people. See also CHINESE COMMUNIST PARTY; DING LING; GREAT LEAP FORWARD; HUNDRED FLOWERS CAMPAIGN; MAO ZEDONG; PEOPLE'S REPUBLIC OF CHINA.

ANYANG　A city in Henan Province near the border of Hebei Province in central China. Today Anyang is a center for regional trade and agriculture and has a population of a half-million. It has become industrialized, but jade carving is still a major economic activity. Anyang is best known for its great historical importance. In 1889 the scholars Liu Er and Wang Yirong ascertained that old tortoise shells sold in traditional medicine shops in Beijing had come from Xiaotun village near Anyang. They had been plowed up for centuries by farmers, who called them dragon bones. The scholars recognized the scratches on the shells as an ancient form of writing. The tortoise shells, as well as the shoulder bones of oxen and sheep with writing on them, had actually been used for divining the future during the Shang dynasty (1750–1040 B.C.) and have thus been termed "oracle bones." These oracle bones had been described by the ancient historian Sima Qian (Ssu-ma Chien, c. 145–90 B.C.) of Yin, the capital of the Shang dynasty, which was supposedly located in this region.

Scientific excavations of Bronze Age sites at Anyang were first made by the Academia Sinica from 1928 to 1937. These and subsequent excavations found objects from the Shang dynasty and also verified the existence of the Xia dynasty (2200–1750 B.C.), China's first prehistoric dynasty. The Xia dynasty marked a transition between the late-Neolithic culture and the urban civilization of the Shang dynasty that replaced the Xia. Around 1380 B.C. Yin, now known as Anyang became the last capital of the Shang dynasty when Pan Geng, the 10th Shang emperor, moved his court there and began constructing palaces, government buildings, temples and mausoleums. The ruins at Anyang include 53 palaces, 13 temples and 11 mausoleums. Excavations of royal tombs at Anyang have yielded thousands of objects that provide information about the daily life of the Shang ruling class and Shang religion, economic activities,

government and diplomatic relations, warfare and so forth. Anyang was a center for bronzeware production—mainly vessels to hold food and wine used in sacred rituals. Excavations are currently being made in the Houjiazhuang and Wuguan areas. Many of the found objects are exhibited at the Historical Museum in Beijing. Permission for foreigners to visit Anyang was formerly given only to historians and archaeologists who have specialized knowledge about the history of the area, but the site is now open to visitors. See also ACADEMIA SINICA; BRONZEWARE; HENAN PROVINCE; JADE; ORACLE BONES; SHANG DYNASTY; SIMA QIAN; XIA DYNASTY.

AOMEN　See MACAO.

ARABS AND CHINA　See SHIPPING AND SHIPBUILDING; SILK ROAD; TALAS, BATTLE OF; TANG DYNASTY.

ARCHAEOLOGY IN CHINA　(*kaoguxue* or *k'ao-ku-hsueh*) Modern archaeological field techniques were introduced in China by Western researchers in the early 20th century. Beginning in the Song dynasty (960–1279), Chinese literati, or scholars, who staffed the imperial bureaucracy had engaged in antiquarianism, which they called the "study of metal and stone" (*jinshuxue* or *chin-shu-hsueh*). They had a great reverence for written texts, such as the classics and books of Confucianism and the histories of previous imperial dynasties, and the arts, such as painting, poetry and calligraphy, which had originated during the Zhou dynasty (1100–256 B.C.). Chinese historians had begun writing about the past as early as the Han dynasty (206 B.C.–A.D. 220), and Sima Qian (Ssu-ma Ch'ien; c. 145–90 B.C.) wrote the first "Official History," *Records of the Historian* (*Shiji* or *Shih-chi*). Historical records kept by all subsequent dynasties have made the dating of events in China from 841 B.C. on relatively easy; datings before that time are not settled.

Chinese legends describe legendary emperors who supposedly taught the Chinese people the skills and arts that formed the basis of Chinese culture. These legends also describe the Xia dynasty, which supposedly lasted from c. 21st–18th century B.C., although archaeologists have found no material evidence from the Xia. The Shang dynasty (1750–1040 B.C.), which claimed to have overthrown the Xia, is the first dynasty from which artifacts have been excavated. The Zhou, in turn, overthrew the Shang. The Chinese emperors and literati were also collectors and connoisseurs of artworks, jades, textiles, lacquerware and bronzeware dating back to the Shang and Zhou. The Song imperial court even published two illustrated catalogues of its collections of antiquities. During the Qing dynasty (1644–1911), scholars began producing more catalogues of ancient objects and relying on these objects to explicate passages in classical Chinese texts.

The traditional Chinese respect for burial sites, based on the practice known as "ancestor worship," meant that most tombs remained untouched until the late 19th century. When the Qing dynasty gave foreign nations concessions to finance and build railroads in the late 19th century, many rich burial sites were unearthed for the first time. The railroad line west from Luoyang to Xi'an, old imperial capital cities, cut through the ancient cradle of Chinese civilization, including some of the largest and wealthiest burial grounds of the ancient Chinese imperial families. This enabled archaeologists for the first time to excavate large quantities of ritual bronze vessels, jade and ceramic objects, and other materials buried with the deceased. Many of these objects have ended up in European museums.

Before World War I, several European expeditions conducted research in western China (Chinese Central Asia). In 1900, workmen repairing the walls in the Buddhist cave temples at Dunhuang in Gansu Province, which had been begun in the fourth century, discovered a library of ancient Chinese and Tibetan Buddhist manuscripts which had been hidden in the 11th century. In 1907 Paul Pelliott, a French archaeologist working in the region, hurried to Dunhuang and selected the best manuscripts. That same year, M. Aurel Stein, a Hungarian who worked for the British government in India, led an expedition to Dunhuang. There he acquired many of the manuscripts, sending most of them to London, where they were exhibited. Many of the most important Dunhuang manuscripts were acquired by the British Museum and other European museums and libraries. The Chinese scholar Luo Zhenyu (1866–1940) in Beijing learned of this great loss to China and sent a telegraph to government officials in the Dunhuang area to stop the foreign acquisition of these texts. In 1910 many of the remaining texts were shipped to Beijing, although many of these were also later acquired by Chinese and European private collectors. Scholars around the world have been cataloguing, photographing and studying the manuscripts from Dunhuang. There are also important Buddhist cave temples and sculptures at Dazu, Longmen and Yunggang.

Some of the most important discoveries in Chinese archaeology were the "oracle bones" dating from the Shang dynasty. Two Chinese professors realized that bones dug up by farmers and sold in herbal medicine shops as "dragon bones" had ancient pictographs inscribed on them. In 1903 scholars began studying the bones, and in 1928–37 excavations were made at Anyang, possibly the last Shang capital, in Henan Province in the Yellow River (Huanghe) valley. Characters on the bones proved to be the earliest form of Chinese writing and had been used for divination purposes by the Shang ruler. Magnificent bronze vessels, weapons, war chariots and other objects excavated from Shang archaeological sites, especially royal tombs, have provided a great deal of information about ancient Chinese culture and imperial government.

Johan Gunnar Andersson (1874–1960), a Swedish geologist, initiated the study of prehistoric archaeology in China. In 1920, while working for the Chinese Geological Survey, he discovered fossils of *homo erectus* at the cave of Zhoukoudian (Chou-k'ou-t'ien), southwest of Beijing (formerly known as Peking). Scholars from around the world began studying the fossils called Peking Man, but they were lost during World War II. Andersson also identified several Neolithic sites in northern China. In 1923 he made excavations at the Yangshao site in Henan Province, for which the Neolithic culture in that region was named. However, later scholarship proved wrong many of his conclusions about dates and Western origins for the Neolithic cultures. In 1930–31, archaeological excavations at Chengziyai in Shandong Province identified the Longshan culture, one of the

two most important Chinese Neolithic cultures along with the Yangshao.

Li Ji (1896–1979) and Liang Siyong (1904–54) at Harvard University were the first Chinese scholars trained in modern field archaeology. In 1928 they became the leaders of the archaeological research sponsored by the Chinese Nationalist (Kuomintang; KMT) government, under the Institute of History and Philology (Lishi Yuyan Yanjiusuo or Li-shih Yu-yan Yan-chi-suo) of the recently founded Academia Sinica (Zhongyang Yanjiuyan or Chung-yang Yan-chi-yuan). In 1934 the Academia Sinica published a report on the site at Chengziyai, which was the first major archaeological report on a prehistoric site in China. They conducted excavations of the palaces and tombs of the Shang kings at Anyang, at which the first generation of Chinese archaeologists received their training. However, this work was brought to a halt by the Japanese invasion of China in 1937 and China's War of Resistance against Japan (1937–45; World War II). A number of Japanese scholars performed archaeological work in northeastern China and Taiwan during the war. In 1932 the writer and historian Guo Moruo (1892–1978) had published an important volume, *Researches on Ancient Chinese Society*. He later became China's minister of culture.

After 1945 the Chinese Nationalists and Chinese Communists resumed fighting their civil war, which the Communists won in 1949. The Nationalists, including some who were members of the Academia Sinica, fled to Taiwan; the Institute of History and Philology was moved to Taiwan, where Li Ji and other scholars published the findings from the Anyang excavations. In 1965–66 archaeologists from National Taiwan University undertook a joint field project in Taiwan, led by K. C. Chang (1931–   ), a Chinese-born American achaeologist. In the mid-1970s the Institute of History and Philology also began conducting field excavations in Taiwan.

The Chinese Communists established the People's Republic of China (PRC) in 1949. Xia Nai (Hsia Nai; d. 1985), who had been trained in England, became director of the Chinese Institute of Archaeology, which was founded in 1950 as part of the new Chinese Academy of Sciences. He also became vice-dean of the Chinese Academy of Social Sciences. Xia Nai established that the Yangshao Neolithic culture (c. 5000–c. 2000 B.C.) was older than Qijia, not the reverse, as Swedish scientist Johan G. Andersson had claimed, and thus he ended the dominance of foreign scholars in Chinese archaeology. He led archaeological excavations in various parts of China and instructed hundreds of students who became China's leading archaeologists.

The robbing of graves and archaeological sites had become a serious problem in China prior to 1949. The PRC government passed a law in May 1950 protecting cultural relics and monuments and forbidding the export of any work of art from China; it also provided a large amount of funds that stimulated archaeological research. Beginning in 1952, departments of archaeology were established at Beijing University and other Chinese universities. The State Bureau of Cultural Relics, under the Ministry of Culture, created a national system for protecting archaeological sites. The Institute of Archaeology established permanent field stations at major sites such as Anyang; Erlitou in Henan Province, an Early Bronze Age site; and the capitals of ancient dynasties near Xi'an in Shaanxi Province and Luoyang in Henan Province. From 1956–58, Xia Nai took part in the excavation of the Ming Tombs outside Beijing. These mausoleums of 13 of the 16 emperors of the Ming dynasty (1368–1644) are open to the public and are a popular tourist atraction. Xia Nai also used newly discovered ancient silk textiles and foreign coins to develop theories about economic and cultural relations between ancient China and regions of central and western Asia, especially Persia (modern Iran), and the Roman Empire, which traded with China along the so-called Silk Road that terminated at Xi'an (formerly known as Chang'an).

After 1949, as China was rebuilding itself a large number of ancient sites all over the country that had archaeological value were unearthed. In 1954 Chinese researchers published a two-volume work on archaeological material recovered during the previous five years. The government expected archaeologists under Guo Moruo, the PRC Minister of Culture, to excavate materials that would confirm the CCP Marxist theory of Chinese history, which held that China developed from a primitive society to a slaveholding society to a feudal society, from which the CCP liberated the Chinese people. During the Cultural Revolution (1966–76), Red Guards destroyed many cultural and historical sites that they condemned as feudal. Chinese schools and universities, museums and reseach institutions were closed, and anyone concerned with traditional Chinese culture was condemned as bourgeois and punished or even killed. As the Cultural Revolution wound down, archaeological journals were permitted to resume publication in 1972, especially since the Chinese government began using archeological exhibitions to improve relations with foreign countries. Fieldwork shifted to an emphasis on finding valuable objects that could be shown off in exhibitions.

Ever since the United States normalized relations with the PRC in 1979 and foreigners began visiting the country in large numbers, many archaeological sites have been turned into popular tourist attractions, such as the spectacular finds around Xi'an. Banpo, the earliest village discovered from the Neolithic Yangshao culture, has been opened to the public. In 1974 peasants digging a well near Xi'an discovered an ancient site of an enormous army of terra-cotta warriors that had been buried with the first emperor, Qin Shi Huangdi (r. 221–210 B.C.). Archaeologists have now excavated 6,000 figures of warriors and horses, close to lifesize, which are lined up in a huge undergound vault now open to tourists. The Shaanxi History Museum, opened in Xi'an in 1992, houses materials dating from Paleolithic Langtian Man, the New Stone Age settlements at Lintong and Banpo (c. 5000–4000 B.C.), and artifacts from the Shang through Qing dynasties.

Since the early 1980s the PRC has pursued a policy of rebuilding and modernizing the country. Institutes of Cultural Relics and Archaeology have been established in all of the Chinese provinces, enabling researchers to concentrate on ancient developments in particular regions rather than having to fit their discoveries into a single unified theory of the development of Chinese culture. Some recent finds have included Neolithic cultures in the coastal areas of northeastern and southeastern China and regional Bronze Age cultures in Sichuan Province and the lower Yangzi River valley.

At the same time, looting of archaeological sites has become widespread and has gone virtually unchecked by the PRC, causing a serious threat to archaeological fieldwork. In 1991 the government eliminated a regulation that had long prevented foreign archaeologists from performing fieldwork in China, and today Chinese archaeologists are attempting to improve their work by setting up joint projects with foreign researchers. See also ACADEMIA SINICA; ANCESTOR WORSHIP; BRONZEWARE; CHANG'AN; CHINESE ACADEMY OF SCIENCES; DAZU CAVE TEMPLES AND SCULPTURES; DUNHUANG CAVE PAINTINGS AND CARVINGS; GUO MORUO; JADE; LITERATI; LONGMEN CAVE TEMPLES AND SCULPTURE; LUOYANG; MING TOMBS; NEOLITHIC PERIOD; ORACLE BONES; PEKING MAN; RAILROADS; SILK ROAD; TERRA-COTTA ARMY, TOMB OF QIN SHI HUANGDI; TOMBS; XIA NAI; XI'AN; YUNGANG CAVE TEMPLES AND SCULPTURES; NAMES OF INDIVIDUAL DYNASTIES.

ARCHITECTURE, TRADITIONAL The Chinese began constructing buildings aboveground as early as 8,000 years ago. Most early Chinese aboveground structures were made of wood. Stone, brick, rammed earth, felt and metals also were used later, although wood always remained the most popular material. A wooden structure built 7,000 years ago and excavated at Hemudu village in Zhejiang Province shows that by then the Chinese had already mastered the technique of building wooden frames joined with a mortise and tenon. Adding strength to a building, a system of wood frames composed of poles and beams tenoned firmly together was invented. Wood frames have some resistance to strong winds and earthquakes, which frequently occur in China. A mortise is a groove or slot, usually rectangular in shape, in a piece of wood into which another piece of wood, the tenon, fits or through which it passes. A mortise-and-tenon joint provides strong structural support. The wooden column is the principal support for the roof. Rather than a column cap, as used in Western architecture, the Chinese invented the *dougong (toukung)* bracket and *queti (ch'ueh-t'i)* cornice, which connect and reinforce columns and beams and are also decorative. The *dougong* bracket is the basic unit of a traditional Chinese building, by which the sizes of all the other parts are measured. *Dou* refers to a block of wood and *gong* to bow-shaped projections. The *dougong* increases a column's load capacity and gives a roof the strength to extend outwards and upwards. Chinese architecture is characterized by heavy upturned roofs, which are often covered with beautifully colored glazed tiles. The *dougong* brackets under the corner beams especially serve to transfer the weight of the roof onto the columns. The *queti* cornice, which became popular during the Ming (1368–1644) and Qing (1644–1911) dynasties, is used to reinforce the column and shorten the span between two beams, and is also decorative.

The Chinese developed the technique of using rammed earth for the foundations and walls of huge imperial palaces, tombs and gardens by the 21st century B.C. Chinese builders prevented a wood structure from rotting due to ground moisture and rainy weather by placing it on a tall platform foundation and topping it with a massive roof. The Shang dynasty (1750–1040 B.C.) is the earliest Chinese dynasty from which archaeologists have excavated artifacts. The Shang kings built palaces with features that became typical of Chinese palace-style architecture. The foundation of the

Shang Palace at Erlitou in Henan Province, an earthen platform 354 feet by 328 feet dating from the 16th century B.C., is the oldest known palace in China. On it stood rectangular timber-framed buildings with main columns that rested on large stones at the bottom of postholes.

The remains of the Shang capital of Ao, discovered in 1950 at Zhengzhou in Henan Province, includes several palace buildings made of rammed earth on earthen platforms. Pillars, crossbeams and ridgepoles were made of wood, and the pillars were placed on stone bases. Bamboo or other wooden material may have been placed between the layers of the rammed earth to absorb moisture. The largest building in ancient China, and perhaps the world, was the Epang Palace, constructed as part of a huge palace complex during the Qin dynasty (221–206 B.C.). The Epang Palace was built on a 717,703-square-yard platform and had floor space of 95,693 square yards.

The use of earthen walls created the two elements that became typical of Chinese architecture: walls that were not weight-bearing, and a roof that had large overhanging eaves. Ancient Chinese palaces had thatched roofs, but in later times they were covered with beautifully colored glazed tiles. Similar Shang palaces and royal tombs have also been excavated at Anyang in Henan. The palace complex at Anyang includes a central group of 21 large halls that were grouped together in three rows on a north-south axis. The central group has three large halls and five gates that point south. All ancient Chinese cities were laid out according to this plan, with the streets forming a grid, or chessboard pattern, and the emperor at the top of the central north-south axis facing south. This can be seen in the old section of the modern city of Xi'an in Shaanxi Province, formerly known as Chang'an, which was the capital of several Chinese dynasties, notably the Tang (618–907). Ancient Chinese cities were surrounded by walls and moats.

Commoners, who were mostly peasants and craftsmen, lived in semi-subterranean homes with floors as deep as nine feet below ground. Such dwellings can be seen at the Neolithic village of Banpo, which has been excavated outside Xi'an. In the vast region of northern China covered by deep deposits of yellow soil known as loess, the Chinese carved homes out of loess cliffs, which are still lived in today. When the Chinese began building homes aboveground, they grouped the rooms around a central courtyard, which provided privacy. The custom of several generations of an extended family living together in a compound is still practiced in many regions of the country. Homes in northern China include a built-in raised platform for living and sleeping, called a *kang* (*k'ang*), which is heated underneath.

A courtyard enclosed by buildings is characteristic of all Chinese architecture, from palaces to ordinary homes. Compounds built for emperors and wealthy Chinese families contained many courtyards, each surrounded by buildings, which were combined in a complex pattern. Builders followed the principles of *feng shui,* or geomancy, the proper placement of buildings and rooms in relation to each other in order to bring good fortune and keep away evil spirits. The head of the family lived in the main hall at the north of a central north-south axis. Younger brothers and their families lived in the side buildings in the main courtyard. More distant relatives such as cousins inhabited courtyards further

south in the complex. Servants lived in buildings along the southern wall near the entrance to the first courtyard. A large screen, made of stone or some other sturdy material, stood inside the entrance to the compound to provide privacy and prevent evil spirits from entering.

By the early Zhou dynasty (1100–256 B.C.), which overthrew the Shang, Chinese architects were using the elaborately decorated wooden brackets typical of Chinese post-and-beam buildings. These spread the weight of sloping roofs whose ends turned upwards, especially heavy ones covered with glazed tiles, over large spaces. In northern China, which is cold and windy, roofs have tended to be thick and heavy and extend only a short amount so that the winter sun can enter the building. In southern China, which is warmer and rainier, roofs tend to have a steeper slope and a higher upturn at the corners of the eaves.

During the Song dynasty (960–1279), wealthy Chinese began designing gardens to complement their living compounds. The gardens, emphasizing the elements of "mountains and water," used rocks and ponds to re-create the natural world on a small scale. Covered walkways, bridges and pavilions were included so people could sit and enjoy the view. Some of the most beautiful Chinese gardens can still be seen in Suzhou in Jiangsu Province.

Temples were built all over China to Confucius (551–479 B.C.), whose thought was accepted as orthodox by the Han dynasty (206 B.C.–A.D. 220) and all subsequent Chinese dynasties. Large Chinese clans also built family temples where they performed rituals to honor their ancestors known as "ancestor worship." Temples were also built in the Daoist tradition. The Buddhist religion, which was introduced into China from India around the first century A.D. and was patronized by many Chinese rulers in the fifth–10th centuries, influenced the building of numerous temples that had one or more main halls and frequently included a pagoda (tall tower). Cave temples filled with stone carvings, sculptures and paintings were also cut into the sides of mountains. The best known Buddhist cave temples are at Dazu, Dunhuang, Longmeng and Yungang. The wooden pagoda built in 516 at Yongning Temple in Luoyang in Henan Province was 449 feet high, one of the tallest ancient buildings in the world. The oldest surviving wooden pagoda in China is in Yingxian, Shanxi Province. Built in 1056, it is 221 feet high. The main hall in Nanchan Temple on Mount Wutai in Shanxi Province, built in the eighth century, is the oldest extant wooden structure in China.

The Chinese began building structures with bricks and arches by the third century B.C., although bricks never replaced wooden frames with earthen walls as the major building material. The Chinese produced large, hollow bricks between the fifth and third centuries B.C., and wedge-shaped bricks with a mortise on one side and a tenon on the other during the Han dynasty. Bricks then were used mainly to build underground tombs and sewer tunnels. In the fifth and sixth centuries A.D., brick was also used to construct structures above ground, such as pagodas and beamless shrines. During the Ming dynasty, brick was used to build walls around Chinese cities and to reconstruct some parts of the Great Wall built across northern China to keep out nomadic invaders. During the Qing, brick was used to build common structures because of its durability and ability to insulate. Metals were used as early as the Warring States Period, as seen in the bronze brackets, lintels and devices to strengthen wooden joints that have been excavated.

The Chinese also used stone, especially for building arch bridges, notably the Zhaozhou Bridge built near Beijing in Hebei Province from 605 to 617. Stone-arch bridges were not built in Europe until many centuries later. The best-known stone structure in China is, of course, the Great Wall. It is actually a series of walls, with a combined total length of about 4,500 miles, that were built over many centuries by various Chinese emperors. Tourists can visit a restored section of the Great Wall at Badaling north of Beijing.

There are three magnificent surviving examples of ancient Chinese architecture, all of which have been restored and opened to the public. The oldest is the Confucian temple at the Kong family mansion, the home of Confucius, in Qufu, Shandong Province. The Forbidden City (Imperial Palace), which was constructed in Beijing by the second emperor of the Ming dynasty (1368–1644), has 10,000 rooms and is the largest ancient building complex in the world. And the imperial summer resort at Chengde, north of Beijing in Hebei Province, was constructed by the Manchu rulers of the Qing dynasty (1644–1911). In addition, the Temple of Heaven near the Forbidden City is a beautiful example of a Chinese imperial religious complex covered with glazed-tile roofs. See also ALLEYS; ANYANG; ARCHAEOLOGY; BRIDGES; CHENGDE; CONFUCIUS; DAZU CAVE TEMPLES AND SCULPTURES; DUNHUANG CAVE PAINTINGS AND CARVINGS; FENG SHUI; FORBIDDEN CITY; FURNITURE, TRADITIONAL; GARDENS; GREAT WALL; LOESS; LONGMEN CAVE TEMPLES AND SCULPTURES; MING TOMBS; PAGODAS; PAVILIONS; QUFU; ROCKS; SHANG DYNASTY; TEMPLE OF HEAVEN; TEMPLES; TILES; GLAZED; XI'AN; YUNGANG CAVE TEMPLES AND SCULPTURES.

ARGUN RIVER AND ARGUN, TREATY OF See AMUR RIVER; HEILONGJIANG PROVINCE.

ARHAT See LUOHAN.

ARMED FORCES See CENTRAL MILITARY COMMISSION; CHINESE COMMUNIST PARTY; CIVIL WAR BETWEEN COMMUNISTS AND NATIONALISTS; EIGHTH ROUTE ARMY; PEOPLE'S LIBERATION ARMY; WAR OF RESISTANCE AGAINST JAPAN.

ARROW WAR (1856–60)   Also known as the Second Opium War and the Anglo-French War of 1856–60; a war initiated by Great Britain to force China to honor the articles of the Treaty of Nanjing (1842), which concluded the Opium War (1839–42). Great Britain had fought the Opium War to force China to open up Chinese cities to foreign trade and residents. The government of the Qing dynasty (1644–1911) that ruled China had restricted foreign trade to the southern port city of Guangzhou (Canton). Foreign traders were required to conduct all of their business in Guangzhou through native Chinese merhants who belonged to a guild known as the Cohong or "Hong" (from *gonghang*, "combined merchant companies") and who made very high profits. The balance of trade had been unfavorable to Great Britain, whose traders bought large quantities of luxury goods such as tea, silk and porcelain from China but could only sell Indian cotton to China. British traders redressed the imbalance by selling large quantities of Indian opium to China, which drained the Chinese economy of silver and demoralized the Chinese people. In 1839 the Qing sent Lin Zexu (Lin Tse-hsu) to eliminate the opium trade. He forced the British to surrender 20,000 chests of opium, which he publicly destroyed, but he could not get the British to pledge that they would stop shipping opium to China. The British withdrew to the island of Hong Kong and continued selling opium to smugglers.

The Opium War began after a group of British sailors killed a Chinese man in Kowloon but the British refused to surrender the sailors to Chinese authorities. A fleet of Chinese junks sailed to Hong Kong to seize the sailors, and the British opened fire on them. From 1840 to 1842 British forces captured several ports between Guangzhou and Shanghai at the mouth of the Yangzi River (Changjiang). The Chinese could not put up a strong defense, and Qing officials sued for peace and signed the Treaty of Nanjing with Great Britain. The 13 articles of the treaty gave the British many privileges and rights in China, including extraterritoriality, meaning the right to try British accused of crimes in China in British rather than Chinese courts. Five treaty ports were opened for foreign residence and trade, and Shanghai soon replaced Guangzhou as China's largest trading port. China also ceded Hong Kong to Great Britain.

Other foreign powers, including the United States, France and Russia, forced China to sign similar treaties with them. These concessions to foreign countries greatly damaged the prestige of the Qing dynasty, which had been founded by Manchus, an ethnic group from Manchuria (modern northeastern China) whose rule was greatly resented by the Han ethnic Chinese who comprised the vast majority of the Chinese population. The Chinese considered the Treaty of Nanjing too harsh, while the foreign powers considered it too lenient and wanted the Qing to open more treaty ports, especially in the Chinese interior. They also wanted the right to establish diplomatic representation in Peking (Beijing), the Chinese capital.

The Arrow War broke out over an altercation in autumn 1856 concerning the *Arrow*, a Chinese-owned river vessel that was registered in Hong Kong and thus flew the British flag (although it was later discovered that the registration had expired). Chinese police boarded the *Arrow*, arrested 12 of the Chinese crew as pirates and pulled down the flag. Harry Parkes, the British consul, considered this an insult to Great Britain, but the Chinese governor-general of Guangzhou, who finally returned the prisoners, refused to offer an apology. In 1858 the British naval force at Guangzhou bombarded and then captured the city. France also joined the war because it had its own grievances with China. In February 1856 Father Chapdelain, a French Roman Catholic missionary in Guangxi, had been tortured and executed. Some of his Chinese converts had been arrested and charged with instigating a rebellion and executed.

British forces led by Lord Elgin and French forces led by Baron Gros moved on Tianjin, a northern port city near Beijing, but the Qing government sued for peace, and they forced the Qing to sign the Treaty of Tianjin. This treaty exacted harsh measures on the Chinese, including a large indemnity and lower tariffs on foreign trade. Its articles included the "most-favored-nation" clause, which gave other foreign powers, such as France, the same benefits in China as Great Britain. It allowed foreigners to travel anywhere in China with valid passports, assured the protection of foreign missionaries, and gave British ships chasing pirates the permission to enter any Chinese port. Six new treaty ports would be opened immediately and four more would be opened on the Yangzi, one of China's two longest rivers, as soon as the Qing government was able to suppress rebellions there. The treaty also gave Britain and France the right to station ministers of their governments in Beijing. However, in 1859 a Chinese court refused to ratify the Treaty of Nanjing and the foreign ministers were not allowed to enter Beijing. Qing forts at Dagu near Tianjin also fired on and sank four British gunboats.

In 1860 the British sent a mission to Beijing to negotiate with the Qing, who then arrested the negotiators and even executed some of them. In retaliation Lord Elgin led British troops into Tianjin and Beijing. Qing emperor Xianfeng (Hsien-feng; r. 1851–61) and his court fled north to the Manchu summer resort at Chengde (Rehol or Jehol). The foreign troops looted the beautiful Summer Palace in Beijing and burned it to the ground, although they did not harm the Forbidden City, which contained the Imperial Palace. Prince Gong (Kung), the emperor's brother, remained in Beijing to deal with the British, who forced him to obey the terms of the 1858 Treaty of Nanjing. They also required him to ratify the Convention of Beijing (1860), which placed an even higher indemnity on China. The Qing government was forced to open 10 more treaty ports to foreign trade and to grant the right of travel and residence in China's interior to foreign missionaries and traders. The Qing also gave permission for Chinese to emigrate on British ships, and thousands of Chinese laborers soon began immigrating overseas to North and South America, Hawaii and Australia. The Convention also ceded the southernmost area of the Kowloon peninsula to Hong Kong, which Great Britain had made a Crown Colony. In 1898 the British also gained the New Territories adjoining Kowloon on the Chinese mainland. Hong Kong, Kowloon and the New Territories reverted to China in 1997. After the Qing awarded all of these benefits to Britain, the British supported the Qing, which was seriously threatened by the Taiping Rebellion (1850–64). Foreign nations preferred to keep the weakened Qing government in power so that they could manipulate it to their advantage, and foreign soldiers took part in the defeat of the Taipings. See also CANTON SYSTEM CHENGDE; GONG, PRINCE; GUANGZHOU; HONG KONG; KOWLOON; LIN ZEXU; MACAO; NANJING, TREATY OF; OPIUM WAR; OVERSEAS CHINESE; QING DYNASTY; SHANGHAI; TAIPING REBELLION; TIANJIN; TIANJIN, TREATY OF; TREATY PORTS; UNEQUAL TREATIES; YANGZI RIVER.

ART See BIRD-AND-FLOWER PAINTING; CALLIGRAPHY; CLOISONNE; EMBROIDERY; ENAMELWARE; FIGURE PAINTING; FORBIDDEN CITY; INK PAINTING; IVORY CARVING; JADE; LACQUERWARE; LANDSCAPE PAINTING; NATIONAL PALACE MUSEUM (TAIPEI); NORTHERN SCHOOL OF PAINTING; PORCELAIN; SILK; SOUTHERN SCHOOL OF PAINTING.

ART OF WAR, THE See SUNZI.

ARTISANS See BRONZEWARE; EMBROIDERY; GOLD AND SILVER; IVORY CARVING; JADE; LACQUERWARE; PORCELAIN; SILK; SOCIAL CLASSES.

ASIAN GAMES, HELD IN BEIJING, 1990 Regional track-and-field competitions for men and women from Asian countries held every year since 1951 and which were held in Beijing in 1990. The Asian Games are sponsored by the International Amateur Athletic Federation (IAAF) and are also under the patronage of the International Olympic Committee (IOC).

The Asian Games were first held in 1951 in New Delhi, India, and since 1954 they have been held every four years. Political controversies, frequently involving China, have troubled many of the Asian Games. Pakistan objected to the Indian site of the first games, and the Communist People's Republic of China (PRC) objected to the inclusion of athletes from Taiwan, the island where the Nationalists (Kuomintang) fled and established a Chinese government when they were defeated by the Chinese Communists in 1949. The PRC objected again when Taiwan was included in the 1962 Asian Games, so the IAAF agreed to exclude Taiwan from those games. Israel was also excluded from the 1962 games due to objections from the Arab nations. In 1966, both Israel and Taiwan were allowed to compete in the Asian Games in Thailand, but the Arab nations boycotted and riots broke out during the games.

In 1963 the Communist countries in Asia had formed Games for the New Emerging Countries (GANEFOL), which held their own games without IAAF sponsorship in 1966 and 1969. The Asian Communist countries decided to rejoin the Asian Games in the 1970s. The XIIth Asian Games were awarded to the PRC and were held in the capital city of Beijing in 1990, one year after the world had censured the PRC for violently crushing the student protest in Beijing known as the Tienanmen Square Massacre; thus, the participation of 36 teams at the Asian Games indicated political acceptance of the PRC by other Asian nations. Competitions were held at 79 stadiums and gymnasiums.

Chinese athletes dominated the sports of volleyball, world table tennis, badminton and basketball and won a majority of medals at the 1990 Asian Games. China had also participated in the Olympic Games in 1932, 1936 and 1948. After 1949, China withdrew from the International Olympic Committee (IOC), but it applied for readmission in 1975. The IOC decided to admit the PRC and to allow Taiwan to participate but not call itself China, so Taiwan protested by withdrawing from the IOC. The PRC returned to full participation in the Olympic Games at the 23rd Olympiad in 1984. See also CIVIL WAR BETWEEN COMMUNISTS AND NATIONALISTS; PEOPLE'S REPUBLIC OF CHINA; SPORTS; TIANANMEN SQUARE MASSACRE.

ASIA-SAT-1 See SPACE INDUSTRY.

ASTROLOGY See ALMANAC; ASTRONOMY AND OBSERVATORIES; CALENDAR; WEDDINGS, TRADITIONAL; ZODIAC, ANIMAL.

ASTRONOMY AND OBSERVATORIES From ancient times, the Chinese placed great importance on the observation of the movement of the planets and stars. Ruling dynasties built observatories in their capital cities so that astronomers could issue the annual official calendar that regulated the agricultural year and sacred ceremonies. An observatory's raised platform derived from an altar and symbolized the Daoist belief that Heaven had granted the emperor his power and authority to rule, known as the Mandate of Heaven (*tianming* or *t'ien-ming*). Astronomical instruments were considered to be sacred ritual implements. The oldest illustration of the Daoist astrological system of 28 constellations surrounding the pole star, or Big Dipper in their center, was found on a wooden chest from the 2,400-year-old tomb of Marquis Yi of Zeng. Ancient Daoist astronomers used the 28 constellations to organize their observations of the movements of the sun, moon and the five planets then known. Scientists in the imperial court kept records of their astronomical observations continuously for more than 2,000 years. Records from the 11th century B.C. to the early 20th century A.D. list more than 1,600 solar eclipses, 1,100 lunar eclipses and 200 occultations, or disappearances, of planetary bodies behind the moon.

By 1000 B.C. Zhou dynasty (1100–256 B.C.) astronomers were able to observe the stars by holding up a jade circumpolar constellation template—a flat disk with a wide opening in the center—with the pole star in the center. Notches around the outer edge of the disk would match the pattern of stars that surrounded the pole star. Different disks were used as the star positions changed during the year. These disks are some of the earliest astronomical instruments in the world. The Chinese developed the equatorial system of astronomy, which was adapted by modern Western astronomers beginning with Tycho Brahe (1576–1601). This system uses an instrument in which the equator is the horizontal circle around the side of the instrument, and the pole star is the top point. The sky is divided into 28 sections, known as "lunar mansions" (*xiu* or *hsiu*), each of which contains certain named constellations of stars. The pole star and the stars around it never set beneath the horizon. During the year Chinese astronomers observed the changing positions of the other visible stars in the sky and were able to determine where the rest of the stars were positioned, even when they set below the horizon.

The Chinese had become highly skilled in making bronzeware during the Shang dynasty (1750–1040 B.C.), and had also invented iron casting, so it was easy for them to make bronze and iron astronomical instruments. These consisted of large metal rings that were precisely marked with the degrees of the circle. Armillary spheres—different rings representing different sky-circles—were joined together at the two points where they crossed each other. One ring represents the equator and the other represents the meridian, a sky-circle that passes directly over the observer's head and also through the pole. Chinese instruments also had sighting-tubes through which astronomers determined the position of different stars by moving the tubes around the equator and noting the degrees of the circle at which stars were seen. Astronomers could draw extremely precise maps of the stars in the sky and show how they fell into arrangements of constellations. During the Han dynasty (206 B.C.–A.D. 220), Zhang Heng (Chang Heng) designed the best-known example of a celestial globe, which had a system of gears turned by water power that slowly turned the globe one revolution

per day. In 52 B.C. the astronomer Geng Shouchang (Keng Shou-ch'ang) invented the first permanently mounted equatorial armillary ring. Later astronomers added more rings.

During the Song dynasty (960–1279) in 1086, Su Song (Su Sung) compiled a book with elaborate illustrations on the armillary sphere and clock (the book has survived). After the Northern Song dynasty fell in 1127 to the Jin dynasty (1115–1234), the Jin rulers moved the astronomical instruments from the Song capital at Kaifeng in modern Henan Province to Beijing (then called Zhongdu or Chung-tu) and placed them in the observatory of the Jin Chief Astronomer. The Song court moved south and established the Southern Song dynasty (1127–1279) at Hangzhou. In 1247 a circular star chart three feet in diameter was carved on a stone pillar in Suzhou that depicts the positions of 1,434 stars and shows the boundaries of the Milky Way.

When the Mongols conquered the Jin dynasty and established the Yuan dynasty (1279–1368) with their capital at Beijing, they built a new observatory just north of the observatory that can be seen today. The astronomer-mathematicians Wang Xun (Wang Hsun) and Guo Shoujing (Kuo Shou-ching) brought Chinese astronomy to its highest development. Guo designed many complicated astronomical instruments and compiled the Shoushi Calendar that was used for many generations. The instruments they designed, which were built by a craftsman from Nepal named Arniko, were used by Chinese astronomers for the next 500 years. The Dengfeng Observatory, built in 1279, is the oldest surviving astronomical structure in China. Astronomers calculated the length of the solar year by measuring the shadow cast by a 105-foot-long stone rod. China is the only country in the world in which astronomers documented all four known supernovae that have appeared in the sky, in 1006, 1054, 1572 and 1604.

When the Ming dynasty (1368–1644) overthrew the Yuan, the first Ming emperors made their capital at Nanjing and moved the astronomical instruments there. In 1421 Ming emperor Yongle (Yung-lo) moved the capital to Beijing but left the instruments in Nanjing because Ming emperor Hongwu (Hung-wu) was buried there. Yongle had a new set of bronze instruments cast in Beijing that were modeled after the ones in Nanjing. A new observatory was built on the site of the watchtower to the southeast of the old capital district of Beijing, the observatory that can be seen today. It was equipped with traditional astronomical instruments including a celestial globe and a water clock. The Beijing Observatory, the largest observatory in the world when it was built, was used continuously from 1442 to 1929, during the Ming and Qing (1644–1911) dynasties, the early days of the Republic of China and the Warlord Period (1916–28). Now open to the public, it looks much the same as when it was built between 1437 and 1446. The large bronze instruments still stand on the large observation platform and adjacent structures.

After the Qing dynasty replaced the Ming in 1644, Qing emperor Kangxi (K'ang-hsi) appointed Ferdinand Verbiest, a Belgian, Roman Catholic Jesuit priest, to introduce European astronomical measurements and instruments in the Imperial Astronomical Bureau. The Jesuits were highly trained in mathematics and science. From 1669 to 1673, Verbiest supervised the construction of six large bronze instruments, including a celestial globe, equatorial armilla, ecliptic armilla, altazimuth, quadrant and sextant. The old Ming bronze instruments were moved to the ground floor and the new ones were installed in their place on the observatory platform. The celestial sphere, built between 1669 and 1683, was the most important Qing instrument in the observatory. Forty years later, another priest named Bernard-Kilian Stumpf supervised the making and installation of the seventh large instrument, the azimuth theodolite. In 1754 the eighth instrument was completed, a new armillary sphere based on a Western model.

When the antiforeign Boxers laid seige to the foreign legation quarters in Beijing in 1900, an allied army of eight foreign powers invaded Beijing and looted all the observatory instruments. The Astronomical Bureau was able to continue making observations using two smaller instruments that were installed in 1905. In 1921 the large bronze instruments were returned to China and the Beijing Observatory was restored. After the Chinese Communists founded the People's Republic of China in 1949, the government took measures to protect the observatory structure. Recently the instruments were repaired and a special exhibition room was opened nearby.

A new observatory, one of China's most important scientific research projects begun in the late 1970s when China began rebuilding after the Cultural Revolution (1966–76), was completed in Yunnan Province in southwestern China in 1983. It is located east of Kunming on the Yunnan-Guizhou Plateau, 6,560 feet above sea level, where there is high atmospheric transparency. Scientists at the Yunnan Observatory perform astrophysics research, including solar physics, stellar physics, celestial mechanics, astrometry and radio astronomy. See also BEIJING; BOXER UPRISING; CALENDAR; JADE; JESUITS; MANDATE OF HEAVEN; ZHOU DYNASTY.

ATHLETICS See MARTIAL ARTS; SPORTS.

AUMEN See MACAO.

AUNG SAN SUU KYI See UNITED NATIONS FOURTH WORLD CONFERENCE ON WOMEN.

AUTONOMOUS REGIONS See GUANGXI-ZHUANG AUTONOMOUS REGION; INNER MONGOLIA AUTONOMOUS REGION; NINGXIA-HUI AUTONOMOUS REGION; PROVINCES, AUTONOMOUS REGIONS AND MUNICIPALITIES; TIBET; XINJIANG-UIGHUR AUTONOMOUS REGION.

AUTUMN HARVEST UPRISING See CHINESE COMMUNIST PARTY; CIVIL WAR BETWEEN COMMUNISTS AND NATIONALISTS; JIANGXI PROVINCE; LONG MARCH; MAO ZEDONG.

AUTUMN MOON FESTIVAL (Zhongqiujie or Chung Ch'iu Chieh, "Eighth Moon Festival") Also known as the Mid-autumn Festival; a celebration held on the 15th day of the eighth month in the lunar calendar (roughly corresponding to September) to honor the harvest moon. The Chinese go out at night to enjoy viewing the autumn moon. Children carry lanterns made of bamboo frames and colorfully decorated paper, and adults sip rice wine and compose poems about the moon. Mirrors are traditionally given as gifts at the Moon Festival to symbolize brightness and intelligence. Everyone eats mooncakes—heavy buns stuffed with a sweet paste made of such ingredients as lotus or watermelon seeds or red dates—that symbolize the fertility of the season. They are stamped on top with pictures of the Moon Goddess Chang E or with auspicious Chinese characters. Mooncakes were supposedly created during the Yuan dynasty (1279–1368) when the Chinese people were unhappy under the rule of the Mongols. A peasant leader named Zhu Yuanzhang (Chu Yuan-chang; 1328–98) started a revolution on the day of the Autumn Moon Festival by having secret messages in mooncakes passed among the villagers. He led the Chinese in overthrowing the Mongols and founded the Ming dynasty (1368–1644), ruling as the first Ming emperor Hongwu (Hung-wu). See also CHANG E; HONGWU, EMPEROR; LANTERNS; YUAN DYNASTY.

AVALOKITESHVARA See AMITABHA; BUDDHISM; DALAI LAMA; GUANYIN; PURE LAND SECT OF BUDDHISM.

AVATAMSAKA SUTRA See FLOWER GARLAND SECT OF BUDDHISM.

AVENUE OF THE ANIMALS See MING TOMBS.

AVG See FLYING TIGERS.

"AX-CUT TEXTURE STROKE" IN PAINTING See LI TANG; MA YUAN; XIA GUI.

AYDINGKOL, LAKE See TURPAN; TURPAN DEPRESSION.

AZALEA See RHODODENDRON.

BA JIN (Pa Chin; 1904–   )   A prolific modern Chinese author. Ba Jin was born in Sichuan Province but moved to Shanghai when he was 19. He wrote during a period when China was seething with revolutionary fervor, especially following the Northern Expedition in 1926 against Chinese warlords. Many Chinese students identified themselves with the characters in his novels and stories. He was influenced by Russian authors, including Ivan Turgenev, in his use of such novelistic devices as drawing up character types, establishing conflict in the story line, and creating scenes that move the plot along.

In 1922 Ba Jin moved to Paris and became an anarchist. There he published his first work, a short novel titled *Destruction,* in 1929. He created his pen name by combining syllables in Chinese from the names of his favorite authors, Bakunin and Kropotkin. When Ba Jin returned to China, he published many other novels and short stories. In the 1930s he published the *Love Trilogy,* which contains the three short novels *Fog, Rain* and *Lightning.* This was followed by the *Swift Current Trilogy,* which includes the novels *Family, Spring* and *Autumn* and describes the struggles of modern Chinese young people against the conservative, Confucian-based patriarchal family system that dominated China for 2,000 years. *Family* (*Jia* or *Chia*) became very famous; critics have compared it to the great 18th-century Chinese novel *Dream of the Red Chamber* (*Hongloumen* or *Hung Lo-men*). In the 1950s a quarter-million copies of this novel were sold in the Soviet Union.

Ba Jin suffered great hardships during the Chinese Cultural Revolution (1966–76), when many artists and intellectuals were attacked. In 1977 he began writing a lengthy work about his own ordeal, which took him eight years to write and was published as *Collected Essays.* The Chinese people call Ba Jin "the conscience of the Chinese intellectuals." *Family* remained a best-seller, especially among young overseas Chinese in Southeast Asia. After nearly two decades of condemnation in the People's Republic of China, the novel was reissued there in 1978. In December 1984, Ba Jin was invited to speak to a meeting of the Chinese Writers Associa-

tion, whose members were concerned about freedom of speech in China. He was too ill to attend, so another writer read his speech. Ba Jin asserted that the time had come for Chinese writers to create new "epic masterpieces" that would equal the *Dream of the Red Chamber* and the poems of the great Tang dynasty (618–907) poets; such authors would be China's Dante, Shakespeare, Goethe and Tolstoy. On January 5, 1985, the Chinese Communist Party issued a new "charter" for writers that promised them "democracy and freedom" but cautioned them to follow Marxist-Leninist thought. Ba Jin's works have been adapted into popular serial dramas for Chinese television. See also DREAM OF THE RED CHAMBER; NORTHERN EXPEDITION.

BABAO   See EIGHT TREASURES.

BACTRIAN CAMEL   See CAMEL CARAVANS.

BADA SHANREN (Pa-ta Shan-jen; 1626–1705)   A painter whom some critics consider the most influential artist in the history of Chinese painting; also known as Zhu Da (Chu Ta), and in English as "Master of the Lotus Garden." He was raised in Jiangsu Province in eastern China. Bada Shanren was a prince in a branch of the royal family of the Ming dynasty (1368–1644). When the Manchus took over the Chinese Empire under the Qing dynasty (1644–1911), he took part in the anti-Manchu resistance but suffered a breakdown and subsequently gave up leading a normal life and stopped painting in the accepted styles. He became a Buddhist monk and spent the rest of his life wandering. He also became a heavy drinker and has been described as painting in a frenzy while drunk.

Bada Shanren painted in the two most common types of Chinese painting: bird-and-flower and landscape. He created his landscapes and other ink paintings in a seemingly careless yet strong and spontaneous manner characteristic of the ink paintings of the Chan (Zen) Buddhist tradition. His compositions were brilliantly designed, with a generous use of space, and he painted the birds, flowers and landscapes with just a few sure, quick brushstrokes. Though his style seems very simple compared to the detail-filled compositions of his contemporaries, his paintings express the essence of the subjects he portrays and maintain a strong element of humor that is in keeping with the Chan tradition. Bada Shanren has been a major influence on 20th-century artists. See also CHAN SECT OF BUDDHISM.

BADAIN JARAN DESERT See TENGGER DESERT.

BADALING See BEIJING; GREAT WALL.

BAGUA See ALCHEMY; BOOK OF CHANGES; EIGHT TRI-GRAMS; FUXI.

BAI Also known as the Minjia; one of China's 55 national minority ethnic groups. The Bai are classified by their language, which belongs to the Tibeto-Burman language group. According to the 1990 census, nearly 1.6 million Bai live in the northwestern region of Yunnan Province, making them one of the largest minority groups in the Tibeto-Burman category. Yunnan lies in southwestern China and borders Tibet and Burma (Myanmar). The ancestors of the Bai were some of the region's original settlers, and excavations have shown that about 3,000 years ago the Bai were making tools from stone and animal bones. In the early eighth century, the Bai in the Dali region of Yunnan defeated Chinese troops of the Tang dynasty (618–907) and established the Nanzhao Kingdom. This kingdom controlled much of southwestern China and later controlled northern Burma as well. The Nanzhao Kingdom was defeated in the mid-13th century by the Mongols led by Khubilai Khan.

Unlike many of the minority groups in southern China who inhabit remote mountainous regions, the Bai live in open plains and are very similar to the Han, the majority Chinese ethnic group; for example, the Bai, like the Han, are farmers who cultivate rice in wet paddy fields and raise animals and silkworms. Although the Bai have been successful in retaining their own language, they are also familiar with the Han spoken and written language, which is standard in China. Bai women begin learning embroidery when they are seven years old and sew colorful designs on clothing, baby carriers, aprons and other items used in daily life. See also EMBROIDERY; MINORITIES, NATIONAL; YUNNAN PROVINCE.

BAI JUYI (Po Chu-yi or Po Chu-i; 772–846) One of the most highly regarded of all Chinese poets. Bai Juyi lived during the Tang dynasty (618–907), considered the "Golden Age" of Chinese culture, and is often classed with two other great Tang poets, Li Bai (Li Po; 701–62) and Du Fu (Tu Fu; 712–70). Seven of Bai Juyi's poems have been included in the classic anthology, *Three Hundred Poems of the Tang Dynasty*. He was born in Hunan Province in central China. His father was often absent, serving in various government positions in Chinese provinces. Bai Juyi began writing poetry when he was quite young. In 800 he passed the examinations, which enabled him to take up a position in the imperial bureaucracy that governed China. In 807 he joined the Hanlin ("Forest of Writing Brushes") or Imperial Academy. His duties included writing official correspondence sent by the emperor to neighboring states. A few years after 809, Bai Juyi was banished to a minor provincial position. In 822 he was appointed governor of the beautiful city of Hangzhou, and many government officials who had retired there became his friends. In 825 he was named governor of Suzhou, another beautiful city, but retired the following year due to illness. He spent the last 17 years of his life in Luoyang, the capital of Hunan Province, serving as governor for two years and then retiring once more due to illness.

Many of Bai Juyi's poems address the social and political problems of his time, and he even indirectly criticized the imperial regime of his day. He became a devout follower of the Buddhist religion, and his poems are filled with Buddhist compassion for the poverty and suffering of others. He believed that a poet has a duty to influence public affairs and morals, and he criticized Li Bai and Du Fu for not writing enough poems about the suffering of the people. Bai Juyi's most famous poem is a ballad, *The Everlasting Wrong* (or *Song of Unending Regret*), about the An Lushan Rebellion in 755, which forced Emperor Xuanzong (r. 712–56) to flee the capital city of Chang'an (modern Xi'an) and caused the death of his beloved concubine Yang Guifei. In the poem, the emperor is so heartbroken by her death that he persuades a magician to search the universe for her, and finally her spirit sends messages to her beloved emperor, but they cannot return to their glorious days in Chang'an. This ballad was sung in teahouses throughout China and became the most beloved of all Chinese poems. Bai Juyi was the first Chinese poet to become known outside China, especially in Japan and Korea. His other most renowned poem is *Song of Piba*, which recounts the sad fate of a courtesan who had once been famous. Both of these poems demonstrate that happiness is fleeting and can be overwhelmed by hopeless circumstances.

Bai Juyi employed a simple style of writing that people of all classes, even the uneducated, could readily understand. He often wrote poems in collaboration with his friend Yuan Zhen (Yuan Chen; 779–831). Many of Bai Juyi's poems have been translated into English. Some of the most beautiful translations have been made by the British scholar Arthur Waley, who preferred Bai Juyi above all other Chinese poets. See also AN LUSHAN REBELLION; BUDDHISM; CHANG'AN; DU FU; HANLIN ACADEMY; HANGZHOU; IMPERIAL BUREAUCRACY; LI BAI; LUOYANG; SUZHOU; TANG DYNASTY; WALEY, ARTHUR; XUANZONG, EMPEROR; YANG GUIFEI.

BAIDUNZI See PORCELAIN.

BAIHUA MOVEMENT See CHEN DUXIU; HU SHI; LAN-GUAGE, CHINESE; NEW CULTURE MOVEMENT.

BAIMASI See WHITE HORSE TEMPLE.

BAMBOO (*zhu* or *chu*) A tall plant that grows mainly in China, Japan and Southeast Asia but is now found throughout the world. The bamboo resembles a tree but is actually a grass with a tall, thick stalk and thin, delicate branches and leaves. There are about 1,000 species of bamboo, 300 of which are found in China, the greatest number of any country, where they cover about 12,350 square miles. Bamboo flourishes mainly in the low mountains and hills south of the

Yangzi River and east of the Yunnan-Guizhou Plateau, such as the Li River area in Guangxi-Zhuang Autonomous Region, where the subtropical climate and abundant rainfall produce lush vegetation. Some species may grow as high as 30 or 40 feet and have a diameter of 2 or 3 feet.

The length of the reproductive cycle differs for each species of bamboo. Some reproduce in one year, while the longest take 120 years; the average is 10 to 15 years. The highest and fastest-growing is Meso Bamboo, which comprises 78 percent of the total bamboo groves in China and requires only two months to develop from shoots into a mature plant. One bamboo plant can spread its underground stems over a large area, and a bamboo grove comprises a stand of one species of the plant. After a species of bamboo flowers and produces seeds, the entire stand of plants dies. Species of Fountain Bamboo grow at heights of 3,300 to 10,000 feet on the slopes of the Qinling Mountain Range, mainly in Sichuan Province in western China, where they have become the staple food of the endangered giant pandas, who suffer deprivation when the bamboo stand dies and have to be moved to new areas or fed bamboo brought from other areas.

The sturdy and pliant bamboo represents strength, endurance and resilience to the Chinese because it bends when the wind blows but always returns to an upright position. The bamboo, plum and pine are known as the "Three Friends of Winter" because all three remain green and flourish in the winter, representing happiness and endurance in old age. A porcelain vase with the "Three Friends" motif is a popular traditional gift symbolizing friendship. Bamboo leaves are often depicted in Chinese designs and paintings. Bamboo is used to make a wide variety of items that are used in daily life, such as chopsticks, umbrellas, hats, baskets, bags and trays, and craft objects such as folding fans, toys and vases. Thin strips of bamboo can be woven together, and the stalks heated and bent to make chairs, beds, chests of drawers, tables and folding screens. Every region of China has developed its own style for weaving and working with bamboo. For example, Fujian Province in the southeast specializes in bamboo carvings of animals and mythical creatures made by weaving delicate strands of bamboo around clay forms coated with lacquer. The Chinese even lash bamboo stalks together to make rafts for fishermen as well as building scaffolds. In ancient China, bamboo tablets were commonly used to write on before paper was invented around the second century B.C. Slats of bamboo stalks were sewn together to make a kind of folding book. Bamboo leaves were traditionally used to make raincoats and thatched roofs. The leaves, seeds, sap and roots are still used in herbal medicines, and tender young bamboo shoots are a common food in the Chinese diet. See also CHOPSTICKS; MEDICINE, HERBAL; PANDA; PLUM.

"BAMBOO NETWORK"   See OVERSEAS CHINESE.

BAN BIAO   See BAN GU AND BAN ZHAO; SIMA QIAN.

BAN CHAO (Pan Ch'ao; A.D. 32–102)   A great general during the Eastern Han Dynasty (25–220). Ban Chao led a large Chinese expedition west to the Caspian Sea and brought most of Central Asia under the control of the Chi-

nese Empire between A.D. 73 and 97. He was born into a famous family of scholars: his brother, Ban Gu (Pan Ku; 32–92), was a well-known historian who produced a history of the Western Han Dynasty (206 B.C.–A.D. 8); their sister, Ban Zhao (Pan Chao; 49–120), completed this work after Ban Gu died and became China's most famous woman scholar, writing poetry and essays as well.

In A.D. 73 Ban Chao led forces to reconquer the Tarim Basin in modern Xinjiang-Uighur Autonomous Region. Han Emperor Wudi (r. 141–87 B.C.) had brought this region of Central Asia into the Chinese Empire, but the Xiongnu and other non-Chinese tribes had taken it back. Ban Chao reestablished Chinese control by getting the tribal factions to fight against each other. In A.D. 91 Ban Chao was appointed governor-general of the empire's western territories and led his expedition nearly 4,000 miles west from the Han capital at Luoyang. Upon reaching the Caspian Sea, he sent his lieutenant, Gan Ying (Kan Ying), further west to make contact with the Roman Empire (called Daqin [Ta Ch'in] by the Chinese). When Gan Ying reached the northeastern shore of the Persian Gulf, sailors there—who did not want to lose the profits they had made transporting goods on the so-called Silk Road between China and the Middle East—warned him that attempting to cross the uncharted gulf would be very dangerous. Gan Ying turned back, and consequently no more attempts were made by the ancient Chinese Empire to reach Rome. However, in 166 the Roman emperor Marcus Aurelius sent an ambassador to the Chinese court at Luoyang with gifts of rhinoceros horn and ivory elephant tusks for the emperor. Arab sea traders reached the southern Chinese port of Guangzhou (Canton) in 147. See also BAN GU; EASTERN HAN DYNASTY; LUOYANG; SILK ROAD; XIONGNU.

BAN GU (Pan Ku; A.D. 32–92) and **BAN ZHAO** (Pan Chao; A.D. 49–120)   A brother and sister who were famous scholars and historians during the Eastern, or Later, Han dynasty (A.D. 25–220). Their father was a scholar named Ban Biao (Pan Piao; A.D. 3–54). Their brother was General Ban Chao (Pan Ch'ao; A.D. 32–102), who led a large Chinese expedition west to the Caspian Sea and brought most of Central Asia under the control of the Han Chinese Empire A.D. 73–97. The Han Dynasty had been interrupted by the brief reign of a usurper named Wang Mang A.D. 9–23, and the first part of the dynasty is known as the Western or Former Han dynasty (206 B.C.–A.D. 8). Ban Gu wrote *The History of the Former Han Dynasty* (*Hanshu*), patterning it on the *Records of the Historian* (*Shiji* or *Shih chi*) by Sima Qian (Ssu-Ma Ch'ien; c. 145–90 B.C.), the first official history of China. Ban Gu's history was written in 100 chapters and was divided into four broad categories: imperial records, biographies, tables, and essays on many topical subjects, such as administrative institutions and criminal laws. His history also included a bibliography that standardized the categorization of the many philosophical schools that had flourished in China during the fifth to third centuries B.C. Ban Gu's work was the first of the so-called dynastic histories, and his topical essays made his dynastic history even more valuable for Chinese scholars than Sima Qian's history. Ban Gu's history became the prototype for histories of later dynasties, which were written by government-sponsored teams of scholars in each succeeding dynasty who used as their sources the daily records kept by the previous dynasty. These histories were compiled for every Chinese dynasty down to the founding of the modern Republic of China in 1912. Ban Gu also wrote many other works of prose and poetry. He died before he finished the Han dynastic history, and his sister, Ban Zhao, completed the work. She also wrote the *Code for Women* as well as poetry and essays and became China's most renowned woman scholar. Biographies of Ban Biao and Ban Gu were composed in the *History of the Later Han Dynasty* (*Hou Hanshu*). See also BAN CHAO; CODE FOR WOMEN; EASTERN HAN DYNASTY; SIMA QIAN; WESTERN HAN DYNASTY.

BAN ZHAO See BAN CHAO; BAN GU AND BAN ZHAO; CODE FOR WOMEN.

BANGZI OPERA See OPERA, BEIJING.

BANK OF CHINA China's main foreign exchange bank and its most profitable state-owned bank. The Bank of China is the foreign exchange arm of the People's Bank of China, the official bank of the People's Republic of China (PRC), founded in 1949 by the Chinese Communist Party (CCP).

The Bank of China, housed in a modern Hong Kong skyscraper designed by world-renowned architect I.M. Pei, supervises foreign exchange for the entire country. S.E. MEYER

The new Communist government nationalized the Chinese banking system and centralized it under the People's Bank of China, which reports to the Ministry of Finance and is a special agency of the State Council. Foreign trade is supervised by the Bank of China, the Ministry of Foreign Trade and Economic Cooperation, and the General Administration of Customs. The Bank of China had been founded in 1912, when the Republic of China (ROC) was founded, with headquarters in Shanghai. It handled foreign trade and currency exchange throughout the republican era. After 1949 its headquarters were moved to Beijing, and its overseas branches broke off into those that supported the PRC and those that retained ties with the Nationalists, who had fled to the island of Taiwan, where they established the ROC government.

The Bank of China handles many dealings in foreign exchange, such as allocating China's foreign exchange reserves, arranging foreign loans, setting exchange rates for China's currency, issuing letters of credit, and handling all financial transactions with foreign companies and individuals. However, in 1984 the permission to deal in foreign currency was also granted to the Agricultural Bank, People's Construction Bank, China Industrial and Commercial Bank, and China International Trust and Investment Corporation (CITIC). The Bank of China provides loans for production and commercial transactions related to exports, maintains relations with hundreds of foreign commercial banks and performs research on international monetary trends. It has offices in Beijing and other Chinese cities that actively export goods, and it maintains overseas offices in major financial centers such as Singapore, New York, London and Luxembourg. The Bank of China headquarters in Hong Kong, the world's largest duty-free port, is a modern skyscraper designed by the world-famous Chinese architect I. M. Pei. Hong Kong, formerly a British Crown Colony, reverted to the PRC in 1997. The Bank of China has 13,863 branches. In 1997 its profits declined 25 percent to $725 million. See also CHINA INTERNATIONAL TRUST AND INVESTMENT CORPORATION; CURRENCY, MODERN; HONG KONG; MINISTRY OF FINANCE; PEI, I.M.; PEOPLE'S BANK OF CHINA.

BANKING See BANK OF CHINA; CURRENCY, MODERN; FOREIGN TRADE AND INVESTMENT; HONG KONG AND SHANGHAI BANKING CORPORATION; PEOPLE'S BANK OF CHINA.

BANNER SYSTEM, MANCHU (*gusai* or *ku-sai*) A system originated by the Manchu leader Nurhachi (1559–1626) to organize the Manchus, a group of seminomadic tribes, into a powerful military force that soon conquered China and established the Qing dynasty (1644–1911). In 1601 Nurhachi began strengthening his power by organizing the Manchus in northeastern China into four "banners," or companies, of warriors for administrative purposes and to build a strong, disciplined army. The banners, which were assigned color designs of yellow, white, blue or red, eventually totaled 24. Beginning in 1601, all Manchus were registered with their local banner, under which they were taxed, conscripted and mobilized for war. Nurhachi used the banner system to break down traditional divisions between different Manchu tribes and to consolidate leadership in his own clan. There were first four and later eight banners. In 1616, Nurhachi declared the founding of the Later Jin dynasty (1616–36), and two years later he declared war against the Chinese Ming dynasty (1368–1644). When he died in 1626, his six sons, a nephew and a grandson controlled the eight Manchu banners, eventually forming the grand council of state. Banners of ethnic Chinese (Han) and Mongols, a seminomadic ethnic minority in northern China, were later added to the system, and by the 1640s there were eight Chinese and eight Mongol banners as well as the eight Manchu banners.

During the Qing dynasty, military officers and soldiers, primarily descendants of the Manchus who had founded the dynasty, held hereditary ranks in the banners that provided the administrative framework for the standing army. Local militias were also raised as necessary to suppress bandits. Some banners were placed around the capital of Beijing in the northeast, and others were stationed at strategic points around the country. From 1646 to 1647, much of northern China was also assigned to the banners. Landowners and peasants were relocated to other regions and many hereditary Manchu-banner families were moved into northern China from Manchuria. The banners enabled the Manchus to maintain their distinct ethnic identity while ruling the Han (ethnic Chinese); thus, the Manchus had changed from raiders along the northern borders into the protectors of the Chinese Empire. The Manchus employed the Chinese to run the imperial bureaucracy or civil service, but provincial governorships and other important positions had to be filled by Chinese who belonged to the banners, denying many able Chinese from rising to high bureaucratic positions. By the middle of the 19th century, the military power of the Manchu banners had declined to the point where they could not suppress rebellions within China or protect the country against foreign invaders. See also MANCHU; NURHACHI; QING DYNASTY.

BANPO VILLAGE See ARCHAEOLOGY; NEOLITHIC PERIOD; SHAANXI PROVINCE; XI'AN; YANGSHAO CULTURE.

BANQUETS (*yanhui*)   Large meals with many courses served at festivals, especially the New Year, the birth of a child, weddings, birthdays, funerals and many other social or business occasions, such as the celebration of scholars passing their examinations, the election of public officials or the entertaining of clients. The Chinese love to celebrate every life event with a banquet adhering to customs that have been practiced for centuries. Chinese families also traditionally offer banquets before the ancestral tablets on their family altars on specified days, and then consume the food.

The official records from the Ming dynasty (1368–1644) contain the earliest detailed description of an imperial feast, served during the 13th year of the reign of the Yongle (Yung-lo) emperor (r. 1403–1424). The famous novel *The Golden Lotus* contains detailed descriptions of Ming ceremonial banquets and shows the importance of food in the ritual life of the Chinese. During the Qing dynasty (1644–1911), when the Han Chinese people were ruled by the Manchus, there were two kinds of imperial feasts: *Manxi* (*Man-hsi*; Manchu), of which there were six basic grades; and *Hanxi* (*Han-shi*; Chinese), of which there were five. A first-class *Manxi* banquet served by an emperor or empress included 34 varieties of meat and fruit and 24 plates of cakes and pastries, with a total of more than 300 dishes.

Chinese traditionally enjoyed dining on "picture" or pleasure boats while sailing on a river or lake, such as scenic West Lake near Hangzhou. Picture boats on the Pearl River in the southern city of Guangzhou (Canton) had a front compartment for socializing, one in the rear for dining, and one in the middle where scholars joined together to compose poems and paint landscapes or calligraphy. Female entertainers were hired to sing and serve dinner.

Today the Chinese usually hold banquets in restaurants or banquet halls rather than in private homes. The host (always male) seats the guests at one or more round tables according to their professional and social status and their age. The seat of the guest of honor is to the right of the host and faces the door. The next most important guest is seated to the left of the host. Each person has his or her own bowl of rice, but the serving dishes are placed in the middle of the table for everyone to share. The host serves large portions of food to the guests on his left and right, but they are not obligated to finish everything. At a formal banquet, before the guests begin eating, the host first pours warm rice wine for everyone and drinks to the health of each guest. At a less formal occasion, he picks up his chopsticks and waves them to the guests on his right and then his left to signal the start of the meal. There are three glasses at the plate of each guest, one for beer, soft drinks or mineral water, another for hot rice wine or grape wine, and a very small one for a clear but strong alcoholic beverage distilled from grain that is drunk when toasts are made. Of the last category, the best known Chinese distilled liquor is *maotai*. During a banquet, the host and guests offer many toasts, ending each one by saying "*ganbei* [*kan-pei*]," literally "a dry [meaning "empty"] glass," a phrase similar to "bottoms up" in English. Speeches may also be given during the banquet. Between courses or after the meal, the Chinese also enjoy playing games such as finger-guessing or finger-matching, where two guests each extend an arm and a certain number of fingers and try to guess the total number of fingers that will be extended. The loser of each round drinks a cup of wine.

In a typical Chinese banquet, a variety of dishes prepared by different cooking methods is served to provide a range of visual and taste sensations. Much of the conversation may have to do with the kinds of food that are served and the regions where the ingredients were grown. The various ingredients, textures and flavors are carefully chosen to complement each other. The first course, which is already on the table when the guests are seated, includes one or more cold plates with smoked or marinated meats, vegetables and seafood arranged in an attractive design such as a flower. The first four dishes brought from the kitchen usually have been stir-fried. Then comes a soup, followed by four "heavier" dishes that have been braised with sauce. There may also be a roasted dish such as Peking duck or a whole fish such as sweet and sour Yellow River carp. A fish is often served, because the word for fish (*yu*) is pronounced the same as the word for abundance. The last dish in this series is usually sweet, especially a sweet soup made from lotus seeds, lotus roots, almonds or water chestnuts. Then come four rice-accompanying dishes (*fancai* or *fan ts'ai*) to settle the stomach, such as mixed vegetables with bean curd, and a plain soup. The guests stop drinking alcoholic beverages when these dishes are set on the table. If Peking duck had been served earlier, duck soup made by simmering the carcass with cabbage will then be served. The banquet ends with a plate of fresh fruit. Tea is served before and after but not during the meal. All of these courses, which may include more than 60 dishes and condiments, are typical for an ordinary Chinese banquet. (A banquet served by a government official will be even longer and more elaborate.) When it is time to end the banquet, the guest of honor stands up to leave and everyone follows him. See also ALCOHOLIC BEVERAGES; ANCESTOR WORSHIP; COOKING, CHINESE; FINGER GUESSING GAMES; GOLDEN LOTUS, THE; MAOTAI; RICE; TEA; WEDDINGS, TRADITIONAL; WOK; NAMES OF INDIVIDUAL INGREDIENTS AND FOODS.

BAO   See DIM SUM; NOODLES.

BAOHUANG HUI   See KANG YOUWEI; LIANG QICHAO.

BAOJIA SYSTEM   See WANG ANSHI.

BAOPUZI   See GE HONG.

BAOTOU   The largest city in Inner Mongolia Autonomous Region in northern China. Baotou is located west of Hohhot, Inner Mongolia's capital, in the steppes of the Ordos Plateau on the northernmost reaches of the Yellow River (Huanghe). The Daqing Mountains lie to the north. Baotou was formerly a small city in a dry, undeveloped region inhabited by nomadic Mongolians who herded sheep, goats, cattle and horses. The name Baotou means "land with deer." After a railroad line to Beijing was completed in 1922, the city began to develop and grew to become the most important commercial center in Inner Mongolia and northwestern China. Wool, furs, clothing, grain and tea were the main articles of trade. After the Chinese Communists founded the People's Republic of China (PRC) in 1949, they constructed large steel mills at Baotou as part of their first Five-Year Plan (1953–57) for China's economic development. The region has large deposits of coal, iron and other minerals. Today Baotou is highly industrialized and is known as the "steel city of the grasslands." Its population of more than one million consists mostly of Han ethnic Chinese who have moved there to work. Experts from the U.S.S.R. supervised the Baotou Iron and Steel Company until relations between the two countries broke down and the Soviets withdrew all their experts from China in 1960. It is possible to take a tour of the steel works. The city also has a steam locomotive museum. Light industries in Baotou include textiles, carpets, leather and furs.

The main tourist attraction is Wudangzhao Monastery (Wu-tang-chao), about 45 miles northeast of Baotou, which was built in the Tibetan style around 1749 by the Yellow Hat Sect of the Tibetan form of Buddhism, known as Lamaism. The Mongols had adopted Lamaism before they conquered China under the Yuan dynasty (1279–1368). Formerly 1,200 monks lived at the monastery, but only a few live there today. The 200-year-old murals in the main halls have retained their bright colors, and many treasures can still be seen in the monastery. Meidaizhao (Mei-tai-chao) is another Yellow Hat monastery close to Baotou. The mausoleum of Genghis Khan (1162–1227), who unified the Mongol tribes and led them to create a vast Mongol empire extending from Korea to Central Asia, is located southwest of Baotou. Tourists who wish to visit the cite must first pass through the Mongol city of Dongsheng. Since the U.S.S.R. collapsed in 1991, the people of Outer Mongolia have elevated Genghis Khan to a virtual deity. Mongolians from both Inner and Outer Mongolia make pilgrimages to his mausoleum, which is now called "Grave of the Leader" (Yijin Horo). He and three of his wives lie in the rear of the main hall, and his fourth son and his wife lie in the east hall; his weapons are exhibited in the west hall. Religious ceremonies are held four times a year at the mausoleum to honor Genghis Khan. The enormous, barren Gobi Desert begins just south of Baotou. About 40 miles south of the city is Resonant Sand Gorge, whose sand dunes rise as high as 131 feet. See also FIVE-YEAR PLANS; GENGHIS KHAN; GOBI DESERT; INNER MONGOLIA AUTONOMOUS REGION; IRON TECHNOLOGY AND STEEL INDUSTRY; LAMAISM; MONGOL; NOMADS AND ANIMAL HUSBANDRY; ORDOS PLATEAU.

BAREFOOT DOCTORS   Peasants, workers and educated young people who have been trained to be grassroots health care workers among China's rural population. So-called barefoot doctors were organized during the Cultural Revolution (1966–76) to help the vast numbers of Chinese farmers in the poor countryside who did not have access to medical treatment. A barefoot doctor is given a three-to-six-month short training course in a hospital and is also given occasional refresher courses. They are paramedics who handle basic illness and other medical problems and refer complicated cases to fully trained doctors. They also educate people about preventive health care and sanitary environmental practices, provide immunizations and train local health care workers to give first aid and care for minor illnesses. Barefoot doctors who have the ability and motivation may be sent to an urban medical center for more advanced training. "Worker doctors" with similar training provide comparable services in industrialized regions. There are also "Red Medical Workers," or unpaid housewives, who provide medical services in local neighborhoods. Local midwives are also given training similar to that of barefoot doctors, and they usually assist at several childbirths per month. See also PEOPLE'S COMMUNE.

BARGES   See GRAND CANAL; SUZHOU; YANGZI RIVER.

BAT   (*fu*)   A traditional Chinese good-luck symbol that is frequently depicted in designs for porcelain, textiles, lacquerware and other crafts. The bat motif is often so ornate that it may resemble a butterfly. In the West the bat has a negative connotation, but in China the animal has a positive meaning because the Chinese word for "red bat" (*hongfu*) sounds similar to the phrase for "abundant good fortune" (*hongfu*; written with different characters; red is the Chinese color for happiness). A decorative motif with five bats is also commonly used because the five bats (*wufu*) symbolize the five types of good fortune (also pronounced *wufu*): good health, wealth, long life, love of virtue and a natural death. An old Chinese herbal medicine text claims that silvery white bats a thousand years old can be found living in caves, and a person who eats them will enjoy long life and good eyesight. Thus bat blood, gall, wings and so forth are sometimes prescribed as ingredients in traditional medicines. See also WRITING SYSTEM; NAMES OF INDIVIDUAL CRAFTS.

BATIK See INDIGO DYEING OF TEXTILES.

BAXIAN See EIGHT IMMORTALS.

BAYANHARSHAN MOUNTAIN RANGE See KUNLUN MOUNTAIN RANGE; QINGHAI PROVINCE.

BEAN CURD See SOYBEANS AND SOY PRODUCTS.

BEANS AND BEAN PRODUCTS Chinese cuisine employs a variety of beans, such as brown and black beans, green mung beans, red beans and white soybeans, which are very nutritious. Products made from them are important ingredients in many Chinese dishes, including desserts and snack foods. Heavily salted and fermented black beans are used in soups and sauces and add flavor to a variety of dishes, such as steamed spareribs with salted black beans. Soybeans, which are extremely nutritious, are processed into bean curd (*dowfu* or *towfu*), known by the Japanese name *tofu* in the West; a beverage known as soy milk; and red and yellow bean pastes for flavoring dishes. Red beans and soybeans are combined with ginger, garlic, salt, sugar, chili pepper and other spices to make the pungent deep-red hoisin sauce. Soy sauce, the most common Chinese seasoning, is made from fermented soybeans combined with salt. Kidney beans, small red beans, known in the West by the Japanese name azuki, and green mung beans are made into a sweet paste filling for steamed buns and sweet glutinous rice buns. Sweet bean paste is also one of the ingredients—along with lotus and almond seeds, sliced red dates and candied fruits—in the sweet rice dish known as "eight precious pudding." At the annual spring Lantern Festival each child up to age 15 is given a piece of mung bean dough filled with a candle in the shape of the animal associated with his or her birth year, according to the 12-year Chinese animal zodiac.

Large and small bean sprouts and the shoots of mung beans and soybeans are all rich in protein and other nutrients. They are served in some Chinese dishes to add a crunchy texture. The Chinese also make noodles from mung bean flour. Long green beans similar to string beans, broad or fava beans and large bean sprouts are stir-fried with oil, garlic and other seasonings and served as an individual vegetable, or cooked with meat and other ingredients. Green vegetables are the favorite food of the majority of the Chinese people. See also COOKING, CHINESE; SEASONINGS FOR FOOD; SOYBEANS AND SOYBEAN PRODUCTS; VEGETABLES AND VEGETARIAN DISHES; ZODIAC, ANIMAL.

BEER See ALCOHOLIC BEVERAGES.

BEI See STONE TABLETS.

BEI RIVER See PEARL RIVER.

BEI SONG DYNASTY See NORTHERN SONG DYNASTY.

BEIBAN RIVER See PEARL RIVER.

BEIDA See BEIJING UNIVERSITY.

BEIDAIHE A resort city with six miles of beaches, located east of Beijing on the Bo Hai Gulf in Hebei Province; its population is about 17,000, Beidaihe was a fishing village until the 1890s, when British engineers who were building the Tianjin-Shanhai Guan railroad began using it as a summer resort. Villas belonging to foreigners and wealthy Chinese were burnt down in the Boxer Rebellion in 1899 but were rebuilt by the government of the Qing dynasty (1644–1911). The government of the People's Republic of China has transformed Beidaihe and its hundreds of villas into a resort for Chinese workers and has constructed sanitoriums and guest homes. Communist leaders have also built villas here, including Jiang Qing, the widow of Mao Zedong and a notorious member of the "Gang of Four." Today foreign tourists also enjoy visiting Beidaihe. Other sight-seeing attractions in the area include Lotus Blossom Stone Park on Dongliang Feng Mountain, the Ancient Temple of Guanyin (Goddess of Mercy), and Eagle Pavilion, which provides a panoramic view of the resort. Shanhaiguan Pass, about 20 miles from Beidaihe, was the most important mountain pass at the eastern end of the Great Wall, which had been erected to defend China from invaders. Shanhaiguan Pass was originally constructed in 1381, and for many centuries it was the control point for traffic between northern and northeastern China. See also BO HAI GULF; BOXER REBELLION; GREAT WALL; HEBEI PROVINCE; JIANG QING; RAILROADS.

BEIHAI PARK (Beihai Gongyuan or Pei-hai Kung-yuan; North Lake Park) A beautiful park in the capital city of Beijing that was the site of pleasure palaces for emperors of the Liao, Jin, Yuan, Ming and Qing dynasties. Beihai Park remains much as it was during the time of the Qian-long emperor (r. 1736–95). Opened to the public in 1915, the park was extensively restored in 1951 and is a popular recreation area, with boating in the summer and ice skating in the winter. An imperial residence was built on this site in the 10th century during the Liao dynasty (947–1125). In the 12th century, rulers of the Jin dynasty (1115–1234) dug the Lake of the Western Flower (Xihua Tan) and formed the dirt into hills and islands. They also erected Gonghan Palace and various pavilions. Khubilai Khan, the first emperor of the Mongol Yuan dynasty (1279–1368), enhanced the park with a magnificent design that impressed the European explorer Marco Polo. During the Ming dynasty (1368–1644), the lake was divided into Beihai and Zhonghai Lakes, and various buildings were constructed that remain today.

Beihai Park's design is based on a legend about a deep place to the east where all the rivers and oceans ran and disappeared, and where there were three islands known as Penglai (the mythical paradise of the Daoist religion) where the immortals live. The park is enclosed by a wall with three gates at the east, south and north. In the southern section lies the Round City (Tuancheng), which was the center of Dadu, as the old capital of the Yuan dynasty was known. The most important building there is the Hall of Receiving Light (Chengguang Dian), containing a 15-foot-high white jade statue of Buddha. In the courtyard there is a jade basin two feet high and five feet in diameter, which was used by Khubilai Khan to serve wine at ceremonial banquets. The front gate, the Gate of Received Light (Chengguangmen), leads to the triple-arched Bridge of Everlasting Peace (Yong'an Qiao, built 1331) that connects the circular wall with Qionghua Island in Lake Beihai. This is one of two bridges connecting the island to the mainland. Located on the island's south side, it has an ornamental gate at each end and was built in the Yuan dynasty. Steps from the bridge lead to the Temple of Eternal Peace (Yong'an Si), built in 1651. The second bridge, on the island's last side, is called Zhishan Qiao.

On the island are many bridges and buildings decorated with colorful glazed tiles. At the center is the 119-foot-high White Dagoba Temple, built A.D. 1651 on the ruins of the original Palace of the Moon (Guangjan). Many of the stones around Qionghua Island were supposedly brought by Jin rulers from Suzhou, where they had been taken from Lake Taihu in Bianling (Kaifeng), the capital of the Northern Song dynasty (960–1127). South of the Dagoba the Pavilion of the Benevolent Voice (Shanyin Dian) provides a magnificent view of Central and South Lakes, Jingshan Park, the Imperial Palace, Tiananmen Square, Chairman Mao Zedong Memorial Hall and Qianmen Gate. Behind the pavilion is the 114-foot-high White Pagoda (Baita), built in 1651 in the Tibetan Buddhist style when the Dalai Lama visited Beijing. A path leading north through artificial caves leads to Yilan Tang, a richly painted covered walkway that runs along the north shore of the island, where Fan Shang Restaurant serves imperial court cuisine. Southwest of the island is the fan-shaped Chamber of Reading the Classics (Yuegu Lou), housing a collection of 495 tablets engraved with inscriptions by famous poets and calligraphers. There are several other buildings and the opened Botanical Garden, whose grounds were formerly part of the Ten Thousand Buddha Tower complex (Wanfo Lo). The famous Nine Dragon Screen (Jiulong Bi), built in 1417 as part of Khubilai Khan's original palace, is a 87-foot-long wall that is more than 15 feet high and decorated with glazed tiles depicting nine dragons chasing a pearl in clouds above the waves. See also BEIJING; JIN DYNASTY; KHUBILAI KHAN; LIAO DYNASTY; PAGODA; POLO, MARCO; QIANLONG, EMPEROR.

BEIJING   Formerly known as Peking, Peiping and Beiping; a city in northern China that served as the capital of several imperial dynasties and is the political and cultural capital of the People's Republic of China (PRC), founded in 1949 by the Chinese Communist Party (CCP). The name *Beijing* means "Northern Capital." Beijing, with a population of about 9 million, lies within Hebei Province, but it is an autonomous administrative municipality. In 1982 the total area of the municipality was increased to more than 11,000 square miles, including 10 city districts and 9 surrounding counties. The city of Tianjin about 60 miles to the southeast serves as the port city for Beijing, connected to the Bo Hai Gulf by the Yongding River. The Yan Mountains (Yanshan) lie to the northeast, and the vast Mongolian plateau begins to the northwest. The Great Wall, originally built to protect China from nomadic invaders, lies north and northeast of Beijing. The Taijang Mountains lie to the west, and the vast North China Plain to the south. The large quantities of dust that blow into the city from the Gobi Desert to the northwest are known as "yellow wind."

The Beijing region was the home of the prehistoric ancestors of the Chinese people. The fossil remains and tools of so-called Peking (Beijing) Man, a prehistoric human who lived about 700,000 years ago, were discovered at Zhoukoudian (Chou-kou-tien) in the southwestern part of modern Beijing. A city called Youdou stood on the site of Beijing about 4,000 years ago. It was succeeded by a city called Ji, situated where all land and water routes converged on northern China, which became the capital of the state of Yan during the Western Zhou dynasty (1100–256 B.C.). When the first emperor unified China under the Qin dynasty (221–207 B.C.), Ji was the administrative center of one of the 36 prefectures of the empire. From the Qin through the Jin dynasties (221 B.C.–A.D. 420), Ji served as the commercial and cultural center for ethnic groups inhabiting northern China. When the Grand Canal was opened during the Sui dynasty, the emperor Yangdi (r. 604–618) sailed to Ji on the Grand Canal and raised a large army to wage campaigns in northeastern China. Emperor Taizong (r. 626–49) of the Tang dynasty marched his troops through Jin when he invaded Korea in 645 and constructed Minzhong Temple (now called Fayuan Temple) there to commemorate Chinese soldiers who died in the campaign.

Ji served as the secondary capital of the Khitan (Qidan) Liao (947–1125) and the Jurchen Jin (1115–1234) dynasties. The Jin renamed the city Zhongdu (Central Capital) and rebuilt it on the model of Kaifeng, the capital of the Northern Song dynasty (960–1127), which they had conquered, with palaces and pleasure gardens. In 1215 the Mongols attacked Zhongdu and burned down the palaces except for Daning outside the city. In 1260 Khubilai Khan, the Mongol founder of the Yuan dynasty (1279–1368), moved to Daning Palace in Zhongdu. With the help of a hydraulic engineer named Guo Shuojing, Khubilai Khan harnessed the rivers and canals and rebuilt the capital as Khanbaliq (Cambaluc; known in Chinese as Dadu or Tatu, or "Great Capital"). Work was begun in 1267 and completed in 1293, by which time a half-million people resided in the capital. The greater city was enclosed by a wall with 11 gates and was 40 miles in circumference. Nine transverse and nine perpendicular streets formed a grid that divided the city's residential area into 50 neighborhoods (*fangs*). Among other projects, Guo built the Tonghui Canal linking Tongxian, the northern terminus of the Grand Canal, with Jishuitan, which enabled barges carrying grain and other goods from southern China to sail into Dadu. The city developed many markets and became the largest trading center in the world at the time. Since the Yuan dynasty, most residents of Beijing have lived in courtyard houses along small winding alleys, known by the Mongol term *hutong*, although these are now slowly being replaced by high-rise apartment buildings.

Emperor Hongwu, who overthrew the Yuan and founded the Ming dynasty (1368–1644), captured the city in 1368, destroyed the magnificent Yuan palaces and renamed the city Beiping (Northern Peace). However, he made his capital at Nanjing. In 1403 Zhudi usurped the throne, reigning as the Yongle emperor (r. 1403–24), renamed the city Beijing (Northern Capital) and made it his secondary capital. In 1421 he moved his court from Nanjing to Beijing and began a massive rebuilding of the city. This was the only time in

Chinese history that the imperial capital was moved from south to north. During the Ming dynasty, Beijing comprised the outer city, the imperial city, and the Forbidden City, each area surrounded by a wall. The Forbidden City contained an immense complex of beautiful palace buildings; these are now open to the public and are one of the most famous tourist attractions in China. The city plan was designed on a straight line that passed from Zhengyangmen or Qianmen (Front Gate) in the south to the Bell and Drum towers in the north, dividing the outer, imperial and Forbidden cities into equal halves. The imperial throne in Taihe Hall, seat of the ruling dynasty, was situated on this central axis. When the outer city was expanded, the line was extended from Qianmen to Yongdingmen (Gate of Eternal Pacification) for a total length of five miles. The materials and workmen for rebuilding Beijing were transported to the city on the Grand Canal. Tribute grain was shipped to the capital by the canal, totaling as much as 200,000 tons annually, and was kept in 56 storehouses in Beijing.

When the Manchus overthrew the Ming in 1644 and founded the Qing dynasty (1644–1911), they made Beijing their capital but changed the city very little. Qing emperors Kangxi and Qianlong constructed a vast complex of imperial gardens on the western outskirts of Beijing, the most famous of which were the Yuanmingyan Gardens. In 1751, to celebrate his mother's auspicious 60th birthday, Qing emperor Qianlong ordered the construction of Qingyiyuan (Park of Clear Ripples), had Wengshan renamed Wanshoushan (Hill of Longevity) and rebuilt Kunming Lake to resemble West Lake in Hangzhou, capital of the Southern Song dynasty (1127–1279). The Qing also built the Yonghegong (Palace of Harmony and Peace) Buddhist monastery and the Temple of Heaven, where the emperors went to offer ritual sacrifices to Heaven.

The Grand Canal, which had been the main supply line to Beijing for nearly a thousand years, silted up and fell into disrepair after the Yellow River (Huanghe) changed its course in 1855. During the 19th century, foreign powers pressured the Qing to open Chinese cities to foreign trade, known as treaty ports. In 1900 the antiforeign Boxer Uprising, assisted by Qing troops, opened fire on the foreign legations in Beijing. Telegraph lines were cut and Beijing was isolated. A combined force of eight foreign powers invaded Beijing, causing the Qing emperor and empress dowager to flee the capital, and burned down the centuries-old Summer Palace (which had been rebuilt by Empress Dowager Cixi [Tz'u Hsi] in 1888 with money that should have gone to the Chinese navy). The Summer Palace, restored after 1949, is today one of Beijing's most popular tourist attractions and resort areas. In 1901 the foreign powers forced the Qing to sign the International Protocol, which, among other things, permitted foreigners to establish embassies, military commands and banks in Beijing.

In 1911, Chinese revolutionaries led by Dr. Sun Yat-sen overthrew the Qing, and on January 1, 1912, Sun was inaugurated as the provisional president of the new Republic of China in Nanjing, where the capital was moved after the last Qing emperor formally abdicated and became known as Henry Puyi. However, three weeks later Sun had to yield the presidency to Yuan Shikai (Yuan Shih-k'ai), who kept the government in Beijing, where it remained until 1926. On May 4, 1919, students from prestigious Beijing University and other universities in the city protested the awarding of the former German concessions in the Chinese province of Shandong to Japan. The May Fourth Movement, as it became known, spread throughout China and inspired Chinese revolutionaries to organize the country against foreign imperialism. China became divided among a number of warlords, and Beijing was threatened after the Japanese invaded Manchuria (northeastern China) and established their puppet state of Manchukuo. In 1937 Japanese and Chinese troops clashed at the Marco Polo Bridge in southwestern Beijing, and China began fighting its War of Resistance against Japan (1937–1945). Formally known as the Lugou Bridge, the bridge had been built during the Jin dynasty and decorated with 485 stone lions. It became known as the Marco Polo Bridge because the famous Italian traveler had mentioned it in his book in the 14th century.

After Japan was defeated in 1945, the Chinese Communists led by Mao Zedong (Mao Tse-tung) and the Nationalists (Kuomintang; KMT) led by Chiang Kai-shek resumed their civil war. In 1949 the CCP defeated the KMT, and on October 1, 1949, Mao stood on the balcony above the Gate of Heavenly Peace, leading to the Forbidden City, in Tiananmen Square in Beijing and proclaimed the founding of the PRC.

Many CCP leaders reside in Zhongnanhai Compound to the west of the Forbidden City, built in the 10th–13th centuries as a resort area for Chinese emperors. The immense Tiananmen Square is the center of modern Beijing, and the Communists have erected several monumental buildings there, including the Great Hall of the People and the Mao Zedong Mausoleum. During the Cultural Revolution (1966–76), Tiananmen Square was the site of massive Communist rallies. During the 1989 pro-democracy movement that was televised around the world, students held the square for two months until CCP leaders declared martial law in the city and ordered the brutal military suppression of the demonstrators.

Some other well-known sites in Beijing include the History Museum and Museum of the Revolution, Military Museum, Natural History Museum, National Library of China, and Capital Museum and Library; the Soong Ching Ling Museum, the residence of the widow of Sun Yat-sen, who became the most prominent woman in modern China; and two museums honoring modern Chinese authors Lu Xun (Lu Hsun) and Xu Beihong (Hsu Pei-hung). Performances of the Beijing Opera are also popular. Jingshan Park and Beihai Park are popular recreation areas, along with many smaller parks. Tiantan Park contains the Ming Temple of Heaven, which has become the symbol of Beijing. Chinese emperors once offered ritual sacrifices to Heaven on the circular altar, but now the temple is open to tourists. The Beijing Zoo is very popular, especially for its pandas. Many temples are open to the public, notably the Lama Temple, the most famous Tibetan Buddhist temple in China. The Confucius Temple is the largest Confucian temple in China outside Qufu, the home of Confucius, and adjoins the Imperial College, which contains a "forest" of stone tablets engraved with the names of scholars who passed the difficult examinations for the imperial bureaucracy. The largest bronze bell in China can be seen at the Great Bell Temple, and many other temples can be visited. The Ancient Observatory can be seen on a watchtower on the old city wall. It was built in the 15th century to help imperial astrologers draw up their charts and to assist the navigation of ships.

Most tourists to Beijing make day-trips out of the city to visit the Ming Tombs and the Great Wall. A section of the wall has been restored at Badaling, about 25 miles north of the city. The Ming Tombs are the burial site of Ming emperors. The tombs of Qing emperors can also be visited at the Western Qing Tombs and Eastern Qing Tombs. The resort area of Western Hills lies close to the Summer Palace. Fragrant Hills Park, the part of the Western Hills closest to Beijing, is the final stop for city buses. Nearby are the Azure Clouds Temple, Temple of the Sleeping Buddha, the Eight Great Temples (known as Badachu) and Xiangshan Botanical Gardens. See also ALLEYS; ASTRONOMY AND OBSERVATORIES; BEIHAI PARK; BEIJING UNIVERSITY; BELLS AND CHIMES; BO HAI GULF; BOXER UPRISING; CIVIL WAR BETWEEN COMMUNISTS AND NATIONALISTS; CIXI, EMPRESS DOWAGER; CONFUCIANISM; FORBIDDEN CITY; GRAND CANAL; GREAT HALL OF THE PEOPLE; GREAT WALL; IMPERIAL EXAMINATION SYSTEM; KHUBILAI KHAN; LU XUN; MAO ZEDONG; POLO MARCO POLO BRIDGE INCIDENT; MAY FOURTH MOVEMENT OF 1919; MING TOMBS; NATIONAL LIBRARY OF CHINA; PANDA; PEKING MAN; PEOPLE'S REPUBLIC OF CHINA; POLO, MARCO; PUYI, HENRY; SOONG QINGLING; STONE TABLETS; SUMMER PALACE; TEMPLES; TIANANMEN SQUARE; TIANANMEN SQUARE MASSACRE; TIANJIN; WAR OF RESISTANCE AGAINST JAPAN; XU BEIHONG; YUAN SHIKAI; ZHONGNANHAI COMPOUND; NAMES OF INDIVIDUAL DYNASTIES.

BEIJING CONFERENCE See UNITED NATIONS FOURTH WORLD CONFERENCE ON WOMEN.

BEIJING (PEKING), CONVENTION OF (1860) A treaty signed between China and Great Britain after the British won the Arrow War (1856–60; Second Opium War). In 1857 the British seized the southern Chinese port city of Guangzhou (Canton) and moved north, taking the strategic Dagu forts in 1858 and threatening Tianjin and Beijing, the capital city. The Qing dynasty (1644–1911) government gave in to British demands and signed the Treaty of Tianjin (1858), which imposed harsh measures on the Chinese. However, the Qing rulers did not want to follow the demands of the treaty, especially the clause allowing ambassadors of foreign nations to live in Beijing. The Qing told the British they would negotiate with them in Shanghai. The British attempted to travel to Beijing to negotiate there, but the Qing had a blockade set up and defeated the British fleet. In 1860 the British sent another mission to Beijing to negotiate with the Qing, who arrested the negotiators and even executed some of them. Lord Elgin led British troops into Tianjin and Beijing, where they burned down the beautiful Summer Palace—although they did not harm the Forbidden City and the Imperial Palace. The emperor had fled to Manchuria (northeastern China) and appointed Prince Gong, his younger brother, to negotiate with the British. Prince Gong agreed to obey the terms of the 1858 Treaty of Tianjin. The British also forced him to sign a Convention of Beijing expressing the "deep regret" of the emperor for attacking the representatives of the British queen. The Convention also

required China to pay a large financial indemnity to Britain, gave permission for Chinese to emigrate on British ships, made Tianjin a treaty port, and ceded the southernmost area of the Kowloon peninsula to Hong Kong, a British Crown Colony. Upon receiving these benefits, the British then supported the Qing, which was seriously threatened by the Taiping Rebellion (1850–64), because they preferred to work with a government that had already given them many concessions rather than having to begin all over again with a new regime. See also ARROW WAR; BEIJING; HONG KONG; KOWLOON; SUMMER PALACE; TAIPING REBELLION; TIANJIN; TIANJIN, TREATY OF; TREATY PORTS.

BEIJING OPERA See OPERA, BEIJING.

BEIJING RESEARCH ACADEMY (BEIJING RESEARCH LABORATORY) See ACADEMIA SINICA; CHINESE ACADEMY OF SCIENCES.

BEIJING UNIVERSITY (Beijing Daxue or Pei-ching Tahsueh; byname Beida or Pei-ta) Formerly known as Peking University; the most prestigious university in China. Located in the capital city of Beijing, the university was founded in 1898 as Yanjing University and was administered by the United States. In 1953, after the founding of the Communist People's Republic of China in 1949, the university, now administered by China and known as Beijing University, moved to its present location. In 1959 it took over the humanities and social studies departments of Qinghua (Tsinghua) University and was reorganized. The Beijing University Library is one of China's greatest university libraries. By the mid-1980s it contained more than 3 million volumes, one-fourth of them in foreign languages. Tuition, books, equipment and medical care at the university are free, and the students, who live in dormitories, receive a government stipend for meals.

Beijing University has played a prominent role in modern Chinese political movements. The May Fourth Movement of 1919, protesting the secret agreement between the Chinese and Japanese governments to award the Chinese province of Shandong to Japan, began as a demonstration by students from Beijing University. Mao Zedong (Mao Tse-tung; 1893–1976), the founder of the People's Republic of China, was then a librarian at Beijing University and became active in the May Fourth Movement. Chancellor Cai Yuanpei (T'sai Yaun-p'ei) brought prominent scholars to the university, including Chen Duxiu (Ch'en Tu-hsiu), who served as dean of letters. Chen also published the influential journal *La Jeunesse* (New Youth). By the mid-1960s Beijing University had 4,300 faculty members and 10,000 students. The Cultural Revolution (1966–76) began on May 25, 1966, when members of the philosophy department at Beijing University put up a "big-character poster" (*dazibao*) criticizing the university's president for suppressing debate on literary compositions by the writer Wu Han (which were actually an attack on the policies of Mao Zedong). Initially the university president was dismissed and Beijing's Communist Party Committee was reorganized, but the debate rapidly spread to schools and universities throughout China. On August 8, 1966, the Communist Central Committee called for a revolutionary movement for the study and application of Mao's works by all Chinese, and within a few months the entire Chinese education system was shut down. Groups of students known as Red Guards traveled around the country, leading the movement to "destroy the old and establish the new." Beijing University closed for three years but was reopened in 1970 with a new curriculum that emphasized practical experience and physical labor. To gain admission, potential students had to have two years' experience working on a farm or in a factory as well as the recommendations of their coworkers, and they had to pass an entrance examination, which could be waived if they had several years of work experience.

After the Cultural Revolution, China's education system had to be restored. Beijing University once again emphasized scholarly research and admitted students who had completed secondary school with high grades. In 1978, a standardized national entrance examination for admission to universities was given to Chinese students for the first time since the Cultural Revolution. Students at Beijing University also played an important part in the antigovernment demonstrations that filled Tiananmen Square in 1989, which ended with the massacre of hundreds—perhaps thousands—of people. Thousands of other students and workers were imprisoned, and some students fled the country. Police also cordoned off the university district in northwestern Beijing. Since then, the beautiful campus of Beijing University has been closed to the public to keep out foreign influences, and the students are kept under close watch. See also BIG-CHARACTER POSTERS; CHEN DUXIU; CULTURAL REVOLUTION; EDUCATION SYSTEM; LI DAZHAO; MAO ZEDONG; MAY FOURTH MOVEMENT; TIANANMEN SQUARE MASSACRE.

BEILING (NORTHERN IMPERIAL TOMB) See ABAHAI; SHENYANG.

BEIYANG ARMY See YUAN SHIKAI.

BEIYANG NAVAL FLEET See QING DYNASTY; SINO-JAPANESE WAR OF 1894–95.

BELLS AND CHIMES Musical instruments made from metal or stone that when struck on the outside with wooden mallets or sticks produce musical sounds. The Chinese classify bells, which are hung on wooden frames, as one of the eight types of musical instruments and associate them with the element of metal in traditional Chinese cosmology. The stone-chime (lithophone), made from pieces of stone or jade tied to a frame and struck similarly to bells, is another of the eight types of instruments and is associated with stone. Bells have been played since ancient times in China. The Chinese made the first bronze bells in the world, and used them to perform ceremonial music, especially during the Shang Dynasty (1750–1040 B.C.) and Zhou dynasty (1100–256 B.C.). Chinese bronze bells are the only instruments in the world dating from the Bronze Age that can still be played. Chinese bronze bells that date back to the 14th century B.C. or even earlier have been excavated. Scholars have attempted to reconstruct the sound of these bells and chimes and the conceptual theory behind the sounds they produce.

The manufacture of ancient Chinese bells by casting an alloy of metals was an amazing technological achievement. Bells were developed from metal scoops used to measure grain and evolved into two forms of hand bell: the *to*, which faces upwards, and the *chung*, which faces downwards. The Chinese used the musical pitches of the *chung* to draw up their entire system of measurements for length, width, weight and volume. Government authorities kept order in a state by regulating the pitches of the bells. Chimes developed from sets of pottery bells that were used as early as the Neolithic period (c. 12,000–2000 B.C.) and have been excavated at a Longshan Culture site in Shaanxi Province. The Chinese turned to bronze and other metals for making bells because the metals were stronger than pottery and also gave the bells a more exact pitch. In ancient China, a set of bells or chimes symbolized the status, wealth and power of the owner, who was usually the lord of a feudal state. The set of bells was played on important occasions such as religious rituals and official banquets, and singing and dancing were were also performed to the music. The technology for producing the bells and chimes developed over the centuries, giving the instruments a wider range and a purer sound. Large bells that produced a deeper tone were also produced and hung individually.

Large bells hung in Buddhist and Confucian temples are struck with long wooden poles to announce the periods for religious rituals. China's largest bronze bell hangs in a bell tower in the Juesheng (Chueh-sheng) Buddhist Temple, also known as the Great Bell Temple, in the northern part of Beijing. It measures 18 feet high and 14.4 feet across at the mouth and weighs 63 tons. The bell was made to commemorate the military men who died in northern campaigns during the reign of Ming emperor Yongle (Yung-lo; r. 1403–24). Seventeen Buddhist sutras (scriptures) in the hand of Ming calligrapher Shen Du (Shen Tu) were cast on the inner and outer surfaces of the bell. The characters are still legible and the bell is free of rust. When struck, its deep musical sound can be heard more than 15 miles away. Buddhist and Daoist priests also ring a small brass handbell with a clapper when they perform rituals.

In 1953 archaeologists discovered a set of three bells from the Shang dynasty at the Yin Ruins in Henan Province. Bronze bells were discovered in the area of the mausoleum of Qin Shi Huangdi (r. 221–210 B.C.), China's first emperor, when his tomb was excavated in the 1970s. In 1978, an archaeological dig in Suixian County in Hubei Province excavated the tomb of Marquis Yi of the state of Zeng. He was a nobleman in the fifth century B.C. who was a contemporary of Confucius, and his tomb was built in 433 B.C. One of the treasures excavated was a perfectly preserved collection of more than 120 musical instruments, most of them still able to be played. Also discovered in the tomb was a set of 65 large bells, known as *zhong (chung)*, weighing a total of four and a half tons, suspended from a three-tiered lacquered wooden frame and tuned to a chromatic 12-tone scale. Each bell can produce two distinct pitches, about one-third of a scale interval apart, and the set has a range of five octaves. The smallest bell weighs 5 pounds and is 8 inches high, and the largest weighs 449 pounds and is 61 inches high. As many as five musicians played the set of bells by striking them on the outside with a hammer. A bell sounds one note if struck in the center and another note if struck to one side. Each bell is inscribed with a long passage detailing what notes it plays and how they fit into a musical scale, and how that scale relates to other scales used for sets of bells in other feudal states at that time. Also excavated from the tomb was a large bell weighing 5,500 pounds.

The Hubei Song and Dance Ensemble, a famous troupe led by a woman named Jiang Guiyang (Chiang Kuei-yang) that performs the folk music and dance of Hubei Province, constructed reproductions of the bronze bells from the tomb of the Marqui of Yi. The troupe studied ancient texts to help re-create the music that was played on these instruments in ancient China and also created dances based on the configurations of ideograms used in ancient poetry, and on artifacts discovered in the dig. The Hubei have performed their re-creation of ancient Chinese music, singing and dancing in a show called the "Imperial Bells in China" in 20 cities across China. In 1989 the troupe toured the United States with this show. See also BRONZEWARE; MUSIC AND DANCE, CEREMONIAL; QIN SHI HUANGDI; SHANG DYNASTY; TEMPLES; ZHOU DYNASTY.

BENEVOLENT ASSOCIATIONS See SIX COMPANIES, CHINESE.

BETHUNE, NORMAN (1890–1939)   A Canadian doctor who went to China and became famous for organizing medical services for the Eighth Route Army of the Chinese Communist Party (CCP), later known as the People's Liberation Army (PLA). He died and was buried in China. Bethune was born in Gravenhurst, Ontario. Following the profession of his grandfather, Bethune trained to become a surgeon. While studying medicine in Toronto, Bethune interrupted his studies from 1911 to 1912 to serve as a laborer-teacher at Frontier College and in 1915 to serve as a stretcher-bearer in World War I in Europe. When he finished medical school he joined the British Royal Navy. After his period of service he took postgraduate medical training in Britain and then entered private practice in Detroit, Michigan. In 1926 Bethune learned that he had contracted pulmonary tuberculosis. His illness influenced him to help other victims of the disease and to practice thoracic surgery, first at the Royal Victoria Hospital in Montreal and then at the Hospital du Sacré-Coeur in Cartierville, Québec. From 1929 to 1936 Bethune invented or redesigned 12 medical and surgical instruments and published 14 articles on thoracic surgical techniques he had invented. He realized that patients often contracted tuberculosis because of poor socioeconomic conditions, and he worked hard to bring about reforms in Canadian health care and medical services.

Bethune visited the U.S.S.R. in 1935 and decided to join the Communist Party. In 1936 he joined the republican cause in the Civil War in Spain, where he organized the first mobile blood-transfusion service, which served a battlefront more than 600 miles long. The next year he returned to Canada to raise money for the Spanish antifascists and became aware of the Chinese Communist resistance to the Japanese troops who had invaded China (War of Resistance against Japan; 1937–45). He maintained that "Spain and China are part of the same battle." In 1938 Bethune traveled to China, where he joined the Communist Eighth Route Army in the region along the border between Shanxi and Hebei Provinces in northern China. He worked ceaselessly to treat wounded soldiers and educate the Chinese about med-

ical practices. In 1939 Bethune accidentally died from septicemia (blood poisoning) and was buried in Shijiazhuang, capital of Hebei, where the hospital that he founded has been named for him. His tomb can still be visited.

CCP leader Mao Zedong (Mao Tse-tung) commemorated Bethune with an essay, "In Memory of Norman Bethune," which challenged all Communists to follow Bethune's selfless example and devote themselves to helping other people. Mao's essay was one of three articles that the CCP required all Chinese to read during the Cultural Revolution (1966–76), and it caused the Chinese people to define Canada in terms of Bethune's personal sacrifice. In 1988 Canadian actor Donald Sutherland starred as Norman Bethune in the film *Norman Bethune: The Making of a Hero*. The film was coproduced by the August First Film Studio, which is connected with the Chinese People's Liberation Army, and Canadian and French companies. See also CHINESE COMMUNIST PARTY; EIGHTH ROUTE ARMY; HEBEI PROVINCE; PEOPLE'S LIBERATION ARMY; WAR OF RESISTANCE AGAINST JAPAN.

BHUTAN See HIMALAYA MOUNTAIN RANGE: SINO-INDIAN BORDER DISPUTE; TIBET.

BI (brush) See CALLIGRAPHY; FOUR TREASURES OF THE STUDY; PAINTING; WRITING SYSTEM, CHINESE.

BI (*pi*)   A flat, round jade disk with a circular opening in the center that is about one-third the size of the whole ring. A *bi* symbolized Heaven (*tian* or *t'ien*) and was also the insignia for princes and nobles of the fourth and fifth ranks in the imperial court. Some scholars believe that the *bi* represented the sun because its shape is the same as the ancient Chinese character for the word "sun." The *bi* was used in ritual sacrifices by the emperor, who was called the "Son of Heaven," and could be given as a gift by him. It was used from ancient times through the Qing, China's last imperial dynasty (1644–1911). The *bi* is often paired with the *zong* (*tsung*), a ring or tubular container which is square on the outside and symbolizes the earth.

The surface of a *bi* is usually decorated, commonly with raised or engraved spirals forming a "grain pattern." Other motifs include dragons (symbolic of the emperor), tigers, birds and fish. The Chinese have always revered jade because it is a very hard, smooth stone and its colors are pure and beautiful, ranging from white to light through dark green, blue, yellow, brown, purple, gray and black. The Chinese word for jade, *yu*, means "a stone that is beautiful." In ancient China white jade was reserved for the emperor. See also DRAGON; EMPEROR; HEAVEN; JADE; TIGER.

BIANFU See BAT.

BICYCLE (*zixingche* or *tzu-hsing-ch'e*)   A two-wheeled vehicle that is the primary means of transportation for millions of Chinese. The bicycle was introduced into China around 1891 by two American world travelers named Allen and Sachtleben, who wrote a book about their journey, *Across Asia on a Bicycle*. The Qing dynasty (1644–1911) court enjoyed the new invention, and Emperor Xuantong (r. 1909–12), the last Qing emperor, who became known as Puyi, rode a bicycle around the Forbidden City in Beijing.

Introduced to China in 1891, the bicycle has become the primary mode of transportation for millions of Chinese. S.E. MEYER

Today it is estimated that there are 370 million bicycles in China, about 7 million in Beijing alone. Most are single-speed with hand brakes. Some Chinese drive tricycles that have a two-wheeled wooden platform on the back for transporting large objects—even couches or refrigerators.

The owner of a bicycle has to have it inspected, similar to the way automobiles are inspected in the United States, and has to acquire a license. Some Chinese cities even issue license plates for bicycles. Bicycle riders who have accidents or ride while under the influence of alcohol can be fined and have their bicycles impounded. Repeat offenders are required to attend "reeduction classes."

China's 600 bicycle factories produce 41 million bicycles per year, making it one of the world's leading bicycle manufacturers. Some are exported but most are purchased by the Chinese. Major brands include Phoenix, Flying Pigeon and Forever. It is true that cars are becoming more popular and cities have bus systems, but bicycles are usually faster and more convenient in China's increasingly congested traffic. Chinese cities have bicycle parking lots guarded by attendants.

BIG-CHARACTER POSTERS (*dazibao*) Also known as "large-character announcements"; large posters hung on walls and billboards in parks, schools, factories and other public places as a means for communicating ideas among the general population. The posters, often written anonymously and by hand by Chinese government officials, stimulate public discussion on timely issues. The posters and the debates they engender also enable the Chinese government to learn what the Chinese people think about their topics of concern. The posters became widespread during the Cultural Revolution (1966–76), which is considered to have begun when members of the philosophy department at Beijing University hung a big-character poster that criticized the university president for suppressing a debate about a play performed in Beijing in 1966. The play was a veiled attack on Mao Zedong's government. Mao responded by hanging his own poster encouraging the "great cultural revolution of the proletariat." The political debate spread like wildfire throughout China. Mao encouraged students to criticize feudalism, and in a short time the country's entire educational system was closed down. The Cultural Revolution ended when Mao died in 1976 and his widow, Jiang Qing, and three others of her closest associates were accused of being the "Gang of Four" who had masterminded the revolution. Big-character posters played an important role during the Cultural Revolution, as well as in the subsequent denunciation of the Gang of Four. These posters have continued to be very popular with the Chinese people, who enjoy debating current events in public places. See also CULTURAL REVOLUTION.

BIG WILD GOOSE PAGODA See BUDDHISM; PAGODA; XI'AN; XUANZANG.

BI-HSI See TORTOISE.

BING XIN (Ping Hsin; 1900–)   A female author whose short stories and poems were very popular in China in the early 1920s; real name Xie Wanying (Hsieh Wan-ying). Bing Xin was born in Fujian Province. She was educated in the Chinese classics and began writing stories as a young girl. She converted to Christianity and went to an American school in Beijing, and her stories began to reflect the Western influences she had acquired. While attending Yenching University in Beijing, she published her first work, *Two Families*, when she was only 19. She published many more short stories and lyrical poems about nature and childhood that brought her great fame. In 1923 Bing published *Letters to My Young Readers*, the first in a series that would give her an international reputation. She won a grant to study at Wellesley College in the United States, where she received an M.A. in 1926. That same year she returned to China, where she married Wu Wenzao (Wu Wen-tsao), a Chinese man she had met in the United States. She also published a collection of 29 articles for young readers, which became a best-seller; it was reprinted 20 times by 1935.

Bing continued to write short stories and poems for several decades. Starting in 1951, she published four more collections of *Letters to Young Readers*. Her most famous works include *More Letters to Young Readers, About Women, T'ao Ch'i's Summer Schedule* and *Miscellaneous Essays*, a collection of essays she wrote between 1959 and 1964. After this period she did not write very much, but she became active in cultural affairs, especially children's literature, for the Chinese Communist government. In 1980 Bing won the Chinese national short story award. Her books are still beloved by young people and used as educational materials in schools in the People's Republic of China, the Republic of China (Taiwan), Hong Kong and for overseas Chinese in Southeast Asia.

BINZANG See FUNERALS.

BIOGAS See ENERGY SOURCES.

BIRD-AND-FLOWER PAINTING (*huaniaohua*)   A category of traditional Chinese painting in which the subjects depicted are birds and flowers. This category combines two broader categories of Chinese painting: birds and animals (*chin-shou*) and flowers (*hua-hui*). Flower painting derived from Buddhist banner paintings, which were brightly deco-

Big-character posters, which communicate current issues by the government, have drawn public interest since the Cultural Revolution.
S.E. MEYER

rated with beautiful flowers. The banners were brought from India and Central Asia after the Buddhist religion was introduced into China from India (circa first century A.D.). Buddhist flower painting became very popular in China during the Tang dynasty (618–907). By the 10th century flower painting (*huahui*) became a distinct category of Chinese painting due to the techniques for brushstrokes and delicate washes of color devised by the artists Huang Chuan and Xu Xi (Hsu Hsi). The Chinese combined their tradition of painting birds and animals with flower painting to form the genre called bird-and-flower painting. The love of birds and flowers also relates to the native Chinese philosophy of Daoism (Taoism), which emphasizes harmony with nature. Another reason that birds and flowers became a specific category is that the parts of birds, such as beaks, claws and feathers, and of flowers, such as petals, leaves and stems, can be painted with the same brushstrokes that are used for writing Chinese characters in calligraphy, which the Chinese consider one of the highest art forms. Certain birds and flowers were often paired, such as river reeds and wild geese or plum blossoms and nightingales. This genre was introduced to Japan, where it culminated in the Kano and Rimpa Schools, around the 14th century. Xu Wei (Hsu Wei; 1521–93) is considered the founder of modern Chinese bird-and-flower painting. See also CALLIGRAPHY.

BIRD ISLAND See QINGHAI, LAKE.

BIRTHDAYS (*shengri* or *sheng-jih*)   A Chinese traditional belief that every person turns one year older on the New Year in the lunar calendar (usually in early February); thus, that day is regarded as everyone's birthday. In China, male children were once preferred (and often still are) and the birth of a son was celebrated with a large banquet for family and friends. Since the infant mortality rate was high and many babies died during the first month of life, a family was happy and grateful if their baby son reached one month of age. To celebrate, the family would give friends and relatives hard-boiled eggs with shells dyed red and slices of pickled ginger. Today red eggs are given out for baby girls as well. A child's first birthday—when he or she reaches one year of age—is also the occasion for a happy banquet. As children grew up, they traditionally had to pay respect to their parents on their birthdays by performing kowtows, a sequence of bows in which they prostrate themselves and touch their foreheads to the floor. Carved images of the Eight Immortals of the Daoist religion are placed on tables at birthday parties. In the carved images, the Eight Immortals are accompanied by two children on water buffaloes, who summon the God of Longevity, who brings the peach of immortality. The Immortals, who are believed to dwell on mountain peaks and bring happiness and humor to human beings, in legend dine together at the Peach Festival to honor the Daoist Goddess Xiwangmu, the Royal Lady (or Mother) of the Western Paradise. Anyone who eats a peach from the Heavenly Peach Orchard next to her palace supposedly gains immortal life. Birthdays are especially important for older people, who are traditionally honored in Chinese culture. Older people are celebrated at the New Year and on their actual birthdays with a banquet at which two dishes are served that symbolize longevity, long noodles made from flour and steamed cakes shaped like peaches. Another traditional birth-

day dish is round dumplings with sweet fillings, which represents happiness and unity.

Women and men celebrate certain years according to the theory of yin and yang. Yin is the female principle and even numbers are considered yin, while yang is the male principle and odd numbers are yang. To gain a balance of yin and yang, women usually have large celebrations on their 51st, 61st, 71st and 81st birthdays, while men celebrate their 50th, 60th, 70th and 80th birthdays. The 60th birthday is also important for men and women because the celebrant has completed the 60-year cycle based on the traditional 12-year animal zodiac and the so-called Five Material Agents. Every year is assigned an animal, such as a tiger or horse, and every person born in that year is considered to share the qualities of that animal. Each cycle of 12 years is assigned one of the five agents or material elements: earth, wood, metal, fire, and water. The five 12-year cycles total 60 years. See also DAOISM; EIGHT IMMORTALS; FIVE MATERIAL AGENTS; KOWTOW; NOODLES; PEACH; XIWANGMU; ZODIAC, ANIMAL.

BITTER WINDS   See WU, HARRY.

BIXI   See TORTOISE.

BIYAN   See SNUFF BOTTLES.

BLACK POTTERY   See LONGSHAN CULTURE.

BLANC DE CHINE   See DEHUA PORCELAIN.

BLUE-AND-WHITE WARE   One of the major types of porcelain produced in China since the 14th century, which had a great influence on porcelain production in the West during the 17th and 18th centuries. The technique of underglaze painting in cobalt blue and copper red originated during the Tang dynasty (618–907) and was perfected during the Ming dynasty (1368–1644). The process entailed painting designs on an unfired piece of porcelain, applying a thin layer of clear glaze, and then firing the piece in a kiln at a high temperature. Because of the high temperatures required for firing porcelain, only cobalt blue, iron, and copper-oxide pigments could be used to decorate them with underglaze painting.

Chinese collectors originally regarded blue-and-white ware as gaudy and vulgar, but the ware's popularity grew during the reign of Ming emperor Chenghua (r. 1465–88). During the Tang dynasty the Chinese originally imported cobalt blue pigments from Persia (modern Iran), and hence the color was called Mohammedan blue after Mohammed, the founder of Islam. Cobalt deposits were later discovered in China and were also used for decorating porcelain, but the coloring was not as deep and vivid as that produced with imported pigments. The color was used infrequently on Tang three-color ware.

The earliest surviving pieces of Chinese blue-and-white ware date from the Mongol Yuan dynasty (1279–1368), when underglazed blue-and-white ware was produced at the imperial kilns at Jingdezhen (Ching-te-chen). Many of the pieces were large, such as storage jars for wine. By the early Ming dynasty the kilns at Jingdezhen were the largest in the world. When the Manchus overthrew the Ming and established the Qing dynasty (1644–1911), the kilns fell into disrepair. They were restored by Qing emperor Kangxi (K'ang-hsi; r. 1661–1722), a great patron of the arts, and large pieces of blue-and-white porcelain were produced once again.

The Chinese exported great quantities of blue-and-white ware to Southeast Asia, India and the Middle East, with two major collections of Chinese export blue-and-white ware at Teheran, Iran and Istanbul, Turkey. The ware was first exported to Europe in the 17th century, during Kangxi's reign, where it was collected by royalty and sold at high prices. European porcelain producers, such as those at Delft, Majolica and Staffordshire in England, began to produce imitations of Chinese blue-and-white ware. English kilns developed a transfer-printing process which made blue-and-white ware that anyone could afford, and Spode created the blue willow design based on a Chinese legend. Since then, blue-and-white ware has remained the most popular type of ceramic in the world. In the 17th century, Japanese and Korean factories also began producing large quantities of blue-and-white ware for the lucrative porcelain trade, notably at Arita, the center of porcelain production in Japan. See also BRITISH EAST INDIA COMPANY; CHINOISERIE; ENAMELWARE; JINGDEZHEN; PORCELAIN; WILLOW.

BO HAI GULF (Gulf of Chihli)   A large inland sea that is an extension of the Yellow Sea (Huanghai) off the northeastern coast of China. The Bo Hai Gulf forms the eastern boundary of the North China Plain. Shandong Province, a large peninsula, lies between the Bo Hai Gulf and the Yellow Sea. The Liaodong Peninsula, part of Liaoning Province, encloses the Bo Hai Gulf on the north. Between the two peninsulas, the Bo Hai Straits control the entrance to the Yellow Sea. The Yellow River (Huanghe), second-longest in China, empties into the Bo Hai Gulf. The province that comprises the broad alluvial plain curving around the gulf is called Hebei, "north of the Yellow River." Tributaries of the Hai River (Haihe) drain southeast from Beijing into the Bo Hai Gulf. Tianjin, Beijing's port city and a major shipping center, lies on the gulf. The Takang oilfield in the Bo Hai Gulf is one of the areas where offshore exploration and drilling for oil have been concentrated. See also HAI RIVER; HEBEI PROVINCE; LIAONING PROVINCE; SHANDONG PROVINCE; TIANJIN; YELLOW RIVER; YELLOW SEA.

BOARD OF RITES   See MINISTRY OF RITES.

BOATS   See CHINA MERCHANTS STEAM NAVIGATION COMPANY; DRAGON BOAT FESTIVAL; GRAND CANAL; JUNK; SHIPPING AND SHIPBUILDING; YANGZI RIVER; YELLOW RIVER; ZHENG HE.

BODHI   See WISDOM.

BODHIDHARMA   An Indian Buddhist monk credited with introducing the Chan (meditation, from the Indian Sanskrit word *dhyana*) sect of Buddhism into China during the Northern and Southern dynasties (420–589). Chan tradition states that he arrived in China during the reign of Emperor Wu (502–49), founder of the Liang dynasty, and became known there as Damo or Tamo. Chan is known around the world as Zen, the Japanese pronunciation of the term, because this sect was introduced to the West by Japanese Zen thinkers, notably Daisetz Teitaro Suzuki (1870–1966). According to Chan texts, the sect originated with teachings supposedly given by the historical Buddha to one of his disciples and then transmitted directly "from mind to mind," that is, from an enlightened teacher, or patriarch, to his disciple in a series, down to Bodhidharma, who was the 28th Indian patriarch. Several centuries after the Chan sect took hold in China and a lineage of Chinese leaders developed, Bodhidharma became known as the first patriarch of Chan Buddhism in China. Huike (Hui-k'o; 487–593) was the second Chinese patriarch. Sengcan (Seng-Ts'an; d. 606) became the third patriarch, Daoxin (Tao-hsin; 580–636) the fourth and Hongren (Hung-jen; 602–675) the fifth. The school then split into a northern branch, headed by Shenxiu (Shen-hsiu; circa 600–706) and a southern one, headed by Huineng (638–713); each of these patriarchs was regarded by his followers as the legitimate sixth patriarch.

A Chan text called *The Record of the Transmission of the Lamp* (*Jingde Chuandenglu*) recounts that while Bodhidharma was sitting in meditation, a man named Shenguang (Shen-kuang), who was discontented with the Chinese religions of Confucianism and Daoism, came to learn from the Indian Buddhist monk the way to end his suffering and despair. Bodhidharma ignored him, but Shenguang, deep in despair about the meaning of life, kept returning until he finally persuaded the monk of his sincerity and determination. Bodhidharma accepted him as his disciple and gave him the name Huike (Hui-k'o). *The Lankavatara Sutra* (a *sutra* is a Buddhist text), supposedly given by Bodhidharma to Huike, contains the religious philosophy of the Chan Sect. In the text a *bodhisattva* ("wise being") named Mahamati leads a discussion of various topics centered on the concept of self-realization of the ultimate truth (*svapratyamagati* in Sanskrit), termed absolute mind or "mind only" (*cittamatra* in Sanskrit). The basic principles of Chan thought are summarized in a poem attributed to Bodhidharma but actually written during the Tang dynasty (618–907), which claims that Chan is transmitted independently of written scriptures and enables one to see into one's own nature and hence attain Buddhahood.

Chan's emphasis is not on the study of scripture, performance of religious ritual or worship of a deity, but the practice of meditation and other techniques that will bring the religious seeker to the realization of his or her own true nature—the Buddha nature that can be awakened within each person.

Chinese legend states that when Bodhidharma came to China, he stayed at the Songshan Shaolin Temple in the Songshan Mountains in central China. There he supposedly spent nine years sitting cross-legged in meditation facing a wall (*biguan* or *pi-kuan*, or "wall gazing") until his legs withered away. He is credited with teaching the Shaolin monks self-defense techniques that were developed into forms of the martial arts. Even today, practitioners of the martial arts respect Bodhidharma, or Damo, as the founder of these arts, which promote physical health and spiritual cultivation and the "martial virtues" (*wudi*) of discipline, humility, self-restraint and respect for life.

Japanese legend claims that after Bodhidharma completed his work in China, he traveled to Japan and appeared in the form of a beggar at Kataoka Yama near the ancient capital of Nara. Shotoku Taishi (574–622), the imperial regent who devised major reforms that centralized the government, supposedly met Bodhidharma there and exchanged poems with him. In Japan, Bodhidharma is known as Daruma. Many Westerners are familiar with the bright red Japanese Daruma dolls, which are legless, with fierce bearded faces and wide bases. If a Daruma doll is tipped over, it rights itself again, just as a Zen practitioner is able to rebound from adversity. In Japan, when someone wishes to attain a goal—such as a politician seeking to be elected—he or she paints in one of Daruma's eyes, and when the wish is fulfilled the other eye is painted in. Many famous Chan paintings depict the powerful figure of Bodhidharma using only a few deft strokes of black ink. See also BUDDHISM; CHAN SECT OF BUDDHISM; INK PAINTING; SHAOLIN TEMPLE.

BODHISATTVA (*pusa* or *p'u sa*)   "Being of wisdom"; a being who has attained enlightenment, or freedom from suffering, according to the Mahayana ("Greater Vehicle") branch of Buddhism, which was introduced into China from India around the first century A.D. A bodhisattva has taken a vow to help all who suffer attain enlightenment as well. Buddhists originally applied the term *bodhisattva* to the Buddha, the man who founded the Buddhist religion after freeing himself from suffering and hence becoming the Buddha. Throughout the many lives and incarnations he supposedly underwent prior to his final incarnation in India in the sixth century B.C. as Siddhartha Gautama, he used the wisdom he had gained through striving for enlightenment to perform great acts of compassion that helped others overcome their suffering. This combination of compassion and wisdom became the ideal in Mahayana Buddhism, whose thinkers contrasted Mahayana with the earlier form of Buddhism called Hinayana ("Lesser Vehicle"), because it maintained that a person can become enlightened only by renouncing the world and becoming a monk or nun. Mahayanists claimed that the Hinayana position was selfish and egotistical, and they emphasized the ideal of the bodhisattva, who does not renounce the world but remains active in it by helping others attain enlightenment.

As Buddhism developed in China and sects such as Pure Land Buddhism emerged, bodhisattvas were frequently worshiped as deities, with offerings given to their painted or sculpted images in temples. The most popular bodhisattva in China was Guanyin (Kuan-yin) (who in India had been the male deity Avalokiteshvara) who later became worshiped as the female Goddess of Mercy. See also BUDDHA; BUDDHISM; GUANYIN; MAITREYA AND MANJUSRI; PURE LAND SECT OF BUDDHISM; TEMPLES.

BOGUE, TREATY OF See MOST FAVORED NATION TRADE STATUS.

BON See KAILAS, MOUNT; LAMAISM.

BONSAI See CONTAINER GARDENS.

BOOK OF CHANGES (*Yijing* or *I Ching*)   An ancient manual used for divining fate through a system of eight tri-grams (*bagua* or *pa-kua*) that represent the basic elements in nature. The *Yijing* was supposedly invented by the legendary emperor Fuxi. The *Book of Changes* became one of the designated Five Classics (*wujing*), or canonical texts, of Confucianism. It is still used by practitioners of Chinese folk religion and has become a popular means of divination in the Western world. By the time of Confucius (551–479 B.C.), the ancient system of eight trigrams had been multiplied to 64 hexagrams. Each trigram is a symbol consisting of three solid or broken lines, which is based on the concept of yin and yang, the universal principles that are believed to be the foundation of all existence. Solid lines represent yang, the male, or active principle, and broken lines represent yin, the female, or passive principle. The 64 hexagrams are formed by placing one trigram on top of another. The eight trigrams symbolize Heaven (*qin*), Earth (*kun*), thunder (*chen*), wind (*sun*), water (*kan*), fire (*li*), mountains (*ken*) and water (*tui*). The first two, Heaven and Earth, were thought to be yang and yin, and as such they are the father and mother of the other trigrams and of all creation.

One method of divining fate is that of throwing dice to determine each line in the symbol that will provide an answer to a posed question, which is usually ambiguous and complex. Doing this several times in a row may, in fact, produce different answers to the same question. The short ancient text of the *Book of Changes* provides clues for interpreting the answer. The longer appendixes (called "wings") that were added centuries later, during the Qin (221–206 B.C.) and Han (206 B.C.–A.D. 220) dynasties, discuss the philosophical meaning of the answers. The book is more than just a fortune-telling manual. The trigrams and hexagrams became imbedded in Chinese culture as the system of symbols that explained the metaphysical principles by which the universe functions. See also DAOISM; EIGHT TRIGRAMS; FIVE CLASSICS OF CONFUCIANISM; FUXI.

BOOK OF DOCUMENTS See BOOK OF HISTORY.

BOOK OF FILIAL PIETY See FILIAL PIETY.

BOOK OF HISTORY (*Shujing* or *Shu-ching*)   Also known as the *Book of Documents;* a collection of speeches, announcements and reports supposedly made by various rulers and their ministers from the times of the mythical emperor Yao (supposedly r. 2357–2256 B.C.) and Emperor Shun (supposedly r. 2255–2206 B.C.,) down to the early Zhou dynasty (1100–256 B.C.), although some actually date from the middle or late Zhou dynasties or even several centuries later. The most recent events referred to in the *Book of History* occurred in 626 B.C. The Chinese have traditionally considered the speeches in the collection to be records of the governing bureaucracy of the ancient sage-kings, and thus these leaders have served as models for all subsequent rulers of China. Until the modern era, the Chinese regarded most of these documents as authentic descriptions of ancient Chinese government and society. They also believed that Confucius (551–479 B.C.) edited the collection and wrote a short introduction to each document. The *Book of History* is one of the Five Classics (*wujing*) of Confucianism and contains the finest examples of the earliest written Chinese prose.

When the leaders of the Zhou clan overthrew the Shang dynasty (1750–1040 B.C.) and established their own rule, they issued decrees, contained in the *Book of History,* that validated their conquest and told the defeated people of Shang why they should submit to their Zhou conquerors. The Zhou rulers based their authority on the concept of the Mandate of Heaven (*tianming* or *t'ien-ming*), arguing that Heaven chose certain men to rule the world and that their heirs may continue to govern with the sanction of Heaven as long as they rule with righteousness, benevolence and wisdom. But if the imperial clan loses these qualities, Heaven could depose them and grant favor to a new ruling clan. The Zhou argued that the Shang rulers had become evil and thus lost the Mandate of Heaven; thus, Heaven sanctioned the Zhou to overthrow the Shang and establish a new dynasty. Shang society was reminded that the founder of the Shang dynasty had himself been sanctioned by Heaven to overthrow the evil ruler of the Xia dynasty. From the Zhou era down to modern China, this concept of dynastic cycles and the Mandate of Heaven has been the accepted interpretation that the Chinese have applied to their history, and the *Book of History* has served as the primary source for all Chinese political thought. It states that there are three sources of political authority, the Mandate of Heaven, the goodwill of the people, and the virtue of the ruler. See also BOOK OF CHANGES; BOOK OF RITES; BOOK OF SONGS; CONFUCIANISM; FIVE CLASSICS; MANDATE OF HEAVEN; SHANG DYNASTY; SHUN, EMPEROR; SPRING AND AUTUMN ANNALS; YAO, EMPEROR.

BOOK OF ODES   See BOOK OF SONGS.

BOOK OF POETRY   See BOOK OF SONGS.

BOOK OF RITES (*Liji* or *Li chi*)   Also known as the *Record of Rites,* and properly known as the *Ritual;* a collection of documents describing ancient rituals and court ceremonies that is one of the Five Classics (*wujing*) of Confucianism. This book is a restoration of the original *Classic of Rites* (*Lijing*) that had been lost in the third century B.C. The documents in the *Book of Rites* were compiled during the Han dynasty (206 B.C.–A.D. 220) and were taken from earlier texts written in the period between the middle or late Zhou dynasty (1100–256 B.C.) and the early Han dynasty. Confucius (551–479 B.C.) was traditionally regarded as the compiler and editor of some of the texts. In the 12th century A.D., two chapters of the *Book of Rites*—the "Great Learning" (*Daxue*) and the "Doctrine of the Mean" (*Zhongyong*)—were taken out and added to two other documents, the *Analects* (Sayings) of Confucius (*Lunyu*) and the *Book of Mencius* (*Mengzi*), to form the Four Books (*Sishu*) of Confucianism. The *Analects,* considered to be the teachings of Confucius himself, repeatedly emphasize the importance of the *Book of Rites* and the *Book of Songs* (*Shijing*).

The *Book of Rites* covers a wide range of subjects, from philosophical statements about the meaning of life to detailed rules for everyday behavior. It teaches that a government can cultivate moral virtue in its citizens by having them follow prescribed rituals and listen to proper music. The *Book of Rites* describes a ceremonial building called the *Mingtang* where the emperor was supposed to conduct religious rituals that would benefit the Chinese state. The most famous passage in the *Book of Rites* is traditionally considered to explain Confucius's concept of an ideal social order, called the Age of Grand Harmony (Datong), a period prior to the rise of imperial dynasties when the Great Way was prevalent in the world and all people worked together for the common good (*Tianxia Weigong*). This latter slogan has been frequently used by the leaders of modern China and is engraved on many public monuments, such as the tomb of Sun Yat-sen (1866–1925), founder of the Republic of China (1911–49).

One of the most important texts in the *Book of Rites* is the *Spring and Autumn Annals* (*Lushu Chunqiu*), which has three sections that are concerned with the three Confucian principles of Heaven, Earth and human beings. The section on Heaven has 12 chapters, corresponding to the months of the year, and describes how the government should act during each month. This almanac demonstrates the way that Chinese culture has combined religion, astronomy, government and ethics. See also ANALECTS CONFUCIAN; BOOK OF CHANGES; BOOK OF HISTORY; BOOK OF SONGS; CONFUCIANISM; DOCTRINE OF THE MEAN; FIVE CLASSICS OF CONFUCIANISM; FOUR BOOKS OF CONFUCIANISM; GREAT LEARNING; MENCIUS; SPRING AND AUTUMN ANNALS; SUN YAT-SEN.

BOOK OF SONGS (*Shijing* or *Shih-ching*)   Known also as the *Book of Odes* or *Book of Poetry;* a collection of 305 ancient folksongs and ceremonial hymns or odes, which is the most important book of the Five Classics (*wujing*) of Confucianism and one of the oldest written texts in the world. The songs were supposedly collected by Confucius (551–479 B.C.) but actually date from around the 10th to the seventh centuries B.C. It has been established that they were a major source in Confucius teaching. The *Analects* (*Sayings*) *of Confucius* (*Lunyu*) repeatedly emphasize the importance of the *Book of Songs* and *Book of Rites* (*Liji*). The Han dynasty (206 B.C.–A.D. 220) declared Confucianism the official government philosophy. In the second century B.C., the songs were arranged into a standard edition of the *Book of Songs* by a Confucian scholar.

The majority of the songs are written in four-syllable lines that rhyme, falling into three general categories: folksongs (*feng*), political poems (*ya*) and ritual hymns (*song*). Their subjects include marriage, military battles and heroes, the greatness of the Zhou dynasty, which ruled China 1100–256 B.C., and ceremonies performed by Zhou rulers, such as religious sacrifices and banquets.

The first song in the collection is known as *Guan Chu* (*Kuan ch'u*), and tradition claims it was performed for the 12th-century B.C. wedding of a prince who was an ancestor of the Zhou dynasty. Members of the ruling class were expected to have an educated knowledge of the *Book of Songs.* In China, to say that someone "did not know the *Guan Chu*" was equivalent to saying that someone "did not know the ABCs." The prominence given to *Book of Songs* laid the foundation for the great regard that the Chinese have always held for poetry.

Allusions to lines in the songs were commonly made in diplomatic messages exchanged by the various feudal states in Zhou times. Confucian scholars traditionally regarded *Book of Songs* as the authoritative source for all questions regarding rituals and moral behavior. These scholars interpreted the songs allegorically to show the moral meanings they contained. See also ANALECTS, CONFUCIAN; BOOK OF CHANGES; BOOK OF HISTORY; BOOK OF RITES; CONFUCIANISM; FIVE CLASSICS; SPRING AND AUTUMN ANNALS.

BOOK OF SPRING AND AUTUMN See SPRING AND AUTUMN ANNALS.

BOOK OF TEA, THE See TEA.

BOOK OF THE WAY AND ITS POWER, THE (BOOK OF THE WAY OF VIRTUE, THE) See DAODEJING.

BOOKS See COMMERCIAL PRESS; DAOIST CLASSICAL TEXTS; FIVE CLASSICS OF CONFUCIANISM; FOUR BOOKS OF CONFUCIANISM; IMPERIAL EXAMINATION SYSTEM; PRINTING IN CHINA; QUOTATIONS FROM CHAIRMAN MAO ZEDONG; SCROLLS; YONGLE ENCYCLOPEDIA.

BORODIN, MIKHAIL (1884–1952)   A professional communist revolutionary who was sent from the Soviet Union to China in 1923 to work with Dr. Sun Yat-sen, the founder of modern China. Borodin helped reorganize Sun's political party, the Chinese Nationalist Party (Kuomintang; KMT), which was then closely cooperating with the newly founded Chinese Communist Party (CCP).

Mikhail Borodin was an alias; he had been born in Belorussia into a Jewish family whose name was Gruzenberg (Grusenberg) and had been raised in Latvia. After the Revolution of 1905 in Russia, Borodin emigrated to the United States. He returned to Russia in 1917, the year of the October Revolution that established the Soviet Union. The next year, Vladimir Lenin sent him as an emissary to the Comintern, the Third Communist International.

In China, Sun Yat-sen had led the Revolution of 1911 that overthrew the Qing dynasty (1644–1911), China's last imperial dynasty, and founded the Republic of China in 1912, with himself as its first president. The republican government was soon taken over by Yuan Shikai (Yuan Shih-k'ai), a northern Chinese warlord based in Beijing, and the country became divided up among contending warlords during the Warlord Period (1916–28). Sun traveled between Shanghai and Guangzhou (Canton) in southern China, attempting to regain control of the Chinese government. In Shanghai he met with Dr. Adolf Joffe, who the U.S.S.R. had sent to negotiate a treaty with the Beijing government, and this opened the way for Soviet assistance to the KMT. The CCP was founded in 1921 by Chen Duxiu (Ch'en Tu-hsiu) and Li Dazhao (Li Ta-chao), who had been leaders of the May Fourth Movement of 1919 and were influenced by the Russian Revolution. The Comintern, begun by Lenin in 1919, sent agents to assist the Chinese in organizing a communist party. One of these, Gregory Voitinsky, met with Li in Beijing and Chen in Shanghai in 1920, and their efforts to recruit Chinese intellectuals resulted in the First Congress of the CCP in Shanghai in July 1921. One of the delegates was Mao Zedong (Mao Tse-tung), who eventually became chairman of the CCP. A Dutch communist named H. Maring (real name, Hendricus Sneevliet) who was sent to China by the Comintern in 1921 enabled the CCP to connect with the KMT, although many members of both parties opposed this connection.

Borodin arrived in Guangzhou in October 1923 as the agent of the Soviets and the Comintern. His mission was to place Chinese Communists in strategic positions in the KMT as a means of furthering the communist revolution in China. Borodin and Sun reorganized the KMT by creating a centralized political party called the Chung-kuo Kuomintang (Zhongguo guomindang in Pinyin), modeled after the Communist Party in the U.S.S.R. Chung-kuo, "Middle Kingdom," is the traditional Chinese name for the country, reflecting the belief that China is the center of the world. The party held its First National Congress in January 1924, at which it adopted a constitution with a five-level structure with power invested in a Central Executive Committee elected by an annual congress of delegates. The party's nationalist and anti-imperialistic ideology was based on Sun's "Three Principles of the People." In 1924 the KMT and the CCP established a military academy at Whampoa, near Guangzhou, to train officers to lead the National Revolutionary Army. The U.S.S.R. initially financed the academy and contributed instructors and weapons. Sun appointed Chiang Kai-shek as director of the academy, and plans for an expedition to northern China were made to remove the warlords. In 1923 Sun had sent Chiang to Moscow for several months to study political and military issues. (Mao Zedong and Zhou Enlai [Chou En-lai], who later became the second-most important person in the CCP, also held positions at the academy.) In 1925 Sun died and Chiang was his replacement as head of the KMT.

That year some members of the KMT Central Executive Committee met near Beijing in the "Western Hills Conference" and voted to expel the Communists from the KMT, punish Wang Jingwei—the leader of the KMT's left wing in Guangzhou—and remove Borodin as party adviser. CCP leader Chen Duxiu offered to have the Communists leave the KMT and to form an alliance between the two parties, but the Comintern opposed this proposal because Communist influence was increasing in the KMT, the leading revolutionary party in China. The Second National Congress of the KMT, held in January 1926, included Communists as about one-third of its delegates but excluded the "Western Hills Clique," which had established a rival party headquarters in Shanghai. The Second Congress expressed gratitude to Borodin and the U.S.S.R. for their assistance. This marked the point of greatest cooperation between the KMT and the CCP.

In March 1926 Chiang Kai-shek, who thought he had uncovered a Communist plot to kidnap him, halted Communist participation in the National Revolutionary Army, placed the Soviet advisers under house arrest, and forced Wang Jingwei, his rival, to leave the KMT. Borodin was in Beijing, negotiating with Feng Yuxiang (Feng Yu-hsiang), the warlord who had taken control there. Borodin returned to Guangzhou in April, and Chiang reassured him that he opposed the right wing of the KMT and still supported Sun's policies of collaborating with the CCP and with the Soviet Union, and developing a mass revolutionary movement in China. Borodin promised to limit Communist influence in the KMT and to support Chiang's schedule for the Northern Expedition against the warlords there, which began in May

1926. The left flank of the expedition took Wuchang (Wuhan) before the end of the year. Wang and other left-wing KMT members established a base at Wuchang with Borodin as one of their advisers. Borodin wanted them to keep moving north to link up with Feng, whose base was in Inner Mongolia and who seemed to be on the Soviet side. However, many of the troops in Wuchang belonged to war-lords who had joined the KMT cause merely to advance their own opportunities for power.

In April 1927 Feng Yuxiang discovered that the Soviet government was conducting subversive revolutionary activities in China, and he had Li Dazhao and 19 other Chinese executed. In June, a telegram from Soviet leader Stalin to a Comintern agent in China that contained orders on how to conduct the Chinese revolution was read to the Politburo of the CCP's Central Committee and shown to Wang Jingwei. The Soviet attempt to dictate policy in China caused the left wing of the KMT to turn against the Soviets and the CCP. They expelled Communists from the KMT, and in April 1927 Chiang ordered an outright massacre of Communists in Shanghai and Nanjing, Chiang Kai-shek's base. Borodin had tried to win the support of Feng Yuxian, but on June 21 Feng told the KMT government in Wuhan that they should join the KMT government in Nanjing and send Borodin back to Russia. On July 23 the KMT based in Wuchang expelled all Communists from the KMT and ordered the CCP to stop its revolutionary activities. On July 24 Wang Jingwei set a telegram to Feng, informing him that the Wuchang KMT had expelled the CCP and Borodin and that he would join the KMT in Nanjing. Borodin and other Comintern agents fled China for the U.S.S.R., although other agents arrived in China to work underground with the CCP. In the 1930s Borodin was arrested during Josef Stalin's Great Purge and was sent to a labor camp in Siberia, where he eventually died. See also CHEN DUXIU; CHIANG KAI-SHEK; CHINESE COMMUNIST PARTY; LI DAZHAO; MAO ZEDONG; MAY FOURTH MOVEMENT OF 1919; MIDDLE KINGDOM; NATIONALIST PARTY; NORTHERN EXPEDITION; SUN YAT-SEN; WANG JINGWEI; WARLORD PERIOD; WHAMPOA MILITARY ACADEMY; WUHAN.

BOUYEI Known also as Zhongjia; one of China's 55 national minority ethnic groups. The Bouyei, who number about 2.5 million, inhabit Guizhou, a remote and sparsely populated province in southwestern China, which is home to many minority groups. Classified on the basis of language with the Dai (Thai) people; a romanized script has even been developed for the Bouyei language. The Bouyei are related to the Zhuang, China's largest minority group, which inhabits Guizhou Province and Guangxi-Zhuang Autonomous Region. In this area the Bouyei build their homes with stone blocks fitted together without plaster and cover them with slates. They are very poor and struggle to get enough to eat. They wear dark clothing trimmed with bright colors, and married women wear distinguishing symbols on their head-cloths. The women are skilled in batik, a technique for dyeing textiles with indigo and other colors. The Bouyei use stone for building and to make food containers. Most Bouyei villages were built like fortresses, because they were often attacked by bandits and government troops. Every February or March, during the first lunar month in the traditional calendar, the Bouyei hold a 10-day festival at Huangguoshu (meaning "Yellow Fruit Tree") Falls, China's most important waterfall. This 280-square-mile region in Guizhou, with 18 waterfalls and 100 caves, was not explored by the Chinese until the 1980s, when they were planning to harness its hydroelectric power. See also DAI; GUIZHOU PROVINCE; INDIGO DYEING OF TEXTILES; MINORITIES, NATIONAL; ZHUANG.

BOWING See ANCESTOR WORSHIP; KOWTOW; TRIBUTE SYSTEM.

BOXER UPRISING A rebellion in northern China against Christian missionaries, foreign diplomats and technology by a secret group, the "Society of Righteous and Harmonious Fists" (Yihequan or I-ho-ch'uan); so named because its members practiced weaponless martial arts as well as secret rituals. Westerners called these martial arts "shadow boxing" and, hence, named members of this society "Boxers." Some of the members claimed that their ability to control their breathing and muscles enabled them to withstand bullets. The society, which later changed its name to the "Righteous and Harmonious Militia" (Yihetuan), was a late offshoot of the White Lotus Secret Society that had led rebellions from 1796 to 1805. The Boxers quickly gained members among Chinese peasants, coolies and craftsmen, but they also attracted many members from among the conservative Confucian-educated literati, or scholar-gentry class, who staffed the imperial bureaucracy of the Qing dynasty (1644–1911). The Boxers, using the slogan "Protect the Qing, destroy the Foreigners," initiated their attacks against foreigners when the Qing gave the concessions of Weihaiwei to Great Britain and Qingdao to Germany. Both concessions were in Shandong Province in northern China, a peninsula close to the capital, Beijing, which controlled access to the strategic Gulf of Bo Hai. Weihaiwei had been occupied by Japan for three years after the defeat of China in the Sino-Japanese War (1894–95). There had already been peasant rebellions against Christian missionaries in six central Chinese provinces in 1896–97, including Shandong, where the people had also suffered from several devastating natural disasters, including drought, famine and the flooding from the Yellow River.

By 1898 the Boxers were attacking Christian missions and telegraph lines. The army of Yuan Shikai (1859–1916), who had been made governor of Shandong in December 1900, was not able to prevent the Boxer Uprising from spreading throughout northern China. In 1900 the Boxers moved into the metropolitan area of Beijing, where they burned churches and railway stations, killed Chinese Christian converts, destroyed electric and telegraph lines and attacked foreign concessions. British and American diplomats pressured the Qing to send troops to put down the Boxer uprising. However, Qing Empress Dowager Cixi (Tz'u Hsi; 1835–1908) decided to use the Boxers for her own gain and permitted Qing troops to help the Boxers attack the foreign Legation Quarter in Beijing. A secretary of the Japanese Legation was murdered on June 16. On June 17, allied forces took the Qing Dagu Fortress at Tianjin. On June 19, the Qing informed the foreign legations that their personnel had to leave Beijing within 24 hours. The next day, Germany's minister, Baron Klemens von Ketteler, was killed while on his way to negotiate with the Zongli (Tsungli) Yamen (Qing foreign office). On June 21, 1900, after the Boxers had attacked foreign legations and burned churches in Beijing for 10 days, Cixi declared war against all foreign powers that had diplomatic contacts with China. The Boxer siege of the foreign legations in Beijing lasted for 56 days, during which time 250 foreigners and many Chinese Christian converts were killed. Governors in central and southern China made agreements with foreign consuls that they would keep a neutral stance and ignore imperial orders issued after June 20.

Meanwhile, every Western power with diplomatic staff in China had sent soldiers to capture the capital. On June 10, 2,000 foreign troops began marching from Tianjin, south of Beijing. Around the same time, an international squadron landed at Tianjin, where a force of 18,000 soldiers from eight nations disembarked to march on the capital. On July 13 they seized Tianjin. On August 14, this international relief force of 20,000 fought their way into Beijing and rescued the foreigners and Chinese Christians who had been beseiged in the foreign Legation Quarters and the Beitang Roman Catholic Cathedral. By easily taking the city with much killing, looting and raping of the civilian population, the foreigners exposed the lack of power of the Qing. On August 15, Cixi and Emperor Guangxu, disguised as peasants, escaped from the palace with Manchu princes and high officials, and fled west to Xi'an in Shaanxi Province. While staying there, the Chinese statesman Li Hongzhang (Li Hung-chang; 1823–1901) conducted negotiations with the foreign powers. On September 7, 1901, only two months before Li's death, all sides signed the "Boxer Protocol." Most of the high Chinese government officials who had led the uprising were forced to commit suicide. Examinations for the imperial bureaucracy were suspended for five years in 45 cities where the Boxers had attacked foreigners. China sent special envoys to Germany and Japan to apologize for the murder of their diplomats. The Dagu Fortress and other Chinese fortifications along the coast protecting Beijing were destroyed. Foreign legations were allowed to station troops in Beijing for their self-defense, and China was forbidden to import foreign weapons for two years. Moreover, China was forced to pay an indemnity of 450 million ounces of silver, about five years of income for the Qing government, which, including interest, would not be paid off until 1940. (The country was already paying a heavy indemnity to Japan after its defeat in the Sino-Japanese War.) The United States and several other countries later returned the outstanding Boxer indemnity to China. After the Boxer Uprising was settled, Russia refused to pull its troops from Manchuria (northeastern China), and this became a major cause of the Russo-Japanese War of 1904–5. When Cixi returned to Beijing, she reactivated many reforms that she had overturned earlier when suppressing the Reform Movement of 1898. During the Chinese Cultural Revolution (1966–76), the anti-Western fanaticism of the Red Guards was compared by many to that of the Boxers at the end of the 19th century. See also BEIJING; BO HAI GULF; CHRISTIANITY; CIXI, EMPRESS DOWAGER; CULTURAL REVOLUTION; LI HONGZHANG; MANCHURIA; MARTIAL ARTS; QING DYNASTY; REFORM MOVEMENT OF 1898; SHANDONG PROVINCE; SINO-JAPANESE WAR OF 1894–95; TIANJIN; WHITE LOTUS SECRET SOCIETY; YUAN SHIKAI; ZONGLI YAMEN.

BOXING   See TAIJIQUAN.

BRAHMAPUTRA RIVER   See HIMALAYA MOUNTAIN RANGE; LHASA; TIBET.

BRIDGES (*qiao* or *chiao*)   Suspension bridges and segmental arch bridges were invented in China. The earliest suspension bridges were ropes, usually made of woven hemp or some other natural fiber, thrown across a gorge or shot across tied to an arrow. (The Chinese invention of the crossbow in the fourth century B.C. provided more power to send heavier ropes across wider gorges.)

Various types of multiple-cable bridges were developed, such as one made from three ropes, in which a person would walk on two ropes and hold the third, overhead, for balance. Sometimes woven mats were attached to the two bottom ropes or cables, making the footing more secure. A Chinese dynastic history from A.D. 90 refers to a suspension bridge made with wooden planks to make the crossing easier. The Chinese began making cable bridges using bamboo. Bamboo cables can stand more than three times the stress that a two-inch-thick hemp rope can stand. A center made from bamboo core was covered with plaited bamboo strips from the outer layers of bamboo.

The best-known Chinese suspension bridge is a catenary bridge, which has a roadway, or platform, that follows the curves of the cables rather than hanging flat. Anlan Bridge at Guanxian in Sichuan Province is a well-known catenary suspension bridge that may have been built as early as the third century B.C. Having eight successive spans with a total length of 1,050 feet, it has thick rope cables and the walking platform is made of wood planking.

Suspension bridges with wrought-iron chains were first constructed in China in the sixth century A.D. and were soon copied in Tibet (which was then independent) and other countries in the Himalaya Mountains. There many rivers originate that flow through steep gorges in China and Southeast Asia. The Chinese developed iron technology much earlier than other countries, and may have used wrought-iron chains for suspension bridges by the first century A.D. They built massive stone abutments to anchor the chains. (Suspension bridges did not appear in Europe until the 18th century, a century after Roman Catholic Jesuits and other Westerners in China described suspension bridges they had seen in Guizhou Province.) The use of wrought-iron chains for a suspension bridge enabled the suspension of a planking walkway that hangs flat rather than following the curve of the chains. The longest Chinese iron-chain suspension bridge was about 430 feet long, at Lushan in Sichuan. The longest bridge of this type that still exists is 361 feet long, spanning the Dadu River at Luding in Sichuan. The chains are buried 40 feet deep in stone pillars on both sides. The present bridge, which replaced an earlier one, was built in 1705. The Luding Bridge is famous in China because Chinese Communists crossed it under difficult conditions during their so-called Long March to escape Chinese Nationalists in 1935.

Suspension bridges have been used mainly in southwestern China, while stone-arch bridges have been used chiefly in northern China. The segmental arch bridge, which requires less material and is stronger than a semicircular arch bridge, was invented in China in the seventh century A.D.

The Great Stone Bridge (Zhaozhou) over the Jiao River, near Shijiazhuang in Hebei Province, is one of the world's oldest segmental arch bridges and is a remarkable feat of engineering. The Chinese are very proud of the Great Stone Bridge, which was depicted on a Chinese postage stamp in 1961. The architect Li Chun built this limestone-block bridge in 610. (Segmental arch bridges were not built in Europe until the 14th century.) It is 165 feet long, 31 feet wide and has a span of 123 feet. Two upper arches on either side provide support and allow floodwaters to pass through without damaging the bridge.

The Marco Polo Bridge over the Yongding River in the southwestern part of Beijing is China's greatest segmental arch bridge; it is named for the famous Italian traveler who saw it in 1290 and wrote a lengthy description. Impressed that 10 mounted men could ride abreast across the bridge, he admired the 283 marble lion heads topping parapets on the carved balustrade. The bridge, built in 1189 and still being crossed by heavy traffic, has a succession of 11 segmental arches and is 700 feet long. The bridge was the site of a clash between Japanese and Chinese troops in 1937, beginning China's War of Resistance against Japan (1937–45; World War II).

There are several other famous bridges in China. Baodai Qiao Bridge is two miles south of Suzhou in the Wuxian district. Built in 806 and restored several times, the bridge is 1,040 feet long and is supported by three stone piles. The Chengyang Wind and Rain Bridge, built in 1916 by master carpenters of the Dong ethnic minority in Guangxi Zhuang Autonomous Region in southern China, is a fine example of Dong timber-frame construction. The bridge has five pavilions that rest upon five stone piles and are connected by covered walkways. The bridge over the Qiantang River in Hangzhou, the capital of Zhejiang Province, was the first double-decker bridge in China, handling both street and railway traffic. It was built in 1937 and is 4,300 feet long. The Yangzi River Bridge at Nanjing in Jiangsu Province is a great accomplishment of the Chinese communists who founded the People's Republic of China (PRC) in 1949. Opened in 1968, the double-decker bridge is one of China's longest, with a 15,000-foot-long road on top and a 22,000-foot-long railway line underneath. The bridge enabled the first direct railway link between Beijing and Shanghai, thus connecting the regions north and south of the river. See also DONG; HIMALAYA MOUNTAIN RANGE; IRON TECHNOLOGY AND STEEL INDUSTRY; LONG MARCH; MARCO POLO BRIDGE INCIDENT; YANGZI RIVER.

BRIEF HISTORY OF CHINESE FICTION, A See LU XUN.

BRITAIN AND CHINA See ARROW WAR; BOXER UPRISING; BRITISH EAST INDIA COMPANY; CANTON SYSTEM; CHINESE MARITIME CUSTOMS SERVICE; CHRISTIANITY; GORDON, CHARLES GEORGE; HONG KONG; INTERNATIONAL SETTLEMENT IN SHANGHAI; MACARTNEY, GEORGE, LORD; OPIUM WAR; SHANGHAI; SINO-BRITISH JOINT DECLARATION ON THE QUESTION OF HONG KONG; TAIPING REBELLION; TREATY PORTS; UNEQUAL TREATIES.

BRITISH EAST INDIA COMPANY A joint-stock company organized in Great Britain in 1599 to conduct trade with India and East Asian countries. Portugal, Spain, Holland and France had already formed companies that engaged in such trade, and, in 1600, merchants in London acquired from Queen Elizabeth I a charter to form the East India Company. The original title of the company was "The Governor and Merchants of London Trading into the East Indies." The Company's first fleet of five ships sailed in 1601. They carried gold and silver coins, iron, tin, lead and woolen broadcloth to Asia and returned with cargoes of spices worth more than one million British pounds, more than three times the value of the British goods the Company had traded. The Portuguese, who had made their Asian base on the island of Macao, and the Dutch, who had a foothold in Indonesia, fought with the British to prevent the East India Company from encroaching on their own lucrative trade in such goods as spices, tea, porcelain and silk. The Portuguese and Dutch forced the British company to limit its trade to India and several neighboring countries. Yet the British East India Company quickly became rich from its own trade, particularly by purchasing cotton in India and selling it in China for tea, silks, spices and other luxury goods—a "three-corner" pattern of trade between Britain, India and China.

The British East India Company armed its ships, known as East Indiamen, and maintained an army with its own officers to defend the company's trading interests both on the sea and in foreign countries where it acquired trading rights. It went so far as to administer foreign territories, make treaties with Asian governments, and maintain harbors, channels and military defenses along the coasts of India and other foreign countries. The Company's ships were often more advanced than the men-of-war built for the British Royal Navy. A trading voyage to Asia and back took each ship two years.

In the late 17th century the British East India Company began trading with China through the southern port city of Guangzhou (Canton), the only city where the Chinese government permitted foreigners to trade. The company established a trading post—known as a "factory" for the company's factor, or agent—in Guangzhou in 1699. The Chinese government established in the 18th century the Canton system to regulate foreign trade, by which Western merchants would have to conduct all of their business through native Chinese merchants in Guangzhou who belonged to a guild known as the Cohong or "Hong" (from *gonghang*, "combined merchant companies"). The *hong* merchants made high profits by regulating the prices for imported and exported goods and by collecting all duties and tariffs on behalf of the Chinese government. Western traders had to confine themselves to an area along the bank of the Pearl River where the residences and offices of the foreign factors were located, known as the "13 Factories." The merchants of the East India Company became very wealthy and lived luxuriously in their factory in Guangzhou, but they could not bring along their wives or enter the gates of the city.

In the mid-18th century the French attacked British trading stations, but the British, led by Robert Clive, defeated the French at Plassey in 1757; this event began British rule in India. In 1772 the British East India Company suffered financial reverses and nearly went bankrupt. The British Parliament lent it £1.5 million and passed an act that placed the administration of British India under a governor-general appointed by the British Crown. The company's army became the largest military force in East Asia and continued to establish trading bases in South and Southeast Asia. In 1793 the British government and the East India Company sent Lord (George) Macartney to China to request the ending of the Canton system, the opening of more Chinese ports to foreign trade and the setting of fair tariffs. The Chinese emperor refused to give in to these requests and informed King George III of Britain that China would not increase its foreign trade because it did not need anything from other countries. In 1799 the Chinese government gave the East India Company permission to move its factory to Guangzhou.

The balance of trade was not favorable to Britain, which, despite selling Indian cotton, was being drained of silver to pay for tea and other goods from China. Hence, the British began importing opium from India to sell in China. The British continued to press China to open the country to foreign trade and sold large quantities of opium to the Chinese, which in turn drained China of large quantities of silver. In 1834 the East India Company was abolished and the British government sent Lord Napier to Guangzhou to replace the company as supervisor of the triangular Britain-India-China trade. The British government commissioned Lord Napier to persuade China to open the country to equal trade with Britain, but he was no more successful than Lord Macartney had been.

The Qing government commissioned Lin Zexu (Lin Tse-hsu) to eliminate the opium trade in Guangzhou, which was demoralizing and impoverishing the country. He arrived there in 1839 and confined the British to the "13 Factories" trading zone and confiscated their opium. These actions led Britain to declare war on China, known as the Opium War (1839–42), in which they defeated China and forced it to sign the Treaty of Nanjing (1842), which, among other things, opened five cities to foreign trade and residents as so-called treaty ports and ceded the island of Hong Kong to Britain. Shanghai quickly replaced Guangzhou as China's largest trading port. See also CANTON SYSTEM; GUANGZHOU; HONG KONG; MACAO; MACARTNEY, LORD GEORGE; NANJING, TREATY OF; OPIUM WAR; SILK; TEA; TREATY PORTS.

BROADCASTING The government of the People's Republic of China (PRC) created the Central Broadcasting Administration in 1954 and renamed it the Ministry of Radio and Television in 1982. After absorbing the Film Bureau from the Ministry of Culture in 1986, the department was renamed the Ministry of Radio, Cinema, and Television (MRCT). The influence of the MRCT has grown as television, now available to large segments of the Chinese population, has replaced the film industry as the principal means of mass communication in China. The MRCT regulates cooperation between the television and filmmaking industries in planning, producing and filming. It also encourages coproduction between Chinese and foreign film studios, such as with Bernardo Bertolucci's Academy Award–winning film *The Last Emperor*, which was co-produced by China, Italy and Great Britain. The MRCT administers many organizations related to broadcasting in the areas of training, talent searches, research, publishing and manufacturing. Three major broadcasting organizations are subordinate to the MRCT. The Central People's Broadcasting Stations provide domestic radio service to all regions of the country. Radio Beijing is China's overseas radio service. China Central Television (CCTV) controls all television broadcasting within China. The Propaganda Department of the Chinese Communist Party (CCP) coordinates the work of the MRCT and the Ministry of Posts and Telecommunications (MPT).

Radio and television broadcasting expanded rapidly in China during the 1980s. By 1985 radio reached 75 percent of the population through 167 radio stations and 215 million radios, as well as an extensive wired loudspeaker system. The Central People's Broadcasting Stations provide radio programs for minority groups in China in such languages as Korean, Manchurian, Tibetan (Zang), Uighur and Kazak, and also direct programs toward Taiwan and overseas Chinese communities. Radio Beijing broadcasts to the world in more than 38 languages and in various Chinese dialects, such as Cantonese, Hakka and Amoy. It also provides English-language news programs for foreign residents in Beijing. In 1985 China had more than 104 television stations, and about 85 percent of the urban population had access to television. In the late 1980s there were only a small number of black-and-white television sets in Chinese homes as a whole, but by 1993 the majority of homes had television sets, about half of them color. By September 1995 there were more than 230 million television sets in China for 1.2 billion people. Popular radio programs include soap operas based on popular Chinese novels, and Chinese and foreign music. Television shows largely provide entertainment, such as feature films, sports, drama, music and dance, and children's shows, although there are also news broadcasts and educational shows. Between 1982 and 1985, six U.S. television companies signed agreements to provide American television programs to China.

In 1985 CCTV, which produces its own programs, began constructing a major new studio in Beijing. The Television University in Beijing produces several weekly educational programs, such as English-language lessons. The New China (Xinhua) News Agency is a government agency that handles domestic and international news and foreign affairs. See also FILM STUDIOS; NEW CHINA NEWS AGENCY; TELECOMMUNICATIONS.

BROCADE See CHENGDU; SILK; TEXTILE INDUSTRY.

BRONZEWARE (*qingtong* or *ch'ing t'ung*) Objects made from an alloy of copper and tin, first produced in China from 1700 to 1500 B.C., during the Shang dynasty (1750–1040 B.C.), the earliest Chinese dynasty from which archaeologists have been able to find artifacts. The Shang, which supposedly replaced the Xia dynasty (2200–1750 B.C.), originated in the Yellow River (Huanghe) valley in modern Honan Province. The Shang were ruled by a king and a small aristocracy who established a centralized government that held power over the common people. Members of the Shang ruling class used bronze containers to conduct sacrificial ceremonies to ensure that the powerful spirits of their ancestors would continue to protect them. These rulers were able to extend their kingdom with the use of bronze weapons, including halberds and knives, and horse-drawn chariots with bronze fittings.

The Shang may possibly have learned the technique of "cold-working" bronze from the Middle East, but they created their own technique for casting bronze objects: pouring molten bronze into pottery molds. No other culture has been able to equal the high quality of ancient Chinese bronze-casting. This technique was based on direct casting, or the use of piece molds to cast the entire container with its surface designs all at once. The negative image of the container's shape and decorations were carved in strips of clay, which were dried, fired in a kiln and joined together to make a complete outer mold for the container with a clay core for its interior. Molten bronze was then poured into the mold and hardened. Then the clay mold and core were removed from the bronze container, which only required a small amount of finishing work to reach its final form.

The Chinese cast bronze containers in a number of different shapes, many of which were based on the shapes of ceramic containers produced during the Neolithic period (12,000–2000 B.C.). Shang bronze containers were made in several types. Food cookers are large round pots with handles and three legs similar to a tripod that enabled them to be placed over cooking fires. The best known food cooker, the *ding* (*ting*), was used to hold sacrificial meats during religious rituals. Other cooking vessels include the *yen* and the *li*. Large bronze food containers, some with lids, include the *gui* (*kuei*), *yu, fu, tou* (*dou*) and *dui* (*tui*). Bronze lidded wine containers include the *yu, fangyi* (*fang-i*), *lei, hu* and *zun* (*tsun*). There are also bronze, three-footed wine warmers that could be placed over a fire, including the *zhia* (*chia*) and *jue* (*chueh*); wine servers, large with a vessels lid, spout and handle, including the *he* (*ho*) and *guang* (*kuang*); and wine goblets, the *zhi* (*chih*) and *gu* (*ku*).

The designs on bronze containers changed over time. Early Shang bronzes were decorated with a narrow band that contained flat, simple geometric patterns and occasionally reliefs of animal heads. The designs became much more complex as Shang bronze technology developed, some motifs in rounded relief and others covering the entire container. Design motifs included bands of dragon and phoenix shapes, squared spirals (*leiwen*), demonic masks (*taotie*), and animal forms such as birds, snakes, cicadas and water buffaloes, which could be realistic or abstract. Many bronze pieces also have inscriptions cast into them, from simple pictograms during the Early Shang, which were also inscribed on "oracle bones" used to divine the future, to dedications to ancestors in the later Shang.

By the end of the Shang dynasty, private families were also using bronze containers in their own ancestral rituals, known as ancestor worship. One of the most important sites where Shang bronzes have been excavated is the later Shang capital at Xiaotun near Anyang in Honan; many splendid royal tombs dating from circa 1400 B.C. to the end of the dynasty in 1040 B.C. can be found there. The bronze ceremonial containers within these tombs are the main material and artistic artifacts from the Shang society and provide a great deal of information about Shang government and society. Bronze weapons and fittings, carvings of jade, stone, ivory and bone, and ceramics were also buried in the tombs.

The Chinese continued to produce bronzeware during the Zhou dynasty (1100–256 B.C.), which overthrew the Shang, and created new types of designs to ornament them that are complex and finely detailed. They also developed techniques to inlay bronzeware with gold, silver, malachite and semiprecious stones. During the Zhou, inscriptions on bronze containers also became much longer, recording information about the historical events that caused wealthy patrons to have the containers cast. These inscriptions tell historians much about Early Zhou government, society and ceremonial practices, and the names of feudal states and their leaders, which helps historians discern the extent of the empire. Rulers of feudal kingdoms under the Zhou had large sets of cast-bronze bells that were suspended on wooden frames and played to symbolize their authority. In 1978 a magnificent set of bronze bells was excavated from the tomb built in 433 B.C. for Marquis Yi of the state of Zeng in modern Hubei Province, where the ancient technique of bronze casting had become highly advanced.

Wealthy Chinese began using bronze containers in daily life as well as for ancestor worship. In the later Zhou, bronze garment hooks and mirrors decorated with inlay and other ornamentation became widely produced. Iron gradually began to replace bronze in China during the fifth to fourth centuries B.C., especially for weapons and agricultural implements such as plows. The unification of the Chinese Empire under the Qin dynasty (221–206 B.C.) marked the close of the Bronze Age in China. See also ANCESTOR WORSHIP; ANYANG; BELLS AND CHIMES; DING; IRON TECHNOLOGY AND STEEL INDUSTRY; IVORY CARVING; JADE; MIRRORS; NEOLITHIC PERIOD; ORACLE BONES; QIN DYNASTY; SHANG DYNASTY; XIA DYNASTY; ZHOU DYNASTY.

BRUSH FOR WRITING AND PAINTING See CALLIGRAPHY; FOUR TREASURES OF THE STUDY; PAPER; WRITING SYSTEM, CHINESE.

BU See ORACLE BONES.

BUCK, PEARL SYDENSTRICKER (1892–1973)   An American author best known for her novels, short stories and articles about China. The first American woman to win the Nobel Prize in literature in 1938 for her novels about China, notably *The Good Earth* (1931), and her biographies of her Presbyterian missionary parents, *The Exile* (1936) and *Fighting Angel* and *Portrait of a Soul* (1936). She was born in West Virginia but her parents, Absalom and Caroline Stulting Sydenstricker, took her to China when she was an infant. She was educated in Shanghai and then attended Randolph-Macon Women's College in Virginia. After college she returned to China and in 1917, she married John Lossing Buck, a missionary and agricultural expert. From 1921 to 1931 she taught at several universities in Nanjing under the Presbyterian Board of Foreign Missionaries. She wrote many articles and stories about life in China that were published in American magazines from 1923 to 1931. She published her first novel, *East Wind, West Wind*, in 1930. Her second novel, *The Good Earth* (1931), brought her international acclaim for its powerful description of the struggles of a Chinese peasant family, and for it she was awarded the Pulitzer Prize in 1932.

In 1933 she resigned from the Presbyterian Board of Foreign Missionaries and returned to the United States, and in 1935 she divorced John Buck. All the while she kept writing, and during her lifetime she wrote about 100 books. In 1935 she married her publisher, Richard J. Walsh. Her interest in East-West relations extended to areas other than writing alone. In 1949 she established the Welcome House agency to arrange adoptions of mixed-race children who had been fathered in Asian countries during and after the Pacific War, and in 1964 she founded the Pearl S. Buck Foundation in Bucks Country, Pennsylvania, to further the work of aiding mixed-race children fathered by servicemen. She herself had one daughter and adopted nine other children. A documentary film about her life, *East Wind, West Wind: Pearl Buck, The Woman Who Embraced the World*, was produced in 1993, the Pearl Buck Centennial Year. That same year her alma mater also held a symposium on her life and work. She won many other literary and humanitarian awards and honorary degrees.

BUDALA GONG   See POTALA PALACE.

BUDDHA   The title for the founder of the Buddhist religion, which was introduced into China from India around the first century A.D. The term *Buddha* is an honorific title in the classical Indian languages of Sanskrit and Pali for "one who has awakened"; that is, a person who has achieved enlightenment or self-realization. *Buddha* is also related etymologically to the Sanskrit/Pali term *buddhi,* meaning "intelligence" and "understanding." Hence one who has awakened is "one who knows." The title *Buddha* became applied to Siddhartha Gautama, the historical founder of Buddhism, who lived in northeastern India (modern Nepal) in the late sixth to early fifth centuries B.C. He is also known as Sakyamuni because he was the son of a chief of the Sakyas, a small tribe in the foothills of the Himalaya Mountains. Few details are known about his actual life but many legends developed. He was married and had a child, but he became so troubled by the problem of human suffering—especially as experienced through disease, old age and death—that he renounced his privileged life and became a wandering monk seeking resolution for the problem of all suffering. After many years of practicing asceticism without resolving the problem for himself, he renounced the ascetic way as well. He then became awakened to the truth he sought, which he called the "Middle Way," and spent the rest of his life teaching and gathering a community of followers. He died at age 80, probably in 486 B.C.

The starting point of the Buddha's teachings is known as the "Four Noble Truths":

1. That life entails suffering.
2. That suffering is due to attachment.
3. That it can be stopped if attachment is stopped.
4. That this can be done by leading a disciplined and moral life and engaging in meditation.

The Buddhist religion grew rapidly, and after several centuries it divided into two branches. The earlier branch, Theravada ("Teaching of the Elders"), taught that awakening could be realized only if one completely gave up ordinary life to became a monk or nun. Later, Buddhists who maintained that every person could become awakened without renouncing ordinary life criticized the selective nature of Theravada and referred to it as Hinayana, or the "Lesser Vehicle." Their branch, which emphasized universal enlightenment, became

A freestanding sculpture of the Buddha awaits worshipers in a Buddhist temple.   S.E. MEYER

known as Mahayana, the "Greater Vehicle." Buddhism died out in India, but Theravada Buddhism took hold in Southeast Asia, while Mahayana spread to China, Korea and Japan.

The Chinese initially adopted the Buddha as a human who had attained divinity, similar to the legendary Yellow Emperor and the philosopher Laozi (Lao Tzu), whom the Chinese believed had attained immortality. Many sects developed within Mahayana in China, and some of them taught that the possibility of release from suffering was through salvation provided by a deity rather than through one's own efforts. Even during his own lifetime, Gautama tended to be worshiped by followers as a god and was considered to be the final Buddha in a series of earlier Buddhas. Mahayana Buddhism developed the concept that more Buddhas would appear on earth in the future, particularly Maitreya, the "Buddha of the Future," whose coming was supposedly foretold by the historical Buddha and whose teaching would purify the world. Mahayana Buddhism also developed the concept of the heavenly Buddha, Amitabha (Omitofo or A-mi-t'o-fo in Chinese; "Immeasurable Light"), the Buddha of Boundless Light who is Lord of the "Pure Land" or Western Paradise and who is associated with the earthly Gautama Buddha. The worship of Amitabha in China grew into the Pure Land sect, the most popular Chinese sect of Buddhism.

Mahayana also reveres bodhisattvas ("beings of wisdom"), who have attained awakening but remain active in the world compassionately using the power of their wisdom to help others become enlightened. Many bodhisattvas are worshiped as deities. The most popular bodhisattva in China has been Guanyin (Kuan-yin), who in India had been the male deity Avalokiteshvara but in China became worshiped as the female Goddess of Mercy. The world's tallest bronze Buddha was recently cast in Nanjing for the Polin Monastery on Lantau Island in Hong Kong, where it stands on a hilltop. Called the Tiantan Buddha, it is 87 feet high and weighs 250 tons. See also AMITABHA; BODHISATTVA; BUDDHISM; GUANYIN; HIMALAYA MOUNTAIN RANGE; PURE LAND SECT OF BUDDHISM.

BUDDHISM   A religion that was introduced into China from northeastern India (modern Nepal) around the first century A.D. and developed there as one of the three main religious traditions, along with Confucianism and Daoism. Siddhartha Gautama is the historical founder of Buddhism.

The starting point of Buddhist teachings is known as the "Four Noble Truths":

1. That life entails suffering.
2. That suffering is due to attachment.
3. That it can be stopped if attachment is stopped.
4. That this can be done by leading a disciplined and moral life and engaging in meditation.

Buddhism developed many techniques, such as meditation, to help people overcome suffering. The religion eventually divided into two main branches, Theravada or Hinayana, which spread to Sri Lanka (Ceylon) and Southeast Asia, and Mahayana, which spread to China, Korea and Japan. Theravada teaches that awakening can only be realized by giving up one's ordinary life and becoming a monk or nun. Later Buddhists, who maintained that every person could become awakened without renouncing ordinary life, developed Mahayana Buddhism, which emphasizes universal enlightenment.

Buddhism entered China along the Silk Road through Central Asia, during the time when the Han dynasty (206 B.C.–A.D. 220) was breaking down and the Chinese Empire was unstable. The Han court had decreed that Confucianism was the orthodox state religion and had developed an imperial bureaucracy or civil service staffed by literati, or scholars educated in the Confucian classical texts. Confucian thought is concerned with ethics, human relationships, harmony in the family and society, and the ruling of the empire. Unlike Buddhism, Confucianism had no abstract metaphysical thought, but Buddhism found an affinity with Daoism, the other native Chinese tradition, which addressed the issues of creation and the nature of the universe.

After the Han dynasty fell, China became divided into a number of different kingdoms, known as the Six Dynasties Period (220–589). These included, at various times in different parts of the country, the Three Kingdoms, the Jin dynasty and the Northern and Southern dynasties. The literati turned to Buddhist and Daoist thought to find meaning in a time of political and social turmoil. Buddhist thought is concerned with liberation from *samsara,* or the world of suffering, impermanence and death. A person continues to be reborn in this world, with each life determined by his or her karma,

or the results of actions performed in past lives. According to Buddhism, selfish desires and ignorance about the cause of suffering keep a person enmeshed in the endless chain of rebirth. The goal is to overcome this ignorance, to break out of the painful cycle of rebirth and achieve a state known as Nirvana, or enlightenment.

Buddhism already had a large canon of sutras, or religious scriptures, and Chinese monks began translating them from Indian Sanskrit into the Chinese language using Daoist terms, a system known as "matching concepts." A Chinese monk named Daoan (Tao-an; A.D. 314–85) recognized that Buddhist texts had to be understood in their own terms rather than in conjunction with Daoism. He learned of Kumarajiva (350–413), who was fluent in Chinese and many languages of India and Central Asia, and had the emperor of the Later Qin dynasty (384–417), which ruled much of northern China, bring him to the court at Chang'an (modern Xi'an in Shaanxi Province) to translate Buddhist texts. Assisted by more than a thousand monks, Kumarajiva completed translations of 98 texts, many of which became the most important sutras for sects of Chinese Buddhism; the most important was the *Lotus Sutra* (formally known as the *Sutra of the Lotus of the Wonderful Law*). He also developed many terms that became central in Chinese Buddhist thought.

A number of Chinese monks made arduous pilgrimages to India to gather Buddhist sutras. The first was Faxian (Fa-hsien; fourth–fifth centuries), who spent 15 years on his journey and wrote a book, *A Record of the Buddhist Countries,* which has provided historians with valuable information about India during this period. The most famous was Xuanzang (Hsuan-tsang; 602–64), who left an important record of his pilgrimage from Chang'an to India, where he studied at the Buddhist University of Nalanda and traveled around the country. He brought back many sutras and translated about 75 of them. Xuanzang's pilgrimage formed the basis for the beloved 16th-century Chinese novel *Journey to the West (Xiyouji* or *Hsi-yu-chi;*), also known as *Monkey* for one of the characters who accompanies Xuanzang to India.

Various rulers during the Six Dynasties Period patronized Buddhism, especially those in the north who were not Han ethnic Chinese but members of various nomadic tribes who had invaded China and become "Sinicized," that is, adopted the Chinese language and customs. Many members of the Han upper classes fled south of the Yangzi River (Changjiang), especially to the region of modern Nanjing, where they attempted to perpetuate Han Confucian culture (although Buddhist scholars had some influence in their courts). The greatest patrons of Buddhism were the Toba Turks (Tuoba or T'o-pa) who established the Northern Wei dynasty (386–534) in northern China, with their first capital at Datong in Shanxi Province and their second at Luoyang in Henan Province, which had been the last capital of the Han dynasty. The Northern Wei sponsored two massive projects of Buddhist stone carvings: the Yungang Cave Temples and Sculptures near Datong and the Longmen Cave Temples and Sculptures near Luoyang. Both sites, which are open to the public today, include numerous grottoes carved into cliffs and filled with sculptures of Buddhist deities, ranging from small to enormous. Some of the earliest Chinese Buddhist sculptures can be seen at Dunhuang in Gansu Province in western

China, where in 366 Buddhist monks began carving magnificent caves, known as the Mogao Grottoes, into cliffs and filling them with carved Buddhist sculptures. Similar Buddhist caves and sculptures can be seen at Dazu in Sichuan Province and at Mount Maiji (Maijishan) and Bingling Si in Gansu.

Sculpture became especially associated with Buddhism in China. In the mid-6th century, sculptors began making freestanding, three-dimensional sculptures of the Buddha; bodhisattvas (*pusa* or *p'u sa* in Chinese; "beings of wisdom"), who were believed to attain enlightenment but remain active in the world, compassionately using the power of their wisdom to help others become enlightened; and Maitreya (*Milofo* in Chinese), the "Buddha of the Future." They produced monumental bronze sculptures during the seventh and eighth centuries, which disappeared in China, but their style has been preserved in Korea and Japan. They also made Buddhist sculptures from clay or from wood that was covered with paint or lacquer, a specially treated tree sap that hardens to an extremely durable finish. Large wooden Buddhist sculptures were usually made of several pieces held together with mortise and tenon joints.

Many Mahayana Buddhist sects developed in China, some of which taught the possibility of release from suffering through salvation provided by a deity rather than through one's own efforts. Mahayana Buddhism developed the concept that more Buddhas would appear on Earth in the future, particularly Maitreya. Mahayana also developed the concept of the heavenly Buddha, Amitabha (Omitofo in Chinese: "Immeasurable Light"), the Buddha of Boundless Light who is Lord of the "Pure Land," or Western Paradise. The worship of Amitabha in China grew into the Pure Land Sect, the most popular Chinese sect of Chinese Buddhism. Mahayana also revered bodhisattvas; the most popular was Guanyin (Kuan-yin), who in India had been the male deity Avalokiteshvara but in China became worshiped as the female Goddess of Mercy. Another popular bodhisattva was Manjusri, the "God of Wisdom." Also depicted in Buddhist art are the numerous *luohan* (*lohan; arhat* in Sanskrit), a group of worthy disciples of the Buddha.

Chinese Buddhist temples were built in the same architectural style as Confucian and Daoist temples and ranged from small buildings to large compounds built around several courtyards. The main hall contained a table with a beautiful sculpture of a seated deity and an altar holding utensils for religious rituals. Attendant deities were placed on the right and left of the main deity. If the temple compound had more than one hall, lesser deities were placed in the first hall and the principal deity in the rear hall. In Chinese popular religion, a temple could house many deities from both the Daoist and Buddhist pantheons, along with deities sacred to the local community. Wealthy Chinese families built and endowed Buddhist temples, sites where monks could continually perform rituals for their benefit. Some temples attracted hundreds of monks and nuns and accumulated a wealth of landholdings and religious art.

The best-known feature of a Chinese Buddhist temple is the pagoda, a tower as high as 15 stories, each with a curved overhanging roof. Pagodas, based on structures in India called stupas, were built to house sutras and religious relics. About 10,000 pagodas have survived in China, the oldest being the pagoda at Songyue Temple near Shaolin Temple.

The wooden pagoda at Fogong Monastery near Datong, built in 1056, is the most important wooden building in Chinese architecture. Two pagodas in Xi'an are famous symbols of China: The Big Wild Goose Pagoda was built in 652 to store sutras brought back from India by Xuanzang, and the Small Wild Goose Pagoda was built in 707–9. White Horse Temple, constructed in A.D. 68 near Luoyang, was the first Buddhist temple of its kind built after Buddhism was introduced into China.

Many Buddhist temples and monasteries were built in the tranquil countryside, alongside lakes or rivers or on the sides of mountains. Four mountains are sacred to Buddhism in China. Each mountain represents one of the four quarters of the universe, and each is the dwelling place of a manifestation of Buddhist enlightenment. Mount Putuo, an island off Zhejiang Province, is the eastern mountain; Mount Wuta in Shanxi Province is the northern; Mount Emei in Sichuan Province is the western; and Mount Jiuhua in Anhui Province is the southern. Many temples, pagodas and monuments, Daoist as well as Buddhist, have been placed on each mountain. There is also a set of five mountains that are sacred to Daoism.

Four major sects of Mahayana Buddhism developed in China, the Tiantai Sect, the Flower Garland Sect (Huayan), the Pure Land Sect (Jingtu or Ching-t'u) and the Chan sect, known in the West by the Japanese name Zen. Tiantai was the first Buddhist sect to originate in China. Its teachings were similar to those of the Flower Garland Sect. Both sects had highly abstract philosophical teachings and maintained that their religious rituals could only be performed by monks who had given up all worldly attachments, so their members came from the upper classes who had the time and education to study the scriptures. Tiantai teachings are based on the *Lotus Sutra*, an Indian text that has remained one of the popular Mahayana Buddhist scriptures throughout Asia. This scripture, supposedly Sakyamuni's final sermon before he entered Nirvana, teaches that all human beings can attain enlightenment if they have faith in the eternal transcendent Buddha, who appeared in the world to help all people become free from suffering. The beautiful lotus flower rising up from the mud symbolizes the way purity and truth rise above evil, and all people have the lotus of the Buddha nature within them. The Flower Garland Sect took as its main scripture the *Avatamsaka Sutra,* an Indian text that teaches that all things are created by the Mind. The goal of this teaching is to become free from suffering by having a calm mind and freeing oneself of passions and false thoughts.

The Pure Land Sect taught that everyone is able to attain salvation through faith, and so it appealed to the masses of Chinese laypeople and became the most widely followed sect in China. The Pure Land is the Western Paradise, the kingdom established by the Bodhisattva Dharmakara when he attained Buddhahood as Amitabha. The Buddha of Boundless Light and Lord of the Western Paradise, he is depicted in Buddhist paintings and sculptures as seated on a lotus throne in the Western Paradise with his attendants at his side. One is Guanyin, the Goddess of Mercy. The *Pure Land Sutra* teaches that anyone who calls on the name of Amitabha, with single-minded devotion, will be saved from suffering and death by being reborn into bliss in the Western Paradise or Pure Land.

The Chan Sect of Buddhism was founded, according to legend, by Bodhidharma, who supposedly traveled to China from India around 520 and sat cross-legged facing a wall in meditation for many years. Bodhidharma is associated with Shaolin Temple, the traditional home of Chinese martial arts (*wushu*). Chan is the Chinese word for *dhyana*, the Indian Sanskrit term for meditation. Bodhidharma taught that a person could overcome suffering by awakening to the realization that the ordinary self which suffers is not a person's "Buddha Nature" or "True Self." Chan Buddhism does not rely on written scriptures or a transcendent deity to be worshiped, but teaches the direct awakening of the True Self. When the Chinese emperor persecuted Buddhists in 845, Chan survived because of its freedom from such things as written texts, religious symbols, sculptures and other representations of deities. The Chan Sect, which values simplicity and spontaneity, became associated with the arts in China, especially ceramics, monochromatic ink painting and poetry, as expressed in the Cold Mountain poems attributed to Han Shan. Liang Kai (Ling K'ai) and Mu Qi (Mu Ch'i), both active in the 13th century, were renowned Chan painters. Chan was also extremely influential in Japan, and many aspects of Japanese culture renowned in the West today derived from Chinese Chan Buddhism.

Tibet developed its own sect of Buddhism, known as Lamaism. Lama means an honored religious master, similar to a guru in India, and the Dalai Lama became the spiritual and temporal head of Tibet. The Potala Palace in Lhasa, the Tibetan capital, is the traditional seat of the Dalai Lama. The Mongols, a nomadic group to the north of China who established the Yuan dynasty (1279–1368), adopted Lamaism, which is still practiced in Inner Mongolia as well as Tibet. However, the Chinese military occupation of Tibet in the 1950s brutally suppressed the Tibetan religion, murdered or imprisoned thousands of monks and destroyed most of the Tibetan temples. The current Dalai Lama and thousands of his followers fled into exile in Dharamsala, India, where he established a Tibetan government-in-exile.

Emperor Wendi (r. 581–604), the founder of the Sui dynasty (581–618) that reunified China after the Six Dynasties period, patronized Buddhism, especially the Tiantai Sect. The Sui was soon overthrown by the Tang dynasty (618–907), and during the first two centuries of the Tang, Buddhism reached its highest point of development in China. Tang Empress Wu (c. 627–705), the only Chinese empress to rule in her own right, supported the Buddhist religion and used it to legitimize her reign. She patronized the carving of the Longmen Cave Temples and Sculptures, which were executed near Luoyang between the late fifth and seventh centuries. Printing was invented in China during the Tang dynasty and developed in conjunction with the Buddhist religion. Chinese Buddhists wanted to have copies of religious charms and the sutras, creating the need for mass production of verses and texts. Moreover, the copying or printing of sutras was considered a great virtue in the Buddhist religion. Buddhist temples required multiple copies of sutras, and by A.D. 800 whole pages were being carved onto large wooden blocks to mass-produce sutra texts. The earliest surviving complete printed book, a Buddhist sutra called the *Diamond Sutra*, dated 868, was discovered at the Dunhuang Cave Temples in western China.

The Tang dynasty also strengthened the Confucian-based imperial bureaucracy. Buddhism coexisted harmoniously with Confucianism and Daoism as the "Three Teachings." Confucianism was closely associated with family rituals, scholarship and the bureaucracy, Daoism with healing and agricultural practices, and Buddhism with funerals and memorial services. But many Chinese criticized Buddhism as a "barbarian" religion that went against the Confucian emphasis on perpetuation of the family. The strong denunciation of Buddhism by the Confucian scholar Han Yu (768–824) influenced Tang Emperor Wuzong (Wu-tsung; r. 840–46) to issue decrees persecuting the Buddhist religion. Thousands of monks and nuns were returned to lay life, monastic estates were confiscated, temples destroyed and bronze sculptures melted down. Wuzong's successor rescinded the persecution decrees in 845, and Buddhism survived in China, especially the Pure Land and Chan Sects, but from then on the religion played a lesser role in Chinese culture.

Confucianism remained strong during the Song dynasty (960–1279), when the literati attained the height of their power in the Chinese government. However, Confucian thinkers such as Zhu Xi (Chu Hsi; 1130–1200) who revived Confucian thought during the Song, known as Neo-Confucianism, adapted Buddhist philosophical concepts. The Mongols who overthrew the Song dynasty patronized Lamaism and suppressed the literati. Zhu Yuanzhang, a rebel leader who overthrew the Mongols and founded the Ming dynasty (1368–1644), was the leader of the Red Turbans, a secret society that was inspired partly by the popular worship of Maitreya, the Buddha of the Future. Zhu ruled as the first Ming Emperor Hongwu (Hung-wu; r. 1368–99). During the Ming and Qing (1644–1911) dynasties, the Chinese literati were not attracted to Buddhism, and so the religion remained active primarily on the popular level, intermixed with Daoist practices. In the late 18th century, the White Lotus Rebellion (1796–1805), an outgrowth of the Maitreya worship of the Red Turbans Rebellion, posed a threat to the Qing dynasty.

Christian missionaries became influential in China during the 19th century. Modern Chinese leaders such as Sun Yat-sen, who led the Revolution of 1911 that overthrew the Qing and established the modern Republic of China (ROC), converted to Christianity and drew upon Western ideas. After the Chinese Communist Party (CCP) founded the People's Republic of China (PRC) in 1949, the Communist ideology espoused by CCP Chairman Mao Zedong (Mao Tse-tung; 1893–1976) replaced Confucian ideology in Chinese government and society. The CCP banned the practice of religion and returned Buddhist monks and nuns to lay life. Many religious buildings were destroyed or put to other uses, such as government offices. During the Cultural Revolution (1966–76), Red Guards attacked everything concerned with traditional Chinese culture and damaged or destroyed religious and historical sites. Since the late 1970s, the Chinese government has been restoring some religious buildings and opening them to the public, and it allows Chinese Buddhists to practice their religion once again.

Buddhist temples flourish in Hong Kong and Taiwan, where the Chinese Nationalists (Kuomintang; KMT) fled ROC after the Communists defeated them in a civil war in

1949. A person may enter a Chinese temple at any time to communicate with the deity, especially to get advice about a personal problem or decision. The worshiper may light several sticks of incense and place them in the incense brazier on the altar, bow or make prostrations before the altar, and offer sacrificial food or burn pretend paper money. The deity's answer is received by divination, such as shaking out of a vase a long slip of bamboo that has a number corresponding to a printed piece of paper, or by interpreting the pattern of two curved wooden blocks dropped on the floor. Temples are crowded at Buddhist festivals, such as the birthday of the deity housed in the temple, when men parade the sculpture of the deity around the neighborhood accompanied by the noise of firecrackers, horns, drums and cymbals. See also AMITABHA; BODHIDHARMA; BODHISATTVA; BUDDHA; CHAN SECT OF BUDDHISM; CHARMS AND AMULETS; CONFUCIANISM; DALAI LAMA; DAOISM; DAZU CAVE TEMPLES AND SCULPTURES; DUNHUANG CAVE PAINTINGS AND CARVINGS; FAMILY STRUCTURE; FAXIAN; FLOWER GARLAND SECT OF BUDDHISM; FOUR SACRED MOUNTAINS OF BUDDHISM; FUNERALS; GANSU PROVINCE; GUANYIN; HAN SHAN; HAN YU; IMPERIAL BUREAUCRACY; INK PAINTING; JOURNEY TO THE WEST; KARMA; KUMARAJIVA; LAMAISM; LIANG KAI; LONGMEN CAVE TEMPLES AND SCULPTURES; LOTUS; LOTUS SUTRA; LUOHAN; MAITREYA AND MANJUSRI; MARTIAL ARTS; MONGOL; MU QI; NEO-CONFUCIANISM; NORTHERN AND SOUTHERN DYNASTIES; NORTHERN WEI DYNASTY; PAGODA; PAPER; POTALA PALACE; PRINTING IN CHINA; PURE LAND SECT OF BUDDHISM; RED TURBANS REBELLION; SCULPTURE; SHAOLIN TEMPLE; SILK ROAD; SINICIZATION; SIX DYNASTIES PERIOD; SUI DYNASTY; TANG DYNASTY; TEMPLES; TIANTAI SECT OF BUDDHISM; TIBET; TIBETAN; VEGETABLES AND VEGETARIAN DISHES; WHITE HORSE TEMPLE; WHITE LOTUS SECRET SOCIETY; WU, EMPRESS; XUANZANG; YUNGANG CAVE TEMPLES AND SCULPTURES; ZHU XI.

BULHADING, TOMB OF See YANGZHOU.

BUND See HUANGPU RIVER; SHANGHAI.

BUREAUCRACY See HAN DYNASTY; IMPERIAL BUREAUCRACY; LITERATI; NINE-RANK SYSTEM; SONG DYNASTY; TANG DYNASTY.

BURGEVINE, HENRY ANDREA See WARD, FREDERICK TOWNSEND.

BURMA ROAD A transportation route built from the railroad terminus at Lashio, Burma, to Siakwan (Hsia-Kuan) in Yunnan Province in southern China to bring supplies to Chinese troops during China's War of Resistance against Japan (1937–45; World War II). A 9-foot-wide single-lane highway 715 miles long, it was built through the mountains of Burma by the hand labor of 200,000 men, women and children. The Burma Road was the only transportation route into and out of China after Japanese troops occupied the major cities of eastern China and Japanese ships blockaded the Chinese coast. Chinese Nationalist (Kuomintang; KMT) forces led by Generalissimo Chiang Kai-shek (1887–1975) had fled to the central Chinese province of Sichuan, which was protected by high mountains, and established their capital at Chongqing (Chungking). Supplies provided by the Allied forces were transported to Nationalist forces along the Burma Road. The Japanese pressured Great Britain, which had colonized Burma, to close the Burma Road, which Great Britain did on July 12, 1940. General Claire Lee Chennault (1890–1958) then organized the Flying Tigers (whose official name was the American Volunteers Group; AVG), a group of American pilots who volunteered to fly missions for China in 1941–42. They flew supplies from India over the "Hump" (the Himalaya Mountains) to China. In 1942 Japanese troops invaded China along the Burma Road, but Chinese troops, supported by Chennault's pilots, halted them in Yunnan. U.S. army engineers, later assisted by Chinese troops, were able to construct the Ledo Road, a 487-mile-long supply route that connected northeastern India with the old Burma Road. The Ledo Road opened to traffic in January 1945. Chiang Kai-shek later renamed this route the Stilwell Road to honor American General Joseph Stilwell (1883–1946), who served as commanding general of all U.S. forces in China, Burma and India during World War II and also served as Chiang's chief of staff. The Ledo Road remains an important transportation route. See also CHIANG KAI-SHEK; CHONGQING; FLYING TIGERS; HIMALAYA MOUNTAIN RANGE; NATIONALIST PARTY; STILWELL, JOSEPH; WAR OF RESISTANCE AGAINST JAPAN.

CAAC See AIRLINES AND AIRPORTS.

CADRE (*ganbu*) A person who has been completely indoctrinated in the revolutionary ideology and methods of the Chinese Communist Party (CCP) and who draws upon this indoctrination in his or her work; more generally, a person holding an administrative or managerial position in either the CCP or the government bureaucracy of the People's Republic of China (PRC), which the Communists founded in 1949. The Communist cadre system in the PRC is comparable to the civil service system in many other countries and to the former Confucian-educated imperial bureaucracy. Since 1949 the CCP has held a monopoly on political power in China and runs every unit in the country. In the 1950s the Communists consolidated their power by sending thousands of cadres into the Chinese countryside to lead the land-reform program under which land was taken away from landlords and wealthy peasants and redistributed to poorer peasants. The CCP controls all job assignments and promotions in the entire country, so every Chinese person who wants to advance his or her career or to work in a professional specialty must join the CCP. Party cadres function as overseers at every level of the Chinese economy and society, all the way down to villages and the neighborhood associations for families living along a common alley in Beijing and other cities.

Party cadres, especially at higher administrative levels, may earn several times more than ordinary Chinese workers, and the government gives them many benefits, such as the best housing, the use of official automobiles and drivers, excellent medical care, vacation trips, and the ability to buy consumer goods not available to the general public. Cadres are also in the best position to benefit from China's traditional informal system of connections (*guanxi* or *kuan-hsi*), in which people cultivate personal relationships to gain favors such as good jobs for themselves and their relatives, entrance into a university, better housing, and so forth.

Since China began modernizing in the late 1970s, party cadres have been taking advantage of the rapid growth of Chinese enterprises and markets and have been functioning as marketing consultants for local work units (*danwei*). In the late 1980s the party and government cadre system was staffed by about 14 million cadres, and reform leaders such as Deng Xiaoping attempted to streamline the bureaucracy by removing tens of thousands of elderly and incompetent cadres. They retired many cadres to advisory positions and took the radical step of abolishing the life-tenure system for state and party cadres and specifying age limits for many government offices. They also emphasized the need to promote younger and better educated cadres and to train them for leadership positions. See also ALLEYS; CHINESE COMMUNIST PARTY; DENG XIAOPING; IMPERIAL BUREAUCRACY; LAND REFORM BY COMMUNISTS; PEOPLE'S REPUBLIC OF CHINA; WORK UNIT.

CAI See AGRICULTURE; COOKING, CHINESE; VEGETABLES AND VEGETARIAN DISHES.

CAI YUANPEI See ACADEMIA SINICA; BEIJING UNIVERSITY.

CAIGUO See WOK.

CAIRO CONFERENCE See WAR OF RESISTANCE AGAINST JAPAN.

CALENDAR Division of a year into specified periods of time, which was important to the ancient Chinese as the means for regulating their agricultural cycle. The calendar was also important because the Chinese believed that the reigning emperor held his throne through the Mandate of Heaven that legitimized his rule. If the emperor proved unable to maintain the harmony between Heaven and Earth, he would lose the mandate. A well-governed empire was associated with regularity in the yearly cycle, and hence the annual calendar drawn up by the emperor's astronomers symbolized the emperor's rule as sanctioned by Heaven. Chinese legends claim that in 2254 B.C., Emperor Yao commanded his astrologers to establish the annual cycle of changing seasons so that farmers would know when to plant crops. This calendar was developed during the Shang dynasty (1750–1040 B.C.), the first dynasty from which archaeologists have found artifacts, and was prepared annually by a board of mathematicians directed by a minister of the imperial government. They drew up a lunar calendar based on the cycles of the moon, which range between 29 and 30 days long, shorter than the months in the Gregorian solar calendar used in the West. Each new Chinese dynasty published a new official annual calendar, and the publication of an unofficial calendar could be considered an act of treason.

In the Chinese lunar calendar, every month had to begin on the day of a new moon. On the first day of each new year, the emperor promulgated an almanac that informed his subjects of the dates for the start of each lunar month and whether an extra month would be added to the calendar that year to reconcile the lunar and solar calendars. The Chinese New Year or Spring Festival, by far the most important Chinese festival, has always been held on the second new moon after the winter solstice, between January 21 and February 20. Chinese astronomers had to reconcile the lunar year, which comprises 12 months having 354 days, with the solar year, which has 365 1/4 days, by adding intercalary or "leap" months to the calendar at certain times, making a 13-month year. Eleven leap months had to be added every 19 years to keep the lunar calendar from falling behind the solar calendar. The lunar years are organized in a cycle of 60 characters, with each year associated with two characters. The first character is one in a series of Ten Celestial Stems, associated with the traditional theory of the Five Material Agents (wood, fire, earth, metal and water), and the second is one of a series of Twelve Hourly Branches, which are also used to identify the 12 two-hour periods into which the Chinese divided a day. Each of the 12 years is associated with a particular animal, and every person born in that same year is believed to possess the traits of that year's animal. The 12-year cycles are further organized into a cycle based on the Five Material Agents, for a total of 60 years.

Since ancient times the Chinese have also used a third calendar, an artificial division of time comprising a series of 60-day periods. They also counted a 10-day cycle, considered one week, which determined the days of rest. The seven-day week was later adopted in China from Central Asia. The Chinese further divided the year into 24 "solar seasons" (qi or ch'i) that were named for the events that occurred during these seasons on the North China Plain, the cradle of Chinese civilization. For example, the spring season begins around February 5 with the New Year Festival, the rainwater season around February 19, insects awaken around March 5, and so forth. The Qing Ming (Ch'ing Ming; "Clear and Bright") Festival, when the Chinese sweep the graves of their ancestors and honor the deceased, is held every April 4 or 5, the 106th day after the winter solstice. The last solar season, known as severe cold, begins around January 21 and is the time when the Chinese busily prepare for the New Year Festival.

Chinese astronomers became highly skilled at studying the movements of the planets in the sky and predicting eclipses of both the sun and moon, and emperors built observatories to further the study of astronomy and astrology. By the end of the Warring States Period (403–221 B.C.), Chinese astronomers had compiled a catalog with 1,464 entries on stars and their positions in the sky. They revised the calendar more than 40 times over a period of 2,000 years (and made 50 more unsuccessful attempts to revise it). In the 16th century, during the Ming dynasty (1368–1644), Roman Catholic Jesuit missionaries went to China and impressed the imperial court with their knowledge of mathematics and science. In 1611 the Chinese Ministry of Rites recommended that the traditional calendar be reformed; the government commissioned a group of Jesuits who served in the Board of Astronomy, led by Joannes Adam Schall von Bell, to revise the calendar. The Qing dynasty (1644–1911), which overthrew the Ming, continued to use the Jesuit calendar, known as the Shixian (Shih-hsien). After Schall died in 1666, another Jesuit, Ferdinand Verbiest, took his place. When the Chinese overthrew the Qing in the Revolution of 1911, they replaced their traditional calendar with the Gregorian calendar used in the West. However, they continue to schedule their traditional festivals according to the lunar calendar.

The agricultural almanac (Tong Shu or T'ung Shu), which dates back more than 4,000 years, is still published annually and is consulted by Chinese all over the world to schedule important events, such as weddings, funerals and business agreements, on days that are astrologically auspicious. The almanac contains the solar and lunar calendars and information about many topics, such as lucky days, weather predictions, horoscopes and feng shui, or the art of geomancy—placing buildings and furniture in positions that will bring good luck. At the front of the almanac is a picture of a farmer with an ox, which contains details that predict the weather for the year. For example, a hat on the farmer indicates that the spring will be cold. See also AGRICULTURE; ALMANAC; ASTRONOMY AND OBSERVATORIES; FENG SHUI; FIVE MATERIAL AGENTS; HEAVEN; JESUITS; MANDATE OF HEAVEN; NATURAL DISASTERS; NEW YEAR FESTIVAL; OX; ZODIAC, ANIMAL.

CALLIGRAPHY (shu)   The art of writing Chinese characters or ideographs with a brush and ink. Calligraphy became a fine art when paper was invented in China around A.D. 200, enabling writers to spend countless hours perfecting their characters. The Chinese have always placed a high value on written texts and the aesthetic creativity of the ideographs, leading them to regard calligraphy as the greatest of the fine arts. The Chinese word for civilization (wen) is pronounced the same as the word for script or pattern. Members of the literati, or scholar-gentry class, were educated to write characters beautifully, and their calligraphy was believed to be a "heart print" (xinyin or hsin-yin), that is, to reveal their moral and spiritual self-cultivation. Calligraphy was one of the subjects in the examinations for the imperial bureaucracy's positions, which were filled by the literati. The tools of the calligrapher were the so-called Four Treasures of the Study, including paper, a pointed writing brush, inkstick and inkstone, which are all still used by Chinese calligraphers and monochrome ink painters. Ink is produced by grinding the inkstick on the inkstone while adding a small amount of water.

The finest Chinese calligraphers became famous, and their works were, and still are, highly valued as fine art. Students copy these works to improve their own calligraphy.

In China, calligraphy is considered the greatest of the fine arts.   COURTESY, MUSEUM OF FINE ARTS, BOSTON

Many Chinese paintings have been enhanced by the brushing of sayings or poems in calligraphy onto them. For the Chinese, the three arts of painting, calligraphy and poetry go together and are considered the "Three Perfections" (*sanjue* or *san chueh*). There are several kinds of inscriptions on paintings: those written by the painter, those written by the painter's friends, and comments about the painting by later collectors or connoisseurs. Those written by friends may praise the painter and his style, describe who was present and what they discussed when he executed the painting, and may include a poem. Some of the greatest Chinese calligraphers include Dong Qichang (Tung Ch'i-ch'ang), He Shaoji (Ho Shao-chi), Huang Tingjian (Huang T'ing-chien), Jin Nong (Chin Nung), Mi Fu, Qi Gong (Ch'i Kung), Wang

Xizhi (Wang Hsi-chih), Xu Wei (Hsu Wei), Yan Zhenqing (Yen Chen-ch'ing), Yu U Jen (Yu Yu-jen), and the so-called Eight Eccentrics of Yangzhou. Many Chinese artists best known for their paintings produced great works of calligraphy as well.

The most ancient form of Chinese writing consists of pictograms engraved into shells and "oracle bones" used for divination during the Shang dynasty (1750–1040 B.C.). They are known as "shell-and-bone characters" (*jiaguwen* or *chia-ku wen*). The number of Chinese written characters increased greatly during the Zhou dynasty (1100–256 B.C.), as seen on inscriptions on bronze objects from that time, and the script started to become stylized. By the end of the Warring States Period (403–221 B.C.), the Chinese were writing on bamboo strips and silk textiles with ink and a bamboo-handled brush with goat or rabbit hair. In the late third century B.C., Emperor Qin Shi Huangdi (r. 221–210 B.C.), the unifier of China, revised the Chinese writing system by getting rid of about half the characters that had been used and restructuring many of the characters that were retained. The Han developed this script into *bafen* (*pa-fen*), an "eight-part script" in which characters were formed by combining eight basic features. This script, with each character consisting of a geometric pattern inside a square shape, became known as "official" or "clerical script" (*lishu*). The formal versions of these characters have kept the same structure for more than 2,000 years, down to the modern era, although informal cursive and abbreviated versions have also been developed. The government of the People's Republic of China, founded in 1949, has made mandatory the use of many abbreviated characters and has created more simplified forms. However, Chinese living in Taiwan and other places outside mainland China continue to use the traditional written characters.

There are four general styles of Chinese calligraphy. Each style requires the writer to handle the brush in a certain way. The calligraphy must have a balance of thick and thin strokes and must be neither too heavy nor too light.

1. **Seal scripts** developed from characters used by ancient scribes. The great seal script (*dazhuan* or *ta-chuan;* also known as *zhouwen* or *chou-wen*) was developed during the Zhou dynasty by a court recorder, also named Zhou, who standardized the various writing systems into a system of 9,000 characters. The characters standardized under Emperor Qin Shihuangdi are known as small seal script (*xiaozhuan* or *hsiao-chuan*). The seal-script style is solemn because every stroke is given the same weight, and it is very difficult to write with a brush. The style became fashionable among some calligraphers in the 17th century and is still used for writing formal verses which are given as presents.

2. **Regular or standard brush scripts** range from the "clerical" or "official script" (*lishu*) standardized during the Han dynasty to the "regular style" upon which modern printed characters are based. This was the first calligraphic style to utilize all the types of strokes that a brush can make, and it is the most difficult and complicated of all the styles of Chinese calligraphy. Many Chinese regard *lishu* as the most important calligraphic style. It is still used for official purposes such as banknotes and street-name signs. The *kaishu* or "regular style," a simplification of *lishu*, became the accepted script for all formal uses since A.D. 200 and is the style taught in Chinese schools today. It is also known as "regular characters" (*zhenshu* or *chen-shu*) and "orthodox characters" (*zhengshu* or *cheng-shu*).

3. **Running script** (*xingshu* or *hsing-shu*) is a simplified cursive version of the *lishu* style that was used to write private and informal letters. The style may have been developed by Wang Xizhi (Wang Hsi-chih; 321–79).

4. **"Grass" script** (*caoshu* or *ts'ao-shu*) is a shorthand of *lishu* with greatly abbreviated and rapidly written characters. The calligrapher is free to change or even eliminate many of the brushstrokes. This style is cursive yet abstract and

intuitive and can only be read by persons who have made a special study of the script. See also BRONZEWARE; FOUR TREASURES OF THE STUDY; HAN DYNASTY; IMPERIAL EXAMINATION SYSTEM; INK PAINTING; LANGUAGE, CHINESE; LITERATI; ORACLE BONES; QIN SHIHUANGDI, EMPEROR; WRITING SYSTEM, CHINESE; NAMES OF INDIVIDUAL CALLIGRAPHERS.

CAMBULAC   See BEIJING; KHUBILAI KHAN; YUAN DYNASTY.

CAMEL CARAVANS   Long trains of pack animals that began traveling west from Chang'an (modern Xi'an in Shaanxi Province), the capital of the Han dynasty (206 B.C.–A.D. 220), carrying luxurious silk to trade in Central Asia and the Middle East on the route that became known as the Silk Road. Camels, which can survive in the desert without water for long periods, were brought to China from Central Asia by the third century B.C.

Central Asians had domesticated two-humped Bactrian camels, which were preferred on the Silk Road because they could keep up a faster pace than one-humped dromedary camels, and each Bactrian could carry as much as 500 pounds of goods. The Bactrian camel grows from 7 to 11 feet long, including the head, and has a tail as long as 30 inches. The camel has a short, dark brown coat in the summer, and grows a long, warm woolly coat in the winter. Camel caravans were the only means of transportation in the desert regions of western and northern China right into the early 20th century; camels are still used today, along with railroads and trucks. For protection against bandit attacks, merchants on the Silk Road formed large caravans that included as many as a thousand camels and were defended by armed guards. Today a small number of camels roam in wild herds in the Gobi Desert, but most camels are domesticated. In the northern Chinese cuisine, camels were consumed at special occasions; camel's hump stew was a delicacy served at the table of the imperial family. See also GOBI DESERT; HAN DYNASTY; SILK; SILK ROAD; TAKLIMAKAN DESERT; ZHANG QIAN.

CAMELLIA   Evergreen shrub belonging to the tea family (*Theacae*) native to mild climates in China and other Asian countries. The camellia has shiny, bright green leaves and waxy, long-lasting white, pink or dark red flowers that may bloom from September through April. The three species of camellia that are commonly cultivated around the world are native to China and Japan. The most important is the *Camellia japonica,* which can grow up to 30 feet high in its native forests. The hardy *Camellia sasanqua* has many varieties. The most famous and beautiful Chinese camellia species, *Camellia reticulata,* is native to the southwestern province of Yunnan. Records from the Ming dynasty (1368–1644) praise Yunnan camellias as "the most beautiful flowers under Heaven." The bushes may grow as high as 20 feet and bear dark pink flowers during winter and spring.

The Chinese are attempting to protect rare camellia species. For example, a reserve for the *Camellia chrysantha* has been established in Fangcheng in Guangxi-Zhuang Autonomous Region in southwestern China. The *Camellia rhytidocarpa,* or "Wrinkled-fruit Camellia," is one of the 10 plant species protected in Huaping Reserve in Guangxhi. The golden camellia, the rarest of the more than 200 varieties of camellia in China, is mostly found in Yunnan Province. See also GUANGXI-ZHUANG AUTONOMOUS REGION; YUNNAN PROVINCE.

CAMPHOR WOOD   Wood of a large evergreen tree known as *Cinnamomum camphora* belonging to the laurel family (*Lauraceae*). Native to warm climates in China, Taiwan, Japan, Java and Sumatra, and Brazil. Camphor wood is a major agricultural product in Taiwan. The Yu Mountains in China have an abundance of tall camphor trees. The Chinese have long stored scrolls and other important documents in cabinets and chests made of camphor wood to protect them from insects. China's oldest government archives, the Imperial Historical Archives (also known as the First Historical Archives) in Beijing preserves documents in 20 camphor-wood chests decorated with imperial dragons and clouds.

Camphor—a strong but sticky, fragrant crystalline compound made by distilling the wood and bark of the camphor tree—makes an excellent repellent for use in mothballs, medicines (especially camphor oil for aching joints) and plastics. See also IMPERIAL HISTORICAL ARCHIVES; TAIWAN.

CANALS   See HANGZHOU; GRAND CANAL; QIN DYNASTY; SUI DYNASTY; SUZHOU; YUAN DYNASTY.

CANTON   See GUANGZHOU; GUANGZHOU (CANTON) FAIR.

CANTON OPERA   See OPERA, GUANGZHOU.

CANTON SYSTEM   The system by which the Chinese government regulated all trade between China and Western nations from the mid-18th century until 1842. The Chinese, who had always considered their empire the center of the world, or the "Middle Kingdom" (Zhongguo or Chung Kuo), had conducted trade with Asian nations by making them pay tribute to China and thus acknowledge the sovereignty of the Chinese emperor or "Son of Heaven" (*tianzi* or *t'ien tzu*). When the Dutch and Portuguese came to China to trade in the 16th century, they tried at first to obtain wider trading privileges but finally agreed to submit to the requirements of the tributary system. In 1760 the Qing dynasty (1644–1911) established the Canton system whereby Western merchants would have to conduct all of their business in the southern Chinese port city of Canton, Guangzhou in Chinese. They would also have to be supervised by native Chinese merchants who belonged to a guild known as the Cohong or "Hong" (from *gonghang*, "combined merchant companies"). The Cohong had been formed in 1720 by Chinese merchants in Canton who wanted to monopolize foreign trade and thus earn higher profits through regulation of prices for imported and exported goods. The 12 or 13 members of the Cohong were held responsible not only for the trade but also for the proper behavior of the Westerners. In 1754 the Qing had ordered the Cohong merchants to "secure" or guarantee every ship that sailed into Canton, and so they became known as the security merchants. They sold the cargo brought by the Western ships, procured the Chinese goods that the Western traders wanted to purchase, and collected all duties and tariffs and turned them over to the Chinese government. They also took care of the needs of the ships' captains and crew. The Chinese merchants forced the Western traders to pay bribes and much higher tariffs than the amounts set by the Chinese government. The traders could not get back any money lost if a Cohong merchant went bankrupt or refused to pay what he owed the traders. The Chinese government subjected the Westerners to many regulations and greatly restricted their activities. Western traders residing in Canton had to confine themselves to an area along the bank of the Pearl River where the residences and offices of the foreign "factors" were located, known as the Thirteen Factories. They were not allowed to bring their wives and families or to study the Chinese language. At the end of the summer trading season each year, they were required to shut down their operations in Canton and move to Macao, a small island the Chinese had ceded to the Portuguese in the mid-16th century. Trade and communication with Qing government officials could only be conducted through members of the Cohong. The profits were so great from trading with China that Western traders submitted to the restrictions placed on them. The British East India Company conducted most of the foreign trade with China at Canton. In 1793 the British government and the East India Company sent Lord George Macartney to China to request the ending of the Canton system, the opening of more Chinese ports to foreign trade and the setting of fair tariffs. The Qing Emperor Qianlong refused to give in to these requests and informed British King George III that China would not increase its foreign trade because it did not need anything from other countries. The British were not satisfied and pressed China harder and harder to open the country to foreign trade, especially by selling large quantities of opium to the Chinese. The Canton system ended in 1842 when Britain defeated China in the Opium War and forced China to sign the Treaty of Nanjing, which abolished the Canton Cohong monopoly system; opened the Chinese cities of Canton, Fuzhou, Xiamen (Amoy), Ningbo and Shanghai to British subjects as so-called treaty ports; and ceded the island of Hong Kong to Britain. See also BRITISH EAST INDIA COMPANY; GUANGZHOU; HONG KONG; MACAO; MIDDLE KINGDOM; NANJING, TREATY OF; OPIUM WAR; PEARL RIVER; TREATY PORTS; TRIBUTE SYSTEM.

CAO CAO   (Ts'ao Ts'ao; A.D. 155–220)   A military general who took power at the end of the Eastern, or Later, Han dynasty (A.D. 25–220) and became the most important leader in northern China. Cao Cao was born to a wealthy aristocratic family; his father had been adopted by a head eunuch in the imperial palace. Cao Cao entered the military and became a general. He put down the Yellow Turbans Rebellion, a peasant uprising that began in A.D. 184 and almost overthrew the Han dynasty (206 B.C.–A.D. 220). During the period of a coup and subsequent anarchy at the end of the Eastern Han, warlords controlled various regions of China, especially in the south. Cao Cao forced the eastern Han emperor to leave the Han capital at Luoyang in central China and move northeast to Yenzhou. Meanwhile, in Luoyang Cao Cao appointed himself chief minister of the Han and thus effectively became the dictator of the Han Empire. With the dream of reunifying China, Cao Cao waged military campaigns against other warlords. By 205 he conquered and unified all of China north of the Yangzi River. He aimed to found a new dynasty but died in 220 before he could do so.

Cao Cao had built up his army from members of the Yellow Turbans Rebellion who had surrendered to the Han. He declared that he would restore the centralized authority of the Han, but although he won the Battle of Guandu, he did not achieve his goal. Cao Cao led his Wei forces against those of the kingdom of Shu in Sichuan Province and those of the kingdom of Wu, a naval power that lay south of the Yangzi in the region of modern Nanjing. Cao Cao was defeated by Shu and Wu forces at the Battle of Chibi on the Yangzi because of the superior naval skills of the southern military. He was forced to accept a division of the country between north and south and to give up his dream of unifying all of China. When Cao Cao died in 220 his son Cao Pi (Ts'ao P'i), deposed the Han puppet emperor and founded the Wei dynasty, which succeeded in briefly conquering the southwest in 263. The kingdoms of Wei, Wu and Shu became locked in a stalemate known as the Three Kingdoms Period (220–80).

Cao Cao's exploits were immortalized in a cycle of folktales that formed the basis for the epic 14th-century historical novel *Romance of the Three Kingdoms* (*Sanguozhi yanyi*). Episodes from this novel are still performed in Beijing opera, and Cao Cao is one of the most frequently staged and best-known characters in the opera. In addition, Cao Cao is famous for his poetry. He and his sons are termed the four royal poets of the Wei dynasty, known collectively as Cao Wei Fu Zi. See also CAO FAMILY OF ROYAL POETS; EASTERN HAN DYNASTY; OPERA, BEIJING; ROMANCE OF THE THREE KINGDOMS; THREE KINGDOMS PERIOD.

CAO FAMILY OF ROYAL POETS (Ts'ao Family)   A family that held the throne of the Kingdom of Wei, one of the so-called Three Kingdoms (Three Kingdoms Period, Sanguo; 220–80) and included four major poets, known collectively as Cao Wei Fu Zi (Ts'ao Wei Fu Tzu): Cao Cao (Ts'ao Ts'ao; 155–220); two of his sons, Cao Pi (Ts'ao P'i; 187–226) and Cao Zhi (Ts'ao Chih; 192–232); and Cao Rui (Ts'ao Jui; 205–239), a son of Cao Pi. When Cao Cao died in 220, his son Cao Pi (Ts'ao Pi) deposed the Han dynasty (206 B.C.– A.D. 220) puppet emperor and founded the Wei (or Cao Wei) dynasty that ruled the Kingdom of Wei (220–65) with its capital at Luoyang. Cao Cao is the most famous of the four because he was also a great military leader who defeated his rivals and unified China north of the Yangzi River. He attempted to conquer the kingdom of Shu to the south but was defeated. Cao Cao is a leading character in the epic 14th-century historical novel, *Romance of the Three Kingdoms* (*Sanguozhi yanyi*). Episodes from this novel are performed in Beijing opera, and Cao Cao, the "villain," is one of the most frequently staged and best-known opera characters. Known as Wei Wendi (Wen-ti), he was a patron of literature as well as a poet and critic. His "Essay on Literature" is the earliest work of Chinese literary criticism. Cao Zhi had vied with Cao Pi for the Wei throne from 211 until 217, when Cao Pi named Cao Zhi his heir apparent. However, Cao Zhi never took the throne, for when Cao Pi died, his son Cao Rui took his place, ruling as Wei Mingdi (Ming-ti; r. 226–239).

The four Cao poets often wrote verses with lines of five or seven characters, a poetic form which later became popular during the Tang dynasty (618–907) and is known as Regulated or New-Style Verse (*shi* or *shih*). Cao Pi's "Song of

Yen," about the separation of a husband and wife, is the oldest seven-character *shi*.

Although Cao Zhi never held a government position, he played an important role in the development of Chinese lyric poetry. Critics regard Cao Zhi as the best of the four poets. He drew upon the anonymous folk ballads (*yufu* or *yueh-fu*) that had become popular in China during the previous four centuries. He wrote most of his poems using five-character lines and favored such imaginative subjects as the luxuries of the Wei court, the Daoist immortal who ascends to Heaven, and the person who wanders through the countryside. Cao Zhi had a great influence on other Chinese poets during his own time and in later periods. See also CAO CAO; REGULATED OR NEW-STYLE VERSE; ROMANCE OF THE THREE KINGDOMS; THREE KINGDOMS PERIOD.

CAO GUO JIU   See EIGHT IMMORTALS.

CAO WEI FU ZI   See CAO CAO; CAO FAMILY OF ROYAL POETS.

CAO XUEQIN   See DREAM OF THE RED CHAMBER.

CAO YU (Ts'ao Yu; 1905–   )   Né Wan Jiabao; a prominent playwright who has written Western-style dramas and has been associated with many prestigious Chinese cultural associations. Cao was born in Tianjin, a major port city near Beijing, but his family was from Hubei Province. He graduated from prestigious Qinghua University in 1931 and became a professor of drama in China and the United States. In April 1935, Cao Yu's first and most famous drama, *Thunderstorm* (*Leiyu*), was given its premiere in Tokyo. It was published in late 1934 in the *Literary Quarterly* (*Wenxue jikan* or *Wen-hsueh chi-k'an*) and in 1935 as a book. In 1935 he wrote *Sunrise* (*Richu* or *Jih-ch'u*), in 1937 *The Wild* and in 1941 *The People of Beijing* (*Beijingren* or *Peking-jen*). He also co-founded the Chinese Drama Society in 1937. After the Chinese Communist Party (CCP) established the People's Republic of China (PRG) in 1949, Cao held a number of important positions in the Central Drama Institute, the Federation of Literature and Art Circles, the Writers' Association, the Association for Cultural Relations with Foreign Countries, Beijing Literature and Art Association, People's Academy of Dramatic Arts and Sino-Soviet Friendship Association's executive board. He also visited Japan and Prague, Czechoslovakia, as a member of peace delegations. In 1965 he became a member of the CCP.

Cao was director of the Beijing People's Art and Drama Institute before the Cultural Revolution (1966–76) and resumed that position in 1979. He was purged in 1966 and did not reappear until 1975, when he became a Hubei deputy to the 46th National People's Congress (NPC), serving until 1988. He also served as a member of the NPC Standing Committee from 1978 to 1983. In 1978 he was vice president of the Chinese Dramatists' Association, and in 1979 he was elected chairman. Since 1979 he has led delegations of playwrights to the United States, Western Europe and Japan. In 1981 he was elected president of the International Theatre Institute's China Center; in 1982, vice president of the PEN Centre; and in 1982, president of the Shakespeare Research Foundation. His dramas since 1949 include *Bright Skies* (*Minglang de tian* or *Ming-lang te t'ien*;

1954) and *Wang Zhaojun* (*Wang Chao-chun*; 1978), about one of the "four famous beauties" of Chinese history, a princess during the Han dynasty (206 B.C.–A.D. 220) who was sent to marry the ruler of Mongolia and is still revered by the Chinese people for her virtue and the great sacrifice she made to bring peace between China and tribes beyond its borders. See also COMMUNIST PARTY; CULTURAL REVOLUTION; DRAMA, CHINESE; NATIONAL PEOPLE'S CONGRESS; PEOPLE'S REPUBLIC OF CHINA; QINGHUA UNIVERSITY; WANG ZHAOJUN.

CAOZHUN See KITCHEN GOD.

CARAVANS See CAMEL CARAVANS; HAN DYNASTY; SILK ROAD.

CARP (*yu, li*) A large freshwater fish that has several meanings in Chinese culture. The carp is a symbol of strength and perserverance. The scales and whiskers of the fish give it a resemblance to the dragon, the greatest symbol of power. According to Chinese legend, a carp that is brave and strong enough to swim up the Yellow River against the current and leap the falls at Dragon Gate (Longmen) will be transformed into a dragon; hence the popular Chinese saying, "The carp becomes a dragon" (*li hua long*). The design motif of a carp leaping over Dragon Gate was a symbol for successfully passing the civil service examinations that would enable a scholar to receive an appointment in the imperial bureaucracy and attain literary distinction. The carp is also a popular design motif on Chinese porcelain.

Fish play a large part in the Chinese diet, especially in southern China where they are abundant in lakes and rivers. The words for fish and abundance are pronounced the same in Chinese (*yu*), so the fish symbolizes wealth. A whole cooked fish, usually a carp, is the central dish at a Chinese banquet. A favorite recipe is a sweet-and-sour dish called West Lake carp that originated in the city of Hangzhou near the famous West Lake.

Fish also symbolize harmony, marital happiness and reproduction because they multiply rapidly and are believed to swim in pairs. Hence fish are some of the traditional gifts that a bride's family expects to receive at a formal betrothal ceremony. At the New Year Festival, "lucky money" is given out in red envelopes decorated with a carp, as well as a peach and pine tree, symbols of long life.

Beautiful varieties of ornamental carp, especially the golden variety, are raised in Chinese ponds and tanks, moving freely without restraint through its watery environment, the fish is an important symbol in the Buddhist religion. Fishtanks are found in the courtyards of Buddhist temples, and a fish is one of the auspicious motifs in designs of the Footprint of the Buddha. See also BANQUETS; BUDDHISM; DRAGON; FISH AND SHELLFISH; IMPERIAL BUREAUCRACY; NEW YEAR FESTIVAL; PORCELAIN; WEDDINGS, TRADITIONAL; WEST LAKE; YELLOW RIVER.

CARPETS (*ditan* or *ti-t'an*) Large, thick floor-coverings woven from sheep or goat wool or camel hair. Carpet weaving in China dates back to the Eastern Han dynasty (A.D. 25–220), when the Chinese Empire expanded north and west to include many nomadic animal-herding tribes, who wove patterned blankets by hand for protection against the cold winters. By the Tang dynasty (618–907), carpet weaving had become a popular craft in China, as seen in the poem *Red Carpet* by the famous Tang poet Bai Juyi (Po Chu-i; 772–846): "The carpet is soft and fragrant/The delicate patterns are too precious to be trampled." In the 10th century, when the Khitan (Qidan) made the city of Youzhou (modern Beijing) the capital of the Liao dynasty (947–1125), numerous carpets were brought to the capital from northwestern China as tribute to the emperors. This stimulated an active handwoven-carpet industry in Youzhou. In 1860, during the Qing dynasty (1644–1911), the Dalai Lamai, the religious and political leader of Tibet, visited China's capital and presented Tibetan carpets to Emperor Xianfeng (Hsien-feng). The emperor greatly admired the carpets and established a carpet-weaving institute with Tibetan artisans as teachers.

Beijing, Tianjin and Suzhou have become the modern Chinese centers for carpet weaving. Beijing carpets have many colorful designs known as "Chinese orthodox" based on ancient imperial patterns and motifs of birds and flowers developed from designs used for traditional Chinese bronze ware, pottery, porcelain, lacquerware, silk textiles, murals, stone carvings and paintings. Some examples are dragons, flying phoenix birds, bats, lotus flowers, the Twelve Symbols of Authority and the Eight Treasures of Buddhism. Some modern Chinese factories also produce carpets designed in the style of other countries such as Persia (modern Iran). Old carpets were dyed with vivid, lasting natural dyes in blue, red and imperial yellow. Modern carpet-makers are not able to reproduce these hues; thus, these authentic old carpets are now extremely rare and expensive.

The craft also remains a thriving industry in Tibet and Xinjiang autonomous regions in western China. Artisans in Gyangze, Tibet, known as the "home of Tibetan carpets," have produced carpets for more than 600 years. About one-third of the city's nearly 8,600 households produce carpets and traditional Tibetan costumes. Bayan Hot in Xinjiang has had a carpet industry for nearly 200 years. Carpets were originally produced for aristocratic families and Buddhist temples, which used handwoven cushions and pillar covers as well as carpets. Nomadic herdsmen also used handwoven saddle rugs, which they also slept on. By the end of the Qing dynasty (1644–1911), there were more than 10 workshops in Bayan Hot, then known as Dingyuanying (Ting-yuan-ying), that produced handwoven carpets and silver and copper wares. In 1965 the Alxa Carpet Factory was established as the largest in the area, with workshops for shearing, washing, spinning, dyeing and weaving wool. In 1991 the company's traditional style of carpet, known as "Mansion" or "Prince's Mansion," won a silver medal at the second international fair in Beijing.

Weaving a carpet by hand requires many steps. In a factory, artists design the carpets, developing about 6 to 10 designs in color every month. The completed design is then given to another designer or copier, who draws it in black on tissue paper that is the actual size of the carpet to be woven. The tissue paper is then pasted onto the cotton warp yarns strung on the loom, and the design is traced onto the yarns to provide a guide for the weaver. A miniature design of the carpet with directions for the colors to be used in each line is also provided. A weaver sits at the loom and ties knots of wool, with each knot bound to two warp threads; trims them with a sharp knife to the depth of pile specified; and pounds them into place with an iron fork-shaped tool. The depth of the carpet's pile ranges from 3/8 to 5/8 of an inch. The longer the pile the softer the carpet. The number of warp yarns may vary from 60 to 120 per square foot, with 90 the most common number for the popular market. A heavy weft or cross-thread is also part of the carpet's structure. Several weavers may work on a large carpet. Large carpets are usually woven in two or three sections which are bound together by the warp threads. See also BAT; DRAGON; EIGHT TREASURES; LIAO DYNASTY; LOTUS; NOMADS AND ANIMAL HUSBANDRY; PHOENIX; TIBET; TWELVE SYMBOLS OF AUTHORITY; XINJIANG-UIGHUR AUTONOMOUS REGION.

CAS See CHINESE ACADEMY OF SCIENCES.

CASTIGLIONE, GIUSEPPE See QING DYNASTY.

CATHAY A name for China, derived from Khitai; also, the Central Asian name for an ethnic group of proto-Mongols known in China as Khitan (Qidan or Ch'i-tan). The Khitan were a confederation of tribes from the areas of Inner Mongolia and western Manchuria. They ruled North China 947–1125 as the Liao dynasty with their capital at Peking (Beijing). After the Liao fell in A.D. 1125, the name Khitai was still used by neighboring peoples for the region that had been ruled by the Liao dynasty. This region was differentiated from China proper, which included Central China, ruled by the Five Dynasties (A.D. 907–60), with its capital at Kaifeng; and South China, ruled by the Southern Song dynasty (1127–1279), with its capital at Hangzhou. The terms Cathay and China were both used by the European explorer Marco Polo (1254–1324), who spent 17 years in China during the Yuan dynasty (1279–1368), which had been established by the Mongols. European geographers believed they were two different regions until the early 17th century, when the Jesuits Matteo Ricci and Bento Goes verified that Cathay and China were the same. Today Khitai remains the preferred name for China in Russia and in Western and Central Asia.

In English literature the name Cathay for China is sometimes used with exotic connotations. See also LIAO DYNASTY; MONGOL; POLO, MARCO; RICCI, MATTEO.

CAVE TEMPLES AND SCULPTURES See BUDDHISM; DAZU CAVE TEMPLES AND SCULPTURES; DUNHUANG CAVE PAINTINGS AND CARVINGS; LONGMEN CAVE TEMPLES AND SCULPTURES.

CAVES OF A THOUSAND BUDDHAS See XINJIANG-UIGHUR AUTONOMOUS REGION.

CCP See CHINESE COMMUNIST PARTY.

CELADON WARE (*qing ciu* or *ch'ing tz'u,* "blue-green porcelain") A type of stoneware coated with a semi-translucent green-gray glaze. The color is caused by the oxidation of iron in the glaze when the ware is fired at a high temperature in a kiln. Production of celadon-type ware originated with the pale-green Yue wares of Zhejiang Province in the third century B.C. They were compared to jade for their color and luminous quality. The high point of celadon production came during the Five Dynasties period (A.D. 907–60) and the Song dynasty (960–1279).

Celadon was the first Chinese ceramic ware brought to Europe. The name was applied to these ceramics by French collectors in the 17th century, after the green-gray ribbons worn by a shepherd named Celadon, the hero of the French play *Astrée* by d'Urfe. The Chinese simply use the term "blue-green ware," and sometimes further identify a piece by the name of the kiln where it was produced. Celadon pieces from kilns in Yaozhou, Shaanxi Province, in northern China are the best known and have an olive-green glaze. Pieces from Longquan kilns in southern Zhejiang Province tend to have a bluish tint due to the white clay used by the potters, which heightens the shiny quality of the glaze.

Celadon ware is frequently decorated with patterns in slight relief that are created by incising or casting the pieces before glazing, so that when the piece is fired the glaze collects in the grooves. Well-known designs from the Song dynasty include lotus and peony flowers and clouds. Some pieces have crackles in the glaze. Originally the crackles happened accidentally, when the glaze shrank faster than the body of a piece while cooling after firing, but potters began producing crackles for a decorative effect. Celadon ware was widely exported to Muslim countries in the Middle East, and also throughout Asia, beginning in the Tang dynasty (618–907). Techniques for producing celadon were adopted by potters in Korea and Japan. Celadon was taught to Korean potters at the end of the 10th century A.D. and became the predominant ware in Korea during the Yi dynasty (1392–1910). In Japan the production of celadon was perfected at the Seto kilns. See also JADE; SONG DYNASTY.

CELESTIAL LAKE See URUMQI.

CENTRAL ASIA See ARCHAEOLOGY; BUDDHISM; CAMEL CARAVANS; HAN DYNASTY; HORSE; KAZAKH; KIRGHIZ; LATTIMORE, OWEN; MUSLIMS; NOMADS AND ANIMAL HUSBANDRY; SILK ROAD; TANG DYNASTY; UIGHUR; XINJIANG-UIGHUR AUTONOMOUS REGION; XIONGNU.

CENTRAL COMMITTEE OF THE CHINESE COMMUNIST PARTY The government organization in which political power is formally vested in the People's Republic of China (PRC), founded by the Chinese Communist Party (CCP) in 1949. The National Party Congress, which is in theory the highest body of the CCP and convenes every five years, elects the members of the Central Committee, which has 30 component departments and functions as the highest political body between meetings of the National Party Congress. Meetings of the Central Committee, known as plenums or plenary sessions, are supposed to be held at least once a year. Central Committee members also hold partial, informal and enlarged meetings where they formulate policies which are then confirmed by a plenum. The Central Committee has the power in plenum to elect a Politburo (Political Bureau) and the chairman of the CCP, as well as its vice chairmen. Mao Zedong (Mao Tse-tung) was chairman of the CCP until he died in 1976 and was succeeded by Hua Guofeng (Hua Kuo-feng). The CCP chairman is also the commander in chief of the People's Liberation Army (PLA).

The Central Committee assigns much of its work to the Politburo and the Standing Committee of the Politburo, whose members are elected by the Central Committee. The Politburo is the major decision-making body in the Chinese government, and the Standing Committee, with about half a dozen members, is its innermost circle of power. In 1962 there were 187 members of the Central Committee, 25 members of the Politburo and 7 members of the Standing Committee. Until the late 1970s, the military had a large representation on the Central Committee and other national-level political bodies. Deng Xiaoping, as part of his reforms to rebuild China after the Cultural Revolution (1966–76), began decreasing military participation in these bodies and reduced military membership in the Central Committee from 30 percent in 1978 to 22 percent in 1982. In May 1982 the Central Committee reorganized its internal structure, cutting staff by 17.3 percent and reducing subordinate bureaus by 11 percent. Nearly half of the members elected to the Central Committee in September 1982 were new members, and 83 percent of the alternate members were newly elected. See also CHINESE COMMUNIST PARTY; GOVERNMENT STRUCTURE; HUA GUOFENG; MAO ZEDONG; NATIONAL PARTY CONGRESS; PEOPLE'S REPUBLIC OF CHINA; POLITBURO.

CENTRAL KINGDOM   See MIDDLE KINGDOM.

CENTRAL MILITARY COMMISSION AND MINISTRY OF NATIONAL DEFENSE   The Communist Party and government bodies responsible for national defense in the People's Republic of China (PRC), founded by the Chinese Communist Party (CCP) in 1949. The Central Military Commission directs the People's Liberation Army (PLA) under the command of the chairman of the CCP, who until 1982 was China's commander in chief, and administers the National Defense Science, Technology and Industry Commission (NDSTIC), which was formed in 1982 by merging several government bodies concerned with defense science and technology. Members of the Central Military Commission are elected by the CCP Central Committee and control the military through the General Political Department of the PLA. The Ministry of National Defense works very closely with the Central Military Commission and draws up plans for implementing the defense and military policies set by the CCP. It also provides military attachés for Chinese embassies, and its Foreign Affairs Bureau deals with foreign attachés and military visitors. It works closely with the Ministry of Foreign Affairs when high-level military and government leaders travel abroad. The ministry's strategic research arm, the Beijing Institute for International Strategic Studies, performs research on military and security issues that affect the PRC's foreign policy. Military courts, the largest group of special courts in China, are independent of civilian courts and directly subordinate to the Ministry of National Defense. Military courts try all treason and espionage cases, and their decisions are reviewed by the Supreme People's Court.

The positions of chairman of the Central Military Commission and of minister of national defense are never filled by the same person, but many members of the Central Military Commission also hold positions in the Ministry of National Defense. The minister of national defense is superior to the chief of staff of the PLA but is under the direct orders of the chairman of the CCP and the premier of the State Council. The ministry operates training programs and military exercises for the PLA, provides the framework for logistical and administrative military activities, and determines strategies and weapons to be used. Leaders of the PRC government reformed the military command structure in 1980, and in 1982 the armed forces were completely reorganized under General Yang Dezhi to transform the PLA from a people's militia trained in revolutionary ideology led by Mao Zedong (Mao Tse-tung) into a disciplined professional army trained in modern warfare. The hierarchy of military ranks and the use of special uniforms for officers, both of which had been abolished during the Cultural Revolution (1966–76), were reinstituted. In 1982, as part of the general reform movement led by Deng Xiaoping, a state Central Military Commission was created under the National People's Congress as a counterpart to the CCP Central Military Commission. The same leader heads both commissions, and the CCP commission retains authority over the state commission. Deng, who wanted to reduce the political role of the military and place it under civilian control, had become chairman of the CCP commission in 1981, and he appointed his supporters to key positions in the CCP commission, the Ministry of National Defense, and the PLA's General Staff Department, General Political Department and General Logistics Department. The 1982 state constitution kept the CCP Military Commission to provide the political direction for military policy, but it established the state Central Military Commission to oversee the appointments of top military leaders, manage PLA financial and material resources, and develop and implement military regulations to make the PLA more professional. It also designated the chairman of the state Central Military Commission as commander in chief of the armed forces. In 1985, to save money, the PRC reduced its army of 4.2 million by one-quarter to 3 million soldiers, still the largest army in the world. The PRC purchased or built a range of modern sophisticated weapons, and by 1988 it had become a manufacturer and supplier of arms to other countries, such as Iraq. Since 1949 a large proportion of the PRC's scientific and technical research and development efforts have been performed for the military and have been kept secret. See also CHINESE COMMUNIST PARTY; NATIONAL PEOPLE'S CONGRESS; PEOPLE'S LIBERATION ARMY; PEOPLE'S REPUBLIC OF CHINA; STATE COUNCIL; SUPREME PEOPLE'S COURT.

CERAMICS   See BLUE-AND-WHITE WARE; CELADON WARE; DEHUA PORCELAIN; DING WARE; ENAMELWARE; JINGDEZHEN; LONGSHAN CULTURE; PORCELAIN; RU WARE; TEMMOKU WARE; THREE-COLOR WARE; WHITE WARE; YANGSHAO CULTURE; YI-XING POTTERY; ZIZHOU WARE.

CHA   See TEA.

CHAIRMAN MAO   See MAO ZEDONG; QUOTATIONS FROM CHAIRMAN MAO ZEDONG.

CHAN SECT OF BUDDHISM   A sect of the Buddhist religion, which was introduced into China from India around the first century A.D., known in the Western world by the Japanese term Zen. "Chan" is the Chinese word for *dhyana* (*zazen* in Japanese), the Indian Sanskrit term for meditation or concentration of the mind, and hence Chan is known as the meditation sect of Buddhism.

Legends attribute the founding of Chan to Bodhidharma (known as Daruma in Japan), who supposedly traveled to China from India around 520 and sat cross-legged facing a wall in meditation for many years. According to legend, he first stayed at Shaolin Temple in central China. Bodhidharma supposedly spent nine years in meditation there, after which time he taught Shaolin monks self-defense techniques that developed into the Chinese martial arts. Legend also has it that a troubled Chinese scholar named Shenguang (Shen-kuang) approached Bodhidharma, desperate to learn the answer to the problem of human suffering, and became his first Chinese student, acquiring the name Huike (Hui-ko). Bodhidharma taught enlightenment—the cessation of suffering—by having the student come to the realization that the ordinary self which suffers is not a person's Buddha Nature or True Self. He claimed to bring a "direct transmission" of the Buddha Nature which had been transmitted from the Buddha himself and passed on from teachers to students.

Chan does not rely on written scriptures or a transcendent god to be worshiped, but teaches the direct awakening of the True Self, as expressed in a famous Chan summary:

> Direct transmission from mind to mind
> No reliance on the written word
> Transmission outside of the [orthodox] religion
> Pointing directly to the human mind and seeing the
> innate nature, one becomes Buddha; this mind is
> already Buddha.

Along with meditation, Chan developed other techniques to help a student gain enlightenment, such as interviews with Chan masters. Chan systematized a body of "public cases" (*gongan* or *kung-an; koan* in Japanese) that describes past encounters between Chan students and teachers and is intensely studied and meditated upon. Many other collections of Chan stories provide a history of the sect.

One of the most important Chan masters was Huineng (638–713), who became the sixth Chan patriarch in a direct line from Bodhidharma and is regarded by many as the actual founder of Chan in China. He taught that the realization of enlightenment is not a gradual process but is experienced all at once by a student who has been grappling with the problem of suffering.

Chan became an established sect in China by the eighth century. Along with meditation and *koan* study, it also emphasized the communal life of monks and nuns in monasteries, and physical work such as cooking, cleaning and gardening. When the Tang dynasty emperor persecuted Buddhists in 845, the Chan Sect survived because of its freedom from such things as written texts, religious symbols, sculptures and other representations of deities. Chan has coexisted harmoniously with Pure Land, the other major sect of Chinese Buddhism. The Chan Sect, which values simplicity and spontaneity, became associated with the arts, especially ceramics, monochromatic ink painting and poetry, as expressed in the poems attributed to Han Shan. Liang Kai (Liang K'ai) and Mu Qi (Mu Ch'i), both active in

the 13th century, are the most renowned Chinese Chan painters.

Chan or Zen was introduced into Japan and gained a firm hold there due to the efforts of Eisai (1141–1215) and Dogen (1200–53), both of whom spent many years studying in Chinese Chan monasteries, and many Chan texts were translated into Japanese (and recently into English). The modern Japanese Zen teacher Shaku Soen (1859–1919) and his student, D. T. Suzuki (1870–1966), introduced Zen to the Western world, where it has become an influential religious sect. The two main Japanese Zen schools, which have taken root in the West, are Soto, derived from the Chinese Caodong (Ts'ao-tung) School, and Rinzai, originated by the Chinese Chan master Linji (Lin-chi; d. 867). The Linji School began the practice of koan study. See also BODHIDHARMA; BUDDHA; BUDDHISM; HAN SHAN; INK PAINTING; LIANG KAI; MARTIAL ARTS; MU QI; PURE LAND SECT OF BUDDHISM; SHAOLIN TEMPLE.

CHANG CHIAO See ALCHEMY; YELLOW TURBANS REBELLION.

CHANG CH'IEN See XIONGNU; ZHANG QIAN.

CHANG CHUEH See YELLOW TURBANS REBELLION.

CHANG CH'UN-CH'IAO See CULTURAL REVOLUTION; GANG OF FOUR; JIANG QING.

CHANG CHUN-CH'IU See ZHANG JUNQIU.

CHANG E The Goddess of the Moon, also known as Heng O. Chang E is associated with the Autumn Moon Festival that takes place on the 15th day of the eighth month—around mid-September—in the traditional Chinese lunar calendar. During the festival, the Chinese view the full moon and imagine they see Chang E flying across it. In Chinese mythology, Chang E was the wife of the famous archer Hou Yi, who was supposedly a member of the Imperial Guard during the reign of the legendary Emperor Yao. One day 10 suns appeared in the sky, causing the people to suffer years of heat and drought. Hou Yi used his magic bow and arrows to shoot down nine suns, leaving only one sun, and saved the earth. He was rewarded with the pill of immortality by the Daoist goddess Xiwangmu, the Royal Lady of the West. While Hou Yi was away on a mission, one of his disciples went into his bedroom to steal the pill, found Chang E admiring it, and threatened to kill her if she did not give it to him. Frightened, she swallowed it instead, and became immortal and flew up to the moon. When she got there she was so exhausted that she spit out the casing of the pill, which became a jade rabbit. Chang E herself became a three-legged toad. All the while Hou Yi had been chasing her across the sky, but his pursuit was hampered by a strong wind. He built a palace on the sun and continued to shoot arrows at her. Symbolized by the moon and the sun, Chang E and Hou Yi see each other on the 15th night of every lunar month, on the night when the moon is fully illuminated by the sun's rays. They represent the principles of feminine and masculine, negative and positive, and *yin* and *yang* that the Chinese believe govern the universe. See also AUTUMN MOON FESTIVAL; XIWANGMU; YAO, EMPEROR; YIN AND YANG.

CHANG HENG   See ZHANG HENG.

CHANG HSUEH-LIANG   See ZHANG XUELIANG.

CHANG, K. C.   See ARCHAEOLOGY.

CHANG KUO LAO   See EIGHT IMMORTALS.

CHANG KUO-T'AO   See ZHANG GUOTAO.

CHANG LING   See MING TOMBS.

CHANG LING   See ZHANG DAOLING.

CHANG LO-HSING   See NIAN REBELLION.

CHANG TA-CH'IEN (Zhang Daqian; 1899–1983)   Also known as Chan Dai-chien and Zhang Yuan (Chang Yuan); a prolific modern Chinese painter, collector and connoisseur. Chang Ta-Ch'ien was born in Sichuan Province to an artistic family and attended boarding school at Chongqing. He was only 12 years old when he received his first commission—to paint a set of divining cards for a fortune teller. At 17, he was captured by bandits while coming home from school. The bandit chief made him write a letter to his family asking for ransom money, and his calligraphy was so beautiful that the chief made him his personal secretary. During the 100 days that he was a captive, Chang read poetry books that the bandits had stolen from wealthy homes.

Chang and his brother, Zhang Shanzi (Chang Shan-tzu), went to Japan to study textiles. When he returned, Chang studied traditional Chinese painting in Shanghai with the famous painters Zeng Xi (Tseng Hsi) and Li Ruiqing (Li Jui-ch'ing), and worked as a painter in Shanghai and Suzhou. In 1940 he went to the Buddhist Dunhuang Cave Temples in the northwestern province of Gansu, where he spent $2\frac{1}{2}$ years copying more than 200 murals in the temples, which date back more than a thousand years. He then visited famous mountains and rivers throughout China, visiting Mount Huang (Huangshan) four times.

Chang became very eccentric, adopting the style of a long robe and beard worn by ancient Chinese scholars, and he had several wives at the same time. After traveling all over the world and spending many years in the United States, India, Argentina and Brazil, Chang settled in Taipei, Taiwan. He frequently made forgeries of paintings by old Chinese masters to fool curators and connoisseurs, which he often did. Many of these paintings probably hang in museums around the world under the names of the original artists, complete with fake red-seal impressions.

Chang Ta-ch'ien was a prolific artist who mastered all the traditional styles of Chinese painting, especially those of the 17th and 18th centuries, and produced about 30,000 paintings of his own. He also developed his painting style on the works of Western abstract expressionists. When he grew older he began losing his eyesight, so he developed a new form of landscape painting by splashing ink and bright blue, green and yellow colors made from minerals onto paper and adding a few final touches with a brush. Eighty-seven of Chang Ta-ch'ien's paintings were exhibited in 1992 at the Arthur M. Sackler Gallery in Washington, D.C., the Asia Society in New York City and the Saint Louis Art Museum. Chang's daughter, Zhang Xinrui (Chang Hsin-jui), became a teacher at the Sichuan Art College. See also DUNHUANG CAVE PAINTINGS AND CARVINGS; HUANG MOUNTAIN RANGE; SEALS.

CHANG TAO-LING   See ZHANG DAOLING.

CHANG TSO-LIN   See ZHANG ZUOLIN.

CHANG TZU-CH'IEN   See ZHAN ZIQIANG.

CHANG YUAN   See CHANG TA-CH'IEN.

CHANG'AN ("Enduring Peace")   The capital of China for more than 1,000 years during 11 dynasties, from the Zhou (1100–256 B.C.) through the Tang (618–907); now known as the modern city of Xi'an, the capital of Shaanxi Province in central China. Chang'an and the city of Luoyang (to the east in Henan Province) frequently alternated as the capitals of successive dynasties. A village from the Neolithic period excavated at the nearby village of Banpo indicates that the Chang'an area, situated in the Wei River valley, was inhabited at least 8,000 years ago. In the mid-11th century B.C., King Wenwang of the Western Zhou dynasty (1100–771 B.C.), which overthrew the Shang dynasty (1750–1040 B.C.), established his capital at Feng, southwest of modern Xi'an, on the west bank of the Feng River. The next Zhou king moved the capital to Hao on the east bank of the river, and this remained the capital until 771 B.C.

Emperor Qin Shi Huangdi, the unifier of China who founded the Qin dynasty (221–206 B.C.), established his capital on the north bank of the Wei River in Xianyang, near modern Xi'an. (In 1974 archaeologists discovered the burial site of Emperor Qin Shi Huangdi. The excavation of the terra-cotta army of 7,000 life-size soldiers, horses, chariots and their trappings that were buried east of his mausoleum has become one of the most popular tourist destinations in China.)

Gaodi, the first emperor of the Han dynasty (206 B.C.–A.D. 220) built his capital farther north of Xianyang. The Han dynasty was weakened by the Yellow Turbans Rebellion. The three most powerful Han generals divided the empire among them. The ensuing period is known as the Three Kingdoms Period (A.D. 220–80) and was characterized by power struggles among several clans that continued for the next 360 years. During this time, Luoyang, Chengdu, and Nanjing were all established as capitals of various dynasties. Wendi, the emperor who founded the Sui dynasty (581–618), unified China under a central government, resolving centuries of conflict, and established his capital southeast of the Han dynasty capital, calling it Daxingzheng, "City of Great Wealth." He then restored Luoyang and moved his capital there.

Gaozu, first emperor of the Tang dynasty (618–907), returned the capital to the original Sui capital at Daxingzheng and named it Chang'an ("Enduring [or Eternal] Peace"). He expanded the city by building palaces, markets, and parks. Chang'an was the final destination on the Silk Road, the network of trade routes along which camel caravans carried silk, porcelains, tea and other Chinese goods through Central Asia to the Middle East and brought West-ern goods, art, and religion into China. During the Tang, Chang'an was the largest and most cosmopolitan city in the world, with a population of one million in the city itself and nearly 2 million in the metropolitan area. It was inhabited by many traders from foreign countries, including thousands from Persia (modern Iran), who were Muslims and estab-lished the Muslim religion (Islam) in China. Some other groups included Central Asian Muslims such as Uighurs, Tibetans, Zoroastrians, and Nestorian Christians. The Bud-dhist religion, which had been introduced from India around the first century A.D., flourished in China during the Tang, as did Chinese art, literature and performing arts.

The marvels of Chang'an, including its magnificent palaces, temples, markets and large population of foreigners, were described in numerous Chinese sources. The city was visited by the Japanese Buddhist monk Ennin (793–864), whose diary is the oldest surviving account of China by a for-eigner. The Japanese city of Kyoto (originally called Heian-kyo, "Capital of Peace and Tranquillity"), established in 794, was modeled on Chang'an. Kyoto was also built on a grid, surrounded by mountains and bisected by a river. Kyoto remained the imperial capital of Japan until 1868 when the emperor moved to Tokyo. Chang'an was built following the principles of *feng shui* or Chinese geomancy, which aligns a site with favorable geographic features. Chang'an has a grid pattern and is surrounded by mountains with a river running through it. During the Tang, Chang'an had 9 main streets running north and south and 12 running east and west. The city was divided into 112 districts for administrative pur-poses. It was surrounded by a 24-mile-long wall with 13 gates, 4 in the north and 3 each in the south, east, and west. Part of the southern wall, known as Xiwang Tai, can still be seen just south of Lianhualu Street in front of Yuxiangmen gate. The Imperial Palace complex was located in the north-ern part of the city. Today the foundations of the palace buildings known as Taiji Gong, Daming Gong and Xinqing Gong can be seen. Government offices were located south of the palace district, considered the inner city. Residences, markets, temples and mosques were located in the outer city. Chang'an began to decline after the fall of the Tang dynasty. It recovered somewhat during the Ming dynasty (1368–1644), when a royal residence was constructed at Chang'an. By then the city was called Xi'an and was only about one-sixth the size of Chang'an during its high point under the Tang. See also CAMEL CARAVANS; ENNIN; FENG SHUI; LUOYANG; MUSLIMS; QIN SHI HUANGDI, EMPEROR; SILK ROAD; XI'AN; YELLOW TURBANS REBELLION; NAMES OF INDI-VIDUAL DYNASTIES.

CHANGBAI MOUNTAIN RANGE (Changbaishan or Chang-pai Shan)   A series of parallel mountain ranges, running northeast to southwest in the southeastern region of Manchuria (northeastern China) along the Chinese border with North Korea. Many rivers originate in the Changbai Mountain Range, including the Yalu, the Sungari (Songhua-jiang) and the Tumen, which flow out of Tianchi Lake ("The Lake of Heaven"). The heavily forested mountains have a dozen year-round snow-covered peaks; hence, they are called Changbai ("eternal white"). Baiyun Peak, 8,830 feet high, is the highest point in Manchuria. The peaks, all more

than 7,500 feet, are volcanoes that have erupted three times since the 16th century, the latest in April 1702. Volcanic eruptions formed Tianchi Lake, which covers an area of 609 square miles and has a depth of 1,224 feet, making it the deepest lake in China. There are hot springs in various parts of the lake, as well. The Changbai Waterfalls, a famous scenic spot in the northern slope of the Changbai range, plunge 223 feet into the Erdaobai River, which flows into the Songhuajiang. The Changbai mountain range has a harsh cli-mate, with strong winds blowing about 270 days a year. About 1,400 varieties of plants grow in the mountains, 800 of which have economic value for the Chinese. The Chang-bai mountain range is China's principal source of timber, as well. The "three treasures" of Manchuria are also found there: ginseng, a root which is used in herbal medicines; the sika deer, whose antlers are also used in medicines; and the sable, a small animal with a beautiful and valuable fur coat. Protected cranes and Manchurian tigers also live in the mountains. In 1961 the Chinese government established the Changbai Mountain Nature Reserve, covering 469,500 acres, the largest in China, and a forest ecology study station. Many Chinese and foreign scientists conduct scientific surveys in the Changbai Mountains, and South Korean tourists also visit the region. See also CRANE; DEER; GINSENG; JILIN PROVINCE; MANCHURIA; SABLE; TIGER; TUMEN RIVER; YALU RIVER.

CHANGCHUN   The capital city since 1954 of Jilin Province, with a population of 1.5. million. Changchun is situated on the Yitong River in the center of China's large northeastern plain, part of the region known as Manchuria. The name Changchun means "Eternal Spring." Changchun was largely developed during the Japanese occupation of Manchuria (1932–45), when it served as capital of the Japan-ese puppet state, Manchukuo (Manzhoughuo in Chinese). Puyi (Xuantong or Hsuan-t'ung), the last emperor of the Qing dynasty (1644–1911), which had been established by the Manchurians, was declared to be Manchukuo's "emperor," but a Japanese government official wielded the actual power. Puyi's former palace is now open to the public as the Changchun Museum. The Japanese gave Changchun the name Xinjing. The South Manchurian Railroad, which Japan used for exploiting the minerals and other resources of Manchuria, ran between Changchun and Dalian, an impor-tant harbor on the southern tip of the Liaodong Peninsula.

Following the war, China's first automobile manufactur-ing plant was constructed in Changchun, which remains the "motor city" of China. Factories still produce cars, trucks, buses, railroad cars, tractors and the famous "Red Flag" lim-ousines for Chinese leaders. Other industries include electric motors, machine tools, textiles and food processing. The Changchun Film Studio (formerly the Northeast Film Stu-dio), which was set up in 1946, is very well known. Also in Changchun are Jilin University, one of 22 institutes of higher learning located there, and the prestigious Chinese Academy of Sciences.

Tourist attractions include South Lake (Nanhu) Park, the Children's Park, and Xinlicheng Reservoir on the upper course of the Yitong River. The Puppet Emperor's (Puyi's) Palace and Exhibit hall are open to the public. See also CHI-NESE ACADEMY OF SCIENCES; FILM STUDIOS; JILIN PROVINCE;

MANCHUKUO; MANCHURIA; PUYI, HENRY; WAR OF RESISTANCE AGAINST JAPAN.

CHANGJIANG AND CHANGJIANG DAQIO BRIDGE
See NANJING; YANGZI RIVER.

CHANG-PAI SHAN   See CHANGBAI MOUNTAIN RANGE.

CHANGSHA
The capital city of Hunan, a densely populated province in south-central China. Changsha is situated on the east bank of the Xiang River and has the largest harbor along the Xiang, enabling goods to be transported by barges. The majority of freight includes grains, coal, timber and construction materials. The alluvial plains around Changsha are among the most fertile regions of China, and major crops include rice, tea, soybeans and grains. Greater Changsha has a population of more than 4 million and has been an important trading center for more than 2,000 years. In 1904 Changsha was opened to foreign trade, and many Europeans and Americans settled in the city. In 1908 a railroad was built linking Changsha with Hankou (now part of the city of Wuhan) and the capital city of Beijing. Today Changsha is one of the three most important stations on the Beijing-Guangzhou railroad line connecting northern and southern China.

Changsha was inhabited at least 5,000 years ago, and written records go back 3,000 years. Three tombs dating from the Western Han dynasty (206 B.C.–A.D. 8) have been excavated at Mawangdui, an eastern suburb of the city. The Hunan Provincial Museum houses archaeological exhibits on the region's history, including rare artifacts from the Mawangdui tombs such as lacquerware and fragments of books copied onto silk. The crafts of metalworking, lacquerware and textiles have been practiced in Changsha since the Spring and Autumn Period (722–481 B.C.). Tourists can visit the Hunan Ceramics Museum and the Museum of Chinese Traditional Painting, Pottery, and Porcelain. During the Song dynasty (960–1279), Changsha was an important center for education. The Yuelu Academy, one of China's four imperial academies of higher education, was founded in Changsha in 976. It is now Hunan University located in Yuelushan Park, where there are teahouses and pavilions from which to view the countryside. Mao Zedong, leader of the Chinese Communist Party and founder of the People's Republic of China in 1949, was born in nearby Shaoshan and moved to Changsha in 1912 to attend Teacher's Training College. He became an active member of the Chinese Communist Party while residing in Changsha. Tourists can visit the many sites associated with Mao, such as his schools and the houses where he resided. From October 1921 to April 1923 he lived with his first wife at Qingshuitang, the former office of the Hunan Party Committee, and one of their children was born there. The Juzi Zhou Tou Memorial Pavilion has been erected in Mao's honor. Every year on June 24, thousands of swimmers reenact Mao's famous swim across the Xiang River in 1959 when he was 65 years old.

Other sites include Kaifu Buddhist Temple, the Changsha Catholic and Protestant churches, and the Muslim Temple. Orange Island is a long sandbank in the middle of the Xiang River that affords a good view of the river traffic. A remnant of Changsha's ancient wall can still be seen. Most of the city was destroyed during the War of Resistance against Japan (1937–45) and was not restored until the 1950s. The city has been industrialized, with major products including textiles, processed foods, machine tools, electronics and chemicals. Lushan Temple on Yuelushan was founded in 268 and is one of the oldest surviving Buddhist temples in China. See also ARCHAEOLOGY; CHINESE COMMUNIST PARTY; HUNAN PROVINCE; MAO ZEDONG; RAILROADS.

CHAN-KUO   See WARRING STATES PERIOD.

CHAO CH'ING   See ZHAO DAN.

CHAO KAO   See EUNUCHS; QIN DYNASTY; QIN SHI HUANGDI, EMPEROR.

CHAO K'UANG-YIN   See NORTHERN SONG DYNASTY.

CHAO MENG-FU   See ZHAO MENGFU AND GUAN DAOSHENG.

CHAO SHAO-ANG   See ZHAO SHAO'ANG.

CHAO TAN   See ZHAO DAN.

CHAO TZU-YANG   See ZHAO ZIYANG.

CHAO YUNG   See ZHAO MENGFU AND GUAN DAOSHENG.

CHAOSHAN   See SHANTOU.

CHAOZHOU   See SHANTOU.

CHAPDELAIN, FATHER   See ARROW WAR.

CHARMS AND AMULETS (fu)
Small objects that the Chinese traditionally wear or carry in the belief that they possess the power to bring good fortune, protect from disease and ward off evil spirits. Amulets are made from a great variety of materials, such as paper, stone, metal and found natural objects. Some are worn on a cord hung around the neck or on the shoulder, chest or back, and others may be placed at specific points in rooms or, if paper, pasted on doors or walls. In China, religious verses may be printed on narrow strips of red or yellow paper and pasted over doors or onto walls to protect a home. Larger paper charms are often decorated with woodcuts—colorful pictures made from hand-carved wooden blocks. Printing, invented in China and stimulated by the Buddhist religion, was introduced from India around the first century A.D. Small pieces of paper were printed in great quantities with Buddhist verses or charms from a canon of thousands of sutras, or scriptures. None of the ancient Chinese paper charms have survived, but many have survived in Japan, where they were printed around A.D. 770 during the reign of the Empress Shotoku to celebrate the end of a civil war. The charms were printed from copper blocks that had been cast from clay models, a technique the Japanese learned from the Chinese.

Another traditional Chinese printed charm was the "swallow ashes charm" (shaohuitunfu or shao hui t'un fu), a spell against evil spirits written on a piece of yellow paper. The person holding the paper charm burns it, then mixes the ashes with water and swallows them. Chinese farmers ensure food harvests by buying special paper charms known as *hushenfu* to keep evil spirits away from growing crops and to protect their pigs and chickens. These charms have brightly colored pictures of the agricultural deities or simply have their names written on them. They include the rain-bringing dragon, or the spirit of the land; the sun-loving phoenix, or the spirit of grain, especially rice; and the deity of the local region. Two words that are frequently inscribed on paper charms are *fu*, meaning prosperity or happiness, and *shou*, meaning long life. *Shou* is often combined with *shuangxi* (*shuang-hsi*), the auspicious character for double happiness. The Chinese like to buy new charms on the first day of the New Year, the most important festival in the Chinese calendar. Paper charms are also important in the native Chinese tradition of Daoism. In popular Daoism, Zhang Daoling (Chang Tao-ling), the first Master of Heaven, created charms and talismans (held objects) to protect humans and animals from evil spirits. He also founded a school of exorcism and faith healing. Paper charms and bronze medals with a picture of Zhang riding a tiger and wielding the magic sword with which he conquered the "Five Poisonous Animals" are also popular in China.

Mirrors have always been considered powerful by the Chinese and play an important role in geomancy or *feng shui*, or the study of the placement of certain objects at crucial places in a room to protect a home. *Feng shui* also relies on charms, including pictures of spirits or "words of power" written on paper scrolls or inscribed on stone tablets. The "old brass mirror" (*gutongjing* or *ku t'ung ching*) supposedly had the power to heal a person who has been made "insane" by the sight of a demon, by simply having the person look at his or her face in the mirror. Wealthy Chinese hung such mirrors in their homes. Traditional brides also protect themselves by wearing the so-called illuminate-demon mirror (*zhaoyaojing* or *chao yao ching*).

Coins or coin-shaped objects have been another popular form of amulet in China. Shopkeepers often hung a picture of two coins, symbolic of the God of Wealth, to attract money. Old brass or copper coins (known as "cash") having a hole in their center were strung on a long piece of iron to form the shape of a sword; this was hung at the head of a bed in the belief that the emperor during whose reign the coins were minted would keep away ghosts and evil spirits. They were especially used in rooms of those who are sick or have committed suicide or died violent deaths.

Traditionally, a tiger's claw amulet (*huzhao* or *hu chao*) supposedly gives the wearer the courage of the tiger. A carved peach-wood or peach-stone amulet supposedly has great power against evil spirits, binds children to life and brings longevity. Children especially have needed protection, since the infant mortality rate has been very high in China, and when babies are born their families acquire charms from their local temples. Many children wear a brass or silver charm shaped like a flat padlocked around their necks, which is believed to chain them to life and protect them against death. Another common charm is a silver dog-collar to make evil spirits think the child is only a dog, considered by many Chinese to be a worthless creature. Chinese boys were often dressed like girls, or wore jade or silver anklets,

for the same reason. Wearing a silver chicken leg ensures that the boy will be able to "scratch" a good living when he grows up. Little boys also wear red threads around their wrists to bring them long life and happy memories. See also BUDDHISM; CURRENCY, HISTORICAL; DAOISM; DOUBLE HAPPINESS AND LONG LIFE; DRAGON; FENG SHUI; MIRRORS; NEW YEAR FESTIVAL; PAPER; PHOENIX; PRINTING; TIGER; WEDDINGS, TRADITIONAL; ZHANG DAOLING.

CHE SCHOOL OF PAINTING See DAI JIN.

CHEKIANG PROVINCE See ZHEJIANG PROVINCE.

CHEN BODA See CULTURAL REVOLUTION.

CHEN DUXIU (Ch'en Tu-hsiu; 1879–1942)

Author who helped reform Chinese literature and who was also a founder and leader of the Chinese Communist Party. Chen was born into a wealthy family in Anhui Province and was given a traditional Chinese education. He also traveled abroad to study in Japan, where he helped in founding several revolutionary societies, and in France, where he was influenced by the history of the French Revolution. After the Republic of China was founded in 1912, Chen was appointed Dean of Letters of Beijing University, China's most prestigious university. In 1915 he founded *New Youth* (*La Jeunesse*), a monthly intellectual journal that acquired a large circulation. In 1919 he wrote a controversial editorial for the magazine that supported social science and democracy in place of Confucian morality and hierarchical Chinese tradition. Chen was a leader, along with Lu Xun and other Chinese authors, of the New Culture Movement, which replaced classical Chinese with the vernacular language, called *baihua* (*pai-hua*), in modern Chinese literature.

Chen was also a leader of the Chinese protest against Japan known as the May Fourth Movement of 1919 and was imprisoned for three months for distributing antigovernment literature, opposing the government of the Republic of China in Beijing that had made a secret agreement to award Japan the concessions in Shandong Province formerly held by Germany. Conservative opponents forced Chen to resign from Beijing University. He moved to Shanghai, a center for Marxist revolutionary activity, where he founded the Chinese Communist Party with Li Dazhao (Li Ta-chao; 1888–1927). Chen served as the first secretary of the Chinese Communist Party 1921–27. Mao Zedong (Mao Tsetung; 1893–1976), who later became party leader, was at the time a delegate to the party's First Congress, which met in Shanghai in 1921. Chen opposed the view of Mao Zedong and other Chinese Communist leaders that they had to work with members of the peasant class in order to overcome Chinese feudalism, and under Chen's leadership the party almost collapsed, especially when he forgave the Nationalist (Kuomintang; KMT) forces who had committed anti-Communist massacres in Shanghai and Wuhan. In 1927 Mao deposed Chen and removed him from the party. The Nationalist government arrested Chen in 1933 and sentenced him to prison. He was pardoned in 1937 and died of cancer in 1942. See also CHINESE COMMUNIST PARTY; LU XUN; MAO ZEDONG; MAY FOURTH MOVEMENT OF 1919; NATIONALIST PARTY; NEW CULTURE MOVEMENT.

CHEN DYNASTY See NORTHERN AND SOUTHERN DYNASTIES.

CHEN HONGSHOU (Ch'en Hung-shou; 1598–1652) A painter who is considered one of the most creative artists during the late Ming dynasty (1368–1644). Chen also used the names Zhanghou (Chang-hou) and Laolian (Lao-lien). He was born in Zhejiang Province in southern China to a family of literati or Confucian-educated scholars who held positions in the imperial bureaucracy. When he was four years old he supposedly painted a mural more than 10 feet high of Guan Yu (Kuan Yu), a great general in the second century who later became worshiped as Guandi (Kuan-ti), the Chinese God of War. Chen's first painting teacher was Lan Ying, a master in the Zhe School of Painting. At age 10, Chen went to Hangzhou, the cultural center of China, to study painting. He progressed so rapidly that he began selling his works when he was only 14 years old. He also studied philosophy with a well-known scholar named Liu Zongzhou (Liu Chung-chou). After his parents both died, he became boisterous and drank heavily, yet he continued to paint. He excelled in all major Chinese art forms, including bird-and-flower, figure and landscape painting. He studied previous masters of these forms but developed his own style, which became more exaggerated as he grew older. His bird-and-flower paintings are filled with vivid colors; his landscape paintings are quite decorative; and his figure paintings are touched with irony. Chen also painted models for woodcuts that were printed to illustrate sets of game cards and three editions of the popular novel *The Romance of the Western Chamber.* He was renowned as well for his calligraphy, the fine art of writing Chinese characters with a brush. In addition, he wrote numerous essays on art, which were compiled by his son under the title, *Collected Writings of the Hall of Precious Silken Threads.*

During the reign of Ming emperor Chongzhen (Chungchen; r. 1628–45), Chen was given an official position as a professional painter in the imperial court in Beijing, where he copied the portraits of emperors from previous dynasties. He became famous in the court, but the corruption of many of its members prevented him from rising to a high position, so he resigned and returned to Zhejiang. In 1644 the Manchus, an ethnic group from Manchuria (northeastern China), overthrew the Ming dynasty and established the Qing (1644–1911). When the Qing army reached Zhejiang, Chen became a Buddhist monk at Yunmen Temple in Shaoxing, 40 miles from Hangzhou, where he took the names Huichi (Hui-ch'ih), Laochi (Lao-ch'ih) and Yunmen Monk. He became ill and died when he was 55 years old. See also BIRD-AND-FLOWER PAINTING; CALLIGRAPHY; FIGURE PAINTING; GUANDI; HANGZHOU; LANDSCAPE PAINTING; MING DYNASTY; QING DYNASTY; WOODCUTS.

CH'EN HUNG-SHU See CHEN HONGSHU.

CH'EN I See CHEN YI.

CHEN KAIGE (Ch'en K'ai-ke; 1953–) One of China's most prominent film directors, Chen's films present realistic portrayals of life in rural Chinese villages. His father, Chen Huai'ai, is also an important film director in the generation of Chinese directors whose films are characterized by socialist realism. When the Cultural Revolution (1966–76) broke out, Chen Kaige had to go to Yunnan Province in southern China to work on a rubber plantation even though he was only 15 years old. He then had to serve in the People's Liberation Army (PLA) and work in a factory, spending a total of eight years in Yunnan. In 1978 Chen was able to become a student in the Directing Department of the newly reopened Beijing Film Academy. His first film was *Yellow Earth* (1985), the tragic story of a young peasant woman who lives on the Loess Plateau in northern Shaanxi Province and is forced into an arranged marriage. Zhang Yimou (Chang Yi-mo), who has become an important film director in his own right, was the cinematographer for this film. Chen and Zhang are considered members of the post–Cultural Revolution Fifth Generation of film directors in China. *Yellow Earth* gained critical acclaim when it was shown at the Ninth Hong Kong International Film Festival in 1985. It was also shown at film festivals in Cannes, Montreal, Tashkent, Edinburgh and Hawaii. Chen's second film was *Big Parade*, about the life of soldiers in the PLA. He next filmed *King of the Children,* which describes the difficult experiences of a high school student who had been sent to work in the countryside for nine years during the Cultural Revolution and who is "recalled" to teach in a poor rural school. It was shown at the 1988 Cannes Film Festival.

In 1987, Chen went to New York to study and work. He was the first Chinese director of his generation to live in a foreign country for a long period, learn English and become friendly with foreign artists. He stated that his experiences there made him want to experiment more in his filmmaking. When Chen returned to China, he wrote and directed *Life on a String* (1990), which tells the story of an elderly master of a one-stringed musical instrument called the *erhu* and his young pupil, both of whom are blind. The master tells the boy that he might be cured of blindness if he will devote his life to music. Chen based the film on a story by Chinese author Shi Tiesheng (Shih T'ieh-sheng), which has been translated into English as "Strings of Life." Chen's wife, Hong Huang (Hung Huang), helped him finance the film by attracting British, German and Japanese investors. They worked through Beijing Film Studio to put together an all-Chinese crew to shoot the film. This was the first film shot in China by a Chinese crew and director that was completely financed by foreign investors.

Chen's best-known film is *Farewell My Concubine*, which won the Best Film award at the Cannes Film Festival in 1993. Based on the popular novel by the Hong Kong author Lilian Lee, this is a modern epic about the difficult friendship of two male stars of the Beijing Opera as they suffer through wars and the Cultural Revolution. One specializes in male roles and the other in female roles, and they often perform a famous opera about a Chinese emperor and his favorite concubine. The relationship between the two stars is tragically changed when one marries a woman, played by the internationally renowned Chinese actress Gong Li (Kung Li). Chen's films have won many international awards and a special prize at the Golden Rooster Awards, China's equivalent to the Academy Awards, or Oscars. His most recent film is *Temptress Moon* (Feng Yue; 1997). See also CONCUBINAGE; CULTURAL REVOLUTION; ERHU; FILM STUDIOS; GONG LI; LOESS; OPERA, BEIJING; PEOPLE'S LIBERATION ARMY; ZHANG YIMOU.

CH'EN PO-TA   See CULTURAL REVOLUTION; DENG XIAOPING.

CHEN SHAOBAI (CH'EN SHAO-PAI)   See SUN YAT-SEN.

CHEN TS'I   See ACUPUNCTURE.

CH'EN TU-HSIU   See CHEN DUXIU.

CHEN YI (Ch'en I; 1901–72)   One of the most important Chinese Communist military leaders during the 1930s and 1940s, who held high positions in the Chinese government. Chen Yi also became a leader of the Chinese Communist Party (CCP) and served as China's foreign minister (1958–67). Born in Sichuan Province, Chen was able to work and study in France (1919–21) through a worker-student program sponsored by the Chinese government. Zhou Enlai (Chou En-lai) and Nie Rongzhen (Nieh Jung-chen), who also became Communist leaders, were with Chen Yi in France. Chen had become politically active in France, and continued to be so after his return home. Back in China, Chen and Zhou held positions at the Whampoa (Huaingpu) Military Academy. In 1927, Chen took part in the Communist Nanchang Uprising. In 1928 he joined the Fourth Red Army recently formed by Mao Zedong (Mao Tse-tung), leader of the CCP, and Zhu De (Chu Teh), founder of the Chinese Communist Army. From 1934 to 1935 the Communists had to move their headquarters from south-central to northwestern China, which they did on the rigorous Long March. While most Communist leaders went on the march, Chen stayed behind in southern China to head the guerrilla movement there. When China went to war with Japan, which had invaded China (War of Resistance against Japan, 1937–45), Chen's guerrilla forces were taken into the New Fourth Army, the main Communist force in central China. This combined force fought the Japanese in the lower valley of the Yangzi River. In 1941 Chen became the acting commander of the New Fourth Army. After Japan was defeated, the Communists and Nationalists (Kuomintang; KMT) engaged in a civil war which the Communists won, establishing the People's Republic of China in 1949. Chen was named mayor of Shanghai, one of China's most important port cities, and he wielded much power in eastern China. He was also head of Shanghai Military Affairs Commission. In 1954 he moved to Beijing, the capital, where he took office as Vice-Premier of Foreign Affairs. In 1956 the Communist Party made Chen a member of the Politburo which governed China, and in 1958 Chen succeeded Zhou Enlai as China's foreign minister. During the Cultural Revolution (1966–76), radical Red Guards took over the Chinese foreign ministry in Beijing in June 1967 and attacked many Chinese officials for being bourgeois "capitalist roaders." The Red Guards forced foreign minister Chen Yi to make a public criticism of himself several times before crowds of hostile students in the presence of his longtime comrade, Premier Zhou Enlai. Chen Yi was thus disgraced and Chinese foreign policy was placed directly under the control of Zhou's office. He was also removed from the Military Affairs Commission, because he opposed radical Lin Biao. The Ninth Party Congress (1969) removed Chen from the Politburo and took away all of his government positions. Chen regained control of the ministry but never recovered his health. Although he was reinstated in the Military Affairs Commission in 1971, he died in 1972. See also CHINESE COMMUNIST PARTY; CIVIL WAR BETWEEN COMMUNISTS AND NATIONALISTS; CULTURAL REVOLUTION; LONG MARCH; POLITBURO; WAR OF RESISTANCE AGAINST JAPAN; ZHOU ENLAI.

CHENG CH'ENG-KUNG   See ZHENG CHENGGONG.

CHENG HO   See ZHENG HE.

CHENG HSIAO-HSU   See MANCHUKUO; PUYI, HENRY.

CHENG MING   See RECTIFICATION OF NAMES.

CHENGDE   A town in Hebei Province in northern China, situated about 150 miles northeast of the capital city of Beijing. Chengde was used as a summer resort by Emperor Kangxi (r. 1661–1722) of the Manchu Qing dynasty (1644–1911). In 1703 Emperor Kangxi (K'ang-hsi) began building his Summer Palace at Chengde, also known as Jehol, which he called "Fleeing-the-Heat Mountain Villa" (Bishu Shanzhuang or Pishu Shanchuang). Emperors Yongzheng (Yung-cheng; r. 1723–35) and Qianlong (Ch'ien-lung; r. 1736–95) added to the Imperial Summer Villa in Chengde until it became as large as the combined areas of both the Forbidden City and the Summer Palace in Beijing. The villa covers 1,383 acres surrounded by a 6-mile-long wall and comprises a complex of palaces, gardens and temples. The temples were built in styles representing the major sects of the Buddhist religion, which were practiced by Tibetans and other foreign dignitaries visiting the court.

The Front Palace of the villa contains the Hall of Simplicity and Sincerity, also known as Nanmu Hall for the kind of aromatic wood used to build it. The hall was the Qing throne room, but is now a museum. It was used as a set for the recent film, *The Last Emperor,* about the last Qing emperor, Xuantong (Hsuan-t'ung; Puyi; r. 1909–12). The Hall of Refreshing Breezes and Hazy Views, also on display, served as the emperor's bedroom. The room's original furnishings are intact. The buildings in the compound were constructed in many styles taken from China's national minority ethnic groups, so that emissaries from those groups would feel comfortable while staying at Chengde.

Putuozongsheng Temple, the largest Buddhist temple at Chengde, is a small version of the Potala Palace in Lhasa, Tibet. It was built as the site on which visiting dignitaries from Tibet, Mongolia, Qinghai and Xinjiang could celebrate Emperor Qianlong's 60th birthday and his mother's 80th. Qianlong supported the Tibetan sect of Buddhism, known as Lamaism, because it was also followed by the Mongols, whom he wished to keep pacified. The Mongols, a nomadic group in northern China, had ruled the Chinese Empire under the Yuan dynasty (1279–1368). Emperor Yongzheng even declared Lamaism the imperial religion of the Qing dynasty.

Most of the compound at Jehol contains lakes, hills, small forests, and gardens, including 72 landscapes that represent the scenery in different regions of China. A grassy area in the northeast section re-creates the Mongolian steppes. Thirty Mongol yurts (felt huts) housed princes and lamas (priests), and horseriding pageants were held there. Today the Mongolian Hotel (Menggubao) occupies this spot as a summer inn for tourists.

Qing emperors and their courts spent six months per year at Chengde. When the British and French burned down the Summer Palace in Beijing during the Arrow War (Second Opium War) in 1860, the Qing royal family fled to Chengde. The area's remote location ensured the preservation of its palaces and gardens. Chengde is now a quiet provincial town with a population of about 200,000. The main industries are tourism, light industry and mining. The government is restoring the Imperial Summer Villa, which is largely in ruins, to promote tourism. See also KANGXI, EMPEROR; LAMAISM; MONGOL; POTALA PALACE; PUYI, HENRY; QIANLONG (EMPEROR); QING DYNASTY; SUMMER PALACE.

CHENGDU
Capital city of Sichuan Province in southwestern China, with a population of about 4 million. Chengdu is situated in the middle of the fertile Sichuan Basin, one of the most important agricultural regions in China, about 170 miles northwest of the city of Chongqing. Sichuan, with a subtropical climate, is the most heavily populated Chinese province and one of the oldest. Chengdu, a center for agricultural trade, is a port city situated on the Jing (Brocade) River, a tributary of the Min River which feeds into the Yangzi River (Changjiang). The city is laid out with broad streets and numerous public parks. In the old quarters a number of traditional stucco houses with balconies of carved wood can still be seen. However, the old city walls were taken down in the early 1960s, and the old Imperial City was destroyed during the Cultural Revolution (1966–76).

Chengdu's history dates back more than 2,500 years and it has been the political, economic and cultural center of Sichuan since 300 B.C. Soon after Chengdu was founded, the smelting of metal and mining of salt deposits became important industries, and irrigation canals were constructed to improve agriculture. During the Eastern Han dynasty (A.D. 25–220) it became known as Jinjiangcheng, "Brocade City," for its flourishing silk industry which was patronized by the imperial court. The industry continues to flourish today. Lacquerware, silver filigree jewelry and bamboo products are other major handicrafts that continue to be produced.

The city became the capital of the state of Shu during the Three Kingdoms Period (A.D. 220–80) under Liu Bei (161–223), who founded the Shu (221–63) with the help of Generals Guan Yu and Zhang Fei and Liu Bei's government minister, Zhuge Liang (d. 234). Their battles against General Cao Cao (Ts'ao Ts'ao; 155–220) have been immortalized in the well-known novel *Romance of the Three Kingdoms*. (Now on video games, its episodes are performed in many Chinese plays and operas.)

Chengdu became a prosperous trading and cultural center during the Tang dynasty (618–907). The first paper money ever issued by a government was minted in Chengdu by the Northern Song dynasty in 1024. The Mongols who invaded China and founded the Yuan dynasty (1279–1368) destroyed the city, but it was rebuilt and in 1368 was named capital of Sichuan Province. After the collapse of the Ming dynasty (1368–1644), Chengdu served as the center of a revolutionary kingdom established by Zhang Xianzhong, which lasted only from 1645 to 1646.

In the modern era, after Japan invaded China in 1937 and while China fought the War of Resistance against Japan (1937–45; World War II), thousands of Chinese fled from the eastern provinces to Chengdu, reestablishing their universities and research institutes in the city. Sichuan Province became a center of Nationalist (Kuomintang; KMT) resistance against Japan, centered in Chongqing. During the civil war in the late 1940s between the Communists and the Nationalists, Chengdu was one of the last Nationalist strongholds. After the Communists took over China in 1949, Chengdu became a major manufacturing and transportation center, with railroad lines and highways merging there and linking Sichuan with other provinces. Important industries include machine manufacturing, metallurgy, coal mining, natural gas, and electronics and computers. Agriculture is another important activity, with the Chengdu region a major producer of rice and wheat. Other crops include sweet potatoes, tea, tobacco and herbs for traditional medicines.

Today Chengdu serves as the educational and cultural center for southwestern China. There are more than 14 institutions of higher education and research institutes, as well as an institute for national minority groups, of which there are many in Sichuan Province. The Sichuan Opera Troupe carries on a tradition nearly 2,000 years old with performances that combine music, dance and acrobatics and comprise a popular entertainment in China. There is also a Children's Opera Troupe with performers and musicians between 5 and 14 years old.

Major tourist sites include Wuhou Temple (Wuhou Ci), a memorial to Zhuge Liang, the great military leader of the state of Shu. Founded in the sixth century, the buildings were reconstructed in 1672 and were recently restored. Du Fu (Tu Fu; 712–70), one of China's greatest poets, retired to a thatched cottage in Chengdu in 759 and wrote 240 poems during the three years that he lived there. Tourists can visit the compound built on the site of Du Fu's cottage in the ninth century, which was expanded over the centuries and has been restored by the Chinese government. Scenic Riverview Pavilion (Wangjianglou) was constructed on the Jing River in the late Ming dynasty and rebuilt in the late 19th century. It contains several pagodas, more than 100 varieties of bamboo and an exhibit of container gardens or miniature landscapes (*penjing*; known in the West by the Japanese term *bonsai*). Chengdu Zoo houses one of the world's best exhibits of giant pandas, which are native to Sichuan. Sichuan Provincial Museum exhibits archaeological objects that explain the history of the province.

The old Chinese area possesses a rich array of religious architecture. Qingyang Gong, also known as Cultural Park, is a large Daoist temple compound founded during the later Han dynasty, although the buildings that survive date from the second half of the Qing dynasty (1644–1911). The viceregal Summer Palace has been recently restored after being destroyed during the Cultural Revolution. The Precious Light Monastery (Baoguangsi), an immense Buddhist temple compound about 12 miles east of Chengdu, was protected from destruction during the Cultural Revolution. Originally founded around the second century A.D., it houses Buddhist sculptures, notably a sculpture of Buddha made from white Burmese jade and a hall with 500 sculptures of Buddhist figures known as Luohan. Other treasures include several paintings by Chinese emperors and a collection of works by contemporary artists. Another Buddhist temple, Wenshu Yuan, founded in Chengdu in the sixth century, is one of the most active Buddhist centers in China today. The present buildings date from 1691.

Teahouses with their fronts open to the streets are very popular in Chengdu, and Chinese opera singers often perform in them. The thousands of peasants who flock into the city each day to sell their produce and goods or to sightsee make the teahouses very lively. Sichuan cuisine is world renowned for its hot, spicy dishes that often contain flower petals and medicinal herbs. Some of the best known dishes are bean curd cooked in spicy meat sauce, duck cooked with herbs, and chicken cooked with orchid petals. An annual lantern festival at the Chinese New Year (late January to early February) has been held in Chengdu for more than 1,300 years. See also BAMBOO; BUDDHISM; CAO CAO; CHONGQING; CIVIL WAR BETWEEN COMMUNISTS AND NATIONALISTS; CONTAINER GARDENS; DU FU; LACQUERWARE; LANTERN FESTIVAL; MINORITIES; NATIONAL; OPERA; PANDA; ROMANCE OF THE THREE KINGDOMS; SICHUAN PROVINCE; SILK; TEA; TEMPLES; DAOIST; WAR OF RESISTANCE AGAINST JAPAN; ZHUGE LIANG.

CH'ENGTU See CHENGDU.

CHENG-TUNG (EMPEROR) See ZHENGTONG (EMPEROR).

CHENNAULT, CLAIRE LEE See BURMA ROAD; FLYING TIGERS.

CHESS, CHINESE (*weiqi* or *wei-ch'i*) A popular board game known in the West by the Japanese name *go*. *Weiqi* may have first been played in India more than 4,000 years ago. Possibly developing from the ancient Chinese game of *yi*, the modern form of *weiqi* seems to have "appeared" during the Tang dynasty (618–907). Before this, *weiqi* was played on boards 17 rows of 17 squares. It was introduced into Korea and Japan in the fifth or sixth century. *Weiqi* is played on a square board that is marked with 19 horizontal and 19 vertical lines dividing it into squares, with the lines having 361 intersections. There are two players, one using 180 white markers or "stones" and the other using 181 black. The black player goes first and places a number of stones on certain points on the board before play begins. *Weiqi* is known as "surrounding stones" because the object of the game is to place enough stones on the board to capture more territory by controlling more squares than the opponent. The game sounds easy but actually involves complicated strategy. Rivalries between master players are followed with great interest.

CHI See WISDOM.

CH'I See QI.

CHI'I HSI See COWHERD AND WEAVER MAID FESTIVAL.

CHI KUNG See QIGONG.

CHI'I PAI-SHIH See QI BAISHI.

CHIA-CHING (EMPEROR) See JIAJING (EMPEROR).

CHIA-CHU See FURNITURE, TRADITIONAL.

CHIANG CHIEH-SHIH See CHIANG KAI-SHEK.

CHIANG CH'ING See JIANG QING.

CHIANG CHING-KUO (Jiang Jingguo; 1910–88) The former president of the Republic of China, which was established on Taiwan Island by the Chinese Nationalists (Kuomintang; KMT) in 1949. He is the son of Nationalist leader Chiang Kai-shek by his first wife. The Chinese Communist Party (CCP) defeated the Nationalists and founded the People's Republic of China (PRC) in 1949, and the Nationalists fled to Taiwan, where Chiang Kai-shek became the first ROC president there. Chiang Ching-kuo, born in Zhejiang Province, became involved in revolutionary activities as a young man. In 1925 he went to Moscow, where he studied at Sun Yat-sen University, founded by the U.S.S.R. to educate Chinese students and named for the founder of the Nationalist Party and the first president of the Republic of China (ROC) established in 1912. Chiang's father was then an important leader of the KMT, which had been cooperating with the recently founded CCP. In 1927 Chiang Kai-shek turned against the CCP and ordered the massacre of many Communists. Chiang Ching-kuo denounced his father and went to Leningrad (St. Petersburg) to study at the Central Tolmachev Military and Political Institute, from which he received a degree. He held several jobs in the U.S.S.R. and married a Russian woman in 1935. Chiang denounced his father's policies once more in 1936, although he later asserted that he had been forced to do so and to stay in the U.S.S.R.

In 1937 Chiang Kai-shek agreed to a KMT-CCP united front when China began fighting its War of Resistance against Japan (1937–45). Chiang Ching-kuo returned to China and was reunited with his father. During the war he held a number of military and administrative positions in the KMT government, and his father relied heavily on his advice. In 1949 both father and son went to Taiwan and established the headquarters of the KMT government, which they continued to call the Republic of China (ROC), as stated in the 1946 constitution. Chiang Ching-kuo became head of the military and security agencies of the ROC government. In 1965 he became Minister of National Defense and commander of the ROC military. In 1972 his father appointed him prime minister. In 1973 he became ROC leader when his father became ill, and he enacted policies to remove corruption from the government and to bring more native-born Taiwanese (whose ancestors had earlier emigrated from China) into the legislative and executive branches of the ROC government, formerly dominated by KMT officials from mainland China.

The United States and many other countries had supported the ROC on Taiwan as the legitimate government of China and had refused to recognize the PRC. However, in 1970s the United States under President Richard Nixon reversed its policy, breaking diplomatic ties with the ROC and establishing diplomatic relations with the PRC. Yet the U.S. Congress passed the Taiwan Relations Act which supported continuing economic ties between the United States and the ROC. The ROC also lost China's seat in the United Nations to the PRC. Chiang Ching-kuo always opposed ROC recognition of the Communist PRC and negotiations for the reunification of Taiwan with mainland China. When Chiang Kai-shek died in 1975, Chiang Ching-kuo became interim president until March 21, 1978, when the National Assembly formally elected him to a six-year term as president. In 1984 he was elected to a second term. Under his leadership, Taiwan developed economically and became very prosperous. Before Chiang died in 1988, he initiated the political process to move Taiwan toward democracy, and he lifted martial law, which had been in force in Taiwan for 44 years. He also liberalized domestic policies and permitted citizens of the ROC to travel to the PRC. When Chiang died he was succeeded by Lee Teng-hui, his chosen vice president, who continued the process of democratic reform. Lee was the first ROC president born on the island of Taiwan. See also CHIANG KAI-SHEK; CIVIL WAR BETWEEN COMMUNISTS AND NATIONALISTS; LEE TENG-HUI; NATIONALIST PARTY; REPUBLIC OF CHINA; SOONG MEI-LING; SUN YAT-SEN; TAIWAN; UNITED NATIONS; WAR OF RESISTANCE AGAINST JAPAN.

CHIANG CHUNG-CHENG   See CHIANG KAI-SHEK.

CHIANG FENG   See JIANG FENG.

CHIANG KAI-SHEK (1887–1975)   Official name Chiang Chung-cheng (Jiang Zhongzheng); the leader of the Chinese Nationalist Party (Kuomintang; KMT) and the president of the Republic of China (ROC), established on Taiwan Island in 1949, until his death in 1975. He is also known as Chiang Chieh-shih (Jiang Jieshi), which is pronounced Chiang Kai-shek in the Cantonese (Guangzhou) or southern Chinese dialect. He acquired the title Generalissimo. His eldest son, Chiang Ching-kuo (Jiang Jingguo; 1910–88) succeeded him as president of the ROC until he died in 1988 and was succeeded by Lee Teng-Hui, the current ROC president. Chiang Kai-shek's second wife was Soong Mei-ling (Soong Mayling, Sung Mei-ling or Song Meiling; 1897–), also known as Madame Chiang Kai-shek, one of the two most prominent Chinese women in the 20th century. The other is her sister, Soong Qingling (Soong Ching-ling; 1893–1981), who married Dr. Sun Yat-sen (1866–1925), the revered founder of modern China. The Soong sisters were born into a wealthy family in Shanghai that had converted to Methodism and they, along with their sister and brother, were educated in the United States. Their father provided much of the financial support for Sun Yat-sen's revolutionary political movement. Soong Qingling married Sun Yat-sen in 1915, and it was at their home in Shanghai that Chiang Kai-shek met Soong Mei-ling. Chiang wanted to marry her even though he was already married and his wife had given him two sons, including Chiang Ching-kuo. They married in 1927 while he was in Japan in brief exile from the KMT. Although she did not hold many official positions, Soong Mei-ling played an important role as Chiang Kai-shek's English interpreter and secretary.

Chiang Kai-shek was born in Zhejiang Province. The Manchu Qing dynasty (1644–1911) that ruled China had been greatly weakened during the 19th century by demands forced on China by Western powers through military defeats and the so-called unequal treaties. The defeat of China by Japan in the Sino-Japanese War of 1894–95 was a further blow to the Qing dynasty. China also suffered from the Russo-Japanese War of 1904–5, which was fought on Chinese land for control of concessions in China. These events made Chiang decide to pursue a military career, and after high school he attended Paoting (Baoding) Military Academy in Hebei Province, which trained Chinese officers in Western military techniques. After graduation the government sent him to Japan for further military training. Many Chinese revolutionary leaders were based in Japan or had widespread support among the large number of Chinese students there. In 1906 Chiang, as did many other Chinese males, cut off his queue, or long braid, as an act of political defiance. The Manchu Qing had forced Han Chinese men to wear their hair in the Manchu style with a long braid in the back. The largest anti-Qing organization was Sun Yat-sen's Revolutionary Alliance (Tongmenghui or T'ung-meng-hui), which Chiang joined. Sun later reorganized this alliance as the Kuomintang (KMT). Sun frequently traveled abroad to raise funds for the alliance, and Chiang met Sun in Japan in 1910.

The Chinese revolution that overthrew the Qing dynasty broke out on October 10, 1911, with the Wuchang Uprising and is hence called the Revolution of 1911. (The ROC on Taiwan still celebrates this date as the anniversary of its founding, known as Double Tenth Day.) After the uprising, Chiang went with other revolutionary-minded Chinese to Shanghai, China's largest port and trading city, to take an active part in the revolution. He led a group in attacking the Qing governor's office at Hangzhou and turning that city over to Sun's new revolutionary government.

On January 1, 1912, Sun became president of the new provisional government of the ROC, which was based at Nanjing. Yuan Shikai (Yuan Shih-k'ai; 1859–1916), the most powerful military official in northern China, persuaded Sun to resign so that he could become ROC president. Sun agreed to do so if Yuan met several conditions, including persuading the last Qing emperor, a young boy who became known as Henry Puyi, to abdicate the throne. The emperor abdicated on February 12, 1912 and Sun resigned the next day. Two days after that Yuan was elected ROC president and made his capital at Beijing, which remained the Chinese capital for 15 years. That summer, Sun went to Beijing and helped establish the Kuomintang (KMT), with himself as director. In 1913 elections were held and the KMT became the majority party in the Chinese national assembly. However, KMT leader Song Jiaoren (Sung Chiao-jen; 1882–1913) was assassinated, and Yuan banned the KMT and dispatched troops to several Chinese provinces which had KMT governors. They even captured Nanjing, the former KMT capital, and the KMT was not able to organize a strong resistance to Yuan. Chiang, who supported Sun and opposed Yuan, had to flee to Japan, as did Sun. While there, the two men became close friends.

In 1916 Yuan died shortly after he had made an unsuccessful attempt to establish a new dynasty with himself as emperor. Li Yuanhong (Li Yuan-hung; 1864–1928) became the new president of the ROC in Beijing. Sun went to Guangzhou, where he established a military government in 1917. But other military leaders there caused Sun to move to

Shanghai in 1918. Yuan's death in 1916 opened the way for many competing warlords to carve up China into regions under their control, known as the Warlord Period (1916–28). In 1921 the parliament in Guangzhou abolished the military government and formed a new government with Sun as president. In 1922, while Sun was in Guangzhou, he was warned of an attempted coup against him and escaped to a gunboat. Chiang joined Sun in Guangzhou and accompanied him to Hong Kong and then to Shanghai.

The Chinese Communist Party (CCP) had been founded in Shanghai in 1921. In 1923 Sun signed an agreement with an official of the U.S.S.R. that the KMT would cooperate with Soviet and Chinese communists. In August 1923 he sent Chiang to the U.S.S.R. as head of a Chinese military mission to procure weapons and study Soviet military organization. When Chiang returned to China he delivered a report on his mission and became a member of the KMT Military Council. The KMT and CCP cooperated in establishing the Whampoa (Huangpu) Military Academy, near Guangzhou, to train officers to lead a military expedition against the warlords who controlled China. Chiang was named the academy's first commandant, in charge of the military training of 2,000 cadets in the first three classes. He worked closely with Zhou Enlai (Chou En-lai; 1898–1976), who later became the second-most important leader in the CCP, and with Mikhail Borodin (1884–1952) and other Russian advisers who had come to China. Many of the officers at the academy later formed the so-called Whampoa clique, one of the most important groups that supported Chiang. The Whampoa Military Academy was later renamed the Central Military Academy and was moved to Nanjing. Chiang remained its director, and graduating officers pledged their loyalty to him.

Political leaders in the north invited Sun to meet with them in Beijing to discuss government affairs. He was very ill with cancer and died in Beijing on March 12, 1925. He was first buried there, but later his body was placed in a splendid mausoleum built for him in Nanjing. Other KMT leaders contended with each other to become Sun's successor. In January 1926 Chiang was elected a member of the KMT Central Executive Committee at the Second National Congress. Three months later he became the most powerful leader in Guangzhou by taking action against the Communists and arresting many Russian advisers. In May the Central Executive Committee of the revolutionary government in Guangzhou approved Chiang's proposal to halt Communist influence in the KMT. In June 1926 Chiang was named commander-in-chief of the National Revolutionary Army, and in July he launched the Northern Expedition to unify China. By March 1927 his forces had regained Chinese territory as far north as Shanghai and Nanjing on the Yangzi River. However, the KMT now had two centers of power, with the left wing, led by Wang Jingwei (Wang Ching-wei; 1883–1944), establishing a government in Wuhan in Hubei Province and the right wing, led by Chiang, establishing a national capital at Nanjing.

Members of the CCP and the left-wing faction of the KMT had done advance work to persuade local peasants and workers to support the Northern Expedition, but Chiang felt that they had become too revolutionary. In April 1927 Chiang abruptly turned against the Communists and sent his troops into Shanghai, where they were organizing workers' strikes, to arrest and execute them. Thousands were killed but some escaped, including Zhou Enlai and his wife, Deng Yingchao (Teng Ying-ch'ao; 1904–92), to join Communist forces at the Soviet base in the Jinggang Mountains on the border between Jiangxi and Anhui provinces in south-central China. However, Chiang's anti-Communist campaign had not been authorized by the Central Committee of the KMT, and the government based in Wuhan removed him as commander in chief. Chiang responded by setting up his own government in Nanjing, but partly members forced him to resign, and he went into exile in Japan. There he married Soong Mei-ling in December 1927. Chiang had converted to Methodism but had not legally divorced his first wife, and the Chinese people strongly disapproved of his new marriage.

In China, left-wing KMT members began to change their opinion of the CCP and agree with Chiang that the Chinese Communists were being controlled by Moscow and that they wanted to eliminate the KMT. Wang Jingwei and his faction decided to begin purging Communists from the KMT. The left- and right-wing factions of the KMT reunited, abolished the KMT government in Nanjing and moved the Wuhan government there, officially naming it the National Government of China. In 1928 Chiang returned to China from Japan. Soong Qingling, his wife's sister, condemned Chiang for betraying Sun Yat-sen's revolutionary principles and joined the Communist side. Chiang once again became KMT commander in chief and led the second stage of the Northern Expedition, with the goal of conquering northern China. Japanese troops stationed in the north interfered with the expedition, but Chiang's troops took Beijing in June 1928, symbolically unifying all of China south of the Great Wall. On October 10, 1928 Chiang became chairman of a new Chinese national government and established his capital at Nanjing. The Communists led a number of uprisings in Chinese cities, all of which were bloodily suppressed by the Nationalists, and Mikhail Borodin and other foreign advisers fled the country. The KMT refused to allow any other political party to have a role in the Nationalist government. From then until 1949, Chiang commanded the majority vote in the standing committee of the Central Executive Committee, the most powerful body in the KMT.

By the end of 1928, Zhang Xueliang (Chang Hsueh-liang; 1898–), the most powerful warlord in Manchuria (northeastern China), agreed to Nationalist rule in Manchuria, although he did not relinquish his actual power there. His father, Zhang Zuolin (Chang Tso-lin; 1873–1928), who had been military governor of Manchuria, had been assassinated earlier that year by Japanese troops stationed in Manchuria. Many members of the CCP, and even dissident generals and political leaders in the KMT, continued to oppose Chiang's government. Warlords in various regions claimed local power for themselves and Chiang sent troops against them, but he still felt it most important to eliminate the Communists. In 1930 Chiang launched the first of five annual major campaigns against Communist forces in south-central China.

In May 1931 opposition leaders formed an alternative government. On September 18, 1931, Japanese forces used the so-called Manchurian Incident as a pretext to launch a full-scale invasion of Manchuria. Chiang felt that his troops could not resist the Japanese and pulled them out of Manchuria, which made the Chinese people regard him as weak and unpatriotic. But he still felt that his most urgent task was to wipe out communism in China. In 1932 the Japanese established a puppet state in Manchuria called Manchukuo (Manzhouguo or Man-chou-kuo in Chinese) and forced Puyi, the last Qing emperor, to serve as its figurehead. The Japanese used Manchukuo as their base to invade China Proper and the rest of Asia. In 1934 the Communists, under bombardment in Jiangxi by Chiang's Nationalist forces, finally decided to escape to the northwest on the epic Long March (1934–35). Led by Mao Zedong (Mao Tse-tung; 1893–1976), Zhou Enlai, and military commander Zhu De (Chu Teh; 1886–1976), the Communists finally established their headquarters at Yan'an in Shaanxi Province. The legendary survivors of the rigorous Long March later became the leaders of the civil war in which the Communists defeated the Nationalists in 1949. Chinese Communists accused Chiang of preferring to fight his own countrymen rather than resist the Japanese who had invaded China, and they urged a KMT-CCP united front against Japan.

In 1935 Chiang ordered the Manchurian warlord Zhang Xueliang to send his troops to fight the Communists at Yan'an. The Manchurian soldiers were angry that they were sent against their own countrymen while the Japanese were occupying their own land, and they stopped fighting. In December 1936 Chiang flew to Zhang Xueliang's headquarters at Xi'an in Shaanxi. A group of KMT and CCP military leaders kidnapped Chiang at the Huaqing Hot Springs outside Xi'an to persuade him to stop fighting the Communists and form a KMT-CCP united front to fight the Japanese; this is known as the Xi'an Incident. Soong Mei-ling and her brother played a major role in the negotiations to have Chiang released by persuading him to agree to the united front. He did so on December 25 and flew back to Nanjing.

In 1937 Japanese troops moved from Manchuria into northern China, where they quickly gained control of the North China Plain, and in August they attacked Shanghai. In November they took Nanjing and committed atrocities against hundreds of thousands of Chinese residents, an episode known as the "Rape of Nanjing." The Chinese began fighting their War of Resistance against Japan (1937–45; World War II). Warlords sent their troops to join Communist and Nationalist forces, but Chinese soldiers were poorly equipped and trained in comparison to the well-equipped Japanese soldiers who were schooled in modern Western military techniques. Guangzhou fell to the Japanese on October 21, 1938, and Hankou, the provisional Nationalist capital after Nanjing had fallen, was captured on October 25. Chiang moved his Nationalist government to Chongqing in Sichuan, a province in southwestern China protected by high mountains. Many Chinese universities and industries also moved there.

Soong Mei-ling made a great contribution to the war effort by appealing to Americans to provide material and military assistance to China. She made many trips to the United States, and in February 1943 she became the first Chinese and the second woman to address a joint session of the U.S. Congress. Still serving as Chiang's English interpreter, she accompanied him to the Cairo Conference in November 1943, where she met personally with U.S. President Franklin. Roosevelt and British Prime Minister Winston Churchill. She also communicated messages between Chiang and U.S. General Joseph Stilwell, who was chief of staff to Chiang and commander in chief of the China-Burma-India theater.

In December 1938 the Japanese persuaded Wang Jingwei to desert the Nationalists and join their side. Wang justified his actions by asserting that China had no chance of winning against Japan and that to continue fighting was suicidal. He had hoped to prevent the Japanese from treating the Chinese too harshly in the areas they occupied, but the Japanese, after installing Wang as "President," merely treated him as their puppet. By the end of 1939 Japan controlled more than half of all the territory and population of China, from Manchuria to the Chinese border with Vietnam (Indochina). World War II broke out in Europe in September 1939, which brought China foreign allies such a Great Britain. The Chinese people were exhausted from the fighting, but the Japanese were spread too thin in China, and the two sides entered a stalemate. Famine was widespread, causing hundreds of thousands of people to starve to death and weakening Japanese forces. A group of U.S. airplane pilots organized themselves into a unit under General Claire Chennault, popularly known as the Flying Tigers, to fly supplies to the Nationalists from India "over the Hump" of the Himalaya Mountains. After Japan bombed the U.S. naval fleet at Pearl Harbor on December 7, 1941, the United States became an official ally of China and sent more military and financial aid. General Stilwell arrived in China in early 1942, with the major objective of keeping the Burma Road open for the transport of supplies from Burma to the Nationalists at Chongqing. He became Chiang's chief of staff but disagreed with his policies and argued that all anti-Japanese factions in China should be armed, including the Communists, whom Chiang still mistrusted. In early 1941 Nationalist troops defeated the Communist New Fourth Army in the lower Yangzi River valley. The Nationalists and Communists were still as much opposed to each other as they were to the Japanese and looked forward to resuming their civil war after the defeat of Japan.

In 1943 Chiang published two books, *China's Destiny* and *Chinese Economic Ideology,* in which he argued for a new Chinese society built on ancient Confucian virtues such as filial piety and loyalty, and a government characterized by democratic centralism. Chiang also promoted the New Life Movement, which aimed to instill such virtues in the Chinese people as discipline and hygiene. Chiang became head of the Nationalist government once more when Lin Sen died in October 1943. He persuaded President Roosevelt to dismiss Stilwell, who was replaced by General Albert Wedemeyer in October 1944.

After the United States dropped the first atomic bomb on Hiroshima, Japan on August 6, 1945, the Soviet army marched into Manchuria and met little resistance from Japanese troops. Japan surrendered to the Allied forces on August 14, 1945, and the Chinese Nationalist government returned to Nanjing. American diplomats attempted to ensure that Japanese troops in northern China and Manchuria would surrender to the Nationalists rather than the Communists, thus making Chiang the dominant leader in postwar China. However, the Soviet troops in Manchuria had dismantled or destroyed many of the industries the Japanese had established there. The Russians then turned over Manchuria and all the weapons the Japanese had surrendered there to the Chinese Communists. The Americans also attempted to negotiate a Nationalist-Communist government to rule all of China, although the U.S. government still supported the Nationalists as the sole legal government of China. Chiang and CCP leader Mao Zedong met for six weeks at Chongqing in the fall of 1945, but nothing came of their negotiations. At the end of 1945 President Harry S Truman sent General of the Army George C. Marshall as his special ambassador to China with the mission of persuading the Communists and Nationalists to form a coalition government, but he did not succeed and blamed both sides for being intransigent. He did arrange a cease-fire in January 1946, but the United States continued to give huge quantities of weapons and supplies to the Nationalists.

After Marshall left China, the Nationalists and Communists began fighting a full-scale civil war, initiated on June 26, 1946, by the Nationalist offensive against areas held by the Communists in Hubei and Henan provinces. The Communists used guerrilla tactics and mobilized peasants to their side by such practices as land reform, in which they took land away from wealthy landowners and gave it to peasants who had little or no land. The Chinese people had become disgusted with the corruption of the Nationalists and were suffering from runaway inflation that made the currency of the Nationalist government worthless. Many Chinese businessmen, who had strongly supported Chiang, began to leave the country. By the end of 1947, the Americans felt that the Nationalists had no chance of winning and withdrew their support for Chiang. In 1948 Soong Mei-ling went to the United States to raise American support for the KMT, but President Truman refused to change the U.S. policy of noninvolvement in China.

The Communists, who had gained much support in northern China, took Manchuria in the fall of 1948, where 300,000 Nationalist troops surrendered to the Communists. They then took northern China, with Nationalist forces offering little resistance. In November 1948, during the second major battle of the civil war, in the Huai River basin north of Nanjing, entire divisions of Nationalist troops deserted to the Communists. On November 29 the Communists launched, in the Beijing-Tianjin area, their third major campaign. In January 1949 the Communists won the Huai River campaign and also took Beijing and Tianjin. On April 23, 1949, the Communists crossed the Yangzi River and took Nanjing, Chiang's Nationalist capital. Shanghai fell to the Communists on May 27 and Guangzhou in October.

In 1949 Chiang retired as president of the ROC and was succeeded by Li Zongren (Li Tsung-jen) as acting president. In the spring of 1949, Chiang began moving Nationalist troops to Taiwan, a large island 100 miles off the southeastern coast of China, which had been governed by the Qing dynasty until Japan occupied it in 1895. Japan surrendered Taiwan to China in 1945. Chiang had already ordered the transfer of China's gold reserve to the island. The Nationalists had also packed hundreds of crates of priceless antiques from the Forbidden City in Beijing, the Imperial Palace where emperors of the Ming (1368–1644) and Qing dynasties had resided, and most of these were sent to Taiwan, where they later formed the collection of the National Palace Museum in Taipei.

On October 1, 1949, Mao Zedong proclaimed the founding of the People's Republic of China (PRC) in Beijing. The Communists took Chongqing in November. Chiang traveled to the Philippine Islands and Korea and several places in China and then fled to Taiwan from Chengdu, Sichuan, on December 10, 1949, the same day that Chengdu fell to the Chinese Communists. In Taiwan, Chiang and his Nationalist supporters established the headquarters of the KMT government, which they continued to call the Republic of China (ROC) and still claimed to be the legitimate government of all of China. (The Communists considered Taiwan a renegade province of China.) On March 1, 1950, Chiang resumed the ROC presidency, which he held until his death. Chiang's son, Chiang Ching-kuo, became head of the military and security agencies of the ROC government, and in 1965 he became minister of national defense and commander of the ROC military. In 1972 his father appointed him prime minister. The next year, when Chiang Kai-shek became ill, his son became acting ROC leader. Soong Mei-ling had stayed in the United States but joined Chiang Kai-shek in Taiwan in 1950. She continued traveling to the U.S. to represent the ROC and its interests, and lived there for many years after Chiang Kai-shek died in 1975. See also BEIJING; BORODIN, MIKHAIL; BURMA ROAD; CHENGDU; CHIANG CHING-KUO; CHINESE COMMUNIST PARTY; CHONGQING; CIVIL WAR BETWEEN COMMUNISTS AND NATIONALISTS; DENG YINGCHAO; DOUBLE TENTH FESTIVAL; FLYING TIGERS; GUANGZHOU; HUAI RIVER; JINGGANG MOUNTAIN RANGE; LAND REFORM BY COMMUNISTS; LONG MARCH; MANCHU; MANCHUKUO; MANCHURIAN INCIDENT; MAO ZEDONG; NANJING; NATIONAL PALACE MUSEUM (TAIPEI); NATIONALIST PARTY; NEW LIFE MOVEMENT; NORTHERN EXPEDITION; PEOPLE'S REPUBLIC OF CHINA; PUYI, HENRY; QING DYNASTY; QUEUE; REPUBLIC OF CHINA; REVOLUTION OF 1911; REVOLUTIONARY ALLIANCE; RUSSO-JAPANESE WAR OF 1904–5 AND CHINA; SHANGHAI; SICHUAN PROVINCE; SINO-JAPANESE WAR OF 1894–95; SONG JIAOREN; SOONG CHING LING; SOONG MEI-LING; STILWELL, JOSEPH; SUN YAT-SEN; TAIWAN; UNEQUAL TREATIES; WANG JINGWEI; WAR OF RESISTANCE AGAINST JAPAN; WARLORD PERIOD; WHAMPOA MILITARY ACADEMY; WUCHANG UPRISING; XI'AN; YAN'AN; YANGZI RIVER; YUAN SHIKAI; ZHANG XUELIANG; ZHOU ENLAI; ZHU DE.

CHIANG TSE-MIN See JIANG ZEMIN.

CHIANG-NAN SCHOOL OF PAINTING See DONG YUAN.

CHIANGSHI PROVINCE See JIANGXI PROVINCE.

CHIAO See BRIDGES.

CH'IAO-HSIANG TIES See CONNECTIONS; OVERSEAS CHINESE.

CHIA-YU-KUAN PASS See GREAT WALL.

CHIBI, BATTLE OF See CAO CAO.

CHICKEN (*xiaoji* or *hsiao-chi*) The most important meat in the Chinese diet, along with pork, since ancient times. Inscriptions on oracle bones dating from the Shang dynasty

(1750–1040 B.C.) frequently mention chicken. Many chicken bones have been found at Anyang, the principle site where oracle bones have been excavated, and at the Banpo Neolithic Village, occupied c. 4500–3750 B.C., near modern Xi'an. Pottery chickens and pigs have been found in many tombs dating from the Han dynasty (206 B.C.–A.D. 220). Chickens were available year-round, while pigs were only butchered shortly before the New Year Festival, the only time they were consumed. This custom continued until the modern era. Government officials have encouraged Chinese peasants to raise these animals because they efficiently convert waste-products into high-quality protein. Thus, the Chinese sick and elderly are fed a larger amount of chicken and eggs than usual. Traditionally, the eldest male member of a family and his wife eat one or two poached eggs for breakfast. After a woman gives birth to a child, she spends a customary confinement period of one month during which she eats at least one poached egg per day and chicken or chicken soup with her other meals. When a child is born, particularly a son, the mother's family sends her gifts of food, including several chickens and a basket of eggs, to help her recover from childbirth. The father's family dyes chicken eggs red and proudly gives them out to relatives and neighbors. A whole chicken or duck may be placed on a family altar as a sacrificial offering to the family's ancestors. The Chinese have traditionally believed that the blood of a rooster chases away ghosts; it is also one of the animals in the 12-year Chinese zodiac. People born in the Year of the Rooster are thought to be confident, dignified, argumentative and critical, good with money and capable but domineering administrators. The most recent Year of the Rooster was 1995.

Chinese cuisine includes a wide variety of recipes for cooking chicken. One of the most popular methods is to cut the chicken into small pieces and then stir-fry them in a wok with vegetables and seasonings such as soy sauce and sherry to make a light sauce. Seasoned pieces of chicken are also fried in oil. Whole chickens may be roasted, braised in soy sauce and other seasonings, steamed, or boiled in water to make a soup. Chicken rubbed with salt and baked is a famous dish of the Hakka people of southern China. A popular dish from northern China, especially in winter, is the fire pot, a round, charcoal-burning stove in the middle of a ring-shaped pot in which clear chicken broth is boiled. Diners select pieces of sliced raw food from large platters, such as chicken, beef, vegetables and bean curd, and cook their own meal in the broth. See also ANCESTOR WORSHIP; COOKING, CHINESE; DUCK; ORACLE BONES; PIG; SEASONINGS FOR FOOD; ZODIAC, ANIMAL.

CHIEN WARE   See TEMMOKU WARE.

CH'IEN-LUNG (EMPEROR)   See QIANLONG (EMPEROR).

CHIEN-WEN (EMPEROR)   See HONGWU (EMPEROR); YONGLE (EMPEROR).

CHIH   See WISDOM.

CHIH-K'AI AND CHIH-YI   See TIANTAI SECT OF BUDDHISM.

CHIHLI, GULF OF   See BO HAI GULF.

CHIH-NU   See COWHERD AND WEAVER MAID FESTIVAL.

CH'I-KUNG   See QIGONG.

CHILDREN IN CHINA   See CHILDREN'S DAY; CHILDREN'S PALACES; EDUCATION SYSTEM; FAMILY STRUCTURE; FILIAL PIETY; ONE-CHILD FAMILY CAMPAIGN; WEDDINGS, TRADITIONAL.

CHILDREN'S DAY   A festival held every June 1 to honor children. The Chinese people adore and take great pride in children and their accomplishments. On this day schoolchildren participate in games and performances of gymnastics, song and dance, plays and puppet shows. Games include Chinese chess, relay races and tugs of war. Some children on Children's Day also become members of the Young Pioneers, a major group for young people affiliated with the Chinese Communist Party. See also CHILDREN'S PALACES; FAMILY STRUCTURE.

CHILDREN'S PALACES (*shaonian gong*)   Government-run schools that provide special training for children age 7 to 17 who have advanced skills in such areas as music, dance, painting, mathematics or technology (professional artists often instruct the classes). Talented children are selected to attend these palaces in addition to their regular schools. Chinese children's palaces were first modeled on those in the Soviet Union and were established in China by Soong Qingling (1893–1981), widow of Sun Yat-sen, founder of modern China. After the communists took over China in 1949, she worked tirelessly for the government to promote the welfare of the Chinese people until she died.

There are 11 children's palaces in Shanghai, China's largest city. The first and biggest is the Shanghai Municipal Children's Palace, which was established in a mansion in 1949 that had been owned by the wealthy Sassoon family, who moved to Hong Kong. Tourists may visit the palaces and watch while classes are in session. See also EDUCATION SYSTEM; SOONG QINGLING.

CH'I-LIN   See QILIN.

CHILUNG   See TAIPEI; TAIWAN.

CH'IN DYNASTY   See QIN DYNASTY.

CHIN NUNG   See JIN NONG.

CH'IN SHIH-HUANG-TI (EMPEROR)   See QIN SHI HUANGDI (EMPEROR).

CHIN, STATE OF   See SPRING AND AUTUMN PERIOD.

CHINA GRASS   See RAMIE; TEXTILE INDUSTRY.

CHINA INTERNATIONAL TRAVEL SERVICE (CITS; LUXINGSHE)   The largest official agency for tourist travel in China, founded in 1954, CITS has about 200 branches and sub-branches throughout the country and also operates sales offices in Hong Kong, Macao and many countries around the world. The agency is also referred to as LUX-

INGSHE, its Chinese acronym. The main office is in the capital city of Beijing. CITS works with foreign tour groups to make all the necessary arrangements for travel within China, including transportation, hotel reservations, meals and sight-seeing. All final decisions about tour itineraries in China are made by CITS. Guides from CITS accompany tour groups and some business delegations. In 1983 the Chinese government gave permission to some municipal and provincial CITS branches to issue visas to foreign groups, as long as the groups spend some of their time touring within that city or province. In 1989 a new division, China International Travel Service (Group) was formed to attract tourists to China and increase the services offered to them. CITS also handles applications from foreigners for individual travel in China, approves itineraries, receives payments, and issues visas. Although embassies are better places to acquire visas, CITS began issuing them to individual travelers in 1985 under its new "China-to-FIT" (Foreign Independent Travel) program.

Other travel services include the China Travel Service (CTS), which offers tours in China mainly to tourists of Chinese descent. It has offices in Hong Kong and many Chinese cities. There are also Overseas Chinese Travel Service (OCTS) offices in major cities as well. Since August 1, 1985, the Chinese government has permitted overseas Chinese to visit China with valid passports from their respective countries only; they do not need visas or exit permits. Finally, the China Youth Travel Service (CYTS) Tours Corporation, an affiliate of the All-China Youth Federation, has become the second-largest tour operator in China next to CITS. It provides most of the same services as CITS and CTS, mainly for tour groups, although it does serve individual tourists as well. See also ALL-CHINA YOUTH FEDERATION; OVERSEAS CHINESE.

CHINA INTERNATIONAL TRUST AND INVESTMENT CORPORATION (CITIC)
An organization founded by businessman Rong Yiren (Jung Yi-jen) in 1979 to promote and assist foreign investment in China. Before the Chinese Communists founded the People's Republic of China in 1949, Rong had managed 24 factories in the textile, printing and dyeing, machinery and flour industries. In 1978 the Chinese government proclaimed China's "open-door" policy for industry and commerce, and Premier Deng Xiaoping asked Rong to contribute his abilities to this purpose.

When Rong founded CITIC, he went to the United States to meet with American bankers and entrepreneurs to encourage them to invest in China, and he signed economic cooperation agreements on CITIC's behalf with many Chinese provinces and municipalities. CITIC borrows and lends money internationally, issues foreign bonds, makes overseas investments, encourages and participates in joint ventures, and imports foreign technology and equipment. One of Rong's first successful projects was the issuing of 10 billion Japanese yen worth of Chinese bonds on the Tokyo Stock Exchange to revive the Yizheng Chemical Fiber Industry Joint Corporation in Jiangsu Province. In 1984 the Chinese government permitted CITIC and three banks to deal in foreign currency, which until then had been handled by the Bank of China (the foreign exchange division of the People's Bank of China).

In 1986, CITIC was renamed CITIC Group and changed its focus to concentrate on energy, metallurgy, and raw materials—Chinese industries which previously had not been very successful in attracting foreign investments. Since 1986, one of the largest investment projects of CITIC has been the Bohai Aluminum Co., Ltd. By the end of 1986 CITIC Group had set up 47 joint ventures, invested in 114 Chinese companies, and issued U.S.$550 million in foreign bonds. That same year the business magazine *Fortune* named Rong Yiren one of the 50 most important figures in the world economy.

The CITIC grew rapidly during the first decade of China's economic reforms. When it was founded in 1979, CITIC had 500,000 yuan. By 1990 its registered capital was 3 billion yuan and its total assets were more than 20 billion yuan. It owned 23 subsidiaries, including a bank that operated in China and abroad, and had invested in 200 other enterprises. Two-thirds of its investments were in energy, raw materials production, transportation, and telecommunications facilities. It also invested in aluminum factories, forestry and pulp mills in the United States, Australia and Canada. One of the major projects of CITIC Hong Kong (Holdings) Ltd. was the recently built Hong Kong–Kowloon cross-harbor tunnel, which includes a highway and an underground railway; it was built with an investment of 4.4 billion Hong Kong dollars. CITIC Hong Kong also acquired 12.5 percent of the shares of Cathay Pacific Airways. See also BANK OF CHINA; FOREIGN TRADE AND INVESTMENT; HONG KONG.

CHINA LEAGUE FOR CIVIL RIGHTS See SOONG QINGLING.

CHINA MEN See KINGSTON, MAXINE HONG.

CHINA MERCHANTS STEAM NAVIGATION COMPANY (CMSN) A company founded in 1872 in the newly developed port city of Shanghai by Li Hongzhang (Li Hungchang), a Qing dynasty (1644–1911) government official, to provide modern steamship transport to compete with the foreign companies that in the mid-19th century had monopolized ocean shipping and controlled transportation on the Yangzi River (Changjiang), thus draining silver from China. Between 1872 and 1884 the China Merchants Steam Navigation Company purchased 50 steamships, which it operated along the Chinese coast and on the Yangzi. In 1873 the company opened sea routes from Shanghai to Japan and other Asian countries. In 1877 it bought out an American firm, Russell and Company, which operated transportation on the Yangzi from Shanghai to Hankou and competed with the British companies of Jardine, Matheson, Dent and Company, and Butterfield and Swire. The Chinese government subsidized the China Merchants Company to carry the tribute rice that was brought north annually from the Yangzi Delta to the capital, Beijing. Long fleets of grain junks (sailing ships) had transported these rice shipments up the Grand Canal since the early 15th century. The new company enabled the rice to be transported quickly by steamship on the Yellow Sea and Bo Hai Gulf from Shanghai to Tianjin, a large port near Beijing. Li Hongzhang was stationed in Tianjin as governor-general of the capital province from 1870 to 1895.

China Merchants Company steamships were fueled by coal from the Kaiping mines that were opened north of Tianjin in 1878. In 1881 the first permanent railroad was built in

China to bring this coal to Tianjin. The first group of Chinese students that went to study in the United States traveled on a China Merchants Company steamship. The China Merchants Company was well directed in the beginning by Tong Jingsing (T'ung Ching-sing), who had been trained in British management practices. However, because the Chinese government controlled the company, it was not developed in a way so as to take advantage of business opportunities, and, unfortunately, its profits were never used to build up the company but instead were pocketed by many of its managers and employees. Thus, it proved unable to compete with British steamship lines. The Kaiping coal mines also lost money and, in 1900, were taken over by foreigners—among them Herbert Hoover, who later became president of the United States.

Nevertheless, the China Merchants Steam Navigation Company remained in business, maintaining a branch in Hong Kong near the southern Chinese port city of Guangzhou (Canton). After the Chinese Communists founded the People's Republic of China (PRC) in 1949, the Hong Kong branch returned to China to help the country in 1950 and was taken over by the PRC government. The company quickly developed its operations and became a holdings company with limited liability, which was formally founded in 1986 under the name China Merchants Holdings Co., Ltd. (CMH). When the PRC government began reforming its economic system in the late 1970s, it established 13 Special Economic Zones (SEZs), opening the first at Shenzhen near Guangzhou. It established an export-oriented industrial development zone on the Shekou Peninsula, which was a part of the Shenzhen SEZ. Yuan Geng (Yuang Keng), executive vice-chairman of CMH in Hong Kong, was appointed director of the management committee of the Shekou Industrial Zone. CMH was one of the four largest organizations funded in Hong Kong by China, and, under Yuan Geng's direction, the CMH brought many Hong Kong entrepreneurs into Shekou. The Japanese Sanyo Electronic Co., Ltd., was the first foreign enterprise to come to Shekou, which grew so rapidly that by 1991 there were 400 enterprises, 76 percent of them foreign funded. Shekou Harbor, completed in 1990, links the Shekou Industrial Zone to an international shipping network. Hong Kong–based CMH has resumed and developed its shipping business and also acts as the general agent of the China Ocean Shipping Company of Beijing and many provincial and municipal Chinese shipping companies in Hong Kong. It has diversified into real estate, finance, trade and travel, and supplies logistic services to foreign oil companies engaged in offshore oil exploration in the South China Sea. See also ENERGY SOURCES; FOREIGN TRADE AND INVESTMENT; GRAND CANAL; HONG KONG; JUNK; RAILROADS; RICE; SHANGHAI; SHIPPING AND SHIPBUILDING; SOUTH CHINA SEA; SPECIAL ECONOMIC ZONES.

CHINA NEWS SERVICE See NEW CHINA NEWS AGENCY.

CHINA OCEAN SHIPPING COMPANY See SHIPPING AND SHIPBUILDING.

CHINA PROPER The term applied to the territory of China that lies within the Great Wall, the vast network of earth, brick and stone barriers built across northern and northwestern China to defend it from nomadic tribes that frequently invaded the country. China Proper, the region populated primarily by Han or ethnic Chinese, traditionally includes 18 historic provinces comprising the modern provinces of Anhui, Fujian, Guangdong, Hebei, Hubei, Hunan, Jiangsu, Qinghai, Shaanxi, Shandong, Shanxi, Sichuan, Yunnan and Zhejiang, as well as Guangxi-Zhuang Autonomous Region. It has been roughly divided into northern and southern China by the Yellow (Huanghe) and Yangzi (Changjiang) rivers, which flow across the country from west to east. The Chinese have always preferred to use the term "Middle (or Central) Kingdom" (Zhongguo or Chung-kuo) for their country, indicating their belief that China is the center of the earth. Another Chinese term for the Middle Kingdom is "all (that is) under heaven" (*tianxia* or *t'ien-hsia*). During the imperial period, which lasted until the overthrow of the Qing dynasty (1644–1911), the remote regions of northern and western China, inhabited by non-Han peoples such as Mongols, Manchus, Tibetans and Uighurs, were known as Outer China. This was so even though the Mongols ruled China under the Yuan dynasty (1279–1368) and the Manchus ruled it under the Qing dynasty. The regions of Outer China include Manchuria (northeastern China, comprising the modern provinces of Heilongjiang, Jilin and Liaoning), Mongolia, Tibet (Xizang), Qinghai, and Xinjiang (formerly known as Chinese Turkestan). All of these regions have been incorporated into the People's Republic of China (PRC), founded in 1949, but have varying degrees of autonomy. See also GEOGRAPHY; GREAT WALL; HAN; INNER MONGOLIA AUTONOMOUS REGION; MANCHURIA; MIDDLE KINGDOM; NOMADS AND ANIMAL HUSBANDRY; TIBET; XINJIANG UIGHUR AUTONOMOUS REGION; NAMES OF INDIVIDUAL PROVINCES.

CHINA PUBLISHING HOUSE See COMMERCIAL PRESS.

CHINA RECONSTRUCTS See SOONG CHING LING.

CHINA SEA See EAST CHINA SEA; SOUTH CHINA SEA.

CHINA TRAVEL SERVICE See CHINA INTERNATIONAL TRAVEL SERVICE.

CHINA WELFARE FUND AND INSTITUTE See SOONG QINGLING.

CHINA YOUTH TRAVEL SERVICE See ALL-CHINA YOUTH FEDERATION; CHINA INTERNATIONAL TRAVEL SERVICE.

CHINA'S DESTINY See CHIANG KAI-SHEK.

"CHINA'S SORROW" See NATURAL DISASTERS; YELLOW RIVER.

CHINATOWNS See OVERSEAS CHINESE; SIX COMPANIES, CHINESE.

CHINESE ACADEMY OF SCIENCES (CAS) The leading institution of learning and comprehensive scientific research in the People's Republic of China (PRC). The CAS was established in 1949, combining research institutes under the former Academia Sinica and Beijing Research Academy (the former Beijing Research Laboratory). It is nominally subordinate to the State Science and Technology Commission but, in practice, reports directly to the State Council. Members of the prestigious CAS include China's most senior and best-known scientists. The CAS has stimulated many fields of research and has played a major role in developing new technologies in China such as computers, robotics, new materials and lasers. CAS programs train Chinese scientists and nurture high-tech industries.

In 1993, the CAS operated 123 institutes and employed 80,000 people in all fields of science. About half of these institutes perform some basic research, and some are well known to scientists in other countries, such as the Institute for High-Energy Physics in Beijing. About 30 percent of CAS activities are devoted to basic research; 30 percent to population, resources and the environment; and 40 percent to technology development.

The CAS also supports the University of Science and Technology of China (USTC); its main campus was moved from Beijing to Hefei in Anhui Province in 1970 during the Cultural Revolution. The CAS was funded directly by the Chinese government until the country recently switched to a market economy, forcing the CAS to gain half of its budget through competition for contracts in government and industrial projects. In 1994, the CAS had an annual income of U.S.$325 million. Most CAS institutes now have to acquire about 60 percent of their funding from outside sources, such as grants, special programs and nongovernmental sources. In 1995 the CAS submitted a development plan for the next 5 to 10 years to the Chinese government, and the scientific community is debating which facilities should be given priority on the basis of scientific value, technical challenge and financial requirements and projected benefits. See also STATE COUNCIL.

CHINESE-AMERICANS See FOREIGN TRADE AND INVESTMENT; OVERSEAS CHINESE; SIX COMPANIES, CHINESE; SUN YAT-SEN.

CHINESE COMMUNIST PARTY (CCP) The political party that founded the People's Republic of China (PRC) in 1949, after defeating the Chinese Nationalist Party (Kuomintang; KMT) in a civil war, and that still controls the PRC government. The CCP was founded in Shanghai, China's largest city and trading port, in July 1921. Chinese communists had been influenced by the Revolution of 1911 and the May Fourth Movement of 1919. In 1911 the Chinese people had overthrown the Manchu Qing dynasty (1644–1911), China's last imperial dynasty. Dr. Sun Yat-sen (1866–1925) had led the revolution, and in 1912 he had been inaugurated first president of the new Republic of China (ROC) at Nanjing. That year Sun also organized the Chinese Nationalist Party, an outgrowth of his Revolutionary Alliance (Tong-menghui or T'ung-meng-hui). However, the northern Chinese warlord Yuan Shikai (Yuan Shih-k'ai; 1859–1916) forced Sun to resign in 1912 so that he could become president of the ROC. After Yuan died in 1916, China was divided among local warlords, and whatever warlord controlled Beijing also controlled the Chinese government.

After World War I, it was revealed that the warlord government in Beijing had made a secret agreement with the Japanese government that Japan would be given the concessions in China that had been held by Germany. The Chinese people were outraged, and on May 4, 1919, Chinese students, led by students from Beijing University, held massive public demonstrations against the Beijing government and Japan. These demonstrations grew into a nationwide political movement that inspired modern Chinese revolutionaries and also stimulated the so-called New Culture Movement among Chinese intellectuals and artists.

In 1917 Russia had undergone its Bolshevik revolution, which established the communist Soviet Union. Many of the Chinese students who had gone abroad to study became members of the Communist Party in Japan, France and other countries. Mao Zedong (Mao Tse-tung; 1893–1976), who eventually became chairman of the CCP, belonged to a Marxist study group in Beijing led by Li Dazhao (Li Ta-chao), whose publication, *New Youth*, praised the Bolshevik revolution and Marxist ideology. In 1920, Gregory Voitinsky, an agent from the Comintern (Communist International) in Moscow, helped the Chinese establish communist cells in Beijing, Shanghai, and Hunan and Hubei provinces. Mao, who had been born in Hunan, led the communist cell there.

In July, 1921, 12 delegates from communist groups in Beijing, Guangzhou, Shanghai, Wuhan, Jinan and Japan met secretly in Shanghai to convene the First National Party Congress of the CCP. Mao attended the congress as an official delegate from Hunan. Zhang Guotao (Chang Kuo-t'ao; 1897–1979), another founder of the CCP, had been a leader of the May Fourth Movement and a member of Mao's study group. Zhu De (Chu Teh; 1886–1976), who later became commander of the Chinese Communist military, was another founder. Chen Duxiu (Ch'en Tu-hsiu; 1879–1942), who was not able to attend the meeting, was elected secretary-general of the CCP.

Soviet advisers went to China to help organize the CCP and reorganize Sun's KMT on the model of the Soviet Communist Party. The most prominent adviser was Comintern agent Mikhail Borodin (1884–1952). In July 1922 the CCP held its Second National Party Congress in Shanghai and accepted the Comintern's instructions that CCP members cooperate with the KMT and join the KMT while keeping their identity as members of the CCP. In 1922 the KMT had 150,000 members and the CCP only 300 members; by 1925 the CCP had 1,500 members. The CCP held its Third National Party Congress in 1923 in Guangzhou in southern China. Mao was elected to the party's nine-member Central Committee. The National Party Congress acknowledged that the KMT was the leading party of the Chinese revolution and decided to cooperate with the KMT, and the two parties formed their First United Front. Mao was elected an alternate member of the KMT Central Executive Committee at its First National Congress, held in Guangzhou in 1924. He also became the acting director of its Central Committee.

The KMT and CCP cooperated to establish the Whampoa (Huangpu) Military Academy near Guangzhou, to train officers for a Northern Expedition against the warlords who controlled China. Chiang Kai-shek (Jiang Jieshi; 1887–1975), whom Sun had sent to Moscow to study military training and organization, was named the academy's first commandant. Chiang worked closely with Zhou Enlai (Chou En-lai; 1898–1976), who served as director of the academy's Political Department. Zhou had joined the Communist Party while a student in France. In 1925, when he returned to China, he married Deng Yingchao (Teng Yingch'ao; 1904–92), another political activist who became an early member of the CCP. Zhou later became the second-most important leader in the CCP, and Deng (not to be confused with Deng Xiaoping) also held high-ranking positions. The CCP held its Fourth National Congress in Shanghai in January 1925. Sun Yat-sen died in March 1925, and the KMT divided into right- and left-wing factions, with Chiang Kai-shek leading the former.

In June 1926 Chiang Kai-shek was named commander in chief of the National Revolutionary Army, and in July he launched the Northern Expedition against the warlords to unify China. By 1927 his forces regained territory as far north as Shanghai and Nanjing on the Yangzi River (Changjiang). The left wing of the KMT, led by Wang Jingwei (Wang Ching-wei; 1883–1944), established a government at Wuhan in Hubei Province, while Chiang's right wing established a Nationalist capital at Nanjing. Members of the CCP and the left-wing faction of the KMT had gone ahead of the Northern Expedition to gain support from local peasants and workers. However, Chiang felt that their emphasis on social and economic reforms had become too revolutionary, and in April 1927 he turned against the Communists and sent his troops into Shanghai to arrest and execute them. Thousands were killed but some escaped, including Zhou Enlai and Deng Yingchao, to join Communist forces in Jiangxi Province in south-central China. At the same time as the purge in Shanghai, the CCP held its Fifth National Congress at Wuhan in April–May 1927. Wang Jingwei and his KMT faction in Wuhan decided that Chiang Kai-shek was correct that the CCP was being controlled by Moscow and planned to eliminate the KMT, and so they also began purging the Communists in July 1927.

Communists in the Chinese countryside attempted several unsuccessful insurrections against the KMT. Zhou Enlai and Zhu De were major organizers of the Nanchang Uprising, the Communist military rebellion against the KMT of August 1, 1927. The CCP considers this date the birth of the Red Army, which later became known as the People's Liberation Army (PLA). The Nationalists put down the uprising, and Zhu De took his troops to Hunan Province and joined with guerrilla forces led there by Mao Zedong. Mao had moved to his home province of Hunan and led the Autumn Harvest Uprising of 1927, an insurrection by Hunan peasants. When it failed, the CCP removed Mao from the Central Committee and other positions. However, Mao recognized that in contradiction to orthodox Marxist theory, in China the peasants rather than the urban workers were the social group that the Chinese Communists should mobilize for their revolution. Peasants formed the vast majority of the Chinese population and had always been a force for social change. Many times in Chinese history, dynasties had been overthrown and new dynasties established by rebellious peasants who believed that the old dynasty had lost the "Mandate of Heaven." The Taiping Rebellion (1850–64), one of the largest rebellions in Chinese history and one which nearly overthrew the Qing dynasty, greatly influenced Mao.

The CCP had to hold its Sixth National Congress in Moscow in the summer of 1928. Li Lisan, who controlled the

meeting, urged that the CCP continue working in Chinese cities and criticized Mao's emphasis on guerrilla warfare and mobilization of peasants. But Mao and Zhu De built up a Communist military force in the Jinggang Mountains on the border of Hunan and Jiangxi Provinces, which had about 10,000 troops by the winter of 1927–28. In 1929 they moved the Red Army south to Ruijin in Jiangxi, where Zhu built up the Red Army to 200,000 troops by 1933. Other Communist leaders joined them there. Mao's skill at guerrilla-fighting tactics and peasant mobilization enabled him to become the dominant CCP leader. In November 1931 Mao was appointed chairman of the government of the Chinese Soviet Republic, and Zhang Guotao was sent to become head of a Soviet in northern China.

In 1928 Chiang Kai-shek led the second phase of the Northern Expedition and took Beijing in June 1928, symbolically unifying all of China south of the Great Wall. On October 10, 1928, Chiang became chairman of a new Chinese Nationalist government (ROC) and established his capital at Nanjing. The KMT refused to allow any other political party to have a role in the ROC government. The Communists led a number of uprisings in Chinese cities, all of which were bloodily suppressed by the Nationalists, and Mikhail Borodin and other foreign advisers fled the country. Beginning in 1930, Chiang sent five annual KMT military campaigns against the Communist forces in south-central China.

On September 18, 1931, Japanese forces invaded Manchuria (northeastern China), but Chiang told his troops not to resist the Japanese and pulled them out. He still felt the most urgent task of the KMT was to wipe out Communists in China. In 1932 the Japanese formed a puppet state in Manchuria called Manchukuo (Manzhouguo or Man-chou-kuo in Chinese) and used it as their base to invade China Proper and the rest of Asia.

Chiang's Nationalist forces encircled the Communist forces in Jiangxi, and in 1934 Mao, Zhou and other CCP leaders decided that their forces should escape to the west. About 100,000 Red Army soldiers and CCP members began the epic Long March (1934–35), which covered 6,000 miles. During the Long March, the CCP held a meeting of the Politburo (Political Bureau) of its Central Committee in January 1935 in Guizhou Province. The party established a new leadership with Mao as chairman, and accepted Mao's ideology of guerrilla warfare. Mao was the first leader of the CCP, and of any Communist Party in the world, who had not been chosen by the Comintern. From 1935 until he died in 1976, the CCP was strongly associated with Mao.

On October 20, 1935, the survivors of the Long March, who only numbered about 7,000, officially ended their march when they met up with the 15th Red Army Corps at Wuqizhen in northern Shaanxi Province. Only about 50 women survived the march, including Deng Yingchao. The legendary survivors became the leaders of the final stage of the civil war between the CCP and the KMT, and high-ranking officials in the PRC government. Two American journalists who spent time with the Communists at Yan'an wrote books that remain important sources about Mao, the Long March and the CCP. Edgar Snow described the life of Mao in *Red Star over China* (1937), and Agnes Smedley wrote the autobiography of Zhu De, published in 1956 as

The Great Road. Both authors published several other books about China and the CCP.

Chiang Kai-shek ordered Zhang Xueliang (Chang Hsuehliang; 1898–), the warlord of Manchuria, to send his troops to fight the Communists in Shaanxi. But the Manchurian soldiers did not want to fight their own countrymen while the Japanese were occupying their land. Mao also wanted to halt the CCP-KMT civil war, and the CCP Politburo called for an "Anti-Japanese National United Front." Chiang flew to Zhang's headquarters at Xi'an in Shaanxi in December 1936. There Zhang and other KMT and CCP leaders kidnapped Chiang to persuade him to stop fighting the Communists and form a KMT-CCP united front to fight the Japanese; this is known as the Xi'an Incident. Chiang agreed to do so and flew back to Nanjing.

In 1937 Japanese troops moved into northern China and quickly took the North China Plain, Shanghai, and Nanjing, where they committed terrible atrocities known as the "Rape of Nanjing." Combined KMT-CCP forces, bolstered by private armies of Chinese warlords, began fighting China's War of Resistance against Japan (1937–45; World War II). The Communist Red Army was renamed the Eighth Route Army of the National Army, with Zhu De serving as commander of all Chinese Communist military operations. Peng Dehuai (P'eng Teh-huai; 1898–1974) served as deputy commander of the Eighth Route Army. Other Communist commanders and political commissars included Liu Bocheng (Liu Po-cheng; 1892–1986), Deng Xiaoping (Teng Hsiao-p'ing; 1904–97), Lin Biao (Lin Piao; 1907–71) and Nie Rongzhen (Nieh Jung-chen; 1899–   ). KMT forces controlled southwestern China, and CCP forces northwestern China. The Communists also led guerrilla forces in Henan, Zhejiang and Shandong Provinces and in other regions between those controlled by Japanese forces, especially in northern China. In 1938 Zhang Guotao defected to the KMT and the CCP purged him for rightist deviation.

In 1938 Canadian surgeon Norman Bethune went to China and organized medical services for the Communist Eighth Route Army in the region along the border between Shanxi and Hebei provinces. He worked ceaselessly to treat wounded soldiers and educate the Chinese about medical practices. In 1939 he died and was buried in Shijiazhuang, the capital of Hebei Province. He became a great hero to the Chinese people. In 1988 Canadian actor Donald Sutherland starred as Bethune in the film *Norman Bethune: The Making of a Hero,* coproduced by the August First Film Studio, which is connected with the PLA, and Canadian and French companies. The film is another important source of information about the CCP.

World War II broke out in Europe in September 1939, which brought China allies such as Great Britain. After Japan bombed the U.S. naval fleet at Pearl Harbor on December 7, 1941, the United States became an official ally of China and sent more military and financial aid. U.S. General Joseph Stilwell became Chiang Kai-shek's chief-of-staff. Chiang had moved the Nationalist government to Chongqing (Chungking) in Sichuan, a province in southwestern China protected by high mountains. Stilwell wanted to arm all factions in China that were fighting the Japanese, including the Communists, but Chiang strongly disagreed and had Stilwell replaced

by General Albert Wedemeyer. The KMT-CCP Second United Front had begun breaking down in 1941 when Nationalist troops defeated the Communist New Fourth Army in the lower Yangzi River valley, known as the New Fourth Army Incident. Although Zhou Enlai was in Chongqing, the two parties barely cooperated for the rest of the war against Japan; they looked forward to resuming their civil war.

The CCP held its Seventh National Party Congress, the first since 1928, in Yan'an in early 1945. It adopted a constitution with a preamble stating that "the thought of Mao Zedong" was the official party ideology. The party confirmed Mao as chairman of the Politburo, the Central Committee and the Secretariat of the Central Committee. He thus had complete control of the CCP by the end of China's War of Resistance against Japan and the resumption of the CCP-KMT civil war.

On August 8, 1945, two days after the United States dropped the first atomic bomb on Hiroshima, Japan, the USSR declared war on Japan and sent a huge army into Manchuria, which met little resistance from Japanese troops there. Japan surrendered to the Allied forces on August 14, 1945, and the Chinese Nationalist government returned to Nanjing. American diplomats attempted to ensure that Japanese troops in northern China and Manchuria would surrender to the Nationalists rather than the Communists, thus making Chiang the dominant leader in postwar China. However, the Soviet troops turned over Manchuria and all the weapons the Japanese had surrendered there to the Chinese Communists in the region, which greatly aided the CCP in the final stages of the civil war.

The Americans also attempted to negotiate a postwar coalition KMT-CCP government that would rule all of China. The CCP now had about 1.2 million members, plus 900,000 soldiers in its military, and controlled an area with a population of 90 million Chinese. CCP leaders Mao and Zhou met with Chiang Kai-shek at Chongqing for six weeks in the fall of 1945, but nothing came of their negotiations. Zhou went to northern Shaanxi to help direct the CCP forces there. U.S. president Harry Truman sent General of the Army George C. Marshall as his special ambassador to China with the mission of persuading the Communists and Nationalists to form a coalition government, but he did not succeed in this and blamed both sides for being intransigent. The United States continued to give the Nationalist government enormous loans, and it ensured that China became a permanent member of the Security Council of the newly formed United Nations.

On May 1, 1946, the CCP officially renamed its military the People's Liberation Army (PLA). On June 26, 1946, Nationalist troops waged an offensive against Communist-held areas in Hubei and Henan provinces. However, the Nationalists were not able to gain support among the Chinese people because of the rampant corruption in their government and runaway inflation, which made the Nationalist currency worthless. By the end of 1947, the Americans saw that the Nationalists had no chance of winning the civil war and withdrew their support for Chiang Kai-shek.

The Communists used guerrilla-fighting tactics and mobilized peasants to their side. One of their most effective techniques was land reform, in which they encouraged peasants to criticize publicly the wealthy landowners who exploited them, and then took away land from the landowners and gave it to peasants who had little or no land. PLA troops launched two major offensives, one in northeastern China and one which moved across the Yellow River in Shandong Province. On September 12, 1948, Lin Biao led a major campaign in Manchuria, where 300,000 Nationalist troops surrendered to the Communists. The PLA took Shenyang (formerly known as Mukden), the capital of Liaoning Province, on November 2. In the second great battle of the civil war, in the Huai River basin in north-central China, the PLA surrounded 66 of the KMT's 200 divisions. A large number of KMT soldiers defected to the CCP or were captured. This campaign ended with a victory for the PLA on January 10, 1949, which to all effects ended the KMT regime on the Chinese mainland. In a third major campaign, the PLA took Tianjin on January 15 and Beijing, without any resistance, on January 31.

Chiang Kai-shek resigned as ROC president and his successor, Li Zongren (Li Tsung-jen), negotiated peace with the Communists. But the CCP demanded unconditional surrender and the punishment of Chiang and other Nationalists they deemed war criminals. The KMT would not agree to these demands, so the Communists resumed their offensive in April 1949 and moved south of the Yangzi to take Nanjing on April 23, Shanghai on May 27 and Guangzhou in October. Chiang moved his Nationalist troops to Taiwan, an island 100 miles off the coast of southeastern China, and transferred China's gold reserve there. He himself fled to Taiwan on December 10, 1949, after the Communists took Chongqing and Chengdu in Sichuan. Chiang established the headquarters of the KMT government on Taiwan, which he still called the Republic of China (ROC) and claimed to be the legitimate government of all of China. He proclaimed that Taipei, the capital of Taiwan, was the temporary capital of China.

From September 20–21, 1949, the CCP held the Chinese People's Political Consultative Conference (CPPCC) in Beijing, which served as the legislative and representative body of the new Communist government they were forming. The CPPCC was originally an organization formed in 1948 by the CCP but it included nearly all other Chinese factions that opposed the KMT. The CCP still permits these political parties, known as the eight democratic parties, to function on a small scale in China. On September 22, 1949, the CPPCC passed an Organic Law, which specified the procedure and structure for government operations. On September 29 the Conference proclaimed its Common Program, which served as the law of the new Communist government until the 1954 state constitution superseded it.

On October 1, 1949, Mao, joined by a large group of CCP leaders and other colleagues, stood on the rostrum above the gate in Tiananmen Square in Beijing and proclaimed the founding of the Communist People's Republic of China (PRC). Several days before, he had been elected chairman of the Central Government of the PRC. The Chinese Communists, who consider Taiwan a renegade province of China, call their civil war with the Nationalists the War of Liberation, and their victory National Liberation. Since 1949, there has been virtually no difference between the CCP and the PRC. In theory, all state power in the PRC belongs to the

people, but, in fact, the government of the PRC is subordinate to the CCP and serves to implement its policies.

Great Britain, the USSR and many Eastern European countries recognized the PRC as *the* legitimate government of China. In 1950 Mao traveled to Moscow and negotiated the Sino-Soviet Treaty of Friendship, Alliance, and Mutual Assistance. After North Korea invaded South Korea in 1950, the United States provided military support to the ROC on Taiwan, and the United States and many other countries recognized the ROC as the legitimate government of China. The PRC sent more than 2.3 million soldiers across the Yalu Tsungpo River into North Korea, which borders Manchuria, to defend against advancing United Nations (UN) troops, which included many U.S. soldiers. The CCP waged a public campaign to mobilize the Chinese people against the United States. The Chinese troops suffered extremely heavy casualties, but the Chinese were proud that for the first time in modern history they had been able to resist foreign troops and prevent them from advancing into Manchuria. In 1950 the PRC also sent troops westward into Tibet (Xizang) and within a year "liberated" this region, according to the CCP. The Tibetans strongly resisted the Chinese troops, and this issue of the Chinese occupation of Tibet has still not been settled.

The CCP continued the process of land reform throughout the countryside. In 1950 the PRC passed the Agrarian Reform Law, which expanded the land-reform program to affect nearly all Chinese citizens by mandating the combining of farms into collectives known as people's communes. The government also passed the Marriage Law of 1950, which intended to free women in China from the old Confucian-based feudal system under which they were forced into marriage and obligated to obey their husbands; the new law also permitted women to divorce under certain conditions. Children were provided some legal protections as well.

In 1951–52 the CCP launched a movement of "class struggle" against landlords, wealthy peasants, intellectuals, and corrupt bureaucrats and businessmen, known as the Three-Anti and Five-Anti Campaigns. Using public mass trials, the CCP purged officials who were considered to be incompetent and not totally loyal to the party. Hundreds of thousands of Chinese were executed and a much larger number were sent to prison or labor camps. In 1953 the CCP announced China's first Five-Year Plan (1953–57), which aimed to develop heavy industry based on the Soviet model. The Chinese government has continued issuing Five-Year Plans for China's economic and industrial development up to the present time. In 1953 China also held its first modern census, which showed the population to be 583 million, much higher than was expected.

In 1954 the PRC passed its first state constitution, which centralized the authority of the government in the National People's Congress (NPC), which superseded the CPPCC. The CPPCC did not disband but has continued functioning as a political consulting body on major state policies of the PRC. The NPC is comparable to the U.S. Congress or the British Parliament and is, in theory, still the highest government body of the PRC. Local congresses elect delegates to provincial congresses, who in turn elect delegates to the

NPC. The NPC elects the president and vice-president of the PRC. The 1954 NPC elected Mao chairman of the PRC, Zhou premier of the State Council and Liu Shaoqi chairman of the Standing Committee of the NPC. Mao was concurrently chairman of the CCP and president of the PRC until 1959, although he remained chairman of the CCP until he died in 1976. The premier of the State Council actually wields more power than the president. Zhou served as premier from 1954 until he died in 1976. Deng Xiaoping, Zhou's protégé, served concurrently as secretary general of the CCP and vice-premier of the State Council.

The CCP has a structure similar to that of the PRC government, and its highest body is the National Party Congress (not to be confused with the NPC). Under it is the CCP Central Committee, whose functions and powers are exercised by the Politburo. The Standing Committee of the Politburo is a select group of about a half-dozen members that forms the inner circle of power in the PRC. Many of China's highest-ranking leaders have held positions concurrently in the CCP and the PRC government.

In the spring of 1956 Mao initiated a movement known as the Hundred Flowers Campaign, or the Double Hundred Campaign, which encouraged intellectual and cultural leaders to criticize publicly the CCP and party cadres (officials). However, these denunciations became so strong that CCP leaders abruptly stopped the campaign in August 1957 by declaring the Anti-Rightist Campaign, in which critics of the party were condemned and punished for being "bourgeois rightists." Again, many Chinese were arrested and sent to prison or labor camps. By the end of this movement, Lui Shaoqi had become Mao's designated successor.

In 1958 Mao announced the Great Leap Forward (1958–60), which aimed to speed up the development of China's heavy industries and mobilize the great masses of unskilled Chinese workers. But the experiment turned out to be a disaster and resulted in severe famine and the erosion of thousands of acres of farmland. In April 1959, the CCP required Mao to step down as chairman of the PRC, and he was replaced by Liu Shaoqi, although Mao remained chairman of the CCP. In 1960 CCP leaders persuaded Mao to cancel the Great Leap Forward and admit that it had failed.

Around 1956 the PRC and the USSR, which had been close allies, began growing apart ideologically in what became known as the Sino-Soviet Conflict. In April 1960 the PRC criticized Soviet leaders for being "revisionist," and in June the USSR stopped all of its aid shipments to the PRC and recalled the thousands of Soviet technical experts who had been working in China. These moves devastated the Chinese economy. By 1962 Mao had denounced the Soviet government as a right-wing dictatorship. Mao wanted to prevent China from turning to capitalism, as he believed the USSR had done; this concern was a major impetus for launching the Cultural Revolution in 1966. By 1963 the two countries were competing to be the leader of the Communist world, and their relations deteriorated to the point where they were fighting border skirmishes in the late 1960s.

In 1962 Mao began an ideological campaign against capitalism and revisionism known as the Socialist Education Movement (1962–65), a precursor to the Cultural Revolution. He also enacted a campaign urging people "to learn from the People's Liberation Army (PLA)." Lin Biao, minister of national defense, compiled the *Quotations from Chairman Mao Zedong,* also known as the "Little Red Book," to indoctrinate PLA recruits with Mao's revolutionary thought. The Socialist Education Movement became a struggle in the CCP between the moderate anti-Mao faction and the pro-Mao radical faction. The moderates seemed to have more power in 1965, and some historians believe that by that time Mao had lost control of the CCP.

Mao launched the Great Proletarian Cultural Revolution in 1966 to purge his opponents, including Liu Shaoqi, and to purify the CCP of reactionary influences. On August 18, 1966, Mao, Zhou, Lin Biao and other CCP officials presided over a massive rally, orchestrated by Jiang Qing (Chiang Ch'ing; 1914–91), Mao's wife, in Beijing's Tiananmen Square in support of the Cultural Revolution. The Red Guards, who became the vanguard of the revolution, first appeared at this rally, and eight massive political demonstrations were held in three months in Tiananmen Square. The Red Guards carried out Mao's orders to oppose feudalism and capitalism by destroying a great deal of property and persecuting and killing numerous Chinese, many of them CCP and government officials. In July 1968 Mao finally abolished the Red Guards, which brought the most radical phase of the Cultural Revolution to an end, although the turmoil continued until Mao's death in 1976.

In 1968 the CCP officially denounced Liu Shaoqi, Mao's designated successor, and formally expelled him from the Party. He was placed under house arrest and died in 1969. Liu was succeeded as chairman by Lin Biao, who was then himself accused of plotting against Mao and, according to the official CCP line, died in a plane crash while attempting to flee China in September 1971. Zhou remained loyal to Mao but attempted to mediate between the radical pro-Mao and moderate anti-Mao factions. Zhou also played a major role in establishing diplomatic relations between the PRC and the United States under President Richard M. Nixon in the early 1970s. On October 25, 1971, the UN passed a resolution to expel the ROC and give China's seat to the PRC. On January 1, 1979, the United States transferred diplomatic recognition from the ROC to the PRC, and many other countries did the same. Yet the United States has maintained close economic ties with the ROC on Taiwan. In January 1975, Zhou addressed the Fourth NPC and advocated the policy of the Four Modernizations to reform and develop China. CCP officials linked this policy with industrialization and the opening up of foreign trade.

Zhou died on January 8, 1976, Zhu De died on July 6, and Mao died on September 9. On October 6, more than 30 radical CCP leaders were arrested and deposed from their official positions by the moderate faction led by Hua Guofeng (Hua Kuo-feng; 1920–   ), who had seized power in the CCP's Central Committee. On October 13, the CCP announced that Hua had been appointed to replace Mao as CCP chairman, chairman of the Party's Central Military Commission, and premier of the State Council. On October 22, 1976, four of the arrested radical leaders were charged with a plot to overthrow the Chinese government. This so-called Gang of Four, including Jiang Qing and three of her closest supporters in the CCP, were blamed for causing the Cultural Revolution and a wide variety of other crimes.

They were formally put on trial in November 1980 and were judged guilty. Mao's body was embalmed and placed on public view in the Chairman Mao Memorial Hall in Tiananmen Square.

In August 1977, at the 11th National Party Congress, Hua Guofeng declared the official end of the Great Proletarian Cultural Revolution. Deng Xiaoping, who had been purged twice, was rehabilitated once and for all, and began consolidating his power as the leader of the movement to reform and modernize China. In December 1978, at the Third Plenary Session of the 11th Central Committee of the CCP, Deng launched a major program for reforming Chinese political, social and economic institutions and even the CCP's Maoist and Communist ideology. Deng's protégé, Hu Yaobang (Hu Yao-pang; 1917–89), was elected secretary-general of the CCP as well as head of the Party's Propaganda Department, and Hu took over the daily operations of the Party. The government encouraged foreign trade and investment by opening four Special Economic Zones (SEZs) in 1979. More SEZs and Coastal Open Cities were soon designated.

The NPC promulgated revised state constitutions in 1975, 1978 and 1982 to help the PRC recover from the Cultural Revolution by reinstating government bodies and institutions that had been suspended. The 1982 constitution transferred administrative power from people's communes, which were disbanded, to local government bodies. It abolished life tenure in the highest government positions and limited national leaders to two consecutive terms in office. In 1980, Hu Yaobang and Zhao Ziyang (Chao Tzu-yang; 1919–), another Deng protégé, were elected to the Standing of the Politburo and the newly restored Party Secretariat. In 1981, Deng had Hua Guofeng demoted as CCP chairman and put Hu Yaobang in this position. In the late 1980s, the CCP Secretariat and the State Council began exercising most of the responsibility for foreign policy decisions, in place of the Politburo. Li Xiannian (Li Hsien-nien; 1905–92) was elected president of the PRC in 1983 and Yang Shangkun (Yang Shang-k'un; 1907–) in 1988. Jiang Zemin (Chiang Tse-min; 1926–) was president as of October 1997, when he visited President Clinton in Washington, D.C.

In 1986, Chinese students held pro-democracy demonstrations in 15 cities demanding free elections and freedom of speech, assembly and the press. Hu Yaobang did not denounced them and their intellectual supporters, and CCP hardliners criticized Hu for being too lenient. In January 1987 the Party demoted Hu from his position as CCP general secretary and replaced him with Zhao Ziyang, former head of the State Council. Li Peng (Li P'eng; 1928–), more conservative than Zhao regarding economic reform, replaced Zhao as prime minister. When Hu was dismissed, Chinese students regarded him as a hero. Hu died on April 15, 1989, and on April 17, pro-democracy demonstrations broke out, which grew into a massive six-week demonstration in Tiananmen Square in Beijing. On the night of June 4, 1989, Li Peng and other CCP hardliners ordered the military to assault the demonstrators; this became known as the Tiananmen Square Massacre. Zhao Ziyang, a moderate, was purged after the massacre. Since then, the CCP has maintained strict control over the country, and relations have been severely strained between the PRC and foreign countries. Deng Xiaoping continued to wield power behind the scenes until his death on February 19, 1997. See also ANTI-RIGHTIST CAMPAIGN; BEIJING; BEIJING UNIVERSITY; BETHUNE, NORMAN; BIG-CHARACTER POSTERS; BORODIN, MIKHAIL; CADRE; CHEN DUXIU; CHIANG KAI-SHEK; CHINESE PEOPLE'S POLITICAL CONSULTATIVE CONFERENCE; CIVIL WAR BETWEEN COMMUNISTS AND NATIONALISTS; CONSTITUTION, STATE, OF 1954; CULTURAL REVOLUTION; DENG XIAOPING; DENG YINGCHAO; EIGHTH ROUTE ARMY; FIVE-YEAR PLANS; FOREIGN TRADE AND INVESTMENT; FOUR MODERNIZATIONS; GANG OF FOUR; GOVERNMENT STRUCTURE; GREAT LEAP FORWARD; HU YAOBANG; HUA GUOFENG; HUNDRED FLOWERS CAMPAIGN; JIANG QING; JIANG ZEMIN; JIANGXI PROVINCE; JINGGANG MOUNTAIN RANGE; KOREAN WAR; LAND REFORM BY COMMUNISTS; LEGAL SYSTEM; LI DAZHAO; LI PENG; LI XIANNIAN; LIBERATION, NATIONAL; LIN BIAO; LIU SHAOQI; LONG MARCH; MARRIAGE LAW OF 1950; MAY FOURTH MOVEMENT OF 1919; NANCHANG; NANJING; NATIONAL PARTY CONGRESS; NATIONAL PEOPLE'S CONGRESS; NATIONALIST PARTY; NEW CULTURE MOVEMENT; NEW FOURTH ARMY INCIDENT; NIXON, U.S. PRESIDENT RICHARD M., VISIT TO CHINA; NORTHERN EXPEDITION; PEASANTS AND PEASANT REBELLIONS; PENG DEHUAI; PENG ZHEN; PEOPLE'S COMMUNE; PEOPLE'S LIBERATION ARMY; PEOPLE'S REPUBLIC OF CHINA; POLITBURO; QUOTATIONS FROM CHAIRMAN MAO ZEDONG; RED GUARDS; REPUBLIC OF CHINA; REVOLUTION OF 1911; REVOLUTIONARY ALLIANCE; SHANGHAI; SINO-INDIAN BORDER DISPUTE; SINO-SOVIET CONFLICT; SMEDLEY, AGNES; SNOW, EDGAR; SOCIALIST EDUCATION MOVEMENT; SPECIAL ECONOMIC ZONES; STATE COUNCIL; SUN YAT-SEN; TAIPING REBELLION; TAIWAN; THREE-ANTI AND FIVE-ANTI CAMPAIGNS; TIANANMEN SQUARE; TIANANMEN SQUARE MASSACRE; TIBET; UNITED NATIONS; VIETNAM WAR AND CHINA; WAR OF RESISTANCE AGAINST JAPAN; WARLORD PERIOD; WHAMPOA MILITARY ACADEMY; YAN'AN; YANG SHANGKUN; YE JIANYING; ZHANG GUOTAO; ZHAO ZIYANG; ZHOU ENLAI; ZHU DE.

CHINESE CONSOLIDATED BENEVOLENT ASSOCIATION See SIX COMPANIES, CHINESE.

CHINESE EASTERN RAILWAY See HARBIN; LIAODONG PROVINCE; RAILROADS.

CHINESE ECONOMIC IDEOLOGY See CHIANG KAI-SHEK.

CHINESE MARITIME CUSTOMS SERVICE An organization established by the Qing dynasty (1644–1911) government in the mid-19th century to control the collection of customs dues at Shanghai, which had recently been opened to Western traders as a so-called treaty port by the Treaty of Nanjing between China and Great Britain in 1842. In 1853, the British consul in Shanghai, Rutherford Alcock, made an agreement with the Qing government to have a foreign inspector oversee the collection of customs dues, control the foreign merchants and hand over the dues to the Chinese government. Another Britisher, H. N. Lay, was appointed as foreign inspector, and by 1861 he was made inspector general of the organization, now fully established as the Chinese Maritime Customs Service. Lay overstepped his authority, and in 1863 he was replaced by Robert Hart (1835–1911), formerly a foreign inspector of customs at the southern port city of Guangzhou (Canton). Hart served in this position until 1908 and gained a reputation for being honest and hardworking. He used the customs network to set up a postal service in 1896, which became independent in 1911. The Qing court relied on the trustworthy Hart for numerous issues having to do with foreign relations.

By 1875 there were more than 400 foreigners, mainly British, employed in the Maritime Customs Service. Many Chinese also held positions in the service, where they acquired a knowledge of Western business methods. In addition to collecting customs dues, the service supervised such activities as charting waterways, dredging channels and maintaining lighthouses, buoys, and wharf and harbor facilities. The service also handled complex financial matters involving foreign loans and indemnities, which the Chinese felt encroached on Chinese sovereignty. This sentiment grew after the foreign powers forced China to pay an enormous indemnity upon crushing the Boxer Uprising in 1900. The total revenues collected by the Maritime Customs Service were not enough to make the required payments, and the Chinese government had to hand over the revenues from the salt tax and other domestic taxes as well. For this the Chinese people strongly resented the foreigners as well as the Qing government, which was overthrown in the Revolution of 1911. A biography of H. B. Morse (1855–1934), who served as Commissioner of the Chinese Maritime Customs Service, was published in 1995. Morse, born in Canada, was recruited from the graduating class of Harvard University to work in the service. He worked and lived throughout China for 35 years, rising through the ranks to Commissioner. After Morse retired, he wrote several histories of China, including *The International Relations of the Chinese Empire (1910–18)*. See also BOXER UPRISING; QING DYNASTY; SHANGHAI; TREATY PORTS.

CHINESE PEOPLE'S POLITICAL CONSULTATIVE CONFERENCE

(CPPCC) The legislative and representative body of the government of the People's Republic of China (PRC) when it was founded by the Chinese Communist Party (CCP) on October 1, 1949, after the defeat of the Nationalist Party (Kuomintang; KMT). The CPPCC was originally an organization formed in 1948 by the united front that was led by the CCP but included nearly all other Chinese factions that opposed the KMT. These political parties, which have continued to function on a small scale in China since 1949, include the Revolutionary Committee of the KMT, the China Democratic League, the China Democratic National Construction Association, the China Association for Promoting Democracy, the China Peasants' and Workers' Democratic Party, China Zhigongdang (Chih Kung Tang), Jiusan (Chiu San) Society and the Taiwan Democratic Self-Government League. On September 22, 1949, the CPPCC passed the Organic Law specifying the procedures and structure for government operations. The Organic Law set up the Central People's Government (CPG) and elected a Central People's Government Council (CPGC), which was to be the highest body in the Chinese national government and which would appoint and remove members of all other government bodies. The Organic Law also defined the functions and powers of the CPGC, which was to act for the CPPCC when it was not in session, and other government organizations.

On September 29, 1949, the CPPCC proclaimed its Common Program, which served as the law of the PRC until it was superceded by the 1954 state constitution. The Common Program was based on the ideas of Communist leader Mao Zedong (Mao Tse-tung) that the new Chinese government would be founded on the anti-KMT and anti-imperialist united front and would include workers, peasants, small property owners, and wealthier businessmen and others who shared the united front's political position. The Program established the general principles for redistributing land, eliminating foreign privileges in China, confiscating property owned by capitalists who favored the right wing of the KMT, and industrializing the country. It also guaranteed women equal rights with men and affirmed the principle of equality among the more than 50 ethnic minority groups in China. The Program specified that the CPPCC was to be a temporary legislative body until the country was secure enough to hold elections for a National People's Congress (NPC; not to be confused with the National Party Congress). It also called for the election of congresses of united front members at the local level. In addition, the Organic Law empowered the CPGC to set up a Government Administration Council (GAC), a People's Revolutionary Military Council, and a Supreme People's Court and Procuratorate. The GAC was to serve as the administrative branch of the government, headed by a premier and including several vice-premiers and all government ministers who directed economic and social affairs in China. The Revolutionary Military Council commanded the armed forces but was controlled by the CPGC, which also had the power to interpret and amend the Organic Law.

In 1954 the functions of the CPPCC were taken over by the National People's Congress (NPC), which remains the highest legislative body in the PRC. In August 1954, local elections were held for deputies to the First NPC, which was held in September. On September 20, 1954, the NPC promulgated the first formal state constitution of the PRC. The CPPCC, which met formally for the second time in 1954, did not disband but continued operating as a political consulting body on major state policies of the PRC. The third CPPCC convened in 1959, the fourth in 1964, the fifth in 1978, the sixth in 1983 and the seventh in 1988. The 1978 CPPCC was the first held since the Cultural Revolution (1966–76), after which Chinese leaders began rebuilding and modernizing the country. Deng Xiaoping (Teng Hsiao-p'ing), who favored economic and political reform, was elected chairman. Since 1978, government leaders who have initiated reforms for modernizing China have made the CPPCC an increasingly important symbol of cooperation among various interests, and reform leaders have given the CPPCC an increasingly prominent role.

The CPPCC has national and local committees and is made up of a variety of groups and individuals, including leaders of the CCP and other political parties that were loyal to the CCP during its civil war with the KMT; mass organizations, such as the All-China Federation of Trade Unions, the All-China Women's Federation, and the Communist Youth League; compatriots from Hong Kong (which reverted to China in 1997), Macao (which will revert to China in 1999) and Taiwan (which the PRC considers one of its provinces); overseas Chinese; and prominent Chinese scientists, educators, medical professionals, journalists, cultural figures, and representatives of China's 55 officially designated national minority ethnic groups. The CPPCC usually holds its national sessions in conjunction with the sessions of the NPC. See also ALL-CHINA FEDERATION OF TRADE UNIONS; ALL-CHINA WOMEN'S FEDERATION; CHINESE COMMUNIST PARTY; CIVIL WAR BETWEEN COMMUNISTS AND NATIONALISTS; COMMUNIST YOUTH LEAGUE; CONSTITUTION, STATE OF 1954; DEMOCRATIC PARTIES; HONG KONG; LAND REFORM BY COMMUNISTS; MACAO; MINORITIES, NATIONAL; NATIONAL PEOPLE'S CONGRESS; TAIWAN.

CHINESE PEOPLE'S VOLUNTEERS　See KOREAN WAR; PEOPLE'S LIBERATION ARMY.

CHINESE SIX COMPANIES　See SIX COMPANIES, CHINESE.

CHINESE TURKESTAN　See XINJIANG-UIGHUR AUTONOMOUS REGION.

CHINESE WORKERS REVIEW　See YEN, YAN YANGCHU JAMES.

CH'ING DYNASTY　See QING DYNASTY.

CH'ING T'UNG　See BRONZEWARE.

CH'INGHAI PROVINCE　See QINGHAI PROVINCE.

CHINGHIS KHAN　See GENGHIS KHAN.

CHING-KANG MOUNTAIN RANGE　See JINGGANG MOUNTAIN RANGE.

CH'ING-T'AN MOVEMENT　See SEVEN SAGES OF THE BAMBOO GROVE.

CH'INGTAO　See QINGDAO.

CHING-TE-CHEN　See JINGDEZHEN.

CHING-T'IEN　See WELL-FIELD SYSTEM OF AGRICULTURE.

CHING-T'U　See AMITABHA; PURE LAND SECT OF BUDDHISM.

CHINLING MOUNTAIN RANGE　See QINLING MOUNTAIN RANGE.

CHINOISERIE　A decorative style popular in Europe during the 17th and 18th centuries. Inspired by elements from Chinese design, it was actually based on the European fantasy of the way "exotic" designs and decorative objects from the Orient were supposed to look. Typical chinoiserie motifs include a bird on a flowering branch, a pavilion in a garden or a uniquely shaped rock. Exquisitely woven silk panels known as *gesu* (*kesi*, or "cut silk"), which the Chinese used to make mountings for fine paintings, covers for Buddhist scriptures and panels for screens, had been imported by Portuguese and Spanish traders during the Ming dynasty (1368–1644); they were also used to make robes worn by Roman Catholic priests. During the late 16th century, European trading companies such as the British East India Company began importing luxurious objects from China and other Asian countries, especially Japan and India, including silk and cotton textiles, porcelains, lacquerware, silverware and furniture. Interest in chinoiserie was stimulated in the late 17th century when 600 lacquered tray tops were imported by England from China and made into tables. (Nevertheless, the British used the term "japan" for lacquerware.) In 1688, John Stalker and George Parker published the influential book, *A Treatise on Japaning and Varnishing,* which described the production of lacquerware and included Oriental design patterns. Because of the popular but erroneous European belief that lacquer came from India, lacquerware was also called India work or Coromandel work, after the Coromandel coast of southeastern India. In France, chinoiserie reached its height during the reign of Louis XIV but continued into the 18th century, when it was adapted into the style known as "Louis XV" or "rococo."

European artisans frequently mounted Chinese porcelain pieces in luxurious gold or silver settings. Chinese artisans began producing textiles, wallpaper and porcelains with decorations that, while Chinese in inspiration, were designed for European tastes. The blue-and-white willow pattern, based on a Chinese folktale about two lovers, became a popular motif for sets of dinnerware. Around 1670, a group of British artisans traveled to China to introduce Chinese craftsmen to patterns in the European taste. Around 1700 another group made a similar trip to India. European porcelain factories eventually mastered Chinese techniques and copied Chinese designs on the dishes they produced. They also learned the secret of kaolin clay, which the Chinese used to manufacture delicate, translucent white porcelains. The growing wealth of the European middle class spurred its craftsmen to produce imitations of all the decorative objects that had been imported from Asia. For example, wooden furniture could be made to look like bamboo, a wood native to Asia. Textile manufacturers in China and Europe alike created patterns that imitated traditional Chinese landscapes painted on silk. The publication of numerous pattern books and manuals further spread the interest in Oriental designs. The Royal Pavilion at Brighton, England, constructed for King George IV, is one of the best-known examples of chinoiserie. It was built by John Nash between 1815 and 1817 and decorated the following three years by John Frederick Cace and 44 artisans. The recently restored pavilion is Indian in its architectural style but mostly Chinese in its interior decoration, including carved golden dragons on the ceiling, red-and-gold landscape murals, and crystal dragons and lotus flowers on a 30-foot chandelier. See also BAMBOO; BRITISH EAST INDIA COMPANY; DRAGON; FURNITURE, TRADITIONAL; LACQUERWARE; LOTUS; PORCELAIN; SILK; TEXTILE INDUSTRY; WILLOW.

CHIN-SHIH　See IMPERIAL BUREAUCRACY; IMPERIAL EXAMINATION SYSTEM; NINE-RANK SYSTEM.

CHIN-T'IEN　See WELL-FIELD SYSTEM OF AGRICULTURE.

CH'IN-TSUNG (EMPEROR)　See GAOZONG (EMPEROR) (SONG); HUIZONG (EMPEROR).

CH'I-SHAN   See LIN ZEXU; OPIUM WAR.

CH'I-TAN   See CATHAY; LIAO DYNASTY.

CHIU   See ALCOHOLIC BEVERAGES.

CHIU-HUA, MOUNT   See FOUR SACRED MOUNTAINS OF BUDDHISM; JIUHUA, MOUNT.

CHIU-LUNG PI   See DATONG; DRAGON.

CHONGDE (EMPEROR)   See ABAHAI; QING DYNASTY.

CHONGMING ISLAND   See YANGZI RIVER.

CHONGQING (Chungking)   The largest city in Sichuan province in central China, with a population of more than 6 million. Chongqing is located on a hilly peninsula at the juncture of Yangzi (Changjiang) and Jialing rivers (Jialingjiang). It is surrounded by mountains called Nanshan, Gele and Jinyun. The city is known as the "Furnace of the Yangzi" because its climate is very hot and humid.

The history of Chongqing dates back more than 2,000 years. It was the capital of the Ba Kingdom by the 12th century B.C. and was a trading center called Bajun during the Qin dynasty (221–206 B.C.). The city was known as Jiangzhou during the Han dynasty (206 B.C.–A.D. 220). During the Tang dynasty (618–907) it was called Yuzhou, and the classic name Yu is still used for the city. During the 12th century it was called Chongqing. Chongqing gained importance in the 19th century. Unequal treaties between China and foreign nations forced Chongqing to open to foreign traders in 1891 and to give the Japanese a concession there in 1901.

During China's War of Resistance against Japan (1937–45; World War II) Chongqing succeeded Wuhan (Hankou) in Hubei Province as the capital of the Nationalist (Kuomintang) government and thus served as the wartime capital of China from 1938 to 1945. It grew rapidly to almost 2 million people as millions of Chinese escaped Japanese troops by fleeing westward from eastern coastal regions. Many factories, universities and government offices were moved to Chongqing. The Japanese bombed the city but were never able to invade Sichuan because of the high mountains protecting the province. During this period, the Nationalists and the Chinese Communists formed a united front to fight the Japanese. The southern office of the Chinese Communist Party was located at Chongqing, and a detachment of the Communist Eighth Route Army was stationed in the city. The home that Communist leader Zhou Enlai rented from 1938 to 1945, which was used as a secret office by the Communists, is now open to tourists as a memorial to Zhou called Red Cliff Village (Hongyancun).

In August 1945 the Communist leader Mao Zedong came to Chongqing to negotiate a truce with the Nationalists but was unsuccessful, and the two sides fought each other in the civil war won by the Communists, who founded the People's Republic of China on October 1, 1949. Since then, Chongqing has been industrialized and is now the most important center for manufacturing in southwestern China. Major industries include steel, shipbuilding, chemicals, tex-

tiles, rubber tires and processed foods. Chongqing has been linked by railroad lines to other important Chinese cities such as Chengdu, also in Sichuan, Shanghai, Wuhan, Kunming, Guiyang and Xi'an. The Yangzi River was made more navigable so that ships of 3,000 tons were able to sail up to Chongqing. Pipelines were put in place to draw natural gas from the deposits in the region. There are several universities and technical schools, the Sichuan Academy of Fine Arts, and the Chongqing Workers' Palace of Culture.

Other tourist sites include the Chongqing City Museum and the Museum of Natural History, Northern Hot Springs (Beiwenquan) and Southern Hot Springs (Nanwenquan), Laojun Dong caves and Jinyun Mountain (Jinyunshan). The public park on Loquat Mountain (Pipashan), the highest point in Chongqing, offers a beautiful view of the city from the tea garden on the summit. Steamship rides on the Yangzi from Chongqing to Wuhan, stopping at Wanxian, are popular. High cliffs may be seen as the ships sail through Qutang, Wushan and Qiling gorges. There are splendid Buddhist cave temples and sculptures at Dazu 120 miles northwest of Chongqing. See also CHENGDU; CIVIL WAR BETWEEN COMMUNISTS AND NATIONALISTS; DAZU CAVE TEMPLES AND SCULPTURES; NATIONALIST PARTY; SICHUAN PROVINCE; WAR OF RESISTANCE AGAINST JAPAN; WUHAN; YANGZI RIVER; ZHOU ENLAI.

CHONGZHEN   (EMPEROR) (Ch'ung-chen;   1611–44) The reigning emperor of the Ming dynasty (1368–1644) when Li Zicheng (Li Tzu-ch'eng; c. 1605–45) led the rebellion that formally ended the Ming, which was replaced by the Manchu Qing dynasty (1644–1911). Chongzhen's personal name was Zhu Yujian, and his temple name as emperor was Sizong; Chongzhen (meaning "Respect for Pillars of State") was his posthumous reign name (r. 1628–44).

Chongzhen was a hard-working emperor who cared for his people, but when he took the throne the Ming dynasty was in an irreversible decline. A terrible famine in Shanxi Province had caused starving peasants to destroy the countryside. Also, Chinese soldiers at garrisons in Shanxi and Manchuria (northeastern China) mutinied because they had not been paid for a long time, and they were soon joined by coolie couriers whom the government had dismissed. That same year, the Manchus, a seminomadic ethnic group in Manchuria, began moving south to attack the Chinese capital city of Beijing. The Ming sent soldiers to fight them off, but these soldiers also mutinied because they had not been paid. Northern China was now beset by rebellions. Li Zicheng became the leader of a large rebel (non-Manchu) force and brought most of northern China under his control. He led his army toward Beijing with the intent of becoming the new emperor. Ming General Wu Sangui (Wu San-Kuei; 1612–78), stationed at the Great Wall to stave off the Manchus, decided to let the Manchus into China to help the Chinese put down the rebellion. Li Zicheng's rebel forces invaded Beijing on April 25, 1644. Emperor Chongzhen had not been told that the rebels were about to enter the city. When they attacked his palace in the Forbidden City, his wife, the empress, committed suicide, and he hanged himself on Coal Mountain behind the Forbidden City. The Manchu army then entered Beijing on June 5, 1644, without further resistance and proclaimed the Qing dynasty, which they had founded in 1636 in Mukden, the ruler of the Chinese Empire. After Emperor Chongzhen committed suicide, Zhu Yousong (Chu Yu-sung), a grandson of the Wanli Emperor (r. 1573–1620), was installed as Ming emperor in Nanjing. The following year, however, the Manchus captured Nanjing and took Zhu to Beijing, where he died soon after. Other members of the imperial family tried to sustain the Ming court, but the dynasty died out in 1661. See also FORBIDDEN CITY; GREAT WALL; LI ZICHENG; MANCHU; MING DYNASTY; QING DYNASTY.

CHOPS See SEALS.

CHOPSTICKS (*guaizi* in pinyin, or *faai jee,* "quick little boys," in Cantonese or Guangzhou dialect)   A pair of stick-like utensils used for eating. "Chopsticks" is the pidgin English translation; "chop chop" in pidgin English means "quick, quick," and *guaizi* came to be known as "chop sticks" because they are manipulated quickly. They are usually about 10 inches long and a $\frac{1}{4}$-inch thick at the top, narrowing to the base. Bamboo and wooden chopsticks are both used for cooking because they can withstand high temperatures and do not alter the taste of the food. They are also used to stir and mix food, beat eggs, lift food from cooking pots, and so forth. For eating, chopsticks made of gold, silver, ivory, jade, coral, horn, bone or plastic as well as bamboo or wood are used. Ivory chopsticks are to the Chinese what sterling silver utensils are to Westerners.

When the food is served at a banquet, the host picks up his chopsticks and says, "*ji guai* (begin using the chopsticks)." Everyone takes their food from common dishes in the center of the table. Food is served either in small pieces or in pieces that can easily be broken apart with chopsticks and picked up easily. Rice is eaten by lifting one's small bowl with the left hand and using chopsticks with the right hand to push the rice into one's mouth. Between courses, chopsticks are laid on small decorative ceramic rest on the table.

Chopsticks are held slightly below the middle of their length, with the smaller tips pointed toward the food. The lower chopstick is held stationary between the thumb and index finger and supported on the third finger. The upper chopstick, which acts as a lever, is held between the tip of the thumb and the crook of the index and middle fingers. When finished eating, the diner places the chopsticks together on the bowl with the small tip pointing away. It is considered impolite to wave chopsticks around or to leave them standing in a bowl of rice, and bad luck to drop a pair of chopsticks. Finding a pair of chopsticks at one's place at the table in which the two sticks are of different lengths means that one will miss one's train, plane or ship. Fine chopsticks are traditionally a required gift from the groom's parents at Chinese weddings to ensure that the couple stay together and produce many children.

Chopsticks have been used in China at least as far back as the Shang dynasty (1750–1040 B.C.), although people then probably ate most food with their fingers. The oldest extant chopsticks, made of bronze, were excavated at sites dating from the fifth century B.C. (late Eastern Zhou to early Warring States periods). Archaeologists have not determined whether they were used for eating or for lifting meat and vegetables from hot soup pots. Chopsticks are mentioned in

the *Qu Li* section of the *Book of Rites* (*Liji,* circa late Zhou period), where they are referred to by the Chinese character that depicts a man holding two pieces of bamboo. Chopsticks are also used in other Asian countries, mainly Japan, North and South Korea and Vietnam. See also BANQUETS; COOKING, CHINESE; CORAL; IVORY CARVING; JADE; RICE.

CHOU, DUKE OF See ZHOU, DUKE OF.

CHOU DYNASTY (A.D. 951–59) See FIVE DYNASTIES PERIOD; ZHOU DYNASTY.

CHOU EN LAI See ZHOU ENLAI.

CHOU-K'OU-T'IEN See ARCHAEOLOGY; PEKING MAN.

CHOW MEIN See NOODLES.

CHOWRY See YAK.

CHRISTIANITY Christianity was introduced into China in three separate forms; Nestorian Christianity, Roman Catholicism and Protestant Christianity. The Nestorian Church traces its beginnings to Nestorious (fl. 428–36; died c. 451), the bishop of Constantinople (modern Istanbul) who was decreed heretical for teaching that Jesus Christ had two distinct personages, human and divine. Nestorian Christianity took strong hold in Persia (modern Iran) in the fifth and sixth centuries. A Persian named Olopan (Alopen) introduced the religion to China in 631 at Chang'an (modern Xi'an), the cosmopolitan capital of the Tang dynasty (618–907). Foreign traders brought many other religions to China, including Judaism, Manichaeism, Zoroastroanism and Islam. The Tang imperial government permitted Nestorian Christians to build churches in Chang'an and all Chinese provinces. Nestorian monks were active in educating people, feeding and clothing the poor, and caring for the sick. A Nestorian monk supposedly saved a Tang emperor from going blind, and the religion became associated with the Tang imperial family. However, it did not gain many Chinese converts and was diminished when Tang Emperor Wuzong (Wu-tsung) persecuted Buddhism, another foreign religion that had been introduced to China, in 845. Small communities of Nestorian Christians existed in China until the Song dynasty (960–1279). The Mongols, who founded the Yuan dynasty (1279–1368), patronized Nestorian Christianity and established a Nestorian bishopric at their capital in modern Beijing in 1275. Many Mongol leaders took their wives and government ministers from the Nestorian Kerait and Ongut tribes of Central Asia, and Khubilai Khan (1214–94), founder of the Yuan, was the son of a Kerait princess who was a Nestorian Christian.

Some Roman Catholics traveled to China along the trade routes in the extensive Mongol Empire, or were taken prisoner while the Mongols were waging campaigns in Europe. King Louis IX of France sent the Dominican William of Rubruck (fl. 1250) to convert the Mongol Khan Mongke, but Mongke was tolerant of all religions. The Roman Catholic pope sent the Franciscan John of Monte Corvino (1246–1328) on a papal mission to Khubilai Khan, who died before the missionary arrived at the Mongol Yuan court in modern Beijing. The father and uncle of the Italian explorer Marco Polo (1254–1324) had visited the court of Khubilai Khan, who asked them to return to China with a hundred Christian priests, letters from the pope, and holy water from Jerusalem. Marco joined them on their return journey to China in 1271, in which they took a letter from the pope and holy water to Khubilai Khan. In 1307 the Yuan emperor appointed him the first archbishop of the Roman Catholic Church in China. The pope also sent an embassy under John Marignolli (fl. 1340) which stayed in China from 1338–46. The year after the Chinese overthrew the Mongol Yuan dynasty and established the Ming dynasty (1368–1644), the archbishop was expelled from Beijing, and Christian missions did not travel to China for 200 years.

Roman Catholic Portuguese traders and missionaries arrived on the coast of Guangdong Province in southern China in 1517. The Ming court ceded the small island of Macao, near the major Chinese port of Guangzhou (Canton), to the Portuguese, who made Macao their trading base in the Far East. (Macao is scheduled to revert to China in 1999.) Matteo Ricci (1552–1610), a member of the Roman Catholic Society of Jesus, known as the Jesuits, received permission from the Ming court to settle in Beijing in 1601. Ricci spent the rest of his life in China, introducing the Christian religion and Western knowledge to the Chinese and acquiring knowledge about Chinese religion, science and government. Other Jesuits soon joined him in China. The Chinese admired the highly-educated Jesuits, especially for their knowledge of mathematics, science and technology. The Chinese court appointed a group of Jesuits headed by Joannes Adam Schall von Bell to head the office of astronomy that determined the official annual calendar, which was extremely important for agriculture and ritual purposes.

Ricci and his successors learned the Chinese language and studied the classical Confucian texts that formed the foundation of the education of the literati, or scholars, who staffed the Chinese imperial bureaucracy. Ricci wrote a book in Chinese, *The True Meaning of the Lord of Heaven*, in which he explained the basic concepts of the Christian religion using Confucian terms, such as "self-cultivation," to appeal to the literati. He used the Chinese term "Lord of Heaven" to translate the Christian term "God." The Jesuits made few Chinese converts, but the reports they sent back to the West about Chinese culture influenced European philosophers and political thinkers, such as Leibniz and Voltaire. Ricci and other Jesuits wore the clothing of the literati and accepted Chinese religious practices such as so-called ancestor worship, the propitiation of deceased relatives. They practiced "accommodation," that is, they accepted Confucianism as a system of ethics and found points of similarity between Christian and Confucian teachings.

When the Manchus overthrew the Ming and established the Qing dynasty (1644–1911), they kept the calendar and retained the Jesuits in important positions. After Schall died in 1666, the Jesuit Ferdinand Verbiest was appointed to head the court observatory. The Jesuit Father Gerbillon negotiated the Treaty of Nerchinsk (1689) between China and Russia. The Qing Kangxi emperor (K'ang-hsi; r. 1661–1722) permitted the first Chinese Catholic bishop to be ordained. In 1692 Kangxi issued an imperial edict tolerating the Christian religion in China, and missionaries of the Dominican and Fran-

ciscan orders also became active in China. They were jealous of the Jesuits and criticized them for being too tolerant of "pagan" practices, which culminated in the Rites Controversy. The Dominicans and Franciscans appealed to Pope Clement I in Rome, and in 1704 he ruled against the Jesuits. Emperor Kangxi immediately banished all Roman Catholic missionaries who did not accept Ricci's tolerant position on Chinese practices. In 1705 the pope sent Cardinal Tournon as papal legate to Beijing to forbid Chinese Christian converts from practicing their traditional rituals. This interference in Chinese affairs angered Kangxi, who expelled the legate. In 1715 the pope issued a bull and sent another legate to Beijing. Qing Emperor Yongzheng (Yung-cheng; r. 1723-35) responded by banning Christianity in China in 1724 and expelling most of the missionaries. He permitted a few to remain in their positions as scientists, architects and artists but forbade them from making converts, and the Roman Catholic Church began to decline in China. The Chinese literati distanced themselves from the church, whose missionaries could work only in secret among poor and uneducated Chinese. The Chinese government did not lift the ban against the Roman Catholic religion until the French forced the Qing to do so in 1846.

In the mid-17th century the Dutch and the British, who were Protestant Christians, also arrived at southern China and sought trading privileges. However, the Qing government did not give them permission to enter the country but restricted their trade through officially designated merchants at Guangzhou. The British attempted to open up China to Western-style trade, resorting to military force in defeating China in the Opium War (1839–42). The Treaty of Nanjing ending the Opium War opened five Chinese cities as so-called treaty ports to foreign traders and Christian missionaries. The right of extraterritoriality was extended to foreigners, meaning that if accused of a crime a foreigner would be tried under the laws of his or her own country rather than those of China. This treaty also ceded the island of Hong Kong to the British, who made it a Crown Colony. (Hong Kong reverted to China in 1997.) The treaty of Tianjin (1858), signed after the Arrow War (also known as the Second Opium War), opened more treaty ports, allowed foreigners to travel anywhere in China with valid passports and extended protection to Western missionaries in China. Many other Western countries signed similar "unequal treaties" with the Qing government.

By the beginning of the 19th century there were perhaps 200,000 Roman Catholics in China. The first Protestant missionary to China, Robert Morrison, was sent by the London Missionary Society and arrived in Guangzhou in 1807. He worked as a translator for the British East India Company and also compiled the first Chinese-English dictionary and translated the Bible into Chinese. A second missionary sent to help him was not allowed to remain in China, so he went to the British port of Malacca in modern Malaysia where he worked with the overseas Chinese community. The first group of Protestant missionaries from the United States was the American Board, belonging to the Congregationalist denomination. Many missionaries from various European and American denominations, Protestant and Catholic, soon followed. Missionaries established schools, hospitals and other projects that contributed to the modernization of China, but they made few converts. In 1850 missionaries established St. Paul's College in Hong Kong to train Chinese ministers.

The Christian religion played a major role in the Taiping Rebellion (1850–64), which nearly overthrew the Qing. Hong Xiuquan (Hung Hsiu-ch'uan; 1813–64), the leader of the rebellion, was given pamphlets in Guangzhou written by the first Chinese convert to Protestant Christianity. In 1843 Hong, after a series of dramatic visions, announced that he was the younger brother of Jesus Christ and that he had been commanded by God to destroy "pagan idols" and bring people to worship the true God. After studying Christianity for two months with Issachar J. Roberts, an American Protestant missionary in Guangzhou, Hong began building up a movement that acquired 30,000 converts in three years. In 1850 his followers began fighting Qing troops and moving north. In September 1851 Hong claimed to have founded a new dynasty and took the title "Heavenly King," of the "Heavenly Kingdom of Great Peace" (Taiping Tiangu or T'ai-p'ing T'ien-ku; Taiping for short). In 1852 the Taipings, who numbered more than one million, moved east across the Yangzi River valley and made their capital at Nanjing. They sent an army north toward the Qing capital at Beijing, but this was halted. Combined Qing and foreign troops finally defeated the Taipings on July 19, 1864. The Taiping Rebellion was a major source of inspiration for the 20th-century Communist leader Mao Zedong (Mao Tse-tung; 1893–1976), who established the People's Republic of China in 1949.

In 1864 there were fewer than 200 Christian missionaries in China, but by 1890 there were about 1,300. By 1900 there were 700 Protestant missionaries in China based at 498 stations. Prior to 1900 most of the Protestant missionaries were active in or near the port cities, where they enjoyed the privileges of extraterritoriality, while the Roman Catholics were active deep in China's interior, as was the China Inland Mission, an evangelical Protestant organization founded in 1865 by Hudson Taylor. Western powers often had to send troops and gunboats to rescue them from attacks by hostile Chinese. In 1898 there were 2,458 Protestant missionaries in China, and only about 80,000 Chinese converts.

The Chinese for the most part did not trust the Christian missionaries. Members of the Confucian-educated literati or scholar class, whose ideology determined Chinese social customs and morality, felt threatened by them. To accept the foreign religion would be to admit that Chinese culture was inferior. Christian missionaries taught that there was only one true religion, that it was revealed by God and that not to believe in it was heresy. The Chinese, to the contrary, had a history of tolerance regarding religious beliefs, and the three religious traditions of Confucianism, Daoism and Buddhism had coexisted in China for two millennia.

Christian missionaries founded schools that helped develop modern Chinese education, such as Yenjing University in Beijing and its associated Harvard-Yenjing (Yenching) Institute, and St. John's University in Shanghai. They opened the first schools for girls in China, as well as Western-style museums, libraries, magazines and newspapers. Missionaries also promoted public health, trained doctors and nurses, established hospitals open to all Chinese, set up orphanages and asylums for the blind and insane, and provided technical training in agriculture and engineering. Timothy Richard (1832–1919) and the Christian Literature Society translated both religious and secular texts into Chinese. Translators used the colloquial written Chinese language rather than the classical literary language used by Chinese scholars, which made a great contribution to modern Chinese culture, especially the post-1915 Chinese literary renaissance known as the New Culture Movement.

The Boxer Uprising erupted in 1899 in part because the Qing granted special privileges to Roman Catholics, which caused a branch of the Boxers to attack Christian churches and missionaries. The Boxers, formally known as the Society of the Righteous and Harmonious Fists, entered Beijing in 1900 and laid seige to the foreign legation quarters. A combined Western force suppressed the Boxers and occupied the city. The Western powers forced the Qing to sign the International Protocol of 1901, which, among other things, gave Westerners in China complete freedom to engage in trade and missionary activities. By 1914 there were more than 250,000 members of Protestant churches and 1.4 million Roman Catholics in China, although the latter counted all members of a household while Protestant counted only those who joined the churches.

Many Chinese Christians took part in the Revolution of 1911, which overthrew the Qing and established the modern Republic of China (ROC) in 1912. Sun Yat-sen (1866–1925), leader of the revolution, had converted to Christianity while studying medicine in Hong Kong. He married Soong Qingling (Song Qingling, Soong Ch'ing-ling or Sung Ch'ing-ling; 1893–1981), whose wealthy father had become a Methodist and who had funded Sun Yat-sen's revolution. Sun also founded the Chinese Nationalist Party (Kuomintang; KMT). His successor, Chiang Kai-shek (1887–1975), converted to the Methodist religion when he married Soong Qingling's sister, Soong Mei-ling (1897–   ). The Soong siblings were all educated in the United States and became very prominent in modern China.

Students at the Chinese Christian schools also joined the antigovernment and anti-Western May Fourth Movement of 1919, which inspired modern Chinese revolutionaries. By 1930 the total number of Christians in China was only about one percent of the population, but they were influential because many leaders of the Chinese Nationalists government were Christians. When the Chinese Communist Party (CCP) defeated the Nationalists in 1949 and founded the People's Republic of China (PRC), they expelled Christian missionaries from China and executed or imprisoned many Chinese Christians. Chiang Kai-shek and the Nationalists had fled to Taiwan and established the ROC government there. In 1954 the PRC government enacted the "Three-Self Patriotic Movement," also known as the "Three-Self Movement." This required religious organizations in China to be self-governing, self-supporting and self-propagating, that is, not to depend on foreign dictation of policy, foreign funds or foreign ideas. In 1957 the Catholic churches united in the Chinese Patriotic Catholic Association. The Catholic Church in China was prevented from being controlled by the Vatican, and this divided the religion into an officially recognized "patriotic" Chinese Catholic Church and an "underground" church whose members were still loyal to the pope. The PRC government has even refused to allow the pope to appoint archbishops in China. In 1980 Monsignor Tang was released after spending 22 years in prison, and the pope appointed him archbishop of Guangzhou, but the official Chinese Church criticized this appointment as "the Pope rudely interfering in the sovereign affairs of the Chinese Church." In 1988 Bishop Zeng Jingmu was released after 35 years' imprisonment; other leading bishops are still being detained. The Vatican maintains official diplomatic relations with the government of the Republic of China (ROC) on Taiwan. Protestant churches in China have mostly supported the Three-Self Movement. Since it was enacted, Bishop K. H. Ting (Ding) has served as the most important liaison between Chinese Protestants and the PRC government. During the Cultural Revolution (1966–76), native and foreign religions alike came under attack and their churches and temples were damaged or destroyed. Since then, many religious buildings have been restored and have resumed holding services. In 1982, according to the official PRC census, there were 5.5 million Protestants and 3.5 million Catholics in China. In 1994 there was a combined total of 10 to 30 million Christians in the country. In 1990, 1.2 million copies of the Bible were printed in the Chinese language. Wenzhou, the largest port and industrial city in southern Zhejiang province, has long been a center for the Christian religion. See also ANCESTOR WORSHIP; ARROW WAR; ASTRONOMY AND OBSERVATORIES; BOXER UPRISING; BUDDHISM; CALENDAR; CHANG'AN; CHIANG KAI-SHEK; CONFUCIANISM; CULTURAL REVOLUTION; DAOISM; HONG XIUQUAN; IMPERIAL BUREAUCRACY; JESUITS; JEWS; LANGUAGE, CHINESE; LITERATI; MACAO; MANICHAEISM AND ZOROASTROANISM; MAY FOURTH MOVEMENT OF 1919; MONGOLS; MUSLIMS; NANJING, TREATY OF; NERCHINSK, TREATY OF; NESTORIAN CHRISTIANITY; NEW CULTURE MOVEMENT; OPIUM WAR; POLO, MARCO; QING DYNASTY; RICCI, MATTEO; RITES CONTROVERSY; SOONG QINGLING; SOONG MEI-LING; SUN YAT-SEN; TAIPING REBELLION; TIANJIN, TREATY OF; TREATY PORTS; UNEQUAL TREATIES; WENZHOU.

CHRYSANTHEMUM (*juhua* or *chu-hua*) A flowering plant native to temperate regions of Asia and Europe that is a favorite subject in Chinese painting. The round, multi-petaled flowers may be gold, white, pink, purple, pale green, or white with red streaks. The chrysanthemum has been cultivated in China for more than 3,000 years, which has resulted in many varieties, some quiet and charming, others flamboyant. The variety of chrysanthemum with a simple, daisylike flower, also known as the China aster, is the one most frequently depicted in Chinese ink painting. Chrysanthemums are often given poetic names, such as "Heaven Full of Stars" or "Jade Saucer Gold Cup." The chrysanthemum is associated with autumn because it blooms hardily at that time despite frost and cold winds. The ninth month in the traditional lunar calendar (roughly corresponding to October) is called "Chrysanthemum Month," when the Chinese enjoy viewing the beautiful blooming plants. The flower also signifies long life, friendship, and the life of a scholar spent in quiet retirement. The poet Tao Yuanming (also known as Tao Qian, 365–427) was poor but turned down the offer of a government position, preferring to devote his life to poetry, music, wine and chrysanthemum growing. The Chinese consider the chrysanthemum one of the "Four Noble Plants," along with the bamboo, plum and orchid. Dried chrysanthemum flowers are used for cosmetic and medicinal purposes and are commonly used to make a wash for sore eyes. Chrysanthemum tea is made from dried petals, which may also be steeped in wine. See also BAMBOO; ORCHID; PLUM; TAO YUANMIMG.

CHU, KINGDOM OF See ANHUI PROVINCE; HUBEI PROVINCE; HUNAN PROVINCE; JIANGSU PROVINCE; TEN KINGDOMS PERIOD.

CHU HSI See ZHU XI.

CHU RIVER See PEARL RIVER.

CHU TA See BADA SHANREN.

CHU TEH See ZHU DE.

CH'U YUAN See QU YUAN.

CHU YUAN-CHANG See HONGWU, EMPEROR; MING DYNASTY; RED TURBANS REBELLION.

CHU YU-CHIEN (EMPEROR) See LI ZICHENG; MING DYNASTY.

CH'UAN-CH'I See DRAMA.

CHUANG TZU See ZHUANGZI.

CHUANQI See DRAMA.

CHU-KO LIANG See ZHUGE LIANG.

CH'UN CHIEH See NEW YEAR FESTIVAL.

CHUN FU See GUO XI.

CHUN JIE See NEW YEAR FESTIVAL.

CH'UN-CH'IU See SPRING AND AUTUMN ANNALS; SPRING AND AUTUMN PERIOD.

CHUNG See LOYALTY.

CH'UNG-CHEN (EMPEROR) See CHONGZHEN (EMPEROR).

CHUNG CH'IU CHIEH See AUTUMN MOON FESTIVAL.

CHUNG K'UEI See ZHONG KUI.

CHUNG-KUO See ALL UNDER HEAVEN; MIDDLE KINGDOM.

CHUNG-KUO KUOMINTANG See BORODIN, MIKHAIL; NATIONALIST PARTY.

CHUNG-LI CHIEN See EIGHT IMMORTALS.

CHUNG NAN-HAI COMPOUND See ZHONGNANHAI COMPOUND.

CH'UNG TEH (EMPEROR) See ABAHAI; QING DYNASTY.

CHUNG WA See MIDDLE KINGDOM.

CHUNG YUNG See DOCTRINE OF THE MEAN; HUMANITY; SUPERIOR MAN.

CHUNGKING See CHONGQING.

CHUNQIU See SPRING AND AUTUMN ANNALS; SPRING AND AUTUMN PERIOD.

CHUNQIU FANLU See DONG ZHONGSHU.

CHUN-TZU See HUMANITY; SUPERIOR MAN.

CHUO CHUNG-T'ANG See TAIPING REBELLION.

CI See LYRIC VERSE.

CIAN, EMPRESS See CIXI, EMPRESS DOWAGER.

CICADA Also known as the katydid; an insect that is common throughout China, especially in the warmer southern regions. The cicada has the longest life span of any insect—up to 17 years or more. It has long been a symbol of regeneration or rebirth for the Chinese because it sheds its skin and renews itself when it becomes mature. Cicadas average one to two inches in length and have broad bodies with transparent wings. Their front wings are larger than the hind wings, and their front legs are also longer than the others. Cicadas may be black, brown or green and may have dark markings on their bodies. Their heads are wide with short antennae and large eyes; both enable them to detect the approach of their enemies, the chief of which is the praying mantis. Because the male cicada makes loud, rhythmic musical sounds to attract females all summer long, the cicada is a symbol of happiness and immortality for the Chinese. The male makes these sounds through the vibration of organs known as timbals located underneath his body on the first segment of the abdomen. A few species vibrate their wings together to produce sounds. Female cicadas lay eggs in trees and shrubs. A young cicada larva drops to the ground and burrows under the earth, where it spends its first four years. Then it returns above ground as a pupa which divides down the back, and the mature cicada emerges.

In ancient times, the Chinese placed cicadas carved from jade in the mouths of the dead buried in tombs because the insects were believed to prevent a corpse from decaying or to be able to speed up the process of a deceased person's rebirth in another world. During the Shang (1750–1040 B.C.) and early Zhou (1100–256 B.C.) dynasties, the cicada was a decorative motif in both realistic and stylized forms on bronzeware. It was also used on bronze and cloisonné objects produced during the 18th and 19th centuries that imitated ancient bronzes. See also BRONZEWARE; CLOISONNE; JADE.

CINEMA See FILM STUDIOS.

CINNABAR Mercuric sulfide, which has a red color and has been used by the Chinese as a pigment. Beginning in the Han dynasty (206 B.C.–A.D. 220), Chinese alchemists in the Daoist tradition concocted many chemical compounds in their attempt to find the pill, or elixir, of immortality (*xiandan* or *hsien tan*), and they used cinnabar as one of their main ingredients. The alchemists classified cinnabar as a "medicine," although it is actually a poison. They used cinnabar and jade as their "great medicines" and combined them with various other ingredients, such as sulfur, saltpeter, ore of cobalt, mica and salt. Heating cinnabar separates the two elements that comprise mercuric sulfide, mercury (quicksilver) and sulfur. The alchemists viewed the two elements in terms of the yin-yang duality they believed underlies everything in the universe. Mercury, a cool silver liquid suggesting the moon, represents the yin, or feminine, polarity; sulfur, a yellow solid suggesting the sun, represented the yang, or masculine, polarity. The alchemists especially valued "returned cinnabar," the substance that is formed by mixing the two elements of "purified" mercury and "purified" sulfur which have been produced by heating mercuric sulfide. Many objects buried in Chinese tombs were covered with cinnabar, which was believed to help the person who has died make the journey to the Western Paradise. Cinnabar is also used to make red lacquerware. This is done by coating a wood base with layers of a tree sap, known as lacquer, that has been mixed with mercuric sulfide. A cinnabar lacquer piece usually has a design in relief, most commonly of birds and flowers, created by carving through the layers of lacquer. The earliest carved cinnabar objects date from the Yuan dynasty (1279–1368). See also ALCHEMY; DAOISM; LACQUERWARE.

CIRCULAR MOUND ALTAR OF HEAVEN See TEMPLE OF HEAVEN.

CITIC See CHINA INTERNATIONAL TRUST AND INVESTMENT CORPORATION.

CITS (CTS) See CHINA INTERNATIONAL TRAVEL SERVICE.

CIVIL AIR TRANSPORT See FLYING TIGERS.

CIVIL SERVICE See CHINESE COMMUNIST PARTY; DONGLIN ACADEMY; GOVERNMENT STRUCTURE; HANLIN ACADEMY; IMPERIAL BUREAUCRACY; IMPERIAL EXAMINATION SYSTEM; LITERATI; NINE-RANK SYSTEM.

CIVIL WAR BETWEEN COMMUNISTS AND NATIONALISTS A war fought between the Chinese Communist Party (PRC), led by Mao Zedong (Mao Tse-tung; 1893–1976) and the Chinese Nationalist Party (Kuomintang; KMT), led by Chiang Kai-shek (Jiang Jieshi; 1887–1975), which ended with the Communist defeat of the Nationalists in 1949. Chiang and his Nationalist supporters fled to the island of Taiwan, while Mao and the Communists proclaimed the founding of the People's Republic of China (PRC) in Beijing on October 1, 1949. The Chinese people had overthrown the Manchu Qing dynasty (1644–1911), China's last imperial dynasty, in 1911, known as the Revolution of 1911. The revolutionary movement had been led by Dr. Sun Yat-sen (1866–1925), the founder of the Revolutionary Alliance (*Tongmenghui* or *T'ung-meng-hui*). Communists and Nationalists alike have always revered Sun as the founder of modern China. Sun frequently traveled abroad to raise funds for the alliance. When he returned to China, on January 1, 1912, he became president of the new provisional government of the Republic of China (ROC), which was based at Nanjing. Sun resigned soon after and the northern warlord Yuan Shikai (Yuan Shih-kai; 1859–1916) replaced him as ROC president, with his capital at Beijing. In the summer of 1912 Sun went to Beijing and helped establish the KMT, with himself as director. In 1913 elections were held and the KMT became the majority party in the Chinese national assembly. However, KMT leader Song Jiaoren (Sung Chiao-jen; 1882–1913) was assassinated, Yuan banned the KMT, and Sun had to flee to Japan. While there he became close friends with Chiang Kai-shek, who had been trained as a military officer in China and Japan.

Yuan died in 1916 and Li Yuanhong (Li Yuan-hung; 1864–1928) became the new president of the ROC in Beijing. Sun attempted to form a military government in Guangzhou in southern China but was forced to move to Shanghai in 1918. China was carved up among various warlords during what is known as the Warlord Period (1916–28). In 1917 China entered World War I by declaring war against Germany in hopes of getting back Shandong Province, which Germany had acquired in concessions from the Qing dynasty but was now controlled by Japan. In 1918 the Beijing government signed a secret agreement with Japan acknowledging Japan's claim to Shandong. This agreement was revealed at the Paris Peace Conference in 1919, and the Chinese people were outraged. On May 4, 1919, Chinese students held massive public demonstrations against the Beijing government and Japan. These culminated in a nationwide political movement known as the May Fourth Movement of 1919, which rekindled revolutionary fervor in China and stimulated the so-called New Culture Movement among Chinese writers and intellectuals.

In 1921 the parliament in Guangzhou abolished the military government and formed a new government with Sun as president. That same year, a small group founded the Chinese Communist Party (CCP) in Shanghai, China's largest city and trading port, with members including Mao Zedong and Zhang Guotao (Chang Kuo-t'ao; 1897–1979). They were advised by Communists who had been sent from the U.S.S.R., which had undergone its Bolshevik Revolution in 1917. Soviet advisers in China also gave support to Sun and the KMT. In 1922, while Sun Yat-sen was in Guangzhou, he was warned of an attempted coup against him and escaped to a gunboat. Chiang Kai-shek joined Sun in Guangzhou and accompanied him to Hong Kong and then to Shanghai. In 1923 Sun signed an agreement with a Soviet official that stated that the KMT would cooperate with Russian and Chinese communists and pledged Soviet assistance for the unification of China. Sun sent Chiang to Moscow to procure weapons and study Russian military organization. Mikhail Borodin (1884–1952), an agent of the Comintern (Communist International), and other Soviet advisers went to China to help reorganize the KMT on the model of the Soviet Communist Party. The Comintern instructed CCP members to cooperate with the KMT and join the KMT while keeping their identity as members of the CCP. In 1922 the KMT had 150,000 members and the CCP only 300 members; by 1925 the CCP had 1,500 members.

Soviet advisers helped the KMT establish a political institute to train members in techniques for propaganda and mass mobilization. The KMT and CCP cooperated to establish the Whampoa (Huangpu) Military Academy near Guangzhou, which would train officers for a Northern Expedition against the warlords who controlled China. Chiang was named the academy's first commandant, and he worked closely with Zhou Enlai (Chou En-lai; 1898–1976), who later became the second-most important leader in the CCP, and with Mikhail Borodin and other Russian advisers.

Sun died of cancer on March 12, 1925, while in Beijing for political meetings and was later buried in a splendid mausoleum built for him in Nanjing. In 1926, Chiang thwarted a kidnaping attempt and became the most powerful leader in the government in Guangzhou by taking action against the Communists and arresting many Russian advisers. In May the Central Executive Committee of the revolutionary government in Guangzhou approved Chiang's proposal to halt Communist influence in the KMT. In June, Chiang was named commander in chief of the National Revolutionary Army, and in July he launched the Northern Expedition against the warlords to unify China. By March 1927 Chiang's forces regained Chinese territory as far north as Shanghai and Nanjing on the Yangzi River (Changjiang). However, the KMT now had two centers of power. The left wing, led by Wang Jingwei (Wang Ching-wei; 1883–1944), moved the government from Guangzhou to Wuhan in Hubei Province, while the right wing, led by Chiang, established a national capital at Nanjing. The warlord regime still existed in Beijing and was recognized by foreign countries as the legitimate government of China.

Members of the CCP and the left-wing faction of the KMT had done advance work to persuade local peasants and workers to support the Northern Expedition. However, Chiang felt that their emphasis on social and economic reforms had grown too revolutionary, especially when they organized workers strikes in urban factories. In April 1927 Chiang abruptly turned against the Communists and sent his troops into Shanghai to arrest and execute them. Thousands were killed but some escaped, including Zhou Enlai and his wife, Deng Yingchao (Teng Ying-ch'ao; 1904–92). The survivors joined Communist Red Army forces at the Soviet base in the Jinggang Mountains, located on the border of Jiangxi Province in south-central China.

Communists in the Chinese countryside attempted several unsuccessful insurrections against the KMT. Zhou Enlai was a main organizer of the Nanchang Uprising, the Communist military rebellion against the KMT on August 1, 1927. The CCP considers this date the birth of the Red Army, which later became known as the People's Liberation Army (PLA). The Nationalists put down the uprising, and Zhu took his troops to Hunan Province and joined with guerrilla forces led by Mao Zedong in Hunan Province. Mao, who had been born to a peasant family in Hunan, led the Autumn Harvest Uprising of 1927, an insurrection by Hunan peasants. Mao recognized that, in contradiction to orthodox Marxist theory, Chinese peasants rather than urban workers were the social group that the Communists should mobilize for their revolution. Peasants formed the vast majority of the Chinese population and had always been a force for social change. Many times in Chinese history, dynasties had been overthrown and new dynasties established by rebellious peasants who believed that the old dynasty had lost the "Mandate of Heaven." Mao's skill at guerrilla-fighting tactics and peasant mobilization enabled him to become chairman of the CCP. He worked with military commander Zhu De (Chu Teh; 1886–1976) to build up a Communist military force on the Jiangxi-Hunan border which had about 10,000 troops by the winter of 1927–28. In 1929 they moved the Red Army to Jiangxi Province, where they established a Soviet (Communist base) and Zhu built up the Red Army to 200,000 troops by 1933.

Chiang's order to massacre the Communists in Shanghai had not been authorized by the Central Committee of the KMT, and the government based in Wuhan removed him as commander in chief. Chiang tried to set up his own government in Nanjing but was forced to go into exile in Japan. While there he married Soong Mei-ling (Soong Mayling, Sung Mei-ling or Song Meiling; 1897–), who became known as Madame Chiang Kai-shek. She was the sister of Soong Qingling, or Song Ch'ing-ling or Sung Ch'ing-ling; 1893–1981), the widow of Sun Yat-sen. Their father had been one of the main financial supporters of Sun's Revolutionary Alliance, and their brother became the Minister of Finance in the ROC government. The two sisters became the two most prominent women in modern China.

In China, left-wing KMT members at Wuhan were shown telegrams and other evidence that convinced them that the Chinese Communists were being controlled by Moscow and that they wanted to eliminate the KMT. Wang Jingwei and his faction decided to begin purging Communists from the KMT. The left- and right-wing factions of the KMT reunited, abolished the KMT government in Nanjing and moved the Wuhan government there, officially naming it the National Government of China. In 1928 Chiang returned to China from Japan. Soong Qinglingcondemned him for betraying Sun Yat-sen's revolutionary principles and joined the Communist side. Chiang once again became KMT commander in chief and led the second stage of the Northern Expedition, with the goal of conquering northern China. His troops took Beijing in June 1928, symbolically unifying all of China south of the Great Wall. On October 10, 1928, Chiang became chairman of a new Chinese national government and established his capital at Nanjing.

The Communist led a number of uprisings in Chinese cities, all of which were bloodily suppressed by the Nationalists, and Mikhail Borodin and other foreign advisers fled the country. The KMT refused to allow any other political party to have a role in the Nationalist government. From then until 1949, Chiang commanded the majority vote in the standing committee of the Central Executive of the KMT. By the end of 1928, Zhang Xueliang (Chang Hsueh-liang; 1898–), the most powerful warlord in Manchuria (northeastern China), agreed to Nationalist rule. His father, Zhang Zuolin (Chang Tso-lin; 1873–1928), who had been military governor of Manchuria, had been assassinated earlier that year by Japanese troops stationed in Manchuria. However, many members of the CCP, and even dissident generals and political leaders in the KMT, continued to oppose Chiang's government. Warlords in various regions claimed local power for themselves and Chiang sent troops against them. However, Chiang still felt that his most important mission

was to eliminate the Communists. In 1930 he launched the first of five annual major campaigns against the Communist Red Army in south-central China.

On September 18, 1931, Japanese forces used the so-called Manchurian Incident as a pretext to launch an invasion of Manchuria. Chiang felt that his troops would not be able to resist the Japanese and pulled them out of Manchuria, which made the Chinese people regard him as weak and unpatriotic. But he still felt that the most urgent task of the KMT was to wipe out communism in China. In 1932 the Japanese established a puppet state in Manchuria called Manchukuo (Manzhouguo, or Man-chou-kuo in Chinese) and used it as their base to invade China Proper and the rest of Asia. Chiang's KMT forces continued their campaigns against the Communist Red Army, and in 1934 Mao, Zhou and other Communist leaders decided that their forces should escape to the northwest, and they set out on the epic Long March (1934–35). About 100,000 soldiers and CCP members began the march. Only about 50 of them were women, including Deng Yingchao. A small number of survivors finally arrived at Yan'an in Shaanxi Province, where CCP leaders established their headquarters. The legendary survivors of the Long March became the leaders of the final stage of the civil war between the CCP and KMT and high-ranking officials in the PRC government.

In 1935 Chiang Kai-shek ordered Zhang Xueliang to send his troops to fight the Communists at Yan'an, but the Manchurian soldiers were angry that they had been sent against their own countrymen while the Japanese were occupying their own land, and they stopped fighting. In December 1936 Chiang flew to Zhang's headquarters at Xi'an in Shaanxi. Zhang and a group of KMT and CCP military leaders kidnapped Chiang to persuade him to stop fighting the Communists and form a KMT-CCP united front to fight the Japanese; this is known as the Xi'an Incident. Chiang agreed to do so on December 25 and flew back to Nanjing. In 1937 Japanese troops moved from Manchuria into northern China and quickly gained control of the North China Plain. In August they attacked Shanghai. In November they took Nanjing and, in what became known as the "Rape of Nanjing," committed atrocities against hundreds of thousands of Chinese residents. The Nationalist government moved to Hankou (Wuhan).

Combined KMT-CCP forces, bolstered by private armies of Chinese warlords, began fighting the Chinese War of Resistance against Japan (1937–45; World War II). The Communist Red Army was renamed the Eighth Route Army of the National Army, with Zhu De serving as commander of all Chinese Communist military operations. Peng Dehuai (P'eng Teh-huai) served as deputy commander of the Eighth Route Army. The army had three divisions, with Liu Bocheng (Liu Po-cheng) as commander of one, the 115th division. Deng Xiaoping (Teng Hsiao-p'ing) served under him as political commissar. Another division was commanded by Lin Biao (Lin Piao), and Nie Rongzhen (Nieh Jung-chen) served as his deputy commander and political commissar. All of these leaders played a major role in the final stages of the CCP-KMT civil war and in the government of the People's Republic of China.

Chinese troops were poorly equipped and trained in comparison to the well-equipped Japanese soldiers who were trained in modern military techniques. The Japanese took Guangzhou on October 21, 1938, and Hankou on October 25. Chiang moved the Nationalist government to Chongqing in Sichuan, a province in southwestern China protected by high mountain ranges. Many Chinese universities and industries also moved there. In December 1938 the Japanese persuaded Wang Jingwei to desert the Nationalists and join their side. He did so because he felt that continued Chinese resistance to the Japanese was suicidal, and he hoped to prevent the Japanese from treating the Chinese too harshly; but the Japanese merely treated Wang as their puppet. In September 1939 war broke out in Europe, which brought China foreign allies such as Great Britain. Canadian surgeon Norman Bethune went to China and organized medical services for the Eighth Route Army. He died in 1939 and was buried in Hebei Province and become a hero to the Chinese people.

After Japan bombed the U.S. naval fleet at Pearl Harbor on December 7, 1941, the United States became an official ally of China and sent more military and financial aid. U.S. President Franklin D. Roosevelt sent General Joseph Stilwell to become Chiang's chief of staff and commander of the China-Burma-India theater. Stilwell disagreed with Chiang's political policies and argued that all anti-Japanese factions in China should be armed, including the Communists, but Chiang still opposed the Communists. In early 1941 Nationalist troops defeated the Communist New Fourth Army in the lower Yangzi River valley, known as the New Fourth Army Incident. This marked the breakdown of the KMT-CCP united front. The KMT and CCP were eager to resume their civil war.

Japan surrendered on August 14, 1945, and the Chinese Nationalist government returned to Nanjing. At the end of the War of Resistance, the Communists controlled a large amount of territory in the regions that had been occupied by the Japanese. American diplomats, who supported Chiang Kai-shek, tried to make sure that Japanese troops in northern China and Manchuria would surrender to the Nationalists rather than the Communists, so that Chiang would be the dominant leader in postwar China. But Russian troops, who had entered Manchuria when the United States dropped the bomb on Hiroshima, Japan, on August 6, turned over Manchuria and all the weapons the Japanese had surrendered there to the Chinese Communists. The Americans, including U.S. ambassador to China Patrick J. Hurley, also attempted to negotiate a coalition KMT-CCP government that would rule all of China. CCP leaders Mao and Zhou met with Chiang at Chongqing for six weeks in the fall of 1945, but nothing came of their negotiations. Zhou went to northern Shaanxi to help direct the CCP forces there. At the end of 1945, U.S. President Harry Truman sent General of the Army George C. Marshall as his special ambassador to China with the mission of persuading the Communists and Nationalists to form a coalition government, but he did not succeed and blamed both sides for being intransigent. Marshall did arrange a cease-fire in January 1946, but the United States continued to give the Nationalist government enormous loans. The United States had supplied $1.5 billion worth of aid to Nationalist China during the War of Resistance, and it gave the Nationalists $2 billion more from 1945 to 1948. The United States also made sure that China became a permanent member of the Security Council of the newly formed United Nations.

The Nationalists and Communists began fighting a full-scale civil war. On May 1, 1946, the CCP officially renamed its military the People's Liberation Army (PLA). On June 26, 1946, Nationalist troops waged an offensive against Communist-held areas in Hubei and Henan Provinces. However, the Nationalists were not able to gain support among the Chinese people because of the rampant corruption in their government and the runaway inflation that rendered the Nationalist currency worthless. Many Chinese businessmen, who had been the core group supporting the KMT, began leaving the country. By the end of 1947, the Americans saw that the Nationalists had no chance of winning the civil war and withdrew their support for Chiang. In 1948 Soong Mei-ling went to the United States to raise American support for the KMT, but President Truman refused to change the U.S. policy of non-involvement in the civil war in China.

The Communists used guerrilla tactics and mobilized peasants to their side by such practices as land reform, in which they encouraged peasants to criticize the wealthy landowners who exploited them and then took land away from the landowners and gave it to peasants who had little or no land. On May 13, 1947, PLA troops commanded by Lin Biao launched a major offensive in northeastern China. On June 30, Liu Bocheng led a large PLA force southwest across the Yellow River in Shandong and began another major offensive. The Communists had gained much support in northern China, and on September 12, 1948, Lin Biao led a major campaign in Manchuria, where 300,000 Nationalist troops surrendered to the Communists in October. The PLA took Shenyang (formerly known as Mukden), the capital of Liaoning Province, on November 2. In the second great battle in the Huai River basin in north-central China, the PLA surrounded 66 of the KMT's 200 divisions. A large number of KMT soldiers defected to the CCP or were captured. On November 29, 1948, the PLA led by Lin Biao launched the Beijing-Tianjin campaign, the third major campaign of the civil war.

On January 10, 1949, the campaign in the Huaihai River basin ended with a victory for the PLA, which to all effects ended the KMT regime on the Chinese mainland. On January 15, 1949, Tianjin fell to the PLA. On January 31 the PLA took Beijing without any resistance. Chiang resigned as ROC president and Li Zongren (Li Tsung-jen), who succeeded him, attempted to negotiate peace with the Communists. The Communists, however, demanded unconditional surrender and the punishment of Chiang and other Nationalists they deemed war criminals. The Nationalists would not agree to these demands, so the Communists resumed their offensive in April 1949 and moved south of the Yangzi to take Nanjing on April 23. They took Shanghai on May 27 and Guangzhou in October.

In the spring of 1949, Chiang began moving Nationalist troops to Taiwan, a large island 100 miles off the southeastern coast of China which had been governed by the Qing dynasty until Japan occupied the island in 1895. (Japan surrendered Taiwan to China in 1945.) Chiang had already ordered the transfer of China's gold reserve to Taiwan. The Nationalists had also packed hundreds of crates of priceless antiques from the Forbidden City in Beijing, the Imperial Palace where emperors of the Ming (1368–1644) and Qing dynasties had resided. The crates were sent to different parts of China, and then the majority of them were shipped to Taiwan, where they later formed the collection of the National Palace Museum in Taipei.

From September 21 to 30, 1949, the CCP held the Chinese People's Political Consultative Conference (CPPCC) in Beijing, which served as the legislative and representative body of the new Communist government they were forming. The CPPCC was originally an organization formed in 1948 by the united front led by the CCP but including nearly all other Chinese factions that opposed the KMT. These political parties, known as the democratic parties, are still permitted to function on a small scale in China. On October 1, 1949, Mao Zedong stood on the rostrum above the gate in Tiananmen Square in Beijing and proclaimed the founding of the People's Republic of China (PRC). The PLA took Chongqing, the wartime Nationalist capital in Sichuan, in November. Chiang fled to Taiwan from Chengdu, Sichuan on December 10, 1949, the same day that Chengdu fell to the Communists. In Taiwan, Chiang and his Nationalist supporters established the headquarters of the KMT government, which they still called the Republic of China (ROC) and claimed to be the legitimate government of all of China. Chiang proclaimed that Taipei, the capital of Taiwan, was the temporary capital of China. The Chinese Communists, who consider Taiwan a renegade province of China, call their civil war with the Nationalists the War of Liberation, and their victory National Liberation. The United States and many other countries cut off diplomatic ties with the government in Beijing and recognized the ROC on Taiwan as the legitimate government of China. On March 1, 1950, Chiang resumed the presidency of the ROC, which he held until his death in 1975. See also BEIJING; BETHUNE, NORMAN; BORODIN, MIKHAIL; CHIANG KAI-SHEK; CHINESE COMMUNIST PARTY; CHINESE PEOPLE'S POLITICAL CONSULTATIVE CONFERENCE; DEMOCRATIC PARTIES; DENG XIAOPING; DENG YINGCHAO; EIGHTH ROUTE ARMY; GUANGZHOU; HUAI RIVER; JIANG QING; JINGGANG MOUNTAIN RANGE; LAND REFORM BY COMMUNISTS; LIBERATION, NATIONAL; LIN BIAO; LIU BOCHENG; LONG MARCH; MANCHUKUO; MANCHURIA; MANCHURIAN INCIDENT; MANDATE OF HEAVEN; MAO ZEDONG; MAY FOURTH MOVEMENT OF 1919; NANCHANG; NANJING; NATIONAL PALACE MUSEUM (TAIPEI); NATIONALIST PARTY; NEW FOURTH ARMY INCIDENT; NIE RONGZHEN; NORTH CHINA PLAIN; NORTHERN EXPEDITION; PEASANTS AND PEASANT REBELLIONS; PENG DEHUAI; PEOPLE'S LIBERATION ARMY; PEOPLE'S REPUBLIC OF CHINA; REPUBLIC OF CHINA; REVOLUTION OF 1911; REVOLUTIONARY ALLIANCE; SHANGHAI; SMEDLEY, AGNES; SNOW, EDGAR; SOONG CHING LING; SOONG MEI-LING; STILWELL, JOSEPH; SUN YAT-SEN; TAIWAN; TIANANMEN SQUARE; UNITED NATIONS; WAR OF RESISTANCE AGAINST JAPAN; WARLORD PERIOD; WHAMPOA MILITARY ACADEMY; WUCHANG UPRISING; XI'AN; YAN'AN; YANGZI RIVER; YUAN SHIKAI; ZHANG GUOTAO; ZHANG XUELIANG; ZHOU ENLAI; ZHU DE.

CIXI, EMPRESS DOWAGER (Tz'u Hsi; 1835–1908) Original name Yehonala; a Manchu concubine in the court of the Qing dynasty (1644–1911) emperor Xianfeng (Hsien-Feng; r. 1851–61), who was the most powerful person in the imperial court during the final half-century of China's last imperial dynasty. The Manchus are an ethnic group from Manchuria (modern northeastern China) who were asked

by a general of the Ming dynasty (1368–1644) to help Ming forces put down a rebellion but who instead took control of the Chinese capital at Beijing, overthrew the Ming and established the Qing dynasty. Yehonala became a palace concubine when she was 16 years old. As Emperor Xianfeng's favorite, she rose to high status in 1856 when she gave birth to his only surviving son, who was made the heir apparent. Educated in the Chinese language, Yehonala began taking an active role in the affairs of state and handling official papers.

The Opium and Arrow Wars, unequal treaties, and rebellions such as the Taiping had greatly eroded the power of the Qing and brought many Western influences into China; Western troops had even burned down the imperial Summer Palace in Beijing in 1860. Emperor Xianfeng, who was humiliated, fled to Chengde (Rehol or Jehol) and gave up his authority to live a life of debauchery, from which he died in the autumn of 1861. Just before he died, eight of his most strictly antiforeign advisers were appointed as joint regents of his son, who was only four years old, and Yehonala was given the rank of empress dowager (mother of the emperor) though deprived of all power. She conspired with Prince Gong (Kung), a Manchu official, to arrest the eight co-regents, three of whom were killed and five of whom were given other punishments. When Xianfeng died in 1861, Cixi became co-regent for her son, who succeeded to the throne as Emperor Tongzhi (T'ung-chih; r. 1862–75). The empress dowager, now known by the title Cixi, and the empress consort, Cian (Tz'u An), the legitimate wife of Emperor Xianfeng, were appointed co-regents of the child-emperor Tongzhi. The affairs of state were conducted by Prince Gong, whom Cixi appointed Prince Counselor, and Li Hongzhang (Li Hung-chang).

Cixi lived in luxurious splendor in the imperial palace in the Forbidden City in Beijing, surrounded by a retinue of powerful eunuchs. She was ambitious and ruthless and used every method she could to increase her own power. In 1865 she removed the rank of Prince Counselor from Prince Gong, although she permitted him to retain his other positions. Emperor Tongzhi supported the Self-Strengthening Movement, which attempted to modernize China by adapting Western technology while retaining Chinese institutions. In 1872 Tongzhi married, which ended the regency, and in 1874 he came of age. Tongzhi died in 1875, when he was only 19 years old, and Cixi maneuvered to have his cousin and her nephew, the son of her sister, who was only four years old, succeed him as Emperor Guangxu (Kuang-hsu; r. 1875–1908). This violated Qing rules of succession, since he belonged to the same generation as Tongzhi, but Cixi did not want her daughter-in-law, Tongzhi's widow, whom she hated, to become empress dowager in her place. Cixi forced her daughter-in-law, who was pregnant, to commit suicide so that no son would be born to interfere with Cixi's scheming. Since Emperor Guangxu was a child, Cixi, who was both his aunt and adoptive mother, ruled as his co-regent. In 1866 Guangxu came of age, but Cixi refused to give up the regency until he married in 1889; after that she still exercised control by reading all official government documents. Cixi played the foreign powers off against each other and did the same with the officials in the Qing government. One of her most notorious acts was to use funds that had been allocated to build a modern Chinese navy to rebuild the Summer Palace, including the marble boat, in Beijing.

The world-famous marble boat at the Summer Palace is one of many luxuries Empress Dowager Cixi afforded herself.   S.E. MEYER

The Qing suffered more setbacks from foreign powers. France won control of Vietnam, traditionally a vassal state of the Chinese tribute system, in the Sino-French War (1884–85). Cixi dismissed Prince Gong in 1884 and replaced him with Prince Chun. China also lost the tributary states of Burma and the Ryukyu (Liu Ch'iu) Islands (Okinawa), which were taken by Japan. Japan, which was now modernized, easily defeated the Chinese navy in the Sino-Japanese War of 1894–95. Japan then took control of Korea, traditionally a tributary state of the Chinese Empire, as well as Port Arthur (part of modern Dalian, a strategic port in Manchuria), Taiwan and the Pescadore Islands.

Emperor Guangxu became influenced by a group of progressive literati or scholars in the imperial bureaucracy who advocated reforms based on the Japanese model of modernization. Most of the reformers belonged to the Han, the majority ethnic group in China, who resented the Manchus. Conservative government officials, particularly the Manchus, felt that the reforms were too radical and advocated gradual change. The Reform Movement of 1898 (also known as the Hundred Days Reform), lasted 103 days from June 11 to September 21, 1898, during which Emperor Guangxu enacted more than 100 reforms intended to modernize Chinese institutions. The Reform Movement was betrayed when Yuan Shikai (Yuan Shih-k'ai), who had been the Chinese military commander during the Sino-Japanese War,

informed Empress Dowager Cixi of a supposed plot to take her prisoner, and on September 21, 1898, she led a coup d'état and placed Emperor Guangxu under house arrest. She canceled his reform edicts, had six of the leading reformers executed and assumed the regency for the rest of her life. The two leading reformers, Kang Youwei (K'ang Yu-wei) and Liang Qichao (Liang Ch'i-ch'ao), fled abroad and founded the Protect the Emperor Society (*Baohuang Hui* or *Pao-huang Hui*). Their goal was to bring about a constitutional monarchy in China, but they never succeeded. Cixi rewarded Yuan Shikai by making him governor of Shandong Province.

The conservatives privately supported a secret society, the Society of Righteousness and Harmony (Yil Yihequan or I-ho-ch'uan), commonly known as the Boxers, who led an antiforeign, anti-Manchu and anti-Christian uprising in northern China. Cixi encouraged the Boxers to lessen their anti-Manchu stance and direct their efforts against Westerners in China. She appointed Yuan Shikai to suppress the Boxer Uprising. In the summer of 1900 the Boxers laid seige to the foreign legation quarters in Beijing and the nearby port city of Tianjin, and eight foreign powers sent a combined force against them. The empress dowager, emperor, Manchu princes and high court officials fled west to Xi'an in Shaanxi Province. The Qing declared war against the foreign powers, who defeated the Boxers and occupied not only Beijing but all of northern China. They exacted a heavy penalty on the Qing, including payment of a large indemnity and the cessation of the examinations for the imperial bureaucracy. The Russians then occupied Manchuria until the Russo-Japanese War of 1904–5, in which Japan defeated Russia and took control of the region.

When Cixi returned to Beijing in January 1902, she allowed many of the reforms that she had previously canceled to be reenacted. In 1905 the Qing government abolished the examination system for the imperial bureaucracy. Western-style schools were established and gained more than a million students. In 1907 the U.S. government allocated the indemnity funds paid to it by China after the Boxer Uprising to fund Chinese students, hundreds of whom went to study in universities in the United States. Cixi had enacted the reforms to preserve the Qing dynasty, which was on the verge of collapse, but they were not sufficient to delay the downfall of the Qing. Chinese revolutionaries were gaining followers, and from 1906–8 there were seven uprisings against the Qing in southern China.

Empress Dowager Cixi, known as the "Old Buddha," died suddenly on November 15, 1908. Emperor Guangxu, her son, had died after a long illness only the day before, apparently poisoned by Cixi before she died. On November 13 she had chosen her grand-nephew to succeed Guangxu. He took the throne when he was only three years old and reigned as Emperor Xuantong (Hsuan-tung; r. 1908–11; now known as Henry Puyi). Three years after Cixi died, the Chinese people, led by Dr. Sun Yat-sen, overthrew the Qing dynasty in the Revolution of 1911. The Forbidden City in Beijing is now open to the pubic and Cixi's throne in the Palace of Gathering Excellence can still be seen. See also BEI-JING; BOXER UPRISING; FORBIDDEN CITY; IMPERIAL EXAMINA-TION SYSTEM; KANG YOUWEI; LI HONGZHANG; MANCHU; PUYI, HENRY; QING DYNASTY; REFORM MOVEMENT OF 1898; REVO-LUTION OF 1911; RUSSO-JAPANESE WAR OF 1904–5; RYUKYU ISLANDS; SELF-STRENGTHENING MOVEMENT; SINO-FRENCH WAR; SINO-JAPANESE WAR OF 1894–95; SUMMER PALACE; TAI-WAN; YUAN SHIKAI.

CLASS STRUCTURE See CADRE; EMPEROR; HAN; IMPERIAL BUREAUCRACY; LITERATI; MINORITIES, NATIONAL; PEASANTS AND PEASANT REBELLIONS; SINICIZATION; SOCIAL CLASSES.

CLANS See ANCESTOR WORSHIP; FAMILY STRUCTURE; SIX COMPANIES, CHINESE; TEMPLES.

CLARIONET See FLUTES AND WIND INSTRUMENTS.

CLASSIC OF FILIAL PIETY See FILIAL PIETY.

CLASSIC OF RITES See BOOK OF RITES.

CLEAR AND BRIGHT FESTIVAL See QING MING FESTIVAL.

CLERICAL SCRIPT See CALLIGRAPHY; LI SI; STONE TABLETS; WRITING SYSTEM, CHINESE.

CLIMATE, CHINESE China, the third-largest country in the world, has many geographical features that give it a wide climatic range, from subarctic in Heilongjiang Province in the northeast (also known as Manchuria) to tropical on Hainan Island in the south. The climate of eastern China, where much of the population is concentrated, is mild to subtropical. The northwestern region is extremely dry, with less than 20 inches of rain per year, and dust blows across China from the Gobi and other deserts. The Qinghai-Tibet Plateau, north of the Himalaya Mountain Range, the highest in the world, forms its own dry and cold climatic region. Several long mountain ranges that run west to east across the middle of the country form the dividing lines between temperate and tropical zones. In general, January is the coldest month in China and July the hottest. Average temperatures vary greatly throughout the country. In January they dip below freezing in the north, and they may drop well below 0 degrees Fahrenheit in the northeast, where rivers freeze over more than 180 days per year. Average winter temperatures increase as the latitude moves south, rising to 60 degrees in the southeastern and southern coastal provinces of Fujian and Guangdong. While winter temperatures vary widely in China, summer temperatures are more uniform among different regions, with an average July temperature of 70 degrees throughout the country. Temperatures have the greatest variation in Manchuria and in Xinjiang-Uighur Autonomous Region in the far northwest.

The Chinese climate is determined largely by monsoon winds that arise because of differences in the capacity to absorb heat between the land and the seas that lie to the east and south. Large air masses accompanied by strong winds move seasonally across the country. From September through April, polar air masses move down from Siberia across Mongolia and North China, causing cold, dry weather; and from April through September, tropical air masses from the Pacific and Indian oceans move into China from the south, bringing hot weather and rainfall. Summer monsoons are the main source of rain in China. The climate of central and north China is determined by the frontal zone where these two air masses meet in North China in the summer, causing heavy rainfall there. In autumn the winds decrease but the frontal zone moves down to central China, where the resultant heavy rainfall frequently causes flooding. The seasonal variations in rainfall cause problems for agriculture in China, and throughout history the Chinese have suffered many disasters due to alternating floods and droughts. Southeastern China also suffers from severe typhoons between July and September, and this region has the highest average annual precipitation, over 250 inches a year. More than 80 percent of China's annual precipitation falls between May and October. This factor, combined with hot temperatures, is beneficial to the cultivation of plants, especially rice, in the eastern and southern regions. Farmers can grow two, or even three, crops in one year. See also GEOGRAPHY; GOBI DESERT; MANCHURIA; NATURAL DISASTERS; QINGHAI-TIBET PLATEAU; RICE; NAMES OF INDIVIDUAL PROVINCES.

CLOISONNÉ (*jingtailan* or *ching-t'ai-lan*) A technique by which bronzeware is decorated with colorful enamels. Intricate patterns such as flowers and leaves are outlined with thin bronze or copper wires soldered onto the bronze or glued on with rice paste; these shapes are known by the French term *cloisons,* or "cells." Artisans paint thick colored enamel pastes in the cells between the wires, which keep the colors separated, and fire the object at a low temperature to harden the enamel. Then they grind the surface smooth with abrasives, polish it to make the colors glossy, and coat the wires with gold. Enamel is made of glass, to which metallic oxides are added to provide the colors. Popular colors used by Chinese cloisonné artisans during the Ming dynasty (1368–1644) include red, yellow, green, black, purple, cobalt blue and turquoise. During the Jing Tai Period (1450–56), the Chinese began to call cloisonné objects "Jing Tai Blue." Today more than 40 colors are available. Different colors require different firing temperatures; thus, repeated firings are necessary, beginning with colors that have higher melting points. From the late Ming dynasty bronze bases were replaced by coppered biscuits with soldered wires.

There are several variant techniques for cloisonné. In champlevé, depressions are carved out of the metal base to make patterns and then filled with enamels. In repoussé, depressions are hammered into the metal before being filled. In painted enamelware, metal bases are completely covered with a coat of opaque enamel—usually white—and a design is painted on with additional coats of colored enamels. The piece is then fired. This technique, originally developed in Limoges, France, was used on both metal and porcelain. The latter is called "foreign porcelain" by the Chinese. Imported into China in the early 18th century, it was produced mostly at Guangzhou (Canton) in southern China on commission by Western traders for export.

Some cloisonné objects may have been made in northeast China toward the end of the Mongol-ruled Yuan dynasty (1279–1368). The earliest known Chinese reference to cloisonné is in a book for art collectors and connoisseurs written in A.D. 1388, where it is referred to as *dashi* ("Muslim") ware. The cloisonné technique with its vivid colors became popular in China during the Ming dynasty. The oldest Chinese pieces that can be positively dated are from the 15th century; these include incense burners, boxes, plates, animal and bird shapes, and ornamental objects for the desks of scholars. See also ENAMELWARE; MING DYNASTY.

CLOTHING See COTTON; DRAGON; EMBROIDERY; INDIGO DYEING OF TEXTILES; NINE-RANK SYSTEM; PHOENIX; RAMIE; SILK; TEXTILE INDUSTRY.

CMSN See CHINA MERCHANTS STEAM NAVIGATION COMPANY.

COAL See ENERGY SOURCES; MINING INDUSTRY.

COASTAL OPEN CITIES See FOREIGN TRADE AND INVESTMENT; SPECIAL ECONOMIC ZONES.

CODE FOR WOMEN (*Nujie* or *Nu-chieh*)   Also known as *Lessons for Women;* a book written to instruct women on proper behavior, written by Ban Zhao (Pan Chao; A.D. 49–120), a famous woman scholar, along with her scholar brother, Ban Gu (Pan Ku; A.D. 32–92). Ban Zhao was a highly educated woman—unusual for her time—who completed her brother's *History of the Former Han Dynasty (Han-*

shu) after he died. In addition, Ban Zhao held the position of governess for an empress of the Han dynasty (206 B.C.–220 A.D.) and her ladies-in-waiting. Her *Lessons for Women* adhered to the Chinese patriarchal system in which women held a lesser position to men and were supposed to obey their father as children, their husbands as wives, and their sons after their husbands died. Girls were expected to marry at age 15, and were forbidden to marry a man with the same family name because they might have an ancestor in common. There were seven grounds on which a husband could divorce a wife: disobeying her husband's parents; not being able to have children; adultery; jealousy; having an incurable disease; talking too much; and stealing. Bhan Zhao argued that women should be given the same education that men (and she herself) received in the classic books of the Confucian tradition, the orthodox school of thought, in imperial China. However, this practice did not become common in China. See also BAN GU AND BAN ZHAO; CONFUCIANISM.

COHONG   See BRITISH EAST INDIA COMPANY; CANTON SYSTEM; MACARTNEY, GEORGE, LORD; OPIUM WAR.

COLD MOUNTAIN AND COLD MOUNTAIN TEMPLE See HAN SHAN; SUZHOU.

COLLECTIVES   See PEOPLE'S COMMUNE.

COLOANE   See MACAO.

COLORS (*yanse*)   Colors have many traditional symbolic meanings in Chinese culture. Since ancient times, the theory of the five material agents or elements that make up all things in the universe has associated certain elements, seasons, directions and powerful creatures with certain colors. Wood is associated with spring, east, green and the green dragon; fire with summer, south, red and the red bird or phoenix, the symbol of the empress; earth with the center, yellow and the yellow dragon, the symbol of the emperor; metal with autumn, west, white and the white tiger; and water with winter, north, black and the black tortoise. Red is the color of happiness and is used on all happy occasions. Yellow, the color of the Chinese Empire, was worn only by the emperor, his sons and lineal descendants, except for his grandsons, who wore purple. The Forbidden City, the imperial palace compound in Beijing where Chinese emperors dwelt from the 14th to 20th centuries, is formally known as the Purple Forbidden City. The walls are red, symbolizing the south, sun, happiness and the *yang,* or masculine, principle. The roofs are bright yellow, symbolizing the earth and the *yin,* or feminine, principle. The color green was associated with the Ming dynasty (1368–1644) and yellow with the Qing dynasty (1644–1911), China's last imperial dynasty. Higher-ranking government officials were carried in blue sedan chairs, lower-ranking ones in green chairs. Members of the imperial bureaucracy or civil service were ranked into nine levels and wore silk patches embroidered with colorful designs to indicate rank. The button atop their cap also indicated rank; for example, a red coral button stood for the first rank, blue stone for the third, purple stone for the fourth, white jade for the sixth, and gold for the seventh through ninth ranks.

At a traditional Chinese wedding, green is associated with the groom and red with the bride, who wears a red robe for good luck. Lucky money is given out at the New Year Festival and many other happy occasions in red envelopes stamped with the gold characters for double happiness. At the New Year, verses are written on red paper and pasted on the doors of homes to bring good luck. Red is the traditional color of virtue, truth and sincerity. The Chinese say that an honest and sincere person has a red heart. White, symbolic of moral purity, is the color for death, funerals and mourning in China, in contrast to the Western custom of wearing black. To the Chinese, black symbolizes guilt, and a depraved person is described as having a black heart.

Chinese arts and crafts employ a wide range of beautiful colors. The Chinese discovered the art of producing silk and dyeing it in bright colors thousands of years ago. Blue has been the most common traditional color for Chinese clothing, especially among the peasants who comprise the majority of the Chinese population and who traditionally wore natural fibers such as hemp, cotton and ramie. The folk art of dyeing textiles a vivid indigo-blue color became highly developed in China.

The most precious types of jade are white in color. The Chinese also carve ivory into elaborate shapes. The first color that Chinese potters were able to produce in ceramics was green, known as celadon ware in the West. Chinese potters discovered the techniques for producing porcelain, a lustrous and delicate white ceramic, and for decorating porcelain objects with green, purple, yellow, brown, black, red or gold enamels. Blue-and-white painted porcelain has also been very popular. The Chinese also learned the art of decorating metal objects with colorful enamels, known as cloisonné. The symbolic meaning of colors plays an important part in Chinese design motifs. A common type of symbol is the rebus, a homophone that contains a secret message or double meaning. For example, red bats are often used to decorate Ming and Qing ceramics because "red bat" (*hongfu*) sounds the same as "abundant good fortune." Goldfish are also used because the word for goldfish (*jinyu*) sounds the same as "gold in abundance" and thus expresses a wish for wealth and prosperity. Bright colors, especially red, are used in traditional Chinese architecture, such as temples, with roofs often covered with brightly colored glazed tiles.

In Beijing Opera and other Chinese regional operas, colors used in face makeup and costumes have symbolic meaning and indicate the rank or character of the person being portrayed. Yellow is for royalty, red for loyal subjects of the emperor, dark red for military chiefs, and pink for young unmarried women. An emperor's robe is yellow and embroidered with coiled dragons winding up and down. High government officials also wear yellow robes, but have dragons flying downward. A black face symbolizes an honest but rough man. A white face indicates a dignified but cunning and dangerous person, and a white patch on the nose indicates a villain. Devils have green faces, and deities gold or yellow faces. See also ARCHITECTURE, TRADITIONAL; BAT; BLUE-AND-WHITE WARE; CELADON WARE; CLOISONNÉ; DOUBLE HAPPINESS AND LONG LIFE; DRAGON; EMBROIDERY; EMPEROR; ENAMELWARE; FIVE MATERIAL AGENTS; FORBIDDEN CITY; INDIGO DYEING OF TEXTILES; IVORY CARVING; JADE; LUCKY MONEY; NEW YEAR FESTIVAL; NINE-RANK SYSTEM; OPERA, BEIJING; PORCELAIN; SILK; TEMPLES; TILES, GLAZED; WEDDINGS, TRADITIONAL; WHITE WARE; YIN AND YANG.

COMMENTS ON PAINTING (HUAYULU) See SHI TAO.

COMMERCIAL PRESS, THE (Shangwu Yinshuguan or Shang-wu Yin-shu-kuan)   The oldest and largest modern publishing house in China, established in Shanghai in 1897. The second oldest, China Publishing House (Zhonghua Shuju or Chung-hua Shu-chu), was established in 1912 by editors, printers and distributors who had worked at the Commercial Press. During its first 85 years, the Commercial Press published more than 20,000 books. The company began as a printing company founded by three printers, Xia Cuifang (Hsia Ts'ui-fang) and the Bao brothers, Bao Xian'en (Pao Hsien-en) and Bao Xianchang (Pao Hsien-ch'ang). The Commercial Press soon became a publishing company that edited, translated, printed and distributed books and periodicals. The company grew so rapidly that in 1902 the partners brought in another member, Zhang Yuanji (Chang Yuan-chi), who at first was chief of the editing and translating department and later became the president of the company. Zhang visited publishing companies in Europe and the United States, where he learned a great deal about how to hire employees and conduct operations for the Commercial Press.

In 1904 the Commercial Press published the *New Textbooks*, the first complete set of textbooks designed for Chinese primary and middle schools. When the Republic of China was established in 1912 after the Revolution of 1911 overthrew the Qing dynasty (1644–1911), the Commercial Press published the *Republican Textbooks*, the set of which was reprinted 2,540 times. *Short Story Magazine* was a popular literary journal that carried the first stories written by some of China's greatest modern authors, including Ba Jin (Pa Chin), Lao She and Ding Ling (Ting Ling). The Press published books edited by the Chinese Literary Society and by other academic organizations. It published both ancient and modern texts and academic and popular books and magazines in the fields of literature, philosophy, history, political science, science, engineering, medicine, agriculture, the arts, music and sports. During many of the years that it has been operating, the Commercial Press has been able to publish a new book every day, and in the 1930s it claimed to be the world's largest publishing house. The Press has published hundreds of reference books in Chinese and foreign languages. It set up a joint venture with the Shogakkan Publishing House in Japan to publish the *Modern Japanese-Chinese Dictionary* and the *Chinese-Japanese Dictionary*. The Commercial Press has specialized in translating and publishing foreign works of philosophy and social sciences, such as Yan Fu's translation of T. H. Huxley's *Evolution and Ethics*, which has had a great influence on modern Chinese philosophy. The Press recently published the *Chinese Translation of the World Famous Academic Works* with 50 titles and 69 volumes in Part I and 50 titles and 64 volumes in Part II. See also BA JIN; DING LING; LAO SHE; PRINTING; YAN FU.

COMMUNE See PEOPLE'S COMMUNE.

COMMUNIST PARTY, CHINESE See CHINESE COMMUNIST PARTY.

COMMUNIST YOUTH LEAGUE Also known as the Young Communist League; a government organization for members of the Chinese Communist Party who are between 15 and 25 years of age. The Communist Youth League indoctrinates and trains these young people to become regular adult members of the party. The League is directed by the United Front Work Department of the Communist Party Central Committee. The League's head, known as the first secretary, is a member of the party's Central Committee. The importance of the Communist Youth League diminished during the Cultural Revolution (1966–76), when Red Guard groups took over many of the League's functions in Chinese schools and universities. In 1987 the Communist Youth League in China had 52 million members in 2.3 million branches, which connect Chinese youth with the Chinese Communist Party. The League has also established connections with youth organizations in other countries. In addition, the Communist League administers the Young Pioneers, the Chinese Communist party organization for children under age 15. Branches of the Young Pioneers hold after-school activities such as games and sports, and also sponsor activities for young people to participate in community service. See also CHINESE COMMUNIST PARTY; RED GUARDS.

COMPASS (*zhinanzhen* or *chi nan chen*) An instrument that indicates geographical and astronomical direction by using a magnetized needle that points or refers to the north–south axis. The compass, which became an important tool for the navigation of ships, was invented in China, where it originated in boards marked with astrological symbols used for divination. The most important part of the compass was the *shi* (*shih*), consisting of two layers, an upper disc representing Heaven (*tian* or *t'ien*) and a lower square representing earth. The stars of the constellation known as the Big Dipper, Plough or Great Bear were marked on the upper layer, and the characters for the directions or points of the compass were marked on both layers. A spoon that represented the Big Dipper was placed on the *shi* with the bowl in the center and the handle pointing toward the symbols written in a circle around the board; sometimes a metal fish was used in place of a spoon. In the fourth century B.C. the Chinese began carving the spoon from lodestone (magnetite) because of its magnetic properties. The spoon's ability to point to the southerly direction gave it the name "south-pointing spoon." Unlike Western compasses, which use north as the primary direction, Chinese compasses commonly use south as the main direction and the character for south is often painted in red.

Sometime between the first and sixth centuries A.D., the Chinese discovered that they could transfer the magnetic ability of lodestone to small iron needles by rubbing a piece of lodestone on the point of a needle. They floated the needles on water in small bowls marked with the directions of the compass. In the eighth or ninth century they discovered the principle of magnetic declination, meaning that they had to compensate for the fact that the magnetic needle does not align precisely along the north–south axis.

Chinese geomancy, known as *feng shui*, still relies on a magnetic compass to determine the best sites for buildings, tombs and even cities. Geomancers were using a compass without a magnetic needle by the second century B.C., and with a magnetic needle by the 11th century A.D. A compass for geomancy has complex markings that indicate the way that a person's date and time of birth and other personal factors are connected with the channels or "veins" in the earth through which positive natural energies (*qi*) that are beneficial to human beings flow. The markings also indicate the relationships of a site to the earth and the position of the planets and other astrological features. The earliest record of the use of the magnetic compass as a navigation aid on Chinese ships is in *Pingzhou* (*P'ingchow*) *Table Talk*, a book written in 1117 by Chu Yu, then governor of the southern port city of Guangzhou (Canton). This was a century before the compass was used by Europeans, who acquired it from the Chinese. The magnetic compass enabled Chinese shipping to increase greatly during the Song dynasty (960–1279), with junks sailing as far as Vietnam, Malaysia, India and the Persian Gulf. During the Ming dynasty, Zheng He (1371–1433) commanded large sailing expeditions to East Africa. See also FENG SHUI; HEAVEN; ZHENG HE.

COMPLETE LIBRARY OF THE FOUR TREASURIES, THE See QIANLONG (EMPEROR).

COMPRADOR (plural *compradores*) Portuguese term for the Chinese general manager of a foreign trading company who handled all of its operations in China. The term was commonly used in the pidgin English that became widespread along the Chinese coast. The comprador was the highest-ranking Chinese employee in these companies, which included such British firms as Jardine, Matheson, which still functions in Hong Kong; Butterfield and Swire; Dent and Company; and the Hongkong and Shanghai Banking Corporation. The best-known American company was Russell and Company, which in 1872 became the China Merchants' Steam Navigation Company, operating steamships on the Yangzi River (Changjiang) between Shanghai and Hankou. The Portuguese were the first Europeans to establish regular trading relations with China, in the 16th century. They made their base at Macao, a small island near the southern Chinese port city of Guangzhou (Canton). The Chinese had traditionally engaged in trade with foreign countries by requiring them to become part of the tribute system, under which they had to send missions to bow before the Chinese emperor, give him presents and acknowledge his suzerainty. European traders did not want to submit to the emperor, so the Chinese restricted their trade to Guangzhou, where they were required to do all of their business through native Chinese merchants who belonged to a guild known as the Cohong or "Hong" (from *gonghang*, "combined merchant companies"). This is known as the Canton system for regulating foreign trade. Western traders were confined to an area in Guangzhou along the bank of the Pearl River where the residences and offices of the factors of foreign companies were located, known as the "13 Factories." Britain attempted to force the Chinese government to open Chinese cities to Western-style trade and finally did so by defeating China in the Opium (1839–42) and Arrow wars (Second Opium War; 1856–60). China opened many cities as so-called treaty ports, and Shanghai quickly replaced Guangzhou as China's largest trading port.

Every foreign company in China had a foreign director, but since knowledge of the Chinese language and connections (*guanxi* or *kuan-hsi*) with Chinese buyers, suppliers and government officials were crucial, the most important employee was actually the comprador. He hired and fired the Chinese employees and served as their guarantor. They ranged from the translators and clerks who staffed the office to the security guards and coolies or laborers in the company warehouses, which were called "godowns." The coolies loaded and unloaded ships and carried the goods between the ships and the godowns. The comprador made arrangements to sell the company's goods to Chinese markets and to purchase Chinese goods that the company would sell abroad. He also acted in many other ways as the company's necessary go-between in the complicated world of Chinese business and society. Western companies did not have to open branches outside of their head offices in the port cities, because the compradores and their Chinese staff were able to do business with a far-ranging Chinese distribution system. Compradores were also trained in Western business practices. Many compradores moved from Guangzhou to Shanghai when it became the preeminent trading city, and they comprised the prominent social class in Shanghai into the early 20th century. See also ARROW WAR; CANTON SYSTEM; CHINA MERCHANTS STEAM NAVIGATION COMPANY; CONNECTIONS; GUANGZHOU; HONG KONG; HONGKONG AND SHANGHAI BANKING CORPORATION; MACAO; OPIUM WAR; PEARL RIVER; SHANGHAI; TREATY PORTS; YANGZI RIVER.

COMPREHENSIVE MIRROR FOR AID IN GOVERNMENT
See SIMA GUANG.

CONCUBINAGE
A system by which a man brings one or more women into his household to cohabit with him in addition to his legal wife. A man's wives, concubines and female servants are collectively known as a harem. Concubinage has been practiced throughout Chinese history, mainly by the wealthy men who could afford it, and primarily as a way to provide many children. Chinese law treated the children of concubines as equal in status and rights to the children of the main wife. If an empress died without having borne a male heir, the son of a high-ranking concubine would be designated the heir to the throne. Chinese emperors had large harems with hundreds of concubines. The two women in Chinese history who wielded the greatest power, Empress Wu (r. 690–705) and Empress Dowager Cixi (Ts'u Hsi; 1835–1908), had been imperial concubines. The Italian explorer Marco Polo described the harem of the Mongol leader Khubilai Khan who founded the Yuan dynasty that ruled China 1279–1368. He had four main wives, each of whom had a household of thousands of servants. Every year, 30 or 40 concubines were chosen for the emperor from 500 girls who were brought to him from all over the Chinese Empire. The residences for Chinese empresses and imperial concubines can still be seen in the harem quarters of the Forbidden City complex in Beijing.

Being selected as an imperial concubine was a very high honor that was sought after by members of the highest-ranking Chinese families. The beloved Chinese novel, *Dream of the Red Chamber* (or *Dream of Red Mansions*), by Cao Xue-qin (Ts'ao Hsueh-ch'in; 1715?–1763) contains an episode in which a female relative becomes an imperial concubine. She is allowed to pay a visit to her home, where her family builds a garden to honor her. Film director Zhang Yimou (1951–) addressed the issue of modern concubinage in *Raise the Red Lantern* (1991) starring Gong Li.

In China, a concubine was ritually and legally defined as a secondary spouse. Her duties were to serve the wife, defined as the principal spouse, and to bear children. Chinese ritual and legal texts clearly defined the status differentiation between wives and concubines. Marriage between people of different social classes was prohibited because this would damage the husband's family, but concubines could be taken from lower social classes.

There were several ways in which a man could bring a concubine into a household. The most common way was for a man to purchase her, by signing a contract. Many concubines were the daughters of tenant farmers or merchants who did business with a wealthy man or high government official, who were eager to have their daughters enter the wealthy households. Many concubines also came from poor families who sold them to become prostitutes or entertainers, known as "sing-song girls," who were trained to read and write, sing, play musical instruments, and hold conversations with wealthy guests at banquets. When such a girl was chosen to be a concubine, the new owner paid a specified price, a portion of which went to the professional entertainment house to which she had belonged and part to the girl herself, who also possessed expensive clothing and jewelry that had been given to her as presents. The man would buy out her contract and pay off any debts that she owed. A concubine could also enter a household by the performance of some but not all of the rituals of a traditional Chinese wedding. Sometimes a maid could be promoted to the position of concubine. A concubine could also be given to a man as a gift or as a grant from the emperor to a meritorious official, especially a military commander, as a reward for loyal service. If a wife died, the husband might make his concubine his legal wife.

The divorce of a husband and wife has traditionally been rare in China because of the disgrace it brings to the family. Even a concubine, once a man brought her into his home, could not be sent out of the home without lengthy negotiations with her own family. A man usually took a concubine after his wife proved unable to bear a son and was about 40 years old. A concubine tended to be much younger than the husband, and her presence often disturbed the normal family relationships. The wife might have resented her, although the concubine always remained subordinate to the wife in the family hierarchy. In addition, the sons or sons-in-law might be sexually attracted to their father's concubine. Frequently, when a husband died, his wife sent his concubines out of the home and they joined other households. When the Chinese Communist Party founded the People's Republic of China, it promulgated the Marriage Law on May 1, 1950, which intended to abolish the "feudal elements" of traditional Chinese family law, including the practice of concubinage. See also FAMILY STRUCTURE; FORBIDDEN CITY; WEDDINGS, TRADITIONAL.

CONDIMENTS
See SEASONINGS FOR FOOD.

CONFERENCE OF NON-ALIGNED NATIONS See ZHOU ENLAI.

CONFUCIANISM (*ruxue* or *ju-hsueh*)   The school of thought founded by Confucius (551–479 B.C.), which became accepted as orthodox by the imperial government of the Han dynasty (206 B.C.–A.D. 220) and all subsequent dynasties. The term *ru* (*ju*) refers to scholars in ancient China, who usually were supported by wealthy families, whom they advised on ceremonial and funeral affairs. After Confucius died, these scholars became organized into an academic group based on his teachings. Confucius lived during the Warring States Period (403–221 B.C.), the final period of the Zhou dynasty (1100–256 B.C.), when feudal states were contending with others for dominance. He was one of many great thinkers of the time, considered the "golden age" of Chinese philosophy, when the so-called Hundred Schools of Thought flourished. Confucius traveled with his students to many different feudal states and was given financial support by the feudal rulers he advised. A conservative, he looked back to the early days of the Zhou dynasty as the ideal period when rulers were benevolent and people lived together in harmony. His ideal was the "superior man," the cultivated man or gentleman (*junzi* or *chuntzu;* "son of a prince"). For Confucius, a person became noble not by birth but through developing five virtues, which became central to his school of thought: humanity or benevolence (*ren* or *jen*); righteousness (*yi*); propriety or proper conduct (*li*); wisdom (*zhi* or *chi*); and trustworthiness (*xin* or *hsin*). Underpinning all of these virtues is the most important one, filial piety (*xiao* or *hsiao*), the respect and obedience of children toward their parents. Confucius maintained that when all family relationships are in order, including those between husband and wife and parents and children, then there will be order in society. His patriarchal view of the family, in which the wife obeys her husband and the children obey their father, became the basis of the Chinese family structure. Sons were especially important, because they carried on the family line and performed the ritual sacrifices to honor their deceased parents and other family ancestors. For Confucius the relationship between fathers and sons is the basic model for both the family and society, in which the ruler should be virtuous and act as a father to his subjects.

According to tradition, Confucius spent the last years of his life compiling and editing the *Book of Songs* (*Shijing* or *Shih-ching*), *Book of History* (*Shujing* or *Shu-ching*), *Book of Rites* (*Liji* or *Li-chih*), *Book of Changes* (*Yijing* or *I-ching*) and the *Spring and Autumn Annals* (*Chunqiu* or *Ch'un Ch'iu*). These texts became the canonical Five Classics of Confucianism (*wujing* or *wuching*). Confucius's own discourses were recorded in the *Analects* (*Sayings; Lun Yu*) by his disciples. This text became one of the canonical Four Books of Confucianism (*sishu* or *ssu-shu*) during the 13th century A.D.

During the three hundred years after Confucius's death, Confucianism was just one of the Hundred Schools of Thought and only become widely accepted during the Han dynasty. Some other important schools of thought included the Legalist School and the Moist School, which was based on the teachings of Mozi (Mo Tzu), who lived in the mid-

fifth century B.C. and may have been a disciple of Confucius. Mozi went beyond Confucius's emphasis on the family and taught the principle of universal love. Daoism, supposedly founded in the sixth century by Laozi (Lao Tzu), became one of the three most important traditions in China, along with Confucianism and Buddhism, which was introduced from India around the first century A.D. After Confucius died, his school divided into eight schools, one of which is represented by Mencius (Mengzi or Meng-tzu; c. 372–289 B.C.), who is considered the successor of Confucius and is thus referred to by the Chinese as the "Second Sage" (*Yasheng*).

Mencius, like Confucius, looked back to the early Zhou feudal system as a model for good government, and he maintained that the genuine ruler has the qualities of humanity and a sense of duty for taking care of his people, the way a father takes care of his family. Mencius asserted that a ruler who does not act properly will lose the Mandate of Heaven (*tianming* or *t'ien-ming*), which legitimizes his reign, and his subjects will be justified in rebelling against him. This concept was the foundation for imperial rule in China, and the Zhou and every subsequent Chinese dynasty claimed that their rule was legitimized by the Mandate of Heaven. Mencius taught that human nature is essentially good, and he emphasized the Confucian concept of righteousness (*yi*), which includes a strong sense of duty and commitment to fulfilling one's obligation to another person. Mencius's disciples recorded his teachings in a book, the *Mencius* (*Mengzi* or *Meng-tzu*), which later became another one of the Four Books of Confucianism.

Xunzi (Hsun Tzu; c. 298–238 B.C.) was the next most important Confucian thinker at the end of the Warring States Period. He disagreed with Mencius that human nature is essentially good and claimed that man must work to cultivate his goodness through education and the performance of rituals, which would bring about order in society. Xunzi, like other Confucianists, emphasized the ceremonial performance or "proper" music and dance (*yueh*). He combined elements from Daoism, which emphasized harmony with nature, and the Legalist School of Thought, which emphasized the absolute power of the ruler and the use of strict rewards and punishments, with the concepts of Confucianism. The two most important Legalist thinkers, Li Si (Li Ssu) and Han Feizi (Han Fei Tzu), were students of Xunzi. Later Confucian thinkers criticized Xunzi for being too Legalist in his own thought.

The Zhou dynasty was brought to an end by Qin Shi Huangdi, the first emperor, who unified China under the Qin dynasty (221–206 B.C.). He was a harsh ruler who subscribed to the Legalist School. The Qin was soon overthrown by the Han dynasty (206 B.C.–A.D. 220), which established many of the institutions that became standard for Chinese government and society for two millennia. The Han developed the centralized government of the Qin into the imperial bureaucracy or civil service staffed by Confucian-educated scholars. Dong Zhongshu (Tung Chung-shu; 179–104 B.C.) led the movement that influenced Han Emperor Wudi (Wu-ti) to accept Confucianism as the ideology of the Chinese imperial government. In 136 B.C., Emperor Wudi proclaimed Confucianism the official state cult. Twelve years later he established an imperial university at the Han capital of Chang'an (modern Xi'an in Shaanxi Province), with a curriculum based on the Five Classics of Confucianism. From the Han through the Qing dynasty (1644–1911), the literati (*wenren* or *wen-jen*), or scholars, who staffed the imperial bureaucracy were educated in the classical texts of Confucianism. Dong helped develop the political philosophy that formed the bureaucracy's foundation of the imperial bureaucracy. He built upon the basic ethical concepts of Confucianism, and also drew upon cosmological concepts held by the Yin-Yang and the Five Material Agents (*wuxing* or *wu-hsing*) schools of thought. Confucianism influenced Daoist philosophy as well. Wang Bie (Wang Pi; A.D. 226–249) attempted to incorporate the social and moral emphasis of Confucianism into Daoist metaphysical thought and wrote a commentary on Confucian texts using terms and concepts from the Daoist tradition. Wang argued that Confucianism shows the origin of all things within the realm of Being, whereas Daoism goes beyond this to the level of the ultimate, which is the *Dao* (*Tao*), the unified principle that underlies all things that exist.

During the Han dynasty, all Chinese government schools began to conduct regular sacrifices to Confucius, who became the patron saint of the imperial bureaucracy. From the Han through every subsequent dynasty, every Chinese emperor paid homage to Confucius, who was awarded the title, "Great Perfect, Most Holy Culture-Spreading Former Teacher Confucius." During the Tang dynasty (618–907), Confucius became worshiped as a deity. In 630, Tang Emperor Taizong (T'ai-tsung; r. 626–49) decreed that a Confucian temple should be established in every province and county of the Chinese Empire. In 647 these temples were made into national shrines to Confucius and to those government officials whose scholarship had best contributed to Confucianism. Tang Emperor Xuanzong (Hsuan-tsung; r. 712–56) founded the Hanlin ("Forest of Writing Brushes") Academy as a group of scholars who could assist the emperor and the imperial court by writing diplomatic letters and literary compositions such as poetry, which enjoyed a golden age during the Tang and has been a highly valued art in China every since. By the Ming dynasty (1368–1644), leading scholars from the Hanlin Academy formed the most important body in the imperial government.

Han Yu (768–824) was a Tang official, famous poet and prose writer, and Confucian scholar who laid the foundation for the revival of Confucian thought during the Song dynasty (960–1279) known as Neo-Confucianism. He also strongly opposed the Buddhist religion, foreshadowing the Tang persecution of Buddhism in 845. Han Yu and other Confucian scholars disliked the Buddhist viewpoint that existence and human personality are an illusion, and condemned such Buddhist practices as celibacy and mortification of the body for going against the Confucian emphasis on respect for one's parents, or filial piety, and continuation of the family line. Despite the brief persecution of the Buddhist religion, Buddhist and Daoist concepts became very influential in Chinese culture. As a reaction, during the Song dynasty, Neo-Confucian thinkers returned the thought of Confucius to its predominant place as the ideology of the imperial government. They also drew upon Buddhist and Daoist concepts such as the Infinite and the Absolute to emphasize the spiritual aspects of Confucian thought. During the Song the

literati class attained its most widespread influence, not only in government, but in the arts, such as calligraphy (the fine art of writing Chinese characters with a brush), ink painting, landscape painting and poetry. The Chinese class calligraphy, painting and poetry together as the "Three Perfections."

Neo-Confucianism is known in Chinese as the Rational School (*Lixue* or *Li-hsueh*). It was originated in the latter half of the 11th century by Zhou Donyi (Chou Tun-i) and the Cheng brothers, Cheng Yi (Ch'eng I) and Cheng Hao (Ch'eng Hao). Neo-Confucian thinkers maintained that the human self and all things in the universe possess the so-called Heavenly Principle (*tianli* or *t'ien-li*), and they were concerned with a person's ability to overcome evil in oneself through moral and spiritual cultivation. They even adapted the practice of meditation from Buddhism, calling it "quiet sitting" (*jingzuo* or *ching-tso*).

Zhu Xi (Chu Hsi; 1130–1200) developed a synthesis of Neo-Confucian thought known as the Rationalist School or the School of Principle or Reason. He created more precise definitions for many important Confucian concepts, basing his thought on a principle central to the Confucian text known as the *Great Learning* (*Daxue* or *Ta-hsueh*), the "investigation of the nature of things and relationships." He maintained that a person's mind is essentially one with the mind of the universe and is hence able to enter into and understand the principles of all created things. The goal in Zhu Xi's thought is to become a sage (*sheng*) by actualizing one's potential as a human being in this life, known as humanity, a central principle of Confucianism. Zhuxi codified four Confucian texts into the canonical Four Books: the *Analects* of Confucius, *Book of Mencius*, *Doctrine of the Mean* (*Zhongyong* or *Chung-yung*) and *Great Learning*. In 1313, the Yuan dynasty (1279–1368) issued an official decree that knowledge of the Four Books and Zhu Xi's commentaries on them would from then on be mandatory for the imperial examination system. Chinese students first memorized the Four Books and then went on to study the Five Classics. During the Qing dynasty (1644–1911) there was a strong revival of interest in the ideas of Zhu Xi.

The second major branch of Neo-Confucianism is the School of Mind or Intuition, known as the Lu-Wang School, after Lu Xiangshan (Lu Hsiang-shan; 1139–93) and his early-16th-century follower, Wang Yangming, the second-most important Neo-Confucian thinker. Wang was influenced by the Chan (Zen; "meditation") Sect of Buddhism. He argued that a person is born with the knowledge of what is good and can put this knowledge into action if he has developed his intuitive knowledge through thinking and meditating. Wang's philosophy influenced early 20th-century Chinese idealists and leaders of the movement to modernize China, including Kang Youwei (K'ang You-wei) and Liang Qichao (Liang Ch'i-ch'ao) in the 19th century and Dr. Sun Yat-sen (1866–1925), the founder of the Republic of China.

Roman Catholic Jesuit missionaries who went to China, beginning with Matteo Ricci (1552–1610), learned the Chinese language and studied the Five Classics and Four Books of Confucianism. The Jesuits introduced Confucian thought to Europe, and in 1687 the *Analects* and the *Doctrine of the Mean* were published in Latin in Paris. Confucianism influenced European philosophers and political thinkers such as Leibniz, especially during the Enlightenment. Voltaire praised

Confucius as an "explicator of truth." Robespierre, a leader of the French Revolution, quoted a phrase from Confucius, "Do not do to others as you would not wish done to yourself..." in the French Declaration of the Rights of Man. The Jesuits in China accepted the Confucian tradition as a system of ethics and found points of similarity between Christian and Confucian teachings. They permitted their Chinese Christian coverts to continue performing the Confucian rituals to honor their ancestors, known as ancestor worship, which led to a conflict between the Chinese emperor and the pope known as the Rites Controversy. In 1724 the emperor banned Christianity in China, although Christian priests continued to work clandestinely in the country until the ban was lifted in 1846 due to French pressure.

Confucianism, and the system of bureaucratic government staffed by Confucian-educated scholars, became extremely influential in other parts of Asia, especially Japan, Korea, Vietnam, Taiwan, Singapore and Hong Kong. In China, the pressure from Western powers that wanted an open system of trade, combined with internal rebellions by Han ethnic Chinese against the Manchus who had established the Qing dynasty, brought down not only the Qing but the entire imperial system of government. In 1905 the Qing ended the examination system for the imperial bureaucracy. In 1911 the Chinese, led by Sun Yat-sen, overthrew the Qing in the Revolution of 1911, and in 1912 they established the Republic of China. The intellectual leaders of the formative May Fourth Movement of 1919, such as Chen Duxiu (Ch'en Tu-hsiu), Li Dazhao (Li Ta-chao), Lu Xun (Lu Hsun) and Wu Yu, strongly criticized the conservative teachings of Confucianism. The Chinese Communist Party (CCP), founded in 1921, also criticized Confucianism as backward and feudalistic. In 1949 the CCP defeated the Chinese Nationalists (Kuomintang; KMT), the party founded by Sun Yat-sen. KMT leader Chiang Kai-shek fled to Taiwan and established the pro-Confucian ROC government there. The CCP founded the People's Republic of China (PRC) with Mao Zedong (Mao Tse-tung) as chairman, and Communist and Maoist ideology replaced Confucian ideology in China. Confucianism was strongly attacked during the Cultural Revolution (1966–76) for being feudalistic. However, during the 1960s the Asian countries that subscribed to Confucian thinking had experienced rapid economic growth and modernization, while the PRC had suffered a complete breakdown of its political, education and social system. During the late 1970s, after the deaths of Mao and Zhou Enlai (Chou En-lai), the Chinese government undertook a program to rebuild and modernize the country. Scholarship on Confucianism became acceptable once more, and books and theses were published on Confucian topics, as well as an academic journal, *Research on Confucius*. Since the government restored the Kong family mansion, cemetery and Confucian temple in Qufu and opened it to the public, there has been a revival of Confucianism in Beijing, the Chinese capital. Several international seminars on Confucius were held in Qufu in the 1980s. The China Confucius Foundation was established in 1984 and has sponsored many academic activities on Confucianism. The Shandong Publishing Commission Office has published the Guide to Confucian Culture, a comprehensive set of books on Confucius's life and the various schools of Confu-

cianism. See also ANCESTOR WORSHIP; BUDDHISM; CALLIGRAPHY; CHAN SECT OF BUDDHISM; CONFUCIUS; DAOISM; DONG ZHONGSHU; FAMILY STRUCTURE; FEUDAL SYSTEM; FILIAL PIETY; FIVE CLASSICS OF CONFUCIANISM; FIVE MATERIAL AGENTS; FOUR BOOKS OF CONFUCIANISM; HAN DYNASTY; HAN YU; HUMANITY; HUNDRED SCHOOLS OF THOUGHT; IMPERIAL BUREAUCRACY; IMPERIAL EXAMINATION SYSTEM; INK PAINTING; JESUITS IN CHINA; LANDSCAPE PAINTING; LEGALIST SCHOOL OF THOUGHT; LITERATI; MENCIUS; MOZI; MUSIC AND DANCE, CEREMONIAL; NEO-CONFUCIANISM; PROPRIETY; QIN DYNASTY; QUFU; RIGHTEOUSNESS; RITES CONTROVERSY; SONG DYNASTY; SUPERIOR MAN; TEMPLES; WANG BIE; WANG YANGMING; WARRING STATES PERIOD; WISDOM; WUDI, EMPEROR; XUNZI; YIN AND YANG; ZHOU DYNASTY; ZHU XI; NAMES OF INDIVIDUAL BOOKS, CLASSICS AND DYNASTIES.

CONFUCIUS (551–479 B.C.) The most important thinker in Chinese history. Confucius is the Latin version of his name, which in Chinese is Kongzi or Kongfuzi (K'ung Tzu or K'ung Fu Tzu; Master Kong or K'ung). His real name was Kong Qiu (K'ung Ch'iu), but Chinese do not refer to him by that name out of respect. The teachings of Confucius, known as Confucianism, were accepted as the orthodox school of thought by the Chinese imperial court from the Han dynasty (206 B.C.–A.D. 220) through the Qing (1644–1911), the last dynasty, and remain influential in China and parts of Asia, especially Taiwan, Singapore, Japan, Korea and Vietnam. His school is officially known as the School of Literati (*ru* or *ju*); the literati (*wenren* or *wen-jen*) are members of the scholar class who staffed the imperial bureaucracy. The teachings of the school are based on nine major texts known as the Five Classics of Confucianism and the Four Books of Confucianism. Down to this century, every educated Chinese has learned these texts, which formed the basis of the examinations for the imperial bureaucracy. According to Chinese tradition, Confucius compiled the *Spring and Autumn Annals* and edited and wrote commentaries on the *Book of Songs* and the *Book of History*. Modern historians question whether Confucius left any of his own writings. One of the five classics, the *Analects*, contains sayings attributed directly to Confucius that were recorded by his disciples.

A biography of Confucius was recorded in the *Shiji* (*Shih Chi*), the first history of China, written by Sima Tan (Ssu-ma T'an) and his son, Sima Qian (Ssu-ma Chien), during the reign of Han Emperor Wudi (Wu-ti; r. 141–87 B.C.). Confucius was born in Nishan, in the feudal state of Lu in modern Shandong Province, about 20 miles from Qufu, where the Kong family built its mansion. Chinese all over the world still celebrate his birthday on September 28. The Kong family mansion, cemetery and Confucian temple in Qufu have been opened to the public. Confucius's teachings were attacked as "feudalistic" during the Cultural Revolution (1966–76) and many buildings and relics in the Kong family compound in Qufu were damaged or destroyed. The Chinese government restored them in the 1980s, and in 1984 ceremonies were held for the unveiling of a restored statue of Confucius in Da Cheng Hall in the Confucian Temple.

The descendants of Confucius have been buried in the cemetery, known as the Confucian Forest, which contains the tomb of Confucius and those of his sons and hundreds of descendants. Family descent is traced from Confucius in an unbroken line through the eldest sons of 77 generations, who all resided at Qufu. The 77th direct descendant of Confucius, K'ung Teh-cheng, now resides in Taiwan, where he fled with the Chinese Nationalists (Kuomintang; KMT) when they were defeated by the Chinese Communists in 1949. At the beginning of 1993 K'ung, age 72, announced his resignation as head of Taiwan's Examination Yuan, the body that conducts examinations for the civil service.

Chinese filmmaker Wu Yigong (Wu Yi-kung) longtime head of the Shanghai Film Studio, made the dramatic film, *A Confucius Family* (1992). It tells the story of Confucius's contemporary descendants, a family with five generations living together, from Kong Xiangbi (K'ung Hsian-pi), the 75th-generation grandson, to Kong Chuixin (K'ung Ch'ui-hsin), the 79th-generation grandson, who still live in the Communist People's Republic of China. In winter 1990, Wu had visited Qufu and was affected by seeing the new tomb of a descendant of Confucius who had been educated and worked in Xinjiang in western China during the 1970s, had died there and was subsequently reburied in Qufu.

Confucius was born to a family of the lower aristocracy in the feudal state of Lu in Shandong. His father died when he was young and his mother raised him. He lived during the Warring States Period (403–221 B.C.), the final period of the Zhou Dynasty (1100–256 B.C.), when feudal states were contending with each other for dominance. This period ended when the first emperor, Qin Shi Huangdi, unified China under the Qin dynasty (221–206 B.C.). Confucius was one of many great thinkers of the time, which is considered the "golden age" of Chinese philosophy, embodied in the so-called Hundred Schools of Thought. He became prime minister of the state of Lu but resigned in 497 B.C. because he disapproved of the ruler's immorality. He became a teacher and attempted to train his students to be good advisers to the rulers they would eventually serve. He also traveled with his students to many different feudal states over a period of 13 years, and was given financial support by the feudal rulers he advised. Confucius was the first teacher in Chinese history to accept commoners as students in addition to members of the aristocracy.

Confucius was a conservative who looked back to the early days of the Zhou dynasty as the ideal period when rulers were benevolent and people lived together in harmony. His ideal human being was the gentleman (*junzi* or *chu-tzu;* "son of a prince"), the cultivated or superior man. For Confucius, a person becomes noble not by birth but through developing the five virtues of humanity or benevolence (*ren* or *jen*), righteousness (*yi*), proper conduct (*li*), wisdom (*zhi* or *chih*) and trustworthiness (*xin* or *hsin*). Confucius maintained that the relationship between fathers and sons is the basic model for both the family and society, in which the ruler should be virtuous and act as a father to his people. For Confucius the most important virtue is filial piety (*xiao* or *hsiao*), the respect and obedience of children toward their parents. When all family relationships are in order, including those between husband and wife and parents and children, then society will be orderly. Mencius (Mengzi or Meng-tzu; c. 372–289 B.C.), who expanded upon the thought of Confucius, became the second-most important Confucian thinker. Xunzi (Hsun Tzu; c. 298–238 B.C.) was another major Confucian thinker.

In 136 B.C. Han Emperor Wudi (Wu Ti) proclaimed Confucianism as the official state cult. During the Han dynasty, (206 B.C.–A.D. 220), all government schools began to conduct regular sacrifices to Confucius, who became the patron saint of the imperial bureaucracy. During the Tang dynasty (618–907), Confucius became worshiped as a deity. In 630 the Tang emperor decreed that a Confucian temple should be established in every province and county of the Chinese Empire, and in 647 these temples were made into national shrines to Confucius and those government officials whose scholarship had best contributed to Confucianism. See also CONFUCIANISM; FILIAL PIETY; FIVE CLASSICS OF CONFUCIANISM; FOUR BOOKS OF CONFUCIANISM; HAN DYNASTY; HUMANITY; HUNDRED SCHOOLS OF THOUGHT; IMPERIAL BUREAUCRACY; IMPERIAL EXAMINATION SYSTEM; LITERATI; MENCIUS; PROPRIETY; QUFU; RIGHTEOUSNESS; SUPERIOR MAN; WARRING STATES PERIOD; WISDOM; XUNZI; ZHOU DYNASTY; NAMES OF INDIVIDUAL BOOKS.

CONNECTIONS (*guanxi* or *kuan-hsi*) A network of friends and acquaintances who can help a person acquire goods, have a service performed, or get a good job or entrance to a school. Personal relations are very important in China, and people try to help each other using their connections with others who are in a position to provide what is needed. The Chinese commonly refer to this use of connections as "going through the back door" (*zouhoumen* or *tsou-hou-men*). Traditionally, the extended family was the basis of the connections network. However, since the founding of the People's Republic of China in 1949, a person's work unit (*danwei*) controls many aspects of his or her life, such as housing and food rations, and permission to marry, have children and travel, change jobs, or enter a university, the army or the Chinese Communist Party. Having good connections is essential for getting these things. Cadres, or people who have been indoctrinated in Communist ideology and methods and who hold responsible positions in the Party, have the best connections and therefore always receive preference. Cadres became the new elite group in Communist China because they were skillful in creating networks of connections, especially by ingratiating themselves with their superiors in the political sphere. Now that China is becoming more capitalist, connections are still extremely important. Many overseas Chinese are investing in their ancestral villages and regions. Their connections are termed the "Bamboo Network." See also CADRE; CHINESE COMMUNIST PARTY; OVERSEAS CHINESE; WORK UNIT.

CONSTITUTION, STATE, OF 1954 The first constitution of the People's Republic of China (PRC), which was founded by the Chinese Communist Party (CCP) in 1949 after it defeated the Chinese Nationalist Party (Kuomintang; KMT), led by Chiang Kai-shek. The first legislative and representative body of the PRC government was the Chinese People's Political Consultative Conference (CPPCC), which passed an Organic Law on September 22, 1949 specifying the procedures and structure for government operations. On September 29, 1949, the CPPCC proclaimed its Common Program, which served as the law of the PRC until 1954. The Common Program specified that the CPPCC was to be a temporary legislative body until the country was secure enough to hold elections for a National People's Congress (NPC). Although Chiang Kai-shek and his KMT supporters fled to Taiwan in 1949, the CCP wanted to make sure that it gained control of the entire country and overcame opposition to its policies throughout China.

The formal adoption of the 1954 state constitution centralized the authority of the government in the National People's Congress (NPC). In ascending order, voters at the local city or county level elected the base-level congress, which elected delegates to the provincial congress, which sent delegates to the NPC, which was elected for four years. In August 1954, the PRC held local elections to choose deputies to the First NPC, held in September. On September 20, 1954, the NPC promulgated the first formal state constitution of the PRC, which was partly modeled after the Soviet Union's 1936 constitution. Soviet legal advisers even helped the Chinese adapt the Soviet legal code in the 1954 constitution by rewriting it to fit Chinese conditions. The Chinese state constitution is a formal expression of the political values of the CCP and contains general statements of policy and outlines for the organization of the government.

The preamble of the 1954 constitution stated that the country was ready for "planned economic construction and gradual transition to socialism." The constitution emphasized the change from production based on private property to production based on various types of collective ownership and national planning. It granted citizens equality before the law and guaranteed women legal rights equal with those of men. It granted Chinese citizens freedom of speech, of correspondence, of demonstration and religious belief; specified that they could vote and could run for election; and granted them the right to an education, work, rest, material assistance in old age, and the ability to bring complaints to government agencies. It also granted them the right to a public trial and to offer a defense aided by a "people's lawyer."

Section IV of Chapter 2 of the constitution provided details on how the country was now divided into a complex bureaucratic hierarchy, listing the duties, terms of office, and powers of local governments and individual officeholders. The 1954 NPC elected Mao Zedong (Mao Tse-tung) chairman of the PRC, Zhou Enlai (Chou En-lai) premier of the State Council and Liu Shaoqi (Liu Shao-ch'i) chairman of the Standing Committee of the NPC. Mao and Zhou remained the two highest leaders of the CCP and the PRC until they both died in 1976. The position of chairman gave Mao most of the country's political power, as detailed in Articles 39 to 46 of the constitution. The premier nominated heads of ministries, who were confirmed by the NPC or its standing committee. The constitution also provided details on the role and operations of the courts and prosecutorial organs of the national government.

The NPC promulgated revised state constitutions in 1975, 1978 and 1982 to help the PRC recover from the Cultural Revolution (1966–76) by re-instating government bodies and institutions that had been suspended, such as the ministry of education. The 1982 constitution restored the posts of president and vice president of the PRC, established a state central military commission, and transferred administrative power from people's communes, which were disbanded, to local government bodies. Furthermore, it abolished life tenure in the highest government positions and limited national leaders to two consecutive terms in office. See also CHINESE COMMUNIST PARTY; CHINESE PEOPLE'S POLITICAL CONSULTATIVE CONFERENCE; GOVERNMENT STRUCTURE; LEGAL SYSTEM; NATIONAL PEOPLE'S CONGRESS; PEOPLE'S COMMUNES; PEOPLE'S REPUBLIC OF CHINA.

CONTAINER GARDENS (*penjing* or *p'en-ching*) Known in the West by the Japanese term *bonsai* ("tray planting;" *pencai* or *p'en-ts'ai* in Chinese); trees in miniature grown in pots using techniques that prevent them from growing very large yet enable them to retain the shape of full-grown trees (not to be confused with Western container gardens). Chinese gardens are designed to create a replica of the natural world in a courtyard inside a walled compound, and a container garden is a miniature version of such a garden. The Chinese invented the art of container gardens more than a thousand years ago, although little is known about its early history. They were probably inspired by stunted trees that were produced by natural conditions on high mountains or along the seacoast, such as strong winds, heavy snow and dry soil.

A container garden can be created by taking a stunted tree from nature and transplanting it into a container, but most are grown from seeds, cuttings or young trees. The container, usually dark in color, has drainage holes and usually has small feet to raise it slightly. The trees are kept small by pruning their branches and roots, pinching off new growth, and repotting them every one to three years. Wires are also wrapped around their branches and trunk to force them gently to grow into a specific shape. There are many different styles, such as an upright trunk; a trunk that grows in a slant; a tree that hangs over the container, twisted or gnarled; or one growing along a rock placed in the container with its roots exposed. Asymmetry is a desired feature in container gardens. Several trees may also be planted in one container to suggest a forest.

Container gardens can live for hundreds of years and may be handed down through the generations of a family. The Chinese also created the art of miniature gardens formed by arranging small stones and plants on trays, known as "tray scenery" (*bonseki* in Japanese). The stones replicate the large rocks with unusual shapes that are a common feature of Chinese landscape gardens.

Container gardens were introduced into Japan during the Kamakura Period (1185–1333) along with a variety of art forms associated with the Chan (Meditation) sect of Buddhism—known in Japan and in the West as Zen. The Japanese refined the art of container gardens, and it was introduced to America in the 1870s, where it has become quite popular. There are two major collections of container gardens, or bonsai, at the National Arboretum in Washington, D.C., and the Brooklyn Botanic Garden in New York City. See also GARDENS; ROCKS.

COOKING, CHINESE Cooking has been developed to a very high degree in China. Pottery remains of containers excavated from the Neolithic period (c. 12,000–2000 B.C.) indicate that steaming and boiling were the first main cooking methods, although stir-frying small pieces of food and seasonings quickly over high heat became another common Chinese-cooking method. These remains also show that even at that early time, grain was the most important food in the Chinese diet. The Chinese word for cooked rice, *fan*, is also the word for a lunch or dinner meal, which is centered around dishes of cooked grain, such as rice or rice products—noodles or dumplings—or steamed bread made from wheat flour. *Fan* is accompanied or "supplemented" by *cai* (*ts'ai*), which literally means "vegetables" but includes any cooked food, such as soybean curd, poultry, fish, seafood and meat, cut into small pieces that can easily be eaten with chopsticks. *Fan* includes all other cooked grains as well as rice, such as millet, wheat, sorghum and barley. Millet and wheat are the principle grains cultivated in northern China, while rice is the main grain in southern China, where the warmer and wetter climate can sustain two or even three crops each year. The Chinese grain-based diet was made possible by living in settled villages where grain and other crops were cultivated. These were some of the main traits by which the Chinese defined themselves as members of the Han Chinese ethnic group, in distinction to people they considered "barbarians," such as the nomadic tribes to the north and northwest who herded sheep, goats and horses. The Chinese also distill alcoholic beverages from grain, notably *maotai* (*mao-t'ai*), a strong drink made from sorghum used in toasts at banquets.

Some of the most important ancient artifacts comprise magnificent large bronze vessels from the Shang (1750–1040 B.C.) and Zhou (1100–256 B.C.) dynasties, such as the three-legged *ding* (*ting*), that were used to hold food and wine for ritual sacrifices. Salt was so vital that for 2,000 years the imperial Chinese government held a monopoly on it. Food and drink have always played a central role in all Chinese customs, festivals and ceremonial occasions, such as birthdays, weddings and funerals. While an ordinary homestyle meal may include grain and two or three dishes, a banquet has many courses that are served in a prescribed order and includes foods that have symbolic and auspicious meanings. The Chinese even prefer to hold banquets to conduct business negotiations. Chinese families traditionally keep a picture of the "Kitchen God" (or "Stove Prince") on their kitchen wall to keep watch over everything the family does. Before the new year, they ask him to say good things about them when he goes up to report to the ruler of heaven. While he is away, the family takes down his picture and puts up a new one of him for the upcoming new year.

The foods that the Chinese eat most frequently, such as rice, wheat, soybeans, cabbage, pork, poultry, and fish raised in fish farms, provide the greatest quantity for the least cost. The same is true of Chinese cooking techniques, which are very economical and fuel-efficient. Chinese cooks use the water in which vegetables have been boiled to make soup, which is consumed at the end of every traditional Chinese meal and is the main source of liquid in the diet. The Chinese infrequently bake or grill foods but prefer to boil or steam them, or stir-fry them quickly in oil in a wok, a large rounded open metal pan with handles. The chief cooking utensils include a wok and bamboo steamers, cleaver with a large rectangular blade, wooden chopping block, ladle and turner, strainers and long chopsticks. Small dishes of food can be steamed on top of rice while it boils in a large covered pot, or steamed in bamboo containers stacked over boiling water in a wok. Some foods are stewed for longer amounts of

time in clay pots, known as "sand pots," or fried in a deep or shallow amount of oil. Pieces of meat or poultry may also be "red stewed" in a large amount of soy sauce and water, with other seasonings such as ginger, scallions or sherry. Another well-known cooking method, especially in northern China, is the Mongolian hot pot, or fire pot, a metal stove with a chimney in the middle in which charcoal is burned. A large metal ring-shaped pan around the chimney holds broiling broth in which diners cook pieces of meat and vegetables to their own taste. After they have cooked all the food, the diners end the meal with the broth served in soup bowls. The Chinese traditionally eat fruit, such as oranges, litchis, plums and peaches, rather than rich desserts, although this habit is now changing. Chinese do not drink tea during but after a meal, and in fact tea is consumed all day long, sometimes accompanied by snacks, such as dumplings, served by street food vendors and in *dim sum* restaurants, especially in southern China.

The Chinese prefer to cook with the freshest seasonal ingredients possible, which, until recently, they purchased every day because they lacked refrigerators. They also preserve some foods, especially fish and vegetables, by salting, pickling or drying. While they prepare some dishes with a variety of seasonings, such as soy sauce, they serve others with small dishes of sauce so that each diner can control the flavor of his or her food.

Chinese cuisine has specific rules for preparing dishes by combining certain ingredients that taste good together, and for preparing a meal by combining certain types of dishes so that there is a variety of complementary tastes, textures, cooking techniques and so forth. The cook usually spends more time cutting or chopping the ingredients than cooking them over heat. The Chinese believe that many foods have medicinal value and keep people healthy. For example, watery soups containing many vegetables are considered a food, beverage and medicine. Both Chinese cooking and traditional Chinese herbal medicine are based on the ancient concept that everything in the universe is made up of two principles, the yin, or feminine, principle and the yang, or masculine, principle, which must be kept in balance. Certain types of food are believed to be able to correct an imbalance of yin and yang. Similarly, the Chinese classify foods as "hot" (yang) or "cold" (yin), not for their temperatures but for their effects on the body. A hot or cold condition in the body can be corrected by consuming food of the opposite type. For example, a fever, caused by eating too much "hot" food such as oily meat or fried and fatty food, can be cured by eating "cold" food such as crabs. In traditional Chinese medicine, a prescribed combination of roots, bark and other natural materials are boiled together in water to make a thin, dark liquid. Ginseng, a root, is one of the most widely used herbs in China.

There are four major regional schools of Chinese cooking. The cooking of the north is centered in Beijing (formerly known as Peking), China's capital since the 13th century, but also includes the styles of Tianjin and Qingdao cities and Shandong Province, the birthplace of Confucius. Chefs moved to Beijing from all parts of China, and the excellent restaurants in the capital area have incorporated many techniques from other regions. Some well-known Beijing dishes include Peking Duck, *mushu* pork, mandarin fish, and noodles and steamed breads made from wheat flour. People in northern China tend to eat more lamb, the preferred meat of the nomadic tribes that frequently invaded China and ruled it under the Yuan (1279–1368) and Qing (1644–1911) dynasties. Shandong Province is also renowned for its cuisine, which includes meat cooked in wine or smoked, sweet and sour dishes, and steamed breads.

The cooking of the east is centered in Shanghai, China's largest city and trading port, and also includes the style of such major cities as Nanjing, Suzhou, Hangzhou, Yangzhou and Ningbo. Shanghai cooking uses large amounts of soy sauce and sugar. Some popular dishes include honey ham, salt-cured chicken, preserved mustard-green soup, scallion fish and a wide variety of fish and seafood dishes. The cooking of the south is centered in Guangdong Province, the capital of which is the major port city of Guangzhou (Canton), and also includes the food of Fujian Province and Guangxi-Zhuang Autonomous Region. The southern is the best-known Chinese-cooking style around the world because large numbers of southern Chinese have emigrated to other countries. The southern Chinese consume a lot of fish and seafood. Some typical dishes include sea bass with black beans, shark fin soup, wonton, roast pork and suckling pig. The fourth style is the cuisine of Sichuan Province in the southwest, a fertile agricultural region known as a "land of abundance." Sichuan cooking tends to be spicy due to the widespread use of anise pepper and hot chili peppers (most families grow their own), but it also has sweet and sour tastes. Condiments with peppers are also available, such as thick hot pepper sauce, pickled hot peppers, chili-flavored oil and a thick broad bean sauce. There are more than 20 main methods of preparing Sichuan dishes. Sichuan dishes made with bean curd are renowned, such as *mapo doufu* (*ma-p'o tou-fu;* "Mrs. Pockmark's bean curd"), which combines white soybean curd cubes with fried ground beef in spices, green garlic shoots and crushed peppercorns. Other popular dishes include Sichuan duck, sliced pork in hoisin sauce, spicy chicken, and hot and sour soup. Hunan Province in south-central China is also known for spicy dishes and seafood, especially carp, a large freshwater fish (*yu*) that is served at most Chinese banquets. The word for fish is pronounced the same as the word for abundance, so the fish symbolizes wealth and good fortune for the Chinese. See also AGRICULTURE; ALCOHOLIC BEVERAGES; ANCESTOR WORSHIP; AUTUMN MOON FESTIVAL; BANQUETS; BEANS AND BEAN PRODUCTS; BRONZEWARE; CARP; CHICKEN; CHOPSTICKS; DIM SUM; DUCK; FISH AND SHELLFISH; FUNERALS; GINSENG; GRAIN; HAN; HUNGRY GHOSTS FESTIVAL; KITCHEN GOD; LITCHI; MAO-TAI; MEDICINE, HERBAL; MUSHROOMS; NEOLITHIC PERIOD; NEW YEAR FESTIVAL; NOMADS AND ANIMAL HUSBANDRY; NOODLES; ORANGE; PEACH; PIG; PLUM; RESTAURANTS AND FOOD STALLS; RICE; SALT MONOPOLY; SEASONINGS FOR FOOD; SOYBEANS AND SOY PRODUCTS; TEA; VEGETABLES AND VEGETARIAN DISHES; WEDDINGS, TRADITIONAL; WOK; YIN AND YANG; NAMES OF INDIVIDUAL CITIES AND PROVINCES.

COOLIE The Western term for a Chinese laborer. (The word *coolie* comes from the Hindi word *kuli,* probably imported from India by the British, to signify an unskilled laborer or porter.) In the treaty ports, which were Chinese cities opened to foreign trade in the mid-19th century, many thousands of coolies worked on the waterfronts. The large population and high birthrate in China provided a constant source of cheap labor. Thousands of coolies were coerced or even kidnapped to work in other countries. They carried goods between the foreign ships and the warehouses, called godowns. The coolies were supervised by compradores, Chinese men hired by foreign companies to manage their business. Many went to the United States and other countries in South America and Asia as credit contract laborers. Foreign shippers paid the fees for their passage and gave them several months' pay in advance for their families. This money would then be deducted in installments from the wages they earned in the country where they labored until the sum was fully repaid. The Chinese Six Companies strictly controlled Chinese laborers who went to the United States. In 1862, the U.S. Congress passed an act prohibiting the coolie trade. See also OVERSEAS CHINESE; SIX COMPANIES, CHINESE; TREATY PORTS.

CORAL (*shanhu*) A natural substance, frequently rosy orange in color, that the Chinese have used to make snuff bottles, carved figures and other decorative objects. Coral is a kind of limestone made by tiny animals known as coral polyps. They live in warm, shallow water and build limestone coatings around themselves for protection. (It takes nearly 10 years for a piece of coral to grow one inch.)

Coral is found in a number of beautiful colors and shapes, such as lacy fans or short, thick branches. There are about 300 varieties of coral in the world. Red is the most valuable. Coral polyps commonly live in groups, or colonies, and many tropical islands are surrounded by thick underwater walls called coral reefs. A coral reef can build up and combine with sand to form a whole island. The Zhoushan Islands in the South China Sea along the coast of Zhejiang Province, which form China's largest archipelago, contain many islands made up of coral reefs, including the Xisha Islands, the Zhongshan Islands and the Spratly (Nansha) Islands. Sparsely inhabited coral islands with large populations of sea birds also stretch for a thousand miles from Hainan Dao Island in southern China. Since ancient times, the Chinese have imported most of their coral from Sri Lanka (Ceylon) and Persia (modern Iran). They believed that coral represents a tree known as the *tieshu* (*t'ieh shu*), which grows at the bottom of the sea and produces flowers only once a century. Coral symbolized longevity and promotion in the Chinese imperial bureaucracy, and officials in the second of the nine ranks in the bureaucracy wore a coral button on their caps. The art of coral carving is similar to jade carving. The Chinese carve pieces of coral into decorative objects such as figurines and vases decorated with bird or flower motifs. See also IMPERIAL BUREAUCRACY; JADE; NINE-RANK SYSTEM; SNUFF BOTTLES; SOUTH CHINA SEA; SPRATLEY ISLANDS.

CORMORANT A large, black waterbird traditionally domesticated by Chinese fishermen to catch fish. Cormorants have been used for fishing for hundreds of years in China, and the practice was mentioned by Odoric of Pordenone (c. 1286–1331), who acted as an emissary between Pope Benedict XII and the Mongol emperor of China during the Yuan dynasty (1279–1368). The cormorants are tied to

Until recently outlawed, domesticated cormorants had been used for fishing for centuries in China.   DENNIS COX

the boats, and hemp ropes are placed around their necks to prevent them from swallowing the fish. They dive into the water and catch fish until their throats are full, then jump back onto the boats and disgorge the fish. Fishermen take the cormorants to fish during the night because the birds are afraid of the dark and will stay close to lanterns placed at the bows of the boats. However, in the past few decades the birds were catching so many fish that they were depleting Chinese fish stocks, so the government outlawed the domestication of cormorants. However, many traditional flocks of fishing cormorants can still be seen, especially on the Li River around the popular tourist city of Guilin in southwestern China.

The largest cormorant colony in China is on Bird Island (Niao Dao) in Qinghai Lake, China's largest salt lake, on the Qinghai-Tibet Plateau in western China. Thousands of the birds breed on the rocky shores or in trees, and feed on the abundant fish in the lake. Cormorants also nest on other plateau lakes in northwestern and southwestern China.

Cormorants lay two to four eggs at a time. The incubation period is 25 days, and baby birds leave the nest when they are 21 days old. See also GUILIN; QINGHAI, LAKE.

COTTON (*mianhua* or *mien-hua*)   One of the main textiles produced in China, along with silk and ramie, which is made from a plant fiber. Cotton is produced from the seed hairs of the cotton plant. The Chinese also use cottonseed oil for cooking. Cotton, which has been cultivated in India for 4,000 years, was introduced into China during the Song dynasty (960–1279), along with sorghum, a grain that became a major crop for food and the production of alcoholic beverages. A Chinese Daoist nun named Huang established the cotton industry in the lower Yangzi River valley. By 1300 the Chinese were using a kind of cotton gin—a machine with two rollers that squeeze the seeds out of raw cotton so that the plant fibers can be spun into yarn. Cotton textiles are sturdy and take colored dyes well. Members of the Chinese nobility and literati, or scholar class, wore silk robes, but the majority of the Chinese were peasants and workers who wore only durable homespun clothing. Until the 14th century such clothing was made from ramie or hemp fiber, but with the use of the cotton gin, they were made from cotton decorated with designs created with blue indigo dyes. Indigo-dyed textiles remain a popular folk craft in China.

During the Ming dynasty (1368–1644), cotton-cloth manufacture was an important cottage industry. Peasant wives spun cotton yarn to supplement the income from family farms. During the Qing dynasty (1644–1911), cotton manufacture became the largest handicraft industry in China. Suzhou, the largest city in the world in the 15th and 16th centuries, become a major center of production for high-quality silk and cotton textiles, which were sold throughout China and exported to Asia, Europe and even the Americas. However, Qing China had frequent shortages of raw cotton because a population boom induced farmers to produce food grains rather than cotton and other crops that had commercial value, and Chinese government policy prevented the import of much cotton from the outside world.

The production of cotton played a major role in the 19th-century Opium Wars in which Great Britain defeated China and forced it to open many more cities to foreign trade. The British traded British textiles with India; Indian cotton was sold to China by the British; and Chinese silks, porcelain and tea were sold by China to England. However, the Chinese did not want Indian cotton, and the British had to expend a great quantity of silver to make up their trade deficit. They decided to force on the Chinese the sale of opium and caused hundreds of thousands to become addicts. This reversed the trade deficit and great quantities of Chinese silver paid for opium were sent to England. Yet a British trade report written in 1866 states that cotton was grown extensively in China and was woven into a coarse, strong cloth worn by peasants and laborers. In the late 19th and early 20th centuries, cotton spinning and weaving was the largest domestic industry in China. After the Communists took over in 1949, the Chinese government reorganized and expanded cotton-textile production. Cotton cultivation increased in the areas around the port cities, which had established spinning centers, including Shanghai, Qingdao, Tianjin and Guangzhou. New spinning and weaving factories were also built near inland regions that grew cotton, such as the North China Plain. In 1983 China produced 4.6 million tons of cotton textiles, more than double the 1978 total. By the early 1990s China was cultivating a surplus of cotton. See also INDIGO DYEING OF TEXTILES; OPIUM WARS; RAMIE; SILK; SUZHOU; TEXTILE INDUSTRY.

COURTYARDS See ARCHITECTURE, TRADITIONAL.

COWHERD AND WEAVER MAID FESTIVAL (Qixi or Ch'i-hsi) Also known as the Double Seven Festival; a romantic festival celebrated on the seventh day of the seventh month in the traditional Chinese lunar calendar (around the beginning of July). It celebrates the legend of Zhinu, the Weaver Maid, the industrious daughter of the King and Queen of Heaven, who was given in marriage to a hard-working cowherd named Niulang from the western river of the "Heavenly Paradise." After they married, they enjoyed being with each other so much that their work did not get done. The disappointed King and Queen separated the two by putting the Milky Way, or "Heavenly River," in the sky and sent the Cowherd back to the west and the Maid back to the east. From then on they were only permitted to see each other once per year, on the seventh night of the seventh lunar month. They meet on the "Great Bird Bridge," formed by compassionate magpies across the Milky Way. The Chinese pray for good weather on this night so that the loving couple can enjoy a happy reunion. If it rains, the lovers are supposedly weeping because the magpies cannot form the bridge and the lovers must endure another year of separation. Based on ancient Chinese Daoist beliefs, Niulang represents agriculture and corresponds to the star Altair in the constellation Aguila. Zhinu symbolizes weaving and the star Vega in the constellation Lyra. At this time of year both stars are bright in the sky. Their two children, a son and a daughter, are the small stars near Vega. Traditionally, at the Cowherd and Weaver Maid Festival unmarried women made offerings to Zhinu, the patron deity of needlework, and held embroidery competitions. The festival has also become very popular in Japan, where it is known as the Star Festival, or *Tanabata*. See also CALENDAR; DAOISM.

COXINGA See ZHENG CHENGGONG.

CPPCC See CHINESE PEOPLE'S POLITICAL CONSULTATIVE CONFERENCE.

CRANE (*he* or *ho*) A graceful bird that is a Chinese symbol for long life and is frequently depicted in designs for textiles and other crafts. It is the second-most important bird in Chinese legend, after the phoenix, the symbol of the empress. The crane, usually shown under a pine tree, is also a symbol of longevity, as are the spotted deer and the tortoise. Legend has it that there are four kinds of crane: the white, the yellow, the blue, and the black, which is supposed to live for centuries. When a black crane turns 600 years old it no longer needs food, only water. According to legend, the crane takes an active role in human affairs, and humans have been transformed into cranes.

Xiwangmu, the beautiful Royal Lady of the West in the Daoist religion, is often depicted riding a white crane. Spirits traditionally ride to the "Western Heaven" on a crane. Thus the figure of a crane with its wings spread out may be placed on a coffin or on a banner in a funeral procession. In the imperial bureaucracy, the white crane was embroidered on the robes of civil officials who belonged to the fourth rank.

Nine of the 15 species of crane can be found in China, where the majority of cranes breed and spend the winter. As many as 2,000 Siberian, or great white cranes have wintered at the nature reserve at Lake Poyang. Rare Japanese, or red-crowned, cranes breed in the wild in several Chinese provinces, especially Heilongjiang, while some are also bred in captivity. Other species found in China include the white-naped, common, demoiselle and hooded cranes. The black-necked crane is the only species of crane which breeds and spends the whole year in the plateau wetlands of Qinghai, Tibet and Gansu provinces. These cranes are also being bred in captivity.

All species of crane build nests of dried grass on open ground near water. They lay one or two eggs, which they incubate for 31 to 33 days. Family groups migrate south during the winter and return to their original breeding grounds in the spring. See also DEER; FUNERALS; IMPERIAL BUREAUCRACY; PHOENIX; POYANG, LAKE; TORTOISE; XIWANGMU.

CUISINE, CHINESE See AGRICULTURE; BANQUETS; BEANS AND BEAN PRODUCTS; CHICKEN; COOKING, CHINESE; DIM SUM; DUCK; GRAIN; PIG; RESTAURANTS AND FOOD STALLS; RICE; SEASONINGS FOR FOOD; SOYBEANS AND SOY PRODUCTS; VEGETABLES AND VEGETARIAN DISHES; WEDDINGS, TRADITIONAL; WOK.

CULTURAL REVOLUTION (1966–76) Formally known as the Great Proletarian Cultural Revolution (*wuchan jieji wenhua da geming*); a movement initiated by Mao Zedong (Mao Tse-tung; 1883–1976) to purge the Chinese Communist Party (CCP) of reactionary influences and opponents of his revolutionary ideology. The U.S.S.R. had been a close ally of the PRC until the late 1950s and helped China develop its heavy industries by sending large numbers of technicians to China. However, around 1956 the two countries began growing apart ideologically and a rift developed, known as the Sino-Soviet Conflict, which contributed to the Cultural Revolution. In 1958 Mao announced the Great Leap Forward (1958–60), which intended to speed up China's development, especially that of heavy industries, in the spirit of the communist revolution that had established the PRC. But the Great Leap Forward turned out to be a disaster and resulted in severe famine and the erosion of thousands of acres of farmland. In April 1959, the CCP required Mao to step down as chairman of the PRC, and he was replaced by Liu Shaoqi (Liu Shao-ch'i; 1898–1969), although Mao remained chairman of the CCP. In September 1959 Mao replaced minister of National Defense Peng Dehuai (P'eng Teh-huai; 1900–), who advocated modernization of the PLA, with Lin Biao (Lin Piao; 1907–71), who emphasized revolutionary purity in the military. In 1960 CCP leaders persuaded Mao to cancel the Great Leap Forward and admit that it had failed. In April 1960 the PRC criticized Soviet leaders for being "revisionist," and in June the U.S.S.R. halted all aid to the PRC and called home the thousands of Soviet experts working in China. This devastated the Chinese economy.

In the early 1960s more moderate CCP officials such as Liu Shaoqi, Deng Xiaoping (Teng Hsiao-p'ing; 1904–97) and Peng Zhen (P'eng Chen; 1902–97) had gained influence in the CCP, and they initiated measures to stabilize the economy. But Mao fought to hold onto power in the Party. By 1962 he had denounced the Soviet government as a right-wing dictatorship which had turned to capitalism. He wanted to prevent the same thing from happening in the PRC, a major reason he launched the Cultural Revolution in 1966. In 1962 Mao began an ideological campaign known as the Socialist Education Movement (1962–65) against what he perceived as a trend toward capitalism and revisionism in the PRC. Many Chinese peasants had turned away from collectives and toward private enterprise, and many cadres (CCP officials) had become corrupt, taken bribes, misappropriated government funds and falsified financial records. Mao enacted a simultaneous campaign urging people "to learn from the People's Liberation Army." Lin Biao, minister of National Defense, urged members of the PLA and the CCP to follow the thought of Chairman Mao, and he compiled the *Quotations from Chairman Mao Zedong,* also known as the "Little Red Book," to indoctrinate PLA recruits with Mao's revolutionary thought. The Socialist Education Movement became a struggle between the moderate anti-Mao faction in the CCP and the pro-Mao radical faction that emphasized class struggle.

In September 1964 Liu Shaoqi, who had been informed about the corruption of CCP members in the Chinese countryside, issued a set of directives that tried to blunt the radical Maoist faction. In 1965 Mao urged the Politburo to begin a campaign to correct dissident intellectuals, but many party officials refused. Lin Biao and four other leaders supported Mao, but Liu Shaoqi and Deng Xiaoping opposed Mao and were supported by five other leaders, and Zhou Enlai abstained. This humiliated Mao, and some historians believe that he had now lost control of the CCP.

Mao retreated to Shanghai, the city where the CCP had begun and still a center for radical party members. Also, Jiang Qing (Chiang Ch'ing; 1914–91), Mao's wife, had been an actress there. From there Mao inaugurated his campaign to purge his opponents, including Liu Shaoqi, and to purify the CCP of reactionary influences. The Cultural Revolution began with an article published in a Shanghai newspaper on November 10, 1965, criticizing Wu Han, the deputy mayor of Beijing. He had written a historical play, *Hai Rui Dismissed from Office,* that seemed to be an indirect criticism of Mao's replacing Peng Dehuai with Lin Biao. Jiang Jing copublished the article with another CCP official named Yao Wenyuan. The article also implicated Peng Zhen, the First CCP Secretary of Beijing, who had allowed the play to be published. Peng Zhen later became the first member of the Politburo to fall in the Cultural Revolution. Chinese newspapers published editorials debating the issue.

By late March 1966 Mao was back in Beijing, where he attacked Peng Zhen at a meeting of the Politburo. On May 1, 1966, at a massive rally to celebrate International Workers Day in Tiananmen Square in Beijing, Zhou Enlai announced the formal start of the Great Proletarian Cultural Revolution. On May 16, the Politburo purged Peng Zhen and established the Cultural Revolution Group (CRG), comprising Jiang Qing and other pro-Mao radicals. The Politburo also called for attacks on "all representatives of the bourgeoisie who have infiltrated the Party, government, army and cultural world."

On August 18, 1966, Mao, Zhou, Lin Biao and other CCP officials presided over a massive rally, orchestrated by Jiang Qing, in Tiananmen Square in support of the Cultural Revolution. The Red Guards made their first public appearance at this rally. They were young Chinese, mainly students in their teens and 20s, who were given free railroad passes to travel to Beijing and other large cities from all over the country. Eleven million went to Beijing alone. Chinese institutions of higher education were closed and did not reopen until the late 1970s. The Red Guards held eight massive political demonstrations in three months in Tiananmen Square. Speeches at the rallies were usually given by Lin Biao, Jiang Qing, Zhou Enlai and Chen Boda (Ch'en Po-ta), Mao's personal secretary. Their subject was the reconstruction of the PRC through destruction of the so-called Four Olds: old ideologies, old culture, old customs and old habits. At each rally, Mao appeared to the Red Guards in person, wearing a Red Guard armband, and they spent hours shouting slogans and singing songs that praised him. One of the best-known songs was the Chinese Communist anthem, *The East Is Red* (*Dongfang hong*) by the composer He Luting (Ho Lu-t'ing; 1902–   ), which compares Mao's appearance in China to the rising of the sun.

On April 20, 1966, Red Guards began criticizing Liu Shaoqi for being a capitalist and destroying "bourgeois and feudal remnants." The Red Guards carried out Mao's orders to oppose feudalism, including Confucian thought, and capitalism. They expressed their revolutionary ideology and their criticisms of reactionaries on big-character posters (*dazibao*) hung on walls in public places.

The Red Guards vandalized bookstores, libraries, religious buildings, museums, historical sites and private homes, and even destroyed family altars and ancestral tablets. They physically beat and killed large numbers of people they accused of being bourgeois, especially those who had had contact with Western people and Western education, and burned their books, artworks and furniture. The great novelist Lao She (1898–1966), best known for *Rickshaw Boy,* was beaten to death in Beijing. Thousands of other Chinese committed suicide or were imprisoned. In 1968–69 about 20 million Chinese students and intellectuals were sent out of the cities to work in the countryside. Many performed manual labor, although the party also encouraged them to serve as primary school teachers, accountants for production teams on people's communes, or so-called barefoot doctors who were trained to provide basic medical services. The Chinese education, health and transportation systems were nearly destroyed, and scientists and archaeologists stopped doing research.

Mao's radical faction in the CCP attacked many Party officials for being revisionist, including State Chairman Liu Shaoqi, Mao's designated successor. Zhou remained loyal to Mao but attempted to mediate between the radical pro-Mao and moderate anti-Mao factions. In December 1966 the Socialist Education Movement was officially merged into the Cultural Revolution. By then every person in China had a copy of *Quotations from Chairman Mao Zedong.* The Red Guards began dividing into factions that fought with each other, and by 1967 China was on the verge of anarchy. In March 1967 the CCP turned to Zhou to conduct the daily affairs of the government. The Red Guards criticized Zhou in conjunction with their attacks on Confucianism, but Zhou survived and maintained his political base. He was never purged from office as were many officials under him, such as Deng Xiaoping and Chen Yi (Ch'en Yi). Deng was a member of the Politburo Standing Committee and general secretary of the CCP Central Committee, but he was arrested and accused of collaborating with Liu Shaoqi and labeled a traitor. By early 1967 Deng was removed from all of his positions except his CCP membership and was arrested and eventually sent to work in a tractor factory in Jiangxi Province.

The PLA high command was purged in early 1967, and regional military forces were ordered to establish military control and maintain order. But many regional commanders supported conservative party and government officials rather than Party radicals, and so the Red Guards attacked them.

Foreign developments helped temper the violent extremes of the Cultural Revolution. The United States was heavily involved in the war in Vietnam, which borders China to the south. In 1966–68 the USSR to the north steadily built up troops along its border with China, and in March 1969 Chinese and Soviet troops clashed in the area they disputed along the Wusuli (Ussuri) River. In 1968 the USSR also invaded Czechoslovakia. On July 28, 1968, Mao and other CCP leaders met with Red Guard leaders, criticized their armed struggles and abolished the Red Guards, which brought the most radical phase of the Cultural Revolution to an end. However, the turmoil did not really stop until Mao died in 1976 and the so-called Gang of Four was arrested and blamed for causing this revolution.

On October 22, 1976, the Party announced that four of the arrested radical leaders had been charged with a plot to overthrow the Chinese government. These included Jiang Qing and three other Politburo members, Yao Wenyuan, Wang Hongwen (Wang Hung-wen) and Zhang Chunqiao (Chang Ch'un-ch'iao). When the Gang of Four were arrested, the CCP was divided over the Cultural Revolution and its causes, and fighting broke out around the country. The government called out troops in January 1977, and in March it executed people it accused of being enemies of the CCP. For two years after the Gang of Four were arrested, CCP leaders continued their nationwide campaign to criticize them and blame them for everything that had gone wrong in China. As time went on, more and more far-fetched accusations were made against them. In death Mao was still so greatly respected that no criticisms were leveled against him; all blame was deflected to his widow and her three closest associates. Their actions were also associated with Lin Biao.

In 1977 the CCP confirmed Hua Guofeng as chairman of the Chinese People's Political Consultative Conference (CPPCC) and its Military Affairs Committee and restored Deng Xiaoping as deputy chairman of the CPPCC, vice premier of the State Council, and many other important positions. Deng became the leader of China's economic and political reforms based on the Four Modernizations that Zhou had advocated. The Party removed the Gang of Four from all of their CCP positions and expelled them from the Party.

In August 1977, at the 11th National Party Congress, Hua Guofeng declared the official end of the Great Proletarian Cultural Revolution. Many leaders who had been purged were rehabilitated and returned, and Deng Xiaoping was raised to the third-highest position in the Politburo, after Hua Guofeng and Ye Jianying. That year, academic and sci-

entific institutions that had been closed were reopened, intellectuals and scientists were brought back from the countryside and restored to their faculties and laboratories, and scientific journals resumed publication. Chinese authors began writing literature once more, and many novels and short stories exposed the abuses of power and the tragic waste of talent that had occurred during the Cultural Revolution, hence called the "literature of the wounded."

On March 5, 1978, the National Party Congress elected Hua Guofeng premier of the State Council, and Deng Xiaoping and others vice premiers. In 1978 the National People's Congress approved a new state constitution and proclaimed the Four Modernizations to rebuild and modernize China. In November 1978, big-character posters began appearing in Chinese cities, criticizing Mao for having supported the Gang of Four. In December 1978, Deng launched a major program for reforming Chinese political, social and economic institutions and even the CCP's Maoist and communist ideology. This became known as China's "Second Revolution." In 1979 the government rehabilitated thousands of Chinese intellectuals, restored them to positions of honor, and began rebuilding the education system. During the late 1970s and early 1980s most of the young people who had been sent to work in the countryside were able to move back to the cities and find jobs in the expanding Chinese economy.

The Gang of Four were not formally put on trial until November 1980, when a 35-judge special court was convened, which issued a 20,000-word indictment against the Gang of Four and 6 of Lin Biao's closest associates. The trial was a momentous event in modern Chinese history and greatly damaged the prestige of Mao and the political system he and his supporters had created. On January 25, 1981, the special court held its last session and rendered a guilty verdict against all 10 defendants. The Gang of Four were even airbrushed out of the photographs of Mao's funeral ceremonies. Jiang Qing refused to confess her guilt and claimed that everything she had done during the Cultural Revolution had been ordered by Mao himself. The court did not want to turn her into a martyr, especially if it were true that she had only carried out Mao's orders, and it commuted the death sentence on Jiang Qing and Zhang Chunqiao to life imprisonment.

In 1981 the CCP issued an official report stating that the chief responsibility for the Cultural Revolution "does indeed lie with Comrade Mao Zedong" and that, because of Mao's emphasis on class struggle, he had "confused right and wrong and the people with the enemy." Hu Yaobang (Hu Yao-pang; 1917–89), the newly elected CCP chairman, issued a statement on the 60th anniversary of the founding of the CCP asserting that "although Comrade Mao Zedong made grave mistakes in his later years, it is clear that if we consider his life work, his contributions to the Chinese revolution far outweigh his errors." Ten years later, Jiang Qing committed suicide on May 14, 1991, supposedly by hanging herself in prison. Some scholars believe that the CCP will eventually reverse her guilty verdict. See also ANCESTRAL TABLETS; BAREFOOT DOCTOR; BEIJING; BIG-CHARACTER POSTERS; CADRE; CHINESE COMMUNIST PARTY; CONFUCIANISM; DENG XIAOPING; EDUCATION SYSTEM; GANG OF FOUR; GOVERNMENT STRUCTURE; HE LUTING; HU YAOBANG; HUA

GUOFENG; INTERNATIONAL WORKERS DAY; JIANG QING; LIN BIAO; LIU SHAOQI; NIXON, RICHARD, U.S. PRESIDENT, VISIT TO CHINA; PENG DEHUAI; PENG ZHEN; PEOPLE'S LIBERATION ARMY; PEOPLE'S REPUBLIC OF CHINA; POLITBURO; QUOTATIONS FROM CHAIRMAN MAO ZEDONG; RED GUARDS; SHANGHAI; SINO-INDIAN BORDER DISPUTE; SINO-SOVIET CONFLICT; SOCIALIST EDUCATION MOVEMENT; STATE COUNCIL; TIANANMEN SQUARE; UNITED NATIONS AND CHINA; VIETNAM WAR; WUSULI RIVER; YE JIANYING; ZHOU ENLAI.

CURRENCY, HISTORICAL   The traditional Chinese system for using metal coins, pieces of printed paper or other objects as money. In the second millennium B.C., strings of cowrie shells were used as money in China. Bronze objects such as tools and weapons then became a medium of exchange, and during the Spring and Autumn Period (772–481 B.C.) and the Warring States Period (403–221 B.C.), different types of bronze coins were minted by various Chinese states. Archaeologists have discovered bronze spades and knives that were used as money. Southern Chinese states used cowrie-shaped pieces of bronze and stamped bars of gold for large transactions.

Qin Shi Huangdi (r. 221–210 B.C.), the first Chinese emperor and unifier of China under the Qin dynasty (221–206 B.C.), standardized a system of currency as well as a system of weights and measures. This system used round coins with square holes in the middle so that they could be collected on strings. These strings of copper coins were called "cash" in Chinese. When Chinese trade increased with the expansion of the empire during the Han dynasty (206 B.C.–A.D. 220), especially along the so-called Silk Road, the Han government took strict control over the minting of coins. The large amounts of copper cash that merchants needed to transport for commercial transactions eventually became unwieldy. Local military governors did not want their provinces to lose their reserves of copper cash, so they sometimes put limits on trading. To resolve the problem, merchants initiated the use of bills of exchange or deposit certificates, which the Chinese imperial court adopted by issuing deposit certificates at a 3-percent interest charge. Merchants could deposit their copper cash with the government and receive a certificate that could be circulated as a form of money. These certificates, and the immense amount of copper needed as trading, increased during the Tang dynasty (618–907), inspiring the Chinese to invent paper money, which was first printed in 1024 in Chengdu in Sichuan Province by the Song dynasty (960–1279). This was the first use of paper money in the world. Paper money rapidly spread throughout the Chinese Empire, even among the peasant class.

The system for printing and circulating paper money during the Mongol Yuan dynasty (1279–1368) was described by the Italian explorer Marco Polo (1254–1324), who spent 17 years serving the Yuan court. The Mongols realized that China could not produce enough copper to make bronze for the large quantity of coins needed to circulate throughout the vast Chinese Empire, so the Yuan dynasty declared that paper money would be the legal currency in China, with bronze coins allowed for small transactions and silver ingots for large ones. Polo was amazed that the small rectangles of paper had the same financial authority as if they were made

of gold or silver. On each piece of paper money, specially appointed government officials wrote their names and impressed their seals or name stamps, and then the head official stamped it with his seal in vermilion to make the paper money authentic. Europeans may have first learned about the technique of printing from this paper money printed in China.

During the Ming dynasty (1368–1644), the use of paper money collapsed in the mid-15th century, but the Chinese economy was saved by imports of silver. Spanish galleons sailing from Acapulco, Mexico, brought enormous quantities of silver bullion from the Americas through Manila in the Philippines to be traded for Chinese silk and porcelains. The Portuguese also traded significant amounts of silver, from both Macao and Japan, with China. These imports of silver, which in some years totaled more than one million Chinese ounces, enabled the late Ming to experience an economic revival which carried over into the Qing dynasty (1644–1911). In the 17th century, China also imported large amounts of copper from Japan to mint coins.

In the 19th century, the Qing had to contend with European nations attempting to open China to foreign trade, which had always been strictly regulated by the Chinese government. China began losing large amounts of silver as the Europeans, especially the British, flooded the country with opium. Qing attempts to control the opium trade and prevent silver from leaving the country resulted in China's defeat by Great Britain in the Opium War (1839–42). The Treaty of Nanjing that concluded the war forced China to open more ports to foreign trade and to pay a large indemnity to Great Britain. China had to make similar agreements with the United States and France, and it entered a century of exploitation by and warfare with foreign powers that destroyed its traditional economy. In the 20th century, the Chinese Nationalists (Kuomintang), whose lengthy civil war with the Chinese Communists was interrupted by the Japanese invasion of China in the 1930s, printed so much paper money that the result was hyperinflation. Chinese money had so little worth that a wheelbarrow of paper money could only buy a small bag of rice, and many Chinese merchants fled the country.

When the Communists defeated the Nationalists and founded the People's Republic of China (PRC) in 1949, the country experienced economic turmoil while people fought to change their paper money into gold. The PRC standardized a system of currency known as *Renminbi* (RMB: "People's Money") which is still being used. See also BANK OF CHINA; BRONZEWARE; CURRENCY, MODERN; MACAO; OPIUM WAR; PAPER; POLO, MARCO; PRINTING; QIN SHI HUANGDI; SEALS; SILK ROAD.

CURRENCY, MODERN (*renminbi*)   The currency of the People's Republic of China (PRC) issued by the People's Bank of China, the Renminbi (RMB; "People's Money"). After the Chinese Communist Party (CCP) founded the PRC in 1949, the government nationalized China's banking system and centralized it under the People's Bank of China, which has a foreign exchange arm known as the Bank of China. In 1951 the government tried to control inflation by unifying the country's monetary system, through the creation of the RMB. The basic unit of RMB is the *yuan*. A *yuan* is divided into 10 *jiao* and 100 *fen*. One *jiao* is equal to 10 *fen*. *Yuan, jiao* and *fen* are issued in paper notes, and coins. *Yuan* notes are issued in denominations of 1, 2, 5, 10 and 50; *jiao* notes in denominations of 1, 2 and 5; and *fen* coins in denominations of 1, 2 and 5. There are also a 1 *yuan* coin, a 5 *jiao* coin, and 1, 2 and 5 *fen* notes. The Chinese government prohibits people from transporting RMB into or out of China, so travelers must convert RMB into foreign currency before leaving the country. The PRC formerly required foreign tourists and Chinese visitors from Hong Hong, Macao and Taiwan to use Foreign Exchange Certificates (FEC), also known as "tourist money," to pay for government hotels, rail and air travel, and international telephone calls and faxes.

FEC were printed in paper notes in denominations of 1, 5, 10, 50 and 100 *yuan* and 1 and 5 *jiao*. Tourists were allowed to pay for other things with RMB. The Chinese government abolished the use of FECs in 1994, so tourists now pay for everything with RMB. In 1994 the *renminbi* was devalued by nearly 50 percent, which had helped keep it strong during the recent Asian financial crisis. See also BANK OF CHINA; CURRENCY, HISTORICAL; PEOPLE'S BANK OF CHINA; PEOPLE'S REPUBLIC OF CHINA.

CYTS See ALL-CHINA YOUTH FEDERATION; CHINA INTERNATIONAL TRAVEL SERVICE.

DABIE MOUNTAIN RANGE A range of forest-covered mountains, running southeast to northwest in Hubei Province and forming Hubei's border with Anhui and Henan Provinces in central China. Like the Qinling Mountain Range to the northwest, the Dabie Mountain Range forms the catchment area between the drainage basins of two major rivers, the Yangzi (Changjiang) and the Huai (Huaihe). It also serves as the boundary between the northern warm-temperate deciduous forest and the southern subtropical evergreen forest. Although the Dabie Mountains are not very high, with the tallest peaks only about 3,300 feet above sea level, they are home to a large variety of animals and plants native to the two regions that they straddle. These include many species of pine, magnolia, camellia, paulownia and bamboo. Two extremely rare plants are the metasequoia, a conifer from the Tertiary era, which elsewhere is usually found only as a fossil, and the ginkgo biloba, which dates back even earlier to the Jurassic era and is now nearly extinct. See also BAMBOO; CAMELLIA; GINKGO; HUAI RIVER; HUBEI PROVINCE; QINLING MOUNTAIN RANGE; YANGZI RIVER.

DADU See BEIJING; HEBEI PROVINCE; KHUBILAI KHAN; YUAN DYNASTY.

DAGU, QING DYNASTY FORTS AT See ARROW WAR; TIANJIN, TREATY OF.

DAI (Tai) One of the main ethnic and linguistic groups among China's 55 national minority groups; also known as the Lu. The Dai linguistic group includes, in addition to the Dai people, the Bouyei, Dong, Gelo, Li, Maonan, Mulam, Primmi, Sui and Zhuang national minorities who inhabit southwestern and southern China. In 1990 there were more than one million Dai living in the southwestern province of Yunnan, mainly in the Xishuangbanna Autonomous District (Prefecture) of the Dai people. *Xishuangbanna* is the Chinese translation of *Sip Sawng Panna,* the Dai name for the region meaning "12 rice-growing districts." The Dai in Yunnan are closely related to the Dai in Thailand, Burma, Vietnam and Laos; the latter three form the southern border of Yunnan. During the Chinese Cultural Revolution (1966–76), many Dai fled across the southern border into Thailand, Burma, Vietnam and Laos. In order to prevent further Dai emigration, after the Cultural Revolution the Chinese government granted them the Xishuangbanna Autonomous District. This district is situated in the southernmost region of Yunnan with its capital located on the Mekong River. The city, formerly known as Jinglan but now called Jinghong, had been the capital of a Dai kingdom in the 13th century. The ruins of many Dai Buddhist temples from that era, a large number of which were destroyed during the Cultural Revolution, are now being restored. The Mongols invaded Yunnan when they ruled China under the Yuan dynasty (1279–1368). The Chinese took the area when they overthrew the Mongols and founded the Ming dynasty (1368–1644).

The Dai in Yunnan live in remote tropical forests in steep mountainous areas. There is also a group of Northern Dai residing in Guangxi and Guizhou provinces, but their language is distinct from Southwestern Dai and they have been highly assimilated so that their culture, clothing and dwellings resemble those of the Han, the majority Chinese ethnic group. The Southwestern Dai wear the long, colorful sarongs worn by Dai in Southeast Asia, practice the religion of Theravada Buddhism, which is dominant in Southeast Asia but not in China, and live in houses built aboveground on high pilings. Their writing system resembles those used in Laos and Burma. The Dai love to attend festivals where they sing and dance. Their main celebration is the Water Splashing Festival for the New Year, held in the spring and so named because the Dai have fun throwing water on each other to symbolize the removal of dirt and unhappiness in the old year and renewal in the new year. See also BOUYEI; DONG; GUIZHOU PROVINCE; MINORITIES, NATIONAL; XISHUANGBANNA AUTONOMOUS PREFECTURE OF THE DAI PEOPLE; YUNNAN PROVINCE; ZHUANG.

DAI AILIAN (1916–) An internationally renowned Chinese dancer and dance educator. Though born to a Chinese merchant family that had emigrated to Trinidad from Guangdong Province in southern China, Dai has lived in China for more than 50 years. She enjoyed dancing as a child and began studying dance at age 5. In 1931 she went to London, where she studied ballet and modern dance for nine years and was introduced to Japanese, Indian and Indonesian dance. In 1940 Dai traveled to Hong Kong, where she fell in love with Ye Qianyu (Yeh Ch'ien-yu), a Chinese painter. They went to Chongqing in Sichuan Province, the capital of Nationalist China during China's War of Resistance against Japan (1937–45; World War II), where Dai taught ballet and modern dance at several government-run schools. She studied the history of Chinese dance and choreographed two dances based on the information she had gathered. Since opera performed in various regions of China, such as Guangdong and Guangxi Provinces, contains many dance movements, Dai traveled to such areas to further her research on Chinese dance. She also studied the dances of several of China's minority ethnic groups, such as the Dais, Naxis, Tibetans and Yis. In 1945, Dai and her husband spent two months at Kangding in Sichuan Province, studying Tibetan folk dances. The following year, she stimulated a great interest in minority folk dances when she and her students performed several of them at a conference in China. They performed in theaters in Chongqing and Shanghai. In 1946–47 Dai and her husband visited the United States and Trinidad. She and her students performed at the Brooklyn Academy of Music in New York City.

After the Chinese Communists founded the People's Republic of China in 1949, Dai became the vice chairman of the Dancers' Association of China and director of the Central Ballet Group and held that position until 1955. Two works she choreographed in the 1950s, "Lotus Dance" and "Flying Apsaras," won international folk dance awards. She also trained a professional group of folk dancers who belonged to China's various ethnic minorities. In 1954 she was appointed president of the Beijing Dance Academy. During the Cultural Revolution (1966–76), she was prevented from doing any artistic work and was forced to labor in the countryside for four years. In 1978 she was once again vice chairman of the Dancer's Association. In 1979 she visited Great Britain, the United States and Trinidad, and in 1979–80 she visited several European countries.

In the 1980s, Dai began using Laban dance notation to record and preserve minority folk dances and wrote two books, *Eight Tibetan Nationality Dances* and *Eight Yi Nationality Dances.* She also established the Everybody Dances Club. In 1982 Dai was elected vice chairman of the International Dance Association Council of UNESCO. In 1983 she was a member of the jury at the International Choreography Competition in Turin, Italy. In 1985 she was Deputy Director of UNESCO's Dance Council. She has spent much of her time traveling throughout Asia, the United States, and Europe to lecture on Chinese dance, attend academic conferences and judge international ballet competitions. See also MINORITIES, NATIONAL; OVERSEAS CHINESE; TIBETAN; YI.

DAI DONGYUAN   See DAI ZHEN.

DAI JIN (Tai Chin; 1388–1455)   Also known as Dai Wenjin (Tai Wen-chin); a landscape painter whose followers became known as the Zhe (Che) School, after his native Zhejiang (Chekiang) Province. Dai Jin was born in Hangzhou in Zhejiang, which was a major cultural center ever since it had been the capital of the Southern Song dynasty (1127–1279). He painted, for a time, in the Academy of the Ming dynasty (1368–1644) court in Beijing, but lost his position when one of his paintings offended the emperor, and he returned to Hangzhou around 1430. Although Dai Jin had been a professional court painter, he and his colleagues in Zhejiang painted in the amateur literati (*wen ren*) or scholarly Southern Song School in which landscape painting was a means of expressing moral views. It was closely associated with the fine art of writing with a brush, as if he were writing calligraphy. He utilized techniques from the earlier Ma-Xia School (named for Ma Yuan and Xia Gui), such as broad ink washes and "ae-cut strokes" (*cun* or *ts'un*), but he also executed many paintings in his own strong and expressive style. His most famous painting is the long horizontal rolled scroll, *Fishermen on the River.* Sadly, Dai Jin died in poverty and without recognition of his greatness, but after his death he gained a reputation as a great painter. Dai Jin's brushwork had a great influence on later painters, in Japan as well as China. See also CALLIGRAPHY; HANGZHOU; LANDSCAPE PAINTING; MA YUAN; SOUTHERN SCHOOL OF PAINTING; XIA GUI.

DAI QING   See THREE GORGES WATER CONSERVANCY PROJECT.

DAI WENJIN   See DAI JIN.

DAI ZHEN (Tai Chen; 1723–77)   Also known as Dai Dongyuan (Tai Tung-yuan); the greatest Chinese philosopher and scholar of the Qing dynasty (1644–1911). He was born to a poor family in southern Anhui Province but was able to acquire an education. It was said that Dai Zhen was so inquisitive that he frequently asked questions that his teachers could not answer. By age 16 he had memorized all the Confucian classical texts and their commentaries. However, he was never able to pass the examinations for the imperial bureaucracy. He taught school for two years, then spent the rest of his life producing scholarly works in a variety of subjects including philosophy, mathematical history, astronomy, philology, phonetics and textual criticism. In 1773 the imperial government appointed Dai Zhen a compiler of the *Four Libraries* (or *Four Treasures*), which position he held until he died at age 54. His greatest works are his *Commentary on the Meaning of Terms in the Book of Mencius* (*Mengzi Ziyi Suzheng* or *Meng-tzu Tzu-yi Su-cheng*) and *An Inquiry on Goodness* (*Yuan Shan*).

Dai Zhen's major philosophical concern was the method by which one could determine the truth, or "principle of things." He opposed the Rationalist School of Neo-Confucianism, whose members, notably Zhu Xi (Chu Hsi; 1130–1200), asserted that the principle of things existed in the human mind and could thus be realized through mental discipline and introspection. Dai Zhen maintained that for the Neo-Confucianists, the principle of things was completely subjective. He argued that principle of things could be found within the things themselves, studied objectively through scientific method, which entails observation and analysis. This mode of study belonged to the so-called Han School of Thought, whose members looked back to the writings of Confucian masters during the Han dynasty (206 B.C.–A.D. 220), before Confucianism was influenced by Daoist and Buddhist ideas. For example, the Rationalists claimed that human beings should use reason to suppress their desires. Dai Zhen argued that the Confucian sages taught that desires and feelings are natural and that people should channel their desires in the proper direction rather than suppress them. See also IMPERIAL EXAMINATION SYSTEM; MENCIUS; NEO-CONFUCIANISM; ZHU XI.

DAIMIAO TEMPLE See TAI, MOUNT.

DAIREN See DALIAN.

DALAI LAMA The leader of the Yellow Hat Sect (*dGe lugs pa*) of the Tibetan form of the Buddhist religion, known as Lamaism, and the religious and political leader of Tibet. In the 16th century the Grand Lama of the Yellow Hat monastery in Lhasa, the capital of Tibet, received the title Dalai, meaning "ocean" or "measureless." He was believed to be an incarnation of Avalokiteshvara, the Buddhist deity of compassion and mercy. Each Dalai Lama is believed to be the reincarnation of the previous one. The Mongols, who ruled China under the Yuan dynasty (1279–1368), supported Tibetan Lamaism after the third Dalai Lama converted the Altan Khan, the most powerful Mongol ruler of his time, to the religion. In 1643 a Mongol leader named Guushi Khan helped the Dalai Lama and his Yellow Hat Sect defeat the older Red Hat Sect of Lamaism, his major opposition, which made the Dalai Lama the undisputed religious leader of Tibet. The fifth Dalai Lama rebuilt the Potala Palace as his residence in Lhasa, the capital of Tibet, and established his political control over much of the country. In 1652, shortly after the Manchus overthrew the Ming dynasty (1368–1644) and established the Qing dynasty (1644–1911), the fifth Dalai Lama traveled from Tibet to Beijing to pay tribute to the Manchu Qing emperor and acknowledge his suzerainty. However, he and his successors continued to support the Mongols against the Qing. In 1720 the Qing removed the Mongolian choice as Dalai Lama and installed their own candidate in this position. By the middle of the 18th century the Qing had established a protectorate in Tibet. China continued to control Tibet and the Dalai Lamas, although in 1906 the British forced China to grant them trading and diplomatic privileges in Tibet. The Communist People's Republic of China (PRC), founded in 1949, made Tibet a Chinese Autonomous Region.

The current Dalai Lama is Tenzin Gyatso (1935–), the 14th Dalai Lama. He was born into a peasant family, but at age 2 he was recognized, following Tibetan tradition, as the reincarnation of the 13th Dalai Lama. He was educated in Tibetan Buddhist studies for 18 years, passed a rigorous set of examinations, with honors, and completed the *Geshe Lharampa*, the highest level of scholarly achievement in Buddhist philosophy, which is comparable to a doctorate. China

sent troops into Tibet in 1950 and signed an agreement in 1951 with the Dalai Lama to allow Tibet's theocratic system to continue but under Chinese control. The Chinese treated the Tibetans brutally, torturing or murdering many of them and destroying their monasteries. The Tibetans rebelled against the Chinese in 1958–59 but were harshly suppressed. The Dalai Lama, along with tens of thousands of Tibetans, fled to northern India, where he established his government-in-exile in Dharamsala. He continues to use this as his base but travels all over the world, teaching Tibetan Buddhist ideas and advocating self-determination for Tibet, gaining many non-Tibetan followers and supporters. In 1988 the Dalai Lama informed the Chinese that he would no longer insist upon Tibet's sovereign independence, but the Chinese government refused to open negotiations with him. The Dalai Lama has always advocated peaceful means for resolving the problem of Tibet's status, and he was awarded the Nobel Peace Prize in 1989.

In 1995, when the Dalai Lama celebrated his 60th birthday—a major occasion for Asian people—with three days of meetings and prayers, the Chinese government denounced him and demanded that the Indian government prevent him from conducting political activities during the celebration. The Indian government replied that it supported the Dalai Lama's freedom of expression. That year the Dalai Lama also became embroiled in a conflict with the Chinese government over the selection of the 11th Panchen Lama, the second-most important Tibetan Lama. He confirmed the selection of a six-year-old boy in the Tibetan village of Nagqu as the reincarnation of the Panchen Lama. However, the Chinese government claimed that it has final authority over the recognition of important lamas, under a 1792 treaty between Tibet and the Qing government, and rejected the validity of the Dalai Lama's choice and selected another boy as Panchen Lama. The issue is still disputed. See also BUDDHISM; LAMAISM; LHASA; POTALA PALACE; QING DYNASTY; TIBET; TIBETAN.

DALI See KUNMING; YUNNAN PROVINCE.

DALIAN (Ta-lien) A city in Liaoning Province in Manchuria (northeastern China) that has played an important role in modern Chinese history and is the largest port in Manchuria; also known as Luda, modern Dalian, formed by combining the cities of Lushun (formerly known as Port Arthur) and Dalian, is strategically located on the southern tip of Liaodong Peninsula, which divides the Bo Hai Gulf from the Yellow Sea. Dalian, the largest port in Manchuria and the second-largest in China, controls the entrance to the Bo Hai Gulf and lies directly across the gulf from Tianjin, the port for the capital city of Beijing. During the Qing dynasty (1644–1911), Dalian was the main base for Chinese coastal defenses.

In the late 19th century, Russia, Britain, France, Germany, Japan and the United States attempted to increase their trade with China by taking control of different regions in the country. Russia built the port at Dalian in 1899 after China gave it concessions in the strategic ports of Port Arthur and Dalian (Luda). Russia sent a large number of troops into Manchuria during the antiforeign Boxer Uprising in 1900 and China allowed them to stay. Japan came into conflict with Russia over Manchuria and Korea and initiated the Russo-Japanese War (1904–5). Japanese troops marched through Korea into Manchuria, landed on Liaodong Peninsula and occupied Dalian, and also took Port Arthur. In May 1905, the Japanese navy destroyed the Russian Baltic fleet in the Battle of Tsushima. Japan forced Russia to hand over its concessions in Port Arthur and Dalian; control of the South Manchuria Railway, and the southern half of Sakhalin Island; and to give Japan exclusive rights in Korea. Japan continued to enlarge the port facilities in Dalian until they were completed in 1930, after which Japanese troops invaded Manchuria and set up the puppet state of Manchukuo (Manzhouguo or Manchou-kuo in Chinese). In 1937 Japan invaded China Proper from Manchuria. After Japan was defeated in 1945, the Chinese Communists and Nationalists resumed their civil war. The Communists won in 1949 and established the People's Republic of China (PRC). They began rebuilding Dalian and other Chinese cities.

Modern Dalian has a population of about 2 million. The broad, deep-water port remains ice-free year-round, and a new harbor was completed in 1976 to accommodate oil tankers. Major products exported through the port include petroleum, coal, timber, grain, machinery, pig iron and steel products. In 1973, the Nianyuwan oil terminal was built to handle oil brought from the Daqing Oil Field through a 604-mile pipeline. The Dalian Shipyard, originally built in 1898 and one of the largest enterprises managed by the China Shipping Industry Corporation, produced China's first 50,000-ton oil tanker and also the first 27,000-ton bulk-cargo freighter designed according to international standards. The Dalian Steel Mill produced one-third of China's annual output of high-speed tool steel in 1985. Dalian is also an important area for fishing and seafood processing, as well as for marine scientific research.

In 1980 the Chinese government established a modern management-training center at Dalian and, in 1984, established the Dalian Economic and Technological Development Zone (EATDZ). This was the first of 15 Chinese EATDZs, smaller than the special Economic Zones (SEZs) but having the same function of encouraging foreign trade, that were opened along the Chinese coast. A new port has been constructed in Dayao Gulf, near Dalian, that is one of China's four largest international transhipment ports.

Today, Japanese companies comprise the largest number of foreign investors in the Dalian zone. Many Dalian residents learned the Japanese language when Japan controlled Manchuria (1932–45). The city has also become a popular health resort because of its mild climate, beaches, seaside parks such as Xinghai (Starfish) Park and sanatoriums. Edible seaweed is cultivated in the waters off Xinghai. See also BO HAI GULF; DAQING OIL FIELD; FISH AND SHELLFISH; IRON TECHNOLOGY AND STEEL INDUSTRY; KOREAN WAR AND CHINA; LIAODONG PENINSULA; LIAONING PROVINCE; MANCHUKUO; MANCHURIA; RUSSO-JAPANESE WAR OF 1904–5; SHIPPING AND SHIPBUILDING; SPECIAL ECONOMIC ZONES; YELLOW SEA.

DALIANG   See KAIFENG.

DAMANSKY ISLAND   See WUSULI INCIDENT; WUSULI RIVER.

DANCE   See ACROBATICS AND VARIETY THEATER; DAI AILIAN; KUNQU; OPERA, BEIJING; OPERA, GUANGZHOU; STILT WALKING; TAIJIQUAN; YANGKO.

DANDIAN   See QI; QIGONG.

DANDONG HARBOR   See YALU TSUNGPO RIVER.

DANWEI   See WORK UNIT.

DAO ZHUN   See JADE EMPEROR.

DAOAN   See BUDDHISM; KUMARAJIVA.

DAODEJING   (*Tao-te ching*)   The most important book in Daoism (Taoism), one of the two native Chinese religious and philosophical traditions, along with Confucianism. *Dao* (*Tao*) means "way," "path," or "road," and *de* (*te*) means "vast virtue," resulting in the English translation *The Book of the Way of Virtue* or *The Way and Its Power*. The book is also known as the *Laozi* (*Lao Tzu*), the name of the supposed author of the *Daodejing*. Legends place Laozi contemporary with the historical figure of Confucius (551–479 B.C.); however, the *Daodejing* is actually a composite work by a number of authors, some of whom may have dated back centuries before Laozi supposedly lived. By the second century A.D., Laozi had been transformed into a superhuman being. His worship was formally organized and supported by the Tang dynasty (618–907), whose emperors claimed to be descended from him, even though this had no basis in historical fact.

The *Daodejing* is a short book composed of brief chapters containing about 5,000 Chinese characters. It uses poetic, symbolic, and paradoxical expressions to describe the ultimate power which animates everything that exists. Many Chinese thinkers have written commentaries on the *Daodejing*. The book has had an enormous influence in Chinese culture, and other cultures as well, as it remains the most widely translated Chinese book.

Whereas the books in the Confucian canon attempt to regulate the behavior of rulers and their subjects, the *Daodejing* argues that the best kind of government is that which governs least. The ideal ruler is a wise man who is in harmony with the Dao, and thus governs effortlessly, so that his people would not even be aware that they were being governed. According to Laozi, wisdom entails studying oneself, and the wise man "takes no action" that interferes with anything, but leaves things alone. This concept of "actionless acting" or "acting without acting" is known as *wu wei*. A person with this ability acts in a yielding manner compared to water, which flows everywhere and seems to be weak yet is actually stronger than anything else. Such a person is in harmony with the *Dao*, the source or "Mother" of all things that exist, which does nothing (*wu wei*) and yet leaves nothing undone.

The *Dao* is said to be eternal, infinite, unchanging, self-sufficient, empty and silent. Laozi compares the Dao to a block of wood that has not yet been carved into a form. The *Dao* is formless and cannot be grasped as an object. It is the fundamental, undivided unity in which is resolved all the contradictions and differentiations that beset everything that exists.

One is able to know the *Dao* through silence and "returning to the root." Laozi advocates that the sage become gentle, like a newborn baby. Although the *Daodejing* presents its own unique theory of government, in China the book became associated with men of the literati, or scholar class, who chose to retire from active government service to live in quiet harmony with the natural world. See also CONFUCIANISM; DAOISM; LAOZI; LITERATI.

DAOFU See SOYBEANS AND SOY PRODUCTS.

DAOGUANG (EMPEROR) See LIN ZEXU.

DAOISM (Taoism) One of the three main religious traditions in China, along with Confucianism and Buddhism. Confucianism and Daoism are native Chinese traditions, whereas Buddhism was introduced into China from India around the first century A.D. The Chinese have a traditional saying that they are Confucianists in public and Daoists in private. The Confucian emphasis on the patriarchal extended family and the practice of honoring deceased ancestors, known as ancestor worship, were two of the most important ways by which the Han ethnic Chinese defined themselves as a people. The government of the Han dynasty (206 B.C.–A.D. 220) decreed that Confucianism was the orthodox state cult, and Confucian temples were established all over the Chinese Empire. But Daoism also appealed to the Chinese because of its emphasis on personal freedom and harmony with nature. According to legend, the founder of Daoism was Laozi (Lao Tzu or Lao Tze, "Old Master; also known as Lao Tan), supposedly a contemporary of Confucius in the sixth century B.C. Laozi is credited with writing the most important Daoist text, the *Daodejing* (*Tao Te Ching;* also known as the *Laozi* or *Lao Tzu*), although the text was actually written down in the third century B.C. By the second century A.D., Laozi had been transformed into a superhuman being whose worship was formally organized. The founder of the Tang dynasty (618–907), Emperor Gaozu (Kao-tsu; r. 618–26), claimed to be descended from Laozi and built an ancestral temple at the site where Laozi was supposedly born.

Dao (*tao*) means "way," "path" or "road," and *de* (*te*) means "vast virtue," so the *Daodejing* (*jing* or *ching* means "book") has been translated into English as *The Book of the Way of Virtue* or *The Way and Its Power.* Whereas the classical texts in the Confucian canon are concerned with regulating the behavior of rulers and their subjects, the *Daodejing* argues that the best kind of government is that which governs least. The ideal ruler is a wise man who is in harmony with the *Dao* and thus governs effortlessly, so that his people are not even be aware of being governed. According to Laozi, wisdom entails studying oneself, and the wise man "takes no action" that interferes with anything but leaves things alone. This concept of "actionless acting" or "acting without acting" is known as *wu wei.* A person with this ability acts in a yielding manner compared to water, which flows everywhere and seems to be weak yet is actually stronger than anything else. Such a person is in harmony with the *Dao,* the source, or "Mother," of all things that exist, which does nothing (*wu wei*) and yet leaves nothing undone. The *Dao* is eternal, infinite, unchanging, self-sufficient, empty and silent; it is also

formless and cannot be grasped as an object. It is the fundamental, undivided unity in which all the contradictions and differentiations that beset everything that exists are resolved. One is able to know the *Dao* through silence and "returning to the root."

The second-most important Daoist thinker was Zhuangzi (Chuang Tzu; 369–286 B.C.), who produced a body of Daoist writings collectively known as the *Zhuangzi* (*Chuang Tzu*), one of the most profound of all Chinese literary and philosophical works. Zhuangzi made his points by using humor, stories, metaphors, allegories and paradox rather than systematic arguments. He expressed the Daoist view that all things are constantly moving and changing, and the wise person knows how to yield and flow with the Dao by "doing nothing," not interfering in the workings of the universe but seeking harmony with nature. In the political sphere, the ideal ruler is one who does not interfere in the working of his kingdom.

After Buddhism was introduced into China, translators of Buddhist texts used many Daoist terms to express Buddhist concepts in the Chinese language. Buddhism had an enormous number of canonical texts, which stimulated Daoists to compile a Daoism canon. However, Daoists traditionally kept these texts hidden from people not initiated into the religion. Modern scholars of Daoism rely on the edition of the Daoist canon, which includes more than 1,400 texts, that was printed during the Ming dynasty (1368–1644) and preserved at the White Cloud Temple in Beijing, formerly the Daoist center in northern China.

Buddhism also had a highly developed system of temples and monasteries administered by priests, monks and nuns. In the second century A.D., Daoists responded to the new religion by organizing their own tradition into a formal religion, known as the Way of Celestial Masters, and establishing the Daoist priesthood. While Confucianists emphasized ethics and political and social organization, Daoist priests were associated with magicians or shamans, known as *wu,* who helped Chinese peasants by performing rituals to gain benefits from good deities and dispel evil spirits, and to make contact with spirits of the deceased. Eventually, popular Daoism became divided into two broad schools, the northern and southern. The northern school, known as "Perfect Truth," is stricter and requires priests to leave their homes and live as ascetics, refrain from consuming alcoholic beverages and certain forbidden foods, and train others to become priests. The more lenient southern school allows priests to marry and have families and to enjoy alcohol and meat when not observing religious fasts. The head, or "Heavenly Master," (*tianshi* or *t'ien-shih*) of the southern school did have some prestige, and remains the head of the religion, but he never had authority over Daoism comparable to that of the pope in Roman Catholicism. The imperial Chinese government issued ordination certificates to Daoist and Buddhist priests. Transmission of the Daoist religion occurred on a personal basis from master to disciple. Daoism developed a close relationship with the Chan (Zen) sect of Buddhism, which also emphasizes the personal transmission of enlightenment from master to disciple.

Chinese popular religion mixed together elements of Daoism and Buddhism. The Daoist pantheon absorbed a large number of Chinese popular deities, the best known of which are the Jade Emperor, Eight Immortals (*baxian* or *pa hsien*), Xiwangmu (Hsi-wang-mu) and Mazipo (Ma Tsu P'o). The Jade Emperor, the August Personage of Jade Yudi (Yu-ti), is the ruler of Heaven and its bureaucracy, which mirrors the imperial bureaucracy on Earth. The Eight Immortals are eight human beings who were believed to have gained immortality through their strenuous efforts in meditating, performing good deeds and making sacrifices. They are not worshiped in temples, but their pictures and symbols have been depicted in murals and wall carvings to represent long life and immortality. They are also a common design motif in many Chinese arts and crafts, and carved images of the Eight Immortals are placed on tables at birthday parties. There are actually 11 figures, for the immortals send 2 children riding water buffaloes to summon the God of Longevity, who carries the peach of immortality.

The Eight Immortals received permission to dine together at the Peach Festival to honor Xiwangmu, the Royal Lady (or Mother) of the Western Paradise, the heavenly realm where one was believed to go after death. Anyone who eats a peach from the Heavenly Peach Orchard next to her palace is believed to gain immortal life. Xiwangmu represents the yin, or female, principle, and her consort, Dong Wanggun (Tung Wang-kun) or Mugong (Mu Kung), the Royal Lord of the East, who keeps the register of the Daoist gods, represents the yang, or male, principle. Li Tieguai (Li T'ieh-kuai), the patron of Chinese herbal medicine doctors, is the most beloved of the Eight Immortals. He was the first to gain immortality, after Xiwangmu cured his leg ulcer, and he is depicted as a crippled beggar with a crutch, carrying a gourd of magic medicine to bring the dead back to life. Mazipo is the Daoist Queen of Heaven and Holy Mother, and she is especially revered by Chinese sailors and fishermen, with many temples to her situated along the southern Chinese coast and in Taiwan and Hong Kong. Mazipo is also associated with Guanyin (Kuan-yin), the Buddhist goddess of mercy, and has been compared to the Virgin Mary in Christianity.

Daoists were also involved in alchemy, the search for a chemical substance known as the elixir or pill of immortality that will bring immortal life when ingested. Traditional Chinese herbal medicine, which is still practiced and is being adopted by Western doctors, is related to Daoist alchemy. The first emperor, Qin Shi Huangdi, who unified China under the Qin dynasty (221–206 B.C.) was obsessed with finding this elixir of immortality. He brought Daoist shamans into his court and made several journeys to the Chinese coast seeking the "Islands of the Blessed" where the Immortals supposedly dwell. He took his imperial title from the Yellow Emperor, Huangdi (Huang-ti), who, according to legend, brought political order to China and taught the Chinese people many things necessary for their survival, and then rose to Heaven (*tian* or *t'ien*) as an immortal. Emperor Qin Shihuangdi traveled to Mount Tai (Taishan) in Shandong Province to make offerings to Heaven to legitimize his reign. Mount Tai, also known as "Eastern Peak" (Dongyue) is the most sacred of the "Five Sacred Mountains of Daoism," also known as the "Five Guardian Peaks" (*wuyue* or *wuyueh*) of the Chinese Empire. These include Mount Tai, the eastern mountain where the sun rises; Mount Heng in Shanxi Province, the northern mountain; Mount Hua in

Shaanxi, the western; Mount Heng in Hunan Province, the southern; and Mount Song in Henan Province, the mountain in the center. Laozi supposedly lived in a cave near Mount Song. Similarly, the Buddhist religion reveres Four Sacred Mountains in China.

Many Chinese emperors, such as Wudi (Wu-ti; r. 141–87 B.C.) of the Han dynasty, patronized Daoist alchemists and consumed numerous chemical substances that they believed would bring them immortality. Between 389 and 404, the emperor of the Northern Wei dynasty (386–534) established at his capital a professorship of Daoism and a Daoist laboratory for preparing medical concoctions. However, many alchemists kept their knowledge a secret, and some even became political subversives. An alchemist and faith healer named Zhang Jiao (Chang Chiao) led the Yellow Turbans Rebellion against the Han dynasty in A.D. 184, which greatly weakened the dynasty. Many Daoist secret societies arose throughout Chinese history and threatened later dynasties, even in recent times, such as the Eight Trigrams Rebellion against the Manchu Qing dynasty (1644–1911). The Eight Trigrams (*bagua* or *pa kua*) comprise an ancient Chinese theory that uses symbols for heaven, earth, thunder, wind, water, fire, mountains and water. The trigrams are themselves based on the ancient theory of yin and yang. These theories are also related to the ancient theory of the "Five Material Agents," associated with the elements of water, fire, wood, metal and earth.

The classical Chinese text, the *Book of Changes* (*Yijing* or *I-ching*), contains a complex system of divination based on the trigrams. This book became a classical Confucian text but was also claimed by the Daoists, who wrote commentaries on it that reflect their attempt to develop a general scientific theory. Ge Hong (Ko Hung; 283–343) is considered the greatest Chinese Daoist alchemical writer. In addition to developing scientific method and such important inventions as gunpowder, Chinese alchemists also developed many respiratory techniques and physical exercises that aim to preserve the body's *qi* (*ch'i*, or energy or vital force). These were incorporated into the Chinese martial arts (*wushu*), such as *gigong* (*ch'i-kung*), *kung fu* (*gongfu*) and *taijiquan* (*t'ai-chi ch'uan*), a slow, dancelike exercise routine that large numbers of Chinese people still practice outdoors every morning.

The writings of Laozi and Zhuangzi became popular with Chinese intellectuals, such as the group known as the Seven Sages of the Bamboo Grove, during the period of disunion between the fall of the Han dynasty in 220 and the reunification of China under the Sui dynasty. The Sui established a Daoist institute for the study of such subjects as astrology and *feng shui* (geomancy), and as a means of controlling the Daoist priests. Knowledge of the Five Classics of Confucianism had been the basis for the examination system by which scholars were selected to staff the imperial bureaucracy or civil service. In 741, under Tang Emperor Xuanzong (Hsuan-tsung; r. 712–56), new imperial examinations were introduced for scholars who chose to be tested on Daoist rather than Confucian texts. The next year he issued a decree stating that the main texts of the Daoist canon had the same status as the classical texts of Confucianism. Emperor Xuanzong himself, a great patron of Chinese arts and scholarship, acquired a diploma certifying his knowledge of Daoist thought. However, while Daoism coexisted with Confucianism, it never displaced Confucian learning as the official Chinese ideology.

Chinese landscape painting, known as *shanshuihua,* or "mountains and water," after its main subjects, was strongly influenced by the Daoist reverence for the natural world. This style of painting attained its full development during the Song dynasty (960–1279) and remained the dominant style into the modern era. Chinese landscape painters depicted human beings—when they included them in their compositions—as tiny figures in a vast expanse of nature. Traditional Chinese gardens also emphasize the Daoist theme of mountains and water, using rocks and ponds to create a microcosm of the mountains and lakes found in nature.

Knowledge of Daoism spread beyond the borders of the Chinese Empire ruled by the Han ethnic Chinese. Several new Daoist sects developed under the Jin dynasty (1115–1234), established by the Jurchens, who ruled northern China until the Mongols displaced them. The two most important new Daoist sects were the Supreme Unity (Taiyi or T'ai-yi) and Perfect Realization (Quanzhen or Ch'uan-chen) sects. The latter preserved Daoist monasticism into the modern era. The Mongol leader Genghis Khan had an interest in the religion and brought a Daoist priest into his court to counsel him on political matters as well as Daoist techniques for immortality. Genghis Khan rewarded the priest by issuing a decree in 1223 that Daoists were exempt from taxation. Buddhist and Daoist leaders vied for imperial favor, and in 1255 the Mongol leader Mongke had them conduct a debate in his presence. It was judged that the Daoists lost, but they refused to accept this decision. Further debates were held in 1256 and 1258, when the Daoists lost again and some of their texts were condemned and burned by Mongol officials at the Mongol capital at modern Beijing. However, Mongol leader Khubilai Khan, who founded the Yuan dynasty (1279–1368), the first non-Han Chinese dynasty to govern all of China, established relations with the head of the Daoist religion in southern China and allowed Daoists some influence in his court.

The Daoist religion continued to be practiced until the present era and still flourishes in Taiwan, Hong Kong and overseas Chinese communities in Southeast Asia and around the world. The 64th Celestial Master Chang lives in exile in Taiwan, where the Chinese Nationalists fled in 1949 after they were defeated by the Chinese Communists, who founded the People's Republic of China (PRC) in 1949. There are still a few Daoist monasteries in the PRC, which permits the religion to function under the Chinese Daoist Association. Daoist priests perform rituals to benefit the well-being of the members of their religion, such as rituals to "request peace and calm" (*qiu pingan* or *ch'iu p'ing-an*) or "improve one's destiny" (*buyun* or *pu-yun*). They "open the eye" (*kaiyan* or *k'ai-yen*) of a wooden statue by invoking the deity to take up residence in the statue and perform the elaborate ritual of renewal (*jiao* or *chiao*), which invokes deities to descend upon a Daoist temple and the village or neighborhood it serves. Such community festivals, which are expensive and require many days to perform, are held regularly in Taiwan and Hong Kong. See also ALCHEMY; BOOK OF CHANGES; BUDDHISM; CHAN SECT OF BUDDHISM; CINNABAR; DAODEJING; DAOIST CLASSICAL TEXTS; EIGHT IMMORTALS; EIGHT TRIGRAMS; EIGHT TRIGRAMS REBELLION; ELIXIR OF IMMORTALITY; FENG SHUI; FIVE MATERIAL AGENTS; FIVE SACRED MOUNTAINS OF DAOISM; GAOZU, EMPEROR; GARDENS; GE HONG; GENGHIS KHAN; GUANYIN; HAN; HONG KONG; ISLANDS OF THE BLESSED; JADE; JIN DYNASTY; KHUBILAI KHAN; KUNG FU; LANDSCAPE PAINTING; LAOZI; MARTIAL ARTS; MAZIPO; MEDICINE, HERBAL; PEACH; QI; QIGONG; QIN SHI HUANGDI, EMPEROR; SEVEN SAGES OF THE BAMBOO GROVE; TAI, MOUNT; TAIJIQUAN; TAIWAN; TEMPLES; XIWANGMU; YELLOW EMPEROR; YELLOW TURBANS REBELLION; YIN AND YANG; ZHUANGZI.

DAOIST (TAOIST) CLASSICAL TEXTS (*Daozang* or *Tao Tsang*)   A collection of documents that became accepted as canonical scriptures in the native Chinese religion of Daoism. In the second century A.D., the Daoist philosopher Wei Boyang (Wei Po-yang; fl. 147–67), wrote *The Kinship of the Three Ways of the Yellow Emperor, Laozi, and the Book of Changes* (*Cantongqi* or *Ts'an-t'ung-ch'i*), in which he attempted to synthesize Daoist thought and alchemy with the ideas of the Yin-Yang school of thought and the *Book of Changes* (*Yijing* or *I Ching*). This book became the source for several Daoist classical scriptures. In the third century, Gohong (Ko Hung; 253–333?) wrote *The Philosopher Who Embraces Simplicity* (*Baopuzi* or *Pao-p'u Tzu*), an important text in the Daoist philosophy of religion, which attempts to combine Daoist alchemical thought with Confucian ethics. When the Daoist canon was first printed in 1116, the texts filled 5,481 paper-bound volumes. However, these texts were traditionally kept hidden from those who were not initiated into the Daoist religion. Modern scholars of Daoism rely on the edition of the Daoist canon, which includes more than 1,400 texts, that was printed during the Ming dynasty (1368–1644) and preserved at the White Cloud Temple in Beijing, formerly the Daoist center in northern China. This collection includes 5,385 books bound in the Chinese style and known as *juan* (*chuan;* literally, "scroll," although they are similar to booklets).

The Daoist canon is divided into two categories known as Three Vaults and Four Supplements. The First Vault is based on texts of the Mao Shan School that were transcribed by Yang Xi (Yang Hsi) during visions that he had from 364 to 370, in which a group of Perfected Ones from the "Heaven of Exalted Purity" (*Shangqing* or *Shang-ch'ing*) dictated the texts to him; they are thus called the *Shangching* scriptures. The Second Vault includes scriptures of the Lingbao (Ling Pao; or "Sacred Jewel") School that supposedly derived from three high-ranking deities known as "Heavenly Reverences" (*Tianzun* or *T'ien-tsun*). The primary text of the Third Vault is the *Scripture of the Three Sovereigns* (*Sanhuangwen*), whose origin is not known but which Daoists associated with the lords of the three cosmic realms: heaven, earth and human. The main scriptures of the Four Supplements were not added to the Daoist canon until the sixth century, but they are actually older than those of the Three Vaults. The First Supplement includes the most important Daoist texts, the *Daodejing* (*Tao te-ching*) and the *Zhuangzi* (*Chuang Tzu*). The *Daodejing,* translated as *The Book of the Way of Virtue* or *The Way and Its Power,* is also known as the *Laozi* (*Lao Tzu,* "Old Master"; also known as Lao Tan), the name of the supposed author of the book. Chinese legends place Laozi in the sixth century B.C., contemporary with the historical figure of Confucius, but the *Daodejing* was actually written down in the third century B.C. The *Zhuangzi* comprises the writings of the Daoist philosopher Zhuangzi (fourth century B.C.). The Second Supplement is the *Scripture of Supreme Peace* (*Daipingjing* or *T'ai-p'ai-ching*), comprising discussions between a "Heavenly Master" and disciples called "Perfected Ones." This scripture influenced members of the Yellow Turban Secret Society, who fought a rebellion against the Han dynasty in the late second century A.D. The Third Supplement includes scriptures on alchemy and the search for the elixir of immortality, and also includes the *Sunzi* (*Sun Tzu*), a military treatise named for its author. The Fourth Supplement comprises scriptures from the oldest Daoist School, the Way of Heavenly Masters. See also ALCHEMY; BOOK OF CHANGES; DAODEJING; DAOISM; ELIXIR OF IMMORTALITY; LAOZI; SUNZI; YIN AND YANG; ZHUANGZI.

DAOJI   See SHI TAO.

DAOZANG   See DAOIST CLASSICAL TEXTS.

DAQING OIL FIELD   China's largest inland oil field, which is located under the city of Daqing in Heilongjiang province in northeastern China (Manchuria), the largest oil producer of all the Chinese provinces. Drilling operations began at Daqing in 1958 with Soviet technical assistance. The Soviet experts left the following year, but the Chinese were able to continue drilling on their own and first struck oil on September 26, 1959. By 1963 Daqing was producing about 2.3 million tons of oil per year. The discovery of major oil fields in Shandong Province, Tianjin special municipality and other regions enabled the Chinese to meet all of their domestic petroleum needs by the mid-1960s. By 1974 they were able to export 6.6 million tons of crude oil to Japan. In the 1970s the Chinese laid their first oil pipeline, from Daqing to the port of Qinhuangdao on the Gulf of Bo Hai in Hebei Province. The pipeline began operating in 1974 and was extended to the capital city of Beijing in 1975. Daqing, formerly a small town, grew rapidly with the construction of apartments to house the families of workers in the petroleum industry there. Daqing produced stable oil yields until 1990. China developed the 45 oil fields at Shengli, in the Huang River delta in northern Shangdong Province, to succeed Daqing. See also BO HAI, GULF; ENERGY SOURCES; HEILONGJIANG PROVINCE.

DARUMA   See BODHIDHARMA.

DATONG   A city in northern Shanxi Province with a population of nearly 1 million. It is a mining and industrial center and a major railroad juncture between Shanxi and Hebei provinces and Inner Mongolian Autonomous Region. Datong's coal industry grew rapidly in the 1920s with the manufacture of coal-burning steam engines, and today Shanxi produces the most coal of any Chinese province. (The only functioning steam-locomotive factory in the world is in Datong.) Other industries have also become important to the city's economy, including agricultural machinery, cement, carpets and shoes. Bronze ware is a famous local product. Datong is located on a dusty, arid plain 4,000 feet

In the hills outside Datong, Buddhist cave temples contain statues and bas-reliefs carved by thousands of sculptors in the fifth century.
DENNIS COX

above sea level, just south of the Great Wall and the border of Inner Mongolia. Datong's importance dates back to the fourth century A.D. when Toba invaders, a Turkic people from Central Asia, conquered northern China and established the Northern Wei dynasty (386–534) with their capital at Datong, then called Binzheng, and adopted Buddhism as their state religion. Buddhist cave temples were carved by thousands of laborers and sculptors at Yungang in the Wuzhou Hills west of Datong, beginning in A.D. 460. Among them were fifty-three caves containing more than 51,000 bas-reliefs and statues of Buddha and other Buddhist deities. The largest statue is 55 feet high. The caves can still be seen, although many statues have been vandalized and taken to foreign museums. Buddhist sites in Datong include Upper Huayan Monastery, Lower Huayan Monastery and Shanhua Monastery. Datong declined in importance when the sixth Northern Wei emperor moved the capital to Luoyang in A.D. 494. The town flourished again under the Liao dynasty (947–1125) when the Liao people made it one of their secondary capitals and gave it the name Datong, meaning "Great Harmony." It remained a strategic fortified town against nomadic invaders on China's frontier, especially against the Mongols during the Ming dynasty (1368–1644).

The renowned Nine Dragon Screen (Jiulong Bi) in the center of Datong is the largest and oldest of its kind in China. It was built for the residence of Zhu Gui, the 13th son of the first Ming emperor, Hongwu (Hung-wu; r. 1368–99) but in 1644 the entire complex burned down except for the screen. Made of colored ceramic tiles, it depicts nine dragons rising from the sea and flying toward the sun. The reflection of the dragons in a small pool in front of the screen makes them seem to writhe when the wind blows. See also ARCHITECTURE, TRADITIONAL; BUDDHISM; DRAGON; GREAT WALL; LIAO DYNASTY; NORTHERN WEI DYNASTY; SHANXI PROVINCE.

DAXUE See GREAT LEARNING.

DAYAN TA See XI'AN; XUANZANG.

DAZIBAO See BIG-CHARACTER POSTERS.

DAZU CAVE TEMPLES AND SCULPTURES (Dazu Shike) A large group of Buddhist cave temples and sculptures carved from stone and scattered around Dazu County about 120 miles northwest of Chongqing in Sichuan province. Dazu County is one of the most important Buddhist archaeological sites in China, especially since the carvings were executed four centuries later than those at other sites in southern China such as Dunhuang and Yungang, which were carved prior to the late Tang dynasty (618–907). The Dazu carvings were created during the Tang and Song (960–1279) dynasties and include the last series of rock sculptures carved in China during the Song. These evince a greater freedom of expression than earlier carvings.

In the Dazu region there are more than 50,000 sculptures divided among 40 sites. Of these, 13 are major, but the largest number of caves and sculptures are located at two sites, on Beishan (Northern Hill; also known as Longgangshan, Dragon Mound Hill) and on Baoding Mountain (Treasure Peak Mountain, Baoding Shan), each of which contains about 10,000 sculptures. At Beishan, the earliest sculptures were carved in 892 into rocks chosen as a military stronghold by Wei Junjing, then the military leader of Sichuan. He is commemorated by an inscription and sculpture at the entrance to Beishan. Wei commanded the construction of the first Buddhist temple at Beishan. Cave 136, the best preserved of the caves at Beishan, depicts Puxian, the patron deity of Mount Emei, riding a white elephant and Guanyin, the Buddhist goddess of mercy. It also has a magnificent carved wheel representing the cycle of life and death in Buddhist thought, along with 20 carvings of Buddhist deities and animals. Cave 125 houses a large sculpture of Guanyin, while Cave 245 contains a splendid portrayal of the "Western Paradise" ruled by the Buddhist deity Amitabha (Omitofo) that includes more than 1,000 small carvings depicting scenes from Buddhist sutras (scriptures). A pagoda on the mountaintop is the sole remnant of the Buddhist monastery that once stood on Beishan.

The sculptures at Mount Baoding, considered the most beautiful of all the carvings at Dazu, were executed between 1179 and 1249. The funds for this work were collected by the monk Zhao Zhifeng, who made Mount Baoding a center of the Mizong Tantric sect of Buddhism. Zhao planned the carvings to be a unified group, and the miniature model he constructed to guide the carvers still exists. The Great Buddha Crescent (Dafowan) is about 545 yards long and reaches 33 yards at its highest point. Here lies the most famous sculpture at Dazu, a 34-yard-long depiction of the Sleeping Buddha entering Nirvana that is 102 feet long and over 16 feet high. Two other important sites in the Dazu region are located at the Southern Mountain (Nanshan), also topped by a pagoda, and at Shimen Mountain (Shimenshan). See also AMITABHA; BUDDHISM; DUNHUANG CAVE PAINTINGS AND CARVINGS; GUANYIN; YUNGANG CAVE TEMPLES AND SCULPTURES.

DEEP SIGNIFICANCE OF THE SPRING AND AUTUMN ANNALS See DONG ZHONGSHU.

DEER (lu) A gentle animal that has an important position in Chinese mythology, art and traditional herbal medicine. The symbolic meanings of the deer are many. The deer symbolizes the salary of a government official, which is also pronounced lu. The Chinese traditionally believed that the deer lived a very long life, and so the animal became a Chinese symbol of longevity associated with Shou Lao, the God of Longevity. This deity is often depicted riding a stag (male deer with antlers), holding the peach of immortality and surrounded by a type of mushroom known as the lingzhu (lingchu) fungus, which also represents immortality. The deer is supposedly the only animal that can find the lingzhu fungus. The deer is also depicted with other symbols of immortality, including the crane, pine tree and tortoise.

There are many species of deer native to China. Among them, a spotted deer known as the Sika or Japanese deer (Cervus nippon) inhabits the forests of mountain ranges in eastern China, especially in the Changbai Mountains of Manchuria (northeastern China). Sika deer are one of the "three treasures" of Manchuria, along with ginseng, a root also used in herbal medicine, and the sable, a small animal with beautiful and valuable fur. The Chinese believe that Sika deer antlers increase one's health and longevity and hence use them to make herbal medicine. The soft inner portion of the antlers is dried, ground into a powder and made into pills, and the other parts of the antlers are boiled to make a jelly or ointment. The Chinese also use the heart, liver, kidney, meat, bones, sinew and skin of the Sika deer. The Sika deer, whose forests are disappearing, is now endangered. So, too, are the Siberian musk deer (Moschus moschiferus), Thorold's, or white-lipped, deer (Cervus albirostris) and the Chinese water deer (Hydropotes inermis). The Chinese government has established the Tiebu Nature Reserve in Sichuan Province to protect the Sika deer. Thorold's deer are protected in the Wolong Nature Reserve, and Chinese water deer in Jiuzhaigou Nature Reserve.

The musk deer inhabits broad-leaved forests throughout China. The male musk deer produces glandular secretions that are used to make perfume and herbal medicine. Other varieties of deer in China include the red deer, or wapiti (Cervus elphus), roe deer (Capreolus capreolus) and tufted deer (Elaphodus cephalophus). The lesser mouse deer (Tragulus javanicus) weighs less than 5 lbs. and is found only in the southern region of Yunnan Province. The Eld's deer (Cervus eldi) is found only on Hainan Island off the southern Chinese coast. Wild herds of Pere David's deer (Elephurus davidi-

anus) were formerly common across the North China Plain and the middle and lower reaches of the Yangzi River, but they were hunted until only one group was left in 1894. This group was captured and taken to England, where they were bred in captivity and their offspring were placed in European zoos and parks. Some Pere David's deer were brought back to China in 1986. See also CHANGBAI MOUNTAIN RANGE; CRANE; HAINAN ISLAND; PEACH; TIAN MOUNTAIN RANGE; TORTOISE.

DEHUA PORCELAIN (Te-hua)

A high-quality, fine white porcelain with a clear glaze that is produced in Dehua County in the southeastern Chinese province of Fujian; known as Jian white or ivory white, and in the West by the 19th-century French term *blanc de Chine* ("white of China"). Although termed white ware, Dehua porcelain ranges from gray-white to ivory in color.

Porcelain has been made in Dehua for more than 1,000 years. Archaeologists have excavated more than 189 kilns dating back to the Song (960–1279) and Yuan (1279–1368) dynasties, many of which produced porcelain for export from China. Dehua porcelain was first exported to Europe through Dutch merchants in the 13th century. The Italian explorer Marco Polo (1254–1324), who sailed home from the major port city of Xiamen in Fujian, brought back many large ivory and blue-and-white Dehua vases. Dehua porcelain became extremely popular during the Ming dynasty (1368–1644). Porcelain has been produced steadily at Dehua up to the present time. A Ceramics Research Institute, a Ceramic Art Society, and several art schools have been established at Dehua to train artists in Dehua techniques. Porcelain made in Dehua is very fine because the area is rich in kaolin—a pure white, plastic clay that Chinese potters first discovered and employed to invent techniques for making porcelain. Dishes, bowls, teacups, teapots and vases are produced at Dehua, but the most popular objects are figures of humans and deities, especially Guanyin (Kuan-yin), the Buddhist goddess of mercy. Many Dehua pieces are decorated with designs in relief that have been carved or made in a mold, and some are also decorated with blue designs, such as birds and flowers. The largest porcelain figures made at Dehua are 5 feet high, and the smallest only 3.5 inches high. A famous Guanyin by the renowned Ming potter He Chaozhong (Ho Ch'ao-chung) is displayed at the Palace Museum in the Forbidden City in Beijing. See also GUANYIN; PORCELAIN; WHITE WARE; XIAMEN.

DEMOCRATIC PARTIES (*minzhu dangpai* or *min-chu tang-p'ai*)

Also known as "satellite parties"; eight political parties that existed before the Chinese Communist Party (CCP) founded the People's Republic of China (PRC) in 1949 and which the CCP permits to continue functioning. The "democratic parties" are small and are not opposition parties to the CCP, which holds the real governing power in China. Even today the CCP supposedly consults with the eight democratic parties, but in fact they must acquiesce to the CCP. The Revolutionary Committee of the Chinese Kuomintang (Chinese Nationalist Party, or the KMT) was founded in 1949 by members of the KMT who disagreed with their party's policies. The China Democratic League was founded in 1941 by Chinese scholars and artists. The China Association for Promoting Democracy was founded in 1945 by intellectuals in the fields of culture, publishing and primary and secondary education. The China Democratic National Construction Association was also founded in 1945 by educators and people in the business world. The Chinese Peasants' and Workers' Democratic Party was founded in 1931 by intellectuals in the fields of medicine, the arts and education. The China Zhigongdang (Chih Kung Tang; Party for Public Interest) was founded in 1925 to gain support from overseas Chinese communities. The Jiusan (Chiu San; September Third) Society was founded in 1945 by college professors and scientists to commemorate the victory of the "international war against fascism," that is, World War II, called by the Chinese the War of Resistance against Japan (1937–45). The Taiwan Democratic Self-Government League was founded in 1947 by "patriotic supporters of democracy who originated in Taiwan and now reside on the mainland."

After World War II ended with Japan's defeat in 1945, the CCP, led by Mao Zedong (Mao Tse-tung), and the Chinese Nationalist Party (Kuomintang; KMT), led by Chiang Kai-shek, resumed their civil war. On May 5, 1948, the eight democratic parties accepted the CCP's invitation to hold the Chinese People's Political Consultative Conference (CPPCC). All of the parties formed a united front to oppose the KMT and imperialism. In 1949 the Communist-led united front defeated the KMT, and Chiang Kai-shek and his followers fled to Taiwan. In September 1949 the CPPCC formally decided to establish the PRC and passed an Organic Law that specified the procedures and structure for government operations. On September 29, 1949, the CPPCC proclaimed its Common Program, which served as the law of the PRC until the 1954 state constitution superseded it. Mao Zedong proclaimed the founding of the PRC in Beijing on October 1, 1949. See also CHINESE COMMUNIST PARTY; CHINESE PEOPLE'S POLITICAL CONSULTATIVE CONFERENCE; CIVIL WAR BETWEEN COMMUNISTS AND NATIONALISTS; CONSTITUTION, STATE, OF 1954; NATIONALIST PARTY; PEOPLE'S REPUBLIC OF CHINA; TAIWAN.

DEMOCRATIC PEOPLE'S REPUBLIC OF KOREA (NORTH KOREA)

See KOREAN WAR; MANCHURIA; UNITED NATIONS; YALU RIVER.

DENG XIAOPING (Teng Hsiao-p'ing; 1904–97)

A prominent official in the Chinese Communist Party (CCP), which founded the People's Republic of China (PRC) in 1949, who was purged and restored to power several times and who had been the major force in the PRC government since the deaths in 1976 of party leaders Mao Zedong (Mao Tse-tung) and Zhou Enlai (Chou En-lai).

Deng was born in Sichuan Province. As a student he became involved in the May Fourth Movement of 1919, which inspired many young Chinese to become political activists. From 1920 to 1925 Deng studied in France, where he joined the Chinese Communist Party in 1924. In 1926 he studied in the U.S.S.R. for several months and then returned to China. The Communist Party of the U.S.S.R., which had sent many members to China to help organize the CCP, assigned Deng to assist Li Lisan, who was then head of the CCP. From 1926 to 1932 Deng worked for the CCP in Shanxi and, then, Guangxi provinces. By 1930 Deng was chief of staff in the Third Army Corps led by Peng Dehuai (P'eng Teh-huai), and in 1931 he was assigned to Ruijin.

Deng organized the Seventh Red (Communist) Army. In 1932 he joined the CCP forces led by Mao Zedong and Zhou Enlai, which had retreated to Jiangxi Province after Chiang Kai-shek, leader of the Chinese Nationalist Party (Kuomintang; KMT), turned against the CCP in 1927 and ordered the massacre of the Communists. When the Communists began their Long March west in 1934–35 to escape the Nationalists, Deng was Director of the First Army Corps Political Department. The CCP made its headquarters in Yan'an in Shaanxi Province, where by 1936 Deng was the Red Army's deputy political commissar.

In 1937, when the Chinese began fighting their War of Resistance against Japan (1937–45; World War II), the CCP forces were reorganized into the Eighth Route Army. Deng was promoted to political commissar of the 129th Division (later the Second Field Army), one of the army's three divisions. After Japan was defeated in 1945, Deng was elected to the CCP's Seventh Central Committee. The CCP and KMT resumed their civil war, and Deng was one of the main leaders of the Huaihai Campaign that ensured the CCP victory in 1949, when the CCP founded the PRC and the KMT fled to Taiwan. From 1950 to 1954 Deng served in Chongqing, Sichuan Province, as the first secretary of the CCP Southwest Regional Bureau, political commissar of the army and the military region under the bureau's control, and vice chairman of the Southwest Administrative Committee. In 1952 he was transferred to Beijing, where he became vice premier under Zhou Enlai and held a crucial position as Zhou's general secretary. From 1953 to 1954 Deng was the only CCP official who served on all three committees set up under the three main CCP leaders—Mao, Zhou and Liu Shaoqi (Liu Shao-ch'i)—to establish a national legislative committee.

From 1953 to 1954 Deng served as minister of finance, and from 1954 to 1959 he was a member of the Standing Committee of the Chinese People's Political Consultative Conference (CPPCC). He was removed from office but won a power struggle and became general secretary of the CCP's Central Committee and served concurrently as vice premier of the State Council. Deng was elected to the Politburo in 1955 and was reelected at the Eighth Party Congress in 1956. In 1956 Deng was appointed to a high-ranking and powerful position, secretary general of the Secretariat, and became a member of the Politburo Standing Committee, the inner circle of power in the CCP.

After the Great Leap Forward of 1958 ended in economic disaster, Mao had to step down as chairman of the PRC and was replaced by Liu Shaoqi in April 1959. Deng, who worked with Liu to rebuild the Chinese economy, became well known for advocating a pragmatic position, which he summed up in his famous saying, "I do not care whether a cat is black or white, the important thing is whether it catches mice." Deng was reappointed vice premier under Zhou in 1959 and vice chairman of the National Defence Council in 1965. In the early 1960s, when relations between the PRC and the U.S.S.R. were deteriorating, Deng, who had maintained connections with the international communist movement, made several trips to Moscow. In 1962 Mao initiated the Socialist Education Movement (1962–65) to halt what he perceived as a capitalist trend in the CCP and bring

a return to orthodox Communist ideology. Liu and Deng, who were moderates, opposed Mao's policy. By mid-1965 Mao regained control of the CCP with the help of Lin Biao, Jiang Qing (Chiang Ch'ing; Mao's fourth wife), and Chen Boda (Ch'en Po-ta), a party theoretician. Mao and his faction began attacking CCP officials, including state chairman Liu Shaoqi. In mid-1966, these attacks had turned into a mass action formally called the great Proletarian Cultural Revolution (1966–76). When it began, even though Deng was a member of the Politburo Standing Committee and general secretary of the CCP Central Committee, he was arrested and accused of collaborating with Liu Shaoqi, who had opposed the Red Guards and was subsequently denounced and purged. Deng was labeled a "renegade, scab, and traitor," and by early 1967 he was removed from all his positions except his membership in the CCP and sent to work in a tractor factory in Jiangxi Province. Liu Shaoqi and other "capitalist roaders" were also purged. Premier Zhou Enlai, Deng's mentor, attempted to reconcile the Mao-Lin Biao and Liu-Deng factions. Zhou persuaded Mao to allow Deng to be brought back to Beijing in 1973, and Deng made a dramatic return to power, becoming vice premier of the State Council under Zhou Enlai, vice chairman of the Standing Committee and chief of staff of the People's Liberation Army (PLA). He joined the Politburo in December 1973, and by early 1975 he was a vice chairman of the Central Committee. Deng appeared to be a possible successor to Mao or Zhou, both of whom were ill and would soon die in 1976.

When Zhou died in January 1976, it was thought that Deng would replace him, but in February Hua Guofeng (Hua Kuo-feng) was named acting premier. After Zhou died, there was a huge public outpouring of grief. In April a massive unauthorized demonstration to commemorate Zhou in Tiananmen Square in Beijing turned into a riot when wreaths laid at the Monument to the People's Heroes (Revolutionary Martyrs) disappeared. The CCP called out the police and military troops and many demonstrators were arrested. The radical faction in the Politburo led by Jiang Qing blamed Deng for the riot and immediately removed him from all of his official positions. They also denounced his emphasis on scientific and technical development by labeling him an "arch unrepentant capitalist-roader in the Party and behind-the-scenes promoter of the right deviationist wing to reverse correct verdicts."

When Mao died on September 9, 1976, a moderate faction took power in the Central Committee and elevated Hua Guofeng to acting chairman of the CCP. In October 1976 the so-called Gang of Four, a group of four radical CCP officials including Jiang Qing, were arrested and blamed for the Cultural Revolution. Deng was reported to have been involved in the investigation of their crimes, and big-character posters calling for Deng's return appeared on walls in Beijing in January 1977. On July 22, 1977, the Party restored Deng to all his previous positions. Public demonstrations in Beijing celebrated his return to power and regional newspapers described him as "respected and beloved."

In August 1977 Deng was elevated to the third-ranking position in the Politburo. At the fourth NPC in March 1978, Hua was reappointed premier, but Deng retained a great deal of influence in the CCP and many members of his faction were placed in or retained important party positions. Hua announced a Ten-Year Plan that reemphasized Zhou's policy of Four Modernizations to develop and modernize China after the Cultural Revolution, and Deng became the leader of China's modernization and economic reform. On March 18, 1978, Deng delivered the opening speech at China's first National Science Conference in Beijing, in which he expressed the new policies of the CCP by asserting that education and training in science and technology were more important than political ideology. He asserted that technically skilled personnel would not be discriminated against, as they had been in the past, on the basis of the distinctions between "mental" and "manual." Agricultural reforms led by Deng in the early 1970s and 1980s greatly increased the food supply for Chinese cities, which encouraged many Chinese to migrate to the cities from rural areas, especially those who had been sent there as punishment during the Cultural Revolution. At the Third Plenum of the Eleventh Central Committee in December 1978, Deng launched a major program for reforming Chinese political, social and economic institutions and even its Communist and Maoist ideology, which became known as China's "Second Revolution." Deng's goal was to have the PRC become a modern, developed nation by the year 2000.

From 1977 to 1980 Deng served as chief of the PLA General Staff and vice premier. From 1978 Deng headed numerous PRC delegations to the United States, Japan and 15 other countries. On January 1, 1979, the United States and the PRC established diplomatic relations, and the United States reaffirmed its agreement that the PRC was the legal government of China and that Taiwan, provisionally governed by the ROC, was in fact a region of China. On January 28, 1979, Deng arrived in Washington, D.C., for an official diplomatic visit, and the United States and the PRC rapidly increased their commercial, technical and cultural relations. In August 1980 Deng resigned from his government positions in order to open the way for younger leaders. However, he retained his Party positions and advocated the policy of "reform and opening," meaning that the Chinese economic system should be reformed and opened to foreign trade.

From 1981 to 1990 Deng served as chairman of the PRC and from 1983 to 1989 he was chairman of the CCP's Central Military Commissions. From 1982 to 1987 he was reelected to the Politburo Standing Committee, 12th Party Congress; in 1987 he served only on the Presidium of the 13th Party Congress. In January 1982 Deng called for a "revolution" in the government bureaucracy to reduce the number of officials, starting with the highest level, to enable younger and better-educated Party cadres to take over leadership as China modernized. The Party created the Central Advisory Commission to facilitate the transfer of power from veterans of the Long March to younger officials and appointed Deng its first chairman. The CCP Central Committee also reorganized and streamlined its staff, and provincial-level party and government structures reorganized as well. In 1982 Deng consolidated his power at the 12th National Party Congress, after which the Party published *The Selected Works of Deng Xiaoping* as the authoritative ideological source for the reforms it was undertaking. In 1985 it issued another volume, *Building Socialism with Chinese Characteristics,* containing Deng's speeches and writings on economic, ideological and foreign policy. An expanded update of this book was issued in 1987 to provide further support for reforms. Deng's approach was summed up in his slogans, "seeking truth from facts" and "socialism with Chinese characteristics."

From 1982 Deng had been honorary president of the Soong Ching Ling (Song Qingling) Foundation, named for the widow of Dr. Sun Yat-sen, the founder of modern China, who became the most prominent woman in China. He oversaw the negotiations that led Great Britain to agree in 1984 that it would return its colony of Hong Kong to China in 1997. In 1987 Deng retired from his CCP positions and required other veterans of the Long March to retire as well. The office of Party Chairman was abolished, and the general secretary was designated Party leader. In 1988 Deng was PLA representative and Presidium member at the Seventh National Party Congress. He wanted to place the PLA under civilian leadership and ordered a purge to change it into a modern, professional military, although the PLA resisted many of his reforms. During the CCP-ordered military suppression of the pro-democracy movement in Tiananmen Square in June 1989, Deng retained his power. However, in November 1989 he formally retired as chairman of the Central Military Commission. Zhao Ziyang, who had been lenient with the Tiananmen Square protesters, was ousted as general secretary of the CCP, and Deng named Jiang Zemin as his successor. Jiang became president, general secretary of the CCP and chairman of the Central Military Commission.

After Deng's formal retirement, he enjoyed great prestige and exercised much power behind the scenes. In 1992 he came out of retirement by making an appearance at Shenzhen Special Economic Zone, just across the border from Hong Kong, where he encouraged the Chinese to "dive into the sea" of capitalist enterprise. Many Chinese then became entrepreneurs and attracted foreign investors in China. Deng's youngest daughter, Deng Rong (Xiao Rong), who served as his official translator, wrote a biography of him, *Deng Xiaoping, My Father.*

Deng died on February 20, 1997, a little more than four months before Britain returned Hong Kong to China. Many ordinary Chinese did not seem upset by his death, since his economic reforms were succeeding and he, unlike Mao Zedong, had discouraged a personality cult. Following the wishes of Deng and his family, the Chinese government held a simple funeral for him in the Great Hall of the People and decreed six days of official mourning. Deng's body did not lie in state, and his remains were cremated and his ashes were scattered into the sea. There had been much speculation as to who would succeed him. At the National Party Congress in September 1997, Jiang Zemin was reconfirmed as president of China and Party secretary. See also BIG-CHARACTER POSTERS; CHINESE COMMUNIST PARTY; CIVIL WAR BETWEEN COMMUNISTS AND NATIONALISTS; CULTURAL REVOLUTION; EIGHTH ROUTE ARMY; FOUR MODERNIZATIONS; GANG OF FOUR; GOVERNMENT STRUCTURE; GREAT HALL OF THE PEOPLE; GREAT LEAP FORWARD; HU YAOBANG; HUA GUOFENG; JIANG ZEMIN; LI XIANNIAN; LIU SHAOQI; LONG MARCH; MAO ZEDONG; MAY FOURTH MOVEMENT OF 1919; NATIONAL PARTY CONGRESS; PENG DEHUAI; PEOPLE'S LIBERATION ARMY; RED GUARDS; SICHUAN PROVINCE; SINO-SOVIET CONFLICT; SOCIALIST EDUCATION MOVEMENT; SOONG QINGLING; SPECIAL ECONOMIC ZONES; TIANANMEN SQUARE MASSACRE; WAR OF RESISTANCE AGAINST JAPAN; ZHAO ZIYANG; ZHOU ENLAI.

DENG YINGCHAO (Teng Ying-ch'ao; 1904–92)   The wife of Chinese Communist premier Zhou Enlai (Chou En-lai; 1898–1976), who was herself a prominent Communist official and activist for women's rights. One of the best-loved and most highly respected people in China, she was commonly known as "Elder Sister Deng"; her name means "Surpassing Brightness." Although she never had children of her own, she was the adoptive mother of Chinese Premier Li Peng and about nine other Chinese who had been war orphans.

She was born Deng Wenshu in Henan Province. Her father, Deng Tingzhong (Teng T'ing-chong), was military governor of Nanning in modern Guangxi-Zhuang Autonomous Region during the final years of the Qing dynasty (1644–1911) but was forced to leave his position and go into exile in Xinjiang in western China. He died there when his daughter was three years old. Her mother, Yang Zhende (Yang Cheng-te), worked as a doctor and teacher, although the family remained poor. Between 1913 and 1920 Deng attended schools in Beijing and Tianjin. In school she was given the name Yingbin ("clever and courteous"), but she later changed it to Yingchao. The Chinese overthrew the Qing in the Revolution of 1911 and established the Republic of China, but the country continued to suffer exploitation by warlords and foreign powers. Deng was attracted to revolutionary activities as a student and took part in the patriotic Chinese May Fourth Movement of 1919. She was also active in the movement to end the traditional Chinese custom of footbinding. Deng and her schoolmates, Guo Longzhen (Kuo Lung-chen) and Liu Qingyang (Liu Ch'ing-yang), organized the Tianjin Patriotic Women's Union and the Tianjin Students Union. Deng later joined with Zhou Enlai and others in founding the progressive Awakening Society. She also founded the Women's Star Society, which published *Women's Star Weekly* and *Women's Daily*.

Deng married Zhou Enlai in 1925 after he returned to China from studying in France. She founded the Tianjin Socialist Youth League and became an early member of the Chinese Communist Party (CCP) in 1925. The CCP and the Chinese Nationalist Party (Kuomintang; KMT) cooperated for a while, during which time Deng represented the CCP in the Central Women's Department of the KMT. After their cooperation fell apart, Deng went underground as a revolutionary activist. She became secretary-general of the CCP's Central Bureau of the Jiangxi Revolution, and she was one of only about 50 women who survived the rigorous Long March westward by the Communists in 1934–35 to escape the Nationalists. In 1938 Deng became a leader in the Chinese branch of the League against International Aggression, and she met frequently with foreigners active in the world peace movement.

During China's War of Resistance against Japan (1937–45; World War II), Deng used her considerable political abilities to mobilize the Chinese united front, which included the CCP and the KMT, against the Japanese. She also encouraged women to join the struggle for democracy in China. After the CCP defeated the KMT in their post–World War II civil war and founded the People's Republic of China in 1949, Deng became vice chairwoman and then honorary chairwoman of the All-China Women's Federation, which she had helped found. She also held various leading positions in the CCP and the PRC government.

During the turbulent Cultural Revolution (1966–76), Deng and Zhou were both able to maintain their public image as revolutionaries while they avoided becoming enmeshed in factional struggles. In 1969 Deng became a member of the Central Committee of the CCP. After the Cultural Revolution, she was elected vice chairwoman of the Standing Committee of the National People's Congress and became a member of the Politburo in 1978. She represented China on many trips to Japan, Southeast Asia and Europe, and was the leader of the CCP's work on women's issues. In 1983, she was elected chairwoman of the Standing Committee of the National Political Consultative Conference. In 1987, at the Third Plenary Session of the 11th Central Party Committee, she became second secretary of the CCP's Central Commission for Discipline Inspection. In 1989 she supported the party leaders' decision to order tanks and troops to fire on pro-democracy demonstrators in Tiananmen Square. See also ALL-CHINA WOMEN'S FEDERATION; CHINESE COMMUNIST PARTY; CIVIL WAR BETWEEN COMMUNISTS AND NATIONALISTS; CULTURAL REVOLUTION; GOVERNMENT STRUCTURE; LI PENG; LONG MARCH; MAY FOURTH MOVEMENT OF 1919; NATIONAL PEOPLE'S CONGRESS; NATIONALIST PARTY; PEOPLE'S REPUBLIC OF CHINA; POLITBURO; TIANANMEN SQUARE MASSACRE; ZHOU ENLAI.

DENGLONG   See LANTERNS.

DESERTS   See DZUNGARIA BASIN; GOBI DESERT; LOESS; TAKLIMAKAN DESERT; TENGGER DESERT; TURPAN DEPRESSION.

DEZONG (EMPEROR)   See TANG DYNASTY.

DIALECTICIANS   Also known as the School of Names (Mingjia or Ming-chia; "School of Semantics"); a classical school of Chinese philosophy which formed one of the so-called Hundred Schools of Thought during the late Zhou dynasty (1100–256 B.C.). Chinese thinkers who fell into this category were interested in logic in its broadest sense, which includes dialectics, sophisms and paradoxes. Like the Greek Sophists, they enjoyed arguing for its own sake and debated such issues as whether a white horse was a horse or whether a hard rock was a rock. Members of other philosophical schools felt that the arguments of the dialecticians were futile because they had nothing to do with human beings and their relationships with each other, the central concern of Confucianists and other major Chinese schools. Dialectical thought contained the seeds of modern logic but it never developed and soon died out, and logic never became an independent discipline in China.

Huishi (Hui Shih; 380–300 B.C.) and Gongsun Lung (Kung-sun Lung; 320–250 B.C.) are the best-known Chinese dialecticians. Huishi was a government minister who wrote a code of laws. He was a friend of the Daoist thinker Zhuangzi (Chuang Tzu; 369–286 B.C.) and wrote a text on logic which has been lost, but chapter three of the *Zhuangzi* preserves a list of 10 of his paradoxes. Some of these are well known, including: (1) The greatest thing has nothing beyond itself; this is called the infinite. The smallest thing has nothing within itself; this is called the infinitesimal. (4) The sun at noon is the sun declining. The creature born is the creature dying. (7) I go to Yue (Yueh) today and arrived there yesterday. (10) Love all things equally, for the heavens and the earth are one composite body. Huishi's 10th paradox, advocating the principle of universal love, is similar to the thought of Mozi (Mo Tzu; c. 470–c. 391 B.C.). Gongsun Lung, a scholar who ran his own school that was patronized by various feudal rulers, was mainly interested in logic and dialectic. His short text, the *Gongsun Lungzi* (*Kung-sun Lung Tzu*), is difficult to understand but filled with stimulating ideas through which he attempted to establish a method of epistemological analysis. Chapter Two develops the paradoxical argument that a white horse is not a horse, Chapter Three discusses the relationship between things and their attributes, and Chapter Five comprises a discourse on the hardness and whiteness of a rock. See also CONFUCIANISM; HUNDRED SCHOOLS OF THOUGHT; MOZI; ZHUANGZI.

DIALECTS See LANGUAGE, CHINESE; MANDARIN; MINORITIES, NATIONAL; NEW CULTURE MOVEMENT; PUTONGHUA.

DIAMOND SUTRA See BUDDHISM; DUNHUANG CAVE PAINTINGS AND CARVINGS; PRINTING.

DIANCHI, LAKE See KUNMING; YUNNAN PROVINCE.

DIANXIN See DIM SUM.

DIAO CHAN (Tiao Chan) The most beautiful woman in the Three Kingdoms Period (San Guo; 220–280) and one of the "four famous beauties" in Chinese history. Diao's father died when she was a girl, so she and her mother became servants in the mansion of a government minister named Wang Yuan. After Diao's mother also died, Wang's wife gave her a refined upbringing. She was not only beautiful but intelligent and fond of studying. At the time, the emperor was being controlled and the people were being oppressed by an evil government official, the imperial rector, who was the rival of Minister Wang. Wang and Diao Chan plotted to overthrow him by creating a rivalry between the rector and his godson, who was also his most powerful general. Wang offered Diao to the rector as a concubine, but Wang also told the general that Diao was his daughter and that she would marry the general. On the wedding day, Wang sent Diao to the rector's home instead, and told the general that the rector had kidnapped her. This infuriated the general, who killed the rector so he could have Diao Chan for himself. This act freed the Chinese people from the evil tyrant. It is not known what happened to Diao Chan, although she may have married the general. Her patriotic story, the subject of many Chinese novels and operas, is titled *The Tangled Rings*. See also CONCUBINES; OPERA; THREE KINGDOMS PERIOD.

DIARY OF A MADMAN See LU XUN.

DIM SUM (*dianxin* in pinyin, *tien-hsin* in Wade-Giles) "Heart's delight"; the term in Guangzhou dialect (Cantonese) for a special meal in the southern Chinese style consisting of various small but delicious portions of food, such as steamed dumplings stuffed with meat or sweet bean paste or spring rolls. Fried meats and vegetables, noodles in broth, and *joak*, a thick rice soup, may also be served. The Chinese enjoy *dim sum* lunches in teahouses, which are used for business meetings as well as for social gatherings between friends and family. The atmosphere of a teahouse is noisy and crowded. There is no menu; servers wheel around pushcarts with the various specialties or carry items on a tray. Diners select as many items as they want and pay for the total number of dishes and steamer baskets at the end. Many restaurants offer 50 or more *dim sum* dishes each day. *Dim sum* is available in Chinese restaurants in many Western countries. See also COOKING, CHINESE; TEA.

DING, BISHOP K. H. See CHRISTIANITY.

DING (*ting*) A large round bronze container with handles and three legs, similar to a tripod that was used to hold sacrificial meats during religious rituals in ancient China. The legs enabled the *ding* to be placed over a fire. The *ding* is one type of bronzeware that was produced especially during the Shang dynasty (1750–1040 B.C.), one of the earliest periods in Chinese history. Other bronze ritual containers from this period include the *zun* (*tsun*), *gui* (*kuei*) and *jia* (*chia*), which was used to heat wine. The vessels were all decorated in relief with masklike faces of supernatural creatures and spiral forms. Bronzeware in the *ding* shape has been excavated from tombs by archaeologists in the region south of the Yangzi River (Changjiang), which marked the southernmost area of Shang culture and sovereignty. Bronze objects, made from an alloy of copper and tin, were first produced in China during the Xia dynasty and became widespread during the Shang. The Chinese may have learned the technique from the Middle East, but they created their own technique for casting bronze objects by pouring molten bronze into pottery molds. The *ding* shape remained important in Chinese culture, and hundreds of years after the Shang dynasty it was produced in other materials, especially a type of greenish gray porcelain known as celadon. See also BRONZEWARE; CELADON; SHANG DYNASTY; XIA DYNASTY.

DING LING See MING TOMBS.

DING LING (Ting Ling; 1904–86) The best-known modern Chinese woman writer. Ding Ling was born in Hunan Province to a family of landowners. Her father, who had studied in Japan, died when she was young. Her widowed mother took her to the cities of Changde and Changsha so that they could both receive a modern education. Her mother, who stopped binding her feet, became a teacher and eventually director of the women's school that they had attended in Changde.

Ding Ling read many new Chinese novels and translations of foreign novels. She graduated from Shanghai University in 1923 and moved to the capital city of Beijing, where she continued reading on her own and audited some classes taught by Lu Xun (Lu Hsun; 1881–1936), the greatest modern Chinese writer. She had some of her articles published in the *Beijing News*. There, she lived with a young writer named Hu Yepin (Hu Yeh-p'in), and the two became friends with Shen Congwen (Shen Ts'ung-wen), who would later become another prominent Chinese writer.

The first story Ding Ling wrote was "Meng Ke." It tells the story of a provincial girl who moves to Shanghai to live with her wealthy relatives and gets a job acting for a film studio. It was published in 1927 in the prestigious *Fiction Monthly*. Her second story, "Diary of Miss Sophie," was featured in the same journal in 1928. Within a few years Ding Ling published three volumes of short stories about independent and adventurous women, which made her famous. In 1928, Ding and Hu moved to Shanghai. With Hu Yepin she founded a small publishing company, the Red and Black Press, and with Shen Congwen she founded a journal, *The Human World*. Lu Xun founded the Left-Wing Writers' League in 1930. During the seven years that the League functioned, Ding Ling was chief editor of its official journal, *The Dipper*, and secretary of its Party and Youth League branch. In 1930 Ding Ling had a son with Hu Yepin, who had become a Communist activist. Hu was arrested by the Nationalists (Kuomintang; KMT) and executed with four other left-wing writers in 1931. Ding was grief-stricken. She joined the Chinese Communist Party in 1933 and worked hard to promote the party, in addition to writing novels, including *Water*, about the disastrous flood of 1931, and her autobiographical novel, *Mother*. The Nationalists arrested her in May 1933 and confined her in private homes for three years to keep her from working for the Communists. They also banned her books.

In 1935 she had a second child with her lover, Feng Da (Feng Ta). The next year, she was able to escape confinement and went to the Communist base at Yan'an in Shaanxi Province in western China. Ding Ling worked for the CCP and continued to write fiction, but also began writing poetry and plays. She joined a theater troupe that performed for soldiers and peasants during China's War of Resistance against Japan (1937–45; World War II). After the war, she moved to Hebei Province to work with the Communists and peasants for land reform. In 1948 she traveled to Budapest as a Chinese Communist delegate to the Second Democratic Women's Federation. She also represented China at a World Congress to Defend Peace in Czechoslovakia. In 1949, while the Communists defeated the Nationalists and founded the People's Republic of China, Ding Ling was the head of the Chinese delegation that went to Moscow for the anniversary of the Bolshevik October Revolution. The Chinese Communist Party (CCP) appointed her to compile the collected edition of the writings of Hu Yepin, honored by the Communists as a martyr. When she returned to China she held several government positions and was elected vice chairman of the Chinese Writers' Association. However, from 1953 on, Ding Ling was subjected to much criticism by the Communists for her past writing, and she lost her professional positions and literary institute. In 1955, she was accused of being the head of an anti-party clique and labeled a Rightist and traitor. However, she never admitted that she was guilty of the charges against her. In 1957 she was expelled from the Communist party and the Writers' Union and sent to work on a farm in Heilongjiang Province in far northeastern China (Manchuria). With the start of the Cultural Revolution (1966–76), she was subjected to physical and psychological abuse. In 1970 she was taken to Beijing and jailed in a maximum-security prison for five years. Her first husband, Chen Ming, a Communist writer whom she had met in Yan'an during the War of Resistance against Japan, was also imprisoned. In 1975, Ding and Chen were labeled counter-revolutionaries and were sent to Shanxi Province, but they were permitted to write once more. In 1979 she was brought back to Beijing, and all the charges that had been raised against her in the 1950s were cleared. Despite being ill with cancer, she addressed the National Congress of Writers and Artists and resumed writing her long novel, *In Bitterly Cold Days*. See also CHINESE COMMUNIST PARTY; YAN'AN.

DING WARE (Ting ware)   A type of ceramic that is one of the "five great wares" of the Song dynasty (960–1279) and the only one of the five that is not classified as a celadon ware. The name *Ding* derives from Dingxian in modern Hebei Province in northern China where it was first produced. Ding ware, the first type of ceramic that is known to have been used at the Song imperial court, evolved from white ceramic wares made in the seventh and eighth centuries. Ding pieces have buff-colored clay bodies, ivory-colored glazes and thin, elegant shapes, indicating that they were developed to replace dishes made of silver. They were decorated with incisions of flowers, such as peonies, and other motifs such as birds and dragons. At first the potters incised the designs by hand, but they later employed molds to impress the designs in order to increase productivity. Such mass-production techniques stimulated the growth of the Chinese ceramic industry but resulted in a lessening of quality, and Ding ware lost the patronage of the court. However, Ding ware continued to be produced through the Yuan dynasty (1279–1368) and perhaps even later. See also SONG DYNASTY.

DITAN   See CARPETS.

DIVINATION   See ALMANAC; BOOK OF CHANGES; BUDDHISM; FENG SHUI; ORACLE BONES; TEMPLES.

DIXIN, KING   See SHANG DYNASTY.

DIZANG BUSA   See JIUHUA, MOUNT.

DOCTRINE OF THE MEAN, THE (*Zhongyong* or *Chungyung*)   An essay on several concepts that are central to Confucian thought, such as the character and social obligations of the genuine human being ("superior man" or "true gentleman"; *junzi* or *chun-tzu*) and the ethical responsibilities of the ruler. The *Doctrine of the Mean*, also known as *The Mean*, is one of the most important texts in the Chinese Confucian canon. It has traditionally been attributed to Confucius's grandson Kong Ji (483–402? B.C.), but it is probably composed of several texts which may date, in part, as late as the early Han dynasty (206 B.C.–A.D. 220). The *Doctrine of the Mean* was originally a chapter in the *Book of Rites* (*Liji*), one of the Five Classics (*wujing*) of Confucianism. The Neo-Confucian scholar Zhu Xi (1130–1200) added this document to three others to form the Four Books (*Sishu*) of Confucianism. The other three documents are the *Great Learning* (*Daxue*; also formerly a chapter in the *Book of Rites*), the *Analects* (*Sayings*) of Confucius (*Lunyu*) and the *Book of Mencius* (*Mengzi*; Mencius, or Mengzi, was a Confucian scholar who lived c. 372–289 B.C.).

The Chinese title of the *Doctrine of the Mean, Zhongyong,* is composed of the terms "centrality" (*zhong*) and "normality" (*yong*). The term used in translation, "The Mean" (or "The Golden Mean," as Confucius called it), indicates the Confucian concept of the primary norm for human action which, if understood and adhered to, will bring human beings into harmony with the the universe as a whole. Another important concept in the book is "sincerity," or "truth" (*cheng*), which means that the fundamental nature of human beings is the same as the fundamental nature of the universe. There is a connection between the moral order and the universal order, and an individual who achieves perfection through moral self-cultivation will experience a harmonious union with the universe. This Confucian concept of the self-realization of unity with all persons and things corresponds to the metaphysical principle called the *Dao,* or the "Way," in the Chinese religion known as Daoism. Scholars in the Neo-Confucian School, which developed in the Song dynasty (960–1279), were influenced by Daoism. They regarded the *Doctrine of the Mean* and the *Great Learning* as the most important sources for their thought. See also ANALECTS, CONFUCIAN; BOOK OF RITES; CONFUCIANISM; DAOISM; FIVE CLASSICS OF CONFUCIANISM; FOUR BOOKS OF CONFUCIANISM; GREAT LEARNING, THE; MENCIUS; NEO-CONFUCIANISM; ZHU XI.

DOG   See LION; ZODIAC, ANIMAL.

DOLLS   See TOYS, TRADITIONAL.

DOLONNUR   See CHENGDE.

DONG   See WINTER FESTIVAL.

DONG   Also known as the Kam; one of China's 55 national minority groups. The Dong belong to the Dai (Tai) ethnic group in southwestern China, who are related to people in Thailand and Burma. The 1990 census recorded 2,514,014 Dong, who are widely spread through Guangxi-Zhuang Autonomous Region and the provinces of Guizhou and Hunan. The Chinese government has given the Dong in Guangxi-Zhuang their own autonomous district, known as Sanjiang Xian. This is a region of mountains covered with dense forests of bamboo, fir, tung and tea oil trees. The Dong have traditionally been crop farmers and loggers in the forests. They build three-story timber-frame houses of more than 100 fir logs fitted together with no nails. The ground floor includes a wood shed and pigsty; the second floor contains the living quarters; and the third floor is used for storing food.

The Dong are famous for building drum towers and bridges. The Dong traditionally kept a large drum to summon village elders to council meetings or to gather the villagers together when an enemy tribe attacked. Chengyang Wind and Rain Bridge (Changyang Fengyu Qiao), the largest covered pavilion bridge in the world, can be seen about 13 miles north of the capital city of Sanjiang. It is a fine example of the Dong style of building. Constructed in 1916, the bridge comprises five wooden pavilions standing on five stone piles and connected by covered wooden walkways. Such bridges are common in regions inhabited by the Dong,

and provide protection from the natural elements and a place to rest and talk.

Every Dong village also has a drum tower built with 300 or more logs, which has from 3 to 13 stories and may be as high as 65 feet. The Dong still gather at drum towers and hold their festivals on the stone-paved area in front of the towers, singing and dancing to the music of the reed pipe, a traditional instrument that the Chinese call *sheng.* See also GUANGXI-ZHUANG AUTONOMOUS REGION; MINORITIES, NATIONAL; SHENG.

DONG BEIYUAN   See DONG YUAN.

DONG BIWU   See UNITED NATIONS.

DONG QICHANG (Tung Ch'i-ch'ang; 1555–1636)   A government minister in the Ming dynasty (1368–1644), and a painter, calligrapher, art collector and theorist who has had enormous influence on Chinese artists and art critics down to the present time. Dong Qichang was a member of the literati class who governed China in the imperial bureaucracy and became tutor to the Crown Prince. He led the return to classical values in landscape painting through the study of great works by scholar-painters in the literati tradition. His direct followers, known as the Orthodox School, include six 17th-century masters: Wang Shimin (1592–1680), Wang Jian (Wang Chien; 1598–1677), Wang Hui (1632–1717), Wang Yuanqi (Wang Yuan-ch'i; 1642–1715), Wu Li (1632–1717) and Yun Shouping (1633–90). Wang Shimin was Dong's pupil, and the National Palace Museum in Taipei, Taiwan has an album of Wang's small copies of Chinese masterpieces with calligraphy inscriptions by Dong. Dong's own monochrome ink landscapes, associated with the Chan (Zen) sect of Buddhism to which he belonged, are very structured and intellectual.

Dong is best known as a critic. He categorized Chinese painting into two opposing schools, the Northern and the Southern. The Northern School comprised court and professional artists who painted in a colorful, decorative style, from the "green-and-blue" masters of the Tang dynasty (618–907) through Ma Yuan (active c. 1190–1225) and Xia Gui (Hsia Kuei; active c. 1180–1224) of the Southern Song dynasty (1127–1279). The Southern School, or *wen ren* (*wen-jen*) tradition, which Dong believed was superior, comprised amateur literati painters for whom landscape painting was a means of expressing their insights on human nature and the natural world. This school began in the Tang dynasty with Dong's favorite painter, Wang Wei (699–761) and came down to Dong's time with the painters Shen Zhou (Shen Chou) and Wen Zhengming (Wen Cheng-ming). There are inconsistencies in the details that Dong uses to present his argument, but his categories of Northern and Southern schools of painting have held a general validity in Chinese culture. Dong and his colleague, Mo Shilung (1540–87), compiled a history of Chinese painting, although Mo died before they completed the work. Dong also wrote a book about painting, *Talking of Painting (Hua Shuo),* which remains one of the most important works on Chinese aesthetics; in it he discusses historic and stylistic periods, connoisseurship and classification of Chinese paintings. See also CALLIGRAPHY; CHAN SECT OF BUDDHISM; INK PAINTING;

LANDSCAPE PAINTING; MA YUAN; NORTHERN SCHOOL OF PAINTING; SOUTHERN SCHOOL OF PAINTING; TANG DYNASTY; WANG WEI; WU LI; XIA GUI.

DONG RIVER   See PEARL RIVER.

DONG SHUDA   See DONG YUAN.

DONG WANGGUN   See XIWANGMU.

DONG YUAN (Tung Yuan; 10th century)   The best-known painter from the Five Dynasties Period (907–60), when Chinese landscape painting developed rapidly as painting techniques were perfected; also known as Dong Shuda (Tung Shu-ta) and Dong Beiyuan (Tung Pei-yuan). Dong Yuan was born in Zhongling (modern Nanchang) in Jiangxi Province. He and his student, the priest Ju Ran (Chu-Jan), founded the Jiangnan (Chiang-nan; "south of the Changjiang" or Yellow River) School of Painting, named for the region where they lived. This school had great influence on the development of Chinese landscape painting down to the modern era. Its paintings, echoing the soft and misty landscapes of southern China, are softer and more freely and loosely executed than the works of many northern Chinese painters, which tended to be angular and austere and to have strong outlines. Dong painted some works in color and others in the monochromatic style of ink painting. He filled his paintings with rivers, lakes, fishing boats, small villages, forests partly hidden by clouds and rain, and finely painted mountains. Chinese critics of the 11th and 12th centuries especially admired the way Dong depicted the atmospheric effects of weather, such as "rivers and lakes in wind and rain" and "trees in the mist." One of Dong's greatest works is the painting on silk *Xiaojiang and Xiangjiang* (Hsiao and Hsiang rivers in Hunan Province), which portrays a broad panoramic scene along a river valley. See also INK PAINTING; JIANGXI PROVINCE; LANDSCAPE PAINTING.

DONG ZHONGSHU (Tung Chung-shu; 179–104 B.C.) A philosopher who led the movement to have the ideas of Confucius (551–479 B.C.) accepted as the official Chinese school of thought. For three centuries after the death of Confucius, his school was one of several that coexisted and vied for official recognition by the rulers of the several Warring States (Zhanguo). Some other major schools included Legalism, Daoism and the school of Mozi. Qin Shi Huangdi, ruler of the state of Qin and a proponent of Legalism, brought about the unification of China in 221 B.C., but his empire lasted only until 206 B.C. By the following century, the efforts of Dong Zhongshu led the Han dynasty (206 B.C.–A.D. 220) to recognize Confucianism as the orthodox religious philosophy of the Chinese imperial government. Dong was named an official adviser to the Han emperor, and he helped to develop the system of political philosophy that formed the foundation of the imperial bureaucracy or civil service. To the basic ethical concepts taught by Confucius and his disciples, Dong added political principles and cosmological concepts held by the Yin-Yang and the Five Material Agents (*wuxing*) schools of thought. Yin and yang refer to the two metaphysical principles that permeate everything in the universe, which is characterized by flowing movement.

Yin is the female, negative, dark principle and yang is the male, positive, light principle. Dong also incorporated the concept of *qi* (*ch'i*), the metaphysical and material power that is the fundamental component of everything in the universe. He stated that it fills the whole universe, surrounding human beings just as water surrounds fish, and unites all created things. His system is contained in the *Deep Significance of the Spring and Autumn Annals* (*Chunqiu Fanlu*), a collection of short essays that had a major influence on the development of Han Confucian thought.

The five agents are metaphysical modes or forces that have been associated with certain periods of time, particularly the changing seasons, in a specified order. Each mode or agent gives rise to its successor in this order: wood (spring, green, the number eight), fire (summer, red, seven), earth (in the center of the calendar, yellow, five), metal (autumn, white, nine) and water (winter, black, six). Each agent also has many other correspondences. Dong argued that the ruler could govern properly only by acknowledging and being in harmony with the order of the five agents, and he associated the agents with the five branches of the imperial government. Wood represents the minister of agriculture, fire the minister of war, earth the minister of works, metal the minister of the interior, and water the minister of justice. See also CONFUCIUS; CONFUCIANISM; HAN DYNASTY; IMPERIAL BUREAUCRACY; LEGALIST SCHOOL OF THOUGHT; MOZI; QIN DYNASTY; WARRING STATES PERIOD; YIN AND YANG.

DONGBEI   See HEILONGJIANG PROVINCE; JILIN PROVINCE; LIAONING PROVINCE; MANCHURIA; SHENYANG.

DONGHAI   See EAST CHINA SEA.

DONGLIN (TUNG-LIN) ACADEMY   An academy of Confucian learning that was reestablished in the late Ming dynasty (1368–1644) at Wuxi in modern Jiangsu Province by conservative scholars who opposed the Neo-Confucian thought of Wang Yangming (1472–1529). (The academy was founded in the 12th century but had ceased operations.) The leaders of the Academy were Gu Xianzheng (Ku Hsien-cheng; 1550–1612) and Gao Panlong (Kao P'an-lung; 1562–1626), who had both openly criticized what they believed to be the immoral behavior of high officials in the Ming imperial bureaucracy. In 1603 they began rebuilding the Donglin Academy as a center for promoting Confucian scholarship and as a meeting place for political activists. Scholars and government officials from throughout the lower Yangzi River valley supported the academy. They developed into a political faction known as the Donglin Movement, whose members played a prominent role in the imperial bureaucracy, in the capital city of Beijing.

Many of the Confucian scholars who taught at Donglin opposed the power of Wei Zhongxian (Wei Chung-hsien), the head eunuch who wielded the real power in the imperial court during the reign of the Ming emperor Xizong (Hsi-tsung; r. 1620–27), known as the Tianqi (T'ien-ch'i) Emperor. From 1625 to 1626 Wei had many of the Donglin scholars arrested, tortured and executed. Gao Panlong had been dismissed from his position in Beijing and returned to the Donglin Academy at Wuxi, but he committed suicide in 1626 to avoid execution. In 1629, after the death of the

Tianqi emperor, the removal of Wei Zhongxian, and the accession of the Chongzhen (Ch'ung-chen) emperor (r. 1628–45), the Donglin scholars were brought into favor once more. They held many high government positions through the rest of the Ming dynasty. See also CONFUCIANISM; EUNUCHS; IMPERIAL BUREAUCRACY; MING DYNASTY; WANG YANGMING; WEI ZHONGXIAN.

DONGLING (EASTERN IMPERIAL TOMB) See NURHACHI; SHENYANG.

DONGSON BRONZE AGE CULTURE See RED RIVER.

DONGTING, LAKE (Dongting Hu)   A lake in northern Hunan Province that has been celebrated by many poets as far back as the third century B.C. Jiang Kui (1155–1235) called Lake Dongting a "jade dish brimming with quicksilver." The lake's fertile basin is known as one of the "rice bowls" of China. Lake Dongting is fed by the Yangzi River (Changjiang), China's longest river, to the north and its major tributaries. Water from the lake flows back into the Yangzi through canals at Yueyang. Lake Dongting has the second-largest surface area of any lake in China, covering 1,500 square miles. It has three sections, the eastern, southern and western lakes; the eastern is the largest. The region around Lake Dongting was the site of a peasant rebellion in 1130–35 led by Zhong Xian; it was put down by the renowned general Yue Fei.

The city of Yueyang is situated next to Lake Dongting. A boat ride from the harbor to the lake provides a splendid view of Yueyang city; the famous 49-foot-high Yueyang tower (Yueyanglou), originally built in A.D. 716 and capped with gold roof tiles; and Junshan Island, covered with wooded hills and terraced tea plantations. See also HUNAN PROVINCE; YANGZI RIVER; YUE FEI; YUEYANG.

DONGTING, MOUNT See TAI, LAKE.

DONGYUE See TAI, MOUNT.

DOOR GODS (menshen)   A pair of gods who guard homes, palaces, temples and other buildings. Their pictures are painted on the doors of a building or printed on pieces of paper that are pasted on the doors. In place of pictures of the door gods, characters representing them may be written on red squares of paper and pasted to the doors. In temples, these gods may be portrayed in gold on the main doors to keep away evil spirits. They are depicted as fierce men in ancient military uniforms holding swords and battle axes on long poles.

Legends differ about the identity of the door gods. One version states that they were the spirits of generals from the Tang dynasty (618–907) who faithfully guarded Emperor Gaozong (Kao-tsung) when he suffered from an illness caused by evil spirits. After the emperor recovered, he ordered the portraits of his loyal generals, Qin Shubao (Ch'in Shu-pao) and Yu Chi Jingde (Yu Ch'ih Ching-te), to be painted on the palace doors to prevent the evil spirits from returning. Another version states that the gods were two brothers, Shen Tu and Lu Lei, who lived during the Five Dynasties Period (907–60). Their stone house was located in a peach orchard, north of which dwelled an evil prince who drank people's blood and ate their hearts. He eventually killed the brothers, but they had been so courageous that the Chinese commemorated them by painting their pictures on the doors of their homes. The brothers were eventually depicted wearing military uniforms similar to those of the Tang dynasty generals.

DORGON (1612–50)   A prince and military leader of the Manchus, an ethnic group in the region that now comprises northeastern China (also known as Manchuria), who overthrew the Ming dynasty (1368–1644) and laid the foundations for the Manchu Qing dynasty (1644–1911). Dorgon was the 14th son of the great Manchu leader Nurhachi (1559–1626) and uncle of Nurhachi's son and successor, Abahai (1592–1643). As the commander of the White Banner, a group within the Manchu Banner System of military organization, he raided 40 cities in northeastern China. When Abahai died, some Manchu leaders wanted to make Dorgon his successor, but Dorgon declined out of respect for traditional Manchu lines of succession. However, he was named regent for Abahai's son Fulin, who was only five years old. Another Manchu leader, Jirgalang, was appointed co-regent.

The Manchus were eager to overthrow the Chinese Ming dynasty (1368–1644), and in 1644 a rebellion led by Li Zicheng (Li Tzu-ch'eng; c. 1605–45) gave them their opportunity. The rebellion confronted Ming General Wu Sangui (Wu San-Kuei) at the Great Wall north of the capital city of Beijing. Wu made an alliance with the Manchus for protection, but when he let the Manchus pass through a gate in the Great Wall, in poured 20,000 Manchu horse-riding soldiers. The rebels fled in panic and Wu pursued them. The rebel forces entered Beijing in April 1644, and the emperor and empress hanged themselves. The Manchus then entered the city unopposed on June 5 and proclaimed their rule over China under the Qing dynasty, which they had established since 1636 at their capital at Mukden. They installed Fulin as emperor, who reigned as Shunzhi (Shun-chih) from 1644 to 1661. Dorgon ruthlessly exercised absolute control and took away the power of the Manchu clan over the Six Ministries of government, and he removed Jirgalang as co-regent in 1647. Dorgon used Ming officials to run the imperial bureaucracy, and he retained most of the Ming government institutions and practices. By 1646, Dorgon's generals had conquered all of the Chinese Empire except the provinces in the southwest, although it took the Manchus four decades to completely end Ming resistance to their rule in southern China. Dorgon died suddenly on the last day of 1650 on a hunting trip when he was only 38 years old. His death left a power vacuum that was filled by some of the Manchu leaders he had suppressed. They disgraced him after his death, but this was reversed by the Qianlong emperor in 1773. See also ABAHAI; BANNER SYSTEM, MANCHU; LI ZICHENG; MANCHU; NURHACHI; QING DYNASTY.

DOUBLE HAPPINESS AND LONG LIFE (Shuangxi or Shuang hsi, Zhou or Shou)   Two popular phrases having auspicious connotations for the Chinese, who write the characters as decorative motifs on lanterns and other objects displayed at important celebrations. Double Happiness, the symbol of the bliss shared by a married couple, is used especially at weddings to ensure the happiness of the bride and groom. The character for Long Life appears on many occasions, especially at birthdays to ensure the longevity of the person celebrating the birthday. The characters for Double Happiness and Long Life are usually accompanied by other Chinese decorative motifs. For example, peaches and figures of the Eight Immortals of the Daoist religion also symbolize longevity and decorate the table at a birthday party. Noodles are served at birthdays and weddings because their length connotes longevity as well. The color red symbolizes happiness and good luck and is widely used at all Chinese celebrations. At traditional weddings, the bride is married in a red robe. Double Happiness is also stamped in gold on red "lucky money" envelopes presented to children and unmarried young women at the New Year Festival and other occasions. See also BIRTHDAYS; COLORS; EIGHT IMMORTALS; LUCKY MONEY; NOODLES; PEACH; WEDDINGS, TRADITIONAL.

DOUBLE HUNDRED CAMPAIGN See HUNDRED FLOWERS CAMPAIGN.

DOUBLE SEVEN FESTIVAL See COWHERD AND WEAVER MAID FESTIVAL.

DOUBLE TENTH FESTIVAL (Shuangshi jie, National Day) A national holiday held in Taiwan on October 10—the 10th day of the 10th month—to commemorate the revolution against the Qing dynasty (1644–1911), which led to the founding of the modern Republic of China in 1912. This revolution began with the uprising that took place on October 10, l911, by army units in Wuchang, the capital of Hubei province. The Double Tenth Festival is not celebrated in mainland China, where October 1 is celebrated as National Day to commemorate the founding of the People's Republic of China (PRC) by Mao Zedong and the Chinese Communist Party on October 1, 1949, in Beijing. When the Communists took over China the Nationalists (Kuomintang), led by Chiang Kai-shek, fled to the island of Taiwan and made Taipei the capital of the Republic of China. Chinese who live outside China or Taiwan express their political alignment by celebrating either the Double Tenth Festival or the PRC's National Day. See also CHIANG KAI-SHEK; NATIONAL DAY; NATIONALIST PARTY; PEOPLE'S REPUBLIC OF CHINA; QING DYNASTY; REPUBLIC OF CHINA; TAIWAN; WUCHANG UPRISING.

DOWFU See SOYBEANS AND SOY PRODUCTS.

DRAGON (long or lung) A mythical creature that holds first place among the four greatest creatures, including the phoenix, tiger and tortoise. Since ancient times in China, the dragon has been the most important symbol of power and has been associated with the emperor. While in the West the dragon is an evil creature, in China the dragon is benevolent and auspicious, the bringer of life-giving rain. The Azure (or Blue) Dragon symbolizes the East and spring. Because the dragon supposedly can bring rain and transform its size and shape and appear or disappear at will, its power to control the forces of nature was believed to be reflected in the power of the emperor on earth. An emperor was required to rule virtuously to ensure rainfall, vital for China's agriculture. The

Book of Rites (Liji), one of the Five Classics of Confucianism, states that in times of drought, an altar is to be erected at the Temple of the Dragon King (Lung Wang Miao).

The dragon motif is very ancient in China. For example, dragons decorate bronzeware from the Shang dynasty (1750–1040 B.C.), such as *ding,* sacrificial food vessels that have legs in the form of dragons. The five-clawed imperial dragon, or *long,* the majestic symbol used only by the emperor, represents the male, positive principle of the universe, known as yang in traditional Chinese thought. There are nine types of dragons: the *long,* an ancient primitive form known as *kui,* the Celestial Dragon, the Spiritual Dragon, the Dragon of the Hidden Treasures, the Winged Dragon, the Horned Dragon, the Coiling Dragon and the Yellow Dragon. Only the emperor was permitted to wear all nine types to decorate his robes. The nine-dragon motif can still be seen on the glazed-tile screen in the Forbidden City (Imperial Palace) in Beijing. Every Chinese dynasty, beginning with the Han (206 B.C.–A.D. 220), used for its coat of arms the motif of a pair of dragons fighting for a pearl and, for the national flag, a five-clawed dragon with the red sun or jewel on a yellow background.

By the arrival of Ming dynasty (1368–1644), members of the imperial court wore colorfully embroidered silk dragon robes to symbolize the feudal system by which China was governed. The designs of these robes were meant to symbolize the order of the universe; thus court officials were ranked by emblems embroidered on their dragon robes. The emperor's robe was bright yellow, and his insignia was composed of four medallions with five-clawed coiling dragons on the front and back. The heir to the throne wore an orange robe embroidered with the same four imperial medallions. Dragons were also portrayed on the emperor's furnishings and possessions and on those of his courtiers.

The Chinese traditionally believed that the legendary emperor Fuxi could assume dragon form. He brought the Great Waters of the universe into order by digging dikes, canals and irrigation ditches to tame the Yellow River (Huanghe). The five-clawed dragon was also worn by the emperor because legends state that the Dragon King moves in all four directions simultaneously; the fifth direction is the Center, where he remains. Chinese maps are drawn with the south at the top. The Azure Dragon of the East is to the left, which is yang, and the White Tiger of the West is to the right, which is yin (negative and feminine).

Feng shui ("wind and water"), the Chinese system of geomancy, is commonly used to determine the proper site, or "Dragon's Head," for building a home. The site is consecrated with offerings in the shape of a dragon, and when the home is completed the dragon is invited to dwell there in a special alcove. The same principles are used for choosing burial sites. In *feng shui* the left and weaker side, guarded by the Azure Dragon, must be higher than the stronger right side, which is guarded by the White Tiger.

The phoenix, symbol of the empress, represents the female principle, or yin. In imperial times the phoenix was embroidered only on the robes of empresses. The phoenix dragon and phoenix still represent the groom and bride in a traditional Chinese wedding. During one of the rituals, the betrothed couple exchanges prescribed gifts and marriage contracts (*longfengdu,* or *lung feng tu*) providing astrological

In China, the dragon is a symbol of benevolence and power.   COURTESY, MUSEUM OF FINE ARTS, BOSTON

details about the dates of their birth; the bridegroom's contract is written on red paper, decorated with a dragon, and the bride's on green paper, decorated with a phoenix. At the formal betrothal, held 10 days before the final wedding ceremony, "Dragon and Phoenix" cakes symbolizing a happy married life are served.

The majestic dragon flying in and out of clouds has been the most important of all design motifs in Chinese arts and crafts, such as paintings, textiles and ceramics. Some of the best known examples are blue dragons on white porcelain produced in the Ming dynasty. A dragon with a pearl in its beard symbolizes the wish for wealth and good luck. The third-century painter Cao Buxing (Ts'ao Pu-hsing) was the first major Chinese artist to specialize in dragons. The greatest dragon painter was Chen Rong (Ch'en Jung; active 1235–60), whose most celebrated painting is *The Nine Dragons* (A.D. 1244), in the collection of the Museum of Fine Arts, Boston.

A scholar named Wang Fu described the dragon, or *long,* in a 10th-century encyclopedia as having "horns like a stag, forehead like a camel, eyes like a demon, neck like a snake, belly like a sea monster, scales like a carp, claws like an eagle, footpads like a tiger, ears like an ox." The dragon has 81 crests on its back, whiskers on each side of its mouth, and vaporous breath that can turn into rain. Embedded in its beard is the shining pearl of wisdom that reflects the emperor's striving for virtue on behalf of his empire. The "flaming pearl," representing the sun, wisdom, power and the imperial treasure, is depicted with the imperial dragon because the dragon guards this pearl under water. Legends describe Dragon Kings as rulers of the waterworld, who supposedly keep their treasures in underwater crystal palaces where they feed upon pearls and opals. There are five Dragon Kings, corresponding to the five sacred mountains, and once per year they rise out of the water and up to heaven to report to the heavenly emperor. In the Daoist religion the

dragon symbolizes the *dao,* the unseen but powerful lifeforce which pervades the universe and represents the North, while the tiger represents the South.

Dragon dances—in which a line of men run while covered by a long, colorful cloth dragon—are a popular feature of parades at the New Year and other festivals. Teams of rowers compete against each other at the Dragon Boat Festival held on the fifth day of the fifth month in the lunar calendar. Longmen Falls (Dragon Gate) is a famous site on the Yellow River. Legends claim that once every year the carp, a powerful fish, swims upstream to compete in leaping Longmen Falls. The successful ones are transformed into dragons and rise up into the sky. Dragons are believed to rise to the sky in spring and to plunge down into the waters in autumn. Scholars who successfully passed the imperial government examinations were described by the phrase *li hua long,* "the carp becomes a dragon." One of the finest Chinese green teas is Dragon Well tea (*longjing*) from Hangzhou in Zhejiang Province.

The dragon is the fifth animal in the traditional 12-year animal zodiac. People born in the Year of the Dragon are thought to be honest, brave and energetic but short-tempered and stubborn. The dragon, the greatest celestial power, brings the five blessings of wealth, harmony, virtue, long life, and living one's allotted life span. Dragon-born men are considered especially fortunate. See also BOOK OF RITES; BLUE-AND-WHITE WARE; BRONZEWARE; CARP; DAOISM; DING; DRAGON BOAT FESTIVAL; EMBROIDERY; EMPEROR; FUXI; FENG SHUI; FORBIDDEN CITY; PEARL; PHOENIX; TEA; TIGER; TORTOISE; WEDDINGS, TRADITIONAL; YELLOW RIVER; YIN AND YANG; ZODIAC, ANIMAL.

DRAGON BOAT FESTIVAL (Duan Wu Jie or Tuan Wu-chieh) Also known as the Fifth Month Festival (Wu Yue Jie) or the Double Fifth; a festival held on the fifth day of the fifth month in the traditional lunar calendar (around the summer solstice in June). Races are held with long, narrow boats with carved wooden dragon heads on the prows. Each boat has 8 to 15 pairs of rowers. Two men stand in the middle, one beating a drum to guide the rowers and the other banging a gong to encourage them. A third man at the prow waves a small red flag and chants to keep the rowers pulling together. Spectators on the riverbanks cheer the teams on, and fireworks are set off. The Dragon Boat Festival developed from ancient rituals held to propitiate the dragon just before the rainy season began in the sixth month, as the dragon was believed to control the rivers and bring life-giving rain.

The festival became associated with Qu Yuan (born c. 343 B.C.), a great poet and patriot of the State of Chu during the Warring States Period (403–221 B.C.). Political intrigue in the court caused the Chu ruler to lose trust in his loyal counselor Qu Yuan. The rival state of Qin then destroyed much of the Chu kingdom. Qu Yuan wrote poems that criticized the new Chu rulers, and they sent him from the capital city of Ying into exile. When the armies of Qin occupied the Chu capital of Ying and razed the imperial palace and ancestral temple in 277 B.C., Qu Yuan committed suicide by jumping into a river on the fifth day of the fifth month. He became the Chinese model of the honest government official. After Qu Yuan's death, people supposedly threw rice-filled bamboo sections into the river to prevent fish from eating his body so that it could be recovered for burial. Many people rowed out to find his body but never found it. At the Dragon Boat Festival people eat *zongzi*, date-filled glutinous rice balls wrapped in bamboo or lotus leaves and tied with natural black tendrils.

Dragon-boat racing actually became widespread during the Tang dynasty (618–907) in the Yangzi River region of South China. The festival remains largely a southern Chinese custom. A large regatta that attracts a quarter of a million people is held in Nanning, about 300 miles west of Guangzhou (Canton). Women's teams now compete as well as men's, and Western teams have recently competed in the dragon-boat races in Hong Kong, and similar races are now held in New York City. See also DRAGON; FIREWORKS AND GUNPOWDER; NANNING; WARRING STATES PERIOD.

DRAMA IN CHINA   Theatrical entertainment has a long history in China, going back to the ancient dramatic ballads. Structured song-and-dance performances developed during the Tang dynasty (618–907). Popular performing arts such as acrobatics and variety theater, comparable to vaudeville in the United States, have always drawn large audiences all over the country. For many centuries, professional storytellers have recited legendary and historical episodes, especially in urban teahouses. Dramatic narratives (*zhugongdiao* or *chu-kungtiao*), a form of prose narrative with interludes of song, developed during the Song dynasty (960–1279). Dramas were not written as literature in China until the Yuan dynasty (1279–1368), which was established by the Mongols, an ethnic group who invaded China from north of the Great Wall. Poetry and Confucian moralistic stories had dominated Chinese literature until the Yuan, when playwrights turned from such elitist literature to produce entertaining works that could be enjoyed by the common people. Confucian-educated Han Chinese literati or scholars had

always staffed the imperial bureaucracy, but the Mongols only allowed a small number of them to hold bureaucratic positions, so some scholars began writing dramas as a leisure activity or to earn money. These dramas became a medium through which the Han ethnic Chinese could express their resentment against their Mongol rulers. However, the dramatic pieces were similar to Western operas because the actors performed them by lyrical singing, dancing and mimetic gestures, accompanied by a traditional orchestra. Action did not become important in Chinese theater until the Beijing Opera developed in the 19th century.

A total of 171 plays have survived from the Yuan dynasty. Major Yuan playwrights include Wang Shifu (Wang Shih-fu), Guan Hanqing (Kuan Han-ch'ing), Ma Zhiyuan (Ma Chi-yuan), Bo Po (Po P'o) and Gao Wenxiu (Kao Wen-hsiu). Chinese playwrights took their plots from novels and stories based on legendary and historical events, especially the *Romance of the Three Kingdoms, Journey to the West* (also known as *Pilgrimage to the West* and *Monkey*), *Outlaws of the Marsh* and *Dream of the Red Chamber.* The oldest school of Chinese drama, which developed in the capital city of Beijing, is known as the Northern School (*zaju,* or "variety plays"). Northern plays usually have four acts (*zhe*), although a fifth act is sometimes added, and have a wide range of themes, including history, religion, lawsuits, military battles, adventure and love stories. Many of the librettos for the arias are, in fact, poems of the highest literary quality. The Southern School (*chuanqi* or *ch'uan-ch'i*) developed during the Ming dynasty (1368–1644), especially around the city of Suzhou. One of the most popular styles of theater, which developed in the 16th and 17th centuries and is still performed today, is a type of opera known as *kunqu.* During the 19th century, the so-called Theater of the Capital (*jingxi* or *ching-hsi,* or *jingju* or *ching-chu*) developed, now known as Beijing Opera. Another popular style of theatrical entertainment is Guangzhou (Canton) Opera.

Chinese scholars began translating Western literature in the late 19th century, and in the 1920s some Chinese authors, stimulated by the May Fourth Movement of 1919 and the New Culture Movement, started writing Western-style dramas. They were especially influenced by the plays of Oscar Wilde, Henrik Ibsen and Eugene O'Neill. Student drama clubs in Chinese cities produced many of the plays. Modern Chinese theater reached its full development in the 1930s and became known as "spoken theater" (*huaju* or *hua-chu*). In 1921 the Popular Theater Society was founded in Shanghai and the monthly journal *Theater* (*Xiju* or *Hsi-chu*) began publication. In 1931 the League of Chinese Left-Wing Dramatists was established.

The best-known modern Chinese playwrights include Cao Yu (Ts'ao Yu) and Hong Shen (Hung Shen), who, like a number of other playwrights, also wrote films. Many authors wrote plays for the patriotic theatrical performances that flourished during China's War of Resistance against Japan (1937–45; World War II), including Guo Moruo (Kuo Mo-jo) and Lao She. Beijing Opera also experienced a revival during this time, especially at Yan'an, the headquarters of the Chinese Communists, who were active in the War of Resistance. Dramatic operas were written based on episodes from historical novels and also on folk tales and songs popular in the Chinese countryside. *The White-Haired Girl* was first performed in Yan'an in April 1945. This new type of theater, which combined the techniques of traditional dramatic operas with folklore and events of daily life, continued to develop after the Communists founded the People's Republic of China in 1949. During the Cultural Revolution (1966–76), Chinese writers were not able to produce and perform their works, but Jiang Qing (Chiang Ch'ing), the wife of Communist chairman Mao Zedong (Mao Tse-tung), created her own type of theater, which combined Western-style singing and ballet with Chinese revolutionary themes such as *The Red Detachment of Women*. Chinese dramatic theater and opera was revived after the Cultural Revolution, along with the Chinese film industry. Foreign plays have also been produced in China, such as Bertold Brecht's *Life of Galileo*, Arthur Miller's *Death of a Salesman* and plays by William Shakespeare. See also ACROBATICS AND VARIETY THEATER; CAO YU; DREAM OF THE RED CHAMBER; FILM STUDIOS; GUAN HANQING; GUO MORUO; HONG SHEN; JIANG QING; JOURNEY TO THE WEST; KUNQU; LAO SHE; MAY FOURTH MOVEMENT OF 1919; NEW CULTURE MOVEMENT; OPERA, BEIJING; OPERA, GUANGZHOU; OUTLAWS OF THE MARSH; ROMANCE OF THE THREE KINGDOMS; STORYTELLING; WANG SHIFU; YUAN DYNASTY.

DREAM OF THE RED CHAMBER (*Hongloumeng* or *Hung Lo-meng*)   Also known as *A Dream of Red Mansions*; a novel by Cao Xueqin (Ts'ao Hsueh-ch'in; 1715–63) which is the greatest and best-loved Chinese work of fiction. Some literary scholars have devoted their entire lives to studying this novel. Various manuscripts and editions of the novel have been preserved; 80 chapters may be original, and 40 more chapters have been revised or added. The complicated story recounts the decline of an extended family belonging to the literati, or scholar-gentry class, whose members are sheltered in the enclosed gardens and living quarters of the Rong (Jung) Mansion, the family compound. Episodes depict the details of daily life and the complicated relationships in such a family during the Ming dynasty (1368–1644). Cao Xueqin drew upon his memories of his own upbringing to write the novel. His family had been personal servants to the Kangxi emperor (r. 1661–1722), having been raised in luxury in Nanjing, but his family became disgraced and impoverished and had to move to Beijing.

The story overflows with sentimental emotions. It centers on two cousins in love with each other; the hero Jia Baoyu (Chia Pao-yu; Precious Jade) and the heroine Lin Daiyu (Lin Tai-yu; Black Jade). Baoyu cannot marry his true love because their grandmother, who dotes on the boy, wants him to marry another girl, Xue Baochai (Hsueh Pao-ch'ai). The family tells him that he is to marry Daiyu, but after the ceremony he discovers that his bride, who had been veiled, is really Baochai. When Daiyu learns that the family has deceived Baoyu, she falls ill and dies of grief. Baoyu, standing tearfully by Daiyu's body, hears the bells of a distant Buddhist monastery and walks out of the Rong family compound, perhaps to renounce the world and become a monk.

In 1989 the novel was made into a serial feature film, *A Dream of Red Mansions*, that required two years of preparation and three years of shooting. The film follows the narrative pattern of the novel; it consists of eight episodes in six parts and runs for 13 hours. It was directed by Xie Tieli, produced by the Beijing Film Studio and financed by the China Film Distribution and Exhibition Corporation. Jia Baoyu and Lin Daiyu were performed by two famous actors from Chinese opera troupes, Xia Qin and Tao Huimin. About 150 of the novel's 900 characters appeared on the screen. See also FAMILY STRUCTURE; KANGXI (EMPEROR); LITERATI; MING DYNASTY; OPERA; WEDDINGS, TRADITIONAL.

DROUGHTS   See AGRICULTURE; CLIMATE OF CHINA, NATURAL DISASTERS.

DRUMS (*gu* or *ku*)   Musical instruments made from round wooden frames covered with the tanned skins of animals, which are beaten with wooden sticks or hands. Drums were one of the earliest types of instruments played in China. Chinese inscriptions on bones dating from about 1300 B.C. to 1050 B.C. (the oracle bones) include characters for drums. The earliest drums were probably made of fired pottery, then filled with bran and covered with skins, and played to encourage bravery in warriors during battles. The Chinese classify drums as one of the eight types of musical instruments and associate them with skin because drumheads are made by stretching animal skins over their frames. Types of Chinese drums include the large barrel drum; the small barrel drum, which is placed horizontally on a frame and played on the ends; and a small flat drum with a skin top and a hollow bottom. The rattle drum (*taogu* or *t'ao ku*) is a small drum with a handle passing through it and two balls hung on strings from each side of the drum barrel. The player holds the handle and twirls the drum to make the balls strike the drumheads. Small rattle drums may be carried by street vendors. The fish drum is a bamboo pipe that has one end covered with snakeskin. Blind fortune-tellers play this drum, which is the symbol of Zhang Guolao (Chang Kuo-lao), one of the Eight Immortals in the Daoist religion. Drums played at Confucian temples may be brightly painted and decorated with red or gold dragons, birds, flowers and other motifs. See also EIGHT IMMORTALS; MUSIC AND DANCE, CEREMONIAL.

DRY LACQUER TECHNIQUE   See SCULPTURE.

DRYSANDRA TREE   See PHOENIX.

DU FU (*Tu Fu*; 712–70)   One of the most renowned poets in Chinese literary history. Du Fu is classed with his friends, the poet Li Bai (Li Po; 701–62) and the poet-painter Wang Wei (699–761), as one of the three greatest poets of the Tang dynasty (618–907), the "Golden Age" of Chinese culture. Another highly regarded Tang poet is Bai Juyi (Po Chu-i; 722–846). The ability to write poetry was highly valued by the Tang government and was a requirement for the educated men selected by examinations to serve in the imperial bureaucracy. During the Tang dynasty the type of poem known as the Regulated Verse, or New Style Verse, was formalized to contain a regulated number of five- and seven-syllable lines.

Du Fu was born at Shaoling near the capital city of Chang'an (modern Xi'an in Shaanxi Province in central China), the eldest son of an aristocratic family. Despite his great talents and ambitions, Du Fu failed the examinations for the imperial bureaucracy, perhaps because his family lacked necessary connections. He had also developed his own complex style of writing that may not have been appreciated by the examination judges.

Du Fu spent many years traveling before and after he took the examinations in 736. During his travel he met Li Bai in 744 or 745. The two became close friends—despite Li Bai's reputation as a drunkard and romantic poet—and they exchanged poems with each other.

Du Fu was able to achieve certain positions in the court by impressing Emperor Xuanzong (Hsuan-tsung; r. 712–56) with his poetry. In 752 he was allowed to take a special examination, which he passed. After the An Lushan Rebellion broke out in 756 and toppled the emperor, Du Fu fled with his family to Sichuan and became a refugee.

Du Fu's poems are filled with melancholy feelings about historical events and his own experiences. He expressed the suffering felt by those who were poverty-stricken, including his own family. The Confucian virtues of moralistic reflection and compassion permeate his work. About 1,500 poems and some prose works by Du Fu have survived. Many English translations have been made of poems by Du Fu and his friends. Some of the most beautiful ones are by the British translator Arthur Waley (1889–1966). See also AN LUSHAN REBELLION; BAI JUYI; CONFUCIANISM; IMPERIAL BUREAUCRACY; LI BAI; REGULATED OR NEW-STYLE VERSE; TANG DYNASTY; WALEY, ARTHUR; WANG WEI; XUANZONG (EMPEROR).

DU WENXIU (Tu Wen-hsiu; d. 1872)   One of the main leaders of the "Panthay Rebellion," a Muslim rebellion that erupted in 1856 in Yunnan Province in southwestern China against the Chinese government under the Qing dynasty (1644–1911). Ma Dexin (Ma Te-hsin; the Grand Priest; d. 1874) and Ma Rulong (Ma Ju-lung; d. 1891) were also leaders of the rebellion. Southwestern China had the largest population of Muslims after the western provinces of Gansu and Shaanxi. The immediate cause of the rebellion was the heavy land taxes and extra levies imposed by the Qing government upon the Muslims in Yunnan. The Muslims and Chinese also fought over the gold and silver mines that were one of Yunnan Province's few sources of wealth. The Chinese had depleted their own mines and tried to take over the Muslim mines. In 1855 rioting in Yunnan led to a major Chinese attack on the Muslims, who defended themselves and in 1856 seized the important city of Dali. Du Wenxiu gave himself the name "Sultan Suleiman" and proclaimed his kingdom, Nanping Gui ("Kingdom of the Pacified South"), with its capital at Dali. This kingdom lasted for 15 years. Ma Rulong defected to the Qing in 1860, which gave them the advantage. The rebellious Muslims placed the city of Kunming under siege and overran it in 1863, but Qing forces quickly took it back. The Qing were able to end the rebellion by persuading some of the Muslim forces to join their side and by building up local militias led by able Chinese generals. In 1873, after heavy fighting, Qing troops under Ma Rulong and Chinese General Cen Yuying (1829–89) took Dali from the Muslims. Du Wenxiu tried to commit suicide but was unsuccessful, and the Qing captured and executed him. See also KUNMING; MUSLIMS; QING DYNASTY; YUNNAN PROVINCE.

DUAN QIRUI   See REPUBLIC OF CHINA; SUN YAT-SEN; WARLORD PERIOD; YUAN SHIKAI; ZHANG ZUOLIN.

DUAN WU JIE   See DRAGON BOAT FESTIVAL.

DUCK (ya)   The waterfowl that represents happiness and is a popular item at Chinese banquets. Mandarin ducks, so named because they have beautiful feathers and are considered superior to other ducks, are believed to mate for life and to die of loneliness if they are separated. Hence, a pair of male and female mandarin ducks symbolizes marital happiness and faithfulness and is a common motif at weddings. The ducks are usually depicted with the lotus flower, a Buddhist symbol for purity. A famous folk poem from the Han dynasty (206 B.C.–A.D. 220) tells of a husband and wife who are forced to commit suicide and are buried together in a common grave; in the tree above them sit two "Birds of True Love," or mandarin ducks.

White domestic ducks are raised in ponds used for irrigating rice paddies, although wild ducks are also consumed. Reddish brown dried ducks hang in Chinese food stores. There are many recipes for roasting or stewing duck with such ingredients as soy sauce, litchi fruit or tangerine peel. Other popular dishes include tea-leaf smoked duck and camphor-smoked duck. The best-known dish is Peking (Beijing) duck, which is prepared by a process of drying and roasting to make the skin crispy. It is served by rolling slices of duck meat and skin in thin pancakes with spring onions and plum sauce. The duck carcass is boiled to make a soup which is consumed at the end of the meal. Other cities have their own versions for preparing duck, such as Nanjing duck. Salted duck is eaten in the winter because the salt preserves it from spoiling. At the Chinese New Year, small pieces of salted dried ducks are added for flavor to pots of boiling soup or rice. A cooked duck is sometimes one of the dishes offered in religious rituals. Duck gizzards, feet, tongue, kidney and liver are delicacies in China.

Duck eggs are preserved by various methods of salting and drying. The famous "one-hundred-year eggs" or "one-thousand-year eggs" are actually prepared by placing them for two months in a mixture of lime, fine ash and salt, and sometimes tea. The chemicals move through the eggshells by osmosis to flavor and preserve the eggs. See also BANQUETS; COOKING, CHINESE; LOTUS; WEDDINGS, TRADITIONAL.

DUKE OF ZHOU   See ZHOU, DUKE OF.

DULCIMER   See STRING INSTRUMENTS.

DULIU RIVER   See PEARL RIVER.

DUMPLINGS   See DIM SUM; NOODLES; RESTAURANTS AND FOOD STALLS.

DUNHUANG CAVE PAINTINGS AND CARVINGS (Dunhuang shihe)   A large complex of cave temples 15 miles southeast of Dunhuang in the northwestern province of Gansu that contain some of the most important Buddhist art in the world. The Mogao Grottoes (Mogao Ku, Thousand Buddha Grottoes; Qianfodong), as they are known, comprise the oldest Buddhist site in China. Tourists may visit 30 of the caves between April and November, and scholars may receive permission to visit about 10 more. There are also 16 West Caves (Western Caves of a Thousand Buddhas, Qianfoxidong) at Nanhutian along the Dong River, the only survivors of another group of Buddhist grottoes. UNESCO has designated Mogao Grottoes a protected site of world patrimony. Dunhuang is situated on the old Silk Road along which camel caravans transported luxurious Chinese goods such as silk, tea and porcelain to the ancient Mediterranean world and brought back Western goods, culture and religions. After Buddhism was introduced into China from India in the first and second centuries A.D., Dunhuang became a center for Indian and Central Asian monks. Yu Zun (Yu Tsun), a monk traveling west through this region, had a vision of 1,000 golden Buddhas at Dunhuang and began carving them in the sandstone cliffs in A.D. 366. For the next thousand years, through eight dynasties, monks and artisans carved hundreds of grottoes along a distance of about 1,750 yards and filled them with wall paintings and carvings. By the time of their completion there were more than 1,000 caves, but slightly less than half have been preserved, containing about 500,000 square feet of frescoes and more than 2,000 painted sculptures. The art at Dunhuang shows Indian, Chinese and Central Asian influences.

During the Five Dynasties Period (907–60) and the early Song dynasty (960–1279), three generations of the family of Cao Yiquan had control of Dunhuang and expanded or restored many of the caves. An academy of painting was established to train artists to work in the caves. While Dunhuang remained a major Buddhist center until the 11th century, the area declined as trade dwindled on the Silk Road. The caves were abandoned by the monks in the 15th century and were rediscovered in 1900 by Wan Yuan, a refugee from famine in Hebei Province. While cleaning Grotto 15 he found the monastery library, hidden by the monks in 1036 when they had to flee the invading Tangut tribe, who founded the Xixia dynasty (1038–1227). The treasures of the library, numbering about 60,000 items, included sutras (scriptures) and historical documents, scrolls, paintings and embroidered textiles. The Chinese Qing dynasty government had no interest in the materials, so Wan Yuan sold a huge amount of them to British and French scholars, who sent them to European museums. The oldest printed text in the world, a 16-foot-long scroll on which the Buddhist *Diamond Sutra* was printed with seven different woodblocks in 868, was discovered at Dunhuang by Sir Aurel Stein and now belongs to the British Museum Library. Western and Japanese collectors and Chinese warlords and soldiers continued to plunder the caves until the People's Republic of China was founded in 1949.

The Chinese government established the Dunhuang Cultural Research Institute in 1961 and designated the Mogao Grottoes and the 16 West Caves as national treasures. Artifacts are exhibited in a museum at the base of the caves. Many grottoes have been ruined by desert sands and erosion, but 492 grottoes carved between the fourth and 14th centuries have been preserved. The frescoes, painted sculptures, and ceiling and pillar decorations have been protected with a chemical coating. The frescoes portray scenes from the entire life of Sakyamuni Buddha, the founder of Buddhism, including his birth, enlightenment, wandering and preaching, and

his entering nirvana. Numerous other subjects are also depicted, such as wild animals, creatures from Chinese legends, geometric patterns, lotus blossoms (a symbol of Buddhism), and scenes of hunters, fishermen and craftsmen. Clothing styles and facial features show a strong Indian influence in the art.

The Mogao Grottoes are laid out in squares or rectangles in five stories, making a kind of honeycomb pattern. Each grotto has a tablet listing its number, date of carving and dynastic period. Balconies were added beginning in the Song dynasty to link the rows of grottoes. Twenty-three caves have been preserved from the early period of carving. Cave 275, built 340–80 and thus one of the oldest at Dunhuang, contains frescoes of Sakyamuni and King Sivi and several sculptures of the Buddhist god Maitreya. The largest group of caves are 213 grottoes dating from the Tang dynasty (618–907) containing splendid paintings and sculptures. Cave 220 has a famous painting of a group of musicians and dancers, along with a Buddhist layman named Vimalakirti who is shown debating with the emperor and his ministers. The largest grotto is 44 feet high, the smallest less than 3 feet. The largest sculpture is 36 feet tall, the smallest about 4 inches. Scholars around the world have recently established the Dunhuang Project to assess manuscripts and art objects from Dunhuang owned by foreign museums and libraries. See also BUDDHISM; GANSU PROVINCE; LOTUS; SILK ROAD; NAMES OF INDIVIDUAL DYNASTIES.

DUTCH IN CHINA   See BRITISH EAST INDIA COMPANY; TAIWAN.

DYNASTY   See EMPEROR; HISTORICAL PERIODS; MANDATE OF HEAVEN; PEASANTS AND PEASANT REBELLIONS.

DZO   See TIBET; YAK.

DZUNGARIA BASIN   An enormous inland drainage basin north of the Tarim Basin in Xinjiang-Uighur Autonomous Region in far northwestern China. The Dzungaria Basin is enclosed by the Tianshan Mountain Range on the south, which divides the Dzungaria from the Tarim Basin; the Altai Mountain Range on the northeast, which divides it from Outer Mongolia; and the Tarbagatai Mountain Range on the northwest, which forms the border between the People's Republic of China and the former republics of the U.S.S.R. The floor of the Dzungaria Basin, which is mainly grassland, has an average altitude of 1,640 feet, which is 2,000 feet lower than the Tarim Basin. The Dzungaria has more rain than the arid Tarim Basin because air masses flow in through several mountain passes bringing moisture, although annual precipitation is less than 10 inches. It is also colder than the Tarim because it receives a strong northwesterly wind in the winter. The Kara-Irtysh River, which flows along the foothills of the Altai Range into Kazakhstan and then western Siberia, is the only river that originates in China and empties into the Arctic Ocean.

The Dzungaria Basin, like the Tarim Basin, played an important role in early contacts between China and the Mediterranean world, because one branch of the Silk Road passed along the northern edge of the Tianshan Mountain Range. Xinjiang is inhabited largely by members of ethnic minority groups, such as Uighurs, Kazakhs and Mongols who have traditionally been nomadic herders of animals, such as sheep, goats and horses. Modern interest in the Dzungaria Basin lies in its large deposits of oil, coal and metallic ores, especially the large Karamai oil field in the west. Gold has been mined in the Altai Mountains since ancient times, and metallic ores have been mined there since 1949. The capital of Xinjiang, Urumqi, is located on a desert plateau 9,000 feet above sea level on the southern edge of the Dzungaria Basin. The Longhai Railroad now links Urumqi with the Chinese capital at Beijing. Many large farms have been established in the Manass River valley, with such major crops as wheat, cotton, grapes, apples and delicious Hami melons, named for the oasis city of Hami. See also ALTAI MOUNTAIN RANGE; ENERGY SOURCES; GEOGRAPHY; HAMI; MINING INDUSTRY; NOMADS AND ANIMAL HUSBANDRY; SILK ROAD; TARIM BASIN; TIAN MOUNTAIN RANGE; URUMQI; XINJIANG-UIGHUR AUTONOMOUS REGION.

EARTHQUAKES See NATURAL DISASTERS; ZHANG HENG.

EAST CHINA SEA (Donghai)   A large body of water lying east of the Chinese mainland and bounded by Taiwan to the south, the southern islands of Japan (Kyushu and Ryukyu islands) to the east, and the Yellow Sea (Huanghai) to the north. The 100-mile-wide Taiwan Strait between Taiwan Island and the coast of southeast China forms part of the East China Sea and is a major shipping area. The East China Sea, which covers an area of about 770,000-square miles and has a maximum depth of about 8,900 feet, is considered a marginal sea of the Pacific Ocean. The main part of the East China Sea along the Chinese coast forms a continental shelf with a depth of no more than 656 feet. It is a rich fishing ground that attracts Japanese fleets. The sea has a rocky coastline with many coves and bays. China's longest and most important waterway, the Yangzi River (Changjiang), empties into the East China Sea. See also RYUKYU ISLANDS; TAIWAN; YANGZI RIVER; YELLOW SEA.

EAST INDIA COMPANY See BRITISH EAST INDIA COMPANY.

EAST IS RED, THE See ANTHEM, NATIONAL; CULTURAL REVOLUTION; HE LUTING.

EAST RIVER See PEARL RIVER.

EASTERN CHOU DYNASTY See SPRING AND AUTUMN PERIOD; WARRING STATES PERIOD.

EASTERN HAN DYNASTY (A.D. 25–220)   Also known as the Later Han dynasty; the final phase of the Han dynasty (206 B.C.–A.D. 220), one of the longest dynasties in Chinese history, and the period when many imperial institutions were established. Han is the name of the ethnic group that forms the majority of the Chinese population. The first phase of the Han dynasty was the Western, or Former, Han dynasty (206 B.C.–A.D. 8), which had its capital at Chang'an (modern Xi'an in Shaanxi Province). This was brought to an end by

Wang Mang, who attempted to usurp the throne and found his own dynasty, known as the Xin (A.D. 9–23) and as the Wang Mang Interregnum. Chinese peasants engaged in widespread rebellions, and in A.D. 23 a band of rebels known as the Red Eyebrows sacked Chang'an and killed Wang Mang. In 25 Liu Xiu (Liu Hsiu), a descendant of the Western Han imperial family, reestablished the Han dynasty and ruled as Emperor Guangwudi (Kuang Wu-ti). In 27 he finally forced the Red Eyebrows to surrender. He returned to the practices of the Western Han dynasty, including the Confucian-based imperial bureaucracy, and the Eastern Han dynasty was strongest under his reign and those of his immediate successors.

Guangwudi established the Han capital at Luoyang in modern Henan Province, east of Chang'an (this is the reason why his dynasty is known as the Eastern Han). He established a Confucian academy there to train scholars or literati (*wenren*, or *wen-jen*) to become high officials in the bureaucracy. Ban Biao (Pan Piao) and his son Ban Gu (Pan Ku) and daughter Ban Zhao (Pan Chao)—all of them prominent scholars—compiled the *History of the Former Han Dynasty* (*Hanshu*). Ban Zhao also wrote the authoritative *Code for Women* (*Nujie*, or *Nu Chieh*). Paper, invented in China and presented at the Han court in 105, was produced on a large scale for bureaucratic record-keeping, especially for tax records. Emperor Guangwudi commissioned the great Han general Ban Chao (Pan Ch'ao), another son of Ban Biao, to lead a large Chinese expedition west to make alliances with Central Asian tribes, especially for defense against a northern nomadic group called the Xiongnu (Hsiung-nu). During the Western Han, China had expanded its borders and had become engaged in the trade of silk and other luxury goods along the Silk Road to Central Asia and the Mediterranean world. Ban Chao got as far as the Caspian Sea and brought much of Central Asia, including the entire Tarim Basin, under Han Chinese control from 73 to 97.

Beginning in the first century A.D., the Han court fell into political struggles among the families of various imperial consorts, as well as government officials and eunuchs, who played a major role in the Han court. From 88 to 144, three powerful families dominated the court. Peasants began rebelling once more, and in 184 a group known as the Yellow Turbans, which took its ideology from the popular cults associated with the Daoist tradition, led an armed rebellion that was suppressed two years later but spurred political conflict throughout China.

The Han Empire became divided among a number of kingdoms, and the military generals who had been commissioned to fight the rebellious peasants turned against the Han. In 190, Dong Zhuo (Tung Chuo) sacked and burned Luoyang, thus destroying the Han archives and imperial library, an act for which he was assassinated. Cao Cao (Ts'ao Ts'ao), a brilliant Han general, became the virtual dictator of the Wei region of China north of the Yangzi River (Changjiang). He remains the character most frequently portrayed in Beijing Opera. After he died in 220, his son, Cao Pi (Ts'ao Pi), forced the last Han emperor, Xiandi (Hsien-ti), to abdicate the throne, and he founded the kingdom of Wei (or Cao Wei). Wei fought with the kingdoms of Shu (or Shu Han), located in modern Sichuan Province, and Wu, located around modern Nanjing south of the Yangzi, during the Three Kingdoms Period (220–80). The period between the downfall of the Han dynasty and the reunification of China under the Sui dynasty (581–618) is known as the Six Dynasties Period (220–589). It includes the Three Kingdoms Period, the Western Jin dynasty (265–316) and Eastern Jin dynasty (317–420), and the Northern and Southern dynasties (420–589). See also BAN CHAO; BAN GU AND BAN ZHAO; BUDDHISM; CAO CAO; CHANG'AN; CODE FOR WOMEN; CONFUCIANISM; EUNUCHS; HAN; IMPERIAL BUREAUCRACY; LUOYANG; OPERA, BEIJING; PAPER; RED EYEBROWS REBELLION; SILK; SILK ROAD; SIX DYNASTIES PERIOD; TARIM BASIN; THREE KINGDOMS PERIOD; WANG MANG; WESTERN HAN DYNASTY; XIONGNU; YELLOW TURBANS REBELLION.

EASTERN IMPERIAL TOMB See NURHACHI; SHENYANG.

EASTERN JIN DYNASTY See WESTERN AND EASTERN JIN DYNASTIES.

EASTERN PEAK See TAI, MOUNT.

EASTERN TURKESTAN REPUBLIC See KASHGAR; MUSLIMS.

EASTERN ZHOU DYNASTY See SPRING AND AUTUMN PERIOD; WARRING STATES PERIOD; ZHOU DYNASTY.

ECHO WALL See TEMPLE OF HEAVEN.

EDUCATION SYSTEM (MODERN) The system for educating Chinese students under the administration of the State Education Commission, which was founded in 1985. Education has been a major goal of the government of the People's Republic of China (PRC), established by the Chinese Communist Party (CCP) in 1949. Prior to 1949, more than half of the Chinese population was illiterate. The traditional education system was based on study of the Confucianist texts known as the Five Classics and the Four Books. Chinese educated under this system belonged to the literati

(*wenren* or *wen-jen*), or scholar class, whose members held positions in the imperial bureaucracy. After the Chinese Revolution of 1911 overthrew the Qing dynasty (1644–1911), the last imperial dynasty, and the Republic of China (ROC) was established in 1912, Chinese authors initiated a movement to write fiction using the vernacular rather than the classical language, known as the New Culture (or New Literature) Movement. Since the Chinese language is written with characters, or ideographs, rather than with an alphabet, learning to read and write Chinese takes many years. The characters have been simplified in the modern era, but students still must copy hundreds of characters over and over again to memorize how to both write and pronounce them.

In the 1950s the PRC adopted the modern education policy and methods of the U.S.S.R. However, in the late 1950s, the PRC government attacked Chinese intellectuals and teachers during the Anti-Rightist Campaign and the Great Leap Forward, which set back the Chinese education system. During the Cultural Revolution (1966–76), Chinese schools and universities were shut down, the education system was nearly destroyed and scientists stopped during research. Since the late 1970s, the PRC government has followed the policy of the Four Modernizations and has once again given education a central position in order to rebuild and modernize the country. Since 1980 the World Bank has given the PRC large loans to increase scientific research in Chinese universities.

Today more than 80 percent of the Chinese population is literate. In April 1986 the National People's Congress (NPC) adopted a law making nine years of education compulsory in Chinese cities and developed areas by 1990 and in the rest of the country by the end of the 20th century. This includes six years of primary school and three years of junior secondary or middle school. Children also attend three years of preschool from ages three to six to provide moral and social training. Many kindergartens are run as boarding schools, with children returning home for weekends and holidays. In 1995 about 96 percent of Chinese primary-school-age children were enrolled in primary schools, which teach moral education, reading and writing the Chinese language, science, arithmetic, geography, history, music, painting and physical education. The last three years of compulsory education comprise the first three years of secondary education.

Fewer girls than boys go to school, especially in rural areas, where the girls are needed to work on farms and in households. Only 6 percent of 15-to-19-year-old Chinese were illiterate by the late 1980s, but 70 percent of them were women, and this held true into the 1990s. Many rural boys and girls drop out after six years of school to work on family farms. Public schools charge fees, and many rural children, who live too far from the schools to attend them on a daily basis, must pay room and board to stay at them. Private charities raise money to pay tuition for girls in poor rural areas, but millions of children are still beyond the current reach of government and private assistance. Teachers in rural areas are also paid far less than teachers in cities.

After the first three years of secondary education, some Chinese students go on to three more years of senior secondary education and then to a technical school, college or university. Entrance examinations for Chinese universities are extremely difficult. Every year about 1.5 to 2 million students take the nationwide entrance examinations for the half-million openings in Chinese universities. Similar competitive examinations are held for students who wish to enter professional and technical schools. In 1987 there were more than 1,000 institutions of higher learning and approximately 18 university students per 10,000 people in China. Every year thousands of Chinese students also travel abroad to study at universities in the United States and other countries.

In 1980 the PRC government designated 98 of China's 675 universities as "national keypoint (*zhongdian*) universities." This number changed through the 1980s but held at 97 by 1990. Twenty-six of these were specially designated as "keypoints among the keypoints." The most prestigious university in China is Beijing University (known as Beida; formerly Peking University), founded in 1898. Its students have played a prominent role in modern Chinese political movements. Mao Zedong (Mao Tse-tung), founder of the PRC, was a librarian at Beijing University before he helped found the Chinese Communist Party. Qinghua University, known as the "cradle of Chinese engineers," is China's second-most prestigious university and emphasizes engineering, science, and economic management. In 1979, China Central Television (CTC) began an "open university program," and television became an important way of providing higher education in China. By 1984 there were "radio and television universities" in more than 300 cities and 1,000 counties throughout 28 Chinese provinces, autonomous regions and special municipalities. See also BEIJING UNIVERSITY; CHINESE ACADEMY OF SCIENCES; CONFUCIANISM; CULTURAL REVOLUTION; FOUR MODERNIZATIONS; IMPERIAL EXAMINATION SYSTEM; NEW CULTURE MOVEMENT; QINGHUA UNIVERSITY; WRITING SYSTEM, CHINESE.

EIGHT DEMOCRATIC PARTIES See DEMOCRATIC PARTIES.

EIGHT ECCENTRICS OF YANGZHOU See YANGZHOU.

EIGHT IMMORTALS (*baxian* or *pa-hsien*) In the Daoist tradition, eight human beings who were believed to have gained immortality through their strenuous efforts in meditating, performing good deeds, and making sacrifices. While dwelling on mountain peaks, they kept their bodily forms and remained in touch with the earthly world. Worshiped in temples, they are believed to be able to bring dead people back to life and to transform any object into gold by using the so-called Philosopher's Stone. The Eight Immortals are Zhong Lijian (Chung Li-chien), Cao Guojiu (Ts'ao Kuochiu), Lan Caihe (Lan Ts'ai-ho), Zhang Guolao (Chang Kuo Lao), Han Xiangzi (Han Hsiang-tzu), Li Tieguai (Li T'iehkuai), He Xiangu (Ho Hsien-ku), and Lu Dongbin (Lu Tung-pin). Folk stories about the Immortals became widespread in China during the Tang (618–907) and Song (960–1279) dynasties. Right up to the present, their pictures and symbols have been portrayed in murals and wall carvings to represent long life and immortality. They are also a common design motif in many arts and crafts, such as in jade carving and on teapots, and even on pastries. Carved images of the Eight Immortals are placed on tables at birthday parties. There are actually 11 figures, for the immortals send two children, riding water buffaloes, to summon the God of Longevity who carries the peach of immortality. The Immor-

tals bring happiness and humor to brighten the lives of human beings. Although the eight did not know each other in human life, they received permission to dine together at the Peach Festival to honor the Daoist goddess Xiwangmu (Hsi Wang-mu), the Royal Lady (or Mother) of the Western Paradise. Anyone who eats a peach from the Heavenly Peach Orchard next to her palace is believed to gain immortal life.

Zhongli Jian is the head of the Eight Immortals and is depicted as a fat man holding a magic fan that revives people who have died. He discovered the secret of the elixir of immortality and invented the powder of transmutation. Cao Guojiu, the patron of actors, belonged to the royal family during the Song dynasty but left the court to seek immortality by practicing the Daoist religion. He is depicted as an imperial official wearing a court robe embroidered with clouds, a symbol of good fortune and wisdom, and carrying a pair of castanets. Lan Caihe is the patron of Chinese florists and is depicted as a young man in a blue robe carrying a basket of flowers.

Zhang Guo Lao, a hermit who lived in the seventh to eight centuries during the Tang dynasty (618–907), was believed to have magic powers and to be able to make himself invisible. He is depicted as an old man riding a white mule. A picture of him offering a son is often hung on the bedroom wall of a newly married couple. His symbol is the Yu Ku, a hollow bamboo musical instrument played with two sticks. Han Xiangzi, a ninth-century scholar, is the patron of Chinese musicians and is depicted playing a jade flute. Li Tieguai is the patron of Chinese herbal medicine doctors and is depicted as a crippled beggar with a crutch who carries a gourd holding magic medicine to bring dead people back to life. The most beloved of the Eight Immortals, he was the first to gain immortality, after he was cured of a leg ulcer by Xiwangmu herself.

Lu Dongbin, the patron of scholars, lived about A.D. 750, also during the Tang. A Daoist hermit, he achieved immortality at the early age of 50. He had been a high government official but was forced to flee the court and hide in the mountains. Lu supposedly had superhuman powers to kill dragons and transform objects. He is usually depicted as a Daoist carrying the evil-destroying sword on his back and a fly-whisk that represents his mastery over space. He Xiangu, who lived during the Tang dynasty, is the only female among the Eight Immortals. She is represented carrying a lotus flower, the Buddhist symbol for purity. See also DAOISM; ELIXIR OF IMMORTALITY; LOTUS; MEDICINE, HERBAL; PEACH; XIWANGMU.

EIGHT-LEGGED ESSAY See IMPERIAL EXAMINATION SYSTEM.

EIGHT TREASURES (*babao* or *pa-pao*) Also known as the Eight Precious Things; a set of eight symbols of good fortune and happiness that are commonly used in Chinese designs on porcelain, embroidered textiles, lacquerware, cloisonné and other crafts. Usually represented as a group, the eight treasures may be depicted alone as well. The Eight Treasures are: a pearl; a coin for warding off evil; a diamond-shaped lozenge taken from ancient headgear worn to symbolize victory; a round mirror that symbolizes the happiness of a married couple; a stone chime, a percussion instrument shaped like an inverted "V"; a pair of books symbolizing learning and the literati or scholars who ruled China in the imperial bureaucracy; a pair of rhinoceros horns representing happiness; and a leaf symbolizing good health and healing through herbal medicine, a popular motif on ceramics from the Qing dynasty (1644–1911). The Eight Treasures also have red ribbons that represent their power.

A different set of eight treasures is associated with Buddhism, which was introduced into China from India around the first century A.D. These symbols, believed to be on the Buddha's foot, are used for Buddhist altar implements and temple murals. They include the wheel of the law taught by the Buddha; the lotus, representing purity; a conch shell, a symbol of royalty whose sound, when blown, is supposed to be the Buddha's voice; a pair of fish representing marital happiness and fidelity; an umbrella; a canopy or flag; an endless knot, symbolizing eternity; and a lidded jar that holds sacred relics or the ashes of a cremated person. The eight Buddhist treasures also have ribbons in their design. Another popular set of symbols is associated with the Eight Immortals in the native Chinese religion of Daoism. These include a sword, fan, lotus, flute, flower basket, gourd, castanets and large bamboo tube also played as a flute. See also BUDDHISM; EIGHT IMMORTALS; LITERATI; LOTUS; MEDICINE, HERBAL; PEARL; WEDDINGS, TRADITIONAL; NAMES OF INDIVIDUAL CRAFTS.

EIGHT TRIGRAMS (*bagua* or *pa kua*)   A Daoist system which uses combinations of broken and solid lines for representing the basic elements in nature, supposedly invented by the legendary Emperor Fuxi (Fu Hsi). The Chinese have used this system to divine fate for thousands of years. It is still used by practitioners of Chinese folk religion and has become a popular means of divination in the Western world as well. The system of eight trigrams was recorded in the *Book of Changes* (*Yijing* or *I Ching*), an ancient manual that became one of the Five Classics (*wujing* or *wu ching*) of Confucianism. Each trigram is a symbol consisting of three solid and/or broken lines. The trigrams are themselves based on the concept of yin and yang, the universal principles the Chinese believe are the foundation of everything that exists. Solid lines represent yang, the male, active principle, and broken lines represent yin, the female, passive principle. The eight trigrams symbolize Heaven (*qin* or *ch'ien*), Earth (*kun*), thunder (*chen*), wind (*sun*), water (*kan*), fire (*li*), mountains (*ken*) and water (*tui*). The first two, Heaven and Earth, were thought to be yang and yin, respectively, and as such they are the father and mother of the other trigrams and of all created things. Each trigram is also associated with many other qualities, such as a virtue, an animal and a direction on the compass; for example, Heaven is, among other things, ceaseless power, the horse and south.

The eight trigrams are arranged in three ranks. By the time of Confucius (551–479 B.C.), the ancient system of eight trigrams had been multiplied to 64 hexagrams. The Chinese accepted the system of trigrams and hexagrams as the symbols that explained the metaphysical principles by which the universe functions. Starting in the 14th century, the eight trigrams became a popular Chinese decorative motif in ceramics, metalwork and other crafts. They are often depicted surrounding the symbol for yin and yang. The Chinese traditionally believe that a person who wears a copper, silver or jade plaque with this motif, or hangs one over the door of his or her home, will be protected from misfortune and be prosperous. See also BOOK OF CHANGES, DAOISM EIGHT TRIGRAMS REBELLION; FIVE CLASSICS OF CONFUCIANISM; FUXI; YIN AND YANG.

EIGHT TRIGRAMS REBELLION   An 1813 uprising against the Manchu Qing dynasty (1644–1911) by a sect that named itself for the traditional Chinese system of categorizing aspects of nature for divination, known as the Eight Trigrams. The Eight Trigrams sect was a revival of the White Lotus Secret Society that led a peasant rebellion from 1796 to 1804. The White Lotus was a Buddhist millenarian sect that taught that Maitreya, the Buddha of the Future, would descend to earth, restore the Chinese Ming dynasty (1368–1644), remove disease, natural disasters and all other suffering in this life, and bring happiness in the next life. These teachings appealed to impoverished Chinese peasants. In 1811 a teacher of the White Lotus Sect, Lin Qing (Lin Ch'ing; 1770–1813), met a similar religious teacher named Li Wencheng (c. 1770–1813). These leaders built up chapters of a new sect—which they named the Eight Trigrams—in the capital city of Beijing and in the regions of southern Zhili (Chih-li), northern Henan Province and western Shandong Province. They promised the men and women who joined them that they would gain high positions and other rewards in the forthcoming millennium. Lin Qing announced that he was the reincarnation of Maitreya and that Li Wencheng was the King of Men. The titles King of Men, King of Heaven and King of Earth, given to leaders of the Eight Trigrams, followed the Chinese view that human beings are placed in between the two extremes of heaven and earth.

Members of the sect wore white cloth sashes and carried knives in preparation for the struggle that would bring about the era of "endless blessings," which would begin on the 15th day of the 9th month in the Chinese lunar calendar (October 8, 1813). They carried banners proclaiming "Entrusted by Heaven to Prepare the Way," similar to the banners carried by the rebels in the popular Ming novel *Outlaws of the Marsh* (also known as *The Water Margin; Shuihuzhuan* or *Shuihuzhuan*), which read "Carry Out the Way on Behalf of Heaven." Like the rebel heroes of this novel, members of the Eight Trigrams Sect believed that the emperor had lost the Mandate of Heaven (*tianming* or *t'ien ming*) that legitimized the reign of his dynasty. They believed they were removing him by Heaven's command.

Lin Qing sent 250 members of the sect to the Forbidden City, the imperial palace in Beijing. There they planned to kill the Jiaqing emperor (Chia-ch'ing; r. 1796–1820) when he returned from a hunting trip. Eighty members got inside the walls of the imperial palace and killed everyone they saw, but the eunuchs, who ran the palace, and the imperial princes fought and overcame them. Qing authorities soon arrested Lin Qing and Li Wencheng. For several months, thousands of members of the Eight Trigrams Sect, who had set up headquarters in Hua city in Henan Province, stirred up trouble and attacked several Chinese cities. The Qing sent an army that took back the regions controlled by the Eight Trigrams and put the sect members under siege in Hua. The army invaded the city and ended the rebel occupation on January 1, 1814. The Eight Trigram Rebellion had no lasting effect on the Qing dynasty, but the teachings of the sect continued to influence Chinese peasants. See also EIGHT TRIGRAMS; FORBIDDEN CITY; MAITREYA AND MANJUSRI; MANDATE OF HEAVEN; OUTLAWS OF THE MARSH; QING DYNASTY.

EIGHTH ROUTE ARMY The name for the army of the Chinese Communist Party (CCP), formerly known as the Red Army, while China fought its War of Resistance against Japan (1937–45; World War II). In 1931 Japan invaded Manchuria and established the puppet state of Manchukuo the following year. Following the Marco Polo Bridge Incident on July 7, 1937, Japan launched a full-scale invasion of China, and China declared war on Japan. On August 22, 1937, the CCP formally reorganized its forces as the Eighth Route Army of the National Army. (Many of its commanders later held top CCP and government positions in the People's Republic of China (PRC), founded by the CCP in 1949.) Zhu De (Chu Teh) was commander of the army and Peng Dehuai (P'eng Teh-huai) was deputy commander. Zhu's wife, Kang Keqing (K'ang K'e-ch'ing), served as director of the political department of the Eighth Route Army. The army had three divisions, with Liu Bocheng (Liu Po-cheng) as commander of one, the 115th division. Deng Xiaoping (Teng Hsiao-ping) served under him as political commissar. Another division was commanded by Lin Biao (Lin Piao), and Nie Rongzhen (Nieh Jung-chen) served as his deputy commander and political commissar. The army's headquarters were in the new Nationalist capital of Chongqing in Sichuan Province, which is protected by high mountains. In 1946, following the defeat of Japan, the army became known as the People's Liberation Army (PLA).

Canadian surgeon Norman Bethune went to China and organized medical services for the Eighth Route Army. The August First Film Studio, connected with the PLA, made a feature film about Bethune and the Eighth Route Army during China's War of Resistance entitled *Norman Bethune: The Making of a Hero* (1988). See also BETHUNE, NORMAN; CHINESE COMMUNIST PARTY; CIVIL WAR BETWEEN COMMUNISTS AND NATIONALISTS; LIN BIAO; LIU BOCHENG; LONG MARCH; MARCO POLO BRIDGE INCIDENT; NATIONALIST PARTY; NIE RONGZHEN; PENG DEHUAI; PEOPLE'S LIBERATION ARMY; WAR OF RESISTANCE AGAINST JAPAN; ZHU DE.

ELECTRIC POWER See ENERGY SOURCES; THREE GORGES WATER CONSERVANCY PROJECT.

ELEPHANT TRUNK MOUNTAIN See GUILIN.

ELGIN, LORD See ARROW WAR; BEIJING, CONVENTION OF; GONG, PRINCE.

ELIXIR OF IMMORTALITY (*xiandan* or *hsientan*) Also known as the pill of immortality; a chemical compound sought by a few alchemists of the royal court who practiced Daoism. This elixir which would give them the secret to immortal life and the ability to make gold. Some Daoists believed that the elixir of immortality could be found on the Island of the Eastern Sea, also known as the Island of the Blessed or Immortals. The Daoist Paradise is Shou Shan, the Hills of Longevity, which has been depicted by Chinese artists as a place of mountains with lakes and rivers, bridges, viewing pavilions, and pine trees, through which the Daoist gods are seen wandering.

The Yellow Emperor of legend, also known as Huangdi (Huang-ti), who supposedly sat on the throne 2697–2597 B.C., is credited with writing a treatise on medicine which contained the secrets immortality and creating gold. Many historical Chinese emperors sought these abilities so as to make themselves equal to the Yellow Emperor. A few Daoist philosophers, who were concerned with immortality and alchemy, revered the Yellow Emperor as the source of their teaching. Even today sculptures of the Yellow Emperor are still placed in Daoist temples. Some of the materials with which Daoist alchemists attempted to create the elixir of immortality included cinnabar, red sulphuret of arsenic, sulphur, yellow sulpheret of arsenic, mother of pearl, peach tree sap, charred mulberry ash, ginseng and various other mineral and herbal substances. They also concocted liquids from gold and jade, known as gold and jade essences. (Ginseng has remained one of the most important elements in Chinese herbal medicine.)

The first Chinese emperor, Qin Shi Huangdi, who unified China under the Qin dynasty (221–206 B.C.), was obsessed with finding the elixir of immortality and sent many people to find the Island of the Immortals. Near the end of his life, he made a grand tour east to the sea, and on the way back he encountered a group of magicians who requested permission to travel to the mystical islands of Penglai to find the elixir of immortality. The emperor sent a large number of young men and women with them, but there is no record of their successful return.

The Monkey King, who is popular in China as the central character in the 16th-century novel *Journey to the West* (*Xiyouji*; also known as *Pilgrimage to the West* and *Monkey*), has many humorous adventures. In one of the novel's best-known episodes, "Monkey Causes Havoc in Heaven," Monkey steals the banquet feast of the gods and makes himself doubly immortal by eating the peaches of immortality and swallowing the pill of immortality, which he has stolen. The elixir of immortality is also associated with the moon. Chang E (also known as Heng O), the Goddess of the Moon, found the pill of immortality in the bedroom of her husband, Hou Yi. He was an archer who saved the world by shooting down 9 of the 10 suns that were burning up the earth, and Xiwangmu, the Daoist Royal Lady of the West, rewarded him with the pill of immortality. Hou Yi's disciple found Chang E holding the pill and threatened to kill her if she did not give it to him. Frightened, she swallowed it, became immortal and flew up to the moon, where she became a three-legged toad. The Chinese see a white rabbit in the moon pounding the herbs to make the elixir of immortality, which Chang E will soon drink. See also ALCHEMY; CHANG E; DAOISM; GINSENG; ISLANDS OF THE BLESSED; JADE; MONKEY; QIN SHI HUANGDI, EMPEROR; XIWANGMU; YELLOW EMPEROR.

EMBLEM, NATIONAL The symbolic picture that officially represents the People's Republic of China (PRC), which was founded in 1949 by the Chinese Communist Party (CCP). The national or state emblem depicts the Gate of Heavenly Peace (Tiananmen or T'ien-an-men) that leads from Tiananmen Square to the Forbidden City (former imperial palace) in Beijing. The enormous gate was built of stone with a wooden roof in 1417 and restored in 1651. A stream flowing at the foot of the gate is crossed by five white marble bridges.

CCP Chairman Mao Zedong (Mao Tse-tung; 1893–1976) stood on the rostrum on top of the gate on October 1, 1949, and proclaimed the founding of the PRC. A huge portrait of Mao hangs on the gate's central portal. On important occasions, CCP leaders make appearances on the rostrum before large crowds that gather in the square.

In the emblem, five yellow, five-pointed stars shine above the gate. One large star represents the PRC and CCP leaders, while four smaller stars in a semicircle beneath it represent the four classes of people in the republic: workers, peasants, small business owners and capitalists loyal to the PRC. Alternately, the four may be considered to represent the four types of workers: farmers, factory workers, white-collar workers and managers. A wreath of ears of grain with a cogwheel at the base surrounds the gate and stars; the wreath symbolizes agriculture and the cogwheel industrial development. The five stars are also placed on the PRC national flag, against a red background. See also CHINESE COMMUNIST PARTY; FLAG, NATIONAL; PEOPLE'S REPUBLIC OF CHINA; TIANANMEN SQUARE.

EMBROIDERY (*cixiu,* or *tz'u-hsiu* "to embroider") The art of hand-sewing beautiful and colorful designs on textiles. In China, the finest embroidery has been done with dyed silk threads on silk fabric, although nylon fabric may be used today. Gold and silver threads are also used. Village peasants have worn clothes made of cotton, hemp or other plant fibers such as flax and decorated them with embroidery motifs similar to those in the folk art of papercutting.

There are two main types of Chinese embroidery. One type uses a long stitch known as the satin stitch, or the combination of a long and short stitch. The other uses the so-called Beijing knot or French knot, also called the seed stitch. Other stitches used include the chain, stem and split stitches, and a technique for anchoring longer stitches with short stitches known as "couching" is often used to outline designs. The fabric being embroidered is placed on a frame which keeps it taut and enables the embroiderer to roll up the work as she completes a section. Paper stencils or cutout patterns are used to transfer the design to the fabric.

Silk weaving and embroidery were (and still are) traditionally women's work in China. Mothers taught their daughters how to weave and embroider, and a girl who was skillful in these arts had higher status and a better chance of finding a good husband. Pattern books were handed down through families as heirlooms. The use of silk was so widespread by the Ming dynasty (1368–1644) that upper-class homes were filled with embroidered objects, including wall hangings, folding screens, tablecloths and bedspreads, as well as clothing. Even children wore embroidered clothing, and every baby boy had tiger shoes and other items embroidered with motifs to protect him from danger. Robes worn by the emperor, his family and members of the imperial court were decorated with elaborate embroidery. Design motifs and colors decorating a person's robes were strictly designated according to his or her rank. The emperor's robe was embroidered with the 12 symbols of his authority, including five-clawed dragons, the sun, moon and stars, a mountain, pheasant, sacrificial goblets, water weed, grain, fire, an ax, and a Fu, or lion-dog. Members of the court wore an appropriate patch on their robes decorated with the ani-

mals, plants and other motifs assigned to the nine levels in the court. An imperial robe may have been embroidered by as many as 12 workers over 5 years.

There are four major embroidery centers in China: Sichuan, Suzhou, Hunan and Guangdong provinces. Sichuan Province in the southwest is the center where large embroidered squares for making quilts and other household items are produced. Weaving and embroidery were begun in Sichuan more than 1,500 years ago. During the Tang (618–907) and Ming dynasties, the "Yue" or Guangdong (Canton) style of embroidery was popular. This is a colorful style that makes use of gold and silver threads, red and green silk threads, and even peacock feathers and seed pearls. Motifs include plum blossoms, peonies and bamboo. Guangdong Province, whose capital is Guangzhou (Canton), the major port in southern China, is still an important center for embroidery. Hunan Province in central China is known for realistic embroideries of landscapes and animals, especially lions and tigers, that have a subtle, shaded look. Many of these are copies of famous paintings. Embroiderers also use a technique that gives the appearance of animal fur.

Suzhou, in Jiangsu Province in central China, is perhaps the best-known center for silk weaving and embroidery. Today, visitors to Suzhou can still see two silk weaving mills and the Museum of Suzhou Embroidery, which has incorporated the Embroidery Research Institute, established in 1954 to preserve traditional Chinese embroidery techniques and to develop new ones. At that time about 20 stitches were used, but many new ones have been added. Artisans at the Institute are famous for their double-sided embroideries that typically portray a Shandong cat, goldfish or lady, with different patterns and colors on each side of the cloth. An embroiderer works with silk thread that has been split into as many as 48 delicate strands. Although some of the works are sold at the institute, most of the fine pieces are placed in exhibitions abroad, given to important diplomatic visitors or used to decorate new hotels. The new museum houses a collection of more than 2,000 embroidered works that date as far back as the Han dynasty (206 B.C.–A.D. 220).

During the last dynasty, the Qing (1644–1911), imperial textiles were made in Weaving Offices (Zhizao Ju) supervised by the imperial palace, known as the Forbidden City, in the capital city of Beijing but located in the cities of Suzhou, Hangzhou and Jiangning, which had famous silk industries. Designs for weaving were created by artisans of the Imperial Household Department and approved by the Board of Rites and the emperor. Hand-woven and embroidered robes were stored in the palace, which still has a collection of about 10,000 robes. See also DRAGON; EMPEROR; FORBIDDEN CITY; NINE-RANK SYSTEM; PAPERCUTTING; SILK; SUZHOU; NAMES OF INDIVIDUAL DESIGN MOTIFS.

EMEI, MOUNT See FOUR SACRED MOUNTAINS OF BUDDHISM.

EMIGRATION See FUJIAN PROVINCE; HONG KONG; OVERSEAS CHINESE; PEARL RIVER; SHIPPING AND SHIPBUILDING; SINGAPORE; SIX COMPANIES, CHINESE; TAIWAN; XIAMEN.

EMPEROR (*huangdi* or *huang-ti*) The head of a dynasty that ruled the Chinese Empire. This term was first used by

King Zhen of the state of Qin, who unified China under the Qin dynasty (221–206 B.C.) and proclaimed himself Emperor Qin Shi Huangdi (Ch'in Shih-huang-ti; r. 221–210 B.C.), the "First Emperor of Qin." He took the name *Huangdi* from the legendary Yellow Emperor, who supposedly founded the Chinese Empire. Ever since the Qin reign, China has been ruled by a series of emperors belonging to dynasties that succeeded each other, except for a few periods when competing dynasties controlled various parts of the empire at the same time. It was forbidden to refer to an emperor by his personal name, not only during his own reign, but during the entire reign of his dynasty. After an emperor died, he was given a posthumous temple name by which he would be referred, preceded by the name of his dynasty. For example, one of the greatest emperors of the Han dynasty (206 B.C.–A.D. 220) was Liu Bang (Liu Pang), who is known as Han Wudi (Wu-ti; r. 141–87 B.C.). The fourth Han emperor, Han Wendi (Wen-ti; r. 180–157 B.C.), was the first to use a reign title, which could be used to refer to a date during his reign, for example, the first year of the Hou Yuan reign. Some emperors used many different reign titles, often changing them in order to reverse bad fortune and bring about good fortune. Students of Chinese history commonly use their dynasties and temple names to refer to Chinese emperors, except for emperors of the Ming and Qing dynasties. During the Ming dynasty (1368–1644), the emperor began to adopt a reign title that was used throughout his reign, and by which he is still known, rather than by his posthumous temple name. For example, Zhu Yuanzhang (Chu Yuan-chang), who founded the Ming and became the first Ming emperor (r. 1368–99), was given the posthumous temple name Taizu (T'ai-tsu). However, he is referred to by the name of his reign, Hongwu (Hung-wu), meaning "Boundless Valor." Technically he should be referred to as the Hongwu emperor. This practice was continued during the Qing dynasty (1644–1911), China's last imperial dynasty. Each Ming and Qing reign name was an expression of hope that the reign would be fortunate, such as Ming emperor Jiajing (Chia'ching; r. 1522–67), "Perpetual Happiness," and Qing emperor Yongle (Yung-lo; r. 1403–24), "Eternal Contentment." These reign names are also used to date porcelain from the Ming and Qing dynasties, because the reign name was written on the bottom of each piece made during a particular emperor's reign.

Individual dynasties had different rules for succession, but, in general, the eldest son inherited the throne, especially if his mother was the first wife of the emperor. Since Chinese emperors had many concubines, the son of a concubine also had a chance to become the next emperor. Many times an emperor was placed on the throne while he was a young boy, so that regents exercised the real power in his name. There are two famous exceptions to the rule that only men were emperors in China. Empress Wu usurped the Tang dynasty throne in 690 but was deposed in 705, and Empress Dowager Cixi (Tz'u Hsi; 1835–1908) wielded the real power during the last half-century of the Qing dynasty. In later dynasties, especially the Ming and Qing, the eunuchs who staffed the imperial palace became very powerful, and some of them ruled as virtual dictators while the emperors were merely figureheads.

Chinese history begins with six legendary emperors. Fuxi (Fu-hsi) supposedly taught the Chinese people how to hunt, fish, domesticate animals, build houses and write using simple characters. Shen Nong (Shen-nung) taught them how to cultivate crops for food and medicine. The Yellow Emperor (Huangdi) organized the universe into Heaven and Earth and created an administrative bureaucracy, the calendar, and many other important aspects of civilization. Yao and Shun are considered to be models of the virtuous ruler as later defined by the Confucian tradition. Yu the Great supposedly founded the first Chinese dynasty, the Xia (c. 2200–1750 B.C.), although no physical remains have been found from the Xia. The Shang dynasty (1750–1040 B.C.), the first from which archaeologists have excavated artifacts, was founded by Tang the Victorious.

The Zhou dynasty (1100–256 B.C.) overthrew the Shang and claimed that they had been given the mandate to rule, which Heaven had given to the Shang but had taken away from them because their rulers were not virtuous. All succeeding dynasties in China legitimized the reigns of their emperors by claiming that they had been given the Mandate of Heaven (*tian ming* or *t'ien-ming*). The Zhou established a feudal system in which a number of kingdoms recognized the Zhou ruler as their overlord. By the end of the dynasty, known as the Warring States Period (403–221 B.C.), the stronger kingdoms conquered weaker ones and contended with each other. The strongest proved to be Qin, and the ruler of Qin unified China under the Qin dynasty and became the first true emperor of China, Qin Shi Huangdi. The Han dynasty (206 B.C.–A.D. 220) established a Confucian-educated imperial bureaucracy, comparable to a civil service in Western countries, which continued to run the Chinese government until the end of the Qing dynasty. The Chinese commonly refer to themselves as Hanren ("People of Han"), the descendants of the Han dynasty. Han is also the name for the majority ethnic group in China. The Han Chinese called their country the Middle Kingdom (Zhongguo or Chung-kuo) and regarded all non-Chinese as "barbarians." They developed the tribute system for regulating trade with foreign peoples by requiring them to send missions to kowtow (bow down) before the Chinese emperor and give him tribute, for which they would receive the right to trade at designated places in China. Chinese emperors built the Great Wall across northern China to keep out nomadic tribes who constantly threatened the Chinese empire. Some tribes, such as the Xiongnu (Hsiung-nu), managed to invade China and establish their own dynasties in various northern regions. Many of them became "Sinicized"—that is, adopted Chinese customs, clothing, the language and writing system and married Chinese women—so that in a few generations they were completely assimilated into China. During the Six Dynasties Period, or Period of Disunion (220–589), the Chinese Empire became divided into many competing dynasties, but it was reunified under the Sui dynasty (581–618) by Sui Emperor Wendi (Wen-ti; r. 581–604). The Sui was soon replaced by the Tang dynasty (618–907), one of the high points of Chinese culture, when many influences from India, Central Asia and other foreign regions were brought into the empire, especially along the so-called Silk Road on which China traded silk, porcelains, tea and other luxury goods. Many Chinese also like to think of themselves as "People of

Emperors ruled China, through successive dynasties, from the third century B.C. until 1912.   COURTESY, MUSEUM OF FINE ARTS, BOSTON

Tang" (Tangren). During the Song dynasty (960–1279), China experienced another high point in its culture, especially painting. The Song was overthrown by the Mongols, an ethnic group who invaded China from the north and

established the Yuan dynasty (1279–1368), the first time the entire Chinese Empire was ruled by non-Chinese people. The founder of the Yuan was the great Mongol leader Khubilai Khan, who had actually founded the Yuan in 1260, before conquering all of China, and reigned as Emperor Yuan Shizu (Shi Tsu; r. 1260–94).

The Han Chinese resented their Mongol rulers, and in 1368 a Chinese rebel leader named Zhu Yuanzhang (Chu Yuan-chang) overthrew the Yuan and established the Ming dynasty. He reigned as the first Ming Emperor Hongwu (Hung-wu; 1368–99). In 1644 the Manchus, an ethnic group based in Manchuria (modern northeastern China), invaded China, overthrew Ming emperor Chongzhen (Chung-chen; r. 1628–45) and established the Qing dynasty, the second time that the entire Chinese Empire was governed by non-Han Chinese. Several members of the Ming imperial family fled south and attempted to continue the dynasty, but it ended with the death of Ming emperor Yongli (r. 1647–61). Chinese emperors had always resided in splendid palaces, and the most magnificent of all was built in Beijing at the start of the Ming, an enormous complex known as the Forbidden City, where Qing emperors also resided. The Qing dynasty began losing its authority in the l9th century when Great Britain and other foreign powers refused to submit to the Chinese emperor in the tribute system and forced China to open cities to foreign residents and trade, known as treaty ports.

The Chinese people overthrew the Manchu Qing in the Revolution of 1911 and established the Republic of China in 1912. Xuantong (Hsuan-t'ung; r. 1909–12), the last Qing emperor, now known as Henry Puyi, resided in the Forbidden City until 1925. The complex is now open to the public and is one of the main tourist attractions in China. The Japanese made Puyi the head of the puppet state that they established in Manchuria in 1932, known as Manchukuo. See also CONCUBINAGE; CONFUCIANISM; EUNUCHS; FORBIDDEN CITY; HAN; HISTORICAL PERIODS; IMPERIAL BUREAUCRACY; KOWTOW; MANDATE OF HEAVEN; MIDDLE KINGDOM; PUYI, HENRY; QIN SHI HUANGDI; SINICIZATION; TREATY PORTS; TRIBUTE SYSTEM; NAMES OF INDIVIDUAL EMPERORS AND DYNASTIES.

EMPRESS DOWAGER   See CIXI, EMPRESS DOWAGER.

ENAMELWARE (*fahua*)   Porcelain objects, such as vases, bowls and plates, that are decorated with polychrome enamels. Porcelain is a fine, delicate type of ceramic made from a body of fused clay, covered with a glaze and then fired in a kiln at a high temperature, usually about 1,280°C. Enamelware is closely related to cloisonné, a technique for decorating bronzeware with polychrome enamel pastes. *Fahua* is the Chinese term for a ceramic version of the cloisonné technique. Chinese potters developed the technique for producing enamelware in the 12th century during the Song dynasty (960–1279) and perfected it during the Ming dynasty (1368–1644).

Enamel is a type of glass which has been colored with metallic oxides; for example, cobalt for blue, copper for green, manganese for purple and antimony for yellow. Enamel fuses at a lower temperature than porcelain, so a porcelain object to be decorated with enamel is first fired in the kiln, with or without an initial porcelain glaze. The enamel is then painted onto the object, which is fired a second time at a lower temperature to fuse the enamel. Song potters originally used iron-red overglaze enamel, which became popular during the Ming dynasty and is known as *rouge de fer*, and yellow overglaze enamel, although they occasionally used other colors such as green and purple. Designs painted with enamel on porcelain objects became more complex during the Ming as styles and tastes changed with each new emperor's reign. Design motifs include ornate flowers, scenes taken from bird-and-flower and landscape paintings, and textile designs. During the Qing dynasty (1644–1911) polychrome enamelware became the most popular type of Chinese ceramic.

Chinese potters developed many colors and technical variations of enamelware. *Famille verte,* which includes several shades of green, became the most popular style during the reign of Qing emperor Kangxi (K'ang-hsi; r. 1661–1722). Other colors are also classified with *famille verte,* including yellow (known as *famille jaune*) purple, deep red with a coral tone, white, deep blue and black (*famille noir*), a composite color produced by covering brown-black pigment with green, purple or clear enamel. The Chinese referred to the colors belonging to *famille verte* as "hard colors" (*yingcai* or *ying-ts'ai*) because they could not be given much gradation or shading. *Famille verte* enamels were sometimes used along with underglaze cobalt-blue painting, and touches of gilt were also added to highlight the design.

Qing potters also revived techniques for monochrome glazing that dated back to the Song. They further developed the copper-red technique to produce a thick deep-red glaze with fine crackles that is known as *sang-de-boeuf* (oxblood; *langyao*). This color was also transmuted to produce peachbloom glaze, a mottled pink glaze called "kidney bean" by the Chinese. The finest peachbloom wares comprise a series of small and elegant objects, such as vases and water droppers, the latter used by scholars for calligraphy. These containers were made in eight standard shapes. Qing potters also produced green, powder blue, yellow and purple monochrome enamel.

Qing porcelains attained their greatest refinement during the reign of the Yongzheng emperor (Yung-cheng; r. 1723–35), when the new *famille rose* enamels became the dominant Chinese style for decorating porcelains. The rose-pink color was derived from colloidal gold and had a wide range of tones, from pale pink to deep ruby. Porcelain painters mixed an opaque white enamel with the colors to modify them, enabling them to use a range of color values for the first time and hence incorporate subtle shading into their designs, similar to the shading in oil paintings. The technique of painting *famille rose* enamels was probably adopted from European painted enamels on gold and copper, which were introduced into China by Roman Catholic Jesuit missionaries. The Chinese term for *famille rose* is "soft colors" (*ruancai* or *juan-ts'ai*) or "foreign colors" (*yangcai* or *yang-ts'ai*). The palette of *famille rose* enamels gave rise to a third category of Qing monochromes, opaque and semiopaque enamels used alone as glazes. The Chinese termed these "colors after the European style" (*xiyang* or *hsi-yang*). See also BIRD-AND-FLOWER PAINTING; CALLIGRAPHY; CLOISONNÉ; JESUITS; LANDSCAPE PAINTING; MING DYNASTY; PORCELAIN; QING DYNASTY; SONG DYNASTY.

ENERGY SOURCES   Coal is, by far, the most important source of primary energy in the People's Republic of China

(PRC), which has around 900 billion metric tons (MT) of identified and recoverable coal resources, more than three times the reserves in the United States or in the former republics of the U.S.S.R. Shanxi Province in northern China ranks first with more than 200 billion tons of coal reserves, followed by Inner Mongolia with more than 190 billion tons and by Shanxi, Guizhou, Ningxia and Anhui, which all have more than 20 billion tons. The abundant coal deposits in Shanxi Province are close to the surface and easy to mine. The capital city of Taiyuan has become a major center for coal production and transportation and is also important for its iron and steel and heavy-machine-building industries. Coal is transported by railroad to the densely populated and industrialized areas in southern and southeastern China, but transportation facilities are inadequate, so the PRC still needs to import coal. During the 1980s the PRC encouraged joint ventures with foreign companies to increase coal mining. Many Chinese provinces and municipalities have cooperated to establish the China National Coal Development Corporation, which has been responsible for developing joint coal-mining ventures with foreign investors. In 1985 Occidental Petroleum signed a 30-year joint-venture agreement with the PRC to develop an open-pit coal mine at Pingshuo in Shanxi, which could become the world's largest; however, Occidental, which had a 25-percent stake in the $650 million venture, withdrew in the mid-1990s.

The PRC also has large oil and gas reserves. In 1959 it struck oil at its largest oil field, under the city of Daqing in Heilongjiang Province in northeastern China (Manchuria). By 1985 Daqing oil field was producing 53 million tons of oil per year, half of China's crude oil output. Major oil fields were also discovered in Shandong Province, Tianjin special municipality and other regions. In the 1970s the PRC laid its first oil pipeline, from Daqing to the port of Qinhuangdao on the Gulf of Bo Hai in Hebei Province. Preliminary exploration showed that the PRC has around 30 to 60 billion tons of oil reserves. There are also large natural gas fields in 20 of China's provinces, autonomous regions and municipalities, although natural gas production is small in relation to its potential reserve base and crude oil production. Forty percent of gas production comes from fields in Sichuan Province.

Large oil and gas basins have been discovered in the South China Sea at the Pearl River (Zhujiang) estuary, Beibu Gulf and on the sea's northern continental shelf. China's petroleum and geological industry began to survey the South China Sea in the early 1960s and expanded this survey in the 1970s. In 1979 the Chinese government, after passing regulations authorizing the China National Oil Corporation (CNOC) to invite tenders from abroad, signed agreements on geophysical prospecting of the South China Sea and the southern part of the Yellow Sea with more than 40 companies from 12 countries. In 1981 the first well was drilled in the South China Sea. In 1982 the State Council drew up the Regulations of the PRC on the Exploitation of Offshore Petroleum Resources in Cooperation with Foreign Enterprises, providing legal protection for China's sovereignty and economic interests, as well as the rights and interests of foreign companies. By 1990 prospectors discovered rich oil and gas reserves across 400,000 square miles of coastal waters, and a wide-ranging series of joint projects with overseas oil companies were initiated. By 1990 CNOC signed contracts

and agreements with 45 companies from 12 companies, attracting investment totaling US $2.65 billion.

In 1983 most of China's large oil refineries were consolidated under Sinopec (China National Petrochemical Corporation), and refineries were upgraded to shift output from fuel oil to more valuable products such as gasoline, kerosene, diesel fuel and components for petrochemicals. China has also greatly increased production of non-energy-use products such as raw materials, lubricants, asphalt, coke, paraffin and solvents. A strategic plan drawn up in 1989 outlined plans for a natural gas development zone in the western part of the South China Sea and for the exploitation of oil resources in the East China Sea Basin, as well as Sino-foreign development of oil refineries and oil-based chemical industries. The PRC is spending billions of dollars to build a pipeline to carry oil east from potentially huge reserves in the Tarim Basin in remote Xinjiang-Uighur Autonomous Region in western China. China has become a huge importer of dollar-priced oil; its imports rose 57 percent in 1997.

The Chinese government has encouraged research into the utilization of biogas or methane, an inflammable gas produced by the fermentation of organic matter such as plants and human and animal wastes. Since the majority of the Chinese people still practice agriculture, this could be a significant energy source. A cubic meter of methane is equivalent to 2,250 grams of coal in caloric value. In the 1930s, China was the first country to use methane, and by the 1980s there were more than 7 million methane-producing tanks in the Chinese countryside. With a volume of 8 to 10 cubic meters, each tank can produce from 1 to 3 cubic meters of gas daily, enough each day for cooking and lighting purposes for a family of four. Methane production also burns up the eggs of parasites, helping to eliminate hookworm disease, snail fever and leptospirosis, which are common in rural areas. Methane is a clean energy source that causes no environmental pollution, and the residues left in the tanks are excellent fertilizers.

Electric power was the fastest-growing form of energy in the PRC during the 1980s yet was the shortest in supply. Chinese industry uses around 80 percent of all electricity generated, and frequent shortages and blackouts severely reduce industrial productivity. The PRC is attempting to alleviate the problem by building hydroelectric stations, thermal plants and substations. China's many large rivers give it a vast hydroelectric potential which the government is now developing, with a number of hydropower projects planned or under construction. These include the world's largest dam at the Three Gorges Water Conservancy Project on the Yangzi River (Changjiang), which is expected to generate 84 billion kilowatt hours annually. The PRC has imported new power plants from the West, which account for about 20 percent of total generating capacity. China also has rich geothermal resources, with a total of more than 2,500 hot springs discovered to date. There are also large steam fields in Yunnan Province, Tibet and other areas.

Nuclear power is another potential energy source. The PRC has the goal of developing nuclear power to a 6,000 MW capacity by 2000, having an additional 6,000 MW under construction by 2000, and bringing on-line an additional 1,200 MW every year after 2000. However, it may have trouble meeting these goals due to a lack of financial and technical resources. See also DAQING OIL FIELDS; GEOGRAPHY; IRON TECHNOLOGY AND STEEL INDUSTRY; RAILROADS; SOUTH CHINA SEA; TARIM BASIN; THREE GORGES WATER CONSERVANCY PROJECT; NAMES OF INDIVIDUAL PROVINCES AND AUTONOMOUS REGIONS.

ENLIGHTENMENT DAILY   See NEW CHINA NEWS AGENCY.

ENNIN (793–864)   A Japanese monk in the Tiantai (T'ien T'ai; known in Japan as Tendai) sect of the Buddhist religion who visited China and whose diary is the oldest surviving report on China by a foreigner. The diary, *Record of Pilgrimage to China in Search of the Holy Law* (*Nitto Gubo Junreiki*), is a valuable resource for historians. It was translated into English by Edwin O. Reischauer, a former U.S. ambassador to Japan (1961–66). Ennin is known in Japan by his posthumous title, Jikaku Daishi. He was a member of the last embassy sent by the Japanese imperial court during the Tang dynasty (618–907), one of the greatest periods in the history of Chinese culture. The embassy traveled to China in 838, and Ennin stayed until 847. As a Buddhist scholar, he knew how to read the Chinese language when he traveled to China. (Buddhism had been introduced into China from India around the first century A.D. and transmitted to Japan from China in the fifth century A.D.) In China, Ennin planned to visit Mount Tiantai in modern Zhejiang province in eastern China, the home of his sect, but did not receive permission from the government. He did visit Chang'an (modern Xi'an in Shaanxi Province in northwestern China), the Tang capital and the largest and most cosmopolitan city in the world at the time. He also visited Mount Wuta (Wutai or Wut'ai), an important center for the Tiantai sect and one of the Four Sacred Mountains of Buddhism in China.

When Ennin arrived in China, Buddhism was at the height of its influence there. However, Emperor Wuzong (Wu-tsung) began issuing edicts in 842 forcing Buddhism monks and nuns to become lay people and appropriating Buddhist temple property for the government. The persecution of Buddhism reached its height in 845. However, Emperor Wuzong died in 846 and his successor relaxed the anti-Buddhist regulations.

When Ennin returned to Japan in 847 he brought back a quantity of Buddhist sutras (scriptures) and religious objects, as well as the diary he kept during his stay in China. It has been compared to the record kept by the Italian explorer Marco Polo (1254–1324), which is quite famous in the Western world, but unfortunately Ennin's diary is not well known in the West. It contains a wealth of detailed information on many aspects of Chinese culture and is especially important for scholars of religion because it provides a first-hand account of the Chinese persecution of Buddhism. When Ennin returned to Japan, he stayed on Mount Hiyei for more than 20 years, during which time he founded the Onjoji Monastery, better known as Miidera, on Lake Biwa at the foot of Mount Hiyei. He was patronized by the emperor and the powerful Fujiwara clan in the nearby capital of Kyoto. See also BUDDHISM; CHANG'AN; FOUR SACRED MOUNTAINS OF BUDDHISM; POLO, MARCO; TANG DYNASTY; TIANTAI SECT OF BUDDHISM.

ERDAOBAI RIVER   See CHANGBAI MOUNTAIN RANGE.

ERHU   A musical instrument, held vertically in the lap, with a long, thin neck and two strings that is played by a bow that fits between the two strings and is pushed across one string and pulled against the other. The instrument has a haunting sound that resembles a human voice. It belongs to the family of string instruments known as the *huqin*, or "barbarian fiddles," so-called because they were introduced into China from nomadic Central Asian tribes. By the Song dynasty (960–1279) the *huqin* were used in China to play popular folk music. Even today they are the main instruments in the orchestras that accompany Beijing Operas. See also OPERA, BEIJING.

ERSHI HUANGDI (EMPEROR)   See LI SI; QIN DYNASTY.

ETIQUETTE   See BANQUETS; MUSIC AND DANCE, CEREMONIAL; PROPRIETY.

EUNUCHS   Castrated men who served the royal family in the Chinese imperial palace. The first mention in official documents of eunuchs as a major faction in the Chinese government dates from the eighth century B.C., during the Zhou dynasty (1100–256 B.C.). However, eunuchs had existed for about five or six centuries prior, when the Chinese marriage system became polygamous and upper-class men began taking many wives and concubines. Enemies captured in battle were often castrated, as were criminals, and the eunuchs were then put to work in the harems, or women's quarters, of rulers and high government officials. The eunuchs guarded the women, educated them and their sons, and performed the duties of servants. Since eunuchs were not able to father children, the royal bloodline would be kept pure. In later dynasties, some poverty-stricken families had their sons and grandsons castrated in hopes that they would be able to enter the emperor's service. During the first imperial dynasty, the Qin (221–206 B.C.), the eunuch Zhao Gao (Chao Kao) placed the second emperor on the throne and got rid of rivals to his power.

During the Han dynasty (206 B.C.–A.D. 220), young emperors who wanted to assert their own power against the power of their mothers' relatives had to make the eunuchs their allies, and these emperors appointed eunuchs to high positions of great responsibility. The eunuchs were the only males with whom Chinese emperors had daily contact. The mother of an emperor, known as the empress dowager, exercised great power through her relatives in the court, especially since many emperors came to the throne while they were still children. The two factions, emperor and eunuchs against empress dowager and relatives, entered into serious conflicts. The eunuchs often won and exiled, imprisoned or even executed the relatives of the empress dowager, especially if she was no longer living. The eunuchs took control of the government and made the emperors their puppets. Every time an emperor died and a new child-emperor took the throne, the new empress dowager served as regent, purged the eunuchs who controlled the previous emperor and placed her relatives in high positions. Then the new emperor would make allies among the eunuchs, and the whole process would be repeated. The third faction in the government, the Confucian-educated literati, or scholars, who staffed the imperial bureaucracy, had no choice but to ally themselves with the empress dowager and her family, because they, unlike the eunuchs, respected Confucian scholarship.

Chinese historians attribute the fall of the Han dynasty, as well as the Tang (618–907) and Ming (1368–1644) dynasties, to the power of the eunuchs in the government. The eunuchs and the literati had their first major conflict starting in A.D. 166, which ended in complete victory for the eunuchs in A.D. 172. Toward the end of the Han dynasty, the eunuchs became so powerful that they brought the military into their political struggles. In A.D. 189 a famous general was assassinated at court, and to avenge him, his troops slaughtered all the eunuchs they could find in the palace. This coup placed the governing power in the hands of the military general Cao Cao (Ts'ao Ts'ao), who became the virtual dictator of northern China. His son forced the last Han emperor to abdicate and founded the Wei dynasty, one of the so-called Three Kingdoms (220–80).

After the several centuries of political turmoil known as the Six Dynasties Period (220–589), China was reunified under the Sui dynasty (581–618). In 835, during the Tang dynasty and the reign of Emperor Wenzong (Wen-tsung), the civil officials in the bureaucracy attempted to purge the eunuchs but were unsuccessful. The eunuchs conducted a large-scale purge of the bureaucracy and from then on played a major role in the Tang imperial government. Eunuch generals were placed in control of military troops after the An Lushan Rebellion in the mid-eighth century, which almost ended the Tang dynasty. By the ninth century, the eunuchs had gained control of the imperial court and government, led by a eunuch council of imperial advisers. They placed emperors on the throne and removed and even murdered them. The eunuchs were not as powerful during the Song dynasty (960–1279), but they still held positions in the court, and they became quite powerful during the Yuan (1279–1368) and Ming dynasties.

At the beginning of the Ming dynasty the imperial palace in Beijing, the enormous complex known as the Forbidden City, was constructed. The buildings in the front of the complex were used for government purposes, and the buildings in the rear housed the emperor, his consorts and women relatives, and thousands of female servants, concubines and eunuchs. In the early 15th century a palace school was established to educate young eunuchs. While many eunuchs functioned in the government bureaucracy, many others joined imperial guard units or fought in defense bastions at the Great Wall that protected the northern Chinese border. The eunuchs exercised their greatest power during the Ming, and several eunuch dictators controlled the Ming government, such as Wang Jin (Wang Chin; d. 1449). He took the emperor onto the battlefield against the Mongols, resulting in the defeat of the Chinese army and the capture of the Ming emperor. The eunuch Wang Zhi (Wang Chih) controlled the government from about 1477 to 1481; Liu Jin (Liu Chin) controlled it from 1506–10; and Wei Zhongxian (Wei Chung-hsien), the most hated of the eunuch dictators, governed China during the reign of Emperor Tianqi (T'ien-ch'i; r. 1620–27) and brutally purged the literati in the Donglin Academy.

During the early Ming dynasty, the Grand Eunuch Zheng He (Cheng Ho)—like many eunuchs, a Muslim—led seven maritime expeditions that sailed as far as the east coast of Africa and brought many foreign kingdoms into China's tribute system. Ming Chinese foreign trade was administered by the imperial household, which was in turn controlled by the palace procurement offices staffed by eunuchs. Every object used in the palace, whether made in imperial workshops or presented as a gift from a foreign kingdom under the tribute system, passed through the hands of eunuchs, who became wealthy under this system. When the Ming dynasty fell in 1644, there were more than 100,000 eunuchs in Beijing.

During the Qing dynasty (1644–1911), established by the Manchus who overthrew the Ming, the eunuchs continued to run the imperial palace. The notorious Empress Dowager Cixi (Tz'u Hsi; 1835–1908) exercised the real power in the court for the final half-century of the Qing, and she was assisted by loyal but corrupt eunuchs. The Chinese overthrew the Qing in the Revolution of 1911 and founded the Republic of China in 1912, the same year that Xuantong (Hsuan-t'ung), the last Qing emperor (later known as Henry Puyi), abdicated the throne. He and his relatives, servants and eunuchs were permitted to reside in the Forbidden City until 1924, when a Chinese warlord forced them to leave. Sun Yaoting (1902–96) was the last surviving eunuch who had served the last Qing emperor and his consort, Empress Wanrong (Wan-jung). Sun was born in Hebei Province. His father secured for him a position in the imperial palace in the Forbidden City, and he remained Empress Wanrong's personal attendant until the emperor and empress left the Forbidden City in 1924. Sun left this position a year later. After the People's Republic of China was founded in 1949, the Chinese government took care of him, and he resided with his stepson in Guang Hua Temple in Beijing. His friends wrote a biography of his life, *The Bittersweet Life of a Eunuch*. See also CIXI, EMPRESS DOWAGER; DONGLIN ACADEMY; EMPEROR; FORBIDDEN CITY; IMPERIAL BUREAUCRACY; PUYI, HENRY; TRIBUTE SYSTEM; WEI ZHONGXIAN; ZHENG HE.

EVEREST, MOUNT (Qomolangma)   The highest mountain in the world, at 29,028 feet. It is named in honor of the Englishman Sir George Everest, the first surveyor of India. *Qomolangma*, the name by which Tibetans and Chinese know the mountain, means "Mother Goddess of the Earth." Mount Everest lies in the Tibet Autonomous Region along China's border with Nepal and is part of the Trans-Himalayan Mountain Range, the world's highest. Glaciers flow from Mount Everest north into Tibet and south into Nepal. The mountain was closed to foreigners until the Dalai Lama, the spiritual and political leader of Tibet, permitted a British expedition led by George H. Leigh-Mallory to explore Everest in 1921. A second expedition in 1922 reached the North Col, nearly 27,300 feet high, and a third climbed the mountain in 1924. There were several expeditions in the 1930s, and the first flight over Everest took place in 1933.

In 1950 China took control of Tibet and closed it to foreigners, but Nepal allowed a climbing party from the United States to approach Everest from the south. Expeditions climbed the mountain in 1952 and 1953. On May 29, 1953, Edmund Hillary (b. 1919) and the Sherpa guide Tenzing Norkay successfully completed the first ascent to the summit of Everest. Hillary, a New Zealand mountaineer and explorer, described this feat in *High Adventure* (1955). A Chinese-Tibetan team probably reached the top of Mount Everest along its northern slope in 1960. In 1963 an expedition from the United States made the first traverse of Everest, up the west ridge and down the South Col. In 1975, Tabei Junko of Japan was the first woman to reach the summit. In 1978 Reinhold Messner of Italy and Peter Habeler of Austria made the first climb without oxygen, and in 1980, without oxygen, Messner made the first solo ascent of Everest. The Chinese government conducted a scientific survey of the mountain for developing its natural resources in 1966 and 1967. The Mount Qomolongma Nature Reserve was established in 1989 on the Chinese side of the border to preserve the area's rare ecosystems and to explore the geological and cultural history of the area. Tibetan farmers and herders also live on the reserve. See also HIMALAYA MOUNTAIN RANGE; TIBET.

"EVERLASTING WRONG, THE"   See BAI JUYI; XUANZONG, EMPEROR; YANG GUIFEI.

EVER-VICTORIOUS ARMY   See GORDON, CHARLES; TAIPING REBELLION; WARD, FREDERICK TOWNSEND; ZENG GUOFAN.

EXTRATERRITORIALITY   See NANJING, TREATY OF; TIANJIN, TREATY OF; TREATY PORTS; UNEQUAL TREATIES.

FAAI JEE See CHOPSTICKS.

FACE (*mianzi* or *mien-tzu*)   The Chinese term for a person's prestige or social standing. Chinese people try hard not to "lose face" in public. They have traditionally compared the social humiliation of losing face to the physical mutilation of a person's eyes, nose or mouth. "Face" is tied to the concept of "connections" (*guanxi* or *kuan-hsi*), which indicates a relationship in which two people exchange favors on a continuing basis, for example, helping each other find a job or a place to live. People who have established a *guanxi* relationship are required to live up to their commitment of reciprocal assistance. A person who fails to do so is socially scorned for losing face. Having face enables a person to develop and enlarge his or her network of *guanxi* relationships. Whenever a Chinese person is asked to help someone else, he or she carefully calculates "face" considerations before making a decision. For example, a man will readily perform a favor for his brother or friend, but will be more cautious about agreeing to help a new acquaintance.

The concepts of face and connections date back thousands of years in China and are rooted in the principles of Confucianism, which are concerned with creating a social hierarchy that will bring about harmony in society. The modern Communist Chinese government tried to eradicate these concepts, regarding them as feudal, but they have survived and are still followed by Chinese in the People's Republic of China, as well as Taiwan, Singapore and overseas Chinese communities. The Chinese are also concerned with keeping face when dealing with foreigners. A foreign tourist who vehemently argues with a Chinese hotel desk clerk about a problem with accommodations will cause the Chinese to lose face, and the latter will not give in to the foreigner's demands. A better solution is to calmly wait and give the hotel management a chance to work out a compromise. See also CONFUCIANISM; CONNECTIONS; OVERSEAS CHINESE.

FA-HSIEN See FAXIAN.

FAHUA See ENAMELWARE; THREE-COLOR WARE.

FAIRBANK, JOHN KING (1907–91)   An American scholar and professor of Chinese history who transformed the field of Chinese studies from a concern with antiquity to a comprehensive study of Chinese history and culture down to the modern era. Born in South Dakota, Fairbank began his college education at the University of Wisconsin before transferring to Harvard University, where he graduated summa cum laude in 1929. As a Rhodes scholar from 1929 through 1932, he traveled to Beijing and taught as a lecturer at Qinghua University. For the next two years he traveled throughout a dozen Chinese provinces as a Rockefeller Foundation Fellow. In 1936 Fairbank joined the faculty at Harvard. When America entered World War II, he spent time working in Washington, D.C., and Chongqing in Sichuan Province, the wartime capital of the Chinese Nationalist government. After the war he returned to Harvard, where he served as director of the East Asian Research Center from 1955 to 1973; in 1959 he was named Francis Lee Higginson Professor of History. Fairbank retired in 1977.

During his years as a professor, he also served as an advisor to the governments of the United States and China. He wrote and edited more than two dozen books; his first, *The United States and China*, was published in 1948. Fairbank wrote several widely used textbooks with Edwin O. Reischauer, a professor of Japanese studies at Harvard who also served as American ambassador to Japan. These include *East Asia: The Great Tradition* and *East Asia, the Modern Transformation*. Before he died he edited his last book, *China: A New History*, which was published in 1992. Fairbank also served as president of both the American Historical Association and the Association for Asian studies.

FAMILLE JAUNE, FAMILLE NOIR, FAMILLE ROSE, FAMILLE VERTE See ENAMELWARE.

FAMILY STRUCTURE   The family has been the basic unit in Chinese society for thousands of years. Its importance is shown in Chinese names, in which the family name is given first, followed by the personal name—the reverse of the Western practice. The traditional Chinese family was an extended family that included several generations, and as many as 50 or more people lived in the same compound. The family had a hierarchical structure based on gender, age, order of birth and degree of relationship, and every person had a strictly defined position within that structure. The Chinese family system was based on the teachings of Confucius (551–479 B.C.), whose school of thought, known as Confucianism, became the orthodox state cult during the Han dynasty (206 B.C.–A.D. 220). Confucius held a patriarchal view of the family in which the wife obeys her husband and the children obey their father. He maintained that when all family relationships are in order, including those between husband and wife and parents and children, then there will be order in society. For Confucius the relationship between fathers and sons is the basic model for both the family and society, and the ruler should act as a father to his subjects. Sons were especially important because they carried on the family line, took care of their parents when they grew old and performed the ritual sacrifices to honor their deceased parents and other family ancestors. The most important Confucian virtue is filial piety (*xiao* or *hsiao*), the respect and obedience of children toward their parents. The eldest son of every Chinese family was obligated to give his parents a proper funeral. If he did not do so, the family would be disgraced and the deceased were believed to become malevolent ghosts.

Every family had an altar with ancestral tablets (*lingwei*) that commemorated deceased ancestors. Ritual offerings and prayers were made to the ancestors daily and at special occasions such as weddings and births. Families with a common ancestor formed a large clan (*zi* or *tsu*), which often had its own temple structure to house the ancestral tablets. The Kong family mansion, the home of Confucius and his descendants in Qufu, Shandong Province now open to the public, includes the family archives, Confucian temple and cemetery where Confucius and all of his descendants are buried. Chinese clans have built temples not only in mainland China but in Hong Kong and in Taiwan, Singapore and other countries where they have emigrated. At the Qing Ming (Ching Ming) Festival in April, Chinese families sweep the graves of their ancestors and make offerings to them.

The Confucian patriarchal and patrilineal family structure is one of the basic elements shared by all members of the Han Chinese ethnic group, who today comprise about 93 percent of the population of China. Members of other ethnic groups who became sinicized, or assimilated into the Han, did so by adopting such Han customs as the Confucian family structure. According to Confucian thought, a woman should be obedient to her parents before marriage, to her husband after marriage and to her son after her husband's death. Families commonly arranged marriages in which the bride and groom never met each other prior to the wedding. A married woman left her own family and moved into her husband's household. According to an old Chinese proverb, "Raising daughters is like raising children for another family." In her husband's home the new wife had to work hard, obey her husband's parents and honor his ancestors. She was frequently tormented by her mother-in-law. Although the eldest male became the titular head of the family, the *daidai* (*tai tai*), his wife or widow, actually controlled the family and had to be respected and obeyed by all of its members. A young wife's only hope for gaining a measure of power in the family was to give birth to a son. As the son grew up, the mother's power increased, especially after he brought a wife into the family whom his mother could dominate.

The Chinese have many traditional customs regarding children that they still practice. Nine days after the first child is born into a family, the maternal grandmother gives the baby many presents, which may include a hand-embroidered hat shaped like the cap worn by ancient Chinese scholars. The hat, symbolic of an intellectual mind, is decorated with bells, tassels, beads, flowers and other designs. A boy's hat is embroidered with a dragon, the symbol of the Chinese emperors, and a girl's with a phoenix, the symbol of the empresses. Because of the high mortality rate, the birth of a child was not celebrated until it was one month old. Red-dyed eggs were sent to friends and relatives to announce the birth of a boy, and today are also sent to announce a girl. A Chinese child is traditionally given many charms to protect his life, and proud mothers and grandmothers embroider colorful tiger slippers and hats for him to wear.

A man whose wife did not bear a son could bring secondary wives or concubines into the household if he could afford the expenses. Wealthy men often had several concubines, and Chinese emperors had large harems with hundreds of concubines to provide numerous children for the imperial family. Although concubines were subordinate to legal wives, Chinese law treated the children of concubines as equal in status and rights to the children of the first wife. Divorce was allowed in some conditions but was very rare, since it brought shame to the families of both the husband and the wife. Indeed, any action that would bring shame, or a loss of face, to a person would bring shame to his or her entire family.

After the Chinese Communist Party (CCP) founded the People's Republic of China (PRC) in 1949, it enacted the Marriage Law of 1950 to free Chinese women from the feudal elements of the traditional Confucian family system. The law affirmed the equality of women with men, gave women equal inheritance rights with men, permitted divorce under certain conditions, ended concubinage and gave children some legal protection that aimed to end the traditional practice of infanticide, especially of girls, and the sale of minors. In 1981 the PRC government enacted a revised marriage law that raised the legal age for marriage for men to 22 and for women to 20. The government also attempted to break down the traditional Chinese family structure by organizing villages into people's communes, in which every member shared work and profits equally, and by organizing people into work units (*danwei*) that controlled most aspects of their lives, including permission to marry and have children. However, people's communes were disbanded in the early 1980s. Most Chinese, whether single or married, continue to live with their parents, who help raise the grandchildren and take care of the home while their children are at work.

China has undergone a population explosion, due mainly to the traditional emphasis on having large families with many sons, and today the Chinese population numbers more than one billion. Since 1979 the PRC government has attempted to control population growth through its one-child family campaign, which limits every family, except for some minority ethnic groups, to one child in the city and two in the countryside. Men are encouraged to wait until age 28 to marry, and women to wait until age 25. The one-child family policy has been very controversial and has not been easy to enforce, especially outside the cities, since peasant families need many people to work the land. The Confucian-based desire for a son to support the parents and continue the family line is still extremely strong, and female infanticide remains a problem. Many Chinese people are now concerned that single children may become tyrannical "little emperors" who get whatever they want from their parents and do not know how to share or get along with others. See also ANCESTOR WORSHIP; ANCESTRAL TABLETS; CHARMS AND AMULETS; CONCUBINAGE; CONFUCIANISM; DRAGON; FACE; FUNERALS; HAN; MINORITIES, NATIONAL; NAMES; ONE-CHILD FAMILY CAMPAIGN; PHOENIX; QING MING FESTIVAL; QUFU; TIGER; WEDDINGS, TRADITIONAL.

FAMINES See AGRICULTURE; NATURAL DISASTERS.

FAN See AGRICULTURE; COOKING, CHINESE; GRAIN; NOODLES; RICE.

FAN CHUNG-CHENG See FAN GUAN.

FAN KUAN (Fan K'uan; c. 950–1050; fl. c. 990–1030) Also known as Fan Zhongzheng (Fan Chung-cheng); one of the greatest landscape painters during the Northern Song dynasty (960–1127). Fan Kuan was a professional court painter who worked in the monumental style of the Northern Song. However, he was shy and spent the later years of his life living as a recluse in the rugged mountains of Shanxi province. His paintings carefully depict the details of a landscape—mountains, trees and streams—in a vigorous and dramatic way. Their composition and style reflect the austere nature of his life. A fine example of Fan Kuan's work is a large black-ink landscape painting on silk, *Traveling among Mountains and Streams*, a hanging scroll owned by the Palace Museum in Taipei, Taiwan. Because of the large mountains that dominate the painting, it is classified as being in the "Master Mountain" style. A sheer rocky cliff rises from a misty ground. Fan Kuan used small brushstrokes to fill in the foreground, and "axe-cut texture strokes" (*cun* or *ts'un*) to paint in the details of the mountain so that it seems very realistic. Some scholars argue that this is the best painting in the early Chinese landscape style of the 10th–11th centuries, and it became a model studied by later painters. Fan Kuan's paintings were so highly regarded that in the early 12th century the imperial collection owned 58 of his paintings, including a set of 12 horizontal rolled scrolls. See also LANDSCAPE PAINTING; NORTHERN SCHOOL OF PAINTING.

FAN K'UAN See FAN KUAN.

FAN ZHONGZHENG See FAN KUAN.

FANCHUAN See JUNK.

FANG LIZHI (Fang Li-chih; 1936–   ) The most famous contemporary Chinese dissident. Fang was born to a working-class family in the beautiful southern city of Hangzhou, where his father was a postal worker. He studied science at prestigious Beijing University, where he joined the Communist Youth League, the organization established for young people by the Chinese Communist Party (CCP). Fang initially believed that the CCP was helping the Chinese people, but he soon began to oppose many of its actions, especially the party's intrusion into scientists' research. In 1957 Fang became a target of the Anti-Rightist Movement, which CCP officials used to oppress Chinese intellectuals and artists, and he was purged and deprived of his CCP membership. Although later rehabilitated, Fang remained outspoken, and during the Cultural Revolution (1966–76) he spent a year in prison before being sent to work in the countryside. While there, the only scientific book he could find was a cosmology text; after rereading it many times, he decided to switch from his field of research of solid-state physics to cosmology.

After Fang was again rehabilitated in 1978, China wanted to reform and modernize to catch up with other countries, so the government sent him to participate in many international conferences on physics. Traveling to the United States, England, Sweden, Italy and Japan made him aware of the intellectual freedom enjoyed in democratic countries and the slowness of change in China. Fang spoke at university campuses across China, bluntly criticizing the CCP and expressing doubts that Deng Xiaoping's plans for reforming and modernizing China would succeed. In 1984 Fang became vice president of the University of Science and Technology in Hefei, the capital of Anhui Province, where he had been a professor. He encouraged academic freedom through his commitment to "science, democracy, creativity and independence." In 1985 Fang became a member of the Chinese Academy of Sciences' Department of Mathematics and Physics, and in 1986 he became vice president of the Astronomical Society.

In autumn 1986, while addressing students at Tongji University in Shanghai, Fang challenged party leaders even more strongly by declaring that CCP policies had failed and by calling for human rights and democracy. Chinese students held protest in the winter of 1986–87, and Deng blamed Fang for influencing them. In January 1987 he was expelled from the CCP and dismissed as vice president of the University of Science and Technology for "bourgeois liberalization."

In January 1989 Fang wrote an open letter to the CCP calling for the release of Wei Jingsheng, an activist in the Democracy Wall movement in 1978 who had been arrested and imprisoned for 10 years. Shortly after Fang published his letter, visiting U.S. President George Bush invited Fang to a state banquet in Beijing, but CCP officials refused to let him attend. In spring 1989, student protesters held massive demonstrations in Tiananmen Square in Beijing, but Fang avoided them because he did not want to be seen as instigating the students. Even so, when party officials authorized the violent suppression of the protesters on June 4, 1989, known as the Tiananmen Square Massacre, they accused him of being the "black hand" behind the democracy movement. Fang and his wife, Li Shuxian (Li Shu-hsien), took refuge in the U.S. embassy in Beijing, where they hid for more than a year while the U.S. and PRC governments negotiated their safe exit from China.

Fang joined the astronomy faculty of Cambridge University in England. In 1991 he took a position as a visiting professor of astrophysics at the Institute for Advanced Study at Princeton University in New Jersey. He and his wife wrote the textbook for his class on cosmology, *Creation of the Universe*, which was never published in China. In 1991 he also published *Bringing Down the Great Wall*, an English-language translation of 32 of his essays, speeches and interviews since 1979 in which he discusses his scientific research in cosmology and the problems of the Communist PRC government. More than 30 other universities offered Fang permanent faculty positions; he chose a tenured position at the University of Arizona, because three of the best astronomical observatories in the United States are located near Tucson. Fang has helped organize the Committee to End the Chinese Gulag, which is working to secure the release of more than 1,000 dissidents in Chinese prisons and work camps (*laogai*). Harry Wu, another famous Chinese dissident, has used videos to document the abuses of prisoners in the *laogai*. See also ANTI-RIGHTIST CAMPAIGN; BEIJING UNIVERSITY; CHINESE ACADEMY OF SCIENCES; CHINESE COMMUNIST PARTY; COMMUNIST YOUTH LEAGUE; CULTURAL REVOLUTION; PEOPLE'S REPUBLIC OF CHINA; TIANANMEN SQUARE MASSACRE; WEI JING-SHENG; WU, HARRY.

FANS (*shanzi* or *shan-chi*; *fengshan*)   Two types of fans have been made by hand in China: the flat fan, which has been used since the Han dynasty (206 B.C.–A.D. 220), and the folding fan, which was invented in Japan in the seventh century A.D. and introduced into China through Korea in the 11th century. Flat fans are made by attaching pieces of paper or silk to wooden handles and decorating them with painting, calligraphy or embroidery. Folding fans are made from small strips or ribs of bamboo or sandalwood that are attached at the base. Traditionally, a man's fan commonly has 20 or 24 ribs and a woman's fan has 30 or more ribs. Scenes are often carved into the wood to make an openwork design. Valuable fans may also be made from ivory, ebony, mother-of-pearl or wood coated with lacquer. Peasants may buy folk-craft fans made from feathers or woven bamboo, dried grasses, palm leaves or wheat straw.

The earliest fans were used in China for ordinary purposes, such as fanning the fire in a stove to keep it burning or to drive away insects. Over time, fans became more beautiful, and most of China's finest artists decorated flat and folding fans with bird-and-flower paintings and calligraphic inscriptions or poems. The painted piece of silk or paper for a fan may even be mounted and framed as a picture for display rather than attached to a handle. Since the Ming dynasty (1368–1644), the folding fan has been the major type of fan used by artists. Members of the literati, or scholar class, often painted flowers and inscribed poems on fans for their friends. The fan is the symbol of Zhong Li Jian, one of the Eight Immortals in the Daoist religion, who is depicted as a fat man holding a magic fan that revives people who have died. See also BAMBOO; BIRD-AND-FLOWER PAINTING; CALLIGRAPHY; EIGHT IMMORTALS; IVORY CARVING; LACQUERWARE; LITERATI; SANDALWOOD; SILK.

FANYING   See MIRRORS.

FAREWELL MY CONCUBINE   See CHEN KAIGE.

FARMING   See AGRICULTURE; ALMANAC; GRAIN; NATURAL DISASTERS; OX.

FATE (*ming*)   The concept that everything that happens in a person's life is determined by the decree or Mandate of Heaven (*tianming* or *t'ien-ming*). The Chinese, especially the Confucianists, conceived of Heaven as the impersonal power that governs all created things, guiding the destinies of human beings and providing rewards and punishments. Men have a moral duty to put themselves in harmony with the will of Heaven. The Chinese term *ming* has the meaning of the verb "to order," "to give" or "to endow." Fate represents the qualities with which Heaven has endowed human lives, especially the length of one's life and one's ultimate success or failure. A person should know what his nature is and do his best to fulfill that nature. The *Doctrine of the Mean* (*Zhong Yong* or *Chung Yung*), one of the Four Books of Confucianism, states that "What Heaven imparts (*ming*) to man is called human nature." Each person should realize this nature by making a sincere effort at moral cultivation. The Confucian philosopher Mencius (Mengzi or Meng Tzu; c. 372–289 B.C.) maintains that a person's goal should be to cultivate his moral life, developed his own self-nature and let nature take its course. The philosopher Mozi (Mo Tzu; c. 470–391 B.C.) criticized the Confucianists for their tendency to fatalism and their skepticism regarding Heaven and spiritual beings. Mozi maintained that Heaven is an active power that manifests love for all human beings, and that humans should follow Heaven by practicing universal love. Fatalism is a major concept in the Confucian thought of Wang Chong (Wang Ch'ung; A.D. 27–97?), which he extended to human beings and countries alike, arguing that the prosperity, life span and downfall of a dynasty are determined by fate.

Some thinkers in the Chinese Daoist tradition also tended toward fatalism. The great Daoist thinker Zhuangzi (Chuang Tzu; 369–286 B.C.) asserted that human beings should cultivate their spirit by "following what is necessary and inevitable." Men can find harmony and peace of mind by "abiding with the nature of things" and letting nature follow its ever-changing yet cyclical course. The *Liehzi* (*Lie Tzu*), attributed to Lieh Yukao (Lie Yu-k'ao; c. 450–375 B.C.) but actually written by a Neo-Taoist thinker in the third century A.D., includes a dialogue between "(Human) Effort" (*li*) and "Destiny" (or Fate; *ming*, which is decreed by heaven). Effort claims that it controls the length of a person's life and his success, position and wealth. Destiny retorts that it is not possible to control or manage such things, because they have already been determined, and even the fate of heaven cannot intentionally change their course. See also CONFUCIANISM; DAOISM; DOCTRINE OF THE MEAN; HEAVEN; KARMA; MOZI; ZHUANGZI.

FAXIAN (Fa-hsien; A.D. fourth–fifth century)   A Chinese Buddhist monk who made a pilgrimage to India in A.D. 399 to collect religious relics and sutras (Buddhist scriptures) and bring them back to China for translation. He was the first and most famous of many Chinese Buddhist monks who did so. Another was Xuanzang (Hsuan-tsang; A.D. 602–64), who left an important record of his pilgrimage from Chang'an (modern Xi'an) in Shaanxi Province in Central Asia to India. The Buddhist religion had been introduced into China from India in the first century A.D.. Faxian spent a total of 15 years on his journey and wrote a book, *A Record of the Buddhist Countries* (*Foguoji* or *Fo-kuo-chi*), which has provided historians with valuable information about India during this period. He took the overland route from Chang'an along the Silk Road across the Gobi Desert through Central Asia, to Gandara in Afghanistan, and down into the north Indian plain. He traveled to every region of India except the Deccan. In A.D. 411 Faxian took a ship from Calcutta on the Ganges River delta to Sri Lanka and Sumatra, and finally landed on the coast of Shandong Province in eastern China. His ship had been headed for Guangzhou (Canton) in southern China but was blown off course. In A.D. 414 Faxian finally returned to Chang'an with the books and relics he had acquired. He moved to Nanjing in A.D. 416 and began the laborious job of translating the sutras from Indian Sanskrit into Chinese and also writing the record of his pilgrimage. See also BUDDHISM; CHANG'AN; GOBI DESERT; SILK ROAD; XUANZANG.

FEN   See CURRENCY, MODERN.

FEN RIVER   See SHANXI PROVINCE; TAIYUAN.

FENG SHUI   "Wind and water"; a system of geomancy that originated in China around the 10th century B.C. *Feng shui* is still commonly used to bring good fortune and ward off bad luck through the proper positioning of tombs, buildings and furnishings to put them in harmony with the world of nature and spirits. Geomancers developed their principles by studying the movement of the planets and stars and their relationship to the earth, the earth's magnetism and topography, and the balance of yin and yang elements. The flowing movement of the universe is symbolized by the Eight Trigrams and the principles of yin (negative, female) and yang (positive, male) that form the basis of the classical text, the *Book of Changes* (*Yijing* or *I Ching*). The Daoists traditionally believe that the earth is a living organism with curving channels similar to the veins and arteries through which blood pulses in a human body. Sites where those channels converge are especially favorable because they emanate *qi* (*ch'i*), or life energy. Curved lines are preferred because evil spirits, known as *sha*, travel along straight lines, and angles prevent the flow of *qi*. The geomancer "reads" the patterns of mountains, plains, rivers and valleys to determine whether a particular site is open to positive or negative influences. He is aided by a magnetic compass, which was invented in China more than 2,000 years ago, and by printed manuals that explain the complex factors involved in *feng shui*.

The Daoists believed that the auspicious siting of a tomb would benefit the heirs of the deceased. As a whole, tombs, buildings, and cities have been oriented toward the south to gain the sun's warmth and shelter from the cold winds that blow from the north. Mountains on the northern side also give protection. Water on the southern side, such as a river or lake, brings good fortune. Mountains are thought to have meridians of prosperity, or "profit lines," based on their physical features, and cities and buildings should be lined up with these meridians. Traditional Chinese compounds are built on a north-south axis, with the major halls facing south directly on the center axis and balanced buildings on both sides. This plan was also used to construct cities such as Chang'an (modern Xi'an), the capital during the Tang dynasty (618–907) and the Forbidden City in Beijing, the capital built by the Ming dynasty (1368–1644). The construction of imperial tombs according to the principles of *feng shui* can be seen in the Ming tombs outside Beijing.

Although the practice of *feng shui* has been forbidden by the government of the People's Republic of China, Chinese people around the world still follow its principles. In the booming city of Hong Kong, nearly all the new skyscrapers have been constructed with the aid of *feng shui*, the practice of which is a multibillion dollar business in that city. Many buildings have open atrium lobbies on the ground floor so the spirits in the mountains will not have their view of the water blocked. Because straight lines are associated with evil influences, and sharp angles are "spirit daggers" that send harmful energy into a building, many corner offices have small mirrors (*bhat gwa*) placed at strategic points to deflect bad energy. Triangles are considered the worst of all angles because in the Cantonese dialect (Guangzhou) the phrase for triangle sounds like the phrase for burial urns, a very bad omen. The roofs of many buildings in Hong Kong have triangles that are trimmed off. To keep out evil spirits, elevators are not located directly inside a building's entrance but are off to the right. Escalators are placed at a diagonal from the entrance to confuse the spirits and to keep money from flowing out of the building. The Cantonese word for "four" sounds similar to the word for death, another bad omen; thus, many buildings, especially hospitals, do not have a fourth floor, just as many Western buildings do not have a 13th floor. The Chinese prefer the ninth floor, because the word for "nine" sounds like the word for immortality; or the 33rd floor, because the word for "three" sounds like the word for life. The most preferred number is eight, because its word sounds like "prosperity."

In the rooms of a home or office, furniture is aligned so that desks face water but do not face doors. Aquariums can supply needed water. Plants are good luck, especially ones with big leaves, which signify imminent prosperity. The *feng shui* geomancer divides a room into nine equal squares using a compass known as a *luopan*, which includes the five elements, eight compass points, and 64 symbols based on the Eight Trigrams. He combines that information with the birthdates of the occupants and other complex factors to analyze whether a room is arranged to best advantage and how to neutralize unlucky points. Colors are also important in *feng shui*. Red is auspicious, while blue is negative. Chinese companies use red in their logos to bring good fortune. See also BEIJING; BOOK OF CHANGES; CHANG'AN; EIGHT TRIGRAMS; FORBIDDEN CITY; FUNERALS; HONG KONG; MING TOMBS; YIN AND YANG.

FENG YU-HSIEN See BORODIN, MIKHAIL; WARLORD PERIOD; ZHANG ZUOLIN.

FENG YUXIANG See BORODIN, MIKHAIL; WARLORD PERIOD; ZHANG ZUOLIN.

FENGHUANG See PHOENIX.

FENGJIAN (FENG-CHIEN) See FEUDAL SYSTEM; ZHOU, DUKE OF.

FERGHANA See HORSE; TARIM BASIN; WESTERN HAN DYNASTY; WUDI, EMPEROR; XIONGNU.

FEUDAL SYSTEM (*fengjian* or *feng-chien*)   A system of political organization created by the Duke of Zhou, the brother of King Wu of the state of Zhou in the Wei River valley. King Wu overthrew the Shang dynasty (1750–1040 B.C.) and established the Zhou dynasty (1100–256 B.C.). Confucius (551–479 B.C.), whose thought became orthodox for the Chinese imperial government, revered the early centuries of the Zhou dynasty as the ideal period of peaceful, orderly government in Chinese history. The Duke of Zhou created a feudal system based on the concept that all land belongs to the king and all people are his subjects. Zhou feudalism, however, differed from a fully developed feudal system based on legal bonds between lords and subjects, because it was relatively decentralized and based largely on family connections. Members of the Zhou royal family and its close allies were given authority over states in northern and central China, but they were required to attend the Zhou court and provide the government with military support. The Zhou capital was at Chang'an (modern Xi'an in Shaanxi Province in central China) on the Wei River. Lands around the capital were controlled directly by the Zhou king. Local governments were placed under the control of territorial lords whose power was hereditary-based. These lords were Zhou royal family members, descendants of Shang nobles, some military generals and government officials, and chiefs of other states that had come under Zhou rule but were allowed to administer their own lands. Laws were passed to regulate the succession of a lord's power after he died, stating that an elder son was superior to a younger and that a legal wife was superior to a concubine, so that an elder son of a legal wife had precedence. The lords were divided into five feudal ranks based on the size of their lands. Feudal lands, or "fiefs," were granted by a lord to his vassals, who in turn were required to fulfill obligations to their lord, which involved paying tributes and performing services.

Agricultural lands were organized by the "well-field system" (*jingtian*) whereby a square piece of land covering about 40 acres was divided by a grid into 9 equal squares of about 4.5 acres. Eight peasant families were each given one square to live on, and they collectively farmed the center square for their lord, to whom it belonged. The important Confucian philosopher Mencius (c. 372–289 B.C.) looked back to the well-field system as the ideal which, if reinstated, would help the peasants of his time, many of whom were impoverished and had to sell their land and work as sharecroppers. The feudal system weakened during the later centuries of the dynasty, as some of the states that were vassals to the Zhou became stronger, and after the eighth century B.C. the power of the Zhou king had been diminished. The feudal system was brought to an end by the state of Qin, which came to control much of northwestern China and eventually unified the country under the Qin dynasty (221–206 B.C.). See also CHANG'AN; CONFUCIUS; WELL-FIELD SYSTEM; ZHOU, DUKE OF; ZHOU DYNASTY.

FICTION See DING LING; DREAM OF THE RED CHAMBER; GOLDEN LOTUS; JOURNEY TO THE WEST; KINGSTON, MAXINE HONG; LAO SHE; LU XUN; NEW CULTURE MOVEMENT; OUTLAWS OF THE MARSH; ROMANCE OF THE THREE KINGDOMS; SCHOLARS, THE; SHEN CONGWEN; SHEN FU; TAN, AMY.

FIFTH-MONTH FESTIVAL See DRAGON BOAT FESTIVAL.

FIGURE PAINTING   A category of painting that includes portraits of human figures and religious paintings, primarily Buddhist, of divine figures. These paintings contrast with Chinese landscape paintings in which humans, when present, are very small in the context of nature. However, figure painting has a longer history than landscape painting in China and originated with portraits of Confucian scholars and other esteemed people, and with illustrations of texts on moral behavior. Paintings of human figures and animals such as houses were executed on the walls of ancient Chinese palaces and tombs. During the Han dynasty (206 B.C.–A.D. 220), when the teachings of Confucius (551–479 B.C.) were accepted as the orthodox school by the imperial court, palace walls were decorated with paintings of Confucian subjects, such as a son caring for his parents, the highest virtue, known as filial piety. Professional court artists also executed portraits of Chinese emperors, imperial concubines, members of the imperial court, scholars and other wealthy clients. Figure paintings emphasized the richly colored clothing worn by the subjects, dignified posture, and the arrangement of figures in hierarchical order within the composition.

Figure painting attained its full development in China during the Tang dynasty (618–907). Along with formal portraits, artists painted scenes of daily life, such as scholars gathered together to study and compose poetry, court ladies dressing their hair or enjoying a garden, and foreign dignitaries bearing tribute to the Chinese emperor. Chinese figure painters have also illustrated well-known poems, folk songs and traditional stories. For example, numerous painters have depicted the prose poem, "The Red Cliff," by Su Shi (Su Shih; also known as Su Dongpo or Su Tung-p'o; 1036–1101), in which the poet and his friends are setting off on a journey, accompanied by the moon and their shadows. Chinese paintings and poems are closely connected, and a painting often has a poem inscribed on it by a close friend of the artist.

Many ancient figure paintings have not survived. One exception is the handscroll *Thirteen Emperors* attributed to Yan Liben (Yan Li-pen; d. 673), now in the Boston Museum of Fine Arts. Wu Daozi (Wu Tao-tzu; active c. 720–60) was the greatest Tang figure painter, although his works have not survived and are only known through description in written records. He painted about 300 paintings on dry plaster walls in Buddhist temples in Chang'an (modern Xi'an), the Tang capital, and Luoyang. After the Tang dynasty, both landscape and ink painting became the most widespread types of painting in China, although some artists continued to produce figure paintings. Li Gonglin (Li Kung-lin; c. 1040–1106) was the greatest figure painter of the Northern Song dynasty (960–1126).

The Buddhist religion, introduced into China from India around the first century A.D., brought with it a complicated iconography of Buddhist bodhisattvas (wise beings) and deities, especially the founder of the religion, who is known as the Buddha (the Awakened One). The Buddha is commonly depicted as a large figure with a smaller bodhisattva or a disciple on each side. In the mid-fourth century, artists began creating wall paintings and sculptures of Buddhist religious figures in Chinese temples and caves. The most famous and best-preserved Chinese Buddhist wall paintings are at the Mogao Caves at Dunhuang in Gansu Province in western China. These murals also include portraits of Chinese noble patrons who provided financial support for the artists. Other major Buddhist sites with wall paintings include the Longmen cave temples and sculptures near Luoyang and the Yungang cave temples and sculptures near Datong. The Chinese government has been attempting to restore cave paintings and sculptures, which provide inspiration for contemporary Chinese artists. See also BODHISATTVA; BUDDHA; BUDDHISM; DUNHUANG CAVE PAINTINGS AND CARVINGS; LI GONGLIN; LONGMEN CAVE TEMPLES AND SCULPTURES; SU SHI; WU DAOZI; YUNGANG CAVE TEMPLES AND SCULPTURES.

FILIAL PIETY (*xiao* or *hsiao*)   One of the most important concepts in the school of thought of Confucius (551–479 B.C.), which became accepted as orthodox by the Chinese imperial government. Filial piety is a virtue that requires a child to have respect for and defer to his or her parents as long as they live, and to provide them a proper funeral when they die. Filial disobedience was considered the worst of all crimes. Even the Chinese emperors were required to practice filial piety. Even after death, parents must be honored by their families with regular ceremonies and offerings, commonly referred to as ancestor worship. In the *Analects* (*Lunyu*)—sayings attributed to Confucius—sons are urged to serve their parents, provide for their needs and treat them with reverence. The concept of filial piety was strongly emphasized by Mencius (372–289 B.C.), the second-most important Confucian philosopher.

The *Book of Filial Piety* (*Xiaojing* or *Hsiao ching*) has been used as a basic text to educate Chinese students from the time of Confucius into the present century. It was composed in the third or second century B.C. but claims to be written by Zengzi (Tseng Tzu), a disciple of Confucius. The book is a dialogue between Confucius and Zengzi in which the former makes filial piety the foundation of all morality, arguing that one can become a citizen who is loyal to the ruler and obeys the government only by first learning how to serve, obey and revere one's parents. Confucian thinkers set up a hierarchy of relationships in the family and in society, and they emphasized three bonds: the chaste virtue of the wife, the filial obedience of the son to the father and the loyalty of the subject to the ruler. The father had autocratic power in the family, and the ruler's power was comparable to that of

the father of his subjects. Owing to the Confucian emphasis on filial piety, the family has always been the strongest social institution in China and even in overseas Chinese communities. See also ANALECTS, CONFUCIAN; ANCESTOR WORSHIP; CONFUCIANISM; FAMILY SYSTEM; MENCIUS.

FILM STUDIOS   The Chinese film industry dates back to the beginning of the century, and during its first 80 years more than 4,000 films and documentaries were produced. The first Chinese film was the drama *Dingjun Mountain* (1905). Early Chinese filmmakers produced dramatic narratives and adapted popular Chinese novels, such as *Dream of the Red Chamber, Journey to the West, Romance of the Three Kingdoms* and *Outlaws of the Marsh*. They also adapted episodes from Beijing Opera, a traditional form of entertainment that relies on exaggerated costumes, makeup and gestures. In 1913 Zheng Zhengqiu (Cheng Cheng-ch'iu) directed the first Chinese feature film, *The Difficult Couple*, adapted from an opera. Unfortunately no prints have survived. The oldest surviving film in China is *The Romance of a Fruit Peddlar* (1922), written by Zheng Zhengqiu and directed by Zhang Shichuan (Chang Shih-ch'uan).

Film studios prior to the founding of the Communist People's Republic of China (PRC) in 1949 were controlled by foreign companies. After 1949, independent Chinese film studios were established. The major studios in China today include the Changchun, Beijing and Shanghai studios; the Pearl River and Xi'an studios are gaining prominence. The Golden Rooster Awards are presented annually in China for the best film, director, actors, and actresses and so forth, comparable to the Academy Awards or Oscars in the United States. The first Chinese Film Festival was held on September 21, 1989. Some of the most important actors in Chinese film history include Hu Die, Lan Ma, Zhao Dan, and Lisa Lu, who moved to the United States.

Changchun Film Studio is the oldest studio in China. It was founded in October 1946 during the civil war between the Chinese Communists and Nationalists (Kuomintang; KMT) after the Communists gained control of the Manchurian Film Studio in April 1946. Originally called Northeast Film Studio, it was renamed the Changchun Film Studio in 1955. It is located in Changchun, capital of Jilin Province in Manchuria (northeastern China). The studio's original mission was to produce newsreels and documentaries about the Communist liberation of Manchuria, which from 1932 to 1945 was a Japanese puppet state called Manchukuo. The studio produced China's first film with puppets, *Dream of the Emperor;* its first cartoon, *To Catch a Turtle in a Jar;* and *Bridge,* the first Chinese feature film to be produced after 1949. By 1981, Changchun Film Studio had produced nearly 300 feature films and those based on Chinese operas, 160 scientific and educational films, and dubbed more than 660 foreign films from more than 30 different countries. The studio trained many film workers who went on to become famous scriptwriters, cinematographers and directors.

The Beijing Film Studio was established in the capital city of Beijing shortly after 1949. Revolutionary artists came from many regions of China to work at the studio, which produced films in three general categories: those based on novels by modern Chinese authors, those adapting episodes from traditional Chinese operas, and those recounting experiences from the Communist revolution. Yu Lan, star of *A Revolutionary Family,* won the best actress award at the Moscow International Film Festival in 1961. *Rickshaw Boy,* based on a famous modern novel by Lao She, and *Border Town,* from a modern novel by Shen Congwen (Shen Ts'ung-wen), both directed by Ling Zifeng (Ling Tzu-feng), also won critical acclaim. With the advent of the Cultural Revolution (1966–76), Beijing Film Studio was forced to shut down production. It reopened in the late 1970s, and in 1980 *The Young Teacher,* a children's film, won the Special Prize at the Golden Rooster Awards and was named an Outstanding Film by the Ministry of Culture. The same studio filmed the most beloved of all Chinese novels, *Dream of The Red Chamber,* in eight parts over five years, the longest feature film ever made in China. It tells the emotional story of members of an extended family who suffer reversals in fortune during the Ming dynasty (1368–1644). Recently the Beijing Film Studio has co-produced films with foreign film companies, including Bernardo Bertolucci's *The Last Emperor* (1987), about Henry Puyi, who had been the last emperor of the Qing dynasty (1644–1911) and was made the puppet emperor of Manchukuo by the Japanese. This film won nine Academy Awards, including one for best picture, in the United States.

The China Children's Film Studio, established in 1981 in the same complex as the Beijing Film Studio, with actress Yu Lan as president, was the first endeavor in China to produce films for children. The studio's first films were *Red Elephant* and *Next Time Port.* Many respected directors came from other studios to make children's films, and the studio, which produced 45 films in its first decade, has gained a reputation for a high level of artistry.

The Shanghai Film Studio, founded in 1949 and one of the largest studios in China, continues the tradition of realist pictures with anti-feudal and anti-imperialist themes that had been filmed in Shanghai prior to 1949. Shanghai is often compared to New York City for its international population and prominence in the fields of entertainment and finance. The studio's excellent production facilities have enabled it to produce films with many international joint ventures, such as Steven Spielberg's *Empire of the Sun* (1987). The studio has established the Mountain Lion Film Corporation to produce films, manage television and film equipment, and train people to work in these areas.

The Pearl River Film Studio, located in the southern city of Guangzhou (Canton), began construction in 1958 and first made newsreels. It started producing feature films in 1959, and by 1961 it was in full operation, making three films per year. One of the most important directors at Pearl River is Lu Jue (Lu Chu-e), who formerly worked at the Shanghai Film Studio. The Cultural Revolution caused Pearl River to stop production from 1966 to 1973, but since 1977 it has been very active. The studio's location close to Hong Kong has enabled it to enter many joint ventures with foreign companies. In 1986 the studio produced a full-length biographical film of Dr. Sun Yat-sen, founder of modern China, to honor the 120th anniversary of his birthday in southern China. This was the most expensive film made in China to date, and it won many prizes at the Seventh Golden Rooster Awards. The studio is now a corporation with departments for making feature, short and animated films

and television programs, a production factory, an acting troupe, an orchestra and a literature department.

In 1984 the Chinese government chose the small local film studio in Xi'an in northwestern Shaanxi Province to introduce the new "responsibility system" for certain government enterprises on an experimental basis. Wu Tianming (Wu T'ien-ming), director of *River without Buoys* and *Life,* was appointed head of the Xi'an Film Studio, then the youngest studio head in China. He encouraged the work of creative young film artists who joined the studio, which emphasizes films set in China's northwestern region. Several films, including *In the Wild Mountains, Horse Thief* and *Black Cannon Incident,* have been highly praised. The internationally famous young Chinese directors Chen Kaige and Zhang Yimou have been associated with Xi'an Film Studio. Gong Li has been the leading actress in Zhang's films. The studio was purged after the Chinese government called out the military against pro-democracy demonstrators in Tiananmen Square in 1989, and Wu moved to Los Angeles.

The August First Film Studio, founded in 1952, is connected with the People's Liberation Army (PLA). One of the largest and oldest Chinese film studios, it produces feature films, documentaries and educational films on military topics, especially the history of the Chinese Communist revolution. The studio's monthly magazine-film, *Life of the PLA,* depicts the training and experiences of PLA soldiers. During the 1950s the studio co-produced documentary films with the Soviet Union, Czechoslovakia and Bulgaria, and in the 1980s it began actively producing films with foreign filmmakers. The best-known such film is *Norman Bethune: The Making of Hero* (1988), co-produced with Canadian and French companies; it is the true story of a Canadian surgeon who went to China and treated wounded Communist soldiers. See also BETHUNE, NORMAN; CHEN KAIGE; CHINESE COMMUNIST PARTY; DREAM OF THE RED CHAMBER; GONG LI; HU DIE; JOURNEY TO THE WEST; LAN MA; LAO SHE; LING ZIFENG; LU, LISA; MANCHURIA; OPERA, BEIJING; OUTLAWS OF THE MARSH; PEOPLE'S LIBERATION ARMY; PEOPLE'S REPUBLIC OF CHINA; PUYI, HENRY; ROMANCE OF THE THREE KINGDOMS; SHAANXI PROVINCE; SHEN CONGWEN; SUN YAT-SEN; XI'AN; ZHANG YIMOU; ZHAO DAN.

FINGER GUESSING GAMES (*huachuan*)   Games played with the hands and fingers that the Chinese like to play while eating and drinking, especially at banquets. Any two people at the table can play the game of "guessing fingers." Each player raises his right forearm, then at a mutual signal extends it and sticks out from zero to five fingers toward the other player while shouting a number from 1 to 10. The player who shouts the number that equals the sum of the fingers that both players stick out wins the round. The loser has to drink a cup of wine or other alchoholic beverage, and his cup is immediately refilled for the next round. When both players guess the wrong number, they raise their arms and extend their fingers again. The game can go on as long as the two people want to keep playing. Several pairs at a table can play the game at the same time, making for a very noisy and amusing banquet.

The Chinese have many variations on this basic finger-guessing game. One of the best known was adopted from the Japanese game of "scissors-paper-stone" (*janken pan*). When the two players lower their forearms at the same time, their hands make the symbols for one of these objects. An open palm represents a piece of paper, a clenched fist a stone, and the extended index and middle fingers a pair of scissors. The winner is determined by the fact that the paper can wrap up the stone, scissors can cut the paper, and the stone can dull the scissors. For example, if one player extends the symbol for scissors and the other extends paper, scissors wins. The loser of each round has to take a drink. If both players extend the same symbol, the round is a draw and they play again. See also ALCOHOLIC BEVERAGES; BANQUETS.

FIREWORKS AND GUNPOWDER

Explosive materials invented in China that are made from sulfur and nitrates. These two materials, first discussed in written records during the Han dynasty (206 B.C.–A.D. 220), were used by Daoist alchemists to concoct elixirs that would supposedly give a person immortal life. The alchemists isolated and refined the three ingredients required to make gunpowder: saltpeter (potassium nitrate), sulfur and carbon, which they acquired from charcoal. Until the 10th century, the Chinese used gunpowder to make fireworks that could be shot up into the sky to make colorful explosive designs. They filled bamboo tubes with gunpowder and threw the tubes into fires to set off the explosions. Various ingredients were added to the gunpowder to make colors, for example, indigo to make blue-green, white lead carbonate to make white, red lead tetroxide to make red, cinnabar to make purple, and arsenical sulfides to make yellow. They also mixed in steel dust or powdered cast-iron shavings to add bright sparkles to the fireworks. Since gunpowder makes a lot of noise when fired, the Chinese also used it to make firecrackers that they set off at the New Year Festival and other special occasions to chase away evil spirits. The Chinese still make excellent fireworks and firecrackers, especially in the town of Liuyang in Hunan Province, which produces more than 300 varieties.

In the 10th century, the Chinese began using gunpowder to make explosive devices for military use. Official chronicles of the Song dynasty (960–1279) and two other documents from that period frequently mention "rocket," "missile," "fire cannon" and "fire ball" (hand grenades and flamethrowers), showing that the Chinese were now commonly using such weapons in warfare. In 994 a besieged city used gunpowder fire-arrows to drive away the huge military force that surrounded them. In the first half of the 11th century the Chinese began using a "thunderclap bomb" that made a great deal of noise because of its high percentage of saltpeter. These bombs could start fires and scare the horses of invading nomads, who were a constant threat to China.

An early form of the gun was invented in China about 905, and a true gun was produced during the 13th century. Archaeologists discovered a bronze gun more than one foot long dating from 1288 in northeastern China. The earliest description of the use of "fire cannon" was given in the account of a battle fought in 1126 against nomadic Jurchen invaders. This device was a bamboo tube filled with gunpowder which was set on fire and hurled as a flaming missile toward the enemy. Such a bamboo tube had to be carried by two soldiers, and it could only be thrown a short distance. The description of a battle in 1132 notes that fire cannons were placed on a platform that was moved next to the wall of a besieged city and were fired over the wall. Gunpowder was adapted and improved for military purposes by the Arabs, and by the 14th century it was being used in Italy; from there it spread to other European countries, which began using gunpowder militarily against China in the 16th century. See also DAOISM; ELIXIR OF IMMORTALITY; JURCHEN; SONG DYNASTY.

FIRST EMPEROR, THE   See QIN SHI HUANGDI (EMPEROR).

FIRST HISTORICAL ARCHIVES   See IMPERIAL HISTORICAL ARCHIVES.

FISH AND SHELLFISH

(yu)   Important sources of protein in the Chinese diet, especially in southern China. The Chinese eat hundreds of varieties of both freshwater and saltwater fish, some similar to Western types, such as catfish, sea bass, cod, trout, salmon, snapper and sole. Shellfish includes shrimp, prawn, crab, lobster, scallops, abalone, sea cucumber, clams and oysters. Fish and shellfish are usually bought alive from large tanks in Chinese markets and kept in containers of water until they are cooked, thus keeping them fresh (most Chinese have not had refrigerators until recently). Some fish, as soon as they are caught, are processed by various techniques for preserving, such as pickling, cooking or drying.

The Chinese have a wide variety of techniques for cooking fish and seafood. Salted fish, for example, is soaked in water, seasoned with ginger and steamed over rice while it is cooking. A more common method is stir-frying in oil in a wok with soy sauce and other seasonings, such as bean paste, wine vinegar, garlic and scallions; other ingredients such as bean curd and vegetables may be added. Baking, boiling and frying are also common cooking methods in China.

The Chinese usually serve fish for auspicious occasions because the word for fish, yu, is pronounced using the same sound as the word for abundance, so fish symbolizes wealth. A whole cooked fish, usually a carp—a large freshwater fish symbolizing strength, courage and perserverance—is often the central dish at a Chinese banquet. The carp's scales and whiskers make it resemble a dragon, the greatest symbol of both power and an emperor. Fish also symbolize marital happiness and reproduction; thus, it plays an important role in traditional Chinese weddings.

About 80 percent of all freshwater fish consumed are raised in fish-farm ponds; the remainder is gathered from rivers and lakes. Approximately 80 percent of saltwater fish consumed in China is caught in the open waters of the Yellow, East China and South China Seas, with the remainder raised in fish farms along the coast. The entire Chinese coast has been developing rapidly, with many hatcheries for abalone, shellfish and breeding kelp, an edible seaweed that is a good source of nourishment. Rongcheng, on eastern Shandong Peninsula and surrounded by the Yellow Sea, is one of China's most important fishing zones. Shidao, a satellite town, is the largest fishing port in northern China. Chinese fisheries grew more than 10 percent per year from 1978–86, especially freshwater fish. See also BANQUETS; CARP; COOKING, CHINESE; DRAGON; EAST CHINA SEA; GEOG-

RAPHY; SEASONINGS FOR FOOD; SOUTH CHINA SEA; WEDDINGS, TRADITIONAL; YELLOW SEA.

FIVE BUSHELS OF RICE SECT (DAOISM) See ZHANG DAOLING.

FIVE CLASSICS OF CONFUCIANISM (*wujing* or *wu-ching*) A collection of five books that form part of the basic canon of the Confucian school of thought, which became accepted as orthodox by the Chinese imperial government during the Han dynasty (206 B.C.–A.D. 220). The *Five Classics* include the *Book of Changes* (*Yijing* or *I Ching*), *Book of History* (or *Book of Documents*; *Shujing* or *Shu-ching*), *Book of Rites* (*Liji* or *Li-chi*), *Book of Songs* (*Shijing* or *Shih-ching*), and *Spring and Autumn Annals* (*Chun Qiu* or *Ch'un Ch'iu*). Originally a manual for divination of the future, the *Book of Changes* became the source for many Chinese philosophical concepts. The *Book of History,* a collection of documents on the history of the Zhou dynasty (1100–256 B.C.), is the source for many Chinese ideas on the right of an emperor to rule and the moral laws by which the country should be governed. The *Book of Rites* is a restoration of the original *Classic of Rites* (*Lijing* or *Li-ching*), which described ancient rituals and court ceremonies, that had been lost in the third century B.C. The *Book of Songs* is a collection of more than 300 folk songs from the Zhou period. The *Spring and Autumn Annals* is a short chronicle of events in the State of Lu (modern Shandong Province), the home of Confucius, from 722 to 481 B.C. Confucian tradition claims that these five documents were written before the time of Confucius (551–479 B.C.) and that Confucius himself had a hand in preserving, editing and writing commentaries on them. The Confucian canon also includes the Four Books of Confucianism (*sishu*): the *Analects* (sayings) of Confucius (*Lunyu*), *Book of Mencius* (*Mengzi* or *Meng Tzu*), *Doctrine of the Mean* (*Zhongyong* or *Chung yung*) and *Great Learning* (*Daxue* or *Ta hsueh*). The last two texts were originally chapters in the *Book of Rites,* but the great Neo-Confucian scholar Zhu Xi (Chu Hsi; 1130–1200) separated them out and combined them with the *Analects* and the *Book of Mencius* to form the Four Books.

Knowledge of the Five Classics and the Four Books of Confucianism was essential for members of the literati, or scholar-gentry class, since these texts formed the basis of the examinations by which applicants from literati families were chosen to staff the imperial bureaucracy, from the founding of the Grand Academy (taixue or t'ai-hsueh) in 124 B.C. by Han Emperor Wudi (Wu-ti; r. 141–87 B.C.) right up to 1905 near the end of the Qing Dynasty (1644–1911). At several times in Chinese history, the texts of the Confucian canon were inscribed on stone columns (stele) and set up in the Grand Academy; many of these are still preserved in Beijing, the capital of China since 1279, and Xi'an, an ancient imperial capital formerly known as Chang'an. After learning how to read and write, a young Chinese student first read aloud and memorized the Four Books, and then studied the Five Classics. From the Han dynasty onward, Confucian scholars constantly wrote critical commentaries on the Five Classics and the Four Books in order to provide a more comprehensive understanding of Confucian ideas. See also CONFUCIUS; CONFUCIANISM; FOUR BOOKS OF CONFUCIANISM; IMPERIAL EXAMINATION SYSTEM; LITERATI; NAMES OF INDIVIDUAL BOOKS.

FIVE DYNASTIES PERIOD (Wu tai; 907–60)   A period of disunity between the Tang (618–907) and Song (960–1279) dynasties when northern China was ruled by five dynasties in rapid succession. During the same period, southern China was ruled by 10 kingdoms, nine of them simultaneously, known as the Ten Kingdoms Period (907–60). In addition, the Khitan (Qidan), a nomadic Altaic (Turkish)-speaking tribe in southern Manchuria (modern northeastern China), invaded China's northeastern frontier. They forced the first ruler of the Later Jin dynasty (936–47) to give them 16 border prefectures within the Great Wall, including the wall's strategic gates in modern Hebei Province and the area that is modern Beijing. In 904 the Khitans formally established their empire, which became known after 947 as the Liao dynasty (947–1125). Toward the end of the Tang dynasty, high taxes were raised against the population, the Chinese Empire became decentralized and military governors claimed large territories for themselves, creating the five dynasties. During the Five Dynasties Period, many literati—members of the scholar class who ran the imperial bureaucracy that governed China—fled south and made a great contribution to the development of Chinese civilization in the southern provinces.

The Five Dynasties in northern China included the Liang (907–23), Tang (923–36), Later Jin (936–46), Han (947–50) and Zhou (951–60). Each was a military dictatorship that was unable to hold out for long against invasions by nomadic tribes. The first, the Liang, was the longest of the five. It was founded by Zhu Wen (known as Taizu or T'ai-tsu; r. 907–12), who aimed to become emperor of all China but failed because his dynasty lacked the necessary resources. He was succeeded by two more Liang emperors. The Tang dynasty had four emperors and was founded by the son of a Turkish mercenary soldier. The first Jin dynasty emperor, Shi Jing-tang (known as Gaozu or Kao-tsu; r. 936–42), lost the 16 northern prefectures to the Khitan, thus destroying China's frontier defense system against nomadic invaders and affecting the Chinese Empire for more than four centuries to come. The Later Han dynasty, with two emperors, was the shortest officially recognized dynasty in Chinese history. When the dynasty fell, the founder's brother founded the Northern Han, the last of the Ten Kingdoms in southern China. The fifth northern dynasty was the Later Zhou, with three emperors. Chai Rong (Ch'ai-Jung), the adopted son of the founder, laid the foundations for the reunification of China under the Song dynasty. However, he died at age 38 and one of his officers, Zhao Kuangyin (Chao K'uang-yin), seized power, proclaimed himself the first Song emperor Taizu (T'ai-tsu; r. 960–76), and united all of China except for the area ruled by the Liao dynasty. See also GREAT WALL; LIAO DYNASTY; LITERATI; SONG DYNASTY; TANG DYNASTY; TEN KINGDOMS PERIOD.

FIVE GUARDIAN PEAKS OF THE CHINESE EMPIRE See FIVE SACRED MOUNTAINS OF DAOISM.

FIVE MATERIAL AGENTS (*wuxing* or *wu hsing*)   Also known as the Five Material Elements; according to ancient

Daoist Chinese thought, five elements that are dynamic qualities or energies that can be perceived in all created things. In order, they are earth, wood, metal, fire and water. The word *xing* (*hsing*), while translated as agent or element, is actually a verb meaning to act or to go. The function of the Five Agents is similar to that of yin and yang, the two fundamental principles that the Chinese traditionally believe control everything in the universe. Yin is female, passive, dark, negative, cold, and yang is male, active, light, positive, hot. These two principles are complementary and succeed each other in a continuing cycle. The Yin-Yang school of thought also expounded the principle of the Five Agents that were believed to control the workings of the universe, especially the changing seasons and periods of time that continually follow each other. These concepts provided the theoretical foundation for scientific thought in China for 2,000 years. The Five Agents have an active nature, and each agent is "overcome" by the next agent in turn; that is, fire overcomes wood, earth overcomes fire, and so on in a never-ending process.

The Five Agents are believed to provide the energy for all other groups of five that are important to the Chinese, such as the Five Virtues in the Confucian school of thought, the Five Government Ministers, the Five Sacred Mountains of the Daoist religion, the Five Musical Notes in the pentatonic scale and the Five Basic Colors—yellow, green, white, red and black. Each agent is associated with elements in the other categories of five. For example, fire belongs to summer, which is red and associated with the Ministry of War. The Five Sacred Mountains are associated with the four geographical directions and the center of the universe. The eastern mountain is green, the southern is red, the central is yellow, the northern is black, and the western is white. Wood is associated with spring, green, the east, and the Minister of Agriculture; fire with summer, red, the south and the Ministry of War; earth has no season of its own but assists the other elements in controlling the four seasons and is associated with yellow, the center and the Ministry of Works; metal with autumn, white, the west, and the Minister of Interior. Many other categories were believed to correspond with the Five Agents, and large charts can be drawn up to list all of the associations.

The agents and colors were applied to ruling dynasties as well. The Xia dynasty (2200–1750 B.C.) had been associated with wood, the Shang dynasty (1750–1040 B.C.) with metal, and the Zhou dynasty (1100–256 B.C.), which was losing its power when the Five Agents theory was developed, was associated with fire and the color red. Hence the dynasty that would succeed it would supposedly be associated with water and the color black. Shi Huangdi (246–210 B.C.), who overthrew the Zhou and established the Qin dynasty (221–206 B.C.), willingly chose water and black as the symbols of his new dynasty.

The source for these ancient beliefs was the *Book of Changes* (*Yijing* or *I Ching*), one of the Five Classics of Confucianism; it was originally meant for divination but contains many philosophical concepts. The Five Agents still play an important role in Chinese culture for fortune-telling and casting horoscopes, both of which are especially important when two people want to get married. The agents are also connected with the animal zodiac which associates every year with a particular animal in a 12-year cycle, and every person born in the same year is believed to share the traits of that animal. Each 12-year cycle is associated with one of the Five Agents, as well as with one of the five colors, directions, seasons and so forth. For example, a person born in 1994 is considered to be a "dog," with the qualities of metal, the west and wood and is honest, well-liked, intelligent and even-tempered. A person who has lived to the age of 60 is especially celebrated for having lived through the complete zodiac cycle of five 12-year cycles. See also BOOK OF CHANGES; CONFUCIANISM; FIVE SACRED MOUNTAINS OF DAOISM; YIN AND YANG; ZODIAC, ANIMAL.

FIVE SACRED MOUNTAINS OF DAOISM Also known as the Five Guardian Peaks (Wuyue or Wu-Yueh) of the Chinese Empire; five mountains sacred to the native Chinese religion of Daoism, where Chinese emperors formerly performed sacrificial rituals for Heaven and Earth. The Five Sacred Mountains of Daoism include Mount Tai in Shandong Province, the eastern mountain where the sun rises; Mount Heng in Shanxi Province, the northern mountain; Mount Hua in Shaanxi, the western; Mount Heng in Hunan Province, the southern; and Mount Song in Henan Province, the mountain in the center. There is also a set of four mountains sacred to the Buddhist religion; this belief was introduced into China from India around the first century A.D. Both religions revere a mountain in each of the four quarters of the universe, with Daoists revering a fifth mountain in the center. Many temples, pagodas and monuments have been placed on the mountains, to which the Chinese of both religions make pilgrimages.

Mount Tai (Taishan) in Shandong, also known as "Eastern Peak" (Dongyue), is the most sacred of the five Daoist mountains and has been revered for more than 2,500 years. Emperor Qin Shi Huangdi, who unified China under the Qin dynasty (221–206 B.C.), traveled to Mount Tai to make offerings to legitimize his reign. More than 250 Daoist, Buddhist and Confucian temples and monuments have been built on the mountain. Daimiao, the temple at the southern foot of Taishan, the starting point for pilgrims climbing the mountain, is where emperors made sacrifices to the Earth. On the summit, where emperors made sacrifices to Heaven, is Yuhuang Dian, a temple dedicated to Yuti, the Jade Emperor, the ruler of Heaven and the highest deity in Daoism. Emperors were carried up the mountain, but pilgrims climb it on a path of nearly 7,000 stone steps that lead to the summit, 5,069 feet above sea level.

Hengshan, in northern Shanxi Province, is situated in an area that was for centuries a frontier zone between nomadic Mongols who established the Yuan dynasty (1279–1368) and Han Chinese to the south. Hence, the mountain was often cut off from the Chinese Empire. The Chinese Ming dynasty (1368–1644) recovered the region and issued an imperial decree naming Mount Heng the "Northern Guardian" (Beiyue or Pei-yueh) of the empire, to which the emperor was to make annual sacrifices. After the Republic of China was established in 1912, imperial sacrifices were abolished, and the pilgrim road and temples on the mountain were neglected. Hengshan, which rises 7,280 feet above sea level, is located about 40 miles southeast of the city of Datong and is still considered the guardian of China's northern frontier.

In Shaanxi Province, Huashan, the western mountain, (also known as "Flower Mountain") is considered the most beautiful of the five sacred mountains. It belongs to the mountain mass Tongguan (T'ung-kuan), itself a branch of the Qingling Mountain Range, which guards the east-west corridor through the provinces of Shaanxi, Shensi and Henan. Huashan is situated just south of the confluence of the Wei and Yellow rivers (Huanghe), near the latter's right-angled, major turn to flow east across China. A cradle of Chinese civilization, this area is the site where ancient emperors made sacrificial offerings to the Daoist gods when they claimed the "Mandate of Heaven" (*tianming* or *t'ien-ming*) that legitimized their reign. Tang the Victorious, founder of the Shang-Yin dynasty, offered sacrifices at Huashan supposedly in 1766 B.C., as did Wu Wang, founder of the Zhou dynasty, supposedly in 1122 B.C. Huashan has five peaks, of which the North Peak is the lowest, at 6,280 feet. The four other peaks, of which the East Peak is the steepest, rise about 2,000 feet higher. The pilgrim path winds up and down each peak and takes several days to complete. The largest temple, the "Palace of Golden Heaven," is on the South Peak. Legend claims that atop Huashan grows a white fungus, which, if eaten, will transform a person into an immortal being, and beans that will satisfy hunger for 49 days. Huashan was painted by many early landscape artists from Chang'an (modern Xi'an), the capital of the Tang dynasty (618–907). Artists of the Song dynasty (960–1279) considered Huashan the embodiment of everything the Chinese love most in nature.

Hungshan, the southern mountain, is located 75 miles south of Zhangsha in the West (Xiang) River valley in Hunan Province and rises 4,500 feet. It is also called Zhurong Feng (Chu-jung Feng), the "Blessed Fire Peak," because it lies in the southern quarter of the universe where the sun is at its highest in summer. The village of Nanyue lies at the foot of the mountain, site of the South Peak Temple (Nanyue Miao), built during the Ming dynasty and one of the finest temples in China. The splendid Great Hall has upturned double roofs covered with imperial-yellow glazed tiles. The pilgrim path begins at the temple's rear gate and leads to the summit, from which, on a clear day, there is a magnificent view of the "Five Dragon Rivers" believed to be fed by the rain god of Heng-shan. Seventy-two lesser peaks surround the mountain's top peak. The beautiful waterfall, Water Curtain Cave (Shuilien Dong or Shui-lien Tung), was visited by Chinese emperors, who rested there in the yellow-tiled pavilion.

Mount Song (Songshan; or "The Lofty"), the central mountain, is located about 20 miles south of the Yellow River in Henan Province. About 5,000 feet high, it belongs to the Qinling Mountain Range, the easternmost extension of the Kunlun Range. The pilgrim path up Songshan begins about three miles south of the town of Dengfeng at the Temple of the Central Guardian Peak (Zhongyue Taishi Songgao or Chung-yueh T'ai-shi Sung-kao). First built 2,000 years ago during the Han dynasty, the temple has been rebuilt several times. In the spring, thousands of pilgrims journey to make offerings at this temple without climbing the mountain. Near Songshan is a cave called Laozhun Dong (Lao-chun Tung), where Laozi (Lao Tzu), the most important Daoist thinker and author of the *Daodejing* (*Tao-te ching*), supposedly lived. The oldest pagoda in China can be seen in one of Songshan's deepest and most spectacular ravines, in the ruins of a Buddhist temple called Songyue Miao (Song-yueh), which had been built in 509. The pagoda has 12 sides and is 15 stories high. Also nearby is Shaolin Monastery, founded in 477; its resident monks were famous for their martial arts skills. Bodhidharma, the legendary teacher who brought Chan (Zen) Buddhism to China, supposedly lived in a cave near Shaolin. See also BODHIDHARMA; BUDDHISM; DAOISM; FOUR SACRED MOUNTAINS OF BUDDHISM; HEAVEN; LANDSCAPE PAINTING; LAOZI; MANDATE OF HEAVEN; QINLING MOUNTAIN RANGE; SHAOLIN TEMPLE; TAI, MOUNT; WEI RIVER.

FIVE SAGE KINGS See JADE EMPEROR; SHUN, EMPEROR; YAO, EMPEROR; YELLOW EMPEROR; YU, EMPEROR.

FIVE VIRTUES OF CONFUCIANISM See CONFUCIUS; FILIAL PIETY; HUMANITY; PROPRIETY; RIGHTEOUSNESS; WISDOM.

FIVE-ANTI CAMPAIGNS See THREE-ANTI AND FIVE-ANTI CAMPAIGNS.

FIVE-YEAR PLANS After the Chinese Communist Party (CCP)—led by Mao Zedong (Mao Tse-tung)—won the civil war against the Nationalist Party (Kuomintang; KMT) and founded the People's Republic of China (PRC) in 1949, it enacted a series of measures to rebuild the country, stimulate economic growth and assist the farmers. In 1953 it announced the First Five-Year Plan, which was intended to consolidate government ownership of factories and businesses and increase production and the tax base. (The idea for five-year plans was taken from the U.S.S.R.) The First Five-Year Plan (1953–57) provided the guidelines for building up Chinese heavy industries. It also called for the mobilization of unskilled laborers both in cities and rural areas to work on construction projects, to build smaller-scale factories and to locate raw materials. Local governments were given more control over their production activities, and more responsibility was given to workers at the local level. The Communist government also attempted to speed up development by an ambitious plan called the Great Leap Forward (1958–60). However, the Great Leap Forward had problems; the economy grew very quickly but unevenly, great strains were placed on transportation networks, and the mobilization of female as well as male workers into the industrial sector caused severe disruption of agriculture. All this led to the policy's failure and cancellation.

In 1960 the U.S.S.R. cut off all aid to China, which was an even greater blow to the development of Chinese industry. However, the newly created system of people's communes as centers for economic and technical development was one of the successes of the Great Leap Forward.

The Chinese government continued to issue five-year plans, although political disruption prevented the Second (1958–62), Third (1966–70), Fourth (1971–75) and Fifth (1976–80) Five-Years Plans from having much effect. The Sixth Five-Year Plan (1981–85) was not so much a guideline as it was an examination of the previous plans. The Seventh Five-Year Plan (1986–90) was intended to carry out economic reforms, but it, too, was disrupted by political dissension; the Ninth is due to end in 2000. See also GREAT LEAP FORWARD; PEOPLE'S COMMUNE; PEOPLE'S REPUBLIC OF CHINA; RUSSIA AND CHINA.

FLAG, NATIONAL   The official flag of the People's Republic of China (PRC), founded in 1949 by the Chinese Communist Party (CCP) under Chairman Mao Zedong (Mao Tse-tung; 1893–1976). The flag's design comprises a field of red with five yellow, five-pointed stars in the upper left corner. The color red symbolizes the communist revolution, although it is also the traditional Chinese color for happiness. The stars symbolize the unity of the revolutionary people under the leadership of the Communist Party. One star is larger; this represents the PRC and CCP leaders. The four smaller stars in a semicircle represent the four classes of people in the PRC (workers, peasants, small business owners and loyal capitalists), or the four types of workers (farmers, factory workers, white-collar workers and managers). These five stars also appear in the PRC's national emblem, shining above the Gate of Heavenly Peace (Tiananmen or T'ien-an-men) in Beijing. See also CHINESE COMMUNIST PARTY; COLORS; EMBLEM, NATIONAL; PEOPLE'S REPUBLIC OF CHINA; TIANANMEN SQUARE.

FLOWER GARLAND SECT OF BUDDHISM (Huayan or Hua-yen Sect)   One of the four most important sects in Chinese Buddhism, along with the Tiantai (T'ien-t'ai), Pure Land and Chan (Zen) Sects. The Buddhist religion was introduced into China from India around the first century A.D. The Flower Garland and Tiantai sects in China were practiced only by monks from the upper classes, since they were based on highly philosophical teachings that could not be followed by the masses of Chinese, who followed Daoism and did not have the education or spare time required to study the scriptures and highly philosophical teachings. The Flower Garland sect had its roots in Indian Buddhist thought but developed as a distinct sect in China. Dushun (Tu-shun; 557–640) was an early teacher but Fazang (Fa-tsang), the "Great Master of Xianshou" (Hsien-shou; 643–712) is considered the sect's actual founder. Therefore this sect is also called the Xianshou School. It took as its main scripture the *Avatamsaka Sutra,* an Indian text that claims to present the teachings of Sakyamuni Buddha, and argues that all things are created by the Mind and that the entire universe arises at the same time. This concept, known as the Universal Causation of the Realm of Law (Dharmadhatu), is similar to the Tiantai sect's concept of "all three thousand realms immanent in an instant of thought." Fazang's well-known lecture, recorded as *Essays on the Golden Lion,* discusses the chain of cause and effect by which all things in the phenomenal world come into being. He claims that these things give the illusion of having existence but are actually "empty," although their emptiness does not negate the fact of their illusory being. The goal of this teaching is to enter Nirvana, or freedom from suffering, which is achieved by having a calm mind and freeing oneself of passions and false thoughts. See also BUDDHISM; TIANTAI SECT OF BUDDHISM.

FLOWERS   See CAMELLIA; CHRYSANTHEMUM; LOTUS; ORCHID; PEONY; PLUM; RHODODENDRON.

FLUTES AND WIND INSTRUMENTS   Musical instruments played by blowing air into them with the mouth and using the fingers to cover or open holes to change the notes.

The Chinese classify the flute as one of the eight types of musical instruments and associate it with bamboo, the type of wood from which it is made. Types of flute include the common flute (*di* or *ti*), small flute (*guan* or *kuan*) and ceremonial flute (*xiao* or *hsiao*), all of which are bamboo tubes held vertically or horizontally; the oboe-like clarinet (*so na*); and panpipes (*paixiao* or *p'ai hsiao*), made from a row of different lengths of bamboo tubes. Another of the eight types of Chinese instruments is a wind instrument called the *sheng,* a mouth organ associated with the gourd, whose shape it resembles. The *sheng* is made from a cluster of 13 or so thin bamboo pipes of varying lengths. Each pipe has, at the bottom, a bronze reed that vibrates to produce a different sound. Another of the eight types of instruments is the vessel-flute, or ocarina (*xuan* or *hsuan*), which is associated with the Earth because it has a round clay body. Flutes and *sheng* are mentioned in Chinese documents as far back as the Zhou dynasty (1100–256 B.C.). See also SHENG.

"FLYING HORSE OF GANSU"   See LANZHOU.

FLYING TIGERS   A group of American pilots who volunteered to fly missions for China in 1941–42, during its War of Resistance against Japan (1937–45; World War II). Its official name was the American Volunteers Group (AVG), and its commander was U.S. General Claire Lee Chennault (1890–1958). The Japanese army had forced the Chinese Nationalist (Kuomintang) army, led by Chiang Kai-shek (1887–1975), to flee west to Sichuan Province, which was protected by high mountains. Although the Japanese were able to conduct bombing raids on Sichuan, the Flying Tigers helped prevent the Japanese military from taking control of the region.

In early 1941, when America still held a neutral position regarding the Pacific war, the U.S. government gave permission for volunteer American pilots to fly missions in P-40 fighter planes, which the United States had sold to the Nationalists under the Lend-Lease Act. The planes carried the insignia of the Chinese Nationalist Army. Members of the AVG, known by the romantic name "Flying Tigers," trained in Burma (Myanmar), a country southwest of China that was once part of the British Empire. They were providing air defense for Nationalist forces in southwestern China and for Allied forces in Burma prior to the Japanese attack on the American naval base at Pearl Harbor, Hawaii, on December 7, 1941, which drew America into the Pacific War. The Flying Tigers disbanded in July 1942, and most of its pilots enlisted in the U.S. Army Air Force.

General Chennault, born in Texas, had joined the U.S. army during World War I and became a flyer in 1919. A pioneer in developing air tactics for fighting wars, he led a fighter squadron in Hawaii for three years before becoming chief of fighter training at Maxwell Field, Alabama. He retired in 1937 and acted as an air adviser to the Chinese Nationalist government, building up their air force with American planes through the lend-lease program. He also recruited and trained the pilots who joined the Flying Tigers, who eventually numbered 100, with about 200 crew members. In April 1942 the U.S. army recalled Chennault, and he served as head of the U.S. air war in China until July 25, 1945. He retired again and returned to China in 1946 to establish the Civil Air Transport for the Nationalists, which he ran until 1958.

In 1991 the U.S. government admitted that the pilots and crew of the Flying Tigers had not been volunteers but were actually on "active duty" in a covert mission during their time of service in the American Volunteers Group. The truth had been kept secret because the group's mission violated the U.S. Neutrality Act, which forbids the U.S. government from taking sides in conflicts between warring countries, and it might have provoked the Japanese against the United States. See also CHIANG KAI-SHEK; NATIONALIST PARTY; SICHUAN PROVINCE; WAR OF RESISTANCE AGAINST JAPAN.

FOLK ART See INDIGO DYEING OF TEXTILES; PAPERCUTTING; TOYS, TRADITIONAL; WOODCUTS.

FOOCHOW See FUZHOU.

FOOD See AGRICULTURE; BANQUETS; BEANS AND BEAN PRODUCTS; CHICKEN; COOKING, CHINESE; DIM SUM; DUCK; GRAIN; NOMADS AND ANIMAL HUSBANDRY; PIG; RICE; RESTAURANTS AND FOOD STALLS; SEASONINGS FOR FOOD; SOYBEANS AND SOY PRODUCTS; VEGETABLES AND VEGETARIAN DISHES; WEDDINGS, TRADITIONAL.

FOOTBINDING   The custom of binding young girls' feet so that they would not grow normally but would instead bend into deformed, three-inch-long arcs. Bound feet were euphemistically called "golden lilies." The custom began among female entertainers and members of the Chinese court during the early Song dynasty (960–1279). By the end of the dynasty, foot binding had spread throughout the families of the literati, or scholar class, who governed China. Women whose feet had been bound wore special tiny shoes that were beautifully embroidered. They could not walk normally and had to be supported while walking and even standing. Their feet caused them to move with a sway that the Chinese considered feminine and graceful.

When a girl was between ages five and eight, her feet were wrapped tightly with long strips of cloth that pushed the four small toes on each foot down around and under the balls of her feet. The binding cloths, changed daily, constantly compressed the feet from front to back, gradually breaking the arches and causing them to turn upwards in an arched shape so that only the back edge of the heels could support the girl's weight. When a girl's feet stopped growing her constant pain stopped, but she still wore the binding cloths to support her feet and to hide their deformity. Her leg muscles also became atrophied from too little use, so her legs were extremely thin.

The custom of footbinding became so widespread in China that small bound feet gave girls a better chance in making a good marriage and getting a higher bride price. Also, women with bound feet could not run away from an unhappy marriage. In addition, the tiny bound feet became sexualized as highly desirable by Chinese men. Eventually women of the peasant class, who had to work hard as farmers, began binding their feet as well. Members of the minority groups in China, including the Mongols who ruled during the Yuan dynasty (1279–1368) and the Manchus who ruled during the Qing dynasty (1644–1911), did not bind

Gradually abolished in the 19th and 20th centuries, footbinding and its effects are seen now only in older generations of Chinese women.   S.E. MEYER

their feet. The custom of footbinding was opposed in the 19th and 20th centuries by members of the Taiping Rebellion and the Nationalist and Communist Parties, as well as by Western missionaries, although women with bound feet were still seen in China into the middle of the 20th century. See also LITERATI; SONG DYNASTY.

FORBIDDEN CITY   A walled area in Beijing, the present capital of China, which contains the palace compound inhabited from 1420 to 1912 by 24 emperors of the Ming (1368–1644) and Qing (1644–1911) dynasties. The largest complex of ancient buildings in China, and in the world, the Forbidden City covers 250 acres and is surrounded by a moat 177 feet wide and a wall 33 feet high. It contains 800 buildings with 9,000 rooms, including 37 palaces, 20 halls and pavilions, 9 monumental gates, and gardens, streams and courtyards large enough to hold banquets for 2,000 people. Commoners were forbidden from entering the compound unless they had special permission, and the emperors left it only for special occasions, such as the performance of rituals at the Temple of Heaven. The Forbidden City is also called "The Great Within" (Ta Nei) and the Old Imperial Palace (Gugong or Ku-kung). The Forbidden City was the residence of the "Son of Heaven," the traditional term for the emperor. Formally known as the Purple Forbidden City (Zijincheng or Tzu-chin-ch'eng), it was so called because purple was the color associated with the polestar, which the Chinese considered the center of the universe. The compound was built on a north-south axis according to the geomantic principles of *feng shui*. The Front Palace (Qianchao) in the southern part of the complex contained the halls of government, and the Inner Palace (Neiting) to the north contained the residences of the emperor, his consorts and harem, and thousands of female servants, concubines and eunuchs. This area also housed storerooms, libraries and a hall of historical archives. The emperors held ceremonial audiences and received foreign tributary missions in the large Outer Court. Over the centuries, fires destroyed the Forbidden City many times; the buildings presently standing were constructed after the 18th century, although their design remains the same as the originals. The compound, which was opened to the public in 1949 as the Palace Museum, is continually being restored.

Ming emperor Yongle (Yung-lo; r. 1403–24) began building the palaces of the Forbidden City in 1407, and they were completed in 1420. The next year he transferred his court from Nanjing to Beijing. Qing emperor Qianlong (Ch'ienlung; r. 1736–95) renovated and extended many of the buildings. The most beautiful garden is named for the Qianlong

emperor. In its center is the Palace of Imperial Peace, with a temple dedicated to the god of fire. The Nine Dragon Wall, about 18 feet high and 90 feet long and decorated with colorful ceramic tiles, was built in 1773 during Qianlong's reign. Just south of the Forbidden City lie the Temple of Heaven, Tiananmen Square and several modern buildings, such as the Great Hall of the People, the Mao Zedong Mausoleum—which houses the former Chinese Communist leader's body—and the Palace Museum, which houses exhibits on the natural history of China and the history of the Chinese Communist revolution.

Visitors enter the Forbidden City through the main gate on the northern side of Tiananmen Square, go through the Meridian Gate (Wumen), cross white-marble bridges over the Golden Water River (Jinshuihe) and ascend a flight of steps leading to the main palace gate, the Gate of Supreme Harmony (Taihemen). This opens onto an immense courtyard bounded on the north by the "Three Great Halls" that stand in the center of the Front Palace: the Hall of Supreme Harmony (Taihedian), the Hall of Complete Harmony (Zhonghedian) and the Hall of Preserving Harmony (Baohedian). Each of the halls is situated on a three-level, white-marble terrace, with each level bounded by a white balustrade with pillars carved with dragons, phoenixes, lotus leaves and cloud patterns. Stairs leading to the successive halls have a marble path in the middle, carved with dragons and other animals, known as the "dragon pavement." Emperors were carried in a litter over this path; no one else was allowed to set foot on

Only with special permission were commoners allowed into the Forbidden City, the emperor's residence from 1420 to 1912. S.E. MEYER

it. The halls are decorated with large bronze sculptures and coffered roofs with golden dragons. The Hall of Supreme Harmony, the largest and most important building in the Forbidden City, was used for major ceremonial occasions, such as enthronement and birthday celebrations of emperors. The magnificent red-and-gold hall contains a highly decorated Dragon Throne of purple-colored wood surrounded by six golden columns with carved dragons. The dragon is the symbol of the Chinese emperor. The square in front of the Gate of Heavenly Purity (Qianqingmen) divides the Forbidden City into the inner and outer courts.

The inner court, containing the former private residences of the imperial family, includes the Palace of Heavenly Purity (Qianqinggong), the Hall of Prosperity (Jiaotaidian) and the Hall of Earthly Peace (Kunninggong). The Imperial Garden (Yuhuayuan) is a large classical Chinese landscaped garden at the northern end of the Forbidden City. Many of the buildings on the western and eastern sides of the Forbidden City are now museums that are also open to visitors. The six Western Palaces, living quarters for the empress and concubines, display their personal possessions. Visitors leave by the north gate, the Gate of Divine Military Genius (Shenwumen).

After the Qing dynasty was overthrown by the Revolution of 1911, the Republican government at Nanjing permitted Henry Puyi—the boy who was the last Qing Emperor, known as Xuantong (Hsuan-t'ung)— and his family to continue living in the Forbidden City and to retain ownership of the imperial art treasures. In 1924 a warlord forced Puyi to flee to Tianjin. The following year the Forbidden City became a museum. The Old Palace Museum (Gugong bowuguan or Ku-kung po-wu-kuan) exhibits paintings, calligraphy, ceramics, bronzeware and jade objects from the imperial art collection. Even though many of the art treasures were stolen or destroyed, the collection still contains nearly one million items. Many of these were brought to the Forbidden City to replace treasures taken to Taiwan by Chinese Nationalists (Kuomintang) escaping the Chinese Communists in 1949 and which are housed in the magnificent National Palace Museum in Taipei. In 1987 UNESCO placed the Forbidden City on its list of the world's cultural and national heritage sites. See also BEIJING; CONCUBINAGE; DRAGON; EMPEROR; EUNUCH; FENG SHUI; GREAT HALL OF THE PEOPLE; MING DYNASTY; NATIONAL PALACE MUSEUM (TAIPEI); PUYI, HENRY; QING DYNASTY; TEMPLE OF HEAVEN; TIANANMEN SQUARE.

FOREIGN AFFAIRS See MINISTRY OF FOREIGN AFFAIRS.

FOREIGN TRADE AND INVESTMENT The People's Republic of China (PRC), founded in 1949 by the Chinese Communist Party (CCP), traded mostly with the USSR and other Communist countries until 1976. After the Cultural Revolution (1966–76), the PRC government moved toward the economic reforms and trade growth promoted by Deng Xiaoping (Tung Hsiao-p'ing). In 1997 China ran a $40 billion trade surplus. By 1998 foreign trade accounted for 20 percent of China's gross domestic product. Economic growth had been 10–14 percent a year but has decreased to about 7 percent.

Contemporary Chinese leaders have realized that foreign trade and technology are necessary for modernizing China. The Chinese government long had a policy of "self-reliance," which restricted and diversified imports and foreign credits

to prevent China from becoming dependent on, or exploited by, any foreign country, as it had been from the mid-19th through mid-20th centuries. The PRC government began liberalizing foreign trade restrictions in 1978 and opened the Chinese economy to foreign investment in 1979. On July 8, 1979, the government acted to bring foreign capital and technology into China by promulgating an equity joint-venture law, which encouraged foreign investment in China. The government also allowed investment in contractual (or cooperative) joint ventures and wholly foreign-owned enterprises. In 1980 the PRC opened four Special Economic Zones (SEZs), at Shenzhen, Zhuhai and Shantou in Guangdong Province and Xiamen in Fujian Province, to facilitate foreign investment and trade and to function as export-processing centers; a fifth was opened on Hainan Island in 1988. The government has enacted other policies to increase exports, such as encouraging the rapid development of factories that assemble imported components into consumer goods for export to hard-currency countries.

In 1986 the PRC formally applied to rejoin the General Agreement on Tariffs and Trade (GATT), which governs much of the world's trade. Many Western countries, however, resist granting membership to the PRC because of its perceived human rights violations, especially the violent suppression of pro-democracy demonstrators in Tiananmen Square in 1989, its imprisonment of dissidents in labor camps (laogai) and its strict government controls on the Chinese economy. The PRC government limits foreign access to the Chinese market through such measures as tariffs, import and export licensing, import substitution regulations and foreign exchange restrictions. It also restricts foreign entry into insurance, banking, accounting and legal service. Moreover, legal and regulatory systems in the PRC are arbitrary and not very well developed and thus hinder the ability of foreign investors to conduct business there.

In 1991, the PRC joined the Asia-Pacific Economic Cooperation (APEC) group, which promotes free trade and cooperation in economic, trade, investment and technology issues. The PRC government eliminated time restrictions on the establishment of joint ventures and allowed foreign partners to become the chairs of joint venture boards. It granted more preferential tax treatment for wholly foreign-owned businesses and contractual ventures and for foreign companies which invest in selected economic zones or in sectors encouraged by the government, such as energy, communications and transportation. It authorized some foreign banks to open branches in Shanghai, China's largest and most commercial city, and allowed foreign investors to purchase special "B" shares of stock in selected companies listed on the Shanghai and Shenzhen securities exchanges (although "B" shares carry no ownership rights in a company).

Hong Kong, the largest outside investor in the PRC at the time of its return to China from Britain in 1997, has been replaced by Taiwan as the largest. During most of the 1980s, Japan was China's second-largest trading partner and the largest supplier of China's imports. China's imports from Japan began increasing sharply in 1992, partly because of the large volume of machinery and equipment imported for the many Japanese investment projects in China. In 1993 China's imports from Japan totaled $17.4 billion, and its exports to Japan totaled $20.7 billion.

The United States was China's third-largest trading partner in the 1980s, following Hong Kong and Japan, but by 1990 the United States had surpassed Japan as China's second-largest partner. From 1979 until the end of 1993, U.S. commitments to directly invest in China reached a total of $14.4 billion. In 1996 China's imports from the United States totaled $12 billion but its exports to the U.S. totaled more than $51 billion. However, before the reversion in June 1997, the PRC considered its exports that were first shipped to Hong Kong in transit to the U.S. as exports to Hong Kong, whereas the United States counted these same Chinese exports that entered the United States through Hong Kong as imports from the PRC, which created a discrepancy in trade statistics. Many companies in the United States, Japan, Taiwan and other countries established subsidiaries or holding companies in Hong Kong to take advantage of the colony's more lenient investment and tax regulations, and these companies coordinated investment in projects in China. Hong Kong companies have played a major role in selling Chinese products such as clothing, footwear and toys, which comprise a large share of total U.S. imports from China. China exports about one-third of its total output to the United States. In 1996 the United States was the largest market for Chinese goods.

In 1980, agricultural products and mineral fuels, mainly crude petroleum, accounted for half of the PRC's exports, and manufactured goods accounted for the other half. By 1991 these shares were 22.5 percent and 77.5 percent, respectively. As for imports, the share of agricultural products and mineral fuels declined from 35 percent in 1980 to 16.9 percent in 1991, and the share of manufactured products increased from 65 percent to 83.1 percent. There have been large increases in the PRC's imports of industrial raw materials, machinery and transportation equipment, partly because many foreign investors have imported their own machinery and equipment as part of their investment. The rapid increase in foreign investment in China has been a major force in the growth of China's domestic economy and the expansion of its foreign trade. During 1992, contracted foreign direct investment in China totaled $58.1 billion. In 1993 it totaled $408.4 billion, nearly as much as the cumulative amount invested in China during the entire period 1979–92. The value of contracts signed by U.S. companies alone in 1993 amounted to 44.3 percent of the total. In 1992, more than 70 countries and independent administrative regions were the source of direct foreign investment in China. Taiwan, the United States and Japan have been the main investors in China, as was Hong Kong before the 1997 reversion.

In 1992 Deng Xiaoping adopted policies that further opened the Chinese economy, thus increasing the types of foreign-funded enterprises that may be established in the PRC, opening more regions of the country through investment incentives and providing more access to economic sectors in which foreign investment had been prohibited or highly restricted. The PRC, which has large onshore and offshore oil deposits, has established special laws and procedures for foreign investment in the exploration and development of its oil resources. It has also approved the establishment of two more types of foreign-funded enterprises: the umbrella enterprise and the limited company. The umbrella company enables a foreign company with two or more projects in China to combine its activities under a parent company, which allows it to set up subsidiaries so that they can integrate various operations, such as manufacturing and the purchase of raw materials, and invest in new subsidiary projects. The limited company, which is a company that is limited by the shares it issues, enables foreign firms to establish a form of investment in China that is similar to a corporation in the United States, that is, an enterprise with legal-person status that raises capital by issuing shares of equal value. Most limited companies in China are held privately rather than publicly, although a few foreign-funded companies do publicly trade their stock, which can be listed on either the Shanghai or the Shenzhen exchange. The recent financial crisis in Asia is decreasing foreign investment in China, 70 percent of which comes from Asia. In 1997, foreign direct investment in China totaled about $14 billion, although the number of foreign-investment contracts in China fell 28 percent from 1996. See also DENG XIAOPING; HONG KONG; MACAO; MINISTRY OF FOREIGN TRADE AND ECONOMIC COOPERATION; MOST FAVORED NATION TRADE STATUS; SHANGHAI; SINGAPORE; SPECIAL ECONOMIC ZONES; TAIWAN; TIANANMEN SQUARE MASSACRE.

"FOREST OF TABLETS" See CONFUCIUS; STONE TABLETS; TAIZONG, EMPEROR (TANG); XI'AN.

"FOREST OF WRITING BRUSHES" See HANLIN ACADEMY.

FORMER HAN DYNASTY See WESTERN HAN DYNASTY.

FORMER SHU KINGDOM (908–925) See TEN KINGDOMS PERIOD.

FORMOSA See TAIWAN.

FORTUNE COOKIES Cookies containing proverbs or amusing phrases written on small pieces of paper. They are made from square pieces of dough twisted into the same enclosed circular shape as a wonton, the popular Chinese noodle dumpling. One fortune is placed inside each cookie before baking. Fortune cookies are not a traditional Chinese custom, but they are given out at the end of a meal in many Chinese restaurants in America, where diners often expect a dessert. They were invented in the 1920s by a worker in the Kay Heong Noodle Factory in San Francisco. Fortune cookies originally contained sayings of Confucius (551–479 B.C), considered to be the most important Chinese thinker.

FOSHUN See GUANGZHOU.

FOUR AUSPICIOUS ANIMALS See DRAGON; PHOENIX; QILIN; TORTOISE.

FOUR BOOKS OF CONFUCIANISM (*sishu* or *ssu-shu*) A collection of four books that forms part of the basic canon of the school of Confucius (551–479 B.C.), which became accepted as orthodox by the Chinese imperial government during the Han dynasty (206 B.C.–A.D. 220). The Four Books include the *Analects* (Sayings) of Confucius (*Lunyu*), *Book of Mencius* (*Mengzi* or *Meng Tzu*), *Doctrine of the Mean* (*Zhongyong* or *Chung Yung*) and *Great Learning* (*Daxue* or *Tahsueh*). The *Great Learning* and the *Doctrine of the Mean* were originally two chapters of the *Book of Rites* (*Liji* or *Li-chi*), one of the Five Classics of Confucianism (*wujing* or *wu-ching*), but the great Neo-Confucian scholar Zhu Xi (Chu Hsi; 1130–1200) separated them out and combined them with the *Analects* and the *Book of Mencius* to form the Four Books. The Five Classics include the *Book of Changes* (*Yijing* or *I Ching*), *Book of History* (or *Book of Documents; Shujing* or *Shu-ching*), *Book of Rites* (*Liji* or *Li-chi*), *Book of Songs* (*Shijing* or *Shih-ching*), and *Spring and Autumn Annals* (*Chun Qiu* or *Ch'un-ch'iu*). Among the Four Books, the *Analects* is a collection of wise sayings and dialogues with students attributed to Confucius. The *Book of Mencius* was written by Mencius (or Mengzi, c. 372–289 B.C.), the second-most important Confucian scholar, who emphasized the basic goodness of human nature and expounded the theory of the Mandate of Heaven (*tianming* or *t'ien-ming*), which legitimizes the rule of emperors as long as they remain virtuous. The *Doctrine of the Mean* is an essay on several important Confucian concepts, such as the ethical responsibilities of the ruler and the nature of the "superior man" or "gentleman" (*junzi* or *chun-tzu*). The *Great Learning* is a short essay that provides a complete system for the education of the individual and the organization of society.

Knowledge of the Four Books and the Five Classics was essential for members of the literati, or scholar-gentry class, since these texts formed the basis of the examinations by which applicants from literati families were chosen to staff the imperial bureaucracy that governed China. These examinations were administered until 1905, near the end of the Qing dynasty (1644–1911). After learning how to read and write, a young Chinese student first read aloud and memorized the Four Books, and then studied the Five Classics. From the Han dynasty onward, Confucian scholars constantly wrote critical commentaries on the Five Classics and the Four Books in order to provide a more comprehensive understanding of Confucian ideas. See also CONFUCIANISM; CONFUCIUS; FIVE CLASSICS OF CONFUCIANISM; IMPERIAL EXAMINATION SYSTEM; LITERATI; MANDATE OF HEAVEN; MENCIUS; SUPERIOR MAN; ZHU XI; NAMES OF INDIVIDUAL BOOKS.

FOUR CLEAN-UPS See MAO ZEDONG; SOCIALIST EDUCATION MOVEMENT.

FOUR FAMOUS BEAUTIES OF CHINA See DIAO CHAN; WANG ZHAOJUN; XI SHI; YANG GUIFEI.

FOUR GREAT NOVELS See GOLDEN LOTUS; JOURNEY TO THE WEST; OUTLAWS OF THE MARSH; ROMANCE OF THE THREE KINGDOMS.

FOUR MODERNIZATIONS, THE A government campaign in the People's Republic of China in the 1970s and 1980s stressing the need to modernize methods of research and production in the critical areas of agriculture, industry, science and technology, and national defense so that China would become a relatively advanced industrialized nation by the year 2000. The origin of the Four Modernizations was a statement that Mao Zedong (Mao Tse-tung) made in 1963, asserting that China had to improve its economy and technology, which "lagged far behind those of imperialist countries." Modernization would assure that China could avoid being pushed around any farther by the more technologically advanced "imperialist" countries. Premier Zhou Enlai (Chou

En-lai) put forth the government's proposal for the Four Modernizations at the third (1964–65) and fourth (1975) sessions of the National People's Congress. At the fifth (1978) session, after the so-called Gang of Four was brought down and Deng Xiaoping was rehabilitated, Communist Party chairman Hua Guofeng announced a 10-year plan for the Four Modernizations. They were adopted as the official party line at the Third Plenum of the 11th Central Committee (December 1978). Hence, in the aftermath of the Cultural Revolution, party leaders switched their goals for the success of the country from the politics of class struggle to economic development. Education, especially in science and technology, was promoted as the foundation of the Four Modernizations. New party policies included giving more authority to managers and economic decision-makers, emphasizing material incentives for workers, and expanding the systems for research and education. Chinese leaders also increased foreign trade and the exchanges of students and experts with industrialized nations. They reformed the commune system and purchased a large amount of industrial equipment from Japan and the West. Chinese economists warned that the country was attempting to do too much at once, and party leaders announced that they would slow the process of modernizing the following year. However, the Four Modernizations remained an important slogan in China into the 1980s and provided the impetus for improvements, especially in scientific and technical education. See also CULTURAL REVOLUTION; DENG XIAOPING; EDUCATION SYSTEM; HUA GUOFENG; NATIONAL PEOPLE'S CONGRESS; PEOPLE'S COMMUNE; PEOPLE'S REPUBLIC OF CHINA.

FOUR NOBLE PLANTS See BAMBOO; CHRYSANTHEMUM; ORCHID; PLUM.

FOUR SACRED MOUNTAINS OF BUDDHISM (Si Da Mingshan or Ssu Ta Mingshan)   Four mountains sacred to the Buddhist religion, which was introduced into China from India around the first century B.C. Each mountain represents one of the four quarters of the universe, and each is the dwelling place of a manifestation of Buddhist enlightenment. Putuoshan, an island off Zhejiang Province, is the eastern mountain; Wutaishan in Shanxi Province is the northern; Emeishan in Sichuan Province is the western; and Jiuhuashan in Anhui Province is the eastern. Many temples, pagodas and monuments, Daoist as well as Buddhist, have been placed on each mountain. (There is also a set of five mountains that are sacred to the native Chinese religion of Daoism.)

Putuoshan (P'u-T'o) is a hilly island about four miles long and three miles wide; its highest point is Buddha's Peak at 939 feet. Putuo is one of more than 100 islands of the Chusan Archipelago in the deep-blue waters of the East China Sea, and it is renowned for its beautiful views, temples and the artist-scholars who have immortalized it in their work. Also known as "Little White Flower Island" (Xiao Baihua or Hsiao Pai-hua Shan) for its beautiful flowers, the island is a wildlife sanctuary protected by Guanyin (Kuan Yin), the Buddhist goddess of mercy. There are two main temples in the north and south, as well as about 100 smaller Buddhist and Daoist shrines, hermitages and scenic spots. The "Front Temple" (Qian Si or Ch'ien Ssu) in the south was built in the 16th century and enlarged in the 17th century. Its Buddhist name is "Stepstone to Universal Salvation" (Puji Si or P'u-chi Ssu). The "Rear" or northern temple (Hou Si or Hou Ssu) is smaller but more charming, as it is built on a series of terraces up the slope of Buddha's Peak. Its official name is "Rain Law Temple" (Youfa Si or Yu-fa Ssu), referring to the way a rainstorm clears the sky and removes the dust, revealing the way to become a Buddha or enlightened being. The Ninth Dragon Hall contains an enormous sculpture of Guanyin made of lacquered wood covered with gold. Both temples were built during the Ming dynasty (1368–1644) and enlarged by Manchu Qing dynasty emperors in the 17th and 18th centuries.

Wutaishan (Wutai, "Five Peaks"), the northern mountain, is 70 miles from Datong in Shanxi Province, close to the Daoist northern mountain, Hengshan, which can be seen from Wutaishan on a clear day. Beiyue (Pei-yueh), the highest of Wutaishan's five peaks, is 9,500 feet above sea level. Wutai is situated at a famous strategic pass known as Yanmen Guan (Yen-men Kuan), where nomadic tribes frequently invaded China from the north. One of the most important battles in Chinese history took place there in A.D. 615, when nomads were driven away by Li Shimin (Li Shih-min), who three years later founded the Tang dynasty (618–907), one of the high points of Chinese culture. The five peaks of Wutaishan have a radius of 13 miles, and there is a monastery on every peak. Making a pilgrimage up and down the path to every peak takes several days. Most of the temples belong to Lamaism, the Tibetan sect of Buddhism that had been adopted by the Mongols, who conquered China from the north and founded the Yuan dynasty (1279–1368). *Busa Ding (Pusa Ting)* is the highest monastery on Central Peak; it is also the main destination of pilgrims to Wutaishan because of its Great White Stupa, a low, round structure containing Buddhist relics. Another important monastery is Xiantong Si (Hsien-t'ung Ssu, "Fine Thread Penetration"), which belongs to the Linji (Lin-chi) Sect of Chan (Zen) Buddhism. It was built 466–500 and enlarged in the 16th century.

Emei Shan (Omei), the Buddhist western mountain in Sichuan Province, is ruled by Puxian (P'u-hsien), "Universal Light"; Samanta Bhadra in Indian Sanskrit. Puxian forms a popular trio of Buddhist figures with Sakyamuni (or Siddhartha), the historical founder of Buddhism, and Manjusri (Wenshu in Chinese; "Transcendental Wisdom"). Emeishan is the highest of all the nine sacred mountains in China, at 11,000 feet. The Peak of the Thousand Buddhas (Qianfo Ding or Ch'ien-fo Ting) is situated in the center of Emeishan's top plateau. The Golden Peak (Jin Ding or Chin Ting), is located on the mountain's eastern side, and the Myriad Buddha Peak on the Western.

Jiuhuashan (or Chiu-Hua, "Nine Flower Mountain"), the southern mountain, is located in southern Anhui Province about 20 miles south of the Yangzi River. Its patron saint is Dizang Busa (Ti-tsang Pusa), a ruler of the Buddhist underworld who releases suffering souls when their families make a pilgrimage to the mountain to pray and make offerings. See also BUDDHISM; CHAN SECT OF BUDDHISM; DAOISM; FIVE SACRED MOUNTAINS OF DAOISM; JIUHUA MOUNT; LAMAISM.

FOUR SUPERNATURAL CREATURES See DRAGON; PHOENIX; TIGER; TORTOISE.

FOUR TREASURES OF THE STUDY (*wengfangsibao* or *wen-wang-wzu-pao*) Four writing implements that were

essential in the study of a member of the literati, or scholar-gentry class, which governed China for more than two millennia in the imperial bureaucracy. The four treasures include paper (*zhi* or *chih*), a writing brush (*bi* or *pi*), inkstick (*hui*) and inkstone (*duan* or *tuan*). These implements are still used for writing Chinese characters and composing monochrome ink paintings, which have always been closely related to calligraphy. Chinese characters are written vertically with a brush. The literati were trained to write in beautiful styles, and excellent calligraphy was and still is believed to show the writer's self-cultivation and spiritual tranquillity. The finest calligraphers became famous, and their works were highly valued as art and as examples for later students to copy.

Paper was invented in China and became widely used there during the Han dynasty (206 B.C.–A.D. 220). It was made from natural fibers—mainly the bark of the mulberry bush, bamboo shoots, and scraps of fabric made from silk and the hemp plant. The fibers were ground into a pulp with water in a trough, and then a screen on a wooden frame was lowered into the pulp and lifted out. The layers of pulp clinging to the screen were dried to form a sheet of paper. Books were written and paintings were composed on vertical paper scrolls that were hung, and on horizontal scrolls that were rolled up.

A writer or painter always prepares fresh ink (*mo*) by grinding a hard inkstick on an inkstone, adding a few drops of water until the desired consistency is achieved (although bottled inks are now commonly sold). Ink can range from thick and black to thin and gray, depending on how much water is mixed with the inkstick grindings. Inksticks were first produced in the late Tang dynasty (618–907). An inkstick is made from refined pine soot or lampblack mixed with animal glue and scents, such as camphor or musk, to mask the smell of the glue. The result of this process, ink, is pressed into small molds that frequently have impressed designs. Gold decoration may also be painted on the finished stick. Good inksticks may be very expensive and handed down as heirlooms. An inkstone is a slab of slate or jade that is carved with a decoration and has a shallow depression at one end where the water is added. Inkstones were first made 1,300 years ago from stone along the Duan River in Guangdong Province.

A brush is made by gluing the hairs of a fox, lamb, or other animal into a bamboo, porcelain or enamel handle so that the hair comes to a fine point, thus allowing the writer or painter to control the brush strokes. The brush is held vertically and is used by moving the wrist, the arm, or, in some cases, the entire body. Brushes are made in a wide range of sizes and thicknesses. Other implements that aid in writing include wrist rests, pots and stands for holding brushes, and small containers that hold water for mixing ink. These implements are made by carving bamboo, wood, jade or ivory into fruits, flowering plants or other decorative objects. Many people from Huizhou, a poor mountainous region of southern Anhui Province in eastern China, traveled around China as peddlers of the four writing implements. They became so successful that they formed guilds of merchants who specialized in pawnshops, moneylending and other businesses that extended far beyond Anhui and flourished through the Qing dynasty (1644–1911). See also CAL-

LIGRAPHY; CAMPHOR WOOD; INK PAINTING; LITERATI; PAPER; SCROLLS; WRITING SYSTEM.

FOURTH RED ARMY See ZHU DE.

FOUSHENG LIUJI (FOU-SHENG LIU-CHI) See SHEN FU.

FRANCE AND CHINA See ARROW WAR; FUZHOU; INTERNATIONAL SETTLEMENT IN SHANGHAI; JESUITS; OPIUM WAR; SINO-FRENCH WAR; UNEQUAL TREATIES; VIETNAM WAR; YUNNAN PROVINCE; ZENG GUOFAN.

FRANCO-CHINESE TREATY See OPIUM WAR.

FRENCH INDOCHINA RAIL LINE See KUNMING; YUNNAN PROVINCE.

FRIENDSHIP STORES Retail stores operated by the government in major Chinese cities and tourist sights to provide convenient shopping and services for foreign visitors. Friendship Stores carry luxury goods of reliable quality that until recently were rarely found in regular Chinese department stores; these include silk, hand-embroidered blouses, jewelry, jade and ivory carvings, cloisonné ware, lacquerware and paintings. Friendship Stores may also carry antiques in places where there are no separate government-run antique shops. Each store carries its own unique selection of goods. Sales clerks often speak foreign languages, and the stores have facilities for packing and shipping purchases abroad. The Chinese people are generally not permitted to shop at Friendship Stores but must use the General Department Stores, which are also open to foreigners. Prices are slightly higher at Friendship Stores. Today Chinese department stores carry a larger variety of items that appeal to foreign tourists. See also NAMES OF INDIVIDUAL CRAFTS.

FTC See MINISTRY OF FOREIGN TRADE AND ECONOMIC COOPERATION.

FU See CHARMS AND AMULETS; LION.

FU See RHYME-PROSE STYLE OF VERSE.

FU CHIEN See SINICIZATION.

FU RIVER See SICHUAN PROVINCE.

FU-HSI, EMPEROR See FUXI, EMPEROR.

FUJIAN See SINICIZATION.

FUJIAN PROVINCE A province on the southeastern coast of China that covers an area of 47,000 square miles and has a population of about 28 million. The capital city, Fuzhou, has a population of about 1.3 million. Xiamen (formerly known as Amoy) is the second-largest city, with a population exceeding 500,000. Fujian Province was originally called Min after the Min River, which flows through the province. The Min dialect is still spoken in Fujian and subdialects are spoken in Fuzhou and Xiamen. The province is very mountainous, with narrow but fertile river valleys and a jagged, rocky coastline. The heavily forested mountains had kept Fujian isolated from the rest of China until the past few centuries. Several national minority groups inhabit the province, such as the She, the Gaoshan, and the Man.

Fujian belonged to the kingdom of Yue until it was conquered by the kingdom of Chu during the Warring States Period (403–221 B.C.). The son of a king of Yue then founded the kingdom of Min Yue. The region was inhabited by the Yue, a fishing people who occupied coastal regions as far south as Vietnam. Fujian was annexed into the Chinese Empire established by Emperor Qin Shi Huangdi under the Qin dynasty (221–206 B.C.). After the Tang dynasty (618–907) was overthrown, a Min kingdom was reestablished with its capital at Fuzhou, but it lasted only from 909 until 946.

Fujian, one of the most important trading regions in China as far back as the Tang and Song dynasties, is situated across the Taiwan Strait from the island of Taiwan (formerly known as Formosa). Shipbuilding has long been a major industry in Fujian, and today luxury yachts are being produced. Ships laden with lucrative goods such as silk, porcelain and tea sailed from Fujian, especially the port city of Quanzhou, for Japan, Korea, and countries in Southeast Asia and the Near East. They brought back to China spices, timber, ivory and herbal medicines. Fujian's coasts were prey to the Japanese pirates known as *woukou* (*wako* in Japanese) from the 14th century until 1570, and smuggling was widely practiced. In the late 16th century, Portuguese and Dutch traders also became active in the region. Fujian was one of the last regions where the Ming dynasty (1368–1644) made a stand against the Manchus, who had invaded China from the north and established the Qing dynasty (1644–1911).

Today Fujian is active in the trade between Taiwan and mainland China. About half the Chinese who now live on Taiwan (the Republic of China) emigrated there from Quanzhou, and the dialect spoken in Taiwan is based on one spoken in southern Fujian. Nationalist (Kuomintang) Chinese troops withdrew to the islands of Mazu and Quemoy, outposts of Taiwan, off the Fujian coast following the Communists victory in 1949. A museum in Quanzhou houses exhibits on the city's maritime trading history. The city has the oldest mosque in China, built in the 11th century for the Arab Muslim traders who had settled there. A large portion of the large overseas Chinese community in Indonesia originated in Fujian.

Fujian Province is China's third-largest producer of sugarcane, bananas, fish and seaweed, and the fourth-largest producer of rubber. It is a significant producer of tea, pears, tropical fruits, seafood and aquatic products. Rice and other grains are grown on more than 80 percent of Fujian's total cultivated area, and salt is produced in coastal areas. Tea had been cultivated in the province since the Tang dynasty, and Fujian was China's main exporter of tea until the mid-19th century, when the British began growing tea plants in Sri Lanka (Ceylon) and Assam, a province of India. The word "tea" derives from *tay,* a word in the dialect spoken in Fujian. Dutch traders introduced tea to Europe in the early 17th century. In addition to shipbuilding, major industries in Fujian are primarily low-technology ones such as processed foods, and traditional ones such as porcelain, paper and handicrafts. Lacquerware produced in Fujian is quite famous. The province includes one of China's four largest forestry regions. See also FUZHOU; LACQUERWARE; MAZIPO;

MUSLIMS; PIRATES; SPECIAL ECONOMIC ZONES; TAIWAN; TEA; TREATY PORTS; XIAMEN.

FUKIEN PROVINCE See FUJIAN PROVINCE.

FULIN See SHUNZHI (EMPEROR).

FULING See NURHACHI; SHENYANG.

FUNERALS (*zangli* or *tsang-li*; *binzang* or *pin-tsang*) Traditional rituals and customs for burying the dead which aim to ensure the deceased person's entry into the spirit world. In the Chinese Confucian tradition, which emphasizes filial piety or respect for one's parents as the greatest virtue, the eldest son of every family is obligated to give his parents a proper funeral. If he does not do so, the family will be disgraced and the deceased will become a malevolent ghost. A proper Chinese funeral has to include a large coffin, a funeral procession, a gravesite chosen according to the principles of *feng shui*, or geomancy, gifts and sacrificial offerings to the deceased, a prescribed period of mourning, and the maintenance of the gravesite and a family shrine for the ancestors. Families sweep the graves of their ancestors and present offerings to them every spring at the Qing Ming Festival. Although the Chinese Communist government discouraged traditional Chinese funerals because of their heavy expense, they are being practiced once again. The government encourages cremation, but the Chinese still prefer ground burial.

Chinese funeral rituals are complicated and filled with symbolic actions intended to prevent the family from being contaminated by evil influences. An elderly person who is dying is moved into the main hall of the home that houses the family shrine; the shrine holds tablets for deceased ancestors, whom the person will join after death. When the person dies, the family washes the corpse and dresses it in "longevity clothes," the style of which dates back to the Han dynasty (206 B.C.–A.D. 220). The family puts on sackcloth and makes wailing sounds for the deceased at specified times. They send white cards to relatives and friends to announce the death; white, rather than black, is the Chinese color for funerals and mourning. Neighbors hang red cloth or paper over their doorways to protect themselves from evil influences and the contagion of death. The family of the deceased places a temporary paper ancestral tablet on the family altar in the main hall. Relatives and friends visit to pay their respects and leave offerings, such as paper money to be burned at the funeral; incense; scrolls on which they have written tributes to the deceased; and real money to help pay for funeral expenses. The family places the deceased in the coffin and waits for the auspicious day chosen for the funeral when the coffin is sealed, transported to the gravesite and buried.

In the procession to the grave—the major event of a Chinese funeral—the coffin is carried by four or more pallbearers or placed on the back of a truck decorated with flowers. Musicians, Buddhist or Daoist priests, and people carrying banners, scrolls, parasols and a picture of the deceased walk in front of the coffin. Family members, led by the eldest son, walk behind the coffin. Brightly colored wreaths of paper flowers on a bamboo frame are placed in front of the gravesite. The coffin is lowered into the grave to the accompaniment of sad music, the chanting of priests and the wailing of mourners. The eldest son then kneels before the grave with the paper ancestral tablet. The head of the clan or another important man takes a brush dipped in vermilion ink and places the final red dot on the written character *ju* (*chu*) to indicate that the soul of the deceased now resides in the ancestral tablet that commemorates the deceased in the family shrine. The tablet is placed on a rice measure in front of the grave, and the clan head makes an offering to it while incense is burned. Finally, the mourners walk around the grave while wailing, and then return home.

The son carries the paper ancestral tablet home and places it on the family altar. The family will later replace it with a permanent wooden ancestral tablet (*lingwei*). Incense is kept burning on the altar in a burner that holds a bit of earth from the grave. The practice of making regular offerings to deceased ancestors is known as ancestor worship. The final ritual of a Chinese funeral is the "joining of the incense burners," in which a pinch of ash from the incense burner of the recently deceased family member is put into the incense burners in front of other ancestral tablets on the family altar to symbolize the unity of the ancestors, the family and clan.

The Buddhist religion has been associated with funerals in China, and a family may arrange for a memorial service to be held in a Buddhist temple within 49 days after the person has died. Devout Buddhists may have services held for the full seven weeks. The Chinese traditionally believe that during the first 49 days after the body dies, the spirit of the deceased remains in its old home and requires offerings of food and the burning of paper money and clothes, known as joss paper, to help it travel to the next world. See also ANCESTOR WORSHIP; ANCESTRAL TABLETS; BUDDHISM; FENG SHUI; FILIAL PIETY; INCENSE; JOSS PAPER; QING MING FESTIVAL.

FUNG YU-LAN (Feng You-lan; 1895–?) The most important Chinese philosopher in the 20th century. Fung was born in Henan Province. He received his undergraduate degree from Beijing University in 1918 and his doctorate in 1923 from Columbia University in New York City, where he studied with John Dewey and Frederick J. E. Woodbridge. After returning to China that same year, Fung taught at Zhongzhou University at Kaifeng, then at Zhongshan University in Guangzhou (Canton), and in 1927 at the Beijing Yanjing University. In 1928 he was appointed dean of the Philosophy Department and dean of the College of Arts at Qinghua (Tsinghua) University in Beijing. In 1933 he lectured on Chinese philosophy at several universities in Britain.

Fung became well known after his *History of Chinese Philosophy* was published in two volumes in 1934. This work was translated into English by Dirk Bodde in 1937, and a revised English translation was published by Princeton University Press in 1952 and 1953. In 1939 Fung published his philosophical system in *New Rational Philosophy* (*Xinlixue* or *Hsin li-hsueh*), which drew upon concepts from 12th-century Chinese philosophers in the Neo-Confucian School of Thought. Fung's method of discussing Chinese philosophy in a logical, systematic manner was a new development, as Chinese philosophers had traditionally employed the methods of asserting their opinions and using metaphors to maintain their positions.

During China's War of Resistance against Japan (1937–45; World War II), Fung was dean of the College of Arts at the Southwestern Associated University in Kunming, Yunnan province. After the war ended, he resumed his positions at Qinghua University. From 1946 to 1947 he was a visiting professor at the University of Pennsylvania. Fung received an honorary Ph.D. in literature from India's New Delhi University and traveled abroad as a member of several Chinese delegations. In 1954 he was director of the Research Department of the History of Chinese Philosophy at Beijing University. In 1955 he was appointed a member of the Department of Philosophical and Social Sciences under the Chinese Academy of Sciences.

In 1957 and 1958, leaders of the Chinese Communist Party, which had founded the People's Republic of China (PRC) in 1949, attacked Fung and thousands of other Chinese intellectuals and artists. They criticized Fung for his revisionist standpoint in philosophy and forced him to reject his philosophy for being idealistic, abstract and without any historical or practical grounding. Even after he did so, from 1957 to 1963 radical Chinese Communist thinkers continued to attack Fung for his "idealistic" system of philosophy. Fung remained a professor at Beijing University. However, during the Cultural Revolution (1966–76), he was publicly denounced by radicals as a counterrevolutionary element, and he disappeared until 1972. He taught at Beijing University in 1973 and disappeared again in 1976, but by the late 1970s he was rehabilitated. In 1981 the New China (Xinhua) News Agency named Fung as "a leading scholar who has made invaluable contributions to the plan for compilation and publication of ancient books."

Fung had published numerous volumes on the history of Chinese philosophy between 1924 and 1964. His work in this field has been an important resource for thinkers in the Western world as well as in China. In 1982 Fung was awarded an honorary doctor of letters degree by Columbia University. In 1983 he was elected a member of the Standing Committee of the Sixth Chinese People's Political Consultative Conference (CPPCC). See also CHINESE ACADEMY OF SCIENCES; CHINESE PEOPLE'S POLITICAL CONSULTATIVE CONFERENCE; CULTURAL REVOLUTION; NEO-CONFUCIANISM.

FURNITURE, TRADITIONAL CHINESE (*jiaju* or *chia-chu*) In ancient times, the Chinese sat cross-legged on the floor in plainly furnished rooms; high-ranking individuals sat on platforms covered with mats. These platforms later developed into the *kang* (*k'ang*), a built-in, brick raised platform that ran across the entire side of most rooms used as common living spaces and was heated underneath and covered with rugs or felt blankets. A low table made of fine wood was placed in the center of the *kang*, and cupboards were placed alongside the *kang* to hold objects that would be commonly used, such as teacups. The *kang* remains a feature of traditional homes in northern China and is used for both sitting during the day and sleeping at night. The *kang* was even built into Chinese palaces, as in the former imperial palace in Beijing known as the Forbidden City. During the Spring and Autumn Period (772–481 B.C.), the Chinese used only a few pieces of furniture, including a *ji* (*chi*), a short table that served as an arm rest; an *an*, a general purpose table; and beds and shelves. Later the Chinese also began using wooden chests, cupboards, divans and platform beds that were usually covered with canopies, giving sleepers some privacy. Quilts for sleeping were placed on the platform bed at night and were folded and stored in the morning. Canopied wooden beds became especially elaborate in southern China.

By the Tang dynasty (618–907), when the Chinese absorbed many influences from Central Asia, they gave up the custom of sitting on floor mats and adopted the foreign custom of sitting on chairs and stools. The use of chairs marked a major turning point in the development of Chinese furniture. Different kinds of chairs were ranked according to their uses. The early Chinese name for one type of chair was *huchuang* (*hu ch'uang*), or "barbarian couch." High-ranking Chinese sat on armchairs with round or square backs, while lower ranks sat on chairs without arms; the lowest ranks used stools or barrel seats. Armchairs were covered with furs such as tiger skins for military officials, or with luxurious textiles, especially silk brocade. In the winter, upholstered cushions were placed on large wing chairs. Portable folding chairs were used by emperors when they were out of doors and by court officials while traveling. A type of lounge chair, with a movable headrest and an extension that can be pulled out for a person to extend the legs and feet, is known as a "drunken lord's chair" (*zuiwengyi* or *tsui weng i*). In the summer, the Chinese used lighter chairs, made of bamboo or rattan with openwork frames. Some chairs had cane seats, which were made by interweaving long strips of cane or raffia and threading them through wooden holes in the wooden frame of the seat. Chinese chairs often had a front stretcher that served as a footrest to keep the feet up off the floor; which typically was large polished-brick slabs not covered with rugs—these could be cold, especially in northern China.

By the Song dynasty (960–1279) the Chinese were using high tables for eating, writing and painting, and altars for family shrines and in religious temples. Long, narrow, formal side tables (*tiaoan* or *t'iao-an*) were placed against the centers of walls to display flower arrangements, porcelain objects and so forth. One type of side table with ends that curve upward is known as an "upturned head" side table (*qiaotou* or *ch'iao-t'ou*). Tables were also used to hold the *qin* (*ch'in*), an instrument similar to a zither, which was played by many Chinese people of the upper and educated classes. A type of square dining table used for banquets, made of plain varnished wood or brightly lacquered wood, is still rented out by Chinese caterers for important occasions such as weddings, birthdays and funerals. It is called the "Eight Immortals table" (*baxianzhuo* or *pa hsien cho*), after the Eight Immortals, or superhuman figures, who represent good fortune in the Daoist tradition. Instead of using desks, the Chinese write and paint on a large flat table, simply called a "painting table" (*huazhuo* or *hua cho*), that accommodates the inkstone, inkstick, water dripper, brushes and brush holders that are used for writing Chinese characters with a brush. These utensils, used for both calligraphy and painting, are known as the Four Treasures of the Study.

The Chinese traditionally arrange furniture in a specific way based on their custom that the most honored position in a room is the farthest into the room, away from the drafts and disruptions at the entrance. At Chinese banquets the guest of honor is seated farthest from the door and facing it. A formal Chinese building is constructed on a north-south axis, with the main entrance in the south wall, and a throne or seat of honor is always placed opposite the entrance and against the north wall, facing the sun. Secondary chairs are commonly placed with a small table between each pair, in formal groups of three, against the rear or side walls. The Chinese like to place pieces of furniture at right angles to each other and parallel to the walls of a room, not in the center of the room in informal groupings as is the custom with modern Western furniture.

The Chinese have used a variety of cupboards or armoires with doors to store clothes and other objects. Even today folded garments are stored in large standing wardrobes or armoires and usually placed two next to each other in pairs. Many types of smaller cupboards are used to store household objects, eating utensils, scrolls, writing utensils and so forth. Frequently wardrobe and cupboard doors are held shut with locks. The Chinese also use cupboards with open shelves and a wide range of small and large locking storage chests that also serve as tables. The chests have metal hinges in the back, handles on each side and a lock shield and hasp for a Chinese padlock on the front. The chests are commonly made of wood, although they may be made of lacquered or painted red leather decorated with red or gold cutout designs. Camphor wood is often used to make storage chests because its strong scent helps to protect the contents from insects. Valuable scrolls and other documents are stored in camphor wood chests, as can be seen at the Imperial Historical Archives in Beijing.

Chinese furniture was designed to reflect the Chinese style of house construction. For example, the round legs and supports of a chair were modeled after the columns and beams of a wooden building. Round, curved parts were always carved by hand, and elaborate designs of flowers and other motifs were often carved into the backs and other large sections. Chinese furniture is made without glue or metal nails; instead, different types of miter and mortise-and-tenon joints are used, which make the pieces quite strong and easy to take apart and reassemble. Floating tongue-and-groove panels enable the pieces of wood to contract and expand with changes in the weather to prevent cracking.

Chinese furniture-making reached its highest development during the early Ming dynasty (1368–1644), and Ming hardwood furniture, with its elegance and simplicity of form, is still prized by collectors. The pieces are made of the finest woods—mostly red sandal, mahogany and *Ormosia henryi,* which are hard and have fine grains and a glossy surface. Hardwoods were transported by ship from southern to northern China and were also imported from foreign countries, especially in Southeast Asia. Craftsmen used woodworking tools with carbonized iron parts, which were especially effective for hardwood processing. During the Ming, high government officials and wealthy merchants settled in Suzhou, Yangzhou and the capital city of Beijing and built large residences and gardens, for which there was a great demand for furniture. The Forbidden City, built in Beijing during the Ming, still contains the magnificently carved thrones and other pieces of furniture used by emperors of the Ming and Qing (1644–1911) dynasties.

The finest pieces of Chinese furniture are made of sandalwood, satinwood or rosewood, which is hard and dark and has a fine grain and fragrant scent. Less expensive furniture was made from pine, walnut, elm, fruit woods and bamboo, which is light but sturdy. Boxwood is used to make inlay designs in furniture made from other types of wood. The Chinese have also made furniture by covering wood pieces with numerous coats of lacquer, the refined sap of the lacquer tree (*Rhus verniciflua*). Chinese emperors and wealthy literati highly prized lacquered furniture. Large quantities of Chinese furniture were exported to Europe in the 17th and 18th century, especially small desks, screens and other pieces decorated with carvings and painted lacquer. They made a major contribution to the European interpretation of Chinese styles, known as chinoiserie. See also ARCHITECTURE, TRADITIONAL; BAMBOO; CAMPHOR WOOD; CHINOISERIE; CLOISONNÉ; EIGHT IMMORTALS; FOUR TREASURES OF THE STUDY; IMPERIAL HISTORICAL ARCHIVES; LACQUERWARE; SANDALWOOD.

FUXI (Fu Hsi; 2953–2838 B.C.)   The first of the three Chinese legendary emperors, known as the Three Divine Sovereigns or Three August Ones. Fuxi supposedly had the body of a serpent, and the first dragon was said to have appeared to him in 2962 B.C. He is credited with teaching the arts of civilization to the Chinese people, including hunting and fishing, cooking, the domestication of animals, music, the writing system, sericulture (the cultivation of silkworms) and the weaving of threads from silkworm cocoons into textiles. According to legend, in 2852 B.C. Fuxi created the eight trigrams (*bagua* or *pa kua*), a set of marks using long and short lines, which are used to divine the future and that also form the basis of calligraphy. The eight trigrams form the basis for the philosophy in the classical text, the *Book of Changes (Yijing* or *I Ching).* Hence, Fuxi has been highly revered by Chinese scholars. In addition, he invented the measuring instrument that legendary Emperor Yu used to measure the universe. The creator goddess Nugua (Nu-kua), who restored order to the world after the monster Gong Gong (Kung Kung) attempted to destroy it, became identified as the sister or wife of Fuxi. By the Han dynasty (206 B.C.–A.D. 220), Fuxi and Nugua were depicted as having human bodies and dragon tails that are intertwined and holding measuring instruments that represent the yang (male) and yin (female) principles that permeate everything in the universe. Fuxi also standardized the contract for marriages and invented an early type of calendar. See also BOOK OF CHANGES; CALLIGRAPHY; DRAGON; EIGHT TRIGRAMS; SILK; YU, EMPEROR.

FUZHOU   The capital city of the province of Fujian, with a population of more than one million. Its name means "wealthy town." Fuzhou is located on the north bank of the Min River (Minjiang), about 25 miles inland from the Taiwan Strait and is surrounded by mountains; the Min River valley is considered one of the most beautiful valleys in China. Another important feature of Fuzhou is its numerous hot springs, from which hot water is piped into many of the city's hotel rooms. Fuzhou is also renowned for its production of beautiful lacquerware and handicrafts, such as painted umbrellas, printed silk, animal-horn combs and stone carvings.

Fuzhou's history can be traced back to 202 B.C., when it was made the capital of the Min Yue kingdom. By the sixth century A.D. the city was heavily populated. It became capital of the Kingdom of Min from 909 to 944. Fuzhou expanded greatly as a trading port during the Northern Song dynasty (960–1126) when overland caravan trade routes between China and Central Asia, known collectively as the Silk Road, were cut off and maritime routes had to be used instead. The city has numerous temples and mosques dedicated to Mazipo, the goddess of the sea. In 1279, Fuzhou and the city of Guangzhou (Canton) became the last places where the Southern Song rulers resisted the invading Mongols who founded the Yuan dynasty (1279–1368).

By the 13th century, Fuzhou had become a prosperous trading center with a diverse population that included Muslims, Jews and Christians. The Treaty of Nanjing in 1842 forced Fuzhou to become one of the five Chinese treaty ports open to foreign trade, and many Westerners began settling near Fuzhou on the south bank of the Min River. Tea was the most important product exported through Fujian. The Mawei shipyards nine miles outside Fuzhou were built with French assistance, and the first Chinese gunboat was launched from there in 1868. In 1898 the Japanese gained a concession in Fuzhou. The city suffered during China's War of Resistance against Japan (1937–45). Since 1949 Fuzhou has been well industrialized, especially after 1956 when it was connected to the main Chinese railroad lines. The Chinese government designated Fuzhou as one of China's "autonomous economic zones" in 1979, and as one of 14 Coastal Open Cities in 1984. An Economic and Technical Development Zone has been established in the town of Mawei.

There are many interesting tourist sites in Fuzhou, many of which are temples. Yushan Hill, a hill rising 190 feet in the middle of the city, is compared to a turtle. Nearby is the 135-foot-high White Pagoda (Baita; Dingguang Ta), which houses the municipal library. It was built of brick covered by wood in 904, but it burned down in 1534. In 1548 it was restored and painted white. Yushan Library is housed in a small temple hall called Baita Si, built in 905 and renovated in the Qing dynasty (1644–1911). The Qigong Ci temple compound commemorates General Qi Jiguang (1528–87), sent by the Ming dynasty in 1562 to Fujian to combat the Japanese pirates along the coast. He won three major battles against them.

Wushi Hill (Wushan), also in the center of Fuzhou, has been a popular site for visitors as early as the Tang dynasty (618–907). There are many stone tablets on the hill with engravings by famous calligraphers. Wuta Pagoda (Wushi Ta), 115 feet high and dating from 941, is called the Black Pagoda. On Pingshan Hill in northern Fuzhou is Hualin Si, a temple built in 965, although most of its buildings date from the Qing dynasty. Drum Mountain (Gushan), at 2,195 feet, lies on the Min River, east of Fuzhou. Yongquan Si, a Buddhist temple, was built on the mountain in 908. This temple houses a number of treasures, including 7,500 volumes of Buddhist sutras (scriptures) and a white jade sculpture of a reclining Buddha. There are two ceramic pagodas—extremely rare in China—that were built in another location in 1082 and brought to this temple in 1972. Xichan Si, a temple on Yishan Mountain 2 miles west of Fuzhou, was built between 1875 and 1908, but it almost completely destroyed during the Cultural Revolution (1966–76). It is now being restored and the resident monks are being supported by contributions from overseas Chinese.

A memorial built in 1905 commemorates Lin Zexu (1785–1850), who was sent by the Qing dynasty in 1839 as chief commissioner to Guangzhou to halt the smuggling of opium into China by the British. He burned 20,000 cases of opium, causing the British to occupy the area and force more ports to be opened to their trade. Lin was removed from office and exiled to the Xinjiang region. However, several years later he was recalled and appointed governor of Yunnan and Guizhou provinces in southern China. His tomb can be seen in a northern suburb of Fuzhou.

The Fujian Museum contains archaeological exhibits on the history of the area. Next to it is a Museum of the Revolution that presents the history of the founding of the People's Republic of China. See also FUJIAN PROVINCE; LACQUERWARE; LIN ZEXU; MAZIPO; NANJING, TREATY OF OPIUM WAR; PIRATES; SPECIAL ECONOMIC ZONES; TEA; TREATY PORTS.

G

GAMES AND GAMBLING See CHESS, CHINESE; FINGER GUESSING GAMES; MAHJONG; PLAYING CARDS.

GAN RIVER See JIANGXI PROVINCE.

GANBEI See BANQUETS; MAOTAI.

GANBU See CADRE.

GANG OF FOUR A group of four Communist leaders who were accused of being responsible for the Cultural Revolution (1966–76). The Cultural Revolution was a mass mobilization of youth that threw China into turmoil, causing many deaths and enormous damage to public and private property—from temples and historical sites to personal furniture and book and art collections—the education system, science and technology, and even personal and social relations. On October 6, 1976, less than one month after the death (September 9) of Mao Zedong (Mao Tse-tung), who had been chairman of the Chinese Communist Party (CCP) and leader of the People's Republic of China (PRC), more than 30 radical Communist leaders were arrested and deposed from their official positions by the moderate leaders who had seized power in the CCP's Central Committee. Two senior Politburo (Political Bureau) members conducted the arrests: Minister of National Defense Ye Jianying (Ye Chian-ying) and Wang Dongxing (Wang Tung-hsing), commander of the elite bodyguard of the CCP. On October 13, the CCP announced that Hua Guofeng (Hua Kuo-feng) had been appointed to replace Mao as CCP chairman, chairman of the Party's Central Military Commission, and premier. On October 22, the CCP then announced that four of the 30 arrested radical leaders, labeled the "Gang of Four," had been charged with a plot to overthrow the Chinese government. The four included Jiang Qing (Chiang Ch'ing), a former actress from Shanghai who was also Mao's widow; Wang Hongwen (Wang Hung-wen), a Shanghai radical who was deputy chairman of the CCP; Zhang Chunjiao (Chang Ch'un-chiao), a vice-premier of the CCP; and Yao Wenyuan, a radical theoretician from Shanghai who had exercised power over the Chinese mass media. The initial accusations against them included attempting to forge all or part of Mao's will; issuing orders and attributing them to Mao; and hiring a gunman to make an attempt on the life of Hua Guofeng, Mao's designated successor. The respect for Mao was still so great that no criticisms were leveled against him; all blame was deflected to his widow and the three radical leaders who were her closest associates. Increasingly, accusations were made against the Gang of Four, some of them rather far-fetched. Their actions were also associated with Lin Biao (Lin Piao), a powerful leader in the early days of the Cultural Revolution who had published the *Quotations of Chairman Mao*, the "little red book" that everyone had waved in mass demonstrations, but who was later discredited.

When the Gang of Four were arrested, the CCP was divided over the Cultural Revolution and its causes. Fighting broke out around the country, especially in the central provinces where farmers still grow much of China's food. In Shanghai, two days after the arrests of the Gang of Four, 30,000 militiamen had to be called up. The CCP waged a campaign to root out supporters of the Gang of Four all over the country, and fighting continued in various places from December 1976 through June 1977. The government called out troops in January 1977 and in March executed people the CCP accused of being its enemies. For two years after their arrest, Chinese leaders continued the nationwide campaign to criticize the Gang of Four and blame them for everything that had gone wrong in China. This campaign replaced the previous Party campaign to criticize Deng Xiaoping (Teng Hsiao-p'ing). The four were eventually brought to trial for "crimes against the people" and were sent to prison; they were even airbrushed out of the photographs of Mao's funeral ceremonies. Chinese leaders who had been criticized and even killed during the Cultural Revolution were now rehabilitated, given back their official positions if they were still alive or, if deceased, having their honor restored. In August 1977 the CCP convened the 11th National Party Congress to bring the moderate position into the forefront, and Hua declared an official end to the Great Proletarian Cultural Revolution. Deng Xiaoping, who had been purged twice during the Cultural Revolution, was rehabilitated once and for all, and he began consolidating his power as the leader of the reform movement. In 1978 the National People's Congress approved a new state constitution and proclaimed the Four Modernizations to rebuild and modernize China. See also CENTRAL COMMITTEE OF THE CHINESE COMMUNIST PARTY; CHINESE COMMUNIST PARTY; CULTURAL REVOLUTION; DENG XIAOPING; FOUR MODERNIZATIONS; HUA GUOFENG; JIANG QING; LIN BIAO; MAO ZEDONG; PEOPLE'S REPUBLIC OF CHINA; QUOTATIONS FROM CHAIRMAN MAO ZEDONG; YE JIANYING; ZHOU ENLAI.

GANSU PROVINCE A narrow, sparsely populated province in northwestern China that covers an area of 150,600 square miles and has a population of about 20 million. The capital city, Lanzhou, stretches along the southern bank of the Huang River, which cuts through the province. Gansu extends 1,000 miles from southeast to northwest, so it has several climatic zones. The Gansu Corridor (Hexi Zoulang) in the west has dry desertlike conditions. The area southeast of the Yellow River (Huanghe) has a cooler climate and forms part of the loess plateau. "Loess," the loose yellow soil that blows in from the Gobi and other deserts in the Inner Mongolia Autonomous Region, builds up fertile plateaus and fills the Yellow River with silt. The largest loess plateau in the world, covering 400,000 square miles, lies in parts of Gansu, Shaanxi and Shanxi provinces and part of the Ningxia-Hui Autonomous Region. Until the past few decades when modern irrigation systems were constructed, crop failure due to drought was a frequent problem in Gansu, causing severe famines. Wheat is now the most important crop, followed by barley, millet, beans and sweet potatoes, and fruit such as pears, peaches, apricots, apples and watermelons. The Qilian Mountains mark the edge of the Qinghai Plateau to the west. Mongols and members of other national minorities raise sheep, horses, goats and cattle in the Gansu highlands. The largest minority ethnic group in Gansu, the Hui, are ethnic Han Chinese who follow the Muslim religion.

Gansu Province is very poor, and its rural population has one of the lowest net per-capita incomes in China. However, it does have rich mineral resources—especially large iron-ore deposits—which are now being mined. Lanzhou has become the main industrialized city and the hub of the railway network in western China. Other industrialized cities in Gansu include Yumen, Jiuquan and Tianshui.

Emperor Shi Huangdi, who unified China under the Qin dynasty (221–206 B.C.), first brought Gansu under Chinese rule. During the Han dynasty (206 B.C.–A.D. 220), Chinese power continued to expand west and controlled the lucra-

The southeastern region of Gansu Province is home to part of the largest loess plateau in the world.   DENNIS COX

tive trade routes to Central Asia and the Mediterranean world known collectively as the Silk Road. Camel caravans traveled through the Gansu Corridor because they could stop at the series of oases that were fed by water from the Qilian Mountains. The caravans carried silk, porcelain and tea to the west through the "Jade Gate" at the western border of Gansu; they returned east through the Gansu Corridor bringing Western goods, art, music and dance, and religions, such as Islam and Buddhism. Several places in Gansu became important centers for Buddhist art. The best known is Dunhuang, at the western end of the Gansu Corridor, where, beginning in A.D. 366, Buddhist monks spent centuries cutting caves into a sandstone wall more than 5,000 feet long and decorating them with paintings and sculptures. The Great Wall, more than 2,000 miles long, ends in northwestern Gansu. Jiayuguan Pass, built in 1372, forms the western end of the Great Wall. See also BUDDHISM; CAMEL CARAVANS; DUNHUANG CAVE PAINTINGS AND CARVINGS; GOBI DESERT; GREAT WALL; HUI; LANZHOU; LOESS; MINORITIES, NATIONAL; MONGOL; MUSLIMS; NOMADS AND ANIMAL HUSBANDRY; QIN DYNASTY; QINGHAI-TIBETAN PLATEAU; SILK ROAD; YELLOW RIVER.

GAO KEGONG (Kao K'o-kung; 1235–1310) Considered to be the greatest Chinese landscape painter during the Yuan dynasty (1279–1368). Gao Kegong was born in Turkestan (part of modern Xinjiang-Uighur Province in western China), but he came to northern China and was educated in Chinese culture. Khubilai Khan, the Mongol who established the Yuan dynasty, welcomed men like Gao Kegong in his court in Beijing because they could bridge the gap between the foreign Mongol rulers and the native Chinese of the literati (*wenren*), or scholar gentry class, who staffed the imperial bureaucracy that governed the country. Although a painter, Gao Kegong was appointed to high court positions, including president of the Board of Punishments. However, he spent many of his later years painting in the southern city of Hangzhou, China's cultural center ever since it had become the capital of the Southern Song dynasty (1127–1279). His paintings from that period portray the misty, fertile climate of the Hangzhou region, an area of many lakes, including West Lake. Gao Kegong's early paintings show an influence from the great landscape painter Mi Fu (1051–1107), stimulating a revival of interest in that painter and painters from the Five Dynasties Period (907–60). He learned from the styles of other painters as well, but he developed his own style of painting, which was emotional and impressionistic. Gao Kegong painted the details of his landscapes, such as trees and mountain peaks, in a realistic way that gives them solidity and makes them seem to come forth from a cloudy mist. See also HANGZHOU; KHUBILAI KHAN; LANDSCAPE PAINTING; MI FU; YUAN DYNASTY.

GAO XIANZHI See TALAS, BATTLE OF.

GAOCHENG See TURPAN; XINJIANG-UIGHUR AUTONOMOUS REGION.

GAODI (EMPEROR) (Kao-ti; 256–195 B.C.) The founder of the Han dynasty (206 B.C.–A.D. 220), one of the longest

and greatest dynasties in Chinese history; also known as Han Gaodi. Gaodi is his posthumous reign name. His real name was Liu Bang (Liu Pang). He was from the former small state of Han in the North China Plain, but became a prominent government official in the state of Chu in the Yangzi River (Changjiang) valley in central China when the harsh Qin dynasty (221–206 B.C.) was losing its power. Liu Bang contended for power with several other leaders, and in 206 B.C., when a number of kingdoms were being founded, he accepted the title of King of Han. He was supported by Xiang Yu (Hsiang Yu), who was from the state of Chu, but they soon became rivals and their factions fought each other during the civil war that followed Qin's downfall. In 202 B.C., Xiang Yu was defeated and killed, and Liu Bang, King of Han, officially became the first emperor of the Chinese Empire ruled by the Han dynasty. As king and then emperor, he reigned from 206 to 196 B.C.

Liu Bang was originally a peasant, the first Chinese ruler who did not come from an aristocratic family. An illiterate, he disliked the scholars who ran the government bureaucracy, but he recognized the need to have educated advisers in the court, and he himself had the ability of a statesman to do the right thing at the right time. The Qin dynasty had been run by adherents of the Legalist school of thought, which emphasized strict punishments and the concentration of absolute power in the emperor. Liu Bang relied on scholars of the Confucian School and thus began the process by which the Chinese Empire became modeled on Confucian principles of government, emphasizing the benevolence of the ruler as the means for encouraging virtue in his subjects. His advisers, led by his chancellor, the renowned statesman Xiao He (Hsiao Ho), did away with the harsh legal system of the Qin government but retained some of its basic institutions, such as the system of provinces in the center of the Chinese Empire. Large areas of the northern and eastern regions were awarded as kingdoms to members of Liu Bang's family. Taxes, paid in grain or textiles, were levied on the population, and a feudal system was instituted on the model of the Zhou dynasty (1100–256 B.C.). Xiao He moved the capital across the Wei River from Xianyang to Chang'an (modern Xi'an in Shaanxi Province in western China), which grew into a large, cosmopolitan city and served as the imperial capital for several later dynasties. See also CHANG'AN; CONFUCIANISM; FEUDAL SYSTEM; HAN DYNASTY; IMPERIAL BUREAUCRACY; LEGALIST SCHOOL OF THOUGHT; QIN DYNASTY.

GAOLING See ALCOHOLIC BEVERAGES.

GAOZONG (EMPEROR) (Kao-tsung; 628–83). The third emperor of the Tang dynasty (618–907). His real name was Li Zhi (Li Chih); Gaozong, meaning "High Ancestor," was his posthumous reign name (r. 649–83). Gaozong was the son of Taizong (T'ai-tsung; his original name was Li Shimin), the second Tang emperor, who consolidated the Tang government and expanded the Chinese Empire. When Gaozong took the throne, he was not strong enough to control the group of elder statesmen who had wielded power during Taizong's reign and still ruled the Tang court. Within a few years he became very ill, and his second wife, Empress Wu Zetian (Wu Tse-t'ien; known as Wu Zhao or Wu Chao;

627?–705), ruthlessly seized the reigns of power when he suffered a stroke in 660. She had been a concubine in Taizong's harem, and she had married Gaozong after having his first wife killed. Empress Wu removed the intended successors to Gaozong, and when he died in 683 she placed her youngest son on the throne as emperor; however, she wielded the actual power as empress dowager, even calling herself Emperor Shengshen. See also TAIZONG, EMPEROR; TANG DYNASTY; WU, EMPRESS.

GAOZONG (EMPEROR) (Kao-tsung; 1107–87)   The first emperor of the Southern Song dynasty (1127–1279). His personal name was Zhao Gou (Chao Kou); Gaozong, meaning "High Ancestor," was his posthumous reign name (r. 1127–62). He was the ninth son of Song emperor Huizong (Hui-tsung; r. 1100–25) and the younger brother of the emperor Qinzong (Ch'in-tsung; 1100–61), Qinzong took the throne after their father abdicated.

The Song dynasty (960–1279) was threatened and eventually sent south to form the Southern Song Dynasty (1127–1279) by the Jurchen. The Jurchen were a nomadic people in northern China who founded the Jin dynasty (1115–1234). In 1123, they overthrew the Khitan Liao dynasty (947–1125) in northeastern China (modern Manchuria). The Song had cooperated with the Jurchen against the Liao, but then went to war against the Jurchen in hopes of gaining territory that had been held by the Liao dynasty. The Song military was weak, however, and in 1126 the Jurchen attacked Kaifeng, the Song capital. Emperor Huizong abdicated the throne to his son, Emperor Qinzong (Ch'in-tsung). The Jurchen forced the Song to sign a humiliating treaty, and fighting, soon broke out again. In the winter of 1126–27 the Jurchen besieged Kaifeng and captured Emperor Qinzong, Huizong, and members of the Song court. Gaozong, then the prince of Kang, was away from Kaifeng on a government mission when it fell. The Song forces that had survived the Jurchen attack proclaimed him emperor on June 12, 1127.

As the new Song emperor, Gaozong fled to Zhenjiang and then further south to Hangzhou, then known as Linan. There he and the remnants of the Song court established the Southern Song dynasty. The Jurchen invaded as far south as Hangzhou, hunting down the Song emperor for four years. Gaozong had to keep moving, and, for a while, even hid on a junk (a Chinese boat) on the East China Sea.

In 1132 the Song forced the Jurchen to retreat north, and Gaozong returned to Hangzhou, which was made the Southern Song capital in 1138. The Song still hoped to return to Kaifeng where the Song imperial tombs were located, but as the Jurchen and the Song continued fighting, Gaozong realized that the Song could not regain their northern territory. In 1141 he had his chief councillor, Qin Gui (Chin K'uei; 1090–1155), negotiate a peace treaty with the Jurchen. This treaty further humiliated the Song, forcing them to pay a large amount of reparations and an annual subsidy of silk and silver to the Jurchen. This effectively made the Song a vassal state of the Jin dynasty. The Huai River, which flows eastward through Henan and Anhui provinces into northern Jiangsu Province, was made the boundary between Jin and Song territories. The peace treaty with the Jurchen forced the Song to remove from authority the highest commanders of

their army; Gaozong had to accuse the great Song general Yue Fei (Yueh Fei; 1103–41) of treason and execute him. Yue Fei's martyrdom made him a hero to the Chinese people, and in 1161 his name was restored to honor and many temples were built to revere him. That same year, near the end of Gaozong's reign, the Song, relying on their navy, beat back another invasion by the Jurchen Jin.

In 1162 Gaozong abdicated the throne to his nephew and spent the remainder of his years in contented retirement. He was a patron of the arts, as his father had been, and he established a National Academy for the artists from his father's Northern Song court who had been able to flee south to Hangzhou. He also established a National University, an Imperial Academy and a School of Medicine. The beautiful city of Hangzhou remained the cultural capital of China for many centuries, even after the Song dynasty was overthrown by the Mongols, who established the Yuan dynasty (1279–1368). See also HANGZHOU; HUAI RIVER; JIN DYNASTY; JURCHEN; KAIFENG; LIAO DYNASTY; NORTHERN SONG DYNASTY; SONG DYNASTY; SOUTHERN SONG DYNASTY; YUE FEI.

GAOZU (EMPEROR) (Kao-tsu; 566–635)   Also known as Tang Gaozu; the founder and first emperor of the Tang dynasty (618–907). His personal name was Li Yuan; Gaozu, meaning "High Progenitor," was his posthumous reign name (r. 618–26). Known as the Duke of Tang, he was related by marriage to the royal families of the Sui (581–618) and Northern Zhou (557–81) dynasties in northern China and held a high position in the Sui government. Northern China was beset by rebellions, and he was given command of the army garrison at Taiyuan that defended the Sui against Turkish nomadic tribes that threatened China from the north. In 617 the Sui emperor fled to his southern capital at Daxingzheng, which became known as Chang'an (modern Xi'an) under the Tang dynasty. Li Yuan, probably encouraged by his son Li Shimin (who became the second Tang emperor, Taizong or T'ai-tsung; r. 626–49), decided to lead a rebel force against the Sui. He took the Sui capital and placed a child prince on the throne as puppet emperor of the Sui. In 618 Li Yuan declared himself the emperor of a new dynasty, the Tang, named for the lands he owned in modern Shanxi Province. Emperor Gaozu, with the help of excellent military generals including his own sons, spent the first 10 years of his reign subduing several other rebel leaders who had also attempted to succeed the Sui dynasty. The Tang were victorious because their capital at Chang'an lay in a protected position surrounded by mountains. However, resistance to the Tang in northeastern China lasted throughout the dynasty.

Emperor Gaozu modeled the Tang government bureaucracy on that of the Sui, and he centralized administrative control in the capital to prevent the independence of the 300 prefectures into which he had divided the Chinese Empire. He continued the Sui system of examinations to select qualified Confucian-trained scholars to run the bureaucracy. He also built a temple at Chang'an dedicated to the great scholar Confucius (551–479 B.C.) and to the Duke of Zhou (Duke of Chou), who established the institutions of the Zhou (Chou) dynasty (1100–256 B.C.), regarded by Confucius as the ideal period of Chinese history. However, Gaozu favored the Daoist tradition and claimed that he was a descendant of

Laozi (Lao Tzu; sixth century B.C.), the traditional founder of Daoism. To ensure that the peasants would have enough to pay their taxes, Gaozu attempted to enact a system of land equalization that gave a specified amount of land to each adult, most of which reverted to the state when the adult turned 60 years of age. However, this system proved impossible to carry out because there was not enough land available. In addition, the peasants were required, in accordance with the corvée system, to supply a specified number of young men to work on government projects. Gaozu established hundreds of local militia units to ensure that his new dynasty would have a reliable supply of soldiers to defend it.

When Gaozu's sons engaged in a feud over who would become the next Tang emperor, Gaozu named Li Shimin, his second son, the heir to the throne. Li Shimin was an able general who had control of the Palace Guard; this gave him the advantage in the struggle for power, and he eventually had his brothers executed. In 826 Gaozu was forced to abdicate the throne to Li Shimin, who consolidated the Tang dynasty and acquired the posthumous reign name Taizong. See also CHANG'AN; CONFUCIUS; IMPERIAL BUREAUCRACY; IMPERIAL EXAMINATION SYSTEM; SUI DYNASTY; TAIZONG, EMPEROR; TANG DYNASTY ZHOU, DUKE OF; ZHOU DYNASTY.

GARDEN OF THE MASTER OF THE FISHING NETS
(Wangshi Yuan) One of the best-known gardens in Suzhou, a city noted for its beautiful gardens. The Master of the Fishing Nets is the smallest garden in Suzhou, covering 1.2 acres, and it is typical of those built by lesser civil bureaucrats. It was originally laid out in A.D. 1140 by a government official named Shi Zhengzhi (Shih Cheng-chih). The garden changed owners many times and was then abandoned until 1770, when another official named Song Zongyuan restored it. The garden, praised for its elegance and harmony, includes a two-story residence with three courtyards and a pond surrounded with rocks, pavilions and a covered walkway. Scholars liked to gather in the Library of Study for literary competitions. In 1981 the Metropolitan Museum of Art in New York City opened the Astor Court, a reproduction of the Hall for Staying Spring (Dianchunyi), one of the buildings and its courtyard that is in the western part of the Garden of the Master of Fishing Nets. See also GARDENS, SUZHOU.

GARDENS (yuan)
Spaces that are designed to reproduce features of the natural world, and a major element of Chinese architecture. Beginning in the Zhou dynasty (1100–256 B.C.), Chinese rulers built beautiful gardens around their palaces. Today the extensive gardens of the Qing dynasty (1644–1911) Summer Palace in Beijing are open to the public and are a popular resort and tourist attraction. Chinese individuals first built private gardens during the Han dynasty (206 B.C.–A.D. 220). This practice increased during the Song dynasty (960–1279) and became widespread during the late Ming dynasty (1368–1644), when the landscape architects Zhang Lian (Chang Lien) and his sons became famous. Between 1631 and 1634, Ri Cheng (Jih Ch'eng) wrote *The Craft of Gardens* (Yuanye or Yuan yeh), which may have been the first Chinese manual on landscape gardening. Numerous garden owners during the late Ming wrote guides to their gardens. Many catalogues of Chinese gardens have also been compiled, beginning with *The Famous Garden of Luoyang* (Luoyang mingyuanji or Lo-yang ming yuan chi) by the Song author Li Gefei (Li Ko-fei). Buddhist monasteries and Daoist temples were frequently built in famous scenic areas, and their gardens incorporated the beautiful features of their surroundings.

Traditional Chinese homes and temples are built around one or more courtyards where the gardens are placed. A garden is enclosed by stone or stucco walls, and the ground is paved with brick or flat paving stones laid in squares or arranged in a complex pattern. Asymmetrical and irregular in shape, a Chinese garden reflects elements in the natural world. The basic parts of a Chinese garden are the same as those of Chinese landscape painting—mountains and water (shan shui), which can be represented in a garden by rocks and evergreen trees to suggest mountains, and a pond and stream to suggest lakes and rivers. The art of designing gardens is known as "piling up stones." Mountains represent the yang, or masculine, element in nature, and water the yin, or feminine, element. Buildings placed in a Chinese garden include pavilions where people can rest and enjoy the view while being protected from the sun and rain; bridges, verandas and covered walks or corridors; and multistoried buildings that frequently house libraries. Gardens also contain flowers and plants that the Chinese consider auspicious and symbolic, such as bamboo, plum, maple, orchid, chrysanthemum, peony, camellia and rhododendron. Large gardens may also contain animals the Chinese consider ornamental, such as deer, cranes, ducks and peacocks. Small carp or goldfish and lotus flowers are frequently raised in garden ponds.

The southern Chinese city of Suzhou in Zhejiang Province became famous for its gardens, most of which were laid out during the Ming and early Qing dynasties. The Garden of the Master of the Fishing Nets is quite famous because a portion of it has been reproduced in the Metropolitan Museum of Art in New York. Many members of the literati, or scholar class, in Suzhou made their garden courtyards into three-dimensional landscape paintings with uniquely shaped trees, rocks and mountains, which were placed in positions where they could be viewed from pavilions and balconies and through latticed windows or openings in the wall such as round "moon gates." The literati enjoyed wandering through the miniature landscapes in their gardens, comparing it to wandering in spirit through a landscape painting. In the beloved Chinese novel, *Dream of the Red Chamber,* a cousin of the main character who has been made an imperial concubine is allowed to visit her family, who creates a new landscape garden to honor her. Late-17th-century accounts of Chinese gardens by Jesuit missionaries influenced the European fashion for natural, informal gardens. The Porcelain Trianon was built in Versailles in 1670 in what the French considered the Chinese style. The Chinese also created the art of container gardens, known in the West by the Japanese term bonsai. This involves pruning and training trees in containers so that they stay miniature in size yet retain their natural features. See also ALLEYS; ARCHITECTURE, TRADITIONAL; CONTAINER GARDENS; DREAM OF THE RED CHAMBER; GARDEN OF THE MASTER OF THE FISHING NETS; JESUITS; LANDSCAPE PAINTING; LITERATI; ROCKS; SUMMER PALACE; SUZHOU; YIN AND YANG; NAMES OF INDIVIDUAL FLOWERS, TREES AND ANIMALS.

GATE OF HEAVENLY PEACE   See EMBLEM, NATIONAL; TIANANMEN SQUARE.

GAUTAMA BUDDHA   See AMITABHA; BUDDHA.

GE HONG (Ko Hung; 283–343)   The greatest Chinese alchemist, who recorded the theory of immortals and of techniques for alchemy, the mystical and proto-scientific search for the so-called pill or elixir of immortality (*xiandan* or *hsien tan*), a substance that would give the person who consumes it immortal life. Chinese alchemy developed within the native Chinese religion of Daoism, which emphasizes harmony with nature. Ge Hong wrote "The Master Who Embraces Simplicity" (*Baopuzi* or *Pao-p'u Tzu*), an important philosophical work in Daoism. His predecessor was the Daoist thinker Wei Boyang (Wei Po-yang; fl. 147–67), who wrote a book in which he tried to synthesize Daoist philosophy and alchemy with the ideas of the Yin-Yang School of Daoist thought and the *Book of Changes* (*Yijing* or *I Ching*), one of the Five Classics of Confucianism. Wei Boyang's text became the foundation of several classical Daoist scriptures. Ge Hong attempted to combine the occult aspect of a small esoteric movement within the Daoist tradition with the ethical concerns of Confucianism. The Daoist theory of immortals claimed that a person could cultivate the body through such practices as physical exercise and control, proper diet, herbal medicine, massage, bathing and breathing exercises to maintain physical and mental health, restore youth, and create a "spirit-body" that would live eternally after the death of the physical body. Alchemists even taught that gold, which is produced by using fire to transform sulphides of mercury, is unchangeable and eternal, so drinking gold fluid would prolong a person's life. Ge Hong provided detailed alchemical formulas, especially for compounding the elixir of immortality from gold and cinnabar, or mercuric sulfide. He also elaborated a system according to which every good or evil action that a person performs will increase or decrease a specified number of days in that person's life span. Ge Hong's concepts became fundamental doctrines in Chinese popular traditions. Ge Hong also wrote a compilation of biographies of Daoist "immortals," entitled *Shenxianquan* (*Shen-hsien-chuan*).   See also ALCHEMY; CINNABAR; CONFUCIANISM; DAOISM; DAOIST CLASSICAL TEXTS; ELIXIR OF IMMORTALITY; YIN AND YANG.

GE WARE   See RU WARE.

GEDOU   See KOWTOW.

GELO   See DAI.

GENERAL STUDY OF LITERARY REMAINS, THE   See MA DUANLIN.

GENGHIS KHAN (Chinghis Khan or Jenghiz Khan; 1162–1227)   A powerful chief of the Mongols, a seminomadic group of tribes who lived north of the Great Wall. The Mongols conquered the Jin dynasty (1115–1234) in 1234, and in 1279 they completely conquered the Song dynasty (960–1279), establishing their rule over the Chinese Empire under the Yuan dynasty (1279–1368), with Khubilai Khan, Genghis Khan's grandson, as the first Yuan emperor. He also established his capital city in Beijing, which is still the capital of China. "Genghis Khan" is a title meaning "Emperor within the Seas"; his real name was Temuchin. His father had been a Mongol chief, and Temuchin quickly ascended to the leadership of the Mongols, assuming the title Genghis Khan in 1206. By then Genghis Khan had 95 military units under his control, each with 1,000 mounted soldiers and their supporting families, who lived on pasturelands assigned to them. At the lead of the Mongol army was the elite Imperial Guard of 10,000 of the best soldiers. Genghis Khan proclaimed that he had a divine mission from Heaven to rule all the peoples of the world. He led Mongol campaigns west into Central Asia and Russia, and east to Manchuria and Korea. All Mongol men learned to ride horses and shoot weapons as boys, so they were always prepared to fight as a well-trained mobile cavalry. In 1209 Genghis Khan led the Mongols south into Chinese territory to assault the kingdom of Xixia (990–1227). In 1211 he invaded the Jin dynasty (1115–1234), with its capital at Beijing, and in 1214 the Jin emperor gave the Mongol leader valuable gifts and fled south to Kaifeng. The Mongols took the Jin capital the following year. Genghis Khan died in August, 1227, while making his final campaign against the Xixia. His sons and grandsons ruled four khanates, respectively, in Persia, South Russia, Central Asia and China. His son Ogotai succeeded him and began the Mongol assault on the Song dynasty which Khubilai Khan completed.   See also HORSE; JIN DYNASTY; KHUBILAI KHAN; MONGOL; SONG DYNASTY; XIXIA, KINGDOM OF; YUAN DYNASTY.

GENTLEMAN   See HUMANITY; SUPERIOR MAN.

GEOGRAPHY   China is the third-largest country in the world and has a very wide range of geographical and climatic features. Covering an area of 3,719,275 square miles, its borders with other countries total more than 117,445 miles. To the east lie North Korea and Russia; to the north, Russia and the People's Republic of Mongolia (outer Mongolia); to the west, Kazakhstan, Kyrgyzstan, Tajikistan, Afghanistan, Pakistan, and India; and to the south, Nepal, Bhutan, Myanmar (Burma), Vietnam and Laos. The eastern coast borders, from north to south, the Bo Hai Gulf, Yellow Sea (Huanghai), East China Sea (Donghai), South China Sea (Nanhai), and Gulf of Tonkin; most of these are marginal seas of the Pacific Ocean to the east. Approximately 5,000 islands lie off the Chinese coast.

China covers 49 degrees of latitude and thus contains very diverse climatic zones, from subarctic in the northwest to tropical in the south. About 66 percent of the land is covered with mountains, hills and steppes. The land surface of China can be divided geographically into three general zones. In the west lies the Qinghai-Tibet Plateau, the largest highland area in the world, bounded in the south by the Himalaya Mountain Range. The plateau averages more than 13,210 feet above sea level and contains many mountain peaks above 26,000 feet high; Mount Everest (Qomolangma), on the border of Tibet Autonomous Region and Nepal, is at 29,028 feet the highest mountain in the world. The Turpan Depression in Xinjiang Autonomous Region is the lowest point in China, with Lake Aiding 505 feet below sea level. East of the Qinghai-

Tibet Plateau lies the Kunlun Mountain Range, whose peaks average about 16,500 feet, with many reaching higher than 23,000 feet. This mountain range divides into several branches as it runs from west to east. Other mountain ranges include the Qinling, Tai, Altai, Nan and Dabie. The Chinese have revered nine mountains as the Four Sacred Mountains of Buddhism and the Five Sacred Mountains of Daoism.

China's second land zone begins east of the Kunlun and includes the Tarim Basin, the semiarid steppes of Inner Mongolia, the immense plateau of yellow soil known as loess in northern China Plain and Sichuan Province, and the Yunnan-Guizhou Plateau. The third zone extends eastward to the coast and is mostly flat, with few elevations higher than 330 feet. This region, the cradle of Chinese civilization, contains most of China's population, agriculture, cities and industries. The North China Plain and the Manchurian Plain in the northeast are highly developed regions.

Many rivers flow across the country from west to east and have been the major routes for transporting people and goods during most of China's history. The longest are the 3,494-mile-long Yangzi River (Changjiang), which empties into the East China Sea near Shanghai; and the 2,903-mile-long Yellow River (Huanghe), which empties into the Yellow Sea in Shandong Province in northeastern China. Other major rivers include the Huai, Huang, Wei, West, Wusuli, Yalu, Mekong and Pearl. The largest lakes include Dongting, Poyang, West and Tai. See also CLIMATE; NAMES OF INDIVIDUAL GEOGRAPHIC FEATURES AND REGIONS.

GEOMANCY See FENG SHUI; ORACLE BONES.

GERMANY AND CHINA See MAY FOURTH MOVEMENT OF 1919; QINGDAO; SHANDONG PROVINCE; UNEQUAL TREATIES; WORLD WAR I.

GEZHOUBA DAM See THREE GORGES WATER CONSERVANCY PROJECT; YANGZI RIVER.

GIBBON See MONKEY.

GINGER See SEASONINGS FOR FOOD.

GINKGO (*yinxing* or *yinhsing*; "silver fruit" or "silver apricot")   A deciduous, dioecious tree with fan-shaped leaves that is native to China. Having existed for almost 200 million years, the ginkgo is the sole survivor of the *Ginkgo* genus of the *Ginkgoacae* family. The Chinese name for the ginkgo means "silver apricot," as its fruit looks like apricots coated with white flour. The ginkgo fruit is oval and has a thin but hard white shell; another Chinese name for it is *baiguo* ("white fruit"). The Chinese also call the ginkgo the "grandfather-and-grandson" tree because it needs 20 to 30 years to grow to maturity—the grandfather plants the tree and the grandson picks the fruit. Ginkgo trees are cultivated in Jiangsu, Anhui and Zhejiang provinces in southeastern China, but they also grow wild from northeastern China to Guangdong and Guangxi provinces in southern China. Ginkgoes were also taken abroad and now grow in parks and gardens all over the world. Many Chinese ginkgo trees are several hundred to 1,000 years old. The largest have tall, thick trunks more than six feet in diameter. Ginkgo seeds are edible when roasted, but they are poisonous if too many are eaten. They are also used to produce herbal medicines to lessen coughing and the production of mucus, especially for asthma sufferers. The skin of the ginkgo fruit contains tannin, which the Chinese extract and use to tan animal hides. They use the wood of the ginkgo, which is light yellow and has a close grain, for building, furniture, wood carving and other handicrafts.

GINSENG (*renshen* or *jen-shen*)   A root plant belonging to either of two species of *Panax*, perennial herbs of the ginseng family (*Araliaceae*), which is used by the Chinese for medicinal purposes and to flavor food and drinks. Asiatic ginseng (*Panax ginseng*) is native to temperate areas of East Asia, with much of the ginseng used in China growing wild in the forests of Manchuria in northeastern China and Korea.

Ginseng is considered one of the "Three Treasures of Manchuria" along with deer antler and sable fur. Ginseng is also cultivated, but the roots that grow wild are considered much more potent. American ginseng (*Panax quinquefolius*) roots have been exported to China since the 18th century. They were shipped through France or England until John Jacob Astor sent the first direct shipment in 1782. Ginseng became so over-harvested in China that a special decree was issued during the reign of Emperor Daoguang (Tao-kuang; 1821–50) to protect the plant from becoming extinct. Until this century, only members of the imperial court and wealthy families were able to use ginseng.

Since ancient times the Chinese have regarded ginseng as having medicinal properties that can treat a wide variety of conditions, including anemia, asthma, colds and fevers, complications from difficult childbirth, diabetes, headaches, indigestion, nervous disorders and rheumatism. Ginseng helps to tone the central nervous system and regulate high blood pressure. It has been shown to contain aluminum, barium, calcium, glucose, iron, manganese, magnesium, phosphorus, potassium, silicon, sodium, titanium and volatile oils. It is used as a general stimulant and tonic for the body's systems to help build up a person's *qi*, or vital force.

Ginseng is prepared in different ways for different conditions. Powdered ginseng is often mixed with various other foods or liquids. Ginseng "essence" is prepared by cooking the root in water until a sediment remains, which then is pressed into a ceramic crock for storage. It must not be prepared or stored in metal bowls. Ginseng wine is made by soaking the root in a very strong alcoholic beverage, such as vodka. The Chinese call ginseng the "man-shaped root" (*renshen*) because the root resembles the human body, with protrusions similar to arms and legs. Ginseng roots are graded according to place of origin, shape, markings, color, taste and texture. See also CHANGBAI MOUNTAIN RANGE; COOKING, CHINESE; MANCHURIA; MEDICINAL, HERBAL.

GLASS See ENAMELWARE; SNUFF BOTTLES.

GMD See NATIONALIST PARTY.

GO See CHESS, CHINESE.

GO-BETWEENS See WEDDINGS, TRADITIONAL.

GOBI DESERT Also known as the Great Gobi; an immense dry, stony region in northwestern China, primarily the northern part of the Inner Mongolia Autonomous Region: It also covers much of the People's Republic of Mongolia (Outer Mongolia). Mongol people inhabit the region. The term *gobi* is Mongol for any shallow, windy desert basin. The Gobi Desert is a vast basin with an average altitude of about 3,000 feet, surrounded by mountains that rise above 6,000 feet. These include the Altai, Holan Shan, Yin Shan and Greater Khingan mountain ranges. The desert is divided from the fertile plain of the Yellow River (Huanghe) to the south by the Yin Mountain Range, which has a number of peaks rising to 6,900 feet. Within the Gobi are many smaller, shallow basins termed *tala* by the Mongols. Numerous streams run down the mountain ranges, mainly in the spring, and disappear in the lower *tala* of the Gobi. One large section of the Gobi runs in a southerly direction west of the huge bend of the Yellow River and contains the Tengri (Tengkoli) Desert sand dunes.

The Gobi Desert affects the climate of Asia. When it heats up in the summer, its low atmospheric pressure sends up air masses which draw violent storms or monsoons from the tropical Pacific Ocean over East Asia. The Gobi averages less than 8 inches of precipitation per year, with less than 2 inches in the center of the desert. Temperatures average 63 degrees F in July and −4 degrees F in winter, but may climb as high as 100 degrees F in summer and drop to −40 degrees F in winter. Fierce northwesterly winds in the winter raise up sandstorms in the central and western Gobi and spread dust storms from the desert throughout northern China. For centuries following the last Ice Age, about 12,000 years ago, cyclonic winds picked up the dusty soil known as loess from the Gobi Desert and dropped it over northwestern China, creating huge, fertile cliffs.

Beginning in the Han dynasty (206 B.C.–A.D. 220), camel caravans transported silk across the Gobi Desert along two routes skirting the Taklimakan Desert, a northern route through the Turpan Depression and a southern one through Hotan (Khotan or Hetian). The Gobi Desert is the region of origin for the Mongol people, who conquered much of the Asian world under Genghis Khan (1162–1227), and for rare animals such as the Mongolian wild horse. Today the population density of the region averages 5.0 persons per square mile in the grasslands of the southeastern fringes and 0.5 persons per square mile in the desert steppes. Inhabitants are nomadic herders who raise mainly sheep, goats and camels. See also ALTAI MOUNTAIN RANGE; CAMEL CARAVANS; GENGHIS KHAN; HOTAN; INNER MONGOLIA AUTONOMOUS REGION; LOESS; MONGOL; SILK ROAD; TAKLIMAKAN DESERT; TURPAN DEPRESSION; YELLOW RIVER.

GODS See AMITABHA; BODHISATTVA; BUDDHA; DOOR GODS; EIGHT IMMORTALS; GUANDI; GUANYIN; KITCHEN GOD; MAITREYA AND MANJUSRI; MAZIPO; SCULPTURE; TEMPLES; XIWANGMU.

GOHONG See DAOIST CLASSICAL TEXTS.

GOLD AND SILVER (*huangjin* or *huang-chin* and *yin*) Two precious metals that have been used since ancient times to mint currency and to make decorative objects. The Chinese use the same character *jin* (*chin*)—meaning metal—to represent both gold and silver. In the systems of *feng shui* and yin-yang, gold or metal is the main element, or agent, of the so-called five material agents, which also include wind, fire, water and earth, that make up everything in the universe. Ancient Chinese alchemists claimed to possess the elixir of immortality with which they could transform ordinary substances into gold and acquire immortal life. Goldfish (*jinyu* or *chin-yu*) symbolize wealth and good fortune for the Chinese because their name sounds like "gold in abundance." The design of a goldfish with a graceful tail is frequently used to decorate ceramics and embroidery. For centuries, Chinese women bound their feet to make them small and delicate, and they were called "golden lilies." This term came from Emperor Donghun Hou (Tung-hun Hou) in the late fifth century, who had water lilies made of gold leaf scattered on the ground for his concubine Pan Fei (P'an Fei) to dance on, which led him to say, "Every step (of hers) makes a lotus grow."

During the Shang (1750–1040 B.C.) and Zhou (1100–256 B.C.) dynasties, the Chinese developed techniques for smelting and working gold, and this precious metal came to represent wealth, power and rank. Emperors wore gold crowns and wealthy women gold ornaments, such as ear pendants and bracelets. Shang gold objects have been discovered in the excavations at Anyang, but goldsmithing became fully developed during the Zhou dynasty; bronze pieces inlaid with gold and silver designs, such as those discovered from the ancient imperial capital at Luoyang, are magnificent. Wealthy Chinese even had the bronze fittings of their chariots decorated with gold, silver and malachite inlay. Gold and silver inlay on bronzeware was popular during the Han dynasty (206 B.C.–A.D. 220), with a common design being silver cloud scrolls on a gilt ground. Typical bronze pieces include vases, containers and incense burners with lids shaped like mountain peaks that represent paradise in Daoism. Bronze pieces were also decorated by the technique of gilding, in which gold or silver was mixed with mercury to form an amalgam or paste that was painted onto the bronze. Heating the piece evaporated the mercury and left the gold or silver on the surface.

Before the development of foreign trade in China, gold and silver had the same value. China was one of the first countries to use gold and silver coins as currency. Cubes of gold weighing 1 catty (a unit of measurement) were used as currency from the 11th to the third centuries B.C. During the Spring and Autumn Period (772–481 B.C.) and the Warring States Period (403–221 B.C.), all the vassal states of the Zhou emperor used knife-shaped, spade-shaped or round bronze coins, except the State of Chu, a wealthy gold producer, which circulated a *yuan* gold coin as well as a bronze shell replica and a bronze coin. A *yuan* coin is shaped like a large flat slab or a disk and is inscribed. The term *yuan* originally meant a measure of the weight of gold, but it came to mean gold money in general. Ancient *yuan* coins were first discovered in Funan County in Anhui Province in 1970, and were later discovered in several other Chinese provinces.

The First Emperor of the Qin dynasty (221–206 B.C.) issued the *yi* gold coin, which weighed 20 *liang* (one *liang* equals $1\frac{1}{3}$ ounce), as the preferred currency of the dynasty. During the reign of Western Han Emperor Wudi (Wu-ti; r.

141–87 B.C.), gold coins were cast in the shape of a horse's hoof and a unicorn's toe. Tang and Song dynasty gold coins were shaped into square or rectangular slabs or disks. During the Qing dynasty, currency was minted in boat-shaped ingots. In ancient China, gold money was not circulated among the common people but used for tax payments and for large financial transactions. Emperors and aristocrats also gave gold coins as presents and rewards.

The cosmopolitan Tang dynasty (618–907), which attained a high point of Chinese culture, is known as China's Golden Age. Many foreign traders settled in the Tang capital of Chang'an (modern Xi'an), and Chinese craftsmen made gold, silver and bronze mirrors, jewelry and containers influenced by metalworking techniques and design motifs introduced from Central Asia and the Middle East. Motifs include flowers and floral scrolls, birds, human figures and hunting scenes. Typical gold pieces include hair ornaments, jewelry and small boxes, especially ones used to hold Buddhist religious objects. Gold and silver wire and foil were often used to make inlay designs on lacquerware. Gold and silver foil were made by beating the metals into very thin sheets. Filigree jewelry was made by twisting and braiding thin gold and silver wire. In the 14th century a technique developed known as *qiangjin* (*ch'iang-chin*), in which the artisan etched designs in lacquer with a needle and filled the spaces with gold. The Chinese also used gold and silver threads in weaving silk brocade textiles. Strips of gold or silver foil backed with paper were commonly used, but for large patterns gold foil that was wound around silk thread was used, which was sturdier.

Large-scale, modern gold mining has been conducted in China since the founding of the People's Republic of China (PRC) in 1949. In 1957 exploration missions discovered gold deposits in all the provinces and autonomous regions, except Shanghai. Large gold mines were opened beginning in 1975, and thousands of "panning centers," where gold was collected in basins in rivers and streams, were built around the country. Today more than 50 percent of China's gold production comes from about 200 mines. Zhaoyuan Gold Mine in Shandong Province is one of the largest in China, and Zhaoyuan County is known as the "city of gold and land of abundance." Recently the largest gold-producing area has been around Mohe in Heilongjiang Province in Manchuria (northeastern China). By 1986 China's gold reserve ranked fourth in the world, after South Africa, the U.S.S.R. and the U.S., and China ranked sixth in the world in gold production. China's gold market was long closed but was partially reopened in 1982. Recently the government of the PRC has issued commemorative sets of engraved gold coins, such as the panda gold coin (face value = 1,000 yuan) issued in 1984. The Chinese, especially in Hong Kong and in Singapore and other Southeast Asian cities, invest their money in gold jewelry such as bracelets and rings. Lately the Chinese on the mainland have also resumed this traditional practice.

Silver has been relatively rare in China, although there are some deposits in southwestern China, and the Chinese have imported the metal from India. Silver is a symbol of brightness and purity to the Chinese. Some Chinese children wear silver lockets to protect them from evil influences. The Chinese poetically call the Milky Way the "silver river," the Moon the "silver sickle" or "silver candle" and the human eye the "silver sea." Silver mining is conducted on a small scale, mainly in Henan, Shandong, Hebei, Sichuan and Yunnan provinces. Silver was used in small amounts in ancient China, in the manufacture of bowls and cups during the Han dynasty, but the Tang dynasty represented the height of Chinese silver-working, which was influenced by Persian, specifically Sassanian, techniques and motifs. Common types of silver objects during the Tang include bowls, boxes and stemmed cups of beaten or cast silver. They are decorated with designs of floral or vine scrolls, animals, birds and hunting scenes.

Silver was not used as legal currency in China until 1197, when Jin Emperor Zhangzong (Chang-tsung) issued five kinds of silver coins that weighed from 1 to 10 *liang*. The Yuan dynasty issued paper money as the only legal tender—since copper production was not sufficient to mint enough coins—but allowed silver in ingots to be used for large transactions. During the reign of Ming emperor Zhentong (r. 1436–50), silver was officially made a common medium of exchange and was allowed to circulate alongside bronze currency, and taxes were paid in silver. Silver currency was commonly produced in shoe-shaped silver ingots or sycee.

After the Portuguese and Spanish began trading with China in the 16th century, the Spanish silver peso or "Mexican dollar" became a coin of currency in China into the 20th century. The Spanish brought huge quantities of New World silver from Acapulco through Manila into Nagasaki, Japan and Fujian Province on the southeastern Chinese coast. During the Qing dynasty (1644–1911), especially in the 1820s and 1830s, when the British smuggled in large amounts of opium, silver began leaving China in large quantities to pay for the opium. When Qing tried to control the opium trade and stop the outflow of silver, the British fought two wars against China known as the Opium Wars. Silver coins were first minted by machine during the reign of Qing Emperor Guangxu (Kuang-hsu; r. 1875–1908), for the Guangxu silver dollar minted in Guangdong Province in 1889. During the reign of Emperor Xuantong (Hsuan-t'ung; r. 1909–12), China's last emperor, the Qing government took back the right to mint coins from the provinces and began to mint the "Silver Dollar of the Great Qing" (*daqing yingbi* or *ta-ch'ing ying-pi*) in 1909. The new dollar went into circulation two years later, the same year that the revolution led by Dr. Sun Yat-sen overthrew the Qing dynasty and established the Republic of China in 1912. See also BRONZEWARE; CURRENCY, HISTORICAL; CURRENCY, MODERN; DAOISM; ELIXIR OF IMMORTALITY; FISH AND SHELLFISH; FOOTBINDING; LACQUERWARE; OPIUM WAR; TANG DYNASTY.

"GOLD BRIDGE," "GOLD CUSTOMS" AND "GOLD CARD" PROGRAMS   See THREE GOLD PROGRAMS.

"GOLD MOUNTAIN" (SAN FRANCISCO)   See OVERSEAS CHINESE.

"GOLDEN LILIES"   See FOOTBINDING; GOLD AND SILVER.

GOLDEN LOTUS, THE (*Jin Ping Mei*)   A famous experimental novel written by an unknown Chinese author in the late 16th century. The novel recounts the adventures of

Ximen Qing (Hsi-men Ch'ing), a merchant in Shandong Province during the Song dynasty (960–1279) who became wealthy by manipulating government officials. The novel vividly presents the details of daily life and the rivalries and intrigues among the members of a large provincial household. It describes in detail Ximen's sexual experiences with his six wives as well as with prostitutes and other women. Golden Lotus is the name of Ximen's fifth wife, who had murdered her first husband and then tried to seduce Ximen's brother before marrying him. Ximen himself finally dies because of his excessive sexual activity, and his household falls apart. The novel's moralistic ending regards the conquest of northern China by "barbarians" during the Song dynasty as retribution for the corruption of Chinese society. See also CONCUBINAGE; FAMILY STRUCTURE; SONG DYNASTY.

GOLDEN MEAN See DOCTRINE OF THE MEAN, THE; HUMANITY; LOYALTY; SUPERIOR MAN.

GOLDEN ROOSTER AWARDS See CHEN KAIGE; FILM STUDIOS; GONG LI; ZHANG YIMOU.

GOLDFISH See CARP.

GONG BAN See GONG XIAN.

GONG, PRINCE (Kung, Prince; 1833–98) Also known as Yixin (I-hsin); a Manchu prince who played an important role in the foreign affairs of the government of the Manchu Qing dynasty during the period when foreign powers forced many concessions from the Qing. The Manchus were an ethnic group from Manchuria (northeastern China) who overthrew the Han Chinese Ming dynasty (1368–1644) and established the Qing dynasty (1644–1911). Their rule was strongly resented by the Han Chinese who have always formed the vast majority of the Chinese population. Prince Gong was the son of Qing Emperor Daoguang (Tao Kuang; r. 1821–50) and the half-brother of Emperor Xianfeng (Hsien Feng; r. 1851–61), with whom he had a close relationship. Prince Gong's father-in-law, Guiliang (Kuei-liang), signed the Treaty of Tianjin (Tientsin) between China and Britain in 1858 which concluded the Arrow War (also known as the Second Opium War; 1856–60), one of several so-called unequal treaties that Western powers forced China to sign. The treaty stated, among other things, that foreign ambassadors would be allowed to reside with their family and staff in the Chinese capital of Beijing. The Qing government, not wanting to honor the demands of this treaty, refused the entrance of foreign ambassadors to Beijing and sent forces that defeated British troops. In 1860 the imperial court fled Beijing when Britain and France retaliated by sending troops into Tianjin and Beijing and burning down the Summer Palace. In September 1860 Emperor Xianfeng appointed Prince Gong, the highest-ranking Qing official still in Beijing, to make peace with the foreign allies, which he did in October after negotiating with Lord Elgin, the British representative. The Qing government had to sign the Convention of Beijing (1860), which gave the British many more benefits in China. Prince Gong also signed treaties with France and with Russia, to whom was ceded the land between the Wusuli (Ussuri) River and the Sea of Japan, thus permitting Russians to trade in the treaty ports that had been opened to foreigners along the Chinese coast.

Prince Gong realized that the Qing would have to establish a government office to handle foreign affairs. For 2,000 years the Chinese imperial government had considered itself the center of power, the "Middle Kingdom" (Zhongguo or Chung-kuo), and had maintained diplomatic and trade relations with other countries by requiring them to become tributaries of China, as part of the so-called tribute system. This system fell apart in the 19th century when Western nations forced China to treat them as equal powers. In 1861 the Qing opened the Zongli Yamen (Tsungli Yamen), an abbreviation of Zongli geguo shiwu yamen (Tsungli ko-kuo shi-wu yamen), the Office for the General Administration of the Affairs of the Different Nations. The *yamen*, as it is commonly called, was placed under the Grand Council in the imperial bureaucracy. The emperor appointed a Controlling Board of five high-ranking officials to govern the *yamen*, and Prince Gong served as its head until 1884. In 1862 he established the Tongwenguan (T'ung-wen-kuan), a school of foreign languages connected to the *yamen*, directed by Robert Hart, the British Inspector-General of the Chinese Maritime Customs Service. Hart and Prince Gong had a strong working relationship. In 1866 the school was upgraded to a college and added departments of chemistry, physics, mathematics, astronomy and international law; in 1898 it was reorganized as Imperial University.

Prince Gong also acted as a co-regent for Emperor Tongzhi (T'ung-chih, r. 1862–75) while he was a minor. When Emperor Xianfeng died in 1861, Prince Gong, Empress Dowager Cixi (Tz'u Hsi; 1835–1908), the new emperor's mother, and Empress Cian (Tz'u An), the deceased emperor's widow, staged a coup d'état that removed the eight official regents and made themselves the new emperor's co-regents. Prince Gong held the title of Prince Counselor but Cixi exercised the real power in the Qing government. The policy of the regents initiated a so-called Restoration (*zhongxing* or *chung-hsing*, the traditional Chinese term for the revival of a dynasty) of the Qing dynasty. Although the Han Chinese opposed opening China to foreigners, the Manchu appeasement of foreign powers, led by Prince Gong and the Empress Dowager, prolonged the life of the Qing for another half-century. By 1865, the Empress Dowager had sufficiently empowered herself to remove the rank of Prince Counselor from Prince Gong, although she allowed him to keep his other offices. When Emperor Tongzhi died in 1875, Cixi placed another boy on the throne, Emperor Guangxu (Kuang-hsu; r. 1875–1908), so that she could continue to be the regent. Empress Dowager Cixi blamed Prince Gong for the Sino-French War (1884–85), which had erupted over control of Vietnam, and removed him from power in 1884. He was called back after China and Japan began fighting the Sino-Japanese War of 1894–95, but it was too late to have an effect in the government. When Prince Gong died in 1898, Emperor Guangxu, advised by reformers led by Kang Youwei (K'ang Yu-wei), attempted to enact a wide range of reforms in the Chinese government, known as the Reform Movement of 1898 (also known as the Hundred Days Reform). Empress Dowager Cixi staged another coup d'état that ended the reforms and placed the emperor under house arrest. See also BEIJING, CONVENTION OF; CHINESE MARITIME CUSTOMS SER-

VICE; CIXI, EMPRESS DOWAGER; QING DYNASTY; REFORM MOVEMENT OF 1898; SINO-FRENCH WAR; SINO-JAPANESE WAR OF 1894–95; SUMMER PALACE; TIANJIN, TREATY OF; TONGZHI, EMPEROR; TREATY PORTS; UNEQUAL TREATIES; ZONGLI YAMEN.

GONG LI (Kung Li; 1965–)   The most prominent contemporary Chinese film actress. Frequently ill as a child, Gong was also lonely because she was much younger than her four brothers and sisters, but in school she showed a talent for singing and dancing. On her third attempt, she was admitted to the Performing Department of the Central Drama College. While in her second year there, Gong was discovered by Zhang Yimou (Chang Yi-mo), a cinematographer who gave her the starring role in *Red Sorghum* (1987), the first film he directed. She has starred in all of Zhang's subsequent films and has also been his partner in private life, even though his wife refused to give him a divorce. *Red Sorghum,* adapted from the novel of the same name by Mou Yan, is about a woman in an arranged marriage and her lover in a sorghum-growing region of Shandong Province. It won the Gold Bear for best film at the 38th Berlin International Film Festival and was the first mainland Chinese film ever shown in the New York Film Festival. In 1988 she acted in two films by other directors, *Empress Dowager Cixi* and *The Terracotta Warrior,* directed by Ching Siu-tung, which made her a screen idol in Hong Kong and attracted film producers from Hong Kong, Taiwan and Japan.

Gong then starred in four films by Zhang Yimou. *Judou* (1990) tells the story of a woman (Gong) who is sold into an unhappy marriage that ends in tragedy. The film was shown at the 1990 Cannes Film Festival, where it won the Luis Buñuel Award and was highly praised by French critics; the film was also nominated in the U.S. for an Academy Award as best foreign film. *Raise the Red Lantern* (1991), based on the short story "Wives and Concubines" by Su Tong (Su T'ung), is about a young woman who is persuaded to become one of the concubines of a wealthy man. It won a Silver Lion at the 48th Venice Film Festival and was nominated for best foreign film at the U.S. Academy Awards; Gong was also nominated for best actress at the David Film Festival in Italy. Zhang adapted *The Story of Qiuju* (1993) from the novel by Chen Yuanbing (Ch'en Yuan-ping). The film is set in a remote mountain village in northwestern China, where a man is injured by the village headman and his strong-willed pregnant wife, played by Gong, goes through many levels of government bureaucracy to sue him. In 1991, the film won the Golden Lion Award for best film, and Gong won the Volbi Cup for best actress at the 49th Venice International Film Festival, the first time a Chinese actress has ever won this award. Her most recent film with Zhang is *Shanghai Triad* (1995), about gangsters in 1930s Shanghai, which has won several international awards. Gong played the heroine in *The King's Parking with His Favorite,* directed by Chen Kaige, another major young Chinese director associated with Xi'an Film Studio. She also played the female lead in Chen's renowned film *Farewell My Concubine* (1993), which won the best film award at the Cannes Film Festival. Based on a popular novel by the Hong Kong author Lilian Lee, it is a modern epic about the difficult friendship between two male stars of the Beijing Opera as they suffer

through wars and the Cultural Revolution (1966–76). Gong also played the leading role in *Soul of a Painter,* directed by the woman director Huang Shuqin (Huan Shu-ch'in), about Pan Yuliang (P'an Yu-liang), a Chinese woman painter who settled in France. This role was extremely difficult because Gong had to play the painter from age 17 to 70. In 1995 Gong Li and Zhang Yimou ended their personal relationship, and in 1996 she married a Singapore business executive. Her most recent movie is *The Chinese Box* (1998). See also CHEN KAIGE; CONCUBINAGE; FAMILY STRUCTURE; FILM STUDIOS; OPERA, BEIJING; ZHANG YIMOU.

GONG XIAN (Kung Hsien; 1620–89)   Also known as Gong Ban (Kung Pan-ch'ien); a painter and calligrapher during the Qing dynasty (1644–1911), founded by the Manchus, a tribal group from Manchuria (modern northeastern China) who overthrew the Ming dynasty (1368–1644). Gong was born in Jiangsu Province and moved to Nanjing, where he resided for most of his life. He was primarily an ink painter and was perhaps the most skilled of all Chinese painters in creating ink landscapes with complex compositions in a wide range of shades of ink from silvery gray to deep black. He frequently painted the same themes, with rugged peaks, cascading waterfalls and broken clouds, but rarely a human figure. When the Manchus overthrew the Ming dynasty Gong continued to support the Ming, and his personal sense of despair, coupled with harassment by political enemies, caused him to retire to the mountains where he could paint and write poetry. His despair is reflected in the dark and gloomy paintings he produced during that period.

In 1655 Gong returned to Nanjing and joined a small group of Ming supporters. He was a contemporary of the painters Bada Shanren (Pata Shan-ren) and Shitao (Shih-t'ao; also known as Daoji or Tao-chi). Gong became well known as a poet, publisher and teacher as well as an artist. His student, Wang Kai, was the main compiler of a definitive book on Chinese painting called the *Mustard Seed Garden Manual of Painting.* During the 1660s Gong built a home known as the Half-Acre Garden and lived there in semiretirement. His ink landscape paintings from this later period of his life are calm and peaceful. He died in poverty in 1689. See also BADA SHANREN; CALLIGRAPHY; INK PAINTING; MUSTARD SEED GARDEN MANUAL OF PAINTING; NANJING; QING DYNASTY; SHI TAO.

GONGFU   See KUNG FU.

GONGHANG   See CANTON SYSTEM.

GONGS AND CHIMES   See BELLS AND CHIMES; BRONZEWARE.

GOOD EARTH, THE   See BUCK, PEARL SYDENSTRICKER.

GORDON, CHARLES GEORGE (1833–85)   A British soldier who fought with the British forces that defeated China in the Arrow War (Second Opium War, 1856–60), and who led a Chinese army against the Taiping Rebellion (1850–64) and defended Shanghai, which had become a major European trading center, against the Taipings. For these exploits he gained the nickname "Chinese" Gordon. He had been commissioned a second lieutenant in the Royal

Engineers in 1852, fought bravely during the Crimean War (1853–56) and was promoted to captain in 1859. The next year Gordon went to China to fight in the Arrow War. When British troops occupied the capital city of Beijing in October 1860, Gordon ordered them to burn down the emperor's Summer Palace. In May 1862, the Taipings were threatening Shanghai, a treaty port opened to Western traders in 1842. Gordon led the corps of engineers who were ordered to build up the city's defenses. In 1863, after the American commander Frederick Townsend Ward was killed in battle, Gordon took command of the "Ever-Victorious Army," a mercenary army of 3,500 Chinese raised by Shanghai's merchants to defend the city. This army was supported by steam-driven gunboats that could navigate shallow waters. For the next year and a half, Gordon's army helped the Qing dynasty (1644–1911) army led by Li Hongzhang (1823–1901) to suppress the Taiping Rebellion by capturing many strategic cities along China's eastern coast.

After Gordon returned to England in January 1865, he spent five years commanding the Royal Engineers at Gravesend, Kent. In 1873 he was appointed governor of the province of Equatoria in the Sudan. He spent more than two years mapping the Upper Nile River and establishing stations along the river south to modern Uganda. He also put down many rebellions and suppressed the slave trade. He had to return to England in 1880 because of illness, but he then spent two years serving in India, China, Mauritius and Cape Colony, South Africa. In 1884 the British government sent Gordon back to the Sudan to evacuate Egyptian forces from Khartoum, which was about to be attacked by Sudanese rebels. He arrived in Khartoum in February 1884, and a month later, before he evacuated the British troops, the rebels put the city under siege. On January 16, 1885, they overran the city and killed all the defenders, including Gordon. This tragedy caused a great outcry among the British people, who revered Gordon as a martyr. See also ARROW WAR; LI HONGZHANG; SHANGHAI; SUMMER PALACE; TAIPING REBELLION; WARD, FREDERICK TOWNSEND.

GOVERNMENT STRUCTURE   The legislative and representative bodies of the government of the People's Republic of China (PRC), founded by the Chinese Communist Party (CCP) in 1949. Although in theory, all state power in China belongs to the people, in fact the government of the PRC is subordinate to the CCP and serves to implement its policies. Eight other small political parties, known as democratic parties, also function in China but do not form opposition parties to the dominant CCP. Starting in 1949, the Chinese People's Political Consultative Conference (CPPCC) served as the legislative and representative body of the PRC government until 1954, when the PRC enacted a state constitution and elected a National People's Congress (NPC). The NPC is a legislative body comparable to the U.S. Congress or the British Parliament and is in theory the PRC's leading government body. The 3,000 deputies (members) of the NPC are elected from local councils and assemblies at the provincial and county levels and serve five-year terms. The NPC meets every year for two weeks, and its Standing Committee handles NPC operations when it is not in session. The NPC elects the president and the vice president of the PRC. The president is the head of state and is responsible to the NPC. Mao Zedong (Mao Tse-tung) was president from 1954 until 1959, when he was replaced by Liu Shaoqi (Liu Shao-ch'ih), although Mao remained chairman of the CCP until he died in 1976. Li Xiannian (Li Hsien-nien) was elected president in 1983 and Yang Shangkun (Yang Shang-k'un) in 1988. Jiang Zemin (Chiang Tse-min) is the current president and general secretary of the CCP; he was reconfirmed in these positions at the National Party Congress in September 1997.

There are four branches of power under the NPC: the State Council (executive branch); the Central Military Commission (military branch); the Supreme People's Court (judicial branch); and the Supreme People's Procuratorates, or inspectors general (procuratorates branch). The State Council is the highest organ of government administration, corresponding to the U.S. president's cabinet. The State Council has a number of functions, including the drafting of legislative bills for submission to the NPC or the NPC Standing Committee. It administers all of the PRC government ministries and many other agencies, commissions, administrations, bureaus, academies and corporations. The State Council is formally responsible to the NPC, but in practice, since senior members of the State Council are also powerful leaders of the CCP, the State Council is mainly responsible to the Secretariat of the CCP, under the Politburo (Political Bureau) and its Standing Committee. The NPC decides on the choice of the premier of the State Council nominated by the chairman (or president) of the PRC, and it has the power to remove members of the State Council from their positions. The premier, comparable to the prime minister in Britain, actually wields more power than the president of the PRC. Zhou Enlai (Chou En-lai) was premier from 1954 until he died in 1976. The conservative Li Peng was appointed to his second five-year term as premier of the State Council, which will end in 1998.

The First Session of the Seventh NPC, held in 1988, was televised live; its meetings and panel discussions were recorded and broadcast the same day; and Chinese and foreign journalists were allowed to attend the panel discussions and question the NPC deputies in press conferences. The Seventh NPC ratified laws and constitutional amendments to legitimize private business and land sales and to encourage foreign investment in China. It restructured the State Council and dissolved 14 ministries and commissions and established 10 new ones: the State Planning Commission and the ministries of personnel, labor, materials, transportation, energy, construction, aeronautics and astronautics industry, water resources, and machine building and electronics industries. Many of the ministries that were dissolved were turned into business enterprises that have the responsibility for their own profits and losses.

Local administrative divisions comprise a three-level system of provinces, counties and townships. At the highest of the three levels, China is divided into 22 provinces, 5 autonomous regions and 3 large municipalities. The structure of the provincial governments are modeled on the structure of the central government. The CCP has a structure similar to that of the PRC government, and its highest body is the National Party Congress (not to be confused with the NPC). See also CENTRAL MILITARY COMMISSION; CHINESE COMMUNIST PARTY; CHINESE PEOPLE'S POLITICAL CONSULTA-

TIVE CONFERENCE; CONSTITUTION, STATE, OF 1954; DEMOC-
RATIC PARTIES; JIANG ZEMIN; LI PENG; MINISTRY OF FINANCE;
MINISTRY OF FOREIGN AFFAIRS; MINISTRY OF FOREIGN TRADE
AND ECONOMIC COOPERATION; NATIONAL PARTY CONGRESS;
NATIONAL PEOPLE'S CONGRESS; PEOPLE'S REPUBLIC OF CHINA;
POLITBURO; PROVINCES, AUTONOMOUS REGIONS AND MUNIC-
IPALITIES; STATE COUNCIL; STATE PLANNING COMMISSION;
SUPREME PEOPLE'S COURT; ZHOU ENLAI.

GRAIN (*fan*)   The most important food type in the Chinese diet, and the most important source of the calories and
protein in the diet. The Chinese word for cooked rice, *fan*, is
also the word for "meal," which is centered around dishes of
cooked grain, such as rice, noodles, dumplings or steamed
bread (*mantou* or *man-t'ou*). The *fan* is accompanied by *cai*
(*ts'ai*), which literally means "vegetables" but also includes
meat, fish, seafood, bean curd or any other cooked food that
is cut into small pieces so that it can be easily eaten with
chopsticks. Each person is served his or her own bowl of
fan, and the *cai* dishes are served in the center of table in
large bowls or dishes for everyone to share. The Chinese eat
this type of meal for lunch and dinner. A typical Chinese
breakfast comprises rice porridge, with small side dishes of
dried fish, pickled vegetables or boiled eggs. Street vendors
also sell sticks or circles of fried dough, sesame biscuits,
steamed buns and dumplings. In southern China, dim sum
restaurants that serve dumplings and other snacks are very
popular.

The Chinese distinguish between grains cooked to a
fluffy consistency (*ganfan* or *kan fan*) and grains cooked
into a porridge or gruel (*xifan* or *hsi fan*), which they consume for breakfast and late-night snacks. *Fan* cooked with
rice is *baimifan* (*pai mi fan*, "white rice *fan*"), to be distinguished from "sorghum" *fan* (*gaoliangmifan* or *kaoliang mi
fan*) or "millet" *fan* (*xiaomifan* or *hsiao mi fan*), which are
also commonly consumed grains. In Chinese dining halls,
fan is also called *zhushi* (*chu shih*), the main or primary
food, and *cai* is called *fushi* (*fu shih*), the supplementary or
secondary food. The word *shi* (*shih*) is also used for food or
a meal in general.

The Chinese have consumed a grain-based diet for thousands of years, which was made possible by living in settled
villages where they could raise grain and other crops. These
were some of the main traits by which they defined themselves as Chinese (that is, members of the Han ethnic
group), as distinct from people they considered "barbarians"
because they did not grow grains. For example, nomadic
tribes to the north and northwest herded sheep, goats and
horses and ate large pieces of grilled meat and fermented
milk products such as yogurt and cheese.

Millet was the major crop of the Chinese Neolithic Yangshao culture (c. 5000–3000 B.C.), which was centered in
northern China. The Yangshao people even used millet to
brew alcoholic beverages. Millet has ever since been the
principal grain consumed in the north, although wheat and
sorghum are also widely consumed and winter wheat has
become the main crop. Potatoes, soybeans, barley, oats,
buckwheat, field peas and beans are also counted as grains
by the Chinese government. The North China Plain, which
extends along several provinces, is the major agricultural
area in northern China. The Chinese also distill a strong

alcoholic beverage from sorghum known as *maotai* (*mao-
t'ai*), which is used to make toasts at banquets. (Zhang
Yimou's award-winning film *Red Sorghum* (1987) was about
a woman in a sorghum-growing region of Shandong
Province.

Rice has always been the major grain crop south of the
Yangzi River (Changjiang), which divides China into north
and south. In the 1980s the highest grain yields in China
were in the lower Yangzi Valley and Sichuan, Guangdong
and Fujian provinces. Southern China has a semitropical climate and abundant rainfall for growing two or even three
crops of rice per year in wet paddy fields. Wet-grown rice
produces more calories per acre and higher amounts of plant
protein than any other grain and is rich in B vitamins. Chinese emperors collected taxes in payments of rice and other
grains and built the Grand Canal and other canals along
which the grain taxes could be transported from the fertile
agricultural regions to the capital cities. Some emperors also
established grain storage facilities around the country to help
the peasants in time of famine caused by frequent natural
disasters such as floods and droughts. Corn was introduced
into China during the 16th century, along with sweet potatoes, peanuts and sugarcane.

Today, China is the world's leading producer of grain,
accounting for 23 percent of world grain production of 1,740
metric tons (MMT) during crop year 1994–95. Rice is the
leading grain, followed by coarse grains—mostly corn and
sorghum, and wheat. The provinces of Heilongjiang, Jilin
and Liaoning in Manchuria (northeastern China) are leading
producers of corn, wheat and soybeans. Consumption of all
grain in China rose by nearly 9 percent from crop year
1990–91 to 1994–95. Rice consumption remained stagnant,
but consumption of wheat and coarse grains, used mostly for
animal feed, increased. However, annual grain production in
China actually fell over the five-year period ending in crop
year 1994–95. During that time, rice production fell, due
largely to changing patterns of consumption by the Chinese
people, who are eating more wheat-based products and
meat.

China has to import grain to feed its population of more
than one billion, partly because of its inadequate and ineffi-
cient railroad and transport facilities along the Yangzi and
Yellow (Huanghe) rivers, which cannot move sufficient grain
from northeast and inland agricultural regions to the coastal
regions where nearly half of the Chinese population resides.
In 1993 China began a five-year, $2-billion grain infrastruc-
ture project to construct a storage network of nearly 40
MMT of grain, located at 370 sites in the northeast and along
the Yangzi. It is also adding grain terminals at major ports
such as Daya Bay and Yinkou in Liaoning Province and
Shanghai at the mouth of the Yangzi. In crop year 1994–95,
China increased net grain imports and became the leading
world import market for wheat, the second global market for
rice, and the sixth market for corn (coarse grain). See also
AGRICULTURE; BANQUETS; BEANS AND BEAN PRODUCTS;
COOKING, CHINESE; DIM SUM; GRAND CANAL; HAN; MAOTAI;
NOMADS AND ANIMAL HUSBANDRY; NOODLES; NORTH CHINA
PLAIN; RICE; SHIPPING AND SHIPBUILDING; SOYBEANS AND SOY
PRODUCTS; YANGSHAO CULTURE; ZHANG YIMOU.

GRAND ACADEMY   See FIVE CLASSICS OF CONFUCIANISM.

GRAND CANAL (Yunlianghe or Yunliang-ho, "Grain Transport River")   A long north-south waterway originally constructed during the Sui dynasty (581–618) to connect the Hai, Huai, Yellow (Huanghe) and Yangzi (Changjiang) rivers, which all flow west to east, so that goods, especially grain, could be transported between southern and northern China. The Grand Canal was expanded by later emperors until it became the longest and oldest manmade waterway in the world. More than 1,200 miles long, the canal is, at its widest, about 200 feet across and ranges from 2 to 15 feet in depth. From north to south it passes through four provinces: Hebei, Shandong, Jiangsu and Zhejiang. The northern terminus of the Grand Canal is Dongzhou, about 15 miles east of the capital city of Beijing, and the southern terminus is Hangzhou, the capital of Zhejiang Province in southeastern China.

The first part of the canal was dug 2,400 years ago from the Yangzi through the city of Yangzhou to Huai'an by the Kingdom of Wu (modern Jiangsu Province) to transport its soldiers north to fight the Kingdom of Qi (modern Shandong Province). The modern city of Suzhou in Jiangsu Province had been the capital of Wu, and it developed rapidly because of the Grand Canal, which still plays a major role in the city's economy. Emperor Qin Shin Huangdi, who unified China under the Qin dynasty (221–206 B.C.), ordered the construction of waterways and canals that enabled water transportation for 1,200 miles from the Yangzi to Guangzhou (Canton), a major port city in southern China.

Between A.D. 605 and 618, Yangdi (Yang-ti; r. 604–18), the second emperor of the Sui dynasty, built a long waterway by connecting many rivers and small canals, thus extending the Grand Canal from Hangzhou north across the Yangzi to Yangzhou, and then northwest to the region of the capital city of Luoyang. By 609 the canal was extended from this far inland point to the region of modern Tianjin and Beijing in northeastern China. By sailing on local streams and lakes as well as the Grand Canal, barges could transport the food produced in the lower Yangzi region up through northern China to strengthen the northern frontier and feed the capital area. Large granaries were built, one able to hold 3.3 million bushels. The entire network of waterways in China extended for about 30,000 miles and created the world's most heavily populated trading area. The Dongji section of the Grand Canal, between Yangzhou (about 15 miles north of Zhejiang) and Banju on the Yellow River, was the first artificial waterway between the Yangzi and the Yellow rivers, China's two most important rivers. After 763, during the Tang dynasty (618–907), the Grand Canal was the lifeline of the Chinese Empire. Kaifeng, the capital city of the Northern Song dynasty (960–1127), was located near the junction of the early Grand Canal and the Yellow River, at the head of barge transport from the lower Yangzi grain basket.

The Grand Canal was completed in 1293 during the Mongol Yuan dynasty (1279–1368). Khubilai Khan, the first Yuan emperor, established his capital at Khanbaliq (modern Beijing) and had the Grand Canal restored and shortened to give it a more direct north–south route, with two new waterways dug through the western region of Shandong Province. Yuan hydraulic engineers were even able to construct a section of the waterway over the top of a mountain to connect the capital with southern China. After completion of the Grand Canal, Wuxi in the Yangzi River delta became a major center for shipping grain to the capital. As the Yuan dynasty grew weak, the Grand Canal fell into disrepair, but the Ming dynasty emperor Yongle (Yung-lo; r. 1403–24) had the canal reconstructed and the channel widened and deepened. In 1411 a Chinese engineer named Song Li solved the problem of water flow by building a mile-long dam with sluice gates, forming a reservoir divided into sections by 14 locks with gates that could be opened and closed to control the water. During the Ming, the Grand Canal was maintained by local corvée labor without any financing from the central government in Beijing. Taxes were paid to Beijing in grain—vital for the survival of the capital region. In the mid-15th century there were 11,775 grain barges sailing the Grand Canal, manned by 121,500 military officers and troops. Although these men were supposed to receive their pay from their army rations, they were in fact seldom paid and were forced to earn money by transporting private cargo in their grain barges. Any natural disaster such as a flood caused a crisis that required the raising of special funds to pay the troops. Grain shipments on the canal were threatened for a while by the White Lotus Secret Society rebellion in Shandong in the late 1700s.

Raw cotton grown in northern China was shipped down the Grand Canal to textile production centers in the lower Yangzi region, especially around Shanghai, which was for a time a leading exporter of cotton yarn to Guangdong Province in southern China. Luxury wares, such as porcelain from the kilns at Jingdezhen, were transported to all directions in China, while brick tea from central China was sent up the Han River to be exchanged at tea-horse markets on the Central Asian frontier. Due to the growth of industrialization in the late 19th century, from 1872 rice was carried by steamship from the Yangzi delta north from Shanghai to Tianjin to feed the capital region. However, after an extensive system of railroads was built in China beginning in the late 19th century, many sections of the Grand Canal fell into disrepair, and the canal had also been damaged by frequent flooding of the Yellow River.

Today the southern half of the Grand Canal is still heavily used by barges to transport goods, especially the section from Hangzhou to the Yangzi River near Zhejiang. North of the Yangzi the canal passes through Yangzhou to the lake district of the Huai Valley and continues northwest to Tsinan. The section of the canal north of Tsinan in western Shandong has not been used since the 18th century because of heavy silting. Closer to Tianjin, the Grand Canal remains a major trade route, with many dams and locks to control water flow and assist the passage of boats. North of Tianjin, the canal flows along the shallow Pai River to Dongzhou. The northern sections of the canal freeze over during the winter.

In 1958 the Chinese government decided to restore the canal and established the Grand Canal Committee under the Minister of Communication as well as an engineering headquarters for the Grand Canal. By 1963, dams had been built on a 250-mile section of the canal in northern Jiangsu Province to facilitate the navigation of boats and to provide drainage, flood control, irrigation and a supply of water. Today mostly coal and industrial goods rather than grain are transported on the canal. See also GRAIN; HAI RIVER;

HANGZHOU; HUAI RIVER; KAIFENG; KHUBILAI KHAN; LUO-YANG; MING DYNASTY; SHANGHAI; SUI DYNASTY; SUZHOU; WHITE LOTUS SECRET SOCIETY; WUXI; YANGDI (EMPEROR); YANGZHOU; YANGZI RIVER; YELLOW RIVER; YUAN DYNASTY.

GRAND SECRETARIAT

GRAND SECRETARIAT (Neige or Nei-ko)   Officially known as the Grand Secretariat of the Cabinet (Neige daxueshi or Nei-ko ta-hsueh-shih); a post created within the imperial bureaucracy, or civil service, during the Ming dynasty (1368–1644). In previous dynasties the imperial bureaucracy's cabinet, comprising the Six Ministries, was headed by a prime minister. The position of prime minister dated as far back as the Shang dynasty (1750–1040 B.C.). Emperor Hongwu (Hung-wu; r. 1368–99), founder of the Ming dynasty, accused three of his prime ministers of treason and had them executed. In 1380 he finally abolished the office of prime minister and placed the cabinet under his direct jurisdiction, thus functioning as his own prime minister.

Beginning in 1426, Ming emperors used the Grand Secretariat to exercise control over the government bureaucracy. The grand secretary superseded the prime minister. At first, the grand secretary was not allowed to make decisions about government policy, but over time the men who held this position gradually acquired more authority. They also increasingly shared power with the eunuchs who ran the imperial palace. A competent grand secretary who was trusted by the emperor was eventually able to function as a virtual prime minister. Emperor Hongwu enlarged the elite Hanlin Academy, which provided him with highly educated men to assist him as grand secretary. The Grand Secretariat oversaw the other government ministries. Other members of the imperial bureaucracy did not trust the grand secretaries, however, because they had spent their careers within the Hanlin Academy and had not acquired the broad experience that had been gained by other high-ranking bureaucracy members. The Grand Secretariat did not receive formal recognition until the mid-16th century, during the reign of Emperor Jiajing (Chia-ching; r. 1522–67), who withdrew from the responsibilities of government and left power in the hands of his highly disliked grand secretary, Yan Song (Yen Sung). The Qing dynasty (1644–1911) that supplanted the Ming continued the post of grand secretariat until 1729, when Emperor Yongzheng (Yung-cheng; r. 1723–35) created the office of Grand Council or Office of Strategic Affairs (Junjiqu or Chun-chi ch'u), which he placed above the Grand Secretariat and supervised himself. He gave the Grand Council powers that until then had been wielded by other government departments, including affairs of the imperial bureaucracy, military affairs, and the writing and issuing of important imperial edicts. The Grand Council determined government policy and the Grand Secretariat was reduced to handling the routine affairs of government administration. See also EMPEROR; HANLIN ACADEMY; HONGWU (EMPEROR); IMPERIAL BUREAUCRACY; JIAJING (EMPEROR); MING DYNASTY; QING DYNASTY.

GREAT BRITAIN AND CHINA

GREAT BRITAIN AND CHINA   See ARROW WAR; BOXER UPRISING; BRITISH EAST INDIA COMPANY; CANTON SYSTEM; CHINESE MARITIME CUSTOMS SERVICE; CHRISTIANITY; GORDON, CHARLES GEORGE; HONG KONG; INTERNATIONAL SETTLEMENT IN SHANGHAI; MACARTNEY, GEORGE, LORD; OPIUM WAR; SHANGHAI; SINO-BRITISH JOINT DECLARATION ON THE QUESTION OF HONG KONG; TAIPING REBELLION; TREATY PORTS; UNEQUAL TREATIES.

GREAT HALL OF THE PEOPLE, THE

GREAT HALL OF THE PEOPLE, THE (Renmin Dahuitang)   A large modern building on the west side of Tiananmen Square in the capital city of Beijing that houses the Offices of the Standing Committee of the National People's Congress (NPC), which meets here periodically. The entrance gates were cast in bronze, and in front are twelve marble columns, each one 80 feet tall. Formerly known as the National People's Congress Building, the Great Hall of the People covers an area of 560,000 square feet and was constructed in 10 months in 1958–59 with the help of many students and workers. There are many rooms and reception areas for important meetings and interviews with foreign diplomats. Each room is named for a Chinese province or autonomous region and is furnished in a distinct style. State guests are entertained in a banquet hall that can seat 5,000 people. Richard Nixon, the first American president to visit the People's Republic of China, was honored with a banquet in the Great Hall of the People in 1972. The Great Hall of the People is open to the public when the NPC is not sitting. A 9,700-seat auditorium is equipped with 12-channel simultaneous interpretation equipment for every seat. See also BANQUETS; NATIONAL PEOPLE'S CONGRESS; NIXON, RICHARD, U.S. PRESIDENT, VISIT TO CHINA; TIANANMEN SQUARE.

"GREAT HELMSMAN"

"GREAT HELMSMAN"   See MAO ZEDONG.

GREAT LEAP FORWARD, 1958–60

GREAT LEAP FORWARD, 1958–60   A campaign initiated by the Chinese government under Mao Zedong to speed up China's development in the spirit of the communist revolution that had established the People's Republic of China in 1949. The Great Leap Forward had the slogan, "General Line for Socialist Construction." People's communes, which had been newly created in the Chinese countryside, were to be the centers for economic and technical progress. There were approximately 23,500 people's communes by the autumn of 1958. Each commune was expected to be self-supporting and was given control of all the means of production for its needs. Mao's intention was to develop China's heavy industries, but he also wanted to mobilize the great masses of unskilled workers in the cities and countryside.

The policy of the Great Leap Forward would doom it to economic failure. Workers on communes were supposed to manufacture industrial goods using materials available locally, but this was not always possible, and the goods that were produced were most often of very bad quality. Manufacturing plants were mismanaged and allowed to deteriorate. Farmers were told to ignore thousands of years of knowledge that the Chinese had accumulated about the best way to grow crops, and the result was severe famine in large areas of the country and the erosion of thousands of acres of farmland. Workers and peasants alike suffered from starvation and exhaustion. In 1959, the Chinese Communist Party admitted that it had exaggerated the success of the Great Leap Forward in its production report for 1958. Mao had to step down as chairman of the People's Republic of China in April 1959, and was replaced by Liu Shaoqi, although Mao remained chairman of the Chinese Communist Party. In

1960, other top Party leaders persuaded Mao to cancel the Great Leap Forward and admit that it had failed. See also MAO ZEDONG; PEOPLE'S COMMUNES; PEOPLE'S REPUBLIC OF CHINA.

GREAT LEARNING, THE (*Daxue* or *Ta-hsueh*   A short story of 1,750 characters that provides a complete system for personal education and social organization. *The Great Learning* has been attributed to various writers, including Confucius's grandson Kong Ji (Kung chi; 483–402? B.C.), his disciple Zheng Shen (Cheng Shen) or another of his students. Some recent scholars have dated the essay as late as 200 B.C., although its basic ideas probably derive from Confucius (551–479 B.C.). *The Great Learning* advises the ruler and his officials about the way good government can be attained through the moral self-cultivation of the ruler and of men in society. The essay offers a method that contains "eight points," three having to do with social activities and five with self-cultivation and personal discipline—the so-called rectification of the mind (or heart.) It asserts that the country can be governed properly by first regulating the family. A person who fulfills his obligations to his parents and his family as the basic social unit, a concept known as filial piety (*xiao* or *hsiao*), is qualified to undertake greater responsibility in the service of society and the state. The goal is a harmonious flow from the perfected individual to the orderly family to the well-governed country so as to bring about a peaceful world.

The Great Learning was originally a chapter in the *Book of Rites* (*Liji* or *Li-chi*), one of the Five Classics (*Wujing* or *Wu-ching*) of Confucianism, but the Neo-Confucian scholar Zhu Xi (Chu Hsi; 1130–1200) added this chapter to three other documents to form the Four Books (*Sishu*) of Confucianism. The other three books are *The Doctrine of the Mean* (*Zhongyong* or *Chung yung*; also formerly a chapter in the *Book of Rites*), the *Analects* (*Sayings*) of Confucius (*Lunyu*) and the *Book of Mencius* (*Mengzi* or *Meng Tzu*; Mencius was a Confucian scholar who lived c. 371–289 B.C.). In 1315, the Chinese government designated Zhu Xi's commentaries on the Five Classics as the orthodox interpretation of the Confucian tradition, and a thorough knowledge of his commentary on the Four Books was required in order to pass the examinations for positions in the imperial bureaucracy. Zhu Xi argued that it is possible for men to overcome their limitations or weaknesses and perfect themselves. He followed the method of the "investigation of the nature of things and relationships" in *The Great Learning*, and asserted that this could be done by acquiring a thorough knowledge of the classic Confucian documents. Wang Yangming (1472–1529), another major Neo-Confucianist scholar, wrote a highly regarded commentary on the *Great Learning*. The principles of the *Great Learning* have had an immense influence in China and in other Asian countries where Confucianism has played an important role, such as Japan and Korea. See also ANALECTS, CONFUCIAN; BOOK OF RITES; CONFUCIANISM; DOCTRINE OF THE MEAN; FILIAL PIETY; FIVE CLASSICS OF CONFUCIANISM; FOUR BOOKS OF CONFUCIANISM; IMPERIAL BUREAUCRACY; MENCIUS; WANG YANGMING; ZHU XI.

GREAT PHARMACOPOEIA, THE   See LI SHIZHEN.

GREAT PROLETARIAN CULTURAL REVOLUTION   See CULTURAL REVOLUTION.

GREAT WALL   Also known as the Wall of 10,000 Li (Wanli Chang Cheng; a *li* is a measure of distance); a series of walls constructed across northern and western China to protect the Chinese Empire from invasions by nomadic tribes. Historians have proven that the existence of a single, continuous "Great Wall" that was built all at once is actually a myth. Many walls, even ones with double or triple sections, had been erected across parts of northern China beginning in the seventh century B.C. Emperor Qin Shi Huangdi (259–210 B.C.), who unified China under the Qin dynasty (221–206 B.C.), was believed to have constructed the Great Wall, and it is true that during his reign, fortification walls that had been built earlier by various warring states were connected to form a wall about 1,650 miles long. This was done by vast armies of workers conscripted as corvée labor, a form of government service in which men were required to work on projects for a certain period of time each year.

There are actually four long walls that were rebuilt or extended, mainly during the Western Han (206 B.C.–A.D. 9), Sui (581–618), Jin (1115–1234) and Ming (1368–1644) dynasties. The extensive wall system with hundreds of watchtowers that can be seen today was built with brick and stone by corvée labor in the 16th century during the Ming dynasty. The Ming continuously renovated the Great Wall. The Great Wall was not always able to keep out the nomadic invaders, but it did serve as a psychological dividing line for the Ming Chinese, supposedly keeping them inside the empire and the nomads outside it. Earlier dynasties had not just tried to shut the nomads out but had sought to blunt the threats they posed by engaging in trade, diplomacy and warfare. The Han dynasty, especially under Emperor Wudi (Wuti; r. 141–87 B.C.), waged many military campaigns against the Xiongnu tribes to the north, gained control of much of Central Asia, and extended the Great Wall to the west through Gansu Province to the Xinjiang-Uighur Autonomous Region to maintain the safety of the trade route known as the Silk Road. The entire Great Wall complex was divided into nine commands that reported to the Ministry of Defense and were directly responsible to the emperor. When a garrison, stationed near the wall, noticed movements by enemy troops, it notified the nearest watchtower by smoke signals or fires, and the alarm was passed along all the watchtowers within the region of the command.

Between its farthest extremities, the Great Wall today stretches more than 4,000 miles from Heilongjiang Province in northeastern China to the desert region of Gansu Province in the northwest. The total combined length of all the walls that have been built is about 31,000 miles. North of the Great Wall lies the Mongolian Plateau, known as the Inner Mongolia Autonomous Region (Nei Menggu). The western terminus of the wall is the massive, thick-walled Jiayu Fort at Jiayuguan Pass ("the Pass of the Pleasant Valley") in Gansu, built during the Han dynasty. The Chinese called the fort "the mouth," and those who passed through it were "outside the mouth," that is, outside imperial protection. The fort was also known as the "Jade Gate" and its last door was poetically called the "Gate of Sighs." At the eastern end of the wall, Shanhaiguan Pass, 20 miles from Beidaihe and

The Great Wall is actually a series of walls, with a combined length of more than 31,000 miles.   S.E. MEYER

200 miles from Beijing on the border between Hebei and Liaoning Provinces near the sea, was the most important pass. It controlled the traffic between the northern and northeastern regions of China. The first gate, named Yaguan, had been erected there in 618, but the present structure dates back to 1639. For many centuries this pass was the site of heavy fighting between the Chinese and nomadic tribes invading from the north. Most visitors to the capital city of Beijing visit the section of the Great Wall at Badaling, about 60 miles to the north, which was repaired in 1957 and is wide enough for 5 horsemen or 10 men to march abreast. Juyong Pass, about 40 miles away, had been of great strategic importance as the checkpoint for entrance to Beijing from the north. Today the pass is well known for its complex of gates dating from the 14th century. Within the gates is a marble terrace from 1345 known as Yuntai ("Cloud Terrace"), all that remains of Tai'an Temple, which burned down in 1702.

The Mongols, who ruled China under the Yuan dynasty (1279–1368), had built Beijing as their capital. After the Ming defeated the Mongols, the second Ming emperor, Yongle, moved his court from Nanjing to Beijing to be near the Great Wall as a defense against other tribes who were threatening from the north. In 1644 the Ming fell to the Manchus when a rebellion led by Li Zicheng threatened the capital, and Ming General Wu Sangui, stationed at Shanhaiguan Pass at the Great Wall, made the mistake of letting the Manchus

come through to help him suppress the rebellion. They quickly took over Beijing, overthrew the Ming and established their own dynasty, the Qing (1644–1911). The Great Wall lost its importance during the Qing because the Manchus attempted to maintain harmonious relations with other tribes on the northern steppes. However, the Great Wall has remained one of China's most important and world-renowned symbols. Recently the China Great Wall Society has conducted archaeological and historical research on the wall. In 1987 UNESCO placed the Great Wall on its list of the world's great national and historical sites. See also BEIJING; COOLIE; GANSU PROVINCE; HAN DYNASTY; LI ZICHENG; MANCHU; MING DYNASTY; MONGOL; NOMADS AND ANIMAL HUSBANDRY; QIN DYNASTY; XIONGNU.

GU   See DRUMS.

GUAN   See TEMPLES.

GUAN CHU   See BOOK OF SONGS.

GUAN DAOSHENG   See ZHAO MENGFU AND GUAN DAOSHENG.

GUAN HANQING (Kuan Han-ch'ing; 1241?–1320?) The most highly regarded playwright in the northern Chinese style of drama that became known as *zaju*, "variety plays" or "miscellany plays," and that flourished during the Yuan dynasty (1279–1368). Many critics in fact regard Guan Hanqing as China's greatest playwright. He was born in Dadu (Ta-tu; modern Beijing), probably to a family of the literati or scholar class. He belonged to a guild for writers of plays for performing groups and wrote more than 60 plays, though only 17 have survived. One of Guan's best-known works is *Injustice Suffered by Dou E* (*Dou E yuan* or *Tou-o yuan*), a tragedy about a widow who is executed after being wrongly convicted of murder, but who comes back as a ghost and is proven innocent. Another is *Butterfly Dream* (*Hudiemeng* or *Hu-tieh meng*) about the Daoist philosopher Zhuangzi (Chuang Tzu; 369–286 B.C.) and his wife, who was unfaithful. He is also famous for *Meeting Enemies Alone* and *Saving a Prostitute*. Guan enjoyed depicting people of the lower social classes, especially women, whom he showed to be intelligent, courageous and honest. His humor and sympathy for his characters underly his portrayals of everyday occurrences, which form the backbone of his plays. See also YUAN DYNASTY.

GUAN YU　See GUANDI; ROMANCE OF THE THREE KINGDOMS.

GUANDI (Kuan Ti)　The God of War, a divinized hero named Guan Yu (Kuan Yu; 162–220) who became a general for the kingdoms of Wei and Shu, two of the Three Kingdoms that contended in the third century A.D. (Three Kingdoms Period, 220–80). This period has been immortalized in the epic 14th-century novel by Luo Guanzhong (Luo Kuan-chung), *Romance of the Three Kingdoms* (*Sanguochi yanyi* or *San-kuo-ch'ih yan-yi*), whose episodes are a mainstay of Chinese operas and dramas. Fighting on the side of Liu Bei (Liu Pei) of Shu and his prime minister, Zhuge Liang (Chu-ke Liang), Guan Yu helped defeat Cao Cao (Ts'ao Ts'ao; 155–220), the founder of the northern kingdom of Wei, in one of the most famous battles in Chinese history. Guan Yu is often depicted with Liu Bei on his right and Zhang Fei (Chang Fei) on his left. They are known as the Three Brothers of the Peach Orchard, after the place in the novel where they swore to be blood brothers and to uphold justice.

Guan Yu became a folk hero to many groups in Chinese society, who variously identified him as the god of loyalty, the god of wealth, the god of literature, the protector of temples, and the patron of actors and of secret societies. In 1614 the Ming dynasty (1368–1644) government awarded Guan Yu imperial rank, designating him as Guandi, the God of War, and in 1725 the imperial government took control of the cult that worshiped him. There were hundreds of temples to Guandi in every county in China, and the Qing dynasty (1644–1911) selected 1,600 of those as official temples. Guandi was revered as the heroic warrior who was loyal to and protected the established government. By 1835 the Qing had elevated the worship of Guandi in the imperial ritual sacrifices to the same level as the worship of Confucius, whose school of thought was the orthodox religion for the Chinese imperial government. Even today the Chinese visit temples built to honor Guandi on the ninth day of the ninth month in the lunar calendar (roughly corresponding to

October) to offer him food and incense. People who want to gain Guandi's protection take oaths of loyalty in front of mediums who become possessed by the god's spirit and enter a trance during which they perform martial arts with swords attached to long poles. Many businessmen worship Guandi because he was an honest man who remained loyal to Liu Bei and Zhang Fei, with whom he became blood brothers; some businessmen may even become blood brothers with Guandi. See also CAO CAO; ROMANCE OF THE THREE KINGDOMS; THREE KINGDOMS PERIOD; ZHUGE LIANG.

GUANDU, BATTLE OF　See CAO CAO.

GUANGDONG PROVINCE　A province in southern China that includes the major port city of Guangzhou (Canton) and three Special Economic Zones (SEZs), Shenzhen, Zhuhai and Shantou. Guangdong Province covers an area of 81,850 square miles and has a population of around 70 million. Guangzhou, the capital, which lies in the Pearl River (Zhujiang) Delta, has a population of more than 3 million. The Special Administrative Region in Hong Kong, a British Crown Colony until it reverted to China in 1997, is situated near Guangzhou and has a population of more than 6 million. Macao (Macau), a Portuguese colony near Hong Kong with a population of about half a million, will revert to China in 1999. Other cities in Guangdong include Zhanjiang, the largest coastal port west of Guangzhou; Zhaoqing, a beautiful site on the Xi (West) River; Foshan, a traditional handicraft center; and Chaozhou, an ancient trading city. Hainan, a large island in the South China Sea close to Vietnam, formerly belonged to Guangdong but was made a separate province in 1988.

Guangdong has a hot, humid tropical climate with an average temperature of 72 degrees F, and suffers from monsoon rains and typhoons in late summer and early autumn. It borders the provinces of Fujian, Jiangxi and Hunan to the east and north and Guangxi-Zhuang Autonomous Region to the west. Southern Guangdong forms a coastline along the South China Sea, the longest coast of all Chinese provinces. Guangdong has long been an important center for mairtime trade with Southeast and South Asia and the Middle East.

The province was brought into the Chinese Empire when Emperor Qin Shi Huangdi (r. 221–210 B.C.), who unified China under the Qin dynasty, sent military expeditions against the Nanyue kingdom. In 111 B.C. Emperor Wudi (Wu-ti; r. 141–87 B.C.) of the Han dynasty established military garrisons in Nanyue. The regions that comprise the modern provinces of Guangdong and Guangxi were combined to make up the independent kingdom of Nanhan from 909 to 971. Han (ethnic) Chinese kept moving south into Guangdong, especially after Jin invaders drove the Song dynasty south in the 12th century and Mongol invaders established the Yuan dynasty (1279–1368). The Han Chinese settled in the fertile Pearl River Delta and pushed local ethnic groups into more remote moutainous regions.

The history of Guangdong Province is largely the history of the port city of Guangzhou. Many foreign traders, including Muslims, Jews and Christians, settled in the city, which has the oldest mosque in China. European trading ships, first Portuguese and the Dutch, appeared in Guangdong waters in the 16th century. British and French traders soon followed. The Chinese government strictly limited European trade to Guangzhou, where it was controlled by a designated group of merchants call the Cohong or Hong; this is known as the Canton system to regulate foreign trade. The British tried unsuccessfully to end this system and to open China to Western-style trade. In the 19th century they defeated China in the Opium War and Arrow War, forcing China to open a number of so-called treaty ports and to cede Hong Kong to Britain.

A number of minority groups still inhabit Guangdong; the largest include the Zhuang, Miao, Hakka, Yao and Li. Hong Xiuquan (Hung Hsiu-ch'uan; 1813–64), a member of the Hakka minority, led the Taiping Rebellion (1850–64), which was the largest uprising in 19th-century China and nearly broguht down the Qing dynasty (1644–1911). Dr. Sun Yat-sen (1866–1925), who led the Revolution of 1911 that overthrew the Qing and established the Republic of China, was a native of Guangdong and found much support for his revolutionary movement in the province. He was also widely supported by overseas Chinese, many of whom had emigrated from Guangdong to Southeast Asia, Australia, Hawaii, and North and South America.

Chinese Nationalists and Communists used Guangdong as a base in the 1920s from which they launched the Northern Expedition against the warlords that controlled China. The Japanese occupied Guangdong during China's War of Resistance against Japan (1937–45; World War II). After Japan's surrender, the Chinese Communists defeated the Nationalists and founded the People's Republic of China (PRC) in 1949. Since then, Guangdong has been heavily industrialized. In 1980 the Chinese government opened four Special Economic Zones, three in Guangdong, to encourage foreign trade and investment in China. Shenzhen (near Guangzhou), Zhuhai (near Macao), Shantou in eastern Guangdong, and Xiamen in neighboring Fujian Province. Shenzhen grew at the amazingly rapid rate of 20 percent a year. Many companies based in Hong Kong opened factories in Guangdong. The Guangzhou (Canton) Trade Fair is held twice annually for businesspeople who want to trade with and invest China.

The tropical climate enables Guangdong farmers to grow two crops of rice per year, and three or even four crops of vegetables. The desnsely populated Pearl River Delta has a large number of fish farms and is one of the largest "rice and fish" regions in China. Major crops include sugar cane, tropical fruit, tobacco, silkworm cocoons, peanuts, spices, maize and cotton. Food processing and textiles are two of Guangdong's main industries. See also ARROW WAR; CANTON SYSTEM; CHRISTIANS; FISH; GUANGZHOU; GUANGZHOU (CANTON) TRADE FAIR; HAINAN ISLAND; HAKKA; HAN; HONG KONG; JEWS; LI; MACAO; MIAO; MUSLIMS; NORTHERN EXPEDITON; OPIUM WAR; OVERSEAS CHINESE; PEARL RIVER; RICE; SILK; SOUTH CHINA SEA; SPECIAL ECONOMIC ZONES; SUN YAT-SEN; TAIPING REBELLION; TEXTILE INDUSTRY; TREATY PORTS; YAO; ZHUANG.

GUANGMING RIBAO   See NEW CHINA NEWS AGENCY.

GUANGWUDI (EMPEROR)   See EASTERN HAN DYNASTY; LIU XIU.

GUANGXI-ZHUANG AUTONOMOUS REGION (Guangxi Zhuangzu Zizhiqu)

A province in southwestern China that is administered as an autonomous region because a large number of its inhabitants belong to various national minority ethnic groups. Nearly all of the approximately 14 million members of the Zhuang, China's largest minority, reside in the Guangxi-Zhuang Autonomous Region and comprise about 35 percent of its population. National minorities in Guangxi also include the Miao, Yi, Dong, Yao, Mulao, Maonan, Jing, Hui (Chinese Muslims) and other smaller groups. However, the Han (ethnic Chinese) now make up the majority of the population. The region first came under Chinese influence when, in 214 B.C., the Qin dynasty sent an army into Guangdong Province and eastern Guangxi. Over the centuries, the various ethnic groups and the Han have struggled for control of the Guangxi region.

Guangxi today has a population of about 37 million and covers 91,500 square miles. The capital city is Nanning, in the south. Northern Guangxi borders Hunan and Guizhou provinces, eastern Guangxi borders Guangdong Province, and western Guangli borders Yunnan Province. Guangxi's southern coast borders the Gulf of Tonkin (Beibu Wan) and receives about 110 inches of rainfall per year, the highest amount in China. The tropical climate enables three crops of rice to be grown each year. Southwestern Guangxi borders Vietnam, and the major routes between China and Vietnam run through Guangxi. Since ancient times, the Chinese and Vietnamese have sent troops against each other through Guangxi.

The Guangxi region is famous for its natural beauty. Guilin, situated on the Li River (Lijiang) in northeast Guangxi, is one of the most popular tourist areas in China because of its karst landscapes. Karst is formed by the erosion and collapse of limestone and other soft rocks, and most of Guangxi sits on a limestone plateau. Numerous oddly shaped rock formations covered with vegetation rise in the middle of the plains around Guilin. Also, there are splendid tropical forests in the area of Longgang. Several rivers form in the mountains of Yunnan and Guizhou provinces and flow southeast through Guangxi. The largest is the Yu River (Yujiang), which flows into Guangdong Province to the east, where it joins the Pearl River delta and empties into the China Sea. Major agricultural products include sugarcane, sweet potatoes, corn, peanuts, tea, tobacco, many types of fruit, spices, wood and cotton. Another important product is ramie, a natural fiber woven from a type of grass that is commonly used to make textiles in China. Guangxi also has rich mineral resources, especially coal and iron, and mining and manufacturing have increased during the last three decades.

One of the most important historical events in Guangxi was the Taiping Rebellion (1850–64), a revolutionary movement against the Qing dynasty (1644–1911) that swept throughout China. It was led by Hong Xiuquan (Hung Hsiuch'uan; 1813–64), who was born in Guangxi to a family of the Hakka, another national minority. During the last half of the 19th century, the British, through Guangdong Province, and the French, through Vietnam, strove to increase their influence in the region, and the cities of Longzhou, Wuzhou and Nanning were opened to foreign trade. Guangxi leaders supported the overthrow of the Qing dynasty by the Revolution of 1911 and the establishment of the Republic of China in 1912. They formed the so-called Guangxi Clique, the main opposition group to Chiang Kai-shek within the Nationalist Party (Kuomintang), and controlled much of Guangdong, Hunan and Hubei Provinces during 1926–37. After the Japanese invaded Guangxi in 1939, terrible fighting took place in the region during China's War of Resistance against Japan (1937–45). See also CHIANG KAI-SHEK; GUILIN; HONG XIUQUAN; MINORITIES, NATIONAL; NANNING; NATIONALIST PARTY; RAMIE; TAIPING REBELLION; VIETNAM WAR AND CHINA; WAR OF RESISTANCE AGAINST JAPAN; NAMES OF INDIVIDUAL NATIONAL MINORITIES.

GUANGXU (EMPEROR) See CIXI, EMPRESS DOWAGER; GONG, PRINCE; REFORM MOVEMENT OF 1898.

GUANGZHOU   Also known as Canton; the capital of Guangdong Province in southern China and one of the oldest and most important cities in the country. Guangzhou, located in the Pearl River (Zhujiang) estuary, has been a port city and one of the main entries into China for more than 1,000 years. There was a town on the site as far back as the Qing dynasty (221–206 B.C.). Indian and Roman traders were traveling to Guangzhou by the second century A.D. to purchase Chinese silk, porcelain, tea, spices and other luxury goods. Arab, Jewish, Christian and Zoroastrian traders settled in Guangzhou during the Tang dynasty (618–907) after the port was declared open to foreigners in 714. Guangzhou soon developed an active trade with South and Southeast Asia and the Middle East. Huaisheng Mosque, built in Guangzhou in 627, is the oldest mosque in China.

The first Europeans arrived in the 16th century, when Portuguese ships put into Guangzhou in 1514 and received permission in 1557 to establish a base on the island of Macao (Macau), about 90 mile south of Guangzhou. Roman Catholic Jesuit missionaries began arriving with Portuguese traders, and in 1582 they were allowed to enter the town of Zhaoqing, northwest of Guangzhou. Matteo Ricci, the first Jesuit in China, was introduced to the Ming dynasty (1368–1644) imperial court in 1598. In 1622 the Dutch attacked Macao but were driven off by the Portuguese. British ships appeared soon after, but the Ming refused to honor the first British request for permission to trade in China in 1625. China had always regulated foreign trade by requiring foreign nations to submit to the sovereignty of the Chinese emperor and pay tribute, for which they would receive permission to trade in specially designated zones along the Chinese border. In 1760 the Qing dynasty (1644–1911) established the so-called Canton system whereby Western merchants would have to conduct all of their business in Canton and would have to be supervised by native Chinese merchants belonging to a guild known as the Cohong or "Hong." The Cohong had been formed in 1720 by Chinese merchants in Canton to gain a monopoly over foreign trade and to increase profits by regulating the prices for imported and exported goods. Western traders residing in Canton had to confine themselves to an area along the bank of the Pearl River where the residences and offices of the foreign "factors" were located, known as the "13 Factories." When the summer trading season ended each year, they had to close their operations in Canton and move to Macao.

In 1793 the British government sent Lord George Macartney to China to request the ending of the Canton system and the opening of more Chinese ports to foreign trade, but Qing emperor Qianlong (Ch'ien-lung; r. 1736–95) refused to give in to these requests. The British continued to pressure China, and by the early 19th century they were selling large quantities of opium to the Chinese, which was demoralizing the country and draining its silver. The Qing sent Lin Zexu (Lin Tse-hsu) to Canton to stop the opium trade but he was unsuccessful. The British defeated China in the Opium War (1839–42) and forced the Qing to sign the Treaty of Nanjing, which among other things, abolished the Canton Cohong monopoly system, opened Canton and four other cities as treaty ports for foreign trade, and ceded the island of Hong Kong to Britain. The British gained further concessions after they defeated China in the Second Opium War, known as the Arrow War (1856–60). In 1847 Chinese laborers began emigrating from Canton in large numbers to North and South America and Australia.

Guangzhou has also played a major role in the political development of modern China. The Taiping Rebellion (1850–64), which nearly overthrew the Qing dynasty, originated in Guangzhou under the leadership of Hong Xiuquan (Hung Hsiu-ch'uan), who was exposed to Protestant Christian beliefs and claimed that he, as Jesus' younger brother, was called by God to destroy the Qing and establish the Kingdom of God on earth. Hong gained many followers among his fellow Hakka, a large ethnic group residing in Guangdong who belong to the Han Chinese majority but speak a different dialect and have their own unique customs. Armed fighting between the Taipings and Qing troops broke out in July 1850, and thousands of impoverished Chinese peasants and laborers, pirates and bandits joined the Taiping movement. The Taiping army marched as far north as Nanjing, where they established their capital. Foreign troops allied with Qing troops placed Nanjing under siege in 1862 and finally defeated the Taipings in 1864.

Dr. Sun Yat-sen (1866–1925), the founder of modern China, was born near Guangzhou. Sun led the Chinese Revolution of 1911 that overthrew the Qing, and in 1912 he was inaugurated as provisional president of the Republic of China in Nanjing, although he soon had to yield the presidency to Yuan Shikai. Sun returned to Guangzhou in July 1917 and tried unsuccessfully to persuade military commanders to join his republican cause. After a local warlord was ousted in 1920, Sun established a Republican government in Guangzhou on May 5, 1921, but this failed and he had to go into exile. In 1923 Sun returned once more to Guangzhou and gained assistance from his brother-in-law Chiang Kai-shek and military and political advisers from the U.S.S.R. Sun reorganized the Nationalist Party, which he had founded in 1900, as the Kuomintang (KMT). The Whampoa (Huangpu) Military Academy was established in Guangzhou in 1924 to train military leaders for the KMT and the recently founded Chinese Community Party (CCP), which were cooperating. In 1924 the CCP also established the National Peasant Movement Institute in Guangzhou to train party cadres. Mao Zedong (Mao Tse-tung) was the institute's director for one year and taught there, as did Zhou Enlai (Chou En-lai) and other party leaders. Sun died in 1925, and Chiang became the leader of the KMT and led the Northern

Expedition in 1926 to overthrow warlords in northern China. Guangzhou was occupied by Japanese troops during China's War of Resistance against Japan (1937–45; World War II). After Japan was defeated in 1945, the KMT, which controlled Guangzhou, fought a civil war with the CCP. On October 14, 1949, two weeks after the CCP founded the PRC, Communist troops took Guangzhou.

Although Guangzhou was no longer the only Chinese city where foreign trade was permitted, it remained one of the country's most important trading centers through the 20th century. Since 1949 Guangzhou has become heavily industrialized and very prosperous. Major industries in Guangzhou include porcelain and silk production, food processing, oil refining and plastics, chemicals and electronics. Major agricultural products include tea, sugarcane, mulberry trees for feeding silkworms, tropical fruit and seafood. In 1980 the Communist government of the People's Republic of China (PRC) established four areas along the Chinese coast as Special Economic Zones (SEZs) to encourage foreign trade and investment in China, increase Chinese exports, and import foreign technology and expertise in management. Three of the four SEZs, Shenzhen, Zhuhai and Shantou, were opened in Guangdong, close to Guangzhou, Macao and Hong Kong, which has become one of the world's largest trading centers. Hong Kong and Macao (which will revert to the PRC in 1999) are linked to Guangzhou by ferries, and a railroad line and toll highway also connect Guangzhou and Hong Kong. The Chinese Export Commodities Fair, also known as the Guangzhou (Canton) Fair, is held in Guangzhou for 20 days twice a year in April and October for business people who want to conduct foreign trade in China. Attendees are invited by China's national foreign trade corporations.

Major tourist sites include Guangzhou Museum; the Peasant Movement Institute, which is now a museum; Memorial Garden to the Martyrs, honoring Communists who were massacred by the KMT in 1927; the Mausoleum of the 72 Martyrs and Memorial of Yellow Flowers, which honors victims of the unsuccessful Canton insurrection of April 27, 1911 (six months prior to the overthrow of the Qing); and Sun Yat-sen Memorial Hall. Religious sites include the Temple of the Six Banyan Trees, Bright Filial Piety Temple, Five Genies Temple, Huaisheng Mosque and Sacred Heart Church, completed by a French architect in 1888. Shamian Island, the site of French and British concessions in the 19th century, is filled with colonial buildings that housed foreign trading offices and residences. Resort areas include Cultural Park, Orchid Park, Liuhua Park, and Haichuang Park in Henan, a southern district of Guangzhou, connected to the north bank of the Pearl River by Renmin Bridge. Yuexiu Park, the largest in Guangzhou, includes the Sun-Yatsen Monument, a five-story pagoda known as the Zhenhai Tower, and the Sculpture of the Five Goats, the symbol of Guangzhou, which is known as the City of Goats after the myth that it is the site where five immortals riding goats brought ears of rice to human beings. The name Guangzhou means "broad region." Other sites include the Guangdong Provincial Museum and the Guangzhou Zoo. Zhongshan University houses the Lu Xun (Lu Hsun) Museum, honoring China's greatest modern writer, who taught at the university in 1927. The Southern Yue Tomb Museum is situated on the

site of the tomb of Emperor Wen, the second ruler of the Southern Yue Kingdom, dating back to 100 B.C.

Tourists enjoy cruises on the Pearl River and excursions to resort areas outside the city, such as White Cloud Hills, Lotus Mountain, Jinsha Park and Conghua Hot Springs. Foshan (Buddha Hill), a town 21 miles southwest of Guangzhou, is a renowned traditional handicraft center, especially for papercutting, pottery, metal casting and silk weaving. Papercuts from Foshan are sold as tourist souvenirs throughout China. The main attraction in Foshan, especially for tour groups from Hong Kong, is the Ancestors Temple, a Daoist temple built in the late 11th century of interlocking beams without nails or metal. See also ARROW WAR; BRITISH EAST INDIA COMPANY; CANTON SYSTEM; CHIANG KAI-SHEK; CHINESE COMMUNIST PARTY; CIVIL WAR BETWEEN COMMUNISTS AND NATIONALISTS; FOREIGN TRADE AND INVESTMENT; GUANGDONG PROVINCE; GUANGZHOU FAIR; HAKKA; HONG KONG; JESUITS; LIN ZEXU; LU XUN; MACAO; MUSLIMS; NATIONALIST PARTY; OPIUM WAR; OVERSEAS CHINESE; PAPERCUTTING; PEARL RIVER; RICCI, MATTEO; SILK; SOUTH CHINA SEA; SPECIAL ECONOMIC ZONES; SUN YAT-SEN; TAIPING REBELLION; TREATY PORTS; TRIBUTE SYSTEM; UNEQUAL TREATIES; WHAMPOA MILITARY ACADEMY.

GUANGZHOU (CANTON) FAIR   Formally known as the Chinese Export Commodities Fair; a trade fair held twice annually in the southern port city of Guangzhou (Canton) to promote the export of Chinese products. Chinese trading corporations at the Guangzhou Fair also purchase commodities for industrial and agricultural production from foreign businesspeople, such as machinery, steel, fertilizers, grains and textile materials. The Guangzhou Fair is the largest annual event in the city next to the New Year Festival and is attended by tens of thousands of people. The fair is one of the most important channels through which foreign businesspeople are able to trade with the People's Republic of China (PRC). It is held in the Guangzhou Foreign Trade Centre, a large exhibition hall between the Guangzhou train station and the Dongfang Hotel, which houses permanent displays of Chinese and foreign products. The spring session of the Fair is held April 15–25 and the autumn session is October 15–25. Nineteen PRC trading delegations participate in the Guangzhou Fair: Cereals, Oils and Foodstuffs; Textiles; Light Industrial Products; Native Produce and Animal By-Products; Arts and Crafts; Silk; Metals and Minerals; Chemicals; Machinery; the United Trade Delegation of Instruments, Technology and Economic Cooperation; Machinery and Equipment; United Trade Delegation of the XINSHIDAI; Medicines and Health Products; Joint Ventures using Chinese and Foreign Investment; Electronics; United Trade Delegation of Nonferrous Metals and Metallurgical; Comprehensive Trade Delegation; Comprehensive Trade Delegation of Service and Culture; and Trade Delegation of Special Economic Zones. The Special Economic Zones (SEZs) are regions along the Chinese coast specially designated by the government to handle foreign trade.

Foreign businesspeople are required to obtain an invitation to attend the Guangzhou Fair. The Guangzhou Foreign Trade Centre issues the invitation cards, although longtime traders with the PRC receive invitations through the China National Foreign Trade Corporations. New clients who wish to attend the fair may apply for an invitation to the Chinese foreign trade corporation with which they may have business. Businesspeople may also acquire invitations at the last minute from the Commercial Section of the Chinese Embassy in their country or from China International Travel Service Company stationed in their country. At the Guangzhou Fair, they may also contact the Foreign Liaison Department for an invitation. Specialized mini-fairs are also frequently held in China by foreign trade corporations at central and local levels. See also CHINA INTERNATIONAL TRAVEL SERVICE; FOREIGN TRADE AND INVESTMENT; GUANGZHOU; MINISTRY OF FOREIGN TRADE AND ECONOMIC COOPERATION, SPECIAL ECONOMIC ZONES.

GUANGZHOU OPERA See OPERA, GUANGZHOU.

GUANHUA ("OFFICIAL LANGUAGE") See LANGUAGE, CHINESE; MANDARIN.

GUAN WARE See KUAN WARE.

GUANXI See CONNECTIONS.

GUANYIN Also known as Kuan Yin; the Goddess of Mercy in the Buddhist religion, which was introduced into China from India around the first century A.D. In India this was a male deity known as Avalokiteshvara, but in China the deity was given a female aspect by the 12th century A.D. She is considered the embodiment of compassion, wisdom and love and is frequently depicted sitting on a lotus flower—the Buddhist symbol of purity—and holding a vase of *lingzi* (*ling-tzu*), a plant which supposedly cures every illness. The Chinese traditionally believe that anyone who prays to Guanyin will be cured of illness. She is also portrayed holding a baby in her arms to show that she can help women to conceive. The name Guanyin means "She Who Hears All Sounds." She is also identified as Miao Shan, who was born the daughter of an emperor on the 19th day of the second month in the traditional lunar calendar. Her father had her killed because she wanted to become a Buddhist nun rather than marry, and she transformed into a holy spirit (*xian* or *hsien*) who was reincarnated as a human being in order to help other humans. Guanyin has been one of the most popular deities in China, particularly in the Pure Land Sect of Buddhism.

Guanyin is an attendant of Amitabha, the Buddhist God of Light and Lord of the Western Paradise. She is often shown accompanied by her two faithful disciples, Gintong and Yunu. Guanyin is so popular that statues of her have been kept not only in Buddhist temples but also in most temples of the Daoist religion, where she is ranked just below Mazipo, the Daoist Queen of Heaven. The 19th day of the second lunar month (roughly corresponding to March in the Western calendar), is the birthday of Guanyin, and devout women make special offerings of food, paper clothing and money to her statues on that day. See also AMITABHA; BUDDHISM; DAOISM; LOTUS; MAZIPO; PURE LAND SECT OF BUDDHISM.

GUGONG BOWUGUAN See FORBIDDEN CITY.

Guanyin, the Goddess of Mercy, symbolizes compassion, wisdom, and love for the Chinese. COURTESY, MUSEUM OF FINE ARTS, BOSTON

GUGONG (MANCHU IMPERIAL PALACE) See SHENYANG.

GUILIN A city in Guangxi-Zhuang Autonomous Region in southwestern China with a population of more than 300,000. One of the country's most popular tourist destinations because of its magnificent limestone karst scenery, Guilin is situated on the Li River (Lijiang), from which tourists riding in boats view the hundreds of oddly shaped mountains rising up individually from the fertile plains around the city. The mountains were formed as wind and water gradually eroded a thick layer of limestone that had been at the bottom of the sea covering the region 300 million years ago until it was thrust upward by geological activity. Each mountain is hollowed out with subterranean caves and rivers. Poets and painters throughout Chinese history have celebrated the beauty of Guilin. The most famous cave is known as Reed Flute Cave, named for the reeds at its opening that were formerly used to make flutes. A 1,600-foot trail through the cave leads past unique stalagmite and stalactite formations. At Zengpiyan Cave, archaeologists have excavated a Stone Age village 10,000 years old.

Elephant Trunk Mountain (Xiangbishan) resembles an elephant drinking from the water. According to legend, the Emperor of Heaven came down to conquer the earth and forced his elephant to work so hard that it became ill. Local farmers saved its life, and the grateful elephant stayed on earth to work for the farmers. The enraged Emperor of Heaven killed the elephant while he was drinking water, and he turned to stone in that position. When the waters of the Li River are high, a boat can pass through Water Moon Hole, a cave between the elephant's trunk and body. Other popular tourist sites in Guilin include a park known as District of the Two Lakes, Fubo Hill and Seven Star Park. The city is known as "Fragrant Blossom Wood" for its cassia trees that bloom in the autumn.

Guilin was founded by Emperor Qin Shi Huangdi, who unified China under the Qin dynasty (221–206 B.C.) and constructed the Ling Canal to join the Li and Xiang rivers, facilitating access between the Yangzi River (Changjiang) and the Pearl River in Guangdong Province. In 1644, the Ming dynasty government, escaping the Manchus who established the Qing dynasty (1644–1911), made Guilin their capital. During the Japanese occupation of China (War of Resistance against Japan, 1937–45), millions of Chinese nationalists and intellectuals fled inland and nearly 1 million settled in Guilin, which served as the national capital in 1936. The karst caves provided protection for hospitals, printing plants and theatrical troupes. The U.S. military built an air base at Guilin.

Many residents of Guilin are Zhuang, a Muslim ethnic group who comprise the largest of China's national minorities. A large portion of the modern city has been constructed since 1960, including hundreds of factories, with major products including textiles, pharmaceuticals, fertilizers and machinery. Traditional products continue to be made, such as wine, candy, bamboo chopsticks and umbrellas. Irrigation projects have made possible the production of rice, grain, bamboo, fruit and by-products of the cassia tree, such as tea and herbal medicine. See also GUANGXI-ZHUANG AUTONOMOUS REGION; LI RIVER AND LING CANAL; MING DYNASTY; WAR OF RESISTANCE AGAINST JAPAN; ZHUANG.

GUIYANG   The subtropical capital city of Guizhou Province in southwestern China, with a population of about 1.4 million. The city was not fully opened to foreign tourists until 1985. Guizhou is a very poor province inhabited by several national minority groups, mainly the Miao and Buyi peoples. Major sites in Guiyang include Qianlingshan Lake and Park, Great Happiness Chan (Zen) Buddhist Temple (*Hongfusi*), Huaxi Park, Nanjiao Park and Hebin Park. Number One Scholar Pavilion was built during the Ming dynasty (1368–1644) to honor scholars. The surrounding countryside is hilly and rocky with the large limestone formations known as karst. Rice, wheat and tea are cultivated in terraced fields on the hillsides. Huangguoshu Waterfall and

Hundreds of odd-shaped limestone mountains rise up from the fertile plains around Guilin.   S.E. MEYER

Dragon Cave (Longgong) are located about 100 miles outside Guiyang. Huangguoshu, 243 feet high, is China's highest waterfall. See also GUIZHOU PROVINCE, MIAO; MINORITIES, NATIONAL.

GUIZHOU PROVINCE

A poor, mountainous province in southwestern China covering an area of 67,200 square miles, with a population of about 29 million. The capital city is Guiyang. Guizhou Province is located on a large plateau that decreases in altitude from the northwest to the southeast. The plateau consists of limestone, slate and red sandstone, with underground rivers and lakes and numerous caves; there are oddly shaped karst formations caused by erosion. The Dalou Mountains rise in the north, and the Miaoling Mountains in the south form the watershed of Guizhou. The mountain ranges give the province a moist climate with warm summers and mild winters. Guizhou Province has the highest amount of rainfall in China, with 274 days of rain per year (except for the southern coast of Guangxi); monsoons strike the southern and eastern regions. Huangguoshu Falls in the Baishui River is, at 243 feet high, the largest waterfall in China. The Wu River (Wujiang), a tributary of the Yangzi River (Changjiang), cuts east to west through Guizhou but is not navigable by large ships. The province is very rich in natural resources, such as coal, iron ore, copper and aluminum. During the past three decades Guizhou has been industrialized, mainly with iron and steel, chemicals, and machine manufacturing. Only 12 percent of the land can sustain crops, primarily rice. Grains and tobacco are grown in the dryer northwest region. A famous product is *Maotai,* a clear alcohol beverage distilled from sorghum which is commonly used for making toasts at banquets throughout China.

Until the modern era, Guizhou was one of the most undeveloped and sparsely populated provinces in China. The original inhabitants of Guizhou were members of various national minority ethnic groups, especially the Miao people. More than half of the 4 million Miao in China today reside in Guizhou. Since 1949, the Chinese government has granted a measure of autonomy to regions with large numbers of national minorities, and in Guizhou these exist in the southeast, where many Miao and Bouyei people live, and the south, home of the Zhuang people. During the Han dynasty (206 B.C.–A.D. 220), Chinese officials established a degree of control over the non-Chinese minorities in Guizhou but penetrated only into the northern and eastern parts of the region. The Ming dynasty (1368–1644) established a provincial government and named the region Guizhou. In 1413 a road was built from remote Yunnan Province through Guizhou to the center of China, which increased government control of the area and encouraged settlement by Han Chinese and other settlers from neighboring provinces. Beginning in the 16th century, many poor Chinese moved into Guizhou, especially the Hakka, another national minority who were pushed out of more fertile regions. In 1726–29 the Qing dynasty (1644–1911) tried to install its own officials in Guizhou, resulting in numerous rebellions. Modernization of the province began in the 1940s when Japanese invading troops pushed the Nationalist (Kuomintang) government forces southwest into the area, and highways and railway lines were constructed. See also BOUYEI; GUIYANG; HAKKA; HAN; MAOTAI; MIAO; NATIONAL MINORITIES; WAR OF RESISTANCE AGAINST JAPAN; YUNNAN PROVINCE; ZHUANG.

GUNPOWDER See FIREWORKS AND GUNPOWDER.

GUO MORUO

(Kuo Mo-jo; 1892–1978) An important modern Chinese poet, essayist, playwright, literary critic and historian; née Kuo Kaichen. Guo was born in Sichuan Province to a merchant and landowning family. From 1897 to 1905 he received a traditional education in Chinese classical texts. After completing this education, he went to Japan in 1914 at age 22 to continue his studies, enrolling in a pre-medical program. Guo's family had forced him to enter an arranged marriage in China in 1912, but in Japan in 1916 he began a common-law relationship with Sato Tomiko, a Japanese woman who would bear him five children. In 1918 Guo entered medical school at Kyushu Imperial University at Fukuoka in southern Japan. In 1921 Guo left the university and went to Shanghai, where he joined the editorial staff of the Taidong (T'ai-tung) Publishing Company. At this time he also began his career in literature, writing romantic and patriotic poetry. His first collection of poems was published as *The Goddesses* (*Nushen;* 1921).

Guo and several friends then returned to Japan, where they founded the Creation Society. Between 1922 and 1924, Guo and his colleagues founded and edited the journals *Creation Quartery, Creation Weekly* and *Creation Daily.* However, the group had a falling out and ended the Creation Society in May 1924. While editing the journals, Guo had also translated a number of foreign books into Chinese, including works by the German authors Goethe and Nietzsche, and poems by German and English Romantic poets. Influenced by the New Culture Movement, he also translated classical Chinese poems into vernacular Chinese, known as *baihua* (*pai-hua*).

After graduating from medical school in April 1923, Guo brought his family to Shanghai, but his Japanese wife disliked China and took their children back to Japan. Guo returned to Japan in 1924, where he translated into Chinese *Social Organization and Social Revolution,* by the Japanese Marxist Kawakami Hajime; this work persuaded Guo to become a Marxist himself. After translating *Virgin Soil,* a novel by the Russian author Ivan Turgenev, into Chinese, Guo decided to return to China and work for the cause of social revolution. In China in 1924 he wrote his most well-known novel, *Fallen Leaves* (*Luoye* or *Lo-yeh*), which was based on the early days of his love affair with his Japanese wife. He lived in Shanghai, where he continued his writing, translating, and political activities. In 1925 he and others revived the Creation Society and began publishing a new journal, *The Flood* (*Hongshui* or *Hung-shui*).

In 1926 Guo became chairman of the Department of Literature at Sun Yat-sen University in Guangzhou (Canton) in southern China. Sun had founded the Chinese Nationalist Party (Kuomintang; KMT), which was cooperating with the recently founded Chinese Communist Party (CCP) to launch a National Revolutionary Army in 1926 against the warlords who controlled many regions of China (the Northern Expedition). Guo became chief of the propaganda section for the National Revolutionary Army. He soon became involved in political differences between different factions of the KMT and the CCP. After the KMT massacred many Chinese Communists in April 1927, Guo took part in the Nanchang Uprising by CCP members on August 1, 1927. Later that year he returned to Shanghai and went into hiding. In 1928 Guo and his family began a 10-year period of exile in Japan. During that time he studied ancient Chinese history and paleontology, including the earliest form of Chinese writing, the inscriptions on "oracle bones" from the Shang dynasty (1750–1040 B.C.). While residing in Japan, Guo wrote dozens of scholarly books, articles, short stories, essays and translations. In 1936 he joined the Writers' Association.

In 1937 Guo returned to China, while his family remained in Japan. That same year Japan invaded China, which began fighting its War of Resistance against Japan (1937–45; World War II). In China, Guo wrote anti-Japanese propaganda and helped found the left-wing newspaper, *Salvation Daily* (*Jiuwangribao* or *Chiu-wang jih-pao*). After Shanghai fell to the Japanese in November 1937, Guo escaped to Hong Kong. From there he went to Guangzhou to seek funding for his newspaper, which resumed publication in 1938. That year Guo went to Hankou, where the KMT had made their capital until they were forced to move to Chongqing in Sichuan Province. Guo stayed in Chongqing from the end of 1938 until 1946. In 1942 and 1943 he wrote five historical plays, including *The Tiger Tally* and *Qu Yuan,* based on historical events that inspired the Chinese people who were defending their country. Guo was also inspired by the American poet Walt Whitman, who had tended wounded and dying soldiers during the American Civil War and whose poems celebrate the human spirit. From 1943 to 1945, Guo produced further studies on the history of ancient China.

In June 1945, shortly before the end of the war, Guo went to the U.S.S.R. for the anniversary celebration of the Russian Academy of Sciences. In 1946 he took part in China's Political Consultative Conference, led by the CCP, and he also participated in the unsuccessful attempt to have the CCP and KMT reconcile their differences. In 1947 Guo resumed his scholarly work and moved to Hong Kong. In 1948 he joined the Chinese Communists in Hubei Province. In 1949, shortly before the CCP defeated the KMT and established the People's Republic of China (PRC), Guo helped found the All-China Federation of Writers and Artists, with himself as chairman. In September 1949, he was elected to the Chinese People's Political Consultative Conference (CPPCC), for which he traveled frequently to Shanghai, Hong Kong and Shenyang.

Guo held a number of high positions in the PRC. However, at the start of the Cultural Revolution in 1966, he was removed from his positions and forced to publicly state that his works should be burned because he had not properly understood the thought of Communist Chairman Mao Zedong (Mao Tse-tung). Guo was rehabilitated after the Cultural Revolution ended in 1976; he died in 1978. In 1982, the Chinese State Council designated the residence of Guo and his third wife, Yu Liqun (Yu Li-ch'un), in Beijing, where he had spent the last 15 years of his life, a historical site under government protection. On June 12, 1988, the 10th anniversary of Guo's death, the residence was opened to the public. The large compound includes houses built around a central courtyard in the traditional Chinese style. All of the rooms remain the same as they were when Guo and Yu lived there. In the formal parlor, Guo had met with friends from foreign countries and discussed government affairs with Chinese Premier Zhou Enlai (Chou En-lai) and major cultural and scientific figures. Guo's relatives have donated to this museum many of his manuscripts, books, calligraphy, paintings, letters and stone rubbings. See also CHINESE PEOPLE'S POLITICAL CONSULTATIVE CONFERENCE; CIVIL WAR BETWEEN CHINESE COMMUNISTS AND NATIONALISTS; CULTURAL REVOLUTION; NANCHANG; NEW CULTURE MOVEMENT; NORTHERN EXPEDITION; ORACLE BONES; PEOPLE'S REPUBLIC OF CHINA; WAR OF RESISTANCE AGAINST JAPAN.

GUO RUOXU See GUO XI; LANDSCAPE PAINTING.

GUO XI (Kuo Hsi; c. 1020–90) A landscape painter in the Northern Song school of painting also known as Chun Fu. Guo Xi was born in Henan Province. He became a professional court painter at the Northern Song capital in Kaifeng and was appointed head of the Imperial Academy of Painting under the patronage of Emperor Shenzong; (r. 1068–85). Guo Xi's colleagues considered him the finest painter of his generation. His style is very forceful and energetic, and his paintings contain complex and realistic details. He executed many monumental paintings that covered walls of rooms and large standing screens.

Guo Xi loved nature and traveled widely around China. His *Early Spring* (1072), a landscape painting on silk, is the best known of his few works that have survived. Guo Xi also wrote a critical work, *Advice on Landscape Painting* (*Shanshui Xun* or *Shan-shui hsun*), which became even more well known than his paintings. His son edited this book and added his own essays. (It has been translated into English.) In it Guo Xi advises artists to study nature, especially the way the four seasons change into each other, and to see how a natural scene can look different in the morning and the evening. He states the importance of painting movement in water and clouds, and of expressing the life force (*qi* or *ch'i*) in mountains. Guo Xi argues that a painting should make the viewer feel as if he were really there in the landscape. He discusses the "virtuous man" in the Confucian sense, who loves landscape paintings because he earnestly performs his duties as a government official and cannot take time off to wander through nature, but who refreshes himself by taking a symbolic journey through the landscape in a painting. See also LANDSCAPE PAINTING; NORTHERN SCHOOL OF PAINTING; QI.

GUOMINDANG See NATIONALIST PARTY.

GUOQING TEMPLE See HAN SHAN; TIANTAI SECT OF BUDDHISM.

GUOYU See PINYIN SYSTEM OF ROMANIZATION; PUTONGHUA.

GUQIN See QIN.

GURI See LACQUERWARE.

GUSAI See BANNER SYSTEM, MANCHU; MANCHU; NURHACHI.

H

HAI RIVER (Haiho He)   A major river that flows from west to east across the North China Plain and empties into the Bo Hai Gulf. Its upper course actually comprises five navigable tributaries that converge about 50 miles west of the Bo Hai Gulf near Tianjin City. Tianjin, China's third-largest city and the main port and industrial center in northern China, lies south of Beijing and stretches along the banks of the Hai River for about 10 miles. The city frequently suffered heavy flooding in the past, but dikes have been constructed to contain the floodwaters. The Hai River drains an area of 164,670 square miles, including the greater part of Hebei Province and parts of Shandong, Shanxi and Honan provinces, as well as the Inner Mongolia Autonomous Region and the Beijing and Tianjin regions. Along with the Grand Canal, the Hai River forms the navigable route from the plain of Hebei Province. See also BO HAI GULF; GRAND CANAL; HEBEI PROVINCE; TIANJIN.

HAIKOU   See HAINAN ISLAND.

HAINAN ISLAND (Hainan Dao)   A large tropical island that is the southernmost point in China. Located in the South China Sea 30 miles south of the Leizhou Peninsula of Guangdong Province, Hainan lies southwest of Hong Kong and close to Vietnam. Formerly administered by Guangdong, in 1988 the Chinese government designated Hainan Island China's 31st province and the largest of China's Special Economic Zones for foreign trade and investment. Hainan covers 13,000 square miles and has a population of more than 6 million. The island's original inhabitants are members of the Li and Miao national minorities who today live mainly in the center of the island and number about one million. The city of Tongshi is the cultural and political center of the Li and Miao autonomous region that has been established on Hainan. Haikou on the northern coast is the capital of Hainan Province.

Hainan was a place of exile for Han dynasty (206 B.C.–A.D. 220) government bureaucrats and others who fell out of favor with the imperial court. The Limu Ling Moun-tains make up one-fourth of the island and are covered with dense tropical forests, including rare woods such as ebony and rosewood. The island is also rich in mineral deposits, mainly iron ore, titanium and rock crystal; rose quartz deposits discovered on the island gave it the name by which it was traditionally known, "Rose-Jeweled Kingdom" (Qiongzhou). Oil deposits were recently discovered off the southwest coast. Hydroelectric power is provided by the Sun and Nandu rivers on Hainan's western side. Rice, sugarcane, coffee, cotton, rubber and tropical fruits are cultivated on the coastal plains. Fishing, sugar refining and food processing are important industries. Pearls are cultivated on the southeast coast. On the eastern coast are lovely beaches and Hainan's largest coconut plantation.

Haikou is Hainan's principal city and chief port for shipping agricultural products to the mainland. It was a busy trading port as far back as the Tang dynasty (618–907). Four development zones have been established around Haikou where hundreds of projects have been put into operation. More than 20 ports have been constructed. China has actively promoted financial investment, especially from Hong Kong, to develop Hainan as a tourist resort. Sanya is the main tourist center on the southern end of the island. International flights land at recently opened Fenghuang Airport in Sanya.During the past four decades, many overseas Chinese from Malaysia, Indonesia and Vietnam have settled on Hainan Island and contributed much to its development. See also MIAO; MINORITIES, NATIONAL; OVERSEAS CHINESE; PEARL; SPECIAL ECONOMIC ZONES; VIETNAM WAR AND CHINA.

HAKKA   Also known as Kejia (K'o-chia); a group of Chinese who belong to the Han ethnic majority but have their own unique dialect, customs and cuisine. The Hakka have settled mainly in southern Jiangsu and Guangdong provinces in southern China, although they originally lived in the north. The Hakka language is a distinct dialect that is closer to Mandarin, the form of Chinese spoken in the north, than the southern Cantonese dialect spoken in Guangdong. The name Hakka means "guest people," "guest families" or "strangers," indicating that they came from far away. In the third century B.C. the Hakka inhabited the Yellow River valley region on the southern border of Shandong Province and the northern border of Anhui and Henan Provinces. Severe persecution during the Qin dynasty (221–206 B.C.) caused them to begin migrating southward toward Zhejiang, Fujian and Jiangsu Provinces. Further persecutions in the fifth century A.D. pushed them further south, and in the 10th–13th centuries a large number of Hakka ended up in Guangdong, where the present families are able to trace their genealogies as far back as 20 generations. There is also a large Hakka community in Hong Kong, especially in the New Territories. In the 19th century many Hakka converted to Christianity; the Taiping Rebellion, which caused great turmoil in China from 1850 to 1864, was led by a Hakka named Hong Xiuquan (Hung Hsiu-chuan; 1813–64), who proclaimed that he was the younger brother of Jesus Christ.

The peasant Hakka women's style of dress is distinct from that of the Cantonese women in Guangdong. They wear a long jacket that comes down nearly to the knees and an unusual wide-brimmed hat without a crown but with a curtain of cloth hanging from the brim. Unlike Han Chinese women, Hakka women never bound their feet, and they have had more freedom than other Chinese women.

Hakka cuisine does not rely heavily on spices, garlic or strong oils but emphasizes fresh, crisp vegetables that are lightly cooked to bring out their delicate flavors. Well-known Hakka dishes include chicken rubbed with salt and baked, and vegetables and bean curd stuffed with minced fish. See also HAN; HONG KONG; HONG XIUQUAN; TAIPING REBELLION.

HALL OF THE IMPERIAL VAULT OF HEAVEN See TEMPLE OF HEAVEN.

HALL OF PRAYER FOR GOOD HARVESTS See TEMPLE OF HEAVEN.

HAMI A city that is the gateway to Xinjiang-Uighur Autonomous Region (formerly known as Chinese Turkestan) in western China. Hami lies in a fault depression about 650 feet below sea level and experiences extreme temperatures ranging from a high of 109 degrees F in summer to a low of -26°F in winter. Formerly known as Yiwu, Yizhou or Kumul, Hami was an important oasis city on the Silk Road along which China traded silk and other luxury goods with the Mediterranean world. In 1986 archaeologists excavated more than 80 tombs around Hami and discovered 50 corpses believed to be more than 3,000 years old. The corpses, well preserved due to the dry desert climate, are dressed in brightly colored woolen clothing, fur hats and leather boots.

The earliest surviving reference to Hami is in a book, made of pieces of bamboo and bound with white silk, that was excavated from a second-century B.C. tomb in Henan province in Central China. It recounts the semilegendary journey of Emperor Mu, the fifth emperor of the Zhou dynasty (1100–256 B.C.), to visit the goddess Xiwangmu (Hsi Wang Mu), the Queen Mother of the West. On his return he supposedly stayed in Hami for three days, and the inhabitants gave him 300 horses and 2,000 sheep and cattle.

The Chinese regarded Hami as the key to access to the northwest, and the city was often taken by various nomadic tribes who inhabited regions to the north and northwest and frequently threatened China. In 73 B.C. General Ban Chao of the Han dynasty (206 B.C.–A.D. 220) defeated an army of the Xiongnu (Hsiung-nu) tribe and established a colony at Hami. Trade along the Silk Road became very active during the Han dynasty. After the Han fell, China became divided into many kingdoms, and in the sixth and early seventh centuries Hami became part of the kingdoms founded by the Eastern and Western Turks. When China was reunified under the Tang dynasty (618–907), Tang Emperor Taizong (Tai-tsung) regained control of Hami and other oasis cities in the Central Asian region. The Chinese Buddhist monk Xuanzang (Hsuan-tsang; 602–64), who made a famous pilgrimage to India to gather Buddhist scriptures, rested for several weeks in Hami. The renowned Italian traveler Marco Polo (1254–1324) traveled through "the province of Kamul" on his journey to the court of Mongol ruler Khubilai Khan, who established the Yuan dynasty (1279–1368) in China. Polo recorded that the inhabitants of Hami were very hospitable. During the Ming dynasty (1368–1644), Hami sent missions to the Chinese emperor in Beijing which acknowledged his suzerainty under the tribute system.

Despite being a vassal of China, Hami was invaded a number of times by the nearby oasis city of Turpan. In 1681, during the Qing dynasty (1644–1911), the Dzungar Mongols took Hami, Turpan and most of eastern Chinese Turkestan. The Qing sent forces to defeat the Dzungars and defeated Galdan, their leader, in 1696. But his descendants continued fighting the Qing, and in 1713 Galdan's nephew captured Hami, although Qing forces soon removed him, and in 1754 they gave the Dzungars their final defeat. From 1697 to 1930, Uighur kings ruled Hami. Initially they sent tribute missions to the Qing, but in the 19th century they became involved in several Muslim rebellions in Xinjiang. In 1880 the Chinese general Zuo Zongtang (Tso Tsung-t'ang) defeated Yakub Beg, the Muslim rebel who ruled Kashgar, and established his headquarters in Hami to oppose Russian forces that had occupied a region west of Hami. After the last Hami king died in 1930, the city was administered by China, but a Muslim rebellion spread through Xinjiang and much of Hami was destroyed.

Today Hami has been rebuilt and has a population of about 300,000, including members of minority ethnic groups such as Uighurs, Kazakhs, Mongols and Hui, Han ethnic Chinese who practice the Muslim religion. Hami is now famous for growing grapes, dates, watermelons and more than 30 varieties of the delicious Hami melons (*Hami gua*), which are also sold in Turpan. The region is irrigated by more than 100 underground water channels that bring water from the melting snows of the Tianshan Mountain Range. Hami also has a number of industries that produce carpets, clothing, plastics, cement and canned fruits. Tourist sites include the tombs of the Hami kings, the tomb of the seventh-century Muslim missionary Gai Si (Kai Ssu), and a museum that exhibits one of the ancient corpses. A 300-foot section of the old palace wall can still be seen. See also BAN CHAO; HUI; KAZAKH; MONGOL; MUSLIMS; POLO, MARCO; SILK ROAD; TAIZONG, EMPEROR (TANG); TIAN MOUNTAIN RANGE; TURPAN; UIGHUR; XINJIANG-UIGHUR AUTONOMOUS REGION; XIONGNU; XUANZANG.

HAN ("Han people," *Han ren* or *Han jen*)   Also known as Han Chinese; the ethnic group to which 91 percent of the Chinese population belongs. This group traditionally includes all people who speak and write the Chinese language, of which there are eight dialects and many subdialects but only a single written form. Han Chinese also subscribe to longstanding Han cultural values and customs, especially for family rituals such as weddings, childbirth, funerals and propitiation of deceased relatives, known as ancestor worship. The name Han, or "people of Han," derives from the Han dynasty (206 B.C.–A.D. 220), when the Chinese people were merged into a unified civilization. However, there are still differences within the Han people because many other groups have been assimilated into the Han over the centuries. Members of these groups have become Han by using the written Chinese language, subscribing to Han values and customs, and practicing agriculture in the manner of Han villages. The largest division among the Han has been between north and south. The eight Han dialects, which are not mutually understood, include Mandarin (the northern dialect, considered the "official" dialect), Wu, Yue, Xiang, Hakka, Gan, Southern Min and Northern Min. The Yue dialect includes speakers of Cantonese, the largest southern group, in Guangdong Province.

Citizens of China who do not belong to the Han ethnic group belong to one of the country's national minorities, 55 of which had been officially designated by the Chinese government as of 1986. Some of these groups have been given a degree of autonomy in their regions, for example, Guangxi-Zhuang Autonomous Region in southern China. Many of the minorities inhabit lands where Han-style agriculture cannot be practiced, such as deserts, mountains or steppes where nomads raise sheep and other animals that require large areas to graze. The Han people have always considered themselves to be "civilized" and have tended to look down upon members of the national minorities. From the Han dynasty until modern times, the Han have always dominated the Chinese government and economy. The modern concept of the Han as a nationality (*Han minzu*) emerged with China's transition from an imperial system to a modern nation with the overthrow of the Qing dynasty and the founding of the Republic of 1911. Sun Yat-sen (1866–1925), leader of the republican movement, maintained that there were "Five Peoples of China," the Han majority, unified into a single group, and the Manchu, the Mongolian, the Tibetan, and the Hui (ethnic Chinese who are Muslim) minority groups. The Communist government that has ruled China since 1949 has retained Sun's emphasis on the Han as a unified group but has expanded the number of minority groups. The government has also sent many Han people to settle in regions dominated by minority groups, adding to the tension between the Han and the minorities. See also AGRICULTURE; ANCESTOR WORSHIP; FUNERALS; HAN DYNASTY; MANDARIN; MINORITIES, NATIONAL; WRITING SYSTEM, CHINESE; WEDDINGS, TRADITIONAL.

HAN DYNASTY (206 B.C.–A.D. 220)   One of the longest dynasties in Chinese history, and the period when many imperial institutions became established, notably the Confucian-based imperial bureaucracy. Han is the name of the ethnic group who form the majority of the Chinese population. The Han replaced the Qin dynasty (221–206 B.C.), which had been founded when King Zheng of Qin overthrew the Zhou dynasty (1100–256 B.C.) and proclaimed himself Qin Shi Huangdi, the "First Emperor" (r. 221–210 B.C.) of a unified Chinese empire. He was a harsh ruler who used the concepts of the Legalist school of thought, which advocated that a ruler should have absolute power. After he died and his son Hu Hai became second emperor, rebellions began breaking out around the empire. Court rivalries forced Hu Hai to commit suicide in 207 B.C. and caused the deaths of his highest advisers. Zi Ying, the First Emperor's nephew, became the third emperor but in less than two months surrendered to a rebel army in 206 B.C., and the Qin Empire fell into civil warfare. The strongest region was the one that claimed to succeed the former Zhou state of Chu, in the Yangzi River (Changjiang) valley. Two Chu leaders, Xiang Yu (Hsiang Yu) and Liu Bang (Liu Pang), contended for power. Liu Bang became king of a region to the west of Chu, defeated the forces of both Qin and Chu led by Xiang Yu, and in 206 B.C. accepted the title of King of Han. In 202 B.C. he proclaimed himself the emperor of the Han dynasty. He is known by his reign name, Emperor Gaodi (Kao-ti; r. 206–195 B.C.).

Gaodi came from the peasant class and was illiterate, yet he recognized the need for educated officials to advise him and to administer the Han Empire. On his top adviser's recommendation, Gaodi moved his capital to Chang'an (modern Xi'an), across the Wei River from the Qin capital of Xianyang. Using the teachings of the classical scholar and teacher Confucius (551–479 B.C.), which emphasize hierarchical order and harmony in society and the family, Gaodi laid the foundations for an imperial bureaucracy that would be carried on through succeeding dynasties. Emperor Qin Shi Huangdi had burned huge number of books, so Han scholars attempted to restore the Chinese classical literature and philosophy that had been recorded during the Zhou dynasty. A collection of books came to be known as the Five Classics of Confucianism, and it formed the basis of the examination system that was used to select bureaucratic officials.

Gaodi was succeeded by his son, known as Emperor Huidi (Hui-ti; r. 195–188 B.C.). When he died, Gaodi's widow, Empress Lu, continued the Liu family line by having infants placed on the throne. When she died in 180 B.C., one of Gaodi's sons took the throne, known as Emperor Wendi (Wen-ti; r. 180–157 B.C.). Chinese historians look to Wendi as the model of a virtuous ruler who is concerned for the well-being of his subjects. He continued his father's efforts to develop a centralized government bureaucracy and absorb former kingdoms into the Han Empire. Wendi was succeeded by Jingdi (Ching-ti; r. 157–141 B.C.), who also continued these policies. The next emperor, known as Han Wudi (Wu-ti; r. 141–87 B.C.), extended the empire to the west and dealt with nomadic tribes on the northern border, especially the Xiongnu (Hsiung-nu), who conducted frequent raids into China. Wudi sent one of his best generals, Zhang Qian (Chang Ch'ien), to form alliances with tribes to the northwest against the Xiongnu. He made several journeys in which he garnered much information about the peoples beyond the Han borders and their desire to trade with China, especially for silk, which gave rise to the so-called Silk Road. China also began purchasing horses from western tribes, especially in Ferghana, for military purposes.

A battle among opposing political factions erupted in Chang'an in 91 B.C., four years before the death of Wudi, and the empress and heir apparent were forced to commit suicide. When Wudi died in 87 B.C., he was succeeded by Emperor Zhaodi (Chao-ti; 87–74 B.C.), but the Han dynasty declined into weakness and factionalism. During the reign of Emperor Chengdi (Ch'eng-ti; r. 33–7 B.C.), the Wang family became powerful, and Wang Mang became regent to the infant Han emperor. He then attempted to replace the Han with his own dynasty; known as Xin. The Xin dynasty lasted from A.D. 9 to 23 and is also known as the Wang Mang Interregnum. It ended when a peasant rebel band known as the Red Eyebrows captured Chang'an and killed Wang Mang in A.D. 23, causing civil war to break out all over China. In A.D. 25 Liu Xiu (Liu Hsiu) restored Han rule, and in A.D. 27 the Red Eyebrows surrendered.

Liu Xiu, known as Emperor Guangwudi (Kuang Wu-ti), established his capital at Luoyang in modern Henan Province. The period before the usurpation of the throne by Wang Mang is known as the Western, or Former, Han dynasty (206 B.C.–A.D. 8) and the period after it as the Eastern, or Later, Han dynasty (A.D. 25–220). Guangwudi returned to the practices of the Western Han dynasty, and the Eastern Han was strongest under his rule and that of his immediate successors. Ban Biao (Pan Piao) and his son Ban Gu (Pan Ku) and daughter Ban Zhao (Pan Chao), all of them prominent scholars, compiled the *History of the Former Han Dynasty* (*Hanshu*), which became the model for histories written by later Chinese dynasties. Ban Zhao also wrote the *Code for Women* (*Nujie* or *Nu-chieh*). Paper was invented in China during the Han dynasty and was produced on a large scale for record-keeping in the imperial bureaucracy. The Han general Ban Chao, another son of Ban Biao, led a large Chinese expedition west to the Caspian Sea and brought most of Central Asia under the control of the Chinese Empire from A.D. 73 to 97.

Beginning in the first century A.D., the Han court fell into political struggles among the families of various imperial concubines, as well as government officials and eunuchs, who played a major role in the court. In A.D. 184, a group known as the Yellow Turbans, which took its ideology from the Daoist tradition, led an armed rebellion which was suppressed in A.D. 196 but sparked political unrest throughout China. The country became divided among a number of kingdoms. Cao Cao (Ts'ao Ts'ao), a brilliant military general under the Han, became the virtual dictator of China north of the Yangzi River (Changjiang). After he died, his son, Cao Pi (Ts'ao P'i) forced the last Han emperor to abdicate the throne in A.D. 200 and founded the kingdom of Wei (or Cao Wei). Wei fought with two other kingdoms, Shu (or Shu Han) and Wu, during the so-called Three Kingdoms Period (220–80). The period between the downfall of the Han dynasty and the reunification of China under the Sui dynasty (581–618) is known as the Six Dynasties Period (220–589). It includes the Three Kingdoms Period, the Western Jin dynasty (265–316) and Eastern Jin dynasty (317–420), and the Northern and Southern dynasties (420–589). See also BAN CHAO; BAN GU AND BAN ZHAO; CAO CAO; CHANG'AN; CODE FOR WOMEN; CONFUCIANISM; EASTERN HAN DYNASTY; EUNUCH; FIVE CLASSICS OF CONFUCIANISM; GAODI, EMPEROR; HAN; HORSE; IMPERIAL BUREAUCRACY; IMPERIAL EXAMINATION SYSTEM; IRON TECHNOLOGY AND STEEL INDUSTRY; LEGALIST SCHOOL OF THOUGHT; LUOYANG; PAPER; QIN DYNASTY; RED EYEBROWS REBELLION; SALT MONOPOLY; SILK ROAD; SIMA QIAN; SIMA TAN; SIX DYNASTIES PERIOD; WENDI, EMPEROR; WESTERN HAN DYNASTY; WANG MANG; WUDI, EMPEROR; XIONGNU; YELLOW TURBANS REBELLION; ZHANG QIAN; NAMES OF INDIVIDUAL DYNASTIES.

HAN DYNASTY (947–950) See FIVE DYNASTIES PERIOD.

HAN FEI TZU See HAN FEI ZI.

HAN FEIZI (Han Fei Tzu; c. 280–233 B.C.) The most important theoretician of the Legalist school of thought, also known as the School of Law. He was born a prince in the ruling family of the state of Han. Han Feizi (*zi* means "master") drew up plans for Han to increase its power, but the Han ministers did not utilize them, so he concentrated on writing essays on his philosophy of government. In 233 B.C. the state of Han sent him on a mission to the neighboring state of Qin, whose power threatened Han, and the Qin king apparently decided to give Han Feizi a position in his own government. One of the Qin king's ministers, Li Si (Li Ssu), removed his rival by imprisoning Han Feizi and forcing him to commit suicide with poison. Han Feizi and Li Si had both been fellow students of Xunzi (Hsun Tzu; c. 298–238 B.C.), then the leading philosopher in the Confucian school of thought. Li Si later became the first prime minister of the Qin dynasty (221–206 B.C.) under Emperor Qin Shi Huangdi, who brutally employed Legalist principles to create a centralized Chinese empire. Confucian scholars attributed the rapid collapse of the Qin to the principles of Legalism, which they despised, although they appreciated the practical recommendations for government put forth in Legalist manuals.

Legalists in turn criticized the Confucian view that people could be educated to be virtuous. Han Feizi and other Legalist thinkers argued that human nature is basically selfish, and thus the social order can be maintained only when the ruler imposes rules his subjects must obey without questioning and enforces them with strict punishments. In Han Feizi's view, "the ruler alone possesses power." The book known as the *Han Feizi* is the most complete explanation of Legalist philosophy. It contains essays written by Han Feizi himself and by other Legalist thinkers, as well as some non-Legalist materials. Some fragments are attributed to Shen Dao (Shen Tao) (fl. 310 B.C.), and the rest to famous ministers of powerful states, such as Guan Zhong of Qi (d. 645 B.C.), Lord Shang Yang of Qin (d. 338 B.C.) and Shen Buhai (Shen Pu-hai) of Han (d. 337 B.C.). The book regards the three essentials of government to be "power" (*shi*), "law" (*fa*) and "performance and title" (*xing ming* or *hsin ming*), the method for controlling government officials by comparing their actions with their precisely defined responsibilities. The concepts of Han Feizi prepared the way for the central bureaucracy that was developed by the Han dynasty (206 B.C.–A.D. 220) to govern China and that continued up to the modern era, through the combination of Legalist and Confucian principles. See also CONFUCIANISM; HAN DYNASTY; IMPERIAL BUREAUCRACY; LEGALIST SCHOOL OF THOUGHT; LI SI; QIN DYNASTY; SHANG YANG, LORD; XUNZI.

HAN HSIANG-TZU See EIGHT IMMORTALS.

HAN RIVER (Han Shui)   The main tributary of the Yangzi (Changjiang), China's largest river. The Han River basin covers 67,875 square miles in Shaanxi, Henan and Hubei provinces. It has a greater discharge than the Yellow River (Huanghe), China's second longest river. The Han originates on the slopes of the Qinling mountain range in central China and flows southeast for about 935 miles, then joins the Yangzi at Wuhan in Hubei Province. Its frequent changes in volume are a constant threat to the dense population and rich agriculture lands of its lower basin. The Han and Huai rivers provide the rough dividing line between North and South China. See also HUAI RIVER; YANGZI RIVER.

HAN SHAN   An unconventional poet during the Tang dynasty (618–907) whose works have been collected in an anthology of more than 300 poems. Han Shan's name literally means "Master of Cold Mountain." The *Han-Shan Shi* (*Poetry of Han Shan*) has been translated into several English versions as *Cold Mountain* and is considered one of the greatest literary works of the Chan sect of Buddhism, known as Zen in Japan, where Han Shan's poetry is greatly admired as the expression of an enlightened Zen layman. The only source of information about Han Shan, apart from facts that can be gleaned from his poems, is a preface to the anthology by Yin Luqiu (Yin Lu-ch'iu), supposedly a Tang government official, which may be spurious. Yin Luqiu states that no one knew where Han Shan came from and that he was a poor, shabbily dressed and eccentric scholar who lived as a recluse at Cold Mountain, 20 miles west of the town of Tangxing, in the Tiantai Mountain Range south of the Bay of Hangzhou in the southeastern Chinese province of Zhejiang. Han Shan frequently visited his friend Shi De (Shih Te), who worked in the kitchen of Guoqing Temple and gave him scraps of food to take home. This site is the center of the prominent Tiantai Sect of Buddhism, active in Japan as the Tendai Sect.

The name Shi De means "The Foundling." The two friends are portrayed in Chan ink paintings as comically grotesque and always laughing together. Yin Liqiu says that he was taken to visit Han Shan and Shi De at the temple by the Chan monk Feng Gan (Feng Kan). The two eccentrics were laughing uproariously in front of the kitchen stove; when they saw Feng Gan, they mocked him for bowing to them. The other monks ran into the kitchen, astonished at their impudence, but Han Shan and Shi De ran out of the temple and returned to Cold Mountain before anyone could catch them. When gifts of clothing and medicine were sent, Han Shan shouted, "Thieves!" and disappeared into a cave. Shi De also vanished. Yin Liuqiu had the monks assist him in collecting the poems that Han Shan had written on trees, rocks and the walls of houses and offices in the town, as well as some poems composed by Shi De.

The bulk of poems in the anthology do appear to be written by one author, an educated farmer who left home because of poverty and family problems and wandered extensively until he retired to Cold Mountain. His poems are written in colloquial language, even the slang of his time. They cover a wide range of subjects and criticize the government bureaucracy, Buddhist priests, and seekers of immortality in the Daoist religion. Most memorable are the poems about his life as a hermit on remote Cold Mountain, replete with Chan Buddhist terms and images. In the introduction to his translation of Han Shan's poems, the famous British scholar Arthur Waley (1889–1966) explains that Cold Mountain is not only a place but a state of mind, the place where the Buddha can be found in one's own self.

The Han Shan Temple (Hanshan Si; Cold Mountain Temple) can be seen about three miles west of the city of Suzhou in Jilin Province in eastern China. Constructed in 503–08, the temple later acquired the name of Han Shan because he resided here for a time. The temple was restored in 1905, and Japanese monks presented a bronze bell to replace the bell that had formerly been taken away by Japanese invaders. See also CHAN SECT OF BUDDHISM; INK PAINTING; TIANTAI SECT OF BUDDHISM; WALEY, ARTHUR.

HAN SUYIN (1917–)   Real name Elizabeth Comber; a best-selling author of books on China and other Asian countries. Han Suyin is a pen name meaning "The Chinese gamble [for liberty]." She is the daughter of a Chinese scholar and engineer named Chow and his French wife, whose family name is Denis. Han Suyin has asserted that she writes as an Asian. Her books have been praised for presenting an honest and objective picture of conditions in contemporary Asia. She was born in Beijing and educated at Yenching University and in Brussels and London, where she earned a degree in medicine. In London she met General Tang, a Chinese diplomat and military attaché. They returned to China, where they married in 1938. He fought with the Nationalist (Kuomintang) Army against the Japanese, who had invaded China (War of Resistance against Japan, 1937–45), and she practiced medicine. The deterioration of China due to Japanese aggression and the corruption of rival Chinese factions became the subject of her first book, *Destination China* (1942), which she wrote with an American woman missionary who remained anonymous. She also gave birth to a daughter named Mei. However, General Tang was killed fighting the Communists in China's civil war. Han Suyin had returned to London during the war to complete her medical studies. She felt a strong duty to help the Chinese people and returned to China, which had become Communist in 1949. However, she was treated as an outsider there, and she did not want to live in a totalitarian state, so she left the country and settled in Hong Kong. From then until 1964 she practiced medicine in Hong Kong, Malaysia and Singapore. She then gave up medicine to spend all her time writing and giving lectures.

In 1953, Han Suyin published her most popular book, *A Many-Splendored Thing*, about her love affair as a Eurasian woman with a Western foreign correspondent, set in the midst of the postwar social and political turmoil in the beautiful city of Hong Kong. Her lover was killed while covering the Korean War. (This book was made into a popular American movie, *Love Is a Many-Splendored Thing* (1955), starring William Holden and Jennifer Jones.) In 1952, Han Suyin married Leonard Comber, a former British policeman who had become a scholar of Asian cultures. By 1957 they were living in Singapore, then part of Malaysia, where she ran a medical clinic and gave lectures to raise money for charities. Her book, *And Rain My Drink*, depicts the conflicts in Malaysia at that time between British colonialism and emerging nationalism. Some of her other best-selling works include *Till Morning Comes, The Mountain Is Young, The Crippled Tree, A Mortal Flower* and *China in the Year 2001.* Between 1956 and 1974 she conducted a series of 11 unprecedented long interviews with Chinese premier Zhou Enlai (Chou En-lai; 1898–1976). Her book, based on these and further interviews with his family and colleagues and research in Chinese archives, was published in 1994 as *Eldest Son: Zhou Enlai and the Making of Modern China, 1898–1976.* See also CIVIL WAR BETWEEN COMMUNISTS AND NATIONALISTS; HONG KONG; NATIONALIST PARTY; PEOPLE'S REPUBLIC OF CHINA; WAR OF RESISTANCE AGAINST JAPAN.

HAN XIANGZI   See EIGHT IMMORTALS.

HAN YU (768–824)   An official during the Tang dynasty (618–907) who was also a famous poet, Confucian scholar, and the greatest prose writer of his time. Han Yu's ideas laid the foundation for the revival of Confucian thought during the Song dynasty (960–1279), known as Neo-Confucianism. He emphasized two Confucian texts, the *Book of Mencius* (*Mengzi* or *Meng Tzu*) and the *Great Learning* (*Daxue* or *Ta Hsueh*), originally a chapter in the *Book of Rites* (*Liji* or *Li-Chi*), one of the canonical Five Classics of Confucianism (*wujing* or *wu-ching*). Influenced by Han Yu, Neo-Confucianists later combined the *Book of Mencius* and the *Great Learning* with two other texts, the *Doctrine of the Mean* (*Zhongyong* or *Chung Yung*) and the *Analects* (Sayings) of Confucius (*Lunyu*), to form the canonical Four Books of Confucianism (*sishu* or *ssu-shu*). Han Yu was also a vigorous opponent of the Buddhist religion, foreshadowing the official Tang government persecution of Buddhism in 845. Owing to centuries of trade with Central Asia along the Silk Road, by the Tang dynasty the Chinese had become open to many foreign cultural influences, including the religion of Buddhism, which had been founded in India and introduced into China around the first century A.D. Han Yu subscribed to the moralistic and humanistic standpoint of Confucianism, which disliked the Buddhist viewpoint that existence and human personality are an illusion and condemned such Buddhist practices as celibacy and mortification of the body for undermining the Confucian emphasis on respect for one's parents (known as "filial piety") and continuation of the family line. In 819 Han Yu wrote an essay, *On the Bone of Buddha,* to protest the display in the imperial palace in Chang'an (the modern city of Xi'an in Shaanxi Province) of a finger bone that was supposedly a relic from the Buddha himself. Denouncing what he believed was the superstitious and subversive nature of the foreign religion, Han Yu argued that the government should destroy the "decayed and rotted bone" and outlaw Buddhism, which he blamed for stirring up trouble ever since the religion had been brought into China. This essay greatly angered Tang emperor Xianzong (Hsien-tsung; r. 805–20), who sent Han Yu into exile in southern China. See also BUDDHISM; CONFUCIANISM; FILIAL PIETY; FIVE CLASSICS OF CONFUCIANISM; FOUR BOOKS OF CONFUCIANISM; GREAT LEARNING, THE; MENCIUS; NEO-CONFUCIANISM; TANG DYNASTY.

HANGZHOU (Hangchow)   The capital city of Zhejiang Province in eastern China and one of the old imperial capitals, along with Xi'an, Luoyang, Kaifeng, Nanjing and Beijing. Hangzhou, located in northern Zhejiang at the southern end of the Grand Canal, and between West Lake (Xihu) and the Qiantang River, has long been renowned for its beauty and attracts many tourists. The Italian traveler Marco Polo (1254–1324) praised Hangzhou as the most beautiful and prosperous city in the world. It was paired with Suzhou, a charming city of canals and gardens in Jilin Province in eastern China, in the famous saying, "In Heaven there is Paradise, on Earth there are Hangzhou and Suzhou." Unfortunately, most of Hangzhou has been rebuilt since 1949, and the only place that preserves its traditional beauty is West Lake, to the west of Hangzhou, a popular tourist attraction. West Lake carp, a large freshwater fish, is a favorite dish in the Chinese cuisine, cooked with a sweet-and-sour recipe that originated in Hangzhou.

Today the city of Hangzhou has a population of about 1.3 million and has been modernized and industrialized. The region was settled in ancient times, but the city did not begin developing until the Grand Canal was completed in 610. In 799 the governor began construction of dikes to protect the city from floods, and this work was continued by Governor Bai Juyi (Po Chu-i; 772–846), who was also one of the three greatest poets of the Tang dynasty (618–907). When the Tang was overthrown, the region of the Yangzi Delta and modern Zhejiang became the kingdom of Wuyue (907–78) with Hangzhou as the capital. Hangzhou flourished after 1126, when the Song dynasty (960–1279) imperial court was forced to flee its capital at Kaifeng due to invasions by the nomadic Jurchen people, and made Hangzhou the capital of the Southern Song dynasty. Numerous artists and literati, or scholars, also settled in the area, and Hangzhou served as China's cultural center for many centuries, even after the Song dynasty was replaced by the Mongol Yuan dynasty (1279–1368). Su Shi (also known as Su Dongpo or Su Tung p'o; 1036–1101), another of China's most important poets, lived in the city. From the 10th through 12th centuries, Hangzhou was also a major center for printing.

When the Mongols overthrew the Song and established the Yuan dynasty, Hangzhou retained its importance and was called by the Mongols, Xingzaisuo ("The Temporary Residence of the Emperor"). Marco Polo, who served the Yuan government for a time, and other Western travelers visited the city during this period. Hangzhou remained wealthy during the Ming (1368–1644) and Qing (1644–1911) dynasties because of its lucrative silk industry and its location in a highly fertile rice-cultivating region. The city has been one of China's main centers for silk production since the Tang dynasty, and today the Hangzhou Silk Printing and Dyeing Complex is the largest of its kind in China. When the Chinese Ming dynasty overthrew the Yuan, Hangzhou began to suffer attacks by pirates in the 16th century. The city was greatly damaged in the 19th century during the Taiping Rebellion (1850–64), and although rebuilt, it never regained its former prominence.

Most of Hangzhou's scenic and historic spots of interest to tourists are found at West Lake, including boat trips on the lake, the Zhejiang Provincial Museum and Library, the Sun Yat-sen Garden, the Shing Yin Si Temple, and a pavilion known as the Autumn Moon on the Calm Lake. Another popular tourist site is the teahouse in the Dinghui Buddhist temple at Running Tiger Spring (Hupao Quan), one of the most famous springs in China. Visitors enjoy the famous Longjing (Dragon Well) tea, which is grown on plantations outside Hangzhou and is named for the Dragon Well, an underground spring which was discovered nearly 2,000 years ago. Other tourist sites include the Qiantang River basin, Liuhe Ta and Baochu Ta pagodas, Qiantangjian Daqiao Bridge over the river, and Wuyun, Beigao Feng and Yuhuang mountains. The Region of the Nine Brooks and Eighteen Bends (Jiuqi Shibajian) is a scenic destination for hikers. The botanical garden west of West Lake is renowned as one of the best in China, with 4,000 species of plants. The Lingyin Si monastery, also known as Yunlinchan Si, is one of the ten most famous Buddhist sites in China. It was supposedly named by the Indian Buddhist monk Huili, who climbed nearby Feilai Feng Mountain in 326. Yuemiao Temple is dedicated to General Yue Fei (1103–41), a great patriot of the Southern Song dynasty who had been falsely accused and then executed by enemies. The emperor commemorated him by building this temple in his honor in 1221. Many people travel to Yanguan, northeast of Hangzhou, to see the spring tide of the Qiantang River, which occurs during the days after the 15th day of the third month in the traditional lunar calendar. The strong pull of the moon's gravity causes the waters to pour up the river from the estuary in a huge wave. See also BAI JUYI; CARP; GRAND CANAL; PIRATES; POLO, MARCO; PRINTING; SILK; SOUTHERN SONG DYNASTY; SU SHI; SUZHOU; TEA; WEST LAKE; YUAN DYNASTY; YUE FEI; ZHEJIANG PROVINCE.

HANI One of China's 55 national minority ethnic groups. The Hani, who number about 1.3 million, inhabit Yunnan Province in southwestern China. Many Hani live in the Honghe Hani-Yi Autonomous Prefecture in Yunnan, which has China's largest deposits of tin ore. They are classified on the basis of language with the Tibeto-Burman group. They reside in remote mountainous areas and cultivate rice, corn, tea and poppies in terraced fields. The Hani claim that they have been growing tea for more than 50 generations, and a tea tree named "King of Trees" (chawang) in Nanluoshan, Yunnan, is supposedly the first tea tree their ancestors planted. Locally grown Pu'er tea is well known. When they come down into towns to trade their goods at weekly markets, one can see Hani women wearing head coverings decorated with antique coins, silver rings, beads and feathers. The Hani wear handwoven clothes commonly dyed indigo or black. A similar Tibeto-Burman group called the Lahu, who number about half a million, reside in the same areas as the Hani. See also MINORITIES, NATIONAL; TIBETAN; YI; YUNNAN PROVINCE.

HANKOU See WUHAN.

HANLIN ACADEMY A national academy of scholars within the imperial bureaucracy that was created by Emperor Xuanzong (Hsuan-tsung; r. 712–56) during the Tang dynasty (618–907) and continued functioning into modern times. Xuanzong was a reformer, scholar and patron of the arts. He founded the Hanlin Academy to establish a group of scholars who could assist the emperor and the imperial court by writing diplomatic letters and literary compositions such as

poetry, which has been a highly valued art in China since Tang times. *Hanlin* literally means "forest of writing brushes," referring to the implement for writing Chinese characters. The imperial bureaucracy was composed of members of the scholar-gentry, or literati class, who were selected through civil service examinations based on the classical texts of Confucianism. However, a talented man such as the renowned poet Li Bai (701–62) could be appointed to the Hanlin Academy without passing the standard examinations. The academy's role was expanded by the Hongwu emperor (Hung-wu; r. 1368–99), who founded the Ming dynasty (1368–1644), which replaced the Mongol Yuan dynasty (1279–1368). He needed a group of highly trained advisers who could help him rebuild the native Chinese government. Under the Ming emperor Yongle (r. 1403–24), the leading scholars from the Hanlin Academy became a powerful coterie who were closer to the emperor than were his chief ministers. By the mid-16th century, this body of secretaries from the Hanlin was formally designated the Grand Secretariat (Neige) of the imperial bureaucracy. However, other members of the bureaucracy resented the members of the Grand Secretariat because they were too closely allied with the emperor, and they had risen through the Hanlin Academy and had not developed their careers by holding a variety of positions within the bureaucracy. See also CALLIGRAPHY; HE SHAOJI; HONGWU (EMPEROR); IMPERIAL BUREAUCRACY; LI BAI; XUANZONG, EMPEROR; YONGLE (EMPEROR).

HANYANG See WUHAN.

HARBIN The capital city of Heilongjiang Province in Manchuria (northeastern China). Harbin has a population of about 3 million and is one of China's most important industrial centers and railway junctions. It lies on the fertile Manchurian Plain along the banks of the Songhua (Sungari) River, a tributary of the Amur River (Heilongjiang), which forms the border between China and Russia. Summers are mild in Harbin but winters are very harsh, lasting about six months. The average January temperature is −2 degrees F but may drop to -36°F. Ships of up to 500 tons sail up the Songhua River to Harbin, but navigation is halted when the river freezes for six months in the winter. A 35-mile dam was built after the Sungari flooded the city in 1957. Jiangpan Gongyuan Park on the south bank of the Songhua, and Sun Island in the middle, are lovely recreation areas. Harbin's ice festival, held in the first month of the traditional Chinese lunar calendar (in early February), is a popular tourist attraction. It is held in Zhaolin Park, named for Li Zhaolin, a Communist hero in China's Civil War who was killed by the Nationalists (Kuomintang) in 1946. Huge ice sculptures are carved in the form of animals, buildings, flowers, lanterns and so forth, and are illuminated at night.

The Heilongjiang Province Museum has exhibits on the historical development of the province and fossils of extinct animals found in the area. Unique specialties in the local cuisine include salmon, bear paw and nose of camel deer. Harbin was settled by ancestors of the Manchu people about 1,000 years ago and was originally called Arjin. It remained a small hunting and fishing village until 1896, when the Russians were given a concession to build the Chinese Eastern Railroad inside Manchuria and chose Harbin as its starting point. The line was linked to Dalian, Vladivostock and the Trans-Siberian Railroad. Because Harbin's location on the Songhua River gave it strategic importance, the city was Russia's most important military base during the Russo-Japanese War (1904–05). The Russians withdrew from Harbin after the Japanese defeated them and took over the city, but in 1917 many Russians came to Harbin as refugees from the Russian Revolution.

The Japanese invaded Manchuria and occupied Harbin in 1932. The Soviet army defeated the Japanese for the Allied forces in August 1945. When they withdrew a year later, Communist forces arrived before the Nationalists and took control of the city. After 1946, most Russians accepted Stalin's offer of amnesty and returned to the Soviet Union. British, French, Germans, Italians and Americans were also economically and politically active in Harbin; thus, the city even today seems more Western than Chinese. Since then, Harbin has developed into one of China's largest manufacturing centers. Major products include machine tools, building materials, agricultural machinery, textiles, helicopters and electronics. Food processing is an important industry, and wheat, corn, soybeans and wood for timber, pulp and paper are brought to Harbin from the entire Manchurian region. The Daqing oil fields near Harbin contain some of China's most important petroleum reserves. See also AMUR RIVER; CLIMATE, CHINESE; ENERGY SOURCES; HEILONGJIANG PROVINCE; MANCHURIA; RAILROADS; SHIPPING AND SHIP-BUILDING; SONGHUA RIVER.

HART, ROBERT See CHINESE MARITIME CUSTOMS SERVICE; GONG, PRINCE.

HATEM, GEORGE See MA HAIDE.

HAWAII See OVERSEAS CHINESE; REVOLUTIONARY ALLIANCE; RYUKYU ISLANDS; SIX COMPANIES, CHINESE; SUN YAT-SEN.

HE LUTING (Ho Lu-t'ing; 1903–) A modern musician and composer who composed the famous Chinese Communist anthem, *The East Is Red* (*Dongfang hong*). He was born in Hunan Province and studied at the Shanghai Conservatory. After 1938 he taught at the Lu Xun Institute of Arts, the school established by the Chinese Communist Party (CCP) in Yan'an in Shaanxi Province, where they made their headquarters after they fled the Nationalists (Kuomintang; KMT) in the Long March of 1934–35. After the CCP defeated the KMT and founded the People's Republic of China in 1949, He participated in the first CCP Central Committee. In 1950 he was vice president of the Central College of Music and the Chinese Musicians' Association and was elected a member of the Federation of Literature and Art Circles. In 1954 he served as a deputy from Shanghai to the First National People's Congress, and he was elected a council member of the Association for Cultural Relations with Foreign Countries. He Luting became president of the Shanghai Conservatory, China's most prestigious music school, but he was purged during the Cultural Revolution (1966–76). Following his rehabilitation by the Party, He served as a member of the Standing Committee of the CCP's Central Committee in 1978 and 1983. Since 1979 he has been vice chairman of the

Federation of Literature and Art Circles. He was director of the Shanghai Conservatory (1979–86) and has been honorary director from 1986 to the present. He also served as vice president of the Chinese Musicians' Association (1979–85) and has been honorary director since 1985. See also CENTRAL COMMITTEE OF THE CHINESE COMMUNIST PARTY; CULTURAL REVOLUTION; NATIONAL PEOPLE'S CONGRESS; YAN'AN.

HE SHAOJI (Ho Shao-chi; 1799–1873) A renowned scholar, poet and calligrapher. He Shaoji was born to a well-known family in Hunan Province. His father, He Linghan (1772–1840), held a high position in the imperial bureaucracy and was renowned for his calligraphy and painting. He's three brothers were also excellent calligraphers. He passed the examinations for the imperial bureaucracy in 1836 and became a member of the Hanlin Academy in the capital city of Beijing in 1839. From that year until 1852 he held a number of positions in the imperial court and also traveled throughout China. He spent the rest of his life in the city of Suzhou. He studied several different forms of calligraphy, from the ancient seal, clerical scripts and inscriptions on stelae (stone columns) in northern China, to modern standard and running scripts. He diligently practiced the art of calligraphy by copying an inscription many times over, each time concentrating on its particular style of brushwork. He was greatly influenced by the standard and running-script styles of the calligrapher Yan Zhenqing (Yen Chen-ch'ing; 709–85). He also copied the style of the epitaph of Zhang Heinu (Chang Hei-Nu), dating from the Northern Wei dynasty (386–534), and made the style well known by the essays in a book he composed on the art of calligraphy. He was most famous for his calligraphy in the clerical, cursive and running scripts, and most of his surviving works are in these scripts. See also CALLIGRAPHY; HANLIN ACADEMY; SUZHOU; YAN ZHENQING.

HE XIANGU See EIGHT IMMORTALS.

HE ZIZHE See LONG MARCH.

HEALTH CARE See ACUPUNCTURE; BAREFOOT DOCTORS; MEDICINE, HERBAL; MOXIBUSTION.

HEAVEN (*tian* or *t'ien*) Sometimes translated as "Sky"; the home of Shangdi (Shangti), the Lord-on-High or highest deity, in ancient Chinese belief. The Chinese traditionally believed that their ancestors also went to live in Heaven after they died, from where they continued to have a strong influence on the lives of their descendants. Heaven came to be regarded as the supreme deity that had a personal interest in the affairs of human beings. The Zhou dynasty (1100–256 B.C.) justified their conquest of the Shang dynasty (1750–1040 B.C.) by claiming that the Shang rulers had lost the "Mandate of Heaven" (*tianming* or *t'ien ming*) which gave them the right to rule, and the Zhou claimed the Mandate for themselves. Subsequent Chinese dynasties legitimized their overthrow of previous dynasties by making the same claims regarding the Mandate of Heaven. The ancient Chinese believed that Heaven and Shangdi exercised similar power over the universe and human beings, but, over time, the character "*di* (ti)" in Shangdi became specifically associated with the emperor, the highest ruler in human society, and the term Heaven became applied to the governing power of the universe as a whole. Hence the Chinese referred to the emperor as the "Son of Heaven" (*tianzi* or *t'ien tzu*). Heaven became a more impersonal and universal concept as the power that governs all created things, and it acquired an ethical connotation as the cosmic moral order and power that guides the destinies of human beings, providing rewards and punishments. The Chinese developed a theory of three levels, Heaven, Earth and man, which has been very influential in the aesthetic sphere, such as landscape painting and flower arrangement. When the Jesuit Christian missionary Matteo Ricci (1552–1610) came to China, he studied the ancient Chinese classical texts for support in his efforts to convert the Chinese to the Christian religion, and he argued that the concepts of heaven and Shangdi were the same as the Christian concept of God. See also EMPEROR; MANDATE OF HEAVEN; RICCI, MATTEO; SHANGDI.

HEAVEN AND EARTH SOCIETY See SMALL SWORD SOCIETY.

"HEAVENLY KINGDOM OF GREAT PEACE" See TAIPING REBELLION.

HEAVENLY MASTER See DAOISM; ZHANG DAOLING.

HEBEI PROVINCE A province in northern China that covers 71,442 square miles and has a population of about 60 million. The name Hebei means "to the north of the river," referring to the Yellow River (Huanghe) which flows through Henan Province to the south. The eastern part of Hebei Province lies on the North China Plain, which also encompasses the provinces of Shandong, Henan, northern Jiangsu and northern Anhui. Northwestern Hebei comprises a plateau ranging about 4,500 feet above sea level. Hebei is also bordered by the provinces of Liaoning to the northeast, Shanxi to the west and Shandong to the southeast, as well as Inner Mongolia Autonomous Region to the north and the Bo Hai Gulf to the east. The capital city, Shijiazhuang, has a population of more than one million; other major cities include Tangshan, Handan, Zhangjiakou and Baoding. Beijing, the capital of China since the Yuan dynasty (1279–1368), and the industrial port city of Tianjin are in Hebei but both are governed as independent municipalities. About 10,000 members of the Mongol national minority ethnic group inhabit Hebei, as well as some half-million members of the Hui nationality (Chinese Muslims).

Hebei has vast mineral deposits, with more than 80 minerals and large coal reserves. Much of Hebei's coal is transported to the major port city of Shanghai. Large oil deposits have been discovered at Daqing, near Tainjin, at Renqiu, and in the Bo Hai Gulf. Since 1949 Hebei province has been highly industrialized. Major products include petroleum, iron, steel, textiles, chemicals, machinery and electricity. Agriculture is also important, and Hebei is one of China's largest producers of wheat, millet and other grains, soybeans, beer, cotton, hemp, tobacco, peanuts, walnuts, sesame, fruit, mutton, fish and shellfish. Hebei is also China's largest producer of salt, taken from salt swamps along the Bo

Hai coast. Sheep and goats are raised in the province's northern region, which is dryer and less irrigated.

In ancient times, Hebei was a frontier area to the Chinese Empire, which resorted to building the Great Wall for protection from nomadic tribes who periodically invaded from the north. Shanhaiguan pass, 20 miles from Beidaihe on the border of Liaoning Province, was the most important pass at the eastern end of the Great Wall. Constructed in 1381, this was for several centuries the control point for movement between the northern and northeastern regions of China; the surviving building dates from 1639. From the Western Han dynasty (206 B.C.–A.D. 8) through the Tang dynasty (618–907), Chinese garrisons were established in Hebei. General An Lushan, commander of the armies in the region of modern Beijing, led a rebellion from 755 to 763 that deposed Emperor Xuanzong (Hsuan-tsung; r. 712–56) and almost brought down the dynasty.

Nomadic tribes called the Khitan invaded Hebei and established the Liao dynasty (947–1125) that controlled northeastern China and Inner Mongolia. When the Mongols conquered China under the Yuan dynasty (1279–1368) and established their capital at Khanbaliq (Cambaluc; modern Beijing), Hebei became the political center of China and has remained so up to the present time.

Shijiazhuang, the capital, was a small village until it began to develop when the Beijing-Hankou (Wuhan) Railroad was built in 1905, and it is still overshadowed by Beijing and Tianjin. Today Shijiazhuang is a major railroad junction. Its most important industries include cotton textiles, chemicals, machinery and minerals. The city served as the northern headquarters of the Chinese Communist Party for two years during the civil war with the Nationalists (the Kuomintang). Dr. Norman Bethune, a Canadian surgeon who organized medical services for the Communist army, is buried in Shijiazhuang, and a hospital has been named for him. To the north, Long Xing Monastery (Long Xing Si) has the oldest temple buildings still standing in China, dating from the 10th to 13th centuries. To the southeast lies the stone Anji Qiao Bridge, the oldest segment-arch bridge in the world, built from 605 to 616.

Chengde, formerly called Rehol (Jehol, or Warm River), was the Summer Residence (Bishushanzhuang) for the Manchu emperors of the Qing dynasty (1644–1911), who spent several months there every year. Chengde, 165 miles from Beijing, thus served as China's secondary capital during the Qing. The palace was built by the Kangxi (K'ang-hsi) emperor beginning in 1703, and eight temples and buildings in the style of many different nationalities were added by the Qianlong (Ch'ien-lung) emperor; the complex was completed in 1790. But the Qing court abandoned Chengde after the Jiaqing (Chia-ch'ing) emperor was killed by lightning near the palace in 1820, although the Xianfeng (Hsien-feng) emperor went to Chengde in 1860 to escape allied English and French forces that invaded Beijing.

Beidaihe is a popular seashore resort on the Bo Hai Gulf. Shanhaiguan is an old walled town that was built at the eastern end of the Great Wall. Eighty miles east of Beijing lies the complex known as Dongling, or Eastern Tombs (Qing Tombs), the burial site of 5 emperors, 15 empresses, 100 imperial concubines and 1 princess of the Qing dynasty (1644–1911). At the center is Xiaoling, mausoleum of the

Shunzhi (Shun-ch'ih) emperor, founder of the Qing dynasty. Yuling is the mausoleum of the Qianlong emperor, whose reign (1736–96) is considered the Qing "golden age." Nearby lies the most important tomb at Dongling, that of Empress Dowager Cixi (Tz'u Hsi). About 25 miles north of Beijing are the Ming Tombs (Shisan Ling, "The Thirteen Tombs"), one of the most popular tourist sites in China. Thirteen mausoleums were constructed for 13 of the 16 emperors of the Ming dynasty (1368–1644) and their wives and concubines.

In 1920, a 500,000-year-old human skull, known as Peking Man, was found in Hebei Province. Handan, in southern Hebei, was settled as early as the Shang dynasty (1750–1040 B.C.). The town served as capital of the state of Zhao from 386–228 B.C. and became a wealthy trading center. It was destroyed at the end of the Qin dynasty (221–206 B.C.) but rebuilt under the Han dynasty (206 B.C.–A.D. 220). Ruins of the ancient city can still be seen southwest of the modern industrial city of Handan. In the same region are the Echo Stone Grottoes (Xiangtang Shiku), caves that were carved into the Shigu Mountains (Shigu Shan) in the sixth century. To the north of Handan lies Luzu Ci Temple (Luweng Ci), established during the Tang and Song dynasties, although the present buildings date from the Ming dynasty. See also AN LUSHAN REBELLION; BEIDAIHE; BEIJING; BETHUNE, NORMAN; BO HAI GULF; CHENGDE; CIVIL WAR BETWEEN COMMUNISTS AND NATIONALISTS; CIXI, EMPRESS DOWAGER; GREAT WALL; HUI; JIN DYNASTY; JURCHEN; KHITAN; LIAO DYNASTY; MING TOMBS; MONGOL; NORTH CHINA PLAIN; PEKING MAN; QING DYNASTY; RAILROADS; SHIJIAZHUANG; TIANJIN; YUAN DYNASTY.

HEFEI The capital city of Anhui Province in eastern China, with a population of more than one million. Hefei is situated in the basin of the great Yangzi River (Changjiang) and is north of Lake Chao. Surrounded by rice paddies and wheat fields, the city was a center for trade and handicrafts until 1949, when it underwent industrial modernization. Principal industries include steel, iron, chemicals and textiles. At the center of Anhui Province, Hefei is also a juncture for railroads and river traffic. In ancient times Hefei was located farther north than the present city. Founded during the Han dynasty (206 B.C.–A.D. 220), it became a military center for the Wei Empire during the Three Kingdoms Period (220–80). One of the most famous battles in Chinese history took place in the vicinity in A.D. 225. The forces led by the famous general and poet Cao Cao (Ts'ao Ts'ao), although greatly outnumbered, defeated a powerful army from the Wu Empire led by Sun Quan. During the Southern Song dynasty (1127–1279), Hefei was the center of defense against the nomadic Jurchen invaders who established the Jin dynasty (1115–1234) in northern China. The Hefei Museum has exhibits on the history of the region. Its treasure is a 2,000-year-old jade burial suit sewn with silver thread. The elite Chinese University of Science and Technology is located in Hefei. See also ANHUI PROVINCE; CAO CAO; JADE; JIN DYNASTY; THREE KINGDOMS PERIOD.

HEILONGJIANG PROVINCE The most northern province in China, and one of three provinces, along with Jilin and Liangdong, that comprise the region known as Manchuria and as Dongbei ("the Northeast"). Heilongjiang is also the largest province in China (there are several autonomous regions that are larger), covering 177,584 square miles, with a population of about 33 million. The capital city is Harbin with a population of about 2 million. Harbin lies on the banks of the Songhua (Sungari) River and is one of China's most important manufacturing and transportation centers; papermaking is one of its major industries. Large ships sail up the Songhua to Harbin, but the river freezes over for six months every year. The ice festival held each winter in Zhaolin Park is a popular tourist attraction for its enormous carved ice sculptures.

Heilongjiang borders Jilin Province to the south and Inner Mongolia Autonomous Region (Nei Menggu) to the west. The province is separated from Russia by the Amur River (Heilongjiang, or the "River of the Black Dragon"), on its northern border and the Wusuli River (Wusulijiang; also known as the Ussuri) on the east. China and Russia have had military standoffs along the border in Heilongjiang at portions of the Amur, Wusuli and Argun Rivers. The Amur, the province's longest river, is a major shipping artery but freezes over 180 days every year. Heilongjiang Province suffers extremely cold winters that last five to eight months, and short warm summers. The average temperature in January is –4 degrees F on the plains and –18 degrees F in the mountains; in July it ranges from 68 degrees to 75 degrees.

The eastern terminus of the Great Wall, built to protect China from invading nomadic tribes, lies in Heilongjiang. The tribal group known as the Jurchen originated in the Amur River valley. They conquered the Liao dynasty (947–1125), founded the Jin dynasty (1115–1234), and nearly conquered the Song dynasty (960–1279), forcing the Chinese emperor to flee south in 1127 and establish the Southern Song dynasty. In the 17th century, under the leadership of Nurhachi (1559–1626) and his son Abahai (1592–1643), the Jurchen changed their name to Manchu, conquered China and established the Qing dynasty (1644–1911), thus joining Manchuria with China. The Treaty of Nerchinsk (1689) between the Manchus and the Russians established the border between Manchuria and Siberia (eastern Russia) along the Amur River. With the Treaty of Argun in 1858, Russia annexed the north bank of the Amur River, and in 1860 Russia took control of all of Manchuria north of the Amur and east of the Wusuli River south to Vladivostock. Heilongjiang began urbanization when Russia constructed the Northeast China Railroad, a branch of the Trans-Siberian Railroad, in 1896–1903 to connect Vladivostock with Moscow. Taking advantage of the disruption caused by the Boxer Rebellion, the Russians fully occupied Heilongjiang in 1900; but they were forced to give up all their rights in Manchuria when Japan defeated Russia in 1905.

The province was then primarily controlled by the Chinese until the Japanese occupied Manchuria in 1931 and set up their puppet state of Manchukuo (Manzhouguo or Manchou-kuo in Chinese) with the deposed Manchu emperor, then known as Puyi, at its head. They exploited Manchuria's vast natural resources and set up manufacturing plants in the region, sending most of the products back to Japan. In August 1945 Russia declared war on Japan, occupied Manchuria and dismantled most of the factories. The civil war between the Nationalists (Kuomintang) and Chinese Communists brought further suffering to the region until the Communists established the People's Republic of China in 1945. In 1954 China claimed substantial Russian territory along the Amur, Wusuli and Argun rivers, and China and Russia massed troops along their border. After numerous military skirmishes, the two countries resumed negotiations in 1987 but still have not resolved their border dispute.

Today the population of Heilongjiang consists largely of Han (ethnic Chinese) who have emigrated to the province. However, there are still many Manchus as well as members of other national minority ethnic groups, including Koreans and Mongols and the Daur, Ewenki, Oroqen, and Hezhe, the smallest group in China.

Heilongjiang Province has extremely large deposits of oil and coal, and a large number of China's coal mines. The largest oilfield in China is near Daqing. The massive Fulareqi steelworks near Qiqihar were built in the 1950s with Russian aid. The northern and eastern regions of the province comprise heavily forested mountain ranges. Heilongjiang is one of China's most important suppliers of timber, including birch, fir and larch, oak, elm, ash, maple and spruce. Tourists come to Heilongjiang to hunt bear, deer and wild boar. In the summer, hundreds of red-crested cranes inhabit the bird sanctuary of Shalong. The volcanic region of Wudalianchi and the forests in the Lake Jingpo region are known for their beauty. The south belongs to the Great Manchurian Plain, a fertile agricultural region. Major crops include soybeans, wheat, corn and sugar beets. Heilongjiang is one of China's main producers of jute and hemp. Cattle are raised on the steppe grasslands of the central plains to provide milk, cheese and butter. See also AMUR RIVER; CRANE; HARBIN; JILIN PROVINCE; JURCHEN; KOREAN; MANCHU; MANCHUKUO; MANCHURIA; MONGOL; MINORITIES, NATIONAL; NERCHINSK, TREATY OF; PUYI; RUSSO-JAPANESE WAR OF 1904–05 AND CHINA; SONGHUA RIVER; WUSULI RIVER.

HEILUNGKIANG PROVINCE AND RIVER See AMUR RIVER; HEILONGJIANG PROVINCE.

HELAN MOUNTAIN RANGE   See TENGGER DESERT.

"HELL MONEY"   See FUNERALS; JOSS PAPER.

HENAN PROVINCE   A province in north-central China that covers an area of about 104,000 square miles and has a population of nearly 87 million. The capital city is Zhengzhou. The name Henan means "South of the Huanghe," or Yellow River. Much of Henan Province belongs to the North China Plain, a flat, fertile region encompassing large regions of Hebei, Shandong and Shanxi provinces. The plain was created by the frequent flooding of the Yellow River (Huanghe), which deposits voluminous amounts of loess silt. For thousands of years, the Chinese have constructed extensive dikes to give some measure of protection against the Yellow River's destructive floods. The Huai River (Huaihe) originates in Henan Province and flows through several lakes to join the Yangzi River (Changjiang) near Yangzhou in Jiangsu Province.

Henan, poetically called the "Flower of the Middle Kingdom," has been an important region in China since prehistoric times. Neolithic artifacts have been excavated at Yangshao Cao village where the Yellow, Wei and Fen Rivers come together; this area is known as the "Cradle of Chinese Civilization." Zhengzhou, the capital, on the Jinshui River just south of the Yellow River, is one of the most ancient towns in China. Excavations have uncovered artifacts from the Shang dynasty (1750–1040 B.C.). Zhengzhou was probably the city of Ao, capital of the 10th Shang emperor. Three of China's major ancient imperial capitals are located in Henan: Anyang, Luoyang and Kaifeng. The Henan Provincial Museum in Zhengzhou has exhibits on the history of the area. Today, Zhengzhou is a major communications center at the intersection of two major Chinese rail lines—the Beijing-Guangzhou line that runs north to south and the Longhai line that travels from Gansu Province in the west to the East China Sea—and has the longest railroad yard in China. It is also an industrialized city and the center of textile production in Henan. Until the 10th century A.D., the imperial capital alternated frequently between Zhengzhou and Chang'an (modern Xi'an in Shaanxi Province) to the west. Near the town of Huaiyang, southwest of Zhengzhou, is a site claimed to be the tomb of Fuxi, a legendary emperor who supposedly taught humans how to hunt, fish and raise animals and developed the eight trigrams (bagua or pa kua) that are found in the Book of Changes (Yijing or I Ching). In northern Henan lies Anyang, another major archaeological site which was the first capital of the Shang dynasty. Numerous tortoise shells and bones that were used by Shang rulers to divine the future have been excavated in Anyang.

The city of Luoyang, about 70 miles west of Zhengzhou, served as the capital of the Eastern Zhou dynasty (771–256 B.C.). Kaifeng, in eastern Henan, became the Chinese imperial capital during the Five Dynasties Period (907–60) and the Northern Song dynasty (960–1126). Kaifeng was an important center for culture, education, printing and trade with western regions of China. Today it is a popular tourist site, especially due to interest in its history as a Jewish center. Several hundred descendants of the Jews who settled there centuries ago live in Kaifeng today; their ancestors may have been traders who entered China on the Silk Road, or else immigrants from a Jewish community in southwestern India.

Henan Province is China's most important producer of wheat, and is a major producer of silk textiles, as well as jute and hemp. Other important crops include rice, peanuts, cotton, sesame, walnuts and tea; much of the tea is exported. Major cities in Henan belong to the Huaihai Economic Zone, which connects the capitals of several provinces economically and by communications with cities and ports along China's coast. See also ANYANG; BOOK OF CHANGES; EIGHT TRIGRAMS; FUXI; HUAI RIVER; KAIFENG; LOESS; LUOYANG; NORTH CHINA PLAIN; ORACLE BONES; RAILROADS; SHANG DYNASTY; YANGSHAO CULTURE; YELLOW RIVER; ZHENGZHOU.

HENG, MOUNT   See FIVE SACRED MOUNTAIN OF DAOISM.

HERBAL MEDICINE   See COOKING, CHINESE; MEDICINE, HERBAL.

HEXAGRAMS   See BOOK OF CHANGES; EIGHT TRIGRAMS.

HIMALAYA MOUNTAIN RANGE The world's highest mountain range, forming China's southwestern border with Nepal, Sikkim, India and Bhutan. *Himalaya* is an Indian Sanskrit word meaning "dwelling place of snow." The Himalaya Mountains were formed about 40 million years ago when the northward movement of the Indo-Australian Plate carried the northern boundary of the Indian Subcontinent beneath the Eurasian continental crust. These two layers of continental crust buckled and folded, creating an area of crust 43 miles thick, and thus, forming the Himalaya Mountain Range. The range, extending from the plains of India to the Qinghai-Tibet Plateau (Qing Zang) in southwestern China, is 1,490 miles long from west to east, between 124 and 186 miles wide from south to north, and averages 19,680 feet high. The Himalayas run along the plateau's southern edge. The range contains 11 of the 17 mountains in the world that are at least 26,000 feet high. Mount Everest, known as Qomolongma, on the border between China and Nepal is the highest mountain in the world, with its peak at 29,028 feet above sea level. Kachenjunga, on the Nepal-Sikkim border, is the third-highest mountain on earth.

The Himalayas are actually a series of parallel ranges: foothills (called the "Piedmont Zone" and the Siwalik Range) are located to the south; the Small Himalaya Range is north of these; and most northerly sits the Great Himalaya Range, which is 31 to 56 miles wide and contains snow-covered peaks. Glaciers within the Chinese border cover 4,268 square miles. The Karakoram Mountain Range to the northwest, in Xinjiang-Uighur Autonomous Province and Kashmir, is also commonly included as part of the Himalayas. Three great rivers rise close together in Tibet north of the Great Himalaya Range, run parallel to it and cut south through the Great and Lesser ranges and the foothills: the Indus, the Sutlej and the Zangbo (also known as the Dihang); the Zangbo is known as the Brahmaputra in India.

The Himalaya and the Kunlun mountain ranges enclose the Qinghai-Tibet (Qing Zang) Plateau, which encompasses most of Tibet and part of Qinghai Province. This is the highest and largest plateau in the world, covering 850,000 square miles—23 percent of all Chinese land area. Called the "Roof of the World," it has elevations averaging more than 13,120 feet above sea level, and its major peaks are more than 23,000 feet high. The plateau has thin air, cold average temperatures, and glaciers, with the soil permanently frozen over much of its area, thus the region's vegetation and population are both extremely sparse. The Yangzi and the Yellow (Huanghe) the two largest rivers in China, both originate in the plateau, where monsoon rains hit the southern side of the Himalayas where they drop all their moisture, and flow all the way to the country's eastern coast.

India and China have had a border dispute in the area where the Aksai Chin area of northeastern Jammu and Kashmir is controlled by China but claimed by India. Running east from Bhutan and north of the Brahmaputra River, a large area is controlled by India but has been claimed by China ever since the 1959 Tibetan revolt. The area was demarcated by the McMahon Line, which the British drew along the Himalayas in 1949 to form the Sino-Indian border; at present, India accepts and China rejects this boundary. In 1980, China made its first attempt in 20 years to settle this border dispute, proposing that India give the Aksai China area to China in return for China's recognition of the McMahon Line, but India rejected this offer. By 1986 the two countries had entered their seventh round of talks but had made little progress, and each side accused the other of making incursions into its territory. The dispute remains unresolved. See also EVEREST, MOUNT; KUNLUN MOUNTAIN RANGE; QINGHAI PROVINCE; QINGHAI-TIBET PLATEAU; TIBET; XINJIANG-UIGHUR AUTONOMOUS REGION.

HISTORICAL PERIODS Chinese history is divided into periods named for the imperial dynasties that ruled China; from the Xia dynasty (2200–1750 B.C.) to the Qing dynasty (1644–1911). The rules of some dynasties overlapped in different parts of the country. During the lengthy Neolithic period (c. 12,000–2000 B.C.) many of the features that were to become central in Chinese culture were developed, including agriculture, walled villages, the patriarchal family system, ceremonial burials, and the propitiation of ancestral

DYNASTIES
Xia (2200–1750 B.C.)
Shang (1750–1040 B.C.)
Zhou (1100–256 B.C.)
Western Zhou (1100–771 B.C.)
Eastern Zhou (771–256 B.C.)
Spring and Autumn Period (772–481 B.C.)
Warring States Period (403–221 B.C.)
Qin (221–206 B.C.)
Han (206 B.C.–A.D. 220)
Western Han (206 B.C.–A.D. 8)
Wang Mang Interregnum (also known as Xin; 9–23)
Eastern Han (25–220)
Three Kingdoms Period (San Guo; 220–80)
Wei (220–65)
Shu (221–63)
Wu (222–80)
Western Jin (265–316)
Eastern Jin (317–420)
Northern and Southern (420–589)
Southern (Disunited)
Northern Wei (386–534)
Sui (581–618)
Tang (618–907)
Five Dynasties Period (North China) (907–60)
Ten Kingdoms (907–60)
Liao (A.D. 947–1125)
Song (960–1279)
Northern Song (960–1126)
Southern Song (1127–1279)
Xixia (1038–1227)
Jin (1115–1234)
Yuan (1279–1368)
Ming (1368–1644)
Qing (1644–1911)

spirits, known as ancestor worship. The most important phases were the Yangshao culture (fifth to third millennia B.C.) and the Longshan culture (c. 3000–2200 B.C.). The modern period following the Qing dynasty includes the Republic of China (1912–49), Warlord Period (1916–28), War of Resistance against Japan (Sino-Japanese War of 1937–45), Civil War between Communists and Nationalists (Kuomintang; 1946–49), and the founding of the Communist People's Republic of China in 1949.

See also EMPEROR; NAMES OF INDIVIDUAL PERIODS AND DYNASTIES.

HMONG See MIAO.

HO HSIEN-KU See EIGHT IMMORTALS.

HO LU-T'ING See HE LUTING.

HO SHAO-CHI See HE SHAOJI.

HOHHOT The capital city of Inner Mongolia Autonomous Region (Nei Menggu) in northern China. Hohhot, meaning "Blue City"—Kuku-Khoto in Mongolian (although many erroneously state that it means "Green City")—is located in a marshy oasis on the Mongolian steppes. The skies are usually blue and the weather sunny, although cold winds whip through the region in the winter. Mongolia is the homeland of the Mongol people, who ruled China under the Yuan dynasty (1279–1368) and now comprise one of the China's 55 national minority ethnic groups. Today about 100,000 Mongols live in Hohhot, which has a population of more than one million, most of whom are Han or ethnic Chinese. The rest of the population is divided among 32 other ethnic groups. Many tribes have lived in Mongolia, including the Xianbei, Khitan (Qidan), Donghu, Nuzhen, Xiongnu and the Turks. The old section of Hohhot was built in 1581 by Altan Kahn, leader of the Tumed tribe, during the Ming dynasty (1368–1644). Altan Khan had become chief of the eastern Mongols in 1543 and led his troops close to the Chinese capital of Beijing in 1550 but was forced to retreat. In Hohhot he established an administrative government for the Mongols based on the Han Chinese system of imperial bureaucracy. The city grew up around Buddhist temples and lamaseries, some of which have been restored.

Han Chinese farmers began settling in the rich farmlands around Hohhot in the 17th century. After another northern tribe, the Manchus, overthrew the Ming and established the Qing dynasty (1644–1911), the Kangxi emperor (r. 1661–1722) sent troops to Mongolia to secure Manchu sovereignty, and a new, Chinese-style city developed in the region of Hohhot. The Mongol and Chinese cities eventually merged into one large city, with the Mongolian section a trading center for animals and animal products, and the Chinese quarter the residential and government district. In 1928 Hohhot was named capital of the new province of Suiyuan. However, the region was under Japanese control from 1937 to 1945. In 1952, after the Chinese Communists established the People's Republic of China (PRC), Inner Mongolia was designated an autonomous region with its capital at Hohhot. The first university in Inner Mongolia was founded in Hohhot in 1957. In the 18th century the city had begun developing into a center for the production of wool textiles, and today there are more than a dozen woolen mills producing hundreds of varieties of textiles. Other main industries include electronics, machinery, construction materials and food products.

There are many religious sites in Hohhot. The White Pagoda Temple (Wanbu Huayanjing Ta Pagoda), 15 miles east of Hohhot, was built between 983 and 1031 and has been restored several times. It contains six stone tablets from the Jin dynasty (1115–1234). The 18th-century Diamond Pagoda is all that remains of the Five-Pagoda Temple (Wutasi). The Great Mosque (Qingzhen Dasi Mosque) dates from the reign of the Qing emperor Qianlong (r. 1736–95). In 1933 the Holy Hall of the Mosque was restored and a minaret was built. Dazhao Monastery was built from 1567 to 1572 by Altan Khan, who had converted the Mongols to the Yellow Hat Sect of the Tibetan Buddhist religion, known as Lamaism. Xiletuzhao Lama Temple was built during the Qing dynasty on the site of a small temple where Huofo Xitituke, a highly educated monk who taught the fourth Dalai Lama, had resided. The large complex contains five courtyards and hall built in the Tibetan style. Its 50-foot-high *dagoba* (pagoda) is considered the most beautiful in Inner Mongolia.

About six miles south of Hohhot stands the tomb of Wang Zhaojun (Wang Chao-chun), built to honor a concubine whom the Chinese emperor Yuandi of the Western Han dynasty gave in marriage to Prince Han Xie (Han Hsieh), *shanyu* (chief) of the Xiongnu, in 33 B.C. to form a diplomatic alliance. He supposedly died two years later, and she became the wife of his successor. There are many Chinese stories and plays about Wang Zhaojun, who came to be revered by the Mongols as a goddess of fertility. Both the Mongols and Han Chinese honor her as a symbol of peace and have high regard for her tomb. An exhibition hall near the tomb tells the story of her life. Dayao, the large site of an advanced Old Stone Age culture a half-million years old, was discovered in 1973 about 20 miles northeast of Hohhot.

Hohhot is the starting point for tourists who wish to visit the Mongolian grasslands and stay overnight in yurts (traditional Mongolian tents). Many tourists come to Hohhot to enjoy Naadam, the traditional Mongolian summer festival. The National Museum of Inner Mongolia has exhibits on the region from prehistoric times. See also INNER MONGOLIA AUTONOMOUS REGION; LAMAISM; MONGOL; NOMADS AND ANIMAL HUSBANDRY; WANG ZHAOJUN; XIONGNU.

HONAN PROVINCE See HENAN PROVINCE.

HONG See CANTON SYSTEM; MACARTNEY, GEORGE, LORD; OPIUM WAR.

HONG KONG (Xianggang in pinyin) A Special Administrative Region of China situated in the South China Sea at the mouth of the Pearl River delta, 80 miles southeast of the southern Chinese port city of Guangzhou (Canton), that was ceded to Great Britain in the 19th century but reverted to the People's Republic of China (PRC) in 1997. A railroad connects Hong Kong with Guangzhou. Hong Kong, the world's

Hong Kong is a major international trade center, with the Bank of China dominating its skyline, and a popular tourist destination.
S.E. MEYER

largest and busiest duty-free port, has a population of 6.5 million, most of them Chinese. The official language is Chinese, but many speak English because it was a British Crown Colony until 1997. It has a tropical climate and suffers from violent typhoons in the late summer. Since the region is mountainous, most residents live on 15 percent of the land area, giving it the highest population density in the world. Hong Kong includes the 35-square-mile island of Hong Kong; the New Territories, including Kowloon Peninsula, on the Chinese mainland; and more than 230 surrounding islands, the largest of which is Lantau (Lan Tao). The total area is 663 square miles. Victoria on the northern edge of Hong Kong Island is the capital city of the region. Most government buildings and the headquarters of banks, such as the Hongkong and Shanghai Banking Corporation and the Bank of China, and commercial trading houses, known as hongs, are located at the foot of Victoria Peak, which rises 1,825 feet. The city of Kowloon is the major commercial center, and most of the industrial development has occurred in the New Territories. Star Ferry boats have been crossing the large natural deepwater harbor between Victoria and Kowloon for nearly a century.

Great Britain acquired the barren island of Hong Kong from China in 1842 under the Treaty of Nanjing, signed after Britain defeated China in the Opium War (1839–42). In 1860, under the Convention of Beijing, China ceded Kowloon to Britain, and in 1898 Britain acquired a 99-year lease over the New Territories adjoining Kowloon. In 1979, Britain and the PRC began negotiations for the reversion of Hong Kong. In 1984 the two sides signed the Sino-British Joint Declaration on the Question of Hong Kong, which stated that Britain was to return Hong Kong to the PRC on July 1, 1997, and that the PRC government was to resume sovereign rights over Hong Kong on the same date. The PRC has designated Hong Kong a Special Administrative Region of China to give the territory a high degree of autonomy and enable it to continue its capitalist economic system; the PRC has dubbed this arrangement "One Country, Two Systems." Hong Kong maintains its own currency and economic and political system.

Hong Kong has grown into one of the world's largest and most prosperous free-trade ports, where investors and merchants have been protected by British law. It is the world's third-largest financial center and 11th-largest trading center. Manufacturing is a major industry, with the main products being electronics goods, textiles, clothing, yarn and fabric, footwear and watches. More clothing is shipped from Hong Kong than from any other world port. Many manufacturing companies have their offices in Hong Kong while their factories operate on the mainland. Re-exports account for 83 percent of Hong Kong's total exports. Hong Kong investments employ more than 6 million Chinese in the PRC. Hong Kong is also a major tourist destination. It is a paradise for shoppers, and food lovers enjoy its many excellent restaurants; Hong Kong is also a popular point of entry to the PRC. The PRC has invested nearly U.S.$30 billion in Hong Kong, and the former colony conducted more than $70 billion in two-way trade with China in 1996. The PRC's Bank of China has built a skyscraper for its headquarters in Hong Kong designed by world-renowned architect I. M. Pei. Lantau Island is a popular day trip for Buddhist pilgrims and tourists to see the world's largest bronze Buddha, at the Po Lin Monastery on top of Ngong Ping Mountain. See also BANK OF CHINA; BEIJING, CONVENTION OF; BRITISH EAST INDIA COMPANY; GUANGZHOU; HAINAN ISLAND; HONGKONG AND SHANGHAI BANKING CORPORATION; KOWLOON; MACAO; NANJING, TREATY OF; PEARL RIVER; PEI, I. M.; SINO-BRITISH JOINT DECLARATION ON THE QUESTION OF HONG KONG; TIANJIN, TREATY OF.

HONG SHEN (Hung Shen; 1894–1955) A playwright who became also one of the first Chinese filmmakers. Hong Shen was born in Jiangsu Province and was educated in Beijing and at Harvard University in the United States. In 1922 he returned to China and taught at several universities in succession. In 1923 he joined the Shanghai Dramatic Society. This marked the beginning of the modern movement in Chinese drama. Hong directed the society's plays, which were written by himself and other modern Chinese authors, as well as plays by Western authors that he had translated, such as *Lady Windermere's Fan* by Oscar Wilde. Hong's play *ZhaoYanwang* (1922) showed an influence from *The Emperor Jones* by American playwright Eugene O'Neill. In 1930 Hong joined the Chinese Star Motion Picture Company and produced one of the first sound films in China, which became extremely popular. In 1932, the company sent him to Hollywood to study film technique.

When he returned to China, Hong produced a very successful propaganda film against Japan, which had been making aggressive moves against China. In 1936, when Japan was about to invade China, Hong joined with other writers in issuing a Manifesto of the Literary Circle, which called for resistance against oppression and freedom of speech. During China's War of Resistance against Japan (1937–45), Hong directed theatrical companies that traveled around the country giving performances to raise the spirits of the Chinese people.

After the Chinese Communist Party founded the People's Republic of China in 1949, Hong played an active role for the government in cultural relations and served as vice chairman of the Chinese Stage Artists. As a member of the Left-Wing Dramatists League, Hong mounted productions that were directly political in meaning. He also drew upon the techniques that he had learned from the Western theater for his plays and films. In traditional Chinese theater, such as Beijing Opera, men played women's roles. Hong Shen saw women acting in plays while he was abroad. Back in China, he took the then radical step of casting actresses in plays he produced. In the late 1930s and 1940s the Chinese Communist Party based at Yan'an (Shaanxi Province) supported the appearance of women in Chinese plays and operas. See also PEOPLE'S REPUBLIC OF CHINA; WAR OF RESISTANCE AGAINST JAPAN.

HONG XIUQUAN (Hung Hsiu-ch'uan; 1813–64) The leader of the Taiping Rebellion (1850–64) against the Manchu Qing dynasty (1644–1911). Hong was born in Guangdong Province in southern China to a poor family of the Hakka minority group. He gained an education but several times failed to pass the provincial examinations in Guangzhou (Canton) for a position in the imperial bureaucracy. In 1837 he became ill, fell into a trance and had dramatic visions. After he recovered, he became a village schoolteacher for six years. In 1843 he read pamphlets written by the first Chinese convert to Protestant Christianity, which he had been given in Guangzhou, and announced that he was the second son of the God Jehovah and the younger brother of Jesus Christ. He claimed that his visions commanded him to cast out demons, destroy "pagan idols" and bring people to worship the true God. In 1847 he studied Christianity for two months with a Protestant missionary in Guangzhou. Hong began destroying ancestral tablets in Confucian temples, which angered the Chinese in Guangzhou, so he and his converts moved north into Jiangsu Province, where they converted thousands more to their movement. Most belonged to the Hakka, Miao and Yao ethnic minorities. Hong preached that he was called by God to destroy demons and establish the Kingdom of God on earth by destroying the Qing dynasty. When armed fighting between the Taipings and Qing troops broke out in July 1850, thousands of impoverished peasants, unemployed laborers, pirates and bandits—many of whom belonged to secret societies such as the Triads—joined the Taiping movement.

In September 1851 Hong claimed the founding of a new dynasty and took the title, "Heavenly king" (*tianwang* or *t'ien-wang*) of the "Heavenly Kingdom of Great Peace" (Taiping tiangu or T'ai-p'ing t'ien-ku). Five other Taiping leaders were also given the title "king." In 1852 Taiping forces marched north through Hunan Province and east through the Yangzi River valley, joined by numerous impoverished peasants and revolutionary bands. In March 1853 they captured Nanjing, the southern capital of the Qing, where they established their headquarters, called "Heavenly Capital" (Tianjing or T'ien-ching). Hong lived as a king in seclusion in his palace, accompanied by concubines. By 1853 the Taipings numbered more than 1 million. They sent an army north toward the Manchu capital at Beijing, but the soldiers from southern China were not used to the cold northern winter weather and were defeated by Qing forces. The Taipings sent another army west to gain control of Jiangsu, Anhui, Hubei and Hunan Provinces, but they were opposed by the forces raised in Hunan by Zeng Guofan (Tseng Kuo-fan). In 1856 one of the Taiping kings plotted to overthrow Hong, but another king assassinated him and murdered thousands of his Taiping supporters. The Taiping king and military commander Shi Dakai (Shih-Ta-k'ai) ended the slaughter and left the Taiping movement in disgust. These events divided and weakened the Taipings, who were now being forced into a defensive position. They had to fight Qing troops led by Zeng Guofan and Li Hongzhang (Li Hung-chang), and the volunteer Chinese and Western "Ever-Victorious Army," led by the American Frederick Ward Townsend until he was killed in 1862, when the Englishman Charles George Gordon took his place. These forces put

Nanjing under siege on May 31, 1862, and finally took the city from the Taipings in July 19, 1864. Hong committed suicide in June. His body, shrouded in a yellow satin cloth embroidered with dragons, which could only be worn by a Chinese emperor, was discovered in a sewer underneath his palace. See also ANCESTRAL TABLETS; CHRISTIANITY; GORDON, CHARLES; HAKKA; LI HONGZHANG; MIAO; NANJING; QING DYNASTY; SHI DAKAI; TAIPING REBELLION; WARD, FREDERICK TOWNSEND; YAO; ZENG GUOFAN.

HONGKONG AND SHANGHAI BANKING CORPORATION
The most powerful financial institution in the Hong Kong Special Administrative Region, and the most prominent and influential bank in Asia. The Hongkong and Shanghai Banking Corporation was founded after Great Britain acquired the island of Hong Kong under the Treaty of Nanjing in 1842. The treaty also opened Shanghai at the mouth of the Yangzi River and five other Chinese cities to foreign residents and traders, known as treaty ports. The bank was based in Shanghai, China's largest trading city, until the Chinese Communist Party (CCP) founded the PRC in 1949 and evicted the bank from its huge granite building in Shanghai's financial district; the bank then moved its headquarters to Hong Kong. The local branch of the CCP moved into the bank building in Shanghai. The top executives and international officers of the Hongkong and Shanghai Banking Corporation are still primarily English and Scots, although the company is now recruiting more Asians. In 1994 Vincent Cheng Hoi Chuen, a Hong Kong Chinese, became the bank's chief financial officer. Until recently, 80 percent of all paper currency minted in Hong Kong carries the image of the modern skyscraper headquarters of the Hongkong and Shanghai Banking Corporation, which opened in 1985. The 52-story building was designed by British architect Norman Foster and may have cost more than U.S.$1 billion. The bank has financed many of the immense fortunes that traders have acquired in Hong Kong, and it has used the profits it has made from recent rapid economic development in the PRC and such Asian countries as Singapore, Taiwan, Thailand and Indonesia to move into Europe, North America and the Middle East. In 1994, investors valued the Hongkong and Shanghai Banking Corporation at $29 billion, making it the world's 13th-largest bank. It had offices in 65 countries, although it still earned two-thirds of its profits in Hong Kong. Midland Bank is the bank's largest acquisition in Great Britain, and Marine Midland its largest in America.

In 1993 the Hongkong and Shanghai Bank earned $3.8 billion before taxes, more than any other bank in the world, on assets of $305 billion. The bank's recently established parent company, HSBC Holdings Plc., based in London, is the world's most profitable bank. HSBC also owns 61.48 percent of the next-largest bank in Hong Kong, the Hang Seng Bank Ltd. It controls dozens of banks and financial institutions in many different countries, as well as a group of investment banks under the Wardley Group and James Capel names, the Hong Kong Bank of Canada and the British Bank of the Middle East.

The Hongkong and Shanghai Banking Corporation provides all of the finance services required for trade, such as export and import letters of credit, loan financing and collections on commercial paper. Every year the bank issues more than 100,000 import letters of credit and more than 200,000 export letters of credit. It is uncertain whether the bank is still able to continue its current operations now that Hong Kong has reverted to China, although the bank's executives are optimistic about the future. The Bank of China, the foreign arm of the PRC's People's Bank of China, has become very competitive in Hong Kong and has won the privilege to mint money. Its headquarters are in another skyscraper directly across from those of the Hongkong and Shanghai Banking Corporation. Hong Kong reverted to the PRC in 1997. See also BANK OF CHINA; FOREIGN TRADE AND INVESTMENT; HONG KONG; OPIUM WAR; PEOPLE'S BANK OF CHINA; TREATY PORTS.

HONGLOUMENG See DREAM OF THE RED CHAMBER.

HONGSHAN CULTURE See NEOLITHIC PERIOD.

HONGSHUI RIVER See WEST RIVER.

HONGWU (EMPEROR) (Hung-wu; 1328–98)   The first emperor of the Ming dynasty (1368–1644). His original name was Zhu Yuanzhang (Chu Yuan-chang); Hongwu, meaning "Vast Military Achievement," is his reign title (r. 1368–98). The previous dynasty, the Yuan (1279–1368), had been founded by the Mongols, an ethnic group to the north of China that invaded the country and overthrown the Southern Song dynasty (1127–1279). The Han ethnic Chinese, the vast majority of China's population, resented the rule of the Mongols. By the middle of the 14th century, China was beset with anti-Mongol rebellions, the largest of which was carried out by a secret society known as the Red Turbans.

Zhu Yuanzhang was an orphaned peasant who became a novice in a Buddhist monastery. In 1352 he joined the private guard of Guo Zixing (Kuo Tzu-hsing), a local Red Turban leader in the Huai River valley who was a subordinate of Han Liner, the Red Turban leader who claimed to be the emperor of a restored Song dynasty. In 1355 Guo died and Zhu, who had married Guo's daughter, took his place. He led his rebel group across the Yangzi River and in 1356 captured the major city of Nanjing and made it his base. (Han Liner drowned suspiciously in 1367 while under Zhu's protection.) In 1361 Zhu took the title Duke of Wu, and, in 1364, the Prince of Wu, showing that he himself intended to establish a dynasty; Wu was the ancient name for this region of China during the Three Kingdoms Period (220–80) and the Five Dynasties Period (907–60). In 1363 Zhu's forces defeated those of Chen Youliang (Ch'en Yu-liang), who controlled the central Yangzi region and claimed to be the leader of the Red Turban movement in the entire region of southern China. The decisive defeat occurred in a naval battle on Lake Poyang in Jiangxi Province. Zhu went on to take control of the entire central China region and then defeated his other rivals for power. The most powerful was Zhang Shicheng (Chang Shih-ch'eng), based at Suzhou, who was defeated by Zhu in 1367.

On January 12, 1368, Zhu proclaimed the restoration of Chinese rule under the Ming ("Radiance") dynasty with himself as emperor. Hongwu became a capable but tyrannical ruler who instituted the practice of corporal punishment of officials in the imperial bureaucracy, who often died from their floggings. In previous dynasties the Six Ministries of the bureaucracy (Rites, Revenue, Personnel, War, Justice and Public Works) had been headed by a prime minister who was highly educated and respected for his personal virtue and who reported to the emperor, but Hongwu abolished the position of prime minister and placed the ministries directly under his control. This system worked well for him, but later Ming emperors did not have his personal authority and left control of the government to the eunuchs who staffed the imperial palace.

In 1380 and 1393 there were two attempted coups against Hongwu, both of which he crushed mercilessly. Some Mongols from the Yuan had stayed in China and continued to hold their positions in the imperial bureaucracy or joined the Ming army. Others returned to the Mongol territory north of the Great Wall but pledged loyalty to the Ming. However, a number of Mongol tribes continued to menace northwestern China, so Hongwu waged military campaigns against them until his troops pushed quite a distance into Mongol territory. Twice they even captured the capital at Karakorum, forcing the Mongol chieftains to sue for peace. Hongwu also brought Yunnan Province to the southwest into the Chinese Empire and thus completed the region known as China Proper. He recognized the importance of a strong navy, since he had won the naval battle on Lake Poyang, so he built up the Chinese navy and sent ships to patrol the coast against the many pirates in Chinese waters. He also undertook a complete census of the population in China and the compilation of land-survey maps and land-tax books, and tried to lessen the influence of wealthy landholding families in southern China by forcing them to move to Nanjing.

Emperor Hongwu's eldest son died in 1392, so he named his eldest grandson as his heir. Known as Emperor Jianwen (Chien-wen; r. 1399–1402), he was an able ruler but was opposed by Hongwu's fourth son, Zhu Di (Chu Ti), the Prince of Yan (Yen), who led a rebellion and removed Jianwen from power. The prince took the throne as Emperor Yongle (Yung-lo; r. 1403–24) and became one of the greatest Ming emperors. See also CHINA PROPER; EUNUCHS; GREAT WALL; HUAI RIVER; IMPERIAL BUREAUCRACY; KARAKORUM; MING DYNASTY; MONGOL; NANJING; PIRATES; POYANG, LAKE; RED TURBANS REBELLION; YONGLE (EMPEROR); YUAN DYNASTY.

HONGZE, LAKE (Hongze Hu)   The third-largest freshwater lake in China, encompassing an area of 1,084 square miles in Jiangsu province. Lake Hongze is located on the Huai River plain, a large alluvial plain that experiences frequent flooding. The Huai River once flowed into the East China Sea, but now a tributary flows first into Lake Hongze, then south into Lake Gaoyou and finally into the Yangzi River (Changjiang). Canals dug from Lake Hongze channel the river's water into the sea. The lake has been dammed on its eastern side, causing its water level to rise above the level of the adjoining Lixia River. See also EAST CHINA SEA; HUAI RIVER; JIANGSU PROVINCE.

HOPEH (HOPEI) PROVINCE   See HEBEI PROVINCE.

HORSE (ma)   An animal that most likely originated in Central Asia and became very important in China. Archaeologists have determined that more than a half-million years ago, early small varieties of the horse were coexisting with humans in central and eastern China. Remains of horses have been excavated from the Neolithic period known as the Yangshao culture (c. 5000–c. 2000 B.C.) along with painted red pottery typical of that culture; and horse remains from the Longshan culture (c. 3000–2200 B.C.) have been found with polished black pottery vessels. At Anyang, capital of the late Shang dynasty (c. 1750–1040 B.C.), remains of two horses with bronze fittings and their carriage driver have been excavated. During the Zhou dynasty (1100–256 B.C.), bronze was used to make implements for horse riding and archery. The armies that unified China under the Qin dynasty (221–206 B.C.) founded by Emperor Qin Shi Huangdi (259–210 B.C.) relied heavily on horses and armored chariots. The pottery and bronze armies that were buried with the emperor near modern Xi'an have been excavated and include armored chariots, horses and riders.

The Chinese Empire was constantly threatened by invasions of nomadic tribes from Central Asia, but it also depended on trade with those same tribes to maintain its lucrative trade along the so-called Silk Road. The main acquisition the Chinese wished from the nomads was the horse. The nomads had excellent horseriding skills that enabled them to maneuver advantageously against their opponents. During the Western Han dynasty (206 B.C.–A.D. 9), the Chinese valued highly the horses raised by tribes in Ferghana to the west (modern Uzbekistan) because they were much bigger, stronger and swifter than native Chinese horses. In A.D. 102, Han Emperor Wudi (Wu-ti) sent an army of 40,000 men to lay siege to Ferghana and capture their horses. The Chinese were defeated, but a second army of 60,000 succeeded in bringing 3,000 horses to the Han capital at Chang'an (modern Xi'an). The Fergehan horse then became famous as "The Heavenly Horse of China" and was portrayed in many Han dynasty paintings, sculptures and tomb tiles. This horse is often depicted in the "flying gallop" position with all four legs off the ground. The Chinese also acquired horses from Kucha and Kushan, and Arabian horses from Bukhara and Samarkand. The Central Asian regions that became absorbed into western and northwestern China, largely comprising steppes and high plateaus that have a dry climate and little vegetation, have favorable conditions for raising horses and other ungulates, including camels, sheep, yaks and goats. China also possesses the last survivors of the endangered Przewalski's horse, which had dwindled to about 400 in zoos around the world. In 1986, the first group of captive Przewalski's horses was released into the wild near Urumqi, the capital of Xinjiang-Uighur Autonomous Region. The Asiatic wild ass inhabits the Qinghai-Tibet Plateau in western China, where the inhabitants, mostly seminomadic Tibetans, herd horses, sheep and yaks. Explorers recently discovered survivors of an ancient horse in Tibet, which they named the Riwoche horse.

Each Chinese dynasty used all available means to acquire horses for military purposes and couriers. In the mid-seventh century, a Tang dynasty emperor sent a Chinese princess to marry the Khan (ruler) of a Turkish tribe for the bride price of 50,000 horses, as well as camels and sheep. During the Sui (581–618) and Tang (618–907) dynasties, a number of towns along the Chinese frontier with Central Asia became trading centers where the Chinese bartered silk—which at that time only they produced because they kept the technique a secret—for horses. In the late Tang, China exchanged the high price of one million bolts of silk for 100,000 horses every year, which strained the empire's treasury. During the Song (960–1279) and Ming (1368–1644) dynasties, tea was another important luxury item that the imperial government used as barter for horses. The Ming established a Horse Trading Office in Shaanxi Province in western China, with branches at Hami and Dunhuang.

Small but sturdy Mongolian ponies were introduced from the Mongol people who lived north of the Great Wall and who ruled China during the Yuan dynasty (1279–1368). The Mongols had established an empire stretching from eastern Europe all the way to China, and they used an enormous number of horses to maintain their efficient horse-messenger service throughout their empire. Mongol armies were highly mobile and able to rapidly encircle enemies because they relied on archers riding lightly armored horses. By at least the fourth century A.D., the Mongols were using iron stirrups, which kept them stable on horseback so they could shoot their iron-tipped arrows with amazing accuracy. Mongol soldiers had learned to ride horses as little boys, and they were used to living in the saddle for days on end.

In China, horse sculptures were made from stone, bronze and pottery and were often buried in tombs, with and without riders. Horses are one of the stone animals that guard walkways to imperial tombs from the Han through the Ming (1368–1644) dynasties. Sculptures of horses also frequently guard temples, along with lions and dogs, and were traditionally believed to come alive at night and gallop about. Horses were also a common subject in Chinese painting. The most famous painters of horses were Han Kang (c. 754) and Zhao Meng Fu (c. 1274). During the Tang dynasty, the horse was one of the most frequent subjects of painting, sculptures and poetry. One of the best-known themes using horses in Chinese art is the "Eight Horses of Emperor Mu Wang." Horses have also been a common motif in China for decorating porcelain, jade carvings and textiles, especially during the Ming and Qing (1644–1911) dynasties.

The Chinese character for horse, *ma*, derives from the ancient character depicting four legs, a tail and a head drawn with three brush strokes. In Chinese mythology, the horse is considered yang, the male, or positive principle, in contrast to yin, the negative, or female principle, and is associated with the element of fire. A bright young Chinese scholar is traditionally called a "thousand *li* colt" (a *li* is one-third of a mile). The horse is one of the 12 animals in the traditional zodiac that assigns an animal to each year. People born in the Year of the Horse are thought to be cheerful, independent, clever, talkative, quick to anger and able to handle money well. The most recent Year of the Horse was 1990, which corresponds to 4688 in the Chinese calendar. See also DOG; HAMI; LION; MONGOL; NOMADS AND ANIMAL HUSBANDRY; QIN SHI HUANGDI, EMPEROR; QINGHAI-TIBET PLATEAU; SILK ROAD; WUDI, EMPEROR; YAK; YIN AND YANG; ZODIAC, ANIMAL.

HOTAN (Khotan)   A city in Xinjiang-Uighur Autonomous Region, the farthest west of any Chinese province. Hotan is situated in the Tarim Basin between the Taklimakan Desert to the north and the Kunlun Mountain Range to the south. It was an important oasis city on the so-called Silk Road estab-

lished in the Han dynasty (206 B.C.–A.D. 220), and was a major exporter of jade to the Chinese Empire. Camel caravans carried Chinese silk, porcelain and tea west through Central Asia to the Mediterranean world, and brought back Western goods, culture and religions. The southern branch of the Silk Road passed through Hotan, and the northern through Turpan, both skirting the Taklimakan Desert. The kingdom of Hotan, which had been established by the Xiongnu nomadic tribe, had been conquered by troops sent by Han Emperor Wudi in 108 B.C. (The Chinese name for Hotan is Yutian.) In the third century A.D. a monk from the Indian province of Kashmir converted the region to the Buddhist religion. Tibetan invaders from the south threatened Hotan at the end of the seventh century, but the region, while a satellite of China, retained its autonomy until the late 10th century when Muslim Turkish nomadic tribes invaded from Central Asia. All of these groups fought to control Hotan for three centuries. In 1760, troops sent by the Qing dynasty (1644–1911) made the region part of the Chinese Empire.

Today Hotan has a population of about 200,000, with the majority belonging to the national minority group ethnic known as Uighurs, who are Muslim nomadic herders. Several other ancient oasis towns lie along the road east from the city into the forbidding Taklimakan Desert. Hotan is famous for colorful handmade carpets, handwoven silk, carved jade, felt (made from boiled wool), and handmade paper. Since the Han era, the main crop has been the mulberry shrub, the leaves of which are fed to silkworms. See also CARPETS; HAN DYNASTY; JADE; KUNLUN MOUNTAIN RANGE; MUSLIMS; PAPER; SILK; SILK ROAD; TAKLIMAKAN DESERT; TARIM BASIN; TIBET; TURPAN DEPRESSION, UIGHUR; XINJIANG-UIGHUR AUTONOMOUS REGION; XIONGNU.

HOU YI (HOU I)   See CHANG E.

HOWE, JAMES WONG (1899–1976)   Original name was Wong Tung Jim; a highly acclaimed Chinese-American cinematographer in the American film industry. Born in the southern Chinese port city of Guangzhou (Canton), Howe emigrated with his family to the United States when he was five years old and lived in Washington and Oregon states. In 1916 Howe moved to Southern California and found work on the many silent films that were being produced there, learning all the filmmaking techniques then in use. When sound became used in films, he invented techniques for overcoming the limitations that sound placed on the movement of the cameras. When shooting *Transatlantic* (1931), Howe was the first cinematographer to use a wide-angle lens and deep focus. He was also one of the earliest cinematographers to use a handheld camera, such as in *Body and Soul* (1947), where he filmed boxing scenes while being pushed around the set on rollerskates. Howe was awarded Academy Awards for cinematography for *The Rose Tattoo* (1955) and *Hud* (1963). He died in Hollywood, California, in 1976. The Chinese-American actress Beulah Quo produced the television documentary *James Wong Howe—The Man and His Movies,* for which she became the first Asian-American woman to win an Emmy Award.

HSI WANG MU   See XIWANGMU.

HSI-SHIH See XI SHI.

HSI-YU-CHI See JOURNEY TO THE WEST; XUANZANG.

HSIA DYNASTY See XIA DYNASTY.

HSIA KUEI See XIA GUI.

HSIA NAI See ARCHAEOLOGY; XIA NAI.

HSIAMEN See XIAMEN.

HSIAO AND HSIAO-CHING See ANCESTOR WORSHIP; FIL-IAL PIETY.

HSIEH HO See SIX CANONS OF PAINTING.

HSIEH LING-YUN See XIE LINGYUN.

HSIEN HSING-HAI See XIAN XINGHAI.

HSIEN-FENG (EMPEROR) See ARROW WAR; CIXI, EMPRESS DOWAGER; GONG, PRINCE; QING DYNASTY.

HSIEN-TI (EMPEROR) See EASTERN HAN DYNASTY.

HSIEN-TSUNG (EMPEROR) See TANG DYNASTY.

HSIN CH'I-CHI See XIN QIJI.

HSIN DYNASTY See WANG MANG.

HSIN NIEN See NEW YEAR FESTIVAL.

HSIN-CHING See CHANGCHUN; MANCHUKUO.

HSIUNG-NU See XIONGNU.

HSU PEI-HUNG See XU BEIHONG.

HSU WEI See XU WEI.

HSUAN-TE (EMPEROR) XUANDE (EMPEROR).

HSUAN-TSANG See XUANZANG.

HSUAN-TSUNG (EMPEROR) See AN LUSHAN REBELLION; TANG DYNASTY; XUANZONG (EMPEROR); YANG GUIFEI.

HSUAN-T'UNG (EMPEROR) See PUYI, HENRY.

HSUN KUAN-NIENG See XUN GUANNIANG.

HSUN TZU See XUNZI.

HU DIE (Hu Tieh; 1908–89) Original name Hu Ruihua (Hu Jui-hua); one of the most popular actresses in Chinese films. She was born in Shanghai, but when she was nine years old her family moved to Guangzhou (Canton). Her father was the general inspector on the Beijing-Fengtian railway line. In 1924, when she was 16, her family moved back to Shanghai, where she became the first student in the China Film School, the first film actors' training school in China. She took the professional name Hu Die, meaning "Butterfly."

Hu Die's first role after graduation was a supporting character in the film *Success*. After this she starred in more than 20 feature films; most of them were produced by the Youlian and Tianyi Film corporations. Her movies, such as *The Sweeping Autumn Fans* and *The Tragic History of the Butterfly Lovers*, embraced classical Chinese themes.

Hu Die had the delicate and dignified look of a "classical" Chinese beauty. In 1928 she joined the Stars Film Corporation, where she starred in the company's most important films. Her first role for Stars was controversial—"Red Aunty," in the second part of *The Burning of Red Lotus Temple*. Hu Die also starred in China's first talking movie, *Red Peony the Songstress*. Her most important film, was *Two Sisters*, directed by Zheng Zhengqiu (Cheng Cheng-ch'iu), who adapted the story from his own stage play, *The Noble and the Crazy*. Hu Die played the double role of twins, Da Bao (Ta Pao) and Er Bao (Erh Pao), who were separated after birth. One became the arrogant wife of a warlord, while the other became the wet nurse for her own sister's child. Hue Die played the two different women so skillfully that even now the film wins acclaim when shown in China and abroad. In 1933 a poll conducted by *Star Daily* named Hu Die "Queen of Screen."

In 1935 she was a member of the Chinese film delegation invited to the Soviet International Film Exhibition in Moscow, where *Two Sisters* was shown. She then traveled to Germany, France, Great Britain and Italy. When she returned to China she starred in *A Flower at Night*, *The Misfortunate Peach Blossom*, *Brothers on a Trip*, *Rights of Women* and *Everlasting Smile*.

In 1937 the Japanese invaded China and attacked Shanghai in August. A fire destroyed the production base of the Stars Film Corporation and Hu Die and her family fled to Hong Kong, which the Japanese invaded the following year. The Japanese intended to take Hu Die to star in a documentary called *Hu Die Touring Tokyo*, but she secretly fled to Chongqing in Sichuan Province, the capital of Nationalist China, and remained there until the war ended, assisting her businessman husband. After the Chinese Communists established the People's Republic of China in 1949, Hu Die starred in *Street Boys*, *Women of Two Generations* and *When the Moon Is Full*. In 1960 she was named best actress at the Seventh Asian Film Festival in Tokyo for her role in *Rear Door*. After Hu Die made *The Woman in the Tower* in 1967, she announced her retirement. In 1975 she moved to Canada, where she spent the rest of her life. See also WAR OF RESISTANCE AGAINST JAPAN.

HU SHI (Hu Shih; 1891–1962) A famous educator, philosopher and diplomat. Hu Shi was born in Shanghai, where his father was a minor official until he died in 1895. He was a brilliant student and won a scholarship to attend Cornell University in Ithaca, New York, where he received a degree in 1914. In 1917 he received his doctorate in philosophy from Columbia University in New York, where he studied under the pragmatist thinker John Dewey. Returning to China that year, Hu Shi was appointed professor of philosophy at Peking (Beijing) University. He joined the new movement in Chinese literature and culture that emphasized *bai-hua* (*pai hua*), the use of vernacular language in literature, and he became well known as a scholar and political thinker associated with the May Fourth Movement of 1919. During the 1920s, journals published Hu Shi's many essays expounding his ideas. He criticized the two main Chinese political parties, the Communists and the Nationalists (the Kuomintang). Even though Japan had invaded Manchuria, he opposed war between China and Japan because he thought it would destroy the reforms that had been enacted to modernized China. In 1938, after war had broken out between the two nations, Hu Shi was appointed Chinese ambassador to the United States, a post he held until 1942. He remained in the United States until the end of World War II, when he returned to China to serve an appointment as chancellor of Peking University from 1946 to 1949. When Chinese Communist forces surrounded the capital city in 1948, he fled to Nanjing. He then returned to the United States to live in semiretirement. In 1958 he was appointed president of the Academia Sinica in Taiwan (the Republic of China). Hu Shi died in Taipei, Taiwan. See also ACADEMIA SINICA; CIVIL WAR BETWEEN COMMUNISTS AND NATIONALISTS; MAY FOURTH MOVEMENT OF 1919; WAR OF RESISTANCE AGAINST JAPAN.

HU TIEH See HU DIE.

HU YAOBANG (Hu Yao-pang; 1917–89)   A Communist official in the People's Republic of China (PRC) whose death triggered the 1989 pro-democracy student demonstrations that ended with the Tiananmen Square Massacre. Hu was born into a poor peasant family in Hunan Province and joined the Chinese Communist Party (CCP) when he was 14. In 1941 he met Deng Xiaoping (Teng Hsiao-p'ing; 1904–97) while serving in the Red (Communist) Army. His career from then on was always tied to Deng's. In the 1950s and '60s, Hu served as head of the Communist Youth League. Hu and Deng were purged by the CCP in 1966, when the Cultural Revolution (1966–76) broke out, and were rehabilitated in 1973, only to be purged yet again. Deng was rehabilitated once more in 1977 and began rising to the leadership of the CCP. As a close associate of Deng, Hu was appointed to important Party positions. Hu became a prominent leader when the CCP began reforming the government and rebuilding the country following the destructive Cultural Revolution. Chairman Mao Zedong (Mao Tse-tung; 1893–1976) and Premier Zhou Enlai (Chou En-lai; 1898–1976), who had been the two highest Party leaders since the Communists founded the PRC in 1949, both died in 1976. After their deaths, Deng Xiaoping, who had been purged twice during the Cultural Revolution, was rehabilitated and led the CCP faction that promoted modernization and economic and political reforms. The CCP abolished the prestigious position of chairman and made the party secretariat the highest body of the Party. The secretary general, the head of the secretariat, thus became one of the most important persons in the CCP, although he did not have the power once held by chairman Mao Zedong. At the third Plenum of the National Party Congress's 11th Central Committee in December 1978, Deng was able to have Hu

Yaobang elected secretary general of the CCP, as well as head of the Party's propaganda department, and Hu took over the daily operations of the Party. This plenum marked the Chinese government's official turn toward modernization following the Cultural Revolution. At the Fifth Plenum of the 11th Central Committee in 1980, Hu Yaobang and another Deng protégé, Zhao Ziyang, were elevated to the Standing Committee of the Politburo (Political Bureau) and the newly restored party secretariat. Hu was made general secretary of the Central Committee, the highest CCP administrative post. In May 1980, General Secretary Hu visited Lhasa, the capital of Tibet, to apologize to the Tibetan people for the terrible harm that the Chinese inflicted on them and their culture during the Cultural Revolution. At the Sixth Plenum of the 11th Central Committee in 1981, Deng was able to have Hua Guofeng demoted as party chairman and to have Hu Yaobang take his place. Hua was given the face-saving position of vice chairman. Deng himself replaced Hua as chairman of the CCP Central Military Commission. Shortly after the plenum closed, at the celebration of the 60th anniversary of the founding of the CCP, new party chairman Hu made a statement that attempted to repair the damage that had been done to the legacy of Mao Zedong and the CCP by the excesses of the Cultural Revolution. Hu declared that although Chairman Mao made serious mistakes in his later years, "his contributions to the Chinese revolution far outweigh his errors. . . . His immense contributions are immortal." Hu also praised Zhou Enlai, Liu Shaoqi (Liu Shao-ch'i), Zhu De (Chu Teh), Peng Dehuai (P'eng Teh-huai) and many leaders who had been considered Mao's enemies during the Cultural Revolution. The CCP used Hu's speech to end debate on the Maoist era and move into a period of modernization.

In November 1983 Hu visited Japan to reassure Japanese leaders who were concerned about the stability of the Chinese government and about who would be Deng's successor. At the meeting of the CCP Central Committee in September 1986, Party hardliners denounced "bourgeois liberalization"—the Party's term for the adaptation of Western political and cultural ideas and the preference for capitalism over socialism. The Central Committee passed a resolution calling for the spiritual reconstruction of socialism. Students and others in China had been promoting democratization and progressive reforms, and large numbers of students held demonstrations in 15 cities demanding free elections and freedom of speech, assembly and the press. Hu did not denounce the demonstrators and the intellectuals who supported them, and he continued to favor political reform by means of bringing "democratization," or pluralism, into the Chinese political system. Party hardliners critized Hu for handling the demonstrators too leniently, and they convinced Deng to oppose such reforms and deal more harshly with the students. Hu had been considered Deng's successor as CCP leader, but members of the Politburo attacked him for creating an atmosphere in which people were encouraged to question the Communist system, for pushing economic reforms too far and for speaking abruptly in public. Deng attempted to influence Hu to correct his errors but Hu supposedly did not do so, and in January 1987 he was demoted from his position as general secretary. Zhao Ziyang, former head of the State Council, replaced Hu as general secretary, and Li Peng, more conservative than Zhao regarding economic reform, replaced Zhao as prime minister. Hu was, however, permitted to keep his seat on the Standing Committee of the Politburo, and in the media he was shown attending important Party meetings.

When Hu was dismissed, Chinese students immediately regarded him as a hero. Hu died on April 15, 1989, and on April 17 prodemocracy demonstrations broke out in Shanghai and Beijing, where students placed wreaths in Tiananmen Square to commemorate him. Two days later the students marched to the Zhongnanhai compound, the residence of many CCP leaders, and held a sit-in, calling for Li Peng to come out and address them. On April 21, 100,000 students held a rally in Tiananmen Square, the same day as the official memorial service for Hu Yaobang. They demanded the posthumous restoration of Hu's honor as well as freedom of speech, assembly and press, increased funding for education, and the publication of the incomes and financial assets of top government leaders. The protestors held the square until the night of June 4, when the government ordered a full-scale military assault against them. See also CHINESE COMMUNIST PARTY; CULTURAL REVOLUTION; DENG XIAOPING; GOVERNMENT STRUCTURE; HUA GUOFENG; LI PENG; TIANANMEN SQUARE MASSACRE; TIBET; ZHAO ZIYANG; ZHONGNANHAI COMPOUND.

HU YAO-PANG See HU YAOBANG.

HUA GUOFENG (Hua Kuo-feng; 1920–) A leading Communist politician who replaced Mao Zedong (Mao Tsetung) as chairman of the Chinese Communist Party (CCP) when Mao died in 1976. Hua was born to a peasant family in Shanxi Province. He joined the CCP as a young man, working as a guerrilla leader and Party secretary at the country level in Shaanxi and Shanxi provinces. When the CCP founded the People's Republic of China (PRC) in 1949, Hua was in Hunan, Mao's home province, where he was active in agriculture and land reform—the redistribution of land from landlords to peasants. From 1952 to 1955 Hua moved up to the district level in the Party bureaucracy and became a leader of the Communist movement to establish agricultural collectives, known as people's communes. In 1956 he became head of the Hunan Culture and Education Office and helped lead the movement to end illiteracy and to adopt a standard dialect, known as *putonghua,* throughout China. In 1957 he became head of the CCP's United Front Department in Hunan. During China's Great Leap Forward (1958–60), he gained attention for his work in establishing agricultural collectives.

Hua was still working at the provincial level during the 1960s, especially in the areas of military preparedness, water conservation, and trade and finance. During the Cultural Revolution (1966–76) he built up his political power, and in 1971 he was transferred to the capital city of Beijing, where he worked in the staff office of the State Council under Premier Zhou Enlai (Chou En-lai). Hua took part in the investigation of Lin Biao (Lin Piao), whom the CCP had designated as Mao's successor as Party chairman. In 1972 the Chinese government announced that Lin had attempted a coup to overthrow Mao but had failed; while trying to escape to the

U.S.S.R., he was killed when his plane crashed. Hua was elected to the Politburo in August 1973 at the National Party Congress. At the National People's Congress in January 1975, Hua was elected a vice-premier, making him sixth in rank in the CCP hierarchy. He was also made Minister of Public Security. He worked closely with Mao and developed a personal relationship with him. When Zhou Enlai died in January 1976, Deng Xiaoping was in position to succeed him as premier. However, radical Party leaders attacked Deng and removed him from all of his official positions in April 1976. They named Hua acting premier and Party vice chairman, the second-highest position in the CCP, placing him just below Mao, who was quoted as telling Hua, "With you in charge, I'm at ease."

When Mao died on September 9, 1976, Hua succeeded him as chairman of the CCP. In October, shortly after Mao's death, Hua ordered Party leaders in Beijing to purge more than 30 radical Party leaders, including Jiang Qing (Mao's widow), Zhang Chunjiao, Yao Wenyuan and Wang Hongwen; they became known as the "Gang of Four" and were brought to trial and blamed for the Cultural Revolution. Party leaders announced that Hua was now chairman of the Politburo, the Central Committee of the CCP; chairman of the Central Military Commission (commander-in-chief of the armed forces); and premier of the State Council. At the National People's Congress in March 1978, Hua was reaffirmed in these positions. When Deng Xiaoping was rehabilitated the next year, he began strengthening his power in the CCP, with his faction opposing the more conservative faction associated with Mao and led by Hua. In September 1980, Hua was replaced as premier by Zhao Ziyang, a provincial Party official and protegée of Deng. In June 1981 Hua resigned as chairman of the Central Committee and was replaced by CCP secretary general Hu Yaobang, another Deng protegée. Hua was allowed to "save face" by accepting the position of vice chairman of the Central Committee, but he was removed as chairman of the Central Military Commission and replaced by Deng Xiaoping. Party leaders were now publicly criticizing Mao for having made serious mistakes, especially during the Cultural Revolution. They praised Hua for having helped defeat the Gang of Four but criticized him for having opposed Deng from 1976 to 1977 and for belonging to the "two whatevers" group, who were to "support whatever policy decisions Chairman Mao made and follow whatever instructions Chairman Mao gave." See also AGRICULTURE; CENTRAL MILITARY COMMISSION AND MINISTRY OF NATIONAL DEFENSE; CULTURAL REVOLUTION; GANG OF FOUR; GOVERNMENT STRUCTURE; HU YAOBANG; LAND REFORM BY COMMUNISTS; MAO ZEDONG; PEOPLE'S COMMUNE; POLITBURO; PUTONGHUA; ZHAO ZIYANG; ZHOU ENLAI.

HUA KUO-FENG See HUA GUOFENG.

HUA, MOUNT See FIVE SACRED MOUNTAINS OF DAOISM.

HUA SHUO See DONG QICHANG.

HUAANGGUOSHU WATERFALL See BOUYEI; GUIYANG; GUIZHOU PROVINCE.

HUAI RIVER (Huaihe)   One of the major rivers of China. The Huai River flows eastward through Henan and Anhui provinces into northern Jiangsu Province. The Huai and Han rivers form a natural boundary between northern and southern China. More than 10 tributaries of the Huai River cross Anhui Province, and they have caused disastrous floods over the centuries. Irrigation projects since 1949 have controlled this flooding. The Huai River and the Yellow River (Huanghe; China's second-longest river) to the south carry so much loess (a type of soil) that over millennia the Chinese coast along the Yellow Sea has been moved several miles east and lakes have been formed. This marshy coastal area, where the Hui empties into the sea, has long been an important source of salt.

However, Huai no longer flows directly into the East China Sea. One tributary flows into Lake Hongze (Hongze Hu), then south into Lake Gaoyou (Gaoyou Hu) and finally into the Yellow River; another flows north from Lake Hongze through two canals into the sea.

Beginning in A.D. 605 and integrated canal system known as the Grand Canal was constructed part of which linked the important city of Luoyang, which frequently served as the capital city, to the Huai River and then to the Yangzi River (Changjiang; China's longest river). Popular rebellions broke out under the last emperor of the Mongol Yuan dynasty (1279–1368), when many peasants suffered from the flooding of the Huai and Yellow rivers and the government used forced labor to repair the broken dams. This was one of the factors bringing Mongol rule of China to an end. See also ANHUI PROVINCE; EAST CHINA SEA; GRAND CANAL; HAN RIVER; HENAN PROVINCE; HONGZE, LAKE; JIANGSU PROVINCE; LOESS; NATURAL DISASTERS; YANGZI RIVER; YELLOW RIVER; YUAN DYNASTY.

HUANG (Huangshan, or "Yellow Mountains")   A range of mountains extending for 160 miles in southern Anhui Province that have been celebrated by Chinese painters and poets for their mystical beauty. Mount Huang (Huangshan), for which the range is named, rises to 7,251 feet; 30 of the 72 peaks in the Huang Range are higher than 5,400 feet. The geological processes of faulting and folding have given the Huang unique shapes with caves and grottoes, jagged peaks, rocks hanging over sheer cliffs, and gnarled pine trees growing from the rock face. Streams flowing through the mountains have many rapids and waterfalls, and there is a hot springs resort at the western base of Mount Huang. Tourists can climb stone steps on the east and west slopes all the way to the top of Mount Huang, where they can stay overnight in two hotels. Cable cars also run to the summit. The Huang Mountains have been a scenic attraction since Tang dynasty emperor Tianbiao (T'ien-piao) named them in 747. Chan (Zen) Buddhist master Zhiman (Chih-man) founded a temple on Mount Huang that became well known as the Xiangfu Si (Hsiang-fu-ssu). In 1990 UNESCO placed Mount Huang on its list of world natural and cultural heritage sites. See also ANHUI PROVINCE; CHAN SECT OF BUDDHISM; GEOGRAPHY.

HUANG CHAO   See PEASANTS AND PEASANT REBELLIONS.

HUANG CHUNG-YING   See ZHAO DAN.

HUANG GONGWANG (Huang Kung-wang; 1269–1354)   One of China's greatest landscape painters. He is known as one of the four great masters of the Yuan period (1279–1368), along with Ni Zan (Ni Tsan), Wang Meng and Wu Zhen (Wu Chen). Their works have the qualities of calm detachment, spiritual purity and the objectivity of a member of the literati (*wen ren*), or scholar, class to which they belonged. Artists who followed the Ma-Xia (Ma Yuan-Xia Gui) School, founded in the 12th century, left much empty space in their compositions, but Huang Gongwang and Wang Meng filled in the entire space of their pictures with details. Rather than making a stark composition, they kept adding cliffs, trees, rocks and mountain peaks until the scene filled the entire scroll. They built up their landscapes—through a careful process of adding brushstrokes, lines and dots—until the mountains, trees and other elements of the scene were completed. Huang Gongwang's masterpiece is the scroll painting *Dwelling in the Fuchun Mountains*, which he completed for a friend in 1350 after three years. He is still greatly admired for his excellent and detailed brushwork.

Huang Gongwang, as a member of the literati who governed China as part of the imperial bureaucracy, was also highly educated and skilled in music and poetry. However, Huang lived during the Yuan dynasty, which had been founded by Mongols from the north who had overthrown the Han or ethnic-Chinese Song dynasty (960–1279). Although some literati still staffed the Yuan bureaucracy, the Mongols forced many of members to retire. Like many literati artists, he was considered an "amateur" painter. (Literati artists were considered "amateurs" in the best sense, in that they expressed themselves through their art.)

Near the end of his life, Huang became a Daoist recluse, wandering in the mountains and sketching the elements of nature that were meaningful for him. Today art historians still cannot agree on a definitive body of work that can be attributed to Huang Gongwang. See also DAOISM; LANDSCAPE PAINTING; LITERATI; NI ZAN.

HUANG HO   See YELLOW RIVER.

HUANG HSING   See REPUBLIC OF CHINA; REVOLUTIONARY ALLIANCE; SUN YAT-SEN.

HUANG KUNG-WANG   See HUANG GONGWANG.

HUANG RIVER   See GANSU PROVINCE; SHAANXI PROVINCE.

HUANG T'ING-CHIEN   See HUANG TINGJIAN.

HUANG TINGJIAN (Huang T'ing-chien; 1045–1105)   A great calligrapher of the Song dynasty (960–1279), as well as an art critic and poet. He is considered one of the Four Great Masters of Song calligraphy and the founder of the Jiangsu school of poetry. Huang Tingjian was born in Jiangsu Province to a family of the literati, or scholar class; he later passed the examinations that gave him a position in the imperial bureaucracy. Huang helped to compile the Veritable Records of the reign of Emperor Shenzong (*Shen-tsung*; r. 1067–85), but for this he was accused of criticizing the policies of the current Song government and was sent into exile in Sichuan Province for six years. During this time he painted his famous *Scroll for Zhang Datong* (*Chang Ta-t'ung*). He was sent into exile a second time in the southern province of Guangxi, where he died.

Huang Tinjian agreed with his literati contemporaries, including Mi Fu and Su Shi, that one's calligraphy expresses one's personality—a concept known as "heart print" (*xinyin* or *hsinyin*). They believed that this was true for landscape painting as well. The important thing was not to make a pictorial representation of the subject but to use the brushstrokes to reveal one's own thoughts and feelings. This concept had a major influence on literati painting. Critics have concluded that the sharp brushstrokes of Huang Tingjian's own calligraphy reveal that he had a strong and determined, even stubborn, character, but that he was also generous to others. See also CALLIGRAPHY; PAINTING; SONG DYNASTY.

HUANG XING See REPUBLIC OF CHINA; REVOLUTIONARY ALLIANCE; SUN YAT-SEN.

HUANG ZHAO See PEASANTS AND PEASANT REBELLIONS; TANG DYNASTY.

HUANG ZONGYING See ZHAO DAN.

HUANGDI See EMPEROR; QIN SHI HUANGDI; YELLOW EMPEROR.

HUANGHAI See YELLOW SEA.

HUANGHE See YELLOW RIVER.

HUANGPU MILITARY ACADEMY See WHAMPOA MILITARY ACADEMY.

HUANGPU RIVER (Whampoa River; Huangpujiang)   A river that flows through the major port city of Shanghai, running north to the Wusong Estuary where it joins the Yangzi River, as it flows into the Yellow Sea. The harbor area extends more than 40 miles through the city along the Huangpu River, whose waterway is 33 feet deep and 730 feet wide. Oceangoing ships of more than 10,000 tons can navigate the river year-round. Goods are shipped from Shanghai to more than 300 ports around the world. By 1985 the port of Shanghai, the largest city in the western Pacific region, was handling 150 million tons of cargo. In the early 1990s at least one-third of all Chinese trade passed through the wharves and shipyards along the Huangpu. Construction of a modern seaway has allowed ships of up to 50,000 tons to sail into the harbor. Tourists can view the port activities by taking a four-hour river cruise to the mouth of the Yangzi River, one of the two largest rivers in China, which lies 10 miles north of Shanghai and empties into the Yellow Sea. Industrial districts and oil refineries line the banks of the Huangpu. The river is Shanghai's major water source even through it is badly polluted by sewage, industrial discharges and waste from ships. Nanpu Bridge, the largest bridge in China when it was opened in 1992, has enabled the rapid development of Pudong New Area on the east bank of Huangpu. The Treaty of Nanjing (1842) opened the port of Shanghai to Western traders and permitted them to lease land on the west bank of the Huangpu River. Westerners constructed large European-style buildings along the central waterfront, a wide avenue known as the Bund, to house their banks, trading houses and consulates. This area was the most active part of the city, with all kinds of boats from Chinese sampans to large cargo ships anchoring there. Today the main wharves are located farther down the Huangpu River and the buildings along the avenue, now called Zhongshan Number One Road East, house Chinese government offices such as the Foreign Trade Corporations and the Trade Union Headquarters. The Customs House, with its tall clock tower, is still in use while the former Cathay Hotel is now the Peace Hotel. Offices of the Shanghai Municipal Government are located in the building that formerly housed the Hongkong and Shanghai Bank. See also NANJING, TREATY OF; PUDONG NEW AREA; SHANGHAI; YANGZI RIVER; YELLOW SEA.

HUANGPU, TREATY OF See UNEQUAL TREATIES.

HUANG-TI See EMPEROR; YELLOW EMPEROR.

HUAQING HOT SPRINGS (Huaqing Chi)   Since ancient times a resort area located about 30 miles east of Xi'an (formerly Chang'an), the capital city of Shaanxi Province in northwestern China. Lying at the foot of scenic Lishan (Black Horse) Mountain, the Huaqing Hot Springs' water maintains a temperature of about 110 degrees F and contains many minerals. For 3,000 years the springs were a recreation area for the exclusive use of the Chinese emperors. Emperor Youwang of the Zhou dynasty (1100–256 B.C.) was the first ruler to build his winter place at Huaqing Hot Springs. Tang emperor Taizong (T'ai-tsung r. A.D. 626–49) also built a place there which was enlarged by Emperor Xuanzong (Hsuan-tsung; r. A.D. 712–56), who added a pond fed by the hot springs. His beautiful concubine Yang Guifei (Yang Kuei-fei) supposedly bathed in the Nine-Dragon Hot Spring and the Guifei Hot Spring. In 936, after the Tang dynasty fell, a Daoist monastery was built on the ruins of the palace. After 1949 the Chinese People's Government extensively renovated the Huaqing Hot Springs, building halls and pavilions in the Tang style around the pond and expanding the pools, and made them a resort for working people.

The Huaqing Hot Springs were the site of the so-called Xi'an Incident on December 12, 1936, when Chiang Kaishek was forced to accept the terms of the Nationalist alliance with the Communist Party. See also CHIANG KAISHEK; CIVIL WAR BETWEEN COMMUNTISTS AND NATIONALISTS; TANG DYNASTY; WAR OF RESISTANCE AGAINST JAPAN; XI'AN; XUANZONG, EMPEROR; YANG GUIFEI.

HUAYAN (HUA-YEN) SECT OF BUDDHISM See BUDDHISM; FLOWER GARLAND SECT OF BUDDHISM.

HUBEI PROVINCE   A province in central China that covers 72,195 square miles and has a population of about 51 million; the capital city, Wuhan, has a population of about 4 million. Other major cities include Huangshi, Shashi, Yichang and Xiangfan. Hubei is bordered by the provinces of Anhui to the east, Henan to the north, Sichuan and Shaanxi to the west and northwest, and Jiangxi and Hunan to the south.

Hubei means "to the north of the lake," referring to Lake Dongting in northern Hunan Province. Hubei is known as

The mineral-rich water at Huaqing Hot Springs maintains an average temperature of 110 degrees F.   S.E. MEYER

"the province with a thousand lakes"; many canals were also built to connect the lakes and rivers. The Yangzi River (Changjiang), one of the two main rivers in China, flows eastward through southern Hubei toward the Yellow Sea. Its position in the middle region of the Yangzi gave Hubei a prominence in Chinese history, although it has also brought disastrous floods, and extensive dikes have recently been constructed to protect the region. The Han River (Hanjiang), the main northern tributary of the Yangzi, flows through northern Hubei. Several mountain ranges cross northern Hubei, including the Wu, where the Yangzi drops through a gorge near Yichang down to the plains that form the eastern two-thirds of Hubei. A large dam built on the Yangzi at Yichang helps regulate flooding and improves navigation on the river. Mount Wudang (Wudangshan), where many Daoist temples have been built, lies in the Wu Range.

Hubei is an important region for both manufacturing and agriculture. Major industries include iron, steel, machinery, shipbuilding and textiles. The province is China's main producer of rolled steel and motor vehicles, second-largest producer of pig iron, and third-largest producer of steel and tractors. The province also has significant mineral deposits. The Jianghan Plain is one of the major rice- and wheat-growing areas in China. Other crops include corn, sorghum, sweet potatoes, fruit, tea, cotton and ramie, a plant used to make fibers. Hubei is China's main producer of sesame and the second-largest producer of hemp, lacquer, freshwater fish and shellfish, and herbal medicines. Pork is another major product.

Hubei Province has a very ancient history. Remains from the Yangshao Neolithic culture have been excavated in Hubei, dating back to c. 4500–3500 B.C. During the Warring States Period (403–221 B.C.), Hubei was part of the state of Chu, then the center of southern Chinese civilization. The remains of the Chu capital can still be seen near Shashi, a region that was incorporated into the Chinese Empire founded by Emperor Qin Shi Huangdi under the Qin dynasty (221–206 B.C.). Toward the end of the Eastern Han Period (A.D. 25–220), Sun Ce (Sun Ts'e) created the state of Wu on the lower Yangzi, and it was "officially inaugurated" as a kingdom by Sun Quan (Sun Ch'uan) in A.D. 222. The capital was established at Wuchang, now part of Wuhan, but was moved to Nanjing in A.D. 229. The kingdom of Wu was one of the chief powers in the Three Kingdoms Period (San Guo; A.D. 220–80), along with the kingdoms of Wei and of Shu, as immortalized in the first Chinese novel, *The Romance of the Three Kingdoms* (*Sanguozhi yanyi*). The three kingdoms were conquered by the Western Jin dynasty (A.D. 265–316).

Hubei formed part of Hunan Province, known as Huguang, from the 13th century until the Qing dynasty (1644–1911) divided Hunan and made Hubei a separate province. Rebellions by the White Lotus Secret Society—a Buddhist religious sect that attracted many peasants—were active in Hubei beginning in the 1780s before they were finally suppressed by the government in 1805. Western nations forced China to open the cities of Hankou, Yichang and Shashi to Western trade in 1860. Tea, tobacco, sesame, cotton and plant oils were the main products exported to the West. Hubei was a major center for the Taiping Rebellion (1850–64), the largest rebellion against the Qing dynasty, which was finally suppressed by Chinese and Western troops.

The industrial city of Wuhan on the Yangzi River is centrally located on the main north-south railroad line between the major cities of Beijing in the north and Guangzhou (Canton) in the south. Large quantities of iron, steel, agricultural machinery, railcars, trucks and machine tools are manufactured in Wuhan. The mile-long bridge built across the Yangzi River at Wuhan in 1957 enabled railroads to connect north and south China for the first time. The city comprises three towns—Wuchang, Hanyang and Hankou—that developed on the banks of three rivers that converge there. During the third century A.D., Wuchang was capital of the state of Wu, and during the Yuan dynasty (1279–1368) it was the capital of a province that extended all the way to the South China Sea. After that period the three towns played a lesser role until the Treaty of Nanjing (1842) opened Wuhan to Western traders. The Revolution of 1911, which overthrew the Qing dynasty (1644–1911), began in Wuhan with what is known as the Wuchang Uprising. The Communists set up the National Peasant Movement, headed by Mao Zedong, in Wuhan in 1927. Today Wuhan is an important military center. The Hubei Provincial Museum houses exhibits on the history of the region. See also AGRICULTURE; DONGTING, LAKE; GRAND CANAL; HAN RIVER; HUNAN PROVINCE; MEDICINE, HERBAL; NANJING, TREATY OF; RAMIE; REVOLUTION OF 1911; ROMANCE OF THE THREE KINGDOMS; TAIPING REBELLION; THREE KINGDOMS PERIOD; WHITE LOTUS SECRET SOCIETY; WUCHANG UPRISING; WUHAN; YANGSHAO CULTURE; YANGZI RIVER.

HUI   Chinese who practice the Muslim religion; one of China's 55 national minority ethnic groups. The Hui speak the Chinese language and are physically the same as the Han Chinese, the major ethnic group, but differ from them by their religious beliefs and dietary practices. In 1993 there were 8.6 million Hui, the second-largest minority in China next to the Zhang. The Hui reside mainly in northwestern China in the provinces of Gansu and Qinghai, Xinjiang-Uighur Autonomous Region and Ningxia-Hui Autonomous Region (Ningxia Huizu Zizhiqu). In Ningxia the Hui were given a measure of self-rule by the Chinese government. The capital city, Yinchuan, located on the west bank of the Yellow River at the foot of the Great Wall, was a center for horse trading from the Tang dynasty (618–907) to the modern era. Many of the Hui are descendants of Arab soldiers who came to China in the eighth century to help defeat the An Lushan Rebellion against the Tang dynasty, and who settled in northwestern China and were given Chinese wives. Others are descendants of Arab traders, large numbers of whom settled in a number of Chinese cities, or of Chinese who converted to Islam. Guangdong Province in southern China, whose capital is the major port city of Guangzhou (Canton), has a Hui population of about 4,500. More than 30,000 Hui reside in Xi'an (formerly Chang'an), the capital of Shaanxi Province in western China, which has six mosques. The most important of these is the Great Mosque (Huajue Xiang), founded in 742. The buildings seen today date from the 14th century

and have been restored several times, most recently in 1987. See also AN LUSHAN REBELLION; MINORITIES, NATIONAL; MUSLIMS; NINGXIA-HUI AUTONOMOUS REGION; XI'AN; YINCHUAN.

HUI   See CALLIGRAPHY; FOUR TREASURES OF THE STUDY.

HUI-TSUNG (EMPEROR)   See HUIZONG EMPEROR.

HUIZONG (EMPEROR) (Hui-tsung; 1082–1135)   Also known as Song Huizong (Sung Hui-tsung); the last emperor of the Northern Song dynasty (960–1126). His real name was Zhao Ji (Chao Chi); Huizong, meaning "Excellent Ancestor," was his posthumous reign name (r. 1100–25). Huizong undertook a number of projects that benefited the Chinese people, such as land reclamation, attempts to control the river flooding that frequently threatened the peasants, and the building of hospitals and schools. He patronized artists and was a poet, calligrapher and painter himself, specializing in bird-and-flower paintings. He founded a painting academy in his court and directed the compilation of the *Xuanhe (Hsuan-ho) Catalogue of Painting,* which contained 6,396 paintings by 231 artists.

In the political sphere, Huizong favored the faction that wanted to continue the reforms that had been enacted by Song government minister Wang Anshi (1021–86), during the reign of Emperor Shenzong (Shen-tsung; r. 1068–85), and he removed 120 of the highest-ranking conservative government officials. He also made the mistake of allocating too much power to several eunuchs, especially Tong Guan (T'ung Kuan; d. 1126), and a self-serving official named Cai Jing (Ts'ai Ching; 1047–1126), all of whom deceived the emperor politically by giving him bad advice and erroneous information about political conditions in the court. Tong Guan even took control of the military. Dissatisfaction with Huizong's rule was aggravated by the heavy taxes that he raised to support his luxurious lifestyle. Rebellions broke out in Zhejiang Province in 1120 and Shandong Province in 1121.

The most serious problem for the Song emperor was the existence of several kingdoms founded by nomadic peoples in northeastern China, which proved to be the downfall of the Song. The Song had never been able to conquer the Khitan (Qidan) Liao dynasty (947–1125). The Jurchen Jin dynasty (1115–1234) had been a vassal state of the Liao, but the Jurchens conquered the Liao dynasty and also established their lordship over several other kingdoms on the Chinese frontier. Emperor Huizong initially cooperated with the Jurchens and made an alliance with them against the Liao, their common enemy, in 1120. In 1123, without asking for Song assistance, the Jin overthrew the Liao. The Song, hoping to gain the territory ruled by the Liao, waged an attack against the Jin dynasty. However, the Song military proved to be weak, and in 1126 the Jurchens attacked Kaifeng, the Song capital. Emperor Huizong abdicated the throne to his son, Emperor Qinzong (Ch'in-tsung; r. 1125–27), and the Song were forced to sign a very unfavorable treaty with the Jin dynasty. Fighting soon broke out again, and the Jin besieged Kaifeng in the winter of 1126–27 and captured Emperor Qinzong, Huizong and members of the Song court. This forced the Song to flee south to Hangzhou, where they established the Southern Song dynasty (1127–1279) at Hangzou in Zhejiang Province. Huizong spent the remainder of his life as a captive of the Jin. See also BIRD-AND-FLOWER PAINTING; EUNUCHS; JIN DYNASTY; JURCHENS; KAIFENG; LIAO DYNASTY; NORTHERN SONG DYNASTY; SONG DYNASTY; SOUTHERN SONG DYNASTY; WANG ANSHI.

HUMANITY (*ren* or *jen*) Also translated as benevolence, perfect virtue, goodness or love; one of the most important concepts of Confucius (551–479 B.C.), whose school became accepted as orthodox by the Chinese imperial government during the Han dynasty (206 B.C.–A.D. 220). Attempting to present a solution for the problems of society and government during his time, Confucius found the answer in the concept of humanity; he argued that if individuals returned to virtue or humanity, society would be saved. To Confucius, the person who has humanity practices the five basic virtues: courtesy, generosity, good faith, diligence and kindness. Humanity is what enables a person to endure adversity and enjoy prosperity. The person who has humanity is an authentic human being, which Confucius defines as the "superior man" or "gentleman" (*junzi* or *chun-tzu*). Such a person lives according to the "Golden Mean" (*Zhongyong* or *Chung Yung*), which is similar to the Golden Rule in Western ethical thought. In Confucius's words, "Do not do to others what you would not want others to do to you." The term Confucius used for the concept of humanity, or *ren*, is a homophone of the Chinese term for "man." Confucius used the written character for *ren* in a way that combines all the moral qualities of the gentleman, or perfect man, including loyalty, the performance of one's duty in good faith, love for family and friends, and courtesy.

Mencius (Mengzi or Meng Tzu; c. 372–289 B.C.), another important Confucian thinker, also based his teachings on the concept of humanity, to which he added a second concept, righteousness (*yi* or *i*), also translated as duty, meaning a strong sense of obligation and commitment in personal and social relationships. Mencius emphasized—even more than Confucius—that humanity is the basis for proper government. To Mencius, the genuine ruler possesses the moral qualities of humanity and a sense of duty, and such a ruler sets the proper example for his subjects. Mencius believed that all people are born with the possibility of humanity and an inclination toward goodness. Humanity is, in fact, the quality that differentiates human beings from animals. Mencius maintained that when each person returns to his original goodness, and the government returns to the goodness and order that existed in ancient times, all evil in the individual and, thus, in society will disappear.

During the Song dynasty (960–1279), a revival of Confucian thought, known as Neo-Confucianism, developed among Chinese scholars. Humanity remained a central concept for such Neo-Confucian thinkers as Zhu Xi (Chu Hsi; 1130–1200), who developed a synthesis of Neo-Confucian philosophy. He argued that through humanity, or *ren*, an individual overcomes selfishness and identifies himself with all things, thereby uniting himself with the mind of the universe, defined as love and creativity. For Zhuxi, humanity is the essential nature of human beings, but it is also the cosmic principle or force that creates and sustains all things. Wang Yangming (1472–1529), another major Neo-Confucian thinker, argued that humanity unites the truly wise person with the whole universe. See also CONFUCIANISM; CONFUCIUS; MENCIUS; NEO-CONFUCIANISM; RIGHTEOUSNESS; SUPERIOR MAN; WANG YANGMING; ZHU XI.

HUNAN PROVINCE A small but densely populated province in south-central China that covers 81,073 square miles and has a population of about 58 million. The capital, Changsha, has a population of more than 2 million; other major cities include Hengyang, Xiangtan and Zhuzhou. Ten percent of the population is comprised of members of the Miao ethnic group. Other national minorities inhabiting Hunan include the Dong, Tujia, Yao and Zhuang.

Hunan Province borders the provinces of Jiangxi to the east, Guangdong and Guanxi to the south, Guizhou and Sichuan to the west and Hubei to the north. Through Hunan the Xiang River flows from south to north and empties into Lake Dongting, the second-largest freshwater lake in China, from which its tributaries flow into the Yangzi River. The name Hunan means "to the south of the lake." Summers in Hunan are hot and damp and winters are cool and short. The Miluo River is where the famous poet Qu Yuan drowned himself about 280 B.C., an event commemorated in southern China each May by the Dragon Boat Festival.

Hunan, a major rice-growing region, is also China's second-largest producer of tea and pork. Ramie, a type of grass used to make fiber, is another important agricultural product. Other products include citrus fruit, tung-oil seed, freshwater fish, shellfish, sugarcane, tobacco, fruit, lumber and lacquer. The cuisine of Hunan is noted for its extensive use of hot chili peppers. The province has large deposits of non-ferrous metals and rare metals, especially antimony, stibium, lead, zinc, mercury, tungsten, copper, coal, and kaolin, which is used in porcelain production. Hunan is one of China's main producers of chemical fertilizers, iron and steel, locomotives and rolling stock.

During the Warring States Period (403–221 B.C.), Hunan belonged to the kingdom of Chu, a powerful state from the seventh to the third centuries B.C., and was sparsely populated by the Miao and Yao peoples. The Changsha region was the center of Chu in the first century B.C. More than 1,000 graves filled with sumptuous goods, some dating back to the Zhou (1100–256 B.C.) and Han (206 B.C.–A.D. 220) dynasties, have been excavated around Changsha. Han (ethnic Chinese) immigrated into Hunan from the north in the third and fourth centuries A.D., pushing the native peoples to the west and southwest. Every time that invading tribes such as the Mongols and Manchus conquered northern China, more Han people would move into Hunan, a process known as sinicization. During the Ming (1368–1644) and Qing (1644–1911) dynasties, Hunan and Hubei provinces formed one province known as Huguang Province, which supplied most of the rice for the Chinese Empire. An elaborate network of canals enabled goods from the region to be transported to other regions along the Yangzi River and the Grand Canal. In the 18th century, the Qing rulers divided Hunan and Hubei into separate provinces.

Hunan Province has played an important role in modern China. During the Taiping Rebellion (1850–64), Zeng Guofan (Tseng Kuo-fan), a native of Hunan, raised the armies to regain imperial control of the territories in the Yangzi Valley. Mao Zedong, chairman of the Chinese Communist Party and founder of the People's Republic of China in 1949, was born

Fishermen return with their daily catch from one of the many rivers in Hunan Province.   S.E. MEYER

in Shaoshan in Hunan in 1893. In 1926 and 1927, Mao organized the revolutionary peasant movement in Hunan and led the Autumn Harvest Uprising of 1927. In 1928 he joined the revolutionary group based in the Jinggangshan, which covers part of Hunan and Jiangxi provinces.

The capital city, Changsha, is situated mostly on the east bank of the Xiang River, which divides the city in half. It has the largest harbor along the Xiang and has been an important trading center for more than 2,000 years, with products being transported by river barge. In 1904 Changsha was opened to foreign trade, and in 1908 a railroad was built linking the city with Hankou and China's capital, Beijing. Major tourist sites include the Juzi Zhou Tou Memorial Pavilion in honor of Mao Zedong, who moved to Changsha in 1912 to attend high school, and the Hunan Provincial Museum. See also CHANGSHA; DONG; DONGTING, LAKE; DRAGON BOAT FESTIVAL; GRAND CANAL; HUBEI PROVINCE; MAO ZEDONG; MIAO; NATIONAL MINORITY; SINICIZATION; TAIPING REBELLION; YAO; ZENG GUOFAN; ZHUANG.

HUNDRED DAYS REFORM   See REFORM MOVEMENT OF 1898.

HUNDRED FLOWERS CAMPAIGN   A movement initiated in the spring of 1956 by Chinese Communist leader Mao Zedong (Mao Tse-tung); also called the Double Hun-

dred Campaign. Mao formed the Hundred Flowers Campaign in response to the rigid position of the Soviet Union, on whom China had relied, and the uprising in Hungary against Soviet rule. Mao wanted to defuse the potential for rebellion in China. He proclaimed the classical slogan, "let a hundred flowers blossom and a hundred schools of thought contend," a reference to the so-called Hundred Schools of Thought that had flourished from the sixth to the third centuries B.C. For Mao, the hundred flowers represented the development of the arts, and the hundred schools the development of science. Mao asserted that truth would grow out of its struggle with falsehood, and that good things and good people will develop by struggling against bad people. Mao began liberalizing the political sphere in China in 1956—only seven years after he founded the People's Republic of China—in order to encourage intellectual and cultural leaders to participate in the government.

The Chinese were cautious at first, but when the Hundred Flowers Movement was announced, a large number of citizens made public criticisms of the practices and policies of the Chinese Communist Party and Party cadres. Many were liberal thinkers rather than Party members, and they especially made the case for academic freedom. Chinese who had been educated in Europe and America were the first to speak out. Legal experts strongly criticized the National People's Congress for being too slow in both passing and enacting laws that had already been drafted. They also charged that Party cadres were badly qualified and interfered with the workings of legal institutions for their own purposes. They denounced Party members who acted as if they were above the law. Scientists complained that political meetings and rallies took too much time away from their scientific work, which was being directed by unqualified Party cadres. The government never expected such a strong response. In August 1957, Communist leaders abruptly stopped the Hundred Flowers Campaign by declaring the Anti-Rightist Campaign, in which critics of the party were condemned and punished for being "bourgeois rightists." See also ANTI-RIGHTIST CAMPAIGN; CHINESE COMMUNIST PARTY; HUNDRED SCHOOLS OF THOUGHT.

HUNDRED SCHOOLS OF THOUGHT   The Chinese phrase for the numerous philosophies that developed in the period 551 to c. 233 B.C. Many of the classical texts that provided the intellectual foundations of Chinese civilization were written during this period. At that time, Chinese philosophers taught students but also traveled from kingdom to kingdom, advising rulers on governing and gathering followers for their schools of thought. Most were members of the literati (*wenren* or *wen-jen*), or scholar-gentry class, and were educated in reading and writing classical texts. Comparable to a civil service, these were the men who governed China in the imperial bureaucracy.

The most important of the Hundred Schools of Thought was founded by Confucius (551–479 B.C.), whose theories became accepted as orthodox by the Chinese imperial government during the Han dynasty (206 B.C.–A.D. 220). Writings associated with Confucius, and with Mencius (Mengzi or Meng Tzu; c. 372–289 B.C.), another important Confucian thinker, became canonical texts in China. In addition to Confucianism, the main philosophies that developed during the Hundred schools of thought Period include Daoism, whose main thinkers were Laozi (Lao Tzu; sixth century B.C.) and Zhuangzi (Chuang Tzu, 369–286 B.C.); Mohism, named for Mozi (also known as Mo Di or Moti; 470–391? B.C.); and the Legalist school of thought, whose main thinkers were Xunzi (Hsun Tzu; c. 298–238 B.C.), Han Feizi (Han Fei Tzu; c. 280–233 B.C.) and Li Si (Li Ssu; d. 208 B.C.). The main emphasis of Daoism is harmony with nature and with the universe, which is constantly changing. Mozi taught that all human beings are equal and that they should practice universal love. The principles of Legalism extolled a centralized authoritarian government and formed the basis for the imperial dynasties that ruled China for two millennia. Another influential school during this period was the School of Yin and Yang and the Five Material Agents, which taught that all created things in the universe are made possible by the opposing energies of two fundamental principles: yin, which is dark, female, cold and negative; and yang, which is light, male, warm and positive. This theory also held that all things are characterized by qualities associated with the Five Material Agents, which include earth, wood, metal, fire and water. See also CONFUCIUS; CONFUCIANISM; DAOISM; FIVE MATERIAL AGENTS; HAN FEI ZI; LAOZI; LEGALIST SCHOOL OF THOUGHT; LITERATI; LI SI; MENCIUS; MOZI; YIN AND YANG; XUNZI; ZHUANGZI.

HUNG HSIU-CH'UAN See HONG XIUQUAN; TAIPING REBELLION.

HUNG LO-MENG See DREAM OF THE RED CHAMBER.

HUNG, MOUNT See FIVE SACRED MOUNTAINS OF DAOISM.

HUNG O See CHANG E.

HUNG SHEN See HONG SHEN.

HUNGRY GHOSTS FESTIVAL (Zhong Yuan Jie or Yulan Hui)   A festival held on the 15th day of the seventh month in the Chinese lunar calendar when families have traditionally made offerings to the god of the earth and the spirits of the underworld. The Hungry Ghosts Festival was introduced into China along with Buddhism from India around the second century A.D.; Buddhists know it as the Magnolia Festival. The Chinese believe that from the first to last day of the seventh lunar month—roughly corresponding to August in the Western calendar—the god of the earth travels to Heaven to report on the good and evil deeds of human beings. At this time the gates of the underworld are open, and the spirits of the dead who do not have anyone still living to make offerings and bring them consolation will wander the earth and possess people who are alive. These spirits can only be pacified by food and the burning of incense sticks, paper clothing and "hell money" (joss paper). The night before the festival, lanterns are hung on long poles outside Buddhist temples, and small lanterns in paper boats are floated on rivers and lakes to inform the wandering spirits that they will be given offerings the following day. The Chinese also believe that these offerings will take away bad luck and help prevent epidemics of disease. On the day of the festival, every family should place auspicious foods in front of the ancestral tablets on the family altar; they include a duck, a watermelon, a dish of noodles, or crabs, the latter symbolizing respect for one's elders (filial piety, or *xiao* or *hsiao*), one of the most important virtues in Chinese culture. Traditionally, married women whose parents had already died were required to return to their own family homes to pay their respects to their deceased parents during the festival. See also ANCESTRAL TABLETS; BUDDHISM; FAMILY STRUCTURE; FILIAL PIETY; FUNERALS; HEAVEN; JOSS STICKS.

HUNGSHUI RIVER See WEST RIVER.

HUNG-WU (EMPEROR) See HONGWU (EMPEROR).

HUPEI (HUPEH) PROVINCE See HUBEI PROVINCE.

HURLEY, PATRICK J., U.S. AMBASSADOR TO CHINA See CIVIL WAR BETWEEN COMMUNISTS AND NATIONALISTS; REPUBLIC OF CHINA; WAR OF RESISTANCE AGAINST JAPAN.

HUTONG See ALLEYS.

I-CHING See BOOK OF CHANGES.

IDEOGRAPHS See WRITING SYSTEM, CHINESE.

I-HO-CH'UAN See BOXER UPRISING.

IMMORTALITY See ALCHEMY; CHANG E; DAOISM; EIGHT IMMORTALS; ELIXIR OF IMMORTALITY; PEACH; XIWANGMU.

IMPERIAL ACADEMY See HANLIN ACADEMY.

IMPERIAL BUREAUCRACY The form of government during China's imperial period from the Han dynasty (206 B.C.–A.D. 220) through the Qing dynasty (1644–1911), comparable to the civil service in Western countries. Members of the bureaucracy are known as *shenshi* or *shenjin* (*shen-shih* or *shen-chin*; literally, "scholars wearing belts with hanging ends"), translated as literati-degree-holders, scholar-bureaucrats or officials, scholar-gentry, or mandarins, as they were called by the Portuguese who went to China to trade in the 16th century. Mandarin became the Western name for the dialect of the Chinese language spoken in northern China, the official dialect of the Chinese imperial government and still the official dialect in the Communist People's Republic of China. Qin Shi Huangdi, who unified China under the Qin dynasty (221–206 B.C.) and reigned as China's first emperor, organized the Chinese Empire into 40 prefectures, centralized the Qin government and forced the rulers of other states to move to the Qin capital. He standardized the Chinese writing system and the system of weights and measures, adopted a single coinage and enacted a set of uniform laws and a tax system for the entire country. All of these were administered by a bureaucracy staffed by educated officials. Qin was an absolute monarch who built his empire on the harsh teachings of the Legalist school of thought. Scholars and government officials, who followed the teachings of the Confucian school of thought, opposed Qin's brutality, and Qin retaliated by ordering that all books except those on practical topics such as agriculture and medicine were to be burned. After the book burning, he supposedly had 460 scholars buried alive. Qin died in 210 B.C., and his dynasty fell four years later to the Han dynasty (206 B.C.–A.D. 220).

Han emperors built on Qin's bureaucracy and established many institutions that continued in China throughout the imperial period, which ended in 1911 with the downfall of the Qing dynasty. Most important was the centralized imperial bureaucracy staffed by scholars or literati educated in the teachings of Confucius (551–479 B.C.). Confucius was concerned with social harmony and advocated government by "superior men" (*junzi* or *chun tzu*), who were educated and had high morals. In 136 B.C., Han Emperor Wudi (Wu-ti; r. 141–87 B.C.) proclaimed Confucianism as the official state cult. In 124 B.C., he founded an imperial university with a curriculum based on the Five Classics of Confucianism. These included the *Book of Changes, Book of History, Book of Rites, Book of Songs* and *Spring and Autumn Annals*. Candidates for the positions in the bureaucracy were selected by examinations, which required memorization of the Confucian classics, beautiful calligraphy (the art of writing Chinese characters with a brush) and the ability to write prose and poetry that contained allusions to ancient Chinese history and literature. The implements used for writing the Chinese language, including paper, a brush, an ink stick and an ink stone, are known as the Four Treasures of the Scholar's Study. The literati (*wenren* or *wen-jen*) eventually replaced the old aristocratic families that had controlled China during the Zhou dynasty (1100–256 B.C.) as the ruling elite in China.

When the Han dynasty fell, China was divided up into a number of competing dynasties in different regions of the country, known as the Six Dynasties Period (220–589). Emperor Wendi (Wen-ti; r. 581–604) reunited the Chinese Empire under the Sui dynasty (581–618). He built his capital at Chang'an (modern Xi'an in Shaanxi Province), centralized and strengthened the government bureaucracy, created a new tax system and promulgated a new law code which served as the model for all later Chinese imperial law codes. The Sui held imperial examinations that were open to all educated men who wanted to take them and used the examinations to select officials not only for the central government but also for the local bureaucracies that governed the Chinese provinces.

The Sui was overthrown by the Tang dynasty (618–907), one of the greatest periods of Chinese culture, when Chang'an became the largest and most cosmopolitan city in the world. The Tang continued the imperial bureaucracy and the imperial examination system and made Confucius the bureaucracy's patron saint. In 630 the Tang emperor decreed that a Confucian temple should be established in every province and county of the Chinese Empire, and in 647 these temples were made into national shrines to Confucius and those government officials whose scholarship had best contributed to the Confucian school of thought. The Tang emperor ruled through two ministries that drew up policy, the Chancellery (Menxiasheng or Men-hsia-sheng) and the Secretariat (Zhongshusheng or Chung-shu-sheng), and through an executive body headed by the Department of State Affairs (Shangshusheng). Under this department were the Six Boards (Linbu or Lin pu), the Nine Courts (Jiusi or Chiu ssu) and other ministries and directorates. The Six Boards handled the affairs of personnel, revenue, rites (religious and ceremonial affairs), defense, justice and public works. During the Tang, when the Chinese population numbered about 50 million, more than 18,000 officials held positions in the Tang bureaucracy, and more than 368,000 men were on the government payroll, including local officials, clerical assistants and army officers. Tang emperor Xuanzong (Hsuan-tsung; r. 712–56) founded the Hanlin ("Forest of Writing Brushes") Academy to establish a group of scholars who could assist the emperor and the imperial court by writing diplomatic letters and literary compositions such as poetry, which enjoyed a golden age during the Tang and has been a highly valued art in China ever since.

During the Song dynasty (960–1279), another great period for Chinese culture, the literati had their greatest influence. They brought their "amateur" style of landscape painting (wenrenhua or wen-jen hua), which is executed with the same brush and ink as calligraphy, to its fullest development. Literati paintings often included poems written in beautiful calligraphy, and the Chinese classify painting, calligraphy and poetry together as the "Three Perfections." The Song literati also advanced the design of Chinese gardens as microcosms of the natural world and were associated with the qin (ch'in), a musical instrument similar to a zither.

The Song selected officials for the imperial bureaucracy by holding examinations at the provincial and metropolitan levels in regular three-year cycles. Woodblock printing, which had been invented in China in the eighth century, developed quickly in the 11th century. It made available large numbers of printed books, thus increasing literacy among the Chinese people and enabling them to become familiar with literature and the Confucian classics. This in turn led to the revival of Confucianism known as Neo-Confucianism (and known in Chinese as the Rational School, Lixue or Li hsueh). The great Neo-Confucian scholar Zhu Xi (Chu Hsi; 1130–1200) combined four texts to form the Four Books of Confucianism, which were added to the curriculum for the imperial examinations. These include the Analects (Sayings)

of Confucius, Book of Mencius, Doctrine of the Mean and Great Learning. Wang Yangming (1472–1529) was the second-most important thinker of the Neo-Confucian School.

The imperial examination system was disrupted during the Yuan dynasty (1279–1368), founded by the Mongols, a nomadic ethnic group that had invaded China from the north. They retained the imperial bureaucracy but staffed it with many of their own people and limited the number of Han ethnic Chinese who could hold high bureaucratic positions. Many literati became discouraged during the Yuan and retired to spend their time painting and writing poetry and dramas, which consequently flourished during this period. Emperor Hongwu (Hung-wu; r. 1368–1399), who overthrew the Mongols and founded the Han Chinese Ming dynasty (1368–1644), reorganized the imperial bureaucracy into a hierarchy of nine ranks. He required officials to wear squares of silk tapestry known as kesi on their robes that had designs identifying the bureaucratic rank to which they belonged. He also abolished the office of the prime minister and expanded the role of the Hanlin Academy because he needed a group of highly educated advisors who could help him rebuild the Han Chinese government. "Grand secretaries" from the Hanlin performed the functions of a prime minister, and eventually becoming the leaders of the entire imperial bureaucracy. Under the Yongle Emperor (Yung-lo; r. 1403–24), the leading Hanlin scholars became a powerful coterie who were closer to the emperor than were his chief ministers.

By the mid-16th century, this cabinet of Hanlin secretaries was formally designated the Grand Secretariat (Neige or Nei-ko) of the Imperial Bureaucracy. Directly under the secretaries were the national academies, comparable to modern think tanks, that performed research and drafted important documents for the emperor; the six departments of rites, personnel, revenue, justice, public works and war; the military boards, which administered military garrisons and special border defenses; and the censorate, which supervised all levels of the bureaucracy by conducting audits, surprise inspections and undercover investigations to control corruption and inefficiency. Beneath the six departments, in descending order, were the provincial governments, the prefectural governments and the country governments. China was divided into about 20 provinces, each headed by a governor and divided into several prefectures, which were further divided into several counties. County magistrates, at the lowest level of the bureaucracy, had the same education as higher government officials and followed the same laws and regulations wherever they were posted throughout the empire. The magistrate's office (yamen) kept large registers which recorded the owners of all land in the county. The registers were also used for collecting taxes, which had been paid with grain until the Ming, when they were paid in silver. The yamen included a courtroom, where Chinese citizens could present petitions and make complaints and where civil and criminal cases were tried, although the government encouraged people to settle civil cases in private. Magistrates also appointed the heads of villages, guilds and neighborhood associations. Magistrates were frequently transferred to different offices around the country, but the yamen employees, such as clerks, policemen and messengers, kept their positions and had a great deal of local power.

In 1603 the Donglin (Tung-lin) Academy, a former academy of Confucian learning, was reestablished by a group of conservative scholars who opposed the Neo-Confucian thought of Wang Yangming and the power of Wei Zhongxian (Wei Chung-hsien), the head eunuch who wielded the real power in the imperial court. Eunuchs staffed the imperial palace, and some acted in the emperor's place and became virtual dictators. In 1625–26 Wei had many of the Donglin scholars arrested, tortured and executed. However, the Donglin scholars came back into favor after Wei Zhongxian was removed from power and the Chongzhen Emperor (Ch'ung-chen; r. 1628–45) took the throne, and they held many high government positions through the rest of the Ming dynasty.

The Hanlin Academy attained its highest power during the Qing dynasty, which was founded by the Manchus, an ethnic group from Manchuria (modern northeastern China) who overthrew the Ming. The Manchus, as had the Mongols, limited the number of Han Chinese literati who could hold positions in the imperial bureaucracy, a policy that increased Han resentment toward the Manchus, especially in southern China. In 1905 the literati completely lost their government support when the Qing abolished the imperial examination system. However, six years later the Chinese overthrew the Qing in the Revolution of 1911 and founded the Republic of China, which ended not only the dynasty but the imperial bureaucracy. Subsequently, Chinese scholars were forced to study at military schools or newly founded Western-style universities, such as Beijing University, and they became active in the modern revolutionary movements that were sweeping 20th-century China.

The People's Republic of China (PRC), founded in 1949 by the Chinese Communist Party (CCP), is governed by a bureaucracy as vast and complex as the imperial bureaucracy. Its members have been trained in Communist ideology rather than Confucianism, although recently the PRC government has turned away from strict communism and has emphasized modernization and economic growth. Confucian ideas are also being revived in Beijing, the capital of China. See also BEIJING UNIVERSITY; CALLIGRAPHY; CONFUCIUS; CONFUCIANISM; DONGLIN ACADEMY; DRAMA; EUNUCHS; FIVE CLASSICS OF CONFUCIANISM; FOUR BOOKS OF CONFUCIANISM; FOUR TREASURES OF THE STUDY; GARDENS; HANLIN ACADEMY; IMPERIAL EXAMINATION SYSTEM; LANDSCAPE PAINTING; LEGALIST SCHOOL OF THOUGHT; LITERATI; MANDARIN; NEO-CONFUCIANISM; PRINTING; QIN; SUPERIOR MAN; WANG YANGMING; WEI ZHONGXIAN; ZHU XI; NAMES OF INDIVIDUAL BOOKS AND DYNASTIES.

IMPERIAL COURT See DRAGON; EMPEROR; FORBIDDEN CITY; IMPERIAL BUREAUCRACY; NINE-RANK SYSTEM; PHOENIX.

IMPERIAL EXAMINATION SYSTEM (*jinshi*, or *chin-shih*) Examinations given to educated men of the literati (*wenren*), or scholar-gentry class, to select the best scholars for positions in the imperial bureaucracy or civil service. Scholars who passed the exam governed China from the Han dynasty (206 B.C.–A.D. 220) through the last dynasty, the Qing (1644–1911). After being selected, the ablest officials rose through the ranks to the highest government positions. The families that produced successful candidates attained power, wealth and the prestige usually held by aristocratic families in other cultures. Eventually all Chinese males were allowed to take the examinations. A man from a poor family had the chance of passing them and achieving high status and wealth for his entire family. The examinations were extremely competitive, and a man who failed them could disgrace his relatives as well as himself, especially if his family had made many sacrifices for him to complete his education. However, many candidates were able to take the examinations repeatedly until they passed them. Those who did not pass were still able to hold local positions as teachers and public servants.

Han Emperor Wudi (Wu-ti; r. 141–87 B.C.) founded a centralized bureaucracy based on the ideas of Confucius (551–479 B.C.), who had advocated government by "superior men" (*junzi* or *chun-tzu*) who were educated and had high morals. An imperial university was established in 124 B.C., in which the classical texts of the Confucian tradition formed the corpus of knowledge on which the examinations were based. Known as the Five Classics (*wujing* or *wu-ching*), these include the *Book of Changes* (*Yijing* or *I Ching*), *Book of History* (*Shujing* or *Shu-ching*), *Book of Rites* (*Liji* or *Li-chi*), *Book of Songs* (*Shijing* or *Shih-ching*), and *Spring and Autumn Annals* (*Chun Qiu* or *Ch'un Ch'iu*). This system survived during the period of disunity following the Han and was employed by subsequent dynasties. Education became more available during the Song dynasty (960–1279), after the government opened schools around the country and the invention of printing enabled large numbers of people to acquire books. The imperial examination system brought officials into the government from all regions of the country, thus increasing the loyalty of residents in those regions and serving as an important means of unifying the whole empire through education in traditional Chinese concepts and values. Beginning in 1487, the examination was dominated by the "eight-legged essay," a literary composition with parallel arguments on a determined subject.

The great Neo-Confucian scholar Zhu Xi (Chu Hsi; 1130–1200) combined four Confucian texts to form the Four Books (*sishu* or *ssu-shu*), which in the 12th century were added to the curriculum for the imperial examinations. These include the *Analects* (*Sayings*) of Confucius (*Lunyu*), *Book of Mencius* (*Mengzi* or *Meng Tzu*), *Doctrine of the Mean* (*Zhongyong* or *Chung-yung*), and *Great Learning* (*Daxue* or *Ta-hsueh*). In 1315, the Ming dynasty (1368–1644) accepted Zhu's interpretation of Confucianism as orthodox. It divided the examination system into three levels. Candidates who passed the examinations administered at the prefectural level were allowed to take the provincial examinations, after which they could accept low government positions or take the metropolitan examinations. Those who succeeded in passing the provincial and metropolitan were assigned ranks by an examination administered by the imperial palace. The elite were appointed to the Hanlin ("Forest of Writing Brushes") Academy and became major advisers to the emperor. The examinations at the provincial level and above were given every three years, and fewer than one percent of the candidates passed them. See also CONFUCIANISM; FIVE CLASSICS OF CONFUCIANISM; FOUR BOOKS OF CONFUCIANISM; HANLIN ACADEMY; IMPERIAL BUREAUCRACY; LITERATI; SUPERIOR MAN; ZHU XI.

IMPERIAL HISTORICAL ARCHIVES (Huangshicheng) A building inside a section of the capital city of Beijing called the Forbidden City, housing official documents, including annals, edicts and genealogical records, from the Ming (1368–1644) and Qing (1644–1911) dynasties. As China's oldest government archives, the collection is also known as the First Historical Archives; the Second Historical Archives in Nanjing houses records from the Republic of 1912 on. The Imperial Historical Archives was constructed in 1534 at the order of Ming emperor Chongzhen (r. 1628–45) and is still in good condition. It is based on the plan of a previous document storehouse, which existed in remote antiquity, mentioned by the historian Sima Qian (c. 145–90 B.C.). The main hall, two side halls and a separate pavilion for storing tablets were built almost completely of stone, to reduce the risk of fire and decomposition; they were restored and open to the public in 1981. Documents have been preserved in 150 chests (*nanmu*) lining the main hall made of camphor wood covered with gilded bronze sheets that are decorated with dragons and clouds (camphor helps protect the documents from insects). There is a conservation laboratory for the restoration of documents and an air-conditioned storage room. The only copy of all 11,095 volumes of the *Yongle Encyclopedia,* compiled during the reign of Ming emperor Yongle (Yung-lo; r. 1403–24), was stored at the Imperial Historical Archives, but the encyclopedia was looted or destroyed when foreign troops took Beijing during the Boxer Uprising in 1900. See also BOXER UPRISING; CAMPHOR WOOD; FORBIDDEN CITY; MING DYNASTY; QING DYNASTY; SIMA QIAN; YONGLE ENCYCLOPEDIA.

IMPERIAL PAINTING ACADEMY An academy founded by Song dynasty Emperor Huizong (Hui-tsung; r. 1101–25) to promote the style of painting he desired his court painters to follow. Paintings executed in this manner, known as the academic style, are delicate, realistic portrayals of elements in nature, especially birds and flowers. The artist carefully paints every detail using bright, jewel-tone pigments. This contrasts with the so-called amateur style of the literati, or scholars, who staffed the imperial bureaucracy and who sought to express themselves by creating spontaneous black-and-white ink paintings of natural scenes that were dominated by mountains. The amateur-literati-style of ink painting is closely related to calligraphy, the art of writing Chinese characters with a brush. The division between the academic and literati styles has lasted in Chinese painting down to the modern era, although the two styles have influenced each other.

Emperor Huizong was himself a talented painter and calligrapher. He elevated the former court-painting bureau into the prestigious Imperial Painting Academy to honor professional court painters, previously considered only craftsmen, by giving them equal status to scholars of history or literature. Huizong was also a collector and brought many of the finest Chinese paintings and works of calligraphy from antiquity to his court and had them catalogued. Sadly, most of these works were destroyed when the Song capital of Kaifeng was sacked by the Jurchens, a nomadic group who had taken control of northern China and established the Jin dynasty (1115–1234). Huizong abdicated the throne to Qinzong (Ch'in-tsung), but both men were captured by the

Jurchens, and the remnants of the Song court fled south and made their new capital at Hangzhou in Zhejiang province (Southern Song dynasty, 1127–1279). Many artists also gathered at Hangzhou, which remained the cultural capital of China for many centuries. The painter Li Tang (c. 1050–c. 1130), who had been head of the Imperial Painting Academy in Kaifeng, was able to reestablish the academy in the Southern Song court. See also BIRD-AND-FLOWER PAINTING; HANGZHOU; HUIZONG, EMPEROR; INK LI TANG; LITERATI; PAINTING; SONG DYNASTY.

IMPERIAL PALACE See CHENGDE; FORBIDDEN CITY; SUMMER PALACE.

IMPERIAL PALACE, MANCHU (GUGONG) See SHENYANG.

IMPERIAL TOMBS, MANCHU See SHENYANG.

IMPERIAL VAULT OF HEAVEN See TEMPLE OF HEAVEN.

INCENSE (*xiang* or *hsiang*) Scented wood, which may be combined with other substances, that is burned to produce a pleasant fragrance. Sandalwood is a popular wood for making incense. Burning incense, commonly in the form of long thin sticks, is used as an offering before sculptures of deities in temples of the Buddhist religion. Incense is also burned in rituals of the native Chinese religion of Daoism. Incense sticks are placed vertically into holes in small metal or ceramic incense burners or into sand in large containers, such as bronze pots. One form of bronze incense burner dating back to the Han dynasty (206 B.C.–A.D. 220) has a lid in the shape of mountain peaks that symbolize paradise in the Daoist religion. The Chinese also burn incense at funerals; for festivals such as the New Year and Qing Ming (Ching Ming), when they sweep the graves of their ancestors; and on their family altars in the practice known as ancestor worship. Wealthy Chinese families traditionally burned incense in their homes to perfume the air while entertaining guests. By the Song dynasty (960–1279), the Chinese imperial government held a monopoly on the manufacture and sale of incense, as well as tea, salt and alcoholic beverages. The Chinese also imported incense and sandalwood from other Asian countries. See also ANCESTOR WORSHIP; BUDDHISM; FUNERALS, TRADITIONAL; NEW YEAR FESTIVAL; QING MING FESTIVAL; SANDALWOOD.

INDIA AND CHINA See BUDDHISM; DALAI LAMA; FAXIAN; HIMALAYA MOUNTAIN RANGE; SILK ROAD; SINO-INDIAN BORDER DISPUTE; TIBET; XUANZANG.

INDIGO DYEING OF TEXTILES The folk art of decorating cotton textiles with complex designs using the deep-blue dye made from indigo plants; also known as batik. The use of cotton became widespread in China during the Song dynasty (960–1279). Aristocrats and wealthy people wore silk clothing, but the vast majority of Chinese were peasant farmers who wore indigo-dyed homespun cotton. The folk art of indigo-dyeing is especially associated with the Miao, Yao, Bai, Yi and other minorities in Yunnan and Guizhou provinces in southwestern China. Historical records dating from the Han (206 B.C.–A.D. 220) and Tang (618–907) dynasties contain references to batik. Indigo dye is made from the fermented leaves of locally grown indigo plants (*polygonum tinctorium*), which are picked in August. Indigo dyeing is done by women to make clothing for their dowries and many items used in daily life, such as cloths used to carry children on women's backs, quilt covers, curtains and scarves.

In the batik process, a woman dips a special knife made of copper into melted wax and then draws a design of wax lines and dots on a piece of white cotton. She commonly uses a waterproof stencil made from oiled paper or parchment to create the design. She then immerses the cloth immersed in a vat of indigo dye; the waxed areas resist the dye while the unwaxed areas turn deep blue. After the cloth is removed from the dye it is boiled in water to remove the wax and then washed; the areas that were covered by the wax have remained white and form the designs. Crackling of the wax in the vat of indigo dye creates so-called "ice lines" in the white areas of the cloth. Common decorative motifs include flowers, fruit, plants, butterflies, birds and fish, all of which have auspicious symbolic meanings. Stylized designs such as double happiness (*shuangxi*) and long life (*zhou*) are also popular. Geometric designs often border the cloth. Traditionally, only dark blue was used for batik, but today, women also use light blue, and other colors such as red and yellow, which are auspicious in Chinese tradition. Large Chinese textile companies often mass-produce batik designs created by peasant women. See also BAI; MIAO; MINORITIES, NATIONAL; TEXTILE INDUSTRY; YAO; YI.

INDUS RIVER   See TIBET.

INK PAINTING   (*shuimohua*, literally "water-ink painting") A style of monochromatic painting executed with simple lines and shapes in black ink (*mo*), diluted with water, on white paper or silk; known in the West by the Japanese term *sumi-e* ("ink pictures"; also called *suibokuga*, Japanese for "water-ink painting"). The Chinese classify ink painting as one type in the art form known as paintings of the literati (*wenrenhua* or *wen-jen-hua*), that is, paintings by "amateurs" belonging to the Confucian-educated members of the literati, or scholar class, who staffed the imperial bureaucracy and who were skilled in the three most admired arts: painting, calligraphy and poetry writing. These arts are interrelated and are all performed with the so-called Four Treasures of the Study: the brush, the inkstick, the inkstone or ink-grinding stone, and the paper.

Chinese painters developed monochromatic techniques during the Tang dynasty (618–907), and ink painting flourished during the Song dynasty (960–1279), one of the greatest eras of Chinese culture. It became especially associated with the Chan Sect of Buddhism, known in the West by the Japanese term Zen Buddhism, which emphasizes simplicity, spontaneity and self-expression. Ink painting was also influenced by the Chinese religion of Daoism, which emphasizes spontaneity and harmony with nature. Favorite subjects of ink painters include elements of nature such as birds, pine trees, bamboo, plum blossoms, chrysanthemums and orchids, whose lines and forms are readily

expressed by skilled brushwork. Chinese painters recognized a wide range of ink values, which they termed "the colors of ink."

The aim of ink painting is to capture, using a minimum of rapid, spontaneous brush strokes and ink washes, the essence of the subject being depicted. This style is also known as *xieyi* (*hsieh i*), literally, "write idea" or "idea writing." Ink paintings are asymmetrical and contain a large proportion of empty space, which has a positive connotation in Chinese art and philosophy because it expresses the "emptiness" out of which all things are created. In the 14th century, painters in Japan adopted Chinese ink painting, and this style became one of the most important and admired painting styles in that country, where Zen Buddhism has also flourished and deeply influenced the arts. Japanese monks who studied in Chinese Buddhist monasteries, beginning in the Tang dynasty (618–907), brought paintings back to Japan. Two of the finest Chinese ink painters, many of whose works have been preserved in Japan, are Liang Kai (early 13th century) and Mu Qi (Mu-Ch'i; late 13th century). See also BAMBOO; BIRD-AND-FLOWER PAINTING; CALLIGRAPHY; CHAN SECT OF BUDDHISM; CHRYSANTHEMUM; DAOISM; FOUR TREASURES OF THE STUDY; LIANG KAI; MU QI; ORCHID; PAPER; PLUM.

INKSTICK   See CALLIGRAPHY; FOUR TREASURES OF THE STUDY; INK PAINTING.

INKSTONE   See CALLIGRAPHY; FOUR TREASURES OF THE STUDY; INK PAINTING.

INNER MONGOLIA AUTONOMOUS REGION
(Neimenggu or Nei Monggol Zizhiqu)   A province in northern China which covers some 456,000 square miles and has a population of approximately 21 million. The capital city is Hohhot (Chinese spelling Huhehaote; "Blue City," called "Green City" by the Chinese), with a population of about one million. Baotou is the largest city and an industrial center. The region borders Outer Mongolia (the Mongolian People's Republic) to the north, and the Chinese provinces of Heilongjiang, Jilin, Liaoning, Hebei, Shanxi, Shaanxi and Ningxia-Hui Autonomous Region. For much of Chinese history, Inner Mongolia lay beyond the frontiers of the Chinese Empire and was inhabited by seminomadic tribes. Tribes of the Xiongnu people controlled the area by the 10th century B.C. and were a threat to neighboring tribes by the fifth century B.C. Fortifications built to defend against the Xiongnu eventually led to the building of the Great Wall. Turkic-speaking tribes invaded Mongolia in the fifth century A.D. In 904 the Khitan tribe established the Liao dynasty (947–1125), which occupied Inner Mongolia and northeast China. The name "Cathay" for China came from the name Khitan.

In 1947, Inner Mongolia was the first Chinese province to be designated an autonomous region, even prior to the founding of the People's Republic of China in 1949, because a large number of its inhabitants still belonged to national minorities. Most important are the three million Mongols, (about 13 percent of the region's population) who originated in this region. The Mongolian leader Genghis Khan (1162–1227) unified the Mongol tribes, invaded China and established the Yuan dynasty (1279–1368). The Mongols built their winter capital at Dadu (modern Beijing in Hebei Province) and their summer capital at Shangdu (modern Dolonnur in Inner Mongolia). The Ming dynasty (1368–1644) forced the last Yuan emperor to flee China and return to Mongolia, and Mongol tribes fought with each other for three centuries until they were reunited by a Mongol leader named Dayan Khan. The Manchus, an ethnic group from northeastern China who founded the Qing dynasty (1644–1911), brought Mongolia into the Chinese Empire, although the region produced frequent rebellions. In 1911 Mongolian fighters made Outer Mongolia a separate region and aligned it with Russia. When the Japanese invaded Inner Mongolia during the 1930s, Mongols organized secret societies which aligned with the Chinese Communists, who were active in northern China and later founded the People's Republic of China in 1949. The Mongols helped the Communists defeat Japan and found the PRC. Hence the Communists gave them autonomy in 1947. Other ethnic minorities in Inner Mongolia today include Hui (Chinese Muslims). The non-Muslim residents are mostly Han (ethnic Chinese) who were brought to the region after 1949 to settle and work in factories and mines. In order to control the Mongols, in 1969 the Chinese government assigned large areas of Inner Mongolia to other provinces, but these areas have been returned since the end of the Cultural Revolution in 1976.

The northern part of Inner Mongolia is covered by the Gobi Desert (also known as the Great Gobi), a huge dry, stony region that also covers much of Outer Mongolia and is the region of origin for the Mongol people. The term *gobi* is a Mongol word for any shallow, windy desert basin. The Gobi Desert has an average altitude of about 3,000 feet and is surrounded by the Altai's Hulanshan, Yinshan, and the greater Khingan mountain ranges. It affects the climate of Asia, sending up hot air masses in the summer that draw violent storms called monsoons, or typhoons, from the tropical Pacific Ocean over East Asia. Loose yellow soil called loess has blown from the Gobi for thousands of years and built up high, fertile plateaus over much of northwestern China. Starting in the Han dynasty (206 B.C.–A.D. 220), camel caravans transported silk, porcelain and tea west across the Gobi Desert along the so-called Silk Road and returned with Western goods, culture and religions.

Inner Mongolia contains 30 percent of China's grassy pasturelands, which extend north from Hohhot across the Daqing Mountain Range. From the Altai Mountain Range in the west, the Mongolian Plateau extends to the Manchurian Plateau in the east. The altitude of the plateau averages about 3,000 feet above sea level, and the climate is dry and cool, although the temperature fluctuates a great deal. In the winter, temperatures can drop to -22°F, and strong winds blow from the north. In the summer, the temperature averages a pleasant 68°F. The sun shines, and the sky is clear and blue almost every day of the year. Nomadic tribes herd sheep, cattle, horses, goats and camels, although they now tend to live in permanent homes and keep their animals in barns. Inner Mongolia is China's second-largest producer of mutton and dairy products. Foreign tourists can visit grasslands settlements in Xilamulun Sumu, Huitengxile and Baiyunhushao.

Agriculture is also practiced, primarily on the Hetao Plain of the Yellow River west of Baotou. Major crops include wheat and other grains, soybeans, flax seeds and sugar beets, and Inner Mongolia has rich mineral deposits, especially coal, and the largest deposits in the world of rare earth metals and niobium deposits. It has the largest in China of natural soda deposits. Since 1949 the region has been industrialized, with major products including iron and steel, machinery, chemicals and electronics. It is also China's third-largest producer of timber.

Hohhot, the starting point for trips to outlying areas of Inner Mongolia, was founded in 1581 by the Tumet nomadic tribe. In 1735 the Qing dynasty constructed a frontier defense town nearby, and the two towns were joined together in the 20th century. Tourist sites include the Tomb of Wang Zhaojun (Wang Shao-chun), a Han dynasty princess who was sent to marry Prince Han Xie Shanyu (Chan Yu), chief of the Xiongnu tribe, in 33 B.C. The marriage was to cement the political relations between the Han and what the Han called "The Northern Boundaries." Wang Zhaojun is a famous "virtuous woman" in Chinese history who has become a symbol of peace and is the subject of many plays and stories. The Museum of Inner Mongolia in Hohhot has exhibits on the history of the region and its peoples, including Ulanhu, a Mongolian leader who became the first governor of Inner Mongolia and was vice president of the People's Republic of China. The Da Zhao Lamasery in Hohhot, belonging to the Yellow Hat Sect of Tibetan Buddhism, was built in the 16th century and is being restored to its former grandeur. The Xilitu Zhao is another Tibetan Buddhist temple undergoing restoration. There are also four mosques in Hohhot. Of these, the largest is the Great Mosque; it was originally built in 1693 and expanded in 1789. See also ALTAI MOUNTAIN RANGE; BAOTOU; BEIJING; CAMEL CARAVANS; CLIMATE; GENGHIS KHAN; GOBI DESERT; HOHHOT; LIAO DYNASTY; LOESS; MANCHURIA; MONGOL; MUSLIMS; MINORITIES, NATIONAL; NOMADS AND ANIMAL HUSBANDRY; QING DYNASTY; SILK ROAD; WANG ZHAOJUN; XIONGNU; YELLOW RIVER; YUAN DYNASTY.

INTERNATIONAL SETTLEMENT IN SHANGHAI (*Shanghai zuji* or *Shanghai tsu-chi*)   The section in the city of Shanghai, on China's east coast, where concessions were held by the British, French and other foreign powers prior to World War II. Shanghai is China's largest city and most important financial and industrial center and one of the world's largest ports. It is located on the Wusongpu and Huangpu (Whampoa) rivers near where the Huangpu flows into the Yangzi River (Changjiang), one of China's two longest rivers and transportation routes. The Yangzi flows into the East China Sea 30 miles beyond that juncture. Shanghai was opened to foreign trade and residents as one of five so-called treaty ports after Great Britain defeated China in the Opium War (1839–42) and forced the Qing dynasty (1644–1911) to sign the Treaty of Nanjing. The British opened a concession in Shanghai in 1841 and the French in 1847. In 1863 an International Settlement was established along the northern bank of the Huangpu by combining the British and American settlements. After Japan defeated China in the Sino-Japanese War of 1894–95, a Japanese Concession (*riben zujie* or *jih-pen tsu-chi*) was also opened in Shanghai on the north bank of the Wusong River. The French Concession (*faguo zujie* or *fa-kuo tsu-chi;* also known as Frenchtown) extended west of the Huangpu between the International Settlement to its north and the old Chinese city to its south, a labyrinth of alleys along which many Chinese still live. The dividing line between the International Settlement, which was dominated by the British, and the French Concession was known as Edward VII on the eastern and Avenue Foch on the western side; it is now called Yan'an Lu. Most of the Bund, the main financial district, lay within the International Settlement, but a strip of the Bund lay within the French concession, south of Yan'an Lu, and was called the Quai de France. Actually, most of the residents of the French Concession were Chinese, and one-third of the residents were White Russian émigrés who owned cafes and tailoring businesses along the central avenue, Huaihai Lu. The French, who had taken control of Vietnam after defeating China in the Sino-French War of 1884–85, used Vietnamese troops to police the French Concession. The British used Sikhs to guard the International Settlement, where there were also many Chinese residents. All of the foreign districts were autonomous and ruled by the laws and police of their respective countries, known as extraterritoriality.

After the Chinese overthrew the Qing dynasty, China's last imperial dynasty, and established the Republic of 1912, foreigners took over the entire administration of Shanghai and even controlled the Chinese customs office. In 1912 the old walls around the Chinese city were also torn down, and today the Chinese city is surrounded by the Zhonghua-Renmin Road. In the 1920s and 1930s Shanghai was Asia's largest and most cosmopolitan city, known as the "Paris of the East." European-style buildings to house banks, trading houses, hotels, businesses and clubs were built on the Bund along the Huangpu River. The British Public Gardens, now called Huangpu Park, are located at the northwestern end of the Bund (the gardens were notorious for a sign forbidding dogs and Chinese from entering them). Foreign ships protected the city, which held the largest single foreign investment in the world, by patrolling the Huangpu and Yangzi rivers and the Chinese coast. By 1935 Shanghai had more than 3.7 million residents, including more than 57,000 foreigners.

Japan invaded China in 1937 and took control of Shanghai. Many refugees from World War II in Europe, especially Russians and Jews, fled to the International Settlement. After Japan was defeated in 1945, the Chinese Communist Party (CCP) and the Nationalist Party (Kuomintang; KMT) fought a civil war. In 1949 the CCP defeated the KMT, who fled to the island of Taiwan, and took control of Shanghai. The Communists attempted to make Shanghai a showcase for the new China, and they converted the European buildings in the International Settlement to new uses. The former clubhouse at the racetrack, one of the oldest buildings in the city, is now the Shanghai Municipal Library. The majestic Hongkong and Shanghai Banking Corporation building now houses the Shanghai People's Municipal Government. See also ALLEYS; HONGKONG AND SHANGHAI BANKING CORPORATION; HUANGPU RIVER; SHANGHAI; NANJING, TREATY OF; OPIUM WAR; TREATY PORTS; UNEQUAL TREATIES; YANGZI RIVER.

INTERNATIONAL STUDIES See MINISTRY OF FOREIGN AFFAIRS.

INTERNATIONAL WORKERS DAY A national holiday for workers in factories and on communes that is celebrated on May 1 in the People's Republic of China. International Workers Day, also known as International Labor Day or May Day, has also been celebrated in most other communist countries around the world, such as the former Soviet Union. On this day, the Chinese people hang flags, banners and posters praising the workers for their hard efforts. They perform plays and dances and participate in organized athletic competitions. Government leaders join the audiences for these public events. Many Chinese families that live in cities travel to the countryside to relax for the day. International Workers Day celebrations conclude with more dancing and fireworks. See also CHINESE COMMUNIST PARTIES; FIREWORKS AND GUNPOWDER; PEOPLE'S COMMUNE.

INTERNATIONAL WORKING WOMEN'S DAY A special celebration on March 8 with which the People's Republic of China, founded in 1949, honors all women, not just mothers. March 8 is celebrated as International Women's Day in many countries around the world. In China, factories, offices and other places of employment give all working women a half-day vacation on this day. Public speakers remind people of the difficulties that women endured in feudal times in China and praise the merits of contemporary women. Children give small handmade gifts to their mothers.

IRON RICE BOWL See WORK UNIT.

IRON TECHNOLOGY AND STEEL INDUSTRY Metals produced by smelting and casting that are used to make a wide variety of tools, weapons and building materials. Steel is made from commercial iron but has a lower carbon content and is malleable. China developed technologies for casting bronze, a metal alloy, during the Shang dynasty (1750–1040 B.C.), and small amounts of wrought iron have been excavated at sites from the late Shang. By the seventh to sixth centuries B.C. the Chinese were commonly using coal-burning blast furnaces to manufacture cast-iron tools, weapons, cooking pots, and even toys and animal figures. The iron sword replaced the bronze dagger-ax, or halberd, as the main weapon. By the Han dynasty (206 B.C.–A.D. 220), Chinese foot soldiers wore iron armor, including face masks. In 119 B.C. the Han emperor nationalized all cast-iron factories so he could monopolize the industry. Cast-iron pots enabled the Chinese to mass-produce salt from evaporated brine, and the imperial government also made salt a lucrative monopoly. The Chinese learned how to deep-drill for natural gas, which they burned to evaporate the salt. Salt and iron became two of the most important items in Chinese trade.

The largest single piece of ancient Chinese cast-iron is the Great Lion of Zangzhou (Tsang-chou) erected in modern Hebei Province in 854 by Tang emperor Shizong (Shih Tsung) to commemorate his military campaign against the Liao dynasty. Standing 20 feet high, at 166 feet in length, and weighing about 40 tons, this statue was made 400 years before cast-iron objects were manufactured in Europe. Several cast-iron pagodas were erected in China, including a 78-

foot-high pagoda built in 1105 in modern Shandong Province, which was cast layer by layer in octagonal sections. After the Mongols acquired iron swords, speartips and arrowtips from the Chinese, they were able to overthrow the Southern Song dynasty (1127–1279) and unify China under the Yuan dynasty (1279–1368). In 1234 they seized the capital of the Jin dynasty (1115–1234) at Kaifeng and took all the Chinese blacksmiths there, whom they forced to make weapons for the Mongol troops. Several years later the Mongols defeated Kievan Russia, and they kept expanding their empire until it stretched from China to the edge of Europe.

In late-19th-century China, iron technology was applied to building steamships and railroads. But iron and steel production barely advanced from then until the Chinese Communists founded the People's Republic of China (PRC) in 1949. At that time, the annual Chinese steel output was only 160,000 tons. Advisers from the U.S.S.R. helped the PRC build up its iron and steel industries, and in 1952 China produced 1.35 million tons of steel. By 1957, annual steel output had increased to 5.35 million tons, and by 1987 China had become the world's fifth-largest producer of iron and steel. In 1989 it produced more than 60 million tons of steel, making it the world's fourth-largest steel producer. The Bayi Steel Company was China's first medium-sized iron and steel complex. The PRC also began construction of two large-scale steel complexes at Wuhan and Baotou. After the economic failure of the Great Leap Forward in the late 1950s, China went through a period of adjustment in the early 1960s, during which the iron and steel industry developed steadily. In 1964, a large steel complex designed and constructed solely by the Chinese opened at Panzhihua in Sichuan Province. The Cultural Revolution (1966–76) interrupted this development, and the industry recovered only in the late 1970s with the so-called Four Modernizations policy, which encouraged economic reform and an open door to foreign trade and investment.

The Chinese government planned to distribute iron and steel production across the country. In 1985 there were about 2,000 state and collective enterprises, ranging from small enterprises producing less than 5,000 tons of steel per year to the large integrated Anshan Steel Company in Liaoning, which in 1982 produced 6.1 million tons of pig iron, 6.8 million tons of steel, and 4.4. million tons of steel products. China had 10 integrated enterprises with a crude-steel-making capacity of 1.0 million tons per year or more, which accounted for 60 percent of total steel production. The largest iron and steel enterprises tend to be located in the northern, northeastern (Manchuria) and south-central regions, close to abundant supplies of iron ore, coal and limestone. The only major exceptions are the Baoshan Iron and Steel Plant near Shanghai, which was begun in 1978 and began operating its blast furnace in 1985 and which will depend on imported ore, and another large enterprise in Shanghai, which uses pig iron transported from other parts of China and in the future would switch to imported materials.

In 1990 the Anshan Iron and Steel Company, founded more than 70 years earlier, was China's largest iron and steel production center. Its three steelworks and 12 steel-processing factories could turn out more than 8 million tons annually. In 1990, of China's 1,200 iron and steel enterprises, 14 had the capacity to produce more than 1.0 million tons of

steel annually. The variety and quality also increased by 1990. That year, the Wuhan Iron and Steel Company was China's largest steel-plate production center. More than 1,000 kinds of rolled and ordinary steel could be produced to more than 20,000 specifications, and 29 percent of the total output met international specifications. During the 1980s China spent U.S.$5 billion buying foreign technology to produce iron and steel. The government also decided to accelerate development by introducing foreign capital, which has helped many companies, such as the Wuhan and Anshan plants, to start modernizing and renovating their equipment. By 1993, the government estimated that China's annual steel output would rise by 5 million tons. By 1998 Baoshan Iron and Steel Group Corp. was among the top 500 companies worldwide, with assets of $9.2 billion. See also BRONZEWARE; PAGODA; RAILROADS; SALT MONOPOLY; SHIPPING AND SHIPBUILDING.

IRTYSH RIVER See DZUNGARIA BASIN.

ISLAM See HUI; MINORITIES, NATIONAL; MUSLIMS; NOMADS AND ANIMAL HUSBANDRY.

ISLANDS OF THE BLESSED (Penglai or P'eng-lai) Also known as the Three Islands of the Immortals, the Islands of the Eastern Sea, or the Fortunate Islands; islands that were believed in the Daoist tradition to be the site of the herb of immortality. They were supposedly located in the East China Sea off the coast of Jiangsu Province. According to legends, the islands were inhabited by immortals with feathers and wings, who consumed precious jewels scattered along the shores and drank from the fountain of life, which flowed from a high rock made of jade. Originally there were five islands that floated freely in the sea. When they bumped against the Chinese coast, the immortals complained to the Emperor of Heaven, who ordered Yuqiang (Yu-ch'iang), the god of the ocean wind, to attach three tortoises to each island to anchor them in place. The Count of Dragons entered the ocean and caught six of the tortoises, causing two of the islands to drift to the north and sink, which angered the Emperor of Heaven. The other three islands remained in place, held by their tortoises, and attracted people who sought immortality. Qin Shi Huangdi, the first emperor who unified China under the Qin dynasty (221–206 B.C.), wanted to live forever and became obsessed with finding the Daoist elixir of immortality. He made several long journeys to the Chinese coast in his quest. In 219 B.C. he sent a group of several thousand young men and women, guided by the Daoist adept Xushi (Hsu Shih), to find the Islands of the Blessed. They supposedly sailed within sight of the islands but were driven back by strong winds. Qin Shi Huangdi died on his final tour to the sea in 210 B.C. It may be that the story of the group he sent east indicates an attempt to colonize the islands of Japan, which lie to the east of China. See also DAOISM; EAST CHINA SEA; ELIXIR OF IMMORTALITY; QIN SHI HUANGDI.

IVORY CARVING A Chinese art form since the Shang dynasty (1750–1040 B.C.). Ivory (*xiangya* or *hsiang-ya*) is a soft material taken from elephant tusks and the teeth and horns of the hippopotamus, rhinoceros, boar, walrus and whale that can be easily be carved into elaborate designs and figures. Ranging in color from pure white to yellow and brown, ivory has a smooth, appealing texture and can be polished to a high gloss. Most Chinese ivory carvings depict humans, animals and flowers. There were also elephants in northern China until the middle of the first millennium B.C. Shang ivory carvings are similar in design to the flat, linear designs of bronze objects that were cast during that period and are a highlight of Shang art. In later centuries, ivory was used mainly to carve small sculptures ranging from a few inches to three feet high. In the 17th century, objects used for writing in their studies by scholars of the literati (*wenren*) class were added to the repertoire of ivory carvings, especially wrist rests and containers to hold writing brushes. Wood and lacquer furniture were also enhanced with inlays of carved ivory. In the 18th and 19th centuries, very large ivory objects that showed the curve of the elephant tusk were also carved. Intricate carvings began in the 19th century, such as chess sets, boats covered with flowers, and decorative concentric spheres in which the interior balls rotate, most of which are usually displayed on stands. The spheres are a specialty of carvers in the Guangzhou (Canton) area in southern China, which has been a major export center for many centuries. See also BRONZEWARE; FURNITURE, TRADITIONAL.

JADE (*yu*)   A very rare and beautiful stone that has been valued as the most precious substance by the Chinese since ancient times. The Chinese traditionally believe that jade has magical and healing qualities because it is so hard as to seem indestructible. Its strength and translucence were connected with the qualities of wisdom, moral courage, power and purity. Jade was also associated with immortality, which was the goal of some alchemists in the Daoist religion. Ancient emperors drank powdered jade mixed in water to try to become immortal. Jade has been worked for thousands of years in China. Jade tools were made as far back as the Neolithic period (c. 12,000–c. 2000 B.C.), including hammerheads, ax-heads and knives. They had a ritual and symbolic function and were often the insignia of a prince. Other jade ritual objects were also made, including the *bi* (*pi*), a disk with a hole cut in the center, a symbol of heaven often awarded to nobles to affirm their status. During the Zhou dynasty (1100–256 B.C.), the practice of including pieces of jade and carvings, especially of the skin-shedding insect called the cicada, with the goods buried in aristocratic tombs became widespread.

Many wealthy Chinese began to use jade implements such as hairpins, earrings, belt hooks, amulets and charms, which they also gave as tokens of friendship. During the Han dynasty (206 B.C.–A.D. 220), emperors wore a hat with nine strings of jade beads. Han nobles were sometimes buried in suits made from pieces of jade sewn together with gold thread. Some of these have been excavated, such as the jade suits for the Han prince Liu Sheng and his wife, and put on display in Chinese museums. Chinese emperors carried a jade scepter as a symbol of their power. Since jade makes a pleasing musical sound when struck, pieces of jade in different sizes were suspended on frames to make musical instruments. After the Buddhist religion was introduced into China around the first century A.D., numerous jade statues were carved of Buddhist deities, especially Guanyin, the goddess of mercy, as well as bowls shaped like lotus flowers, the Buddhist symbol of purity.

There are actually two types of stone that are commonly called jade. Both are found in remote regions of China and Myanmar (Burma), and in past centuries both were transported to inner China with immense difficulty, increasing their value even more. Jadeite is a silicate of sodium and aluminum, and is found in a hilly region in northern Myanmar, which lies south of Yunnan Province in southwestern China. The Chinese did not use jadeite until the 18th century. Nephrite is a silicate of calcium, magnesium and aluminum, and comes from Eastern Turkestan (part of modern Xinjiang-Uygur Autonomous Region in western China), around Hotan and Yarkand. Nephrite stones are found lying loose in the beds of the Green Jade and White Jade rivers in Xinjiang. Jade is usually thought of as bright green, but jadeite and nephrite both have a wide range of colors and shades. The Chinese divide nephrite into nine colors, including moss green, yellow, dark blue, bright blue, black, deep red, bright red, "clear water," and opaque white or "mutton fat." They divide jadeite into eight colors, including translucent grass-green, light green with bright-green markings, clouded, dark green, brownish red, translucent white, opaque white, and green-black.

The Chinese have used jade to make a great variety of beautiful objects, including bowls, plates, cups and chopsticks; writing implements such as containers and rests for brushes, table screens and signature seals; figures of plants, humans and animals, especially horses, and oxen, flowers and fruits; the Eight Immortals, gods in the Daoist religion; and "boulder carvings," elaborate landscapes with mountains, trees, waterfalls, and so forth, displayed as decorative pieces. Jade is much too hard to be carved or cut directly. It must be slowly worn down using an abrasive, such as powdered stones, crushed garnets, corundum, or quartz sand, and iron or bronze saws, drills and wheels. The abrasive must be continually moistened with water. Holes are drilled in jade using diamonds. A steel tube is used to hollow out vases and make cavities. This slow, painstaking process for carving jade also increases its value. Emperors of the Qing dynasty (1644–1911) valued jade so highly that imperial workshops were established in the capital city of Beijing, and the best jade craftsmen were brought there from around the country. In 1958 the jade carvers' cooperatives in the city were organized into the Beijing Jade Studios, where more than a thousand carvers still work and young people are trained as apprentices. Jade is also produced in other cities, but Beijing remains the center for jade carving.

JADE EMPEROR Yu Huang or Yu Di (Yu Ti), the "August Personage of Jade"; the supreme deity of the Daoist religion, who presides over Heaven, and a major figure in Chinese folklore. The Chinese traditionally believe that jade, which is rare, beautiful and so hard as to seem indestructible, has magical and healing qualities. The Jade Emperor is associated with these qualities and is also a symbol of purity and nature. He is sometimes referred to as the "Pearly Emperor." The Jade Emperor is one of the "Three Pure Ones," a trio of Daoist deities that includes Dao Zhun (Tao Chun), who controls the relations between the universal principles of yin and yang; and Laozi (Lao Tzu), the most proficient writer on Daoism and author of the most important Daoist text, the *Daodejing* (*Tao-te Ching, The Way and Its Power*). The Chinese celebrate the Jade Emperor's birthday on the 19th day of the first month in the traditional lunar calendar, around mid-February. Known as the "Festival of the Gathering of the 100 Gods," this is when the lower gods appear at the Jade Emperor's heavenly court to inform him of human activities on Earth. One week before the New Year Festival, the most important holiday in the Chinese calendar, the Kitchen God (Caozhun or Ts'ao-chun) is believed to travel to Heaven to report to the Jade Emperor about what has happened on earth during the year.

Legends recount that the Jade Emperor's mother, Bao Yu (who represents the moon) and his father, Jing De (the sun), asked a Daoist priest to help them conceive a son. His mother saw a vision of Laozi riding a dragon and carrying a male child. She then gave birth to this child, Yu Huang. His body gave out a bright light, and he was intelligent and compassionate and aided poor and sick people. After he became emperor, he abdicated the throne and retired to the hills of Buming to spend his time meditating. When he perfected himself he ascended to Heaven to rule forever as the Jade Emperor. However, he came back to Earth hundreds of times to instruct people, cure the sick and aid the country.

According to legend, the Jade Emperor has a heavenly court that reflects the Chinese imperial court bureaucracy on earth. He dwells in the same type of palace as the earthly emperor and has ministers to govern the various departments that are concerned with every aspect of human life on Earth. The Jade Emperor himself is directly involved only with the affairs of the earthly emperor. After the Jade Emperor supposedly appeared twice to emperors of the Song dynasty (960–1279), he was given official recognition as the supreme deity by Emperor Zhenzong (Chen-tsung) of the Liao dynasty in 1005. Chinese emperors made sacrifices to the Jade Emperor twice a year at the Altar of Heaven in the capital city of Beijing. The Jade Emperor's deputy is Dongyu Dadi (Tung-yo ta-ti), the Great Emperor of the Eastern Peak, the birthplace of the yang (masculine, positive) universal principle. The wife of the Jade Emperor is Wangmu Niang-Niang, a variant of the name Xiwangmu (Hsi Wang Mu), the Daoist goddess who presides over the West.

The beloved Chinese 16th-century novel, *Journey to the West* (*Xiyouji* or *Hsi-yu-chi*), has a famous episode set in the heavenly court of the Jade Emperor known as "Monkey Causes Havoc in Heaven." The Monkey King, a trickster who has supernatural powers, becomes drunk at a banquet given in his honor by the Dragon King of the Eastern Sea. Servants of the King of Hell take Monkey prisoner, but he escapes, steals the book in which judgments are recorded, and deletes his name and the names of all monkeys. The Monkey King is sent to Heaven to explain his actions, but he steals the banquet feast that the gods are planning to enjoy and makes himself doubly immortal by eating the peaches of immortality and swallowing the pill of immortality, which he has stolen. See also DAOISM; EMPEROR; JADE; JOURNEY TO THE WEST; KITCHEN GOD; LAOZI; MONKEY XIWANGMU.

JAPAN AND CHINA See CHAN SECT OF BUDDHISM; CONFUCIANISM; ENNIN; FOREIGN TRADE AND INVESTMENT; INTERNATIONAL SETTLEMENT IN SHANGHAI; MANCHUKUO; MANCHURIAN INCIDENT; MARCO POLO BRIDGE INCIDENT; MAY FOURTH MOVEMENT OF 1919; MING DYNASTY; NANJING; PIRATES; PURE LAND SECT OF BUDDHISM; PUYI, HENRY; RUSSO-JAPANESE WAR OF 1904–05; RYUKYU ISLANDS; SCULPTURE; SHANDONG PROVINCE; SINO-JAPANESE WAR OF 1894–95; TAIWAN; TANG DYNASTY; TREATY PORTS; TWENTY-ONE DEMANDS ON CHINA; UNEQUAL TREATIES; WAR OF RESISTANCE AGAINST JAPAN.

JEHOL See CHENGDE.

JEN See HUMANITY.

JEN I See REN BONIAN.

JEN PO-NIEN See REN BONIAN.

JESUITS Members of the Roman Catholic Society of Jesus, who entered China as missionaries in the 17th century. Catholic missionaries had gone to China as early as the 13th century, but the Jesuits were the first to have a major impact in the country. They traveled along the sea route used by Portuguese and Spanish traders. The Portuguese had a base at Macao, a small island near the southern Chinese port city of Guangzhou (Canton). The Jesuits entered China from Macao through Guangzhou. The first Jesuit in China was Matteo Ricci (1552–1610), who received permission from the Ming dynasty (1368–1644) court to settle in Beijing in 1600. The highly educated Jesuits intrigued the Chinese with their knowledge of mathematics, science and technology, especially astronomy, cartography, hydraulic engineering, and European clockworks and weapons such as cannons. Ricci's world atlas informed the Chinese of many countries in the world that they had not known about. In 1644 the Chinese court appointed the Jesuit Ferdinand Verbiest to introduce European astronomical measurement and instrument in the Imperial Astronomical Bureau. Jesuits continued to head the office of astronomy that determined the official annual calendar, which was extremely important for agriculture and ritual purposes, and a group of Jesuits headed by Joannes Adam Schall von Bell developed an improved Chinese calendar. Jesuit artists also influenced

Chinese painters in Western painting styles and techniques. Jesuits who went to China made a lifetime commitment, for the Chinese court would not give them permission to leave the country.

When the Manchus overthrew the Ming and established the Qing dynasty (1644–1911), they kept the calendar and retained the Jesuits in important positions. After Schall died in 1666, Verbiest, was appointed to head the court observatory. Jesuits also played a diplomatic role in the court, and a Jesuit negotiated the Treaty of Nerchinsk (1689) between China and Russia. Ricci and his successors learned the Chinese language and studied the classical Confucian texts that were the basic texts in the education of the literati, or scholars, who staffed the Chinese imperial bureaucracy. The Jesuits translated into Chinese more than 100 treatises on Western science and technology, beginning with Euclid's *Geometry*. During the 17th and 18th centuries, some 80 Jesuit missionaries produced Chinese translations of more than 400 Western works, with more than half of these on the Christian religion and about a third on science. The reports on China that the Jesuits sent back to Europe influenced European philosophers and political thinkers, especially during the 18th-century Enlightenment. The German philosopher Leibniz (1646–1716) was greatly influenced by Chinese Confucian ideas. The Jesuits also stimulated the popularity of European decorative art styles known collectively as chinoiserie.

The Jesuits practiced "accommodation," that is, they accepted the Confucian tradition as a system of ethics, finding points of similarity between Christian and Confucian teachings, and permitted their Chinese converts to continue performing the Confucian rituals to honor their ancestors, known as "ancestor worship." This brought the Jesuits into conflict with other Catholic missionaries in France, notably the Franciscans and Dominicans, who complained to the pope in Rome. The pope attempted to stop the Jesuits from accommodating Confucian practices; this created the conflict known as the Rites Controversy. The emperor of China did not like having the Christian pope tell him what to do, so he banned Christianity in China in 1724. In 1773 the pope dissolved the Society of Jesus. The Chinese ban against Christianity was not lifted until the French forced the Qing to do so in 1846, although Christian priests had continued to work in the meantime clandestinely in China. See also ASTRONOMY AND OBSERVATORIES; BEIJING; CALENDAR; CHINOISERIE; CHRISTIANITY; CONFUCIANISM; IMPERIAL BUREAUCRACY; LITERATI; NERCHINSK, TREATY OF; RICCI, MATTEO; RITES CONTROVERSY.

JEWELRY   See GOLD AND SILVER; JADE; KINGFISHER.

JEWS   People who practiced the religion of Judaism were residing in China by the middle of the Tang dynasty (618–907), when many foreign traders, including Persian (Iranian) and Arab Muslims, settled in the country. Most foreigners resided in the capital city of Chang'an (modern Xi'an in Shaanxi Province), the southern port of Guangzhou (Canton) and the southeastern port of Quanzhou near Xiamen. The Chinese term for Jews is *tiaojinjiao* (*t'iao-chin-chiao,* "the religion that extracts the sinews"). The only records left by Jews in China came from Kaifeng in modern Henan Province, which was the capital of the Northern Song dynasty (960–1126) and the home of the largest community of Jews in China. These Jews may have come to Kaifeng along the Silk Road through Central Asia, although Chinese historians maintain that they were descendants of members of Jewish communities on the southwestern coast of India who immigrated to China. Jews built a synagogue (*qingzhensi* or *ch'ing-chen-ssu* in Chinese) in Kaifeng in 1163. The Jewish community flourished in Kaifeng until the 18th century and survived on a small scale into the 20th.

During the Ming (1368–1644) and early Qing (1644–1911) dynasties, Jews held positions as government officials, military officers and physicians. In 1615, a Catholic priest named Nicola Trigault translated and published the diaries of Matteo Ricci (1552–1610), the first Jesuit priest who had been permitted to reside in China. These diaries include the account of a meeting between Ricci and a Jew from Kiafeng, who said that there were about a dozen Jewish families in Kaifeng, which had a large synagogue containing scrolls of the Jewish scripture known as the five books of Moses. Several hundred descendants of the original Jewish community still live in Kaifeng, although they have not retained many Jewish practices. The original synagogue was destroyed when the Yellow River flooded in 1642, and was rebuilt but destroyed again by floods in the 1850s. Christian missionaries saved the Jewish scrolls and prayer books, which are now housed in libraries in Israel, the United States and Canada, including a Chinese-Hebrew Memorial Book of the Dead owned by Hebrew Union College in Cincinnati, Ohio. The Jewish community in Kaifeng plans to rebuild the synagogue and open a Jewish museum. During World War II, thousands of Jews fled from Europe and the U.S.S.R. to Shanghai, China's largest city. The government of the People's Republic of China (PRC) has officially designated Jews as one of China's 55 national minority ethnic groups. Western scholars have recently formed an association to promote the study of the history of the Jews in China. See also KAIFENG; MINORITIES, NATIONAL; MUSLIMS; SHANGHAI; SILK ROAD.

JIAJING (EMPEROR) (Chia-ching; 1507–67)   The 12th emperor of the Ming dynasty (1368–1644); grandson of the Ming emperor Chenghua (r. 1465–88). His personal name was Zhu Houcong (Chu Hou-ts'ung), and he reigned under the name Shizong (Shih-chung); Jiajing (Chi-ching), meaning "Prosperous Tranquility," is his reign name (r. 1522–67). After the first half of his reign, the Jiajing emperor became obsessed with the practices of the Daoist religion, which he believed would bring him longevity. This was of particular concern to him since the six preceding emperors had all died before turning 40 years of age. He withdrew himself from an active role in the government for long periods of time, entrusting decisions to the Grand Secretaries, such as Yen Song (Yen Sung), who was strongly disliked. During Jiajing's reign, the Grand Secretariat (Neige or Nei-ko) was given formal recognition.

The economy and defenses of the Chinese Empire had been declining for some time, and they worsened during Jiajing's reign. Pirates (*woko*) harassed the coast without much Chinese resistance. Troops stationed on the northern frontier to ward off invading nomadic tribes put a strain on the imperial treasury, which was also reduced by widespread tax evasion by members of the literati, or scholar-gentry class, who staffed the imperial bureaucracy. The Mongols, who had ruled China under the Yuan dynasty (1279–1368) but had been driven north by the founder of the Ming dynasty, began increasing their attacks on the Chinese frontier. Twice the Mongols sent emissaries to the Ming court to establish a tributary relationship, but the Chinese killed them, which further antagonized the Mongols. In 1541 and 1542 they invaded modern Shanxi Province, where they killed or captured several hundred thousand Chinese, along with their animals. In 1550 the Mongol chief, Altan Khan, led a major invasion of China. The Chinese general at Datong was able to prevent an attack by bribing the Mongol forces and promising them trading rights. But Altan moved east, broke through the Great Wall near Beijing and put the capital under siege for three days. His forces also plundered the other cities in this region. In 1551 Altan Khan again asked the Ming court to grant the Mongols a trading relationship, and they agreed to this, but the two sides mistrusted each other and the Chinese placed difficult requirements on the Mongol trade. The Mongols continued to wage raids for plunder across the northern Chinese frontier. During the 1550s and 1560s many Chinese peasants impoverished by taxes and exploitation also fled north of the Great Wall.

During the reign of Jiajing, who became a follower of Daoism, a change was made in the revering of Confucius (551–479 B.C.), whose school of thought was orthodoxy for the Chinese imperial government. The emperor approved the proposal made in 1530 that the veneration paid to Confucius should be reduced. Confucius would no longer have the title of prince (*wang*); buildings where ceremonies were conducted in his honor would be called halls rather than temples; and the images of Confucius would be destroyed and replaced by tablets. The Portuguese, the first Europeans to sail to Asia in quest of trade, received permission during Jiajing's reign name to settle and trade in the Pearl River (Zhujiang) estuary in southern China. Around 1565 they acquired the island of Macao near the Chinese port of Guangzhou (Canton). Emperor Jiajing was succeeded by his son, whose reign name was Longqing (Lung-ch'ing), meaning "Abundant Blessings" (r. 1567–72). See also CONFUCIUS; CONFUCIANISM; GRAND SECRETARIAT; GREAT WALL; MACAO; MING DYNASTY; MONGOLS; PIRATES; TRIBUTE SYSTEM.

JIALING RIVER   See SICHUAN PROVINCE.

JIAN WARE   See TEMMOKU WARE.

JIANG FENG (Chiang Feng; 1910–82)   Original name Zhou Xi (Chou Hsih); the most important artist in China during the 1950s and a leading figure in the Anti-Rightist Campaign of 1957. Jiang was born into a working-class family in Shanghai, China's largest and most Westernized city. He did not have much formal education, but he learned painting and joined an art club that met in the evenings, where he met many Chinese students, artists and intellectuals. By the time Jiang was 21 years old he had become active in left-wing politics. In the summer of 1931, he was one of 13 young artists chosen for a woodblock-print class taught by Lu Xun (Lu Hsun), the leading radical Chinese author

and artist. This class was influential in making woodblock prints, or woodcuts, which became the favorite artistic medium for conveying the revolutionary message in China. Jiang spent the next 20 years producing woodcuts. He joined the CCP in 1932 and became friendly with Feng Xuefeng (Feng Hsueh-feng), a Communist writer closely associated with Lu Xun. Shortly after, Jiang and several of his revolutionary friends were arrested and imprisoned. Jiang was released from prison in 1933 but was soon rearrested. Lu Xun encouraged his artistic activities in prison by sending him a book of German expressionist prints. Jiang was not the best woodcut artist, but he excelled as an art teacher and administrator.

Jiang's circle had little interest in the traditional style of art taught in art academies operated by the Nationalist (Kuomintang; KMT) government, especially the academy in Hangzhou, which had been China's cultural center ever since the Southern Song dynasty (1127–1279) had made the beautiful city its capital. After Japan invaded China in 1937, Jiang became the administrator of woodcut propaganda artists at the Lu Xun Academy of Arts, which the Communists had established at Yan'an in Shaanxi Province, where they made their headquarters after they escaped the Nationalists on the so-called Long March (1934–35). Jiang became very interested in oil paintings in the style of Soviet socialist realism, which he maintained were as popular in the U.S.S.R. as colorful woodcuts (*nianhua*) for the New Year Festival were in China.

After the Communists defeated the Nationalists in 1949, Jiang played a major role in reorganizing traditional Chinese painting academies into modern art academies based on the Soviet model. He directed the reorganization of the National Hangzhou Art College (1949–51) and was the most important leader in the Central Academy of Fine Arts in Beijing (1951–57). From 1955 to 1957, the Central Academy held a postgraduate class in oil painting taught by Konstantin M. Maksimov, the only Soviet painter who ever taught in China as an official foreign expert. Between 1953 and 1957, Jiang held the highest positions in the Chinese government's art administration, which gave him the most influence in determining art policy and made him the CCP spokesman for art. He was acting director and Party secretary of the Central Academy of Fine Arts in Beijing, and first vice chairman and Party secretary of the national Chinese Artists Association.

In 1956–57 Communist chairman Mao Zedong (Mao Tse-tung) encouraged Chinese intellectuals and artists to criticize the Party's policies and programs openly, in the Hundred Flowers Campaign. But in August 1957, CCP leaders abruptly ended this campaign by declaring the Anti-Rightist Campaign, in which they condemned critics of the Party as "bourgeois rightists" and "class enemies." The government sent tens of thousands of intellectuals, writers and scientists to labor camps or placed them under surveillance. Jiang had reorganized the Chinese art-education system on behalf of the CCP, but when the Party criticized him, he refused to agree that he had made mistakes, and the Party punished him by labeling him "Number One Rightist in the Art World." Many artists supported Jiang at first, so the Party then convicted him of organizing an "anti-Party group." One reason he may have been attacked was because of his association with followers of Lu Xun, who were purged by their enemies in the Ministry of Culture and Central Propaganda Department. Also, Party bureaucrats in Zhejiang Province resented Jiang's reorganization of the painting academy in Hangzhou and placing it under the authority of the Central Academy of Fine Arts in Beijing.

The Ministry of Culture forced many artists to testify that Jiang favored Western-style art over the traditional Chinese style of ink painting. In autumn 1957 Mao gave a speech in which he linked Jiang with the authors Hu Feng, who had been condemned and committed suicide, and Ding Ling (Ting Ling) and Feng Xuefeng, who had also been denounced by the Party as anticommunists. Artists who refused to criticize Jiang were themselves condemned by the Party: thus, many artists saved their own careers by giving in to pressure to denounce Jiang, who was replaced by Cai Ruohong (Ts'ai Jo-hung). Although Jiang lost his official positions in the CCP, he remained active in the Chinese art world and never gave up his revolutionary concept of art. In 1978 he quoted Lu Xun's opinion that art must be divided into the "art of the oppressors and the art of the oppressed," which expressed his view that traditional Chinese art belongs in the former category and Western-style realistic art in the latter category. See also ANTI-RIGHTIST CAMPAIGN; CHINESE COMMUNIST PARTY; DING LING; HUNDRED FLOWERS CAMPAIGN; LU XUN; WOODCUTS; XU BEIHONG.

JIANG JIESHI See CHIANG KAI-SHEK.

JIANG JINGGUO See CHIANG CHING-KUO.

JIANG QING (Chiang Ch'ing; 1914–91) Also known as Madame Mao Zedong (Mao Tse-tung); original name Li Jin; the fourth wife of Chinese Communist Party (CCP) chairman Mao Zedong, and a member of the so-called Gang of Four—four CCP leaders who were arrested in 1976 and convicted of causing the tumultuous Cultural Revolution (1966–76). Jiang was born to a poor family in Shandong Province. She studied traditional Chinese opera and then modern drama, auditing classes at Qingdao University. She joined the CCP in 1933. During the 1930s she became a film actress in Shanghai, China's largest and most Westernized city and international port, where the CCP had been very active since its founding in 1921. In 1937 she traveled to CCP headquarters in Yan'an in Shaanxi Province, where the Communists had ended their Long March (1934–35) to escape the Nationalists (Kuomintang; KMT).

In 1939 Jiang married Communist leader Mao Zedong when he was 45 years old. Mao had been married three times before. His family had arranged his first marriage when he was only 14 years old. His second wife had been executed in Hunan Province in 1930. His third wife had been one of the few women to survive the Long March, but in Yan'an they separated and Mao sent her to Moscow, ostensibly to receive medical treatment. Other CCP leaders opposed Mao's marriage to Jiang, but they accepted it on condition that she would play no role in politics, to which she agreed. Mao gave her the name Jiang Qing, meaning "Lapis River." She had one child by Mao, a daughter named Li Na. In 1948, when the CP was fighting a civil war with the Chinese Nationalists, Jiang was head of the film office of the CCP Propaganda Department. The CCP defeated the KMT and founded the People's Republic of China in 1949.

In the early 1960s Jiang inaugurated a radical reform of Beijing Opera and ballet, and in April 1963 she issued a circular, "On Suspending the Performance of Ghost Plays," calling for a ban on traditional Chinese drama. In 1964 she organized the Festival of Beijing Opera in Contemporary Themes, which inaugurated new theatrical forms combining traditional opera techniques with Western music and contemporary scenery, costumes and makeup. "Model" works that were first performed at this festival included *Taking the Bandit's Stronghold*, later called *Taking Tiger Mountain by Strategy*. Jiang's revolutionary ballet, *The Red Detachment of Women*, was televised in the United States on February 2–20, 1966. Jiang, following the instructions of CCP official Lin Biao (Lin Piao), convened "The Forum on the Work in Literature and Art in the Armed Forces" in Shanghai.

In the summer of 1966 Jiang initiated the Cultural Revolution when she and Yao Wenyuan (Yao Wen-yuan), another CCP official later accused of being one of the Gang of Four, published an article denouncing *Hai Rui Dismissed from Office*, a supposedly historical play that had been recently performed, for being a veiled criticism of Mao's actions. Yao had published an article in late 1965 criticizing Wu Han, the mayor of Beijing. In 1966 Mao and his faction purged or attacked many CCP officials, including State Chairman Liu Shaoqi (Liu Shao-ch'i). Premier Zhou Enlai (Chou En-lai), a longtime colleague of Mao who remained loyal to him, still attempted to mediate between the two party factions. Jiang's faction opposed Zhou's pragmatic position and called for an increased political role for the "revolutionary masses." On August 20, 1966, the young CCP radicals known as the Red Guards in Beijing began destroying "bourgeois and feudal remnants," and they began to criticize Liu Shaoqi, Mao's designated successor, for being a capitalist.

In the early 1970s Jiang supposedly led the attacks by Party radicals on Deng Xiaoping (Teng Hsiao-p'ing) and other Party leaders who advocated economic reforms. Mao died on September 9, 1976. On October 6, more than 30 radical CCP leaders were arrested and deposed from their official positions by the moderate faction led by Hua Guofeng (Hua Kuo-feng) who had seized power in the CCP's Central Committee. Jiang Qing and three other Politburo members, Wang Hongwen (Wang Hung-wen), Yao Wenyuan and Zhang Chunjiao (Chang Ch'un-chiao) were imprisoned and accused of being the "Gang of Four" who had caused the Cultural Revolution. The CCP publicly announced that the four radical leaders had been charged with a plot to overthrow the Chinese government.

On October 24 the CCP held an enormous demonstration in Tiananmen Square to support Hua Guofeng (Hua Kuo-feng), Mao's designated successor as CCP chairman, and to criticize the Gang of Four. Wu De (Wu Teh) condemned the Gang of Four for attempting to divide the CCP and seize power. As time went on, more and more extreme accusations were leveled against the four. Mao was still so highly respected that no one criticized him; all blame was deflected to his widow and the three radical leaders who were her closest associates.

On July 21, 1977, the Third Plenum of the Tenth Chinese People's Political Consultative Conference (CPPCC) confirmed Hua Guofeng as chairman of the CPPCC and its military affairs commission. It also restored Deng Xiaoping to deputy chairman of the CPPCC, and expelled the Gang of Four from the CCP and removed them from all of their Party positions. The Party accused Jiang of being a "bourgeois careerist, conspirator, counterrevolutionary double-dealer and renegade." In December 1977 a group in the Ministry of Education charged that the Gang of Four had "wrought havoc to our educational cause and the level of education as a whole" and thus retarded the four modernizations advocated by Deng—the modernization of Chinese agriculture, industry, national defense and science.

The Gang of Four was not formally put on trial until November 1980, when a 35-judge special court was convened and issued a 20,000-word indictment against the Gang of Four and six of Lin Biao's closest associates. The court charged them with sedition, conspiring to overthrow the government, persecution of Party and government leaders, plotting to murder Mao, suppression of the masses, persecuting 34,380 people to death, and fomenting an armed rebellion in Shanghai. In December 1980, near the end of the trial, Jiang Qing shouted out in court: "It is more glorious to have my head chopped off than to yield to accusers. I dare you to sentence me to death in front of one million people in Tiananmen Square." On January 25, 1981, the special court held its last session and rendered a guilty verdict against all 10 defendants. It condemned Jiang and Zhang Chunjiao to death with a two-year suspension, Wang Hongwen to life imprisonment, Yao Wenyuan to a 20-years imprisonment and the others to lengthy prison terms. The Gang of Four was even airbrushed out of the photographs of Mao's funeral ceremonies. When the court read out her death sentence, Jiang cried out, "I am prepared to die" and was taken out of the court. She refused to confess her guilt and claimed that everything she had done during the Cultural Revolution had been ordered by Mao himself. The court was in a difficult position because, while it stated that Jiang had not shown "sufficient repentance," it did not want to turn her into a martyr, especially if it were true that she had only carried out Mao's orders. On January 25, 1983, the death sentences on Jiang and Zhang Chunjiao were commuted to life imprisonments. Jiang committed suicide on May 14, 1991, supposedly by hanging herself in prison. The Chinese government did not announce her death until after June 4, 1991, the second anniversary of the government-ordered massacre of prodemocracy demonstrators in Tiananmen Square in 1989. Some scholars believe that the CCP will eventually reverse Jiang's guilty verdict. See also BEIJING; CHINESE COMMUNIST PARTY; CIVIL WAR BETWEEN COMMUNISTS AND NATIONALISTS; CULTURAL REVOLUTION; DENG XIAOPING; FOUR MODERNIZATIONS; GANG OF FOUR; GOVERNMENT STRUCTURE; HUA GUOFENG; LIN BAO; LIU SHAOQI; LONG MARCH; MAO ZEDONG; PEOPLE'S DAILY; RED GUARDS; SHANGHAI; TIANANMEN SQUARE; TIANANMEN SQUARE MASSACRE; YAN'AN; YE JIANYING.

JIANG ZEMIN (Chiang Tse-min; 1926–) The president of the People's Republic of China (PRC), founded in 1949 by the Chinese Communist Party (CCP), and chairman of the CCP Politburo (Political Bureau). Jiang joined the CCP in 1946. The following year he received a degree in electrical engineering from Jiaofong University in Shanghai. By 1950 he was director of the Northeast Military Region's Military Engineering Department. In 1955 he spent a year in Moscow as commercial councillor in the Chinese embassy to the U.S.S.R., which at that time had close ties with the PRC. When Jiang returned to China, he held a number of administrative positions in the Party in the areas of electronics and heavy industry. In 1980–82 he was vice minister of the Administrative Commission for Import and Export Affairs, and in 1981–82 he was also vice minister, State Foreign Investment Commission. In 1982 he was also elected to the 12th CCP Central Committee, and in 1983 he became minister of the Electronics Industry. From 1985–88 Jiang served as a mayor of Shanghai, China's largest and most Westernized city, and helped open Shanghai to investments from foreign companies. In 1988 he stepped down as mayor of Shanghai, but kept the position of Shanghai municipal CCP secretary.

In 1989, when the Party declared martial law to end the student protests in Tiananmen Square, Jiang gained the support of CCP leader Deng Xiaoping (Teng Hsiao-p'ing) when he closed down the liberal newspaper *World Economic Herald*. On June 24, 1989, Jiang was elected a member of the Politburo and was appointed to replace Zhao Ziyang as secretary-general, the highest position within the CCP. Zhao was removed from office because of his leniency with the Tiananmen Square demonstrators. In 1989 Deng resigned as chairman of the CCP Central Committee's Military Commission and was replaced by Jiang Zemin, and in 1990 Jiang also replaced Deng as chairman of the State Military Commission. In addition, Jiang became president of China. Since 1990, he has been criticized by foreign leaders for not improving human rights in China. In 1992 Jiang paid a goodwill visit to Japan, where he praised Japan's successful economic development as a model for China, which, under Deng's leadership, has been attempting to reform and modernize its economy. In mid-1994 Jiang promoted 19 senior military officers to full generals to consolidate his power in the People's Liberation Army.

Jiang addressed the United Nations in New York for the organization's 50th anniversary session in October 1995, giving a hard-line speech on Taiwan and human rights issues. The PRC considers Taiwan a province of China and wants to reintegrate it into the country. Jiang also met with U.S. President Bill Clinton in New York, although relations between the PRC and the United States had been strained since June 1995, when the United States government granted a visa permitting Taiwan's President, Lee Teng-hui, to visit the country to accept an honorary doctorate from Cornell University, his alma mater.

Jiang has attempted to consolidate his position as CCP leader since the death of Deng Xiaoping in February 1997, and he has built a network of officials in the military and security forces who are loyal to him. Jiang is referred to as the "third-generation leadership" after Mao and Deng. In 1993 Jiang appointed a former colleague from Shanghai as head of the People's Armed Police, a force of 800,000 that was formed as a second military organization, in addition to the People's Liberation Army, to prevent public assemblies from turning into huge antigovernment demonstrations such as the one at Tiananmen Square in 1989.

Since Jiang's influence depended on his relationship to Deng, it was not certain that it would last after Deng passed away. The situation was similar to that of Hua Guofeng, who was the designated successor to Chairman Mao Zedong but who was removed from power soon after Mao died in 1976. However, at the National Party Congress in September 1997, Jiang was reconfirmed as president of China and general secretary of the CCP. The Chinese people have appeared to be satisfied with the country's economic progress under Jiang's leadership. Some speculate that Jiang wants to revive the position of chairman of the CCP. In November 1997 he traveled to the United States for an official state visit with President Clinton. See also CHINESE COMMUNIST PARTY; DENG XIAOPING; GOVERNMENT STRUCTURE; HUA GUOFENG; LEE TENG-HUI; NATIONAL PARTY CONGRESS; SHANGHAI; TAIWAN; TIANANMEN SQUARE MASSACRE.

JIANG ZHONGZHENG See CHIANG KAI-SHEK.

JIANGLING See YANGZI RIVER.

JIANGNAN SCHOOL OF PAINTING See DONG YUAN.

JIANGSU PROVINCE A province on China's east coast with a population of about 64 million that covers 38,610 square miles. Its capital city, Nanjing (Nanking), is one of the most important cities in China, with a population of about 2.5 million; other major cities include Wuxi, Suzhou, Wuxi, Yangzhou, Xuzhou, Changzhou and Yancheng. The major port city of Shanghai, China's largest city, lies in southern Jiangsu but forms its own administrative region. Jiangsu is bordered on the east by the East China Sea and the provinces of Shandong to the north, Anhui to the west, and Zhejiang to the south.

Jiangsu is known as the "land of water" because of the rivers, lakes and ponds and the Grand Canal. The Yellow River (Huanghe) runs through the north of the province and the Yangzi River (Changjiang) through the south. Both carry huge quantities of soil and deposit it in their deltas and, thus, have moved the coastline of Jiangsu east by about 30 miles during the past 2,000 years. This process has also formed several major lakes, such as Hongze and Tai. Dikes have been constructed for protection from frequent flooding of the rivers. In the 1950s, projects redirected the course of the Yellow River from flowing directly into the East China Sea, causing it to flow first into Lake Hongze, then into Lake Gaoyou and then into the Yangzi River. Two canals also channel the Yellow River northward from Lake Hongze into the East China Sea.

Soil deposited by the rivers makes Jiangsu a fertile agricultural region. Numerous boats and barges distribute the products on the canals to other regions of China.

During the Neolithic period, an advanced culture, the Xia (2200–1750 B.C.), thrived in the Jiangsu region. The lower Yangzi Valley, especially around Nanjing, was a major center for the manufacture of bronzeware between 2200 and 500 B.C. In the late sixth century B.C. the kingdom of Wu in Jiangsu became powerful through the trading and shipping of products by boats. Wu came in conflict with the kingdom of Chu in the mid-Yangzi region, and also with the kingdom of Yue in the region of modern Zhejiang Province. In 506

B.C. the king of Wu captured the Chu capital at Ying. The conflict in the fifth century B.C. between the kings of Wu and Yue became legendary. Goujian, the Yue king, defeated his rival by sending Xi Shi (Hsi Shih), one of the "Four Famous Beauties of China," to entertain Fucha, the Wu King, making him neglect his duties.

When the Buddhist religion was introduced into China from India in the first century A.D., Jiangsu was one of the first places to accommodate the new religion. Records tell that a Buddhist community was established at Pengcheng by 65 A.D. In the eighth or ninth century A.D., the method of growing rice in flooded fields known as paddies became utilized in the lower Yangzi Valley, which provided regular harvests and enabled the population to increase rapidly. Jiangsu became highly developed after the 12th century, when the Northern Song dynasty's (960–1127) court fled south to escape Mongols invading from the north and established its capital at Hangzhou in Zhejiang Province, stimulating the commerce and culture of the lower Yangzi region. The Mongols founded the Yuan dynasty (1279–1368) but were overthrown by the Ming dynasty (1368–1644), whose rulers established their capital at Nanjing in Jiangsu. Nanjing served as the Ming capital until 1421, when the Ming court moved north to Beijing (Peking).

Many Western traders, especially British, came to China during the Qing dynasty (1644–1911), mainly through the ports of Shanghai and Guangzhou (Canton) in the south. During the 19th century, China and Great Britain fought two wars because the British, to put the balance of trade in their favor, brought large quantities of opium into China and caused the addiction of many Chinese people. The Chinese also resented their being forced to open some of their cities to Westerners as so-called Treaty Ports open to foreign trade and residents. Nanjing became one of the strongholds of the native Chinese Taiping Rebellion (1850–64), but the city was recaptured by Chinese imperial troops in 1864, thus ending the rebellion.

In the 20th century, the Chinese overthrew the Qing dynasty and established the Republic of China in 1912 under Sun Yat-sen (1866–1925). Sun was soon replaced by the warlord Yuan Shikai (1859–1916) and the capital was supposed to be transferred from Beijing to Nanjing, although this did not happen for 15 years. Jiangsu, on the Chinese Coast close to Shanghai, China's largest city and trading port, suffered from the invasion of China by Japan in 1931, the War of Resistance against Japan (1937–45; World War II), and the civil war between the Communists and the Nationalists (the Kuomintang) in the 1940s.

After the Communists took over in 1949 the province rapidly became modernized and industrialized. Major industries today include textiles, chemicals, mining and metal-cutting equipment, radios and televisions, bicycles and household appliances. Jiangsu is also one of China's most important producers of agricultural products, including rice, wheat and barley, vegetable oil, peanuts, pears, grapes, fish, shellfish, pork, mutton and jasmine (to flavor tea). Mulberry trees are grown to feed the leaves to silkworms.

Nanjing, formerly known as Jiankang and Jinling, is one of the oldest cities in China, dating back to the Eastern Zhou dynasty (771–256 B.C.). It served over a period of 2,000 years as the capital of eight dynasties, including the Ming.

The city walls and the tomb of the founder of the Ming, Emperor Hongwu (Hung-wu), were damaged during the Taiping Rebellion but can still be seen. The Mausoleum of Sun Yat-sen commemorates the founder of the modern Republic of China. The Jiangsu Provincial Museum exhibits art and archaeological artifacts from the region. Other tourist sites include the monumental bridge constructed over the Yangzi River in the 1960s, the Drum Tower and Great Bell Pavillion, the Museum of the Taiping Rebellion, Linggu Buddhist Temple, Xuanwu Lake and Qixia Mountain. Colorful brocade produced in Nanjing, a type of woven silk also known as cloud brocade, is one of the three finest brocades made in China.

Suzhou, with a population of nearly one million, is a beautiful city of canals and gardens situated on Lake Taihu, connected with the Grand Canal. A section of The Garden of the Master of the Fishing Nets in Suzhou has been recreated in the Metropolitan Museum of Art in New York City. Another tourist site is Bao Dai Bridge just outside Suzhou, which dates from the Tang dynasty (618–907). Suzhou is renowned for its silk and embroidery industries. Tiger Hill, an artificial hill 118 feet high, is on the site of the birthplace of the king of Wu, who founded Suzhou around 600 B.C. He is buried near the top of the hill.

The city of Yangzhou, situated on the Grand Canal, is another beautiful city of canals and gardens that attracted many scholars, poets and artist to retire. The works of the so-called Eight Eccentrics of Yangzhou are exhibited in the Municipal Museum. The city became a major trading center during the Tang dynasty. Its traditional handicrafts are still renowned, such as lacquerware, jade carvings, embroidery, papercuttings, woodblock prints, and container gardens (known by the Japanese term *bonsai* in the West). The Western trader Marco Polo (1254–1324) served for a time as the governor of Yangzhou under the Yuan dynasty.

Wuxi, located on the Grand Canal on the northern shore of Taihu, is one of the oldest cities in the Yangzi Delta. The Donglin ("Eastern Grove") Academy for Confucian studies was established here in the 17th century. This beautiful city, with a population of about one million, is a popular holiday resort. See also BRONZEWARE; CONFUCIANISM; CONTAINER GARDENS; EAST CHINA SEA; CIVIL WAR BETWEEN COMMUNISTS AND NATIONALISTS; EMBROIDERY; GARDEN OF THE MASTER OF THE FISHING NETS; GRAND CANAL; HONGZE, LAKE; JADE; LACQUERWARE; NANJING; OPIUM WAR; PAPERCUTTING; POLO, MARCO; SILK; SUN YAT-SEN; SUZHOU; TAIHU; TAIPING REBELLION; WOODCUTS; WUXI; XI SHI; YANGZHOU; YELLOW RIVER; YUAN SHIKAI.

JIANGXI PROVINCE   A province in south-central China that covers an area of 64,350 square miles and has a population of about 36 million. The capital city, Nanchang, has a population of about two million; other major cities include Pingxiang, Xinyu and Jingdezhen. The Yangzi River (Changjiang) forms part of the northern border of Jiangxi, which also borders Anhui, Zhejiang, Fujian, Guangdong, Hunan and Hubei provinces. Lake Poyang in northern Jiangxi is the largest freshwater lake in China, with an area of about 2,000 square miles. Several famous mountains rise from the lakeshore, including Lushan, one of the five sacred mountains of China. The Jiuling, Wugong, Jinggang and

Xikuang Mountains enclose the province. The Gan River (Ganjiang), which crosses Jiangxi from south to north and flows into Lake Poyang and the Yangzi River, has always been a major route for transporting goods. The large plains of Jiangxi are very fertile regions for growing rice, and many farmers can harvest two crops per year. Other agricultural products include tea, sugarcane, sweet potatoes and citrus fruit, notably mandarin oranges. Jiangxi is China's third-largest producer of marine shellfish and is a significant producer of freshwater fish and shellfish. Forestry products are also important, including timber and pine resin. Jiangxi has large mineral deposits, including coal, tantalum, nickel and the largest copper reserves in China. Its tungsten deposits may be the largest in the world. Since 1949, the province has been industrialized and is China's largest producer of ferro-alloy and third-largest producer of generators.

Porcelains produced at factories in Jingdezhen (Ching-te-chen), for centuries the most important porcelain center in China, have long been world-famous, especially blue and white ware. The porcelain is made with a fine type of white clay called kaolin that comes from Gaoling, a village about 35 miles outside Jingdezhen. Ceramics were first produced in this area during the Han dynasty (206 B.C.–220 A.D.), when the city was called Xinping. The introduction of high-firing kilns during the Tang dynasty (618–907) enabled the production of great quantities of fine porcelain. An edict issued by Emperor Jingde (r. 1004–7) proclaimed Xinping the porcelain production center for the imperial court. The city then acquired the name Jingdezhen from the name of this emperor's reign, and it has continued to be a center for porcelain production, with more than 14 porcelain factories operating today.

Jiangxi belonged to the kingdom of Chu during the Zhou dynasty (1100–256 B.C.) and was inhabited by members of groups other than ethnic Chinese, or Han people. The region was brought into the unified Chinese Empire (221–206 B.C.) by Qin Shi Huangdi. Han Chinese began settling in Jiangxi during the third to sixth centuries to escape nomadic tribes invading northern China. The current borders of the province were established during the Ming dynasty (1368–1644).

Nanchang's history dates back to the second century B.C. The city was always an administrative and trading center, and it became a major distribution center for porcelain produced at Jingdezhen. The Jiangxi Provincial Museum and an exhibition hall for paintings and calligraphy by the 17th-century artist Zhu Da (Chu Ta) are major tourist sites.

Jiangxi Province became prominent in the 20th century as the birthplace of the Communist People's Liberation Army. The Nanchang Uprising on August 1, 1927, marked the first battle fought by an organized military force commanded by the Chinese Communist Party. The Communists initiated the Nanchang Uprising against the Nationalists (Kuomintang; KMT) because in April 1927 KMT leader Chiang Kai-shek had ordered the KMT to massacre Chinese Communists, with whom the KMT had been cooperating. Many Communists fled to the Soviet base in Jiangxi Province. A peasant army of 30,000 under Communist leaders Zhou Enlai (Chou En-lai) and Zhu De (Chu Teh) defeated Nationalist (Kuomintang) forces led by Chiang Kai-shek and held Nanchang for several days. The former headquarters of the uprising have been turned into a museum. Communist leader Mao Zedong (Mao Tse-tung) also led the Autumn Harvest Uprising at the same time. After the failure of the Autumn Harvest Uprising of 1927, Mao Zedong, soon to become head of the Communist Party, fled to the Jinggang Mountain Range along the border of Jiangxi and Hunan provinces and began working with military commander Zhu De to organize the peasants into a guerrilla army. By that winter there were 10,000 troops. However, Chiang Kai-shek waged five annual KMT military campaigns against the Communists in Jiangxi, who were forced to flee the Nationalists. In October 1934, the Communist Red Army set forth on its Long March. About 100,000 troops started on their circuitous retreat that went for 8,000 miles through 11 provinces in southwestern and northwestern China, but only 8,000 survivors reached Mao's final destination in southern Shaanxi Province, where he set up Communist headquarters for 10 years at Yan'an. The Chinese Communist Party regards August 1, 1927, the date of the Nanchang Uprising in Jiangxi Province, as the birth date of the Communist Army, now called the People's Liberation Army (PLA). See also BLUE-AND-WHITE WARE; CIVIL WAR BETWEEN COMMUNISTS AND NATIONALISTS; JINGDEZHEN; JINGGANG MOUNTAIN RANGE; LONG MARCH; MAO ZEDONG; NANCHANG; PEOPLE'S LIBERATION ARMY; POYANG, LAKE; YANGZI RIVER.

JIANKANG See NANJING; WESTERN AND EASTERN JIN DYNASTIES.

JIANKING See JIANGSU PROVINCE; NANJING.

JIANWEN (EMPEROR) See HONGWU (EMPEROR); YONGLE (EMPEROR).

JIAO See CURRENCY, MODERN.

JIAOHE See TURPAN; XINJIANG-UIGHUR AUTONOMOUS REGION.

JIAYUGUAN PASS See GANSU PROVINCE; GREAT WALL.

JIE, KING See SHANG DYNASTY; XIA DYNASTY.

JIEFANGJUN BAO See NEW CHINA NEWS AGENCY; PEOPLE'S LIBERATION ARMY.

JILIN PROVINCE A province in the center of northeastern China (a region known as Dongbei and also as Manchuria), that covers 69,485 square miles and has a population of about 24 million. The name Jilin means "Forests of Happiness." The capital city, Changchun, has a population of more than 2 million; other major cities include Jilin and Hunjiang. Jilin borders North Korea to the east and the Chinese provinces of Heilongjiang, Liaoning and the Inner Mongolian Autonomous Region to the north, south and west. Jilin has long, cold winters when the temperature can average as low as 0 degrees F, but the summers are warm with an average temperature of 75 degrees F. Most of the rain falls between May and September. The province has three geographic regions: the east, which is mountainous and covered with forests, the hilly central region and the western plains.

Three major rivers have their source in the Changbai Mountain Range that borders North Korea in eastern Jilin: the Yalu, the Tumen and the Songhua (Songhuajiang), the most important river in the province. The Changbai Nature Reserve is the second-largest reserve in China. It contains a volcanic crater lake called Lake Tian (Lake of Heaven).

Jilin is a major region for the growing of grain, including rice, maize, millet and sorghum, as well as soybeans and sugarbeets. The province is China's second-largest producer of corn and lumber. Jilin also produces the so-called three treasures of northeastern China, ginseng, sable fur and deer antlers (used in herbal medicine). Ninety percent of all Chinese ginseng comes from Jilin. Horses, cattle and sheep are raised, primarily by members of the Mongol ethnic group.

Jilin was always on the border of the Chinese Empire. In the eighth century it was part of the powerful Bohai state, which was destroyed in 927 by the Khitan, a group of primarily Mongol tribes who established the Liao dynasty (947–1125) that controlled much of northeastern China. In the 12th century the Jurchen people in central Jilin and Heilongjiang founded an independent state that brought down the Liao dynasty in 1125 and conquered all of northern China. In 1234 the Jurchens were defeated by the Mongols who established their own control in this region and ruled China under the Yuan dynasty (1279–1368). During the Chinese Ming dynasty (1368–1644), Jilin was a tributary state of China. In the late 16th century the Jurchens grew powerful once more, and in 1616 they founded an independent state in Manchuria that took the name Manchu in 1633. In 1644 the Manchus defeated the Ming dynasty and established the Qing (1644–1911).

In 1860 the Russians occupied the region north of the Amur River, which separates Manchuria and Siberia. Jilin was founded as a province only in 1907 when Manchu restrictions on Han Chinese settlement in Manchuria were lifted. Jilin City, on the banks of the Songhua River and surrounded by the Changbai Mountains, was the capital of the province until 1954, when Changchun was made the capital. The Japanese invaded Jilin in 1931. In 1932 they made Changchun the capital of Manzhouguo (Manchuria; Manchukuo in Japanese), their puppet state in northeastern China, and renamed the city Xinjing. After Japan's defeat in 1945, Russian troops invaded the province, followed by Chinese Nationalist (Kuomintang) troops, who were, in turn, defeated in 1948 by Chinese Communist Party forces. The city also has important universities and research institutes. Visitors can see the former residence of Puyi, the last emperor of the Qing dynasty (1644–1911), whom the Japanese forced to be the figurehead of Manchukuo.

Jilin Province has been greatly industrialized since 1949, with major products including chemicals and construction equipment. The province is China's main producer of optical instruments and motor vehicles and has the second-largest papermaking industry in the country. Changchun lies on the banks of the Yitong River and has been the most important Chinese city for motor-vehicle production since China's first automobile factory was established there in 1953. See also AMUR RIVER; CHANGBAI MOUNTAIN RANGE; CHANGCHUN; CIVIL WAR BETWEEN COMMUNISTS AND NATIONALISTS; GINSENG; JILIN; JURCHEN; LIAO DYNASTY; MANCHU; MANCHUKUO; MANCHURIA; MONGOL;

PUYI, HENRY; SONGHUA RIVER; TUMEN RIVER; WAR OF RESIS-
TANCE AGAINST JAPAN; YALU RIVER.

JIN DYNASTY (1115–1234)   A dynasty founded in China
by the Jurchen, a tribe of Tatar people in northern
Manchuria (modern northeastern China) who were the
ancestors of the Manchus who ruled China under the Qing
dynasty (1644–1911). (This Jin dynasty is not to be confused with the Western Jin dynasty [265–316] or the Eastern
Jin dynasty [317–420].) The Jurchens paid tribute to the
Liao dynasty (947–1125) that had been founded by the Khitan (Qidan) people. In 1112 the Jurchen chief Aguda (A-ku-
ta) refused to cooperate when the Liao emperor paid his
annual visit to the Manchurian border. Jurchen men were
raised to live and fight on horseback, and they formed a
highly effective mobile fighting force. Aguda quickly gained
leadership over the local tribes and led his troops to defeat
the Liao army soundly in 1114. In 1115 Aguda established
the Jin ("Golden") dynasty. In 1125 he finally overthrew the
Liao dynasty and drove the Khitan west. The Jurchen also
established lordship over the Koreans in northeastern Asia,
the Uighurs in western China, and the Tibetans of the kingdom of Xixia, also in western China. From 1126 to 1127 the
Jurchens besieged Kaifeng, the capital of the Chinese Song
dynasty (960–1279), captured the emperor and forced the
Song to flee south to Hangzhou, where they established the
Southern Song dynasty (1127–1279).

The boundary between Jin and Song territories ran along
the Huai River between the Yellow and the Yangzi Rivers.
These were China's two longest and most important rivers,
with the Yellow River and the fertile and heavily populated
North China Plain coming under Jin rule. This was the first
time in Chinese history that a large percentage of the Han
(ethnic Chinese) population was brought under the rule of
non-Chinese. The Jin leaders found that they could only
govern their territory by adapting the Chinese system of an
imperial bureaucracy staffed by scholars educated in the
Confucian classics. However, the Han Chinese scholars had
to be trained in the Jurchen language, and the Jurchen leaders in the tribe's homelands in northern Manchuria still
maintained control over the territory. The Jin attempted to
conquer the Southern Song and invaded the region south of
the Yangzi River in 1129–30, but when they attempted to
retreat, the Song forces—led by General Yue Fei—blocked
them with armed junks (Chinese boats). Song leaders were
divided about how to deal with the Jin dynasty. In 1142 they
decided to sign a peace treaty with the Jin, in which the Song
paid a quantity of silver and silk as tribute and declared itself
a vassal state of Jin. This agreement lasted until 1164, when
Jin was divided by internal political differences. The Song
were then able to have their tribute lessened and to be considered equal by the Jin. In 1153 the Jurchen moved the Jin
capital to the region that is modern Beijing.

The Mongols, a tribal people to the north with highly
effective cavalry forces, were a continuous threat to the Jin
dynasty, but serious internal problems delayed the Jin from
dealing with them. In 1194 the Yellow River overflowed its
banks and changed its course, destroying the homes and
crops of many Chinese. The Jin economy was also beset by
inflation caused by the system of paper money that the Jin
had taken on when they conquered the Northern Song

dynasty and by the expense of sending military campaigns
against the Southern Song. The Jin emperor Madaku (Zhangzong or Chang-tsung; r. 1190–1208) sent a diplomatic mission to the Mongol court, who realized the threat to the Jin
from the Mongols. The Mongol leader Genghis Khan first
conquered the kingdom of Xixia and then turned against the
Jin dynasty in 1211 and 1212, resulting in a Jin coup in
which a military general murdered the emperor and put
another person on the throne. The Mongols invaded a large
portion of Jin territory in 1213–14 but pulled back when the
Jin gave them a large quantity of goods. The Jin emperor
moved his capital from Beijing to Kaifeng to protect himself.
The Mongols soon put Beijing under siege and slaughtered
thousands of its residents. The Jin were by now suffering
from constant rebellions and famine, but for the time being
Genghis Khan turned to other conquests. In 1217 he began
his final campaign against the Jin, but they fought him off for
more than a decade. The Jin were also fighting the Southern
Song because they had stopped making their tribute payments. In 1233 the Mongols attacked Kaifeng and brought
down the Jin dynasty. They went on to conquer the Southern
Song and ruled China under the Yuan dynasty (1279–1368).
See also GENGHIS KHAN; JURCHEN; KAIFENG; LIAO DYNASTY;
MONGOL; NORTH CHINA PLAIN; SONG DYNASTY; SOUTHERN
SONG DYNASTY; YANGZI RIVER; YUE FEI.

JIN NONG (Chin Nung; 1687–1764)   An important calligrapher, painter, collector, poet and bibliophile during
the Qing dynasty (1644–1911). Jin Nong is classed among the
group of major 18tn-century Chinese painters termed the Eight
Eccentrics of Yangzhou (Yangchow). He was born in Qiantang
in Zhejiang Province but spent many years of his life in
Yangzhou. He had an extensive collection of rubbings of
inscriptions taken from ancient bronzeware and tomb
objects, which influenced his own style of calligraphy, a
heavy, square clerical script. In contrast to his calligraphy, Jin
Nong's paintings have a light and playful quality. He made
many ink paintings of bamboo, birds or flowers such as
plum blossoms. Some of the latter were painted for him by
two of his students, Lo Bing (Lo P'ing; 1733–99) and Xiang
Zhun (Hsiang Chun; c. 1740–80), which Jin Nong then
signed as his own. Since Jin Nong did not hold government
positions, as did many calligraphers and painters of the
literati (scholar class), for a time he had to earn money by
painting decorations on lanterns. See also BIRD-AND-FLOWER
PAINTING; CALLIGRAPHY; LANTERNS; STONE RUBBINGS.

JIN PING MEI   See GOLDEN LOTUS.

JIN, STATE OF   See SPRING AND AUTUMN PERIOD.

JI'NAN   The capital city of Shandong Province and a major
industrial, transportation, and military center. Ji'nan, with a
population of about 2 million, lies in a valley 217 miles
south of Beijing between the Yellow River (Huanghe) to the
north and the Taishan Mountain Range to the south. It is
called the "City of Springs," of which some of the most
famous are Black Tiger Spring, Pearl Spring and Five Dragons Pool. The largest of Ji'nan's 100 springs is Spurting
Spring, in a park in the city center, which continually sends
pure water into the air from three underground spots. An

ancient saying describes Ji'nan as having "springs and willow trees in every courtyard." Daming Lake Park includes Xiayuan Garden, laid out in 1909; Beiji Ge Daoist Temple, built during the Yuan dynasty (1279–1368); and Tingyuan Garden, designed in 1792 with streams and covered walkways, where poets and writers formerly gathered for banquets and discussions. On the outskirts of Ji'nan, the Thousand Buddha Hill offers a good view of the city and the Yellow River in the distance. Many sculptures of Buddha were carved into the cliffs (581–600), but most were demolished during the Cultural Revolution (1966–76). Other scenic attractions in the Ji'nan area include the Temple of Prosperous Country, Dragon Spring Cave and Pavilion for a Panoramic View. The sixth-century Four Gate Pagoda may be the oldest stone pagoda in China.

The Shandong Provincial Museum in Ji'nan has two sections on the history and the natural history of the province. It possesses a calendar from 143 B.C. that is supposedly the oldest extant Chinese calendar. Ji'nan is one of the oldest areas of human settlement in China, and archaeologists have found remains from the Neolithic period (c. 12,000–2000 B.C.). During the Shang (1750–1040 B.C.) and Zhou (1100–256 B.C.) dynasties it was a fortified town known as Luo. During the Han dynasty (206 B.C.–A.D. 220) it gained its present name, Ji'nan, meaning "south of the River Ji." This river, which has disappeared, flowed near what has become the lower reaches of the Yellow River. Because of the river and access to the Yellow Sea, Ji'nan was a prosperous town during the Tang (618–907) and Northern Song (960–1127) dynasties, and it was made the capital of Shandong Province in the 12th century.

The modern development of Ji'nan began in 1852 when the Yellow River changed its course toward the north, giving Ji'nan access to the waterways of northern Shandong and southern Hebei provinces. The city became a major trading center for such agricultural products as grains, cotton, peanuts and tobacco. Ji'nan's economic and industrial development was furthered by a system of railroads, beginning in 1904 when a railway line was constructed by Germans to Qingdao, a port on the Yellow Sea, which was then a German concession. In 1912 this line was connected to the line linking Tianjin, Beijing and central China. The Germans, British, and Japanese opened many textile mills and other factories and built numerous European-style buildings, which have remained. The dikes that protect Ji'nan from disastrous flooding by the Yellow River may be seen about a half-hour outside the city. An embankment and pumping station allows the river to be used for agricultural irrigation. See also QINGDAO; RAILROADS; SHANDONG PROVINCE; YELLOW RIVER.

JING RIVER See CHENGDU; SHAANXI PROVINCE.

JING TAI BLUE See CLOISONNÉ.

JINGDEZHEN (Ching-te-chen) A city in Jiangxi Province in southeastern China that for hundreds of years was the most important center in the world for the production of fine porcelain. Located on the Chang River in the northeastern region of the province, Jingdezhen was the site of pottery production as early as the Han dynasty (206

B.C.–A.D. 220), when the town was called Xinping. The beautiful white porcelain manufactured there during the Tang dynasty (618–907) was praised with the name "artificial jade." Porcelain is a type of ceramic that is thin, hard and translucent white, made from the mixture of a very refined white clay called kaolin and a white powder called "China clay" or petuntse (from the Chinese word for clay, *baidunzi* or *pai-tun-tzu*). There are large deposits of kaolin about 35 miles outside Jingdezhen, at the village of Gaoling, from which the name kaolin was taken. Minerals to make high-quality glazes for the porcelain are also acquired nearby. Boats have traditionally transported the materials upstream to the harbor at Jingdezhen and the finished products downstream to the coast for shipping to markets all over China and around the world.

During the Song dynasty (960–1279), the kilns at Jingdezhen produced extremely fine white porcelain, notably bluish-white Qingbai (Ch'ing-Pai) ware and an imitation of a northern type known as Dingyao (Ting-yâo). By the beginning of the 14th century, the potters at Jingdezhen were experimenting with new techniques. The Northern Song emperor Jingde (r. 1004–7) issued an edict proclaiming that Jingdezhen would be the official production center for porcelain for the imperial court. Each piece manufactured there had "made in the Jingde period" printed on the bottom. The city acquired the name Jingdezhen from this emperor's reign name.

Shufu ("privy council") ware was the first porcelain to be made at Jingdezhen on imperial order. The majority of these pieces are bowls and dishes that are decorated by incising lines in the clay, pressing the clay into molds or painting it with liquid clay called slip, under a bluish-white (Qingbai) glaze. The decorations are usually flowers, lotus leaves, or phoenixes among clouds, and they often include the words *shufu* or auspicious words such as happiness (*fu*) or long life (*shou*). *Shufu* ware also includes cups with stems, ewers, bottles and jars decorated with applied reliefs, and statues of Buddhist figures such as bodhisattvas (wise beings) and Guanyin (the Goddess of Mercy) made for placement in home shrines. The pieces were made in many stages by a large group of artisans who specialized in shaping the pieces on the wheel, polishing, painting and glazing, and firing them in the kiln. As many as 80 different craftsmen may have worked on one piece of porcelain.

After the Mongols conquered all the lands from the Near East to China, where they established the Yuan dynasty (1279–1368), the Chinese began exporting large quantities of a type of porcelain known as blue-and-white ware (white porcelain decorated with blue cobalt underglaze) to the Near East, where it was highly valued. The pieces were decorated in blue or red with designs of dragons, phoenix birds, fish and flowers, and many of the designs were adapted from the Muslim cultures to which the pieces were exported. In the 16th century the Portuguese began importing blue-and-white porcelain from China to Europe, where it was even more highly regarded and was associated with the Holy Family in the Christian religion. By the 17th century, Europeans had such a demand for Jingdezhen porcelain that Western agents were stationed in Guangzhou (Canton), the major port in southern China, to place orders for porcelain designed specifically for European tastes. Jingdezhen factories also shipped large quantities of plain white porcelain to be decorated in Guangzhou.

In 1369 Hongwu, the first emperor of the Ming dynasty (1368–1644), had designated certain kilns at Jingdezhen to be used solely for imperial production, and from then on those imperial kilns supplied all of the vast quantities of porcelain used in the Ming and Qing (1644–1911) courts. By the early Ming dynasty, Jingdezhen was the largest center for porcelain production in the world, with several hundred craftsmen and 300 kiln complexes. During the reign of the Wanli emperor (1572–1620) there was a decline in the quality of the porcelain. After the death of Wanli in 1620, the turmoil caused by civil war and bandits further harmed the porcelain industry at Jingdezhen. Also, kilns in Japan such as those at Arita were producing fine porcelains known as Imari ware that captured many markets in Southeast Asia and Europe.

In 1675 the imperial porcelain factories at Jingdezhen were destroyed by rebels, but they were rebuilt several years later. In 1682 the Kangxi (K'ang-hsi) emperor appointed Cang Yingxuan (Ts'ang Ying-hsuan) director of the imperial kilns at Jingdezhen. He and his two successors revived the porcelain industry, and the fine pieces continued to be manufactured through the Qing dynasty. The Ming taste was for colorful enameled floral motifs and cobalt-blue and copper-red ("oxblood") underglazes. Porcelain from the Song and Ming dynasties were reproduced at Jingdezhen during the Qing dynasty and widely exported. New enamel colors, known as *famille rose* and *famille verte,* were also developed. However, European factories had learned how to produce porcelain that imitated the pieces made at Jingdezhen and the market for fine Chinese porcelain declined. In addition, the Dutch sent their own models to be copied at Jingdezhen and at Arita in Japan.

Sadly, Jingdezhen was destroyed in 1853 during the Taiping Rebellion, although a few kilns were later able to resume production. During the 20th century, China suffered so much turmoil from the Japanese occupation during World War II and from the civil war between the Chinese Communists and Nationalists that ended in 1949, that few pottery kilns were in operation around the country. However, since 1949 the Chinese government has encouraged the revival of porcelain production. Today Jingdezhen has nearly two dozen government-run porcelain factories producing more than 350 million pieces per year and is once again the most important center in China for porcelain production. Traditional blue-and-white ware and porcelain with a translucent pattern of grains of rice are the most popular types. The Jingdezhen Museum of Ceramic History houses exhibits on the history of the city's porcelain production. See also BLUE-AND-WHITE WARE; CHINOISERIE; DRAGON; ENAMELWARE; GUANGZHOU; JIANGXI PROVINCE; PHOENIX; PORCELAIN.

JINGGANG MOUNTAIN RANGE (Jinggangshan; Chingkang Shan) A mountain range along the border between Hunan and Jiangxi Provinces in southern China. Jinggang Mountains run from east to west and cover an area of 443 square miles.

In these mountains the Chinese Communist Party (CCP) established its first revolutionary base in 1927. The Commu-

nists fled to the Jinggang Mountains after the Nanchang Uprising on August 1, 1927, in which CCP leaders Zhu De (Chu Teh) and Zhou Enlai (Chou En-lai) led a rebellion against the first united front between the CCP and the Nationalists (Kuomintang; KMT) who had massacred many Communists, when the united front between the two groups had fallen apart earlier that year. Survivors of the Nanchang Uprising and other unsuccessful Communist insurrections, including the Autumn Harvest Uprising led by Mao Zedong (Mao Tse-tung), escaped to the Jinggang Mountains. Various groups who gathered there, including Communists, KMT deserters, impoverished peasants and bandits, joined together under the leadership of Mao and Zhu to form the military branch of the CCP, known as the First Workers' and Peasants' Army, or the Red Army. This force later became known as the People's Liberation Army (PLA). Army headquarters were established at Ciping (Tz'u-p'ing) in the center of the Jinggang Mountain Range. The Red Army used guerrilla tactics to survive several campaigns waged against it by the larger and more powerful KMT forces. Eventually the Communists had to abandon their base in the Jinggang Mountains and escape the KMT forces by going on the rigorous Long March of 1934–35, at the end of which they established their new headquarters in Yan'an in Shaanxi Province in western China.

Today the beautiful Jinggang Mountains are a popular tourist area. The main town, Ciping, is located on a narrow strip of flat land surrounded by mountain peaks. A stream flows through the area, and Lake Yicui has lovely bridges and pavilions and flower gardens surrounding it and on its islands. On a mountain peak in a park south of Ciping, a group of carvings depicts the Communist battles in the Jinggang Mountains. Dragon Pool, another scenic spot near Ciping, has 18 waterfalls and 5 pools. One 220-foot-high waterfall is named for Guanyin, the Buddhist Goddess of Mercy. Numerous rock formations are said to resemble humans, animals, pavilions and pagodas. Yangmei Peak to the southwest of Ciping is famous for its pine trees and groves of rhododendron bushes, which burst into color in April. Shiyan Cave, 55 miles northeast of Ciping, has many underground caverns with bats, stalagmites and stalagtites. The caverns cover a total length of 3,280 feet and a depth of 360 feet. See also CHINESE COMMUNIST PARTY; GUANYIN; LONG MARCH; MAO ZEDONG; NANCHANG; PAGODA; PAVILIONS; PEOPLE'S LIBERATION ARMY; RHODODENDRON; ZHOU ENLAI; ZHU DE.

JINGLUO See MEDICINE, HERBAL; TAIJIQUAN.

JINGNAN KINGDOM (913–63) See TEN KINGDOMS PERIOD.

JINGTIAN See WELL-FIELD SYSTEM OF AGRICULTURE.

JINGTU See AMITABHA; PURE LAND SECT OF BUDDHISM.

JINLING See JIANGSU PROVINCE; NANJING.

JINSHA RIVER See YANGZI RIVER.

JINSHI See IMPERIAL BUREAUCRACY; IMPERIAL EXAMINATION SYSTEM; NINE-RANK SYSTEM.

JINYANG See TAIYUAN.

JIU See ALCOHOLIC BEVERAGES.

JIUHUA, MOUNT (*Jiuhuashan* or *Chiu-Hua Shan;* "Nine Flower Mountain") A mountain in Anhui Province in eastern China; one of the Four Sacred Mountains of the Buddhist religion, which had been introduced into China from India around the first century A.D. The other three sacred mountains are Mount Wutai (Wu-t'ai) in Shanxi Province, the Buddhist northern mountain; Mount Putuo (P'u-T'o), an island off Zhejiang Province, the eastern mountain; and Mount Emei, or Puxian (P'u-hsien), in Sichuan Province, the western mountain. Mount Jiuhua, the Buddhist southern mountain, is located in southern Anhui about 20 miles south of the Yangzi River. Its patron saint is Dizang Busa (Ti-tsang Pusa), the Chinese name for the Indian Sanskrit name Kshitigarbha Bodhisattva. Dizang Busa was a ruler of the Buddhist underworld. He carries a magic staff with which he opens the door that free the suffering souls who have been imprisoned. Every September, October and November, thousands of pilgrims journey to Mount Jiuhua to free their deceased relatives. Kim Kiao Kak, a Korean Buddhist monk, went to Mount Jiuhua in 720 and established a temple there for the worship of Dizang Busa. Every year pilgrims journey to Jiuhua for a festival that commemorates the monk's death. One of Dizang Busa's incarnations was supposedly on Mount Jiuhua, as Prince Jin Xianying (Chin Hsien-ying), who took the religious name of Qiaojue (Ch'iao-chueh), "Exalted Awakening." He died on the mountain in 794 at the age of 99, and his mausoleum is located on the wooded hilltop in the hollow surrounded by the mountain's peaks. The principle monastery on Mount Jiuhua was supposedly built on a site chosen by Beidu (Pei-tu), an Indian monk who went to the mountain in 401. An imperial decree in 780 gave the monastery its present name, Huacheng Si (Hua-ch'eng Ssu), "City Temple of Transformation." The monastery was destroyed during the Taiping Rebellion (1850–64) but was later rebuilt. During the Tang dynasty (618–907) there were more than 300 temples and monasteries in the vicinity of Jiuhua with more than 5,000 monks and nuns, but today only about 70 temples and monasteries remain. See also BUDDHISM; FOUR SACRED MOUNTAINS OF BUDDHISM.

JIULONG BI See DATONG; DRAGON.

JIULONG RIVER See XIAMEN.

JIUZHAIGOU NATURE RESERVE See MONKEY.

JOAK See DIM SUM; RICE.

JOFFE, ADOLF See BORODIN, MIKHAIL; SUN YAT-SEN.

JOHN OF MONTE CORVINO See CHRISTIANITY.

JOINT VENTURES See FOREIGN TRADE AND INVESTMENT; SPECIAL ECONOMIC ZONES.

JOSS PAPER Paper in the form of money, clothes, food and other necessities that is burned in large quantities at Chinese funerals so the spirit of the deceased will have everything it needs as it travels to the next world. The Chinese traditionally believe that the spirit world is parallel to the human world and that when the paper objects are burned, they transform into real objects as they pass through the smoke into the spirit world. Joss paper money is made from small pieces of paper, about four inches square, with patches of gold leaf or tinfoil attached to the center to represent gold and silver money. It is often made in the shape of ingots. The Chinese also burn many bundles of "bank notes" in various denominations issued by the "Hell Bank," a legendary bank that issues money to finance evil. In Hong Kong and other prosperous communities they may even burn luxuries such as paper automobiles. The bonfire for the paper objects is built beside the grave. Once the funeral ceremony ends, the mourners leave when the flames die down. See also CURRENCY; FUNERALS.

JOSS STICKS See ANCESTRAL TABLETS; FUNERALS.

JOURNEY TO THE WEST (*Xiyouji* or *Hsi-yu-chi*) Also known by the names *Pilgrimage to the West* and *Monkey;* a humorous novel published in 1592, attributed to Wu Chen'gen (1506?–82?), that is one of the most beloved books in Chinese literature. It tells the story of the magical Monkey King, who converts from the native Chinese religion of Daoism to the imported religion of Buddhism and assists a Buddhist monk named Xuanzang on his journey to the west. The story is based on the actual pilgrimage to India in 629–45 made by the Chinese Buddhist monk Xuanzang (Hsuang-tsang; 602–64) to gather sutras (religious scriptures) for translation. When Xuanzang returned to China he presented the emperor a written account of his journey, *Record of the Western Regions* (*Xiyuji*). The 16th-century novel was compiled from a number of oral and written sources containing folk legends and Buddhist miracle stories that had accumulated around the figure of Xuanzang over the centuries.

Xuanzang is also protected on his journey by other characters with supernatural powers, including a pig and a dark spirit of the sands. Along the way, they have a number of adventures fighting battles with supernatural figures. Monkey King is strong-willed and mischievous and is said to be able to cover 18,000 *li* (about 6,000 miles) in one bound. He is forced to wear a tight iron helmet to help him control his wild impulses. One of the best-known episodes in the novel is known as "Monkey Causes Havoc in Heaven." Monkey steals the banquet feast that the gods are planning to enjoy and makes himself doubly immortal by eating the peaches of immortality and swallowing the stolen pill of immortality. There are several English translations of *Monkey* or *Journey to the West.* See also BUDDHISM; MONKEY; PEACH; XUANZANG.

JOY LUCK CLUB, THE See TAN, AMY.

JU DA See BADA SHANREN.

JU WARE See RU WARE.

JUANZHOU See SCROLLS.

JUCHEN   See JURCHEN.

JUDICIAL SYSTEM   See LEGAL SYSTEM; SUPREME PEOPLE'S COURT.

JUDOU   See GONG LI; ZHANG YIMOU.

JU-HSUEH   See CONFUCIANISM.

JUHUA   See CHRYSANTHEMUM.

JUNE FOURTH MASSACRE   See TIANANMEN SQUARE MASSACRE.

JUNG YI-JEN   See RONG YIREN.

JUNK (*fanchuan*)   A type of wooden sailing boat used in China and Southeast Asia; its ancient design was based on a raft that was traditionally made from short sections of bamboo that were bound together. Junk is the Malay word for ship. The junk has a flat or slightly curved bottom, sides that curve upward and a bow and stern that are wide but squared off. It has no keel, sternpost or stempost, but it does have a large rudder that can be raised and lowered. The junk is not built with internal skeletal ribs—the common design for many types of boat—but with solid partitions known as bulkheads that make the junk very strong and provide it with watertight compartments. The four-sided sails, or lugsails, made from panels of cloth or woven mats, are attached to horizontal bamboo poles known as battens and are mounted on one to five masts. The design of the junk was described by the Italian explorer Marco Polo (1254–1324) in his memoir of his journey to China, but this design was not utilized by Western naval engineers until the 18th century.

The junk has been used in China primarily to transport cargo. In the 16th century, the Chinese developed a type of boat known as the articulated junk to sail on the Grand Canal. It was a long narrow barge with two sections that could separate in order for the ship to move through curving channels that had become quite shallow due to silt deposits.

The boatmen are very strong and work hard for little pay. Trackers are men who walk along a riverbank pulling boats with ropes through long difficult passages on a river. There was a guild for prosperous junkmasters. In Shanghai, which became a major port after it was opened to foreigners in 1842, and other areas, these guilds were subdivided into specific guilds for junkmen who performed various functions, such as ocean-going sailors, rice shippers and tea shippers. In the 1920s in the city of Chongqing, there were 22 different guilds just for the river system in Sichuan Province. Each guild had its own guildhall, and business was conducted there and in public teahouses. People who live on junks form a separate subculture in China. In the lower reaches of the Yangzi (Changjiang) and other major rivers, along the coasts of Fujian and Guangdong Province in southeastern China, on the Pearl River up to Guangzhou (Canton), and in

Hong Kong and Macao, many people spend their whole lives on boats. They are frowned upon by the rest of the population, but they intermarry within their group and have their own unique culture, customs and religious beliefs. (For example, they avoid placing their chopsticks across a bowl in a position that would suggest a junk that has run aground.) See also GRAND CANAL; PEARL RIVER; POLO, MARCO; SHANGHAI; SHIPPING AND SHIPBUILDING; TEA; YANGZI RIVER.

JUNSHAN ISLAND   See DONGTIN, LAKE; YUEYANG.

JUNZI   See HUMANITY; SUPERIOR MAN.

JURCHEN (Jurched, Juchen, or Nu-chih)   A tribe of Tatar people who were nomadic hunters in the forests and plains of northern Manchuria (modern northeastern China) and spoke a Tungusic language. The Jurchens founded the Jin dynasty (1115–1234)—not to be confused with the Western Jin dynasty (265–316) or the Eastern Jin dynasty (317–420)—in northern China and were the ancestors of the Manchus who ruled China under the Qing dynasty (1644–1911), the last Chinese imperial dynasty. The Jurchens lived east of the region controlled by the Khitan people under the Liao dynasty (947–1125) and paid tribute to them. In 1112 the Jurchen chief, Aguda (A-ku-ta), refused to cooperate when the Liao emperor paid his annual visit to the Manchurian border, and Aguda soon gained leadership over the other local tribes. He severely defeated a large Liao army in 1114, and the following year he established a Jurchen empire named Jin ("Golden"). In 1120 he gained control of half the Liao empire, foreshadowing the collapse of the Liao in 1125. As a result, the Khitan headed west to set up the state of Kara or Black Khitan in eastern Turkestan (modern Xinjiang-Uighur Autonomous Region), which lasted until the Mongols conquered China and ruled it under the Yuan dynasty (1279–1368). The Jurchens went on to besiege Kaifeng, capital of the Chinese Northern Song Dynasty (960–1126), where they captured the emperor and forced the Song to flee south to Hangzhou where they established the Southern Song dynasty (1127–1279).

The Jin rulers gradually abandoned their Jurchen customs, clothing and language for Chinese ones, especially after they moved their capital to Kaifeng from the city that is modern Beijing. During the Chinese Ming dynasty (1368–1644), the Jurchens agreed to abandon their nomadic traditions; they settled in walled towns and farmed, and soon developed small states. By joining the Chinese tribute system that regulated trade, the Jurchens benefited financially and culturally from the trade with China in luxury goods. The Ming Chinese established Jurchen garrisons on the northern frontier, and the state where the Manchus developed their power had been the region of the first Jurchen guard to be formed by the Chinese. See also GENGHIS KHAN; JIN DYNASTY; KAIFENG; LIAO DYNASTY; MANCHU; MANCHURIA; NORTHERN SONG DYNASTY; TRIBUTE SYSTEM.

KAIFENG   A city in Henan Province in central China that
served as the capital of the Northern Song dynasty
(960–1126) and six other dynasties. Today Kaifeng is a modern city with a population of about 300,000 and is the agricultural center of Henan. It is located just south of the Yellow
River (Huanghe) and east of the city of Zhengzhou, capital of
the province. Since 1949 Kaifeng has been industrialized, with
major products including chemicals, agricultural machinery,
electronics, flour and cooking oils. The city is famous for its
traditional crafts, especially silk and embroidery.

Kaifeng has a very ancient history. It became the adminis-
trative center of the powerful state of Wei as early as 362
B.C., when it was known as Daliang. The city was destroyed
by troops of the Qin dynasty in the third century B.C. When
the Grand Canal was constructed in the seventh century A.D.
Kaifeng grew in importance. During the Three Kingdoms
Period (A.D. 220–80) it served as capital of the Wei Kingdom
(220–65). The city also became the capital in turn of the late
Jing, Han and Zhou dynasties during the Five Dynasties
Period (907–59).

Kaifeng reached the height of its influence when it was
chosen to be capital of the Northern Song dynasty by Taizu,
the first Song emperor. Situated on the Grand Canal, the
main route for the transport of goods from southern to
northern China, it soon outgrew the former imperial capital
of Chang'an (modern Xi'an) and Luoyang. During the Song
dynasty, Kaifeng was known as Bianjing or Dongjing. In
1105, its population is estimated to have been more than one
million, making it the largest city in the world at that time.
During the Northern Song, Kaifeng was a major center for
printing and for scientific inventions in medicine, astronomy, mechanical engineering and fireworks. A 17-foot-long
scroll painted by the Song artist Zhang Zeduan (Chang Tse-
tuan), *On the River at Qingming* (*Qingming Shanghe Tu*), portrays details of life in Kaifeng in the 11th century during the
Qing Ming Festival, when families tend the graves of their
ancestors.

Thousands of traders, many of them Jews and Muslims,
as well as scholars and Buddhist monks migrated to the city
from other regions of China and from other Asian and Central Asian countries. In the 12th century, a large population
of Jews, who had immigrated to China from the Middle East
around the seventh century A.D., moved from Hangzhou to
Kaifeng. During the 14th and 15th centuries, there were
more than a thousand Jewish traders and bankers in Kaifeng
who held great influence in the city. A synagogue
(*qingzhensi*) was built in 1163. The Jewish community is
commemorated in Kaifeng by three pillars that are dated
1489, 1512 and 1619. However, the synagogue disappeared
by 1866 and by the late 19th century there were few Jews left
in the city. Today many tourists visit Kaifeng because of their
interest in its Jewish history.

Kaifeng lost its importance after nomadic invaders called
the Jin or Jurchen (later called the Manchus; founders of the
Qing dynasty), destroyed the city and caused the Song court
to flee south in 1127. The city also suffered from damaging
floods after 1194 when the Yellow River changed its course
southward because of vast deposits of silt. Flooding of the
Yellow River has been a constant problem throughout the
history of Kaifeng. In 1642 Kaifeng suffered from heavy
flooding of the river. In 1644, invading Manchus (who overthrew the Ming dynasty that year) threatened Kaifeng. City
leaders tried to defend it by opening the dikes of the Yellow
River, but this caused an enormous flood that killed more
than 300,000 people.

During the Nationalist Period (1928–49), Kaifeng served
as the capital of Henan Province. In 1954 Henan's capital was
moved to Zhengzhou. Many of Kaifeng's major historic sites
can be seen inside the old city walls, which were built after
the floods of 1642 and 1644. The Dragon Pavilion (Long-
ting), a pyramid-shaped building with several large terraces,
was built on the site of the Song dynasty palace in 1692. A
huge stone carved with dragons in the center of the pavilion
may once have supported the imperial throne. When Kaifeng
was the Northern Song capital, the examinations for positions in the imperial bureaucracy were administered here to
candidates who came from all over China. A double staircase
in the Dragon Pavilion is aligned on the north-south axis of

the old city, along which the emperor traveled to perform religious ceremonies at the Temple of Heaven (Yanqing Daoist Temple) in the southern part of the city at the summer and winter solstices.

Yuwangtai Gongyuan Park holds Old Music Terrace, or King Yu's Terrace (Yuwangtai), where famous Tang dynasty (618–907) poets such as Du Fu (Tu Fu) and Li Bai (Li Po) gathered to drink wine and recite poetry. Xiangguo Si, a Buddhist monastery founded in the sixth century, houses a beautiful sculpture of Guanyin, the Goddess of Mercy. The monastery was originally built in A.D. 555 and rebuilt several times after being destroyed by floods. The buildings seen today date from 1766 and have been recently restored. Also in Kaifeng, Iron Pagoda (Tieta) is a lovely 13-story pagoda, 175 feet high, that was built in 1049 and restored after World War II. The pagoda is covered with brown and green glazed tiles and decorated with mythical beasts, flowers and Buddhist figures. Dong Da Mosque, in Kaifeng, one of the most active Muslim centers in Henan Province, was rebuilt in 1922 after a flood destroyed much of the city. The city also has a recently built a museum on the history of Kaifeng. Many bronze objects from the Shang dynasty (c. 1750–1040 B.C.) have been excavated in the region. See also BRONZEWARE; GRAND CANAL; HENAN PROVINCE; IMPERIAL EXAMINATION SYSTEM; JEWS; JURCHEN; MUSLIMS; NORTHERN SONG DYNASTY; QING MING FESTIVAL; YELLOW RIVER; ZHENGZHOU.

KAILAS, MOUNT Also known as Mount Kailash; a mountain in the Tibet Autonomous Region (Xizang Zizhiqu) in western China that is the most sacred mountain in Asia. Tibetans call the mountain Kang (or Gang) Rimpoche, meaning "Blessed Jewel of the Snow." Mount Kailas is believed to be the home of deities in three religions: Hinduism, the main religion of India; Buddhism, which was founded in India but taken to China and other Asian and Southeast Asian countries; and Bon, the ancient Tibetan religion that influenced the Tibetan sect of Buddhism, known as Lamaism. Bon includes the practices of shamanism, exorcism rituals and the worship of various beneficent and harmful deities. The first Buddhist monastery was established in Tibet near the end of the eighth century, and by the 12th century, Lamaism had become the national religion of the Tibetan people. Hindus believe that Mount Kailas is the home of Shiva, the god of destruction and the patron deity of ascetics. Tibetan Buddhists believe that it is the home of the terrifying deity, Demchog.

Mount Kailas is located in the sparsely populated, rugged, windswept plateau of western Tibet. The mountain is 22,028 feet high and belongs to the Himalaya Mountain Range, the highest in the world. Nearby Lake Manasarovar, the sister lake of Mount Kailas and the highest body of fresh water in the world, is believed to have been born from the mind of Brahma, the Hindu god of preservation. Pilgrims walk around the sacred lake. Few Western travelers have visited this holy mountain and completed the *kora*, the 32-mile circuit that pilgrims walk around it, which ascends nearly 5,000 feet during its course. Asians have been making the pilgrimage to honor the gods at Mount Kailas for more than a 1,000 years. They begin at the settlement of Darchen at the base of the mountain and stop to pray at many sites along the *kora* dedicated to religious masters and supernatural beings. Orthodox Buddhists circle the mountain in a clockwise direction, but Bon pilgrims walk counterclockwise. Most pilgrims take two and a half days to complete the *kora*, but some Tibetans can complete it in one day. Those who wish to perform a pilgrimage of the highest devotion constantly prostrate themselves around the mountain, which can take more than 13 days. Pilgrims sleep at guesthouses run by monasteries on the mountain. The highest point of the *kora* reaches a mountain pass at 18,600 feet, marked by prayer flags on a sacred pile of rocks, where pilgrims shout "Victory to the Gods!" ("Lha Gyalo!"). No one climbs above this point because they do not want to violate the sacred mountain peak. See also BUDDHISM; HIMALAYA MOUNTAIN RANGE; LAMAISM; TIBET.

KAIPING COAL MINES See CHINA MERCHANTS STEAM NAVIGATION COMPANY.

KAISHU (K'AI-SHU) See CALLIGRAPHY; WRITING SYSTEM, CHINESE.

KAI-TSU (EMPEROR) See GAOZU (EMPEROR).

KAM See DONG.

KAN, YUE-SAI (1948–) A Chinese-American woman television producer and entrepreneur who owns a sole-proprietorship company called Yue-Sai Kan, Inc., which is the only wholly owned foreign subsidiary in China. She was born in Guilin in Guangxi, the eldest of four daughters. When she was one year old, the Chinese Communists defeated the Nationalists (Kuomintang) and her wealthy family fled to Hong Kong, where she was educated at an exclusive Catholic school for girls and learned French. She went to the United States for college, attending the Oahu campus of Brigham Young University and the University of Hawaii. Kan trained as a concert pianist but chose not to pursue this career. In 1971 she moved to New York City and got a job as a fund raiser, and in 1975 she became an American citizen. That same year, she and her sister Vicki set up an import-export business between China and America. She also began producing television shows for a Chinese cable station in New York, and in 1980 she started her own television production company. Her first project was a series about Asia called *Looking East*. Kan became famous in 1984 when she translated and narrated the script for a joint venture between the Boston public television station WNET and the People's Republic of China's Central China TV (CCTV) on the 35th anniversary of the Chinese Communist Revolution. CCTV officials were so impressed with her that they asked her to produce and host a series called *One World* that they had developed to inform the Chinese people about the outside world. Kan became a celebrity in China and was made an honorary citizen. She produced an Emmy-winning documentary on Christianity in China called *China: Walls and Bridges* and a series of videos for Northwest Airlines called *Doing Business in Asia*. She also wrote several books, including *Layman's Guide to Traditional Chinese Medicine*, and a column for Northwest Airlines' inflight magazine. She also began selling her own line of cosmetics in China, which were developed by American chemists but are mixed in her own factory in southern China with ingredients that include Chinese herbal extracts. To promote them she produced a television series in Mandarin, Cantonese and English called *Yue-Sai's World*. In 1990 she married James McManus, an American businessman. The couple made their home in New York. See also BROADCASTING.

KANCHENJUNGA, MOUNT See HIMALAYA MOUNTAIN RANGE.

KANG (K'ANG) See ARCHITECTURE, TRADITIONAL; FURNITURE, TRADITIONAL.

KANG KEQING (K'ANG KE-CHING) See EIGHTH ROUTE ARMY; ZHU DE.

KANG YOUWEI (K'ang Yu-wei; 1858–1927)   A prominent scholar and reformer who led the Reform Movement in 1898. Born in Guangzhou province in southern China, Kang was a philosopher who taught Western learning. He became famous when he published a controversial study of the classical Chinese philosopher Confucius, portraying him as a reformer. Kang's work was criticized for being revolutionary and had to be withdrawn. One of Kang's students was Liang Qichao (Liang Ch'i-ch'ao; 1873–1929), who joined him in his reform efforts against the Qing dynasty (1644–1911). The two scholars advocated social and institutional changes in China. In 1895, after the Sino-Japanese War of 1894–95, they moved to the Chinese capital city of Beijing. Kang urged the emperor to enact reforms, and he gained the support of many government officials for adding a constitutional form of government to the monarchy. This so-called Reform Movement of 1898 lasted only three months, however, for the Empress Dowager Cixi (Tz'u Hsi; 1835–1908) led a coup that harshly ended the reform movement and wrested power from the Guangxu (Kuang-hsu) emperor for herself. British diplomats helped Kang escape arrest and execution. He lived abroad for the next 15 years, all the while advocating reforms in China, while the country suffered the Boxer Rebellion and revolutionary turmoil. Liang had escaped to Japan. The two founded the Protect the Emperor Society (Baohuang Hui or Pao huang Hui) to promote the establishment of a constitutional monarchy in China. Kang strongly disagreed with Sun Yat-sen (1866–1925), who advocated the overthrow of the Qing dynasty and the founding of a Chinese republic. After Sun established the Republic of China in 1912, Kang returned to China in 1913. He continued to work for the restoration of imperial rule and helped lead the temporary and unsuccessful Restoration of 1917. See also BOXER UPRISING; CIXI, EMPRESS DOWAGER; LIANG QICHAO; QING DYNASTY; REFORM MOVEMENT OF 1898; REPUBLIC OF CHINA; SUN YAT-SEN.

K'ANG YU-WEI See KANG YOUWEI.

K'ANG-HSI (EMPEROR) See KANGXI (EMPEROR).

KANGXI (EMPEROR) (K'ang-hsi; 1645–1722)   An emperor of the Manchu Qing dynasty (1644–1911) whose reign is not only the longest but also one of the greatest in the history of China. His personal name was Xuanyue (Hsuan yueh); Kangxi, meaning "Lasting Peace," is his posthumous reign name (r. 1661–1722). He became emperor when he was only six, with regents acting in his stead, but when he turned 15 in 1669 he removed the regents and took full control of the Qing government. When he died in December 1722 he was succeeded by his fourth son, Yinzhen (Yin-chen; 1678–1735), known as the Yongzheng Emperor (Yung-chen; r. 1722–36). Yongzheng and his son and successor, known as the Qianlong Emperor (Ch'ien-lung; r. 1736–95), were also great emperors, and Qianlong's reign is often termed China's "golden age."

The Manchus who established the Qing dynasty were a seminomadic tribe that had invaded China from the northeast (the modern Chinese region of Manchuria) and overthrown the Ming dynasty (1368–1644). Kangxi and his successors became students and patrons of the Chinese language and culture and developed an imperial government that unified the Manchu rulers and their Chinese subjects. Kangxi studied the Confucian classical texts, Chinese literature, geography, astronomy, mathematics and music. He commissioned the compilation of a comprehensive collection of poetry from the Tang dynasty (618–907); collections of works on the Confucian classics, history, philosophy and other subjects; various dictionaries and encyclopedias; and the *Kangxi Dictionary*, which became the standard dictionary of the Chinese language for more than 200 years. In 1700 he ordered the compilation of an encyclopedia, *A Collection of Books and Illustrations of Ancient and Modern Times* (*Gujin tushu jicheng* or *Ku-chin t'u-shu chi-ch'eng*), which when completed in 1725 was the largest work ever printed in the world.

When Kangxi took the throne, pro-Ming factions in southern China were still resisting Manchu rule. He suppressed them in 1681 with the help of Chinese commanders loyal to him. In 1683, with the assistance of the Dutch, he conquered the final center of Ming resistance on the island of Taiwan, which he brought into the Chinese Empire. Kangxi and his successors also annexed northern and western regions including Mongolia, Dzungaria, Turkestan (modern Xinjiang-Uighur Autonomous Region) and Tibet. Kangxi himself sometimes led the Qing military campaigns. To the south, the Miao ethnic group was brought under Chinese control, and Burma and Vietnam submitted to Chinese suzerainty under the tribute system. Kangxi made six inspection tours to southern China. In 1684 he made a pilgrimage to Qufu in Shandong Province to visit the shrine of Confucius (551–479 B.C.), whose school of thought had been orthodox for the Chinese imperial government for nearly two millennia. He also climbed Mount Tai (Taishan), the most revered of the Five Sacred Mountains of Daoism. He supervised the construction of the Qing Summer Palace at Chengde, about 100 miles northeast of Beijing.

Kangxi sent forces against the Russians, who had claimed Chinese territory along the Amur River in Manchuria. In 1689 he signed the Treaty of Nerchinsk with the Russian czar Peter the Great, which divided up Manchuria between the Chinese and the Russians and opened the way for annual Russian trading caravans to Beijing. The Roman Catholic Jesuit priests Gerbillon and Pereira acted as translators during the negotiations. Jesuit missionaries had been allowed into China, beginning with Matteo Ricci in 1600. The Jesuits were very knowledgeable about modern science and technology, and the Kangxi emperor appointed Jesuits to administer the Imperial Board of Astronomy; the Jesuit observatory can still be seen in Beijing. In 1708 Kangxi sent Jesuits to all regions of China to make a geographical survey, the results of which were recorded in *The Complete Atlas of the Empire* (*Huangyu chuanlantu* or *Huang-yu chuan-lan t'u*), completed in 1715. He also gave the Jesuits permission to preach Christianity to the Chinese. However, in 1715 Pope Clement XI sent a letter to Kangxi, demanding that Chinese Christian converts give up their Confucian practice of ancestor worship. Kangxi was furious at the Pope's attempt to interfere with his authority and with his attack on Confucian tradition, and he forbade the teaching of Christianity in China. See also ASTRONOMY AND OBSERVATORIES; CHENGDE; CONFUCIUS; JESUITS; MANCHU; MIAO; MING DYNASTY; NERCHINSK, TREATY OF; QIANLONG, EMPEROR; QING DYNASTY; QUFU; RITES CONTROVERSY; TAI, MOUNT; TAIWAN; TRIBUTE SYSTEM; YONGZHENG, EMPEROR.

KAN-PEI   See BANQUETS; MAOTAI.

KAN-PU   See CADRE.

KANSU PROVINCE   See GANSU PROVINCE.

KAO HSIEN-CHIH   See TALAS, BATTLE OF.

KAO KO-KUNG   See GAO KEGONG.

KAOLIN   See JINGDEZHEN; PORCELAIN.

KAO-TI (EMPEROR)   See GAODI (EMPEROR).

KAO-TSUNG (EMPEROR)   See GAOZONG (EMPEROR).

KARAKORUM   The capital city of the Mongol people, begun by Genghis Khan (1162–1227) and completed by his third grandson, Ogodei (d. 1241), in 1235. Karakorum was built on the banks of the Orhon River, 200 miles west of Ulan Bator, the present capital of the Mongolian People's Republic (Outer Mongolia), which lies between China and Russia. The Mongols were a nomadic tribe who invaded China from the north and ruled under the Yuan dynasty (1279–1368). Karakorum was for 45 years (1190–1235) the capital of the great empire that the Mongols controlled from the Middle East to China. Some remnants of the city can still be seen, including one of the four large stone tortoises that were believed to protect the city from floods.

In 1260, Khubilai Khan (1214–94), another grandson of Genghis Khan, declared himself the Great Khan (ruler of the Mongol Empire) at Chengde (Shang–tu), his summer residence. Khubilai Khan's brother, who had control of the Mongolian lands, proclaimed himself the khan at Karakorum. Their conflict ended in 1264 when Khubilai Khan defeated and captured his brother. In 1267 Khubilai Khan established his winter capital at Beijing, which he called Khanbalik ("the town of the Khan"), but the Chinese called Dadu ("Great Capital"). This was the beginning of Mongol control in China. Karakorum then lost its prominence, although it remained the seat of the governor of Mongolia proper. When the Chinese Ming dynasty (1368–1644) overthrew the Yuan

dynasty, the Mongols were driven out of China and returned to Karakorum. After the family line of Khubilai Khan died out in the 15th century, the city lost its importance altogether. In the 17th century, Karakorum was destroyed by invading forces of the Manchu, another northern nomadic tribe, who conquered China and ruled under the Qing dynasty (1644–1911).

A number of Western travelers visited Karakorum. A Flemish Franciscan monk, William of Rubruck, visited the city in 1254 and wrote a description of its Buddhist temples, Muslim mosques, a Nestorian Christian church and the khan's palace and storehouses. Marco Polo (1254–1324) traveled to Karakorum in 1275 while he was serving in Khubilai Khan's government, and also described the city. In this century, Karakorum has been excavated by Mongolian and Russian archaeologists, who uncovered a number of palaces and residences. Near Karakorum is the oldest Buddhist monastery in Mongolia, Erdene Dzuu, which was built at the end of the 16th century and contains some columns, sculptures and other objects that had been taken from the ruins of Karakorum. The temple's architecture combines Mongolian, Chinese and Tibetan styles (the Mongols practiced the Tibetan form of Buddhism, known as Lamaism). See also BEIJING; CHENGDE; GENGHIS KHAN; INNER MONGOLIA AUTONOMOUS REGION; KHUBILAI KHAN; LAMAISM; MONGOL; POLO, MARCO; YUAN DYNASTY.

KARAKORUM MOUNTAIN RANGE   See HIMALAYA MOUNTAIN RANGE; QINGHAI-TIBET PLATEAU.

KARATE   See KUNG FU; MARTIAL ARTS.

KARMA   The Buddhist belief that the events in a person's current life are caused by his or her actions in previous lives. The Buddhist religion was introduced into China from India around the first century A.D. In Buddhism, karma is connected with the concept of reincarnation, the belief that a person undergoes continuing cycles of birth, death and rebirth until he or she becomes liberated from the cycle and enters into the bliss of nirvana. Karma might be thought of as the seeds that are sown by a person's actions in past lives, the causes that have later effects. According to Buddhism, ordinary human life is characterized by suffering, disease, the pains of growing old and death. These experiences are caused by the human ego's selfish attachments or desires. Ignorance about the cause of suffering keeps a person enmeshed in the endless chain of rebirth. Many Buddhists have believed in a system of merits and demerits whereby performing good deeds and religious practices in this life works off the karma of bad deeds performed in previous lives and ensures rebirth in better circumstances. The various Buddhist sects offer different methods for breaking out of the painful cycle of rebirth by achieving wisdom or salvation. See also BUDDHISM; FATE.

KARST   See GUANGXI-ZHUANG AUTONOMOUS REGION; GUILIN; GUIZHOU PROVINCE; KUNMING.

KASHGAR (Kashi)   The westernmost city in China, in the Xinjiang-Uighur Autonomous Region. It has a population of about 200,000, comprised mainly of Muslim national minorities such as Uighurs, Kirghiz, Uzbeks and Tadzhiks. To the north of Kashgar is the Tianshan Mountain Range, to the west the Pamir Mountain Range, and to the east the Taklimakan Desert. The Tuman River flows through the city and past East Lake. Kashgar sits 4,232 feet above sea level. It receives less than four inches of rain a year, but water is brought from the snow-covered mountains.

Opened to foreign visitors only in 1985, Kashgar is very much a Central Asian city with relatively little Chinese influence. Known in ancient times as Shule, Kashgar was one of the most important oasis towns on the Silk Road between China and the Middle East, at the point where the northern and southern branches of the route joined west of the Taklimakan Desert. The earliest settlers in Kashgar were Indo-Europeans who brought Indian and Persian culture. The Han Chinese defeated them and took control of Shule in 76 B.C. In 640 A.D., Tang-dynasty China made Kashgar one of the "Four Garrisons" of western China, but the city was hard to defend against Turkish nomadic tribes, Tibetans, and Arabs who successively came to the region. The Buddhist religion became prominent but was replaced by Islam in the 10th century A.D. Uighurs founded a kingdom with Kashgar as their capital, but it was defeated by the Han Chinese in 1120 A.D.

Genghis Khan led the Mongols to conquer Kashgar in the 13th century, and his son Jagatai ruled the city. It was razed by the Mongol emperor Tamerlane (Timur) in 1289–90, but its fortifications were rebuilt in the 16th century. Muslim factions fought each other there in the 17th century. In 1759 the Qing dynasty incorporated Xinjiang into the Chinese empire. In 1860 Kashgar was opened to Russian trade. Yakub Beg, a Muslim leader, took Kashgar in 1864–65 and established an independent kingdom, but when he died in 1877 the Chinese regained the region. In 1884 the Qing made Xinjiang a province of China. In the 20th century the British, Russians and Japanese vied for power in this area. In 1934 a Muslim rebel raised armies in Kashgar, and in 1954 Muslim dissidents briefly established the Eastern Turkestan Republic. In 1955 the People's Republic of China established the Xinjiang-Uighur Autonomous Region with Kashgar, the main city in the region's southwest, as its capital.

There are nearly 100 mosques in Kashgar. The Id Kah (Great) Mosque, one of the largest in China, faces a large square near the city center. The Tomb of Abakh Hoja (or Huja Abbak) is a domed mausoleum for five generations of the family of Xiangfei, a beautiful concubine of Emperor Qianlong (Ch'ien-lung; 1711–99). Kashgar's Sunday bazaar attracts around 150,000 people each week; metal ware, Yengisar knives, jewelry, carpets, pottery, musical instruments, spices and melons are some of the most important items for sale. The city is a starting point for expeditions climbing the Himalaya Mountains. See also GENGHIS KHAN; HIMALAYA MOUNTAIN RANGE; MINORITIES, NATIONAL; MONGOL; MUSLIMS; SILK ROAD; TAKLIMAKAN DESERT; TAMERLANE; TIANMOUNTAIN RANGE; UIGHUR; XINJIANG-UIGHUR AUTONOMOUS REGION.

KATYDID See CICADA.

KAZAKH   Also spelled as Kazak; one of China's national minority groups. In 1993 there were 1,111,718 Kazakhs in China. They belong to the Turkic-speaking group of the Altaic languages group. Kazakhs inhabit Xinjiang-Uighur Autonomous Region (formerly known as Chinese Turkestan), the westernmost part of China; Qinghai and Gansu provinces; and the Republic of Kazakhstan across the border. Xinjiang became a province of China in 1884. The Chinese Communists, who founded the People's Republic of China in 1949, designated Xinjiang an autonomous region. Xinjiang includes Ili Kazakh Autonomous Prefecture, Mori Kazakh Autonomous Counties and Barkol Kazakh Autonomous County. The Kazakhs are nomadic people who herd sheep and horses and practice the Muslim religion. Their Ili and Barkol horses are famous throughout China. Kazakhs live in round felt tents called yurts, decorated inside with colorful embroidered textiles. Their traditional clothing is made of fur and leather, with owl feathers in their caps for good luck. They love to hunt, sing and dance. Minstrels, known as *akunse* (*aken*), play a two-stringed instrument called the *dongbera* (*dongbula*) and perform traditional songs and recite stories.

In 1962, Chinese government policies forced members of minority ethnic groups in China to grow crops instead of herding animals and reduced state subsidies, causing a rebellion in Xinjiang. Sixty thousand Kazakh herders fled across the border to Kazakhstan, then part of the Soviet Union. More recently, the Chinese government has enacted policies that are favorable to national minorities. See also MINORITIES, NATIONAL; NOMADS AND ANIMAL HUSBANDRY; XINJIANG-UIGHUR AUTONOMOUS REGION.

KEELUNG   See TAIPEI; TAIWAN.

KEJIA   See HAKKA.

KESI   See SILK.

KHANBALIK   See BEIJING; HEBEI PROVINCE; KHUBILAI KHAN; YUAN DYNASTY.

KHITAI   See CATHAY.

KHITAN   See CATHAY; FIVE DYNASTIES PERIOD; LIAO DYNASTY.

KHOTAN   See HOTAN.

KHUBILAI KHAN   (also spelled Kublai or Kubla; 1214–94) Known as Yuan Shizu (Yuan Shih-tsu) in Chinese histories; a Mongol leader who became first emperor of the Yuan dynasty (1279–1368), making him the first non-Chinese to rule the entire Chinese Empire. The grandson of the great Mongol leader Genghis Khan (1162–1227), Khubilai Khan reigned as the chief of the Mongol world from 1260 to 1294. In 1259 he was fighting a campaign against the Chinese Song dynasty (960–1279) under his uncle Ogodei (Ogodai or Ogotai) when Mongke (Mangu or Mongka), the Mongol chief, died. He hurried back to the Mongol base in northern China and bested his rivals to win the title of Great Khan. In 1271 he adopted the dynastic name Yuan ("Original") and proceeded to conquer the Southern Song dynasty (1127–1279), which had its capital at Hangzhou in eastern

China. In 1263 Khubilai Khan moved his capital to the site of modern Beijing in northern China, calling it Khanbalik ("City of the Khan"; Cambaluc in Mongol; the Chinese later called it Dadu (Tatu); "Great Capital." He then led his fierce Mongol warriors through Sichuan Province to Vietnam, south of China, turned northeast, moved down the Yangzi River and defeated the Song navy, the last organized Chinese opposition to the Mongols. In 1279 the last Song emperor jumped off a ship and drowned.

As the new emperor of China, Khubilai Khan ordered public works projects to help stabilize the country economically and politically. He rebuilt the Grand Canal, the major route for transporting rice and other agricultural products from southern to northern China. He also had engineers change the course of the Yellow River (Huanghe), which tended to overflow its banks and cause widespread damage. He organized Chinese peasants into communities of 50 to 100 farms each, so they could help each other and increase agricultural production. Khubilai Khan allowed the Chinese to practice their native religions of Confucianism and Daoism and tried to persuade Chinese artists to move to the Mongol court. However, the Chinese people always resented him and other Yuan rulers as barbarian foreigners who had taken over their country. Chinese emperors had staffed their bureaucracies with Confucian-trained Chinese scholars or literati, but Khubilai Khan staffed his government with Mongols and other non-Chinese, such as Persians, Turks, Uighurs and other Central Asian and Middle Eastern Muslims. The Yuan government enacted laws that strongly discriminated against the ethnic Chinese population. The Song dynasty had been a high point in Chinese culture, but the Mongols repressed Chinese scholars and artists, considering teachers no better than beggars, so there was little cultural development during the Yuan. The only Chinese art that thrived was drama. Khubilai Khan practiced religious tolerance but favored the Tibetan branch of Buddhism, known as Lamaism.

The father and uncle of the Italian explorer Marco Polo (1254–1324) had traveled together in 1260 from Europe to the Mongol court. In 1265 Khubilai Khan, some of whose family members were Nestorian Christians, sent them back with letters for the Roman Catholic pope. They returned to China in 1271, bringing with them Marco and letters from Pope Gregory X to Khubilai Khan. The khan liked Marco Polo, who served for 17 years in the Mongol government, including three years as an official in the city of Yangzhou. When he returned to Europe, Marco Polo wrote a book that described what he had seen and experienced in China, including descriptions of Khubilai Khan, his palaces and government.

Khubilai Khan strained his military resources by sending expeditions to conquer Japan, Vietnam, Burma and the Indonesian island of Java. His attempted invasions of Japan through Korea in 1274 and 1281 were both destroyed by typhoons, which gave the Japanese the belief that their country was protected from foreign attack by "divine winds" (*kamikaze*). The two Mongol invasions of Java in 1281 and 1292 also failed. However, Mongol diplomatic missions in the 1280s brought many small kingdoms in South and Southeast Asia into the tribute system by which they acknowledged Yuan suzerainty. After Khubilai Khan died in

1294, he was canonized with the name Shizu (Shih-tsu). The Mongol Yuan dynasty rapidly declined and was overthrown less than a century later and replaced by the Chinese Ming dynasty (1368–1644). See also BEIJING; DRAMA; GRAND CANAL; GENGHIS KHAN; KARAKORUM; LAMAISM; LITERATI; MONGOL; POLO, MARCO; SONG DYNASTY; SOUTHERN SONG DYNASTY; TRIBUTE SYSTEM; YANGZI RIVER; YELLOW RIVER; YUAN DYNASTY.

KIAKHTA, TREATY OF   See YONGZHENG (EMPEROR).

KIANGSI PROVINCE   See JIANGXI PROVINCE.

KIANGSU PROVINCE   See JIANGSU PROVINCE.

KINGFISHER   A bird whose beautiful blue feathers are applied to silver or copper to make pictures and screens with landscape and floral designs, decorations, jewelry and hair ornaments. The common kingfisher, which is often seen darting into rivers, is found over plains and around the waters of low mountains all over China. Pied kingfishers, lesser pied kingfishers, ruddy kingfishers, white-breasted kingfishers and black-capped kingfishers are usually found near low mountain creeks in southern China. The lesser pied kingfisher usually hovers over the water before diving. The white-breasted kingfisher is commonly seen away from the water's edge where it catches insects, crabs and lizards. Kingfishers, which nest alone or in pairs, dig holes deep into firm banks to make their nest; they gather fishbones to line a chamber where they lay up to eight eggs.

Delicate objects decorated with kingfisher feathers are produced mainly in Beijing and Guangzhou. They are made by alternating blue feathers in shades of azure, ultramarine and sapphire with filagree flowers and dragons interspersed with artificial pearls and enamel on a silver or copper base. The Chinese believe that kingfisher feathers resemble the colors of the sky and the blue-green tints of distant hills. They symbolize the colorful traditional clothing worn by women and the beauty of the women themselves. Ornate wedding chairs in which brides are carried to the homes of their new husbands are decorated with kingfisher feathers, auspicious symbols of beauty, good luck and marital happiness. See also ENAMELWARE; PEARL; WEDDINGS, TRADITIONAL.

KINGSTON, MAXINE HONG (1940–)   A best-selling Chinese-American author. Kingston was born in Stockton, California, the eldest of six children born in America to parents who had emigrated from China (two children had also been born and died in China). Her father named her Maxine after a lucky blond woman who frequented a gambling parlor he managed; her Chinese name is Ting Ting. Maxine Hong Kingston received her undergraduate degree from the University of California at Berkeley in 1962 and her teaching certificate in 1965. She taught English, language arts and mathematics in California from 1965 to 1967 and in Hawaii from 1967 to 1977, and became a visiting associate professor of English at the University of Hawaii–Honolulu in 1977. Her first book was *The Woman Warrior: Memoirs of a Girlhood among Ghosts* (1976). It is classified as nonfiction but combines true stories, fairytales and myths told to her by her family, especially her mother and other Chinese-Americans while she was growing up in Stockton. She won the National Book Critics Circle Award for general nonfiction in 1976, the *Mademoiselle* Magazine Award in 1977, and the Anisfield-Wolf Race Relations Award in 1978. In 1979 *Time* magazine named *The Woman Warrior* one of the top 10 nonfiction works of the decade. Her second book, *China Men* (1980), comprises an equally powerful combination of true stories and mythology but concentrates on her father and other Chinese men who immigrated to work in North America and Hawaii. This book was named to the American Library Association Notable Books List in 1980. That same year, Kingston was named a Living Treasure of Hawaii and became a National Education Association writing fellow. In 1981 she won the American Book Award for general nonfiction for *China Men*, as well as the Stockton (California) Arts Commission Award. In 1983 she won the Hawaii Writers Award. In 1987 she published *Hawaii One Summer.* In 1988 she published *Tripmaster Monkey: His Fake Book*, a humorous novel that combines Chinese-American history and mythology to tell the story of Wittman Ah Sing, a young Chinese-American man who lives by doing whatever he wants without regard for the consequences. Maxine Hong Kingston has also published short stories and articles in numerous periodicals, including the *New York Times Magazine, New Yorker, Ms.* and *American Heritage.* She married Earll Kingston, an actor, in 1962 and has a son, Joseph Lawrence Chung Mei. See also OVERSEAS CHINESE.

KIRGHIZ   One of China's 55 officially designated national minority ethnic groups. The Kirghiz belong to the Turkic ethnic group and follow the Muslim religion. In 1993 there were 141,000 Kirghiz inhabiting Xinjiang-Uighur Autonomous Region in far northwestern China, 80 percent of them in the Kizilsu Kirghiz Autonomous Prefecture in Southwestern Xinjiang. They also inhabit Kyrgyzstan, a former republic of the U.S.S.R. north of the Xinjiang border. Although some Kirghiz live in cities, they are traditionally nomadic herders of sheep, goats and cattle, living on the lower slopes of mountains in winter and moving to higher pasture lands in warmer weather. Their traditional home is the *boziwuyi*, a round tent similar to a Mongolian yurt decorated with beautiful embroidered curtains. The Kirghiz folk epic, *Manasi*, is considered, along with the Mongolian and Tibetan, as one of the three great folk epics of China's minorities. It is a narrative poem in eight parts about generations of the ancient Manasi family. The present recorded versions has about 200,000 lines. In 840 the Kirghiz moved down from western Siberia and attacked the Uighurs, an ethnic group in outer Mongolia, and forced them out of that region. The Uighurs became the dominant ethnic group in Xinjiang, formerly known as Chinese Turkestan, which is also inhabited by a nomadic Muslim ethnic group called the Kazakhs. The Kirghiz were later overtaken by the Mongols, who ruled China under the Yuan dynasty (1279–1368). See also KAZAKH; MINORITIES, NATIONAL; MUSLIMS; NOMADS AND ANIMAL HUSBANDRY; UIGHURS; XINJIANG-UIGHUR AUTONOMOUS REGION.

KIRIN PROVINCE   See JILIN PROVINCE.

KITCHEN GOD   (Caozhun or Ts'ao-chun; "Stove Prince") The most important deity in traditional Chinese homes. The Kitchen God is believed to observe the good and evil done by every person in the household. A piece of red paper decorated with a picture of the Kitchen God, or inscribed with the words, "Seat of the Kitchen God," is hung in a small shrine or niche over the kitchen stove. Offerings are made to him twice a month.

Several rituals and beliefs surround the Kitchen God. At the end of each year, on the 23rd day of the 12th moon in the Chinese lunar calendar (usually in January, one week before the New Year Festival), the Kitchen God supposedly travels to Heaven to make his report to the God of Heaven about what has happened on Earth during the year. On this day the male household members conduct a special ceremony to give the Kitchen God a proper send-off. (Women are not allowed to take part in rituals worshiping the Kitchen God.) He is offered cakes made from sticky rice containing sweet fillings so that he will make a favorable report about family members. After the ceremony his paper image is taken down and burned with joss paper, and firecrackers are set off to speed him on his journey. The Kitchen God's niche remains empty while he is away for a week, during which time the household makes final preparations for celebrating the New Year. He is welcomed back to the home on New Year's Eve, the 30th night of the 12th moon, and a new image of him is hung above the stove. That night the family enjoys a banquet before fasting on New Year's Day.

According to Chinese legend, the Kitchen God was once a man who became so poor that he finally had to sell his wife to another man who was wealthy. One day he had to work for his wife's new husband, and he did not recognize his wife in her new house. But she still cared for him, and baked him sesame cakes with money inside. He took them along when he finished his job and, not realizing that she had put money in them, sold the cakes to a man he met along the way. When he later discovered what his wife had done for him out of love, he felt unworthy to live any longer and killed himself. But the God of Heaven saw that the man was good and honest, and transformed him into the Kitchen God. This deity has become known to Westerners through the novel *The Kitchen God's Wife* (1991), by the Chinese-American author Amy Tan. See also BANQUETS; HEAVEN; NEW YEAR FESTIVAL; TAN, AMY.

KITES   Kites have been made in China since ancient times, when they were called "paper birds" (*zhi yuan*). They are constructed of frames made of thin pieces of wood or bamboo that are tied together and covered with brightly painted paper. Kites were flown in China as early as the fifth or fourth century B.C. According to legend, Kongshu Pan (K'ung-shu P'an), the god of artisans, built kites in bird shapes. For many centuries, the Chinese used kites to send messages and ask for help during military campaigns. In the 10th century A.D. a Chinese man named Li Ye supposedly flew a kite with a small piece of bamboo attached to it by a silk ribbon, and the vibration of the wind on the ribbon caused the kite to make a musical or whistling sound. Since then, the Chinese have called kites "aeolian harps" (*fengzheng* or *feng-cheng*). Today kites are flown for enjoyment, but in past times they had other uses. During the fourth century B.C., there were attempts to fly people using kites, and a prince of the Wei kingdom supposedly flew for about two miles. By the 13th century A.D., the use of kites to lift up humans was practiced throughout China. It was described by the Italian explorer Marco Polo (1254–1324), who said that this was done before a ship went on a voyage. If the kite flew straight up successfully, the voyage would also be successful, but if not, merchants would be afraid to sail on the ship. During the sixth century A.D., cities under siege by enemy troops flew kites to send military signals. In some parts of China, kites were believed to have healing powers, and they were flown to draw fevers out of patients. In the capital city of Beijing, competitions were held in which teams of men and boys attempted to fly the most splendid kites. Kite flying today is a popular recreation all over China enjoyed especially by children. Chinese kites are made in great variety of shapes and colors. Some of the most popular designs are human and mythical figures, flowers, birds, fish, worms, bats, dragonflies and the Monkey King. Kites are categorized by the way they are made, with either a "hard wing" or a "soft wing." The frame of a "soft wing" kite can be taken apart so the kite can be stored in a box. A "hard wing" kite is constructed with the body, head and wings in one piece and is covered with stronger paper or silk fabric. This type of kite can be flown in strong winds and kept in the air for a long time. Kites in southern China tend to be delicate while those in the north are strong and boldly decorated. The city of Weifang in Shandong Province has been famous for its kite makers and fliers since the Ming dynasty (1368–1644). Every year it hosts the Weifang International Kite Festival. See also BAMBOO; PAPER; SILK.

KMT   See NATIONALIST PARTY.

KO HUNG   See DAOIST CLASSICAL TEXTS; GE HONG.

K'O-CHIA   See HAKKA.

KONG FUZI   See CONFUCIUS.

KONGLIN   See QUFU.

KONGMIAO TEMPLE   See QUFU.

KONGZI   See CONFUCIUS.

KOO, V. K. WELLINGTON (Ku Wei-chun; 1887–1985)   A Chinese diplomat who served as ambassador to Great Britain and the United States and who represented China in signing the United Nations charter in 1945. Koo was born to a wealthy family in Shanghai. He received B.A. and M.A. degrees from St. John's University, a British school in Shanghai, and then went to the United States, where he received B.A., M.A. and Ph.D. degrees from Columbia University in New York. In 1912 he returned to China and held various positions in the government of the Republic of China (ROC), which had just been established under the leadership of Dr. Sun Yat-sen after the Revolution of 1911 overthrew the Qing dynasty (1644–1911), China's last imperial dynasty. In 1915 the ROC government appointed Koo minister to Mexico, and shortly after, minister to the United States.

In 1919 Koo was a member of the Chinese delegation to the Paris Peace Conference that concluded World War I.

China had entered the war in 1917 by declaring war on Germany in hope of getting back Shandong Province, where Germany had held concessions until Japan, which had joined the war on the Allied side, claimed Shandong for itself. At the Paris Peace Conference, it was revealed that the Chinese government in Beijing had made a secret agreement with Japan giving Shandong to Japan. The Treaty of Versailles, drawn up at the conference, contained an international agreement to award to Japan all of Germany's former concessions in China. This infuriated the Chinese people and led to the nationwide Chinese protest against Japan known as the May Fourth Movement of 1919. Koo played a major role in the Chinese decision not to sign the Treaty of Versailles.

Koo's career as a diplomat spanned 40 years, during which he served as China's ambassador to Great Britain, France and the United States, as foreign minister, and in a number of other positions. He became associated with Zhang Zuolin (Chang Tso-lin), a warlord in Manchuria (northeastern China) who controlled Beijing from 1926 until 1928. That year Chiang Kai-shek, who later became head of the Chinese Nationalist Party (Kuomintang; KMT) that controlled the ROC, led the Northern Expedition against the Chinese warlords. Chiang drove Zhang Zuolin out of Beijing and issued an order for Koo's arrest, although this was later rescinded. Koo then became an adviser to Zhang Xueliang (Chang Hsueh-liang), Zhang Zuolin's son, who had succeeded him as warlord of Manchuria. Japan invaded Manchuria in 1931, defeating some of Zhang's troops and causing others to retreat, and established a puppet state there in 1932. Koo returned to his career as international diplomat, serving at the same time as China's ambassador to France and chief delegate to the League of Nations, the forerunner of the United Nations.

In 1937 Japan invaded China Proper, and China began fighting its War of Resistance against Japan (1937–45; World War II). In 1941, Koo became China's ambassador to Britain. He negotiated several treaties between China and Britain, including the abolition of extraterritoriality in 1943. Extraterritoriality was a right that China had granted to Britain and other foreign nations after Britain had defeated China in the Opium War (1839–42) and forced it to open a number of cities, known as treaty ports, to foreign trade and residents; it meant that foreigners accused of crimes in those ports would be tried under the laws of their own countries rather than the laws of China.

Near the end of World War II in 1945, the United Nations was established, and Koo represented China in signing the United Nations Charter on June 26, 1945, less than two months before Japan surrendered. In May 1946 he became China's ambassador to the United States. The KMT and the Chinese Communist Party (CCP), which had fought each other but had formed a united front against Japan, now resumed their civil war. Koo influenced the United States to support the KMT. He also took part in the attempt to have the KMT and CCP make a peace agreement in 1949, but this did not succeed. The CCP defeated the KMT, whose members fled to Taiwan Island, where they established the provisional government of the ROC.

On October 1, 1949 the CCP proclaimed the founding of the People's Republic of China (PRC) as the government of mainland China. Koo served as ROC ambassador to the United States until 1956, and from 1957 to 1967 he served on the International Court of Justice at The Hague in the Netherlands. He then spent his remaining years living in retirement in the United States. See also CIVIL WAR BETWEEN COMMUNISTS AND NATIONALISTS; LEAGUE OF NATIONS; NATIONALIST PARTY; REPUBLIC OF CHINA; UNITED NATIONS; WARLORD PERIOD; WORLD WAR I; ZHANG XUELIANG; ZHANG ZUOLIN.

KOREA AND CHINA See BUDDHISM; CONFUCIANISM; KOREAN WAR; MANCHURIA; MING DYNASTY; RUSSO-JAPANESE WAR OF 1904–05; SCULPTURE; SINO-JAPANESE WAR OF 1894–95; TIANJIN, CONVENTION OF; TRIBUTE SYSTEM; TUMEN RIVER; UNITED NATIONS; YALU RIVER; YANGDI, EMPEROR.

KOREAN (Chao Xian or Chao Shin, in Chinese)   One of China's 55 officially designated national minority ethnic groups. The Korean people in China speak the same language and have the same culture as the people of Korea. They are concentrated in Manchuria (northeastern China) in the eastern region of Jilin Province and the southeastern region of Heilongjiang Province, near the Tumen and Yalu rivers that form the boundary between China and North Korea. This area is very sensitive politically. Koreans also reside in the Manchurian province of Liaoning. In 1993 there were 1.9 million Koreans in China, 40 percent residing in the Yangbian Korean Autonomous Prefecture and the area around the Changbai Mountains in Jilin.

Many Koreans were brought to China as laborers by the Japanese after they invaded Manchuria in the 1930s and established the puppet state of Manchukuo (Manzhouguo in China) in 1932. Japan had annexed Korea as a colony in 1910. However, China and Korea already had a long history of interaction. During the reign of Emperor Wudi (Wu-ti; r. 141–87 B.C.) of the Han dynasty, the Chinese established colonies in northern Korea where there were already settlements of Chinese refugees. These colonies lasted until about 313 to 316, when the Korean Koguryo state took control of the area from the Chinese. Later Chinese emperors made unsuccessful attempts to take back regions of Korea, although Korea was brought into the Chinese Empire by the Mongols during the Yuan dynasty (1279–1368) and by the Manchus, a nomadic tribe based in Manchuria, during the Qing dynasty (1644–1911).

Chinese culture was a strong influence on Korean culture. The Koreans spoke a language that differed from Chinese, but they used classical Chinese characters to write their official documents and classical literary works. In the 15th century an alphabet for native Korean words was invented. This alphabet is combined with Han Chinese characters for the numerous loan-words from Han Chinese in Korean. The Korean Folk Customs Museum in Longjin, Jilin, preserves a traditional Korean-style home and articles used in daily life, such as furniture, clothing, porcelain and eating utensils. One room contains books with detailed information about 310 Korean surnames. Korean customs and festivals are similar to those of the Chinese. The Koreans love to sing, dance, and hold sporting events, especially wrestling for boys and swinging on high swings for girls. See

also CHANGBAI MOUNTAIN RANGE; KOREAN WAR; MANCHURIA; MINORITIES, NATIONAL.

KOREAN WAR   A war fought between North and South Korea, which the Communist People's Republic of China (PRC) entered on the side of North Korea in 1950. It was only one year after the PRC had been founded by the Chinese Communist Party (CCP).

The Korean War broke out on June 5, 1950, when forces of the Democratic People's Republic of Korea (DPRK), commonly known as North Korea, armed by the U.S.S.R., moved south across the 38th parallel to attack South Korea. On June 27, U.S. president Harry Truman ordered the Seventh Fleet of the U.S. Navy to patrol the Taiwan Strait that lies between mainland China and the island of Taiwan, where the Nationalists (Kuomintang; KMT) led by Chiang Kai-shek had fled when the CCP defeated them in 1949. Truman entered the conflict on South Korea's side to defeat communism on the Korean Peninsula. He also began pressuring European countries to increase the economic embargo that had already been initiated against the PRC. United Nations forces supported South Korea. The UN and the United States recognized the Nationalist government of the Republic of China (ROC) on Taiwan rather than the Communist PRC government, as the legitimate government of China. North Korea asked the PRC for help when UN forces, primarily U.S. troops, crossed the 38th parallel into North Korea and began advancing toward the border with China. China then sent many warnings to the United States but they were ignored. On October 25, China sent more than 2.3 million Chinese People's Volunteers, who were actually members of the People's Liberation Army (PLA), to defend North Korea against the UN troops advancing toward the Yalu River. The Yalu (Yalujiang) forms the border between North Korea and northeastern China. The Chinese forces included about two-thirds of all China's field army, artillery and air force and all of its tanks. They suffered extremely heavy casualties in North Korea but prevented UN forces from crossing the Yalu into China and drove them back to the 38th parallel. The war ground into a stalemate. The U.S.S.R., which in February 1950 had signed the Treaty of Friendship, Alliance, and Mutual Assistance with the PRC, gave China some military and technical assistance, but the war placed a serious drain on Chinese resources.

During the Korean War the PRC also waged a domestic campaign to mobilize the Chinese people against enemies of the country, with the slogan "Resist America, Aid Korea." This campaign channeled the initial enthusiasm of the Chinese for the CCP after 1949, when the party proved effective in cleaning up Chinese cities, removing beggars and crime, controlling inflation, and getting the Chinese people to rebuild the country, control disease and end illiteracy. From 1951 to 1952 the Chinese government held mass trials that attacked foreigners and Christian missionaries as U.S. agents, and it launched a movement of "class struggle" against landlords, wealthy peasants, intellectuals, and corrupt bureaucrats and businessmen, known as the Three-Anti and Five-Anti Campaigns.

In 1951 the UN declared that China was an aggressor in Korea and sanctioned a global embargo on the shipment of arms and other war materials to China. This embargo actually strengthened the relationship between the PRC and the U.S.S.R. China's entry into the Korean War prevented the PRC from gaining the seat for China in the UN; the seat was given instead to Taiwan (Republic of China; ROC). The Korean War was also a major factor in the negative relationship between China and the United States until the early 1970s, with the United States maintaining travel restrictions and a trade embargo with China and providing military aid to Taiwan.

The Korean War ended in a draw. Truce talks were held at Panmunjom, and an armistice was signed in July 1953. The Chinese people were proud of what their new country had done, and asserted that they had won a victory of sorts. For the first time in the modern era, the Chinese had been able to fight foreign powers, holding them off militarily and preventing them from advancing into Manchuria. Meanwhile, during the Korean conflict, China had also sent troops westward into Tibet (Xizang) and within a year "liberated" this region. Although Tibet had longstanding political ties with China, the Tibetan people strongly opposed the incursion of Chinese troops into their territory. See also CIVIL WAR BETWEEN COMMUNISTS AND NATIONALISTS; PEOPLE'S LIBERATION ARMY; PEOPLE'S REPUBLIC OF CHINA; THREE-ANTI AND FIVE-ANTI CAMPAIGNS; TIBET; UNITED NATIONS; YALU RIVER.

KO-SSU   See SILK.

KOTIE (K'O-T'IEH)   See STONE RUBBINGS.

KOTO   See QIN.

KOUKOU NOR   See QINGHAI, LAKE.

KOWLOON   (Jiulong, in pinyin)   A peninsula on the Chinese mainland that comprised part of the former British Crown Colony of Hong Kong, located at the mouth of the Pearl River Delta. This colony also included Hong Kong Island and adjacent islets, south of Kowloon, and the so-called New Territories, which extended north from Kowloon and bordered the People's Republic of China (PRC). The major Chinese port city of Guangzhou (Canton) in Guangdong Province lies about 90 miles to the northwest. The British moved to Hong Kong Island after they were expelled from the Portuguese colony of Macao, and China ceded the island to Great Britain under the Treaty of Nanjing after they defeated China in the Opium War (1839–42). In 1860 China ceded Kowloon to Britain under the Beijing Convention of 1860. In 1898 Britain acquired from China a 99-year lease over the New Territories, which greatly increased the size of its Hong Kong colony. The two countries agreed that in 1997 all of Hong Kong, including Kowloon and the New Territories, would revert to China. Kowloon Peninsula and nearby Stonecutter's Island have a combined area of 3.75 square miles. The Kowloon Mountain Range divides the peninsula's harbor and commercial, industrial and residential districts on the southern tip (known as Tsimshatsui, "Pointed Sandspit") from the agricultural area to the north. Hong Kong's extensive port facilities are centered in Kowloon, and many tourist hotels and shopping centers are located there, including the famous Peninsula Hotel. The main street is Nathan Road, named for Sir Matthew Nathan, who became governor

of Hong Kong in 1904. The Kowloon-Guangzhou Railway runs for 22 miles from the southern tip of Kowloon Peninsula to the point where it crosses the former border of the PRC at Lowu. Frequent passenger and car ferries connect Kowloon to Hong Kong Island. The runway for Kai Tak airport extends into Kowloon Bay. See also BEIJING CONVENTION OF 1860; HONG KONG; MACAO; NANJING, TREATY OF; NEW TERRITORIES.

KOWTOW   (gedou or ke-tou)   A formal way of bowing that demonstrates deep respect to a superior. The kowtow is known as "three kneelings and nine prostrations" because a person had to get down on his or her knees three times and touch the forehead to the floor three times each time he or she kneeled. Government ministers kowtowed in front of the emperor, commoners before government officials, children before their parents, and family members before their ancestors. The kowtow was performed by members of diplomatic and trading missions from foreign tributary states such as Burma and Thailand when they were granted an audience with the emperor once a year as members of the Chinese tribute system that regulated foreign trade. The Chinese considered the emperor to be the "Son of Heaven" (tianzi or t'ien-tzu) and China to be the "Middle Kingdom" (Zhongguo or Chung-kuo) the center of the world. See also ANCESTOR WORSHIP; MIDDLE KINGDOM; TRIBUTE SYSTEM.

KOXINGA   See ZHENG CHENGGONG.

KU   See DRUMS.

KU WEI-CHUN   See KOO, V. K. WELLINGTON.

KUAN   See TEMPLES.

KUAN CH'U   See BOOK OF SONGS.

KUAN HAN-CH'ING   See GUAN HANQING.

KUAN TAO-SHENG   See ZHAO MENGFU AND GUAN DAOSHENG.

KUAN TI   See GUANDI.

KUAN YIN   See GUANYIN.

KUANG WU-TI (EMPEROR)   See EASTERN HAN DYNASTY.

KUANG-HSU (EMPEROR)   See CIXI, EMPRESS DOWAGER; GONG, PRINCE; REFORM MOVEMENT OF 1898; QING DYNASTY.

KUAN-HSI   See CONNECTIONS.

KUANWARE   (Guan ware)   A type of ceramic that is known as one of the "five great wares" of the Song dynasty (960–1279). It is characterized as a "celadon" ware because of the green-blue color of its thick, opaque glaze, which tended to crackle. Celadon pieces usually have a light blue or green color. However, Kuanware was also produced in colors ranging from brownish gray to gray to pale lavender-blue. Kuanware was produced mainly for members of the

Song imperial court and literati, or scholars, who staffed the imperial bureaucracy, with typical pieces including dishes, teacups, and utensils for the scholar's study such as calligraphy brush holders and water droppers. See also CELADON WARE; FOUR TREASURES OF THE STUDY; LITERATI; SONG DYNASTY.

KUBILAI KHAN See KHUBILAI KHAN.

KUEICHOU PROVINCE See GUIZHOU PROVINCE.

KUELIN See GUILIN.

KU-KUNG PO-WU-KUAN See FORBIDDEN CITY.

KUMARAJIVA (350–413) A central Asian Buddhist monk who made translations of many important Buddhist texts into the Chinese language. The religion of Buddhism, which had been founded in India in the fifth century B.C., was introduced into China around the first century A.D. and by A.D. 166 was patronized by the reigning emperor of the Han dynasty (206 B.C.–A.D. 220). In the fourth century many Chinese belonging to the Confucian-educated literati, or scholar class, took a strong interest in Buddhist concepts, which had some elements similar to the native Chinese tradition of Daoism, which also appealed to fourth-century literati. Buddhism had accumulated an enormous number of sutras (scriptures) and other texts, which the literati studied to find concepts that would help them understand concepts in the Daoist classical texts. A Chinese monk named Daoan (Tao-an; 314–385) maintained that Buddhist texts had to be understood on their own rather than in conjunction with Daoism, and he drew up guidelines by which scholars could make accurate translations. He also compiled the first catalogue of the 611 Buddhist scriptures that had been translated into Chinese by that time. In 399 a Chinese Buddhist monk named Faxian (Fa-hsien) left the capital city of Chang'an (modern Xi'an in Shaanxi Province) on a pilgrimage to India to collect Buddhist manuscripts; he arrived back in China in 414. Other pilgrims and foreign monks brought many other Buddhist texts to China.

Daoan learned of Kumarajiva, who was fluent in Chinese and many languages of India and Central Asia. He had been born in Kucha in the Tarim Basin of Central Asia and had studied Buddhism in Kashmir and Kashgoe. He had spent 17 years as a prisoner in Gansu Province when his region was absorbed by a northern Chinese military leader. Daoan persuaded Emperor Yaochang (Yao Ch'ang) of the Later Qin dynasty (384–417) that ruled much of northern China to bring Kumarajiva to Chang'an, where he would receive imperial support to translate Buddhist texts. In 401 Kumarajiva arrived in Chang'an, where he led a team of more than 1,000 monks in copying and revising old translations and producing new ones. Kumarajiva completed beautiful, precise translations of 98 texts, many of which became the most important sutras for Chinese sects of Buddhism, and he originated many religious and philosophical terms that became standard in Chinese Buddhism. The most important text was the *Lotus Sutra,* the most revered sutra in Mahayana, the branch of Buddhism that took root in China due to Kumarajiva's efforts.

Kumarajiva also delivered lectures on his translations to thousands of Chinese Buddhist monks, who then wrote commentaries on his translations. Due largely to his efforts, Buddhism became popular all over China by the end of the fifth century. See also BUDDHISM; CHANG'AN; DAOISM; DAOIST CLASSICAL TEXTS; FAXIAN; LITERATI; LOTUS SUTRA; TARIM BASIN.

KUMQUAT See ORANGE.

K'UN-CH'U See KUNQU.

KUNG, PRINCE See ARROW WAR; GONG, PRINCE.

KUNG FU (*kongfu* or *gongfu*) A martial art (*wushu*) that uses hand and foot movements and fighting without weapons, similar to the Japanese martial art known as karate. There are two systems of Chinese kung fu, the "hard style" and the "soft style." The hard style requires power, strong kicks, and an "iron hand," meaning strong fists that can strike hard objects. The soft style emphasizes quick and agile movements and a "poison hand," that is, the ability to strike vulnerable places in an opponent's body. Both systems of kung fu begin their movements with a position known as the "horse stance," in which the feet are far apart, the knees are slightly bent, the back is straight, and the arms are bent to place the fists with knuckles up at hip level. Students of kung fu must practice for many years to gain proficiency in the many different movements taught by their schools. Unlike schools of karate, most kung fu schools do not hold competitions or tournaments and do not rank their students by colored belts. However, in the 1980s some kung fu schools did begin awarding colored belts or patches to students. Chinese movies with actors who fight using kung fu movements are very popular around the world; especially those made in Hong Kong. Their movements are made more dramatic by the use of sound effects, stunt men and other special effects. In China, kung fu masters had a reputation for having superhuman powers. The Chinese weaponless martial arts, especially a slow-moving form known as *taijiquan* (tai chi ch'uan), supposedly originated at Shaolin Si, a Chan (Zen) Buddhist temple about 55 miles southwest of the city of Zhengzhou in Henan Province. Shaolin Temple is associated with Bodhidharma (known in Chinese as Tamo). The founder of Chan Buddhism, Bodhidharma was credited with originating the training techniques that developed into the Chinese weaponless martial arts. See also BODHIDHARMA; FILM STUDIOS; MARTIAL ARTS; SHAOLIN TEMPLE; TAIJIQUAN.

K'UNG FU TZU See CONFUCIUS.

KUNG HSIEN See GONG XIAN.

KUNG PAN-CH'IEN See GONG XIAN.

K'UNG TEH-CHENG See CONFUCIUS.

K'UNG TZU See CONFUCIUS.

KUNG-HANG See CANTON SYSTEM.

KUNLUN MOUNTAIN RANGE (Kunlunshan)　A range of high mountains that forms the southern boundary of Xinjiang-Uighur Autonomous Region and the north wall of the Qinghai-Tibet Plateau in western China. The Kunlun Mountains stretch 1,550 miles between the Pamir Mountain Range to the west and the Qinghai-Tibet Plateau to the east, along the Tarim Basin in Xinjiang and the southern fringe of the Qaidam Basin in Qinghai Province. Traces remain of the southern route of the old Silk Road between China and the West where it cut through the Kunlun Mountain Range. The mountains have an average height of about 16,500 feet, and many peaks rise to more than 23,000 feet. There are many glaciers in the western section, but the eastern section has a very dry climate. The range's volcanic zone contains 11 extinct volcanoes. The Kunlun Mountain Range divides into several branches as it runs eastward from the Pamir Mountains into the Sichuan Basin in central China. The northern branches, the Altunshan and the Qilianshan, circle the Tibetan Plateau and border the Qaidam Basin, a swampy region with numerous salt lakes. A southern branch, the Qin, divides the watersheds of the two major rivers in China, the Yangzi River (Changjiang) and the Yellow River (Huanghe). See also GANSU PROVINCE; QINGHAI-TIBET PLATEAU; SILK ROAD; TARIM BASIN; TIBET; XINJIANG-UIGHUR AUTONOMOUS REGION; YANGZI RIVER; YELLOW RIVER.

KUNMING　The capital city of the southwestern province of Yunnan. Kunming lies the farthest southwest of any major city in China, and has a population of about 2 million. Formerly isolated and backward, it has been connected by railroad and air travel with the important cities of Chengdu in Sichuan Province and Guangzhou in Guangdong Province. Members of 22 national minority ethnic groups, the greatest number in China, inhabit Yunnan Province, and a rich variety of minorities wearing colorful clothing can be seen in Kunming, such as the Bai, Hani, Hui, Miao and Yi. Many of these people are related to ethnic groups in Myanmar (Burma) Laos and Vietnam, which border Yunnan to the south.

Kunming is located in the center of Yunnan on a fertile plain with an altitude of 6,200 feet. Because it has the most temperate climate of any Chinese city and flowers bloom all year round, Kunming is called the "City of Perpetual Spring." Mountains surround the city on the east, north and west. Lake Dian (Dian chi) and Daquang Park lie just outside the southwestern edge of the city. The lake covers more than 200 square miles and is the sixth-largest freshwater lake in China. Ten miles southwest of Kunming, the Western Hills (Xishan) overlooking Lake Dianchi host the Dragon Gate (Longmen), a group of caves and statues carved into the rock in the 18th and 19th centuries. There are also the Huating Temple, the largest in Kunming, and the San Qing Pavilions, built as part of a summer resort for the imperial family during the Yuan dynasty (1279–1368).

Kunming's origin dates to 279 B.C. when troops from the kingdom of Chu moved into the region around Lake Dian. A city called Kuzhou was established near modern Kunming in A.D. 109. In the eighth century the Nanzhao Kingdom in Yunnan took Kunming and made the city its secondary capital, after Dali to the northwest. In 1274, the Mongols took Kunming and the rest of Yunnan. The Mongols ruled China under the Yuan dynasty. Toward the end of the Yuan dynasty this area was named Kunming County. The Ming dynasty (1368–1644), which overthrew the Yuan, called the area Yunnanfu and built a walled town there. When the Manchus invaded China, overthrew the Ming and founded the Qing dynasty (1644–1911), the final Ming resistance to the Manchus held out in Kunming in the 1650s. General Wu Sangui (Wu San-kuei) led his own anti-Qing rebellion until he died on 1678. The Qing defeated Wu's successor. A walled city was built in the area in 1832, which became Kunming municipality in 1928. Du Wenxiu (Tu Wen-hsiu), who led a Muslim rebellion in Yunnan, placed Kunming under siege several times between 1858 and 1873. The Qing finally put down the rebellion in 1873. The French Indochina Rail Line from Vietnam to Kunming was completed in 1910 and still provides service between Kunming and the Vietnam border.

After the Japanese invaded China in 1937, Nationalist forces (Kuomintang; KMT) moved their capital to Chongqing in Sichuan Province, and many refugees from eastern China ended up in Kunming during the China's War of Resistance against Japan (1937–45; World War II). During the war, thousands of Yunnan peasants also came into the city to work in newly built factories. Many American soldiers and advisers, including the U.S. Air Force's "Flying Tigers," were based in Kunming. The famous Burma Road built during the war still serves the city. Since the war, Kunming has continued to modernize and industrialize. Major products include steel, machinery, mining equipment, chemicals, motor vehicles, textiles, and consumer goods. The city also has 11 colleges and universities, including the Institute for Nationalities, where folk dance performances are sometimes given.

A portion of the old walled city can still be seen in the northeast section of Kunming. The city has many temples dating from the Yuan dynasty, as well as the Ming dynasty Daoist Gold Temple on Phoenix Song Hill. In addition, Kunming is a base for many tours to nearby sites. Other tourist sites include Green Lake and Yuantong Park and Zoo. Seven miles west of the city lies Bamboo Temple (Qiongzhu Si), which is 700 years old and houses 500 wooden statues of Buddha carved by a sculptor between 1883 and 1890. Eighty miles southeast from Kunming is the Stone Forest, a large area of oddly shaped peaks made of karst (limestone that has been eroded by underground streams). The scenic walled town of Dali can be seen on a lake along the old Burma Road. See also BAI; BURMA ROAD; DU WENXIU; FLYING TIGERS; HANI; HUI; MIAO; MUSLIMS; MINORITIES, NATIONAL; QING DYNASTY; WAR OF RESISTANCE WITH JAPAN; YI; YUNNAN PROVINCE.

KUNMING LAKE　See SUMMER PALACE.

KUNQU (K'un-Ch'u)　A form of Chinese opera that originated 400 years ago during the Ming dynasty (1368–1644) and has remained to this day the most important theatrical form in China. Kunqu, which literally means "Kun tunes," is named after the Chinese city of Kun-shan. The opera developed in the area around Suzhou in Jiangsu Province, the economic and cultural center of the Lower Yangzi (Changjiang) River valley. Kunqu Opera has influenced Beijing (Peking) Opera, which developed later but is better known in the West. Some of the greatest Kunqu operas include the *The*

Peony Pavilion by Tang Xianzu (T'ang Hsian-tsu; 1550–1617), a love story; *The Peach Blossom Fan* by Kong Shangren (K'ung Shang-jen; 1648–1718), a tragic depiction of the Ming dynasty's overthrow by the Manchus who founded the Qing dynasty (1644–1911); and *The Palace of Eternal Youth* by Hong Sheng (Hung Sheng; c. 1645–1704), the famous story of the tragic love of Tang emperor Xuanzong (Hsuan-tsung; r. 712–56) for his concubine Yang Guifei (Yang Kuei-fei).

Kunqu performers sing, dance and recite dialogue written by poets during the Ming and Qing dynasties. Thus every performer has to be highly trained in all three performing arts of singing, dancing and acting. The stage for a Kunqu performance has no sets and a minimum of props. The colorful, elaborate costumes and makeup worn by the performers convey the emotions and drama of the opera. The orchestra sits to the left of the performers. A bamboo flute is the principal musical instrument. Musicians also play other wind and string instruments, such as a Chinese-style oboe, a one-string *erhu,* and a three-string *sanxian* (*san-hsien*), as well as a small drum, a pair of wooden clappers that set the rhythm for the performers, and gongs and cymbals, which are struck to accent the performers' words and actions. Kunqu is now being performed in the United States by companies such as the Kunqu Society, Inc., based in Hartsdale, New York, whose members formerly belonged to the prestigious Shanghai Kun Opera Company. See also DRAMA; DRUMS; ERHU; FLUTES AND WIND INSTRUMENTS; MING DYNASTY; OPERA; QING DYNASTY; SANXIAN; YANG GUIFEI.

KUO HSI   See GUO XI.

KUO JUO-HSU   See LANDSCAPE PAINTING.

KUO MO-JO (KUO MO-RUO)   See GUO MORUO.

KUOMINTANG   See NATIONALIST PARTY.

KU-SAI   See BANNER SYSTEM, MANCHU.

KWANGSI PROVINCE   See GUANGXI-ZHUANG AUTONOMOUS REGION.

KWANGTUNG PROVINCE   See GUANGDONG PROVINCE.

KWEICHOW PROVINCE   See GUIZHOU PROVINCE.

KYOTO   See CHANG'AN; TANG DYNASTY.

LABORERS See ALL-CHINA FEDERATION OF TRADE UNIONS; COOLIE; SIX COMPANIES, CHINESE; WORK UNIT.

LACQUERWARE (*qiqi* or *ch'i-ch'i*)   Decorative yet useful objects made from a core of wood, bamboo, paper or fabric coated with layers of sap from the lacquer tree (*Rhus verniciflua*), which is native to China and grows wild in the central and southern areas of the country. The Chinese were practicing the art of lacquerware by the 13th century B.C., as seen in the perfectly preserved objects excavated from ancient Chinese tombs. In 1976 archaeologists at Anyang excavated the tomb of Queen Fu Hao, who was buried in a lacquer coffin. By the Han dynasty (206 B.C.–A.D. 220), lacquer production was organized and controlled by the government bureaucracy. The industry was centered in Sichuan Province, where there were two imperial lacquer factories. Individual artisans made the wooden bases, refined the lacquer, brushed on the coatings, applied the decorations, and polished the objects. As many as eight artisans might work on a single piece of lacquerware. Hardened lacquer is waterproof and extremely durable, so the Chinese used it to cover boats, leather, weapons and food utensils. Lacquer production techniques were introduced from China to Korea, Southeast Asia, the Ryuku Islands (Okinawa) and Japan, where artisans brought the art of lacquerware to a very high level, which is still practiced today. In the West, lacquerware became known as "Japan ware."

The lacquer tree is a variety of sumac closely related to poison ivy, so raw lacquer is toxic and artisans must handle the materials carefully. First the sap is tapped from the lacquer tree and refined. Pigments may be added to color the lacquer red, black, yellow, brown, white or green. Red lacquer is made from cinnabar, or mercuric sulfide, which played an important role in Chinese alchemy. Numerous layers of lacquer are then brushed onto the core material, as many as 200 for a finely lacquered object. This is a very time-consuming process because each layer has to harden thoroughly, which can take weeks, and must be ground and polished before the next one can be applied. Lacquer objects may also be beautifully decorated with designs such as flowers made from inlays of small pieces of jade, mother-of-pearl, ivory, tortoiseshell, gold, silver and semiprecious stones. Designs are also produced by carving through the thick layers of lacquer that cover an object. Carved lacquerware became popular during the Southern Song dynasty (1127–1279). Many coats of lacquer are applied to a wood or bamboo base, usually red and yellow, with the final layers brown-black. Deep grooves are then cut into the lacquer to make a design that reveals the layers of contrasting colors. This type of carved lacquer is called *tixi* (*t'i-hsi*) in Chinese but is known in the West by its Japanese name, *guri*.

A wide variety of objects are made from lacquer, including boxes for writing equipment and paper, serving dishes and food containers, trays, cosmetic boxes and even religious sculptures, furniture and musical instruments such as the zither-like *qin* (*ch'in*). Gold lacquer may also be used to repair broken or cracked ceramics. After the 17th century the Chinese art of "Coromandel lacquer" became very popular in Europe, especially for furniture and screens. Layers of black lacquer are applied to a white claylike base and then carved through to create a black linear design against a white background. Lacquerware is still produced in China, and Fuzhou, the capital of Fujian Province, is especially famous for its beautiful and lightweight "bodiless" lacquerware. The Fujian Provincial Arts and Crafts Research Institute trains artisans in complex lacquer production techniques. See also BAMBOO; CINNABAR; FURNITURE, TRADITIONAL; QIN; RYUKYU ISLANDS.

LAMAISM   The popular name for the form of the Buddhist religion practiced in Tibet Autonomous Region (Xizang Zizhiqu). Lamaism is a complex system that developed through the combination of esoteric Indian Buddhist practices, known as Tantrism, with a native form of Tibetan religion, known as Bon, which practices shamanism, exorcism rituals and the worship of various beneficent and harmful deities. There are seven main schools of Lamaism, the most important of which is the Yellow Hat Sect (*dGe lugs pa*). The Dalai Lama, head of the Yellow Hat Sect, is the spiritual and temporal leader of Tibet and is believed by Tibetans to be an incarnation of the Buddhist deity Avalokiteshvara, the patron deity of Tibet. The current Dalai Lama is Tenzin Gyatso (1935–), the 14th Dalai Lama. The word lama is a title for a highly respected religious teacher or monk, called a guru in Indian Sanskrit. Tibetan lamas are celibate and live in strictly organized communities in Buddhist temples and monasteries. They study and chant Buddhist sutras and perform rituals and sacred dances. According to tradition, Buddhism was brought to Tibet in the early seventh century from India and China, during the reign of King Srong btsan sgam po (c. 620–629). He patronized the religion and ordered scholars to create a system of writing so that Buddhist sutras (scriptures) could be translated into the Tibetan language. The first monastery was established in Tibet near the end of the eighth century. By the 12th century, Lamaism had become the national religion of the Tibetan people. Tibetans revere Mount Kailas as their most sacred mountain.

In the mid-13th century the Mongol ruler Mongke appointed a Tibetan lama named Namo to administer all Buddhist affairs throughout the entire Mongol empire. The Mongols were a group of nomadic tribes that originated in Mongolia, north of the Great Wall, and established a vast empire, ruling China under the Yuan dynasty (1279–1368). The Mongols patronized Lamaism and awarded millions of acres of land to the most important Lamaist monasteries. In 1557 the third Dalai Lama converted the Altan Khan, during his time the most powerful Mongol ruler. After the Mongol Yuan dynasty was overthrown by the Han Chinese Ming dynasty (1368–1644), the Mongols continued to practice Lamaism. The religion underwent a reform in the 15th century, which gave birth to a new sect, founded by Tsong-kha-pa (d. 1419), known as the Yellow Hat Sect, in contrast to the older Red Hat Sect. His leadership later became divided into two lines of succession from his first and second disciples, the Dalai Lamas and the Panchen Lamas. Each new Dalai Lama and Panchen Lama was supposedly the reincarnation of the previous one. When one of them died, the head lamas searched among newborn Tibetans to find the boy in whom he was reincarnated. The Dalai Lama and Panchen Lama were considered equivalent spiritually, but the Dalai Lama always had more political power in Tibet.

Lamaism was also adopted by the Manchus, an ethnic group from Manchuria (modern northeastern China) that ruled China under the Qing dynasty (1644–1911). Qing emperor Yongzheng (Yung-cheng; r. 1723–36) turned the palace where he resided in Beijing, the Chinese capital, into a Lamaistic temple, which can still be seen today. Qing rulers greatly expanded the Mongol Empire in China until it reached its greatest size during the reign of Qianlong (Ch'ien-lung; r. 1736–95). The Dalai Lama visited the Qing court in Beijing in 1652, bringing tribute to the emperor, who gave him the gold symbols of authority held by the ruler of a vassal state within China's tribute system. He rebuilt the Potala Palace in Lhasa, the capital of Tibet, to be the residence for himself and subsequent Dalai Lamas.

In 1717 the Dzungars invaded Tibet and captured Lhasa. In 1720 the Qing sent two armies into Tibet that forced the Dzungars out and installed the seventh Dalai Lama in the Potala Palace. The Qing intervened in Tibet several more times in the 18th century. During Qianlong's reign the Yellow Hat Sect, led by the fifth Dalai Lama, defeated the Red Sect of Lamaism with the aid of a Mongol leader named Guushi Khan. After an intervention in 1750, Emperor Qianlong decreed that the Dalai Lama would be the sole political ruler of Tibet and that a council of Qing ministers would be formed in Lhasa to advise him. The Panchen Lama was ordered to stay at Shigatse, west of Lhasa. Tibet remained a vassal state throughout the Qing dynasty.

In the 20th century, Tibetans attempted to assert their independence. After the Chinese Communist Party (CCP) founded the People's Republic of China (PRC) in 1949, they declared Tibet an autonomous region of the PRC and sent troops into the region in 1950. The Tibetans rebelled against the Chinese in 1958–59 but were harshly suppressed. The current Dalai Lama, along with tens of thousands of Tibetans, fled to India, where he established the Tibetan government-in-exile. He has always advocated peaceful means for resolving the problem of Tibet's status, and in 1989 he was awarded the Nobel Peace Prize. During the Cultural Revolution (1966–76), Red Guards destroyed thousands of Tibetan Buddhist temples, monasteries, religious objects and scriptures and killed a great number of lamas. Since 1980 the Chinese government has restored some of the monasteries, including the Potala Palace. Tibetans in exile in India, Nepal and other countries still practice Lamaism. In 1995 the Dalai Lama became embroiled in a still-unresolved controversy with the PRC government over the reincarnation of the Panchen Lama in a six-year-old boy. The PRC refused to recognized the boy confirmed by the Dalai Lama and selected another boy as the reincarnation. See also BUDDHISM; CULTURAL REVOLUTION; DALAI LAMA; KAILAS, MOUNT; MONGOLS; QING DYNASTY; TEMPLES; TIBET; TIBETAN; TRIBUTE SYSTEM; YUAN DYNASTY.

LAN CAIHE See EIGHT IMMORTALS.

LAN MA (1915–1976) Original name Dong Shixiong (Tung Shi-hsiung); one of China's greatest male film actors, and the most famous Chinese film actor from the 1930s to the 1950s. Lan Ma was born into a family of doctors. As a child he became interested in acting through some neighbors who were in show business, and he began acting on the stage in primary school. At age 16 he became a professional actor and changed his name to Lan Ma. Because of his gentle and easygoing nature, his friends gave him the nickname "Lazy Horse," which is also pronounced Lan Ma. He was a charming and versatile actor who played about one hundred different characters during his career. In 1939 he played a slow but kindhearted salesman in his first film, *Paradise on an Isolated Island*. Some of his other films include *Dreaming in Paradise, Sons and Daughters in a Troubled World, Hope in the Human World* and *Three Women*. Lan Ma's greatest role was the male lead, Hu Zhiqing, in *Myriads of Lights*. Hu is an honest white-collar worker who tries to support his family during the difficult period following China's War of Resistance against Japan (1937–45; World War II), which was marked by government corruption and economic and social turmoil. Audiences felt great sympathy for the man, who loses his job, sees his family break apart, is hurt in a traffic accident, and feels anger and sorrow because despite all his efforts he has been prevented from taking care of his family. This film, one of the classics of the Chinese cinema, was shown abroad in the early 1990s to critical acclaim. See also WAR OF RESISTANCE AGAINST JAPAN.

LAN TAO ISLAND   See HONG KONG.

LAN TS'AI-HO   See EIGHT IMMORTALS.

LANCANG RIVER   See MEKONG RIVER.

LANCHOU   See LANZHOU.

LAND REFORM BY COMMUNISTS   A process for confiscating land from landowners and wealthy peasants and redistributing it to poorer peasants, which the Chinese Communist Party (CCP) used to advance its cause in modern China. The Communists began this practice in their soviet base in Jiangxi Province during the late 1920s and early 1930s and used it in the villages they brought under their control in northern China during their civil war with the Nationalists (Kuomintang; KMT). After the Communists defeated the KMT and founded the People's Republic of China (PRC) in 1949, they passed the Agrarian Reform Law of June 28, 1951, under which they expanded the land reform program to affect nearly all Chinese citizens. They mobilized hundreds of thousands of cadres (*ganbu* or *kan-pu*; party officials) to spread out through villages in the vast Chinese countryside, where they established peasant associations and led lower and middle peasants in testifying against landlords and wealthy peasants. They encouraged the peasants to speak out at public demonstrations, called "struggle meetings" because their goal was to foment a class struggle, about how much they had suffered from landlord exploitation. The worst landlords and wealthiest peasants were publicly paraded before a People's Court to be denounced, humiliated and even beaten or killed. Some were allowed to be reeducated or rehabilitated through physical labor. Two million Chinese may have died in the slave labor system during the first five years of the PRC and more than one million may have been executed. Many people committed suicide to avoid being subjected to such punishment.

Peasant organizations were set up to redistribute the land. They took some or all of the land from landlords and wealthy peasants who farmed part and leased part of their land. They let middle peasants keep the land they were already farming. And they alloted new land to poor peasants and landless farm workers. Altogether, titles to about 45 percent of China's arable land were redistributed to the 60 to 70 percent of farm families that had previously owned very little or no land. After the Communists completed land reform in an area, they encouraged farmers to form small "mutual aid teams" of six or seven households that would cooperate in some aspects of agricultural production. The process of land reform also displaced former village leaders in favor of new leaders, whom the CCP further indoctrinated in revolutionary activity. By the end of 1953 the Communists had demolished the traditional structure under which landlords and wealthy peasants controlled rural China, and they had redistributed parcels of land and material goods to more than 100 million poorer

families. Land reform did not remove land from private ownership, between 1949 and 1958. By that year, after the Communists had consolidated the national government of the PRC, they began combining farms into collectives known as people's communes. See also AGRICULTURE; CADRE; CHINESE COMMUNIST PARTY; CIVIL WAR BETWEEN COMMUNISTS AND NATIONALISTS; PEASANTS AND PEASANT REBELLIONS; PEOPLE'S COMMUNE; PEOPLE'S REPUBLIC OF CHINA.

LANDSCAPE PAINTING   (*shanshuihua*)   One of the main types of traditional Chinese painting, literally called "mountains and water" (*shanshui*) after its two main subjects. Other types of Chinese painting include bird-and-flower, figure and ink painting. Landscape painting was influenced by the Daoist tradition, which emphasizes nature and man's harmony with it. Human figures, when included in a landscape painting, were very small. Several elements are standard in Chinese landscape paintings, such as rugged mountains partly covered with misty clouds, a waterfall, groups of trees, and perhaps a valley with a lake or river, a bridge, a boat and a hut alongside the water. The paintings have no fixed perspective, as does Western painting. Some Chinese paintings were mounted on large vertical hanging scrolls, which were hung only for a few days at a time. However, more were executed on horizontal rolling handscrolls, which enable the viewer to move through the landscape, enjoying different aspects while the scroll is rolled open a few feet at a time from right to left. The earliest Chinese landscape paintings were done on silk, but later artists used highly absorbent paper as well as silk.

Chinese landscape painting originated during the Three Kingdoms Period (220–80), but natural scenes were painted only as the background for figure paintings or portraits. During the Sui (581–618) and Tang (618–907) dynasties, artists began making paintings that had natural landscapes as their central theme. During the Tang, the literati (*wenren* or *wen-jen*), or Confucian-educated scholars who staffed the imperial bureaucracy or civil service, had the time and freedom to paint. The great painters Wu Daozi (Wu Tao-tzu; active c. 720–60) and Li Sixun (Li Ssu-hsun; 651–716) developed landscape painting as a distinct type of painting. Wang Wei (699–761), who was also influenced by the Buddhist religion, is credited with inventing monochrome ink landscape painting, and Li Sixun and his son Li Zhaodao (Li Chao-tao; active c. 670–730) with developing colored landscape painting, which later became known as the "blue and green" tradition. Landscape painting became closely associated with calligraphy, the fine art of writing Chinese characters with a brush and ink. Landscape painting employs water-based black and colored inks and has four main approaches: ink and wash (*shuimo*); light crimson (*qianjiang* or *ch'ian-chiang*), a method to achieve light-colored landscape paintings by adding strokes in reddish brown to a wash-painting base; blue and green (*qinglu* or *ch'ing-lu*), which uses these colors, produced from minerals; and golden and green (*jinbi* or *chin-pi*), which adds gold to *qinglu* paintings. *Shuimo*, the basis of the other three techniques, uses only ink and water to depict natural scenes. Light and dark effects are produced by varying the brushwork and the use of the ink and water. The artist must move his brush confidently without wavering or stopping and, unlike Western oil painters, cannot alter the lines already drawn.

During the Five Dynasties Period (907–960), Chinese landscape painting matured and many excellent landscape artists were active. Landscape painting reached its full development during the Northern Song dynasty (960–1126) and remained the dominant style of traditional Chinese painting into the modern era. It became especially associated with the literati, who considered themselves "amateurs," in the best sense of the word, in contrast to the professional painters of the imperial court. For them, painting was a means of meditating and expressing their self-cultivation. They were also influenced by Buddhism, especially the Chan ("meditation") Sect, known in the West by the Japanese name Zen Buddhism. Literati painting, called *wenrenhua (wen-jen-hua)*, originated in the group of artists around the poet Su Shi (Su Shih; also known as Su Dongpo or Su Tung-p'o; 1036–1101). Landscape painting, calligraphy and poetry are all executed with the same brush, ink and other utensils, known as the Four Treasures of the Scholar's Study. Poems were often inscribed in calligraphy in empty spaces on the paintings, usually by the artists or their friends. The Chinese classify these three arts together as the "Three Perfections" (*sanjue* or *san-chueh*). Landscape painting also became associated with gardening, another literati activity, which emphasized mountains and water, and harmony between the human and the natural world. Elements of nature have symbolic meaning in Chinese landscape paintings; for example, pine trees and cranes symbolize long life, bamboo loyalty and plum blossoms purity.

The Spirit of the Brush, a collection of essays by Chinese painters between 317 and 960, expresses their intentions as artists and their criteria for evaluating paintings. Chinese landscape painting developed into two schools, both of which used primarily blue and green in their work. The Northern School includes painters during the first part of the Song dynasty, known as the Northern Song dynasty, which had its capital at Kaifeng in Henan Province. In 1127 Kaifeng was captured by the Jurchen, an ethnic group from Manchuria (modern northeastern China) who established the Jin dynasty (1115–1234) in northern China. The Song court fled south and established its capital at the beautiful city of Hangzhou, south of the Yangzi River (Changjiang) in Zhejiang Province (Southern Song dynasty, 1127–1279). Many artists moved to Hangzhou and continued the landscape painting tradition. The Northern School of Painting is characterized by strong, rough brushstrokes. The Southern School is characterized by flowing, elegant brushstrokes.

Some of the most important Northern Song painters include Su Shi, Mi Fu (also known as Mi Fei), Li Cheng, Fan Kuan (Fan K'uan), Liu Songnian (Liu Sung-nien), Li Sixun (Li-hsun), Guo Xi (Kuo Hsi) and his son Guo Ruoxu (Kuo Juo-hsu), Xu Daoning (Hsu Tao-ning), Ma Yuan and Xia Gui (Hsia Kuei). The latter two originated their own style, using bold "ax-cut-texture strokes," in which the angles of the brush strokes seem to hack out the shapes of the rocks. They had been associated with the Northern School but moved to the Southern court at Hangzhou, where their style became known as the Ma-Xia (Ma-Hsia) School. Other Southern painters include Li Tang (Li T'ang), Dong Yuan (Tung Yuan), Mu Qi (Mu Ch'i) and Liang Kai (Liang K'ai).

Most Chinese painters still lived in the Yangzi River valley during the Yuan (1279–1368) and Ming (1368–1644) dynasties, when the capital was moved north to Beijing, widening the division between literati and professional court painters. Great painters during the Yuan include Gao Kegong (Kao K'o-kung), Huang Gongwang (Huang Kung-wang), Zhao Mengfu (Chao Meng-fu), Wu Chen (Wu Ch'en), Wang Meng and Ni Zan (Ni Tsan). During the Ming, Chinese painting was dominated by the Wu and Zhe (Che) schools. The foremost painter was Shen Zhou (Shen Chou). His best-known student was Wen Zhengming (Wen Cheng-ming). Other major Ming painters include Dai Jin (Tai Chin), Cheng Hongshu (Ch'en Hung-shu), Dong Qichang (Tung Ch'i-ch'ang) and Xu Wei (Hsu Wei). Dong Qichang was also an art critic and historian who devised the categories of Northern and Southern Schools of Painting. His student, Wang Gai (Wang Kai), was the main compiler of *The Mustard Seed Garden Manual of Painting,* an important text on Chinese painting. During the Qing dynasty (1644–1911), major painters include Wu Li, Gong Xian (Kung Hsien), Bada Shanren (Pa-ta Shan-jen; also known as Ju Da or Chu Ta), Shitao (Shih-t'ao; also known as Daoji or Tao-chi) and Wu Changshi (Wu Ch'ang-shih). Ren Bonian (Jen Po-nien; also known as Ren Yi or Jen I; 1840–96) is considered by many the most interesting of the late Qing artists. Important painters during the modern era include Qi Baishi (Ch'i Pai-shih), Chang Ta-ch'ien (Zhang Daqian) and Zhao Shao-ang (Chao Shao-ang). Huang Binhong (Huang Pin-hung) was one of the last of the great Wu school painters. See also BIRD-AND-FLOWER PAINTING; CALLIGRAPHY; CHAN SECT OF BUDDHISM; CONFUCIANISM; DAOISM; FIGURE PAINTING; FOUR TREASURES OF THE STUDY; GARDENS; HANGZHOU; INK PAINTING; LITERATI; MUSTARD SEED GARDEN MANUAL OF PAINTING; NORTHERN SCHOOL OF PAINTING; PAPER; SCROLLS; SILK; SOUTHERN SCHOOL OF PAINTING; WU SCHOOL OF PAINTING; INDIVIDUAL ARTISTS.

LANGUAGE, CHINESE   The language spoken by members of the Han ethnic group who comprise about 92 percent of China's population, and by Chinese who reside in Taiwan, Singapore and other countries. Chinese is the major language in the Sino-Tibetan linguistic group, which also includes the languages of Tibet, Vietnam, Thailand, Laos and Burma. There are at least seven major families of the Chinese language, including Mandarin, Cantonese, Wu, Hakka, Gan, Xiang and Min (including Taiwanese). These are commonly termed dialects, but they differ from each other so much that a person who can speak only the southern dialect of Cantonese, for example, cannot understand a person who speaks the northern dialect of Mandarin. The seven language families are further divided into dialects and subdialects. However, all Chinese dialects have nearly the same grammar, and everyone who speaks Chinese, no matter what dialect, uses the same system of ideographs or characters for writing the language. Since the early 20th century, Chinese officials have promoted Mandarin, especially the dialect spoken in the capital city of Beijing, as the national spoken language. Mandarin, the Western name for the northern Chinese dialect, is now spoken by about three-fourths of all Chinese citizens. The classical Chinese term for the Mandarin dialect is *guanhua,* "official language," because when imperial government officials were sent from the capital at Beijing to the Chinese provinces, they spoke Mandarin and communicated with people in those regions through interpreters. Today most Chinese speak Mandarin and also their own regional dialects. Members of China's 55 officially designated national minority ethnic groups study the Chinese language but are also permitted to use their own languages. The Chinese call spoken Mandarin *putonghua*, "common speech." In 1956 the Chinese government introduced *putonghua* as the language to be used by teachers in schools and in the national broadcast media.

Cantonese, which is spoken in Guangdong Province, Guangxi-Zhuang Autonomous Region and Hong Kong, is the second-most common dialect in China. Since most Chinese immigrants to America came from Guangdong and most immigrants to Great Britain came from Hong Kong, Cantonese is also spoken by most Chinese in those countries. The Wu dialect of Shanghai and the Min dialect of Fujian Province are also spoken by many people. The Chinese further distinguish between *baihua*, "vernacular language," and *wenyan*, "classical language." The latter was the language used in the imperial bureaucracy and is not spoken but used only in writing. It has fallen out of use since the May Fourth Movement of 1919, which stimulated an interest by Chinese writers in using vernacular, the daily language of ordinary people, rather than classical language. This is known as the New Culture Movement. Scholars still learn the classical language in order to study the classical texts of Chinese literature.

Chinese is a tonal language in which one syllable can be pronounced with different voice pitches or rising or falling notes to convey different meanings. It contains a great number of homonyms, words that are pronounced the same but have different meanings, so tones are necessary for conveying the meaning of words. For example, the syllable written *mai* and pronounced "my" can mean either "to buy" or "to sell," depending on whether the speaker's tone rises or falls. *Ma* can mean "mother," "hemp," "horse" or "to scold." *Putonghua* has four tones: a high pitch, rising tone, falling-rising tone and falling tone. The Cantonese dialect has six tones with variations within the six, making it even more difficult to speak than Mandarin.

Chinese grammar is fairly simple. Sentences are constructed in the order of subject-verb-object, the same as English. Adjectives precede nouns and adverbs precede verbs. Word order is very important. Chinese has no articles such as "a" or "the," no verb tenses, no plurals and no gender. These are discerned from the grammatical and situational contexts of sentences. The Chinese language is monosyllabic. When it is written, each word has its meaning represented by an ideograph, of which there are about 60,000, although most of these are not used. In the modern era, however, many polysyllabic words are being formed by putting two characters together. More than 30 systems have been devised over the past several centuries for transcribing Chinese into a phonetic script using the Roman alphabet. The Wade-Giles System has been employed for more than a century and is still commonly used in the Western world. In 1958 the Chinese government adopted the pinyin system, which is now also used in the West. Scholars and others who are concerned with China must be familiar with both sys-

tems even if they prefer one of the two. See also CALLIGRAPHY; HAN; MANDARIN; MAY FOURTH MOVEMENT OF 1919; PINYIN SYSTEM OF ROMANIZATION; POPULATION, CHINESE; PUTONGHUA; WADE-GILES SYSTEM OF ROMANIZATION; WRITING SYSTEM, CHINESE.

LANGYAO　See ENAMELWARE.

LANKAVATARA SUTRA　See BODHIDHARMA.

LANTAU ISLAND　See HONG KONG.

LANTERN FESTIVAL (Yuan Xiao Jie or Yuan Hsiao Chieh, "Feast of the First Full Moon")　A festival held in North China on the full moon that falls on the 15th day of the first month in the traditional lunar calendar (around mid-February in the Western calendar). The Lantern Festival closes the two-week New Year Festival. Children carry candlelit paper lanterns with many colors and designs, such as red circles, goldfish, dragons, monkeys and boats. Houses and shops are also decorated with lanterns. Firecrackers are set off to scare away evil spirits. Many villages hold stilt dances or parades with dragon and lion dances during the New Year and Lantern festivals. Special foods are eaten, such as boiled taro, wheat flour cooked to resemble cotton balls, or glutinous rice balls with sweet fillings. A traditional game among the educated classes is "guess the lantern's riddle" (*cai deng mi* or *ts'ai teng mi*); the riddles, usually literary allusions very difficult to guess, are pasted on hanging lanterns. The Lantern Festival is mentioned in historical records dating as far back as the Han dynasty (206 B.C.–A.D. 220). At that time the festival was marked by sacrificial rituals for Tai Yi, the God of the Polar Star, who was thought to embody the two universal principles of yin and yang. See also DRAGON; LANTERNS; LION; NEW YEAR FESTIVAL; STILT WALKING; YIN AND YANG.

LANTERNS (*denglong* or *teng-lung*; *tideng* or *t'i-teng*) Lanterns are made from thin bamboo or wooden frames covered with paper or silk, although other materials may be used, such as sheepskin or glass. The paper may be painted or cut into openwork designs, and the silk may be painted or embroidered. Farmers also make lantern frames from wire or rice stalks. Lanterns can have a great variety of shapes, such as a sphere, square or thin oblong; people, gods, boats or flowers; and animals or supernatural creatures, such as dragons, phoenixes or cranes. For example, Guanyin (Kuan-yin), the Buddhist Goddess of Mercy, may be depicted holding a child in her arms. Rabbit lanterns are popular with Chinese children because they traditionally see a rabbit-in-the-moon rather than a man-in-the-moon. Some lanterns even have mechanical devices that allow them to move like a flying bird or a swimming fish. "galloping horse lanterns" (*zoumadeng* or *chou-ma-teng*) keep spinning around because a burning candle heats the air, which turns a wheel hidden inside them. So-called "magic lanterns" have revolving panels that tell a story, such as Monkey King defeating a demon. Lanterns are hung on a wall, carried on a pole or placed on a stand. They are lit by burning a candle or oil inside them and are brightly decorated.

Red, black and yellow are the predominant colors used to decorate lanterns. Red symbolizes happiness for the Chinese, so red is commonly used at Chinese festivals and other happy occasions such as birthdays and weddings. Some lanterns are made with red paper with small holes punched in them to illuminate an auspicious character, such as long life or double happiness. A pair of red lanterns is traditionally hung at a family's gate to celebrate a wedding. People in the far north make lanterns by freezing layers of ice and placing red candles inside them. Chinese lanterns often have long red tassels hanging from them, as well as other decorations, such as pearls and carved jade pendants. The frames may also be elaborately carved with openwork scenes and designs. The most expensive lanterns are made with white silk or gauze on which is painted auspicious characters or objects, or famous scenes from Chinese history. Lanterns made in the city of Suzhou from painted silk with sandalwood, boxwood or mahogany frames, are considered the most beautiful and elegant. The Chinese display lanterns for all happy occasions, and cities hang red lanterns in city squares to celebrate the Spring Festival (which usually falls in early February) and national holidays such as May Day (May 1) and National Day (October 1). See also BAMBOO; DOUBLE HAPPINESS AND LONG LIFE; LANTERN FESTIVAL; PAPER; WEDDINGS, TRADITIONAL; INDIVIDUAL ANIMALS AND SUPERNATURAL CREATURES.

LANTIAN See NEOLITHIC PERIOD.

LANZHOU The capital city of Gansu Province and the second-largest city in northwestern China, with a population of more than 2 million. The climate is warm in summer but very cold and dry in winter, and strong winds blow in the spring. Lanzhou lies on the upper reaches of the Yellow River (Huanghe) in the eastern part of the Gansu Corridor, a narrow desert area that connects northeastern China and Xinjiang-Uighur Autonomous Region. For more than 2,000 years Lanzhou served as an oasis for caravans; it was also a key garrison town. It was also an important oasis town on the Silk Road along which silk-laden camel caravans traveled across Asia to the Middle East. It was a strategic supply depot for the Chinese struggle against Japanese occupation during the War of Resistance against Japan (1937–45, World War II).

Lanzhou's history goes back at least to 81 B.C., when it was known as Jizheng, "Gold City." But the surrounding area remained very poor until after 1949 when industrial modernization took place. Chinese nuclear power research has been centered in Lanzhou since 1960. Major industries include petrochemicals, machinery, railway cars and engines, textiles, metal working, and leather and wool processing. A dam on the Yellow River west of Lanzhou provides electric power, as well as water necessary for the city's uranium-enriching plant. Unfortunately, Lanzhou has become badly polluted. The city is an important center for trade between northwestern and southwestern China and the Central Plains of Gansu. Railway lines also make the city a major link between northwestern China and the eastern China coast. Many national minorities live in the Lanzhou area, most of them Muslim, including Uighurs, Mongols, Hui people; and Tibetans, who are Buddhist. They are aided by the National Minorities Institute in Lanzhou. Gansu Province Museum has exhibits on the history of the area, including cultural relics of the Silk Road. Its *Flying Horse of Gansu* is one of the most reproduced sculptures of China. Other sites include White Pagoda Mountain and Five Springs Park. Binglingsi Grottoes to the south were built in the fourth century and added to during many dynasties. They include 183 caves and an 88-foot high statue of Maitreya, the Buddha of the Future. See also GANSU PROVINCE; MAITREYA AND MANJUSRI; MINORITIES, NATIONAL; SILK ROAD; WAR OF RESISTANCE AGAINST JAPAN.

LAO SHE (Lao Sheh; 1899–1966) An author who became famous for his humor and his depictions of traditional life in the capital city of Beijing. Lao She was not a Han or ethnic Chinese but a Manchu, one of China's national minority ethnic groups. When he was born, the Manchus were ruling China under the Qing dynasty (1644–1911), which was overthrown and replaced by the modern Republic of China (1912–49). He bacame a schoolteacher and published the novel *Lao Zhang's Philsosophy*. In the 1920s, Lao She taught in London and became influenced by British writers, especially Charles Dickens, whose eccentric characters are reflected in Lao She's early works. He was also influenced by D. H. Lawrence and Joseph Conrad, and he drew upon *Gulliver's Travels* by Jonathan Swift for his novel *Cat Country*. This was a satirical allegory, published serially in 1931–32, about the difficult conditions in China, which was being wracked by war between the Communists and the Nationalists (Kuomintang) while the Japanese were building a military force there. This work inspired patriotic Chinese students against Japan and helped the Communist cause. In 1925 Lao She began writing fiction in the unique vernacular language of Beijing and produced many novels, including *Biography of Niu Dianze (Tientse)*, *Divorce*, *Four Generations under One Roof* and *Rickshaw Boy* (1937), his best and most popular novel. He realistically described the life of a man who suffered, working like a horse by pulling passengers in a two-wheeled rickshaw through crowded city streets. Lao She also wrote many Western-style plays, including *The Problem of Face*. He moved to New York City in 1946 and became very famous in the United States due to the English translation of *Rickshaw Boy* and his play *Camel Xiangzi*. He returned to China in 1950, after the Communists had won the civil war and founded the People's Republic of China in 1949, even though his friends warned him that life there might be very difficult. Lao She was chosen to "polish" the autobiography supposedly written by Puyi (1906–67), the last Manchu emperor of the Qing dynasty under the reign-title Xuantong, whom the Japanese made head of Manchukuo, the puppet state they established in northeastern China (Manchuria). The book was actually written by a number of Chinese authors. Lao She died tragically during the Cultural Revolution (1966–76) when Red Guards severely beat him for being influenced by the West, and he consequently committed suicide. Since then, his plays have been revived in China and his novels have been serialized for television dramas. In 1984 the Chinese film director Ling Zifeng adapted Lao She's famous novel to make the film *Rickshaw Boy*. The 16-volume *Collected Works of Lao She* has been translated into many languages. See also BEIJING; CIVIL WAR BETWEEN COMMUNISTS AND NATIONALISTS; CULTURAL REVOLUTION; FACE; MANCHU; MANCHUKUO; PUYI, HENRY.

LAO TAN See LAOZI.

LAO TZU See LAOZI.

LAOGAI See FANG LIZHI; MOST-FAVORED-NATION TRADE STATUS; WEI JINGSHENG; WU, HARRY.

LAOZI (Lao Tzu, "Old Master"; also known as Lao Tan) The supposed author of the *Daodejing* (*Tao Te Ching*, "The Way and Its Power"), the basic text of Daoism, one of the two major Chinese philosophical traditions, along with Confucianism. Although legends place Laozi in the sixth century B.C., the *Daodejing* was actually written down in the third century B.C., *Dao* means "way," "path" or "road." In Daoist thought, the *Dao* represents the fundamental principle that pervades the universe and all things in it, including human beings. Since all things are constantly moving and changing, the wise person knows how to yield and flow with the *Dao*, described by the *Daodejing* using the metaphors of woman, child and water. Whereas Confucianism emphasizes social obligations and the need to act according to specified behaviors, Daoism emphasizes "doing nothing" (*wu wei*), not interfering in the workings of the universe and being humble and spontaneous like a child.

The name Laozi is first mentioned in documents attributed to Zhuangzi (Chuang Tzu, 369–286 B.C.), a great Daoist thinker. These documents claim that Laozi was contemporary of, but somewhat older than, Confucius (551–479 B.C.). By the first century B.C., so many legends had accumulated around Laozi that it became impossible to identify him with any historical person. By the second century A.D. he had been transformed by myth into a superhuman being, the worship of whom was organized and was even supported by the Tang dynasty (618–907), because Tang emperors claimed to be descended from him. One legend states that Laozi's mother carried him in the womb for 62 years and that he was born as a white-haired old man who spoke at birth, pointing to a plum tree and taking the surname Li (plum). Another story contends that he was a government official in Luoyang, capital of the Zhou dynasty (1100–256 B.C.), and had a son who became a soldier. When Laozi was 160 years old, he rejected the corruption of the Tang dynasty and traveled west toward Central Asia. He is usually portrayed riding west on his ox. According to legend, while Laozi was making his journey, the official at the Hangu mountain pass asked him to write a book, and so he recorded the *Daodejing*. When he finished, he continued on his way and was never seen again.

The Buddhist religion, founded in India in the sixth century B.C., was introduced into China around the first century B.C. through Central Asia, and hence some Chinese argued that Laozi was actually the Buddha or one of Buddha's disciples. Daoists in turn claimed that Laozi had taught the "western barbarians" (the Buddhists) only a simplified version of his philosophy on his journey west. In fact, Buddhist sutras (scriptures) were translated into Chinese using many terms from Daoist thought. See also BUDDHISM; CONFUCIANISM; DAODEJING; DAOISM; OX; ZHUANGZI.

LAST EMPEROR, THE See PUYI, HENRY.

LATER HAN DYNASTY See EASTERN HAN DYNASTY.

LATER JIN DYNASTY See FIVE DYNASTIES PERIOD; NURHACHI.

LATER SHU KINGDOM See TEN KINGDOMS PERIOD.

LATTIMORE, OWEN (1900–1989) A renowned American scholar of Central Asian history and culture specializing in the Chinese provinces of Mongolia, Manchuria and Xinjiang (formerly Chinese Turkestan). Lattimore was born in Washington, D.C. but raised in China. He was educated in Switzerland and England, but returned to China in 1919. He traveled to Mongolia and Xinjiang from 1926 to 1927. During the 1920s he worked as a businessman and journalist in Beijing, Shanghai and Tianjin. During this time he became interested in the cultures of Mongolia, Manchuria and the border regions of inner Asia where Turkic languages are spoken. Throughout his life, Lattimore frequently visited and wrote pioneering scholarly works about these areas. His wife, Eleanor Holgate Lattimore, accompanied him and was the first American woman to travel overland from Beijing to India. She wrote about their adventurous honeymoon in *Turkestan Reunion* (1934). He received support from the Harvard-Yenching Institute, the John Simon Guggenheim Memorial Foundation and the Institute for Pacific Relations. Lattimore attended graduate school at Harvard University but never completed a degree. Between 1933 and 1941 he served as editor of the journal *Pacific Affairs*. In 1938 he was named director of the Walter Hines Page School of International Relations at Johns Hopkins University. He wrote dozens of journal articles and books, including *The Desert Road to Turkestan* (1928), *High Tartary* (1930), *Manchuria, Cradle of Conflict* (1932), *The Mongols of Manchuria* (1934), *Inner Asian Frontiers of China* (1940) and *Mongol Journeys* (1941).

During World War II, the U.S. government assigned him to be a political adviser to General Chiang Kai-shek (1887–1975), leader of the Nationalist Chinese (Kuomintang; KMT) government. Lattimore served at Chiang's headquarters from 1941 to 1942. He served as deputy director of Pacific operations for the U.S. Office of War Information (1942–44) and with the Reparations Commission in Occupied Japan (1945–46). After the war he returned to academia and published *Solution in Asia* (1945), *The Situation in Asia* (1949) and *Pivot of Asia* (1950). He and Eleanor Lattimore wrote *The Making of Modern China, A Short History* (1944).

In 1950 Senator Joseph McCarthy accused Lattimore of being the main Soviet espionage agent in the United States and of being a Chinese Communist sympathizer who conspired to destroy American support for Chiang Kai-shek so that Mao Zedong (Mao Tse-tung; 1893–1976) could bring the Communists to power in China. Lattimore defended himself before the Senate Foreign Relations Committee and denounced McCarthy's charges as false. The committee agreed that Lattimore had never been a communist and never acted at the direction of a foreign power. He then published *Ordeal by Slander* (1950). However, for two years the Senate Internal Security Committee under Senator Pat McCarran debated the question, "Who Lost China?" and concluded that Lattimore had directed a group of prominent American scholars and government officials who had attempted to direct American policy to benefit Chinese communism. Federal courts dismissed Justice Department indictments against Lattimore because the FBI could not find one reliable witness to testify against him. But this controversy forced Lattimore to resign as director of the Page School at Johns Hopkins. He then worked for the United Nations, lectured in Europe and traveled in Central Asia.

From 1963 to 1970, Lattimore was a highly regarded professor of Chinese studies at Leeds University in England. He wrote *Nationalism and Revolution in Mongolia* (1955), *Nomads and Commissars: Mongolia* (1962), *Studies in Frontier History* (1962), *History and Revelation in China* (1974) and, with Eleanor Lattimore, *Silks, Spices and Empire* (1968). He also translated and edited, with Fujiko Isono, *The Diluv Khutagt: Memoirs and Autobiography of a Mongol Buddhist Reincarnation in Religion and Revolution* (1982). After his death, Lattimore's papers were given to the Library of Congress by the Lattimore Institute for Mongolian Studies. In 1992, the University of California Press published *Owen Lattimore and the "Loss" of China* by Robert P. Newman. See also CHIANG KAI-SHEK; MAO ZEDONG; MANCHURIA; MONGOLIA; PEOPLE'S REPUBLIC OF CHINA; XINJIANG-UIGHUR AUTONOMOUS REGION.

LAW, SCHOOL OF   See LEGALIST SCHOOL OF THOUGHT.

LAWS   See CONSTITUTION, STATE, OF 1954; LEGAL SYSTEM; SUPREME PEOPLE'S COURT.

LEAGUE OF LEFT-WING WRITERS   See LU XUN.

LEAGUE OF NATIONS   The League of Nations was an international association established by the Treaty of Versailles following World War I (1914–18) to discuss disputes between nations and to work out agreements that would prevent wars. China had entered World War I in 1917 by declaring war on Germany in hopes of getting back Shandong Province, which was then controlled by Japan. The Qing dynasty (1644–1911), China's last imperial dynasty, had given Germany concessions in Shandong in the late 19th century. Japan joined World War I on the Allied side and seized German holdings in Shandong and Pacific islands. In 1918 the Chinese government in Beijing signed a secret agreement with Japan affirming Japan's claim to Shandong. In 1919, at the Paris Peace Conference at Versailles, this secret deal was made public and the Chinese people were furious. Massive student demonstrations against the Chinese government and Japan broke out on May 4, 1919, and escalated into a nationwide opposition in China known as the May Fourth Movement. Chinese students closed down the schools and universities and boycotted Japanese goods, and merchants and workers supported the boycott. The Chinese government finally told the Chinese delegates at Versailles to walk out and not sign the peace treaty. The League of Nations held its first meeting in 1920 in Geneva, Switzerland, with representatives from 41 member nations. The problem of Shandong Province was settled at the Washington Conference of 1921–22, where a bilateral treaty between Japan and China returned Shandong to Chinese control.

In 1931 Japan invaded Manchuria (northeastern China), and China requested assistance from the League of Nations and the United States. The Western powers gave China verbal and moral support as stated in the so-called Stimson Doctrine, which the League of Nations incorporated in a res-

olution proposed by Great Britain. In November 1931 the league sent a commission to China, headed by Great Britain's Lord Lytton, to investigate the dispute between China and Japan. In February 1932, Japan declared Manchuria's independence from China, and in March it established the puppet state of Manchukuo. Japanese forces also attempted to take the major Chinese port city of Shanghai. In October 1932 the commission issued the *Lytton Report,* which criticized Japan's actions in China for violating international treaties. However, the commission saw that Japan could not be forced to leave Manchuria, so the report recommended that Manchuria be governed by an autonomous administration under Chinese sovereignty that made special provision for Japan's economic interests in the region, which is rich in minerals, timber and other natural resources. The League of Nations was unable to act against Japanese aggression in China because, while not wanting to legitimize Japan's actions, it did not want to directly condemn Japan and force it to break off diplomatic relations with the Western powers.

After much debate, the league adopted the *Lytton Report* in February 1933. Japan withdrew from the league the following day and sent military forces to occupy the northern Chinese province of Jehol (Rehol), which it annexed to Manchukuo, as well as a strip of land in Hubei Province between the Chinese capital of Beijing and its port city of Tianjin. In 1937 China declared war on Japan, now known as the War of Resistance against Japan (1937–45; World War II). The League of Nations disbanded during World War II, and after the war it was replaced by the United Nations (U.N.) See also LYTTON COMMISSION; MANCHUKUO; MAY FOURTH MOVEMENT OF 1919; SHANDONG PROVINCE; UNITED NATIONS; WORLD WAR I.

LEE KUAN-YU (LEE KUAN YEW)   See SINGAPORE.

LEE TENG-HUI (1923–   )   The president of the Republic of China (ROC) on Taiwan Island, which lies 100 miles off the southeastern coast of China. The Chinese Nationalist Party (Kuomintang; KMT) established the provisional government of the ROC on Taiwan when the Nationalists fled there after being defeated in 1949 by the Chinese Communist Party (CCP), which founded the People's Republic of China (PRC) on the Chinese mainland. Nationalist leader Chiang Kai-shek served as ROC president until he died in 1975. His son, Chiang Ching-kuo, served as president from 1978 to 1988. Lee Teng-hui was the chosen vice president of Chiang Ching-kuo, whom he succeeded as president when Chiang died in 1988. Lee is the first ROC president who was born on Taiwan rather than the Chinese mainland. He was born to a Christian family in a rice-growing village near Taipei, the capital of Taiwan, during the time that Taiwan was a colony of Japan. He was an excellent student at his Japanese-run high school and won a scholarship to study at prestigious Kyoto Imperial University in Japan. In 1945, after Japan was defeated in World War II, it relinquished control of Taiwan, and the Nationalists took over the island and removed from office all Taiwanese who had held positions under Japanese rule. Lee, who spoke Taiwanese and Japanese, began studying Mandarin Chinese, the language of government officials in mainland China, which is spoken by KMT members. He went to the United States to study agricultural economics and received a master's degree from Iowa State University and a Ph.D. from Cornell University in 1968. When he returned to Taiwan he taught at Taiwan National University and served as an adviser to the ROC government on rural development. In 1972 he became minister without portfolio for the ROC's promotion of agriculture in developing countries.

In 1978 Lee became mayor of Taipei, and three years later, when he was 58, he became governor of Taiwan. In 1984, KMT leaders in Taiwan's National Assembly appointed Lee vice president of Taiwan. When Chiang Ching-kuo died in 1988, Lee served as president for the last two years of the term and as chairman of the KMT. In 1990, KMT leaders appointed him president in his own right. When the United Nations was founded after World War II, the ROC held China's seat in the U.N. and was a veto-holding member of the U.N. Security Council. After 1949 it continued to hold the seat even though the PRC sent a delegation to the U.N. to claim the seat. The U.N. reversed its position in 1971 when it passed a resolution to expel the ROC and give China's seat to the PRC. The PRC maintains that Taiwan is a province of China, and both PRC and KMT leaders claim that they seek the reunification of Taiwan with China. Lee claims to agree with the goal of unification, but he foresees Taiwan as an equal to mainland China and wants Taiwan to have a seat in the United Nations as a step toward bringing the two Chinas together.

On July 10, 1995, Lee received a visa from the United States to visit Cornell University, which awarded him an honorary doctorate. This was the first visit to the United States by a leader of Taiwan since 1979, when the United States dropped its "Two Chinas Policy" and recognized the PRC as the only legitimate government of China. Lee's visit caused the PRC government to become angry with the U.S. government, especially after Lee gave a speech at Cornell praising democracy. The U.S. State Department stated that Lee's visit represented no change in the administration's China policy, but the PRC government, which considers Taiwan a renegade province, recalled its Washington ambassador, Li Daoyu, and canceled a series of diplomatic meetings. The PRC also halted military cooperation with the Pentagon and began testing missiles only 85 miles off Taiwan. Negotiations between the PRC and the United States led to the return of Li Daoyu to his post as ambassador in October 1995.

In 1996, the KMT scheduled Taiwan's first presidential election for March 23 and Lee was expected to win. Several weeks before the election, the PRC began staging intensive war games in the Taiwan Strait to discredit Lee and intimidate the Taiwanese from voting for their country's independence. However, this made the Taiwanese support Lee even more strongly, and he won the election by a decisive majority of 54 percent of the vote. Lee was recently nominated for the Nobel Peace Prize. See also CHIANG CHING-KUO; CHIANG KAI-SHEK; CIVIL WAR BETWEEN COMMUNISTS AND NATIONALISTS; NATIONALIST PARTY; REPUBLIC OF CHINA; TAIWAN; UNITED NATIONS.

LEGAL SYSTEM   The system for investigating crimes and prosecuting criminal cases in the People's Republic of China (PRC), which was founded in 1949 by the Chinese Commu-

nist Party (CCP). The types of law in the PRC today include the state constitution, litigation procedures, economic, civil and criminal laws, and administrative decrees. The laws are established by the Standing Committee of the National People's Congress (NPC). The state constitution was ratified in 1954 and has been revised several times, most recently in 1982. The legal system of the PRC includes three branches: the public security organs, which investigate crimes and detain suspects; the procuratorate for approving arrests, establishing an a priori case against suspects and making prosecutions; and the courts, which pass judgments. The Supreme People's Court is the highest judicial body in the country and is directly responsible to the Standing Committee of the National People's Congress (NPC), the highest legislative body. The Supreme People's Court has jurisdiction over all lower and special courts and serves as the ultimate appellate court. The courts beneath the Supreme People's Court, in descending order, include the higher, intermediate and basic. There are also Special People's Courts, under the jurisdiction of the Supreme People's Court, which handle treason and espionage cases. The majority of Special People's Courts are military courts, which are independent of civilian courts and directly responsible to the Ministry of National Defense. The Supreme People's Procuratorate is also directly responsible to the Standing Committee of the NPC. Underneath it are the higher, intermediate, basic and special people's procuratorates.

The Chinese legal system is oriented toward settling cases at lower judicial levels, often by mediation that keeps a case from even being brought into court, so cases are rarely taken all the way to the Supreme People's Court. Most people who appear before courts in the PRC are convicted, and the role of their defense lawyers is not to establish their innocence, as in the U.S. legal system, but to get their punishments reduced. Throughout their history, the Chinese people have tried to settle disputes through private mediation and to avoid entering courts. There have been only a small number of lawyers, who have had little power or social status. The CCP encouraged Chinese peasants to form associations, which evolved into formal village mediation groups set up to resolve local feuds. After the CCP founded the PRC in 1949, it made people's mediation committees an important part of the country's new legal system. The state constitution clearly defined the role of these committees as grass-roots organizations through which people can participate in managing government and social affairs.

Members of people's mediation committees are elected by the village, neighborhood or workplace that they serve, and they serve without pay. They are responsible for explaining the law and mediating civil disputes and minor criminal cases, and they help enforce community solidarity. Many people's mediation committees are composed largely of women. After the committee members are elected they attend formal courses in the Chinese legal system and law enforcement methods, which are taught by senior members of the PRC's justice department. Since the mediators lessen the case loads of lawyers and judges, enabling them to concentrate on more difficult cases, legal professionals willingly provide training and help the mediators handle complex disputes. The justice department requires mediators to list the main problems in a dispute, suggest ways in which they might be solved, and take a continuing interest in the case to prevent feuds from escalating. People's mediation committees resolve about 90 percent of China's civil disputes and some minor criminal cases, with no cost to the parties involved. There are more than 800,000 such committees in the PRC.

The Chinese legal system was almost completely destroyed during the Cultural Revolution (1966–76), but was re-established in 1978 and greatly expanded beyond covering criminal matters during the 1980s. In 1982 the first civil procedure law was promulgated for provisional use in the PRC. The new Administrative Procedure Law allows Chinese citizens to sue government officials for abuse of authority or malfeasance. The new civil law addresses many kinds of civil matters, including family law and divorce, contract law and commercial law, especially since the PRC government has encouraged foreign trade and investment in China. There are now many civil disputes in such areas as joint ventures, patent rights, trademarks, copyright, maritime transportation, capital construction and insurance. Many more Chinese are becoming lawyers with expertise in foreign legal systems so that they can handle these cases. The NPC has passed statutes that aim to assure foreigners doing business with Chinese companies that agreements and contracts will be honored. See also CONSTITUTION, STATE, OF 1954; FOREIGN TRADE AND INVESTMENT; MARRIAGE LAW OF 1950; NATIONAL PEOPLE'S CONGRESS; PEOPLE'S REPUBLIC OF CHINA; SUPREME PEOPLE'S COURT.

LEGALIST SCHOOL OF THOUGHT   Also known as the School of Law; the term applied to a diverse group of thinkers during the Warring States Period (403–221 B.C.) who devised concepts and strategies for solving the problems of society and government. Legalism was one of the four most important schools among the "Hundred Schools of Thought" that developed during a period of socio-political ferment. (The three other main schools were Confucianism, Daoism and Moism.)

The greatest Legalist thinker was Han Feizi (Han Fei Tzu; c. 280–233 B.C.). He argued that human nature is basically selfish and that the social order can be maintained only when the ruler imposes strict rules that his subjects obey without questioning and that the ruler enforces with strict punishments. In Han Feizi's view, "the ruler alone possesses power." Following the Warring States Period, the state of Qin was able to unify China under the Qin dynasty (221–206 B.C.) because its strongest leaders, Lord Shang Yang (d. 338 B.C.) and the first emperor of China, Qin Shi Huangdi, brutally employed Legalist principles. These principles were expounded by the legalist thinker Xunzi (Hsun Tzu; c. 298–238 B.C.). Li Si (Li Ssu; 280–208 B.C.), the first prime minister of the Qin dynasty, who had been a student of Xunzi along with Han Feizi, was also a strong advocate of the Legalistic approach in the Qin government. However, the Qin dynasty collapsed quickly, and Confucian scholars, who emphasized the goodness of human nature and self-cultivation through education, attributed to the dynasty's downfall to the errors of Legalism. While Confucian principles were utilized by the Han dynasty (206 B.C.–A.D. 220) that succeeded the Qin and became one of the greatest Chinese dynasties, the Han also employed some Legalist views on the

organization of government and society. See also CONFUCIANISM; HAN DYNASTY; HAN FEIZI; HUNDRED SCHOOLS OF THOUGHT; LI SI; QIN DYNASTY; QIN SHI HUANGDI; SHANG YANG, LORD; XUNZI.

LEIZU (LEI-TSU)   See SILK; YELLOW EMPEROR.

LEOPARD   See SNOW LEOPARD.

LEPROSY   See MA HAIDE.

LESSONS FOR WOMEN   See CODE FOR WOMEN.

LHASA   The capital of Tibet, an autonomous region in western China called Xizang Zizhiqu in Chinese. Lhasa has been the political, cultural and economic center of Tibet for more than 350 years. The city, with a population of more than 100,000, lies in a valley on the banks of the Lhasa, River, a tributary of the Brahmaputra (Tsanpo) River. The Himalaya Mountain Range, the highest in the world, forms the southern border of Tibet; Lhasa, situated on a plateau, has an altitude of 12,040 feet above sea level. The city is divided into two sections, with the newer and larger section settled mostly by Han, or ethnic, Chinese. The older is the Tibetan section, with the Jokhang (Dazhao in Chinese) Temple in the center. This temple, one of the most sacred shrines in Tibet, was built in 651 to house a golden statue of the Buddha brought by the Tang dynasty (618–907) Chinese princess Wencheng when she married King Songzan Gambo (Songtsen Gampo) of Tibet. Other buildings have been constructed around the main temple. The Jokhang is filled with sumptuous Buddhist sculptures and paintings, including an 85-foot-high statue of the Buddha. Pilgrims from all over Tibet visit Lhasa to make a clockwise circuit, called the Barkhor, around Jokhang Temple. The area surrounding Jokhang is a busy market with shops, vendors and teahouses.

The most important site in Lhasa is the magnificent Potala Palace, now a museum but formerly the headquarters of the Dalai Lama, the religious and secular head of Tibet. The Tibetan form of Buddhism is called Lamaism. The Potala Palace is 13 stories high and contains more than 1,000 rooms and Buddhist shrines filled with 200,000 sculptures and miles of wall paintings. The current Dalai Lama, the 14th, fled south into India with many lamas and other followers when Tibetans rebelled against their harsh treatment by the Chinese between 1958 and 1959, but his living quarters can be seen in the Red Palace at Potala. The tombs of eight Dalai Lamas can also be seen. Since 1976, the Chinese government has spent millions of dollars to renovate the Potala.

An Exhibition Hall at the foot of the Potala displays exhibits on the history and culture of Tibet. The Norbu Lingka, about two miles west of the Potala Palace, is the former summer palace of the Dalai Lama. The original building was erected in 1755 and pavilions were added by succeeding Dalai Lamas. Now the Norbu Lingka is a public park with gardens, small palaces and shrines, and a zoo. Drepung (Zhebang) Monastery, about four miles outside of Lhasa, is active as one of Tibet's 10 remaining Buddhist monasteries and houses about 300 lamas. The large stone buildings were erected in 1416. Drepung, at one time the largest monastery in the world, was home to the fifth Dalai Lama before the Potala was built. Sera (Sela) Monastery about three miles north of Lhasa is another active monastery that houses about 150 lamas. Founded in 1419, it includes a large prayer hall and three rooms housing archives. See also DALAI LAMA; LAMAISM; POTALA PALACE; TIBET.

LI   An ethnic group that is one of the largest of the 55 officially designated national minority groups in China. The Li are farmers who inhabit rural, mountainous areas in Guangdong Province and Hainan Island in southern China. Most are farmers who reside in the Hainan Li-Miao Autonomous Prefecture. Their population numbered 1,110,900 according to the 1990 census. The Li belong to the Dai (Tai) ethnic and linguistic group, which includes, among others, the Bouyei, Dai, Dong and Zhuang, the largest of China's national minorities. The Li migrated from Guangdong to Hainan about 3,000 years ago and are thus considered the aborigines on the island. They conducted many rebellions against the Han, the dominant Chinese ethnic group. However, the Li on Hainan assisted the Chinese Communists during China's War of Resistance against Japan (1937–45; World War II). After the Communists established the People's Republic of China in 1949, they designated the Limuling Mountain Range (Limulingshan) in the center of Hainan, the territory inhabited by the Li people, an autonomous region. Central Hainan is also inhabited by the Miao, another large minority group. Li women formerly had their bodies tattooed when they were 12 or 13 years old. They are famous for their handwoven brocade textiles. Today most Li wear Western-style clothing, although they bury their dead in traditional Li clothing so that the ancestors will welcome the newly deceased person. The Li hold a traditional festival on the third day of the third month in their lunar calendar (around April). At the festival they sing and display their handicrafts, and young people select marriage partners. See also BOUYEI; DAI; DONG; GUANGDONG PROVINCE; HAINAN ISLAND; HAN; MIAO; ZHUANG.

LI   See CARP.

LI   See PROPRIETY.

LI BAI (Li Po; 701–62)   One of the most renowned poets in Chinese history. Li Bai is classed with his friends, the poet Du Fu (Tu Fu; 712–70) and poet-painter Wang Wei (699–761), as one of the three greatest poets of the Tang dynasty (618–907), the "golden age" of Chinese culture. During this period, the type of poem known as the Regulated Verse or New Style Verse was formalized to contain a regulated number of five- and seven-syllable lines. The ability to write poetry was highly valued by the Tang government and was a requirement for the educated men selected by examinations to serve in the imperial bureaucracy.

According to his family tradition, Li Bai was born in Gansu Province (far Western China) or in Central Asia. By the time Li Bai was five years old, his family, who may have been traders, had settled in Sichuan Province. He was well educated but refused to take the examinations that would provide him a position in the imperial bureaucracy. Yet from 742 to 744 he held a position in the court at Chang'an (mod-

ern Xi'an in Shaanxi province), as a member of the Hanlin ("Forest of Writing Brushes") or Imperial Academy. However, his reputation as a heavy drinker kept Li Bai from gaining any position of responsibility, and he spent much of his life wandering from place to place. During the An Lushan rebellion in 755 that toppled Emperor Xuanzong, he was arrested for having a connection with some rebels and was nearly executed.

In 744 or 745 Li Bai met Du Fu. The two became close friends and exchanged poems with each other. Whereas Du Fu was a Confucian moralist, Li Bai valued spontaneity and naturalness, which aligned him with the Daoist and Chan (Zen) Buddhist traditions. Even though he spent much of his life reading and studying, he satirized the moral and intellectual values of Confucianism, such as literary scholarship. One of his favorite subjects was the alchemical search for the "Elixir of Immortality."

Li Bai is known as a "romantic" poet, and many of his poems are based on dreams or journeys of the spirit. His drunkenness was associated by the Chinese with openness to divine inspiration. The light of the moon's reflection is a common image in Li Bai's poetry, and his best-known poem describes his drinking in the company of the moon and his shadow. Li Bai is said to have died when he was drunk because he fell out of a boat while trying to grasp the moon's reflection in the water.

Li Bai's best-known poems are written in an old folk-ballad style known as *yuefu* (*yueh-fu*), which had fewer rules than did the new regulated style about the length of lines and number of syllables in a poem. Twenty-six of Li Bai's poems are included in the Chinese anthology, *Three Hundred Poems of the Tang Dynasty*. Many of his poems have been translated into English, notably by the British translator Arthur Waley in *The Poetry and Career of Li Po* (1950). See also AN LUSHAN REBELLION; CHAN SECT OF BUDDHISM; CONFUCIANISM; DAOISM; DU FU; ELIXIR OF IMMORTALITY; HANLIN ACADEMY; IMPERIAL BUREAUCRACY; LI BAI; REGULATED OR NEW STYLE VERSE; TANG DYNASTY; WALEY, ARTHUR; WANG WEI.

LI CHAO-TAO   See LANDSCAPE PAINTING; LI SIXUN.

LI CHI   See ARCHAEOLOGY.

LI CH'ING-CHAO   See LI QINGZHAO.

LI CHUN FESTIVAL   See ALMANAC; OX.

LI DAZHAO (Li Ta-chao; 1888–1927)   A cofounder of the Chinese Communist Party (CCP). Li Dazhao was born to a peasant family in Hebei Province and was educated at a military academy in Tianjin and at Waseda University in Tokyo, where he was introduced to Marxist thought. When he returned to China, Li became an editor for *New Youth*, a journal that had been founded by Chen Duxiu (Ch'en Tu-hsiu; 1879–1942), dean of letters of Beijing University, to serve as a voice for the new Chinese movement that was interested in Western literature and culture.

In 1918 Li became head librarian at prestigious Beijing University, and in 1920 he also became a professor of history there. The 1917 Russian Revolution, which had given birth to the Soviet Union, influenced Li to give lectures on Marxist thought at the university. Many of his students went on to play important roles in the Communist Party, including Mao Zedong (Mao Tse-tung; 1893–1976), a clerk in the library who eventually founded the People's Republic of China.

In July 1921 the groups Li had established to study Marxist thought were organized into the Chinese Communist Party, with Li Dazhao as party leader. Li served as a liaison between the Communist Party and the Nationalist Party (Kuomintang; KMT) founded by Sun Yat-sen, but his most important function was to develop political theory for the Chinese Communists. According to Marxist thought, China would be liberated after the Western world underwent a revolution by the proletariat, or working class, against the capitalist class that oppressed them. Li maintained that China could not wait for the Western revolution and that the Chinese urban working class was too small to carry out a revolution on its own. Li theorized that China's peasants, by far the largest class in the country, would be the ones to carry out the revolution, and that it would be a nationalistic revolution by the Chinese people against the foreign imperialists who had oppressed and exploited them. Mao Zedong based his own revolutionary ideas and strategy upon Li's concepts.

Li was a leader of the May Fourth Movement of 1919, a nationwide protest against the governments of China and Japan for their secret agreement that awarded the Chinese province of Shandong to Japan. He later became embroiled in political confrontation with the warlord Zhang Zuolin (Chang Tso-lin) in Manchuria (northeastern China), who was strongly anti-Communist. Li and his companions took refuge at the Soviet Embassy in Beijing. However, in April 1927 the warlord took him and 19 others from the embassy and executed them. See also BEIJING UNIVERSITY; CHEN DUXIU; CHINESE COMMUNIST PARTY; MAO ZEDONG; MAY FOURTH MOVEMENT OF 1919; ZHANG ZUOLIN.

LI DELUN (? –) A world-famous symphonic orchestra conductor. Before the Chinese Communists established the People's Republic of China (PRC) in 1949, Li was conductor of the Central Orchestra in Yan'an, Shaanxi Province, in western China, which had been the communist headquarters. After 1949, Li brought his orchestra to Beijing, the capital city. In 1953 he went to the Soviet Union, where he studied under the prominent Soviet conductor, N. Anosov. Li made his Soviet debut in 1957 when he and his teacher conducted the first symphony concert of Moscow's Sixth World Youth Festival. Returning to China that year, Li was appointed conductor of the Central Symphony Orchestra in Beijing. In 1959 he celebrated the 10th anniversary of the founding of the PRC by conducting an orchestra of 500 musicians in a performance of *Prelude to the Spring Festival* by the Chinese composer Li Huanzhi in the Great Hall of the People. In 1960 he was director of the Central Philharmonic Orchestra. He disappeared from 1966 to 1973 during the Cultural Revolution. After that, he went abroad several times with Chinese Cultural delegations. In 1978, 12,000 people attended the performance he conducted of *From the New World* by Antonin Dvorak at the Workers Gymnasium in Beijing. In 1983, he was again chief conductor of the Central Philharmonic Orchestra. In 1985, he was elected vice-chairman of the Chinese Musicians' Association. One of Li's

proudest moments was the "Spring of Symphonic Music,' a concert by 800 musicians in the Gymnasium on March 1, 1987. Thirty-six thousand people attended the performance, which included works by Li Huanzhi, Tchaikovsky and other composers.

During the 1980s, Li conducted more than 300 concerts throughout China. He led the movement for the construction of the Beijing Concert Hall, which was completed in 1985, and assisted in establishing symphony orchestras in Shandong Province and Inner Mongolia Autonomous Region. He has promoted an interest in symphonic music in China by giving many lectures in schools, factories and areas outside Beijing. In 1987 he joined Teng Ch'ang-kuo (Deng Changguo), a famous conductor from Taiwan, in conducting a concert in San Francisco. Li has conducted in several foreign countries and has performed with famous Western musicians such as violinists Isaac Stern and Yehudi Menuhin. In 1980 the Chinese Ministry of Culture awarded Li a certificate of honor, and in 1986 the government of Hungary awarded him the Liszt Medal. Li has served as vice president of the Chinese Musicians' Association, as a member of the State Education Commission's Art Committee, as art director of the Central Philharmonic Society and as conductor of the Central Philharmonic Orchestra. See also GREAT HALL OF THE PEOPLE; YAN'AN.

LI GONGLIN (Li Kung-lin; c. 1040–1106) The most outstanding figure painter during the Northern Song dynasty (960–1126). Li was born into a wealthy literati, or scholar, family in Anhui Province. He was educated in the classics of Confucianism and Chinese history, and he also studied his father's extensive collection of art works. Li taught himself painting and calligraphy, the fine art of writing Chinese characters, especially poetry, with a brush. In 1070 he passed the examination for the imperial bureaucracy, or civil service, in which he held various official positions. In 1100 he retired from the bureaucracy and moved to the countryside to concentrate on art. Li's painting was influenced by previous masters such as Wang Wei, Wu Daozi (Wu Tao-tzu) and Gu Kaizhi (Ku K'ai-chih). Li played an important role in the development of the theory of literati painting, considered "amateur" because literati who painted in this style did so as a means of self-expression, in contrast to professional painters in the imperial court who painted in a more realistic style. His painting style has much in common with calligraphy, using thin lines of ink and little color, and this became the dominant style of literati figure painters. See also CALLIGRAPHY; FIGURE PAINTING; IMPERIAL BUREAUCRACY; LITERATI; WANG WEI; WU DAOZI.

LI GUIFEN See LU, LISA.

LI HE (Li Ho; 790–816) A major poet of the Tang dynasty (618–907). He was born in Gansu Province, but his family moved to their estate in Henan Province. Upon completing his education, in 609 he passed the Prefectural Examination by which literati or scholars were selected for positions in the imperial bureaucracy. He also met and became the protegé of the famous poet and essay writer Han Yu (768–824). Li He went to the capital city of Chang'an (modern Xi'an) to take the literary examination that would award him the title of *jinshi* (*chin-shih*; "advanced scholar"), but he was forbidden to take this examination because his deceased father's given name, Li Jinsu (Li Chin-su), was pronounced the same as *jinshi*, a taboo to the Chinese government of the time. Li He was allowed to hold only a low-level position as supervisor of ritual at the Court of Imperial Sacrifices. He held this office from 811 to 814, returned home for a short time, and then became a member of the staff of a military general. His health had been declining ever since he had been prevented from taking the literary examination, and in 816 he returned home to die. Li He's poetry is filled with unusual and even eccentric images, which he drew from Chinese mythology and the Daoist and shamanist traditions. His complex poems contain many allusions to the restrictions suffered by the literati, whom the government often neglected in preference to those with a military or moneymaking bent. Li He used mystical imagery to make critical comments about the political and social conditions of his day. See also DAOISM; HAN YU; IMPERIAL EXAMINATION SYSTEM; LYRIC VERSE.

LI HO See LI HE.

LI HONGZHANG (Li Hung-chang; 1823–1901) A leading Han Chinese military commander and diplomat under the Manchu Qing dynasty (1644–1911). A native of Anhui province, he became a protegé of the military commander and statesman Zeng Guofan (Tseng Kuo-fan; 1811–72). During the Taiping Rebellion (1850–64), Li Hongzhang organized the army in Anhui, which joined with the army from Hunan Province led by Zeng Guofan to defeat the Taiping rebels at their headquarters in Nanjing. After this, Li was appointed governor-general of Liangjiang, which included the modern provinces of Anhui, Jiangsu and Jiangxi. The Qing court appointed Zeng to suppress the Nian Rebellion, but he had disbanded a large number of his best troops and had to rely on Li's troops from Anhui. They were not fully loyal to Zeng, however, so the court reversed Li and Zeng's positions, making Zeng the governor-general of Liangjiang and Li the commander of the military campaign against the Nian bandits. His soldiers finally brought the rebellion to an end in 1868. The Qing raised Li to the rank of a noble and gave him the honorific title, Grand Guardian of the Heir Apparent. Zeng Guofan, who had been ennobled after defeating the Taipings at Nanjing, died in 1872. Li remained one of the most powerful government officials in China for the next three decades, holding the position of governor-general of northeastern China at Tianjin.

Li Hongzhang supported the Self-Strengthening Movement by which the Chinese government adopted elements of Western science and technology in order to strengthen the country's defenses, and he initiated many of its projects. He founded the China Merchant Steamship Navigation Company, greatly expanded the Kaiping coal mines near Tianjin to provide fuel for Chinese ships, founded a large cotton mill at Shanghai to reduce Chinese imports of textiles, developed arsenals in Tianjin to manufacture ammunition for the guns he began purchasing from Western powers, and constructed dock facilities at the Manchurian city of Lushun (modern Dalian). He also sent the first group of Chinese boys to study in the United States and Europe. Li negotiated for China with foreign powers regarding many diplomatic issues. In the 1870s he negotiated with Japan over the status of the Ryukyu Islands (Okinawa) and Korea. The Japanese annexed the Ryukyus in 1879, but Li prevented them from annexing Korea by having the Korean king sign treaties with Western nations.

In the 1880s Li attempted to build up the Chinese navy, but a Qing official diverted the funds for the navy to build a new summer palace for Empress Dowager Cixi (Tz'u Hsi). When French forces quickly destroyed the Chinese naval base at Fuzhou during the Sino-French War (1884–85), Li led the faction in the Qing court that wanted China to negotiate for peace with France, which China did in 1885. The Japanese military intervened in Korea in 1894, claiming they were suppressing Korean rebels, and in Korea they routed Li's North China army and his naval fleet on the Yalu River. Li's provincial North China army and naval fleet had been the only Chinese forces sent against the Japanese military. This was China's first modern war, and the country was poorly prepared for it. After Japan soundly defeated China in the Sino-Japanese War (1894–95), Li negotiated the Treaty of Shimonoseki with Japan, the terms of which were very harsh for China.

Many Chinese officials argued that the country now had to enact drastic reforms quickly to modernize itself or it would not survive. They rejected Li Hongzhang's position that China should modernize carefully and gradually. Li also lost influence in the Qing government after the Japanese defeat of China. During the Reform Movement of 1898, also known as the Hundred Days Reform, Emperor Guangxu (Kuang-hsu; r. 1875–1908) dismissed Li from the Zongli Yamen (Tsung-li Ya-men), the Chinese government office that dealt with foreign nations. The emperor had initiated the Reform Movement. However, Empress Dowager Cixi harshly ended the Reform Movement after a hundred days, imprisoned the emperor, and took power herself. In 1900, Li was assigned the task of negotiating with foreign powers the protocol that concluded the Boxer Uprising in Beijing and Tianjin. China had declared war on the foreign nations that defended themselves against the Boxers, but the foreign troops routed the Chinese forces, and the emperor and Empress Dowager Cixi fled west to Xi'an. The Boxer Protocol, signed in 1901 by Li Hongzhang and Prince Gong (Kung), the highest Qing prince, with 11 foreign nations, included the payment of heavy reparations by China, punishment of war criminals, permission for foreign soldiers to maintain permanent garrisons in Beijing, and a 5-percent tariff on imports in treaty ports. The day before he died from illness in 1901, Li Hongzhang chose Yuan Shikai (Yuan Shih-k'ai; 1859–1916) to be his successor as governor-general and the trainer of China's New Army. Yuan became a powerful warlord who would replace Sun Yat-sen as president of the Republic of China, which was founded with the overthrow of the Qing dynasty in 1911. See also BOXER UPRISING; CHINA MERCHANTS STEAM NAVIGATION COMPANY; GONG, PRINCE; NIAN REBELLION; QING DYNASTY; RYUKYU ISLANDS; SELF-STRENGTHENING MOVEMENT; SHIMONOSEKI, TREATY OF; SINO-FRENCH WAR (1884–85); SINO-JAPANESE WAR (1894–95); TAIPING REBELLION; TIANJIN; TREATY PORTS; YUAN SHIKAI; ZONGLI YAMEN.

LI HOUJU (HOU-CHU) See LI YU.

LI HSIEN-NIEN See LI XIANNIAN.

LI HUA LONG (LI HUA LUNG) See DRAGON.

LI HUNG-CHANG See LI HONGZHANG.

LI JI See ARCHAEOLOGY.

LI KUCHAN (Li K'u-ch'an; 1898–1983) A prominent modern Chinese painter and calligrapher. Li Kuchan was born into a poor family in Shandong Province, and was influenced by a painter in his hometown to study painting himself. At age 21, he studied with the famous Chinese painters Xu Beihong (Hsu Pei-hung) and Qi Baishi (Ch'i Pai-shih) while earning money pulling rickshaws. By age 28 he became a teacher of painting. Li was also politically active and became involved in the patriotic Chinese May Fourth Movement of 1919. During China's War of Resistance against Japan (1937–45; World War II), he refused to work for the Japanese, who had invaded China, and they imprisoned and tortured him.

During the six decades that he was a painter, Li traveled all over China. He believed that painters should work from live models and, while their style should not be totally realistic, should express the life of their subjects. He drew upon traditional Chinese motifs for symbolic expression, especially in bird-and-flower painting. Some of his most famous works include *Lotus, Eagles, Orchids* and *Bamboo*. When Li was 81 he painted the enormous work, *The Height of Summer*, which was hung in the central hall of the Great Hall of the People in Beijing, the Chinese capital. At age 83 he painted *Sturdy Bamboo*, the largest ink painting of bamboo executed in China since the Tang dynasty (618–907), for the Great Hall of the People. Li also practiced calligraphy, the art of writing Chinese ideographs with a brush and ink, every day, because he believed that Chinese painting and calligraphy are bound together. After Li died, his family donated about 400 of his works to his hometown of Ji'nan, the capital of Shandong, where the Li Kuchan Museum was opened in the Bamboo Park to exhibit them. The museum, in the colorful classical Chinese style, has 180 rooms built around gardens and courtyards. See also BAMBOO; BIRD-AND-FLOWER PAINTING; CALLIGRAPHY; GREAT HALL OF THE PEOPLE; JI'NAN; LOTUS; MAY FOURTH MOVEMENT OF 1919; ORCHID; QI BAISHI; WAR OF RESISTANCE AGAINST JAPAN; XU BEIHONG.

LI KUEI-FEN See LU, LISA.

LI KUNG-LIN See LI GONGLIN.

LI LIWENG See MUSTARD SEED GARDEN MANUAL OF PAINTING.

LI MADOU (LI MA-TOU) See RICCI, MATTEO.

LI PENG (Li P'eng; 1928–) Formerly the premier of the State Council of the People's Republic of China (PRC), founded by the Chinese Communist Party (CCP) in 1949. Li Peng was born in Sichuan Province. When he was only three years old, he became an orphan when the Nationalists (Kuomintang; KMT) executed his father for taking part in

the Nanchang Uprising, a rebellion in August 1927 against Nationalist troops by Communist forces led by CCP leaders Zhou Enlai (Chou En-lai; 1898–1976) and Zhu De (Chu Teh; 1886–1976). The Nationalists had cooperated with the newly founded CCP, but in April 1927 they turned against the party and massacred many Communists. The Nanchang Uprising ended the CCP-KMT united front against Chinese warlords. When Li was 11 he was adopted by Zhou and his wife, Deng Yingchao (Teng Ying-ch'ao), who both became prominent CCP leaders. After China's War of Resistance against Japan (1937–45; World War II), in 1948 Li went to Moscow to be educated as a hydroelectric engineer. He returned to China in 1954 and held various positions in the energy industry. In 1979 he became vice minister of the power ministry, and in 1981–82 minister of the power ministry. In 1982–83 he served as vice minister of the newly established Ministry of Water Conservation and Power.

Li has been a member of the CCP Central Committee from 1982 to the present. From 1983 to 1988 he served as vice premier of the State Council. In 1984–88 he was head of four State Council leading groups, and in 1986–88 he was head of Central Flood Control Headquarters. Flooding has always been a devastating problem in China, especially along the Yangzi (Chiangjiang) and Yellow (Huanghe) rivers, and recently the Chinese government has undertaken massive flood control projects such as the Three Gorges Dam Water Conservancy Project. In 1987 Li served on the Presidium Standing Committee and was elected to the Politburo Standing Committee, the inner circle of power in the CCP. Since 1984 he has been chairman of the Environmental Protection Committee and since 1985 chairman of the State Education Commission; he has also been minister of the State Commission for Restructuring the Economic System. From the early 1980s Li has represented the PRC on state visits to the United States, Canada, Japan, Western and Eastern Europe and Africa. In foreign affairs he is a specialist in relations with Russia and Eastern Europe.

In 1988 Li became premier of the State Council. On April 17, 1989, Chinese students held a massive pro-democracy demonstration in Tiananmen Square in Beijing, two days after the death of Hu Yaobang, whom they considered a hero after he was dismissed as CCP general secretary. Zhao Ziyang replaced Hu as general secretary, and Li Peng, more conservative than Zhao regarding economic reform, replaced Zhao as prime minister. On April 19, the students marched to the Zhongnanhai compound, the residence of many CCP leaders, where they held a sit-in and called for Li Peng to come out and address them. The protesters held Tiananmen Square, and Li Peng announced the imposition of martial law on May 20. The students demanded that CCP leaders Li Peng and Deng Xiaoping step down from their positions. On June 4, 1989, Party officials ordered a full-scale military assault against the demonstrators in Tiananmen Square. Li Peng is considered the leader most responsible for ordering the brutal military suppression of the pro-democracy movement. However, he remained in power and was considered a possible successor to Deng Xiaoping.

In November 1989, Deng resigned from his positions and designated Jiang Zemin his successor. Jiang became president of China, general secretary of the CCP, and chairman of the Central Military Commission, and so Li Peng had to share power with him. The Chinese constitution requires Li to resign as premier in 1998 after his second five-year term ends. He was replaced by Zhu Ronji. Some believe that he wishes to replace Jiang as president or Qiao Shi as chairman of the National Party Congress. See also CENTRAL COMMIT-TEE OF THE CHINESE COMMUNIST PARTY; CHINESE COMMU-NIST PARTY; DENG XIAOPING; DENG YINGCHAO; ENERGY SOURCES; GOVERNMENT STRUCTURE; HU YAOBANG; JIANG ZEMIN; NANCHANG UPRISING; POLITBURO; STATE COUNCIL; THREE GORGES DAM WATER CONSERVANCY PROJECT; TIANAN-MEN SQUARE MASSACRE; ZHOLI ENLAI.

LI PO   See LI BAI.

LI QINGZHAO   (Li Ch'ing-chao; 1081–1143)   The great-est female poet in Chinese history. Li Qingzhao was born into a family of the literati (scholar) class in Shandong Province. In 1101 she married a scholar named Zhao Mingcheng (Chao Ming-ch'eng; 1081–1129). They were happy together and enjoyed sharing their intellectual knowl-edge and writing poems for each other, although their friends agreed that her poems were much finer than his. They also compiled the *Catalogue of Inscriptions on Stone and Bone* (*Jinshilu* or *Chin-shih lu*), which records 2,000 ancient documents. Sadly, Zhao died while they were fleeing the Jurchen people, rulers of the Jin dynasty (1115–1234), who took Kaifeng, the capital of the Northern Song dynasty (960–1126). She traveled on to Hangzhou in Zhejiang Province, where the Song had moved their capital (Southern Song dynasty, 1127–1279). After two years there, she trav-eled again to Jinhui, also in Zhejiang, where she spent the remainder of her life. As a woman alone in a male-dominated culture, Li Qingzhao was not accepted by the literati and died unhappily in poverty. However, after her death, the greatness of her poems was recognized. During her life, she wrote six volumes of poetry and seven volumes of essays. She wrote her poems in the delicate lyric form known as *ci* (*tz'u*), which was the most widely used poetic form during the Song dynasty. Only fragments of her poems have sur-vived, but her poetry maintains its high reputation even today. See also HANGZHOU; JURCHEN; KAIFENG; LITERATI; LYRIC VERSE; NORTHERN SONG DYNASTY; SOUTHERN SONG DYNASTY.

LI RIVER AND LING CANAL   (Lijiang and Lingqu)   An important river and manmade canal in Guangxi-Zhuang Autonomous Region in southwestern China. The 271-mile-long Li River (Lijiang) connects to Guangdong Province through the Gui River (Guijiang), and to the South China Sea via West River (Xijiang). The longest river in southern China, the Xijiang flows through Guangxi and Guangdong provinces and empties into the South China Sea. The Ling

Some of China's most spectacular scenery, admired since ancient times, can be seen along the Li River.   S.E. MEYER

canal was constructed to connect the Li and West rivers. Two smaller canals were built along with the main section, called the Nanqu, that linked the two rivers.

Construction on the Ling Canal was begun around 215 B.C. by Emperor Qin Shi Huangdi, founder of the Qin dynasty (221–206 B.C.). To bypass an unnavigable section of the Li River, the canal was built 17 miles long from a location near Guilin until it reached the point where the Li empties into the Gui River (Guijiang). The canal enabled Qin troops to be transported from the region of the Yangzi River (Changjiang) in Hunan south to Guangdong Province, where they made an unsuccessful attempt to conquer the kingdom of Nanyue. The Ling Canal remained the main transportation route between central and southern China until about A.D. 50 and was later replaced by the Grand Canal, a shorter route that was constructed through Jiangsu Province. By the early ninth century the Ling Canal was in such disrepair that it was no longer navigable. In 825 the canal was reconstructed with a system of locks to raise and lower boats along the waterway, and by the 12th century these locks had been replaced with 36 new locks that allowed larger boats carrying 1,000 bushels to sail the canal. The Ling Canal is still used today but can be navigated only by small boats and is used primarily as a source of water for irrigating crops.

The beauty of the Lijiang around the region of Guilin city, one of the most popular destinations in China, has been celebrated by poets and painters since ancient times. The Chinese compare the 51.5-mile stretch of the Li River from Guilin to Yangshuo to a landscape painting on a scroll. The most spectacular scenery is at Huangbu Shoal, where seven mountain peaks are reflected on the smooth surface of the water. The river is often misty due to the humid climate, but on clear days the beautiful landscape is reflected in the water. Tourists enjoy boat rides to view the hundreds of oddly shaped mountains that rise up from the fertile plains along the river. Known as karst, these mountains and their subterranean caves were formed by the erosion of a thick layer of limestone that had been thrust upward from the bottom of the sea by geological activity 300 million years ago. Many fishing families live on their small, flat-bottomed boats on the Li River, and they often use large black birds known as cormorants to catch fish. See also CORMORANT; GRAND CANAL; GUILIN; LANDSCAPE PAINTING; QIN DYNASTY; WEST RIVER.

LI SAO   See QU YUAN; TAN DUN.

LI SHANGYIN (813–858)   A major Chinese poet during the Tang dynasty (618–907) whose works influenced a number of later poets; also known as "Scholar of the Jade Stream" (Yuxi Sheng; Yu-hsi Sheng). Li Shangyin was born in Henan Province, the son of a government official, and he held positions under military governors in many different regions, including the modern provinces of Shandong, Shanxi, Gansu and Sichuan. However, he never rose to a high government position. As a young man his poetic talents were already evident. Li Shangyin composed his poems in many different styles, ranging from ancient forms to the colloquial language of his time, and he employed complex sensual images and structures, especially his "Untitled" poems

in Regulated or New-Style Verse (shi). About 600 of his poems have survived, which fall into three categories. The first includes "untitled" poems, or shih which are ambiguous and sensual. The second includes poems written for friends and relatives, and refers to events in his life. The third includes poems that are concerned with contemporary social and political events, although some are written as if they refer to events in the past.

LI SHIH-CHEN   See LI SHIZHEN.

LI SHIMIN   See TAIZONG (EMPEROR) (TANG).

LI SHIZHEN (Li Shih-chen; 1518–1595)   The most famous practitioner of herbal medicine during the Ming dynasty (1368–1644). Li Shizhen became interested in herbal medicine as a boy when he went to the hillsides with his father to gather plants that had healing properties. He was educated in the Confucian classics and passed the examinations that qualified him to be assigned a post in the imperial bureaucracy, but he maintained his strong interest in the use of plants for herbal medicine. At the age of 35, Li Shizhen began compiling a monumental reference work, which took him 27 years to complete. Published in 1596 with beautiful plates as *The Great Pharmacopoeia* (*Bencao Gang Mu* or *Pen-ts'ao kang-mu*; also known as *Materia Medica Ordered on the Basis of Monographs and Individual Characteristics*), this book has 50 chapters and describes in detail about 1,000 plants and 1,000 animals, classifying them into 62 divisions according to their characteristics. An appendix lists more than 8,000 prescriptions for herbal medicine. Li Shizhen also quotes 952 previous Chinese sources in this field. His book is considered the greatest scientific work of the Ming dynasty. No other Chinese scholar has produced any comparable work. The book has been translated into English, German and other languages. See also IMPERIAL EXAMINATION SYSTEM; MEDICINE, HERBAL.

LI SI (Li Ssu; 280–208 B.C.)   The chancellor (*changxiang* or *ch'ang-hsiang* to King Zheng (Cheng), ruler of the state of Qin, who unified China under the Qin dynasty (221–206 B.C.). During Li Si's time, Qin was one of many states that were contending with each other. Qin's location in the Wei River Valley in the Central China Plain protected it from invaders and gave it fertile soil for agriculture. The capital city was Xianyang (later known as Chang'an; modern Xi'an). After unifying China, Zheng called himself Qin Shi Huangdi ("First Sovereign Qin Emperor"), associating himself with the legendary Yellow Emperor, known as Huangdi ("Emperor"), whom the Chinese believed had the power of immortality.

Li Si was a clerk in the state of Chu but saw that Qin was becoming the strongest state and moved there in 247 B.C., the year before Zheng became king of Qin. He gained favor with Zheng and was promoted to high positions in which he provided the strategy by which Zheng ruthlessly conquered all neighboring states. When Zheng proclaimed the unification of the empire under his reign as Emperor Qin Shi Huangdi, he appointed Li Si chancellor. From then until the emperor died in 210 B.C., Li Si remained the most powerful government minister in the dynasty. He convinced Qin Shi Huangdi that all power should remain centralized under the emperor and gave him the rationale for his brutal regime. Li Si followed the ideas of the Legalist School of Thought, which he had studied under the Confucian philosopher Xunzi (Hsun Tzu; c. 298–238 B.C.), who, contrary to some Confucian scholars, taught that human nature is evil and that people have to be controlled by harsh laws. His fellow student was Han Feizi (Han Fei Tzu; c. 280–233 B.C.), who became the most important Legalist philosopher. Han Feizi was also given a position in the Qin government, but the ruthless Li Si imprisoned his rival and forced him to commit suicide with poison. Emperor Qin was so ruthless that stirrings of opposition began among members of his court, especially among the literati, or scholars. In 213 B.C. Li Si advised him to burn their Confucian and philosophical books and the official histories of the other states that he had conquered. He did: This was a great tragedy for Chinese scholarship. In 212 B.C. the emperor further terrorized the scholars by having 460 of them buried alive (although some believe that this number was exaggerated).

Li Si was responsible for the standardization of Chinese writing into one system of characters, known as "Small Seal" script, which became used throughout the empire and was the basis for the "Clerk" style and later developments in written Chinese. He also standardized the system of weights and measures. Lines of defense that had been made from earthworks along the empire's northern border were organized into a coordinated system that formed the basis for the "Great Wall of China." Men were conscripted to fight invading tribes, mainly the Xiongnu (Hsiung-nu).

Emperor Qin Shi Huangdi went on many journeys seeking the Elixir of Immortality, and in 211 B.C. he made his final trip, southeast to the sea, accompanied by an entourage that included Li Si and the head of the court eunuchs, Zhao Gao (Chao Kao). The emperor died on the way back after naming Fu Su, his eldest son, his successor. But Li Si helped Zhao Gao place Huhai, the younger son, on the throne as the second emperor, Ershi Huangdi. The new emperor had many of the palace guards and soldiers put to death. Chief eunuch Zhao Gao wanted Li Si removed from power, and he influenced the emperor to kill Li Si in 208 B.C. Ershi Huangdi's reign lasted only two years, and the dynasty fell under the succeeding emperor in 206 B.C. See also CHANG'AN; EUNUCHS; GREAT WALL; HAN FEIZI; LEGALIST SCHOOL OF THOUGHT; QIN DYNASTY; QIN SHI HUANGDI, EMPEROR; WEI RIVER; WRITING SYSTEM, CHINESE; XIONGNU; XUNZI.

LI SIXUN (Li Ssu-hsun; 651–716)   A landscape painter during the Tang dynasty (618–907) who was regarded as the main practitioner of the decoratively colored style of landscape painting. Li Sixun was also the founder of the so-called Northern School of professional court painters, in contrast to the Southern School of literati, or scholar-painters, which was founded by Wang Wei (699–761). The style of the Northern School, which has continued into the modern era, is characterized by severity of form and an emphasis on balanced design, precise lines and detailed workmanship. Li distinguished himself by painting his landscapes with deep, rich colors.

Li Sixun was related to the Tang imperial family and, despite being exiled for a time due to political intrigue, was awarded an honorary rank in the imperial court. Li Sixun's son, Li Zhaodao (Li Chao-tao; active c. 670–730), painted in his father's style and became known as Little General Li, as his father was called Big General Li. No works have survived that can be conclusively attributed to father or son, but it is known that both painted in a highly decorative and detailed style. They were especially fond of using the colors blue and green (called *qinglu* or *ch'ing-lu*, the "blue and green tradition"), as well as white and gold. See also LANDSCAPE PAINTING; LITERATI; NORTHERN SCHOOL OF PAINTING; SOUTHERN SCHOOL OF PAINTING; TANG DYNASTY; WANG WEI.

LI SSU   See LI SI.

LI SSU-HSUN   See LI SIXUN.

LI TA-CHAO   See LI DAZHAO.

LI TANG (Li T'ang; c. 1050–c. 1130)   A painter during the Song dynasty (960–1279) who developed a style of painting that provided the foundation for the Southern Song (1127–1279) school of landscape painting. Li Tang was born in Henan Province in central China and eventually became head of the imperial painting academy in the capital city of Kaifeng under Emperor Huizong (Hui-tsung). He is associated with the Northern School of landscape painting that had originated with Li Sixun (Li Ssu-hsun; 651–716). Li Tang's powerful style has been described as being based on the "ax-cut texture stroke" (*fupi cun* or *fu-p'i ts'un*), in which the angles on the rocks in his landscapes appear to have been hacked out by the sides of his painting brush. A landscape painting in this style on a silk fan, *A Myriad of Trees on Strange Peaks*, held by the National Palace Museum in Taipei, Taiwan, is attributed to Li Tang and dated 1124 but is probably a later copy. Sadly, it is likely that none of Li's original works have survived. They were destroyed when Kaifeng fell to Jurchen invaders in 1127. However, copies of his paintings, works attributed to him, and aesthetic writings from the time indicate that Li was the most influential Chinese painter in the 12th century.

When Li fled south to Hangzhou, capital of the Southern Song dynasty, after the Jurchen invasion he joined the formal Academy of Painting known as Huayuan that had been established under Emperor Gaozong (Kao-tsung). The finest Northern painters were given positions in the academy to continue the tradition of court painting in the new Song capital. Li is credited with transmitting the monumental, realistic Northern style of painting to the gentler Southern Song style known as the Ma-Xia (Ma-Hsia) school. See also HANGZHOU; KAIFENG; LANDSCAPE PAINTING; LI SIXUN; NORTHERN SCHOOL OF PAINTING; SONG DYNASTY; SOUTHERN SCHOOL OF PAINTING.

LI TIEGUAI (LI T'IEH-KUAI)   See EIGHT IMMORTALS.

LI TSUNG-JEN   See CHIANG KAI-SHEK; REPUBLIC OF CHINA.

LI TZ'U-CHENG   See LI ZICHENG.

LI XIANNIAN (Li Hsien-nien; 1905–1992)   A leading official in the Chinese Communist Party (CCP), which founded the People's Republic of China (PRC) in 1949, who served as president of the PRC 1983–86. Li was born in Hubei Province and was trained to be a carpenter. In 1926 he joined the Northern Expedition conducted by the Chinese Nationalists (Kuomintang; KMT) against the warlords who controlled northern China. The Nationalists had been cooperating with the newly founded CCP, but in 1927 they turned on the Communists and brutally attacked them. This caused Li to become a member of the CCP. When the Communists made their Long March to Shaanxi Province in 1934–35 to escape the Nationalists, Li served as army captain and political commissar. He later became commander of the Central China Military Committee and then deputy commander of the Fourth Field Army. After the Communists defeated the Nationalists and founded the PRC in 1949, Li held prominent CCP positions in central-south China 1949–54. In 1954 he was elected a deputy from Hubei Province to the first National People's Congress. From 1956 to 1987 he served as a member of the Politburo (Political Bureau). He also served as minister of finance, 1957–75. Among his other positions, he was a member of the CCP Secretariat from 1958 until the Cultural Revolution broke out (1966–76); director of the State Financial and Economic Affairs Bureau from 1959 until the Cultural Revolution; vice chairman of the State Planning Commission, 1962–72; a member of the Standing Committee of the Politburo, 1977–87; and vice chairman of the State Financial and Economic Commission, 1979–81. From 1983 to 1986 Li served as president of the PRC. In 1988 he was executive chairman of the Presidium and chairman of the National Committee of the Seventh CCP Central Committee. Since 1978 Li also visited 30 countries as a representative of the PRC, including the United States, Canada, Romania, Yugoslavia and many nations in Africa, Asia and the Pacific region. See also CHINESE COMMUNIST PARTY; CIVIL WAR BETWEEN COMMUNISTS AND NATIONALISTS; GOVERNMENT STRUCTURE; LONG MARCH; MINISTRY OF FINANCE; NATIONALIST PARTY; NORTHERN EXPEDITION; PEOPLE'S REPUBLIC OF CHINA.

LI YU (937–978; r. 961–975)   Also known as Li Houju (Li Hou-chu); the third and final ruler of the brief Southern Tang dynasty (one of the kingdoms during the Five Dynasties and Ten Kingdoms Period (907–60). Li Yu lost his throne in 975 to the Song dynasty (960–1279) and was taken captive to the Song capital (the modern city of Kaifeng in Henan Province). As the Southern Tang ruler, Li Yu encouraged the arts and the Buddhist religion, making his court very cultured. He himself is best remembered as an accomplished poet, calligrapher and painter. These arts provided him a refuge from the burdens of ruling his kingdom and from the tragedies of the death of his beautiful, talented wife and their young son. While in captivity he wrote many fine lyric poems (ci or tz'u) in which he expressed his deep grief over his personal tragedies with a melancholy, delicate quality. His poems gave this form of poetry a new, more personal style. Li Yu was forced by the Song emperor to commit suicide. However, some of the men from his Southern Tang court played a role in developing the highly refined artistic culture of the Song court. See also CALLIGRAPHY; FIVE DYNASTIES PERIOD; KAIFENG; LANDSCAPE PAINTING; LYRIC VERSE; SONG DYNASTY.

LI YUANHAO   See XIXIA, KINGDOM OF.

LI YUANHONG (Li Yuan-hung; 1864–1928)   A military commander who became the only president of the Republic of China (ROC) at Beijing to serve two terms. Li became a divisional commander of a brigade in the modernized New Army of the Manchu Qing dynasty (1644–1911) and was stationed in Wuchang (now part of the modern city of Wuhan, along with Hankou and Hanyang) in Hubei Province in central China. On October 10, 1911, the anti-Qing Revolution broke out among army units in Wuchang that had been infiltrated by radicals. Dr. Sun Yat-sen (1866–1925), the leader of the Revolutionary Alliance (Tongmenghui or Tung-meng hui), the dominant group in the anti-imperial movement, was in the United States at the time, raising funds from overseas Chinese to support the revolution in China. When the uprising broke out, the governor-general and the commander of the local garrison decided to flee rather than fight the rebels. Li was the only person of high rank who remained in Wuchang, and his troops forced him to become the military governor of the new military government they established, even though he had not been associated with the revolutionaries. The revolution spread successfully to other Chinese cities and members of the Revolutionary Alliance demonstrated throughout China in support of the troops that had revolted at Wuchang, which made Li feel more favorable about his position of leadership. By the end of November 1911, 15 of China's 24 provinces, including most of the provinces south of the Yangzi River, declared that they were independent of the Qing. When Sun returned to China, he was inaugurated as president of the Republic of China in Nanjing on January 1, 1912. Li was inaugurated as vice president and continued to hold that position after Sun had to step down in March to be replaced by Yuan Shikai (Yuan Shih-kai; 1859–1916), former commander in chief of the imperial army in Beijing, where political power was concentrated. When Yuan died in June 1916, Li succeeded him as president and held that office until the last Qing emperor, Xuantong (Hsuan-tung; r. 1909–12; later known as Henry Puyi) was restored to the throne briefly in July 1917. In 1922 Li was persuaded to become president of the republic once again, but in September 1923 he had to resign. After Yuan died, China had been divided by warlords, and Li was unable to reunite the country through negotiation rather than the use of military force. See also QING DYNASTY; PUYI, HENRY; REPUBLIC OF CHINA; REVOLUTION OF 1911; REVOLUTIONARY ALLIANCE; SUN YAT-SEN; WARLORD PERIOD; WUCHANG UPRISING; YUAN SHIKAI.

LI ZHAODAO   See LANDSCAPE PAINTING; LI SIXUN.

LI ZICHENG (Li Tz'u-cheng; c. 1605–1645)   The leader of a rebellion that formally ended the Ming dynasty (1368–1644). Li Zicheng was a native of Shaanxi Province in northwestern China where there had been popular uprisings due to famine, epidemics, economic hardship and neglect of the region by the Ming government, which angered military generals in the frontier region. In late 1640, while the Ming were preoccupied with defending themselves on their northeastern border against the Manchus, Li Zicheng gathered a large army in Henan Province, where people were suffering from famine, and captured the major city of Luoyang. The rebellion gained momentum when it was joined by Li Yen, a member of the literati, or scholar class, that governed China in its imperial bureaucracy. In 1642 the rebels laid siege to Kaifeng, another major city, where they cut the Yellow River dikes and several thousand people died from drowning and starvation. At the end of 1643, Li Zicheng moved to Xi'an in Shaanxi, where he changed the city's name back to Chang'an, as it had been called when it was the capital of the Tang dynasty (618–907). In 1644 Li proclaimed the establishment of a new dynasty, called the Great Shun, and began marching toward the Ming capital at Beijing. The imperial court there was defenseless but refused to lose face by fleeing south to the city of Nanjing.

Marching his army east, Li Zicheng occupied the high points along the Great Wall north of Beijing, as well as the area of the Imperial Tombs. The Ming army led by General Wu Sangui (Wu San-Kuiei; 1612–78) was positioned inside the Great Wall, holding off the Manchus. Wu decided to ask the Manchus to help the Ming fight off Li Zicheng's rebels. Li Zicheng was not aware of Wu's alliance with the Manchus, and he marched his army to the pass in the Great Wall known as Shanhaiguan, bringing with him Wu's father and the emperor's son. Wu's father pleaded with Wu to surrender and save his life, but Wu declared that he was loyal to the Ming, and the rebels killed the father in front of Wu, making Wu even more determined to defeat them. He opened the gate at Shanhaiguan and let the Manchus in. Twenty thousand Manchu soldiers riding horses with iron breastplates galloped into the rebel army, which panicked and fled. Wu pursued the rebels instead of rushing to defend Beijing. Li Zicheng entered Beijing in April 1644, when the eunuchs who ran the Forbidden City (Imperial Palace) opened a gate and let the rebel troops in. The empress hanged herself in the palace, and Emperor Chongzhen (Ch'ung-chen) wandered about the grounds in despair and then hanged himself on Coal Hill on the north side of the palace compound. The Manchus, led by their chief Dorgon (1612–50), entered Beijing unopposed on June 5, 1644. They proclaimed their new dynasty, the Qing (which they had established since 1636 in their capital at Mukden in Manchuria and which ruled the Chinese Empire from 1644 to 1911), as the successor to the Ming dynasty and installed their seven-year-old king as the first Qing emperor, Shunzhi (Shun-chih; r. 1644–61). Li Zicheng and his rebel army joined the Manchus. Wu attempted to lead a rebellion against the Qing from 1673 to 1683, but it failed because the Chinese were not eager to support him. See also BEIJING; GREAT WALL; KAIFENG; LUOYANG; MANCHU; MING DYNASTY; QING DYNASTY; SHAANXI PROVINCE; SHUNZHI, EMPEROR.

LI ZONGREN   See CHIANG KAI-SHEK; REPUBLIC OF CHINA.

LIANG CH'I-CH'AO   See LIANG QICHAO.

LIANG DYNASTY   See FIVE DYNASTIES PERIOD; NORTHERN AND SOUTHERN DYNASTIES.

LIANG KAI (Liang K'ai; early 13th century A.D.)   A painter who exerted great influence over later Chan (Zen in Japanese) Buddhist painters in China and Japan and over Chinese academic painters as well. The only source of information about Liang Kai's life is a Chinese text called the *Precious Mirror of Pictures* (*Tu Hui Bao Jian* or *T'u-hui Pao-chien*). He was trained at the Southern Song Imperial Painting Academy during the period in Chinese art history called *Kai* (A.D. 1201–04). Liang Kai painted in the style of Xia Gui (Hsia Kuei; active, c. 1180–1224). Liang Kai rose to the top rank of painter-in-attendance at the academy and was awarded the Golden Belt for his mastery of brushwork. However, he did not keep the belt for himself, but hung it in the academy and left to spend the rest of his life in Chan monasteries in and near Hangzhou, the beautiful capital of the Southern Song dynasty (1127–1279). He preferred the freedom to live as "the Crazy Liang," as he called himself, and was very fond of drinking wine. The works by Liang Kai that remain are in a style of ink painting known as the "abbreviated brush," in which the emphasis is not on careful depiction of detail but on spontaneous presentation of the subject as a whole with rough irregularity. Most of his paintings have been taken to Japan, where he is known as Ryokai. Some of his best-known works with Buddhist subject matter are *Sakyamuni [Buddha] Descending the Mountain, Dancing Budai, The Sixth Patriarch Cutting Bamboo, The Sixth Patriarch Destroying the Sutra, Hanshan and Shide* and *Sage of Yaotai*. His *Landscape in Snow* and *Intoxicated Old Man* are also well-known. Perhaps Liang Kai's most famous painting is a portrait of the great Tang dynasty poet, *Li Bai* (Li Po). Several of these paintings are in the Tokyo National Museum. See also CHAN SECT OF BUDDHISM; INK PAINTING; LI BAI; XIA GUI.

LIANG QICHAO (Liang Ch'i-ch'ao; 1873–1929)   A prominent Chinese scholar, journalist and reformer; born near the southern city of Guangzhou (Canton). He was an excellent student and passed the provincial examinations for the imperial bureaucracy at age 16. He later studied Western learning, such as philosophy and political science, under Kang Youwei (K'ang Yu-wei; 1858–1927), a philosopher in Guangzhou who led the reform movement against the Qing dynasty (1644–1911). Liang joined Kang in advocating social and institutional changes in China. In 1895, at the end of the Sino-Japanese War, the two scholars went to the Chinese capital city of Beijing. Liang assisted Kang in organizing Chinese opposition to the Treaty of Shimonoseki that concluded the war, which was unfavorable to China. The Chinese imperial government awarded Liang an official rank in the bureaucracy, where he became a leader of the political and social changes known as the Hundred Days of Reform (1898). The Empress Dowager Cixi (Tz'u Hsi; 1835–1908) harshly ended this reform movement and led a coup to wrest power from the emperor, who had supported it, causing Liang to flee to Japan. There he continued to advocate reforms in China based on a constitution. In Japan he founded a journal that greatly influenced Chinese intellectuals, and he was very active in writing books and articles that promoted China's modernization. Sun Yat-sen (1866–1925), the leader of the anti-Qing movement and later the founder of the Republic of China, was also in Japan and tried to bring Liang to his side. However, the two factions supporting Sun and Liang became rivals, with Sun's faction advocating the overthrow of the Qing dynasty and the founding of a Chinese republic, and Liang's faction advocating constitutional monarchy. The Association for the Protection of the Emperor (Baohuang Hui or Pao-huang-hui), a monarchist society founded in Japan by Kang and Liang, sent Liang to Southeast Asia and the United States.

After the Revolution of 1911 brought down the Qing and founded the Republic of China (ROC), Liang returned to China, where he held various government positions and organized the Progressive political party in 1913. At first, his party supported President Yuan Shikai (Yuan Shih-k'ai; 1859–1916), who in 1912 replaced Sun Yat-sen as president of the ROC, but opposed his attempt to become a new emperor. Liang also opposed the Twenty-One Demands made on China by Japan in 1915, as well as the brief imperial Restoration of 1917; Kang Youwei supported the latter. Liang retired from politics in 1918 and traveled to Europe, which was recovering from World War I, as an unofficial delegate to the Paris Peace Conference. This trip diminished his enthusiasm for Western culture and Marxist thought. In 1920 Liang returned to China and became a professor of Chinese history at Nankai University in Tianjin. He also continued to produce works of scholarship until he died in Beijing. See also CIXI, EMPRESS DOWAGER; KANG YOUWEI; QING DYNASTY; REPUBLIC OF CHINA; SHIMONOSEKI, TREATY OF; SUN YAT-SEN; TWENTY-ONE DEMANDS ON CHINA; YUAN SHIKAI.

LIANG SIYONG See ARCHAEOLOGY.

LIAO DYNASTY (947–1125) A dynasty founded by the Khitan (Qidan), a confederation of nomadic peoples in western Manchuria (modern northeastern China) and Inner Mongolia. Yelu Agaoji (Yeh-lu A-pao-chi; 872–926) led the Khitan to create an empire in northern Asia. In 907 Yelu declared himself emperor and formally established the Khitan Empire. Known as Emperor Taizu (T'ai-tsu; r. 907–926), he encouraged Chinese to immigrate to Khitan territory and developed an economy that was based on nomadic animal husbandry in the north and Chinese settled agriculture in the south. He also created a Khitan script by simplifying Chinese characters. When Taizu died in 926 the Khitan held suzerainty over kingdoms from the Ordos Plateau, including the Xixia, to Korea in the east. Lands belonging to the Khitan Empire included Manchuria, Inner Mongolia and the northern Chinese prefectures of Hebei and Hedong. Taizu and his successor, Taizong (T'ai-tsung; r. 926–947), developed a government that combined the Tang Chinese bureaucratic system with nomadic tribal customs, the former holding sway from the southern capital at modern Beijing over the Chinese who lived in the south and latter ruling from the Supreme Capital in southern Rehol (Jehol) over nomadic tribes in the north. In 947, with the reign of Emperor Shizong (Shih-tsung; 947–951), the Khitan formally adopted the Chinese name Liao for their dynasty. The Liao had nine emperors altogether. The Chinese Song dynasty waged unsuccessful military campaigns against the Liao in 979 and 986. In order to prevent invasion by the Liao, in 1005 the Song signed the Treaty of Shanyuan with the Liao, which gave the Liao diplomatic equality with the Song and required the Song to pay an annual subsidy of silver and silk to the Liao. An additional treaty in 1042 forced the Song to pay a higher subsidy. In 1115 the Jurchen, a nomadic tribe in

Manchuria who were vassals of the Liao, began attacking the Khitans and brought down the Liao dynasty in 1125. A member of the Liao imperial family escaped west to the Ili valley in modern Xinjiang and established a new Khitan empire, known as the Kara (Black) Khitay, in Central Asia. (The Chinese called it the Western Liao.) This empire lasted until the Mongols conquered China in the next century and established the Yuan dynasty (1279–1368). The name Khitay is the source of the name Kitai for China in Russia and the Middle East, and the name Cathay for China in the Western world. See also BEIJING; CATHAY; IMPERIAL BUREAUCRACY; JURCHEN; NOMADS AND ANIMAL HUSBANDRY; SONG DYNASTY; XIXIA, KINGDOM OF.

LIAODONG PENINSULA A peninsula that forms the southern region of Liaoning Province in northeastern China. Lioning is one of three Chinese provinces known collectively as Manchuria. The Liaodong Peninsula has a rugged, rocky coastline with numerous inlets and harbors, and mountains that range from 1,000 to 3,000 feet high. It borders the Yellow Sea, the Bo Hai Gulf and the Korea Bay of the Yellow Sea, and lies across the Bo Hai Straits from the peninsula that forms the northeastern region of Shandong Province. At the tip of the Liaodong Peninsula, the port city of Dalian (also known as Luda) has a harbor that remains free of ice all year long and is deep and wide enough for large oceangoing ships. Hence Dalian plays a major role in waterborne traffic between northeastern China and the lower Yangzi River (Changjiang) and southeastern coastal areas of China. The city has a strategic location, controlling the entrance to the Bo Hai Gulf, the seaway to northeastern China, and access to the major industrial port of Tianjin. Dalians with a total population of about 5 million, is also a popular tourist and health resort because of its nice beaches and relatively mild climate. It was the center of Chinese coastal defense during the Qing dynasty (1644–1911). In 1878, Lushun, now part of Dalian but then known as Port Arthur, was chosen to be the home port for the Beijing Fleet, China's first modern naval force.

At the end of the 19th century, Lushun became involved in the conflict between Russia, which wanted the port for access to the Pacific Ocean, and Japan, which wanted it for access to Manchuria. After the Russians completed a railroad line to Lushun in 1903 and established a large naval base, Russia and Japan went to war in 1904–05. The Treaty of Portsmouth in 1905 concluding the Russo-Japanese War returned the sovereignty of Manchuria to China but gave Japan the lease on the Liaodong Peninsula. The Russians, who had developed Dalian into a prosperous city, had to concede it to the Japanese as well, who developed it into a modern port and industrial city and connected it to the newly built Northeastern China Railway. Japan held the peninsula until the end of World War II in 1945.

After the Chinese Communists established the People's Republic of China in 1949, Dalian developed rapidly and is now one of China's most important fishing ports. The combined cities of Dalian and Lushun are also called Luda. The Liaodong Peninsula is the center of apple cultivation in China. Other major crops include corn, soybeans, peanuts and cotton. Important industrial products include steel, ships, locomotives and railway rolling-stock, machinery, chemicals and textiles. See also BO HAI GULF; DALIAN; LIAO-NING PROVINCE; LUDA; MANCHURIA; RAILROADS; RUSSO-JAPANESE WAR OF 1904–05; YELLOW SEA.

LIAONING PROVINCE A province in northeastern China; one of three provinces, along with Heilongjiang and Jilin, collectively known as Manchuria. It covers 54,047 square miles and has a population of about 38 million. The capital of Liaoning is Shenyang, called Mukden in the Manchurian language, and it has a population of about 5 million. Other major cities include Anshan, Benxi, Beipiao, Fushun, Fuxin and Dalian (also known as Luda). Liaoning is bordered by North Korea to the east, Jilin Province to the northeast, Hebei Province to the southwest, and Inner Mongolia Autonomous Region to the west. Liaodong Peninsula, the southern part of the Province, juts into the Bo Hai Gulf, which borders the province on the south. Summers are short but warm and rainy, and winters are very cold with an average temperature of 14 degrees F. The vast Songliao (Sungari) Plain, irrigated by the Liao River (Liaohe), is very fertile. Major crops include sorghum, wheat, rice, peanuts, cotton, tussor (wild silk) and tobacco. Liaoning produces 40 percent of China's wild silk, made by untended silkworms. The province is China's largest producer of shellfish and second-largest producer of apples and seaweed. Fishing and sea-salt resources are also significant. Ginseng is harvested for herbal medicines.

Highly industrialized, Liaoning is China's main producer of steel, with about one-fifth of the country's total production; the third-largest producer of natural gas and crude oil; and the largest producer of mining equipment and metal-cutting machine tools. The province has one-third of China's total oil refining capacity. Other manufacturing includes machinery, fuel, electricity, oil refining, and light industrial products such as textiles, bicycles, televisions and sewing machines. The province has one-quarter of China's iron ore deposits and its largest deposits of talcum and boron.

Liaoning Province lies beyond the Great Wall that had been built by the Han Chinese to prevent incursions from non-Han (non-ethnic Chinese) nomadic tribes in the north and west. In ancient times, the Han had established the kingdom of the Northern Yan in Liaoning in 409, but it lasted only until 439. The non-Han tribes regained control until the Tang dynasty (618–907) again brought the region under Chinese control, and the Ming dynasty (1368–1644) established military settlements there. A native tribe called the Jurchen, who began calling themselves Manchu, expanded in the late 16th to early 17th centuries. Nurhachi (1559–1626) consolidated his power as leader of the Manchus, and from 1625 to 1644 Shenyang was the Manchu capital. Nurhachi's grandson Abahai (1592–1643) defeated the Ming and founded the Qing dynasty (1644–1911).

In the 19th century, Russia and other Western powers vied over Liaoning for its enormous natural resources, especially minerals. The Russians built the Northeast China Railroad in 1896–1903, linking the port city of Dalian with Changchun, Harbin and Jilin in Heilongjiang province and Vladivostok in Russia. This provided the Russians access to the ice-free port at Lushun (also known as Port Arthur; port of modern Dalian) in Liaoning. Japan had claimed the Liao-

ding Peninsula after it defeated China in the Sino-Japanese War of 1894–95 but was forced to return it to China by Russia, Germany and France. Russia quickly took control of the peninsula and increased its influence during the disruption caused by the anti-foreign Boxer Uprising in China in 1900. The Russo-Japanese War began when Japanese submarines attacked the Russian fleet in Port Arthur on February 7 and 8, 1904. Japan virtually destroyed the Russian Baltic fleet in the Battle of Tsushima at Port Arthur, and went on to win the war. The Treaty of Portsmouth (1905) forced Russia to give Japan all rights in Manchuria.

In 1931 the Japanese completely occupied Liaoning and the rest of Manchuria and in 1932 they set up their puppet state of Manchukuo (Manzhouguo or Man-chou-kuo in Chinese) with the deposed Manchu emperor, then known as Henry Puyi, at its head. They quickly industrialized the region. However, bombing during World War II and Soviet occupation and withdrawal after the war damaged much of Liaoning's manufacturing infrastructure. Later, during China's civil war, Liaoning was held by the Nationalists (Kuomintang; KMT) until it fell to the Chinese Communists on November 2, 1948. Its population today comprises 29 national minority ethnic groups, such as Manchu, Hui, Xiba and Korean, along with the Han, who are the majority. The Communist government has invested a great deal in Liaoning's heavy industries.

Shenyang, originally Mukden, was the capital of the Manchus. Nurhachi built his imperial palace at Mukden in 1625 through 1636. In 1644 the Manchu capital was moved to Beijing, which remains the capital of China. The Manchu imperial palace and three imperial tombs can be seen in Shenyang. Largely constructed within the last 50 years, Shenyang is today one of China's largest and most important cities and is a major culture and communications center with 28 institutions of higher learning. Luda is an important industrial port formed by combining the naval base at Lushun with Dalian; it still has traces of its former occupations by the Russians and the Japanese. See also BO HAI GULF; BOXER UPRISING; CIVIL WAR BETWEEN COMMUNISTS AND NATIONALISTS; DALIAN; GREAT WALL; JURCHEN; LIAODONG PENINSULA; MANCHU; MANCHUKUO; MANCHURIA; NURHACHI; PUYI, HENRY; QING DYNASTY; RUSSO-JAPANESE WAR OF 1904–5; SHENYANG; SINO-JAPANESE WAR OF 1894–95; WAR OF RESISTANCE AGAINST JAPAN.

LIAOTUNG PENINSULA See LIAODONG PENINSULA.

LIBERATION, NATIONAL The official term in the People's Republic of China (PRC) for the victory of the Chinese Communist Party (CCP) over the Chinese Nationalist Party (Kuomintang; KMT) and the founding of the PRC in 1949. The two parties had cooperated after the CCP was established in the early 1920s, but in 1927 KMT leader Chiang Kai-shek (1887–1975) turned against the CCP and had many communists massacred. After several years of fighting, the Communist Red Army (later known as the People's Liberation Army; PLA) led by Mao Zedong (Mao Tse-tung; 1893–1976) made its famous Long March to western China in 1934–35 to escape the Nationalists. They made their headquarters at Yan'an in Shaanxi Province. The CCP and KMT formed another united front during China's War of

Resistance against Japan (1937–45; World War II), but after Japan was defeated in 1945 they resumed their civil war. The Communists eventually gained the advantage, especially through the use of guerrilla tactics and land reform, a process by which they took land from landowners and wealthy peasants and redistributed it to peasants who owned little land.

On January 15, 1949, the PLA took the port city of Tianjin, and on January 31 it peacefully took Beijing. Nanjing, Chiang Kai-shek's Nationalist capital, fell to the PLA on April 23, and Shanghai on May 27. Chiang and the Nationalists fled to Taiwan Island, where they established the provisional government of the Republic of China (ROC). The CCP held the Chinese People's Political Consultative Conference (CPPCC) in Beijing on September 21–30, which served as the legislative and representative body of the PRC government. On September 29 the CPPCC adopted the Common Program, a provisional constitution that contained the policies of the Central People's Government (CPG). Based on the ideas of CCP chairman Mao Zedong, it served as China's law until it was superseded by the state constitution passed by the National People's Congress in 1954. On October 1, 1949, the CCP formally established the PRC. The same day the CPG held its first meeting and appointed Mao as chairman of the CPG's Revolutionary Military Affairs Committee, Zhou Enlai (Chou En-lai; 1898–1976) as premier of the Government Administrative Council and minister of foreign affairs, and Zhu De (Chu Teh; 1886–1976) as commander-in-chief of the PLA. Mao and Zhou remained the top two leaders in the PRC until they died in 1976. The official newspaper of the PLA is still published under the name *Liberation Army Daily* (*Jiefangjun Bao*). See also CHINESE COMMUNIST PARTY; CHINESE PEOPLE'S POLITICAL CONSULTATIVE CONFERENCE; CIVIL WAR BETWEEN COMMUNISTS AND NATIONALISTS; GOVERNMENT STRUCTURE; LAND REFORM BY COMMUNISTS; LONG MARCH; MAO ZEDONG; NATIONAL PEOPLE'S CONGRESS; NATIONALIST PARTY; PEOPLE'S LIBERATION ARMY; PEOPLE'S REPUBLIC OF CHINA; YAN'AN.

LIBERATION ARMY DAILY See NEW CHINA NEWS AGENCY; PEOPLE'S LIBERATION ARMY.

LIBRARIES See NATIONAL LIBRARY OF CHINA; NINGBO; SHANGHAI; STONE TABLETS.

LIEHZI (LIE TZU) See FATE.

LI-HSUEH See NEO-CONFUCIANISM.

LI-ITO AGREEMENT See SINO-JAPANESE WAR OF 1894–95.

LIJI See BOOK OF RITES.

LIJIANG See LI RIVER AND LING CANAL.

LIJING (LI-CHING) See BOOK OF RITES.

LILY See FOOTBINDING; LOTUS.

LIN BIAO (Lin Piao; 1907–1971) A Chinese Communist military commander designated the successor to Mao

Zedong (Mao Tse-tung; 1893–1976) during the Cultural Revolution (1966–76) but who was later discredited. Lin was born in Hubei Province but moved to Shanghai, where he joined the Socialist Youth League in 1925. He enrolled in the Whampoa (Huangpu) Military Academy in Guangzhou (Canton), where he became known to Zhou Enlai (Chou En-lai; 1898–1976), a future Communist leader who was then deputy director of the academy's political department. In 1926 Lin joined the Northern Expedition, a military campaign to eliminate the power of warlords. In 1927 he joined the Chinese Communist Party. That year the Nationalists (Kuomintang; KMT), who had cooperated with the CCP, turned on the Communists and massacred many of them. Lin took part in the retaliatory Nanchang Uprising on August 1, 1927 by the Communists against the Nationalists, which historians regard as the birth of the Red Army (later known as the People's Liberation Army; PLA). He then joined the Communist forces led by Mao on the border between Hunan and Jiangxi provinces. He went on the Long March (1934–35) by Communist forces under Mao's leadership through central and western China to escape the Nationalist forces, which were fighting a civil war against the Communists. Lin became head of the military academy that the Communists established at their new headquarters at Yan'an in Shaanxi Province.

When China fought its War of Resistance against Japan (1937–45; World War II), Lin became commander of the Communist Fourth Field Army. The Communists and Nationalists formed a united front to fight the Japanese, but their alliance did not last. After Japan was defeated the two parties engaged in a full-scale civil war. In October 1945 Lin was sent to Manchuria (northeastern China) to accept the surrender of Japanese troops and to work with troops from the Soviet Union, who had crossed the border into Manchuria after the U.S.S.R. declared war on Japan on August 8. The Soviet support of Lin's troops, who were given weapons surrendered by the Japanese, enabled the Communists to defeat the Nationalists in Manchuria. When Lin captured the city of Mukden (now known as Shenyang) on November 1, 1948, the Nationalists began to collapse. In January 1949 Lin captured the strategic cities of Tianjin and Beijing. The Nationalists fled to Taiwan and the Communists took other Chinese cities and founded the PRC in Beijing on October 1, 1949. Lin became a member of the Communist Government Council. In 1950, Chinese forces led by units of his Fourth Field Army crossed the Yalu River and entered the Korean War against United Nations forces. Lin rose steadily in the military and in the Communist Party, and in 1959 he replaced Peng Dehuai (P'eng Teh-huai; 1898–1974), who advocated the modernization of the Chinese military, as minister of national defense. Li advocated revolutionary purity over professionalism, and he brought the PLA under stricter control by the Communist Party. In 1965 the Chinese government published Lin's essay, "Long Live the Victory of People's War!" defending China's support of revolutionary movements in Third World countries.

In 1966 the Cultural Revolution began, throwing China into 10 years of turmoil. During the Cultural Revolution, Lin took the place of Liu Shaoqi (Liu Shao-ch'i; 1900–69), who had been purged as state chairman by early 1967. In April 1969 the Ninth Party Congress passed a new party constitution that designated Marshal Lin Biao as CCP vice chairman and Mao's successor. The PLA, however, was divided on policy issues. Lin's faction argued that politics should be in command and that China should continue its struggle against the U.S.S.R. and the United States. From 1970 to 1971 Zhou Enlai built a coalition with a group of PLA regional military commanders who disagreed with some of Lin's radical leftist policies and who were concerned about his political ambitions, which they believed would hamper economic development and the modernization of the military. Also in opposition to the radical position of Lin's faction, behind the scenes, the PRC was attempting to reestablish ties with the United States. In 1972, the same year that U.S. president Richard Nixon visited China and the two countries resumed diplomatic relations, the Chinese government announced that Lin Biao had died in September 1971. It claimed that Lin had attempted a coup to overthrow Mao but had failed and tried to escape to the U.S.S.R.—and his plane had crashed. The government purged the close supporters of Lin Biao. These events marked the turning point in the Cultural Revolution, which finally ended in 1976. In 1980 the government held a notorious trial that indicted Lin Biao's closest supporters and the so-called Gang of Four, who were blamed for the excesses of the Cultural Revolution. See also CHINESE COMMUNIST PARTY; CIVIL WAR BETWEEN COMMUNISTS AND NATIONALISTS; CULTURAL REVOLUTION; GANG OF FOUR; KOREAN WAR; LIU SHAOQI; LONG MARCH; MANCHURIA; MAO ZEDONG; NATIONALIST PARTY; NIXON, RICHARD, U.S. PRESIDENT, VISIT TO CHINA; NORTHERN EXPEDITION; PENG DEHUAI; PEOPLE'S LIBERATION ARMY; PEOPLE'S REPUBLIC OF CHINA; YAN'AN; ZHOU ENLAI.

LIN PIAO See LIN BIAO.

LIN SEN See CHIANG KAI-SHEK.

LIN SHU (1852–1924) A translator of more than 171 Western works of literature into Chinese including works by Daniel Defoe, Charles Dickens, Alexander Dumas, Victor Hugo, Sir Walter Scott, Henrik Ibsen and Miguel Cervantes. Lin Shu was born in Fujian Province. He never traveled to other countries or even learned another language, but listened to oral interpretations of the works by his friends or employees. He then wrote down his adaptations of these novels. Many of Lin Shu's contemporaries were writing in a new style using vernacular Chinese, but he scorned this literary movement and wrote in a beautiful classical Chinese style for which he was praised. His translations have been criticized for containing many errors, but they played an important role in introducing Western literature to the Chinese people. Lin became famous in the late 19th century for his translation of La Dame aux camélias by Dumas. Lin Shu himself especially admired the understanding of people that the British writer Charles Dickens expressed in his novels. The Chinese scholar Yan Fu (1853–1921) was translating Western works into Chinese at the same time as Lin Shu, but Yan Fu concentrated on nonfiction in such areas as political science and philosophy while Lin Shu specialized in fiction. See also YAN FU.

LIN ZEXU (Lin Tse-hsu; 1785–1850) A government official during the Manchu Qing dynasty (1644–1911) who attempted to prevent opium smuggling into China and who played an important role in the Opium War (1839–1942) in which Great Britain defeated China. Beginning in 1829 the Qing had unsuccessfully attempted to prohibit opium traffic in China. By the time of the Opium War, more than 30,000 chests of opium per year were being brought into the country, many Chinese were addicted to the drug, and great quantities of silver bullion were flowing out of China to pay for the opium. In 1838 Emperor Daoguang (Tao-kuang; r. 1821–50) appointed Lin Zexu, who was governor of Hubei and Hunan provinces, as imperial commissioner in the southern port city of Guangzhou (Canton) and ordered him to end the opium trade "once and for all." Lin's strong measures had greatly reduced opium traffic in Hubei and Hunan. He asserted that if China did not stop the opium traffic altogether, the country would keep becoming poorer and its people weaker. Eventually there would not be enough money to support an army nor would there be any competent soldiers.

When Lin arrived in Guangzhou in the spring of 1839, he issued a strong warning to the Chinese merchants in the Cohong, the organization that held an official monopoly on foreign trade in Guangzhou under the so-called Canton System of Trade, that they would be punished if the opium trade continued. He ordered all foreign traders to give up their opium, which they did after he blockaded the foreign warehouse section outside Guangzhou, known as the Thirteen Factories, and he destroyed more than 20,000 chests of opium in public. Lin wrote a letter to Britain's Queen Victoria appealing to moral principles and asking Britain to give up the opium trade, which it controlled. He had copies made so that every European ship returning home could deliver this message. But the British refused to guarantee that they would stop shipping opium into China, and Lin as a result threatened to ban all foreign commerce in China. In July 1839, a group of English sailors in Kowloon, across from Hong Kong Island, killed a Chinese man. Lin demanded that the accused sailors surrender to the Chinese government, but the British refused, and this increased tensions between the two countries.

Lin ordered the expulsion of all British residents from the island of Macao, where foreign traders were required to live during the time that they were not trading in Guangzhou. Lin had the Qing issue an imperial edict on December 13, 1839, which completely banned British trade in China. In response, the British sailed up the Chinese coast, taking Amoy (modern Xiamen), Ningbo and Jusan (Chu Shan) Island and reaching Tianjin, where they began to negotiate with the Manchu Qing official Qishan (Ch'i-shan), whose policy was the opposite of Lin's hard line. The British complained that Lin had dealt too harshly with them, so in September 1840 the Qing appointed Qishan to take Lin's place as imperial commissioner and to handle the negotiations to conclude the Opium War. Among other demands, the British forced the defeated Qing government to strip Lin of his rank and title, to reimburse Britain for the opium Lin had destroyed, and to send him into exile in Xinjiang in western China. Lin spent three years there and was then brought back east to handle other matters for the Qing government. Lin was responsible for much of the material in the *Illustrated Handbook of Maritime Countries* (*Haiguotuji* or *Hai-*

Kuo t'u-chih) published in 1844 by Wei Yuan and reprinted with additions in 1847 and 1852. It advocated that China adopt the superior weapons and military technology of the Western powers. The book was translated into Japanese in 1854–56 and greatly influenced Japan's modernization movement. In 1850 the Qing appointed Lin imperial commissioner for suppression of the Taiping Rebellion (1850–64), but he died before he could take up the position. See also CANTON SYSTEM; OPIUM WAR; QING DYNASTY; TAIPING REBELLION.

LINCOLN, ABRAHAM See THREE PRINCIPLES OF THE PEOPLE.

LING CANAL See LI RIVER AND LING CANAL.

LING PAO SCHOOL See DAOIST CLASSICAL TEXTS.

LING ZIFENG (Ling Tzu-feng; 1917–) One of China's most prominent film directors. Ling was born in Sichuan Province in 1917. He graduated from the Sculpture Department of Beijing Art College in 1934 and from the National Drama College in Nanjing in 1937, the same year that China began fighting Japanese invaders (War of Resistance against Japan, 1937–45; World War II). Ling worked in many positions in the Chinese film industry, including actor, scriptwriter, art designer and director. Since 1959 he has been a general director for the Beijing Film Studio. Most of the films he has directed are adaptations from novels by modern Chinese authors such as Shen Congwen (Shen Ts'ung-wen), who wrote *Border Town,* and Lao She, who wrote *Rickshaw Boy,* which became well-known in the Western world as well as in China. Ling's most important films include *Daughters of China* (1949), which won a Freedom Prize at the Czechoslovak International Film Festival; *Mother* (1956); *Keep the Red Flag Flying* (1960); *Geologist Li Siguang* (1979), which won the Outstanding Film Prize from the Chinese Ministry of Culture; *Rickshaw Boy* (1981), which won numerous awards, including Best Film, Best Actress, Best Art Director and Best Props at the Third Golden Rooster Awards (similar to the Academy Awards or Oscars in China); *Border Town* (1984), which won the Best Film award at the Fifth Golden Rooster Awards and Best Director at the New Stage Film Awards; and *A Woman for Two* (1988), which also won many awards, including the Best Film award at the First Chinese Film Festival. Ling recently directed *Wave over Dead Waters.* See also FILM STUDIOS; LAO SHE; SHEN CONGWEN.

LINGBAO SCHOOL See DAOIST CLASSICAL TEXTS.

LING-CHU FUNGUS See DEER.

LINGNAN SCHOOL OF PAINTING See ZHAO SHAO'ANG.

LINGQU See LI RIVER AND LING CANAL.

LINGWEI See ANCESTOR WORSHIP; ANCESTRAL TABLETS; FUNERALS.

LINGZHU FUNGUS See DEER.

LION (*shizi* or *shih-tzu*) A popular symbol in Chinese art and culture, the lion is often depicted as a cross between a dog and a lion. Lions are not native to China, although some had been sent as gifts to Chinese emperors, so the lion came to be portrayed in a stylized way with a short, thick body, curly mane, bulging eyes, and a wide mouth. The lion is associated with the religion of Buddhism, which had been introduced into China from India in about the first century A.D. Buddhists regarded the lion as the defender of the religion and the protector of sacred buildings; and hence stone sculptures of lions squatting on their hind legs were often placed in front of the gates to temples and palaces. The Chinese consider it lucky to rub the paw of a lion sculpture. A male lion usually has a brocade ball under its right paw and a female lion has a cub. The lion is also called the Fu dog or Fu lion since Fu means Buddha.

The Manchus who ruled China under the Qing dynasty (1644–1911) emphasized the similarities between their palace dogs and the Buddhist lion. They did so because the name Manchu derives from the Buddhist deity Manjusri (Wen Shu in Chinese), who was commonly portrayed in Chinese art as riding a lion. The lamas (priests) of

Buddhists regard the lion as the defender of their religion and the protector of sacred buildings. DENNIS COX

Lamaism, the Tibetan sect of Buddhism, patronized by the Manchus, sent lionlike dogs as tribute gifts to the Manchu court in Beijing. These dogs have become known in the West as Pekingese after the original anglicized name of Beijing (Peking). The Empress Dowager Cixi (Tz'u Hsi; 1835–1908) strongly emphasized the connection between her Pekingese dogs and the Buddhist lion in order to strengthen the connection between her Manchu court and Tibetan Buddhism.

Lion dances are performed in China and in overseas Chinese communities at festivals, especially during the New Year (Spring) Festival, and other happy occasions. A lion dancer wears a large costume with long yellow fur that shakes when he dances and a mouth that he can open and close. He performs acrobatic movements to the music of loud drums and gongs. The best dancers can even climb up on a large ball and roll it with their feet. Another dancer will hold up a ball on a pole in front of the lion to coax it. During the Song dynasty (960–1279), lion dances were performed to chase away enemy armies by scaring their horses and elephants with the loud noises to make the animals panic and run away. Lion dances are said to have become popular in China after villagers in Guangdong Province during the Ming dynasty (1368–1644) performed them to scare away a vicious beast that had killed many people and livestock. Thus lion dances are also believed to chase away evil spirits. See also BUDDHISM; CIXI, EMPRESS DOWAGER; LAMAISM; MAITREYA AND MANJUSRI; NEW YEAR FESTIVAL; OVERSEAS CHINESE; QING DYNASTY.

LISHU See CALLIGRAPHY; STONE TABLETS; WRITING SYSTEM, CHINESE.

LISU An ethnic group that is one of the 55 official national minorities in China, with a population of 574,856, according to the 1990 census. The Lisu are farmers who inhabit the rural and mountainous Nu (Nujiang), Mekong (Lancang) and Jinsha river valleys along the Chinese border of Burma. These valleys in Yunnan Province are in southwestern China. Most Lisu inhabit the Nujiang Lisu Autonomous Prefecture in Yunnan. Some Lisu also reside in Sichuan Province. They belong to the Tibeto-Burman ethnic and linguistic group, which includes the Bai, Hani, Tibetan and Yi groups, among others. They are farmers who practice an animistic religion, similar to the Yi ethnic minority. They enjoy drinking *sheijiu*, an alcoholic beverage distilled from grains. A romanized script has been created for the Lisu language and has been used to publish newspapers, magazines and books. The Lisu are divided into two groups according to their traditional clothing. One group wears black clothes with bands of red, yellow and blue, while the other group dresses in brightly colored clothes. The women decorate their clothing with silver ornaments and jewelry. The Lisu hold their traditional Knife Ladder Festival in March. Eight barefoot young men climb a 50-foot-high pole, on which 30 knives have been tied with their blades pointing upward. At festivals the men also compete using the crossbow and catapult, while the women compete in games on swings. See also BAI; HANI; MEKONG RIVER; TIBETAN; YI; YUNNAN.

LITCHI (*lizi* or *li tze*) Also known as lychee; a round fruit about one inch in diameter that has a sweet but delicate taste. Litchis grow in clusters on trees in the semitropical climate of southern China. The smooth white fruit has a thick, dark red hull that must be removed. Litchis are sold fresh in the summer and in dried form and in cans packed with syrup all year round, and are now available in Western markets. The Chinese especially enjoy litchis as a dessert. Similar fruits are the longan (*longyen* or *lung yen*), loquat (*piba* or *p'i pa*) and rambutan (*shaozi* or *shao tzu*). Litchis and longans were new and exotic fruits to the Han dynasty (206 B.C.–A.D. 220) court in northern China, which had them brought from Guangdong Province by special fast horses. Litchis were also grown in Fujian and Sichuan provinces. During the reign of Emperor Shun (r. 126–44), the poet Wang Yi wrote a verse praising the litchi as the leading fruit given as tribute to the emperor by foreign missions. Yang Guifei (Yang Kuei-fei), the famous and beloved concubine of Emperor Xuanzong (Hsuan-tsung; r. 712–56) who was blamed for his overthrow, was extremely fond of litchis and supposedly had them delivered to the Tang court at Chang'an (modern Xi'an in Shaanxi Province) by fast-riding horse couriers. Merchants made large profits selling litchis. The Chinese believed that eating litchis was a remedy for drinking too much wine. Large festivals were held in Guangzhou (Canton) in late summer to celebrate the ripened litchis. In the eighth century the poet and government official Zhang Jiu-ling (Chang Chiu-ling) wrote that although the litchi was compared with the longan and with table grapes, which had been introduced from Central Asia, there was really no comparison. He claimed that the litchi was worth serving to kings and nobles and was even worth being included in the food offerings made to family ancestors, a heretical view since the litchi was not a classical Chinese food. See also ANCESTOR WORSHIP; YANG GUIFEI.

LITERACY PROGRAM See YEN, YAN YANGCHU JAMES.

LITERATI (*wenren* or *wen-jen*; *shi* or *shih*) Members of the scholar class who were educated in the classics of Confucianism and held positions in the imperial bureaucracy; comparable to a civil service. The bureaucracy was established during the Han dynasty (206 B.C.–A.D. 220) and lasted through the Qing dynasty. Han emperor Wudi (Wu-ti; r. 141–87 B.C.) established a central bureaucracy based on the ideas of Confucius (551–479 B.C.), who had advocated government by "superior men" (*junzi* or *chun-tzu*) who were educated and had high morals. The Han dynasty established an imperial university in 124 B.C. with a curriculum based on the Five Classics of Confucianism, which were concerned with social harmony. Examinations were held to select men to staff the bureaucracy. Candidates had to have beautiful calligraphy, the art of writing Chinese characters with a brush; had to memorize the Confucian classical texts; and had to be able to write prose and poetry that contained allusions to ancient Chinese history and literature. The implements used for writing the Chinese language, including paper, a brush, an ink stick and an ink stone, are known as the Four Treasures of the Scholar's Study. The Chinese invented paper about 2,000 years ago. Those men who passed the examinations were given official bureaucratic positions and their families were given an elite social status. The bureaucracy had a complicated set of grades and orders of rank, which later became known as the Nine-Rank System, and members wore robes decorated with embroidered motifs that indicated their rank.

Members of the bureaucracy were known as *shenshi* or *shenjin* (*shen-shih* or *shen-chin;* literally, "scholars wearing belts with hanging ends"), which is translated as literati, degree-holders, scholar-bureaucrats or officials, scholar-gentry or mandarins. Mandarin is the dialect of the Chinese language spoken in northern China, which became the official dialect of the Chinese government. The literati eventually replaced the old aristocratic families as the ruling elite in China. They had their greatest influence during the Song dynasty (960–1279), when the invention of printing in China enabled large numbers of people to acquire books and the government opened schools around the country to make education available to more Chinese. The imperial examinations were open to scholars from all over China, from poor as well as wealthy families, although they were closed to sons of merchants. This system served as an important means for unifying the Chinese Empire through educating its citizens in traditional Confucian-based concepts and values. Confucian thought experienced a revival during the Song, known as Neo-Confucianism. Zhu Xi (Chu Hsi), the greatest Neo-Confucian scholar, combined four Confucian texts to form the Four Books of Confucianism, which were added to the curriculum for the imperial examinations. Scholars who passed the prefectural, provincial and metropolitan levels of the examinations were permitted to take the examination administered by the imperial palace. The elite were appointed to the Hanlin ("Forest of Writing Brushes") Academy and became advisers to the emperor.

During the Song dynasty, the literati brought their "amateur" style of landscape painting (*wenrenhua* or *wen-jen hua*), which is executed with the same brush and ink as calligraphy, to its fullest development. Literati paintings often included poems written in beautiful calligraphy, and the Chinese classify painting, calligraphy and poetry together as the "Three Perfections." The Chinese believe that the subtle and understated literati style of painting expresses the personality of the artist, who often took up painting after retiring from public life. The literati also advanced the design of gardens as calm, restful microcosms of the natural world. Chinese gardens and landscape paintings share the same subject, "mountains and water." The literati are also associated with the *qin* (*ch'in*), a musical instrument similar to a zither, which they enjoyed playing at parties where they drank wine and composed poems.

The position of the literati declined during the Qing dynasty and changed greatly in the 20th century. The Qing dynasty was founded by Manchus, an ethnic group from Manchuria (modern northeastern China) that was vastly outnumbered by the Han Chinese ethnic majority. Yet the Qing reserved half of the positions in the imperial bureaucracy for Manchus, which meant that many Han literati, however well qualified, would never be able to hold official positions. This increased Han Chinese resentment toward the Manchus, especially in heavily populated southern China. In 1905 the literati lost their government support when the Qing dynasty abolished the imperial examinations. The Chinese anti-Manchu revolutionary movement came to a head when the dynasty was overthrown by the Revolution of 1911. Chinese scholars then had to begin studying at military schools, which taught mathematics and science, and at newly founded Western-style universities, such as Beijing University. Some also traveled abroad to study at universities in Japan, the United States and Europe, and they brought back to China such Western intellectual concepts as Darwinism and Marxism-Leninism.

Chinese students and intellectuals played a prominent role in the Revolution of 1911 and the May Fourth Movement of 1919, which were the source of modern Chinese revolutionary movements. In 1919 there was also a movement in China to use *baihua* (*Pai-hua*), the Chinese vernacular language, rather than the classical Chinese that had always been used in schools, business and the government bureaucracy. This became known as the New Literature, or New Culture, Movement. In the early 1920s, many intellectuals helped found the Chinese Communist Party (CCP), which established the People's Republic of China (PRC) in 1949. Mao Zedong (Mao Tse-tung), who served as CCP leader for decades, was a librarian at Beijing University when he joined the party. Zhou Enlai (Chou En-lai), the second most important CCP leader, was born to a literati family. The PRC is governed by a bureaucracy as vast and complex as the imperial bureaucracy, although its members have been trained in Communist ideology rather than Confucianism. Chinese students today take difficult and highly competitive examinations, comparable to the examinations for the imperial bureaucracy, which admit only a small number of them to universities and other Chinese institutions of higher learning. See also BEIJING UNIVERSITY; CALLIGRAPHY; CONFUCIANISM; FIVE CLASSICS OF CONFUCIANISM; FOUR BOOKS OF CONFUCIANISM; FOUR TREASURES OF THE STUDY; HANLIN ACADEMY; IMPERIAL BUREAUCRACY; IMPERIAL EXAMINATION SYSTEM; INK PAINTING; LANDSCAPE PAINTING; LANGUAGE, CHINESE; MANDARIN; MAY FOURTH MOVEMENT OF 1919; NEO-CONFUCIANISM; NEW CULTURE MOVEMENT; NINE-RANK SYSTEM; QIN; SUPERIOR MAN; WRITING SYSTEM, CHINESE; ZHU XI.

"LITTLE EMPERORS" See FAMILY STRUCTURE; ONE-CHILD FAMILY CAMPAIGN.

"LITTLE RED BOOK" See QUOTATIONS FROM CHAIRMAN MAO ZEDONG.

LIU BANG See GAODI (EMPEROR).

LIU BEI See GUANDI; ROMANCE OF THE THREE KINGDOMS; ZHUGE LIANG.

LIU BINYAN (Liu P'in-yen; 1925–) A well-known modern Chinese author and dissident. Liu was born in Harbin, the capital of Heilongjiang, China's most northeastern province. His parents separated when he was young, which forced him to leave school. But he wanted to be a writer and published his first story in 1939, when he was only a teenager. He worked as a teacher in Tianjin and joined the Chinese Communist Party (CCP) in 1949, during China's War of Resistance against Japan (World War II; 1937–45). The CCP defeated the Nationalist Party (Kuomintang; KMT) and founded the People's Republic of China (PRC) in 1949. In 1951, Liu took a position with *Youth Daily*, published in the capital city of Beijing. He then became a roving reporter for the *People's Daily*, the official CCP newspaper, and began writing pieces in a unique style that has been termed "reportage fiction," using fiction techniques to describe the actual working and living conditions of the Chinese people. In the so-called Hundred Flowers Movement, CCP leaders encouraged people to openly criticize the party bureaucracy, so Liu wrote *On the Bridge Construction Site*, in which a young work leader saves part of the bridge his team is building when a flood threatens to destroy it. But his boss, an older party cadre (administrator), accuses the young man of being arrogant because he used his own initiative to save the bridge and demotes him to another, lower-level job. *An Inside Story* describes a young woman reporter who tells the truth about how Communist bureaucracy wastes resources and harms workers; for example, miners are forced to work in dangerous conditions and are prevented from getting enough sleep because they have to attend frequent political meetings. But the corrupt and uncaring party cadres who run her newspaper will not print her stories, and they refuse to give her membership in the CCP, which would provide her many benefits, because she supports the workers over the cadres.

Liu himself was punished for telling the truth. In 1958, as a result of the CCP Anti-Rightist Campaign to punish the artists and intellectuals who had openly criticized the party during the Hundred Flowers Movement, Liu was sent to work in the countryside and denounced as a "mouthpiece of the bourgeois rightists." He was released but soon arrested again, and between 1958 and 1979 he was a prisoner for all but two months when he was allowed to visit his family. But he never stopped writing, and in 1979 he published his most famous work, *Between Me and Monsters*, a strong criticism of the Cultural Revolution (1966–76) and the CCP system under the leadership of Chairman Mao Zedong (Mao Tse-tung). It tells the story of a paymaster of a coal company in the highly industrialized northeastern region (Manchuria) who builds a lucrative organized crime network with the support of the local heads of the CCP. When the book was published, people wrote to Liu from all over China telling him that he had portrayed a true picture of conditions in the country.

Liu was rehabilitated after 1979 and returned to his work as a reporter. In 1983–85 he served as secretary of the Chinese Writers' Association, and in 1985 he was appointed vice chairman. In 1987 he was expelled from the CCP for "bourgeois liberalization," but he remained vice chairman of the Chinese Writers' Association. He left China in 1989 during the crisis caused by the student pro-democracy demonstrations in Tiananmen Square in Beijing, but continued to write. He became famous in the Western world and published *Speaking Out Is Better than Silence* (1980), *Mud under the White Coat* (1984) and *The Second Kind of Loyalty* (1985). See also ANTI-RIGHTIST CAMPAIGN; CADRE; CHINESE COMMUNIST PARTY; HUNDRED FLOWERS CAMPAIGN; MANCHURIA; PEOPLE'S DAILY; TIANANMEN SQUARE MASSACRE.

LIU BOCHENG (Liu Po-ch'eng; 1892–1986)   A veteran military leader who held high official positions in the People's Republic of China (PRC), founded in 1949 by the Chinese Communist Party (CCP). Liu was born in Sichuan Province. His father was a traveling musician who educated Liu in classical Chinese culture. Liu attended military school, graduating in 1911, and in 1926 he joined the recently formed CCP. In August 1927 he took part in the Nanchang Uprising. From 1928 to 1930 he studied at the Red Army Military Academy in the U.S.S.R. Liu was an excellent soldier who was highly skilled in guerrilla warfare, which the Communists used against the Chinese Nationalists (Kuomintang; KMT). In 1931 he joined the Communist forces led by Zhu De (Chu Teh) and Mao Zedong (Mao Tse-tung), and became concurrently chief of staff, Armed Forces Headquarters, and head of the Red (Communist) Army Academy in Ruijin. When the Communists made their Long March in 1934–35 to escape the Nationalists, Liu served as chief of staff of the Communist First Front Army. When China fought its War of Resistance against Japan (1937–45; World War II), Liu became commander of the 115th Division, one of the three divisions of the Eighth Route Army. In 1941 the 115th Division occupied the provinces of Hebei, Henan and Shandong, where a regional government was established with Deng Xiaoping (Teng Hsiao-p'ing) as political commissar.

In 1947, during the civil war between the CCP and KMT, Liu's troops drove a wedge between KMT forces in Wuhan and Nanjing in central China. Liu was one of the most effective Communist military leaders, especially through the use of guerrilla tactics. In 1949, the year that the CCP defeated the KMT, Liu joined his forces with those of CCP commander Chen Yi and took Nanning, where Liu became mayor and chairman of the Nanning Military Control Commission. When the CCP founded the PRC, Liu became a member of the Central People's Government Council (then the highest government organ) and the People's Revolutionary Military Commission. He led his troops southwest into Yunnan Province, where he served as one of the three leading figures in the Southwest Military Region until 1954. He also led forces into Tibet when China invaded that region in 1950–51.

Liu served as president of the PLA (People's Liberation Army, formerly the Red Army) Military Academy in Nanjing from 1951 to 1957. In 1954 he was elected a member of the Standing Committee of the First National People's Congress (NPC). From 1959 to 1979 he served as vice chairman of the Standing Committees of the Second-Fifth NPC. From 1954 to 1957 he was also director of the PLA General Training Department. In 1961 he was a member of the Standing Committee of the CCP Military Affairs Commission. Liu was appointed marshal and decorated with the Orders of August First, Independence and Freedom, and Liberation. In 1955, when the PLA awarded military ranks, Liu was named as one of China's 10 marshals, the highest rank. In 1956 he was elected to the Politburo (Political Bureau) and held this position until 1982, and he was selected as a vice chairman of the NPC. Liu, a strong advocate of professionalization within China's military, was also a prolific writer and translated many military works from Russian. Although he did not appear in public after 1977 because of failed eyesight, Liu continued to hold great prestige in the PRC. See also CHEN

YI; CHINESE COMMUNIST PARTY; CIVIL WAR BETWEEN COMMUNISTS AND NATIONALISTS; DENG XIAOPING; EIGHTH ROUTE ARMY; LONG MARCH; NANCHANG UPRISING; NATIONAL PEOPLE'S CONGRESS; PEOPLE'S LIBERATION ARMY; PEOPLE'S REPUBLIC OF CHINA; POLITBURO; TIBET; WAR OF RESISTANCE AGAINST JAPAN.

LIU CHIN See EUNUCHS.

LIU CH'IU ISLANDS See RYUKYU ISLANDS.

LIU FA See SIX CANONS OF PAINTING.

LIU HAI A god of wealth and successful undertakings. According to legend, Liu Hai was a government minister in the 10th century who also became an adept in alchemy, with which he attained supernatural powers. Stories claim that he owned a magical three-legged toad, a symbol of making money, on which he could ride anywhere. The toad would sometimes run away and disappear down a well, but it loved money so much that Liu Hai could always catch it by putting a string down the well on which were tied gold coins (called "cash"). Another version of the story states that the toad lived in a deep pond and sent out a poisonous gas that harmed people. Liu Hai caught the toad with a gold coin and destroyed it, illustrating the moral that the desire for money can ruin people. Liu Hai is commonly depicted with one foot on the toad and holding a string of five gold coins. This design, known as "Liu Hai Sporting with the Toad," is believed by the Chinese to be the most auspicious monetary symbol for a person.

LIU HSI-CHUN See ZHANG QIAN.

LIU JIN See EUNUCHS.

LIU LICHUAN See SMALL SWORD SOCIETY.

LIU PANG See GAOZU (EMPEROR).

LIU PEI See GUANDI; ROMANCE OF THE THREE KINGDOMS; ZHUGE LIANG.

LIU P'IN-YEN See LIU BINYAN.

LIU PO-CH'ENG See LIU BOCHENG.

LIU SHAO-CH'I See LIU SHAOQI.

LIU SHAOQI (Liu Shao-ch'i; 1898–1969) A leader of the Chinese Communist Party (CCP). Liu was born in Hunan Province and was educated at the First Normal School in Jangsha where Mao Zedong (Mao Tse-tung; 1893–1976), the future leader of the Communist People's Republic of China, was also a student. Liu moved to Shanghai, where he joined the Socialist Youth League in 1920. That winter he was sent to Moscow in the Soviet Union with a group of Chinese students to attend the Communist University for the Toilers of the East. The Chinese Communist Party held its First National Congress in Shanghai in July 1921. Liu, who was still abroad, joined the Moscow branch of the CCP. In 1922

he returned to China and spent several years organizing Chinese coal miners and other workers. In 1923 he went south to Guangzhou (Canton), where the Communists were preparing to form an alliance with the Nationalist (Kuomintang) Party. In 1925 Liu was elected vice chairman of the All-China Federation of Labor. In 1927 he was elected to the Central Committee of the CCP, and general secretary of the All-China Federation of Labor. That year the Nationalists began purging the Communists and attempted to destroy the CCP, and Liu went into hiding. In 1930 he reappeared in Shanghai, working with Communist leader Zhou Enlai (Chou En-lai; 1898–1976) to organize labor unions. In 1932 Liu moved to Mao's Communist base in the mountains of Jiangsu Province. The following year Liu joined the Long March (1934–35) westward by the Communists to escape the Nationalists, but he left the march to go underground once again.

From 1936 until 1942 Liu continued working as a Communist organizer in north and central China and served as head of the bureaus of those regions for the CCP Central Committee. During that time he also traveled to Yan'an in Shaanxi Province, where Mao had established Communist headquarters. In 1937 the Communists and Nationalists had formed a shaky alliance to fight the Japanese, who had invaded China (War of Resistance against Japan; 1937–45). Liu, one of the chief theorists of the CCP, continued rising in the party hierarchy during the war, and in 1945 the CCP designated him its third-ranking member after Mao and Zhu De (Chu Teh; 1886–1976).

When the Communists established the PRC on October 1, 1949, Liu became the second chairman of the government, again following Mao and Zhu De. Liu wrote the book, *How to Be a Good Communist,* which became required reading for everyone in China. The First National People's Congress, held in 1954, formally elected Mao chairman (or president) of the PRC and elected Liu chairman of the Standing Committee of the National People's Congress. By the time of the Hundred Flowers Movement in 1957, Liu was Mao's designated successor. In December 1958, due to the failure of the country's Great Leap Forward, Mao announced that he was stepping down as chairman of the PRC, and in April 1959 Liu was elected to this position. In the early 1960s the CCP was beset by struggles between radical and pragmatic factions over the political and economic policies that the country should follow. In September 1964 Liu, who had been informed about the corruption of CCP members in the Chinese countryside, issued a set of directives that quoted Mao's writings but actually tried to blunt the radical Maoists. Mao attempted to purge his opposition from the party by inaugurating the Cultural Revolution (1966–76). He accused Liu and his colleagues of following a "revisionist" policy and demanded that they be removed from their positions. In 1967 Mao persuaded the Politburo Standing Committee to censure Liu. Red Guards attacked Liu as an anti-Mao counterrevolutionary who was "China's number one capitalist roader," the phrase Mao's faction used to attack anyone whom they felt was not a good Communist and should be purged. They kidnapped Liu's wife, Wang Guangmei (Wang Kuang-mei), who also held a high position in the party. Any Chinese who was caught reading Liu's book was also denounced as a "capitalist roader." The Twelfth Plenary

Session of the CCP in October 1968 officially denounced Liu and formally expelled him from the party, and in 1969 it replaced him as chairman with Lin Biao (Lin Piao; 1907–71). Liu remained in disgrace until he died in detention in 1969. In 1980 the CCP rehabilitated Liu posthumously and held memorial services for him throughout the country. See also CHINESE COMMUNIST PARTY; CIVIL WAR BETWEEN COMMUNISTS AND NATIONALISTS; CULTURAL REVOLUTION; LIN BIAO; LONG MARCH; MAO ZEDONG; NATIONALIST PARTY; PEOPLE'S REPUBLIC OF CHINA; ZHOU ENLAI; ZHU DE.

LIU TSUNG-YUAN See LIU ZONGYUAN.

LIU XIJUN See ZHANG QIAN.

LIU XIU (Liu Hsiu; d. A.D. 57)   Known by his posthumous title of Guangwudi (Kuang Wu-ti); founder of the Eastern or Later Han dynasty (A.D. 25–220), after the period when the Western or Former Han dynasty (206 B.C.–A.D. 8) was nearly overthrown by the insurrection of Wang Mang, known as the Wang Mang Interregnum (A.D. 9–23). Liu Xiu, the cousin of the last Western Han emperor and a ninth-generation descendant of the founder of the Han dynasty, was a native of the Nanyang district (in modern Henan Province). His father had been a country magistrate, but Liu Xiu became an orphan at age 9 and was raised by his uncle, a powerful landlord who sent him to the capital at Chang'an (modern Xi'an in Shaanxi Province) to study the classical books of Confucianism, which provided the model for the Han imperial bureaucracy. Liu Xiu also served as an administrator in the countryside, performing such duties as selling grain in a district where there was a food shortage. His Confucian training and his rural experience taught him that the Chinese Empire would remain stable only if the physical needs of the peasants were met by the government.

Wang Mang, the Han regent, seized the throne in A.D. 9 and attempted to make government reforms, but his economic programs were not successful and peasant rebellions broke out. In A.D. 22 a famine in Nanyang caused the landlords to lead their angry peasants in a revolt, and Liu Xiu joined their cause. Wang Mang was killed the next year, and the rebel warlords engaged in a struggle for control of the throne, with the main factions including the Red Eyebrows and the Green Woodsmen. It took 12 years of fighting for Liu Xiu to defeat his rivals and bring all of the Chinese Empire under his control, although in A.D. 24 he had already proclaimed himself the emperor of the restored Han dynasty. The city of Chang'an had been devastated by the fighting and was still in the hands of the Red Eyebrows, so in A.D. 25 Liu Xiu, flying red imperial banners in place of the yellow banners of the Western Han, moved the capital of his new Eastern or Later Han dynasty to Luoyang in Henan Province. In A.D. 54 the members of his court encouraged Liu Xiu to offer sacrifices to Heaven on Mount Tai (Taishan). Performing these rituals was confirmation that the emperor had been given the Mandate of Heaven (tianming or t'ien-ming) that legitimized his reign. Liu Xiu preferred to wait until he was sure that his subjects were content with his rule, and he performed the rituals at Mount Tai in A.D. 56. The Eastern Han Dynasty was strongest during the reigns of Liu Xiu, its founding emperor, and his son and successor, Liu Zhuang,

known as Emperor Mingdi (Ming-ti). They reduced taxes, ended monopolies on important commodities, and issued edicts to free slaves. See also CHANG'AN; CONFUCIANISM; EASTERN HAN DYNASTY; LUOYANG; MANDATE OF HEAVEN; PEASANTS AND PEASANT REBELLIONS; TAI, MOUNT; WANG MANG; WESTERN HAN DYNASTY.

LIU ZONGYUAN (Liu Tsung-yuan; 773–819)   A poet and essayist active in the literary movement to revive a freer style in Chinese prose writing during the Tang dynasty (618–907). The movement created the poetic form known as regulated or new-style verse (shi or shih). Liu Zongyuan was born and raised in Chang'an (modern Xi'an), the cosmopolitan Tang capital. Even as a young man he was a talented writer, but after completing his education he entered the imperial bureaucracy that governed China. He quickly rose to high position and was known for his honesty. However, Liu gained political enemies who caused him to fall out of favor, and in 805 was assigned to a minor government position in a rural district in modern Hunan Province. After 10 years he was appointed to the position of prefect in Guangxi, a remote province in southern China then inhabited largely by ethnic minorities. The poems that Liu wrote describe his feelings as a northern Chinese who has been exiled from the imperial court and who is struggling to cope with his isolation in the village life of southern China. His poems show that over time he came to feel more comfortable in his new surroundings. As a prose writer, Liu supported his contemporary Han Yu (768–824), another scholar and government official, in the movement to free Chinese writers from "parallel prose" (pianwen or p'ien-wen), a highly formal and restricted style used by the literati or scholars for nearly 1,000 years. Liu and Han attempted to revive the clarity and simplicity of the so-called "ancient style" or "Han style" (Han dynasty, 206 B.C.–A.D. 220) of Chinese classical prose, which was used by the famous historians Sima Qian (Ssu-ma Ch'ien) and Ban Gu (Pan Ku). Liu wrote many essays in this beautiful style, describing the scenery of southern China, that have been beloved by the Chinese people. See also CHANG'AN; HAN YU; IMPERIAL BUREAUCRACY; LITERATI; REGULATED OR NEW-STYLE VERSE.

LIUQIU (LIU-CH'IU) See RYUKYU ISLANDS.

LIU-SONG DYNASTY See NORTHERN AND SOUTHERN DYNASTIES.

LIXUE See NEO-CONFUCIANISM.

LOESS   A yellowish-brown soil that blows through northern China from desert regions, especially from the plateau of the Inner Mongolia Autonomous Region, which lies north of the Great Wall. Inner Mongolia lies south of the largest loess plateau in the world, covering about 400,000 square miles in Shaanxi Province, areas of Gansu, Shanxi, Hebei and Henan Provinces, and part of Ningxia Hui Autonomous Region. Loess is composed mostly of quartz, feldspar and mica and is very dusty and easily carried on the wind and dropped. In some places in Shaanxi Province, loess deposits are more than 200 feet thick. This soil is very fertile, and also can be used for building; many Chinese still live in homes that have been cut into the faces of loess cliffs. However, loess erodes easily.

The Yellow River (Huanghe) is so named because it carries large quantities of eroded loess. The middle section of the Yellow River runs for 500 miles through loess land. It has created the fertile North China Plain, which covers part of the provinces of Hebei, Henan, Shandong and Shanxi by flooding. Each time the river floods and breaks its dikes, which it has done hundreds of times in recorded history, it deposits a new layer of loess over thousands of square miles and then carves a new path to the sea. Neolithic farmers began cultivating millet along these fertile river terraces 7,000 years ago, and this area has become heavily settled and cultivated. The main crops today are wheat, sorghum, millet and corn. Loess hills along the Yellow River have been terraced in order to control erosion and create new land for agriculture.

Due to loess deposits, the mouth of the Yellow River has shifted markedly over the centuries, sometimes emptying into the Bo Hai Gulf north of Shandong Province and sometimes into the Yellow Sea south of it. The famous pottery army at Emperor Qin Shi Huangdi's mausoleum, which was excavated near Xi'an in 1974, was buried under loess soil for 2,200 years. A famous dessert made with pureed chestnuts is named Peking Dust, after the soil blown into Beijing by swirling winds at the end of a dry summer. See also AGRICULTURE; BO HAI GULF; GANSU PROVINCE; GRAIN; HEBEI PROVINCE; HENAN PROVINCE; INNER MONGOLIA AUTONOMOUS REGION; NINGXIA-HUI AUTONOMOUS REGION; SHAANXI PROVINCE; SHANDONG PROVINCE; SHANXI PROVINCE; TERRA-COTTA ARMY, TOMB OF EMPEROR QIN SHI-HUANGDI; XI'AN; YELLOW RIVER; YELLOW SEA.

LO-HAN See LUOHAN.

LOLO See YI.

LONG See DRAGON.

LONG LIFE See DOUBLE HAPPINESS AND LONG LIFE.

LONG MARCH, THE (1934–1935) A yearlong trek to northwestern China by a large branch of the Red Army, the military arm of the Chinese Communist Party (CCP), to escape the army of the Nationalist Party (Kuomintang; KMT), against whom they were fighting a civil war. The CCP and KMT had cooperated in the 1920s, but in April the KMT led by Chiang Kai-shek had massacred a large number of Communists in Shanghai, and many other Communists fled to the countryside. In August 1927 the Communists retaliated against the KMT with the Nanchang Uprising led by Zhu De (Chu Teh) and Zhou Enlai (Chou En-lai) and the Autumn Harvest Uprising led by Mao Zedong (Mao Tse-tung). Many Communists fled to the Soviet base area that had been established in the Jinggang Mountain Range along the border between Hunan and Jiangxi provinces. There the Communists joined with poor peasants, KMT deserters and local bandits to form the First Workers' and Peasants' Army, or Red Army (later known as the People's Liberation Army; PLA).

From 1927 until 1934, the Red Army fought KMT forces by using guerrilla tactics that made Mao a world-famous military strategist. However, the Red Army was forced into a defensive position that it was not able to maintain because it ran short of medical supplies and weapons. In 1928 Chiang Kai-shek became the chairman of a new KMT government with his capital at Nanjing. In 1930 he launched the first of five annual major campaigns against the Communists in Jiangxi. When the Communists began to run out of food and ammunition in the spring of 1934, they made contingency plans to move from Jiangxi to places where other Communist soviets were surviving, either in Sichuan Province in western China or Shaanxi Province in northwestern China.

By the end of 1934 the Red Army had to retreat, and it was able to evacuate many people before the KMT realized what was happening. About 100,000 Communists left the Jiangxi base and began their rigorous trek to northwestern China; this became known as the Long March. Some Communist troops remained in Jiangxi as decoys. The sick, elderly and very young also had to stay there, including two children born to Mao's companion He Zizhe (Ho Tzuche), who accompanied him on the march. The Red Army retreat took one year and covered more than 4,000 miles, crossing 24 rivers and 18 mountain ranges and passing through 12 provinces, fighting along much of the route. Some members were left at villages along the way to organize Chinese revolutionaries. The Red Army moved west through the southwestern province of Guizhou. In January 1935 the Communist army stopped to rest in Zunyi, Guizhou Province. There Mao and other CCP leaders held a conference, and Mao was elected chairman of the CCP Politburo. The army took a twisting route that skirted Guilin in Guizhou and Kunming in Yunnan Province, and then moved north along the borderlands of Tibet and through Gansu Province (west of Chengdu in Sichuan) to Shaanxi. There in 1935 Mao and the approximately 7,000 (estimates range from 4,000 to 8,000) survivors of the Long March from the Jiangxi base joined with the Fourth Army led by Zhang Guotao (Chang Kuo-t'ao), one of the founders of the CCP. In 1931, Zhang Guotao had become the head of a Soviet base in northern China. He had established a base in the Dabie Mountain Range northeast of Wuhan but in 1933 had to move it to northern Sichuan. When they met, there were many more troops under Zhang than under Mao. Mao and his colleagues would not accept Zhang's claims to leadership, and when they heard that a small CCP army from the Dabie Mountains had set up a base in Shaanxi near the Great Wall, Mao and the Jiangxi Red Army moved there. Zhang marched his 4th Army north by a different route. By October 20, 1935, Mao's forces joined the 15th Red Army Corps in Shaanxi, where they were safe from KMT troops. They had regrouped around Baoan village, between the Great Wall and Xi'an, a very poor and mountainous region of China. With Yan'an as their headquarters, they established a base and began to organize the area. The Red Army gained members from local peasants, Muslims and members of secret societies. Zhang's army had suffered heavy losses, so the CCP put him on trial in 1937 and ordered him to undertake "rectification study," meaning ideological indoctrination. Zhang then broke away from Mao's faction and went over to the KMT side.

Only the Red Army leaders and a very small proportion of the troops traveled the entire length of the Long March. The military commanders were carried most of the way on litters each day, after staying up each night to deal with army intelligence, logistics, and personnel to prepare for the following day of marching and fighting. About 50 women survived the Long March, including Jiang Qing (Chiang Ch'ing), who became Mao's wife; Deng Yingchao (Teng Yingch'ao), the wife of Zhou Enlai; and Ding Ling (Ting Ling), a famous author. In Yan'an Ding Ling was assigned to work on editing the historical records of the Long March. When the Communists began their march, Zhou outranked Mao. But Mao's insistence on guerrilla warfare tactics proved successful, and on the Long March Mao regained his power as party leader and became chairman of the Politburo. From that time on, Mao held the most powerful position in the CCP and Zhou functioned as Mao's second-in-command.

The Red Army was still very vulnerable in Shaanxi, as KMT troops loyal to Chiang Kai-shek were massing at Xi'an to fight what they hoped would be their final campaign to eliminate the Communists. The Japanese had invaded Manchuria and set up a puppet state there in 1932, and were preparing to invade China Proper. The Chinese Communists tried to survive by promoting a nationwide anti-Japanese United Front. On December 9, 1935, students in Beijing staged a huge anti-Japanese rally, and Chinese all over the country supported them. The Communists persuaded KMT military commanders Zhang Xueliang and Yang Hucheng to form a national front with them against the Japanese. On December 12, 1936, they kidnapped Chiang Kai-shek at the Huaqing Hot Springs outside Xi'an. After heavy negotiations, Chiang was released two weeks later when he agreed to stop fighting the Communists and to lead the entire country in an anti-Japanese united front. This agreement not only spared the Communists but also gave them a patriotic image.

The Long March was a definitive event in modern Chinese history. In Yan'an the Communists developed their ideology, guerrilla tactics and indoctrination methods. The veterans of the Long March became the elite in the CCP and held major positions in the government of the People's Republic of China (PRC) founded by the Communists in 1949. When the Cultural Revolution (1966–76) broke out in China, it presented an experience for the young Chinese who had been born after 1949 that was comparable to the famous Long March of 1935. In the 1980s, the Chinese government began the process of transferring power from members of the Long March generation to younger officials. See also CHIANG KAI-SHEK; CHINESE COMMUNIST PARTY; CULTURAL REVOLUTION; DENG YINGCHAO; DING LING; HUAQING HOT SPRINGS; JIANG QING; JIANGXI PROVINCE; JINGGANG MOUNTAIN RANGE; MAO ZEDONG; PEOPLE'S LIBERATION ARMY; POLITBURO; SHAANXI PROVINCE; YAN'AN; ZHANG GUOTAO; ZHANG XUELIANG; ZHOU ENLAI; ZHU DE.

LONGAN   See LITCHI.

LONGEVITY HILL   See SUMMER PALACE.

LONGMEN CAVE TEMPLES AND SCULPTURES (Longmen Shiku)   A group of Buddhist caves carved into mountains located on both sides of the Yi River nine miles south of Luoyang in Henan Province in north-central China. Longmen Mountain (also called West Mountain, Xishan) rises on the west bank and Xiang Mountain (also called East Mountain, Dongshan) rises on the river's east bank. Longmen means "Dragon Gate." An ancient legend states that at this site there was a mountain behind which a destructive dragon lived in a large body of water. Legendary emperor Yu got rid of the dragon by splitting the mountain open and giving it passage to the sea.

At Longmen there are more than 1,300 caves containing over 2,100 grottoes and niches, about 100,000 sculptures, several pagodas and numerous inscriptions. The carving began at Longmen in 494 during the Northern Wei dynasty (386–534) and continued into the seventh century. The Northern Wei rulers made Buddhism their state religion and had already commanded the carving of caves at Datong, their first capital. They moved the capital to Luoyang in 494 and began a similar project there. It is claimed that a total of 800,000 craftsmen created the Longmen Buddhist cave temples and sculptures, which rank with those at Dunhuang in Gansu Province and Datong in Shanxi Province as high points of Chinese Buddhist artistic expression. The Buddhist religion was introduced into China from India and had originally been brought to Luoyang in 68.

The Buddhist art at Longmen progressed through different styles. The Guyang Cave, begun in 495 and the oldest at Longmen, contains rock paintings and bas-relief wall carvings of *apsaras*, winged heavenly beings commonly depicted playing musical instruments or carrying flowers and incense. The best example of the elongated, two-dimensional yet energetic Northern Wei style is contained in the Central Pingying Cave, which houses 11 large sculptures of the Buddha and several smaller sculptures of the Buddha and his disciples. The Shikusi Cave contains impressive scenes of processions.

The majority of the caves and sculptures, and the finest, were carved from 713 to 741 during the Tang dynasty. The best example is the Fengxian Temple Cave, which contains a 55-foot-high sculpture of the Buddha as well as sculptures of other Buddhist deities. Throughout the caves are many carvings of lotus flowers, which symbolize purity in Buddhism; the most beautiful are on the ceilings of the Central Pingyang and Lotus Flower caves. The Cave of the Medical Prescriptions is interesting for its carved pillars, which are inscribed with more than 120 cures for the diseases suffered by people in this area in the sixth century.

Also at Longmen is the Temple of Guandi, rebuilt during the Ming dynasty (1368–1644). It commemorates General Guan Yu (Kuan Yu) who lived during the Three Kingdoms Period (220–80). One of the main characters in the popular epic novel, *Romance of the Three Kingdoms*, Guan Yu was deified as the god of war under the name of Guandi (Emperor Guan). On top of Xiangshan can be seen the tomb of Bai Juyi (Po Chu-yi; 772–846), one of the greatest poets in Chinese history. See also BAI JUYI; BUDDHISM; DATONG; DUNHUANG CAVE PAINTINGS AND CARVINGS; GUANDI; LOTUS; LUOYANG; NORTHERN WEI DYNASTY.

LONGMEN FALLS   See CARP; DRAGON; YELLOW RIVER.

LONGSHAN CULTURE (c. 3000–2200 B.C.) One of the two main cultures in China during the Neolithic period. The Yangshao was an earlier civilization dating from 5000 to c. 2000 B.C. The Longshan culture is named for Mount Long (Longshan, "Dragon Mountain") in Shandong Province where artifacts from the culture were first identified in 1929. This site, Chengziyai, actually represents a late phase in the history of the Longshan culture, which extended along the whole length of China's eastern coast. The Xia dynasty, formerly thought to be legendary, may have developed from the Longshan Culture, and archaeologists anticipate finding Xia artifacts at Longshan sites.

Its unique thin pottery is one of Longshan's distinguishing features; it has a shiny black or gray surface with very little decoration and frequently as thin as an eggshell. The pieces were made with an iron-rich clay that turned black from smoke and high temperatures when fired in sealed kilns. The Longshan pieces were the first Chinese pottery to be formed on a potter's wheel. Objects made for ceremonial use include bowls on tall flaring stems, delicate wine cups on pierced stands, and vessels with three legs like a tripod. Longshan potters also produced hand-formed earthenware in gray, red and black for everyday use. The Yangshao culture had its own type of ceramics; red earthenware decorated with plants, fish and spiral designs in black and occasionally white. Many ceremonial objects made from bronze during the Bronze Age period following the Longshan evidence a continuation of Longshan pottery forms, especially the tripod vessel, known as a *ding*. Longshan people also knew how to work jade, a very hard stone that has been highly valued throughout Chinese history for its durability, color, markings and symbolic meaning. Jade forms produced during the Longshan include the *bi*, a flat disc with a hole in the center, and the *zong*, a cylindrical tube, both of which have been found in Bronze Age artifacts. The connection between the two periods is also seen in some late Longshan ax forms that were later cast in bronze.

Longshan villages were surrounded by walls of firmly packed earth for defense against enemies. The villages developed into walled cities by the Shang dynasty (1750–1040 B.C.), and this method of protection continued throughout Chinese history. Several centers of power in China emerged from the Longshan period. The Longshan culture in Shaanxi Province in western China produced the Zhou dynasty (1100–256 B.C.), in Shandong the powerful state of Qi, and in the Yangzi River (Changjiang) delta in eastern China the powerful states of Yue and Wu. Longshan burial practices show that social distinctions developed during the Longshan culture, with more elaborate burials for members of upper classes. Objects found in Longshan graves indicate an increasing differentiation among social classes and a patriarchal system characterized by the propitiation of male ancestral spirits. Longshan graves typically contain a male skeleton lying stretched out on its back, with one or more female skeletons on their sides facing the male, with their knees and waists bent in deference to him. In contrast, the Yangshao culture was apparently matriarchal. Other Longshan religious practices include rituals to benefit agriculture and divination of the future by the use of oracle bones. Known as scapulamancy, this was a system by which the shoulder-blades of oxen, sheep and pigs were heated and drilled with holes to produce cracks that were interpreted as answers to questions about the future. See also ANCESTOR WORSHIP; BI; BRONZEWARE; DING; JADE; NEOLITHIC PERIOD; ORACLE BONES; SHANG DYNASTY; XIA DYNASTY; YANGSHAO CULTURE; ZHOU DYNASTY.

LONGYANG DAM See YELLOW RIVER.

LOPNOR, LAKE See TARIM BASIN.

LOQUAT See LITCHI.

LORD OF SHANG See TANG, KING.

LORD SHANG See SHANG YANG, LORD.

LOTUS (*lian* or *lien, he* or *ho*) A flowering plant, similar to the water lily, with broad, flat leaves and round multi-petaled white flowers; it grows in the water and represents the summer season for the Chinese. The Sixth Moon in the traditional Chinese lunar calendar (roughly corresponding to the month of July in the Western calendar) is poetically called the Lotus Moon. The birthday of the lotus is celebrated on the 24th day of the Sixth Moon, at the time when summer rains are expected to begin falling in northern China. Lotus blossoms in the ponds and moats of the old imperial capital of Beijing are a sign that prayers to the Dragon Prince, who brings the rain necessary for an abundant harvest, have been successful. People crowd the lakes of the Winter Palace to view the beautiful pink blossoms.

The Chinese name for the lotus sounds similar to Chinese phrases for fertility and prosperity, and so the lotus became a popular design motif indicating these qualities in Chinese crafts such as ceramics, embroidery and carpets. "Lotus panels," a design of stylized leaves, were used to provide frames for flowers and other painted motifs, carpets and embroidery. The phrase *hebing* (*ho-p'ing*), "lotus vase," sounds like the Chinese word for peace, and thus a lotus vase represents the wish for peace and tranquillity. Chinese artists often paint a series of pictures depicting the four seasons, with plum blossoms for winter, the peony for spring, the lotus for summer and the chrysanthemum for autumn.

The lotus is the symbol of purity in the Buddhist religion because it grows up from the mud of a pond yet produces a beautiful white flower. The flower's wheel-like shape also symbolizes the Wheel of Life to Buddhists. The Buddha's throne is depicted as a large lotus blossom with many petals flattened outward. Other Buddhist deities, such as Guanyin, the popular goddess of mercy, are also placed on lotus flowers. The Lotus Sutra is one of the most important scriptures in the Buddhist religion. Similarly, in the Daoist religion, the lotus is the emblem of He Xiangu, (Ho Hsien-Ku), the "Immortal Lady," one of the "Eight Immortals." She holds a lotus stem and seed pod, whose large number of seeds make the lotus a fertility symbol. She is sometimes represented on a floating lotus petal.

The Chinese rarely cut lotus flowers because they look most beautiful in their natural setting. The roots, fruit and leaves of the lotus are used in Chinese cuisine. Lotus seeds are used for medicinal purposes and are eaten at wedding banquets. The seeds are also used to make sweets for banquets and fillings for mooncakes served at the Autumn Moon Festival. See also AUTUMN MOON FESTIVAL; BUDDHISM; CHRYSANTHEMUM; DAOISM; EIGHT IMMORTALS; GUANYIN; LOTUS SUTRA; PEONY; PLUM.

LOTUS SUTRA   One of the most important scriptures of the Mahayana branch of the Buddhist religion; formally known as the *Sutra of the Lotus of the Wonderful Law* (*Saddharmapundarika Sutra*). Buddhism, which was introduced into China from India about 2,000 years ago, imparts its beliefs through the sutras or teachings. Sutra is the Indian Sanskrit term for scripture. The first translation of the Lotus Sutra from Sanskrit into Chinese was made in the third century A.D. This scripture claims to relate the final sermon that Shakyamuni (also known as Siddhartha Gautama), the historical Buddha, gave to his followers before he entered Nirvana. It teaches that all human beings can attain enlightenment if they have faith in the eternal, transcendent Buddha, who appeared in the world to help every person become free from suffering. This universal outlook is the main principle of Mahayana Buddhism and is symbolized by the lotus flower. Just as the beautiful lotus rises up from the mud, so do purity and truth rise above evil. According to Mahayana Buddhists, all people have the lotus of the Buddha nature within them.

The Lotus Sutra is the basic scriptural text of the Tiantai (T'ien-t'ai) sect of Buddhism. Founded by the Chinese Buddhist monk, Zhikai (Chih-k'ai; also known as Zhiyi or Chi-i; 538–597) and named for the Tiantai (T'ien-t'ai; "Heavenly Mountain") in Zhejiang Province where he taught, this was the first native Chinese sect of the Buddhist religion. The sect attempted to harmonize the conflicting doctrines of various devotional and intellectual schools of Buddhist thought using the teachings of the Lotus Sutra. This scripture also became very popular in Japan after the Japanese monk Saicho (767–822) studied Tiantai teachings in China and founded the Tendai (Tiantai) Buddhist sect in Japan, where the Lotus Sutra is called *Hokke Kyo*. See also BUDDHISM; LOTUS; TIANTAI SECT OF BUDDHISM.

LOVE IS A MANY-SPLENDORED THING   See HAN SUYIN.

LOYALTY (*zhong* or *chung*)   A virtue in the Confucian tradition that entails performing a required duty with one's total ability and dedication. Confucius (551–479 B.C.) associated loyalty with the virtue of reciprocity (*shu*). Both are necessary when one interacts with other people, and both are based on the principle of humanity (*ren* or *jen*), also translated as benevolence or goodness. In the *Analects* (*Sayings; Lunyu*) of Confucius, one of the Four Books of Confucianism, Confucius's disciple Tseng Tzu is quoted as saying that his master's teaching can be summed up in the two concepts of loyalty and reciprocity. Confucius maintained that one should be loyal to performing one's duty, and that this duty is prescribed by humanity (or, in Western terms, conscience). Loyalty should be given not only to the ruler, but also to the principles and duties that help all men. Both principles of loyalty and reciprocity determine the relationships one has with others. A person of genuine humanity, whom Confucius calls the "superior man" or "gentleman" (*junzi* or *chuntzu*), lives according to the Golden Mean (*Zhongyong* or *Chung yung*), similar to the Golden Rule in Western ethics: In Confucius's words, "Do not do to others what you would not want others to do to you." The result is, presumably, peace among human beings. See also ANALECTS, CONFUCIAN; CONFUCIANISM; HUMANITY.

LOYANG   See LUOYANG.

LU   See DEER.

LU (MINORITY GROUP)   See DAI.

LU DONGBIN   See EIGHT IMMORTALS.

LU HAODENG (HAO-TENG)   See SUN YAT-SEN.

LU HSIANG-SHAN   See NEO-CONFUCIANISM.

LU HSUN   See LU XUN.

LU JI   (Lu Chi; 261–303)   An important literary critic and poet from the southern Chinese kingdom of Wu (222–80), one of the so-called Three Kingdoms. His grandfather was a founder of the Wu kingdom and his father was commander of the Wu army. Lu Ji wrote many poems in the rhyme-prose style of rhapsodic verse known as *fu*, which actually combines poetry and prose. His most influential work of literary criticism is his "*Fu* on Literature" (*Wen fu*), which discusses the methods involved in composing *fu* poetry. This work itself is written in the *fu* form. The Western Jin dynasty (265–316) conquered the kingdom of Wu, and in 290 Lu Ji moved to the Jin capital of Luoyang, where he was named the head of the national university. He ascended to even higher posts in the imperial bureaucracy or civil service, and was even awarded a noble title. However, he became caught up in a political rebellion that planned to attack Luoyang and overthrow the Jin emperor, and in 303 he was executed. See also RHYME-PROSE STYLE OF VERSE; THREE KINGDOMS PERIOD.

LU, LISA   (? –)   A Chinese-American actress who became a famous Hollywood movie star. Lu was born into a family connected with the Peking (Beijing) Opera. Her father, Lu Jialai (Lu Chia-lai), was a strong supporter of the opera, and her mother, Li Guifen (Li Kuei-fen), was a Peking Opera star in the 1920s who was famous throughout China and was praised by Peking Opera master Mei Lanfang. After Lu's father died, she and her mother lived in Mei's home for nine years, and Lu studied opera with her mother and Mei.

In 1947, Lu began attending the University of Hawaii, majoring in financial administration but also taking drama and speech classes. She married, and with her husband moved to California. There she studied acting at the Pasadena Playhouse, from which she graduated in 1958. Lu acted in many plays and won her first leading role opposite Marlon Brando in *Teahouse of the August Moon*. She has acted in more than 200 films and television shows, including *The King and I* (1956) with Yul Brynner and *The Mountain Road* with James Stewart. In 1970 Lu received Taiwan's Golden Horse Award for best actress for her role in *The Arch*. In 1974 she received the same award for her role as Qing Empress

Dowager Cixi (Tx'u Hsi; 1835–1908) in *The Empress Dowager,* a Hong Kong production directed by Li Hanxiang (Li Han-hsiang). She also won the award for best supporting actress for her role in *The Fourteen Amazons.*

Lu has helped introduce Peking Opera to the United States by translating several works and by directing the Lu An'qi Peking Opera Troupe that her mother established in California. The troupe is composed of Peking Opera fans who practice singing, dancing and acting twice a week and perform full-length operas for Chinese festivals. In 1991, Mayor Tom Bradley of Los Angeles gave Lu a special award for the contributions she has made to the art of acting. In 1992, Lu went to China to help the Shanghai People's Art Theater stage *Plaza Suite* by the Broadway playwright Neil Simon. She then made plans to produce *Teahouse* by Chinese author and playwright Lao She on Broadway. In 1993 in *The Joy Luck Club* and *Temptation of a Monk.* See also CIXI, EMPRESS DOWAGER; LAO SHJE; MEI LANFANG; OPERA, BEIJING.

LU, STATE OF See CONFUCIUS; QUFU; SHANDONG PROVINCE; SPRING AND AUTUMN ANNALS.

LU TUNG-PIN See EIGHT IMMORTALS.

LU XIANGSHAN See NEO-CONFUCIANISM.

LU XUN (Lu Hsun; 1881–1936) The first Chinese author of modern novels and the first major Chinese author to write in the vernacular. His real name was Zhou Shuren (Chou Shu-jen). He first used the pen name Lu Xun when he published "Diary of a Madman" in 1918. Lu Xun was born in Shandong Province. His grandfather had been an official in the imperial bureaucracy during the Qing dynasty (1644–1911) and his father was a scholar. When Lu Xun was 13, his grandfather was imprisoned for political reasons, so Lu Xun and his mother went to his grandmother's home in the countryside near Shaoxing in Zhejiang Province. There he learned of the oppression and suffering of Chinese peasant families, which became a major theme in his works. His father died when he was 16 and his family became impoverished. At age 18, Lu Xun attended the Naval Academy in Nanjing, which charged no tuition. There he was introduced to Western concepts of democracy, science and capitalism, notably Darwin's theory of evolution, which influenced him to join the Chinese struggle against imperialism and feudalism. The next year he transferred to the School of Railways and Mines at the Jiangnan Army Academy, from which he graduated in 1901.

In 1902 Lu Xun went to study at Kobun School in Tokyo, Japan, and in 1904 he attended medical college in Sendai, Japan. While in Japan, Lu Xun became patriotic and dedicated himself to helping China, as he expressed in his poem, "An Inscription to a Self-Portrait." In 1904 he joined the Revive China Society (*Guangfuhui* or *Kuang Fu Hui*) and became active in the movement to overthrow the Qing dynasty, which included many Chinese young people studying in Japan.

In 1906 Lu Xun decided to transfer from medical studies to literature as a means of changing the Chinese people's view of life. He wrote several essays in Japan to introduce Chinese readers to the natural and social sciences and world literature. He also translated foreign literature into Chinese, mainly patriotic works by authors in Russia and other oppressed countries, to encourage Chinese revolutionaries. He published these works in 1909 as *Stories from Other Lands,* with some stories translated by his brother Zhou Zuoren (Chou Tso-jen).

In the summer of 1909, Lu returned to China and taught at the Zhejiang Normal School. He became dean and then principal of the Shaoxing Middle School. After the Revolution of 1911 overthrew the Qing dynasty, Lu published *Remembering the Past,* a story in classical Chinese. After the Republic of China established its provisional government at Nanjing in 1912, Lu Xun was appointed a member of the Ministry of Education. He moved to Beijing when the government moved there. The republic did not succeed in eliminating Chinese warlords, however, and Lu Xun became disillusioned with the government. The October Revolution of 1917 in Russia introduced the Chinese to the communist ideas of Marx and Lenin, which influenced Lu Xun. In 1918 he published "Diary of a Madman" the first short story in vernacular Chinese, which made him famous. The story portrays the oppression and exploitation of the majority of the Chinese people by the small group of educated officials in the highest social class, which Lu Xun maintained should be overthrown.

Between 1918 and 1924, Lu Xun wrote 25 short stories, published as *Wandering* and *Call to Arms.* His most famous story was "The True Story of Ah Q," published in 1923, about a character named Ah Q who symbolized Chinese bureaucrats who ran the Republic of China but who turned out to be failures. Lu Xun's vernacular style grew out of the May Fourth Movement of 1919, in which radical Chinese intellectuals wanted to move away from what they believed was the stifling nature of classical, literary Chinese writing. They attempted to create a new, modern literature by using traditional Chinese characters to write down the language used by the Chinese in ordinary life. This is known as the New Literature Movement, which was part of the New Culture Movement.

Between 1918 and 1927, Lu Xun held teaching positions at Beijing University, the Beijing Girls' Normal College, Xiamen University, and Sun Yat-sen University in Guangzhou (Canton). During the 1920s and 1930s he wrote stories of the highest quality that compare with those of the best-known authors from other countries. These works concentrate on the social and political conflicts in China during the Warlord Period (1916–28), when factions led by rival warlords of different regions in China contended with each other.

In 1927, Chiang Kai-shek, leader of the Chinese Nationalist Party (Kuomintang; KMT), ordered the massacre of Chinese Communists in Shanghai and other cities, who were his rivals. Lu Xun tried but failed to save students from Sun Yat-sen University who were arrested and executed, so he resigned from his teaching position in protest. He moved to Shanghai on October 3, 1927, where he lived until his death in 1936. There he studied Marxist-Leninist thought and joined the Chinese Communist revolution. In 1930 Lu Xun was a founder of the China Freedom League and the China League of Left-Wing Writers. This movement subscribed to the Russian Soviet doctrine known as socialist realism, which holds that art should portray contemporary events as they really are by showing the problems of feudal society, and thus art will give hope for the future in a socialist society. In 1933 Lu joined Soong Qingling, widow of Sun Yatsen, the founder of modern China, and others in organizing the China League for Civil Rights. He also helped organize the International Anti-Imperialist, Anti-Fascist Conference in Shanghai and was elected honorary chairman of its presidium.

Lu Xun's critical work, *A Brief History of Chinese Fiction*, written in 1924 and revised in 1930 and translated into English in 1959, was the first book of its type in China. In it he discusses Chinese fiction from the myths and legends of ancient times through the beginning of the modern period at the close of the Qing dynasty. His *Outline of the History of Han Literature*, written in 1926, was another formative work on Chinese literary history. Lu Xun's complete works, numbering 900, have been published in several editions. The 1981 edition includes his letters, diaries, and prefaces and postscripts to ancient books and to his translations. Some of his stories have been adapted into operas, dramas and films, such as *The New Year Sacrifice* in the Yue Opera repertoire and *Regret for the Past*, produced by the Beijing Film Studio. The Lu Xun Museum, where he lived in Shanghai from 1927 to 1936 and was buried, is open to the public. See also CHINESE COMMUNIST PARTY; LANGUAGE, CHINESE; MAY FOURTH MOVEMENT OF 1919; NATIONALIST PARTY; NEW CULTURE MOVEMENT; QING DYNASTY; REVOLUTION OF 1911; REPUBLIC OF CHINA; SOONG QINGLING; WARLORD PERIOD.

LU YOU (Lu Yu; 1125–1210)   An important and prolific poet during the Southern Song dynasty (1127–1279). Lu You was born in Shanyin in Zhejiang Province to a family of the literati, or scholar-gentry class. His father taught him to write poetry when he was very young. During his long life, Lu You wrote about 20,000 poems, mostly in the form known as regulated or new-style verse (*shi* or *shih*). More than 9,000 have been preserved. Many of these express his patriotic desire to fight and drive back to the desert the nomadic "barbarians," the Jurchens, who had overthrown the Northern Song dynasty (960–1127) two years after Lu You's birth. The Jurchens forced the Song imperial court to move its capital south from Kaifeng to Hangzhou. Lu You's poems fall into three periods: those he wrote as a young man when he was developing his art; those he wrote in middle age with an expressive, vigorous style; and those he wrote in retirement, many of which have a tranquil tone.

Lu You's personal life was sad for many years. As a young man he married a woman he loved very much, but his mother forced him to divorce her. He passed the examinations for the imperial bureaucracy in Hangzhou, but the prime minister took a disliking to him and prevented him from being given any appointments in the bureaucracy. After the prime minister died in 1160, Lu You was summoned back to Hangzhou and appointed assistant commissioner in the Grand Court of Appeal and compiler in the Privy Council. However, he lost this position in 1166 because he was openly critical of government policies. In 1170 he was sent west to Sichuan Province as a government administrator, and was able to travel to army garrisons in frontier regions. He subsequently held administrative positions in Fujian, Jiangsu and Zhejiang Provinces. During this time Lu You

also became famous for his poetry. He returned to Hangzhou twice, in 1202 to help compile imperial historical records and in 1204 for an audience with Emperor Ningzong (Ningtsung; r. 1195–1224). As an old man, Lu You gave himself the artistic name Fangweng, or "Emancipated Old Man." See also HANGZHOU; IMPERIAL BUREAUCRACY; SOUTHERN SONG DYNASTY;

LUCKY MONEY (*hongbao* or *hang-pao*)   Money that is given in red envelopes to children, unmarried girls and service people, such as delivery boys, at the New Year or Spring Festival and on other occasions such as birthdays. The red envelopes are sold in stationery stores and are stamped with gold designs, which usually include the characters for Double Happiness (*Xi* or *Hsi*), Great Fortune (*Da Ji* or *Ta Chi*) and Great Advantage (*Dali* or *Ta Li*). Also depicted on the envelopes are the peach and the pine tree, both representing longevity, and the carp, a large fish symbolizing success through endeavor. In southern China the cypress tree is often portrayed instead of the pine. Families stock up on large quantities of red envelopes for lucky money. At weddings, when the bride leaves her parents' home, the bridesmaids give her lucky money envelopes for pocket money. Red envelopes are also offered between families of the bride and groom with amounts strictly defined by custom. At funerals, white mourning envelopes are sent to people who have contributed money to help the family pay the funeral expenses; the mourning family returns half the amount that people had contributed. See also BIRTHDAYS; CARP; DOUBLE HAPPINESS AND LONG LIFE; FUNERALS; NEW YEAR FESTIVAL; PEACH; PINE; WEDDINGS, TRADITIONAL.

LUDA   See DALIAN.

LULIANG MOUNTAIN RANGE   See SHANXI PROVINCE.

LUNG   See DRAGON.

LUNYU   See ANALECTS, CONFUCIAN.

LUOHAN (Lohan)   An important figure in the Buddhist religion, which was introduced into China from India around the first century A.D.; literally, a "worthy." Luohan is the Chinese term for the Sanskrit *Arhat* (*Arhant*), "destroyer of the enemy [i.e., desires]," "deserving and worthy" or "worthy." A luohan has supposedly moved through all the stages of the Buddhist "eightfold path," has conquered all the desires that enmesh a person in the continuous cycle of birth and death and hence will no longer be reborn. He is regarded as a saint who has already attained Nirvana and is attributed with supernatural powers. In China, an important Buddhist motif is the Eighteen Luohan, who are considered the personal disciples of the Buddha and the patrons and guardians of his religion. When Maitreya, the Buddha of the Future, comes to Earth, the Luohan will collect all the relics of the Buddha, build a splendid pagoda to house them, and then vanish into Nirvana. Sixteen of the Eighteen Luohan originated in India, and two were added by Chinese Buddhists. Sculptures of the Eighteen Luohan line the side walls of the second or main hall of a typical Chinese Buddhist monastery. Each Luohan is depicted in a prescribed pose with his particular symbol, all of which were developed by Buddhist painters during the Tang dynasty (618–907). For example, the first of the Eighteen, Pindola the Bharadvaja (Bindulu Bolotuoshe or Pin-tu-lo Po-lo-to-she), sits with an open book on his right knee and holds a beggar's staff. The sixth luohan, Tamra Bhadra (Danmolo Botuo or Tan-mo-lo-Po-t'o), a cousin of the Buddha, sits in a position of worship and holds a Buddhist rosary (*mala* in Sanskrit) with 108 prayer beads. The 18th luohan, Bolotuoshe (Po-lo-t'o-she), who may be another form of the first luohan, is shown riding a tiger to symbolize his power to overcome evil. Sometimes Emperor Liang Wudi (Liang Wu-ti; r. 502–549), first emperor of the Liang dynasty in southern China and a great patron of the Buddhist religion, is included as one of the Eighteen Luohan. Each of the Eighteen Luohan has a retinue of 500 to 1,600 luohan under him. Chinese Buddhists also refer to the Five Hundred Luohan, to whom a famous Buddhist temple is dedicated in the southern city of Guangzhou (Canton). See also BUDDHA; BUDDHISM; PAGODA; TEMPLES.

LUOYANG   A city in Henan Province in north-central China that in ancient times served as the capital and cultural center for 10 dynasties of the Chinese Empire. Luoyang, with a population today of more than one million, is situated south of the Yellow River (Huanghe) on the east-west railroad line that links Zhengzhou and Xian.

Heavily populated as far back as the Neolithic period (12,000–2000 B.C.), Luoyang was the imperial capital for nearly 1,000 years, beginning with the Eastern Zhou dynasty (771–256 B.C.) when it was called Chengzhou. It was destroyed by wars and rebuilt many times. The city remained an important center during the Qin dynasty (221–206 B.C.) and Han dynasty, especially the Eastern Han (A.D. 25–220), when it became the imperial capital. During the Han, Luoyang's growth was stimulated by the invention of paper and the introduction of the Buddhist religion from India. At its peak, it was home to tens of thousands of scholars because of its prestigious imperial university and library. Luoyang was destroyed between 189 and 190 near the end of the Han dynasty, but was rebuilt by the Wei kingdom (220–65). During the Northern Wei dynasty (386–534), there were more than 1,300 Buddhist temples in the city, and work was begun carving the Longmen cave temples and sculptures nine miles south of Luoyang. When the Sui dynasty (581–618) conquered the Wei, Luoyang was completely destroyed, but a new city was constructed on a grid pattern. Two canals through the city enabled barges weighing up to 800 tons to transport goods between Luoyang and cities in northern and southern China. Luoyang, called Dongdu by the Sui, reached its height as a commercial hub, and many foreign merchants settled in the city, swelling the population to one million.

During the Tang dynasty (618–907) Luoyang was overshadowed by the new capital at Chang'an (modern Xi'an) in Shaanxi Province, but its continued prestige as a center for scholars attracted the finest Tang poets, notably Du Fu (Tu Fu), Li Bai (Li Po) and Bai Juyi (Po Chu-i). The infamous Empress Wu Zetian (r. 690–705) preferred Luoyang. In 937 the Jin, one of the Five Dynasties (907–60) in northern China, moved their capital to Kaifeng in eastern Henan, initiating Luoyang's decline. The city finally lost its importance when the Song dynasty (960–1279) was forced by invaders to move south to the Yangzi River (Changjiang) valley in the 13th century.

Since 1949 Luoyang has been modernized and industrialized, with major products including machinery, plate glass and tractors. The city's location on the Yellow River has subjected it to disastrous flooding over the centuries. Recently, dikes and canals have been constructed to help control the flooding. The Yellow River carries vast quantities of a type of soil known as loess that is blown from China's desert regions. The UNESCO International Silt Research and Training Center, which studies problems caused by river silts, is located in Luoyang.

Since the Tang dynasty, Luoyang has been known as the "City of Peonies" for its beautiful peony flowers. Major tourist sites include the Luoyang Museum, which houses artifacts discovered during the 1950s when farmers in the area began digging terraces on which to grow crops. The museum's treasures include bronzeware from the Shang and Zhou dynasties. Royal Town (Wangcheng) Park contains two underground Han dynasty tombs decorated with frescoes and bas-relief carvings. Lanterns, a traditional product of Luoyang, are hung in the park during the New Year Festival. The White Horse (Baimasi) Temple of the Chan (Zen) Sect of Buddhism, five miles northeast of Luoyang, is the oldest Buddhist temple in China. Nearby stands the 13-story Qigongta Pagoda, possibly built during the Tang and restored in 1175 during the Song dynasty. The nearby Longmen (Dragon Gate) caves are numbered at more than 1,300 and contain more than 2,100 carved grottoes and niches, about 100,000 Buddhist sculptures, and several pagodas. See also BAI JUYI; BRONZEWARE; DU FU; HENAN PROVINCE; LANTERNS; LI BAI; LOESS; LONGMEN CAVE TEMPLES AND SCULPTURES; PAGODA; PEONY; WHITE HORSE TEMPLE; YELLOW RIVER; WU, EMPRESS; INDIVIDUAL DYNASTIES.

LUSHU CHUNQIU   See BOOK OF RITES.

LUSHUN   See DALIAN; LIAODONG PENINSULA; LIAONING PROVINCE.

LUTE   See PIPA.

LU-WANG SCHOOL   See NEO-CONFUCIANISM.

LUXINGSHE   See CHINA INTERNATIONAL TRAVEL SERVICE.

LYCHEE   See LITCHI.

LYRIC VERSE   (*ci* or *tz'u*)   A form of poetry that is written to music that has already been composed; *ci* means "words [for singing]." The poet would select a tune or compose one himself and then write the *ci* to fit the tune. The *ci* would not have its own name but would be given the name of the tune for which it was written. The lines of a *ci* are unequal in length, in contrast to the poetic form known as regulated or new-style verse (*shi*), in which all the lines have the same length. The *ci* form probably originated during the Tang dynasty (618–907), but it became widely used by Chinese poets during the Five Dynasties Period (907–60) and the Song dynasty (960–1279). It first appeared in the pleasure quarters of cities, where women entertainers performed songs in which each line had a specific number of characters, ranging from two to nine. The words to such a song were called *ci*. Eventually the finest Chinese poets began writing *ci* to the songs from the pleasure quarters; the *ci* became an accepted form of poetry. The first great *ci* poet was Li Yu (937–78; r. 961–75), the final ruler of the brief Southern Tang dynasty, one of the so-called Five Dynasties. He lost his throne to the Song dynasty and was taken captive to the Song capital of Kaifeng, where he wrote many beautiful and melancholy *ci* expressing his deep grief over his personal tragedies. The finest *ci* poets of the Song dynasty include Ouyang Xiu (Ou-yang Hsiu; 1007–72), Wang Anshi (1021–86), Su Shi (also known as Su Dongpo or Su Tung-p'o; 1036–1101), Lu You (Lu Yu; 1125–1210), Xin Qiji (Hsin Ch'i-chi; 1140–1207) and a woman named Li Qingzhao (Li Ch'ing-chao; 1081–1143). See also FIVE DYNASTIES PERIOD; LI QINGZHAO; LI YU; LU YOU; OUYANG XIU; REGULATED OR NEW-STYLE VERSE; SONG DYNASTY; SU SHI; WANG ANSHI; XIN QIJI.

LYTTON COMMISSION A commission of inquiry formed at China's request by the League of Nations and headed by Great Britain's Lord Lytton (Edward Robert Bulwer Lytton, the second Earl of Lytton; 1876–1947) to pressure Japan regarding its invasion of China.

Japanese troops had been stationed in Manchuria (northeastern China) before the so-called Manchurian Incident on September 18, 1931, when the Japanese set off a bomb on the South Manchurian Railway line outside of Mukden (modern Shenyang) and blamed it on the Chinese. The Japanese Guandong (Kwantung) Army then occupied Mukden in "self-defense," making it their base for taking over all of Manchuria, a region rich in natural resources. The military occupation also gave Japan a strategic advantage against the Soviet Union, which bordered Manchuria and had concessions in the region. China requested assistance from the League of Nations and the United States. The United States, while not willing to undertake military intervention in China, tried to influence other foreign powers to take a firm position against Japan. The Western powers gave China verbal and moral support as stated in the so-called Stimson Doctrine, composed by American secretary of state Henry L. Stimson, which maintained "official nonrecognition of conquests or settlements [in China] by other than peaceful means." The League of Nations incorporated the Stimson Doctrine in a resolution proposed by Great Britain, and in November 1931 the league ordered Lord Lytton to investigate the situation and sent the Lytton Commission to Manchuria to investigate the dispute between China and Japan.

On February 18, 1932, Japan declared Manchuria's independence from China, and in March it established the puppet state of Manchukuo (Manzhouguo or Man-Chou-kuo in Chinese) with Henry Puyi (1906–67), the last emperor of the Qing dynasty (1644–1911), as its token leader. In 1932 Japanese forces attempted to take the major Chinese port city of Shanghai but were driven back by the Chinese Nineteenth Route Army. In October 1932 the commission issued its report, known as the *Lytton Report,* in which it criticized Japan's military actions in China as "unwarranted" and in violation of international treaties. The report recognized that Japan's actions could not be undone, so it recommended that Manchuria be governed by an autonomous administration under Chinese sovereignty that made special provision for Japan's economic interests in the region. The league did not want to directly condemn Japanese aggression and force it to break off relations with Western powers, but it also did not want to legitimize Japan's actions. After much debate, the league adopted the *Lytton Report* in February 1933. The following day, the Japanese delegate to the League of Nations delivered a speech defending Japan's actions and warning the other foreign powers—and Japan withdrew from the league. Japanese troops then occupied the northern Chinese province of Jehol and annexed it to Manchukuo. They also moved into Hebei Province and established a 30-to-40-mile-wide demilitarized zone between the Chinese capital of Beijing and the port city of Tianjin, which Chinese troops could not enter without Japanese permission. Japanese aggression in China escalated into China's War of Resistance against Japan (1937–45; World War II). See also LEAGUE OF NATIONS; MANCHUKUO; MANCHURIAN INCIDENT; PUYI, HENRY.

M

MA, YO-YO (1955–) A world-renowned cello player whom many critics regard as the greatest cellist of his generation. Yo-Yo Ma was born to Chinese parents in Paris. His father, Ma Hiao-Tsiun, was a musicologist, violinist and composer from a town near Shanghai who had moved to Paris in the 1930s. His mother was a mezzo-soprano opera singer from Hong Kong. Yo-Yo Ma's older sister, Yeou-Cheng Ma, studied the violin but later became a pediatrician. He decided to study the cello when he was a little boy, and his father was his first teacher. Ma played his first public recital at the University of Paris when he was only six years old. The next year his family moved to New York City, where his father took a teaching job. There the great violinist Isaac Stern heard Yo-Yo Ma play the cello, which brought him to the attention of the renowned cello players and teachers Leonard Rose and Pablo Casals, who praised him highly. Ma studied at the Juilliard School in New York from age 9 to 16 with Leonard Rose and Janos Scholz. Rose said that by the time Ma was 12 years old he knew all of the most difficult studies for cello, and he had one of the greatest techniques of any cello player. In 1963 Leonard Bernstein invited Yo-Yo Ma to perform on a nationally televised show to raise funds to build the John F. Kennedy Center for the Performing Arts in Washington, D.C. The next year Ma made his New York City debut at Carnegie Hall.

Yo-Yo Ma attended the Professional Children's School in New York City and, even though he skipped two years, graduated at age 15. He enrolled in Juilliard's college division but then decided to attend Columbia University. After he visited his sister, who was studying in Cambridge, Massachusetts, he transferred to Harvard University, where he studied music history, theory and criticism as well as cello playing techniques. He also continued to give performances on and off campus and in large cities when he had the time. In 1971 he played at Carnegie Hall in a benefit for the Children's Orchestra, which his father had founded. Ma received a B.A. degree in humanities from Harvard and became a professional musician. In 1978 he was selected as sole winner of the Avery Fisher Prize, a very prestigious award that enables

young classical musicians to perform with major symphony orchestras. That year he also married Jill Hornor, an American woman who taught German literature at Harvard.

Ma has performed the repertoire of classical cello compositions with major orchestras all over the world, and he often plays more than 100 concerts a year. He also performs solo recitals and chamber music concerts with other important musicians, such as the violinists Itzhak Perlman and Young-Uck Kim and the pianist Emanuel Ax. He began his own series, "Yo-yo Ma and Friends," at Lincoln Center in New York City. Ma has recorded all of the major classical works composed for the cello and has won nine Grammy awards.

He also enjoys playing contemporary works and experimenting with other musical styles. Since 1990, Ma has played the premiere performances of 11 new compositions for cello and has also commissioned and performed new works for the cello by contemporary composers, including Leon Kirchner's *Music for Cello and Orchestra* (1992), Christopher Rouse's *Violoncello Concerto* (1992) and Richard Danielpour's *Concerto for Cello and Orchestra* (1994). The *Boston Globe* has said of Yo-Yo Ma that "there is hardly any virtuoso of any instrument who is as complete, profound, passionate, and humane a musician." In 1993 Ma introduced a new instrument called the hypercello, an electronic form of the cello invented by the composer Tod Machover. Ma issued *Hush*, an imaginative recording of music by classical composers, with the American singer and musician Bobby McFerrin, which became a best-seller. Ma also worked on a documentary film about the music of the people of the Kalahari Desert in Africa. He has appeared on American television shows including the popular children's program, "Sesame Street."

MA DUANLIN (Ma Tuan-lin; c. 1250–1319) The author of *The General Study of Literary Remains* (*Wenxian Tongkao* or *Wen-hsien t'ung-k'ao*), considered one of the three greatest works of Chinese dynastic and bureaucratic history, along with the *General Treatises* (*Tongzhi* or *T'ung chih*) by Zheng Qiao (Cheng Ch'iao; 1108–66) and the *Comprehensive Mirror* *for Aid in Government* (*Zishi tongjian* or *T'ung tien*) by Sima Guang (Ssu-ma Kuang; 1019–85). These three encyclopedic works, known collectively as the Three *Tong* (*T'ung*), served as models for numerous histories compiled by later Chinese scholars.

Ma Duanlin spent 20 years writing his *General Study,* which concludes with the year 1254, and he drew upon material in the two other works. He felt it necessary, as did Zheng Qiao, to compile a comprehensive survey of the entire span of Chinese history. Ma's book contains 348 chapters and covers 24 themes, beginning with a study of the systems of land taxation throughout the various dynasties, thus showing the importance of land and taxes to the Chinese. Other topics include the population of China, religious practices, education, the examination system for the imperial bureaucracy, currency, commerce and finance, and the criminal justice system. Ma Duanlin presented the issues in favor of the changes that had been made to Chinese institutions during the reigns of various emperors and the issues opposed to them, and frequently added his own commentaries. Ma divided Chinese history into two categories—political and institutional (or bureaucratic). He agreed with the opinion of Zheng Quao that while political history falls into distinct periods, the history of the imperial bureaucracy must be studied as a whole. See also HISTORICAL PERIODS; IMPERIAL BUREAUCRACY; IMPERIAL EXAMINATION SYSTEM; SIMA GUANG.

MA HAIDE (Ma Hai-te; 1910–)   A highly esteemed American doctor who went to China in 1923 and remained there, providing medical care for the Chinese people and becoming a Chinese citizen; real name George Hatem. Ma was born in Buffalo, New York, to parents who had emigrated from Lebanon. He studied at the University of North Carolina and in Beirut and Switzerland, where he received a medical degree from the University of Geneva Medical School in 1933. He was interested in studying tropical diseases and heard that China needed doctors, so he went to Shanghai in 1933 and opened a medical practice. He met members of the Chinese Communist Party (CCP) and was eager to take part in their revolutionary activities. He took the Chinese name Ma Haide and became the first foreigner admitted into the CCP. Underground CCP members often used his Shanghai clinic as a rendezvous. Soong Qingling, widow of Dr. Sun Yat-sen, the founder of modern China, helped Ma and American journalist Edgar Snow travel to the Communist base in Yan'an in Shaanxi Province in western China. They arrived in 1936, and Ma joined the CCP the following year and took the Chinese name Ma Haide. During China's War of Resistance against Japan (1937–45; World War II) and the civil war between the Chinese Communists and Nationalists (Kuomintang; KMT), Ma tended the wounded Communist troops along with Canadian doctor Norman Bethune and an Indian medical team, which had also come to help the Chinese. Between 1944 and 1947, Ma took care of more than 40,000 wounded. Communist leader Mao Zedong (Mao Tse-tung) appointed Ma adviser to the Health Ministry of the Central Military Commission, the Central Foreign Affairs Department and the New China (Xinhua) News Agency.

After the Communists established the People's Republic of China in 1949, Ma formally became a Chinese citizen. He worked with the Ministry of Health as a counselor and at the Dermatology and Venereal Disease Research Institute under the Chinese Academy of Medical Science. Ma aimed to eliminate venereal disease and leprosy in China, and his research, which frequently took him to remote villages and border areas such as Xinjiang, Qinghai and Inner Mongolia, helped China nearly eradicate venereal disease in the early 1960s. Ma's research on leprosy was interrupted by the Cultural Revolution (1966–76), but the Chinese government reinstated it after the Cultural Revolution ended. In 1981, the State Council declared that China should eliminate leprosy by the end of the century, and Ma devoted all his energies to accomplishing that goal. In April 1983, Ma was awarded the 1982 prize from the Damien-Dutton Leprosy Society of the United States for his work to eliminate that disease.

In 1971, Ma had led a Chinese medical team to care for Edgar Snow before he died. In 1978, he and his Chinese wife Zhou Sufei (Chou Su-fei) visited his relatives in the United States. In 1979, Ma headed a Chinese delegation to Canada to commemorate the 40th anniversary of the death of Norman Bethune. On November 22, 1983, Premier Deng Xiaoping and other Chinese government leaders met with Ma to congratulate him for 50 years of service to China. See also BETHUNE, NORMAN; CHINESE COMMUNIST PARTY; CIVIL WAR BETWEEN COMMUNISTS AND NATIONALISTS; CULTURAL REVOLUTION; NEW CHINA NEWS AGENCY; PEOPLE'S REPUBLIC OF CHINA; SNOW, EDGAR; SOONG QINGLING; WAR OF RESISTANCE AGAINST JAPAN.

MA HAI-TE   See MA HAIDE.

MA TSU P'O   See MAZIPO.

MA TUAN-LIN   See MA DUANLIN.

MA YUAN (fl. c. 1190–1225)   A prominent landscape painter and the cofounder, with Xia Gui (Hsia Kuei; fl. c. 1180–1224), of the Ma-Xia (Ma-Hsia) school of landscape painting. Born into a family of painters, Ma Yuan held a position in the painting division of the Hanlin Academy, the national academy of scholars within the imperial bureaucracy, and achieved the rank of *daizhao* (*tai-chao*), "painter in attendance." The academy was located in Hangzhou, the capital of the Southern Song dynasty (1127–1279) and the cultural center of China after the Song court had to leave its northern capital at Kaifeng to the Jurchen in 1127.

Ma and Xia specialized in monochrome ink paintings. They belonged to the Northern Song school of landscape painting but developed a new style by using the bold "ax-cut texture stroke" (*fupi cun* or *fu-p'i ts'un*) that had been developed by Li Tang (Li T'ang; c. 1050–c. 1130), whose style of painting laid the foundation for the Southern school of painting. With this technique, the angles of the brush strokes seem to hack out rocks in painting. This style contrasts with the delicate brushwork of the Northern Song school. Ma and Xia simplified the composition by opening up more space and providing a new freedom of movement. Ma Yuan became known as "one-corner Ma" because he tended to emphasize one corner of the composition in his landscapes, leaving much empty space that seemed to stretch into infinity. Ma's style was much imitated by painters who came after him. The Ma-Xia school was influential not only in China but also in Japan, where it inspired the monochrome ink landscape paintings of the Muromachi Period (1338–1573). See also HANGZHOU; HANLIN ACADEMY; INK PAINTING; LANDSCAPE PAINTING; LI TANG; SOUTHERN SONG DYNASTY; XIA GUI.

MA ZI PO   See MAZIPO.

MACAO (Macau; Aomen)   A Portuguese colony at the most southwesterly point of the Pearl River estuary where it empties into the South China Sea, about 45 miles west of Hong Kong and 90 miles from the major Chinese port city of Guangzhou (Canton). Macao comprises a peninsula of 2.1 square miles joined to a large delta island, as well as the islands of Taipa (1.4 square miles) and Coloane (2.6 square miles), for a combined total area of 6.1 square miles. A bridge links Macao Peninsula to Taipa Island. Out of a population of half a million, about 98 percent are Chinese.

Macao became a province of Portugal in 1951; in 1976 it was granted broad powers of autonomy. The Portuguese received permission from the Chinese government to occupy Macao in 1557, and they made it the first European settlement on the Chinese coast. From their base at Macao, the Portuguese became the first Westerners to trade with China, establishing a monopoly on foreign trade in Guangzhou. By the 1660s, following the Chinese emperor's ban on direct trade by Chinese merchants with Japan, Portuguese traders were making fortunes as middlemen between China and Japan. They bought Chinese silk and shipped it to Japan, where they traded it for silver from Japanese mines. The Portuguese used this silver, valued more highly in China than in Japan, to buy ever larger quantities of Chinese silk. Luxury goods were also sent West by the Portuguese, including silk, porcelain, spices, sandalwood, pearls, ivory and carpets.

Roman Catholic Jesuits traveled to Asia as missionaries to convert the local population. Matteo Ricci, the first Jesuit to enter China, did so through Macao.

In the 1620s the Portuguese explored the island of Taiwan and gave it the name "Ilha Formosa" ("Beautiful Isle"), but they did not settle there, preferring to retain Macao as their main base of operations in East Asia. During the 1660s, Qing dynasty (1644–1911) Chinese naval forces blockaded Macao. All Chinese were ordered to leave the city, and Portuguese ships were banned. The Chinese also threatened to destroy the Portuguese buildings, but local Qing officials declined to carry out these orders, which would have damaged Macao's economy. The Portuguese sent diplomatic embassies and used the Jesuits in the capital city of Beijing to gain Qing permission for them to keep Macao. In the 1730s the Qing attempted to regulate the growing trade between China and Western nations, especially Britain, by setting up the "Canton system," under which foreign traders had to reside in Macao and trade only at Guangzhou with Chinese merchants licensed by the Qing to engage in international trade. Chinese were allowed to settle in Macao in large numbers starting in 1793. In the 1800s, British merchants were

trafficking in opium in China, and the Chinese official Lin Zexu drove them from Guangzhou and Macao. The British, led by Charles Elliot, then settled on the nearly uninhabited island of Hong Kong. China ceded Macao to Portugal under a treaty in 1887.

During World War II, Macao was known as the "Lisbon of the Orient," because it was a lively center of political intrigue, gambling and gold smuggling. Today there are six authorized gambling casinos in Macao, as well as jai alai, greyhound racing, horse racing, and the annual Macao Grand Prix for drivers from all over Asia. Gambling produces about one-third of Macao's gross domestic product and is expected to continue to do so after the city reverts to China. Macao is thus known as the "Monaco of the East." Jetfoil boats bring tourists from Hong Kong, many of whom are gamblers, in less than an hour. An enormously wealthy Chinese man named Stanley Ho owns Macao's casinos and its ferry service to Hong Kong. In 1995 Macao opened an international airport. The Chinese government under Deng Xiaoping engaged in negotiations with Portugal in 1985 for the return of Macao to China. In 1987 the two countries agreed to the Joint Declaration on the Question of Macao. Macao will become a special administrative region of China on December 20, 1999—two years after Britain's return of Hong Kong—the date when Portugal is scheduled to complete the transfer of governmental authority.

The inner harbor on the western side of Macao is the city's main commercial and manufacturing district, especially for textiles. Tourism is Macao's major economic activity. The most famous site in Macao is the ruins of St. Paul's Church, comprising a five-story stone facade and grand staircase built in the early 17th century by the Jesuits using Japanese Christians and local artisans. The church and the college next to it burned down in 1835. The chapel of the Jesuit missionary St. Francis Xavier displays the bones of his right arm. Another major site is the Monte Fort, whose guns fought off the Dutch when they attempted to invade Macao in 1522. Tourists can also visit the 600-year-old Ma Kok (also called A-Ma) Temple, from which Macao took its name, and the 350-year-old Kum Iam Temple. The Piyi Temple, also known as the Temple of the (Buddhist) goddess Guanyin, was built during the Yuan dynasty (1279–1368) and is one of the most popular tourist attractions in Macao. See also HONG KONG; JESUITS; PORTUGUESE; RICCI, MATTEO; SILK.

MACARTNEY, GEORGE, LORD (1737–1806)   Viscount Macartney of Dervock, the first British ambassador to China; full name George Macartney, Earl, Baron Macartney of Parkhurst and of Auchinleck, also called (from 1776) Baron of Lissanoure. Macartney was born to a Scots-Irish family in Northern Ireland and studied at Trinity College in Dublin. The British Crown knighted him and appointed him envoy extraordinary to Russia in 1764. When he returned, he entered Parliament and served as chief secretary for Ireland from 1769 to 1792. In 1775 he became governor of the Caribbee Islands (Grenada, the Grenadines and Tobago). In 1776 he was made an Irish baron. From 1780 to 1786 he served as governor of Madras, India. Upon making him a viscount in 1792, the British government sent him to the Qing dynasty (1644–1911) court in Beijing to protest against trade restrictions and to persuade the Qing to open more ports to foreign trade, reduce tariffs and permit the British to establish an embassy in Beijing. The British East India Company had dominated Western trade with China, which was limited to southern Chinese ports. In 1757 Emperor Qianlong (Ch'ien-lung; r. 1736–95) had issued a decree that all foreign nations except Russia must restrict their trade with China to the southern port city of Canton (modern Guangzhou). The Cohong or Hong, a corporation of nine merchants in Canton, was formed to monopolize trade with the Western nations. This became known as the Canton System of foreign trade.

The British mission arrived in China in August 1793, and the Qianlong emperor gave Macartney two audiences at his Summer Palace in Rehol (Jehol; also known as Chengde), a hunting preserve north of Beijing where Qing emperors spent the summer months. The second audience took place on Qianlong's 83rd birthday. Macartney refused to obey the Chinese command to kowtow, that is, to perform the ritual prostrations in front of the emperor required of all ambassadors from countries that submitted to China's tribute system. He knelt only on one knee before the Chinese emperor, the same as he did before the British king. Macartney presented the Qianlong emperor with King George's written request for more satisfactory trade arrangements for Great Britain and for a British embassy in Beijing. Qianlong declared that the Chinese Empire was "self-sufficient" and did not need anything that could be traded by other nations; China permitted only a small amount of foreign trade as a special favor to other countries. Macartney had brought gifts to the Chinese, including a planetarium, telescope, ship models, six small cannon and a horse carriage with glass windows and gilt carvings. Qianlong issued an edict that thanked King George III for his "tribute presents," making it seem as if Britain were just another small foreign nation that was submitting to become part of China's tribute system, and rejected British requests for greater trading opportunities. The condescending Chinese attitude toward the British culminated in the 19th-century Opium Wars in which Britain forced the Qing to open Chinese cities to foreign trade.

Despite Macartney's unsuccessful mission to China, he became an earl in the Irish peerage in 1794 and was elevated to the rank of baron in the English peerage in 1796. He was then appointed governor of the new British colony of the Cape of Good Hope in southern Africa. Macartney retired due to illness in 1798 and died in 1806. He was married but produced no surviving heirs, so his titles became extinct when he died. See also BRITISH EAST INDIA COMPANY; CANTON SYSTEM TO REGULATE FOREIGN TRADE; CHENGDE; KOWTOW; OPIUM WAR; QIANLONG, EMPEROR; QING DYNASTY; TRIBUTE SYSTEM.

MCMAHON LINE See HIMALAYA MOUNTAIN RANGE; SINO-INDIAN BORDER DISPUTE.

MADAME MAO ZEDONG (MAO TSE-TUNG) See JIANG QING.

MAGNETIC COMPASS See COMPASS; FENG SHUI.

MAGNOLIA FESTIVAL See HUNGRY GHOSTS FESTIVAL.

MAHAYANA BUDDHISM See AMITABHA; BODHISATTVA; BUDDHA; BUDDHISM; CHAN SECT OF BUDDHISM; DALAI LAMA; DAZU CAVE TEMPLES AND SCULPTURES; DUNHUANG CAVE PAINTINGS AND CARVINGS; FAXIAN; FLOWER GARLAND SECT OF BUDDHISM; FOUR SACRED MOUNTAINS OF BUDDHISM; GUANYIN; HAN SHAN; INK PAINTING; KARMA; KUMARAJIVA; LONGMEN CAVE TEMPLES AND SCULPTURES; LOTUS; LOTUS SUTRA; LUOHAN; MAITREYA AND MANJUSRI; NORTHERN WEI DYNASTY; PAGODA; POTALA PALACE; PURE LAND SECT OF BUDDHISM; SCULPTURE IN CHINA; SHAOLIN TEMPLE; TEMPLES; TIANTAI SECT OF BUDDHISM; XUANZANG; YUNGANG CAVE TEMPLES AND SCULPTURES;

MAHJONG *(majiang)* A game played by four people using dice and 136 tiles similar to dominoes; formally called *ma chueh*. The two Chinese characters for mahjong literally mean "house sparrow," which may refer to the bird-like sound of the tiles being shuffled. Mahjong developed from a card game called *ma tiao* that may have been based on tarot cards and introduced into China from Europe, perhaps in the 16th century. The card game was widely played in China until the late 18th century. Today the mahjong tiles are usually made of plastic, although they may be made of ivory or bone backed by bamboo. They are marked with 34 kinds of symbols, four tiles having the same symbol. There are five series: the *wan* (the Chinese cardinal number for 10,000) series, the circle series and the stick series, each of which have nine different symbols; the wind series, with four symbols for East, South, West and North; and the prime series, with three symbols for red, green and white. The circle and stick symbols derive from coin and string symbols. The symbols for wind comprise the four cardinal directions. In the prime series, red is marked with the character for hitting a jackpot and green with the character for prosperity. There is also a series of eight flower tiles, which are rarely used now.

To begin play, the tiles are lined up in a "wall." Three players pick up 13 tiles each. The fourth or "east" player picks up 14 tiles and makes the first discard. Each player continues to take a turn choosing a tile from the wall and discarding an unwanted one. The goal of the game is to acquire a completed hand: four sets of three tiles each and an identical pair, called mahjong. The numerical score of a completed hand depends on the particular combination of tiles in the hand, with rarer combinations bringing higher scores. Both men and women in every social class have enjoyed playing mahjong in China and in other countries where the Chinese have emigrated. The game was brought into the United States during the 1920s, where it became quite popular. However, the complex rules proved too difficult for American players, who simplified the rules to the point where mahjong may have lost much of its appeal.

MA-HSIA SCHOOL OF LANDSCAPE PAINTING See MA YUAN; MU QI; XIA GUI.

MAITREYA AND MANJUSRI (Mili and Wenshu in Chinese) Two of the most important figures in the Mahayana branch of the Buddhist religion, which was introduced into China from India around the first century A.D. Maitreya is the "Buddha of the Future," the Buddha who will return to the Earth 5,000 years in the future as supposedly predicted by the historical Buddha who founded the Buddhist religion. The Indian Sanskrit term "Maitreya" ("the Merciful One") is called Mili in Chinese. He is portrayed as a stout man with a bare chest and round belly carrying a bag, and is also called the "Laughing Buddha" because of his laughing expression. A sculpture of Maitreya stands in the first hall of a Buddhist monastery. In China, Budai Heshang (Pu Tai Ho Shang), one of the Buddhist *luohan* (*arhat* in Sanskrit), or personal disciples of the Buddha, is believed to be a reincarnation of Maitreya or of Amitabha (Avalokitesvara in Sanskrit), the Buddha of Boundless Light who is Lord of the Western Paradise, associated with the "Pure Land" of Maitreya. Many of the sculptures in the temples carved at Longmen near Luoyang in Henan Province during the sixth and seventh centuries are inscribed with prayers for rebirth in the Pure Land or Western Paradise. The Pure Land Sect became the most popular Buddhist sect in China. The worship of Maitreya in popular Chinese Buddhism influenced Han Chinese revolts against their Mongol rulers in the 14th century, such as the Red Turbans Rebellion, one of whose leaders overthrew the Mongols and established the Ming dynasty (1368–1644). It also influenced the White Lotus Rebellion in the late 18th century against the Manchu Qing dynasty (1644–1911).

Manjusri is a bodhisattva ("being of wisdom"; *pusa* or *p'u sa* in Chinese) who has attained enlightenment and has taken a vow to help all other suffering beings attain enlightenment as well. In China Manjusri became worshiped as the god of wisdom and is popularly depicted as riding on a golden-haired lion, the symbol of bravery, signifying his power over life and death. Manjusri is usually shown wearing a blue robe with a red collar, with a long flowing beard and his hair in a top-knot. He holds a sword in his right hand to cut down religious ignorance, and in his left hand a lotus flower, the symbol of Buddhism, on which is a sacred book of Buddhist sutras (scriptures). A sculpture of Manjusri stands in the second hall of a Buddhist monastery, next to the image of Sakyamuni Buddha, the historical Buddha. Chinese Buddhists revere Manjusri as one of the three greatest bodhisattvas or "Three Great Beings" (*Sandashi* or *San Ta Shih*), along with Wen Shu and Guanyin (Kuan Yin; Avalokiteshvara in Sanskrit), the Buddhist Goddess of Mercy.

The Indian Sanskrit name Manjusri means "Wonderful Virtue" or "Lucky Omen." He is filled with benevolence, and brings happiness and good fortune, and personifies knowledge. Indian Buddhists also referred to Manjusri as "the Singing Buddha," Mahamati ("Great Wisdom") and Kumararaja ("King of Teaching"), who supposedly has a thousand arms and a hundred begging bowls. According to Buddhist legends, he was an Indian king in the late 10th century who went to China but was chased away by scheming monks. Manjusri is very important in Lamaism, the Tibetan sect of Buddhism that was adopted by the Mongols, who ruled China under the Yuan dynasty (1279–1368). He is associated with Mount Wuta (Wutai) near Datong in Shenxi Province in northern China, one of the Four Sacred Mountains of Buddhism. A large white pagoda there is believed to contain one of Manjusri's hairs from the time he appeared there in the form of an old man. Most of the temples on Mount Wuta belong to Lamaism. See also AMITABHA; BODHISATTVA; BUDDHA; BUDDHISM IN CHINA; FOUR SACRED MOUNTAINS OF BUD-

DHISM; GUANYIN; LAMAISM; LONGMEN CAVE TEMPLES AND SCULPTURES; PAGODA; PURE LAND SECT OF BUDDHISM; RED TURBANS REBELLION; SCULPTURE; WHITE LOTUS REBELLION.

MAN ZU See MANCHU.

MAN-CHOU-KUO See MANCHUKUO.

MANCHU (Manzu or Man-tsu in Chinese) One of China's 55 officially designated national minority ethnic groups. The Manchus actually ruled China when they overthrew the Ming dynasty (1368–1644) and established the Qing dynasty (1644–1911), China's last imperial dynasty. Their homeland, Manchuria, became the northeastern region of the Chinese Empire when they took the throne. The Qing expanded the empire to its greatest extent. Because Manchuria is rich in natural resources, Russia and Japan fought for control of this region in the Russo-Japanese War of 1904–5. Japan won the Russian concessions there but Russia refused to withdraw all of its troops. In 1931 Japan invaded Manchuria and established a puppet state called Manchukuo, with Henry Puyi as token head of state. He had been the last Qing ruler, known as Xuantong (Hsuan-tung; r. 1909–12). Manchuria was returned to Chinese control when Japan was defeated in World War II.

The Manchus are descendants of the Jurchen (Jurched), a Tungusic people from Manchuria. The Jurchen defeated the Khitan (Qidan), who had established the Liao dynasty (947–1125), and founded the Jin dynasty (1115–1234) in northern China. The Manchu tribes were organized into a military and political power by Nurhachi (1559–1626). His son Abahai (1592–1643), who named his dynasty the Qing and proclaimed himself emperor, controlled much of the land north of the Great Wall by the early 1640s. In 1644, when the Ming general Wu Sangui (Wu San-kuei) asked the Manchus to help the Ming defeat a peasant rebel army that had attacked the capital city of Beijing, the Manchus captured Beijing and established themselves as the rulers of all China. Members of the Han Chinese ethnic group, which comprises more than 90 percent of the population of China, greatly resented their Manchu masters, especially the southern Chinese. They eventually overthrew the Manchus in the Revolution of 1911.

During the Qing dynasty, the Manchus forbade the Han Chinese from traveling into the Manchu homeland and from trading or intermarrying with Manchus. They even forced Han men to wear the Manchu hairstyle, with the front hairs shaved off and the back hairs woven into a long braid, which humiliated the Han. Manchu women did not follow the Han Chinese custom of painfully binding their feet to make them stay small. In the 20th century the Manchus have become largely assimilated and physically resemble the Han, especially since many Han immigrated to Manchuria in the early part of the century after the Qing fell. The Manchus are distinguished only by their language, a form of the Altaic language, which has been declining, and their religion, Lamaism (Tibetan Buddhism), to which they had been converted before 1644. According to the 1990 census, more than 9.8 million Manchus, mostly farmers, resided in Manchuria and Hebei and other provinces in northern China. See also ABAHAI; JIN DYNASTY; JURCHEN; LAMAISM; LIAO DYNASTY;

MANCHURIA; MINORITIES, NATIONAL; NURHACHI; PUYI, HENRY; QING DYNASTY; RUSSO-JAPANESE WAR OF 1904–5.

MANCHUKUO Known as Manzhouguo (Man-chou-kuo) in Chinese; the puppet state that Japan established in Manchuria (northeastern China) in 1932. Many historians consider this action by Japan as the first step toward World War II. Japan had already defeated China in the Sino-Japanese War of 1894–95 and had taken over Russian concessions in Manchuria at the conclusion of the Russo-Japanese War of 1904–5. In September 1931 the Japanese used the so-called Manchurian Incident as a pretext to seize the city of Mukden (modern Shenyang), the capital of Liaoning Province in Manchuria, and used Mukden as a base to rapidly take control over the entire region, which is rich in natural resources. Japan's actions shocked the Chinese people, who held massive demonstrations against Japan and boycotted Japanese goods. Chiang Kai-shek, leader of the Chinese Nationalists (Kuomintang; KMT), the party that had established the Republic of China (ROC) in 1912, was fighting a civil war against the Chinese Communist Party (CCP) when Japan invaded Manchuria. He stopped the KMT campaign against the CCP and returned to the KMT capital in Nanjing to deal with the Japanese crisis. Chiang did not want to go to war with Japan but preferred to ask the League of Nations to assist China. He ordered KMT military commander Zhang Xueliang (Chang Hsueh-liang), whose forces in Manchuria still outnumbered those of the Japanese and had the ability to resist them, not to fight. By the end of 1931 the Japanese had routed all of Zhang's KMT troops from Manchuria. The United States and other Western nations gave China their moral support, and in November the League of Nations sent the Lytton Commission to investigate the situation in Manchuria.

On February 18, 1932, Japan declared Manchuria's independence from China, and in March it established the puppet state of Manchukuo with Henry Puyi as its token leader. Puyi had ruled China as Emperor Xuantong (Hsuan-t'ung; r. 1909–12), the last emperor of the Qing dynasty (1644–1911), which had been established by the Manchus when they overthrew the Ming dynasty (1368–1644). Japanese agents forcibly took Puyi to Manchukuo from his residence in Tianjin. Japanese troops attempted to take the major Chinese port city of Shanghai but were driven back by the Chinese 19th Route Army.

In October 1932 the Lytton Commission issued its report, which criticized Japan for violating international treaties but recommended that Manchuria be governed by an autonomous administration under Chinese sovereignty that made special provision for Japan's economic interests in the region. The League of Nations did not want to directly condemn Japan but also did not want to legitimize Japan's actions in Manchuria, and in February 1933 it adopted the *Lytton Report.* The next day, Japan withdrew from the League of Nations and issued a warning to the other foreign powers. Japanese troops then occupied the northern Chinese province of Rehol (Jehol) and annexed it to Manchukuo. They also moved into Hubei Province, where they established the 30–40-mile-wide East Hebei Autonomous Region between the Chinese capital of Beijing and the port city of Tianjin.

In May 1933 the Nationalists signed the Tanku truce with Japan, under which they agreed to withdraw from the Beijing-Tianjin area where, according to the Protocol signed to end the Boxer Uprising in 1900, Japan was allowed to station troops, which it did. Japan continued its drive to bring all of North China under its control, and in 1935 it created a North China Autonomous Region consisting of five Chinese provinces, Hebei, Shandong, Shanxi, Chahar and Suiyuan. On July 7, 1937, Chinese troops fought the Japanese in the so-called Marco Polo Bridge Incident. In August, Japan attacked Shanghai once again, and China began fighting its War of Resistance against Japan (1937–45; World War II). Japan expanded militarily throughout China and other Asian countries until it was finally defeated in 1945. See also BOXER UPRISING; CHIANG KAI-SHEK; HEBEI PROVINCE; LEAGUE OF NATIONS AND CHINA; LYTTON COMMISSION; MANCHURIA; MANCHURIAN INCIDENT; MARCO POLO BRIDGE INCIDENT; PUYI, HENRY; RUSSO-JAPANESE WAR OF 1904–5; SHENYANG; SINO-JAPANESE WAR OF 1894–95; WAR OF RESISTANCE AGAINST JAPAN; ZHANG XUELIANG.

MANCHURIA Also known as Dongbei ("the northeast"); the northeastern region of China, comprising the provinces of Jilin, Liaoning and Heilongjiang. The region has long, cold winters but temperate summers. Manchuria lies beyond the Great Wall that was built by the Han ethnic Chinese to prevent incursions from non-Han peoples in the north and west. The Tang dynasty (618–907) brought Manchuria under its control, and the Ming dynasty (1368–1644) established military settlements there. Manchuria is the homeland of the Manchus, an ethnic group descended from the ancient Jurchens, who founded an independent state in Manchuria in 1616 and took the name Manchu in 1633. In 1644 the Manchus moved south into Beijing, the Chinese capital, overthrew the Ming Dynasty and established the Qing dynasty (1644–1911), China's last imperial dynasty, thus joining Manchuria to China. The region is rich in minerals, timber and other natural resources, and in the 19th century foreign powers, especially Russia and Japan, began contending for control of Manchuria. The Treaty of Nerchinsk (1689) between the Manchus and the Russians established the border between Manchuria and Siberia (eastern Russia) along the Amur River. In 1860 Russian forces occupied the region in Jilin Province north of the Amur River, and in 1900, during the Boxer Uprising, they fully occupied Heilongjiang Province.

The city of Shenyang, called Mukden in the Manchurian language, was the Manchu capital and is now the capital of Liaoning Province. North Korea borders Liaoning to the east. Liaodong Peninsula juts south into the Bo Hai Gulf. At its southern tip is a strategic harbor formerly known as Port Arthur and now part of modern Dalian. Japan defeated China in the Sino-Japanese War of 1894–95 and claimed the Liaodong Peninsula, but other foreign powers forced Japan to return it to China. Russia then took control of the peninsula and in 1896–1903 built the Northeast China Railroad, a branch of the Trans-Siberian Railroad, giving it access to Port Arthur. Japan gained all Russian concessions in Manchuria after it destroyed the Russian fleet in the Russo-Japanese War of 1904–5. The Chinese nominally controlled Manchuria until 1931, when Japan used the so-called Manchurian Incident as a pretext to send troops to occupy Liaoning Province. In 1932 Japan established its puppet state in Manchuria, called Manchukuo (Manzhouguo or Man-chou-kuo in Chinese), with the deposed, last Manchu Qing emperor, known as Henry Puyi, at its head. The Japanese made Changchun in Jilin Province the capital of Manchukuo and renamed it Xinjing. Japan was defeated in 1945, and the Chinese Nationalists (Kuomintang; KMT) held Liaoning until the Chinese Communists took it on November 2, 1948, a year before they established the People's Republic of China (PRC). In 1950, during the Korean War, the PRC sent more than two million troops across the Yalu River into North Korea to prevent the United Nations forces from crossing the border into Manchuria. This was the first time in modern history that the Chinese had been able to fight foreign powers and prevent them from advancing into China.

The Sungari (Songliao) Plain, irrigated by the Liao River (Liaohe), is a major agricultural region, especially for sorghum, wheat, apples and wild silk. Liaoning also has large fishing, seaweed and sea-salt industries, and ginseng is harvested for herbal medicines. The province is also highly industrialized and is China's main producer of steel, mining equipment and machine tools, and a large producer of natural gas, crude oil and iron ore. The PRC government has made large investments in Liaoning's heavy industries.

Jilin Province, with its capital at Changchun, also borders North Korea to the east. The province's eastern region is mountainous and heavily forested and a source of lumber and the "three treasures of Manchuria," ginseng, sable fur and deer antlers (used in herbal medicine). Three major rivers have their source in the Changbai Mountain Range, the Yalu, the Tumen and the Songhua River, the most important river in the province. The western plains of Jilin are a major region for the growing of grain, soybeans, sugar beets and corn. Jilin has also become industrialized, with its main products being motor vehicles, optical instruments, chemicals, construction equipment and paper.

Heilongjiang Province is the largest and most northern province in China (there are several autonomous regions that are larger). Its capital is Harbin, a major port on the banks of the Songhua River. Heilongjiang is separated from Russia by the Amur River (Heilongjiang) on its northern border and the Wusuli River (Wusulijiang; also known as the Ussuri) on the east. China and Russia have had military standoffs along the Heilongjiang border. The eastern terminus of the Great Wall lies in Heilongjiang. The Jurchens, ancestors of the Manchus, originated in the Amur River valley. They conquered the Liao dynasty (947–1125), founded the Jin dynasty (1115–1234) and nearly conquered the Song dynasty (960–1279), forcing the Chinese emperor to flee south in 1127 and establish the Southern Song dynasty. Heilongjiang has large oil and coal deposits, including China's largest oilfield, near Daqing, and is industrialized, with steel as a major product. The province is also one of China's most important suppliers of timber. The bird sanctuary of Shalong is the summer home for hundreds of red-crested cranes. The southern part of the province belongs to a fertile agricultural region known as the Great Manchurian Plain. Major crops include soybeans, wheat, corn and sugar beets, as well as jute and hemp, which are used to make such products as fibers and rope.

Many Han Chinese have settled in Manchuria, but there are still many Manchus and members of other national minority ethnic groups, including Korean, Mongol and Hezhe, the smallest minority group in China. See also AMUR RIVER; BO HAI GULF; CHANGCHUN; CHANGBAI MOUNTAIN RANGE; CRANE; DAQING OIL FIELD; DEER; GINSENG; GREAT WALL; HAN; HARBIN; HEILONGJIANG PROVINCE; IRON TECHNOLOGY AND STEEL INDUSTRY; JILIN PROVINCE; JURCHEN; KOREAN; KOREAN WAR; LIAODONG PENINSULA; LIAONING PROVINCE; MANCHU; MANCHUKUO; MANCHURIAN INCIDENT; MINORITIES, NATIONAL; NERCHINSK, TREATY OF; PUYI, HENRY; QING DYNASTY; RUSSO-JAPANESE WAR OF 1904–5; SABLE; SHENYANG; SINO-JAPANESE WAR OF 1894–95; SONGHUA RIVER; TUMEN RIVER; WUSULI RIVER; YALU TSUNGPO RIVER.

MANCHURIAN INCIDENT   The seizure of the city of Mukden, the capital of Liaoning Province in Manchuria (northeastern China), by Japanese troops in September 1931. The Japanese used Mukden, called Shenyang in Chinese, as a base from which they rapidly brought all of Manchuria under their control. The Chinese came to regard the Manchurian Incident as the beginning of World War II and the root cause of their War of Resistance against Japan (1937–45).

Because Liaoning has vast natural resources, Western powers had vied for its control during the 19th century. In 1898 Russia took control of the Liaodong Peninsula, made Shenyang its base and built the Northeast China Railroad in 1896–1903. Japan and Great Britain allied themselves against Russia, and Japan defeated Russia in the Russo-Japanese War of 1904–05, during which the battle of Mukden was fought February 19–March 10, 1905. Russia had to cede its rights to southern Manchuria to Japan, which used Mukden as its base for exploiting Manchuria's mineral resources and building factories. After the Republic of China was founded in 1912, the Japanese allowed several Chinese warlords to operate out of Mukden. Zhang Zuolin (Chang Tso-lin) ruled the northern Chinese provinces from 1916 until he was assassinated in 1928. The area was further troubled in 1931, when Chinese and Korean farmers in the area had a violent dispute over land rights, which led to anti-Chinese riots in Korea and Japan in which several hundred Chinese were killed or injured. The Chinese began to boycott goods made in Japan, and harsh feelings increased on both sides.

The Manchurian Incident occurred when Chinese soldiers murdered a Japanese captain named Nakamura in northwestern Manchuria. The Japanese used this event as an excuse to increase their power in Manchuria. On the night of September 18, 1931, Japanese troops set off a bomb on the Southern Manchurian Railroad track outside Mukden and seized the city with the pretext of protecting the railroad from a Chinese attack. The Chinese people were shocked by this incident and held further anti-Japanese demonstrations and boycotts. Chiang Kai-shek, leader of the Chinese Nationalist forces, which had been fighting the Chinese Communists, halted the civil war and addressed the Manchurian crisis. He decided to take China's case against Japan to the League of Nations, and commanded Zhang Xueliang (Chang Hsueh-liang), whose Chinese forces in

Manchuria outnumbered the Japanese troops there, not to fight the Japanese, because Chiang wanted to use the Chinese troops to fight the Chinese Communists. The Japanese drove Zhang's troops out of Manchuria before the end of 1931 and occupied all of Manchuria, where they established their puppet state of Manchukuo (Manzhouguo in Chinese) in 1932 with the capital at Changchun. They rejected the League of Nations judgment against them and claimed that they were maintaining Manchuria's internal peace and security. See also CHANGCHUN; CHIANG KAI-SHEK; LEAGUE OF NATIONS; LIAODONG PENINSULA; LIAONING PROVINCE; MANCHURIA; SHENYANG; WAR OF RESISTANCE AGAINST JAPAN; ZHANG ZUOLIN.

MANDALA   A complex, colorful picture that is a symbolic representation of the universe. It is used for meditation and ritual purposes in the Tantric sects of the Hindu and Buddhist religions. The mandala is now associated mainly with the Tibetan form of Buddhism, known as Lamaism. Mandala is the Indian Sanskrit word for "circle." The Tibetan word for a mandala painted on a cloth scroll is *tanka* (*thang-ka*). Mandalas may be painted on cloth or paper or created in a temporary form using colored threads, sand or rice powder. A *tanka* is designed in the form of an outer square that encloses one or more concentric circles, which enclose a square divided into four triangles by lines that run from the center to the four corners. Five circles at the center and inside the four triangles contain images or symbols of Buddhist deities, usually the five so-called "self-born" Buddhas. Other Buddhist images and symbols fill the *tanka* or mandala in a hierarchical design. The outside borders are also symbolic. A ring of fire represents the burning away of spiritual ignorance and prevents uninitiated persons from entering the mandala. Next in turn, a ring of diamonds represents spiritual illumination; a circle of eight graveyards represents the eight aspects of intellectual thought; and a ring of lotus leaves symbolizes Buddhist enlightenment. The beautiful lotus is the sacred flower of Buddhism because it rises from the mud and thus represents purity. A person meditating on a mandala visualizes himself going into the mandala and making his way through the levels of images until he arrives at the center. Buddhists believe that mandala meditation helps concentrate spiritual power and bring freedom from suffering. See also BUDDHISM; LAMAISM.

MANDARIN   The Western term for a member of the literati (*wenren; wen jen*), or scholar-gentry, class that staffed the Chinese imperial bureaucracy, which functioned as a civil service from the Han (206 B.C.–220 A.D.) through Qing (1644–1911) dynasties. The word comes from the Portuguese *mandar,* "to govern," which was taken in turn from a Malay word, *mantri,* "government minister." Portuguese officials, who first went to China to trade in the 16th century, applied the name *mandar* to Chinese government officials. The rank of mandarins in the imperial bureaucracy was denoted by a rigid and complex system of robe colors they wore, as well as the design motifs of embroidered patches sewn onto the robes. This is known as the "Nine-Rank System."

Mandarin is also the Western name for the dialect of the Chinese language spoken in northern China, which became predominant and is now spoken by about three-fourths of all Chinese citizens. The Chinese term for the Mandarin dialect is *guauhua,* "official language," because when imperial government officials were sent from the capital at Beijing to the provinces throughout China, they were required to speak this dialect and to communicate with people in those regions through Mandarin interpreters. See also IMPERIAL BUREAUCRACY; LANGUAGE, CHINESE; LITERATI; NINE-RANK SYSTEM.

MANDARIN DUCK   See DUCK.

MANDATE OF HEAVEN (*tianming* or *t'ien ming*)   The concept that a ruler had the approval of heaven (*tian* or *t'ien*) as long as he was virtuous, but that he lost heaven's approval and the right to his throne if he became unjust. The greater part of Chinese history falls into periods defined by the dynasties that ruled the country under an emperor, whom the Chinese referred to as the "Son of Heaven" (*tianzi* or *t'ien tzu*). The concept of the Mandate of Heaven originated with the Zhou dynasty (1100–256 B.C.). The duke of Zhou (Zhou Gong or Chou Kong) justified the Zhou conquest of the Shang dynasty (1700–1027 B.C.) by asserting that the Shang rulers had lost the Mandate of Heaven, which gave them the right to rule, and the Zhou claimed the Mandate for themselves. The Zhou rulers told the Shang that the same process had occurred when they had overthrown the Xia dynasty (2200–1750 B.C.). The Zhou claimed that their right to rule came not from their clan ancestors but from a broad, impersonal deity—Heaven (*tian*)—whose mandate (*tianming*) might be conferred on any family that was morally worthy of the responsibility. After the Zhou defeated the Shang, the duke of Zhou gave a speech to the Shang nobles asking them to submit to the will of Heaven, which had decreed that the Shang had broken the laws of Heaven and deserved to be punished. His speech, handed down orally and written down several centuries later, was the earliest statement of the Chinese theory of the Mandate of Heaven. This doctrine asserted that the ruler was accountable to a supreme moral force that guides the human sphere, and it established moral criteria for holding power by asserting that a wise and benevolent ruler would retain the mandate.

All subsequent Chinese dynasties legitimized their overthrow of previous dynasties by making the same claims regarding the Mandate of Heaven. The basic ideology of the Confucian-based Chinese state was that the ruler's exemplary and benevolent conduct manifesting his personal virtue (*de* or *teh*) made his people follow him and gave him the Mandate. Chinese historians viewed the history of their country as a continuous cycle of revival and decline as each dynasty rose and fell in turn. The official historians of each new dynasty were given the task of writing the history of the previous dynasty, which had been overthrown. Chinese chronicles recorded that natural disasters such as earthquakes and floods and celestial events such as comets and eclipses increased in frequency toward the end of each dynasty, and these were regarded as signs that the unjust actions of the ruler were causing him to lose the Mandate of Heaven. The historians and other members of the imperial bureaucracy that governed China belonged to the literati (scholar) class. Once the literati were persuaded that a dynasty had lost its moral claim to the throne, that dynasty could not be saved. For example, Sui emperor Yangdi (Yangti; r. 604–618) attempted to conquer Korea but exhausted the treasury. His defeat was a major cause of rebellions against his rule, based on the belief that he had lost the Mandate of Heaven.

The military men who founded dynasties felt that they had received the Mandate of Heaven when the Chinese stopped resisting them. The literati in their bureaucracies looked down upon these men of violence (*wu*) as lacking in self-cultivation (*wen*), a central Confucian concept. The Chinese term for the country, Middle Kingdom (Zhongguo or Chung-kuo), indicates that the chieftains of non-Chinese peoples were required to acknowledge China's superiority by bowing down (*kowtow*) before the Chinese emperor, who held Heaven's Mandate to govern China and whose magnificent benevolence and compassion naturally attracted outsiders to enter and be transformed by Chinese civilization. Tribal peoples who invaded China and established their own dynasties, including the Jurchens who founded the Jin dynasty (1115–1234), the Mongols who founded the Yuan dynasty (1279–1368), and the Manchus who founded the Qing dynasty (1644–1911), adopted the concepts of Confucianism, especially that of the Mandate of Heaven, and used them to maintain their political control. See also EMPEROR; HEAVEN; IMPERIAL BUREAUCRACY; KOWTOW; LITERATI; MIDDLE KINGDOM; ZHOU, DUKE OF; ZHOU DYNASTY.

MANICHAEISM AND ZOROASTRIANISM Two foreign religions of the many that were introduced into China during the Tang dynasty (618–907), when many foreign traders settled in the large, cosmopolitan capital city of Chang'an (modern Xi'an). Other foreign religions introduced during that time include Judaism, Nestorian Christianity and Islam, whose followers are called Muslims. The Buddhist religion had already been introduced into China from India around the first century A.D. and had gained many Chinese converts. During the reign of the second Tang emperor, Taizong (T'ai-tsung; r. 626–649), the Silk Road—the great trade route across Central Asia to the Middle East—was established, and China openly welcomed those who brought foreign culture, art objects, music and dance, and religion. Members of foreign religions were permitted to live in their own communities and follow their own customs and laws.

Manichaeism was founded in Persia (modern Iran) by Mani (c. 216–274), who taught that there are two opposing principles: good, which is associated with light, and evil, which is associated with darkness. The human body and the created world belong to the principle of evil or darkness, whereas the human spirit belongs to the principle of good or light. Time has three phases. In the first phase, good and evil are separate, in the second phase they are mingled, and in the third phase they will be separated again. Human beings exist in the second phase of time as both body and spirit. They must purify themselves of evil so that when the third phase of time will begin, they will be able to dwell in the light rather than in the darkness. Manichaeans regarded themselves as members of the same family. Their strict morality included giving alms to the poor and avoiding alcohol, meat and cheese. Lay members were allowed to marry, but the clergy had to be celibate and to perform periods of fasting.

Manichaeism spread eastward through Central Asia. Persian traders brought the religion to China in the late seventh century, and a century later the religion began to spread throughout the country. The Uighurs, a tribe on China's northern frontier that had helped the Chinese suppress the An Lushan Rebellion around 762, converted to Manichaeism in 763. This influenced many Chinese to convert to the religion as well. In 768 a Manichaean temple was built in Chang'an; around 771 temples were built in four other cities; and in 807 they were built in Luoyang and Taiyuan, showing that the religion was gaining converts to the east. By the 12th century, there were many Manichaean communities in southeastern China. After this time, however, the religion began to decline, and many of its members turned to sects of Buddhism or to the native Chinese philosophy of Daoism, especially secret societies in the southern Chinese provinces of Fujian and Zhejiang.

Zoroastrianism was founded in Persia (modern Iran) by Zoroaster (c. 600 B.C.), who taught that there is a cosmic battle between good and evil. Its practices included the worship of the "fire *xian*" (*huoxian* or *huo-hsien*) twice a year. Persian embassies brought the religion to northern China c. 516–519, where they influenced the Empress Dowager Ling. By the time of the Sui dynasty (581–618), Zoroastrian tent leaders or clergy (*sabao* or *sa-pao*) were established in Chang'an. In 621 a Zoroastrian shrine for Persian foreigners was established in Chang'an, and in 631 a (*muhu*), or Zoroastrian priest, was accepted at the Tang court. The Tang government gave the Zoroastrian church official recognition and treated its clergy as equals to Chinese who held the fifth and seventh ranks of the imperial bureaucracy or civil service. However, Chinese were forbidden to take part in Zoroastrian sacrificial ceremonies, and the scriptures of the religion were not translated into Chinese. By the eighth century, there were as many as five Zoroastrian shrines in Chang'an, three in Luoyang, three in Kaifeng, and others in many other Chinese cities.

Manichaeism and Zoroastrianism were both severely persecuted, along with the Buddhist religion, by Emperor Wuzong (Wu-tsung; r. 840–846) in 845. He ordered the monks of all three religions to return to secular life. Zoroastrian magis were murdered in Khanfu (modern Guangzhou) in 878. Manichaeism also declined with the decline of the Uighurs, who had been attacked in 840 by the Kirghiz, a tribe from western Siberia. In 842 the Uighurs made many raids into China to gain much-needed food. The Chinese sent a military campaign against them and executed several hundred members of the Uighur community in Chang'an. Manichaean beliefs regarding the end of the second phase of time and the imminent arrival of the third phase may have influenced the White Lotus Secret Society, which led rebellions against the Ming dynasty (1368–1644) and Qing dynasty (1644–1911). Zoroastrianism died out in China probably by the 13th century. See also BUDDHISM; CHANG'AN; JEWS; MUSLIMS; NESTORIAN CHRISTIANITY; SILK ROAD; TAIZONG (EMPEROR); TANG DYNASTY; UIGHUR; WHITE LOTUS SECRET SOCIETY; WUZONG (EMPEROR).

MANJUSRI See BODHISATTVA; LION; MAITREYA AND MANJUSRI.

MANTOU See NOODLES.

MANUFACTURING See FOREIGN TRADE AND INVESTMENT; FOUR MODERNIZATIONS; SPECIAL ECONOMIC ZONES.

MANY-SPLENDORED THING, A See HAN SUYIN.

MANZHOUGUO See MANCHUKUO.

MANZU See MANCHU.

MAO DUN (Mao Tun; 1896–1981) A famous modern Chinese novelist and pioneer of China's revolutionary culture. Mao Dun, which means "contradiction," is the pen name of Shen Yanbing (Shen Yen-ping), whose name was originally Shen Dehong (Shen Te-hung). Born in Zhejiang Province, Shen entered Beijing University in 1913, but had to interrupt his education in 1916 to earn money. He became a proofreader at the Commercial Press in Shanghai, and quickly became an editor and translator. He played an active role in the May Fourth Movement of 1919 and became one of the earliest members of the Chinese Communist Party (CCP). In 1920 Shen joined other young Chinese writers in founding the "Literary Society." They took over *Short-Story Magazine* (*Xiaoshuo Yuebao* or *Hsiao-shuo Yueh-pao*) and used it to publish current literature. Shen was the magazine's editor until 1923.

In 1926 he joined the Northern Expedition against the warlords, serving as secretary to the propaganda department of the Nationalist (Kuomintang) Central Executive Committee. Conflict between the socialist branch of the Nationalist Party and the CCP caused Shen to leave the Nationalists and resume writing fiction. In 1930 Shen joined with Lu Xun (Lu Hsun) in helping to found the League of Left-Wing Writers. That same year he published a trilogy of three short novels called *Eclipse* (*Shi* or *Shih*) under the pen name Mao Dun, about his experiences with the Northern Expedition. The trilogy made him famous. Western critics praised the psychological realism of the trilogy, but Chinese Marxist critics criticized the work on ideological grounds. Mao published *Midnight* (*Ziyue* or *Tzu-yueh*) in 1933, and Chinese Marxist critics praised it for its social realism. Like his contemporaries such as Ba Jin (Pa Chin; b. 1904), Mao Dun wrote about characters who were fired with revolutionary fervor and was influenced by Russian writers such as Turgenev.

During China's War of Resistance against Japan (1937–45), Mao Dun founded and edited two literary journals to help the Chinese patriotic cause. After the Communists established the People's Republic of China (PRC) in 1949, he stopped writing fiction in order to work for the government in Beijing, serving on a number of literary and cultural committees. He was elected to many positions, including chairman of the All-China Literary Workers Association (now the Chinese Writers' Association). In 1949 he was appointed the PRC's first minister of culture, but he was dismissed from that position in 1964 when Mao Zedong purged many artists and intellectuals during the Socialist Education Movement. In the 1970s he was vice president of the Chinese Writers' Association and edited a magazine of literature for children. In 1978, after suffering for a decade during the Cultural Revolution (1966–76), he resumed his

activities in the Communist government. Other works by Mao Dun include *Rainbow, Spring Silkworms, The Lin Family Shop, The Frosted Leaves Are Red as Flowers in February,* and *Around Qingming Festival.* Many of his works have been translated into foreign languages. He also began writing his memoirs but did not complete them before he died in 1981. See also BA JIN; COMMERCIAL PRESS, THE; CULTURAL REVOLUTION; NATIONALIST PARTY; NORTHERN EXPEDITION; PEOPLE'S REPUBLIC OF CHINA; WAR OF RESISTANCE AGAINST JAPAN.

MAO SHAN SCHOOL See DAOIST CLASSICAL TEXTS.

MAO TSE-MIN See URUMQI.

MAO TSE-TUNG See MAO ZEDONG.

MAO TUN See MAO DUN.

MAO ZEDONG (Mao Tse-tung; 1893–1976) Also known as Chairman Mao; the founder of the Chinese Communist Party (CCP), which established the People's Republic of China in 1949, and the leader of the CCP from 1935 until his death in 1976. Mao was the eldest of four children born to a fairly prosperous peasant family in Shaoshan, Hunan Province, in central China. After attending primary school, he worked on his family's farm for several years and then went back to school in 1909. On his own, he also read widely in traditional Chinese literature and translations of Western works on philosophy, politics and economics. In 1918 Mao graduated from the Fourth (later called the First) Teacher's Training School in Changsha, the capital of Hunan. He then went to Beijing, the capital of China, where he worked as a librarian under the brilliant revolutionary thinker Li Dazhao (Li Ta-chao) at prestigious Beijing University. Mao's family had arranged for him to marry a local girl while he was only 14 years old, but she remained in Hunan.

In 1911, under the leadership of Dr. Sun Yat-sen, the Chinese people had overthrown the Manchu Qing dynasty (1644–1911), China's last imperial dynasty, and established the Republic of China (ROC) at Nanjing in 1912. That year Sun also organized the Chinese Nationalist Party (Kuomintang; KMT), an outgrowth of his Revolutionary Alliance (*Tongmenghui* or *T'ung-meng-hui*). Despite the founding of the ROC, warlords in Beijing continued to control the Chinese government.

Mao became active in student revolutionary causes. After World War I, it had been revealed that the warlord government in Beijing had made a secret agreement with Japan that Japan would be given the concessions in China that had been held by Germany. The Chinese people were outraged, and on May 4, 1919, Chinese students, led by students from Beijing University, held massive public demonstrations against the Beijing government and Japan. These culminated in a nationwide political movement known as the May Fourth Movement of 1919, which rekindled revolutionary fervor in China. This movement inspired all modern Chinese revolutionaries and also stimulated the so-called New Culture Movement among Chinese intellectuals and artists. Mao studied Marxist theory, and by 1920, three years after the Bolshevik October Revolution of 1917 in Russia, he defined himself as a Marxist.

In addition to Beijing, Mao spent time in Shanghai, China's largest port and trading city, and Hunan Province, organizing Chinese students according to Marxist principles. For a time he also taught in Changsha. In July 1921, 12 delegates from Communist groups in Beijing, Guangzhou, Shanghai, Wuhan, Jinan and Japan met in Shanghai to convene the First National Party Congress of the Chinese Communist Party. The CCP regards this as the official date of its founding. Shanghai was an active center for worker's movements. Mao attended the congress as an official delegate from the Communist group in Hunan.

Soviet advisers went to China to help organize the CCP and reorganize Sun Yat-sen's KMT on the model of the Communist Party in the U.S.S.R. The most prominent adviser was Mikhail Borodin (1884–1952), an agent of the Comintern (Communist International). The Comintern instructed CCP members to cooperate with the KMT and join the KMT while keeping their identity as members of the CCP. In 1922 the KMT had 150,000 members and the CCP only 300 members; by 1925 the CCP had 1,500 members. From 1921 to 1923 Mao worked for the CCP, organizing labor unions and labor strikes.

At the CCP Third National Party Congress in 1923, held in Guangzhou in southern China, Mao was elected to the party's nine-member Central Committee. The National Party Congress acknowledged that the KMT was the leading party of the Chinese revolution and decided to cooperate with the KMT, and the two parties formed their First United Front. Mao held several positions in the KMT, including director of the Peasant Movement Training Institute in 1926. Mao was elected an alternate member of the KMT Central Executive Committee at the KMT's First National Congress, held in Guangzhou in 1924. He also became the acting director of its Central Committee. The KMT and CCP cooperated to establish the Whampoa (Huangpu) Military Academy near Guangzhou, to train officers for a Northern Expedition against the warlords who controlled China. Chiang Kai-shek (Jiang Jieshi; 1887–1975) was named the academy's first commandant. He worked closely with Zhou Enlai (Chou Enlai; 1898–1976), who served as director of the academy's Political Department. Zhou had joined the Communist Party while a student in France; he later became the second-most important leader in the CCP.

In 1925 Mao was active in Hunan organizing peasants. After a strike he organized was suppressed, Mao fled to Guangzhou, where he became secretary of the propaganda department of the KMT. Upon Sun Yat-sen's death in 1925, KMT leaders vied to become head of the party; Chiang Kai-shek eventually won out. In June 1926 Chiang was named commander-in-chief of the National Revolutionary Army, and in July he launched the Northern Expedition against the warlords to unify China. By 1927 his forces had regained territory as far north as Shanghai and Nanjing. Members of the CCP and the left-wing faction of the KMT had gone ahead of the expedition to persuade local peasants and workers to support it. However, Chiang felt that their emphasis on social and economic reforms had become too revolutionary, especially when they organized workers' strikes in urban factories.

Mao attended the KMT's Central Executive Committee meeting in Wuhan in March 1927, and the CCP's Fifth NPC

Chairman Mao, a founder of the Chinese Communist Party (CCP), served as its leader until his death in 1976.   LU HOUMIN

in April–May 1927. Chiang had already begun purging Communists from the KMT in Guangzhou, and in April 1927 Chiang sent his troops into Shanghai to arrest and execute the Communists there. Thousands were killed but some escaped, including Zhou Enlai and his wife Deng Yingchao, to join Communist forces at the Soviet base on the border of Jiangxi Province in south-central China.

Communists in the Chinese countryside attempted several unsuccessful insurrections against the KMT. Zhou Enlai and Lin Biao helped organize the Nanchang Uprising, the Communist military rebellion against the KMT on August 1, 1927. The CCP considers this date the birth of the Communist Red Army, which later became known as the People's Liberation Army (PLA). The Nationalists put down the uprising, and Zhu De took his troops to Hunan Province and joined Mao, who was leading guerrilla forces in Hunan. Mao led the Autumn Harvest Uprising of 1927, an insurrection by Hunan peasants. By this time Mao was convinced that, in contradiction to orthodox Marxist-Leninist theory, in China the peasants rather than the urban workers were the social group that the Chinese Communists should mobilize for their revolution. Peasants formed the vast majority of the Chinese population and had always been a force for social change. Many times in Chinese history, dynasties had been overthrown and new dynasties established by rebellious peasants who believed that the old dynasty had lost the "Mandate of Heaven." Mao and Zhu realized that it was more important for the Communists to control the countryside than to expend a lot of troops to try and take over large cities.

Mao and Zhu built up a Communist military force in the Jinggang Mountain Range on the border of Hunan and Jiangxi provinces, which had about 10,000 troops by the winter of 1927–28. In 1929 they moved the Red Army to Ruijin in southeastern Jiangxi Province, where they established a Soviet (communist base) and Zhu built up the Red Army to 200,000 troops by 1933. Other Communist leaders joined them in Jiangxi. Zhou Enlai, who spent several years as head of the CCP military department and became political commissar of the Red Army, disagreed with Mao and other CCP officials about military strategies. However, Mao's skill at guerrilla fighting tactics and peasant mobilization enabled him to become the dominant CCP leader.

In 1928 Chiang Kai-shek led the second phase of the Northern Expedition and took Beijing in June 1928, symbolically unifying all of China south of the Great Wall. On October 10, 1928, Chiang became chairman of a new Chinese Nationalist government (ROC) and established his capital at Nanjing. The KMT refused to allow any other political party to have a role in the ROC government. The Communists led a number of uprisings in Chinese cities, all of which were bloodily suppressed by the Nationalists, and Mikhail Borodin and other foreign advisers fled the country. Beginning in 1930, Chiang sent five annual KMT military campaigns against the Communist forces in south-central China.

On September 18, 1931, Japanese forces launched a full-scale invasion of Manchuria (northeastern China), but Chiang told his troops not to resist the Japanese and pulled them out of Manchuria. Chiang still felt the most urgent task of the KMT was to wipe out communism in China. In November 1931 Mao was appointed chairman of the government of the Chinese Soviet Republic, and Zhang Guotao was sent to become the head of a Soviet in northern China. In 1932 the Japanese formed a puppet state in Manchuria called Manchukuo (Manzhouguo or Man-chou-kuo in Chinese) and used it as their base to invade China Proper and the rest of Asia. Despite the Japanese threat, Chiang's KMT forces continued their campaigns against the Communist Red Army and encircled the Soviet in Jiangxi.

In 1934 Mao, Zhou Enlai, Zhu De and other CCP leaders decided that their forces should escape to the west. About 100,000 soldiers and CCP members began the epic Long March (1934–35), which covered 6,000 miles. During the Long March, the CCP held a meeting of the Politburo (Political Bureau) of its Central Committee in January 1935 in Guizhou Province. The party established a new leadership with Mao as CCP chairman. Mao was the first leader of the CCP, and of any Communist Party in the world, who had not been chosen by the Comintern. In June 1935, Red Army troops led by Mao and Zhu met up with Zhang Guotao's 50,000 Red Army troops in Sichuan Province. Zhang asserted that he should be the leader of the combined Red Army, but as Mao had recently been elected head of the CCP, he and his supporters rejected Zhang's claim. Most of the Red Army troops left with Mao to continue their rigorous march to join other CCP troops in northern Shaanxi. A smaller number of troops went with Zhang and Zhu De to remote southwestern China near the Tibetan border.

On October 20, 1935, the survivors of the Long March under Mao, who numbered only about 7,000, officially ended their march when they met up with the 15th Red Army Corps at Wuqizhen in northern Shaanxi Province. The legendary survivors became the leaders of the final stage of the civil war between the CCP and KMT and later became high-ranking officials in the PRC government. Only about 50 women survived the march, including Deng Yingchao and Mao's third wife. His second wife had been executed in Hunan in 1930. In late 1936, CCP leaders moved their headquarters to Yan'an in Shaanxi Province. Mao and his third wife separated at Yan'an, and he sent her to Moscow, ostensibly to receive medical treatment. Mao married his fourth wife, Jiang Qing (Chiang Ch'ing; 1914–91), at Yan'an in 1939 when he was 45 years old. An actress and political activist from Shanghai, she was later blamed for the Cultural Revolution (1966–76).

Zhang Xueliang (Chang Hsueh-liang; 1898–), the warlord of Manchuria, had pledged his loyalty to Chiang Kai-shek and the KMT. In 1935 Chiang ordered Zhang to send his troops to fight Mao's Communist Red Army at Yan'an. However, the Manchurian soldiers were angry that they had been sent against their own countrymen while the Japanese were occupying their land, and they did not want to fight. Mao also wanted to halt the CCP-KMT civil war, and on December 25, 1935, the CCP Politburo called for an "Anti-Japanese National United Front," although this did not end the war. In December 1936 Chiang flew to Zhang's headquarters at Xi'an in Shaanxi. Zhang, Zhou Enlai and other KMT and CCP military leaders kidnapped Chiang to persuade him to stop fighting the Communists and form a KMT-CCP united front to fight the Japanese; this is known as the Xi'an Incident. Chiang agreed to do so and flew back to his capital at Nanjing. In 1937 Japanese troops moved from Manchuria into northern China and quickly took the North China Plain. In August they attacked Shanghai. In November 1937 they took Nanjing and committed atrocities against hundreds of thousands of Chinese residents, an incident known as the "Rape of Nanjing."

Combined KMT-CCP forces, bolstered by private armies of Chinese warlords, began fighting the War of Resistance against Japan. The Communist Red Army was renamed the Eighth Route Army of the National Army, with Zhu De serving as commander of all Chinese Communist military operations. Peng Dehuai (P'eng Teh-huai) served as deputy commander of the Eighth Route Army. Other commanders and political commissars included Liu Bocheng (Liu Po-cheng), Deng Xiaoping (Teng Hsiao-p'ing), Lin Biao (Lin Piao) and Nie Rongzhen (Nieh Jung-chen). KMT forces controlled southwestern China, and CCP forces northwestern China. The Communists also led guerrilla forces in Henan, Zhejiang and Shandong provinces and in other regions between the areas controlled by Japanese forces, especially in northern China.

Mao began planning the new Chinese Communist government that he expected to form after the War of Resistance ended, and in 1940 he drew up an outline of its program. In early 1941 the KMT-CCP united front began breaking down when Nationalist troops defeated the Communist New

Fourth Army in the lower Yangzi River valley, an event known as the New Fourth Army Incident. Both sides looked forward to resuming their civil war. During the early 1940s Mao consolidated his position as leader of the CCP, and in 1943 and 1944 the party elected him chairman of the Central Committee and of the Politburo. The CCP held its Seventh National Party Congress, the first since 1928, in Yan'an in early 1945. It adopted a constitution with a preamble stating that "the thought of Mao Zedong" was the official party ideology. Mao had complete control of the CCP by the end of the War of Resistance.

After Japan surrendered on August 14, 1945, the United States attempted to negotiate a coalition KMT-CCP government that would rule all of China. The CCP now had about 1.2 million members, plus 900,000 soldiers in its military, and controlled an area with a population of 90 million Chinese. Mao and Zhou met with Chiang at Chongqing for six weeks in the fall of 1945, but nothing came of their negotiations. Zhou went to northern Shaanxi to help direct the CCP forces there. The United States also attempted to have all Japanese troops in China surrender to the Nationalists rather than the Communists, so that Chiang Kai-shek would be the dominant political leader in postwar China. But Russian troops had entered Manchuria on August 8, 1945, and they turned over Manchuria and all the weapons the Japanese had surrendered there to the Chinese Communists, which greatly helped the CCP cause. The United States continued to give the Nationalist government enormous loans and made sure that China became a permanent member of the newly-formed United Nations.

On May 1, 1946, the CCP officially renamed its military the People's Liberation Army (PLA). On June 26, 1946, Nationalist troops waged an offensive against Communist-held areas in Hubei and Henan provinces, which marked the resumption of the civil war. However, the Nationalist government could not gain support from the Chinese people because of rampant corruption and inflation. Chinese businessmen, who had been the core supporters of the KMT, began leaving the country. By the end of 1947, the Americans saw that the Nationalists had no chance of winning the civil war and withdrew their support for Chiang Kai-shek.

The Communists used guerrilla tactics and mobilized Chinese peasants to their side by such practices as land reform, in which they encouraged peasants to criticize the wealthy landowners who exploited them and then took land away from the landowners and gave it to peasants who had little or no land. The Communists continued to gain support in northern China, and Lin Biao led a major campaign in Manchuria, where 300,000 Nationalist troops surrendered to the Communists in October 1948. In the second great battle of the civil war, in the Huai River basin in north-central China, the PLA surrounded 66 of the KMT's 200 divisions. A large number of KMT soldiers defected to the CCP or were captured. The PLA won this campaign on January 10, 1949, which to all effects ended the Nationalist regime on the Chinese mainland.

From September 21 to 30, 1949, the CCP held the Chinese Political Consultative Conference (CPPCC) in Beijing, which served as the legislative and representative body of the new Communist government. The CPPCC was originally an organization formed in 1948 by the united front led by the CCP but including nearly all other Chinese factions that opposed the KMT. These eight political parties, known as the democratic parties, are still permitted to function on a small scale in China. On September 22, 1949, the CPPCC passed an Organic Law that specified the procedure and structure for government operations. On September 29, it proclaimed its Common Program, which served as the law of the new government until the 1954 state constitution superseded it. On October 1, 1949, Mao, joined by a large group of CCP leaders and other colleagues, stood on the rostrum above the gate in Tiananmen Square in Beijing and proclaimed the founding of the Communist People's Republic of China (PRC). Several days before, he had been elected chairman of the Central Government of the PRC.

In December 1949 Mao went to Moscow and met with Stalin on his first trip outside China. After 1949, Great Britain, the U.S.S.R. and many Eastern European countries recognized the PRC. In 1950 Mao made another trip to Moscow, where he negotiated the Sino-Soviet Treaty of Friendship, Alliance, and Mutual Assistance. The United States had withdrawn support for the Nationalist government when it fled to Taiwan, but after North Korea invaded South Korea in 1950, the United States changed its policy and provided military support to the ROC. The United States and many other countries accepted the ROC on Taiwan as the legitimate government of China and refused to give diplomatic recognition to the Communist PRC. The PRC supported North Korea and sent more than 2.3 million soldiers across the Yalu Tsungpo River to defend against advancing UN troops. They suffered extremely heavy casualties, including the death of Mao's eldest son, Mao Anying, and the war ground into a stalemate. Truce talks began in July 1951 and an armistice was signed in July 1953.

The CCP waged a public campaign to mobilize the Chinese people against the United States, whose troops fought for South Korea, and it continued the process of land reform throughout the countryside. Then it began combining farms into collectives known as people's communes. In 1951–52 the CCP launched a movement of "class struggle" against landlords, wealthy peasants, intellectuals, and corrupt bureaucrats and businessmen, known as the Three-Anti and Five-Anti Campaigns. Using public mass trials, the CCP purged officials who were incompetent and not totally loyal to the party. Hundreds of thousands of Chinese were executed and a much larger number were sent to prison or labor camps. In 1953 the CCP announced China's first Five-Year Plan (1953–57), which aimed to develop heavy industry based on the U.S.S.R. model. The government has continued issuing Five-Year Plans for China's economic and industrial development up to the present time. In 1953 China also held its first modern census, which showed the population to be 583 million, much higher than was expected.

In 1954 the PRC passed its first state constitution, which centralized the authority of the government in the National People's Congress (NPC), which superseded the CPPCC. The 1954 NPC elected Mao chairman of the PRC, Zhou premier of the State Council and Liu Shaoqi chairman of the Standing Committee of the NPC. The position of chairman gave Mao most of the country's political power, as detailed in Articles 39 to 46 of the constitution. Deng Xiaoping, Zhou's protege, served concurrently as secretary general of the CCP and vice premier of the State Council.

In the spring of 1956 Mao initiated a movement known as the Hundred Flowers Campaign or the Double Hundred Campaign, which encouraged intellectual and cultural leaders to make public criticisms of the CCP and party cadres (officials). But they became so strong in their denunciations that CCP leaders abruptly stopped the campaign in August 1957 by declaring the Anti-Rightist Campaign, in which critics of the party were condemned and punished for being "bourgeois rightists." Again, many Chinese were arrested and sent to prison or labor camps. By the end of this movement, Liu Shaoqi had become Mao's designated successor.

In November 1957 Mao led a Chinese delegation to the U.S.S.R. In 1958 he announced the Great Leap Forward (1958–60), which intended to speed up China's development in the spirit of the communist revolution that had established the PRC. Mao wanted to develop China's heavy industries and at the same time mobilize the great masses of unskilled Chinese workers. But the Great Leap Forward turned out to be a disaster that resulted in severe famine and the erosion of thousands of acres of farmland. In April 1959 the CCP required Mao to step down as chairman of the PRC, and he was replaced by Liu Shaoqi, although Mao remained chairman of the CCP. In September 1959 Mao replaced minister of national defense Peng Dehuai (P'eng Teh-huai), who advocated modernization of the PLA, with Lin Biao, who emphasized revolutionary purity in the military. In 1960 party leaders persuaded Mao to cancel the Great Leap Forward and admit that it had failed.

The U.S.S.R. had been a close ally of the PRC until the late 1950s and had signed a treaty providing for the Soviet defense of China against Japan and its allies. The U.S.S.R. helped China develop its heavy industries and sent large numbers of technicians to China, and many Chinese went to the U.S.S.R. for training. However, around 1956 the two countries began growing apart ideologically, a split that became known as the Sino-Soviet Conflict. Soviet leader Nikita Khrushchev criticized Mao's Great Leap Forward, which angered Mao, who resented what he perceived as the U.S.S.R.'s attempt to control China. Mao rejected Khrushchev's proposal for a joint Pacific fleet and a Russian communications complex on the east coast of China. The U.S.S.R. supported India in the Sino-Indian border skirmishes. In April 1960 the PRC criticized Soviet leaders for being "revisionist," and in June the U.S.S.R. stopped all of its aid to the PRC and called home the thousands of Soviet experts working in China. This devastated the Chinese economy.

By 1962 Mao had also denounced the government of the U.S.S.R. as a right-wing dictatorship. Mao wanted to prevent China from turning to capitalism, as he thought the U.S.S.R. had done, and this was a major reason he launched the Cultural Revolution in 1966. By 1963 the two countries were competing to be the leader of the Communist world, and their relations deteriorated even further during the Vietnam War. In 1968 Mao and Zhou condemned the Soviet invasion of Czechoslovakia and called the U.S.S.R. China's most dangerous enemy. The U.S.S.R. built up a huge military force along China's northern border, and the two countries fought border skirmishes in the late 1960s.

In the early 1960s more moderate CCP officials such as Liu Shaoqi, Deng Xiaoping and Peng Zhen had gained influence in the party, and they initiated measures to stabilize the Chinese economy. In 1962, two years after the failure of the Great Leap Forward, Mao began an ideological campaign known as the Socialist Education Movement (1962–65) against what he perceived as a trend toward capitalism and revisionism in the PRC. This movement, considered a precursor of the Cultural Revolution, is also known as the "Four Clean-ups" because it intended to remove corruption among party cadres in the four areas of accounts, granaries, property and the work-points awarded to peasants. Mao enacted a simultaneous campaign urging people "to learn from the People's Liberation Army (PLA)." Lin Biao, minister of national defense, urged members of the PLA and the CCP to follow the thought of Chairman Mao, and he compiled the *Quotations from Chairman Mao Zedong,* also known as the "Little Red Book," to indoctrinate PLA recruits with Mao's revolutionary thought. The Socialist Education Movement became a struggle between the moderate anti-Mao faction in the CCP and the pro-Mao radical faction that emphasized class struggle.

In September 1964 Liu Shaoqi, who had been informed about the corruption of CCP members in the Chinese countryside, issued a set of directives that tried to blunt the radical Maoist faction. In 1965 Mao urged the Politburo to begin a campaign to correct dissident intellectuals, but many party officials refused. Lin Biao and four other leaders supported Mao, but Liu Shaoqi and Deng Xiaoping opposed Mao and were supported by five other leaders, and Zhou Enlai abstained. This humiliated Mao, and some historians believe that he had then lost control of the CCP.

Mao retreated to Shanghai, the city where the CCP had begun and still a center for radical party members. From there, in 1966 he inaugurated his campaign to purge his opponents, including Liu Shaoqi, and to purify the CCP of reactionary influences. The Cultural Revolution officially began in May 1966 with an article published in a Shanghai newspaper criticizing Wu Han, the deputy mayor of Beijing, who had written a historical play that seemed to be an indirect criticism of Mao. On May 1, 1966, at a massive rally for International Workers Day in Tiananmen Square, Zhou announced the formal start of the Great Proletarian Cultural Revolution. On July 16, with great publicity, Mao took a famous swim in the Yangzi River at Wuhan to counter rumors that he was ill and to show that he was willing and able to lead the Cultural Revolution.

On August 18, 1966, Mao, Zhou, Lin Biao and other CCP officials presided over a massive rally, orchestrated by Jiang Qing, in Tiananmen Square in support of the Cultural Revolution. The Red Guards first appeared in public at this rally, and they held eight massive political demonstrations in three months in Tiananmen Square. At each rally, Mao appeared to them in person, wearing a Red Guard armband, and they spent hours shouting slogans and singing songs that praised him. At later demonstrations the Red Guards were televised all over the world waving copies of the "Little Red Book."

Mao and his radical faction attacked many CCP officials whom he accused of being revisionist, including State Chairman Liu Shaoqi, Mao's designated successor. Zhou remained loyal to Mao but attempted to mediate between the radical pro-Mao and moderate anti-Mao factions. In October 1968 the CCP officially denounced Liu Shaoqi and formally expelled him from the party. He was placed under house arrest and died in 1969. Liu was succeeded as chairman by Lin Biao, who was then himself accused of plotting against Mao and, according to the official party line, died in a plane crash while attempting to flee China in September 1971.

The Red Guards carried out Mao's orders to oppose feudalism and capitalism, and they destroyed a great deal of property and persecuted and killed numerous Chinese, many of them government and party officials. By 1967 China was on the verge of anarchy, and Mao finally called out the PLA to control the Red Guards. On July 28, 1968, Mao and other CCP leaders abolished the Red Guards, which brought the most radical phase of the Cultural Revolution to an end. However, the turmoil of the Cultural Revolution did not really end until Mao died in 1976 and the so-called Gang of Four, including Jiang Qing, was arrested and blamed for causing the revolution. In the early 1970s, Jiang Qing supposedly led the attacks by party radicals on Deng Xiaoping and other party leaders who advocated economic reforms.

In the early 1970s, the United States under President Richard M. Nixon reversed its policy and began opening up relations with the PRC. On October 25, 1971, the U.N. passed a resolution to expel the ROC and give China's seat to the PRC. On February 22, 1972, President Nixon visited China and met with Mao and Zhou. On February 28 the two countries issued a joint Sino-U.S. communique, known as the "Shanghai Communique," which, among other things, stated that the United States would withdraw its military forces from Taiwan and that Taiwan was a part of China. On January 1, 1979, the United States transferred diplomatic recognition from the ROC to the PRC, and many other countries did the same. In January 1975, Zhou addressed the Fourth NPC and advocated that China should undertake efforts to reform and develop the country, a policy known as the Four Modernizations. CCP officials linked this policy with industrialization and the opening up of foreign trade.

Zhou died on January 8, 1976, and in April the Chinese held mass demonstrations in Tiananmen Square at which they commemorated Zhou and criticized the close associates of Mao who had opposed Zhou. Military commander Zhu De died on July 6. In July a strong earthquake destroyed the city of Tangshan in Hebei Province, killing and wounding hundreds of thousands. The Chinese people had always regarded such natural disasters as portents of the impending downfall of a ruling dynasty, as symbols that it had lost the Mandate of Heaven, and this earthquake seemed a precursor of the end of the Maoist era.

Indeed, Mao died on September 9, 1976. On October 6, more than 30 radical CCP leaders were arrested and deposed from their official positions by the moderate faction led by Hua Guofeng (Hua Kuo-feng; 1920–), who had seized power in the CCP's Central Committee. On October 13, the CCP announced that Hua had been appointed to replace Mao as CCP chairman, chairman of the party's Central Military Commission, and premier of the State Council. On October 22, the party announced that four of the arrested radical leaders, known as the Gang of Four, had been charged with a plot to overthrow the Chinese government. These included Jiang Qing and three other Politburo members, Wang Hongwen (Wang Hung-wen), Yao Wenyuan and Zhang Chunjiao (Chang Ch'un-chao). They were initially

accused of attempting to forge all or part of Mao's will, issuing orders and attributing them to Mao, and hiring a gunman to make an attempt on the life of Hua Guofeng. As time went on, more and more accusations were made against them, some of them rather far-fetched. Mao was still so greatly respected that no criticisms were leveled against him; all blame was deflected to his widow and her three closest associates. Their actions were also associated with Lin Biao.

The Gang of Four were formally put on trial for "crimes against the people" in November 1980. Their trial, a momentous political event, greatly damaged the prestige of Mao, who had been revered as the "Great Helmsman" of the PRC, and the political system he and his supporters had created. The four were imprisoned and even airbrushed out of the photographs of Mao's funeral ceremonies. Mao's body was embalmed and placed on public view in the Chairman Mao Memorial Hall, a modern mausoleum built for him in Tiananmen Square. An enormous picture of Mao has hung in the square for four decades. Mao's family home at Shaoshan in Hunan and his headquarters at Yan'an in Shaanxi have been opened to the public. In 1993 Shaoshan celebrated the hundredth anniversary of Mao's birth.

In August 1977, at the 11th National Party Congress, Hua Guofeng declared the official end of the Great Proletarian Cultural Revolution. Deng Xiaoping, who had been purged twice during the Cultural Revolution, was rehabilitated once and for all, and began consolidating his power as the leader of the movement to reform and modernize China. By late fall in 1978, big-character posters were being publicly displayed in Chinese cities criticizing Mao and connecting him to the wrongdoing of the Gang of Four. In December 1978, at the Third Plenary Session of the 11th Central Committee of the CCP, Deng Xiaoping launched a major program for reforming Chinese political, social and economic institutions and even the CCP's Maoist and Communist ideology. In 1981 the CCP issued an official report on the Cultural Revolution stating that Mao's emphasis on class struggle had led to "the confusing of right and wrong" and to "confusing the people with the enemy." See also ANTI-RIGHTIST CAMPAIGN; BEIJING; BEIJING UNIVERSITY; BIG-CHARACTER POSTERS; BORODIN, MIKHAIL; CADRE; CHEN DUXIU; CHIANG KAI-SHEK; CHINESE COMMUNIST PARTY; CHINESE PEOPLE'S POLITICAL CONSULTATIVE CONFERENCE; CIVIL WAR BETWEEN COMMUNISTS AND NATIONALISTS; CONSTITUTION, STATE, OF 1954; CULTURAL REVOLUTION; DENG XIAOPING; DENG YINGCHAO; EIGHTH ROUTE ARMY; FIVE-YEAR PLANS; FOUR MODERNIZATIONS; GANG OF FOUR; GOVERNMENT STRUCTURE; GREAT LEAP FORWARD; HUA GUOFENG; HUNAN PROVINCE; HUNDRED FLOWERS CAMPAIGN; INTERNATIONAL WORKERS DAY; JIANG QING; JIANGXI PROVINCE; JINGGANG MOUNTAIN RANGE; KOREAN WAR; LAND REFORM BY COMMUNISTS; LI DAZHAO; LI PENG; LIBERATION, NATIONAL; LIN BIAO; LIU SHAOQI; LONG MARCH; MANDATE OF HEAVEN; MAY FOURTH MOVEMENT OF 1919; NANCHANG UPRISING; NANJING; NATIONAL PARTY CONGRESS; NATIONAL PEOPLE'S CONGRESS; NATIONALIST PARTY; NATURAL DISASTERS; NEW CULTURE MOVEMENT; NEW FOURTH ARMY INCIDENT; NIE RONGZHEN; NIXON, U.S. PRESIDENT RICHARD M., VISIT TO CHINA; NORTHERN EXPEDITION; PEASANTS AND PEASANT REBELLIONS; PENG DEHUAI; PENG ZHEN; PEOPLE'S COMMUNE; PEOPLE'S LIBERATION ARMY; PEOPLE'S REPUBLIC OF CHINA; POLITBURO; QUOTATIONS FROM

CHAIRMAN MAO ZEDONG; RED GUARDS; REPUBLIC OF CHINA; REVOLUTION OF 1911; SHAANXI PROVINCE; SHANGHAI; SINO-INDIAN BORDER DISPUTE; SINO-SOVIET CONFLICT; SMEDLEY, AGNES; SNOW, EDGAR; SOCIALIST EDUCATION MOVEMENT; STILWELL, JOSEPH; SUN YAT-SEN; THREE-ANTI AND FIVE-ANTI CAMPAIGNS; TIANANMEN SQUARE; UNITED NATIONS; VIETNAM WAR; WAR OF RESISTANCE AGAINST JAPAN; WARLORD PERIOD, WHAMPOA MILITARY ACADEMY; XI'AN; YAN'AN; ZHANG GUO-TAO; ZHOU ENLAI; ZHU DE.

MAO ZEMIN See URUMQI.

MAONAN See DAI.

MAOTAI A strong alcoholic beverage similar to vodka, traditionally drunk while making toasts at Chinese banquets. Glasses of maotai are raised to toast the health of the host and guests after the host's opening speech, and toasts are also made during the many courses of food served at a typical banquet. Maotai is made in the town of Maotai in Guizhou Province, using a type of sorghum grain grown in northern China. The liquor is processed by cooking the grain to produce a liquid, which is then fermented eight times and distilled seven times until crystal clear. This process takes one year, after which the maotai is aged for several years. The Chinese government operates the state-run maotai distillery. Maotai became famous in the West when it was drunk for a toast made by Mao Zedong for U.S. president Richard Nixon when the president visited China in 1972. See also BANQUETS; BEVERAGES, ALCOHOLIC; NIXON, RICHARD, U.S. PRESIDENT, VISIT TO CHINA.

MARBLE BOAT OF EMPRESS DOWAGER CIZI (Tz'u Hsi) See SUMMER PALACE.

"MARCH OF THE VOLUNTEERS" See ANTHEM, NATIONAL.

MARCO POLO BRIDGE INCIDENT (1937) A military skirmish between Chinese and Japanese troops that became the first battle in the Chinese War of Resistance against Japan (1937–45; World War II). The Japanese military had already established itself in Manchuria (northeastern China), with a puppet state known as Manchukuo, and in Hebei Province. Chinese troops stationed around the 800-year-old beautiful stone bridge across the Yongding River, about 10 miles west of the capital city of Beijing, began strengthening their defenses in 1937.

The bridge was known as the Marco Polo Bridge (Lugouqiao or Lukouchiao) because the 13th-century traveler after whom the bridge was named had admired it. A railroad bridge next to the Marco Polo Bridge was strategically important because it linked southern railway lines with Wanping, a major railway junction that provided access to Tianjin and other cities. On July 7, 1937, Japanese troops made a night maneuver to the bridge and fired blank cartridges. Chinese troops then fired onto the Japanese but did not injure anyone. However, when the Japanese discovered a soldier missing at role call, the Japanese commander assumed that the Chinese had captured him and ordered his troops to attack Wanping. The Chinese troops fought back but were ineffectual. Both sides decided to stop fighting, and uncoordinated negotiations were attempted at many levels between Chinese and Japanese leaders. Japan decided to mobilize five troop divisions in case they were needed in China. Chiang Kai-shek, leader of the Chinese Nationalists (Kuomintang), sent four divisions to Baoding in southern Hebei. The Japanese premier blamed the Chinese for the incident and called for a Chinese apology. Military commanders in the area prepared to withdraw their troops, but fighting broke out once more around the Marco Polo Bridge. Japanese troops succeeded in taking control of the region around Beijing and Tianjin. Chiang Kai-shek decided to attack the Japanese troops in Shanghai, a major port city in central China. Japan responded by sending 15 troop divisions into China, and the two sides began fighting a full-scale war known as the War of Resistance Against Japan. See also CHIANG KAI-SHEK; HEBEI PROVINCE; MANCHUKUO; NATIONALIST PARTY; WAR OF RESISTANCE AGAINST JAPAN.

MARIGNOLLI, JOHN See CHRISTIANITY.

MARITCHI See MAZIPO.

MARITIME SILK ROAD See FUJIAN PROVINCE; GUANGDONG PROVINCE; PORCELAIN; SHIPPING AND SHIPBUILDING; XIAMEN; ZHENG HE.

MARQUIS YI OF ZENG See ARCHAEOLOGY; BELLS AND CHIMES; BRONZEWARE.

MARRIAGE See CONCUBINAGE; DRAGON; FAMILY STRUCTURE; MARRIAGE LAW OF 1950; ONE-CHILD FAMILY CAMPAIGN; PHOENIX; WEDDINGS, TRADITIONAL.

MARRIAGE LAW OF 1950 A comprehensive law regarding marriage promulgated on May 1, 1950, by the government of the People's Republic of China (PRC), which was founded in 1949 by the Chinese Communist Party (CCP). This new law intended to free women in China from the old feudal system under which they had been forced into marriage and had to obey their husbands, who were often abusive, and also to permit them to divorce under certain conditions. The law also intended to give children some legal protection that would end the traditional practice of infanticide, especially of girls, and the sale of minors. The feudal system was based on the teachings of Confucianism, which maintained that a woman should be obedient to her parents before marriage, to her husband after marriage and to her son after her husband's death. Families commonly arranged marriages without giving the intended spouses any say in the matter, and they held extremely elaborate and costly wedding celebrations. Many women were bought by men as secondary wives or concubines, and they had even fewer rights than first wives, who did exercise some authority within the household, especially over their daughters-in-law and their husbands' concubines.

The Constitution of the PRC states that there should be complete equality between men and women, both in the home and in the workplace, and the Marriage Law of 1950 affirmed this principle. The law gave women equal inheritance rights with men. Many Chinese men opposed the new law but it did provide some benefits for women. Nearly one million divorces from feudal-style marriages were granted within a year of the enactment of the Marriage Law. On September 10, 1981, the NPC approved the revised Marriage Law of the PRC. One of its main points was to raise the legal age for marriage for men to 22 and for women to 20. Article 2 of the law states that "the lawful rights and interests of women, children and the aged are protected." Article 3 states that "within the family, maltreatment and desertion are prohibited." Articles 15–21 define the rights and duties of parents and children. Parents have the duty to raise and educate their children, and children have the duty to support and assist their parents, especially when they become elderly or disabled. The 1981 law also discusses relationships between grandparents and grandchildren and between brothers and sisters. All family members are charged with helping all others, especially when the parents are deceased. The law seeks to base the relationships in Chinese families on equality and mutual respect and assistance.

Today a Chinese couple is legally married by completing the process of registering with the government. A couple who wants to marry must each first get a letter from his or her workplace listing his or her marital status, sex, date of birth, ethnic group, the identity of the intended spouse, and whether they have any close blood ties. The man and woman take these letters to the local marriage registration office and fill in a marriage application form. They must also bring proof of their places of residence, medical certificates, and small photographs of themselves, which will be placed in the marriage certificate, similar to a passport. Divorced persons have to show their divorce certificates. Marriage is denied if the applicants have not reached the age for marriage stipulated in the Marriage Law; if either person does not freely consent to the marriage; if one of them already has a spouse; if they are close blood relations; or if either one has leprosy or venereal disease. There are special regulations for Chinese citizens who wish to marry foreigners, Chinese expatriates and residents of Macao, which will revert to the PRC in 1999. When a marriage receives official approval, each spouse is given a marriage certificate in a red folder with the characters in gold for "Marriage Certificate" on the front and "Double Happiness" on the back. Double Happiness is the traditional Chinese symbol for auspicious occasions. See also CONCUBINAGE; DOUBLE HAPPINESS AND LONG LIFE; FAMILY STRUCTURE; WEDDINGS, TRADITIONAL.

MARTEN See SABLE.

MARTIAL ARTS (*wushu*) Arts of combat or self-defense, now mainly used as methods of exercise. Martial arts employ stylized movements of attack and defense and require the coordination of hands, feet and eyes; however, there are martial arts styles that can be practiced by people of any age, even the elderly. The many systems of martial arts in China fall into the broad categories of empty-hand boxing, weapons training, training in pairs, sparring, and group exercises. The best known style of empty-hand boxing (*nei-jia* or *nei chia*) is taijiquan (*tai chi ch'uan*), the practice of slow and gentle routines that resemble a dance. Every morning in China, large groups of people, especially the elderly, practice *taijiquan* in parks and other public places. Related

styles include *xingyiquan* (*hsing yi chuan*), which is more vigorous, and *baguazhang* (*pa kua chang*), which emphasizes the coordination of a variety of hand movements and unique footwork, such as walking in small circles. *Baguazhang* is based on the eight trigrams (*bagua* or *pa kua*) that represent the ancient Chinese theory of yin and yang and the eight directions of the universe. Other martial arts styles include long boxing (*changquan* or *ch'ang ch'uan*), which includes the quick and powerful styles known *shaolin* and *zha* (*cha*). Weapons training uses many types of equipment, such as a sword, spear, staff, chain with a pointed tip, and an iron ball on a rope. Training in pairs may be done with empty-handed styles or with a combination of empty hands and weapons. Group exercises entail a demonstration performed by more than six athletes.

Chinese martial arts techniques and weapons developed from ancient farming and hunting methods and implements. The martial arts were highly developed by the Han dynasty (206 B.C.–A.D 220). At the end of the Han, a famous physician named Hua Tuo developed a system of exercises to keep the body flexible and delay the aging process, known as the "Five Animal Forms," which imitated the movements of the deer, bear, monkey, tiger and crane. Several styles practiced today developed from those ancient styles, including the monkey style, snake style and eagle claw style. The Chinese martial arts became especially associated with the Shaolin Chan (Zen) Buddhist monastery (Shaolin Si), which was built in 495 near Zhengzhou in Henan Province. Bodhidharma, the legendary founder of the Chan sect of the Buddhist religion in China, supposedly went to Shaolin and created methods for physical training for the monks, which developed into the Shaolin Quan, a style of boxing that has become world famous under the name *kung fu* (*gongfu*).

During the Tang dynasty (618–907), the Chinese government established a system for selecting military officials through martial arts tests and competitions. In the Song dynasty (960–1279), the government established rules for open challenges to martial arts contests. Frequent competitions encouraged the development of the martial arts during the Ming dynasty (1368–1644), when the classic book on martial arts, *Treatise on Armament Technology,* was published. During the Ming, the variety of martial arts techniques were organized into systems or "schools." The schools south of the Yangzi River (Changjiang), known as *nanquan* (*nan ch'uan*), emphasized hand techniques, while schools in the north emphasized kicking forms. When the "soft" method known as *taijiquan* developed during the Ming, the martial arts moved beyond an emphasis on physical combat to a concern with improving health and longevity. This method is based on the theories of unblocking the flow of energy (*qi* or *ch'i*) through the body, which also form the basis of traditional Chinese herbal medicine, related healing techniques such as acupuncture and moxibustion, and a system of breathing exercises and movements known as *qigong* (*ch'i kung*).

After the Chinese Communists founded the People's Republic of China (PRC) in 1949, the government encouraged the practice of the martial arts. By 1956 the State Physical Culture and Sports Commission formally designated martial arts as a competitive sport, and martial arts training and research departments were established in schools and institutes of physical culture. Martial arts have been included

The martial arts, practiced throughout China and much of the world today, were developed from ancient farming and hunting methods.
S.E. MEYER

in national games, and seven kinds of national martial arts competitions are held annually. These include team A and team B, free sparring, trials for selecting the best martial arts artists, *taijiquan* and sword, and traditional routines.

Chinese martial arts have become famous all over the world, especially due to the genre of films produced in Hong Kong that uses actors skilled in the martial arts, and schools have been established in many countries. Since 1983 the PRC has sent martial arts teams and coaches to perform and teach in foreign countries and has accepted foreigners to study in China. Many countries and regions now have their own teams. Asia, Europe, South America and Oceania have established intercontinental martial arts organizations and hold international tournaments. Martial arts were included in the formal events of the 11th Asian Games in 1990. That year the International Wushu (Martial Arts) Association, joined by 38 countries and regions, was founded. The First World Wushu Championships were held in Beijing, the Chinese capital, in 1991. More than 400 martial arts masters from 41 countries and regions took part in three competitions—routine competition, exhibition and free-style combat (*sanshou*)—with judges from the PRC and 12 other countries. Some of the best competitors outside the PRC came from Hong Kong (which reverted to the PRC in 1997), Japan and the Philippine Islands.

Seven basic routines incorporating traditional movements have been established for the World Wushu Championships:

1. Modern long-range boxing, with simple and vigorous yet graceful movements.
2. Southern-style boxing, with vigorous, sudden movements and steady steps.
3. *Taijiquan*, which employs smooth, continuous movement, guided by a quiet mind and accompanied by natural breathing.
4. Broadsword, which uses swift, bold and powerful movements and a heroic manner. A single-broadsword performer usually holds the broadsword in one hand and does complementary movements with the other hand.
5. The sword, a short double-edged weapon, is manipulated with brisk, quick, graceful and flexible movements.
6. The cudgel, a long, edgeless weapon, known as "the forefather of weapons," which is handled with movements that are bold, swift and powerful.
7. The spear, one of the four famous ancient weapons in China, known as "the king of weapons." It is first used for pricking, then for blocking and capturing an opponent. The fighter must hold the spear flat and prick straight in and out with quick, powerful movements.

See also ACUPUNCTURE; BODHIDHARMA; EIGHT TRIGRAMS; KUNG FU; MEDICINE, HERBAL; MOXIBUSTION; QI; QIGONG; SHAOLIN TEMPLE; SPORTS; TAIJIQUAN; YIN AND YANG.

MATCHMAKERS   See WEDDINGS, TRADITIONAL.

MATSU ISLAND   See FUJIAN PROVINCE.

MAWANGDUI, HAN TOMBS AT   See CHANGSHA.

MA-XIA SCHOOL OF LANDSCAPE PAINTING   See MA YUAN; MU QI; XIA GUI.

MAY DAY   See INTERNATIONAL WORKERS DAY.

MAY FOURTH MOVEMENT OF 1919   Widespread demonstrations by the Chinese against the governments of China and Japan for their secret agreement awarding the Chinese province of Shandong to Japan. Germany had held concessions in Shandong since the end of the 19th century. When World War I broke out in Europe in 1914, Japan joined the Allied side against Germany and seized German holdings in Shandong. In 1915 Japan issued its Twenty-one Demands to the Chinese warlord government in Beijing, which rejected some of the demands but allowed Japan to keep the Shandong territory it already held. In 1917, Britain, France and Italy also agreed to the Japanese claim on Shandong in exchange for Japanese naval action against Germany. In 1917 China declared war on Germany with hopes of regaining Shandong from Japan, and sent 100,000 laborers to work with the Allied Powers in western Europe. However, in 1918 the Chinese government made a secret deal with Japan, agreeing with the latter's claim on Shandong. This became public knowledge when the Versailles Peace Conference in 1919 awarded Japan the treaty rights in Shandong formerly held by Germany. The Chinese people were infuriated by this betrayal, especially since they had suffered a humiliating defeat in the Sino-Japanese war of 1894–95.

On May 4, 1919, student representatives from 13 Beijing universities and colleges met and drew up five resolutions protesting the Shandong agreement, calling for the awakening of the Chinese masses to the country's problem, proposing a mass meeting of people in Beijing, urging the formation of a Beijing student union, and calling for a protest demonstration that afternoon. Three thousand students gathered in front of the Gate of Heavenly Peace in Tiananmen Square and gave out handbills asserting that the Chinese people refused to accept the way traitors had sold out China's sovereign rights. They marched to the foreign legation headquarters where they left letters for the foreign ministers, and then moved on to confront the three cabinet-level Chinese officials who had made the secret agreement with Japan. The crowd beat the Chinese minister to Japan, and set the house of the minister of communications on fire. The police arrested 32 students. The entire country immediately erupted in protests, strikes and shop closings, and newspapers reiterated the students' demands.

This movement grew into a year-long boycott of Japanese goods. Student unions were quickly formed in many Chinese cities. The Chinese government released the student demon-

strators, dismissed the three officials and forced the cabinet to resign, and the Chinese delegation at Versailles refused to sign the peace treaty concluding the war. The United States settled the problem by calling the Washington Conference, in which Japan withdrew its claims to Shandong as contained in the secret agreement. The nations involved signed the Nine-Powers Pact of the Washington Conference in 1922. The May Fourth Movement took place in the context of an intellectual movement from 1917 to 1923 known as the New Culture Movement, and the two terms are sometimes used interchangeably. The May Fourth Movement brought many Chinese intellectuals into the Marxist fold, including Mao Zedong (Mao Tse-tung). Mao, the founder of the Communist People's Republic of China in 1949, was working as a librarian at Beijing University when the movement broke out. The first general meetings of the Chinese Communist Party were held in 1921. See also CHINESE COMMUNIST PARTY; MAO ZEDONG; NEW CULTURE MOVEMENT; TWENTY-ONE DEMANDS ON CHINA; WARLORD PERIOD (1916–28); WORLD WAR I.

MAZIPO   (Ma Tsu P'o)   The Queen of Heaven and Holy Mother in the Daoist religion; also known as Tianhou (T'ien Hou). According to Chinese legend, Mazipo was originally a maiden named Lin, the daughter of a fisherman who lived near Fuzhou city in southeastern Fujian Province, one of China's most important maritime regions. Every day she chanted long prayers to protect her parents while they were out to sea fishing. One day she fell into a trance and foresaw that their boat would be overcome by huge waves. She ran to the shore and used her spiritual powers to bring them back safely. She continued to rescue people from the sea and died in the course of her efforts. From then on, she was worshiped as a goddess by the Chinese.

In particular, sailors and their families worship Mazipo. Called boat people because they live their whole lives on their boats (known as junks), these people burn candles to Mazipo. When they make new nets or mend old ones, they spread the nets out and make offerings to her. Models of fishing boats may be given to her temples in gratitude for her protection. When a junk is going to sail on a long trip, a statue of Mazipo is carried in a procession to a temple, where many offerings are then made to her. When the junk sails out of the harbor, imitation paper money is thrown from its stern (back end). Many temples and shrines have been built to Mazipo along the Chinese coast. The most important religious ceremony of the year for the boat people is the ritual performed for Mazipo on the 23rd day of the third moon in the traditional lunar calendar, around the end of April, before sailors go to sea on their first fishing trip of the year. Incense and candles are lighted, prayers are chanted, and offerings of roasted pork and chicken are made to ask her to bring the sailors good weather, successful fishing, and protection against disaster.

Mazipo is sometimes associated with the Buddhist goddess Maritchi, the "Mother of the Measure (of rice)," who is depicted with eight arms holding weapons and religious objects. She is believed to live in the stars of the constellation Ursa Major (Great Bear), also called the Big Dipper (the words "measure" and "constellation" are pronounced the same way in Chinese). Mazipo has also been identified with

Guanyin (Kuan Yin), the Buddhist goddess of mercy, and sculptures of Guanyin are commonly found in shrines to Mazipo. Scholars have compared her with the Virgin Mary in the Christian religion. Two deities serve as attendants to Mazipo, "Thousand Mile Eyes" and "Fair Wind Ears," who supposedly have supernatural powers, respectively, of seeing and hearing. See also DAOISM; FUJIAN PROVINCE; GRAND CANAL; GUANYIN; JUNK.

MAZU ISLAND See FUJIAN PROVINCE.

MEDIATION See LEGAL SYSTEM.

MEDICINE, HERBAL The use of plants to produce medicines, one of the major methods traditionally used by the Daoists to treat illness, along with such techniques as acupuncture and moxibustion. The traditional Daoist view of health is that it is a state of balance between the human body and the natural world and between various components within the body. This view is based on the Daoist tenet that everything in the world is composed of the universal aspects of yin (feminine) and yang (masculine), and on the theory of qi (ch'i), the vital energy that flows throughout the body and the universe. If channels in the body through which qi flows are blocked, a person will become ill. Acupuncture and moxibustion apply small needles and burning cones of herbs to points on those channels, known as meridians, where a doctor discovers a blockage. A person may also enhance qi by practicing a form of slow, rhythmic movements known as taijiquan (t'ai ch'i ch'uan). The basic theory of Chinese medicine also includes the concepts of the five material agents (wuxing or wu-hsing), the four methods of diagnosis (sizhen or ssu-chen), the eight principal syndromes (bagang or pa-kang), the analysis of disease by the study of energy, nourishment and the blood (weiqiyingxue or wei-ch'i-ying-hsueh), and the five solid viscera (suzang or su-tsang) and six hollow viscera (liufu), all of which embody the organic Chinese concept of the human body.

The traditional art of medical diagnosis has been very highly developed in China and employs four methods for diagnosis: 1) inspecting the patient's general physical condition, behavior, feelings, complexion, eyes, tongue and excreta; 2) listening to the patient's voice, breathing and coughing, and smelling the odor of the body, breath and excreta; 3) asking the patient questions about when the illness appeared, what may have caused it, and the patient's medical history; 4) palpation of the patient's body with light pressure to detect abnormalities, and measurement of the patient's pulse at three different points on the wrist. The condition of the tongue and the pulse provide the doctor a great deal of information about the patient's condition.

When the illness is diagnosed, the doctor writes a prescription for a combination of herbs that will improve the patient's health. The patient purchases the herbs in packets specially put together for him or her. Each packet is usually boiled in water for around half an hour to produce a dark, thick liquid that the patient drinks. The herbal treatment may continue for several weeks or more. Herbal medicines are also available in other forms such as large pellets, capsules and prepared tonics. Unlike Western drugs, which aggressively treat a disease, Chinese herbal medicines aim to restore the balance in the patient's body and bring about slow but steady improvement. Many foods are also considered to have medicinal value. For example, fresh ginger is eaten to treat stomachache and diarrhea, and chicken soup is a common remedy for colds. Medicines made from the root known as ginseng are popular. Deer antler is also thought to have medicinal value.

China has an enormous variety of medicinal herbs, which are produced by pharmaceutical factories all over the country. Chinese medicines are usually classified under one of three categories: 1) Xingwei (hsing-wei), which includes all herbal medicines that can alter conditions caused by cold or febrile factors, or that have a medical effect based on their flavor; 2) Gujing (ku-ching), medicines that can affect the body's internal channels and are based on the theory of internal organs (fuzang or fu-tsang) and channels and collaterals (jingluo or ching-luo), which maintains that cures taken from different plants have close ties with specific internal organs; 3) Shengjiangfuchen (sheng-chiang-fu-ch'en), literally "raise-lower-float-sink." This latter category includes medicines that induce vomiting ("raise"), defecation ("lower"), night sweating ("float") and relief from spots or boils on the surface of the skin ("sink").

Chinese researchers discovered that the potency of medicinal herbs could be increased through treating them with various methods such as roasting, baking or simmering in water. Such processing also removes toxic elements from poisonous plants and leaves their curative elements. Most herbal remedies are prepared by grinding with a mortar and pestle, washing and treating with water, baking, or a combination of water treatment and baking. Today, herbal doctors can draw upon 8,000 different kinds of traditional Chinese medicines, which are available as pills, powders, poultices or dans (processed herbs). Scientists continue to research ways in which to increase the quality of many traditional medicines and to develop and manufacture new ones.

Medical records were inscribed on bones and tortoise shells excavated from tombs of the Shang dynasty (1750–1040 B.C.). There is a huge library of works on traditional Chinese medicine, comprising about 30,000 titles. The first Chinese medical treatise, *The Yellow Emperor's Canon of Medicine*, written more than 2,000 years ago, laid the theoretical foundation for Chinese medicine. It describes the physiology and pathology of the human body and promotes the principle of diagnosis and treatment through the theories of yin and yang and the five material agents of water, fire, metal, wood and earth. It also discusses the medicinal value of food. The first systematic treatise on the origins of Chinese medicines is *Huai Nan Zixiu (Huai-nan-tzu-hsiu)*, dating from the Han dynasty (206 B.C.–A.D. 220), which documents the work of a farmer who tasted hundreds of herbs. Between 100 and 180 A.D., Shen Nong wrote the first work that recorded medical herbs systematically, *Shen Nong's Canon of Materia Medica*, which lists 365 plant species. *The Treatise on Febrile and Other Diseases*, written by Zhang Zhongjing (Chang Chung-ching) in the second century A.D., maintains that "diagnosis and treatment must be based on an overall analysis of the illness and the patient's condition." Mi Huangfu (265–317) wrote the first book on acupuncture and moxibustion. Chao Yuanfang (581–618) wrote *The Source of Diseases*. In the Tang dynasty, Sun Simiao

Chinese herbal medicines are used, in conjunction with acupuncture and other techniques, to restore the body's balance.   DENNIS COX

collected most of the medical prescriptions that had been used to date and compiled *Golden Prescriptions*, which had a great influence on the development of Chinese medicine. In the Ming dynasty, Li Shizhen (Li Shih-Chen; 1518–95) wrote the well-known *Compendium of Materia Medica* (*Bencao gang mu* or *Pen-tsao kang mu*), the first book on botany and materia medica in the world, which describes 1,892 herbs used for medicinal purposes.

Western medicine was introduced to China in the Ming (1368–1644) and Qing (1644–1911) dynasties, and the two medical systems became complementary in China. Since 1949, the PRC government has drawn up a series of policies encouraging the development of Chinese medicine and pharmacology. In 1990 China had 65 universities, colleges and schools and 60 research institutes of Chinese medicine and pharmacology, 2,000 hospitals of traditional Chinese medicine, and about one million professional medical workers. Huqingyutang (Hu-ch'ing yu-t'ang) in Hangzhou is one of the most famous herbal pharmacies in China. It was supposedly the predecessor of the first state traditional Chinese medicine administration, established during the Southern Song dynasty (1127–79). The pharmacy's present buildings date back to 1874, when Hu Xueyan (Hu Hsueh-yan), an official in the Qing dynasty bureaucracy, founded the present Huqingyutang. The pharmacy produces about 300 medicines, many of which are sold overseas as well as in China. It

authorized a group of famous Chinese doctors to collect its prescriptions in a book, *A Collection of Huqingyutang Medicinal Boluses, Powders, Ointments and Pellets*. The pharmacy cooperates with hospital and medical research institutes to discover new forms and applications for herbal remedies. It has its own herbal medicine and tonic research institute and has developed dozens of new medicines.

Pillows filled with medicinal herbs are a traditional Chinese remedy for maintaining health and curing some illnesses. Most of these medicinal herbs are picked on the snow-covered Yaowangtai Peak of the Taibai Mountain Range in Shaanxi Province. The Chinese believe that breathing the scent of the herbs and absorbing them through the skin will regulate the functions of the internal organs, stimulate blood circulation, reduce blood pressure, relax the muscles and joints, kill pain, cure colds and promote restful sleep. Medicated pillows for children are believed to help them resist colds, kill pain, enhance their eyesight and hearing, and promote growth. See also ACUPUNCTURE; CHICKEN; DEER; GINSENG; LI SHIZHEN; MARTIAL ARTS; MOXIBUSTION; QI; TAIJIQUAN; YELLOW EMPEROR.

MEDITATION See BODHIDHARMA; BUDDHISM; CHAN SECT OF BUDDHISM; NEO-CONFUCIANISM; WANG YANGMING.

MEI See PLUM.

MEI LANFANG (1894–1961)   A master of the Beijing (Peking) Opera who specialized in female roles (*qingyi* or *ch'ing-i*) and who introduced traditional Chinese opera to foreign countries. Many critics consider Mei one of the greatest performers of Chinese opera, which combines singing, acting and dancing, in Chinese history. The son and grandson of famous opera performers, Mei began studying in the Peking (Beijing) Opera company when he was eight years old and made his stage debut when he was 12, playing a weaving girl. Men traditionally performed women's roles in the Beijing Opera. Mei played many female roles throughout his career and was especially acclaimed for his performances of the "Flower-Shattering Diva." When he was 14, he joined the Xiliencheng (Hsi-lien-ch'eng) Theatrical Company and performed in many localities, including Shanghai, which made him nationally famous. Mei toured Japan in 1919 and 1924, the United States in 1930, the Soviet Union in 1932 and 1935 and Korea in 1953. Two American universities awarded him honorary doctoral degrees in literature. Mei moved to Hong Kong when China began fighting its War of Resistance against Japan (1937–45; World War II) but then moved to Shanghai, which was occupied by the Japanese, and stopped performing until 1946.

Mei studied the various local operas that are performed in different regions of China, such as *Kunqu* in Jiangsu Province, and adopted performing concepts and techniques from all of them. He opened his own school of Beijing Opera based on his own style of dance, called the "Mei Lanfang School" and taught more than 200 students who went on to perform throughout China and many other countries. While introducing Beijing Opera abroad, Mei also influenced foreign drama. He got to know many famous foreign playwrights, writers, singers, dancers and painters, including Maxim Gorky, Konstantin Stanislavsky, S. M. Eisenstein, Bertolt Brecht, George Bernard Shaw, Charles Chaplin and Paul Robeson. Mei continued to promote cultural exchanges between China and other countries until he died. After the Chinese Communist Party (CCP) founded the People's Republic of China in 1949, Mei and other performers revived several *Kunqu* operas and adapted the operas *Broken Bridge* and *Peony Pavilion* into films. An active member of the CCP, he became the director of several Chinese cultural organizations. On August 8, 1981, the 20th anniversary of Mei Lanfang's death, six Chinese organizations, including the Ministry of Culture and the Beijing and Shanghai chapters of the Chinese Dramatists' Association held commemorative performances of Peking Opera. Mei's son, Mei Baojiu (Mei Pao-chiu), performed in *The Great Reunion* with Yu Zhenfei (Yu Chen-fei), a friend of Mei Lanfang who had performed this opera with him many times. See also KUNQU; OPERA, BEIJING.

MEIN   See NOODLES.

MEISSEN POTTERY   See YIXING POTTERY.

MEKONG RIVER   A river that originates in Tibet Autonomous Region (Xizang Zizhiqu) and flows southeast for 2,600 miles; also known as the Lancang in Chinese. The Mekong River cuts through the mountains of Yunnan Province in a narrow valley with steep gorges for 1,150 miles. The river then forms the border between Laos and Burma, descends from the mountains and crosses the Korat Plateau between Laos and Thailand. It finally flows into Cambodia, where fertile alluvial plains extend out from both its shores, and empties into the South China Sea through a large delta. Many channels also flow from the river into Vietnam, where they deposit silt that enlarges the delta. The Mekong River can be navigated from the South China Sea as far as Phnom Penh, the capital of Cambodia. Along with the Mekong, the Yangzi (Changjiang), Red, and Salween rivers all originate in the Himalaya Mountain Range in eastern Tibet or in its foothills to the east, and flow in steep valleys parallel to each other through southwestern China. Then they diverge to flow through China, Vietnam and Burma and empty into the East China Sea, the South China Sea and the Bay of Bengal. See also HIMALAYA MOUNTAIN RANGE; RED RIVER; SALWEEN RIVER; TIBET; YANGZI RIVER; YUNNAN PROVINCE.

MENCIUS (Mengzi or Meng Tzu, "Master Meng"; c. 372–289 B.C.)   The second-most important thinker in the Confucian tradition, next to Confucius (551–479 B.C.). The Chinese thus call Mencius the "Second Sage of Confucianism." He was born in the state of Lu in modern Shandong Province, also the home state of Confucius, and he studied with a follower of Zisi (Tzu Ssu), the grandson of Confucius. Mencius lived toward the end of the Zhou dynasty (1100–256 B.C.), when the dynasty had lost its power and its vassal feudal states were fighting with each other, a time known as the Warring States Period (403–221 B.C.). As Confucius had done, Mencius traveled to several of these rival states, teaching his philosophy and unsuccessfully trying to find a feudal lord who would follow his principles of good government. He argued that the people who perform manual labor should be governed, and the people who work with their minds should govern.

Mencius looked back to the early centuries of the Zhou dynasty, which Confucianists regarded as a "golden age," and claimed that his view of government came from the humanistic attitude of King Wen of the Zhou, who lived 700 years earlier than Mencius. In the early Zhou feudal system, peasant families owned parcels of agricultural lands that were organized by the so-called "well-field system" (*jintian* or *chin-t'ien*) whereby a square piece of land was divided into nine equal squares, one for each of eight families and the ninth to be farmed collectively for the feudal lord. Mencius regarded the well-field system as the ideal, which the governments of his time should reinstate to help the many peasants who had become impoverished. For him, the genuine ruler has the qualities of humanity (*ren* or *jen;* also translated as benevolence) and a sense of duty for taking care of his people. The ruler of a country is like the father of a family. He should educate the people, ensure that their physical needs are cared for, and set an example by being virtuous himself. According to Mencius, if a ruler does not act the way he should, he will lose the Mandate of Heaven (*tianming* or *t'ien-ming*), which legitimizes his reign, and his subjects will be justified in rebelling against him.

In the idealistic teachings of Mencius, all evil will disappear when individuals recover their original goodness and the government returns to the benevolent policies of ancient rulers. He taught that human nature is essentially good and that this capacity for goodness is what distinguishes human beings from animals. He disagreed with two philosophers of his time: Yang Zhu (Yang Chu), who taught that every person should live according to his own self-interest; and Mozi (Mo Tzu; c. 470–391 B.C.), who taught that one should love all people equally. Mencius added the concept of righteousness (*yi*) to the teachings of Confucius. He argued that each person's position in the social hierarchy determines the way that other people should love that person and perform duties owed to him. Righteousness includes a strong sense of duty and commitment to fulfilling one's obligation to another person. The disciples of Mencius recorded his teachings in a book known as the *Discourses of Mencius* or simply the *Mencius* (*Mengzi*). The Neo-Confucian scholar Zhu Xi (Chu Hsi; 1130–1200) added the *Mencius* to three other Confucian texts to form the Four Books of Confucianism, which became the fundamental texts studied by Chinese scholars and the basis of the examinations for positions in the imperial bureaucracy. See also CONFUCIANISM; FOUR BOOKS OF CONFUCIANISM; HUMANITY; IMPERIAL EXAMINATION SYSTEM; MANDATE OF HEAVEN; MOZI; RIGHTEOUSNESS; WARRING STATES PERIOD; WELL-FIELD SYSTEM; ZHOU DYNASTY; ZHU XI.

MENG-TZU   See MENCIUS.

MENGZI   See BOOK OF MENCIUS; MENCIUS.

MENSHEN   See DOOR GODS.

MERIDIAN POINTS   See ACUPUNCTURE; MOXIBUSTION; QI.

METALS   See MINING INDUSTRY.

MI FU   (Mi Fei; 1051–1107)   A landscape painter who is considered one of the four Great Masters of the Northern Song dynasty (960–1126) as well as the finest Song calligrapher, noted for his use of the cursive form of script. Mi Fu belonged to a group that included two other painters, Weng Tong (Wen T'ung) and Li Gonglin (Li Kung-lin), the calligrapher Huang Tingjian (Huang T'ing-chien) and the poet Su Shi (also known as Su Dongpo or Su Tung-p'o). All of those artists did not wish to portray nature realistically but wished to use their art as a means of self-expression (*xieyi* or *hsieh i*; "to write ideas"). Mi Fu's painting falls into the category of literati or amateur scholar-gentry painting (*wenren hua; wenjen hua*), which later became classified as the Southern School. This school contrasted with the professional court painters, known as the Northern School. Mi Fu invented the technique known as "splashed ink" (*pomo*), or "Mi dots," that uses small blobs of ink made with the side of the brush to build up shapes of mountains and rocks. He was also fond of portraying mist and clouds, and because he used washes without outlines around the figures painted, his paintings had what has been called a "boneless" quality. Mi Fu's son Mi Yuren (Mi Yu-jen) further developed this style.

Mi Fu was born into a family of high status and was raised in the imperial court. As an adult he held many positions in the imperial bureaucracy, but his independent, eccentric nature kept him from rising to high office. In 1104 he became a teacher of painting and calligraphy in the Northern Song capital at Kaifeng (in modern Henan Province). His last position was that of a military governor in modern Jiangsu Province, where he died and was buried.

In addition to being a painter and calligrapher, Mi Fu wrote a book of poetry and several works of critical writings based on collections of painting and calligraphy owned by himself and several others. Unfortunately, no paintings have survived that can be definitely attributed to Mi Fu, although several museums own scrolls that may have been painted by him. His work is known through written descriptions of it and through the work of his son and others who followed his style. See also CALLIGRAPHY; LANDSCAPE PAINTING; NORTHERN SCHOOL OF PAINTING; SOUTHERN SCHOOL OF PAINTING; SU SHI.

MI YU-JEN   See MI FU.

MI YUREN   See MI FU.

MIANZI   See FACE.

MIAO   Also known as the Hmong; one of China's national minority ethnic groups. The 1990 Chinese census showed that there are about 7.4 million Miao living in the southwestern provinces of Guizhou, Yunnan, Hunan and Guanxi-Zhuang Autonomous Region. Their language belongs to the Miao-Yao linguistic group and is divided into several dialects. The Miao, who also inhabit Vietnam, Laos and Thailand to the south of China, live in remote mountainous areas and practice slash-and-burn agriculture. When they use up all the land around a village, the entire village has to move to a new place. Their main crops are maize, rice and opium poppies. The Miao practice a traditional form of spirit worship through which they believe they maintain contact with their ancestors.

For centuries there were conflicts between the Han Chinese, the dominant ethnic group, and the Miao. During the late 1700s, massive immigration of Han people into western Hunan sparked widespread rebellions by the Miao inhabitants. The government of the Qing dynasty (1644–1911) harshly suppressed these uprisings.

The Miao gather on the eighth day of their fourth lunar month (around mid-May) to offer sacrifices to their ancestors and cultural heroes. This was the day that these heroes, Ya Yi and Ya Nu, were killed in battle while stopping a cruel ruler from carrying out his annual custom of forcing the Miao to choose one of their beautiful young women to be his concubine. At this festival the Miao sing, play reed pipes (called *lusheng* in Chinese) and bronze drums, and dance to honor their ancestors, drive away evil spirits and ensure a good harvest. On festive occasions, Miao women wear large amounts of silver necklaces, bracelets and headdresses, which shake when they dance. The jewelry is handed down as a family heirloom. Miao women are renowned for their beautifully embroidered clothes. See also GUANXI-ZHUANG AUTONOMOUS REGION; GUIZHOU PROVINCE; HUNAN PROVINCE; MINORITIES, NATIONAL; SHENG; YAO; YUNNAN PROVINCE.

MIAO   See TEMPLES.

MID-AUTUMN FESTIVAL   See AUTUMN MOON FESTIVAL.

MIDDLE KINGDOM (Zhongguo or Chung-kuo) The name that the Chinese have traditionally preferred to use for their country. It is written with a character made of a square with a vertical line through the center. The word *zhong* (*chung*), "middle" or "central," is also used in the term for the Chinese language: *zhong wen*, which means "middle language." The words originate from ancient times, as kingdoms of northern China started to become unified and the people living there believed that they lived in the center, or middle, of the world. Another term for the Middle Kingdom or Central Nation is "all (that is) under Heaven" (*tianxia* or *t'ien-hsia*). The Chinese believed that only those persons residing in the Middle Kingdom under the rule of the Chinese emperor, whose court on Earth represented the heavenly court, were civilized; those who lived beyond the country's borders were considered uncivilized barbarians. This China-centered viewpoint is termed sinocentrism. When camel caravans began to travel west from China to the Mediterranean world on the Silk Road around the first century A.D., they passed through the so-called Jade Gate that took them out of Gansu Province and into Xianjiang, then considered the "New Frontier." Many of the people outside the borders of the Chinese Empire entered into a tributary relationship with China that granted them trading privileges.

Over the centuries, the unification of China spread to incorporate northern, central and coastal southern regions of China, and people formerly considered barbarians were absorbed and eventually accepted as Chinese, a process known as sinicization. Nomadic invaders who established dynasties in China also became sinicized by adopting Han Chinese customs, clothing, cuisine and Confucian ideology. When Europeans first appeared in the 16th century and attempted to engage in trade, the Chinese government forced them to follow the elaborate rituals of the tribute system that were applied to trade missions from "barbarian" countries. However, while the Chinese maintained that their empire was the center of the Earth, or Middle Kingdom, Europeans refused to acknowledge this or to pay tribute to the Chinese emperor as his vassals. In the 19th century, Britain and other European countries used military force to weaken the Chinese tribute system. This began with the British defeat of China in the Opium War (1839–42), and eventually resulted in the overthrow of the Qing dynasty (1644–1911).

The name China as used by Westerners derives from the Qin (Ch'in) dynasty (221–206) B.C., when China was first unified by Emperor Qin Shi Huangdi. However, many modern Chinese still use the term Middle Kingdom for their country. See also ALL UNDER HEAVEN; CHINA PROPER; EMPEROR; OPIUM WAR; QIN DYNASTY; SINICIZATION; TRIBUTE SYSTEM.

MIEN-TZU See FACE.

MILITARY See CENTRAL MILITARY COMMISSION AND MINISTRY OF NATIONAL DEFENSE; CIVIL WAR BETWEEN COMMUNISTS AND NATIONALISTS; EIGHTH ROUTE ARMY; LONG MARCH; MAO ZEDONG; PEOPLE'S LIBERATION ARMY; WAR OF RESISTANCE AGAINST JAPAN; WHAMPOA MILITARY ACADEMY; YE JIANYING; ZHU DE.

MILLET See AGRICULTURE; GRAIN; YANGSHAO CULTURE.

MILOFO See MAITREYA AND MANJUSRI.

MIN BAO (MINBAO OR MIN PAO) See REVOLUTION OF 1911; REVOLUTIONARY ALLIANCE; SUN YAT-SEN.

MIN KINGDOM (909–945) See TEN KINGDOMS PERIOD.

MIN RIVER See CHENGDU; FUJIAN PROVINCE; FUZHOU; SICHUAN PROVINCE; YANGZI RIVER.

MING See FATE.

MING DYNASTY (1368–1644) The dynasty that overthrew the Yuan dynasty (1279–1368), which had been founded by the Mongols, an ethnic group from the region north of China Proper whose members were the first non-Han ethnic Chinese to rule the Chinese Empire. The founder of the Ming dynasty was Zhu Yuanzhang (Chu Yuan-chang), who reigned as the first Ming emperor, Hongwu (Hung-wu; r. 1368–98). He became a leader in the Red Turban secret society that conducted uprisings against the Mongols, who were greatly resented by their Han subjects, who comprised the vast majority of the Chinese population. He defeated the other Red Turban leaders and in 1368 proclaimed the restoration of Han Chinese rule under the Ming ("Radiance") dynasty with himself as emperor. Emperors of previous dynasties are referred to by their posthumous temple names. However, Hongwu is referred to by the name of his reign; Hongwu means "Boundless Valor" or "Vast Military Achievement." Technically he should be referred to as the Hongwu emperor. This practice of assigning each emperor's reign a glorious name was continued through the Ming and Qing (1644–1911) dynasties.

Hongwu made his capital at Nanjing on the Yangzi River (Changjiang). He restored the imperial bureaucracy or civil service, which had been diminished under the Yuan, and the examination system by which Confucian-education scholars were selected to staff it. He also established a nationwide school system subsidized by the Ming government. A capable but tyrannical ruler, Emperor Hongwu abolished the position of prime minister and placed the government ministries directly under his control. Later Ming emperors did not have his personal authority and left control of the government to the eunuchs who staffed the imperial palace, some of whom became virtual dictators. Hongwu waged military campaigns against a number of Mongol tribes that continued to menace northwestern China, and he forced the Mongol chieftains to sue for peace. He also brought the southwestern province of Yunnan into the empire and thus completed the region known as China Proper. He built up the Chinese navy and sent ship patrols against the many pirates that threatened the Chinese coast. A hydraulic engineer named Song Li (Sung Li) led the completion of the Grand Canal that enabled grain, sent as tax payments, and other goods to be transported by barges from southern to northern China.

Hongwu was succeeded by his eldest grandson, known as Emperor Jianwen (Chien-wen, "Establishing Culture"; r. 1398–1402). However, Hongwu's fourth son, Zhu Di (Chu Ti), the prince of Yan (Yen), led a rebellion and removed Jianwen from power. He took the throne as Emperor Yongle

(Yung-lo, "Eternal Contentment"; r. 1403–24) and became one of the greatest Ming emperors. Yongle had been based at the former Yuan capital city of Dadu (Tatu; called Khan-baliq or Cambaluc, "City of the Khan," by the Mongols) in northern China, only 40 miles south of the Great Wall that separated China from the Mongols and other nomadic tribes. He recognized the need to strengthen China's northern defenses, so he moved the capital there in 1421 after rebuilding it and renaming it Beijing, "Northern Capital." Nanjing ("Southern Capital") remained the Ming auxiliary capital. In Beijing Yongle constructed the Inner City, the Imperial City where court officials resided, and the Forbidden City or Imperial Palace, now known as the Palace Museum and one of the most popular tourist sites in China. The Forbidden City is the largest complex of ancient buildings, not only in China but also in the entire world. It served as the residence of Yongle and all subsequent Ming and Qing emperors, their families and concubines, and thousands of female servants and eunuchs who staffed the imperial palace. Emperors held ceremonial audiences and received foreign tributary missions in the large Outer Court. Yongle also chose a propitious site outside Beijing for his tomb and those of subsequent Ming emperors. The Ming Tombs were restored in the 1950s and have become another popular tourist site.

Yongle gave high positions in the imperial bureaucracy to Confucian-educated scholars from the prestigious Hanlin ("Forest of Writing Brushes") Academy, who came to be known as Grand Secretaries. He ordered the compilation of a comprehensive manuscript containing the essential subjects in Chinese scholarship, known as the *Yongle Encyclopedia* (*Yongle dadian* or *Yung-lo ta-tien*), which was completed in 11,095 volumes by more than 2,000 scholars. In 1404 Yongle commissioned the Muslim eunuch Zheng He (Cheng Ho) to construct and sail a large fleet of ships on seven naval expeditions, which brought many foreign states into the Ming tribute system that rewarded states submitting to Chinese suzerainty and gave them permission to trade with China. After Zheng He's expeditions, however, the Ming halted further maritime missions, perhaps due to opposition by Confucian scholars in the bureaucracy who resented the increasing power of the eunuchs. Inland sailing on China's canals and many large rivers took precedence as China turned inward, although some merchants defied government orders and continued to trade with countries in Southeast Asia.

In 1407–08 Ming forces annexed Tonkin (northern Vietnam), which lies south of China, and in 1413 China created the southern province of Guizhou. The Mongols threatened China once more, although the powerful Mongol leader Tamerlane had died in 1405 before Chinese troops had to face him. In 1408 Yongle sent a military campaign against the Mongols, who crushed the Chinese forces. The next year, Yongle personally led a huge Ming army that defeated the combined Mongol forces in western China. In 1421 Yongle moved the Ming court to Beijing. Four years later he was succeeded by Emperor Hongxi (Hung-hsi; r. 1425–26), who was soon replaced by Emperor Xuande (Hsuan-te; r. 1426–36).

During the Ming dynasty China enjoyed peace internally, the population grew to about 250 million people, many became wealthy from trade, and Chinese culture reached a high level of attainment, especially in literature, ceramics and painting. The most famous and beloved Chinese novels were published during the Ming. *The Romance of the Three Kingdoms* and *Outlaws of the Marsh* (also known as *The Water Margin* and *All Men Are Brothers*) were written in the late 14th century. *Journey to the West* (also known as *Monkey*) was written in the 16th century and was based on stories about the Chinese Buddhist monk Xuanzang (Hsuan-tsang), who made a famous pilgrimage to India in the seventh century. *The Golden Lotus* was written in 1610. Most Ming Chinese painters were literati who lived in the Yangzi Valley, especially in the vicinity of Hangzhou, which had been the capital of the Southern Song Dynasty (1127–1279) and remained the cultural center of China. Famous Ming painters include Dong Qichang (Tung Ch'i-ch'ang), Huang Gongwang (Huang Kung-wang), Ni Zan (Ni Tsan), Shen Zhou (Shen Chou) and Wen Zhengming (Wang Cheng-ming). Colorfully decorated porcelain is perhaps the most famous product of the Ming, especially blue-and-white ware. The most beautiful Ming porcelains were produced at the imperial kilns at Jingdezhen (Ching-te-chen).

Chinese scholarship also advanced during the Ming. The most important thinker was Wang Yangming (also known as Wang Shouren or Wang Shou-jen; 1472–1529), a general who was also a major Neo-Confucian philosopher. He belonged to the School of the Mind or Intuition, and criticized the concepts of the earlier prominent Neo-Confucian thinker, Zhu Xi (Chu Hsi; 1130–1200), who belonged to the Rationalist School or the School of Reason. Wang Yangming maintained that a person could develop his intuitive knowledge through thinking and meditating, and that knowledge and action are united. His philosophy became influential all over Asia, especially in Japan, and influenced Dr. Sun Yat-sen (1866–1925), the founder of modern China. Li Shizhen (Li Shih-chen; 1518–95) compiled a *Compendium of Materia Medica* (*Bencao gangmu* or *Pen-ts'ao Kangmu*) or book of herbal medicine, detailing about 1,000 plants and 1,000 animals, which is considered the greatest scientific work of the Ming dynasty. It remains the basic source for traditional Chinese herbal medicine and has been translated into English, German and other languages.

After the reign of the Yongle emperor, the Ming dynasty began a gradual decline. Emperors increasingly relied on their eunuchs, who increased their power by controlling the secret police. Literati opposed the power of the eunuchs but also fought each other in struggles between factions in the imperial bureaucracy. Despite the thriving economy, the luxurious habits of Ming emperors, campaigns against the Mongols and pirates, and bureaucratic corruption placed a drain on the government treasury. Giving up the lucrative maritime trade also removed a major source of revenue. Large numbers of Chinese subjects had found ways to avoid paying taxes, but after 1522, Ming government officials reformed and simplified the tax system by combining all dues into one payment, to be collected at one or two fixed dates. The Chinese called this the Single-Whip Reform, because the characters for "single whip" are pronounced the same as the characters for "combination in one item" or "under one head" (*yitiaobian* or *i-ti'ao-p'ien*). The government also changed the payment of taxes from grain to silver, which could be more easily transported to the capital.

The Ming also had to deal with Europeans, who began arriving in greater numbers seeking to force the Ming to open up China to Western-style trade. In 1514 the first Portuguese trading ships put in at Guangzhou, but the Portuguese crews clashed with the Chinese until 1557, when China leased Portugal the small island of Macao near Guangzhou as a trading base. (Macao is still a Portuguese colony but will revert to China in 1999.) In 1622 Dutch ships attacked Macao but the Portuguese beat them off. The Dutch then attacked cities on the Chinese coast and established an enclave on the island of Taiwan, 100 miles off the southeast Chinese coast. English ships arrived in Chinese waters soon after. In 1592 and 1597, Ming forces also had to fight in Korea, which they defended against Japanese invasion forces led by Toyotomi Hideyoshi.

The Portuguese were the first Europeans to establish systematic diplomatic and trading relations with China. Roman Catholic Jesuit missionaries accompanied them. The first was Matteo Ricci, who entered China from Macao in 1583. In 1598 Ricci was introduced at the Ming imperial court, where he impressed Emperor Wanli (r. 1573–1620) and court officials, and in 1601 he was given permission to reside in Beijing with an imperial stipend as a Western scholar. More Jesuits followed Ricci to China. They adopted the clothing and customs of the Confucian-educated literati and permitted their Chinese converts to continue practicing their traditional rituals, known as ancestor worship, which led to later conflict with the Pope in Rome, known as the Rites Controversy. The Ming court was impressed with the Jesuits' knowledge of mathematics and science, especially astronomy, and placed them in charge of the imperial observatory, which made the astronomical calculations for drawing up the annual calendar, which was extremely important to Chinese farmers and bolstered the emperor's reign.

The Ming dynasty was in decline by the time Ricci arrived in Beijing, and peasant rebellions were beginning to break out, especially in regions affected by natural disasters such as floods and droughts. The largest rebellion was led by a bandit named Li Zicheng (Li Tzu-ch'eng) in northwestern China in 1628. By 1643 Li controlled three Chinese provinces. The next year he led a large rebel army against the Ming in Beijing and reached the area of the Great Wall where the Ming general Wu Sangui (Wu San-kuei) was stationed to keep the Manchus out of China. The Manchus, formerly known as the Jurchen, were an ethnic group based in Manchuria (modern northeastern China) who had been organized into a tribal confederation by Nurhachi. They began to expand their territory and took control of Korea in 1637. When Li Zicheng's army arrived in 1644, General Wu made the mistake of asking the Manchus help him fight off the rebels, and he allowed them through the pass in the Great Wall. Li's army marched on Beijing, where eunuchs opened the gates of the Forbidden City in April 1644. The Ming emperor Chongzhen (Ch'ung-chen; r. 1628–44) and his empress hanged themselves. The Manchus pursued Li Zicheng's rebel forces, and on June 5, 1644, the Manchu chieftain, Dorgon, led his forces unopposed into Beijing. He proclaimed that their dynasty, the Qing (which the Manchus had actually established in 1636), had now replaced the Ming.

Some members of the Ming court had been able to flee south, where they attempted to continue the Ming dynasty and drive out the Manchus. These included Emperors Hongguang (Hung-Kuang; r. 1645), Longwu, (Lung-wu; r. 1646) and Yongli (Yung-li; r. 1647–61). The Ming loyalists in southern China were supported by Zheng Chenggong (Cheng Ch'eng-kung; 1624–62), popularly known as Coxinga (Koxinga), who drove the Dutch off Taiwan, established a government there and promoted emigration from the Chinese mainland. After he died his successors fell into opposing factions, and in 1683 the Qing attacked Taiwan, defeated the final Ming resistors and incorporated Taiwan as a Qing prefecture. In 1886 they made Taiwan a province of China. See also ASTRONOMY AND OBSERVATORIES; BEIJING; BLUE-AND-WHITE WARE; CALENDAR; CHINA PROPER; CHONGZHEN (EMPEROR); DONG QICHANG; DONGLIN ACADEMY; DORGON; EMPEROR; ENAMEL WARE; EUNUCHS; FORBIDDEN CITY; GOLD AND SILVER; GOLDEN LOTUS, THE; GRAND CANAL; GREAT WALL; HAN; HANGZHOU; HANLIN ACADEMY; HONGWU, EMPEROR; IMPERIAL BUREAUCRACY; IMPERIAL EXAMINATION SYSTEM; JESUITS; JIAJING (EMPEROR); JINGDEZHEN; JOURNEY TO THE WEST; LANDSCAPE PAINTING; LI SHIZHEN; LI ZICHENG; LITERATI; MACAO; MANCHU; MANCHURIA; MEDICINE, HERBAL; MING TOMBS; MONGOL; NANJING; NATURAL DISASTERS; NURHACHI; OUTLAWS OF THE MARSH; PIRATES; PORCELAIN; QING DYNASTY; RED TURBANS REBELLION; RICCI, MATTEO; ROMANCE OF THE THREE KINGDOMS; SONG DYNASTY; TAIWAN; TAMERLANE; TRIBUTE SYSTEM; WANG YANGMING; WANLI (EMPEROR); WEI ZHONGXIAN; XUANZONG (EMPEROR); YANGZI RIVER; YONGLE (EMPEROR); YONGLE ENCYCLOPEDIA; YUAN DYNASTY; ZHENG CHENGGONG; ZHENG HE.

MING TOMBS (Shisan Ling, "The Thirteen Tombs") Thirteen mausoleums constructed for 13 of the 16 emperors of the Ming dynasty (1368–1644) and their wives and second wives. The emperors chose the location and design of their tombs while they were still alive, based on the principles of *feng shui* (geomancy). Each burial site contained three parts: the building where sacrifices were offered, the stele (tower) where prayers were chanted, and the mound that covered the underground burial chamber. The Ming tombs are located about 25 miles north of the capital city of Beijing in a valley protected by the Tianshoushan (Tian Shou Mountains). Although only three of the 13 tombs have been excavated, the Ming Tombs are a popular tourist attraction.

In 1955–58 archaeologists opened up Dingling, the tomb of the 13th Ming emperor, Zhu Yijun (r. 1572–1620), commonly referred to by his reign name, Wanli. Also known as the "Underground Palace," this was the first imperial tomb to be excavated in China. It has five vaulted stone chambers. The coffins of the emperor and his two empresses are displayed, and more than 3,000 objects are also exhibited in the tomb and two small museums, including a gold crown and gold wine containers. The buildings on the ground above Dingling have also been restored. Changling, the burial site of the third Ming emperor, Yongle (Yung-lo; r. 1403–24), the first emperor to be buried in the Ming Tombs, has also been excavated. His wife, Empress Xu (Hsu; d. 1407), is also buried there. Supposedly 16 concubines were buried with Yongle. Zhaoling, the tomb of Emperor Longqing (Lung-ch'ing; r. 1567–72) and three of his wives, was opened to the public in 1989. Archaeologists are still working on Changling and Zhaoling.

The Ming tombs are approached by the Sacred Way (Shendan), four miles long, which is entered through a white marble portico that has five gateways with carved pillars. The entrance to the sacred burial area is guarded by the 120-foot-high Great Red Gate (Da Hong Men) (which actually has three gateways). Living emperors walked through the two gateways on each side; dead emperors were carried through the central gateway into the burial area, which was formerly surrounded by a wall. After the Great Red Gate is the double-roofed Stele Pavilion (Pei Ting), at the center of which is a 30-foot-high column on the back of a 6-foot-high tortoise sculpture. Beyond this lies the Avenue of the Animals, a row of 24 carved stone animals in standing and kneeling pairs on each side of the road. They include a lion, the mythical *xiezhi,* a camel, an elephant, the mythical *qilin* and a horse. There are also six pairs of sculptures of military and civil bureaucrats. The Dragon Phoenix Gate (Longfeng Men) with three arches leads to the 13 tomb sites. See also EMPEROR; FENG SHUI; MING DYNASTY; WANLI (EMPEROR); YONGLE (EMPEROR).

MINGDI (MING-TI) EMPEROR See EASTERN HAN DYNASTY; LIU XIU.

MINGHUANG (EMPEROR) See XUANZONG (EMPEROR).

MINGJIA (MING-CHIA) See DIALECTICIANS.

MINGZHOU See NINGBO.

MINING INDUSTRY China has large deposits of coal, iron ore and other important minerals. It also has some of the world's largest deposits of rare earth minerals, copper, lead, tin, zinc, mercury, nickel, aluminum, manganese, antimony, tungsten, molybdenum, vanadium, titanium, pyrite, gypsum, barite, phosphorus, asbestos, borax, fluorite and magnesite. However, it has been difficult for the Chinese to extract enough of these minerals for industrial purposes because they do not have sufficient means to transport them from mines to factories and they lack enough modern equipment to mine, smelt and refine them. China has had to import such materials as steel, pig iron, copper and aluminum. China does have large uranium deposits, which are relatively easy to mine. It also produces sufficient quantities of nonmetallic minerals for domestic use, such as salt, talc, graphite, magnesite, phosphates, pyrite, sulfur, fluorite and barite.

Coal is China's most important source of primary energy. In 1987 it was used to meet more than 70 percent of the country's total energy demand. The Chinese began mining coal in large quantities after foreign powers began building railroads in China in the late l9th and early 20th centuries. The Daye mine in Hubei Province was opened in 1891 to supply the first modern steelworks at Hanyang. Coal mining was one of China's most developed industries in the first half

Three of the original 13 Ming Tombs have been excavated, drawing thousands of tourists each year to view 15th- to 17th-century imperial artifacts. S.E. MEYER

of the 20th century, with major mines at Datong, Fushun and Kailuan in northeastern China producing much of the coal used for Chinese railroads, shipping and industry. Japan, which invaded Manchuria (northeastern China) in 1931, exploited the coal and other resources in that region and northern China until it was defeated in 1945. After the Communists founded the People's Republic of China (PRC) in 1949, the government made heavy investments in modern mining equipment and in developing large, mechanized mines.

China has around 900 billion metric tons (MT) of identified and recoverable coal reserves. About 80 percent of the known coal deposits are in the northern and northwestern regions but are hard to exploit because they are located far from the most industrialized regions of the country. For example, there are extremely large deposits of coal and metallic ores in the remote Tian Shan Mountain Range in western China. Since opening the country to foreign investment in the 1980s, China has been using foreign capital to develop large mining projects. In 1989–91 the Chinese mined over one billion metric tons of coal. Even so, China has to import coal to meet the need for it in industrialized regions in southern China, because it is difficult to ship coal from the regions in northern and central China where it is mined.

The Chinese have known how to manufacture iron weapons and other objects for more than 2,000 years. China has large iron ore deposits in about two-thirds of its provinces and autonomous regions, but they are of relatively poor quality. Also, it is difficult to transport and refine the ore to produce sufficient quantities of iron, and in the 1980s China had to import iron. China has also had to import foreign iron- and steel-making equipment, which is more technologically advanced than its domestically produced equipment.

Since 1949, geologists have conducted explorations in China that have located deposits of more than 130 useful minerals, although they believe that the country's metal and mineral resources are still largely unexplored. China has the largest deposits of rare-earth metals in the world, at least five times the total found in other countries. Bayan Obo in Inner Mongolia Autonomous Region in northern China, the first rare-earth mining area that was "tapped" in China, was in 1982 still considered to have the largest supply in the country. Rare-earth minerals are called the "fraternal fifteen" or lanthanides. They exist naturally together and are difficult to extract. More than 200 varieties have been found but only a small number have industrial value. The Chinese have been able to produce sufficient quantities of beryllium, tungsten, molybdenum, barium, manganese, mercury, niobium, zirconium and titanium, but lack sufficient quantities of chromium, platinum and gold. Rare-earth metals are commonly used in atomic energy, national defense, agriculture, chemical, metallurgical, oil and light industries, and in the manufacture of optical instruments and medicines. Baotou, a city hundreds of miles from Bayan Obo, established China's largest rare-earth production and research center. By the mid-1980s China was exporting rare metals used in the aerospace and electronics industries. See also ENERGY SOURCES; IRON TECHNOLOGY AND STEEL INDUSTRY; RAILROADS; SHIPPING AND SHIPBUILDING.

MINISTRIES OF THE STATE COUNCIL See STATE COUNCIL.

MINISTRY OF FINANCE (MOF)   The government organ of the People's Republic of China (PRC) that controls all Chinese financial services, credit and the money supply. After the Chinese Communist Party (CCP) founded the PRC in 1949, it centralized the banking system in the People's Bank of China under the MOF; this was the first state sector to be completely socialized. The MOF reports to the State Council and works closely with the People's Bank of China and its foreign exchange arm, the Bank of China. It keeps watch over the use and disbursement of funds to units of production, including local industrial enterprises, and their profit targets and costs. It maintains units and branches in every locality in the PRC, and it plays an important role in planning the Chinese economy. The MOF works with the General Office of the Central Committee of the CCP to prepare the annual state budget. See also BANK OF CHINA; CENTRAL COMMITTEE; PEOPLE'S BANK OF CHINA; STATE COUNCIL.

MINISTRY OF FOREIGN AFFAIRS (MFA)   One of the most important ministries in the government of the Communist People's Republic of China (PRC), which was founded in 1949. The MFA administers the PRC's diplomatic relations with 138 countries and its representation in the United Nations and other international organizations. The MFA has five regional vice ministers and 15 functional offices, which oversee the various areas of foreign relations, divided either geographically or functionally. For example, one vice minister is responsible for North American and Oceanian Affairs and one is responsible for Asian Affairs. Four important subordinate institutes conduct the ministry's long-term research and planning. The Chinese People's Institute of Foreign Affairs provides information about foreign visitors to senior policymakers and analyzes policy issues pertaining to foreign affairs. The Foreign Affairs College trains all Chinese diplomats, who may also receive training at the College of International Relations, Beijing Foreign Languages Institute, and international studies departments in major universities. The Institute of International Studies is the principal internal research facility of the MFA. Staff members include full-time researchers and diplomats who are assigned there for a one- or two-year assignment. The Chinese People's Association for Friendship with Foreign Countries is a national organization that seeks to promote bilateral exchanges on an unofficial basis. Specialists from other PRC ministries also serve abroad in PRC embassies and consulates, such as military attaches from the Ministry of National Defense, which administers the People's Liberation Army (PLA), and commercial officers from the Ministry of Foreign Trade and Economic Cooperation. See also GOVERNMENT STRUCTURE; MINISTRY OF FOREIGN TRADE AND ECONOMIC COOPERATION; PEOPLE'S REPUBLIC OF CHINA.

MINISTRY OF FOREIGN TRADE AND ECONOMIC COOPERATION (MOFTEC)   A ministry of the government of the People's Republic of China (PRC) that oversees foreign trade and investment. Foreign trade was formerly a government monopoly, but since 1979 the central government has decentralized foreign trade management authorities to provinces, autonomous regions, municipalities and industrial ministries. In 1979 the Chinese government set up four Special Economic Zones (SEZs) where foreign investors are given preferential treatment. In 1984 it opened 14 coastal cities to foreign investment, with preferential treatment similar to the SEZs. By the early 1980s, about a thousand foreign trading corporations (FTCs) had been granted trading rights in China, although they were strictly regulated as to the goods traded, the methods and types of trade, and the companies with which they could conduct trade. By 1994 the Chinese government had granted trading rights to about 6,000 FTCs, large- and medium-scale production enterprises and research institutions.

About 300 specialized FTCs remain under the direct control of MOFTEC. Some specialize in just a few products or commodities. For example, China's import system requires that all grain purchases be channeled through a single state FTC, the China National Cereals and Oils Import and Export Corporation. Some FTCs, such as the China National Pharmaceutical Import and Export Corporation, are permitted to export and import only the products used in their particular industry. However, most general trading corporations are not directly controlled by MOFTEC and are permitted to trade nearly any product as the agent for a factory or enterprise. They can also buy and sell for their own account.

In the late 1980s the Chinese government granted trading rights to non-FTCs, such as manufacturing enterprises. By 1993, 839 large and medium enterprises had foreign trading rights. However, smaller enterprises often continue to use their links to FTCs to handle imports and exports. Large companies tend to establish trading offices offshore in order to gain greater access to markets outside China. The Chinese government has also given trading rights to newly formed enterprise groups in such areas as chemicals, electronics, metals, minerals, petroleum products and textiles.

Although the Chinese government has largely opened up the country to foreign trade, MOFTEC still develops foreign trade plans in consultation with the State Planning Commission, although mandatory plans are issued only for the country's most critical trade. While the decrease in central planning is constantly creating more opportunities for foreign companies to establish direct contacts with Chinese buyers and sellers, it is also creating a complicated and even confusing market for foreign companies. Even so, the People's Republic of China is one of the world's fastest-growing economies. In 1992 its gross national product (GNP) increased 12.8 percent and it is projected to grow at 8 to 9 percent annually through the 1990s. The five-year plan for 1991 through 1995 called for China to spend $70–80 billion a year on imports. China is also spending about $30 billion between 1993 and 2000 to import foreign technology and equipment for 210 large projects in 23 industries. Chinese exports have also increased dramatically. Exports to the United States, China's number-one market, grew from $592 million in 1979 to $25.7 billion in 1992, making China the fifth-largest exporter to the United States that year. See also SPECIAL ECONOMIC ZONES.

MINISTRY OF NATIONAL DEFENSE See CENTRAL MILITARY COMMISSION AND MINISTRY OF NATIONAL DEFENSE.

MINISTRY OF RADIO, CINEMA AND TELEVISION See BROADCASTING.

MINISTRY OF RITES   The department in the Chinese imperial bureaucracy responsible for the proper performance of imperial activities, such as enthronement and funerals of emperors and annual ritual sacrifices; also known as the Board of Rites. The emperor was revered as the Son of Heaven (*Tianzi* or *T'ien tzu*), Heaven's representative on Earth. The imperial rituals were prescribed by the Confucian tradition, which became the orthodox school of thought for the Chinese imperial government during the Han dynasty (206 B.C.–A.D. 220). The *Book of Rites* (*Lijing* or *Li Ching*) is one of the Five Classics of Confucianism. Sui emperor Yangdi (Yang-ti; r. 604–618), who sponsored a revival of Confucian learning, formally established the Ministry of Rites. He also developed the competitive examination system by which Confucian-educated scholars were chosen for positions in the imperial bureaucracy.

In 694, Empress Wu (r. 690–705), who patronized the Buddhist religion, placed Buddhism under the jurisdiction of the Bureau of National Sacrifice within the Ministry of Rites. The ministry came to control the priests of Buddhism and the native Chinese religion of Daoism by administering central registries through which the priests had to be examined and certified. From the Tang (618–907 A.D.) through the Ming dynasty (1368–1644), the Ministry of Rites was responsible not only for religious rituals but also for matters that may be termed foreign affairs, such as handling protocol for missions from vassal states that brought tribute to the Chinese Empire. Members of these missions were required to perform the ritual *kowtow*, or prostrations, before the Chinese emperor.

During the Manchu Qing dynasty (1644–1911), the Board of Rites was one of the six major departments in the imperial bureaucracy. Along with important ritual activities, it handled relations with tributary states such as Korea, Annam (Vietnam), Burma and the Ryukyu (Liuqiu or Liu Ch'iu) Islands (modern Okinawa). An office known as the *Li Fan Yuan* handled relations between the Manchu imperial court and the Mongol princes; the Mongols, like the Manchus a foreign nomadic ethnic group, had invaded and ruled China during the Yuan dynasty (1279–1368). This office also handled relations with Russia, Tibet and the region in western China that is modern Xinjiang-Uighur Autonomous Region. European traders, who began arriving in China in the 16th century, did not wish to submit to the Chinese tribute system or to the strict Chinese regulations, which limited them to trade through official agents in the southern city of Canton (Guangzhou) (the Canton System for foreign trade). The British, who dominated Western trade with China and were especially unhappy with Chinese trade restrictions, defeated China in the Opium War (1839–42) and Arrow War (1856–60) and forced China to open more cities to foreign trade. The Chinese government had no secular office to handle foreign affairs until the late 19th century, when Europeans demanded such an office to receive their diplomats. China responded by establishing the *Zongli Yamen*. See also BOOK OF RITES; CANTON SYSTEM TO REGULATE FOREIGN TRADE; CONFUCIANISM; EMPEROR; FIVE CLASSICS OF CONFUCIANISM; IMPERIAL BUREAUCRACY; KOWTOW; RYUKYU ISLANDS; TRIBUTE SYSTEM; ZONGLI YAMEN.

MINJIA See BAI.

MINORITIES, NATIONAL Members of the 55 ethnic groups officialy designated by the Chinese government as national minorities (*shaoshu minzu* in Chinese), that is, groups not belonging to the dominant Han ethnic group. The government defines a nationality as a group of people of common origin who live in a common area, use a common language, and identify with the same group in their economic and social organization and behavior. The difference between the minorities and the Han is not so much racial as cultural and linguistic.

The Chinese state constitution of 1954 guarantees equal treatment of the minorities. In 1959 the government constructed the Nationalities' Cultural Palace in Beijing to serve as a center for national minorities. According to the 1990 census, national minorities comprise about 90 million people, 8 percent of China's total population, but they occupied about 60 percent of China's total land area.

The minorities fall into 15 major linguistic regions that correspond to their geographic distribution. Many of them live in regions not suited to Chinese-style agriculture, such as the remote and mountainous areas of southwestern China and the steppes and arid deserts of northern and northwestern China. The Chinese government has designated five regions with large minority populations as autonomous regions that have the status of provinces. These include Guangxi-Zhuang Autonomous Region in the southwest, and Tibet, Ningxia-Hui, Xinjiang-Uighur and Inner Mongolia autonomous regions in the west and northwest. There are also 29 autonomous districts, such as the Xishuangbanna Autonomous District of the Dai nationality in Yunnan Province.

The Chinese government works to maintain stable relations with the minorities because many of them live in politically sensitive areas bordering other countries inhabited by ethnic groups related to the minorities in China, or live in regions with large deposits of strategic minerals and oil. Tibet (Xizang) is a highly sensitive area, especially since the 1950s when the Tibetans rebelled against China. In 1958 their leader, the Dalai Lama, fled to India with a large number of followers. Today the Tibetans in China number about four million, but the Chinese government has been sending large numbers of Han to settle in Tibet and other minority regions. The largest ethnic minority group is the Zhuang, with a population of 15.5 million concentrated in Guangxi-Zhuang, Yunnan and Guangdong Provinces in south-central China. However, the Zhuang have been partly assimilated with the Han and do not cause problems for the government. The second-largest group is the Hui, about 9 million Han Chinese who follow the Muslim religion. The third-largest is the Uighur, a group of about 6 million Muslim Turkic people who inhabit Xinjiang. Other major national minorities include the Bai, Bouyei, Dai, Hani, Kazakh, Kirghiz, Korean, Manchu, Miao, Mongol and Yao.

During the Cultural Revolution (1966–76), minority languages, cultures and religions were discriminated against and Red Guards committed violence against some minority peoples. In 1980 the Chinese government adopted a number of measures to provide economic and financial assistance to minority areas, which greatly improved their standard of living and gave them more autonomy. The government allows minority children to be educated in their own languages and cultures as well as in the Han Chinese language. Typically, ethnic minorities are allowed to marry earlier than members of the Han ethnic majority and to have more children. The government generally exempts them from the one-child-per-family campaign. Minority children can get into universities with lower examination scores than those required of Han students, and model members of minorities are chosen for prominent government positions. Because of this affirmative action policy, some families that formerly had tried to assimilate into the Han majority are now applying for declarations that they are members of a minority group and not Han. The Han have tended to look down on minorities, but recently there has been an increase in intermarriage between members of the Han and national minority groups. See also CONSTITUTION, STATE, OF 1954; HAN; MUSLIMS; NATIONALITIES CULTURAL PALACE; NOMADS AND ANIMAL HUSBANDRY; ONE-CHILD FAMILY CAMPAIGN; POPULATION, CHINESE; INDIVIDUAL GROUPS AND PROVINCES.

MINZHU DANGPAI See DEMOCRATIC PARTIES.

MIRRORS (*jingzi; fanying*) In ancient China, mirrors possessed various symbolic meanings as well as magical power. Round cast-bronze discs had fronts with highly polished, reflective images and decorated backs. The technique for casting bronzeware became highly developed during the Shang dynasty (1750–1040 B.C.). During the Han dynasty (206 B.C.–A.D. 220), the backs of mirrors became decorated with the so-called "TLV" pattern in which certain marks resemble these letters. Such bronze mirrors were produced through the Tang dynasty (618–907), although by that time only the "V" mark was being used. In the seventh century, mirrors were also being produced from silver.

These ancient mirrors were believed to have the power to protect their owners from evil, make hidden spirits visible and reveal the secrets of the future. A person who has been scared by a ghost supposedly could be healed by looking in such a mirror. In ancient China these mirrors were often hung on the ceilings of burial chambers. Wealthy Chinese still hang them in their homes for protection.

Bands around mirrors were often decorated with symbols based on ancient Chinese cosmological beliefs. These symbols include the 12 animals in the 12-year zodiac cycle; the dragon, phoenix, tiger and tortoise (creatures associated with the four directions); depictions of the eight trigrams (*bagua*), used to foretell the future; and the Eight Immortals, deities in the Daoist religion. The round mirror is one of the Eight Treasures, a popular Chinese design motif. It is also a symbol of unbroken marital happiness. A mirror is placed on the bride's chair at a wedding, and may be used to flash the rays of the sun on her. See also BRONZEWARE; DRAGON; EIGHT IMMORTALS; EIGHT TREASURES; EIGHT TRIGRAMS; PHOENIX; TIGER; TORTOISE; ZODIAC, ANIMAL.

MISSIONARIES See JESUITS; NESTORIAN CHRISTIANITY; RICCI, MATTEO; TAIPING REBELLION; CHRISTIANITY.

MO SHILUNG See DONG QICHANG.

MO TO See MOZI.

MO TZU See MOZI.

MOCHI (MO-CH'I) See WANG WEI.

MODI See MOZI.

MOGAO GROTTOES See DUNHUANG CAVE PAINTINGS AND CARVINGS.

MOHISM See MOZI.

MOKKEI See MU QI.

MONEY See CURRENCY, HISTORICAL; CURRENCY, MODERN.

MONGOL One of China's 55 officially designated national minority ethnic groups. The Mongols ruled China under the Yuan dynasty (1279–1368), which was established by Khubilai Khan (1214–94), who reigned as the first Yuan emperor, Shizu (Shih-tsu). The Mongols originated as a group of nomadic tribes in the region north and northwest of the Great Wall known as Mongolia. Today Mongolia is divided into Inner Mongolia (Nei Monggol), an autonomous region within the People's Republic of China, and the independent Mongolian People's Republic. Mongol boys were raised to ride horses all day long and to live and fight in the saddle. Mongol girls were also trained to ride. The women and children constantly migrated across the steppe lands, herding sheep and goats, with horses pulling their tents and belongings in large wagons. Their religion was originally a form of shamanism, but many Mongols married women who practiced Nestorian Christianity, and Mongol leaders converted to Lamaism (Tibetan Buddhism). Genghis Khan (1162–1227), the grandfather of Khubilai Khan, unified the Mongol tribes and organized them into a powerful military force highly skilled in cavalry techniques. In less than a century the Mongols established the largest empire the world had ever seen, covering most of Asia and stretching all the way into Europe. Although nomadic tribes had long invaded China, the Mongols were the first "barbarians," that is, not belonging to the Han ethnic group, who conquered all of China, and they strongly discriminated against the Han. The Ming dynasty (1368–1644) overthrew the Mongols and pushed them back to the northern steppes. The Manchus, who overthrew the Ming and established the Qing dynasty (1644–1911), conquered Inner Mongolia and made it their vassal state even before they founded the Qing. In 1697 Emperor Kangxi (K'ang-hsi; r. 1661–1722) led an army to Outer Mongolia, where in 1707 he destroyed the power of the Mongols and made that region a vassal state as well. However, the Mongols ruled a kingdom west of Outer Mongolia, named Dzungaria, which at the height of its power in the 1670s included Chinese Turkestan (part of modern Xinjiang-Uighur Autonomous Region), the Ili River valley and the Altai Mountains. The Qing finally conquered this Mongol kingdom in 1757 and brutally killed most of the Dzungars. When the Chinese overthrew the Qing during the Revolution of 1911, the Mongols revolted against the Qing

and reestablished their theocratic monarchy, which continued until 1924 when the last Mongol Buddhist leader died.

The Mongols are a branch of the Altaic ethnic group whose members inhabit an area stretching from Siberia to the Mediterranean Sea and also include the Turkic and Tungusic (including Manchu) peoples. According to the 1992 census, about 4.8 million Mongolians reside in China, mainly in Inner Mongolia, Gansu and Qinghai provinces in western China, Hebei Province in northern China, and in Manchuria (northeastern China, the home of the Manchus). Many Mongols still live as nomadic animal herders. Foreign tourists visit Inner Mongolia, often staying overnight in the round, wool tents known as yurts (*ger* in Mongolian). Every July and August, Mongols gather to hold *namdan*, a traditional sporting event that includes horseracing, archery and wrestling. Mongols learn to ride horses as small children, and many Mongolian dances imitate the movement of horses. See also GENGHIS KHAN; GREAT WALL; HORSE; INNER MONGOLIA AUTONOMOUS REGION; KHUBILAI KHAN; LAMAISM; MANCHUS; MINORITIES, NATIONAL; NESTORIAN CHRISTIANITY; NOMADS AND ANIMAL HUSBANDRY; YUAN DYNASTY.

MONKEY (*hou*) There are several species of monkey native to China. The most common Chinese monkey is the brown-and-red rhesus macaque, which lives in groups of about 10 primarily in southern mountain forests. They can also be found as far north as Hebei Province. The stumptailed monkey inhabits the high mountains in southwestern and southern China. This species has long beards and looks very human. The black leaf monkey and gray leaf monkey have long forelegs and long tails that help them climb steep rocks and swing from tree to tree. The beautiful golden monkey is an endangered species protected by Chinese law. Its long, thick, golden brown fur was considered quite valuable in China; for a while only members of the imperial family were allowed to wear it. The golden monkey inhabits Sichuan and southern Gansu and Shaanxi Provinces. Its forest habitat has dwindled due to logging and the clearing of forests for agriculture, so it now resides mainly in the Jiuzhaigou Nature Reserve in Sichuan Province and the Wolong Nature Reserve where northwestern Sichuan meets Gansu and Shaanxi Provinces. It lives in small groups in high mountains about 9,800 feet above sea level. The golden monkey's head and body have a total length of about 24 to 33 inches, and its tail is nearly as long.

Two endangered species of monkey inhabit southwestern China. Biet's snub-nosed monkey is found in northwestern Yunnan Province, and Brelich's snub-nosed monkey resides in Guizhou Province. Both have dark fur but may be related to the golden monkey. Three species of gibbons inhabit tropical forests in southern Yunnan Province and Hainan Island: the white-browed or Hoolock gibbon, the Lar or common gibbon, and the concolor, crested or white-cheeked gibbon. These gibbons weigh about 11 to 28 pounds each and have long, powerful forelimbs that help them swing rapidly from tree to tree. Gibbons are social and communicative—and quite entertaining to watch.

In China, the monkey is a popular character known as the Monkey King in folk tales, dramas and opera. In his rousing encounters with the Jade Emperor, ruler of Heaven,

Monkey King always wins. He is a trickster but helps people by keeping away evil spirits that cause illness. Strong-willed, always in motion, impulsive and mischievous, Monkey King is the central character in *Journey to the West* (*Xiyouji* or *Hsi-yu-chi;* also known as *Pilgrimage to the West* and *Monkey*), a humorous 16th-century novel beloved by the Chinese. It has been translated into English, and tells the story of the magical Monkey King, who converts from the native Chinese religion of Daoism to Buddhism. The Monkey King accompanies the Buddhist monk Xuanzang (Hsuang-tsang) on his journey to the west. The story is based on the actual pilgrimage to India from 629 to 645 made by Xuanzang to gather sutras (religious scriptures) for translation. He is protected by several characters with supernatural powers, including Monkey King, a pig and a dark spirit of the sands.

Monkey King is said to be able to cover 18,000 *li* (about 6,000 miles) in one bound, and he wears a tight iron helmet to help him control his wild impulses. His Buddhist name in the *Journey to the West* is Sun Wukong (Sun Wu-k'ung), "Aware of the Emptiness of All Things." One of the novel's best-known episodes is known as "Monkey Causes Havoc in Heaven." Monkey King steals the banquet feast of the gods and makes himself doubly immortal by eating the peaches of immortality and swallowing the pill of immortality.

Actors who portray Monkey on stage are very agile and perform many acrobatics. Monkey King has become a familiar character in the West and was even featured in the American children's television special, "Big Bird Goes to China."

The monkey is one of the animals in the traditional 12-year cycle known as the animal zodiac. People born in the Year of the Monkey are believed to be clever, successful, good with money, competitive, selfish and lovable. The most recent Year of the Monkey was 1992. See also BUDDHISM; JOURNEY TO THE WEST; PEACH; XUANZANG; ZODIAC, ANIMAL.

MONUMENT TO THE PEOPLE'S HEROES (REVOLUTIONARY MARTYRS) See CULTURAL REVOLUTION; TIANANMEN SQUARE; ZHOU ENLAI.

MOON See AUTUMN MOON FESTIVAL; CHANG E; RABBIT; YIN AND YANG.

MOONCAKES See AUTUMN MOON FESTIVAL; LOTUS; PHOENIX.

MORRISON, ROBERT See CHRISTIANITY.

MORSE, H. B. See CHINESE MARITIME CUSTOMS SERVICE.

MOST-FAVORED-NATION (MFN) TRADE STATUS MFN status represents a commitment by a country that it will extend to another country the lowest tariff rates it applies to any third country. The U.S. government has extended MFN status to China. MFN status had first been applied in China in the l9th century, when Britain and other foreign powers forced China to open some of its cities to foreign residents and trade as so-called "treaty ports." The Treaty of the Bogue (1843) signed by China and Britain, a supplement to the Treaty of Nanjing (1842) that concluded the Opium War (1839–42) in which Britain defeated China, contained the first use of the MFN clause with China. The clause was

included in most of the treaties that foreign powers signed with China, known as "unequal treaties," so that any right that China gave to another foreign power, even at a date later than the signing of the particular treaty, would also be given automatically to the power with which China had signed the treaty.

The United States recognized the Communist People's Republic of China (PRC) and normalized trade relations in the 1970s. The reciprocal granting of MFN treatment was the most important point in the U.S.-China Trade Agreement signed in 1979, which initiated normal commercial relations between the United States and China. Since China is a non–market economy country, its MFN status must be renewed annually by a U.S. presidential waiver stipulating that China meets the freedom-of-emigration requirements set forth in the Jackson-Vanik amendment to the Trade Act of 1974. The United States gave China the waiver routinely until 1989, when human rights became a major issue after the Chinese government authorized the brutal crackdown on student pro-democracy demonstrators in Tiananmen Square in June 1989. After the Tiananmen Square massacre, the presidential waiver for China continued, but the U.S. Congress began to strongly oppose MFN renewal and began debating whether to link the renewal of China's MFN status to the improvement of human rights conditions in China. In 1991 and 1992, Congress voted to place conditions on MFN renewal for China, but the administration of President George Bush vetoed those conditions, arguing that the U.S. relationship with China was important and the MFN status was not the proper means for placing pressure on China and would isolate it from the world community.

The United States does not want to isolate China because it is the world's most populous nation and fastest growing major economy, and it is a permanent member of the United Nations Security Council. In 1993 U.S. imports from China totaled $31.5 billion, while U.S. exports to China totaled $8.8 billion. When President Clinton succeeded George Bush, he was committed to linking the renewal of China's MFN trade status with an improvement in China's human rights conditions. The U.S. government has also complained about human rights abuses in Chinese prison factories or work camps, known as *laogai,* and has not wanted to sanction the purchase of products made by prisoners. The conditions in the *laogai* are inhumane and prisoners are commonly tortured, as Chinese dissident Harry Wu has documented. China has refused to compromise on this issue and has threatened to disrupt relations with the United States, so the United States has been reluctant to press China too hard. The laws of the United States prohibit importation of prison labor products, and in fact the laws of the PRC prohibit exporting them. In August 1992, the United States and China signed the prison labor memorandum of understanding (MOU) providing the exchange of information between both countries regarding conditions in their respective prison facilities, and they signed a separate statement of cooperation that specified terms for implementing the MOU in March 1994.

In May 1993 President Clinton signed an executive order adding a requirement for his administration to review China's compliance with the August 7, 1992, U.S.-China prison labor MOU as part of his annual assessment of

China's MFN status. On May 28, 1993, Clinton announced a unified congressional and executive branch policy whose central principle would be the insistence upon significant progress in human rights in China. He signed an Executive Order that extended China's MFN status for 12 months and stated that extension of MFN in 1994 would depend on whether China made significant progress in improving human rights. The order specified particular areas that would be examined in 1994, including the release of citizens imprisoned for the nonviolent expression of their political beliefs and the Universal Declaration of Human Rights. The United States has also been concerned about trade and arms proliferation, and the president's Executive Order directed the secretary of state and other officials to take all legislative and executive actions to ensure that China follows international standards. For example, if any nation has violated the international guidelines for weapons sales by supplying them to countries forbidden by international agreements, U.S. laws provide for placing strict sanctions against that nation. On May 26, 1994, President Clinton decided to renew the granting of MFN status to China for another year, based on the U.S. State Department's positive assessment of China's emigration policies and on reviewing progress under the prison labor MOU. The debates continued in 1995, 1996 and 1998. Cina continues to enjoy MFN status despite concerns about human rights violations there. See also FOREIGN TRADE AND INVESTMENT; TIANANMEN SQUARE MASSACRE; UNEQUAL TREATIES; WU, HARRY.

MOUTH ORGAN See SHENG.

MOVIES See CHEN KAIGE; FILM STUDIOS; GONG LI; LU, LISA; ZHANG YIMOU.

MOXIBUSTION Also known as moxa cautery; a traditional Chinese method for treating illness in which herbs are rolled into a small cone-shaped lump, placed on the patient, ignited and left to burn down slowly. The cone does not touch the patient's skin directly but is placed on a piece of ginger or garlic or on a layer of salt on the skin. A doctor commonly places several cones at crucial points on the patient at the same time. The herb used in moxibustion is mugwort wormwood (*aiyen*; Latin name, *Artemisia vulgaris*) in the form of powdered moxa, which is considered effective in treating such conditions as severe diarrhea, arthritis, menstrual disturbances and pain in childbirth. Even young children are treated with moxibustion for such conditions as mild conjunctivitis; the herbal cone is placed on their hands in the space between their middle and index fingers. Moxibustion is often practiced in conjunction with acupuncture, a traditional treatment involving the placement of tiny needles in designated points on the patient's body to open up blocked channels of energy or *qi* (*ch'i*). Chinese doctors rely on charts of the human body that illustrate these channels and specify the points where acupuncture needles or moxibustion should be applied. The Chinese term for acupuncture, zhenjiu (*chen chiu*), literally means "needles and moxa." The theory underlying the therapeutic application of heat in moxibustion is the need to bring the yin or feminine element and the yang or masculine element back into proper balance in the patient's body. According to traditional Chinese thought, yin and yang

are the basis of all created things in the universe. The oldest surviving text on moxibustion and acupuncture is *The Yellow Emperor's Canon of Medicine* (*Niejing Suwen* or *Nieh-ching suwen*), written during the Warring States Period (403–221 B.C.). Huangbu Mi, a physician during the Western Jin dynasty (A.D. 265–316) wrote the influential text *A Classic of Acupuncture and Moxibustion*. See also ACUPUNCTURE; MEDICINE, HERBAL; QI; YIN AND YANG.

MOZI (Mo Tzu; c. 470–391 B.C.)   A philosopher whose school of thought, known as Mohism, was one of the four main Chinese philosophies prior to the suppression of "the Hundred Schools of Thought" by Emperor Qin Shi Huangdi in 213 B.C.; also known as Modi (Mo Ti). Confucianism, Daoism and Legalism continued to play a central role in Chinese culture but Mohism disappeared, although some of its ideas were taken up by the Legalists. Mozi was the first Chinese thinker to rival Confucius (551–479 B.C.). The book of essays expounding Mohism, known as the *Mozi*, strove to put forth new ideas that broke with traditional Chinese practice. Confucius had adapted to his teaching the moral tradition that had already developed in China.

Mozi was born into a humble family, perhaps in the state of Lu in Shandong Province during the Eastern Zhou Period (771–256 B.C.). He may have been a carpenter. He became an engineer and an expert in defensive strategy, and held a high government position in the state of Song and finally directed a school back in Lu. He traveled to many neighboring states, teaching a philosophy based on universal love. Mozi held up as his utopian ideal the mythologized Xia dynasty (2200–1750 B.C.), when all people supposedly cared for each other as one family and treated all children as their own. His mottoes were, "the man of Chu is my brother," "love for everyone (*jian'ai*)," and "all men are equal before Heaven." This concept of love was not abstract, but required the fulfillment of everyone's material needs, starting with food, clothing and housing.

Mozi had been educated in the classic texts of Confucianism, but he criticized the Confucian emphasis on family relationships as socially divisive. He attempted to develop methods for improving government and tried to prevent rulers from committing wars of aggression.

He and his students put Mohist ideas into practical usage by mediating in political disagreements and assisting states that had been attacked to defend themselves under siege. Mohists also criticized Confucianists for impractical activities such as elaborate rituals, large court orchestras and long periods of mourning. They further believed, in contrast to the Confucian emphasis on social position through birthright, that all qualified men should be appointed to government positions without regard for their class. See also CONFUCIANISM; LEGALIST SCHOOL OF THOUGHT; QIN SHI HUANGDI, EMPEROR.

MRCT (MINISTRY OF RADIO, CINEMA AND TELEVISION) See BROADCASTING; FILM STUDIOS.

MU QI (Mu-ch'i; late 13th to mid-14th century A.D.)   One of the greatest Chinese masters of Chan (Zen) Buddhist monochrome ink painting. His real name was Faqiang (Fa-ch'iang), but he took the art name Mu Qi as his artistic identity. A native of Sichuan Province, he moved to Hangzhou, the beautiful capital city of the Southern Song dynasty (1127–1279) in Zhejiang Province. There he rebuilt the ruined monastery of Lui Tongsi alongside West Lake. Mu Qi died between 1335 and 1340. Few details are known about his career as a painter. He was trained in the style of painting taught by Xia Gui (Hsia Kuei) and Ma Yuan, known as the Ma-Xia (Ma-Hsia) School, which for many critics and connoisseurs represents the apex of Chinese landscape painting. This style also had a great influence on the development of landscape painting in Japan. Its qualities include mastery of brushwork, depth of feeling, poetic sadness, austerity, simplicity, and a sense of space created by painting the landscape in one corner of the canvas in order to suggest an unlimited perspective.

Mu Qi's greatest works took the Ma-Xia foundation to a new extreme, the Chan style of ink painting known as the "abbreviated brush." This technique does not depict subjects with careful detail but gives a spontaneous presentation of the subject with irregular brushwork. In this way he painted a great variety of subjects, including dragons, tigers, monkeys, birds, landscapes, trees, stones, and Buddhist and human figures. As was done with the paintings of Liang Kai (Liang K'ai; fl. early 13th century), another important Chan ink painter, many of Mu Qi's paintings have been taken to Japan, where he is known as Mokkei. There he has been much more appreciated than in China. *Guanyin, Monkeys, and Crane* is a famous set of three vertical scrolls by Mu Qi that hangs in Daitokuji, a prominent Zen Buddhist temple in Kyoto, Japan. In the center scroll is the White-Robed Guanyin (Kuanyin; Kannon in Japanese), the Buddhist goddess of mercy, seated in meditation. On one side is a crane in a bamboo grove; on the other, gibbons in a pine tree. *Six Persimmons*, perhaps the most highly regarded painting attributed to Mu Qi, is also in the Daitokuji collection. This simple portrayal of six persimmon fruits, in the Chan Buddhist view, is a more profound representation of the true Buddha nature than paintings of formal, idealized Buddha images. *Dragon and Tiger* and *Chestnuts* are owned by Daitokuji as well. Other paintings by Mu Qi, some of which are owned by Japanese museums, include *Bodhidharma* (the First Patriarch of Chan Buddhism; Daruma in Japanese), *Lao Tzu*, *Baba Bird on an Old Pine Tree*, *Kingfisher on a Dry Reed*, *Wagtail on a Lotus Leaf*, *Swallow on a Lotus Pond*, *Swallows and Willow*, *Wild Geese among Reeds*, *Peony*, *Sunrise*, *Sunset in a Fishing Village*, *Autumn Moon over Lake Dongting*, *Night Rain at Xiaoxiang*, and *Evening of Snow* from *Eight Views of Xiaoxiang*. See also BODHIDHARMA; CHAN SECT OF BUDDHISM; GUANYIN; INK PAINTING; LIANG KAI; WEST LAKE.

MU US DESERT See ORDOS PLATEAU.

MUKDEN See SHENYANG.

MULAM See DAI.

MUNICIPALITIES See BEIJING; PROVINCES, AUTONOMOUS REGIONS AND MUNICIPALITIES; SHANGHAI; TIANJIN.

MUSEUM OF CHINESE HISTORY See TIANANMEN SQUARE.

MUSEUM OF CHINESE IN THE AMERICAS See OVERSEAS CHINESE.

MUSEUM OF THE CHINESE REVOLUTION See TIANANMEN SQUARE.

MUSHROOMS (*mogu* or *mo-ku*) Commonly called funguses or fungi; a food consumed as a vegetable, usually dark brown in color, that grows in wild forests and is also cultivated. The consumption of mushrooms was recorded in Chinese historical documents more than 3,000 years ago. In 1996 China produced 600,000 tons of mushrooms, making it the world's leading producer. China has 60 percent of the world's mushroom varieties. Today mushrooms are frequently sold dried and have to be soaked in water to soften before cooking. They are most often chopped into pieces and added to dishes with other sliced vegetables and meats that are stir-fried in a wok. About 350 species of edible fungus are found in China. The shiitake (*donggu* or *tung ku* in Chinese) grows wild in the southern provinces of Jiangxi, Fujian, Guangdong and Guangxi and is cultivated in more than 10 provinces. It is a central ingredient in vegetarian and many other dishes. In the autumn, numerous oyster mushrooms, yellow oyster mushrooms, tricholoma matsutake and other varieties grow abundantly in Manchuria (northeastern China). The first two grow on broadleaf tree stumps and are eaten fresh or dried. The third grows on the roots of pine trees in the Changbai Mountain Range in Manchuria, as well as in the pine forests of Sichuan, Yunnan and Guizhou provinces. Other northeastern favorites include honey fungus (*Armillaria mellea*) and *Lepista sodida*.

The Kalgan mushroom grows on the grasslands of Inner Mongolia, and dried Kalgans command a very high price. Stone-shaped puffball mushrooms grow in Xinjiang in northwestern China. The round yellow monkey head mushroom (*Hericium erinaceus*) grows high on tree trunks in Henan and southern Shanxi provinces. The wild paddy mushroom grows in Guangdong, Fujian and Hunan and has become one of the most widely grown edible fungi in the world. The boletus grows in the forests of Sichuan, Yunnan and Guizhou, and different species of boletus grow in northern pine forests. Dried boletus, called pine mushroom, is popular among urban Chinese. The termite mushroom grows near termite nests in dark hillside forests in southwestern provinces and is delicious cooked in chicken or meat broth. The chanterelle and russula grow in Yunnan and Guizhou. The giant russula is found in Fujian forests.

The white or silver fungus and wood ear (*muer* or *mu erh*; also known as cloud ears, *yuner* or *yun erh*) fungus have long been consumed by the Chinese as food and as medicines and are cultivated in large quantities. The Chinese cultivated wood ear more than 1,300 years ago. The best wood ear is grown in Hubei, Shaanxi, Henan, Guangxi and Heilongjiang provinces. White fungus is extensively cultivated in Fujian and other southern provinces and on the island of Taiwan. The Chinese consider the white fungus a medicinal food that aids the lungs, stomach and immune system, and they also enjoy its delicate flavor and somewhat crunchy texture. A sweet soup containing white fungus is served at the end of a banquet for the New Year Festival and on other festive occasions. See also COOKING, CHINESE; SEASONINGS FOR FOOD; VEGETABLES AND VEGETARIAN DISHES.

MUSIC AND DANCE, CEREMONIAL (yue or yueh)

Elegant ritual movements, sounds and rhythms performed for ceremonies in the classical Chinese tradition of the early Zhou dynasty (1100–256 B.C.). These music-dance compositions were called "Proper Music" in the school of thought founded by Confucius (551–479 B.C.), which became the orthodox philosophy of the Chinese imperial government. Confucius placed a great emphasis on propriety (li), which was expressed in solemn rituals that created order and harmony among all human beings and between humans and Heaven. He maintained that music is the highest art form because it expresses human feelings and virtues. One of the Five Classics, supposedly edited by Confucius, is the *Book of Songs* (*Shijing* or *Shih-ching*), an anthology of poems that were folk songs or songs performed at banquets or at ritual sacrifices made by members of the Chinese aristocracy. The philosopher Xunzi (Hsun Tzu; c. 298–238 B.C.) developed the Confucian concept of ceremonial music into a complex theory on the nature and purpose of music. He argued that a ruler could cultivate his subjects to be virtuous by having them listen to the proper music, and that this would bring happiness to his kingdom. According to Xunzi, the tones that produce music are based upon the responses of the human heart to the external things that it encounters. Hence a well-governed kingdom will create music that is peaceful and filled with joy. In Chinese classical texts, the written character for music, yue, can also be read as le, meaning joy.

The instruments in a Chinese classical orchestra include drums, *sheng* (mouth organs), *xun* (ocarinas), flutes, *qin* (zithers), bronze bells of different sizes suspended on frames and struck to produce musical tones, and sounding stones or stone chimes (lithophones). Chinese archaeologists have excavated a number of ancient bronze and stone instruments, and musicians have recreated the musical compositions played on them. According to Chinese mythology, the cabinet in the bureaucracy of legendary emperor Shun included a minister of music (Kui or K'uei) whose duties were to teach music to the eldest sons of the aristocratic families so as to instill wisdom and harmony in them. The imperial bureaucracy during the Han dynasty (206 B.C.– A.D.220) included a Bureau of Music (*yuefu*), which was especially favored by Han Wudi (Wu-ti; r. 141–87 B.C.), the most powerful Han emperor. During his reign the Bureau of Music collected songs, trained orchestras and choirs, and performed music and dance at official ceremonies such as banquets and religious rituals. Court ceremonies were greatly reduced after Wudi's death, and in 7 B.C. the Bureau of Music was abolished. See also BELLS AND CHIMES; BOOK OF SONGS; CONFUCIANISM; CONFUCIUS; DRUMS; FLUTES; HEAVEN; IMPERIAL BUREAUCRACY; PROPRIETY; SHENG; XUNZI.

MUSICAL INSTRUMENTS

See BELLS AND CHIMES; DRUMS; ERHU; FLUTES AND WIND INSTRUMENTS; KUNQU; OPERA, BEIJING; OPERA, GUANGZHOU; PIPA; QIN; SANXIAN; SHENG; STORYTELLING; STRING INSTRUMENTS; YANGKO.

MUSLIMS

In China, members of ethnic minority groups who practice the religion known as Islam (meaning "peace" or "surrender to God"; *yisilan jiao* in Chinese), and who number more than 35 million. Some of the largest Muslim (Moslem) groups in China include the Uighur, Kazakh and Kirghiz minorities. There is also a minority group, the Hui, who speak the Chinese language and are physically the same as the Han Chinese, the majority ethnic group in China, but who practice the Muslim religion. According to the 1990 census, there are more than 7 million Uighurs, 1 million Kazakhs, 140,000 Kirghiz and 8 million Hui in China. Muslims believe that there is one God, Allah, and they practice dietary restrictions, such as not eating pork, which is a mainstay of the Han Chinese diet. Muslims worship Allah in mosques led by clergy called mullahs or imams. The Muslim religion was founded by Mohammed, who was born in Arabia around A.D. 570 and died in 632. His teachings included the concepts of monotheism and universal brotherhood. Within a century after his death, Arab Muslims had extended their empire from Persia (modern Iran) to Spain.

The Muslim religion was brought to China peacefully during the Tang dynasty (618–907) by traders from Persia (modern Iran) and the Middle East, many of whom settled in Chang'an (modern Xi'an in Shaanxi Province), the capital city, and in the major southern Chinese trading ports of Guangzhou and Quangzhou. During the Tang, trading of Chinese luxury goods such as silk, porcelain and tea was very active along the overland and maritime Silk Road. Many of the Hui are descendants of Arab soldiers who came to China in the eighth century to help the Chinese defeat the An Lushan Rebellion against the Tang dynasty. The Hui reside in Xinjiang and Ningxia-Hui autonomous regions, and in the western provinces of Gansu and Qinghai. The Muslim religion was also brought by Turkish-speaking nomadic groups from central Asia, such as the Uighurs and Kazakhs, who invaded northwestern and western China and settled in Xinjiang. Muslims also reside in Yunnan Province in southwestern China. There are mosques in many Chinese cities, and a large mosque in Xi'an (ancient Chang'an) has recently been restored.

During the Song (960–1279) and Yuan (1279–1368) dynasties, tens of thousands of Muslims settled in the Quanzhou region near the port of Xiamen in Fujian Province on the southeastern Chinese coast. Quanzhou has been designated by UNESCO as one of the key areas for investigating the maritime Silk Road and as the center for all relevant research in China. During the Song and Yuan, Quanzhou was an active religious center, with Islam the most important of the foreign religions practiced there. An Arab with the surname Ding settled in Quanzhou during the Yuan, and today more than 17,000 members of the Muslim Hui minority share the surname Ding and still inhabit the town of Chendai; about 13,000 more live elsewhere in China and more than 10,000 have migrated to Hong Kong (which reverted to China in 1997), Macao, Taiwan and other countries. All have preserved their Muslim religious customs, although they have been assimilated to the Han Chinese in other aspects of life.

The Uighurs, Kazakhs and Kirghiz inhabit politically and militarily sensitive regions of western China that border former Soviet republics that also have a majority of Uighurs, Kazakhs, Kirghiz and other Muslims. Muslims in Xinjiang rebelled against the Qing dynasty (1644–1911) from 1868 to 1873 to protest discrimination against Muslims in Shaanxi and Gansu; and in Yunnan Province from 1856 to 1873 in a conflict between local Muslims and Han Chinese known as the Panthay Rebellion. To retain the loyalty of the Muslims, the Communist government of the People's Republic of China (PRC) has given them some measure of autonomous rule in Xinjiang and Ningxia Hui. It has also exempted them from the campaign to limit Chinese families to one child each, so the Muslim populations have been growing at a faster rate than the Han majority. See also CHANG'AN; GUANGZHOU; HAN; HUI; KAZAKH; KIRGHIZ; MINORITIES, NATIONAL; NINGXIA HUI AUTONOMOUS REGION; ONE-CHILD FAMILY CAMPAIGN; POPULATION OF CHINA; SILK ROAD; UIGHUR; XIAMEN; XINJIANG-UIGHUR AUTONOMOUS REGION.

MUSTARD SEED GARDEN MANUAL OF PAINTING (*Jieziyuanhuazhuan* or *Chieh-tzu yuan hua chuan*) A manual published in 1679 by Li Liweng that provides instruction on how to paint in the traditional Chinese style. Li printed a series of color prints in his small garden in Nanjing, which he said was "as large as a grain of mustard seed," and so he named his collection of prints "the painting manual of the mustard seed garden." Around 1685 an expanded collection of the prints was published in Suzhou. This edition was brought to Europe in 1692 by the German doctor E. Kaempfer, who had traveled to Japan with a Dutch embassy, and most of the prints from Kaempfer's set were finally acquired by the British Museum in London. The Hamburg Museum in Germany owns the sheet on arts and crafts. *The Mustard Seed Garden Manual of Painting* has been published in numerous Chinese editions and has been translated into English. It remains the most important source on techniques for all students of traditional Chinese painting. The manual is divided into books on particular subjects that are commonly found in Chinese landscapes and other paintings, such as trees, rocks, bamboo, orchids, butterflies, boats, human figures and so forth.

MYTHOLOGY See CHANG E; EIGHT IMMORTALS; ISLANDS OF THE BLESSED; JADE EMPEROR; KITCHEN GOD; MAZIPO; MONKEY; NE ZHA; PANGU; SHEN NONG; SHUN, EMPEROR; XIWANGMU; YAO, EMPEROR; YELLOW EMPEROR; YU, EMPEROR.

N

NAMCO, LAKE See KAILAS, MOUNT; TIBET.

NAMES, CHINESE The Chinese address a person with the surname or family name (*xingming* or *hsing-ming*) first, followed by the given name, the reverse of Western custom; this method indicates the dominance of the family in Chinese society. An ancient text credits the legendary emperor Fuxi with establishing a system of 100 family names, and the Chinese use the phrase "the hundred family names" to mean "the people" in the general sense of "everyone." Ancient China was matriarchal and the mother's family name served as the family name, but by the 12th century B.C., the father's family name was used. Names were taken from various sources, such as the name of the reigning dynasty, a city or village, a district, feudal territory, scenic rest stop, historical person, title, government official, clan or trade. Today, according to a Chinese post office handbook, there are 5,730 different Chinese family names, the most common of which include Wang, Zhao, Liu, Chen, Li, Zhang, Huang and He. A family name usually comprises one written character, although there may be two, such as Ao-yang. People with the same family name belong to the same clan and belong to the same ancestral temple, where they gather for social occasions and hold ceremonies to honor their ancestors. For important ceremonies and celebrations, the Chinese write their family names on lanterns, which are placed at the main entrances of their homes. Since the family or clan name symbolizes one's ancestral home, it is carved on a tombstone to indicate the return to one's source.

The constitution enacted by the Communist government of the People's Republic of China (PRC) gives women and men equal rights. Article II of the Marriage Law of 1950 states that husband and wife have the right to use either his or her own family name, "so a woman can keep her own name after marriage." Article 16 of the revised Marriage Law of 1980 states that "children may adopt either their father's or their mother's family name."

A person's given name usually has two characters. Some names are used for males, some for females, and others can be used for both. The Chinese believe that the given name assigned to a new baby will represent his or her character and destiny, so they create the name very carefully to have a positive connotation and embody the parents' aspirations for the child. The name must also sound pleasant when pronounced, and the written characters must be easy to write and have an aesthetic appeal. Some examples of auspicious given names are Jiazhu, "Pillar of the Family"; Weiguo, "To Have Authority over the Country"; and Wende, "Respectable Scholar."

Families of the upper and literati (scholar) classes may have generation names, which originated when the ancestor of a clan assigned a character to each generation succeeding him. Usually these characters were taken from a family poem, and each person in the same generation of a family has the same word character from the poem as the first character in his or her name. The next character in the poem is then used for the first character in the names of all members of the next generation. As this practice is continued through the generations, knowledge of the family poem will enable one to recognize which generation each person in the family belongs to. The second character in a family member's given name will distinguish that person from the other members of the same generation. See also FAMILY SYSTEM; FUXI; LANGUAGE, CHINESE; LITERATI; MARRIAGE LAW OF 1950; WRITING SYSTEM, CHINESE.

NAMRI SONGZAN (NAMRI SONGTSEN), KING See TIBET.

NAN MOUNTAIN RANGES (Nanshan) The general name for a large complex of mountain ranges that run northwest to southeast in northwestern China. The mountains have an average height of 13,000 to 16,500 feet, although many peaks are higher than 20,000 feet and are covered with snow and glaciers. Keke Lake lies in a large depression between some of the mountains. The Nan Mountain Range lies between the Zaidamu Basin in Qinghai Province and the plateau of northwestern Gansu Province, and it marks the southeastern boundary of Xinjiang Uighur Autonomous

Region. The western region of the Nan Mountains is extremely dry and large areas are completely barren or have sparse vegetation. The eastern region receives more rainfall and is covered with a variety of vegetation, such as spruce forests and alpine meadows. The Nan Mountain Range is also sparsely populated, with large areas completely uninhabited. The people who do live in the mountains are seminomadic herders belonging to the Tibetan and Mongol ethnic groups. See also GANSU PROVINCE; MONGOL; QINGHAI PROVINCE; TIBETAN; XINJIANG-UIGHUR AUTONOMOUS REGION.

NANCHANG The capital city of Jiangxi Province in southeastern China, with a population of about 1.6 million and a subtropical climate. Nanchang's history dates back 2,000 years. The city is located on the east bank of the Gan River, which runs north–south through Jiangxi. It has always been a junction for river traffic, a market for agricultural products, and an administrative center. Rice has been a fertile crop in this area since the eighth century. Nanchang was also a storage and distribution center for kaolin pottery and porcelain from the kilns at Jingdezhen, about 125 miles away, which was for centuries the main site of Chinese porcelain production.

Nanchang also has political and historical importance as the site of the Nanchang Uprising on August 1, 1927. This event has traditionally marked the beginning of the Chinese Communist People's Liberation Army (PLA). The uprising was a successful rebellion led by Communist Party leaders Zhu De and Zhou Enlai against the Nationalist Party (Kuomintang) leader Chiang Kai-shek's troops. Chiang Kai-shek had effectively suppressed Communist power earlier that year. Zhu De and Zhou Enlai were attempting to recapture power by controlling Nanchang, where the Kuomintang army was stationed. They were not successful, but some of the retreating Communist army, led by Zhu De, joined Mao Zedong's army. The combined forces became known as the First Workers' and Peasants' Army, or Red Army. August 1, 1927, is considered the official date for the founding of the Red Army, which became known as the People's Liberation Army in 1946, and the date is celebrated each year in the People's Republic of China.

Many of Nanchang's important sites commemorate the Nanchang Uprising, including the August 1st Park, the Museum of the Revolution, the Memorial Pagoda of the Nanchang Uprising, the Martyrs Memorial and the Former Stronghold of the Nanchang Uprising (now a museum). The Historical Museum of Jiangxi Province houses exhibits on ancient China. Other sites include the Sa'an Si Temple, the Youminsi Tongzhong Bronze Bell dating from A.D. 967, the Peach Orchard (a favorite place for picnics) and Qingyunpu Temple. After 1949 Nanchang also underwent industrial development. Major products today include tractors, diesel engines, textiles, chemicals and processed foods. See also CIVIL WAR BETWEEN COMMUNISTS AND NATIONALISTS; JIANGXI PROVINCE; JINGDEZHEN; NANCHANG UPRISING; PEOPLE'S LIBERATION ARMY; ZHOU ENLAI; ZHU DE.

NANCHAO, KINGDOM OF See AN LUSHAN REBELLION; BAI; TALAS, BATTLE OF; TANG DYNASTY; YUNNAN PROVINCE.

NANHAI See SOUTH CHINA SEA.

NANJING Formerly known as Nanking; a city with a population of about 4.5 million that is the capital of Jiangsu Province in eastern China. Nanjing is one of China's four ancient capital cities and has also been the modern capital of the country. It has a strategic location on the southern bank of the Yangzi River (Changjiang), one of China's two longest rivers and major transportation routes, and lies 150 miles west of Shanghai, China's largest city and port. The Qinhuai River flows through Nanjing Proper, and Zijinshan (Purple Mountain) lies to the east of the city. Nanjing has many universities, notably Nanjing University and Nanjing Normal University, and has become an important industrial center for the automobile, electronics and machine tool industries.

Nanjing lies between two fertile plains, the Jiangnan Plain to the south and the Huai River (Huaihe) Plain to the north. The Yangzi River valley was a cradle of Chinese civilization. About 200 sites dating from the Shang (1750–1040 B.C.) and Zhou (1100–256 B.C.) dynasties have been excavated in the Nanjing area. In the Spring and Autumn (772–481 B.C.) and Warring States Periods (403–221 B.C.), Nanjing was considered "a home of emperors and kings." The city is also called Jinling (Golden Ridge) because in 333 B.C., after the king of the Chu conquered the kingdom of Yue, he ordered men to bury gold on a hillside at Nanjing to propitiate the spirits and keep him in power. In the third century A.D., Sun Quan, the king of Wu, one of the three contending Kingdoms during the Three Kingdoms Period (220–80) moved his capital south from Wuchang to Nanjing and renamed it Stone City. The court of the Eastern Jin dynasty (317–420) settled there after fleeing from northern invaders. Four brief dynasties in succession made it their capital, the Song (420–79), the Qi (479–502), the Liang (502–57) and the Chen (557–89). It was also the capital of the Southern Tang (923–36), one of the 10 states during the Five Dynasties Period (907–60). Many wealthy and powerful northern Chinese families moved to the Nanjing region and several industries developed there, including papermaking, porcelain, copper smelting and silk brocade weaving.

In 1368 Zhu Yuanzhang (Chu Yuan-chang), the leader of a peasant rebellion, overthrew the Yuan dynasty and founded the Ming dynasty (1368–1644); he is known as Emperor Hongwu (Hung-wu). He chose Yingtian Prefecture, located on the Yangzi and the Grand Canal, as his capital, which he renamed Nanjing (Southern Capital). He made Beijing to the north, the former Yuan capital, his secondary capital. Hongwu brought thousands of workmen to build, over a period of 21 years, what became the world's largest city at the time. They built a 26-mile-long city wall 46 feet wide at its base, 13 to 26 feet thick on top and 39 feet high. This is the longest city wall ever built, and most of it still stands today, including Jubao Gate, now known as Zhonghua Gate, which has remained intact through numerous wars. Zhudi (Chu Ti), known as Ming emperor Yongle (Yung-lo), moved the capital to Beijing in 1420 and Nanjing suffered a decline in influence. When the Ming fell to the Manchus who established the Qing dynasty (1644–1911) at Beijing, several pretenders to the Ming throne attempted to continue the dynasty in Nanjing and other southern locations but were eventually defeated. However, during the Qing, Nanjing remained a major commercial and cultural center and enjoyed two centuries of peace.

In the 19th century, Great Britain fought two Opium Wars to open China to foreign trade. In 1842 a British naval squadron of 80 ships sailed up the Yangzi, took the city of Zhenjiang, and went as far as Nanjing, where they threatened to attack the city. The Qing government capitulated and signed the Treaty of Nanjing, the first of the so-called "unequal treaties" that it was forced to sign with foreign powers, opening Chinese cities to foreign traders and residents as treaty ports. Among other things, the treaty ceded the island of Hong Kong to Great Britain. Nanjing was declared a treaty port in 1858 but not opened to foreigners until 1899. A powerful anti-Qing and anti-foreign movement known as the Taiping Rebellion (1850–64) developed in southern China, and the Taiping army moved as far north as Nanjing, where it made its capital. The British and other foreign powers allied themselves with the Qing against the Taipings and besieged and attacked Nanjing for seven months in 1864. They finally took the city and killed the Taipings, ending the rebellion.

The Chinese people overthrew the Qing in the Revolution of 1911, and in 1912 Dr. Sun Yat-sen was inaugurated as the provisional president of the new Republic of China (ROC) in Nanjing. Sun soon had to yield the presidency to Yuan Shikai, who kept the capital in Beijing. That same year Sun founded the Nationalist Party (Kuomintang; KMT) and Yuan sent troops to take Nanjing and destroy the KMT. Sun fled to Japan and then went to Guangzhou (Canton) in southern China, where he established a military government and built up a movement to defeat the warlords in northern China. He died of cancer in 1925 and was later buried in a magnificent mausoleum in Nanjing, which today is a major tourist site. Chiang Kai-shek became the leader of the KMT and cooperated with the recently founded Chinese Communist Party (CCP), but in 1927 he turned against the CCP and ordered the massacre of Communists in several cities, including Nanjing. From 1928 to 1937 Nanjing served as the KMT capital.

In 1937 Japanese troops, which had invaded Manchuria (northeastern China) in 1931 and had continued into China Proper, captured Nanjing and committed a terrible slaughter of the residents, known as the "Rape of Nanjing." Chinese estimates place the number of victims at about 300,000. The KMT and CCP formed a united front to fight the Japanese, which became known as China's War of Resistance against Japan (1937–45; World War II). After Japan was defeated in 1945, the KMT government, which had fled west to Sichuan Province, returned to Nanjing in 1946. In 1946–47 the KMT and CCP held peace talks, but the two parties resumed their civil war. When Nanjing fell to the CCP in April 1949 the city was in ruins. Chiang Kai-shek and his KMT followers fled to Taiwan Island, where they established the provisional government of the ROC, and CCP chairman Mao Zedong (Mao Tse-tung) proclaimed the founding of the People's Republic of China (PRC) in Beijing on October 1, 1949.

Nanjing has been rebuilt, and large-scale campaigns to plant trees and flowers have earned it the nickname Jiali, "Beautiful City." There are many public parks and gardens, and Xuanwu and Mochou lakes are popular recreation areas in the center of the city's two most famous parks. The dou-ble-decker Yangzi River bridge, which opened in 1968, is one of the longest bridges in China and a great feat of Chinese Communist engineering. The road for automobiles on top is 14,760 feet long and the railway line below is 21,976 feet long. Before this bridge opened, there was no direct railroad connection between Beijing and Shanghai, China's largest city and port.

In the center of Nanjing is the Drum Tower, built in 1382, and the Bell Tower, which houses a huge bronze bell cast in 1388. Chaotian Palace, built during the Ming as a school for children of the imperial court, was reconstructed in 1866. The Taiping Museum, built next to a garden belonging to the first Ming emperor, displays artifacts and copies of documents, maps and books relating to the Taiping Rebellion and the siege of Nanjing in 1864. The Memorial of the Nanjing Massacre displays pictures of the Japanese massacre of Chinese residents during the Rape of Nanjing in 1937, and it has a viewing hall built over a grave where victims were buried. The Nanjing Museum houses exhibits on the region from prehistoric times to the PRC.

The Temple of Confucius in Fuzimiao in the southern part of Nanjing was a center of Confucian learning for more than 1,500 years. The buildings seen today are reconstructions. Nearby are the Imperial Examination Halls where Confucian-trained scholars studied for the examinations to gain positions in the imperial bureaucracy. Fuzimiao is now the main entertainment center in Nanjing, crowded with restaurants, souvenir shops and other attractions.

The tomb of Hongwu, the first Ming emperor, lies on the southern slope of Zijinshan. Also located there is the Sun Yat-sen Mausoleum, a pilgrimage site for the Chinese because Communists and Nationalists alike honor Sun as the founder of modern China. A stone stairway more than one thousand feet long and 230 feet wide leads to Sun's crypt at the top. Also on Zijinshan are the Beamless Hall, a temple built entirely of bricks in 1381; Pine Wind Pavilion, originally dedicated to Guanyin (Kuan Yin), the Buddhist Goddess of Mercy; and the Linggu Buddhist Temple and Pagoda. Zhongshan Mountain outside Nanjing is especially beautiful in early spring when thousands of plum trees blossom. Qianliang Mountain is heavily forested. The Stone City built on it by the kingdom of Wu during the Three Kingdoms Period is open to the public as a natural park. See also CIVIL WAR BETWEEN COMMUNISTS AND NATIONALISTS; CONFUCIANISM; HONGWU, EMPEROR; IMPERIAL EXAMINATION SYSTEM; JIANGSU PROVINCE; NANJING, TREATY OF; NATIONALIST PARTY; OPIUM WAR; REPUBLIC OF CHINA; SUN YAT-SEN; TAIPING REBELLION; TEN KINGDOMS PERIOD; THREE KINGDOMS PERIOD; TREATY PORTS; UNEQUAL TREATIES; WAR OF RESISTANCE AGAINST JAPAN; YANGZI RIVER; NAMES OF INDIVIDUAL DYNASTIES.

NANJING, TREATY OF (1842) The treaty between Great Britain and the Manchu Qing dynasty (1644–1911) that ended the Opium War (1839–42), which the British had started in order to force the Qing to open China to Western-style trading. Britain defeated the Qing and forced them to sign the treaty. This treaty, along with supplementary treaties signed in 1843, gave Britain privileges and rights in China, many of which had originally been requested by Lord (George) Macartney when he led the first British mission to China in 1793.

Prior to the Opium War, China had maintained a tribute system under which foreign countries wanting to engage in trade sent missions to the Chinese capital to submit to the sovereignty of the Chinese emperor. When Britain and other Western nations began demanding permission to trade with China without submitting to the tribute system, China regulated their trade by forcing foreign traders to conduct their business through officially designated Chinese merchants, the Cohong (or "Hong") in the southern port city of Guangzhou (Canton). This was known as the Canton System to Regulate Foreign Trade.

The British wanted to force the Qing to open up the country to Western-style trade. Yet the Chinese people had no interest in purchasing British-made goods in sufficient amounts to make up the deficit created by British purchases of silk, porcelain, tea and other Chinese luxury goods. The only thing the British could get the Chinese to buy in large quantities was opium, an illegal drug, with which they soon began flooding the country. The opium trade drained China of large quantities of silver, used as payment for the drug. The Qing's several attempts to halt the British opium trade resulted in the Opium War.

The Treaty of Nanjing, which contained 13 articles, and supplementary treaties included the following provisions favorable to Britain:

1. An indemnity to be paid to Britain by China of 21 million Mexican silver dollars as compensation for war expenses, opium confiscated by the Chinese government, and debts owed by the Cohong merchants in Guangzhou to British merchants. Britain had already received six million dollars as ransom for the opium that had been confiscated by Lin Zexu, the Qing commissioner.
2. The opening of the five so-called treaty ports of Guangzhou, Xiamen, Fuzhou, Ningbo and Shanghai for foreign residence and trade.
3. The abolition of the Cohong and the establishment of a moderate fixed tariff on imports and exports, which China could not alter without British consent.
4. Britain awarded most-favored-nation treatment by China, meaning that Britain would automatically be given any privilege that China might later extend to any other nation.
5. The appointment of foreign consuls at treaty ports who would be able to communicate directly with officials of equal rank in the Qing government. This included the principle of extraterritoriality in civil and criminal cases. British consuls would have jurisdiction over British subjects accused of crimes or involved in disputes with Chinese citizens. British citizens would be tried, by the consul, under British law, while Chinese citizens would be tried under the Chinese laws of China. This principle, exempting the British from Chinese laws, violated China's judicial powers.
7. The cession of Hong Kong, a barren island near Guangzhou, to Britain in perpetuity. Under the Conventions of Beijing in 1860, China ceded Kowloon, on the mainland across from Hong Kong, to Britain as well. In 1898 Britain acquired a 99-year lease over the New Territories adjoining Kowloon. Hong Kong, Kowloon and the New Territories reverted to China in 1997.

Neither the Chinese nor the British fully accepted the items of the Treaty of Nanjing, and the Qing government was caught in an impossible position between the demands made by foreign powers and the strong anti-foreign feelings of the Chinese people. The Chinese also hated the Qing, who were Manchus, an ethnic group from Manchuria (modern northeastern China) that had invaded China and overthrown the Chinese Ming dynasty (1368–1644). Foreign demands greatly damaged the prestige of the Qing. The British and French fought another war against China, known as the Arrow War (Second Opium War, 1856–60), and secured further concessions at Nanjing in 1858 and in the Beijing Convention of 1860. The United States and other foreign powers pressured China for similar concessions. The treaties China signed with foreign powers giving them favorable rights and privileges in China became known by the Chinese as "unequal treaties." See also ARROW WAR; BEIJING, CONVENTIONS OF (1860); CANTON SYSTEM TO REGULATE FOREIGN TRADE; GUANGZHOU; HONG KONG; KOWLOON; MACARTNEY, LORD GEORGE; NEW TERRITORIES; OPIUM WAR; QING DYNASTY; SINO-BRITISH JOINT DECLARATION ON THE QUESTION OF HONG KONG; TREATY PORTS; TRIBUTE SYSTEM; UNEQUAL TREATIES.

NANKING See NANJING.

NANLING MOUNTAIN RANGE A series of granite mountains that run west to east for 870 miles in a wide belt across southern China. The mountains are fairly low, with few peaks higher than 3,300 feet. The Nanling range forms the divide and watershed between Hunan and Jiangsu provinces and the Yangzi River basin, which lie north of the range, and Guangxi-Zhuang Autonomous Region, Guangdong Province and the West River valley, which lie to the south. The Nanling range also protects southern China from the cold north winds that blow across the Asian continent; they give the region a semi-tropical climate, which allows farmers to grow crops all year round.

Until the 12th century, the Nanling Mountains also formed a cultural barrier. The area south of the Nanling range, called Lingwai ("Beyond the Ranges") or Lingnan ("South of the Ranges"), was relatively undeveloped and separated from the highly developed area north of the Nanling. The passes through the Nanling Mountains were crucial for communication and transport between northern and southern China, especially after northern nomadic invaders forced the Song dynasty (960–1279) court to flee south in the 12th century. During the Qin dynasty (221–206 B.C.), which unified China, the Xingan Canal was built through the passes in northeastern Guangxi-Zhuang to connect the Yangzi and Pearl rivers. The Nanling Mountain Range has been an important source of minerals. Hundreds of years ago, silver was taken from the mountains, and now tin, copper, iron, zinc, antimony, tungsten and wolfram are mined. There are also small coal deposits in the central area of the mountains in Guangdong Province. See also PEARL RIVER; YANGZI RIVER; INDIVIDUAL PROVINCES.

NANNING The capital city of the Guangxi-Zhuang Autonomous Region in southwestern China, with a population of about 2.5 million. This region is the home of the

Zhuang people, China's largest national minority, who are Muslim and number more than 15 million. Eleven other national minorities live in the region, such as the Miao, Yao and Shi, so a National Minorities Institute was established in Nanning in 1952.

Nanning lies 310 miles west of Guangzhou (Canton) on the Yong River near the meeting point of the Yu and Zuo rivers. It is China's southernmost city, founded during the Yuan dynasty (1279–1368) as an agricultural market center on trade routes south to Indochina and west to the Himalaya Mountains. Rice, sugarcane and subtropical fruits are the main crops. The city has also become industrialized after railways began to connect the south and west of China after 1949. Major industries today include sugar refining, food processing, printing, tanning of leather, and mining. The area leads China in producing tung oil, which is used in varnishes and paints. Since Nanning is close to the Vietnam border, it was a strategic military staging and supply center during the Vietnam conflict in the 1960s and 1970s, and also during China's confrontation with Vietnam in 1979. The Museum of the Guangxi Zhuang Autonomous Region displays exhibits on the history of the area. The Dragon Boat Festival, held on the fifth day of the fifth lunar month (around June in the Western calendar), attracts thousands of people each year. Teams of boats decorated with dragon heads compete in lively races. See also DRAGON BOAT FESTIVAL; GUANGXI ZHUANG AUTONOMOUS REGION; MIAO; MINORITIES, NATIONAL; YAO; ZHUANG.

NANSEI ISLANDS (Nansei Shoto) See RYUKYU ISLANDS.

NANSHA ISLANDS See SOUTH CHINA SEA; SPRATLY ISLANDS.

NANYUE, KINGDOM OF See LI RIVER AND LING CANAL.

NANZHAO, KINGDOM OF See AN LUSHAN REBELLION; BAI; TALAS, BATTLE OF; TANG DYNASTY; YUNNAN PROVINCE.

NAPIER, LORD See BRITISH EAST INDIA COMPANY; QING DYNASTY.

NATIONAL DAY A public holiday that celebrates the founding of the People's Republic of China on October 1, 1949. On this day the Chinese Communist People's Liberation Army led by Mao Zedong, which had defeated the Nationalist Party (Kuomintang; KMT) led by Chiang Kai-shek in a bitterly fought civil war, triumphantly entered the capital city of Beijing. Mao addressed the enormous crowd that met him in Tiananmen Square and proclaimed a new government in China. It was supposed to be a united front composed of various political parties and other groups who had fought together against the KMT, but the Chinese Communist Party (CCP) became the real governing power. The Communists call their victory in 1949 "National Liberation." During the two-day celebration for National Day, held on October 1 and 2 of each year, the Chinese people cook festive dishes, dress in their best clothes, and crowd city squares and parks that are decorated with colored lights and banners. Cities hold massive parades and rallies in public squares and sports stadiums, where thousands of people cre-

ate "placard art" by holding up different colored cards on cue to create pictures and sayings in Chinese calligraphy. See also CHINESE COMMUNIST PARTY; CIVIL WAR BETWEEN COMMUNISTS AND NATIONALISTS; LIBERATION, NATIONAL; MAO ZEDONG; PEOPLE'S LIBERATION ARMY; PEOPLE'S REPUBLIC OF CHINA.

NATIONAL DEFENSE SCIENCE, TECHNOLOGY AND INDUSTRY COMMISSION (NDSTIC) See CENTRAL MILITARY COMMISSION AND MINISTRY OF NATIONAL DEFENSE.

NATIONAL LIBERATION See LIBERATION, NATIONAL.

NATIONAL LIBRARY OF CHINA China's only national library, located in the capital city of Beijing, which upon its opening in 1987 was the largest library in Asia and the second-largest library in the world after the U.S. Library of Congress. The National Library succeeded the Qing Dynasty Imperial Library, which was opened to the public in 1912 after the Revolution of 1911 established the Republic of China. It was renamed the National Library of Beijing in 1928. After the founding of the Communist People's Republic of China (PRC) in 1949, the library was moved to the west of Beihai Park and renamed the National Library of China. The recently constructed library, located near Purple Bamboo Park (Zizhuyuan), covers 18 acres and comprises a complex of 13 buildings. The H-shaped building housing the book stacks has 22 stories, three of them underground, and can store 19 million volumes. The library includes more than 30 reading and reference rooms, a catalog hall with an automated information and retrieval system, a microfilm-reading room, five audio-visual rooms, an exhibition room, and a lecture hall with 1,200 seats and facilities for simultaneous translation and closed-circuit television. By 1995 all of the library's books and documents were handled automatically. The old library building has been made a branch of the National Library. The National Library of China has exchange relations with more than 1,600 libraries and academic institutions in more than 100 countries and regions. See also BEIJING.

NATIONAL PALACE MUSEUM (Taipei) A museum in Taipei, the capital of the Republic of China (ROC) on Taiwan Island, that houses the world's largest collection of Chinese art. Chinese emperors on the mainland began collecting these objects, some of them dating back more than 3,000 years, in the 10th century. Emperors of the Qing dynasty (1644–1911) consolidated the collection. When the Revolution of 1911 ended the dynasty, the treasures remained in the hands of the last Qing emperor, Xuantong (Hsuan-t'ung, r. 1909–12; later known as Henry Puyi), who continued to reside in the Forbidden City (imperial palace) in Beijing. He was evicted from the Forbidden City in 1924, and in 1925 the collection was opened to the public as the Peking (Beijing) Palace Museum. After the Japanese army invaded Manchuria in 1931 and prepared to invade China Proper, the Chinese Nationalists (Kuomintang; KMT), led by Chiang Kai-shek, packed 15,000 crates of treasures from the Palace Museum. They intended to take them to Nanjing, the Nationalist capital. The treasures were divided into five groups, transported on different routes around China by trucks and riverboats and even stored in caves. The collection was later taken to Chongqing, the Nationalist capital in Sichuan Province during China's War of Resistance against Japan (1937–45; World War II). After Japan surrendered in 1945, the collection was again moved when the Nationalist capital returned to Nanjing. The following year the Chinese Communists and Nationalists began fighting a civil war.

In 1949, when the Chinese Communists defeated the Nationalists and founded the People's Republic of China (PRC), Chiang Kai-shek and his Nationalist supporters fled to Taiwan, where they established the provisional government of the ROC. Many of the imperial art treasures were finally brought to Taiwan in 4,000 crates; thousands of other crates had to be left in mainland China, including about 700 crates that had to be abandoned to make room on a ship for Chinese Nationalists escaping the Communists. The objects that did arrive in Taiwan all survived without damage and were the very best pieces from the imperial collection. The last ones finally arrived in the ROC in the early 1960s. The Chinese Communists have accused the Nationalists of stealing these objects, but the Nationalists claim that they have preserved them from destruction by the Communists, especially during the Cultural Revolution (1966–76).

Some pieces belonging to the collection were sent to the United States in 1961 for an exhibition called "Chinese Art Treasures." The National Palace Museum was built in Taipei in 1965 to house the imperial collection. It holds more than 700,000 art objects in enormous, hidden underground vaults. Only about one percent of the collection can be shown at any one time. Some objects are on permanent display, but collections of paintings, calligraphy, porcelain, jade, imperial robes, bronzeware and rare books are rotated regularly. In 1996 the National Palace Museum sent a sample of its treasures for a temporary exhibit at the Metropolitan Museum of Art in New York City and museums in other American cities, "Splendors of Imperial China." See also BRONZEWARE; CALLIGRAPHY; CIVIL WAR BETWEEN COMMUNISTS AND NATIONALISTS; FIGURE PAINTING; FORBIDDEN CITY; INK PAINTING; JADE; LANDSCAPE PAINTING; PORCELAIN; PUYI, HENRY; QING DYNASTY; TAIPEI; TAIWAN; WAR OF RESISTANCE AGAINST JAPAN.

NATIONAL PARTY CONGRESS The highest political body of the Chinese Communist Party (CCP), which founded the People's Republic of China (PRC) in 1949. The National Party Congress (not to be confused with the National People's Congress, China's highest legislative body) is convened every five years. Local CCP members at the county level elect county party congresses, which elect the delegates to the National Party Congress. The National Party Congress in turn elects the members of the Central Committee of the CCP, which has 30 component departments and functions as the highest political body between meetings of the National Party Congress. The Central Committee elects members of the Politburo (Political Bureau) and the Politburo's Standing Committee; the latter is the inner circle of power in the PRC. The CCP constitution adopted at the Seventh National Party Congress in 1945, when Mao Zedong (Mao Tse-tung) assumed total control of the party as chairman of the Central Committee, the Politburo and the Secretariat, was still in force in 1949. The CCP held its Eighth

National Party Congress in 1956, at which a new party constitution was promulgated. The Ninth National Party Congress convened in 1969 and issued a third constitution. The 10th congress in 1973 issued a fourth constitution and the 11th in 1977 issued a fifth constitution. The 12th congress was held in 1982, with 1,545 delegates, and the 13th in 1987.

The National Party Congress reviews reports on CCP activities since the previous session, revises the party constitution, ratifies the party's program for a specified period of time, and elects the Central Committee. The congress does not have the power to generate legislative bills or to provide checks and balances for the various party and government departments, and serves mainly to approve policies already drawn up by party leaders. But it does provide a forum at the national level for cadres (CCP officials) from all across China who are rising in the party hierarchy.

When Communist leaders began introducing reforms to rebuild the country after the Cultural Revolution (1966–76), at the 12th National Party Congress in September 1982 they institutionalized the process of removing unwanted leaders from power. Deng Xiaoping (Teng Hsiao-p'ing), who consolidated his power as a reformer at this congress, created and became head of the party's new central body, the Central Advisory Commission, consisting of party members who had served the CCP for at least 40 years. These elderly heroes of the Communist revolution were made consultants to the party and the government, which gave them some authority but kept them out of real positions of power. The new constitution passed by the 12th National Party Congress formalized the pragmatic approach to economic development and modernization promoted by Deng and Zhao Ziyang (Chao Tzu-yang), a major architect of China's economic reform. The congress denied that class struggle, a central precept of Communist thought, was important in modern China; restructured the CCP organization to remove the Maoist "personality cult"; and abolished the position of party chairman and replaced it with that of general secretary, a less grandiose title, although the power of the position remained the same. The most recent party congress and the first since the death of party leader Deng Xiaoping was the 15th, held in September 1997. At the congress, Jiang Zemin was reconfirmed as president of the PRC; he emphasized the need for China to continue its economic development. See also CENTRAL COMMITTEE OF THE CHINESE COMMUNIST PARTY; CHINESE COMMUNIST PARTY; CONSTITUTION, STATE, OF 1954; DENG XIAOPING; GOVERNMENT ORGANIZATION; MAO ZEDONG; NATIONAL PEOPLE'S CONGRESS; POLITBURO; ZHAO ZIYANG.

NATIONAL PEASANT MOVEMENT INSTITUTE See MAO ZEDONG; WUHAN.

NATIONAL PEOPLE'S CONGRESS (NPC) The highest legislative body in the People's Republic of China (PRC), which was founded by the Chinese Communist Party (PRC) in 1949. Although the NPC saw an increase in its role during the 1980s, it has always played a consultative role and serves as a symbol of the Communist government's legitimacy; political decisions have always been handled by the CCP through its National Party Congress, the highest political body of the CCP. The National People's Congress (NPC) has several main functions: to amend the PRC state constitution and enact laws; to supervise the enforcement of the constitution and the laws; to elect the president and vice president of the PRC: to decide on the choice of the premier of the State Council nominated by the president; to elect the highest government officials; to elect the chairman and other members of the Central Military Commission; to elect the president of the Supreme People's Court and the procurator-general of the Supreme People's Procuratorate; to approve the national economic plan and budget; to decide on matters of war and peace; and to approve the establishment of special administrative regions and their governing systems. In addition, the NPC has the power to remove the most important government leaders from office, including the president and vice president and members of the State Council and the state Central Military Commission.

The NPC has 3,000 members who meet once a year and serve five-year terms. People's congresses at the provincial level and the People's Liberation Army (PLA) elect delegates to the NPC. The NPC functions through the Standing Committee, a permanent body whose members, numbering fewer than 200, it elects. The Standing Committee presides over NPC sessions, for which it determines the agenda, routing of legislation and nominations for offices. It also handles many other functions, such as conducting the election of NPC delegates; interpreting the state constitution and laws; supervising the executive and judicial bodies and the state Central Military Commission; deciding on the appointment and removal of State Council members based on the premier's recommendations; approving and removing senior judicial and diplomatic officials; ruling on the ratification and abrogation of treaties; and deciding on the proclamation of a state of war when the NPC is not in session. The NPC also has six permanent committees, one each for ethnic minorities, law, finance, foreign affairs, and overseas Chinese; and one for education, science, culture and health.

In 1954 the NPC replaced the Chinese People's Political Consultative Conference (CPPCC), the original legislative and representative body of the PRC. The first session of the first NPC was held in September 1954, after local elections for deputies had been held in August. On September 20, 1954, the NPC promulgated the first formal state constitution of the PRC. The constitution gave the Standing Committee of the NPC the power to appoint and dismiss judicial personnel and to enact legal codes. The first NPC also formally elected Mao Zedong (Mao Tse-tung) chairman (or president) of the PRC; elected Liu Shaoqi (Liu Shao-ch'i) chairman of the Standing Committee of the NPC; and named Zhou Enlai (Chou En-lai) premier of the new State Council, the main government organization under the NPC. The NPC took over the functions of the Chinese People's Political Consultative Conference (CPPCC), which since 1949 had been the legislative body and representative organ of the PRC government and became an essentially advisory body. People's representative congresses down to the village level were established under the NPC. Members of people's congresses were elected at the local level, and each congress in turn voted to send a specified number of its members to the congress at the next level above it. Delegates to the NPC include not only members of the dominant Han ethnic

group, who comprise about 97 percent of China's population, but also representatives from the 55 officially designated national minority ethnic groups. At the 1985 NPC, minority deputies comprised 13.5 percent of all representatives. Policy comes down through the lower levels from the NPC, but is influenced by the opinions of delegates at lower-level congresses. Real power remains vested in the leaders of the CCP, notably the Central Committee and the Politburo and its Standing Committee.

In 1959 Mao Zedong had to take responsibility for the failures of the Great Leap Forward, and he stepped down from his position as chairman of the PRC. The NPC elected Liu Shaoqi as Mao's successor, although Mao remained chairman of the CCP. At the fourth NPC in 1975, Zhou Enlai outlined the so-called Four Modernizations, a program for modernizing the four sectors of agriculture, industry, national defense, and science and technology. The fifth NPC in 1978, held when China was trying to rebuild after the Cultural Revolution (1966–76) and the deaths in 1976 of China's three great leaders, Mao, Zhou and Zhu De (Chu Te), reflected the conflict between radicals headed by Hua Guofeng (Hua Kuo-feng) and moderate reformers led by Deng Xiaoping (Teng Hsiao-p'ing). In 1978 the new Chinese policy for rapid economic growth and foreign trade was solidified by the 10-year plan presented by Hua Guofeng at the fifth NPC. Many people who had been purged during the 1950s and the Cultural Revolution, especially those sympathetic to Deng's position, were rehabilitated. A new state constitution was adopted at the fifth NPC in 1978, with legal reforms that would prevent the radicals from returning to power and that would provide the legal structure under which China could be developed economically. The NPC also mandated the need for new criminal, procedural, civil and economic codes, and these were drawn up beginning in 1979. Deng consolidated his power at the 12th National Party Congress in September 1982 and the NPC in December 1982, where a new state constitution was adopted. See also CENTRAL COMMITTEE OF THE CHINESE COMMUNIST PARTY; CENTRAL MILITARY COMMISSION AND MINISTRY OF NATIONAL DEFENSE; CHINESE COMMUNIST PARTY; CHINESE PEOPLE'S POLITICAL CONSULTATIVE CONFERENCE; CONSTITUTION, STATE, OF 1954; DENG XIAOPING; FOUR MODERNIZATIONS; GOVERNMENT STRUCTURE; HUA GUOFENG; LEGAL SYSTEM; LIU SHAOQI; MAO ZEDONG; NATIONAL PARTY CONGRESS; PEOPLE'S REPUBLIC OF CHINA; POLITBURO; STATE COUNCIL; ZHOU ENLAI; ZHU DE.

NATIONALIST PARTY Also known as the Chinese Nationalist Party, and formally known as the National People's Party (Kuomintang; KMT); a political party founded in August 1912 by Dr. Sun Yat-sen (1866–1925), leader of the Chinese revolutionary movement known as the Revolution of 1911, which overthrew the Manchu Qing dynasty (1644–1911). The KMT was the successor to the Revolutionary Alliance (*Tongmenghui* or *T'ung-meng hui*), also known as the Revolutionary League or Alliance Society, which Sun had founded with Huang Xing (Huang Hsing) in Tokyo, Japan, in 1905 with the goal of overthrowing the Qing and establishing a modern Chinese republic. The Revolutionary Alliance was a coalition of several Chinese revolutionary groups whose members had fled to Japan or had gone there to study in Japanese universities. At that time there were thousands of Chinese students in Japan. Sun based his movement on what he termed the Three Principles of the People (*sanminzhuyi* or *san-min-chu-i*): nationalism, democracy, and people's livelihood." Sun also received a great deal of support from overseas Chinese communities in Southeast Asia, Hawaii, and North and South America, and he frequently traveled abroad to raise funds. In China, young military officers supported Sun's revolution as a way to advance their careers and to ensure that China became a strong, modern nation.

While Sun was in the United States, his followers, who had infiltrated Qing troops stationed in Wuchang (later known as Wuhan) in Hubei Province, decided to stage an uprising there on October 10, 1911, by attacking the governor-general's office. This date is still celebrated by the Republic of China (ROC) on Taiwan as Double Tenth Day, the beginning of the Chinese revolution. The success of the Wuchang Uprising encouraged revolutionaries in other Chinese cities and provinces, and by the end of November 1911, 15 of the 24 Chinese provinces were independent of the Qing. When the revolutionaries captured the major city of Nanjing, the first capital of the Ming dynasty (1368–1644), which the Qing had overthrown, the Qing sent Yuan Shikai (Yuan Shih-k'ai; 1859–1916) to suppress them. But he secretly negotiated with the revolutionaries to remove the Manchu Qing and establish a republican government, with the hope that he would become its president. The national assembly in Beijing, the Qing capital, elected Yuan Shikai prime minister on November 8, 1911.

Sun went to Britain and France to gain diplomatic and financial support for the new government he planned to establish. He then returned to China, and on January 1, 1912, the Revolutionary Alliance inaugurated Sun as the first president of the Provisional Government of the Chinese Republic, with its capital at Nanjing. Li Yuanhong (Li Yuanhung; 1864–1928) was named vice president. Yuan demanded that Sun hand over the presidency of the Republic of China to him so that the country could be united under a government based in Beijing. Sun agreed to do so if Yuan could persuade the Qing emperor to abdicate, which he did on February 12, 1912. Yuan was sworn in as provisional president of the Republic of China on March 10, 1912, in Beijing.

Sun formed the National People's Party (KMT) in August 1912 by merging his Revolutionary Alliance with several other revolutionary groups in hopes of gaining enough seats in the new national assembly to control Yuan Shikai. Song Jiaoren (Sung Chiao-jen; 1882–1913) was made head of the KMT, while Sun became active in China's economic reconstruction, especially the building of railroads. Elections for the new bicameral parliament were held in February 1913 and the KMT won a major victory. However, Yuan increased his opposition to the KMT and to parliamentary government, and the KMT divided into factions. Yuan had Song assassinated in March 1913, dismissed government officials not loyal to him, and split up the KMT. Seven southern Chinese provinces rebelled against Yuan but he suppressed the rebellion, and Sun and other revolutionary leaders had to flee to Japan. Yuan became a virtual dictator and formally dissolved the KMT on January 10, 1914, and had its members removed from the national assembly and provincial

assemblies. While in Japan, Sun planned to overthrow Yuan Shikai, but Yuan brought about his own downfall by attempting to establish a new dynasty with himself as emperor. He died in 1916, and Sun returned to China and settled in Shanghai, China's largest port and trading city. China became divided up among a number of warlords, during a time known as the Warlord Period (1916–28). The government of China was controlled by whatever warlord controlled Beijing.

Sun briefly became head of a military government in Guangzhou in southern China but was forced to return to Shanghai. After World War I, it was publicly revealed that the Beijing government had made a secret agreement with Japan to award all of Germany's former concessions in China to Japan. The Chinese people were outraged, and Chinese students led a massive demonstration known as the May Fourth Movement of 1919, which has inspired all modern Chinese revolutionaries. Sun did not play a leading role in the movement, but he drew upon the support of the students and made contacts with most of the Chinese warlords. In October 1919 Sun and his followers reestablished the KMT to oppose the government in Beijing.

In November 1920 Sun returned to Guangzhou, where he was elected president of the ROC by the extraordinary parliament there. But the warlord of Guangzhou soon drove Sun out of the city. He was able to return there once again in February 1923. Mikhail Borodin (1884–1952), a Soviet adviser, joined Sun in Guangzhou and helped him reorganize the KMT, with Sun's Three Principles of the People as the foundation of the party's doctrine. Many Soviet advisers had come to China to help the Chinese Communist Party (CCP), which had been founded in Shanghai in 1921, and they also supported the KMT. The CCP and KMT cooperated in the early 1920s with the common goal of overcoming the warlords.

In January 1924 the reorganized KMT held its first National Congress in Guangzhou, and adopted the constitution that Borodin had drawn up. The party also adopted the so-called "Three New Policies," which included an alliance with the U.S.S.R., support for workers' and peasants' movements, and collaboration with the CCP, although this last policy was controversial and opposed by some of Sun's colleagues. In May 1924 the KMT and CCP established the Whampoa (Huangpu) Military Academy near Guangzhou to train military officers to lead a Northern Expedition against the warlords. Chiang Kai-shek (Jiang Jieshi; 1887–1975), one of Sun's lieutenants, was made head of the academy. In 1924 Sun completed his *Outline of National Reconstruction*, which predicted that China's reconstruction would undergo three stages, from direct military government to leadership by the KMT and finally to a democratic form of government.

Some of the soldiers in the armies loyal to Sun in Guangzhou treated the merchants of the city badly, and the merchants organized a terribly destructive armed revolt against Sun, which lost him many supporters. In late 1924, following a coup in Beijing, Sun was invited there to help reorganize the government; however, Sun was very sick with cancer and died in Beijing on March 12, 1925.

After Sun died, other KMT leaders contended to become his successor. In January 1926 the KMT held its second National Congress in Guangzhou, and Chiang Kai-shek was elected a member of the KMT Central Executive Committee. Three months later he became the most powerful leader in Guangzhou by taking action against the Communists and arresting many Russian advisers. In May the Central Executive Committee of the revolutionary government in Guangzhou approved Chiang's proposal to halt Communist influence in the KMT.

In June 1926 Chiang was named commander-in-chief of the National Revolutionary Army, and in July he launched the Northern Expedition to remove the warlords and unify China. By March 1927 his forces had regained Chinese territory as far north as Shanghai and Nanjing on the Yangzi River (Changjiang). The KMT now established two centers of power. The left-wing faction, led by Wang Jingwei (Wang Ching-wei; 1883–1944), formed a government in Wuhan. The right-wing faction, led by Chiang, established a national capital at Nanjing. The warlord government still functioned in Beijing and was recognized by foreign countries as the legitimate government of China. In April 1927 Chiang turned against the Communists and sent his troops into Shanghai to arrest and execute them. Thousands were killed but some escaped to join Communist forces at the Soviet base in the Jinggang Mountain Range on the border of Jiangxi Province in south-central China. The Communists staged the Nanchang Uprising on August 1, 1927, which marked the beginning of the civil war between the CCP and the KMT.

The Central Committee of the KMT had not authorized Chiang's anti-Communist campaign in Shanghai, and the KMT government based in Wuhan removed him as commander-in-chief. Chiang responded by setting up his own government in Nanjing, but party members forced him to resign, and he went into exile in Japan. However, left-wing KMT members began to agree with Chiang that the Chinese Communists were being controlled by Moscow and that they wanted to eliminate the KMT, and Wang Jingwei and his faction began to purge Communists from the KMT. The left- and right-wing factions of the KMT reunited, abolished the KMT government in Nanjing and moved the Wuhan government there, officially naming it the National Government of China.

In 1928 Chiang returned to China from Japan. He became KMT commander-in-chief once again and completed the second stage of the Northern Expedition. His troops took Beijing in June 1928, symbolically unifying all of China south of the Great Wall. On October 10, 1928, Chiang became chairman of a new Chinese Nationalist government and established his capital at Nanjing. The KMT refused to allow any other political party to have a role in the Nationalist government. From then until 1949, Chiang commanded the majority vote in the standing committee of the Central Executive Committee, the most powerful body in the KMT.

In March 1929 the KMT held its third National Congress in Nanjing, despite protest by dissident members of the KMT, including Wang Jingwei. The dissidents held an "enlarged Congress of the KMT" in Beijing in August 1930 and established an alternative Nationalist government led by Yen Hsi-shan), with Wang Jingwei as new leader of the KMT. But this fell apart by November 1930. In February 1931, Chiang placed Hu Han-min, an important KMT official, under house arrest in Nanjing, and other KMT leaders called for Chiang's impeachment. In May an opposition KMT government was formed in Guangzhou.

In September 1931, Japan used the so-called Manchurian Incident as a pretext to invade Manchuria, which created a national emergency in China. But Chiang was more concerned with eliminating the Chinese Communists than fighting the Japanese invaders, and in 1930 he had launched the first of five annual major campaigns against Communist forces in south-central China. In 1932 the Japanese established a puppet state in Manchuria called Manchukuo (Manzhouguo or Man-chou-kuo in Chinese) and used it as their base to invade China Proper and the rest of China. The KMT and CCP continued fighting their civil war, and in 1934–35 the Communists escaped to the northwest on their epic Long March and established their headquarters at Yan'an in Shaanxi Province. In December 1936, while Chiang Kai-shek was at Xi'an in Shaanxi, KMT and CCP military leaders kidnapped him to persuade him to form a KMT-CCP united front against the Japanese, and he agreed to do so. In 1937 the Japanese took the North China Plain, Shanghai and Nanjing, where they committed atrocities against hundreds of thousands of Chinese, known as the "Rape of Nanjing." The Chinese began fighting their War of Resistance against Japan (1937–45; World War II).

After Nanjing fell, Chiang moved the Nationalist capital to Hankou on the Yangzi, but the Japanese took this on October 25, 1938, shortly after they took Guangzhou. Chiang moved his Nationalist government to Chongqing in Sichuan, a province in southwestern China protected by high mountain ranges. In December 1938 the Japanese persuaded Wang Jingwei to desert the Nationalists and join their side. He asserted that continued Chinese resistance to the Japanese was suicidal, and he attempted to prevent the Japanese from treating the Chinese too harshly in the areas they occupied. World War II broke out in Europe in September 1939, which brought China allies such as Great Britain. The United States entered the war after Japan bombed the U.S. naval fleet at Pearl Harbor on December 7, 1941. General Joseph Stillwell, USA, became Chiang Kai-shek's chief-of-staff, although he disagreed with Chiang's policies and wanted to arm all Chinese factions that opposed the Japanese, including the CCP. The KMT-CCP united front had begun breaking down in early 1941 when Nationalist troops defeated the Communist New Fourth Army in the lower Yangzi River valley, and the two sides looked forward to resuming their civil war.

Japan surrendered on August 14, 1945, and American diplomats tried to negotiate a KMT-CCP government to rule all of China, although the U.S. government still supported the Nationalists. Nothing came of these negotiations, and the United States continued to give huge loans to the Nationalists. Full-scale civil war erupted on June 26, 1946, with a Nationalist offensive against areas held by the Communists in Hubei and Henan provinces. They CCP had gained much support in China, especially since the KMT Nationalist government was marked by rampant corruption and inflation. By the end of 1947, the Americans saw that the Nationalists had no chance of winning the war and withdrew their support for Chiang Kai-shek. In 1949 the Communists took Beijing, Nanjing, Shanghai, Guangzhou and Chongqing. On October 1, 1949, Communist leader Mao Zedong (Mao Tsetung; 1893–1976) proclaimed the founding of the People's

Republic of China (PRC) in Beijing. In spring 1949 Chiang Kai-shek began moving Nationalist troops to Taiwan Island, and in December he fled to Taiwan. More than two million Nationalists also moved to Taiwan, where the KMT established its provisional government, which it still called the Republic of China (ROC) and claimed to be the legitimate government of all of China.

Chiang Kai-shek resumed the ROC presidency on March 1, 1950, and held it until his death in 1975. After 1949, Great Britain and the U.S.S.R. recognized the PRC, but after the Korean War broke out in 1950, the United States and many other countries accepted the ROC on Taiwan as the legitimate government of China. However, in the 1970s the United States reversed its policy, and on January 1, 1979, it transferred diplomatic recognition from the ROC to the PRC, although it has maintained close economic ties with the ROC. Chiang's son, Ching-kuo (Jiang Jingguo; 1910–88), succeeded him as president and led the ROC's economic development and progress toward democratic reform. Chiang Ching-kuo was succeeded by his chosen vice president, Lee Teng-hui (1923–   ), the current president of the ROC, who was born on Taiwan. The ROC held open presidential elections in March 1996, but Lee won a major victory and the KMT remains the dominant political power. The KMT maintains that it seeks reunification of the ROC with the PRC, but many people in Taiwan prefer that the ROC become independent.

In the PRC, the CCP has allowed eight so-called Democratic Parties to continue functioning on a small scale. One of these parties is the Revolutionary Committee of the Chinese Kuomintang, which was founded in 1948 by dissident members of the KMT. The PRC regards Taiwan as a renegade province and claims that it seeks reunification. Prior to the 1996 elections, the PRC harassed the ROC by holding military exercises in the Strait of Taiwan off the southeastern Chinese coast. See also BEIJING; BORODIN, MIKHAIL; CHIANG CHING-KUO; CHIANG KAI-SHEK; CHINESE COMMUNIST PARTY; CHONGQING; CIVIL WAR BETWEEN COMMUNISTS AND NATIONALISTS; DOUBLE TENTH DAY; GUANGZHOU; LEE TENG-HUI; LONG MARCH; MANCHU; MANCHUKUO; MANCHURIA; MANCHURIAN INCIDENT; MARCO POLO BRIDGE INCIDENT; MAY FOURTH MOVEMENT OF 1919; NANCHANG UPRISING; NANJING; NORTHERN EXPEDITION; PUYI, HENRY; QING DYNASTY; REPUBLIC OF CHINA; REVOLUTION OF 1911; REVOLUTIONARY ALLIANCE; RUSSO-JAPANESE WAR OF 1904–5; SHANGHAI; SINO-JAPANESE WAR OF 1894–95; STILWELL, JOSEPH; SUN YAT-SEN; TAIWAN; THREE PRINCIPLES OF THE PEOPLE; UNITED NATIONS; WAR OF RESISTANCE AGAINST JAPAN; WARLORD PERIOD; WHAMPOA MILITARY ACADEMY; WORLD WAR I; WUCHANG UPRISING; YUAN SHIKAI; ZHANG XUELIANG.

NATIONALITIES CULTURAL PALACE (Fuchengmennei Dajie)   A cultural center built in Beijing for China's 55 national minority groups. The Han people, or ethnic Chinese, comprise about 94 percent of China's population, but the national minorities inhabit nearly 60 percent of all Chinese territory. The palace is located just west of Tiananmen Square and was constructed in 1959 on the 10th anniversary of the founding of the People's Republic of China. The white building is trimmed in green with a turquoise glazed-tile roof and is 13 stories high. It contains a cultural center,

a museum with exhibition halls, 44 hotel rooms on 6 floors, and a library with hundreds of thousands of books and magazines in the minority languages, as well as rare old documents such as village histories and religious scriptures. A restaurant serves dishes eaten by the minorities, and a gift shop sells beautiful minority textiles, clothing and craft objects that are particular to each of China's various cultures. The East Wing houses an auditorium with seating for 1,000 people, with ultrasonic simultaneous translation equipment for seven minority languages. Concerts and other performances are frequently held there. The West Wing contains a dance hall, club, indoor sports facilities, dining room and Muslim kitchen (since many of the national minorities are Muslim). See also MINORITIES, NATIONAL; MUSLIMS.

NATURAL DISASTERS   Floods, droughts, famines and earthquakes, which have frequently caused terrible suffering for large numbers of people in China, especially the peasant farmers who have always comprised the majority of the population. The Chinese often interpreted natural disasters as signs that the ruling dynasty had lost the Mandate of Heaven (*Tianming* or *T'ien-ming*), which legitimized the reign of an emperor in the Confucian system, and that the dynasty deserved to be overthrown. Peasant rebellions commonly broke out in regions where the people had become impoverished and suffered famines from natural disasters. Many secret societies based on the beliefs of Daoism and Buddhism led rebellions, some of which overthrew dynasties and established new ones. Before the modern Republic of China (ROC) was founded in 1912, Chinese imperial dynasties wrote dynastic histories over a period of 2,117 years in which were recorded 1,621 serious floods and 1,392 serious droughts. These averaged out to 1.42 disasters each year.

Projects to control flooding and provide irrigation for growing crops have been the most crucial public works in China. According to Chinese legend, Emperor Yu (third millennium B.C.) spent years constructing water-control projects, such as reservoirs, irrigation channels and drainage works that ended floods and irrigated the fields. Many historical emperors continued these works and also built canals for the transport of grain and granaries to store food for the peasants in times of famine. The earliest recorded project was the Peony Dam at Shouxian in modern Anhui Province, built in the early sixth century B.C. Qin Shi Huangdi, the first emperor, who unified China under the Qin dynasty (221–206 B.C.), constructed such works as the Zhengguo Canals, which took water from the Jing River to irrigate the area north of the capital city of Chang'an (modern Xi'an in Shaanxi Province). The two emperors of the Sui dynasty (581–618) built the Grand Canal, which formed a major transportation route between southern and northern China.

The longest and most important rivers in China are the Yellow River (Huanghe), which cuts across the North China Plain and was the cradle of Chinese civilization; and the Yangzi River (Changjiang), the longest river in China and the third-longest river in the world, which divides northern and southern China. The Yellow River and its tributaries carry enormous quantities of silt, a yellow earth known as loess that is blown in from the deserts to the north and northwest and falls in very deep but fertile deposits, known as the Loess Plateau. Silt deposits in Chinese rivers cause them to frequently overflow their banks and sometimes even change course; hence the Yellow River is called "China's Sorrow." Heavy rains in the summer can cause it to overflow its banks, which have been built up in eastern China to protect against floods. In some areas the Yellow River flows on a bed that is 12 feet higher than the countryside. In the 2,000 years before 1949 the lower section of the Yellow River underwent 26 major changes of course and broke through its dikes more than 1,500 times. The final stretch of the river swung back and forth so frequently that it often created a flood area of 250,000 square miles, causing terrible disasters. The Yellow River formerly emptied into the Yellow Sea in southern Shandong Province, but it changed its course in 1898, submerging much of the Shandong plain east of the city of Ji'nan, and now empties into the Bo Hai Gulf in northern Shandong.

Northern China is very dry and depends on the Yellow River and its tributaries for irrigation of crops, especially millet, wheat, sorghum and other grains. The small amount of rain falls mostly during the three summer months, and the winter climate is harsh and freezes the ground for nearly three months. Intense summer rains, which can last more than a week, may cause floods that carry away the crops. Farmers in northern China spend a lot of their time maintaining the dikes and river banks. Southern China has a semitropical climate and abundant rainfall, so it has not suffered as much from the extreme conditions that plague the north, although flooding of the Yangzi and other rivers can be a serious problem. The chief southern crop is rice, which is grown in wet paddy fields. Farmers can get two or even three crops a year. They have built an extensive system of narrow dikes, which also serve as paths for people to walk on and push wheelbarrows. The fields are irrigated by a complex network of canals and streams.

Because of the constant threat of famine, Chinese families taught their children to be frugal and to eat every grain of rice in their bowl. Because they also developed very efficient farming techniques and consumed a grain-based diet, they did not raise many grazing animals but instead grew grain and vegetables, which are more nutritious and provide more calories at less cost. When they did consume meat it was usually pork and poultry, which are also more economical and do not require grazing. Moreover, the Chinese practiced extensive fish farming in ponds and along the seacoast. These techniques commonly were not enough to prevent famine, which has been frequent even in the 20th century. In 1920, a famine killed 500,000 Chinese people; one in 1925 took 580,000 lives; and one in 1935 killed 3 million people.

Since the Chinese Communist Party (CCP) founded the People's Republic of China (PRC) in 1949, it has undertaken many projects to control flooding and conserve water. In 1950 the Yellow River experienced a large flood that affected more than 13 million people, the first major flood since the founding of the PRC. In the early 1950s, masses of Chinese people began harnessing the Yellow River by building more than 5,000 reservoirs on the river's mainstream and tributaries. Water detention gates were built at natural lakes, such as Hongze, and embankments were built or strengthened

along the river. The Northern Jiangsu Irrigation Trunk Canal was dug and the river course to the sea was dredged, making it capable of discharging 20,000 cubic meters of flood water per second. By 1991, more than 4,000 irrigation and drainage stations had been erected along the Yellow River and 800 irrigated areas formed. Over the last four decades more than 35.6 billion cubic meters of earth and stone have been removed from the Yellow River. The Chinese government has planned to complete the eastern route, a project starting on the lower Yellow River to divert water from south to north, which will alleviate water shortages in Beijing, Tianjin and the North China Plain and revive the Beijing-Hangzhou Grand Canal.

In 1958 the CCP enacted the Great Leap Forward with the intent of building up heavy industries in China, but it turned out to be a catastrophe. In the three years after it began, a terrible drought, combined with CCP policies that refused to follow time-honored agricultural practices and that caused the erosion of thousands of acres of land, resulted in the worst disaster in the Chinese countryside since the famine of 1897. This famine killed as many as 20 to 40 million people, possibly more than died in China's War of Resistance against Japan (1937–45; World War II). In 1960 the government rescinded the Great Leap Forward, but China was not able to progress during the next decade because of the tumultuous Cultural Revolution (1966–76). In the late 1970s the government was able to begin rebuilding and modernizing the country and to encourage foreign trade and investment.

In the summer of 1981, the second-largest flood in 100 years occurred in the upper reaches of the Yangzi River (Changjiang). It washed away the homes of 1.1 million people, closed down 3,000 factories, mines and businesses, and affected more than 20 million people, especially in the southwestern Chinese province of Sichuan. In 1990 the Yangzi and Yellow rivers both suffered catastrophic floods caused by torrential rains. The provinces of Anhui, Jiangsu, Hunan, Hubei and Guizhou especially suffered great loss of property and farmland. Fortunately the death toll was only 2,300. The Chinese government is constructing the Three Gorges Water Conservancy Project—including the world's largest dam—on the upper Yangzi to control flooding, generate electricity and divert water for irrigating crops.

China has also experienced a great number of earthquakes, especially since it has many high mountain ranges with steep cliffs and deep river gorges. Zhang Heng (Cheng Heng), a royal astronomer in the second century A.D., invented the first seismograph. It registered an earthquake when a bronze ball dropped from a bronze vessel into the open mouth of one of the bronze toads that were arranged in a circle around the vessel. The direction of the toad indicated the direction from the capital city where the earthquake had occurred, so the emperor could send troops to help those who had suffered the disaster. In the 20th century, two of the three earthquakes registering over 8.5 on the Richter scale took place in China: the 8.6-magnitude quake in Haiyuan, in the Ningxia-Hui Autonomous Region in 1920, and the 8.6-magnitude quake in Zayu, Tibet, in 1950. Of the more than one million deaths attributed to earthquakes worldwide in the 20th century up to 1993, 550,000 occurred in China. Two severe earthquakes, the 8.6

earthquake in Haiyuan in 1920 and a 7.8-magnitude quake in Tangshan in July 1976, resulted in more than 200,000 deaths each. The latter was the worst earthquake since the founding of the PRC in 1949 and had not been predicted. It destroyed Tangshan, a mining and industrial center about 110 miles east of the capital city of Beijing, and killed 242,000 people and injured 164,000.

The Chinese government has attempted to develop measures for predicting earthquakes, and has successfully predicted some quakes, although this problem is not resolved. In 1971 the PRC government established the State Seismological Bureau and set up seismological organizations at the provincial level. More than 800 earthquake monitoring stations, as well as numerous mobile observation posts, have been set up in seismic regions. China leads the world in the amount of data on earthquakes it has collected and observations it has made. A new nationwide seismic zoning map was plotted in 1990.

Environmental pollution has recently become a very serious problem in China and is aggravating natural disasters. The Chinese economy doubled between 1980 and 1995 and is expected to continue growing at the rate of about 10 percent a year. With China's rapid industrialization, many companies are using up a great amount of water that would normally be used to irrigate crops, and they are polluting the air and rivers by discharging their untreated toxic wastes. Pesticides also contaminate the waterways. The air is so polluted in most Chinese cities that a large number of people now suffer from lung cancer and respiratory diseases. Factories use so much water that rivers are drying up and more than 300 cities have inadequate water supplies. The Yellow River has been reduced to a trickle in the northern provinces and has dried up as far as 60 miles inland from where it is supposed to empty into the Bo Hai Gulf. Groundwater levels are falling, causing land levels to sink, and near the coast, saltwater seeps into drinking water. The Ministry of Water Resources estimates that every day, China needs at least 400 million gallons of water more than it can provide.

The Chinese population, already numbering 1.2 billion, is still growing rapidly and is creating the need for more food. Economic prosperity is also allowing more Chinese to consume fewer vegetables and more meat, hence requiring higher grain output to feed livestock. Tourism, foreign trade and investment have resulted in large plots of land formerly cultivated for crops being converted to hotels, resorts and golf courses as well as factories. Problems are also caused by deforestation and desertification in the western provinces, meaning the loss of much arable land and more dust being blown into the air. For example, the advance of the Gobi, Tengger and Badain Jaran deserts has caused the loss of more than half of the arable land in Gansu Province in western China. Nomadic minority ethnic groups in the north and northwest who raise herds of animals such as sheep and goats have also overgrazed the land and contributed to environmental problems. See also AGRICULTURE; CLIMATE, CHINESE; GEOGRAPHY; GRAIN; GRAND CANAL; LOESS; GREAT LEAP FORWARD; MANDATE OF HEAVEN; NOMADS AND ANIMAL HUSBANDRY; NORTH CHINA PLAIN; PEASANTS AND PEASANT REBELLIONS; PEOPLE'S REPUBLIC OF CHINA; THREE GORGES WATER CONSERVANCY PROJECT; YANGZI RIVER; YELLOW RIVER; YU, EMPEROR; INDIVIDUAL PROVINCES AND REGIONS.

NAVIGATION See COMPASS; GRAND CANAL; JUNK; SHIPPING AND SHIPBUILDING; ZHENG HE.

NDSTIC (National Defense Science, Technology and Industry Commission) See CENTRAL MILITARY COMMISSION AND MINISTRY OF NATIONAL DEFENSE.

NE ZHA (No Cha) A popular deity depicted as a child with magical powers, holding a large magic ring and spear and perched on wheels of fire. Ne Zha was believed to perform many miracles with the help of the golden bracelet that was on his right wrist when he was born. This bracelet he could enlarge to use as a weapon to defend the emperor. According to Chinese mythology, Ne Zha was the son of the pagoda god Li Jing (Li Ching), the Prime Minister of Heaven. One popular story holds that one day while Ne Zha was bathing in the ocean, he accidentally killed the son of the Dragon King, Long Wang (Lung Wang). The Dragon King put the blame on Ne Zha's father, accusing him of not raising his son correctly, and made a report to the Jade Emperor who rules Heaven. Ne Zha committed suicide to show that he and not his father was responsible. His martial arts teacher made a statue of Ne Zha, which was supposedly entered by his spirit. Ne Zha was believed to answer every prayer addressed to the statue. See also DRAGON; JADE EMPEROR.

NEEDHAM, JOSEPH (1900–1995) A British scholar who was chief editor and author of the highly praised encyclopedic work, *Science and Civilisation in China;* full name Noel Joseph Terence Montgomery Needham. Needham was born in London, where his father was a doctor who gave him an interest in medicine and science. He studied biochemistry at Cambridge University, receiving a Ph.D. in 1925 and an Sc.D. in 1932. He joined the university faculty and served as president of Gonville and Caius College at Cambridge (1959–66), Master of the College (1966–76), then became a senior fellow there. In 1924 Needham married Dorothy Mary Moyle, also a biochemist at Cambridge, but their marriage later ended. In 1959 he married Lu Gwei-djen. Needham first became interested in China, and began learning the Chinese language as a hobby, when three young Chinese scientists went to Cambridge in 1936. During World War II, Needham was sent to China as head of the British Scientific Mission in China and counselor at the British Embassy in Chongqing, Sichuan Province, where the Chinese Nationalists had moved their capital. From 1942 to 1946 he served as an adviser to the Chinese National Resources Commission and military services, providing a link between the Allied powers and the scientists and technologists of China. The Chinese scientific community had been isolated from the outside world by Japanese forces. Needham traveled throughout China to deliver needed scientific and medical supplies and books. After the war he spent two years as director of the department of natural sciences of UNESCO, and then returned to his fellowship at Cambridge University.

In 1952 he was a member of the International Commission for the Investigation of Bacteriological Warfare in China and Korea. In 1958 he became chairman of the Ceylon (Sri Lanka) Government University Policy Commission. Needham held memberships in many professional societies and served as president of the International Union of the History of Sciences from 1972 to 1975. He was a foreign member of the National Academy of China and a fellow of the Royal Society in London. In 1980 he was named an honorary professor at the Institute of the History of Science, National Academy, Beijing, and in 1983 an honorary professor of the Chinese Academy of Social Science. Needham won numerous science awards and was given honorary doctoral degrees by many universities around the world. In 1984 he received the Science Award (first class) from the National Science Commission of China. He also was received into the Order of the Brilliant Star (third class with sash) in China. Needham wrote more than two dozen books and monographs, by himself or with other authors, as well as articles in many periodicals, in addition to the seven-volume *Science and Civilisation in China*. The first volume was published in 1954. More than 20 authors assisted Needham in writing the encyclopedia, which many reviewers have regarded as one of the most important works of the 20th century. It was abridged by Colin A. Ronan and published by Cambridge University Press as *The Shorter Science and Civilisation in China* (1978–86).

NEI MONGOL AUTONOMOUS REGION See INNER MONGOLIA AUTONOMOUS REGION.

NEIGE See GRAND SECRETARIAT.

NEI-KO See GRAND SECRETARIAT.

NEIMENGGU See INNER MONGOLIA AUTONOMOUS REGION.

NEO-CONFUCIANISM Known in Chinese as the Rational School (Lixue or Li-hsueh); a philosophical school based on the classical teachings of Confucius (551–479 B.C.) that developed during the Song dynasty (960–1279). Confucianism had been the orthodox imperial school of thought since the Han dynasty (206 B.C.–A.D. 220), but the native Chinese tradition of Daoism and the Buddhist religion, which had been introduced from India, had also gained influence in Chinese culture. Neo-Confucianist thinkers returned the thought of Confucius to its predominant place as the ideology of the imperial government, and, drawing upon Daoist and Buddhist ideas, they renewed Confucianism by emphasizing its spiritual aspects. The Confucian-educated literati (wenren or wen-jen) or scholar class, which staffed the imperial bureaucracy, attained its most widespread influence during the Song dynasty. The questions in the examinations by which officials were selected to staff the bureaucracy were based on the Five Classics of Confucianism (wujing or wu-ching). These ancient texts, which were supposedly compiled and edited by Confucius, are concerned with harmonious hierarchal relations in the family and society.

Confucius and Mencius (c. 372–289 B.C.), the second-most important Confucian thinker, did not address the abstract philosophical issues of metaphysics or cosmology. Song Confucian scholars began to do so by borrowing terms such as the Infinite and the Absolute from Daoism and Buddhism, as well as the concern of these traditions with self-transformation. Neo-Confucianists even adapted the practice

of meditation from Buddhism, calling it "quiet sitting" (jingzuo or ching-tso).

Neo-Confucianism originated in the second half of the 11th century with Zhou Donyi (Chou Tun-i) and the Cheng brothers, Cheng Yi (Ch'eng I) and Cheng Hao (Ch'eng Hao), who sought to describe the principle that is the foundation of everything that exists. Zhou called it the Great Ultimate. Neo-Confucian thinkers maintained that the human self and all things in the universe possess the Heavenly Principle (tianli or t'ien-li), which they contrasted with the material "life force" (qi or ch'i) of physical things, which is a Daoist concept. They were also concerned with the psychology of human desires and a person's ability to overcome evil in oneself through moral and spiritual cultivation.

Zhu Xi (Chu Hsi; 1130–1200), the greatest Neo-Confucian thinker, developed a synthesis of Neo-Confucian thought known as the Rationalist School or the School of Principle or Reason. Alongside this school developed the Confucian School of the Mind or Intuition, which reached its highest point during the Ming dynasty in the thought of Wang Yangming (1472–1529). Zhu Xi created more precise definitions for many important Chinese concepts, such as the Great Ultimate, human nature, the mind, qi and propriety (li). He based his thought on a principle central to the Great Learning, the "investigation of the nature of things and relationships." He maintained that man's mind is essentially one with the mind of the universe and is hence able to enter into and understand the principles of all created things. One should investigate one's self and then investigate the nature of things in the world. The goal is to become a sage (sheng) by actualizing one's potential as a human being in this life, known as humanity (ren or jen), a central principle of Confucianism.

Zhu Xi codified the Four Books of Confucianism (Sishu) as part of the Confucian canon and the foundation for the Chinese educational system. These books include the *Analects (Sayings) of Confucius (Lunyu)*, *Book of Mencius (Mengzi or Meng-tzu)*, *Doctrine of the Mean (Zhongyong or Chung-yung)* and *Great Learning (Daxue or Ta-hsueh)*. In 1313, the Yuan dynasty issued an official decree that knowledge of the Four Books of Confucianism and Zhu Xi's commentaries on them would from then on be mandatory for the imperial examination system. These texts remained the basis of the imperial examinations until the examination system was ended by the Qing dynasty in 1905. Chinese students first memorized the Four Books and then went on to study the Five Classics of Confucianism. During the Qing dynasty (1644–1911) there was a strong revival of interest in the ideas of Zhu Xi.

The second major branch of Neo-Confucianism is the School of the Mind or Intuition, known as the Lu-Wang School, after Lu Xiangshan (Lu Hsiang-shan; 1139–93) and his early 16th-century follower, Wang Yangming. Wang, who was influenced by the Chan (Zen) Sect of Buddhism, argued that man is born with the knowledge of what is good and that he can put this knowledge into action if he has a pure mind. A person can develop his intuitive knowledge through thinking and meditating, and this will guide his actions. For Wang, "Knowledge is the beginning of action and action is the completion of knowledge." Wang's philosophy influenced early 20th-century Chinese idealists and leaders of the movement to modernize China, including Kang Youwei (K'ang Yu-wei) and Liang Qichao (Liang Ch'i-ch'ao) in the 19th century and Dr. Sun Yat-sen (1866–1925), the founder of the modern Republic of China in 1912. It also influenced Japanese leaders of the movement to modernize Japan in the late 19th century. See also BUDDHISM; CHAN SECT OF BUDDHISM; CONFUCIANISM; CONFUCIUS; DAOISM; FIVE CLASSICS OF CONFUCIANISM; FOUR BOOKS OF CONFUCIANISM; QI; SONG DYNASTY; WANG YANGMING; ZHU XI.

NEOLITHIC PERIOD (c. 12,000–2000 B.C.) The period during which the early human inhabitants of China developed various practices that became typically Chinese, such as food cultivation, social organization, and the production of beautiful objects such as decorated pottery, jade and silk. Proto-humans had inhabited China for about half a million years. In 1927 archaeologists discovered bones dating back to about 500,000 B.C. in limestone caves at Zhoukoudian (Chou-k'ou-tien) in Hebei Province, near Beijing, which they called Peking Man. In 1963, they discovered fossil remains of a similar hominid, perhaps about 100,000 years older than Peking Man, at Lantian in Shaanxi Province in western China. Remains of Neanderthals (200,000–100,000 B.C.) and *Homo sapiens* (100,000–25,000 B.C.), the direct ancestor of modern humans, have been found at many sites throughout China. The fertile valley of the Yellow River (Huanghe) in the North China Plain was the region where prehistoric Chinese people began making cultural advances.

The earliest Neolithic cultures that archaeologists have discovered in Henan, Shaanxi and Gansu Provinces in the Yellow River valley date back to 6500–5000 B.C. Artifacts include unpainted pottery decorated with markings made by cords and incisions, and implements for agriculture and food preparation such as serrated knives, grinding stones, and mortars and pestles. People at the Peiligang site in Henan raised crops, stored grain in subterranean pits, spun hemp and silk and wove them into textiles, domesticated dogs and pigs, and buried the dead with goods associated with them.

Beginning in approximately 5000 B.C. the Neolithic period in China fell into two main cultures, the Yangshao and the Longshan. The earliest, the Yangshao, dates from the fifth to the third millennium B.C. and was the earliest settled culture in China. It was discovered in the 1920s at various sites along the valleys of the Wei River and the middle Yellow River (Huanghe) in northern China. Archaeologists have discovered hundreds of Yangshao sites in Henan, Shaanxi and Gansu. The Yangshao people were formerly hunter-gatherer tribes who settled into villages divided into areas for dwelling, making pottery by firing clay pieces in kilns, and burying the dead. The daily life of a Yangshao village can be seen in the village that archaeologists have excavated at Banpo, near modern Xi'an in Shaanxi Province. The Yangshao lived in semi-subterranean pounded-earth houses; domesticated pigs, dogs, sheep and cattle; fished with nets; raised silkworms to produce silk textiles; made red pottery with painted decorations; gathered fruits and nuts; and grew millet, which they ground into flour with mortars and pestles. They cultivated millet in the fertile plateaus along the rivers formed by deposits of loess, a yellow soil that blows into China from deserts to the north. Millet remains the principal grain consumed in northern China, in distinction

to rice, which has been cultivated throughout southern China since the Neolithic period. Artifacts excavated from Yangshao sites include spinning wheels; stone implements for growing and preparing food; stone, shell and bone ornaments; and animal bones used for divination. The Hongshan culture (c. 4500–2500 B.C.), related to the Yangshao, has been discovered at sites in the eastern region of Liaoning Province in Manchuria (northeastern China) and in neighboring regions. Beautiful carved and polished jade objects from the Hongshan are the earliest that have been discovered in China. Some Hongshan tombs contain a large number of valuable objects, indicating a strong differentiation between social classes.

The second main Neolithic culture, the Longshan, was centered in modern Shandong Province but extended along the whole length of China's eastern coast, with the earliest sites dating from around 3000 B.C. and the culture continuing until the start of the Bronze Age (2200–500 B.C.). Longshan culture is distinguished by its unique thin black or gray pottery, the first pieces of Chinese pottery to be formed on a potter's wheel. Longshan people also knew how to work jade, a very hard stone that has been highly valued throughout Chinese history for its durability, color and symbolic meaning. Longshan jade forms include the *bi* (*pi*), a flat disc with a hole in the center, and the *zong* (*tsung*), a cylindrical tube. Longshan people built earthen walls around their villages for protection; the Chinese people typically lived in walled villages until the modern era. Longshan graves contained more valuable goods than those of the Yangshao, which indicates that the differentiation among social classes had increased, as had the amount of property held by individual clans. There may also have been a shift from a matriarchal to a patriarchal form of social organization.

The Neolithic period was followed by the Xia dynasty, which has been dated about 2200–1750 B.C. but is considered semilegendary. The succeeding dynasty, the Shang (1750–1040 B.C.), is the first historic dynasty in China from which archaeologists have excavated artifacts. The Shang were highly skilled at making bronzeware. A type of large three-footed bowl made by Yangshao and Longshan potters served as the prototype for a type of bronze pot called a *ding* (*ting*) made for ritual purposes by the Shang. They also made bronze *bi* and *zong* based on Longshan jade forms. Another practice during the Shang that derived from the Longshan was divination by the use of oracle bones. The shoulder blades of animals were heated, and the resulting cracks were interpreted as answers to questions about the future. See also AGRICULTURE; BI; BRONZEWARE; DING; JADE; LOESS; LONGSHAN CULTURE; NORTH CHINA PLAIN; ORACLE BONES; PEKING MAN; SHANG DYNASTY; SILK; XIA DYNASTY; XI'AN; YANGSHAO CULTURE; YELLOW RIVER.

NEPAL See HIMALAYA MOUNTAIN RANGE; SINO-INDIAN BORDER DISPUTE; TIBET.

NEPHRITE See JADE.

NERCHINSK, TREATY OF (1689) A treaty between China and Russia that established the border between the two countries. This was the first treaty that China signed with a Western country. In the late 16th century, Russian fur trappers, traders and explorers had entered Siberia and begun moving toward the border of Manchuria, today the provinces of northeastern China. This region was the homeland of the Tungusic tribes, who had accepted as their sovereigns the Manchu people, who ruled China under the Qing dynasty (1644–1911). In 1644 the Russians entered the Amur River valley, and Emperor Kangxi (K'ang-hsi; r. 1661–1722) sent troops led by the Manchu Songgotu to oppose them. The power of the Chinese military convinced the Russians to sign the Treaty of Nerchinsk in 1689. The boundary was drawn across the mountain peaks that separate the Amur and Lena river valleys, to the Sea of Okhotsk, placing the Amur River completely within Chinese territory. The treaty also provided for some overland trade between the two countries. Roman Catholic Jesuit missionaries, who served as interpreters and foreign advisers to the Chinese emperors and imperial bureaucracy, helped write the six articles of the treaty. It was signed by Songgotu on behalf of Emperor Kangxi, and by Fedor Aleksevitch Govolin for Emperor Peter the Great. The Treaty of Nerchinsk was modified by the Treaty of Kiakhta (1728) and was superseded by the Treaties of Aigun (1858) and Peking (1860). During the 19th century the Qing Manchu rulers had become so weak that Russia and other Western powers gained many territorial concessions in China, including a number of treaty ports. These affected the border between Russia and China, which is still in dispute. See also AMUR RIVER; JESUITS; KANGXI (EMPEROR); MANCHU; TREATY PORTS.

NESTORIAN CHRISTIANITY

A Middle Eastern form of the Christian religion that a Syrian named Olopan (Alopen) introduced to China in 631 at Chang'an (modern Xi'an), the cosmopolitan capital of the Tang dynasty (618–907). Nestorianism, the first form of Christianity to be brought to China, took its name from Nestorius (fl. 428–436), the bishop of Constantinople (modern Istanbul), who was decreed heretical for teaching that Jesus Christ had two distinct persons, human and divine. His followers established the Nestorian Christian religion, which became widespread in Persia (modern Iran) in the fifth and sixth centuries. Nestorian churches in Persia and Syria sent missionaries to India and China between the 6th and 10th centuries. A major source on Nestorianism in China is a stone stela excavated near Xi'an in 1623. Engraved with a cross in the center of coiling dragons, the stela was erected by Tang emperor Dezong (Tetsung; r. 780–805) in 781. The stela is also engraved with a text in Chinese and Syrian called *The Spread of Syrian Nestorianism in China*, which describes the activities of Nestorian Christians in China during the seventh and eighth centuries. It states that in 635, a Syrian priest named A-lo-pen brought the Nestorian Bible, which had 27 chapters, to China, and Tang emperor Taizong (T'ai-tsung; r. 626–649) ordered a government minister to give him an audience. The emperor studied Nestorian teachings and "concluded that they were beneficial to men and the world." The Tang government officially tolerated all religions and gave Nestorian Christians permission to build their first church in Chang'an in 638. The stela states that during the reign of Tang emperor Gaozong (Kao-tsung; r. 649–83), Nestorian churches were built in all Chinese provinces. Other sources for Nestorianism include a list of Chinese Christian books among the manuscripts discovered at Dunhuang and the mention of Syrian Christians in Tang imperial edicts of 683, 745 and 845.

Nestorian Christians were active in educating people, feeding and clothing the poor, and giving medical care to the sick. Nestorian monks became renowned as medical doctors, and one even saved a Tang emperor from going blind. The monks were not allowed to own private property or slaves. They held worship services every seventh day and sang hymns seven times every day. Tang emperor Xuanzong (Hsuan-tsung; r. 712–56) commanded his four brothers to worship in the Nestorian church in Chang'an, and ordered that his image and those of the four previous emperors should be kept in the church. He awarded Nestorian monks government ranks, and gave them incense and a banquet every Christmas Day. Nestorian Christianity became associated with the Tang imperial family. Few Chinese converted to the religion, and when Emperor Wuzong (Wu-tsung) persecuted Buddhism in 845, 3,000 Nestorian monks were required to return to private life. Small communities of Nestorian Christians existed in China until the Song dynasty (960–1279) and persisted after that time in Central Asia.

The Mongols, who preferred the Tibetan Buddhist sect known as Lamaism for political reasons, to oppose the Chinese Confucians, tolerated many different religions, including Nestorianism. Mongol leader Khubilai Khan (1214–94), founder of the Yuan dynasty (1279–1368), was the son of a Kerait princess who was a Nestorian Christian. Many Mongol leaders took their wives and government ministers from the Nestorian Kerait and Ongut tribes of Central Asia. The Mongols established a Nestorian bishopric at their capital in modern Beijing in 1275. When Khubilai Khan was emperor of China, he sent a Chinese Nestorian Christian ambassador named Rabban Bar Sauma to Europe in 1287–88. He met with King Philip the Fair in Paris and celebrated Christian mass in front of the Roman Catholic Pope in Rome. In 1289 Khubilai Khan created a special government office for Nestorian Christian affairs, which was ranked on the same level as the office for the native Chinese religion of Daoism. See also CHANG'AN; CHRISTIANITY; DUNHUANG CAVE PAINTINGS AND CARVINGS; KHUBILAI KHAN; MONGOL.

NEW CHINA (*XINHUA*) NEWS AGENCY

A Chinese government agency that is the main source for domestic news about China, and the only source for international news published in Chinese newspapers and broadcast on Chinese radio and television stations. The New China News Agency belongs to the Propaganda Committee, an organization of the Chinese Communist Party (CCP) Central Committee, which includes the Central Broadcasting Administration. This committee publishes several papers, notably the *People's Daily* (*Renmin Ribao*), the official party newspaper. Other major newspapers include the *Enlightenment Daily* (*Guangming Ribao*), which covers science, education and culture; and the *Liberation Army Daily* (*Jiefangjun Bao*), the official paper of the People's Liberation Army. The China News Service (*Zhongguo Xinwenshe*) is another news agency that provides news stories and photographs to domestic Chinese newspapers and to radio and television stations in foreign countries.

The New China News Agency has departments that handle domestic news, international news, domestic news for foreign news services, and foreign affairs. The agency has a widespread network of correspondents in more than 90 overseas bureaus. It also releases the *News Bulletin* in English, French, Spanish, Arabic and several other languages, and provides special features to newspapers and magazines in more than 100 countries. The agency maintains an international telecommunications network with major cities around the world and files news reports to foreign countries via an international communications satellite. See also CENTRAL COMMITTEE OF THE CHINESE COMMUNIST PARTY; PEOPLE'S DAILY; PEOPLE'S LIBERATION ARMY.

NEW CULTURE MOVEMENT   A movement among Chinese scholars in the early 20th century to reevaluate the Confucian-based institutions and beliefs that had defined the Chinese cultural tradition for two millennia. Until this time, scholars, or members of the literati class, were educated in the Confucian classics and staffed the Chinese imperial bureaucracy or civil service. After the Qing dynasty (1644–1911) was overthrown and the modern Republic of China was founded in 1912, many scholars chose to avoid taking government positions and worked instead on creating a new Chinese culture. They hoped to remove the elements that had prevented China from becoming a modern power, and uphold elements from Chinese tradition that could still be useful. One important aspect of the New Culture Movement was an attempt to write literature in the vernacular or everyday language of the Chinese people, known as *baihua* (*pai-hua*), rather than use classical written Chinese (*wenyan* or *ren-yen*), which dated back to about 200 B.C. and was extremely complex and difficult to learn. The leader of the *baihua* movement was Hu Shi (1891–1962), who had studied abroad under the Western philosopher John Dewey and was a professor at prestigious Beijing University. Hu was also a leader of the movement to use scientific methods to critically analyze Chinese legends, myths, folklore, classical texts, and novels written during the Ming (1368–1644) and Qing dynasties.

Many members of the New Culture Movement were also involved in the May Fourth Movement of 1919, a nationwide protest of the Chinese people against the secret agreement between the governments of China and Japan to award the Chinese province of Shandong to Japan. The May Fourth Movement was also a reaction against the so-called Twenty-One Demands that Japan had issued to China in 1915. The terms May Fourth Movement and New Culture Movement are sometimes used interchangeably. Some May Fourth leaders decided to take an active political role and joined the Chinese Communist Party when it was founded in 1921. Others chose to continue their work as scholars of Chinese culture and history within the New Culture Movement. These scholars were also influenced by revolutionary movements in the West such as those concerned with socialism and the rights of women and working people. See also HU SHI; LANGUAGE, CHINESE; MAY FOURTH MOVEMENT OF 1919.

NEW FOURTH ARMY INCIDENT   An ambush of several thousand Chinese Communist Party (CCP) New Fourth Army troops in the lower Yangzi River valley by Nationalist (Kuomintang; KMT) forces in January 1941. The Communists and Nationalists had been fighting against each other but made an alliance to resist the Japanese when they invaded China in 1937 (War of Resistance against Japan, 1937–45; World War II). In December 1940, Chiang Kai-shek, commander of the Nationalist forces, decreed that all Eighth Route Army troops south of the Yangzi had to cross over to the river's north bank by January 31, 1941. Commanders of the New Fourth Army delayed, and between January 7 and January 13, 1941, Nationalist forces ambushed the southern wing of the New Fourth Army. They killed about 3,000 Communist troops and executed many more after arresting them. The CCP regrouped the rest of the New Fourth Army in six areas north of the Yangzi, and was soon able to establish a large guerrilla base south of the Yangzi as well. The CCP gained supporters because of the vicious Nationalist ambush. Although the Communists and Nationalists did not end their alliance against the Japanese, the New Fourth Army Incident marked the breakdown of their united front, and both sides became more concerned with resuming their fight against each other than with fighting the Japanese. This was especially true after the United States joined the war on China's side after Japan attacked the American naval base at Pearl Harbor on December 7, 1941. See also CHIANG KAI-SHEK; CHINESE COMMUNIST PARTY; CIVIL WAR BETWEEN COMMUNISTS AND NATIONALISTS; NATIONALIST PARTY; PEOPLE'S LIBERATION ARMY; WAR OF RESISTANCE AGAINST JAPAN.

NEW KOWLOON   See HONG KONG; KOWLOON; NEW TERRITORIES.

NEW LIFE MOVEMENT   A movement initiated by Chiang Kai-shek, leader of the Chinese Nationalist Party (Kuomintang; KMT), on February 19, 1934, to promote the virtues of Confucianism and modern hygienic practices among the Chinese people. The KMT controlled the government of the Republic of China (ROC), which had been established in 1912. Chiang began the New Life Movement to counter the success of the Chinese Communist Party (CCP), the enemy of the KMT, whose members emphasized class struggle and worked with peasants to help improve the conditions of their daily life. Between February 19 and March 26, 1934, while Chiang was leading the KMT military campaign against CCP forces in southern Jiangxi Province, he gave five speeches on the principles of the New Life Movement. The KMT and the Nationalist government sponsored and directed the movement and held mass demonstrations to publicize it. In 1935 George Shepherd, a Christian missionary and reformer from New Zealand, was appointed head of the New Life Movement. By the end of 1935, the movement had been established in branch associations in 19 provinces of China.

Chiang's motive for initiating the New Life Movement was to mobilize the Chinese people to work for the Nationalist cause. He felt that the Chinese lacked discipline and a sense of public morale and social consciousness. Their traditional attitude of *suibian* (*sui-pien*), or laziness and a fatalistic attitude toward life, was, in Chiang's view, a major reason China had been unable to attain equality with other nations. He aimed to replace this attitude with an emphasis on discipline, cleanliness and personal hygiene, based on the concept of an alert mind in a healthy body. The movement had as its model the common people in Western nations, who believed that "cleanliness is next to godliness," but it also found these virtues in the Chinese Confucian tradition. Confucius (551–479 B.C.), whose school of thought had been orthodox for the Chinese imperial government for 2,000 years, taught that a person is inherently good and can cultivate his or her good nature through education and moral practices. His ideal human being is the "superior man" or gentleman (*junzi* or *chun-tzu*; "son of a prince"), who becomes noble not by birth but through self-cultivation.

Chiang promoted the Confucian virtues of humanity or benevolence (*ren* or *jen*), justice or righteousness (*yi*), proper conduct (*li*), understanding (*zhi* or *chi*), honesty (*lian* or *lien*), self-respect (*chi* or *ch'ih*) and trustworthiness (*xin* or *hsin*). The mottoes of the New Life Movement were "from self to others" and "from simple to complex." Chiang promoted 95 rules to guide people's conduct, which ranged from abstract principles such as self-sacrifice to concrete rules such as not spitting in public. The New Life Movement aimed to create a new type of Chinese citizen who would be willing to work hard and make personal sacrifices for the good of the Chinese nation.

After 1936 Soong Mei-ling, Chiang Kai-shek's wife, who belonged to the Methodist Church, played a major role in promoting the New Life Movement. However, the movement did not have much effect on the Chinese people because it relied on traditional concepts that did not seem to relate to modern times and because the KMT leaders imposed it from above in an authoritarian manner yet did not seem to possess the Confucian virtues themselves. The New Life Movement dwindled away after the Japanese invaded China in 1937 and the KMT and CCP formed a united front to fight China's War of Resistance against Japan (1937–45; World War II). However, the emphasis of the New Life Movement on discipline and hygiene was adapted by the government of the People's Republic of China (PRC), which the CCP established in 1949 after defeating the KMT. See also CHIANG KAI-SHEK; CONFUCIANISM; NATIONALIST PARTY; PEOPLE'S REPUBLIC OF CHINA; SOONG MEI-LING; NAMES OF INDIVIDUAL VIRTUES.

NEW LITERATURE MOVEMENT See LANGUAGE, CHINESE; MAY FOURTH MOVEMENT OF 1919; NEW CULTURE MOVEMENT.

NEW STYLE VERSE See REGULATED OR NEW STYLE VERSE.

NEW TERRITORIES The name formerly applied to the area on mainland China north of the peninsula of Kowloon (Jiulong in pinyin); also known as New Kowloon. The New Territories and Kowloon were part of the former British Crown Colony of Hong Kong, located at the mouth of the Pearl River delta in southern China. The colony also included Hong Kong Island and adjacent islets and Stonecutters Island. The New Territories, which comprised 90 percent of Hong Kong's total area, consisted partly of territory on the Chinese mainland and partly of more than 230 islands, with a total area of about 366 square miles. The major Chinese port city of Guangzhou (Canton) in Guangdong Province lies 90 miles to the northwest.

The British moved to Hong Kong island after they were expelled from the Portuguese colony of Macao (which will revert to China in 1999). The Chinese ceded Hong Kong to Great Britain after the latter defeated China in the Opium War (1839–42). In 1898 the British acquired a 99-year lease over the so-called New Territories of Kowloon, which greatly increased the size of their Hong Kong colony. In 1997 Britain ceded control over all of Hong Kong, including Kowloon and the New Territories, to China. Until recently the New Territories were largely agricultural, with rice and vegetables the main crops. Fishing is another important economic activity, and people live on boats in the numerous harbors. The area has been undergoing recent development, especially as ties have grown stronger between Hong Kong and the mainland; textile manufacturing has become important. The inhabitants of the former New Territories are mostly Cantonese (Han Chinese from Guangdong Province) or Hakka, one of China's national minority ethnic groups. There is also a population of Hoklo (the name means that they came from Fujian Province in China) who are traditionally skilled boatmen. See also GUANGDONG PROVINCE; GUANGZHOU; HAKKA; HONG KONG; KOWLOON; MACAO; OPIUM WAR; PEARL RIVER.

NEW YEAR FESTIVAL (Yuan Dan [Yuantan] or Xin Nian [Hsin Nien])   Also called the Spring Festival (Chun Jie or Ch'un Chieh); the most important festival in the Chinese year. The New Year is celebrated in late January or early February, according to the traditional Chinese lunar calendar, and lasts for 15 days. This festival starts a new cycle and celebrates the arrival of spring. People who live away from home return to spend the holiday with their families. For several weeks before the New Year begins, Chinese send red cards with good wishes to their friends and relatives. Activities during the New Year festival include paying respectful visits to elders, writing poems, hanging red strips of paper, and enjoying banquets with many courses. The Chinese also display brightly colored woodcuts in the folk art tradition that depict happy children, beautiful women, good harvests and folk heroes.

The Chinese carefully clean their homes for the festival. They traditionally believe that one week before the New Year festival, the Kitchen God (Caozhun or Ts'aochun; "Stove Prince") travels to Heaven to report what has happened on Earth during the year. Male members of the family make offerings to the Kitchen God and then take down the piece of red paper decorated with his picture from the shrine over the kitchen stove. After a week, when members of the household have completed their preparations for the festival, a new picture of the Kitchen God is hung above the stove on New Year's Eve, the 30th night of the Twelfth Moon. Then all the members of the family share a reunion dinner to reinforce their harmonious relations. Special foods with symbolic meanings are served. For example, abalone represents abundance; bean sprouts, black seaweed, soybeans and pork represent prosperity; dumplings symbolize unity and happiness; oysters foretell good business; and carp, a large fish, symbolizes success. Special foods are also offered on the altar to the family's ancestors, including ground nuts and lotus seeds, which represent childbirth and continuity; lichees, which indicate success; and longan, a sweet, round fruit that symbolizes unity and happiness.

During the New Year period, the Chinese continue to eat and drink together and pay visits to friends and family members. They traditionally try to pay off old debts by the New Year. They also hold lion dances and set off strings of noisy firecrackers to chase away evil spirits. The New Year Festival was traditionally believed to have begun in ancient times, when a wild beast called nian (nien) ate many people in a certain village at the end of every winter. One year the villagers scared the beast away by beating gongs and drums and setting off firecrackers. This practice then spread throughout China. The New Year Festival closes with the Lantern Festival on the 15th day, the first full moon of the first lunar month. Beautiful paper lanterns are hung to decorate houses and shops and are carried by children. See also ANCESTOR WORSHIP; BANQUETS; CARP; FIREWORKS AND GUNPOWDER; KITCHEN GOD; LANTERN FESTIVAL; LION AND LION DANCE; WOODCUTS.

NEW YOUTH (LA JEUNESSE) See CHINESE COMMUNIST PARTY; LI DAZHAO.

NEWSPAPERS See NEW CHINA NEWS AGENCY; PEOPLE'S DAILY; RED FLAG.

NGO FORUM See UNITED NATIONS FOURTH WORLD CONFERENCE ON WOMEN.

NI TSAN See NI ZAN.

NI ZAN (Ni Tsan; 1301–74) One of the greatest landscape painters in Chinese history. Ni Zan is considered one of the "Four Great Masters of the Yuan Dynasty," along with Huang Gongwang (Huang Kung-wang; 1269–1354), Wu Zhen (Wu Chen; 1280–1354) and Wang Meng (c. 1309–85). These artists rejected the romanticism and lyricism found in paintings of the Southern Song style. Reflecting their distaste for the Mongol Yuan dynasty, which had overcome the Song in 1279, they attempted to develop a new style of painting that was objective and detached. Beginning in 1331 they inaugurated a new period in the history of Chinese art.

Ni Zan also wrote lyric poetry. He was born to a high-level family in Wuxi on the Grand Canal in eastern China. He married and had a family, and enjoyed all the fine things available to a wealthy, educated man, including a beautiful garden, a library and an extensive collection of paintings, jade objects and bronzeware. He became a renowned poet and painter, but he refused to come to the Yuan dynasty (1279–1368) court because it was run by Mongols—an ethnic group that had invaded China from the north and overthrown the highly cultured Song dynasty (960–1279)—and the Yuan court had denied privileges to members of the Han Chinese educated class. Ni Zan even refused a commission by the ruler of his district to paint a picture. Over time he freed himself of his wealth and possessions to live as a Daoist, close to nature and entirely devoted to his art.

Ni Zan actually became a painter relatively late in his life, around 1338. After this, he completed many paintings as he wandered around the countryside. His compositions are simple and sparse, lacking the high mountains, huge gnarled trees and pounding waterfalls that can be seen in many Chinese landscape paintings. They usually contain a few thin trees, a lake and some low hills. Ni Zan used ink in a very restrained manner. He never included human beings in his landscapes, investing his paintings with a sense of spaciousness and solitude. See also DAOISM; HUANG GONGWANG; LANDSCAPE PAINTING; YUAN DYNASTY.

NIAN (NIEN) REBELLION A peasant rebellion against the Manchu Qing dynasty (1644–1911) in the mid-19th century. The Nian Rebellion officially broke out in 1852, but its roots went back to bandit groups in the 1790s who terrorized areas north of the Huai River and south of the Yellow River, especially in the border region along southwestern Shandong, northwestern Jiangsu, east-central Henan and northern Anhui provinces. The term Nian may refer to these highly mobile bandit groups, or to their martial costumes or the twisted paper torches they carried at night on their raids. The Nian grew during the 19th century despite their lack of central leadership or political and religious ideology. Some members did have connections with other rebel groups, such as the White Lotus, Eight Trigrams or Triad societies. However, the majority of Nian were simply impoverished peasants. Nian bands raided villages for their crops, kidnapped wealthy land owners for ransom, and held up government salt transports. Heavy flooding in northern Jiangsu in 1851 brought more hardships to the peasants and brought many more members into the Nian groups. That year the Qing government officially declared the Nian to be rebels. Around the same time, the Taiping Rebellion (1850–64) was also posing a serious threat to the dynasty, and the Taiping seized the important city of Nanjing in 1853. The leaders of the Taiping Rebellion did not coordinate their uprising with the Nian Rebellion; the combined movements might have been able to topple the Qing.

Hardships caused by severe flooding of the Yellow River brought even more peasants into the Nian. By 1853, the leaders of 18 Nian bands came to an agreement that their leader was Zhang Luoxing (Chang Lo-hsing), a landowner from northern Anhui who controlled salt smuggling and sheep stealing in the area. In 1856 they declared Zhang "Lord of the Alliance" and gave him the honorific title, "Great Han Prince with the Heavenly Mandate." The Nian bands organized themselves into five groups called banners, named for the colors associated with each group. By now the powerful Nian forces numbered 30,000 to 50,000, and they were able to cut off communications between Beijing, the Qing capital, and Qing forces attempting to take back Nanjing from the Taiping. The Nian built dozens of fortified villages north of the Huai River from which they staged their raids on other villages.

In 1860 the Qing ordered General Senggelinqin to defeat the Nian rebels. He was a Mongol who had defeated a Taiping army near Tianjin in 1853 and had helped repel British forces from Dagu in 1859 but who had allowed the British into Beijing in 1860. Using highly trained Manchu and Mongol cavalry forces, he killed Zhang Luoxing and terrorized both the Nian and the Chinese people in the region. Other Nian leaders took over the rebellion and led successful guerrilla attacks against the Qing troops, eventually ambushing and killing General Senggelinqin and most of his troops. The Qing next sent General Zeng Guofan (Tseng Kuo-fan), who had helped defeat the Taiping in Nanjing, against the Nian, but he was not successful either. His protegé, Li Hongzhang (Li Hung-chang), was then made commander, but he also had trouble suppressing the Nian at first. He persisted against them, using gunboats on the rivers and foreign-made rifles and artillery that gradually gave him an advantage. By August 1868, Li's troops had decisively defeated the Nian in Shandong and executed all the Nian they captured. The Qing raised Li Hongzhang to a noble rank, as they had done with Zeng Guofan when he took back Nanjing. See also EIGHT TRIGRAMS REBELLION; HUAI RIVER; LI HONGZHANG; QING DYNASTY; TAIPING REBELLION; WHITE LOTUS SECRET SOCIETY; YELLOW RIVER; ZENG GUOFAN.

NIE RONGZHEN (Nieh Jung-chen; 1899–?) A Communist military leader who held high-ranking offices in the People's Republic of China (PRC), founded by the Chinese Communist Party (CCP) in 1949. Nie was born in Sichuan Province and was a boyhood friend of Deng Xiaoping (Teng Hsiao-p'ing), the former CCP leader who died in 1997. Nie took part in the demonstrations known as the May Fourth Movement of 1919 and joined the Communist Youth League in 1922 and the CCP in 1923. He studied engineering in France and also went to Belgium and the U.S.S.R., where he studied at the Red Army Academy in Moscow in 1924–25. When he returned to China he worked under Zhou Enlai (Chou En-lai) in the Military Committee of the Guangdong Communist Party in Guangzhou, and was an instructor and secretary-general of the Political Department at Whampoa (Huangpu) Military Academy in 1925–26. In 1926 Nie took part in the Northern Expedition by the Nationalist Party (Kuomintang; KMT) against the warlords that controlled northern China. He helped plan the Nanchang Uprising in August 1927 in which KMT soldiers revolted against KMT leaders after they had turned against the CCP, with which the KMT had been cooperating, and massacred many Communists. He held high-ranking positions in the Communist army and was elected to the Central Executive Committee. Nie joined the Communists on their Long March to escape the Nationalists in 1934–35 and gained a reputation for his many heroic deeds.

When the Communist army reorganized as the Eighth Route Army, Nie was appointed the deputy commander to Lin Biao (Lin P'iao) and political commissar in 1937. In 1943, during China's War of Resistance against Japan (1937–45; World War II), Nie was transferred to CCP headquarters in Yan'an in Shaanxi Province. In 1945 he was elected a member of the CCP Central Committee and held this position until he resigned in 1985. During the civil war between the CCP and the KMT, he led the Communist takeover of the strategically important town of Shijiazhuang and helped consolidate the North China Military Region for the Communists and became its commander. Nie and Lin Biao were the two most important commanders in the Communist takeover of the capital city of Beijing in 1949, when the CCP founded the PRC. Nei served as commander of the Beijing-Tianjin Garrison in 1949–50, mayor of Beijing in 1949–51 and chairman of the Beijing Military Control Commission. He was active in establishing the CCP Central Committee, of which he became a member, and the Central People's Government Council, which administered China until the National People's Congress (NPC) met in 1954. Nie

also served as acting chief of staff of the Revolutionary Military Council from 1949 to 1954. Among his many positions, he was a member of the Standing Committee of the first NPC in 1954; Sichuan deputy at the second and third NPC, 1958–75; and vice chairman of the Standing Committee, fourth and fifth NPC, 1975–80. In 1955 Nie was appointed one of the 10 highest ranking marshals in the People's Liberation Army (PLA; formerly the Red Army) and was awarded the decorations of August First, Independence and Freedom, and Liberation first class. In the late 1950s he represented the PRC on many visits to Moscow, London, Berne, Prague and Eastern European countries.

Nie was elected vice premier of the State Council, 1956–74; appointed chairman of the State Council's Scientific Planning Commission (Science and Technology Commission), 1957–66; chairman of the State Council's Science and Technology Commission for National Defence in 1967; and vice chairman of the CCP Central Military Commission, 1961–88, and of the NPC Central Military Commission, 1983–88. He is known as the father of the PRC's nuclear program. Nie served on the Politburo (Political Bureau) from 1967 to 1969, but was purged by the Red Guards during the Cultural Revolution (1966–76). In 1973 he was rehabilitated and in 1974 he was restored to his position on the Military Affairs Commission. He was also restored to the Politburo in 1977 and 1982. In 1980 he served on the Constitution Revision Committee. Nie resigned from the Politburo and the Central Committee in 1985, but in 1987 he became a Presidium member of the 13th National Party Congress. He was a powerful leader of the conservative faction in the CCP that opposed Deng Xiaoping's policies for reform and modernization. See also CHINESE COMMUNIST PARTY; CIVIL WAR BETWEEN COMMUNISTS AND NATIONALISTS; COMMUNIST YOUTH LEAGUE; DENG XIAOPING; EIGHTH ROUTE ARMY; GOVERNMENT STRUCTURE; LIN BIAO; LONG MARCH; MAY FOURTH MOVEMENT OF 1919; NATIONALIST PARTY; NORTHERN EXPEDITION; PEOPLE'S LIBERATION ARMY; WAR OF RESISTANCE AGAINST JAPAN; WHAMPOA MILITARY ACADEMY.

NIEH JUNG-CHEN See NIE RONGZHEN.

NINE DRAGON SCREEN See DATONG; DRAGON.

NINE DRAGON WALL See FORBIDDEN CITY.

NINE-RANK SYSTEM A system by which Emperor Hongwu (Hung-wu; r. 1368–98), founder of the Ming dynasty (1368–1644), required court and military officials to wear badges on their robes that identified which of the ranks they belonged to in the imperial bureaucracy. Members of the bureaucracy were selected by a rigorous examination system. They were known as *shenshi* or *shenjin* (shen-shih or shen-chin; literally, "scholars wearing belts with hanging ends"), which is translated as degree-holders, literati, scholar-bureaucrats or officials, scholar-gentry, or mandarins. The highest level of degree-holders is known as *jinshi* (chin-shih). The examination system had been disrupted during the Yuan dynasty (1279–1368), which had been founded by the Mongols, a nomadic group that invaded China from the north, but was reestablished by the Ming. Mongol courtiers had worn on their robes large plaques decorated with animals and flowers, which may also have been symbols of rank.

Badges worn by Chinese courtiers during the Ming and Qing (1644–1911) dynasties are squares of colorful silk beautifully embroidered with brightly colored images of birds and animals, each of which is a powerful symbol that held political and cultural meaning for the Chinese. These include the pheasant, peacock, duck, crane, quail, tiger, leopard, panther and *qilin* (*ch'i-lin*), a mythological beast with a dragon's head and horns. Elements from nature such as waves, clouds, rocks and trees, as well as design motifs such as one or more of the so-called Eight Treasures, are also embroidered on the badges. The combination of symbols on a badge often forms a pun or rebus that can be understood only by persons who have a thorough knowledge of the Chinese language. The nine ranks of officials were also distinguished by a button or ball of stone, glass or metal, and of a specified color, which they wore on top of their caps. For the first rank, the button was of red coral, the third of blue stone, the fourth of purple stone, the fifth of crystal, the sixth of white jade, and the seventh through ninth of gold. The largest badges are 14 inches square. During the Qing dynasty, the badges were reduced to 11 inches square and became more subdued in color and design. The Revolution of 1911 that overthrew the Qing and ended the imperial system made the nine-rank badges obsolete in China, but 20th-century Western scholars and tourists have been collecting them for their beauty and the historical and cultural information they provide. See also EIGHT TREASURES; EMBROIDERY; IMPERIAL BUREAUCRACY; IMPERIAL EXAMINATION SYSTEM; LITERATI; MANDARIN; MING DYNASTY; REVOLUTION OF 1911; NAMES OF INDIVIDUAL ANIMALS.

NINGBO A city in Zhejiang Province in eastern China. Ningbo has a population of more than 1 million, and is located at the confluence of the Feng, Yu and Yong rivers. It lies at the center of the sea lanes on which goods are shipped along China's coast. The excellent deepwater harbor remains free of ice and silt throughout the year, making shipping, fishing and shipbuilding Ningbo's major industries for nine centuries. The waters off Ningbo's coast around the Zhoushan Islands, near where the Yangzi, Qian, Qiantang and Yong rivers flow into the East China Sea, are rich fishing grounds. Ships also leave Ningbo for Mount Putuo (Putuoshan), another island, which is traditionally believed to be the home of the goddess Guanyin (Kuan-yin). Putuoshan has been a famous Buddhist pilgrimage site since the 10th century. Mount Putuo on the island is one of the four sacred mountains of the Buddhist religion. On the island there are three Buddhist monasteries and 88 temples where 3,000 monks and nuns reside, and beautiful beaches as well.

During the Tang dynasty (618–907), Ningbo became a center for trade along China's coast and with foreign countries. During the Song dynasty (960–1279) the Chinese lost their ability to trade with the West along the overland Silk Road when Central Asian nomadic tribes became powerful. As a result, foreign trade along sea routes became even more important. Ningbo, then known as Mingzhou, became especially predominant after 1127 when the Song capital was moved to the nearby city of Hangzhou. Ningbo became the center for the trade of goods between coastal cities and the capital, and between China and Japan. China sent silk, porcelain and other valuable items to Japan, and in return received gold, silver and copper. Silk production is still a major industry in Zhejiang Province; it is known as the "Home of Silk."

Ningbo declined when the Chinese government limited overseas trade during the Ming dynasty (1368–1644). However, foreign trade was stimulated again with the arrival of Portuguese, Dutch and British ships in the late 16th century. After Britain defeated China in the first Opium War (1839–42), the Treaty of Nanjing made Ningbo a "treaty port"—open to foreign traders and residents—along with Guangzhou, Shanghai, Xiamen and Fuzhou. This treaty also gave Hong Kong to Britain. Ningbo was occupied in 1861 by forces of the Chinese anti-foreign Taiping Rebellion, but British and French armies expelled them a year later. In 1885 the city was placed under siege by France's Admiral Courbet to force China to assent to the French presence in Vietnam and in the Gulf of Tonkin. Ningbo remained a trading port but became secondary to the city of Shanghai to the north. Since 1949 Ningbo has been industrialized, and a dredging project has connected the port to the Grand Canal and China's extensive network of inland waterways.

Major tourist sites in Ningbo include the Tianyi Ge Pavilion, the oldest private library or document storehouse in China. It was constructed in 1561 by Fan Qin, a military official during the Ming dynasty, and served as the model for the seven imperial libraries built by the Qing emperor Qianlong (Ch'ien-lung; r. 1736–95). The Tianfeng Pagoda, the highest structure in Ningbo, was originally constructed 800 years ago, although the present building was rebuilt in 1330. It offers a good view of the city. Moon Lake, a famous scenic spot for more than 1,300 years, has been described by many poets. Sheli Pagoda at the fifth-century Ayuwang Temple east of Ningbo is another well-known site. Sheli means "Buddhist relic," and the pagoda is believed to contain a piece of bone from Sakyamuni, the founder of the Buddhist religion. The temple exhibits calligraphy from emperors of the Song dynasty. Tiantong Si, a famous monastery about 80 miles east of Ningbo, sits on Mount Taibai, one of the five sacred mountains of the Chan (Zen) sect of Buddhism. See also BUDDHISM; GRAND CANAL; GUANYIN; OPIUM WAR; PAGODA; PORCELAIN; SHANGHAI; SILK; TAIPING REBELLION; TREATY PORTS; ZHEJIANG PROVINCE.

NINGXIA-HUI AUTONOMOUS REGION (Ninghsia Hui or Ningxia Huizu Zizhiqu) A province in northwestern China that since 1958 has been administered as an autonomous region because a large number of its inhabitants belong to national minorities, primarily the Hui, ethnic Chinese who follow the Muslim religion. Other minorities include Mongols and Manchus. Its borders have been changed many times, but today Ningxia covers about 40,000 square miles and has a population of about 4.5 million. The capital city is Yinchuan, with a population of about 500,000. The northern two-thirds of Ningxia consists of deserts surrounded by mountains. The southern third lies on the Mongolian plateau, through which the Yellow River (Huanghe) flows at a high altitude ranging between 3,600 and 4,000 feet above sea level. The plateau has been formed from loess, loose yellow soil that blows in from the Gobi and other deserts in northwestern China, builds up fertile plateaus and fills the Yellow River with silt. The largest loess plateau in the world, covering 600,000 square miles, it lies in part of the Ningxia Hui Autonomous Region and parts of Gansu, Shaanxi and Shanxi Provinces.

Ningxia borders the Inner Mongolia Autonomous Region to the north, Gansu Province to the south and west, and Shaanxi Province to the east. The region has little rainfall, and the temperature ranges from 73 degrees F in summer to about 20 degrees F in winter. Irrigation channels, initially constructed during the Western Han dynasty (206 B.C–A.D. 8), provide water for agriculture. The Yinchuan Plain is an important producer of wheat, rice, sorghum and other grains, as well as cotton, sesame, apricots and other fruits. A dam at Qingtongxia, a city south of Yinchuan on the Yellow River, provides hydroelectric power. Nomadic tribes herd sheep and other livestock on the steppes, and Ningxia is China's main producer of sheep fleece. There are large deposits of mineral resources, especially coal, and a coal industry has been developed along the Helan Mountains.

The city of Yinchuan lies on the west bank of the Yellow River and east of the Helan Mountains. The Lanzhou-Beijing railroad connects Yinchuan with the rest of China. Originally known as Xingqing, Yinchuan has been a center for horse trading from the Tang dynasty (618–907) to the modern era. The city was the capital of the Xixia dynasty (1038–1227). This dynasty was ruled by the Tangut, a nomadic tribe related to the Tibetans. Under the Tangut ruler Li Yuango (d. 1048), Xixia rivaled the Song and Liao dynasties until the Mongols under Genghis Khan destroyed it. Another major city in Ningxia is Zhongwei, a market town southwest of Yinchuan. See also GANSU PROVINCE; GENGHIS KHAN; HUI; INNER MONGOLIA AUTONOMOUS REGION; LOESS; MINORITIES, NATIONAL; MONGOL; MUSLIMS; NOMADS AND ANIMAL HUSBANDRY; XIXIA, KINGDOM OF; YELLOW RIVER; YINCHUAN.

NIRVANA See BODHISATTVA; BUDDHA; BUDDHISM; CHAN SECT OF BUDDHISM; FLOWER GARLAND SECT OF BUDDHISM; PURE LAND SECT OF BUDDHISM; TIANTAI SECT OF BUDDHISM.

NIULANG See COWHERD AND WEAVER MAID FESTIVAL.

NIXON, RICHARD, U.S. PRESIDENT, VISIT TO CHINA (1972) The first official visit by a U.S. president to China. Nixon's visit was especially important since the United States had opposed the Chinese Communist Party (CCP), which founded the People's Republic of China (PRC) in 1949. The leaders of the Cultural Revolution that had erupted in China in 1966, especially Lin Biao (Lin Piao), wanted to keep China from having relations with the United States and the U.S.S.R. However, many Chinese Communist leaders realized that the country could not continue in isolation, and it especially needed help in developing its technology. The Chinese government secretly began making contact with the U.S. government. In December 1970 it sent a message through the government of Pakistan to Henry Kissinger, Nixon's national security adviser. This opened the way for private negotiations between the United States and China. In April 1971 the Chinese invited the U.S. table-tennis team, then competing in Japan, to visit China. This move gained

the humorous nickname of "Ping-Pong diplomacy." In July 1971, Kissinger made a top-secret visit to China to meet with Premier Zhou Enlai (Chou En-lai) and lay the plans for a visit by President Nixon. China was still criticizing the United States for its involvement in Vietnam and the bombing of Cambodia, and at the time the U.S. State Department wanted to prevent China from joining the United Nations. Even so, Kissinger's visit was a success. U.S.-China negotiations were bolstered by the United States ending its ban on the transfer of U.S. dollars to China, which allowed Chinese-Americans to send money to their families in China. Moreover, the United States allowed Chinese goods to be exported into the United States for the first time since the Korean War, and it permitted American-owned ships that sailed under foreign flags to carry goods to China.

On July 15, 1971, President Nixon broadcast the news that before May 1972 he would personally visit China. Taiwan, formally known as the Republic of China (ROC), a strong ally of the United States, suffered from this announcement. The Nationalist Party (Kuomintang; KMT) led by Chiang Kai-shek, who had lost the civil war to the Communists in 1949, had fled to the island of Taiwan, where it established the ROC. On August 2, 1971, the United States announced that it would support the movement in the United Nations to seat the PRC, although it would oppose the expulsion of the ROC, which was holding the seat for China. On October 25, the U.N. voted to expel the ROC and give the Chinese seat to the PRC. On February 21, 1972, President Richard Nixon arrived in Beijing, the capital of China. He was greeted at the airport by Zhou Enlai and some other leaders, but no crowds lined the streets to cheer his motorcade. That afternoon he met formally with Chairman Mao Zedong (Mao Tse-tung). Nixon was also taken to visit the Great Wall and the Ming Tombs and was honored with banquets at which numerous toasts were made with *maotai* (a potent Chinese liquor). Chinese and American negotiators worked behind the scenes to forge a political agreement on U.S.-Chinese relations that addressed the issue of Taiwan. On February 28, while Nixon was in Shanghai, the two countries issued the "Shanghai Communiqué" signed by Nixon and Zhou Enlai. The document did not resolve the differences between the United States and China, but it did enable them to begin the process of normalizing their relations. The U.S. Congress voted to continue providing military aid to Taiwan and to continue trading with it. In 1973, the United States and China opened liaison offices in Beijing and Washington, D.C., respectively. The Nixon visit to China became the subject of an opera by the American composer John Adams, titled *Nixon in China*, first produced in 1987. See also MAO ZEDONG; MAOTAI; NATIONALIST PARTY; PEOPLE'S REPUBLIC OF CHINA; TAIWAN; ZHOU ENLAI.

NO CHA See NE ZHA.

NOBLE MAN See SUPERIOR MAN.

NOMADS AND ANIMAL HUSBANDRY A number of China's 55 officially designated minority ethnic groups inhabit grassy steplands in the north, northwest and west and traditionally herd animals—mainly sheep, goats and horses. In contrast, the Han, the majority Chinese ethnic group, traditionally live in settled villages and practice agriculture. According to the 1990 census of the People's Republic of China (PRC), national minorities comprised about 90 million people, 8 percent of China's total population, but they occupied about 60 percent of China's total land area. A number of minorities do practice agriculture, but some of the largest groups are nomadic herders by tradition, including the Mongols, Manchus, Tibetans, Uighurs and Kazakhs. Nomadic tribes to the north and northwest have threatened China ever since the first emperor, Qin Shi Huangdi, unified the country under the Qin dynasty (221–206 B.C.). He began constructing the Great Wall across northern China to defend the Han Chinese from non-Chinese invaders. The Great Wall is actually a series of connected fortifications built by many Chinese emperors over the centuries. It did not always keep out nomadic invaders, but it did serve as a psychological dividing line for the Chinese, who considered all non-Han peoples "barbarians." The Chinese also tried to lessen the threats from nomadic peoples by engaging in trade, diplomacy and warfare. The Han dynasty (206 B.C.–A.D. 220) waged many military campaigns against the Xiongnu (Hsiungnu) tribes to the north and gained control of much of Central Asia. Chinese emperors instituted the tribute system whereby foreign peoples could receive permission to trade with China by sending missions to the Chinese capital to bow before the emperor and offer him gifts.

Many nomadic tribes established kingdoms in northern China when the Chinese empire became fragmented during the Six Dynasties Period (220–589). They became assimilated by adopting the Han Chinese government bureaucracy, institutions, language, social customs and ways of thinking, a process known as sinicization. Five major nomadic "barbarian" tribes invaded China. The Xiongnu, Xianbei (Hsien-pei) and Jie (Chieh), who moved down from the northern steppes, spoke languages related to Turkish, Mongolian and Tungusic. The Qiang (Ch'iang) and the Di (Ti) came from mountainous regions to the west and spoke languages similar to Tibetan and Tangut. Their invasions caused many Han Chinese to migrate south of the Yangzi River (Changjiang), especially wealthy aristocrats. However, many Han remained in northern China and cooperated with the sinicized invaders. Successive waves of nomadic invaders became absorbed into the Han Chinese culture.

The Tibetans did not assimilate into the Han. They inhabit Tibet Autonomous Region (Xizang Zizhiqu) in western China, which is surrounded by the Himalaya Mountain Range, the highest in the world. The Tibetans have tried to maintain their independence and have staged several uprisings since 1949, which the Chinese government has brutally suppressed. Tibetans herd yaks, large bisonlike animals with thick wool.

The Uighurs, a Turkic group of about six million people who comprise China's third-largest minority group, inhabit Xinjiang Uighur Autonomous Region in remote western China, north of Tibet. The ancient Silk Road, along which China traded silk and other luxury goods with the Mediterranean world, went through Xinjiang, formerly known as Chinese Turkestan. The Uighurs and Kazakhs, another Turkic group who also inhabit Xinjiang, follow the Muslim religion and herd sheep, goats and horses. The Chinese emperors

bought large numbers of horses for military purposes from the Uighurs and neighboring peoples.

The Mongols, who founded the Yuan dynasty (1279–1368), were the first non-Han people to rule all of China. Originally a group of nomadic Altaic tribes from the region north and northwest of the Great Wall known as Mongolia, they established a vast empire that stretched all the way from China to eastern Europe. Mongol boys were raised to live and fight in the saddle, and Mongol girls were also taught how to ride. The women and children constantly migrated across the steppe lands, herding sheep and goats, with horses pulling their tents (*ger* in Mongolian; commonly known as yurts) and belongings in large wagons. The Mongols adopted the Tibetan form of the Buddhist religion, known as Lamaism. The Han Chinese overthrew the Mongol Yuan and established the Ming dynasty (1368–1644). Today Mongolia is divided into Inner Mongolia Autonomous Region within the PRC and the independent Mongolian People's Republic, also known as Outer Mongolia.

The Manchus, a nomadic group based in Manchuria (modern northeastern China), are descendants of the Jurchen (Jurched), a Tungusic people who defeated the Khitans (Qidans), founders of the Liao dynasty (947–1125), and established the Jin dynasty (1115–1234) in northern China. In 1644 the Manchus overthrew the Ming dynasty and founded the Qing dynasty (1644–1911), China's last imperial dynasty. The Manchus also adopted Lamaism. Today nearly 10 million Manchus reside in Manchuria and Hebei Province, and have become largely assimilated into the Han population. See also AGRICULTURE; GREAT WALL; HAN; HORSE; INNER MONGOLIA AUTONOMOUS REGION; KAZAKH; LAMAISM; MANCHU; MANCHURIA; MINORITIES, NATIONAL; MONGOL; MUSLIMS IN CHINA; SINICIZATION; SIX DYNASTIES PERIOD; TIBET; TIBETAN; TRIBUTE SYSTEM; UIGHUR; XINJIANG-UIGHUR AUTONOMOUS REGION; XIONGNU; YAK.

NONGOVERNMENTAL ORGANIZATION (NGO) FORUM
See UNITED NATIONS FOURTH WORLD CONFERENCE ON WOMEN.

NOODLES (*mein*)   A food that is prepared from a dough of flour and water that is made into long strands. Skilled chefs can spin the dough in the air and cut it many times in a row to make long, thin noodles similar to spaghetti. Noodles are usually considered a Chinese invention, although no one knows for certain, and were first consumed in China during the Han dynasty (206 B.C.–A.D. 220), when techniques for grinding large amounts of grain into flour were developed. Chinese noodles can range in width from very thin to wide and flat. The flour for noodles may be made from wheat, millet, mung beans, buckwheat, rice or other grains. In Guangzhou (Canton) in southern China, egg is often added to the dough. The Chinese classify noodles as *fan*, a grain food.

Noodles are cooked by boiling them in water and then rinsing them in cold water. They are then added to other ingredients, especially large bowls of broth containing green vegetables, slices of roasted pork and other meats and flavorings. Noodle dishes are commonly eaten for lunch and as snacks, and are sold in noodle shops and by street vendors with carts. They can also be stir-fried with meat and vegeta-

Skilled chefs can spin dough in the air and cut it several times to make long, thin noodles.   S.E. MEYER

bles, a dish popularly known in the West as *chow mein*. Noodles are usually not served at dinner, except for birthday banquets, when their length is a symbol of long life. Instant noodle soups known as *ramen* (*larmen* in Chinese) have become so popular that in 1994 three billion servings were sold in China.

Besides noodles, the Chinese also make and consume other foods made from a dough of flour and water, such as bread (*mantou*), heavy steamed buns filled with ground meat or fruits (*bao* or *pao*), and filled dumplings in a variety of shapes, which are usually enjoyed at a snack meal known as *dim sum*. Small noodle factories often make the thin skins called *won ton* used to wrap dumplings. See also COOKING, CHINESE; DIM SUM.

NORBU LINGKA See LHASA.

NORTH CHINA PLAIN An alluvial plain, the largest in China, which has been formed in northern China by the Yellow (Huanghe), Huai and Hai rivers. The North China Plain lies in Shanxi, Henan, Hebei and Shandong provinces and is one of China's most densely populated areas. The plain is a continuation of the Manchurian (Dongbei) Plain in northeastern China but is separated from it by the Bo Hai Gulf, an extension of the Yellow Sea (Huanghai). The Qinling mountain range in central China and the Taihang in north China

border the plain, and the Qinling separates it from the Yangzi River (Changjiang) delta to the south. The Yellow River carries a huge amount of soil known as loess from the loess plateau in northern China and deposits it on the North China Plain. In fact, the river has deposited so much soil that it has changed its course many times throughout Chinese history, causing disastrous floods. The soil deposits, however, are rich and fertile. Combined with high temperatures and abundant rainfall in the summer, they make the North China Plain one of China's major agricultural areas.

The region produces half the country's cotton and more than half its wheat, which is the staple food in northern China (rice is consumed mainly in the south). Other grains are also grown, such as corn, sorghum and millet, as well as fruits and vegetables. The Yellow River flows slowly through the plain, and the silt has raised the riverbed 13 to 16 feet above its original banks, so the Chinese have had to build dikes to contain the river. In this region, they call the Yellow River the "Above-Ground River." The dikes have to be continuously repaired. The Chinese have also constructed many irrigation systems on the plain, especially since the late 1960s.

The North China Plain is the cradle of Chinese civilization. Archaeologists have excavated many sites in this region dating back to the Neolithic period (c. 12,000–2000 B.C.) and the Bronze Age Xia (about 2200–1750 B.C.) and Shang

(1750–1040 B.C.) dynasties. The state of Qin on the North China Plain unified China into an empire under the Qin dynasty (221–206 B.C.), and the plain remained China's political and cultural center through several dynasties. Over many centuries the Chinese built the Grand Canal to connect China's major rivers, including the Yellow, to enable barge transportation of grain and other goods to the imperial capital cities of Kaifeng, Luoyang and Beijing, also the modern capital. See also AGRICULTURE; GRAND CANAL; LOESS; NATURAL DISASTERS; QINLING MOUNTAIN RANGE; YELLOW RIVER; NAMES OF INDIVIDUAL DYNASTIES, PROVINCES AND CITIES.

NORTH KOREA See KOREAN WAR; MANCHURIA; UNITED NATIONS; YALU TSUNGPO RIVER.

NORTH LAKE PARK See BEIHAI PARK.

NORTH RIVER See PEARL RIVER.

NORTHEAST CHINA RAILROAD (NORTHEASTERN CHINA RAILWAY) See HEILONGJIANG PROVINCE; LIAODONG PENINSULA; LIAONING PROVINCE; MANCHURIA; RAILROADS.

NORTHERN AND SOUTHERN DYNASTIES (420–589) A period in Chinese history when China was divided into many kingdoms before being reunified under the Sui dynasty (581–618). The Northern and Southern dynasties comprised the final division of the Six Dynasties Period (220–589), which began with the overthrow of the Han dynasty (206 B.C.–A.D. 220) and includes the Three Kingdoms Period (220–280), the Western Jin dynasty (265–316) and Eastern Jin dynasty (317–420), and the Northern and Southern dynasties. In 265 Sima Yan (Ssu-ma Yan) briefly unified China under the Western Jin dynasty. However, foreign nomadic tribes such as the Xiongnu (Hsiung-nu) and Xianbei (Hsien-pei) settled inside the Great Wall, even though it had been built across northern China as protection from nomadic invaders, and they helped bring down the dynasty. In 304 a Xiongnu named Liu Yuan proclaimed himself king of Han and conquered most of northern China. In 316 Sima Yan's descendants fled to Jiankang (modern Nanjing in eastern China) and founded the Eastern Jin dynasty. After the Western Jin fell in 316 and the great imperial cities of Luoyang and Chang'an (modern Xi'an) were sacked, China became fragmented among a succession of short-lived dynasties in the north and south until 589.

During the Eastern Jin dynasty, large numbers of Chinese, including many aristocrats, Confucian-educated scholars and government officials, migrated south of the Yangzi River (Changjiang) and colonized southern China. They became concentrated in the Eastern Jin capital at modern Nanjing. Attempts by northern rulers to take over the south were stopped by the Battle of Feishui in 383, and a line of partition was drawn across China that generally paralleled the northern border of the southern Chinese region where rice was cultivated in wet paddy fields.

In 420 the Eastern Jin dynasty was overthrown by one of its generals, Liu Yu, who declared himself the first emperor of the Liu-Song dynasty (420–79). The Liu-Song was one of the Southern Dynasties, which also included the Wu

(222–230) that had been conquered by the Wei; the Eastern Jin (317–420), a continuation in the south of the Eastern Jin that had briefly reunited China; the Southern Qi (479–502); the Liang (502–557); and the Chen (557–589), which became absorbed by the Sui dynasty when it reunified China. The Buddhist religion, which had been introduced into China from India, grew rapidly during this period. The Liang dynasty's Emperor Liang Wudi (Liang Wu-ti; 502–49) was the greatest southern patron of Buddhism. According to Buddhist legend, he is the emperor with whom Bodhidharma, the founder of the Chan Sect of Buddhism (known in the West by its Japanese name, Zen), had an audience when he first came to China. During the long period of relative peace during his reign, trade and commerce increased in the cities along the Yangzi River and in Guangzhou (Canton), and many foreign merchants settled in these cities. Liang was overthrown by the Chen dynasty, but the Chen in turn fell to the Sui dynasty.

Some of the Northern Dynasties were established by nomadic invaders who became sinicized, that is, who adopted Chinese names and customs and married Chinese wives, so that after two or three generations they were indistinguishable from the Han ethnic Chinese. A branch of the Xianbei known as the Tuoba Tartars invaded China from the north and established the Northern Wei dynasty. The Northern Dynasties that followed the downfall of the Western Jin included the Northern Wei (386–534; not to be confused with the kingdom of Wei), which became divided into the Eastern Wei (534–550) and the Western Wei (537–557); the Northern Qi (550–577); and the Northern Zhou (557–581), which brought down the Northern Qi in 577.

In the 490s Emperor Xiao Wendi (Hsiao Wen-ti; r. 471–499) moved his capital from modern Datong to Luoyang and controlled a region that extended from Dunhuang in western China to Korea in the northeast. He insisted that his subjects adopt Chinese customs and clothing, but he also patronized Buddhism and authorized the carving of the Buddhist cave temples at Longmen. In 581 the Northern Zhou was overthrown by one of its sinicized generals, Yang Jian (Yang Chien), who became the first emperor of the Sui dynasty, known as Emperor Wendi (Wen-ti; r. 581–604). In 589 he took Nanjing, conquered the south and reunified China. See also BODHIDHARMA; BUDDHISM; GREAT WALL; HAN DYNASTY; LONGMEN CAVE TEMPLES AND SCULPTURES; LUOYANG; NANJING; NORTHERN WEI DYNASTY; SINICIZATION; SIX DYNASTIES PERIOD; SUI DYNASTY; TANG DYNASTY; THREE KINGDOMS PERIOD; WENDI, EMPEROR; WESTERN JIN DYNASTY AND EASTERN JIN DYNASTY.

NORTHERN EXPEDITION A military campaign launched in July 1926 under Chiang Kai-shek (1887–1975), commander in chief of the National Revolutionary Army, against the warlords that had controlled China since 1916. It moved north from Guangdong Province in southern China. The army included forces of the Chinese Nationalist Party (Kuomintang; KMT) and of the recently founded Chinese Communist Party (CCP). The campaign finally attained the goal of reunifying China in 1928 when it took Beijing, the traditional capital, in northern China. The major units of the National Revolutionary Army had Russian military advisers. In July 1925 the Nationalist Party had proclaimed the Nationalist government in Guangzhou (Canton) in southern China to rival the warlord government. The CCP and the KMT had made an alliance and joined forces to reunify China, and Chiang had replaced Sun Yat-sen as head of the alliance when the latter died in 1925. However, after Sun's death, the CCP-KMT alliance began to fall apart, partly because the Communists did not want to have a Nationalist leader. At the end of 1926, the Nationalist government moved north from Guangzhou to Wuhan, the capital of Hubei Province in northern China. Behind the scenes, this government was controlled by the Russian adviser Michael Borodin (1884–1952), Chinese Communists, and the left wing of the KMT led by Wang Jingwei (Wang Ching-wei). The first phase of the Northern Expedition succeeded in defeating or incorporating the forces of 34 warlords in southern China. During the second phase of the Northern Expedition, Chiang's forces took the important financial centers of Hankou, Nanjing and Shanghai in the Yangzi River valley in eastern China.

On April 12, 1927, Chiang decided to purge all left-wingers, and his troops assaulted the Communists in all Chinese cities controlled by the KMT. In doing so, Chiang destroyed the infrastructure of the CCP. The CCP-KMT united front ended. After the massacre, the left-wing KMT faction led by Wang Jingwei condemned Chiang and expelled him from the KMT. Although Chiang was dismissed as commander in chief of the National Revolutionary Army, he established his own rival Nationalist government at Nanjing on April 18, 1927. In response, the government based in Wuhan launched its own northern military campaign to gather more troops to combat Chiang. However, the northern warlords who had favored the reunification of China, and whose support had been counted on by the Wuhan Nationalist government, did not want to cooperate with a Communist-influenced government. The Nationalists in the Wuhan government removed the Communists from the Nationalist Party, and on August 1, an uprising by Communist-led troops against Nationalist troops at Nanchang, the capital of Jiangxi Province, turned into a violent anti-Communist purge. Later Communists celebrated August 1, 1927, as the birth date of the People's Liberation Army (PLA). After the Communists attempted an unsuccessful coup at Guangzhou in December 1927, they had to flee to mountainous areas in rural China, especially in Jiangxi. The Wuhan Nationalist government joined with that at Nanjing, made Nanjing the seat of government, and formally reinstated Chiang as commander-in-chief. In the spring of 1928, Chiang continued his campaign to conquer China north of the Yangzi. When Nationalist forces closed in on Beijing, the warlord Zhang Zuolin (Chang Tso-lin; 1873–1928) withdrew from the city, which was taken by Nationalist troops led by Yan Xishan (Yen Hsi-shan; 1883–1960) on June 8, 1928. This completed the Northern Expedition and reunified China after warlords had controlled the country for a dozen years. See also BORODIN, MIKHAIL; CHIANG KAI-SHEK; CHINESE COMMUNIST PARTY; JIANGXI PROVINCE; NANCHANG; NANJING; NATIONALIST PARTY; WANG JINGWEI; WARLORD PERIOD; WUHAN; ZHANG ZUOLIN.

NORTHERN HAN KINGDOM (951–979) See TEN KINGDOMS PERIOD.

NORTHERN IMPERIAL TOMB See ABAHAI; SHENYANG.

NORTHERN QI DYNASTY See NORTHERN AND SOUTHERN DYNASTIES.

NORTHERN SCHOOL OF PAINTING A style of painting practiced during the Northern Song dynasty (960–1126), which had its capital at Kaifeng in modern Henan Province. Painters in the Northern style had a great influence on the subsequent development of painting and also porcelain, in Japan as well as in China. Kaifeng was captured in 1127 by an ethnic group known as the Jurchen, who had established the Jin dynasty (1115–1234), and the Song court fled south and made Hangzhou in Zhejiang Province the capital of the Southern Song dynasty. Many artists moved to Hangzhou, which was for many centuries the cultural center of China, even after the Southern Song dynasty was overthrown by the Mongols, who founded the Yuan dynasty (1279–1368). Song emperors patronized the arts, and the Northern School became identified with professional painters, especially in the imperial court. Northern painters specialized in bird-and-flower paintings and landscapes and employed a style that is academic, detailed, delicate, precise, colorful and decorative. Northern painters preferred to paint on vertical hanging scrolls, although they also used horizontal rolling scrolls. The painters were trained in the imperial academy that had been established during the Tang dynasty (618–907). Huizong (Hui-tsung; r. 1100–25), the last Northern Song emperor, was a painter who gathered a talented group of artists around him. Some of the greatest Northern Song painters include Li Cheng (Li Ch'eng), Fan Kuan (Fan K'uan), Guo Xi (Kuo Hsi) and his son Guo Ruoxu (Kuo Jo-hsu), Xu Daoning (Hsu Tao-ning) and Li Tang (Li T'ang).

The Southern School became associated with "amateurs" belonging to the Confucian-educated literati, or scholar class (*wenren* or *wen-jen*), who staffed the imperial bureaucracy. The division of Chinese painting into two opposing schools, Northern and Southern, was devised by Dong Qichang (Tung Ch'i-ch'ang; 1555–1636), a calligrapher and art cataloguer, to assert the superiority of paintings by self-expressive scholars in the Southern School. In the Northern School, Dong included such painters as Li Sixun (Li Ssu-hsun), Liu Songnian (Liu Sung-nien), Ma Yuan and Xia Gui (Hsia Kuei). The latter two originated their own style of monochrome ink painting, using bold "ax-cut texture strokes" (*fupi cun* or *fu-pi ts'un*) of the paintbrush that had been developed by Li Tang, in which the angles of the brush strokes seem to hack out the shapes of the rocks in their landscapes. Their style became known as the Ma-Xia School. See also BIRD-AND-FLOWER PAINTING; INK PAINTING; KAIFENG; LANDSCAPE PAINTING; NORTHERN SONG DYNASTY; SCROLLS; SOUTHERN SCHOOL OF PAINTING; NAMES OF INDIVIDUAL PAINTERS.

NORTHERN SONG DYNASTY (Northern Sung; 960–1126) Also known as the Bei Song dynasty; the first period of the Song dynasty (960–1279), the last major Chinese dynasty that was founded by a coup d'état. The second period of the Song, known as the Southern Song dynasty (1127–1279), began after the Jurchen, an ethnic group based in Manchuria (modern northeastern China), captured the Northern Song capital at Kaifeng in modern Henan Province and the survivors of the Song court fled south and established their capital at Hangzhou. The founder of the Song dynasty, Zhao Kuangyin (Chao K'uang-yin), was born to a military family in northeastern China. He became the military commander of the area that included the capital city of Kaifeng and inspector general of the imperial forces under Emperor Shizong (Shih-tsung) of the Later Zhou dynasty (951–960), one of a dozen kingdoms into which China had been divided during the Five Dynasties Period (907–960). When the emperor died, his successor was only seven years old, and the Palace Corps mutinied and placed Zhao on the throne. Zhao became the first Song emperor and is known as Emperor Taizu (T'ai-tsu; r. 960–976). He brought all but two of the independent kingdoms under Song control. Unlike the founders of previous dynasties, who had destroyed their military rivals, Taizu persuaded them to relinquish their military commands, and in return he gave them honorary titles and offices and large pensions. By doing so he reduced their military power and kept them loyal to the Song. Taizu realized that the Chinese people were exhausted from a long period of military campaigns, so he emphasized the reunification of the country under a restored imperial bureaucracy modeled on that of the Tang dynasty (618–907). He also restored the Confucian-based examination system by which officials were selected to serve in the bureaucracy. They belonged to the literati (*wenren* or *wen-jen*), or scholar class, which had its most extensive influence during the Song dynasty.

The Song capital at Kaifeng, then known as Bianjing or Dongjing, is located at the head of the Grand Canal in the Yellow River valley. The canal and river were major arteries for the transport of rice and other agricultural products, textiles, lumber and handicrafts from southern to northern China. Kaifeng quickly grew to have a population of more than one million. Today many tourists visit Kaifeng because of their interest in the large Jewish community that became established there during the Song. Kaifeng became a center for woodblock printing, which had been invented in China in the eighth century and quickly developed starting in the 11th century. The large number of printed books put into circulation during the Song increased literacy among the Chinese people and gave them familiarity with Chinese literature and the classical texts of Confucianism. This led to the Song revival of Confucianism, known as Neo-Confucianism.

The Song dynasty became the most culturally active period in Chinese history. Arts such as landscape and ink painting, calligraphy and poetry flourished during the Song, and painting, like the dynasty, became divided into the Northern School and the Southern School. Fan Kuan (Fan Guan) was the greatest painter in the Northern School. The Chinese have termed painting, calligraphy and poetry the "three perfections" (*sanjue* or *san-chueh*). An interest in designing gardens accompanied the interest in landscape painting, as both were concerned primarily with "mountains and water." Some of the greatest Song poets were Ouyang Xiu (You-yang Hsiu) and Su Shi (Su Shih; also known as Su Dongpo or Su Tung-p'o). The Song upper classes became wealthy and purchased luxury goods such as silk and porcelain, which made the merchant class wealthy. New technologies were invented, such as water clocks, thread-spinning

machines to make textiles, and agricultural machines, and rice production greatly increased.

Taizu's younger brother, Zhao Kuangyi (Chao K'uang-yi), succeeded him as emperor and is known as Emperor Taizong (T'ai-tsung; r. 976–997). He centralized the government and conquered the final two independent kingdoms, Wuyue in 978 and Northern Han in 979. However, the Song were never able to bring under their control the region in northern and northeastern China, including part of the North China Plain inside the Great Wall, that was ruled by the Khitan (Qidan) under the Liao dynasty (947–1125). In 1005 the Song signed a treaty that acknowledged Liao control of that region.

During the reign of Emperor Shenzong (Shen-tsung; r. 1067–85), Prime Minister Wang Anshi initiated many institutional reforms in the economic, educational and military spheres, but the bureaucracy became divided into pro-reform and anti-reform conservative factions. After Shenzong died, the conservative faction, led by the renowned historian Sima Guang (Ssu-ma Kuang), took power and did away with the reforms. The reformers regained power in 1093 but did not receive the support they formerly had in the bureaucracy.

Emperor Huizong (Hui-tsung; r. 1100–25) was the last ruler of the Northern Song dynasty. He was an excellent painter and calligrapher and patronized court artists. However, Huizong has been blamed for the downfall of the Song dynasty. During his rule the population was heavily taxed to pay for military campaigns and the luxurious lifestyle of the court, and rebellions broke out in Zhejiang Province in 1120 and Shandong Province in 1121. The Song had also been paying heavy tribute to the Liao and to the kingdom of Xixia on its northwestern border because it had not been able to control them with its military. The Jurchens in Manchuria (modern northeastern China) had been vassals of the Liao dynasty, but they broke away and founded the Jin dynasty (1115–1234). The Song made an alliance with the Jin against the Liao, and in 1123 the Jin defeated the Liao on their own. The Song, intending to regain the northern part of modern Hebei Province, which had been occupied by the Liao, attacked the Jin but proved weak militarily. The Jin attacked the Song capital of Kaifeng in 1126. Song emperor Huizong abdicated the throne to his son, known as Emperor Qinzong (Ch'in-tsung), and the Jin forced the Song to sign a humiliating treaty.

In the winter of 1126–27 the Jin laid siege to Kaifeng and captured it and took control of northern China. Huizong, Qinzong and 3,000 officials of the Song court were taken captive, and Huizong lived in captivity until he died in 1135. The prince of Kang, the ninth son of Huizong, was away from Kaifeng when it fell to the Jin, and he was able to escape to the south and restore the Song dynasty. Known as Emperor Gaozong (Kao-tsung; r. 1127–62), the first Southern Song emperor, he made temporary headquarters at two places and finally established the Song capital at Hangzhou, a beautiful city that is the capital of modern Zhejiang Province. See also CALLIGRAPHY; FIVE DYNASTIES PERIOD; GAOZONG, EMPEROR; GARDENS; GRAND CANAL; HUIZONG, EMPEROR; IMPERIAL BUREAUCRACY; IMPERIAL EXAMINATION SYSTEM; JEWS; JIN DYNASTY; JURCHEN; KAIFENG; LIAO DYNASTY; LITERATI; NEO-CONFUCIANISM; NORTH CHINA PLAIN; NORTHERN SCHOOL OF PAINTING; OUYANG XIU; PORCELAIN; PRINTING; SIMA GUANG;

SOUTHERN SONG DYNASTY; SU SHI; TAIZONG, EMPEROR; TAIZU, EMPEROR; WANG ANSHI; XIXIA, KINGDOM OF; YELLOW RIVER.

NORTHERN WEI DYNASTY (386–534) A dynasty established in north China by the Toba Turks (Tuoba or T'o-pa), a branch of the nomadic tribe known as the Xianbei (Hsien-pei), who had settled in the region of modern Shanxi Province after the fall of the Han dynasty (206 B.C.-A.D. 220). The Northern Wei reunified north China, which had broken down into the so-called Sixteen Kingdoms after the Han fell. Their first capital was at Datong in northern Shanxi. In 494 the great Northern Wei ruler Xiaowendi (Hsiao-wen-ti; r. 471–99) moved the capital to Luoyang, south of the Yellow River, which had been the Eastern Han capital. He and his grandmother, the Dowager Empress Feng, decreed that the non-Han subjects of the Northern Wei dynasty had to adapt Han Chinese culture and bureaucratic government. The Northern Wei spoke only the Chinese language in their court, wore Chinese clothing, took Chinese surnames and intermarried with the Chinese families in the area. Xiaowendi brought prosperity to his kingdom by enacting land reforms, reducing taxes and increasing agricultural production. He and other Northern Wei rulers also supported the Buddhist religion, which had been introduced into China from India around the first century A.D. They sponsored two massive projects of Buddhist stone carvings, the Yungang Cave Temples and Sculptures near Datong and the Longmen Cave Temples and Sculptures near Luoyang, both of which can be seen today. The nomadic tribes on Wei's northern frontier resented the adaptation of Chinese culture and rebelled against the Northern Wei dynasty beginning in 524. The nomadic tribes were subdued by another tribal group called the Erzhu, which took Luoyang, the Northern Wei capital, and ruled north China for a short time. At this time, the Northern Wei dynasty divided into two branches. The Eastern Wei was ruled by Gao Huan, who moved his capital from Luoyang to Ye (Anyang in modern Henan Province). The Western Wei was ruled by Yuwen Tai, who made his capital at Chang'an (modern Xi'an). The Eastern Wei was overthrown in 550, and the Western Wei in 557. See also BUDDHISM IN CHINA; DATONG; LONGMEN CAVE TEMPLES AND SCULPTURES; LUOYANG; YUNGANG CAVE TEMPLES AND SCULPTURES.

NORTHERN ZHOU DYNASTY See NORTHERN AND SOUTHERN DYNASTIES.

NPC See NATIONAL PEOPLE'S CONGRESS.

NU RIVER See TIBET.

NU-CHIEH See CODE FOR WOMEN.

NUCLEAR POWER See ENERGY SOURCES.

NUGUA See FUXI.

NUJIE (NU-CHIN) See CODE FOR WOMEN.

NU-KUA See FUXI.

NURHACHI (1559–1626) The unifier of the Tungusic Sushis, a tribe of the Jurchen ethnic group that had established the Jin dynasty (1115–1234). Controlling eastern and southeastern Manchuria, which is now the northeastern part of China, the Jurchens later became known as the Manchus and ruled China under the Qing dynasty (1644–1911), which was founded by Nurhachi's son Abahai (1592–1643).

Nurhachi's father was a tribal chieftain who was killed in battle. Over several decades Nurhachi consolidated his power by employing the so-called "banner" system (*gusai*), dividing his army into four (eventually expanded to 24) companies of warriors, each with its own banner in a distinctive color, for administrative purposes and to build a disciplined army. Nurhachi initially paid tribute to the Chinese Ming dynasty (1368–1644) in Beijing, and in 1608 signed a boundary treaty with the Ming, all the while preparing his army to fight against them. In 1616 Nurhachi declared the founding of the Later Jin dynasty (1616–36); two years later he announced his "Seven Grievances" against the Ming and declared open warfare. The Ming sent an army of 200,000 to Manchuria, but Nurhachi's troops, outnumbered but hardened fighters, defeated them. In a few years he conquered all territory formerly held by the Ming east of the Liao River. In 1625 the Manchus made Shenyang, the capital of Liaoning Province, their capital and gave it the Manchurian name Mukden. Nurhachi used Chinese civil bureaucrats whom he had taken prisoner to set up a bureaucracy in Mukden.

Nurhachi died in 1626 in a battle against forces of the Ming dynasty outside the fortified Ming city of Ningyuan. Dongling (Eastern Imperial Tomb), today officially called Fuling, was constructed northeast of Mukden in 1629–51 to house the remains of Nurhachi and his wife. See also BANNER SYSTEM, MANCHU; JIN DYNASTY; LIAODONG PENINSULA; LIAONING PROVINCE; MANCHU; MANCHURIA; QING DYNASTY; SHENYANG.

OBSERVATORIES See ASTRONOMY AND OBSERVATORIES; JESUITS.

OCARINA See FLUTES AND WIND INSTRUMENTS.

OCTS See CHINA INTERNATIONAL TRAVEL SERVICE.

OGODAI (OGODEI, OGOTAI) See GENGHIS KHAN; KARAKORUM.

OIL See BO HAI GULF; DAQING OIL FIELDS; DZUNGARIA BASIN; ENERGY SOURCES; SOUTH CHINA SEA; SPRATLY ISLANDS.

OIRAT MONGOLS See ZHENGTONG, EMPEROR.

OKINAWA See RYUKYU ISLANDS.

OLD PALACE MUSEUM See FORBIDDEN CITY.

OLYMPIC GAMES See SPORTS; WEI JINGSHENG.

OMEI, MOUNT See FOUR SACRED MOUNTAINS OF BUDDHISM.

OMITOFO See AMITABHA.

ONE-CHILD FAMILY CAMPAIGN A policy announced by the Chinese government in 1979 to limit population growth by allowing each married couple to have only one child in the city and two children in the countryside. Chinese families traditionally had large numbers of children, and they especially wanted sons to carry on the family line and take care of the parents and ancestral spirits, in keeping with the teachings of Confucianism. After the Chinese Communist Party (CCP) founded the People's Republic of China (PRC) in 1949, the Ministry of Public Health introduced various family planning campaigns and programs to control population growth, but these did little to alter Chinese fertility. In the early 1960s the government attempted another campaign, which succeeded in cutting the birth rate in half in the cities in 1963–66. The tumultuous Cultural Revolution (1966–76) interrupted this campaign, but the government resumed its efforts to control population growth in the early 1970s. So-called "barefoot doctors," lay people trained in basic medical techniques to treat people in the countryside, distributed birth control information and contraceptives to residents of people's communes. After the Cultural Revolution the CCP initiated new policies to reform and modernize the country, and in 1979 it enacted the one-child policy under which most families were restricted to having only one child. This policy has been very controversial and has been hard to enforce uniformly around the country. For the most part it has not been applied to members of China's 55 national minority ethnic groups. They comprise only about 7 percent of the population, but the Chinese government wishes to have good relations with them to ensure political stability, since most of them inhabit sensitive border regions.

As part of the one-child family campaign, the Chinese government encouraged couples to delay marrying, as late as age 28 for men and 25 for women. The Revised Marriage Law enacted in 1982 set the legal age for marriage for Chinese men at age 22 and women at age 20. A woman who delays marriage until after 25 is entitled to a longer maternity leave when she gives birth to her child. Recently the government has encouraged couples in the cities to sign a one-child pledge by offering them an extra month's salary every year until the child turns 14, plus housing usually given to a family of four, although a shortage of housing makes this promise difficult to carry out. If the couple has a second child these privileges are eliminated, and the man and woman may be demoted at work or even lose their jobs. A woman who has an abortion is entitled to a vacation with pay. Some incentives used in the countryside include giving a farm couple who have only one child a double-sized plot of land. All birth control methods are free in China. The ones most commonly used are the IUD, female sterilization and abortion. In some areas, officials force women to have abortions, and they also

Since 1979, the Chinese government has attempted through the One-Child Family Campaign to restrict urban couples to one child and rural couples to two. S.E. MEYER

record erroneous figures to make sure their areas meet the birth quotas. Neighborhood committees administered by the CCP, consisting mainly of older women, strongly pressure Chinese couples in their neighborhood to obey the government policy and have only one or two children.

The one-child campaign has been fairly successful in Chinese cities, but not as much in the countryside, where peasants still wish to have many children who can help with farm work. Some pregnant women hide in the countryside until after their children are born, but they can be penalized with steep fines, loss of jobs, and other drastic punishments such as the destruction of their house and furniture. The Confucian-based desire for a son to continue the family is still so strong in China that female infanticide remains a problem, and some areas have a population imbalance of many more boys than girls.

In the 1980s, about 80 percent of the parents of single children were between 30 to 40 years old, had grown up during the Cultural Revolution and had received almost no education because the schools had shut down. Hence they were driven to ensure that their children got every possible advantage in life. The Chinese have recently criticized single children, who are indulged and obsessed over by their parents, have strong wills, are rude, dislike manual labor and constantly want to be given presents. Chinese journalist Han Yi coined the term "Little Emperors" to describe them. This term refers to the custom in imperial China of placing a deceased emperor's heir on the throne even if he was just a child. A "little emperor" had all his wishes indulged and was given the same homage as an adult emperor.

In 1989 the Chinese population numbered 1.1 billion. China has 22 percent of the world's population living on just 7 percent of the world's arable land. In 1971 the annual population increase in China was 2.3 percent, which would have doubled the country's population in 30 years. By 1994 the increase was down to 1.4 percent, although that would still double the population in 48 years. In 1987 the birthrate was 23.3 births per thousand, and in 1990 it was down to 18.2 per thousand. With the one-child policy, the Chinese government hopes that the population will peak at 1.9 billion in the mid-21st century, then stabilize and begin to decline. In October 1995, the Chinese government, recognizing that its one-child family campaign was failing to halt rapid population growth, offered farmers financial incentives to stop having children. Farmers who stick to the policy will be given priority in getting welfare, loans and development funds from the government. Recently many Chinese illegal immigrants to the United States have requested political asylum by claiming that the one-child policy has oppressed them, especially the women who have undergone forced abortions and sterilization. They fear that if they are sent back to China, they will be given prison terms or fines and will be politically harassed. See also ANCESTOR WORSHIP; BAREFOOT DOCTORS; CONFUCIANISM; FAMILY STRUCTURE; FILIAL PIETY; MINORITIES, NATIONAL.

ONE-HUNDRED- AND ONE-THOUSAND-YEAR EGGS
See DUCK.

OPEN DOOR POLICY
A policy that gives all nations of the world equal access to trade in a particular country. The Open Door policy is most commonly associated with the United States' reaction to the relations between China and several foreign powers in the 19th century. China had been forced to sign unequal treaties by Britain, France, Germany, Russia and Japan, giving the various countries trade advantages and concessions of land. Each country gained its own "sphere of influence" in China in which it had exclusive rights for building railroads and telegraph systems and mining mineral resources. In 1899 U.S. secretary of state John Hay formally announced the doctrine that became known as the Open Door policy. He sent Open Door notes to the governments of Britain, Germany, Russia, Japan, Italy and France that implied that the United States would not accept any monopoly rights of foreign nations in their spheres of influence in China. This action seemed as if the United States, which did not want to claim Chinese territory for itself, was attempting to preserve China's integrity by preventing it from being partitioned by foreign powers. Actually, the Open Door was developed to give the United States an "equal opportunity" alongside the other foreign powers to conduct trade and exploit resources anywhere it wanted to in China.

In 1900, the Boxer Uprising, by a Chinese faction that opposed privileges for foreigners in China, presented a challenge to the Open Door. Russia used the Boxers as an excuse to move into Manchuria (northeastern China) and attempted to move into northern China as well, but Britain warned Russia to stay out of that region. At the same time, Germany also wanted to increase its spheres of influence. In July 1900, while Russian troops were entering Manchuria, Hay sent another Open Door note to Britain, France, Germany, Japan and Russia, maintaining that the principle of equal trade rights depended on the integrity of China's territory. The note stated that the United States sought a "collective guarantee" from the foreign powers "which may bring about permanent safety and peace in China, [and] preserve Chinese territorial and administrative entity." This solution would also "protect all rights guaranteed to friendly Powers by treaty and international law, and safeguard for the world the principle of equal and impartial trade with all parts of the Chinese Empire." None of the foreign powers replied to this note except Britain, and the United States did not want to commit its military power to enforce the Open Door policy in China.

The division of China among the foreign powers was halted for a time, not by America's policy but by the rivalry among the foreign powers. The Chinese valued the Open Door policy as a sign of support from the United States, however, and for 50 years regarded the United States as the only foreign power that they could trust because it did not want to take Chinese territory for itself. At the Washington Conference in 1921–22 following World War I, all the powers attending the conference signed the Nine Power Open Door Treaty, which required that the powers other than China "respect the sovereignty, the independence, and the territorial integrity of China" and "to use their influence for the purpose of effectually establishing and maintaining the principle of equal opportunity for the commerce and industry of all nations throughout the territory of China." Although the treaty was written in abstract language and did not provide economic or military sanctions to be applied to any power that violated the treaty, China was satisfied with concessions that it gained from foreign powers at the conference. The Open Door remained a pillar of American policy toward China until the Chinese Communists defeated the Nationalists in 1949 and closed China to foreign exploitation. See also BOXER UPRISING; CIVIL WAR BETWEEN COMMUNISTS AND NATIONALISTS; TREATY PORTS; UNEQUAL TREATIES; WORLD WAR I.

OPERA, BEIJING
Also known as Peking Opera; a popular form of theater that combines acting, singing, dancing and acrobatics accompanied by a traditional Chinese orchestra comprised mainly of loud percussion instruments and two-string fiddles, known as *erhu* and *huqin* (*hu-ch'in*). Other instruments include the *pipa,* similar to a lute; the *sheng* or reed pipe; and the *yueqin* (*yueh-ch'in*), similar to a moon-shaped guitar. Wooden clappers accentuate the actions on stage. The actors wear elaborate, colorful costumes and stylized masks or painted faces that represent the particular types of roles they are playing. They sing in loud voices, because the operas were originally performed in crowded outdoor settings, and the songs have clearly defined rhythms.

Beijing Opera was originally known as *pihuang* or *luantuan,* "plucking at random" (on a stringed instrument). It originated in Anhui and Hubei provinces to the south of Beijing. For the celebration of the 55th year of the reign of Qing emperor Qianlong (Ch'ien-lung) and his 80th birthday in 1790, some artists from those regions first performed this style of opera in Beijing. Performers began drawing upon Kunqu (K'un-ch'u), Qin and Yi styles of opera that had been performed in the imperial court and at Beijing theaters during the 16th and 17th centuries, and by the early 19th century they had developed the distinctive style of Beijing Opera. This opera has a much more colorful repertoire with a greater emphasis on acrobatics than other styles of Chinese opera.

Beijing Opera has four types of characters, male (*sheng*), female (*dan* or *tan*), the "painted face" (*jing* or *ching*) and clown (*chou* or *ch'ou*). Male roles include such characters as scholars and government officials, called *wensheng,* and warriors (*wusheng*), who are highly trained in acrobatics. The category of male roles is subdivided into the bearded *laosheng* who portray old men and the *xiaosheng* (*hsiaosheng*) who portray young men. The female roles were traditionally performed by men but are now performed by women. They include elderly, dignified women such as mothers and widows (*laodan* or *lao-tan*); elegant aristocratic women (*qingyi* or *ch'ing-i*); ladies' maids (*huadan* or *huatan*), who wear brightly colored costumes; women warriors (*daomadan* or *tao-ma-tan*); and women comedians (*caidan* or *ts'ai-tan*). Painted face roles include warriors, noble heroes, adventurers and demons. Their opposite are the clowns.

Though traditionally all roles in the Beijing Opera were performed by men, female roles are now given to women as well.   S.E. MEYER

Actors use very few props and convey the meaning of their words and songs through gestures, movements, mime and facial expressions.

The stories in Beijing Opera were taken from plays performed earlier in China and from traditional stories and novels. One of the most popular is the novel, *Romance of the Three Kingdoms,* based on the actual conflict between three Chinese kingdoms in the third century A.D. General Cao Cao (Ts'ao Ts'ao; 155–220), a historical figure who is one of the novel's main characters, is perhaps the character most frequently portrayed in Beijing Opera performances. Mei Lanfang (1894–1961) was one of the greatest modern performers who introduced Beijing Opera to other countries. He was one of the last traditional male performers in the *dan* or female roles. Beijing Opera is still popular after 200 years and there are many professional companies, including four troupes of the National Beijing Opera Theater under the Ministry of Culture, four more troupes of the Beijing Opera Theater, the Experimental Beijing Opera Theater and the Fenglei Beijing Opera Troupe. There are also many amateur troupes organized by various associations and cultural centers. Beijing Opera performers and fans hold frequent gatherings to sing opera in their homes. Retired Chinese also love to gather in city parks and sing opera passages, accompanied by the *erhu.*

There are 365 styles of traditional Chinese opera. Guangzhou (Canton) Opera, one of the best known, is per-formed in southern China, and since many Chinese immigrants to other countries came from the south, it is also popular in overseas Chinese communities. Huangmei Opera originated in the villages where the provinces of Anhui, Hubei and Jiangxi meet. It evolved out of popular tea picking songs (*caichadiao* or *ts'ai ch'a-tiao*) in Huangmei County, Hubei Province, and incorporated folk songs and portions of songs from Qingyang Opera. It then spread to Anqing in Anhui Province, where it developed into local songs in the Anqing dialect, now known as *Fuqiang,* Anqing Prefecture opera or *Huaiqing.* Huangmei songs are soft and sweet, and the opera's singing and dancing have an appealing simplicity of style. A Huangmei Opera theater was built in 1982 that involves hundreds of people in writing operas, training performers and organizing performances.

Bangzi (Pang-chi) Opera originated from the folk songs of Shaanxi and Gansu provinces in western China during the Ming dynasty (1368–1644), and eventually spread east to Henan, Hebei and Shanxi provinces. It has become the most popular performing art in the Hebei countryside, and there are dozens of troupes in the province. The Hebei School of Art has a Bangzi department with about 50 teachers and more than 300 students. Bangzi Opera is characterized by high-pitched music, accented by the beating of wooden clappers (*bangzi*). See also ACROBATICS AND VARIETY THEATER; BIWA; CAO CAO; DRUMS; ERHU; KUNQU; MEI LANFANG;

OPERA, GUANGZHOU; PIPA; ROMANCE OF THE THREE KINGDOMS; STRING INSTRUMENTS.

OPERA, GUANGZHOU (CANTON)

The most popular opera form in the southern Chinese province of Guangdong, of which Guangzhou is the capital city, and one of the best-known forms of traditional Chinese opera, along with Beijing Opera and Kunqu. Since many Chinese began emigrating from Guangzhou, a major port city, in the 19th century, Guangzhou (Cantonese) Opera has been popular in many overseas Chinese communities in Southeast Asia and North and South America. Guangzhou and other forms of Chinese opera combine acting, singing, dancing and acrobatics performed by highly skilled actors wearing brightly colored costumes and makeup. The first Guangzhou Opera guild was formed during the reign of Ming emperor Wanli (r. 1573–1620). Around 1770, during the reign of Qing emperor Qianlong (Ch'ien-lung; r. 1736–96), opera troupes from the Chinese provinces of Hunan, Jianxi, Anhui, Fujian, Jiangsu and Zhejiang moved to Guangzhou. Contemporary Guangzhou Opera blends the opera styles from those provinces with the music and folk songs of Guangdong Province.

Guangzhou Opera originally had 10 types of roles, including the male role (*sheng*), female role (*dan* or *tan*), painted-face role (*jing* or *ching*) and clown (*chou* or *ch'ou*), and modern performers are reviving the traditional roles. Each type of role is characterized by a particular style of makeup, costumes, body and eye movements, and voices. Makeup for Guangzhou Opera covers the neck as well as the face. Guangzhou Opera was originally sung in classical Chinese in high-pitched melodies with loud accompaniment by musical instruments. Later the performers began using the vernacular dialect, and the melodies were sung in lower keys that are more pleasant to hear. Opera masters are permitted to improvise on the melodies they perform and hence create their own unique singing styles. The singing styles of master performers Xue Juesheng (Hsueh Chueh-sheng) and Ma Shizeng (Ma Shih-tseng) remain popular today. Spoken dialogues and monologues are also performed in the vernacular Guangzhou dialect. Acrobatics are based on the style of martial arts popular in southern China and include the use of weapons such as swords and spears, hand-to-hand combat, somersaults and movements from a weaponless, dance-like martial art known as *taijiquan* (*t'ai chi ch'uan*). Traditional orchestras include such instruments as the *sanxian* (*san-hsien*), a three-stringed banjo-like instrument known to the West by the Japanese term *samisen;* moon-shaped guitars (*yueqin* or *yueh-ch'in*); two-stringed guitars (*erxian* or *erh-hsien*); and drums, gongs and cymbals, which are played to accent the performers' movements. Guangzhou orchestras have also incorporated Western instruments such as the violin and now have a total of 11 musicians.

The Guangzhou Opera repertoire comprises about 9,000 traditional and modern themes, many of which are based on historical legends, stories from classical Chinese literature or folk tales. Some are even based on historical events or adapted from foreign stories, plays and films. Since the founding of the Communist People's Republic of China (PRC) in 1949, the Chinese government has encouraged Guangzhou Opera artists to improve their repertoire, performing skills, music, and scenery and props, and a number of new operas have been created. The Guangzhou Opera Troupe has toured Hong Kong, Macao, Singapore, the United States and Canada. See also GUANGDONG PROVINCE; GUANGZHOU; KUNQU; OPERA, BEIJING; OVERSEAS CHINESE; TAIJIQUAN.

OPIUM WAR (1839–42)

A war initiated by Great Britain to force China to open up to the Western-style system of trade. For centuries China had maintained a tribute system whereby foreign countries wanting to conduct trade first had to send missions to the Chinese capital bearing tribute for the Chinese emperor, before whom they bowed in a series of prostrations known as *kowtow* (*gaodao* or *kao-tao*). This symbolized the submission of their country to Chinese suzerainty, for which they received permission to trade in specified regions in China. European trading ships began arriving at the southern Chinese port city of Guangzhou (Canton) in the late 16th century, and the British East India Company, established in 1600, soon came to dominate European trade with China. In the 18th century the government of the Qing dynasty (1644–1911) that ruled China established the Canton system to regulate foreign trade: Western merchants now had to conduct all of their business through native Chinese merchants in Guangzhou who belonged to a guild known as the *Cohong* or "*Hong*" (from *gonghang*, "combined merchant companies"). The *hong* merchants made high profits by regulating the prices for imported and exported goods and by collecting all duties and tariffs on behalf of the Chinese government. Western traders were confined to an area along the bank of the Pearl River where the residences and offices of the factors of foreign companies were located, an area known as the "13 Factories."

The British East India Company nearly went bankrupt in 1772, but the British parliament loaned it £1.5 million and passed an act that placed the administration of British-held India under a governor-general appointed by the British Crown. The company's army became the largest military force in East Asia. In 1793 the British government sent Lord (George) Macartney to China to request the ending of the Canton system, the opening of more Chinese ports to foreign trade, and the setting of fair tariffs. Emperor Qianlong (r. 1736–95) gave Macartney two audiences at his Summer Palace north of Beijing. Macartney refused to obey the Chinese command to *kowtow* and knelt only on one knee before the emperor, the same as he did before the British king. He presented gifts to the emperor, but Emperor Qianlong considered them "tribute presents" and refused to give in to the British requests, stating that China would not increase its foreign trade because it did not need anything from other countries.

In 1799 the Qing government gave the British East India Company permission to move its factory to Guangzhou. However, the balance of trade was not favorable to Britain, whose traders sold Indian cotton to China but bought luxury goods such as tea, silk and porcelain from China, which drained silver from the British economy. The British continued pressuring the Qing government to open the country to foreign trade, and they also began selling large quantities of opium to China, which drained China of silver and demoralized the Chinese people. There was widespread smuggling of opium into the country, especially along the coast north of Guangzhou. In 1816 Britain sent another mission to China, headed by Lord Amherst, but if fared no better than Macartney. In 1834 the British government abolished the East India Company and sent Lord Napier to Guangzhou to supervise the triangular Britain-India-China trade and to continue pressuring the Qing government.

The Qing responded by commissioning Lin Zexu (Lin Tse-hsu) to eliminate the opium trade in Guangzhou. He arrived there in 1839 and blockaded the 13 Factories and confined 350 foreign traders for six weeks, until the British surrendered 20,000 chests of opium, which he publicly destroyed. The British refused to pledge that they would stop shipping opium to China, so Lin threatened to ban all commercial traffic. Qing officials also refused to deal directly with Captain Charles Elliot, the British government's official supervisor of British trade at Guangzhou. The British withdrew to Macao and the island of Hong Kong and continued to supply opium to smugglers, many of them members of secret societies, while acquiring Chinese tea through American companies doing business in China. In July 1839 a group of British sailors killed a Chinese man in Kowloon on the Chinese mainland across from Hong Kong, but the British refused to surrender the sailors to Lin. When a fleet of Chinese war junks sailed toward the British fleet at Hong Kong to seize the sailors, the British fired on them and the Opium War began.

The British dispatched a military force with armed steamships that were able to maneuver in the shallow estuaries and harbors of southern China. From 1840 to 1842 they captured several ports between Guangzhou and Shanghai at the mouth of the Yangzi River (Changjiang), one of China's two largest rivers. The Chinese were not able to put up a strong defense, and after the British threatened to take Nanjing, the Qing secondary capital on the Yangzi, Qing officials sued for peace and began negotiating with the British near Tianjin, a port close to the Chinese capital of Beijing. Lin Zexu was removed from office for his failure to stop the British, although he was later reinstated. The British forced the Qing government to sign the Treaty of Nanjing in 1842. The 13 articles of this treaty, along with supplementary treaties signed in 1843, gave Britain many privileges and rights in China. Five treaty ports were opened for foreign residence and trade: Guangzhou, Amoy (Xiamen), Fuzhou, Ningbo and Shanghai, which soon replaced Guangzhou as China's largest trading port. China awarded Britain most-favored-nation status, meaning that Britain would automatically be given any privilege that China might later extend to any other nation. The British were allowed to appoint foreign consuls at treaty ports who could deal directly with Qing government officials, and they were given extraterritoriality in civil and criminal cases. This meant that British subjects accused of crimes or involved in disputes with Chinese citizens would be tried, by the consul, under British law; this principle actually violated China's judicial powers. China ceded Hong Kong to Britain in perpetuity. In 1860 Britain gained Kowloon, and in 1898 it acquired a 99-year lease over the New Territories adjoining Kowloon. Hong Kong, Kowloon and the New Territories peacefully reverted to China in 1997. The Portuguese will return Macao to China in 1999.

These concessions to Britain greatly damaged the prestige of the Qing dynasty in the eyes of the Han Chinese people, who resented the Manchus, an ethnic group from Manchuria (northeastern China) that had overthrown the Chinese Ming dynasty (1368–1644) and founded the Qing. The Manchus were buffeted by the demands made by Britain and other foreign powers and by the strong anti-foreign and anti-Manchu feelings of the Han, the vast majority of the Chinese people. Other foreign powers forced the Qing to sign treaties with them similar to the Treaty of Nanjing, granting the right of extraterritoriality and most-favored-nation status, such as the Treaty of Wangxia (Wang-hsia) signed in 1844 with the United States and the Franco-Chinese Treaty signed in 1844. The Qing government did not want to honor these treaties, considered "unequal treaties" by the Chinese, and did not want to open more treaty ports to foreigners. Britain soon entered another war with China, known as the Arrow War (also known as the Second Opium War; 1856–60). See also ARROW WAR; BRITISH EAST INDIA COMPANY; CANTON SYSTEM TO REGULATE FOREIGN TRADE; GUANGZHOU; HONG KONG; JUNK; KOWLOON; KOWTOW; LIN ZEXU; MACAO; MACARTNEY, GEORGE, LORD; NANJING, TREATY OF; PEARL RIVER; QIANLONG, EMPEROR; QING DYNASTY; SHANGHAI; TREATY PORTS; TRIBUTE SYSTEM; UNEQUAL TREATIES.

ORACLE BONES (*jiaguwen* or *chia ku wen*, "shell and bone writing")   Animal bones and tortoise shells that were used for divining the future during the Shang dynasty (1750–1040 B.C.). They were originally dug up by farmers in the region around Anyang in Henan Province in central China, who called them dragon bones. They were sold in traditional medicine shops as far away as the capital city of Beijing. In 1889 two scholars, Liu Er and Wang Yirong, realized that the tortoise shells in these shops had scratches on them that were an ancient form of writing. Scientific excavations of Bronze Age sites at Anyang were first made by the Academia Sinica from 1928 to 1937. These and subsequent excavations turned up objects from the Shang dynasty and also seem to verify the existence of the Xia dynasty (2200–1750 B.C.), China's first Neolithic dynasty. Xia and Shang rulers followed the practice of seeking information about the future from their gods and ancestors by means of oracle bones. The shoulder bones of oxen and sheep and the bottom shells of tortoises were used. The point of a heated bronze tool was applied to the bones and shells until hairline cracks appeared in them, and the ways the cracks formed were believed to provide positive or negative answers to the questions asked. Priest-scribes were trained to analyze the cracks in the bones and shells. The Chinese word for divination, *bu* or *pu*, was written by showing two hairline cracks joining to form an angle.

More than 100,000 oracle bones have been excavated near Anyang. By the early 1980s about 1,300 distinct marks had been discerned, which can be compared with modern written Chinese characters, and a similar number are still to be deciphered. More than 1.6 million characters have been found on oracle bones at Anyang, providing comprehensive information about the Shang dynasty. Thus Chinese writing developed through several stages in a direct line from oracle bone inscriptions to the present forms. The markings on oracle bones—pictographs, which were usually inscribed with a tool made of bronze or jade—are the earliest known form of Chinese writing. This writing style was at its peak between 1700 and 1100 B.C., but the fact that it was so complex and highly developed indicates that the written Chinese language had originated at least by 2000 B.C. Twentieth-century Chinese writers have been able to reconstruct the ancient oracle "shell and bone" style of writing and have made it an accepted style in the art form of Chinese calligraphy. See also ANYANG; CALLIGRAPHY; WRITING SYSTEM, CHINESE.

ORANGE (*juzi* or *chu-tzu*)   A small, round citrus fruit that is extremely popular in China, where many species are grown in the south. The most popular and sweetest is the tangerine or mandarin orange (*Zhongguo ganju* or *Chung-kuo kan-chu*), which includes "bitterpeel" and "sweetpeel" varieties. The kumquat is a winter-ripening variety of golden bitterpeel tangerine. Related fruits, the pomelo (*yu*) and the bitter citron (*juyuan* or *chu-yuan*), were introduced into ancient China from Vietnam. Chinese oranges were also introduced to the Western world. The Canton orange (*zheng* or *cheng*), also known as the coolie orange, was introduced to the Arabs who controlled much of Central Asia in the 9th and 10th centuries, and it eventually arrived in Spain, where it is known as the Seville orange and is used to make excellent marmalade. A sweeter variety of this orange was brought to Europe by Crusaders in the 14th century and was developed into Valencia and navel oranges.

Oranges symbolize good fortune and are commonly included in food offerings made to ancestors in Chinese homes and to religious deities in Chinese temples. Usually four oranges are placed on a plate among the offerings. Oranges were included in sacrifices to Heaven performed by the Chinese emperor at the New Year, and tribute payments of oranges were sent from Fuzhou in Fujian Province to the imperial capital at Beijing for this purpose. The Chinese serve oranges at the New Year Festival in early February or late January, the most important Chinese festival. Giving someone a gift of oranges at this time expresses a wish for their happiness and prosperity in the coming year.

In Chinese herbal medicine, a tincture of orange peel, especially the bitterpeel tangerine, is widely used as a sedative, expectorant and digestive. The dried fruit and seeds are also used medicinally. Pharmacists and grocers sell large quantities of dried and fresh pieces of orange peel, which are also used in Chinese cooking for fish and meat dishes such as roasted duck with orange peel. Dried peel is soaked in water to soften before cooking. Oranges preserved in salt are a traditional Chinese remedy for drinking too much wine. See also HEAVEN; MEDICINE, HERBAL; NEW YEAR FESTIVAL.

ORCHID (*lanhua*)   A perennial plant that grows in temperate and tropical regions. The orchid has flowers with delicate, curling petals and long, thin, graceful leaves. Many varieties are native to China, the most common being the *Aglaia odorata*, a small green species with a beautiful scent. There are nearly one thousand species of Chinese orchids. Today about 200 varieties are cultivated. Chinese orchids are divided into two general classes, spring blooming and autumn blooming. The fragrant orchid, according to the philosopher Confucius (Kongfuzi; 551–479 B.C.), represents the superior man of moral virtue and refinement, whose rep-

utation precedes him like perfume. The orchid is also a symbol of spring, love and a woman's beauty. Orchids are hence popular subjects in Chinese painting. The delicate flowers and leaves especially lend themselves to the Chinese style of monochrome ink painting, which is related to the calligraphic method of writing in strokes with a brush. A noted 17th-century manual of floral painting techniques, *The Mustard Seed Garden Painting Manual,* states that orchid leaves should be painted in a few broad strokes and should have a floating grace that moves in rhythm with the wind; and that the heart of the orchid is like the eyes of a beautiful woman. The Chinese consider the orchid one of the "Four Noble Plants," along with the bamboo, plum and chrysanthemum. Orchid Flowers are used to make tea and herbal medicine. See also BAMBOO; BIRD-AND-FLOWER PAINTING; CALLIGRAPHY; CHRYSANTHEMUM; CONFUCIUS; INK PAINTING; MUSTARD SEED GARDEN MANUAL OF PAINTING; PAINTING; PLUM.

ORDOS PLATEAU   An arid region in northwest China that lies south of the Yellow River in the Inner Mongolia Autonomous Region and extends south into Shaanxi Province. The grasslands of the Ordos Plateau are isolated from the North China Plain by the Great Wall to the south and southeast, which cuts across the large northern bend of the Yellow River (Huanghe). The Ordos region contains sparse grassland that dwindles into large areas of sand dunes and stony desert, such as the Mu Us Desert near the Great Wall, which has become increasingly dry over the past thousand years. The desert has been spreading to the southeast, and in the 1960s various measures were taken to contain the shifting sand, such as planting a line of hardy trees parallel to the Great Wall. The kingdom of Xixia was founded in the Ordos Plateau in A.D. 990 by the Tangut Tibetan tribal confederation. Today the region is sparsely populated by nomadic Mongol herders. Vast coal deposits in the Ordos Plateau have contributed to the development of the modern industrial city of Baotou on the Yellow River, where there is a large steelworks. See also BAOTOU; GREAT WALL; INNER MONGOLIA AUTONOMOUS REGION; MONGOL; SHAANXI PROVINCE; XIXIA, KINGDOM OF; YELLOW RIVER.

OUTER MONGOLIA   See ALTAI MOUNTAIN RANGE; INNER MONGOLIA AUTONOMOUS REGION; MONGOL; XINJIANG-UIGHUR AUTONOMOUS REGION.

OUTLAWS OF THE MARSH (*Shuihuzhuan* or *Shi-hu-chuan*)   One of the most important Chinese works of historical fiction; also known as *The Water Margin.* The novel tells the story of the bandit Song Jiang (Sung Chiang), who led a minor rebellion between A.D. 1120 and 1121 at the end of the Northern Song dynasty (960–1126). His band of 108 rebels initially fought against government forces to right the wrongs of oppression and injustice, similar to Robin Hood and his band of men. However, because they ravaged the countryside and captured many cities in the process, they gained other enemies and had to defend themselves against them as well. By the end of the story, each of the bandits has met his death.

Legends and plays about heroic rebels accumulated into a massive manuscript that eventually contained 120 chapters. The version that became standard is a compilation of stories and plays dating from the 13th and 14th centuries made by Shi Naian and Lo Guanzhong. This version underwent many revisions during the 16th and 17th centuries. The popularly accepted version, which has only 70 chapters, was produced in 1644 by the author Jin Shengtan (Chin Sheng-t'an; d. 1661), who actually rewrote the book. Mao Zedong (Mao Tse-tung; 1893–1976), the Chinese Communist leader who founded the People's Republic of China, greatly admired *Outlaws of the Marsh*. The American author Pearl Buck translated the book into English under the title *All Men Are Brothers* (1933). See also BUCK, PEARL; MAO ZEDONG; NORTHERN SONG DYNASTY; PEASANTS AND PEASANT REBELLIONS.

OUTLINE OF NATIONAL RECONSTRUCTION See NATIONALIST PARTY; SUN YAT-SEN.

OUYANG XIU (Ou-yang Hsiu; 1007–1072)   An important government official, historian and poet during the Song dynasty (960–1279). Born in Sichuan Province, Ouyang was one of the first southern Chinese to become prominent in the Northern Song court at Kaifeng. As a young man he took an administrative position in Luoyang after completing his education in 1030. A high-placed government official then sponsored him for a position in the Imperial Academy in Kaifeng. The most prestigious work a Chinese scholar could complete was an officially commissioned history of the previous dynasty, the Tang (618–907). The Song emperor rejected the Tang history written by Liu Xu (Liu Hsu; c. 885–944) and ordered Ouyang, the most prominent scholar at the time, and another scholar named Song Qi (Sung Ch'i; 998–1061) to write a new one. The two scholars took 17 years to complete their work, known as the *New History of the Tang* (*Xin Tangshu* or *Hsin T'ang shu*). After he completed this, Ouyang became involved in a political struggle and was banished to Yiling. There he wrote the *New History of the Five Dynasties* (*Xin wudaishi* or *Hsin wu-tai shih*; 907–959) to replace a history written by another scholar.

Ouyang wrote in the so-called "ancient style," which he discovered in the writings of the Tang essayist Han Yu (768–824) and emulated because he thought it was beautiful. He brought about a revival of this style by requiring his proteges to write in it as well. Ouyang was accomplished in many fields and took the pen name Liuyi (Liu-i) or "six ones," referring to one library, one archaeological collection, one musical instrument, one set of Chinese chess, one container of wine and one old man (himself) who enjoyed all of them.

In 1060 Ouyang returned to the capital but was exiled again in 1068 to Anhui Province because he opposed the controversial reforms being enacted by Prime Minister Wang Anshi (Wang An-shih; 1021–86). Ouyang had been a reformer in his earlier days and had sponsored Wang as a young man. The entire court was divided over Wang's policies, and eventually his reforms were abolished after the death of Emperor Shenzong (Shen-tsung; r. 1067–85) who supported him. Wang's reforms were also opposed by a close friend of Ouyang's, the government official and important historian Sima Guang (Ssu-ma Kuang; 1019–85), who replaced Wang Anshi as prime minister after Emperor Shenzong died in 1085. See also HAN YU; IMPERIAL BUREAUCRACY; KAIFENG; NORTHERN SONG DYNASTY; SIMA GUANG; TANG DYNASTY; WANG ANSHI.

OVERSEAS CHINESE (*huaqiao* or *hua ch'iao*; literally, "Chinese sojourner")   The term for all Han ethnic Chinese people who live outside mainland China (the Communist People's Republic of China; PRC), and especially for Chinese living in Southeast Asia, which includes the Indochina Peninsula, Malaysia, Indonesia, Singapore and the Philippines. The Han Chinese have defined themselves for more than 2,000 years as sharing certain traits and customs, including the ideas and practices of Confucianism; the propitiation of deceased relatives, known as ancestor worship; a cuisine centered on grain dishes, primarily rice, wheat or millet, accompanied by dishes of vegetables and protein foods; and a patriarchal and patrilineal family structure. During the past two centuries, Chinese have emigrated all over the world yet have retained many of their traditional customs. There are large overseas Chinese communities in Australia, North and South America, the Pacific and Caribbean Islands, Europe, the Middle East and Central Asia. Districts in foreign cities that have many Chinese residents, stores, restaurants and businesses are known as Chinatowns. Most overseas Chinese came from the southern Chinese province of Guangdong, mainly the region of the Pearl River delta, or the southeastern province of Fujian, or have ancestors who emigrated from those two provinces.

More than 90 percent of all foreign tourists who visit the PRC today are overseas Chinese. In the PRC, the term overseas Chinese is also applied to Chinese citizens who have spent time abroad studying or working and have then returned to China. Residents of Hong Kong, the former British Crown Colony ceded by China to Britain in 1842 and returned to China in 1997, and Macao, a Portuguese colony ceded by China in the 16th century, were referred to as "compatriots" (*tongbao* or *t'ung pao*) rather than overseas Chinese. Macao will revert to China in 1999. The PRC considers the island of Taiwan, governed by the Republic of China (ROC), a province of China, so the Chinese on Taiwan are not considered overseas Chinese. The Chinese Nationalists (Kuomintang; KMT) who control the ROC fled to Taiwan after the Chinese Communists defeated them in a civil war in 1949.

Although the largest number of Chinese emigrated abroad in the 19th and early 20th centuries, Chinese traders have traveled abroad on maritime trade routes since ancient times. From the Han dynasty (206 B.C.–A.D. 220) to the mid-19th century, the Chinese imperial government controlled foreign trade with China through the tribute system, which required foreign nations to send missions to give gifts to the Chinese emperor and bow down to him and acknowledge his suzerainty. During the Tang dynasty (618–907), many Chinese traders emigrated on the overland and maritime Silk Road. By the 10th century, large Chinese merchant ships known as junks were trading at ports throughout Southeast Asia and the East Indies (modern Indonesia). The Ming dynasty (1368–1644) sent Admiral Zheng He (Cheng Ho) on expeditions in 1405–33 that sailed across Southeast and South Asia and reached the east coast of Africa. Two major trade routes during the Ming went down the coast of modern Malaysia to the Strait of Malacca and through the Philippine

Islands to the East Indies. Chinese traders established agents at all of the ports on these routes, and overseas Chinese communities developed in them, with many Chinese becoming wealthy entrepreneurs.

European countries began trading in Asia in the 16th century and established colonies in the region, where the Chinese settlers were protected by European laws. In Southeast Asia, the Chinese served as tax collectors and provided services such as markets, ferries and bridges. They established fraternal organizations based on their places of origin in China; secret societies such as the Triad Society; and trading guilds and temples to protect their business interests. Even though the Ming and Qing (1644–1911) dynasties banned overseas trade and emigration, about 100 large southern Chinese junks traded every year with ports in Southeast Asia. Their main port in China was Xiamen (formerly known as Amoy) in Fujian Province, close to the ports of Fuzhou and Quanzhou but not supervised by government offices of merchant shipping as those cities were. In 1959 the Xiamen Overseas Chinese Museum was opened and was supported by Tan Kah Kee, a wealthy Chinese merchant living in Malaysia.

Emigration from China increased rapidly in the mid-19th century due to several factors, including pressure by Western powers on the Qing government to abandon the tribute system and open China to Western-style trade. Britain defeated China in the Opium War (1839–42) and Arrow War (Second Opium War; 1856–60), and the Qing had to sign so-called unequal treaties with Britain and other Western countries granting them many rights and concessions in China and opening many cities as treaty ports. The internal pressures of overpopulation and insufficient agricultural production also caused many Chinese to emigrate. Around 1845 a network was organized at Xiamen in Fujian and Shantou (formerly known as Swatow) in Guangdong for Chinese coolies (laborers) to immigrate to the Americas, especially to work in the silver mines in Peru and on the sugar cane plantations of Cuba. They were crowded onto cargo ships on which many of them died before even reaching their destinations.

Chinese emigration increased from 1850 to 1873 with the expansion of gold production. Gold was discovered in California in 1848, and many coolies soon began immigrating there. They called California "the old mountains of gold" (*jiujinshan* or *chiu-chin-shan*) or simply "gold mountain" (*gam saan*). They also immigrated to Australia, where gold was discovered in 1851, and called it "the new mountains of gold" (*xinjinshan* or *hsin-chin-shan*). Indentured Chinese coolies supplied much-needed labor in Southeast Asia, Hawaii, North and South America, Australia and Africa to work mines and plantations and to build cities, ports and railways, especially after the African slave trade was banned. Many Chinese worked in tin mines in Malaysia and Indonesia. The Qing government permitted the Western powers to recruit as many Chinese coolies as they wanted, and 100,000 left the country every year. Construction of the transcontinental Pacific railway in the United States began in 1863, with most of the laborers Chinese. Thousands of them died from the heavy work and difficult conditions. Chinese also helped build the transcontinental Pacific railway in Canada.

About 46,000 Chinese immigrated to Hawaii in the second half of the 19th century and about 380,000 to the U.S. mainland between 1849 and 1930. The so-called Six Companies controlled Chinese immigration to the United States. Established along the lines of traditional clan and regional associations in China, the Six Companies assisted their immigrant members to find jobs and housing, helped the sick and poor, and arranged to send the bodies of deceased Chinese back to China. In their halls, members could perform the rituals of ancestor worship and conduct business negotiations. Their leaders promoted Confucian education and virtues in America to legitimize their authority. Chinese merchants in the United States also established a body of officials elected from the Six Companies to deal with issues that were important to the Chinese in the United States as a whole. White laborers resented the Chinese, who had to endure terrible acts of violence and discriminatory laws, which the Six Companies protested. In 1882 and 1884 the U.S. government passed Exclusion Acts to prohibit the entry of Chinese laborers into the country, and in 1892 it passed the Geary Act, which suspended Chinese immigration for 10 more years. The Six Companies attempted to fight these and the Deficiency Act passed in 1904 that prevented Chinese from immigrating to Hawaii and the Philippine Islands, which were now U.S. possessions. In 1905 the mainland Chinese protested by organizing a boycott against American goods.

The earthquake that devastated San Francisco on April 18, 1906, destroyed most of the municipal records, which actually benefited the Chinese in the United States. Most of the immigrants had been men, and after the earthquake they were able to claim that they had been born in the United States, which allowed them to bring their wives into the country. About 10,000 Chinese women immigrated to the United States between 1907 and 1924. Many young Chinese males also entered the country as "paper sons," meaning that they had bought the legal or forged birth certificates of U.S. citizens born in China and claimed that they were their sons and hence citizens as well. By 1940 there were 77,504 Chinese on the U.S. mainland. The Museum of Chinese in the Americas, in New York City, has exhibits on the history of Chinese emigration.

During the first half of the 20th century, Chinese immigration to Southeast Asia greatly increased, growing about 50–60 percent between 1900 and 1930. Singapore, Malacca and Penang in Malaysia, and Cholon, a suburb of Saigon in Vietnam (Indochina), became Chinese cities, and nearly half the population of the Malay Peninsula became Chinese. Most of the immigrants were small buinessmen, artisans or laborers on farms and plantations, but they worked very hard and some became extremely wealthy. In 1917–18, during World War I, some 140,000 Chinese laborers also went to France to dig trenches for the Allies and bury dead bodies.

The overseas Chinese communities were a major source of support for Dr. Sun Yat-sen (1866–1925), who founded the Revolutionary Alliance (Tongmenghui or T'ung-meng-hui) that led the Revolution of 1911, which overthrew the Qing dynasty and established the modern Republic of China (ROC). Sun also established the Chinese Nationalist Party (Kuomintang; KMT), which controlled the ROC government. During China's War of Resistance against Japan (1937–45; World War II), overseas Chinese sent large donations to China, bought Chinese government bonds, boycotted Japanese goods and went to China to join the military forces fighting the Japanese.

After 1949, when the Communists defeated the Nationalists and established the People's Republic of China (PRC) while the Nationalists fled to Taiwan, overseas Chinese communities became divided in their loyalties to mainland China and the ROC government. Many, including members of the Six Companies in the United States, tended to be conservative and anticommunist and to support traditional Chinese values, so they supported the Nationalist ROC government on Taiwan. However, some overseas Chinese supported the new Communist PRC government. The Chinese Communist Party (CCP) permitted eight so-called democratic parties to continue functioning on a small scale in China, including the Party for Public Interest (*China Zhi Gong Dang*), which had been founded in 1925 to gain the support of overseas Chinese. Within the PRC government, the United Front Work Department, which was established in the 1940s, has been responsible for maintaining relations with overseas Chinese. It reports to the Central Committee of the CCP. After the PRC enacted its first state constitution in 1954, overseas Chinese deputies attended the First National People's Congress (NPC), the highest government body in the PRC. The United States and most other countries recognized the ROC as the legitimate government of China until the late 1970s, when they switched diplomatic recognition to the PRC. However, most countries have also maintained economic relations with the ROC, which rapidly developed into an economic power.

After World War II, the natives of the British, French and Dutch colonies in Malaysia, Vietnam and Indonesia fought to gain their independence. The success of the overseas Chinese in those countries, and their association with the former colonial masters, brought them resentment and discrimination by the native peoples. In the 1960s, the Chinese city of Singapore separated from Malaysia and became an independent country. Today the ethnic Chinese who live in Asia outside mainland China—in Taiwan, Singapore and the rest of Southeast Asia—number about 40 million and produce $600 billion in goods and services. Hong Kong, which was a British Crown Colony until it reverted to the PRC in 1997, is the world's busiest container port. The overseas Chinese family-controlled enterprises are known as the "bamboo network." The total assets of public companies in Asia controlled by overseas Chinese total more than $500 billion. The ethnic Chinese of Indonesia comprise the largest single group of ethnic Chinese in Southeast Asia. In Malaysia they comprise more than one-third of the population. Thailand, which was never colonized, also has a large Chinese population.

A group of about 55 million overseas Chinese living in Asia, the United States and Canada provided 80 percent of all direct foreign investment in the PRC before 1998. They financed the current economic boom that has made China the third-largest market in the world after the United States and Japan. Much of their investment has been in the officially designated Special Economic Zones (SEZs) and Coastal Open Cities along the Chinese coast and on Hainan Island, a province of the PRC in the South China Sea near Guangdong Province. Perhaps more important, they have maintained close connections with their home districts or villages in China, known as *qiaoxiang* (*ch'iao-hsiang*) ties. The PRC government appealed to these ties when it was rebuilding and modernizing China during the 1980s. It encouraged overseas Chinese to contribute money to charities, temples and public works in their home districts. In return, overseas Chinese entrepreneurs have doors opened to them in the Chinese government and economy. Overseas Chinese also control the commerce in nearly every country of the Pacific Rim. Many believe that there will soon be an economic and cultural "Greater China" created by combining mainland China and Taiwan. See also ANCESTOR WORSHIP; ARROW WAR; CHINESE COMMUNIST PARTY; CHINESE NATIONALIST PARTY; CIVIL WAR BETWEEN COMMUNISTS AND NATIONALISTS; CONFUCIANISM; CONNECTIONS; COOKING, CHINESE; COOLIES; DEMOCRATIC PARTIES; FAMILY STRUCTURE; FOREIGN TRADE AND INVESTMENT; FORTUNE COOKIE; FUJIAN PROVINCE; GUANGDONG PROVINCE; GUANGZHOU; HAINAN ISLAND; HAN; HONG KONG; JUNK; MACAO; NATIONAL PEOPLE'S CONGRESS; OPIUM WAR; PEARL RIVER; PEOPLE'S REPUBLIC OF CHINA; QING DYNASTY; REPUBLIC OF CHINA; REVOLUTION OF 1911; REVOLUTIONARY ALLIANCE; SHIPPING AND SHIPBUILDING; SILK ROAD; SINGAPORE; SIX COMPANIES; SPECIAL ECONOMIC ZONES; SUN YAT-SEN; SWATOW WARE; TAIWAN; TREATY PORTS; TRIBUTE SYSTEM; UNEQUAL TREATIES; XIAMEN.

OVERSEAS CHINESE TRAVEL SERVICE See CHINA INTERNATIONAL TRAVEL SERVICE.

OX (*gongniu* or *kung-niu*)   A large animal similar to a bull; also known as the water buffalo and traditionally used by Chinese farmers to pull carts and plough the land for planting crops. Tibetans also raise an animal called the dzo, which is a cross between the ox and the yak, a large, shaggy animal similar to a bison. There are many legends about the ox, which symbolizes spring and agriculture for the Chinese. One such legend involves the "meeting of the spring" (Li Chun Festival), falling around February 5, during which the Chinese hold a ceremonial ploughing and beat a spring ox made of clay to hasten the return of spring. During the imperial period, the emperor would plough a sacred field, turning over eight furrows with an ox-drawn plough, and plant rice and millet seeds. After the field was ploughed, the ox was broken into pieces. These pieces, in addition to hundreds of other small ox statues, were placed in the farmers' fields to ensure a good harvest. In ancient times an ox was slaughtered as a ritual sacrifice at this festival, but was later replaced by a clay, straw and finally a paper model of an ox that was burned. The first page of the traditional almanac (*Tong Shu* or *T'ung Shu*), an annual publication containing information on a wide variety of topics including weather predictions and solar lunar calendars, shows a farmer (Niu lang; also called the Spirit Driver or Meng Shen) leading his spring ox (Chun niu), a symbol of the Li Chun Festival. The details and colors in the picture all provide information about the weather that is predicted for the coming year, so that farmers will have some idea of the outcome of their efforts.

The ox, known as water buffalo in southern China, symbolizes spring and agriculture for the Chinese.   DENNIS COX

According to other legends, the ox was originally a star deity. The Jade Emperor, ruler of Heaven, sent him to Earth to tell people that if they worked hard, they would always be able to eat food every third day. But the ox misunderstood and told people that the emperor had decreed that they should eat three times every day. Because of his mistake, the Emperor of Heaven sent the ox back to Earth to help farmers with their ploughing, for without his help they would never have been able to grow enough food to eat three times a day. The Chinese have regarded oxen as kind, beneficial animals who have helped people in many ways.

The Cowherd and Weaver Maid Festival (Qi Xi or Ch'i Hsi), also known as the Double Seven Festival, as it is held on the seventh day of the seventh Chinese lunar month (around the beginning of July), is very popular in China. It celebrates the legend of the Weaver Maid Zhinu (Chih Nu), daughter of the Heavenly King, who was married to a hard-working cowherd named Niulang from the western river of the Heavenly Paradise. They enjoyed each other so much that they neglected their work, forcing the king to send the cowherd back to the west and the maid back to the east. They were permitted to see each other only once a year, on the seventh night of the seventh lunar month. Based on ancient Chinese beliefs, Niulang represents agriculture and the star Altair, and Zhinu symbolizes weaving and the star Vega. Both stars are bright in the sky in early July.

The ox is the second of the 12 animals in the traditional animal zodiac, which has a different creature corresponding to each year in a 12-year cycle. People born in the Year of the Ox are thought to be patient, hard-working, stubborn, trustworthy and calm.

Shoulder blades of oxen and sheep, as well as tortoise shells, were used for divination during the Shang dynasty (1750–1040 B.C.). Known as oracle bones, they were incised with written characters and heated in a fire. The resultant cracks in the bones were analyzed for information they were believed to provide about the future. See also AGRICULTURE; ALMANAC; COWHERD AND WEAVER MAID FESTIVAL; EMPEROR; ORACLE BONES; ZODIAC, ANIMAL.

P

PA CHIN See BA JIN.

PA KUA See ALCHEMY; BOOK OF CHANGES; EIGHT TRIGRAMS; FUXI.

PAGODA (*ta* or *t'a*)   A towerlike building associated with temple compounds of the Buddhist religion, which was founded in India in the sixth century B.C. and introduced into China around the first century A.D. Pagodas commonly are made of wood, brick or stone and have as many as 15 stories, each with an upcurved overhanging roof. Built around a central interior staircase, pagodas can have many shapes. They include three parts, the base, the body and the top, which usually is in the form of a miniature pagoda. Chinese pagodas derive from the low, round brick structures in India known as stupas, which enshrine sutras (Buddhist scriptures) and relics of the Buddha, founder of the religion. In China the pagoda changed its shape, taking elements from Chinese pavilions and towers, but kept its function as a storage place for sacred objects.

Chinese pagodas were first built of wood in square shapes, but in the early 13th century they began to be constructed of bricks in hexagonal or octagonal shapes. From the Yuan through Qing dynasties (1279–1911), pagodas also were built in circular, cross and 12-sided shapes with such materials as clay, stone, bronze, iron and glazed tiles. Most of the wooden pagodas were destroyed by fire. About 10,000 Chinese pagodas survive, most made of brick and stone. Buddhism has declined in China, and many pagodas and other religious structures were destroyed during the Cultural Revolution (1966–76); some have been rebuilt. The many old pagodas around the country indicate how Buddhism spread through ancient China. Often pagodas were built on a mountain outside a city or village after a natural disaster, to pacify the spirits and prevent a recurrence. The beauty of their design also enhanced the landscape. Brick good-luck pagodas also were built to ward off bad luck from neighboring villages.

Ancient records state that the first Chinese pagoda was constructed near Nanjing in the middle of the third century,

but it has not survived. The oldest surviving brick pagoda in China, built in 532, is the 131-foot-high pagoda at Songyue Temple 7 miles from the famous Shaolin Temple on Mount Song in Henan Province. Shaolin monks have traditionally

Besides housing sacred objects, Chinese pagodas are often built to pacify spirits after a natural disaster. S.E. MEYER

375

been buried in the Pagoda Forest, a complex of 220 brick-and-stone pagodas that were built between A.D. 791 and 1830. The pagoda at Fogong Monastery at Yinxiang near Datong, built in 1056, is the only surviving wooden pagoda still standing in China and one of the oldest wooden buildings in the world. Another famous pagoda is the octagonal Fo Guan Si in Shanxi Province, constructed from wood in the 11th century. It stands more than 230 feet high and houses a large sculpture of Guanyin (Kuanyin), the Buddhist Goddess of Mercy. Two pagodas in Xi'an (the capital city, known as Chang'an, during the Tang dynasty; 618–907) are well known. The Big Wild Goose Pagoda (Dayanta) was built in 652 to store Buddhist manuscripts brought back from India by the pilgrim monk Xuanzang (Hsuan-tsang; 602–664). In 704 the five-story pagoda was reconstructed into a seven-story Buddhist temple 210 feet high, and a monastery with 897 rooms was built next to it. The 141-foot-high Small Wild Goose Pagoda (Xiaoyanta) was built between 707 and 709. It was destroyed by war and earthquakes but repaired and opened to the public in 1977. The 13th-century white pagoda at Miaoyin Monastery in Beijing is the earliest pagoda in China built in the shape of the ancient Indian stupa. See also BUDDHISM; PAVILION; SHAOLIN TEMPLE; TEMPLES; TILES, GLAZED; XI'AN; XUANZANG.

PA-HSIEN See EIGHT IMMORTALS.

PAI MA SSU See WHITE HORSE TEMPLE.

PAI-HUA MOVEMENT See CHEN DUXIU; HU SHI; LANGUAGE, CHINESE; NEW CULTURE MOVEMENT.

PAINTING See BIRD-AND-FLOWER PAINTING; CALLIGRAPHY; FOUR TREASURES OF THE STUDY; INK PAINTING; LANDSCAPE PAINTING; MUSTARD SEED GARDEN MANUAL OF PAINTING; NORTHERN SCHOOL OF PAINTING; PAPER; SCROLLS; SILK; SIX CANONS OF PAINTING; SOUTHERN SCHOOL OF PAINTING; WU SCHOOL OF PAINTING.

PALACES See ARCHAEOLOGY; ARCHITECTURE, TRADITIONAL; CHENGDE; EMPEROR; FORBIDDEN CITY; SUMMER PALACE.

PALEOLITHIC PERIOD See PEKING MAN.

PAMIR MOUNTAIN RANGE See KASHGAR; KUNLUN MOUNTAIN RANGE; SILK ROAD; XINJIANG-UIGHUR AUTONOMOUS REGION.

PAN CHAO See BAN GU AND BAN ZHAO; CODE FOR WOMEN.

PAN CH'AO See BAN CHAO.

PAN KU See BAN GU AND BAN ZHAO; SIMA QIAN.

P'AN KU See PANGU.

PAN PIAO See BAN GU AND BAN ZHAO; SIMA QIAN.

PAN PIPES See FLUTES AND WIND INSTRUMENTS.

PANCHEN LAMA See DALAI LAMA; LAMAISM; TIBET.

PANDA (*xiongmao* or *hsiung-mao*) A large black-and-white mammal related to the bear. The best-known species is the Giant Panda, whose distinctive coloring and doll-like appearance make them very appealing to humans. Indigenous to China, pandas inhabit bamboo forests in cold, high mountain areas. Near extinction today, only a few hundred pandas remain in their natural habitat, mainly in the Wolong Panda Reserve and other protected areas in western Sichuan, Shaanxi and Gansu provinces. Pandas are nonaggressive, solitary and rarely seen by humans in the wild. They communicate with other pandas by scent signals and occasional vocal sounds, making social contact only during their brief mating season. An adult panda weighs about 220 pounds; a baby, only about 3.5 ounces. Pandas reproduce infrequently and the babies are not well developed physically at birth. They mature at age 6 or 7 and usually live into their 20s.

A panda spends its time eating, resting and traveling slowly through the forest. It uses a thumblike outgrowth of its wrist bone like a sixth finger to grasp and manipulate the 30 pounds of bamboo leaves and stems it eats daily, mainly

Today only a few hundred pandas remain in their natural habitat, despite efforts by the Chinese and international conservation communities to restore the population. DENNIS COX

of the type known as fountain bamboo. The panda's dependence on bamboo is problematic because the bamboo plant has a reproductive cycle as long as 100 years. After it flowers, an entire stand of bamboo dies, thus depriving the pandas of their food source until a new bamboo stand grows.

Two centuries ago pandas occupied a widespread area of central and southern China, but human population growth, logging, farming, development and poaching have severely reduced their habitat area. Pandas are now endangered but protected in China. In 1980 the Ministry of Forestry and the World Wide Fund for Nature established the Research Center for Giant Pandas in Wolong Nature Reserve in Sichuan. The center promotes conservation of the Giant Pandas, surveys the remaining populations and studies their habits in the wild. The American naturalist George Schaller has encouraged the establishment of a panda reserve the size of Great Britain in the Tibetan plateau.

There have been many recent efforts to protect the panda. In 1983 large areas of fountain bamboo flowered and died in China, and 64 pandas were taken into captivity to try to save them, although only 46 survived. In 1985 a breeding center for pandas was established in the nature reserve at Baishui River. In 1991 China set up its 14th panda reserve, in western Gansu Province. Zoos around the world have attempted to breed pandas in captivity with some success, but not enough are born to make up for those that die in the wild. Between 1984 and 1991 Chinese courts handled 123 cases involving poaching of Giant Pandas. The main market for panda skins has been among businessmen from Japan, Hong Kong and Taiwan. China's threat to execute poachers resulted in a 60 percent drop in poaching cases in 1991.

The People's Republic of China gave two Giant Pandas, Ling-Ling and Hsing-Hsing, to the National Zoo in Washington, D.C. after U.S. president Richard Nixon visited China in 1972. Ling-Ling gave birth five times but none of her cubs survived. The pandas drew 3 million visitors a year, but Ling-Ling died suddenly at age 23 in 1993. As of January 1993, only 95 Giant Pandas remained in zoos, with Hsing-Hsing the only one in the United States.

The Red, or Lesser, Panda, a raccoonlike animal belonging to a different family from the Giant Panda, is indigenous to southwest China and countries of Southeast Asia. It has dark red-brown fur, short legs and a long tail, and black-and-white facial markings similar to the Giant Panda. The Red Panda eats bamboo stems and leaves, fruit and birds' eggs. See also BAMBOO; NIXON, RICHARD, U.S. PRESIDENT, VISIT TO CHINA (1972); SICHUAN PROVINCE.

PANG-CHI OPERA See OPERA, BEIJING.

PANGU (P'an ku)   The First Man; in Chinese mythology, the creator of the universe. Different versions of the creation story state that Pangu was born either from a rock or from the Egg of Chaos, and was formed from the two universal principles in Daoist thought, yin (feminine) and yang (masculine). According to one version, the universe was a mixture of gases and matter that looked like an enormous hen's egg and was not separated into Heaven and Earth. A giant named Pangu slept inside the egg. He awoke one day after 18,000 years of sleep and could see nothing but darkness. He

took a huge ax and chopped the great egg in half. The lighter gas kept rising higher to form Heaven and the heavier matter sank to form Earth. Pangu kept growing until he filled the space between Heaven and Earth. When he died at a very old age, his left eye became the sun and his right eye the moon. Other parts of his body became the stars, wind and clouds, mountains, and all other things in the visible universe. His blood flowed as rivers and his flesh became rice fields. Trees grew out of the hair on his body, his bones became metal and stone, and his sweat became the rain and dew. Pangu is often depicted in Chinese art as a strong man carrying an ax. See also YIN AND YANG.

PANTHAY REBELLION See DU WENXIU.

PAO See DIM SUM; NOODLES.

PAODING (P'AO-TING) MILITARY SCHOOL See YUAN SHIKAI.

PAO-HUANG HUI See KANG YOUWEI; LIANG QICHAO.

PA-PAO See EIGHT TREASURES.

PAPER (zhi or chih)   A Chinese invention, usually attributed to the first century A.D. However, archaeologists have discovered fragments of paper made from raw silk, preserved in the Gobi Desert, that date back to the second and first centuries B.C. Written documents record that a eunuch named Cai Lun (Ts'ai Lun) presented paper to the Han dynasty imperial court in A.D. 105, the traditional Chinese date for its invention. By the fourth century, paper was used commonly in China, supplanting the sewn-together wooden and bamboo strips previously used for writing. Silk was used to a lesser degree. The Chinese made paper by grinding various natural fibers—mainly the bark of the mulberry bush, bamboo shoots and scraps of fabric made from the hemp plant—into pulp with water in a trough. A screen on a wooden frame was lowered into the pulp and lifted out; the layers of pulp that clung to the screen were dried, forming a sheet of paper. The final step was to "size" the paper, traditionally by coating it with a salt called alum and glue made from animals, so that the ink and colored paints would not spread when brushed onto the paper.

The use of paper became widespread during the Han dynasty (206 B.C.–A.D. 220), but many books written on paper then did not last, so little information about this period has survived. However, the use of paper during this dynasty encouraged the development of many different styles of calligraphy, which became a specialized and highly regarded art form in China. Paper is one of the Four Treasures of the Study of a member of the literati, or scholar, class that governed China's imperial bureaucracy. The other three are a brush, inkstick and inkstone on which the stick is rubbed with water to make ink. The Chinese traditionally write books and compose paintings on vertical paper scrolls that are hung and on horizontal scrolls that are rolled up. The latter are made by pasting sheets of paper together to make a continuous roll that is mounted on a wooden roller. One scroll typically contains the text of one chapter of a book. The use of paper made possible the copying and translation of scriptures of the Buddhist religion, which was introduced into China from India around the first century A.D. Thousands of Buddhist scrolls made of fine paper were found in 1907 in a walled-up library in the complex of cave temples and sculptures at Dunhuang in western China. Some have dates indicating that they were written during the fifth century A.D.

The Chinese bureaucracy also benefited from the invention of paper and used it in vast quantities. For example, by the time of the Tang dynasty (618–907), the Board of Finance was using about 500,000 sheets of paper each year just to make tax assessments. Paper money also was invented in China and was first printed in 1024 in Chengdu in Sichuan Province.

Printing also was invented in China. Some scholars believe that Europeans first learned about printing from Chinese printed paper money. Paper was not used in Europe until around the 11th century; one route of transmission was through Muslim Arabs, by whom Chinese forces were disastrously defeated at the Battle of Talas in 751 in what is now Afghanistan. The Arabs captured many workers in a Chinese paper mill at Talas, thus learning the technique of papermaking. Within a few decades the Arabs were manufacturing paper in Baghdad (in modern Syria). They kept the technique a secret and sold paper to the Europeans at very high prices. The Europeans did not learn to make paper themselves until more than three centuries later.

In China, papermaking increased greatly when nomadic invasions forced the Song dynasty to flee south to southern China, and the city of Hangzhou, the Southern Song capital, became the center of Chinese arts and culture. The literati, who highly valued reading and writing, had their greatest influence in China at this time. The use of paper money also increased when the Mongols conquered China under the Yuan dynasty (1279–1368). The Chinese had mainly used bronze coins for currency, but the Mongols realized that China could not produce enough copper to make the large quantity of coins needed in such an enormous country, so they made paper money the only legal currency.

Besides providing the raw material for literature, works of art and money, paper has been put to many other uses in China. The folk art of papercutting, in which thin sheets of paper are cut into intricate shapes by hand to make colorful decorations, is often employed for festivals and other celebrations. Paper also is used to make flat and folding fans, which have been a major handicraft in China since the Tang dynasty. Stone rubbings are made by placing a sheet of paper over a stone that has been engraved with a text or picture, and rubbing ink over the paper to make a copy of the engraving. At Buddhist funerals, mourners burn large quantities of paper in the form of money, clothes, food and other necessities to provide the spirit of the deceased with everything it will need while traveling to the next world. The Chinese traditionally believe that burning the paper objects, known as joss paper, transforms them into real objects as they pass through the smoke into the spirit world. See also CALLIGRAPHY; CURRENCY; DUNHUANG; FANS; FOUR TREASURES OF THE STUDY; HANGZHOU; INK PRINTING; JOSS PAPER; LITERATI; PAINTING; PAPERCUTTING; PRINTING; SCROLLS; STONE RUBBINGS; TALAS, BATTLE OF; WRITING, CHINESE.

"PAPER SONS" See OVERSEAS CHINESE.

PAPERCUTTING The Chinese folk art of cutting thin sheets of paper into intricate shapes by hand. The resulting creations are used as decorations for festivals and celebrations. The Chinese hang brightly colored papercuts, also known as window flowers, on windows, walls, doors, mirrors, lamps and lanterns. They also give them as gifts. Red paper is preferred for papercuts because it symbolizes life. At the New Year or Spring Festival, papercuts are hung at entrances to bring the family good luck. Some popular motifs include the butterfly, peony flower, chrysanthemum, bat (a good-luck symbol) and latticework. Each region of China produces a special type of papercut. For example, those from northern China are strong and boldly outlined, while those from the south are delicate and complex. Foshan in Guangdong Province is renowned for latticework papercuts of landscapes and human figures and for floral designs made from colorful paper and gold or silver foil.

Papercuts can be made with either scissors or a knife. When sharp, pointed scissors with large round handles are used, up to eight sheets of paper are fastened together and the design is cut into all the sheets at once. With a knife, a stack of paper sheets is laid in a box frame on a soft foundation made from a mixture of fat, ashes and beeswax or paraffin. A pattern is placed on top through which the design is cut into the paper with sharp knives of various sizes held vertically. Punches and chisels also are used. Knife papercuts commonly are made in sets of four, six or eight designs related to one subject, such as birds and flowers or a folktale. Papercutters may follow a pattern or work freehand. In the Chinese countryside, the art of papercutting has been practiced by women and girls, and brides often were judged by how well they could cut paper designs. Farm families handed down treasured papercuts through the generations. Professional papercutting artists in workshops are usually men.

The Chinese had invented paper by 200 B.C., although it took several centuries to develop the technology for mass-producing good-quality paper from hemp or mulberry bark. Paper was used widely throughout China by A.D. 200 primarily for writing and painting, but also for making craft objects such as fans, lanterns and umbrellas. Archaeologists have discovered papercuts from the sixth century, and this art probably originated several centuries earlier. Papercuts also served an important function as patterns for embroidery and lacquerware. At Chinese funerals, paper shapes representing necessities for the dead spirit as it travels to the next world, such as food and clothing, are burned beside the grave. See also BAT; CHRYSANTHEMUM; EMBROIDERY; FAN; FUNERAL; JOSS PAPER; LACQUERWARE; LANTERN; NEW YEAR FESTIVAL; PAPER; PEONY; UMBRELLA.

PA-P'U TZU See GE HONG.

PARACEL ISLANDS See SOUTH CHINA SEA; SPRATLY ISLANDS.

PA-TA SHAN-JEN See BADA SHANREN.

PAVILIONS (*tingzi* or *t'ing-tzu*) Buildings that are erected in Chinese gardens and at scenic spots for people to rest and enjoy nature. Pavilions are one of the main features in Chinese gardens, along with long corridors or covered walkways and bridges over lakes, ponds or streams. Pavilions even may be built on bridges, and a bridge may be constructed like a covered walkway. Many different styles of pavilions and corridors exist in China. Corridors may be straight, curving or zigzag, high or low, and even be constructed climbing a hill or along a shoreline. Pavilions may be square, round, multisided or shaped like a familiar form, such as a fan or a plum blossom. The Li or Hat-shaped Pavilion in the Humble Administrator's Garden in Suzhou, a city famous for its gardens, has a cone-shaped roof resembling a bamboo hat. Different construction styles include the rustic thatched pavilion, elegant bamboo pavilion, noble stone pavilion and projecting wood-frame pavilion. Many pavilions have roofs that slope upward and are covered with tiles. Pavilions, corridors and bridges are designed to enhance their natural settings. A large garden may contain many pavilions at various sites that offer different views, for example, by a lake or stream, on a hillside, in a grove of trees or next to a bed of flowers. The West Garden in Suzhou has a pavilion in the middle of its lake. Some pavilions are best enjoyed at certain times of the year, such as a pavilion from which to view blooming peonies in the spring or a snow-covered landscape in the winter. The Five Pavilions in Jingshan Park in Beijing provide a majestic view of the capital city. Beihai Park, a popular traditional resort area in Beijing, includes the Five Dragon Pavilions along the shore of its lake. See also ARCHITECTURE, TRADITIONAL; BEHAI PARK; BRIDGES; GARDENS; SUZHOU.

PEACH (*taozi* or *t'ao-tzu*)   A soft, sweet fruit that grows on trees, believed to have originated in China. The peach has a vast range of symbolic meanings for the Chinese. It represents spring, immortality and marriage as well as the second month of the year in the traditional lunar calendar (roughly corresponding to March in the Western calendar). It is the fruit of the gods in Chinese folklore. Shouxing (Shou Hsing), the Chinese God of Longevity and the star Canopus in the southern constellation Argus, often is depicted emerging from or holding the round peach of immortality (Pan Tao). The Heavenly Peach Orchard of the Jade Emperor, ruler of heaven, produces the peach of immortality. Supposedly, this orchard grows next to the beautiful palace on the Kunlun Mountains that is the home of Xiwangmu (Hsi Wang-mu), the Royal Lady (or Mother) of the West. The peach tree of immortality is said to bloom only once every 3,000 years; its fruit takes another 3,000 years to ripen. Legends claim that peaches from this tree give immortal life to anyone who eats them. When the fruit ripens, Shou Xing and the Eight Immortal Gods have a banquet at Xiwangmu's court to celebrate her birthday and make themselves young again. At Chinese birthday parties, images of these deities are displayed with those of the peach of immortality so that the person celebrating the birthday will gain longevity. In the humorous 16th-century novel *Journey to the West,* the character Monkey gets revenge for not being invited to the heavenly birthday party by stealing the entire feast. He makes himself doubly immortal by eating all the peaches and swallowing the pill of immortality, which he had stolen earlier.

Priests of the Daoist religion, mainly in Taiwan and other Chinese settlements outside the People's Republic of China, use wood from peach trees to make charms and amulets. The peach fruit is a main ingredient of the Daoist Elixir of Immortality. Peach stones are carved in the shape of padlocks to make amulets that protect children from kidnapping and death. At the New Year Festival in February, a branch of peach blossoms is placed at the door of a Chinese home to keep evil from entering. The first new moon of the new year, when the peach trees are in bloom, is considered the most auspicious time to hold a wedding.

The peach also is used in traditional herbal medicine. The fruit is thought to provide help for respiratory diseases. Peach stones are used to treat coughs and rheumatism; its flowers are used as a laxative; its bark for jaundice, dropsy, asthma and other problems; and its sap, drawn from cuts in the tree bark, as a sedative or an astringent. See also BIRTHDAYS; CALENDAR; CHARMS AND AMULETS; DAOISM; EIGHT IMMORTALS; ELIXIR OF IMMORTALITY; JOURNEY TO THE WEST; MONKEY; NEW YEAR FESTIVAL; XIWANGMU.

"PEACH GARDEN" OATH OF LOYALTY   See ROMANCE OF THE THREE KINGDOMS; YELLOW TURBAN REBELLION.

PEACHBLOOM GLAZE   See ENAMELWARE.

PEARL (*zhenzhu* or *chen-chu*)   A round, luminous gem formed inside the shell of an oyster. A pearl forms when the oyster secretes a substance called nacre that coats an irritant that has entered its shell. The nacre builds up many layers and solidifies. This process can happen naturally, but today most pearls used for jewelry are cultivated by placing small mother-of-pearl beads inside oysters that are kept in frames in the ocean. The pearls are harvested when they are sufficiently large. Today, pearls are usually imported into China from Japan, where many are cultivated, and from other Asian countries and Australia. Pearls symbolize feminine beauty and purity to the Chinese. Chinese women use face creams and powders made from ground pearls in the belief that their skin will be more beautiful.

In Chinese art, a flaming pearl representing the sun is often depicted with the imperial dragon, the most powerful of all creatures. The dragon flying through the clouds has been one of the most important design motifs in Chinese arts and crafts, such as paintings, ceramics and textiles. A dragon with a pearl symbolizes wealth and good luck. When men perform dragon dances at the New Year and other festivals, one man holds a large pearl on a pole in front of the dragon. In Chinese mythology, pearls are guarded by the five Dragon Kings, who reside in underwater palaces made of crystal and dine on pearls and opals. The pearl is also associated with the moon and is thought to provide protection against fire. It is one of the common symbols in the Eight Treasures (*ba bao* or *pa pao*), a traditional design motif. Buddhist legends also classify the wonder-working pearl as one of the Seven Treasures that signify a Chakravarti, or universal ruler.

One of China's most important rivers is named after the pearl. The Pearl River (Zhujiang) flows through Guangdong Province and empties into the South China Sea at Guangzhou (Canton), one of China's largest cities and the major port through which Western goods and traders entered China, starting in the 16th century. Nearly all of the Chinese who immigrated to North America before World War II came from the Pearl River Delta. See also DRAGON; EIGHT TREASURES; PEARL RIVER.

PEARL RIVER (Zhujiang)   A river in Guangdong Province in southern China formed by the convergence of the three major rivers that comprise the Pearl River system, the West (Xi), the North (Bei) and the East (Dong). Together the three are properly called the Pearl River Delta. The Pearl was the name given to the lower course of the West River after this convergence. The Pearl River Delta covers about 3,500 square miles, is the largest river in southern China and drains half the area of Guangdong Province. Counting its tributaries, dredged channels and canals, the river's total length is 1,500 miles. It originates as the 1,300-mile-long West River in Yunnan Province in southwestern China. The rivers that form the Pearl River Delta are fed by heavy rains that have extreme seasonal fluctuations in southern China, and they collect so much water that the Pearl River system discharges six and a half times as much water each year as the Yellow River (Huanghe), one of China's two largest rivers, even though its basin is only about half as large as that of the Yellow. Two major tributaries of the Pearl River Delta, the Beiban and the Duliu, flow southeast into Jiangsu Province.

The soil in the Pearl River Delta is very rich due to the 2 billion cubic feet of alluvial deposits carried by the West River each year. The river system advances Guangzhou's coastline by about 350 feet annually. The Pearl River Delta comprises a network of canals and streams that flow between paddies, the wet fields where rice is cultivated. The 12-month growing season in Guangdong's subtropical climate supports three rice crops a year. Other crops include tropical fruit, vegetables, sugarcane, tobacco and oil-bearing plants. The raising of silkworm cocoons and fish farming are other major economic activities in the delta.

Guangzhou (Canton), the capital of Guangdong Province, with a population of about 3.5 million, is located on the north bank of the Pearl River and has long been one of China's most important port cities. The 20-acre Cultural Park, one block from the river, is the site of most of Guangzhou's cultural events, and has an aquarium, exhibition halls, gardens, open air theaters, an opera house, concert hall and teahouse. The island port cities of Hong Kong and Macao are situated south of Guangzhou and just east of the Pearl River estuary where it empties into the South China Sea. The river is navigable for 10,000-ton ships as far as Huangpu, nine miles south of Guangzhou. Ships of 2,000 tons can sail to Wuzhou, 220 miles beyond Guangzhou. Large junks can sail up to Nanning in Guangxhi Zhuang Autonomous Region, west of Guangdong, to the Li River. A tributary of the West River, the Li then leads to the popular tourist city of Guilin. The Pearl River system has the second-largest amount of water traffic after the Yangzi River (Changjiang). Guangdong has more than 1,300 rivers throughout the province, and their drainage basins cover about 400,000 square miles. The Han River is second in importance to the Pearl system in Guangdong. See also FISH AND SEAFOOD; GUANGDONG PROVINCE; GUANGZHOU; HAN RIVER; HONG KONG; JUNK; LI RIVER AND LING CANAL; MACAO; RICE; SOUTH CHINA SEA; WEST RIVER.

PEARLY EMPEROR   See JADE EMPEROR.

PEASANTS AND PEASANT REBELLIONS   Uprisings led by Chinese peasants (*nong* or *nung*), one of the four social classes in the traditional Chinese Confucian system, which became accepted as the orthodox state ideology during the Han dynasty (206 B.C.–A.D. 220). The highest social class included the emperor, members of the imperial court and the literati (*shi* or *shih*), or Confucian-educated scholars who staffed the imperial bureaucracy. The class under them was composed of the peasants who farmed the land, by far the greatest percentage of the Chinese population. Artisans (*gong* or *kung*) comprised the third class, and merchants (*hong* or *hung*), the fourth and lowest class. The practice of agriculture, living in settled villages and consuming a grain-based diet were some of the main traits by which the Han ethnic Chinese people always have characterized themselves. Agriculture and settled villages had appeared in China around 7000 B.C., especially in the lower valley of the Yellow River (Huanghe). This region is made up of deep deposits of loess, loose yellow soil that blows into China from deserts to the north and northwest. The Yellow River carries vast deposits of loess, which have made it flood many times throughout Chinese history and cause massive destruction. The peasants built and maintained dikes as high as 20 feet above ground level along the river to help contain it. The Yellow River, which empties into the Bo Hai Gulf in Shandong Province, has changed its course drastically several times over the centuries, killing thousands of people and destroying vast areas of fertile farmland.

Natural disasters, including floods, droughts and famines, often have affected peasants throughout China. Many times the people interpreted such disasters as signs that the ruling dynasty had lost the Mandate of Heaven (*tianming* or *t'ien-ming*), which legitimized the reign of an emperor in the Confucian system, and that the dynasty deserved to be overthrown. While in theory the peasants formed the second class, actually they were at the bottom of Chinese society, poor, illiterate and hardworking, and were exploited by the educated class that owned most of the land. The peasants also were subjected to heavy taxation, especially grain payments, and conscripted into the military and into forced labor, known as corvee labor, to build public works projects such as the Grand Canal and the Great Wall to keep out invading nomads from the north. While the literati maintained the cult of Confucianism, the peasants turned to the popular mystical traditions of Daoism and Buddhism, which were intermixed at the popular level and had large pantheons of deities to whom people could pray for help and consolation. Many secret societies based on Daoist and Buddhist beliefs gained members from the peasant class and led rebellions against the ruling class. Several of these secret societies overthrew Chinese dynasties and established new ones. The Confucianists pragmatically accepted the leader of a successful rebellion as the new emperor of the new dynasty, who had gained the Mandate of Heaven. At times the literati even supported the rebellions.

Some Chinese emperors built large state granaries to store food that could be used to feed the peasants in times of famine, and they expanded and maintained the system of dikes and canals to provide irrigation for crops and prevent rivers from flooding. However, these measures were not always sufficient. The Chinese empire was unified during the Qin dynasty (221 B.C.–206 B.C.), which was soon overthrown by the Han dynasty (206 B.C.–A.D. 220). During the Han dynasty, one of China's longest and most important, many Chinese institutions became established, including the cult of Confucius and the imperial bureaucracy. In A.D. 9, Wang Mang (d. A.D. 23) usurped the throne and set up his own Xin dynasty (9–23), also known as the Wang Mang Interregnum. At this time the Chinese peasants were suffering terribly from famine and the disastrous flooding of the Yellow River. Wang Mang attempted to make economic reforms but was unable to help the peasants, who turned to a secret society in Shandong Province known as the Red Eyebrows for the way they made up their faces to look like demons. Hundreds of thousands of peasants joined the Red Eyebrows Rebellion against Wang Mang, as did many Han nobles. The Red Eyebrows took the Han capital city of Chang'an (modern Xi'an in Shaanxi Province), killed Wang Mang and sacked the city.

In 25 Liu Xiu (Liu Hsiu), a descendant of the Han imperial family, reestablished the Han dynasty and moved his capital east from Chang'an to Luoyang in Henan Province. His dynasty is hence called the Eastern Han dynasty (also known as the Latter Han dynasty; 25–220). Ruling as the Han emperor, he finally suppressed the Red Eyebrows Rebellion in 27. However, new peasant rebellions broke out. Zhang Daoling (Chang Tao-ling), a faith healer who lived in the second century A.D. in modern Sichuan Province, was the first Celestial Master or Heavenly Teacher of the organized Daoist religion. He established a semiindependent state inhabited by his followers on the border of Sichuan and Shaanxi provinces. Many other leaders established similar movements in the Chinese countryside.

The largest anti-Han rebellion was led by the Yellow Turbans, also known as the Daoist Sect of the Great Peace (Taipingdao or T'ai-p'ing-t'ao), a religious sect in modern Hubei Province led by a Daoist faith healer. Their armed rebellion gained many followers in central China between the Yellow and Yangzi rivers and spread as far as Manchuria (modern northeastern China) and Fujian Province in the southeast. In 196 the Eastern Han dynasty finally suppressed the Yellow Turbans, but the dynasty ended less than three decades later, due to continuing peasant rebellions and the increasing power of local military leaders and wealthy landowners.

China broke apart into many contending kingdoms but was reunified by the Sui dynasty (581–618), whose two emperors conscripted hundreds of thousands of peasants to build the Grand Canal and repair and extend the Great Wall. The Sui was soon replaced by the Tang dynasty (618–907), one of the most glorious periods in Chinese history. However, the Tang was nearly brought down by a rebellion in 755 led by a military general named An Lushan. Chinese peasants had suffered several years of famine prior to the outbreak of this rebellion, but An Lushan's forces were mainly professional soldiers who had been stationed at the northern frontier. Famines in northern China in the late ninth century caused peasants to form rebellious bands and take many provinces. More than a half-million of them, led by Huang Zhao (Huang Chao), occupied Luoyang in 880 and Chang'an, the Tang capital, in 881. Troops loyal to the

Tang routed the rebels, but the city was destroyed and warlords took control of the Chinese empire, ending the dynasty in 907.

Much of China was reunified under the Song dynasty (960–1279), another high point for Chinese culture and the power of the literati. The Jurchens, an ethnic group to the north of China, took the Song capital at Kaifeng in 1127 and forced the Song court to flee south and establish its court at Hangzhou. The Song is thus divided into the Northern Song dynasty (960–1127) and Southern Song dynasty (1127–1279). A minor peasant rebellion led by Song Jiang (Sung Ch'iang) in 1120–21, near the end of the Northern Song, gave rise to popular stories about his rebel band that came to symbolize the values of rebels in Chinese culture. Plays were written about this rebellion in the 13th and 14th century, and the stories eventually were brought together in one large cycle, known as the *Shuihuzhuan* (*Shui-hui-chuan*), which was written down in several versions in the 16th and 17th centuries. In 1644 the author Jin Shengtan (Chin Sheng-t'an) published a condensed version, which became one of the most popular novels in China, under the title *Outlaws of the Marsh* or *The Water Margin*. The American author Pearl Buck (1892–1973), who had been raised in a missionary family in China, made a famous English translation called *All Men Are Brothers*.

The Southern Song fell to the Mongols, another ethnic group from the north who established a vast empire extending from China to the edge of Europe and ruled China under the Yuan dynasty (1279–1368). The Mongols were the first non-Han Chinese to rule the whole Chinese empire, and they were greatly resented by the Han Chinese people. The White Lotus sect originated during the Yuan and attracted many peasants as a symbol of Han Chinese resistance to foreign domination. The sect led a rebellion that even cut off the Grand Canal, the major transportation route in China, especially for the transport of grain to the capital at Beijing. The White Lotus appealed to impoverished peasants by promising them that Maitreya, the Buddha of the Future, would descend to Earth, restore Han Chinese rule, remove disease, natural disasters and all other suffering in this life, and bring happiness in the future.

By the 1340s another sect known as the Red Turbans or Red Scarves had spread from the middle Yangzi River region to Shandong Province. The sect's ideology blended elements from the cult of Maitreya with native Confucian and Daoist beliefs and the Manichaean religion, which had entered China from Central Asia. Zhu Yuanzhang (Chu Yuan-chang), a poor orphan whose family had died from drought and famine, became leader of this secret society. He led the Red Turbans Rebellion that overthrew the Mongols and established the Ming dynasty (1368–1644). Zhu reigned as the first Ming emperor, Hongwu (Hung-wu; r. 1368–98).

The suffering of the peasants continued after the restoration of Chinese rule, and rebellions continued. In 1627–28 peasants suffered terrible famine from droughts in northern Shanxi Province. They became militant and were joined by soldiers who had been let go from the army or who had deserted from Manchuria, where an ethnic group called the Manchus were threatening the Ming. The rebels rampaged through Shaanxi, Hebei and other Chinese provinces. Li Zicheng (Li Tzu-ch'eng) became their commander and attempted to conquer the Ming dynasty. He marched his rebel army to Beijing, the undefended Ming capital, and the Ming emperor hanged himself. Ming general Wu Sangui, who was stationed at the Great Wall to keep the Manchus out of China, asked the Manchus to help him defend against Li Zicheng's rebels. He let the Manchus, led by Dorgon, pass through the gate in the wall. They continued on to Beijing, took the city and proclaimed themselves the new rulers of China under the Qing dynasty (1644–1911).

The Han Chinese resented the Manchus, the second foreign group to rule the whole Chinese Empire. Many Han began moving south, where they cultivated large areas of land but came into conflict with members of the minority ethnic groups that inhabited these areas. These minorities, such as the Miao in western Hunan, led rebellions in the second half of the 18th century. The Han also began conducting large-scale rebellions against the Qing. One of the first was led by the White Lotus Secret Society. The Qing had forbidden the Chinese to join that and other religious sects, so the sects became secret societies. The White Lotus Rebellion (1796–1805) broke out in Hubei, Sichuan and Shaanxi provinces. It gained many followers among poor, uneducated peasants in the area north of the Huai River (modern Anhui Province), which the Qing recently had opened to settlement, and the poor migrants there led a desperate existence. Qing military forces finally suppressed the White Lotus rebel bands by taking control over the food supply and cutting off their source of recruits. However, the rebellion seriously damaged the Qing.

The population of China grew rapidly in the 18th century, creating a land shortage and increasing tensions between wealthy landowners and farmers who worked very hard to grow sufficient food on land that they rarely owned. In 1813 an offshoot of the White Lotus, another secret society known as the Eight Trigrams, led a peasant uprising in northern China that actually sent forces to try to invade the Forbidden City, the imperial palace in Beijing, but Qing troops suppressed them. Secret societies gained adherents, especially in southern China, where the Triad Society (Sanhehui or San-ho-hui; also known as Tiandihui or T'ien-ti-hui) became strong. The numerous anti-Qing uprisings in the 19th century shared the slogan Overthrow the Qing.

Between 1840 and 1850 there were more than 100 armed uprisings in China. One was the Small Sword Society Uprising (1853–55) in the region of Shanghai, China's largest port and trading city. Britain and other foreign powers handed the Qing military defeats in the mid-19th century and forced them to open Chinese cities as treaty ports to foreign traders and residents. This further humiliated and weakened the Manchu Qing and strengthened the resolve of the Han Chinese people to overthrow them.

The Taiping Rebellion (1850–64) was the largest uprising in 19th-century China and nearly overthrew the Manchu Qing dynasty. The leader, Hong Xiuquan (Hung Hsiu-ch'uan; 1813–64), was influenced by Christian ideas, which Western missionaries were spreading in China. Hong claimed that he was the younger brother of Jesus Christ and that God had called him to establish the Kingdom of God on Earth by overthrowing the Qing. Thousands of peasants, laborers, bandits and members of secret societies joined his movement. In 1852 Taiping forces marched down the Yangzi River

valley, and in 1853 they captured Nanjing, where they established their capital. By this time the Taipings numbered more than one million. They captured 600 Chinese walled cities and attempted unsuccessfully to take the Qing capital at Beijing. Combined Qing and Western forces finally defeated the Taipings in 1864. Other rebellions took place in China around the same time, including the Nian Rebellion (1852–68) and uprisings by Muslims who inhabited regions in China's northwest and southwest.

At the end of the 19th century, many northern Chinese peasants joined the antiforeign and anti-Qing Boxer movement, formally known as the Society of Righteous and Harmonious Fists, which was distantly related to the White Lotus Secret Society. In 1900 the Boxers laid siege to the foreign legation quarters in Beijing and forced the Qing emperor and empress dowager, who wielded the real power, to flee the city. Combined foreign forces finally suppressed the Boxers and took control of the city. In 1911 the Chinese people, led by Dr. Sun Yat-sen (1866–1925), overthrew the Qing in the Revolution of 1911 and established the Republic of China (ROC). Sun also established the Chinese Nationalist Party (Kuomintang; KMT) that controlled the ROC.

The Chinese Communist Party (CCP) was founded in Shanghai in 1921 with the goal of overcoming Chinese Confucian feudal traditions and creating a classless society. Mao Zedong (Mao Tse-tung; 1893–1976) was able to become dominant in the CCP because he recognized that the Chinese Communists should mobilize the Chinese peasants rather than urban workers, contrary to orthodox Marxist ideology, for their revolution. Mao was inspired by the rebel band in *Outlaws of the Marsh* and by the Taiping Rebellion. He and Zhou Enlai (Chou En-lai; 1898–1976), who became second-in-command under Mao, saw that it was more important for the Communists to control the countryside than to lose troops trying to take over large cities. The CCP defeated the Chinese Nationalists in a civil war and established the People's Republic of China (PRC) in 1949. The Communists mobilized the peasants to their cause, especially in northern China, by enacting land reform policies under which they encouraged peasants to criticize the landowners who exploited them, then took away land from wealthy landowners and gave it to peasants who had little or no land. They also organized peasant villages into people's communes in which every member was supposed to share work and profits equally. However, the CCP disbanded the people's communes in the early 1980s when it began building up the Chinese economy and encouraging foreign trade and investment. Nevertheless, today more than half of the Chinese labor force is still engaged in agriculture, and China has the world's largest agricultural economy. Farmers have to grow enough crops to feed a population of 1.2 billion, even though only about 10 percent of the land is suitable for cultivation.

The Good Earth, a famous novel by Pearl Buck, describes the desperate lives of Chinese peasants in the late 19th and early 20th centuries. Her novel was made into a film. Peasants also have been the subject of several recent Chinese films that have been widely shown in the West. *Yellow Earth*, directed by Chen Kaige (Ch'en K'ai-ke) and filmed by Zhang Yimou (Chang I-mo), portrays the difficult life of peasants on the loess plateau in northwestern China. *Old Well*, filmed by and also starring Zhang, tells the story of residents of a drought-stricken village looking for water. *Red Sorghum,* the first film that Zhang directed, is about a woman in an arranged marriage and her lover in a sorghum-growing region of Shandong Province. *The Story of Qiuju,* set in a mountain village in northwestern China, tells the story of a man who is injured by the village headman and whose strong-willed pregnant wife goes through many levels of government bureaucracy to gain justice for her husband. See also AGRICULTURE; AN LUSHAN REBELLION; BOXER UPRISING; BUCK, PEARL; BUDDHISM; CHEN KAIGE; CHINESE COMMUNIST PARTY; CIVIL WAR BETWEEN COMMUNISTS AND SOCIALISTS; CONFUCIANISM; COOLIE; DAOISM; EIGHT TRIGRAMS REBELLION; EMPEROR; GRAIN; GRAND CANAL; GREAT WALL; HAN DYNASTY; HONGWU, EMPEROR; LAND REFORM BY COMMUNISTS; LI ZICHENG; LOESS; MAITREYA AND MANJUSRI; MANDATE OF HEAVEN; MAO ZEDONG; MINORITIES, NATIONAL; NATURAL DISASTERS; NIAN REBELLION; OUTLAWS OF THE MARSH; PEOPLE'S COMMUNE; PEOPLE'S REPUBLIC OF CHINA; RED EYEBROWS REBELLION; RED TURBANS REBELLION; REVOLUTION OF 1911; SMALL SWORD SOCIETY; SOCIAL CLASSES; TAIPING REBELLION; WANG MANG; WHITE LOTUS SECRET SOCIETY; YANGZI RIVER; YELLOW RIVER; YELLOW TURBANS REBELLION; ZHANG DAOLING; ZHANG YIMOU; NAMES OF INDIVIDUAL DYNASTIES.

PEI See STONE TABLETS.

PEI, I. M. (1917–)   Full name Ieoh Ming Pei; a Chinese-American who is one of the world's most famous architects and has made modernism the official style for institutional buildings in the United States. Pei was born in the beautiful Chinese city of Suzhou, where his family home still stands. His father was a wealthy banker and his mother was a flutist and poet. Pei was raised in the cosmopolitan Chinese city of Shanghai, which has many 19th-century European buildings. He moved to the United States in 1935 to study architecture at the University of Pennsylvania, but transferred to the Massachusetts Institute of Technology (MIT). He studied architecture at Harvard University with European refugees Walter Gropius and Marcel Breuer, who had brought the Bauhaus style to America. Pei received his masters degree in architecture in 1946 and became an instructor and assistant professor in 1945–48. He did not return to China, and in 1954 he became an American citizen.

In 1948 Pei became a partner of the bombastic New York real estate developer William Zeckendorf, who fell into bankruptcy in the 1960s. In 1958 Pei established his own architectural firm, I.M. Pei and Associates, later called I.M. Pei and Partners. Many leading architects joined his firm, as did two of his sons. In 1964 Pei secured from Jacqueline Kennedy his first monumental commission, the John F. Kennedy Library in Boston (1979). Pei's architectural style is known for the way he integrates structures with their environments. Some of Pei's most important buildings include the Mile High Center in Denver (1957); National Airlines Terminal at Kennedy International Airport, Long Island (1971); Hancock Tower in Boston; East Wing of the National Gallery of Art, Washington, D.C. (1978); Jacob K. Javits Convention Center (New York Convention and Exhibition Center; 1979); and West Wing of the Museum of Fine Arts,

Boston (1981). In 1989 Pei designed the two-stage expansion and renovation of the Louvre Museum in Paris (completed in 1993), including its controversial glass pyramid, which is now regarded as the symbol of the new Paris architecture. He also designed the Morton H. Meyerson Symphony Center in Dallas (1989); the Luce Chapel in Taichung, Taiwan; the Fragrant Hill Hotel near Beijing, China's capital (1989); the 70-story Bank of China Tower in Hong Kong (1989); and the Rock & Roll Hall of Fame and Museum in Cleveland (1995).

In 1989 Pei's firm was renamed Pei Cobb Freed and Partners. He retired from the firm in 1990 but remained active with such works as the Miho Museum in Shiga, Japan; the Goulandris Museum in Athens; and the new Schauhaus addition to the German Historical Museum in Berlin. Pei has won many prestigious awards, including the Gold Medal of the American Institute of Architects (1979), La Grand Medaille d'Or from the French Academy of Architecture (1981), the Pritzker Architecture Prize (1983), and the Japanese Praemium Imperiale (1989). In 1997 he selected the U.S. Library of Congress as the major repository for his personal and professional papers. See also BANK OF CHINA; SHANGHAI; SUZHOU.

PEILIGANG See NEOLITHIC PERIOD.

PEIPING See BEIJING.

PEI-TA See BEIJING UNIVERSITY.

PEI-YANG ARMY See YUAN SHIKAI.

PEI-YANG NAVAL FLEET See QING DYNASTY; SINO-JAPANESE WAR OF 1894–95.

PEKING See BEIJING.

PEKING DUST See LOESS.

PEKING MAN (*Pithecanthropus pekinensis* or *homo erectus pekinensis; Sinanthropus pithecus*)   Hominid bones, including a skull fragment, dating to about 500,000 B.C., which were found in 1927 in limestone caves at Zhoukoudian (Chou-k'ou-tien) in Hebei Province, about 29 miles southwest of the capital city of Beijing, (at that time called Peking). When they were discovered, these were the oldest fossil remains of hominids ever found. They included the remains of more than 40 humans, who stood upright, had a cranial capacity about two-thirds that of modern humans, made and used tools and cooked meals over a fire. The skull's shovel-shaped incisor teeth, typical of members of the Mongoloid race, suggest that Peking Man may have been a distant ancestor of the modern Chinese. The fossils of Peking Man were lost during the Japanese invasion of China in the 1930s. However, similar fossils have since been excavated in the same area and have been dated to 500,000 to 210,000 B.C. In 1963 fossil remains of a slightly more primitive but similar hominid, perhaps about 100,000 years older than Peking Man, were found at Lantian in Shanxi Province. This hominid, named *Sinanthropus lantianensis* or Lantian Man, had a brain somewhat smaller than that of Peking Man but still much larger than that of the most advanced human-like ape.

PEKING OPERA   See OPERA, BEIJING.

PEKINGESE DOG   See LION.

P'ENG CHEN   See PENG ZHEN.

PENG DEHUAI (P'eng Teh-huai; 1898–1974)   A government leader in the People's Republic of China (PRC) who was purged for rightist deviation in 1959. Peng Dehuai was born in Hunan Province. As a young man he joined the Nationalist (Kuomintang) army, but in 1927 he deserted the Nationalists and joined the army of the Chinese Communist Party. The following year he led a Communist rebellion against the Nationalists.

Peng was an important member of the Long March that Communist forces made to escape the Nationalists from 1934 to 1935. During China's War of Resistance against Japan (1937–45; World War II), he served as deputy commander of the Eighth Route Army, continuing to hold this position during the civil war between the Communists and Nationalists. In 1949 the Communists defeated the Nationalists and established the PRC. During the Korean War (1950–53), Peng served as head of the Chinese forces in Korea. He was then named minister of defense and pushed for the modernization of the Chinese armed forces.

At the Politburo Conference held at Lushan in 1959, Peng led an attack against the Great Leap Forward that had been promoted by party chairman Mao Zedong (Mao Tse-tung), because he thought it would hinder the military's modernization. Mao feared that Peng's attack showed that the military wanted to take control of the Communist Party, so he brought other military leaders to his side, including the ideological Maoist Lin Biao (Lin Piao). Mao dismissed Peng from office and named Lin Biao minister of defense. Peng was not denounced publicly, however, and he was permitted to travel around China to evaluate the results of the Great Leap Forward. In 1962 Peng tried to win reinstatement as minister of defense, but Mao refused to allow this.

When the Cultural Revolution (1966–76) began, Peng was believed to belong to the faction that opposed Mao. In fact, the Cultural Revolution began as a debate about academic essays and a play written by Wu Han, the vice-mayor of Beijing, that were a disguised attack on Mao's dismissal of Peng in 1959. The plays had to do with Hai Rui (Hai Jui), a government official during the Ming dynasty (1368–1644) who was unjustly dismissed from office because he publicly criticized the emperor. Wu Han's essays and play were widely debated by academics, and members of Beijing University's Philosophy Department put up a "big-character poster" (wall poster, *dazibao*) criticizing the university president for suppressing debate on this issue. The political struggle sparked by this issue spread throughout the country. All Chinese schools were shut down and the students were urged to join the Red Guards in attacking "old" ideas and culture. Mao's wife, Jiang Qing (Chiang Ch'ing), had Peng arrested and brought from Chengdu to Beijing and put on public trial by the Red Guards. He disappeared from the public eye and died before the end of the Cultural Revolution. See also BEIJING UNIVERSITY; BIG-CHARACTER POSTERS; CHINESE COMMUNIST PARTY; CULTURAL REVOLUTION; EIGHTH ROUTE ARMY; GREAT LEAP FORWARD; KOREAN WAR; LIN BIAO; LONG MARCH; MAO ZEDONG; RED GUARDS; WAR OF RESISTANCE AGAINST JAPAN.

P'ENG TEH-HUAI   See PENG DEHUAI.

PENG ZHEN (P'eng Chen; 1902–97)   The first member of the Politburo in the People's Republic of China (PRC) to become a victim of the Cultural Revolution (1966–76). Peng had joined the newly formed Chinese Communist Party (CCP) in the 1920s and was active in organizing urban workers to join the party. During the 1920s and 1930s he was imprisoned for his revolutionary activities for a total of six years. In the mid-1930s Peng became lieutenant to Liu Shaoqi (Liu Shao-ch'i), later designated a successor to Communist leader Mao Zedong (Mao Tse-tung), in the North China Bureau of the CCP. During China's War of Resistance against Japan (1937–45) and the civil war between the CCP and the Nationalist Party (Kuomintang; KMT), Peng held various positions within the CCP. In 1949, after the Communists founded the PRC, Peng became secretary of the Beijing Municipal Communist Party. Two years later he became mayor of Beijing, the Chinese capital city.

In Beijing, Peng became involved in a conflict with the CCP. In the mid-1950s some CCP leaders and Mao supported the role of intellectuals who were not members of the party but collaborated with it. Peng and Liu led the faction of hard-liners who placed party unity and orthodoxy of thought above all else. In 1956 Mao's faction encouraged the intellectuals to criticize the Communist Party in the so-called Hundred Flowers Campaign. When they did so in 1957, they were severely punished by the Anti-Rightist Campaign, which had grown out of Peng's conservative faction.

From 1958 to 1960 China suffered economic and agricultural disaster with the failure of the Maoist policy for economic development known as the Great Leap Forward, and it ended its previous close relationship with the U.S.S.R. Leading intellectuals in the CCP began criticizing PRC Chairman Mao, especially in Beijing, where Peng was the leader of the Beijing CCP Committee. Lin Biao (Lin Piao), who supported Mao's revolutionary fervor, took the place of Marshal Peng Dehuai (P'eng Teh-huai) as Chinese minister of national defense in 1959 and brought the People's Liberation Army (PLA) under stricter control of the Communist Party.

Over the next 10 years, party factionalism escalated into the Cultural Revolution. This movement, led by Mao, broke out in Beijing in 1966 when Wu Han, the city's vice-mayor, published a play about an ancient emperor who was criticized for improperly dismissing a government official. Mao, interpreting this as a criticism of his own dismissal of Marshal Peng Dehuai in 1959, attacked Wu Han. Peng Zhen (who was not related to Peng Dehuai), the leading CCP official in Beijing as well as a member of the national Politburo, felt that Mao's attack on Wu Han was an attack on himself. An investigation in Beijing concluded that Peng Zhen was innocent; Mao then convened a forum in Shanghai where party leaders denounced Peng Zhen. They removed him from office in April 1966. Peng was forced to spend many years in prison while the Cultural Revolution grew into a mass movement that tore China apart.

After the Cultural Revolution ended in 1976, Peng was released from prison and rehabilitated. In the late 1970s he was made head of the Legal Affairs Commission, which drew up a new comprehensive legal system for China that was put into effect on January 1, 1980. The new laws promulgated under Peng reduced the power exercised by public security authorities and increased the power of the police and the courts, giving people accused of crimes the right to legal counsel and to appeal their sentences. In November 1979 Peng was appointed secretary general of the Standing Committee of the Fifth National People's Congress (NPC), which enabled him to control the reconstruction of the Chinese legal system. The Standing Committee presided over sessions of the NPC, set the agenda and handled the routing of legislation and nominations for political offices. In 1987, while Peng held this position, the Standing Committee also was given the power to "enact and amend laws with the exception of those which should be enacted by the NPC." Throughout the 1980s Peng, also a member of the Politburo, remained a conservative within the CCP who emphasized party unity and gradual political change, in opposition to the rapid economic and political reforms emphasized by Chairman Deng Xiaoping (Teng Hsiao-p'ing). From 1981 to 1988 he served as chairman of the NPC. See also ANTI-RIGHTIST CAMPAIGN; CHINESE COMMUNIST PARTY; CULTURAL REVOLUTION; DENG XIAOPING; HUNDRED FLOWERS CAMPAIGN; LEGAL SYSTEM; LIU SHAOQI; NATIONAL PEOPLE'S CONGRESS; POLITBURO.

P'ENG-CHING See CONTAINER GARDENS.

PENGHU ISLANDS See SHIMONOSEKI, TREATY OF; SINO-FRENCH WAR; SINO-JAPANESE WAR OF 1894–95.

PENGJING See CONTAINER GARDENS.

PENGLAI (P'ENG-LAI) See ISLANDS OF THE BLESSED.

PEONY (*fuguihua* or *fu-kuei-hua*) The favorite flower of the Chinese people and, like the orchid, a symbol of spring and of female beauty. The peony also symbolizes good fortune and nobility; the Chinese name for the peony, *fuguiha,* means "flower of wealth and honor." The peony grows in small bushes and produces in late spring many large, round, fragrant white, pink or red flowers with numerous petals.

The Chinese cultivate peonies in many areas of the country, but they consider those grown in Luoyang in Henan Province the finest because of ideal climate and soil conditions. About 200 varieties of peony flourish in Luoyang today. In Beijing, peony blossoms are illuminated at night for viewing. Often Chinese artists make a series of paintings depicting the four seasons, with the plum blossom for winter, the peony for spring, the lotus for summer and the chrysanthemum for autumn. Peony flowers are a popular design motif in Chinese arts and crafts, such as painting, porcelain, embroidery, cloisonné and papercuts. See also CHRYSANTHEMUM; LOTUS; LUOYANG; ORCHID; PLUM; NAMES OF INDIVIDUAL CRAFTS.

PEOPLE OF CHINA See HAN; MINORITIES, NATIONAL; POPULATION.

PEOPLE'S BANK OF CHINA The official bank of the People's Republic of China (PRC), founded by the Chinese Communist Party (CCP) after they defeated the Chinese Nationalists in 1949. The Communists established the People's Bank in 1948, when Communist forces were winning battles throughout northern China. China was beset by chronic inflation and fiscal chaos, and the Communists wanted to centralize and stabilize the country's monetary system. After 1949 the People's Bank, with headquarters in Beijing, became the PRC's central note-issuing bank, handling all banking, financial and credit activities in China. The banking system was the first sector in the PRC to become completely socialized. The People's Bank of China was given the sole responsibility for issuing currency and controlling the Chinese money supply, and it acted quickly to stop raging inflation. In 1950 the Communist government required all state agencies and enterprises, including retail outlets, to deposit most of their accumulated cash with the People's Bank of China. The bank, which reports to the Ministry of Finance and is a special agency of the State Council, grew into the world's largest single banking entity.

The People's Bank of China functions both as a national central bank—supervising the monetary system and controlling the state budget—and as a commercial and savings bank. It serves as the government treasury, the clearing center for financial transactions, the main source of credit for economic units, the holder of enterprise deposits and the national savings bank. The State Planning Commission works with the People's Bank of China, the State Economic Commission, State Statistical Bureau, economic ministries and other government organs to draw up annual and multi-year plans, including the Five-Year Plans, for the future direction and goals of the Chinese economy. The People's Bank of China expects to issue 200 million credit cards to consumers by the year 2000, which will result in a large consumer database. It is currently remodeling itself after the U.S. Federal Reserve System.

The Bank of China is the foreign exchange arm of the People's Bank of China. The PRC's foreign trade is supervised by the Bank of China, the Ministry of Foreign Trade and Economic Cooperation, and the General Administration of Customs. See also BANK OF CHINA; CURRENCY, MODERN; FIVE-YEAR PLANS; MINISTRY OF FINANCE; STATE COUNCIL; STATE PLANNING COMMISSION.

PEOPLE'S COMMUNE (*gongshe*) A collective unit under the system for organizing agricultural collectives established by the Chinese Communist Party (CCP) after it founded the People's Republic of China (PRC) in October 1949. Even before that date, the CCP had brought about land reform in much of northern China, taking it away from wealthy landowners and distributing it to peasants who had little or no land of their own. The vast majority of the Chinese people are peasants who farm the land. After 1949 the CCP first made Chinese farmers form rural cooperatives to combine their resources for growing and selling crops. After several years, under the program known as the Great Leap Forward (1958–60), these cooperatives were turned into much larger people's communes, in which the land was owned in common by all commune members.

On April 29, 1958, the PRC's first people's commune, the Sputnik Federated Co-operative, was established in Henan

Province in central China. Altogether 26,000 people's communes were established, each of which combined an average of 20 to 30 cooperatives, with an average of 5,000 households and about 10,000 acres in each commune. Officials in the State Planning Commission told the commune members what crops to raise and how much to produce each year. At year's end, the commune's profits were distributed to its members based on how many "work points" they had accumulated during that year. A peasant family's income depended on how many people it provided to work in the collective fields.

From 1958 to 1982, people's communes were the largest collective units and the highest of three administrative levels for agriculture in rural China. The two levels beneath communes were production brigades and, at the bottom, production teams, which were the basic accounting and farm production units in communes. A production brigade was equivalent to a traditional village, and a production team usually included about 30 families and about 100 to 250 members. A commune was self-sufficient and handled all the means of production for its members, and also small local industry, education of its children, marketing of its crops and other products and security, which was maintained by militia organizations. Each commune had kitchens, dining halls and nurseries that all members shared. For a short time, some communes even had dormitories where members lived instead of private homes. Communes also provided some workers for large-scale projects, such as building hydroelectric dams and irrigation systems, which would further the development of both agriculture and industry.

The Great Leap Forward proved to be an economic disaster, one result of which was a shortage of food, and the CCP had to modify the commune system by decentralizing some of its control over the communes and providing some material incentives to farmers. However, the basic commune system remained unchanged through the 1970s, when the CCP, after the death in 1976 of Communist leader Mao Zedong (Mao Tse-tung) and the end of the Cultural Revolution, began initiating reform programs for modernizing China and improving its economy.

In the winter of 1982–83, the CCP abolished people's communes and enacted the "responsibility system" in agriculture, under which individual farm families hold long-term leases on land that they farm themselves. The Chinese government still sets quotas for some crops, such as grain, cotton and oil seeds, and each family grows the amount of crops required by the government and sells them to the state for a fixed price. The family is free to grow any other crops that it chooses and sell them at free-market prices. Many Chinese farm families, especially those near urban areas, have greatly increased their incomes under this system, and many specialize in certain crops that form an important part of the Chinese diet, such as vegetables, pork, ducks and fish raised in artificial ponds.

People's communes were replaced by townships (*xiang*), the basic government administrative unit below the county level in rural areas. Each township, which is about the same size as the people's commune that it replaced, has a people's congress and an elected chairman. Production brigades were turned into townships or villages, and most production teams were disbanded and replaced by villages. Villages (*nongcun*) are the lowest level in the Chinese Communist system of government. Their duties include administering welfare payments and settling disputes. Branches of the CCP also are organized at the village level. See also AGRICULTURE; CHINESE COMMUNIST PARTY; GREAT LEAP FORWARD; LAND REFORM BY COMMUNISTS; PEOPLE'S REPUBLIC OF CHINA.

PEOPLE'S COURTS See LEGAL SYSTEM; SUPREME PEOPLE'S COURT.

PEOPLE'S DAILY (*Renmin Ribao*) The official national newspaper of the Chinese Communist Party (CCP), which has governed the People's Republic of China (PRC) since 1949, when the newspaper began publication. The *People's Daily* is the only national newspaper in China; all others are considered local and usually are not distributed outside of their own provinces or regions. The paper is administered by the Propaganda Committee of the CCP Central Committee and receives the domestic and foreign news it prints through the New China (*Xinhua*) News Agency (also part of the Propaganda Committee). The content of the *People's Daily* is controlled directly by Politburo leaders. Editorials represent the Communist Party's own political decrees and on important occasions may be published jointly in *Red Flag* (recently renamed *Seeking Truth*), the paper of the CCP, and *Liberation Army Daily,* the paper of the People's Liberation Army (PLA). Hu Jiwei has been chief editor of the *People's Daily* since 1977. Public indexes to the newspaper since 1949 have been made available to libraries in other countries. See also CHINESE COMMUNIST PARTY; NEW CHINA NEWS AGENCY; POLITBURO.

PEOPLE'S JOURNAL, THE See REVOLUTIONARY ALLIANCE; REVOLUTION OF 1911; SUN YAT-SEN.

PEOPLE'S LIBERATION ARMY (PLA) Formerly known as the Red Army; the army of the Chinese Communist Party (CCP), which founded the People's Republic of China (PRC) in 1949. The PLA includes the ground force, the navy, the air force and the strategic nuclear forces. The PLA publishes its own newspaper, *Liberation Army Daily* (*Jiefangjun Bao*), which has a large circulation, and has its own film studio, the August First Film Studio. The PLA is directed by the Central Military Commission under the command of the chairman of the CCP, who until 1982 was China's commander-in-chief. The Central Military Commission administers the National Defense Science, Technology and Industry Commission (NDSTIC), which was formed in 1982 by merging several government bodies concerned with defense science and technology. Members of the Central Military Commission control the military through the General Political Department of the PLA. The Ministry of National Defense, which works very closely with the Central Military Commission, draws up plans for implementing the defense and military policies set by the CCP and provides military attachés for Chinese embassies. It also operates training programs and military exercises for the PLA, provides the framework for logistical and administrative military activities and determines strategies and weapons to be used. The minister of national defense is superior to the chief of staff of the PLA but is under the direct orders of the chairman of the CCP and the premier of the State Council.

The PLA was formed in 1927 as the "Red Army." The Chinese Nationalist Party (Kuomintang; KMT), led by Chiang Kai-shek since 1925, had cooperated with the CCP, which was founded in 1921. The two parties had established the Whampoa (Huangpu) Military Academy near Guangzhou (Canton) to train officers to lead an expedition against the northern warlords who controlled much of China. Mao Zedong (Mao Tse-tung) and Zhou Enlai (Chou En-lai), who became the two highest leaders in the CCP, were connected with that military academy. The Northern Expedition was launched by the Nationalists in 1926 and was successful. But in 1927 Chiang turned against the Communists, expelling them from the KMT and ordering their massacre in Shanghai in April. Some Communist leaders, including Lin Biao (Lin Piao) and Mao Zedong, tried to organize uprisings in the countryside, but the KMT suppressed them. Mao fled to the Soviet base in the Jinggang Mountains on the border between Hunan and Jiangxi provinces. Chinese Soviets also were established in Hubei, Hunan, Sichuan and Shaanxi provinces. From 1928 to 1934 Mao led the Communist guerrillas in mobilizing peasant forces in the Jiangxi Soviet area. He succeeded because he was familiar with the peasants and the conditions of their daily lives, and he was supported loyally by military commander Zhu De (Chu Teh) and his forces, which became the Red Army.

Chiang Kai-shek led KMT forces against the Communist forces led by Mao in Jiangxi, and in 1934 the Communists decided to escape to the west. In the autumn of 1934 they began their famous Long March, in which they covered 6,000 miles in a little more than a year, losing many soldiers in the process. They finally made their headquarters at Yan'an in Shaanxi Province in western China. There the Red Army consolidated, trained its forces and won over the local peasants. After Japan invaded China in 1937, the CCP and the KMT formed a united front to fight the War of Resistance against Japan (1937–45; World War II). On August 22, 1937, the CCP formally reorganized its forces as the Eighth Route Army of the National Army. Many of the Eighth Route commanders and political commissars later held top CCP positions in the People's Republic of China (PRC), founded by the CCP in 1949, including Mao Zedong, Zhou Enlai, Lin Biao, Zhu De, Peng Dehuai (P'eng Teh-huai), Liu Bocheng (Liu Po-cheng), Deng Xiaoping (Teng Hsiao-p'ing) and Nie Rongzhen (Nieh Jung-chen).

During the war the KMT became more preoccupied with defeating the Communists than resisting the Japanese. While Japanese forces controlled most of northern China, the Eighth Route Army supported the Shanxi-Hebei-Chahar Border Region Government. From there the Communist guerrilla soldiers moved east across the Yellow River (Huanghe) into the North China Plain and on to Shandong Province. Toward the end of the war they controlled large areas of China north of the Yangzi River. After Japan was defeated in 1945, the CCP and the KMT resumed their civil war. The CCP won a major victory in Manchuria (northeastern China), where the retreating Soviet forces handed their supplies over to them and the Japanese troops surrendered to them rather than to the KMT. The second major CCP victory was in the Huai River basin in north-central China, where the Red Army, by now known as the People's Liberation Army, surrounded 66 out of 200 KMT divisions and ended

Chiang Kai-shek's Nationalist regime on the Chinese mainland. In April 1949 the Communists moved south of the Yangzi, taking Shanghai in May and Guangzhou later in 1949. On October 1 Mao proclaimed the founding of the PRC in Beijing, and in December Chiang and his Nationalist government fled to Taiwan Island.

When the CCP founded the PRC in 1949, many Chinese were willing to accept the new government because the Nationalist regime had been as corrupt as those of the warlords, while the PLA soldiers were disciplined and worked to help the Chinese people. In 1950 the Korean War broke out, North Korea borders Manchuria, China's most industrialized region, and the PRC feared that advancing United Nations forces would cross the border, so in October 1950 it sent PLA forces across the Yalu River into North Korea to respond to that nation's request for assistance. These PLA units were called the Chinese People's Volunteers. At the same time, the government sent PLA forces into Tibet (Xizang) in western China, which had been independent since the Qing dynasty (1644–1911) fell. The Tibetans fiercely resisted the PLA forces for nearly a decade, but finally the Dalai Lama, Tibet's spiritual and temporal leader, had to flee to northern India with thousands of his followers. In 1951 the United Nations declared that the PRC was an aggressor in Korea and sanctioned a global embargo on the shipment of arms and other war materials to the PRC. This helped to keep the PRC isolated and prevented it from taking China's seat in the United Nations, which was held by the KMT's Republic of China (ROC) on Taiwan.

In the early 1960s Mao Zedong began a movement to remove what he perceived as capitalist and antisocialist forces from the CCP and restore its ideological purity. This developed into the Cultural Revolution (1966–76), a decade of turmoil during which thousands of Chinese students became Red Guards who traveled all over the country, enforcing Mao's position by holding massive political demonstrations, criticizing and even beating and killing people they deemed counterrevolutionary, including CCP officials, and damaging many historical sites, libraries and art collections. During the Cultural Revolution, the PLA abolished the hierarchy of military ranks and the use of distinctive uniforms for officers. Mao's faction in the CCP, which included Lin Biao, was supported by the PLA. The opposing faction was led by Liu Shaoqi (Liu Shao-ch'i) and Deng Xiaoping. Premier Zhou Enlai attempted to mediate between the two factions. China came close to anarchy, and the PLA, the only government organization that was able to restore order, became the de facto political authority. PLA regional military commanders went against Mao's orders to support the leftist radicals. In 1967 the PLA organized revolutionary committees, a new form of local governing body that replaced local CCP committees and administrative bodies, and in which PLA commanders held the greatest power. In late 1968 Mao finally realized that continuing the revolutionary violence would serve no purpose.

In 1968–69 the U.S.S.R. invaded Czechoslovakia and built up its forces along the PRC border. In March 1969 PLA troops clashed with Soviet forces on Zhenbao Island in the disputed Wusuli (Ussuri) River border area. Tensions with the Soviet Union helped tone down Chinese political factionalism. In 1971 Mao removed Liu Shaoqi, his possible successor, and replaced him with Lin Biao, then marshal of the PLA. In 1972 the government reported that Lin Biao had plotted against Mao, had been discovered in 1971, and he, his family and several PLA leaders had been killed in a plane crash while trying to escape to the U.S.S.R. Lin's supporters were purged from the PLA, which increased its efforts to make the military more professional and less political.

In 1975 the PRC embarked on a program to enact the "Four Modernizations," announced by Zhou Enlai and supported by Deng Xiaoping, to rebuild and modernize the country. The fourth modernization was to establish a professional military force equipped with modern weapons. Since 1978 the PLA has demobilized about 3 million men and women and has adopted modern methods for recruitment and manpower, strategy and education and training. In 1980 the PLA military command structure was reformed, and in 1982 General Yang Dezhi (Yang Teh-chih) completely reorganized the PLA so that it would be changed from Mao's ideology-dominated people's militia into a disciplined professional army with high morale that was trained in handling modern weapons. Military ranks and special uniforms for officers were restored.

In 1982, as part of the general reform movement led by Deng Xiaoping, a state Central Military Commission was created under the National People's Congress (NPC) as a counterpart to the CCP Central Military Commission. The same leader heads both commissions, and the CCP Central Military Commission retains authority over the state commission. In 1984, 40 top PLA officers holding the rank of general who were over 60 years old were retired. Marshal Ye Jianying (Yeh Chian-ying) was retained in key CCP positions because he had served the PLA with distinction since the Long March. In 1985 the PLA was reduced from 4.2 million members to 3.3 million, still the largest military in the world. In 1988 the PLA adopted, as part of its modernization and regularization, a new system of military ranking and new insignia. The officers were divided into 11 ranks, with general, first class, being the highest. Seventeen senior PLA officers were awarded the rank of general. Regular soldiers were divided into seven ranks. The status of active-service officers in scientific research, medicine, athletics, literature and art was changed to nonmilitary. Those people switched from uniforms to civilian clothes but remained at their posts. In 1993 there were about 3.3 million men and women in the PLA. The government planned to continue upgrading equipment and training and to make further troop cuts, especially for the navy and air force.

In 1989 Chinese students held a massive pro-democracy demonstration in Tiananmen Square in Beijing, China's capital. CCP hard-liners finally called out PLA forces to brutally suppress the demonstration, which was televised around the world. The Chinese people were shocked, and the country entered a period of political and social repression. In 1996 the PLA held intensive military exercises in the 100-mile-wide Taiwan Strait to intimidate the Taiwanese people just before they held their first public election for president of the ROC. They were not intimidated and elected Lee Teng-hui, the incumbent president. See also CENTRAL MILITARY COMMISSION AND MINISTRY OF NATIONAL DEFENSE; CHIANG KAI-SHEK; CHINESE COMMUNIST PARTY; CIVIL WAR BETWEEN COMMUNISTS AND NATIONALISTS; CULTURAL REVOLUTION;

EIGHTH ROUTE ARMY; FILM STUDIOS; FOUR MODERNIZATIONS; LIN BIAO; LIU BOCHENG; LIU SHAOQI; LONG MARCH; MAO ZEDONG; NIE RONGZHEN; NORTHERN EXPEDITION; PEOPLE'S REPUBLIC OF CHINA; REPUBLIC OF CHINA; TIANANMEN SQUARE MASSACRE; WAR OF RESISTANCE AGAINST JAPAN; WHAMPOA MILITARY ACADEMY; YAN'AN; YE JIANYING; ZHU DE.

PEOPLE'S REPUBLIC OF CHINA (PRC)   The present government of mainland China, which was established in 1949 by the Chinese Communist Party (CCP) after it defeated the Chinese Nationalist Party (Kuomintang; KMT), led by Chiang Kai-shek. When the PRC was founded, the Chinese People's Political Consultative Conference (CPPCC) was the government's legislative and representative body. The CPPCC had been formed in 1948 by the united front led by the CCP and other Chinese factions that opposed the KMT. On September 22, 1949, the CPPCC passed an Organic Law specifying the procedures and structure for government operations. On September 29 the CPPCC proclaimed its Common Program, which served as the law of the PRC until the 1954 state constitution superseded it. On October 1 CCP Chairman Mao Zedong (Mao Tse-tung; 1893–1976) proclaimed the founding of the PRC in Tiananmen Square in Beijing, which remains the capital city. In theory, all state power in the PRC belongs to the people, but in fact the government of the PRC is subordinate to the CCP and serves to implement its policies. Eight other small political parties, known as democratic parties, which had belonged to the CPPCC are still permitted to function in the PRC, although they do not form opposition parties.

In 1954 the PRC enacted a state constitution and elected a National People's Congress (NPC), comparable to the U.S. Congress or the British Parliament and in theory still the highest government body of the PRC. Local congresses elect delegates to provincial congresses, who in turn elect delegates to the NPC. The NPC elects the PRC's president and vice president. The president is the head of state and is responsible to the NPC. Mao was chairman of the CCP and president of the PRC concurrently from 1954 until 1959, when he was replaced as president by Liu Shaoqi (Liu Shao-ch'ih), although Mao remained CCP chairman until he died in 1976. As of early 1998 Jiang Zemin (Chiang Tse-min) was president. There are four branches of power under the NPC: the State Council (executive branch), the Central Military Commission (judicial branch), the Supreme People's Court (judicial branch) and the Supreme People's Procuratorates, or inspectors general (procurates branch). The State Council is the highest organ of government administration, comparable to the U.S. president's cabinet. It drafts legislative bills for submission to the NPC and administers all of the government ministries as well as many other agencies, commissions, administrations, bureaus, academies and corporations. Senior members of the State Council are also powerful CCP leaders.

The CCP has a structure similar to that of the PRC government, and its highest body is the National Party Congress (not to be confused with the NPC). Under it is the CCP Central Committee, whose functions and powers are exercised by the Politburo (Political Bureau). The Standing Committee of the Politburo is a select group of about six members that forms the inner circle of power in the PRC. The Politburo was considered the major decision-making body in the PRC until the late 1980s, when the CCP Secretariat and the State Council began exercising most of the responsibility for foreign policy decisions. The NPC decides on the choice of the premier of the State Council nominated by the chairman (or president) of the PRC, and it has the power to remove State Council members from their positions. The premier of the State Council actually wields more power than the president. Zhou Enlai (Chou En-lai) served as premier from 1954 until he died in 1976. As of early 1998, the conservative Li Peng was premier. The official currency of the PRC is *Renmenbi* ("People's Money"), with its basic unit known as the *yuan*.

After the Chinese Communists founded the PRC in 1949, Great Britain and the U.S.S.R. recognized it as the legitimate government of mainland China, but the United States and many other countries recognized the Nationalist government of the ROC on Taiwan. Taiwan held China's seat in the United Nations until 1971, when the PRC was admitted to the United Nations and Taiwan was expelled, and many countries switched their diplomatic ties from the Nationalists to the Communists. In 1972 U.S. President Richard M. Nixon reversed his position on China and visited the PRC. On January 1, 1979, the United States ended diplomatic relations with Taiwan and gave diplomatic recognition to the PRC. However, the U.S. government continues to give Taiwan military support and maintains economic ties. The PRC considers Taiwan a renegade province of China and seeks to have it reunited with the mainland.

The PRC includes more territory than did the Chinese empire during any of the dynasties that controlled China for more than 2,000 years. Its total land area covers 3,719,275 square miles, and its border with other countries totals more than 117,445 miles. China covers 49 degrees of latitude and thus contains very diverse climatic zones, from subarctic to tropical. The PRC comprises 22 provinces, five autonomous regions and three centrally governed special municipalities, Beijing, Tianjin and Shanghai. In 1997 the British Crown Colony of Hong Kong reverted to the PRC as a Special Administrative Region of China; the Portuguese colony of Macao will revert in 1999. The Chinese provinces, traditionally known as China Proper, fall into rough geographic regions, the northeast (Manchuria), the region north of the Yangzi River (Changjiang), that south of the Yangzi, and the western and southwestern regions. Most provinces are located in the eastern half of the country. The autonomous regions lie in the farthest northern, western and southwestern regions: and have been given some autonomy because they are inhabited by many members of China's 55 officially designated national minority ethnic groups, especially the Mongols, Uighurs, Tibetans and Zhuang, the largest minority. National minorities comprise about 7 percent of the population, while the Han Chinese ethnic majority comprises about 93 percent of the population. The Han are united by their common language and writing system, Confucian heritage, family system and cuisine. Over the centuries many non-Han peoples adopted the Han Chinese language and customs and became assimilated into the Han, a process known as Sinicization. See also BEIJING; CENTRAL COMMITTEE OF THE CHINESE COMMUNIST PARTY; CHINA PROPER; CHINESE COMMUNIST PARTY; CHINESE PEOPLE'S POLITICAL CONSULTATIVE CONFERENCE; CIVIL WAR BETWEEN COMMU-NISTS AND NATIONALISTS; CLIMATE; CONSTITUTION, STATE, OF 1954; CULTURAL REVOLUTION; CURRENCY (MODERN); DEMOCRATIC PARTIES; GEOGRAPHY; GOVERNMENT STRUCTURE; HAN; LANGUAGE, CHINESE; LEGAL SYSTEM; MAO ZEDONG; MINORITIES, NATIONAL; NIXON, RICHARD M., U.S. PRESIDENT, VISIT TO CHINA; PEOPLE'S LIBERATION ARMY; POLITBURO; POPULATION; PROVINCES, AUTONOMOUS REGIONS AND MUNICIPALITIES; SINICIZATION; UNITED NATIONS; ZHOU ENLAI; NAMES OF INDIVIDUAL CITIES AND PROVINCES.

PERFORMING ARTS See ACROBATICS AND VARIETY THEATER; FILM STUDIOS; KUNQU; OPERA, BEIJING; OPERA, GUANGZHOU; STILT WALKING; STORYTELLING; YANGKO.

PESCADORE ISLANDS See SHIMONOSEKI, TREATY OF; SINO-FRENCH WAR; SINO-JAPANESE WAR OF 1894–95.

PETROLEUM See BO HAI GULF; DAQING OIL FIELDS; DZUNGARIA BASIN; ENERGY SOURCES; SOUTH CHINA SEA; SPRATLY ISLANDS.

PETUNTSE See JINGDEZHEN; PORCELAIN.

PHARMACOLOGY See ELIXIR OF IMMORTALITY; LI SHIZHEN; MEDICINE, HERBAL.

PHOENIX (*fenghuang*) A mythical long-tailed bird that represents the female principle, or yin, and symbolizes women. The five colors of the tail feathers stand for the five cardinal virtues of righteousness, propriety, wisdom, humanity and sincerity. The phoenix is second among the four superintelligent creatures, along with the dragon, tiger and tortoise. It is believed to rule over the south and symbolizes the sun's warmth and the summer harvest. Born from fire, often it is portrayed rising from flames or perched on the sun. Thus many times it is called the Red Bird of the South.

The phoenix is the symbol of the Chinese empress and frequently is depicted together with the dragon, the symbol of the emperor and the male principle, or yang. Traditionally the dragon and phoenix were embroidered only on robes of emperors and empresses. Manchu empresses during the Qing dynasty (1644–1911) wore a heavy black headdress with a phoenix in the center. As one stage of a traditional Chinese wedding, the bride and groom exchange marriage contracts that provide their horoscopes, accompanied by prescribed gifts. The bridegroom's contract is written on red paper, decorated with a dragon, and the bride's on green paper, decorated with a phoenix. At the formal betrothal ceremony, held 10 days before the actual wedding ceremony, "Dragon and Phoenix" cakes symbolizing a happy married life are served. At weddings, the phoenix is stamped in gold with the "Double Happiness" character on lucky money envelopes and other objects used in the ceremony.

The phoenix resembles a pheasant but has long, graceful tailfeathers similar to a peacock. It is a popular design motif in textiles and ceramics and commonly is depicted with the peony flower, the symbol of good fortune and nobility. The bird is believed to alight on the drysandra tree (*wutong*), an ornamental tree with bell-shape flowers that are white on the outside and reddish-brown inside. Drysandra seeds often are used to make paste fillings for mooncakes eaten at the Autumn Moon Festival. The home of the phoenix is in the mythical Vermilion Hills. Chinese traditions hold that the phoenix appears in the world only in times of peace; hence it also symbolizes harmony and order in the world. It was supposedly seen at the birth of the great Chinese philosopher Confucius (551–479 B.C.). See also AUTUMN MOON FESTIVAL; CLOTHING, TRADITIONAL; DOUBLE HAPPINESS; DRAGON; PEONY; TIGER; TORTOISE; WEDDINGS; YIN AND YANG.

PI See BI.

PICKLES See SEASONINGS FOR FOOD; VEGETABLES AND VEGETARIAN DISHES.

PIEN FU See BAT.

PIG (*zhu* or *chu*) One of the most important animals in the Chinese diet and culture. The written character for family or home is comprised of a pig under a roof. Pigs and dogs were the earliest domesticated animals in China. Many pig remains have been excavated at sites of the Yangshao (5000–3000 B.C.) and Longshan (3000–2200 B.C.) Neolithic cultures and have been found at all sites dating from the Shang (1750–1040 B.C.) and Zhou (1100–256 B.C.) dynasties. Cooked pig meat, or pork, has been offered in Chinese religious sacrifices since ancient times. Pottery sculptures of pigs and pig houses have been found in tombs of the Han dynasty (206 B.C.–A.D. 220). From that time down to the modern era, rural Chinese butchered pigs once a year, a few days before the New Year Festival in late January or early February. The Chinese have numerous ways of cooking pork. Small pieces are used in stir-fry dishes or fried to make sweet and sour pork. Ground pork is used in many dishes, such as the filling for dumplings, which are enjoyed year-round as appetizers or snacks (dim sum) but are a special treat at the New Year Festival. Large cuts of pork are braised with soy sauce to make "red-cooked" pork. The meat also can be steamed or braised with hoisin sauce, scallions and other flavorings. Pork can be used to make soup stock, and pork meatballs or slices of barbecued pork may be added to soups. Pork sausage and pork spareribs cooked with soy and seasonings are also Chinese favorites. Even pig's feet have a place in Chinese cuisine. A whole roast pig provided by the bride's family is served at a traditional Chinese wedding. Cooked pork also is offered to ancestors at traditional family altars, after which it is consumed by living family members.

The Chinese export the bristles of the black hog, which are used to manufacture brushes and sturdy thread for sewing shoes and harnesses. Pig intestines are exported for use as sausage containers. The wild boar, which has long tusks, still can be found in Chinese forests, although its habitat has been greatly reduced by hunting and the country's expanding population, which is converting forests into farmland. Large numbers of wild boar live on the wide reed beds of the Tarim River catchment area in Xinjiang-Uighur Autonomous Region in western China. A pig is one of the main characters in the beloved and humorous 16th-century Chinese novel, *Journey to the West* (*Xiyouji* or *Hsi-yu chi*; also translated as *Pilgrimage to the West* and *Monkey*), based on the actual pilgrimage of the Chinese Buddhist monk Xuan-

zang (Hsuan-tsang; 602–664) to India to collect scriptures for translation. The pig or boar is one of the animals in the 12-year zodiac. The Chinese believe that people born in the Year of the Boar are honest, courageous, loyal and hardworking. The most recent Year of the Boar was 1995. See also COOKING, CHINESE; DIM SUM; JOURNEY TO THE WEST; NEW YEAR FESTIVAL; SEASONINGS FOR FOOD; WEDDINGS, TRADITIONAL; ZODIAC, ANIMAL.

PILL OF IMMORTALITY See ALCHEMY; ELIXIR OF IMMORTALITY.

PING HSIN See BING XIN.

PING SHENG YEN CHIN See YEN, YAN YANGCHU JAMES.

PINGNAN, SULTANATE OF See DU WENXIU; YUNNAN PROVINCE.

"PING-PONG DIPLOMACY" See NIXON, RICHARD, U.S. PRESIDENT, VISIT TO CHINA.

PINGTAN (P'ING-T'AN) See STORYTELLING.

PINGYANG, PRINCESS (P'ing-yang; 600–623) The daughter of Li Yuan, known as Emperor Gaozu (566–635; r. 618–26), founder of the Tang dynasty (618–907). Princess Pingyang became a famous figure in Chinese history for her military leadership, which helped her father found the new dynasty. During the reign of Emperor Yangdi (Yang-ti; r. 604–18) of the Sui dynasty (589–618), Li Yuan was a duke and military commander in the state of Tang in modern Shanxi Province in northern China. Yangdi had drained the economy and conscripted huge numbers of Chinese to build the Grand Canal and his capital in Luoyang. His cruelty caused peasant rebellions to break out all over China, and many members of the aristocracy and the literati, or scholar class that staffed the imperial bureaucracy, joined the opposition to the emperor. Yangdi intended to imprison Li Yuan, whose military power presented a threat to the throne. To stop Yangdi from doing so, in 617 Li Yuan sent a message to his sons and to Pingyang's husband, Cai Shao (Ts'ai Shao), who was a bodyguard to the crown prince, that they should join him immediately in a rebellion against Yangdi. Cai Shao joined his father-in-law, and Pingyang fled to her family's country estate in Huxian County outside the capital, where she found peasants dying of starvation. She opened her family's grain reserves to feed them and raised an army of several hundred men to fight the emperor's troops. This force came to be known as the Woman's Army because she was their leader. Princess Pingyang's brother also joined their father's cause. The princess joined her army with that of several other leaders of peasant armies who also wanted to overthrow the tyrannical Yangdi. One was Shi Wanbao (Shih Wan-pao), a local leader skilled in the martial arts, whose friend was a cousin of Pingyang's father. Another was He Panren (Ho Ban-jen), leader of an army of 10,000, who abducted Yangdi's prime minister and placed him second-in-command of his own army. These three armies formed into one army with Princess Pingyang as their commander and captured the capital of Huxian County. She maintained strict discipline among the troops and forbade them from pillaging.

The Sui generals did not think Princess Pingyang's rebellion was a threat because she was a woman. Only after she had built up an army of 70,000 did they finally wage a campaign against her. Her army defeated them, and meanwhile Li Yuan's army also had many victories against Sui troops. He ordered the husband of Princess Pingyang to take his cavalry unit to assist her forces. She marched north with 10,000 of her best soldiers to help her brother, leading a small group of rebels, defeat the imperial troops in his area, the region of modern Xi'an in Shaanxi Province. In late 617 Princess Pingyang and her father dealt the final blows to the Sui army and took the capital city of Daxingzheng (known as Chang'an during the Tang; modern Xi'an). Li Yuan placed a Sui boy prince on the throne as puppet emperor, but in the fifth month of 618 he proclaimed himself emperor of a new dynasty, the Tang, named for his fiefdom in Shanxi. He awarded his daughter the title of marshal, a rank that previously had been given to imperial princes, and made her the head of an army. A steep mountain pass that she once had guarded was renamed the Young Lady's Pass in her honor.

When Princess Pingyang died at age 23, Emperor Gaozu ordered a magnificent funeral procession for her, including musicians and flag-carrying military officers dressed for battle, which could be given only for loyal government ministers and famous generals. He also gave her the posthumous honorary title *zhao (chao)*, awarded only to very distinguished people. The Tang dynasty became one of the greatest eras of Chinese civilization, and today many Chinese still proudly refer to themselves as Men of Tang (*Tangren*). See also GAOZU, EMPEROR; PEASANTS AND PEASANT REBELLIONS; SUI DYNASTY; TANG DYNASTY; YANGDI, EMPEROR.

PINGYAO

One of the best-preserved ancient walled cities in China. Pingyao is located on the banks of the Feng River (Fenghe) in Shanxi Province in northern China. It was settled more than 2,000 years ago during the Western Zhou dynasty (1100–771 B.C.) and was surrounded by walls made of rammed earth. In 1370, at the start of the Ming dynasty (1368–1644), the city was enlarged and its wall were rebuilt. Since then they have been restored several times. The city wall, covered with brick, is 20,318 feet long and 20 to 33 feet high, with its top surface ranging from 10 to 20 feet wide. Each of the six gates is enclosed for defense. The Wenchang and Kuixing pavilions on top of the wall are dedicated to the Chinese god of literature, and a watchtower stands at each corner of the wall. Another 72 small watchtowers symbolize the best disciples of the great teacher, Confucius (551–479 B.C.). The layout of Pingyao is the same as it was during the Ming dynasty, with a grid of four large streets, eight small ones and 72 alleys. The Jinjin bazaar, where vendors sell goods at stalls in the early morning, at noon and in the evening, is located in the center of the city. Two-story shops made of wood and brick with heavily decorated facades line the streets of Pingyao. Private homes are surrounded by high brick walls that have ornately decorated main gates.

Pingyao has been a business and financial center for centuries. During the Qing dynasty (1644–1911), banks known as *piaohao*, operated by Shanxi money dealers to handle transfers of money, were based in Pingyao. Richly decorated lacquerware produced in Pingyao, including large screens, altars, chests and jewelry boxes, has been famous for more than 1,000 years.

The city has many important historical sites. The 10,000-Buddha Hall in Zhengguo Buddhist Temple, constructed in 963, is one of the oldest buildings in China. Shuanglin Temple is famous for its collection of brightly colored sculptures of Buddhist deities dating from the Song (960–1279) through Qing dynasties. Cixiang Temple was built during the Song. The Hall of Great Achievements in the Confucian Temple dates back 800 years. Other sites include the Huiji Bridge and a brick pagoda dating back to the Jin dynasty (1115–1234). See also ALLEYS AND COURTYARDS; CONFUCIUS; LACQUERWARE; PAGODA; SHANXI PROVINCE; TEMPLES, BUDDHIST.

PIN-TSANG See FUNERALS.

PINYIN SYSTEM OF ROMANIZATION
A standardized system for translating the Chinese language into English and other European languages that employ the roman alphabet. Romanization of Chinese is difficult and tends to be only approximate, because written Chinese characters generally represent the meaning of a word rather than its pronunciation.

The Wade-Giles system developed by two British scholars, Sir Thomas Francis Wade and Herbert Allan Giles, in the 19th century was the first standard system of Chinese romanization and the one most widely employed for more than a century. It is still used in Taiwan and many other countries, as well as for catalogs and indexes in many libraries, museums and other institutions. In 1953 the government of the People's Republic of China (PRC) devised its own phonetic system, known as pinyin (*Han yu pinyin fang-an*, Chinese Language Transcription Proposal). The pinyin system was approved by the National People's Congress in 1958, with the intention of aiding the spread of *putonghua* ("common language") throughout China. *Putonghua*, also called *guoyu* ("national language"), is the common spoken language now used by most people in China, who also speak their own regional dialects.

Words often are pronounced the same in the Wade-Giles and pinyin systems. The main difference lies in the words' spelling. For example, Mao Tse-tung in Wade-Giles is Mao Zedong in pinyin. Scholars must be familiar with both systems as well as with the so-called Postal System, which was devised by the Chinese Postal Administration in 1906 for spelling Chinese geographical names. At that time it was commonly used on maps, gazetteers and other geographical resources. In 1979 the Chinese government banned the use of the Postal System, but it is still used in Taiwan and some other countries. The pinyin system for romanizing Chinese personal and place-names recently has gained widespread used in Western publications, media and libraries, including the U.S. Congress. See also LANGUAGE, CHINESE; PUTONGHUA; WADE-GILES SYSTEM OF ROMANIZATION (and table).

PIPA (*p'i-p'a*)
A musical instrument similar to the lute that has a round body, short neck and four strings. The *pipa* is named for its resemblance to the round loquat fruit of the same name. The body of the *pipa* and the long neck, which has a slight bend, are made of paulownia wood. A musician holds the instrument vertically on the lap and uses the left hand to

Introduced in China around the fourth century, the lyrical pipa *usually accompanies literary or military compositions.*   S.E. MEYER

press down the strings. Originally the right hand strummed the strings with a large pick, but since the Tang dynasty (618–907) the hand has been used to pluck and strum the strings. The *pipa* is one of the most important musical instruments in China, where it often was played as a solo instrument, although it also has been used in orchestras accompanying various forms of theatrical entertainment. There are two types of songs in the *pipa* repertoire, literary and military. One of the most famous literary compositions is a gentle, lyrical song, "Ancient Tune of Spring." Famous military pieces include "Ambush" and "The Conqueror Sheds His Armor."

The *pipa* was brought into China in the fourth to sixth centuries from the nomadic tribes of Central Asia. Another such instrument acquired from those tribes is the two-string *erhu* (erh-hu), which is held vertically and played with a bow. The *pipa* derived from the Turkish *barbat*, which had developed from the ancient Greek *barbatos*. The *pipa* is depicted in many murals at the Buddhist cave temples, known as the Mogao Grottoes, at Dunhuang in Gansu Province in western China. The famous Tang poet Bai Juyi (Po Chu-i; 722–846) wrote a long narrative poem, *The Pipa Player.* In China the *pipa* is especially associated with the Manchu, Mongol and Naxi ethnic groups. From China the *pipa* entered Japan, where it is played in musical ensembles and is also used to accompany singers. The Japanese term for the instrument is *biwa.* See also BAI JUYU; DUNHUANG CAVE PAINTINGS AND CARVINGS; ERHU; MANCHU; MONGOL; NAXI.

PIRATES (*wokou*)   Raiders who threatened the Chinese coast, especially during the Ming dynasty (1368–1644), although they had been a problem in China as early as the Song dynasty (960–1279). During the Yuan (1279–1368) and early Ming dynasties, grain paid as tribute to the imperial government was transported from southern to northern China by coastal fleets, which often were attacked by pirates. With the completion of the new Grand Canal in 1415, grain was transported securely along inland waterways. The Ming Chinese commonly referred to the coastal pirates as Japanese, but they also included many Chinese. Pirate raids became widespread during the Ming due to the tribute system under which China conducted much of its trade with foreign countries. In 1401 Japan sent its first tribute mission to China, which began a trading relationship, conducted through the Chinese city of Ningbo in Zhejiang Province, that was highly profitable to both countries. However, disagreements soon marred the trading relationship. In the 1430s the Ming government tried to resolve the problem by decreeing that Japan could send just one tribute mission every 10 years, that each mission could be comprised of only two ships and 200 people, and that members of the mission had to be authorized representatives of the Japanese government. Various feudal lords in Japan each sent their own missions to Ningbo, and Chinese officials there had to decide which mission they should recognize. Often they selected the one that paid them the largest bribe and sent the others back to Japan. Those who were rejected, and thus prevented from trading with China legally, began smuggling goods between the two countries, with the collaboration of Chinese traders. This smuggling proved so lucrative that many other Japanese also decided to become smugglers. When the Chinese government tried to stop them, the smugglers retaliated by attacking villages along the Chinese coast.

In 1387 the Ming built a network of fortifications along China's eastern and southern coasts to defend against the pirates. Early Ming emperors also built up the Chinese navy to patrol coastal waters. However, the pirates traveled in small squadrons of quick-sailing ships that often could evade Ming defenses. Despite officially allowing only one Japanese mission every 10 years, the Chinese did allow some regular trade between Japan and China, controlled by a system that licensed authorized delegations to trade at specified Chinese ports. However, piracy increased as Japan fell into civil war during the 16th century. In 1523 pirates burned Ningbo, and in 1552 a pirate squadron sailed up the Yangzi River and attacked cities along its shores. In 1555 pirates besieged the major city of Nanjing on the Yangzi and plundered a port in Fujian Province. Not until 1563 were Ming forces able to drive the pirate invaders out of Fujian. Piracy was reduced when the Chinese government then eased its embargo on all trade along the Chinese coast, and Western countries as well as Japan and other Asian countries were able to trade actively with China. See also FUJIAN PROVINCE; MING DYNASTY; NINGBO; TRIBUTE SYSTEM; YANGZI RIVER.

PLA   See PEOPLE'S LIBERATION ARMY.

PLAYING CARDS (*yezi* or *yeh-tzu*)   Sets of cards made from thick, stiff paper and decorated with numbers and pictures that are used to play various games. Paper was invented in China and widely used there by A.D. 200, and playing cards were invented in China during the Tang dynasty (618–907). In the ninth century a Chinese woman wrote the first known book on playing card games, but it has not survived. Ouyang Xiu (Ouyang Hsiu), an 11th-century government official, recorded that the Chinese began using playing cards when they changed their way of making books from paper rolls (scrolls) to bound sheets of paper. The sets of playing cards, many of which have survived, were about $\frac{3}{4}$ inch wide and $2\frac{1}{2}$ inches long. They were printed with colorful pictures using hand-carved blocks of wood, a method used in China for printing both written texts and popular works of art. Artists often colored the pictures by hand. Designs on the backs of the cards often depicted characters from the famous Chinese novel *Outlaws of the Marsh* (also known as *The Water Margin; Shuihuzhuan* or *Shui-hu-chuan*), a compilation of stories and plays dating back to the 13th and 14th centuries but based on legends about a band of rebels in the 12th century at the end of the Northern Song dynasty (960–1127).

Playing cards were introduced into Europe by the late 14th century and likely had traveled through the empire established by the Mongols that stretched from China, which they ruled under the Yuan dynasty (960–1279), all the way to the edge of Eastern Europe. The earliest complete sets of playing cards that have survived in China are literary cards dating from the 17th century. They are similar to a later type of playing card known as money cards (*zhipai* or *chi-p'ai*), which has suits in different denominations of traditional Chinese money, with nine cards in each suit plus four special cards. During the 18th century the government of the Qing dynasty (1644–1911) passed laws forbidding government officials from gambling and against the manufacture and sale of more than 1,000 playing cards by a single person.

Many Chinese people all over the world still enjoy playing card games, both Chinese and Western styles, as well as many other types of gambling games, especially *mahjong* (*majiang* or *ma-chiang*), played with tiles, and dominoes (*tianjiu* or *t'ien-chiu*). They also have played board games since ancient times, and Chinese chess (*weiqi* or *wei-ch'i*), played on a grid using black and white stones or markers, is still very popular. This game was introduced into Japan, where it is known as *go*, and lately has become popular in the Western world. At banquets the Chinese enjoy playing many types of guessing games using their fingers, such as "scissors, paper and stone." See also CHESS, CHINESE; FINGER-GUESSING GAMES; MAHJONG; OUTLAWS OF THE MARSH; PAPER; PRINTING; WOODCUTS.

PLUM (*lizi* or *li-tzu; mei*)   A type of fruit tree with gnarled, sturdy branches that bear delicate blossoms in the winter despite frost and snow. The plum is associated with winter, and as such welcomes the new year and heralds the return of spring. The plum blossom is the national flower of China, representing purity, strength, courage and perseverance. It symbolizes a person who is able to stand firm against adversity. The plum blossom has five petals, representing long life, happiness, health, prosperity and the natural passing of life. Since the Tang dynasty (618–907) the plum also has been associated with poetry and learning. Plum blossoms have been a favorite subject in Chinese painting. Their form is well suited to depiction in monochrome ink painting, which is closely related to calligraphic writing with ink and brush. The plum, bamboo and pine, all of which thrive in the winter, are called the Three Friends. They have been painted together often, particularly on long horizontal hand scrolls. The plum, bamboo, orchid and chrysanthemum are considered the Four Noble Plants. Hua Guang (Hua Kuang), an 11th-century Daoist painter, was supposedly the first to create monochrome ink paintings of plum blossoms. His *Book of the Plum* (*Mei Pu*) presents artistic, philosophical and horticultural instruction about the plum. One of the most famous hand-scroll paintings depicting plum blossoms in the moonlight in great variation is by Qian Lu (Ch'ien Lu; fl. mid-15th century). In China, plum trees grow wild and also are cultivated. The smooth-skinned oval fruit is enjoyed by the Chinese, as is a type of apricot that often also is referred to as a plum. Plums have been used for flavoring in Chinese cooking since ancient times. Plum sauce, which is at once sweet, sour and tangy, is well known in the West. The plum also has a place in traditional Chinese herbal medicine, with its seeds used for treating coughs and its root-bark for fevers. See also BAMBOO; CHRYSANTHEMUM; INK PAINTING; MEDICINE, HERBAL; ORCHID.

PO CHU-I (PO CHU-YI)   See BAI JUYI.

POETRY   See BAI JUYI; CALLIGRAPHY; CAO FAMILY OF ROYAL POETS; DRAMA; DU FU; LANDSCAPE PAINTING; LI BAI; LI

SHANGYIN; LYRIC VERSE; QU YUAN; REGULATED OR NEW-STYLE VERSE; RHYME-PROSE STYLE OF VERSE; SIMA XIANGRU; TAO YUANMING; WALEY, ARTHUR; WANG GUOWEI; WANG WEI; XIE LINGYUN; YUAN HAOWEN.

POIBA See TIBETAN.

POLITBURO Formally known as the Political Bureau; an organ in the government of the People's Republic of China (PRC), which was founded by the Chinese Communist Party (CCP) in 1949. The Politburo is a smaller elite body within the CCP Central Committee, an organ under the National Party Congress. Since the Central Committee convenes only every five years, the Politburo exercises the Central Committee's functions and powers. The Politburo's Standing Committee is an even more select group of about six members that forms the inner circle of power in Chinese government. In 1949 the central leadership of the CCP was vested in the Politburo, the Secretariat and the Central Committee. The Politburo originally had 11 members, including Chairman Mao Zedong (Mao Tse-tung), Zhou Enlai (Chou En-lai), Liu Shaoqi (Liu Shao-ch'i) and Zhu De (Chu Teh). In the next four years, Lin Biao (Lin Piao), Peng Zhen (P'eng Chen), Peng Dehuai (P'eng Te-huai) and Deng Xiaoping (Teng Hsiao-p'ing) were added. These men all held prominent positions in the CCP for the rest of their lives. In 1956 the CCP constitution of the Eighth National Party Congress introduced the Politburo's Standing Committee, with Mao, Zhou, Liu, Zhu, Lin, Deng and Chen Yun (also a member of the Politburo). Until the early 1980s, members of the Politburo nominated the members of the Central Committee, which in turn oversees the election of delegates to provincial party congresses, who help select the delegates to local party congresses.

The Politburo was considered the major decision-making body in the PRC government until the late 1980s. In 1980 the CCP Secretariat was reestablished with supervisory authority over the various departments of the Central Committee. The Secretariat provides expertise to the Politburo and its presiding Standing Committee in making policy decisions, drafts the major policy resolutions for deliberation by the Politburo and supervises the implementation of CCP policy. In 1982 the party constitution abolished the position of party chairman and expanded the base of political authority to include a number of top CCP leaders, including the Standing Committee of the Politburo. By the late 1980s the Secretariat and the State Council, rather than the Politburo, were exercising most of the responsibility for foreign policy decisions. The State Council refers major decisions to the Secretariat for resolution and then to the Political Bureau for ratification. See also CENTRAL COMMITTEE OF THE CHINESE COMMUNIST PARTY; CHINESE COMMUNIST PARTY; GOVERNMENT STRUCTURE; NATIONAL PARTY CONGRESS; NAMES OF INDIVIDUAL LEADERS.

POLITICAL BUREAU See CENTRAL COMMITTEE OF THE CHINESE COMMUNIST PARTY; POLITBURO.

POLITICAL PARTIES See CHINESE COMMUNIST PARTY; DEMOCRATIC PARTIES; GOVERNMENT STRUCTURE.

POLO, MARCO (1254–1324)   A Venetian merchant who became the most famous traveler to China during the pre-Renaissance period, and perhaps the only one of the European merchants who traveled across Asia at that time who left a record of his trip.

Niccolo and Maffeo Polo, Marco's father and uncle, were Venetian traders who made the journey in 1260 from the Turkish city of Constantinople to the Mongol Empire in Asia ruled by Khubilai Khan (1214–94), known as the Great Khan. In 1265 the two returned to Europe with letters from the Khan for the Roman Catholic Pope. They arrived back in Venice in 1269 and began another journey to Asia in 1271, taking Marco with them and carrying letters from Pope Gregory X to Khubilai Khan. The Polos stayed in China, then known to the West as Cathay, for 17 years (1275–92). They had traveled there along the Silk Road, an overland route through Central Asia over which camel caravans had carried silk from China to the Roman Empire since the Han dynasty (206 B.C.–220 A.D.).

In 1295, shortly after Marco Polo returned home to Venice, the 41-year-old became a prisoner of war in a sea battle between Venice and Genoa. While imprisoned in Genoa, he dictated to another prisoner, a romance writer named Rusticiano, his observations about his time in China; these memoirs are known as *Description of the World* or *The Travels of Marco Polo*. The book was widely circulated in handwritten manuscripts because printing was not yet available in Europe. It has been translated into many languages. About 140 manuscripts survive, but there is no definitive text. His observations, generally accurate but containing some exaggerations, are an invaluable source for historians of China. Polo's book, the first consistent description of the geography, government, economy, advanced technology and refined culture of China, astounded the Europeans of his time. Christopher Columbus had a copy in which he made notes. The trip across the Silk Road took the Polos three and a half years and ended at the Mongol capitals of Shang-tu (Xanadu), the summer capital north of the Great Wall of Khubilai Khan, and Cambaluc (called by the Mongols Khanbaliq, "City of the Khan"), now the city of Beijing. Marco Polo was there when Mongol forces defeated the last remnants of the Song dynasty (960–1279) navy to make the Great Khan the ruler of all China under the Yuan dynasty (1279–1368). Polo's writings give a fascinating portrait of the Khan as a highly intelligent man who wanted to conquer yet was interested in the needs of his subjects. However, as Polo frequently observed during his travels, the Chinese people greatly resented the Mongols, who ruled their country with an iron fist.

Marco Polo served in the Khan's government and wrote reports for him. The highest position he held was as an official in the Yangzhou city administration for three years in the 1280s. He traveled widely; his destinations included Yunnan Province in southwest China, possibly Burma and the beautiful southern Chinese city of Hangzhou (then known as Qinsai). Polo was intrigued by the Chinese use of paper money, asbestos, coal to provide heat, military fire-bombs and projectile grenades. The art of printing was brought from China to Europe soon after, due perhaps to Europeans examining printed paper money Polo brought back from China. In 1292 the Polos left China for home by the sea route around China, Southeast Asia and India. They traveled in the entourage of a Mongol princess who was to be married in Persia (modern Iran). Khubilai Khan was very old, so the changing political climate around his imminent death may have influenced the Polos' decision to leave. When Marco Polo was released from prison around 1299, he returned to Venice to resume trading activities, married and had three daughters. He supposedly stated on his deathbed, "I did not tell half of what I saw [in China], because I knew I would not be believed." Some scholars, including Frances Wood in *Did Marco Polo Go to China?* (1996), now question whether Marco Polo actually traveled to China. See also BEIJING; CAMEL CARAVANS; CATHAY; CURRENCY; HANGZHOU; KHUBILAI KHAN; MONGOLS; PRINTING; SILK ROAD; YUAN DYNASTY; YUNNAN.

POMEGRANATE (*shiliu*) A beautiful flowering shrub native to Southwest Asia but not to China that produces red or yellow round fruits with many edible seeds. The pomegranate fruit has become a symbol in China of fertility and prosperity. As such, it usually is depicted in Chinese art as half open, bursting with seeds. The same Chinese character represents "seed" and "sons"; thus the pomegranate represents the strong traditional Chinese wish to have many sons to perpetuate the family. Pillowcases embroidered with pomegranates are a popular wedding gift. Pomegranate flowers may range from white to pale pink to dark red and may be single or double. They are associated with the sixth month in the traditional lunar calendar, roughly corresponding to June. The pomegranate plant grows 10 to 30 feet high and has smooth, shiny leaves more than 3 inches long. The fruit is actually a berry about 2 to 5 inches in diameter, with a red, yellow or white pulp.

Zhang Qian (Chang Ch'ien), who helped open up the Silk Road, is credited with bringing the pomegranate to China from Kabul, Afghanistan in 126 B.C. The Chinese have cultivated it ever since, with the finest varieties produced in Shandong, Hubei and Henan provinces. Pomegranate flowers are used to make a hair dye, the root is used to prepare a medicinal tonic, and the bark and dried peel of the fruit are used to treat dysentery, eye diseases, typhoid, tuberculosis bacilli and rheumatism. Since the peel contains tannic acid, it is used to tan animal hides and to dye silk, cotton, wool and linen textiles.

POMELO See ORANGE.

POMO See MI FU; WANG WEI.

POPULATION, CHINESE According to the official figures for 1992, the population of the People's Republic of China (PRC) consisted of 1.158 billion people, the largest population in the world. About one-quarter live in cities, while three-quarters are peasants who live in villages, although many villages have grown so much that they may be reclassified as cities. The government has restricted migration to urban areas since the late 1950s. In 1986 the population density was about 165 people per square mile. However, much of the population is concentrated in the regions along the eastern and southeastern coast, where population density is more than 450 people per square mile, while much of the

far northern, northwestern and western regions are sparsely populated, with about 15 persons per square mile. Sichuan Province in central China has by far the largest population, about 105 million in 1987. Other heavily populated provinces include Henan, Shandong, Jiangsu, Guangdong, Hunan, Hebei, Anhui, Hubei, Zhejiang and Yunnan. The three largest cities, Shanghai, Beijing and Tianjin, are administered as autonomous municipalities. Shanghai has a population of about 14 million, making it one of the largest and most densely populated cities in the world. There are also large populations of Han Chinese (the ethnic majority) in Hong Kong, Macao and Taiwan. Hong Kong, with a population of about 6 million, reverted to the PRC in 1997, and Macao will revert to the PRC in 1999. The PRC considers Taiwan one of its provinces, although the government on Taiwan, the Republic of China (ROC), was established there by Chinese Nationalists (Kuomintang; KMT) after they were defeated by the Chinese Communist Party (CCP) in 1949. The ROC and PRC both claim to seek the reunification of Taiwan, which has a population of more than 21 million, with mainland China.

According to the 1982 census, about one-third of the Chinese population was under 15 years of age. By 1991 the average life span in China had reached nearly 69 years, a fairly high figure when compared to the country's economic development. About 93 percent of the population is made up of the Han majority ethnic group; 55 officially designated national minority groups make up the other 7 percent. These minorities inhabit about 60 percent of the total land area of China, much of it in politically and militarily sensitive border regions, so the government has given the minorities some political autonomy and other concessions to maintain their loyalty. The largest minority group is the Zhuang, who inhabit Guangxi-Zhuang Autonomous Region in southwestern China. The second-largest group is the Hui, primarily in the western provinces, who physically resemble the Han Chinese but practice the Muslim religion. Some other large ethnic groups include the Muslim Uighurs in Xinjiang Autonomous Region in western China; the Yi (Lolo) in southwestern China; the Manchus, who ruled China under the Qing dynasty (1644–1911) and who inhabit the three northeastern provinces collectively known as Manchuria; the Mongols, who ruled China under the Yuan dynasty (1279–1368) and who inhabit Inner Mongolia Autonomous Region in northern China; and the Tibetans, who inhabit Tibet Autonomous Region in western China.

Since less than 20 percent of all land in the PRC is arable, the country finds it difficult to produce sufficient food, especially since frequent floods and droughts affect agriculture. The Chinese population doubled in the 18th century, and by 1850 it had reached 350 million. Many Chinese immigrated to work in other countries, but the country still had a high growth rate, due largely to the Confucian emphasis on continuing the family line, especially through the birth of sons. The government of the PRC has instituted various policies to limit population growth, including raising the age of legal marriage, birth control and the one-child family campaign that limits urban families to one child each and peasant families to two children each. Despite this campaign, in February 1995 China's population had already reached 1.2 billion, which had been the government's target for the end of the century, placing a great strain on the country's resources. The PRC hopes to hold its natural population growth rate below 10 per 1,000 and the total population to within 1.3 billion by the year 2000 to ensure sustainable social and economic development. The growth rate had fallen from 25 per 1,000 in the 1970s to 11 per 1,000 in 1993. The government set the growth rate target to have a population of not more than 1.4 billion by 2010 and 1.5 billion to 1.6 billion by 2040. The PRC must achieve zero growth after the population reaches 1.6 billion because its resources cannot support more people. Chinese provinces and autonomous regions are individually responsible for controlling their population growth. Those with the highest birth rates are the western autonomous regions of Tibet and Xingjiang, where the large ethnic minority populations have been excluded from the one-child policy. In the mid-1990s, however, the national government found it necessary to encourage birth control in those regions. See also AGRICULTURE; FAMILY STRUCTURE; GEOGRAPHY; HAN; MINORITIES, NATIONAL; MUSLIMS; NOMADS AND ANIMAL HUSBANDRY; ONE-CHILD FAMILY CAMPAIGN; OVERSEAS CHINESE; PEASANTS AND PEASANT REBELLIONS; NAMES OF INDIVIDUAL CITIES, PROVINCES AND ETHNIC GROUPS.

PORCELAIN (*ciqi* or *tz'u ch'i*)   A fine, delicate type of ceramic made from a body of fused clay covered by a glaze and fired in a kiln at a high temperature, usually about 2,336 degrees F. Ordinary pottery, known as earthenware, is made from clay fired at much lower temperatures. Porcelain is unique because it is made with a pure clay, called kaolin or China clay, which when fired at a high temperature undergoes a physical change called vitrification, making it translucent and unable to be penetrated by water. Chinese potters invented porcelain because they had readily available quantities of kaolin and were able to build high-temperature kilns. Chinese porcelain makers mix pure kaolin with "porcelain stone," called *baidunzi* or *pai-tun-tzu*, which has a high percentage of feldspar; this helps the kaolin vitrify at a lower temperature and increases the translucence of the porcelain. *Baidunzi* also is used to make glazes that turn into a lustrous glass when fired at a high temperature, thus forming porcelain.

Pottery containers were commonly made during the Neolithic period in China as early as 8,000 to 9,000 years ago. Chinese potters invented porcelain in the 16th century B.C., when Shang dynasty potters produced the first protoporcelain, which was lustrous and made of kaolin clay, but did not have the fusion of the clay with feldspar and quartz, which characterizes true porcelain. Archaeologists have found true Chinese porcelain dating back to the first century A.D. The earliest porcelain ware, in simple forms such as containers and vases, was painted with glossy vitreous blue glaze and made a ringing sound when struck. Porcelain technology developed rapidly in modern Zhejiang Province during the late Eastern Han dynasty (A.D. 25–220). The blue porcelain ware of this period spread over a wide area and practically replaced bronzeware and lacquerware for daily use. The Chinese found that porcelain was less expensive than those wares, stronger than earthenware and made of readily available materials. During the Han dynasty, potters developed the ability to make more evenly shaped objects

Invented in China around the 16th century B.C., the process of making porcelain remained a Chinese secret until a German factory was able to reproduce it in the 18th century.   COURTESY, MUSEUM OF FINE ARTS, BOSTON

and a thicker, more even glaze. By the end of the sixth century A.D., porcelain was being produced all over the country. Pure white porcelain appeared for the first time, as did underglaze decoration, mainly pale green under white or pale yellow glaze .

The white bisque protecting glaze for porcelain was invented during the Sui dynasty (581–618). New techniques were developed during the Tang dynasty (618–907) for decorating the perfect white glaze with brightly colored designs by painting, mold printing and stamped decoration. The 6th to 10th centuries were an important transition period for Chinese porcelain. The best-known styles of the time included Yue celadon, the painted underglaze ware of the Changsha kilns and the white porcelain of Xing. Pale blue-green Yue celadons were the finest type of ceramic produced during the Tang and were reserved by Prince Qian of the state of Wuyue for exclusive use as tribute to the imperial house. The Changsha kilns were the first to use iron oxide and copper oxide as coloring agents to produce a new type of porcelain, which was brownish green with underglaze decorations of flowers, birds, animals or other designs. Black-glazed and colored porcelains were also popular in northern China during the Tang. Colored porcelain was made by applying a coat of changeable glaze over a monochrome ground of black, brown or white underglaze, which produced an effect of spots tinged with sky blue or moon-white.

After the eighth century, Chinese porcelain was exported along the Silk Road and the maritime sea route to Japan and Korea; Southeast, South and Central Asia; the Mediterranean coast; and North and East Africa. The sea route, in fact, became known as the Porcelain Road. In the 11th century, Chinese porcelain techniques were brought to Persia (modern Iran), then to the Middle East, Turkey and Egypt. The Chinese imported cobalt blue pigments from Persia, and blue-and-white ware became the most popular type of Chinese decorated ceramic, especially for export to other countries. In 1470 Chinese porcelain arrived in Venice and spread from there to the rest of Europe, where it became extremely popular. In the 16th century Portuguese trading galleons began acquiring Chinese porcelains in Manila in the Philippine Islands and bringing them to Europe. The Chinese kept the techniques for making porcelain a strictly guarded secret. Only in 1520 was a sample of kaolin clay brought to Europe by the Portuguese. Europeans searched for local deposits of kaolin, but they were not aware of all the other technical requirements for making porcelain. Factories in Dresden, Germany finally were able to produce porcelain in the 18th century. The Japanese also began manufacturing Chinese-style porcelain, which became known as Arita ware or Imari ware, mainly for the European market.

In China, regional styles emerged during the Song dynasty (960–1279), when porcelain reached its highest refinement. The five greatest Song porcelains were ivory-white *ding* (*ting*) ware from Hebei Province, elegant blue *ru* (*ju*) ware from Henan, the beautiful transmuted *jun* (*chun*) style from Henan, the crackled *ge* (*ke* or *ko*) porcelain of Zhejiang and delicate black wares with purple rims made at the imperial kilns in Hangzhou. The best-known Yuan dynasty (1279–1368) styles include the elegant blue-and-white *qinghua* (*ch'ing-hua*) and the deep color of the *youlihong* (*yu-li-hung*), tinted with red underglaze.

Jingdezhen (Ching-te-chen) became one of the four most famous porcelain-producing towns of the Song, and its exquisite bluish-white porcelain, as fine and delicate as jade, became popular throughout China. Typical varieties had sky blue patterns, a glossy glaze and thin white biscuit. During the Ming dynasty (1368–1644), Jingdezhen became the Chinese national center for porcelain production, partly because of unlimited supplies of local kaolin, pine wood to fuel the kilns and river transport facilities, and partly because master craftsmen moved there from all over China because of the fame of its porcelain products. The imperial kiln was established at high cost in 1402 to fill the strict requirements of the palace and cater to the personal taste of the emperor. There were also many public kilns supplying less expensive porcelain for ordinary citizens. Porcelain manufacturing became a highly organized activity at Jingdezhen, with teams of workers specializing in one step of the process, such as washing the clay, forming the objects, covering them with glazes and so forth. Kilns were built up the slopes of hills and could fire thousands of pieces at the same time. By the late 17th century, European trading companies had agents in

Jingdezhen ordering porcelain produced specifically for European tastes.

During the Ming dynasty, bright colors were used, including deep red, ruby, jade green, bright yellow and peacock blue. *Duocai* (*tuo-ts'ai*) types used blue-and-white underglaze with multicolored glaze, while *wucai* (*wu-ts'ai*) or polychrome wares had bright colors and sharp contrasts. Chinese porcelain makers perfected the technique of decorating porcelain with underglaze painting in cobalt blue and copper red. These techniques included transparent overglaze enamel painting, enamel glazes, glazes over carved coatings known as slips and combinations of painting and carving techniques. Bold floral patterns were very popular.

During the Qing dynasty (1644–1911), artisans imitated earlier styles but also developed new colors for enamel painting, such as *famille rose* and *famille verte,* which gives porcelain a three-dimensional appearance. Porcelain designs became quite elaborate during the 19th century, with entire objects frequently covered with enamel painting and gold lines. Porcelain manufacture declined as China fell into a century of warfare and disruption. Since the founding of the People's Republic of China (PRC) in 1949, the Chinese government reopened many old ceramic manufacturing sites, and Jingdezhen has again become China's most important porcelain production center. See also BLUE-AND-WHITE WARE; CELADON; DING WARE; ENAMELWARE; JINGDEZHEN; RU WARE; SILK ROAD; WHITE WARE.

PORK See PIG.

PORT ARTHUR See DALIAN; LIAODONG PENINSULA; RUSSO-JAPANESE WAR OF 1904–5; SINO-JAPANESE WAR OF 1894–95.

PORTSMOUTH, TREATY OF See HEILONGJIANG PROVINCE; JILIN PROVINCE; LIAODONG PENINSULA; LIAONING PROVINCE; MANCHURIA; RUSSO-JAPANESE WAR OF 1904–5.

PORTUGUESE See CHRISTIANITY; COMPRADOR; JESUITS; MACAO; RICCI, MATTEO.

POSTAL SERVICE The system for delivering mail, which is administered by the Ministry of Posts and Telecommunications. Postal service in China dates back more than 2,000 years, but in the past it mainly served the imperial court and government bureaucracy. Private mail services were established during the Ming dynasty (1368–1644). During the 19th century, mail was also handled by customs posts and foreign postal services in the Chinese cities that had been opened to foreign nations as treaty ports. In 1877 the Qing dynasty (1644–1911) established a modern postal service, and in 1896 it established the Imperial Post Office under the foreign inspector-general of customs. In 1914 China joined the Universal Postal Union. However, postal service in China developed slowly. When the People's Republic of China (PRC) was founded in 1949, the country had only about 330,000 miles of postal routes and only one post office for every 220 square miles. By 1975, when the main links in the postal and telegraphic systems had been completed, there were more than two million miles of postal routes. Post and telegraphic offices had multiplied nine times between 1949 and 1975, and much of the development had been in the more remote provinces. By 1987 the Chinese postal service employed more than 12 million people and handled per year 5.479 billion pieces of mail and more than 25 billion newspapers and magazines, whose subscriptions it also handled. About half of all Chinese mail is transported by trucks on the highways, about a quarter by railroads and a quarter by air mail. Mail delivery is quite rapid, and a letter sent to a destination in the same city may be delivered the same day. In 1971 China joined the Universal Postal Union once again, after its isolation during the Cultural Revolution, which began in 1966. In 1973 the Ministry of Posts and Telecommunications was reestablished, after a period of two years when the ministry had been downgraded to a subministry and its postal and telecommunications functions had been separated. In 1987 the postal service implemented the use of six-digit postal codes. China has postal and telegraphic connections with more than 100 countries. It reestablished its connection with the United States in the late 1970s. In 1998 China announced that it would merge the Ministries of Posts and Telecommunications and Electronics Industry into a new Ministry of Information Industry. See also CULTURAL REVOLUTION; TREATY PORTS.

POSTAL SYSTEM OF ROMANIZATION See PINYIN SYSTEM OF ROMANIZATION; WADE-GILES SYSTEM OF ROMANIZATION.

POTALA PALACE (Budala Gong or Pu-ta-la Kung)   An enormous building in the center of Lhasa, the capital of Tibet, an autonomous region in western China called Xizang by the Chinese. The Potala Palace was built in the 17th century on the site where a building had been erected in the 7th century. It is composed of 13 stories, 1,000 rooms and 10,000 Buddhist chapels decorated with statues and wall paintings. The Red Palace in the center was formerly Tibet's religious and political headquarters but is now a museum. Visitors also can see the White Palace, the private living quarters of the Dalai Lama, Tibet's religious and secular leader, who fled into exile in India when the Tibetans revolted against the Chinese from 1958 to 1959. The Tibetan branch of the Buddhist religion is known as Lamaism. Many previous Dalai Lamas have been buried in jewel-encrusted gold crypts in the Red Palace. Every day thousands of Tibetan Buddhist pilgrims file through the Potala Palace while chanting, bowing on the floor and making offerings of yak butter or pieces of ceremonial cloth known as *khata*. The Potala is also a major attraction for non-Tibetan tourists. Since 1976 the Chinese government has spent about $2.5 million to restore the Potala Palace and other important sites in Lhasa, many of which were damaged during the Cultural Revolution (1966–76). See also DALAI LAMA; LAMAISM; LHASA, TIBET.

POTTERY ARMY See TERRA-COTTA ARMY, TOMB OF EMPEROR QIN SHI HUANGDI.

POYANG, LAKE (Poyanghu)   The largest freshwater lake in China, with an area of about 2,000 square miles. Located in Jiangxi Province, Lake Poyang is fed by the greatest tributary of the Yangzi River (Changjiang). The lake contains sev-

eral scenic islands. The most famous, Xieshan (Shoe Mountain), takes its name from the legend of a goddess who washed her feet in Lake Poyang but dropped her shoe into the water; the shoe turned into the island. A number of famous mountains rise from the shores of Lake Poyang, including Lushan and Shizhong Shan. The latter, which lies on the southern bank of the Yangzi, has been celebrated as far back as the Han dynasty (206 B.C.–A.D. 220) by numerous poets, calligraphers and government bureaucrats. Shizhong Mountain also played a significant military role in ancient Chinese wars. Yilan Ting is a famous pavilion on the cliffs above the Yangzi River that provides a good observation point.

Lake Poyang was for centuries a major center for shipping goods between the lower Yangzi River valley and the southern city of Guangzhou (Canton). The plain surrounding the lake is one of the two "rice bowls" of China, along with that around Lake Dongting (Dongting Hu); in both areas two crops of rice grow annually. Cotton and tea are also important crops that thrive in the environs of Lake Poyang. A famous naval battle took place in the Lake in 1360 between Zhu Yuanzhang (Chu Yuan-Chang; 1328–99), founder of the Ming dynasty (1368–1644), known as Emperor Hongwu, and a rival leader who controlled the middle region of the Yangzi, including Jiangxi. See also DONGTING; LAKE; HONGWU, EMPEROR; JIANGXI PROVINCE; RICE; YANGZI RIVER.

PRC See PEOPLE'S REPUBLIC OF CHINA.

PREHISTORIC PERIOD See ARCHAEOLOGY; LONGSHAN CULTURE; NEOLITHIC PERIOD; XIA DYNASTY; YANGSHAO CULTURE.

PRIMMI See DAI.

PRINTING   The technique for producing multiple copies of documents, which was invented in China. The earliest form of printing in China was the use of seals, pieces of stone or other materials carved on one end with the characters of a person's name. A seal was dipped in red ink paste and pressed onto a piece of silk or other material to print the name. Another early form of printing was stone rubbings. In 175 the standard Confucian texts, the Five Classics, were carved on large standing stones, or stele. Copies were made by affixing pieces of paper to the stones and rubbing ink into the paper to make an impression of the characters. Paper was invented in China by 200 B.C. and was mass-produced from mulberry bark or hemp by the second century A.D. Books were first made in scroll form, with sheets of paper pasted together to form a long continuous roll that was mounted on a wooden roller. Accordion-folded booklets were invented later, using thin paper printed on one side only with a double page divided by a center panel along which the page was folded with the blank side folded in. The doubled sheets were sewn together at the outer margin to make a book. A large book was made of several volumes, which were kept together in a stiff cover similar to a modern slipcase. Accordion books were later replaced by books bound with string and enclosed in cardboard wrappers.

Printing with woodblocks was invented in China between 680 and 750, during the Tang dynasty (618–907). The development of printing was closely associated with the Buddhist religion, which had been introduced into China from India and had a large canon of sutras, or scriptures. Buddhists wanted to have copies of religious charms and sutras, which created the need for mass production. Moreover, the copying or printing of sutras was a great virtue in the Buddhist religion. The earliest blocks for printing resembled large seals, with Chinese characters carved in reverse onto the surface of the blocks; when coated with ink and pressed on paper, the characters were printed in readable form. Since Buddhist temples needed multiple copies of the sutras, by 800 whole pages were carved onto large blocks to mass-produce the texts. A block made of a good fine-grained hardwood, such as pear or jujube, could be used to make several thousand impressions before wearing out, and a cut block could be stored and reused when needed over many decades or longer.

Block printing also contributed to the spread of literacy and the flowering of Chinese literature, especially poetry, during the Tang dynasty. By the ninth century there were book markets in Chang'an, Luoyang and other Chinese cities. Printing was first mentioned in Chinese records in 835. In 848 the life story of a famous Daoist alchemist was printed. The earliest surviving complete printed book, a Buddhist text called the *Diamond Sutra,* dated 868, was discovered at the Dunhuang Cave Temples in western China. Between 932 and 953 the Confucian classics were printed with woodblocks. These texts formed the basis of the examinations that were administered to select officials for the imperial bureaucracy, comparable to a civil service in Western countries. The bureaucracy ran the Chinese government for more than 2,000 years, through the Qing dynasty (1644–1911). The complete canon of Buddhist sutras, known as the *Tripitaka,* was first published between 971 and 983 and required the cutting of 130,000 woodblocks. Soon several other editions were published. The complete canon of texts for the native Chinese religion known as Daoism was printed three times between 1019 and the end of the 13th century. A great variety of other publications, including literary works, medical texts and many other topics, also were printed. In addition, artists used woodblocks to make colorful prints, known as woodcuts.

In the early 11th century, movable type was first used in China, employing type made of wood, porcelain or copper. Bi Sheng invented movable-type printing around 1040 by using porcelain characters set on an iron form in a mixture of wax and resin; the characters could be reused. Metal movable type was perfected in Korea during the early 15th century. Since the Chinese language is written not with an alphabet but with thousands of characters that each represent one word, movable type was not necessarily a faster process than printing from woodblocks. Every character had to be made individually and at a high cost. Further, a great deal of skilled labor and time was required to sort, store and reset a type font that included several thousand different characters. Often carving new double-page blocks for each printed book was quicker and easier. This remained true into the 20th century, when typewriters had the same problem of handling thousands of Chinese characters and were slow and difficult to use. Until recently it was still easier to write Chinese documents by hand and copy them with mimeograph or photocopying machines. Computer software has made printing in the Chinese language much easier.

The increased circulation of printed books during the Song dynasty (960–1279) made education available to a larger group of people, and the literati, or scholar class that staffed the imperial bureaucracy, had their greatest influence during this time. Mass-production of printed books also aided the scholars who had to prepare for the examinations for positions in the bureaucracy. The Chinese always have revered the written word, and people who could read and write had high status. Calligraphy, the fine art of writing Chinese with a brush, is considered the highest art form and is classed with poetry and painting as the Three Perfections. The cities of Kaifeng and Hangzhou and Sichuan Province were Song centers for the fine printing of beautiful books using woodblocks. Song emperors commissioned the government publication of standard Chinese works. Every Chinese dynasty had produced a history of the preceding dynasty, and all of these histories were printed over a period of 70 years during the Song.

The Mongols who founded the Yuan dynasty (1279–1368) made printed paper money the legal currency of the Chinese empire. By the 16th century commercial printers in China were producing great numbers of publications at lower costs, mainly from woodblocks, which further increased the availability of books and the expansion of schools throughout the country. The greatest accomplishment of metal movable-type printing in China was the 18th-century imperial encyclopedia *Tushu jicheng* (*T'u-shu chi-ch'eng,*) which totaled 800,000 pages. The casting in copper of the required quarter-million characters took nine years alone. Unfortunately, the characters later were melted down to make copper coins. Western printing techniques were introduced into China in the late 19th century, when China was revising its traditional curriculum and establishing Western-style institutions of higher learning. The Commercial Press was established in Shanghai at that time; by the 1930s it was the world's largest printing house. It is still in operation. The Communist government of the People's Republic of China is likely the largest publisher in the world today, with provincial and national presses printing hundreds of thousands of copies of books in many fields, ranging from politics and technology to leisure activities. Some works, such as the collected writings of Chairman Mao Zedong (Mao Tse-tung), have been printed in millions of copies. Woodblock printing has become a fine handicraft in China. See also BUDDHISM; CALLIGRAPHY; COMMERCIAL PRESS; CURRENCY, HISTORICAL; DUNHUANG CAVE TEMPLES AND SCULPTURES; FIVE CLASSICS OF CONFUCIANISM; LITERATI; PAPER; SCROLLS; STONE RUBBINGS; WOODCUTS; WRITING SYSTEM, CHINESE.

PRODUCTION BRIGADE AND PRODUCTION TEAM
See PEOPLE'S COMMUNE.

PROPRIETY (*li*)   One of the most important concepts in the school of thought founded by Confucius (551–479 B.C.), which became accepted as orthodox by the Chinese imperial government during the Han dynasty (206 B.C.–A.D. 220). Confucius claimed that he was not an innovator but a transmitter of tradition, which for him was embodied in the concept of *li,* meaning "propriety" or "proper behavior according to status" but usually translated as "rites," "ritual," or "etiquette." In the Confucian sense, propriety refers to the good manners and courtesy exhibited by a cultured person, who is called the "superior man," "noble man" or "gentleman" (*junzi* or *chun tzu*). More than simply rules for politeness, propriety means the entire way in which a cultivated person acts and thinks properly. Enough propriety gives a person moral authority.

Connected with *li* are ancient ceremonial music and dances (*yue* or *yueh,* "proper music") performed in a ritualistic manner from the time of the early Zhou dynasty (1100–256 B.C.). Confucius regarded this period as a time of peace and social order established by wise and virtuous leaders. Their *li* and *yue*—their rituals, music and dances—are visible expressions of wisdom, virtue and a hierarchically organized society. According to Confucian belief, society's health is revived by the performance of *yue.* Chinese scholars recently have researched these ancient rituals, music and dances, which have been recreated at the Kong family mansion, the home of Confucius in Qufu, Shandong Province, now restored and open to tourists.

Also closely connected with *li* or propriety is another Confucian virtue: filial piety (*xiao* or *hsiao*), the respect for and deference to parents by children. After venerating their parents during their lifetimes, children must give them a proper funeral, mourn them for three years and honor them on a regular basis with ceremonies and offerings. All these actions are commonly referred to as ancestor worship. That the rules of propriety have a religious basis is illustrated by the written character for *li,* which has two parts that depict communication with supernatural forces and a sacrificial container.

The guidelines for *li* were recorded in ancient records that became the canonical texts or classics of the Confucian tradition. Originally they were applied to members of the upper classes, especially the literati (*wenren* or *wen jen*), or scholar class, that ran the government bureaucracy. Over time the guidelines became important for Chinese of all classes. Confucius taught that if the ruler behaves according to the rules of propriety, he will have moral prestige that will favorably influence his subjects, and his government will function properly. See also CONFUCIANISM; CONFUCIUS; FILIAL PIETY; FIVE CLASSICS OF CONFUCIANISM; FOUR BOOKS OF CONFUCIANISM; LITERATI; MUSIC AND DANCE, CEREMONIAL; QUFU; SUPERIOR MAN.

PROTECT THE EMPEROR SOCIETY See KANG YOUWEI; LIANG QICHAO.

PROVINCES, AUTONOMOUS REGIONS AND MUNICIPALITIES   The highest level of administrative divisions in the People's Republic of China (PRC), comparable to states in the United States. The PRC has 22 provinces and five autonomous regions. The capital city of Beijing and the large commercial port cities of Tianjin and Shanghai comprise three centrally governed special municipalities. The Chinese provinces fall into rough geographic regions, and most of them are located in the eastern part of the country. The northeastern provinces (Dongbei; also known as Manchuria), which border North Korea and Russia, include Liaoning, Jilin and Heilongjiang, the largest of all Chinese provinces, although several autonomous regions are larger. Manchuria is the homeland of the Manchus, an ethnic group that invaded China Proper and established the Qing dynasty (1644–1911), China's last imperial dynasty. The provinces north of the Yangzi River (Changjiang), one of China's two largest rivers and a major transportation artery, include Hebei, Shanxi, Shandong, Henan, Jiangsu, Anhui and Hubei. The North China Plain, one of China's most densely populated areas, lies in Shanxi, Henan, Hebei and Shandong provinces. The provinces south of the Yangzi include Zhejiang, Jiangxi, Hunan, Fujian and Guangdong. Hainan Island off the southern tip of Guangdong recently was made a province. The provinces of southwestern China include Sichuan, Guizhou and Yunnan, which borders Vietnam, Laos and Burma. The provinces of northwestern China include Shaanxi, Gansu and Qinghai.

China's provinces are inhabited mostly by Han ethnic Chinese, who comprise about 93 percent of the country's population. The PRC government has given some autonomy to regions that are inhabited mostly by members of some of the largest of China's 55 officially designated national minority ethnic groups, with whom the government wishes to have good relations. These include the Mongols, Hui (ethnic Chinese who practice the Muslim religion), Uighurs, Tibetans and Zhuang, the largest minority group. The autonomous regions are also politically and militarily sensitive because they border several other countries with which China has strained relations, including former republics of the U.S.S.R., Afghanistan, Pakistan, India, Nepal, Bhutan and Vietnam. Inner Mongolia (Nei Menggu or Nei Monggol) Autonomous Region stretches across much of China north of the Great Wall that had been built over the centuries by Han Chinese emperors to keep out nomadic groups such as the Mongols, who invaded China and established the Yuan dynasty (1279–1368). Ningxia Hui Autonomous Region lies between Inner Mongolia and Gansu Province. Xinjiang-Uighur Autonomous Region in the far northwest, formerly known as Chinese Turkestan, is China's largest autonomous region. Tibet Autonomous Region (Xizang Zizhiqu) lies south of Xinjiang and north of the Himalayas, the highest mountains in the world. The Tibetans have strongly resisted domination by the PRC, which was established in 1949 by the Chinese Communist Party (CCP). The Dalai Lama, the temporal and spiritual leader of Tibet, fled with tens of thousands of Tibetans to northern India, where he established the Tibetan government-in-exile. Guangxi-Zhuang Autonomous Region in southern China borders Vietnam to the southwest.

The administrative division beneath that of provinces, autonomous regions and municipalities contains autonomous prefectures, counties, autonomous counties, cities and municipal districts. The level beneath them contains townships and villages, which the CCP combined into people's communes. The CCP disbanded communes in the early 1980s. See also CHINA PROPER; DALAI LAMA; GEOGRAPHY; HAN; HUI; MINORITIES, NATIONAL; MONGOL; MUSLIMS; NOMADS AND ANIMAL HUSBANDRY; NORTH CHINA PLAIN; PEOPLE'S COMMUNE; TIBETAN; UIGHUR; YANGZI RIVER; ZHUANG;

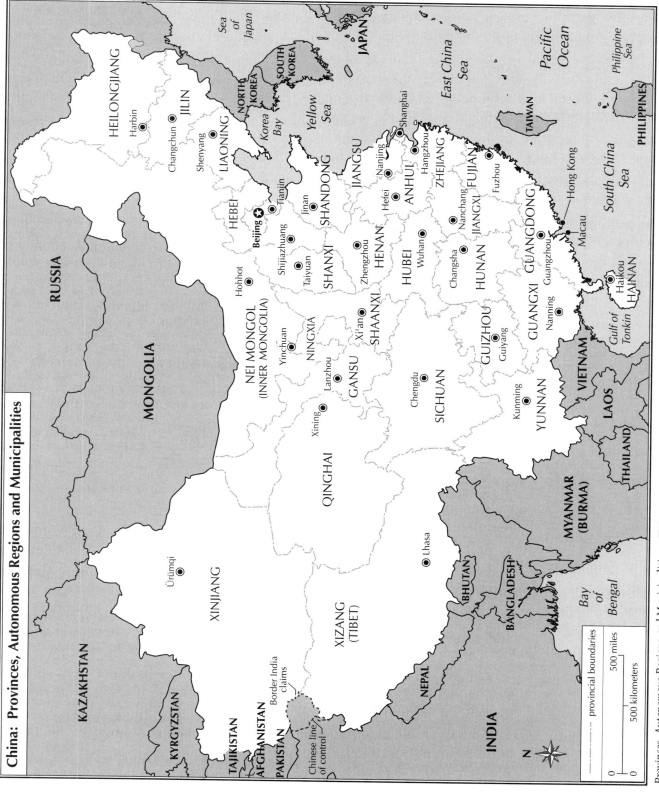

China: Provinces, Autonomous Regions and Municipalities

RUSSIA

KAZAKHSTAN

KYRGYZSTAN

TAJIKISTAN

AFGHANISTAN

PAKISTAN

MONGOLIA

HEILONGJIANG

Harbin

JILIN

Changchun

Shenyang

LIAONING

NORTH
KOREA

SOUTH
KOREA

*Sea
of
Japan*

JAPAN

*Korea
Bay*

*Yellow
Sea*

*East China
Sea*

TAIWAN

*Pacific
Ocean*

*Philippine
Sea*

PHILIPPINES

HEBEI

Beijing

Tianjin

Jinan

SHANDONG

JIANGSU

Nanjing

Shanghai

Hangzhou

ZHEJIANG

Shijiazhuang

Hohhot

Taiyuan

SHANXI

Zhengzhou

HENAN

Hefei

ANHUI

Wuhan

HUBEI

FUJIAN

Fuzhou

Hong Kong

Macau

*South China
Sea*

Haikou

HAINAN

NEI MONGOL
(INNER MONGOLIA)

Yinchuan

NINGXIA

Xi'an

SHAANXI

Lanzhou

GANSU

Chengdu

SICHUAN

Changsha

HUNAN

Nanchang

JIANGXI

GUANGDONG

Guangzhou

Guiyang

GUIZHOU

GUANGXI

Nanning

*Gulf of
Tonkin*

Xining

QINGHAI

Kunming

YUNNAN

VIETNAM

LAOS

THAILAND

MYANMAR
(BURMA)

Ürümqi

XINJIANG

XIZANG
(TIBET)

Lhasa

Border India
claims

Chinese line
of control

BHUTAN

BANGLADESH

NEPAL

INDIA

*Bay
of
Bengal*

THE MOSCHOVITIS GROUP

Provinces, Autonomous Regions and Municipalities

— — — provincial boundaries

0   500 miles

0   500 kilometers

N

NAMES OF INDIVIDUAL PROVINCES, AUTONOMOUS REGIONS AND MUNICIPALITIES.

PRZEWALSKI'S HORSE   See HORSE.

PUBLIC HEALTH   See BAREFOOT DOCTORS; MA HAIDE; ONE-CHILD FAMILY CAMPAIGN.

PU-CHIEH   See PUYI, HENRY.

PUDONG NEW AREA, SHANGHAI   An area in the major port city of Shanghai designated for economic development by the Chinese government in 1990. Shanghai was opened to foreign trade as a treaty port in the mid-19th century. In 1984 the Chinese government, after establishing four Special Economic Zones (SEZs) for foreign investment and trade in southern China, designated Shanghai one of 14 coastal cities open to foreign investment and trade. The Pudong New Area comprises seven development zones in a triangle of about 217 square miles on the east side of the Huangpu River and has a population of about 1.5 million. The Huangpu River is the main waterway through the city and includes Shanghai Harbor and the Bund, the trading center built by Europeans when Shanghai became a treaty port. Each zone having a different development objective: finance and commerce, export processing, free trade, heavy industry, and science and education. The Shanghai municipal government has issued a series of regulations pertaining to the development of the area. The Regulations of Shanghai Municipality for the Encouragement of Foreign Investment specifies the incentives that the government offers to foreign companies willing to invest in Pudong. These are similar to government incentives offered to foreign investors in the SEZs. Numerous foreign companies have sent representatives to Shanghai to develop projects for the Pudong New Area. Shanghai is one of China's main centers for technical expertise and the source of more than 15 percent of China's total industrial production. Pudong has China's tallest skyscraper. However, about 70 percent of the area's office buildings stand empty and property prices have dropped by 50 percent between 1996 and 1998. See also HUANGPU RIVER; SHANGHAI; SPECIAL ECONOMIC ZONES.

PUJIE   See PUYI, HENRY.

PURE BRIGHTNESS FESTIVAL   See QING MING FESTIVAL.

PURE LAND SECT OF BUDDHISM   (Jingtu or Ching-t'u; Sukhavati in Sanskrit)   A sect in the Mahayana ("Greater Vehicle") branch of the Buddhist religion. Buddhism was introduced into China from India around the first century A.D. The Pure Land Sect can be traced back to India but developed in China and became one of the four influential sects of Chinese Buddhism, along with the Chan (Zen), Flower Garland (Huayan) and Tiantai (T'ien-t'ai) sects. Unlike the Flower Garland and Tiantai sects, which taught complex philosophies that could be studied only by educated members of the upper classes who became monks, Pure Land taught that everyone is able to attain salvation through faith. This made the sect appealing to the masses of Chinese laypeople.

The Pure Land is the kingdom or Western Paradise established by the Bodhisattva Dharmakara to fulfill his vows when he attained Buddhahood as Amitabha (Omitofo or A-mi-t'o-fo in Chinese; "Immeasurable Light"). Also known as Amitayus and Amita, Amitabha is one of the most important Buddhist deities. He is the Buddha of Boundless Light and Lord of the Western Paradise, and is depicted in Buddhist paintings and sculptures as seated on a lotus throne in the Western Paradise with his attendants at his side. The lotus, a beautiful flower that rises up from the mud, is the Buddhist symbol of purity. One of Amitabha's attendants is Guanyin (Kuan Yin), who was worshiped in India as the male deity Avalokiteshvara ("The Lord Who Looks Down"), a powerful and compassionate deity. In China, Guanyin was transformed into the Goddess of Mercy, the most popular deity in Pure Land and Chinese folk religion. The *Pure Land Scripture* (*Sukhavativyuha* in Indian Sanskrit; *Wuliangshoujing* in Chinese) teaches that anyone who calls on the name of Amitabha with single-minded devotion will be saved from suffering and death by being reborn into bliss in the Western Paradise or Pure Land.

The Chinese were worshiping Amitabha by the end of the fourth century A.D. Huiyuan (344–416) was the first patriarch of the Pure Land Sect. In 404 he wrote a famous defense of the Buddhist religion against its Chinese critics. Many centuries later, members of the White Lotus Secret Society claimed Huiyuan as their founder. Pure Land teachers such as Daochuo (Tao-ch'o; 562–645) originated popular devotional practices, including the use of a Buddhist rosary that enabled worshipers to count the number of times they invoked the name of Amitabha. Worship entailed the frequent repetition of the sacred phrase "Hail to Amitabha Buddha!" ("*Nanmo Omitofo*"). Shandao (Shan-tao; 613–81), Daochuo's disciple, helped make Pure Land the most widespread Buddhist sect in China. Other Chinese Buddhist sects absorbed the practice of devotion to Amitabha, and the Pure Land and Chan sects developed a close relationship. See also AMITABHA; BUDDHISM; CHAN SECT OF BUDDHISM; GUANYIN; WHITE LOTUS SECRET SOCIETY.

PURPLE FORBIDDEN CITY   See FORBIDDEN CITY.

PUSA   (P'U SA)   See BODHISATTVA.

P'U-T'O   See FOUR SACRED MOUNTAINS OF BUDDHISM.

PUTONGHUA   "Common speech"; the common spoken language of China, also called *guoyu* ("national language"). The government of the People's Republic of China has made *putonghua* the country's official spoken language because it is used in various forms by more than 70 percent of the population of China. This language utilizes 420 distinctly pronounced syllables. Since there are more than 40,000 characters in the Chinese writing system, and some words sound like others, a single spoken word can represent as many as 100 or more different written characters. When Chinese talk with each other, they may trace the character for a certain word with the finger of one hand on the palm of the other.

The government began promoting the use of *putonghua* in 1956 to standardize the spoken language used by the Han people, who comprise 93 percent of the population of China. This policy was promoted by Hua Guofeng, then head of the Hunan Culture and Education Office, as a means of ending illiteracy. *Putonghua* is based on the northern Chinese dialect, with Beijing (the capital) pronunciation as its standard. In the West this language traditionally has been known as Mandarin. Individuals speak *putonghua* and also the dialects of their native regions. See also HAN; HUA GUOFENG; LANGUAGE, CHINESE; MANDARIN.

PUTUO, MOUNT See FOUR SACRED MOUNTAINS OF BUDDHISM; NINGBO.

PUYI, HENRY (1906–1967) Formerly known as Emperor Xuantong (Hsuan-t'ung; r. 1909–12), the last emperor of the Qing dynasty (1644–1911), China's last imperial dynasty. Henry Puyi (P'u-yi) was his personal name. Led by Dr. Sun Yat-sen, the Chinese overthrew the Qing in the Revolution of 1911 and established the Republic of China (ROC; 1912–49). Sun became the first president of the ROC and head of the Chinese Nationalist Party (Kuomintang; KMT). On November 14, 1908, Qing emperor Guangxu (Kuang-hsu; r. 1875–1908) died suddenly and suspiciously less than 24 hours after Cixi (Tz'u-hsi), the empress dowager who had controlled the imperial throne, also died. On November 13 she had chosen her grandnephew Xuantong to succeed his uncle Guangxu; he became the emperor of China when he was only three years old. Although Xuantong's reign is often dated 1909 (at the start of the new lunar year) to 1911, he formally abdicated the throne on February 12, 1912, ending more than 2,000 years of imperial rule in China. He was permitted to retain his title, his imperial residence in the Forbidden City in Beijing and an annual allowance of about $3 million to maintain his residence. Sun also resigned as provisional president of the ROC in 1912 and was replaced by military general Yuan Shikai (Yuan Shih-k'ai).

Puyi continued to live in seclusion in the Forbidden City, the residence of Chinese emperors since the Ming dynasty (1368–1644). Monarchists sought his return to the Manchu throne, and in 1917 General Zhang Xun (Chang Hsun) captured Beijing and restored the dynasty with Puyi as emperor. However, the Restoration of 1917 lasted only 12 days, and the Nationalists resumed power. In 1924 the Chinese Christian General Feng Yuxiang (Feng Yu-hsiang) forced Puyi to leave the Forbidden City, so he fled to the home of his father, Prince Chun (Ch'un), in Tianjin, a major port city near Beijing. Puyi later sought refuge in the Japanese Concession in Tianjin and resided there from February 1925 until November 1931. After the Russo-Japanese War of 1904–5 the Japanese had won the Russian concessions in Manchuria (northeastern China), the homeland of the Manchus who

had established the Qing dynasty. In 1928 the Nationalists captured Beijing. In 1931 Puyi sailed on a Japanese ship to Port Arthur (part of modern Dalian) on the Liaoning Peninsula in Manchuria.

In 1931 Japan invaded Manchuria, where it established the puppet state of Manchukuo (Manzhouguo or Man-chou-kuo in Chinese) in March 1932 to use as its base to invade China Proper. The Japanese asked Puyi to become the first "chief executive" of the state of Manchukuo. Japanese agents took Puyi to Changchun in Jilin Province, the capital of Manchukuo, which they renamed Xinjing (Hsin-ching). On March 9 Japan installed Puyi as chief executive and Zheng Xiaoxu (Cheng Hsiao-hsu) as premier. After two years the Japanese elevated Puyi to emperor, the third time that he had assumed this title. However, being emperor of Manchukuo made him an enemy of the Chinese state and a war criminal. In 1937 China declared war and began fighting its War of Resistance against Japan (1937–45; World War II). On August 18, 1945, after Japan surrendered, the Soviets kidnapped Puyi from Mukden (modern Shenyang) and held him prisoner in the U.S.S.R. for five years. During that time he went to Tokyo and appeared as a prosecution witness in the war crimes trial held by the Allies following World War II.

On August 1, 1950, the Soviets repatriated Puyi to the People's Republic of China (PRC), which the Chinese Communist Party (CCP) had founded in 1949 after it defeated the Nationalists, who fled to Taiwan Island. The PRC government imprisoned Puyi and put him through a process of "reeducation" that transformed him from imperialistic emperor to Communist citizen. In 1959 Puyi was granted amnesty and released from prison, as was his brother Pujie (Pu-chieh), after which he worked as a gardener and librarian and told his life story to a ghostwriter, Li Wenda. His supposed biography, translated into English as *From Emperor to Citizen,* was in fact written by many Chinese authors and "polished" by Lao She, the famous author of *Rickshaw Boy.* In 1962 Puyi, whose Manchu wife Wan Jung (Wan Chung; known as Elizabeth) had died in Manchukuo during the war, married a Chinese woman, Li Shuxien (Li Shu-hsien), who survives him. He died of cancer in Beijing in 1967 at the age of 61. Italian film director Bernardo Bertolucci told the story of Henry Puyi and his wife and concubines in the feature film *The Last Emperor* (1987), with Chinese-American actor John Lone playing Puyi as an adult. In 1988 the film won nine Academy Awards in the United States. A series on Puyi was also broadcast on Chinese television. See also CHANGCHUN; CHINESE COMMUNIST PARTY; DALIAN; FORBIDDEN CITY; LAO SHE; MANCHU; MANCHUKUO; MANCHURIA; QING DYNASTY; REPUBLIC OF CHINA; REVOLUTION OF 1911; RUSSO-JAPANESE WAR OF 1904–5; SUN YAT-SEN; TIANJIN; WAR OF RESISTANCE AGAINST JAPAN; YUAN SHIKAI.

Q

QAIDAM BASIN See QINGHAI PROVINCE.

QI (ch'i)   The vital energy or life force within each person that the Chinese traditionally consider the basic force of the universe. *Qi* often is translated into English as "material force" or "matter-energy." The human body is believed to center and concentrate *qi* in a place called the *dandian* (*tan tien*), about two inches below the navel in the lower abdomen, which is also the body's center of gravity. The deep breathing that properly moves *qi* through the body should come from the *dandian*. *Qi* flows through the human body in 12 channels called meridians, the most important of which pass through the vital organs. A person can become ill when the flow of *qi* is blocked, so the deep breathing and the movements practiced in the martial arts (*wushu*) such as *qigong* (Ch'i Kung; "energy work") and *taijiquan* (*t'ai-chi-ch'uan*; "supreme polarity boxing") help remove blockages that impede the flow of *qi*. Some causes—or results—of blockage include injury, tension and aging.

Qi was a major concept in Chinese thought at least as early as the Han dynasty (206 B.C.–A.D. 220), especially among some Daoists who sought immortality. Breathing techniques to enhance the flow of *qi* and increase longevity date back even earlier than the Han and were combined with meditation techniques practiced by followers of the Buddhist religion, which was introduced from India into China about the first century A.D. Philosophers of Confucianism, the religious tradition deemed orthodox by the Chinese imperial government, theorized about *qi* as well. The Han Confucianist Dong Zhongshu (Tung Chung-shu; 179–104 B.C.) described *qi* as a clear substance that fills the universe, unites all created things and surrounds human beings the way that water surrounds fish. Zhang Zai (Chang Tsai; also known as Zhang Hengqiu or Chang Heng-ch'u; 1021–77) elaborated on *qi* as a single fundamental substance that comprises the entire universe. He made the concept of *qi* the basis of his philosophical system. In Zhang's view, all things that exist are manifestations of *qi*, their original source. Cheng Yi (Ch'eng Yi; 1033–1107) subscribed to Zhang Zai's concept of *qi* and

added to it the concept of *li*, "principle," meaning the eternal laws that give definition to all created things. He argued that *qi* and *li* exist together. Similar ideas were developed by his brother, Cheng Hao (Ch'eng Hao; 1032–85). The great Neo-Confucian thinker Zhu Xi (Chu Hsi; 1130–1200) built on Cheng Yi's philosophy and provided a more complete definition of *qi*. In his view, *li* (principle) comes before *qi* (material force), but the two cannot be separated from each other, and both are necessary in the process by which all things are created. See also CONFUCIANISM; DAOISM; MEDICINE, TRADITIONAL; MEDITATION; QI GONG; TAIJIQUAN; ZHU XI.

QI BAISHI (Ch'i Pai-shih; 1863–1957)   Also called Qi Huang (Ch'i Huang); a painter who, along with Zhang Dajian (Chang Ta-chien, b. 1889), is considered one of the last great painters in the traditional Chinese style. Qi Baishi is considered one of the Four Great Masters of 20th-century Chinese painting, with Zhang Dajian, Wu Changshi (Wu Ch'ang-shih; 1844–1927) and Xu Beihong (Hsu Pei-hung; 1894–1953). Qi Baishi was born into a poor family in Hunan Province and had to drop out of school. At age 12 he became an apprentice to a relative who taught him carpentry and furniture-making. Qi educated himself by studying the popular Chinese work on art, the *Mustard Seed Garden Manual of Painting*, and became skilled in the arts of painting, calligraphy and poetry. At age 27 Qi studied painting and classical literature with a teacher, and two professional artists taught him to paint portraits. Qi became especially famous as a painter of birds, flowers, insects, crabs and shrimps, showing his interest in painting small things rather than large landscapes. He developed a special technique, using a lot of water in the brush, to paint strokes having a transparent quality.

At age 32 Qi organized a group of 7 students to study poetry, known as the Longshan shishe (Lung-shan shih-she). A member introduced him to the art of carving seals (known as chops in the West) that the Chinese use to stamp their names on important documents. In 1900 Qi began building a house in the Hunan countryside, where he resided for 20

years, until he moved to Beijing. In 1902 he accepted an offer to teach painting in Xi'an in central China. During the next seven years Qi traveled to many provinces to see the famous cities, mountains, rivers and lakes that had been portrayed by many Chinese artists. He also visited important scholars and government officials who had an interest in his paintings. After these travels Qi returned to Hunan, built two more houses and continued to paint the landscapes he had seen, design furniture, write poems and engrave seals.

Qi went to Beijing briefly in 1917 and then moved there in 1920. There he met many prominent artists and scholars and became famous for his art. Qi produced a large number of works, specializing in decorative paintings and portraits. He developed his own style, which combined delicacy in painting small things such as insects with bold, spontaneous strokes in the style associated with the Chan (Zen) Sect of Buddhism. He also composed many poems, which he wrote on his paintings. Toward the end of his career, Qi experimented with methods of flinging and splashing ink that resemble the modern Western abstract expressionists, although he remained a traditional Chinese painter.

Before the Japanese invaded China in 1937, Qi lectured on Chinese painting at the Beijing Academy of Art. He remained in Beijing during China's War of Resistance against Japan (1937–45; World War II). In 1946 he traveled to Nanjing and Shanghai, where his paintings were exhibited by a number of art organizations, including the All-China Art Association. In 1949 Qi was a sponsor of the Chinese Painting Society, which intended to preserve traditional methods of Chinese painting, and in 1953 he became honorary president of the society. He also held several other positions, including honorary professor at the Central Academy of Fine Arts. In 1955 the World Peace Council in Stockholm, Sweden awarded Qi the International Peace Prize. He used half his prize money to establish the Qi Baishi scholarship for the advancement of traditional Chinese painting. When Qi died in 1957, he left to the Chinese government all the artwork in his collection, including paintings, calligraphy, seals, poems and other writings. He is estimated to have executed more than 10,000 paintings alone during his life. A memorial museum exhibiting his work was opened to the public at one of his homes in Beijing. Many collections of Qi's paintings and seal impressions also were published. Qi had married twice and left seven sons and six daughters, several of whom became painters and seal engravers. See also CALLIGRAPHY; CHAN SECT OF BUDDHISM; FIGURE PAINTING; INK PAINTING; LANDSCAPE PAINTING; MUSTARD SEED GARDEN MANUAL OF PAINTING; SEALS.

QIANLING See TANG IMPERIAL TOMBS.

QIANLONG (EMPEROR) (Ch'ien-lung; 1711–1799)   An emperor of the Manchu Qing dynasty (1644–1911) whose long reign from 1736 to 1795 is considered one of the greatest periods of Chinese history. The fourth son of Emperor Yongzheng (Yung-cheng; r. 1723–36), his name during his reign was Hongli (Hung-li); Qianlong, meaning "Heavenly Exalted," is his posthumous reign name. The early years of his reign were dominated by two officials who had also advised his father, Oertai (O-erh-t'ai), who died in 1745, and Zhang Tingyu (Chang T'ing-yu), who retired in 1749. From then on, Qianlong dominated the Qing government, following the example of his father and his grandfather, the great emperor Kangxi (K'ang-hsi; r. 1661–1722). He lived frugally, devoted many hours each day to administrative concerns, and was a painter, poet, calligrapher and patron of Chinese literature and scholarship. Qianlong was the first Manchu Qing emperor to be fully acquainted with Han Chinese culture. The middle years of Qianlong's reign were a high point for China, with the country enjoying its greatest prosperity, administrative stability and cultural activity. The imperial treasury was so full that Qianlong canceled tax payments four times during his reign. He ordered a collection to be made of all important works in every subject, whether printed, out-of-print or hand-copied. Scholars performed this immense task from 1773 to 1782, resulting in a collection of 3,457 entries in 93,556 fascicles titled *The Complete Library of the Four Treasuries* (*Sikuchuanshu* or *Ssu-k'u ch'uan-shu*). This compilation was even larger than the famous *Yongle* (*Yung-lo*) *Encyclopedia* commissioned by the Ming emperor Yongle (r. 1403–24). However, works even slightly critical of the Manchus were destroyed in the process. Seven handwritten copies of the Qianlong collection were made and housed in seven newly built libraries. Dai Zhen (Tai Chen; 1723–77), one of the greatest Confucian scholars of the Qing dynasty, lived during Qianlong's reign. Great literary works written during his reign include *Dream of the Red Chamber* by Cao Xueqin (Ts'ao Hsueh-ch'in) and *Six Chapters of a Floating Life* by Shen Fu (fl. 1786).

The Qianlong emperor enlarged the Chinese Empire to its widest extent, covering an area of more than 4 million square miles. His armies defeated potential enemies along China's borders, including Mongols and Muslim tribes in Chinese Turkestan (modern Xinjiang-Uighur Autonomous Region). His troops also put down uprisings by the Miao ethnic group in Guizhou in southern China. He brought Vietnam, Burma and Nepal into the tribute system as vassals of the Chinese empire. The Chinese population and the area of land being cultivated both increased dramatically, with the population of China Proper more than doubling between 1749 and 1793. During his reign, Qianlong made six inspection tours of his empire. Qing emperors had attempted to expand their influence in Tibet, today an autonomous region in western China, and had sent armies into Tibet to intervene in the civil wars there and to expel the Dzungars who had taken control of the country. In 1750 the Qing restored order in Tibet after several political leaders were murdered, and the Qianlong emperor decreed that the Dalai Lama would be Tibet's only ruler, advised by a newly created council of ministers. Qianlong stationed Qing troops and ministers in Lhasa, Tibet's capital, to maintain order and advise the Dalai Lama, the spiritual and temporal ruler. By these means, China kept Tibet as a protectorate throughout the rest of the Qing dynasty.

Roman Catholic Jesuit missionaries had been allowed into China, beginning with Matteo Ricci, who arrived in 1600.

Many of them became imperial advisers. But disputes among members of different Catholic orders in China caused Emperor Qianlong to expel most missionaries from the country. The only ones permitted to stay were scientists, architects and artists, and they were forbidden to make Chinese converts to their religion. European Jesuits designed the Yuan Ming Yuan, Qianlong's Summer Palace. In 1773 the Roman Catholic Church dissolved the Society of Jesus, mainly because of the continuing Jesuit practice, which a papal legate to Beijing in 1705 had forbidden, of allowing Chinese converts to continue practicing ancestor and other traditional Chinese rituals. This is known as the Rites Controversy.

From 1792 to 1793, Lord Macartney led a mission to the Qing court as the first British ambassador to China and was given two audiences with Qianlong at Rehol (Jehol; also known as Chengde), the hunting preserve north of Beijing where Qing emperors spent the summer months. Qianlong received Macartney politely but refused to end government restrictions on international trade. In 1730, in order to regulate foreign trade, the Qing had restricted the transaction of all foreign trade to Guangzhou (Canton) in southern China through a number of licensed Chinese merchants, known as the Canton System. Macartney was unable to persuade the Qianlong emperor to establish diplomatic relations or to negotiate a trade treaty between China and Great Britain. The Chinese attitude toward the British culminated in the 19th-century Opium Wars in which Britain forced the Qing to open Chinese cities to foreign trade.

During the later years of Qianlong's reign, corruption and inefficiency in the Qing government caused a strong anti-Qing feeling among the Chinese people, which resulted in the rebellion led by the White Lotus Secret Society (1796–1805). Qianlong's favorite adviser, a Manchu named Heshen (Ho-shen; 1750–99), who served as grand chancellor for 20 years, had acquired an immense fortune through his corruption. Qianlong's military campaigns and six tours also had placed a burden on the treasury. By the time the White Lotus Rebellion began in 1796, Qianlong had abdicated his throne to Emperor Jiaqing (Chia-ch'ing; r. 1796–1820) but he and Heshen wielded the real power until Qianlong died three years later. Heshen was then arrested and ordered to commit suicide. See also CANTON SYSTEM TO REGULATE FOREIGN TRADE; CHENGDE; DAI ZHEN; DALAI LAMA; DREAM OF THE RED CHAMBER; GUANGZHOU; JESUITS; KANGXI, EMPEROR; MACARTNEY, GEORGE, LORD; OPIUM WAR; QING DYNASTY; SHEN FU; TIBET; TRIBUTE SYSTEM; YONGLE ENCYCLOPEDIA; YONGZHENG, EMPEROR.

QIANMEN (SOUTH GATE)   See TIANANMEN SQUARE.

QIANTANG RIVER   See HANGZHOU; ZHEJIANG PROVINCE.

QIAO   See BRIDGES.

QIAOXIANG TIES   See CONNECTIONS; OVERSEAS CHINESE.

QIDAN   See CATHAY; FIVE DYNASTIES PERIOD; LIAO DYNASTY.

QIGONG (*chi kung*)   "Energy work"; a martial art (*wushu*) originating in China that consists of deep breathing and exercises performed while standing in place or moving very slowly. *Qigong* exercises probably started as ancient therapeutic exercises called *daoyin* (*tao-yin*) that date back at least to 700 B.C. However, the sequence of *qigong* exercises practiced today was for the most part formalized in the 20th century. The routine helps the practitioners breathe deeply and naturally, and harmonizes and concentrates the mind. Most Chinese practice *qigong* along with other martial arts such as *taijiquan* (*t'ai-chi-ch'uan*) and *kung fu* (*gongfu*). The goal of *qigong* is to improve the flow of *qi* (*ch'i*), the vital energy or life force within each person that the Chinese consider the basic force in the universe. The human body centers and concentrates *qi* in a place called the *dandian* (*tan tien*), about two inches below the navel in the lower abdomen. The deep breathing that moves *qi* through the body should come from the *dandian,* which is also the body's center of gravity. *Qi* flows through the human body in 12 channels called meridians, the most important of which pass through the vital organs. A person can become ill when the flow of *qi* is blocked; the deep breathing and the movements practiced in *qigong* and other martial arts help remove blockages that impede the flow of *qi*. Some causes of blockage include injury, tension and aging. The exercises can aid in the healing of many types of pain and illness. The first World Conference for Academic Exchanges in Medical *Qigong* was held in China in 1988, with more than 600 scholars from 19 countries participating. The conference set up a World *Qigong* Federation in Beijing. *Qigong* movements are gentle and can be practiced even by elderly persons. See also KUNG FU; QI; TAIJIQUAN.

QIJIA CULTURE See ARCHAEOLOGY; NEOLITHIC PERIOD; XIA NAI.

QILIAN MOUNTAIN RANGE See GANSU PROVINCE; KUN-LUN MOUNTAIN RANGE; QINGHAI-TIBET PLATEAU.

QILIN (*ch'ilin*)   A mythical animal that symbolizes benevolence and kindness for the Chinese. Since the *qilin* is believed to live for 1,000 years, it also symbolizes longevity. The *qilin* supposedly has the body of a deer, the tail of a cow, the neck of a wolf, the head of a dragon and the legs and hooves of a horse. It has yellow fur and a horn on its head, similar to a unicorn. The Chinese believe that the *qilin* appears only when the country is peaceful and prosperous. In the Confucian tradition, the dragon, phoenix, tortoise and *qilin* are the four auspicious animals that bring good luck to Chinese emperors. Chinese legends state that the *qilin* often appeared during the time of the sage emperors Yao and Shun. In the *Book of Songs,* China's oldest collection of folk songs, a poem praises the *qilin* by comparing its kindness, benevolence and cleverness to that of Jifa (Chi-fa), first emperor of the Western Zhou dynasty, in the 11th century B.C. He got these good qualities from his mother, Tai Si (T'ai Ssu), who is compared to a *qilin*. Legends state that when the great thinker and teacher Confucius (551–479 B.C.) was born, a *qilin* appeared in his hometown of Qufu and spit out a "sacred book." Benevolence or humanity (*ren or jen*), represented by the *qilin,* is one of the main virtues in the Confucian tradition.

To this day some Chinese believe that the kind and gentle *qilin* sends children to families. They often hang on their doorways folk art pictures of the *qilin* with a beautiful child riding on its back as it is being delivered to a family. Some pictures depict the *qilin* accompanied by the goddess and her maidservants who send children. Other pictures show a sacred book hanging from the *qilin's* horn. The *qilin* is a common decorative motif on Chinese ceramics and embroidery. See also BOOK OF SONGS; CONFUCIUS; DRAGON; HUMANITY; PHOENIX; SHUN, EMPEROR; TORTOISE; YAO, EMPEROR.

QIN (*ch'in; guqin* or *ku-ch'in*)   A musical instrument similar to a zither that is made from a long box of lacquered wood with two holes in the back for resonance; properly known today as the *guqin* (ancient *qin*). The front of the *qin* is made from tung wood and the back from Chinese catalpa wood. Traditionally the seven strings that run lengthwise along the top of the instrument were made of silk; now they are made of nylon and steel. The body of the *qin* is lacquered and inlaid with 13 small disks indicating pitch positions. A musician places the *qin* horizontally on a table, plucks the strings with the right hand and presses down the strings with the left hand, moving the fingers to different positions along the strings to alter the pitch. There are more than 200 different finger positions. The traditional system of musical notes for playing the *qin* uses complex symbols that instruct the musician on the string points to press, the fingers to use and the ways in which the strings should be plucked. The *qin* has a range of four octaves, and each string has 13 overtones.

The *qin,* which originally had five strings, originated more than 3,000 years ago and is considered the most elegant of all Chinese instruments. It was played in ensembles in the imperial court and at religious rituals, and also as a solo instrument. Members of the literati, the class of educated scholar-bureaucrats, were expected to know how to play the *qin*. Playing was considered a spiritual activity through which a musician could express feelings and refine personality. Nearly 1,000 musical compositions can be played on the *qin,* about half of which also have lyrics that can be sung. The oldest of these is the melancholy "Lament for the Past" by the famous poet Jiang Baishi (Chiang Paishih) of the Song dynasty (960–1279). Some pieces for the *qin* were composed as early as the first century B.C., and 150 date from the Tang dynasty (618–907). The two best-known solo pieces are "Flowing Water" and "Guanglingsan." Also popular is a love song, "The Courtship of the Phoenixes," as well as a song based on a farewell poem by the famous poet Wang Wei (699–761), "Parting Song at the Yang Guan Pass." Chinese scholars have written many books about the instrument, such as *Drills for the Qin,* attributed to Cai Yong (133–92), which lists the titles of nearly 50 compositions at that time that could be played on the *qin* as solos or to accompany singing.

Professional musicians today play some ancient musical instruments. These include several *qin* excavated in Hubei Province from the Warring States period (403–221 B.C.) and one found in Hunan Province from the Western Han dynasty (first century B.C.). The Palace Museum preserves a *qin* made by the Lei Wei brothers, master *qin* makers during the Tang dynasty whose instruments have become valuable treasures. Some musicians have performed much research on the *qin* and rendered ancient *qin* music into modern notation.

A 26-stringed zither-like instrument called a *se* used in ancient China is no longer played. However, a 13-stringed zither called a *zheng* (*cheng*) is still played in southern and southwestern China. It is the prototype of the Japanese musical instrument called the *koto,* which performs a comparable role in Japan to the *qin* in China. See also LITERATI; WANG WEI.

QIN DYNASTY (221–206 B.C.)   The dynasty that replaced the Zhou dynasty (1100–256 B.C.) and whose ruler proclaimed himself the First Emperor of the unified Chinese empire. The First Emperor gave himself the name Qin Shi Huangdi; Huangdi is the Chinese name for the legendary Yellow Emperor, who supposedly unified China and gave the Chinese many important inventions, such as pottery, an agricultural calendar and herbal medicine. Qin had been one of seven feudal states under the Zhou; eventually it conquered all the other Zhou feudal states. The state of Qin had grown strong under the leadership of Shang Yang, Lord Shang (d. 338 B.C.), who had created a new military aristocracy to replace the hereditary noble families. Qin Shi Huangdi took the throne in 236 B.C. as King Zheng (Cheng) of Qin. He made Li Si (Li Ssu), who belonged to the Legalist School of Thought and had been a fellow student of Legalist thinker Han Feizi (Han Fei-tzu), his chief adviser, the Chancellor of the Left. The Legalists taught that a ruler should have absolute power and that he should control his subjects through harsh laws and punishments. King Zheng proceeded to conquer the six remaining states, unifying China in 221 B.C.

When he became emperor, Qin Shi Huangdi embarked on an ambitious program to organize and extend the Chinese empire. He set up 40 prefectures (comparable to states in the United States) in the country and divided each into several counties. Eventually the prefecture as an administrative division disappeared in China; the county has continued to the present day. He weakened the power of rulers of other states by forcing them to move to the Qin capital and centralized the Qin government by appointing the governors of the newly created prefectures. He standardized weights and measures, enacted a set of uniform laws and a tax system for the entire country, and adopted a single coinage, using round copper coins with a square hole in the center so they could be strung together. Known as cash, these coins remained standard currency in China up to the modern era. The Chinese writing system also became standardized during the Qin dynasty.

Qin Shi Huangdi also forced thousands of families to move to colonize different regions and to provide men for military service and hard labor, under which hundreds of thousands died. The emperor conscripted huge numbers of workers to build palaces, especially his magnificent palace at Afang, roads and canals for irrigation and transportation. He also built a long defensive wall across the northern frontier, the prototype of the Great Wall, to keep out invading nomads such as the Xiongnu (Hsiung-nu). He sent troops south as far as Vietnam and absorbed territories in the modern provinces of Sichuan, Guangxi and Fujian into the Chinese empire.

Peasants, scholars and government officials greatly resented the First Emperor's authoritarian rule. In 213 B.C. some scholars and officials attempted to persuade him to decentralize some of his power by allowing feudal states to have a degree of autonomy. Li Si, speaking for the emperor, replied that scholars who study the past to criticize the present create only chaos. He drew up an order from Emperor Qin Shi Huangdi that all books except those written about practical topics such as agriculture, medicine and divination were to be burned. Scholars who disobeyed this order were to be executed, and not long after the book burning, 460 scholars supposedly were buried alive. Even the emperor's eldest son and presumed heir, Fu Su, opposed this brutal act, and the emperor sent him to exile in the northern frontier near the Great Wall.

On his last journey to the sea, Qin Shi Huangdi realized he was dying, and wrote a letter to his son Fu Su implying that he would become emperor. But the chief eunuch, Zhao Gao (Chao Kao), had his own plans for succession and never sent the letter. When Qin Shi Huangdi died on the journey, Zhao Gao and Li Si kept his corpse hidden and issued decrees as if they had come from the emperor. They conspired to place Hu Hai, another son of the First Emperor, on the throne as the Second Emperor, and they forged a letter from the emperor to Fu Su ordering him to commit suicide, which he did. The First Emperor was buried in a pyramid-shaped burial mound about 20 miles east of modern Xi'an.

Hu Hai was a weak man, and rebellions began breaking out, starting in 209 B.C. Zhao Gao and Li Si soon came into conflict, and Li Si was executed in 208 B.C. The Second Emperor was forced to commit suicide in 207 B.C., and Zhao Gao was assassinated. Zi Ying, the First Emperor's nephew, became Third Emperor but ruled for less than two months before surrendering to a rebel army in 206 B.C. Various local leaders asserted their control over small regions, and the Qin empire fell into civil warfare. The strongest region was the one that claimed to succeed the former Zhou kingdom of Chu, in the Yangzi River (Changjiang) valley. Two leaders of Chu, Xiang Yu (Hsiang Yu) and Liu Bang (Liu Pang), struggled for power. Xiang Yu was from an old aristocratic family and wanted to be the ruler of Chu while allowing 17 other kingdoms to exist autonomously. Liu Bang became king of a region in the west of Chu and wanted to establish a new centralized government to rule China as Qin Shi Huangdi had done, with himself as the new emperor. Liu Bang defeated the forces of Qin and of Chu led by Xiang Yu, and in 206 B.C. he accepted the title of King of Han. In 202 B.C. he proclaimed himself the emperor of the Han dynasty, which lasted until A.D. 220. Liu Bang is known by his posthumous reign title, Gaodi (Kao-ti). See also ALCHEMY; ALL UNDER HEAVEN; ELIXIR OF IMMORTALITY; EUNUCHS; GAODI, EMPEROR; HAN DYNASTY; HAN FEIZI; LEGALIST SCHOOL OF THOUGHT; LI SI; MAO ZEDONG; QIN SHI HUANGDI; SHANG YANG, LORD; TAI, MOUNT; TERRA-COTTA ARMY, TOMB OF QIN SHI HUANGDI; WARRING STATES PERIOD; XIONGNU; YELLOW EMPEROR; ZHOU DYNASTY.

QIN SHI HUANGDI (EMPEROR) (Ch'in Shih-huang-ti, 259–210 B.C.; r. 221–210 B.C.)   The ruler of the state of Qin, who overthrew the states that had been vassals of the Zhou dynasty (1100–256 B.C.) and unified China under the Qin dynasty (221–206 B.C.). The main source for the life of Emperor Qin Shi Huangdi is the *Records of the Historian* (*Shiji* or *Shih-chi*) by Sima Qian (Ssu-ma Chien; c. 145–90

B.C.), an official historian of the Han dynasty (206 B.C.–A.D. 220), which replaced the Qin dynasty. Qin Shi Huangdi was the illegitimate son of a courtesan and was only 13 years old when he ascended the throne as King Zheng (Cheng) of the state of Qin. At that time Qin was one of the seven remaining states that had been vassals of the Zhou. These seven had defeated the many other Zhou vassal states in the final part of the Zhou dynasty, known as the Warring States Period (403–221 B.C.). The Qin had taken over the former Zhou territory and made their capital at Xianyang (later known as Chang'an; modern Xi'an in Shaanxi Province in western China). The state of Qin had grown strong under the leadership of Shang Yang, Lord Shang (d. 338 B.C.). Lu Buwei (Lu Pu-wei), a former merchant who was the court adviser, was rumored to be King Zheng's real father. His mother and Lu Buwei acted as his regents until he reached the age of 21, in 238 B.C. An informant told King Zheng of a planned rebellion by Lu Buwei, and the king removed him from office and forced him to commit suicide. He then made Li Si (Li Ssu), who belonged to the Legalist school of thought, his chief adviser, the Chancellor of the Left. The Legalists taught that a ruler should have absolute power and that his subjects should be controlled with a harsh system of laws and punishments.

King Zheng completed the conquest of the other Chinese states in 221 B.C. and proclaimed himself Shi Huangdi, the "First Emperor." He took the name Huangdi from the Yellow Emperor. He was the legendary emperor who supposedly founded the Chinese Empire; invented many things used by humans, such as pottery, boats and carts; drew up an agricultural calendar; and is associated with medicine and alchemy. Qin Shi Huangdi set up 40 prefectures (comparable to states in the United States) in the country and divided each into several counties. Eventually the prefecture as an administrative division disappeared in China, but the counties continue to the present day. He weakened the power of the rulers of the states he had conquered by forcing them to move to the Qin capital. He standardized weights and measures, enacted a set of uniform laws and a tax system for the entire country, and adopted a single coinage using round copper coins with a square central hole. Known as cash, these coins remained standard currency in China up to the modern era. The Chinese writing system also became standardized during the Qin dynasty.

Qin Shi Huangdi conscripted a large number of workers to build palaces, especially his magnificent palace at Afang, roads and canals for irrigation and transportation. He also built a long defensive wall across the northern frontier, the prototype of the Great Wall, to keep out invading nomads. He also extended the borders of his empire south as far as Vietnam and absorbed territories in modern Sichuan, Guangxi and Fujian provinces.

Qin Shi Huangdi was a strong-willed, ruthless and egocentric man who also had a deep interest in supernatural studies. He became consumed with the alchemical quest by certain court members who claimed to be Daoists to gain immortal life by ingesting herbs and chemicals that might be the so-called elixir of immortality. In 227 B.C. an assassin made an attempt on his life, which intensified his paranoia and his religious endeavors. He was the first ruler to climb Taishan (Mount Tai), a mountain in modern Shandong Province long believed sacred by the Chinese, to offer sacrifices to Heaven. He left a stone monument on Mount Tai declaring that he had unified China and that "All under Heaven" now had a single order and a single law. He traveled on to the east coast, where he could view the Penglai Islands, believed to be the home of the Daoist Immortals. On his journey home he met a group of magicians who asked his permission to make an expedition to the Penglai Islands to find the elixir of immortality. Qin Shi Huangdi sent them with thousands of young men and women he had conscripted for this purpose, but they never returned, and legends claim that they settled the islands of Japan. He made two more trips to the east coast in 218 B.C. and 215 B.C. to find the elixir of immortality. His journeys combined religion and politics, as he stopped in many regions along the way to offer religious sacrifices and to meet with local officials, thus asserting his authority throughout his empire.

The peasants, scholars and government officials alike greatly resented the authoritarian rule of Emperor Qin Shi Huangdi. He forced thousands of families to settle in different regions and to provide men for military services and hard labor, under which hundreds of thousands died. In 213 B.C. some scholars and officials tried to persuade him to loosen his control and decentralize some of his power by allowing feudal states to have a degree of autonomy. Li Si replied on the emperor's behalf that the Qin dynasty was a new era and that scholars who study the past to criticize the present create only chaos. He drew up an order from the emperor that all books except those written about practical topics such as agriculture, medicine and divination were to be burned. Scholars who disobeyed this order were to be executed, and not long after the book burning, the emperor supposedly had 460 scholars buried alive. Even the emperor's eldest son, Fu Su, opposed this act, for which the emperor sent him into exile.

Qin Shi Huangdi became even more terrified when he was informed of ill omens portending his downfall, and in 211 B.C. he decided to make another tour of his empire to seek immortality. This time he followed a southern route, accompanied by a royal entourage with Li Si, concubines and eunuchs, including the head eunuch Zhao Gao (Chao Kao). After eight months, the emperor decided to return to his capital, but he became deathly ill and realized he would die. He wrote a letter to his son, Fu Su, asking him to meet his funeral cortege at Xianyang and bury him there, implying that Fu Su would be his father's successor. He asked Zhao Gao to deliver the letter, but Zhao Gao had his own plans to succeed Qin Shi Huangdi and never delivered it. The emperor died soon after, and Li Si, Zhao Ghao and Hu Hai, another son of the emperor, decided to conceal his death on the return journey. They transported his corpse in a covered chariot and brought food to it and issued decrees from it as if the emperor were still alive. They also plotted to make Hu Hai the next emperor, and sent a forged letter from the emperor to Fu Su demanding that he commit suicide, which he did. When they arrived at the Qin capital, Hu Hai was proclaimed the second emperor. The First Emperor was buried in a pyramid-shape burial mound at the foot of Mount Li (Lishan) on the Huishui River, about 20 miles east of modern Xi'an.

In 1958 Mao Zedong (Mao Tse-tung), chairman of the Communist People's Republic of China (PRC), praised

Emperor Qin Shi Huangdi for exterminating people who "used the past to criticize the present," as the Chinese Communists had done. In September 1971 enemies of Mao made an attempt on his life because they claimed he was a "feudal tyrant" and "a contemporary Qin Shi Huangdi." Mao's supporters launched a nationwide campaign to show that the First Emperor had been a wise ruler who, like Mao, had achieved the unification of China. Beginning in 1972, laudatory biographies of Qin Shi Huangdi were published in the PRC and sold millions of copies. In 1974 farmers drilling a well near the First Emperor's burial mound discovered some ancient pottery figures. Archaeologists began excavations and discovered an enormous underground army of thousands of soldiers, horses and chariots that had been buried with Qin Shi Huangdi to protect him. This terra-cotta army has become one of the most famous tourist sites in China. See also ALCHEMY; ALL UNDER HEAVEN; CHANG'AN; ELIXIR OF IMMORTALITY; EUNUCHS; GREAT WALL; LEGALIST SCHOOL OF THOUGHT; LI SI; MAO ZEDONG; QIN DYNASTY; SHANG YANG, LORD; TAI, MOUNT; TERRA-COTTA ARMY, TOMB OF QIN SHI HUANGDI; WARRING STATES PERIOD; YELLOW EMPEROR; ZHOU DYNASTY.

QING DYNASTY (1644–1911)

The dynasty founded by the Manchus, formerly known as the Jurchen, an ethnic group based in Manchuria (modern northeastern China) that overthrew the Ming dynasty (1368–1644). The Qing was China's last imperial dynasty; it was overthrown by the Revolution of 1911, which established the Republic of China (ROC) in 1912. The Manchu tribes had been united into a confederation by Nurhachi (1559–1626), who had founded the later Jin dynasty in 1616 and organized all of the Manchus into military units, known as banners. In 1627 Nurhachi's son Abahai (1592–1643) succeeded him as Jin ruler, and in 1636 he changed the dynasty's name to Qing and declared himself emperor with the reign name Chongde (Ch'ung Te; r. 1636–43). Ming and Qing emperors are referred to by their reign names, and technically Abahai should be referred to as the Chongde emperor. Since Abahai never ruled the Chinese Empire in the capital city of Beijing, Chinese historians consider his son and successor, who took the reign title Shunzhi (Shun-chih; r. 1644–61), the first Qing emperor. Before Abahai died, he had brought Mongolia under Manchu control and had sent several armies to invade northern China. The Mongols had ruled China under the Yuan dynasty (1279–1368), which had been overthrown by the Ming. The Mongols were the first non-Han Chinese ethnic group to rule the Chinese Empire, and the Manchus were the second. The Han Chinese, who comprised the vast majority of the population of China, resented the Mongols and the Manchus.

In 1640 a Chinese rebel leader named Li Zicheng (Li Tz'u-cheng) gathered a large army in Henan Province and captured several major cities. In 1643 he proclaimed himself the emperor of a new dynasty, the Great Shun, with its capital at Chang'an (modern Xi'an). He then marched toward Beijing, where the Ming imperial court was defenseless but refused to flee south to its auxiliary capital at Nanjing. Li's army occupied the high points along the Great Wall north of Beijing that had been built to protect the Chinese against northern nomadic tribes. The Ming army led by General Wu Sangui (Wu San-kuei) was positioned inside the Great Wall to keep the Manchus from invading, but Wu made the mistake of asking the Manchus to help his Ming forces fight off Li Zicheng's rebels. He opened the gate at Shanhaiguan and 20,000 Manchus riding horses with armor poured into China and routed the rebel army. Wu pursued the rebels instead of defending Beijing, and Li Zicheng led his forces into Beijing in April 1644. Ming emperor Chongzhen (Ch'ung-chen; r. 1628–44) and his empress hanged themselves. On June 5, 1644, the Manchus, led by their chief Dorgon (1612–50), entered Beijing unopposed, proclaimed the Qing dynasty as the successor to the Ming dynasty and installed their seven-year-old king as the first Qing emperor, Shunzi.

Some members of the Ming court were able to flee south, where they attempted to continue the Ming dynasty and drive out the Manchus. Ming loyalists in southern China were supported by a Chinese adventurer named Zheng Chenggong (Cheng Ch'eng-kung; 1624–62), popularly known as Koxinga or Coxinga. He established a government on Taiwan Island and promoted immigration there from the Chinese mainland. After he died his successors fell into opposing factions, and in 1683 the Qing attacked Taiwan, defeated the final Ming resistors and incorporated Taiwan as a Qing prefecture. In 1886 the Qing made Taiwan a province of China. In 1673 Wu Sangui, who had driven Ming supporters to southern Chinese provinces and had made a base for himself in the southwest, attempted to make his territory independent of the Qing. Two other Chinese generals joined his rebellion, known as the Revolt of the Three Feudatories. Qing forces finally suppressed them in 1681.

The Qing emperors took up residence in the imperial palace in Beijing, a massive complex known as the Forbidden City, which had been built by the third Ming emperor, who moved the capital there from Nanjing in 1420. The next three Qing emperors enjoyed long reigns, which many historians consider the greatest period in premodern Chinese history. The Kangxi emperor (K'ang-hsi; r. 1661–1722) was one of the greatest rulers in Chinese history. He was succeeded by his fourth son, who ruled as the Yongzheng emperor (Yung-cheng; r. 1723–36). His fourth son in turn reigned as the Qianlong emperor (Ch'ien-lung; r. 1736–95), whose reign often is termed China's "golden age." The Manchus retained the imperial bureaucracy or civil service, which had governed China for more than 1,000 years. The bureaucracy was staffed by Confucian-educated Han Chinese literati, or scholars, who were selected by a rigorous examination system. Qing rulers placed Manchus in about half of the highest offices in Beijing. This lessened the chances of Han literati rising to high levels in the bureaucracy and increased their resentment toward the Manchus. Each Chinese province was governed by both a Manchu governor general and a Chinese governor. The Manchus forced Chinese men to wear their hair in the Manchu style, a long braid known as a queue, and they forbade marriages between Manchus and Han Chinese. They aimed to keep Manchuria as a special area for pure-blooded Manchus by forbidding Han Chinese to settle there. However, the Manchus did levy lighter taxes against Chinese farmers than did rulers of previous dynasties.

The Mongols had adopted Lamaism, the Tibetan sect of the Buddhist religion, after the third Dalai Lama, the leader of the Yellow Hat Sect of Lamaism, converted the Altan Khan. In 1643 a Mongol leader helped the Dalai Lama and his Yellow Hat Sect defeat the rival Red Hat Sect, which made the Dalai Lama the undisputed religious leader of Tibet, a large region to the west of China. In 1652, shortly after the Manchus founded the Qing dynasty, the fifth Dalai Lama visited Beijing bearing tribute, and the emperor gave him the gold symbols of authority customarily awarded to a tributary ruler within the Chinese tribute system. However, the Dalai Lama and his successors continued to support the Mongols against the Qing. In 1720 the Qing removed the Mongolian choice as Dalai Lama and installed their own candidate in this position. By the middle of the 18th century the Qing had established a protectorate in Tibet.

Kangxi and his successors annexed other regions to the north and west, including Mongolia, Dzungaria and Chinese Turkestan (modern Xinjiang-Uighur Autonomous Region). Kangxi personally commanded a large Chinese force that got as far as Urga in Outer Mongolia and defeated a powerful khan of the Western Mongols. In 1644 the Russians had entered the Amur River valley, which borders Manchuria, and Qing emperor Kangxi sent troops to oppose them. The power of the Chinese military convinced the Russians to sign the Treaty of Nerchinsk in 1689, which drew a border placing the Amur River completely within Chinese territory. The treaty also provided for some overland trade between China and Russia. To the south, Kangxi brought the Miao ethnic group under Chinese control, and Burma and Vietnam submitted to Chinese suzerainty under the tribute system. He built the Qing Summer Palace at Chengde (Rehol or Jehol) north of Beijing, where the Manchu court could enjoy hunting. He made several inspection tours to southern China, where he could maintain personal contacts with the many literati who resided there and also could check on the maintenance of the Grand Canal, along which rice was transported as tax payments to Beijing, and water conservancy projects on major Chinese rivers.

In 1684 the Kangxi emperor made a pilgrimage to Qufu in Shandong Province to visit the shrine of Confucius (551–479 B.C.), whose school of thought had been orthodox for the Chinese imperial government for nearly two millennia. Kangxi also climbed Mount Tai (Taishan), the most revered of the Five Sacred Mountains of Daoism. He bolstered the examination system to encourage Confucian scholars to join the imperial bureaucracy, and he supported Confucianism, sponsored scholarly research projects and patronized the arts. Scholarly projects included the *Kangxi Dictionary* of about 40,000 characters, which became the standard dictionary of the Chinese language for more than 200 years; a collection of writings on calligraphy and painting; a comprehensive volume on geography based on surveys made by Jesuits, who traveled to all regions of China; and a complete edition of the works of the neo-Confucian thinker Zhu Xi (Chu Hsi; 1130–1200). In 1700 Kangxi ordered the compilation of an encyclopedia that, when completed in 1725, was the largest work ever printed in the world. In 1670 he issued the Sacred Edict, a commentary on imperial maxims from the 14th century during the Ming dynasty, which encouraged the Chinese people to be thrifty, follow the orthodox teachings of Confucius, honor their parents (the prime Confucian virtue of filial piety), respect

the law and pay their taxes. Kangxi also was interested in sciences such as astronomy and cartography, and he continued the imperial patronage of the Jesuits that had begun during the Ming.

The Jesuits and the Qing became embroiled with the Pope in Rome over the Jesuit acceptance of traditional Chinese practices. Known as the Rites Controversy, this came to a head with the issue of the most suitable translation for the name of God. The Jesuits favored Heaven (*tian* or *t'ien*) or Ruler on High (*shangdi* or *shang-ti*), terms used in the Chinese classics, and Kangxi supported them, which angered the pope, who felt that the Chinese emperor was interfering in Christian affairs. He issued a papal bull in 1715 demanding that Chinese Christian converts give up their Confucian practice of ancestor worship. This angered Kangxi, who did not like the pope interfering in matters of Chinese language and religion, especially Confucianism. Other Catholic missionaries had become active in China, mainly those of the Franciscan and Dominican orders, and they condemned the "heathen" practices of Chinese ancestor worship that the Jesuits allowed. Papal legates attempted to work out a compromise with the Qing, but in 1724 Kangxi's successor, Emperor Yongzheng, added a sentence to the Sacred Edict stating that Christianity was a heterodox sect. Some missionaries were expelled from China, although the Jesuits were allowed to stay at the court and continue administering the imperial observatory. Some Jesuits, including the court painter Brother Giuseppe Castiglione, laid out the gardens and constructed buildings and fountains for the magnificent Summer Palace near Beijing.

Toward the end of Kangxi's long and glorious reign, Manchu princes fought each other over who would succeed him, and Kangxi died in mysterious circumstances in 1722. Military factions placed one of his sons on the throne as the Yongzheng emperor. A conscientious ruler, he centralized government authority under his own control. In 1736 his son succeeded him as the Qianlong emperor. Qianlong also patronized scholarship, including an enormous collection known as the *The Complete Library of the Four Treasuries*, which was completed in 1789. It contained seven sets of 36,000 volumes containing 3,450 works, under the four traditional categories of Chinese literature: classics (*jing* or *ching*), history (*shi* or *shih*), philosophy (*zhe* or *che*) and belles lettres (*ji* or *chi*). This undertaking, which employed a great number of Han Chinese Confucian-educated scholars, helped legitimize the Manchus as rulers who were civilized gentlemen ("superior men," *junzi* or *chun-tzu*) in the Confucian tradition. The Manchu adoption of Chinese culture, a process known as Sinicization, helped preserve the stability of the Qing empire through the 18th century. The daily life of a wealthy family during the Qing forms the theme of one of the most beloved of all Chinese novels, *Dream of the Red Chamber*, written in the 18th century by Cao Xueqin (Ts'ao Hsueh-ch'in). Shen Fu wrote another popular novel, *Six Chapters of a Floating Life*.

The Qianlong emperor sent several expeditions west beyond the Ural Mountain Range to the Ili River region between 1755 and 1759 and gained control of all of Chinese Turkestan (modern Xinjiang-Uighur Autonomous Region). The Qing sent political prisoners to colonize the region and appointed a military governor to rule it. Qianlong thus enlarged the Chinese Empire to its widest extent, covering an area of more than 4 million square miles. He brought Vietnam, Burma and Nepal into the tribute system. The Chinese economy prospered, the area of land under cultivation greatly increased and the population of China Proper more than doubled between 1749 and 1793. However, peasant rebellions broke out against the Qing in the late 18th century, especially in Henan and Hubei Provinces. They were led by the White Lotus secret society, which had originated during the Mongol Yuan dynasty and became a symbol of Han Chinese resistance to foreign domination. During the Manchu Qing dynasty the White Lotus appealed to Chinese peasants by promising them that Maitreya, the Buddha of the Future, would descend to Earth, restore the Han Chinese Ming dynasty, remove disease, natural disasters and all other suffering in this life, and bring happiness in the next life. The White Lotus Rebellion began in 1796 to protest the collection of taxes. Qianlong died in 1799, and his successor, the Jiajing emperor (Chia-ching; r. 1796–1820), was able to organize the Qing military to fight the White Lotus rebels and regain control of the regions where they were active. The rebellion dwindled to an end by 1805, but it had seriously damaged the Qing and inspired other anti-Qing rebellions, such as that of the Eight Trigrams secret society in 1813.

The Qing also became weakened by the actions of foreign governments that wanted to force China to end the tribute system and open up the country to Western-style free trade. Many European nations and the United States were engaged in lucrative trade with China through the southern port of Guangzhou (Canton). The British East India Company dominated this trade. The Qing required Western traders to conduct all of their business through native Chinese merchants in Guangzhou who belonged to a guild known as the Cohong or Hong, who made high profits by regulating the prices for imported and exported goods. This is known as the Canton system for regulating trade. When the annual trading season was over, all foreign traders had to withdraw to the small island of Macao, a Portuguese colony near Guangzhou. In 1793 the British government and the East India Company sent Lord (George) Macartney to China to request the ending of the Canton system, the opening of more Chinese ports to foreign trade and the setting of fair tariffs. The Qianlong emperor refused to give in to these requests. The balance of trade was not favorable to Britain, which sold Indian cotton in China but was being drained of silver to pay for tea and other luxury goods such as silk and porcelain. The British began importing opium from India to sell in China, which in turn started draining China of large quantities of silver and demoralizing the Chinese population. In 1834 the British commissioned Lord Napier to persuade China to open the country to equal trade with Britain, but he was no more successful than Lord Macartney.

The Qing government commissioned Lin Zexu (Lin Tse-hsu) to eliminate the opium trade in Guangzhou. He arrived there in 1839 and confined the British to the "13 Factories" trading zone and confiscated their opium. These actions led Britain to declare war on China, known as the Opium War (1839–42). Britain defeated China and forced it to sign the Treaty of Nanjing, which contained 13 articles that, among other things, required China to pay a large indemnity to Britain, abolish the Canton system and open five treaty ports

for foreign residence and trade, and cede the island of Hong Kong, near Guangzhou, to Britain. The treaty ports included Guangzhou, Xiamen, Fuzhou, Ningbo and Shanghai, at the mouth of the Yangzi River, which quickly replaced Guangzhou as China's largest trading port. These demands by a foreign power greatly damaged the prestige of the Qing, who did not want to honor the articles of the treaty.

The British and French fought another war with China, known as the Arrow War (Second Opium War, 1856–60), and defeated China once again. In 1860 the Qing arrested British negotiators sent to Beijing and even executed some; in retaliation, Lord Elgin led British troops into Tianjin and Beijing, where they burned down the Summer Palace. Qing emperor Xianfeng fled to Manchuria and appointed Prince Gong (Kung) to negotiate with the British, who made him sign the Convention of Beijing (1860), the terms of which included an apology by China to Britain and a large Chinese indemnity, made Tianjin a treaty port and ceded Kowloon, on the Chinese mainland across from Hong Kong, to Britain. In 1898 Britain acquired a 99-year lease over the New Territories adjoining Kowloon. In 1997 the British Crown Colony of Hong Kong, including Kowloon and the New Territories, reverted to China. Macao will revert to China in 1999. After the Convention of Beijing, the United States and other foreign powers pressured China for similar concessions and signed treaties with the Qing that the Chinese people felt were "unequal." The convention also gave permission for Chinese to emigrate on British ships, and thousands of Chinese laborers began immigrating overseas to North and South America, Hawaii and Australia.

The Qing dynasty also was seriously threatened by the Taiping Rebellion (1850–64), which broke out in southern China. The leader of the rebellion was Hong Xiuquan (Hung Hsiu-ch'uan; 1813–64), a member of the Hakka ethnic minority group, who received a Chinese Confucian education but also was exposed to Christian ideas taught by Protestant missionaries in Guangzhou. Hong had dramatic visions that led him to announce that he was the younger brother of Jesus Christ and that God had commanded him to bring the Chinese people to worship the true God and to establish the Kingdom of God on Earth. He and his followers moved north into Jiangsu Province, where they attracted 30,000 converts in three years. In 1850 his forces fought Qing troops for the first time, and thousands joined his movement, including peasants, laborers, pirates and bandits, many of whom belonged to anti-Qing secret societies such as the Triad Society. In 1851 Hong claimed to found a new dynasty and took the title "Heavenly King" of the "Heavenly Kingdom of Great Peace" (*Taiping tiangu* or *T'ai-p'ing T'ien-ku; Taiping* for short). He also awarded the title "king" to five other Taiping leaders. Hong claimed that the Taipings would establish a new order in which peasants owned and farmed the land in common and equally shared money, food and clothing; women would be equal to men; and many harmful practices would be eliminated, such as slavery, concubinage, arranged marriage, footbinding, prostitution, opium smoking and torture by legal officials.

In 1852 Taiping forces marched into the Yangzi River valley, where thousands more Chinese joined them, and in 1853 they captured Nanjing, the Qing auxiliary capital on the Yangzi, where they established their headquarters. The Taiping now numbered more than one million, and they captured 600 Chinese cities and sent an army north toward the Qing capital at Beijing. In 1855 Qing forces defeated them in Shandong Province, and a Taiping army sent to the west was opposed by the forces raised in Hunan Province by a Han Chinese government official named Zeng Guofan (Tseng Kuo-fan). In Nanjing one of the "kings" plotted to overthrow Hong, which ended in a massive slaughter that divided and weakened the Taiping. Qing troops led by Zeng Guofan, Li Hongzhang (Li Hung-chang) and Zuo Zongtang (Chuo Chung-t'ang) forced Taiping troops into a defensive position. Zeng's forces were assisted by the volunteer army led by the American Frederick Townsend Ward until he was killed in 1862, when the Englishman Charles George Gordon took his place. Foreign powers initially had supported the Taiping, but they soon realized that the religion was actually a dangerous revolutionary movement, and they preferred to keep the weak Qing government in power because they could manipulate it to their advantage. Combined Qing and Western forces placed Nanjing under siege in 1862 and finally took the city from the Taiping in 1864. None of the Taiping survived. Many other armed rebellions occurred in China around the same time, including the Nian Rebellion, the Small Sword Society Rebellion and uprisings by Muslims in the northwest and south. The Taiping Rebellion was a major source of inspiration for Chinese Communists in the 20th century.

The period of peace in China that followed the Taiping Rebellion is known as the Tongzhi Restoration, the reign of Qing emperor Tongzhi (T'ung-chih; r. 1862–75). He took the throne when he was only five years old, after the death of his father, the Xianfeng emperor (Hsien-feng; r. 1851–61). Tongzhi's mother was the ruthless Cixi (Tz'u Hsi), who became empress dowager upon his accession and wielded the actual power for the last half-century of the Qing dynasty. Cixi, who had been Xianfeng's favorite concubine, served as co-regent with his widowed empress Cian (Ts'u-an) during Tongzhi's reign. Prince Gong also served as imperial adviser, along with several other princes. He convinced the Qing to set up the Zongli Yamen (Tsungli Yamen; Office for General Affairs) to deal with Western diplomats, who did not subscribe to the traditional tribute system. In the 1860s and 1870s government officials supported the Self-Strengthening Movement, under which China aimed to preserve its traditional culture while it acquired Western technology to strengthen its military, built steamships and set up telegraphic communications between Chinese cities. The Qing organized the Chinese Maritime Customs Service to control the collection of customs dues at Shanghai, under which a postal service was also established. In 1872 Li Hongzhang founded the China Merchants Steam Navigation Company in Shanghai to provide modern steamship transport to compete with foreign companies, which in the mid-19th century had monopolized ocean shipping and controlled transportation on the Yangzi, one of China's two largest rivers. The Kaiping coal mines in northern China were expanded to provide fuel for the ships, and the first permanent railway was completed in 1881 to transport the coal. Chinese scholars studied Western languages and translated Western books, and Chinese students were sent to the United States and European countries for military and technical training.

The Self-Strengthening Movement failed to turn China into a modern power because it did not transform the imperial bureaucracy and other traditional Chinese institutions. The limitations of China, a very large country, became obvious when the much smaller country of France defeated it in the Sino-French War (1884–85), fought over the control of Vietnam. Li Hongzhang, who held a government position equal to a prime minister, knew that the Chinese navy was weak and urged that China avoid war by negotiating a settlement with France. But a faction of Chinese and Manchu officials wanted to make a strong stand against the French, and Qing troops fought the French in the Vietnamese regions of Annam and Tonkin. The French fleet destroyed the Chinese fleet, arsenal and docks in Fuzhou and the Chinese fortress on Taiwan, and occupied the Pescadore Islands. France gained complete control of Vietnam, and the French naval victory made China even more vulnerable and open to attacks by foreign powers.

In 1894 Japan, which had modernized its government and military on European models, became the first Asian power to defeat China. Japan went to war over control of Korea, long a tributary of China, in the Sino-Japanese War of 1894–95. Once again Li Hongzhang tried to avoid war by negotiations, but a rebellion in Korea in 1894 brought more Japanese and Chinese troops onto Korean soil. Chinese troops could not hold their own against the modern Japanese army, and the Japanese naval fleet destroyed the Chinese Beiyang (Pei-yang) fleet. Japanese troops also invaded Manchuria (northeastern China) and seized the strategic port of Port Arthur (part of modern Dalian) on the southern tip of the Liaodong Peninsula. Japan and China signed the Treaty of Shimonoseki in 1895, which exacted harsh terms from China, including payment of a huge indemnity; allowing Japanese industries in four Chinese treaty ports; the ceding to Japan of Taiwan, the Pescadore Islands and the Liaodong Peninsula; and recognition of the independence of Korea. China lost control of several other countries that had been vassal states under the tribute system, including Burma and the Ryukyu Islands (Liuqiu or Liu-ch'iu; modern Okinawa). However, Western powers forced Japan to give up its demand for the Liaodong Peninsula.

This humiliating defeat of China by the small Asian nation of Japan caused the Western powers to attempt to gain even more control in China. Germany forced China to give it concessions in Shandong Province in 1897. Russia angered Japan by gaining concessions to build a railroad through Manchuria, and in 1904 Japan went to war with Russia over the control of Manchuria, known as the Russo-Japanese War of 1904–5. Japan made Korea a Japanese protectorate in 1907 and annexed it as a colony in 1910. Japan continued to build up its military, and in 1931 it invaded Manchuria and set up a puppet state there from which it invaded China and the rest of Asia. The Chinese call this their War of Resistance against Japan (1937–45; World War II).

China's defeat by Japan in 1895 also spurred a faction in the Chinese government, led by Kang Youwei (K'ang Yuwei), that wanted to enact reforms to modernize the country, resulting in the Reform Movement of 1898 (also known as the Hundred Days Reform). Kang Youwei and Liang Qichao (Ch'i-chao) presented a memorial (petition) to Emperor Guangxu (Kuangsu; r. 1875–1908) after the Sino-Japanese

War, arguing that China should modernize by enacting a wide range of economic, industrial and administrative reforms. Emperor Guangxu issued 40 reform decrees intended to modernize the Chinese imperial bureaucracy, education system, legal system, economy and technology, military and police system. This was the first time in Chinese history that a Chinese emperor enacted a systematic body of reforms. However, many Qing officials felt that the reforms threatened their positions. Yuan Shikai (Yuan Shih-k'ai), who had been Chinese military commander during the Sino-Japanese War, informed Empress Dowager Cixi, Guangxu's aunt and adoptive mother, of a supposed plot to take her prisoner. On September 21, 1898, she staged a coup d'état, placed Emperor Guangxu under house arrest, executed six radical leaders of the reform movement and assumed the regency until her death. Kang and Liang escaped to Japan, where they founded the Protect the Emperor Society, but Cixi's actions ended the Reform Movement of 1898.

Conservatives in the Qing government supported an anti-Manchu and antiforeign secret society, the Society of Righteousness and Harmony (Yihequan or Yi-ho-ch'uan), a late offshoot of the White Lotus Secret Society commonly known as the Boxers. In 1900 the Boxer Uprising placed the foreign legation quarters in Beijing and Tianjin under siege. Combined forces of eight foreign powers defeated the Boxers and took control of China. The empress dowager, emperor and many court members fled west to Xi'an for two years. Many Chinese now supported a genuine revolution to remove the imperial system altogether and establish a new form of government. The revolutionary movement led by Dr. Sun Yat-sen (1866–1925) gained many followers both in China, especially in the south, and in overseas Chinese communities.

Cixi returned to Beijing in 1902 and enacted many of the reforms that she had previously canceled, in order to preserve the Qing dynasty, now on the verge of collapse. In 1905 the Qing government abolished the examination system for the imperial bureaucracy. In 1905 Sun Yat-sen organized the Revolutionary Alliance (Tongmenghui or T'ung-meng-hui), which aimed to overthrow the Qing and establish a republican government in China. Sun planned five uprisings between 1906 and 1908, which failed but gave him hope that the weakened Qing dynasty would soon fall.

On November 15, 1908 Empress Dowager Cixi suddenly died the day after Emperor Guangxu died, and she was suspected of having him poisoned. On November 13 Cixi had chosen her grand-nephew to succeed Guangxu. He took the throne when he was only three years old and reigned as Emperor Xuantong (Hsuan-tung; r. 1909–12; now known as Henry Puyi). Chinese revolutionary leaders planned an uprising in Guangzhou in April 1911, but it failed and the leaders were executed. The revolutionary movement gained momentum when the Qing government nationalized the Chinese railroads in 1911, which threatened the autonomy of the Chinese provinces, and strikes broke out around the country. The Qing discovered that an uprising was planned in Hankou on October 16. Sun's followers, who had infiltrated government troops in Wuchang (Wuhan) in central China, decided to stage an uprising on October 10. This date is still celebrated by Chinese Nationalists in the Republic of China (ROC; Taiwan) as Double Tenth, the beginning of the

Chinese revolution. The success of the Wuchang Uprising encouraged revolutionaries in other Chinese cities and provinces, and by the end of November 1911, 14 of the 15 Chinese provinces had declared their independence from the Qing. Sun had been in the United States raising funds during the Wuchang Uprising. After he returned to China, on January 1, 1912 he was inaugurated as the first president of the Provisional Government of the Chinese Republic at Nanjing. An open political party called the Chinese Nationalist Party (Kuomintang; KMT) was formed in 1912 as the successor to the Revolutionary Alliance. Emperor Xuantong was permitted to continue residing in the Forbidden City. Warlords later forced him to leave Beijing, after which the Japanese protected him and made him the head of Manchukuo, the puppet state they established in Manchuria in 1932. See also ABAHAI; AMUR RIVER; ANCESTOR WORSHIP; ARROW WAR; ASTRONOMY AND OBSERVATORIES; BANNER SYSTEM, MANCHU; BEIJING; BEIJING, CONVENTION OF; BOXER UPRISING; BRITISH EAST INDIA COMPANY; CANTON SYSTEM FOR REGULATING TRADE; CHENGDE; CHINA MERCHANTS STEAM NAVIGATION COMPANY; CHINA PROPER; CHINESE MARITIME CUSTOMS SERVICE; CHRISTIANITY; CIXI, EMPRESS DOWAGER; CONFUCIANISM; DALAI LAMA; DALIAN; DORGON; DREAM OF THE RED CHAMBER; EIGHT TRIGRAMS REBELLION; EUNUCHS; FORBIDDEN CITY; GOLD AND SILVER; GONG, PRINCE; GORDON, CHARLES GEORGE; GREAT WALL; GUANGZHOU; HAKKA; HAN; HONG KONG; HONG XIUQUAN; JESUITS; KANG YOUWEI; KANGXI (EMPEROR); LI HONGZHANG; LI ZICHENG; LIAODONG PENINSULA; LIANG QICHAO; LIN ZEXU; MACAO; MACARTNEY, LORD GEORGE; MAITREYA AND MANJUSRI; MANCHU; MANCHURIA; MING DYNASTY; MONGOL; MUSLIMS; NANJING; NANJING, TREATY OF; NATIONALIST PARTY; NERCHINSK, TREATY OF; NIAN REBELLION; NURHACHI; OPIUM WAR; OVERSEAS CHINESE; PORCELAIN; PUYI, HENRY; QIANLONG EMPEROR; QUFU; RAILROADS; REFORM MOVEMENT OF 1898; REPUBLIC OF CHINA; REVOLUTION OF 1911; REVOLUTIONARY ALLIANCE; RITES CONTROVERSY; RUSSO-JAPANESE WAR OF 1904–5 AND CHINA; SELF-STRENGTHENING MOVEMENT; SHANGHAI; SHEN FU; SHENYANG; SHIMONOSEKI, TREATY OF; SHUNZHI (EMPEROR); SILK; SINO-FRENCH WAR; SINO-JAPANESE WAR OF 1894–95; SMALL SWORD SOCIETY; SUMMER PALACE; SUN YAT-SEN; TAIPING REBELLION; TAISHAN, MOUNT; TAIWAN; TEA; TIANJIN; TIBET; TONGZHI (EMPEROR); TREATY PORTS; TRIAD SOCIETY; TRIBUTE SYSTEM; UNEQUAL TREATIES; WARD, FREDERICK TOWNSEND; WHITE LOTUS SECRET SOCIETY; WUCHANG UPRISING; XINJIANG-UIGHUR AUTONOMOUS REGION; YONGZHENG (EMPEROR); YUAN DYNASTY; YUAN SHIKAI; ZENG GUOFAN; ZHENG CHENGGONG; ZONGLI YAMEN.

QING MING FESTIVAL (Ch'ing Ming)   A festival held on April 4 or 5, the 106th day after the winter solstice, to honor the dead. Translated as the "Pure Brightness" or "Clear and Bright" Festival, it originally was held to celebrate the greening of nature in the spring after the long winter. Traditional Chinese beliefs hold that the spirit survives the body after death and remains at the grave, keeping watch on people still living. The Chinese began to hold annual ceremonies at gravesites to pacify these spirits at the same time that the beginning of spring was celebrated. The festival is associated with Emperor Jin Wen Gong (Jin dynasty; 1115–1234), who honored the spirit of his faithful servant Za Zi Tui, who had saved the emperor's life and became a "wandering spirit" after he died. On the morning of Qing Ming, families sweep the graves of their ancestors. They place yellow ribbons at the graves to keep away malevolent spirits of the deceased who were neglected by their descendants or who died in a manner that made recovery of their bodies for proper burial impossible. Families offer food, wine and tea to their ancestors on semicircular altars at the sites and then eat the food in a shared banquet. The eldest son of each family conducts a ceremony to honor the ancestors' spirits; it is believed that if these rituals are not carried out, ancestral spirits will adversely affect the family's fortunes. Mourners burn incense, candles and paper money (joss money), and male family members kowtow—perform three sets of prostrations and three bows—while firecrackers are set off. When the family returns home, the ceremony is repeated at the family altar. Under Communist rule, families usually cremate rather than bury the deceased, and in the cities there are only a few government-run public graveyards where Qing Ming ceremonies are held. The Communists use the festival to honor martyrs of Communist liberation, and schoolchildren visit memorial statues to hear stories about the martyrs. However, traditional Qing Ming ceremonies are still held in rural areas and in overseas Chinese communities. See also ANCESTOR WORSHIP; CALENDAR; FAMILY STRUCTURE; JOSS PAPER; KOWTOW; OVERSEAS CHINESE.

QING ZANG   See QINGHAI-TIBET PLATEAU.

QINGDAO   The most important industrial city in Shandong Province in eastern China. Qingdao is located on the Yellow Sea on the southern coast of the Shandong Peninsula and is a busy port and the most popular seashore resort in China. The Yellow Sea and the Bay of Jiaozhou surround the city on three sides, and Mount Lao (Laoshan), 3,717 feet high, lies to the northeast. Six large bays east of the Qingdao Pier have beautiful sand beaches. An island known as Little Qingdao (Xiao Qingdao) was first used as a lighthouse by Germany in 1900 and served as a military station until 1987. Today the lighthouse and adjoining gardens are open to tourists, who can see the rare Qingdao white lily, which blooms only in southern Shandong Province. The Qingdao Art Museum houses a large collection of paintings from the Yuan, Ming and Qing dynasties (13th–19th centuries) and archaeological exhibits on the region. Zhanqiao Pavilion exhibits paintings and crafts, many of which are exported abroad. Lu Xun Park, named for one of China's most famous modern authors, contains the Oceanography Museum and an aquarium. Other famous sites in the Qingdao region include the Daoist temples Taiqing Gong, Taiping Gong, Shangqing Gong and Hualong Gong, and the Buddhist temples Zhanshan Si and Huayan Si.

Today Qingdao has a population of about 1.4 million, but until the late 19th century it was just a small fishing village. In 1891 the Qing dynasty government recognized Qingdao's strategic importance and built a fort and naval station there. In 1895 Germany took over the city as a treaty port open to foreign residents and trade and used it as a coaling station for steamships. The Germans rapidly developed Qingdao into a deep-water harbor and constructed many large buildings of European design. They also founded a brewery that

still produces China's best-known beer, Qingdao, or Tsingtao as it is marketed around the world, which is made with the famous mineral water from springs on Mount Lao.

Qingdao, since gaining notice in the last century, changed hands many times. Japan took over the city during World War I, after which Qingdao was again taken over by the Nationalists (Kuomintang; KMT). The Japanese occupied Qingdao once again after they invaded China in 1937. After World War II the Nationalists regained it, but in 1946 the U.S Army occupied the city for 18 months. In 1948, during China's civil war, the Communists gained final control of Qingdao. Today the Chinese government has built up the city's heavy and light industries, with major products including steel, diesel locomotives, automobiles, tractors, textiles, television sets and electronic products. Workers enjoy seaside vacations at the many sanatoriums built for them in Qingdao. In 1984 the Chinese government designated Qingdao as one of China's 14 Coastal Open Cities, open to foreign investment and trade. Yellow Island, a peninsula southeast of Qingdao, has been declared a Special Economic (SEZ) Zone to promote joint ventures between Chinese and foreign companies. See also ALCOHOLIC BEVERAGES; LU XUN; SHANDONG PROVINCE; SPECIAL ECONOMIC ZONES; YELLOW SEA.

QINGHAI, LAKE   (Qinghai Hu, "Blue Lake")   The largest inland lake in China, covering an area of 1,720 square miles. Lake Qinghai, also known by its Mongol name of Koko Nor, is a salt lake located in the northeast region of Qinghai Province, a high plateau north of Tibet. The lake's ancient name is the Western Sea. The lake, from which Qinghai Province takes its name, lies at an altitude of 10,479 feet and has a circumference of about 560 miles and maximum depth of 125 feet. It was formed when a fault appeared in the Earth's surface about 1 million years ago. A mountain ridge runs along the bottom of the lake, and four peaks rise above the surface as islets, the largest being Haixin Hill. Lake Qinghai is surrounded by mountains, and more than 50 rivers flow into it. The lake is drained by the Yellow (Huanghe) River and its tributaries. Lake Qinghai is the largest breeding ground for migratory birds in China. Bird Island (Niao Dao) near its northwest bank is thickly covered with bird nests. More than 100,000 birds belonging to more than 12 species migrate there from India and southern China to breed. See also QINGHAI PROVINCE; YELLOW RIVER.

QINGHAI PROVINCE   A large, inaccessible province in western China that covers 280,000 square miles and has a population of about 4 million. Qinghai's population density of only about 14 persons per square mile makes it the second-least-populated province in China, after Tibet Autonomous Region (Xizang Zizhiqu). Qinghai borders Tibet to the southwest, and most of the province is an extension of the Tibetan Plateau, with an average altitude of 10,000 feet. The province is named for Lake Qinghai, a large salt lake in the northeast known by its Mongol name, Koko Nor, which is China's largest inland lake. The southern half of Qinghai Province is a mountainous region where the eastern end of the Kunlun Mountain Range runs into the Bayanharshan Mountain Range, with numerous peaks more than 16,000 feet high. It has virtually no inhabitants. In this area, the two greatest rivers in China, the Yellow (Huanghe) and the Yangzi (Changjiang), have their source, as does the Mekong River (Lancanjiang in Chinese). In the northern half of Qinghai there are two basins surrounded by mountains: the Qaidam (Tsaidam) Basin and Lake Qinghai

The province borders Sichuan and Gansu provinces to the east and the Xinjiang-Uighur Autonomous Region to the northwest. Han (ethnic Chinese) have settled in the more temperate valleys, but Qinghai is populated largely by Tibetans and other national minorities, such as Mongols, Hui (Chinese Muslims), Kazakhs, Tu and Salar (Turkish-speaking Muslims). Many of these people are descendants of the Tuyuhun, horse breeders who came from southern Manchuria in the fourth century, and the Tangut, a nomadic tribe that founded the Xixia (Western Xia) dynasty (1038–1227). Many inhabitants of Qinghai herd sheep, horses, camels and yaks, which provide milk, butter, shoe leather and hair that is woven to make tents in which the nomads dwell. Yak hair also is used to make fly whisks and the beards worn by Beijing Opera performers. Yaks are the only means of transporting goods in the otherwise inaccessible high plateau.

Xining in eastern Qinghai Province is the capital city. It has a population of about 500,000 and sits at an altitude of 7,415 feet. Since ancient times it was a stopover for caravans between China and Tibet. The Tibetan monastery of Ta'er (Kumbum in Tibetan), belonging to the Lamaist Sect of Buddhism, is located 17 miles outside of Xining. Founded in 1560, it was the birthplace of Tsong Kha-pa (1355–1417), founder of the Yellow Hat (Gelugpa) Sect of Buddhism. The monastery organizes four great festivals each year. Except for the region around Xining, Qinghai was brought into the Chinese Empire only after the Manchu Qing dynasty (1644–1911) conquered Tibet in the early 18th century. Railroads link Xining with Lanzhou in Gansu Province and Haiyan and are being constructed through the mountains to Lhasa, the capital of Tibet. There are few highways, and the main road through Qinghai from Lanzhou to Xining and Lhasa was completed only in 1954. Deposits of coal and oil have been found in Qinghai, but the traditional industry is salt-mining from the beds of the many salt lakes in the northeast. See also KAZAKH; KUNLUN MOUNTAIN RANGE; LHASA; MEKONG RIVER; MINORITIES, NATIONAL; MONGOL; NOMADS AND ANIMAL HUSBANDRY; QINGHAI, LAKE; TIBET; TIBETAN; XIXIA, KINGDOM OF; YANGZI RIVER; YELLOW RIVER.

QINGHAI-TIBET PLATEAU (Qing Zang)

A plateau in Qinghai Province and Tibet Autonomous Region (Xizang Zizhiqu) in western China that is the highest and largest plateau in the world. It covers 850,000 square miles and 23 percent of all Chinese land area. The Himalaya Mountain Range, including 11 of the 17 mountains in the world that are over 26.000 feet high, borders the plateau's southern edge. The Kunlun and Qilian Mountain ranges border its northern edge, and the Pamir and Karakoram Mountain ranges lie to the west. The highest mountain is Everest (known in Tibetan as Qomolongma) in the Himalayas, with its peak at 29,028 feet above sea level. The mountains and the plateau were formed about 40 million years ago when two plates of the Earth's crust collided, causing them to buckle. This thrust up an area of crust 43 miles thick, capped by mountain peaks.

The Qinghai-Tibet Plateau is called the Roof of the World because it has elevations averaging more than 13,210 feet above sea level. Its highest peaks are more than 23,000 feet high. It has thin air, cold average temperatures and glaciers. Like the Arctic tundra, much of the area's soil is permanently frozen. The wind howls across the treeless, stony landscape, where the climate is very dry. The plateau's annual precipitation is only eight inches, because monsoon rains from India are all halted when they hit the southern side of the Himalayas.

There are basins and lakes in the plateau's interior, including Lake Qinghai, which covers 1,720 square miles and is the largest in China. The Yangzi (Changjiang) and Yellow (Huanghe) rivers, the two largest rivers in China, both originate in the Qinghai-Tibet Plateau and flow all the way to the country's eastern coast.

The vegetation and population of the plateau are both extremely sparse. Tibet and Qinghai are the two least populated provinces in China. Most of the plateau's inhabitants are seminomadic Tibetans who herd sheep, goats and yaks. Most of the region is unsettled. The main town on the plateau is Yushu (formerly known as Jiegu or Chiehku), a collection center and market for wool and sheepskins. Wild animals in the region include the yak, Mongolian and Tibetan gazelles, Bactrian camel, Tibetan antelope, Asiatic wild ass and white-lipped deer, although hunting and overgrazing of their habitats have caused a serious decline in the numbers of these animals. The rare snow leopard lives only in Tibet. Wild birds include the black-necked crane, Tibetan snowcock and snow finches. See also CRANE; HIMALAYA MOUNTAIN RANGE; KUNLUN MOUNTAIN RANGE; QINGHAI, LAKE; QINGHAI PROVINCE; SNOW LEOPARD; TIBET; YANGZI RIVER; YELLOW RIVER.

QINGHUA (TSING HUA) UNIVERSITY

A prestigious university in Beijing that is known as the cradle of Chinese engineers. The university developed from the Qinghua School. In 1908 the U.S. Congress allocated $12 million, about half of the indemnity China had paid the United States following the Boxer Uprising in 1900, to establish a government program for training Chinese students in the United States. In 1911 the funds were used to found the Qinghua School in Beijing, a preparatory school for Chinese students who planned to study in the United States. In 1928 the school was reconstructed into the government-operated Qinghua University. Today Qinghua is a modern university offering courses that emphasize engineering, science, economic management and liberal arts. Many Nobel laureates, famous scientists, writers, educators and government leaders have graduated from Qinghua University, as have a large percentage of the engineers and businessmen who have been active in China's recent development.

Qinghua students took part in anti-imperialist movements, such as the May Fourth Movement of 1919 and the 1935 December Ninth Movement against Japanese aggression. By 1929, 1,268 Chinese scholars from Qinghua University had gone to the United States. During China's War of Resistance against Japan (1937–45; World War II), when the Nationalists (Kuomintang; KMT) fled west to escape the Japanese invaders and set up their capital in Sichuan Province, many schools and factories moved west as well.

Qinghua and Beijing universities and Nankai University from Tianjin joined together to set up the Southwest China Associated University at Kunming in Yunnan Province. Qinghua moved back to Beijing after 1945 and resumed the name Qinghua University.

When the Chinese Communists defeated the Nationalists and founded the People's Republic of China (PRC) in 1949, Communist leader Mao Zedong (Mao Tse-tung) issued instructions for the protection of Qinghua University. The university was geared to combine education and scientific research with practical activities for the socialist reconstruction of China. During the 1960s teachers and students from Qinghua designed and constructed many major projects in China, such as the Miyun Reservoir. After the Cultural Revolution (1966–76) broke out, on August 18, 1966, at the first of eight rallies of more than 1 million people in Tiananmen Square in Beijing, Mao Zedong wore the armband of a group from Qinghua University called the Red Guards (Hongweibing). After this, Red Guard units were formed at universities and schools throughout China. Millions of Red Guards began traveling around the country with free railroad passes, destroying or damaging Chinese temples, cultural artifacts, books and other symbols of so-called bourgeois society. After the Cultural Revolution ended, Chinese universities and schools, which had been closed, reopened and began rebuilding their educational programs.

Today Qinghua University has 17,000 teachers and students, and includes 5 colleges, 28 departments, 38 research institutes and centers, 142 laboratories, more than 100 centers that confer master's and doctoral degrees and 11 stations for postdoctoral research. The national government assigned graduates of Chinese universities to jobs until 1985, when reforms were introduced giving universities and colleges more independence. Qinghua and several other universities began using a system by which graduates could accept jobs offered to them or could look for jobs on their own. See also BOXER UPRISING; EDUCATION SYSTEM; PEOPLE'S REPUBLIC OF CHINA; RED GUARDS; WAR OF RESISTANCE AGAINST JAPAN.

QINGTAN MOVEMENT See SEVEN SAGES OF THE BAMBOO GROVE.

QINGTONG See BRONZEWARE.

QINHUAI RIVER See NANJING.

QINIANDIAN See TEMPLE OF HEAVEN.

QINLING MOUNTAIN RANGE A range of mountains running east to west across central China, primarily through Gansu and Shaanxi provinces. The Qinling Range lies south of the loess plateau that was formed by vast deposits of loose yellow soil, known as loess, blown in from desert regions. Its western end reaches the Qinghai-Tibet Plateau in western China, forming the southwestern border of the North China Plain as it runs east. The mountains average between 6,560 and 9,840 feet high, and the highest peak, Mount Taibai, rises 12,360 feet above sea level. The northern slopes lie in a warm, temperate climatic zone. The southern slopes lie in the subtropical zone, which begins at the latitude of 34 degrees N and extends south almost to the Tropic of Cancer,

just north of the major port city of Guangzhou (Canton). The Qinling Mountain Range is the dividing line between the two zones, the former of which is characterized by deciduous broad-leaved forests, and the latter of which contains subtropical evergreen broad-leaved forests. Thus, the range hosts a wide variety of native animals and plants. Much of the vegetation comprises forests and deciduous trees, primarily sawtooth oaks and Chinese cork oaks. The mountains are inhabited by more than 40 species of mammals, reptiles and amphibians and more than 230 species of birds. Giant Pandas, found mainly in the mountains of Sichuan Province, also inhabit the Qinling Mountains in Shaanxi Province. The Japanese ibis, another rare species, also can be found there. Wildlife preservation areas have been established on Mount Taibai and in Foping in Shaanxi. The Qinling Mountains also form the catchment area between the drainage basins of China's two largest rivers, the Yellow (Huanghe), which flows across northern China, and the Yangzi (Changjiang), which flows across central China. See also LOESS; NORTH CHINA PLAIN; PANDA; QINGHAI-TIBET PLATEAU; YANGZI RIVER; YELLOW RIVER.

QINSAI See HANGZHOU.

QINZONG (EMPEROR) See GAOZONG (EMPEROR) (SONG); HUIZONG (EMPEROR); SOUTHERN SONG DYNASTY.

QISHAN See LIN ZEXU; OPIUM WAR.

QIU JUN See ZHEJIANG PROVINCE.

QIUJU, THE STORY OF See GONG LI; ZHANG YIMOU.

QIXI See COWHERD AND WEAVER MAID FESTIVAL.

QOMOLONGMA See EVEREST, MOUNT; HIMALAYA MOUNTAIN RANGE; TIBET.

QU YUAN (Ch'u Yuan; c. 343–278 B.C.)   The first prominent poet in Chinese history. Twenty-five of his poems survive, the best known of which are the *Lisao, The Nine Songs, The Nine Declarations, Heaven Questioned* and *Summoning the Soul.* They were collected in a major anthology called *Chuchi* ("Songs of the South"), which also contains poems by poets with similar styles writing between the third century B.C. and the first century A.D. Qu Yuan's *Nine Songs,* which actually number 11, are religious songs written to praise the various gods of the state of Qu.

Qu Yuan was born to an aristocratic family in the southern state of Qu in the Yangzi River (Changjiang) valley, which had a highly developed culture and a rich mythological tradition. He was very bright and talented but led a tragic life. Although he held a high position at court, he was slandered by enemies and was banished. Political intrigues between Qu and the state of Qin caused the king of Qu to be captured. Soon after, Qin captured the Qu capital of Ying. At this, Qu Yuan became so disconsolate that he drowned himself. His poem, *The Nine Declarations,* written just before he died, expresses his personal grief over losing favor with the king and the tragedy of the people of Qu when their capital was overtaken. Some critics consider the *Lisao* to be the finest Chinese poem ever written. Translated as "The Lament," "Encountering Sorrow" or "A Song on the Sorrows of Departure," it is an autobiographical poem that recounts the sad history of Qu Yuan's life, his travels, his appreciation of the beauty of nature, his encounter with a wise shaman and an imaginary account of a journey to Heaven. In the poem, the poet is not comforted by any of these things and finally decides to end his life.

QUANZHOU See FUJIAN PROVINCE; MUSLIMS; OVERSEAS CHINESE; SHIPPING AND SHIPBUILDING; XIAMEN.

QUEEN OF HEAVEN See MAZIPO.

QUEMOY ISLAND See FUJIAN PROVINCE.

QUEUE   A hairstyle that men belonging to the Han ethnic majority in China were forced to wear as a symbol of their submission to the non-Chinese Manchus who ruled China under the Qing dynasty (1644–1911). Chinese men had to shave their front hair and comb their back hair into a long pigtail braided with black silk or horsehair. The queue was the hairstyle worn by Manchu men, who considered it a mark of manhood and dignity. Pulling a man's queue was a serious insult. The Chinese felt this foreign hairstyle was a symbol of shame and submission to the Manchus. The traditional Chinese man's hairstyle, dating back to at least the third century B.C., was a topknot, often covered with a black cloth cap. Under the Manchus, priests of the Daoist religion were allowed to continue wearing the topknot and Buddhist priests were allowed to continue the practice of shaving their heads. When Sun Yat-sen (1866–1925), founder of modern China, escaped to Japan in 1895 after his revolutionary plot was discovered, he rebelled against Qing rule by cutting off his queue, wearing Western clothes and growing a mustache. Chiang Kai-shek (1887–1975), who became the leader of the Chinese Nationalist Party (Kuomintang; KMT), also rebelled by cutting off his queue. He did so to force his family to allow him to go to Japan to study. Some Chinese revolutionaries cut off their queues at public anti-Qing demonstrations. When the Chinese overthrew the Qing in the Revolution of 1911, all Chinese men abandoned the queue. See also CHIANG KAI-SHEK; MANCHU; QING DYNASTY; SUN YAT-SEN.

QUFU   A city in Shandong Province in northeastern China that is the birthplace of Confucius (551–479 B.C.), a philosopher whose school of thought was designated by the imperial government of the Han dynasty (206 B.C.–A.D. 220) as the country's orthodox religion; it remained so through the Qing (1644–1911), China's last imperial dynasty. Confucius is properly called Kongfuzi or Kongzi (K'ung Fu-tzu or K'ung-tzu), Master Kong. When he was born, Qufu was the capital of the state of Lu. Even before he died, Confucius was revered as a wise man. One year after his death, Duke Ai of Lu decreed that the home of Confucius should be turned into a temple. The Han emperor Wudi decreed in 205 B.C. that Confucianism was the official religion of China and built a temple to Confucius at Qufu that was expanded by every subsequent dynasty to rule China. The descendants of Confucius became a powerful clan, and by the Yuan dynasty (1279–1368) they were high-level advisers to the emperor.

They were allowed to have control over Qufu and were awarded "living allowances" by the Chinese emperors as long as they performed rituals that would benefit the emperors' health. The Kong family mansion eventually included 463 buildings.

When the Qing dynasty was overthrown by the Revolution of 1911, benefits from the imperial court were stopped and the city suffered financial decline. In 1948, during the civil war between the Chinese Communists and the Nationalists (Kuomintang; KMT), most of the Kong family fled their mansion, and the Nationalists took what the family left behind when they moved to the island of Taiwan. The Communist government that took control of China in 1949 has been renovating the buildings in Qufu, and a Confucius Foundation was established in 1961. The temple buildings and grounds were restored in the early 1980s, and Qufu has been actively recruiting tourists.

Qufu has a very ancient history, with legends claiming that Emperor Shaohao, one of China's mythical rulers, lived there in 6000 B.C. Shaohao's supposed tomb, built during the Song dynasty (960–1279), is located just outside the city. By 2000 B.C., during China's Bronze Age, the Yi people had established a kingdom in this area. In Qufu may be seen the ruins of the Halo Palace, which was at the center of the capital of the state of Lu; the capital was known as Luguo Gucheng. Lu controlled Qufu during Confucius's time. The *Spring and Autumn Annals* (*Chunqiu* or *Ch'un-ch'iu*), the annals of the Lu kingdom, were the source of the name for the period during the Zhou dynasty (1100–256 B.C.) called the Spring and Autumn Period (772–481 B.C.). In 256 the kingdom of Lu was captured by the state of Chu, which was absorbed in turn by the state of Qin, which unified China under the Qin dynasty (221–206 B.C.).

The ancient city of Qufu was laid out in a grid pattern about 3.5 miles by 5 miles and was surrounded by a wall with 11 gates. Seven streets ran east to west and six ran north to south. The history of Qufu is largely the history of the Kong family. Today the city has a population of more than 500,000. About 100,000 members of the Kong family still live in the Qufu area, although they are just ordinary citizens without wealth or privilege. Since the early 1980s Qufu has been actively recruiting tourists and restoring temples, tombs and the old canal around the city.

The Confucius Temple (Kongmiao or K'ung-miao) consists of a series of interlocking courtyards entered by large gates. The entire complex covers almost a mile of buildings, which have red walls and gold roofs similar to the Forbidden City (Imperial Palace) in Beijing. One courtyard contains the Thirteen Pavilions of the Imperial Pillars (Shisan Yubei Ting or Shih-san Yu-pei T'ing), which were intended to protect the 53 stone pillars engraved with calligraphy by Chinese emperors from the Han through Qing dynasties (206 B.C. to 1911). The oldest pillar, or stele, actually dates from 668. Ginkgo Pavilion (Xingtan or Hsing-t'an) in the adjoining courtyard is supposedly where Confucius instructed his disciples under a ginkgo tree. In the center of the temple complex is Dachengdian (Ta-cheng Tien), a large hall built in the 11th century that is supported by stone pillars carved with dragons. This is where ritual sacrifices were offered to Confucius. Shengjidian Hall (Sheng-chi Tien), dating from the 16th century, contains 120 stones carved with scenes from

Confucius's life. Many other halls in the complex exhibit ritual implements, musical instruments and other objects associated with the cult of Confucius. A five-day Confucian Festival is held every year in the middle of the seventh month in the Chinese lunar calendar (August or September), and many tourists attend the performances of traditional rituals and dances during the festival.

The Kong Family Mansion (Kongfu or Kung-fu) consists of a large complex of courtyards, pavilions, storehouses and residences, some of which still have their original furniture, that was inhabited by members of the Kong family until 1937. Begun in 1068, it was enlarged over the years. The Main Gate (*Damen* or *Ta-men*), built during the Ming dynasty (1368–1644) and inscribed with the phrase "Sacred Residence" (*Sheng Fu*), leads to the central area of the mansion. In front of the Great Hall (*Datang* or *Ta-t'ang*) lies the 16th-century Chongguangmen gate (Ch'ung-k'uang-men), which was opened with a 13-gun salute only for a visit from the emperor or other important ceremonial occasions that were held in Datang Hall. Other buildings were used for instruction, private occasions and as residences for family members and servants. Banquets and ceremonies for weddings and funerals were held in the lavishly decorated hall called Qianshangfang (Ch'ien-shang-fang). There is also a private garden named Iron Mountains Garden (Tieshan Yuan). The so-called Apricot Altar supposedly stands on the site of the school that Confucius ran. The front courtyard contains the Kong Family Records Offices and Archives that date from 1534 to 1948. The traditional guest quarters in the mansion, built around 1550, have been renovated to serve as a 60-room hotel for tourists.

The Confucius Forest (Konglin or K'ung-lin), just north of the city, is the family cemetery for 79 generations of Confucius's descendants. It has more than 600,000 tombs and covers more than 500 acres, the largest family cemetery in the world. All descendants of Confucius, whether they are government officials, aristocrats or commoners, must be buried there. To the Chinese people, the Confucian Forest symbolizes the ancient and unchanging culture of China. The oldest graves were constructed for Confucius and his wife during the Song dynasty (960–1279), 1,000 years after his death. His tomb, known as Kongzi Mu (K'ung-tzu Mu), is located in the northwestern section of the cemetery among graves dating from the Eastern Zhou Period (771–256 B.C.). However, it cannot be said with certainty that Confucius is actually buried there. The tomb of his son, Kong Li (K'ung Li), lies east of this grave, and the tomb of his grandson, Kong Ji (K'ung Chi), lies to the south. Kaiting Pavilion was built in the 16th century to honor Zi Gong (Tzu Kung), a student of Confucius who lived in a hut at this site for six years to mourn his teacher. Three pavilions also were erected in honor of three emperors from various dynasties who visited Confucius's grave.

The Temple of the Duke of Zhou is a small temple in eastern Qufu that commemorates the Duke of Zhou, whom Confucius regarded as the finest example of a proper ruler. He was the brother of Emperor Wu, founder of the Zhou dynasty. Yanmiao Temple, just north of the Confucius Temple, was built to commemorate Yan Hui, Confucius's favorite student, who died tragically at the age of 32. Five of the rooms now exhibit archaeological finds from the Qufu area. See also CONFUCIANISM; CONFUCIUS; DRAGON; FUNERALS; GINKGO; SHANDONG PROVINCE; SPRING AND AUTUMN PERIOD; ZHOU, DUKE OF; ZHOU DYNASTY.

QUOTATIONS FROM CHAIRMAN MAO ZEDONG
(*Mao zhuxi yulu*)   A book published in Shanghai in September 1966, during the Cultural Revolution (1966–76), containing quotations from Mao Zedong (Mao Tse-tung), chairman of the Chinese Communist Party and leader of the People's Republic of China (PRC). Also known as the "Little Red Book," it was compiled by Lin Biao (Lin Piao), a marshal in the People's Liberation Army (PLA) who became China's minister of defense. Lin Biao put together a simple edition of Mao's ideas that could be used to indoctrinate PLA recruits, who usually were not highly educated.

Mao had developed his ideas from Soviet Marxism-Leninism while he was staying at Yan'an in Shaanxi Province, where the Communists made their headquarters in 1936 after their two-and-a-half-year "Long March" during their civil war with the Chinese Nationalists (Kuomintang; KMT). Unlike the Soviet Communists, Mao emphasized that the peasants were the basis of the society. As the main force of Mao's army, the Chinese peasants were victorious in 1949, when Mao proclaimed the People's Republic of China. During the Cultural Revolution that took place under Maoist China, Chinese schools and universities were shut down, and millions of teenagers joined the Red Guards. In 1966 the PLA and the Cultural Revolution Groups organized six huge rallies in the capital city of Beijing between August 18 and November 26, and 10 million Red Guards from all over China were given free railroad transportation there. The Red Guards always carried their copies of the *Quotations from Chairman Mao Zedong*. Westerners saw vivid images on television and in newspapers and magazines of the Red Guards waving high their copies of the "Little Red Book." See also CIVIL WAR BETWEEN COMMUNISTS AND NATIONALISTS; CULTURAL REVOLUTION; LIN BIAO; MAO ZEDONG; PEOPLE'S LIBERATION ARMY; PEOPLE'S REPUBLIC OF CHINA; RED GUARDS.

QUTANG GORGE   See THREE GORGES WATER CONSERVANCY PROJECT; YANGZI RIVER.

R

RABBIT (or hare; *tuzi* or *yetu*)   An animal that the Chinese traditionally associate with the Moon. Traditionalists believe that a rabbit lives on the Moon, where it pounds the herbs that make up the elixir of immortality in the Daoist tradition. In the Buddhist tradition, the rabbit was willing to sacrifice its life for the Buddha, founder of the religion, and was rewarded by being reborn on the Moon. The Chinese also believe that Change E (also known as Heng O) became the Goddess of the Moon after she accidentally swallowed the pill of immortality, became immortal and flew up to the moon, where she became a three-legged toad. She coughed out the pill, which became the jade rabbit. Further, the Chinese believe that a bearded old man lives on the Moon and arranges marriages between humans on Earth. All three of these beings are thus associated with the Moon—the old man, toad and rabbit. At the Autumn Moon Festival, on the 15th day of the eighth month (around September) in the traditional lunar calendar, the Chinese, especially in the south, hang or carry paper lanterns, many of them shaped like rabbits. The rabbit on the Moon pounds the elixir under a cassia tree, which is always in flower around the time of the festival, and cassia bark is one of the ingredients in the elixir of immortality. The cassia tree is associated with scholars. Chinese children like to play with toy rabbits, which they honor by calling Mister Rabbit. In northern China the rabbits are made of clay and are dressed as a scholar in the imperial bureaucracy or as a warrior. The rabbit, the symbol of longevity, is a common decorative motif on Chinese porcelain. The rabbit is also one of the animals in the 12-year Chinese animal zodiac. People born in the Year of the Rabbit are believed to be kind, graceful, peaceful, artistic and good scholars. See also AUTUMN MOON FESTIVAL; CHANG E; ELIXIR OF IMMORTALITY; PORCELAIN; WEDDINGS, TRADITIONAL; ZODIAC, ANIMAL.

RADICALS IN WRITTEN CHARACTERS   See WRITING SYSTEM, CHINESE.

RADIO   See BROADCASTING.

RAFFLES, SIR STAMFORD   See SINGAPORE.

RAILROADS   The first railroad was constructed in China in 1876 by a British firm, Jardine Matheson and Co., which built a 10-mile-long, narrow-track railway from Shanghai to Wusongkou at the mouth of the Yangzi River (Changjiang). The Chinese people opposed the railroad, claiming that it disturbed nature, and forced the Qing dynasty (1644–1911) government to dismantle it after less than a year. Five years later, educated Chinese who argued that China should modernize by adopting Western technology pleaded with the government to build its own railroads. The first domestically built railroad in China was a 10-mile-long railway from Tangshan to Xugezhuang in Hebei Province, constructed with funds from the Kaiping Coal Mining Administration. The first locomotive was built at the same time. In 1882 the first domestically made locomotive "dragon" (engine) ran on the Tangshan-Xugezhuang Railway. Railway building became a major activity in China after it was defeated by Japan in the Sino-Japanese War of 1894–95. The Chinese government was too poor to finance railroad construction, so it gave foreign powers concessions in different regions: Russia in Manchuria (modern northeastern China) and northern China, Germany in Shandong Province, Great Britain in the Yangzi River valley down to the Burma border, Japan in Fujian Province and France in Yunnan and Guangxi, the southwestern provinces that border Vietnam (Indochina). After Japan defeated Russia in the Russo-Japanese War of 1904–5, it claimed Russian concessions in Manchuria. Chinese entrepreneurs opposed the carving up of the country by foreign powers and persuaded the Chinese government to build railroad lines in their particular provinces, financed by local investors. Such railroads were built in Sichuan Province in 1903 and in Hubei, Hunan and Guangdong provinces. In 1904 two major railways running north-south and east-west opened in China. Their intersection at Zhengzhou in Henan Province was named "the railways' heart." By 1986 the railyard at Zhengzhou had become the largest in China, receiving or sending off a train every 3.3 minutes and breaking down and recoupling an average of 20,000 cars a day.

In 1905 the Chinese railway engineer Zhan Tianyou (Chan T'ien-yu), who had graduated from the Civil Engineering Department of Yale University, designed and built the ambitious 150-mile-long Beijing-Zhangjiakou Railway, which was opened to traffic in 1909. Later lines were built, including the Jinghan (Beijing to Hankou), Huguang (Hankou to Guangzhou) and Jinpu (Tianjin to Pukou). Chinese provincial leaders were not able to raise enough funds to continue building railroads, so in 1911 the Qing minister of communications nationalized all the railroad trunk lines, for which he would seek foreign loans and technical assistance, and left only the branch lines open to funding by provincial financiers. Provincial leaders organized the Railway Protection Movement, which included a boycott against the government and refusal to pay taxes, and anti-Qing demonstrations broke out in Sichuan that ended in violence. The demonstrations quickly spread to other provinces and helped bring down the Qing dynasty, which fell to the Revolution of 1911.

The Chinese Nationalist Party (Kuomintang; KMT) that controlled the Republic of China continued to build railroads. In 1936 the Wuhan-Guangzhou (Wuchang-Canton) line was completed, so that the capital city of Beijing in the north, which had a line to Wuhan, was indirectly linked with the major ports of Guangzhou and Hong Kong in the south. Railroad building was interrupted and many lines were damaged during China's War of Resistance against Japan (1937–45; World War II) and the civil war between the KMT and the Chinese Communist Party (CCP), which the latter won in 1949 and established the People's Republic of China (PRC). By 1949 about 15,000 miles of railroad lines had been laid in the coastal plains and the industrialized northeastern region, but only about 7,500 miles were opened to traffic. The first line to be built after 1949 was the Sichuan trunk line. Much of the pre-1949 railway system also was repaired or rebuilt. From 1949 to 1984 the PRC laid about 20,000 miles of new railroad track, so that China's railway system expanded to about 32,000 miles of freight and passenger lines, reaching all of China's provinces, municipalities and autonomous regions, major cities and towns and important production bases, except Tibet (Xizang Autonomous Region). In 1984 more than 70 percent of China's total shipping volume—including ground, air, water and pipeline transport—reached its destination by rail. Rail links connect the resource-rich northwestern and southwestern regions with the coastal regions, which have large populations and many port cities.

In 1957 the road-railway bridge over the Yangzi River (Changjiang) at Wuhan was formally opened, linking the Beijing-Wuhan and Wuhan-Guangzhou lines and thus creating the Beijing-Guangzhou railway linking northern and southern China. In 1968 the rail section of the bridge over the Yangzi at Nanjing was opened to traffic, creating a shorter and faster railway link between Beijing and Guangzhou. The completion of the Lanzhou-Xinjiang Railway made the Lianyunkang-Urumqi line an important trunk line connecting China's eastern and western regions. Many major railroad lines cross this trunk line, so goods can be transported from Chinese ports to Xinjiang in western China and then on to Europe, a shorter route through Central Asia than the Trans-Siberian railway from China through Russia. In 1985 construction began on the Northern Xinjiang Railway from Urumqi to Ala Col; it was completed several years later.

The railroad network operated by the PRC government forms the spine of the Chinese freight system. During the 1980s much of the Chinese railroad system was improved, with the upgrading or conversion to double track of heavily used stretches and the construction of several key new lines to relieve congestion. In 1984 China's longest electrified double-track railroad, between Beijing and Datong in Shanxi Province, was opened for operation. In the period from 1980 to 1985, railroads accounted for more than two-thirds of the total ton-kilometers and more than half of the passenger-kilometers in China's transportation systems. However, the economy has been growing so rapidly that China still has a problem in providing enough rail transport to move goods between cities, and the government has continued to make the upgrading of railroads one of its main concerns.

Most Chinese locomotives used outdated and polluting coal-fueled steam engines into the 1980s, when several railroad districts converted to more modern and efficient diesel or electric locomotives, some of which were imported, although China also increased its production of locomotives. In 1993 China's railroads had a total of about 33,500 miles of common carrier lines; 33,100 miles of 1.435-meter standard gauge; 400 miles of 1.000-meter gauge; all single track except 6,950 miles of double track on standard-gauge lines; 4,000 miles electrified; and 6,200 miles of industrial lines. (Gauges range from 0.762 to 1.067 meters.) China's first subways opened in Beijing in 1970 and Tianjin in 1980, and subway systems have been under construction in Shanghai, Guangzhou and Harbin since the 1980s. By 1985 the Beijing subway carried about 280,000 passengers on an average day and 450,000 on a peak day, still only a small percent of the city's 9 million commuters. Lines were extended to accommodate the estimated 20 percent annual increase in passenger traffic. See also MANCHURIA; NANJING; PEOPLE'S REPUBLIC OF CHINA; QING DYNASTY; REPUBLIC OF CHINA; RUSSO-JAPANESE WAR OF 1904–5; SINO-JAPANESE WAR OF 1894–95; NAMES OF INDIVIDUAL CITIES AND PROVINCES.

RAILWAY PROTECTION LEAGUE See RAILROADS.

RAISE THE RED LANTERN See GONG LI; ZHANG YIMOU.

RAIZONG See ABAHAI.

RAMBUTAN See LITCHI.

RAMEN See NOODLES.

RAMIE A perennial plant of the nettle family that the Chinese cultivate to make textiles. Ramie fiber, also called China grass, is strong and flexible, has a luster and resists mildew. Textiles made from ramie take colored dyes readily and do not stretch or shrink when wet. Native to China, Japan and Malaysia, ramie was first cultivated in China around 1000

B.C. and is now grown in the provinces of Hunan, Hubei, Sichuan, Guangdong and Guizhou and in the Guangxi-Zhuang Autonomous Region. The stems of the ramie plant, from which the fiber is taken, grow three to eight feet tall. They are harvested when they turn yellow and most of the leaves have fallen off the plant. Up to four crops of ramie can be harvested each year. Ramie fiber is scraped from the stems, and then the gum, which comprises up to 30 percent of the raw fiber, is removed by various methods that heat the fiber, expose it to chemicals, crush it and finally wash and dry it. Processed ramie fibers, which are long, white and smooth, are spun into threads that can be woven into textiles for clothing, upholstery and tablecloths and napkins. Many textiles are made by combining ramie with cotton, wool or rayon threads. The Chinese also use ramie fibers to make fish nets, fish lines, paper and packing materials. See also TEXTILE INDUSTRY.

RATIONAL SCHOOL See NEO-CONFUCIANISM.

RECIPROCITY See LOYALTY.

RECORD OF RITES See BOOK OF RITES.

RECORD OF THE TRANSMISSION OF THE LAMP See BODHIDHARMA.

RECORDS OF THE HISTORIAN See BAN GU AND BAN ZHAO; SIMA QIAN.

RECTIFICATION OF NAMES (*Zheng Ming* or *Cheng Ming*) A central concept in the Confucian School of Thought, as expounded by Confucius (551–479 B.C.) in Chapter 12 of his *Analects* (*Sayings, Lunyu*). According to Confucius, the Rectification of Names should be the guiding principle for society. Everything should correspond to the name given to it, and every person should correspond to his or her name or position in life. Each name "conforms to Heaven (*Tian* or *T'ien*)," and conforming to one's name will place one in conformity with Heaven. Confucius looked back to an ideal time when rulers were really rulers, government ministers were really ministers, fathers were really fathers and sons were really sons. He taught that investigation into the nature of things will bring about a sincere will, which will lead to moral integrity, which in turn will create a well-established family and hence a well-ordered country. The final result will be peace in the world. The concept of the Rectification of Names thus has an ethical and social emphasis. Xunzi (Hsun Tzu; c. 298–238 B.C.), the most important Confucian philosopher at the close of the Warring States Period (403–221 B.C.), elaborated on this concept. Neo-Confucian philosophers such as Zhu Xi (Chu Hsi; 1130–1200) and Wang Yangming (1472–1529) strongly emphasized the unity between knowledge and actions that is the goal of the doctrine of the Rectification of Names. See also ANALECTS, CONFUCIAN; CONFUCIANISM; CONFUCIUS; HEAVEN; NEO-CONFUCIANISM; WANG YANGMING; XUNZI; ZHU XI.

RED ARMY See CHINESE COMMUNIST PARTY; CIVIL WAR BETWEEN COMMUNISTS AND NATIONALISTS; EIGHTH ROUTE ARMY; PEOPLE'S LIBERATION ARMY; WAR OF RESISTANCE AGAINST JAPAN; ZHU DE.

RED BIRD OF THE SOUTH See PHOENIX.

RED DETACHMENT OF WOMEN, THE See DRAMA; JIANG QING.

RED EGGS See BIRTHDAYS; FAMILY STRUCTURE.

RED EYEBROWS REBELLION A rebellion by a group of rebel peasant bands during the Han dynasty (206 B.C.–A.D. 220) that devastated the Han capital of Chang'an (modern Xi'an in Shaanxi Province). In A.D. 18 the Red Eyebrows (Chimei or Ch'ih-mei) led a rebellion against Wang Mang (d. A.D. 23), who had usurped the Han dynasty and set up his own Xin dynasty (A.D. 9–23). Also known as the Wang Mang Interregnum, this period divided the Han into the Western or Former Han (206 B.C.–A.D. 8) and the Eastern or Later Han dynasties (A.D. 25–220). The Red Eyebrows were a secret society based in Shandong Province that, as happened so many times throughout Chinese history, arose in response to the suffering of the peasants, caused by famine, Wang Mang's inability to redistribute land from landowners to peasants and the disastrous flooding of the Yellow River (Huanghe). The Red Eyebrows took their name from the way they made up their faces to appear like demons. Hundreds of thousands of peasants quickly joined their rebellion, and the Han nobility also joined the peasant opposition to Wang Mang. The Red Eyebrows, along with other groups such as the Green Foresters, moved into Chang'an in A.D. 23 and defeated and killed Wang Mang. They sacked the city and triggered widespread fighting among the population. In 25, Liu Xiu (Liu Hsiu), a descendant of the Han imperial family, established the Eastern Han dynasty and served as its first emperor, known by his posthumous reign name Guangwudi (Kuang Wu-ti; r. 25–57). He moved the Han capital east from the devastated city of Chang'an to Luoyang. Liu Xiu finally suppressed the Red Eyebrows and forced them to surrender in 27. See also CHANG'AN; EASTERN HAN DYNASTY; LIU XIU; PEASANTS AND PEASANT REBELLIONS; WANG MANG; YELLOW RIVER.

RED FLAG (*Hongqi*) The journal published by the Central Committee of the Chinese Communist Party (CCP). First published monthly, since December 1979 it has been published twice a month. It recently has been renamed *Seeking Truth*. *Red Flag* expresses the party's position on current political issues in light of Marxist analysis and discusses methods for carrying out the party's mandates. For important events, the editorials of the *People's Daily* (*Renmin Ribao*), the official national newspaper of the CCP, are printed jointly with *Red Flag* and the *Liberation Army Daily*, the newspaper of the People's Liberation Army. *Red Flag* supported the radical position that promoted the Cultural Revolution (1966–76) and kept China in turmoil for a decade. After the revolution, however, *Red Flag* criticized the Chinese who opposed the new government policy emphasizing incentives for peasants and workers in the countryside. See also CENTRAL COMMITTEE OF THE CHINESE COMMUNIST PARTY; PEOPLE'S DAILY; PEOPLE'S LIBERATION ARMY.

RED GUARDS Young Chinese, mainly students in their teens and 20s, who supported the left wing of the Chinese Communist Party (CCP), led by Mao Zedong (Mao Tse-tung) and Lin Biao (Lin Piao), in its political struggle against Liu Shaoqi (Liu Shao-ch'i), Deng Xiaoping (Teng Hsiao-p'ing) and their supporters in the government during the Cultural Revolution (1966–76). Students all over China were given free railroad passes, and they poured into the capital city of Beijing and other large cities to wage revolution; 11 million went to Beijing alone. Chinese institutions of higher education were closed and did not reopen until the 1970s. The Red Guards, who wore red armbands on which "Red Guard" was written, held eight massive political demonstrations in three months in Tiananmen Square in Beijing. The first demonstration, organized by Mao's wife, Jiang Qing (Chiang Ch'ing), was held on August 18, 1966. At each demonstration, Mao appeared to the Red Guards in person, wearing a red armband himself, and they spent hours shouting slogans and singing songs that praised him. At later demonstrations the Red Guards were televised all over the world waving copies of the "Little Red Book," *Quotations from Chairman Mao Zedong.*

The Red Guards served as the "soldiers" of the Cultural Revolution who opposed what its leaders called "feudalism, capitalism and revisionism" and the "Four Olds": old customs, old habits, old culture and old thinking. They expressed their revolutionary ideology and criticisms of accused reactionaries on big-character posters (*dazibao*) hung on walls in public places. The Red Guards began to vandalize bookstores, libraries, private homes, churches and other religious buildings and to forbid people to wear certain kinds of clothing and read certain types of literature. During their rampages the Red Guards physically beat and killed large numbers of people they accused of being bourgeois and burned their books, artworks and furniture.

In February 1967 the CCP ordered the Red Guards to return home, but millions continued to travel around China, visiting famous sites from the Communist revolution. Red Guards closed Chinese museums and destroyed many archaeological sites, ancient buildings and cultural artifacts all over the country. They denounced any interest in traditional Chinese culture as bourgeois and demanded that intellectuals and local CCP leaders make self-criticisms. Many intellectuals were beaten to death or committed suicide, and the rest were imprisoned or sent to the countryside to perform hard labor for 3 to 10 years. Millions of Chinese students also were sent out of the cities to work in the countryside. In August 1967 Red Guards burned down the main building of the British embassy in Beijing.

Fighting broke out among many of the factions that emerged within the Red Guards based on the schools they had attended or their parents' status, or the desire of certain Red Guards to become leaders of the revolutionary movement. Although the military had tried not to get involved and was itself divided by ideological factions, Mao finally called out the People's Liberation Army (PLA) to control the Red Guards. On July 28, 1968, Mao and other CCP leaders met with Red Guard leaders, criticized their armed struggles and abolished the Red Guards. This meeting brought the most radical phase of the Cultural Revolution to an end. However, the turmoil of the Cultural Revolution did not really end until Mao died in 1976 and the so-called Gang of Four was arrested and blamed for causing the revolution. Liu Shaoqi was treated so badly that he died in 1969, although the CCP reinstated him posthumously in 1980. Many other prominent party leaders also were attacked. See also BIG-CHARACTER POSTERS; CHINESE COMMUNIST PARTY; CULTURAL REVOLUTION; DENG XIAOPING; GANG OF FOUR; JIANG QING; LIN BIAO; LIU SHAOQI; MAO ZEDONG; QUOTATIONS FROM CHAIRMAN MAO ZEDONG; TIANANMEN SQUARE.

RED HAT SECT OF LAMAISM See DALAI LAMA; LAMAISM.

RED MEDICAL WORKERS See BAREFOOT DOCTORS.

RED PANDA See PANDA.

RED POTTERY See YANGSHAO CULTURE.

RED RIVER A river that originates in Yunnan Province in southwestern China, flows southeast for about 750 miles and becomes the main river of northern Vietnam, where it is called the Hong (formerly the Coi) River. It is known as the Yuan River (Yuanhe) in China. Iron oxides suspended in the water give the river a reddish color and its name. The river originates near Lake Erhai, on a plateau more than 6,500 feet above sea level, and cuts through Yunnan in a narrow valley with steep gorges. It flows parallel to the Mekong, Yangzi (Changjiang) and Salween Rivers, all of which originate in the mountains of eastern Tibet or in the foothills to the east, flow in parallel lines through southwestern China and then diverge to flow across China and down to Vietnam and Burma. After the Red River passes into Vietnam it receives its two principal tributaries, the Black River and the Clear River. It then flows past the city of Hanoi, opening into a wide delta that is the most fertile rice-growing region in northern Vietnam, and empties into the Gulf of Tonkin. The port city of Haiphong is located on the northern section of the delta. In China, the Bronze Age Dongson culture that has been excavated in the Red River valley in Yunnan Province dates back at least 2,500 years. See also BRONZE AGE; HIMALAYA MOUNTAIN RANGE; MEKONG RIVER; TIBET; YANGZI RIVER; YUNNAN PROVINCE.

RED SORGHUM See GONG LI; ZHANG YIMOU.

RED STAR OVER CHINA See CHINESE COMMUNIST PARTY; CIVIL WAR BETWEEN COMMUNISTS AND NATIONALISTS; MAO ZEDONG; SNOW, EDGAR.

RED TURBANS REBELLION The largest of many rebellions in the second quarter of the 14th century by the Han Chinese against the Mongols who ruled China under the Yuan dynasty (1279–1368). The Red Turbans Rebellion led to the formation of the Ming dynasty (1368–1644). By the 1340s the rebellion had spread from the middle Yangzi River region to Shandong Province in eastern China. The Red Turbans, also known as the Red Scarves, were a peasant secret society whose leaders aimed to restore the Song dynasty (960–1279), which the Mongols had overthrown. Their ideology blended elements from the cult of Maitreya, the Buddha who was predicted to come to Earth in the future in popular Buddhism; the Manichaean religion, which had entered China from Central Asia; and native Confucianism and Daoism.

The most important leader of the Red Turbans proved to be Zhu Yuanzhang (Chu Yuan-chang; 1328–99). His whole family had died of famine and disease when he was 17, after which he became a novice in a Buddhist monastery. In 1352 Zhu joined the military band led by Guo Zixing (Kuo Tzu-hsing) that was subservient to Han Liner (Han Lin-erh), the Red Turban "Little Prince of Radiance," who claimed to be restoring the Song dynasty. When Guo died in 1355, Zhu took his place and led his forces across the Yangzi River. In 1356 Zhu took the city of Nanjing and made it his military base. In 1361 Zhu took the title of duke of Wu, and in 1364 he called himself the prince of Wu, showing that he intended not only to overthrow the Mongols but to found his own dynasty. In 1363 Zhu defeated Chen Youliang (Ch'en Yu-liang; 1320–63) in a naval battle on Lake Poyang in Jiangxi Province. Chen had controlled the middle Yangzi region and was the leader of the southern half of the Red Turbans movement. After this victory, Zhu proceeded to take control of all of central China as far west as the gorges on the Yangzi and conquered all of his rivals, including Zhang Shicheng (Chang Shih-ch'eng), the most powerful one, who had his base at Suzhou. Zhu developed a bureaucratic government to administer his territory in central China. In 1367 Han Liner died of a suspicious drowning while he was in Zhu's custody. On January 23, 1368 (New Year's Day in the Chinese lunar calendar), Zhu proclaimed the Ming ("Bright" or "Radiance") dynasty, with himself as the first Ming emperor Taizu (T'ai-tsu, "Grand Ancestor"). Sometimes called the Beggar King, he reigned until 1399 and was given the posthumous reign name Hongwu (Hung-wu, "Vast Military Achievement"). He forced the Yuan emperor to leave the capital city of Beijing, thus ending the Yuan dynasty, and drove the Mongols to the Gobi Desert north of the Great Wall. The Ming dynasty lasted until 1644, when it was overthrown by the Manchus, who ruled China under the Qing dynasty (1644–1911). See also HONGWU, EMPEROR; MING DYNASTY; NANJING; POYANG, LAKE; SONG DYNASTY; YANGZI RIVER; YUAN DYNASTY.

REED PIPE See SHENG.

REFORM MOVEMENT OF 1898   Also known as the Hundred Days Reform; a series of social and institutional reforms enacted by Qing emperor Guangxu (Kuang-hsu; r. 1875–1908) during the 103 days from June 11 to September 21, 1898. Guangxu was influenced to enact the reforms of Kang Youwei (K'ang Yo-wei) and Liang Qichao (Liang Ch'i-chao), two leading scholars who had presented a memorial (petitioned) to the throne in 1895 after Japan had defeated China in the Sino-Japanese War of 1894–95. Japan had forced China to sign the Treaty of Shimonoseki, which was very unfavorable to China, but the reform leaders urged China to continue to resist Japan. They also recognized that Japan was strong because it had modernized and adopted many Western institutions, and they argued that the Chinese government also should modernize by enacting a wide range of economic, industrial and administrative reforms. Emperor Guangxu complied by issuing 40 reform decrees intended to modernize the Chinese government bureaucracy, the education and legal systems, economy and technology, and military and police systems. Many of these reforms had been advocated by scholars for decades, for example, in the Self-Strengthening Movement that developed in the 1860s. But the Reform Movement of 1898 was the first time in Chinese history that a Chinese emperor enacted a systematic body of reforms. Most of the reformers belonged to the Han, the majority ethnic group in China, who resented the Manchus, who had invaded China and founded the Qing dynasty. Conservative government officials, particularly those who were Manchu, believed that the reforms were too radical and preferred gradual change.

The main goals of the imperial edicts were to end government corruption; to revise the legal, postal and military systems, the government structure and the examination system that selected scholars for positions in the imperial bureaucracy; to modernize Chinese agriculture, mining, medicine and railroads; and to encourage the study of practical subjects such as economics rather than Neo-Confucian philosophy, the traditional subject of the imperial examinations. This angered many Confucian-trained Han members of the imperial bureaucracy. The reforms called for the establishment of Western-style schools, modern banks, a free press and a military trained by modern Western methods using modern weapons. The Qing government made plans to send Chinese students abroad to study foreign science and technology and to have direct experience of foreign political and social systems. Some reforms attempted to improve economic development by ordering local officials to coordinate reforms in commerce, manufacturing and agriculture, and to increase the production of tea and silk for export. The emperor asked the ministry of revenue to design an annual budget for the entire country. Several reform leaders, including Kang, were appointed secretaries in the Grand Council (Zongli Yamen or Tsung-li-Yamen), the government office that handled foreign affairs.

Emperor Guangxu's aunt and adoptive mother, Empress Dowager Cixi (Tz'u Hsi), exercised the real power in the Qing court. Most of the radical reforms that Guangxu decreed were not actually put into practice, as Qing officials waited to see what Cixi would do. She waited until most of the officials felt that the reforms threatened their positions. On September 14, 1898 Emperor Guangxu issued a decree stating that bannermen, members of the Manchu banner (military) system who had been supported by the Qing government, would have to earn their own living. This especially angered the Manchu members of the Qing court. Yuan Shikai (Yuan Shih-k'ai), who had been the Chinese military commander during the Sino-Japanese War, betrayed the reform movement by informing Cixi of a supposed plot to take her prisoner. On September 21 she staged a coup d'état, placed Emperor Guangxu under house arrest, executed six radical leaders and assumed the regency, which she had held while Guangxu was a minor, for the rest of her life. Kang and Liang escaped to Japan, where they founded the Protect the Emperor Society (Baohuang Hui or Pao-huang Hui), although they never achieved their goal of bringing about a constitutional monarchy in China based on that in Japan. Cixi's dramatic actions put a swift end to the Reform Movement of 1898.

The conservatives in the government supported an anti-Manchu and antiforeign secret society, the Society of Righteousness and Harmony (Yihequan), commonly known as the Boxers. In 1900 the Boxer Uprising placed the foreign legation quarters in Beijing and nearby Tianjin under siege. Foreign troops defeated them and took control of China. The empress dowager, emperor and many court members fled west to Xi'an for two years. The failure of the Reform Movement of 1898 and of the Boxer Uprising caused many Chinese to believe that a genuine revolution was necessary to remove the old imperial system and establish a new form of government. The revolutionary movement led by Dr. Sun Yat-sen gained many followers, and in 1911, three years after the death of Empress Dowager Cixi in 1908, the Chinese overthrew the Qing dynasty. In 1912 Sun established the Republic of China. See also BANNER SYSTEM; BOXER UPRISING; CIXI, EMPRESS DOWAGER; IMPERIAL EXAMINATION SYSTEM; KANG YOUWEI; LIANG QICHAO; NEO-CONFUCIANISM; QING DYNASTY; REPUBLIC OF CHINA; REVOLUTION OF 1911; SELF-STRENGTHENING MOVEMENT; SINO-JAPANESE WAR OF 1894–95; SUN YAT-SEN; YUAN SHIKAI; ZONGLI YAMEN.

REGULATED OR NEW-STYLE VERSE (shi or shih)
A form of poetry that has regular meters and lines of equal length. A shi poem consists of eight lines, all of which have either five or seven syllables. In a five-syllable poem, rhyme is used at the end of the second, fourth, sixth and eighth lines. In a seven-syllable poem, rhyme is used at the end of the first, second, fourth, sixth and eighth lines. The four lines in the middle of the poem form two antithetical couplets. These couplets may be multiplied as many times as the poet desires to form a poetic sequence known as "regulated verses in a row" (pailu or "p'ai lu). On the other hand, four lines of a regulated verse can comprise a poem in themselves, known as "stop-short lines" (juezhu or chueh chu). The shi form developed during the Tang dynasty (618–907), considered the Golden Age of Chinese poetry. Nearly all Chinese poems from that era are composed in the shi form. The greatest Tang poets include Du Fu (Tu Fu; 712–70), Li Bai (Li Po; 701–62), Bai Juyi (Po Chu-i; 772–846) and Li Shangyin (813–58). See also BAI JUYI; DU FU; LI BAI; LI SHANGYIN; TANG DYNASTY.

REHOL See CHENGDE.

RELIGION
See ANCESTOR WORSHIP; BUDDHISM; CHAN SECT OF BUDDHISM; CHRISTIANITY; CONFUCIANISM; CONFUCIUS; DALAI LAMA; DAOISM; DAOIST CLASSICAL TEXTS; FLOWER GARLAND SECT OF BUDDHISM; FUNERALS; JESUITS; JEWS; KARMA; LAMAISM; MANDALA; MANICHAEISM AND ZOROASTRIANISM; MUSLIMS; NESTORIAN CHRISTIANITY; PAGODA; PURE LAND SECT OF BUDDHISM; RICCI, MATTEO; RITES CONTROVERSY; SCULPTURE; TAI, MOUNT; TIANTAI SECT OF BUDDHISM; TEMPLE OF HEAVEN; TEMPLES; WEDDINGS, TRADITIONAL.

REN See HUMANITY.

REN BONIAN (Jen Po-nien; 1840–96)
The best-known Chinese painter during the late Qing dynasty (1644–1911). Ren was born in Zhejiang Province and moved to the port city of Shanghai, which was a major artistic center during the 19th century. There he became a leading member of the White Lotus Society of painters, specializing in decorative, richly colored bird-and-flower paintings (huaniaohua). Critics have described some of Jen's paintings as full of "ripened flavor" (shu), meaning that his brushstrokes were too per-

fect. He painted with quick, sharp strokes and developed his own unique, vigorous style. Ren was influenced both by colorful Chinese popular art and by the bold and restless energy that Western influences were bringing into Shanghai since it had become a treaty port open to foreign powers. See also BIRD-AND-FLOWER PAINTINGS; SHANGHAI; TREATY PORT.

REN YI See REN BONIAN.

RENMIN DAHUITANG (REN-MIN TA-HUI-T'ANG) See GREAT HALL OF THE PEOPLE.

RENMIN RIBAO See PEOPLE'S DAILY.

RENMINBI See CURRENCY, MODERN.

RENSHEN See GINSENG.

REPUBLIC OF CHINA (ROC)
Also known as the Nationalist or Chinese Nationalist government; the government formed by the revolutionary movement led by Dr. Sun Yat-sen (1866–1925) after it overthrew the Manchu Qing dynasty (1644–1911), China's last imperial dynasty. The ROC has been dominated by the Chinese Nationalist Party (Kuomintang; KMT), which was founded by Sun. Since 1949 the ROC has been the government on Taiwan Island, which lies 100 miles off the southeastern coast of China; mainland China has been governed by the People's Republic of China (PRC), which the Chinese Communist Party (CCP) established in 1949 after it defeated the KMT in a civil war and forced the Nationalists to flee to Taiwan. The Qing dynasty had been founded by the Manchus, an ethnic group from Manchuria (northeastern China) that had overthrown the Han Chinese Ming dynasty (1368–1644). The Han ethnic Chinese, who comprised the vast majority of the population of China, greatly resented their foreign rulers. After two centuries of expansion, in the mid-19th century the Qing empire had been seriously weakened by the Opium and Arrow wars and unequal treaties, which gave foreign powers many concessions in China, and by native Chinese uprisings such as the Taiping Rebellion (1850–64). China was defeated by Japan in the Sino-Japanese War of 1894–95 and lost control of several countries that had been vassal states under the Chinese tribute system, including Vietnam, Burma, Korea and the Ryukyu Islands (Liuqiu or Liu-ch'iu; modern Okinawa). Some Chinese officials attempted to strengthen and modernize the country, and their efforts culminated in the Reform Movement of 1898 (also known as the Hundred Days Reform), a series of social and institutional reforms enacted by Qing emperor Guangxu (Kuang Hsu; r. 1875–1908) during the 103 days from June 11 to September 21, 1898.

The Reform Movement was swiftly ended by a coup d'état led by Empress Dowager Cixi (Tz'u Hsi; 1835–1908), who exercised the real power in the Qing court. She placed Emperor Guangxu under house arrest, executed six reform leaders and assumed the regency, which she had held while Guangxu was a minor, until she died in 1908. After the emperor and empress dowager both died in 1908, Prince Chun, the emperor's father, adhered to the constitutional schedule set by the reformers, and the Qing court announced that the Chinese National Assembly would be convened in 1913, three years ahead of schedule. A young boy was placed on the throne as Qing emperor Xuantong (Hsuan-t'ung; r. 1909–11). After the Qing dynasty was overthrown, he became known by his personal name, Henry Puyi.

Many revolutionary societies had been operating in China, most based on secret societies, which for centuries had led anti-imperial peasant rebellions. The main revolutionary group at the end of the Qing was the Revolutionary Alliance (Tongmenhui or T'ung-men-hui; also known as the Revolutionary League or Alliance Society) founded in Tokyo, Japan in 1905 by Sun Yat-sen and Huang Xing (Huang Hsing) with the goal of overthrowing the Qing and establishing a modern Chinese republic. The Revolutionary Alliance was a coalition of several Chinese revolutionary groups whose members had fled to Japan or had gone there to study in Japanese universities. There were thousands of Chinese students in Japan at the time. Sun based his movement on what he termed the Three Principles of the People (San-minzhuyi or San-min-chu-i): "nationalism, democracy and people's livelihood." Sun also received a great deal of support from overseas Chinese communities in Southeast Asia, Hawaii and North and South America. Young military officers in China also supported his revolution as a way to advance their careers and to ensure that China became a strong, modern nation.

In Wuchang (later known as Wuhan) in Hubei Province, Sun's followers, who had infiltrated Qing troops stationed there, decided to stage an uprising on October 10, 1911, by attacking the governor-general's office. The ROC on Taiwan still celebrates this date as Double Tenth Day, the beginning of the Chinese revolution. The success of the Wuchang Uprising encouraged revolutionaries in other Chinese cities and provinces to take action. In some places they won military victories, and in others the governors and governors-general proclaimed their independence from the Qing and threw their support to the revolution. By the end of November 1911, 15 of the 24 Chinese provinces were independent of the Qing.

Sun had been in the United States raising funds during the Wuchang Uprising but soon returned to China. On January 1, 1912 he was inaugurated as the first president of the Provisional Government of the Chinese Republic at Nanjing on the Yangzi River (Changjiang), which had been the first capital of the Ming dynasty. Li Yuanhong (Li Yuan-hung; 1864–1928) was named vice president. Yuan Shikai (Yuan Shih-k'ai; 1859–1916), the commander-in-chief of the Qing imperial army, who had been elected prime minister by the National Assembly on November 8, 1911, held power in Beijing, the capital of the Ming and Qing dynasties. He demanded that Sun hand over the presidency of the Republic of China to him so that the country could be united under a government based in Beijing. Sun agreed to do so if Yuan could persuade the Qing emperor to abdicate. Emperor Xuantong formally abdicated the throne on February 12, 1912. He was permitted to retain his title, a stipend and his imperial residence in the Forbidden City in Beijing. Yuan was sworn in as provisional president of the Republic of China on March 10 in Beijing.

An open political party called the Chinese Nationalist Party (Kuomintang; KMT) was formed in 1912 as the successor to the Revolutionary Alliance, with Song Jiaoren (Sung Chiao-jen; 1882–1913), an associate of Sun, as its head. Elections were held in February 1913 for the new bicameral parliament. Song campaigned against the Yuan government, and his party won a majority of seats, but Yuan had Song assassinated in March 1913. Yuan dismissed government officials not loyal to him and split up the KMT. That summer seven southern Chinese provinces rebelled against Yuan but he suppressed the rebellion, and Sun and other revolutionary leaders had to flee to Japan. Yuan became a virtual dictator; he formally dissolved the KMT on January 10, 1914 and had its members removed from the National Assembly.

In 1915 Sun married Soong Qingling (Song Qingling or Soong Ch'ing-ling or Sung Ch'ing-ling; 1893–1981), who had been educated in the United States. Her wealthy father, Charles Jones Soong (1866–1918), had converted to the Methodist religion and had funded Sun's Revolutionary Alliance, and she had become Sun's personal secretary in 1913.

While in Japan, Sun planned to overthrow Yuan Shikai, but Yuan destroyed himself by attempting to establish a new dynasty with himself as emperor, and he died in 1916. Sun returned to China and settled with his wife in Shanghai, China's largest port and trading city. After Yuan died, China became divided up among a number of warlords, in what became known as the Warlord Period (1916–28). The government of China was controlled by whatever warlord controlled Beijing. In 1917 Sun went to Guangzhou in southern China and became head of a military government there that claimed to be the legal government of all China, but other leaders in the city forced him to retire and return to Shanghai.

China entered World War I on the Allied side in 1917 in hopes of getting back Shandong Province, which Germany had gained as a concession from the Qing. At the Paris Peace Conference that concluded the war, it was revealed that the Beijing government had made a secret agreement with Japan to award all of Germany's former concessions in China to Japan. The Chinese people were outraged, and Chinese students led a massive demonstration against the Beijing government and Japan, known as the May Fourth Movement of 1919. Sun did not play a leading role in the movement, but that year he and his followers reestablished the KMT to oppose the warlord government in Beijing. At the same time, a warlord sympathetic to Sun took control of Beijing.

Sun and his wife returned to Guangzhou in November 1920. He was elected president of the ROC by the extraordinary parliament there. But Sun and the warlord of Guangzhou soon clashed, and troops loyal to the warlord drove Sun out of the city. In August 1922 Sun and his wife returned to Shanghai, where he became a central figure in the negotiations by civil and military officials to reorganize the government in Beijing. The military situation in Guangzhou changed and Sun was able to return there in February 1923. Mikhail Borodin (1884–1952), a Soviet adviser, joined Sun in Guangzhou and helped him reorganize the KMT, with Sun's "Three Principles of the People" as the foundation of the party's doctrine. The U.S.S.R. had undergone its Bolshevik Revolution in 1917, and many Soviet advisers had come to China to help the Chinese Communist Party (CCP), which had been founded in Shanghai in 1921. The CCP and KMT cooperated in the early 1920s. The reorganized KMT held its first national congress in January 1924. In May 1924 the KMT and CCP established the Whampoa (Huangpu) Military Academy near Guangzhou to train military officers to lead a Northern Expedition against the warlords. Chiang Kai-shek (Jiang Jieshi; 1887–1975), one of Sun's lieutenants, was made head of the academy. Chiang became leader of the KMT after Sun died in 1925, and in 1927 he married Soong Mei-ling (Soong Mayling, Sung Mei-ling or Song Meiling; 1898–), the sister of Sun Yat-sen's wife. Their brother, T.V. Soong (Sung Tzu-wen or Song Zuwen; 1894–1971), who was educated at Harvard University, became a financial adviser to Sun and the KMT. He held a number of high positions in the ROC government and was a crucial link between ROC officials and bankers and businessmen in Shanghai.

In late 1924, following a coup in Beijing, Sun was invited to go there to help reorganize the government. He died of cancer in Beijing in 1925. Sun was buried outside the city, but his body was later moved to a splendid mausoleum built for him in Nanjing. Nationalists and Communists alike revere Sun as the founder of modern China. In 1926 Chiang Kai-shek launched the Northern Expedition, and by March 1927 his forces regained Chinese territory as far north as Shanghai and Nanjing. However, the KMT now had two centers of power. The left-wing faction, led by Wang Jingwei (Wang Ching-wei; 1883–1944), established a government at Wuhan in Hubei Province. The right wing, led by Chiang, established a national capital at Nanjing.

In April 1927 Chiang turned against the Communists and sent his troops into Shanghai to arrest and execute them. Thousands were killed, but some escaped to join Communist forces at the Soviet base in the Jinggang Mountain Range in south-central China. The CCP and KMT began fighting their civil war. The Central Committee of the KMT had not authorized Chiang's anti-Communist campaign, and the government based in Wuhan removed him as commander-in-chief. Chiang set up his own government in Nanjing, but KMT members forced him to resign, and he went into exile in Japan. Left-wing KMT members were shown evidence that convinced them that Chiang was correct that the CCP was being controlled by Moscow and that it wanted to eliminate the KMT. Wang Jingwei and his faction began purging Communists from the KMT and reunited with the right-wing faction of the KMT. They abolished the KMT government in Nanjing and moved the Wuhan government there, officially naming it the National Government of China.

In 1928 Chiang returned to China and began leading the second stage of the Northern Expedition. His troops took Beijing in June 1928, symbolically unifying all of China south of the Great Wall. On October 10, 1928 Chiang became chairman of a new Chinese Nationalist government and established his capital at Nanjing. The KMT refused to allow any other political party to have a role in the government. From then until 1949, Chiang commanded the majority vote in the standing committee of the Central Executive Committee, the most powerful body in the KMT.

However, many CCP members, and even dissident generals and KMT political leaders, continued to oppose Chiang's government. In 1930 Chiang launched the first of five annual major KMT campaigns against Communist forces in south-central China. In May 1931 KMT opposition leaders formed an alternative government in Guangzhou. On September 18, 1931 Japanese forces used the so-called Manchurian Incident as a pretext to launch a full-scale invasion of Manchuria. In 1932 the Japanese established a puppet state in Manchuria called Manchukuo (Manzhouguo or Man-chou-kuo in Chinese) and used it as their base to invade China Proper and the rest of Asia. Despite the Japanese threat, Chiang still felt it more important to eliminate the Communists, who escaped from the Nationalists on their epic Long March (1934–35) to northwestern China. Led by Mao Zedong (Mao Tse-tung; 1893–1976), the Communists made their headquarters at Yan'an in Shaanxi Province.

In December 1936, while Chiang was at Xi'an in Shaanxi, CCP and KMT leaders kidnaped him to persuade him to stop fighting the Communists and form a KMT-CCP united front to fight the Japanese; this is known as the Xi'an Incident. Chiang agreed to do so on December 25 and flew back to Nanjing. In 1937 Japanese troops took control of the North China Plain, and in August they attacked Shanghai. In November they took Nanjing and committed atrocities against hundreds of thousands of Chinese residents, known as the Rape of Nanjing. The Chinese began fighting their War of Resistance against Japan (1937–45; World War II). After Nanjing fell, the Nationalists made Hankou, situated on the Yangzi in Hubei Province, their provisional capital. The Japanese took Guangzhou on October 21, 1938 and Hankou on October 25. Chiang moved his Nationalist government to Chongqing (Chungking) in Sichuan, a province in southwestern China protected by high mountain ranges. Many Chinese universities and industries also moved there.

In December 1938 the Japanese persuaded Wang Jingwei to desert the Nationalists and join their side, and installed him as "president" in Nanjing. Wang justified his actions by asserting that China had no chance of winning against Japan and that to continue fighting was suicidal. He hoped to prevent the Japanese from treating the Chinese too harshly in the areas they controlled; this he was able to do to some extent, although the Japanese treated Wang as their puppet.

World War II broke out in Europe in September 1939 and brought China foreign allies such as Great Britain. Chinese and Japanese forces were exhausted from fighting and entered a stalemate. The United States entered the war as an official ally of China after Japan bombed the American naval fleet at Pearl Harbor on December 7, 1941. U.S. General Joseph Stilwell arrived in China in early 1942 and served as Chiang's chief-of-staff and also held several other positions, including Commanding General of U.S. forces in the China-Burma-India Theater. Many American diplomats, military advisers and academic "China experts" also worked at the U.S. Embassy in Chongqing. Chiang still opposed the Communists, but Stilwell disagreed with him and wanted to arm all Chinese forces fighting the Japanese, including the Communists. The KMT-CCP united front had started breaking down in 1941, and the two parties looked forward to resuming their civil war after the defeat of Japan.

Japan surrendered to the Allied forces on August 14, 1945, and Chiang returned his Nationalist government to Nanjing. The Americans, including U.S. ambassador Patrick J. Hurley, attempted to negotiate a postwar KMT-CCP coalition government that would rule all of China. CCP leaders Mao Zedong and Zhou Enlai (Chou Enlai; 1898–1976) met with Chiang at Chongqing for six weeks in the fall of 1945, but nothing came of their negotiations. U.S. president Harry Truman sent General of the Army George C. Marshall as his special ambassador to China with the mission of persuading the CCP and KMT to form a coalition government, but he did not succeed. He arranged a cease-fire in January 1946, but the United States continued to give the Nationalist government enormous loans. The United States also made sure that the ROC held China's seat in the newly formed United Nations and became a veto-holding permanent member of the Security Council of the UN.

On June 26, 1946, Nationalist troops waged an offensive against Communist-held areas in Hubei and Henan provinces. However, the Nationalists were not able to gain support among the Chinese people because of the rampant corruption in the government and runaway inflation, which made the Nationalist currency worthless. Many Chinese businessmen, who had been the core group supporting the Nationalist government, began leaving the country. By the end of 1947, the Americans saw that the Nationalists had no chance of winning their civil war with the Communists, and they withdrew their support for Chiang Kai-shek. The Communists had gained much support in regions the Japanese had held, especially in northern China. The PLA won major battles during which large numbers of Nationalist troops surrendered or were captured. On January 10, 1949 the PLA won its major campaign in the Huai River basin, which to all intents ended the Nationalist regime on the Chinese mainland. On January 15 the major port city of Tianjin fell to the PLA. On January 31 the PLA took Beijing without any resistance.

Chiang resigned as ROC president, and Li Zongren (Li Tsung-jen) succeeded him. Li negotiated peace with the Communists, but they demanded unconditional surrender and the punishment of Chiang and other Nationalists they deemed war criminals. The Nationalists would not agree to these demands, so the Communists resumed their offensive and moved south of the Yangzi to take Nanjing on April 23. They took Shanghai on May 27 and Guangzhou in October. In the spring of 1949, Chiang began moving Nationalist troops to Taiwan, which Japan had surrendered in 1945. Chiang had already ordered the transfer of China's gold reserve to Taiwan.

On October 1, 1949 Mao Zedong proclaimed the founding of the Communist People's Republic of China (PRC) in Beijing. The PLA took Chongqing, the wartime Nationalist capital in Sichuan, in November. Chiang fled to Taiwan from Chengdu, Sichuan on December 10, the same day that Chengdu fell to the Communists. More than 2 million Nationalists fled to Taiwan. On Taiwan, Chiang and his Nationalist supporters established the headquarters of the KMT government, which they continued to call the Republic of China (ROC) and still claimed to be the legitimate government of all of China. They proclaimed Taipei, the capital of Taiwan, to be the temporary capital of China. Since then the Communists have considered Taiwan a renegade province of China.

On March 1, 1950 Chiang resumed the ROC presidency, which he held until his death in 1975. Chiang Ching-kuo (Jiang Jingguo; 1910–88), Chiang Kai-shek's son by his first wife, became head of the military and security agencies of

the ROC government. In 1965 he became minister of national defense and commander of the ROC military. In 1972 his father appointed him prime minister. The next year Chiang Kai-shek became ill and his son became acting ROC leader. Until Chiang Ching-kuo took office, KMT officials from mainland China dominated the ROC government. Chiang enacted policies to remove corruption from the government and to bring more native-born Taiwanese (whose ancestors had earlier emigrated from mainland China) into the legislative and executive branches of the government.

After 1949 Great Britain, the U.S.S.R. and many Eastern European countries recognized the PRC, and India supported the seating of the PRC in the United Nations. The United States had withdrawn support for the Nationalist government when it fled to Taiwan, but after North Korea invaded South Korea in 1950, the United States changed its policy and provided military support to the ROC. The United States and many other countries accepted the ROC on Taiwan as the legitimate government of China and refused to give diplomatic recognition to the Communist PRC. The U.N. voted to let the ROC retain China's seat. However, in the 1970s the United States under President Richard M. Nixon reversed its policy, breaking diplomatic ties with the ROC and establishing diplomatic relations with the PRC. On October 18, 1971 the U.N. opened debate on the question of seating the PRC in place of the ROC, and on October 25 it passed a resolution to expel the ROC and give China's seat to the PRC. On January 1, 1979 the United States transferred diplomatic recognition from the ROC to the PRC. Many other countries did the same. Yet the U.S. Congress passed the Taiwan Relations Act, which supported continuing economic ties between the United States and the ROC. Chiang Ching-kuo always opposed ROC recognition of the Communist PRC and negotiations for the reunification of Taiwan with the mainland.

When Chiang Kai-shek died in 1975, Chiang Ching-kuo became interim president until March 21, 1978, when the National Assembly formally elected him to a six-year term as president. In 1984 he was elected to a second term. Under his leadership, the ROC developed economically and became very prosperous. Before Chiang died in 1988, he lifted martial law, which had been in force in Taiwan for 44 years. He also allowed an opposition political party to win seats in an open election, liberalized domestic policies and permitted citizens of the ROC to travel to the PRC. When Chiang died, he was succeeded by Lee Teng-hui (1923–   ), his chosen vice president, who continued the process of democratic reform. Lee was the first ROC president born on the island of Taiwan. In 1990 the ROC parliament opened, the first in 40 years to have elected representatives. In 1991 President Lee restored constitutional rule and opened the way for free elections.

The KMT, which remains the dominant political party of the ROC, prefers reunification with China to independence for Taiwan. However, Lee regards Taiwan as equal to the PRC and seeks a seat for Taiwan in the U.N. as a step toward bringing the two Chinas together. In 1995 the first air link between Taiwan and the PRC was initiated after 46 years. By 1995 the ROC was the world's 13th-largest trading economy and had built up $90 billion in cash reserves, second only to Japan. The ROC held elections on March 23, 1996, and President Lee easily won another term despite harassment by the PRC, which conducted military exercises in the Strait of Taiwan prior to the election. See also BEIJING; BORODIN, MIKHAIL; CHIANG CHING-KUO; CHIANG KAI-SHEK; CHINESE COMMUNIST PARTY; CHONGQING; CIVIL WAR BETWEEN COMMUNISTS AND NATIONALISTS; CIXI, EMPRESS DOWAGER; DOUBLE TENTH DAY; EIGHTH ROUTE ARMY; FLYING TIGERS; GUANGDONG PROVINCE; GUANGZHOU; HONG KONG; KOREAN WAR AND CHINA; LEE TENG-HUI; LI YUANHONG; LONG MARCH; MANCHUKUO; MANCHURIA; MANCHURIAN INCIDENT; MAO ZEDONG; MARCO POLO BRIDGE INCIDENT; MAY FOURTH MOVEMENT OF 1919; NANCHANG UPRISING; NANJING; NATIONALIST PARTY; NEW FOURTH ARMY INCIDENT; NORTHERN EXPEDITION; OVERSEAS CHINESE; PEOPLE'S LIBERATION ARMY; PEOPLE'S REPUBLIC OF CHINA; PUYI, HENRY; QING DYNASTY; REFORM MOVEMENT OF 1898; REVOLUTION OF 1911; REVOLUTIONARY ALLIANCE; RUSSO-JAPANESE WAR OF 1904–5; SHANGHAI; SINO-JAPANESE WAR OF 1894–95; SOONG MEI LING; SOONG QINGLING; STILWELL, GENERAL JOSEPH; SUN YAT-SEN; TAIWAN; THREE PRINCIPLES OF THE PEOPLE; UNITED NATIONS; WANG JINGWEI; WAR OF RESISTANCE AGAINST JAPAN; WARLORD PERIOD; WHAMPOA MILITARY ACADEMY; WORD WAR I; WUCHANG UPRISING; XI'AN INCIDENT; YAN'AN; YUAN SHIKAI; ZHANG XUELIANG; ZHOU ENLAI; ZHU DE.

RESPONSIBILITY SYSTEM   See AGRICULTURE.

RESTAURANTS AND FOOD STALLS   Places that serve a wide variety of foods ranging from multicourse banquets, to ordinary meals, to individual dishes and snacks. Chinese restaurants are typically crowded and noisy and have limited menus. Many are small, although the Chinese government operates large restaurants in many cities that seat hundreds of people at a time. Diners sit at wooden tables. Foreign tourists in China usually eat in hotel restaurants. When tourists go to large Chinese restaurants they are usually seated in private dining rooms, but they may eat in crowded public restaurants if they choose. The Chinese generally do not entertain at home but hold banquets in restaurants. The fixed meal (*feng fan; fan* is the Chinese term for both grain and a meal) is the most economical way to eat in a Chinese restaurant. An ordinary meal usually includes rice, wheat noodles or buns or other grain food, accompanied by several dishes of vegetables, seafood, poultry, meat or soybean curd prepared in a variety of ways to have different flavors and textures. Different regions have their own specialties; for example, spicy food in Sichuan and Hunan provinces, seafood in the southern city of Guangzhou (Canton), and Beijing duck in the capital city. Beer and other alcoholic beverages such as *maotai* are served during the meal, and tea is served afterward. Large Chinese cities have restaurants that serve Western-style meals, and Western-style cakes and pastries are available. Some American fast food restaurants also are becoming popular in China.

A great variety of food is available besides the large portions that are served in typical Chinese restaurants. In southern China many restaurants and teahouses serve small portions of food known as dim sum (*dianxin* or *tien-hsin*), such as steamed dumplings or steamed buns with various fillings. Around the country, some restaurants and food vendors specialize in noodles, especially large bowls of soup broth containing noodles and other ingredients, such as vegetables and meat. The Chinese people love to eat many kinds of foods bought from vendors who have stalls on the streets. In Beijing many food vendors used to do business on Menkuang Alley outside Qianmen Gate on the south side of Tiananmen Square, although they can be found all over the city, including the alleys where many people still reside. Food served at street stalls is traditionally known as teatime food, since it is consumed between the regular meals. Beijing vendors sell more than 200 varieties of snack foods. Most are made from wheat flour, although they also may include grains, beans, meat, milk, eggs and nuts. Certain foods are popular in different seasons. For example, in autumn and winter the residents of Beijing enjoy filled dumplings, glutinous millet cakes, starch sausage, jellied bean curd, baked wheat cakes, deep-fried dough cakes, deep-fried twisted dough sticks, wonton soup, chopped sheep entrails in sauce, quick-boiled tripe and roasted sweet potatoes. Other specialties include *douzhi* (*tou-chih*), a fermented drink made from ground soybeans, and *saqima* (*sa-ch'i-ma*), fried noodles coated with honey and pressed together. In the spring they enjoy pea flour cake and *aiwowo*, glutinous rice stuffed with sesame and sugar, and in the summer, a kind of firm jelly made from beans. Vendors around the country sell similar kinds of snacks, fresh and sweetened fruits and beverages that are popular in their local regions. Many kinds of prepared food can be bought to serve at home, such as roasted duck, barbecued pork ribs and sausages. See also ALLEYS; BANQUETS; COOKING, CHINESE; DIM SUM; GRAINS; MAOTAI; NOODLES; TEA.

RESTORATION OF 1917   See LIANG QICHAO; PUYI, HENRY.

REVIVE CHINA ASSOCIATION   See SUN YAT-SEN.

REVOLT OF THE THREE FEUDATORIES   See QING DYNASTY.

REVOLUTION OF 1911   A revolution led by Dr. Sun Yat-sen, the founder of modern China, which overthrew the Qing dynasty (1644–1911) and ended more than 2,000 years of imperial rule in China. The Qing had been founded by the Manchus, an ethnic group from Manchuria (modern northeastern China) that had overthrown the Han Chinese Ming dynasty (1368–1644). After two centuries of expansion, the Qing Empire had been seriously weakened in the mid-19th century by the Opium and Arrow wars and unequal treaties, which gave foreign powers many concessions in China, and by native Chinese uprisings such as the Taiping Rebellion (1850–64). China was defeated by Japan in the Sino-Japanese War of 1894–95 and lost control of several countries that had been vassal states under the Chinese tribute system, including Vietnam, Burma, Korea and the Ryukyu Islands (Liuqiu or Liu-ch'iu; modern Okinawa).

Some Chinese leaders had advocated the modernization of China through the adoption of Western science and technology, starting with the Self-Strengthening Movement in the 1860s. These efforts culminated in the Reform Movement of 1898 (also known as the Hundred Days Reform), a series of social and institutional reforms enacted by Qing emperor Guangxu (Kuang-hsu; r. 1875–1908) during the 103 days from June 11 to September 21, 1898. Guangxu issued 40 reform decrees that aimed to modernize the Chinese government bureaucracy, economy and technology, and education, legal, military and police systems. The Reform Movement was swiftly ended by a coup d'état led by Empress Dowager Cixi (Tz'u Hsi; 1835–1908), who exercised the real power in the Qing court. She placed Emperor Guangxu under house arrest, executed six reform leaders and assumed the regency, which she had held while Guangxu was a minor, until she died in 1908. Reform leaders Kang Youwei (K'ang Yo-wei) and Liang Qichao (Liang Ch'i-ch'ao) escaped to Japan, where they founded the Protect the Emperor Society (Baohuang Hui or Pao-huang Hui), with the goal of bringing about a constitutional monarchy in China similar to that in Japan.

In 1900 Beijing suffered an uprising by an anti-Manchu and antiforeign secret society, the Society of Righteous and Harmonious Fists (Yihequan or Ii-ho-ch'uan), commonly known as the Boxers. They placed under siege the foreign legation quarters in Beijing and nearby Tianjin, and a combined foreign force defeated them and took control of northern China. The empress dowager, emperor, Manchu princes and court members fled west to Xi'an in Shaanxi Province. When Cixi returned to Beijing in January 1902, she allowed many of the reforms that she had previously canceled to be reenacted as a means of preserving the Qing dynasty, which was on the verge of collapse. In 1905 the Qing abolished the Confucian-based examination system for the imperial bureaucracy, angering conservative members of the bureaucracy.

From 1906 to 1908 there were seven uprisings against the Qing in southern China. In 1907 the Qing government announced that China would have a National Assembly and assemblies at provincial and local levels. Cixi died suddenly on November 15, 1908, the day after Emperor Guangxu died, apparently poisoned by Cixi. On November 13 she had chosen her grand-nephew, who was only three years old, to succeed Guangxu. He reigned as Emperor Xuantong (Hsuan-tung; r. 1909–12; now known as Henry Puyi). In August 1908 the Qing issued a draft constitution that copied the Japanese constitution but, unlike the Japanese one, vested all power in the Chinese emperor and stated that the executive, legislature and judiciary were merely advisory bodies. The Qing planned to introduce constitutional government gradually over nine years. After the emperor and empress dowager died in 1908, Prince Chun, the emperor's father, adhered to the constitutional schedule, and the court announced that the National Assembly would be convened in 1913, three years ahead of schedule.

Numerous revolutionary societies also were operating in China, many based on secret societies, which for centuries had led Chinese peasant rebellions. The main revolutionary group was the Revolutionary Alliance (Tongmenhui or T'ung-men-hui; also known as the Revolutionary League or Alliance Society) founded in Tokyo, Japan in 1905 by Dr. Sun Yat-sen and Huang Xing (Huan Hsing) with the goal of overthrowing the Manchu Qing dynasty and establishing a modern Chinese republic. Sun had founded his first revolutionary society, the Society to Rejuvenate China, in 1894 in Hawaii. The Revolutionary Alliance, which spread its ideology through its publication *The People's Journal* (*Min Bao* or *Min Pao*), was a coalition of several Chinese revolutionary groups whose members had fled to Japan or had gone there to study in Japanese universities. There were thousands of Chinese students in Japan at the time. Sun based his movement on the Three Principles of the People (Sanminzhuyi or San-min-chu-i): "nationalism, democracy and people's livelihood." Nationalism meant overthrowing the Qing and removing all foreign control from China. Democracy referred to a popularly elected republican form of government. People's livelihood, or socialism, meant helping the common people by regulating ownership of land and means of production.

Sun's support came not only from Chinese intellectuals who had studied abroad but also from overseas Chinese communities in Southeast Asia, Hawaii and North and South America. Younger officers in the Chinese military also supported revolution as a way to advance their careers and to ensure that China became a strong, modern nation. By 1911 the Revolutionary Alliance had nearly 10,000 members, many of whom had been students in Japan and had returned to China, where they continued their revolutionary work in secret. Some were soldiers or officers in the Chinese New Army or members of the new provincial assemblies. Under Sun's leadership, there were eight attempted coups and uprisings in southern China, six in Guangdong Province, one in Jiangxi Province and one in Yunnan Province. Sun's last unsuccessful coup attempt was in spring 1911 when a group of rebels attacked the office of the governor-general of Guangzhou (Canton). His followers then moved north to Wuchang (Wuhan), the capital of Hubei Province.

The revolutionary movement gained impetus when the Qing government nationalized the railroads in 1911, which threatened the autonomy of the Chinese provinces. Students and revolutionaries held demonstrations in which they called for an end to the Manchu Qing dynasty. In Sichuan Province a general strike was called in all the railroads and industries related to their operations. This sparked a desire for rebellion in other Chinese provinces. Revolutionary groups in Shanghai and Hankou planned to hold an uprising in Hankou on October 16, but the government discovered the plot when an ammunition dump blew up. In Wuchang, Sun's followers, who had infiltrated the Manchu troops, decided to stage an uprising on October 10, 1911 by attacking the governor-general's office. This date is still celebrated by Chinese Nationalists on Taiwan as Double Tenth Day, the beginning of the Chinese revolution. The governor-general and military commander fled, and the troops forced Li Yuanhong (Li Yuan-hung) to become their commander. The success of the Wuchang Uprising encouraged revolutionaries in other Chinese cities and provinces to take action. In some places they won military victories, and in others the governors and governors-general proclaimed their independence from the Qing and threw their support to the revolution. By the end of November 1911, 15 of the 24 Chinese provinces asserted that they were independent of the Qing, although foreign powers still recognized the Qing.

Sun had been in the United States raising funds during the Wuchang Uprising. After he returned to China, he was inaugurated on January 1, 1912 as the first president of the Provisional Government of the Chinese Republic at Nanjing. This was the official end of the Qing in the international sphere. Li Yuanhong was named vice president. An open political party called the Chinese Nationalist Party (Kuomintang; KMT) was formed in 1912 as the successor to the Revolutionary Alliance. Yuan Shikai, the commander-in-chief of the Qing imperial army who had been elected prime minister by the National Assembly on November 8, 1911, held power in Beijing. He demanded that Sun hand over the presidency of the republic to him so that China could be united under a government based in Beijing. Sun agreed if Yuan could persuade the last Qing emperor to abdicate. Emperor Xuantong formally abdicated the throne on February 12, 1912. He was permitted to retain his title, his imperial residence in the Forbidden City in Beijing and an annual allowance of about $3 million to maintain his residence. He lived in seclusion in the Forbidden City until a warlord forced him to leave in 1924; he then went to his father's home in Tianjin. The Japanese, who invaded Manchuria (northeastern China) in 1931, established the puppet state of Manchukuo in 1932 and made Puyi its head. Yuan was sworn in as provisional president of the Republic of China on March 10, 1912 in Beijing. See also BEIJING; DOUBLE TENTH FESTIVAL; EMPEROR; FORBIDDEN CITY; KANG YOUWEI; LI YUANHONG; LIANG QICHAO; NATIONALIST PARTY; OVERSEAS CHINESE; PUYI, HENRY; QING DYNASTY; REFORM MOVEMENT OF 1898; REPUBLIC OF CHINA; REVOLUTIONARY ALLIANCE; SUN YAT-SEN; WUCHANG UPRISING; YUAN SHIKAI.

REVOLUTIONARY ALLIANCE (Tongmenghui or T'ung-meng-hui)

The Chinese revolutionary party founded in Tokyo, Japan in 1905 by Dr. Sun Yat-sen (1866–1925) with the goal of overthrowing the Manchu Qing dynasty that had ruled China since 1644; also known as the Revolutionary League or Alliance Society. The alliance spread its ideology through its publication, *The People's Journal* (*Min Bao* or *Min Pao*). It was a coalition of several Chinese revolutionary groups whose members had fled to Japan or had gone there to study in Japanese universities. In fact, there were thousands of Chinese students in Japan at the time. Sun Yat-sen, who had also studied in Europe, openly advocated revolutionary military activism to overthrow the Qing dynasty and establish a modern Chinese republic. He had many supporters who belonged to secret societies in southern China and Hawaii, where he spent part of his youth and had been inducted into the local branch of a Chinese secret society, the Triad Society. His supporters also included overseas Chinese in Singapore and North America. Sun sold bonds to supporters of the regime he hoped to establish in China, promising a tenfold return on their purchase price when his political goals were attained. Many young Chinese women were members of the alliance, and they were going against Chinese tradition by seeking a higher education and refusing to bind their feet. By 1911 the Revolutionary Alliance had nearly 10,000 members, many of whom had been students in Japan and had returned to China, where they continued their revolutionary work in secret. Some were soldiers or officers in the Chinese New Army or members of the new provincial assemblies. Their activities instigated at least seven uprisings against the Qing dynasty and culminated in the Wuchang Uprising of October 10, 1911 that began the Republican Revolution of 1911. Leaders of the Revolutionary Alliance played a prominent role in establishing the Provisional Republican Government in Nanjing on January 12, 1912 with Sun Yat-sen as provisional president.

After the Qing emperor was forced to abdicate the throne on February 12, 1912, several other political parties joined with the Revolutionary Alliance to form the Nationalist (Kuomintang; KMT) Party, the precursor of the Chinese Nationalist Party (Chung-kuo Kuomintang). See also NATIONALIST PARTY; QING DYNASTY; REPUBLIC OF CHINA; SUN YAT-SEN; WUCHANG UPRISING.

RHODODENDRON

With 600 species native to China, this popular flowering shrub is now widely cultivated in the West, including plants known as azaleas. The rhododendron grows at high altitudes in mountainous regions in China, especially in the provinces of Yunnan, Sichuan, Qinghai, Jiangxi, Guizhou, Fujian, Guangdong and Liaoning, and on the island of Taiwan. Most of the native Chinese species can be found in the Hengduan Mountain Range in Sichuan and Yunnan in western China, where they dominate the landscape at 11,000 feet or more above sea level. Larger species of rhododendrons grow about 33 feet high; shorter ones grow as bushes or cling vinelike to the trunks of spruce and fir trees. The delicate cupped flowers bloom in clusters and may be red, pink, white, purple or yellow. In the spring the blooming rhododendrons carpet the Chinese mountains with vivid colors.

RHYME-PROSE STYLE OF VERSE (*fu*)

A form of poetic literature that was created by Qu Yuan (Ch'u Yuan; c. 343–278 B.C.), the first major Chinese poet, and became fully developed during the Han dynasty (206 B.C.–A.D. 220). Qu Yuan's most famous poem, "On Encountering Sorrow" (*Lisao*), tells how he, who had served his king loyally but became estranged from him, traveled through a world of spirits in a flying chariot. The poem is an allegory that associates beautiful women and flowers with the good qualities of particular government officials. During the Western Han dynasty (206 B.C.–A.D. 8), *fu* poems were written in the imperial courts for the emperor and the imperial princes. *Fu*, which became the preferred literary form during the Han, is completely rhymed and has a regular meter, although the Chinese always have considered it closer to prose than to poetry. They contrast the *fu* with the poetic form known as regulated or new-style verse (*shi* or *shih*), which also developed during the Han. The term *shi* was first used for the songs in the classical text *Book of Songs* (*Shijing* or *Shih-ching*) and refers to verses that could be sung. *Fu* poems are never sung. They comprise a longer and more intricate poetic form than *shi*, and writing rhapsodic *fu* verses presented an exhausting challenge to a Chinese poet. A *fu* poem could be on any subject and of any length. The greatest *fu* poet of the Han dynasty was Sima Xiangru (Ssu-ma Hsiang-ju; d. 117 B.C.). Zhang Heng (Chang Heng; A.D. 78–139) was another accomplished *fu* poet during the Han, as well as a versatile scholar and scientist who invented a seismograph to register earthquakes. The poet Lu Ji (Lu Chi; 261–303) even composed a work of literary criticism that is itself written in the *fu* form. See also HAN DYNASTY; LU JI; LYRIC VERSE; QU YUAN; REGULATED OR NEW-STYLE VERSE; SIMA XIANGRU; ZHANG HENG.

RICCI, MATTEO (1552–1610)

The first Roman Catholic Jesuit priest to establish a mission in China, and who was followed there by a number of Jesuits who gained some influence with the Chinese government. Ricci spent much of his life in China, introducing the Christian religion and Western knowledge to the Chinese and acquiring knowledge about Chinese religion, science and government.

Ricci was born in 1552 in Macerata, Italy and went to Rome in 1568 to study law. He became a novice in the Society of Jesus (Jesuits) in 1571 and studied at Jesuit colleges in Florence and Rome. In 1577 he traveled to Portugal to study Portuguese, and the next year he sailed to Goa, a Portuguese colony in southern India. He also lived in Cochin and Malacca (Malaysia) before arriving in Macao, a Portuguese colony on an island next to Hong Kong just south of Guangzhou (Canton), in 1582. The Portuguese were the first Europeans to establish systematic diplomatic and trading relations with China. Ricci arrived in China in 1583 but was not introduced at the imperial court in Beijing by the eunuchs who controlled the Chinese government until 1598. He impressed Emperor Wanli (r. 1572–1620) and senior government officials, and in 1601 he was given permission to reside in Beijing with an imperial stipend as a Western scholar. Ricci was skilled in drawing maps and fixing clocks, and the gifts he had presented the emperor included two clocks and a world atlas, so he was named science tutor to the emperor's son.

Ricci took the Chinese name Li Madou (Li Ma-tou). He learned the Chinese language, developed his own system for romanizing Chinese and compiled a dictionary. He wrote a book in Chinese, *The True Meaning of the Lord of Heaven*, with the assistance of Chinese literati, members of the scholar class who governed China in the imperial bureaucracy, in which he explained the basic concepts of the Christian religion. He drew upon concepts of the great Chinese thinker Confucius, whose thought had become the orthodox Chinese philosophy. Ricci used the concept of "self-cultivation," the central principle in Confucianism, to explain how the "superior man" can cultivate himself by worshiping God, the Lord of Heaven. He also appealed to Confucian scholars by quoting from the classic Confucian texts and by criticizing the native Chinese Daoist religion and the Buddhist religion, which had been introduced into China from India and were not favored by the literati. Ricci's book remained in print in numerous editions in China continuously until the 1940s and was translated into English. Although a Christian missionary, Ricci wore the clothing of the literati and accepted Chinese religious practices such as so-called ancestor worship, the propitiation of deceased relatives. Ricci made few converts but sent positive reports about China back to the West. He also kept a detailed diary that has provided important information about China during the Ming dynasty (1368–1644) and influenced Western thinkers such as Leibniz and Voltaire. Jesuits were highly trained in philosophy, mathematics and science, and Ricci's Jesuit successors in China were given charge of the Bureau of Astronomy that determined the official annual calendar. Ricci was buried outside Fucheng Gate in Beijing by imperial order. The memorial tablet marking his tomb can still be seen. See also ANCESTOR WORSHIP; CONFUCIANISM; IMPERIAL BUREAUCRACY; JESUITS; LITERATI; MING DYNASTY; PORTUGUESE; SUPERIOR MAN.

RICE (*dao* or *tao*)   A grain that is the staple food for most Chinese, especially in central and southern China. Wheat and other grains such as millet and sorghum are the staple food in the dry regions of northern China. The Chinese differentiate between rice and other grain foods—such as noodles, dumplings and steamed bread—all of which they call *fan;* and vegetable and meat dishes prepared to accompany *fan,* which they call *cai* (*ts'ai*). A balanced meal requires a proper amount of both *fan* and *cai* dishes. *Fan* is served separately to each diner, while *cai* dishes are placed in the center of the table for everyone to share. A rice cooker (*fan kuo*) is used only to prepare rice, while *cai* dishes are cooked in a wok (*caiguo* or *ts'ai kuo*). Chinese children are praised for being able to eat larger amounts of *fan* than *cai* dishes. Chinese people commonly greet each other with the question "Have you eaten *fan?*" The Chinese prefer short-grain rice, which absorbs less water and is softer after cooking than long-grain rice. They prepare rice in three ways. First is a congee, a soupy dish in which rice is cooked in a large amount of water for several hours and consumed with salted eggs or other flavorful foods, such as morsels of chicken, pork, beef or fish. Congee is eaten for breakfast and late-night snacks. The second way of cooking rice is to boil it in a lesser amount of water and to add other ingredients to make a thicker soup. The third method is to boil or steam the rice in a large covered pot with less water until all the moisture has evaporated and the rice grains have become fluffy and just soft enough to eat from a bowl with chopsticks. Today rice can be cooked and kept hot all day in automatic electric rice cookers. Short-grained glutinous rice with a sweet flavor, often called sticky rice, is a main ingredient in fillings and desserts and in alcoholic beverages. Cooked glutinous rice is pounded to a paste to make special rice cakes for the New Year and other festivals. Rice is also processed into thin noodles, which are sold dry and cooked like spaghetti.

Rice has been cultivated in the hot, humid climate of central and southern China for thousands of years. In 1978 archaeologists discovered rice remains at Hemudu, south of Hangzhou Bay in Zhejiang Province, which have been dated to about 4000 B.C. Although varieties of rice are grown in dry conditions, most Chinese rice is grown in flooded fields known as paddies, which the Chinese call *shuitian* (*shui-t'ien*), "water fields." Wet-grown rice produces more calories per acre than any other crop with a high nutritional value, and it can sustain large population growth such as China has experienced. China is in fact the world's largest producer of rice.

By the first or second century B.C., the southern Chinese had learned that they could gain a higher yield in their rice crops by sowing rice in seed beds and then transplanting the seedlings to paddies. They also learned to use irrigation pools for raising ducks and growing water chestnuts, beans and cucumbers. Mulberry trees were grown along the banks of irrigation channels to provide leaves for silkworms to eat. The Chinese emperors built a system of canals, notably the Grand Canal, beginning in the Sui dynasty (581–618), to provide water for the irrigation channels. Rice stored in huge granaries along the canals was transported from the south by barges to large cities. Large shipments of rice were used to pay taxes to the imperial government.

By the Song dynasty (960–1279), the largest rice-producing areas were the Yangzi River delta, the river valleys in Jiangsu and Hunan provinces, the Sichuan Basin and the Pearl River area in Guangdong Province. During this time a strain of rice was imported from Champa (modern Vietnam and Cambodia) that matured in 100 days. By the 12th century, Chinese farmers had developed rice strains that matured in just 60 days, which greatly increased rice production. Rice cultivation by double-cropping (growing two crops in one year) spread throughout Hubei and Hunan provinces, which have remained important centers of rice cultivation. During the 18th century, Chinese farmers developed rice strains that required only 40 days for cultivation. Today Jiangsu and Zhejiang Provinces are called "the rice bowl of China."

Many Chinese proverbs have to do with rice. "Even a clever daughter-in-law can't cook without rice" is similar to the American proverb, "You can't make something out of nothing." "The rice has been cooked" refers to a decision that cannot be changed, just as cooked rice cannot be returned to its uncooked state. "Drawing pictures of rice cakes won't stop hunger" means that a person has to perform hard work to acquire the necessities of life. "If you eat his rice, you must obey him" means that you have to obey your boss's orders. "Every ladle strikes the edge of the rice pot once in a while" means that every family is bound to have disagreements. The Chinese consider it very unlucky to knock over a container of rice. See also ALCOHOLIC BEVERAGES; BANQUETS; CHOPSTICKS; COOKING, CHINESE; GRAINS; GRAND CANAL; WOK.

RICHARD, TIMOTHY See CHRISTIANITY.

RICKSHAW BOY See LAO SHE; LING ZIFENG.

RIGHTEOUS AND HARMONIOUS MILITIA See BOXER UPRISING.

RIGHTEOUSNESS (*yi*)   A concept added to the teachings of Confucius (551–479 B.C.) by Mencius (Mengzi or Meng Tzu; c. 372–289 B.C.), the second most important Confucian thinker. Righteousness, also translated as "propriety" or "duty," means loving other people according to one's relationship with them. According to Mencius, righteousness includes a strong sense of duty and commitment to fulfilling one's obligation to another person. Mencius was responding to Mozi (Mo Tzu; c. 470–391 B.C.), another major Chinese thinker, who argued that one should love all people equally. According to Mencius, this was not possible because each person's position in the social hierarchy determines the way that one should love that person and perform duties owed to him or her. The principle of righteousness was also espoused by the Neo-Confucian philosopher Zhu Xi (Chu Hsi; 1130–1200). He argued that the basic Confucian principles, including righteousness, humanity (also translated as benevolence; *ren* or *jen*), propriety (*li*) and wisdom (*zhi* or *chih*), are rooted in the mind, which includes a person's nature and feelings. For Zhu Xi, righteousness and wisdom are expressions of humanity, which is the primary Confucian concept. Zhu Xi agreed with Mencius that the mind is what distinguishes human beings from animals. These thinkers also agreed, as did most Confucianists, that human nature is basically good and that this goodness can be cultivated in a person. See also CONFUCIUS; HUMANITY; MENCIUS; NEO-CONFUCIANISM; PROPRIETY; WISDOM; ZHU XI.

RITES CONTROVERSY   A religious controversy that developed in the Roman Catholic Church in the 17th and 18th centuries over the tolerance of traditional Chinese practices by missionaries of the Jesuit order (Society of Jesus) in China. The Jesuits had gained positions of influence in the Ming Chinese court, starting with Matteo Ricci (1552–1610), who received permission to stay in the capital of Beijing in 1602. He and later Jesuits were learned in mathematics, astronomy, physics and geography, and they were accepted by the Ming emperors as equivalent to the Confucian-educated literati, or scholars, who staffed the imperial bureaucracy. Among other positions, Jesuits were appointed to staff the Chinese Bureau of Astronomy. When the Manchus overthrew the Ming and established the Qing dynasty (1644–1911), Ricci's successor, Adam Schall von Bell (1591–1666), was accepted by the new Qing emperor and became president of the Board for Calendar Regulation in 1645. The Kangxi Emperor (r. 1661–1722) respected Schall's fellow Jesuit, Ferdinand Verbiest (1617–88), and the emperor permitted the Jesuits to ordain the first Chinese Catholic bishop. When Kangxi issued an imperial edict tolerating the Christian religion in 1692, the Dominican and Franciscan orders began to send missionaries to China, who worked with the poor people rather than with scholars. They discovered that the Jesuits had decided that the Chinese practice of ancestor worship and other traditional rites, such as ceremonies to honor Confucius, did not conflict with the Christian religion. They were jealous of the Jesuit success in China, which they felt the Jesuits had achieved by being too tolerant of "pagan" practices. Their opposition to the Jesuits resulted in a controversy known as the Rites Controversy.

The Rites Controversy raged among the rival orders between 1693 and 1705. The Dominicans and Franciscans appealed to Pope Clement I in Rome to decide which position was correct. In 1704 he ruled against the Jesuits. Kangxi immediately banished all Catholic missionaries who did not accept Matteo Ricci's tolerant position on Chinese practices. In 1705 the Pope sent Cardinal Tournon as papal legate to Beijing to forbid Chinese Christian converts from practicing their traditional rituals. This further angered the Kangxi Emperor, who supported the Jesuits and did not want his subjects to have to take orders from the Pope in Rome, and he expelled the legate. The Pope issued a bull (edict) against Jesuit practices in China and sent another legate to Beijing in 1715.

Missionaries belonging to other Catholic orders continued to work in China. The Jesuits retained their positions as court astronomers and mathematicians, but the Rites Controversy caused the Catholic Church to decline in China. The Pope issued another anti-Jesuit bull in 1742 and dissolved the Jesuit order in China in 1773, although Jesuits continued to work there. The most serious result was that the Chinese literati distanced themselves from the Roman

Catholic Church, whose missionaries could then work only among poor and uneducated Chinese. In 1939 the papacy reversed its prohibition against Chinese ancestor worship and ceremonies to honor Confucius. See also ANCESTOR WORSHIP; ASTRONOMY AND OBSERVATORIES; CONFUCIANISM; IMPERIAL BUREAUCRACY; JESUITS; KANGXI, EMPEROR; LITERATI; MISSIONARIES; RICCI, MATTEO.

RITTENBERG, SIDNEY An American who joined the Communist cause in China and became the highest-ranking foreigner in the Chinese Communist Party (CCP), which founded the People's Republic of China (PRC) in 1949. Rittenberg was born to a wealthy family in Charleston, South Carolina. He attended the University of North Carolina, where he joined the Communist Party in 1940, which he admired for its advocacy of civil rights and its antiwar position. He worked for the party, organizing coal miners and workers in the textile and steel industries and attempting to improve the condition of black people in the South. In 1942, after the United States had entered World War II following the Japanese bombing of Pearl Harbor, Rittenberg was drafted into the U.S. Army. He was taught the Chinese language and sent to Kunming in the southwestern Chinese province of Yunnan, where he served as an interpreter in the judge advocate's office. China had been fighting its War of Resistance against Japan since 1937. The poverty of the Chinese people made Rittenberg decide to stay in China after the war to work for the United Nations Relief and Rehabilitation Administration. He believed that the CCP, in contrast to the corrupt Chinese Nationalist Party (Kuomintang; KMT) led by Chiang Kai-shek, was succeeding in helping the Chinese, who had suffered from nearly a century of warfare.

Rittenberg traveled to Yan'an in the province of Shaanxi, where CCP leaders had made their headquarters after they fled west on the Long March in 1934–35 to escape the Nationalists. He joined the CCP and became an adviser to the party's English-language broadcast news service. Many Soviet Communists had come from the U.S.S.R. to help the CCP, and in 1949, the year that the CCP defeated the KMT and founded the PRC, Soviet leader Joseph Stalin ordered the CCP to arrest Rittenberg as an American spy. While he was kept in solitary confinement for five years, he studied the classical Chinese language and the works of CCP chairman Mao Zedong (Mao Tse-tung). In 1955 the party released him and admitted that it had made a mistake in imprisoning him. Nevertheless, Rittenberg still believed in Chinese Communism and decided to remain in China with other foreigners who had gone there because they believed that the Communists were creating a new society. The CCP always treated those foreigners as outsiders; Rittenberg, who went along with party orders to condemn Chinese intellectuals in the Anti-Rightist Campaign of 1957–59, rose to high levels in the party bureaucracy. In 1955 Rittenberg had joined the CCP broadcast administration in Beijing and was given access to classified cables read only by top party officials. In 1963–64, just prior to the Cultural Revolution (1966–76), he was the only foreigner given party clearance to make English translations of the polemics issued by the CCP, which was engaged in an ideological struggle with the U.S.S.R. He also had married a Chinese woman named Yulin.

When Mao inaugurated the Cultural Revolution in 1966 to purify the party of its counterrevolutionary tendencies, Rittenberg supported Mao, even criticizing his own actions and volunteering to do physical labor. He led the purge of the people he worked with in the broadcast administration and then joined the radical faction led by Jiang Qing (Chiang Ch'ing), Mao's wife, to purge the people he had helped put in power. In February 1967 Rittenberg was appointed head of the broadcast administration. The Cultural Revolution became so disruptive that Chinese schools were closed and tens of thousands of students were sent from the cities to work in the countryside. Red Guards roamed the country, attacking people and destroying cultural sites and artifacts. The CCP fell into factions, one led by Mao and Lin Biao (Lin Piao) and supported by the People's Liberation Army (PLA), and the other led by Liu Shaoqi (Liu Shao-ch'i) and Deng Xiaoping (Teng Hsiao-p'ing). Mao turned on many people within the party. Rittenberg was arrested on Christmas Day 1967 and made a scapegoat for the turmoil that had been unleashed. He was kept in solitary confinement until his release in 1977. Mao had died in September 1976, and a month later Jiang Qing and some other CCP leaders had been arrested and accused of being responsible for the Cultural Revolution. Rittenberg's wife and children told him about the horrors that had occurred in China while he was in prison, but at first he refused to believe them or to criticize Mao. After a few years of critical reflection, Rittenberg finally questioned not only Mao but also the communist ideas of Marx and Lenin, and in 1980 he brought his family to the United States. Yet he continued to believe that the CCP had done much to improve the feudal conditions under which the Chinese people had suffered, despite the terrible famine-causing failure of the Great Leap Forward in the 1950s and the anarchy of the Cultural Revolution. In 1993 Rittenberg published his autobiography, titled *The Man Who Stayed Behind*. See also CHINESE COMMUNIST PARTY; CIVIL WAR BETWEEN COMMUNISTS AND NATIONALISTS; CULTURAL REVOLUTION; GANG OF FOUR; JIANG QING; KUNMING; MAO ZEDONG; NATIONALIST PARTY; PEOPLE'S REPUBLIC OF CHINA; YAN'AN.

RITUAL, THE See BOOK OF RITES.

RIVER DOLPHIN, CHINESE A mammal that lives in water and is indigenous to China; also known as the whitefin dolphin (Latin name *Lipotes vexillifer*). The Chinese river dolphin is one of the world's four rare species of freshwater dolphins. It lives only in a few sections of the middle and lower reaches of the Yangzi River (Changjiang), China's longest river, and is the only aquatic animal powerful enough to live in the surging Yangzi waters. An endangered species, it is even rarer than the Giant Panda. In 1990 there were only 200 to 300 river dolphins in China. Recently the Chinese have been attempting to save the species, which is vulnerable to water pollution, fishing and ship propellors. In 1987 a breeding center was established in Anhui Province and a reserve area was defined in the Yangzi. The Institute of Aquatic Organisms at Wuhan has been attempting to breed river dolphins in captivity.

They usually mate and travel together in pairs. The Chinese river dolphin weighs 220 pounds or more. It has a fish-shaped body without gills; a long, flat snout, or "beak"; and a domed head with a small blowhole on top and very small eyes on both sides. The eyes have degenerated because of its long existence in the silt-filled Yangzi water. It swallows its food whole without chewing, although it has sharp teeth, and it breathes with lungs. The river dolphin evolved from a land mammal that, because of changes in land conditions, adapted to life in the water about 20 million years ago. Its forelimbs modified into dorsal fins and its hind limbs degenerated and merged to form a tail. It surfaces to breathe every few dozen seconds, but it remains underwater for several minutes when it is startled. The river dolphin has a large, complex brain and a highly developed sonar system, which it uses to locate food, underwater objects and potential predators. It is very sensitive to weather changes, and if it appears frequently on the surface of the water, a rainstorm is imminent. Chinese fishermen used to believe that it was a "sacred fish" that could summon wind and rain. See also PANDA; YANGZI RIVER.

RMB See CURRENCY, MODERN.

ROBES See EMBROIDERY; NINE-RANK SYSTEM; SILK.

ROC See REPUBLIC OF CHINA.

ROCKETS See SPACE INDUSTRY.

ROCKS (*panshi* or *p'an-shih*)   Important elements in traditional Chinese gardens. Large rocks with unusual shapes symbolizing mountains often are placed in Chinese gardens, which are designed to create a replica of the natural world in the courtyard inside a walled compound. Chinese gardens and landscape painting are both known primarily for combining "mountains and water" (*shanshui*), the literal name for Chinese landscape painting. In traditional Chinese thought, rocks symbolize the yang principle, which is masculine, positive, hard and unyielding. Water symbolizes the yin principle, which is feminine, negative, soft and yielding. The poetic Chinese term for creating a garden is "piling up rocks." The painter Shitao (Shih T'ao, also known as Daoji or Tao-chi; 1641–c. 1710) became famous for his technique of depicting rocky mountains with exaggerated brushstrokes; eventually he retired from painting and turned to designing gardens. In a Chinese garden, scenic views are created by placing many rocks together to construct artificial mountain peaks, caves and overhanging cliffs. A single large rock, known as a "strange" or "fantastic" rock (*qishi* or *ch'i shih*) or a *taihu* (great) rock, also can be displayed as a decorative object to set off its uniqueness or to enhance the view. Such a rock can be placed in the middle of a courtyard, facing a doorway or window or circular opening known as a "moon gate," at a bend in the garden path or in the middle of a pond. Climbing plants usually are placed next to rocks to represent vines that grow on mountain cliffs.

In China, great value is placed on unusually shaped rocks, or taihu *rocks, often displayed in gardens to symbolize strength.*   S.E. MEYER

The use of rocks to represent mountain peaks dates back to the Tang dynasty (618–907). Each time he was dismissed from an official government post, the poet and social critic Bai Juyi (Po Chu-i; 772–846) brought back a rock from the place and stood it in his garden to make a political statement. Numerous rocks were brought from distant regions at great hardship for placement in the famous Gen Yu palace garden constructed during the Northern Song dynasty (960–1127). A manual for garden design written during the Ming dynasty (1368–1644) asserts that "A single rock may evoke many feelings." During the Qing dynasty (1644–1911), four aesthetic qualities were established for choosing a rock for a garden, including perforation (*lou*), slimness (*shou*), transparency (*tou* or *t'ou*) and corrugation (*zhou* or *chou*). The Liu Garden in Suzhou, a city famous for its gardens, contained 12 rocks forming mountain "peaks" that were taken from the region of Lake Tai (Taihu), the derivation of the name *taihu* rock. Three of the original 12 rocks remain in the Liu Garden today, the largest of the many beautiful *taihu* rocks in Suzhou gardens. The Chinese also created the related art of miniature gardens formed by arranging small stones and plants on trays, known as "tray scenery," a variation of container gardens (known in the West by the Japanese term *bonsai*). See also ALLEYS; BAI JUYI; CONTAINER GARDENS; GARDENS; LANDSCAPE PAINTING; SHI-TAO; SUZHOU; TAI, LAKE.

ROMAN CATHOLICISM See CHRISTIANITY; JESUITS; RICCI, MATTEO; RITES CONTROVERSY.

ROMAN EMPIRE See BAN CHAO; SILK ROAD.

ROMANCE OF THE THREE KINGDOMS (*Sanguozhi yanyi* or *San-kuo-chih yen-i*) An epic historical novel attributed to the dramatist Luo Guanzhong (Lo Kuan-chung; c. 1330–c. 1400), about whom no personal details are known. The novel's description of a "broken empire" refers to the breaking up by civil war of the Later Han dynasty into the so-called Three Kingdoms (220–80), the Wei, Shu and Wu. Although the government record from the late third century proclaimed the legitimacy of the kingdom of Wei, the folktales that later developed around the story became more partial to the kingdom of Shu. *The Romance of the Three Kingdoms* is based on narratives compiled in the Song dynasty (960–1279) that derive from earlier legends about the events in a 97-year period, from the so-called Peach Garden oath of loyalty in 184 that began the Yellow Turbans Rebellion (184–96), to the fall of the kingdom of Wu (280). The novel was written in the late Yuan dynasty (1279–1368) or early Ming dynasty (1368–1644) and was revised into its final and well-known form, containing 120 chapters, by Mao Zonggang (Mo Tsung-kang) in the late 17th century (Qing dynasty, 1644–1911).

The novel belongs to the category of Chinese popular literature during the Ming and Qing dynasties called Ming-Qing novels and is considered one of the Four Great Novels in China, along with *Journey to the West*, *The Golden Lotus* and *Outlaws of the Marsh*. About two-thirds of the episodes in *The Romance of the Three Kingdoms* are historical fact, and one-third are fiction but seem to be factual. The earliest surviving edition was written in 1494 and has 24 books and 242 chapters. The main characters in the novel, historical figures whose lives have been aggrandized with legendary traits and adventures, are some of the most beloved heroes in Chinese culture. Episodes of the novel have been adapted into numerous dramas and operas.

In the novel Liu Bei (Liu Pei), who rules the Kingdom of Shu (221–263), takes the "Peach Orchard" oath of loyalty with Guan Yu (Kuan Yu) and Zhang Fei (Chang Fei). They swear to be blood brothers and to defend each other even to their deaths. Guan Yu, a cunning general who fought for both the kingdoms of Wei and Shu, came to be worshiped in China as the god of war, Guandi (Kuan Ti). Zhuge Liang (Chu-ko Liang) is the prime minister of the kingdom of Shu. His brilliant strategies enable Shu to defend itself against Cao Cao (Ts'ao Ts'ao; 155–220), the general of the kingdom of Wei, Shu's principal enemy. Wei was situated to the north and east of the Yangzi River (Changjiang). The kingdom of Shu was to the southwest and included the modern province of Sichuan. The third kingdom, Wu, extended south of the Yangzi. The novel describes the conflict between Shu and Wei, culminating in one of the most famous battles in Chinese history. Cao Cao, who had founded the state of Wei (220–65) with its capital at Luoyang and defeated many warlords until he brought all of northern China under his control, attempted to conquer southern and southwestern China as well. In 208 he faced the southern army led by Zhuge Liang, the final block to his unification of China. The southern generals were able to outmaneuver Cao Cao and force him to fight a naval battle, in which he was less experienced, at Chibi on the Yangzi River in modern Anhui Province. The southerners soundly defeated Cao Cao's forces, and for the time being he had to give up his campaign to unify China. See also CAO CAO; GOLDEN LOTUS; GUANDI; HAN DYNASTY; JOURNEY TO THE WEST; OUTLAWS OF THE MARSH; THREE KINGDOMS PERIOD; YANGZI RIVER; YELLOW TURBANS REBELLION.

ROMANCE OF THE WESTERN CHAMBER See WANG SHIFU.

ROMANIZATION OF THE CHINESE LANGUAGE See PINYIN SYSTEM OF ROMANIZATION; WADE-GILES SYSTEM OF ROMANIZATION.

RONG YIREN (Jung Yi-jen; 1916–) The founder and chairman from 1979 to the present of the China International Trust and Investment Corporation (CITIC), which promotes and assists foreign investment in China. Rong is one of seven sons born to a wealthy family in Jiangsu Province that owned textile, flour and banking businesses. He received a degree from the British St. John's University in Shanghai. Before the Chinese Communist Party (CCP) founded the People's Republic of China (PRC) in 1949, Rong had managed 24 factories in the textile, printing and dyeing, machinery and flour industries. He remained in Shanghai when the Communists took over the country, while four of his brothers fled the country. The Communists asked Rong and other capitalists to help them rebuild the Chinese economy, which had been devastated by decades of war. Rong served as deputy director of Sangsong Cotton Mills and Fuxin Flour Company, both owned by his family.

From 1950 to 1954 he served as a member of the Finance and Economic Affairs Committee of the East China Military and Administrative Council (called the Administrative Council after 1952). In 1950 he was also elected a member of the Shanghai People's Government Council (called the Shanghai People's Council after 1955). In 1952 he was appointed director of the Sangsong Cotton Mills Administrative Council. In 1954 Rong was elected vice chairman of the Shanghai Federation of Industry and Commerce. He served as a Shanghai deputy to the National People's Congresses (NPC) from 1954 until the Cultural Revolution (1966–76) and as vice minister of the textile industry from 1959 until the Cultural Revolution. In 1957 he was appointed a deputy mayor of Shanghai. Rong was a member of the Standing Committee of the Chinese People's Political Consultative Conference (CPPCC) from 1959 to the Cultural Revolution and from 1972 to 1983. During the Cultural Revolution he was beaten by Red Guards and forced to spend seven years performing menial labor.

When China began modernizing after the disastrous Cultural Revolution, in 1978 the government proclaimed China's "open-door" policy for industry and commerce, and Premier Deng Xiaoping (Teng Hsiao-p'ing) asked Rong to assist the country in this purpose. Rong founded the CITIC in 1979 and traveled to the United States to meet with American bankers and entrepreneurs to encourage them to invest in the PRC. The CITIC borrows and lends money internationally, issues foreign bonds, makes overseas investments, encourages and participates in joint ventures and imports foreign technology and equipment. In 1984 the Chinese government permitted the CITIC and three banks to deal in foreign currency, which until then had been handled by the Bank of China. CITIC opened an office in New York City in June 1985. In 1986 the business magazine *Fortune* named Rong one of the 50 most important figures in the world economy.

Rong also resumed holding government positions. He was vice president of the fifth CPPCC from 1978 to 1983 and again served as a Shanghai deputy to the NPC from 1975 to the present. He was Presidium executive chairman and Standing Committee vice chairman at the NPC in 1983 and 1988. He served as vice chairman of the Federation of Industry and Commerce from 1978 to 1988 and chairman from 1988 to the present, and as managing director of the Bank of China, the foreign exchange arm of the People's Bank of China, from 1979 to 1988. In 1980 he was a member of the Constitution Revision Committee. Hong was awarded an honorary doctorate by Hofstra University in New York in 1986 and has served as vice chairman of the Soong Qingling Foundation from 1982 to the present. Soong was the wife of Dr. Sun Yat-sen, the founder of modern China, and she became the most prominent woman in the PRC. He was chairman of Jinan University from 1986 to the present and honorary chairman of China International Economic Consultants Inc. from 1986 to the present. During the 1980s Rong led many economic and trade delegations for the PRC to North and South America, Europe, the Middle East, Africa, Japan and Singapore. See also CHINA INTERNATIONAL TRUST AND INVESTMENT CORPORATION; CULTURAL REVOLUTION; FOREIGN TRADE AND INVESTMENT; GOVERNMENT STRUCTURE; PEOPLE'S REPUBLIC OF CHINA; SOONG CHING LING.

"ROOF OF THE WORLD" See HIMALAYA MOUNTAIN RANGE; QINGHAI-TIBET PLATEAU; TIBET.

ROOF TILES See TILES, GLAZED.

ROOSTER See CHICKEN.

ROSARY, BUDDHIST See AMITABHA; LUOHAN.

ROYAL LADY (OR MOTHER) OF THE WESTERN PARADISE See XIWANGMU.

ROYAL LORD OF THE EAST See XIWANGMU.

RU WARE (Ju Ware) A type of ceramic that is the most famous of the so-called five great wares of the Song dynasty (960–1279). It is characterized as a celadon ware because of the color of its thick blue-gray glaze, which tends to crackle. Ru ware is named for the district in modern Henan Province where it was first developed. It was produced from about 1080 to the early 12th century for courts of the Song emperors Zhezong (Che-tsung; r. 1086–1101) and Huizong (Huitsung; r. 1101–25). Pieces of Ru ware have simple but elegant and perfectly balanced shapes. The delicate cracks in the glaze, known as crazing, were created on purpose and were caused by the different rates of expansion of the clay body and the glaze when the pieces were fired in kilns. The Ru workshop was destroyed when a nomadic tribe known as the Jurchen invaded China and besieged the Song capital at Kaifeng in 1126–27, forcing the court to flee south and establish a new capital at Hangzhou. Although Ru ware was produced for only a short time, it influenced the production of Kuan (Guan) and Ge (Ko) wares, two of the other five great Song wares. Pieces of Ru ware are some of the rarest and most expensive Chinese ceramics that have survived. See also CELADON; KAIFENG; KUANWARE; SONG DYNASTY.

RUGS See CARPETS.

RUIJIN See CHINESE COMMUNIST PARTY; LIU BOCHENG; MAO ZEDONG; PEOPLE'S LIBERATION ARMY; ZHU DE.

RULIN WAISHI See SCHOLARS, THE.

RUNNING SCRIPT STYLE OF CALLIGRAPHY See CALLIGRAPHY; WANG XIZHI.

RUSSIA AND CHINA See BORODIN, MIKHAIL; CHIANG CHING-KUO; CHIANG KAI-SHEK; CHINESE COMMUNIST PARTY; CIVIL WAR BETWEEN COMMUNISTS AND NATIONALISTS; GEOGRAPHY; HEILONGJIANG PROVINCE; MANCHURIA; MAO ZEDONG; NATIONALIST PARTY; NERCHINSK, TREATY OF; RUSSO-JAPANESE WAR OF 1904–5; SINO-SOVIET CONFLICT; SUN YAT-SEN; TIANANMEN SQUARE MASSACRE; UNEQUAL TREATIES; WAR OF RESISTANCE AGAINST JAPAN; WUSULI INCIDENT; YONGZHENG, EMPEROR.

RUSSO-JAPANESE WAR OF 1904–5 A war fought between Japan and Russia for control of Korea and Manchuria (northeastern China), the homeland of the

Manchus who ruled China under the Qing dynasty (1644–1911). Japan had defeated China in the Sino-Japanese War of 1894–95 and ended Chinese suzerainty over the Korean peninsula. However, Japan had been prevented from establishing its own control over Korea when the tripartite intervention of Russia, Germany and France forced it to return the Liaodong Peninsula, part of southern Manchuria, to China. Russia obtained concessions in the strategic ports of Port Arthur and Dalian at the tip of Liaodong. Russia also responded to the antiforeign Chinese Boxer Uprising in 1900 by sending a large number of troops into Manchuria, and gained Chinese permission to keep them there.

In 1902 Japan and Britain agreed to the Anglo-Japanese Alliance, which did not recognize Japan's control over Korea but affirmed that Japan could oppose Russia without Western-power intervention. In 1903 Russia rejected Japan's proposal that it recognize Japan's special interests in Korea in return for Japanese recognition of Russia's special interests in Manchuria. Russia promised to remove all of its troops from Manchuria but removed only a third of them; prominent Japanese leaders asserted that Japan should use its military to force Russia out of Manchuria. Japan had built up a strong military using the indemnity it had exacted from China at the end of the Sino-Japanese War and loans from Britain and the United States. Japan and Russia attempted further negotiations, but these did not succeed.

Japan broke off diplomatic relations with Russia on February 6, 1904. On February 8 the Japanese navy surrounded the Russian fleet at Port Arthur, and Japan declared war on Russia two days later. Japanese troops landed in Korea and marched north across the Yalu River into Manchuria. A second Japanese army landed on the Liaodong Peninsula and occupied Dalian, and a third army took Port Arthur in January 1905. In March the Japanese crushed the Russians in the massive Battle of Mukden (modern Shenyang), although they were not able to rout the Russian troops completely. The Japanese military had reached its limit, and the Russians began sending more troops into Manchuria, so Japan decided to negotiate with Russia. In May, after the Japanese navy destroyed the Russian Baltic Fleet in the Battle of Tsushima, Japan secretly asked U.S. president Theodore Roosevelt to mediate.

Japan and Russia held negotiations in August 1905 at Portsmouth, New Hampshire and signed the Treaty of Portsmouth on September 5. Russia ceded to Japan the southern half of Sakhalin Island and gave Japan exclusive rights in Korea, its concessions in Port Arthur and Dalian and control of the South Manchuria Railway. These terms were subject to the approval of the Chinese government, which Japan received at the Beijing Conference in late 1905. At this conference, the weakened Qing dynasty gave Japan even greater rights in Manchuria than the treaty had specified. This was the first time that Japan had acquired rights and concessions on Chinese land, and it enabled Japan to begin competing with the Western powers that had interests in East Asia. The Russo-Japanese War also had a dampening effect on the Chinese nationalist movement that had been growing against the Qing dynasty, although this movement eventually did overthrow the Qing in the Revolution of 1911. In 1915 Japan presented China with its so-called Twenty-One Demands that extracted more concessions from

China. In 1932 Japan established a puppet state in Manchuria known as Manchukuo (Manzhouguo or Manchou-kuo in Chinese), and used it as a base for invading China and the rest of Asia. Full-scale military conflict broke out, called by the Chinese the War of Resistance against Japan (1937–45; World War II). See also DALIAN; LIAODONG PENINSULA; LUDA; MANCHUKUO; MANCHURIA; QING DYNASTY; REVOLUTION OF 1911; SINO-JAPANESE WAR OF 1894–95; TWENTY-ONE DEMANDS ON CHINA BY JAPAN; WAR OF RESISTANCE AGAINST JAPAN.

RUXUE   See CONFUCIANISM.

RYOKAI   See LIANG KAI.

RYUKYU ISLANDS (Liuqiu or Liu-Ch'iu)   A chain of more than 70 islands that extend for 800 miles between Kyushu, the southernmost of the four main islands of Japan, and the island of Taiwan (Republic of China). The Ryukyu Islands are also known as the Nansei Islands (Nansei Shoto, "Southern Islands") in Japanese. Ryukyu is the Japanese pronunciation of Liuqiu, the name given to these islands by the Chinese Ming dynasty (1368–1644), to which Ryukyu paid tribute as a vassal state in exchange for trading privileges. The islands have a population of more than one million and cover about 866 square miles, of which Okinawa, the largest island, comprises 53 percent. The next largest islands are Iriomote, which is covered by forests and is known for the Iriomote Wild Cat, and Ishigaki. The Ryukyu Islands fall into three groups from north to south: the Okinawa Island group, the Miyako Island group and the Yaeyama group. These subtropical islands, surrounded by coral reefs, are often struck by violent typhoons in late summer and autumn.

Ryukyu was settled in prehistoric times. In 1372 Satto, king of Chuzan (Central Okinawa), established a tributary relationship with China. In 1406 the first Sho dynasty was founded in Chuzan and the capital was moved to Shuri, around which the city of Naha, the modern capital, developed. Ryukyu was organized into three kingdoms in the 15th century. The second Sho dynasty, founded in 1470, lasted until Ryukyu became the modern Japanese prefecture of Okinawa in 1879. For five centuries Ryukyu was a great trading kingdom and the hub of trade among China, Korea, Southeast Asia and Japan. Goods exchanged by Ryukyu traders included Chinese raw silk, silk textiles, pottery, Japanese swords and copper, and Southeast Asian spices. The Chinese and Ryukyu courts sent annual diplomatic and trading missions to each other's kingdoms.

In 1609 the Shimazu clan of Satsuma Province (the modern Japanese prefecture of Kagoshima) on southern Kyushu took control of Ryukyu, but permitted Ryukyu to continue paying tribute to China because they wanted to benefit from the lucrative trade. Many cultural items were introduced into Japan from Ryukyu, including a complex tie-dye weaving technique known as *kasuri* (*ikat*), sweet potatoes and a banjo-like instrument called the *sanxian* (*san-hsien*) in China and *shamisen* in Japan. Ryukyu became famous for its colorful lacquerware, pottery and textiles as well as its strong tradition of classical court and folk music and dances.

In 1816 European ships first appeared in Ryukyu ports. U.S. Commodore Matthew Perry visited Ryukyu twice in

1853 and 1854 when he attempted to open Japan to Western trade. In 1871, 54 Ryukyu Islanders were shipwrecked on Taiwan and killed and eaten by aborigines. Japan asserted that Ryukyu was its vassal state and demanded that China punish the aborigines, but China declared that this was a purely internal Chinese affair. Japan sent a military expedition that occupied a strip of land on the northern Taiwan coast. China threatened to send a larger force to Taiwan. The Qing dynasty (1644–1911) that ruled China was weak, however, and gave in to Japanese demands. It paid an indemnity and signed the treaty of 1874 that recognized Japan's claim as protector of the Ryukyu Islands and referred to the people of Ryukyu as "people belonging to Japan."

The last Ryukyu ambassador to China paid tribute in 1875, when Japan took over the islands directly. In 1879 Japan deposed the Ryukyu king and designated the islands the Japanese prefecture of Okinawa. China's weakness encouraged Japan to wrest other countries, such as Korea, from Chinese suzerainty and to continue expanding throughout Asia until the end of World War II in 1945. Under direct Japanese rule, the Okinawan people became so impoverished that many of them immigrated to Hawaii, the Philippine Islands and South America. Okinawa Island was devastated in 1945 during the final battle between Japan and the Allied Powers in World War II. The United States administered the islands until 1972, when it finally agreed to return them to Japan, although it still maintains military bases on Okinawa. The Japanese government established the Okinawa Development Agency, which has enabled the Ryukyu Islands to make an economic recovery and become a popular resort area. In 1996 the Okinawan people voted to oust the American bases from their land. This issue has not been resolved. See also LACQUERWARE; PORCELAIN; SANXIAN; SILK; TAIWAN; TRIBUTE SYSTEM.

S

SABLE Also known as the marten (Latin name *Martes zibellina*); a small mammal with beautiful brown fur that is one of the "three treasures," or highly prized products, of Manchuria (northeastern China), along with ginseng (a root used in herbal medicine) and sika deer antlers. The sable inhabits northern Asia, from the Ural River to the Pacific Ocean. In China it lives at the foot of the Changbai Mountain Range on the upper reaches of the Second Songhua River, where the climate is cold and snowy much of the year. A sable weighs between $1\frac{3}{4}$ and 4 pounds. The length of its head and body averages 15 to 18 inches and its tail 5 to 8 inches. It feeds on rodents, fish, frogs and pinecones. The sable has a ferocious nature and lives a solitary life except during the short mating season. Wild sables have become nearly extinct, but they are raised in captivity for their fur. As soon as a male and female have mated, they are returned to their own cages, or else they will fight each other viciously. The Chinese call the soft, smooth, waterproof fur of the sable "soft gold." Sable fur coats are very luxurious and are sold for a high price around the world. See also CHANGBAI MOUNTAIN RANGE; DEER; GINSENG; MANCHURIA; SONGHUA RIVER.

SACRED WAY See MING TOMBS; SCULPTURE.

SAGE KINGS See JADE EMPEROR; SHUN, EMPEROR; YAO, EMPEROR; YELLOW EMPEROR; YU, EMPEROR.

SAKHALIN ISLAND See AMUR RIVER.

SAKYAMUNI See BUDDHA; DUNHUANG CAVE PAINTINGS AND CARVINGS.

SALT MONOPOLY Control of the production, distribution and sale of salt (sodium chloride) by the Chinese government in order to raise revenues. The Chinese have processed salt for more than 30 centuries, and Chinese records dating as early as the seventh century B.C. mention the salt industry. The ancient state of Chu became especially wealthy and powerful because of its lucrative salt trade. There are huge salt deposits in modern Sichuan Province in western China, which the Chinese first mined by deep borehole drilling in the first century B.C. during the Han dynasty (206 B.C.–A.D. 220). Natural gas, which they also learned to use very early, was a by-product of this drilling. Today about three-quarters of the common salt in China is produced from seawater, about 16 percent from boreholed brine, about 5 percent from salt lakes and a small amount from rock salt and as a by-product from gypsum mining. The Chinese employ several methods to extract salt from seawater, such as evaporating brine in the sun or boiling dried seaweed to refine the brine.

Emperor Wudi (Wu-ti; r. 141–87 B.C.) of the Han dynasty established a centralized imperial bureaucracy in China, and this government held monopolies to control strategic products such as salt, which was used to preserve as well as flavor food, and iron, which was used to produce weapons. In 119 B.C. 86 commissions were established at Chinese iron and salt mines and on the seacoast, which were authorized to conscript workers to produce and distribute the salt and iron. A tax added to the prices at which they were sold went directly into the government treasury. Taxes on salt remained a major means by which the imperial government raised needed revenues throughout Chinese history. Only a few merchants were permitted to engage in the salt trade. During the Tang dynasty (618–907), a monopoly tax on salt proved to be the only emergency measure for raising money that was successful over a long period. During the Song dynasty (960–1279), the government established monopolies on tea and wine as well as salt. The salt monopoly was fully established by 1230, and during the Mongol Yuan dynasty (1279–1368) it was the government's most profitable source of income. Salt processing was one of the industries, along with shipbuilding, papermaking and printing, that the Chinese conducted on a larger scale than any other country in the world before the 18th century. The occupation of salt producer was hereditary to ensure a continuous supply of workers for this important industry.

Merchants in Yangzhou, at the junction of the Grand Canal and the Yangzi River in modern Jiangsu Province, who were licensed by the government to engage in the salt monopoly became extremely wealthy. During the Qing dynasty (1644–1911), Yangzhou served as headquarters for the Liang-Huai Salt Administration, which controlled the production and distribution of salt in much of eastern and central China. The Grand Canal and Yangzi River were major transportation routes for the shipment of salt, rice and other necessary goods. Salt smugglers were also active in China, and they comprised many members of the 19th century Han Chinese Nian Rebellion against the Qing Dynasty.

The Han Chinese resented the Manchus who ruled them under the Qing dynasty. They overthrew the Qing in the Revolution of 1911 and inaugurated the Republic of China. The warlord Yuan Shikai (Yuan Shih-k'ai; 1859–1916), who became president of the republic, had a strong connection with Britain and other foreign powers that had gained many concessions in China. Yuan dissolved the Chinese parliament, which opposed him; revised the Chinese constitution to make himself president for life; and secured a "Reorganization Loan" from the foreign powers, in return for which he gave them supervision of the salt revenues. When Yuan declared himself emperor of China on December 15 (his reign to begin in 1916), strong resistance broke out. He restored the republic but died soon after, and China became carved up by competing warlords. They vied to capture the capital city of Beijing so as to gain recognition by foreign powers and surplus funds from the foreign-controlled Salt Administration. After decades of civil war and the War of Resistance against Japan (1937–45; World War II), the Chinese Communist Party established the People's Republic of China in 1949 and took control of salt and other strategic Chinese industries. Today China is one of the world's largest producers of salt. See also GRAND CANAL; IMPERIAL BUREAUCRACY; NIAN REBELLION; REPUBLIC OF CHINA; SICHUAN PROVINCE; WUDI, EMPEROR; YANGZI RIVER; YUAN SHIKAI; NAMES OF INDIVIDUAL DYNASTIES.

SALWEEN RIVER   See MEKONG RIVER; RED RIVER.

SAN FRANCISCO   See SIX COMPANIES, CHINESE.

SAN GUO PERIOD   See THREE KINGDOMS PERIOD.

SAN HSIEN   See SANXIAN.

SAN KUO PERIOD   See THREE KINGDOMS PERIOD.

SAN MIN CHUYI   See THREE PRINCIPLES OF THE PEOPLE.

SANCAI   See THREE-COLOR WARE.

SANDALWOOD (*tanxiang* or *t'an-hsiang*)   A fragrant hardwood tree belonging to the family *Santalaceae* and native to southern India and Southeast Asian countries such as Malaysia. Sandalwood trees, which can grow to 40 feet high, have hairy oval leaves and flowers that turn from pale yellow to deep red in color. Many of the trees are semiparasitic on the roots of other plants. Sandalwood has long been a major item of trade throughout Asia. The main source of sandalwood is *Santalum album,* a small evergreen tree native to India, whose yellow-brown wood is very hard and has a fine grain. The tree's fragrance comes from an oil, concentrated in the roots, which Indians distill from the roots and heartwood chips and use to make perfume. Sandalwood is commonly used throughout India and China to make folding fans, boxes, screens and other objects decorated with carvings. Buddhists also use sandalwood to make incense for religious ceremonies and funeral pyres for cremating dead bodies. Red sandalwood comes from *Pterocarpus santalinus,* a small tree native to southern India, Sri Lanka (Ceylon) and the Philippine Islands, and is used to make a red-brown dye for wool. See also FANS; INCENSE.

SANFAN MOVEMENT   See THREE-ANTI AND FIVE-ANTI CAMPAIGNS.

SANG DE BOEF   See ENAMELWARE.

SANGUOZHI YANYI   See ROMANCE OF THE THREE KINGDOMS.

SAN-KUO-CHI YAN-YI   See ROMANCE OF THE THREE KINGDOMS.

SANMINZHUYI   See THREE PRINCIPLES OF THE PEOPLE.

SAN-TS'AI   See THREE-COLOR WARE.

SANXIAN (*san hsien*)   A musical instrument similar to a banjo. The *sanxian,* which probably originated in China, is about $3\frac{1}{2}$ to $4\frac{1}{2}$ feet long and has a round body, long neck and three fretless strings. The frame is made of wood, the front and back of the round body are covered with the skin of dogs or cats and the strings are silk or nylon. The three pegs at the end of the neck that hold the strings are made of ivory, wood or plastic. The musician tunes the instrument by turning the pegs to tighten or loosen the strings, and plays it by plucking the strings with a plectrum made from ivory, tortoiseshell or plastic. The *sanxian* was taken to the Ryukyu Islands (Okinawa), a tributary of China for 500 years that now belongs to Japan, where it is called the *sanshin* or *jamisen* and is covered with snakeskin, and from there to Japan, where it is called the *shamisen* or *samisen.* The *sanxian* makes a lively, twanging sound that associates it with popular entertainment and the pleasure quarters of cities, in contrast to the refined sound made by other Chinese instruments that are played by plucking strings, zithers known as *qin* and *zheng.* See also QIN; RYUKYU ISLANDS.

SATELLITES   See SPACE INDUSTRY; TELECOMMUNICATIONS.

SAYINGS OF CONFUCIUS   See ANALECTS, CONFUCIAN.

SCHALL VON BELL, JOANNES ADAM   See CALENDAR; JESUITS; RITES CONTROVERSY.

SCHOLARS, THE (*Rulin waishi* or *Ju-lin wai-shih*)   Also known as *The Anecdotal History of Men and Letters* or *An*

Unofficial History of the Literati; one of the greatest Chinese classic novels. Written by Wu Jingzi (Wu Ching-tzu; 1701–54), *The Scholars* was the first work of satiric realism to be published in China. The author used realistic and humorous portrayals of his characters to point out the problems of greed and hypocrisy in Chinese society. The title refers to members of the literati, or scholar-gentry class, that governed China in the imperial bureaucracy. Wu Jingzi criticized them for shallowly being concerned only with passing the examinations that would provide them positions in the bureaucracy and bring them official honors. The novel reflects his opinion that the examination system stifled genuine learning and talent and rewarded incompetency. He wrote from personal experience, as he had been born in Anhui Province into a well-off family that lost its wealth. When he was 32 he moved to the city of Nanjing. There he lived in poverty after giving the remainder of his money to restore a temple dedicated to the legendary founder of the state of Wu. He died in the city of Yangzhou. Wu Jingzi modeled the central characters in *The Scholars* after himself and his family members. See also IMPERIAL BUREAUCRACY; IMPERIAL EXAMINATION SYSTEM; LITERATI; NANJING.

SCHOOL OF LAW See LEGALIST SCHOOL OF THOUGHT.

SCHOOL OF MIND OR INTUITION See NEO-CONFUCIANISM.

SCHOOL OF NAMES See DIALECTICIANS.

SCHOOLS See BEIJING UNIVERSITY; EDUCATION SYSTEM (MODERN); IMPERIAL EXAMINATION SYSTEM; LITERATI; QINGHAI UNIVERSITY; WRITING SYSTEM, CHINESE.

SCIENCE AND CIVILIZATION IN CHINA See NEEDHAM, JOSEPH.

SCIENCE SOCIETY OF CHINA See ACADEMIA SINICA.

SCISSORS-PAPER-STONE See FINGER-GUESSING GAMES.

SCROLLS (*juanzhou* or *chuan-chou*) Rolls of paper or cloth that are painted or inscribed with calligraphy. There are two types of scrolls, the hand scroll, which is opened by rolling it horizontally, and the vertical hanging scroll, which is hung on a hook and rolled up when not in use. Hanging scrolls can be changed to set a mood or to reflect the season of the year. A hanging scroll, which can range in size from small to more than 10 feet long, is made by pasting a paper backing on a rectangle of silk or paper and a border of silk or brocade. The top border is much longer than the bottom one. Several more layers are added in a process of pasting and drying that can take as long as several months. The paste is made from wheat starch from which the gluten has been removed so that the scroll will not become stiff and brittle. The mounting is expected to last for 200 years. A stave is added to the top and a wooden roller to the bottom of a hanging scroll. Hand scrolls are made by pasting together rectangles of paper or silk in a sequence that can be as long as 30 feet. The scroll is viewed or read from right to left by unrolling a portion of it that can be held comfortably in two hands, about 18 inches, similar to reading a book, and continuing this process until the entire scroll has been viewed. A hand scroll has an outer brocade cover, an inner silk cover and a title section that introduces the painting or text. Scrolls originated in China during the Tang dynasty (618–907). See also BROCADE; CALLIGRAPHY; INK PAINTING; LANDSCAPE PAINTING; PAPER; PRINTING; SILK.

SCULPTURE (*diaoke* or *tiao-ko*) Figures of humans, animals and deities made of a variety of materials and ranging in size from small carvings to enormous Buddhist deities carved into the sides of cliffs. Nearly all Chinese sculpture was created by anonymous artists; usually it was produced for religious purposes, such as figures placed in tombs and statues of deities in the Buddhist and Daoist traditions. However, other types of Chinese sculptures were produced, such as ornamental figures on the roofs of traditional buildings. The most ancient Chinese sculptures were made of stone, especially marble, and were small carvings with strong, solid designs of human figures and animals such as tigers and buffalos. During the Shang dynasty (1750–1040 B.C.), the Chinese produced magnificent bronze vessels decorated with motifs in relief such as geometric patterns and fierce animal masks. Most of the bronze pieces were containers to hold food and drink during ritual offerings, but some were large bronze figures, such as tigers, decorated with similar patterns. The Chinese continued to produce bronzeware during the Zhou dynasty (1100–256 B.C.), and powerful Chinese rulers had large sets of bronze bells cast and suspended on wooden frames as a display of their authority. Gradually, however, bronze pieces were replaced by ceramics, which the Chinese had been making since the Neolithic period (c. 12,000–2000 B.C.). Yue (Yueh) ware, a type of highly fired brown glaze pottery developed during the late Zhou, was the prototype of the beautiful celadon wares that the Chinese produced a millennium later. The Chinese also invented the techniques for making porcelain, a beautiful thin and lustrous ceramic fired in the kiln at a very high temperature, and porcelain figures became popular export items.

The Shang practiced human sacrifice at funerals and buried attendants with deceased rulers. During the Zhou, human sacrifices were replaced by objects known as *mingqi* (*ming-ch'i*), which were models of things the deceased had enjoyed in life and of human beings, animals and horses and chariots. These were the prototypes of the highly developed figures that were buried in tombs during the Han (206 B.C.–A.D. 220) and Tang (618–907) dynasties. Such figures included models of buildings and watchtowers, boats, carts and scenes of everyday life. Some were hand-modeled, but others were mass-produced with molds, especially around the Eastern Han capital of Luoyang.

The first emperor, Qin Shi Huangdi, who unified China under the Qin dynasty (221–206 B.C.), was buried in a large mausoleum outside the modern city of Xi'an in Shaanxi Province. In 1974 Chinese peasants digging a well nearby discovered what proved to be a huge army of near life-size terracotta warriors, horses and chariots buried underground to guard the first emperor after he died. An enormous underground vault containing 6,000 of these figures that have been restored is one of the most popular tourist attractions in China.

Stone sculptures were not produced during the Zhou dynasty but were made once again during the Han. Monumental three-dimensional sculptures of animals such as horses and lions and mythical beasts such as winged chimeras were placed along the "spirit ways" (*shendao* or *shen-tao*) leading to Han tombs. During this time, sculptors also began carving bas-reliefs to decorate the walls of underground stone chambers, and their style more closely resembled paintings than sculptures.

Chinese sculpture became closely associated with the religion of Buddhism, which was introduced into China from India around the first century A.D. The earliest Buddhist sculptures were monumental and formal, showing a link with Han stone relief carvings. They were made of stone, bronze, gilded bronze, wood and pottery. Wood and clay figures often were decorated with paint, lacquer or gilt. Most Buddhist sculptures are of the human form and depict the founder of the religion, Siddhartha Gautama, also called Sakyamuni, who became known as the Buddha or "enlightened one"; bodhisattvas and luohans, enlightened beings and disciples who work to help others overcome suffering; and the many deities in the Buddhist pantheon. Some of the most popular deities were Amitabha, who rules the Western Paradise where Buddhists believed they would go after they died; Guanyin (Kuan Yin), the goddess of mercy; and Maitreya, the Buddha who is expected to come to Earth in the future. Buddhism is also associated with figure painting, one of the main styles of traditional Chinese painting.

Sculptures also were produced in the native Chinese tradition of Daoism, which also has a large pantheon. However, Daoist sculptures do not portray a wide variety of deities, as do Buddhist sculptures. They usually depict the Yellow Emperor, a mythical figure who supposedly brought order to Chinese society and taught the Chinese people many things necessary for survival, or Laozi, the legendary founder of the Daoist religion, with two attendants. Daoist art was strongly influenced by Buddhist art, and temples in Chinese folk religion included both Daoist and Buddhist figures as well as figures of deities who played an important role in local agricultural communities.

In a Buddhist temple, a beautifully decorated sculpture of a deity, commonly made of gilded bronze or of wood, is placed on a table or throne in the main hall with an altar holding utensils for religious rituals. Sculptures of attendant deities are placed to the right and left of the main deity. If the temple compound has more than one hall, sculptures of lesser deities are placed in the first hall and the principal deity in the rear hall.

Some of the earliest Buddhist sculptures can be seen at Dunhuang in Gansu Province in western China, where in A.D. 366 Buddhist monks began carving magnificent caves, known as the Mogao Grottoes, into cliffs and filling them with carvings of Buddhist deities. The Turkish-speaking tribes that founded the Northern Wei dynasty (386—534) patronized the foreign religion and sponsored the carving of Buddhist cave temples and sculptures into the southern cliffs of Mount Wuzhou at Yungang, near their capital at Datong in Shanxi Province. Most of the Yungang caves were carved between 460 and 494. The sculptures there are typical of the earliest Chinese Buddhist style of stone sculpture. Similar Buddhist caves and sculptures can be seen at Dazu in Sichuan Province and Longmen near Luoyang in Henan Province. Mount Maiji (Maijishan) in southern Gansu has one of the largest groups of Buddhist temple caves and sculptures in China, which were begun during the Northern Wei and were recently discovered. Because the cave walls were too soft to carve, clay and stone figures were placed in the caves. The Bingling Si caves, which were carved into a canyon 197 feet high along a reservoir in the Yellow River (Huanghe), also are in Gansu. They include an 89-foot-high seated sculpture of Maitreya. There are other large Buddhist carvings in different regions of China, such as the Great Buddha of Leshan, carved on a slope of Mount Lingyu (Lingyushan) in Sichuan Province. The 233-foot-high sculpture of the seated Maitreya was completed in 803.

In the mid-sixth century, Chinese sculptors began making free-standing three-dimensional sculptures of the Buddha, bodhisattvas and Maitreya. Great Buddhist bronze sculptures were produced during the seventh and eighth centuries, but were melted down during the persecution of the religion in 845 or lost in later times. Their style still can be seen in the Buddhist sculptures in the temples in Nara, the ancient capital of Japan. The Buddhist religion was introduced from China to Korea and Japan, where many beautiful sculptures in the style of early Chinese Buddhism have been preserved. Perhaps the finest example is a bronze Buddha altarpiece in Horyuji Temple in Nara, Japan, which was made by an immigrant Korean sculptor in 623 in the style of the Chinese mid-sixth century.

Because wood is perishable, very few wood sculptures have survived in China from earlier than the Tang. The earliest are from tombs in the state of Chu and originally were covered with paint or lacquer. In the dry lacquer technique (*jiazhu* or *chia-chu*), a figure is shaped from cloth soaked in lacquer. After it dries and hardens, many more coats of lacquer are applied. Sculptors using this technique could make large, very lightweight figures. By the late Tang, sculptors were producing large Buddhist figures, most made of several parts held together with mortise and tenon joints. They covered the wood with thin plaster or gesso and painted or lacquered it, sometimes adding gold features. This type of Buddhist sculpture was made into the Ming dynasty (1368–1644). During the Ming, sculptors also began making small free-standing secular figures of painted or lacquered wood. They also produced wooden objects for scholars to keep on their desks, such as bamboo brush containers and wrist rests, and small carvings of fruits and flowers.

During the Tang dynasty, Buddhist sculpture became more delicate and graceful. Tang Buddhist sculptures typically have a curved torso with one hip thrust to the side, showing influence from the Hellenic style of sculpture in Afghanistan, which Alexander the Great had conquered in the fourth century B.C. There are Buddhist cave temples and sculptures at Bamiyan, Afghanistan and other sites in Central Asia. Most surviving Tang dynasty Buddhist sculptures are made of stone, although some Chinese pieces dating from that era made of bronze, wood, clay and dry lacquer have been preserved in Japan. Sculptural objects placed in tombs attained their greatest development during the Tang. The Tang capital at Chang'an (modern Xi'an) was the terminus of the Silk Road, and many foreign traders settled in the city. Their influence is shown by the figures of bearded foreigners, camels, horses, soldiers, dancing girls and musicians that were placed in Tang tombs. Most were decorated with colored glazes in the ceramic style known as three-color ware (*sancai* or *san-ts'ai*). Tomb figures declined in artistry after the Tang.

The Tang persecuted Buddhism in 845, closing thousands of monasteries and forcing Buddhist monks and nuns to return to lay life. This was a setback to Buddhist art, but the religion recovered, especially the Pure Land and Chan (Zen) Sects. Other Buddhist sects in China include the Flower Garland and Tiantai Sects and the Tibetan form of Buddhism, known as Lamaism. Although Buddhism continued to be practiced in China up to the modern era, it declined during the Song dynasty, when Confucianism became predominant; and the Yuan dynasty (1279–1368), when China was ruled by the Mongols, a foreign ethnic group that invaded from the north, except for Lamaism, which the Mongols favored. Buddhist sculpture declined with the religion. During the Ming dynasty, however, sculpture was revived, especially the large figures that guard the "spirit way" to the tombs of Ming emperors outside Nanjing and Beijing. Ceramic figures with brightly colored glazes, a revival of the three-color style, were widely used, especially on the roof ridges of palaces and temples, which also were covered with bright yellow, blue and green glazed tiles.

The decorative arts were highly developed during the Ming and Qing (1644–1911) dynasties, including the production of beautiful figures made of porcelain or carved ivory or jade. The Chinese had been carving small figures of ivory and jade, two materials that they valued very highly, since before the Shang dynasty. Some of the most beautiful porcelain figures were produced in Dehua ware, a lustrous white porcelain known in the West, where it was heavily exported, as *blanc de Chine* ("white of China"). These include figures of humans and deities, especially Guanyin, the Buddhist goddess of mercy. See also AMITABHA; ARCHAEOLOGY; ARCHITECTURE, TRADITIONAL; BAMBOO; BELLS AND CHIMES; BODHISATTVA; BRONZEWARE; BUDDHA; BUDDHISM; CELADON; CONFUCIANISM; DAOISM; DAZU CAVE TEMPLES AND SCULPTURES; DEHUA WARE; DUNHUANG CAVE TEMPLES AND CARVINGS; FIGURE PAINTING; GANSU PROVINCE; GUANYIN; IVORY CARVING; JADE; LACQUERWARE; LAOZI; LONGMEN CAVE TEMPLES AND SCULPTURES; LUOHAN; MAITREYA AND MANJUSRI; MING TOMBS; NORTHERN WEI DYNASTY; PORCELAIN; TEMPLES; TERRA-COTTA ARMY, TOMB OF QIN SHI HUANGDI; THREE-COLOR WARE; TILES, GLAZED; WHITE WARE; YELLOW EMPEROR; YUNGANG CAVE TEMPLES AND SCULPTURES.

SE See QIN.

SEAFOOD See FISH AND SEAFOOD.

SEALS (*tuzhang* or *t'u-chang*)   Known in the West as chops; small objects with the ends carved in relief or intaglio with personal or artistic names. The owner of a seal dips the carved end into a small dish of thick red paste and impresses his or her name onto a piece of paper or a scroll to "sign" it. Seals have many different shapes and sizes and are made from a variety of materials, such as jade, stone, wood, metal, animal horn or bone, glass, porcelain or ivory. The carving of seals originated in the Zhou dynasty (1100–256 B.C.) and

has become a separate art form in China. The characters of a person's name have to be laid out in a complex and balanced design within a small square, circle or oval. Seal carvers usually employ the calligraphic style known as Small Seal, which developed from incisions marked on bronze and stone in ancient times. Unlike other styles of calligraphy, Small Seal is characterized by lines of equal thickness and rounded corners rather than sharp angles. Seal signatures can be positive, or yang, carved in relief so that the characters are impressed in red on a white background; negative, or yin, carved in intaglio to impress white characters on a red background; or a combination of positive and negative. The body of the seal is usually a smooth column; it can be decorated with painting, or the opposite end can be carved into a shape, such as an animal. The red seal paste, which was invented in A.D. 450, is made by mixing cinnabar and mineral oil into a pad of raw silk.

Starting in the Song dynasty (960–1279), every government official had his own seal with which to sign papers. The highest officials used oblong seals made of silver, magistrates used square silver seals and officials below them used wooden seals. The seal represented the power of an official's authority, and if it was lost the official could lose his job. Traditionally the official entrusted the seal to his wife for safekeeping. Until the end of the Song dynasty, painters usually wrote small and inconspicuous signatures on their paintings. However, beginning in the Yuan dynasty (1279–1368), painters and their friends began writing inscriptions on the paintings and signing them with their personal or artistic names by impressing red seals on the corners of paintings. Owners of paintings also impressed their seals on the paintings; thus a painting that had been owned in succession by several collectors could be decorated with many seals. The imperial seals used by emperors commonly were impressed in the center of paintings. Seal marks on paintings have given art historians much useful information about the artists and the collectors who owned the works. See also CINNABAR; INK PAINTING; YIN AND YANG.

SEASONINGS FOR FOOD   A variety of ingredients that are commonly used to add flavor to food in the Chinese cuisine and also are believed to benefit one's health. Chinese meals include a range of dishes cooked by various methods so that they have different flavors and textures to interest the diners. The food is served in small pieces that can be eaten easily with chopsticks. The main dish is always grain (*fan*), usually rice in southern China and noodles or other wheat products in northern China, accompanied by vegetables and small portions of soybean curd (known as tofu in the West), fish, chicken, pork or other meats. Some of the seasonings most frequently used in Chinese cooking, especially in soups and dishes cooked by stir-frying in vegetable oil in a wok, include soy sauce, ginger, garlic, scallions, rice vinegar, oil made from sesame seeds and an alcoholic beverage made by fermenting malted millet, rice or sorghum, which usually is called rice wine in English. Pieces of meat and other foods to be cooked may be marinated first in soy sauce and other ingredients. Soy sauce is an extract of fermented soybeans combined with salt. Ginger is a gnarled root that is peeled and sliced or grated. Ginseng root, one of the main ingredients in Chinese herbal medicine, sometimes is used in cooking. Scallions are small, mild onions with long, green stalks that are cut into small pieces. Three types of vinegar are made from rice, light amber, dark black and red; they are also used to preserve or pickle foods. All of these ingredients may be combined in various ways to make dipping sauces, which are served individually so that each diner can flavor the food to taste. Thick sauces also may be served, such as purple hoisin sauce, a combination of soybean flour, red beans, ginger, garlic, salt chili, sugar and other spices; and orange plum sauce, also known as duck sauce, which has a sweet-and-sour flavor.

Other seasonings in Chinese cooking include sugar, honey, star anise, black and brown pepper, chili peppers, hot sauce made from chili peppers, oil flavored with chili peppers, oyster sauce, star anise, shrimp paste, dried shrimp, tangerine peel, tea leaves and five spices powder, made from star anise, cinnamon, fennel or aniseed, pepper and cloves. Chinese cooks also use a variety of products made from beans, including black salted fermented beans and bean sauce or paste, which may be brown and pungent or yellow and mild. The Chinese have devised many unique methods to cook and season food, such as smoking a whole chicken with tea leaves in a covered wok. The Chinese have adapted some seasonings imported from countries in Southeast Asia and other regions, including cardamom, sweet basil, mustard seed, licorice, coriander, dill and saffron. See also ALCOHOLIC BEVERAGES; BANQUETS; BEANS AND BEAN PRODUCTS; CHOPSTICKS; COOKING, CHINESE; GINSENG; SOYBEANS AND SOY PRODUCTS; WOK.

SECOND OPIUM WAR   See ARROW WAR.

SECOND SINO-JAPANESE WAR   See WAR OF RESISTANCE AGAINST JAPAN.

SEEKING TRUTH   See RED FLAG.

SEISMOGRAPH AND SEISMOLOGY   See NATURAL DISASTERS; ZHANG HENG.

SELF-STRENGTHENING MOVEMENT (Ziqiang or Tzu Ch'iang)   A movement in China in the 1860s and 1870s to modernize and strengthen the country by adapting Western technology. China under the Qing dynasty (1644–1911) had been exposed as weak and vulnerable by its defeat by Britain in the Opium War (1839–42), the unequal treaties it was then forced to sign with foreign powers and several major rebellions in the mid-19th century. The name of the Self-Strengthening Movement was taken from one of the classic Confucian texts, the *Book of Changes:* "Heaven moves on strongly; the gentlemen ["superior men," *junzi* or *chun-tzu*] therefore strengthen themselves." Government leaders who promoted the movement quoted the classics to deflect criticism and to show that they intended to maintain China's cultural tradition while borrowing Western technology to build up the country's military strength. Feng Guifen (Feng Kuei-fen; 1809–74) led the movement, quoting the Chinese scholar Wei Yuan (1795–1856) that China should "learn the superior barbarian [non-Chinese] techniques to control the barbarians." Important Chinese supporters included Prince Gong (Kung), Zeng Guofan (Tseng Kuo-fan) and Li Hongzhang (Li Hung-chang).

One of the most important effects of the Self-Strengthening Movement was the establishment of the *Zongli yamen* (*Tsung-li yamen;* foreign office) in Beijing in 1861 and its language school in 1862. Major projects included the building of arsenals at Jiangnan and Nanjing, a dockyard at Fuzhou and a machine factory in Tianjin. The Chinese Merchants Steam Navigation Company was founded in 1872 to offset the dominance of foreign countries in China's coastal shipping. The Beiyang (Pei-yang) Fleet, the official Chinese naval fleet in waters off northern China, was founded in 1888. The Kaiping coal mines were greatly expanded to provide fuel for the ships, and the first permanent railway was completed in 1881 to transport the coal. Chinese scholars studied Western languages and science and Chinese students were sent to the United States. These students had to return to China in 1881, but the best ones were sent to Britain, France and Germany for advanced military and technical training.

Projects undertaken by the Self-Strengthening Movement did not succeed in making China a modern power, however, because they did not transform traditional Chinese institutions, such as the imperial bureaucracy. The limits of the movement became evident when China, a very large country, was easily defeated by the much smaller countries of France in the Sino-French War (1884–85) and Japan in the Sino-Japanese War (1894–95). When a number of Chinese leaders persuaded the emperor to issue edicts intended to modernize China during the so-called Reform Movement of 1898, also known as the Hundred Days Reform, the empress dowager staged a coup that abruptly ended the movement. Many of the reforms addressed in the edicts issued by the emperor during the Reform Movement had already been suggested by the leaders of the Self-Strengthening Movement. See also BOOK OF CHANGES; LI HONGZHANG; OPIUM WAR; REFORM MOVEMENT OF 1898; SINO-FRENCH WAR; SINO-JAPANESE WAR; ZENG GUOFAN; ZONGLI YAMEN.

SETO WARE   See CELADON WARE.

SEVEN SAGES OF THE BAMBOO GROVE (Zhulin Qixian or Chu-lin Ch'i Hsien)   Also known as the Seven Worthies of the Bamboo Grove; a group of scholars and poets during the mid- to late third century A.D. who fled the dangers of the imperial court and retired to the bamboo groves north of Luoyang, capital of the state of Wei, where they enjoyed drinking wine, writing poetry and discussing ideas. Such gatherings were popular with members of the literati (scholar) class from the third through the sixth centuries. Although the literati were educated in the classics of Confucianism, men who joined such groups had turned to the religion of Daoism, which emphasized nonaction and harmony with nature. Frequently joined by Buddhist monks, they were associated with the Daoist *qingtan* (*ch'ing-t'an,* or "pure conversation") movement, which advocated the freedom of expression and escape from the political intrigues of the imperial court.

The Seven Sages of the Bamboo Grove were the best known of these groups. The most famous of the Seven Sages was the eccentric poet Ruan Ji (Juan Chi; 210–63). Another sage, Xiang Xiu (Hsiang Hsiu; c. 230–80) was the coauthor of a well-known commentary on the work of the Daoist thinker Zhuangzi (Chuang Tzu). Other members of the group included Liu Ling, Shan Tao (Shan T'ao), Wang Rong

(Wang Jung) and the musician Yuan Xian (Yuan Hsien). The seventh member, Xi Kang (Hsi K'ang, 223–62), hosted the group. He was a fine writer who criticized the court so strongly that the imperial government condemned him to death even though he had thousands of supporters. The Seven Sages became models for Chinese scholars in later times who also were forced to retire because of political turmoil. See also CONFUCIANISM; DAOISM; LITERATI.

SEVENTY-TWO MARTYRS OF HUANG HUAGANG See SUN YAT-SEN.

SEZ See SPECIAL ECONOMIC ZONES.

SHAANXI PROVINCE A province in western China that covers an area of 75,696 square miles and has a population of about 31 million. Major cities include Xi'an, the capital, with a population of about 1.6 million, and Xianyang. This region, especially the Wei River valley, was settled as far back as the pre-Yangshao era of the Neolithic period (c. 12,000–2000 B.C.). The excavated village at Banpo near Xi'an dates from about 6,000 years ago and belongs to the Yangshao Culture (c. 5000–3000 B.C.). For the first 2,000 years of recorded history in China, Chinese capital cities were located in Shaanxi, especially in the Wei River valley. Xi'an, the site of the ancient city known as Chang'an, was the capital of 11 Chinese dynasties for a total of 1,080 years, alternating with Luoyang and other cities to the east and north. Rulers of the Zhou dynasty (1100–256 B.C.) lived in the city of Hao in the Wei valley near modern Xi'an until they had to flee in 771 B.C. As the Zhou declined in this region, the state of Qin developed, until Qin Shi Huangdi unified China under the Qin dynasty (221–206 B.C.) with his capital in the same area, known as Xianyang. The large terracotta army that was buried with him has been excavated near Xi'an and is one of China's most important tourist sites.

During the Han dynasty (206 B.C.–A.D. 220), the city was the terminus of the so-called Silk Road along which Chinese silk and other luxury goods were traded to the Roman empire. During the Tang dynasty (618–907), one of the greatest periods in Chinese culture, Chang'an was the largest and most cosmopolitan city in the world.

Shaanxi declined after the imperial capitals moved east and north following the Tang dynasty, until it became one of China's poorest regions. It suffered from peasant rebellions and wars into the modern era. Severe droughts and resultant famines from 1876 to 1878 and in 1928 caused about 8 million people to die. Since the founding of the People's Republic of China in 1949, Xi'an has become an industrialized city and is one of the most important economic and cultural centers in northwestern China.

Major sites in Xi'an allow tourists to experience much of its long history. Streets in the section of the city that was originally Chang'an were laid out in a north-south grid pattern that still remains. Foundations of ancient imperial palaces can be seen, as well as the Bell Tower (Zhonglou), where a bell sounded the time each day, and Drum Tower (Gulou). The Large Wild-Goose Pagoda (Dayan Ta) and Small Wild-Goose Pagoda (Xiaoyan Ta) are important Buddhist sites, as are two temples, Guangren Si and Daxingshan Si. The Forest of Steles (Xi'an Beilin) houses the largest and

oldest Chinese collection of stone columns engraved with calligraphy, some dating as far back as the Han dynasty. The Shaanxi Provincial Museum has excellent exhibits on the history of the area from prehistoric times through the Qing dynasty (1644–1911). The Qingzhen Si or Huajue Si Mosque Complex reflects the fact that thousands of Muslim traders settled in the city over the centuries. Confucian and Daoist temples include Dongyue Miao, the Temple of the Eight Immortals (baxianan), and the City God's Temple (Chenghuang Miao). Several sites lie outside the city in addition to the Banpo village excavation and the tomb and terra-cotta army of Emperor Qin Shi Huangdi. Huaqing Hot Springs at the foot of Mount Li, about 30 miles east of Xi'an, was an imperial resort area since ancient times. The Tang Imperial Tombs include the burial places of 19 of the 20 emperors of the Tang dynasty, including Gaozu (Kao-tsu), the first Tang emperor (given name Li Yuan; r. 618–26), who gave the city of Chang'an its name, meaning "Eternal Peace."

Along Shaanxi's northeastern border, the Yellow River (Huanghe), with its tributary the Wei, forms the borders of Shaanxi, Shanxi and Henan provinces. To the south lie the provinces of Hubei and Sichuan; to the west lie Gansu Province and Ningxia Hui Autonomous Region; and to the north lies Inner Mongolia Autonomous Region (Nei Menggu). Shaanxi is divided into three geographic regions. In the north is part of the vast loess plateau that covers about 204,633 square miles of northern China. Loess is a loose yellow soil that blows across China and builds up deposits that are fertile for agriculture. The Yellow River, one of China's two most important rivers, and its tributaries the Wei and the Jing, cross northern Shaanxi. The Chinese Communists used Yan'an in northern Shaanxi as their headquarters between 1936 and 1947 following the conclusion of the two-and-a-half-year Long March. In the center of the province lies the Wei River valley and the Xi'an region. In the south lies the Qinling Mountain Range, which separates and protects the Wei River valley from the upper basin of the Han River. Here is also found Mount Hua (Huashan), one of the Five Sacred Mountains of the Daoist religion. Ancient emperors made sacrificial offerings here to the Daoist gods when they claimed the "Mandate of Heaven" (tianming or t'ien-ming) that legitimized their reign.

Today Shaanxi Province is a major center for machine-building, textile production and electronics manufacturing. It is also China's largest producer of lacquerware, an ancient and beautiful craft. The province has large mineral deposits, including coal, molybdenum, aluminum, vanadium, mercury and nickel. Major agricultural products include grains, primarily corn, millet and sorghum, as well as walnuts, grapes, soybeans, cotton, tobacco, dairy animals and silkworm cocoons. The Jingjiang valley north of Xi'an was a major horse breeding area as far back as the Tang dynasty. Sheep and cattle also are raised in this region. See also CHANG'AN; FIVE SACRED MOUNTAINS OF DAOISM; HORSE; HUAQING HOT SPRINGS; LACQUERWARE; LOESS; MUSLIMS IN CHINA; NEOLITHIC PERIOD; QIN DYNASTY; QINLING MOUNTAIN RANGE; SILK ROAD; TANG DYNASTY; TANG IMPERIAL TOMBS; TERRACOTTA ARMY, TOMB OF QIN SHI HUANGDI; WEI RIVER; XI'AN; YAN'AN; YANGSHAO CULTURE; YELLOW RIVER; ZHOU DYNASTY.

SHADOW BOXING See BOXER UPRISING; TAIJIQUAN.

SHALONG BIRD SANCTUARY See CRANE; MANCHURIA.

SHAMANS See ALCHEMY.

SHAMISEN See SANXIAN.

SHAN-CHI See FANS.

SHANDONG PROVINCE A densely populated and industrialized province on the east coast of China. Shandong covers an area of 59,072 square miles and has a population of about 80 million. The capital city is Jinan, with a population of about 2.15 million. Other major cities include Zibo, Zaozhuang, Taian, Qingdao, Weifang, Ji'ning, Yantai and Dongying. Shandong's eastern region comprises a peninsula that divides the Yellow Sea from the Bo Hai Gulf. It is bordered by the provinces of Hebei to the northwest, Henan to the west, and Anhui and Jiangsu to the south. Shandong lies in the foothills of the Li Mountain Range just south of the Yellow River (Huanghe), one of China's two most important rivers. Mountain caves near Jinan contain Buddhist sculptures dating back to the Northern Wei dynasty (386–534), such as those of One Thousand Buddha Mountain. South of Jinan, Mount Tai (Taishan) is the most sacred of the five sacred Daoist mountains in China and the site of ritual sacrifices to Heaven performed by Chinese emperors. Shandong's southern region has a range of rugged mountains with Mount Tai as their highest point at 5,000 feet. Its eastern region is jutting into the Yellow Sea, a peninsula that contains low mountains with jagged slopes. The western and northern regions form a flat alluvial plain extending from the Yellow River. The land is fertile but dry, subject to long periods of drought. Also, the river has changed its course many times over the centuries, causing frequent disasters for the farmers who work the land.

Shandong has rich mineral and energy resources including coal, iron, gold, diamonds, aluminum and petroleum. Major industries include iron and steel, chemicals, machinery, motor vehicles, trains, ceramics and textiles. The province is famous for a type of heavy woven silk known by the old spelling of the province's name, Shantung. Shandong is China's largest producer of fertilizer and second largest producer of crude oil and salt. Major agricultural products include beer, grain, tobacco, silkworm cocoons, shellfish, marine and freshwater products, pork, mutton and dairy animals. Shandong is China's largest producer of corn, cotton, peanuts and other oil-bearing crops, and apples; it is the second-largest producer of pears, grapes, wheat and soybeans.

Shandong has an ancient history and was the site of the Neolithic culture known as Longshan ("Black Pottery"; c. 3000–c. 2200 B.C.). The state of Lu, home of the great philosophers Confucius (551–479 B.C.) and Mencius (c. 372–289 B.C.), developed in southern Shandong. Confucius (Kong Fuzi or K'ung Fu Tzu), the most important thinker in Chinese history, was born and taught in the city of Qufu. Until the 1930s the Kong family lived in the family compound in Qufu; recently the Chinese government has restored it and opened it to tourists. It includes the splendid Kongmiao Temple built to honor Confucius, with features similar to the Imperial Palace (Forbidden City) in Beijing. The graves of Confucius and 78 generations of his descendants may be seen in the Confucius Forest (Konglin) just north of Qufu.

By the fourth century A.D., due to its location on the Yellow Sea and the Yellow River, Shandong had become a major navigation center for goods being shipped between southern China (modern Guangdong and Fujian provinces) and regions to the north and west. During the 19th century, Shandong suffered from heavy flooding of the Yellow River, which changed its course toward the north in 1852, and from incursions of British, Japanese and German traders and military forces. In the treaty of 1898, the weak Chinese government gave Germany a 99-year lease to an area in Shandong and permission to build a port and railroad in Qingdao on the Yellow Sea. Until 1914 Germans controlled Shandong's economy. Qingdao, with a population of about 1.4 million, is now the most industrialized city in Shandong as well as the most popular seashore resort in China. The Germans constructed a deepwater harbor and large European buildings and founded a brewery, which still produces China's best-known beer, Qingdao, or Tsingtao, as it is marketed around the world. Japan occupied Qingdao during World War I and the War of Resistance against Japan (1937–45; World War II). Chinese Nationalists (Kuomintang; KMT) held Qingdao between the wars. In 1948, during China's civil war, the Communists gained final control of Qingdao and began developing the city's heavy and light industries. In 1984 the Chinese government designated Qingdao as one of China's 14 Coastal Open Cities for foreign trade and investment. Yellow Island, a peninsula southeast of Qingdao, has been declared a Special Economic Zone to promote joint ventures between Chinese and foreign companies.

Ji'nan, 217 miles south of Beijing between the Yellow River and the Taishan Mountain Range, is a major industrial, transportation and military center as well as the capital of Shandong. It is also famous for its hot springs and scenic tourist sites. Ji'nan developed rapidly after 1904, when Germans constructed a railway line to Qingdao. In 1912 this was connected to the major railroad line linking Tianjin, Beijing and central China. Many textile mills were put into operation, and European-style buildings were constructed that still can be seen. See also ALCOHOLIC BEVERAGES; BO HAI GULF; JI'NAN; LONGSHAN CULTURE; QINGDAO; QUFU; RAILROADS; SPECIAL ECONOMIC ZONES; TAI, MOUNT; YELLOW RIVER; YELLOW SEA.

SHANG DYNASTY (1750–1040 B.C.) The first dynasty in Chinese history from which have been excavated artifacts and written records. The Shang succeeded the Xia dynasty (2200–1750 B.C.) when Tang the Victorious overthrew the Xia king Jie (Chieh), who supposedly was a tyrant, and founded the Shang dynasty. Tang the Victorious first conquered many other tribes by persuading them to switch their loyalty from the Xia dynasty to the Shang. He finally captured the Xia capital, near modern Zhengzhou in Henan Province. Tang exiled the Xia king and proclaimed the Shang dynasty. Ancient Chinese documents contain only a few mentions of these two earliest dynasties, and scholars have doubted the historical existence of the Xia, so it is considered semilegendary. Archaeologists have found numerous artifacts from the Shang dynasty, and inscriptions on oracle bones and bronzeware excavated at Anyang, the final Shang capital, in modern Henan Province, provide some information about the Shang dynasty. The first Shang capital was at Xibo on the Luo River (Luohe), close to the Yellow River (Huanghe), 10 miles east of Luoyang; Luoyang served as the capital for several later Chinese dynasties. Archaeologists discovered and excavated the ruins of Xibo in the 1980s. The second Shang capital was at Zhengzhou, south of the Yellow River in Henan, where the 16th-century-B.C. palace building has been reconstructed. Originally the Shang were a nomadic tribe; after they settled in Henan, they gradually began practicing agriculture, with millet, wheat and rice as their main crops.

Some scholars maintain that Chinese civilization emerged during the Shang, with the development of a writing system, an accurate calendar, the organization of tribes into a system of centralized rule under a king, the organized worship of ancestors, a religious system with a pantheon of gods, elaborate burials in tombs filled with goods, horse-drawn chariots for warfare and crafts such as jade carving and silk weaving. Many artistic developments occurred, such as the discovery of glazes to decorate pottery and techniques for working jade. Shang craftsmen took bronze working to its highest technical and aesthetic level, which has never been surpassed. They made a variety of large containers, such as the *ding* (*ting*), which were used mainly to hold food and wine for ceremonial purposes and funeral rituals. The bronze vessels were cast with complex decorations on their surfaces, some of them geometric designs and others suggesting the faces of animals. Shang kings and aristocrats were buried with huge quantities of bronze vessels and pottery and jade implements, as well as with human and animal sacrifices. The humans were mostly prisoners who had been captured from nomadic tribes on the Shang's western borders.

The Chinese acquired wheat, goats and chariots from the Middle East around 1300 B.C., which spurred Chinese agriculture and warfare and the emergence of a military ruling class. Bronze chariots, daggers, halberds and axes were used in battles. Most of the people were peasants who practiced agriculture and lived much as Chinese did during the Neolithic period (c. 12,000–2000 B.C.). Thousands of objects have been excavated from tombs at the last Shang capital, near Anyang in modern Henan Province. Oracle bones were used to divine the answers provided by ancestors of the Shang royal line to questions regarding important state matters. Royal priests took the shoulder blades of ritually sacrificed sheep and cattle and tortoiseshells and cracked them by applying hot metal rods, then interpreted the shapes of the cracks as positive or negative answers to the questions. The priests inscribed the questions and answers on the bones or shells in an archaic script, known as the Shell-Bone Script (*jiaguwen* or *chia-ku wen*), which predates classical Chinese written characters, and stored them in pits. More than 100,000 oracle bones have been excavated, and scholars have published the results of research on about 15,000 of them.

The Shang dynasty was overthrown by the Zhou people, who settled in the Wei River valley and made their capital at Chang'an (modern Xi'an in Shaanxi Province). Zhou had been a vassal state of the Shang, charged with defending the western borders, but Zhou kings Wen and Wu rebelled against the Shang ruler. The Zhou destroyed the Shang capital at Anyang, with the help of Shang slaves they had persuaded to revolt. The duke of Zhou, son of King Wen and younger brother of King Wu, had spent many years in the Shang court. After the Zhou defeated the Shang, the duke of Zhou gave a speech to the Shang nobles telling them that Heaven (*Tian* or *T'ien*) had decreed that the Shang king Dixin (Ti-hsin) was immoral, had broken Heaven's laws and deserved to be punished by being overthrown. This was the first statement of the theory of the Mandate of Heaven (*Tianming* or *T'ien-ming*), which each succeeding Chinese dynasty used to legitimize its overthrow of the previous dynasty. See also ANCESTOR WORSHIP; ANYANG; BRONZEWARE; DING; HENAN PROVINCE; JADE; LUOYANG; MANDATE OF HEAVEN; NEOLITHIC PERIOD; ORACLE BONES; SILK; WEN, KING, AND WU, KING; WRITING SYSTEM, CHINESE; XIA DYNASTY; YELLOW RIVER; ZHENGZHOU; ZHOU DYNASTY.

SHANG YANG, LORD (390–338 B.C.)   A statesman who became the prime minister of the state of Qin, laying the foundation for the unification of China by Emperor Qin Shi Huangdi (259–210 B.C.) under the Qin dynasty (221–206 B.C.). Shang Yang, originally called Gongsun Yang (Kung-sun Yang), was raised in the neighboring state of Wei and was the descendant of a royal concubine. He served the prime minister of Wei, who recommended to the king that Shang Yang be his successor. However, the king did not appoint him to this position, and in 356 B.C. Shang Yang was recruited by King Xiao of Qin. The state of Qin had been a small fiefdom west of the royal domain of the Zhou dynasty (1100–256 B.C.). It was one of the contending independent states that increased in power during the Warring States Period (403–221 B.C.). Qin was located in the upper Wei River valley and was easily defended because enemies could approach only through a few strategic mountain passes. The Qin army always had to be on alert against invading nomadic tribes.

As prime minister, Shang Yang built up Qin into a powerful military machine following the principles of the Legalist School of Thought. He centralized the administration of the counties within the state and divided the population into groups of families that had to provide prescribed numbers of young men to serve in the army. He attracted immigrants from other states by raising the status of peasants through such policies as allowing them to buy and sell land. The subsequent growth of Qin's population provided more soldiers for its army. Shang Yang enacted new laws that exacted harsh punishments, but he also established a generous system of rewards and honorary ranks for those who performed exemplary military service. He built up a professional military class and weakened the power of the traditional aristocratic clans. Shang Yang also persuaded King Xiao (Hsiao) to order the burning of two documents that later became classics in the Confucian canon, the Book of Songs (*Shijing* or *Shih-ching*) and the Book of History (*Shujing* or *Shu-ching*), foreshadowing the massive burning of books by Emperor Qin Shi Huangdi.

Shang Yang's theories and government reforms were laid out in the Book of Lord Shang (*Shangjunshu* or *Shang-chun-shu*), which was compiled by his close followers. His policies made him disliked and feared by both nobles and commoners, but he was safe as long as Xiao remained king of Qin. After King Xiao died in 338 B.C., Shang Yang's enemies immediately had him arrested. He escaped to the lands he owned at Shang and prepared to resist but was captured and killed. His corpse was torn apart by chariots, and the members of his family were also killed. However, successors continued Shang Yang's policies because they knew the benefits to Qin of a centralized government bureaucracy and a strong army. After Shang Yang's death, three dukes ruled Qin for a total of 107 years, and during their long reigns they increased Qin's power through military might and strategic alliances. In 330 B.C. Qin extended its eastern border to the Yellow River, taking lands from the state of Wei. In 316 B.C. it moved southwest to annex the state of Shu, which covered a large area of modern Sichuan Province. See also LEGALIST SCHOOL OF THOUGHT; QIN DYNASTY; QIN SHI HUANGDI, EMPEROR; WARRING STATES PERIOD; WEI RIVER.

SHANGDI (Shang-ti) The Lord on High; the deity who controls the way the universe works and who keeps watch over human beings. According to Chinese legend, Shangdi resides in Heaven (tian or t'ien; sometimes translated as "Sky"). The other gods are placed under his rule, especially those who govern natural phenomena such as the Sun, Moon, stars, wind, rain and certain mountains and rivers. All these deities were thought to have a direct effect on the agricultural economy of China. The Chinese traditionally believed that their ancestors also went to live in Heaven after they died, from where the ancestors continued to have a strong influence on the lives of their descendants.

In prehistoric times Shangdi originally may have been the chief god of a ruling clan, likely an ancestor who became worshiped as divine; he may have gained preeminence as the clan's power increased. By the time of the Zhou dynasty (1100–256 B.C.), Shangdi had such a high position that only the Zhou kings were permitted to make the required ritual sacrifices to him. The Zhou justified their conquest of the Shang dynasty (1750–1040 B.C.) by claiming that the Shang rulers had lost the Mandate of Heaven (tianming or t'ien ming) that gave them their right to rule, and the Zhou claimed it for themselves.

In ancient China the concept of Heaven was connected with that of Shangdi in terms of the similar power they exercised over the universe and humans, and the two terms seem to have meant the same thing. Over time, however, the character "di" in the name Shangdi became specifically associated with the emperor, the highest ruler in human society. The term "Heaven" became applied to the governing power of the universe as a whole. Up to the modern era, the Chinese called the emperor "Son of Heaven" (tianzi or t'ien tzu). They believed that Shangdi rules in Heaven in exactly the same was as the emperor rules on Earth, assisted by the gods as the emperor is assisted by ministries in his bureaucratic government. See also EMPEROR; HEAVEN; IMPERIAL BUREAUCRACY; MANDATE OF HEAVEN; SON OF HEAVEN; ZHOU DYNASTY.

SHANGDU See CHENGDE; KARAKORUM; KHUBILAI KHAN; POLO, MARCO; YUAN DYNASTY.

SHANGHAI The largest city in China, with a metropolitan population of about 14 million, and one of the most densely populated areas in the world. Shanghai, which covers 2,350 square miles, lies between Jiangsu and Zhejiang provinces but is governed as an autonomous municipality with 10 urban boroughs and 10 rural counties. Shanghai is China's most important financial and industrial center and also one of the world's largest ports, due to its location at the mouth of the Yangzi River (Changjiang), where it flows into the East China Sea. The Huangpu (Whampoa) River flows through the center of the city and into the Yangzi. The name Shanghai means "To Go toward the Sea." More than 2,000 oceangoing ships and 15,000 river steamships put in at Shanghai every year. Major industries include textiles, electronics, shipbuilding, machinery, chemicals, steel and metallurgy, bicycles, home appliances and processed foods.

Until the mid-19th century Shanghai was a center for fishing and textile weaving, and it was walled to keep out pirates. After the British defeated China in the Opium War (1839–42), they forced the Manchu Qing government (1644–1911) to sign the Treaty of Nanjing, whose conditions included the opening of five Chinese cities, including Shanghai, as so-called treaty ports to Western traders and residents. The British opened a concession in Shanghai in 1842 and the French in 1847, and in 1863 an International Settlement was established in the city. After Japan defeated China in the Sino-Japanese War of 1894–95, a Japanese concession also was opened in Shanghai on the north bank of the Wusong River. All of the foreign districts were autonomous and ruled by the laws and police of their respective countries, a principle known as extraterritoriality. After Shanghai became a treaty port, Chinese from all over the country began pouring into the city to work as traders and laborers, and by 1900, one million people lived in the city. The Taiping Rebellion (1850–64) benefited Shanghai because it caused most of China's foreign trade, which had formerly been conducted in the southern city of Guangzhou (Canton), to be redirected to Shanghai. The China Merchants Steam Navigation Company was established in Shanghai in 1872.

The International Settlement in Shanghai was located north of the old Chinese city, a labyrinth of alleys along which many Chinese still live today, although they are being replaced by high-rise apartment buildings. The combination of Western financing and expertise with Chinese entrepreneurship and labor transformed Shanghai into Asia's largest and most cosmopolitan city in the 1920s and 1930s, known as the Paris of the East. Wealthy financial houses established headquarters in Shanghai, including the Hongkong and Shanghai Banking Corporation, the Chartered Bank of India, Australia and China, Chase Manhattan Bank and National City Bank of New York, as did powerful British trading firms such as Jardine and Matheson and Sassoon. European-style buildings to house banks, trading houses, hotels, businesses and clubs were erected on the Bund along the Huangpu River, mainly during the 1920s, and are still used today. The British imported the Anglo-Indian word "Bund," meaning the embankment of a muddy waterfront, from similar waterfronts in colonial India. (The Chinese call the Bund waitan.) Today Chinese and foreigners throng to the area to perform taijiquan and martial arts in the morning and shop and socialize in the day and evening. The British Public Gardens, now called Huangpu Park, are located at the northwestern end of the Bund. The Hongkong and Shanghai Banking Corporation building, completed in 1921 and one of Asia's most impressive colonial buildings, now houses the Shanghai People's Municipal Government. The Customs House at 13 Zhongshan Dongyi Road, completed in 1927, still operates. Money invested in Shanghai became the largest single foreign investment in the world. Foreign ships protected the city by patrolling the Huangpu and Yangzi rivers and the Chinese coast. Shanghai became notorious not only for its wealth and its factories, employing more than 200,000 workers, but also for its dance halls, brothels, and gambling and opium dens.

The Chinese people overthrew the Qing dynasty in the Revolution of 1911, led by Dr. Sun Yat-sen, the founder of modern China. In 1912 he was inaugurated as provisional president of the Republic of China (ROC), although he soon had to yield the presidency to Yuan Shikai. Sun went into exile in Japan but returned by ship to Shanghai in 1916 and spent several years shuttling between Shanghai and Guangzhou, trying to get military support for his republican leadership. The Chinese Communist Party (CCP), which founded the People's Republic of China (PRC) in 1949, was organized in Shanghai in July 1921. The small red-brick building at 76 Xingye Road near Fuxing Park where the first CCP meeting was held can still be seen. The Communists were very active in organizing workers in Shanghai, and they cooperated with the Nationalist Party (Kuomintang; KMT) established by Sun Yat-sen.

After Sun died in 1925, his brother-in-law Chiang Kai-shek became head of the KMT. In March 1927 workers in Shanghai began an armed revolution and a general strike and set up a workers' government. On March 22 Chiang led the army of the Northern Expedition into Shanghai, and on April 12 Chiang, cooperating with foreign police and factory owners in the city, turned against the CCP and ordered the KMT to massacre Communists. CCP members who survived fled to the countryside and joined Communist forces that fought the KMT. Japanese troops occupied Shanghai in 1937 during China's War of Resistance against Japan (1937–45; World War II). After Japan was defeated, the CCP and KMT resumed their civil war. In 1949 the CCP defeated the KMT, whose leaders and many members fled to Taiwan, and the CCP founded the People's Republic of China (PRC). The Communists worked hard to "clean up" Shanghai and make it a showcase for their new government. The turbulent Cultural Revolution (1966–76) began when CCP leader Mao Zedong (Mao Tse-tung) published a polemical article in a Shanghai newspaper, and many violent confrontations took place in the city. The so-called Gang of Four, four high CCP officials who were arrested in October 1976, less than a month after Mao died, and blamed for causing the Cultural Revolution, had their power base in Shanghai. Jiang Qing (Chiang Ch'ing), Mao's widow and the accused leader of the Gang of Four, had been an actress in Shanghai in the 1930s. Today the Shanghai Film Studio is one of the leading film studios in China.

Following the Cultural Revolution, Deng Xiaoping (Teng Hsiao-p'ing) led the movement to reform and modernize the PRC and encourage foreign trade once more. In 1984 the PRC government, after establishing four Special Economic Zones (SEZs) in southern China for foreign investment and trade, designated Shanghai one of 14 coastal open cities also open to foreign investment and trade. The Shanghai munici-

pal government is developing Pudong New Area, a triangle of about 217 square miles on the east side of the Huangpu River, into five zones that handle finance and commerce, export processing, free trade, heavy industry, and science and education. The Shanghai stock exchange, which had been closed in 1949, was reopened on September 26, 1986. Many current political and economic leaders are from Shanghai. Rong Yiren (Jung Yi-jen), who founded the China International Trust and Investment Corporation (CITIC) in 1979, belongs to a wealthy Shanghai business family. CCP general secretary Jiang Zemin (Chiang Tse-min) served as mayor of Shanghai from 1985 to 1988 and secretary of the Shanghai branch of the CCP from 1987 to 1989. Shanghai has undergone an economic boom, with highways and skyscrapers being constructed all over the city. The Shanghai World Financial Center, 1,510 feet high, is scheduled to be completed in 2001. A Japanese construction magnate recently announced plans to build the tallest building in the world in Shanghai.

Nanjing Road East (Nanjing Donglu), between the Peace and Park hotels, is Shanghai's busiest shopping center, attracting hundreds of thousands of shoppers on the weekends. The Peace Hotel is the most magnificent pre-1949 hotel in the city. Other major shopping areas include Huaihai Zhonglu, Ruijin Lu, Sichuan Beilu, Jinling Donglu and Nanjing Xilu. The Friendship Store for foreigners was located in the former British consulate on the Bund but has moved to a new building nearby. The Shanghai Antique and Curios Store also is visited by many tourists. The former clubhouse at the racetrack in Renmin Park, one of the oldest buildings in the city, is now the Shanghai Municipal Library. The Shanghai Museum was recently renovated and exhibits Chinese art and archaeological artifacts. The governor of Sichuan Province, named Yu, laid out the Mandarin Gardens (Yuyuan) between 1559 and 1577 for his parents. In 1853 the gardens served as the headquarters for the Small Sword Society, which revolted against the Qing and foreigners in China. The gardens are located in a crowded bazaar filled with shops and restaurants, the popular Wuxingtong Teahouse and the Temple of the Town Gods. The city has a wide range of theaters, movie houses and other entertainment venues, and nightly shows at the Shanghai Acrobatics Theatre are very popular.

A major site in Shanghai is the residence of Sun Yat-sen, where he lived for six years. After he died in 1925, his widow, Soong Qingling, the most prominent woman in modern China, continued to reside there until Japan invaded China in 1937. The tomb of Lu Xun (Lu Hsun), modern China's greatest writer, is located on Sichuan Beilu in Hongkou Park, along with the Lu Xun Museum and residence. The Jade Buddha Temple houses a 6½-foot-high jade sculpture of the seated Buddha, covered with jewels, and is a popular site for overseas Chinese tour groups. The pagoda at Longhua Temple, built during the Song dynasty (960–1279), is the oldest structure in Shanghai; it has been restored several times.

Outside of the city center can be seen the Longhua Pagoda, St. Ignatius Cathedral, the Shanghai Exhibition Center, Huzhou Pagoda and Sassoon Villas, the former residence of the wealthy Sassoon family, which now houses the Shanghai Municipal Children's Palace. The Shanghai Botanical Gardens has a collection of 9,000 container gardens, miniature trees and plants known in the West by the Japanese term *bonsai*. Boat trips depart from the dock on the Bund to make a 40-mile round trip on the Huangpu River to its junction with the Yangzi River. See also ACROBATICS AND VARIETY THEATER; ALLEYS; CHILDREN'S PALACES; CHINA MERCHANTS STEAM NAVIGATION COMPANY; CHINESE COMMUNIST PARTY; CONTAINER GARDENS; CULTURAL REVOLUTION; EAST CHINA SEA; FILM STUDIOS; GANG OF FOUR; HONGKONG AND SHANG-HAI BANKING CORPORATION; HUANGPU RIVER; INTERNATIONAL SETTLEMENT IN SHANGHAI; JIANG QING; JIANG ZEMIN; LU XUN; NANJING, TREATY OF; NORTHERN EXPEDITION; OPIUM WAR; PUDONG NEW AREA, SHANGHAI; RONG YIREN; SHIPPING AND SHIPBUILDING; SMALL SWORD SOCIETY; SOONG QINGLING; SPECIAL ECONOMIC ZONES; SUN YAT-SEN; TAIPING REBELLION; TEXTILE INDUSTRY; TREATY PORTS; YANGZI RIVER.

SHANGHAI COMMUNIQUÉ See NIXON, RICHARD M., U.S. PRESIDENT, VISIT TO CHINA.

SHANGHAI TRIAD See GONG LI; ZHANG YIMOU.

SHANGHUNSHU See SHANG YANG, LORD SHANG.

SHANG-TI See SHANGDI.

SHANG-TU See CHENGDE; KARAKORUM; KHUBILAI KHAN; POLO, MARCO; YUAN DYNASTY.

SHANHAIGUAN (SHAN-HAI-KUAN) PASS See BEIDAIHE; GREAT WALL; HEBEI PROVINCE; QING DYNASTY.

SHANSHUIHUA See LANDSCAPE PAINTING.

SHANSI PROVINCE See SHANXI PROVINCE.

SHANTOU Formerly known as Swatow (Swatou); the second-largest city and port, next to Guangzhou (Canton), in the southern Chinese province of Guangdong. Located on a peninsula in the estuary of the Rong and Dagang rivers, Shantou was a small fishing village when the British East India Company built a station on an island outside the harbor in the 18th century. During the 16th and 17th centuries, large quantities of colorful ceramics made in nearby Fujian Province were exported to Japan, Southeast Asia, Indonesia and India through Shantou, then called Swatow, and thus became known as Swatow ware. In 1860 Shantou was opened to foreign trade as a so-called treaty port by the Treaty of Tianjin that concluded the Arrow War (Second Opium War, 1856–60) between China and Great Britain. Shantou became one of the ports from which Chinese laborers, known as coolies, immigrated to North and South America in the mid-19th century, to build railways or to work in silver mines in Peru.

Today the city has a population of about 500,000 and is a fishing port with food processing and electronics industries. It has undergone economic development since 1979, when the Chinese government designated Shantou one of four Special Economic Zones (SEZs) to encourage foreign trade and investment. Tourist sites include Sun Yat-sen Park, dedicated to the founder of modern China; Zhongshan Park; and

Mayu Island at the entrance to Shantou Harbor, which is being developed as a beach resort. Many residents of Shantou speak the Hakka language or the local dialect. Hakkas belong to the Han Chinese ethnic majority but have their own customs and language.

Chaozhou lies 25 miles away from Shantou at the foot of Mount Lingnan (Lingnanshan) in a plain where farmers produce three crops of rice each year. The history of the city goes back more than 2,000 years; it is one of the so-called four famous ancient towns of China. During the Tang dynasty (618–907), government officials who fell out of favor were exiled to Chaozhou. Embroidery is a famous handicraft of the town, which is also famous for its distinctive cuisine. Tourist sites include West Lake Park, Xiangzi Bridge, Phoenix Pagoda and Wenggong Temple, which was built during the Han dynasty (206 B.C.–A.D. 220). Kaiyuan Buddhist temple, built in 738, has been restored and is now a museum. The combined region of Shantou and Chaozhou often is called Chaoshan. Many overseas Chinese now living in Thailand came from this area. See also BRITISH EAST INDIA COMPANY; COOLIE; GUANGDONG; GUANGZHOU; HAKKA; OVERSEAS CHINESE; SPECIAL ECONOMIC ZONES; SWATOW WARE; TIANJIN, TREATY OF; TREATY PORTS.

SHANTUNG See SHANDONG PROVINCE.

SHANXI PROVINCE A province in northern China that covers an area of 60,602 square miles and has a population of about 30 million. The northern boundary of the province is actually the Great Wall, which runs for 1,500 miles east to west across northern China, and the southern boundary is the Yellow River (Huanghe). Shanxi borders Hebei Province to the east, Henan Province to the south, Shaanxi Province to the west and Inner Mongolia Autonomous Region to the north. The name Shanxi means "west of the mountain," referring to the Taihang Mountain Range to the east, with an altitude of over 3,000 feet. To the west lies the Luliang Mountain Range. The capital of Shanxi is Taiyuan, an industrialized city in the center of the province at the northern end of the fertile Taiyuan Basin, which had been a lake until about 5,000 years ago. Shanxi has China's largest deposits of coal and aluminum and the second-largest deposits of titanium as well as huge quantities of other mineral resources. The province is a major center for heavy industry and has one of the largest iron- and steel-producing factory complexes in China. Other important industries include machinery and textiles. During the War of Resistance against Japan (1937–45; World War II), a great deal of fighting took place in Shanxi as invading Japanese troops exploited the coal mining and other industries around Taiyuan. The Communists, who took control of China in 1949, have continued to develop Taiyuan's industrialization.

Two-thirds of Shanxi Province belongs to the largest loess plateau in the world, which covers 600,000 square miles and includes parts of Gansu, Henan and Shaanxi provinces as well as parts of the Ningxia-Hui and Inner Mongolia Autonomous Regions. Loess is loose yellow soil that blows in from the Gobi and other deserts in western China, building up fertile plateaus and filling the Yellow River (Huanghe) with silt. Dry winds from the northwest cause frequent droughts in Shanxi, and famines were a serious problem before modern irrigation systems were constructed. Most of the rain falls between June and September. The majority of Shanxi's population are farmers whose main crops are wheat, sorghum, millet and cotton.

Taiyuan is situated on the Fen River (Fenhe), a tributary of the Yellow River. To the north, the province opens onto the Mongolian plateau, making Shanxi a corridor through which various nomadic tribes have invaded over the centuries, including the Xiongnu, the Xianbei and the Mongols. The Great Wall had been built as protection against these nomads, but they broke through and moved down the Fen River valley to the heart of the Chinese Empire. In Taiyuan, the Shanxi Provincial Museum houses exhibits on the region's history. The industrialized city of Datong, just south of the Great Wall, long served as a trading center. It sits at the center of Shanxi's coal mining region, on the main railroad line between Beijing and Inner Mongolia. Nearby, Yungang is famous for 53 caves that were carved in the fifth century A.D. and include a 55-foot-high statue of Sakyamuni, founder of the Buddhist religion. This is the oldest collection of Buddhist stone carvings in China.

The southern region of Shanxi played a significant role in the development of Chinese civilization. The state of Qin became a powerful center in the Fen valley during the Western Zhou dynasty (1100–771 B.C.). Several other states vied for power during the Spring and Autumn Period (770–481 B.C.). The kingdom of Jin, with Yi as its capital, gained supremacy between 632 and 597 B.C. In the mid-fifth century, at the beginning of the Warring States Period (403–221 B.C.), Jin was divided into three kingdoms: the Wei in the lower Fen valley; the Han to the south of the imperial domain of the Zhou, centered at Luoyang; and the Zhao with their center at Taiyuan (then called Jinyang). These three kingdoms belonged to Qixong, the Seven Powers, which were unified under Qin in 221 B.C. (Qin dynasty; 221–206 B.C.). Following unification, northern Shanxi played a crucial role in defending the Chinese empire against northern invaders, although the foreign tribes were able to establish several dynasties from the third through the sixth centuries A.D. The Toba founded the Northern Wei dynasty, which controlled northern China from 386 to 534. This region was also the power base for the founding of the Tang dynasty (618–907) and was a strategic area in the Tang defense against invading Turkish tribes. See also DATONG; GREAT WALL; LOESS; MINING INDUSTRY; MONGOL; NORTHERN WEI DYNASTY; QIN DYNASTY; SPRING AND AUTUMN PERIOD; TAIYUAN; TANG DYNASTY; WAR OF RESISTANCE AGAINST JAPAN; WARRING STATES PERIOD; WESTERN ZHOU DYNASTY; XIONGNU; YELLOW RIVER; YUNGANG CAVE TEMPLES AND SCULPTURES.

SHANZI See FANS.

SHAO HSING See ALCOHOLIC BEVERAGES; ZHEJIANG PROVINCE.

SHAOLIN TEMPLE (Shaolin Si) A Chan (Zen) Buddhist monastery that is reputedly where Chinese martial arts (*wushu*), especially the slow-moving weaponless form known as *taijiquan* (t'ai-chi-ch'uan), originated. Shaolin Tem-ple is located about 55 miles southwest of the city of Zhengzhou in Henan Province, and was built in 495 during the Northern Wei dynasty. The Indian Buddhist monk Tuoba supposedly came to China during this period, and Emperor Xiaowen (Hsiao-wen) had Shaolin Temple built for him. According to Chan tradition, Bodhidharma (known in China as Damo or Tamo) came to China from India in 527 during the reign of Emperor Wu (502–549) and founded the Chan Sect of Buddhism at Shaolin Temple. Bodhidharma is credited with developing techniques for training the monks, known as Shaolin Quan, so they could concentrate their minds during their long periods of meditation. These techniques were believed to be the source for *taijiquan* and other methods of fighting without weapons, such as *kung fu* (*gongfu*). These methods also spread to Korea and Japan, where they are known as *karate*, and recently have become popular in the West.

Shaolin Temple was destroyed in 617 but rebuilt in 627. It gained prominence during the Tang dynasty (618–907) when 13 of its monks fought on behalf of Li Shimin (Li Shih-min), who founded the Tang, against his enemy Wang Shi-chong (Wang Shih-ch'ung). The second Tang emperor, known as Taizong (T'ai-tsung; r. 626–49), rewarded the monks by donating large sums of money and land to the temple. Shaolin Temple became so wealthy and famous that sometimes as many as 1,000 monks resided there. The Shaolin monastery complex was destroyed and rebuilt several times. The current buildings date back to the Ming (1368–1644) and Qing (1644–1911) dynasties. The floors of the temple's main hall, Thousand Buddha Hall (Qianfo Dian), show wear from the many monks who practiced their fighting techniques there. Murals in the Baiyi Pavilion depict the fighting monks. The hall contains a beautifully carved jade sculpture of the Buddhist deity Amitabha and a wall painting of 500 *lohan* ("worthies") covers three sides of the hall. Shaolin monks are buried in the 220 pagodas in the compound. A "forest of stelae" (stone tablets or columns) contains inscriptions by many famous calligraphers, including Su Shi (also known as Su Dongpo or Su Tung-p'o; 1036–1101) and Mi Fu (Mi Fei; 1051–1107). Bodhidharma Pavilion was built in the complex to honor the Chan founder and his successor, the second Chan patriarch, Huige (Huike or Hui-k'o; 487–593). There is a cave near the monastery where Bodhidharma supposedly spent many years in meditation. See also BODHIDHARMA; CHAN SECT OF BUDDHISM; KUNG FU; LI SHIMIN; LUOHAN; MARTIAL ARTS; MI FU; STONE TABLETS; SU SHI; TAIJIQUAN; TANG DYNASTY; TEMPLES.

SHAONIAN GONG See CHILDREN'S PALACES.

SHAOSHAN, HUNAN PROVINCE See MAO ZEDONG.

SHAOSHU MINZU See MINORITIES, NATIONAL.

SHAOXING See ALCOHOLIC BEVERAGES; ZHEJIANG PROVINCE.

SHEKOU INDUSTRIAL ZONES See CHINA MERCHANTS STEAM NAVIGATION COMPANY; SPECIAL ECONOMIC ZONES.

SHELL AND BONE WRITING See ORACLE BONES.

SHEN CHOU See SHEN ZHOU.

SHEN CONGWEN (Shen Ts'ung-wen; 1902–88) A modern Chinese author who wrote more than three dozen works of fiction. Shen was born in Hunan Province in central China and had ancestors in the Miao and Tuji minority ethnic groups. When he was 14, his family suffered setbacks and he had to take a job as a scribe with a military unit. He joined a regiment in Yuanling in southern China, the site of border skirmishes with local members of the Miao ethnic group. He first became known as an author for the short stories he wrote about his experiences there. In 1922 Shen went to Beijing, the capital of China, and became a fiction writer; in a single decade he wrote more than 20 volumes. He spent much of his life producing novels and short stories.

Shen set many of his books on the banks of the Wuhui River, which flows through his hometown of Fenghuang. He wrote in a beautiful vernacular style that was influenced by Chinese translations of Western works of fiction. However, he also drew upon the techniques of classical Chinese literature. Shen wrote his finest novel, *The Long River* (*Changhe* or *Ch'ang ho*), while China was fighting its War of Resistance against Japan (1937–45; World War II). During that time he also taught Chinese literature at several universities. His most important collections of short stories are *Lamp of Spring* (*Zhunji* or *Ch'un-teng chi*) and *Black Phoenix* (*Heifengji* or *Hei-feng chi*). In his fiction, Shen depicted the difficult lives of peasants in the Chinese countryside, especially in western Hunan Province. He also became well known for his descriptions of army clerks, shopkeepers, boatmen and Miao people. He wrote *Western Hunan, Hunan Travelogues* and *Border Town* about his native province. In the preface to *Border Town*, Shen wrote that he had an "indescribable affection for peasants and soldiers," who were "upright and honest." Shen is China's best known modern writer of "literature of the countryside." Altogether he wrote more than 4 million words in his novels and in his autobiography, translated as *Autobiography of Congwen*. Shen's works have been translated into many foreign languages.

After the Chinese Communists defeated the Nationalists and established the People's Republic of China (PRC) in 1949, the Communists subjected Shen, who had not been involved in politics, and many other Chinese artists and intellectuals to so-called thought reform. This caused Shen to suffer a nervous breakdown. Thereafter he no longer wrote fiction. However, in 1955 he recovered his health and was given a position on the staff of the Palace Museum in Beijing, where he wrote nonfiction and performed a great deal of historical research. Shen's first historical work, *Study of Ancient Chinese Costumes*, was published in 1981. He also wrote *The Bronze Mirrors of the Tang and Song Dynasties, Designs of Chinese Silk, Ming Brocade* and *Lacquerware of the Warring States Period*. See also BRONZEWARE; CIVIL WAR BETWEEN COMMUNISTS AND NATIONALISTS; FORBIDDEN CITY: HUNAN PROVINCE; LACQUERWARE; MIAO; MINORITIES, NATIONAL; PEASANTS AND PEASANT REBELLIONS; SILK.

SHEN FU (fl. 1786) An author who is famous for his autobiographical work, *Six Chapters of a Floating Life* (*Fousheng liuji* or *Fou-sheng liu-chi*). Only four of the six chapters have survived. Shen Fu wrote in a clear, strong form of the classical Chinese language used by writers during the late Ming dynasty (1368–1644). Very little is known about Shen Fu apart from this book, which presents a charming description of married life. The husband is a poor, unsuccessful member of the literati, or scholar-gentry class. Literati men were educated in the Confucian classics and took highly competitive government-sponsored examinations to gain positions in the imperial bureaucracy or civil service. The book's first chapter details the happiness the husband enjoys with his wife, even though they were brought together by an arranged marriage. The pleasures they share include taking boat rides on moonlit evenings and planting flowers in their garden. Sadly, their relationship is hampered by a misunderstanding between his wife and his parents, and also by their poverty. The book ends tragically when his wife dies at a young age. See also BUDDHISM; DAOISM; IMPERIAL EXAMINATION SYSTEM; LITERATI.

SHEN NONG (Shen Nung) "Divine Husbandman"; the second of the first three Chinese legendary emperors (Three Divine Sovereigns; Three August Ones). His formal name is Yandi (Yen Ti). Ancient legends recount that Shen Nong was born in the 28th century B.C. and that he had the body of a man but the head of a bull. Supposedly he could speak three days after he was born, walk within one week and plow a field when he was three years old. Shen Nong is credited with founding agriculture in China, by taming the ox, yoking the horse and inventing the plow and the cart. He taught the people how to plow the fields and how to use fire to burn away wild plants in order to clear the land for planting (known as slash-and-burn agriculture). Thus he is known as the god of the "burning wind." During his reign, the people suffered from a terrible drought and were saved by Zhi Songzi (Chih Sung-tzu), who then became the Lord of Rain. Shen Nong also supposedly compiled a catalog of 365 species of plants that could be used for medicine, forming the foundation for traditional Chinese herbal medicine. See also AGRICULTURE; HORSE; MEDICINE, HERBAL; OX.

SHEN NUNG See SHEN NONG.

SHEN SHITIAN (SHIH-T'IEN) See SHEN ZHOU.

SHEN TS'UNG-WEN See SHEN CONGWEN.

SHEN ZHOU (Shen Chou, also known as Shen Shitian or Shen Shih-t'ien; 1427–1509) A painter who is considered the greatest of the Four Great Masters of the Ming Dynasty, along with Tang Yin (T'ang Yin; 1470–1527), Wen Zhengming (Wen Cheng-ming; 1470–1559) and Qiu Ying (Ch'iu Ying; c. 1494–1552). They were all members of the literati class of scholar-painters who lived in Suzhou, for many centuries the cultural center of China. Collectively, their style of painting, known as the Wu School for the Wu district surrounding Suzhou, is considered by many the finest expression of painting in the Ming dynasty (1368–1644).

Shen Zhou was born in Suzhou to a wealthy family of the literati class. His grandfather had been a friend of the famous painter Wang Meng, and Shen's family owned many valuable works of painting and calligraphy. Shen never held an official court position but belonged to a group of scholar-painters and art collectors. He practiced all the arts of the brush, including painting, especially landscapes, calligraphy and poetry. In his early years he studied with Liu Que (Liu Chueh) and experimented with styles from the Southern Song dynasty (11th century) and Yuan dynasty (14th century). As part of his training he painted landscapes in the style of Ni Zan (Ni Tsan; 1301–74), although Shen's works have stronger and less delicate brushstrokes than Ni's. He eventually developed his own original style—avoiding the colorful, decorative style of "professional" painters—working in the "amateur" style of the literati, in which painting is considered a means of self-expression and landscapes are portrayed with simple, flowing strokes of black ink.

Many works have survived from each phase of Shen's development as a painter, and his own writings provide further insights into his art. His paintings became popular with fellow members of his literati class and are still valued by modern collectors. Although he painted many different subjects, he especially enjoyed making small landscapes of scenes on his family's estate. One fine example is "Walking with a Staff in the Mountains," held by the National Palace Museum in Taipei, Taiwan. He was the first painter to place a human figure in most of his paintings, which gives the viewer a point of identification. An example is a painting of a flute player on a cliff top, owned by the Nelson Gallery in Kansas City, Missouri. Shen's most famous student was the great painter and calligrapher Wen Zhengming. See also LANDSCAPE PAINTING; LITERATI; MING DYNASTY; NI ZAN; SUZHOU; WEN ZHENGMING.

SHEN-CHIN See IMPERIAL BUREAUCRACY; LITERATI.

SHENDAN See MING TOMBS.

SHENG   A wind instrument that has about 13 thin bamboo tubes of different lengths clustered in a bowl-shaped container that serves as a wind-chest. The bottom end of each tube has a bronze reed that vibrates when the musician blows into a thick bamboo tube that carries air into the wind-chest and causes particular reeds to vibrate when a small hole above each reed is covered, producing the desired sound. Many notes can be sounded at the same time to play chords, and hence the *sheng* usually is called a mouth organ. The instrument produces an ethereal, mysterious sound. In ancient China, beginning with the Zhou dynasty (1100–256 B.C.), the *sheng* was one of the instruments played in orchestras of the royal court. The court orchestra was introduced into Japan in the eighth century A.D. and still performs for the Japanese imperial family. In Japan the *sheng* has 17 bamboo tubes and is called the *sho*.

Several of China's national minority ethnic groups, such as the Miao, Dong, Yao and Yi play a reed pipe similar to the *sheng*, which was known 2,600 years ago. The instrument is made of a single wooden cylinder, one to six bamboo sound pipes, a copper reed and a resonator. The reed pipe is played at festivals, weddings, funerals and other communal events, and its music is danced to.

SHENG-JIH See BIRTHDAYS.

SHENGRI See BIRTHDAYS.

SHENJIN See IMPERIAL BUREAUCRACY; LITERATI.

SHENSHI (SHEN-SHIH)   See IMPERIAL BUREAUCRACY; LITERATI.

SHENSI PROVINCE See SHAANXI PROVINCE.

SHEN-TSUNG (EMPEROR)   See SIMA GUANG; WANG ANSHI.

SHENYANG   The capital city of Liaoning Province in northeastern China, also known as Manchuria, with a population of about 6 million. Shenyang is located on the Hun River (Hunhe), a tributary of the Liao River (Liaohe). It is called Mukden in the Manchurian language. It was the capital of the Manchus, who defeated the Chinese Ming dynasty and founded the Qing dynasty (1644–1911). Nurhachi (1559–1626), who unified the Manchus, began building his imperial palace at Mukden in 1625. In 1644 the Manchu capital was moved to Beijing, which remains the capital of China.

The Manchu Imperial Palace (Gugong) still can be seen in the Chinese Old City in Shenyang. It resembles the Imperial Palace (the Forbidden City) in Beijing but is smaller and thus is known as the Small Imperial Palace (Xiao Gugong). The walled complex is entered through several gates, with the main gate (Daqing Men) in the south, and is divided into east, central and west districts. In the east, the octagonal hall called Cazheng Dian has a yellow ceramic tile roof and bright red columns supporting the colorfully decorated ceiling, two of them wound with gold dragons, the symbol of imperial power. There are also five smaller, square pavilions. In the center is the Main Hall (Congzheng Dian), also with a yellow ceramic tile roof and red columns, two on the left and right with gold dragons. The sumptuous imperial throne sits in the center between these columns in front of a screen also decorated with gold dragons. The ceremony was held here to mark the founding of the Qing dynasty. Manchu emperors held conferences and banquets in the three-story Phoenix Tower (Fenghuang Lou).

Three Manchu Imperial Tombs are located north of the Old City. The largest is Beiling, the North Tomb (also known as Zhaoling), the tomb of Huang Taiji (1592–1643), or Raizong, also known as Abahai, son of Nurhachi and founder of the Qing dynasty. The East Tomb, also known as Fuling, is located eight miles northeast of Shenyang on the Hun River at the foot of Tianzhu Mountain. These are the burial grounds for Nurhachi and his mistress. Nurhachi's posthumous title is Taizu (T'ai-tsu).

Shenyang's history dates back 2,000 years. During the Han dynasty (206 B.C.–A.D. 220), many Han (ethnic Chinese) immigrated to the Shenyang region from Shandong and Hebei provinces. In the 10th century the Khitan, a nomadic tribe in northern China who established the Liao dynasty (947–1125), made Shenyang a major military base. They were followed by the Jin and then the Mongols, who established the Yuan dynasty (1279–1368). The city acquired the name Shenyang, meaning "to the north of the Shen River," in the 13th century. In the 17th century the Manchus, called the Jurchen until 1635, were united by Nurhachi and captured Manchuria. They captured Shenyang in 1621 and made it their capital, giving it the name Mukden in 1625. From there they conquered all of China. When the Manchus founded the Qing dynasty, they moved their main capital to Beijing, but they continued to use Shenyang as a second capital because of the lucrative trade in that region of ginseng, a root widely used in Chinese herbal medicine.

During the 19th century Western powers vied in Liaoning Province for its vast natural resources. The Russians took control of the Liaodong Peninsula, made Shenyang their base in Manchuria and built the Northeast China Railroad between 1896 and 1903. Japan and Great Britain allied themselves against Russia, and Japan defeated Russia in the Russo-Japanese War of 1904–5, during which the Battle of Mukden was fought from February 19 to March 10, 1905. Russia was forced to give up its rights to southern Manchuria to Japan, which used Mukden (Shenyang) as the base for exploiting Manchuria's mineral resources and building many factories. After the Republic of China was founded in 1912, Mukden served as the center for several warlords, notably Zhang Zuolin, who ruled the northern provinces from 1916 until he was assassinated in 1928. In September 1931 a Japanese captain was murdered in an event now known as the Mukden Incident, causing the Japanese to attack Mukden and occupy all of Manchuria. They established their puppet state of Manchukuo (Manzhouguo in Chinese) in Manchuria and turned the region into an industrial base whose resources were sent to Japan. They invaded China Proper in 1937, causing China's War of Resistance against Japan (1937–45; World War II). On August 8, 1945 the U.S.S.R. declared war on Japan, captured Mukden shortly thereafter and began dismantling the factories.

During China's civil war, Chinese Nationalist (Kuomintang; KMT) troops occupied Mukden in spring 1946, but Communist troops took the city on October 30, 1948. From 1949 to 1954 the Communists made Mukden, called Shenyang once again, the capital of Dongbei, the northeastern region of China that formed one of the country's six large administrative regions at that time. Dongbei became somewhat autonomous under the powerful local leader Gao Gang (Kao Kang), but he was removed from power in 1954, and the region was divided into the three provinces of Liaoning, Jilin and Heilongjiang. Shenyang was made the capital of Liaoning.

Most of Shenyang has been constructed within the last 50 years. It is one of China's largest and most important cities and a major culture, communications and education center, with 28 institutions of higher learning. The city has a famous government-supported acrobatic troupe. Acrobatics has been one of the most popular forms of entertainment in China for many centuries. Shenyang and the cities of Anshan, Benxi and Fushun comprise the most important industrial region of China, especially in machine manufacturing. Other important products include chemicals, textiles, electricity, metals and processed foods. See also ABAHAI; ACROBATICS AND VARIETY THEATER; DRAGON; HEILONGJIANG PROVINCE; JILIN PROVINCE; JURCHEN; LIAONING PROVINCE: MANCHU; MANCHUKUO; MANCHURIA; NURHACHI; WAR OF RESISTANCE AGAINST JAPAN; ZHANG ZUOLIN.

SHENZHEN See SPECIAL ECONOMIC ZONES.

SHENZONG (EMPEROR) See SIMA GUANG; WANG ANSHI.

SHI (SHIH) See LITERATI; REGULATED OR NEW-STYLE VERSE.

SHI DAKAI (Shih Ta-k'ai; 1831–1863) A leader of the Taiping Rebellion (1850–64) against the Manchus who ruled China under the Qing dynasty (1644–1911), and the greatest Taiping general. Shi was born in modern Guangxi-Zhuang Autonomous Region in southern China to the family of a wealthy landlord. The Taipings originated in eastern Guangxi under the leadership of Hong Xiuquan (Hung Hsiu-ch'uan; 1813–64). Shi joined the Taipings when he was 19 years old, and he brought many of his family members into the movement, which benefited from their financial contributions. Shi was one of the five original leaders of the Taipings and gained the title "assistant king" (*yiwang* or *i-wang*).

The Taiping Rebellion grew very rapidly and moved as far north as Nanjing on the Yangzi River, from which they made two unsuccessful attempts to conquer northern China in 1852–53. After this, Hong began withdrawing into seclusion, and Yang Xiuqing (Yang Hsiu-ch'ing), the "eastern king," increased his power until he threatened to usurp Hong's position as supreme Taiping leader. In 1856 Hong and Shi asked the "western king" to murder Yang in Nanjing. Unfortunately, he murdered not only Yang but other Taiping leaders and thousands of Taiping followers as well. Shi was the only Taiping leader belonging to the literati, or scholar class, to survive. He protested the massacre, discovered Yang's plan to kill him and escaped from the city. Hong retaliated to the massacre by having the "western king" executed. Shi, by then disgusted with the Taipings, left the movement and went to modern Sichuan Province in central China, taking many Taipings with him, including some of the best military commanders. The Qing government offered Shi a high-ranking position and a large financial reward, but he refused to join them and criticized them for cooperating with foreign powers. He attempted to establish an independent kingdom in Sichuan, but Qing forces caught him there and executed him in June 1863. In the early 20th century, Shi Dakai became a hero to Chinese nationalists who fought against the foreign powers that attempted to dominate China. See also GUANGXI-ZHUANG AUTONOMOUS REGION; HONG XIUQUAN; NANJING; QING DYNASTY; SICHUAN PROVINCE; TAIPING REBELLION.

SHI DE See HAN SHAN.

SHI HUI (Shih Hui; 1915–1957) One of China's greatest film actors and directors. Shi was born in Yangliuqing near Tianjin, but his family moved to Beijing while he was a baby. His father was a school clerk but the family had little money. To make a living, Shi took various jobs, such as railroad steward and dental apprentice. He loved attending movies and stage plays and decided to become an actor. He performed with the Beijing Drama Troupe and then moved to Shanghai, where he joined the China Touring Ensemble. He also appeared with the Shanghai Drama Art Society and the Hard-Working Troupe. His performances in *Big Circus, Night Inn, Autumn Crab Apple* and other plays earned Shi the reputation of "king of the theater" in Shanghai. His acting was influenced by New Year woodcuts from Yangliuqing, variety shows at Tianqiao and various local styles of Chinese operas and music. Shi's father was a fan of the Beijing Opera, and from childhood Shi would act out many parts from the operas. He also drew upon his wide variety of experiences, especially among people of the lower classes, and was able to play many different roles.

In 1941 Shi began to act in films, beginning with *Glory in Turmoil* and *Scenes in Chaotic Years*, in which he played a greedy bank manager and financial speculator. Between 1947 and 1951 he starred in 12 films for the Shanghai Wenhua Film Company, including *False Phoenix,* in which his comic portrayal of a hairdresser delighted Chinese audiences. He also directed three films. Shi directed and starred in his greatest film, *This Life of Mine,* about a policeman in old Beijing. His character lives through the many changes that China experienced from the end of the feudal era under the Qing dynasty (1644–1911) to the founding of the Communist People's Republic of China (PRC) in 1949. The policeman is honest, cares for people of the lower classes and feels despair over the injustices of society. At the end he dies filled with despair and sorrow. Chinese audiences felt great empathy with the character, as they still do when the film is revived, and the Chinese Ministry of Culture gave it the Outstanding Film Award. The Communist government awarded Shi the title "veteran actor," and he was elected a people's representative of Shanghai Municipality. During the 1950s Shi wrote screenplays and directed and performed in a number of films, including *Corrosion, Lieutenant Guan, Stand Up, Sisters, Splendor, A Glimpse of America, Song Jingshi (Sung Ching-shi)* and *Lingering Bond.* He directed *A Feathered-Letter, Sailing on a Foggy Night* and the opera-based *Marriage of the Fairy Princess,* all of which gained a popular audience.

Shi Hui never married. In 1957 he openly criticized several aspects of the Chinese arts when the government encouraged artists and intellectuals to speak out during the so-called Hundred Flowers Campaign. Shi, like many others who had the courage to speak out, was then condemned by the government for being a "Rightist." Crushed, he committed suicide by drowning in 1957. More than 20 years later the government restored his reputation. See also ANTI-RIGHTIST CAMPAIGN; BEIJING; FILM STUDIOS; HUNDRED FLOWERS CAMPAIGN; OPERA, BEIJING; PEOPLE'S REPUBLIC OF CHINA; SHANGHAI.

SHI-CHING See BOOK OF SONGS.

SHIGATSE See TIBET.

SHIH CHI See SIMA QIAN.

SHIH CHING See BOOK OF SONGS.

SHIH HUANG-TI See QIN SHI HUANGDI.

SHIH TA-K'AI See SHI DAKAI.

SHIH TEH See HAN SHAN.

SHIH-T'AO See SHITAO.

SHIH-TSUNG (EMPEROR) See GAOZONG (EMPEROR); HUZONG (EMPEROR); SOUTHERN SONG DYNASTY.

SHIH-TZU See LION.

SHIJI See SIMA QIAN.

SHIJIAZHUANG   The capital city of Hebei Province in northern China. Shijiazhuang, with a population of more than one million, sits at the foot of the Taihang Mountain Range (Taihangshan) that separates the plain of Hebei from Shanxi Province to the west. The city, until recently just a small village, is overshadowed by Beijing and Tianjin, both also in Hebei but governed as independent municipalities. Construction of the Beijing-Hankou (Wuhan) Railroad in 1905 spurred the development of Shijiazhuang. Today it is a major junction for the Beijing-Guangzhou and Taiyuan-Dezhou railway lines. Cotton textiles, chemicals, machinery and mining are its most important industries.

Shijiazhuang served as the northern headquarters of the Chinese Communist Party during the Northern Campaign against the Nationalist Party (Kuomintang; KMT) from 1947 to 1949, from the fall of Communist headquarters in Yan'an to the Nationalists until the capture of Beijing by the Communists. Dr. Norman Bethune, a Canadian surgeon who organized the medical services for the Communist People's Liberation Army starting in 1938, is buried in the Cemetery of Martyrs, the military cemetery in Shijiazhuang. A hospital built in the city in 1937 is named for Dr. Bethune and contains memorial halls to him and Dr. Kortis, an Indian who was the hospital's first director.

About 35 miles north of the city can be seen the Long Xing Monastery (*Long Xing Si*), whose temples date from the 10th to 13th centuries, among the oldest temple buildings still standing in China. The enormous Temple of Great Mercy (*Da Bei Ge*) houses a 70-foot-tall bronze statue of Guanyin, the Buddhist Goddess of Mercy. There the Pavilion of the Rotating Library (Zhuan Lun Zang Dian) is a repository for Buddhist sutras (scriptures); the library holding the sutras revolves within the pavilion. About 25 miles southeast of Shijiazhuang lies Zhaozhou Bridge, one of the oldest segment arch bridges in the world. Built of stone between 605 and 616, the bridge is 55 yards long and spans 40 feet. See also BEIJING; BETHUNE, NORMAN; BRIDGES; BUDDHISM; CIVIL WAR BETWEEN COMMUNISTS AND NATIONALISTS; HEBEI PROVINCE; RAILROADS; YAN'AN.

SHIJING See BOOK OF SONGS.

SHIMONOSEKI, TREATY OF (1895)   The treaty that concluded Japan's defeat of China in the Sino-Japanese War of 1894–95. The treaty was negotiated when China sued for peace and was signed on April 17, 1895. The Treaty of Shimonoseki was named for the city where it was negotiated on the southwestern tip of the main Japanese island of Honshu, where Western ships passed through the Strait of Shimonoseki. Since 1868 Japan had been growing into a modern industrialized nation, and now it wanted to prove itself equal to the Western powers. At first, Japan presented extremely harsh terms to China. Li Hongzhang (Li Hung-chang), the Chinese statesman who served as negotiator, was shot by a fanatic on March 24, leading to apologies by the Japanese and more lenient treaty terms. Li survived but his nephew and adopted son took his place as negotiator. Provisions of the treaty forced China to cede the Liaodong Peninsula, the island of Taiwan, and the Penghu (Pescadore) Islands to

Japan; pay Japan an enormous indemnity; allow Japanese industries to be established in four treaty ports in China, giving Japan the most-favored-nation status that Western powers enjoyed; and recognize the independence of Korea, which had been a protectorate of China. The terms of the treaty were very harsh to China and caused the Chinese people to resent Japan, especially as they could see that Japan really intended to conquer all of China. As it happened, Japan also had designs on Korea, and annexed that country in 1910.

The Treaty of Shimonoseki between Japan and China was Japan's first step in its acquisition of an empire. Russia wanted the Liaodong Peninsula for itself because of its two excellent harbors at Port Arthur and Darien (modern Dalian), so it demanded that Japan return the peninsula to China, which Japan agreed to do for a sum of money paid by China. The Chinese allowed the Russians to construct a railroad through Manchuria to their port at Vladivostok. Seeing China's weakness, the Western powers also moved to control more of China following the Sino-Japanese War, and the Germans forced the Chinese to give them concessions in Shandong Province in 1897. A decade later Japan and Russia fought the Russo-Japanese War of 1904–5, in which the Japanese soundly defeated Russia by destroying its Baltic naval fleet. In 1915 Japan presented its Twenty-One Demands to Chinese president Yuan Shikai (Yuan Shih-k'ai), whose acceptance of them would make China a protectorate of Japan. See also DALIAN; LI HONGZHANG; LIAODONG PENINSULA; MANCHURIA; SINO-JAPANESE WAR OF 1894–95; TREATY PORTS; TWENTY-ONE DEMANDS ON CHINA.

SHIPPING AND SHIPBUILDING

Historically China was an advanced country in shipbuilding and navigation. Ancient boat models show that China was the first country to use rudders on ships. The Chinese also invented leeboards, watertight compartments for ships' hulls, single masts and square sails. They used fore-and-aft rigging, which aligned the sails along the length of the ship rather than across it at right angles and enabled ships to sail into the wind 2,000 years before European ships were able to do this. (Only by copying Chinese ship designs did Europeans achieve this.) Chinese sails were made of bamboo battens with matting stretched between them and could be rolled up and down easily, similar to Venetian blinds; Western canvas sails, in contrast, required sailors to climb along yardarms to furl or unfurl the sails every time the wind changed. The ancient Chinese sailing ship known as a junk is still used today. The Chinese also invented the magnetic compass in the fourth century B.C., which greatly aided navigation. The Chinese used paddle-wheel boats as early as A.D. 418, as recorded in the account of a naval battle under the command of Admiral Wang Zhen-e (Wang Chen-O) of the Liu Song dynasty (420–479). Later shipbuilders made improvements to their design, and swift-moving, rudderless paddle-wheel warships came into widespread use during the Song dynasty (960–1279).

Domestic shipping was very active along China's 3,100-mile coastline and its many rivers and man-made canals. Coastal trade was taking place between northern China and the Yangzi River (Changjiang) area as early as the fifth century B.C., and by the second century B.C. Chinese ships sailed along the southern Chinese coast as far as Annam

(northern Vietnam). China's two longest rivers, the Yellow River (Huanghe) and the Yangzi, flow across the country from west to east and have long been major transportation arteries. The Chinese built many canals, starting in the fifth century B.C., to link the rivers and their many tributaries. Sui emperor Wendi (Wen-ti; r. 581–604) began building the Grand Canal, along which large fleets of junks transported rice and other goods from southern China to northern cities. Subsequent emperors improved and expanded this canal, and lines of barges still carry goods today along sections of it. In Sichuan, large rafts made of bamboo with shallow drafts have long been used to carry up to seven tons of cargo each while navigating waters on which heavier ships are unable to sail.

The Chinese had a maritime as well as an overland Silk Road, along which Chinese goods were transported to other countries. The maritime route started at Hepu (modern Beihai), in Guangxi-Zhuang Autonomous Region in southwestern China. During the Han dynasty (206 B.C.–A.D. 220), ships sailed from Hepu for the Indian Ocean. At Beihai, archaeologists have discovered objects from the Roman Empire, the Middle East and Southeast Asia. The Chinese Buddhist monk Faxian (Fa-hsien), who left China in 399 to walk to India to collect Buddhist scriptures, wrote a record of his sea voyage home across the Bay of Bengal to Sri Lanka, Indonesia and Guangzhou (Canton), although a storm forced his ship to land in Shandong Province instead of Guangzhou. From the Qin dynasty (221–206 B.C.) up to the seventh century A.D., Chinese envoys sailed from Hepu and Xuwen (around modern Zhanjiang in Guangdong Province) past Vietnam, Malaysia and Burma and arrived at southeastern India and Sri Lanka (Ceylon). The Roman Empire, Persia (modern Iran) and some Arabic countries also developed a large sea trade across the Indian Ocean. Guangzhou became the largest harbor in China and remained so until the mid-19th century. By the late eighth century, nearly 4,000 foreign ships arrived in Guangzhou each year.

After the middle of the Tang dynasty (618–907) through the Song (960–1279) and Yuan (1279–1368) dynasties, shipping increased on Chinese sea routes, especially due to the decline of the overland Silk Road because of warfare in Central Asia. From ports at Hepu, Guangzhou and Quanzhou in Fujian Province, Chinese ships sailed south to the Philippines and Indonesia, and through the Straits of Malacca to reach the Indian Peninsula and points farther west. The Silk Road on the sea also was named the silk and porcelain road or ceramic road, after China's major exports, and also was known as the road of spice because China imported spices on this sea route. Guangzhou, Quanzhou, Yangzhou and Mingzhou (modern Ningbo in Zhejiang Province) became international trade ports where Chinese shipbuilding was also very active. Arab traders preferred to use Chinese ships to transport their freight because they were sturdy and seaworthy. Korean and Japanese ships also carried on an active trade with China.

In the 15th century, Ming emperor Yongle (Yung-lo; r. 1403–24) commissioned Admiral Zheng He (Cheng Ho) to build and command fleets that made seven voyages to more than 30 countries and regions as far west as the Persian Gulf, the Red Sea and the east coast of Africa. He brought many foreign states into China's tribute system. However,

Though China uses large modern vessels for shipping cargo, many traditional designs—including the four-sided lugsail—are still in wide use today.   S.E.MEYER

after his voyages the Ming retreated from maritime shipping and placed an embargo on trade along the Chinese coast, which was also threatened by pirates. They had been a problem as early as the Song dynasty but became especially active during the Ming (1368–1644). During the Qing dynasty (1644–1911), Western trading ships began appearing in Chinese waters in large numbers. The Qing government restricted foreign trade to Guangzhou and forced foreigners to conduct all their business through officially designated Chinese merchants; this is known as the Canton system for regulating foreign trade. The British made several unsuccessful attempts to force the Qing to open China to Western trade, and finally did so by military means. The British, using powerful steamships, defeated China in the Opium War (1839–42) and forced the Qing to open Guangzhou, Xiamen (Amoy), Fuzhou, Ningbo and Shanghai to foreign residence and trade. Shanghai, situated on the Huangpu (Whampoa) River in the Yangzi delta region, quickly replaced Guangzhou as China's largest trading port. Britain defeated China once more in the Arrow War (Second Opium War; 1856–60) and forced the Qing to open more treaty ports. Other Western powers, including France, Germany, the United States and Russia, also gained the right to establish foreign traders and residents in the treaty ports. Steamships began carrying grain north along the Chinese coast from 1868.

Some Chinese officials pushed the Qing government to modernize China by adapting Western technology, known as the Self-Strengthening Movement. In 1872 Li Hongzhang (Li Hung-chang), a Qing official, founded the China Merchants Steam Navigation Company (CMSN) in Shanghai to provide modern steamship transport to compete with the foreign companies that had monopolized ocean shipping and controlled transportation on the Yangzi. The company was well directed in the beginning but proved unable to compete with British steamship lines. However, the CMSN remained in business, maintaining a branch in Hong Kong near Guangzhou.

Tensions increased between France and China over control of Vietnam, and France defeated China in the Sino-French War of 1884–85, during which the French navy destroyed the Chinese fleet, arsenal and dockyards in Fuzhou. The French naval victory made China even more vulnerable to foreign attack, and Japan defeated China in the Sino-Japanese War of 1894–95. China's ocean shipping declined as foreign powers reduced the country to semicolonial status. The Chinese people overthrew the Qing in the Revolution of 1911 and established the Republic of China (ROC) in 1912, but the country remained too poor to develop its shipping industry, especially after it was invaded by Japan in 1937 and fought its War of Resistance against Japan (1937–45; World War II). After 1945 the Chinese

Communists and Chinese Nationalists (Kuomintang; KMT) resumed their civil war, and by 1949, when the Communists won and established the People's Republic of China (PRC), China's shipping industry trade was almost nonexistent.

In 1950 the Hong Kong branch of the CMSN returned to China to help the country, and it was taken over by the PRC government. The company quickly developed its operations and became a holdings company with limited liability. The PRC began independent ocean shipping in the early 1960s and rapidly developed its oceangoing fleet in the 1970s. Between 1961 and 1987, China's maritime fleet grew faster than that of any other country, and its merchant fleet tonnage increased by an average 13.6 percent per year. At the end of 1985, about 17 percent of China's merchant fleet was built domestically. By 1984 the fleet's deadweight capacity totaled 8 million tons and the volume of goods transported yearly increased 50 times over that of 20 years previous. Chinese ships traveled to more than 420 ports in more than 100 countries and regions. In the 1980s China accelerated port construction along its coastline and the Yangzi River to meet the needs of its ocean shipping. In 1984 more than 80 percent of China's import and export goods were transported by sea. The PRC opened four shipping lines starting from Shanghai, Guangzhou, Qingdao, Tianjin and Dalian and branching out to ports to the east, west, south and north. By 1984 the China Ocean Shipping Company in Beijing had branches in Shanghai, Guangzhou, Tianjin, Qingdao and Dalian. Each branch established an office or agent in many countries around the world.

In the late 1970s the PRC established 13 Special Economic Zones (SEZs) along the Chinese coast to encourage foreign trade. Major Chinese ports today include Dalian, Guangzhou, Huangpu, Ningbo, Qingdao, Qinhuangdao, Shanghai, Shantou, Tanggu, Xiamen, Xingang and Zhanjiang. In 1993 the Merchant Marine of the PRC had 1,421 ships (1,000 gross registered tons [GRT] or more) totaling 14 million GRT/21 million deadweight tons (DWT). The PRC also directly and indirectly owned an additional 183 ships (1,000 GRT or over) totaling about 6 million DWT that operated under Maltese and Liberian registry.

By 1987 China had about 74,000 miles of navigable waterways, 40,000 of which were more than 3.3 feet deep. The Yangzi River is still by far China's most important river system and transportation artery. In 1986 Yangzi ports handled 133 million tons of cargo, most of it grain, coal and other materials for the steel industry. Engineers blasted away rocks that impeded navigation in the Yangzi River gorges, and steamships can sail up to Chongqing in Sichuan Province. The PRC is now constructing the enormous Three Gorges Water Conservancy Project, including the world's largest dam, to improve shipping in the upper Yangzi. The Songhua (Sungari) River system in Manchuria (northeastern China) and Pearl River (Zhujiang) in southern China are also major transportation arteries. Attempts to increase shipping in the Yellow River have not been very successful because the river carries huge quantities of silt deposits. See also ARROW WAR; CANTON SYSTEM FOR REGULATING FOREIGN TRADE; CHINA MERCHANTS STEAM NAVIGATION COMPANY; COMPASS; FAXIAN; GRAND CANAL; GUANGZHOU; HUANGPU RIVER; JUNK; OPIUM WAR; PEARL RIVER; PIRATES; SHANGHAI; SILK ROAD; SINO-FRENCH WAR; SINO-JAPANESE WAR OF 1894–95; SONGHUA RIVER; SPECIAL ECONOMIC ZONES; THREE GORGES WATER CONSERVANCY PROJECT; TREATY PORTS; YANGZI RIVER; YELLOW RIVER; ZHENG HE; NAMES OF INDIVIDUAL DYNASTIES AND PORT CITIES.

SHISAN LING See MING TOMBS.

SHITAO (Shih-t'ao; 1641–c. 1710)   Also known by his Buddhist name Daoji (Tao-chi); a painter and critic who, along with Bada Shanren (Pa-ta Shan-jen; also known as Zhuda or Chu Ta), was one of the best known of the so-called Individualist painters of the Manchu Qing dynasty (1644–1911). Chinese scholars link these two painters as the Two Stones (*Ershi* or *Erh Shih*). Shitao and Bada were both born into the imperial family of the Chinese Ming dynasty (1368–1644), which was overthrown by the Manchus when they were children. Both became Buddhist monks, but Shitao led the normal life of an educated upper-class gentleman while Bada became an eccentric. Shitao, who was born in Jiangsu Province in southern China, moved to Hangzhou in 1657 and spent most of his life in Jiangsu and Anhui provinces. He became acquainted with a great many Chinese and Manchu scholars and painters and traveled widely throughout China with them. He spent nearly three years painting in the capital city of Beijing and then settled in Yangzhou, where he left the Buddhist community and became a professional painter. In Yangzhou, famous for beautiful gardens, Shitao also became a designer of gardens, an art known as "piling up stones" because rocks and stones that represent mountains are a prominent feature of Chinese gardens. The Garden of Ten Thousand Rocks that he designed for the Yu family in Yangzhou is considered his masterpiece.

Shitao painted his works very expressively and in a wide range of styles. While many of his contemporaries painted imitations of works by previous Chinese masters, Shitao studied the old works but went beyond them to create original forms of expression. Shitao's individualism also characterizes his essays, such as "Comments on Painting" ("*Huayulu*" or "*Hua-yu-lu*"), in which he uses Buddhist and Daoist terms to discuss art and its relationship to the human and natural worlds. He argues that painting is an activity that parallels the forces that create and give momentum to all living things. The important thing about a painting is not its final appearance but whether it expresses the painter's creativity and vital force. Shitao created the "one-line method" by which an artist can express oneness with nature through the single continuous line painted by the brush. Some of his most famous paintings are *The Peach Blossom Spring,* the illustration of a story by Tao Yuanming (T'ao Yuan-ming), and *A Man in a House Beneath a Cliff.* See also BADA SHANREN; GARDENS; LANDSCAPE PAINTING; ROCKS.

SHIZI See LION.

SHO See SHENG.

SHOSOIN See TANG DYNASTY.

SHOU See DOUBLE HAPPINESS AND LONG LIFE.

SHU See LOYALTY.

SHU (SHU HAN), KINGDOM OF   See CAO CAO; CHENGDU; ROMANCE OF THE THREE KINGDOMS: SICHUAN PROVINCE; WESTERN AND EASTERN JIN DYNASTIES.

SHUANGXI (SHUANG HSI) See DOUBLE HAPPINESS AND LONG LIFE.

SHUFU WARE   A type of porcelain ware, mainly bowls and small dishes, that was produced during the Yuan dynasty (1279–1368). *Shufu* ware is made of fine, white porcelain; the pieces are covered with a thick, opaque glaze that has a light blue-green tint. This type of glaze developed from the *Qingbai* (*Ch'ing-pai*) porcelains produced during the early Yuan, which themselves derived from wares produced during the Song dynasty (960–1279) that have pale-blue translucent glazes. Chingbai porcelains were produced only until the middle of the 14th century, while *shufu* porcelains were made until the end of the century. *Shufu* ware is named for the two characters *shu* and *fu*, meaning "privy council," indicating that they were made for use in the imperial palace. Potters used molds to impress the two characters in low relief under the opaque glaze as part of the designs decorating the insides of *shufu* bowls and dishes. Some scholars maintain that the characters *shu* and *fu* on these pieces are combinations of the auspicious words *fu* ("happiness"), *shou* ("longevity") and *lu* ("prosperity"). Some pieces of *shufu* ware have impressed or incised designs on the reverse or outer side as well. The term "*shufu* ware" often is applied to porcelain wares that have mold-impressed designs and thick, light blue-green opaque glazes but do not have the characters *shu* and *fu* in relief. See also PORCELAIN.

SHUIHUZHUAN (SHUI-HU-CHUAN) See OUTLAWS OF THE MARSH.

SHUIMOHUA See INK PAINTING.

SHUN, EMPEROR   The second of the three legendary Sage-Kings praised in Chinese culture for being wise and virtuous rulers. The first was Yao, who supposedly controlled the flood waters of the Yellow River (Huanghe) and the third was Yu, founder of the Xia dynasty (2200–1750 B.C.). Shun was believed to have come to the throne c. 2255 B.C. and was credited with inventing the writing brush. Confucius (551–479 B.C.) included Shun and Yao among the ideal rulers that he held up as standards for rulers in his own time. Mencius (Mengzi or Meng-tzu; c. 372–289 B.C.), another important Confucian thinker, presents the most complete description of Shun and Yao. Confucianists emphasize that the legitimacy of a ruler depends on his virtue, wisdom and humility. They believe that these traits were possessed originally by emperors Yao and Shun and were found also in rulers of great ancient dynasties including the Zhou, Han, Tang and Song.

According to legend, Emperor Yao decided that none of his own 10 sons was worthy to be the next ruler, so he abdicated the throne to Shun, a farmer highly regarded for the way he took care of his parents and brother, demonstrating filial piety (*xiao* or *hsiao*), one of the most important Confucian virtues. Yao gave Shun his two daughters as wives. In turn, Shun himself found his own son unworthy to succeed him, and handed the throne to Yu of Xia, also known as Yu the Great. See also CONFUCIUS; EMPEROR; FILIAL PIETY; MENCIUS; YAO, EMPEROR; YU, EMPEROR.

SHUN-CHIH (EMPEROR) See SHUNZHI (EMPEROR).

SHUNDI (EMPEROR) (Shun-ti; 1333–1368)   The last emperor of the Mongol Yuan dynasty (1279–1368); personal name Toghon Temur. Shundi became emperor when he was just a child. His reign lasted for 35 years, much longer than the reigns of most Yuan emperors. Although a Mongol, Shundi had been given a Chinese education, and as emperor he actively promoted Chinese culture. He continued the activities of the previous Yuan emperor, who had painted, written poetry and calligraphy in the Chinese literati (scholar) style and founded an academy for Chinese arts. Shundi's chief minister attempted to remove Chinese influence from the Yuan court but failed to do so, and under Shundi the court became a center for traditional Chinese literary and fine arts.

The ethnic Han Chinese engaged in many rebellions against their Mongol rulers; these revolts greatly increased during the 1340s, led by the White Lotus Secret Society that developed among poor, uneducated peasants in the area north of the Huai River (modern Anhui Province). The White Lotus became a symbol of Chinese resistance to domination by foreign rulers. The White Lotus rebels even stopped the crucial shipments of grain on the Grand Canal to the Yuan capital of Khanbaliq (Cambaluc; Dadu or Tatu in Chinese; modern Beijing). The rebels were pacified in 1362, but by then the authority of Emperor Shundi had been limited to the capital and remote regions such as Yunnan Province. Zhu Yuanzhang (Chu Yuan-chang; 1328–99), a Chinese rebel leader, defeated rival Chinese rebel leaders in 1367 and gathered enough forces to overthrow Shundi in 1368. Zhu Yuanzhang sent 250,000 Chinese troops to Khanbaliq. Shundi fled to his ancestral homeland in Mongolia before the rebel forces arrived, and the Mongol forces defending the capital collapsed in the face of the rebels. From Mongolia he attempted to raise a Mongol army to reconquer China but did not succeed. Zhu Yuanzhang founded the Ming dynasty (1368–1644) and ruled China as Emperor Taizu (T'ai-tzu; r. 1368–98), gaining the posthumous reign name Hongwu (Hung-wu). See also GRAND CANAL; HONGWU, EMPEROR; MING DYNASTY; MONGOL; WHITE LOTUS SECRET SOCIETY; YUAN DYNASTY.

SHUN TI (EMPEROR) See SHUNDI (EMPEROR).

SHUNZHI (EMPEROR) (Shun-chih; 1638–1661)   The first emperor of the Manchu Qing dynasty (1644–1911); personal name Fulin. He was the son of the Manchu leader Abahai (1592–1643) and succeeded him as leader when he died. Dorgon (1612–50), Abahai's brother, had been offered the Manchu throne but declined it and served the six-year-old Fulin as coregent along with Jirgalang, another Manchu leader. When Dorgon's army took Beijing in 1644, the Manchus overthrew the Ming dynasty (1368–1644) and proclaimed the Qing dynasty with Fulin as emperor of China under the reign name Shunzhi (Shun-chih; r. 1644–61).

Dorgon soon demoted Jirgalang to the position of assistant regent, and he exercised the actual power in establishing the Qing government. Dorgon adapted the Ming Chinese imperial bureaucracy and persuaded many Ming officials to work for the Qing. In 1647 Dorgon removed Jirgalang from his position and sent him to put down a rebellion in southwestern China. With power consolidated in his hands, Dorgon took the title of Imperial Father Regent. When he died unexpectedly on a hunting trip in 1650, a group of Manchu princes and high officials who had been alienated by his policies disgraced Dorgon posthumously, executed some of his supporters and abolished the position of regent. Emperor Shunzhi then ruled directly, advised by Jirgalang and other high-placed Manchus.

During Shunzhi's reign, the Manchus had to eliminate pockets of Ming resistance, especially in southern China, and establish control over the territories of China. The Ming had installed an emperor in Nanjing but the Manchus took the city in 1645, and they also defeated several other Ming loyalists who had attempted to continue the Ming dynasty. The Qing faced their largest threat in Koxinga (Coxinga; Zheng Chenggong or Cheng Ch'eng-kung), the son of a Chinese pirate, who had become wealthy and influential defending the Chinese coast against pirates for the Ming. By 1655 Koxinga had gathered a large number of military and civil supporters, centered in the coastal area of Fujian Province. He led raids on cities along the coast and the Yangzi River and fought a major battle against the Qing at Nanjing, where he suffered heavy losses and had to retreat. In 1660 Koxinga defended his base in Fujian against a large Qing attack, and he was still in power there at the end of Shunzhi's reign.

Emperor Shunzhi learned the Chinese language and acquired a taste for Chinese novels and drama. While a teenager he was influenced by James Adam Schall von Bell, a Jesuit missionary whom Dorgon had appointed to head the Imperial Board of Astronomy. Schall also had healed Shunzhi's mother of a serious illness. Shunzhi relied on the priest for advice but never converted to Christianity. Instead, he developed a strong interest in the Buddhist religion, especially the Chan (Zen) sect. When his favorite consort died in 1660, he was so grief-stricken that he wanted to become a Buddhist priest, but his advisers prevented him from doing so. Shunzhi suffered from ill health, probably from tuberculosis. In 1661 he contracted smallpox and died at age 22. He was succeeded by his third son out of the 14 children he fathered, whose reign name was the Kangxi (K'ang-hsi) Emperor (r. 1661–1722) and whose reign was one of the high points of the Qing dynasty. See also BUDDHISM; CHAN SECT OF BUDDHISM; DORGON; JESUITS; KANGXI, EMPEROR; MANCHU; PIRATES; QING DYNASTY; ZHENG CHENGGONG.

SI See TEMPLES.

SI DA MINGSHAN See FOUR SACRED MOUNTAINS OF BUDDHISM.

SIAN See XI'AN.

SIBERIA See AMUR RIVER.

SICHUAN PROVINCE A large province in southwestern China that covers an area of 218,909 square miles and has a population of about 100 million. The largest city, Chongqing (Chunking), has a population of more than 6 million and is growing rapidly. The capital city is Chengdu, with a population of about 4 million. It is situated in the fertile Sichuan Basin, one of the most important agricultural regions in China, about 170 miles northwest of Chongqing. Other major cities include Suining, Leshan, Zigong, Mianyang, Guangyuan, Deyang and Panzhihua. Sichuan is the most heavily populated Chinese province and one of the oldest, with settlements dating back to the Han dynasty (206 B.C.–A.D. 220). It is bordered by the provinces of Hubei and Hunan to the east, Qinghai, Gansu and Shaanxi to the north, Yunnan and Guizhou-Hui Autonomous Region to the south and Tibet to the west. The name Sichuan means "four streams," referring to the four most important tributaries of the Yangzi River (Changjiang) that flow north to south through the province, the Min, Tuo, Fu and Jialing rivers. Sichuan is surrounded by high mountain peaks that give it a subtropical climate and make it fairly remote and inaccessible. This region was formerly known as Shu Ba, the Kingdom of Shu Han, and a number of other names, before it acquired the name Sichuan during the Song dynasty (960–1279). Although it became a province of the Chinese Empire during the Qing dynasty (1644–1911), Sichuan always has been relatively autonomous because of its remote location.

During China's War of Resistance against Japan (1937–45; World War II), the Nationalist (Kuomintang; KMT) government moved inland from eastern China, and Chongqing succeeded Wuhan (Hankou) in Hubei Province as the wartime capital of China from 1938 to 1945. The city grew rapidly as millions of Chinese fled westward, and many factories, universities and government offices were moved to Chongqing and Chengdu. The Japanese bombed the cities but never invaded Sichuan because of the high mountains. When the Nationalists and the Chinese Communists formed a united front to fight the Japanese, the southern Communist office was located at Chongqing, where a detachment of the Communist Eighth Route Army was stationed. At the war's end in August 1945, Communist leader Mao Zedong went to Chongqing to negotiate a truce with the Nationalists. He was unsuccessful, and the two sides fought a civil war that was won by the Communists, who established the People's Republic of China in 1949. Since then Chongqing has been industrialized and is now the most important manufacturing center in southwestern China. The city was linked to other major Chinese cities by railroad lines, and the Yangzi River was made more navigable so that ships of 3,000 tons can sail up to Chongqing. The city has many universities and technical schools and is the location of the Sichuan Academy of Fine Arts. Tourist sites include museums, hot springs and steamship rides through gorges on the Yangzi. The PRC government is constructing the Three Gorges Water Conservancy Project to enable oceangoing ships to sail up the Yangzi to Chongqing. Splendid Buddhist cave temples and sculptures can be seen at Dazu 120 miles northwest of Chongqing.

Chengdu, a port city on the Jing (Brocade) River, is a center for agricultural trade. The city's history dates back more than 2,500 years, and it has been the political, economic and cultural center of Sichuan since 300 B.C. Its flourishing silk industry was patronized by the imperial court of the Zhou dynasty (1100–256 B.C.). Silk and other handicrafts are still produced, including lacquerware, silver filigree jewelry and bamboo products. Chengdu was the capital of the state of Shu during the Three Kingdoms Period (220–280). The battles of Shu leaders against General Cao Cao (Ts'ao Ts'ao; 155–220) have been immortalized in the famous Chinese novel, *Romance of the Three Kingdoms.* During the Tang Dynasty (618–907) Chengdu became a prosperous trading center. The first paper money ever issued by a government was issued in Chengdu in 1024. Chengdu was destroyed by invading Mongols, who founded the Yuan dynasty (1279–1368), but was rebuilt and became capital of Sichuan Province, which it remained through the Ming dynasty (1368–1644). From 1645 to 1646 it was the center of a revolutionary kingdom established by Zhang Xianzhong (Chang Hsien-chung). After 1949 Chengdu became a major manufacturing and transportation center. Agriculture remains an important activity there, with rice and wheat the main crops. Chengdu is also the educational and cultural center for southwestern China, with institutions of higher education, an institute for the many national minority groups who reside in Sichuan and the Sichuan Opera Troupe, which is nearly 2,000 years old. The many tourist sites include museums, temples and pavilions, and the thatched cottage where Du Fu (Tu Fu; 712–770), one of China's greatest poets, lived for three years. Teahouses where Chinese opera singers often entertain are very popular in Chengdu. The city's annual lantern festival at the lunar New Year has been held for more than 1,300 years.

Sichuan is one of China's richest provinces because of its numerous mineral deposits and favorable conditions for agriculture, with two crops a year. In eastern Sichuan the Red Basin, an inland sea millions of years ago and now irrigated by the Yangzi River and its tributaries, is the site of intensive terrace farming. Major crops grown there include corn, sorghum, sweet potatoes, wheat, sugar cane, cotton, peanuts, citrus fruits and tea. Rice is cultivated in the plains around Chengdu. A reliable irrigation system was constructed originally in the third century B.C. There are also large grassland pastures, and Sichuan is China's leading producer of pork and the second producer of beef. Sichuan cuisine is world famous for its hot, spicy dishes that often contain flower petals and medicinal herbs. Some of the most popular dishes are bean curd cooked in spicy meat sauce, duck cooked with herbs and chicken cooked with orchid petals.

The western half of the province is sparsely populated because it is divided by many mountain ranges. The highest peak is Mount Gongga (Gonggashan), at 24,790 feet above sea level. Mount Emei (Emeishan), one of the Four Sacred Mountains of Buddhism, is located in Sichuan. At 10,167 feet above sea level, it is the highest of all the nine sacred mountains in China. Wolong Nature Reserve in Sichuan is now the home of most of the Giant Pandas, which are threatened with extinction. Sichuan is heavily forested and thus one of China's most important sources of lumber and paper. Large mineral deposits include iron ore, copper, gold, silver, aluminum, phosphorus, salt, coal, asbestos, marble and petroleum. See also CHENGDU; CHONGQING; CIVIL WAR

BETWEEN COMMUNISTS AND NATIONALISTS; DAZU CAVE TEMPLES AND SCULPTURES; DU FU; FOUR SACRED MOUNTAINS OF BUDDHISM; MINORITIES, NATIONAL; PANDA; PAPER; ROMANCE OF THE THREE KINGDOMS; SILK; THREE GORGES WATER CONSERVANCY PROJECT; THREE KINGDOMS PERIOD; WAR OF RESISTANCE AGAINST JAPAN; YANGZI RIVER.

SIDDHARTHA GAUTAMA   See BUDDHA.

SIKA DEER   See CHANGBAI MOUNTAIN RANGE; DEER.

SILK (*si* or *ssu*)   A beautiful and delicate but strong fabric made from the cocoons of silkworms. The production of silk, known as sericulture, was invented in China. The Chinese kept its techniques secret for centuries, although eventually they were smuggled out of the country. Italy, France, Japan, Korea and other countries developed silk industries, but China remained the world's largest silk producer until the early 20th century, when Japan surpassed it. Recently Chinese silk production has increased while that of other countries has declined or disappeared. In 1977 China became number one again, producing 18,000 tons of silk. Jiangsu and Zhejiang provinces in eastern China are the main regions for silk production. In 1991 China's raw silk production was 60 percent of the world's total, its raw silk exports comprised 90 percent of the world's raw silk trade and its silk and satin exports were 50 percent of the world's silk product trade. Silk factories have been concentrated in eastern cities such as Shanghai and Suzhou, but nearly all Chinese provinces, autonomous regions and municipalities, except for Qinghai and Tibet, have silk factories. In 1992 China had 1,506 silk enterprises with 800,000 workers. About 40,000 varieties of silk products have been developed. Some are varieties of traditional silk products, such as silk crepe, twill silk and habutai, and some are produced by new techniques, such as sand washing of silk. Pure silk knitwear, developed in the early 1980s, was the first breakthrough in silk production in 1,000 years. Special finishing processes to increase the softness, elasticity and luxurious look of silk also have been developed.

Silkworms are fed the young leaves of mulberry trees, which are grown on hillsides in the same areas as tea is cultivated. The northern Chinese provinces also have many tussah trees, which are used to raise tussah silkworms. In some regions of China sericulture is combined with fish farming. Mulberry trees are planted around ponds in which carp are raised, and the fish feed on the silkworm droppings. Women in China always have performed the complicated tasks of raising silkworms, gathering their cocoons and spinning the silk threads. By the late Neolithic period (c. 12,000–2000 B.C.) the Chinese knew the techniques for raising silkworms, softening the cocoons in boiling water and unwinding them, and spinning, dyeing, weaving and embroidering with silk threads. According to Chinese legend, Leizu (Lei-tsu), the wife of the Yellow Emperor, developed the techniques of sericulture and taught them to Chinese women. While sitting in her garden, she heard leaves rustling in the trees and saw silkworms spinning their cocoons with silken thread, which she discovered how to weave into fabric.

Silk is produced by incubating the eggs of silkworms for 12 days. When they hatch into thin, tiny larvae, they are

The production of silk, a fabric made from silkworm cocoons, was invented in China.   COURTESY, MUSEUM OF FINE ARTS, BOSTON

placed on round bamboo trays, which are stacked on shelves, and fed fresh mulberry leaves that have been gathered by hand. Silkworms eat continuously for 24 to 28 days and must be fed fresh leaves every two hours around the clock. Then they spin cocoons of fine thread. After three to five days, the cocoons are boiled to dissolve the sericin, a sticky substance on the thread. The long, fine silk fiber of the cocoon is then unreeled into a continuous length of thread that can be dyed and woven.

During the Zhou dynasty (1100–256 B.C.), before the Chinese invented paper, they wrote official documents on rolls of silk and ordinary texts on thin strips of wood that were bound into rolls. Paper was invented in China by 200 B.C. but was not produced in large quantities until about A.D. 200. Chinese artists always have painted and written calligraphy on silk as well as paper, even into the modern era. By the Han dynasty (206 B.C.–A.D. 220), Chinese weavers were using foot-powered multiharness looms and jacquard looms, which required an assistant to move the parts. Silk weaving and embroidery became organized craft industries, with imperial workshops in the capital and many other workshops throughout the country that employed thousands of skilled artisans.

At the start of the agricultural cycle, Chinese emperors performed sacred rituals to ensure that heaven would provide a good harvest. Empresses performed similar rituals at the beginning of the annual cultivation of silkworms. Large quantities of silk textiles were paid as taxes, so that an emperor could present bolts of silk to foreign diplomatic missions that came to pay tribute to him and also to generals and government officials who served him well. Members of the imperial family and court wore long silk robes decorated with colorful designs in silk embroidery that symbolized their rank. Emperors wore robes embroidered with nine dragons. Members of the imperial bureaucracy became divided into nine ranks, known as the Nine-Rank System, and wore squares of tightly woven silk designs on their robes, a form of tapestry known as *kesi* (*k'o-ssu;* "cut silk") or "mandarin squares." *Kesi* also was used to mount fine paintings on scrolls, and to make panels for screens and wall hangings and covers for Buddhist sutras (scriptures). Young

women who knew how to weave and embroider with silk traditionally gained higher status when they married. They could work at home on pieces from private and imperial workshops. Only the wealthy upper classes wore silk clothing, while the peasants, who made up most of the Chinese population, wore clothing made of hemp, ramie and other fibers. They also wore cotton after it was introduced during the Ming dynasty (1368–1644).

Silk is woven on looms that can range from simple frames to complex jacquard or automated looms. Large drawlooms were invented in China and enable the weaver to create intricate patterns in the silk fabric. Warp threads are attached to the loom lengthwise, and weft threads are moved over and under the warp threads to create the fabric. There are thousands of different ways to interweave weft and warp threads. The simplest is the plain "tabby" weave, in which one weft thread moves over one warp thread and under the next in a continuous movement. Brocades and damasks are fabrics that have patterns woven into them. Many different effects are created by using threads of different weights or thicknesses, by using colored threads to weave in designs such as flowers and by mixing weaves.

During the Ming dynasty an imperial weaving workshop was established in Suzhou in Jiangsu Province to produce the emperor's dragon robes. An imperial brocade workshop was established in Hangzhou in Zhejiang Province. Suzhou is still famous for silk tapestry and embroidery, and Hangzhou remains famous for colorful silk damasks, sheer silks and satin brocades with gold threads woven into them. Today Chinese designers are studying brocade-weaving techniques of the Tang, Song and Ming dynasties so that silk weavers can reproduce them. An imperial workshop for brocades using gold and silver threads was established in Nanjing in Jiangsu Province during the Ming. Chengdu in Sichuan Province is called the City of Brocade for the Brocade River running through the city, where silk brocades were washed. A silk weaving and embroidery workshop was established in Chengdu more than 1,500 years ago.

In the middle of the Zhou dynasty, China began exporting silk along caravan trails to the Middle East. During the

Han dynasty, Emperor Wudi (Wu-ti; r. 141–87 B.C.) sent Zhang Qian (Chang Ch'ien) to form alliances with tribes in Central Asia, and he learned that they had a great demand for silk. His expeditions helped open up the so-called Silk Road along which silk, tea, porcelain and other Chinese goods were traded as far west as the Mediterranean world. In the Roman Empire, senators and upper-class women wore delicate Chinese silk and referred to China as the land of the Seres, or "silk people." One pound of raw silk was worth one pound of gold. China also exported these goods on the maritime Silk Road to Japan, Southeast Asia and India. Chinese emperors made many alliances with nomadic tribes along China's northern and western frontiers to try to prevent them from invading the country; the terms of these alliances included large payments of Chinese silk textiles to the nomads.

Some Europeans made the long overland journey to China along the Silk Road; the most famous is Marco Polo (1254–1324). William of Rubruck (fl. 1250) was the first Westerner to identify Cathay, as China was then called in the West, as the land of the Seres, and he informed Westerners of the enormous quantities of silk in China. During the Ming dynasty, *kesi* panels were exported to Europe, where they were used on vestments worn by priests in Roman Catholic cathedrals. In the 16th century Europeans began sending trading ships to China to acquire silk, porcelain, tea and other luxury goods, but the Chinese government restricted them by requiring them to trade only with officially designated merchants in the southern Chinese port city of Guangzhou (Canton). This was known as the Canton system of trade. During the 17th and 18th centuries huge quantities of Chinese patterned silk textiles were exported to the West, where they helped influence the European interpretation of Chinese designs, known as chinoiserie. In the 19th century Great Britain and other European powers forced China to open a number of cities as treaty ports where foreigners could reside and trade. See also BRITISH EAST INDIA COMPANY; CALLIGRAPHY; CANTON SYSTEM OF TRADE; CATHAY; CHENGDU; CHINOISERIE; COTTON; DRAGON; EMBROIDERY; HANGZHOU; INK PAINTING; LANDSCAPE PAINTING; NANJING; NINE-RANK SYSTEM; RAMIE; SILK ROAD; SUZHOU; TEXTILE INDUSTRY; TREATY PORTS; TRIBUTE SYSTEM.

SILK ROAD A network of overland trade routes that ran west from China through Central Asia, to Syria in the Middle East on the Mediterranean Sea. The German geographer Ferdinand von Richthofen gave these routes the name Silk Road in the 1870s. Silk and other Chinese luxury goods such as porcelain, tea, gemstones, incense and spices were transported along the Silk Road in caravans of Bactrian camels, which have two humps and were domesticated in Central Asia. During the Han dynasty (206 B.C.–A.D. 220), the Chinese became acquainted with camels when they extended their military lines westward to defend against invasions by the Xiongnu nomadic tribe. General Zhang Qian (Chang Ch'ien; d. 114 B.C.) went as far west as Bactria (modern Afghanistan) and eventually returned to China with the information that countries to the west wanted to trade with the Han empire, primarily for silk.

The Romans had first seen silk in 53 B.C. when legions led by the governor of the Roman province of Syria were defeated in a battle against Parthian troops, who had flown colorful silk banners. Gifts of silk from Chinese embassies to other countries also had ended up in the Roman Empire. The Romans were very eager to buy large quantities of the beautiful fabric, the production of which had been kept a strict secret for centuries by the Chinese. The silk trade was much more important to the Romans than to the Chinese economy, and Romans were willing to pay one ounce of gold for one ounce of silk, which placed a drain on their economy. When political conditions were stable, even more silk was transported to Rome on the sea route from China by way of Sri Lanka (Ceylon) and the Red Sea. There were also overland trade routes from China to India through modern Yunnan Province and Burma, although the main overland routes for the transport of silk to India from China went along the Tarim Basin, Hotan and Kashmir. Foreign goods and cultural influences were introduced into China along these trade routes, especially the Buddhist religion, which had been founded in India in the sixth century B.C. and brought into China in the first century A.D. Buddhism entered China through Dunhuang in Gansu Province, where a large complex of cave temples and sculptures can still be seen.

From A.D. 73 to 97, Han general Ban Chao (Pan Ch'ao; 32–102) led a large Chinese expedition west to the Caspian Sea and brought most of Central Asia under the control of the Chinese Empire. He sent his lieutenant, Gan Ying (Kan Ying), farther west to make contact with the Roman Empire, called Daqin (Ta Ch'in) by the Chinese. At the Persian Gulf, local sailors, who did not want to lose their profits transporting goods on the Silk Road, persuaded Gan Ying that it was too dangerous for him to sail across. He turned back, and the Chinese never again attempted to make direct contact with the Roman Empire. Caravans with hundreds of men and as many as 1,000 camels traveled westward in stages each year from the Han capital at Chang'an (modern Xi'an in Shaanxi Province). Each camel carried 400 to 500 pounds of cargo, food and drink. They passed through the "Jade Gate," the Chinese euphemism for their western border in modern Gansu Province, and entered the "New Frontier," modern Xinjiang Uighur Autonomous Region (formerly known as Chinese Turkestan). This area was not officially brought into the Chinese Empire until the Qing dynasty (1644–1911). The Silk Road traveled through desert regions where camel caravans were the only possible means of transportation and have remained so even when the Silk Road was closed. Today camels still are used, along with trains and trucks. Traders did not usually travel the entire route. Rather, the goods were traded in several stages between China and Rome, with their price being marked up at each stage, until they were quite costly by the time they reached their destination.

Moving west from Chang'an, at Anxi beyond the Great Wall on the eastern edge of the Taklimakan Desert, the Silk Road divided into a northern and a southern route to skirt the desert. The northern route took caravans through the Jade Gate Pass (Yumenguan or Yumen-kuan) northwest of Dunhuang and along the southern foothills of the Tian Mountain Range. At Hami the northern route divided into two, one route going west from Dunhuang south of the Tian and Pamir Mountain Ranges through Kashgar, the other going north of the Tian and Pamir ranges through Tashkent, Samarkand and Bukhara. The southern route took caravans between the Taklimakan Desert and the Kunlun Mountain Range, turned north beyond the Taklimakan and joined the route through Kashgar. This route joined with the northernmost route at Merv, then continued on to Baghdad and then divided into routes to Damascus, Constantinople (modern Istanbul in Turkey) and other cities in the Roman Empire. Trade moved along one route or another depending on how safe conditions were. The caravans faced constant danger, including punishing heat and lack of water in the desert, blinding sandstorms, blizzards and altitude sickness in the mountains, and bandits.

Emperor Taizong (T'ai-tsung; r. 626–49) of the Tang dynasty (618–907) also sent military expeditions west to secure the Silk Road. The Tang dynasty became one of the greatest periods in Chinese history, due largely to the thousands of foreign traders who settled in China, bringing their own cultures and religions, which the Tang Chinese eagerly incorporated into their own culture. The foreigners included Turks, Arabs, Persians and many other Muslims, Jews, Armenians and Indians. The Tang capital at Chang'an became the largest and most cosmopolitan city in the world. The Silk Road began to decline during the Tang dynasty, however. The Persians learned the art of making silk; moreover, by the end of the eighth century, the sea routes from the southern port of Guangzhou (Canton) to the Middle East were transporting many goods and often were safer than the dangerous overland routes. The Silk Road became more open to Chinese trade with the West during the Yuan dynasty (1279–1368), founded by the Mongol leader Khubilai Khan; the Mongol empire extended all the way to the edges of Europe. Some Europeans, such as the Italian explorer Marco Polo (1254–1324), traveled the Silk Road to China. But with the ascent of the Ming dynasty (1368–1644), the Chinese government severely limited foreign trade, and activity along the Silk Road decreased greatly. Trade remained limited during the Qing dynasty (1644–1911). The Qing restricted Western traders solely to the southern port city of Guangzhou (Canton). This restriction caused Great Britain to wage two Opium Wars against China in the mid-19th century to open China to foreign trade.

In the early 19th century, Russia sent campaigns against the khanates, Muslim rulers, in Central Asia and thus blocked the Silk Road to all but local trade. Muslim rebellions also broke out against Qing control in Gansu and Shaanxi provinces. Britain defeated the Qing in two so-called Opium Wars (1839–42 and 1856–60) and opened many Chinese cities as treaty ports for foreign trade. The Chinese overthrew the Qing in the Revolution of 1911.

In the late 19th and early 20th centuries, Western explorers excavated ancient cities along the Silk Road. Sir Aurel Stein (1862–1943) completed three major Central Asian expeditions between 1900 and 1916 and discovered the vast collection of paintings and manuscripts in the hidden library at Dunhuang, many of which were acquired by the British Museum in London. Other important explorers included the German Albert von Le Coq (1860–1930), the French Paul Pelliot (1879–1945), and Russian, Japanese and American explorers. Chinese trade was disrupted as the country suffered from military occupation by Japan (1937–45), World War II and civil war between Chinese Communists and Nationalists, which the Communists won in 1949. They established the People's Republic of China in 1949. The country was closed to most foreign trade and visitors until the late 1970s. Recently some Western travelers have received permission to travel along the Silk Road and have published accounts of their experiences. See also BAN CHAO; BUDDHISM; CAMEL CARAVANS; CHANG'AN; DUNHUANG CAVE TEMPLES AND SCULPTURES; GANSU PROVINCE; GREAT WALL; HAMI; HAN DYNASTY; HOTAN; JEWS; KASHGAR; KUNLUN MOUNTAIN RANGE; MUSLIMS; POLO, MARCO; PORCELAIN; SILK; TAKLIMAKAN DESERT; TANG DYNASTY; TARIM BASIN; TEA; TIAN MOUNTAIN RANGE; TURPAN; XINJIANG-UIGHUR AUTONOMOUS REGION; XIONGNU; YUAN DYNASTY; ZHANG QIAN.

SILVER   See CURRENCY, HISTORICAL; GOLD AND SILVER.

SIMA GUANG (Ssu-Ma Kuang; 1019–85)   A Confucian scholar, historian and statesman during the Northern Song dynasty (960–1126). Sima Guang is best known for writing the *Comprehensive Mirror for Aid in Government* (*Zishi tongjian* or *Tzu-shih-t'ung-chien*), a monumental history in 354 chapters of the period in China from 403 B.C. to A.D. 959. His main sources were the official histories recorded by preceding dynasties. Sima Guang arranged the material in chronological order, adding his own comments about the events and doctrines that he compiled. This work has remained one of the most authoritative and widely studied histories of China. Sima Guang was a close friend of Ouyang Xiu (1007–72), an important Song official, historian and poet. Sima Guang was also the leader of the conservative faction that opposed the economic, military and educational reforms instituted by Song minister Wang Anshi (1021–86) under Emperor Shenzong (Shen-tsung; r. 1067–85). After Shenzong died, Sima Guang took Wang Anshi's place as prime minister and did away with his reforms. Sima Guang died soon after, and the reformists regained power briefly in 1093 but were not able to develop widespread support. See also NORTHERN SONG DYNASTY; OUYANG XIU; WANG ANSHI.

SIMA QIAN (Ssu-Ma Ch'ien; c. 145–90 B.C.)   A court historian during the Han dynasty (206 B.C.–A.D. 220) who compiled *Records of the Historian* (*Shiji* or *Shi-chi*), the first official history of China. The Han dynasty unified China as a nation and culture. Sima Qian succeeded his father, Sima Tan (Ssu-ma t'an; c. 170–110 B.C.), who had been Grand Historian under Emperor Wudi (Wu-ti; r. 141–87 B.C.) and who began writing China's first comprehensive history. Sima Qian completed his father's work using documents stored in the imperial archives. The *Records of the Historian* contains 130 chapters and covers the history of China from the legendary Yellow Emperor up to c. 90 B.C. The work is a compilation of all documents recording Chinese traditions and legends that were available to Sima Qian.

He divided the material into five sections: Basic Annals, Chronological Tables, Treatises, Hereditary Houses and Memoirs. All later Chinese official historians have followed this same general format, although Basic Annals are better termed Imperial Annals because they record the acts of reigning emperors. The Chronological Tables list in chronological order the kings of the states of China prior to the country's unification, and the nobles and politicians of the Han dynasty. The Treatises are essays on subjects important to the government, such as rituals, music, the calendar and astronomy, the Yellow River and canals, and economics. The Hereditary Houses provides accounts of the major families during China's feudal era. The Memoirs record the lives of military leaders, politicians, philosophers and other famous men. Sima Qian criticized the great Daoist philosopher Zhuangzi (Chuang Tzu; 369–286 B.C.) for having a selfish view of life that is useless in the governing of the country. The Memoirs also discuss non-Chinese lands and people, such as Korea. The final chapter of the *Records* provides a biography of the historians. Sima Qian held a standard of objectivity and accuracy in using his sources unequaled by any other ancient writer. He even placed some of his own subtle criticisms of Emperor Wudi in the text.

Sima Qian's *Records of the Historian* was rewritten and added to by Ban Biao (Pan Piao; A.D. 3–54) and his son Ban Gu (Pan Ku d. 92), historians during the Later Han dynasty. The new volume was called *History of the Former Han Dynasty* (*Han shu*). These scholars set a pattern whereby the history of a dynasty was written by scholars in the succeeding dynasty, although in their own case, they wrote about the first half of their own dynasty, the Western Han. A series of 25 standard histories of China have been written, from Sima Qian's Han history to a history of the Qing dynasty (1644–1911). See also BAN GU AND BAN ZHAO; HAN DYNASTY; SIMA TAN; WUDI, EMPEROR; YELLOW EMPEROR; ZHUANGZI.

SIMA TAN (Ssu-Ma T'an; c. 170–110 B.C.)   The writer of China's first comprehensive history under Emperor Wudi (Wu-ti; r. 141–187 B.C.) whose title was Grand Historian. His son, Sima Qian (145–c. 90 B.C.) completed this work, known as the *Records of the Historian* (*Shiji* or *Shi-chi*). The few details that are known about Sima Tan's life come from his son's autobiography of him in the *Shiji*. In one section of this work, the "Discussion of the Six Schools," Sima Tan discusses the six traditional schools of philosophy that developed in the late Zhou dynasty (1100–256 B.C.) and promotes the superiority of the concepts of the Daoism. He argues that Daoism has incorporated the good points from the Yin-Yang, Confucian, Moist, Legalist and Logical schools of thought and that it teaches how to live a life of meditative awareness and to act in harmony with the universe. Under Emperor Wudi, however, Confucianism became the dominant philosophy in China. See also CONFUCIANISM; DAOISM; LEGALIST SCHOOL OF THOUGHT; MOZI; SIMA QIAN; WUDI, EMPEROR; YIN AND YANG.

SIMA XIANGRU (Ssu-ma Hsiang-ju; 179–117 B.C.)   The greatest Chinese poet of the Han dynasty (206 B.C.–A.D. 220), who wrote in a lengthy, descriptive form of poetry known as the rhyme-prose (*fu*) style. Sima Xiangru was also a fencer and an imperial bodyguard to Emperor Jingyi (Ching I). He joined the court of Prince Xiao (Hsiao) of Liang, where he began writing his famous *fu* poem, "Master Nil" (*Zixu fu* or *Tzu Hsu fu*), in which three speakers describe how much they enjoy hunting. After Prince Xiao died, Sima Xiangru returned to the imperial court, where he eloped with a wealthy widow. Her father opposed the marriage but finally agreed to it because of Sima's connection

with the court. A friend of Sima showed his "Master Nil" poem to Emperor Han Wudi (Wu-ti; r. 141–87 B.C.), who liked it so much that he asked Sima to compose a *fu* poem about the imperial hunt. Sima creatively reworked the poem into a *fu* praising the emperor called "Supreme Park" (*Shanglin fu*). The emperor liked it so much that he gave Sima a court position. Sima spent the rest of his life writing poetry while supported by his wife's fortune. His famous poems include "Laments of Changmen" (*Changmen fu*), about a scorned mistress, and "Refutation to the Sichuan Elders" (*Nan Shu fulao*), which addresses the problem of complaints about taxation. Only 29 of Sima's *fu* and four of his prose works have survived. See also RHYME-PROSE STYLE OF VERSE.

SIMAO   See XISHUANGBANNA AUTONOMOUS DISTRICT OF THE DAI PEOPLE.

SIMLA AGREEMENT   See SINO-INDIAN BORDER DISPUTE.

SINGAPORE   Official name the Republic of Singapore; a small Southeast Asian country at the tip of the peninsula of Malaysia that has a population of more than 3 million, about three-quarters of whom are Chinese, one of the largest and wealthiest groups of overseas Chinese in the world. Recently many of them have made large economic investments in the People's Republic of China (PRC). Trade relations between Singapore and the PRC have become very strong since the two countries established diplomatic relations in 1990. Because of its rapid economic growth, today Singapore is called one of the Four Tigers (or "Four Little Dragons") along with Hong Kong, Taiwan and South Korea. Singapore's other main population groups include Malaysians, Indians and Pakistanis, as well as some Europeans and Eurasians. English is the official language, although Chinese, Malay and Tamil are also spoken. Singapore consists of one main island, Singapore Island, with an area of about 210 square miles, and about 40 smaller ones with a combined area of about 15 square miles. The country has a strategic location on the most important shipping route between the Indian Ocean and the Pacific Ocean. Its main city and capital, also named Singapore, has one of the best-protected harbors in the world and has become one of the world's largest ports. Singapore is thus called the Gateway of the Pacific. Located about one degree north of the equator, Singapore has a tropical climate and vegetation, with an average temperature of about 80°F and nearly 100 inches of rainfall each year. The island has sandy beaches and coral reefs, and tourist sites include the beautiful Botanical Gardens. Mount Faber Hill provides a scenic view of the area. World-famous Raffles Hotel is named for Singapore's founder.

Singapore grew up around an ancient seaport, known as Temasek (Tumasik; Malay for "Old Sea Town"), founded in 1297 as one of the three kingdoms of Srivijaya, a trading empire based in south Sumatra, Indonesia. Singapore traders gathered products from all over Southeast Asia, such as spices, rubber, tin, sugar, copra and lumber, and shipped them to markets worldwide. Modern Singapore was founded in 1819 by Sir Thomas Stamford Raffles, who recognized Singapore's strategic location and began negotiations with local rulers to establish a base there for the British East India

Company. The world-famous Raffles Hotel is named for him. In 1824 Great Britain purchased Singapore and developed the harbor and the city. The name Singapore comes from the Indian Sanskrit words *singa* and *pura,* together meaning "Lion City." Singapore joined with Penang and Malacca, two Malayan states, to form the Straits Settlements. In 1867 these settlements became a crown colony administered by the British Colonial Office. Singapore developed as a prosperous trading center after the Suez Canal was opened in 1869 and steamships were put into use, and large numbers of Chinese immigrated to work there. Japan, which had invaded China in 1937 and sent its troops throughout Asia, occupied Singapore in 1942 during World War II. British forces reoccupied the island in 1945.

In 1946 Singapore became a separate crown colony, and in 1948 it held elections for members of the Legislative Council, the first step toward self-government. In June 1959 it became a self-governing territory under a new constitution. In 1961 the prime minister of Malaya suggested a Federation of Malaysia that would include the state of Singapore, the Federation of Malaya, and the colonies of Sabah (North Borneo) and Sarawak. Malaysia was proclaimed on September 16, 1963, in spite of opposition from Indonesia. The Singapore government had economic and political differences with Malaysia, which put heavy pressure on it, and Singapore separated from the federation in August 1965. Singapore remains connected to the mainland of Malaysia by a causeway for cars and trains. Singapore was admitted to the United Nations as a sovereign state and became a republic on December 22, 1965. It has a unicameral parliament established by the constitution. The president, a ceremonial office, was formerly elected by parliament. The prime minister has been the leader of the majority party. The ruling People's Action Party was founded in the 1950s by Lee Kuan-Yu (Lee Kuan Yew), who served as prime minister for 31 years from 1959 to 1990. Many believe that he still controls the government behind the scenes even though Goh Chok Tong, his designated successor, became prime minister in 1990. The Singapore constitution has been changed to make the presidency a popularly elected office. See also BRITISH EAST INDIA COMPANY; HONG KONG; OVERSEAS CHINESE; TAIWAN.

SINGLE-WHIP TAX REFORM See MING DYNASTY.

SING-SONG GIRLS See CONCUBINAGE; WILLOW.

SINICIZATION The process by which ethnic groups that invaded China and became rulers of the Han Chinese majority ethnic group adopted the government bureaucracy, institutions, language, social customs, cuisine, clothing and ways of thinking of their Han Chinese subjects. The Han referred to these invaders as barbarians. Many of them were nomadic tribes that invaded China from the north and northwest, and Chinese rulers built and enlarged the so-called Great Wall to attempt to keep them out of China. The non-Han invaders eventually realized that they would profit more from becoming sinicized and taxing the Han, who lived in settled communities and practiced agriculture, than they would from killing them and destroying the tax base. Many Han also inhabited large cities where lucrative art objects and handi-

crafts were produced, especially painting, calligraphy, silk and porcelain.

Sinicization also occurred as the Han Chinese moved into southern China. The earliest center of Han Chinese civilization was along the Yellow River (Huanghe), which flows across northern China. The Han regarded the people who lived to the south in the lower Yangzi River (Changjiang) valley as barbarians who practiced such customs as tattooing their bodies, cutting their hair short and clearing forested areas to build villages. During the second half of the Zhou dynasty (1100–256 B.C.) the Han began moving south to escape warfare among rival kingdoms. By the end of the sixth century B.C. the people in the state of Ch'u that had developed in the lower Yangzi had adopted many Chinese customs, although "civilized" Hans to the north still considered them barbarians. This gradual process of Han southward migration continued over the centuries, with some local ethnic groups being absorbed into the Han and others retaining their own identity and customs. Even today there are many minority ethnic groups in southern and southwestern China, including the largest group, the Zhuang, whose homeland has been designated Guangxi-Zhuang Autonomous Region by the government of the People's Republic of China.

Nomadic groups to the north and northwest, such as the Xiongnu (Hsiung-nu) and Xianbei (Hsien-pei), posed a threat to the Han dynasty (206 B.C.–A.D. 220). Han emperors dealt with them by various means, including strengthening frontier fortifications, making alliances with other tribes in Central Asia against their common enemies and paying tribute in money and material goods to the threatening groups. The process of sinicization largely took place during the Six Dynasties Period (220–589), when the Chinese Empire fragmented into many kingdoms following the overthrow of the Han dynasty. The Six Dynasties Period includes the Three Kingdoms Period (220–80), the Western Jin dynasty (265–316) and Eastern Jin dynasty (317–420), and the Northern and Southern dynasties (420–589). Five major tribes considered barbarians by the Han invaded China. The Xiongnu, Xianbei and Jie (Chieh) who moved down from the northern steppes spoke languages related to Turkish, Mongolian and Tungusic. The Qiang (Ch'iang) and the Di (Ti) came from the mountainous regions to the west and spoke languages similar to Tibetan and Tangut. Their invasions caused many Chinese to migrate south, especially wealthy aristocrats.

From the third to fifth century, the number of Han Chinese in the region south of the Yangzi River increased greatly and took over the lands inhabited by local tribes, some of which became Sinicized and lived under the rule of Han aristocrats. During the sixth century Nanjing and other cities along the Yangzi grew in importance, as did the southern port city of Guangzhou (Canton). However, a large number of Han remained in the regions north of the Yangzi and coexisted with the invaders, who adopted the Han Chinese language, literature, philosophy, cuisine and customs. Alien rulers in China even studied the classical texts of Confucianism and patronized Chinese scholars. They took Chinese names, and many of them married Han Chinese women, particularly in the upper classes, and raised their children as Han, so that after two or three generations there was virtually no difference between the invaders and the Han Chinese.

The first major sinicized ruler was Fujian (Fu Chien), who belonged to an ethnic tribe racially related to modern Tibetans. He unified northern China under the Former Qin dynasty (350–94) and extended his empire from southern Manchuria (modern northeastern China) to modern Xinjiang-Uighur Autonomous Region in the west and south to the Yangzi River basin. In 383 he led an army of one million men to conquer southern China, but his inexperienced troops were thoroughly defeated and his empire fell apart. This was a turning point in Chinese history, when the country could have been reunified under one ruling dynasty. Instead, the various tribes in northern China broke away from Fujian's rule and entered into conflict with each other.

The Toba Turks (Tuoba or T'o-pa), a branch of the Xianbei, who had settled in the region of modern Shanxi Province, did succeed in reunifying northern China under the Northern Wei dynasty (386–534). In 494 the Northern Wei ruler Xiaowendi (Hsiao-wen-ti; r. 471–99) moved his capital from Datong to Luoyang, which had been the capital of the Eastern Han dynasty. He decreed that his subjects had to adapt Chinese culture and bureaucratic government and that the educated ones had to study Confucianism. The Northern Wei spoke only the Chinese language in their court, wore Chinese clothing, took Chinese surnames and intermarried with local Chinese families. They also patronized the Buddhist religion, which had been introduced into China from India. Buddhism itself became Sinicized as it spread throughout China, losing its complex Indian metaphysical speculation as new Chinese sects developed, especially the Pure Land and Chan (Zen) Sects. Nomadic tribes on Wei's northern frontier began rebelling against the sinicized Northern Wei Dynasty in 524, and the dynasty divided into two branches. Other dynasties were founded by invaders in northern China after the Northern Wei adopted its sinicization policies. Hence the successive waves of nomadic invaders became absorbed into the Han Chinese culture. See also AGRICULTURE; BUDDHISM; CONFUCIANISM; GREAT WALL; HAN; MINORITIES, NATIONAL; NOMADS AND ANIMAL HUSBANDRY; SIX DYNASTIES PERIOD; XIONGNU; NAMES OF INDIVIDUAL DYNASTIES.

SINKIANG   See XINJIANG-UIGHUR AUTONOMOUS REGION.

SINO-BRITISH JOINT DECLARATION ON THE QUESTION OF HONG KONG   An agreement on the future status of Hong Kong, signed in Beijing on December 19, 1984, by Prime Minister Zhao Ziyang (Chao Tzu-yang) of the People's Republic of China (PRC) and Margaret Thatcher, prime minister of Great Britain. Also present at the signing were Deng Xiaoping, chairman of the Central Advisory Commission of the Chinese Communist Party, Li Xiannian (Li Hsien-nien), president of the PRC, and British foreign secretary Sir Geoffrey Howe. Great Britain had acquired Hong Kong in 1842, as part of the Treaty of Nanjing, which concluded the Opium War (1839–42) in which Britain defeated China; the Hong Kong territory rapidly became an important financial and trading center. In 1860 Britain acquired the southern part of Kowloon Peninsula on the Chinese mainland across from Hong Kong Island. In 1898 the British colony of Hong Kong obtained a

99-year lease on the new territories north of Kowloon and on 235 neighboring islands. By the end of 1995 the British Crown Colony of Hong Kong was the world's third-largest financial center and 11th-largest trading economy.

The Joint Declaration stated that the British government would return Hong Kong to the PRC on July 1, 1997 and that the PRC government would resume sovereign rights over Hong Kong on the same date. It also stated that Hong Kong would "enjoy a high degree of autonomy, except in foreign or defense affairs" and "executive, legislative and independent judicial power," with little change in its current laws, which ensure rights and freedoms of such matters as speech, press assembly, religious belief and travel. The PRC would designate Hong Kong a "Special Administrative Region of China," giving it a high degree of autonomy and enabling it to continue its capitalist economic system. This is known as the "One Country, Two Systems" policy.

As the date approached for the return of the new territories to China, the Chinese and British governments engaged in 22 rounds of negotiations over two years, which resulted in their signing the joint declaration. Chinese and British representatives initialed a draft agreement of the Joint Declaration in September 26, 1984 in the Great Hall of the People in Beijing. The Legislative Council in Hong Kong and the British Parliament approved the draft, and the final accord was signed on December 19, 1994. In December 1995 the PRC announced the list of 150 members appointed to the Preparatory Committee that would work out the details of the Chinese takeover of Hong Kong. Of the 150 committee seats, 94 went to Hong Kong leaders, including businessmen, government officials, church leaders, legislators, academics and a member of the Hong Kong government's Executive Council, or cabinet; 56 went to PRC members, mainly government officials and academics. Residents of Hong Kong are concerned about their future freedoms because none of the seats went to members of Hong Kong's largest political party—the Democrats—who have actively criticized the PRC on human rights issues, especially the Tiananmen Square massacre of 1989. Many Hong Kong residents have moved to Australia and Canada, which belong to the British Commonwealth. See also DENG XIAOPING; HONG KONG; NANJING, TREATY OF; OPIUM WAR; TIANANMEN SQUARE MASSACRE.

SINO-FRENCH WAR   (1884–85)   A war between China and France for the control of Vietnam, which lies to the south of China. China's military forces had been shown to be weak by its defeat by Britain in the Opium War (1839–42), making it vulnerable to foreign attacks. In 1860 the French and the British occupied Beijing, China's capital, defeating China in the Arrow War (1856–60; Second Opium War). The country was also weakened by internal uprisings such as the Taiping Rebellion (1850–64) and the Nian Rebellion. China claimed special rights in Vietnam, regarding that country as a tributary of China, but in 1880 the French expanded their colonial empire by occupying the Vietnamese cities of Hanoi and Haiphong in northern Vietnam (then called Annam). They then pressured China to give them further concessions in Vietnam. Li Hongzhang (Li Hung-chang), who wielded power in the Qing dynasty (1644–1911) government equal to a prime minister, and who had led many projects to modernize and westernize China, knew that the Chinese navy

was weak and urged that China negotiate a settlement rather than go to war against France. However, Chinese and Manchus belonging to the Qingliu (Ch'ing-liu; "Purists") faction wanted the Qing to make a strong stand against the French. In 1884 Li began negotiations, but meanwhile the Qing fought the French in Annam and the neighboring state of Tonkin. The French admiral whose fleet was in the South China Sea sailed his eight warships and two torpedo boats into the harbor at the southeastern Chinese port city of Fuzhou. Negotiations between the two countries broke down in August 1884. The French fleet began firing on the Chinese fleet, which consisted of 11 ships, a few old war junks and rowboats. Within one hour the French destroyed the Chinese fleet, arsenal and docks in Fuzhou. They also had destroyed the Chinese Jilong (Keelung) Fortress on the island of Taiwan and occupied the Pescadore Islands. China won some minor land battles in Vietnam, but the French naval victory made China even more vulnerable and open to attacks by foreign powers than it had been. China and France signed a formal treaty in June 1885 giving France complete control of Vietnam. See also FRANCE AND CHINA; FUZHOU; LI HONGZHANG; VIETNAM AND CHINA.

SINO-INDIAN BORDER DISPUTE (1962) A conflict between China and India over two regions that border China: Kashmir (eastern Ladakh) and a region at the eastern end of the Himalaya Mountain Range between Bhutan and Burma. Kashmir borders Tibet, an autonomous region in western China called Xizang in Chinese. In the early 20th century the British had moved far into Tibet, which the weakened Qing dynasty (1644–1911) could not protect. Since then both India and the successive governments of China have claimed this territory, known as Aksai Chin, which the British carved out of Tibet. In 1950 the People's Republic of China (PRC) reaffirmed Chinese control over Tibet, leading to the Tibetan rebellion against China from 1958 to 1959. In 1958 the Dalai Lama, the religious and secular head of Tibet, fled with thousands of his followers across the border to India. Meanwhile, relations between India and China worsened, and there were several border skirmishes in 1959.

The dispute over the other territory dates back to 1914, when a meeting was held in Simla, India. The British representative, Sir Arthur McMahon, established the border by drawing a line on a map from Bhutan to Burma, over the Himalaya Mountains. This became known as the McMahon line. The government of the Republic of China, which had been established in 1912, refused to ratify the Simla Agreement, arguing that the border should be drawn farther south since this territory was ethnically part of China. The government of the PRC, established in 1949, agreed with this position.

After India became independent from Britain following World War II, it made the same claim on these two territories. India and China each escalated their claims to the territories, and in 1962 the two countries engaged in open warfare, although it ended very quickly without resolving the conflict. China has continued to hold the disputed territory in Kashmir and has built a strategic highway connecting Tibet with Xinjiang-Uighur Autonomous Region. India continued to lay claim to the disputed territory south of the

McMahon Line in the Himalayas, near Arunachal Pradesh, the northeast Indian state bordering Tibet (Xizang Autonomous Region) in China. India and China had another military confrontation in this area in 1986 and have continued to station forces there. The Sino-Indian Border Dispute has affected international relations. During the 1962 conflict, the United States and the U.S.S.R. both supported India. However, India gradually turned away from the United States and toward the U.S.S.R., resulting in the Soviet-Indian treaty of friendship in 1971. That same year India and Pakistan went to war, with the U.S.S.R. backing India and China backing Pakistan. Pakistan was defeated, resulting in the creation of the new state of Bangladesh. See also HIMALAYA MOUNTAIN RANGE; TIBET.

SINO-JAPANESE WAR OF 1894–95 A war fought between China and Japan over control of Korea, which lies between the two countries. Korea had a long history of political association with China under the Chinese tribute system. Japan, which had modernized rapidly by adapting Western institutions and military methods, wanted to seize control of Korea, and in 1874 it concluded a treaty with Korea without seeking China's approval. The treaty opened two Korean ports to Japanese trade and recognized Korea's independence from China. China responded by persuading Korea to open its ports to all Western countries, so that their influence could offset that of Japan. Korea became divided between two political factions, a progressive one led by Korean students who had studied in Japan and wanted Korea to enact reforms to modernize and a conservative one led by officials close to the Korean king who had Chinese support. In 1884 these two factions began fighting each other, and both China and Japan sent troops into Korea. The Chinese forces, led by Yuan Shikai (Yuan Shih-k'ai), routed the Japanese and placed the conservative Korean faction in power. In 1885 the Chinese statesman Li Hongzhang (Li Hung-chang) met with the Japanese statesman Ito Hirobumi to negotiate the conflict, and they signed the Li-Ito Agreement, which specified that if future disturbances erupted in Korea, each country would inform the other before sending troops into Korea. China wanted to keep Korea as a vassal state because if Japan gained control of Korea, it could cross the northern Korean border and invade northeastern China, known as Manchuria.

In 1894 a rebellion broke out that affected much of southern Korea. Korea asked China for assistance in suppressing it. China, after informing Japan of its intention, sent troops into Korea. Japan also sent troops there and seized control of Seoul, Korea's capital. The Japanese deposed the Korean king and put his father on the throne; this new king signed a treaty of alliance with Japan and asked it to eliminate the Chinese troops from Korea. War formally broke out between China and Japan. The Chinese troops could not hold their own against the Japanese army, which was trained in modern methods of warfare and equipped with modern weapons. In a naval battle, the Japanese fleet sank or crippled all of the warships in the Chinese Beiyang (Pei-yang) fleet. Japanese troops invaded Manchuria (northeastern China) from Korea and seized Port Arthur (part of modern Dalian), a strategic port at the southern tip of the Liaodong Peninsula.

The war was concluded in 1895 when Li Hongzhang sued for peace on China's behalf and met with Ito Hirobumi in the spring of 1895. The two statesmen negotiated the Treaty of Shimonoseki, which was signed in Japan on April 17, 1895. The treaty was named for the city where it was negotiated, on the southwestern tip of the main Japanese island of Honshu, where Western ships passed through the Strait of Shimonoseki. Japan initially presented extremely harsh terms to China. However, when Li Hongzhang was wounded by a Japanese citizen in an assassination attempt on March 24, Japan apologized and made the terms of the treaty slightly more lenient. Japan required China to cede to Japan Taiwan Island, the Penghu (Pescadore) Islands and the Liaodong Peninsula in Manchuria, which has a strategic port at its southern tip; pay Japan an enormous indemnity; allow Japanese industries to be established in four Chinese treaty ports, giving Japan the most-favored-nation status that China had already granted to Western powers; and recognize the independence of Korea, which had been a protectorate of China. Japan would have demanded even more except for pressure from Russia, Germany and France, which wanted to gain more Chinese concessions for themselves. They forced Japan to give up its demand to the Liaodong Peninsula in return for a larger indemnity.

China's humiliating defeat by a much smaller nation during the Sino-Japanese War convinced the Chinese people that Japan really intended to conquer all of China. It also spurred the faction in the Chinese government, led by Kang Youwei (K'ang Yu-wei), that wanted to enact reforms to modernize the country, resulting in the Reform Movement of 1898 (also known as the Hundred Days Reform). Following China's defeat by Japan, Western powers attempted to gain more control in China, and Germany forced China to give it concessions in Shandong Province in 1897. Russia angered Japan by gaining concessions from China to build a railroad through Manchuria, and in 1904–5 Japan went to war with Russia over the control of Manchuria. Japan made Korea a Japanese protectorate in 1907 and annexed it as a colony in 1910. Japan continued to build up its military, invaded Manchuria in 1931 and used it as the base from which it invaded China and the rest of Asia. In 1937 China and Japan formally began fighting their second war, which the Chinese call the War of Resistance against Japan (1937–45; World War II). See also DALIAN; LI HONGZHANG; LIAODONG PENINSULA; MANCHURIA; REFORM MOVEMENT OF 1898; RUSSO-JAPANESE WAR OF 1904–5; SHIMONOSEKI, TREATY OF; WAR OF RESISTANCE AGAINST JAPAN; YUAN SHIKAI.

SINO-SOVIET CONFLICT   A conflict between the People's Republic of China (PRC), founded by the Chinese Communist Party (CCP) in 1949, and the U.S.S.R., which was a close ally of the PRC until the late 1950s. The two countries share a very long border. After the October Revolution of 1917 in Russia, Soviet Communists went to China to help organize the CCP, which was founded officially in 1921. In February 1949, shortly before the CCP defeated the Chinese Nationalists (Kuomintang; KMT) and established the PRC on October 1, 1949, CCP Chairman Mao Zedong (Mao Tse-tung) signed a 30-year treaty of alliance with the U.S.S.R. in Moscow. The treaty, known as the Sino-Soviet Alliance, provided for the Soviet defense of China against Japan and

any ally associated with Japan, a reference to the United States. The Sino-Soviet alliance gave China some security against possible attack by the United States, which supported the KMT. It gave the U.S.S.R. special rights in Xinjiang in western China and Manchuria in northeastern China, although the PRC ended these rights in 1954. In addition to providing military support, the U.S.S.R. helped China develop its heavy industries and sent large numbers of technicians to China; many Chinese went to the U.S.S.R. for training. The CCP borrowed the Soviet models for its government bureaucracy, economy, military, education and social welfare systems, and scientific research.

After Soviet leader Joseph Stalin died in 1953, the Chinese became more independent of the Soviets. That year the U.S.S.R. gave up joint control of the railways in Manchuria (northeastern China), which it had held since Japan was defeated in 1945. Two years later it turned over the naval base at Port Arthur (now part of the city of Dalian) to the PRC without requiring the Chinese to pay compensation. Around 1956 China and the U.S.S.R. began growing apart ideologically. The Chinese felt that the Soviets were falling away from the revolutionary dogma of Marx and Lenin, being too conciliatory toward the West, and favoring technocrats and consumerism. Soviet leader Nikita Khrushchev criticized the Great Leap Forward, Mao's program for the economic and agricultural development of China, which angered Mao, who rejected Khrushchev's proposal for a joint Pacific fleet and a Soviet communications complex on the east coast of China. Mao resented what he perceived as the U.S.S.R.'s attempt to control China. In 1959 Khrushchev decided not to give the PRC a sample atomic bomb as promised, and he supported India in the Sino-Indian border skirmishes.

In April 1960 the PRC criticized Soviet leaders for being "revisionist," and in June the U.S.S.R. stopped all aid to the PRC and recalled the thousands of Soviet experts then working in China. This action, combined with the terrible failure of the Great Leap Forward, devastated the Chinese economy. By 1962 Mao also had denounced the government of the U.S.S.R. as a right-wing dictatorship. In Mao's view, capitalism had been restored in the U.S.S.R., and to prevent China from "changing color" in this way, he initiated the Cultural Revolution (1966–76) in the PRC. Relations between the two countries further deteriorated when China fought with India, known as the Sino-Indian Border Dispute. In addition, the U.S.S.R. refused to support the PRC in its dispute with the Nationalist government of the Republic of China (ROC), which had been defeated by the CCP in 1949 and had established itself on Taiwan Island. By 1963 the PRC and the U.S.S.R. were in competition to lead the Communist world, and their relations deteriorated even further during the Vietnam War. In 1968 Mao and Chinese premier Zhou Enlai (Chou En-lai) condemned the Soviet invasion of Czechoslovakia as an act of aggressive imperialism and called the U.S.S.R. China's most dangerous enemy. The Soviets built up a huge military force near China's northern border.

Between 1971 and 1972 the United States, with Richard Nixon as president, began negotiations to establish diplomatic relations with the PRC. During the 1970s the conflict between the PRC and the U.S.S.R. affected the global balance between the two superpowers, the United States and the

U.S.S.R. The Chinese believed that the Soviet Union was trying to surround it strategically. This view was confirmed by Soviet assistance to Vietnam, which invaded and occupied Cambodia in 1978, and by the Soviet invasion of Afghanistan in 1979. Moreover, the newly deployed Soviet Pacific Fleet added to the military threat to China already posed by Soviet forces along China's northern border.

After the Cultural Revolution and the deaths of Mao and Zhou in 1976, CCP leaders drew up new policies to reform and modernize China that were less concerned with ideology than Mao's policies had been. By 1982 the Chinese felt less threatened by the U.S.S.R., which was bogged down in Afghanistan and suffering from a declining economy, so CCP leaders altered their foreign policy and began improving relations and expanding trade with the U.S.S.R. By 1989 the U.S.S.R. was withdrawing troops from Afghanistan, pressuring Vietnam to withdraw from Cambodia and reducing its forces in the Far East. In May 1989 the PRC and the U.S.S.R. held a Sino-Soviet summit meeting to begin normalizing relations between the two countries, and Soviet chairman Mikhail Gorbachev visited the PRC. At the same time, Chinese students were holding a massive prodemocracy demonstration in Tiananmen Square in the capital city of Beijing. The demonstrators had been influenced in part by recent trends toward reform in the U.S.S.R., known as *glasnost* and *perestroika*. CCP officials finally called out the military to force the demonstrators out of Tiananmen Square and instituted martial law. In November 1997 Soviet leader Boris Yeltsin went to China, where he and Chinese president Jiang Zemin signed a declaration on the final demarcation of the 2,500-mile border between Russia and China. They announced that they would pursue closer economic and political ties but did not revive their formal alliance of the 1950s. See also CHINESE COMMUNIST PARTY; CIVIL WAR BETWEEN COMMUNISTS AND NATIONALISTS; CULTURAL REVOLUTION; DALIAN; GREAT LEAP FORWARD; MAO ZEDONG; PEOPLE'S REPUBLIC OF CHINA; REPUBLIC OF CHINA; SINO-INDIAN BORDER DISPUTE; TIANANMEN SQUARE MASSACRE.

SISHU See FOUR BOOKS OF CONFUCIANISM.

SIWALIK MOUNTAIN RANGE See HIMALAYA MOUNTAIN RANGE.

SIX BOARDS See IMPERIAL BUREAUCRACY.

SIX CANONS OF PAINTING (*liu fa*) Also known as the Six Principles of Painting; the basic principles used to judge painters and their works, which were systematized by the figure painter and art critic Xie He (Hsieh Ho) during the late fifth century A.D. These six principles became the standards for evaluating paintings in China and have remained the basis for Chinese art criticism down to the present time. Most of the concepts in Xie He's text had already been expounded in the theories of earlier painters and critics, notably the poet Xiao Tong (Hsiao T'ung) and the painter Gu Kaizhi (Ku K'ai-chih), but Xie He organized the principles into a comprehensive system, known as the *Ancient Painters' Classified Record* (*Guhua Pinlu* or *Ku hua p'in lu*).

The first of the six principles is *qiyunshengdong* (*ch'i yun sheng tung*), or rhythmic vitality, also translated as spirit har-

mony—animating the spirit of the subject in a painting, portraying its vitality. Second is *gufayongbi* (*ku fa yung pi*), or structure ("bone manner") in brushwork, that is, the structural method in using the brush in both painting and calligraphy, the art of writing with a brush. Third is *yingwuxiangxing* (*ying wu hsiang hsing*), or modeling from an object, meaning faithfulness to the object being portrayed. Fourth is *suileifucai* (*sui lei fu ts'ai*), or coloring adaptation—applying colors in conformity with the characteristics of the objects. Fifth is *jingyingweizhi* (*ching ying wei chih*), or careful composition, which is the appropriate placing of elements in a painting. Sixth is *chuanyimuxie* (*ch'uan i mu hsieh*), or the imitation or copying of ancient paintings that serve as models for the education of a painter. The Chinese have always considered the copying of great paintings as a valuable exercise, not only for training a painter in the repertoire of Chinese styles and techniques but also for the preservation of these paintings and the cultivation of respect for tradition. In China, later painters tended to work in the style of earlier painters rather than attempting to develop completely new styles of their own. To them, originality lay not in the style but in the "spirit" of a painting. The first of the six principles, rhythmic vitality, spirit harmony or spirit consonance (*qi yun* or *ch'i yun*), evinces a painter's spirit. *Qi* (*ch'i*, literally, "breath") is the life force or cosmic energy that the Chinese believe gives energy and life to everything that exists. The artist must achieve harmony with *qi* so that its energy fills him and inspires his paintings. See also FIGURE PAINTING; PAINTING; QI.

SIX CHAPTERS OF A FLOATING LIFE See SHEN FU.

SIX COMPANIES, CHINESE A group of six organizations in San Francisco that assisted the many Chinese laborers who immigrated to the United States in the 19th century, protected them and helped them find jobs, mainly building the railroads or working in laundries. The Qing dynasty (1644–1911) that governed China formally agreed to permit Chinese to emigrate after the Arrow War (1856–60), the Second Opium War in which Britain defeated China. In fact, many Chinese laborers had already immigrated to work in Southeast Asia, Australia, Hawaii, North and South America and other foreign areas. Most were from Guangdong Province in southern China. About 46,000 Chinese immigrated to Hawaii in the second half of the 19th century and about 380,000 to the U.S. mainland between 1849, the start of the California Gold Rush, and 1930. Most of the Chinese immigrants to the United States borrowed money from brokers to pay their passage, which they had to repay with interest. The Six Companies were established along the lines of traditional clan and regional associations in China, where all the members of a single clan claiming a common ancestor usually resided in one village or a cluster of adjacent villages. When Chinese laborers immigrated to the United States, they maintained their lineage connections and established clan and regional associations, known as *hui-gan* (*hui-kuan*), for self-protection. These became known as the Chinese Six Companies. The first company was the Zhonghua Gongsuo (Chung-hua Kung-so; Public Hall of the Middle Kingdom), established by Chinese immigrants on Sacramento Street in San Francisco. When a ship arrived from China, the company sent an interpreter to greet the immigrants and to offer them free rooms, water and fuel for about a month, until they could find jobs. By the early 1850s there were so many Chinese in San Francisco that the company could not take care of everyone, so members of various clans organized their own companies to help relatives who emigrated from their own districts in China.

In 1853 the heads of the various Chinese associations formed an umbrella organization called the Four Houses. Other groups continued to organize, and in 1862 two more joined the Four Houses, which changed its Chinese name to the Zhonghua huiguan (Chung-hua hui-kuan), known in English as the Chinese Consolidated Benevolent Association, although Americans called it the Chinese Six Companies. The *huiguan* kept this composition until 1898. Chinese merchants also established the Zaoyi gongso (Tsao-i kung-so), a body of officials elected from the Six Companies, to deal with issues that were important to the Chinese in the United States as a whole. The Six Companies included the Sam Yap Company (Sanyi huiguan or San-i hui-kuan), Yeong Wo Company (Yanghe huiguan or Yang-ho hui-kuan), the Kong Chow Company (Gangzhou huiguan or Kang-chou hui-kuan), Yan Hop Company (Renhe huiguan or Jen-ho hui-kuan), Hop Wo Company (Hehe huiguan or Ho-ho hui-kuan) and Ning Yeung Company (Ningyang huiguan or Ning-yang hui-kuan). By the 1870s the Ning Yeung Company was the largest, followed by the Hop Wo Company. The Six Companies assisted their immigrant members, helped the sick and poor and arranged to send the bodies of deceased Chinese back to China. In their halls, members could perform rituals to honor their deceased ancestors in China, known as ancestor worship, and could conduct business negotiations. The Six Companies usually elected as their leaders Chinese businessmen who were successful in the United States, could speak English and could serve as liaisons between the Chinese and American communities. Merchants did not have much social status in China and were considered the lowest of the four traditional social classes, while the Confucian-educated scholars, or literati, who ran the imperial bureaucracy belonged to the highest class. Therefore, the leaders of the Six Companies promoted Confucian education and virtues in the United States to legitimize their authority.

In 1868, when China and the United States were negotiating a treaty, the Six Companies lobbied for provisions to protect Chinese immigrants in the United States, and they hired an American lawyer to assist these efforts. As a result, the 1868 Burlingame Treaty recognized the "free migration and emigration" of the Chinese to the United States and the rights of Chinese in the United States to "enjoy the same privileges, immunities, and exemptions in respect to travel or residence, as may there be enjoyed as the citizens or subjects of the most favored nation." This encouraged Chinese merchants to lobby for federal legislation to abolish discriminatory state laws. The 1870 Civil Rights Act contained provisions that protected both blacks and Chinese. However, the treaty and laws were not able to prevent discrimination and violence against the Chinese, whom many American accused of providing cheap labor and taking jobs from Irish, Italian and other working-class European immigrants. In 1875 the Page Act was passed to prevent Chinese prostitutes from entering the United States, but it effectively kept out

Chinese wives as well. White laborers resented their Chinese counterparts, and the Chinese endured many acts of violence and discriminatory laws passed against them, which the Chinese Six Companies protested. In 1876 the Six Companies sent a letter to U.S. president Ulysses S. Grant, declaring that the United States always had welcomed immigrants from all countries and that the Chinese had responded by crossing the ocean to the United States. They listed the contributions of the Chinese, such as building the railroads and working in factories, which "increase the riches of this country." Many Chinese also went into U.S. courts to fight for their civil rights.

Before the Qing government established a Chinese legation in Washington, D.C. in 1878, the Six Companies served as diplomatic representatives for the entire Chinese population in the United States. When the Qing legation arrived, the Six Companies worked closely with it to manage the affairs in San Francisco's Chinatown. Americans who opposed Chinese immigration accused the Six Companies of bringing coolies and prostitutes under contract into the country, running gambling and opium dens, extorting money from Chinese immigrants and maintaining their own secret tribunals and laws. In 1882 the U.S. government passed the Exclusion Act to prohibit the entry of Chinese laborers, and in 1884 it passed a second Exclusion Act. Even these acts did not stop violent acts against the Chinese, such as the 1885 massacre of Chinese in Rock Springs, Wyoming Territory.

In 1888 the U.S. Congress passed the Scott bill, which prevented all Chinese laborers who had left the country from returning, even with legally issued certificates of identity. The Six Companies raised money to test the constitutionality of the bill, but the U.S. Supreme Court upheld it. In 1892 Congress passed the Geary Act, which extended the suspension of immigration by Chinese laborers for 10 more years and denied bail to Chinese in habeas corpus proceedings. It also required that all Chinese in the United States apply for a certificate of residence and that all those without a certificate be deported. The Six Companies hired attorneys to have this act declared unconstitutional, and a Chinese Civil Rights League was established in New York; but the Supreme Court ruled in 1893 that Congress had the right to exclude or expel aliens and to provide a system of registration and identification of aliens within the United States. The Six Companies also attempted to fight the Deficiency Act passed by Congress in 1904 that prevented Chinese from immigrating to Hawaii and the Philippine Islands, which were now U.S. possessions.

The earthquake that devastated San Francisco on April 18, 1906 destroyed most of the municipal records, which benefited the Chinese. Prior to the earthquake, only about 5 percent of the Chinese there had been women. After the earthquake, Chinese men in the city were able to claim that they had been born there, and as U.S. citizens they were allowed to bring their wives to the United States. About 10,000 Chinese female immigrants arrived between 1907 and 1924, when Congress passed an immigration act that severely restricted their entry, so they could not establish families in the United States. This act was repealed in 1930, when women comprised 20 percent of the Chinese population in the United States, so they were able to build Chinese-

American families. Chinese sons also had been immigrating to the United States, because according to U.S. law, the children of U.S. citizens were automatically citizens of the United States, even when they had been born in a foreign country. Some young men came as "paper sons," meaning that they had bought the birth certificates of U.S. citizens born in China and claimed they were citizens, so they could enter the country. After the earthquake, many Chinese men in the United States forged certificates saying that they had been born in the United States and then went back to China and returned with four or five young men they claimed were their sons. The "paper sons" had to memorize information about their "fathers" and their families so they could pass identity tests at Angel Island, where immigrants were detained before being permitted to enter San Francisco.

By 1940 there were 77,504 Chinese on the U.S. mainland, with 57 percent living in the Pacific states, 21 percent in the mid-Atlantic states and the rest elsewhere. In 1949, when the Chinese Communist Party (CCP) defeated the Chinese Nationalist Party (Kuomintang; KMT) and founded the People's Republic of China (PRC), the Nationalists fled to Taiwan, where they established the Republic of China (ROC). Chinese Americans were divided in their loyalties to mainland China and Taiwan; members of the Six Companies, who tended to be conservative and emphasize traditional Chinese Confucian values, supported the Nationalists in Taiwan. See also ARROW WAR; CIVIL WAR BETWEEN COMMUNISTS AND NATIONALISTS; CONFUCIANISM; COOLIES; NATIONALIST PARTY; OVERSEAS CHINESE; SOCIAL CLASSES; TAIWAN.

SIX DYNASTIES PERIOD (220–589)   The period in Chinese history between the downfall of the Han dynasty (206 B.C.–A.D. 220), one of China's longest and most important dynasties, and the reunification of the country under the Sui dynasty (589–618). During the Six Dynasties Period, China became divided among a number of kingdoms and competing dynasties, including the Three Kingdoms Period (San Guo or San Kuo; 220–80), the Western Jin dynasty (265–316) and Eastern Jin dynasty (317–420), and the Northern and Southern dynasties (420–589). The Three Kingdoms Period began in 220 when the last Han emperor abdicated the throne to Cao Pi (Ts'ao P'i), who founded the kingdom of Wei (or Cao Wei). Cao Cao (Ts'ao Ts'ao; 155–220), Cao Pi's father and a brilliant military general, had laid the foundations for the kingdom of Wei, which conquered the southwestern kingdom of Shu (or Shu Han) in 263. Cao Cao is one of the most famous figures in Chinese history, and his character is one of the most frequently portrayed in the popular theatrical form known as Beijing Opera. The kingdoms of Wei became locked in a stalemate with the kingdoms of Shu and Wu, which had made a political alliance for self-defense, but in 263 Wei general Sima Zhao (Ssu-ma Chao) led a surprise attack on Shu and took over the Shu kingdom. He soon died, and his son, Sima Yan (Ssu-ma Yan), proclaimed himself emperor of the Jin dynasty (265–316) and absorbed the other two kingdoms into Jin. The Three Kingdoms Period generated a cycle of folktales that formed the basis for the epic historical novel *Romance of the Three Kingdoms,* written in the 14th century and considered one of the Four Great Novels in China.

Sima Yan's brief reunification of China under the (Western) Jin dynasty enabled the ancient, original empire in the center of China, known as the Middle Kingdom (Zhongguo or Chung-kuo), to reestablish its control over the developing regions to the south and southwest. However, foreign nomadic tribes such as the Xiongnu (Hsiung-nu) and Xianbei (Hsien-pei) were allowed to settle inside the Great Wall, which had been built to protect China from nomadic invaders, and this contributed to the dynasty's downfall. After Sima Yan died, the Jin central government collapsed, and the nomadic tribes took advantage of the chaos. In 304 a Xiongnu named Liu Yuan proclaimed himself king of Han and conquered most of northern China, sacking the old capital cities of Luoyang and Chang'an (modern Xi'an). In 316 Sima Yan's descendants fled to Jiankang and founded the Eastern Jin dynasty, with Sima Rui (Ssu-ma Jui) as its first emperor.

After the Western Jin fell in 316, China became fragmented among a succession of short dynasties from 304 to 589. During the Eastern Jin dynasty, large numbers of Chinese, including many aristocrats, migrated south of the Yangzi River (Changjiang) and colonized southern China. In 420 the Jin dynasty was overthrown by its general, Liu Yu, who declared himself the first emperor of the Liu-Song dynasty. The Liu-Song was one of the Southern dynasties, which also included the Wu (222–30), which had been conquered by the Wei; the Eastern Jin (317–420), a continuation in the south of the Eastern Jin that had briefly reunited China; the Southern Qi (479–502); the Liang (502–57); and the Chen (557–89), which became absorbed by the Sui when it reunified China. The Northern dynasties following the Western Jin included, among others, the Northern Wei (386–534; not to be confused with the kingdom of Wei), which divided into the Eastern Wei (534–50) and the Western Wei (537–57); and the Northern Qi (550–77) and the Northern Zhou (557–89), which were replaced by the Sui (589–618). Some of the Northern dynasties were founded by nomadic invaders who became sinicized, that is, adopted Chinese names and customs and married Chinese wives, so that after two or three generations they were indistinguishable from the Han ethnic Chinese.

Although the Six Dynasties Period was a time of widespread military conflict, it also gave rise to great cultural activity, and many consider sculptures and calligraphy from this period the finest ever produced in China. The Buddhist religion, which had been introduced from India around the first century A.D., became practiced widely in China in the sixth century, and thousands of Buddhist monasteries were built. The religion was patronized by the emperors of various dynasties including the Sui. The cities along the Yangzi and the southern port city of Guangzhou (Canton) grew in importance. Many foreign merchants settled in the country, and the foundation was laid for the great expansion of Chinese trade during the Tang dynasty (618–907). See also BUDDHISM; CAO CAO; GREAT WALL; HAN DYNASTY; MIDDLE KINGDOM; NORTHERN AND SOUTHERN DYNASTIES; NORTHERN WEI DYNASTY; OPERA, BEIJING; ROMANCE OF THE THREE KINGDOMS; SINICIZATION; SUI DYNASTY; THREE KINGDOMS PERIOD; WESTERN JIN AND EASTERN JIN DYNASTIES; XIONGNU.

SIX PRINCIPLES OF PAINTING   See SIX CANONS OF PAINTING.

SMALL SEAL SCRIPT See LI SI; WRITING SYSTEM, CHINESE.

SMALL SWORD SOCIETY A branch of the secret society known as the Triads, or Heaven and Earth Society (*Tiandihui* or *T'ien-ti-hui*), which staged a rebellion against the Manchu Qing dynasty (1644–1911) in the major port city of Shanghai and its surrounding region from 1853 to 1855. The Small Sword Society was founded in Xiamen (Amoy) about 1850, but it opened a branch in Shanghai, drawing its members from craftsmen and unemployed sailors. It soon had seven branches, located in Shanghai, and in Fujian, Zhejiang and Guangdong provinces. Liu Lichuan (d. 1855), a Cantonese, was the society's leader.

The society arose at the time when Shanghai was opened to foreign trade, which adversely affected the local economy, as did corruption in the local grain tribute tax. In 1853, during the Taiping Rebellion that nearly brought down the Qing dynasty, members of the Small Sword Society infiltrated the militias raised to defend Shanghai. On September 5, 1853, the society attacked the nearby city of Jiading. Two days later they captured Shanghai. They soon took the cities of Chuanshu and Qingpu as well. They declared a new regime called "the Great Ming" (*Da Mingguo*), a symbol among the Triads of the restoration of Chinese rule, harking back to the Ming dynasty (1368–1644). The society later gave up this regime in favor of joining with the government that Taiping rebels had established in Nanjing. Qing government officials met with the consuls of France, Great Britain and the United States, which resulted in French cooperation with the Qing in 1855 to launch a joint military force that quickly took back Shanghai. Liu Lichuan was killed when Small Sword Society members were forced to retreat. See also QING DYNASTY; SHANGHAI; TAIPING REBELLION; TRIADS.

SMALL WILD GOOSE PAGODA See BUDDHISM; PAGODA; XI'AN.

SMEDLEY, AGNES (1892–1950) An American journalist who spent many years covering the Chinese Communist Party (CCP) during its civil war against the Nationalist Party (Kuomintang; KMT) and the Chinese War of Resistance against Japan (1937–1945; World War II). Smedley was born into a poor family in Missouri and was educated at a charity school. She worked at a number of jobs and felt a close affinity with working people all her life. When she became a journalist, she wrote many articles exposing the abuse and exploitation of American workers. During the 1920s Smedley developed a strong interest in China. She spent eight years in Germany, where she did research into the history of China and India and became active in the political movements of those two countries.

In 1928 Smedley went to China, where she became a special correspondent for the German *Frankfurter Zeitung* and then the British *Manchester Guardian*. She held deep sympathy for the CCP led by Mao Zedong (Mao Tse-tung), which was struggling to overcome the feudalistic abuses and corruption rampant in China. The CCP had cooperated with the KMT since the CCP's founding in 1921, but the reactionary wing of the KMT massacred thousands of Chinese Communists in 1927. A civil war ensued. After the KMT

killed five young writers in February 1931, Lu Xun (Lu Hsun; 1881–1936), China's greatest modern author and himself a revolutionary, wrote "The Present Condition of Art in Darkest China" denouncing the KMT's persecution and execution of writers. Smedley translated this article into English and sent it to be published in the U.S. magazine *New Masses*. She also helped finance Lu Xun's publication of an album of woodcuts by the German artist Kathe Kollwitz.

In January 1937 Smedley made the arduous journey to Yan'an in Shaanxi Province, where the Central Committee of the CCP had made its headquarters following its Long March to escape the KMT between 1934 and 1935. While there she decided to write the autobiography of Zhu De (Chu Teh), commander-in-chief of the CCP's Red Army. He spent several evenings a week providing her stories and information for the projected book, *The Great Road*. After China's anti-Japanese war began in July 1937, Smedley joined Zhu at the front and spent more than a year gathering information about him and meeting with other Red Army generals. She was not able to begin writing the book until after the war ended in 1945. Since its publication in 1956, it has been considered an essential source, along with *Red Star over China* by Edgar Snow, for the study of 20th-century Chinese history and the CCP. Smedley wrote several other books on the Chinese Communist revolution, including *China's Destinies* (1933), *China's Red Army Marches* (1934), *China Fights Back* (1938) and *Battle Hymn of China* (1943). Her books gave people in the United States and Great Britain many insights about the roots and goals of the Chinese Communist Revolution. During China's War of Resistance against Japan, American General Joseph Stilwell, who was head of the U.S. and KMT forces, frequently met with Smedley to talk about the Chinese Communists. She introduced him to Communist leader Zhou Enlai (Chou En-lai), who was second in command after Mao Zedong, and Ye Jianying (Yeh Chien-ying), the Communist chief of staff.

In 1941 Smedley, who was ill, had to leave China via Hong Kong to return to the United States for medical treatment. While there, she continued her revolutionary activities. Accused of being an "enemy spy" or "enemy agent" in 1949, Smedley was forced to leave the United States for England, even though she was still sick. She had planned to return to China and finish *The Great Road*, of which she had already written 380,000 words, but sadly, in 1950 she died in Oxford, England after an operation. Her will requested that her ashes be buried on Chinese soil, and they were buried in a granite tomb outside Beijing, the Chinese capital, in the Babaoshan cemetery for revolutionaries. For her efforts, Smedley is still beloved by the Chinese people. The gray marble headstone is inscribed with these words written by Zhu De on February 16, 1951: "In memory of Agnes Smedley, American revolutionary writer and friend of the Chinese people." See also CHINESE COMMUNIST PARTY; CIVIL WAR BETWEEN COMMUNISTS AND NATIONALISTS; MAO ZEDONG; NATIONALIST PARTY; SNOW, EDGAR; STILWELL, JOSEPH W.; WAR OF RESISTANCE AGAINST JAPAN; YAN'AN; ZHOU ENLAI; ZHU DE.

SNOW, EDGAR (1905–1972) An American journalist best known for his coverage of the Chinese Communist Party (CCP) during its resistance against Japanese and

Nationalist (Kuomintang; KMT) forces in the 1930s. Snow was born in Kansas City, Missouri in 1905 and attended the Missouri School of Journalism. In 1928 he traveled to Shanghai, China and stayed in Asia for 13 years. He spent time in northwestern China, which was suffering from famine, and from 1930 to 1931 he traveled through Southeast Asia. In 1932, as a correspondent for the *Saturday Evening Post,* Snow reported on conditions in Shanghai prior to China's War of Resistance against Japan (1937–45; World War II). That same year Snow and his wife moved to the capital city of Beijing and became acquainted with leaders of the movement by Chinese intellectuals and students against Japanese aggression in Manchuria (northeastern China), an account of which Snow published in *Far Eastern Front.* He taught at Yenjing University and also edited a translation of modern Chinese short stories, *Living China.* Snow was an idealistic supporter of the Chinese Communist revolution. In 1936 he joined the Communists in northwestern China, where they had fled under the leadership of Mao Zedong (Mao Tse-tung) on their Long March to escape the Japanese and Nationalist forces. Snow was the first Western journalist to make contact with the Communist leaders and report on them. He brought with him to Communist headquarters at Yan'an in Shaanxi Province an introduction from Madame Sun Yat-sen (Soong Qingling), widow of the founder of the modern Republic of China.

Snow is best known for his book *Red Star over China,* published in 1937, which describes the Chinese Communist revolutionary movement and its leaders, including Mao Zedong's personal account of his life to Snow. After the Communists won their civil war against the Nationalists and founded the People's Republic of China (PRC) in 1949, anti-Communist Americans criticized Snow for being a Communist sympathizer, but he continued to support the Chinese leaders in the PRC. His second major work on China, *The Other Side of the River, Red China Today,* published in 1962, was a commercial failure. Snow remained friends with Mao Zedong and stood with him on the balcony in Tiananmen Square in Beijing in 1970. Mao and Zhou Enlai (Chou En-lai) relayed through Snow a message to the U.S. government requesting a U.S.-PRC dialogue. Snow died four days before President Richard Nixon made his historic trip to the PRC in 1972. See also CHINESE COMMUNIST PARTY; CIVIL WAR BETWEEN COMMUNISTS AND NATIONALISTS; MAO ZEDONG; NIXON, RICHARD, U.S. PRESIDENT, VISIT TO CHINA; REPUBLIC OF CHINA; SOONG QINGLING; SUN YAT-SEN.

SNOW LEOPARD (*bao* or *pao*)   A rarely seen animal native to Tibet Autonomous Region (Xizang Zizhiqu) and other cold mountainous regions of western Chinese provinces, including Sichuan, Qinghai, Gansu and Xinjiang-Uighur Autonomous Region (Xinjiang-Uighur Zizhiqu). The snow leopard lives at altitudes ranging from 9,840 to 19,680 feet. It is protected by a very thick coat that actually comprises two layers, a thick long outer coat and an undercoat of shorter, softer fur. The coat appears grayish-white with clusters of black spots. The snow leopard is built like an ordinary leopard, with a body about 51 inches long and weighing about 440 pounds. It has a long, thick tail and huge paws that help it regain its balance after it makes extremely long leaps on the mountainsides. Snow leopards live in caves that become covered with thick mats of shed fur. Solitary animals that hunt alone, snow leopards leave their parents when they are one year old. They are fierce hunters of blue sheep, mountain hares, rodents and antelopes and can kill animals three times their size. They hunt at night and are most active at dawn and sunset. The snow leopard, whose Latin name is *Panthera uncia,* has been designated a protected species. The Chinese Ministry of Forestry and the World Wide Fund for Nature have been conducting joint research to help preserve the species. Snow leopards have been bred successfully in captivity at the Xining city zoo in Qinghai Province. See also HIMALAYA MOUNTAINS; QINGHAI-TIBET PLATEAU.

SNUFF BOTTLES   Small containers used to contain snuff (*biyan*), tobacco that is finely ground into a powder inhaled through the nose. Snuff bottles were widely produced in China during the 18th and 19th centuries, after the Manchus who ruled China under the Qing dynasty (1644–1911) introduced the habit of taking snuff into China. The practice was a social custom among the Qing court nobles and wealthy people, but after smoking tobacco was banned in China in 1837, the common people also began taking snuff. The custom decreased after the Republic of China was established in 1912. Initially snuff was considered a medicine, but it became considered a pleasurable experience, and ground spices and herbs often were added to the tobacco to give it an appealing taste and smell. Tobacco and snuff may have been brought to Asia originally by Westerners, who stored snuff in small boxes, but China's humid climate made airtight containers necessary. Traditional Chinese medicine bottles were put to use as snuff containers, and they soon became works of art on which craftsmen spent many painstaking hours. The most common material for snuff bottles was glass, although porcelain, jade, ivory, animal horn, tortoiseshell and numerous other materials also were used. The bottles have tiny stoppers also made from a wide variety of materials, including gems or other precious or semi-precious materials. The stoppers have corks that fit into the necks of the bottles. Tiny spoons of ivory, silver, bone or other materials were attached to the stoppers for dipping out the snuff. The bottles could be smooth and look like precious stones, have carvings in relief or have miniature landscapes or scenes painted on the inside that show through the clear glass. Chinese design motifs based on folklore and mythological and cosmological beliefs were used to decorate the bottles, and auspicious symbols of happiness and good fortune were popular decorations. This art form was a specialty of artists in Beijing and Boshan, Shandong Province. Snuff bottles soon played a role in international relations, presented as gifts to foreign governments and their emissaries from Chinese emperors, and to emperors from the foreign missions. Members of the Manchu court also collected snuff bottles as works of art. In the 20th century, many Westerners also began collecting snuff bottles, and they are displayed by many Western museums. See also MANCHU; QING DYNASTY.

SOCIAL CLASSES   In the traditional Chinese Confucian system, the Chinese people were divided into four social classes. At the top were the emperor, members of the imperial court and the literati (*shi* or *shih*), or Confucian-educated scholars who served the emperor as members of the imperial bureaucracy at all levels—central, provincial and local. They were able to read and write the classical Chinese language used in official documents and were selected for official positions through a highly competitive examination system. During the Han dynasty (206 B.C.–A.D. 220), the imperial government decreed Confucianism the orthodox ideology, so the literati also controlled the performance of public rituals on behalf of the state cult. The literati gradually replaced the old aristocratic families that had controlled the earliest Chinese dynasties. In addition, they came to own most of the land in China.

Beneath the literati were the peasants (*nong*) who farmed the land, by far the greatest number of Chinese people. Agriculture and settled villages had appeared in China around 7000 B.C. From 5000 to 1900 B.C., some regions developed hierarchical societies, with a small group of wealthy nobles ruling the much larger number of poor people who farmed the land. The system of four classes became standard by the Han dynasty. Beneath the peasants were the artisans (*gong* or *kung*), who produced items necessary for daily life and handicrafts. At the bottom were the merchants (*shang*), who produced nothing themselves but acted as middlemen in the buying and selling of food and goods produced by others. The merchants often became wealthy and exercised great power in Chinese society despite their low social status. The military was not included in the four-class system, although China always had a large military. Since the imperial examination system was open to all Chinese males who could gain an education, families in the merchant, peasant and military classes encouraged their sons to join the imperial bureaucracy so that they could raise their social status. Another group not included in the four-class system that actually became quite powerful were the eunuchs who staffed the imperial palace. Chinese emperors began allowing them to handle affairs of state, and by the Ming dynasty (1368–1644) some eunuchs became virtual dictators.

The members of the four traditional social classes belonged to the Han ethnic Chinese group. The Han people were unified by beliefs and practices common to all Han throughout the Chinese Empire, including Confucianism, family structure, ancestor worship, cuisine, clothing, language and system of writing with ideographs, and living in settled villages and farming the land. To the north and northwest of China lived nomadic tribes of various ethnic groups that herded animals such as sheep, goats and horses, and that frequently invaded China and even established dynasties that ruled part or all of the country. These included the Mongols, who founded the Yuan dynasty (1279–1368), and the Manchus, who founded the Qing dynasty (1644–1911), China's last imperial dynasty. Over the centuries Chinese emperors added to the Great Wall built across northern China as an attempt to keep the nomadic invaders out. Other ethnic minorities, some of whom practiced agriculture, also inhabited China, especially the southern and southwestern regions. Some of the non-Han ethnic groups became assimilated into the Han through the process of sinicization, the adoption of Han practices and customs.

The traditional Chinese four-class system began breaking down during the Qing dynasty due to pressure from Western traders, who actually provided more power and respectability to the Chinese merchant class, and from Christian missionaries, who competed with the Confucian literati. These Western influences contributed to the Revolution of 1911, in which the Chinese overthrew the Manchu Qing, and to the founding of the modern Republic of China (ROC) in 1912. The modern revolutionary movements also began breaking down the power of the literati class. When the Chinese Communists founded the People's Republic of China (PRC) in 1949, they professed the aim of overcoming Chinese Confucian feudal traditions and creating a classless society. They enacted land reform policies that took land away from wealthy landowners and gave it to peasants, and they organized peasant villages into people's communes in which everyone was supposed to share work and profits equally. The Chinese people also were organized into work units (*danwei*) that controlled all aspects of their lives, including housing; food rations; and permission to travel, marry, have children, enter the army, university or the Chinese Communist Party (CCP) or change jobs. Fifty-five ethnic groups were officially designated as national minorities and given some measure of autonomy. However, CCP members, known as cadres, became the most powerful and prestigious members of Chinese society because of their connections (*guanxi* or *kuan-hsi*). Today the PRC government is stressing economic development, and merchants are becoming powerful once again, with the gap widening between rich and poor. See also AGRICULTURE; CADRE; CHINESE COMMUNIST PARTY; CHRISTIANITY; CONFUCIANISM; CONNECTIONS; EUNUCHS; FAMILY STRUCTURE; HAN; IMPERIAL BUREAUCRACY; IMPERIAL EXAMINATION SYSTEM; LAND REFORM BY COMMUNISTS; LANGUAGE, CHINESE; LITERATI; MINORITIES, NATIONAL; NOMADS AND ANIMAL HUSBANDRY; PEASANTS AND PEASANT REBELLIONS; PEOPLE'S COMMUNE; REPUBLIC OF CHINA; REVOLUTION OF 1911; SINICIZATION; WORK UNIT.

SOCIALIST EDUCATION MOVEMENT (1962–65)   An ideological campaign initiated by Chinese Communist leader Mao Zedong (Mao Tse-tung; 1893–1976) against what he perceived as a trend toward capitalism and revisionism in the People's Republic of China (PRC). Mao also intended to end the elitism of Chinese scholars, intellectuals and artists, who traditionally tended to look down on physical labor, and to bring workers and peasants and people in the cities and countryside closer together. The Socialist Education Movement is considered a precursor of the Cultural Revolution (1966–76). It began two years after the Great Leap Forward (1958–60), which was supposed to speed up China's development but ended up an economic disaster. Mao had to step down as chairman of the PRC in 1959, although he remained chairman of the Chinese Communist Party (CCP). By 1962 Mao felt a need to purify the party of its growing capitalist tendencies, which developed as the party relaxed its radical policies to help the Chinese economy recover from the Great Leap Forward. Mao believed that the material incentives reenacted to motivate the peasants and workers were corrupting and counterrevolutionary. Many peasants had turned away from collectives and toward private enterprise. Many cadres (party officials) had become corrupt, taken bribes, misappropriated government funds and falsified financial records. Hence Mao inaugurated the Socialist Education Movement at the 10th Plenum of the Eighth National Party

Congress Central Committee. This movement also became known as the Four Clean-ups because it intended to remove corruption among cadres at the local level in the four areas of accounts, granaries, property and the work points awarded to peasants.

Mao aimed to increase the ideological "correctness" of both CCP cadres and the general Chinese population, especially in the countryside, where suffering from the failure of the Great Leap Forward had demoralized the peasants. His methods for this campaign were opposed by moderates in the CCP led by Liu Shaoqi (Liu Shao-ch'i) and Deng Xiaoping (Teng Hsiao-p'ing). Mao enacted another campaign in conjunction with the Socialist Education Movement, which had the theme "to learn from the People's Liberation Army" (PLA). Lin Biao (Lin Piao), minister of national defense, urged members of the PLA and the CCP to follow the thought of Chairman Mao, and he quickly rose to the center of power. He compiled *Quotations from Chairman Mao Zedong,* also known as the "Little Red Book," to indoctrinate PLA recruits with Mao's revolutionary thought. The Socialist Education Movement became a struggle between the moderate faction in the CCP and the pro-Mao radical faction that emphasized class struggle. The Chinese education system was completely reformed to fit in with the work schedule of communes and factories, thus attempting a work-study program known as *xiafang.* This reform intended to provide education for the Chinese masses at a lower cost and to reeducate scholars, intellectuals and artists by drafting them to perform manual labor. In December 1966 the Socialist Education Movement was officially merged into the Cultural Revolution. By then every person in China had a copy of *Quotations from Chairman Mao Zedong.* See also CADRE; CHINESE COMMUNIST PARTY; CULTURAL REVOLUTION; DENG XIAOPING; GREAT LEAP FORWARD; LIN BIAO; LIU SHAOQI; MAO ZEDONG; PEOPLE'S COMMUNE; PEOPLE'S REPUBLIC OF CHINA; QUOTATIONS FROM CHAIRMAN MAO ZEDONG.

SOCIETY FOR THE REBIRTH OF CHINA (Xingzhonghui or Hsing Chung Hui)   A revolutionary secret society established by Sun Yat-sen (1866–1925), the founder of modern China; also known as the Society for the Revival (or Development) of China. While practicing as a medical doctor in the southern Chinese port city of Guangzhou (Canton), Sun met many young Chinese patriots who shared his conviction that the Chinese had to wage a revolution against the Manchus who ruled China under the Qing dynasty (1644–1911). In 1894 Sun returned to Hawaii, where he had attended school for three years as a teenager. There he founded the Society for the Rebirth of China on November 24, 1894, with the secret goal of overthrowing the Qing. His publicly stated goal was to found institutions such as schools and newspapers to help the Chinese people. The following year Sun returned to China and established the society's headquarters in the British crown colony of Hong Kong, near Guangzhou.

Sun had received his medical degree from a British mission hospital in Hong Kong in 1892. After founding the society, he stopped practicing medicine and devoted himself to the revolutionary cause, traveling frequently to Japan, Hawaii, the United States and Europe to raise money and attract members among the overseas Chinese communities.

In 1895 the society planned to initiate the anti-Qing revolution by seizing government offices in Guangzhou. However, the government discovered the plot and captured and executed 46 society members. Sun escaped through Hong Kong and went to Japan, where he began using a different name and wearing Western clothing to disguise himself. He then traveled once more to Hawaii, the United States and England, where he was kidnapped and held at the Chinese embassy but was released after an international outcry. From then on, people around the world regarded Sun as the principal leader of the Chinese revolution.

Sun Yat-sen spent two years in England studying Western political thought and developed a revolutionary doctrine based on what he called the Three Principles of the People (Sanminzhuyi or San-min-chu-i): people's rights or democracy (establish a constitutional monarchy), people's livelihood (equitable distribution of land and wealth) and people's nationalism (let the Chinese rule China). Sun traveled between 1900 and 1905, and the Society for the Rebirth of China gained many overseas Chinese branches. In July 1905 the society joined with other Chinese revolutionary organizations based in Japan to form the Revolutionary Alliance (Tongmenghui or T'ung Meng Hui). When the Revolution of 1911 overthrew the Qing dynasty, Sun was named the first president of the Republic of China (1912–49). See also OVERSEAS CHINESE; QING DYNASTY; REVOLUTION OF 1911; REVOLUTIONARY ALLIANCE; SUN YAT-SEN; THREE PRINCIPLES OF THE PEOPLE.

SOCIETY OF RIGHTEOUS AND HARMONIOUS FISTS See BOXER UPRISING.

SON OF HEAVEN See ALL UNDER HEAVEN; EMPEROR; HEAVEN; MANDATE OF HEAVEN.

SONG, MOUNT See FIVE SACRED MOUNTAINS OF DAOISM.

SONG DYNASTY (960–1279)   The dynasty that reunified China after the Five Dynasties Period (907–59), when China had been divided into 12 rival kingdoms controlled by their militaries. The Song dynasty fell into two periods. The first, which ended when the Jurchens captured the Song capital at Kaifeng in modern Henan Province, is known as the Northern Song dynasty (960–1126). Survivors of the Song court fled south and established their capital at Hangzhou in modern Zhejiang Province; this period is known as the Southern Song dynasty (1127–1279). Zhao Kuangyin (Chao K'uang-yin) founded the Song dynasty. He was born to a military family in northeastern China and became commander of the Palace Corps under Emperor Shizong (Shih-tsung) of the Later Zhou dynasty (951–60) in 959. When the emperor died in 960, his designated successor was only seven years old, and the Palace Corps mutinied and placed Zhao on the throne. He reigned as the first Song emperor and is known as Emperor Taizu (T'ai-tsu; r. 960–76). Taizu brought nearly all of the rival kingdoms and their militaries under his control before he died. He also restored the examination system to select officials for the imperial bureaucracy. These officials belonged to the literati (*wenren* or *wen-jen*), or scholar class, which had its greatest influence during the Song. The Song capital at Kaifeng, then known as Bianjing or Dongjing, is located at the head of the Grand Canal in the Yellow River valley in modern Henan Province. The city quickly grew to have a population of more than one million.

Taizu's younger brother, Zhao Kuangyi (Chao K'uang-yi), succeeded him as emperor and is known as Emperor Taizong (T'ai-tsung; r. 976–97). He centralized the government and conquered the final two independent kingdoms, Wuyue in 978 and Northern Han in 979. The Song rulers were never able to bring under their control the region in northern and northeastern China ruled by the Khitan (Qidan) under the Liao dynasty (947–1125). During the reign of Emperor Shenzong (Shen-tsung; r. 1068–85), Prime Minister Wang Anshi initiated many institutional reforms in the economic, educational and military spheres. However, after Shenzong died, the conservative faction, led by the great historian Sima Guang (Ssu-ma Kuang), took power and did away with the reforms. The reformers regained power in 1093 but did not receive the support they formerly had in the bureaucracy.

Emperor Huizong (Hui-tsung; r. 1100–25) was the last ruler of the Northern Song dynasty. During his rule the population was heavily taxed and rebellions broke out, starting in 1120. The Song had been paying heavy tribute to the Liao and to the kingdom of Xixia on its western border because its military had not been able to control them. The Song made an alliance with the Jurchen Jin dynasty (1115–1234) in Manchuria (modern northeastern China) against the Liao dynasty, and in 1123 the Jurchen Jin defeated the Liao on their own. The Song attacked the Jin with the aim of regaining the northern part of modern Hebei Province, which had been occupied by the Liao, but its military was too weak. The Jurchen Jin attacked the Song capital of Kaifeng in 1126. Song emperor Huizong abdicated the throne to his son, known as Emperor Qinzong (Ch'in-tsung), and the Jin forced the Song to sign a humiliating treaty. In the winter of 1126–27 the Jin captured Kaifeng and took control of northern China. Huizong, Qinzong and the Song court were taken captive, and Huizong lived in captivity until he died in 1135.

The prince of Kang, a son of Huizong, was away from Kaifeng when it fell to the Jin, and he was able to flee south to restore the Song dynasty. Known as Emperor Gaozong (Kao-tsung; r. 1127–62), the first Southern Song emperor, he went to two other cities and then finally established his capital at the beautiful city of Hangzhou. However, the Song continued to feel that Kaifeng was their true capital. The Jin and Song fought for more than a decade, with General Yue Fei leading the Song troops, but the two sides finally signed a peace treaty in 1141. Their boundary was drawn at the Huai River valley. The Mongols invaded northern China in 1209, attacked the Jin dynasty in 1214–15 and crushed it in 1234. They kept moving south and attacked the Song, and in 1279 the last member of the Southern Song imperial family died in a sea battle. The Mongols completed their conquest of China and established the Yuan dynasty (1279–1368), with their capital at modern Beijing in northern China.

Despite all the political and military turmoil, the Song dynasty was one of the greatest periods for Chinese culture, and Hangzhou long remained the cultural center of China. Woodblock printing, which had been invented in China in the eighth century, developed quickly starting in the 11th century. Numerous printed books were put into circulation, which increased literacy among the Chinese people and enabled them to become familiar with literature and the Confucian classics. This in turn led to the revival of Confucianism, known as Neo-Confucianism, with Zhu Xi (Chu Hsi; 1130–1200) its most important thinker. Landscape and ink painting and poetry writing flourished. The Southern Song based at Hangzhou attained a high standard of living, and many workshops were established to produce paper, porcelain and other ceramics, silk, lacquerware and other luxury goods. Merchant guilds and clan associations were formed, and wealthy officials and merchants built mansions and beautiful gardens. See also CALLIGRAPHY; FIVE DYNASTIES PERIOD; GAOZONG, EMPEROR; GARDENS; GRAND CANAL; HANGZHOU; HUAI RIVER; HUIZONG (EMPEROR); IMPERIAL BUREAUCRACY; IMPERIAL EXAMINATION SYSTEM; INK PAINTING; JIN DYNASTY; KAIFENG; LANDSCAPE PAINTING; LIAO DYNASTY; LITERATI; LYRIC VERSE; MONGOL; NEO-CONFUCIANISM; NORTHERN SCHOOL OF PAINTING; NORTHERN SONG DYNASTY; PORCELAIN; PRINTING; REGULATED OR NEW-STYLE VERSE; SIMA GUANG; SOUTHERN SCHOOL OF PAINTING; SOUTHERN SONG DYNASTY; TAIZONG (EMPEROR); TAIZU (EMPEROR); XIXIA, KINGDOM OF; YUAN DYNASTY; YUE FEI; ZHU XI.

SONG JIANG   See OUTLAWS OF THE MARSH.

SONG JIAOREN (Sung Chiao-jen; 1882–1913)   The founder of China's National Party, usually called the Nationalist Party (Kuomintang; KMT). Song was born in Hunan Province and became a revolutionary while a young student, for which he was expelled from school. In 1904 he went to Japan to study. In Tokyo he joined the Alliance Society or Revolutionary Alliance (Tongmenhui; T'ung Meng Hui) founded by Sun Yat-sen (1866–1925) and became head of the society's Tokyo office. Following the Revolution of 1911 that overthrew the Qing dynasty, Sun was inaugurated in Nanjing as the president of the Republic of China on January 1, 1912.

However, Yuan Shikai (Yuan Shih-k'ai; 1859–1916), the powerful commander-in-chief of the Chinese imperial army, had already taken the reins of power in the capital city of Beijing. Sun, in order to protect the new republic and prevent civil war, acceded to Yuan's demand to unite China under a government in Beijing with himself as its head. On February 12, 1912, the last Qing emperor abdicated the throne, and on March 10 Yuan Shikai became the provisional president of the Republic of China. A provisional constitution was promulgated the following day.

Song Jiaoren, an outspoken critic of Yuan Shikai, founded the KMT in August 1912 by merging Sun Yat-sen's Alliance Society with four smaller political parties. KMT leaders hoped to gain the majority of seats in the new two-chamber parliament so that the legislative branch of the republican government could control Yuan Shikai. Elections for the Chinese National Assembly were held in February 1913, and the KMT led by Song Jiaoren won 269 of the 596 seats. Song expected to become premier of the republic's new single-party cabinet and move the Chinese constitution closer to the British model. Yuan Shikai responded by having Song assassinated in Shanghai in March 1913 and banning the KMT. He already had ordered the assassination of several generals who had supported the revolution. Yuan also sent military troops to several provinces with KMT governors that had rebelled against him. The KMT fought the so-called second revolution of 1913 to attempt to remove Yuan but did not succeed. KMT resistance fell apart and Sun Yat-sen and other KMT leaders fled to Japan. Yuan became the virtual dictator of China and attempted to establish a new imperial dynasty. In 1923 Sun reorganized the KMT. See also NATION-ALIST PARTY; REPUBLIC OF CHINA; REVOLUTION OF 1911; SUN YAT-SEN; YUAN SHIKAI.

SONG LI   See GRAND CANAL; MING DYNASTY.

SONG MEILING   See SOONG MEI-LING.

"SONG OF PIBA"   See BAI JUYI.

"SONG OF UNENDING REGRET"   See BAI JUYI; XUAN-ZONG (EMPEROR); YANG GUIFEI.

SONG QINGLING   See SOONG QINGLING.

SONG ZUWEN   See REPUBLIC OF CHINA.

SONGHUA RIVER   A river in Heilongjiang and Jilin provinces that is the largest river in China's northeast region of Manchuria; also known as the Sungari River. The name Songhua means "Heavenly River" in Manchurian. The river is 1,215 miles long and is the main tributary flowing into the Amur River (Heilongjiang), which forms the border between China and Russia. The Songhua River originates in the Changbai Mountain Range near the Korean border and flows northwest, then turns sharply northeast, flows past the city of Harbin and joins the Amur River at the Russian border. The Songhua drains an area of 201,930 square miles, which includes the largest coal deposits in Manchuria, the richest forests in China and one of the main agricultural regions of China, often referred to as the Manchurian Plain. In 1959 vast oil reserves were discovered in the Songhuajiang-Liaohe Basin, and the Daqing oil field went into operation in 1960. The Songhua River is navigable for steamships from Harbin to its mouth and has enormous hydroelectric potential. Songhua Lake (Songhuahu), a man-made lake fed by the Songhua River, lies about 16 miles southeast of the city of Jilin. As well as being a popular recreation area, the lake has fish hatcheries and provides irrigation for the surrounding farmland. See also AMUR RIVER; CHANGBAI MOUNTAIN RANGE; HARBIN; HEILONGJIANG PROVINCE; JILIN PROVINCE; MANCHURIA.

SONGLIAO PLAIN   See MANCHURIA.

SONGSHAN SHAOLIN TEMPLE   See SHAOLIN TEMPLE.

SONGZAN (SONGTSEN) GAMBO   See TIBET.

SONS AND DAUGHTERS OF THE STORM   See ANTHEM, NATIONAL.

SOONG, CHARLES JONES   See REPUBLIC OF CHINA; SOONG QINGLING; SOONG MEI-LING; SUN YAT-SEN.

SOONG AI-LING   See SOONG MEI-LING.

SOONG CHING LING   See SOONG QINGLING.

SOONG MEI-LING   (Soong Mayling or Sung Mei-ling or Song Meiling; 1897–   )   Also known as Madame Chiang Kai-shek; the wife of Chiang Kai-shek, who became head of the Chinese Nationalist Party (Kuomintang; KMT) and president of the provisional government of the Republic of China (ROC) on Taiwan Island. Her sister, Soong Qingling, was the wife of Dr. Sun Yat-sen, the founder of the KMT, although after Sun died in 1925 Soong Qingling broke with the KMT and supported the Chinese Communist Party (CCP). Soong Mei-ling and Soong Qingling became the two most important women in modern Chinese history. They were born in Shanghai into a wealthy family that had come from Wen-chang County on Hainan Island in southern China and had converted to the Methodist denomination of Christianity. Their oldest sister, Soong Ai-ling, went to the United States to study at Wesleyan College for Women in Macon, Georgia. Their father, Sung Yao-ju, who used the Americanized name Charles Jones Soong, had been educated in the United States. A businessman who published Bibles in Chinese, he was a close friend of Sun Yat-sen. In 1908 Soong Qingling also went to study at Wesleyan College; Soong Mei-ling stud-ied privately in Shanghai, then in 1913 attended Wellesley College in Massachusetts to be close to her brother, T.V. Soong (Soong Tse-wen), then a student at Harvard Univer-sity. He later held high positions in the KMT government including minister of finance. Soong Mei-ling graduated from Wellesley in 1917.

She returned to Shanghai, where she met Chiang Kai-shek, then a military officer serving Sun Yat-sen, at the home of her sister Soong Qingling and Sun Yat-sen, who had mar-ried in 1915. Soong Ai-ling had married H.H. Kung (Kung Hsiang-hsi), a prominent Chinese banker who was a direct descendant of Confucius. Chiang wanted to marry Soong Mei-ling but her family was opposed because he was 10 years older than she, was already married to another woman who had borne him two sons and was not a Christian. He persuaded her family to agree to the marriage by promising to convert to Christianity. Soong Qingling remained opposed to the marriage, however. Chiang divorced his wife, and on December 1, 1927 he married Soong Mei-ling in Japan while he was in brief exile from the KMT. He was also baptized into the Methodist Church, although he continued to follow Confucian teachings and did not publicly practice Christian-ity. Although she did not hold many official positions, Soong Mei-ling played an important role as Chiang Kai-shek's Eng-lish interpreter and secretary.

Under Sun's leadership, the KMT had cooperated with the recently founded CCP until Sun died in 1925. In 1926 Chiang led the Northern Expedition against the warlords who controlled China. In April 1927 he turned against the CCP and ordered the KMT to massacre Communists, who fled Chinese cities into the countryside and raised forces to fight the KMT. Japan invaded Manchuria (northeastern China) in 1931 and established a puppet state there called Manchukuo in 1932, which it used as a base to invade China Proper and the rest of Asia. In 1936 CCP and KMT military leaders kidnapped Chiang Kai-shek at Huaqing Hot Springs outside Xi'an to persuade him to stop fighting the Communists and form a KMT-CCP united front to fight the Japanese; this is known as the Xi'an Incident. Soong Mei-ling played a major role in the negotiations to have Chiang released by having him agree to this demand.

During China's War of Resistance against Japan (1937–45; World War II), Soong Mei-ling made a great contribution to the Chinese war effort by appealing to Americans to provide China material and military assistance. She made many trips to the United States and in February 1943 she became the first Chinese and the second woman to address a joint session of the U.S. Congress. Continuing to serve as Chiang's English interpreter, she accompanied him to the Cairo Conference in November 1943, when Chiang met personally with U.S. president Franklin Delano Roosevelt and British prime minister Winston Churchill. The three leaders agreed that Japan should give up control of all the territories it had conquered, that Manchuria and Taiwan Island should be returned to China and that Korea should be given its independence. In China, Soong Mei-ling also carried messages between Chiang and U.S. general Joseph Stilwell, who was helping the Chinese fight Japan. She served as the director-general of the New Life Movement and was the first woman to be decorated by the Chinese government.

After Japan was defeated in 1945, the KMT and CCP resumed fighting a civil war. In 1948 Soong Mei-ling traveled to the United States once again to raise American support for the KMT, but President Harry Truman refused to change the U.S. policy of noninvolvement in the events in China. She remained in the United States until 1950, when she joined Chiang in Taiwan. The CCP had defeated the KMT in 1949, and Chiang and his KMT supporters had fled to Taiwan, where they established the provisional government of the Republic of China (ROC). Soong Mei-ling continued traveling to the United States to represent the ROC and its interests. After Chiang died in 1975 she resided in the United States, but in 1986 she returned to Taiwan. She wrote many magazine articles and books, including *Sian (Xi'an: A Coup d'Etat* (1937), *This Is Our China* (1940), *China Shall Rise Again* (1942) and *The Sure Victory* (1955). Her name was included on American lists of the 10 most admired women in the world for nearly 25 years. See also CHIANG KAI-SHEK; CIVIL WAR BETWEEN COMMUNISTS AND NATIONALISTS; NATIONALIST PARTY; NEW LIFE MOVEMENT; REPUBLIC OF CHINA; SOONG QINGLING; STILWELL, JOSEPH; TAIWAN; WAR OF RESISTANCE AGAINST JAPAN.

SOONG QINGLING (Soong Ching-ling or Sung Ch'ing-ling; 1893–1981)   The most prominent woman in modern China. Soong was the wife of Dr. Sun Yat-sen (1866–1925), the founder of modern China. She carried on his revolutionary activities after he died and became a leader of the People's Republic of China (PRC). She was a pioneer in the Chinese women's movement and, after the Chinese Communists founded the People's Republic of China (PRC) in 1949, became honorary president of the All-China Women's Federation. Soong was born in Shanghai into a wealthy family that had come from Wenchang County on Hainan Island in southern China and had converted to the Methodist denomination of Christianity. Sun Yat-sen was a friend of her parents, and her father had funded Sun's Revolutionary Alliance (*Tongmenghui* or *Tung-meng hui*). In 1908 Soong went to the United States to study at Wesleyan College for women in Macon, Georgia, where she received a B.A. in 1913. While she was a student there, Sun Yat-sen led the Chinese in overthrowing the Qing dynasty (1644–1911) in the Revolution of 1911 and in establishing the Republic of China (1912–49). When Soong graduated, she returned to China and became Sun's personal secretary. In 1915 she married him against the wishes of her family. At that time Sun was in exile in Tokyo, Japan, because the warlord Yuan Shikai (Yuan Shih-k'ai) had taken over Sun's position as president of China. While in Japan, Sun organized the Kuomintang Party (KMT).

After Yuan died in 1916, Sun and Soong returned to China, which was divided among many warlords. In 1917 Sun became head of a military government in Guangzhou (Canton) in southern China to oppose the warlords in northern China. This effort did not succeed, and Sun and Soong moved to Shanghai in 1918. They returned to Guangzhou in 1920, where Sun was elected president of the Republic of China, but troops loyal to another leader drove Sun out of the city and destroyed his books and manuscripts. During this period, Soong suffered a miscarriage, and she remained childless. In August 1922 Sun and Soong returned to Shanghai, where he developed contacts with many Chinese civil and military officials and accepted assistance from representatives of the U.S.S.R. Sun returned to Guangzhou in February 1923, where he reorganized the KMT to combine the previous KMT and the recently founded Chinese Communist Party (CCP). The new political organization adopted Sun's "Three Principles of the People." In 1924 the KMT established the Whampoa Military Academy near Guangzhong, with Chiang Kai-shek (1887–1975) at its head. In 1925 Sun died of cancer in Beijing, where he had traveled in his ongoing attempt to unite the many Chinese factions in the struggle for the country's freedom. Soong gave him a Christian funeral.

In January 1926, at the Second National Congress of the Kuomintang, Soong joined with members of the CCP in condemning the rightist "Western Hills clique" of the KMT for abandoning Sun's principles. She returned to Guangzhou and helped prepare the Northern Expedition (1926–27) against the warlords. In 1927 a workers' uprising freed Shanghai from warlord rule, but Chiang Kai-shek, who had just been named KMT military commander, betrayed the revolutionaries by leading a massacre of Communists, members of trade unions and revolutionary intellectuals and students. KMT officials based in Wuhan led by Wang Jingwei did the same, killing many members of the revolutionary peasant organizations as well. Soong, along with other left-wing KMT members and CCP leaders, issued joint messages denouncing the actions of Chiang and the Wang government.

On August 1, 1927, KMT troops led by CCP leaders Zhou Enlai (Chou En-lai) and Zhu De (Chu Te) held an insurrection, known as the Nanchang Uprising, in which Communist forces attempted to take over the KMT headquarters. On the same day Zhou Enlai and other leaders formed a revolutionary committee and elected Soong to the seven-member presidium of the committee, even though she was not in Nanchang at the time. Soong broke with the

KMT, which had been founded by her husband, in support of the Chinese Communists, peasants and workers. Forces of the Nanchang Uprising and forces of the Autumn Harvest Uprising led by Mao Zedong (Mao Tse-tung) fled to the Jinggang Mountain Range on the Jiangsu-Anhui border and established a military base. CCP and KMT forces fought a civil war from 1927 to 1937.

On December 1, 1927, Chiang Kai-shek married Soong Qingling's sister, Soong Mei-ling (Soong Mayling). During the first two years of the CCP-KMT civil war, Soong traveled to the U.S.S.R. and France on behalf of China. She was also prominent in the Anti-Imperialist League, which had its headquarters in Brussels, Belgium. In 1929 Soong was elected honorary chairman of the second congress of the Anti-Imperialist League and became a leader of the international antifascist movement. When she returned to China in 1931, Soong supported the CCP's proposal to end its civil war with the Nationalists and form a national united front against the Japanese, who had invaded Manchuria (northeastern China) and were planning to move down through mainland China. She criticized Chiang Kai-shek for not resisting Japan's invasion of China and for terrorizing the Chinese people. In 1932 Soong was active in providing aid for the wounded of the 19th Route Army, which fought off the much better equipped Japanese army in the Battle of Shanghai. Soong joined with revolutionary writer Lu Xun (Lu Hsun) and other important figures to form the China League for Civil Rights, to protect and rescue CCP members and other Chinese who opposed Chiang Kai-shek. She bravely continued her activities despite many threats to her life, and addressed the international antiwar congress that met secretly in Shanghai. In 1936, after the CCP army completed its rigorous Long March westward to escape KMT forces, Communist leaders took Chiang Kai-shek hostage in Xi'an to force him to join them in fighting against the Japanese invaders. Based on his pledge to do so, Soong took part in the negotiations to release him.

When China began fighting its War of Resistance against Japan (1937–45; World War II), Soong did not go to Chongqing in Sichuan Province, where the government of the KMT, also known as the Nationalists, had fled from the Japanese and established its capital, but went south to Guangzhou and Hong Kong. There she founded the China Defence League to gather donations and medical supplies from well-known foreigners and overseas Chinese who supported China against Japan. She supported the CCP and criticized the KMT for compromising with and capitulating to Japan. During the war Soong maintained two goals: to preserve and enlarge the national united front against Japan and to ensure equal treatment for all forces of the Chinese resistance. She finally went to KMT headquarters in Chongqing at the end of 1941, where she met with foreigners who were working hard to support the Chinese revolutionary cause, including Ma Haide (George Hatem), Agnes Smedley and Edgar Snow.

After the War of Resistance ended and Chiang resumed the civil war between the KMT and the CCP, Soong continued directing the China Defence League, now renamed the China Welfare Fund, in Shanghai. It had the urgent goal of providing relief for working people in that city, especially in the areas of maternal and infant health, literacy and educa-tion. Soong also gathered many supplies to aid the CCP and the Communist forces, now known as the People's Liberation Army (PLA). When the CCP defeated the KMT in 1949, the KMT fled to Taiwan Island, where it established the Republic of China with Chiang as its president.

In September 1949, after the Communists liberated Beijing, Soong attended the First Plenary Session of the Chinese People's Political Consultative Conference, at which the Communists founded the People's Republic of China. Soong was elected vice chairman of the Central People's Government. In 1952 she was awarded the Stalin International Peace Award, and she donated the money from that award and the royalties from her book, *Striving for New China,* to organizations in China that assisted children and education. In 1954 Soong was elected vice chairman of the Standing Committee of the National People's Congress. In 1957 she accompanied Mao Zedong to the Moscow Meeting of Representatives of Communist and Workers' Parties. Soong was elected vice chairman of the PRC in 1959 and again in 1965. In 1975 she was once again elected vice chairman of the National People's Congress Standing Committee. As a leader of the PRC, Soong represented the Chinese people at home and abroad and visited the U.S.S.R., India, Pakistan, Ceylon, Indonesia and Burma. In China she was especially concerned with women's work and the health and education of children and young people. For many years Soong was head of the People's Relief Administration of China and the Red Cross Society of China. On May 15, 1981, just before Soong died, the Politburo unanimously voted to accept her as a full member of the CCP. On May 16 the Standing Committee of the National People's Congress conferred on her the title of honorary president of the People's Republic of China. After she died, the government held a memorial meeting for her in the Great Hall of the People on June 3. Her ashes were buried in the Soong family graveyard in the Wanguo Cemetery in Shanghai.

In 1982, to commemorate the first anniversary of Soong's death, the Chinese government held a memorial meeting at the compound that had been her residence in Beijing from 1963 until she died in 1981 and that belonged to the imperial family during the Qing dynasty. The government declared Soong's residence a historical landmark and opened it to visitors. Two halls now house a museum of Soong's life where her photographs, letters, books and articles are displayed. In addition to her government work, Soong had produced a large body of writing, including articles for the periodical, *China Reconstructs,* which is published and distributed around the world in editions in seven different languages. Her writings were published as *The Selected Works of Soong Ching Ling* and translated into other languages. The China Welfare Institute continues the work that she had initiated with the China Defence League. See also ALL-CHINA WOMEN'S FEDERATION; CHIANG KAI-SHEK; CHINESE COMMUNIST PARTY; CHONGQING; CIVIL WAR BETWEEN COMMUNISTS AND NATIONALISTS; GOVERNMENT STRUCTURE; GREAT HALL OF THE PEOPLE; LU XUN; MA HAIDE; NANCHANG UPRISING; NORTHERN EXPEDITION; PEOPLE'S REPUBLIC OF CHINA; REPUBLIC OF CHINA; REVOLUTION OF 1911; REVOLUTIONARY ALLIANCE; SMEDLEY, AGNES; SNOW, EDGAR; SOONG MEI-LING; SUN YAT-SEN; THREE PRINCIPLES OF THE PEOPLE; WANG JINGWEI; WAR OF RESISTANCE

AGAINST JAPAN; WHAMPOA MILITARY ACADEMY; YUAN SHIKAI.

SOONG TSE-WEN (T.V. SOONG) See REPUBLIC OF CHINA; SOONG MEI-LING.

SORGHUM See AGRICULTURE; GRAIN; MAOTAI; ZHANG YIMOU.

SOUTH CHINA SEA (*Nanhai*)   A deep-sea basin that is a marginal sea of the Pacific Ocean, as are the Yellow and East China seas, surrounded in part by the Chinese continent. The South China Sea covers an area of approximately 1.8 million square miles and has an average depth of 4,000 feet. Along the continental shelf, the sea is about 600 feet deep. Located in the tropical zone, the sea has a high salt content and a warm temperature. The region is subject to violent typhoons in the summer and autumn. The Taiwan Strait, between the island of Taiwan and mainland China, separates the South China Sea from the East China Sea. The South China Sea borders the Chinese provinces of Fujian and Guangdong and the island of Hong Kong, just south of Guangzhou (Canton), the capital of Guangdong. It also borders Taiwan, Vietnam, Cambodia, Thailand, the Malay Peninsula, Borneo, the small islands of Indonesia and the Philippine Islands. The Luzon Strait connects the South China Sea with the Philippine Sea to the east; the Mindoro and Balabac Straits with the Sulu Sea to the southeast; the Karimata Strait with the Java Sea to the south; and the Strait of Malacca with the Andaman Sea to the west. Today nearly one-quarter of the world's maritime freight passes through the South China Sea.

Most of the numerous small islands in the South China Sea, such as the Xisha (Paracel) Islands, the Zhongshan Islands and the Spratly (Nansha) Islands, are composed of coral reefs. The coral islands that cover a distance of 930 miles from Hainan Island almost down to the equator have few human inhabitants but are home to large numbers of seabirds, such as terns and boobies (similar to gannets), that build nests there to lay their eggs. The sea is inhabited by tropical fish, sharks, dolphins and green turtles.

The South China Sea was the major route by which Europeans first approached China. In the early 16th century, Portuguese trading ships sailing south around Africa and India appeared in the South China Sea. In 1557 the Portuguese received permission from China to establish a colony at Macao, a small island in the Pearl River Delta near Guangzhou. The Portuguese were soon followed by Spanish, Dutch and English ships, all eager to trade with China. Today the South China Sea continues to hold major strategic and economic importance for China. Offshore exploration and drilling for oil has been undertaken since the early 1970s in the 200-nautical-mile zone that is China's exclusive economic zone in the South China Sea. In 1974 Chinese forces took control of three Xisha (Paracel) Islands, which lie close to Hainan Island and Vietnam and had been occupied by troops from the Republic of Vietnam (South Vietnam). China also made claims to the Spratly (Nansha) Islands in the southernmost region of the South China Sea, which are also claimed by Vietnam and Taiwan. These two countries also claim sovereignty over the Xishus. Offshore oil deposits

also have been discovered near Hainan Island, now a province of China. In the 1980s China enlarged its fleet in the South China Sea, especially since the disputed islands lie on the strategic shipping route between Hong Kong and Singapore. See also CLIMATE; ENERGY SOURCES; GEOGRAPHY; GUANGZHOU; HAINAN ISLAND; HONG KONG; MACAO; PEARL RIVER; SPRATLY ISLANDS; TAIWAN.

SOUTH MANCHURIA RAILROAD See CHANGCHUN; DALIAN; RUSSO-JAPANESE WAR OF 1904–5.

SOUTHERN DYNASTIES See NORTHERN AND SOUTHERN DYNASTIES.

SOUTHERN HAN KINGDOM (907–71) See TEN KINGDOMS PERIOD.

SOUTHERN QI DYNASTY See NORTHERN AND SOUTHERN DYNASTIES.

SOUTHERN SCHOOL OF PAINTING (*Wenrenhua* or *wen-jen-hua*)   A style of painting that developed during the Southern Song dynasty (1127–1279) and is contrasted with the Northern School of Painting, which developed during the Northern Song dynasty (960–1126). The Northern Song had its capital at Kaifeng, in modern Henan Province. An ethnic group known as the Jurchen, who had established the Jin dynasty, captured Kaifeng in 1127. The Song court fled south and established their capital at Hangzhou, a beautiful city in Zhejiang Province. Many artists moved to Hangzhou, which remained China's cultural capital for many centuries, even after the Southern Song dynasty was overthrown by the Mongols, who ruled China under the Yuan dynasty (1279–1368). Gaozong (Kao-tsung), the first Southern Song emperor, reestablished the imperial painting academy at Hangzhou, and artists continued to paint landscapes, bird-and-flower paintings and scenes of daily life in the imperial palace. The Northern School became identified with professional painters, especially in the imperial court. The Southern School became associated with "amateurs" belonging to the Confucian-educated literati, or scholar class (*wenren* or *wen-jen*), who staffed the imperial bureaucracy.

The division of Chinese painting into two opposing schools, Northern and Southern, was devised by Dong Qichang (Tung Ch'i-ch'ang; 1555–1636), a calligrapher and art cataloger, to assert the superiority of Southern painters. Dong was himself a member of the literati and became tutor to the crown prince. He led the return to classical Confucian values in landscape painting that was inspired by studying great literati works. The Southern School included literati painters for whom landscape painting was not a decorative art but a method for expressing their subjective moral views on human nature and the natural world. Dong traced the origins of the school back to his favorite painter, a Tang dynasty artist named Wang Wei (699–761).

Literati painting (*wenrenhua* or *wen-jen-hua*) is closely associated with calligraphy, the art of writing Chinese characters with a brush and ink, and with poetry. A literati painting frequently includes a poem inscribed in calligraphy in an otherwise empty space. Southern painting has a spontaneous aspect that is influenced by the southern school of the Chan

(Zen) Sect of the Buddhist religion, which teaches the sudden and spontaneous enlightenment of the individual self. Some of the greatest Chan ink painters include Mu Qi (Mu Ch'i) and Liang Kai (Liang K'ai), both of whom lived in the 13th century and whose works are greatly admired by the Chinese and Japanese alike. Ma Yuan and Xia Gui (Hsia Kuei) had been associated with the Northern School, but they moved to the Southern court at Hangzhou and originated a style known as the Ma-Xia School. See also CALLIGRAPHY; CHAN SECT OF BUDDHISM; GAOZONG, EMPEROR (SONG); HANGZHOU; INK PAINTING; LANDSCAPE PAINTING; LITERATI; NORTHERN SCHOOL OF PAINTING; POETRY; SCROLLS; SOUTHERN SONG DYNASTY; NAMES OF INDIVIDUAL PAINTERS.

SOUTHERN SONG (SUNG) DYNASTY (1127–1279)

The second period of the Song dynasty (960–1279), when Chinese culture attained what many consider its highest development. The first period of the Song is known as the Northern Song dynasty (960–1126). The Song dynasty was founded by Zhao Kuangyin (Chao K'uang-yin), the commander of the imperial forces under Emperor Shizong (Shih-tsung) of the Later Zhou dynasty (951–60). When Shizong died in 959, his successor was only seven years old, and the Palace Corps mutinied and placed Zhao on the throne. He proclaimed the Song dynasty and became the first Song emperor, known as Emperor Taizu (T'ai-tsu; r. 960–76). The Song capital was located at Kaifeng in the Yellow River valley in modern Henan Province. The Song reunified much of China after it had been fragmented into independent kingdoms during the Five Dynasties Period (907–59). However, they were not able to bring under their control the region in northern and northeastern China that was ruled by the Khitan (Qidan) under the Liao dynasty (907–1125).

The downfall of the Northern Song dynasty occurred during the reign of Emperor Huizong (Hui-tsung; r. 1101–25). The Jurchens, an ethnic group in Manchuria (modern northeastern China), had been vassals of the Liao dynasty, but they broke away and founded the Jin dynasty (1115–1234). The Song made an alliance with the Jin against the Liao, and in 1123 the Jin defeated the Liao on their own. The Song tried to regain the northern part of modern Hebei Province, which had been occupied by the Liao, by attacking the Jin. However, the Song military was weak and the Jin attacked the Song capital of Kaifeng in 1126. Huizong abdicated the throne to his son, known as Emperor Qinzong (Ch'in-tsung), and the Jin forced the Song to sign a humiliating treaty.

In the winter of 1126–27 Jin forces captured Kaifeng and took control of northern China. Huizong, Qinzong and 3,000 court officials were captured. The prince of Kang, the ninth son of Huizong, was away from Kaifeng when the Jin took it, and he was able to escape to the south and restore the Song dynasty. He is known as Emperor Gaozong (Kao-tsung; r. 1127–62), the first Southern Song emperor. Gaozong made his headquarters at two places and then finally established the Song capital at Hangzhou, a beautiful city that is the capital of modern Zhejiang Province. However, the Song always considered Hangzhou their temporary capital and felt that Kaifeng was their true capital. The Jin and Song fought for more than a decade, with General Yue Fei commanding the Song troops. The Song realized that they could not defeat the Jin, and so the two sides finally signed a peace treaty in 1141. However, Yue Fei was wrongly accused of treason and executed, after which he became a national hero for the Chinese people. The boundary between the Song and the Jin was drawn at the Huai River.

The Southern Song dynasty was perhaps the greatest period for Chinese art and culture. Many artists moved south to Hangzhou, and landscape and ink painting, calligraphy and poetry writing flourished. The Chinese consider painting, calligraphy and poetry the "Three Perfections" (*sanjue* or *san-chueh*). Emperor Gaozong reestablished the imperial painting academy in Hangzhou that had been founded at Kaifeng. As in the Song dynasty, painting came to be divided into two branches, the Northern School and the Southern School. The latter became identified with the literati (*wenren* or *wen-jen*), or scholars who staffed the imperial bureaucracy. Many of them had the wealth and leisure to become "amateur" painters. Landscape gardening also thrived in conjunction with landscape painting, as both were concerned with subjects in nature called by the Chinese "mountains and water." Some of the greatest Southern Song painters include Li Tang, Mu Qi (Mu Ch'i), Liang Kai (Liang K'ai) and Mi Fei (also known as Mi Fu). Ma Yuan and Xia Gui (Hsia Kuei) had been associated with the Northern School, but they moved to the Southern court at Hangzhou and originated a style of painting known as the Ma-Xia (Ma-Hsia) School. The literati were educated in the classics of Confucianism, the school of thought that had been founded by Confucius (551–479 B.C.). During the Song there was a revival of Confucian thought, known as Neo-Confucianism, with Zhu Xi (Chu Hsi; 1130–1200) as the most important Neo-Confucian thinker.

The wealthy Song upper classes purchased luxury goods such as silk and porcelain, which made the merchant class wealthy. Since Hangzhou was located on the Chinese coast, Song China developed an active trade exporting porcelains, silk, tea and other luxury goods to countries in Asia, Southeast Asia and India along the so-called maritime Silk Road. Chinese porcelains were exported as far west as the Persian Gulf, and Chinese copper coins became standard currency all over Southeast Asia. Hangzhou also was connected by canals to the Yangzi River (Changjiang), one of the two largest rivers to China and a major route for transporting agricultural products and other goods. The Yangzi River valley was a fertile agricultural area that provided sufficient food for the Southern Song. The population of Hangzhou grew to more than 1.5 million, and merchants formed guilds and clans formed associations to provide assistance for their members.

While art and culture were thriving under the Southern Song, the Mongols to the north of the Great Wall, led by Genghis Khan (1162–1227), were building their vast empire. They invaded northern China in 1209, attacked the Jin dynasty in 1214–15 and crushed it in 1234. They kept moving south and attacked the Song. Khubilai Khan (1214–94), Genghis Khan's grandson, was made Great Khan in 1260 and took the title emperor of China in 1271. In 1279 the last member of the Southern Song imperial family died in a sea battle, and the Mongols completed their conquest of China. They established the Yuan dynasty (1279–1368) with their capital at Beijing in northern China. They did not destroy Hangzhou, as the Jin had sacked Kaifeng, and the city remained the cultural center of China for several centuries. See also CALLIGRAPHY; GAOZONG (EMPEROR); GARDENS; HANGZHOU; HUAI RIVER; HUIZONG (EMPEROR); INK PAINTING; JIN DYNASTY; KAIFENG; LANDSCAPE PAINTING; LYRIC VERSE; MONGOL; NEO-CONFUCIANISM; NORTHERN SCHOOL OF PAINTING; PORCELAIN; REGULATED OR NEW-STYLE VERSE; SILK; SILK ROAD; SONG DYNASTY; SOUTHERN SCHOOL OF PAINTING; SOUTHERN SONG DYNASTY; TEA; YUAN DYNASTY; YUE FEI; ZHU XI; NAMES OF INDIVIDUAL PAINTERS AND POETS.

SOUTHERN TANG KINGDOM (937–75) See LI YU; TEN KINGDOMS PERIOD.

SOVIET UNION AND CHINA See BORODIN, MIKHAIL; CHIANG CHING-KUO; CHIANG KAI-SHEK; CHINESE COMMUNIST PARTY; CIVIL WAR BETWEEN COMMUNISTS AND NATIONALISTS; MAO ZEDONG; SINO-SOVIET CONFLICT; SUN YAT-SEN; TIANANMEN SQUARE MASSACRE; VIETNAM WAR; WAR OF RESISTANCE AGAINST JAPAN; WUSULI INCIDENT; ZHOU ENLAI.

SOY SAUCE See SEASONINGS FOR FOOD; SOYBEANS AND SOY PRODUCTS.

SOYBEANS AND SOY PRODUCTS Soybeans are small yellow, brown, blue or green beans that have a very high protein content and thus are widely consumed by the Chinese in place of meat. The Chinese have cultivated soybeans for 5,000 years. They consume soybeans and also feed them to animals. Soybeans can be boiled and eaten as snacks, but they are most commonly processed into bean curd (*dowfu*), known in the West by its Japanese name, *tofu*. Bean curd looks like cheese and is sold in small, flat white cakes about three inches square by one inch thick. The cakes must be stored in water and should be cooked soon after purchasing. Bean curd has been processed in China since ancient times. It is made by cooking soybeans, grinding them into a pulpy mixture and adding a coagulating agent to the pulp. Most of the liquid is drained off, and the thick mixture is then pressed down until it is flat and the excess liquid has drained out. Bean curd is also sold in a fried form, in a very pungent fermented form and in dried sheets, which keep for a long time and must be soaked before cooking. To cook bean curd, the cakes are cut into smaller pieces and stir-fried in oil with vegetables and small portions of meat, or added to soups. Bean curd skin, which is skimmed off the pulp before coagulation, is dried and used to wrap around rice or other fillings. Because the Buddhist religion, which was introduced into China from India around the first century A.D., forbids the consumption of animals, Chinese vegetarian chefs became very skilled at preparing bean curd to resemble the texture and flavor of pork and other meats. The liquid produced by mixing soybean flour with water, known as soybean milk, is a popular Chinese drink. Cooked soybeans also are mashed and fermented to make strong-tasting red and yellow pastes that add flavor to cooked dishes. Another common product made from fermented soybeans is soy sauce (*jiangyu, chiangyu, shihyu* or *siyau*), which is added in small quantities to most Chinese cooked dishes to enhance the flavor. Soy sauce is processed by mixing soybean flour or soybeans with ground wheat, barley or another grain and a microorganism such as *Aspergillus* that stimulates the fermenting process. The resulting product is fermented again with a bacteria called *Lactobacillus* and yeast. Many steps are involved in the fermenting process. The final product is a dark liquid that is strained and bottled. Soybeans also are used in sprout form, which are added to many Chinese dishes, especially those that are stir-fried with oil. The Chinese also consume many other types of beans. See also BEANS AND BEAN PRODUCTS; COOKING, CHINESE.

SPACE INDUSTRY China's industry devoted to launching rockets and satellites into space. After the Chinese Communists founded the People's Republic of China (PRC) in 1949, the country inaugurated its space industry. Since the country was very poor and suffered a technological blockade by other countries, Chinese scientists had to rely on their own efforts to develop a space industry. In 1967 China established the Xi'an Satellite Monitoring Center in Shaanxi Province in western China, which has remained the center of the country's space monitoring program. The Xi'an center monitors and controls all Chinese satellites, communicates with them and recovers ones that have completed their missions. China launched its first satellite on April 24, 1970, from the Jiuquan Satellite Launching Center. That year mobile satellite monitoring stations also were established at Nanning in Guangxi-Zhuang Autonomous Region, Changchun in Jilin Province, western Fujian Province and Kashi in Xinjiang-Uighur Autonomous Region. In December 1975 China became the third country in the world to launch and recover a satellite. By the mid-1980s many Chinese space scientists and technicians had been trained, and China was able to establish three satellite launching centers. The country had relatively sophisticated satellite monitoring technology and facilities but still needed to develop its carrier rockets and satellite recovery system. In May 1980 China launched a long-distance carrier rocket over the Pacific Ocean, and in April 1984 it launched a geostationary satellite.

In October 1985 the Chinese government announced that its Long March series of rockets was available to launch satellites into space for customers from other countries. China signed its first satellite launching contract in 1987. Among other things, China launched a Swedish scientific experimental satellite into orbit, as well as microgravity experimental equipment from France and West Germany. In 1990 China used a Long March-3 carrier rocket to launch the Asia No. 1 Communications Satellite, known as AsiaSat 1. In August and December of 1992, China used Long March-2E carrier rockets, which had been designed by a team led by Wang Dechen (Wang Te-ch'en), to launch two Australian satellites, known as AuSat, from the Xichang Launching Center. The Australian Optus BI telecommunications satellite, made by Hughes Aircraft Corporation of the United States and sent into orbit by China from the Xichang Space Center on August 14, 1992, was the 33rd satellite launched by China. In the 1990s China also began exporting some satellite equipment. Chinese Television relies on satellites to broadcast programs. Central Television transmits by Chinese satellite and microwave, and China Educational Television uses the international satellite known as Intelsat. See also BROADCASTING.

SPECIAL ECONOMIC ZONES (SEZs) Four areas along the Chinese coast that the government established in 1980 to encourage foreign trade and investment in China, increase Chinese exports and import foreign technology and expertise in management. The SEZs, which the government highly restricts, include manufacturing plants and housing for Chinese workers and foreign personnel. Three of the four SEZs—Shenzhen, Zhuhai and Shantou—were opened in Guangdong Province in southern China. Shenzhen is near the major port city of Guangzhou (Canton) and Hong Kong, a center for world trade. Zhuhai is near Macao, a small but active financial center owned by the Portuguese that is scheduled to revert to China in 1999. The fourth SEZ was opened at Xiamen in Fujian Province, across the strait from the island of Taiwan. The SEZs were administered by the Special Economic Zones Office of the State Council.

In 1984 the Chinese government designated 14 "coastal open cities" along the east coast for the same purpose as SEZs. However, in 1985 the government decided to concentrate its resources on four of the 14 cities, the major port cities of Shanghai, Tianjin, Guangzhou and Dalian. Most of the SEZs and coastal open cities had once been so-called treaty ports controlled by foreign powers but were now controlled by the Chinese government. Foreign companies that invest in SEZs receive many benefits. For example, they pay lower corporate taxes than companies elsewhere in China, and they are allowed to send all or most of their after-tax profits to their own countries. They also may renew their land leases at favorable rates. By 1986 there were more than 6,200 foreign-funded businesses in China, including thousands of joint ventures with Chinese companies. In 1996 China gained nearly $40 billion in capital from abroad, the highest amount of foreign investment in any developing nation. By the beginning of 1997, joint ventures accounted for 38 percent of China's economy. However, these businesses have encountered many problems. Chinese labor is available at low wages but often lacks skills, a huge amount of paperwork is required, and often it is difficult for joint ventures to send the foreign investors' profits back to their home countries. Also, since international trade is conducted according to contract law, Chinese lawyers had to be trained to deal with disputes between foreign and Chinese companies. New codes had to be published for contracts, litigation and accounting practices. Shenzhen became a center for the smuggling of imported goods into China and a black market for foreign currency. The population of Shenzhen is growing rapidly, at 20 percent a year, so it soon will be one of the largest cities in China. Its economy is growing at the staggering rate of 45 percent a year. The city has a special residential area for wealthy overseas Chinese who have invested in businesses in Shenzhen. See also GUANGDONG PROVINCE; HONG KONG; OVERSEAS CHINESE; STATE COUNCIL; TAIWAN; TREATY PORTS.

"SPHERES OF INFLUENCE" See OPEN-DOOR POLICY.

SPIRIT OF THE BRUSH, THE See LANDSCAPE PAINTING.

"SPIRIT WAY" OR SPIRIT ROAD See MING TOMBS; SCULPTURE; TANG IMPERIAL TOMBS.

SPIRITS See ANCESTOR WORSHIP; FENG SHUI; HUNGRY GHOSTS FESTIVAL.

SPORTS Forms of physical exercise and competition encouraged by the government of the People's Republic of China (PRC). Sports were not popular in China until the Chinese Communist Party (CCP) founded the PRC in 1949. CCP Chairman Mao Zedong (Mao Tse-tung) taught that the Chinese people should use their hands and bodies as well as their intellects, by practicing sports under the motto for good sportsmanship, "friendship first, competition second." Mao's own enjoyment of swimming inspired many Chinese to take up that sport. The PRC government established the All-China Sports Federation and the State Physical Culture and Sports Commission, which has a Scientific Research Institute. The Beijing Sports Research Institute was established in the late 1970s with four research groups to evaluate physical functions, diagnose specific physical techniques and give advice on training and athlete selection. At the 23rd Summer Olympic Games in Los Angeles in 1984, a marksman named Xu Haifeng won China's first Olympic gold medal, in the free pistol shooting event. In 1990 the 11th Asian Games were held in Beijing, the capital of China. All major sports in China have their own associations. Sports have become popular leisure activities, especially those that require little equipment, such as Ping-Pong (table tennis), soccer, badminton, volleyball and basketball. These are also popular spectator sports, and large cities have stadiums where thousands of people can watch soccer, basketball and ice hockey games.

The most popular sports in China are the martial arts (wushu), traditional methods of exercise that employ stylized movements of attack and defense. The many systems of martial arts fall into the broad categories of empty-hand boxing, weapons training, training in pairs, sparring and group exercises. The best-known style of empty-hand boxing is taijiquan (t'ai chi ch'uan), the practice of slow and gentle routines that resemble a dance. Every morning in China many people, including the elderly, practice taijiquan in parks and other public places. By 1956 the State Physical Culture and Sports Commission formally designated martial arts as a competitive sport and established martial arts training and research departments in schools and institutes of physical culture. Martial arts have been included in Chinese national games, and seven kinds of national martial arts competitions are held annually in China. In 1990 martial arts were included in the formal events of the 11th Asian Games, and the International Wushu (Martial Arts) Association, joined by 38 countries and regions, was established. The First World Wushu Championships were held in Beijing in 1991.

Factories and schools take breaks for taijiquan and other exercises. Factories also organize their own teams to compete in such sports as Ping-Pong and badminton. In the winter in northern China, high school and university students ice skate during their lunch hour. A Chinese woman, Chen Lu, was a medal winner in the figure-skating event during the 1994 and 1988 Winter Olympic Games. Chinese children enjoy sports in schools and youth centers, especially gymnastics. Students who are very skilled at gymnastics are transferred to special schools where they spend hours each day training, and the best students become members of national teams that represent China in world competitions. Members of the ethnic groups that make up China's 55 officially designated national minorities also enjoy their own traditional sports. For example, Mongolians, who are trained to ride horses from childhood, love horse races and other competitive events on horseback. Mongol boys and men also enjoy a traditional form of wrestling. Tibetans enjoy a fast-paced type of folk dancing.

In the early 1970s the Chinese government used Ping-Pong to open up relations with the United States, which had refused to recognize the PRC as the legitimate government of China after the Chinese Communists founded it in 1949. The United States gave diplomatic recognition instead to the Nationalist (Kuomintang; KMT) government of the Republic of China (ROC) on Taiwan. China had participated in the Olympic Games in 1932, 1936 and 1948, but after 1949, disagreement as to whether the PRC or the ROC should represent China led to the PRC's withdrawal from the International Olympic Committee (IOC) in 1959. In 1971, after the Chinese team competed in the world table tennis championships in Japan, the PRC invited the U.S. team to visit China to play a series of matches, a signal that the PRC government wished to hold talks with the U.S. government. This so-called Ping-Pong diplomacy resulted in U.S. president Richard M. Nixon visiting the PRC in 1972. The PRC applied for readmission to the IOC in 1975, and by 1979 Taiwan was told it could participate in the Olympics but not under the name of China. Taiwan withdrew in protest, and hence the PRC now represents China in the Olympics. Since 1981 China has participated in a large number of regional and world athletic competitions, and Chinese athletes dominate the Asian Games. See also ASIAN GAMES, HELD IN BEIJING 1990; MARTIAL ARTS; NIXON, RICHARD, U.S. PRESIDENT, VISIT TO CHINA; TAIJIQUAN.

SPRATLY ISLANDS   Also known as the Nansha Islands; a group of islands in the southernmost region of the South China Sea over which the People's Republic of China (PRC), Taiwan, Vietnam, the Philippines, Malaysia and Brunei all claim sovereignty. Some of these countries also claim the Xisha (Paracel) Islands, which lie close to Vietnam and to Hainan Island. Hainan formerly had been administered by Guangdong Province, but the PRC made the island a separate province in 1988. The PRC now occupies most of the Xisha Islands. In January 1974 naval forces of the PRC's People's Liberation Army (PLA) skirmished with South Vietnamese naval forces over three of the Xisha Islands that had been occupied by South Vietnamese troops. The PLA held a joint amphibious operation in which they seized control of the islands.

Zengmu Reef at the southern edge of the Spratly Islands is the southernmost point of all territory claimed by the PRC. The Spratly Islands, which lie astride the major shipping lanes between Taiwan and Singapore, one of the world's busiest ports, are the most dangerous trouble spot in Asia south of the Korean peninsula. The PRC is contesting its claim to the Spratly and Xisha islands because offshore oil deposits have been discovered in the South China Sea, mainly through explorations by joint ventures between foreign oil companies and the government-owned China National Offshore Oil Company. Just west of the Spratly Islands, Vietnam's Big Bear oil field has gone into production with an estimated 500 million barrels of reserves. The Chinese navy has built ports, runways and radar stations on the Spratly and Xisha islands that China has claimed. The PRC recently warned Vietnam that if it "attempts to encroach on China's sovereignty and territorial integrity," it will respond with a counterstrike. In early 1995, Chinese troops ejected Filipino fishermen from Mischief Reef which lies in an economic zone claimed by the Philippine Islands. China fortified the reef and stationed naval ships nearby. This was the first major clash between China and a Southeast Asian nation. The PRC currently is building up the PLA naval fleet in the South China Sea, conducting naval exercises there and strengthening its naval facilities and deployments in the Xisha Islands. Chinese fishermen also use the Spratly and Xisha islands as bases. The islands are uninhabited coral reefs where turtles breed on the beaches and many birds nest and lay their eggs, creating large deposits of guano that also have economic value as fertilizer. See also ENERGY SOURCES; HAINAN ISLAND; SINGAPORE; SOUTH CHINA SEA; TAIWAN; VIETNAM WAR.

SPRING AND AUTUMN ANNALS (*Chunqiu* or *Ch'un ch'iu*)   The historical records officially compiled by the feudal state of Lu (in modern Shandong Province), the home of Confucius (551–479 B.C.), the preeminent Chinese scholar and philosopher. The entries, supposedly compiled by Confucius himself, chronicle the events in Lu from 722 to 479 B.C. After his death, the *Spring and Autumn Annals* gained a prominent place in the Confucian school of thought as one of the *Five Classics* (*Wujing* or *Wu-ching*); the other four are the *Book of Changes, Book of History, Book of Songs* and *Book of Rites*. Confucian scholars wrote commentaries on the *Spring and Autumn Annals* that expounded on the hidden moralistic ideas they believed Confucius had written into the book. On this basis they claimed that Confucius was not merely a great teacher but a "king."

The phrase "Spring and Autumn" actually refers to the four seasons of the year. The name of the Spring and Autumn Period (722–481 B.C.) in Chinese history derives from these annals. The Spring and Autumn Period is the middle of three periods into which historians usually divide the Zhou dynasty, which lasted altogether from 1100 to 256 B.C. Neighboring feudal states at that time also produced official chronicles, but only those of Lu have survived. See also BOOK OF CHANGES; BOOK OF HISTORY; BOOK OF RITES; BOOK OF SONGS; CONFUCIANISM; CONFUCIUS; EASTERN ZHOU DYNASTY; SHANDONG PROVINCE; SPRING AND AUTUMN PERIOD; WARRING STATES PERIOD; WESTERN ZHOU DYNASTY.

SPRING AND AUTUMN OF MR. LU   See BOOK OF RITES.

SPRING AND AUTUMN PERIOD (Chunqiu or Ch'un-ch'iu; 772–481 B.C.)   A period of history during the Zhou dynasty, the longest dynasty in Chinese history. Historians divide the Zhou into two general periods, the Western Zhou (1100–771 B.C.) and the Eastern Zhou (771–256 B.C.), which they subdivide into the Spring and Autumn Period and the Warring States Period (403–221 B.C.). Zhou rulers established a system of feudal states whose rulers pledged loyalty and support to the Zhou but had the authority to administer their own states. By the time of the Spring and Autumn Period there were about 170 feudal states, over which the Zhou rulers had decreasing control. In 771 B.C.

invaders allied themselves with disaffected vassals of the Zhou, took the Zhou capital and killed the king, and forced the Zhou to leave their homeland and move east. The Spring and Autumn Period began when they established the Eastern Zhou dynasty in the region of modern Luoyang in Henan Province, just south of the Yellow River (Huanghe). The Zhou kings continued to serve a symbolic and ritual function, since they were the only ones who had the right to offer ritual sacrifices to Heaven (tian or t'ien) on behalf of the Chinese people, but they had no power to keep their vassal states from fighting each other and expanding their territories by conquering smaller ones.

The Spring and Autumn Period is named after the *Spring and Autumn Annals* (*Chunqiu* or *Ch'un-ch'iu*), the historical records officially compiled by the feudal state of Lu (in modern Shandong Province), the home of Confucius (551–479 B.C.), the most important Chinese thinker. According to tradition, Confucius himself compiled this set of records, which chronicle the events in Lu from 722 to 479 B.C. This marked the beginning of the Chinese tradition of recorded histories for individual states and, after the country was unified under the rule of an emperor, for each ruling dynasty.

The Spring and Autumn Period was a time of constant warfare among the various feudal states and also of the flowering of classical Chinese culture. Many philosophical schools emerged, known as the Hundred Schools of Thought; two became dominant in China, Confucianism, the school that grew out of the teachings of Confucius, and Daoism. Confucianism, which emphasizes hierarchical order and harmony in society and in the family, became accepted as the orthodox school of thought by the imperial court of the Han dynasty (206 B.C.–A.D. 220). It remains influential today, not only in China but in other Asian countries, especially Japan, Taiwan, Korea and Vietnam. Confucius regarded the early days of the Zhou dynasty as the ideal period of peaceful, orderly government in Chinese history and considered the Duke of Zhou and Zhou founders King Wen and King Wu the best examples of loyal government officials who administered their kingdoms wisely. Confucian teachings are contained in five texts, the Five Classics (*wujing* or *wu-ching*); they include the *Book of Changes, Book of History, Book of Rites, Book of Songs* and *Spring and Autumn Annals*.

Daoism emphasizes individual freedom and harmony with nature. According to legend, Laozi (Lao Tzu), a contemporary of Confucius, was the author of the best-known Daoist text, the *Daodejing* (*Tao Te Ching*). These two schools of thought, the pragmatic Confucian school concerned with social order and moral self-cultivation and the mystical Daoist school concerned with personal experience and self-expression, remained the two dominant philosophical schools throughout Chinese history. Both are concerned with human beings and the way humans can harmonize themselves with the universe. During the Warring States Period, a third major school emerged, known as Legalism, which emphasized the absolute power of the ruler and a harsh system of laws and punishments. This became the official school during the Qin dynasty (221–206 B.C.), which ended the Zhou dynasty and unified the Chinese Empire.

The end of the Spring and Autumn Period usually is dated by the decline of the state of Jin; although powerful enough to defeat the state of Chu in the seventh century

B.C., during the first half of the fifth century B.C. it became divided by internal rivalries and civil war. After the chief minister of Jin, the count of Zhi, was assassinated in 453 B.C., Jin broke up into three states, Han, Wei and Zhao (known as the three Jin). The Warring States Period was characterized by various states forming alliances and contending with each other, and some conquering others. Eventually only seven major states remained—Qin, Wei, Han, Zhao, Chu, Yan and Qi. The strongest proved to be Qin, which had taken control of the Western Zhou state centered at Chang'an (modern Xi'an in Shaanxi Province). The Qin leader unified China under the Qin dynasty and proclaimed himself the "First Emperor," Qin Shi Huangdi (r. 221–210 B.C.). See also CONFUCIANISM; CONFUCIUS; DAODEJING; DAOISM; FIVE CLASSICS OF CONFUCIANISM; HUNDRED SCHOOLS OF THOUGHT; LAOZI; LEGALIST SCHOOL OF THOUGHT; QIN DYNASTY; WARRING STATES PERIOD; ZHOU DYNASTY.

SPRING FESTIVAL See NEW YEAR FESTIVAL.

SSU See TEMPLES.

SSU TA MINGSHAN See FOUR SACRED MOUNTAINS OF BUDDHISM.

SSU-MA CH'IEN See SIMA QIAN.

SSU-MA HSIANG-JU See SIMA XIANGRU.

SSU-MA KUANG See SIMA GUANG.

SSU-MA T'AN See SIMA TAN.

STANDING COMMITTEE See POLITBURO.

STAR FESTIVAL See COWHERD AND WEAVER MAID FESTIVAL.

STATE COUNCIL The highest executive body of the government of the People's Republic of China (PRC), founded in 1949 by the Chinese Communist Party (CCP). The State Council is equivalent to the cabinet or council of ministers in the governments of many other countries. The State Council is formally responsible to the National People's Congress (NPC; not to be confused with the National Party Congress), the highest legislative body in the PRC. In practice, because senior members of the State Council are also powerful leaders of the CCP, the State Council is mainly responsible to the Secretariat of the CCP, under the Politburo (Political Bureau) and its Standing Committee. The NPC decides on the choice of the premier of the State Council nominated by the chairman (or president) of the PRC, and it has the power to remove members of the State Council from their positions. At the First National People's Congress, held in 1954, Premier Zhou Enlai (Chou En-lai) was elected premier of the newly organized State Council, and he held this position until he died in 1976. Each premier since then also has been premier of the State Council. The State Council meets once a month; its standing committee meets twice a week and includes the premier, vice premiers, a secretary and state councilors. The functions of the State Council include drawing up administrative measures; issuing decisions and orders and monitoring their implementation; drafting legislative bills for submission to the NPC or the NPC Standing Committee; and preparing the economic plan and the state budget that the NPC will deliberate and approve.

The State Council administers all of the PRC government ministries and many other agencies, commissions, administrations, bureaus, academies and corporations. Some of the most important have to do with the Chinese economy and foreign policy, such as the Ministry of Foreign Trade and Economic Cooperation, the State Planning Commission, the Special Economic Zones Office, the Ministry of Finance, the Bank of China, the Chinese Academy of Sciences and the Macao Affairs Office. (Macao will revert to China in 1999.) The State Council's offices, commissions and special agencies deal with a wide range of concerns, such as science and technology, national defense and its related industries, environmental protection, civil aviation, Chinese and foreign-language publishing, written Chinese language reform, geology, meteorology, cartography and administration of cultural relics. See also CHINESE ACADEMY OF SCIENCES; GOVERNMENT STRUCTURE; HONG KONG; MACAO; MINISTRY OF FOREIGN TRADE AND ECONOMIC COOPERATION; NATIONAL PEOPLE'S CONGRESS; PEOPLE'S REPUBLIC OF CHINA; POLITBURO; SPECIAL ECONOMIC ZONES; STATE PLANNING COMMISSION; ZHOU ENLAI.

STATE ECONOMIC COMMISSION See STATE PLANNING COMMISSION.

STATE PLANNING COMMISSION A commission administered by the State Council, the highest executive body of the government of the People's Republic of China (PRC), that sets the government policy for annual and long-term economic and agricultural plans for the country, known as Five-Year Plans. Sometimes it even formulates plans for 10-year periods. The State Planning Commission collects and compiles information about the plans drawn up by all government ministries and provincial officials and determines the goals for industrial output and the supply-and-demand relationships for sectors and enterprises critical to the national economy. Below the State Planning Commissions are planning departments in the government ministries, planning bureaus in each of the provinces and planning units in smaller regions down to individual enterprises. The State Planning Commission works with other governmental bodies under the State Council that help it draw up its plans, such as the Bank of China, the Ministry of Foreign Trade and Economic Cooperation, the Ministry of Finance and other economic ministries, the State Statistical Bureau, the State Economic Commission and the People's Bank of China. The PRC government announced in 1998 that it would change the commission's name to State Department and Planning Commission. See also BANK OF CHINA; FIVE-YEAR PLANS; MINISTRY OF FINANCE; MINISTRY OF FOREIGN AND ECONOMIC COOPERATION; STATE COUNCIL.

STATE STATISTICAL BUREAU See STATE PLANNING COMMISSION.

STEEL INDUSTRY See IRON TECHNOLOGY AND STEEL INDUSTRY.

STEIN, AUREL See DUNHUANG CAVE PAINTINGS AND CARVINGS; SILK ROAD.

STELES See STONE TABLETS.

STILT WALKING (*wen* or *wu*) A traditional folk art performed by dancers on tall, thin wooden sticks; very popular at Chinese festivals, especially in northern China. Stilt walking often is performed with *yangko,* a traditional Chinese folk dance also popular at festivals. Stilt walking combines elements from acrobatics, folk dancing and the stylized movements of Chinese opera. Stilt walkers wear the colorful makeup, props and costumes of traditional characters from operas and folktales: emperors, generals, scholars and famous beautiful women. They perform on wooden stilts ranging from 16 inches to 5 feet high.

Stilt walking is classified as *wen* or *wu,* depending on the height of the stilts. In *wen,* the stilts are about three to five feet high and the performers dance gracefully in two or four lines, with men on the left and women on the right, moving through a sequence of complex formations. Energetic music and drumming accompany the dance. The *suono,* a wind instrument similar to a horn, always is played. In *wu,* the stilts are about 16 inches to 3 feet high and the performers execute spectacular movements such as somersaults, jumps, splits and full-circle turns. A stilt-walking performance always follows the same order. The first part, *touqiao* (*t'ou-ch'iao;* "leading stilts"), uses exaggerated gestures and whistle-blowing to direct the dancers and musicians. Next comes *erqiao* (*erh-ch'iao;* "second stilts"), featuring dancers who represent opera characters. At the end comes *yadigu* (*ya-ti-ku;* "last stilts"), which includes the most talented performers. At festival times, especially the New Year or Spring Festival and the Lantern Festival in February, the northern Chinese enjoy lively competitions between groups of stilt walkers from different towns and villages. See also LANTERN FESTIVAL; NEW YEAR FESTIVAL; OPERA, CHINESE; YANGKO.

STILWELL, JOSEPH WARREN (1883–1946) An American general who served as head of the U.S. and Chinese Nationalist (Kuomintang; KMT) forces during China's War of Resistance against Japan (1937–45; World War II). Stilwell graduated from the U.S. Military Academy at West Point in 1904 and was assigned to the Philippine Islands. From 1906 until 1910 he was an instructor at West Point and spent several summers in Latin America. In 1911 Stilwell married Winifred A. Smith and returned to the Philippines after first touring Japan. He visited China in 1911, while the country was undergoing the revolution that established modern China. During World War I he served with the American Expeditionary Force in Europe. In 1919 Stilwell studied the Chinese language in California and then went to Beijing, where he served as a military attaché from 1920 to 1923. He was assigned to Tianjin from 1926 to 1929 and Beijing from 1935 to 1939. By 1932 Japan had established a puppet state called Manchukuo in Manchuria (northeastern China) and had begun sending troops south into China. In 1937 China declared war against Japan. Chiang Kai-shek (1887–1975), leader of the Nationalist Chinese forces, asked Stilwell to be his chief of staff. Stilwell, who arrived in China early in 1942, was given command of the Chinese Fifth and

Sixth armies in Burma, which bordered China on the south. During the war, Stilwell was Commanding General of U.S. forces in the China-Burma-India theater, Deputy Supreme Allied Commander in Southeast Asia, Commanding General of the Chinese Army in India and its field commander in Burma, nominal Chief of Staff to Chiang Kai-shek for the China theater, Chief of the Chinese Training and Combat Command and Administrator of Lend-Lease to China.

In 1942 Japanese troops drove Stilwell's troops from Burma and attempted to invade China along the Burma Road but were stopped by Chinese troops with support from the Flying Tigers (American volunteer pilots). Stilwell and his men made an arduous 140-mile trek on foot through the jungle into India. Stilwell, who was nicknamed "Vinegar Joe" for his stubborn forthrightness, gave priority to defeating the Japanese. Therefore he wanted to supply arms to all Chinese forces, the Communists as well as the Nationalists, but Chiang disagreed. The Nationalists and Communists had been fighting a civil war when China declared war against Japan. Although the two parties made a united front to fight the Japanese, their alliance started breaking down. Chiang eventually requested Stilwell's dismissal, and in October 1944 U.S. President Franklin D. Roosevelt sent General Albert Wedemeyer to replace him. After Japan surrendered in August 1945, the Nationalists and Communists resumed their civil war. In 1949 the Communists defeated the Nationalists, who fled to the island of Taiwan, where they established the Republic of China.

During the war, the Burma Road had been built to transport supplies to the Nationalists, who had been cut off from the outside world after the Japanese forced them to flee to Chongqing in Sichuan Province in southwestern China. After the Burma Road was closed in 1940, General Claire Lee Chennault organized the Flying Tigers (officially named the American Volunteers Group; AVG) to fly supplies to the Nationalists from India over "the Hump" (the Himalaya Mountain Range) in southwestern China. U.S. army engineers, assisted by Chinese troops, constructed the Ledo Road, a supply route connecting northeastern India with the old Burma Road that opened in January 1945. Chiang Kai-shek renamed this route the Stilwell Road to honor the American general. After leaving China in 1944, Stilwell had returned to the United States, where he was awarded the Legion of Merit and the Oak Leaf Cluster of the DSM. In May 1945 he went back to Asia during the Battle of Okinawa and was appointed commander of the U.S. 10th Army in the Pacific theater. He was present at the formal surrender by Japan on September 2 and at the surrender of more than 1,000 Japanese troops in the Ryukyu Islands (Okinawa) on September 7. He wanted to return to China, but Chiang Kai-shek would not give him permission to do so, so he went back to the United States in October 1945. In January 1946 Stilwell was assigned to San Francisco as commander of the Sixth Army in charge of the Western Defense Command. He died there in October 1946. See also BURMA ROAD; CHIANG KAI-SHEK; CHONGQING; CIVIL WAR BETWEEN COMMUNISTS AND NATIONALISTS; FLYING TIGERS; NATIONALIST PARTY; WAR OF RESISTANCE AGAINST JAPAN.

STIMSON DOCTRINE See LYTTON COMMISSION.

STONE RUBBINGS (*kotie* or *k'o-t'ieh*)   Reproductions of calligraphy engraved on stone. The rubbings are made with ink and paper. The paper used for stone rubbings is made from a plant fiber, such as mulberry or bamboo, and is the same kind used for the arts of calligraphy and painting. The ink, also used for those arts, is made by grinding an ink stick on an inkstone and mixing in drops of water to produce exactly the right consistency. The paper, ink stick and inkstone are three of the Four Treasures in a traditional Chinese scholar's study. The fourth is a writing brush.

A stone rubbing is made by pressing a piece of thin paper to the stone and fixing it in place by coating it with a paste made from rice starch and water. The paper then is tamped over its surface with a round cloth pad filled with ink. This process turns black all the areas that are fixed to the stone and leaves white the engraved or carved areas. The paper is peeled off the stone and allowed to dry. The stone rubbing creates a reverse print in which the surface is black and the written characters are white. Since ancient times, the works of famous Chinese calligraphers have been carved onto stone columns, and Chinese scholars purposely made stone rubbings of these works to preserve and copy beautiful and historical calligraphy. They developed their own skills in calligraphy by copying the works of famous masters. By the ninth century, the stone rubbing technique for reproduction was combined with a reproduction method known as the seal stamp technique to create the block-print method for printing books. See also CALLIGRAPHY; FOUR TREASURES OF THE STUDY; PAPER; PRINTING; STONE TABLETS.

STONE TABLETS (*bei* or *pei*)   Stone blocks, columns or pillars that are carved in Chinese ideographs with imperial edicts, the Five Classics of Confucianism, poems or other important texts; known as steles or stelae. Steles were produced as early as the Zhou dynasty (1100–256 B.C.) to disseminate these texts to the population. The strong, formal clerical style (*lishu*) of writing, which developed during the Han dynasty (206 B.C.–A.D. 220), is the style of calligraphy that Chinese have preferred for carving inscriptions on stone tablets.

The Shaanxi Provincial Museum in the former Confucian temple in Xi'an houses China's largest collection of engraved stone tablets. This collection, known as the Forest of Steles, includes more than 1,000 double-sided stone blocks dating from the Han dynasty to the Qing dynasty (1644–1911). Most of these steles were engraved with the Confucian classical texts in 837, during the reign of Tang emperor Wenzong (Wen-tsung; r. 826–40), and were deposited at the Imperial College, where renowned scholars wrote commentaries on them. One of the most important tablets in the collection is the Nestorian Stele, whose engraving describes the arrival of Nestorian Christianity in China in 635 and the religion's development during the seventh and eighth centuries in Xi'an, then known as Chang'an, the capital of the Tang dynasty (618–907). The text includes 1,900 Chinese characters and 50 words in the Syriac language. It also lists 72 names of Nestorian priests and leaders in an old script known as Estrangela.

The Chinese often make paper-and-ink copies of steles, known as stone rubbings. Students also learn calligraphy, the art of writing Chinese characters with a brush, by copying ancient masters whose works are preserved on stone rubbings. The Imperial College in Beijing, which has been restored and converted to public libraries, exhibits 189 large stone tablets that were carved with the texts of the Confucian classics by Jiang Heng (Chiang Heng) from 1726 to 1795. The courtyard of the Confucian Temple (now the Beijing Museum) in the Imperial College contains 198 stone tablets carved with the names of the 51,624 scholars who passed the imperial examinations during the Yuan, Ming, and Qing dynasties (1279–1911). The final tablet lists the successful candidates in the last imperial examination, held in 1904. See also CALLIGRAPHY; CHANG'AN; FIVE CLASSICS OF CONFUCIANISM; FOUR BOOKS OF CONFUCIANISM; IMPERIAL EXAMINATION SYSTEM; NESTORIAN CHRISTIANITY; STONE RUBBINGS; WRITING, CHINESE; XI'AN.

STORY OF QIUJU, THE   See GONG LI; ZHANG YIMOU.

STORYTELLING (*pingtan* or *p'ing-t'an*)   A performing art that dates back more than 400 years in China and combines *pinghua* (*p'ing-hua*), spoken storytelling without music, and *tanci* (*t'an-tz'u*), which is both spoken and sung. *Pinghua* mainly includes stories about historical battles, legal cases or heroic events in popular Chinese historical novels, such as *The Romance of the Three Kingdoms* and *Outlaws of the Marsh* (also known as *The Water Margin*). *Tanci*, which includes stories about love and everyday life, originated as the art of recitation and gradually developed melodies. A traditional Chinese storyteller may accompany him- or herself on a three-stringed instrument called the *sanxian* (*san-hsien*; known in the West by the Japanese term *samisen*) or a five-stringed *pipa* (*p'i-p'a*), or on a folk instrument such as a drum made from a bamboo tube (*zhuqin* or *chu-ch'in*). Each singer has a distinctive style—based on a distinctive dialect from a particular region of China—which expresses the full range of human emotion. Many humorous touches are included to involve the audience. A complete performance of a *pingtan* cycle is told in daily one- or two-hour episodes that may take as long as four to six months to complete. Audiences attend the theater every day so they can hear every episode. Performances by the Shanghai Pingtan Troupe, which is sponsored by the Chinese government, are very popular. Its members have revised and edited many traditional Chinese stories and also have composed many stories about Chinese life based on modern novels and short stories, such as "Harness the Huai River at All Costs." Storytellers also perform in traditional Chinese teahouses, although this custom is dying out. A famous open-air teahouse with storytellers in the People's Park in Chengdu in Sichuan Province, a city famous for its teahouses, seats 300 people. See also CHENGDU; OUTLAWS OF THE MARSH; PIPA; ROMANCE OF THE THREE KINGDOMS; SANXIAN; TEA.

STOVE PRINCE   See KITCHEN GOD.

STRING INSTRUMENTS   Musical instruments made with wooden frames and two or more strings that are plucked or played with a bow. The Chinese classify string instruments as one of the eight types of musical instruments and associate them with silk, from which the strings traditionally are made. Chinese string instruments generally have a melancholy sound, which is believed to strengthen the mind and give rise to pure and faithful thoughts. The string instru-

ments that are held vertically on the lap and played with a bow are classified as *huqin* (*hu-ch'in*; "barbarian fiddles"). The term *hu*, "barbarian," indicates that these instruments were brought to China by outsiders, perhaps nomadic Turkish or Mongolian tribes. They originated during the Tang dynasty (618–907) and were being played in China by the 13th century. The *huqin*, of which the two-string *erhu* is perhaps the best known, are the most important instruments in the orchestras that accompany Chinese operas. The zither (*qin* or *ch'in*) is the most refined of the Chinese instruments and is associated with members of the Confucian-educated literati, or scholar-gentry class. It originated in ancient times and had five strings, but later seven strings were used. The 26-string zither (*se*) is no longer played, but the 13-string zither (*zheng* or *cheng*) is still popular in southern and southwestern China. In Japan this instrument is called the *koto*. The *pipa* (*p'i p'a*) is a four-string pear-shaped lute that originated in the Middle East and was brought across Asia into China and Japan, where it is called the *biwa*. The *sanxian* (*san hsien*) is a three-string banjo that was introduced to the Ryukyu Islands and Japan, where it is called the *samisen*. Other Chinese string instruments include the moon guitar (*yueqin* or *yueh ch'in*) and the harpsichord or dulcimer (*yangqin* or *yang ch'in*). See also ERHU; OPERA, CHINESE; PIPA; SANXIAN; ZITHER.

STRIVING FOR NEW CHINA   See SOONG QINGLING.

STUPA   See PAGODA.

SU DONGPO   See SU SHI; WEST LAKE.

SU SHI (Su Shih; 1036–1101)   Also known as Su Dongpo (Su Tung-p'o); a highly praised poet, essayist, painter, calligrapher and member of the Song dynasty (960–1279) imperial bureaucracy. Su Shi was born to a literary family in Sichuan Province and was educated by his mother. He is classed along with his father, Su Xun (Su Hsun), and his younger brother, Su Che (Su Ch'e), among the so-called Eight Prose Masters of the Tang and Song Dynasties. As a calligrapher, Su Shi also is considered one of the Four Great Masters of the Northern Song dynasty, all of whom specialized in the "running-standard" or "informal regular" script (*xingkai* or *hsing-k'ai*), one of the styles of Chinese calligraphy. He held a number of bureaucratic positions but was banished from court several times because of his conservative opposition to reforms made by the prime minister, Wang Anshi.

Su Shi's poetry has been praised for its natural, flowing quality. He is best known for his lyrics (*ci* or *tz'u*) and prose poetry (*fu*). He was active in reviving classicism in Song dynasty literature. Su Shi's calligraphy, notably his scroll "The Red Cliff," inspired calligraphers during the Ming dynasty (1368–1644) who revived the Song style. See also CALLIGRAPHY; IMPERIAL BUREAUCRACY; LYRIC VERSE; RHYME-PROSE STYLE OF VERSE; WANG ANSHI.

SU TUNG-P'O   See SU SHI.

SUANBAN (SUAN PAN)   See ABACUS.

SUBWAYS   See RAILROADS.

SUI (MINORITY GROUP) See DAI.

SUI DYNASTY (581–618) A brief but powerful dynasty that reunified the Chinese Empire, which had broken up into many regional kingdoms after the fall of the Han dynasty (206 B.C.–A.D. 220). Although there were only two Sui emperors, this short-lived dynasty paved the way for the Tang dynasty (618–907), considered the Golden Age of Chinese culture. The Sui dynasty was founded by Yang Jian (Yang Chien), the duke of Sui, who became Sui emperor Wendi (Wen-ti; r. 581–604) after he usurped the throne of the Northern Zhou (Chou) dynasty. By 589 Wendi captured the Chen Yi capital (modern Nanjing) on the Yangzi River and conquered all eight of the other so-called Northern and Southern dynasties that had ruled China between 420 and 588. Emperor Wendi built his capital city at Chang'an (modern Xi'an in Shaanxi Province), near the site of the old capital of the Western Han dynasty. During the Tang dynasty, Chang'an would become the largest and most cosmopolitan city in the world. Wendi centralized and strengthened the government bureaucracy, created a more effective system for taxation and promulgated a new law code that served as the model for all later Chinese imperial law codes. He conscripted millions of Chinese to begin construction of a canal to transport grain and other agricultural products from the lower Yangzi River valley to Chang'an in western China. He also had granaries constructed at several strategic sites to help his subjects in times of famine. He supported the religion of Buddhism, which had been introduced into China from India around the first century A.D., as well as the native Chinese tradition of Confucianism, which he used to legitimize his reign.

In 604 Wendi was killed by his second son, Yang Kuang, who had also killed his elder brother, the crown prince; these two deaths enabled him to become the second Sui emperor Yangdi (Yang-ti; r. 604–18). Yangdi continued to develop the imperial bureaucracy and the examination system by which Confucian-educated scholars, or literati, were selected for government positions. Like his father, he conscripted his subjects to extend the canal system, which became known as the Grand Canal, and to labor on many other projects, including the reinforcement of the Great Wall, the building of roads and imperial palaces and the construction of an alternate capital at Luoyang to the east of Chang'an. Yangdi sent forces west and north to bring local tribes into China's tribute system. He also sent three military expeditions to conquer the Korean peninsula. All three failed, causing the deaths of thousands of Chinese soldiers and the bankruptcy of the royal treasury. Rebellions against the Sui broke out around Luoyang. Emperor Yangdi fled to his southern capital at Jiangdu (modern Yangzhou), where he spent his time in Buddhist meditation until one of his bodyguards killed him and his son. Li Shimin (Li Shih-min), son of a high-ranking Sui government official, led an army that defeated all rivals for the throne and made his father the first Tang emperor, Gaozu (Kao-tsu; r. 618–26). Li Shimin succeeded his father as the second Tang emperor, Taizong (T'ai-tsung; r. 626–49). See also BUDDHISM; CHANG'AN; CONFUCIANISM; GAOZU, EMPEROR; GRAND CANAL; NORTHERN AND SOUTHERN DYNASTIES PERIOD; TAIZONG, EMPEROR; TANG DYNASTY; TRIBUTE SYSTEM; WENDI, EMPEROR; YANGDI, EMPEROR; YANGZHOU.

SUIBOKUGA (SUI-PO-KU-K'A) See INK PAINTING.

SUMI-E See INK PAINTING.

SUMMER PALACE (Yiheyuan; "Garden of Good Health and Harmony") A large complex of buildings and gardens built in 1888 to commemorate the 60th birthday of Empress Dowager Cixi (Tz'u Hsi; 1835–1908) of the Qing dynasty (1644–1911). The Summer Palace is located six miles northwest of the center of Beijing, the capital city, and covers more than 800 acres. It was erected on the site of the original palace that had been built when Wan Yanliang, the first emperor of the Jin dynasty (1115–1234), established his capital in the Beijing vicinity and built his so-called Gold Mountain Traveling Palace at Longevity Hill. Another Jin emperor diverted the water from Jade Spring to the Gold Mountain Palace. Emperors of the Yuan (1279–1368) and Ming (1368–1644) dynasties also used this site.

The layout of the palace grounds was designed according to the principles of *feng shui* (geomancy; literally, "wind and water"), which brings good luck to a building. Longevity Hill protects the palace on the north side. On the south side, Kunming Lake, designed to imitate the famous West Lake in the former capital city of Hangzhou, represents good fortune. The Painted Gallery, a long covered wooden walkway running along the southern shore of the lake, is decorated with auspicious symbols and landscape paintings on the beams. At the western end of the lake is the famous marble boat that was built with money intended for building a modern Chinese navy. The Octagonal Tower Pavilion (Fa Xing Gui) symbolizes long life. The palace grounds contain more than 100 traditional structures. Visitors enter the complex through the East Palace Gate, guarded by a bronze lion, and come to the buildings that had been the living quarters of the imperial family. They are poetically named the Hall of Benevolence and Longevity (Renshoudian), the Garden of Virtuous Harmony (Deheyuan), the Hall of Happiness and Longevity (Leshantang) and the Hall of Jade Billows (Yulantang). The summit of Longevity Hill offers a scenic view of Beijing and a restaurant serving Beijing cuisine in the Listening to the Orioles Pavilion.

The Summer Palace was destroyed during the Boxer Uprising of 1900 but was restored in 1903. After the Qing dynasty was brought down by the Revolution of 1911, the Summer Palace was made the private property of the deposed last emperor, Xuantong (Hsuan-tung; r. 1909–12; later known as Henry Puyi). In 1924 Puyi was forced to leave by General Feng Yuxiang (Feng Yu-hsiang), and the gardens were opened to the public at a very high price of admission. The following years were marked by struggles between Chinese Nationalists (Kuomintang; KMT), Chinese Communists and Japanese invaders, and the Summer Palace was wrecked, pillaged and its treasures taken out of the country. In 1949 the palace was renovated to its former splendor and reopened to the public. Today Chinese and foreign tourists enjoy strolling through the palace grounds and swimming, boating and ice skating on the lake. Admission is free on May Day (May 1) and National Day (October 1).

Another Summer Palace, Yuanmingyuan ("Garden of Perfect Brightness"; also known as the Old Summer Palace), had been built in this area for the Qianlong emperor (r.

Open to the public today, the 19th-century Summer Palace was the Empress Dowager's 60th-birthday present to herself.   S.E. MEYER

1736–95) during the Qing dynasty. A complex of three large gardens was completed over a period of 150 years. It was badly damaged by British and French troops in 1860 and totally destroyed by the Eight-Power Allied Forces in 1900, although the ruins still can be seen. See also BEIJING; BOXER UPRISING; CIXI; FENG SHUI; GARDENS; JIN DYNASTY; NATIONAL DAY; PUYI, HENRY; QIANLONG EMPEROR; QING DYNASTY; REVOLUTION OF 1911; WEST LAKE.

SUN TZU   See SUNZI.

SUN WU   See SUNZI.

SUN YAOTING (SUN YAO-T'ING)   See EUNUCHS.

SUN YAT-SEN (Sun Yixian or Sun I-hsien: 1866–1925) The leader of the revolutionary movement that overthrew the Qing dynasty (1644–1911), China's last imperial dynasty, and established the Republic of China (ROC). Sun is highly regarded by all Chinese as the founder of modern China. He was born to a peasant family in Guangdong Province in southern China. His original name was Sun Wen but he became known by his Cantonese name, Sun Yat-sen. He received a Chinese education at a village school but also took English lessons from an American Christian missionary. The Taiping Rebellion (1850–64), which almost overthrew the Qing dynasty, had originated in Guangdong, and Sun

heard many stories about it while growing up. When Sun was 12, his elder brother, Sun Mei, returned home from Hawaii, where he had started a small business. The next year the family sent Sun Yat-sen to Hawaii with his brother. This early exposure to the outside world gave Sun an interest in Western learning. In Hawaii he attended a school run by the British Anglican Church, graduating in 1882. He also became a Christian, although his brother refused to let him be baptized and sent him back to China. In 1883 Sun went to Hong Kong, where he attended the Queen's College and was baptized. In 1884 he entered a marriage arranged by his family, but for the next eight years he studied while his wife remained at home in their village. After a trip to Hawaii in 1886, he began studying medicine at a Presbyterian hospital in Guangzhou (Canton).

In 1885 China and France fought the Sino-French War over control of Vietnam, and China's humiliating defeat made Sun decide that the Qing dynasty had to be overthrown. The Qing had been founded by Manchus, an ethnic group from Manchuria who had overthrown the Han Chinese Ming dynasty (1368–1644). In Guangzhou Sun became friends with Zheng Shiliang (Cheng Shih-liang), who belonged to one of many Chinese anti-Manchu secret societies, known as the Triads in English. Sun believed that such societies could play a major role in overthrowing the Qing. In 1887 he returned to Hong Kong to continue his study of medicine with a British doctor named Cantlie. But he also became active studying and promoting revolutionary ideas, and he frequently traveled between Hong Kong and Macao with three revolutionary friends. In 1892 Sun, who had completed his medical studies, set up an office in Macao and gained a large number of patients. He used his earnings to finance his revolutionary political activities. He stayed in contact with Zheng Shiliang, who organized secret societies and made contacts with Chinese government troops. Sun also formed an organization that became known as the Revive China Association (Xingjunghui or Hsing Chung Hui), which he later formally established in Hawaii.

In 1894 Sun had to stop practicing medicine in Macao, a Portuguese colony, because he did not have Portuguese certification, so he made a journey to northern China with another friend, Lu Haodeng (Lu Hao-teng). Sun wrote a memorial (official petition) to the powerful statesman Li Hongzhang (Li Hung-chang), a Qing government official and a leader of the Self-Strengthening Movement to reform and modernize China. Sun recommended a number of reforms that the Chinese government should undertake, such as the use of modern machines for farming, free public education, the abolition of barriers to foreign trade, new networks for transportation and communication and methods

Dr. Sun Yat-sen, a powerful leader of the Chinese revolution, is honored today by both the PRC and the ROC as the founder of modern China. DENNIS COX

for developing natural resources. Li refused to meet Sun or accept his memorial, which convinced Sun that China could progress only by overthrowing the Qing.

The Sino-Japanese War of 1894–95 broke out soon after, with China suffering a humiliating defeat by Japan. In 1895 Li Hongzhang signed the Treaty of Shimonoseki, which concluded the war and made harsh demands on China. Sun returned to Hawaii, where he organized the Revive China Association among the Chinese living there and began serious efforts to raise funds and purchase weapons for an anti-Qing rebellion. Sun's brother made a significant donation, and Sun realized that he could gain much support from overseas Chinese communities. He organized another branch of his association in Hong Kong and then went to Guangzhou to plan a rebellion that included secret society members, overseas Chinese, bandits, Christians and some Qing soldiers. But a crucial arms shipment did not arrive in time and the revolutionary plot was exposed. Sun was able to escape to Hong Kong, but Lu Haodeng was captured and beheaded. Sun then had to flee Hong Kong for Japan, where he made a symbolic revolutionary gesture by cutting off his queue, the pigtail that the Manchus forced the Han Chinese to wear. He also grew a mustache and began wearing Western clothing.

Sun traveled to the United States, where he spoke to many Chinese communities. On October 1, 1896, he arrived in London and met his former teacher, Dr. Cantlie. Soon after, Qing government agents kidnapped Sun and imprisoned him in the Chinese embassy with the intention of sending him back to China to be tortured and executed. Sun was able to smuggle out a message to Dr. Cantlie, who gained his release by appealing to the British Foreign Office and publicizing Sun's plight in the newspapers. This incident made Sun an international celebrity and strengthened his resolve to lead an anti-Qing revolution. He stayed in Europe for two years, studying Western culture and political ideas such as socialism in libraries and museums.

In 1899 Sun went back to Japan, where his friend Chen Shaobai (Ch'en Shao-pai) had been organizing the Chinese revolutionary movement. In Japan Sun formed close relationships with several Japanese who were sympathetic to his cause. Sun sent Chen to Hong Kong, where he began publishing a newspaper. Another of Sun's colleagues made contacts with secret societies in Guangzhou and the cities in the Yangzi River (Changjiang) valley. Sun established his headquarters in Yokohama, Japan, which had a large Chinese community, although many Chinese there were sympathetic to reform leader Kang Youwei (K'ang Yu-wei), Sun's rival. In 1898 Kang persuaded the Qing emperor to enact a series of reforms, known as the Reform Movement of 1898 or the Hundred Days Reform, but Empress Dowager Cixi (Tz'u Hsi) suppressed the reforms and placed the emperor under house arrest. In 1900 the antiforeign Boxer Uprising took control of North China and attacked the foreign legation quarters in Beijing. A combined force of foreign troops ended the uprising and laid harsh terms on the Qing, which turned the Han Chinese people even more strongly against their Manchu rulers. That year Sun directed Zheng Shiliang to lead the Huizhou rising of October 1900, but it failed.

Sun spent two more years in Yokohama. In 1903 he traveled to Vietnam, Hawaii, the United States and Europe. There he found many Chinese students whom the Qing dynasty recently had permitted to study abroad. They were sympathetic to his movement and formed several branches of his Revive China Association. While addressing Chinese students in Brussels, Sun first used the slogan "Three Principles of the People" to summarize his political and social concepts. These principles referred to Chinese nationalism, democracy and people's livelihood or social welfare. He also outlined his plan for a republican government in China that would have five main branches, including the legislative, executive and judicial bodies of Western governments but also traditional Chinese features, such as a system of examinations to select bureaucratic officials.

Sun returned to Japan just after it had defeated Russia in the Russo-Japanese War of 1904–5, the first time that an Asian nation had defeated a European power. Thousands of Chinese students had gone to Japan to learn the methods by which that country had succeeded so that they could apply them at home. In September 1905 Sun organized a new association, the Revolutionary Alliance (*Tongmenghui* or *T'ung-meng-hui*), which had the goals of overthrowing the Qing and establishing a republican government in China. The alliance elected Sun president and began publishing a newspaper, the *People's Paper* (*Minbao* or *Min-pao*). Within a year it had 10,000 members and branches in every Chinese province and many overseas Chinese communities. Sun became extremely active in planning five uprisings between 1906 and 1908. Even though they failed, he was optimistic that the Qing dynasty was so weak that it would soon fall.

In 1907 the Qing forced Japan to expel Sun, although the Japanese gave him a large sum of money and implied that he would be able to return soon. Sun moved to Hanoi in Vietnam, which was a French colony, but the French expelled him as well. He then moved to the Malay Peninsula (Malaysia). Between 1908 and 1911 Sun's Revolutionary Alliance conducted three of the four major uprisings against the Qing dynasty. In November 1908 Empress Dowager Cixi died the day after the emperor died, and she was suspected of having him poisoned. She had wielded the real power in the Qing, and her death seriously weakened the dynasty.

In 1909 Sun traveled to Europe once more to raise money. The next year the Revolutionary Alliance suffered failures that discouraged Sun's followers, so he traveled back through the United States to Singapore and Malaya, where he met with the revolutionary leaders. They drew up plans for the Guangzhou uprising of April 1911. This revolution nearly succeeded, but the leaders were caught and executed by the Qing government. They became known as the 72 Martyrs of Huang Huagang (Huang Hua Kang).

In September 1911, while traveling in the United States once again, Sun received an encoded message from China, which he neglected to decipher for two weeks. It was a request for funds for an uprising planned for the city of Wuchang (Wuhan) in central China. Before Sun replied to the cable, he read in the newspaper that the Wuchang Uprising had taken place in China. Qing authorities had discovered the revolutionary plot, and a bomb explosion on October 9, one week before the planned uprising, caused them to discover a list of the names of the people involved in it. The revolutionaries who had infiltrated the Wuchang garrison of the Qing army decided to act immediately. On the night of October 10, 1911 they rebelled and forced the gov-

ernor and troops loyal to him to flee. Revolutionary forces also took Hanyang and Hankou. The rebels established a military government and forced Colonel Li Yuanhong (Li Yuan-hung) to be their leader. Many Chinese provinces declared their independence from the Qing, and on November 11 the Chinese navy joined the revolutionary side.

When the revolutionaries captured the major city of Nanjing, the former capital of the Ming dynasty, the Qing sent the military commander Yuan Shikai (Yuan Shih-kai) to suppress them. But Yuan moved to increase his own power by secretly negotiating with the revolutionaries to remove the Manchus and establish a republican government, with the hope that he would become its president.

Sun Yat-sen, a powerful symbolic leader of the Chinese revolution, did not return immediately to China but first went to Britain. He persuaded the British to block their loan to the Manchus to build a railroad and to agree to consider making a loan to Sun's government when it was established. Sun also met with the premier of France. He arrived back in China on December 24, 1911, and five days later he was elected provisional president of the newly established Republic of China. He formally assumed the presidency on January 1, 1912. Sun promised Yuan Shikai that if the Manchu emperor abdicated the throne, he would yield the presidency to Yuan. Qing emperor Xuantong (Hsuan-tung; r. 1909–12; later known as Henry Puyi) abdicated one month later, and Yuan became president of the republic.

The Revolutionary Alliance joined with several other revolutionary groups in 1912 to form the National People's Party, also known as the Nationalist Party (Kuomintang; KMT). Rather than serve as leader of this party, Sun became active in China's economic reconstruction, especially the building of railroads. The KMT was led by Song Jiaoren (Sung Chiao-jen), one of Sun's associates. Elections were held in February 1913 for the new bicameral parliament. Song campaigned against the Yuan government, and his party won a majority of seats, but Yuan had Song assassinated in March 1913. Yuan did not favor parliamentary government, and he attempted to increase his own power by dismissing government officials not loyal to him and splitting up the KMT. That summer seven southern Chinese provinces rebelled against Yuan, but the rebellion was suppressed, and Sun and other revolutionary leaders had to flee to Japan. Yuan became a virtual dictator, formally dissolving the KMT on January 10, 1914 and having its members removed from parliament.

In 1915 Sun married Soong Qingling (Soong Ching Ling or Soong Ch'ing-ling or Sung Ch'ing-ling; 1893–1981), a Chinese Christian who had been educated at Wesleyan College for Women in Macon, Georgia. Her wealthy father had funded Sun's Revolutionary Alliance, and when she returned to China in 1913 she became Sun's personal secretary. Sun planned to overthrow Yuan Shikai, but Yuan destroyed himself by attempting to establish a new dynasty with himself as emperor. He died in June 1916. Sun was then able to return to China, where he and his wife settled in Shanghai, and he lectured and wrote. After Yuan died, China was divided up among a number of warlords, known as the Warlord Period (1916–28). The Chinese government was controlled by whatever warlord controlled Beijing. In 1917 a government led by Duan Qirui (Tuan Ch'i-jui) decided that China would enter World War I on the allied side. Sun opposed that decision, but Chinese leaders hoped that an allied victory in the war would return the concessions held by Germany in Shandong Province to China.

From August to September 1917 an "extraordinary parliament" made up of some members of the old National Assembly was held in Guangzhou. Sun was elected grand marshal of a military government that claimed to be the legal government of all China. But some members of the extraordinary parliament challenged Sun's leadership, so he retired and returned to Shanghai, where he and his wife lived from May 1918 to late 1920. He wrote up his memoirs and drew up detailed plans for the economic development of China, which he claimed would be assisted by money from foreign powers. At the Paris Peace Conference that concluded World War I, it was revealed that the Beijing government had made a secret agreement with Japan to award Japan all of Germany's former concessions in China. The Chinese people were outraged, and Chinese students led a massive demonstration against the agreement, known as the May Fourth Movement of 1919. Sun did not play a leading role in this movement but he drew upon the support of Chinese students. He contacted most of the Chinese warlords, and in October 1919 he and his followers reestablished the KMT to oppose the government in Beijing. At the same time, Guangzhou was taken by a warlord sympathetic to Sun. Sun and his wife returned there in November 1920, where he was elected president of the Chinese republic by the extraordinary parliament. But Sun and the warlord in Guangzhou soon clashed, and troops loyal to the warlord drove Sun out of the city. Sun's books and notes were destroyed, and his wife suffered a miscarriage, after which they never had a child. In August 1922 they returned to Shanghai, where he became a central figure in the negotiations by civil and military officials to reorganize the government in Beijing. He also received support from representatives of the U.S.S.R., which had undergone a revolution in 1917.

The military situation in Guangzhou changed and Sun was able to return in February 1923. Mikhail Borodin, a Soviet adviser, joined Sun there and helped him reorganize the KMT. The party adopted Sun's Three Principles of the People as the foundation of its doctrine: nationalism, democracy and people's livelihood. At this time the KMT and the newly founded Chinese Communist Party (CCP) were cooperating. The first national congress of the reorganized KMT was held in January 1924. It adopted the so-called Three New Policies, which included an alliance with the U.S.S.R., support for workers' and peasants' movements and collaboration with the CCP, although this last policy was controversial and opposed by some of Sun's colleagues.

In May 1924 a military academy was established at Whampoa (Huangpu), near Guangzhou. Chiang Kai-shek (1887–1975), one of Sun's lieutenants, whom Sun had sent to the U.S.S.R. to study, was made head of the academy. Two years later Chiang would lead the Northern Expedition against the warlords to unify China. In 1927 Chiang would marry Soong Mei-ling, the sister of Sun's wife, Soong Qingling. Sun lectured to the cadets at the military academy on his Three Principles, and a book compiled from his notes for those lectures remains the best source for Sun's thought. In 1924 Sun also completed his *Outline of National Reconstruction*, which foresaw that China's reconstruction would undergo three stages, from direct military government to leadership by the KMT and finally to a democratic form of government. However, the merchants of Guangzhou, who were heavily taxed and badly treated by some soldiers in armies loyal to Sun, organized an armed revolt against Sun that caused a great number of deaths and the destruction of much property. Sun lost many supporters, both within China and among the overseas Chinese.

In late 1924, following a coup in Beijing, Sun was invited to go there to help reorganize the government. He stopped in Shanghai and Japan and was well received in both places, but he was very sick with cancer when he arrived in Beijing on December 31, 1924. There he found out that the politicians and military leaders already had made an agreement with the foreign powers to once again respect the "unequal treaties" that the foreign powers had forced on China in the 19th century. This was the opposite of everything that Sun had worked for. However, the Chinese public was still sympathetic to Sun, who died on March 12, 1925. His wife gave him a Christian funeral, and then his body lay in state in the Forbidden City, the former imperial palace in Beijing, for three weeks. Thousands of people went to pay him their last respects, and he was eulogized all over China. His body was placed in an old temple in the Western Hills outside Beijing for five years and then was moved to a splendid mausoleum built near the tomb of the first emperor of the Ming dynasty in Nanjing, which became the KMT capital.

After Sun died, Chiang Kai-shek and the KMT violently turned against the Communists, and the two parties began fighting a civil war. They formed a united front to oppose the Japanese invasion, known as China's War of Resistance against Japan (1937–45; World War II), but then resumed their civil war. The CCP defeated the KMT in 1949, and Chiang Kai-shek and his followers fled to Taiwan island, where they established the provisional government of the Republic of China (ROC). The CCP founded the People's Republic of China (PRC) on the Chinese mainland. To this day, both governments claim to be the true heir of Sun Yat-sen's legacy as the founder of modern China. Soong Qingling carried on Sun's revolutionary activities after he died; she joined the CCP and became the most prominent woman in the PRC. See also CHIANG KAI-SHEK; CHINESE COMMUNIST PARTY; CIXI, EMPRESS DOWAGER; GUANGDONG PROVINCE; GUANGZHOU; HONG KONG; KANG YOUWEI; LI HONGZHANG; MACAO; MAY FOURTH MOVEMENT OF 1919; NANJING; NATIONALIST PARTY; OVERSEAS CHINESE; PUYI, HENRY; QING DYNASTY; QUEUE; REFORM MOVEMENT OF 1898; REPUBLIC OF CHINA; REVOLUTION OF 1911; REVOLUTIONARY ALLIANCE; RUSSO-JAPANESE WAR OF 1904–5; SELF-STRENGTHENING MOVEMENT; SHIMONOSEKI, TREATY OF; SINO-FRENCH WAR; SINO-JAPANESE WAR OF 1894–95; SOONG MEI-LING; SOONG QINGLING; TAIPING REBELLION; THREE PRINCIPLES OF THE PEOPLE; UNEQUAL TREATIES; WARLORD PERIOD; WHAMPOA MILITARY ACADEMY; WORLD WAR I; WUCHANG UPRISING; YUAN SHIKAI.

SUN YIXIAN   See SUN YAT-SEN.

SUNG, MOUNT   See FIVE SACRED MOUNTAINS OF DAOISM.

SUNG AI-LING   See SOONG MEI-LING.

SUNG CHAI-JEN See SONG JIAOREN.

SUNG CHIANG See OUTLAWS OF THE MARSH.

SUNG CHING-LING See SOONG QINLING.

SUNG DYNASTY See NORTHERN SONG DYNASTY; SONG DYNASTY; SOUTHERN SONG DYNASTY.

SUNG LI See GRAND CANAL; MING DYNASTY.

SUNG MEI-LING (SUNG MAY-LING) See SOONG MEI-LING.

SUNG TZU-WEN See REPUBLIC OF CHINA.

SUNG YAO-JU (CHARLES JONES SOONG) See REPUBLIC OF CHINA; SOONG MEI-LING; SOONG QINGLING; SUN YAT-SEN.

SUNGARI RIVER See SONGHUA RIVER.

SUNZI (Sun Tzu; fourth century B.C.) A military strategist, also known as Sun Wu, who is attributed with writing the classical Chinese treatise on the art of war and strategy, known as *The Art of War, The Military Science of Sunzi,* or simply the *Sunzi* (*Sun Tzu; Master Sun*). This text actually was compiled in the fourth century B.C. It was later incorporated into the canon of the Daoist religion, a collection of 1,400 texts printed in 1445 known as the *Daozang* (*Tao Tsung*). Bamboo slips bearing the text of the *Sunzi* were discovered in tombs on Yinque Mountain dating from the Han dynasty (206 B.C.–A.D. 220).

Sunzi was born to a military family in modern Huimin County, in the state of Qi in modern Shandong Province, and he studied military science. He began his text on the art of war by arguing that war is the most important matter to a government, determining the survival or death of the state. Some of the 13 chapters are titled "The Strategy of Attack," "Disposition of Military Strength," "Use of Energy," "Weaknesses and Strengths," "Maneuvering," "Variation of Tactics" and "The Use of Spies." Sunzi maintained that the way to victory is to work in harmony with nature rather than simply to employ brute force, and to outwit the enemy and win by deceit without having to fight a battle. He told the story of a general who tricked his enemy into believing an undefended city really was protected by a large army by leaving the city gates open and leisurely playing a musical instrument on the city walls. Sunzi taught that if a battle is necessary, it should be fought quickly, with surprise attacks that strike at the enemy's weak point, to force a quick victory.

Sunzi's work, which was compiled sometime between 400 and 320 B.C., was widely read at the end of the Warring States Period (403–221 B.C.), when many feudal states in China were contending with each other for power. It was certainly studied by the First Emperor, Qin Shi Huangdi, a harsh ruler who unified China under the Qin dynasty (221–206 B.C.). The *Sunzi* continued to influence Chinese military leaders, scholars and strategists, such as the great general Cao Cao (Ts'ao Ts'ao; 155–220), who wrote commentaries on the text. The modern Chinese Communist leader Mao Zedong (Mao Tse-tung) drew upon the ideas of Sunzi while developing his strategy for the Chinese Communist People's Liberation Army (PLA), which in 1949 defeated the Chinese Nationalist (Kuomintang; KMT) army led by Chiang Kai-shek, enabling the Chinese Communist Party (CCP) to found the People's Republic of China (PRC). In the eighth century the *Sunzi* was introduced to Japan and other foreign countries. In 1772 the work was introduced to Europe through a translation by a French Jesuit priest published in Paris, and it was studied by Napoleon Bonaparte. The work has now been translated into more than 12 languages.

In 1992 the Academy of Classical Learning of Sunzi was opened at Huimin in Shandong. The PRC has held several international symposiums on the military science of Sunzi, with scholars discussing such concepts as the application of Sunzi's principles to modern business management. Books on this topic have been published in Chinese, Japanese and English. Contemporary military leaders around the world have studied Sunzi's teachings on the art of war. During the Persian Gulf War in 1991, the chief commander of the U.S. Marine Corps required all marine officials to read an English translation of the *Sunzi*. See also CAO CAO; DAOISM; DAOIST CLASSICAL TEXTS; JESUITS; MAO ZEDONG; PEOPLE'S LIBERATION ARMY; QIN SHI HUANGDI; WARRING STATES PERIOD.

SUPERIOR MAN (*junzi* or *chun-tzu*) An important concept in the thought of Confucius (551–479 B.C.), whose school became accepted as orthodox by the Han imperial government (206 B.C.–A.D. 220). Up to his time, the term "superior man" literally meant superiority in bloodline, that is, the son of a ruler. Confucius changed the term to mean superiority in character, giving it an ethical connotation that did not depend on one's position in society. This was a radical change that scholars believe contributed to the decline of the feudal system in China, which ended in the third century B.C. According to Confucius, the "superior man" or "gentleman" has the quality of humanity (*ren* or *jen*), also translated as benevolence, perfect virtue, goodness or love, which makes him an authentic human being. The superior man is always calm and contented no matter what his circumstances, because he is always in harmony with the universe—in contrast to the inferior man, who is always worried and upset. The Chinese character that Confucius used for humanity or *ren* combines all the moral qualities of the superior man, including loyalty, the performance of duty, love for family and friends, kindness and courtesy. The superior man lives according to the "Golden Mean" (*zhongyong* or *chung yung*), which is similar to the Golden Rule in Western ethical thought; in Confucius's words, "Do not do to others what you would not want others to do to you." See also CONFUCIANISM; CONFUCIUS; FEUDAL SYSTEM; HUMANITY.

SUPREME PEOPLE'S COURT The highest judicial body in the People's Republic of China (PRC), which was founded by the Chinese Communist Party (CCP) led by Mao Zedong (Mao Tse-tung; 1893–1976) in 1949. The Supreme People's Court was first placed under the Central People's Government Council, with Mao as chairman, exercising the highest executive, legislative and judicial powers until the PRC's state constitution was promulgated in September 1954. This constitution formally established the Supreme People's Court and made it directly responsible to the National People's Congress Standing Committee. The president of the Supreme People's Court is the only high government appointment made by the National People's Congress rather than by the direct initiative of the CCP. The court, located in the capital city of Beijing, has jurisdiction over all lower and special courts and serves as the ultimate appellate court. It is authorized to deal with final appeals from lower courts and cases dealing with treason, subversion and international law. However, the Chinese legal system is oriented toward settling cases at lower judicial levels, often by mediation that keeps them from even being brought into court; cases are rarely taken all the way to the Supreme People's Court. Treason and espionage cases usually are handled by Special People's Courts, which are under the jurisdiction of the Supreme People's Court. Military courts, independent of civilian courts and directly subordinate to the Ministry of National Defense, comprise the majority of special courts. The Supreme People's Court reviews the decisions made by military courts. See also CONSTITUTION, STATE; LEGAL SYSTEM; NATIONAL PEOPLE'S CONGRESS; PEOPLE'S REPUBLIC OF CHINA.

SUPREME PEOPLE'S PROCURATORATES See GOVERNMENT STRUCTURE; LEGAL SYSTEM.

SUTRAS (BUDDHIST SCRIPTURES) See BUDDHISM; DUNHUANG; KUMARAJIVA; LOTUS SUTRA; PAGODA; TIANTAI SECT OF BUDDHISM; WHITE HORSE TEMPLE; XUANZANG.

SU-TSUNG (EMPEROR) See AN LUSHAN REBELLION; TANG DYNASTY; XUANZONG (EMPEROR).

SUZHOU   A city in Jilin Province in eastern China that is renowned for its beautiful canals and gardens. Located on the Grand Canal, which connects with the shore of Lake Tai, Suzhou is called the Venice of the East. It is paired with Hangzhou, the beautiful capital city of Zhejiang Province to the south, in the famous saying "In Heaven there is Paradise, on earth there are Hangzhou and Suzhou." Suzhou has a population of about 600,000, but millions of Chinese and overseas tourists visit the city each year.

Suzhou was settled at least 2,500 years ago. Historical records show that iron was smelted in the area during the Spring and Autumn Period (772–481 B.C.). The city became the capital of the state of Wu in 484 B.C. Suzhou developed into an important commercial center when the Grand Canal was built during the Sui dynasty (581–618). The Grand Canal is the longest waterway constructed by humans in the world. Even today lines of barges carry agricultural and manufactured goods along the Grand Canal and the many smaller canals that cross Suzhou. The Bridge of the Precious Belt, four miles outside the city, was built during the Tang dynasty (618–907) by a governor who donated his jade ceremonial belt to help finance the construction. The bridge has 53 arches that extend more than 110 yards across the canal; it is decorated with statues of lions. Marco Polo (1254–1324) visited Suzhou and praised it as a noble city with 6,000 stone bridges.

Suzhou flourished as a center for artists, scholars and financiers down through the Qing dynasty (1644–1911). It attracted numerous high-ranking government officials and wealthy merchants and landowners, many of whom built gardens around their villas where they could enjoy a peaceful retirement. The gardens, many of which are open to tourists today, were designed to be small replicas of the world of nature, with ponds and hills representing famous lakes and mountains. Goldfish and songbirds were placed in the gardens, as were large limestone rocks with unusual shapes taken from West Mountain Island in Lake Tai. The gardens include villas, courtyards, covered walkways, terraces, pavilions and towers, and are surrounded by walls for privacy.

From 1860 to 1863 troops of the Taiping Rebellion occupied Suzhou and damaged it badly. One of the Taiping kings, Fuwang, made his residence in the estate of a Qing official in Suzhou, which can still be seen. The city was rebuilt after imperial troops suppressed the rebellion, but it yielded its prominence as a trading center to the nearby city of Shanghai, one of China's two major ports. During the 20th century Suzhou suffered from the Japanese occupation, the War of Resistance against Japan (1937–45; World War II) and the civil war between the Communists and Nationalists (Kuomintang; KMT). Since 1949 the city has been industrialized. The government has also taken an active role in restoring the gardens and opening them to the public.

A section of the Garden of the Master of the Fishing Nets (Wangshiyuan) has been re-created in the Metropolitan Museum of Art in New York City. The smallest garden in Suzhou, it was originally built in 1140 at the residence of a high government official named Shi Zhengzhi (Shih Cheng-chih). The garden was his "net" to catch intelligent scholars with whom he liked to spend his time. The garden was restored in 1770.

The Surging Wave Garden and Pavilion (Canglangting) was built by a poet named Su Shenqing (Su Shen-ch'ing), who purchased a villa on the site in 1044; it is one of the oldest gardens in Suzhou, although it has been damaged and reconstructed several times. In 1954 the garden was restored and opened to the public. Lion Grove (Shizilin) was established at the rear of a temple that was built on the site by a Buddhist monk named Tianru (T'ien-chu) between 1341 and 1367. It contains large stones from Lake Tai, many of which are thought to resemble lions, thus giving the garden its name.

The Humble Administrator's Garden (Zhuozhengyuan), the largest garden in Suzhou, was built in 1513 by Wang Xianchen. (Wang Hsien-ch'en), a government official who retired to the city. Beautiful ponds cover more than half of the garden's four hectares. The garden is divided into three sections. The central part contains a lovely pavilion, a lotus pond with two artificial islands and the Hall of the Thirty-six Mandarin Ducks (Sanshiliu Yuanyang Guan) with real ducks swimming in the adjacent pond.

The Tarrying Garden (Liuyuan) was built during the Ming dynasty and reconstructed as a public garden in 1876. There are many courtyards and covered walkways as well as flower gardens, areas planted with trees to represent forests and scenic points that provide panoramic views. The focus of the garden is a 21-foot-high, 400-year-old rock from Lake Tai named the Cloud-Capped Peak. The Tarrying Garden and the Humble Administrator's Garden are two of China's four nationally protected gardens, along with the Summer Palace in Beijing and the Imperial Mountain Resort in Chengde in Hebei Province.

Xiyuan Garden, on the opposite side of the street from Tarrying Garden but originally connected with it, was owned by a Ming government official named Xu Shitai. His son built a Buddhist temple on the present site of Xiyuan, and several buildings and hundreds of Buddhist sculptures can still be seen. The Garden of Harmony (Yiyuan), with many flowers and ponds, is the most peaceful and natural of all the gardens in Suzhou. It is located where the villa of government minister Wu Kuan originally stood in the 15th century. A Qing government official purchased it in 1876 and enlarged the garden into two sections. The eastern half contains pavilions, halls and covered walkways housing rare paintings and calligraphy. The western half has lakes and artificial hills with pavilions.

Another famous Suzhou attraction is the Beisi Ta Pagoda, built during the Liang dynasty (502–57). It is the tallest pagoda south of the Yangzi River. The teahouse behind the pagoda is a meeting place for bird lovers who bring along their pet birds in cages. Tiger Hill (Huqiu) is a 117-foot-high hill constructed two miles northwest of Suzhou 2,500 years ago by the king of Wu as the tomb for his father. The Yunyan Pagoda on its peak was completed in 961. Cold Mountain Temple (Hanshan Si) can be seen about three miles west of Suzhou. It was constructed between 503 and 508 and later acquired the name of Hanshan, after an eccentric Chan (Zen) Buddhist monk and poet who resided here for a time in the seventh century. The temple was restored in 1905, and Japanese monks presented a bronze bell to replace the bell that earlier had been stolen by Japanese invaders. The Museum of Steles contains 1,000 engraved stone pillars and 10,000 stone rubbings. The Museum of Numismatics is the first of its kind in China. The Opera Museum contains an opera theater for performances. The Museum of Folk Customs has exhibits on daily life in Suzhou.

Suzhou is famous for its silk and silk embroidery, which were developed industries at least by the Five Dynasties Period (907–60) and reached their height during the Song dynasty (960–1279). The Suzhou Museum of Embroidery incorporates the Suzhou National Embroidery Research Institute, which was established in 1957 to train embroiderers, to study the history of the development of silk embroidery, which the Chinese consider an art form, and to display examples of the art. Silk and sandalwood fans and wood carvings are other famous local crafts. Several famous opera and drama companies are based in Suzhou; a traditional form of storytelling called *pingtan* is common there as well. The performers recite stories or sing them while playing a musical instrument and use a few simple props such as fans. The world-famous architect I. M. Pei was born in Suzhou in 1917. See also EMBROIDERY; FANS; GARDEN OF THE MASTER OF THE FISHING NETS; GARDENS; GRAND CANAL; HANGZHOU; JILIN PROVINCE; PAGODA; PEI, I.M.; ROCKS; SILK; STONE RUBBINGS; STONE TABLETS; STORYTELLING; TAI, LAKE; TAIPING REBELLION.

SUZONG, EMPEROR See AN LUSHAN REBELLION; TANG DYNASTY; XUANZONG (EMPEROR).

SWATOW WARE A type of sturdy ceramic produced in Fujian Province in southeastern China. Swatow pieces typically are large and have a rough finish. Many are brightly decorated with red, turquoise and black enamel. Others have pale-blue or celadon-type (blue-green) glazes with decorations made by applying slip (a mixture of clay and water) before firing in a kiln. Swatow ware was exported in large quantities to Japan, Southeast Asia, Indonesia and India during the 16th and 17th centuries. Swatow is the Western name for a major port city in Guangdong Province in southern China through which the ware was exported, called Shantou (Shan-t'ou) in Chinese. In the 18th century the British East India Company, which traded many Chinese goods to Europe, had a station on an island outside Swatow harbor. See also BRITISH EAST INDIA COMPANY; CELADON; ENAMELWARE; GUANGDONG PROVINCE; SHANTOU.

SWEET DEW INCIDENT See EUNUCHS; TANG DYNASTY.

SYNAGOGUES See JEWS; KAIFENG.

SZECHWAN (SZECH'UAN) PROVINCE See SICHUAN PROVINCE.

T

TA (T'A) See PAGODA.

TADZHIK See KASHGAR; MINORITIES, NATIONAL.

TA-HSUEH See GREAT LEARNING.

TAI (MINORITY GROUP) See DAI; DONG; ZHUANG.

TAI CHEN See DAI ZHEN.

TAI CHIN See DAI JIN.

TAI TUNG-YUAN See DAI ZHEN.

TAI WEN-CHIN See DAI JIN.

TAI YI See LANTERN FESTIVAL; YIN AND YANG.

T'AI-CHI-CH'UAN See TAIJIQUAN.

TAIHOKU See TAIPEI; TAIWAN.

TAIHU The third-largest lake in China, with an area covering about 8,000 square feet and an average depth of 6.5 feet. Taihu is located on the border between Zhejiang and Jiangsu provinces on China's eastern coast. There are 90 islands in Taihu. The largest is Xidong Tingshan, a lovely mountain 1,100 feet high, a popular tourist spot that has been celebrated by many poets. In Jiangsu Province, the city of Wuxi along the Grand Canal on the north shore of Taihu is a busy vacation resort where tourists enjoy boat rides. Ninqu Ta pagoda provides a panoramic view of the lake, which is surrounded by hills on which tea and a variety of fruits are grown. Freshwater fishing is an important activity. A large alluvial plain extends north from Taihu in Jiangsu Province, which has been heavily settled and cultivated since at least the sixth century. The major port of Shanghai, just east of Taihu, is connected with the lake by an extensive network of rivers and canals.

In Zhejiang Province, the Zhejiang Plain extends south from Taihu and is covered with a network of waterways and irrigation channels, notably the Grand Canal. Rice is the major crop, and wheat, beans, cotton, jute and tobacco also are cultivated. Huzhou (Wuxing) on the southern shore of Taihu is a major rice market and has a long-established silk industry. See also GRAND CANAL; JIANGSU PROVINCE; RICE; WUXI; ZHEJIANG PROVINCE.

TAIHU (T'AI-HI) ROCKS See ROCKS.

TAIJIQUAN (*t'ai-chi-ch'uan*) A martial art (*wushu*) that was developed in the 17th century by Chen Wangtin, a renowned martial arts master and military general who lived in Chenjiagou in Henan Province in central China. *Taijiquan* literally means "Supreme Pole Boxing." *Tai* means "supreme" or "ultimate." *Ji* means "polarity" in the sense of yin and yang, the two principles that the Daoist Chinese believe permeate everything in the universe. Yin is the female, dark, delicate principle; yang is the male, light, strong principle. *Quan* refers to the fist and is translated as boxing or "the fist way" of fighting. Master Chen created *taijiquan* by combining the traditional Chinese techniques of boxing (*quanshu*) and deep natural breathing with the medical theory known as *jingluo,* which is concerned with the flow of *qi* (*ch'i*) throughout the human body. *Qi* is the vital energy or life force within each person that the Chinese consider the basic force in the universe. This energy is believed to flow throughout the human body in 12 channels called meridians. Illness can result when the flow of *qi* is blocked, so the goal of *taijiquan* and other martial arts is to remove blockages that impede the flow of *qi*. A martial art called *qi gong* (*ch'i kung,* "energy work") that emphasizes deep breathing and slow, gentle movements often is practiced along with *taijiquan.* Although *taijiquan* movements are slow as well, the art originally was developed as a form of self-defense. However, the use of firearms in fighting diminished the military role of *taijiquan,* and eventually it was practiced as a means of promoting physical and mental well-being.

The Chinese people like to gather together early in the day to practice taijiquan *and other martial arts in public parks and lakesides.*
S.E. MEYER

Taijiquan exercises involve slow, curving movements of the arms, head, torso and legs. They require the harmonious coordination of all parts of the body and the concentration of the mind. The graceful movements combine artistic gestures used in Chinese operas and acrobatics, two stylized forms of traditional entertainment. The soft and yielding quality of the movements is paradoxically a form of strength. A person who practices *taijiquan* will take a firm stand and yield when attacked, rather than directly oppose the attacker. This strategy incorporates the attacker's own aggressive force and unbalances him or her. The defender remains in control and calmly repels the attacker's energy by pushing, throwing, or using pressure on the joints or sensitive points of the attacker's body.

The Chinese people like to gather together early in the morning to practice *taijiquan* under the trees in public places such as parks, riverbanks and lakesides. The gentle movements can be practiced even by people who are elderly or have chronic illnesses, such as high blood pressure and asthma. *Taijiquan* has been proven to enhance the performance of the body's circulatory, respiratory and metabolic systems. The movements also can be practiced as a form of spiritual meditation. Several different schools of *taijiquan* emerged, including Yang, Chen, Wu, Wu (written with a different Chinese character) and Sun. In 1956 a simplified set of *taijiquan* movements based on the exercises of the Yang School became widely accepted by practitioners of

the art. See also DAOISM; MARTIAL ARTS; QIQONG; YIN AND YANG.

TAI-MIAO TEMPLE See TAI, MOUNT.

TAIPA See MACAO.

TAIPEI The capital city and economic and cultural center of the Republic of China (ROC) on the island of Taiwan (formerly known as Formosa). Taipei is located across the 100-mile-wide Taiwan Strait from the People's Republic of China (PRC), which considers Taiwan one of its provinces. Chinese Nationalist leader Chiang Kai-shek established the ROC on Taiwan in 1949 when the Chinese Communists defeated the Nationalists (Kuomintang; KMT) and more than 2 million Nationalists fled to the island. Taipei had been founded in 1708 by Chinese immigrants, and it became a center for overseas trade in the 19th century. Japan acquired Taiwan after defeating China in the Sino-Japanese War of 1894–95 and made Taipei the capital, calling it Taihoku. In 1945, after Japan was defeated in World War II, Taiwan was returned to China. In December 1949 Taipei became the provisional capital of the Chinese Nationalist government. Today Taipei has a population of about 3 million. The city is part of a large industrial area, with the main products being textiles, electronic parts, electrical machinery and appliances, wires and cables, and refrigeration equipment. The nearby port of

Keelung (Chilung), east of Taipei, has a large shipbuilding industry. Taipei lies midway between two of the world's largest ports, Shanghai and Hong Kong, and has become a major trading center.

Popular tourist sites in Taipei include the Presidential Mansion, Taiwan Jinja Shrine, the 15th-century Kentengi Chinese Temple and Buddhist temples at Lion Head Mountain. The National Palace Museum houses one of the world's largest collections of Chinese paintings, calligraphy, porcelain and ancient artifacts, most of which were brought from mainland China by fleeing Nationalists. The museum contains the Chiang Kai-shek Memorial Hall, built in the classical Chinese style. Dragon Mountan (Longshan or Lungshan) Temple, dedicated to Guanyin (Kuan Yin), the Buddhist Goddess of Mercy, is the finest example of Chinese temple architecture in Taiwan. Mount Yang-min nearby is a popular recreation area with many hot springs. See also CHIANG KAI-SHEK; CIVIL WAR BETWEEN COMMUNISTS AND NATIONALISTS; NATIONAL PALACE MUSEUM; NATIONALIST PARTY; REPUBLIC OF CHINA; TAIWAN; TEMPLES.

TAIPING REBELLION (1850–64) The largest uprising in mid-19th century China, which nearly overthrew the Manchu Qing dynasty (1644–1911). The leader of the Taiping Rebellion was Hong Xiuquan (Hung Hsiu-ch'uan; 1813–64), who was born in Guangdong Province in southern China to a poor family belonging to the Hakka, a group within the Han ethnic majority that speaks a different dialect and practices its own customs. Hong was able to gain an education but failed in several attempts to pass the examinations in Guangzhou (Canton) for a position in the imperial bureaucracy. While in Guangzhou he was given pamphlets written by the first Chinese convert to Protestant Christianity. In 1837 Hong became ill, fell into a trance and had dramatic visions, but he recovered and became a village schoolteacher for six years. In 1843 he read the Christian pamphlets, which caused him to announce that he was the younger brother of Jesus Christ and that he had been commanded by God to destroy "pagan idols" and bring people to worship the true God. After Hong studied Christianity for two months with Issachar J. Roberts, an American Protestant missionary in Guangzhou, he began destroying ancestral tablets in Confucian temples, which angered many Chinese, although some joined his cause. Hong and his followers moved north into Jiangsu Province, where they converted thousands to their movement, most of them belonging to the Hakka, Miao and Yao ethnic minorities, women as well as men. Hakka and minority women did not bind their feet, as did Han Chinese women, so they were able to march and fight. In three years 30,000 converts joined Hong's movement, which he called the Worship God Society (Baishangdihui or Pai Shang Ti Hui). He preached that God had called him to establish the Kingdom of God on Earth by overthrowing the Manchu Qing dynasty.

In July 1850 the Taipings fought Qing troops for the first time, and thousands of impoverished peasants, unemployed laborers, pirates and bandits, many of whom belonged to anti-Qing secret societies such as the Triads, joined the Taiping movement. The southern Chinese were especially opposed to the Manchus, a tribal group that had entered China from Manchuria (modern northeastern China) and overthrown the Han Chinese Ming dynasty (1368–1644). In

the mid-19th century China suffered terrible natural disasters, including floods and droughts that caused widespread famine. In addition, Great Britain and other Western powers had defeated the Qing in the Opium Wars and forced them to open several Chinese cities as treaty ports to foreign traders and residents. This disrupted the Chinese economy and put many Chinese laborers out of work.

In September 1851 Hong claimed to found a new dynasty and took the title "Heavenly king" (tianwang or t'ien-wang) of the "Heavenly Kingdom of Great Peace" (Taiping Tiangu or T'ai-p'ing T'ien-ku; Taiping for short). He also awarded the title "king" to five other Taiping leaders and appointed one of the kings, a general named Yang Xiuqing (Yang Hsiuch'ing), commander in chief. Hong advocated many radical social reforms that alienated the Confucian-educated Han Chinese literati, or scholars, who staffed the imperial government. He claimed that the Taipings would establish a new order in which peasants owned and farmed the land in common; money, food and clothing would be shared equally; women would be equal to men; and many practices that caused the Chinese great suffering would be eliminated, including slavery, concubinage, arranged marriage, footbinding, prostitution, opium smoking and torture by legal officials. Although men and women were strictly segregated, many women fought in Taiping battles and held official positions in the Taiping government.

In 1852 Taiping forces marched north through Hunan Province and east down the Yangzi River (Changjiang) valley. Thousands more impoverished peasants and revolutionary bands joined them. In March 1853 the Taipings captured Nanjing, the capital of the Ming and southern capital of the Qing on the Yangzi River. There they established their headquarters, called "Heavenly capital" (tianjing or t'ien-ching). By this time the Taipings numbered more than 1 million. Hong lived like a king in seclusion in his palace in Nanjing, accompanied by concubines, despite his own teachings. Altogether the Taipings captured 600 Chinese walled cities, and they sent an army north toward the Qing capital at Beijing. In 1855 the Yellow River (Huanghe) caused destructive floods in northern China when it changed its course, as it had done many times before, and made its way to the sea north of the Shandong Peninsula rather than south of it. The Taipings sent north were defeated by Qing forces in Shandong in 1855, partly because the southern Chinese soldiers were not used to the cold northern winter weather. The Taipings sent another army west to gain control of Jiangsu, Anhui, Hubei and Hunan provinces, but this army was opposed by forces raised in Hunan by a Han Chinese government official named Zeng Guofan (Tseng Kuo-fan).

As Hong Xiuquan became more reclusive, Taiping king Yang Xiuching took power into his own hands. In 1856 he plotted to overthrow Hong, but another king assassinated Yang and murdered thousands of his supporters. The Taiping king and military commander Shi Dakai (Shih Ta-k'ai) put an end to the slaughter and left the Taiping movement in disgust. These events divided and weakened the Taipings, who were now being forced into a defensive position by Qing troops led by Zeng Guofan, Li Hongzhang (Li Hung-chang) and Zuo Zongtang (Chuo Chung-t'ang). In 1860 the Qing appointed Zeng Guofan imperial commissioner and governor-general of the Taiping-controlled territories and made him commander of the Qing anti-Taiping forces. The success of Zeng's Hunan army increased the power of the Han literati and further weakened the Manchus. Zeng's forces were assisted by the volunteer Chinese and Western "Ever-Victorious Army," led by the American Frederick Ward Townsend. When Townsend was killed in 1862, the Englishman Charles George Gordon took his place. Initially Westerners had been hopeful about Hong's Christian ideals, but they soon realized that his religion was actually a dangerous revolutionary movement, and they preferred to keep the Qing government in power because it was weak and could be manipulated to their advantage.

From 1860 to 1864 bitter fighting took place between Taiping forces and combined Qing and Western forces in the lower Yangzi valley, especially for control of Shanghai, a recently established treaty port at the mouth of the river. The combined Qing and Western forces placed Nanjing under siege on May 31, 1862. Troops led by Zeng Guofan's younger brother, Zeng Guochuan (Tseng Kuo-ch'uan), finally took the city from the Taipings on July 19, 1864, after a 15-day battle. Hong had committed suicide in June. His son and successor escaped from Nanjing but was later captured. None of the Taipings surrendered; they were all slaughtered or burned to death. During the 14 years of the Taiping Rebellion, more than 30 million people were killed in China.

Other rebellions took place in China around the same time as the Taiping Rebellion, including the Nian Rebellion (1852–68) and uprisings by Muslims in the northwest and southwest. In fact, there were more than 100 armed uprisings in China from 1840 to 1850. The Taiping Rebellion was a major source of inspiration for the 20th-century Communist guerrilla leader Mao Zedong (Mao Tse-tung), who became chairman of the Chinese Communist Party (CCP), which founded the People's Republic of China (PRC) in 1949. See also ANCESTRAL TABLETS; CHINESE COMMUNIST PARTY; CHRISTIANITY; CONCUBINAGE; FOOTBINDING; GORDON, CHARLES; GUANGZHOU; HAKKA; HONG XIUQUAN; LI HONGZHANG; MANCHU; MAO ZEDONG; MUSLIMS; NANJING; NIAN REBELLION; PEASANTS AND PEASANT REBELLIONS; QING DYNASTY; SHI DAKAI; TREATY PORTS; WARD, FREDERICK TOWNSEND; YAO; ZENG GUOFAN.

TAIPINGDAO (T'AI-P'ING-T'AO) See YELLOW TURBANS REBELLION.

TAIREN See DALIAN.

TAISHAN A mountain in Shandong Province in eastern China considered the most important of the five sacred mountains of the Daoist religion where Chinese emperors formerly performed sacrificial rituals for Heaven and Earth there. It is also known as Eastern Peak (Dongyue). Since it was the farthest east of the sacred mountains, the Chinese believed that the sun began its daily journey westward from Taishan. The mountain has been revered as sacred for more than 2,500 years. Emperor Qin Shi Huangdi, who unified China under the Qin dynasty (221–206 B.C.), traveled to Taishan to make offerings. During the Song dynasty (960–1279), Emperor Zhenzong (Chen-tsung) glorified the mountain with the rank of "Equal with Heaven." Many columns along the path to the summit are inscribed with prayers offered to the mountain's deity. Over the centuries more than 250 temples and monuments were built on the mountain by members of the Confucian, Daoist and Buddhist religions. Daimiao Temple, at the southern foot of Taishan, the starting point for those climbing the mountain, is where emperors made sacrifices to the Earth. Records from the 12th century state that the temple compound then included several hundred buildings and towers, but only a few buildings have survived. The main hall of Daimiao, Tiankuang Dian, was built in 1009 and restored in 1956. Various emperors placed 157 engraved stone pillars, the oldest dating from 209 B.C., in the grounds.

Pilgrims travel to Taishan on a 15-mile-long road leading north from Tai'an city. Most pilgrims come in February and March, before the season for sowing crops. They climb a path of nearly 7,000 stone steps that lead to the summit 5,069 feet above sea level. Emperors were carried up the steps on a chair. There are teahouses along the path for refreshment and guest houses where visitors can stay overnight. Pilgrims sometimes schedule their climbs to arrive at the summit in time to watch the sunrise on Sunrise Peak (Riguan Feng). The highest peak is called Jiding or Yuhuang Ding. The top half of Taishan often is hidden in clouds.

Confucius (551–479 B.C.), whose philosophy was accepted as the orthodox religion by the Chinese imperial government during the Han dynasty (206 B.C.–A.D. 220), was born at Qufu in the state of Lu, 40 miles south of Taishan. When he climbed the mountain, he remarked that the world appeared very small from the summit, which gave him an important lesson in humility. A memorial arch to Confucius has been erected on Taishan near the First Heavenly Gate, before the arch to the Steps to Heaven and the Red Gate.

Farther up the mountain, Sanguan Miao Temple was built to honor the Three Rulers of Daoism, the deities of Heaven, Earth and Water. The largest monument on Taishan is the Ten-Thousand-Foot Tablet (Wanzhang Bei), which can be seen from the plain below that extends from the mountain. It is engraved with a long poem by the Qianlong emperor (1711–99), a great calligrapher and literary patron, that praises Taishan. His son and successor, the Jiajing emperor (r. 1796–1820), planted 22,000 pine trees higher up, at the beginning of the final climb leading to the South Heavenly Gate (Nantianmen). The gate is guarded by a sculpture of Guandi, the God of War. Near the top is the Azure Clouds Temple (Bixiaci) dedicated to Bixia Yuanzhun, a Chinese deity known as the Original Princess of the Purple and Azure Clouds. On the top of Taishan is Yuhuang Dian, a temple dedicated to the Jade Emperor, the ruler of Heaven and the highest god in Daoism. In 1987 UNESCO placed Taishan on its list of world natural and cultural heritage sites. The Chinese have been preserving 25 ancient buildings, more than 200 engraved stone tablets and 1,100 rock carvings on Taishan. See also CONFUCIUS; DAOISM; FIVE SACRED MOUNTAINS OF DAOISM; FOUR SACRED MOUNTAINS OF BUDDHISM; GUANDI; JADE EMPEROR; STONE TABLETS; TEMPLES.

T'AI-TSUNG, EMPEROR (TANG) See TAIZONG (EMPEROR) (TANG).

T'AI-TSUNG, EMPEROR (SONG) See TAIZONG (EMPEROR) (SONG).

TAIWAN Formerly known as Formosa; an island across the 100-mile-wide Taiwan Strait from mainland China that since 1949 has been the seat of government of the Republic of China (ROC). Taiwan has a population of more than 21 million, most of whom live on the fertile plain along the west coast. The capital city of Taipei is located at the northern tip of the island, which is about 250 miles long and 90 miles wide, with a chain of high mountains running north to south, and has a subtropical climate. Taiwan experiences many earthquakes and, in the late summer, violent typhoons. It is covered with forests, and camphor wood has been one of its traditional exports. Taiwan's main ports are Keelung (Chilung), near Taipei, and Kaohsiung, a highly industrialized city in the south. Other cities include Taichung, Tainan and Changhua. The main agricultural products are rice, sugar, tea and bananas. Fishing and food processing are important industries.

Chinese Nationalist (Kuomintang; KMT) leader Chiang Kai-shek (1887–1975) established the ROC on Taiwan in 1949 when the Chinese Communists defeated the Nationalists, and more than 2 million Nationalists fled to the island. The Chinese Communist Party (CCP) established the People's Republic of China (PRC) on the mainland. The Chinese had known of the island as early as the seventh century. Taiwan had a small population of natives but remained an undeveloped frontier region until several centuries ago. In the 1500s Portuguese sailors named the island Ilha Formosa ("Beautiful Island"), so foreigners called it Formosa, while the Chinese called it Taiwan. In 1624 the Dutch took control of the southwestern area of the island, brought many Chinese settlers there and taught them modern farming methods. In 1661 the Dutch were forced to give Taiwan back to China by Zheng Chenggong (Cheng Ch'eng-kung; 1624–62), popularly known as Coxinga (Koxinga), a Chinese adventurer who supported the faction trying to keep alive the Ming dynasty (1368–1644) after it was overthrown by the Manchus, who established the Qing dynasty (1644–1911). Coxinga established a government on Taiwan and promoted emigration from the Chinese mainland. After he died in 1662 his successors fell into opposing factions, and in 1683 the Qing attacked Taiwan, defeated the final Ming resistors and incorporated Taiwan as a Qing prefecture. In 1886 the Qing made Taiwan a province of China. Japan acquired Taiwan after defeating China in the Sino-Japanese War of 1894–95 and made Taipei the capital, calling it Taihoku. Japan modernized and industrialized Taiwan and used it as the main staging area for its invasion of the Philippines and Southeast Asia in 1941. In 1945, after Japan was defeated in World War II, Taiwan was returned to China. In December 1949 Taipei became the provisional capital of the Chinese Nationalist government. The Nationalists brought to Taiwan thousands of art objects from the imperial collection in China. These are exhibited by the National Palace Museum in Taipei.

Chiang Kai-shek served as president of the ROC until he died in 1975, when his son Chiang Ching-kuo became president. The United States had withdrawn support for the Nationalist government when it fled to Taiwan, but after North Korea invaded South Korea in 1950, the United States changed its policy and provided military support to the ROC. Many other countries also supported the Nationalists as the legitimate government of China and opposed the Communist PRC government. However, in 1971 the PRC was admitted to the United Nations and Taiwan was expelled, and many countries switched their diplomatic ties from the Nationalist ROC to the Communist PRC. On January 1, 1979 the United States ended diplomatic relations with Taiwan and gave diplomatic recognition to the PRC. However, the U.S. Congress passed the Taiwan Relations Act under which the United States continued to give Taiwan military support and maintain economic ties.

Chiang Ching-kuo introduced political changes in Taiwan that would lead to a democratic government. The Nationalist government had put martial law into effect on Taiwan in 1949, but in 1987 martial law was lifted and an opposition political party was allowed to win seats in open elections. After Chiang Ching-kuo died in 1988, his nominee Lee Teng-hui was elected president. In 1990 the parliament opened, the first in 40 years to have elected representatives. In 1991 President Lee restored constitutional rule and opened the way for free elections. Lee is Taiwan's first president born on the island rather than the Chinese mainland. The dominant KMT Party prefers reunification with China to independence. Lee regards Taiwan as an equal to the PRC and seeks a seat for Taiwan in the United Nations as a step toward bringing the two Chinas together. In 1995 the first air link between Taiwan and China was initiated after 46 years, with Air Macau flying from Taiwan to Macau (Macao) and then to Beijing. That same year the U.S. government granted President Lee a visa to visit his alma mater, Cornell University. In protest, the PRC government, which also seeks reunification with Taiwan, recalled its U.S. ambassador, halted military cooperation with the Pentagon and began testing missiles only 85 miles off Taiwan. The PRC conducted further military exercises off the island in the spring of 1996 to intimidate the country before its election on March 23. The election was held and Lee was elected president by a solid majority.

Taiwan's economy has developed rapidly since World War II. The ROC government has maintained economic relations with the PRC that had a total value of $2.5 billion in 1988. Taiwan has many factories and big infrastructure projects. It has become a major trading center, due to its location south of Japan between the major international ports of Shanghai and Hong Kong. Manufactured goods include textiles, chemical fertilizers, electronics and petroleum. By 1995 Taiwan was the world's 13th-largest trading economy and had built up $90 billion in cash reserves, second only to Japan. In January 1996 its per capita gross domestic product made Taiwan the 25th richest country in the world, with household income averaging $28,000 a year. See also CAMPHOR; CHIANG CHING-KUO; CHIANG KAI-SHEK; CIVIL WAR BETWEEN COMMUNISTS AND NATIONALISTS; KOREAN WAR; LEE TENG-HUI; MACAO; NATIONAL PALACE MUSEUM; NATIONALIST PARTY; REPUBLIC OF CHINA; TAIPEI; UNITED NATIONS; ZHENG CHENGGONG.

TAIWAN RELATIONS ACT See REPUBLIC OF CHINA; TAIWAN.

TAIXUE (T'AI-HSUEH) See FIVE CLASSICS OF CONFUCIANISM.

TAIYUAN The capital city of Shanxi Province in northern China, with a population of more than 2 million. Taiyuan, located on the Fen River, is a major industrial center due to the vast deposits of coal and iron in the Taiyuan Basin, which was a lake until about 5,000 years ago. The soil is also very rich, composed of layers of loess, a fine yellow dust that blows in from desert regions to the west. Westerners developed Taiyuan between 1889 and 1909, building a railway, installing electricity and telegraph and telephone lines, and establishing a university and a military academy. After 1949 industrialization was furthered, with steel, chemicals and textiles becoming the major products.

Taiyuan is historically important. A town named Jinyang was built in this area during the Western Zhou dynasty (1100–771 B.C.). It was situated in the corridor through which waves of nomadic invaders poured into the central Chinese plain from the northern steppes over many centuries to conquer the Chinese Empire. The city changed hands many times and became strongly fortified with the best imperial troops stationed there to hold off the invaders. Some Chinese generals also used Taiyuan (still called Jinyang) as a base from which to attempt the overthrow of ruling dynasties. A general named Li Yuan, who had been sent to Taiyuan to suppress a peasant revolt, toppled the Sui dynasty (581–618) and founded the Tang dynasty (618–907). During the Song dynasty (960–1279), the city was held by the Northern Han, a royal house that did not want to submit to the Song. In 979 the Song forced the city to surrender and then destroyed it completely, diverting the waters of the Jin and Fen rivers to wash away the ashes. The survivors settled in a nearby village and developed a new city, which became a prosperous center for trading and crafts; the first official government pottery kilns were established here during the Song dynasty. The city, which later became modern Taiyuan, was taken by rulers of the Jin (1115–1234) and Mongol Yuan (1279–1368) dynasties.

In 1644 the peasant leader Li Zicheng (Li Tzu-cheng) attempted to found a new dynasty at Taiyuan, but the city was conquered by the newly founded Qing dynasty (1644–1911). Li Zicheng is still commemorated in Taiyuan at the lunar New Year Festival. Secret rebel societies, such as the White Lotus, existed in Taiyuan at least since the 11th century. The city played a role in the Boxer Uprising of 1900 against the Qing dynasty. Following the Revolution of 1911, the northern warlord Yan Xishan (Yan Hsi-shan) ruled as a dictator from Taiyuan until the Chinese Communist Party took power in 1949. Shanxi Museum houses exhibits on the historical development of the area.

Fifteen miles southeast of Taiyuan can be found Jinci Temple, a group of temple buildings erected by the Jin family during the Northern Wei dynasty (386–535). Mount Wutai (Wutaishan; also known as Cold Clear Mountain), about 110 miles northeast of Taiyuan, is one of the four sacred mountains of Chinese Buddhism and is believed to be the site where Manjusri, the Bodhisattva of Wisdom, appeared in China. See also BOXER UPRISING; FOUR SACRED MOUNTAINS OF BUDDHISM; LI ZICHENG; LOESS; PEASANTS AND PEASANT REBELLIONS; SHANXI PROVINCE; SONG DYNASTY; TANG DYNASTY; WARLORD PERIOD; WESTERN ZHOU DYNASTY; WHITE LOTUS SECRET SOCIETY.

TAIZONG (EMPEROR) (T'ai-tsung; 600–649)   Known as Tang Taizong; the second emperor of the Tang dynasty (618–907). His personal name was Li Shimin; Taizong, meaning "Grand Ancestor," was his posthumous reign name (r. 626–49). Li Shimin came from a military family and helped put his father, Li Yuan, on the throne as the first Tang emperor Gaozu (Kao-tsu, "High Progenitor"; r. 618–26). The second son of Gaozu, Li Shimin served as a general during the campaign that brought eastern China into the Tang empire. However, his father and brothers made several attempts to kill him because of his strong power base. He then killed his brothers, forced his father to abdicate in 626 and took the throne himself, becoming one of the greatest emperors in Chinese history.

In 630 Emperor Taizong finally halted the incursions into China by nomadic Turkish tribes from the north. He expanded the Tang empire westward into Central Asia and revived the trade routes collectively known as the Silk Road, which terminated at the Tang capital city of Chang'an (modern Xi'an). Foreign traders of many different nationalities settled in Chang'an, which became the largest and most cosmopolitan city in the world.

During Taizong's reign, the Chinese Buddhist monk Xuanzang (Hsuan-tsang; c. 602–64) made a pilgrimage from 629 to 645 to Buddhist centers in India, where he collected scriptures and brought them back to Chang'an for translation. Emperor Taizong built him a retreat called the Great Wild Goose Pagoda, which can still be seen in Xi'an. While Taizong was sympathetic to Buddhism, he supported Confucianism as the state religion and ordered the building of temples dedicated to Confucius (551–479 B.C.) in every Chinese province and county. In 647 he decreed that all of those temples were national shrines commemorating not only Confucius but also great Confucian scholars, whose names were inscribed on stone tablets, or steles. Many of these steles can be seen in the Forest of Tablets (Beilin or Pei-lin) at Xi'an. Taizong also institutionalized the examination system, begun by the Han dynasty emperor Wudi (Wu-ti; r. 141–87 B.C.), to select the men best educated in Confucian scholarship to serve in the imperial bureaucracy. Taizong selected excellent men to serve as government ministers, especially prime minister Wei Zheng (580–643), who was not afraid to criticize Taizong's policies if they were not in accord with the Confucian ideal that a ruler should benefit his people. When Taizong died in 649, his ninth son succeeded him as Emperor Gaozong, whose wife ruled the Tang dynasty as the notorious Empress Wu. See also BUDDHISM IN CHINA; CHANG'AN; CONFUCIANISM; CONFUCIUS; GAOZONG (EMPEROR); GAOZU (EMPEROR); IMPERIAL EXAMINATION SYSTEM; SILK ROAD; TANG DYNASTY; WU, EMPRESS; XI'AN.

TAIZONG (EMPEROR) (T'ai-tsung; 939–997)   Also known as Song Taizong (Sung T'ai-tsung); the second emperor of the Song dynasty (960–1279). Taizong, the younger brother of Taizu (T'ai-tsu), founder of the dynasty, finished the process of reunifying China and centralizing government control that his brother had begun. Taizong's real name was Zhao Kuangyi (Chao K'uang-yi); Taizong, meaning "Grand Ancestor," was his posthumous reign name. He made his career in the military, as had his father and his brother Taizu, who appointed Taizong commander of the Palace Corps during his reign. When Taizu died in 976, Taizong took power and reigned as Song emperor from 976 to 997. His brother had not been able to bring all of China under Song rule, but Taizong completed the reunification of China by conquering the state of Wuyue in 978 and the state of Northern Han in 979. The only territory that Taizong was not able to conquer was that held by the Khitan (Qidan), a nomadic group in the northeast that had established the Liao dynasty (947–1125). He sent many military expeditions against the Khitan, but they always fought back the Chinese, and in 979 they handed him a disastrous defeat at Gaolinghe near modern Beijing. Taizong centralized the Song government by relying on the examinations for the imperial bureaucracy or civil service to find qualified civilian literati, or Confucian scholars, to replace the military people who had held government positions. He was a writer and calligrapher himself, and a patron of scholarship. He also strengthened the Song government's control of taxation and currency. During his reign the Song capital city of Kaifeng grew rapidly as a center for commerce and communications. See also IMPERIAL BUREAUCRACY; IMPERIAL EXAMINATION SYSTEM; KAIFENG; LIAO DYNASTY; LITERATI; SONG DYNASTY; TAIZU, EMPEROR.

TAIZU (EMPEROR) (T'ai-tsu; 928–976) Also known as Song Taizu (Sung T'ai-tsu); the founder and first emperor of the Song dynasty (960–1279). His personal name was Zhao Kuangyin (Chao K'uang-yin); Taizu, meaning "Grand Progenitor," was his posthumous reign name (r. 960–76). Taizu's greatest accomplishment was the reunification of China, thus ending the country's division into many small kingdoms during the so-called Five Dynasties Period (907–60) and Ten Kingdoms Period (907–59). Zhao Kuangyin, like his father, had made his career in the military. In 959 he was appointed commander of the Palace Corps by Emperor Shizong (Shihtsung; r. 954–59) of the Later Zhou dynasty. Shizong chose him because he was honest and had a respect for books and learning. When the emperor died, his seven-year-old heir was deposed by a mutiny of the Palace Corps, who placed Zhao Kuangyin on the throne as the new emperor of the new Song dynasty. Taizu set about bringing all of the Chinese kingdoms under Song control and succeeded in conquering all but two by the time he died in 976. He also weakened the power of the provincial military, which was especially strong in northeastern China, and persuaded many high-ranking military commanders to retire to their provincial estates. He reorganized the imperial bureaucracy, or civil service, by centralizing government control in the Song capital city of Kaifeng. Civilian scholars, or literati, were selected by Confucian-based examinations to hold positions in the imperial bureaucracy. The Song inherited this system from the Tang dynasty (618–907) but greatly increased the number of scholars chosen. They were appointed to replace military men who had been holding government positions, especially in the provinces. Taizu prevented rivalries after his death by appointing his brother to succeed him as emperor. Known as Emperor Taizong (T'ai-tsung; r. 976–97), he continued his brother's policies of centralizing and building up the literati-run imperial bureaucracy. Taizong also sent expeditions against the Khitan, who controlled a large kingdom in northeastern China (modern Manchuria and part of Hebei Province) under the Liao dynasty (947–1125), but was never able to conquer them. Taizu had avoided military confrontations with the Khitan in

order to consolidate his power as ruler of the Chinese Empire. See also CONFUCIANISM; IMPERIAL BUREAUCRACY; IMPERIAL EXAMINATION SYSTEM; KAIFENG; LIAO DYNASTY; SONG DYNASTY; TAIZONG (EMPEROR).

TAKIN A large animal native to Chinese forests that has become an endangered species. Scientists classify the takin (*Budorcas taxicolor*) as kin to the sheep and the ox and as similar to the native North American musk ox. The takin and the musk ox are ancient ungulates. The adult takin is about seven feet long and weighs from 440 to 660 pounds (a weight comparable to that of a yak or water buffalo). The takin has a sheeplike body, a short tail, a large, wide face with a long beard, and horns that twist up and out in an unusual shape. It uses its horns to attack predators. There are four subspecies of takin: the golden takin inhabits the Qinling Mountain Range in Shaanxi Province; the yellow-brown Sichuan takin inhabits Sichuan Province; the Bhutan takin inhabits the Himalaya Mountain Range in Tibet, Nepal and Bhutan, and has black or dark brown hair; and the Mishmi takin inhabits India, Myanmar (Burma) and Yunnan Province in China. The takin dwells in coniferous and broadleaf forests and alpine meadows at altitudes of about 5,000 to 15,000 feet above sea level. In the winter it descends to slightly lower elevations in search of food. In the summer it consumes 40 varieties of grasses, while in the winter it subsists mostly on bamboo leaves, lichens and the bark of fir trees. It licks rock salt in caves or from the soil for its mineral needs. Takins live in groups that commonly contain 10 to 40 animals, although a male takin frequently lives by himself. The animals mate during August and September, and the calves are born in February and March. The Chinese government has established 10 nature preserves in Sichuan and Shaanxi provinces to preserve the takin. Two other endangered species, the Giant Panda and the golden monkey, also inhabit these regions. See also HIMALAYA MOUNTAIN RANGE; MONKEY; OX; PANDA; QINLING MOUNTAIN RANGE; SICHUAN PROVINCE; YAK.

TAKLIMAKAN DESERT The largest desert in China, lying at the center of the Tarim Basin, a huge wasteland that covers about half of Xinjiang-Uighur Autonomous Region in northwestern China. Known as the Sea of Death, the Taklimakan is the second largest desert in the world after the Sahara. It covers 248 miles north to south and 620 miles east to west. The name Taklimakan means "the place you cannot leave" in Uighur. The basin is surrounded by mountains, from which numerous streams drain down into the sands of the Taklimakan Desert. The Tarim River, the longest inland river in China, flows from the Kunlun Mountains through the center of the desert for 438 miles and disappears in the eastern region of the Tarim Basin. The Taklimakan Desert covers about 126,120 square miles, nearly half of the total desert area in China. It receives less than four inches of rain a year, the least amount of rainfall in China. When rain does fall, it evaporates before it reaches the ground because the desert is so hot. The temperature of the sand has been recorded at 183°F. In the winter temperatures fall well below 0°F. On windy days, especially in the spring, sandstorms turn the sky as dark as if it were night. Most of the desert comprises moving sand dunes that, due to winds from the northeast and northwest, tend to drift southward. There is no vegetation, except for tamarisk bushes, poplars and other bushes that grow around the edge of the desert and along the few riverbanks. Huge deposits of oil, natural gas and minerals have been discovered in the Taklimakan Desert.

The only animals that can cross this desert are wild asses and camels. The so-called Silk Road, the ancient routes along which Chinese silk, porcelain and other goods were sent by camel caravans to the Mediterranean world and Western technology and culture were brought to China, crossed the Tarim Basin. Both the northern route, which passed through the city of Turpan, and the southern route, which passed through Hotan, skirt the desert. Today these cities and the other small oases that ring the desert are populated mainly by a Muslim national minority group known as the Uighurs. See also HOTAN; KUNLUIN MOUNTAIN RANGE; SILK ROAD; TARIM BASIN; TURPAN; UIGHUR; XINJIANG-UIGHUR AUTONOMOUS REGION.

TALAS, BATTLE OF   A major battle in 751 in which Chinese forces of the Tang dynasty (618–907) led by Korean-born General Gao Xianzhi (Kao Hsien-chih) were disastrously defeated by Muslim Arab forces near the Talas River in modern Afghanistan. The Arabs had spread rapidly westward across North Africa to the Iberian Peninsula (modern Spain) and eastward to Central Asia in the seventh century. The defeat at Talas meant that the Chinese lost control over the land route through Central Asia, known as the Silk Road, and lost the region around the city of Kashgar known as Western Turkestan (part of modern Xinjiang-Uighur Autonomous Region). However, the Battle of Talas also marked the end of Arab expansion eastward. Thus scholars consider it one of the decisive battles in world history.

In 738 the Chinese had taken back from the Tibetans the Tarim Basin region in Xinjiang. States beyond the Pamir Mountain Range had agreed to be vassals of the Chinese Empire for protection against the threat of Arab invasion. In 747 General Gao also had defeated the Tibetans in this same region. But the Chinese defeat at Talas returned the Tarim Basin to Tibetan control, and shortly after this entire region fell permanently into Muslim hands. Around the same time, Tang forces suffered a severe defeat in southwestern China. In 750 the Kingdom of Nanzhao (Nanchao) in modern Yunnan Province had a dispute with the imperial Chinese that flared up into warfare, and Tang forces were soundly beaten in 751 and 754, giving rise to an independent Nanzhao kingdom that lasted five centuries.

The military defeats in northwestern and southwestern China may have contributed to the rebellion by An Lushan (703–57) in 755 that nearly brought down the Tang dynasty and decisively weakened it. Another result of the Battle of Talas was that the Arab world learned the technique of papermaking, which had been invented by the Chinese at least by the second century B.C. The Arabs captured many workers in Chinese paper factories at Talas, and within several decades paper was being made in Baghdad (modern Syria). Europeans did not learn how to make paper until more than three centuries later because the Arabs kept the technique a secret and sold paper to the Europeans at very high prices. See also AN LUSHAN; KASHGAR; PAPER; SILK ROAD; TARIM BASIN; XINJIANG-UIGHUR AUTONOMOUS REGION.

TA-LIEN   See DALIAN.

TALKING OF PAINTING   See DONG QICHANG.

TAMERLANE (Timur Leng; c. 1336–1405)   A leader of the Mongols, a seminomadic ethnic group north of the Great Wall that frequently invaded China and that ruled the country under the Yuan dynasty (1279–1368), which was overthrown by the Ming dynasty (1368–1644). Tamerlane was a successful conqueror whose goal was to restore the Mongol empire to its previous power. He achieved victories as far away as Eastern Europe and the Middle East. The Ming emperor Hongwu (Hung-wu; r. 1368–98), who had forced out the Mongols and founded the Ming dynasty, had to spend much of his reign sending armies against the Mongols whom they had expelled. By then most of Central Asia had become part of the Mongol empire that still threatened China. The emperor reinforced the Great Wall and had strong garrisons stationed along it. Subsequent Ming emperors also sent armies against the Mongols. The Hongwu emperor also sent a mission to Tamerlane to attempt to maintain diplomatic relations with him. The Yongle emperor (r. 1403–24) also sent missions, but he offended Tamerlane by calling himself the Son of Heaven, the traditional Chinese name for the emperor, and in so doing he addressed Tamerlane as a subordinate. However, in their negotiations, Tamerlane forced the Chinese emperor to address him as an equal. Tamerlane planned a massive invasion of China to restore Mongol rule there. However, he died on the eve of the planned invasion in 1405, and the Yongle emperor was spared from having to contend with the Mongol forces of one of the greatest military leaders in history. See also MING DYNASTY; MONGOL; YONGLE EMPEROR; YUAN DYNASTY.

TAMO   See BODHIDHARMA; SHAOLIN TEMPLE.

TAN, AMY (1952–)   A best-selling Chinese-American author. She was born in Oakland, California a few years after her parents immigrated to the United States from China. Amy Tan, whose Chinese name, An-mei, means "Blessing from America," was raised in several California communities. After her father and her older brother died eight months apart, her mother took Amy and her younger brother to Europe, where they traveled and then settled in Montreux, Switzerland. She completed high school in Europe, and then her family returned to the San Francisco Bay area. Her parents had wanted her to be a neurosurgeon, but she majored in English and linguistics and received her B.A. and M.A. from San Jose State University. She then began working toward a doctorate at the University of California at Santa Cruz and at Berkeley, but she left school in 1976 and worked as a language-development consultant for people with mental retardation. She then directed a training project for developmentally disabled children. In the early 1980s she became a freelance business writer, but she worked as many as 90 hours a week, so for therapy she learned to play jazz piano and began reading fiction by modern women writers.

Amy Tan's first short story, "Endgame," about a brilliant young chess champion who battles with her Chinese mother, was published in FM and Seventeen magazines. In 1987 she entrusted her first collection of short stories to her literary agent and then visited China, where she met her half sisters, who had been born to her mother while she was married to her first husband there. Amy Tan said of this trip: "As soon as my feet touched China, I became Chinese." When she returned home, she was astounded to learn that the publisher G.P. Putnam's would pay her a $50,000 advance for her first book. She turned her short stories into a novel, *The Joy Luck Club,* about four Chinese mothers in San Francisco who tell each other the tragic stories of their lives in China while they play a game called mahjong. The book became a best-seller in 1989 and won the Bay Area Book Reviewers Award for fiction and the Commonwealth Club Gold Award. It was also nominated for the National Book Award for fiction and the National Book Critics Circle Award and was turned into a movie.

Her second novel, *The Kitchen God's Wife* (1991), tells the story of her mother's terrible experiences while married to her abusive first husband in China. This book also received critical acclaim and became a best-seller. In 1992 she published a popular children's book, *The Moon Lady.* Her most recent novel, *The Hundred Secret Senses,* was published in 1995. It tells the story of a Chinese-American woman, Olivia, and her half sister, Kwan, who had been born in China to their father's first wife and who moves to the United States; Kwan deeply affects Olivia. Amy Tan lives in San Francisco with her husband, Louis De Mattei, a tax attorney. See also EMIGRATION OF CHINESE; FAMILY STRUCTURE; KITCHEN GOD; MAHJONG; OVERSEAS CHINESE.

TAN DUN (T'an Tun; 1957–) A prominent contemporary Chinese composer whose works are related to the countercultural and experimental Western musical tradition. Tan was born in Hunan Province. During the Cultural Revolution (1966–76), he was sent to work in rice paddies in the Chinese countryside, but in his spare time he also composed music. In 1976 the Chinese Communist Party (CCP) sent him to work with a Beijing opera troupe as composer, arranger and instrumentalist. In 1978 Tan was able to move to Beijing, the capital of China, to pursue his music studies. There he decided to become a composer and attended the Central Conservatory. In 1980 he composed his first orchestral work, a symphony in four movements for large orchestra, titled *Li Sao,* after a lamentation on the sorrows of parting by the fourth-century Chinese poet Qu Yuan (Ch'u Yuan; 343–278 B.C.). Tan became famous because his symphony was more original and technically more developed than symphonies written by older Chinese composers, and it experimented with the expressive qualities of the Western-style symphony orchestra. He won the prize in the competition for which he had written *Li Sao.* Many young Chinese composers regarded *Li Sao* as an expression of farewell to the era of the Cultural Revolution, when all of Chinese culture had been subjected to political censorship and isolation from the Western world. They followed Tan in writing modern symphonies, although none of their pieces matched his own.

Tan continued to compose avant-garde orchestral works, and in 1983 he was awarded the Weber Prize in a competition in Dresden, Germany for his string quartet *Feng-Ya-Song.* This brought him great prestige in China because, although conservative Chinese music critics did not appreciate his works, he had given his country a place in the inter-

national music world. He was the first Chinese to receive a major European compositional prize since 1949.

Many young Chinese began traveling to Western countries to study and gain exposure to foreign cultures. Tan went to New York, where he first earned money by playing the violin as a street performer. One of Tan's most important compositions, "On Taoism," composed in 1985 for voice and orchestra, was performed at the First Contemporary Chinese Composers Festival in Hong Kong in June 1986. Daoism (Taoism) is a native Chinese religious tradition that is concerned with harmony between human beings and the natural world. "On Taoism" expresses the spiritual calm of Daoist temples but is punctuated with drum rolls and shouts of fearful excitement. The festival in Hong Kong brought together Chinese composers from Hong Kong, the People's Republic of China, Macao, Taiwan, Australia, Canada and the United States. Tan's music also was performed to full houses in Beijing.

In his compositions, Tan has attempted to make Western instruments such as the violin, piccolo and harp sound Chinese. He developed close ties with the BBC Scottish Orchestra in Glasgow, Scotland, which premiered his "Orchestral Theater" (1990), in which the musicians play their Western instruments in a Chinese style and also sing and shout. Tan's works also have been performed in other Western cities such as New York, where his experimental and ritualistic work "Soundshape" (1989) was performed by seven musicians on a variety of handmade ceramic instruments at La Mama's Annex Theater. Tan described his philosophy of composing in an epigraph in which he wrote that "Each day, spirit and environment become more polluted. Humanity grows colder, more ignorant, not respecting even itself." He attempts to compose music that will help offset this, and the melancholy beauty of his compositions makes them seem to invoke the natural world. Tan's "Ghost Opera" (1994) has been performed around the world by the Kronos Quartet. His "Symphony 1997" was first performed at the ceremonies for the reversion of Hong Kong to China on July 1, 1997. On November 8, 1997 Tan conducted the American premiere of his "Marco Polo" at the New York City Opera. It had already been performed in Munich, Amsterdam and Hong Kong. Tan has lived in New York since 1986 and is married to Shanghai-born Jane Huang, a magazine editor. See also CULTURAL REVOLUTION; DAOISM; POLO, MARCO; QU YUAN.

TAN TIEN See QI; QI GONG.

TANG, KING Known as the Lord of Shang; the founder of the Shang dynasty (1750–1040 B.C.), China's earliest historical dynasty. According to ancient Chinese historical records, King Tang conquered Jie, the cruel tyrant who was the last king of the semimythological Xia dynasty (2200–1750 B.C.), in a massive battle and established the Shang dynasty. He named the dynasty for Shang, his vassal state in central China. Shang rulers claimed that Heaven (*Tian* or *T'ien*) had given King Tang its mandate to overthrow the Xia dynasty, because the Xia king was evil. Twenty-nine Shang emperors sat on the throne until the dynasty was overthrown by the Zhou, who themselves claimed the Mandate of Heaven (*tian-ming* or *t'ien-ming*) and established the Zhou dynasty (1100–256 B.C.). The historical records state that Tang was an excellent ruler who followed the fine examples set by the legendary Chinese emperors Yao, Shun and Yu. During Tang's reign, his people suffered famine caused by a seven-year drought. Tang believed that this was an omen that Heaven was displeased with him, so he put on white robes (the color of mourning in China) and made sacrifices to Heaven at the foot of a high mountain. When he finished, Heaven sent rain to revive the crops of the Shang people. Tang persuaded Yi Yin (I Yin), who was knowledgeable about cultivating crops, to become prime minister. Yi Yin taught the peasants how to plant and irrigate seeds in shallow holes. He was also a skilled chef and may have influenced the great rituals that the Shang conducted using large bronze ceremonial containers, such as the three-footed *ding* (*ting*).

Archaeologists conducted excavations at Erlitou in Henan Province between 1959 and 1964. The palace compounds and bronzeware that they found suggested to some that this site may have been Po, King Tang's capital. Others argued that Erlitou was the capital of the earlier Xia dynasty. Fine black pottery also has been excavated at Erlitou. It is related to Xia. In 1970 archaeologists resumed excavations, which continue today. See also ARCHAEOLOGY; BRONZEWARE; DING; MANDATE OF HEAVEN; SHANG DYNASTY; SHUN, EMPEROR; XIA DYNASTY; YAO, EMPEROR; YU, EMPEROR.

TANG, MONSIGNOR See CHRISTIANITY.

T'ANG CHIA-YAO See YUNNAN PROVINCE.

TANG DYNASTY (618–907)   A period in Chinese history, following the reunification of China under the Sui dynasty (581–618), that is considered the golden age of Chinese culture. Many Chinese like to refer to themselves as Tangren, "People of Tang." The dynasty was founded by Li Yuan, a high official in the Sui government who was related by marriage to the royal families of the Sui and the Northern Zhou dynasties. Rebellions in northern China caused the Sui emperor to flee to his southern capital in 617. Li Yuan led a coup and took the Sui capital at Daxingzheng, which became the Tang capital of Chang'an (modern Xi'an in Shaanxi Province). In 618 Li Yuan proclaimed a new dynasty, which he named Tang for his fiefdom in modern Shanxi Province, with himself as emperor. Known as Emperor Gaozu (Kao-tsu; r. 618–26), he organized an imperial bureaucracy similar to that of the Sui government. Beneath the Tang emperor were two ministries, the Chancellery and Secretariat, and an executive body headed by the Department of State Affairs, which controlled the Six Boards, the Nine Courts and various other ministries. The Censorate oversaw government operations as a whole. Officials were selected for the imperial bureaucracy through examinations based on the teachings of the Confucian School of Thought. In 624 Emperor Gaozu issued a system of administrative laws that formed the foundation for the Tang government.

Li Shimin, Gaozu's second son, succeeded him and is known as Emperor Taizong (T'ai-tsung; r. 626–49). He consolidated the Tang bureaucracy and appointed excellent ministers with whom he had a close working relationship. In 630 Taizong dealt a final defeat to the Turkish tribes that had threatened northern China for half a century. He then sent military campaigns southwest against the peoples in the Tibetan borderlands, west into the Tarim Basin to gain control of the Silk Road and northeast against the Korean kingdom of Koguryo. By the end of Taizong's reign, Chinese control was established in the Tarim and Dzungaria basins, and the Tang dynasty was established as a great power that had diplomatic ties with Byzantium, the Sassanian Empire in Iran, the recently founded Tibetan kingdom and with many peoples all over Asia. The Tang Empire covered a greater amount of territory than had the Han dynasty (206 B.C.–A.D. 220). The Tang equipped their military forces with thousands of horses purchased from tribes in Central Asia.

The Tang Empire became the most open society in Chinese history, and the Tang capital at Chang'an became the largest and most cosmopolitan city in the world, with a population of more than one million. Traders of many nationalities settled in China, especially in Chang'an and Luoyang and southern ports such as Guangzhou (Canton), Yangzhou and cities in modern Fujian Province. These included Muslims from Persia (modern Iran), Arabs, Uighurs and Jews. Such foreigners brought the religions of Islam, Judaism, Nestorian Christianity, Manichaeism and Zoroastrianism to China. Foreigners also brought their own types of food, music, dance and poetry, which deeply influenced Tang culture. The Tang was the golden age of Chinese poetry. Some of the most famous poets include Bai Juyi (Po Chu-i; 772–846), Li Bai (Li Po; 701–62), Du Fu (Tu Fu; 712–70) and Wang Wei (699–761), who was also an influential painter. Paper and printing had been invented in China, and the development of block printing made written works available to large numbers of people during the Tang.

During the Tang the Chinese created new styles in ceramics and metalwork, which was influenced by Central Asian styles. A colorful type of pottery known as three-color ware (*sancai* or *san-ts'ai*) became very popular, and many figures in this style excavated from Tang tombs, such as camels, dancers and musicians, provide a vivid picture of life during the Tang. Tea, which had been considered a medicinal drink, now became a popular beverage in China. Tea, beautiful silk textiles, porcelains and other luxury goods produced in Tang China were highly desired by other countries and were traded extensively along overland and maritime routes. Camel caravans plied the overland Silk Road until the 760s, when Arab forces disrupted the Central Asian routes, and the maritime routes from Guangzhou and Yangzhou quickly gained large foreign populations and became extremely important. Chinese goods were shipped to countries all over Asia and Southeast Asia, India, Sri Lanka and the Middle East. Japan and Korea became centralized states that modeled themselves after the Tang dynasty, used the Chinese written language and adopted many aspects of Tang culture. They sent many trading missions to Chang'an, and numerous Japanese and Korean students traveled to the city to study the Chinese language and culture. The Japanese imperial city of Kyoto (formerly known as Heian) was constructed on the rectangular grid model of Chang'an. Many beautiful Tang objects, including pottery, metalwork and musical instruments, have been preserved in the Shosoin, a treasury presented in 756 to Todaiji Temple in Nara, Japan by the widow of a Japanese emperor.

The Buddhist religion, which had been introduced into China from India around the first century A.D. and was patronized by various Chinese emperors, flourished during the Tang and native Chinese sects of the religion developed, especially Chan (Zen) and Pure Land. Many foreign Buddhist monks visited China, and Chinese monks such as Xuanzang (Hsuan-tsang; 602–64) made pilgrimages to India to gather Buddhist sutras (scriptures). Chinese monasteries attracted thousands of monks and nuns and became very wealthy and powerful, until they were suppressed in the mid-ninth century. Han Yu (768–824), a prominent anti-Buddhist Confucian philosopher, influenced Tang emperor Wuzong (Wu-tsung), who issued decrees in 845 that shut down Buddhist monasteries and temples and returned the monks and nuns to secular life. The persecution lasted for nine months. Although the succeeding emperor was more lenient toward the religion, Buddhism played a subordinate role to Confucianism in Chinese government and society from then on.

Emperor Taizong was succeeded by Gaozong (Kao-tsung; r. 649–83), a weak leader who was dominated by his second empress, Wu Zhao (Wu Chao). In 660, after the emperor suffered a stroke, Empress Wu began handling the Tang affairs of state. After Gaozong died in 683 she removed her husband's successors, including one of her own sons, placed her youngest son on the throne but kept him a prisoner, and wielded all imperial power as empress dowager. She moved the imperial capital east from Chang'an to Luoyang, which weakened the power of the old aristocratic families. In 688 she ordered her secret police to crush a revolt by Tang princes and murder government officials and many members of the Tang royal family. In 689 she held several ceremonies that made her the official ruler of China. A female ruler was entirely against the tradition of Confucianism, the orthodox state cult, but she justified her rule by using Buddhist scriptures. She was a patron of the Buddhist cave temples and sculptures carved at Longmen near Luoyang between the late fifth and seventh centuries. In 690 Empress Wu proclaimed herself the emperor of a new dynasty, the Zhou. She was the only female to rule in her own right in Chinese history. Only when she became very ill and died in 705 were her opponents able to restore the Tang dynasty. She was succeeded by two brief reigns of Tang emperors Zhongzong (Chung-tsung) and Ruizong (Rui-tsung), which were marked by corruption and factional struggles for power.

In 713 Xuanzong (Hsuan-tsung; r. 712–56) led a coup and took the throne for himself. Commonly referred to by his reign name Minghuang ("Brilliant Emperor"), Emperor Xuanzong's reign was one of the greatest eras in the history of Chinese culture. He was a patron of the arts, poetry, music and dance as well as a scholar of Buddhism and the native Chinese tradition of Daoism. He took measures to reduce corruption, reform the imperial bureaucracy, increase government revenues and strengthen defenses along China's borders, where he stationed large permanent armies. He also reorganized the system by which grain was transported on canals, especially the Grand Canal that the Sui emperors had begun constructing, so that the capital cities of Chang'an and Luoyang would have adequate food supplies. However, Tang power became seriously threatened during Xuanzong's reign, due partly to

domestic economic instability and to the defeat of Tang forces in 750 by Arabs at the Battle of Talas in Central Asia. This battle has historical importance because the Arabs captured the workers in a Chinese papermaking factory, and thus brought the techniques for making paper to the Arab world.

A rebellion in 755 against Tang emperor Xuanzong led by An Lushan nearly overthrew the dynasty. An Lushan was a general who had become a favorite of Xuanzong and Yang Guifei (Yang Kuei-fei), his beautiful and beloved concubine, who became one of the most famous women in Chinese history. Chang'an and Luoyang fell to An Lushan, but Xuanzong and Yang Guifei were able to escape. However, the soldiers accompanying them blamed them for the rebellion and forced Xuanzong to order Yang Guifei to commit suicide. The broken-hearted emperor abdicated the throne to the crown prince, who ruled as Tang emperor Suzong (Su-tsung) and spent the rest of his life mourning his beloved concubine. Their story has been immortalized by Chinese painters and poets, notably Bai Juyi in "Song of Unending Regret" (*Changhenge* or *Ch'ang-hen ko*). An Lushan's second son assassinated him in January 757, and Tang troops suppressed the rebellion and finally defeated the rebels in 763. The Tang dynasty continued until 907 but never recovered its former glory. Millions of Chinese had died, especially in the rich regions that comprise modern Henan and Hebei provinces, and millions more fled south. During the eighth and ninth centuries the Yangzi River (Changjiang) valley became China's most populated and richest region.

Emperor Dezong (Te-tsung; r. 780–805) attempted to gain back power that the governors of various Chinese provinces had taken for themselves. They had become virtually autonomous, especially those in northern China, and refused to pay taxes to the central Tang government. Dezong enacted a tax reform that was collected in two levies—in summer, after the wheat harvest, and autumn, after the rice harvest. Subsequent Chinese dynasties through the 16th century retained this tax system. Provincial governors felt threatened by Dezong's tax reform and his attempts to end their practice of hereditary succession and to reduce their armies, and they led rebellions that once again nearly brought down the Tang.

Rebellions continued during the reign of Emperor Xianzong (Hsien-tsung; r. 805–20) but were suppressed, largely due to the growth of powerful palace armies commanded by eunuch generals. Since 780 eunuchs had gained positions in every level of the Tang central government. In the ninth century they formed a eunuch council of imperial advisers and began taking part in court factions and even controlling the succession to the throne. In 835 Emperor Wenzong (Wen-tsung) and loyal government officials attempted to purge the eunuchs in an action known as the Sweet Dew Incident. However, they did not succeed, and the eunuchs gained a permanent position of power in the court by purging many officials from the imperial bureaucracy.

During the 830s the Yangzi River valley began to suffer many natural disasters, including floods, droughts and epidemics. The suffering and heavy taxes placed on them by the Tang central government caused the Chinese people to become discontented. Northern and western China had few defenses after the An Lushan rebellion forced the Tang to defend itself by calling back troops from the frontiers. In 763

Tibetans took the modern province of Gansu and Tang outposts in the Tarim Basin in modern Xinjiang. The Uighurs, an ethnic tribe to the north of China, helped the Tang fight the Tibetans and sold them much-needed horses. The Tibetan kingdom collapsed around 840. However, the powerful kingdom of Nanzhao in modern Yunnan Province in southern China invaded Sichuan Province and Annam (Tonkin; northern Vietnam), which was then a province of China. Continual warfare in southern China during the 850s and 860s placed a great strain on the Chinese military.

Rebellions and bandit actions in the Yangzi region and mutinies in the provincial armies occurred in the next two decades. In 880 the southern bandit leader Huang Zhao (Huang Chao) led his forces north, took Chang'an and drove the Tang emperor into exile in Sichuan. Huang Zhao was so brutal that his own forces turned against him and forced him to flee to the east, where he was killed in 884. The Tang emperor returned to Chang'an, but the rebellion had damaged the capital and thrown the Tang government into chaos from which it could not recover. During the dynasty's last two decades, generals fought for control of the central government, and the Tang Empire became divided up into many kingdoms, known as the Five Dynasties and Ten Kingdoms Period (907–60). The northeastern region that had been An Lushan's base was ruled by the Khitan (Qidan) Liao dynasty (947–1125). In 960 the Chinese Empire was reunified under the Song dynasty (960–1279), which built upon many Tang institutions and became another high point of Chinese culture. See also AN LUSHAN; BAI JUYI; BUDDHISM; CAMEL CARAVANS; CHAN SECT OF BUDDHISM; CHANG'AN; CONFUCIANISM; DU FU; EUNUCHS; FIVE DYNASTIES PERIOD; GAOZONG, EMPEROR (TANG); GAOZU, EMPEROR (TANG); GRAND CANAL; GUANGZHOU; HAN YU; HORSE; IMPERIAL BUREAUCRACY; IMPERIAL EXAMINATION SYSTEM; JEWS; LI BAI; LIAO DYNASTY; LONGMEN CAVE TEMPLES AND SCULPTURES; LUOYANG; LYRIC VERSE; MANICHAEISM AND ZOROASTRIANISM; MUSLIMS; NESTORIAN CHRISTIANITY; NORTHERN AND SOUTHERN DYNASTIES; PAPER; PORCELAIN; PRINTING; PURE LAND SECT OF BUDDHISM; REGULATED OR NEW-STYLE VERSE; SILK; SILK ROAD; SUI DYNASTY; TAIZONG, EMPEROR (TANG); TALAS, BATTLE OF; TARIM BASIN; TEA; TEN KINGDOMS PERIOD; THREE-COLOR WARE; TIBETAN; UIGHUR; WANG WEI; WU, EMPRESS; WUZONG, EMPEROR; XUANZANG; XUANZONG, EMPEROR; YANG GUIFEI; YANGZI RIVER.

TANG DYNASTY (923–36) See FIVE DYNASTIES PERIOD.

TANG IMPERIAL TOMBS Tombs that are the burial places of 19 of the 20 emperors of the Tang dynasty (618–907) near the modern city of Xi'an in Shaanxi Province in western China. Xi'an was formerly known as Chang'an and served as the ancient imperial capital of China for more than 1,000 years during 11 dynasties, frequently alternating with Luoying to the east. Gaozu (Kaots'u), the first Tang emperor (given name Li Yuan; 566–635; r. 618–26), returned the capital to Chang'an and gave the city this name, which means "Eternal Peace." Chang'an was the final destination in China for the network of overland trade routes through Central Asia collectively known as the Silk Road. The city was the largest in the world at that time,

with a population of more than 1 million, including thousands of traders from Persia (modern Iran) and other countries west of China.

Two of the largest Tang Imperial Tombs are Qianling and Zhaoling. Qianling, about 65 miles northwest of Xi'an, is the burial site of Gaozong (Kao-tsung), the third Tang emperor (628–83; r. 649–83), and his wife, the infamous Empress Wu (Wuzhou or Wu Zetian; c. 627), who killed one of her sons, a general and probably her father in order to gain power. The approach to the tomb is a "spirit road" lined with stone sculptures of ostriches, flying horses, courtiers and foreign envoys who attended Gaozong's funeral. The tomb complex, located on the slopes of Mount Liang (Liangshan) and having a circumference of 26 miles, has not been entirely excavated. Seventeen tombs adjoin Gaozong's; his relatives and high court officials were buried there. Six of these tombs have been excavated, one of which is the tomb of Prince Zhanghuai (Chang-huai; Tang Zhanghuai Taizi Mu), the emperor's second son. Chinese scientists opened this tomb for examination in 1971 and discovered excellent mural paintings that provided extremely valuable information about daily life and political intrigues of the time. The tomb already had been plundered, but some funerary objects, mostly ceramic, were still in place. Another excavated tomb is that of Princess Yongtai (Yung-t'ai; Yongtai Gongzhu Mu; d. 701), granddaughter of Gaozong, and her husband. The very large tomb also is decorated with murals. Thirteen hundred funerary objects were found, including gold and silver objects, ceramics and clay figures, many of which are on display in the Qianling Museum.

Zhaoling, near Liquan about 40 miles northwest of Xi'an, is the tomb of Li Shimin, the second Tang emperor, known as Taizong (T'ai-tsung; 600–49; r. 626–49), who ruled during one of China's greatest periods of cultural and political accomplishment. Covering 49,420 acres, the compound is the most extensive tomb complex in China and includes the secondary graves of 177 princes, concubines, court officials and military generals. Built on Mount Juizong (Juizongshan), this was the first imperial tomb in China to be constructed on the side of a mountain rather than as a mound on flat land. The tomb has been made into an underground museum opened in 1979. Zhaoling Museum exhibits objects found in the graves, including painted ceramic figurines, paintings and a set of engraved stone tablets and pillars known as a "forest of steles" that provide important information on the peasant uprisings and wars of unification that occurred at the end of the Sui dynasty (581–618) and the beginning of the Tang. See also CHANG'AN; LI SHIMIN; SILK ROAD; STONE TABLETS; TANG DYNASTY; WU, EMPRESS.

TANG JIAYAO See YUNNAN PROVINCE.

TANG THE VICTORIOUS See SHANG DYNASTY.

TANGGULA MOUNTAIN RANGE See THREE GORGES WATER CONSERVANCY PROJECT; YANGZI RIVER.

TANGSHAN See NATURAL DISASTERS; TIANJIN.

TANGUT See NINGXIA HUI AUTONOMOUS REGION; XIXIA, KINGDOM OF; YINCHUAN.

TANKA See MANDALA.

TANKU TRUCE See MANCHUKUO.

TANTRIC BUDDHISM See DAZU CAVE TEMPLES AND SCULPTURES; LAMAISM.

TAN-WEI See WORK UNIT.

T'AO CH'IEN See TAO YUANMING.

TAO CHUN See JADE EMPEROR.

TAO TANG See DAOIST CLASSICAL TEXTS.

TAO YUANMING (T'ao Yuan-ming; 365–427) The finest Chinese poet during the period of disunity between the fall of the Han dynasty in 220 and the rise of the Sui dynasty in 589; also known as Tao Qian (T'ao Ch'ien). Tao Qian became the model of the poet-recluse whose life of scholarly seclusion was admired by both the Daoist and Buddhist religious traditions. After he completed his education, he held several minor government positions, but he soon retired from active life. He gave himself the name Tao Qian ("Tao the hidden or secluded person") and wrote poems about living in close harmony with nature, the main emphasis of Daoism. Two of his favorite images were wine and chrysanthemum flowers, which the Chinese associate with autumn because they bloom at that time despite cold weather. Because of the simplicity of Tao Qian's poems, he did not receive critical acclaim during his lifetime, but he was greatly admired during the Tang (618–907) and Song (960–1279) dynasties, the high points of Chinese culture. Tao Qian's most famous poem, "Peach Blossom Spring," recalls a lost utopia that contrasts with the political instability of his own era. It tells the story of a lone fisherman who sees a beautiful orchard of blooming peach trees along a riverbank and finds a stream flowing from the opening to a cave. He discovers that the cave opens onto a valley where a group of people have been living for 500 years since escaping turmoil during the Han dynasty. This poem greatly appealed to later scholars such as Wang Wei (699–761), who wrote his own poem based on Tao Qian's story. Tao Qian's poems have been translated into English. See also DAOISM; POETRY; WANG WEI.

TAO-AN See BUDDHISM; KUMARAJIVA.

TAO-CHI See SHITAO.

TAOISM See DAOISM.

TAO-KUANG (EMPEROR) See LIN ZEXU.

TAO-TE CHING See DAODEJING.

TARBAGATAI MOUNTAIN RANGE See DZUNGARIA BASIN.

TARIM BASIN An immense, very sparsely populated, barren wasteland that covers about half of Xinjiang-Uighur Autonomous Region in northwestern China north of Tibet, and is the largest inland basin in the world. The Tianshan Mountain Range divides Xinjiang into two regions, with the Tarim Basin to the south and the Dzungaria Basin to the north bordering Kazakhstan and Outer Mongolia. The Tarim Basin is a flat depression about 3,200 feet about sea level and surrounded by the high peaks of the Tianshan, Pamir and Kunlun mountain ranges. Numerous streams drain down from the mountains into the sands of the Taklimakan Desert, which lies in the center of the basin. On the northern side the streams flow into the Tarim River (Tarimhe), the largest river in Xinjiang and the world's longest inland river, which flows east into Lake Lopnor with its vast salt marsh. In 1991 China established the Tarim River Administrative Bureau and began building a large irrigation project on the Tarim River. The Tarim Basin is extremely arid, receiving less than four inches of rain per year. The city of Kashgar lies at the western edge of the Tarim Basin. In 100 B.C., as part of Emperor Wudi's decision to bring all of Central Asia under Chinese domination, a 60,000-man army was sent across the Tarim Basin to conquer the king of Ferghana (near Tashkent). This enabled the so-called Silk Road to be established, whereby Chinese silk was sent by camel caravans to Persia and the Middle East and Western technology and ideas were brought to China. There remain a few oases around the Tarim Basin, populated now mainly by Uighurs, which were important stops on the ancient Silk Road. The Uighurs moved into east and south Xinjiang during the 10th century A.D. and were autonomous until conquered by the Mongols in the 12th century. Melting snows and artificial irrigation allow them to cultivate crops such as grains and fruits. Great reserves of potassium in the Tarim Basin now are being used for modern fertilizers. Grasslands in the foothills surrounding the basin support the herding of sheep and horses. See also DZUNGARIA BASIN; KASHGAR; SILK ROAD; TAKLIMAKAN DESERT; TIANSHAN MOUNTAIN RANGE; UIGHUR; XINJIANG-UIGHUR AUTONOMOUS REGION.

TARRYING GARDEN See SUZHOU.

TARTAR PEOPLE See JIN DYNASTY; JURCHEN.

TATU See BEIJING; KHUBILAI KHAN; YUAN DYNASTY.

TEA (cha) A beverage made by pouring hot water over leaves from the tea shrub, a type of camellia known as *Camellia sinensis*. Tea has been drunk for more than 2,000 years in China. The custom began in southern China perhaps before the Han dynasty (206 B.C.–A.D. 220), and had spread to the north by the Tang dynasty (618–907). There are more than 250 varieties of Chinese tea, all of which have flavors that differ according to many factors, such as the place where they were grown, the time of day and season that the leaves were picked and the methods for processing and brewing the tea leaves. Chinese tea is classified into three main types: unfermented green, fermented black and semifermented red (called black in English). The color classification is based on the method of processing the leaves. As a first step, tea leaves are dried and gently rolled to bring out the chemicals that provide flavor. Green tea leaves are steamed or lightly fired in a pan. Green or black oolong (*wulong* or *wu lung*, "Black Dragon") tea leaves are 30 to 70 percent oxidized by being cured in humid conditions. The

Tea is drunk throughout the day in China, with teahouses serving as popular gathering spots.   DENNIS COX

three types of tea are divided further into two grades, whole and broken. Broken tea leaves usually produce a darker, stronger beverage. All three varieties can be sold as loose tea leaves or compressed into cakes or bricks. Chrysanthemum and jasmine flowers and orange-flower buds may be added to some green teas, and rose flowers to some black teas. Other flavoring ingredients include ginger and tangerine peel. A special variety known as *pu erh* or *bolei* is a green tea that is fermented by introducing bacteria and then aging the leaves for up to 60 years.

Most Chinese tea is grown in the country's southern provinces and autonomous regions, especially Sichuan, Guizhou, Yunnan, Guangdong, Guangxi, Hunan, Anhui, Jiangxi, Fujian and Zhejiang, where the climate is tropical or subtropical, the rainfall abundant and the soil fertile. Oolong and Keemun black are some of the most popular black varieties of Chinese tea. The most popular green teas are Dragon's Well (*Longjing* or *Lung Ching*) from the West Lake region outside Hangzhou, Pilochun from the Lake Tai region, Junshan Silver Needles from Hunan Province and Huangshan Maofeng and Liu-an Guapian from Anhui Province.

Many Chinese people are connoisseurs of tea and are very particular about the color, fragrance and flavor of teas, their place of origin, the way they are stored and the water used to brew the tea. The finest Chinese teas have a pale yellow color when brewed and a delicate aroma without any bitterness. Tea is brewed by putting tea leaves in a heated ceramic teapot, heating fresh water to the boiling point, pouring the water over the leaves and letting the tea sit for five to 10 minutes. About two tablespoons of tea are used for four cups of water. Pouring hot water over the tea leaves a second time brings out the flavor of the tea. Yixing pottery teapots, made from red clay, are quite famous. Tea also may be brewed in individual porcelain cups with lids. Tea leaves should be stored in a can or other container with a tight lid to keep out moisture.

The Chinese do not serve tea with a meal, but after the food is eaten. They drink tea all through the day and always offer tea to visitors. Often snacks are served with afternoon tea, such as rice cakes or almond cakes. Teahouses have been popular gathering places in China for hundreds of years, not only in cities but also in scenic places such as alongside lakes and waterfalls. The city of Chengdu in Sichuan Province is especially noted for its lively teahouse culture. The custom is also popular in Guangzhou (Canton), where the first "two-penny" teahouses opened more than a century ago. The best-known teahouses in Guangzhou today date back to that time.

According to ancient chronicles, the cultivation of tea began in Sichuan in southwestern China. *The Book of Tea*, written by Lu Yu in 760, notes that wild tea trees grew in abundance in the southern Sichuan basin. The Chinese people believe that tea drinking provides many health benefits, such as clearing the mind, stimulating the nervous system and aiding digestion. Scientists have identified about 400 chemical compounds in tea that have proven medicinal value. According to the *Shen Nong Materia Medica,* compiled during the Western Han dynasty (206 B.C.–A.D. 8), tea drinking calms people and increases their longevity. The Chinese include tea in their ritual offerings to ancestors, known as ancestor worship. The custom of drinking tea was spread by Buddhist monks, who found that tea kept them awake and helped them spend long hours meditating. The Chinese began exporting tea to other Asian and Southeast Asian countries during the Western Han dynasty.

Tea was introduced to the Western world in the 17th century, most of it imported by the British East India Company, which held a monopoly on importing tea into England until 1833. Clipper ships raced each other to bring tea from China to London and American cities through the end of the 19th century. The English word *tea* derives from the pronunciation of the word for tea, *tay,* in Fujian Province. The Chinese generally use the word *cha,* a word that comes from Guangdong Province in southern China. See also ANCESTOR WORSHIP; BRITISH EAST INDIA COMPANY; CHENGDU; CHRYSANTHEMUM; TEAHOUSE; YIXING POTTERY.

TE-HUA PORCELAIN   See DEHUA PORCELAIN.

TELECOMMUNICATIONS   Telecommunications in China are administered by the Ministry of Posts and Telecommunications (MPT), which is attempting to develop a modern, sophisticated system to unify the country and serve as the central control for postal services. During the 1970s, China was linked to the international telecommunications network by the installation of communications satellite ground stations and the construction of coaxial cables that linked Guangdong Province in southern China with Hong Kong and Macao. Satellite ground stations originally were installed in 1972 to provide live coverage of the visits to China of U.S. president Richard M. Nixon and Japanese prime minister Kakuei Tanaka. Microwave radio relay lines and buried cable lines were constructed to create a network of wideband carrier trunk lines across the country.

In April 1984 China launched an experimental communications satellite, and in February 1986 it launched its first fully operational telecommunications and broadcast satellite. By 1987 China had joined Intelsat and had linked up with satellites over the Pacific and Indian oceans. By 1995, China had established 23 ground satellite telecommunications stations, cut more than 22 fiber-optic cable backbones, and completed more than 31,000 miles of digital microwave systems.

The MPT now employs several million people to draft and implement construction and financial plans for telecommunications in the capital city of Beijing, control nationwide communication services, research and develop communication technology and provide local support and maintenance technicians for China's telecommunications system. Senior MPT officials have announced the immediate goals of modernizing the telecommunication system, improving long-distance telecommunications capacity, overcoming shortages of telephones in urban areas and expanding national telecommunications and broadcasting satellite systems. In 1986 the MPT established 10 business syndicates under its control to oversee the development of microwave equipment, optical fibers and digital communications.

In December 1989 China had only 11 million telephones, but by 1994 China's telecommunications network had increased its long distance capacity by 63 percent and added 10.8 million subscribers. The government planned to spend the equivalent of $14.4 billion to modernize Chinese phone lines to handle interactive functions. China recently has been buying and installing the equivalent of Bell Atlantic's entire network every year, and will do so for at least a decade. The Chinese government expects that by the year 2000, 78 million telephones, 9 million cellular phones and 25 million pagers will be in use around the country. The government has encouraged the formation of joint ventures between China and foreign telecommunications companies to acquire necessary components. AT&T alone has invested $30 million in eight joint ventures in China that manufacture a range of products including fiber-optic cable, transmission equipment and switching systems. AT&T has had more than $1 billion in sales to China since 1993. Other telecommunications companies doing business with China include Siemens, Nortel, Alcatel, Ericsson and Fujitsu.

The New China (Xinhua) News Agency, a government agency that handles domestic and international news, has established an international telecommunications network linking Beijing with major foreign cities such as Tokyo, Hong Kong, New York, London and Paris. Xinhua also has rented an international communications satellite to file news to foreign countries and exchange news with foreign news agencies. Domestic branches of Xinhua are able to communicate with the head office in Beijing over microwave communications. High-speed fiber-optic networks are being implemented throughout China to link to Japan and the United States via SprintNet. China now has more than 20 national networks, such as CHINAPAC, CHINADDN and CERNET. There are also many local networks, such as APTLIN, the Library and Information Network of the Chinese Academy of Sciences, which links Beijing University and Qinghua University. In Taiwan, the Taiwan Academic Network, known as TAN, provides World Wide Web access to the Academia Sinica Institutes, the national Central Library and other Web servers. The Academia Sinica has input the 25 Chinese dynastic histories (about 40 million written characters) and many other titles, such as the Confucian classical texts with commentaries. See also ACADEMIA SINICA; BROADCASTING; NEW CHINA NEWS AGENCY; NIXON, RICHARD M., U.S. PRESIDENT, VISIT TO CHINA; POSTAL SERVICE; TAIWAN.

TELEVISION   See BROADCASTING.

TEMMOKU WARE   (*jian* or *chien* ware)   A type of pottery primarily used for making tea bowls, and known in the West by the Japanese name, *temmoku. Temmoku* is the Japanese pronunciation of the name Tianmushan, a mountain in Zhejiang Province in China where several Chan (Zen) Buddhist temples were located. During the Song dynasty (960–1279), Chan Buddhists used only this type of tea bowl in a tea ceremony that the Japanese adopted and developed. *Temmoku* ware was produced near Jian-Yang in Fujian Province in southeast China. The shiny glaze can vary in color from dark brown to black. It is frequently thin on the rim of the tea bowl, which is then given a metal binding. The glaze often gathers in thick drips near the unglazed foot of the bowl. *Temmoku* bowls commonly have streaks or patches, which are created during firing in the kiln by iron oxide in the glaze; such effects are termed "rabbit's fur," which has brown streaks; "oil spot," with silver streaks; or "partridge feather." Masters of the Japanese tea ceremony have greatly admired *temmoku* tea bowls, and Japanese potters have produced their own versions of *temmoku* ware, notably at the Seto pottery kiln in Owari Province. Vases, small cylindrical containers for ground tea leaves and large jars for storing tea leaves also may be made of *temmoku* ware. See also CHAN SECT OF BUDDHISM; TEA.

TEMPLE OF HEAVEN (Tiantan or T'ien-t'an Park)   A large walled park covering 6,670 acres in the capital city of Beijing that contains three major buildings where the emperor, or "Son of Heaven" (*tianzi* or *t'ien-tzu*), went to offer prayers and sacrifices to Heaven (*tian*) on behalf of the Chinese people. The structures were built with circular forms corresponding to the shape of Heaven and were laid out on a north-south axis. Each has a deep blue glazed tile roof with a gold spire and three white marble platforms with three tiers, totaling nine tiers, the number that represents Heaven in traditional Chinese beliefs. The structures include the Hall of Prayer for Good Harvests (Qiniandian) to the north; the Hall of the Imperial Vault of Heaven (Huangqiongyu) in the center; and the Circular Mound Altar of Heaven (Huanqiu Tan) to the south. The Bridge of Cinnabar Steps (Danbiqiao), a stone walkway 1 foot high and 131 feet long, connects the three structures. The northern section of the temple is enclosed by a semicircular wall and the southern by a square wall, based on the belief that Heaven is round and the Earth is square. Two walls divide the temple into an inner section containing the important sacrificial structures and an outer section that contains several auxiliary buildings.

This complex is the largest surviving sacrificial temple in China. Construction of the Temple of Heaven was begun in 1406 during the reign of the Yongle (Yung-lo) Emperor and required 14 years for completion. It was expanded under the Qianlong (Ch'ien-lung; r. 1736–95) and Jiaqing (Chia-ch'ing; r. 1796–1820) emperors. The emperor went to the Temple of Heaven every year at the winter solstice to pray for a good harvest and to offer homage to Heaven. The day before the ceremony, he left the Forbidden City (Imperial Palace) and was carried on a litter by 36 men in a grand procession to the temple, during which all the city's residents had to remain indoors and keep silent. This was done until the fall of the Qing dynasty in 1911. The Warlord Yuan Shikai (Yuan Shih-k'ai; 1859–1916), who had ambitions to become emperor of China, was the last person to hold a ceremony at the temple, in 1913. The emperor also performed a similar ritual at the spring equinox. He entered the Temple of Heaven through the Front Gate (Qianmen). The emperor spent the night before the ritual fasting in the Hall of Abstinence, a square building surrounded by a moat and a high wall. The temple also contained facilities for the office of divine music, which trained the musicians who performed during the rituals, and for the preparation of animals for ritual sacrifices.

The Chinese government made the temple a public park in 1949 and added entrances on the other three sides. Tourists now enter through the Western Heavenly Gate (Xitianmen). A long grove of cypress trees leads to the Hall of Prayer for Good Harvests, which had burned down in 1889 and was rebuilt. The hall is 100 feet high and 100 feet in diameter and was built of wood without any nails. The triple cone-shaped roof has 50,000 blue glazed tiles and is supported by 28 wooden pillars. The ceiling vault is brightly painted. The four central columns, known as the Dragon Well Pillars, represent the four seasons. Around them are two rings of 12 columns each, the inner representing the months of the year and the outer the units of time in one day according to traditional Chinese calculation. A slab or marble in the middle of the floor is carved with the symbols of the emperor and empress and is thus known as the Dragon and Phoenix Stone (Longfeng Shi). The three tiers surrounding the hall have rails with a total of 360 white marble balustrades.

The Imperial Vault of Heaven, also with a cone-shaped blue tile roof and brightly painted vault, stored the ceremonial tablets that were used during the rituals. It is surrounded by Echo Wall (Huiyin Bi), a circular brick wall with the acoustical ability to enable two people standing at opposite

The Temple of Heaven, completed in 1420, is the largest surviving sacrificial temple in China.   S.E. MEYER

points to hear each other whispering. The Circular Mound Altar of Heaven is a three-tiered stone terrace enclosed by an inner circular wall and an outer square wall. The terraces represent Earth, the human world and Heaven. The altar is constructed on the basis of the number nine, with stone slabs in multiples of nine. The 27th and final ring of the lower tier is made of 243 stone slabs. At this altar the emperor offered sacrifices to Heaven and prayed for good harvests. See also BEIJING; DRAGON; FORBIDDEN CITY; HEAVEN; MUSIC AND DANCE, CEREMONIAL; PHOENIX; SON OF HEAVEN; TEMPLES.

TEMPLES   Buildings sacred to the native Chinese traditions of Confucianism and Daoism and to the Buddhist religion, which was introduced into China from India around the first century A.D. The three religions have coexisted in China, except for a period of persecution of Buddhism in the mid-ninth century. A Confucian temple is known as a *miao,* a Daoist temple, *guan (kuan)* and a Buddhist temple, *si (ssu).* Every Chinese village and subsection of a town or city has its own community temple, used not only for religious purposes but also as a schoolroom, town hall, children's playground and gathering place for the elderly.

Chinese temples range from small, simple structures to compounds that include a number of buildings grouped together around courtyards and connected by walkways. They all share the same elements common to Chinese secular architecture. The temple is situated in a compound surrounded by a wall that has its main entrance in the south face. The entrance is a triple gate raised above ground level on stone steps. The picture of a pair of guardian door gods (*menshen*) is painted or pasted on the entrance door to keep away evil spirits. The main halls of a temple lie along a north-south axis in the center of the courtyard, and subsidiary buildings run along the east and west sides. The buildings are wooden frames with outer walls of brick and inner walls of brick or wood. The most distinctive feature is the roof, which is structurally independent of the building, with curved eaves that extend beyond the building like a canopy. The curving of the eaves is pronounced in southern China, and decorative ceramic figures of mythical creatures and legendary humans are placed along the ridge and the eaves. The roof often is covered with beautifully colored glazed tiles.

The interior walls and ceiling of the building are decorated with bright colors, especially red, blue, green, gold, white and black, and the posts are bright red. A beautifully decorated sculpture of a deity sits on a table or throne in the main hall with an altar holding utensils for religious rituals. Attendant deities are placed on the right and left of the main deity. If the temple compound has more than one hall, lesser deities are placed in the first hall and the principal deity in the rear hall. In Chinese popular religion, a temple may house many deities from both the Daoist and Buddhist pantheons, along with deities sacred to the local community.

The doors of a Chinese temple are always open, and a person may enter at any time to communicate with the deity, especially to get advice about a personal problem or decision. The person lights several sticks of incense and places them in the incense brazier on the altar, bows or makes prostrations before the altar, and offers sacrificial food or burns pretend paper money (joss money). The deity's answer is gotten by divination, such as shaking a long slip of bamboo out of a vase, which has a number on it, corresponding to a numbered piece of paper printed with an answer. Another method is to drop two curved wooden blocks on the floor and interpret the pattern they make. There is usually a huge bronze vessel filled with sand in the courtyard where worshipers place sticks of burning incense. Temples are crowded on festivals, such as the birthday of the deity housed in the temple. Men parade the statue of the deity around the neighborhood accompanied by the noise of firecrackers, horns, drums and cymbals.

Chinese homes traditionally have an altar that holds the wooden tablets that commemorate deceased family members. Sacrifices are offered regularly to the ancestors, known as ancestor worship in the Confucian tradition, and family members also bow to the ancestors on important occasions, such as weddings. Large Chinese clans have their own temples to house their clan altars and ancestral tablets. The Kong family mansion, home of the great Chinese thinker Confucius (Kong Fuzi or K'ung Futzu; 551–479 B.C.) in Qufu in Shandong Province, has a magnificent temple dedicated to Confucius. Confucianism became the orthodox school of thought in China during the Han dynasty (206 B.C.–A.D. 220). In 630 Tang dynasty (618–907) emperor Taizong (T'ai-tsung) decreed that a Confucian temple should be established in every province and county of the Chinese Empire. In 647 these temples were made into national shrines to Confucius and to government officials who contributed to Confucian scholarship. Major sacrifices were held in these temples in the spring and autumn. Tablets were placed on altars to Confucius until the eighth century, when Confucian temples adopted the Buddhist practice of using sculptures to represent the figure honored in the temple. Confucian temples also began using images of the so-called 10 Wise Ones and the 72 disciples of Confucius, similar to Buddhist sculptures of Buddhas, bodhisattvas (wise beings) and luohan (worthy disciples). There are also large Confucian temples and clan temples in Taiwan, Hong Kong, Singapore and other overseas Chinese communities.

The Temple of Heaven (Tiantan or T'ien-t'an) in the capital city of Beijing contains three major structures where, starting in the late 14th century, the reigning Chinese emperor or "Son of Heaven" (*tianzi* or *t'ien-tzu*) went to offer prayers and sacrifices to Heaven (*Qian* or *t'ien*) on behalf of the Chinese people. The structures were built with circular forms corresponding to the shape of Heaven and were laid out on a north-south axis. Each structure has a deep blue glazed tile roof with a gold spire and three white marble platforms with three tiers, totaling nine tiers, the number that represents Heaven in traditional Chinese beliefs. The structures include the Hall of Prayer for Good Harvests to the north; the Hall of the Imperial Vault of Heaven in the center; and the Circular Mound Altar of Heaven to the south.

Many Chinese temples also have been built in the tranquil countryside, on the sides of mountains or alongside lakes or rivers. The Five Sacred Mountains of Daoism and the Four Sacred Mountains of Buddhism have many temples on their slopes and peaks. Again, these range from small huts to large monastery compounds housing hundreds of monks. The most distinctive building in a Buddhist temple complex is a pagoda (*ta* or *t'a*), a tall structure that derived from low, round brick structures in India known as stupas, which enshrine sutras (Buddhist scriptures) and relics of the Buddha. In China the pagoda changed shape, taking elements from Chinese pavilions and towers, but kept its function as a sacred storage place. Chinese pagodas commonly are made of wood, brick or stone and have as many as 15 stories, each with an upcurved overhanging roof. About 10,000 pagodas survive in China, most made of brick and stone. The oldest is the 131-foot-high pagoda at Songyue Temple near Shaolin Temple. The wooden pagoda at Fogong Monastery near Datong, built in 1056, is the most important wooden building in Chinese architecture. Two pagodas in Xi'an in Shaanxi Province (the capital city of Chang'an during the Tang dynasty) are famous symbols of China. The Big Wild Goose Pagoda (Dayan Ta) was built in 652 to store sutras brought back from India by the Chinese pilgrim monk Xuanzang (Hsuan-tsang; 602–64), and a large monastery was built next to it. The Small Wild Goose Pagoda (Xi'aoyan Ta) was built between 707 and 709 and restored in 1977.

White Horse Temple (Baima Si), seven miles east of Luoyang in Henan Province, is the first Buddhist temple of its kind built after Buddhim was introduced into China. The second emperor of the Eastern Han dynasty (A.D. 25–220) constructed it in 68 to honor two eminent Indian Buddhist monks who brought sculptures and sutras on the back of a white horse. Shaolin Temple, a Chan (Zen) Buddhist monastery near Zhengzhou in Henan Province, is supposedly the place where Chan founder Bodhidharma originated Chinese martial arts (*wushu*). It was built in 495, destroyed in 617 and rebuilt in 627.

Perhaps the most unique temples in China are the cave temples and sculptures carved in cliffs in several regions. The largest are the Dunhuang cave temples and sculptures in Gansu Province in northwestern China, which contain some of the most important Buddhist art in the world. The Mogao Grottoes, as they are known, comprise the oldest Buddhist site in China. A Buddhist monk named Yu Zun began carving them in 366, and for the next 1,000 years, monks and artisans carved hundreds of grottoes and filled them with wall paintings and carvings. There are also impressive cave temples and sculptures at Longmen near Luoyang in Henan Province, dating from the early fifth to the early seventh centuries; Yungang near Datong in Shanxi Province, dating from 460 until the mid-sixth century; and Dazu, about 120 miles northwest of Chongqing in Sichuan Province, dating from the 9th to the 13th centuries. See also ANCESTOR WORSHIP; ANCESTRAL TABLETS; ARCHITECTURE, TRADITIONAL; BODHISATTVA; BUDDHA; BUDDHISM; CONFUCIANISM; CONFUCIUS; DAOISM; DAZU CAVE TEMPLES AND SCULPTURES; DOOR GODS; DUNHUANG CAVE PAINTINGS AND CARVINGS; FIVE SACRED MOUNTAINS OF DAOISM; FOUR SACRED MOUNTAINS OF BUDDHISM; INCENSE; LONGMEN CAVE TEMPLES AND SCULPTURES; LUOHAN; PAGODA; ROOF TILES; SCULPTURE; SHAOLIN TEMPLE; TEMPLE OF HEAVEN; WHITE HORSE TEMPLE; XI'AN; YUNGANG CAVE TEMPLES AND SCULPTURES.

TEMUCHIN See GENGHIS KHAN.

TEN KINGDOMS PERIOD (907–960) A period of disunity between the Tang (618–907) and Song (960–1279) dynasties when southern China was ruled by 10 kingdoms, nine of them coexisting simultaneously. During the same period, northern China was ruled by five dynasties that rapidly succeeded each other, known as the Five Dynasties Period (Wutai; 907–60), and by the Liao dynasty (947–1125) established by nomadic invaders called the Khitan (Qidan). The 10 kingdoms in the south maintained a balance of power because, unlike the northern five dynasties, the rulers maintained their kingdoms as independent and did not engage in destructive warfare or attempt to bring all of the empire under their control. In addition, the rulers established bonds of interdependence through marriages contracted with the families of the other kingdoms. They also established diplomatic, economic and cultural relations with each other and made agreements that in times of famine, a common problem in China, they would provide mutual assistance.

Seven of the 10 kingdoms were located in the Yangzi River (Changjiang) valley: Wu (902–37), Southern Tang (937–75), Wuyue (908–78), Jingnan (913–63), Chu (907–51), Former Shu (908–25) and Later Shu (934–65). The Min (909–45) was located at Fuzhou in modern Fujian Province; the Southern Han (907–71) in modern Guangdong Province and Guangxi-Hui Autonomous Region, with its capital at the port city of Guangzhou (Canton); and the Northern Han (951–79) in modern Shanxi Province. With the downfall of the Tang dynasty, many literati—members of the scholar class who ran the imperial bureaucracy that governed China—had fled south and contributed greatly to the development of Chinese civilization in the southern provinces. The kingdoms in the Yangzi valley were the main areas for the preservation of Tang culture. The Southern Tang in the Yangzi delta was especially fortunate to have three highly educated and cultured rulers. The Wuyue Kingdom lasted the longest of all the 10 kingdoms and five dynasties. Its founder was Qian Liu (902–31), a common soldier who had risen through the ranks during the Tang dynasty to become a military governor. He was also the longest in power of all the rulers during this period. The Min Kingdom on the southeastern coast of China became wealthy from its seagoing trade with the northern and southern Chinese coastal regions, Korea and Southeast Asia, but suffered from political instability. The Southern Han Kingdom in Guangdong and Guangxi had remained under Tang dynasty imperial administration longer than any other region of China, and many senior Tang officials and their families had settled in this kingdom. The kingdom became a prosperous center for trade with Southeast Asia. See also FIVE DYNASTIES PERIOD; FUJIAN PROVINCE; GUANGDONG PROVINCE; LIAO DYNASTY; SONG DYNASTY; TANG DYNASTY; YANGZI RIVER.

TENDAI SECT OF BUDDHISM See TIANTAI SECT OF BUDDHISM.

TENG HSIAO-P'ING See DENG XIAOPING.

TENG YING-CH'AO See DENG YINGCHAO.

TENGGER DESERT A large, sandy, arid region covering 34,750 square miles that lies between southwestern Inner Mongolia Autonomous Region and central Gansu Province in northwestern China. *Tengger* is a Mongolian term for "the heavens," indicating the vast area of the desert. According to local legend, a long time ago the sun god fell in love with a beautiful young woman, and they had several children. The Jade Emperor, the ruler of Heaven, resented their love and sent the woman into exile in the heart of the Tengger Desert, where her blood turned into "black gold" and her sons became the wailing winds that sweep the desert, calling to their mother and crying for their parents' reunion.

The Tengger is one of a series of deserts that cover northern and northwestern China, the best known of which are the Gobi and the Taklimakan. The Tengger begins at the Helan Mountain Range in the east, stretches south past the Great Wall, and joins the Badain Jaran Desert in the northwest. During the Mesozoic Era (170–80 million years ago), this region was covered with forests of sago palms, pines and cypress trees. Two thousand years ago there were grasslands and lakes, and a large river flowed through the region. Caravans carrying luxurious trade goods between China and Central Asia traveled along the riverbanks. The Tengger Desert was formed after cold weather moved down from the Arctic and then enormous quantities of yellow sand, known as loess, blew in, filling the river and lakes and burying trees and plants. Sandstorms from the Tengger continue to cause devastation in nearby regions, and every year the sand moves 33 feet deeper into farmland and pastures, blocking roads and filling the Yellow River (Huanghe). Since 1949 the Chinese have been planting trees and plants, especially along the southern edge of the desert, to keep the sand from encroaching. In 1959 they opened a railroad line between Baotou and Lanzhou, the first one in China to run through a desert. The railway has never been stopped by sand. Layers of rock-bearing petroleum lie under the Tengger Desert, and in the late 1980s, seven oil prospecting teams conducted tests there and determined the location of a large oil field now being drilled. See also ENERGY SOURCES; GOBI DESERT; GREAT WALL; LOESS; TAKLIMAKAN DESERT.

TENGRI DESERT (TENGKOLI)   See GOBI DESERT.

TENZIN GYATSO See DALAI LAMA.

TENZING NORKAY See EVEREST, MOUNT.

TERRA-COTTA ARMY, TOMB OF EMPEROR QIN SHI HUANGDI (Bingmayong) The tomb of Qin (259–210 B.C.), the first emperor, who unified China under the Qin dynasty (221–206 B.C.). The tomb includes a mausoleum and an underground complex in which was buried a terra-cotta (pottery) army with thousands of life-size soldiers, horses and chariots. The whole burial complex lies about 20 miles east of Xi'an in Shaanxi Province in western China. This city, formerly known as Chang'an, was the site of the Qin dynasty capital and remained the imperial capital for several dynasties. Emperor Qin's mausoleum was declared a national monument in 1961 but has not been excavated. The emperor had ordered its construction in 246 B.C., and 700,000 workers and craftsmen spent 36 years building it, although they did not complete the work because the emperor died unexpectedly. His grave lies in a pyramid-shaped burial mound at the foot of Mount Li (Lishan) on the

Emperor Qin Shi Huangdi's burial complex outside Xi'an is "protected" by thousands of life-size soldiers in a terra-cotta army.
DENNIS COX

Huishui River. It was built on a north-south axis and was enclosed by an inner and an outer wall. The location was carefully chosen according to the principles of geomancy, known as *feng shui*.

In spring 1974 farmers drilling a well 1,340 yards east of the burial mound discovered the buried terra-cotta army, which was lined up in rows in battle formation to protect the emperor's tomb. Three pits have been excavated and opened to the public, and a large hall has been built to protect them. The life-size figures were constructed from separate pieces of gray clay that were fired in kilns and then assembled. They include warriors, archers and footsoldiers. Each soldier is unique and has distinctive facial features, and the weapons and armor are authentic, providing a wealth of information for military historians. The first pit contains about 6,000 figures facing east in battle formation and covers an area of 172,000 square feet. The second pit, excavated in 1976, contains about 1,000 warriors in the chariot cavalry corps and covers about 64,500 square feet. The third pit, which covers only about 5,000 square feet, contains 68 statues of high-ranking officers. A fourth pit remained empty, perhaps because the emperor died before the figures could be constructed. The craftsmen who assembled these figures must have constituted an army in themselves to plan and lay out the complex, transport the materials, dig the pits, build and fire the pottery statues, paint the soldiers, and build the chariots from wood and then lacquer them. A museum next to the underground complex exhibits a number of statues to illustrate the hierarchical organization of the emperor's army, the weapons and battle strategies. See also CHANG'AN; FENG SHUI; QIN DYNASTY; QIN SHI HUANGDI (EMPEROR); XI'AN.

TE-TSUNG, EMPEROR   See TANG DYNASTY.

TEXTILE INDUSTRY   One of China's most important industries from ancient times to the contemporary era, both for domestic use and export to foreign countries. In the 1980s China was one of the world's leading producers of textiles, especially silk. The Chinese knew how to spin and weave silk, made from silkworm cocoons, and plant fibers, such as hemp, more than 5,000 years ago. During the Han dynasty (206 B.C.–A.D. 220), China began exporting silk to Central Asia and the Mediterranean world along the so-called Silk Road. The Chinese government kept the techniques for producing silk, known as sericulture, a strict secret until they were smuggled to the Western world around the sixth century. The Chinese first cultivated ramie, also known as China grass, a perennial plant of the nettle family, around 1000 B.C. They used it to make textiles, fishing lines and fishing nets. Upper-class Chinese wore clothing made of silk, while peasants and workers, the majority of the population, wore rougher fibers made from such plants as ramie, hemp and cotton, which was introduced from India and became widely used during the Song dynasty (960–1279). By the late 19th century, cotton spinning and weaving was the largest industry in China. Chinese women, especially those belonging to ethnic minorities in the south and southwest, developed batik, the folk art of decorating cotton textiles with complex designs using deep-blue dye made from indigo plants. Today they also use other colors, such as light blue, red and yellow. Large Chinese textile companies often mass-produce batik designs created by peasant women.

Carpet weaving originated in China during the Eastern Han dynasty (25–220), when the Chinese Empire expanded north and west and incorporated many nomadic animal-herding tribes, who hand-wove patterned blankets for protection against the cold, windy winter weather. By the Tang dynasty (618–907), carpet weaving became a major craft in China. The Khitan (Qidan), who established the Liao dynasty (947–1125) with their capital at the modern city of Beijing, began a handwoven-carpet industry there that still flourishes. The cities of Beijing, Tianjin and Suzhou are the modern Chinese centers for carpet weaving; it is also a major industry in Tibet and Xinjiang autonomous regions in western China.

Silk cultivation, spinning and weaving were major industries in China as early as the Zhou dynasty (1100–256 B.C.). The Chinese wrote official documents on rolls of silk. Even though paper was invented in China by 200 B.C., calligraphers and painters continued to use silk as well as paper into the modern era. By the Han dynasty, Chinese weavers were using foot-powered multiharness looms and jacquard looms,

and silk weaving and embroidery became organized craft industries. The imperial government established workshops in the capital and throughout the country to produce the beautiful silk textiles worn by the wealthy upper classes. Silk brocades also were used to mount fine paintings on scrolls and to make panels for screens and wall hangings and covers for Buddhist sutras (scriptures). Young Chinese women who knew how to weave and embroider silk gained higher status when they married. Many worked at home on pieces from private and imperial workshops. During the Ming dynasty (1368–1644), imperial workshops were established in Suzhou, Hangzhou and Nanjing in eastern China, and these cities are still famous for silk tapestry, embroidery, damasks and satin brocades woven with gold threads. The Museum of Suzhou Embroidery was established in 1954 to preserve traditional Chinese embroidery techniques and to develop new ones. The museum houses a collection of more than 2,000 embroidered works that date back to the Han dynasty. Chengdu in Sichuan Province, known as the City of Brocade, has a silk weaving and embroidery workshop that originated more than 1,500 years ago. Shanghai, which became China's largest city and trading port after Britain defeated China in the Opium War (1839–42), is a major center for mechanized textile factories.

China began exporting silk to the Middle East along caravan trails during the Zhou dynasty, and during the Han dynasty the Silk Road—actually a series of routes to the Mediterranean world—became fully developed. The wealthy upper classes in the Roman Empire were willing to pay a pound of gold for a pound of Chinese raw silk. China also exported silk textiles on the maritime Silk Road to Japan, Southeast Asia and India. Chinese emperors made many alliances with nomadic tribes to the north and west to try to prevent them from invading the country, the terms of which included the payment of large quantities of Chinese silk textiles to the nomads.

Europeans began entering China along the Silk Road, and during the Ming dynasty, brocade panels were exported to Europe for use on vestments by priests in Roman Catholic cathedrals. In the 16th century Europeans, starting with the Portuguese, began sending trading ships to China to acquire silk, porcelain, tea and other luxury goods. The Chinese government restricted them to trading only through officially designated merchants in the southern port city of Guangzhou (Canton), known as the Canton system to regulate foreign trade. During the 17th and 18th century, enormous amounts of patterned silk textiles were exported from China to the West, where they influenced the European interpretation of Chinese designs, known as chinoiserie. In the 19th century Great Britain, France and other foreign powers forced China to open cities to foreign trade and residents as so-called treaty ports.

China remained the world's largest producer of silk textiles until the early 20th century, when Japan surpassed China. The Chinese textile industry declined in the first half of the 20th century due to civil wars and the Japanese invasion that resulted in China's War of Resistance against Japan (1937–45; World War II). The Chinese Communist Party (CCP), which founded the People's Republic of China (PRC) in 1949, made the rebuilding of the textile industry an economic priority. Recently Chinese silk production has increased while that of other countries has declined or disappeared. China became the world's largest silk producer once again in 1977, when it produced 18,000 tons of silk, mainly in Jiangsu and Zhejiang provinces.

In 1979 the Chinese government established Special Economic Zones (SEZs) along the coast to encourage foreign trade and investment. Many factories in the SEZs and in the 14 coastal cities designated "open cities" in 1984 produce textiles and clothing for companies located outside of China, especially in Hong Kong. Shandong, Liaoning, Hubei and Hebei provinces are also major textile-producing regions, and Shanghai, Qingdao, Tianjin and Guangzhou are major centers for spinning cotton. From 1979 to 1984 the output value of the Chinese textile industry rose about 13 percent each year. In 1984 China had about 12,000 enterprises producing textiles and textile machinery, and textile production was 15.4 percent of the country's total industrial output value. By 1986 textiles replaced oil as China's leading earner of foreign exchange. In 1987 China produced 56,000 tons (50,800 metric tons) of silk fiber, 5.02 billion feet of silk fabric and 55.683 billion feet of other fabric. In 1991 China produced 60 percent of the world's total raw silk; its raw silk exports comprised 90 percent of the world's raw silk trade, and its silk and satin exports were 50 percent of the world's silk product trade. See also BRITISH EAST INDIA COMPANY; CAMEL CARAVANS; CANTON SYSTEM TO REGULATE FOREIGN TRADE; CARPETS; CHINOISERIE; COTTON; EMBROIDERY; INDIGO DYEING OF TEXTILES; MINORITIES, NATIONAL; NOMADS AND ANIMAL HUSBANDRY; RAMIE; SILK; SILK ROAD; SPECIAL ECONOMIC ZONES; SUZHOU; TREATY PORTS.

THAI See DAI.

THEATER See ACROBATICS AND VARIETY THEATER; DRAMA; FILM STUDIOS; HONG SHEN; KUNQU; OPERA, BEIJING; OPERA, GUANGZHOU; STORYTELLING.

THEORY OF THE THREE WORLDS See UNITED NATIONS.

THERAVADA BUDDHISM See BUDDHISM.

THIRTEEN FACTORIES See CANTON SYSTEM TO REGULATE FOREIGN TRADE; OPIUM WAR.

THOUSAND-BUDDHA CAVES See TURPAN.

THREE-ANTI AND FIVE-ANTI CAMPAIGNS (*wu fan* and *san fan* movements) Campaigns promulgated in 1951 and 1952 by the government of the People's Republic of China, which had been founded by the Chinese Communist Party (CCP) in 1949. The Three-Anti Campaign intended to purge businessmen and industrialists who were accused by the Communist government of "tax evasion, bribery, cheating in government contracts, thefts of economic intelligence and stealing of state assets." The CCP charged that these men comprised a highly organized group that was corrupting Communist cadres, the name for officials in the Communist Party and government. It then extended this accusation to all members of the bourgeoisie or urban business class in China, many of whom had joined the CCP or developed ties with party officials for their own personal gain. Workers

were encouraged to accuse the people who employed them. The CCP claimed that the Five-Anti Campaign was created to get rid of "corruption, waste and bureaucratism." However, the campaign's actual goal was to make the government bureaucracy efficient and disciplined by removing officials who were incompetent and not completely loyal to the CCP. Only a small number of the accused were tried in formal courts. The Chinese police and other government agencies held public mass trials during which crowds of spectators shouted accusations at those brought to trial. Some historians estimate that millions of Chinese were affected by the Three-Anti and Five-Anti Campaigns, with hundreds of thousands being executed and a much larger number being sent to prison or labor camps. In Shanghai alone, one of China's largest commercial and industrial cities, 140,000 of the 164,000 companies operating there were found guilty. See also CADRE; CHINESE COMMUNIST PARTY; PEOPLE'S REPUBLIC OF CHINA.

THREE-COLOR WARE (*sancai* or *san-ts'ai*) A technique for producing brightly colored ceramic figurines used for burial in tombs of the Tang dynasty (618–907). The clay figurines were covered with a glaze that was usually cream-colored, fired in a kiln, coated with paint and finally layered with three types of colored lead silicate glaze. The term "three-color" refers to the technique rather than to the actual number of colors used, which could vary from two to six and included yellow, brown, green, white, blue and deep amber. Figurines took the form of animals, such as camels and horses; human figures, such as dancers, musicians and soldiers; and buildings, such as houses and granaries. Such figurines were grouped together in tombs. Three-color ware flourished in the seventh century and reached its peak in the eighth century, but stopped being used in tombs in the ninth century. Potters under the Liao dynasty (947–1125), which was established in northern China by a Mongol people named the Qidan (Khitan), produced ceramics in the style of the Tang three-color ware. The term "three-color ware" is also applied to a type of decorated porcelain produced during the Chinese Ming dynasty (1368–1644) commonly called *fahua*. The decorative motifs were painted onto the porcelain in colored lead silicate enamels and outlined with lines of slip (a mixture of clay and water) or incised lines that separate the colors from each other, similar to the way copper wires separate the colors in cloisonne enamel. Three-color ware has become the type of Chinese ceramic best known in the West. See also CERAMICS; CLOISONNE; ENAMELWARE; LIAO DYNASTY; TANG DYNASTY.

"THREE FRIENDS OF WINTER" See BAMBOO; PINE; PLUM.

THREE GOLD PROGRAMS A $1 billion initiative announced by the Chinese government in 1993 to develop the country's information, telecommunication and economic systems.

The "Gold Bridge" program has the goal of completing by 1998 a national information highway to link the central government in Beijing with 400 major cities and 1,000 of the country's largest enterprises. In 1995 the Chinese government announced that Windows 95, a computer software system produced by the American company Microsoft, would be the official computer software in China.

The "Gold Customs" program aims to establish a special telecommunications and information network geared to foreign trade. The government has encouraged joint ventures between foreign and Chinese companies and has established Special Economic Zones (SEZs) to encourage these ventures. The Chinese electronics industry has undergone especially rapid growth. Among China's 200,000 electronics enterprises, more than 8,000 have joint ventures with foreign investors. In 1994 China completed the world's longest fiber-optical transmitting system (2,914 miles) as well as a seabed optical system between China and Japan. The government's eighth Five-Year Plan includes plans to establish 22 fiber-optical transmitting lines. The American company AT&T has set up eight joint ventures in China to manufacture optical cables, digital transmitters, copper cable and exchange systems. AT&T plans to buy $250 million in components from China in the year 2000. The U.S. computer company Compaq began official operations in China in 1993 and became the number-one computer hardware supplier there by 1995, with almost 23 percent market share. The company built a joint venture production facility in Shenzhen SEZ in 1994 and expected to sell 1 million personal computers in China in 1995.

Finally, the "Gold Card" program intends to promote the use of credit cards, or "plastic money," by 300 million residents of Chinese cities. In absolute terms, China now has the world's third-largest economy behind the United States and Japan, although in per capita terms it is still classified as a developing country. See also FIVE-YEAR PLANS; SPECIAL ECONOMIC ZONES; TELECOMMUNICATIONS.

THREE GORGES WATER CONSERVANCY PROJECT A monumental dam that is being constructed on the Yangzi River (Yangtze; known in China as the Changjiang, "Long River"), the longest and most important river in China and the third longest river in the world. The Three Gorges Dam is located just below the mountain gorges where the Yangzi River flows onto the flat plain of eastern China. It will create the world's largest water storage reservoir and hydroelectric plant. The Yangzi flows from west to east for 3,494 miles through major economic centers and provides the main transportation route across heavily populated central China. The river originates in the Tanggula Mountains on the border between Tibet Autonomous Region and Qinghai Province and drops more than 21,600 feet from its source to its estuary near Shanghai on China's east coast. The Yangzi flows down through the valleys of high mountain ranges in Qinghai, Tibet, and Yunnan Province, turns northeast from Shigu in Yunnan, and drops 660 feet in one 10-mile stretch. It then flows through the provinces of Sichuan, Hubei, Hunan, Hiangxi, Anhui and Jiangsu, where it empties into the East China Sea. The river broadens in eastern China and provides much-needed irrigation for agriculture, but it has overflowed its banks many times and caused great destruction and loss of life. Over the centuries the Chinese built dikes to contain the river and to divert excess water into lakes and marshes. The Three Gorges Water Conservancy Project aims to halt the flooding of the Yangzi as well as provide hydroelectric power and improve navigation on the river.

In 1952 the Chinese Communist Party (CCP), which had taken control of China in 1949, formed the Yangzi Valley Planning Office (YVPO) to oversee the development of the Yangzi River resources. The Three Gorges Dam is now under construction on the Yangzi at the scenic Three Gorges (Sanxia) site in Hubei Province in central China. On November 8, 1997, Chinese engineers and workers diverted the Yangzi from its natural course, clearing the way for the dam's construction. At this point, about 800 miles upriver from Shanghai, the distance between the banks of the Yangzi sometimes becomes as narrow as 150 feet. The Gezhouba Dam, 27 miles downstream from the Three Gorges site and four miles upstream from the city of Yichang, was completed in 1989.

The name Three Gorges refers to an area 125 miles long that includes Qutang, Wuxia, and Xiling gorges. This area begins at Baidicheng in Sichuan Province and ends at Nanjingquan in Hubei Province. The Three Gorges comprise a majestic natural site comparable to the Grand Canyon in the United States and have been celebrated over the centuries by Chinese poets and painters. Tourists on passenger ships enjoy beautiful views of the blue-white limestone cliffs. According to Chinese legends, the scenic river channels were carved into the mountains by the goddess Yaoji (Yao Chi) to divert the river around the petrified remains of a dozen dragons she had slain to stop them from harassing Chinese peasants. Every rock in the gorges has a poetic name, such as Upside Down Monkey or Climbing Dragon, and has legends associated with it. The dam, which will be 606 feet high and 1.8 miles wide, will be completed in 2009. It will raise the water level about 175 feet in the gorges and submerge many of their features.

The Three Gorges Dam will be the largest engineering project in the world since the first Chinese emperor, Qin Shi Huangdi (r. 221–210 B.C.), began building the Great Wall. The dam, which had been envisioned initially in the 1920s by Sun Yat-sen (1866–1925), the founder of modern China, is planned to provide more than 17 million kilowatts of electricity a day, equal to 10 nuclear power plants and three times as much power as that generated by the Grand Coulee Dam in the United States. This power will help the Chinese reduce their use of coal, which has caused serious air pollution, and will end the periodic extended blackouts that shut down businesses and factories. However, the project will submerge some of China's most magnificent scenery and hundreds of ancient tombs, temples and rock carvings that date as far back as 10,000 B.C. It also will create a lake 350 miles long, submerging about 1,500 cities and villages and forcing the resettlement of 1.3 million people who live along a 375-mile stretch of the riverbank.

Construction of Gezhouba Dam had been initiated in 1970 but was interrupted by the Cultural Revolution (1966–76). The first phase of the project was completed in 1981, when power generation began and locks were opened to ships. Between 1983 and 1984, famous Chinese writers and scientists led a movement to protest the Three Gorges Dam. Groups opposed to the project lobbied to prevent the World Bank from funding it. In 1988 Dai Qing, a newspaper reporter in Beijing whose editor prevented her from writing about the dam controversy, interviewed all the Chinese scientists who opposed the project because of the harm it might cause to China's environment, economy and political stability. She published the interviews and official documents in a book, *Yangtze! Yangtze!* (1997). The scientists noted that the dam will flood farmland that now yields 40 percent of China's agricultural products, and asserted that the enormous dam would seriously degrade the environment and become clogged with silt. Since the dam was being built in an area that has many earthquakes and landslides, if it broke it would create the worst flood in modern times and inundate cities downstream such as Wuhan, which has a population of one million. Dai's book caused the Chinese government to delay the project for further discussion of its environmental impact. However, after the Tiananmen Square Massacre in 1989 the government began a general crackdown on dissidents, and Dai was jailed for 10 months and her book was banned. That year the government forbade all further public debate about the Three Gorges Dam and similar issues.

In 1992 Premier Li Peng placed the dam issue before the National People's Congress, which usually supports government policies, yet more than one-third of the delegates voted against the dam or abstained from voting for it. Since then, however, Chinese officials have become so eager to increase the economic output of central China, so that it can catch up with the booming coastal regions, that they now support the conservancy project. The Chinese government approved the start-up of the conservancy project in 1992. In 1996, 56 leading Chinese scholars and cultural and political figures petitioned President Jiang Zemin to preserve the Yangzi's cultural treasures, and a 30-volume rescue plan was presented to the project's construction office. However, no preservation was done. The government also plans to build a 730-mile canal to divert water from the Yangzi to Beijing and the dry North China Plain. This project would utilize much of the route of the Grand Canal, which was begun more than 1,000 years ago. See also AGRICULTURE; EAST CHINA SEA; ENERGY SOURCES; GRAND CANAL; GREAT WALL; HUBEI PROVINCE; NATURAL DISASTERS; NORTH CHINA PLAIN; QINGHAI-TIBET PLATEAU; SHANGHAI; TARIM BASIN; YANGZI RIVER; YELLOW RIVER.

THREE KINGDOMS PERIOD (San Guo or San Kuo; 220–280)

A period following the breakup of the Chinese Empire at the end of the Eastern Han dynasty (25–220), when civil war disrupted China and three kingdoms dominated the country. This period began in 220 when the last Han emperor, Xiandi (Hsien-ti), abdicated the throne to Cao Pi (Ts'ao P'i), who founded the kingdom of Wei. Wei (or Cao Wei) was situated to the north and east of the Yangzi River (Changjiang) and included the modern city of Nanjing. The foundations for Wei had been laid by Cao Pi's father, Cao Cao (Ts'ao Ts'ao; 155–220), a brilliant general who had waged military campaigns against other warlords and conquered and unified all of northern China. The second kingdom, Shu, was located to the southwest and included the modern province of Sichuan. The third kingdom, Wu, extended south of the Yangzi. Cao Cao attempted to unite northern and southern China, and fought Wu on the Yangzi in 208, but lost the battle because of Wu's superior naval skills.

The kingdom of Wei had its capital at Luoyang in modern Henan Province. In 263 Wei conquered the southwestern kingdom of Shu (or Shu Han). Shu, the last of the three kingdoms to form, had been founded in 221 by Liu Bei (Liu Pei; 161–223). Shu's heartland, the Red River Basin in Sichuan, was protected from attackers by high mountain ranges that nearly surrounded it. The kingdom of Wu was founded by Sun Ce (Sun Ts'e; 175–200), and in 229 his brother Sun Quan (Sun Ch'uan; 182–252) led the Sun family in declaring itself as the imperial house of Wu. Wu became a naval power, as its region contained many rivers and lakes on which trade goods could be transported. The capital city at modern Nanjing was at that time called Jiankang or Jinling. Zhuge Liang (Chu-ko Liang; 181–234), a brilliant strategist who was prime minister of Shu, made a political alliance with Wu for self-defense. The three kingdoms remained locked in a stalemate until 263, when the Wei general Sima Zhao (Ssu-ma Chao) led a surprise military campaign against Shu by attacking through a remote mountainous region, and he quickly took over the Shu kingdom. He soon died, and his son, Sima Yan (Ssu-ma Yan), proclaimed himself emperor of the Jin dynasty, which lasted from 265 to 316. In 265 Jin absorbed the other two kingdoms.

The Three Kingdoms Period generated a cycle of folktales that formed the basis for the epic historical novel *Romance of the Three Kingdoms* (*Sanguo yanyi* or *San-kuo-yen-i*), attributed to Luo Guanzhong (Lo Kuan-chung c. 1330–c. 1400). This is considered one of the Four Great Novels in China, and many of its episodes still are performed in Beijing Opera. It describes the conflict between Shu and Wei, culminating in the battle in which the southerners defeat Cao Cao. See also CAO CAO; CAO FAMILY OF ROYAL POETS; HAN DYNASTY; LUOYANG; OPERA, BEIJING; ROMANCE OF THE THREE KINGDOMS; ZHUGE LIANG.

THREE PERFECTIONS See CALLIGRAPHY.

THREE PRINCIPLES OF THE PEOPLE (Sanminzhuyi or San min chuyi)

A central concept in the political philosophy of Sun Yat-sen (1866–1925), the leader of the Revolution of 1911 against the Manchu Qing dynasty (1644–1911) and founder of the Republic of China (1912). Sun developed these principles while in Japan in 1897 and first presented them publicly in Tokyo in 1905 when he formed the Revolutionary Alliance (also known as the Alliance Society; Tongmenghui or T'ung-meng hui). The Three Principles of the People refer to "people's nationalism, people's democracy and people's livelihood."

The principle of nationalism calls for the Han Chinese people to overthrow the Manchus who ruled them under the Qing dynasty and to end foreign power hegemony over China. The principle of democracy refers to a popularly elected republican form of government. Sun asserted the need to bring about democracy in China through a constitution embodying the five powers: executive; legislative and judicial powers, which comprise Western governments; and the traditional Chinese powers of examination and censorship. He argued that such a five-power government would be the best and most complete in the world and, quoting Abraham Lincoln, that a Chinese state with this type of government "will indeed be of the people, by the people and for the people." The principle of livelihood, often referred to as socialism, refers to the regulation of the ownership of land

and the means of production, in order to help the common people. Sun did not derive this principle from communist thinker Karl Marx but from Henry George, an American thinker who proposed a tax plan intended to prevent people from making excess profits on land.

Sun also called for a government that would ensure that a greater percentage of food grown by peasants will go directly to them for their own sustenance rather than to their landlords. In 1924 Sun gave a series of lectures in Guangzhou (Canton) that were later compiled into one volume under the title, *Three Principles of the People*. This and other volumes of his talks formed the ideological basis for the National Party (Kuomintang; KMT) led by Chiang Kai-shek. See also NATIONALIST PARTY; QING DYNASTY; REPUBLIC OF CHINA; REVOLUTION OF 1911; REVOLUTIONARY ALLIANCE; SUN YAT-SEN.

THREE-SELF MOVEMENT   See CHRISTIANITY.

THREE   TEACHINGS See   BUDDHISM;   CONFUCIANISM; DAOISM.

"THREE TONG (T'UNG)"   See MA DUANLIN.

THREE TREASURES OF MANCHURIA   See DEER; GINSENG; SABLE.

TIAN   See HEAVEN.

TIAN, LAKE   See JILIN PROVINCE.

TIANANMEN SQUARE   A 100-acre square in the capital city of Beijing that is one of the largest public squares in the world. Tiananmen Square originally comprised 27 acres enclosed within the imperial palace (Gugong), commonly known as the Forbidden City, during the Ming (1368–1644) and Qing (1644–1911) dynasties. The Communist government of the People's Republic of China (PRC) quadrupled the square to its present size with a massive reconstruction program in 1958. The government holds ceremonial gatherings in the square that often number more than a million people. Each flagstone is numbered so that parade units can be lined up in proper order. Tiananmen (T'ienanmen), the "Gate of Heavenly Peace," is a massive stone gate with a wooden roof that was built in 1412 and restored in 1651. It served as the front gate of the Forbidden City and the first entrance into the imperial palace. The gate is 110 feet high and has five arched gateways under the gate tower. Formerly only Chinese emperors were allowed to walk through the middle arch. Five carved white marble bridges span a stream at the foot of the gate, which overlooks Tiananmen Square.

Tiananmen Square was opened to the public after the Revolution of 1911 overthrew the Qing dynasty and led to the founding of the Republic of China in 1912. When the Chinese Communists defeated the Nationalists in a civil war,

Tiananmen Square, known most recently for the 1989 student protest and massacre, is one of the largest public squares in the world.   S.E. MEYER

Communist chairman Mao Zedong (Mao Tse-tung) stood on the rostrum in Tiananmen Square on October 1, 1949, and proclaimed the founding of the PRC. An enormous portrait of Mao Zedong has hung in Tiananmen's central portal for four decades. During special events, Chinese government leaders make public appearances on the rostrum on top of the gate. The Monument to the People's Heroes is a 118-foot-high obelisk placed in the center of the square to honor the heroes who died for the cause of National Liberation in 1949. Just behind the monument and facing the Gate of Heavenly Peace is the Chairman Mao Zedong Memorial Hall, the mausoleum where Mao's body, preserved in a crystal coffin, is viewed by thousands of Chinese and foreign tourists daily. The building covers 200,000 square feet, stands over 100 feet high, and has a flat roof supported by 44 granite pillars.

The Great Hall of the People houses the National People's Congress of the Chinese Communist Party and is the site of official receptions and banquets for up to 5,000 people. Qianmen, the South Gate of Tiananmen Square, was built in the 15th century by the Ming dynasty emperor Yongle. At every winter solstice the reigning emperor traveled through this gate to pray at Tiantan, the Temple of Heaven (Tiantan or T'ien-t'an). During the Qing dynasty, the gate connected the northern, Tatar district and the southern, Chinese district of Beijing. On the east side of Tiananmen Square are two museums. The Museum of Chinese History covers the period up to 1919, and the Museum of the Chinese Revolution covers the founding and development of the Chinese Communist Party during the post-1919 period. Many demonstrations for and against government leaders have been held in Tiananmen Square, including the May Fourth Movement of 1919 and the demonstration against Japanese aggression on December 9, 1935. Enormous rallies of Chinese youth, including Red Guards, were held in Tiananmen during the disruptive Cultural Revolution (1966–76). On April 5, 1976, a million people gathered in the square to mourn the death of Communist leader Zhou Enlai (Chou En-lai). In 1989 a massive anti-government protest in the square, led by university students and televised around the world, ended with a violent military crackdown, known as the Tiananmen Square Massacre. See also CHOU ENLAI; CULTURAL REVOLUTION; FORBIDDEN CITY; GREAT HALL OF THE PEOPLE; IMPERIAL PALACE; LIBERATION, NATIONAL; MAO ZEDONG; MAY FOURTH MOVEMENT OF 1919; MING DYNASTY; REVOLUTION OF 1911; TEMPLE OF HEAVEN; TIANANMEN SQUARE MASSACRE; ZHOU ENLAI.

TIANANMEN SQUARE MASSACRE   Also known as the Tiananmen Square Incident, the Beijing Massacre and the June Fourth Massacre; the brutal suppression in 1989 by the Communist leaders of the People's Republic of China (PRC) of pro-democracy demonstrators in Tiananmen Square in Beijing, the Chinese capital. The huge 100-acre square is located in front of the Forbidden City, also known as the Imperial Palace, the residence of Chinese emperors during the Ming (1368–1644) and Qing (1644–1911) dynasties. Tiananmen (T'ienanmen), the "Gate of Heavenly Peace," is a massive stone gate with a wooden roof that was built in 1412 and restored in 1651. In 1949 Mao Zedong (Mao Tse-tung; 1893–1976), chairman of the Chinese Communist Party

(CCP), stood on the rostrum on top of Tiananmen and proclaimed the founding of the PRC. An enormous portrait of Mao has hung in the gate's central portal for four decades, and Mao's embalmed body is on public view in a large mausoleum built in the square. During special events, such as the anniversary of the founding of the PRC, CCP leaders make public appearances on the rostrum. The Communists have held many mass demonstrations in Tiananmen Square, which can hold a million people, especially during the Cultural Revolution (1966–76). In the center of the square is the Monument to the People's Heroes.

Pro-democracy demonstrations began in Tiananmen Square after Hu Yaobang (Hu Yao-pang; 1917–89), a member of the powerful Standing Committee of the Politburo of the CCP, died suddenly on April 15, 1989. Hu was a symbol of political reform to Chinese students. The CCP had been gradually introducing reforms to rebuild and modernize China after it had been devastated by the Cultural Revolution. But in 1986, CCP hardliners denounced "bourgeois liberalization," their term for the adaptation of Western political and cultural ideas and the preference of capitalism over socialism. The CCP Central Committee passed a resolution calling for the spiritual reconstruction of socialism. Students and others in China had advocated democratization and progressive reforms, and large numbers of students held demonstrations in 15 cities demanding free elections and freedom of speech, assembly and the press. Hu Yaobang, the general secretary of the CCP, did not denounce the demonstrators and the intellectuals who supported them, and he continued to favor political reform through "democratization" of the Chinese political system. Party hardliners criticized Hu for being too lenient with the demonstrators and convinced CCP leader Deng Xiaoping (Teng Hsiao-p'ing) to oppose such reforms and deal harshly with the students. Hu had been considered Deng's successor, but members of the Politburo attacked him, and in 1987 they demoted Hu from his position as general secretary. Zhao Ziyang (Chao Tzu-yang) replaced Hu as general secretary, and the conservative Li Peng (Li P'eng) replaced Zhao as prime minister.

When Hu was dismissed in 1987, Chinese students immediately regarded him as a hero. He died on April 15, 1989, and two days later pro-democracy demonstrations broke out in Shanghai and Beijing, where students placed wreaths in Tiananmen Square to commemorate him. On April 19 the students marched to the Zhongnanhai Compound, the residence of many CCP leaders in Beijing, where they held a sit-in and demanded that Li Peng come out and respond to their demands. On April 22, the day of the official memorial service for Hu Yaobang, 100,000 students held a rally in Tiananmen Square. They demanded the posthumous restoration of Hu's honor; freedom of speech, assembly and press; increased funding for education; and the publication of the incomes and financial assets of CCP leaders. The demonstrations were led by students from prestigious Beijing University, who felt that they were acting in the tradition of Beijing University students who led the May Fourth Movement of 1919, which inspired modern Chinese revolutionaries.

For six weeks in the spring of 1989, students came from nearly all the provinces of China to occupy Tiananmen

Square, where they lived in tents. Students in other Chinese cities also held demonstrations demanding freedom of the press, more democracy, and an end to corruption in the government. In Tiananmen Square, the protestors waved banners and flags inscribed with demands for democracy and an end to corruption. Day and night, they shouted their demands into megaphones, spoke to journalists and asked people to sign petitions. Many residents of Beijing, including organizations of workers, supported the student protestors, bringing them food and drink, and carrying banners with sympathetic slogans. On May 13 about 1,000 students began a hunger strike. On May 18 Li Peng held a televised meeting with student leaders of the demonstration at the Great Hall of the People, also located in Tiananmen Square. On May 19 Zhao Ziyang appeared in the square to express sympathy with the hunger strikers. This was his last public appearance before the massacre, and he was not seen for a long time after it.

CCP leaders tolerated the demonstration at first. However, Mikhail Gorbachev, leader of the U.S.S.R., was scheduled to visit the PRC in the middle of May, and many foreign journalists and broadcasters were in Beijing for the event. The Chinese government did not want to have bad publicity from the demonstration and requested that the students leave Tiananmen Square, but they refused. The events in the square, including the massacre, were broadcast around the world by the American Cable News Network, known as CNN. On May 30 the protestors erected a 40-foot-high statue of the "Goddess of Freedom and Democracy," modeled on the Statue of Liberty in New York City.

On May 20 the hardline faction of the CCP, led by Li Peng, imposed martial law in Beijing. Older Chinese intellectuals, many of whom had been Red Guards during the Cultural Revolution and knew that the government would resort to violence, advised the demonstrators to leave, but the idealistic young students would not give in. The government brought troops of the 27th Army of the People's Liberation Army (PLA) and the People's Armed Police into the city, but tens of thousands of Beijing residents rushed into the streets and erected barricades to block the troops from reaching Tiananmen Square. They held back the troops for more than two weeks, and many soldiers declared that they would never open fire on the student demonstrators. Yet on the night of June 3, loudspeakers in Tiananmen Square warned everyone to go home or else they would suffer serious consequences. Troops and tanks headed toward the square, and soldiers shot people who were blocking their way as well as students who were trying to flee the square. Hundreds were killed and many more were wounded. By the middle of the day on June 4, the troops had sealed off Tiananmen Square. That same day, PLA troops advanced on protestors in Chengdu in Sichuan Province and killed about 300 of them. More protestors were killed in Shanghai on June 6. On June 9 Deng Xiaoping and some other CCP leaders appeared on television and praised the military action for suppressing "counter-revolutionaries trying to overthrow the CCP." Many Chinese people were shocked by the massacre since students have always been highly respected in China as the future leaders of the country. However, the majority of Chinese resent the privileges enjoyed by the students at Beijing University and approved of the government crackdown after the demonstrators failed to disperse.

Thousands of demonstrators were arrested and imprisoned. Some were able to flee abroad. The Chinese government issued a verdict branding the demonstrations as "counter-revolutionary rebellion." Estimates number the victims at more than 2,000, although the exact toll is still not known because the government has refused to release the number or names of people killed in the massacre. Demonstrators who remain in China have been under constant surveillance, and the government has cordoned off Beijing University and other universities. In Hong Kong, which reverted to the PRC in 1997, as many as a million residents took part in public demonstrations in 1989 to protest the massacre and political suppression in the PRC.

After the massacre a number of dissidents hid in the American Embassy in Beijing, including Fang Lizhi (Fang Li-chih), an astrophysicist who had actively demanded democratic reforms, and his wife. They have since moved to the United States. On June 5, 1989, U.S. president George Bush announced the suspension of all government-to-government sales and commercial export of weapons, and of all visits between senior American and Chinese military officials. Relations were strained between the two countries for 18 months. Countries all over the world condemned the massacre, and the PRC endured nearly three years of political isolation and economic sanctions. However, the government continued to pursue a policy of strict repression of dissent. In 1994 it refused to allow the Chinese people to commemorate the fifth anniversary of the massacre publicly. In Hong Kong, where many of the protestors had fled, thousands of Chinese held a public candlelit commemoration of the massacre and chanted "End One-Party Rule." See also BEIJING; BEIJING UNIVERSITY; CHINESE COMMUNIST PARTY; CULTURAL REVOLUTION; DENG XIAOPING; FANG LIZHI; HONG KONG; HU YAOBANG; LI PENG; MAY FOURTH MOVEMENT OF 1919; PEOPLE'S LIBERATION ARMY; PEOPLE'S REPUBLIC OF CHINA; RED GUARDS; TIANANMEN SQUARE; ZHAO ZIYANG; ZHONGNANHAI COMPOUND.

TIANCHI LAKE   See CHANGBAI MOUNTAIN RANGE.

TIANHOU   See MAZIPO.

TIANJIN (Tientsin)   The third-largest city in China, which has a population of about 8.4 million, covers an area of 4,200 square miles and is governed as a separate administrative municipality. Tianjin is located in the northern Chinese province of Hebei, about 90 miles south of Beijing, the capital of China and also a separate administrative municipality. About 1.5 million inhabitants of Tianjin belong to national minority groups such as the Manchus, Mongols, Hui (Chinese Muslims) and Koreans. China's largest artificial harbor has been constructed at Tianjin where ships displacing up to 10,000 tons can berth. The city extends for 10 miles along the Hai River (Haihe), which empties into the Bo Hai Gulf 30 miles to the east. Only 16 feet above sea level, the city has suffered from frequent flooding in the past, but the recent construction of dike systems has greatly reduced this threat. Tianjin is a major railroad hub and transportation center for the heavily populated North China Plain, one of China's major regions for manufacturing and agriculture.

The Tangshan earthquake in August 1976 devastated Tianjin and Tangshan cities and killed hundreds of thousands of people, but the Chinese soon began rebuilding. Many Chinese believed that this natural disaster was an omen predicting the end of the ruling power held by Communist leader Mao Zedong (Mao Tse-tung), and he did in fact die in September 1976. In 1984 the government designated Tianjin as one of China's 14 Coastal Open Cities, and in 1986 it was one of the four urban areas (including Shanghai, Guangzhou [Canton] and Dalian) approved for accelerated economic development and the encouragement of joint ventures with foreign companies. The entire city has been open to foreign investors. It has a large population of scientists and research personnel, with 28 institutions of higher learning and more than 150 independent scientific research institutes. Some of Tianjin's most important products include textiles, machinery, elevators, bicycles, petroleum, natural gas, coal, soda ash, shellfish and sea salt. Tianjin carpets are famous, as are handicrafts such as colorful clay figurines and kites. Agricultural products in the region include wheat, corn, rice, fruit and dairy products.

The history of the Tianjin region dates back to the Warring States Period (403–221 B.C.), but it was not heavily settled until about eight centuries ago, when it was called Zhigu ("buying and selling"). In 1368 the Chinese sent troops to establish a frontier garrison on this site, and its location on the Grand Canal made it a center for the shipping of grain from southern China to Beijing. The city walls were constructed in 1404, but they were destroyed in 1900 during the Boxer Uprising. The Treaty of Tianjin, which ended the Arrow War of 1856–60, the second "Opium War" between Britain and China, demanded that China open more ports to foreign trade, regularize diplomatic relations between China and Western powers, allow Western nations to collect Chinese customs duties, guarantee the rights of missionaries and grant all Westerners the right to be tried in foreign-run rather than Chinese courts. The Qing dynasty (1644–1911) government refused to agree to these demands, so the British and French bombarded Tianjin, landed troops there and marched to Beijing, where they burned the Summer Palace and forced the Chinese to give them the concessions they demanded. In 1900 British and French forces occupied Tianjin during the Boxer Uprising.

By 1915, Tianjin had been divided into enclaves belonging to nine foreign countries, including Britain, France, Germany, Italy, Belgium, Austria-Hungary, the United States, Japan and Russia. The United States never administered its concession, but when it gave up its land at the turn of the century, it did not return the land to China but handed it over to the British. Altogether the foreign concessions in Tianjin were eight times as large as the Chinese area. The city took on a European look as many office buildings and residences were constructed in the Western style, and many of these have been restored since the earthquake. The Japanese occupied Tianjin during the War of Resistance against Japan (1937–45; World War II). After the founding of the People's Republic of China in 1949 the city was developed to become China's most important industrial city after Shanghai.

Major tourist sites include Ancient Culture Street, the oldest residential area in Tianjin. Located along the Hai River, it was first inhabited by fishermen. Buildings on the street have been restored to the Ming (1368–1644) and Qing dynasties, and many shops sell crafts, books, porcelain and carpets. The Temple of Lin Mo Niang, built in 1326, was dedicated to the goddess who protected fishermen. Today it houses a Folk Museum and a stage for performing arts. Tourists can visit the large carpet factories where hundreds of women weave carpets by hand and then etch designs in them using scissors. Arts and crafts may be purchased at the Yanglin Art Society.

Other sites include the Tianjin Art Museum, the Industrial Exhibition Hall and the Zhou Enlai Memorial Hall honoring one of the most important Communist leaders. Zhongshan Park, built in 1905, honors Dr. Sun Yat-sen (Sun Zhongshan), founder of modern China. The Park on the Water (Shuishang Gongyuan) contains a museum of Ming and Qing paintings and a lake where boats can be rented. The Grand Mosque (Qingzhen Dasi), the largest and oldest in the city, was built in 1644. The Dule Si Buddhist Temple, built during the Tang dynasty (618–907) and restored in 984, is one of the oldest wooden buildings in China and remarkably has not been damaged by earthquakes. The Buddhist Temple of Grand Mercy (Dabei Yuan) was built in 1656. Two important universities, Nankai and Beiyang, are located in Tianjin. The beautiful Panshan Mountains are a popular tourist site outside the city. See also ARROW WAR; BO HAI GULF; BOXER UPRISING; CARPETS; GRAND CANAL; HAI RIVER; HEBEI PROVINCE; MINORITIES, NATIONAL; NATURAL DISASTERS; NORTH CHINA PLAIN; QING DYNASTY; SUMMER PALACE; SUN YAT-SEN; TIANJIN; TIANJIN, TREATY OF; TREATY PORTS; ZHOU ENLAI.

TIANJIN (TIENTSIN), CONVENTION OF (1885) An agreement between China and Japan that the two countries would respect the neutrality of Korea and that neither country would intervene in Korea without the permission of the other. Korea is a peninsula jutting from the northeastern region of the Chinese mainland, and is separated from Japan by the Korea Strait. The country, which had been a vassal state of the Qing dynasty (1644–1911), suffered from an internal political crisis beginning in 1876 between conservative and reformist factions. The conservatives asked China to intervene in the crisis, and the reformers asked Japan to do so. In 1882 and 1884, Japan sent military forces into Korea, but both times they were checked by large numbers of Chinese troops that had also been sent there. In 1884 the reformers revolted against the Korean monarchy with Japan's help. The conservatives asked China for assistance, and Yuan Shikai (Yuan Shih-k'ai; 1859–1916), a warlord who later became president of the modern Republic of China, helped the Korean monarchy put down the rebellion. Some Japanese leaders wanted to strike against China. However, Ito Hirobumi (1841–1909), the Japanese foreign minister, agreed to meet with the Qing Chinese diplomat Li Hongzhang (Li Hung-chang; 1823–1901) at the Chinese city of Tianjin, where they negotiated the convention of neutrality for Korea. To prevent Japan from taking over Korea, Li Hongzhang had the king of Korea sign treaties with Britain, France, Germany and the United States. The Qing also established the senior post of Chinese "resident" in Seoul, the Korean capital, to maintain good relations between the

Korean court and the Chinese, who had been given a privileged status in Korea. In 1894 another rebellion attempted to overthrow the Korean monarch, who asked the Chinese for help, and China claimed sovereignty over Korea. Japan and China sent troops into Korea, and the two countries fought the Sino-Japanese War of 1894–95, in which Japan severely defeated China and took control of Korea. See also JAPAN AND CHINA; LI HONGZHANG; SINO-JAPANESE WAR OF 1894–95; YUAN SHIKAI.

TIANJIN (TIENTSIN), TREATY OF (1858) A treaty between China and Great Britain signed during the Arrow War (1856–60; Second Opium War). In 1857 the British seized the southern Chinese port city of Guangzhou (Canton) and moved north, taking the strategic Dagu forts in 1858 and threatening Tianjin, a large industrial city and port, and Beijing, the capital city. The Qing dynasty (1644–1911) gave in to British demands and signed the Treaty of Tianjin (1858), which exacted harsh measures on the Chinese. The treaty contained a most-favored-nation clause that meant other foreign powers, such as France, would receive the same rights and concessions as Britain. The treaty stated that a British ambassador would be allowed to reside in Beijing with his family and staff. The preaching of the Christian religion by foreign missionaries would be protected. Foreigners would be permitted to travel anywhere in China with valid passports, and within 30 miles of treaty ports (cities open to foreign trade) without passports. Official Chinese documents would no longer use the character for barbarian (yi; the common Chinese term for all foreigners) to refer to the British. All Chinese ports and customshouses would use standard weights and measures, official communications would be in English, and British ships chasing pirates would be allowed to enter any Chinese port. As soon as the internal rebellions then raging in China were put down, foreigners would be allowed to trade up the Yangzi River as far as Hankou, and four new treaty ports would be opened on the Yangzi; Hankou, Jiujiang, Nanjing and Zhenjiang. Six more treaty ports were to be opened right away: one in Manchuria (northeastern China), one in Shandong Province, one in Guangdong Province, two on the island of Taiwan, and one on Hainan Island. In these places, a flat fee of 2.5 percent would be charged on foreign imports, in place of interior transit taxes. A supplementary clause specified the conditions for the sale of opium in China by foreigners, even though the Chinese penal code prohibited the sale and use of opium. In return for all of these benefits, the British pulled their troops out of Tianjin and gave the Dagu forts back to the Qing. Although the Qing rulers had signed the Treaty of Tianjin, they did not want to follow its demands, especially the clause that allowed ambassadors of foreign nations to live in Beijing. They handed the British a military defeat, but in 1860 British and French troops moved into Tianjin and Beijing and burned down the Summer Palace. The Qing signed the Convention of Beijing (1860) giving the British many more benefits. See also ARROW WAR; BEIJING, CONVENTION OF (1860); MISSIONARIES; OPIUM WAR; TIANJIN; TREATY PORTS; UNEQUAL TREATIES.

TIANMING See BOOK OF HISTORY; MANDATE OF HEAVEN.

TIANQI (EMPEROR) See DONGLIN ACADEMY; EUNUCHS; WEI ZHONGXIAN.

TIANSHAN MOUNTAIN RANGE ("Heavenly Mountains") A very large range of mountains in western China and Central Asia that extends for 1,553 miles from the Kyzyl Kum Desert in Uzbekistan to the western edge of the Gobi Desert in China near the border of Xinjiang-Uighur Autonomous Region and Gansu Province with Outer Mongolia. The eastern hills surround the Turpan Depression. The Tianshan range includes more than 20 parallel ranges and valleys that run east to west. The Tianshan and the Yin are China's most northerly mountain ranges. There are 6,896 glaciers on the Tianshan peaks that cover an area of 3,687 square miles. More than 200 rivers, including some very long ones, originate in the Tianshan range, and cities north and south of the range have built hydroelectric power plants fueled by them. Abundant rainfall due to moist air from the Arctic Ocean supports a great variety of vegetation on the mountain slopes, with about 2,500 species of trees, shrubs and grasses. Deer inhabit the forests of the northern slopes, and wild sheep known as Argalis inhabit the high rocky peaks.

Most of the Tianshan range lies within China and covers one-fifth of Xinjiang's total area. The range creates a division between the Dzungaria Basin to the north and the Tarim Basin to the south. It is divided into a western and an eastern section by a gap south of the city of Urumqi in Xinjiang. Many of the Tianshan ridges are between 9,840 to 13,120 feet above sea level and some peaks in the eastern section rise above 14,000 feet. The highest peaks are in the western section. On Xinjiang's western border, Pobeda ("Victory") Peak is 24,506 feet high and Khan Tegri is 22,949 feet. Here is found the westernmost point of China, at a longitude of about 73°E in the Tianshan range at the western tip of Xinjiang. The range's highest mountain is Tuomuer Peak, 24,394 feet high. The Tianshan within China contains petroleum deposits and may have mineral deposits such as lead, zinc, tin, copper and iron. Meltwater from glaciers on the northern side of the Tianshan range flows into the Urumqi River, which provides water for Urumqi, the capital of Xinjiang. In 1959 the Chinese Academy of Sciences established the Tianshan Mountains Glacial Station to survey and analyze the glaciers. See also GANSU PROVINCE; GOBI DESERT; TARIM BASIN; TURPAN DEPRESSION; XINJIANG-UIGHUR AUTONOMOUS REGION.

TIANTAI SECT OF BUDDHISM (T'ien-t'ai) A sect in the Mahayana ("Greater Vehicle") branch of the Buddhist religion. Buddhism was introduced into China from India around the first century A.D. Tiantai, the first Buddhist sect to originate in China, became one of the four influential sects of Chinese Buddhism, along with the Chan (Zen), Flower Garland and Pure Land Sects. The teachings of the Tiantai sect are similar to those of the Huayan Sect. Both sects taught that their religious rituals could be performed only by monks who had given up all worldly attachments and completely devoted themselves to the religion. Tiantai was founded by the Chinese Buddhist monk Zhikai (Chih-k'ai, also known as Zhiyi or Chih-yi; 538–97) and named for Tiantai ("Heavenly Terrace") Mountain in modern Zhejiang

Province where he taught. Teachings of the Tiantai Sect are based on the scripture the *Lotus Sutra* (formally known as the *Sutra of the Lotus of the Wonderful Law; Saddharmapundarika Sutra*), an Indian text that has remained one of the most popular Mahayana Buddhist scriptures. Several translations were made of the *Lotus Sutra* from Sanskrit into Chinese, beginning in the third century A.D. This scripture claims to be the record of the final sermon that Sakyamuni (also known as Siddhartha Gautama), the historical Buddha who lived in northern India in the sixth century B.C., gave to his followers before he entered Nirvana. It teaches that all human beings can attain enlightenment if they have faith in the eternal transcendent Buddha, who appeared in the world to help everyone become free from suffering. The beautiful lotus flower, which rises up from the mud, symbolizes the way purity and truth rise above evil, and all people have the lotus of the Buddha nature within them. The Tiantai Sect used the teachings of the *Lotus Sutra* to develop a complex philosophy that attempted to harmonize the various conflicting doctrines held by different schools of Buddhist thought. Since only those who had leisure time and education were able to study Tiantai philosophy, the sect's members tended to come from the upper classes. In the sixth century A.D. the Japanese Buddhist monk Saicho (767–822) introduced the Tiantai Sect into Japan, where it flourished under the name Tendai. See also BUDDHISM; FLOWER GARLAND SECT OF BUDDHISM, LOTUS SUTRA.

TIANTAN PARK See TEMPLE OF HEAVEN.

TIANXIA See ALL UNDER HEAVEN.

TIANZI See ALL UNDER HEAVEN; EMPEROR; HEAVEN; MANDATE OF HEAVEN.

TIAO CHAN See DIAO CHAN.

TIBET (Xizang)   Properly known as Tibet Autonomous Region (Xizang Zizhiqu); a large region in western China that covers 480,000 square miles, one-eighth of China's total territory. Tibet is located on the vast, empty, wind-swept Qinghai-Tibet Plateau and averages more than 13,200 feet above sea level. The Zangbu River (Zangbujiang; also known as the upper Brahmaputra) flows near Mount Kailas (Tise in Tibetan) in southwestern Tibet, the most sacred mountain in Asia. Tibet is bordered by Yunnan and Sichuan provinces to the east, Qinghai Province to the northeast, Xinjiang Uighur Autonomous Region to the north, India to the west and Nepal, Bhutan and India to the south. Tibet is called the "Roof of the World" because its southern border comprises the Himalaya Mountain Range, with more than 50 mountain peaks over 23,100 feet in elevation, including a dozen higher than 26,400 feet. Mount Everest (Qomolongma in Chinese and Tibetan; "Mother Goddess of the World") is the highest mountain in the world. Several other high mountain ranges also lie in Tibet. The Yarlung Zangbo River (also known as the Brahmaputra) flows across Tibet's southern region, 15,543 feet above sea level. Many rivers originate in Tibet, including the Yellow River (Huanghe) and the Yangzi River (Changjiang), China's two longest rivers; the Mekong River (Lancanjiang in Chinese) and the Salween River (Nujiang in

Chinese), which flow into Southeast Asia; and the Brahmaputra and Indus rivers, which flow into India and Pakistan. Tibet has 1,500 lakes, about 30 percent of the total lake area in China. Lake Namco, 15,543 feet above sea level, is China's second-largest saltwater lake and Lake Yamzho Yumco, 13,000 feet above sea level, is Tibet's most important fishing area.

Tibet has a population of about 2 million, giving it a population density of less than three inhabitants per square mile. The majority are Tibetans, who comprise one of the largest of China's officially designated national minority ethnic groups. Tibetans, who call themselves the "Poiba," belong to the Tibeto-Burman linguistic group. Many Han Chinese, the ethnic majority in China, have recently moved into the region, including a large number of soldiers. Tibet has about 140 million acres of arable land, making it one of the largest farming regions in China. Major crops include barley, rye, millet, buckwheat, wheat and fruits and vegetables. Animal husbandry is an important economic activity. Nomadic Tibetans raise yak, goats, sheep and dzo (a cross between a yak and a cow) in the high steppes and summer pasturelands. Tibet is a major producer of meat and dairy products, fur, leather, wool and wool carpets. The region also has large forests and is rich in mineral and water resources and geothermal heat, with more than 4,000 kinds of mineral products and the greatest reserves of lithium and borax in the world. It has a hydropower potential of 200 million kilowatts and abundant solar and wind energy, and it leads China in geothermal resources. Tibet is very remote and transportation is not well developed, but industry and communications have developed rapidly since 1980.

Tibet became a protectorate of China only during the Qing dynasty (1644–1911). The region was first unified in the sixth century by King Namri Songzan (Namri Songtsen), ruler of the kingdom of Yarlung in southeastern Tibet near modern Bhutan. He brought many tribes under his control as far as Nepal. Songzan Gambo (Songtsen Gampo; 617–650) completed the unification of Tibet, Nepal and part of modern Yunnan Province, and established his capital in Lhasa, where he built a palace on the hill where the Potala Palace now stands. He ordered Tumi Sanbujia to develop a phonetic Tibetan alphabet based on north Indian and western Chinese languages. Tibetan culture prospered, especially between the 10th and 16th centuries, and many religious and scholarly books were printed in the Tibetan language. In 634 King Songzan Gambo sent an envoy to the Chinese Tang dynasty (618–907) court asking to marry a Tang princess. Seven years later, Tang princess Wencheng arrived in Tibet, and their marriage created a blood tie between the Tibetans and the Han Chinese. She brought with her a sculpture of the Buddha Sakyamuni, founder of the Buddhist religion; it is still displayed at the Rasa Tsoglak (Jokhan) Monastery in Lhasa, which was completed in 648 to house the sculpture. This marriage brought Tibet into the tribute system whereby foreign countries were permitted to trade with China if they sent missions to the capital to bow before the Chinese emperor and declare themselves his vassals. Young Tibetans went to study in the Tang capital at Chang'an (modern Xi'an in Shaanxi Province), then the largest and most cosmopolitan city in the world.

The Tibetans were fierce fighters, and in 763, Tibetan armies moved north into Gansu and Ningxia and took control of the Silk Road, including the city of Kashgar, along which China traded silk and other goods with the Mediterranean world. Tang Chinese troops occupied Xinjiang, and in response the Tibetans sacked Chang'an. In 821 the Tang signed a treaty with Tibet affirming that the Tibetans occupied Gansu and that they were independent of China. In 842 the Tibetan king was assassinated and the Tibetans retreated to their own country, protected by the high mountains.

The Tibetans continued to practice the Buddhist religion, and Buddhist missionaries traveled to Tibet from India. The Tibetans developed their own sect of Buddhism, known as Lamaism, which incorporated many aspects of the ancient Tibetan Bon religion. Lamaism flourished in Tibet between the 13th and 16th centuries, especially the Yellow Hat Sect, and temples and pagodas were built all over the country. The third Dalai Lama, the head of the Yellow Hat Sect, converted the Altan Khan, the powerful ruler of the Mongols, an ethnic group north of China, to Lamaism. The Mongols ruled China under the Yuan dynasty (1279–1368) and established an empire that extended all the way to eastern Europe. In the 16th century the Grand Lama of the Yellow Hat Monastery in Lhasa received the title Dalai, meaning "ocean" or "measurelessness" in Mongolian. Lama is the title for an honored religious master, similar to guru in India. Each Dalai Lama is believed to be a reincarnation of the previous one. In 1643 a Mongol leader helped the Dalai Lama and his Yellow Hat Sect defeat the older Red Hat Sect of Lamaism, his major opposition, and this made the Dalai Lama the undisputed religious leader of Tibet. The fifth Dalai Lama rebuilt the Potala Palace to be his residence in Lhasa and established his political control over much of Tibet.

In 1368 the Han Chinese had overthrown the Mongol Yuan and established the Ming dynasty. In 1644 the Manchus, an ethnic group based in Manchuria (modern northeastern China), overthrew the Ming and established the Qing dynasty. The Manchus also patronized Lamaism. In 1652 the fifth Dalai Lama traveled from Tibet to the Manchu Qing capital at Beijing, where he paid tribute to the Qing emperor. However, this Dalai Lama and his successors continued to support the Mongols against the Manchus, and the Mongols continued to select the Dalai Lamas. Qing emperor Kangxi (K'ang-hsi) sent troops to Lhasa from 1705 to 1706 but the Tibetans drove them off. In 1720 the Manchu Qing government removed the Mongolian choice as Dalai Lama and installed their own candidate in this position. By the middle of the 18th century the Qing had established a protectorate in Tibet. China continued to control Tibet and the Dalai Lamas, but the Qing became weak in the 19th century, especially due to wars begun by Western powers to open China to foreign trade. The Tibetans attempted to recover their independence while dealing with the British, Russians and Chinese. In 1906 the British forced the Qing to grant them trading and diplomatic privileges in Tibet. In 1910 the Qing sent troops into Tibet and the Dalai Lama fled to India, but the Qing Dynasty was overthrown in the Revolution of 1911 and the Chinese people became preoccupied with establishing the modern Republic of China, so he returned to Tibet in 1912.

China still claimed that Tibet was a Chinese province, and in 1923 the Panchen Lama, the second-most important Tibetan leader, sought refuge in China. However, Tibet remained relatively independent after 1912. When the Chinese Communist Party (CCP) founded the People's Republic of China (PRC) in 1949, it made Tibet an Autonomous Region of China. The PRC sent troops into Tibet in 1950, and in 1951 it signed an agreement with the current Dalai Lama, the 14th, Tenzin Gyatso (1935–   ), to allow Tibet's theocratic system to continue, albeit under Chinese control. However, the Chinese treated the Tibetans brutally, torturing or murdering thousands of them and destroying their monasteries. The PRC also banned the public and private practice of Lamaism. The Tibetans rebelled against the Chinese between 1958 and 1959 but were harshly suppressed, and the Dalai Lama, along with 80,000 Tibetans, fled south to India, where he established his government-in-exile in Dharamsala.

During the Cultural Revolution (1966–76), rampaging Chinese Red Guards destroyed most of the thousands of Tibetan Buddhist monasteries and temples. Altogether between 1950 and 1976 the Chinese killed 1.2 million Tibetans and destroyed all but 13 of their 6,254 monasteries. Recently a few have been restored. The Tibetans are still very religious and make pilgrimages to Buddhist temples, especially for traditional festivals. The Tibetans have been the most resistant to assimilation of any ethnic group in China, and they rebelled against the PRC in 1987 and 1989. The PRC has sent many Chinese troops and police to occupy Tibet, and has also encouraged Han Chinese to settle there and intermarry with the Tibetans. Tibet is a politically sensitive area because the PRC has had border skirmishes with Nepal, Bhutan and India. The Aksai Chin area of northeastern Jammu and Kashmir on Tibet's western border is controlled by the PRC but claimed by India. A large area east of Bhutan and north of the Brahmaputra River is controlled by India but claimed by the PRC.

The Dalai Lama has always advocated peaceful means for resolving the problem of Tibet's status. In 1988 he informed the PRC government that he would no longer insist upon Tibet's sovereign independence, but the government refused to open negotiations with him. In 1989 the Dalai Lama was awarded the Nobel Peace Prize. In 1995 he became embroiled in a conflict with the PRC government over the selection of the 11th Panchen Lama (the 10th had died in 1989). The PRC government rejected the validity of the Tibetan boy chosen by the Dalai Lama and chose another Tibetan boy, claiming that it has final authority over the recognition of important lamas, under a 1792 treaty between Tibet and the Qing government. The PRC government has accused the Dalai Lama of being a "splitist."

The PRC limits tourism in Tibet, although a small number of foreign travelers are able to visit the region each year. Lhasa, the capital city, lies 11,800 feet above sea level. Gangdise Mountain lies to the south and the Nyainqentanglha Mountains to the north. The Lhasa River, a branch of the Yarlung Zangpo, flows through the city in the south. The Potala Palace, with 1,000 rooms, is the traditional residence of the Dalai Lama. The palace is now a museum and was recently restored by the PRC government. An Exhibition Hall at the foot of the palace houses displays on Buddhist monastic life and Tibetan daily life and handicrafts. Jokhang Temple, built 1,300 years ago to commemorate the marriage of King Songzan Gambo and Princess Wencheng, houses the gold statue of the Buddha that she brought to Tibet and is one of the region's holiest shrines. The Barkhor is a pilgrimage circuit and marketplace around Jokhang Temple. Norbu Lingka, two miles west of the Potala Palace, is the former summer residence of the Dalai Lama. Three monasteries outside Lhasa were important sites for the Tibetan government, including the Drepung, Sera and Ganden. They were destroyed during the Cultural Revolution and the monks were killed, but recently the PRC has begun restoring them.

The Yarlung River Valley, about 115 miles southeast of Lhasa, is considered the birthplace of Tibetan culture. Samye Monastery was constructed in 775 as the first Buddhist monastery in Tibet. Yumbu Lhakang is supposedly the oldest building in Tibet. The city of Shigatse (Xigaze in Chinese) is Tibet's second largest urban center. Tashilhunpo Monastery, the seat of the Panchen Lama, was built in 1447. It contains a statue of Maitreya Buddha nearly 90 feet high and a Grand Hall that contains the tomb of the fourth Panchen Lama, decorated with a large amount of gold and jewels. Sakya Monastery about 100 miles west of Shigatse, the most powerful monastery in Tibet 700 years ago, contains one of the most beautiful collections of religious relics that remains in Tibet. Some travelers visit the Rongbuk Monastery, Mount Kailas, and the base camp at Mount Everest. See also BUDDHISM; CULTURAL REVOLUTION; DALAI LAMA; EVEREST, MOUNT, GEOGRAPHY; HIMALAYA MOUNTAIN RANGE; KAILAS, MOUNT; KASHGAR; LAMAISM; LHASA; MINORITIES, NATIONAL; MONGOL; PEOPLE'S REPUBLIC OF CHINA; POTALA PALACE; QING DYNASTY; QINGHAI-TIBET PLATEAU; SILK ROAD; SINO-INDIAN BORDER DISPUTE; TIBETAN; TRIBUTE SYSTEM; YAK; YUAN DYNASTY.

TIBETAN (Zang) The native people of Tibet Autonomous Region (Xizang Zizhiqu), who comprise one of the largest of China's officially designated 55 national minority ethnic groups. According to the 1990 census, about 4.6 million Tibetans reside in Tibet and the provinces of Qinghai, Gansu, Sichuan and Yunnan. Tibet is known as the Roof of the World because its southern border comprises the Himalaya Mountain Range, the world's highest mountains. Tibetans, who call themselves the "Poiba," herd animals, especially the yak, and grow some crops such as barley. The yak, a large animal with long shaggy hair similar to an ox or buffalo, provides meat, milk, hair for weaving textiles and transportation. Prior to the Qin dynasty (221–206 B.C.) in China, the ancestors of the Tibetans herded animals in the central valley of the Yarlung Zangpo River. The Tibetan language belongs to the Tibeto-Burman linguistic group. It is divided into three regional dialects: Weizan, Kang and Anduo. Tibetan king Songzan Gambo (Songtsen Gampo; 617–650) ordered Tumi Sanbujia to develop a phonetic alphabet based on north Indian and western Chinese languages. Tibetan culture prospered from the 10th through 16th centuries, and many religious and scholarly books were produced in the Tibetan language.

The recorded history of the Tibetan people began in the seventh century, when Tibetan armies under King Songzan Gambo occupied Nepal and made part of Yunnan Province their vassal state. After he died, Tibetan armies moved north and took control of the Silk Road, including the city of Kash-

gar. Chinese troops of the Tang dynasty (618–907) occupied Xinjiang, and the Tibetans sacked the Tang capital of Chang'an (modern Xi'an). In 842 the Tibetan king was assassinated and the Tibetans halted their expansion and remained within the borders of their mountainous country from then on. Tang Chinese emperors sent princesses to marry Tibetan kings, one reason why the Chinese claim that Tibet has been a tributary state of China for more than 1,000 years.

The Tibetans have practiced the Buddhist religion ever since it was brought into Tibet from India in the seventh century. Buddhism flourished in Tibet from the 13th through the 16th centuries, and temples and pagodas, especially those of the Yellow Hat Sect of Lamaism, were built all over the country. The Dalai Lama, head of the Yellow Hat Sect, is the religious and political head of Tibet. He formerly resided in the Potala Palace in Lhasa. The current Dalai Lama, the 14th, Tenzin Gyatso, resides in exile in Dharamsala, India, where he fled with 80,000 Tibetans who fled when the Communist People's Republic of China (PRC) sent troops into Tibet in 1959. During the Cultural Revolution (1966–76), most Tibetan Buddhist monasteries and temples were destroyed, although a few have been restored. The Tibetans are still very religious and make pilgrimages to Buddhist temples, especially for traditional festivals. Song and dance are popular among Tibetans, and native Tibetan dramas are performed by masked actors and actresses who sing and dance to the accompaniment of a traditional orchestra.

The Tibetans have resisted assimilation more than any other minority group in China, and they rebelled against the PRC again in 1987 and 1989. The PRC has sent large numbers of Chinese troops and police to occupy Tibet, and has also encouraged many Han Chinese to settle there and intermarry with the Tibetans to dilute their racial stock. Tibet is a politically sensitive area because it borders Nepal, Bhutan and India, with which the PRC has had border skirmishes. See also BUDDHISM; DALAI LAMA; GEOGRAPHY; HIMALAYA MOUNTAIN RANGE; LAMAISM; LHASA; MINORITIES, NATIONAL; POTALA PALACE; QINGHAI-TIBET PLATEAU, SILK ROAD; SINO-INDIAN BORDER DISPUTE; TIBET; YAK.

T'IEN See HEAVEN.

T'IEN HOU See MAZIPO.

T'IEN TZU See ALL UNDER HEAVEN; EMPEROR; HEAVEN; MANDATE OF HEAVEN.

T'IEN-CH'I (EMPEROR) See DONGLIN ACADEMY; EUNUCHS; WEI ZHONGXIAN.

T'IEN-HSIA See ALL UNDER HEAVEN.

TIEN-HSIN See DIM SUM.

T'IEN-MING See MANDATE OF HEAVEN.

T'IEN-T'AI SECT OF BUDDHISM See LOTUS SUTRA; TIANTAI SECT OF BUDDHISM.

T'IEN-TAN PARK See TEMPLE OF HEAVEN.

TIENTSIN See TIANJIN.

TIGER (*hu*) The tiger has been common in the southern provinces of China and in Manchuria in northeast China and revered by the Chinese as a creature with many symbolic attributes. Each direction of the compass is traditionally believed to be ruled by a mythical creature; the White Tiger is the ruler of the West. The tiger is also associated with autumn, when it comes down from the mountains into villages, and is personified by the constellation Orion, which is prominent in autumn. In Chinese astrology, the star Alpha of the Great Bear constellation gave birth to the first tiger. The tiger represents the masculine principle in nature and is king of all the animals, as shown by the four stripes on his forehead which form the character Wang, or Prince. The tiger is regarded as one of the four super-intelligent creatures, along with the dragon, phoenix and tortoise; for centuries, the four have been a major design motif in Chinese art. In southern China, on the tiger's birthday on the second moon in the lunar calendar, fixed in the Western calendar as March 6, women worship the White Tiger. They place paper images of the tiger in their homes to keep away rats and snakes and prevent quarrels. On this date, effigies of the tiger are also put in front of temple buildings for people to make offerings. The God of Wealth, the deified Marshal Chao Gongming (Ch'ao Kung-ming), is depicted riding a black tiger and holding a silver ingot. The Chinese call an able general a "tiger general" and a brave soldier a "tiger warrior."

In Chinese folktales, tigers kill evil men and protect good men. Tiger charms are used to keep away disease and evil, and babies are given colorfully embroidered tiger shoes for protection. Tigers frequently decorate children's clothing and toys. The "Tiger's Claw" (*hu chao*) amulet is believed to ward off sudden fright and give the wearer the courage of the tiger. Because the tiger wards off disasters, it is popular as one of the nine gods worshiped at the New Year Festival. Tiger images are painted on the walls of homes and temples to keep away evil spirits. Dragon-Tiger Mountain is the name for the palace of the hereditary head of the Daoist religion, located in the Dragon Tiger Mountains of Jiangxi Province, east of the capital city of Nanchang. Zhang Daoling (Chang Tao-ling), the "First Master of Heaven" in the Daoist religion, is depicted riding a tiger and carrying a demon-dispelling sword as he escorts the dead to their final destination. A Daoist legend tells of two brothers who took on the role of protecting human beings by capturing demons and throwing them to tigers.

As the enemies of evil spirits, especially those who torment the dead, tigers are carved on tombs and monuments. The Chinese system of *feng shui* (geomancy) requires that a burial site be higher on the right side, the stronger side of the body, so the White Tiger can guard it; the Azure Dragon guards the left side, the body's weaker side. The tiger is the third animal in the 12-year animal zodiac. People born in the Year of the Tiger are thought to be brave, strong, stubborn and sympathetic. The tiger represents the greatest earthly power as well as protection over human life. It chases away the so-called "three disasters": fire, thieves and ghosts. See also DAOISM; DRAGON; FENG SHUI; NEW YEAR FESTIVAL; PHOENIX; TORTOISE; ZHANG DAOLING; ZODIAC, ANIMAL.

TI-HSIN, KING See SHANG DYNASTY.

TILES, GLAZED Porcelain tiles decorated with yellow, blue-green and yellow-brown glazes that were used in imperial palaces and temples from the Tang dynasty (618–907) through the Qing dynasty (1644–1911), China's last imperial dynasty. Prior to the Tang dynasty, Chinese potters produced less-refined, single-color wares, typically black, white or pale green. Chinese roofs were originally covered with thatching. During the Zhou dynasty (1100–256 B.C.), thatched roofs were replaced by roofs made from semi-circular terracotta tiles, which were formed in molds that created designs in relief on their surfaces. Technical developments during the Tang dynasty enabled potters to produce delicate, lustrous porcelain wares that were painted with colored glazes and then fired in a kiln. This technique is known as three-color ware (*sancai* or *san-ts'ai*). Artists placed three-colored glazed tiles together to create large mosaic wall murals. Potters also used the three-color technique to produce sculptures of entertainers, soldiers, horses, camels and other figures that were placed in Tang tombs. The Mongols, who ruled China under the Yuan dynasty (1279–1368), had a strong preference for glazed tile decorations, which influenced subsequent Chinese architecture. Architects during the Ming (1368–1644) and the Qing followed the Yuan model of decorating roofs and walls with tiles in bright colors. Beautiful glazed tiles can still be seen at imperial sites in the capital city of Beijing. One example is the multicolored Nine Dragon Screen built in 1773 in the former imperial palace grounds, known as the Forbidden City. The Temple of Heaven (Tiantan or T'en-t'an), the site where emperors offered sacrifices to Heaven and which has become the symbol of Beijing, has brilliant blue tiles covering the outside walls of the building that encloses the circular Altar of Heaven. Contemporary Chinese artists, notably Wu Yongfan, who graduated from the Central Academy of Arts and Crafts in 1982, have been studying the ancient techniques for coloring, glazing and firing porcelain tiles. They use them to create beautiful tiled mosaic murals and wall decorations employing traditional motifs, such as flowers, fans and Beijing Opera masks, but with a modern look. See also ARCHITECTURE, TRADITIONAL; DRAGON; FORBIDDEN CITY; PORCELAIN; TEMPLE OF HEAVEN; THREE-COLOR WARE.

TIMUR LENG See TAMERLANE.

TING See BRONZEWARE; DING.

TING, BISHOP K. H. See CHRISTIANITY.

TING LING See DING LING.

TING WARE See DING WARE.

TI-T'AN See CARPETS.

TI-TSANG PUSA See JIUHUA, MOUNT.

TOASTS See BANQUETS; MAOTAI; WEDDINGS, TRADITIONAL.

TOBA TURKS See BUDDHISM; DATONG; NORTHERN WEI DYNASTY; SHANXI PROVINCE; SINICIZATION.

TOFU See SOYBEANS AND SOY PRODUCTS.

TOMBS AND TOMB FIGURES See ARCHAEOLOGY; EASTERN IMPERIAL TOMB; MING TOMBS; NORTHERN IMPERIAL TOMB; SCULPTURE; TANG IMPERIAL TOMBS; TERRACOTTA ARMY, TOMB OF EMPEROR QIN SHI HUANGDI; THREE-COLOR WARE.

TONG SHU See ALMANAC; OX.

TONGBAO See OVERSEAS CHINESE.

TONGMENGHUI See REVOLUTIONARY ALLIANCE.

TONGSHI See HAINAN ISLAND.

TONGZHI (EMPEROR) (T'ung-chih; 1856–75) An emperor of the Manchu Qing dynasty (1644–1911) whose reign (1862–75) is known as the Tongzhi Restoration. His personal name was Zaichun (Tsai-ch'un); Tongzhi, meaning "Govern Together," is his posthumous reign name. When he was five years old he succeeded his father, the sickly Xiangfeng (Hsien-feng) emperor (r. 1851–61), whose reign had witnessed China's defeat by Great Britain in the Arrow War (Second Opium War, 1856–60) and devastating rebellions by the Taipings, Nian bandits, Small Sword Society and Muslims. Tongzhi's mother was the ruthless Cixi (Tz'u Hsi), who became empress dowager upon his accession and wielded the actual power for 47 years at the end of the Qing dynasty. Cixi, who had been Xiangfeng's favorite concubine, served as co-regent with his widowed empress Cian (Tz'u-an) during Tongzhi's reign. Prince Gong (Kung; 1833–98) also served as imperial adviser, along with several other princes. Tongzhi was completely dominated by his mother. When he died at age 19, Cixi placed her three-year-old nephew on the throne, known as the Guangxu (Kuang-hsu) Emperor (r. 1875–1908), and she became sole regent when Cian died in 1881.

During Tongzhi's reign, following Prince Gong's advice, in 1861 the Qing set up the Zongli Yamen (Tsungli Yamen; Office for General Affairs) to deal with foreign diplomats, especially those from the Western powers that had forced China to open up many cities as so-called treaty ports. The government also finally suppressed the Taipings in 1864. Under the Self-Strengthening Movement, China acquired Western technology to increase its military power, built ships, organized the China Merchants' Steam Navigation Company and set up telegraphic communications between major Chinese cities. However, there was also a revival of Confucianism during the Tongzhi Restoration, which may have delayed China's modernization in the 19th century. See also ARROW WAR; CHINA MERCHANTS' STEAM NAVIGATION COMPANY; CIXI, EMPRESS DOWAGER; CONFUCIANISM; GONG, PRINCE; NIAN REBELLION; QING DYNASTY; SELF-STRENGTHEN-ING MOVEMENT; SMALL SWORD SOCIETY; TAIPING REBELLION; TREATY PORTS; ZONGLI YAMEN.

TONKIN, GULF OF See GUANGXI-ZHUANG AUTONOMOUS REGION.

TORTOISE (*wugui* or *wu-kuei*) The tortoise or turtle is considered by the Chinese to be one of the four super-intelli-gent animals, along with the dragon, phoenix and tiger. Each direction of the compass is traditionally believed to be ruled by a mythical creature; the tortoise, known as the "Black Warrior," rules the North and represents winter. It is also a symbol of strength, endurance and longevity. The tortoise represents the universe, with the markings on its upper shell supposedly corresponding to the constellations in the sky, and the lines on its lower shell to the Earth. The tortoise is traditionally believed to live for more than 3,000 years without food and air. A type of tortoise called *yuan* is believed to combine the qualities of the tortoise and the dragon, the most powerful of all creatures, and is the attendant of the God of the Waters. The *bixi* (*pi-hsi*) is a river god portrayed as a tortoise with supernatural strength. Many stone pillars are carved with this mighty tortoise at the base holding up the massive stone tablets that are the foundations of the universe.

Chinese creation myths state that originally there were five islands floating in the Eastern Sea. They bumped into mainland China and disturbed the gods, who complained to the Jade Emperor, ruler of Heaven. He ordered the god of the ocean wind to stabilize them by attaching each island to three huge tortoises that took turns holding the island in place, each tortoise serving as an anchor for 60,000 years at a time. A giant who was fishing in the sea caught six tortoises, causing the two islands they were holding to drift to the north and sink. The Jade Emperor angrily retaliated by making all giants smaller than they were. The three islands that were still anchored by tortoises remained in place and drew to them people seeking immortality. They are known as the Islands of the Blessed.

Divination was practiced in the Shang dynasty (1750–1040 B.C.) by heating tortoise shells and shoulder blades of oxen and sheep, collectively called oracle bones, until they cracked. Characters were scratched on the shells and bones to interpret the omens. Farmers near Anyang in Henan Province had been digging up oracle bones for centuries and selling them as "dragon bones," to be ground up in herbal medicines. In 1889 scholars recognized that the scratches on them were an ancient form of writing. Several scientific excavations at the site have turned up a great quantity of tortoise shells and bones, and translations have been made of the oracles written on them.

The written character for tortoise is a pictogram for the animal, with a snakelike head on top, the claws on the left, the shell on the right and the tail at the bottom. Tortoises are found in the warm-temperate zone in China up to its northern limit at 41°N latitude, although one species, Horsfield's Tortoise, lives in the deserts in the northwestern region of Xinjiang-Uighur Autonomous Region. The tortoise is commonly eaten by the Chinese, boiled or cooked in a stew. Since ancient times, the meat of soft-shelled turtles has been a main ingredient in soups in both northern and southern China. A gelatinous essence from the tropical green turtle is highly valued in the finest soups. Turtle eggs are also consumed. See also ANYANG; COOKING, CHINESE; DRAGON; ISLANDS OF THE BLESSED; JADE EMPEROR; ORACLE BONES; PHOENIX; TIGER.

TOYS, TRADITIONAL Objects for children to play with that are made by hand from a wide variety of materials, including clay, dough, bamboo, wood, straw and cloth. Many traditional Chinese toys are made to look like animals or mythical creatures, such as tigers and dragons. Toys are a Chinese folk art and were frequently made by peasants to sell at rural markets at the time of traditional festivals. The Chinese still make folk toys, which are sold by street peddlers and at stalls at local fairs and festivals. The toys are distinct in different regions of the country, and some have been made the same way for hundreds of years. Artisans south of the Yangzi River (Changjiang) usually make toys from bamboo, reeds or grass. They are more delicate than the bold and sturdy toys north of the Yangzi, which are usually made of clay or wood.

One popular southern Chinese toy is the jointed dragon made of sections of bamboo strung together with wires. A stick under the body is turned to make the dragon twist and move in a realistic way. In Zhejiang Province on the southeastern Chinese coast, small figures are carved from boxwood, which has a smooth grain and a golden color. They depict things that children see in their daily lives, such as oxcarts, water buffalos, fishermen, and peasants sowing or winnowing grain. Chubby, brightly painted clay dolls made in Wuxi in Jiangsu Province in eastern China represent happy children. Toy tigers of stuffed and embroidered yellow silk are made in Shandong Province. The brave tiger, king of all the animals, is believed to kill evil men and protect good men. Chinese children wear colorful handmade tiger shoes, hats and charms to keep away disease and evil spirits. In Shaanxi Province in western China, terracotta whistles are made to look like human figures, mainly characters from the traditional opera.

Wooden stick dolls are made in Beijing, the capital city in northern China. Such a doll is carved from a single piece of wood and has a movable head with a round humorous face. During the Autumn Moon Festival, peddlars in Beijing sell clay models of the rabbit that the Chinese traditionally believe lives on the moon. These rabbits are one to three feet high and may be scholar rabbits wearing robes and carrying umbrellas or warrior rabbits wearing traditional military clothing with helmets and banners. Beijing folk artists also make miniature figures by coloring wheat dough and rolling and shaping it into the figures of animals, fat children and characters from the Beijing Opera. Kites and papercuts, brightly colored pictures cut by hand from paper, are folk arts related to folk toys. See also BAMBOO; CHARMS AND AMULETS; EMBROIDERY; KITES; MOON; OPERA, BEIJING; PAPERCUTTING; RABBIT; TIGER.

TRADE UNIONS See ALL-CHINA FEDERATION OF TRADE UNIONS; INTERNATIONAL WORKERS DAY; WORK UNIT.

TRANSLATION OF THE CHINESE LANGUAGE See PINYIN SYSTEM OF ROMANIZATION; WADE-GILES SYSTEM OF ROMANIZATION; WALEY, ARTHUR.

TRANSPORTATION See AIRLINES AND AIRPORTS; BICYCLE; CHINA INTERNATIONAL TRAVEL SERVICE; CHINA MERCHANTS STEAM NAVIGATION COMPANY; GRAND CANAL; JUNK; RAILROADS; SHIPPING AND SHIPBUILDING; YANGZI RIVER; YELLOW RIVER.

TRAY SCENERY See CONTAINER GARDENS; ROCKS.

TREATIES See AMUR RIVER; BEIJING, CONVENTION OF; NANJING, TREATY OF; NERCHINSK, TREATY OF; OPIUM WAR; RUSSO-JAPANESE WAR OF 1904–5; SHIMONOSEKI, TREATY OF; SINO-JAPANESE WAR OF 1894–95; TIANJIN, TREATY OF; TREATY PORTS; UNEQUAL TREATIES.

TREATY PORTS Chinese cities that foreign powers forced the government of the Manchu Qing dynasty (1644–1911) that ruled China to open to foreign residents and trade in the mid-19th century. Prior to then, every Chinese dynasty had permitted foreign countries to trade with China only if they became part of the tribute system. Countries wanting to engage in trade had to send missions to the Chinese capital to submit to the sovereignty of the Chinese emperor, the "Son of Heaven" (*Tianzi* or *T'ien tzu*), by performing a series of prostrations known as kowtow. In return they were given permission to trade for a specified number of days at designated places along the Chinese border. In 1793 Great Britain sent Lord Macartney to China to request the right to engage in open Western-style trade. When the British refused to submit to the Qing emperor, the Chinese responded by forcing foreign traders to conduct their business through officially designated Chinese merchants, the Cohong, in the southern port city of Guangzhou (Canton); this is known as the Canton system of trade. The British used military means to end this system. They defeated China in the Opium War (1839–42) and forced the Qing government to sign the Treaty of Nanjing, the first of many so-called unequal treaties forced on China by Western powers. The Treaty of Nanjing gave the British and other foreign powers many rights and privileges in China, including the opening of five treaty ports, Guangzhou, Xiamen, Fuzhou, Ningbo and Shanghai, to foreign residence and trade. Shanghai, situated on the Huangpu (Whampoa) River in the Yangzi River (Changjiang) delta on China's east coast, rapidly grew into one of the world's most important ports and China's largest city. Xiamen (formerly called Amoy), located in Fujian province on China's southeastern coast across the strait from Taiwan Island, had been a busy trading port for centuries. After the British took over the port, Xiamen became a center for Chinese immigration to Southeast Asia and the Americas. Fuzhou, the capital of Fujian, was also an active port. Ningbo, in Zhejiang Province south of Shanghai, was an important port for fishing as well as trade. The Treaty of Nanjing also ceded Hong Kong, a barren island near Guangzhou, to the British, who developed it into a major center for international trade. Hong Kong reverted to China in 1997.

After the first five treaty ports were opened, Britain continued to pressure the Qing. British and French troops defeated China once again in the Arrow War (also known as the Second Opium War; 1856–60). The Treaty of Tianjin (Tientsin; 1858) that Britain forced the Qing to sign stated that six more treaty ports would be immediately opened to foreign trade: one in Manchuria (northeastern China), one in Shandong Province, one in Guangdong Province, two on Taiwan Island and one on Hainan Island. It added that as soon as the internal rebellions raging in China were put down, foreigners would also be allowed to trade in four more ports, Hankou, Jiujiang, Nanjing and Zhenjiang. The Treaty of Tianjin also gave Westerners the right to collect Chinese customs duties, regularized diplomatic relations between the Qing and Western powers, permitted a British ambassador to reside in the capital city of Beijing, guaranteed the rights of foreign missionaries in China and granted all Westerners accused of committing crimes in China the right to be tried in foreign-run courts under foreign laws rather than in Chinese courts (a principle known as extraterritoriality). The Qing emperor did not want to implement the treaty, and his troops actually handed Britain a military defeat, so in 1860 the British sent an army to attack Beijing, where it burned down the imperial Summer Palace. The Qing then signed the Convention of Beijing (1860) giving the British even more benefits and ceding the southernmost area of the Kowloon peninsula to Hong Kong, which the British had made a Crown Colony. Altogether the Treaty of Tianjin and the Convention of Beijing opened 11 treaty ports: Danshui (Tamsui), Hankou, Jiongzhou, Jiujiang, Nanjing, Niuzhuang, Shantou (Swatow), Tainan, Tianjin (the port for Beijing), Zhenjiang and Zhifu (Chefoo). By the end of the Qing dynasty there were about 50 treaty ports.

The treaty ports continued to prosper after the Revolution of 1911 overthrew the Qing. In 1980 the Communist government of the modern People's Republic of China (PRC) designated four highly restricted areas along the Chinese coast as Special Economic Zones (SEZs) to encourage foreign trade and investment in China, increase Chinese exports and import foreign technology and management expertise. Xiamen is one of these SEZs, and the other three are located near Guangzhou. In 1984 the government designated 14 "coastal open cities" for the same purpose. Many of these were former treaty ports, including Shanghai, Guangzhou and Tianjin. See also ARROW WAR; BEIJING, CONVENTION OF; CANTON SYSTEM TO REGULATE FOREIGN TRADE; EMPEROR; HEAVEN; HONG KONG; HUANGPU RIVER; KOWTOW; MACARTNEY, LORD GEORGE; NANJING, TREATY OF; OPIUM WAR; QING DYNASTY; SPECIAL ECONOMIC ZONES; TIANJIN, TREATY OF; TRIBUTE SYSTEM; UNEQUAL TREATIES; NAMES OF INDIVIDUAL CITIES.

TRIAD SOCIETY See OVERSEAS CHINESE; PEASANTS AND PEASANT REBELLIONS; REVOLUTIONARY ALLIANCE; SMALL SWORD SOCIETY; SUN YAT-SEN.

TRIBUTE SYSTEM A system under which foreign states submitted to Chinese suzerainty by exchanging gifts for trading privileges in China. The tribute system was developed by the court of the Han dynasty (206 B.C.–A.D. 220) to maintain peace with non-Han ethnic groups in distant regions. These Han had incorporated into the Chinese Empire, including part of modern Xinjiang-Uighur Autonomous Region and parts of northern Vietnam and northern Korea. The Han allowed non-Chinese states to retain their autonomy if they agreed to the symbolic sovereignty of the Han, through exchanges of gifts such as silk and intermarriages. Many Han princesses were sent to marry non-Han rulers to strengthen the ties between China and other groups. The Chinese called their country the "Middle

[or Central] Kingdom" (Zhongguo or Chung-kuo), meaning that it is the center of the Earth. They referred to their emperor as the "Son of Heaven" (tianzi or t'ien tzu) and believed that his absolute power on Earth was legitimized by the Mandate of Heaven (tianming or t'ien ming), a concept that originated in the Xia dynasty (2200–1750 B.C.). Each successive dynasty claimed the Mandate of Heaven for itself, arguing that the previous dynasty had become evil and lost the favor of Heaven, and thus deserved to be overthrown.

Every Chinese emperor in every dynasty, as the Son of Heaven, demanded submission under the tribute system from those outside the empire, whom they considered "barbarians." Under the tribute system, foreign countries wanting to engage in trade sent missions to the Chinese capital to submit to the sovereignty of the Chinese emperor. Members of the foreign missions had to perform kowtow (gedou or ke-tou) before the emperor, a ritual that entailed kneeling three times and making three prostrations with each kneel. In return they were given permission to trade for a specified number of days at designated places along the Chinese border.

The tribute system was also the chief means for expanding the Chinese Empire. When the Ming dynasty (1368–1644) expanded the empire to the southwestern regions of Sichuan, Yunnan and Guizhou, the emperors used the tribute system to absorb the native peoples. The emperors legitimized the power of the tribal chiefs over their local domains and gave them Chinese official titles, but allowed them to govern their people in their traditional way. The chiefs, however, had to go to the court to submit to the emperor in person. The chiefs also had to send tribute on a regular basis. In exchange they received luxurious and prestigious gifts from the Chinese court and the privilege of engaging in lucrative trade with China. During the Ming dynasty, China had tributary trading relationships with a large number of vassal states throughout East, Southeast and South Asia. Many of these were brought into the tribute system by Zheng He (Cheng Ho), whom the Ming emperor Yongle (Yung-lo) appointed to lead seven maritime expeditions from 1405 to 1431 that reached as far west as the coast of Africa.

The Manchus who overthrew the Ming and established the Qing dynasty (1644–1911) continued the tribute system based on the belief that the emperor was the Son of Heaven. During the Qing, Western nations began demanding permission to trade with China without submitting to the tribute system. George, Lord Macartney led the first British mission to China in 1793 to request the right to engage in open Western-style trade. The British who ran a great trading empire were insulted when the Chinese regarded their country on the same level as Annam (northern Vietnam) and Burma, both of which had recently entered a tributary relationship with China. The British refused to submit to the Chinese emperor. China responded by strictly regulating foreign trade, forcing foreign traders to conduct their business through officially designated Chinese merchants, the Cohong, in the southern port city of Guangzhou (Canton); this is known as the Canton system of trade. The British used military means to end this system, by defeating China in the Opium War (1839–42) and forcing it to sign the Treaty of Nanjing (1842), which opened five so-called treaty ports to foreign traders: Guangzhou, Xiamen (Amoy), Fuzhou, Ningbo and Shanghai. Britain and other foreign powers then forced China to sign more treaties, called "unequal treaties" by the Chinese, opening more treaty ports and giving foreigners more concessions. This humiliated the Qing and was a major factor in the downfall of the Qing dynasty and the end of the Chinese imperial system with the Revolution of 1911.

Japan also dealt a blow to the tribute system when it occupied the Ryukyu Islands (Liuqiu or Liu-Ch'iu in Chinese), which had been a vassal state of China for five centuries. In 1874, Japan forced China to sign a treaty recognizing Japan's claim as protector of the Ryukyu Islands. The lord of Satsuma in southern Japan had actually occupied the Ryukyus in 1609 but had the islands continue the lucrative trade with China. The last Ryukyu ambassador to China paid tribute in 1875. Japan deposed the Ryukyu king in 1879 and designated the islands the Japanese prefecture of Okinawa. Japan went on to annex Korea and other countries that had accepted Chinese suzerainty, expanding throughout Asia until the end of World War II in 1945. See also CANTON SYSTEM OF TRADE; EMPEROR; HEAVEN; IMPERIAL COURT; KOREA AND JAPAN; KOWTOW; MACARTNEY, LORD GEORGE; MANDATE OF HEAVEN; MIDDLE KINGDOM; QING DYNASTY; REVOLUTION OF 1911; RYUKYU ISLANDS; TREATY PORTS; UNEQUAL TREATIES; ZHENG HE.

TRIGRAMS   See BOOK OF CHANGES; EIGHT TRIGRAMS.

"TRUE STORY OF AH Q, THE"   See LU XUN.

TS'AI   See COOKING, CHINESE; VEGETABLES AND VEGETARIAN DISHES.

TSAIDAM BASIN   See QINGHAI PROVINCE.

TS'AI-KUO   See WOK.

TS'AO FAMILY   See CAO FAMILY OF ROYAL POETS.

TS'AO HSUEH-CH'IN   See DREAM OF THE RED CHAMBER.

TS'AO KUO-CHIU   See EIGHT IMMORTALS.

TS'AO P'I   See CAO CAO; CAO FAMILY OF ROYAL POETS.

TS'AO TS'AO   See CAO CAO.

TS'AO WEI, KINGDOM OF   See CAO CAO; THREE KINGDOMS PERIOD.

TS'AO YU   See CAO YU.

TS'AO-CHUN   See KITCHEN GOD.

TSENG KUO-CH'UAN   See TAIPING REBELLION.

TSENG KUO-FAN   See ZENG GUOFAN.

TSIMSHATSUI   See HONG KONG; KOWLOON.

TSINGHAI PROVINCE   See QINGHAI PROVINCE.

TSINGHUA UNIVERSITY   See QINGHUA UNIVERSITY.

TSINGTAO   See BEER; QINGDAO.

TSUNGLI YAMEN   See ZONGLI YAMEN.

TSUSHIMA, BATTLE OF   See RUSSO-JAPANESE WAR OF 1904–5.

TU FU   See DU FU.

TU WEN-HSIU   See DU WENXIU.

TUAN CH'I-JUI   See REPUBLIC OF CHINA; SUN YAT-SEN; WARLORD PERIOD; YUAN SHIKAI; ZHANG ZUOLIN.

TUAN WU-CHIEH   See DRAGON BOAT FESTIVAL.

TUJIA   An ethnic group that inhabits Hunan and Hubei provinces and ls one of the largest of China's officially designated 55 national minority groups. The Tujia belong to the Tibeto-Burman ethnic group. According to the 1990 census, there were 5,704,223 Tujia in China. Many reside in the Xiangxi Tujia-Miao Autonomous Prefecture in Hunan Province. The Chinese government has also designated several counties in southwestern Hubei as Tujia autonomous counties.

The Tujia claim descent from the ancient Ba people, who around 1100 B.C. helped topple the Shang dynasty and established their own dynasty in the Three Gorges region of the Yangzi River (Changjiang), where they had long controlled salt production. They were subjugated in 316 B.C. by the Qin, who unified China in 221 B.C. Since then, the Tujia have been strongly influenced by the culture of the Han, the Chinese ethnic majority. Most Tujia are farmers who live in two-story homes made of wooden frame covered with the bark of fir trees or pottery tiles. They reside on the second floor, and keep a pigpen and toilet on the ground floor. They eat sour, spicy food and drink large amounts of tea and wine. Tujia women dress in long skirts and tunics embroidered with floral borders. They wear round hats or head cloths, and the men wrap black or white cloths around their heads. The Tujia still practice their traditional wedding and funeral customs. They perform the Changyang Bashan Dance, a graceful funeral dance accompanied by drums, around the coffin, which is placed in an open area. See also HUBEI PROVINCE; MINORITIES, NATIONAL.

TULUFAN   See TURPAN.

TUMEN RIVER   A river that forms part of the border between China and North Korea (Democratic People's Republic of Korea). The Tumen River rises on the eastern slopes of the Changbai Mountains in Jilin Province in northeastern China (also known as Manchuria) that divide China from North Korea. The river flows northeast for 324 miles, then turns southeast and empties into the Sea of Japan. Near its delta the Tumen River forms the border between North Korea and Russia, only about 10 miles long. The river flows through a major lumbering and coal-mining region, and logs are floated down it in the summer. It freezes over during the winter, and is navigable only in its lower portion even in the summer. In North Korea there are large iron ore deposits along the Tumen River, and large hydroelectric plants have been constructed where it falls between Musan and Hoeryong. See also CHANGBAI MOUNTAIN RANGE; JILIN PROVINCE.

TUNG CH'I-CH'ANG   See DONG QICHANG.

TUNG CHUNG-SHU   See DONG ZHONGSHU.

TUNG LING (T'ung Ling; 1933?–)   An internationally renowned Chinese orchestra conductor. Tung was born in Shanghai. His parents had met in the United States, where his father was a professor of educational psychology at Columbia University in New York and his mother, a graduate of Wellesley College in Massachusetts, was a pianist working at the New England Conservatory of Music. They returned to Shanghai, China in the 1930s, where he taught and she directed a children's music conservatory. They also had four children. In 1947 Tung's parents divorced, and his mother took her musically talented children to the United States, while his father remained in Shanghai as head of the Shanghai Teachers College. The children never saw their father again because he died during the Cultural Revolution (1966–76) after spending five years in prison, accused of the crime of being an American-educated intellectual.

Tung Ling and his brother, Tung Yuan, studied at the Curtis Institute of Music in Philadelphia. They joined the Philadelphia Orchestra in 1954, but Tung Yuan moved to the St. Louis Symphony Orchestra. One sister, Tung Quang-Quang, became a pianist and teacher. The other sister became a violinist who married a professor at Cornell University in Ithaca, New York. Tung Ling was drafted into the U.S. army and became director of the U.S. Seventh Army symphony in Germany. He then returned to play violin with the Philadelphia Orchestra. He gained financial backing to found the Camden (New Jersey) Philharmonic, soon called the Philharmonia, which he conducted in concerts at Philadelphia's Academy of Music. In the mid-1970s he also served as artistic adviser for the Temple University Festival. Tung Ling began conducting symphony orchestras around the world and was the first Chinese to conduct the Japan Philharmonic. He and his wife, Margo, founded the Grand Teton Music Festival in Wyoming.

In 1979 Tung Ling was appointed head of the Hong Kong Philharmonic. He closed his Philharmonia but continued to live in the Philadelphia region. In 1980 he returned to China when he was invited to conduct the Shanghai Symphony Orchestra and the Central Philharmonic in Beijing. Back in his home city after 33 years, he visited the family housekeeper who had helped raise him and found his father's collection of about 1,000 old 78-rpm records. He also learned how Chinese musicians had been persecuted during the Cultural Revolution, and that his father had remarried and had a daughter, Tung Niby. She had studied piano in a Shanghai conservatory and, when it was closed during the Cultural Revolution, taught herself to play the violin at home. When Tung Ling met her she was a violinist with the Shanghai Opera Orchestra. Conducting the Shanghai Symphony Orchestra was an emotional experience for him, since it was the first orchestra he had known as a boy and many of its members were friends of his parents. See also CULTURAL REVOLUTION; SHANGHAI.

T'UNG PAO   See OVERSEAS CHINESE.

TUNG PEI-YUAN   See DONG YUAN.

TUNG PI-WU   See UNITED NATIONS.

T'UNG SHU   See ALMANAC; OX.

TUNG SHU-TA   See DONG YUAN.

TUNG WANG-KUN   See XIWANGMU.

TUNG YUAN   See DONG YUAN.

T'UNG-CHIH (EMPEROR)   See TONGZHI (EMPEROR).

TUNG-LIN ACADEMY   See DONGLIN ACADEMY; IMPERIAL BUREAUCRACY.

T'UNG-MENG-HUI   See REVOLUTIONARY ALLIANCE.

TUNGUSIC SUSHIS   See JIN DYNASTY; JURCHEN; MANCHU; NURHACHI.

TUN-HUANG   See DUNHUANG CAVE PAINTINGS AND CARVINGS.

TUO RIVER   See SICHUAN PROVINCE.

TUOMUER PEAK   See TIANSHAN MOUNTAIN RANGE.

TURFAN AND TURFAN DEPRESSION   See TURPAN; TURPAN DEPRESSION.

TURKESTAN, CHINESE   See XINJIANG-UIGHUR AUTONOMOUS REGION.

TURKISH TRIBES   See BUDDHISM; DATONG; HOHHOT; KAZAKH; KIRGHIZ; MUSLIMS; NOMADS AND ANIMAL HUSBANDRY; NORTHERN WEI DYNASTY; SHANXI PROVINCE; SINICIZATION; UIGHUR; XINJIANG-UIGHUR AUTONOMOUS REGION; XIONGNU.

TURPAN (Turfan or Tulufan)   A town in Xinjiang-Uighur Autonomous Province in northwestern China that was a major oasis town on the Silk Road between China and the Middle East. Today Turpan is an agricultural center famous for melons, dates and grapes, which are made into raisins and wine. Underground irrigation channels, called *karezes,* bring melted snow from the eastern edge of the Tianshan Mountain Range. One of the town's earliest names was "Land of Fire" (Huozhou) for its summer heat, which reaches 104 degrees F. Also known as the "Storehouse of Wind" for its blustering winds that blow one-third of the days of the year, Turpan's winter temperature averages a bitterly cold 5 degrees to 14 degrees F. Rainfall averages only .63 inches a year. Located about three-and-a-half hours southeast of the provincial capital of Urumqi, Turpan has a busy bazaar, especially on Sundays, with colorful silk dresses a specialty item. The town is located on the northern edge of the arid Turpan Depression and lies 260 feet below sea level; Lake Aiding nearby is 505 feet below sea level. The population of Turpan, about 200,000, is about 60 percent Uighur, one of the main national minorities, and about 10 percent Hui, another minority. The Uighurs were originally a Central Asian Turkish tribe that converted to Islam.

Often called the "Bright Pearl of the Silk Road," Turpan was founded in the first century B.C. on the northern branch of the Silk Road. The ruins of the ancient town of Gaochang (Karakhoja, Khocho) lie 30 miles east of Turpan. The Han dynasty (206 B.C.–A.D. 220) sent soldiers to Gaochang and added it to a chain of military command posts, giving the Chinese control of the gateway to Central Asia. Gaochang became an important oasis on the Silk Road. However, it was abandoned about the end of the second century A.D. and the Turpan-Gaochang region was successively controlled by various Central Asian dynasties. Turpan was also attacked by the Xiongnu (Hsiung-nu), absorbed cultural influences from India and Persia (Iran), and became a center for the religions of Theravada Buddhism, Manichaeism and Nestorian Christianity. In 640 A.D. the Chinese defeated the Turkish tribes in the region and absorbed Gaochang into the Tang Chinese Empire, calling the town Xizhou. In the eighth century the Chinese made an alliance with a kingdom of Uighur Turks to repel the Tibetans from Xinjiang, and in the ninth century Gaochang became the capital of the Uighurs when they settled in Xinjiang. The Uighurs held Gaochang until the Mongols under Genghis Khan conquered the region in the 13th century.

Many 20th-century Western explorers and archaeologists came to excavate the ancient caves in the Turpan region, such as the German Albert von Le Coq and the British Sir Aurel Stein, and they shipped crateloads of sculptures, frescoes and other treasures back to Europe. However, some objects and documents remain on display in Turpan's museum. The Thousand-Buddha Caves (Qianfodong), carved in a cliff, are located east of Turpan at Bezeklik. West of Turpan lies the ruins of Jiaohe (Yarkhoto), where about 90 B.C. the Han Chinese emperor Wudi (Wu-ti; r. 141–87 B.C.) built a citadel; it was destroyed by Mongols in the 13th century A.D. Near Gaochang lies Astana, the burial ground for that city, which has several decorated tombs open to visitors. Suleiman's Minaret (Sugong Ta), built from 1776 to 1779, can be seen next to a large mosque in the eastern part of Turpan. See also HUI; MINORITIES, NATIONAL; MUSLIMS; SILK ROAD; TIANSHAN MOUNTAIN RANGE; TURPAN DEPRESSION; UIGHUR; URUMQI; XINJIAN-UIGHUR AUTONOMOUS REGION.

TURPAN DEPRESSION   The lowest land area in China, situated at 501 feet below sea level. Lake Aiding (Aydingkol) at its deepest level, 505 feet below sea level, is the second-lowest area in the world after the Dead Sea. The Turpan Depression lies about 100 miles east of the city of Urumqi in Xinjiang-Uighur Autonomous Region. It covers 9,300 square miles. The depression is surrounded by the Pamir, Kunlun and Karakoram mountain ranges, branches of the Tianshan Mountain Range. Almost no rain falls in the Turpan Depression, and it is the hottest place in China, with an average July temperature of 93°F, but sometimes reaching as high as 122°F; hence it is called the "oasis of fire." The Hami Depression, about 640 feet above sea level, lies nearby and is a center for coal mining. To the south is the Taklimakan Desert,

the second-largest desert in the world, after the Sahara. The Turpan Depression lies along the northern branch of the Silk Road, and ruins of ancient marketplaces can be found in the region. Gaochang, southeast of present-day Turpan County, was an important town along the Silk Road and a political, economic and cultural center in Xinjiang. It was founded in the first century B.C., thrived for 1,500 years, and was abandoned in the 14th century A.D. Today fruits, especially melons and grapes dried as raisins, cotton and grains are grown by artificial irrigation. Wells and underground canals have been built to divert melting snow from the Tianshan Mountain Range to the area. See also KUNLUN MOUNTAIN RANGE; PAMIR MOUNTAIN RANGE; TAKLIMAKAN DESERT; TIANSHAN MOUNTAIN RANGE; TURPAN; URUMQI; XINJIAN-UIGHUR AUTONOMOUS REGION.

TURTLE   See TORTOISE.

TWELVE SYMBOLS OF AUTHORITY   A set of 12 symbols that as a group represent the universe. These symbols have been common design motifs in China, especially on the robes of emperors and officials in the government bureaucracy, who were ranked into nine levels symbolized by embroidered squares sewn onto their robes. Only the emperor was permitted to wear all 12 symbols together on his robes, as they comprised the symbolic totality of the universe and of the emperor as ruler of the universe.

The 12 symbols of authority are the most ancient set of symbols in China, dating back thousands of years. They may be portrayed alone or in combinations, and are used to decorate porcelains and other art objects as well as textiles. The symbols include the sun disk, moon disk, and a constellation of three circles symbolizing stars that form a triangle, all of which represent Heaven; mountains, representing Earth; a dragon, which is believed to be able to transform itself, representing the emperor, adaptability, rain and water; a pheasant (related to the phoenix), representing the empress and scholarly refinement; bronze sacrificial goblets, representing filial piety, or respect for one's parents and ancestors, the most important Confucian virtue; water weed, representing purity; grains of rice, representing the ability to feed the people; fire, representing brilliance; an ax, representing the power of punishment; and a geometric design known as the *fu* sign, representing the power of judgment. The symbols for fire and the ax could be used only by the emperor, as they symbolized his absolute authority to judge and punish his subjects. The sun disk is usually red and contains the picture of a three-legged crow. The moon disk is pale blue or green and contains a picture of the rabbit in the moon who pounds the elixir of immortality. The dragon and pheasant together represent animals and birds, or living creatures. The bronze sacrificial cups, water weed, grain, fire and mountain together represent the Five Material Agents (or elements) in traditional Chinese thought: metal, water, wood (plant life), fire and earth. See also DRAGON; ELIXIR OF IMMORTALITY; FILIAL PIETY; FIVE MATERIAL AGENTS; FIVE SACRED MOUNTAINS OF DAOISM; FOUR SACRED MOUNTAINS OF BUDDHISM; HEAVEN; NINE-RANK SYSTEM; RICE.

TWELVE TERRESTRIAL (EARTH) BRANCHES OR TWELVE CYCLICAL SIGNS   See ZODIAC, ANIMAL.

TWENTY-ONE DEMANDS ON CHINA A set of demands that the Japanese government made to Chinese president Yuan Shikai (Yuan Shih-k'ai; 1859–1916) in 1915. China's acceptance of the Twenty-one Demands would make China a protectorate of Japan. There were five groups of demands, with the fifth group being the harshest. The first group required the transformation of Shandong Province from a German sphere of influence into a Japanese one. In 1914 Japan had joined the Allied side against Germany in World War I and seized German holdings in Shandong. The second group would give Japan extensive commercial, industrial and residential rights in South Manchuria and eastern Inner Mongolia. It would also extend Japan's lease of Port Arthur and Dalian (Dairen; modern Luda) on the Liaodong Peninsula from 25 to 99 years. The third group demanded that the Han-yeh-ping Company, the largest iron mining and smelting operation in Hubei Province, be made into a Sino-Japanese joint enterprise, with the Japanese actually controlling the company. The fourth group told the Chinese not to cede or lease to any power other than Japan any harbor, bay or island along the Chinese coast. The fifth group would bring the entire country of China under the control of Japan. Its major demands included: 1) the use of Japanese political, financial and military advisers in the Chinese central government; 2) the owning of Chinese land on which the Japanese would build schools, temples and hospitals; 3) the joint Japanese-Chinese control of the Chinese police force; 4) the purchase of Japanese weapons by China and the establishment of ammunition factories in China jointly controlled by the Chinese and Japanese; 5) the granting of railroad construction rights to Japan in central China; 6) the need for China to consult Japan if it wanted to borrow foreign money for such economic activities as building railroads, mining and the improvement of harbors in Fujian Province; and 7) the granting to Japan of the right to "preach religion" in China.

The whole world was amazed when Japan made the Twenty-one Demands on China. The Chinese already had strong anti-Japanese feelings due to the Sino-Japanese War of 1894–95. But the Chinese had to negotiate with Japan, because China was weak and disunited following the overthrow of the Qing dynasty in the Revolution of 1911, and Japan had a strong, Western-style military. Also, in 1910, Japan had made Korea, which borders northeastern China (Manchuria), its colony.

While Chinese and Japanese leaders were negotiating the demands, Japanese naval fleets sailed into Chinese harbors and the Japanese army greatly increased its presence in Shandong Province and South Manchuria. Japan's intense pressure forced Yuan Shikai to agree to all demands in the fourth group and to the demand relating to Fujian in the fifth group. However, China strongly rejected all other demands in the fifth group. The Japanese dropped these demands for the time being in the face of Chinese resistance. The Chinese government did recognize Japan's authority over southern Manchuria and eastern Inner Mongolia. In 1917, Britain, France and Italy secretly agreed to this Japanese claim in exchange for Japanese naval warfare against Germany. America also agreed to let Japan have a "special interest in China." That same year, China declared war on Germany with hopes of recovering Shandong. In 1918, however, the Chinese government in Beijing made a secret agreement giving Shandong to Japan. This became public knowledge at the Paris peace conference in Versailles in 1919, and the Chinese people were outraged. Three months after Japan made its Twenty-One Demands on China in 1915, Yuan Shikai had also declared himself emperor. All of these events gave rise to a widespread student protest movement in China, which culminated in the May Fourth Movement of 1919. See also DALIAN; LIAODONG PENINSULA; MANCHURIA; MAY FOURTH MOVEMENT OF 1919; SHANDONG PROVINCE; SINO-JAPANESE WAR OF 1894–95; WORLD WAR I; YUAN SHIKAI.

TZ'U See LYRIC VERSE.

TZ'U AN, EMPRESS See CIXI, EMPRESS DOWAGER.

TZU CH'IANG See SELF-STRENGTHENING MOVEMENT.

TZ'U HSI, EMPRESS DOWAGER See CIXI, EMPRESS DOWAGER.

TZU-CHIN-CH'ENG See FORBIDDEN CITY.

TZ'U-CHOU WARE See ZIZHOU WARE.

TZU-SHIH T'UNG-CHIEN See SIMA GUANG.

UIGHUR (Uygur)   One of the largest national minority ethnic groups in China, and the major population of the Xinjiang-Uighur Autonomous Region in western China. Xinjiang was absorbed into the Chinese Empire during the Qing dynasty (1644–1911). The Uighurs, who number more than 7 million today, belong to the Sunni branch of the Muslim religion and speak Turkic languages belonging to the Altaic family. They are descendants of Turkic peoples who established a number of kingdoms in the steppes of Central Asia during the Chinese Tang dynasty (618–907).

When the Tibetans invaded China and took all of the Chinese imperial stud horses in 763, the Tang government gave the Uighurs the privilege of official horse trading for China in return for their military help against the Tibetans. In the mid-ninth century, heavy snowstorms and Kirghiz invaders forced many Uighurs to move west. Some settled in Turpan and Kashgar in Xinjiang. The Id Kah Mosque in Kashgar is the largest mosque in China, with a capacity of 8,000 people. Many Uighur scholars and intellectuals have been residents of Kashgar. During the 13th century, the Uighurs became advisers to the Mongols who ruled China under the Yuan dynasty (1279–1368). Today the Uighurs are farmers who cultivate the oases around the desert region of the Tarim Basin south of the Tianshan Mountain Range. Their main crops are cotton, wheat, corn, rice and fruit, especially melons, dates and grapes. They irrigate their crops with a network of underground channels called the Karez System. All Uighurs, men and women, wear a beautiful four-cornered skullcap called *duopa*, often embroidered with a black or gold peach motif on white cloth. Women wear their long hair in braids. The Uighurs have a long tradition of oral literature and love to sing and dance. See also HORSE; KASHGAR; KIRGHIZ; MINORITIES, NATIONAL; MUSLIMS; TANG DYNASTY; TARIM BASIN; TIANSHAN MOUNTAIN RANGE; TURPAN; XINJIANG-UIGHUR AUTONOMOUS REGION; YUAN DYNASTY.

ULANHOU   See INNER MONGOLIA AUTONOMOUS REGION.

UMBRELLA   The umbrella was invented in China at the end of the fourth century A.D. during the Northern Wei dynasty (A.D. 386–534). It was originally made with a circular wooden or bamboo frame with spokes radiating from a hub, and covered with paper made from the bark of the mulberry bush (erroneously called rice paper in the West) that was coated with oil to make it waterproof. The Chinese used umbrellas for protection from the hot sun as well as rain. During the Eastern, or Later, Han dynasty (A.D. 25–220), a type of silk umbrella, more like a canopy, had been used to cover chariots when it rained. Silk canopies or umbrellas were also carried in ceremonial processions. The Wei emperors were covered by ceremonial umbrellas of red, an auspicious and happy color to the Chinese, and yellow, the imperial color. Commoners were permitted to carry blue umbrellas. An umbrella or canopy, representing protection and shelter, is one of the Eight Treasures of the Buddhist religion.

Although paper umbrellas continued to be used in China, silk umbrellas became popular by the 14th century. In 1368 the Ming dynasty (1368–1644) imperial government issued a decree that silk umbrellas could be used only by members of the royal family. By then, umbrellas had a largely ceremonial function, and they were carried in processions and ceremonies for important royal events such as weddings and birthdays. Ming emperors also presented umbrellas on which they had written their signatures to worthy government officials. In the modern era, a respected government official who retires may be given an "Umbrella of Ten Thousand People," covered with red silk on which the donors' names are written in calligraphy with gold characters. Such an umbrella symbolizes high office, dignity, respect and purity. Colorful hand-painted paper and silk umbrellas, especially with designs of birds and flowers, are still produced in China, especially in Wenzhou in Zhejiang Province in eastern China. See also BAMBOO; BIRD-AND-FLOWER PAINTING; CALLIGRAPHY; EIGHT TREASURES; PAPER; SILK.

UNEQUAL TREATIES   Treaties that Western powers forced the Manchu Qing dynasty (1644–1911), which ruled

China, to sign in the late 19th and early 20th centuries, giving Westerners many rights and privileges in China. Among other things, the unequal treaties placed heavy indemnities on China; forced the Qing government to open many cities to foreign residents and trade as so-called treaty ports and ceded Hong Kong and Kowloon to Great Britain; gave Western powers most-favored-nation status, meaning that any privilege granted to one would be equally granted to all; and gave control of the collection of Chinese customs duties to foreigners. The unequal treaties also granted foreigners the right of extraterritoriality, meaning that foreigners accused of committing crimes in China would be tried by foreign courts under foreign law, rather than by Chinese courts under Chinese law.

The first unequal treaty was the Treaty of Nanjing (1842), signed after Britain defeated China in the Opium War (1839–42). Britain had sought the right to engage in open Western-style trade in China, and it had resorted to military means to end the tribute system and the Canton system by which Chinese emperors strictly regulated foreign trade. In 1844 China signed the Treaty of Wanghia with the United States and the Treaty of Huangpu (Whampoa) with France.

After the Treaty of Nanjing opened the five treaty ports of Guangzhou, Shanghai, Xiamen (Amoy), Fuzhou and Ningbo, Britain continued to pressure the Qing, and British and French troops defeated China once again in the Arrow War (also known as the Second Opium War; 1856–60). The Treaty of Tianjin (Tientsin; 1858) that Britain forced the Qing to sign opened six more treaty ports and promised the opening of four more. It also gave Westerners the right to collect Chinese customs duties, regularized diplomatic relations between the Qing and Western powers, permitted a British ambassador to reside in the capital city of Beijing, guaranteed the rights of foreign missionaries in China and granted extraterritoriality to all Westerners. A clause in the treaty called for a revision every 10 years. When the Qing emperor resisted implementing the Treaty of Nanjing, Britain and France sent an army to attack Beijing, and it burned down the imperial Summer Palace. The Qing were forced to sign the Convention of Beijing (1860) granting even more benefits to the British, including a huge indemnity, more treaty ports and the granting of permission for Chinese to emigrate on British ships.

France, Germany, the United States and Russia also signed unequal treaties with the Qing and received most-favored-nation status. The treaty concluding France's defeat of China in the Sino-French War (1884–85) gave France complete control of Vietnam, ending that country's long relationship with China under the imperial Chinese tribute system. Germany won concessions in Shandong Province, and Russia won concessions in Manchuria (northeastern China). In 1900, after the Chinese forces of the Boxer Uprising entered Beijing and laid siege to the foreign quarters, a combined force of troops from Britain, France, Germany, Italy, Austria, the United States, Russia and Japan defeated the Boxers and occupied Beijing. The governments of these countries forced the Qing to sign another unequal treaty, the International Protocol of 1901, which exacted huge indemnities from China and gave Western powers the complete freedom to pursue their trading and missionizing in China.

In return, the Western powers supported the Qing dynasty, because it was weak and they could manipulate it to their advantage. The Chinese people responded by overthrowing the Qing in the Revolution of 1911. The Republic of China was formed in 1912 under the leadership of Dr. Sun Yat-sen, but warlords soon exerted their control over many regions of the country.

In 1919 the government of the U.S.S.R., which had taken power in Russia after the October Revolution of 1917 overthrew the Russian czar, repudiated the treaties that the czar's government had signed with China and asserted that it wanted to establish equal relations with China. This strongly influenced the Chinese people, many of whom had become active in the May Fourth Movement of 1919, to protest China's exploitation by Japan and Western powers. In 1928 the Nationalist government of the Republic of China (ROC) announced that it wanted to revise or abolish all the unequal treaties that China had signed. It engaged in several years of negotiation with Western powers, but without success. It decided to act on its own and passed a law on January 1, 1932, that unilaterally abolished these treaties, but the Japanese invasion of Manchuria prevented the implementation of this law. On January 11, 1943, Britain and the United States signed new treaties with China that abolished rights such as extraterritoriality that China had granted these countries in the unequal treaties. See also ARROW WAR; BEIJING, CONVENTION OF; BOXER UPRISING; CANTON SYSTEM TO REGULATE TRADE; MANCHURIA; NANJING, TREATY OF; OPIUM WAR; QING DYNASTY; REPUBLIC OF CHINA; REVOLUTION OF 1911; SHANDONG PROVINCE; SINO-FRENCH WAR; SUMMER PALACE; TIANJIN, TREATY OF; TREATY PORTS; TRIBUTE SYSTEM; NAMES OF INDIVIDUAL PORTS.

UNITED NATIONS The United Nations (U.N.) is an international organization founded in 1945 after World War II, with headquarters in New York City, to promote cooperation among nations on issues such as security and development. China sent a delegation of 10 representatives from the Nationalist (Kuomintang; KMT) government and from nongovernmental parties to attend the U.N. conference in San Francisco, where the U.N. charter was drawn up. On October 24, 1945, 51 member states including China signed the charter and the U.N. officially came into existence. V. K. Wellington Koo signed the charter for China. Huang Ha was China's first-term permanent representative to the U.N. Dong Biwu (Tung Pi-wu), the representative from the Chinese Communist Party (CCP), which in 1949 would defeat the Nationalists and establish the People's Republic of China (PRC), was present and signed the U.N. charter. In 1945 the Republic of China (ROC), which had been established by the Nationalists in 1912, held China's seat in the U.N. and was a veto-holding member of the U.N. Security Council.

When the CCP defeated the Nationalists and founded the PRC in 1949, the Nationalists, led by Chiang Kai-shek, fled to the island of Taiwan, where they established the provisional government of the Republic of China (ROC). The PRC government sent a delegation to the U.N. to claim the Chinese seat. Great Britain, the U.S.S.R. and many Eastern European countries had given diplomatic recognition to the PRC government, and India supported the seating of the

PRC in the U.N. However, the United States and many of its allies supported the Nationalists. Hence the U.N. voted to let the ROC retain China's seat.

When the Democratic People's Republic of Korea (North Korea) invaded South Korea in 1950, a U.N. force comprised largely of American troops joined the fight to push back North Korean troops. The PRC issued many warnings to the U.N. force, and it finally responded to a North Korean call for assistance by sending troops into North Korea. The Chinese troops prevented U.N. forces from crossing the Yalu River into Manchuria (northeastern China) and pushed them back south. In 1951 the U.N. declared that China was an aggressor in Korea and sanctioned a global embargo on shipping arms and war materials to China. A truce was called in 1951 and an armistice was signed in 1953 that kept the 38th parallel as the dividing line between North and South Korea. China's actions in the Korean War ensured that, for the time being, it would not replace the ROC as a member of the U.N. It also intensified U.S. antagonism toward the PRC, and the two countries had no diplomatic contact for two decades.

In 1971, U.S. president Richard M. Nixon announced that he had changed his position on China and planned to pay an official visit to government leaders in the PRC. He proposed that the U.N. admit the PRC while allowing the ROC to remain a member. On October 18, 1971, the U.N. opened debate on the question of seating the PRC, and on October 25 it passed a resolution to expel the ROC and give China's seat to the PRC. In 1974, PRC official Deng Xiaoping (Teng Hsiao-p'ing) presented the Theory of the Three Worlds, developed by PRC chairman Mao Zedong (Mao Tse-tung), at U.N. headquarters in New York City. This theory, which became widely accepted around the world, called for a change in the world's power structure. It claims that the First World includes the two superpowers, the United States and the U.S.S.R., which are "imperialist aggressors" whose rivalry will lead to world war; the Second World includes developed countries such as Japan and those of Europe; and the Third World includes developing countries, which oppose superpower hegemony and are the main force in international affairs.

On January 1, 1979, the United States transferred diplomatic recognition from the ROC to the PRC, although it maintained economic ties with the ROC and continued to give it military support. During the 1980s the PRC became an active participant in U.N. scientific activities. The UNESCO International Silt Research and Training Center was established in Luoyang in the PRC to study the problem of river silts, a serious problem in China. On October 14, 1985, Chinese premier Zhao Ziyang (Chao Tzu-yang) spoke at the special session held in New York to celebrate the U.N.'s 40th birthday. See also CHINESE COMMUNIST PARTY; CIVIL WAR BETWEEN COMMUNISTS AND NATIONALISTS; KOO, V. K. WELLINGTON; KOREAN WAR; NATIONALIST PARTY; PEOPLE'S REPUBLIC OF CHINA; REPUBLIC OF CHINA; TAIWAN; ZHAO ZIYANG.

UNITED NATIONS FOURTH WORLD CONFERENCE ON WOMEN Commonly known as the Beijing Conference; a conference sponsored by the United Nations (U.N.) and held in Beijing, the capital of the People's Republic of China, from August 30 to September 8, 1995, that addressed issues concerning women around the world. The Nongovernmental Organization (NGO) Forum was held in China in conjunction with the official U.N. conference. The Chinese government moved the site of the NGO Forum from Beijing to the suburb of Huairou, about 35 miles outside the city, and denied visas to 10,000 women delegates, yet the NGO Forum was the largest gathering of women in the history of the world. Men attended the Forum as well. The principal goal of the NGO Forum was "to bring together women and men to challenge, create and transform global structures and processes at all levels through the empowerment and celebration of women." More than 2,500 panels lasting two hours each were held on topics related to issues concerning women, such as education, health, religion, peace, arts and culture, science and technology, race and ethnicity, youth and human relations. Burmese pro-democracy leader Aung San Suu Kyi, a woman who was awarded the Nobel Peace Prize, delivered the keynote address at the conference, by means of a videotape that a delegate smuggled into the conference. U.S. first lady Hillary Rodham Clinton addressed the conference and participated in forums held by the World Health Organization and the United Nations Development Fund for Women. Conference delegates agreed to a document that set forth a 12-point plan of action for helping women around the world. NGO delegates had much more input into the final document than at previous United Nations conferences on women. See also BEIJING; UNITED NATIONS.

UNITED STATES AND CHINA See BURMA ROAD; CHINA MERCHANTS STEAM NAVIGATION COMPANY; CHRISTIANITY; FLYING TIGERS; FOREIGN TRADE AND INVESTMENT; KOREAN WAR; LYTTON COMMISSION; MOST-FAVORED-NATION TRADE STATUS; NIXON, RICHARD M., U.S. PRESIDENT, VISIT TO CHINA; OPEN-DOOR POLICY; OVERSEAS CHINESE; REPUBLIC OF CHINA; RUSSO-JAPANESE WAR OF 1904–5; SIX COMPANIES, CHINESE; SPECIAL ECONOMIC ZONES; STILWELL, JOSEPH; TAIWAN; TREATY PORTS; UNEQUAL TREATIES; VIETNAM WAR; WAR OF RESISTANCE AGAINST JAPAN.

UNIVERSITY OF SCIENCE AND TECHNOLOGY OF CHINA See CHINESE ACADEMY OF SCIENCES.

UNOFFICIAL HISTORY OF THE LITERATI, AN See SCHOLARS, THE.

URGA, BATTLE OF (1696) A battle in which the army of the Manchu Qing dynasty that ruled China from 1644 to 1911 defeated the army of the Mongols led by Galdan. The Manchus, an ethnic group for which Manchuria (northeastern China) is named, conquered China after subjugating Korea and Inner Mongolia. They then turned their attention to Outer Mongolia on China's northwestern frontier, home of the Mongols, a nomadic tribe that had ruled China under the Yuan dynasty (1279–1368) and continued to pose a threat to the Chinese Empire. The Mongols were one of many nomadic groups that had invaded the Chinese frontier on horseback over two millennia. Mongols learned to ride horses as boys and were used to living and fighting in the saddle. Emperor Kangxi (K'ang-hsi; r. 1661–1722) personally led the Manchu Qing army of 80,000 soldiers, equipped with Western-style artillery, to Outer Mongolia. In the battle near Urga (modern Ulan Bator), the Qing army destroyed the power of the Mongols and made Outer Mongolia a vassal state of the Qing dynasty. Galdan presumably committed suicide after the battle. Most historians agree that the Battle of Urga ended the nomadic threat to the Chinese frontier. The Mongol kingdom of Dzungaria, to the west of Outer Mongolia, proved much harder for the Qing to subdue, but they finally succeeded after a three-year military campaign between 1755 and 1757. See also KANGXI, EMPEROR; MONGOL; QING DYNASTY.

URUMQI (Urumchi) The capital and largest city of Xinjiang-Uighur Autonomous Region in northwestern China, with a population of 950,000. The name Urumqi means "Beautiful Pasture" in the Mongolian language. Urumqi is the home of 14 ethnic groups, the majority of which are Muslim, including members of the Uighur, Mongol, Hui and Kazakh national minorities. There are 30 mosques in the city. In recent years a large number of Han Chinese people have also settled in Urumqi. It is located in an oasis at the northern foot of the Tianshan Mountain Range. Urumqi lies farther inland, away from any major body of water, than any other city in the world. Rainfall is scarce, but water for irrigation is brought from the snows of the Tianshan Mountains. The climate is bitterly cold in winter but pleasant in summer, and the city has been ringed with trees to help keep out strong winds and dirt blown from the deserts.

Urumqi is an industrial center benefiting from Xinjiang's natural resources of coal, petroleum and minerals, especially iron ore. Major products include steel, oil, chemicals and farm machinery. Local handicrafts include carpets, embroidered caps, long-handled knives and jade carved from the extensive jade deposits of Xinjiang. The Urumqi Museum has exhibits on the development of the Xinjiang region. A memorial hall honors martyrs of the Communist Eighth Route Army Headquarters, which used Urumqi as a headquarters in the 1930s and 1940s. Mao Zemin (Mao Tse-Min), brother of Communist leader Mao Zedong (Mao Tse-tung), was a political activist in Urumqi until a local warlord executed him in 1943. Red Mountain (Hangshan) offers a beautiful view of the city. Other sites include People's Park on the west bank of the Urumqi River (Urumqi He) and the Precious Pagoda of the Red Mountain (Hong Shan Baota), supposedly built during the Tang dynasty (618–907). "Swallows' Nest" (Yan'er Wo) is a popular recreation area south of the city. It has a high waterfall, and many swallows nest here in the spring. Baiyang Gou is a scenic area about 40 miles south of Urumqi in a valley of the Tianshan Mountains. A beautiful site three hours east of Urumqi is the Celestial Lake (Tianchi), which lies at an altitude of 6,500 feet on the slopes of 18,000-foot-high Bogda Mountain. It is possible to visit nomadic Kazakhs at their mountainous summer pasture at Nanshan, 40 miles away from Urumqi. See also CARPETS; EIGHTH ROUTE ARMY; HAN HUI; JADE; KAZAKH; KIRGHIZ; LOESS; MINORITIES, NATIONAL; TIANSHAN MOUNTAIN RANGE; UIGHUR; XINJIANG-UIGHUR AUTONOMOUS REGION.

USSURI RIVER See WUSULI RIVER.

UTILITARIANISM See MOZI.

UYGUR See UIGHUR; XINJIANG-UIGHUR AUTONOMOUS REGION.

UZBEK See KASHGAR; MINORITIES, NATIONAL.

V

VEGETABLES AND VEGETARIAN DISHES (*cai* or *ts'ai*) Some of the most important foods in the Chinese diet. A Chinese meal is centered around grain, and the word for cooked rice, *fan,* is also the word for a meal. *Fan,* which also includes other grain dishes—such as noodles, dumplings or steamed bread, and even potatoes, soybeans and other beans—is accompanied by *cai,* which literally means "vegetables" but also includes meat, fish, seafood, soybean curd and any other cooked food that is cut into small pieces that can be eaten with chopsticks. Each person is served his or her own bowl of *fan,* and the *cai* dishes are served in the center of the table in large bowls or dishes for all the diners to share. While the Chinese consume great quantities of grain, most of them say that vegetables are their favorite type of food. Until recently, most Chinese gained 85 to 95 percent of the calories in their diet from grain, and the rest from vegetables. They consumed small quantities of fish and seafood but ate very little poultry or meat, apart from major occasions such as weddings, funerals, the New Year and other festivals. Pork has been the most frequently eaten meat in Chinese cuisine, followed by lamb, the preferred meat of the nomadic herders who inhabit northern and northwestern China. The Chinese traditionally prefer not to eat beef, since farmers use oxen to work their fields.

One of the most commonly eaten vegetables in China is cabbage. Other common plant foods native to China include mushrooms, water spinach, Chinese green onions, leeks, mustard greens, chives, white radishes, bamboo shoots and winter melons, which are cooked as a vegetable. Many other vegetables were introduced to China from other parts of Asia, such as cucumbers, carrots, eggplants, green beans, squash, lettuce, ginger, garlic and large onions. Vegetables native to the Americas were introduced through foreign traders, including white and sweet potatoes, tomatoes, peanuts, corn and peppers. Chili peppers, used heavily in some regions such as Hunan and Sichuan provinces, provide vitamins A and C and some minerals.

One of the most common Chinese methods for cooking vegetables is to quickly stir-fry them in oil in a wok, either alone or in combination with small pieces of other foods such as soybean curd, seafood, poultry or pork, along with soy sauce and other seasonings. Steaming is another popular cooking technique that preserves vitamins and minerals. Pickled vegetables—sliced vegetables prepared by marinating in salted water and spices—are also widely consumed, especially pickled cabbage and radishes. The Chinese have developed a unique method for preparing soybean curd and wheat gluten to imitate meats in vegetarian dishes. This method was influenced by the Buddhist religion, which was introduced into China from India around the first century A.D.

The Chinese also like to eat fruit, especially for dessert, such as peaches, plums, litchis and oranges or tangerines. They also enjoy fruits introduced from other Asian regions, including pineapples, papayas, guavas and bananas. See also AGRICULTURE; BAMBOO; BEANS AND BEAN PRODUCTS; COOKING, CHINESE; GRAIN; LITCHI; MUSHROOMS; NOMADS AND ANIMAL HUSBANDRY; ORANGE; PEACH; PLUM; SEASONINGS FOR FOOD; SOYBEANS AND SOY PRODUCT; WOK.

VENEREAL DISEASE See MA HAIDE.

VERBIEST, FERDINAND See ASTRONOMY AND OBSERVATORIES; CALENDAR; JESUITS; RITES CONTROVERSY.

VERMILION HILLS See PHOENIX.

VERSAILLES, TREATY OF See MAY FOURTH MOVEMENT OF 1919; WORLD WAR I.

VICTORIA See HONG KONG.

VIETNAM AND CHINA See MEKONG RIVER; MING DYNASTY; OVERSEAS CHINESE; QING DYNASTY; RED RIVER; SHIPPING AND SHIPBUILDING; SINO-FRENCH WAR; SPRATLY ISLANDS; TRIBUTE SYSTEM; VIETNAM WAR; XUANDE, EMPEROR; ZHOU ENLAI.

VIETNAM WAR A war between the Communist Democratic Republic of Vietnam (DRV), commonly known as

North Vietnam, and the Republic of South Vietnam in the 1960s and 1970s, in which the Communist People's Republic of China (PRC) supported North Vietnam and the United States supported South Vietnam. China has held military and cultural dominance over Vietnam throughout most of Chinese history since the Qin dynasty (221–206 B.C.), which sent troops south into Vietnam. Armies of the Western Han dynasty (206 B.C.–A.D. 8) invaded and annexed parts of North Vietnam and North Korea, and Chinese Confucian-based culture took root in those regions. The area of Vietnam formerly called Annam was conquered by the Tang dynasty (618–907) in the seventh century (Annam means "pacify the south" in Chinese), and some Chinese immigrated into Vietnam. Vietnam became independent in the 10th century, but the Mongols, who ruled China under the Yuan dynasty (1279–1368), sent four expeditions against Annam and Burma in the late 13th century and brought many Southeast and South Asia kingdoms into their tribute system as vassals. The Ming (1368–1644) and Qing (1644–1911) dynasties also brought Vietnam into their tribute system. In the 19th century the French took control of Vietnam during the Sino-French War of 1884–85. Vietnam was occupied by Japan during World War II until Japan was defeated in 1945, after which Vietnam fought a war of liberation and defeated France in the battle of Dienbienphu in 1954.

North Vietnam then began fighting a long and destructive civil war against South Vietnam, with the PRC assisting the north and the United States and some of its allies assisting the south. However, the Chinese never sent troops into battle in Vietnam, as the Americans did. The Tet offensive in February 1968 caused enormous losses to both North and South Vietnam and its American allies, and the United States began increasing its military campaign to help the south defeat the north. Large numbers of Americans began actively opposing U.S. involvement in the war, and many other countries disapproved of U.S. military actions there. In 1970 Prince Sihanouk of Cambodia (Kampuchea) was overthrown and the United States invaded Cambodia.

The United States had refused to recognize the PRC when it was founded by the Chinese Communist Party (CCP) in 1949, and had supported the Chinese Nationalists (Kuomintang; KMT), who had been defeated by the CCP and fled to Taiwan Island, as the legitimate government of China. The PRC and the United States had fought on opposing sides in the Korean War in the 1950s, with the PRC sending troops to assist North Korea and the United States sending troops to assist South Korea. Despite this situation and the PRC's support of North Vietnam, during the late 1960s the United States attempted to improve its heretofore hostile relations with the PRC. The PRC also became more hostile to North Vietnam because of Vietnam's ties with the U.S.S.R., with which it had bad relations at the time. In 1968 the PRC had condemned the Soviet invasion of Czechoslovakia as an act of imperialist aggression, and in 1969 it had fought border skirmishes with the U.S.S.R. In 1971 U.S. president Richard Nixon announced that he now favored the PRC, and that he intended to visit China. Nixon's announcement helped the PRC replace Taiwan in the China Seat in the United Nations Security Council and General Assembly in 1971. It also encouraged many countries that had previously withheld recognition of the PRC to establish diplomatic relations with the Chinese government in Beijing. North Vietnam became very concerned about the detente between the United States and the PRC, and China had to reassure North Vietnam, as well as North Korea and Laos, that it was still friendly toward them. The PRC maintained good relations with North Korea and Laos, but Vietnam benefited from playing the U.S.S.R. and the PRC against each other.

On February 22, 1972, Nixon arrived in China and met with Mao Zedong (Mao Tse-tung) and other PRC leaders. On February 28, the United States and the PRC issued the Shanghai Communique, which called for closer contacts between them. On March 30, North Vietnam began a major military offensive in South Vietnam, and in July 1972 the last U.S. ground combat forces left Vietnam. From October 8 to 11, 1972, U.S. secretary of state Henry Kissinger and Le Duc Tho negotiated to end the Vietnam War. On January 27, 1973, the United States and the DRV signed the Paris agreements for disengagement from Vietnam. Mao and Zhou Enlai (Chou En-lai), the second-highest ranking PRC leader, both died in 1976, and China began a new era of reform and modernization led by Deng Xiaoping (Teng Hsiao-p'ing).

In December 1978 Vietnam invaded Kampuchea (Cambodia), overthrew the brutal PRC-supported Pol Pot regime and occupied the country. In 1979 Deng visited the United States. On February 17, 1979, after Deng returned to Beijing, the PRC waged a large-scale military campaign across the Vietnam border to punish Vietnam for not showing gratitude for continued Chinese aid; for the sacrifice of Chinese lives, in its wars against France and the United States; for concluding a treaty with the U.S.S.R.; for asserting control over Laos, invading Kampuchea (Cambodia), with Soviet support, and overthrowing the Pol Pot regime; and for mistreating Chinese who resided in Vietnam. The Vietnamese put up a strong resistance, and the Chinese forces withdrew one month after they had begun their limited, ground-force campaign. The PRC claimed victory but the People's Liberation Army (PLA) had performed badly on the battlefield and suffered heavy casualties, showing China's need for a modern, professional army. During the 1980s the U.S.S.R. provided military support to Vietnam, and Vietnam and the PRC deployed troops along their border and had many border incidents, although they avoided going to war. The PRC still disputes the sovereignty of the Xisha (Paracel) and Spratly Islands in the South China Sea with Vietnam and Taiwan. See also KOREAN WAR; NIXON, RICHARD, U.S. PRESIDENT, VISIT TO CHINA; PEOPLE'S LIBERATION ARMY; SINO-FRENCH WAR; SINO-SOVIET CONFLICT; SOUTH CHINA SEA; SPRATLY ISLANDS; TRIBUTE SYSTEM; UNITED NATIONS.

W

WADE-GILES SYSTEM OF ROMANIZATION A system used for translating the Chinese language into English and other European languages that employ the Roman alphabet. Romanization of Chinese is difficult and tends to be only approximate because Chinese written characters generally represent the meaning of a word rather than its pronunciation. The Wade-Giles System was created in 1859 by Sir Thomas Francis Wade (1818–95), a British diplomat and professor of Chinese at Cambridge University, and revised by Herbert Allen Giles (1845–1935), his successor, in 1892. Wade-Giles was the first standard for the romanization of Chinese and was widely employed for more than 100 years. In 1953 the government of the People's Republic of China (PRC) devised its own standard, known as pinyin (*Han-yu p'in-yin,* "Chinese Spelling"), which is becoming more widely accepted; however, the Wade-Giles System is still used in Taiwan, Hong Kong and many other countries. Hong Kong reverted to the PRC and the use of pinyin in 1997. Until recently, all materials published on China in English used the Wade-Giles System, and it is still the standard for catalogs and indexes in many libraries, museums and other institutions although the U.S. Library of Congress has announced that it will convert from the Wade-Giles System to pinyin. The Wade-Giles System is accompanied by the so-called Postal System, devised by the Chinese Postal Administration in 1906, for spelling Chinese geographical names, and is commonly used on maps, gazetteers, etc. Students of China must be familiar with all three systems of romanization. See also LANGUAGE, CHINESE; PINYIN SYSTEM OF ROMANIZATION (AND TABLE).

WALEY, ARTHUR (1889–1966)   Born Arthur David Schloss; he was a British translator who introduced classical Chinese and Japanese literature to the West. Waley attended Rugby and began but did not complete a classical course of study at King's College, Cambridge University. He taught himself to read the classical Chinese and Japanese languages and began making translations while working at the British Museum in London. He lived a very private life, and little is known about him apart from his published works. Waley never held a regular university appointment or traveled to Asia, but he received an honorary LL.D. from Aberdeen University. From 1912 to 1930 he was assistant keeper of the Department of Prints and Drawings in the British Museum, during which time he began making his translations. In 1930, he also became Additional Lecturer in the museum's School of Oriental Studies. Waley's first translation from Chinese was *Chinese Poems,* which he published privately in 1916. Waley is best known for his series of translations of Chinese lyric poems, known as *ci* (*tz'u*); the first of many volumes was published in 1918 under the title, *A Hundred and Seventy Chinese Poems.*

Many of Waley's English translations of Chinese poems were first published in magazines such as *Poetry* before being collected in volumes. He also published *More Translations from the Chinese* (1919), *An Introduction to the Study of Chinese Painting* (1923), *Poems from the Chinese* (1927), *The Way and Its Power* (1934), *The Book of Songs* (1937), *The Analects of Confucius* (1938), *Three Ways of Thought in Ancient China* (1939), *The Life and Times of Po Chu-i* (Bai Juyi; 1949) and *The Poetry and Career of Li Po* (Li Bai; 1950). The renowned poet Bai Juyi (772–846) was the first Chinese poet to become famous outside China, and his works became very popular in Korea and Japan. *The Book of Songs* and the *Analects of Confucius* are two of the most important texts in the canon of the Confucian school of thought, which was orthodox in China for more than 2,000 years. Confucian texts formed the foundation of the Chinese education system, which was geared toward examinations to select officials to staff the imperial bureaucracy, comparable to a civil service. *The Way and Its Power* is Waley's English translation of the *Daodejing* (*Tao Te Ching*) by Laozi (Lao Tzu), the most important text in Daoism (Taoism), the Chinese school of thought that flourished along with Confucianism and had a strong influence on Chinese poetry, painting and other forms of culture. Many scholars consider Waley's version of the *Daodejing* the definitive English translation. Waley based his translation, not on medieval commentaries of the text, as

WADE-GILES TO PINYIN

Wade-Giles	Pinyin	Wade-Giles	Pinyin	Wade-Giles	Pinyin	Wade-Giles	Pinyin	Wade-Giles	Pinyin	Wade-Giles	Pinyin
a	a	chū	ju	hsieh	xie	k'en	ken	lun	lun	pai	bai
ai	ai	ch'ū	qu	hsien	xian	keng	geng	lung	long	p'ai	pai
an	an	chua	zhua	hsin	xin	k'eng	keng	ma	ma	pan	ban
ang	ang	ch'ua	chua	hsing	xing	ko	ge	mai	mai	p'an	pan
ao	ao	chuai	zhuai	hsiu	xiu	k'o	ke	man	man	pang	bang
		ch'uai	chuai	hsiung	xiong	kou	gou	mang	mang	p'ang	pang
cha	zha	chuan	zhuan	hsū	xu	k'ou	kou	mao	mao	pao	bao
ch'a	cha	ch'uan	chuan	hsūan	xuan	ku	gu	mei	mei	p'ao	pao
chai	zhai	chūan	juan	hsūeh	xue	k'u	ku	men	men	pei	bei
ch'ai	chai	ch'ūan	quan	hsūn	xun	kua	gua	meng	meng	p'ei	pei
chan	zhan	chuang	zhuang	hu	hu	k'ua	kua	mi	mi	pen	ben
ch'an	chan	ch'uang	chuang	hua	hua	kuai	guai	miao	miao	p'en	pen
chang	zhang	chūeh	jue	huai	huai	k'uai	kuai	mieh	mie	peng	beng
ch'ang	chang	ch'ūeh	que	huan	huan	kuan	guan	mien	mian	p'eng	peng
chao	zhao	chui	zhui	huang	huang	k'uan	kuan	min	min	pi	bi
ch'ao	chao	ch'ui	chui	hui	hui	kuang	guang	ming	ming	p'i	pi
che	zhe	chun	zhun	hun	hun	k'uang	kuang	miu	miu	piao	biao
ch'e	che	ch'un	chun	hung	hong	kuei	gui	mo	mo	p'iao	piao
chen	zhen	chūn	jun	huo	huo	k'uei	kui	mou	mou	pieh	bie
ch'en	chen	ch'ūn	qun			kun	gun	mu	mu	p'ieh	pie
cheng	zheng	chung	zhong			k'un	kun			pien	bian
ch'eng	cheng	ch'ung	chong	i	yi	kung	gong	na	na	p'ien	pian
chi	ji			jan	ran	k'ung	kong	nai	nai	pin	bin
ch'i	qi	en	en	jang	rang	kuo	guo	nan	nan	p'in	pin
chia	jia	erh	er	jao	rao	k'uo	kuo	nang	nang	ping	bing
ch'ia	qia			je	re			nao	nao	p'ing	ping
chiang	jiang	fa	fa	jen	ren	la	la	nei	nei	po	bo
ch'iang	qiang	fan	fan	jeng	reng	lai	lai	nen	nen	p'o	po
chiao	jiao	fang	fang	jih	ri	lan	lan	neng	neng	pou	bou
ch'iao	qiao	fei	fei	jo	ruo	lang	lang	ni	ni	p'ou	pou
chieh	jie	fen	fen	jou	rou	lao	lao	niang	niang	pu	bu
ch'ieh	qie	feng	feng	ju	ru	le	le	niao	niao	p'u	pu
chien	jian	fo	fo	juan	ruan	lei	lei	nieh	nie		
ch'ien	qian	fou	fou	jui	rui	leng	leng	nien	nian	sa	sa
chih	zhi	fu	fu	jun	run	li	li	nin	nin	sai	sai
ch'ih	chi			jung	rong	lia	lia	ning	ning	san	san
chin	jin	ha	ha			liang	liang	niu	niu	sang	sang
ch'in	qin	hai	hai	ka	ga	liao	liao	no	nuo	sao	sao
ching	jing	han	han	k'a	ka	lieh	lie	nou	nou	se	se
ch'ing	qing	hang	hang	kai	gai	lien	lian	nu	nu	sen	sen
chiu	jiu	hao	hao	k'ai	kai	lin	lin	nū	nū	seng	seng
ch'iu	qiu	hei	hei	kan	gan	ling	ling	nuan	nuan	sha	sha
chiung	jiong	hen	hen	k'an	kan	liu	liu	nūeh	nūe	shai	shai
ch'iung	qiong	heng	heng	kang	gang	lo	luo	nung	nong	shan	shan
cho	zhuo	ho	he	k'ang	kang	lou	lou			shang	shang
ch'o	chuo	hou	hou	kao	gao	lu	lu	o	e	shao	shao
chou	zhou	hsi	xi	k'ao	kao	lū	lū	ou	ou	she	she
ch'ou	chou	hsia	xia	kei	gei	luan	luan			shen	shen
chu	zhu	hsiang	xiang	k'ei	kei	lūan	lūan	pa	ba	sheng	sheng
ch'u	chu	hsiao	xiao	ken	gen	lūeh	lūe	p'a	pa	shih	shi

(Table continues)

WADE-GILES TO PINYIN *(Continued)*

Wade-Giles	Pinyin	Wade-Giles	Pinyin	Wade-Giles	Pinyin	Wade-Giles	Pinyin	Wade-Giles	Pinyin	Wade-Giles	Pinyin
shou	shou	tai	dai	ting	ding	tsen	zen	tuan	duan		
shu	shu	t'ai	tai	t'ing	ting	ts'en	cen	t'uan	tuan	ya	ya
shua	shua	tan	dan	tiu	diu	tseng	zeng	tui	dui	yai	yai
shuai	shuai	t'an	tan	to	duo	ts'eng	ceng	t'ui	tui	yang	yang
shuan	shuan	tang	dang	t'o	tuo	tso	zuo	tun	dun	yao	yao
shuang	shuang	t'ang	tang	tou	dou	ts'o	cuo	t'un	tun	yeh	ye
shui	shui	tao	dao	t'ou	tou	tsou	zou	tung	dong	yen	yan
shun	shun	t'ao	tao	tsa	za	ts'ou	cou	t'ung	tong	yin	yin
shuo	shuo	te	de	ts'a	ca	tsu	zu	tsu	zi	ying	ying
so	suo	t'e	te	tsai	zai	ts'u	cu	tz'u	ci	yu	you
sou	sou	teng	deng	ts'ai	cai	tsuan	zuan			yū	yu
ssu	si	t'eng	teng	tsan	zan	ts'uan	cuan	wa	wa	yūan	yuan
su	su	ti	di	ts'an	can	tsui	zui	wai	wai	yūeh	yue
suan	suan	t'i	ti	tsang	zang	ts'ui	cui	wan	wan	yūn	yun
sui	sui	tiao	diao	ts'ang	cang	tsun	zun	wang	wang	yung	yong
sun	sun	t'iao	tiao	tsao	zao	ts'un	cun	wei	wei		
sung	song	tieh	die	ts'ao	cao	tsung	zong	wen	wen		
		t'ieh	tie	tse	ze	ts'ung	cong	weng	weng		
ta	da	tien	dian	ts'e	ce	tu	du	wo	wo		
t'a	ta	t'ien	tian	tsei	zei	t'u	tu	wu	wu		

Source: *People's Republic of China: Administrative Atlas* (Washington, D.C.: Central Intelligence Agency, 1975), 46–47.

other translators had done, but on a close study of all the early Chinese literature.

Waley is also famous for his translations from Japanese, especially the novel *The Tale of Genji* (*Genji Monogatari*; 1925–33), the world's first novel, written by an 11th-century woman, Murasaki Shikibu. Other Japanese works that Waley translated include *Japanese Poetry: The "Uta"* (1919), *The No Plays of Japan* (1921), *The Pillow Book of Sei Shonagon* (1928) and "The Lady Who Loved Insects" (1929), a story from a Japanese collection. He also wrote many essays on Japanese art and on the Zen (Chan in Chinese) Sect of Buddhism. Waley's English translations of Chinese and Japanese works became popular with the general public. They were translated into other Western languages and influenced modern Western writers, such as Bertolt Brecht. Scholars have criticized Waley for not producing accurate reproductions of the original texts, but Waley's translations are still admired for the beauty of their language. See also ANALECTS, CONFUCIAN; BAI JUYI; BOOK OF SONGS; CHAN SECT OF BUDDHISM; CONFUCIANISM; DAODEJING; DAOISM; IMPERIAL EXAMINATION SYSTEM; LI BAI; LYRIC VERSE.

WALL OF TEN THOUSAND LI   See GREAT WALL.

WALL POSTERS   See BIG-CHARACTER POSTERS.

WAN LI (1916–   )   A high-ranking official in the government of the People's Republic of China (PRC), founded in 1949 by the Chinese Communist Party (CCP). Wan was educated in China but also studied in France as a young man, as did many Chinese who became prominent in the CCP, which was founded in 1921. During the post-1945 civil war between the CCP and and the Chinese Nationalist Party (Kuomintang; KMT), Wan was active in the Communist liberation of Nanjing and Chongqing, the KMT capitals. After 1949 he held important financial positions in these two cities. In Chongqing, Sichuan Province, Wan served on the Finance and Economics Committee headed by Deng Xiaoping (Teng Hsiao-p'ing). He was also a member of the Southwest Military and Administrative Committee and deputy director of the Industry Department. In 1952 Wan was transferred to Beijing, the Chinese capital, where he served as vice minister of the new Ministry of Building from 1952 to 1956 and director of the Urban Construction General Bureau from 1955 to 1956. When the bureau was upgraded to a ministry, Wan served as minister until 1958. He became secretary of the Beijing branch of the CCP and was elected vice mayor of Beijing in 1958. In both of these posts he was subordinate to Peng Zhen (P'eng Chen). Wan served as Beijing deputy to the second National People's Congress (NPC) in 1958 and the third NPC in 1964.

During the Cultural Revolution (1966–76), Wan disappeared twice, first from 1966 to 1971. He returned to public life in high positions in Beijing from 1971 to 1974, and served as Beijing CP secretary from 1974 to 1975 and minister of railways from 1975 to 1976. Wan disappeared the second time from 1976 to 1977. In 1977 he was rehabilitated and elected a member of the Central Committee of the 11th

Party Congress, a position he continued to hold into the 1990s. He also held several high CCP positions in Anhui Province from 1977 to 1980. In 1980 Wan became a member of the Constitution Revision Committee. He served as vice premier from 1980 to 1988 and as acting premier for brief periods in 1982 and 1983. He became a member of the CCP Secretariat from 1980 to 1982 and a member of the Politburo from 1982 to the present. In the 1980s he also held several positions in agricultural administration and other government areas.

In 1987 Wan became a member of the Presidium Standing Committee of the 13th National Party Congress. At the Seventh National People's Congress (NPC) in 1988, Wan, a political moderate, was selected to replace Peng Zhen as chairman of the Standing Committee. The Chinese government was attempting to rebuild and modernize the country, and Peng, a conservative, had blocked or delayed many important pieces of reformist legislation. Wan also became executive chairman of the NPC Presidium. He has been honored with many other titles, such as honorary president of the Bridge Foundation, Tennis Society, Urban Science Society and Literature Foundation. In 1985 he became a member of the Organizing Committee for the 11th Asian Games, which were held in Beijing in 1990. Since 1978 he has also led Chinese delegations to Japan, the United States, the former U.S.S.R. and Romania. See also ASIAN GAMES, 1990; CULTURAL REVOLUTION; DENG XIAOPING; GOVERNMENT STRUCTURE; NATIONAL PEOPLE'S CONGRESS; PENG ZHEN; POLITBURO.

WANG ANSHI (Wang An-shih; 1021–86) A prime minister during the Song dynasty (960–1279) who enacted major reforms in the imperial bureaucracy and the examination systems by which government officials were selected. The bureaucracy became divided into factions supporting and opposing these reforms. The conflict continued even after Wang died, preventing the Song government from facing up to the dangers posed to it by a group of nomadic invaders from the north called the Jurchen.

In 1068 Emperor Shenzong (Shen-tsung; r. 1067–85) decided to support Wang, who was governor of Nanjing at the time. Wang came to the court in Kaifeng and filled the bureaucracy with his supporters so he could carry out his so-called New Policies, which aimed to get rid of corruption in the civil service at both the local and national levels and economic disparities. He organized the Chinese people into groups that would maintain control over landholding and the accumulation of private wealth.

Wang accused the people who opposed his policies of being immoral. His policies were quite radical, but he legitimized them by claiming that they were contained in the classical texts of the Confucian tradition. He argued that all Chinese people should depend on their government, hold the same values, and have stronger ties with their communities than with their families. His reforms caused great turmoil because they attacked the families that were wealthy enough to have their sons educated to take the bureaucratic examinations. Wang increased the number of government schools so that more candidates could prepare for the examinations. He also required that the examination questions be concerned with practical administrative and technical issues rather than simply with knowledge of classical Confucian literature and philosophy.

Wang developed a state marketing system that stabilized the prices of grains and other necessary goods that were transported to the capital as payment of tribute to the government. He also instituted "Green Crop Money," a system for lending money to peasants to buy what they needed to grow crops in the spring and to pay it back at the harvest. The interest rate charged the peasants by the government was lower than that charged by moneylenders, so it aimed to protect the peasants and bring revenue into the government treasury. Wang also instituted a new system of land registration and tax assessment. One of his most successful reforms was the replacement of the standing professional armies, which had poor recruits and were not very effective, with militia forces, known as the *baojia* (*pao-chia*) system. Families were organized into units of ten, which had to provide a certain number of men for their local militias for self-policing and defense.

The statesman and historian Sima Guang (Ssu-ma Kuang; 1019–85) led the conservative faction that opposed Wang Anshi's reforms. The emperor continued to support Wang, but Wang was forced to resign in 1074. The emperor restored him a year later, but Wang had to retire from the court again in 1076. He was sent back to Nanjing and given several lesser positions, and retired from government service with the honorary title of duke. After the emperor died in 1085, his grandmother, the empress dowager, took over as regent and started to dismantle Wang's reforms. Sima Guang took Wang Anshi's place as prime minister and did away with his reforms. Sima Guang's conservative position aimed to keep the imperial Confucian bureaucratic system intact; this had a lasting effect on the Chinese government because the system ran the government through all succeeding dynasties to the end of the Qing (1644–1911). Wang's policies were also opposed by the veteran government official Ouyang Xiu (Ou-yang Hsiu; 1007–72), who had been a reformer early in his career and had sponsored Wang as a young man. The famous statesman and poet Su Shi (Su Shih; also known as Su Dongpo or Si Tung-p'o; 1036–1101) also opposed Wang's reforms and was banished from the court several times and sent in exile to Hainan Island in 1097. See also CONFUCIANISM; IMPERIAL BUREAUCRACY; IMPERIAL EXAMINATION SYSTEM; JURCHEN; OUYANG XIU; SIMA GUANG; SONG DYNASTY; SU SHI.

WANG BIE (Wang Pi; 226–249) A metaphysical thinker in the Daoist tradition who tried to reconcile the differences between Confucius and Laozi (Lao Tzu; the founder associated with Daoism), the two most important Chinese thinkers. Both lived in the sixth century B.C. Wang Bie attempted to assimilate the social and moral emphasis of Confucianism into Daoist thought. He wrote a commentary on Confucian texts using terms and concepts from the Daoist tradition. He also wrote a commentary on the text attributed to Laozi, known as the *Laozi* (*Lao Tzu*) or *Daodejing* (*Tao-te ching*). In this he discussed the concept that all things that have Being belong to the Dao, which he described as Nothingness that is actually a creative power that includes everything that exist. Dao transforms Being into infinite perfection.

His philosophy was one that embraced constant change, or dynamic being. Wang Bie argued that Confucianism shows the origin of all things within the realm of Being, whereas Daoism includes a concept beyond Being, which is Nothing. Wang Bie described "Nothing," or Dao, not as one particular thing as opposed to another, but as the infinite substance that contains everything that has Being. Wang Bie termed Dao "original non-being" (*p'enwu*). He argued that it remains beyond all distinctions or descriptions that can be made, and is the unified principle that underlies all existing things. In keeping with Confucian ideals, however, Wang Bie concluded that the truly wise person does not retire from life as a hermit, the path of many Daoist thinkers, but acts in the social and political sphere by following the Daoist principle of *wuwei*, meaning "nonaction" or "taking no unnatural action." He Yan (Ho Yen; d. 249) and Guo Xiang (Kuo Hsiang; d. 312) were two other important Daoist thinkers who attempted a similar synthesis of Daoism and Confucianism. See also CONFUCIANISM; DAODE-JING; DAOISM; LAOZI.

WANG CHAO-CHUN   See WANG ZHAOJUN.

WANG CHIH   See EUNUCHS.

WANG CHIN   See EUNUCHS.

WANG CHING-WEI   See WANG JINGWEI.

WANG CHONG (CH'UNG)   See FATE.

WANG DONGXING   See GANG OF FOUR; JIANG QING.

WANG FANGYU   (1913–97)   A teacher, scholar, painter, calligrapher and connoisseur of Chinese art. Wang was born in Beijing but spent much of his life in the United States, where he was known as Fred Wang. In China he was educated in the Confucian classics and calligraphy as well as regular academic subjects and received a bachelor's degree from the Catholic University. In 1944 he immigrated to the United States, and the following year he completed a master's degree at Columbia University in New York. Between 1945 and 1965 Wang taught Chinese language and literature at Yale University in New Haven, Connecticut. He wrote several books on the Chinese spoken language and writing system that remain important sources; two of the best-known are *Chinese Dialogues* (1953) and *Introduction to Chinese Cursive Scripts* (1958). In 1965 Wang became chairman of the Asian Studies Department and curator of the Oriental Art Collection at Seton Hall University in New Jersey. There he began compiling a two-volume Chinese-English/English-Chinese dictionary and developing the first computer system to teach the Chinese language.

As a scholar of Chinese paintings and calligraphy, Wang specialized in the work of Bada Shanren (Pa-ta Shan-jen; 1626–1705), a Buddhist monk and the best-known artist of the Qing dynasty (1644–1911). Wang published more than 20 articles in Chinese and English on Bada Shanren's calligraphy, poetry, paintings and relation to other Chinese artists. In 1990 Wang and Richard Barnhart produced the major exhibition and accompanying catalogue, *Master of the Lotus Garden: The Life and Art of Bada Shanren,* the most complete English-language study of the artist's life and works.

In 1974, Wang displayed his calligraphy in a group show at Seton Hall and won first prize. He continued to take part in solo and group exhibitions throughout the United States, China, Canada, Switzerland, Germany and South Korea, often giving lectures and demonstrations to accompany them. He compiled two catalogues with commentary of his calligraphic paintings, *Dancing Ink* and *Dancing Ink II.* In autumn 1997, shortly before he died at age 80, he took part in two exhibitions in New York, one at the Taipei Gallery and another organized by Elizabeth Wang. Wang and his wife, Wang Sum Wai, who died in 1996, gathered an extensive collection of Chinese art, ceramics, scrolls, jade and writing implements dating from ancient times to the 20th century. See also BADA SHANREN; CALLIGRAPHY; INK PAINTING; LANGUAGE, CHINESE; WRITING SYSTEM, CHINESE.

WANG GAI   See DONG QICHANG; LANDSCAPE PAINTING; MUSTARD SEED GARDEN MANUAL OF PAINTING.

WANG GUANGMEI   See CULTURAL REVOLUTION; LIU SHAOQI.

WANG GUOWEI   (Wang Kuo-wei; 1877–1927)   A major Chinese poet, literary and dramatic critic and philosopher. Wang Guowei studied Japanese and Western languages in Shanghai, and in 1902 he went to study in Japan but was not able to stay long because of ill health. He returned to China and taught for several years in Shanghai and Suzhou. He published his first collection of poems in the lyric form (*ci* or *tz'u*) in 1906, and they garnered the highest praise from critics, who called them the finest lyric poems to be published since the Song dynasty (960–1279), one of the high periods of Chinese culture. In 1910 he published a critical work, *Poetry Talks of the Human World,* which was the first work of Chinese literary criticism that quoted Western as well as Chinese sources. Wang had studied the Western philosophies of Kant, Nietzsche and Schopenhauer and had translated some of their works into Chinese. He also drew upon Western philosophy to write the first major modern Chinese critical work on the 18th-century novel, *Dream of the Red Chamber (Hongloumeng),* the most important work of fiction in Chinese history. Wang married and had a family, and they moved to Japan when the Revolution of 1911 broke out that overthrew the Qing dynasty and established the Republic of China. When they returned to China in 1915, he pursued a successful career as a teacher, researcher and writer, and held faculty positions at two universities in Beijing. Sadly, he committed suicide in 1927. A collection of 115 of Wang's finest lyric poems, most of them written between 1905 and 1909, was published under the title *Tiaohua Ci (T'iao-hua tz'u).* See also DREAM OF THE RED CHAMBER; LYRIC VERSE.

WANG HONGWEN (HUNG-WEN)   See CULTURAL REVOLUTION; GANG OF FOUR; JIANG QING.

WANG HSI-CHIH   See WANG XIZHI.

WANG HSIEN-CHIH   See WANG XIZHI.

WANG JIN See EUNUCHS.

WANG JINGWEI (Wang Ching-wei; 1883–1944) A leader of the Chinese Nationalist Party (Kuomintang; KMT) who defected to the Japanese side during China's War of Resistance against Japan (1937–45; World War II) and became head of the pro-Japanese puppet government in Nanjing. Wang won a Chinese government scholarship to study in Japan in 1904 and received his degree at Tokyo Law College in 1906. In Japan he became an officer in the Revolutionary Alliance (Tongmenghui or T'ung-meng-hui) that revolutionary Chinese leader Sun Yat-sen (1866–1925) had founded to oppose the Manchu Qing dynasty (1644–1911). Wang traveled with Sun in 1907 and gave speeches on behalf of the Revolutionary Alliance in Singapore and other Southeast Asian cities with large, wealthy overseas Chinese populations that were a major source of support for the society. In China Wang became nationally famous in 1910 when he took part in a plot to assassinate the Manchu prince regent, the father of Puyi, Qing emperor Xuantong (Hsuan-t'ung). The Qing government discovered the plot and imprisoned Wang in chains for life, but he was spared execution and released after the Wuchang Uprising triggered the Revolution of 1911. Wang then went to France but returned to China in 1917 and took a position on Sun Yat-sen's staff. Sun founded the Republic of China in 1912 and served as its first president. Wang composed Sun's political testament, which Sun signed shortly before he died in March 1925.

Wang led the left wing of the Nationalist Party, which wanted the Nationalists to cooperate with the Chinese Communist Party (CCP) that had recently been founded. Chiang Kai-shek (1887–1975), who later became head of the Nationalist Party, was leader of the party's right wing. In 1927 Wang led the coalition Nationalist government at Wuhan, which opposed Chiang's Nationalist government at Nanjing. When Wang learned that Soviet leader Joseph Stalin had ordered the Chinese Communists to take control of the Nationalists and get rid of those who opposed the Communists, he ended his cooperation with the Communists and purged them from the Nationalist Party. The Nationalist factions were forced to join together when Japan invaded Manchuria (northeastern China) in 1931 and established their puppet state, which they called Manchukuo.

Wang became head of the Nationalist government in Nanjing from 1932 to 1935 while Chiang led the Nationalist military forces that were attempting to eliminate the Communists altogether. Because Wang had to negotiate with Japan for the restoration of railroad and postal service between China and Manchukuo, the Chinese regarded him as a collaborator. An assassin wounded Wang in November 1935, and he left China for a year to receive medical treatment. When China went to war against Japan in 1937, Wang believed that China would not be able to defeat Japan and would actually destroy itself by resisting the Japanese. He also resented having to take second place to Chiang Kai-shek in the Nationalist Party. In December 1938 Wang flew to Hanoi, Vietnam and sent a telegram to Chiang at Chongqing in Sichuan Province, where the Nationalist government had fled from the Japanese, urging Chiang to stop fighting and make peace with Japan. Another assassination attempt spared Wang but killed one of his colleagues. Wang then went to Shanghai and joined the Chinese there who were collaborating with the Japanese.

In 1938 Japan established a puppet "Reform Government" at Nanjing. The Japanese persuaded Wang to defect to their side and in March 1940 installed him as head of a "Reorganized Nationalist Government" at Nanjing. This puppet government signed a peace treaty with Japan in late 1940 but had little authority. On January 9, 1943, Wang's government declared war on the United States and Britain, who were allies against Japan, and it signed a new treaty of alliance with Japan on October 30, 1943. In 1944 Wang traveled to Japan for medical treatment, where he died in Nagoya on November 10. See also CHIANG KAI-SHEK; CHINESE COMMUNIST PARTY; MANCHUKUO; NATIONALIST PARTY; REPUBLIC OF CHINA; REVOLUTION OF 1911; REVOLUTIONARY ALLIANCE; SUN YAT-SEN; WAR OF RESISTANCE AGAINST JAPAN.

WANG KAI See DONG QICHANG; GONG XIAN; MUSTARD SEED GARDEN MANUAL OF PAINTING.

WANG KYO-WEI See WANG GUOWEI.

WANG MANG (d. A.D. 23) A regent of the Western or Former Han dynasty (206 B.C.–A.D. 8) who seized the throne in A.D. 9. Wang Mang attempted to make government reforms, but his economic reforms were not successful and peasant rebellions broke out. He was killed in A.D. 23 and the Han dynasty was restored by Liu Xiu (known as Guangwudi or Kuang Wu-ti) as the Eastern or Later Han dynasty (25–220). This period of interruption of the Han dynasty is known as the Wang Mang Interregnum (A.D. 9–23). Wang Mang was a nephew of a Han princess who became empress dowager, and he married one of his daughters to an emperor. He became regent in 1 B.C., a position that three of his uncles and one cousin had also held for a total of 28 years. By the time of Wang Mang's regency, the Han court, more than 200 years old, was weak, losing its control over the population, and having trouble collecting excessively high taxes; members of the imperial bureaucracy or civil service were discouraged. Wang Mang declared himself emperor in A.D. 9 and called his dynasty the Xin (Hsin, "New"), of which he was the only ruler. His reforms included redistribution of land to limit the wealth of powerful families and provide land to families that formerly owned none; taxation of slave owners; and the replacement of circulating gold coins with bronze ones, allowing the imperial treasury to accumulate a huge hoard of gold. He also patronized education in the Confucian classics, which had provided the model for the Han bureaucracy, and built dormitories in the Han capital at Chang'an (modern Xi'an in Shaanxi Province) to house 10,000 students. Wang Mang himself had a reputation as a Confucian scholar, and he defended his attempted reforms by quoting Confucius and the duke of Zhou, a regent during the early Zhou Dynasty (1100–256 B.C.) whom Confucius admired as the ideal administrator.

Wang Mang thought he would be able to make many more reforms by issuing decrees in the capital and having them carried out all over the Chinese empire, but this did not happen. He placed new people in the aristocratic class but made few changes in the bureaucracy, and many officials continued to resent him for having disrupted the Han dynasty.

Wang Mang's economic programs also proved unable to help the majority of peasants, and rebellions broke out led by powerful landlords, whose factions included the Red Eyebrows and the Green Woodsmen. Liu Xiu, who was to restore the Han dynasty, joined the fighting in A.D. 22. Wang Mang was killed a year later, and in A.D. 25 Liu Xiu proclaimed himself emperor of the Eastern or Later Han dynasty. Although not successful during his lifetime, many of Wang Mang's reforms served as guidelines for later Chinese emperors. See also CONFUCIANISM; EASTERN HAN DYNASTY; IMPERIAL BUREAUCRACY; LIU XIU; RED EYEBROWS REBELLION; WESTERN HAN DYNASTY; ZHOU, DUKE OF.

WANG MU NIANG-NIANG See JADE EMPEROR; XIWANGMU.

WANG PI See WANG BI.

WANG SHIFU (Wang Shih-fu; c. 1250–c. 1337) The most important playwright during the Mongol Yuan dynasty (1279–1368), which has been called the Golden Age of Chinese drama. Wang was born in the Mongol Yuan capital of Dadu (modern Beijing) in northern China. He supposedly wrote 14 plays but only three have survived. His *Romance of the Western Chamber* (*Xixiangji* or *Hsi-hsiang chi*) remains the most popular musical drama in the Chinese theater. It tells the story of a young man studying for the imperial examination who falls in love with the girl whose family lives next to the Buddhist temple where he is staying. He is able to romance her with the cunning help of her maid. When their love affair is discovered, the girl's mother refuses to allow them to marry unless he passes the examination. The young man goes to the capital to take the examination, and in the end he marries his beloved. Wang wrote this play in the theatrical form known as *zazhu* (*tsa-chu*; northern drama), the most popular form during the Yuan dynasty; but he made several innovations, especially in giving singing parts to all of the major characters rather than just to one. He also wrote excellent dialogue for the play, which takes place in five books with four acts each and is much longer than a standard *zazhu*. Wang's play is thus a precursor of the type known as *chuanqi* (*ch'uan-ch'i*), which became the dominant theatrical form during the Ming (1368–1644) and Qing (1644–1911) dynasties. See also DRAMA; IMPERIAL EXAMINATION SYSTEM; YUAN DYNASTY.

WANG SHIMIN (Wang Shih-min; 1592–1680) A landscape painter known as one of the Six Great Masters of the Qing dynasty (1644–1911). He also used the names Xunzhi (Hsun-chih), Yanke (Yen-k'o), Xilulaoren (Hsi-lu lao-jen) and Xitianjuren (Hsi-t'ien chu-jen). Wang was born in Jiangsu Province to a wealthy family that served as officials in the imperial bureaucracy. During the Ming dynasty (1368–1644) his grandfather, Wang Xijue, had been grand secretary and minister of state, and his father, Wang Heng, belonged to the prestigious Hanlin Academy. During the reign of Emperor Chongzhen (Ch'ung-chen; r. 1628–44), Wang Shimin also served in the bureaucracy as vice president of the Court of Imperial Sacrifices. After 1644, when the Manchus overthrew the Ming and founded the Qing dynasty (1644–1911), Wang retired from the bureaucracy and spent all of his time paint-

ing. He had learned how to paint traditional Chinese landscapes as a boy and had been instructed by the prominent painter Dong Qichang (Tung Ch'i-ch'ang; 1555–1636). The National Palace Museum in Taipei, Taiwan, holds an album of small copies of Chinese masterpieces painted by Wang with inscriptions by Dong. Wang's family owned many famous paintings, which he was able to study. He especially admired the works of Huang Gongwang (Huang Kung-wang; 1269–1354), and some of his greatest works include a series of landscapes in Huang's style.

During the early Qing, the poet Wu Weiye (Wu Wei-yo) composed the verse, "The Nine Friends of Painting," in which he associated Wang Shimin with the great painters of the previous generation, including Dong Qichang, Li Lufang and Zhang Xuezeng (Chang Hsueh-tseng). Wang was equally famous for his calligraphy, the fine art of writing Chinese characters with a brush, especially in the clerical script, and he also wrote poetry and prose in the ancient classical Chinese style. The Chinese classify painting, calligraphy and poetry together as the "Three Perfections." Many temples in the countryside asked Wang to inscribe their name plaques with his beautiful calligraphy. Wang Shimin is classified as one of the "Four Wangs," which also include Wang Jian (Wang Chien; 1598–1677), Wang Hui (1632–1717) and Wang Yuanqi (Wang Yuan-ch'i; 1642–1715; Wang Shimin's grandson). These four are also included with Wu Li (1632–1718) and Yun Shouping (Yun Shou-p'ing; 1633–90) as the "Six Masters of the Qing." Wang Shimin, revered in his lifetime as the "grand old man of painting," instructed the other five painters. See also CALLIGRAPHY; DONG QICHANG; HUANG GONGWANG; LANDSCAPE PAINTING; NATIONAL PALACE MUSEUM; POETRY; QING DYNASTY; WU LI.

WANG SHOUREN (WANG SHOU-JEN) See WANG YANG-MING.

WANG TUNG-HSING See GANG OF FOUR; JIANG QING.

WANG WEI (699–761) Also known as Mochi (Mo-ch'i); a painter and poet who was a great inspiration to later Chinese landscape painters, especially those in the so-called Southern School of painting. A talented musician and scholar as well as an artist, Wang Wei was admitted to the upper level of the Tang dynasty (618–907) court in the capital city of Chang'an (modern Xi'an in Shaanxi Province in western China), but he also enjoyed spending time at his country home, Wangchuan. Later painters praised his long horizontal rolling scroll painting of this estate, but only rough copies of this have survived. The original has not been found. He was most admired by his own colleagues for his paintings of snowy landscapes. Wang Wei was a student of the Buddhist religion, and developed a deeper interest in the religion after his wife died. He was the first Chinese artist to paint only landscapes, and the first to express the spiritual quality of his scenes. Instead of the brightly colored and detailed paintings produced by many other artists during the Tang dynasty, Wang Wei worked mostly with black ink, sometimes adding light colors. This style of monochrome ink painting has been especially associated with the Chan (Zen) Sect of Buddhism. It also evidences the connection of Wang Wei's style of painting with calligraphy, the fine art of writing Chinese characters with a brush and black ink. The painting technique known as "broken" or "splashed" ink (*pomo*) has been attributed to Wang Wei, although it dates back to the seventh century. It entails the use of broad up-and-down strokes with the brush and the application of ink in patches or washes that leave white spaces on the paper or silk being painted. An essay on painting landscapes, supposedly written by Wang Wei, was later claimed to have been discovered by Zhang Yanyuan. In it, Wang Wei advises artists to use their instinct more than their brushes, and states that there is no need to put complete details on features painted in the distance. According to Wang Wei, clouds should cover the middle of mountains, waterfalls should cover part of large rocks, trees should cover pavilions and towers, and human and animal figures should cover roads. Morning is to be depicted by light mists in the dawn over the mountains, and evening by the sun setting behind the mountains. Wang Wei also wrote poetry in the classical Chinese style, with an excellent technique and a personal, reflective aspect. He has been praised for "putting painting into his poetry and poetry into his painting." However, his poems lack the political depth of Du Fu (Tu Fu) or the full lyricism of Li Bai (Li Po), the two greatest Tang poets. See also CALLIGRAPHY; INK PAINTING; LANDSCAPE PAINTING; SOUTHERN SCHOOL OF PAINTING.

WANG XIANZHI See WANG XIZHI.

WANG XIZHI (Wang Hsi-chih; 321–79) The most highly regarded calligrapher in Chinese history, termed the "sage of calligraphy." His style has had a great influence on all calligraphers who came after him, and his works have been copied by students of calligraphy up to the present time. Unfortunately, scholars believe that no original works by Wang remain, only copies that have been traced from his works and rubbings. Wang Xizhi was born into a famous family of calligraphers in Shandong Province during the Eastern Jin dynasty (317–420). He held various government posts and then retired in 355 to live in the Shanyin region of Zhejiang Province. The admiration for the calligraphy of Wang Xizhi is illustrated by the fact that even Chinese emperors collected his works. Emperor Taizong (T'ai Tsung), second emperor of the Tang dynasty (618–907) and himself an accomplished calligrapher, spent a great deal of money to collect Wang's calligraphy and required his courtiers to do the same.

Wang Xizhi is credited with developing the fluid "running script" style of calligraphy (*xingshu* or *hsing shu*). He is also famous for writing in the more abbreviated and abstract cursive or "grass style" of calligraphy (*caoshu* or *ts'ao shu*). Wang's best known work of calligraphy is "Preface to the Poems Composed at the Orchard Pavilion" (*Lanting shu* or *Lan-t'ing hsu*), which describes a gathering of 42 famous literary figures to enjoy writing poems and drinking at the Spring Purification Festival in 353. Written in the "running script" style, this work by Wang has become the Chinese standard for that style of calligraphy. The gathering later became a popular subject for paintings, especially during the Ming dynasty (1368–1644) revival of classicism. Wang recorded his theories about the composition of calligraphy in *Eight Components of the Character "Yung."* His youngest son,

Wang Xianzhi (Wang Hsien-chih; 344–86), became a famous calligrapher as well. See also CALLIGRAPHY.

WANG YANGMING (1472–1529) Also known as Wang Shouren (Wang Shou-jen, his real name); a statesman, military general, and major philosopher of Neo-Confucianism, the revival of Confucian thought that began in the Song (960–1279) and continued in the Ming (1368–1644) dynasties. The son of a prominent scholar-official, Wang held many government positions including that of provincial governor. He crushed a revolt led by an imperial prince against the Ming dynasty for levying heavy taxes to finance palace construction. In 1506, Wang protested the imprisonment of a good government official and was punished himself by being beaten and sent into exile at the Chinese frontier for about three years. While there he developed the Neo-Confucian philosophy for which he became famous. After he returned from exile, the Ming gave him an imperial order to put down several rebellions in southwestern China between 1517 and 1519. Although he followed orders, the court did not reward him because he had strongly criticized government corruption as well as the teachings of his rival Confucian philosopher, Zhu Xi (Chu Hsi; 1130–1200). Neo-Confucian thought had been accepted as orthodox by the Chinese government. In 1521 Wang developed his doctrine of the extension of innate knowledge. By this he meant that man is born with the knowledge of what is good and can put this knowledge into action if he has a pure mind. For the next six years Wang retired from the government and spent his time giving lectures on such Confucian topics as sincerity and purposefulness.

Wang Yangming belonged to the Neo-Confucian School of the Mind or Intuition, while Zhu Xi belonged to the Rationalist School or the School of Principle or Reason. Zhu Xi had standardized the Four Books of Confucianism, which became the basis of the Chinese educational system and the examinations for the imperial bureaucracy, and had produced a synthesis of Song dynasty Neo-Confucian thought. He taught that human beings are able to rise above their limitations and weaknesses and are able to enter into and understand the principles of all created things. By created things he meant practical activities such as societal relations and politics. For Zhu Xi, moral action resided in the investigation of principles through the study of the Confucian classics.

Wang Yangming challenged Zhu Xi's emphasis on book learning and taught that through thinking and meditating, a person could develop his intuitive knowledge, which would guide his actions. For Wang, knowledge and action were united: "Knowledge is the beginning of action and action is the completion of knowledge." Wang's theory that every person has innate goodness, based on the ancient Confucian concept that every man could become a sage, was influential in loosening the class structure of Chinese society. Many of Wang's followers established private academies where they opened the public lectures to all men no matter what their social class. Wang's thought also stimulated greater intellectual freedom in China. There was a reaction by some Chinese scholars against Wang's thought after his death. However, Wang Yangming's Neo-Confucian philosophy has been influential throughout Asia, especially in Japan, where many leaders of the movement to modernize Japan subscribed to Wang's thought. His concepts also influenced early 20th-century Chinese idealists and Dr. Sun Yat-sen (1866–1925), the founder of modern China. See also CONFUCIANISM; FIVE CLASSICS OF CONFUCIANISM; FOUR BOOKS OF CONFUCIANISM; NEO-CONFUCIANISM; SUN YAT-SEN.

WANG YANI (1975–)   A contemporary young female painter who became famous in China and the West as a prodigy. She was born in Gongcheng in the southern Chinese province of Guangxi, near the beautiful Li River. Her father, Wang Shiqiang, was a successful painter but gave up his career in 1983 so he would not influence her work. Wang Yani began drawing when she was only two years old. The first exhibition of her paintings, executed in the traditional Chinese style, was held in Shanghai when she was four, organized by nearly two dozen respected elderly painters who were impressed by her talent. By age six she had painted 4,000 pictures and her works were exhibited in Guangzhou, Beijing and Hong Kong. Wang Yani especially loved to paint monkeys, and the Chinese government reproduced one of her early monkey paintings, *Scratching an Itch for Mother,* as a postage stamp. Her style is known in Chinese as *xieyi* (*hsieh-i*), "idea writing" or the spontaneous mixing of ink and pigment, in contrast to *gongbi* (*kung-pi*), "skillful brush" or controlled painting in which pigments are carefully applied to the paper. She became world famous through exhibitions of her paintings in Japan, Hong Kong, Germany, Great Britain and the United States. The Nelson-Atkins Museum of Art organized the show, "Yani: The Brush of Innocence," which was displayed at the Smithsonian Institution in Washington, D.C. in 1989 and museums in other American cities. The youngest artist ever to have a one-person show at the Smithsonian, Wang Yani attended in person and demonstrated her painting ability. In 1991 Zheng Zhensun, a Chinese journalist and photographer, and Alice Low, an American children's-book author and art teacher, published *A Young Painter,* which contains numerous illustrations of Wang Yani's work and describes her career as an artist. See also INK PAINTING; LI RIVER.

WANG YUANQI (Wang Yuan-ch'i; 1642–1715)   Also known as Wang Lutai (Wang Lu-t'ai); the greatest of the group of painters during the Qing dynasty (1644–1911) known as the Four Wangs. Wang Yuanqi was the grandson and student of Wang Shimin (Wang Shih-min; 1592–1680), the earliest of the four, who had studied landscape painting with the great master Dong Qichang (Tung Ch'i-ch'ang; 1555–1636). Wang Shimin also taught the other two Wangs, Wang Jian (Wang Chien; 1598–1677) and Wang Hui (1632–1717). Wang Yuanqi is also known as one of the Six Masters of the Qing, which include the four Wangs plus Wu Li (1632–1718) and Yun Shouping (Yun Shou-p'ing; 1633–90). Wang Hui was the most prolific and successful of the four Wangs during his lifetime, but since then, critics have preferred the work of Wang Yuanqi.

Wang Yuanqi rose to high official positions in the Qing imperial bureaucracy and became senior vice president of the Board of Finance and chancellor of the Hanlin Academy, the most prestigious body in the bureaucracy. Qing emperor Kangxi (K'ang-hsi; r. 1661–1722) favored Wang Yuanqi and

often requested him to paint a landscape in front of him. Kangxi appointed him as one of the editors of an anthology of painting and calligraphy that he commissioned in 1708, known as the *Peiwenzhai Shuhuapu* (*P'ei-wen-chai shu-hua-p'u*). Although Wang was associated with the imperial court, his paintings were quite original. He took his subjects from works by Ni Zan (Ni Tsan; 1301–74) and other masters of the Yuan dynasty (1279–1368), and he painted angular rocks and stark trees in the style of the Ming dynasty painters Dong Qichang. Wang's style is more abstract than typical Chinese landscape paintings. He seems to separate the rocks and mountains into their individual forms, which has caused some Western critics to compare him to Cezanne. Wang's style appears to be simple but is actually quite complex and difficult to execute. He also added colors to his paintings that make them appear modern in comparison to many Chinese paintings, which were made with black ink on a white background. See also HANLIN ACADEMY; KANGXI, EMPEROR; LANDSCAPE PAINTING; NI ZAN; WANG SHIMIN; WU LI.

WANG ZHAOJUN (Wang Chao-chun)   A princess of the Han dynasty (206 B.C.–A.D. 220) who is considered one of the Four Famous Beauties of Chinese history. She was born around 53 B.C. and was so beautiful and talented that she was chosen to be a concubine in the palace of Han emperor Yuandi (Yuan-ti). The court painter, Mao Yen Sho, took bribes from the concubines to make them look even more beautiful in their paintings so the emperor would favor them. However, Wang Zhaojun would not pay him a bribe, so he made her look ugly and even painted a mole on her face, a sign of ill fortune for the Chinese. Prince Hu Han Xie Shanyu (Hsieh Chan Yu), ruler of the Xiongnu (Hsiung-nu), a powerful nomadic tribe in Mongolia on China's northwestern frontier, paid a state visit to the emperor in the capital city of Chang-an (modern Xi'an in Shaanxi Province). In order to cement political relations between the Han Chinese and the Xiongnu, the emperor agreed to give Hu Han Xie Shanyu one of his own concubines. He chose Wang Zhaojun because she was so ugly in her portrait. At the ceremony when he presented her to the so-called "northern barbarian," the emperor realized how beautiful she really was. But he had to honor his promise in order to keep peace for China, so he sent her to Mongolia. Afterward, he had the deceitful painter killed.

On Wang's long journey to her new home, she felt lonely and often looked back with sorrow at her homeland, realizing that she would probably never return to China. She played her *pipa,* a musical instrument similar to a lute, and sang unhappy songs. She remained in Mongolia, bore the ruler a son, and brought Chinese culture to the Xiongnu court. The Chinese traditionally believed that a person who dies in a foreign country is cursed, so they felt a great debt to Wan Zhaojun for the great sacrifice she made to bring peace between China and the borderland tribes. The tomb of Wang Zhaojun can be seen in Hohhot, the capital city of the Inner Mongolia Autonomous Region (Neimenggu) in northwestern China. She has become a symbol of peace and is the subject of many Chinese paintings, plays and poems. See also CONCUBINAGE; HAN DYNASTY; HOHHOT; INNER MONGOLIA AUTONOMOUS REGION; PIPA; XIONGNU.

WANG ZHI See EUNUCHS.

WANGSHIYUAN See GARDEN OF THE MASTER OF THE FISHING NETS.

WANGXIA (WANG-HSIA), TREATY OF See OPIUM WAR.

WANLI CHANG CHENG See GREAT WALL.

WANLI (EMPEROR) (1563–1620) The 14th emperor of the Ming dynasty (1368–1644). He was the grandson of the Jiajing emperor (Chia-ching; r. 1522–67). His real name was Zhu Yijun (Chu Yi-chun), and he ruled under the name Shenzong (Shen-tsung); Wanli is the name of his reign (r. 1573–1620), the longest of the Ming dynasty. During the first decade of his reign, Chief Grand Secretary Zhang Juzheng (Chang Chu-cheng) acted as the young emperor's guardian and wielded the power of a virtual prime minister. He placed his supporters in high positions, maintained control over the government ministries, and even corresponded with provincial governors about administrative problems. He also enacted reforms to trim the budget and increase tax revenues. After Zhang Juzheng died suddenly in 1582, the officials he had banished came back into power and allied themselves with officials who believed that he had abused his power. They purged those he had placed in the government and suspended his austerity programs. Wanli supported their claims and ordered the posthumous stripping of Zhang Juzheng's honors and titles. However, around 1587 the factions that emerged during this struggle began criticizing the emperor, accusing him of laziness, extravagance and improper handling of his succession. He supported the mother of his third son, his favorite concubine, and refused to have his first son, Zhu Changluo (Chu Ch'ang-lo), formally installed as heir apparent according to Ming dynastic tradition. In 1601 Wanli finally gave in and declared that Changluo was the imperial heir. However, this did not put an end to the political fighting and attempted murders that troubled the court. After Zhu Changluo succeeded his father in 1620 as the 14th Ming emperor Taichang, he died within a month, apparently due to the wrong medicine being prescribed by a physician. For the remaining 24 years of the dynasty, the court suffered from the fighting of political factions.

During the second half of his reign, Wanli withdrew from contact with the grand secretaries and other government officials, communicating with them through the eunuchs who ran the imperial palace in the Forbidden City. This strengthened the power of the eunuchs and weakened the imperial bureaucracy. Matteo Ricci (1552–1610), the first Roman Catholic Jesuit priest to establish a mission, arrived in China in 1583 during Wanli's reign. The eunuchs finally had him introduced at the imperial court in Beijing in 1598. Ricci impressed Wanli and senior government officials, and in 1601 they gave him permission to reside in Beijing with an imperial stipend, and named him science tutor to the emperor's son. The Ming had to send military forces to Korea in 1592 and 1597 to fight the invading Japanese forces sent by Toyotomi Hideyoshi, which posed a threat to China. While the Japanese were never decisively defeated, Chinese forces held out against them until Hideyoshi died in 1598

and they were called back to Japan. The campaigns in Korea cost the Ming a great deal of money and they had to increases taxes in China. This, combined with the extravagance of the court, harmed the Chinese economy. In April 1619, shortly before Wanli's death, the army of 100,000 that he had sent against the Manchu leader Nurhachi in Manchuria (modern northeastern China) was defeated. Nurhachi identified the weaknesses of the Ming, and in 1644 he overthrew the Ming and founded the Qing dynasty (1644–1911).

Many historians believe that the decline of the Ming dynasty began during the reign of Wanli. They estimate that the construction and furnishing of Wanli's tomb cost one-half of an entire year's national income. The tomb belongs to the group of mausoleums north of Beijing where 13 of the Ming emperors are buried, a popular tourist site known as the Ming Tombs. Chinese archaeologists began excavating Wanli's tomb in 1955 and discovered numerous gold objects, including a headdress and gold dishes, basins and other containers, some of which were decorated with filigree or repoussé. Visitors can enter the tomb, which contains an entrance room, an antechamber, a chamber for religious sacrifices, Wanli's burial room and two rooms where the two empresses were buried. See also IMPERIAL BUREAUCRACY; MING DYNASTY; MING TOMBS; NURHACHI; QING DYNASTY; RICCI, MATTEO.

WAR OF RESISTANCE AGAINST JAPAN (1937–45) Also known as the Second Sino-Japanese War; a war fought by China against Japan, whose troops invaded Manchuria (northeastern China) in 1931 and used it as a base to invade China Proper and the rest of Asia. When the War of Resistance broke out, China was being governed by the Chinese Nationalist Party (Kuomintang; KMT), led by Chiang Kai-shek (Jiang Jieshi; 1887–1975). The KMT had been founded by Dr. Sun Yat-sen (1866–1925), who had led the revolutionary movement under which the Chinese people overthrew the Qing dynasty (1644–1911), China's last imperial dynasty; this is known as the Revolution of 1911. From 1916 to 1928, warlords controlled many regions of China. The Chinese Communist Party (CCP) had been founded by Mao Zedong (Mao Tse-tung; 1893–1976) and others in 1921 in Shanghai, China's largest port and trading city. Members of the CCP and KMT worked together at first. They established the Whampoa (Huangpu) Military Academy outside Guangzhou in southern China to train military officers to lead a Northern Expedition against the warlords beginning in July 1926, led by Chiang Kai-shek.

In April 1927 Chiang turned against the Communists and sent his troops into Shanghai, where thousands were killed but some escaped, including Zhou Enlai (Chou En-lai; 1898–1976) and his wife, Deng Yingchao (Teng Ying-ch'ao; 1904–92), to join Communist forces at the Soviet base in the Jinggang Mountain Range on the border of Jiangxi Province in south-central China. The KMT and CCP continued to fight their civil war. On October 10, 1928, Chiang, who had taken Beijing in June, became chairman of a new Chinese Nationalist government and established his capital at Nanjing.

Japan had gained concessions in Manchuria following its war with Russia from 1904 to 1905, known as the Russo-Japanese War. By the end of 1928, Zhang Xueliang (Chang

Hsueh-liang; 1898–), the most powerful warlord in Manchuria (northeastern China), agreed to Nationalist rule in Manchuria, although he did not relinquish his actual power there. His father, Zhang Zuolin (Chang Tso-lin; 1873–1928), had been military governor of Manchuria until he was killed in early 1928 when Japanese troops stationed in the region blew up his train. Manchuria has vast natural resources, and during the 19th century Western powers had vied for control of Liaoning Province in southern Manchuria. The city of Dalian, formerly called Port Arthur, at the southern tip of Liaoning is a strategic port that controls access to the Bo Hai Gulf and the cities of Tianjin and Beijing, the Chinese capital.

The Japanese had defeated China in the Sino-Japanese War of 1894–95, fought over control of Korea, which borders Manchuria. In the Treaty of Shimonoseki, which concluded the war, Japan exacted harsh terms on China, including the ceding of Taiwan Island, the Penghu (Pescadore) Islands and the Liaoning Peninsula to Japan. Japan made Korea a Japanese protectorate, and in 1910 it annexed Korea as a colony. Japan continued to build up its military and stationed troops in Manchuria and northern China. After the ROC was founded in 1912, the Japanese allowed several Chinese warlords to operate out of Mukden (known as Shenyang in Chinese), the capital of Liaoning. Zhang Zuolin controlled not only Manchuria but also the northern provinces of China Proper from 1916 until he was assassinated in 1928.

In 1931 Japan used the so-called Manchurian Incident as a pretext to launch a full-scale invasion of Manchuria. On the night of September 18, Japanese troops set off a bomb on the Southern Manchurian Railroad track outside Mukden and seized the city. The Chinese people held anti-Japanese demonstrations and boycotts, and Chiang Kai-shek took China's case against Japan to the League of Nations. The Japanese drove Zhang's troops out of Manchuria before the end of 1931 and rapidly brought all of Manchuria under their control. The Chinese regard the Manchurian Incident as the root cause of their War of Resistance against Japan and the beginning of World War II.

In February 1932, Japan declared Manchuria's independence from China, and in March 1932 it established a puppet state in Manchuria called Manchukuo (Manzhouguo or Man-chou-kuo in Chinese) with the capital at Changchun in Jilin Province. They renamed the city Xinjing (Hsin-ching). The Japanese had been protecting Henry Puyi, the last emperor of the Qing dynasty, and they forced him to serve as the figurehead of Manchukuo. In 1934 they elevated Puyi to emperor of Manchukuo, which made him an enemy of the Chinese state and a war criminal.

At China's request, the League of Nations formed a Commission of Inquiry headed by Britain's Lord Lytton, known as the Lytton Commission, to pressure Japan regarding its invasion of China. Western powers and the League of Nations gave China verbal and moral support. The Lytton Commission report, issued in October 1932, criticized Japan's actions in Manchuria but recognized that they could not be undone. The League of Nations neither wanted to legitimize Japan's actions nor directly condemn its aggression and force it to break off relations with Western powers. The league adopted the *Lytton Report* in February 1933, and the next day Japan,

claiming that it was maintaining Manchuria's internal peace and security, withdrew from the League of Nations. Japanese troops then occupied Jehol, a province in northern China, and annexed it to Manchukuo. They also moved into Hebei Province and established the 30- to 40-mile-wide East Hebei Autonomous Region, a demilitarized zone between Beijing and the port city of Tianjin, which Chinese troops could not enter without Japanese permission. In May 1933 the Nationalists signed the Tanku truce with Japan, under which they agreed to withdraw from the Beijing-Tianjin area. Japan continued its drive to bring all of northern China under its control, and in 1935 it created a North China Autonomous Region consisting of five Chinese provinces: Hebei, Shandong, Shanxi, Chahar and Suiyan.

Meanwhile, Chiang Kai-shek had been sending Nationalist troops against Communist forces in south-central China in five annual campaigns since 1930. In 1934 the Communists in Jiangxi decided to escape the Nationalists by moving to the northwest on the epic Long March (1934–35). Led by Mao Zedong, Zhou Enlai and military commander Zhu De (Chu Teh; 1886–1976), the Communists finally established their headquarters at Yan'an in Shaanxi Province. Chinese Communists accused Chiang of preferring to fight his own countrymen rather than resist the Japanese who had invaded China, and they urged a KMT-CCP united front against Japan. In 1936 Chiang ordered the Manchurian warlord Zhang Xueliang to send his troops to fight the Communists at Yan'an. But the Manchurian soldiers were angry that they had to fight Chinese troops while Japanese troops were occupying their own land, and they stopped fighting. In December 1936 Chiang flew to Zhang Xueliang's headquarters at Xi'an in Shaanxi. Zhang and a group of KMT and CCP military leaders kidnapped Chiang at the Huaqing Hot Springs outside Xi'an and persuaded him to stop fighting the Communists and form a united front; this is known as the Xi'an Incident.

On July 7, 1937, Japanese troops made a night maneuver at the Marco Polo Bridge (Lugouqiao or Lukouchiao) outside Beijing that triggered the first battle in the Chinese War of Resistance against Japan. Chinese troops had been stationed at the beautiful 800-year-old stone bridge because a railroad bridge next to it was strategically important, linking southern railway lines with Wanping, a major railway junction that provided access to Tianjin and other cities. That night Japanese troops fired blank cartridges at the bridge, and Chinese troops fired onto the Japanese but did not injure anyone. However, the Japanese commander discovered a soldier missing at role call and assumed that the Chinese had captured him. He ordered his troops to attack Wanping, and the Chinese troops fought back but were ineffectual. Both sides decided to stop fighting and attempted to negotiate a settlement. Yet Japan mobilized five troop divisions in case they were needed in China, and Chiang Kai-shek sent four divisions to Baoding in southern Hebei Province, north of the Yellow River (Huanghe). The premier of Japan blamed the Chinese for the incident and called for China to apologize. Military commanders in the area prepared to withdraw their troops, but fighting broke out once more around the Marco Polo Bridge, and Japanese troops took control of the region around Beijing and Tianjin. Chiang Kai-shek decided to attack the Japanese troops stationed in Shanghai. Japan responded by sending 15 troop divisions into China in July 1937, and the two sides began fighting a full-scale war. Japan did not declare war on China and referred to its military operation there as the China Incident or the China Affair.

Japanese forces quickly gained control of the North China Plain, and in August 1937 they attacked Shanghai. On August 22, 1937, the CCP formally reorganized its forces as the Eighth Route Army of the National Army. Many of its commanders later held high-ranking positions in the People's Republic of China (PRC). Zhu De was commander of the army and Peng Dehuai (P'eng Teh-huai) was deputy commander. Zhu's wife, Kang Keqing (K'ang K'e-ch'ing), served as director of the political department of the Eighth Route Army. The army had three divisions, with Liu Bocheng (Liu Po-cheng) as commander of one, the 115th division. Deng Xiaoping (Teng Hsiao-p'ing) served under him as political commissar. Another division was commanded by Lin Biao (Lin Piao), and Nie Rongzhen (Nieh Jung-chen) served as his deputy commander and political commissar.

In November 1937 the Japanese took Nanjing and committed atrocities against hundreds of thousands of Chinese residents, known as the "Rape of Nanjing." After Nanjing fell, Chiang Kai-shek established a provisional Nationalist capital at Hankou (Wuhan) in Hubei Province, farther up the Yangzi River. Warlords sent their troops to join Communist and Nationalist forces, but Chinese soldiers were poorly equipped and trained in comparison to the well-equipped Japanese soldiers who were trained in modern Western military techniques. By the end of 1937, Japan proclaimed that the entire coast of China was under blockade, except for Qingdao in Shandong Province and Hong Kong off the coast of southern China. The illegal blockade prevented the delivery of shipments of wartime supplies from Europe to China.

In 1938 Japan announced that its goal was to establish a "New Order in East Asia" (later known as the "Greater East Asia Co-prosperity Sphere") that would save China from the Communist threat and from "improper white influences" that threatened China's territorial integrity. On June 7, 1938, Nationalist troops burst the dikes on the Yellow River near Zhengzhou in Henan Province. They did so to stop Japanese troops, but the drastic action resulted in the deaths of millions of Chinese people and enormous damage to Chinese property and agriculture while having little effect on the military effort. Japanese forces took Guangzhou on October 21, 1938, and Hankou on October 25. Chiang moved his Nationalist government to Chongqing in Sichuan, a province in southwestern China protected by high mountain ranges. Many Chinese universities and industries also moved there. The Japanese sent bombing raids against Chongqing but never invaded Sichuan. KMT forces controlled southwestern China, and CCP forces northwestern China. The Communists also led guerrilla forces in Henan, Zhejiang and Shandong provinces and in other regions between the areas controlled by Japanese forces, especially in northern China.

In 1938 Canadian surgeon Norman Bethune went to China and organized medical services for the Communist Eighth Route Army in the region along the border between Shanxi and Hebei provinces in northern China. In 1936 he had joined the antifascist cause in the civil war in Spain, where he organized the first mobile blood-transfusion service, and he maintained that "Spain and China are part of the

same battle." In China Bethune worked ceaselessly to treat wounded soldiers and educate the Chinese about medical practices. In 1939 he died accidentally from septicemia (blood poisoning) and was buried in Shijiazhuang, the capital of Hebei Province, where the hospital that he founded has been named for him. He became a great hero to the Chinese people.

In December 1938 the Japanese persuaded Nationalist official Wang Jingwei (Wang Ching-wei; 1883–1944) to desert the Nationalists and join their side. Wang justified his actions by asserting that China had no chance of winning against Japan and that to continue fighting was suicidal. He had hoped to prevent the Japanese from treating the Chinese too harshly in the areas they occupied, and was able to do so to some extent, but the Japanese, after installing Wang as "President," treated him as their puppet. By the end of 1939 Japan controlled more than half of all of the territory and population of China, from Manchuria to the southern Chinese border with Vietnam (Indochina).

World War II broke out in Europe in September 1939, which brought China foreign allies such as Great Britain. The Chinese people were exhausted from fighting the Japanese, but the Japanese were spread too thin in China to win the war, and the two sides entered a stalemate. Famine was widespread and hundreds of thousands of people starved to death. A group of U.S. air pilots organized themselves into the American Volunteers Group (AVG) under General Claire Chennault, popularly known as the Flying Tigers, to fly supplies to the Nationalists from India "over the Hump" of the Himalaya Mountain Range. After Japan bombed the U.S. naval fleet at Pearl Harbor on December 7, 1941, the United States became an official ally of China and sent more military and financial aid. China made a formal declaration of war against Japan on December 9, 1941. At Chiang's request, U.S. president Franklin Delano Roosevelt sent General Joseph Stilwell (1883–1946) to serve as Chiang's chief-of-staff. Stilwell was given command of the Chinese Fifth and Sixth Armies in Burma, which borders China on the south, and also served as commanding general of U.S. forces in the China-Burma-India Theater, deputy supreme Allied commander in Southeast Asia, commanding general of the Chinese Army in India and its field commander in Burma, and chief of the Chinese Training and Combat Command and administrator of Lend-Lease to China.

In 1942 Japanese troops drove Stilwell's troops from Burma and attempted to invade China along the Burma Road, which had been built to transport supplies to the Nationalists in China. Chinese troops, supported by the Flying Tigers, stopped the Japanese troops from advancing. Stilwell and Chiang Kai-shek strongly disagreed about military policy. Stilwell wanted to supply weapons to all factions in China fighting the Japanese, including the Communists, but Chiang still mistrusted the Communists and did not want to arm them. In 1941 the KMT-CCP united front had started breaking down when Nationalist troops defeated the Communist New Fourth Army in the lower Yangzi River valley, known as the New Fourth Army Incident.

Soong Mei-ling (Soong Mayling, Sung Mei-ling or Song Meiling), the wife of Chiang Kai-shek, made a great contribution to the war effort by appealing to Americans to provide material and military assistance to China. She made many trips to the United States, and in February 1943 she became the first Chinese and the second woman to address a joint session of the U.S. Congress. She had been educated in the United States and served as Chiang's English interpreter. In November 1943 she accompanied Chiang to the Cairo Conference, where he met personally with U.S. president Roosevelt and British prime minister Winston Churchill. The Cairo Declaration stated that Manchuria and Taiwan would be restored to China after the war and that Korea would eventually become free and independent. Soong Mei-ling also communicated messages between Chiang and General Stilwell, who was nicknamed "Vinegar Joe" for his forthright attitude.

The disagreement between the two military leaders came to a head when Chiang requested Stilwell's dismissal, and in October 1944 President Roosevelt sent General Albert Wedemeyer to replace him. Chiang got along much better with Wedemeyer. U.S. army engineers, assisted by Chinese troops, constructed the Ledo Road, a supply route connecting northeastern India with the old Burma Road that opened in January 1945. Chiang renamed this route the Stilwell Road to honor the American general. In 1945 there were 70,000 American troops stationed in China, half at Kunming in Yunnan Province in southwestern China. There were also many American military advisers, diplomats and academic "China experts" working at the U.S. embassy in Chongqing. However, the United States was concentrating its military efforts on island-hopping in the Pacific Ocean to reach the main islands of Japan. The Chinese War of Resistance tied down 1.28 million Japanese troops in China that would otherwise have been sent against the Americans in the Pacific.

At the Yalta Conference in February 1945, Roosevelt and Churchill agreed to Stalin's demands that if the U.S.S.R. entered the war against Japan after the defeat of Germany, then the U.S.S.R. would be given back the concessions in Manchuria that Russia had formerly held but had been taken by Japan after the Russo-Japanese War of 1904–5. The European leaders kept this agreement secret from Chiang Kaishek and hence made decisions about future control of Chinese territory without involving the Chinese Nationalist government.

The United States dropped the first atomic bomb on Hiroshima, Japan on August 6, 1945. Two days later the U.S.S.R. declared war on Japan and sent a huge army into Manchuria, which met little resistance from Japanese troops there. After Japan surrendered to the Allied forces on August 14, 1945, the Chinese Nationalist government returned to Nanjing. American diplomats attempted to ensure that Japanese troops in northern China and Manchuria would surrender to the Nationalists rather than the Communists, thus making Chiang the dominant leader in postwar China. However, the Russian troops in Manchuria dismantled or destroyed many of the industries that the Japanese had established there, and then turned over Manchuria and all the weapons the Japanese had surrendered there to the Chinese Communists in the region.

On August 18, 1945, the Russians kidnapped Puyi from Mukden (Shenyang) and held him prisoner in the U.S.S.R. for five years. During that time he went to Tokyo and appeared as a prosecution witness in the war crimes trial held by the Allies following World War II. On August 1,

1950, the Russians repatriated Puyi to the PRC, where the government imprisoned Puyi and "reeducated" him. See also BEIJING; BETHUNE, NORMAN; BURMA ROAD; CHANGCHUN; CHIANG KAI-SHEK; CHINESE COMMUNIST PARTY; CHONGQING; CIVIL WAR BETWEEN COMMUNISTS AND NATIONALISTS; DENG XIAOPING; DENG YINGCHAO; EIGHTH ROUTE ARMY; FLYING TIGERS; GUANGZHOU; HIMALAYA MOUNTAIN RANGE; LIN BIAO; LIU BOCHENG; LYTTON COMMISSION; MANCHU; MANCHUKUO; MANCHURIA; MANCHURIAN INCIDENT; MAO ZEDONG; NANJING; MARCO POLO BRIDGE INCIDENT; NATIONALIST PARTY; NEW FOURTH ARMY INCIDENT; NIE RONGZHEN; NORTH CHINA PLAIN; NORTHERN EXPEDITION; PENG DEHUAI; PEOPLE'S LIBERATION ARMY; QING DYNASTY; REPUBLIC OF CHINA; REVOLUTION OF 1911; RUSSO-JAPANESE WAR OF 1905–5; SHANGHAI; SHENYANG; SHIMONOSEKI, TREATY OF; SICHUAN PROVINCE; SINO-JAPANESE WAR OF 1894–95; SOONG MEI-LING; STILWELL, GENERAL JOSEPH; SUN YAT-SEN; TAIWAN; TIANJIN; UNITED NATIONS; WANG JINGWEI; WHAMPOA MILITARY ACADEMY; XI'AN; YAN'AN; YANGZI RIVER; ZHANG XUELIANG; ZHANG ZUOLIN; ZHOU ENLAI; ZHU DE.

WARD, FREDERICK TOWNSEND (1831–1862) An American soldier of fortune who went to China in 1859 and became head of the army of the Manchu Qing dynasty (1644–1911) that put down the Taiping Rebellion (1850–64). Ward was born in Salem, Massachusetts, a town that had actively engaged in trade with China ever since a Salem ship had helped open the trade route between the United States and China in the 18th century. He wanted to become a soldier, but he was not able to get into the U.S. Military Academy at West Point. When he was 15 years old his father, to punish him for truancy, signed him up to work on the clipper ship *Hamilton* that was sailing to Hong Kong. Ward returned from China in 1847 and entered but did not graduate from a military school in Vermont. In 1849 he sailed as first mate on another ship, and from 1849 to 1858 he traveled seeking adventure and joined several armies as a mercenary. He fought with American mercenary William Walker when he invaded Mexico, with Giuseppe Garibaldi in Italy, and with the French Army in the Crimean War. These experiences gave him courage and concern for his fellow soldiers, and taught him new techniques for arming soldiers and fighting wars. In 1859 Ward traveled to Shanghai, a major port city that the British had forced China to open to foreign trade as a treaty port. In 1857, Britain and France had attacked major Chinese port cities to force the Qing government to increase trade with foreign powers, starting a military conflict known as the Arrow War (Second Opium War, 1856–60). The Qing were also being attacked by the Taipings, a messianic peasant sect that had begun in southern China under the leadership of Hong Xiuquan (Hung Hsiu-chuan; 1813–64). By 1859 the Taipings had established their headquarters in Nanjing and were threatening to march on Shanghai and the capital city of Beijing. Ward, a brilliant tactician, began building a disciplined army of Chinese and foreign soldiers drilled in Western military maneuvers, which was privately financed by wealthy Chinese merchants in Shanghai. Because of its victories, the Qing government called this army the "Ever Victorious Army." By 1862, it had grown to more than 3,000 men. The success of Ward's army in the Shanghai region caused the British and French to switch from supporting the Taipings to fighting on behalf of the Qing.

The Qing honored Ward and his lieutenant, Henry Andrea Burgevine, both of whom had become naturalized citizens of China, by awarding them the position of mandarin, fourth rank, which entitled them to wear a mandarin's cap with a blue button and an embroidered tiger patch. A few days later he and Burgevine were awarded the button of the third rank. Ward was also permitted to wear a peacock's feather and was made a brigadier general in the Qing army. These honors made Ward the most honored American in Chinese history. He shocked the foreign community in Shanghai by marrying a widowed Chinese woman named Chang Mei who was the daughter of Taki, a Shanghai financier who had helped to finance Ward's army. Ward received at least 15 serious wounds in battle, but he was so courageous that he always remained on the battlefield. He was killed during a battle at Tzeki, near Ningbo, when he was 30 years old and was buried with the full honors of a Chinese general. British Major Charles Gordon replaced him as head of the "Ever Victorious Army," which helped Qing forces to finally defeat the Taipings in 1864. See also ARROW WAR; GORDON, CHARLES; HONG XIUQUAN; MANDARIN; NINE-RANK SYSTEM; QING DYNASTY; TAIPING REBELLION; TREATY PORTS.

WARLORD PERIOD (1916–28)
A period in the modern history of China when the country was divided among dozens of contending semi-autonomous military commanders who controlled local regions. The Chinese people had overthrown the Qing dynasty (1644–1911), China's last imperial dynasty, with the Revolution of 1911. Under the leadership of Dr. Sun Yat-sen (1866–1925), the Republic of China was established in 1912. Sun was the first president of the republic, but he was pressured by the northern warlord Yuan Shikai (Yuan Shih-k'ai; 1859–1916) to yield the presidency. Sun agreed to do so if Yuan could persuade the last Qing emperor, Xuantong (Hsuan-t'ung; r. 1909–12; later known as Henry Puyi), to abdicate. The emperor did so one month later and Yuan became president of the Republic of China. All of the warlords in China had been trained under Yuan Shikai or had some connection with him. Yuan was the only Chinese leader who was able to secure loans from foreign countries that helped pay for the modern military weapons the warlords needed to equip their armies.

Sun's revolutionary party joined with several others to form the National People's Party, also known as the Nationalist Party (Kuomintang; KMT), led by Song Jiaoren (Sung Chiao-jen; 1882–1913). Elections were held in February 1913 for the republic's new bicameral parliament. Song campaigned against the Yuan government, and his party won a majority of seats, but Yuan, who opposed parliamentary government, had Song assassinated in March 1913. Yuan dismissed government officials not loyal to him, became a virtual dictator, and formally dissolved the KMT in 1914 and had its members removed from parliament. However, Yuan met his downfall when he attempted to establish a new dynasty with himself as emperor, and he died in June 1916. Yuan was succeeded as president of the republic by Li Yuanhong (Li Yuan-hung; 1864–1928), who had been vice presi-

dent, and Li appointed Duan Qirui (Tuan Ch'i-jui; 1865–1936) premier.

In 1915 Japan had presented the Beijing government with its so-called Twenty-One Demands, which intended to make China a protectorate of Japan. The Chinese government rejected some of the demands but allowed Japan to keep the concessions in Shandong Province that had been held by Germany. In 1917 the Beijing government led by Duan Qirui, who had forced Li Yuanhong to retire and replaced him with general Feng Guozhang (Feng Kuo-chang; 1859–1919), entered World War I on the Allied side with hopes of getting back Shandong. At the Paris Peace Conference that concluded World War I, it was revealed that the Beijing government had made a secret agreement with foreign powers to award Japan the former German concessions in Shandong. The Chinese people were outraged, and Chinese students led a demonstration against the agreement, known as the May Fourth Movement of 1919, that became a nationwide protest.

Sun Yat-sen had made contacts with most of the other Chinese warlords, and in October 1919 he and his followers reestablished the KMT to oppose the Beijing government. At the same time, Guangzhou (Canton) in southern China was captured by a warlord sympathetic to Sun, and he went there in November 1920. Sun was elected president of the Chinese republic by an "extraordinary parliament." But Sun and the warlord soon clashed, and troops loyal to the warlord drove Sun out of Guangzhou. He went to Shanghai and became a central figure in the negotiations by civil and military officials to reorganize the government in Beijing. Although Beijing and Guangzhou remained the two seats of power in China until 1927, much of the country remained divided among the many regional warlords.

The military situation in Guangzhou changed and Sun returned there in February 1923. The Western democracies had continued to regard the Beijing government as the legitimate government of China and would not support Sun, so Sun accepted help from the Soviet Union, which had undergone its own revolution in 1917. Mikhail Borodin, a Soviet adviser, helped Sun reorganize the KMT, which cooperated with the newly founded Chinese Communist Party (CCP). In January 1924 the reorganized KMT held its first national Congress. In May 1924 the KMT and CCP established a military academy at Whampoa (Huangpu), near Guangzhou, directed by Chiang Kai-shek (1887–1975). Sun had sent Chiang, one of his lieutenants, to study military and political issues in the Soviet Union. Chiang also became Sun's brother-in-law when he married Soong Mei-ling, the sister of Sun's wife, Soong Qingling.

The merchants of Guangzhou organized an armed rebellion against Sun, which caused him to lose many of his supporters. In late 1924, following a coup in Beijing by the Chinese "Christian general" Feng Yuxiang (Feng Yu-hsiang; 1882–1948), Sun was invited there to help reorganize the government. He was very ill with cancer when he arrived in Beijing on December 31, 1924. He discovered that the politicians and military leaders there had already made an agreement with the foreign powers to respect the "unequal treaties" that the foreign powers had forced on China in the 19th century. Sun died on March 12, 1925, and Chiang Kai-shek succeeded him as head of the KMT. In the summer of

1925, Chiang began preparing to lead the Northern Expedition against the warlords in northern China. By 1926 the KMT had divided into radical and conservative factions, and the number of Communists in the party was increasing. After Chiang defeated an attempt to kidnap him, he dismissed his advisers from the Soviet Union, restricted CCP members from becoming leaders in the KMT, and consolidated his own position as KMT leader. In July 1926 Chiang began the Northern Expedition and within nine months his forces captured half of China.

In early 1927 the alliance between the KMT and the CCP ruptured. The CCP and the left wing of the KMT led by Wang Jingwei (Wang Ching-wei; 1883–1944) moved the Nationalist government to Wuchang (Wuhan) in Hubei Province in central China, where the Revolution of 1911 had erupted with the Wuchang Uprising in October 1911. Chiang turned his KMT forces against the CCP and ordered them to massacre Communists and labor organizers in Shanghai on April 12, 1927. He established his anti-Communist Nationalist government at Nanjing, the former capital of the Ming dynasty (1368–1644). Now there were three Chinese capitals, at Wuchang, Nanjing and Beijing. Nanjing remained the capital of the right-wing Nationalist government until China began fighting its War of Resistance against Japan (1937–45; World War II), when the Nationalists fled inland to Chongqing in Sichuan Province.

After the 1927 massacre, the Communists made unsuccessful attempts to capture several Chinese cities, and peasants led by Mao Zedong (Mao Tse-tung; 1893–1976), one of the founders of the CCP, staged an unsuccessful armed insurrection in Hunan Province, known as the Autumn Harvest Uprising. By the middle of 1927, Wang Jingwei and the left-wing members of the KMT expelled the Communists from Wuhan, but in turn Wang's faction was expelled by a military regime. Both Wang's supporters and the Communists made their last stand in Guangzhou, but warlord troops took back the city. The last remaining Chinese warlord was Zhang Zuolin (Chang Tso-lin; 1873–1928), who was forced to retreat to his base in Manchuria (northeastern China). By 1928 Chiang Kai-shek nominally controlled all of China, thus ending the Warlord Period, and foreign countries recognized his Nationalist government in Nanjing as the sole legitimate government of China. The KMT continued to oppose the Communists, who had fled to the countryside, and to consolidate its power until Japan invaded China Proper from Manchuria in 1937. See also BEIJING; CHIANG KAI-SHEK; CHINESE COMMUNIST PARTY; GUANGZHOU; MAY FOURTH MOVEMENT OF 1919; NANJING; NATIONALIST PARTY; NORTHERN EXPEDITION; PUYI, HENRY; REPUBLIC OF CHINA; REVOLUTION OF 1911; REVOLUTIONARY ALLIANCE; SOONG QINGLING; SOONG MEI-LING; SUN YAT-SEN; TWENTY-ONE DEMANDS ON CHINA; UNEQUAL TREATIES; WANG JINGWEI; WAR OF RESISTANCE AGAINST JAPAN; WHAMPOA MILITARY ACADEMY; WORLD WAR I; WUCHANG UPRISING; YUAN SHIKAI; ZHANG ZUOLIN.

WARRING STATES PERIOD (Zhanguo or Chang-kuo; 403–221 B.C.)   The final period of the Zhou dynasty, the longest dynasty in Chinese history. Historians divide the Zhou dynasty into two general periods, the Western Zhou dynasty (1100–771 B.C.) and the Eastern Zhou dynasty (771–256 B.C.), which they subdivide into the Spring and Autumn Period (772–481 B.C.) and the Warring States Period. The Zhou had established a feudal system under which local rulers administered their states but pledged loyalty and military assistance to the Zhou. After several centuries the authority of the Zhou declined as various states began asserting their power and fighting among each other. In 771 B.C. the Zhou capital at Chang'an (modern Xia'n in Shaanxi Province) was sacked, and the Zhou fled east and established the Eastern Zhou Dynasty in the region of modern Luoyang in Henan Province, just south of the Yellow River (Huanghe). The former Zhou domain was taken over by the rulers of Qin, and the Zhou kings served a symbolic function as the "Sons of Heaven," (tianzi or t'ien-Tzu), the only ones permitted to offer ritual sacrifices to Heaven on behalf of the subjects of the dynasty.

The Eastern Zhou dynasty was a time of warfare but also the period when the two most important Chinese philosophical schools developed, Confucianism and Daoism. The ruler of each state under the Zhou dynasty developed a highly cultured court within a walled town, with complicated rules for etiquette and diplomacy, ceremonial music and dance, religious rituals, and poetry and other literary and fine arts. Craftsmen who worked in bronze, jade, lacquer and other materials settled in or near the towns. Women were required to raise silkworms and weave textiles, some of which were given to the state as tax payments. Some rulers had large sets of bronze bells, known as zhong (chung), cast and suspended on wooden frames, to be played as symbols of their power and enormous wealth. In 1978 archaeologists excavated a set of 65 bells from the tomb of the marquis of Yi of the state of Zeng, who was a contemporary of the great Chinese philosopher Confucius (551–479 B.C.). The marquis's tomb also contained a large bell weighing, 5,500 pounds. During the Zhou dynasty, coins made primarily of bronze were minted, and a new class of merchants emerged who traded not only luxury goods such as jade and silk, but also commodities such as salt. There were also developments in warfare, including a new reliance on foot soldiers and cavalry instead of chariots, the invention of mass-produced crossbows around 400 B.C., and the use of long cast-iron swords in place of bronze daggers. The majority of the population were peasants, who improved agricultural techniques to yield more crops. Irrigation systems and fortifications were built in areas ruled by the Zhou.

During the Warring States Period, Chinese philosophers developed many new schools, known as the Hundred Schools of Thought. The Legalist school of thought, which taught that the ruler should have absolute power and that his subjects should be controlled by harsh laws and punishments, was adopted by the Qin dynasty (221–206 B.C.), which replaced the Zhou. The most important Legalist thinker was Han Feizi (Han Fei Tzu; c. 280–233 B.C.). Mencius (Mengzi or Meng Tzu; c. 372–289 B.C.) and Xunzi (Hsun Tzu; c. 298–238 B.C.) were the most important Confucian thinkers after Confucius himself. Zhuangzi (Chuang Tzu; 369–286 B.C.) is attributed with compiling the most important philosophical text in the Daoist tradition, also known as the Zhuangzi. Qu Yuan (Ch'u Yuan; c. 343–278 B.C.), the first great Chinese poet who can be personally identified, also practiced Daoism and became associated with the esoteric alchemical quest for the so-called Elixir of Immortality.

The transition from the Spring and Autumn to the Warring States Period occurred with the decline of the state of Jin, which had been powerful enough to conquer the state of Chu but became divided by internal rivalries and civil war during the first half of the fifth century B.C. The chief minister of Jin, the count of Zhi, was assassinated in 453 B.C., and Jin broke up into three states, Han, Wei and Zhao. The state of Wu, on the lower Yangzi River, became a major power in 482 B.C. but was soon defeated by the state of Yue in modern Zhejiang Province. In 334 B.C. the state of Chu defeated Yue. Eventually only seven states remained: Qin, Wei, Han, Zhao, Chu, Yan and Qi. They entered their final stage of conflict after Qin defeated the Zhou and killed the last Zhou king in 256 B.C., thus ending the Zhou dynasty. The ruler of each state wanted to unify China once again under his own dynasty. The ruler of Qin in the Wei River valley, who had adopted the ideas of the Legalist school of thought, proved to be the strongest leader. He finally defeated his last two rivals, the states of Qi to the northeast and Chu in the Yangzi River (Changjiang) valley, each of which had claimed to have an army of more than one million. He succeeded in reunifying China under the Qin dynasty and proclaimed himself the "First Emperor," Shi Huangdi (r. 221–210 B.C.). See also ALCHEMY; BELLS AND CHIMES; BRONZEWARE; CONFUCIANISM; DAOISM; ELIXIR OF IMMORTALITY; EMPEROR; HEAVEN; HUNDRED SCHOOLS OF THOUGHT; IRON TECHNOLOGY AND STEEL INDUSTRY; JADE; LACQUERWARE; LEGALIST SCHOOL OF THOUGHT; MUSIC AND DANCE, CEREMONIAL; QIN DYNASTY; QIN SHI HUANGDI (EMPEROR); QU YUAN; SILK; SPRING AND AUTUMN PERIOD; ZHOU DYNASTY; ZHUANGZI.

WASHINGTON CONFERENCE OF 1921–22 See LEAGUE OF NATIONS; MAY FOURTH MOVEMENT OF 1919; OPEN-DOOR POLICY.

WATER BUFFALO See EIGHT IMMORTALS; OX; RICE.

WATER CONSERVANCY AND IRRIGATION See AGRICULTURE; GRAND CANAL; NATURAL DISASTERS; RICE; THREE GORGES WATER CONSERVANCY PROJECT; YANGZI RIVER; YELLOW RIVER.

WATER MARGIN, THE See OUTLAWS OF THE MARSH.

WATER SPLASHING FESTIVAL See DAI; XISHUANGBANNA AUTONOMOUS DISTRICT OF THE DAI PEOPLE.

WAY, THE See DAODEJING; DAOISM; DOCTRINE OF THE MEAN.

WAY AND ITS POWER, THE See DAODEJING; WALEY, ARTHUR.

WEAPONS See BRONZEWARE; FIREWORKS AND GUNPOWDER; HORSE; IRON AND STEEL INDUSTRY; MARTIAL ARTS; TERRACOTTA ARMY, TOMB OF EMPEROR QIN SHIHUANGDI.

WEAVER MAID FESTIVAL See COWHERD AND WEAVER MAID FESTIVAL.

WEAVING See SILK; TEXTILE INDUSTRY.

WEDDINGS, TRADITIONAL Elaborate ceremonies performed to unite a man and woman in marriage. The customs for a traditional wedding have been similar all over China and comprise one of the things that have identified the Han ethnic Chinese people, in distinction to non-Han peoples, whom they considered "barbarians." Over the centuries many non-Han became assimilated into the Han through sinicization, that is, the adoption of the Chinese language, cuisine, clothing, Confucian concepts and customs such as weddings and funerals. Many of these customs are still practiced not only in mainland China, Hong Kong and Taiwan but also in the large overseas Chinese communities in Singapore and other Southeast Asian countries, and by Chinese who have emigrated all over the world. When a Chinese woman married, according to the customs of Confucianism, she completely left her own family and became a member of her husband's family. The patriarchal Confucian family system has required many sons, who perform the traditional rituals to honor deceased ancestors, known as ancestor worship.

Formerly the couple usually did not know each other before the wedding, but were brought together by a professional go-between or matchmaker (*meiren* or *mei-jen*). Both families had to approve of the prospective bride and groom, and once the families made their decision, the couple had no choice but to accept their marriage. Today the man and woman usually know each other before marriage, but the matchmaker, who is frequently a friend or relative rather than a professional matchmaker, still plays an important role. The families of the prospective bride and groom traditionally engaged in lengthy negotiations through the matchmaker to determine what items each side would contribute to the marriage. The two families exchanged lists (*menhudia* or *men hu tieh*) that provided the details of each family's social status. When these were found acceptable, the families exchanged "Eight Character" certificates, which provided the hour, day, month and year of birth of the man and woman. The Chinese traditionally believe that Yuelaoye (Yueh Lao Yeh), the old man with a gray beard who lives on the moon, decides who should marry on Earth. He provides and ties the knot in the red cord that binds the married couple together for life. Families hired an astrologer to determine whether the horoscopes of the prospective bride and groom were compatible. The Chinese have a traditional 12-year animal zodiac, in which every person born in a particular year is believed to have the traits of the animal associated with that year. The years are also associated with one of the five material agents or elements, comprising a cycle of 60 years. The animals and elements in the horoscopes of the man and woman must be compatible, or else they must not marry. These are summed up in proverbs, such as "the sheep and the rat soon separate" and "the rooster starts crying when it sees a dog."

If the astrologer found that the horoscopes were compatible and the marriage was auspicious, the parents of the groom sent engagement gifts (*dingli* or *ting li*) such as clothing to the bride's home. The groom's family set the date of the wedding on an auspicious day and wrote a formal announcement (*dongshu* or *tung shu*) on red paper that was sent out a month or more before the wedding. Next the families exchanged marriage contracts (*longfengtu* or *lung feng t'u*) stating the ages and dates of the couple, which marked the formal betrothal. The letter containing the groom's contract was written on red paper, decorated with a dragon, and the bride's reply was written on green paper, decorated with a phoenix. The groom also sent money and gifts with his letter, including food, such as pork, chickens and wine; clothing; ornaments; and furniture. "Dragon and phoenix" cakes symbolizing a happy married life were sent to relatives and friends to inform them of the upcoming wedding. The dragon (*long* or *lung*) is the Chinese symbol of the emperor and the masculine principle in the universe. The phoenix (*feng*)—a mythological bird symbolizing female beauty, virtue and the empress—is a symbol of joy and happiness that appears throughout a traditional Chinese wedding. Brides wear a phoenix crown, phoenix hairpins, shawls with phoenix designs and a pleated silk skirt embroidered with phoenixes. Even today many Chinese women are given the name "Phoenix." Wedding guests wish the bridal couple good fortune with the phrase, "prosperity brought by dragon and phoenix." Wild geese flying in pairs have been another symbol of happy marriage because they mate for life.

Traditionally a wedding was the most important ceremony in a Chinese girl's life, and she spent years sewing and embroidering her red wedding robe, trousseau and items for her new household. As part of her dowry, her family purchased boxes made of polished wood decorated with colorful designs. The groom's family provided necessary items as well, which in recent years have included such things as a sewing machine and a bicycle. The groom also had to provide presents for the bride's family members, such as food items. On the wedding day, the bride was dressed in a red robe, a color symbolizing good luck, with a red veil covering her face. Her feet did not touch the ground after she was dressed for the wedding, to prevent bad luck in the future. Before leaving her home, the bride performed ceremonial prostrations known as kowtow (*gedou* or *ke-tou*) to the ancestral tablets on her family altar. She also kowtowed to her parents and thanked them for taking care of her. The bride cried on her wedding day because she had to leave her own family and become a member of the groom's family. Her bridesmaids gave her "lucky money" in red envelopes and helped her out the door of her home.

The bride was carried to the groom's house riding inside a covered red chair ornately decorated with auspicious symbols such as kingfisher feathers, a symbol of beauty and martial happiness. Small mirrors were hung on the edges of the chair to scare away ghosts and evil spirits, which turn away when they see themselves in a mirror. At times during a wedding the rays of the sun were flashed on the bride with a mirror to bring her good luck. A small round mirror was also hung on the curtains of her marriage bed to keep away evil. Four men carried the bride's chair in a procession through the streets to the groom's home while musicians played loudly. This journey symbolized the bride's passage from childhood to adult responsibilities and from her own family to that of her husband. Her wedding boxes were also carried in the procession to show off her dowry. Traditionally the bride's parents did not accompany her to the wedding but stayed home and held a banquet for their close relatives and friends. The go-between and bridesmaids accompanied the bride in their place.

Firecrackers were set off when the bride reached the groom's house to drive away ghosts and evil spirits and to let everyone know she has arrived. A lucky woman, who had several sons and had not been widowed, helped the bride down from her chair. The groom tapped the bride on the head with a fan and then used the fan to lift her red veil. This was the first time that the bride and groom saw each other. Her dowry and trousseau were displayed in the groom's home for the wedding guests. The bride served ceremonial tea to the groom's mother. In northern China she also presented her new mother-in-law slippers that she had sewn herself to show off her embroidery skills. In return the bride was given a piece of the family's jewelry. The matchmaker provided a large tray that held rice, wine, oil and a sample of the wedding gifts. There were many elaborate rituals for the exchange of gifts between the two families and friends and relatives. The bride also kowtowed before the groom's family and family altar and made offerings to his ancestors. Large Chinese clans have temples that house the clan's altar and ancestral tablets.

The highlight of a Chinese wedding has always been a lavish multicourse banquet that includes many dishes with symbolic meaning. Fish is always served because the Chinese word for fish (*yu*) is pronounced the same as the word for "abundance." Sweet date soup is served because the word for date (*zao* or *tsao*) is pronounced the same as the word for "early (birth of a) son." Round balls of sweetened rice symbolize a life of unbroken harmony for the couple. The banquet room is decorated with the Chinese characters for double happiness (*shuangxi* or *shuang-hsi*) and long life (*shou*). Banquet guests sit at round tables and share the dishes that are served. Today the go-between and many friends and relatives offer toasts to the newly married couple. The couple also goes to each table to toast the guests, and is toasted in return.

On the third day after the wedding ceremony, the bride traditionally returned to visit her own family, wearing the red silk skirt symbolizing her new status as a wife and a black silk jacket to display all her jewelry, including gold rings, bracelets and necklaces. Before leaving her husband's home, she bowed before his family altar, and at her parent's home she also bowed before their family altar. She brought her parents gifts of food from the groom, especially two roast pigs, which they carved in a ritual way. Parts of the pigs were placed on a tray with two oranges and three kinds of vegetables for good luck, symbolizing a wish for three generations to continue the family line. They sent the tray back to the groom's family as a return present. The bride's family sent slices of the pork to all the relatives and friends who sent her wedding presents.

Husbands and wives rarely divorced in China because it brought disgrace to both of their families. A Chinese man was formerly permitted to take secondary wives or concubines in addition to his wife, if he could afford the expense. A man would be especially inclined to take a concubine if his first wife had not given birth to a son. The most common way for a man to acquire a concubine was to purchase her. A maid could also be promoted to the position of concubine. A concubine always remained subordinate to the wife in the family hierarchy, although wives usually resented concubines and sent them out of the home after their husbands died.

Many Chinese peasants went into debt or even became bankrupt paying for traditional weddings for their children. The Chinese Communist Party (CCP), which founded the People's Republic of China (PRC) in 1949, encouraged the Chinese people to give up expensive traditional wedding customs and marry in civil ceremonies. The CCP promulgated the Marriage Law of 1950 to abolish the "feudal elements" of traditional Chinese family law, including the practice of concubinage. International Workers Day, a public holiday celebrated on May 1 in the PRC, became a favorite day for Chinese couples to marry. Work places commonly sponsored group weddings for more than a dozen couples at a time. Although the CCP discouraged elaborate and costly weddings, since the early 1980s China has undergone rapid economic growth, and many Chinese people have returned to the custom of extravagant weddings as a way of showing off their prosperity and social position. See also ANCESTOR WORSHIP; ANCESTRAL TABLETS; BANQUETS; CONCUBINAGE; DOUBLE HAPPINESS AND LONG LIFE; EMBROIDERY; FAMILY STRUCTURE; FIREWORKS AND GUNPOWDER; FISH AND SEAFOOD; KINGFISHER; KOWTOW; LUCKY MONEY; MARRIAGE LAW OF 1950; MIRROR; PHOENIX.

WEI, KINGDOM OF See CAO CAO; GRAND CANAL; ROMANCE OF THE THREE KINGDOMS; SHANXI PROVINCE; THREE KINGDOMS PERIOD; WARRING STATES PERIOD; WESTERN AND EASTERN JIN DYNASTIES.

WEI BOYANG See ALCHEMY; DAOIST CLASSICAL TEXTS.

WEI CHING-SHENG See WEI JINGSHENG.

WEI CHUNG-HSIEN See WEI ZHONGXIAN.

WEI DYNASTY See NORTHERN AND SOUTHERN DYNASTIES; NORTHERN WEI DYNASTY.

WEI JINGSHENG (Wei Ching-sheng; 1949–) The leading dissident in the People's Republic of China (PRC), which was founded by the Chinese Communist Party (CCP) in 1949. Wei was a Red Guard during the Cultural Revolution (1966–76), which had been initiated by CCP chairman Mao Zedong (Mao Tse-tung) to eliminate counterrevolutionary elements in the CCP. Chinese schools and universities were closed and millions of students traveled to Beijing, the Chinese capital, where they held massive demonstrations. Many students became Red Guards who traveled all over China brutally opposing "feudalism, capitalism and revisionism." China came to the brink of anarchy, so in 1968 Mao abolished the Red Guards, although the turmoil of the Cultural Revolution did not end until Mao died in 1976. CCP leaders then embarked on a campaign to rebuild and modernize China, based on a program known as the Four Modernizations. From 1969 to 1973 Wei was in the army. He then became an electrician in the Beijing Zoo.

During the autumn of 1978, "big-character" posters (dazibao or ta-tzu-pao) began appearing on public walls in Beijing calling for a "fifth modernization," democracy. Wei himself wrote such a poster, which he and his friends later published in a journal. These posters gained a lot of attention, and similar ones were hung on university campuses and in other Chinese cities. They criticized the authoritarian system of government under Mao and called for the Chinese government to institute a democratic multi-party system, free elections, an independent judiciary and freedom of information and publishing. Many underground journals were also published promoting these democratic ideas. Deng Xiaoping (Teng Hsiao-p'ing) and members of his political faction in the CCP tolerated the pro-democracy movement as a way of opposing Hua Guofeng (Hua Kuo-feng) and his faction, who were accused of being "whateverists" because they claimed that whatever Chairman Mao had said was correct. However, in the spring of 1979 the CCP suddenly ended the pro-democracy movement by removing the wall posters and arresting and imprisoning the most outspoken critics of the government. Wei Jingsheng was the most prominent of these critics, and he was arrested and sentenced to 15 years of prison for "counterrevolutionary activity."

In 1982 Deng consolidated his power at the 12th National Party Congress, which marked the beginning of China's post-Mao reform era and placed Deng's supporters in many leadership positions in the CCP. In September 1993 Wei was released after spending $14\frac{1}{2}$ years in prison. The Chinese government, which had been criticized for human rights abuses, released Wei as part of its attempt to persuade the Olympic Committee to hold the Olympic Games in Beijing, although it did not succeed in winning the Olympics. Wei had refused to leave prison without copies of the letters he had written while incarcerated, so the government agreed to give him copies of more than 80 letters and released him from prison. The government ordered Wei not to engage in political activities, but he ignored the spies from State Security who always followed him and openly campaigned for democracy in China. Wei published an article in the *New York Times* on November 18, 1993, in which he stated that the present leaders of China did not understand or listen to reason and that they had no intention of carrying out their former promises about human rights and democracy.

In the spring of 1994, Wei gave a Chinese friend a copy of the letters he had written from prison to his family and to Deng Xiaoping between 1979 and 1993. The friend smuggled the letters out of China and took them to Philip J. Cunningham, a writer in Tokyo, Japan, who translated them into English for publication. Wei's letters to Deng have a harsh, sarcastic tone. He informed Deng that conditions in prison are so brutal that life there is worse than the life of a barnyard animal or a slave: "It's a sub-human existence." Wei had been kept in isolation for long periods of time and had been physically abused and lost many of his teeth. In his letters to Deng, Wei also attacked General Secretary Jiang Zemin and Prime Minister Li Peng, who harshly suppressed the 1989 pro-democracy demonstration in Tiananmen Square in Beijing by calling out the Chinese military. Deng Xiaoping never replied to Wei's letters, although he did refer to them in a secret speech in 1987 that was later leaked to the public, stating that "People [like Wei] who confuse truth and falsehood or black and white, and who start rumors, must not be tolerated."

Shortly after Wei gave his friend his prison correspondence in 1994, the Chinese government arrested Wei again and attempted to silence him by confiscating his notes and computer files. Wei was cut off from the outside world and was not able to write the autobiography he had planned with an American publisher. Yet Wei was nominated for the Nobel Peace Prize. Chinese intellectuals respected Wei's honest and fearless criticisms of the Chinese government, but since the official Chinese news media rarely mentioned him, few of the peasants who comprise two-thirds of the Chinese population knew anything about him. The publication of Wei's letters informed the Western world about his political activism and punishment by the Chinese government.

In 1995 the government put Wei on trial on charges of attempting to overthrow the government. At the closed trial he was sentenced to a further term of 14 years in prison. Wei became very ill in prison but rejected the idea of a medical release if it meant permanent exile from China. In 1997 his writings were translated into English under the title *The Courage to Stand Alone: Letters from Prison and Other Writings by Wei Jingsheng.*

On November 16, 1997, one month after PRC president Jiang Zemin visited the United States—which had been pressuring the PRC about human rights—the government released Wei from prison and allowed him to travel to the United States for medical treatment, calling it "medical parole." Wei underwent medical tests at Henry Ford Hospital in Detroit, Michigan, where he was joined by his youngest sister and her daughter, who live in Germany. The group Human Rights in China invited Wei to New York City, where he was treated for a number of prison-related ailments at the Columbia Presbyterian Medical Center. Wei accepted an appointment to lecture and give workshops as a visiting scholar at Columbia University's School of International Affairs in New York.

Harry Wu is another Chinese dissident who is well known in the West for his documentation of human rights abuses in Chinese prison labor camps, known as *laogai*. He himself was a prisoner for many years, but he has recently been released and has become an American citizen. International human rights groups estimate that more than 1,000 dissidents remain in jail in the PRC. See also BIG-CHARACTER POSTERS; CULTURAL REVOLUTION; DENG XIAOPING; FOUR MODERNIZATIONS; MAO ZEDONG; PEOPLE'S REPUBLIC OF CHINA; RED GUARDS; TIANANMEN SQUARE MASSACRE; WU, HARRY.

WEI PO-YANG   See ALCHEMY; DAOIST CLASSICAL TEXTS.

WEI RIVER (Weihe)   An important river in Shaanxi Province in north-central China that is a major tributary of the Yellow River (Huanghe). The Wei River originates in the plateau of Gansu Province to the west of Shaanxi, flows southeast and then turns east to join the Yellow River where that river makes its major bend from south to east toward the North China Plain. The Wei River is 435 miles long and has a drainage area of about 22,400 square miles. It can be navigated by small boats for 150 miles of its length. The main tributary of the Wei River is the Jing River, which joins the Wei near modern Xi'an, formerly known as Chang'an and the ancient capital city of China for many centuries.

The fertile loess plateaus of Shaanxi Province adjoin the Wei River valley. Loess is a loose, dusty soil that has been blown in from desert regions over hundreds of years and deposited in plateaus that are more than 200 feet deep in some places. Many Chinese farmers still live in homes carved into the faces of loess cliffs. The Yellow River carries an enormous quantity of loess as it flows eastward, and the Wei River carries away about 150 millions tons of loess each year.

The Wei River valley, about 200 miles long, has played a central role in Chinese history. Today it remains the center for agriculture and manufacturing in Shaanxi Province. The Wei Valley and the North China Plain that it adjoins are the traditional heartland of China. Chinese civilization originated in the Wei and Yellow River valleys with the Neolithic culture known as Yangshao. Since ancient times the Wei Valley has also been the main route between China and Central Asia. The Zhou people migrated down the Jing River and founded the state of Zhou in the Wei River valley. They overthrew the Shang dynasty (1750–1040 B.C.) and established the Zhou dynasty (1100–256 B.C.), which lasted the longest of any Chinese dynasty. From about 1000 B.C. to A.D. 1000, the capital of China alternated between Chang'an in the Wei Valley and Luoyang in Henan Province to the east. Also in the Wei Valley, the brutal ruler of the state of Qin defeated his rivals and unified China under the Qin dynasty (221–206 B.C.), calling himself Qin Shi Huangdi, the First Emperor.

The Wei River valley is also the site of the first major irrigation system in China, constructed in the third century B.C. The system was abandoned after the ninth century A.D. but was reconstructed in the 1930s and further repaired after the founding of the People's Republic of China in 1949. More than half of the land in the Wei Valley is under cultivation, with major crops being rice, wheat and other grains, tobacco, cotton, hemp and sesame. See also CHANG'AN; LOESS; NORTH CHINA PLAIN; QIN DYNASTY; SHAANXI PROVINCE; YANGSHAO; YELLOW RIVER; ZHOU DYNASTY.

WEI ZHONGXIAN (Wei Chung-hsien; 1568–1627)   A powerful eunuch in the imperial palace in the Forbidden City in Beijing who became the virtual dictator of China from 1624 to 1627 during the reign of the Ming dynasty emperor Tianqi (T'ien-chi; r. 1620–27). Wei began his service in the palace as a butler for the mother of future emperor Tianqi, then called Zhu Yujiao (Chu Yu-chiao). He gained Zhu's confidence by becoming close to his nursemaid. When Zhu took the throne at 15 years of age, he appointed Wei to a high government position. In 1623 he made Wei head of the Eastern Depot, the headquarters of the imperial palace secret service. Zhu proved to be a weak ruler, and Wei ruthlessly took the reins of power himself by rewarding government officials who were loyal to him and punishing those who opposed him. The governors of many Chinese provinces even erected temples to honor the "grand" eunuch Wei Zhongxian. In imperial rituals Wei was even ranked equal to Confucius (551–479 B.C.), the great scholar whose thought had been designated as orthodox by the Chinese imperial government. The illiterate Wei terrorized the Confucian-trained scholars who staffed the imperial bureaucracy and forced them to be servile to him. He installed a division of eunuch troops to control the imperial palace, set up a network of secret police throughout China, and raised taxes to exorbitant levels in the provinces. Scholars who belonged to the Donglin (Tung-lin) Academy, a center for Confucianism in Zhejiang Province, protested against Wei's dictatorial policies. In 1625 he purged the Donglin scholars and had many of them arrested, tortured and executed. Wei, hated by many Chinese, met his downfall when the young Tianqi emperor died suddenly in 1627. The conscientious new emperor, Tianqi's brother, banished Wei, who hanged himself rather than face trial and punishment for what he had done. The Donglin scholars were rehabilitated in 1629. See also DONGLIN ACADEMY; EUNUCH; FORBIDDEN CITY; MING DYNASTY.

WEIQI (WEI-CH'I) See CHESS, CHINESE.

WELL-FIELD SYSTEM OF AGRICULTURE (*Jingtian* or *Ching-t'ien*) A system in ancient China by which peasant families were organized to farm the land for their feudal lords. A "well" consisted of a square piece of land covering about 40 acres. The square was divided by a grid into nine equal squares of about four and a half acres, with the center square belonging to the lord. Eight families were each given one square to live on, and the eight collectively farmed the center square for their lord. Over time the well-field system gave way to private ownership of land by farmers, who had to pay taxes on their land. The important Confucian philosopher Mencius (c. 372–289 B.C.) looked back to the well-field system, which had been practiced during the early Zhou dynasty (1100–256 B.C.), as the ideal system that should be adopted once again to help the peasants, many of whom in Mencius's time had become impoverished and were forced to sell their land and farm as tenants or sharecroppers. The notions of collective farming, and a group of people working together for the good of the ruler, have been influential in China up to the present time. See also AGRICULTURE; MENCIUS; ZHOU DYNASTY.

WEN, KING, AND WU, KING (Wenwang and Wuwang) The founders of the Zhou dynasty (1100–256 B.C.), the longest-lived dynasty in Chinese history. The Zhou people were a semi-nomadic tribe who inhabited the region of the upper Jing River in northwestern China. They moved south to the region where the Jing meets the Wei River, near the modern city of Xi'an in Shaanxi Province, where they encountered the Shang dynasty (1750–1040 B.C.). At first the Zhou pledged their loyalty to the Shang, who awarded Wen the title Count of the West. However, the Shang later imprisoned Wen on false charges. Wu, son and successor of King Wen (known as the Duke of Zhou; Zhou Gong or Chou Kung), led the Zhou people to overthrow the Shang. Many Chinese tribes had already changed their loyalty from Shang to Zhou when Wu formally declared war on the Shang two years after Wen died. After killing Shang king Zouxin (Tsouhsin), Wu gave himself the title Wuwang ("Martial King") and founded the Zhou dynasty, which he named for his father's dukedom. The name Wenwang was also a title given to Wen after his death. The Zhou asserted that the last Shang king, Zouxin, had lost the mandate that Heaven bestows on a virtuous ruler and takes away from an unjust ruler, and they claimed that the Mandate of Heaven had been given to their own dynasty. Wu built the Zhou capital at Hao, just south of Xi'an. Wu's brother Dan (Tan), who inherited the title Duke of Zhou from his father, was a great scholar who served as the prime minister and general of his brother's new

dynasty. After Wu died, the Duke of Zhou did not claim the throne for himself but acted as regent for his young nephew, Wuwang's son, who became the new king. The Chinese have always revered the Duke of Zhou as a great sage. See also MANDATE OF HEAVEN; WEI RIVER; XI'AN; ZHOU, DUKE OF; ZHOU DYNASTY.

WEN CHENG-MING See WEN ZHENGMING.

WEN JEN See LITERATI.

WEN SHU See BODHISATTVA; GUANYIN; MAITREYA AND MANJUSRI.

WEN ZHENGMING (Wen Cheng-ming; 1470–1559) A painter and calligrapher who is termed one of the Four Great Masters of the Ming Dynasty (1368–1644), along with Shen Zhou (Shen Chou; 1427–1509), Tang Yin (T'ang Yin; 1470–1527) and Qiu Ying (Ch'iu Ying; c. 1494–1552). Wen Zhengming was a student of Shen Zhou, considered the greatest of these four masters. The four were members of the literati class of scholar-painters who lived in Suzhou, for many centuries the cultural center of China. Their style of painting, known as the Wu School for the Wu district surrounding Suzhou, is regarded by many as the finest expression of Ming painting. Literati painters were regarded as "amateurs" in contrast to professional painters who were paid by the court to produce decorative works. Wen was adept in painting in the styles from many different periods of Chinese history. Rather than simply copying them, however, he adapted them with his own precise and elegant style, which was continued by members of his family for several generations. Wen himself taught many students. His calligraphy, the artistic way of writing Chinese characters with a brush and ink, is also highly regarded by connoisseurs.

Wen was a highly literate and cultured man, but despite many attempts he was never able to pass the examinations administered by the Chinese government to select candidates for positions in the imperial bureaucracy. He did not enjoy painting for members of the wealthy upper classes as much as he preferred to give his works to poor people who appreciated them and helped take care of his daily needs. Chinese critics have asserted that the vitality and austerity in Wen's paintings and calligraphy reflect the forthrightness and high principles of his own personality. From Wen's time on, the literati style of painting became the predominant one in China. See also CALLIGRAPHY; LITERATI; SHEN ZHOU.

WENCHENG, PRINCESS See TIBET.

WENCHOW See WENZHOU.

WENDI (EMPEROR) (Wen-ti; r. 180–157 B.C.) Also known as Han Wendi; an emperor of the Han dynasty (206 B.C.–A.D. 220). He was a son of Emperor Gaodi (Kao-ti; also known as Gaozu or Kao-tsu; r. 206–195 B.C.), the founder of the Han, one of the greatest and longest dynasties in Chinese history. Gaodi was a peasant who became the first Chinese ruler not born to an aristocratic family. He was succeeded by his son, Emperor Huidi (Hui-ti; r. 195–188 B.C.), but after Huidi died, Gaodi's widow, known as the Empress Lu, tried to place members of her own family on the throne. Upon her death in 180 B.C., the throne returned to Gaodi's family with the succession of another of his sons, whose posthumous reign title is Wendi. Since his time, many Chinese historians have praised Wendi as an example of an ethical Confucian ruler who lived frugally and dedicated himself to strengthening the Chinese empire and benefiting his subjects.

Jia Yi (Chia Yi), one of his advisers, persuaded him to avoid the policies that had destroyed the Qin dynasty (221–206 B.C.), China's first dynasty, which had fallen quickly and been replaced by the Han dynasty. The Qin dynasty had been governed according to the principles of the Legalist School of Thought, which advocated harsh measures for controlling the population. In contrast, Emperor Gaodi had made Confucian-educated scholars his advisers. Wendi established the process by which Confucian principles and rituals formed the basis of the Chinese imperial government, and he placed Confucian scholars in the highest government offices. He also patronized the native Chinese religion of Daoism. Wendi did away with cruel Qin methods of punishment, freed slaves, provided famine relief and instituted pensions for the elderly. His policies enabled the Chinese economy to prosper. Wendi continued Gaodi's policies of centralizing the government and absorbing more territory into the Chinese empire. He was succeeded by Emperor Jingdi (Ching-ti; r. 157–141 B.C.), who put down a rebellion and further centralized the Han government. Jingdi was succeeded by Emperor Wudi (Wu-ti; r. 141–87 B.C.), the most powerful of all the Han emperors. See also CONFUCIANISM; DAOISM; GAODI (EMPEROR); HAN DYNASTY; QIN DYNASTY; WUDI (EMPEROR).

WENDI (EMPEROR) (Wen-ti; 541–604)   Also known as Sui Wendi; the founder and first emperor of the Sui dynasty (581–618), which reunified China after three centuries of disunity following the collapse of the Han dynasty (206 B.C.–A.D. 220). Wendi, meaning "Cultured Emperor," is his reign name; his personal name was Yang Jian (Yang Chien). Wendi had been a general under the Northern Zhou dynasty, which had overthrown the western branch of the Northern Wei dynasty. For two centuries, members of his family had held positions in the governments of dynasties that had been founded by various non-Chinese ethnic groups in northern China, and they had intermarried with noble Turkish and Mongol families. In 557 he married a woman of the Dugu, an aristocratic non-Chinese clan. In 568 he became Duke Sui under the Northern Zhou. His daughter married the Northern Zhou crown prince, who became emperor in 578 and in 579 conquered the Northern Qi dynasty, which had supplanted the eastern branch of the Northern Wei, thus reunifying northern China. When he died in 580, Wendi overthrew the Northern Zhou and proclaimed himself emperor.

Upon establishing the Sui dynasty in northern China, Wendi proceeded to conquer the south. He reunified China in 589 when his military and naval forces took the southern capital of the Chen Yi Kingdom in the region of modern Nanjing (then known as Jian kang) on the Yangzi River (Changjiang). Wendi built his capital, Chang'an (modern Xi'an in Shaanxi Province), near the old Han capital, which had also been called Chang'an. The city, the largest in the world at the time, included residences for the imperial fam-

ily, government offices, and a residential section with two markets. Wendi established a government administration called the "Three Department" (*sansheng*) system, which included Six Ministries and was based on the Han imperial bureaucracy. He developed a new law code and enacted measures to reform land ownership and and tax collection. He also undertook massive public works projects, especially the construction of the Grand Canal and of grain storages throughout the empire to stabilize grain prices and protect his people against famine.

Wendi supported Confucianism and Daoism, the native Chinese traditions, as well as Buddhism, which had been introduced into China from India around the first century A.D. In 593 he commanded the printing of Buddhist scriptures; this was the first recorded mention of printing in Chinese history. Later in his reign, however, he promoted Confucianism to stem the growing influence of Buddhism. In 595 Wendi made the journey to Taishan (Mount Tai), the sacred mountain where emperors traditionally performed rituals to legitimize their reign as the Son of Heaven. Wendi and his wife, Empress Dugu (Tu-hu), had a falling out with their eldest son, the crown prince. This conflict may have been caused by their second son, Yuan Guang (Yuan Kuang; 569–618), who may also have been responsible for Wendi's death in 604. Yuan Guang took the throne as the second Sui emperor Yangdi (Yang-ti; r. 6054–618). See also BUDDHISM; CHANG'AN; CONFUCIANISM; DAOISM; EMPEROR; NORTHERN WEI DYNASTY; PRINTING; SUI DYNASTY; TAISHAN; YANGDI, EMPEROR.

WENREN   See LITERATI.

WEN-TI (EMPEROR) (HAN)   See WENDI (EMPEROR) (HAN).

WEN-TI (EMPEROR) (SUI)   See WENDI, EMPEROR (SUI).

WEN-TSUNG (EMPEROR)   See TANG DYNASTY.

WENWANG   See WEN, KING, AND WU, KING.

WENYAN   See LANGUAGE, CHINESE.

WENZHOU   A city in Zhejiang Province on China's eastern coast that has been a port since ancient times. Wenzhou is located on the Ou River, 12 miles from the East China Sea. In the second century B.C., this region was the kingdom of Dong'ou (Tung'ou). Wenzhou, founded in the fourth century A.D., has long been a center of the Christian religion in China. Nestorian Christians were active in Wenzhou during the Yuan dynasty (1279–1368). Roman Catholic missionaries arrived in Wenzhou in the 17th century, and Protestant missionaries in 1867. There are still hundreds of thousands of Chinese Christians in the city. In 1877 the Qing dynasty (1644–1911) government that ruled China opened the port of Wenzhou as a so-called treaty port to foreign traders. More recently, in 1984 the Chinese government designated Wenzhou as one of 14 Coastal Open Cities, comparable to the Special Economic Zones (SEZs) it had already established to encourage foreign trade and investment.

Wenzhou was opened to foreign tourists in 1985. Since then it has developed rapidly, with a population of more

Wendi was the founder of the Sui dynasty (581–618). He reunited China after four centuries of political division. COURTESY, MUSEUM OF FINE ARTS, BOSTON

than half a million, and has become the largest trading port and industrial city in southern Zhejiang. Ferries link Wenzhou with Shanghai and other cities, and an airport was opened in 1990. The city's main industries include food processing, paper manufacturing and machine-building. Other export items include tea, timber, jute, alum, bricks and tiles. Local handicrafts include seashell carvings and ceramics. Nearby Qiaotou Village has a button market that sells locally manufactured buttons to buyers from all over the country.

Wenzhou has retained much of its charm, with old houses on narrow streets and an old waterfront. Jiangxin (Chiang-hsin) Temple, built between 861 and 874, is located on an island in the Ou River. The Wenzhou (Wen-chou) Museum, originally Wen Tianxiang (Wen T'ien-hsiang) Temple, built on another island in 1482 and later reconstructed, has exhibits of local archaeological remains and art works. The two islands have been joined and a temple built between them. Miaoguo (Miao-kuo) Temple at the foot of Mount Songtai was built during the Tang and restored in 1988. Outside the city, the Yandang Mountain Range has beautiful scenery, and tourists may visit the Lingyan and Lingfeng temples. Rice, vegetables and tangerines are grown on the fertile plain surrounding Wenzhou, which enjoys a subtropical climate. See also CHRISTIANITY; EAST CHINA SEA; NESTORIAN CHRISTIANITY; SPECIAL ECONOMIC ZONES; ZHEJIANG PROVINCE.

WENZONG (EMPEROR)   See TANG DYNASTY.

WEST LAKE (Xihu)   A famous lake west of the beautiful city of Hangzhou in Zhejiang Province, located on the east-central coast of the China Sea. The lake has an area of about 1,240 acres and an average depth of 6 feet. It is about two miles long and two miles wide at its widest point. West Lake was formed when the Qiantang River delta became filled with silt, causing a small bay to become a fresh-water inland lake. West Lake carp, a large fresh-water fish, is a favorite dish in the Chinese cuisine. It is cooked whole using a sweet-and-sour recipe that originated in Hangzhou. The lake is a popular tourist site, and visitors and Hangzhou natives alike enjoy watching the sun rise over the lake. Beautiful groves of plum, acacia and peach trees planted around the lake bloom at different times of the year, and lotus flowers cover the lake in summer.

West Lake is crossed by two dikes or causeways that divide the lake into three parts. The Baidi Causeway is named for the poet Bai Juyi (Po Chu-i; 772–846), who was governor of Hangzhou in the ninth century and built the lake's first dike in 821. The Sudi Causeway, named for the poet Su Shi (Su Dongpo or Tsu Tung-po; 1036–1101), who was appointed governor of Hangzhou in 1089, has six bridges and is thus called the Six Bridge Dike. After 1130, West Lake became the residence of emperors of the Southern Song dynasty (1127–1279). Emperors of the Qing dynasty (1644–1911) also favored the lake.

There are four islands in West Lake. The largest is Solitary Hill (Gushan), on which are located the Zhejian Provincial Museum and Library, the Sun Yat-sen Garden, the Xiling Seal Engravers Society and a pavilion known as the Autumn Moon on the Calm Lake. The Shing Yin Si Temple is dedicated to the memory of the Provincial Revolutionary Army, which brought about the Revolution of 1911 that overthrew the Qing dynasty and installed Sun Yat-sen as president of China. Among the several tombs on the island are those of the Song dynasty poet Lin He Qing (Lin Ho Ch'ing) and the fifth-century legendary beauty Su Xiaoxiao (Su Hsiao-hsiao). See also BAI JUYI; CARP; COOKING, CHINESE; HANGZHOU; REVOLUTION OF 1911; SOUTHERN SONG DYNASTY; SU SHI; SUN YAT-SEN.

WEST RIVER (Xijiang)   The longest river in southern China, with a total length of 1,373 miles, including the Hongshui River. The West River originates on Maxiong Mountain in Yunnan Province. It is called by the names Nan-pan, Hongshui, Qian and Xun at different places in Guizhou Province and Guangxi Zhuang Autonomous Region, and is called the West River below Wuzhou in Guangxi. The West River's main stream rises at the meeting point of the Hong-shui and You rivers, which originate in Yunnan Province and come together at Guiping in Guangxi; Guangxi largely comprises the basin of the West River system. There are more than 20 scenic and historical spots in the West River Basin, including Dinghu Mountain near the city of Zhaoqing; Lingyang Gorge, which forms the passage linking the upper reaches of the West River with Guangzhou (Canton); and the limestone caves and peaks, known as karst, around Fengkai. The West River flows east through Guangxi and Guangdong provinces and empties into the South China Sea, forming a large delta to the west of Guangzhou and Hong Kong, which are situated in the Pearl River (Zhujiang) Delta. The proximity of these two major river deltas, the West and the Pearl, makes southern Guangdong Province one of China's most important regions for growing rice in flooded fields, known as paddies, and for fish farming. Boats can navigate the West River from the sea to Guiping when the waters are high. See also FISH AND SEAFOOD; GUANGDONG PROVINCE; GUANGXI ZHUANG AUTONOMOUS REGION; RICE; SOUTH CHINA SEA.

WESTERN (265–316) AND EASTERN (317–420) JIN DYNASTIES   The Western Jin dynasty was established by Sima Yan (Ssu-ma Yan; 236–290), who ended the struggle between the three kings of Wei, Shu Han and Wu of the Three Kingdoms Period (220–280). Sima Yan took control of the kingdom of Wei around 250. In 263 Wei conquered the kingdom of Shu, and in 265 Wei defeated the kingdom of Wu. Sima Yan thus reunified China for a short time under the Western Jin Dynasty, enabling the ancient, original empire in the center of China, known as the Middle Kingdom (Zhongguo or Chung-kuo), to reestablish its control over the developing regions to the south and southwest.

The Western Jin dynasty's military power was strengthened by enhanced agricultural productivity and transportation on China's network of waterways. However, Sima Yan allowed some foreign nomadic tribes such as the Xiongnu (Hsiung-nu) and Xianbei (Hsien-pei) to settle inside the Great Wall, which had been built to protect China from nomadic invaders, and this policy eventually brought down the dynasty. He also installed his 25 sons as military governors of different regions. After he died in 290, they went to war against each other. The dynasty's central government collapsed, peasants suffered from famine and impoverishment, bandit groups formed and the nomadic tribes took advantage of the chaos to gain a foothold in the empire.

In 304 a Xiongnu named Liu Yuan proclaimed himself to be the king of Han and conquered most of northern China. In 311 the capital city of Luoyang was sacked by the invaders, and in 316 the old capital city of Chang'an (modern Xi'an) was sacked and the last Western Jin emperor was taken prisoner. The remaining descendants of Sima Yan fled to Jiankang and in 317 founded the Eastern Jin dynasty.

Sima Rui (Ssu-ma Jui), the military governor of Jiankang, became the first emperor of the Eastern Jin. Many scholars and government officials also fled to this region, where they helped preserve traditional Chinese culture. They also joined with monks of the Buddhist religion, which had been introduced into China from India around the first century A.D., to develop Buddhism in a way that would appeal to members of the literati or scholar class who governed in the imperial bureaucracy. Various scripts used in the art of calligraphy also developed rapidly during the Eastern Jin in the fourth century, especially through the efforts of renowned calligrapher Wang Xizhi (Wang Hsi-chih; 321–379).

After the Western Jin fell in 316, China remained fragmented among a succession of short dynasties during a period that lasted from 304 to 589. The colonization and development of southern China increased during the Eastern Jin, with a great rise in population south of the Yangzi River. Military generals waged three campaigns to recover northern China from 313 to 321, 352 to 365 and 416 to 418, but the Jin rulers did not completely support them and they failed. The Jin overcame their rivalries in 383 to halt an invasion of combined infantry and nomad cavalry forces led by a Tibetan general, thereby maintaining the independence of the Chinese south of the Huai River valley. Four brief dynasties succeeded each other in the region after 420, when the Jin dynasty was overthrown by its general, Liu Yu, who declared himself the first emperor of Liu-Song, one of four brief dynasties in southern China following the Jin. See also BUDDHISM; CALLIGRAPHY; GREAT WALL; MIDDLE KINGDOM; NORTHERN AND SOUTHERN DYNASTIES; THREE KINGDOMS PERIOD; WANG XIZHI; XIONGNU; YANGZI RIVER.

WESTERN CHOU DYNASTY See WESTERN ZHOU DYNASTY.

WESTERN HAN DYNASTY (206 B.C.–A.D. 8) Also known as the Former Han dynasty; the first period within the Han dynasty (206 B.C.–A.D. 220), one of the longest dynasties in Chinese history, during which many institutions were established that were adopted by later imperial dynasties that ruled China. Han is the name of the ethnic group that forms the majority of the Chinese population. The Han dynasty was founded by Liu Bang (Liu Pang; 256–195 B.C.), who led a rebellion against the short-lived Qin dynasty (221–206 B.C.). The Qin dynasty had been founded by King Zheng of Qin, who overthrew the Zhou dynasty (1100–256 B.C.), China's longest dynasty, and proclaimed himself Qin Shi Huangdi, the First Emperor (r. 221–210 B.C.) of a unified Chinese empire. He died in 210 B.C. and his son and nephew became the succeeding Qin emperors, but the Chinese people rose up against the harshness of Qin rule and China fell into civil warfare. Liu Bang was a peasant from the region that claimed to succeed the former Zhou state of Chu, in the Yangzi River (Changjiang) valley. He eventually became king of a region to the west of Chu and defeated the remaining forces of Qin and of Chu led by Xiang Yu (Hsiang Yu). In 206 B.C. Liu Bang took the title of King of Han, and in 202 B.C. he proclaimed himself the emperor of the Han dynasty. He is known by his reign name, Emperor Gaodi (Kao-ti).

Gaodi was illiterate but recognized that he needed educated officials to advise him and to administer the Han empire. He appointed as his chief adviser Xiao He (Hsiao Ho; d. 193 B.C.), who persuaded him to move the Han capital to Chang'an (modern Xi'an in Shaanxi Province), across the Wei River from the Qin capital of Xianyang. Gaodi laid the foundations for an imperial bureaucracy based on the teachings of the classical scholar Confucius (551–479 B.C.), which emphasized hierarchical order and harmony in society and the family. Han scholars attempted to restore Chinese classical literature and philosophical texts that had been recorded during the Zhou dynasty but largely destroyed when Emperor Qin Shi Huangdi burned huge numbers of books in 213 B.C. A collection of books on ancient history, poetry and rituals came to be known as the Five Classics of Confucianism. They formed the basis of the examination system that the Han instituted to select officials for the imperial bureaucracy. Confucianism was accepted as the orthodox school of thought from the Han dynasty through the Qing dynasty (1644–1911), and it remains influential in China and other Asian countries, especially Taiwan, Singapore, Japan, Korea and Vietnam.

Gaodi rejected the brutal Legalist system of the Qin, but he built the Han empire using the Legalist doctrine of centralizing government power. He also began extending the borders of the Han Empire. Gaodi was succeeded by his son, known as Emperor Huidi (Hui-ti; r. 195–188 B.C.). After he died, Empress Lu, Gaodi's widow, continued the Liu family line by having infants placed on the throne. She also tried to place members of the Lu family in high government positions, but she died in 180 B.C. and one of Gaodi's sons took the throne, known as Emperor Wendi (Wen-ti; r. 180–157 B.C.). Chinese historians have always regarded Wendi as the model of a virtuous ruler who is concerned for the well-being of his subjects. He continued his father's efforts to develop a centralized government bureaucracy and to absorb former kingdoms into the Han Empire. Wendi was succeeded by Jingdi (Ching-ti; r. 157–141 B.C.), who also continued these policies.

The next Han emperor, known as Han Wudi (Wu-ti, the "Martial Emperor"; r. 141–87 B.C.), greatly expanded the Han empire by incorporating territories on the borders of China. During his reign, Chinese Confucian-based culture was adopted in Vietnam and Korea. Wudi sent forces to the northern frontier to contain the Xiongnu (Hsiung-nu), a group of nomadic tribes that frequently raided China. He also expanded the line of fortifications across the north, known as the Great Wall, that Emperor Qin Shi Huangdi had built. He sent one of his best generals, Zhang Qian (Chang Ch'ien), to the northwest to form alliances with local tribes against the Xiongnu. Zhang Qian made several long journeys on which he acquired a great deal of information about the people beyond the Han borders. He learned that they were eager to trade with China, especially for silk, a luxurious textile that only the Chinese knew how to produce. Camel caravans began transporting trade goods from Chang'an to Central Asia; their route became known as the Silk Road. The Han Chinese also began acquiring horses from western tribes, especially in Ferghana (mordern Uzbekistan), for military purposes.

In 119 B.C. Emperor Wudi established state monopolies for the crucial iron and salt industries and placed strict state control over the minting of coins. He also established a Bureau of Music to promote Confucian ritual music and dance (*yue* or *yueh*; "proper music") in the Han court. In 136 B.C., at the urging of Confucian scholar Dong Zhongshu

(Tung Chung-shu), Emperor Wudi proclaimed Confucianism as the official state cult, and 12 years later, he established an imperial university known as *taixue* (*t'ai-hsueh*; "grand school") in Chang'an with a curriculum based on the Five Classics of Confucianism. By the end of the Han dynasty, the university had more than 10,000 students. During the Han, all government schools began to conduct regular sacrifices to Confucius, who became the patron saint of the imperial bureaucracy. The Chinese writing system had been standardized during the Qin dynasty, which greatly aided scholarship and calligraphy, the art of writing Chinese characters with a brush. The rhyme-prose style of poetry (*fu*) became the most important type of literature during the Han dynasty. Sima Tan (Ssu-mat'an) and his son, Sima Qian (Ssu-ma Qian), compiled the *Historical Records* (*Shiji* or *Shih-chi*), a 130-chapter book that recorded Chinese prehistory and history up to 90 B.C. This was the first of the 26 Standard (or Dynastic) Histories that were compiled throughout Chinese history and were modeled on the *Historical Records.*

By 90 B.C. Han troops were losing their ability to contain the Xiongnu, and the government treasury was nearly depleted, so Wudi had to give up his expansionist policy. In 91 B.C. political factions began fighting in Chang'an, and the empress and the heir apparent were forced to commit suicide. Wudi had arranged for his youngest son to succeed him, which he did when Wudi died in 87 B.C. The reign of the new emperor, Zhaodi (Chao-ti; r. 87–74 B.C.), was also beset by factional struggles, as were the reigns of the following Han emperors. During the reign of Emperor Chengdi (Ch'eng-ti; r. 33–7 B.C.), the Wang family grew powerful. Wang Mang served as regent for the last infant emperor of the Western Han dynasty, and in A.D. 9 he attempted to usurp the throne and found his own dynasty, known as the Xin. The Xin dynasty (A.D. 9–23) is also known as the Wang Mang Interregnum. The general populace also rebelled against the hardships they had been suffering under the Han, and in A.D. 23 a band of peasant rebels known as the Red Eyebrows took Chang'an and killed Wang Mang. Liu Xiu (Liu Hsiu) was able to suppress the rebellion and formally reestablish the Han dynasty in A.D. 25 with himself as emperor. He is known as Emperor Guangwudi (Kuang Wu-ti) and his dynasty is known as the Eastern or Later Han dynasty (A.D. 25–220). See also CAMEL CARAVANS; CHANG'AN; CONFUCIANISM; DONG ZHONGSHU; EASTERN HAN DYNASTY; FIVE CLASSICS OF CONFUCIANISM; GAODI, EMPEROR; GREAT WALL; HAN; HORSE; IMPERIAL BUREAUCRACY; IMPERIAL EXAMINATION SYSTEM; IRON TECHNOLOGY AND STEEL INDUSTRY; LEGALIST SCHOOL OF THOUGHT; MUSIC AND DANCE, CONFUCIAN; NOMADS AND ANIMAL HUSBANDRY; QIN DYNASTY; RED EYEBROWS REBELLION; RHYME-PROSE STYLE OF VERSE; SALT MONOPOLY; SILK ROAD; SIMA QIAN; SIMA TAN; WANG MANG; WENDI, EMPEROR; WRITING SYSTEM, CHINESE; WUDI, EMPEROR; XIONGNU; ZHANG QIAN; ZHOU DYNASTY.

WESTERN LIAO DYNASTY   See LIAO DYNASTY.

WESTERN XIA DYNASTY   See NINGXIA HUI AUTONOMOUS REGION; XIXIA, KINGDOM OF; YINCHUAN.

WESTERN ZHOU DYNASTY (1100–771 B.C.)   The first of two general periods of the Zhou dynasty (1100–256 B.C.),

the longest dynasty in Chinese history. The Zhou dynasty was founded by King Wen (Wenwang) and his son, King Wu (Wuwang). The actual date of its founding is not certain, and some scholars set it at 1027 B.C. or 1122 B.C., although it might even be 1040 B.C. or in the decade preceding that date. The Zhou were a seminomadic tribe who inhabited the region of the upper Jing River in northwestern China. They moved south to the region where the Jing meets the Wei River, near the modern city of Xi'an in Shaanxi Province, where they encountered the Shang dynasty (1750–1040 B.C.). The Zhou pledged their loyalty as vassals of the Shang, but the Shang later imprisoned King Wen of the Zhou on false charges. By then, many vassal states had changed their loyalty from the Shang to the Zhou, and King Wu formally declared war on the Shang and overthrew the dynasty. He established the Zhou dynasty capital at Hao (later known as Chang'an; modern Xi'an), and this city served as the imperial capital for several later dynasties, notably the Tang dynasty (618–907). King Wen's name became synonymous for the Chinese people with "culture" or "civilization."

The Duke of Zhou, King Wen's son and King Wu's younger brother, consolidated the Zhou kingdom while governing as regent for the third king, Wu's son, King Cheng (Ch'eng), while he was a minor. After the Zhou defeated the Shang, the Duke of Zhou gave a speech to the Shang nobles asserting that because they were immoral and had broken the laws of Heaven (*tian* or *t'ien*), the last Shang ruler, Zouxin (Tsou-hsin), had lost the mandate that Heaven bestows on a virtuous ruler, and that it had been given to the Zhou dynasty. Every succeeding Chinese dynasty has used this theory of the Mandate of Heaven (*tianming* or *t'ien-ming*) to justify its own rule. The Zhou permitted a member of the Shang royal clan to be the ruler of a small feudal state so that he could continue offering ritual sacrifices to placate the Shang ancestors. The Duke of Zhou created a feudal system (*fengjian* or *feng-chien*) under the concept that all land belongs to the king and all people are his subjects. The Zhou royal family gave its relatives and close allies the authority to administer states in northern and central China, but it required them to attend the royal court at the Zhou capital in Chang'an and to provide military support to the Zhou. Five feudal ranks were established comparable to the British ranks of duke, marquis, earl, viscount and baron.

Each feudal state under the Zhou had a walled town in which were built temples to ancestors, altars of soil and grain, and palaces for the noble families. The animistic tradition of the Shang was supplanted by the Zhou emphasis on continuing family lines and propitiating the ancestors, known as ancestor worship. The Chinese people have practiced these rituals into the modern era. The Zhou followed the Shang in practicing divination for important occasions by using oracle bones, the bones of animals that were heated to produce cracks, which were interpreted as answers to important questions about the dynasty. However, the Zhou gradually shifted from using oracle bones to relying on a written text known as the *Book of Changes* (*Yijing* or *I-ching*). The Zhou also practiced ancient annual rituals that regulated the agricultural year.

During the Western Zhou Dynasty, artisans such as bronze and jade workers and potters lived in or just outside the towns. Bronze working, which had reached its high point during the Shang dynasty, was adapted by the Zhou. Peasants, the majority of the population, farmed the countryside. Cultivated fields were organized under the "well-field system" in which areas of land were divided into nine squares, with eight families farming one square each for themselves and the center square collectively for their feudal lord. The residents of a feudal state had to pay heavy taxes and were not allowed to move to another state, and adult men were required to provide physical labor and military service. Women had to raise silkworms and weave silk textiles, some of which they had to give to the state in which they resided.

The Zhou strictly controlled the feudal states in the North China Plain and the Wei River valley in the center of its territory, known as the "Middle Kingdom" (Zhongguo or Chung-kuo), the modern name for the country of China, but it had less control over the states at the edges of its territory. The Zhou ruling house actually held power for less than three centuries. In 771 B.C. invaders allied themselves with disaffected vassals of the Zhou, took the Zhou capital and killed the king, and forced the Zhou to leave their homeland and move east. The Zhou crown prince established the Eastern Zhou dynasty (771–256 B.C.) at the city that had been the Zhou subordinate capital, in the region of modern Luoyang in Henan Province, just south of the Yellow River (Huanghe). The former Zhou domain was taken over by the rulers of Qin, who theoretically remained vassals of the Zhou even though they had displaced them. From then on, the Zhou kings served a ritual function but had no power to keep their vassal states from fighting each other. The Zhou and their vassals were finally conquered by the ruler of Qin, who unified China under the Qin dynasty (221–206 B.C.) and proclaimed himself the "First Emperor," Qin Shi Huangdi (Shih Huang-ti; r. 221–210 B.C.).

Confucius (551–479 B.C.), who lived during the Spring and Autumn Period (772–481 B.C.), a division of the Eastern Zhou dynasty, and whose thought later become the orthodox school for the Chinese imperial government, revered the Zhou dynasty. So did Mencius (c. 372–289 B.C.), the second most important Confucian thinker. Confucius regarded the first few centuries of the Western Zhou dynasty as the ideal period of peaceful, orderly government in Chinese history. He considered the Duke of Zhou and Kings Wen and Wu the best examples of loyal government officials for later rulers to emulate. See also BOOK OF CHANGES; BRONZEWARE; CHANG'AN; CONFUCIUS; EASTERN ZHOU DYNASTY; FEUDAL SYSTEM; MANDATE OF HEAVEN; MENCIUS; MIDDLE KINGDOM; NORTH CHINA PLAIN; ORACLE BONES; QIN DYNASTY; QIN SHI HUANGDI; SILK; SPRING AND AUTUMN ANNALS; SPRING AND AUTUMN PERIOD; WARRING STATES PERIOD; WEI RIVER; WELL-FIELD SYSTEM OF AGRICULTURE; WEN, KING, AND WU, KING; ZHOU, DUKE OF.

WESTERNIZATION MOVEMENT (*Yangwu Yundong* or *Yang-wu Yun-tung*) Also known as the Yangwu Movement; a Chinese attempt in the second half of the 19th century to adapt Western technology in such areas as weapons making, shipbuilding and shipping, mining, railways and telegraphy. Some Chinese leaders argued that this was the way to make China powerful and able to stand up to the Western powers, especially Great Britain, France and Germany, which were involved in China. The Yangwu Movement is equivalent to

the Self-Strengthening Movement (*Ziqiang* or *Tzu ch'iang*) under which China instituted many modernization projects between 1861 and 1895. Yangwu is commonly translated as "foreign matters" to distinguish it from "foreign affairs" in the field of diplomacy. See also SELF-STRENGTHENING MOVEMENT.

WHAMPOA, TREATY OF See UNEQUAL TREATIES.

WHAMPOA (HUANGPU) MILITARY ACADEMY A military academy established in June 1924 by the Chinese Nationalist Party (Kuomintang; KMT) at Whampoa near the southern city of Guangzhou (Canton) in modern Guangdong Province. The KMT had been founded by Dr. Sun Yatsen (1866–1925), first president of the modern Republic of China (ROC; f. 1912). With the help of Soviet advisers from the Communist International (Comintern) and members of the recently founded Chinese Communist Party (CCP), the KMT intended for the academy to educate revolutionary army leaders who were patriotic and honest, in contrast to the greedy and violent warlords who controlled China from 1916 to 1928. The warlords had forced Sun to flee to Guangzhou, where he reestablished his government in 1923. In the summer of 1923, Sun sent Chiang Kai-shek (1887–1975), who later became head of the KMT, to the Soviet Union for three months. When Chiang returned to China he was named the first commandant of Whampoa Military Academy.

Another famous Chinese leader associated with the academy was Zhou Enlai (Chou En-lai; 1898–1976), who held high positions in the CCP and later became premier of the People's Republic of China (PRC). When Zhou returned to China from studying in France in 1924, during the period in the 1920s when the KMT and CCP were cooperating, he was made vice director of the political training department at the academy. This placed him under Chiang Kai-shek. From 1923 to 1927, KMT and CCP members worked together at the academy to train soldiers and political leaders. Graduates belonging to each party fought alongside each other against warlords who controlled local regions of China, helping to consolidate the Guangdong (Province) Revolutionary Base Area. Whampoa graduates also undertook the successful 1926 Northern Expedition to free northern China from warlords.

In April 1927, Zhou was CCP leader in Shanghai when the KMT, led by Chiang, turned against the CCP and massacred many Communists in that city, betraying Sun Yat-sen's revolution. Zhou was a leader of the anti-KMT Nanchang Uprising in August 1927, which Communists consider the birth of the Red Army (now known as the People's Liberation Army). The Communists fled to rural Jiangxi Province and began building up a peasant-based guerrilla army. Chiang Kai-shek continued to build up a professional-based army. The Whampoa Military Academy closed in 1934, shortly after Japan invaded Manchuria (northeastern China) and established a puppet state there called Manchukuo (Manzhouguo or Man-chou-kuo in Chinese). The KMT and CCP cooperated for a second time during China's War of Resistance against Japan (1937–45; World War II), but their united front eventually fell apart. After that war the two sides fought a civil war in which the CCP defeated the KMT, whose leaders fled to Taiwan, and founded the People's Republic of China (PRC) in 1949.

Although the academy did not reopen, in 1984 the 60th anniversary of the Whampoa Military Academy was commemorated by a meeting in Beijing attended by Communist leaders and academy alumni from China and abroad. The Whampoa Military Academy Alumni Association was formed at the meeting with Xu Xiangqian (Hsu Hsiang-ch'ien) as its first president. In 1989 the Chinese National Archives Publishing House published a 12-volume "History of the Huangpu (Whampoa) Military Academy (Draft)," which includes the history of the academy, the first KMT-CCP cooperation, and the Northern Expedition; details about major Chinese events between 1924 and 1934; speeches, telegrams and important papers by Sun Yat-sen and other KMT leaders; 750 historical photographs and 30 tactical maps of famous battles involving Whampoa graduates; the names of students at the academy during 21 terms; and the names of the tens of thousands of Chinese who died during the Northern Expedition. These volumes, an important source for modern Chinese history, had been edited by the Whampoa Military Academy committee of administrative affairs and completed in 1936 but until 1989 had never been published. Lin Sen, chairman of the KMT government, wrote the preface and the cover inscription. See also CHIANG KAI-SHEK; CHINESE COMMUNIST PARTY; NANCHANG UPRISING; NATIONALIST PARTY; NORTHERN EXPEDITION; PEOPLE'S LIBERATION ARMY; SUN YAT-SEN; WARLORD PEROID; ZHOU ENLAI.

WHAMPOA RIVER　See HUANGPU RIVER.

WHITE HORSE TEMPLE　(Baimasi or Pai Ma Ssu)　One of the first Buddhist temples built in China after the Buddhist religion was introduced into China from India around the first century A.D. The White Horse Temple is located seven miles east of Luoyang, the capital of 10 ancient Chinese dynasties, in Henan Province. Historical records state that in A.D. 67, the second emperor of the Eastern Han dynasty (A.D. 25–220) sent the scholars Cai Yin (Ts'ai Yin) and Qin Jing (Ch'in Ching) to Tianzhou in modern India to gather Buddhist sutras (scriptures). In the region of modern Afghanistan they met two eminent Indian Buddhist monks, Kasyapamatanga and Sharmaranya, whom they brought back to Luoyang. The monks brought with them, reputedly on the back of a white horse, sculptures and the Sutra of 42 Articles, supposedly the first canonical Buddhist text translated into Chinese. In A.D. 68 the emperor ordered a temple to be built in the monks' honor at the place where their horses had stopped. The monks lived there, translated sutras, and lectured on the Buddhist religion, and were buried there when they died. Their tombs can still be seen at the temple, which has been damaged and restored several times. The renovation done in 1556 forms the foundation for the buildings seen at White Horse Temple today. In 1961 the Chinese government put the temple under its protection as a cultural relic. Red Guards sacked the temple during the Cultural Revolution (1966–76), but then it was restored again and sculptures were brought there from other places. The temple's four main halls contain many sculptures of Buddhist deities and bodhisattvas, as well as stone tablets inscribed with the writing of renowned calligraphers. Two white horses made of

stone stand in front of the temple. Qiyun Tan, an elegant 13-story pagoda, stands about 550 yards away from White Horse Temple. It was probably constructed between the 10th and 12th centuries during the Northern Song dynasty (960–1127). See also BODHISATTVA; BUDDHISM; EASTERN HAN DYNASTY; LUOYANG; STONE TABLETS; TEMPLES.

WHITE LOTUS SECRET SOCIETY　A Buddhist religious sect that led a peasant rebellion against the Manchu Qing dynasty (1644–1911) in Hubei, Shanxi and Sichuan provinces from 1796 to 1804. The rebellion occurred during the final years of the reign of the Qianlong Emperor (Ch'ien-lung; r. 1736–95). The White Lotus and other religious sects had been forbidden by the Qing government, so they became secret societies. The White Lotus secret society originated during the Mongol Yuan dynasty (1279–1368) among poor, uneducated peasants in the area north of the Huai River (modern Anhui Province) and became a symbol of Han Chinese resistance to foreign domination. The secret society led a rebellion during the Yuan that even cut off the Grand Canal, the major transportation route in China. The White Lotus appealed to impoverished peasants by promising them that Maitreya, the Buddha of the Future, would descend to Earth, restore the Han Chinese Ming dynasty that had overthrown the Mongols in 1368 but had been overthrown by the Manchus in 1644, remove disease, natural disasters and all other suffering in this life and bring happiness in the next life. The region where the White Lotus took hold in the 16th century was secluded and mountainous. The Qing dynasty had only recently opened this area to settlement, and the poor migrants there lived a desperate existence. Leaders of the White Lotus added an anti-Manchu racial position to their ideology.

The White Lotus Rebellion began in 1796 to protest the collection of taxes. Imperial forces were not able to quell the many uprisings along the Han River and the upper reaches of the Yangzi River. The peasants were well-organized to defend themselves and had stockpiled food and weapons, so they could quickly hide in the mountains before imperial troops arrived to stop them. Qing military forces were also demoralized by a lack of supplies due to corruption in the imperial government. The Qianlong emperor, who had been senile for several years, died in 1799. His successor, the Jiaqing emperor (Chia-ching; r. 1796–1820), was able to organize the Qing military to fight the White Lotus rebels and gain control over the regions where they were active. Qing troops helped local villagers build hundreds of walled enclosures and organize themselves into militias so they could protect themselves. In addition, they gave amnesty to peasants who had been forced into the White Lotus rebel bands. In the end, Qing commanders defeated the rebels by taking control over the food supply and cutting off their source of recruits.

The White Lotus Rebellion dwindled to an end by 1804. However, the Qing dynasty had been seriously damaged by the rebellion, not only from the high expenses of fighting the rebels, but also because the weakness of the formerly powerful Manchu banner troops had been exposed. Also, many weapons had to be reclaimed from local militia members. In 1813 an offshoot of the White Lotus, another secret society known as the Eight Trigrams, led a peasant uprising in North

China and actually sent forces to try to invade the Forbidden City (Imperial Palace) in the capital city of Beijing. See also BANNER SYSTEM, MANCHU; EIGHT TRIGRAMS REBELLION; GRAND CANAL; QIANLONG, EMPEROR; QING DYNASTY; YUAN DYNASTY.

WHITE WARE   Ceramic objects coated with white glaze, a color that has many traditional meanings in China. White (*baide* or *pai-te*) is the color of autumn and the West quadrant of the universe, which is symbolized by the tiger (*hu*), the king of all the animals and the representative of the masculine principle (yang) in nature. In China, white is also the color of death and funerals, in contrast to the Western custom of wearing black for mourning. In addition, white is associated with the Buddhist religion, which was introduced into China from India around the first century B.C. White is the color of the lotus blossom, the Buddhist symbol of purity, because the beautiful white lotus rises from the mud of a pond. The finest pieces of jade, a hard stone that has been revered by the Chinese for thousands of years, are pale white or cream-colored. The Chinese have long made carvings of jade and ivory, another beautiful white substance. The Chinese began producing white earthenware objects for ceremonial use during the Shang dynasty (1750–1040 B.C.). Shang potters discovered the process of coating earthenware with glazes, made primarily of silica, which forms a glass if fired in a kiln at a high temperature.

After the Shang, Chinese potters did not develop white ware until the Six Dynasties Period (A.D. 220–589). Various white ceramic vessels were buried in tombs dating from late in the period. Six Dynasties white ware formed the basis for white ceramics that have been produced continuously in China up to the present time. During the Tang dynasty (618–907), silver vessels influenced by Indian, Scythian, Sassanian and Byzantine styles were produced in China, and their designs, such as leaves, flowers and scrolls, influenced white ceramic objects made in China during the late Tang and Song (960–1279) dynasties. The linear and pictorial designs made on silver by chasing and tracing were reproduced in ceramics by impressing the clay with molds or by hand-incising the clay before it was glazed and fired in a kiln. White ceramics are mentioned in the famous eighth-century *Book of Tea* (*Chajing* or *Ch'a-ching*). However, most Tang ceramics are colorful, especially the popular three-color ware (*sancai* or *san-ts'ai*).

White ware became popular during the Song dynasty, when it was produced at many kilns in both northern and southern China. *Ding* (*ting*) ware, which evolved from white ceramic wares produced in the seventh and eighth centuries, was the first type of ceramic known to have been used in the Song imperial court. *Ding* pieces, developed to replace silver dishes, have ivory-colored glazes and incised decorations of flowers and other motifs. Members of the Song court appreciated the refined understatement of white ware. Imperial kilns established at Jingdezhen (Ching-te-chen) in Fujian Province in southeastern China began producing white porcelain wares during the Song. *Ding* pieces were also decorated by molds and incisions, and the glaze commonly accumulated in so-called "tear drops."

Chinese white-bodied porcelain wares became extremely popular not only in China but also in countries all over the world. Porcelain is made with kaolin, a pure white, plastic clay that Chinese potters first discovered. White served as both a monochromatic glaze and as a background glaze for ceramics decorated with painting designs made from cobalt, iron and copper. White porcelain bodies formed the background for decorations made with underglaze, especially in red and blue-and-white ware, and overglaze painted enamel decorations, such as *famille verte* and *famille rose*. During the early Ming, a white ware was also produced at Jingdezhen with a delicate hidden decoration (*anhua*), which is very lightly incised and can be seen by holding the piece so that light shines through it from behind. *Yingqing* (*ying-ch'ing*) ware, a type of white ware also produced in Dehua County, was a forerunner of *blanc de Chine* ("white of China"), an extremely popular porcelain that is fired at 2500° Centigrade, the highest of all Chinese porcelains. *Blanc de Chine* glaze has a delicate blue tint, especially where it accumulates in the depressions of a piece, and is hence named "shadow blue." These pieces were also decorated by molds and hand incisions. Large quantities of *blanc de Chine* ware were exported to Europe and were also sold to wealthy Chinese government officials and merchants. Many pieces are Buddhist figures such as Guanyin (Kuan Yin), the Goddess of Mercy, and Bodhidharma, the legendary founder of the Chan (Zen) Sect of Buddhism. See also CERAMICS; DEHUA WARE; DING WARE; ENAMELWARE; GOLD AND SILVER; IVORY CARVING; JADE; JINGDEZHEN; PORCELAIN.

WHITEFIN DOLPHIN   See RIVER DOLPHIN, CHINESE.

WHITE-HAIRED GIRL, THE   See DRAMA.

WILD GOOSE PAGODAS   See PAGODA; TAIZONG, EMPEROR (TANG); XI'AN; XUANZANG.

WILLIAM OF RUBRUCK   See CHRISTIANITY; KARAKORUM; SILK.

WILLOW (*liushu*)   A tree associated with female beauty because of its long, thin branches that sway gracefully. The willow specifically represents the "singsong" girls, or courtesans, who lived and worked in the so-called "willow quarters" of Chinese cities. The willow tree is also a traditional symbol of friendship; a person going on a trip was given willow branches upon leaving. The Chinese believe that the willow has cleansing powers, so they use clusters of willow branches to brush off the tombs of ancestors at the Qingming Festival held in April to honor the dead. The willow is also associated with the coming of spring. Willow branches may be hung over the front door of a Chinese home to bring good fortune. Powerful healers known as shamans use carved images of willow wood to communicate with the spirit world. The willow is a symbol of humility in the Buddhist religion. Willow branches are woven together to make baskets and ropes. Poor people who cannot afford tea may brew a drink with willow leaves, which contain a large amount of tannin, similar to tea leaves. The leaves and bark of certain willow species are used in herbal medicines to treat bruises, dysentery and rheumatism.

The willow tree was a common motif in Chinese poetry, landscape painting and on porcelains. In the late 18th century, willow pattern ceramics were produced in England based on Chinese Ming dynasty (1368–1644) blue and white ware, and became commonly used throughout the West. The famous English potter Thomas Minton engraved the willow pattern on copper in 1780 for porcelain production in his factory. The willow ware pattern derived from a traditional Chinese story about two lovers whose parents refused to let them marry, so they fled across a bridge to an island where they would die together. Their souls became two doves that flew up together over a willow tree, free from obstacles to their love. In Chinese art, a particular flower or tree is usually paired with a particular bird; the willow is traditionally painted with the swallow. See also BLUE AND WHITE WARE; MEDICINE, HERBAL; QING MING FESTIVAL.

"WIND AND WATER" See FENG SHUI.

WIND INSTRUMENTS See FLUTES AND WIND INSTRUMENTS.

WINE See ALCOHOLIC BEVERAGES.

WINTER FESTIVAL (Dong or Tung) The last festival of the Chinese lunar year, held in late December or early January, one month before the New Year Festival. The Winter Festival is held just after the winter solstice and celebrates the fact that the days are becoming longer after the short, dark days of winter. The festival dates back to the Zhou dynasty (1100–256 B.C.), when the Chinese prepared round dumplings of glutinous rice and offered them to their ancestors at this time of year. Chinese families traditionally celebrate the Winter Festival by enjoying large banquets with many courses of specially prepared food and by praying to the gods for a good New Year Festival. Friends also give each other presents as tokens of a good year to come. See also BANQUETS; CALENDAR; NEW YEAR FESTIVAL; RICE.

WISDOM (*zhi* or *chih*) A central concept in the Confucian School of Thought. Wisdom is a virtue associated with the other Confucian virtues of humanity (also translated as benevolence; *ren* or *jen*), righteousness (*yi*) and propriety (*li*). It thus has an ethical connotation and is associated with a person's actions. Wisdom comes from examining and cultivating oneself in order to become a genuine human being. Some Confucian thinkers regard humanity as the primary virtue, and wisdom, righteousness and propriety as aspects of humanity. The important Confucian thinker Mencius (Mengzi or Meng Tzu; c. 372–289 B.C.) stated that the virtues of humanity, righteousness, propriety and wisdom are innate in human nature, and that they are manifested in a person's emotional responses, such as commiserating with other people, being ashamed of and disliking actions that are dishonorable, being modest and yielding to other people, and having a sense of right and wrong. The Confucian philosopher Dong Zhongshu (Tung Chung-shu; c. 179–c. 104 B.C.) maintained that "wisdom is to know." He thus regarded wisdom as moral understanding that forms the basis for actions. He defined wisdom as acting in accordance with the words one has spoken. A man should first use his wisdom to measure the actions he must take, and then he will be able to understand what is beneficial or harmful and what the end

result of an action will be. Such a man will act properly according to the relationships in which he is engaged. Wisdom is also an important concept in the religion of Buddhism, introduced into China from India around the first century A.D., which terms wisdom *bodhi* or enlightenment. See also BUDDHISM; CONFUCIANISM; DONG ZHONGSHU; HUMANITY; MENCIUS; PROPRIETY; RIGHTEOUSNESS.

WOK (*caiguo* or *ts'ai-kuo*) The Cantonese (Guangdong Province dialect) term for a large bowl-shaped metal cooking utensil with handles whose high sides slope toward a central well. This design is very ancient yet efficient for cooking. A wok can be made of iron, steel, aluminum or copper. A new wok must be "seasoned" before use by rubbing cooking oil into it. A wok 14 inches in diameter is practical for most home cooking. It is used for many methods of cooking food, including stir-frying, braising, deep-frying and steaming. The wok is placed on a ring over the fire or stove to hold it steady while cooking. Very little oil is needed to cook with a wok because the oil collects in the center where the heat is concentrated. Food is turned and removed with long chopsticks, spatulas or strainers. When food is steamed in a wok, a dome-shaped cover is used, which causes condensed steam to run down the inside of the cover rather than drip directly onto the food being cooked. Food to be steamed is placed on racks above the water inside the cover. Some types of food, such as filled dumplings, can also be steamed in stacking bamboo steamers with their own lids. Several different foods can be cooked at the same time this way, saving time, space and fuel. See also CHOPSTICKS; COOKING, CHINESE.

WOKOU See PIRATES.

WOLONG NATURE RESERVE See MONKEY; PANDA; SICHUAN PROVINCE.

WOMAN WARRIOR, THE See KINGSTON, MAXINE HONG.

WOMEN IN CHINA See ALL-CHINA WOMEN'S FEDERATION; BAN GU AND BAN ZHAO; BAREFOOT DOCTOR; BUCK, PEARL SYDENSTRICKER; CIXI, EMPRESS DOWAGER; CODE FOR WOMEN; CONCUBINAGE; DAI ALIAN; DENG YINGCHAO; DIAO CHAN; DING LING; FAMILY STRUCTURE; FILM STUDIOS; FOOTBINDING; GONG LI; HAN SUYIN; HU DIE; INTERNATIONAL WORKING WOMEN'S DAY; JIANG QING; KAN YUE-SAI; KINGSTON, MAXINE HONG; LI QINGZHAO; LU, LISA; MARRIAGE LAW OF 1950; ONE-CHILD FAMILY CAMPAIGN; PHOENIX; PINYANG, PRINCESS; SMEDLEY, AGNES; SOONG QINGLING; SOONG MEI-LING; TAN, AMY; THREE GORGES WATER CONSERVANCY PROJECT; WANG YANI; WANG ZHAOJUN; WEDDINGS, TRADITIONAL; WU, EMPRESS; XISHI; XUN GUANNIANG; YANG GUIFEI; ZHAO MENGFU AND GUAN DAOSHENG.

WOODBLOCK PRINTING See PRINTING; WOODCUTS.

WOODCUT (*muke*) An art form that has become very popular in China. Woodcuts are prints made by cutting a picture or design into a block of wood and pressing it onto paper using paint in one or more colors. Although the Chinese had been printing texts with carved wooden blocks for centuries, woodcut pictures were introduced into China only in the 1920s, when Chinese artists and writers were caught up in the revolutionary fervor sweeping Chinese cities. In 1931 the great revolutionary writer Lu Xun (Lu Hsun) established a woodcut study group that encouraged the growth of this new art form in China. Chinese woodcut artists were initially influenced by Western designs, but when the Chinese Communists established an art academy at their headquarters at Yan'an in Shaanxi Province in the 1930s, woodcut artists began adapting traditional Chinese folk designs. Woodcuts, relatively easy and inexpensive to make, proved a good medium for artists to spread their revolutionary message in a form that Chinese peasants and workers could appreciate. The small black and white prints depicted their struggles to end the social conditions that subjected them to lives of hard labor and suffering. After the Chinese Communists founded the People's Republic of China in 1949, woodcut artists began working in colors and incorporating a wider range of subjects, such as landscapes.

Three major schools of woodcuts have developed since the 1920s. The Sichuan school depicts the lives of people belonging to China's national minority ethnic groups, especially nomadic herders. The Jiangsu school portrays the lives and customs of people inhabiting the areas around the rivers and lakes south of the Yangzi River (Changjiang). The third school, known for using strong colors, depicts forests and snow-covered landscapes of northern China. New woodcut schools are also beginning to develop. In 1980, Chinese woodcut artists founded the China Graphic Art Association, which enables artists to share information and sponsors academic discussions of woodcuts. The Chinese like to hang colorful folk-art woodcuts during the New Year Festival (also called the Spring Festival). They originated during the Ming dynasty (1368–1644) with Tang Yin, a scholar who retired to the Taohuawu district of Suzhou in Jiangsu Province. Many New Year woodcut workshops became established in Taohuawu. They still produce woodcuts that depict the daily lives of Chinese people south of the Yangzi River. See also CIVIL WAR BETWEEN COMMUNISTS AND NATIONALISTS; LU XUN; MINORITIES, NATIONAL; NEW YEAR FESTIVAL; PRINTING.

WORK UNIT (*danwei*)   A system by which the Communist government of the People's Republic of China, founded in 1949, organized Chinese workers to handle all aspects of their lives. The work unit is the primary organization through which the Chinese government controls its citizens politically, economically and socially. Workers must go through their work units to get housing permits in cities and leases for land in the countryside; ration coupons for food and other necessary items; permission to change jobs, marry and have a child; entrance to schools and hospitals; and passports to travel or study in other cities or countries. Large work units also offer social services for workers such as day care, recreation facilities, medical clinics and schools. The work unit in modern China performs many functions comparable to the traditional extended family or clan, which was formerly the group with which individuals identified.

Government work units give jobs in administrative offices, research institutes and large factories, and provide their workers with stable salaries and lifetime employment, free health care and pensions. Collective work units staff the entire agricultural sphere as well as smaller factories and workshops. Their members usually make lower salaries and do not always receive health care, pensions and other benefits that government workers do. However, all work units care for people who have chronic illnesses, old people with no families to care for them and families whose chief wage earner is injured or severely ill. Workers commonly belong to the same work unit their entire lives. One village may comprise a work unit. People are either born into their work units or enter them when they begin their first jobs. The system of lifetime membership in a work unit has been called the "iron rice bowl." However, the rapid growth of the private sector in the 1990s has begun breaking down the work unit system. Layoffs are climbing and official urban unemployment rose above 3 percent in 1997. State enterprises plan to cut more than 30 million jobs. See also PEOPLE'S REPUBLIC OF CHINA.

WORLD WAR I   World War I broke out in 1914 in Europe between the Allied forces and Germany. Yuan Shikai (Yuan Shih-k'ai; 1859–1916), a Chinese warlord who had become president of the Republic of China, established in 1912, immediately declared China's neutrality. Japan joined the Allied forces in 1914, declared war on Germany, and seized Shandong Province in China. The Qing dynasty (1644–1911), China's last imperial dynasty, had given Germany concessions in Shandong in the late 19th century, and Japan claimed these concessions for itself when it joined the war. Japan had defeated China in the Sino-Japanese War of 1894–95. In 1915 Japan sent Yuan Shikai a secret document listing 21 demands, known as the Twenty-One Demands on China, which were very harsh and would make China a protectorate of Japan. Yuan Shikai, whom Japan promised to support, gave in to these demands, which not only angered the Chinese people but also shocked the whole world. Japan sent a large number of troops into Shandong and the southern part of Manchuria (northeastern China), and Japanese naval fleets sailed into Chinese harbors. However, the Chinese resisted so strongly that Japan dropped many of the Twenty-One Demands for the time being, although the Chinese government did recognize Japan's authority over southern Manchuria and eastern Inner Mongolia. In 1917, Britain, France and Italy secretly agreed to the Japanese claim on Chinese territory in exchange for Japanese naval support against Germany. The United States also agreed to let Japan have a "special interest in China." These foreign powers felt that having Japan as an ally would help counter the power of the Bolsheviks who had taken over Russia in the October Revolution of 1917.

Yuan Shikai had declared himself the new Chinese emperor on January 1, 1916, but Chinese and foreign opposition convinced him to restore republican rule on March 22. He died on June 6, 1916. After an unsuccessful attempt to restore the last Qing emperor, China became divided among warlords until Chiang Kai-shek (1887–1975) established the Nationalist (Kuomintang; KMT) government at Nanjing in 1928. Meanwhile, in 1916 Duan Qirui (Tuan Ch'i-jui; 1865–1936) succeeded Yuan Shikai as the Chinese premier in Beijing. China entered World War I in 1917 by declaring war on Germany in hopes of getting back Shandong, but in 1918, the Chinese government in Beijing made a secret agreement with Japan giving Shandong to Japan. In 1919 this agreement was made public at the Paris Peace Conference. The Treaty of Versailles contained an international agreement to award

Japan all of Germany's former concessions in China, which made the Chinese people furious. On May 4, 1919, Chinese students held massive demonstrations that escalated into the nationwide protest against Japan known as the May Fourth Movement. The Chinese government finally recognized the validity of the protest and instructed the Chinese delegates at Versailles to walk out and not sign the peace treaty. The problem of Shandong Province was finally settled at the Washington Conference of 1921–22, where a bilateral treaty between Japan and China returned Shandong to Chinese control. See also LEAGUE OF NATIONS AND CHINA; MANCHURIA; MAY FOURTH MOVEMENT OF 1919; SHANDONG PROVINCE; SINO-JAPANESE WAR OF 1894–95; TWENTY-ONE DEMANDS ON CHINA; WARLORD PERIOD; YUAN SHIKAI.

WORLD WAR II See BETHUNE, NORMAN; BURMA ROAD; CHIANG KAI-SHEK; CHINESE COMMUNIST PARTY; CHONGQING; CIVIL WAR BETWEEN COMMUNISTS AND NATIONALISTS; EIGHTH ROUTE ARMY; FLYING TIGERS; LIN BIAO; LIU BOCHENG; MANCHUKUO; MANCHURIAN INCIDENT; MAO ZEDONG; MARCO POLO BRIDGE INCIDENT; NATIONALIST PARTY; PENG DEHUAI; STILWELL, JOSEPH; UNITED NATIONS AND CHINA; WANG JINGWEI; WAR OF RESISTANCE AGAINST JAPAN; ZHU DE.

WOUKOU See PIRATES.

WRITING SYSTEM, CHINESE The Chinese language is written with characters that are pictorial symbols, or ideographs, not with a phonetic alphabet. The characters are traditionally written with a brush and ink using a specified number and order of brush strokes, ranging from one to 24, and are composed in vertical columns from right to left. Members of the literati or scholar-gentry class that staffed the imperial bureaucracy kept in their studies the so-called Four Treasures necessary for writing, which include the brush, paper, an inkstick and an inkstone on which the inkstick is rubbed to produce grounds that are mixed with water to make ink. Fine writing or calligraphy is a highly appreciated art in China, along with landscape painting and poetry, all of which are composed with a brush and ink. Calligraphy has an aesthetic beauty but is also believed to express the inner nature of the person who writes it.

Legendary emperor Fuxi (Fu Hsi; according to legend 2953–2838 B.C.) is credited with inventing the Chinese system for writing using pictorial symbols. The oldest surviving characters date from the 18th century B.C. and are ideographs scratched onto tortoise shells used to divine the future. Ancient characters were simple pictographs with a few lines that resembled the things they represented. Over the centuries the art of calligraphy became more complex as the written characters became more abstract. The various systems for writing characters used in different states in China were unified into one standard system by Emperor Qin Shi Huangdi (259–210 B.C.), who unified China politically under the Qin dynasty (221–206 B.C.). During the next few centuries, several different types of script were developed, ranging from a square clerical style to an informal cursive, or "running," style. A dictionary called *The Explanation of Writing* (*Shuo Wen*), compiled around A.D. 100, classified written characters by their "radicals," or basic pictures that

convey meaning. Altogether the Chinese written language has 214 radicals, examples of which are man, woman, child, heart and water. This system of radicals is still used in Chinese dictionaries. A character is found by picking out the radical, which is usually on the left, top or bottom of the character, and then counting the total number of strokes added to the radical. Some characters have two radicals in them, so finding them in a dictionary can be very difficult. The single writing system has remained the same throughout all of China, despite the many dialects spoken in different regions. The two largest dialects are Mandarin in the north and Cantonese in Guangdong Province in southern China. Chinese people who speak different dialects and thus cannot understand each other orally can readily communicate by writing. Chinese students learn to write by arduously copying characters over and over again to memorize both how to write and to pronounce them. They also copy works of calligraphy by great past masters. See also CALLIGRAPHY; FOUR TREASURES OF THE STUDY; LANGUAGE, CHINESE.

WU, EMPRESS (Wu Zhao or Wu Chao; c. 627–705)   The only woman who ever ruled China in her own right; also known as Wu Zetian (Wu Tse-t'ien). Empress Wu has a controversial reputation as a skillful but ruthless ruler. She was born Wu Zetian to a wealthy family. She married Li Zhi (Li Chih), the third emperor of the Tang dynasty (618–907), known as Emperor Gaozong (Kao-tsung; r. 649–83), after having his wife killed. She had been a concubine in the harem of his father, Emperor Taizong (T'ai-tsung). Her father had assisted Li Shimin, the founder of the Tang dynasty, and had been minister of public works. After marrying, Empress Wu gave birth to four sons, which secured her position as empress. She began handling the affairs of state when the emperor suffered a stroke in 660. Because Empress Wu's husband was weak, she wielded the actual power through him and then through the young rulers who succeeded him, after ruthlessly getting rid of all the government ministers who opposed her. When he died in 683, his will asserted that all important matters should be decided by Empress Wu. After removing several of her husband's successors in turn, including one of her sons, she placed her youngest son on the throne as emperor, but kept him a prisoner and placed all imperial power in her own hands, ruling as empress dowager for six years.

Empress Wu moved the imperial capital east from Chang'an (modern Xi'an) to Luoyang. The old aristocratic families of the Tang were from the Chang'an region in northwestern China, and this move weakened their power. Empress Wu's nephew became head of the faction that aimed to establish a new dynasty with her as ruler. She decreed that her ancestors had royal rank and built an imperial ancestral temple for them at Luoyang. This sparked a revolt against her, which she crushed within three months. To prevent further rebellions, she established a system of secret police and informers. She also broadened her power base among the intellectuals who ran the imperial bureaucracy by promoting men from the lower classes who had passed the examinations, thus further weakening the aristocratic clans. These examination graduates became a small elite, loyal to her, within the government.

In 688, Empress Wu and her secret police crushed a revolt of Tang princes who plotted against her and got rid of nearly all members of the imperial family. In 689 she held several ceremonies that made her the official ruler of China. A women ruler was entirely against the tradition of Confucius, which was the orthodox school of thought, but justification for her rule was found in the scriptures of Buddhism, a religion that had been introduced into China from India around the first century A.D. Empress Wu was a patron of the Buddhist cave temples and sculptures that were carved at Longmen south of the imperial capital of Luoyang between the late fifth and seventh centuries. On September 24, 690, she was proclaimed the emperor of a new Zhou dynasty. She raised the members of her clan to princely rank and promoted the government officials who supported her. Only when she became very ill were those who supported the restoration of the Tang dynasty able to do so. They placed Empress Wu's third son on the throne, and his younger brother succeeded him. Empress Wu died a natural death, and the records of her unique reign were never destroyed. See also BUDDHISM; CHANGAN; CONCUBINE; EMPEROR; LI SHIMIN; LONGMEN CAVE TEMPLES AND SCULPTURES; LUOYANG; TANG DYNASTY.

WU, GORDON Y. S. (1935–) A wealthy Hong Kong businessman who is the biggest single investor in the People's Republic of China (PRC). Until it reverted to China in 1997, Hong Kong was a Crown Colony of Great Britain, which acquired the island after it defeated China in the Opium War (1839–42). Wu was the seventh of nine children of a wealthy Hong Kong businessman, but he built his own financial empire. He received an engineering degree from Princeton University in New Jersey in 1958. When his father retired in 1969, Wu persuaded him to give him a bank guarantee so that he could arrange a loan from the Hongkong and Shanghai Banking Corporation to start his own business. Wu eventually became one of the wealthiest men in Hong Kong.

Wu built the first superhighway in the PRC, in the southern province of Guangdong, which includes the major port city of Guangzhou (Canton) and three Special Economic Zones (SEZs) established by the PRC government in 1980 to encourage foreign trade and investment in China. Companies in Hong Kong, located in the Pearl River delta 80 miles southeast of Guangzhou, employ about 6 million Chinese in the PRC, mainly as factory workers. Wu's highway and a railroad line connect Hong Kong and Guangzhou. Wu has also developed major electric power projects in the PRC and across Asia as far as Pakistan. He has built a mass-transit system in Bangkok, Thailand, and has financial interests in numerous hotel, office and residential properties. In 1995 Wu promised $100 million to the engineering school at Princeton, the largest single gift ever given to the university. He had already given Princeton large donations that totaled about $14 million. See also GUANGDONG PROVINCE; GUANGZHOU; HONG KONG; HONGKONG AND SHANGHAI BANKING CORPORATION; OVERSEAS CHINESE; PEARL RIVER; SPECIAL ECONOMIC ZONES.

WU, HARRY (1934–) A famous contemporary Chinese activist for human rights. Wu was born to a wealthy family in Shanghai, where his father was a banker. In April 1960, when he was a senior at the Geology Institute in Beijing, Chinese Communist authorities arrested him and forced him to spend 19 years in 12 different prison labor camps, known collectively as the Laogai (literally, "Reform through Work"). Chinese prisoners are subjected to routine starvation, torture and forced labor, including the manufacture of many products sold in the United States; the Laogai comprise the world's largest system of forced labor camps.

Wu was released from prison in 1979 and moved to the United States. He recorded his experiences in two memoirs, *Bitter Winds* and *Troublemaker*, and also wrote a book on Chinese prisons, *Laogai—The Chinese Gulag*. He risked his life by returning to the People's Republic of China (PRC) four times to expose the prison labor camps by documenting them with films and photographs. He took a video camera and recorded prison interviews and undercover footage of factories in the camps. Wu's video, *Chinese Prison Labor: Inside China's Gulag,* televised in the United States, shows how China sells hundreds of millions of dollars of goods to the West that have been produced in its system of 2,000 Laogai. He documented the imprisonment, brainwashing and torture that the Chinese government still inflicts on more than a half-million Chinese political prisoners to "reform their thoughts." Wu also appeared on the television shows *60 Minutes* and *20/20*. On June 19, 1995, he was arrested as he attempted to enter the PRC once more through Kazakhstan, which borders Xinjiang-Uighur Autonomous Region in western China. The Chinese government tried and convicted him of stealing state secrets and sentenced him to 15 years in prison, but on August 23 expelled him from the country. The United States had made Wu's release a condition during trade negotiations with the People's Republic of China. Wu returned to the United States, where he continued his struggle for civil rights in China. He established the Laogai Research Foundation, of which he is the executive director, in Washington, D.C. On September 8, 1995, Wu and his wife, Ching Lee Wu, who led the campaign for his release from detention in China in 1995, testified at a hearing before a committee of the U.S. House of Representatives investigating political repression in the PRC. She also LEGAL SYSTEM; PEOPLE'S REPUBLIC OF CHINA; XINJIANG-UIGHUR AUTONOMOUS REGION.

WU, KINGDOM OF (222–280) See JIANGSU PROVINCE; NANJING; ROMANCE OF THE THREE KINGDOMS; THREE KINGDOMS PERIOD; WESTERN AND EASTERN JIN DYNASTIES; WUHAN; XI SHI; YANGZHOU.

WU, KINGDOM OF (902–937) See TEN KINGDOMS PERIOD.

WU CHANGSHI (Wu Ch'ang-shih; 1844–1927) A prominent calligrapher and painter who specialized in painting flowers. Wu Changshi was born to a family of the literati or scholar class in Zhejiang Province. He passed the examinations for the imperial bureaucracy and held official positions for a short time. From the time he was a young man, Wu carved seals that people used to print their names in red ink. He drew upon seal calligraphy styles from the Qin (221–206 B.C.) and Han (206 B.C.–A.D. 220) dynasties for his own seal script. He specialized in a style taken from the "Stone Drum Inscriptions," an example of the ancient Great Seal (*Dazhuan* or *Ta-Chuan*) script, which has been influential on modern carvers, as has Wu's own work. These drums inscribed with calligraphy were found in Shaanxi Province. Wu also wrote calligraphy in the informal, abbreviated style known as running script. He also used calligraphic brushstrokes in his famous paintings of flowers such as winter plum. Critics regard his flower paintings as some of the finest that have been done since the so-called Eight Eccentrics of Yangzhou. See also BIRD-AND-FLOWER PAINTING; CALLIGRAPHY; EIGHT ECCENTRICS OF YANGZHOU; INK PAINTING; SEALS.

WU CHAO See WU, EMPRESS.

WU CHING-TZU See SCHOLARS, THE.

WU DAOZI (Wu Tao-tzu; c. 700–c. 770) The greatest painter of the Tang dynasty (618–907). However, none of his works have survived because he was a member of the Buddhist religion, which had been introduced into China from India and was persecuted by the Chinese in the ninth century. Wu Daozi was praised in critical works by Zhang Yanyuan (Chang Yen-yuan), who asserted that Wu was the only artist who had completely mastered all the principles of painting, and that Wu's art was characterized by the utmost creative vitality. Wu certainly helped bring about a new style in Chinese landscape painting. It has been recorded that he painted freely with bold brush strokes, in contrast to the delicate brushwork of early Tang painters; thus, Chinese critics described his style as "violent," like the arrival of a sudden storm. Some paintings that are supposedly copies of Wu's works have survived, but their veracity is questionable. The same is true for stone engravings that were said to be taken from his drawings. A stone engraving in the Santai Cave at Nanjing was supposedly taken from Wu's portrait of Wen Guanyin, the Buddhist goddess of mercy. Wall paintings in Horyuji Temple in Nara, Japan, were associated with the art of Wu Daozi, but these were damaged by fire after World War II and thus their attribution cannot be determined. Altogether Wu painted 300 frescoes in Buddhist temples, but these have disappeared along with his other works. Some of the frescoes in the cave temples at Dunhuang in the Chinese province of Gansu may show influence from Wu. According to records, Wu also executed a painting on silk of the legendary Yellow Emperor that was hung on the wall like a fresco. See BUDDHISM; DUNHUANG CAVE PAINTINGS AND CARVINGS.

WU JINGZI See SCHOLARS, THE.

WU LI (1632–1718) A landscape painter from Jiangsu Province in eastern China who is considered one of the Six Great Masters of the Qing dynasty (1644–1911). These painters worked in the style of the literati (wenren) or scholar gentry class, following the example of paintings by Dong Qichang (Tung Ch'i-ch'ang; 1555–1636), and practiced calligraphy and poetry as well. Their works contain many details from paintings of earlier centuries, notably the Southern Song School. However, Wu Li also produced some paintings that are more personally expressive, and others that are very realistic in their portrayal of typical landscape features such as hills and valleys. The mountains in his

landscape paintings are often strongly painted as vertical piles of large boulders or as complex and twisted forms. When Wu Li was in his 40s he converted to Christianity, which had been introduced to China by Roman Catholic Jesuit missionaries, and studied Christian theology for six years in Macao, an island just south of Guangzhou (Canton) where the Portuguese were established. He was ordained a Jesuit priest in 1688 when he was 56 years old, and spent the rest of his life working as a missionary in Jiangsu.

Wu Li's religious beliefs never altered the Chinese style of his paintings. He gave himself the art name "Daoist of the Inkwell" (Mojing Daoren or Mo-ching Tao-jen) after the native Chinese religion of Daoism. He stopped painting for a while following his Christian conversion, but then resumed painting in the literati style until he died. See also CHRISTIANITY; DAOISM; DONG QICHANG; JESUITS; LANDSCAPE PAINTING; LITERATI.

WU RIVER See GUIZHOU PROVINCE.

WU SANGUI (SAN-KUEI), GENERAL See DORGON; GREAT WALL; LI ZICHENG; QING DYNASTY.

WU SCHOOL OF PAINTING The most important group of Chinese landscape painters during the late 15th and early 16th centuries (Ming dynasty; 1368–1644). The school was named for Wu County (Wuxian or Wu-hsien) in the region of modern Suzhou, the city in Jiangsu Province where the artists worked, at that time the artistic center of China. Shen Zhou (Shen Chou; 1427–1509) is considered the founder of the Wu School, although he is the most prominent in a long line of painters in Wu that can be traced back to the Tang dynasty (618–907). Shen's student, Wen Zhengming (Wen Cheng-ming; 1470–1559), was another major Wu artist. Members of the Wu School belonged to the literati, or scholar class that staffed the imperial bureaucracy, and painted in the style of "literati painting" (wenrenhua or wen-jen-hua). Serious painters, they were termed "amateurs" to distinguish them from professional court painters. Many of them had retired from government positions and spent their lives quietly dedicated to painting, calligraphy, poetry writing and gardening. The Chinese have always considered calligraphy, writing with a brush and ink, a fine art. Members of the Wu School were inspired by the expressive styles of earlier Chinese artists such as the so-called Four Masters of the Yuan dynasty (1279–1368), which included Ni Zan (Ni Tsan; 1301–74) and Huang Gongwang (Huang Kung-wang; 1269–1354). Paintings by members of the Wu School are characterized by delicate and subtle complexity and allusions to Chinese classical texts. The painters or their friends frequently inscribed poems on the paintings to enhance the mood or theme that was expressed. See also CALLIGRAPHY; HUANG GONGWANG; INK PAINTING; LANDSCAPE PAINTING; LITERATI; NI ZAN; SHEN ZHOU; SUZHOU; WEN ZHENMING.

WU TAI (WU T'AI) See FIVE DYNASTIES PERIOD.

WU TAO-TZU See WU DAOZI.

WU TSE-T'IEN, EMPRESS See WU, EMPRESS.

WU WEI (1459–1508)   One of the finest painters of Chinese landscapes in the style of the Southern Song School. He also used the names Shiying (Shih-ying), Lufu and Ciweng (Tz'u-weng). Wu Wei was born in Hubei Province. He had a very unhappy childhood. At age 17 he traveled to Nanjing, which had been the first capital of the Ming dynasty (1368–1644). He became notorious for his eccentric, carefree behavior, yet he was able to gain a position in the private secretariat of Zhuyi, Duke of the State of Cheng. Emperor Chenghua (1465–88) brought Wu Wei to the capital at Beijing to serve as a professional painter in the Ming imperial court, which tolerated his heavy drinking and unusual manners. Once, while drunk, he painted a remarkable scene of mountain peaks, pine trees and clouds by pouring ink onto a silk scroll and smearing it until the images appeared. The emperor praised him by saying that it was the work of an "Immortal." While the emperor admired Wu Wei's art, the eunuchs who staffed the imperial palace treated him badly because he would not give them free paintings, so he left Beijing and went back to Nanjing. Emperor Hongzhi (Hung-chih; r. 1488–1506) brought him back to the court in Beijing and even awarded him a seal inscribed "Foremost Painter." Yet Wu Wei preferred to return to Nanjing and spent most of his life there among the common people, who gave him the inspiration for his art.

Wu Wei was expert at both figure and landscape paintings and was skilled at using a variety of brush techniques. He specialized in painting human figures in his landscapes, particularly scenes of fishing villages. He is associated with the Zhe (Che) school, named for Zhejiang Province, the home of the major landscape painter Dai Jin (Tai Chin; 1388–1455). Members of the Zhe school employed the techniques and forms of the Ma-Xia (Ma-Hsia) school of painting, named for Ma Yuan (fl. c. 1190–1225) and Xia Gui (Hsia Kuei; fl. c. 1180–1224), but exercised more freedom of expression. Wu Wei's own style is very strong, dynamic and bold, the same as his personality. See also DAI JIN; FIGURE PAINTING; LANDSCAPE PAINTING; MING DYNASTY; SOUTHERN SCHOOL OF PAINTING.

WU WEI   See DAODEJING; DAOISM; LAOZI; ZHUANGZI.

WU ZETIAN, EMPRESS   See WU, EMPRESS.

WU ZHAO   See WU, EMPRESS.

WUCHANG   See WUHAN.

WUCHANG UPRISING   An uprising on October 10, 1911, in Wuchang (part of modern Wuhan), the capital of Hubei Province in central China, which marked the start of the revolution that overthrew the Qing dynasty (1644–1911) and established the Republic of China (1912–49). There had already been many demonstrations and brief uprisings against the Qing throughout China. The Wuchang Uprising was led by radical members of the modernized Chinese New Army of the Qing dynasty. Many of the radicals who had joined the New Army in Wuchang and the nearby city of Hankou were young students who had studied in Japan; some were members of the Revolutionary Alliance (Tongmenghui or T'ung-meng-hui) led by Sun Yat-sen (1866–1925).

On October 9 a bomb accidentally exploded while revolutionaries were making bombs in Hankou. The Qing government discovered the revolutionary soldiers' ammunition dump and got hold of a secret list of army officers who had been planning to lead an anti-Qing uprising. To prevent their being arrested or killed, the revolutionary soldiers in Wuchang decided to act immediately. On October 10 the Wuchang Eighth Engineer Battalion seized the Qing ammunition dump and attacked the office of the governor-general of Hubei. Transport and artillery units stationed nearby joined in the mutiny. The governor-general and the commander of the local garrison decided to flee rather than fight the rebels. The revolutionaries forced Li Yuanhong (Li Yuanhung), a commander of a brigade of the Hubei New Army, to become military governor. They had won a greater victory than they had ever expected. Their revolt spread to other Chinese cities, and members of the Revolutionary Alliance demonstrated all over China in support of the troops that had revolted at Wuchang. By the end of November, 15 of China's 24 provinces, including most of the provinces south of the Yangzi River, declared that they were independent of the Qing. On January 1, 1912, Sun was inaugurated in Nanjing as the provisional president of the Republic of China, and Li Yuanhong was inaugurated as the vice president. See also HUBEI PROVINCE; QING DYNASTY; REPUBLIC OF CHINA; REVOLUTIONARY ALLIANCE; SUN YAT-SEN.

WU-CHING   See FIVE CLASSICS OF CONFUCIANISM.

WUDANG, MOUNT   See FIVE SACRED MOUNTAINS OF DAOISM; HUBEI PROVINCE.

WUDI (EMPEROR) (Wu-ti; r. 141–87 B.C.)   Known as Han Wudi; the fifth and most powerful emperor of the Han dynasty (206 B.C.–A.D. 220). His real name was Liu Che; Wudi, meaning "Martial Emperor," is his reign name. Wudi completed the process by which Han emperors broke down the power of the old aristocratic families that had controlled the Chinese feudal states. Their authority was replaced by a complex imperial bureaucracy developed to govern the Chinese empire. Confucianism, the school of thought founded by Confucius (551–479 B.C.), became predominant in China during Wudi's reign. In 136 B.C. Wudi took the advice of the Confucian thinker Dong Zhongshu (Tung Chung-shu; c. 179–104 B.C.) and proclaimed Confucianism the official philosophy of the Chinese state. Wudi also developed the system of examinations used to select scholars educated in the Five Classics of Confucianism for positions in the imperial bureaucracy, and in 124 B.C. he established a Confucian imperial university in the Han capital of Chang'an (modern Xi'an) to train scholars to become the highest government officials. Sima Qian (Ssu-ma Ch'ien; c. 145–90 B.C.), the first great Chinese historian, wrote a comprehensive history of China up to the time of Wudi, which became a model for later Chinese historians. Poetry flourished during Wudi's reign, and the emperor patronized the poet Sima Xiangru (Ssu-ma Hsiang-ju; 179–117 B.C.). Wudi made three pilgrimages to Taishan (Mount Tai), the sacred mountain in modern Shandong Province, to offer sacrifices to Heaven, which legitimized the reign of a virtuous emperor by giving him the so-called Mandate of Heaven.

Emperor Wudi subscribed to the Confucian view that the ruler should benefit his people. He stabilized food prices by constructing public granaries and ordering government officials in the provinces to buy grain when the price was low and sell it when there was a famine. Wudi had to deal with nomadic tribes to the north of the Great Wall, especially the Xiongnu (Hsiung-nu), who made frequent raids south into China. His military forces spent a half-century fighting the nomads, which nearly bankrupted the Chinese economy. The Han Chinese emperors had been presenting expensive gifts to the Xiongnu to coerce them to patrol the lands along the Great Wall, but Wudi abandoned this policy. When this did not stop the nomadic raids, he sent troops to fight them. He raised money for his army by making salt and iron imperial monopolies. Zhang Qian (Chang Ch'ien; d. 114 B.C.), a Han envoy sent westward to mobilize Central Asian tribes against the Xiongnu, got as far as modern Afghanistan and brought back information about the region, such as descriptions of the horses bred there that the Chinese could use for military purposes. His explorations enabled the opening of the Silk Road along which the Chinese traded valuable goods with Central Asia and the Middle East. Zhang Qian was sent on a second mission to the horse-breeding tribes of Central Asia, which gained 1,000 horses for the Chinese. Emperor Wudi then sent a military expedition that extended the Chinese empire westward to the Ferghana Basin beyond the Pamir Mountain Range. He also sent military expeditions south as far as modern Vietnam and brought the regions of Sichuan, Tibet, Yunnan and Guizhou, as well as the southern kingdom of Nanyue around modern Guangzhou (Canton), under Chinese suzerainty; and northeast, where garrisons were established to protect overland trade routes to the Korean peninsula and a Han government was established in Korea. Wudi extended the Han Empire to its greatest size, but after he died the Han went into decline. His youngest son Zhao Di (Chao-ti) succeeded him as Emperor Zhaodi (r. 87–74 B.C.). See also CONFUCIANISM; DONG ZHONGSHU; FIVE CLASSICS OF CONFUCIANISM; HAN DYNASTY; HORSE; IMPERIAL BUREAUCRACY; IMPERIAL EXAMINATION SYSTEM; MANDATE OF HEAVEN; SILK ROAD; SIMA QIAN; SIMA XIANGRU; TAISHAN; XIONGNU.

WUFAN MOVEMENT See THREE-ANTI AND FIVE-ANTI CAMPAIGNS.

WUGUI See TORTOISE.

WUHAN The capital city of Hubei Province in central China, with a population of more than 3 million. Wuhan is an extremely important city because of its location on the Yangzi River (Changjiang). Although 600 miles upriver from Shanghai, Wuhan is a port for oceangoing ships of up to 8,000 tons. Wuhan lies about halfway between the major southern city of Guangzhou (Canton) and the northern capital city of Beijing, and has a central position on the main east-west water route and on the major north-south railway line. It is one of the few industrial cities in China's interior. Industrial sites were constructed in Wuhan as part of China's First Five-Year Plan (1953–57). Great quantities of iron and steel are produced in Wuhan and made into agricultural machinery, rail cars, trucks and machine tools. Other important products include chemi-cals, building materials, textiles, bicycles, electronics and processed foods. Rice, wheat, tea and cotton are cultivated.

Wuhan is actually a combination of three towns—Wuchang, Hanyang and Hankou—that developed on the banks of three rivers that join at this point: the Yangzi, the Han and the Xiang. The name Wuhan is composed of a character taken from the name Wuchang and one that is shared by Hanyang and Hankou. The towns were connected in 1957 by the Changjiang Bridge across the Yangzi. This bridge enabled north and south China to be connected by railroads for the first time. The mile-long bridge is 280 feet high and has two levels, one for trains and one for cars and trucks. Flooding of the river was a serious problem before dikes were reinforced to protect the city. Winters are mild but summers are extremely hot and humid, giving Wuhan the reputation of being a "Furnace of the Yangzi."

Settlement of this area goes back more than 3,000 years. During the third century A.D., Wuchang, on the right bank of the Yangzi, was capital of the state of Wu; during the Yuan dynasty (1279–1368) it was capital of a large provincial region that extended all the way to the South China Sea. In the Ming dynasty (1368–1644) it remained a provincial capital but with a much reduced area. Hanyang, directly opposite Wuchang on the Yangzi's left bank, was a walled town with a history going back 1,300 years. Hankou, also on the left bank but on the other side of the Han River, was a small fishing village until concessions given to European powers caused it to develop after the Treaty of Nanjing (1868), which ended the Opium Wars in which Great Britain defeated China. Today Wuhan is the third-most important military center in China. The Revolution of 1911 against the Qing dynasty (1644–1911) led by Dr. Sun Yat-sen began in Wuhan (Wuchang), when a revolutionary bomb went off there ahead of schedule and rioting broke out, which triggered uprisings all over China. The Chinese Communists set up the National Peasant Movement Institute in Wuhan for political training; Mao Zedong (Mao Tse-tung) headed it in 1927. In 1949, battles in which Chinese Communists defeated Chinese Nationalist (Kuomintang) forces led to the final victory of the Communists. The Hubei Provincial Museum has exhibits on the history of the region, including the revolutionary activities there. Tourist sites in Wuhan include Sun Yat-sen Park, Red Hill Park, Snake Hill, the Temple of Eternal Spring, East Lake, Tortoise Hill, Guiyuan Buddhist Temple and the Terrace of the Ancient Lute. See also CIVIL WAR BETWEEN COMMUNISTS AND NATIONALISTS; FIVE-YEAR PLANS; HAN RIVER; HUBEI PROVINCE; REVOLUTION OF 1911; SHIPPING AND SHIPBUILDING; TREATY OF NANJING; YANGZI RIVER.

WU-HSING See FIVE MATERIAL AGENTS.

WUHU See ANHUI PROVINCE.

WUJING See FIVE CLASSICS OF CONFUCIANISM.

WU-KUEI See TORTOISE.

WUSHU See KUNG FU; MARTIAL ARTS.

WUSULI INCIDENT (1969) A conflict between China and the U.S.S.R. over the possession of Zhenbao Island in the Wusuli River (Wusulujiang), also known as the Ussuri River. The conflict is also known as the Ussuri incident.

The Wusuli forms the eastern border between Heilongjiang Province in Manchuria (northeastern China) and present-day Russia. During the 19th century, the Qing dynasty (1644–1911) that governed China was weak and Russia was able to take large territories from China. In 1860 Russia claimed all of Manchuria north of the Heilong River (Heilongjiang) and east of the Wusuli River. The U.S.S.R. maintained that a treaty it had signed with China in 1860 placed the border along the Chinese bank of the Wusuli River. In 1954, the Chinese claimed that the border ran along the center of the main channel of the river, giving China navigation rights. Both countries also claimed possession of several hundred islands in the river, including Zhenbao Island.

The government of the People's Republic of China, established in 1949, demanded that the U.S.S.R. admit that it had seized these territories unfairly. The Soviet government refused and immediately changed all Chinese names in the disputed territories to Russian. Starting in the 1960s China and the U.S.S.R. sent military forces to their 4,000-mile border, resulting in occasional conflicts. The Soviet invasion of Czechoslovakia in 1968 made the Chinese very apprehensive about their own border. In March 1969 the dispute came to a head when Chinese and Soviet troops fought two battles over the disputed Zhenbao Island (called Damansky Island by the Russians) in the Wusuli River. In the summer they fought another battle over a border pass in Xinjiang-Uighur Autonomous Region in western China. The two governments held back from further fighting when Soviet premier Alexei Kosygin flew to Beijing to meet with Chinese premier Zhou Enlai (Chou En-lai). China and the U.S.S.R. agreed to hold talks about their border. These discussions began in Beijing in October 1969. Talks were held on and off for many years without reaching a decisive agreement. In a speech in September 1986, Soviet leader Mikhail S. Gorbachev was more conciliatory to the Chinese and agreed with their claim that the border did run along the main channel of the river. See also SINO-SOVIET CONFLICT; WUSULI RIVER.

WUSULI RIVER (Wusulijiang)   Also known as the Ussuri River; a river that forms the eastern border between Heilongjiang Province in northeastern China, a region known as Manchuria, and Russia. The Wusuli River begins where the Ulakhe and Daubikhe Rivers join in Russia, and it flows north-northeast for 365 miles until it joins the Amur River (Heilongjiang) near the Russian city of Kabarovsk. The climate of Manchuria is very harsh and the Wusuli freezes over from mid-November through mid-April. When it is navigable, logs that have been cut in the vast forests are sent down the river. The river has many species of fish; Amur sturgeon is widely fished.

In 1860 Russia took control of all of Manchuria east of the Wusuli River and north of the Amur River. In 1954 China claimed substantial Russian territory along the Wusuli, Amur and Argun rivers, and both countries massed troops along their border, resulting in many clashes. China also claimed the right to navigate the Wusuli. Starting in the 1960s, China and the U.S.S.R. also had many border con-

flicts over islands in the Wusuli River, and in 1969 their troops fought on Zhenbao Island (called Damansky Island by the Russians). In 1987 the two sides finally resumed negotiations about their border dispute although. In November 1997 Russia and China signed a declaration on the final demarcation of their 2,500-mile border. See also AMUR RIVER; HEILONGJIANG PROVINCE; MANCHURIA; SINO-SOVIET CONFLICT.

WUTA (WUTAI), MOUNT   See FOUR SACRED MOUNTAINS OF BUDDHISM.

WU-TI (EMPEROR)   See WUDI, EMPEROR.

WU-TSUNG (EMPEROR) (TANG)   See ENNIN; WUZONG (EMPEROR) (TANG).

WUWANG   See WEN, KING, AND WU, KING.

WUXI   A city on the northern shore of Lake Tai in southern Jiangsu Province that is one of the oldest cities in the Yangzi River (Changjiang) delta. The name Wuxi means "tinless." Tin was mined in this area from the Zhou (1100–256 B.C.) through Han (206 B.C.–220 A.D.) dynasties until it ran out near the end of the Han. The Grand Canal, which runs through the center of Wuxi, was completed in the 13th century and enabled the city to become a distribution center for grain shipped by barge to the capital city of Hangzhou. Merchants grew wealthy as Wuxi developed into one of China's largest grain markets. Although the Grand Canal declined, railroad lines constructed in the 20th century enabled Wuxi to continue as a major trading center. Silk and cotton textiles have long been important industries in Wuxi. The city now has a population of about one million and is also a holiday resort.

The Donglin (Tung-lin; "Eastern Grove") Academy, a center of Confucian studies that had been founded in the 12th century, was reestablished at Wuxi during the 17th century (Ming dynasty; 1368–1644) by a group of scholars opposed to the teachings of the Neo-Confucianist thinker Wang Yangming (1472–1529). Donglin scholars became dominant in the imperial bureaucracy in the capital city of Beijing, but they were brutally purged from the government in 1625 after they ran into conflicts with the eunuch-dictator Wei Zhongxian (Wei Chung-hsien; 1568–1627) under the reign of the Tianqi Emperor (T'ien-ch'i). The group was rehabilitated with the accession of the new emperor in 1629 and held important government positions until the academy was closed when the Qing overthrew the Ming in 1644. Wuxi is also the birthplace of Ni Zan (Ni Tsan; 1301–74), one of the most famous of the literati painters.

Major tourist sites include Xihui Park, which includes two mountains named for the tin was formerly mined here. They are the source for the Second Spring under the Heavens, a famous spring with very pure water that was sent as tribute to the Imperial Court during the Song dynasty (960–1279). Clay figurines are produced here in the shapes of theatrical heroes and masks, peasants and children. Beautiful Plum Garden (Meiyuan) belonged to a high-ranking official of the Qing dynasty (1644–1911) but was purchased in 1911 by the Rong, the wealthiest family in Wuxi. Dragon

Light (Longguang) pagoda offers a panoramic view of Lake Tai. "Turtle's Head" Island (Guitouzhu) and Liyuan Garden are other popular sites. Boat rides on the Grand Canal and Lake Tai are available. The cuisine of Wuxi is famous, especially for eel and crabs from Lake Tai. See also GRAND CANAL; IMPERIAL BUREAUCRACY; JIANGSU PROVINCE; MING DYNASTY; NI ZAN; WANG YANGMING ; YANGZI RIVER.

WUXIA GORGE See THREE GORGES WATER CONSERVANCY PROJECT; YANGZI RIVER.

WUXING See TAI, LAKE; ZHEJIANG PROVINCE.

WUYUE (WU-YUEH) See FIVE SACRED MOUNTAINS OF DAOISM.

WUYUE KINGDOM (908–978) See HANGZHOU; TEN KINGDOMS PERIOD.

WUZING See FIVE MATERIAL AGENTS.

WUZONG (EMPEROR) (Wu-tsung; r. 840–846) An emperor of the Tang dynasty (618–907) best known for his persecution of Buddhists from 841 to 845. Wuzong's predecessor was Emperor Wenzong (Wen-tsung), who died in 840 when he was only 30 years old. Wenzong had attempted to reduce the power of the eunuchs who ran the imperial palace, but the eunuch generals who commanded the palace army had fought back and executed the three chief government ministers and many other high officials. When Wenzong died, the eunuchs did not put the crown prince on the throne but upheld their own candidate, Wuzong, who was the younger brother of Wenzong.

The Buddhist religion had been introduced into China from India around the first century B.C., where it had flourished and produced several native Chinese Buddhist sects.

Confucian-educated scholars who staffed the imperial bureaucracy disliked the foreign religion, especially for its great wealth and its monasticism, which required members to leave their families and give up everything to become monks and nuns. Leaders of the native Chinese religion of Daoism also resented Buddhism's growing influence. Some emperors in previous dynasties had patronized Buddhism as a means of increasing their own power, but in 624 Fu Yi (555–639), the court astrologer, had requested Emperor Gaozu (Kao-tsu), founder of the Tang dynasty, to abolish Buddhism. Tang scholar Han Yu (768–824) had strongly criticized the religion for what he regarded as its superstitious and harmful practices. His criticisms influenced Emperor Wuzong's advisers, who persuaded him to shut down Buddhist monasteries, shrines and temples, some of which were very large, and confiscate Buddhist property. The census for the year 845 records that there were 260,000 Buddhist monks, 4,600 temples and 40,000 shrines. Wuzong forced most of the monks and nuns to return to secular life and become taxpayers, and he destroyed many Buddhist buildings, allowing only one temple in each major prefecture and four at the two capital cities. Huge numbers of Buddhist sculptures, bells and other metal objects were melted down and made into coins, which benefited the Chinese economy. Wuzong's persecution of Buddhism lasted only nine months, but it permanently removed its influence from the Chinese government and gave it the status of a foreign religion once more. The Pure Land and Chan Sects of Buddhism were the best able to survive the persecutions. Other foreign religions in China were also suppressed by Wuzong, such as Nestorian Christianity, Manichaeism and Zoroastrianism. Wuzong died the year after the Buddhist persecution and was succeeded by his uncle, Emperor Xuanzong (Hsuan-tsung). See also BUDDHISM; CHAN SECT OF BUDDHISM; CONFUCIANISM; EUNUCH; HAN YU; MANICHAEISM; NESTORIAN CHRISTIANITY; PURE LAND SECT OF BUDDHISM; TANG DYNASTY.

XANADU See KHUBILAI KHAN; MARCO POLO.

XAVIER, ST. FRANCIS See JESUITS; MACAO.

XI RIVER See LI RIVER AND LING CANAL; WEST RIVER.

XI SHI (Hsi-shih)   A woman in the fifth century B.C. considered the most beautiful of the Four Famous Beauties in Chinese history. Xi Shi lived during the time of Confucius in the Spring and Autumn Period (772–481 B.C.). Her village, Zhuji in modern Zhejiang Province, belonged to the kingdom of Yue on China's east coast, which had been defeated by the powerful kingdom of Wu, and the king of Yue had been made a slave in the Wu court. When he was allowed to return home, he harbored bitter feelings of shame and plotted with his ministers to regain control of the kingdom. One minister scoured the countryside for girls to send to the king of Wu. Finding the beautiful Xi Shi and her friends washing silk in the village stream, he took them to the palace and had them trained for three years in singing, dancing and politics.

Xi Shi was sent as a concubine to the king of Wu with the instructions to use her beauty and talents to distract him from political matters while the kingdom of Yue prepared the people to fight against Wu for their freedom. She lived with the king for 18 years and he fell deeply in love with her. He even built a splendid palace for her with a special hall for her to dance in. The king enjoyed her performances, drank to excess and forgot about a possible threat from the kingdom of Yue. The day came when the Yue army defeated the kingdom of Wu and killed the king. Xi Shi's feelings were torn, because she had spent all those years in Wu working on behalf of her own kingdom yet enjoying a relationship with the king of Wu. Upon learning he had been killed, she consented to return to Yue. The Chinese have greatly respected her for doing her duty out of loyalty to her own country. They have a saying, "Each girl's lover thinks she is as beautiful as Xi Shi." A temple built in Zhuji to honor Xu Shi can still be seen. In 1991 the Xi Shi Palace was built near Xi Shi Pavilion and the site where she washed silk in the river for a living. See also CONCUBINAGE; SPRING AND AUTUMN PERIOD.

XI WANG MU See XIWANGMU.

XIA, WESTERN, DYNASTY (1038–1227) See XIXIA, KINGDOM OF.

XIA DYNASTY   The first Chinese dynasty, with the traditional dates 2200–1750 B.C.. The Xia dynasty is usually thought to be legendary, but now archaeologists do not discount the possibility of unearthing actual Xia artifacts at Neolithic sites such as Longshan. There are also ancient genealogical records that provide the names of 17 rulers who were supposedly Xia emperors. The final emperor is described as a cruel tyrant named Jie, who was overthrown by Tang, first emperor of the Shang dynasty (1750–1040 B.C.). The Shang argued that the Xia deserved to be overthrown because they were no longer virtuous and had therefore lost the "Mandate of Heaven (*tianming* or *t'ien-ming*)." Every subsequent Chinese dynasty employed this concept to validate their overthrow of the previous dynasty.

The founding of the Xia dynasty is attributed to Yu the Great, the third of the mythical Five Emperors who reportedly taught the arts of civilization to the Chinese people. Yu contained the waters of the Great Flood and organized the Chinese to construct water control projects in the Yellow River (Huanghe) Basin, the cradle of Chinese civilization. Little is known about the Xia kings, but they were apparently powerful enough to build large palaces and royal tombs and to extend their sovereignty over part of the North China Plain. In this region, towns had developed into cities by about 2250 B.C. and social classes had emerged with a hierarchy of warrior-rulers, religious leaders, craftsmen and farmers. The kingdom of Xia arose near the modern city of Zhengzhou, the capital of Henan Province in central China. During this era the Chinese moved from the Neolithic period (c. 12,000–2000 B.C.) into the Bronze Age (2200–500 B.C.) as they learned how to cast bronze, an alloy of copper and tin, in pottery molds to make weapons and containers to hold offerings of wine, meat and grain in religious rituals. The Xia and Shang emperors divined the future by reading cracks produced by heating tortoise shells and the shoulder bones of oxen or sheep, known collectively as oracle bones. Many of these have been excavated near Anyang in Henan.

The philosopher Mozi (Mo Tzu; c. 470–391 B.C.), who founded one of the four main schools of thought in ancient China, held up the Xia dynasty as a utopian ideal, when all people supposedly cared for each other as one family. (The Xia dynasty is not to be confused with the Western Xia dynasty [A.D. 1038–1227].) See also ANYANG; BRONZEWARE; HENAN PROVINCE; MANDATE OF HEAVEN; MO ZI; NEOLITHIC PERIOD; NORTH CHINA PLAIN; TANG, KING; YELLOW RIVER; YU, EMPEROR; ZENGZHOU.

XIA GUI (Hsia Kuei; fl. c. 1180–1224)   One of the greatest landscape painters in Chinese history, and the cofounder, with Ma Yuan (fl. c. 1190–1225), of the Ma-Xia (Ma-Hsia) School of painting. The dates of Xia Gui's birth and death are not known. He was born in the vicinity of Hangzhou, the capital of the Southern Song dynasty (1127–1279) and the cultural center of China after the Song court had to flee its northern capital at Kaifeng. Xia Gui served with distinction in the painting division of the Hanlin Academy, the national academy of scholars within the imper-

Thirteenth-century artist Xia Gui is best known for his landscape paintings on handscrolls and on album leaves—like this Sailboat in Rainstorm.   COURTESY, MUSEUM OF FINE ARTS, BOSTON

ial bureaucracy, from about 1200 to 1240. He achieved the rank of *daizhao* (*tai-chao*), "painter in attendance," and was awarded the academy's highest honor, the Golden Belt.

Nothing is known about Xia's artistic training, but he certainly followed the painter Li Tang (Li T'ang; c. 1050–c. 1130), who had developed a powerful style of painting based on the "ax-cut texture stroke" (*fupi cun* or *fu-pi ts'un*), in which the angles of his brush strokes on the rocks in his landscapes seem to have been hacked out by the sides of his painting brush. Xia and Ma Yuan belonged to the Northern Song School of landscape painting but developed a new style by using the bold "ax-cut" brush stroke, in contrast to the delicate brushwork of the Northern Song School. The two painters retained the strength of the Northern style but simplified the composition by opening up more space and providing a new freedom of movement. Xia's strong, energetic style of monochrome ink painting, associated with the Chan (Zen) Sect of Buddhism, had a strong influence on the famous Chan painter Liang Kai (Liang K'ai; early 13th century). Xia's style was extremely important not only in China into the 17th century but also in Japan, where it inspired the monochrome ink landscape paintings of the Muromachi Period (1338–1573), notably those by the great Japanese artist Sesshu (1420–1506). Xia Gui is best known for his paintings on handscrolls and album leaves, the latter of which comprise most of his surviving works. His most famous painting is on a handscroll nearly 30 feet long, "Pure and Remote View of Streams and Mountains," owned by the National Palace Museum in Taipei, Taiwan. See also CHAN SECT OF BUDDHISM; HANGZHOU; HANLIN ACADEMY; INK PAINTING; LANDSCAPE PAINTING; LI TANG; LIANG KAI; MA YUAN; SCROLLS; SOUTHERN SONG DYNASTY.

XIA NAI (Hsia Nai; c. 1910–1985)   A prominent archaeologist who for more than 30 years after the Chinese Communists founded the People's Republic of China (PRC) in 1949 led modern China's archaeological work as director of the Chinese Institute of Archaeology and vice-dean of the Chinese Academy of Social Sciences. After Xia Nai completed his Chinese education, he went to England to study modern archaeological theory and method. During China's War of Resistance against Japan (1937–45; World War II), he undertook excavations in northwestern China. In 1945 he discovered painted pottery shards from the Yangshao Neolithic culture (c. 5000–c. 3000 B.C.) at Qijia Culture tombs in Yangwawan and Ningding, Gansu Province. He was able to establish that Yangshao was older than Qijia, the opposite of the system for dating Gansu's Neolithic culture that Swedish scientist Johan Gunnar Andersson had established. He thus ended the dominance of foreign scholars in Chinese archaeology.

In 1950, the year the Chinese Institute of Archaeology was founded, Xia Nai led the team that began its first excavation, in Huixian County in Henan Province, where they uncovered the remains of 19 wooden chariots from the Warring States Period (403–221 B.C.). Xia Nai later took his team to conduct surveys and excavations in Zhengzhou, Changgao and Mianchi in Henan and in Changsha in Hunan Province. From 1952 to 1955, he organized and conducted four archaeological seminars in the capital city of Beijing and lectured on field archaeology in Luoyang and Zhengzhou. The hundreds of students who attended his lectures went on to become China's leading archaeologists.

From 1956 to 1958, Xia Nai took part in the excavation of the Ming Tombs outside Beijing, the mausoleums of 13 of the 16 emperors of the Ming dynasty (1368–1644), which have since become a popular tourist attraction. For the next two decades, he wrote major scholarly papers and completed important research projects, mainly on the history of Chinese science and technology and the history of China's interaction with other countries. He relied upon new discoveries of ancient silk textiles and foreign coins to develop theories about economic and cultural relations between ancient China and regions of Central and Western Asia, especially Persia (modern Iran) and eastern regions of the Roman empire, which traded with China along the so-called Silk Road. He also used artifacts to explain ancient Chinese developments in mathematics, astrology, chemistry, metallurgy—especially bronzeware—and textile production.

Under Xia Nai's leadership, Chinese archaeology advanced quickly. Chinese scientists began conducting archaeological surveys and excavations all over the country. Xia Nai received many foreign honors for his work and was awarded more honorary titles from foreign academic institutions than any other Chinese scholar. He was elected to the English Academy of Archaeology, the German Institute of Archaeology, the Swedish Royal Academy of Literature, History and Archaeology, the American Academy of Sciences, the Third World Academy of Sciences, and the Italian Near and Far East Institute. He stated that all these honors were given not only to him personally but also to all Chinese archaeologists. See also ARCHAEOLOGY; BRONZEWARE; CHINESE ACADEMY OF SOCIAL SCIENCES; MING TOMBS; NEOLITHIC PERIOD; SILK; SILK ROAD; YANGSHAO CULTURE.

XIAMEN   Known as Amoy in the local dialect; a city of about one million people in Fujian Province on the southeastern Chinese coast directly across the Strait of Taiwan from the island of Taiwan, the Republic of China (formerly known as Formosa). Xiamen, known as the "Garden of the Sea," is actually an island with an area of 47.8 square miles connected to the mainland by a three-mile causeway. Located where the Jiulong (Nine Dragon) River flows into the East China Sea, Xiamen's excellent deepwater harbor has made the city a major trading port and a center for boat building since the 15th century.

Xiamen was first settled during the Southern Song dynasty (1127–1279) and was known as Jiahe Yu (Good Grain Island) for the fertile agricultural region in which it is situated. In the 16th century, Japanese pirates known as *wokou* (*wako* in Japanese) made Xiamen their base, from which they attacked the coasts of China, Korea, the Philippines, Vietnam and Borneo until 1570. In the 17th century, the Ming general Zheng Chenggong (Cheng Ch'eng-kung; also known as Coxinga or Koxinga) led troops across the Strait of Taiwan to drive out the Dutch, who had occupied Taiwan Island in 1624. When China lost the first Opium War in 1842, the Treaty of Nanjing forced the country to open Xiamen and four other so-called Treaty Ports to Western trade and to cede Hong Kong Island to Great Britain. Many Western traders then settled in Xiamen and a large number of Chinese immigrated to Southeast Asian countries through the port. They continue to emigrate today but keep close ties with relatives in Xiamen, and many return to spend their retirement there. Money sent back by overseas Chinese has greatly increased Xiamen's development.

In 1979 Xiamen was designated one of China's four Special Economic Zones (SEZs), along with Shenzhen, Zhuhai and Shantou in Guangdong Province. The zones were designed to attract foreign investment, technology and expertise, and to increase Chinese exports. Xiamen International Airlines is based in the city, and there is a new international airport. Passenger cargo boats sail between other Chinese cities, Hong Kong, Taiwan and Japan. Major tourist sites include the tropical plants in Yuanlin Botanical Gardens and Zhongshan Park, which contains several monasteries and a marble column erected to honor Sun Yat-sen, founder of the Republic of China in 1912. Nanputuo is a thousand-year-old Buddhist temple on Mount Wulao three miles from the city. Gulang Island near Xiamen is a beautiful resort covered with forests.

The renowned writer and revolutionary Lu Xun taught in Xiamen from 1926 to 1927 and is commemorated in a museum on the campus. Jimei, the hometown of Tan Kahkee, a famous overseas Chinese patriot who lived in Singapore as a young man, lies on the mainland north of Xiamen. In 1921 he founded several schools in Jimei, including Xiamen University, which is still supported by overseas Chinese. Visitors can see his mausoleum and monument at Turtle Park, schools that he helped to found, and the Overseas Chinese Museum established in 1959. Northeast of Xiamen lies Quanzhou, the most important Chinese port from the 12th to 15th centuries, which was called Zaiton (Zaitun or Zaytun). Marco Polo sailed from Quanzhou around 1290 when he returned home to Italy after 17 years in China. During the Ming dynasty (1368–1644), Chinese admiral Zheng He (Cheng Ho; 1371–1433) sailed from Quanzhou on seven voyages that took his fleet as far west as the east coast of Africa. See also FUJIAN PROVINCE; LU XUN; NANJING, TREATY OF; OPIUM WAR; OVERSEAS CHINESE; PIRATES; SPECIAL ECONOMIC ZONES; SUN YAT-SEN; TAIWAN; ZHENG CHENGGONG; ZHENG HE.

XI'AN   A city with a population of about 3 million that is the capital of Shaanxi Province in western China. Modern Xi'an lies in the middle of the Guanzhong Plain near the confluence of the Wei and Jing Rivers, on the site of the ancient city of Chang'an, built by Emperor Wendi (Wen-ti; r. 581–604) as the capital of the Sui dynasty (581–618). The Xi'an area, in fact, has been the site of human settlements as far back as China's Neolithic Period (c. 12,000 B.C.–c. 2000 B.C.). Banpo Neolithic Village, which has been excavated and opened to tourists, was inhabited from 4500 B.C. to approximately 3750 B.C. Xi'an served as the capital, at one time or another, of 12 dynasties over the course of 1,190 years. The Chinese thus call it the "City of Capitals." Northern Shaanxi was the home of the Zhou people who conquered the Shang dynasty (1750–1040 B.C.) and established the Zhou dynasty (1100–256 B.C.), with their capital near modern Xi'an. It was also the home of the Qin people, who established the Qin dynasty (221–206 B.C.), the first imperial dynasty to rule all of eastern China, with Qin Shi Huangdi ruling as the first Chinese emperor. The Qin capital was at Xianyang near Xi'an. The capital of the Western Han dynasty (206 B.C.–A.D. 8) was built in this area as well. The Sui capital of Chang'an, built on the site of the Han capital, also

served as the capital of the Tang dynasty (618–907). The starting point of the Silk Road along which trade was conducted between China and the Middle East, Chang'an became the world's largest and most cosmopolitan city.

After the fall of the Tang and the breakup of China into independent states, Chang'an lost its prominence, and later dynasties located their capitals in eastern provinces. By the 19th century, the city now known as Xi'an was an isolated provincial town. In 1930 a railway line was built to Xi'an from Zhengzhou, and after 1949, the Communist government began industrializing the city. However, many ancient sites can still be seen, making Xi'an a major destination for tourists in China.

Xi'an is laid out on the same rectangular grid plan as Chang'an, and the old city walls can still be seen. They were built by Hongwu (Hung-wu), first emperor of the Ming dynasty (1368–1644), on the site of Chang'an's Forbidden City or imperial complex and are the best-preserved city walls in the world. The walls have gateways, defensive towers, and a watchtower at each of the four corners. In the middle of Xi'an sits a huge Bell Tower (Zhonglou), built in the late 14th century but reconstructed in 1739. The tower now houses a waxwork exhibit on ancient Chinese emperors. Nearby is the smaller Drum Tower (Gulou), at the entrance to the Muslim quarter of Xi'an. Beginning in Tang times, many Muslim diplomats, traders and soldiers came to China and settled in the city. Xian's Great Mosque, northwest of the Drum Tower, is one of the oldest and largest mosques in the country. The Buddhist religion became popular in China after it was introduced from India around the first century A.D. In Xi'an several Buddhist pagodas can be seen. The Big Wild Goose Pagoda (Dayanta) was originally built in 652 by Tang emperor Xuanzong to house the Buddhist scriptures brought back from India by the Chinese monk Xuanzang (Hsuan-tsang; 602–664). The pagoda has been enlarged and restored several times. The Little Wild Goose Pagoda (Xiaoyanta), constructed from 707 to 709 to house Buddhist scriptures, stands in the grounds of Jianfu Temple, originally built in 684 to house prayers for the spirit of Tang emperor Gaozong (Kao-tsung; r. 649–83). The Temple of the Eight Immortals (*baxianan*) is the largest temple in Xi'an belonging to the native Chinese religion of Daoism. The former Temple of Confucius, dating from 1374, is now the Shaanxi Provincial Museum, which houses exhibits on the history of the region. It contains the Forest of Steles, a collection of 2,300 engraved stone columns, some dating back to the Han dynasty. The Shaanxi History Museum, which opened in 1992, also houses exhibits on the history of the region displayed in chronological order. The Memorial Hall of the Xi'an Office of the Eighth Route Army is an important site for the Chinese Communist Party.

Outside the city, tourists can visit Banpo Neolithic Village and the immense terra-cotta army (Bingmayon) that was buried to protect the tomb of Emperor Qin Shi Huangdi. The tomb itself lies within a mound of earth that has not been excavated. In 1974, local peasants digging a well nearby discovered an underground vault that contained 6,000 life-size terra-cotta soldiers and horses lined up for battle. Archaeologists have restored the figures and placed them on exhibit inside the vault. More than a dozen other imperial tombs are located outside Xi'an. The Zhao Tomb (Zhaoling) was built for the second Tang emperor Taizong (T'ai-tsung; r. 626–49).

Visitors can also see the ruins of Daming Palace built by Taizong northeast of Xi'an. The Qian Tomb (Qianling) houses the remains of Tang emperor Gaozong and Empress Wu, the only woman who ever ruled China in her own right. Many smaller tombs surround the Qian Tomb, but only five have been excavated, including that of Prince Zhang Huai, second son of Emperor Gaozong and Empress Wu; that of Princess Yong Tai, a granddaughter of Emperor Gaozong and daughter of Emperor Zhongzong (Chung-tsung), which contains wall paintings of servants; and the Mao Tomb (*Maoling*), which houses the remains of Emperor Wudi (Wu-ti; r. 141–87 B.C.), the most powerful emperor of the Han dynasty. The tomb of Yang Guifei (Yang Kuei-fei) houses the remains of the famous concubine beloved by Tang emperor Xuanzong (Hsuan-tsung; r. 712–756). The Tomb of the Yellow Emperor (Huangdi Ling) supposedly contains the remains of the legendary emperor who is considered "father" of the Chinese people.

Twenty miles east of Xi'an, at the foot of Mount Li (Lishan) lies Huaqing Hot Springs (Huaqing Chi), originally a resort for Tang emperors but now open to the public. Fourteen miles east of Xi'an, Xingjiao Temple, an important Buddhist monastery during the Tang dynasty, is the burial place of the Chinese monk Xuanzang (Hsuang-tsang; 602–664) who made a pilgrimage to India. Eighty miles east of Xi'an lies Huashan (Mount Hua), one of the five sacred mountains of Daoism. About 80 miles northwest of Xi'an can be seen Famen Temple (Famen Si), a Buddhist temple built in 300. After heavy rains caused the western side of the temple's 12-story pagoda to collapse in 1981, archaeologists discovered more than a thousand sacred objects and offerings donated by the imperial court, such as coins, gold and silver objects, and stones inscribed with Buddhist scriptures. These are now exhibited in a museum next to the temple. See also BUDDHISM; CHANG'AN; FIVE SACRED MOUNTAINS OF DAOISM; HAN DYNASTY; HUAQING HOT SPRINGS; NEOLITHIC PERIOD; PAGODA; QIN SHI HUANGDI (EMPEROR); SHAANXI PROVINCE; SILK ROAD; SUI DYNASTY; TANG DYNASTY; TERRACOTTA ARMY, TOMB OF EMPEROR QIN SHI HUANGDI; WEI RIVER; XUANZANG; YANG GUIFEI; YELLOW EMPEROR; ZHOU DYNASTY.

XI'AN INCIDENT See CHIANG KAI-SHEK; CIVIL WAR BETWEEN COMMUNISTS AND NATIONALISTS; HUAQING HOT SPRINGS.

XIAN XINGHAI (Hsien Hsing-hai; 1905–45) A composer whose most famous work is the *Yellow River Cantata.* Xian Xinghai was born in Guangdong Province in southern China. When he completed his Chinese schooling he studied music in France. He returned to China in 1935 and became head of the Music Department at the Lu Xun Art Academy in Yan'an in Shaanxi Province in 1939, the same year that he joined the Chinese Communist Party (CCP). He also worked as a composer for two Chinese film companies. In 1940 the CCP Central Committee sent him to the Soviet Union to compose scores for films. He died in the U.S.S.R. in 1945. There he wrote his final piece, *War in a Noble Cause.* His ashes had been kept in the Soviet Union, but in 1983 the Soviet Union honored his family's request and turned his ashes over to China. A memorial ceremony was held at Beijing airport. Chinese artists and musicians held another

memorial for Xian in Beijing on February 2, 1983, to honor him. An orchestra and choir performed the *Yellow River Cantata,* which Xian wrote in 1939, during China's War of Resistance against Japan (1937–45; World War II), to praise the unbending spirit of the Chinese people in resisting Japanese aggression. The cantata, named for China's second-longest river and the cradle of its ancient civilization, has remained one of the most popular modern musical works in China. See also WAR OF RESISTANCE AGAINST JAPAN; YELLOW RIVER.

XIANBEI TRIBES See NORTHERN WEI DYNASTY; SHANXI PROVINCE; SINICIZATION; SIX DYNASTIES PERIOD; WESTERN AND EASTERN JIN DYNASTIES; XIONGNU.

XIANDAN See ALCHEMY; CINNABAR; ELIXIR OF IMMORTALITY.

XIANDI (EMPEROR) See EASTERN HAN DYNASTY.

XIANFENG (EMPEROR) See ARROW WAR; CIXI, EMPRESS DOWAGER; GONG, PRINCE; QING DYNASTY.

XIANG RIVER See CHANGSHA; HUNAN PROVINCE.

XIANGFEI See KASHGAR; QIANLONG (EMPEROR).

XIANGGANG See HONG KONG.

XIANSHOU SCHOOL See FLOWER GARLAND SECT OF BUDDHISM.

XIANYANG See CHANG'AN; QIN SHI HUANGDI (EMPEROR); SHAANXI PROVINCE; XI'AN.

XIANZONG (EMPEROR) See TANG DYNASTY.

XIAO AND XIAJING See ANCESTOR WORSHIP; FILIAL PIETY.

XIAO GUGONG (SMALL IMPERIAL PALACE) See SHENYANG.

XIAO WENDI (EMPEROR) See NORTHERN AND SOUTHERN DYNASTIES.

XIAOTUN VILLAGE See ANYANG.

XIAOWENDI (EMPEROR) See NORTHERN WEI DYNASTY; SINICIZATION.

XIBA See LIAONING PROVINCE; MINORITIES, NATIONAL.

XIBO See SHANG DYNASTY.

XIE HE See SIX CANONS OF PAINTING.

XIE LINGYUN (Hsieh Ling-yun; 385–433) A poet whom many critics regard as the first Chinese nature poet. Xie Lingyun was born to a wealthy aristocratic family and held the title of duke of Kanglo. In addition to poetry, he was skilled at calligraphy and painting. He held several government positions and was expected to have a successful career in the Chinese court. However, in 422 Xie became involved in political intrigue that damaged his career. He supported his friend Liu Yizhen (Liu I-chen; also known as the Prince of Luling) in his attempt to become emperor. However, his opponents murdered the prince and demoted Xie to the position of magistrate in the remote area of Yungjia (Yung-chia). He stayed there for about one year and then retired to his family estate in Zhejiang Province, where he became active in landscape gardening.

During his year as magistrate, Xie wrote some of his best poems, many of which express his feelings about government injustices. While attempting to deal with his demotion, he became interested in the Daoist tradition, which emphasizes harmony with nature and freedom from the concerns of the world. His finest poems, written after 422, describe the beautiful mountains, lakes and rivers of southern China. Many of them describe his sense of losing himself in the landscape. He composed the poems in the rhyme-prose style known as *fu*. One of his most admired poems is "Rhyme-prose on Dwelling in the Mountains" ("*Shanju fu*" or "*Shan-chu fu*").

Xie did come out of retirement to hold a few more government positions but did not carry out his duties properly. In 431 he was exiled again to a position in southern China. There he led an uprising against the government and was nearly executed. He was exiled once more to the region of modern Guangzhou (Canton), and in 433 the government accused him of rebellion and executed him. Nearly one hundred of his poems have survived. See also DAOISM; RHYME-PROSE STYLE OF VERSE.

XIGAZE   See TIBET.

XIHU   See WEST LAKE.

XIJIANG   See WEST RIVER.

XILING GORGE   See THREE GORGES WATER CONSERVANCY PROJECT.

XIN DYNASTY   (A.D. 9–23)   See WANG MANG.

XIN NIAN   See NEW YEAR FESTIVAL.

XIN QIJI   (Hsin Ch'i-chi; 1140–1207)   A military leader who was one of the greatest poets of the Southern Song dynasty (1127–1279). Xin Qiji was born in Shandong Province. Raised as a soldier, he became a brilliant tactician by the time he was 20 years old. When he captured the leader of a rebellion, Xin was given an audience with Emperor Gaozong (Kao-tsung). Xin wanted to avenge the defeat of the Song Chinese in 1127 by the Jurchens, a nomadic tribe who had forced the Song to move their imperial capital from Kaifeng south to Hangzhou. However, the Chinese and the Jurchens negotiated a peace treaty in 1164, forcing Xin to give up this goal. Over the next three decades he held various civil and military posts in several provinces.

In 1194 Xin Qiji retired and built a beautiful country retreat near the border between Fujian and Jiangsu provinces, where he was able to read extensively and to write the poems that made him famous. Many friends visited him

there, including the important Neo-Confucian philosopher Zhu Xi (Chu Hsi; 1130–1200). Xin composed 623 poems, mostly in the lyric *ci* (*tz'u*) form, giving them an emotional content that had not yet been employed in Chinese poetry and that was imitated by many poets after his death. Some of his poems expressed his patriotic sentiments. He also wrote amusing love songs and rustic poems. Xin's poems were collected in an artistic block-print edition between 1188 and 1203. See also JURCHEN; POETRY; SOUTHERN SONG DYNASTY; ZHUXI.

XINGAN CANAL   See NANLING MOUNTAIN RANGE.

XINGJUNGHUI   See SUN YAT-SEN.

XINGQING   See CHANGCHUN; JILIN PROVINCE; MANCHUKUO; NINGXIA HUI AUTONOMOUS REGION; YINCHUAN.

XINGZHONGHUI   See SOCIETY FOR THE REBIRTH OF CHINA.

XINHUA NEWS AGENCY   See NEW CHINA NEWS AGENCY.

XINING   The capital city of Qinghai Province in northwestern China with a population of about 500,000. Xining lies on the banks of the Huangshui River, a tributary of the Yellow River (Huanghe), in the northeastern region of the Qinghai-Tibet Plateau, in a fertile plain 7,000 feet above sea level. The city was a center for the caravans that traveled between China and Tibet (Xizang), which lies south of Qinghai and has been incorporated into China as a so-called autonomous region. Since 1949, Xining, the only large city in Qinghai, has been modernized and industrialized, and has been connected by railroad to Lanzhou, the capital city of Gansu Province to the east. Mountain climbers stop at Xining on their way to ascend Mount A'nyemaqen, 20,610 feet high, in eastern Qinghai. Lake Qinghai (Qinghaihu, "Blue Lake"; also known as Kou Kou Nor), the largest inland lake in China, lies 86 miles west of Xining.

Ta'er Si (Kumbum in Tibetan), one of the largest and most famous monasteries of the Yellow Hat Sect of Lamaism (Tibetan Buddhism; *dGe lugs pa*), is located 12 miles from Xining in Lusha'er. This town claims to be the birthplace of Zongkaba (Tsong Kha-pa; 1355–1417), founder of the Yellow Hat Sect. In former times as many as 4,000 monks resided in Ta'er monastery, which was constructed in the Tibetan style beginning in 1560 and renovated in 1979. There are also some buildings in the Han Chinese style, notably Gold Roof Hall (Serkhang Chenmo, Great Golden House), the main building. Another hall in the compound houses a beautiful gilded sculpture of Zongkaba. The monastery holds four major festivals every year. The most important is the Lantern Festival on the 15th day of the first month in the lunar calendar, around mid-February. Pilgrims can see large sculptures made from yak butter by 10 monks. Also in Xining can be seen the Buddhist Beishan Temple and the Muslim Great Mosque; the latter was built in the late 14th century and is one of the largest in northwestern China. See also LAMAISM; QINGHAI, LAKE; QINGHAI PROVINCE; QINGHAI-TIBET PLATEAU.

XINJIANG-UIGHUR AUTONOMOUS REGION (Xinjiang Uighur Zizhiqu)   The largest and most northwestern province in China. Xinjiang covers 635,830 square miles, 16 percent of the land total of China, and has a population of about 13 million. The capital city is Urumqi, with a population of about 1.13 million, which became Xinjiang's most important city when the railroad was completed in 1963. Xinjiang is strategically important for China, as it borders the Indian state of Kashmir and the republics of Kazakhstan, Kyrgyzstan and Tajikistan to the west; Outer Mongolia (the Mongolian People's Republic) to the northeast; the Chinese provinces of Gansu and Qinghai to the east; and Tibet Autonomous Region (Xizang Zizhiqu) to the south. Xinjiang was formerly known as Chinese Turkestan. It was designated an autonomous region in 1955 because a large number of its population are members of China's national minorities, primarily Muslim Turkish-speaking peoples from Central Asia such as Uighurs, Kazakhs, Kirghiz and Uzbeks. Many are nomadic herders who still live in tents or yurts. Islam is the dominant religion in Xinjiang, and numerous mosques can be seen in Urumqi and other cities.

Xinjiang is the autonomous region in China second in importance demographically and politically to Tibet. Although the Chinese government has settled many Han (ethnic Chinese) in Xinjiang, about 60 percent of the population still belongs to minority groups, with more than 6 million Uighurs and about one million Kazakhs. Continuing ethnic tensions in this strategic and volatile border region have prompted the government to make concessions to the ethnic minorities. A political rebellion in Xinjiang in 1962 caused about 60,000 Kazakh herders to flee across the border to the Soviet Union. Since the Sino-Indian border dispute of 1962, China has strengthened its military control in the region by building a strategic highway linking Xinjiang and Tibet.

Much of Xinjiang consists of barren desert areas with sparse rainfall. The region is divided by the Tianshan Range, which runs east to west. About half of Xinjiang is covered by the large, flat depression known as the Tarim Basin, which lies south of the Tianshan Range and north of the Kunlunshan Range on the border with Qinghai Province. The Dzungaria Basin lies north of the Tianshan Range and south of the Altaishan Range, which borders Outer Mongolia. The Turpan Depression in western Xinjiang, east of the city of Kashgar, is the lowest land area in China and the second-lowest in the world. It receives almost no rain and is the hottest place in China.

Recently Xinjiang has undergone agricultural and industrial development. There are rich deposits of 122 kinds of minerals, including coal, gold and jade, comprising 80 percent of China's total. There are large oil and gas reserves in the Tarim and Dzungaria Basins. Major industries include mining and the manufacture of iron, steel and machinery. Agriculture is made possible by a modern irrigation system that brings water from the Tianshan Range. Xinjiang is China's largest producer of grapes and the third-largest of sugarbeets. Other major crops include cotton, grains, apples and melons. Goods are transported mostly by trucks over the thousands of miles of recently paved highways. Xinjiang consists primarily of pasture land, and the nomadic population has a tradition of herding animals, especially sheep and horses. Mutton and milk are important products.

The city of Turpan was a major oasis on the Silk Road along which camel caravans traveled between ancient China and the Mediterranean world, beginning in the Han dynasty (206 B.C.–A.D. 220). Today Turpan is an agricultural center. Kashgar, the westernmost city in China, was another well-known Silk Road oasis. The caravans carried silk, porcelain and tea to the west and returned east bringing Western goods, art, music and dance, and religions such as Islam and Buddhism. The Caves of the Thousand Buddhas (Qianfu Dong; also known as the Caves of Bezeklik, "place of the frescoes") were built northeast of Turpan between the 6th and 14th centuries. The huge mural paintings were partly destroyed by Muslim invaders, and many more were taken by German explorers to Berlin in the 19th century, only to be destroyed by Allied bombing in World War II. The Caves of the Thousand Buddhas near Gaocheng, an old market town east of Turpan, were built in the third and fourth centuries.

In the first century B.C., Xinjiang was ruled by the Xiongnu (Hsiung-nu), but they were conquered by the Han dynasty Chinese. In 100 B.C., Emperor Wudi (Wu-ti) decided to bring all of Central Asia under Chinese domination and sent an army across the Tarim Basin, which enabled the Silk Road to be established. As the Han dynasty weakened, the individual oasis centers regained their autonomy and provided defenses against invading waves of Tibetans, Huns, Turks and Mongols. In 657, Xinjiang became part of the Chinese empire ruled by the Tang dynasty (618–907). Gaocheng and Jiaohe were major cities on the Silk Road during the Tang dynasty, but in the 14th century Gaocheng was abandoned and Jiaohe declined. Uighurs settled in eastern and southern Xinjiang during the 10th century. See also ALTAISHAN RANGE; CAMEL CARAVANS; DZUNGARIA BASIN; GANSU PROVINCE; HAN DYNASTY; KASHGAR; KAZAKH; KIRGHIZ; MINORITIES, NATIONAL; MUSLIMS; NOMADS AND ANIMAL HUSBANDRY; SILK ROAD; SINO-INDIAN BORDER DISPUTE; TARIM BASIN; TIANSHAN RANGE; TIBET; TURPAN; TURPAN DEPRESSION; UIGHUR; URUMQI; WUDI, EMPEROR; XIONGNU.

XINJING   See CHANGCHUN; MANCHUKUO.

XIONGNU (Hsiung-nu)   A group of Altaic (Turkish) speaking nomadic tribes who lived north of the Great Wall in modern Inner Mongolia Autonomous Region and invaded China frequently during its early imperial period. Emperor Qin Shi Huangdi, who unified China under the Qin dynasty (221–206 B.C.), built the Great Wall, which extended about 2,600 miles from modern Gansu Province in the west to the Liaodong Peninsula in the east, to defend his empire against the Xiongnu. One reason for the downfall of the Qin was the heavy burden placed on the Chinese population to provide labor for the wall's construction. The wall did not completely stop the nomadic invasions, and the Chinese had to further protect themselves by presenting a lavish amount of gifts to the Xiongnu each year, for which the tribal chieftains promised to keep control over the steppe grasslands along the northern Chinese border.

The Xiongnu had formed a confederation of 24 tribes and extended for 1,500 miles from the edge of Manchuria in northeastern China to the steppes in the west. Records of the Han dynasty (206 B.C.–A.D. 220) state that in 200 B.C. the Xiongnu sent more than 300,000 mounted warriors to besiege Liu Bang (Liu Pang), founder of the Han dynasty. The numbers may have been exaggerated, but the Xiongnu were capable of sending 100,000 men into battle, grouped in smaller formations that could be coordinated over a large area. The nomadic men learned to ride horses as boys and lived in the saddle, always on the move and ready to use their tools as battle weapons. The Han dynasty, especially under Emperor Wudi (Wu-ti; r. 141–87 B.C.), fought and won many battles against the Xiongnu yet never completely ended their invasions of China. Some Han emperors had also used a policy of "peace and kinship" (*heqin* or *ho-ch'in*) whereby they gave luxurious gifts, especially silk, to the Xiongnu chieftains and married Han Chinese princesses to them. However, this arrangement proved too expensive and ineffective for the Han and was abandoned by Wudi's time. Wudi and other emperors also sent Han officers west to form strategic alliances against the Xiongnu with other tribes in Central Asia. For example, in 138 B.C. Zhang Qian (Chang Ch'ien; d. 114 B.C.) was given this mission, and after being captured by the Xiongnu and held captive for 10 years, he continued farther west and laid the foundation for the Silk Road along which the Chinese traded silk with Central Asia. Zhang Qian made a second trip in 119–115 B.C. and made an alliance with the Wusun tribe. He brought back a great amount of useful military information about the lands and peoples he had visited. Further western missions were dispatched, which also enabled the Chinese to acquire many of the large, sturdy horses bred by the nomadic peoples.

The Han decisively defeated the Western Horde of the Xiongnu in 121 B.C., and in 100 B.C. a large Chinese army forced the king of Ferghana (modern Uzbekistan) to submit to Chinese control and to send 3,000 horses to the Han capital at Chang'an (modern Xi'an in Shaanxi Province).

In 72 B.C. the Chinese had sent another military force against the Xiongnu. Chinese policy included attempting to divide the Xiongnu, and around 55 B.C. the Xiongnu split into five factions that began fighting each other. The southern branch eventually agreed to come under Chinese control, and the Han were able to decrease the number of Chinese troops stationed along the northern frontier. During the Eastern Han dynasty (A.D. 25–220), the Xiongnu were less of a threat to the empire. However, the Han sent two forces against them in A.D. 73 and A.D. 89. Han, General Ban Chao (Pan Ch'ao; 32–102) forged relationships with western tribes, and he managed to bring most of Central Asia under the influence of the Chinese empire between 73 and 97. However, Han forces caused the nomads to begin moving west, which may have set in motion the subsequent waves of nomadic invasions that culminated in the Huns invading Rome in the fifth century. Some scholars in fact associate the Xiongnu with the Huns, while others dispute this. During the period from 221 to 589, following the downfall of the Han, the Chinese Empire was broken up into many different dynasties, and the Xiongnu were able to control much of northern China. In 304, Liu Yuan, a Sinicized Xiongnu, took power and proclaimed himself king of Han. He captured the major Chinese cities of Luoyang in 311 and Chang'an in 316. In 391 the Northern Wei dynasty (386–534) or Toba

Wei, under Emperor Taba Gui, severely defeated a Xiongnu tribe and killed thousands of members of the ruling noble families. He sent the surviving Xiongnu to the Yellow River region near modern Baotou, the capital of Innger Mongolia, and forced them to give up their nomadic ways and live like the Chinese in permanent settlements where they had to practice agriculture. By the Tang dynasty (618–907) the Xiongnu tribes and culture had disappeared. See also BAN CHAO; GREAT WALL; HAN DYNASTY; HORSE; INNER MONGOLIA AUTONOMOUS REGION; LIU BANG; NOMADS AND ANIMAL HUSBANDRY; NORTHERN WEI DYNASTY; WUDI, EMPEROR; ZHANG QIAN.

XISHA ISLANDS See SOUTH CHINA SEA; SPRATLY ISLANDS.

XISHUANGBANNA AUTONOMOUS DISTRICT OF THE DAI PEOPLE A subtropical mountainous region on the lower reaches of the Mekong River in the southern part of Yunnan Province in southwestern China next to the borders of Myanmar (Burma) and Laos. Xishuangbanna is inhabited by about 650,000 people belonging to 13 different national minority groups. The Dai comprise the largest number, about 35 percent of the total population. They are related to Dai people in Burma, Laos and Thailand, which lie south of Yunnan. Some other minority groups include the Aini, Bulang, Hani, Kucong, Kinuo, Lahu, Miao, Zhuang and Yao. The Xishuangbanna Autonomous District covers about 7,700 square miles. According to Dai legend, it was discovered thousands of years ago by hunters who were chasing a golden deer. In the 13th century the Mongols invaded China and the Buddhist Dais fled south to this region, which was soon annexed by the Chinese empire. Today the Xishuangbanna Autonomous District has been somewhat assimilated into modern China, but the national minority groups continue to speak their own languages, wear their own styles of clothing and practice their own customs.

The Xishuangbanna Autonomous District has been opened to tourists, who can take a boat ride on the Mekong River (known as the Lancang River or Lancanjiang in Chinese) and visit Buddhist temples and pagodas built in the Burmese style. During the Cultural Revolution (1966–76) many Buddhist temples in the area were destroyed, but some have been rebuilt. The Daimenglong Bamboo Shoot Pagoda is seven centuries old. The capital of the district is the small town of Yunjinghong on the Mekong River, which was the capital of a Dai kingdom in the 13th century known as Jinglan. Tourists can visit the 13th-century Mange Buddhist monastery, which has been restored, and the Tropical Plant Research Institute, which was founded in 1953. Members of various national minorities sell their produce and arts and crafts at a market held every Sunday. Outside the town, tourists can visit other temples and pagodas, as well as Manjinglina, a Dai village of bamboo huts erected above the ground on poles. The largest city in the district is Simao, which has a population of about 50,000 and is 350 miles from the city of Kunming, the capital of Yunnan. The most important annual event in the district is the Water Splashing Festival, the Dai New Year, which is held for three days in mid-April. On the first day, thousands of people wearing their native costumes gather on the banks of the Mekong River to watch races between dragon-shaped boats and performances of dances and plays. On the second and third days, all the celebrants fill bowls and other containers with river water and splash each other to commemorate the conquest of a fire demon by seven Dai maidens. A fair is held on the third day.

The district is covered with dense jungles filled with valuable trees such as mahogany, sandalwood, teak and camphor. There are large nature preserves covered with tropical rain forests. Native animals include wild elephants, tigers, panthers, monkeys, bears, peacocks and boa constrictors. The 5,000 plants native to the region include banyan trees with widespread roots, giant waterlilies on which a child can sit without sinking and huge palm trees. Mountain slopes between 4,000 and 6,000 feet above sea level have been cultivated with tea plants, especially the famous Pu'er variety, which the Chinese believe aids the digestion. Three crops of rice can be harvested each year in the valleys. Other crops include tropical fruits such as pineapples and mangoes, sugar cane, cocoa, camphor and quinine, used to treat malaria. The region is the second largest producer of rubber in China. See also DAI; MEKONG RIVER; MINORITIES, NATIONAL; TEA; YUNNAN PROVINCE.

XIWANGMU (Hsi Wang Mu) The Royal Lady (or Mother) of the Western Paradise; a goddess in the Daoist religion who dwells on the Kunlun Mountain Range in western China. Xiwangmu is depicted as a beautiful and gracious princess riding on a white crane, which symbolizes long life. She is attended by two girls who hold a large fan and a basket of the peaches of immortality. She also has five fairy handmaidens who correspond to the colors associated with the four compass directions and the center of the compass. Blue-winged birds also act as her messengers. Some Chinese legends also state that she has a consort, Dong Wang Gun (Tung Wang Kun) or Mu Gong (Mu Kung), the Royal Lord of the East, who keeps the register of the Daoist gods. She represents the yin, or female principle of the universe, and the yang, or male principle. They have 9 sons and 24 daughters.

Her beautiful palace is surrounded by golden walls with a magic fountain on the shore of the Lake of Gems or Green Jade Lake. The Heavenly Peach Orchard of the Jade Emperor, Tianzi (T'ien-tzu), ruler of Heaven, grows next to her palace. Anyone who eats one of these peaches will gain immortal life. The trees take 3,000 years to bloom and another 3,000 years for the fruit to ripen. When this happens, the Daoist gods visit the palace of Xiwangmu to celebrate her birthday and to renew themselves by eating the fruit. In her garden there is also an enormous tree on which grows a type of red jade known as *giong* whose flowers and leaves, if eaten, are supposed to confer immortality as well.

The most beloved of the Eight Immortals in Daoism, Li Tieguai (Li T'ieh-kuai), was the first of the eight to gain immortality because he became the student of Xiwangmu herself after she cured an ulcer in his leg. He is portrayed as a lame beggar with an iron crutch and is the patron deity of herbal healers and exorcists. According to legends, the famous archer Hou Yi was awarded the pill of immortality by Xiwangmu after he saved the Earth from being burned up by the 10 suns. While admiring the pill, his wife, Chang E, was threatened by one of his disciples. She swallowed the pill in

fright and flew up to the moon, where she supposedly still dwells. See also CHANG E; CRANE; DAOISM; EIGHT IMMORTALS; JADE; KUNLUN MOUNTAIN RANGE; PEACH.

XIXIA, KINGDOM OF An empire founded by Li Yuanhao (1003–48) in the region of modern Ningxia and Gansu Provinces in northwestern China. The kingdom of Xixia ("Western Xia") lasted from around 990 to 1227. It lay on the so-called Silk Road, the path of caravans between China and the Middle East. Thus it had regular income in its position as middleman. The main ethnic group was the Tanguts, related to the Tibetan ethnic group. Little is known about the Tanguts, especially since the Mongols destroyed their capital at Kara-Khoto in 1227. They had their own script but scholars have not yet been able to decipher it. Their territory had been a tributary state of the Khitan (Qidan) who established the Liao dynasty (947–1125) in northern China.

In the 1030s, a Tangut named Li Yuanhao fought against the Chinese Song dynasty (960–1279). In 1038, he proclaimed himself emperor of a new dynasty of the independent kingdom of Xixia, which continued to rely on the Liao dynasty to protect it from the larger Chinese Song dynasty. Li also negotiated a treaty with the Song in 1044 that was very favorable to the kingdom of Xixia, which became a vassal of the Song in exchange for large quantities of silver, silk and tea. However, Xixia and Song engaged in conflicts from 1068 through the next several decades. While the Jurchen people were attacking the Liao dynasty in the early 12th century, Song made unsuccessful attacks on Xixia from 1115 to 1119. Although Xixia had a relatively light population, it had a powerful army based on highly mobile and heavily armed cavalry units. The Jurchen, who founded the Jin dynasty (1115–1234), ended direct contact between Xixia and Song but maintained good relations with Xixia until the kingdom was harshly destroyed by the Mongols between 1225 and 1227. See also JIN DYNASTY; JURCHEN; LIAO DYNASTY; MONGOL; SILK ROAD; SONG DYNASTY.

XIXIA LINGMU (ROYAL TOMBS OF WESTERN XIA) See YINCHUAN.

XIYOUJI See JOURNEY TO THE WEST; XUANZANG.

XIZANG ZIZHIQU See TIBET AUTONOMOUS REGION.

XIZHOU See TURPAN.

XU BEIHONG (Hsu Pei-hung; 1895–1953) A painter who made a major contribution to the development of fine arts in modern China. Xu Beihong was born to a poor family in Jiangsu Province. His father was a scholar of traditional Chinese painting, which he taught Xu. At age 19, Xu moved to Shanghai and studied at Aurora University, run by the French. His portrait of Cang Jie (Ts'ang Chieh), the legendary inventor of Chinese written characters, won first place in a painting competition. Xu used the prize money to travel to Japan, and then to Paris, where he studied sketching and oil painting at the Academy of Fine Arts. He spent eight years in Europe, traveling through France, Germany, Britain, Belgium, Italy and Switzerland and acquiring a broad knowledge of Western art. When he returned to China in

1927, he became a professor at the Central Chinese Academy of Fine Arts in Guilin, and later its director. He was also president of the Chinese Painters Association. Xu incorporated Western painting techniques in his art. He gave his students a fresh approach and taught them to portray people and nature as truthfully as they possibly could. One of his favorite subjects was horses, because of their gentleness, loyalty, courage and ability to work hard.

Xu's works have been exhibited in China and foreign countries such as Canada. On the first anniversary of his death, an inscription written by Chinese premier Zhou Enlai (Chou En-lai) was placed over the entrance of Xu's former residence, which had been converted into the Xu Beihong Memorial Hall, and his rooms were maintained as they had been when he was alive. In 1957, four years after Xu died, his widow, Liao Jingwen (Liao Ching-wen), who had worked closely with him, was appointed head of the Xu Beihong Memorial Hall. In October 1966, the original Memorial Hall was torn down for construction of the Beijing subway. In 1983, the present Xu Beihong Memorial Hall was constructed in the northwestern sector of the city, with seven rooms exhibiting many of Xu's sketches and paintings as well as an introduction to his life and work. The fourth room preserves Xu's painting studio and sitting room. His brushes and paints sit on a table ready to use, and an unfinished oil painting stands on the easel, as it did when he died. Xu left more than 1,200 of his own paintings and sketches, more than 1,200 works by other famous Chinese painters throughout history, and 10,000 rare books, illustrations and stone rubbings to the Chinese people. See also STONE RUBBING.

XU WEI (Hsu Wei; 1521–1593)   A calligrapher, painter, poet, author and playwright during the Ming dynasty (1368–1644). Xu Wei was born in Zhejiang Province. Upon completing his education he passed the first level of examinations for the imperial bureaucy but failed in eight attempts to pass the higher provincial examinations. In 1547 he moved to the city of Shaoxing, where he wrote poetry, essays and plays in a studio called "Twig Hall" (Yizhitang). Xu Wei had a tumultuous life. From 1557 to 1562 he held a position as a military commander, but he was later dishonored and made an unsuccessful attempt to commit suicide. In 1566 he was sentenced to seven years in prison because he beat his third wife to death. After he left prison in 1573 he began painting flowers with ink-wash in a free and spontaneous style that influenced flower painters during the Qing dynasty (1644–1911). Xu Wei, however, maintained that his calligraphy, which was also very spirited, was of a higher artistic quality than his painting. See also CALLIGRAPHY; INK PAINTING.

XUANDE (EMPEROR) (Hsuan-te; 1399–1435)   The fifth emperor of the Ming dynasty (1368–1644). His given name was Zhu Zhanji (Chu Chan-chi) and his name during his reign was Xuanzong (Hsuan-tsung); Xuande, meaning "Radiant Virtue," is his posthumous reign name (r. 1426–35). He was the eldest son of Emperor Hongxi (Hung-hsi; r. 1425–26), who died after less than a year on the throne. Emperor Xuande had served as imperial deputy at Nanjing during his father's reign and felt a strong sense of responsibility for the well-being of his subjects. He followed the example of wise emperors in ancient China by making frequent tours to inspect conditions in the countryside where the majority of Chinese lived and worked as farmers. Xuande also had excellent Confucian-educated officials in his government, notably the elder statesmen known as the "three Yangs," whose name later stood for good government officials in China. Xuande was very mild-mannered and granted pardons or reduced the punishments for many criminals. His uncle led an uprising against him after he took the throne, but Xuande treated him leniently by keeping him under house arrest in the capital city of Beijing.

International affairs did not turn out as well. In 1428, Ming Chinese troops were defeated by local forces in Annam (Vietnam), to the south of China, and China had to give up its claim to that country. Uprisings by native peoples in the southern Chinese provinces of Sichuan, Guizhou and Jiangxi also constantly engaged Ming forces, as did raids by Mongol tribes on China's northern frontier. Many soldiers began deserting the Ming army because they were badly treated by their officers, forcing the government to send inspectors to frontier garrisons. The prestige of being a soldier also lessened after the government began putting convicts in the army. The Chinese navy declined as well during Xuande's reign. Large ships commanded by Admiral Zheng He (Cheng Ho; 1371–1433) had made several long-distance expeditions to gather tribute from foreign peoples, but Xuande's father had put a halt to them. One last voyage was made between 1431 and 1432 during Xuande's reign. The Ming lost prestige with foreign countries after it had to retreat from Annam, which dropped the value of Chinese currency and lessened the profits in foreign trade conducted by the government. Private traders took over.

Emperor Xuande supported the arts and was himself a talented painter. During his reign, beautiful porcelain objects were produced at the imperial kilns at Jingdezhen (Ching-te-chen) in Jiangxi Province. Some of the finest pieces of cloisonné enamelware were also produced during his reign. When Xuande died in his early 30s, his eldest son, only seven years old, took the throne. The eunuch Wang Zhen (Wang Chen; d. 1499) wielded power for the young emperor, becoming the first of many eunuchs during the Ming dynasty who functioned as virtual dictators of the Chinese empire and who in large part caused the decline of the Ming. See also CLOISONNE; EUNUCH; JINGDEZHEN; MING DYNASTY; MONGOL; ZHENG HE.

XUANTONG (EMPEROR)   See PUYI, HENRY.

XUANZANG (Hsuang-tsang; 602–664)   A Chinese Buddhist monk who went on a pilgrimage to India in 629–645 to collect sutras (Buddhist scriptures). The record of his journey is a valuable source of information about Buddhist kingdoms in Central Asia, which were conquered by Muslim nomadic tribes over the next few centuries. Buddhism had been introduced from India into China in the first century A.D. The first Chinese monk to make a pilgrimage to India to collect sutras for translation from Indian Sanskrit into Chinese was Faxian (Fa-hsien; fourth to fifth centuries), who also wrote an important book about his journey. Both monks set out from Chang'an (modern Xi'an in Shaanxi Province), then the largest city in the world.

When Xuanzang returned to China in April 645, he was welcomed by a great crowd of monks, government officials and common people. He was then received at Luoyang by the Tang emperor Taizong (T'ai-tsung), who gave him gifts, wrote a letter commending him, and later converted to Buddhism himself. Xuanzang then spent 19 years leading a team in translating the Buddhist sutras. The Big Wild Goose Pagoda (Dayan Ta) in Xi'an was built at the Temple of Great Good Will (Ci'en Si) by Emperor Gaozong in 652 at Xuanzang's request to store the 657 manuscripts he had gathered. The pagoda was enlarged to 10 stories between 701 and 704 and restored in the 1950s. Three stories were lost over the centuries, but the pagoda is much as it was 1,200 years ago. On display is an ink rubbing of a carved stone depicting Xuanzang on his journey carrying a large backpack and holding a fly whisk and lantern. The pilgrimage of Xuanzang was the inspiration for the novel, *Journey to the West* (*Xiyou Ji* or *Hsi-yu Chi*) by Wu Chengen (1500–82), one of the most widely read books in Chinese literature. In the story the magical Monkey King converts from the Daoist religion to Buddhism and helps Xuanzang on his pilgrimage. See also BUDDHISM; CHANG'AN; FAXIAN; JOURNEY TO THE WEST; MONKEY; XI'AN.

XUANZONG (EMPEROR) (Hsuan-tsung; 685–761) An emperor during the Tang dynasty (618–907) whose reign was a high point of Tang culture and power; known as Tang Xuanzong. Xuanzong, whose real name was Li Longji (Li Lung-chi), is also commonly referred to by his posthumous title Minghuang, "The Brilliant Emperor"; Xuanzong, meaning "Mysterious Ancestor," was his reign name (r. 712–56). Xuanzong, who took the throne after his father Ruizong (Jui-tsung; r. 684 and 710–12) abdicated, ended the tumultuous period that beset the Tang after the downfall of the notorious Empress Wu (c. 627–705), who was his grandmother. His own downfall was caused by the rebellion in 755 led by An Lushan, a Turkish general who commanded imperial troops in northeastern China.

When Xuanzong took the throne, he enacted badly needed reforms of the taxation system and the imperial bureaucracy, and strengthened the Chinese empire's defenses along its borders. He also reorganized the system by which grain was transported on the canals to the Tang capital at Chang'an (modern Xi'an in Shaanxi Province). Xuanzong subscribed to the Confucian ideal that the ruler should do all he can to benefit his people. He was a great patron of the fine arts, poetry, music, dance and scholarship and created the Hanlin ("Forest of Writing Brushes") Academy, whose members, the greatest scholars of their time, served as advisers to the emperor. Some of the finest Chinese poets flourished during the reign of Xuanzong, including Li Bai (Li Po; 701–62), Du Fu (Tu Fu; 712–70) and Wang Wei (699–761), who was also a painter. Chang'an became the thriving cultural center of China. Xuanzong also supported the Buddhist religion, which had been introduced into China around the first century A.D., and the native Chinese religion of Daoism.

In 737 Xuanzong gave up his active role in government and entrusted matters to chief minister Li Linfu (d. 752). He devoted himself to his favorite concubine, Yang Guifei (Yang Kuei-fei, a title meaning "Yang, Imperial Concubine of Highest Rank"; also known as Yang Yuhuan, "Jade Circlet"). She became one of the most famous women in Chinese history,

not only because of Xuanzong's love for her but also for her association with General An Lushan, who led the anti-Tang rebellion. In 751 Yang Guifei adopted An Lushan as her son. Her cousin Yang Guozhong (Yang Kuo-chung) succeeded Li Linfu as prime minister. Emperor Xuanzong appointed An Lushan governor-general of modern Hubei Province. In 755 An Lushan, who had come into conflict with Yang Guifei's cousin, led his troops westward and captured the city of Luoyang, and in 756 he took Chang'an. The imperial court fled the city, hoping to settle in Sichuan Province, but at a postal station outside the city the troops that accompanied them refused to go any farther until the people who had caused this tragic situation were punished. The soldiers murdered Yang Guozhong and then demanded the death of Yang Guifei. The emperor acceded to their demands, and she hanged herself from a tree. The heir apparent fled west to Lingwu and usurped the throne; he is referred to by his posthumous reign name Suzong (Su-tsung). Xuanzong abdicated and spent the rest of his life tearfully mourning Yang Guifei. The acclaimed Chinese poet Bai Juyi (Po Chu-yi or Po Chu-i; 772–846) commemorated their tragedy in a ballad, *The Everlasting Wrong* (or *Song of Unending Regret*). Tang troops suppressed the rebellion in 757, when An Lushan was murdered by his son, but fighting continued under various leaders until 763 and tragically weakened the Tang dynasty. See also AN LUSHAN; BAI JUYI; BUDDHISM; CHANG'AN; DAOISM; DU FU; GRAND CANAL; HANLIN ACADEMY; LI BAI; TANG DYNASTY; WANG WEI; WU, EMPRESS; YANG GUIFEI.

XUN GUANNIANG (Hsun Kuan-nieng; fourth century) A young woman warrior who became famous for saving her city from attack when she was only 13 years old. Xun Guanniang's story is included in the official *Historical Records of the Jin Dynasty*. The Jin dynasty was one of several during the Six Dynasties Period (220–589). Her grandfather had been commander-in-chief of the army of the Wei State (220–65) during the Three Kingdoms Period. Her father, Xun Song (Hsun Sung), served as Wei's minister of personnel and then as general of the army. Xun Song had two sons, who became scholars, and a daughter, Guanniang. She did not want to practice sewing, which was the expected activity for girls, but insisted on learning the martial arts.

When Xun Song was stationed in the city of Wancheng in modern Shaanxi Province, a treacherous military leader named Du Zeng (Tu Tseng) requested to be stationed there under him. Before long, Du rebelled and had his troops put Wancheng under siege. Xun Song's troops attempted to drive away Du's troops but were defeated. The closed city gates prevented Du from entering Wancheng, but Xun Song only had a small number of troops left and the grain supplies were low. He attempted to send messengers to request aid from his friend Shi Lan, a military official in Xiangyang, but none could get through the enemy lines. Guanniang had been pleading with her father to join the battle, and since none of his male soldiers had been able to break the siege, he finally agreed to let her make the attempt. After midnight she led a dozen soldiers out of the city. Du Zeng was drunk but attempted to fight Guanniang. She guided her troops into a forest, through which they escaped, and took Xun Song's letter to Shi Lan, who ordered Zhou Fang (Chou Fang), a military leader in a nearby city, to send aid. Zhou

Fang's son and Shi Lan joined their troops and marched toward Wancheng. When Du Zeng heard that reinforcements were on the way, he fled in fear. The people of Wancheng welcomed Guanniang back to the city as a great hero. See also MARTIAL ARTS; SIX DYNASTIES PERIOD.

XUNZI (Hsun Tzu; c. 298–238 B.C.)   The most important Confucian scholar at the close of the Warring States Period (403–221 B.C.). Xunzi held high government positions in the states of Qi and Chu. During his life, the Zhou dynasty (1100–256 B.C.) reached the end of its power and the powerful state of Qin conquered its rival feudal states, culminating in the unification of China under the Qin dynasty (221–206 B.C.). Xunzi thus could not share the optimism of earlier Confucianists, and he disagreed with the view held by the prominent Confucian scholar Mencius (Mengzi or Meng Tzu; c. 372–289 B.C.) that human nature is essentially good. According to Xunzi, man must cultivate his goodness through education and the performance of rituals, and this would bring about order in society. As did other Confucianists, Xunzi emphasized the ceremonial performance of "proper" music and dance (*yue* or *yueh*). Whereas earlier thinkers had ascribed to Heaven (*Tian* or *T'ien*) an ethical nature that rewarded good rulers and punished evil ones, Xunzi argued that Heaven is morally neutral and is not affected by human actions. He maintained that human beings form a triad with Heaven and Earth and associated humans with government, the Earth with its resources, and Heaven with the seasons. Xunzi combined elements from the Daoist philosophy, which emphasizes harmony with nature, and the Legalist School of Thought, which maintains that rulers must be harsh in dealing out rewards and punishments, with the concepts of Confucianism. The two most important Legalist thinkers, Li Si (Li Su) and Han Feizi (Han Fei Tzu), upon whose ideas the Qin dynasty was established, were his students. Later Confucian thinkers criticized Xunzi for being too Legalist in his own thinking. Xunzi wrote critiques of the concepts developed within the so-called Hundred Schools of Thought, the many philosophical schools that had arisen during the Zhou dynasty. He published his ideas in a 32-chapter work known as the *Xunzi* (*Hsun Tzu*). He was influential during the Han dynasty (206 B.C.–A.D. 220), but by the Tang dynasty (618–907) the ideas of Mencius had been accepted as orthodox in the Confucian tradition. See also CONFUCIANISM; DAOISM; HAN FEIZI; LEGALIST SCHOOL OF THOUGHT; LI SI; MENCIUS; MUSIC AND DANCE, CEREMONIAL.

Y

YAK (*maoniu*) A large animal similar to a bison that roams wild in herds of more than 100 in the Qinghai-Tibet Plateau (Xing Zang) in western China. The plateau is called the "Roof of the World" because it has elevations averaging more than 13,210 feet above sea level. The air is thin, dry and cold, and the soil is permanently frozen over much of the plateau, similar to Arctic tundra. The yak is a large species of ox. The yak, which has been domesticated by Tibetans, has long dark brown hair that grows longer to hang down over its legs in winter to keep the animal warm in the bitter climate. It has a large hump on the back, a horselike tail and a pair of curving horns that can grow as long as three feet on a male. Tibetans, one of China's national minority ethnic groups, raise yak, sheep, goats and dzo, a cross between a yak and a cow, in the high steppes and summer pastures of the Kunlun Mountain Range and the Trans-Himalaya Mountain Range. Tibetans often lead a semi-nomadic life, taking millions of animals to pasturelands in the summer, where they stay through the autumn, and returning them to stables for the winter. In the spring they slaughter the animals to use for meat, leather fur coats and tents woven from yak hair. Tibetans also drink yak milk, which they ferment and churn into butter that they mix with tea. The long, thin, silky yak hair is woven with wool to make textiles that are smooth, thick, warm and water-repellant. Tibetan herdsmen weave yak hair to make tents and clothes, and make leather from yak hides. Yak milk and meat are a major source of protein for the Tibetans.

The yak was traditionally called *sibuxiang* (*ssu-pu-hsiang*) for the four animals from which it was thought to have borrowed its oddly shaped body: horns from the deer, hooves from the ox, neck from the camel and tail from the donkey. Ancient wise men are depicted holding a yak's tail, or chowry; yak tails are used as whisks to chase away flies. This whisk was frequently held by Buddhist priests as a symbol of their authority. The wise men carried fly whisks as a sign of their leadership over other human beings, just as a herd of deer is believed to be guided by the movements of a yak's tail. Monks in the Buddhist and Daoist religions still carry yak-tail fly whisks to keep their bodies free from dust and worldly contamination. Daoists also regard the fly whisk as magical. See also BUDDHISM; DAOISM; HIMALAYA MOUNTAIN RANGE; KUNLUN MOUNTAIN RANGE; QINGHAI-TIBET PLATEAU; TIBETAN.

YAKUB BEG See HAMI; KASHGAR.

YALU RIVER (Yalujiang) A 500-mile-long river in Liaoning and Jilin Provinces in northeastern China (Manchuria) that, along with the Tumen River, forms the border between China and Korea. The Yalu River, with a drainage area of over 24,250 square miles, originates in Lake Tianchi in the Changbai Mountain Range and flows southwest for 493 miles along the border between China and Korea and empties into the Korea Bay. It flows swiftly and is navigable for large ships for only about 15 miles in the lower reaches. Dandong is an important city on the Chinese side at the mouth of the Yalu; Sinuiju, on the Korean side. Dandong harbor remains ice-free in the winter and accommodates large ships. Bridges across the Yalu link the Chinese cities of Dandong, Ji'an and Shanghekou with the Korean cities of Sinuiju, Manpu and Supung. Hydroelectric plants along the Yalu River provide much of the electricity for Manchuria, China's most heavily industrialized region.

In 1950, units of the Chinese People's Liberation Army (PLA), responding to a perceived threat to the industrial region of northeastern China by United Nations (U.N.) forces that were advancing in North Korea (Democratic People's Republic of Korea), crossed the Yalu River at the request of Communist North Korea. In 1951 the U.N. charged China with being an aggressor in Korea. Chinese forces fought the U.N. forces to a stalemate, and the final settlement returned Korea to its prewar state of division between North and South. See also CHANGBAI MOUNTAIN RANGE; JILIN PROVINCE; LIAONING PROVINCE; UNITED NATIONS; YELLOW SEA.

YAMEN See IMPERIAL BUREAUCRACY; ZONGLI YAMEN.

YAMZHO YUMCO, LAKE See TIBET.

YAN FU (Yen Fu; 1853–1921)   A scholar who translated important works by Western thinkers into Chinese. Yan Fu was born in Fuzhou in Fujian Province. He was educated in Chinese classical literature and then was educated in the Fuzhou shipyard school. He was among the first Chinese students who traveled to Europe, especially Great Britain and France, to continue their studies. In 1877 he went to Britain to enroll in the naval schools at Portsmouth and Greenwich to study British naval technology, the most advanced in the world. He quickly became interested in British government, law, economics and sociology, and read widely in Western political theory. He was especially influenced by the "Social Darwinists" who tried to apply Charles Darwin's theories of the evolution of species and "survival of the fittest" to social units. Returning to China in 1879, Yan took a position as an academic administrator in the Beiyang naval academy established by Li Hongzhang (Li Hung-chang), becoming superintendent of the academy in 1890.

Yan's interest in the modern reform of China became stronger after China suffered a humiliating defeat by Japan in the Sino-Japanese War of 1894–95. He translated such Western liberal classics as Thomas Huxley's *Evolution and Ethics*, Adam Smith's *Wealth of Nations*, Montesquieu's *Defense of the Spirit of the Laws*, Herbert Spencer's *The Study of Sociology* and John Stuart Mill's *On Liberty*, which were circulated widely throughout China. Yan wanted to show the Chinese that the source of the wealth and power of Western nations was not technology, but rather ideas and institutions. He believed that liberal institutions would strengthen the Chinese state, and he argued that Western-style individualism would help support the Chinese state, not oppose it. His translations of works on Social Darwinism influenced the greatest modern Chinese author, Lu Xun (Lu Hsun; 1881–1936). Yan's translation of Huxley's book, to which he gave a nationalistic emphasis, had an enormous impact on Chinese scholars during the late Qing dynasty (1644–1911) and the early days of the republic, which was founded in 1912. Yan argued that in the struggle for survival, social groups struggle with each other, and the strong and clever ones overcome the weak and stupid ones. Reformers such as Liang Qichao (Liang Ch'i-ch'ao) used this concept of social evolution to argue that the Chinese could strengthen and improve themselves to ensure the survival of their country. Mao Zedong (Mao Tse-tung), the founder of Communist China, was also influenced by Yan's translations. In 1911 Yan Fu became the first head of modern Beijing University, the most prestigious university in China, and he held this position for five years. The chaos of the early years of the Chinese Republic, founded after the Revolution of 1911, and the terrible bloodshed of World War I in Europe caused Yan Fu to lose his enthusiasm for the Western evolutionary theories he had translated and to become more interested in ancient Chinese culture. He wrote poetry in addition to making translations, and two collections of his poems were published after he died. See also LI HONGZHANG; LIANG QICHAO; LU XUN; MAO ZEDONG; REVOLUTION OF 1911; SINO-JAPANESE WAR OF 1894–95.

YAN HSI-SHAN See TAIYUAN

YAN XISHAN See NORTHERN EXPEDITION; TAIYUAN.

YAN ZHENQING (Yen Chen-ch'ing; 709–85)   A talented calligrapher during the Tang dynasty (618–907) who had a great influence on later developments in calligraphy. The Chinese have always valued calligraphy as one of the highest art forms. Yan was a member of the Tang government and was a high-ranking official in the army as well as a calligrapher. His writing is noted for strong strokes of the brush and a creative manner of leaving space between characters. Yan's characters seem filled with the energy of his strong and honest nature. Chinese critics have described Yan's calligraphy as having a "virile beauty." Yan is considered the "second prophet" of Chinese calligraphy after Wang Xizhi (Wang Hsi-chih; 321–79), who has been called the "first prophet." However, Yan and Wang have had equal influence in the development of Chinese calligraphic scripts. Many later calligraphers based their styles on Yan Zhenqing's standard, running and cursive scripts. Even today, students of calligraphy master the standard or *kaishu* style by copying the writing of Yan Zhenqing. See also CALLIGRAPHY; WANG XIZHI.

YAN'AN   A city of about 150,000 people situated on the Yan River 168 miles north of Xi'an in Shaanxi Province. Yan'an is a very important site for the People's Republic of China because from 1936 to 1947 it served as the general headquarters of the Chinese Communist Party (CCP). At the time, the CCP was fighting the Japanese, who had invaded China in the 1930s, and also fighting the forces of the Nationalist Party (Kuomintang; KMT) army in a bitter civil war. In 1936 the Communist Eighth Route Army reached Yan'an at the end of its remarkable 8,000-mile, two-and-a-half-year Long March through central and western China to escape the Nationalists. During the march, Mao Zedong (Mao Tse-tung; 1893–1976) was able to consolidate his position as Communist leader. More than 90 percent of the original Communist forces had perished along the route, leaving only 27,000. However, Mao, Zhou Enlai (Chou En-lai) and other Communist leaders spent their time in Yan'an developing the strategies that would enable the Communists to become victorious by appealing to the Chinese peasants, and eventually to establish the People's Republic of China in 1949. Tourists may visit the former offices and homes of the Communists in Yan'an. Mao had to move several times because of bombing raids by the Japanese. His four sparsely furnished cave dwellings, known as the Four Residences of Mao Zedong, have been made into museums. They form part of the former Revolutionary Headquarters, which are open to the public. The Yan'an Revolutionary Museum has also been opened.

Yan'an University became a major center for training government leaders. Yan'an Pagoda, originally built on a nearby mountain during the Song dynasty (960–1279), became a symbol of the country after 1949. It was restored in the 1950s. The Yan River has cut deeply down into the plateaus of loess, the soil that has blown in from deserts to the west for thousands of years. The Ten Thousand Buddha Cave was built into cliffs along the river. People in the area have cut cave homes into the sides of the loess mountains and have built terraced hills for growing crops, mainly wheat, potatoes and corn. Cave homes are cool in summer and warm in winter. Since 1949 Yan'an has been industrialized. See also CIVIL WAR BETWEEN COMMUNISTS AND NATIONALISTS; LOESS; LONG MARCH; MAO ZEDONG; PAGODA; SHAANXI PROVINCE; WAR OF RESISTANCE AGAINST JAPAN.

YANG See YIN AND YANG.

YANG CH'IN See STRING INSTRUMENTS.

YANG CHU SCHOOL OF THOUGHT See YANGZHU SCHOOL OF THOUGHT.

YANG DEZHI See PEOPLE'S LIBERATION ARMY.

YANG GUIFEI (Yang Kuei-fei; d. 755) "Honorable Consort Yang"; the favorite concubine of the Tang dynasty's (618–907) Emperor Xuanzong (Hsuan-tsung; r. 712–56), and the person who was blamed for the An Lushan rebellion that temporarily deposed the emperor and nearly brought down the Tang dynasty. Yang Guifei is considered one of the Four Great Beauties of China (*Si Mei Ren*).

She was the daughter of a commoner, but the emperor became so enamored of her that he designated her number one among his thousands of concubines. He pledged his eternal love to her every year at the romantic Festival of the Cowherd and Weaver Maid on the seventh day of the seventh lunar month (around August). He brought hundreds of musicians and dancers to court to entertain her. Yang Guifei liked litchi fruit so much that mounted couriers rode day and night between the Tang capital at Chang'an (modern Xi'an) and Guangzhou (Canton), more than 1,500 miles to the south, to bring litchis to the court. Xuanzong was so obsessed with Yang Guifei that he devoted all his wealth and time to her and neglected his duties of state. He gave her inordinate power and raised her male relatives to the court ranks of duke and count, and they became embroiled in factional struggles. Her cousin Yang Guozhong (Yang Kuo-chung) became prime minister.

An Lushan (703–57), a regional commander of Turkish origin, became powerful at court through the patronage of Yang Guifei. She even adopted him as her legal son, but he came into conflict with her cousin and led a revolt in 755. An Lushan's army took Chang'an and he proclaimed himself the new emperor. Emperor Xuanzong fled for Sichuan Province and took Yang Guifei with him, but on the way his troops insisted on the deaths of her and her cousin, blaming them for the disaster. They forced the emperor to order Yang Guifei to die, and she hanged herself on a tree with a silken cord the emperor gave her. An Lushan was murdered by his own son in 757, and armies loyal to the emperor put the rebellion down and restored order by 762. However, the distraught emperor abdicated the throne to one of his sons and spent the rest of his life wandering around the palace lost in mourning for his beloved Yang Guifei. This story became a popular subject in Chinese painting and poetry, notably "Eternal Sorrows" or "Song of Unending Regret"

(*Changhenke* or *Ch'ang-hen ko*) by the renowned Tang poet Bai Juyi (Po Chu-yi or Po Chu-i; 772–846). See also AN LUSHAN; BAI JUYI; CONCUBINAGE; COWHERD AND WEAVER MAID FESTIVAL; LITCHI; TANG DYNASTY; XI'AN; XUANZONG, EMPEROR.

YANG HSIU-CH'ING See SHI DAKAI; TAIPING REBELLION.

YANG KUEI-FEI See AN LUSHAN REBELLION; XUANZONG, EMPEROR; YANG GUIFEI.

YANG SHANGKUN (Yang Shang-k'un; 1907–) The former president of the People's Republic of China (PRC), founded in 1949 by the Chinese Communist Party (CCP). Yang was born in Sichuan Province, where he joined the Communist Youth League, the CCP organization for young people, in 1925. The next year he studied at the Sino-French Institute, which was operated in Chongqing by the Nationalist (Kuomintang; KMT) Party, with which the newly founded CCP was then cooperating. Yang became a member of the CCP in 1927. He studied in Shanghai and worked as a labor organizer under Zhou Enlai (Chou En-lai; 1898–1976), who later became the second highest leader in the CCP. From 1927 to 1931 Yang attended Sun Yatsen University in Moscow, established by the U.S.S.R. for visiting Chinese Communist students. When he returned to China he worked underground in Shanghai for the CCP from 1931 to 1932. Between 1933 and 1937 he served as director of the CCP Political Department under Zhou in the First Red (Communist) Army, except for the period between 1934 and 1935 when the Communists made their Long March west to Yan'an in Shaanxi Province to escape the Nationalists, who had turned on the Communists and brutally attacked them in 1927.

Over the next five decades Yang held a number of positions in the CCP. During China's War of Resistance against Japan (1937–45; World War II), from 1940 to 1946 he was secretary-general at the Eighth Route Army headquarters in Yan'an. In 1945 he began a two-decade term as head of the CCP Central Committee's General Office. After the Communists defeated the Nationalists and founded the PRC in 1949, with the capital at Beijing, Yang was a member of the executive board of the Sino-Soviet Friendship Association. He was elected to the Standing Committee of the CCP Central Committee from 1954 to 1964. In 1956 he was elected to the Central Committee and Secretariat under Deng Xiaoping (Teng Hsiao-p'ing; 1904–97). In 1966, when the Cultural Revolution (1966–76) broke out, Yang was accused of being a counter-revolutionary revisionist. He was later rehabilitated. From 1970 to 1979 Yang was second CCP secretary and vice-chairman of the Guangdong Provincial Revolutionary Committee. In 1979 he was elected a member of the CCP Central Committee's Standing Committee. From 1979 to 1980 he served as vice-governor of Guangdong Province and then as first political commissar, Guangdong Military District. From 1980 to 1983 he was elected Guangdong deputy, Presidium member, vice chairman and secretary-general of the Fifth National Party Congress. From 1981 to 1982 he also served as secretary-general of the Central Committee's Central Military Commission.

In 1982 and 1987 Yang was elected to the Central Committee and Politburo of the 12th and 13th National Party Congresses. In 1982 he was elected permanent vice chairman of the CCP Central Military Commission and in 1983, vice chairman of the PRC State Central Military Commission. In 1988 Yang was elected president of the PRC. He played a major role in the party's use of the military to harshly suppress the pro-democracy student demonstrations in Tiananmen Square in Beijing in 1989. Since 1979 Yang has also been the head of PRC delegations that have visited Japan, North Korea, the Federal Republic of Germany, Austria, Romania and the Philippines. He stepped down as president of the PRC in 1990. See also CHINESE COMMUNIST PARTY; CIVIL WAR BETWEEN COMMUNISTS AND NATIONALISTS; COMMUNIST YOUTH LEAGUE; CULTURAL REVOLUTION; EIGHTH ROUTE ARMY; GOVERNMENT STRUCTURE; PEOPLE'S REPUBLIC OF CHINA; WAR OF RESISTANCE AGAINST JAPAN; YAN'AN; ZHOU ENLAI.

YANG TEH-CHIH   See PEOPLE'S LIBERATION ARMY.

YANG XIUQING   See SHI DAKAI; TAIPING REBELLION.

YANG YU-HUAN   See YANG GUIFEI.

YANG ZHU (YANG CHU) SCHOOL OF THOUGHT
One of the so-called "Hundred Schools of Thought" in ancient China; also known as Yangism. The school was named for Yang Zhu (Yang Chu; 440–c. 360 B.C.), one of the first thinkers in the philosophical tradition known as Daoism (Taoism). Only a few fragments of Yang Zhu's writings have survived. Followers of the Yang Zhu school of thought were concerned with the health and longevity of the body and the avoidance of attachment to worldly things. Mencius (Mengzi or Meng Tzu; c. 372–289 B.C.), the second-most important Confucian philosopher, attacked Yang Zhu for supposedly teaching the principles of "every man for himself" and hedonism. Confucianists maintained that the good person should take action in society to help bring about good government, and Mencius argued that Yang Zhu was so egoistical that he would not perform even the simple action of plucking one hair to help the whole world. However, as a Daoist, Yang Zhu advocated the principle of naturalism whereby one has to let life "have its own way" or freely run its course. One should live naturally and pleasurably with neither strict self-restraint nor self-indulgence and without being concerned about wealth and fame or life and death. A chapter in the Daoist work *Liezi* (*Lieh Tzu*), composed around the third century A.D., has been erroneously attributed to Yang Zhu. The chapter presents a pessimistic view of life, arguing that no matter how long or short one lives or whether one is wise and good or stupid and criminal, everyone dies and turns to rotted bones. Therefore, one should enjoy life with perfect happiness and freedom while one can. See also DAOISM; HUNDRED SCHOOLS OF THOUGHT; MENCIUS.

YANGCHOW   See YANGZHOU.

YANGDI (EMPEROR)   (Yang-ti; 569–618)   Also known as Sui Yangdi; the second emperor of the Sui dynasty (581–618), which reunified China after three centuries of disunity following the collapse of the Han dynasty (206 B.C.–A.D. 220). Yangdi was born Yuan Guang (Yuan Kuang), the second son of Wendi (Wen-ti; 541–604), the first Sui emperor. Yangdi reigned as Sui emperor 604–618. His reign name, Yangdi, means "Emblazoned Emperor." When only 13 years old he was married into a royal family in southern China. He served for 10 years as viceroy of the southern territory with his seat at Jiangdu (modern Yangzhou) on the Yangzi River (Changjiang). He became emperor because his eldest brother, the crown prince, had a falling out with their mother, Empress Dugu (Tu-hu). Yangdi may have caused his father's death to become emperor himself. He was an active emperor who expanded many institutions that had been established by his father, such as the imperial bureaucracy or civil service and its system for education and examinations. Confucian scholarship was revived during his reign. He sent military forces to bring under Chinese control oasis cities on the Silk Road to the west; nomadic Turkish tribes to the north; northern Vietnam, which lay south of China; and the Cham ethnic group in southern China. He also opened diplomatic relations with Japan.

Yangdi undertook massive public works projects, such as the reinforcement of the Great Wall and the building of roads and canals between major cities that became links in the Grand Canal, and the construction of two enormous grain storages. Yangdi kept Chang'an (modern Xi'an in Shaanxi Province) as the center of his government, but he reconstructed the capital city of Luoyang to the east and built luxurious palaces there. The Chinese people began to resent Yangdi's conscription of millions of laborers on these projects, many of whom died, and the high taxes he imposed to raise money for these projects and his military expeditions. When Yangdi sent three huge but unsuccessful military expeditions to conquer the north Korean kingdom of Koguryo, peasant rebellions broke out across northern China. Yangdi retreated by sailing to his southern capital at Jiangdu, where he was assassinated in 618. He has a reputation as one of the harshest of all Chinese emperors. However, his accomplishments laid the foundation for the Tang (618–907), considered by many historians the greatest of all Chinese dynasties. See also CHANG'AN; CONFUCIANISM; GRAND CANAL; GREAT WALL; IMPERIAL EXAMINATION SYSTEM; LUOYANG; SILK ROAD; SUI DYNASTY; TANG DYNASTY; WENDI (EMPEROR).

YANGGE   (*yang-k'o*)   A type of folk dance popular in many regions of China. *Yangge* originated as a form of entertainment for farmers as they performed the back-breaking labor of transplanting rice shoots (*yang*). Performers traditionally sang and danced in the fields to the loud accompaniment of drums and gongs. The dance is still performed at rice-transplanting time by members of several ethnic minority groups in China, such as the Bai and the Tujia in southwestern China. The Han Chinese, who comprise about 93 percent of the country's population, enjoy *yangge* performances at temple fairs and festivals, especially at the New Year or Spring Festival in late January or early February. In northern Chinese villages, a *yangko* group commonly dances from door to door to wish the residents a happy New Year. The costumed dancers perform graceful movements while waving silk fans and colorful handkerchiefs. Formerly men played the female dancers' parts, but now women participate in the dance. *Yangge* is usually performed with an acrobatic form of entertainment known as stilt walking. See also BAI; DRUMS; MINORITIES, NATIONAL; NEW YEAR FESTIVAL; RICE; STILT WALKING; TUJIA.

YANGQIN   See STRING INSTRUMENTS.

YANGSHAO CULTURE   One of the earliest Neolithic settled cultures in China, dating from the fifth to the third millennium B.C. The Yangshao culture developed during the Neolithic period (c. 12,000– c. 2000 B.C.) along the valleys of the Wei River and the middle Yellow River (Huanghe) in northern China and is named for Yangshao village in Henan Province where artifacts from the culture were first identified in 1921.

Formerly hunter-gatherer tribes, the Yangshao people settled into villages divided into areas for dwelling, making pottery by firing clay pieces in kilns and burying the dead. The excavation of a Yangshao village at Banpo near modern Xi'an in Shaanxi Province has revealed the daily life in a Yangshao village with about 500 to 600 inhabitants. The people lived in round thatched homes with pigs and dogs that they had domesticated, fished with nets, gathered fruits and nuts, made pottery with painted decorations, raised silkworms and grew millet that they ground into flour with mortars and pestles. The major crop of the Yangshao culture, millet has ever since been the principal grain consumed in northern China, in contrast to rice, which is cultivated throughout southern China. Yangshao people buried their dead in round pits, and food and utensils placed in the graves are evidence of the early beginnings of so-called ancestor worship, the provision of necessary items for the spirit as it journeys to the next world. Frequently a female corpse was placed in the center of the grave, along with her finest pottery and other possessions, indicating a matriarchal society.

Yangshao culture is characterized by red painted pottery that is one of the two major ceramic types produced in China during the Neolithic period. The second type is a fine black ware from the Longshan culture (c. 3000–c. 2200 B.C.) in modern Shandong Province in eastern China. Before 2000 B.C. Yangshao potters were making coiled red earthenware that was fired in kilns and decorated with plants, fish and spiral or curvilinear designs using black and occasionally white pigments. These pieces were produced for burial in graves and included tall rounded jars, flaring bowls and three-footed bowls whose form was the prototype for a type of bronze pot called a *ding* (ting) that was widely produced for ritual purposes during the Shang dynasty (1750–1040 B.C.). Fish designs were especially prominent in the Wei River valley. See also ANCESTOR WORSHIP; ARCHAEOLOGY; BRONZEWARE; DING; LONGSHAN CULTURE; NEOLITHIC PERIOD; XI'AN.

YANG-TI, EMPEROR   See YANGDI (EMPEROR).

YANGTZE (YANGTSE) RIVER   See YANGZI RIVER.

YANGUO GORGE POWER STATION   See YELLOW RIVER.

YANGWU MOVEMENT   See WESTERNIZATION MOVEMENT.

YANGZHOU   A city in Jiangsu Province at the meeting point of the Huai and Yangzi (Chiangjiang) Rivers. Yangzhou lies on the site of an ancient fortress called Hancheng that during the Warring States Period (403–221 B.C.) was a base for attacks by the state of Wu on states of the Central China Plain. The town that grew up here became important when construction of the Grand Canal began during the reign of Emperor Yangdi (Yang-ti; A.D. 569–618) to ship grain from the fertile south to the arid north. He made Yangzhou the southern capital of the Sui dynasty (581–618), second to the main capital at Luoyang. The Grand Canal flows through the center of the city in a maze of interlinked waterways into the Yangzi River.

By the Tang dynasty (618–907), Yangzhou had become a major commercial center. Many Arab and Persian merchants settled there when it was opened to foreign trade, but were massacred during the An Lushan Rebellion in 760. A famous Tang native of the city was the Buddhist monk Jian Zhen (Chien Chen), who took the Buddhist religion as well as Chinese art, culture and medicine to Japan. Poets such as Li Bai (Li Po) and Du Fu (Tu Fu) came to Yangzhou often and wrote hundreds of poems praising its beauty.

Yangzhou was a large commercial city when Marco Polo, a Venetian trader who served the Yuan dynasty (1279–1368) government, became its governor for three years from 1282 to 1285. In the 17th century the city was viciously attacked because it resisted the Manchus who invaded China and established the Qing dynasty (1644–1911). It recovered, and from the early 18th to early 19th centuries the salt trade was a lucrative enterprise in Yangzhou. Salt merchants were wealthy patrons to the many scholars and artists who flocked to the city and added to its fame, notably the so-called Eight Eccentrics of Yangzhou. Their works are exhibited in the Municipal Museum. Other sites include Slender West (Shou Xi) Lake Park, Fajing Temple (formerly known as Daming Temple), Flat Hills Hall, the Pavilion of Flourishing Culture and the Tomb of Puhaddin (a 16th-century descendant of Muhammad who settled in Yangzhou).

Yangzhou has more than 180 gardens, including He Garden, Yechun Garden and Ge Garden and Yangzhou City Museum. Yangzhou is known for its local arts and crafts, such as lacquerware, jade carvings, embroidery, papercuttings, container gardens (known by the Japanese term *bonsai* in the West) and woodblock reproductions of ancient books. Lacquer work goes back more than 2,000 years in Yangzhou. Recently, Yangzhou has been developing into an international trading city and has built a new port on the Yangzi that can accommodate 10,000-ton ships. See also AN LUSHAN REBELLION; DU FU; GRAND CANAL; EIGHT ECCENTRICS OF YANGZHOU; HUAI RIVER; JIANGSU PROVINCE; LI BAI; POLO, MARCO; YANGZI RIVER.

YANGZI RIVER   (Changjiang, "Long River"; Yangtze or Yangtse)   The longest and most important river in China and in all of Asia, and the third-longest river in the world. The Yangzi River flows west to east for 3,494 miles through some of China's major economic centers and provides the main transportation route across central China, one of the most densely populated areas in the world. It has a catchment area of 450,000 square miles, and its annual flow to the sea averages 3.4585 U.S. billion cubic feet. The mean volume of water discharged at the mouth of the river is estimated at 770,000 cubic feet per second, while the sediment deposited at the mouth totals about 6,428 million cubic feet annually. The Yangzi has 700 tributaries and its drainage basin covers 20 percent of China's total land area. One in 13 people on Earth lives in the Yangzi Basin. The dry, wheat and millet-growing area of North China and the moist rice-growing area of the South divide along the 33rd parallel, about halfway between the Yangzi and the Yellow River (Huanghe) to the north. Rice cultivation is the major agricultural activity throughout the Yangzi River valley and southern China. The Qinlingshan Range divides the Yangzi from the North China Plain.

The Yangzi originates in the Tanggulashan on the border of Tibet and Qinghai Autonomous Regions and drops more than 21,600 feet from its source to its estuary. It flows down through the valleys of high mountain ranges in Qinghai, Tibet and Yunnan Provinces. After it turns northeast from Shigu in Yunnan, the river drops 660 feet in one 10-mile stretch, creating great turbulence. It then crosses the provinces of Sichuan, Hubei, Hunan, Jiangxi, Anhui and Jiangsu, and empties into the East China Sea at Chongming Island near the major port city of Shanghai.

The Yangzi River previously entered the sea at a point farther south, on a course that crossed Lake Tai, the third-largest lake in China, and Hangzhou Bay. Along the middle and lower reaches of the river are found the largest number of deepwater lakes in China. Lotus plants grow abundantly in the shallow lakes along the Yangzi and are harvested for their edible roots and seeds. Lake Poyang, the largest fresh-water lake, and Lake Dongting, the second largest, lie in the middle reach of the Yangzi. Lake Poyang was for many centuries a major center for shipping goods between the Yangzi valley and the large southern port city of Guangzhou (Canton). Thousands of migratory birds, including the Japanese crane, migrate annually to Lake Poyang.

The 1,440 mile section of the Yangzi from Yushu in southern Qinghai to Yibin City in Sichuan is called the Jinsha River. The Yangzi River proper begins at the confluence of the Min and Jinsha Rivers at Yibin, where they enter the Sichuan Basin. In Hubei and Hunan Provinces the Yangzi flows calmly and makes many curving turns. The river is navigable by river steamer along the lower half of its length, and river steamships of 5,000 to 10,000 deadweight-ton capacity can sail inland as far as Hankou (Wuhan) in Hubei Province. At Nanjing, which lies on the south bank of the Yangzi, a bridge was built between 1960 and 1968 over the river to connect the regions north and south of the Yangzi. The Chinese are very proud of the Changjiang Daqio Bridge, which spans the river for 568 feet and has two levels, the upper level for automobiles, bicycles and pedestrians, and the lower for railroad trains. At its delta the Yangzi has formed a wide plain known as "The Land of Fish and Rice" for the abundant species of fish and rice that flourish there. The delta is 50 miles across at its widest point.

The Yangzi was named for the ancient kingdom of Yang (c. 1000 B.C.), which was located along its present lower course. Discoveries at sites from the Neolithic period (c. 12,000–c. 2000 B.C.) indicate settlements where agriculture was practiced. Pottery deposits from the Yangshao and Longshan cultures have been excavated in areas on the North China Plain and along the Yellow River and Lower Yangzi. After the Zhou dynasty (1100–256 B.C.) conquered the east-

ern Chinese plain, the Zhou expanded their power by defeating nomads in the northwest and by moving south into the Han and Yangzi river areas and southeast along the Huai River. Lacquer, made from the sap of the lac tree that is used to make beautiful waterproof wood products, was discovered in the Yangzi valley during the Zhou dynasty. Emperor Qin Shi Huangdi, founder of the Qin dynasty (221–206 B.C.), had waterways and canals constructed to allow transportation by water for 1,200 miles from the Yangzi to Guangzhou. The Sui dynasty (581–618) extended south along the Yangzi. The second Sui emperor Sui Yangdi (Yang-ti) extended the Grand Canal from Hangzhou north across the Yangzi to Yangzhou and then northwest from the Yangzi delta to the capital region at Chang'an (modern Xi'an in Shaanxi Province). By 609 the Grand Canal was extended from this far inland point to the region of Tianjin and Beijing on China's northeastern coast. Barges could then transport food and goods from the lower Yangzi River valley up through North China to supply troops on the northern frontier and to feed the population in the capital region. By the Tang dynasty (618–907), the Yangzi River delta had become the center of economic power in China, due to centuries of human labor that had drained the marshes and constructed the canals, irrigation channels and terrace fields for the cultivation and shipping of rice.

Kaifeng, the capital of the Northern Song dynasty (960–1126), was located near the junction of the early Grand Canal and the Yellow River, the culminating point for barge transportation of rice from the Lower Yangzi. The network of waterways extended for about 30,000 miles. After the Northern Song fell to the Jin in 1127, the Southern Song dynasty (1127–1279) established its capital at Hangzhou, and the Yangzi valley and areas to the south grew rapidly both in population and rice cultivation. Many new dikes were also built along the river to protect against flooding. During the Southern Song the wealthy families in the Yangzi River valley dominated the cultural, intellectual and economic activities in the Chinese Empire.

By 1800 the Yangzi River system supported more than 200 million people. Today about 300 million people live along the middle and lower reaches of the river. During China's War of Resistance against Japan (1937–45; World War II), Chinese Nationalists (Kuomintang; KMT) under General Chiang Kai-shek retreated up the Yangzi River to Sichuan Province and established their capital at Chongqing on the river. During the civil war with the Chinese Communists that followed, the Nationalists made their last stand north of Nanjing on the Yangzi River, and they lost the civil war after Communist forces under Mao Zedong (Mao Tsetung) crossed the Yangzi in 1949 and took every city in their path to Beijing.

The Yangzi has an enormous potential to generate hydroelectric power, and at present it generates nearly half of China's total output (China has the greatest potential for hydroelectric power in the world). Although the Yangzi widens greatly east of Yichang, the water brought in by several tributary rivers that enter at Jiangling causes frequent flooding. The traditional Chinese way of dealing with destructive floods had been to build dikes to contain the river and to divert the water into lakes and marshes. After 1949 the Chinese government planned major projects in the

Yangzi valley for flood control, power and irrigation, although these have been slowed down by political controversy. In 1952 a major flood-control project was completed in the Jiangling area. That year, the Yangzi Valley Planning Office (YVPO) was formed to oversee the development of the Yangzi River resources proposed by the Chinese government, including a huge hydroelectric plant to be constructed on the river at the Three Gorges about four miles above Yichang. Another project was planned to divert the water from the upper portion of the Yangzi to the Yellow River in Qinghai Province to provide irrigation water for northwestern China, especially the Tarim Basin. Construction of a huge dam at the Three Gorges, known as Gezhou Dam, was begun in 1970 but was interrupted by the Cultural Revolution (1966–76). The first phase of the dam was completed in 1981, and power generation was begun and locks were open to ships. Between 1983 and 1984, famous Chinese writers and scientists led a movement to protest the monumental Three Gorges Water Conservancy Project, which would flood the region, burying numerous natural and historical sites and forcing the relocation of 1.3 million people. Groups opposed to the project lobbied the World Bank against funding it. However, the second phase was completed by the late 1980s. After the Tiananmen Square massacre in 1989, the Chinese government forbade all further public debate about the project. In 1992 despite the opposition of many officials, the government approved the start-up of the project. In November 1997 the Yangzi was diverted from its natural course to enable construction of the Three Gorges Dam, planned to be 606 feet high and nearly two miles wide. The government also plans to divert water from the Yangzi to Beijing and the dry North China Plain, and to northwestern China, especially the Tarim Basin. See also CHONGQING; CIVIL WAR BETWEEN COMMUNISTS AND NATIONALISTS; DONGTING, LAKE; GRAND CANAL; HANGZHOU; LACQUERWARE; NANJING; POYANG, LAKE; QINLING MOUNTAIN RANGE; RICE; SHANGHAI; SICHUAN PROVINCE; SOUTHERN SONG DYNASTY; TAI, LAKE; YELLOW RIVER.

YANHUI See BANQUETS.

YAO One of China's 55 national minority ethnic groups. The 1990 Chinese census showed that there were 2,134,013 Yao living in the southern provinces of Hunan, Yunnan, Guangdong and Guizhou, and in Guangxi-Zhuang Autonomous Region, where most of them are concentrated. Yao people also reside in Thailand to the south of China. The Yao ethnic group includes more than 30 sub-groups, such as the Beitou, Baiku, Chashan and Hualan. Each has its own distinct customs and clothing styles. After 1949 the names of these groups were unified as the Yao. The Yao belong to the Miao-Yao linguistic group, but they have been influenced by the Chinese language and culture for many centuries. They still use their own language and wear their own native clothing. They practice an animistic form of religion in which they believe that inanimate things are inhabited by spirits. Like the Miao, the Yao generally live in remote mountainous regions and practice slash-and-burn agriculture, having to move a whole village when the land around the village is used up. Their main crops are dry rice, maize and vegetables. They also raise pigs and water buffaloes. The Yao hold their

harvest festival on the 14th day of the seventh month in their lunar calendar. See also GUANGXI-ZHUANG AUTONOMOUS REGION; MIAO; MINORITIES, NATIONAL.

YAO, EMPEROR (r. 2357–2256 B.C. [legendary]) The fourth of Five Emperors or Sage-Kings in the prehistoric period who reputedly taught the arts of civilization to the Chinese people, and the successor to the Yellow Emperor. Legends praise Yao for bringing peace and prosperity to his subjects, and scholars of Confucianism have idealized Yao as a ruler of great virtue. Yao is discussed in the *Book of History* (*Shujing* or *Shu Ching*), one of the Five Classics of the Confucian canon. Yao decided that his own son was not worthy to inherit the throne, so he named Shun to be his successor (Shun became the fifth of the Five Emperors). According to legend, this caused such a violent rebellion that all 10 suns appeared together in the sky. The world would have been burned up, but Emperor Shun sent Yi, the Good Archer and husband of the moon goddess Chang-E, to shoot down nine of them and thus save the world. See also BOOK OF HISTORY; CHANG E; CONFUCIANISM; EMPEROR; SHUN, EMPEROR; YELLOW EMPEROR.

YAO WENYUAN See CULTURAL REVOLUTION; GANG OF FOUR.

YARLUNG, KINGDOM OF, AND YARLUNG RIVER See HIMALAYA MOUNTAIN RANGE; TIBET.

YE JIANYING (Yeh Chien-ying; 1897–1986) A prominent Chinese Communist military commander and leader in the government of the People's Republic of China (PRC). Ye was born in Guangdong Province in southern China and lived in Singapore and Hanoi, Vietnam when he was young. Back in China, he graduated from the Yunnan (Province) Military Academy. Ye helped Sun Yat-sen, the founder of modern China, establish the Whampoa Military Academy near the southern Chinese city of Guangzhou (Canton) in 1924. Ye took part in several expeditions against Chinese warlords, including the 1926 Northern Expedition. From 1928 to 1931, he studied military science in Moscow. In the 1920s the Nationalist Party (Kuomintang; KMT), founded by Sun and later led by Chiang Kai-shek, had made an alliance with the newly founded Chinese Communist Party (CCP), but in 1927 the Nationalists purged the CCP and massacred many Communists. In protest, Zhou Enlai (Chou En-lai) and other Communists staged the 1927 Nanchang Uprising, which Ye supported. In the late 1920s, Ye led a Communist uprising in Guangzhou and became a general of the Red Army (forerunner of the People's Liberation Army; PLA), serving as president and political commissar of a Red Army training school. In the early 1930s, he became commander of the Fujian (Province) Army Units and chief of general staff of the CCP Central Military Commission. When the main force of the First Front Army of the Communist Red Army began the rigorous Long March west to escape the Nationalists in 1935, Ye commanded the column of soldiers from the Central Military Commission, and he helped chief of general staff Liu Bocheng (Liu Po-ch'eng) organize a Communist campaign to break through the Nationalist line on the Wu River and seize Zunyi. There the CCP Central Committee held a meeting that proved important to the eventual success of the Chinese Communist revolution. When the Red Army established its new headquarters at Yan'an in northern Shaanxi Province, Ye helped Communist leaders Mao Zedong (Mao Tse-tung) and Peng Dehuai (P'eng Teh-huai) win two victories in the area.

In December 1936, several KMT leaders placed Chiang Kai-shek under house arrest at Huaqing Hot Springs near Xi'an to force him to make the KMT cooperate with the CCP to fight the Japanese who had invaded China; this is known as the Xi'an Incident. Ye assisted Zhou Enlai in negotiating with the KMT, which resulted in a new KMT-CCP united front to fight China's War of Resistance against Japan (1937–45; World War II). During this war, the Communists reorganized the Red Army into the Eighth Route Army and the New Fourth Army. Ye returned to Yan'an and became chief of general staff of the Eighth Route Army, working with Mao and Commander in Chief Zhu De (Chu Teh) to make strategic plans for the entire CCP and its armies. After Japan surrendered in 1945, the CCP and KMT agreed to stop fighting their civil war, but Ye learned that the KMT planned to resume its civil war with the CCP. The CCP called Ye back to its Central Military Commission in Yan'an, where he served as deputy chief of staff of the CCP army. In 1949 the CCP defeated the KMT, who fled to Taiwan Island and established the Republic of China (ROC) under Chiang Kai-shek's leadership. On mainland China, the CCP established the People's Republic of China (PRC) under Mao Zedong's leadership. Ye held important positions in the PRC government. In 1955, he was promoted to marshal, the highest rank in the PRC, and was awarded the orders of August 1st, Independence and Freedom, first class.

In 1966 the Cultural Revolution erupted and threw China into turmoil for 10 years. In 1976, less than a month after Mao died, Ye, who was minister of national defense, and Wang Dongxing (Wang Tung-hsing), commander of the elite bodyguard of the CCP, arrested Jiang Qing (Chiang Ch'ing) 2, Mao's wife, and three other CCP members charging them with instigating the Cultural Revolution; they became known as the Gang of Four. A few days later, Hua Guofeng was named party chairman, chairman of the party's Central Military Commission, and premier. At the 11th National Party Congress from August 12 to 19, 1977, Ye, Wang Dongxing, Deng Xiaoping (Teng Hsiao-p'ing) and Li Xiannian (Li Hsien-nien) were elected vice chairmen of the CCP. This congress proclaimed that the Cultural Revolution had formally ended, blamed it on the Gang of Four, and asserted that the current task for the CCP was to build China into a modern, powerful country. At the September 1979 Fourth Plenum of the Eleventh Central Committee, CCP vice chairman Ye proclaimed that the Cultural Revolution had been "an appalling catastrophe" and a severe setback to the socialist cause. After Deng Xiaoping became chairman of the newly created CCP Central Military Commission in l982, Ye Jianying and other military leaders criticized Deng's policies for cultural liberalization and industrial and agricultural reform, but Deng was able to blunt their criticisms. At the sixth National People's Congress in 1983, Ye was honored for serving as chairman of the Standing Committee of the fifth National People's Congress. In 1985 Ye resigned his position on the select Politburo's Standing Committee, and died a

year later. His wife, Zeng Xianchi (Tseng Hsien-ch'ih), also died in 1986. See also CHINESE COMMUNIST PARTY; CIVIL WAR BETWEEN COMMUNISTS AND NATIONALISTS; CULTURAL REVOLUTION; DENG XIAOPING; EIGHTH ROUTE ARMY; GANG OF FOUR; HUA GUOFENG; HUAQING HOT SPRINGS; JIANG QING; LONG MARCH; MAO ZEDONG; NATIONAL PEOPLE'S CONGRESS; NORTHERN EXPEDITION; PENG DEHUAI; PEOPLE'S LIBERATION ARMY; PEOPLE'S REPUBLIC OF CHINA; POLITBURO; WAR OF RESISTANCE AGAINST JAPAN; WHAMPOA MILITARY ACADEMY; YAN'AN; ZHOU ENLAI; ZHU DE.

YEH CHIEN-YING   See YE JIANYING.

YEH-LU CH'U-TS'AI   See YELU CHUCAI.

YEHONALA   See CIXI, EMPRESS DOWAGER.

YELLOW EARTH   See CHEN KAIGE; ZHANG YIMOU.

YELLOW EMPEROR   Also known as Huangdi (Huang-ti); the first of the legendary Five Emperors. According to legend, the Yellow Emperor sat on the throne 2697–2597 B.C., and was followed by legendary emperor Shen Nong (Shen-nung). Ancient Chinese legends claim that he invented astrology, alchemy, an agricultural calendar, the chariot wheel, potter's wheel, magnetic compass, armor, boats and coins for money, which replaced cowry shells as the unit of exchange. His minister invented the first written symbols. The Yellow Emperor wrote *The Yellow Emperor's Classic of Medicine* (*Niejing Suwen* or *Nieh-ching su-wen*), a treatise on medicine that supposedly contained the secrets of how to become immortal and to make gold. Many historical Chinese emperors sought to gain these abilities and make themselves equal to the Yellow Emperor. Philosophers in the Daoist tradition, who were also concerned with immortality and alchemy, revered the Yellow Emperor as the source of their teachings. Sculptures of the Yellow Emperor are placed in some Daoist temples. The Chinese traditionally believed that their clan and family names derived from the 12 names he gave to his sons. The Yellow Emperor's wife, Leizu (Lei-tsu), was a skilled housekeeper and taught the Chinese sericulture, the cultivation of silkworms and the weaving of silk textiles from their cocoons.

According to legends, the Yellow Emperor defeated the Miao people, a tribe from the south, and thus enabled the Chinese race, known as the Han people, to settle in the central Yellow River valley in North China. His minister Zhiyu (Chih-yu) invented warfare and weapons and rebelled against him, but Huangdi was able to defeat the minister by using his inventions. He also asked for help from Pa, the goddess of drought, who drove off the wind and rain summoned by Zhiyu but stayed on Earth after the minister was defeated. Huangdi finally had to send Pa into exile to save the human race.

The Yellow Emperor was associated with the Mandate of Heaven (*tianming* or *t'ien-ming*), the concept that the emperor is permitted by heaven (*tian* or *t'ien*) to sit on the throne only if he remains virtuous. This concept was used throughout Chinese history to legitimize the reign of emperors and the founding of new dynasties. Legends claim that after the Yellow Emperor organized his kingdom, he ascended into the sky as an immortal being. King Zheng of Qin, the unifier of the Chinese Empire under the Qin dynasty (221–206 B.C.), gave himself the title Qin Shi Huangdi ("First Sovereign Qin Emperor") to associate himself with the supernatural powers attributed to Huangdi. He built himself a splendid mausoleum at Mount Li in anticipation of joining the band of immortals after he died on Earth. See also DAOISM; ELIXIR OF IMMORTALITY; EMPEROR; HAN; MANDATE OF HEAVEN; QIN SHI HUANGDI; SHEN NONG, EMPEROR; SILK.

YELLOW HAT SECT OF LAMAISM See DALAI LAMA; LAMAISM; TIBET; XINING.

YELLOW ISLAND See QINGDAO; SHANDONG PROVINCE; SPECIAL ECONOMIC ZONES.

YELLOW RIVER (Huanghe)   The second-longest river in China, next to the Yangzi River (Changjiang). The Yellow River flows for about 2,903 miles across northern China, roughly paralleling the Yangzi to the south. The Qinling Mountain Range divides the watersheds between these two great rivers. The Yellow River originates in the Bayan Harshan Mountains of the Qinghai-Tibet Plateau in western China. The Yellow River-Huangshui Basin forms one section of the Qinghai-Tibet Plateau. The Yellow River flows in a winding course east and then northeast through the provinces of Qinghai, Gansu, Ningxia and Inner Mongolia Autonomous Region, then turns to flow south to form the border between Shaanxi and Shanxi Provinces, and finally turns east to flow through Henan and Shandong Provinces, emptying into the Bo Hai Gulf. The name Henan Province means "South of the (Yellow) River." The Yellow River has enormous hydroelectric potential, and since 1949 many hydroelectric power plants have been constructed on the upper reaches of the river. Upstream dams and irrigation canals along the river have helped control the river's flow. The largest dam is Longyang Dam in Qinghai Province, an important power source. In Shanxi Province, where the Yellow River pours through the Longmen Mountains, it has created some spectacular canyons and the Hukou Waterfall.

The Chinese called the Yellow River "China's Sorrow" because of its tendency to flood. Every year the river carries 1,600 million tons of silt from deposits of soil known as

Several stations, including this one at San Men Gorge, have been built along the 2,903-mile-long Yellow River to tap into its enormous hydroelectric power potential.   HAN XUE ZHANG

loess in western China. The silt builds up the riverbed, causing the water to overflow the riverbanks and flood the surrounding countryside. Chinese peasants have had to build dikes along the river for protection from flooding, and throughout Chinese history they have continually had to make the dikes higher. The waterborne loess deposits of the Yellow River are still building up the broad floodplain, which extends from Shanxi Province to the sea. Two hundred miles inland, great earthen dikes as high as 20 feet above ground level attempt to prevent the turbulent river from overflowing and submerging land. The plain built up by the Yellow River is very fertile and supports thriving agriculture. This region produces about half of China's cotton and more than half of China's wheat.

The lower Yellow River valley is considered the birthplace of Chinese civilization. Archaeologists have excavated thousands of sites from the Neolithic period (c. 12,000–c. 2000 B.C.) that show that settled agriculture besan in China below the southern bend of the Yellow River. The best known of these sites is Banpo Village near modern Xi'an, which dates from about 4000 B.C. Deposits of pottery from the Yangshao culture (c. 5000–3000 B.C.) and the Longshan culture (c. 3000–2200 B.C.) have been found in numerous places on the North China Plain and along the Yellow River and Lower Yangzi. The Shang dynasty, which overthrew the Xia dynasty (2200–1750 B.C.), flourished in the lower Yellow River valley from 1750 to 1040 B.C.

The Grand Canal was built over many centuries to connect the main rivers of China, including the Yellow River, to enable the transportation of grain and other goods from the south to China's imperial capital cities of Kaifeng, Luoyang and Beijing. Kaifeng, the capital of the Northern Song dynasty (960–1127), was situated near the junction of the early Grand Canal and the Yellow River, at the head of barge transport from the major grain-producing region of the lower Yangzi.

The Yellow River has also changed its course many times, with disastrous effects for millions of people. The People's Republic of China (PRC) has been planting trees and damming the tributaries in the watershed of the Yellow River to help contain the river. Toward the end of the Mongol Yuan dynasty (1279–1368), the Yellow River changed its course from northern to southern Shandong Province and flooded more than 300 square miles. The Chinese believed this disaster was an omen that the Mongols had lost the "Mandate of Heaven" legitimizing a dynasty's rule, and peasant rebellions broke out. From 1853 to 1855 the river reverted to flowing through northern Shandong once more, destroying the northern section of the Grand Canal and flooding vast areas of farmland. Between 602 B.C. and 1938 the Yellow River breached its banks 1,590 times and changed its course 26 times.

While China was being torn apart by the anti-Western Boxer Uprising in 1898–1900, especially in Shandong Province, the Yellow River flooded in 1898 with disastrous results. The flood was followed by a lengthy drought that brought famine to millions of Chinese, and North China was ready to explode. This gave impetus to the overthrow of the Manchu Qing dynasty (1644–1911) and the founding of the modern Republic of China. In April 1938, during China's War of Resistance against Japan (1937–45; World War II), Chiang Kai-shek ordered his Nationalist troops to blow up the dikes along the Yellow River in Huayankou in Henan Province, to halt the advancing Japanese troops. This dire act resulted in the drowning of one million Chinese, and another 11 million Chinese were made homeless and without food. The dike was repaired with American help in 1947. In 1955 the government of the People's Republic of China (PRC) developed a plan to control the Yellow River and generate power, which included large-scale water conservation projects on the river's upper reaches. The Yanguo Gorge Power Station began operating in 1962. Many other power stations were constructed. In the late 1980s, the Longyang Gorge Power Station, including a 584-foot dam, was built across the upper reaches of the Yellow River. See also AGRICULTURE; BO HAI GULF; BOXER UPRISING; LOESS; LONGSHAN CULTURE; MANDATE OF HEAVEN; NATURAL DISASTERS; NEOLITHIC PERIOD; NORTH CHINA PLAIN; QINGHAI-TIBET PLATEAU; QINLING MOUNTAIN RANGE; SHANG DYNASTY; WAR OF RESISTANCE AGAINST JAPAN; XI'AN; YANGSHAO CULTURE; YANGZI RIVER; YUAN DYNASTY; NAMES OF INDIVIDUAL PROVINCES.

YELLO RIVER CANTATA See XIAN XINGHAI.

YELLOW SEA (Huanghai)   A partially enclosed sea off the northeastern coast of China that is one of the farthest west extensions of the Pacific Ocean. The Yellow Sea is about 400 miles long and 400 miles wide and covers an area of about 209,000 square miles. It is shallow, with an average depth of 145 feet, although a trench that runs from southeast to northwest in the middle of the sea has a depth of 260 feet. The western coast of the Yellow Sea borders the Chinese provinces of Shandong and Jiangsu, and the eastern coast borders the Korean peninsula. The southern edge of the Yellow Sea borders the East China Sea (Donghai). Major Chinese rivers flowing into the Yellow Sea and Bo Hai Gulf include the Yellow Huai, Liao, Bai and Yalu; major Korean rivers include the Han and Taedong. Some of the major Chinese ports located on the Yellow Sea include Qingdao and Yantai in Shandong, Lianyungang (Xinpu) in Jiangsu, and Dalian (Luda or Lushun, formerly known as Port Arthur) in Liaoning Province. Inchon in South Korea and Chinnampo in North Korea also lie on the Yellow Sea.

Widespread deposits of a type of soil known as loess carried by the Yellow River (Huanghe), which formerly flowed into the Yellow Sea but now flows into the Bo Hai Gulf, have flattened the coastline. China has always suffered from frequent flooding of the Yellow River, one of the two major rivers in China. At the end of the 12th century the river changed its course from northern Shandong Province, a peninsula that divides the Yellow Sea from the Bo Hai Gulf to the north, and began flowing into the Yellow Sea south of the peninsula. From 1853 to 1855 the river reverted to flowing through northern Shandong into the Bo Hai Gulf once more, destroying the northern section of the Grand Canal and flooding immense areas of fertile farmland. The Yellow Sea and the Bo Hai Gulf are connected by the Bo Hai Strait, which lies between Shandong and Liaoning Provinces. See also BO HAI GULF; DALIAN; EAST CHINA SEA; GRAND CANAL; HUAI RIVER; JIANGSU PROVINCE; LIAO RIVER; LOESS; LUDA; QINGDAO; SHANDONG PROVINCE; YALU RIVER; YELLOW RIVER.

YELLOW TURBANS REBELLION   A peasant uprising that broke out in A.D. 184 against the Eastern Han dynasty (25–220). The Yellow Turbans (Huangjin or Huang-chin), also known as the Daoist Sect of the Great Peace (Taipingdao or T'ai-p'ing-tao), were a religious sect that had a communal organization. They preached a messianic faith in the age of "Great Well-Being," which they believed was about to begin. The sect's leaders, including Zhang Jue (Chang Chueh), also promoted faith healing through the use of charms and magical chants. Many of these beliefs and practices derived from popular Chinese religion in the Daoist tradition. The Yellow Turbans Sect originated in modern Hubei Province and gained many adherents in the central Chinese region between the Yellow (Huanghe) and Yangzi (Changjiang) rivers. By 184, the sect had 360,000 armed members. Their armed rebellion spread as far as modern Manchuria in northeastern China and Fujian Province in the southeast. In 196 the Eastern Han dynasty finally suppressed the Yellow Turbans rebellion and killed or captured most of its leaders, and the sect fell apart. The Eastern Han dynasty ended less than three decades after the end of the Yellow Turban rebellion. This was due to continuing peasant rebellions, but also to the fact that the military leaders and wealthy landowners who fought the Yellow Turbans had become more powerful than the Han emperors. By 205, the great military commander Cao Cao (Ts'ao Ts'ao; 155–220) unified the area north of the Yangzi River, then the most important region in China. His son, Cao Pi (Ts'ao P'i; 187–226), deposed the Eastern Han dynasty puppet emperor and founded the Wei (or Cao Wei) dynasty that ruled the kingdom of Wei from 220 to 265. See also CAO CAO; DAOISM; EASTERN HAN DYNASTY.

YELU CHUCAI (Yeh-lu Ch'u-ts'ai; 1190–1244)   A member of the royal family of the Khitan (Qidan) ethnic group who served the powerful Mongol leaders Genghis Khan (1162–1227) and his son Ogodei Khan. The Khitan had founded the Liao dynasty (947–1125), which included Inner Mongolia, Manchuria and the northern Chinese prefectures of Hebei and Hedong. Yelu Chucai served as an official in the Jin dynasty (1115–1234) government, founded by the Jurchen, former subjects of the Liao who had rebelled. In 1215, Yelu Chucai had been taken prisoner by the Mongols when they captured the city (modern Beijing) in northeastern China that had been the capital of the Khitan Liao dynasty. In 1218 Genghis Khan brought him to the Mongol capital at Karakorum, where he became Genghis Khan's secretary-astrologer and then his chief minister. Yelu Chucai had been sinicized, that is, had assimilated characteristics of the ethnic Han Chinese culture. He established a Chinese-style government bureaucracy that selected people by examinations based on Confucian teachings. He also organized a census of North China that provided information for a system of taxation. The Mongols conquered the Chinese empire. In 1279, Genghis Khan's grandson Khubilai Khan established the Yuan dynasty (1279–1368) with himself as the first Yuan emperor.

Before they had established the Yuan Empire, Mongol generals wanted to slaughter the northern Chinese people, who relied on agriculture, and turn their farmlands into empty pastures for animals raised by the nomadic Mongols, such as horses, sheep and goats. Yelu Chucai dissuaded the Mongols from doing this, thus saving millions of lives, by persuading the Mongols that they would profit much more from taxing than from killing the Chinese. He also reformed the system of currency, which had relied on paper money but then become dependent on silver ingots, by reestablishing the use of paper currency throughout China. Yelu Chucai made remarkable accomplishments in guiding the Mongols from being nomadic horse-riding conquerors to settled rulers of a vast, wealthy empire. Ogodei Khan died prematurely from dissipation in 1241 and his widow became the regent for their son Guyug, against Ogodei Khan's wishes. She dismissed from government several of his finest foreign advisers, including Yelu Chucai, who died of grief soon after. See also CURRENCY, HISTORICAL; GENGHIS KHAN; IMPERIAL EXAMINATION SYSTEM; JIN DYNASTY; KARAKORUM; KHITAN; LIAO DYNASTY; MONGOL; NOMADS AND ANIMAL HUSBANDRY; NORTH CHINA PLAIN; SINICIZATION; YUAN DYNASTY.

YEN, JIMMY (Yan Yangchu; James; 1893–1990)   A famous Chinese educator and pioneer of adult literacy programs who spent his life promoting universal education in China, which had a very high rate of illiteracy, and in the United States. Yen was born in Sichuan Province in central China. After completing his education, he went to the United States. and received a doctoral degree from Yale University. He then went to France, where he worked with illiterate Chinese who were employed as laborers there during World War I. Yen developed a course to teach adult literacy and founded the *Chinese Workers Review,* which used a small number of basic written characters that the workers could read. In the 1920s he returned to China and devoted his energies to improving rural education. In 1922 he successfully tested his adult literacy program in Changsha, the capital of Hunan Province. Yen led the Mass Education Movement, which published readers that used 1,200 basic Chinese characters and enabled graduates of a four- to six-week literacy program to read and write. Programs based on the one developed by Yen were used to educate people all over China during the 1920s and 1930s. Yen became so famous that a group of American academics elected him one of the 10 most influential people in the world.

In the 1950s, after the Chinese Communist Party founded the People's Republic of China (PRC), Yen immigrated to the United States, where he continued his work in rural education. At age 94 he returned to China to tour the country, lecture and evaluate educational reforms made by the Chinese government in the 1980s. One of the people accompanying him was Ping Sheng Yen Chin, founder of the Association for Students Returned from the West (to China). The daughter of a famous Chinese diplomat, she had also immigrated to the United States and worked with Professor Yen for more than 40 years. The association made Yen its honorary president and Ping Sheng Yen Chin an honorary member of its council. Yen's friend and colleague Liang Suming, who had belonged to the same group of Chinese democratic revolutionary intellectuals in the early 20th century, had remained in China. See also OVERSEAS CHINESE; WRITING SYSTEM, CHINESE.

YEN FU   See YAN FU.

YEN HSI-SHAN See NORTHERN EXPEDITION.

YENAN See YAN'AN.

YENJING See BEIJING; YUAN DYNASTY.

YI Also known as the Lolo; one of the largest national minority groups in China. The Yi people are farmers who number about 6.5 million, most of whom inhabit Yunnan and Sichuan provinces in southwestern China. More than one million Yi inhabit Liangshan Yi Autonomous Prefecture in Sichuan. Some Yi also reside in Guizhou Province and Guangxi-Zhuang Autonomous Region in southern China. The Yi live in mountainous regions where they grow cash crops and gather wild plants for herbal medicine. The history of the Yi nationality goes back at least 2,000 years. The Yi speak six dialects belonging to the Tibeto-Burman group of the Sino-Tibetan linguistic family. They had a native system of writing in which each letter represented a syllable, but they no longer use this script. The Yi developed their own solar calendar and 12-year animal zodiac. They practice an animistic religion, believing that all things have good or bad spirits in them. There were traditionally two castes among the Yi, the Black Yi and the White Yi. The Black Yi formed the higher caste who held all property and governed the villages. The White Yi, along with Han Chinese, were slaves who formed the lower caste. The Yi in the Liangshan Ranges in Sichuan practiced slavery until 1949. Even today the Black Yi and White Yi maintain a strict distinction. The Yi were traditionally warriors, and some scholars argue that the people who founded the state of Qin, which unified China under the Qin dynasty (221–206 B.C.), were a branch of the Yi people. See also MEDICINE, HERBAL; MINORITIES, NATIONAL; QIN DYNASTY; SICHUAN PROVINCE; YUNNAN PROVINCE.

YI See RIGHTEOUSNESS.

YICHANG See HUBEI PROVINCE; THREE GORGES WATER CONSERVANCY PROJECT; YANGZI RIVER.

YIHEQUAN See BOXER UPRISING.

YIHEYUAN See SUMMER PALACE.

YI-HSING POTTERY See YIXING POTTERY.

YIJING See BOOK OF CHANGES.

YIN AND YANG Two principles that since ancient times in China were considered to be the fundamental principles that control everything in the universe. Yin is considered female, passive, weak, low, earth, water, the moon, rest, dark, cold and negative. Yang is considered male, active, strong, high, heaven, fire, the sun, motion, light, hot and positive. The two principles are complementary and succeed each other in the continuing cycle by which all things grow and change. The Yin-Yang school of thought developed during the Warring States Period (403–221 B.C.). The school also expounded the concept of Five Material Agents (or Five Elements; *wuxing* or *wu-hsing*) that were also thought to control the workings of the universe, especially the changing sea-

sons and periods of time that continually follow each other. The Five Material Agents are earth, wood, metal, fire and water, and they are said to activate all other groups of five, such as the Five Colors (yellow, green, white, red and black).

The concepts of yin and yang and the Five Material Agents provided the theoretical foundation for scientific thought in China for 4,200 years. Only fragments of the writings by members of the Yin-Yang School have survived, but their ideas were assimilated by Confucian and Daoist thinkers. The principles of yin and yang formed the foundation for the *Book of Changes* (*Yijing* or *I-ching*), which became canonized as one of the Five Classics of the Confucian tradition. Although yin and yang are said to be complementary and interdependent, these principles were used by Chinese moralists to tell women that they had to obey and be subordinate to men. See also BOOK OF CHANGES; FIVE MATERIAL AGENTS; HEAVEN.

YIN DYNASTY See SHANG DYNASTY.

YIN MOUNTAIN RANGE See GOBI DESERT; TIANSHAN MOUNTAIN RANGE.

YINCHUAN The capital city of Ningxia Hui Autonomous region, a province in northwestern China that since 1958 has been administered as an autonomous region because many of its inhabitants belong to national minorities. The largest number are Hui, ethnic Chinese who practice the Muslim religion. Yinchuan, with a population of more than a half-million, lies on the west bank of the Yellow River (Huanghe) near the Great Wall. The Helanshan range to the west shelters Yinchuan from the Mongolian deserts. The Lanzhou-Baotou railroad connects the city with the rest of China. The region around Yinchuan is an important producer of wheat, rice, sorghum and other grains, hemp, cotton, sesame and fruits, especially apricots. Crops are watered by an extensive irrigation network that dates back to the Han dynasty (206 B.C.–A.D. 220). Electric power is provided by a dam at Qingtongxia on the Yellow River. Modern industries include textiles, chemicals, machine manufacturing and metal working. Local products include carvings made from stone from the nearby Helan Mountains and wool blankets. Nomadic tribes herd sheep and other livestock on the Ningxia steppes.

Yinchuan, originally known as Xingqing, was a center for horse trading from the Tang dynasty (618–907) to the modern era. It served as the capital of the Kingdom of Xixia (Western Xia dynasty; 1038–1227) between 1036 and 1227. This dynasty was established by the Tangut, a nomadic tribe from Qinhai whose empire rivaled the Song and Liao dynasties until invading Mongols led by Genghis Khan (1162–1227) destroyed the Tangut Empire.

Tourist sites in Yinchuan include the Regional Museum, with West Pagoda (Chengtian Xita) in its courtyard, and North Pagoda (Beita), which is over one hundred feet high and provides a good view of the city. Yuhuang Pavilion, 400 years old, also has a small museum. Streets in the city radiate outward from the Drum Tower in the center. Twenty miles west of Yinchuan are the Royal Tombs of Western Xia (Xixia Lingmu). The site contains eight royal tombs and more than 70 lesser tombs from the Xixia kingdom. See also GENGHIS KHAN; GREAT WALL; HUI; MINORITIES, NATIONAL; MONGOL;

MUSLIMS; NINGXIA HUI AUTONOMOUS REGION; XIXIA, KINGDOM OF; YELLOW RIVER.

YING RIVER See ANHUI PROVINCE; HUAI RIVER.

YINGQING (YING-CH'ING) WARE See WHITE WARE.

YITONG RIVER See CHANGCHUN.

YIXING POTTERY (Yi-hsing) A renowned type of pottery produced in Dingshuzhen in Yixing County, Jiangsu Province in southeastern China. The rich local clay is fired in kilns at high temperatures, turning the Yixing pottery a dark red or brown. Potters sometimes mix in colored pigments made from minerals. The pottery is usually unglazed, although blue or polychrome enamel glazes may be used. The pots are made by hand in a wide variety of interesting shapes, from bold round ones to pots imitating bamboo, tree trunks or flowers such as chrysanthemums. They may also be decorated with objects from nature, such as insects, frogs, fruit or nuts. The finest pieces are taken to Hong Kong where they are sold by department stores and dealers. Yixing pottery, notably teapots (*zisha* or *tzu-sha*), was first produced during the Northern Song dynasty (960–1127). From the mid–17th century, Yixing teapots were widely exported to Thailand, Japan and Europe. The first director of the famous Meissen pottery factory in Germany had his craftsmen develop a red stoneware based on Yixing pottery.

Yixing teapots are still highly prized by tea drinkers and art collectors the world over as the best pots for retaining the flavor and scent of tea brewed in them, even when the tea sits overnight. Potters smooth the outside of the teapots with a buffalo horn spatula, which compresses the particles close to the surface and enables the teapots to retain heat for long periods. The lids also fit very tightly, slowing down the oxidation process, which reduces the tea's flavor. A Yixing teapot absorbs the tea's flavor, so only one type of tea should be brewed in a particular pot to prevent contamination of a fine tea's flavor. The pots should be cleaned out only with cold water, not detergent. See also TEA.

YONGLE (EMPEROR) (Yung-lo; 1360–1424) Known as Ming Yongle; one of the greatest emperors of the Ming dynasty (1368–1644). The fourth son of the first Ming emperor Hongwu (Hung-wu; r. 1368–99), his real name was Zhu Di (Chu Ti); Yongle, meaning "Perpetual Happiness," is his reign name (r. 1403–24). Zhu Di usurped the throne by overthrowing his young nephew Zhu Yunwen (Chuyun-wen; 1377–1402), during whose short reign as Emperor Jianwen (Chien-wen) the Chinese fought a civil war. Jianwen escaped and became a Buddhist monk, but Emperor Yongle murdered hundreds of members of princely families so that no one would attempt to overthrow him. He moved the capital from Nanjing to Beijing, capital of the Mongol Yuan dynasty (1279–1368), which the Ming had overthrown, to strengthen the Ming hold over northern China. The Mongols had called the city Khanbaliq ("City of the Khan"; Cambaluc in Chinese), while the Chinese called it Dadu (Ta-tu, "Great Capital"). Yongle gave it the name Beiping ("Northern Capital"). Beijing lies only 40 miles south of the Great Wall that separated China from the Mongols and other nomadic tribes.

There Yongle built the Inner City, the Imperial City where court officials resided, and the Forbidden City or Imperial Palace, now known as the Palace Museum, which is open to tourists. He also had a propitious site outside Beijing selected for his tomb and those of the Ming emperors who would succeed him. Today the Ming Tombs, about 32 miles northwest of Beijing, are visited by many tourists. Yongle gave positions of authority in the imperial bureaucracy to Confucian-educated scholars from the prestigious Hanlin Academy, who came to be known as Grand Secretaries. He is best remembered for ordering the compilation of a comprehensive manuscript containing the essential subjects in Chinese scholarship, known as the *Yongle Encyclopedia* (*Yongle dadian* or *Yung-lo ta-tien*). More than 2,000 scholars worked on the encyclopedia from 1403 until it was completed with 11,095 handwritten volumes in 1407.

Yongle placed a number of eunuchs in high government positions. In 1404 he appointed the Muslim eunuch Zheng He (Cheng Ho; 1371–1433), who had suppressed a rebellion in his native province of Yunnan in southern China, superintendent of the office of eunuchs and ordered him to oversee the construction of a fleet of large ships. He then made Zheng He the commander in chief of the seven naval expeditions the Ming sent westward to bring more foreign states into the tribute system that rewarded the states that submitted to Chinese suzerainty. Yongle also sent diplomatic embassies westward on the overland routes to Central Asia, which had recently reopened, to encourage trade and tribute. From 1407 to 1408 Ming forces annexed Tonkin (northern Vietnam), which lies south of China. In 1408 Yongle had to wage a military campaign against the Mongols, who threatened the Chinese empire from the north and west. He had already stopped a Mongol attack against China in 1396, before he became emperor, by leading his forces north of the Great Wall. The powerful Mongol leader Tamerlane posed a serious threat to the Chinese empire, but he died in 1405 before Chinese troops had to face him. However, the Mongols crushed the Chinese expedition sent against them by the Ming in 1408. The next year, Yongle personally led an army of half a million soldiers that defeated the combined Mongol forces in western China. He was able to move his court to Beijing upon the completion of the Ming imperial complex in 1421. Nanjing remained the auxiliary Ming capital. Yongle was succeeded by Emperor Hongxi (Hung-shi; r. 1425–26), who was soon replaced by Emperor Xuande (Hsuan-te; r. 1426–36). See also BEIJING; EUNUCH; FORBIDDEN CITY; HANLIN ACADEMY; IMPERIAL BUREAUCRACY; MING DYNASTY; MING TOMBS; MONGOL; TRIBUTE SYSTEM; YONGLE ENCYCLOPEDIA; ZHENG HE.

YONGLE ENCYCLOPEDIA (*Yongle dadian* or *Yung-lo ta-tien*) An enormous manuscript compiled from 1403 to 1407 by a team of more than 2,000 scholars containing all that they deemed to be essential in Chinese scholarship, including the Confucian classics, philosophy, history and other subjects. It was sponsored by the third emperor of the Ming dynasty (1368–1644), known by his reign name as the Yongle (Yung-lo, "Eternal Joy") emperor (r. 1403–24). The manuscript had a total of 22,877 "chapters" (*juan* or *chuan*) or scrolls in 11,000 volumes. The encyclopedia was intended to be printed in book form, but the cost proved too high for this to be done. Three handwritten copies of the manuscript were made; two were kept in the capital at Beijing and one at Nanjing. The various manuscripts disappeared or were dispersed by the 20th century, and today only about 400 volumes have survived. See also FIVE CLASSICS OF CONFUCIANISM; FOUR BOOKS OF CONFUCIANISM; YONGLE (EMPEROR).

YONGTAI, PRINCESS (YONGTAI GONGZHU MU) See TANG IMPERIAL TOMBS.

YONGZHENG (EMPEROR) (Yung-cheng; 1678–1736)
The third emperor of the Qing dynasty (1644–1911). The fourth son of the renowned Qing emperor Kangxi (K'ang-hsi), his real name was Yinzhen (Yin-chen); Yongzheng, meaning "Kind and Proper," is his reign name (r. 1723–36). Yongzheng was a hard-working and frugal administrator. His main accomplishment was to reform the imperial bureaucracy, making the Chinese government more centralized and efficient and less corrupt. He encouraged hydraulic projects that would help prevent the flooding of the Yellow River (Huanghe), a frequent threat to Chinese peasants, and he made reforms in the country's financial system. Yongzheng also brought the military more closely under his control by changing the rules that had allowed some Manchu princes to keep control of their own Banners, or military divisions. However, the death of his father, which brought him to the throne, had been so suspicious that in 1730 Yongzheng defended himself by publicly announcing that he had not murdered his father. Moreover, he persecuted and imprisoned all those who might present a challenge to the throne, including several of his own brothers, two of whom died in prison in 1726 and a third in 1732. He developed an extensive secret police network to spy on members of the bureaucracy. In 1728 Yongzheng signed the Treaty of Kiakhta with Russia and sent two diplomatic embassies to Moscow. In 1729 he established the Grand Council, consisting of five or six appointees with whom he could discuss important administrative and military issues in depth, which supplanted the Grand Secretariat as the most important organ in the Chinese government. Yongzheng's administrative abilities paved the way for the reign of his fourth son, who succeeded him as the great Qing emperor Qianlong (Ch'ien-lung; r. 1736–95). See also BANNER SYSTEM, MANCHU; IMPERIAL BUREAUCRACY; KANGXI, EMPEROR; QIANLONG, EMPEROR; QING DYNASTY; YELLOW RIVER.

YOU RIVER See WEST RIVER.

YOUNG PIONEERS See COMMUNIST YOUTH LEAGUE.

YU See CARP; FISH AND SEAFOOD.

YU See JADE.

YU (YUZHOU) See CHONGQING.

YU, EMPEROR Also known as Yu the Great; a legendary emperor and founder of the Xia dynasty (2200–1750 B.C.), the third of the Five Emperors who gave the arts of civilization to the Chinese people. Yu is credited with containing the waters of the Great Flood that threatened the entire world. Yu spent 13 years without seeing his family, "mastering the great waters," so that he could organize his subjects to construct extensive water-control projects in the Yellow River (Huanghe) basin, the cradle of Chinese civilization. The floods were stopped and the fields were provided the necessary amount of irrigation to grow crops. From ancient China to the modern era, an emperor's ability to remain in favor with his subjects largely depended on public works such as drainage projects, water reservoirs and irrigation channels. The devastation of crops by floods or drought was believed to be a sign that an emperor had lost the "Mandate of Heaven" (tianming or t'ien-ming), which legitimized his rule, and peasant rebellions would spring up against him. Emperor Yu was associated with an ancient river god and was often depicted with a dragon's tail instead of legs. In China the dragon symbolizes the power of the emperor and life-giving rain. Yu is also known as the blacksmith who mastered the element of metal, cast the Nine Cauldrons, and mapped the universe. According to legend, each of the nine cauldrons was decorated with the symbols of a particular region ruled by the Xia dynasty and contained all the creatures and products of that region. See also AGRICULTURE; DRAGON; MANDATE OF HEAVEN; XIA DYNASTY; YELLOW RIVER.

YU HUANG See JADE EMPEROR.

YU RIVER See GUANGDONG PROVINCE; GUANGXI-ZHUANG AUTONOMOUS REGION; PEARL RIVER.

YU TI See JADE EMPEROR.

YUAN See CURRENCY, MODERN.

YUAN See GARDENS.

YUAN See TORTOISE.

YUAN DAN See NEW YEAR FESTIVAL.

YUAN DYNASTY (1279–1368) The dynasty established by the Mongols, an ethnic group to the north of China who invaded the country and overthrew the Southern Song dynasty (1127–1279), which had its capital at Hangzhou. The Yuan was the first non-ethnic-Chinese dynasty to rule the entire country. Genghis Khan (1162–1227) had unified the Mongol tribes of the northern steppe, known as Mongolia, in 1206 and had conquered part of northern China in 1215. His grandson Khubilai Khan (1214–94) conquered the rest of China in 1276–80 and reigned concurrently as the first Yuan emperor (r. 1260–94) and the Great Khan of the Mongol Empire, although Mongol princes disputed the latter title. In 1271 Khubilai Khan had already taken the title Emperor of China and called his dynasty the Yuan ("Original Dynasty"). The Mongols rapidly established an empire that extended from Manchuria (modern northeastern China) in the east to the Danube River in the west. Khubilai moved the Mongol imperial court from Mongolia south to two capitals in China: Dadu (modern Beijing), the winter capital, and Shangdu (Dolonnur in the modern Inner Mongolia Autonomous Region), the summer capital. Dadu was called

Khanbaliq (Cambaluc in Mongol; later Dadu [Tatu] in Chinese). Khubilai Khan had an astronomical observatory built in Khanbaliq that was then the finest in the world.

Khubilai Khan had Chinese advisers and adopted Chinese institutions that had developed under previous dynasties, such as the imperial bureaucracy or civil service whose officials were selected from the literati, or scholar class, by examinations based on Confucian classical texts. However, the Mongols retained their own tribal military form of government as well, and administration of the empire was bilingual, using both the Mongol and Chinese languages. Mongols and Han Chinese were forbidden to intermarry and were required to speak their own languages, wear their own styles of clothing and practice their own customs. The Mongols divided the population of China into four classes, with Mongols at the top. Next were Central Asian allies of the Mongols, such as the Uighurs and Turks. Below them were the *Hanren*, northern Han Chinese and non-Chinese subjects of the former Liao and Jin dynasties such as the Jurchens and Khitans (Qidan). At the bottom were the *Nanren*, Han Chinese who inhabited the region formerly ruled by the Southern Song dynasty. Since the majority of the literati belonged to this category and the highest government positions were reserved for Mongols and other non-Han Chinese, they had limited opportunities to rise in the bureaucracy and resented their Mongol rulers. Many Persians (Iranians) and Central Asian Muslims held government positions and helped the Muslim religion to grow in China. The Mongols tolerated all religions, Chinese and non-Chinese, and became patrons of the Tibetan form of Buddhism, known as Lamaism.

Chinese landscape painters and calligraphers continued to work in the styles that had developed during the Southern Song dynasty. In fact, some of the greatest Chinese painters lived during the Yuan, including Zhao Mengfu (Chao Meng-fu) and Ni Zan (Ni Tsan). Chinese short stories, novels and dramas in the vernacular flourished, especially since they were not censored by the Yuan and served as the medium through which the Han Chinese could express their negative feelings about the Mongols. The type of popular entertainment that became known as Beijing Opera, which combines acting, singing and dancing with musical accompaniment and colorful costumes and makeup, originated during the Yuan.

Under Mongol rule the Grand Canal was repaired and a new branch was built between the capital and Hangzhou so that grain could be transported by barges from southern China to the capital region. Trade within China and between China and foreign countries thrived during the Yuan. The Mongols realized that China could not produce enough copper to mint coins in the quantities needed throughout the Chinese empire, so they issued paper money as the legal tender. Bronze coins, known as cash, were used on a smaller scale and silver ingots were used for large transactions. The Mongols sent expeditions to conquer Japan, Java, Champa, Annam (Vietnam) and northern Burma, which were mostly unsuccessful. Europeans began traveling to China along the trade routes, especially the overland Silk Road. In 1342 the Yuan emperor received John of Marignola, a legate from the pope, at Shangdu. The Italian traveler Marco Polo spent two decades in China from about 1271 to 1292 and later wrote a famous book about his experiences there that provides much information about the Yuan dynasty.

After the reign of Khubilai Khan, Mongol princes engaged in frequent struggles to control the throne, and sometimes two pretenders competed to become emperor. Between 1320 and 1329 alone there were four Yuan emperors. Several emperors were placed on the throne as boys so that de facto power was wielded by regents. The last Yuan emperor was Toghon Temur, known as Emperor Shundi (Shun-ti; r. 1333–68). During his reign, Chinese peasants suffered greatly from disastrous floods of the Yellow (Huanghe) and Huai rivers, and many rebellions broke out against the Mongols, led by secret societies such as the White Lotus and the Red Turbans. Shundi was overthrown by Zhu Yuanzhang (Chu Yuan-chang), who established the Ming dynasty (1368–1644) with himself as the first Ming emperor, known as Emperor Hongwu (Hung-wu; r. 1368–99). Shundi fled to Mongolia and attempted to take back control of China but did not succeed and died in 1370. Every year at the Autumn Moon Festival, the Chinese commemorate Zhu's rebellion against the Mongols, which began when secret messages in mooncakes—heavy buns stuffed with sweet paste—were passed among Han villagers. See also ASTRONOMY AND OBSERVATORIES; AUTUMN MOON FESTIVAL; BEIJING; CURRENCY, HISTORICAL; DRAMA; GENGHIS KHAN; GRAND CANAL; HONGWU (EMPEROR); IMPERIAL BUREAUCRACY; INNER MONGOLIA AUTONOMOUS REGION; KHUBILAI KHAN; LAMAISM; LITERATI; MING DYNASTY; MONGOL; MUSLIMS; NATURAL DISASTERS; NI ZAN; OPERA, BEIJING; PEASANTS AND PEASANT REBELLIONS; POLO, MARCO; RED TURBANS REBELLION; SHUNDI (EMPEROR); SOUTHERN SCHOOL OF PAINTING; SOUTHERN SONG DYNASTY; WHITE LOTUS SECRET SOCIETY; ZHAO MENGFU.

YUAN HAOWEN (1190–1257)   A Jurchen author during the Jin dynasty (1115–1234) who was the greatest Jin poet as well as a prose writer. Born in Shanxi Province in northern China, upon completing his education in 1219 Yuan joined the Jin government and held high-level positions. However, when the Mongols conquered the Jin in 1234, he left the government to pursue his literary interests and do historical research. The Mongols went on to conquer the Chinese Southern Song dynasty (1127–1279) and united China under the Yuan dynasty (1279–1368). In addition to writing poetry in lyric and traditional forms, Yuan wrote a critical study in verse, "On Poetry, Three Quatrains," which is an important work in the history of Chinese literary criticism. He also compiled an anthology of poems by 240 Jin poets, *Collection of the Central Plains* (*Zhongzhouji* or *Chung-chou chi*), and critical studies of the great Chinese poets Du Fu (Tu Fu; 712–70) and Su Shi (Su Shih; 1036–1101). He also wrote biographical sketches of the author Zhao Bingwen (Chao Ping-wen; 1159–1232) and Wang Ruoxu (Wang Jo-hsu; 1174–1243), a scholar of Chinese history and classical texts. See also JIN DYNASTY; JURCHEN; POETRY.

YUAN RIVER (YUANHE) See RED RIVER.

YUAN SHIH-K'AI See YUAN SHIKAI.

YUAN SHIH-TSU See KHUBILAI KHAN.

YUAN SHIKAI (Yuan Shih-k'ai; 1859–1916)   A military official in the Manchu Qing dynasty (1644–1911) who became the second provisional president of the Republic of China (ROC) in 1912 and proclaimed himself emperor shortly before he died. Several members of Yuan's family had been Qing officials, and he was given a Confucian-based education, although he failed the examinations for a position in the imperial bureaucracy. In 1880 he bought a military title. By 1884 a power struggle erupted between China and Japan over Korea, just across the border from Manchuria (northeastern China), the homeland of the Manchus, who had founded the Qing dynasty but were hated by the Han ethnic Chinese who comprised most of China's population. Korea had ancient historical ties with China as a vassal state under the imperial tribute system. In 1884 the conservative faction in Korea, which wanted to retain ties with China, was opposed by the progressive faction of young Koreans who had studied in Japan and wanted to enact reforms based on the Japanese model. Japan and China both sent troops into Korea, ostensibly to restore order, with Yuan Shikai commanding the Chinese force of 3,000 troops. In April 1885 Japan and China signed the Convention of Tianjin (Tientsin) under which both countries withdrew their troops from Korea and agreed to inform the other before sending forces into Korea again. China attempted to keep Korea in its influence by making it a Chinese protectorate, and Yuan was sent back to Korea as Chinese commissioner of commerce there. He left in July 1894, shortly before increasing tensions between Japan and China over Korea resulted in the Sino-Japanese War of 1894–95. Yuan served with distinction in the war but China was defeated by Japan, which declared Korea's independence. Japan later made Korea its protectorate in 1907 and formally annexed it in 1910. The Qing government recognized the inadequacy of its army and appointed Yuan to organize and train a modern Chinese military.

In 1898 Qing emperor Guangxu (Kuang-hsu; r. 1875–1908), following the advice of Kang Youwei (K'ang Yu-wei), Liang Qichao (Liang Ch'i-ch'ao) and other Qing officials who wanted to reform the government, enacted a series of reforms known as the Reform Movement of 1898 or the Hundred Days' Reform. Some reformers even wanted to stage a coup against Empress Dowager Cixi (Tz'u Hsi; 1835–1908), who actually controlled the emperor, and one of them asked Yuan, whose troops were stationed at Tianjin south of Beijing, to carry out the coup. But Yuan informed the empress dowager of the plot, and she halted the reform movement by leading her own coup and placing the emperor under confinement. She appointed Yuan governor of Shandong Province, south of Beijing.

When the Boxer Uprising broke out in 1898, Yuan's army forced the Boxers out of Shandong. After the Boxers put the foreign legations in Beijing under siege in 1900 and caused the emperor and empress dowager to flee the city, a combined force of foreign troops suppressed the rebels all over North China. Yuan was appointed governor of Chihli (modern Hubei Province) and commissioner of the northern ports after the prominent Qing official Li Hongzhang (Li Hung-chang) died in 1901, and he became the most powerful military commander in North China. In 1903, when Japan and Russia were about to go to war over Manchuria (Russo-Japanese War of 1904–5), Yuan was appointed commissioner

of the Army Reorganization Council. He built up his own military force, the Beiyang (Pei-yang) Army, consisting of about 70,000 soldiers in six divisions, and trained officers in his own academy, the Paoding (P'ao-ting) military school. One of the graduates was Chiang Kai-shek (1887–1975), who later became the leader of the Chinese Nationalist (Kuomintang; KMT) government. Military leaders in other parts of China copied Yuan's army. However, when the empress dowager, who had returned with the emperor to Beijing, died in 1908, Yuan was forced to retire.

Revolution against the Qing broke out on October 10, 1911, at Wuchang (Wuhan in Hubei Province), known as the Wuchang Uprising. The Qing recalled Yuan and appointed him governor-general of Hubei and Hunan provinces. He agreed to return to service only when the Qing consented to establish a cabinet and a national assembly and appoint him military commander of all Qing forces. Yuan also demanded legal recognition for the Revolutionary Alliance (Tongmenghui or T'ung-meng hui) founded by Sun Yat-sen. The Qing agreed and appointed him prime minister with the authority to form his own cabinet in November 1911. He immediately removed all Manchus from high government positions and brought military pressure against the rebels at Wuchang, whose leaders negotiated a truce with Yuan.

The provisional government of the Republic of China was proclaimed in Nanjing on December 29, 1911, and Sun Yat-sen was inaugurated as its provisional president on January 1, 1912. Yuan, who wanted to keep power for himself, quickly forced Sun to resign and hand the presidency over to him. Sun agreed to do so if several conditions were met, including the abdication of five-year-old Emperor Xuantong (Hsuan-t'ung; r. 1909–12), the last Qing emperor, now known as Henry Puyi, and the establishment of a republican government in Nanjing. The emperor abdicated on February 12, 1912, Sun resigned the next day, and Yuan was unanimously elected president on February 15, 1912.

Yuan wanted to remain in Beijing, the seat of his power, so he was inaugurated provisional president there on March 12, 1912, and made Beijing the capital of the provisional republic. He placed his underlings in the highest cabinet posts. Sun traveled to Beijing that summer and helped found the Nationalist Party, known as the Kuomintang (KMT). In early 1913 elections were held for a bicameral parliament, and the KMT party became the majority party. But KMT leader Song Jiaoren (Sung Chiao-jen; 1882–1913) was assassinated without interference from Yuan, who dismissed three KMT governors and sent his troops into their provinces and banned all KMT members from parliament. The KMT was too disorganized to resist.

In 1914, when World War I broke out in Europe, Japan declared war on Germany and took possession of the German concessions in Shandong Province. In January 1915, Japan presented Yuan with the so-called Twenty-one Demands on China. The demands, which were so extensive that they would in fact make China a protectorate of Japan, shocked not only the Chinese but also the whole world. Japanese naval fleets sailed into Chinese harbors and large numbers of Japanese troops moved into Shandong and South Manchuria. This intense pressure caused Yuan to agree to most of Japan's demands in May 1915.

Yuan had already decided to establish a new imperial dynasty with himself as emperor. He restored the examination system for the imperial bureaucracy, and on the winter solstice in December 1914 he had offered imperial sacrifices at the Temple of Heaven in Beijing, which former emperors, regarded as the "Son of Heaven" (*tianzi* or *t'ien-tzu*), had performed to gain Heaven's favor. By 1915 Yuan had been declared president for life. In December 1915, military commanders in Yunnan Province in southwestern China sent Yuan a telegram asserting their independence from his rule. Commanders in other regions did the same, and Yuan was not able to suppress their opposition. Nevertheless, he proclaimed his new dynasty on January 1, 1916; but opposition from Liang Qichao and other Chinese military leaders and foreign powers that had concessions in China forced him to restore republican rule on March 22, 1916. Yuan died of uremia on June 6, 1916, and Duan Qirui (Tuan Ch'i-jui; 1865–1936) succeeded him as premier. China entered a period in which it was divided by contending warlords, all of whom had been trained by or associated with Yuan Shikai. In 1917 China entered World War I by declaring war on Germany in hopes of recovering Shandong. See also BEIJING; BOXER UPRISING; CHIANG KAI-SHEK; CIXI, EMPRESS DOWAGER; EMPEROR; HEAVEN; MANCHURIA; PUYI, HENRY; QING DYNASTY; REFORM MOVEMENT OF 1898; REPUBLIC OF CHINA; REVOLUTION OF 1911; RUSSO-JAPANESE WAR OF 1904–5; SHANDONG PROVINCE; SINO-JAPANESE WAR OF 1894–95; SONG JIAOREN; SUN YAT-SEN; TEMPLE OF HEAVEN; TIANJIN, CONVENTION OF; TRIBUTE SYSTEM; TWENTY-ONE DEMANDS ON CHINA; WARLORD PERIOD; WORLD WAR I; WUCHANG UPRISING.

YUAN ZHIZU See KHUBILAI KHAN.

YUAN XIAO JIE See LANTERN FESTIVAL.

YUANDAN (YUANTAN) See NEW YEAR FESTIVAL.

YUANMINGYUAN See SUMMER PALACE.

YUDI See JADE EMPEROR.

YUE (YUEH) See MUSIC AND DANCE, CEREMONIAL.

YUE, KINGDOM OF See JIANGSU PROVINCE; ZHEJIANG PROVINCE.

YUE FEI (Yueh Fei; 1103–1141) A warrior from the peasant class who rose to the rank of military general during the Southern Song dynasty (1127–1279) and became a national hero after winning many battles against Jurchen invaders under the Jin dynasty (1115–1234). In 1127, the Jurchen captured the Song dynasty capital of Kaifeng in northern China. The Song court fled south and established the Southern Song capital at Hangzhou in Zhejiang Province. Yue Fei led the Song in fighting the Jurchen for more than a decade. However, members of the pro-peace faction in the Southern Song court opposed Yue Fei's actions. Prime Minister Chi Gui (Ch'i Kuei; 1086–1151), jealous of Yue Fei's fame and fearful that his military campaigns would incite the northern warriors to destroy the Southern Song dynasty, falsely accused Yue Fei of treason and had him executed. Twenty

years later, Yue Fei's name was restored to honor and he became revered as a martyr. Many temples were built to him. Worship of Yue Fei was pronounced in the 19th century when the Chinese wanted to remove the Manchus, descendants of the Jurchen, who ruled the country under the Qing dynasty (1644–1911). Legends claim that Yue Fei gained his heroism and patriotism from his mother, who tattooed words on his back that reminded him to be loyal to his country. See also JIN DYNASTY; JURCHEN; KAIFENG; MANCHU; SONG DYNASTY; SOUTHERN SONG DYNASTY.

YUE (YUEH) WARE See CELADON WARE.

YUEH FEI See YUE FEI.

YUELAOYE (YUEH LAO YEH) See WEDDINGS, TRADITIONAL.

YUEYANG A city in Hunan Province in southern China along the shore of Lake Dongting (Dongtinghu), the second-largest lake in China. The Yangzi River (Changjiang) and its major tributaries feed the lake, and water from the lake flows back into the Yangzi through canals at Yueyang. The region around Lake Dongting is one of China's main rice-growing areas, and lines of barges transport rice and other goods on the canals to the Yangzi for shipment to other regions of China. Yueyang is a port of call for ferries between Wuhan and Chongqing on the Yangzi, and tour boats ride from Yueyang harbor to Junshan island in Lake Dongting. The island has a nature preserve and tea bushes that produce "silver-needle" tea, which is famous throughout China and was formerly reserved for Chinese emperors. Yueyang has a population of about 200,000 and lies on the main north-south railroad line between Beijing and Guangzhou (Canton). Yueyang was a fortified city during the Han dynasty (206 B.C.–A.D. 220). During the Song dynasty (960–1279) it served as the headquarters of Yueyang military prefecture. During the 12th century the region suffered from a brutal peasant uprising that was suppressed in 1135 by the renowned general Yue Fei (Yueh Fei).

Yueyang Pavilion is a park and temple compound originally built during the Tang dynasty (618–907) and later reconstructed. Many Japanese tourists visit the park because of a famous poem praising it, which they were taught in school. Many Chinese poets have written of Lake Dongting's beauty, including Li Bai (Li Po; 701–62) and Du Fu (Tu Fu; 712–70). Du Fu died on a boat on the lake in 770, and a stone pillar was erected in 1962 to commemorate him, inscribed with calligraphy by Communist marshal Zhu De (Chu Teh; 1886–1976). Yueyang Tower (Yueyanglou), one of the most famous landmarks in southern China, was built in 716 during the reign of Tang emperor Xuanzong (Hsuantsung; r. 712–56) on the site of a structure known as the watergate where the ruler of the kingdom of Wu reviewed his navy during the Three Kingdoms Period (220–80). Even earlier, there had been a cemetery at this location where warriors of the Bazi kingdom, during the Warring States Period (403–221 B.C.), had been buried. The wooden tower is 49 feet high and has a gold-tiled triple roof with edges curving upward. Cishi Pagoda, a brick pagoda built near the eastern shore of Lake Dongting during the Tang dynasty, is another famous landmark of Yueyang. South of Yueyang flows the

Miluoi River, where the poet Qu Yuan (Ch'u Yuan) committed suicide c. 278 B.C. and dragon-boat races are held every year on the fifth day of the fifth month in the lunar calendar. See also DONGTING, LAKE; DRAGON BOAT FESTIVAL; DU FU; LI BAI; PAGODA; QU YUAN; THREE KINGDOMS PERIOD; YANGZI RIVER; YUE FEI.

YUN See FATE.

YUN-CH'U CHU-HUNG   See YUNQU ZHUHONG.

YUNG   See COURAGE.

YUNGANG CAVE TEMPLES AND SCULPTURES   Fifty-three caves carved by Buddhist monks into the sandstone slopes of the Wuzhou Hills about 10 miles west of Datong in the northern Chinese province of Shanxi. Similar cave temples and sculptures can be seen at Dunhuang in the northwestern province of Gansu, but they were carved from terracotta, while those at Yungang are the earliest examples in China of stone carvings.

Datong lies just south of the border of Inner Mongolia and the Great Wall, which had been built to protect China from Central Asian nomadic invaders. In the fourth century A.D., Turkish tribes known as the Toba conquered northern China and established the Northern Wei dynasty (386–534) with their capital at Datong, then called Binzheng. The Toba adopted Buddhism, which had been founded in India in the fifth century B.C., as their official religion. In 460 the Northern Wei emperor Taiwu (r. 424–52) commissioned a renowned Buddhist monk named Tanyao to carve five huge statues of Buddha in caves 16 through 20. Thousands of laborers and sculptors were brought to Yungang to continue the work of carving. The monks at Yungang began their work in A.D. 460 and continued until 494, carving 21 large and 32 smaller caves and filling them with more than 51,000 bas-reliefs and statues of Buddha and other Buddhist figures. The caves extend for close to a mile, and the largest is 55 feet high.

The Yungang cave temples are divided into three groups by geographic location, the eastern caves (1–4), the middle (5–13) and the western (14–53). The most important caves are 5 and 6, 9 through 13 and 16 through 20; 16 through 20 are the oldest caves at Yungang. Today 51,000 statues remain out of an estimated total of 100,000. The largest sculpture is 55 feet high and the smallest is about half an inch. The style of the carvings combines influences from traditions brought into China along the so-called Silk Road from India, Persia (Iran) and the Hellenic (Greco-Roman) region. Cave 3 is the largest and houses three sculptures of a seated Buddha attended by a bodhisattva (wise being) on each side. Their graceful style indicates that they were carved later, during the Sui (581–618) or early Tang (618–907) dynasties. Next to the eastern group of caves there is a monastery built in 1651, known as the Old Monastery of the Stone Buddhas (*Shifogusi*), which is the only survivor of 10 monasteries that once thrived at Yungang.

The Yungang caves can be visited by tourists, who usually begin with cave 5, which has been protected by the monastery buildings and houses the largest sculpture of all the caves, a seated Buddha 56 feet high and 52 feet wide at the base. The temple's walls and ceilings are decorated with carved reliefs. Caves 5 and 6 contain some of the best-preserved sculptures at Yungang. Cave 6 also houses a two-story pagoda decorated with carvings of Buddhist figures. Reliefs on the walls depict major events in the life of the Buddha. Unfortunately, many of the caves at Yungang were vandalized and at least 1,400 sculptures were stolen or sold, especially in the early 20th century, and taken to museums in Europe, North America and Japan. Since 1949, the Chinese government has designated the Yungang cave temples and sculptures as historic monuments and has been restoring them. See also BUDDHISM; DATONG; DUNHUANG CAVE PAINTINGS AND CARVINGS; GREAT WALL; NORTHERN WEI DYNASTY; PAGODA; SHANXI PROVINCE; SILK ROAD.

YUNG-CHENG (EMPEROR)   See YONGZHENG (EMPEROR).

YUNG-LO (EMPEROR)   See YONGLE (EMPEROR).

YUNNAN PROVINCE   A province in southwestern China that covers an area of 150,500 square miles and has a population of about 34 million. The capital city is Kunming with a population close to 2 million. Yunnan is inhabited by members of 21 of China's 55 national minority ethnic groups, the widest variety in China, although the Han (ethnic Chinese) now comprise two-thirds of Yunnan's population. Minorities in Yunnan include the Hui (Chinese Muslims) and the Dai (Thai), Bai, Hani, Miao and Yi, many of whom are related to ethnic groups in Burma, Thailand and Laos on the southern border of Yunnan. To the east, north and west, Yunnan borders the Chinese provinces of Guizhou and Sichuan and the autonomous regions of Guangxi Zhuang and Tibet. The Xishuangbanna Autonomous District of the Dai People, on the border with Burma and Laos, is home to members of 10 different national minorities and contains tropical forests with elephants, gibbons and 58 other species of animals and 400 types of birds.

The Yangzi River (Changjiang) forms part of Yunnan's northern border. Chains of mountain ranges connect with those in Tibet to the west, with deep river valleys and peaks that reach as high as 16,000 feet. The central Ailao Mountain Range divides Yunnan into two large eastern and western regions. Eastern Yunnan comprises a limestone plateau over 6,000 feet high with Lake Dianchi, China's sixth-largest freshwater lake, in the center. Yunnan has a very high amount of rainfall, averaging more than 93 inches each year, mostly during the monsoon season between May and October. There are enormous forests in western Yunnan and tropical jungles in the southwest. The province has rich mineral resources, with China's largest deposits of tin, lead and zinc and substantial deposits of copper, coal and iron. Manufacturing has been developed since 1949, and major products include nonferrous metals, chemicals, machinery, processed foods, textiles and paper. Agriculture is also important, with rice, tea, fruit and sugarcane being important crops. Yunnan is China's main producer of walnuts and tobacco.

Kunming, in the center of Yunnan, is called the "City of Perpetual Spring" because of its beautiful climate. Lake Dianchi lies just outside the city, and the limestone formations known as the Stone Forest lie 80 miles to the southeast. The Institute for Nationalities in Kunming is a center for the national minority groups. The city was formerly isolated and backward but has been modernized and is connected to other major cities by railroads and airlines. The French Indochina Rail Line, completed in 1910, still provides service between Kunming and the Vietnam border.

Yunnan was originally inhabited only by minority peoples ruled by local chieftains. The Bai people established the Nanzhao Empire (738–902), which was succeeded by the state of Dali (937–1253). Invading Mongols conquered the state of Dali in 1253 and joined Yunnan to their rapidly growing empire, which became established as the Yuan dynasty (1279–1368). Yunnan suffered from further fighting as Muslims from other Central Asian tribes moved into the region. The Ming dynasty (1368–1644) encouraged Han Chinese to settle in Yunnan to increase its control over the province. This caused many ethnic conflicts, which resulted in the Muslim uprising from 1855 to 1873 under the Muslim leader Du Wenxiu (Tu Wen-hsiu), who established the sultanate of Pingnan. The Qing dynasty (1644–1911) brutally ended the rebellion.

In the early 20th century, Yunnan suffered from the rivalry between the French, who had a base in Vietnam, and the British in Burma. The French built a railroad from Hanoi, Vietnam to Kunming to exploit Yunnan's copper resources. Yunnan maintained its independence under the warlord Tang Jiayao (T'ang Chia-yao; 1882–1927), who was supported by the Japanese and the French. After the Japanese invaded China in 1937, Chinese Nationalist forces (Kuomintang; KMT) moved their headquarters to Chongqing in Sichuan Province, and many refugees from eastern China flocked to Yunnan during the War of Resistance against Japan (1937–45; World War II). Many Chinese factories, universities and government offices were moved to the safer Yunnan region. The famous "Burma Road" built during the war still serves Kunming. In 1949, Yunnan became part of the People's Republic of China (PRC), which has developed and industrialized the province and has attempted to work with the minorities to ensure its political stability. See also BAI; BURMA ROAD; DAI; HANI; KUNMING; MIAO; MINORITIES, NATIONAL; MONGOL; WAR OF RESISTANCE AGAINST JAPAN; WARLORD PERIOD; YANGZI RIVER; YI.

YUNQU ZHUHONG (Yun-ch'u Chu-hung; 1535–1615) The most prominent Buddhist monk of the Ming dynasty (1368–1644), who organized the various traditions of the Chinese Buddhist religion into a comprehensive system that has survived into the modern era. Yunqu became a Buddhist monk at age 32, after his mother died. He traveled to study with a number of masters at different temples, a common practice among monks. In southern China he was impressed with the beautiful scenery around Hangzhou, the capital of the Southern Song dynasty (1127–1279) and for many centuries following the cultural and political capital of China, and decided to found a monastery there. Buddhist monks had turned to the arts practiced by members of the literati, or scholar class, including painting, calligraphy and poetry writing, and had turned away from moral observances. Yunqu Zhuhong attempted to revive Buddhist morality by instituting a set of strict rules for his monks. He maintained that lay people could also practice Buddhism, and he prescribed actions that his lay followers could perform with compassion to benefit society, thus bringing some of the social concerns of the Confucian tradition into Buddhism. He was concerned with relieving the suffering of animals as well as human beings. Yunqu Zhuhong compiled his rules in a text known as the *Record of Self-Knowledge* (*Zizhi Lu* or *Tzu-chih*). See also BUDDHISM.

YUNU See GUANYIN.

YURT See MONGOL.

YU-TI See JADE EMPEROR.

Z

ZAJI See ACROBATICS AND VARIETY THEATER.

ZAJU See DRAMA.

ZANG See TIBETAN.

ZANGBU RIVER See KAILAS, MOUNT; TIBET.

ZANGLI See FUNERALS.

ZEN SECT OF BUDDHISM See BODHIDHARMA; CHAN SECT OF BUDDHISM; SHAOLIN TEMPLE.

ZENG GUOCHUAN See TAIPING REBELLION.

ZENG GUOFAN (Tseng Kuo-fan; 1811–72) A leading Han Chinese intellectual, statesman and military commander who suppressed the Taiping Rebellion (1850–64) during the late Manchu Qing dynasty (1644–1911). Zeng was born in Hunan Province. He was educated in the Confucian classics and passed the examinations for the imperial bureaucracy. He received an appointment to the Hanlin Academy, and in 1849 he became junior vice-president of the Board of Rites. The Taiping Rebellion against the Manchus who ruled China under the Qing dynasty erupted in southern China under the leadership of Hong Xiuquan (Hung Hsiu-ch'uan; 1813–64). The Taipings fought their way north until they took the major city of Nanjing, which enabled them to control a large area in the central and lower Yangzi River valley, the richest region in China.

In 1860 the Qing appointed Zeng imperial commissioner and governor-general of the Liangjiang provinces, territories controlled by the Taiping Rebellion, and gave him command of the military forces that opposed the rebels. Zeng regarded the Christian-influenced Taipings as a serious threat to the Confucian tradition that was the foundation of Chinese government and culture. He studied military strategy and raised a powerful and effective temporary known as the "Hunan Braves" or the "Hunan Army" (Xiangjun or Hsien chun) led by his brother and other generals belonging to the Han Chinese literati, or scholar class. He also set up a small navy on the Yangzi River. Zeng's protégé Li Hongzhang (Li Hung-chang; 1823–1901), who also became a leading statesman, raised an army in Anhui Province. These forces fought alongside the Qing regular army and a foreign-led force that was eventually commanded by the British officer Charles Gordon. After laying siege to the Taipings in Nanjing, Zeng Guofan took the city on July 19, 1864. Hong Xiuquan had already died, and most of his followers were killed. Zeng stayed in Nanjing as governor-general of Liangjiang, disbanded most of his Hunan Army and ordered the reprinting of classical Confucian works that had been destroyed during the rebellion. He supported the "Self-Strengthening Movement" (*Ziqiang* or *Tzu Ch'iang*) under which the Chinese government adapted Western technology to modernize the country during the 1860s and 1870s. In 1870, the Qing appointed Zeng to investigate an anti-foreign and anti-Christian riot in Tianjin known as the Tianjin (T'ientsin) Massacre. When confronted by a Chinese mob, the French consul, Henri Fontanier, had shot and killed a Chinese man. The mob rioted and killed 10 French Catholic nuns and two priests and other foreigners. Zeng attempted to be conciliatory but was heavily criticized by the foreigners. He was replaced by Li Hongzhang, who leveled heavy fines on the Chinese perpetrators and sent a Chinese mission to apologize to France. See also CONFUCIANISM; GORDON, CHARLES; LI HONGZHANG; MISSIONARIES; QING DYNASTY; SELF-STRENGTHENING MOVEMENT; TAIPING REBELLION.

ZENGMU REEF See SPRATLY ISLANDS.

ZHAN ZIQIAN (Chan Tzu-ch'ien; c. 550–618) A painter whose work, *Spring Outing*, in the collection of the Palace Museum in the Forbidden City in Beijing, is the earliest surviving Chinese landscape scroll. Zhan Ziqian was born in Bohai (modern Yangxin) in Shandong Province. He held a position in the bureaucracy of the Sui dynasty (589–618) but also became a skilled painter, specializing in figures of the

Buddhist and Daoist tradition, finely detailed landscapes, pavilions, horses and carriages, as well as murals. Chinese records attribute to Zhan a number of wall paintings in temples and monasteries in Chang'an (modern Xi'an) and Luoyang. Zhan painted *Spring Outing* on a silk scroll about one foot wide by about three feet long. It depicts a number of people traveling through a beautiful landscape that includes trees, a lake with a bridge and hills on which there are temples. The heavily colored yet harmonious work is relatively simple; its features became typical of Chinese landscape painting. Zhan's style had a great influence on landscape painters during the Tang dynasty (618–907), and especially upon Li Sixun (Li Ssu-hsun) and his son Li Zhaodao (Li Chao-tao). See also FIGURE PAINTING; FORBIDDEN CITY; LANDSCAPE PAINTING; LI SIXUN; SCROLLS; SUI DYNASTY.

ZHANG CHUNQIAO See CULTURAL REVOLUTION; GANG OF FOUR; JIANG QING.

ZHANG DAOLING (Chang Tao-ling; c. second century) Also known as Zhang Ling (Chang Ling); the historical founder of the Daoist (Taoist) religious organization. The Daoist tradition went back thousands of years to at least the sixth century B.C. Laozi (Lao Tzu), who supposedly lived in the sixth century B.C., was the purported author of the first Daoist text, the *Daodejing* (*Tao-te ching*), which has been translated into English as *The Book of the Way of Virtue* or *The Way and Its Power.* Daoism emphasized spiritual freedom and harmony with nature, but it also developed an occult tradition through which a small number of seekers attempted to gain immortality through divination and alchemy. In the second century A.D., Zhang Daoling was able to combine elements of the popular Daoist tradition into a formal religion. He lived and studied Daoism in the area of modern Sichuan Province and wrote a Daoist text to attract followers to his religious organization, which he called the Daoism of the Heavenly Master (*Tianshidao* or *Ti'en-shih Tao*). It acquired the name the Way (*Dao* or *Tao*) of Five Bushels of Rice (*Wudomidao* or *Wu-tou mitao*) because his followers and the patients that he healed were each required to give him five bushels of rice every year to support the organization. Many common people were attracted to Zhang Daoling's religion by his method for healing through magic charms and spells and faith healing. He taught that illness was caused by evil in the mind and could be cured by making a confession to a Daoist priest. The resulting spiritual purification would supposedly bring about physical health. Zhang's title of Heavenly Master passed to his son, Zhang Heng (Chang Heng), and then to his grandson, Zhang Lu (Chang Lu), and became hereditary. Zhang's organization, and a similar movement in east China formally called the *Taipingdao* but popularly known as the Yellow Turbans, staged armed uprisings against the government of the Eastern Han dynasty (25–220). The government suppressed the Yellow Turbans, but Zhang Lu was able to maintain his grandfather's Daoist organization by negotiating a surrender to the Han government in 215. The Heavenly Teacher has been called the "Pope" of the Daoist religion, but he has been a symbolic rather than actual leader and has not controlled Daoist priests. All subsequent Daoist groups that

were organized in China looked back to Zhang Daoling as their founder, even if their leaders were not descendants in his lineage. In 1015 the Daoism of the Heavenly Master was granted a large domain in central China where the Heavenly Master resided in the so-called Dragon and Tiger Mountain. In 1276 the Southern Song dynasty (1127–79) emperor gave official approval to the title Heavenly Teacher. In 1368 the Ming dynasty (1368–1644) emperor legally abolished the title, but it has continued to the present day in popular Daoist religion. The current Heavenly Master, who resides in Taiwan, is the 64th in his lineage. See also DAODEJING; DAOISM; LAOZI; YELLOW TURBANS REBELLION.

ZHANG DAQIAN See CHANG TA-CH'IEN.

ZHANG FEI See GUANDI; ROMANCE OF THE THREE KINGDOMS; ZHUGE LIANG.

ZHANG GUO LAO See EIGHT IMMORTALS.

ZHANG GUOTAO (Chang Kuo-t'ao; 1897–1979) A founder and early leader of the Chinese Communist Party (CCP). Zhang was born near the border between Jiangxi and Hunan provinces to a family of the Hakka ethnic minority group. In his teens he worked for the revolutionary organizations led by Sun Yat-sen (1866–1925), the founder of the modern Republic of China (ROC). Zhang became a student activist and was a leader of the May Fourth Movement of 1919, which protested the secret agreement between the Chinese and Japanese governments to give Shandong Province to Japan. At first he was an anarchist, but he became influenced by Marxist thought while attending a study group at Beijing University led by Li Dazhao (Li Ta-chao; 1888–1927) that was also attended by Mao Zedong (Mao Tse-tung; 1893–1976), who later became the leader of Communist China. In July 1921, Zhang participated with Mao and other Marxists in the meeting that is regarded as the official founding of the Chinese Communist Party. Zhang worked as a Communist organizer and led the Beijing-Hankou Railroad strike that was brutally ended on February 7, 1923, by the warlord Wu Beifu (Wu P'ei-fu). When the Chinese Communist Party made an alliance with the Nationalist Party (Kuomintang; KMT) founded by Sun Yat-sen, Zhang became an official of the Nationalist Party. This alliance broke down, however, after Nationalist forces massacred Communists in April 1927. Zhang took part with other Communists in the uprising at Nanchang on August 1, 1927, considered the official founding of the Chinese Red Army (later known as the People's Liberation Army; PLA). Zhang then traveled to the Soviet Union, where he stayed until the CCP directed him in 1931 to become the head of a Communist Soviet in northern China. Nationalist troops forced Zhang to move his headquarters several times. He first made his base in the Dabie Mountain Range northeast of Wuhan, but in 1933 he moved it to northern Sichuan Province.

In June 1935, toward the end of their Long March, the Red Army troops led by Mao Zedong from their base at Jiangxi joined with Zhang's 50,000 Red Army troops in Sichuan. Zhang asserted that he should be the leader of the combined Red Army, but Mao had recently been elected head of the CCP, and he and his supporters rejected Zhang's claim. Most of the Red Army troops left with Mao to join CCP troops in northern Shaanxi Province. A smaller number of troops went with Zhang and the Communist military leader Zhu De (Chu Teh; 1886–1976) to southwestern China near the Tibetan border. They were isolated there, and in 1937 Zhang and Zhu finally had to lead their troops back to Mao's base in Shaanxi. By then Zhang had lost influence as a Communist leader. When the party sent him in 1938 to attend a conference between Communists and Nationalists, he defected to the Nationalist Party. The CCP purged him for rightist deviation. Zhang remained in the Nationalist capital at Chongqing in Sichuan Province for the remainder of China's War of Resistance against Japan (1937–45; World War II). In 1949 the Communists led by Mao won the civil war they had been fighting with the Nationalists, and Zhang fled to Hong Kong, which was then a British Crown Colony. He died in Toronto, Canada. See also CHINESE COMMUNIST PARTY; CIVIL WAR BETWEEN COMMUNISTS AND NATIONALISTS; HAKKA; LI DAZHAO; LONG MARCH; MAO ZEDONG; MAY FOURTH MOVEMENT OF 1919; NATIONALIST PARTY; WAR OF RESISTANCE AGAINST JAPAN; ZHU DE.

ZHANG HENG (Chang Heng; 78–139)   A famous scientist who invented the telescope and an early seismograph, a device for detecting and recording earthquakes. The seismograph was a bronze container, eight feet in diameter, with a dome-shaped cover and eight dragon heads around its surface, with a bronze ball in the mouth of each dragon. Eight bronze toads with open mouths were placed on the ground around the container, and a distant earthquake would shake a ball out of the dragon's mouth, causing it to drop into the toad's mouth. By this method, even minor shocks and the direction in which they had occurred could be registered. The Chinese government wanted to keep track of earthquakes because they often resulted in rebellions or food riots, and troops would have to be dispatched quickly to prevent disasters. The success of Zhang Heng's seismograph astonished the imperial court. It has been reconstructed by modern scientists.

Zhang Heng was born into a poor family, but he was so brilliant that he was able to acquire an education and become an astronomer. He was also renowned for his poetry and calligraphy, highly valued arts in Chinese culture. When he was 57, Zhang Heng was appointed the government official in charge of the department that studied the heavenly bodies. Using his telescope, he plotted the positions of planets and stars and recorded lunar eclipses. Chinese astronomical observations, so accurate that they are still being used by modern astronomers, date back to 1300 B.C. During the Han dynasty (206 B.C.–A.D. 220) Chinese scientists hotly debated differing astronomical speculations about the structure of the universe. Zhang Heng favored the ecliptical theory (Hun Tian or Hun T'ien) that "Heaven is like an egg and earth is like the yolk wrapped inside the egg." He wrote several books, but only fragments of one book remain, Spiritual Constitution of the Universe. It shows that he visualized the Earth as a sphere with nine continents suspended in infinite space. See also ASTRONOMY AND OBSERVATORIES; NATURAL DISASTERS.

ZHANG JIAO   See ALCHEMY; YELLOW TURBANS REBELLION.

ZHANG JUE   See YELLOW TURBANS REBELLION.

ZHANG JUNQIU (Chang Chun-ch'iu; 1921–)   A renowned performer of Beijing Opera, specializing in the type of role known as the demure female (qingyi or ch'ing-yi). Zhang was born into a poor family, but his mother was a star of the type of opera performed in Hebei Province. When he was 13, Zhang began to study the female role (dan or tan) with Li Lingfeng, an actor in the Beijing Opera who had studied with Wang Yaoqing (Wang Yao-ch'ing), a famous Beijing Opera master. Wang recognized Zhang's talent and later took him on as his personal student. Zhang first appeared on stage in Revival when he was 15 years old. In 1936, he began appearing with troupes run by several famous opera masters and gained critical acclaim in Beijing, Tianjin and Shanghai, with audiences selecting him as one of the four best young performers of female roles. In 1937 he became an apprentice of the great Beijing Opera performer Mei Lanfang, who introduced the opera to foreign countries. In 1942 Zhang founded his own Beijing Opera Troupe, which revived such pieces as Kindness and Enmity in Turbulent Days, Poverty and Wealth and Scrambling for Imperial Power. In 1948, during China's civil war between the Chinese Communist Party (CCP) and the Nationalist Party (Kuomintang; KMT), Zhang went to Hong Kong, where he lived and performed until 1951—two years after the Communists won the war and founded the People's Republic of China (PRC). When he returned to China, during the 1950s and 1960s he staged operas, including contemporary works and operas adapted from episodes in Chinese history. He paid special attention to the costumes and makeup worn by the performers. Zhang also appeared with other leading performers in the film adaptation of the Beijing Opera, The Fate of an Ungrateful Man.

In 1963 Zhang made a trip to Hong Kong to perform as a representative of the PRC. He had to stop performing during the Cultural Revolution (1966–76) but began acting once again in the late 1970s. Since then he has concentrated on consolidating the repertoire he had already performed and on training young opera performers. By 1993 he had more than 160 students in China and foreign countries. In addition to Hong Kong, Zhang has performed in Japan, Canada and the United States, where in 1990 he was awarded an honorary doctorate in liberal arts by Lincoln University and given an award for lifelong achievement in the arts by the Lincoln Center in New York City. In January 1993 the Chinese Ministry of Culture held a ceremony in Beijing to celebrate Zhang's 60-year acting career. His students and fans from all over China, Hong Kong, Taiwan and the United States traveled to Beijing for the ceremony. Liu Xuetao (Liu Hsueh-t'ao), a famous performer of young men roles (xiaosheng or hsiao-sheng), who acted with Zhang for more than 40 years, came from Europe to take part in the ceremony. See also MEI LANFANG; OPERA, BEIJING.

ZHANG LING   See ZHANG DAOLING.

ZHANG LUOXING   See NIAN REBELLION.

ZHANG QIAN (Chang Ch'ien; d. 114 B.C.)   A general during the reign of Han emperor Wudi (Wu-ti; r. 141–87 B.C.) who in 139 B.C. took a military force to the "Western

Regions" (*xiyu* or *hsi-yu*) to negotiate an alliance with a tribe called the Tocharians (Yuezhi or Yueh-chih) against their common enemy, the Xiongnu (Hsiung-nu). But before Zhang Qian reached his destination, he was captured by the Xiongnu and held captive for 10 years. He escaped, but instead of returning to China he continued to search for tribes friendly to the Han. He found that the Tocharians had moved west and were trying to gain control of a region in Bactria (modern Afghanistan) that was still ruled by descendants of the Greek conqueror Alexander the Great (356–323 B.C.). Zhang Qian spent a year trying to work out an alliance with them against the Xiongnu but was unsuccessful and returned to China in 126 B.C. He brought back two products new to China, walnuts and grapevines, as well as news that kingdoms to the west wanted to trade with the Han Empire, especially for silk. Thus Zhang Qian was not only the first Chinese to make contact with leaders of Central Asian tribes, but he also laid the foundation for establishing the Silk Road, a network of routes along which camel caravans transported silk and other luxury goods, such as porcelain and tea, from China to the Mediterranean world.

Zhang Qian also brought back knowledge about the customs of various Central Asian tribes and geographical information that was of military importance to the Han. He informed the Han that they could acquire horses in the west that were large enough to carry heavily armed men, which the Chinese could use to defend against the Xiongnu, who rode smaller Mongolian ponies. Zhang Qian made a second trip from 119 to 115 B.C. to the horse-breeding peoples of Central Asia and made alliance with the Wusun, a nomadic tribe in the Ili Valley (modern Xinjiang-Uighur Autonomous Region). He also visited Ferghana once more, and also Sogdiana and oases in Central Asia. He returned home even more convinced that people in these regions were eager to trade with China, especially for silk. See also HAN DYNASTY; HORSE; SILK; SILK ROAD; XIONGNU.

ZHANG XUELIANG (Chang Hsueh-liang; 1898–) A warlord who controlled Manchuria (northeastern China) when Japan invaded the region in 1931 to establish the puppet state of Manchukuo (*Manzhouguo* or *Man-chou-kuo* in Chinese) in 1932. Zhang Xueliang is known as the "Young Marshal" to distinguish him from his father, the "Old Marshal," Zhang Zuolin (Chang Tso-lin; 1873–1928), whom he succeeded as warlord. Zhang Xueliang had been trained for a military career and joined his father's army in 1917. In 1919 he attained the rank of colonel. Zhang took part in some of the battles and political maneuvering that characterized the warlord period from 1916 to 1928. In late 1925, he was implicated in an attempt by the warlord Feng Yuxiang (Feng Yu-hsiang) to overthrow Zhang Zuolin, who became so angry with his son that he nearly had him executed. In 1926 and in 1928, however, Zhang Xueliang helped his father fight forces of the Northern Expedition against warlords, which was commanded by Nationalist (Kuomintang; KMT) Chinese leader Chiang Kai-shek (1887–1975).

Zhang Zuolin had been acting as de facto head of China in Beijing, but in 1928 the Northern Expedition drove Zhang's forces out of Beijing. Zhang returned to Mukden (modern Shenyang), his capital in Manchuria, on June 3, 1928, but the next day a Japanese bomb blew up his private railway car. He died several days later and Zhang Xueliang succeeded him, although the elder Zhang's death was kept secret for several weeks.

In December 1928, seeking to maintain his independence from the Soviet Union and Japan, which were vying for control of Manchuria, Zhang Xueliang declared his allegiance to the Nationalist Chinese government, now based in Nanjing. In 1929 the Nationalist government gained Zhang's assistance in opposing Soviet influence in Manchuria. Zhang's police raided the Soviet Consulate General in the city of Harbin, and they seized the Chinese Eastern Railway and removed the Soviet railway officials. The Soviets protested and then used military troops to take back the railroad. In 1930 Zhang occupied Beijing on behalf of the Nationalists and suppressed a revolt by local military commanders against Nationalist headquarters in Nanjing.

Japanese forces in Manchuria wanted to limit Chiang Kai-shek's growing influence in China, and they wanted to drive Zhang Xueliang out of Manchuria into northern China so that they could take over Manchuria, which was rich in natural resources. In the so-called Manchurian Incident on September 18, 1931, the Japanese set off a bomb on the railway line outside of Mukden and blamed it on the Chinese. The Japanese Army then occupied Mukden as a first step in taking over all of Manchuria. The Nationalist government ordered Zhang not to oppose the Japanese with military force, and it pulled Nationalist troops out of Manchuria. Chiang Kai-shek believed that it was more important to fight the Chinese Communists than to fight the Japanese. Zhang obeyed Chiang's order, but his troops were demoralized and some were defeated by the Japanese while others retreated into Soviet territory or northern China. After the Japanese established Manchukuo, they began marching toward Inner Mongolia, and Zhang was unable to stop them.

When Japan invaded China, the Nationalists were fighting a civil war with the Chinese Communists. In 1935 the Nationalists sent Zhang's troops to fight Chinese Communist forces, which had made their base in Shaanxi Province in northwestern China after their Long March (1934–35). But his soldiers did not want to fight other Chinese, especially since Japanese troops had occupied their Manchurian homeland, so Zhang and Communist leaders decided on a truce. Zhang played a major role in the so-called Xi'an Incident on the night of December 11, 1936, in which he and General Yang Hucheng, commander of the Nationalist army in Shaanxi Province, placed Chiang Kai-shek under house arrest at his headquarters at the Huaqing Hot Springs outside Xi'an. They organized secret negotiations with Chiang, a Nationalist group from Nanjing including Chiang's wife, Soong Mei-ling (b. 1897), and a Communist delegation led by Zhou Enlai (Chou En-lai; 1898–1976). Chiang finally agreed on December 24 that the Nationalists would stop fighting the Communists for the time being and that both sides would form a united front to fight the Japanese. Zhang could then have joined the Communists led by Mao Zedong (Mao Tse-tung; 1893–1976), but he spared Chiang public humiliation by taking him out of Xi'an and accompanying him to the Nationalist capital in Nanjing. The Chinese people were relieved that Chiang was released from detention and gave him their support. Zhang was tried by a military court and placed under house arrest, which lasted for half a century. He was held in Guizhou Province in southwestern China during most of China's War of Resistance against Japan (1937–45; World War II). In 1946 the Nationalists and Communists resumed their civil war, and in 1948, Zhang was taken to the island of Taiwan with Nationalists who were escaping the impending Communist victory in mainland China. In January 1949, Li Tsung-jen, acting president of the Republic of China on Taiwan, ordered Zhang's captors to free him, but they did not obey his order. Only in 1991 was Zhang finally released from house arrest. He became a symbol of Chinese patriotism for both Nationalists and Communists. See also CHIANG KAI-SHEK; CHINESE COMMUNIST PARTY; CIVIL WAR BETWEEN COMMUNISTS AND NATIONALISTS; HUAQING HOT SPRINGS; MANCHUKUO; MANCHURIA; MANCHURIAN INCIDENT; NORTHERN EXPEDITION; SHENYANG; SOONG MEI-LING; WAR OF RESISTANCE AGAINST JAPAN; ZHANG ZUOLIN; ZHOU ENLAI.

ZHANG YIMOU (Chang Yi-mo; 1951–) One of the most prominent contemporary Chinese film directors, who has also worked as a cinematographer and actor. Zhang was born into a middle-class family in Xi'an, the capital of Shaanxi Province in western China. His father was a government official who had been a major in Chiang Kai-shek's Nationalist (Kuomintang; KMT) army and his mother was a doctor. During the Cultural Revolution (1966–76), Zhang was sent to work in the countryside for three years and as a janitor in a textile factory for seven years. In his spare time he took up painting and saved his money to buy a camera and teach himself photography. In 1978 the Beijing Film Academy reopened, and he attempted to sign up for the entrance examinations. By then he was 27, and the academy's age limit was 22, but he sent his photographs to the Chinese Ministry of Culture and persuaded them to allow him to attend the academy. Zhang studied cinematography and graduated in 1982. He and three colleagues were assigned to the small and remote Guangxi Film Studio in Nanning in southern China. There they were able to use experimental techniques to make their first film, *One and Eight,* about prisoners of war during China's War of Resistance against Japan (1937–45; World War II). This was the first film made by the young post–Cultural Revolution Fifth Generation of Chinese film makers, and it gained a lot of attention in China. Zhang used similar film techniques in *Yellow Earth* (1985), directed by Shen Kaige (Ch'en K'ai-ke), another prominent young Chinese film maker, for which Zhang was director of photography. This film, about the difficult life of peasants on the loess plateau in northwestern China, won the Chinese Golden Rooster Award and was shown at several international film festivals. Zhang then served as cinematographer for *Big Military Parade,* directed by Chen Kaige, a film about soldiers in training. Zhang's next film as cinematographer was *The Old Well* (1987), about residents of a drought-stricken village looking for water. The director, Wu Tianming, who was also the head of the Xi'an Film Studio, gave Zhang the male lead as well, for which he won the best actor award at the second Tokyo International Film Festival. *Old Well* was named best film.

Zhang made his debut as a director with *Red Sorghum* (1987), about a woman in an arranged marriage and her lover in a sorghum-growing region of Shandong Province, which was adapted from the novel of the same name by Mou Yan. It won the Golden Bear for best film at the 38th Berlin International Film Festival and was the first mainland Chinese film ever shown in the New York Film Festival. Gong Li (Kung Li) was the leading actress in this and all subsequent films Zhang has directed. She also became his partner in private life, even though Zhang's wife refused to give him a divorce. In 1996, Gong Li married a Singapore businessman, one year after she and Zhang underwent an emotional breakup. Zhang made a commercial action film, *Operation Cougar* (1989), about a hijacking set against the background of Taiwan's reunification with the People's Republic of China. The Xi'an Film Studio was purged after the Tiananmen Square Massacre of 1989, but Zhang continued to make art films, partly by gaining foreign investors. *Judou* (1990), a Chinese and Japanese co-production, tells the story of a woman named Judou who is sold into an unhappy marriage that ends in tragedy. The film was shown at the 1990 Cannes Film Festival, where it won the Luis Bunuel Award and was highly praised by French critics, and was nominated for an Academy Award (Oscar) for best foreign film in the United States.

Raise the Red Lantern (1991), based on the short story "Wives and Concubines" by Su Tong (Su T'ung), is about a young woman who is persuaded to become one of a wealthy man's several concubines. It won a Silver Lion at the 48th Venice Film Festival and a nomination for best foreign film at the U.S. Academy Awards. Gong Li was also nominated for best actress at the David Film Festival in Italy. Zhang adapted *The Story of Qiuju* (1992) from the novel by Chen Yuanbing. The film is set in a mountain village in northwestern China, where a man is injured by the village headman and his strong-willed pregnant wife goes through many levels of government bureaucracy to sue the headman. The film won the Golden Lion Award for best film, and Gong Li won the Volbi Cup for best actress at the 49th Venice International Film Festival, the first time a Chinese actress has ever won this award. Zhang's most recent film is *Shanghai Triad* (1995), about gangsters in 1930s Shanghai, which has won several international awards. In 1996 the opera house in Florence, Italy announced that Zhang would direct Puccini's "Turandot." See also CHEN KAIGE; CULTURAL REVOLUTION; FILM STUDIOS; GONG LI; LOESS; SHANGHAI; SORGHUM; TIANANMEN SQUARE MASSACRE.

ZHANG YUAN See CHANG TA-CH'IEN.

ZHANG ZUOLIN (Chang Tso-lin; 1873–1928) A powerful warlord who controlled Manchuria (northeastern China) from 1919 until he was killed by a Japanese bomb in 1928. Zhang Zuolin is known as the "Old Marshal," while his son and successor, Zhang Xueliang (Chang Hsueh-liang; 1898–), is known as the "Young Marshal." Zhang Zuolin was born in Fengtian (Fengtien; modern Liaoning Province). He fought in the Sino-Japanese War of 1894–95 and then returned to Fengtian and built up his own army. During the Russo-Japanese War of 1904–5, Zhang's forces fought on the Japanese side. After the war, his troops were taken into the imperial armies of the Manchu Qing dynasty (1644–1911) that ruled China. When the Chinese Revolution of 1911 that overthrew the Qing began with the Wuchang Uprising on October 10, 1911, Zhang suppressed a military rebellion and maintained order in Manchuria.

When the Republic of China was established in 1912 and Yuan Shikai (Yuan Shih-k'ai; 1859–1916) replaced Sun Yat-sen (1866–1925) as president, Manchuria was nominally ruled by the Chinese government in Beijing. However, Zhang Zuolin became so powerful that by 1919 he was the virtual ruler of an autonomous Manchuria. In July 1920 he assisted Wu Peifu (1874–1939), a divisional commander in Hunan Province, in defeating Duan Qirui (Tuan Ch'i-jui; 1865–1936) outside Beijing. Duan, based in Beijing as premier of the Republic of China, had attempted to bring all of China under his control. After defeating Duan, Wu and Zhang fought each other for control of northern China. In the spring of 1922, Zhang took Beijing but was then driven out by Wu, so Zhang retreated to Manchuria. In 1924 Zhang joined a movement to defeat Wu Peifu. Wu moved his troops north toward Manchuria and ordered his general Feng Yuxian (Feng Yu-hsien; 1882–1948) to move westward to prevent Zhang from circling around and coming through the mountain passes to attack Wu from behind. But Feng disobeyed Wu and took control of Beijing instead.

On May 31, 1924, China and the Soviet Union signed the Sino-Soviet Treaty, which defined the rights of China and the U.S.S.R. in the operation of the Chinese Eastern Railway in Manchuria. But Zhang refused to honor the treaty as valid, and signed his own agreement with the U.S.S.R. in September 1924. The Chinese government in Beijing protested to both Zhang and the U.S.S.R. but received no response. In December 1924, Zhang and two other northern warlords invited Sun Yat-sen to Beijing to negotiate the peaceful unification of China. Sun was very ill when he went to Beijing, and he died there on March 12, 1925, before negotiations were completed. Sun's death created a power struggle among his followers in the Chinese Nationalist Party (Kuomintang; KMT).

Chinese warlords fought each other in the period from 1916 to 1928. By 1925 Zhang had advanced his troops as far south as the lower Yangzi River valley, although he soon had to retreat back north. In July 1926, Nationalist Chinese leader Chiang Kai-shek (1887–1975) initiated the Northern Expedition against the warlords with the intent of unifying China. Zhang Zuolin held Beijing in early 1927, after Duan Qirui, the final president of the Republic of China in that city, had been forced to resign in April 1926. Zhang attempted to make himself the legitimate successor of Yuan Shikai but was not accepted as such. Although Zhang dealt with foreign diplomats in Beijing, for more than two years there was in fact no legitimate Chinese head of state. Chiang Kai-shek's Northern Expedition went into its final phase in April 1928 and drove Zhang Zuolin's forces out of Beijing. Zhang Zuolin left Beijing to return to Mukden (modern Shenyang), his capital in Manchuria, on June 3, but the next day a Japanese bomb blew up his private railway car. Zhang died several days later and was succeeded by his son, Zhang Xueliang, who declared his allegiance to the Nationalist government. In 1931 Japan invaded Manchuria and turned it into a puppet state called Manchukuo (*Manzhouguo* or *Man-chou-kuo* in Chinese). See also CHIANG KAI-SHEK; MANCHUKUO; MANCHURIA; NORTHERN EXPEDITION; QING DYNASTY; REPUBLIC OF CHINA; REVOLUTION OF 1911; SHENYANG; SINO-SOVIET WAR OF 1894–95; SUN YAT-SEN; WUCHANG UPRISING; YUAN SHIKAI; ZHANG XUELIANG.

ZHANGHUAI, PRINCE See TANG IMPERIAL TOMBS.

ZHANGUO See WARRING STATES PERIOD.

ZHAO DAN (Chao Tan; 1915–80)   Original name Zhao Fenggao (Chao Feng-kao); one of China's greatest film actors. Zhao was born in Shandong Province but his family soon moved to Jiangsu Province. His father was a fan of Chinese opera and ran a theater, and as a boy Zhao often put on opera performances with his friends. Zhao also practiced painting and calligraphy and became a student at the Academy of Fine Arts in Shanghai. He then decided to become an actor as a way of expressing his feelings, and in 1932 he joined the China Left-Wing Dramatists' Association. His performance as Tihon in 1936 in Ostrovsky's *The Storm,* a strong criticism of feudalism in Russia produced by the Shanghai Amateur Players' Association, made him famous in the city. In the play, Tihon obeys his mother's command to persecute his wife, who becomes so miserable that she drowns herself. Zhao then played Romeo in Shakespeare's *Romeo and Juliet,* also produced by the Shanghai Amateur Players' Association. He began acting in films as well. His first role was a dying man in *The Spring Dream of the Lute.* Appearing in dozens of other films, he played a newspaper proofreader in *Crossroads* and a trumpet player in *Street Angel* in 1936, which made him famous throughout the country.

After China began fighting its War of Resistance against Japan (1937–45; World War II), Zhao joined other actors in forming the Shanghai Theatrical Troupe for National Salvation Number 3. They performed anti-Japanese political dramas at many cities along the Yangzi River (Changjiang). In Wuhan, they performed a play by Yang Hansheng, *Storm over the Great Wall,* in 1938. Zhao went on to Chongqing in Sichuan Province, wartime capital of Nationalist China, where he was given a position at the Central Film Studio. In 1939 Zhao, three other actors and their families traveled west to Xinjiang, where they believed they would be able to develop pro-Chinese operas to help the war effort, but they were all arrested and imprisoned by a Nationalist (Kuomintang; KMT) warlord. Popular outrage finally secured Zhao's release in 1944. He returned to Chongqing and performed in a play by Mao Dun (Mao Tun), *Before and After the Qingming Festival.*

With the war's end in 1945, Zhao returned to Shanghai and played leading roles in *Crows and Sparrows* and several other films. After the Communists founded the People's Republic of China in 1949, Zhao was elected a deputy to the National People's Congress and given membership in the Chinese Communist Party (CCP). He remained an active performer during the 1950s. One of his greatest roles was in *Li Shizhen* (Li Shih-chen), the true story of a pharmacologist during the Ming dynasty (1368–1644). The hero of the story wrote China's most important text on medicinal plants, which is still consulted by doctors of herbal medicine. In another film he played Lin Zexu (Lin Tse-hsu), an imperial commissioner during the Qing dynasty (1644–1911) who tried to thwart the opium trade that Britain was forcing on China in the early 1800s. Zhao also played Nie Er, a famous composer of the 1930s who composed China's national anthem, in *Nie Er* (*Nieh Erh*); and Xu Yunfeng (Hsu Yun-feng), an underground revolutionary member of the Communist Party and friend of Zhao, in *Red Crag.*

By the 1960s, Zhao had become China's most important film actor and his career was reaching artistic maturity. Sadly, the Cultural Revolution (1966–76) broke out, and he was sentenced to five and a half years in solitary confinement. In 1976 he was released and planned to make more films, but was never able to do so. Zhao described his experiences in the books, *Portraying of Film Figures* and *The Gate of Hell*. He spent his final years creating several hundred works of painting and calligraphy in the traditional Chinese style. His essay, "Too Much Interference Brings No Hope to Our Literature and Art," was published just before he died in 1980. Zhao's wife, Huang Zongying (Huang Tsung-ying), was a well-known film actress and screenplay writer. Their daughter, Zhao Qing (Chao Ch'ing), became a famous dancer. See also ANTHEM, NATIONAL; CALLIGRAPHY; CHINESE COMMUNIST PARTY; CULTURAL REVOLUTION; LI SHIZHENG; LIN ZEXU; MAO DUN; NATIONAL PEOPLE'S CONGRESS; NATIONALIST PARTY; OPIUM WAR; PAINTING; PEOPLE'S REPUBLIC OF CHINA; WAR OF RESISTANCE AGAINST JAPAN.

ZHAO GAO   See EUNUCHS; QIN DYNASTY; QIN SHIHUANGDI, EMPEROR.

ZHAO KUANGYIN   See NORTHERN SONG DYNASTY.

ZHAO MENGFU (Chao Meng-fu; 1254–1322) and **GUAN DAOSHENG** (Kuan Tao-sheng)   A highly talented painter, calligrapher, scholar and government official, and his wife, one of the greatest female painters in China. Guan Daosheng was especially renowned for her paintings of bamboo. Zhao Meng-fu was born in Zhejiang Province into a distant branch of the Song imperial family during the Southern Song dynasty (1127–1279), which had its capital at Hangzhou in southern China. He held government positions in the Song imperial bureaucracy until the Mongols led by Khubilai Khan overthrew the Song and established the Yuan dynasty (1279–1368). For 10 years the Yuan pressured Zhao to join its bureaucracy. In 1286 he finally agreed to move to the court at Khanbaliq (called Dadu or Tatu by the Chinese; modern Beijing), the capital built by Khubilai Khan in northern China. There he was appointed to the Hanlin Academy. Zhao served in the Yuan government until 1295 and was such a capable government administrator that he rose to the rank of cabinet minister, secretary to the academy and confidential adviser to the emperor. However, because he joined the Mongol government he was scorned by the Chinese literati or scholars of his time, although he furthered the adoption of Chinese civilization by the Mongols.

Zhao studied the paintings of earlier Chinese masters and revived their styles, especially those of the Tang dynasty (618–907). He painted many different subjects but is especially famous for his paintings of horses, which were very important to the Mongols, a nomadic tribe whose men lived and fought in the saddle. One of Zhao's most famous paintings simply portrays a sheep and a goat, with a beautiful calligraphic inscription along the left side of the paper explaining that he made this painting at the request of a friend. Zhao mastered all the styles of Chinese calligraphy but developed his own individual style, based on the regular, or *kaishu*, style, which became a standard style during the Yuan. He also helped further the emphasis on training in styles used in earlier dynasties and the study of the historical tradition of calligraphy as an art form. One of the best-known examples of Zhao's calligraphy is *Twin Pines against a Flat Vista*, a handscroll painting with the inscription written on the left side. Zhao is also noted for his landscape painting; the finest surviving one is a horizontal scroll titled *Autumn Colours on the Chiao and Hua Mountains*, which has a realistic and austere quality that is not seen in the works of earlier masters. Zhao's work greatly influenced painters of the Ming (1368–1644) and Qing (1644–1911) dynasties. Zhao Meng-fu retired to southern China and brought back a large number of paintings and calligraphic works from earlier dynasties that he had collected while in the north. His son, Zhao Yung (Chao Yung 1289–c. 1363), also became a well-known painter and calligrapher. See also BAMBOO; CALLIGRAPHY; HANLIN ACADEMY; HORSE; IMPERIAL BUREAUCRACY; INK PAINTING; LANDSCAPE PAINTING; SCROLLS; YUAN DYNASTY.

ZHAO QING   See ZHAO DAN.

ZHAO SHAO'ANG (Chao Shao-ang; 1905–)   A modern Chinese painter and teacher belonging to the Lingnan School of painting. Zhao was born in Guangzhou (Canton) in southern China. His father died when he was very young, but his mother worked to earn enough money to send him to school. When Zhao was 16, he was apprenticed to Gao Qifeng (Kao Ch'i-feng), a master in the Lingnan School. The school was founded in the second half of the 19th century by two brothers, Ju Lian (Chu Lian) and Ju Chao (Chu Ch'ao), who developed a detailed yet colorful style for painting birds, flowers and insects. At the turn of the century, the style was further developed by another set of brothers, Gao Jianfu (Kao Chien-fu) and Gao Qifeng, who revived traditional Chinese painting by adapting Japanese and Western techniques and using vivid colors.

Li's beautiful paintings became so famous that when he was 26 he was awarded a gold medal at the World's Fair in Belgium. Li was in Hong Kong when China began fighting its War of Resistance against Japan (1937–45; World War II). When Hong Kong fell to the Japanese, Li escaped on a fishing boat to the nearby island of Macao, from which he struggled to get into Guangzhou. From there he traveled to Chongqing in Sichuan Province in central China, where the Chinese Nationalists (Kuomintang; KMT) had fled to escape the Japanese who had taken control of eastern China. After the war, Zhao settled in Hong Kong, where he lived a simple life and devoted himself to painting, without concern for being rich and famous. The renowned Chinese painter Xu Beihong (Hsu Pei-hong) praised Zhao: "His paintings are lovely, but his character is even more admirable." Zhao is skilled at painting a variety of traditional subjects, including landscapes, human figures, birds, fish and insects, but he is especially admired for his paintings of flowers and animals. Two of his best-known works are *Frog in a Spring Pond* and *The Moon Shines over the Lotus Pond* (1981). Zhao's painting style is gentle and elegant yet complex and full of life. See also BIRD-AND-FLOWER PAINTING; CHONGQING; PAINTING; WAR OF RESISTANCE AGAINST JAPAN; XU BEIHONG.

ZHAO YUNG See ZHAO MENGFU AND GUAN DAOSHENG.

ZHAO ZIYANG (Chao Tzu-yang; 1919–) A Communist leader who succeeded Hu Yaobang as general secretary of the Chinese Communist Party (CCP) in 1987 but was purged in 1989 after the pro-democracy demonstrations and Tiananmen Square Massacre in Beijing. Zhao was born to a prosperous land-owning family in Henan Province in central China. He joined the CCP when he was 19 and fought with Communist guerrillas during China's War of Resistance against Japan (1937–45; World War II). After the Communists established the People's Republic of China (PRC) in 1949, Zhao became an important CCP cadre in Guangdong Province in southern China, where he gained important experience in managing agricultural issues. He was purged in 1967 during the Cultural Revolution (1966–76) because he supported the policies of Deng Xiaoping (Teng Xiaop'ing) and other opponents of Mao Zedong (Mao Tse-tung). In 1972 Zhao was rehabilitated and sent to successive posts in Inner Mongolia and Guangdong. In 1975, when Deng Xiaoping's power grew strong, Zhao became Communist party secretary and political commissar in Sichuan Province in central China, where he directed the so-called "Sichuan miracle" by ending the severe famine there and using the "responsibility system" to increase agricultural production. This system, begun in 1981, required local managers to be responsible for the profits and losses of their collective farms or businesses. Zhao also reduced central planning by Chinese Communist officials in Beijing. He used various incentive systems, such as allowing factories to keep some of their profits and give bonuses to employees, to improve Sichuan's industrial and economic output. Industrial production increased 80 percent in Sichuan between 1976 and 1979.

Zhao's successes made him famous, and the Chinese government adopted some of his methods for the country as a whole. The CCP gave Zhao a position on its 11th Central Committee, and in 1980 he succeeded Hua Guofeng as premier of the State Council. Zhao, in his first speech as premier, supported Deng's new economic guidelines for modernizing and decentralizing China. While Zhao was premier, China began accepting bids from foreign companies for offshore petroleum drilling, and he promised that China would not nationalize any of its large oilfields. In May and June of 1984, Zhao visited nine European countries to stimulate trade relations and foreign investment in China and toured Africa to publicize China's support for Third World countries. He also made a diplomatic visit to the United States, and President Ronald Reagan visited China, where he met with Zhao and other party leaders. On December 19, 1984, Zhao and British prime minister Margaret Thatcher signed the final accord stating that Britain would restore Hong Kong to Chinese sovereignty on July 1, 1997.

When Zhao succeeded Hu Yaobang as general secretary of the Communist Party in 1987, he also became first vice-chairman of the Military Affairs Commission, which was chaired by Deng Xiaoping. Chinese students strongly supported Hu, and when he died in April 1989, pro-democracy demonstrations broke out in Shanghai and Beijing, where they escalated into a massive movement for political and social reform that was televised around the world. Zhao and Li Peng visited fasting students who had to be hospitalized.

In May the five members of the Politburo Standing Committee underwent a power struggle debating how to handle the demonstration; Zhao said that they should take only moderate measures against the students. However, the hardline faction of the Politburo Standing Committee decided to enact martial law. When Li Peng announced it on May 20, residents of Beijing and other cities flooded the streets in support of the demonstrators. The government brought in soldiers and Zhao was stripped of all his powers and placed under house arrest. The soldiers were ordered to fire on the protesters and remove them from the streets. Many were killed or wounded. After the Tiananmen Square Massacre in June, the Chinese government removed Zhao from all his positions to punish him for supporting the "counterrevolutionary rebellion." Li Peng replaced Zhao, who had been Deng Xiaoping's heir apparent, as premier. Since then Zhao has not been seen in public, and he did not attend Deng's funeral in February 1997. He is believed to be living under house arrest in Beijing and waiting for the opportunity to make a political comeback. See also CENTRAL COMMITTEE OF THE CHINESE COMMUNIST PARTY; CHINESE COMMUNIST PARTY; CULTURAL REVOLUTION; DENG XIAOPING; GOVERNMENT STRUCTURE; HU YAOGANG; HUA GUOFENG; PEOPLE'S REPUBLIC OF CHINA; SICHUAN PROVINCE; STATE COUNCIL; TIANANMEN SQUARE MASSACRE; WAR OF RESISTANCE AGAINST JAPAN.

ZHAOLING See ABAHAI; MUKDEN; SHENYANG; TANG IMPERIAL TOMBS.

ZHAOZHOU BRIDGE See BRIDGES.

ZHE SCHOOL OF PAINTING See DAI JIN.

ZHEJIANG PROVINCE A province on the east-central coast that covers an area of 38,614 square miles, the smallest of all the Chinese provinces, and has a population of about 40 million. The capital city is Hangzhou with a population of about 1.3 million. Other major cities include Ningbo, Shaoxing, Jiaxing, Zhoushan and Wenzhou. Zhejiang (also known as the Qiantang) is the name of the main river that flows through the province, which is crossed by thousands of canals and rivers. The Qiantang divides the province into two parts. The northern region belongs to the delta of the Yangzi River (Changjiang) and includes Lake Tai, one of the largest lakes in China. The fertile soil makes this region a prime rice-growing area with two crops a year. Other major agricultural products include tea, with some of the finest Chinese teas being grown around the beautiful old capital city of Hangzhou; mulberry trees, whose leaves are fed to silkworms; jute, a plant used to make such products as rope and fibers; and fish farming. The southern region, another alluvial plain, includes the busy port of Ningbo that provides the outlet to the East China Sea for Shaoxing city. Mountain ranges are covered with forests.

Zhejiang's rugged coastline has made it a haven for pirates since at least the fifth century. In the mid-14th century, when Mongols ruled China under the Yuan dynasty (1279–1368), pirates and workers from the Zhejiang salt mines made joint attacks on the Mongols, who were hated by the Han (ethnic Chinese), and helped overthrow them.

Zhejiang, a major rice-, tea- and mulberry-growing region, is the smallest Chinese province, with around 40 million people.   DENNIS COX

Zhejiang, always heavily populated, was also a center for rebellions by peasants, miners and sailors against burdensome policies of the Northern Song dynasty in the early 12th century and the Ming dynasty in the 15th and 16th centuries. During the Ming, Japanese pirates called *wokou* (*wako* in Japanese) made numerous raids on the Zhejiang coast until they were suppressed in 1570.

During the Warring States Period (403–221 B.C.), Zhejiang was divided between the kingdoms of Wu in the west, and Yue in the east. They competed with each other for trade with kingdoms farther inland along the Yangzi River, and Yue eventually defeated Wu in the fifth century B.C. Yue was conquered in 334 B.C. by the kingdom of Chu and in 223 B.C. by Qin Shi Huangdi, who created the first unified Chinese empire under the Qin dynasty (221–206 B.C.). Another kingdom of Wu was revived during the Three Kingdoms Period (A.D. 220–280) and became more powerful, with its capital first at Wuchang and then at Nanjing. When the Song dynasty emperor was forced to flee south to Zhejiang to escape invading nomadic tribes in the north and made the Song capital at Hangzhou (Southern Song dynasty, 1127–1279), the province enjoyed a period of great prosperity and cultural influence that continued until the Taiping Rebellion in the late 19th century. Zhejiang also experienced the turmoil of the Japanese occupation during the War of Resistance against Japan (1937–45; World War II) and the civil war between the Communists and Nationalists that

ended with the founding of the People's Republic of China in 1949.

Textiles have long been a major industry in Zhejiang, which is known as the "Home of Silk." The province also produces most of the yellow wine in China, notably Shaoxing wine, as well as the highest-grade industrial paper, and is a major producer of machine tools, generators, home appliances and processed foods. There are large natural gas fields in the coastal plain.

The city of Hangzhou is located on the Grand Canal in northern Zhejiang between beautiful West Lake and the Qiantang River. As the thriving capital of the Southern Song dynasty, the city became the cultural center of China and attracted many poets and scholars. It is often paired with Suzhou, a lovely city of canals in Jiangsu Province; "Heaven above, Hangzhou and Suzhou below" is a famous Chinese saying. Shaoxing is the birthplace of Lu Xun (Lu Hsun; 1881–1936), the most famous modern Chinese writer, who is commemorated with a museum. The city is also the home of Qiu Jin (Ch'iu Chin), an early female revolutionary. Outside the city are the supposed tomb and temple of Yu, the legendary founder of the Xia dynasty (2200–1750 B.C.). See also ALCOHOLIC BEVERAGES; GRAND CANAL; HANGZHOU; LU XUN; NINGBO; PIRATES; RICE; SILK; SOUTHERN SONG DYNASTY; TEA; WEST LAKE; YANGZI RIVER; YU, EMPEROR.

ZHENBAO ISLAND   See WUSULI INCIDENT; WUSULI RIVER.

ZHENCI   See ACUPUNCTURE.

ZHENG   See QIN.

ZHENG CHENGGONG (Cheng Ch'eng-kung; 1624–62) Known as Koxinga (Coxinga); a Chinese general and famous military hero who forced the Dutch to give back Taiwan, which they had seized from China in 1624. Coxinga was born in Shijing, a small town in Fujian Province on China's southeastern coast. Shijing was located directly across the straits from Taiwan, an island to which many southeastern Chinese had immigrated. Coxinga's father, Cheng Xilun (Ch'eng Chih-lun), was a pirate who accepted bribes from the Ming dynasty in 1627 and agreed to patrol the coast, shortly before the Ming fell to the Qing dynasty (1644–1911). He became a Ming official who controlled the lucrative overseas and coastal trade in Fujian. When troops of the Manchus, who founded the Qing in 1644, took the city of Nanjing, Coxinga and his father consolidated their forces in Fujian and supported the prince of Tang (T'ang) as pretender to the Ming throne. When Manchu troops marched to southeastern China in 1646, they bribed Coxinga's father, who surrendered his men and ships to gain their favor.

Zheng felt disgraced by his father's surrender, and gathered a group of followers who pledged to support the Ming despite the surrender of many Chinese generals and troops to the Qing. Between 1651 and 1659, Coxinga attacked cities along the coast of Fujian and Zhejiang provinces, refusing all Qing requests to surrender. In 1659 he decided to invade the lower Yangzi River (Changjiang) valley. He landed his troops near modern Shanghai and put Nanjing under siege. A large number of Chinese troops from Anhui Province joined Coxinga's cause. The Manchus sent reinforcements from Beijing, so Zheng retreated from the lower Yangzi valley and returned south to Xiamen (formerly known as Amoy).

After this defeat, Coxinga began building up Chinese land and sea forces in the coastal cities of Shijing, Xiamen and Jinmen so that he could take over Taiwan and use it as the final rallying place for all forces still loyal to the Ming. Two years later, in 1661, he led a fleet of more than 300 warships carrying thousands of Chinese soldiers to Taiwan, where he defeated the Dutch and took control of the island. He established a new government staffed by Chinese literati (scholar-bureaucrats), opened schools and promoted emigration from the Chinese mainland. Coxinga died suddenly, possibly by suicide, in 1662, and opposing factions developed among his successors. His son eventually won, ruling Taiwan until he died in 1681. In 1683 the Qing attacked Taiwan, defeating the final Ming resistors, and incorporated Taiwan as a Qing prefecture. The island remained under Chinese jurisdiction until Japan seized control after defeating China in the Sino-Japanese War of 1894–95.

Coxinga's rebellion against the Qing inspired the growth of many new anti-Qing secret societies in China, notably the Hong (Hung) League, named for the first Ming emperor Hongwu (Hung-wu; r. 1368–98). Everyone in China knew the patriotic slogan of the Hong league, "Down with the Qing and up with the Ming! (*Fan Qing fu Ming*)." A new Zheng Chenggong Memorial Hall was constructed in Shijing in the 1980s, financed by overseas Chinese whose ancestors had emigrated from the region. The former Zheng Chenggong Memorial Hall was the ancestral temple of the Zheng family. The site in Shijing where Zheng inspected his troops before he launched his military campaign is commemorated by large engraved stones. See also FUJIAN PROVINCE; MING DYNASTY; NANJING; OVERSEAS CHINESE; PIRATES; QING DYNASTY; TAIWAN; XIAMEN.

ZHENG HE (Cheng Ho; 1371–1433)   The grand admiral of the Chinese navy who led seven maritime expeditions between 1405 and 1433 for the Ming dynasty emperor Yongle (Yung-lo; r. 1403–24) to Southeast Asia, India, the Persian Gulf, the Red Sea and the east coast of Africa as far south as the Cape of Good Hope. Zheng He, whose original surname was Ma, was born to a Muslim family in the southwestern province of Yunnan. He was captured by Ming troops in Yunnan and forced to become a eunuch in the Forbidden City (imperial palace) in Beijing. When Yongle took the throne, he appointed Zheng He head of eunuchs in charge of general affairs in the palace. Yongle decided to send a Chinese fleet westward to cultivate relations and trade with foreign countries, and chose Zheng He to be its commander. His expeditions took place prior to the great age of European maritime exploration and showed the superior ability of the Chinese to build large ships and navigate them over vast distances.

Zheng He's first expedition sailed from Fujian Province on the southeastern Chinese coast on July 11, 1405, with 62 ships carrying 27,800 men, and traveled to Southeast Asia and India. The Chinese were skilled in navigating with a compass because they had been using the compass, which they had invented in the fourth century B.C., to determine the proper sites for burials. Zheng He's ships were built in Nanjing and were the largest that had ever been sailed in the world, with some of them more than 500 feet long and more than 200 feet wide. In each place where they made port, the Chinese demanded that the inhabitants submit to the "Son of Heaven" (*tianzi* or *t'ien-tzu*; the Chinese emperor). Local leaders who cooperated were rewarded with silk, gold and other valuable gifts. After the first expedition was successfully completed, China sent out six more on an equally grand scale, most of which sailed to the Persian Gulf or to Aden on the southeastern tip of the Red Sea. The outcome of the expeditions was that 36 countries in what the Chinese called the "Western Ocean" agreed to a tributary relationship with China, with the Ming dynasty as their overlord. These included 8 countries in Southeast Asia, 11 in India and Ceylon (Sri Lanka), 5 in Persia (Iran) and Arabia, and five on the east coast of Africa. The most important thing to China was not the material goods sent by tributaries but the acknowledgment by those other countries of China's sovereignty. Chinese porcelain and other goods have been excavated in nearly all the regions where Zheng He's fleet visited.

Zheng He's expeditions were the only large-scale maritime explorations ever sent out by the Chinese government. They enabled China to greatly extend its political influence and trading relationships but were so costly that any further expeditions were cancelled. Other members of the imperial bureaucracy also resented Zheng He's power. China returned to a policy of isolation and lost its momentum as a maritime power. However, there are temples in Southeast Asian countries that continue to honor the memory of Grand Admiral

Zheng He. *See also* EUNUCHS; FUJIAN PROVINCE; SON OF HEAVEN; TRIBUTE SYSTEM; YONGLE (EMPEROR).

ZHENG MING *See* RECTIFICATION OF NAMES.

ZHENG XIAOXU *See* MANCHUKUO; PUYI, HENRY.

ZHENGTONG (EMPEROR) (Cheng-tung; 1427–64)   The sixth emperor of the Ming dynasty (1368–1644). His given name was Zhu Qizhen (Chu Ch'i-chen), and he ruled under the name Emperor Yingzong (Ying-chung); Zhengtong, meaning "Correct Government," is his posthumous reign name (r. 1436–50 and 1457–65; held captive 1449–50). The eldest son of Emperor Xuande (Hsuan-te; r. 1426–36), Zhengtong was only seven years old when he took the throne. Government power became consolidated in Wang Zhen (Wang Chen), the first of many eunuchs who became virtual dictators during the Ming dynasty. During Zhengtong's reign, the Ming appropriated an enormous amount of money from the national treasury to build a mausoleum for the deceased Emperor Xuande, as well as to support the imperial princes, even though they played no role in the Ming government. Increasingly large sums were also channeled into supporting the army.

Meanwhile, the peasants were exploited by the upper classes, who were able to avoid paying taxes, and since there was no strong imperial figure to maintain social order, the peasants began joining bandit gangs and rebellions. The worst rebellions broke out in 1448 in Zhejiang and Fujian provinces, at the same time as the Chinese Empire was fighting local tribes in Yunnan and being threatened with invasion by the Oirat, a Mongol tribe to the north. The Mongols had ruled China during the Yuan dynasty (1279–1368) but were overthrown by the Ming. That same year a disastrous flooding of the Yellow River (Huanghe) made millions of Chinese homeless. The next year the country faced an even greater crisis. The Oirats had pressured the Ming to open markets on the northern Chinese frontier where they could sell their horses. However, the Chinese angered the Oirats by refusing to sell them weapons, iron or copper and paying low prices for their horses. In 1449 the Oirats, led by their chieftain Esen-tayisi, invaded China, reached the capital city of Beijing, and captured the Zhengtong emperor, whom Wang Zheng had advised to go onto the battlefield even though the emperor had no military training. This caused the downfall of the powerful eunuch, who was killed during the battle at Tumu.

Yu Qian (Yu Ch'ien), the minister of war, who had prevented the Mongols from taking Beijing, took the reins of power and placed Zhengtong's younger brother on the throne. The Mongols had planned to demand a large ransom for the return of the Zhengtong emperor, but they decided to send him back to the Chinese, who were humiliated by the Mongol capture and release without ransom of their emperor. Zhengtong's brother reigned for seven more years but then became ill, and Zhengtong staged a coup d'etat to regain the throne. During the decade after they returned the emperor to Beijing, the Mongols continued to fight the demoralized Chinese all along the Great Wall. The Chinese also suffered from a severe shortage of food. In just a few decades the Ming dynasty had fallen far from the glorious reign of the Yongle Emperor (Yung-lo; 1403–24). *See also* BEIJING; EUNUCHS; GREAT WALL; MING DYNASTY; MONGOL; YELLOW RIVER; YUAN DYNASTY.

ZHENGZHOU   The capital city of Henan Province in north-central China. Zhengzhou, located on the Jinshui River about 15 miles south of the Yellow River (Huanghe), has a population of about 2 million. Henan has been an important region since prehistoric times, and Zhengzhou is one of the most ancient towns in China. It was settled at least as far back as 2100 B.C. Excavations have uncovered part of the city wall, foundations of houses, pottery kilns, bronze foundries and artifacts from the Shang dynasty (c. 1750–1040 B.C.). Bronze vessels, ceramics and carved jade and ivory objects have been found in large tombs in the region. Zhengzhou was probably the site of the city of Ao, capital of the 10th Shang king and the second of the seven successive Shang capitals. Until the 10th century A.D., the imperial capital alternated frequently between Zhengzhou and Chang'an (modern Xi'an) in modern Shaanxi Province to the West. In 605, during the Sui dynasty (581–618), the city acquired the name Zhengzhou. The Sui and the Tang (618–907) dynasties made their capital at Chang'an. In the 10th century, the Jin dynasty (1115–1234) moved their capital to Kaifeng in Henan. From then on, Zhengzhou declined until the Chinese Communists founded the People's Republic of China in 1949, when it became the capital of Henan because of its importance as a railway junction.

Zhengzhou suffered greatly after the Japanese invaded China in 1937, especially in 1938 when the Chinese Nationalists (Kuomintang; KMT) opened a breach in the flood dikes holding back the Yellow River. This caused such extensive flooding that nearly one million people died and 12 million had to be evacuated. Today the committee for the development of the Yellow River region has its offices in Zhengzhou.

Since the 1950s, Zhengzhou has become a modern industrialized city and a major communications center at the intersection of the two major Chinese railroads, the Beijing-Guangzhou line that runs north to south and the Longhai line that travels from Gansu Province in the west to the East China Sea. These lines were begun in 1898. Zhengzhou is also the center of textile production in Henan, especially cotton. Other products include agricultural and electrical equipment, chemicals such as fertilizers and aluminum goods.

The Henan Provincial Museum, located in Zhengzhou, has an exhibit commemorating the railroad workers' strike on February 7, 1923, which was brutally ended by the warlord Wu Peifu. The town of Huaiyang, southwest of Zhengzhou, claims to have the tomb of Fuxi, a legendary emperor who supposedly taught humans how to hunt, fish and raise animals, and who developed the eight trigrams (*bagua* or *pa-kua*) that are found in the *Book of Changes* (*Yijing* or *I-ching*). There are two tombs from the Han dynasty (206 B.C.–A.D. 220) in Dahuting Village, also southwest of Zhengzhou. *See also* BOOK OF CHANGES; CHANG'AN; EIGHT TRIGRAMS; FUXI; HENAN PROVINCE; KAIFENG; LUOYANG; RAILROADS; YELLOW RIVER.

ZHI *See* WISDOM.

ZHIKAI See TIANTAI SECT OF BUDDHISM.

ZHINU See COWHERD AND WEAVER MAID FESTIVAL.

ZHIYI See TIANTAI SECT OF BUDDHISM.

ZHONG See BELLS AND CHIMES.

ZHONG See LOYALTY.

ZHONG KUI (Chung K'uei) A physician during the Tang dynasty (618–907) whose picture is drawn on doorways to keep away evil spirits. Zhong Kui is depicted as a heavy man with a fierce expression and thick eyebrows, and is often shown brandishing a sword. An ambitious man, he set out for the capital to take the examinations for a position in the imperial bureaucracy. However, when he spent the night at a Buddhist temple, he got drunk and insulted the monk who had invited him there. The Buddha punished Zhong Kui by transforming him into an ugly man. Even though he passed the examination, Emperor Xuanzong (Hsuan-tsung; r. 712–756) was so disgusted by Zhong Kui's looks that he refused to give him a position. In despair, Zhong Kui protested his unjust treatment by committing suicide on the steps of the imperial palace. His ghost later appeared and cured the emperor of a fever. In gratitude the emperor had Zhong Kui's corpse reburied wearing the green robes of the imperial family, and had him canonized as "Great Chaser of Demons for the Whole Chinese Empire" at the head of an army charged with killing demons that prey on human beings. See also IMPERIAL BUREAUCRACY; XUAN-ZONG, EMPEROR.

ZHONG LI JIAN See EIGHT IMMORTALS.

ZHONG QIU JIE See AUTUMN MOON FESTIVAL.

ZHONGDU See BEIJING; JIN DYNASTY.

ZHONGGUO See ALL UNDER HEAVEN; MIDDLE KINGDOM.

ZHONGGUO GUOMINDANG See BORODIN, MIKHAIL; NATIONALIST PARTY.

ZHONGGUO XINWENSHE See NEW CHINA NEWS AGENCY; PEOPLE'S LIBERATION ARMY.

ZHONGJIA See BOUYEI.

ZHONGLI JIAN See EIGHT IMMORTALS.

ZHONGNANHAI COMPOUND (Chung Nan-hai) A compound in Beijing, just west of the Forbidden City where Chinese emperors lived, which contains the residences of many top Communist officials of the People's Republic of China (PRC). The name Zhongnanhai means "the central and south seas," referring to the two large lakes in the compound. The main entrance, guarded by People's Liberation Army (PLA) soldiers, is the Gate of New China (Xinhuamen). The gate was built in 1758 and was originally called the Tower of the Treasured Moon. The compound was built between the 10th and 13th centuries as a recreation area for Chinese emperors and their courtiers. It was enlarged during the Ming dynasty (1368–1644), but most of the buildings that survive were constructed during the Qing dynasty (1644–1911). During the imperial era, Zhongnanhai was the place where every spring the emperor plowed the first symbolic furrow in a field to begin the annual agricultural cycle. Imperial banquets and the highest examinations in the martial arts were also held there. The notorious Qing empress dowager Cixi (Tz'u Hsi; 1835–1908) resided in the compound for a time, and when she led a coup that ended the Reform Movement of 1898, she imprisoned Qing emperor Guangxu (Kuang-hsu; r. 1875–1908) in the Hall of Impregnating Vitality in Zhongnanhai, where he later died.

When the Revolution of 1911 overthrew the Qing and established the Republic of China, the Zhongnanhai compound became the presidential palace. Yuan Shikai (Yuan Shih-k'ai; 1859–1916), president of the Chinese republic from 1912 to 1916, used the compound for ceremonial occasions, and his vice president resided in the hall where Emperor Guangxu had died. Since the Chinese Communist Party (CCP) founded the PRC in 1949, the highest-ranking party leaders have maintained their residences in Zhongnanhai, including Mao Zedong (Mao Tse-tung), Zhou Enlai (Chou En-lai), Liu Shaoqi (Liu Shao-ch'i), Zhu De (Chu Teh) and Li Peng. Also located in the compound are the offices of the CCP Central Committee, the State Council, the Central Military Commission and the Central People's Government.

In 1989, student protesters held pro-democracy demonstrations in Beijing and other cities following the dismissal of Hu Yaobang (Hu Yao-pang) as general secretary of the CCP and his death on April 15. On April 19, 1989 protesters in Beijing marched from Tiananmen Square to the Zhongnanhai compound and held a sit-in. They tried to force the prime minister to come out of the compound and address them by shouting, "Come out, come out, Li Peng!" The protesters returned to Tiananmen Square and held it until the night of June 4, when party leaders called out the military to attack them (the Tiananmen Square Massacre). See also CHINESE COMMUNIST PARTY; CIXI, EMPRESS DOWAGER; FORBIDDEN CITY; GOVERNMENT STRUCTURE; PEOPLE'S REPUBLIC OF CHINA; TIANANMEN SQUARE MASSACRE.

ZHONGSHAN ISLANDS See SOUTH CHINA SEA; SPRATLY ISLANDS.

ZHONGSHAN MOUNTAIN See NANJING.

ZHONGYONG See DOCTRINE OF THE MEAN; HUMANITY; SUPERIOR MAN.

ZHOU, DUKE OF (Zhou Gong or Chou Kung) The brother of King Wu of the state of Zhou in the Wei River valley, who rebelled against the emperor of the Shang dynasty (1750–1040 B.C.) and founded the Zhou dynasty (1100–256 B.C.), which became the longest of all Chinese dynasties. The Duke of Zhou consolidated the Zhou kingdom while governing as regent for the third king, Wu's son, King Cheng (Ch'eng), during the time he was a minor. Confucius (551–479 B.C.), whose thought became orthodox for the

Chinese imperial government, revered the Zhou dynasty, particularly its first few centuries (Western Zhou dynasty, 1100–771 B.C.), as the ideal period of peaceful, orderly government in Chinese history. He considered the Duke of Zhou to be the best example of the loyal government official, along with Kings Wen (d. 1129 B.C.) and Wu (d. 1115 B.C.). Wu, the father of Wen, built up the state of Zhou when it was still a dependency of the Shang dynasty. Wen's name became synonymous for the Chinese with "culture" or "civilization." Confucius believed that these three rulers embodied the humanity and virtue that were the cornerstones of his philosophy, and that their policies represented everything wise and beneficial in Chinese history. After the Zhou defeated the Shang, the Duke of Zhou gave a speech to the Shang nobles asking them to submit to the will of Heaven, which had decreed that the Shang had broken Heaven's laws and deserved to be punished. The speech, which was handed down orally and not written down until several centuries later, was the first statement of the Chinese theory of the Mandate of Heaven (*Tianming* or *T'ien-ming*), which became used by each successive dynasty to legitimize its overthrow of the previous dynasty.

The Duke of Zhou had spent many years in the Shang court and had maintained close relations with the Shang nobles. He was therefore able to put down a counterrebellion against the Zhou led by the survivors of the Shang government who had formed an alliance with some members of Zhou's royal family. Perhaps the duke's greatest achievement was the creation of a feudal system (*fengjian* or *feng-chien*), using the concept that all land belongs to the king and all people are his subjects. Family members and close allies of the Zhou royal family were given authority over states in northern and central China but had to attend the Zhou court and provide the Zhou military support. The Zhou state had its capital at Chang'an (modern Xi'an in western Shaanxi Province) on the Wei River. This city served as the imperial capital for several later dynasties, notably the Tang dynasty (618–907).

In A.D. 59 the emperor of the Eastern Han dynasty (A.D. 25–220) decreed that sacrifices should be made to Confucius and to the Duke of Zhou in schools throughout the Chinese Empire. This practice continued until the seventh century A.D., when Tang emperor Li Yuan built a temple at Chang'an that was dedicated to Confucius but put the official Yuan Hui in place of the Duke of Zhou and added ancestral tablets of other disciples of Confucius. A work known as the *Zhou Institutions* (*Zhou guan* or *Chou kuan*) records the accomplishments of the Duke of Zhou, but historians doubt that the work is authentic. However, it is certain that the Duke of Zhou was a skilled administrator who made a great contribution to the establishment of early Zhou institutions. The *Book of Changes* (*Yijing* or *I-ching*), one of the Five Classics in the Confucian canon, has been attributed to King Wen and the Duke of Zhou, but they probably had no connection with this book. See also ANCESTRAL TABLETS; BOOK OF CHANGES; CHANG'AN; CONFUCIANISM; CONFUCIUS; FEUDAL SYSTEM; MANDATE OF HEAVEN; SHANG DYNASTY; WEI RIVER; WEN, KING AND WU, KING; ZHOU DYNASTY.

ZHOU DYNASTY (1100–256 B.C.)   The longest dynasty in Chinese history, and one of the earliest. Historians divide the Zhou dynasty into two general periods, the Western Zhou dynasty (1100–771 B.C.) and the Eastern Zhou dynasty (771–256 B.C.), which they subdivide into the Spring and Autumn Period (772–481 B.C.) and the Warring States Period (403–221 B.C.). The Zhou dynasty was founded by King Wen (d. 1129 B.C.) and his son, King Wu (d. 1115 B.C.), of the state of Zhou in the Wei River valley. Zhou was a dependent state of the Shang dynasty (1750–1040 B.C.), but Kings Wen and Wu built up the Zhou state, rebelled against the Shang emperor and overthrew the dynasty. They established the Zhou dynasty capital at Hao (later known as Chang'an; modern Xi'an in Shaanxi Province in western China) on the Wei River. This city served as the imperial capital for several later dynasties, notably the Tang dynasty (618–907). King Wen's name became synonymous for the Chinese people with "culture" or "civilization."

The Duke of Zhou, King Wu's younger brother and King Wen's son, consolidated the Zhou kingdom while governing as regent for the third Zhou king, Wu's son, King Cheng (Ch'eng), while he was a minor. The Duke of Zhou had spent many years in the Shang court and had maintained close relations with the Shang nobles. After the Zhou defeated the Shang, the Duke of Zhou gave a speech to the Shang nobles asking them to submit to the will of Heaven (*Tian* or *T'ien*), which had decreed that the Shang were immoral and had broken Heaven's laws and deserved to be punished. The speech, which was handed down orally and not written down until several centuries later, was the first statement of the Chinese theory of the Mandate of Heaven (*Tianming* or *T'ien-ming*), which was used by each successive dynasty in Chinese history to legitimize its overthrow of the previous dynasty.

The Duke of Zhou created a feudal system (*fengjian* or *feng-chien*) under the concept that all land belongs to the king and all people are his subjects. The Zhou royal family gave relatives and close allies authority over states in northern and central China, but required them to attend the Zhou court and to provide the Zhou military support. Each state had a walled town in which were built temples to the ancestors, altars of soil and grain, and palaces for the aristocrats. The animistic tradition of the Shang was supplanted by a Zhou emphasis on continuing family lines and propitiating the ancestors, known as ancestor worship. Craftsmen such as bronze and jade workers and potters lived in or just outside the towns, and peasants farmed the countryside. Cultivated fields were organized under the "well-field system" in which areas of land were divided into nine squares, with eight families farming one square each for themselves and the center square collectively for their feudal lord.

In 771 B.C. invaders allied themselves with some disaffected vassals of the Zhou, took the Zhou capital and killed the king, and forced the Zhou to leave their homeland and move east. The Zhou established the Eastern Zhou dynasty in the region of modern Luoyang in Henan Province, just south of the Yellow River (Huanghe). The former Zhou domain was taken over by the rulers of Qin, who were theoretically still vassals of the Zhou. From then on, the Zhou kings served a ritual function but had no power to keep their vassal states from fighting each other and expanding their territories by conquering smaller states. By the end of the Zhou dynasty, there were only seven powerful states. The strongest proved to be Qin, whose leader unified China under the Qin dynasty (221–206 B.C.) and proclaimed himself the first emperor, Qin Shi Huangdi (r. 221–210 B.C.).

The Spring and Autumn Period, the first subdivision of the Eastern Zhou dynasty, is named for a state chronicle, a classical historical work called the *Spring and Autumn Annals* (*Chun Qiu* or *Ch'un Ch'iu*). The second subdivision is named the Warring States Period after a collection of anecdotes from the Zhou imperial court, *Strategy of the Warring States* (*Zhanguo* or *Chan-kuo*). Although the Eastern Zhou was a time of strife among the various feudal states, it was also a period of intellectual flowering, known as the Hundred Schools of Thought. The great classical thinkers of the time, whose ideas remained influential in China down to the modern era, include Confucius, Mencius (Mengzi or Meng-tzu) and Laozi (Lao-tzu). The latter supposedly wrote the *Daodejing* (*Tao-teching*), the most important text in the Chinese tradition known as Daoism. The thought of Confucius (551–479 B.C.), known as Confucianism, became the orthodox school of Chinese thought during the Han dynasty (206 B.C.–A.D. 220) and remained so through the Qing dynasty (1644–1911). Mencius is the second most important Confucian thinker. The Legalist School of Thought had a great influence on the Qin dynasty.

Confucius revered the Zhou dynasty, particularly its first few centuries during the Western Zhou, as the ideal period of peaceful, orderly government in Chinese history. He considered the Duke of Zhou and Kings Wen and Wu the best examples of the loyal government official, models whom rulers should emulate. See also ANCESTOR WORSHIP; CHANG'AN; CONFUCIANISM; CONFUCIUS; DAODEJING; DAOISM; FEUDAL SYSTEM; HUNDRED SCHOOLS OF THOUGHT; LEGALIST SCHOOL OF THOUGHT; LUOYANG; MANDATE OF HEAVEN; MENCIUS; QIN DYNASTY; QIN SHI HUANGDI; SHANG DYNASTY; SPRING AND AUTUMN ANNALS; SPRING AND AUTUMN PERIOD; WEI RIVER; WELL-FIELD SYSTEM OF AGRICULTURE; WEN, KING, AND WU, KING; WESTERN ZHOU DYNASTY; ZHOU, DUKE OF.

ZHOU DYNASTY (951–959) See FIVE DYNASTIES PERIOD.

ZHOU ENLAI (Chou En-lai; 1898–1976) The second-most important Chinese official after Mao Zedong (Mao Tse-tung; 1893–1976) since the Chinese Communist Party (CCP) founded the People's Republic of China (PRC) in 1949. Zhou served as premier of the State Council from 1949 until his death in 1976. Zhou was born to a wealthy family in Jiangsu Province who belonged to the literati, or scholar class, that staffed the imperial bureaucracy. He attended a Christian Middle School in Tianjin, a large port city near the capital city of Beijing, and began to study Marxism while a university student. Between 1917 and 1918 Zhou studied in Japan, but he returned to China to take part in the May Fourth Movement of 1919, which inspired many young Chinese to become political activists. The editor of a student newspaper in Tianjin, Zhou was arrested and imprisoned. After he was released in 1920, Zhou studied in France and Germany from 1920 to 1924. He joined the Communist party in 1922 and brought many Chinese students studying abroad into the revolutionary movement. In 1925, after Zhou returned from France, he married Deng Yingchao

Mao Zedong and Zhou Enlai at the 24th conference of the Central People's Government of China. LU HOUMIN

(Teng Ying-ch'ao; 1904–92), another political activist who became an early member of the CCP in 1925. She too became a leading official in the PRC who was revered by the Chinese people as "Elder Sister Deng." Zhou held leading CCP and administrative positions in Guangdong Province in southern China and served as director of the Political Department at Whampoa (Huangpu) Military Academy, which trained many military leaders for the CCP and the Nationalist Party (Kuomintang; KMT). The recently founded CCP and the KMT were cooperating in the 1920s. The efforts of Mao and Zhou to organize peasants in Guangdong are commemorated by the National Peasant Movement Institute in the province's capital city of Guangzhou (Canton).

In the winter of 1926 Zhou and Deng went to Shanghai, China's largest city, where the CCP was actively organizing laborers, and worked with the CCP Central Committee. Zhou then became secretary of the Central Committee's Military Commission. He took his first official position in the CCP when he was elected to the Politburo in 1927. He was one of the three top leaders of the Shanghai workers' and peasants' uprising in 1927. The CCP and KMT had been cooperating, but in April 1927 KMT leader Chiang Kai-shek turned against the CCP and ordered the KMT to massacre Communists. Zhou and Deng narrowly escaped being killed and went underground. Zhou was one of the main organizers of the Nanchang Uprising, the Communist military uprising against the KMT on August 1, 1927, which the CCP considers the birth of the Red Army, later known as the People's

Liberation Army (PLA). For several years Zhou served as head of the CCP military department and frequently disagreed with Mao Zedong and other party leaders. In early 1930 Zhou appeared in Moscow as head of the CCP delegation to the Comintern (Communist International).

In 1931 Zhou returned to China and took a leading position at the soviet (base) that Mao had established in Jiangxi Province. There he debated military strategies with Mao, who developed guerrilla tactics that the CCP would rely upon. In May 1933 Zhou became political commissar of the Chinese Red (Communist) Army. In January 1935 Mao became the unchallenged leader of the CCP, and from that time until his death, Zhou held the secondary position in the party leadership. Zhou and Mao organized and led the so-called Long March of 1934–35 by the CCP to escape the KMT, which ended at Yan'an in the northwestern province of Shaanxi, where the CCP established its headquarters. Deng Yingchao was one of only about 50 women who survived the Long March, and she became very active mobilizing the Chinese united front during China's War of Resistance against Japan (1937–45; World War II).

In December 1936 Zhou met with Zhang Xueliang (Chang Hsueh-liang), the KMT military commander of the Manchurian army in northeastern China whom Chiang Kai-shek had ordered to Shaanxi to fight the Communists. The two agreed that the CCP and KMT should stop fighting and combine their efforts to fight Japan, which had invaded Manchuria in 1931 and was sending troops into China Proper. In 1936 Zhou was the CCP negotiator in the so-called "Xi'an Incident" in which Chiang Kai-shek was kidnapped at Huaqing Hot Springs outside Xi'an by Zhang Xueliang and other KMT military commanders. Zhang and Zhou released Chiang after he agreed to a united front between the CCP and the KMT to fight Japan. In the spring of 1937 Zhou held a series of meetings with Chiang Kai-shek and his staff, which formalized the cooperation between the CCP and the KMT.

During the War of Resistance against Japan, Zhou was based in Nanjing and Chongqing, the successive Nationalist capitals. Zhou and Deng never had children of their own, but they adopted about 10 Chinese who had been war orphans, including Li Peng (Li P'eng; 1928–), who became premier of the State Council of the PRC in 1988. After Japan was defeated in 1945, Zhou and Mao negotiated with KMT leaders in Chongqing to attempt to prevent their fighting a civil war. These talks broke off in 1947. Zhou went to northern Shaanxi to help direct the CCP forces. The CCP defeated the KMT in 1949, and Chiang Kai-shek and his KMT followers fled to Taiwan Island, where they established the provisional government of the Republic of China (ROC).

When the CCP founded the PRC in Beijing on October 1, 1949, Zhou was named premier of the State Administrative Council (which later became the State Council) and concurrently foreign minister, a post he held until 1958. He remained premier until he died in 1976. Deng Yingchao helped found the All-China Women's Federation and became a prominent CCP official in her own right.

The U.S.S.R., which had helped organize the CCP, recognized the PRC the day after it was founded. In 1950, Mao and Zhou went to Moscow to negotiate an agreement for Soviet assistance to China, and on February 14, 1950, they signed the Sino-Soviet Treaty of Friendship, Alliance and Mutual Assistance. In the early 1950s Zhou helped prevent a direct confrontation between the PRC and the United States, which supported Chiang Kai-shek's ROC on Taiwan as the legitimate government of China. The United States and the PRC took opposing positions during the Korean War, which broke out in 1950, with the United States sending troops to support South Korea and the PRC sending military forces across the Yalu River to support the Democratic People's Republic of Korea (North Korea).

In 1952 Deng Xiaoping (Teng Hsiao-p'ing; 1904–97), who had been a CCP official in Sichuan Province, was transferred to Beijing, where he became vice premier under Zhou Enlai and held a crucial position as Zhou's general secretary. Deng remained Zhou's protege during his turbulent career in which he was purged and rehabilitated several times and finally, from the late 1970s into the 1990s, became the most powerful CCP leader after the deaths of Zhou and Mao. In 1954, the First National People's Congress formally named Zhou premier of the new State Council and elected Mao chairman (or president) of the PRC and Liu Shaoqi (Liu Shao-ch'i; 1898–1969) chairman of the Standing Committee of the NPC. Deng Xiaoping served concurrently as secretary general of the CCP and vice premier of the State Council.

In 1954 Zhou played a prominent role in the negotiations held in Geneva between Vietnam (also known as Indochina) and France, which had made Vietnam, a tributary state of China, its colony after defeating China in the Sino-French War of 1884–85. After World War II, Vietnam began fighting a war of independence. While the Geneva Conference was being held, Vietnamese forces defeated the French forces at Dienbienphu; consequently, France and its U.S. allies had to accept a settlement with Vietnam, known as the Final Declaration of the Geneva Conference on Indochina. Zhou had by far the most experience of any CCP leader in foreign policy. Beginning in the summer of 1954, Zhou traveled to India and other Asian and African countries in hopes of forming a united international front. He worked out the Five Principles for Peaceful Coexistence with Indian prime minister Jawaharlal Nehru. In 1955 Zhou attended the Conference of Non-Aligned Nations at Bandung, a historic meeting of 29 Asian and African states; no Western nations sent representatives to the conference.

In 1954 Zhou was elected to the National People's Congress. He was elected to the Central Committee at the Fifth National Party Congress and at all subsequent National Party Congresses. In 1956 the First Plenum of the Eighth Chinese People's Political Consultative Conference (CPPCC) elected Zhou, Liu Shaoqi, Zhu De (Chu Teh) and Chen Yun as deputy chairmen of the CPPCC, and Deng Xiaoping as secretary-general. The de-Stalinization campaign taking place in the U.S.S.R. that year raised the possibility of mass uprisings in Communist Eastern Europe. Zhou traveled to Poland and Hungary on a peacemaking mission that marked the high point of Chinese influence within the Communist bloc. After this, the relationship between the U.S.S.R. and the PRC deteriorated, especially after Nikita Khrushchev consolidated his power as leader of the U.S.S.R.

Following Khrushchev's ouster by Leonid Brezhnev in 1964, Zhou went to Moscow to meet with him in hopes of improving relations but returned home disappointed. The

Sino-Soviet Conflict resulted in border skirmishes in the late 1960s. Zhou stepped down as foreign minister in 1958 and was replaced by Chen Yi, but Zhou continued to lead diplomatic missions to other countries until 1966, when the Cultural Revolution (1966–76) broke out. In December 1963 Zhou and Chen Yi visited the United Arab Republic, Algeria and Morocco as part of a large-scale tour of Arica from 1963 to 1964. In June 1965 Zhou visited Pakistan and Tanzania.

In China, Mao was inaugurating a campaign to purify the CCP of reactionary influences. On May 1, 1966, at a massive rally to celebrate International Workers Day in Tiananmen Square in Beijing, Zhou announced the formal start of the Great Proletarian Cultural Revolution. On August 18, 1966, Zhou, Mao, Lin Biao (Lin Piao) and other CCP officials presided over a massive rally in Tiananmen Square in support of the Cultural Revolution. The Red Guards, who were at the forefront of the destructive revolution until mid-1968, first appeared in public at this rally. By 1967 China was on the verge of anarchy. The Red Guards had destroyed a great deal of property and persecuted numerous individuals, many government and party officials had been condemned and removed from their positions, and the education and transportation systems were at the point of breaking down. In March 1967 the party turned to Zhou to conduct the daily affairs of the government. The Red Guards criticized Zhou and even placed him under siege for a time, but he was never purged from office as were many officials under him, such as Deng Xiaoping and Chen Yi. Zhou also became a target of the anti-Confucius campaign but survived that as well and maintained his political base. In 1969 Zhou was elected to the Standing Committee at the Ninth CPPCC. From 1970 to 1971 Zhou was able to form a center-right alliance with a group of PLA regional military commanders who had disagreed with some of Lin Biao's policies. This coalition enabled more moderate officials to take control of the party and government in the late 1970s and 1980s. Zhou's leadership also enabled many intellectuals who had been purged to be restored to their former positions. Jiang Qing (Chiang Ch'ing, Mao's fourth wife; 1914–91) became the leader of a radical faction in the CCP that emphasized ideological purity and class struggle. They opposed the moderate faction comprised of Long March veterans led by Zhou Enlai, Liu Shaoqi and Deng, and Liu and Deng were purged. Zhou persuaded Mao to allow Deng to be brought back to Beijing in 1973, and Deng made a dramatic return to power, becoming vice premier of the State Council under Zhou Enlai, vice chairman of the Standing Committee, chief of staff of the PLA and a member of the Politburo.

Zhou played a major role in the negotiations to open up relations between the PRC and the United States in the late 1960s and early 1970s. After the KMT had fled to Taiwan in 1949, the United States had supported the KMT government as the legitimate government of China and had refused to recognize the Communist government of the People's Republic of China. In the 1960s the United States sent forces to support South Vietnam in its war against North Vietnam, which was supported by the PRC. Despite these differences, the United States and the PRC agreed to open up relations. On February 22, 1972, U.S. president Richard M. Nixon traveled to the PRC to meet with Mao and Zhou, and Zhou greeted Nixon when his airplane landed in Beijing. On February 28

the two countries issued a joint Sino-U.S. communiqué, known as the "Shanghai Communiqué," which, among other things, stated that the United States would withdraw its military forces from Taiwan and that Taiwan was a part of China.

In early 1972 Zhou learned that he had stomach cancer, but he continued to fulfill his official duties. On August 24, 1973, on the first day of the 10th National Party Congress, Zhou delivered the official CCP version regarding the aborted coup against Mao by Lin Biao in 1971 and his death in a plane crash when he attempted to flee to the U.S.S.R. This congress formally confirmed the policy for modernization advocated by Zhou and Deng and made Deng a member of the CCP Central Committee. On August 30, 1973, the First Plenum of the 10th CPPCC elected Zhou a deputy chairman. In January 1975, Zhou addressed the Fourth NPC and advocated that China should undertake efforts to reform and develop the country by the end of the century. This policy is known as the Four Modernizations, whose goal was to modernize Chinese agriculture, industry, national defense and science and technology. CCP officials linked the Four Modernizations with industrialization and the opening up of foreign trade.

Zhou died of cancer on January 8, 1976. In April 1976, at the time of the Qing Ming Festival, a traditional Chinese festival to honor deceased ancestors, wreaths to commemorate Zhou were placed at the Monument to the People's Heroes (Revolutionary Martyrs) in Tiananmen Square. The wreaths disappeared, apparently by order of the PRC government, and more wreaths were laid during a massive unauthorized demonstration in the square. A riot erupted; a large group of protestors set fire to a government building; and CCP officials called out troops to suppress the demonstrators, many of whom were arrested. Jiang Qing's faction blamed Deng Xiaoping for the riot and immediately removed him from all of his official positions except his CCP membership. Mao died on September 9, 1976, after which Jiang Qing and her so-called Gang of Four were arrested and blamed for causing the Cultural Revolution. Acting premier Hua Guofeng (Hua Kuo-feng; 1920–   ) was elevated to replace Zhou as premier. Deng was restored to all of his positions in 1977, and he became the leader of China's economic and political reforms based on the Four Modernizations that Zhou had advocated. See also BEIJING; CHIANG KAI-SHEK; CHINESE COMMUNIST PARTY; CIVIL WAR BETWEEN COMMUNISTS AND NATIONALISTS; CULTURAL REVOLUTION; DENG XIAOPING; DENG YINGCHAO; FOUR MODERNIZATIONS; GANG OF FOUR; GOVERNMENT STRUCTURE; GUANGDONG PROVINCE; GUANGZHOU; HUA GUOFENG; INTERNATIONAL WORKERS DAY; JIANG QING; KOREAN WAR; LI PENG; LONG MARCH; MAO ZEDONG; MAY FOURTH MOVEMENT OF 1919; MINISTRY OF FOREIGN AFFAIRS; NATIONALIST PARTY; NIXON, RICHARD, U.S. PRESIDENT, VISIT TO CHINA; PEOPLE'S REPUBLIC OF CHINA; RED GUARDS; SINO-SOVIET CONFLICT; TIANANMEN SQUARE; WAR OF RESISTANCE AGAINST JAPAN; WHAMPOA MILITARY ACADEMY; ZHANG XUELIANG; ZHU DE.

ZHOU GONG See ZHOU, DUKE OF.

ZHOUKOUDIAN See ARCHAEOLOGY; PEKING MAN.

ZHOUSHAN ISLANDS See NINGBO.

ZHU See BAMBOO.

ZHU DA See BADA SHANREN.

ZHU DE (Chu Teh; 1886–1976) A great modern military leader who founded the Chinese Communist Army. Zhu De was born into a peasant family. After working as a physical education instructor, he attended the Yunnan Military Academy and graduated in 1911. That year he participated in the revolution that overthrew the Qing dynasty (1644–1911) and established the modern Republic of China. He served as an officer for 10 years in the armies of warlords in Yunnan and Sichuan provinces. In 1922 he traveled to Europe and studied in Berlin and at the University of Göttingen in Germany, where he also became a member of the Chinese Communist Party (CCP). The German government expelled him from the country because of his Communist political activities.

In 1926 Zhu returned to China but kept his Communist affiliation hidden and became an officer in the Nationalist (Kuomintang; KMT) army. In August 1927 he took part in the Nanchang Uprising led by Chinese Communists against the Nationalists, which Communists consider the birth of the Chinese Red Army (later known as the People's Liberation Army; PLA). The Nationalists put down the uprising, and Zhu took his troops to Hunan Province and joined with guerrilla forces led by Mao Zedong (Mao Tse-tung; 1893–1976). Zhu served as commander and Mao as political commissar of these combined forces, which they called the Fourth Red Army. In 1929 they moved to Jiangxi Province, where they established a soviet (Communist base). There, Zhu built up the Red Army to 200,000 troops by 1933. Mao and Zhu based their strategies for modern large-scale war on the principles of guerrilla warfare, defeating their enemies by wearing them down in small attacks rather than by fighting large battles with great numbers of troops. They also realized that since most of the Chinese were peasant farmers, it was more important for the Communists to control the countryside than to expend a lot of troops to try and take over large cities. Under Zhu's command, the Red Army defended its Jiangxi soviet from four Nationalist attacks. Zhu, who became a member of the Communist Politburo in 1934, led the Red Army on its 6,000-mile Long March (1934–35) northwest to Shaanxi Province. When the Japanese invaded China in 1937, the Communists made an alliance with the Nationalists to fight them, with Zhu commanding the Red Army's northern forces, now called the Eighth Route Army. During China's War of Resistance against Japan (1937–45; World War II), Zhu served as the commander of all Chinese Communist military operations. Japan surrendered in 1945, and in 1946 the Communists and Nationalists began fighting their civil war once again, with Zhu commanding the Communist army, now called the People's Liberation Army (PLA). After the Communists decisively defeated the Nationalists and founded the People's Republic of China in 1949, Zhu commanded the PLA until 1954 and was made a marshal. In 1959 he became chairman of the Standing Committee of the National People's Congress. See also CHINESE COMMUNIST PARTY; CIVIL WAR BETWEEN COMMUNISTS AND NATIONALISTS; LONG MARCH; MAO ZEDONG; NATIONAL PEOPLE'S CONGRESS; NATIONALIST PARTY; PEOPLE'S LIBERATION ARMY; POLITBURO; REVOLUTION OF 1911; WARLORD PERIOD.

ZHU WEN, EMPEROR See FIVE DYNASTIES PERIOD.

ZHU XI (Chu Hsi; 1130–1200) The most important philosopher of the Song dynasty (960–1279) school of Neo-Confucianism, whose thought became accepted as orthodox by the Chinese imperial government. Zhu Xi's thought is known as the Rationalist School or the School of Principle or Reason. Alongside this school developed the Neo-Confucian School of the Mind or Intuition, which reached its highest point during the Ming dynasty (1368–1644) in the philosophy of Wang Yangming (1472–1529). Zhu Xi's synthesis of Neo-Confucian thought was a great achievement and proved to be the most influential aspect of Chinese culture throughout all Asian countries, down to the 20th century.

Zhu Xi was born in modern Fujian Province in southeastern China, where his father held a position as magistrate. He studied the religious and philosophical thought of Daoism and Buddhism, but at age 30 he renounced them and began a serious study of Confucianism. Having passed the examinations for the imperial bureaucracy when he was 19, he held a number of government positions during his life. Zhu Xi also wrote commentaries on the classical Confucian texts, headed the group of scholars who condensed the extremely important 354-chapter history of China written by Sima Guang (Ssu-ma Kuang; 1019–85), and became a well-known teacher. Unfortunately, before he died he was unjustly disgraced due to intrigues in the imperial court.

Zhu Xi codified Neo-Confucian thought by combining the ideas of many previous thinkers into a unified whole. His synthesis of Neo-Confucianism appealed to Chinese scholars, who played an active role in governing the country by staffing the imperial bureaucracy or civil service. Zhu Xi also codified the Four Books of Confucianism (Sishu) as part of the Confucian canon and the foundation for the Chinese educational system. They include the Analects (Sayings) of Confucius (Lunyu), Book of Mencius (Mengzi or Meng-tzu), Doctrine of the Mean (Zhongyong or Chung-yung) and Great Learning (Daxue or Ta-hsueh). Knowledge of these books and Zhu Xi's commentaries on them became mandatory for the imperial examination system. Chinese students first memorized the Four Books and then went on to study the Five Classics of Confucianism.

Zhu Xi also worked out more precise definitions for many important Chinese philosophical concepts, such as the Great Ultimate, human nature, the mind, material-force (qi or ch'i) and propriety (li). He taught that human beings had the ability to rise above their limitations or weaknesses. He advocated a principle central to the Great Learning, the "investigation of the nature of things and relationships," and argued that man's mind is essentially one with the mind of the universe and hence able to enter into and understand the principles of all created things. By "things," Zhu Xi meant practical activities that benefit society, such as social relations and politics. Studying the Confucian texts will enable a person to develop his genuine humanity (ren or jen), one of the most important Confucian concepts. During the Qing dynasty (1644–1911), there was a strong revival of interest in the philosophy of Zhu Xi. See also CONFUCIANISM; FIVE CLASSICS OF CONFUCIANISM; FOUR BOOKS OF CONFUCIANISM; GREAT LEARNING; HUMANITY; IMPERIAL EXAMINATION SYSTEM; NEO-CONFUCIANISM; PROPRIETY; QI; WANG YANGMING.

ZHU YOUJIAN, EMPEROR See LI ZICHENG; MING DYNASTY.

ZHU YUANZHANG See HONGWU (EMPEROR); MING DYNASTY; RED TURBANS REBELLION.

ZHUANG The most populous of China's 55 national minority ethnic groups. The Zhuang practice the Muslim religion and belong to the Northern Dai (Tai) ethnic group in southwestern China, who are related to people in Thailand and Burma. The 1990 census recorded 15,489,630 Zhuang in China, with most inhabiting Guangxi-Zhuang Autonomous Region, although some reside in Yunnan and Guangdong Provinces. Guangxi-Zhuang is one of the autonomous regions, established by the Chinese government since 1949, where national minorities with large populations have been given a degree of autonomy in their local affairs. The capital city is Nanning, with a population of about a half-million, located very close to the Vietnam border. The city of Guilin, also in the region, is a popular tourist stop for boat rides on the scenic Li River.

The Zhuang have long been highly assimilated into Chinese culture and resemble the Han or ethnic Chinese. They have their own Northern Dai writing system, which they traditionally used only for certain purposes such as prayers and songs, but it is rapidly dying out. A romanized script has been created for the Zhuang language in which a number of books and magazines have been published. Zhuang women are highly skilled in weaving brightly colored brocade. The Zhuang love to sing, and every spring they hold a song festival. The Zhuang, who cultivate rice, were known to have inhabited Guangxi-Zhuang as far back as the Zhou dynasty (1100–256 B.C.). Their region was annexed in 214 B.C. by the Qin dynasty (221–206 B.C.), but soon after, they established the independent state of Nanyue, only to be reconquered by the Han dynasty (206 B.C.–A.D. 220) between 113 and 111 B.C.. Over the centuries many people of the Yao national minority group migrated into the region, resulting in many military conflicts. In 1052, a Zhuang rebellion led by Nong Zhigao (Nung Chih-kao) attempted to establish an independent kingdom, but it was defeated a year later. The Yao fought a disastrous battle with Ming dynasty (1368–1644) troops near Guiping in 1465. The Taiping Rebellion, which devastated much of China, also broke out near Guiping in 1850. See also DAI; GUANGXI-ZHUANG AUTONOMOUS REGION; GUILIN; MINORITIES, NATIONAL; MUSLIMS; NANNING; RICE; YAO.

ZHUANGZI (Chuang Tzu, "Master Chuang"; 369–286 B.C.) The first Chinese literary artist known by name, and the second-most important thinker in the Daoist tradition, after Laozi (Lao Tzu; sixth century B.C.), the supposed author of the *Daodejing* (*Tao Te Ching, The Way and Its Power*). Zhuangzi's writings, in fact, were the first to mention Laozi. *Dao* means "way," "path" or "road." In Daoist thought, the *Dao* represents the fundamental principle that pervades the universe and everything in it. Since all things are constantly moving and changing, the wise person knows how to yield and flow with the *Dao* by "doing nothing" (*wu wei*), not interfering in the workings of the universe but seeking harmony with nature. For many scholars, Daoism formed an appealing contrast to the strict moral and social emphasis of Confucianism, which became accepted as orthodox by the Chinese imperial government.

Zhuangzi, a librarian and member of the court of the important state of Chu, was offered the position of premier by Chu's ruler. However, Zhuangzi turned down the offer, preferring to remain free from political entanglements and giving him a reputation as a recluse. He was a contemporary of Mencius (Mengzi or Meng-tzu; c. 372–289 B.C.), the second-most important Confucian thinker. Zhuangzi produced a number of writings dealing with Daoist themes, known collectively as the *Zhuangzi* (*Chuang Tzu*). His method relies on humor, stories, metaphors and allegories rather than on systematic arguments, and it is based on paradox, the realization of the unifying principle that underlies all opposites. The person who achieves this will find true freedom, becoming one with the *Dao* and acting spontaneously. For example, one chapter is a discussion on "Making Things Equal," and another is called "Free and Easy Wandering."

A famous passage in the *Zhuangzi* states that after Zhuangzi's wife died, a friend found him singing and pounding on a tub, and asked how he could do that instead of mourning her properly. Zhuangzi replied that when she first died, he did grieve. But he thought back to the time before she was born and realized that a change occurred when she acquired a spirit and a body, and now another change has come about with her death, like the natural progression of the seasons. To continue crying would show that he did not understand fate and the inevitability of change. Zhuangzi's most famous passage tells how he dreamed that he was a butterfly. Then he woke up suddenly and could not tell whether he had been Zhuangzi dreaming that he was a butterfly or if he was now a butterfly dreaming that he was Zhuangzi. He termed this the "transformation of things." See also CONFUCIANISM; DAODEJING; DAOISM; LAOZI.

ZHUGE LIANG (Chu-ko Liang; 181–234) The prime minister of the kingdom of Shu (221–263), one of the three kingdoms, along with Wei and Wu, that vied for power during the Three Kingdoms Period (Sanguo; 220–280). Zhuge Liang was also a prominant scholar, inventor and mathematician. As prime minister he was a brilliant strategist who strengthened Shu's defenses by making a political alliance with the kingdom of Wu. The great military general Cao Cao (Ts'ao Ts'ao; 155–220) had unified China north of the Yangzi River (Changjiang) and attempted to unite northern and southern China by attacking Wu, which lay south of the Yangzi. Wu's superior naval skills enabled it to defeat Cao Cao's forces in 208. When Cao Cao died in 220, his son Cao Pi (Ts'ao P'i) removed the Han dynasty (206 B.C.–A.D. 220) puppet emperor and founded the kingdom of Wei. The three kingdoms of Shu, Wu and Wei became locked in a stalemate until 263. Shu was the last of the three kingdoms to form. It was founded in 221 by Liu Bei (Liu Pei), a distant member of the Han ruling family, who claimed that his kingdom was the legitimate successor to the Han dynasty. Shu's heartland was the Red River basin in southwestern China (modern Sichuan Province), which was protected from attack by his mountain ranges that nearly surround it. Prime minister Zhuge Liang's policies enabled Shu to develop its natural resources and to widen its control over southwestern China. He once boldly repelled an enemy army sent by Wei by sitting in the gate tower of the city walls, playing a zither and singing. The Wei general assumed that this was a trick by Shu forces to trap the Wei army, so he ordered his soldiers to retreat. After Zhuge Liang died in 234, Shu was able to persist for three decades even though it was the smallest of the three kingdoms. However, in 263 the Wei general Sima Zhao (Ssu-ma Chao) led a surprise military attack through a remote mountainous region and defeated Shu. The rivalries of the Three Kingdoms Period generated a cycle of folktales that formed the basis for the 14th-century epic historical novel, *Romance of the Three Kingdoms* (*Sanguo Yanyi* or *San-kuo yen-yi*). See also CAO CAO; ROMANCE OF THE THREE KINGDOMS; SICHUAN PROVINCE; THREE KINGDOMS PERIOD; YANGZI RIVER.

ZHUHAI   See SPECIAL ECONOMIC ZONES.

ZHUJIANG   See PEARL RIVER.

ZI   See FAMILY STRUCTURE.

ZIJINCHENG   See FORBIDDEN CITY.

ZIQIANG   See SELF-STRENGTHENING MOVEMENT.

ZISHA   See TEA; YIXING POTTERY.

ZISHI TONGJIAN   See SIMA GUANG.

ZITHER   See QIN.

ZIZHOU WARE (Tz'u-chou ware)   A large group of stoneware types first made in Hubei Province in northern China. Zizhou stoneware has a heavy, gray body coated with white glaze, and is decorated by painting colored slip under the glaze or by incising lines through colored slip, a thick liquid made by mixing clay and water. The monochrome white or creamy glazes are made by combining feldspar with metallic oxide. The technique of underglaze painting was mastered by Zizhou potters during the Song dynasty (960–1279) and gives the pieces a subdued but beautifully executed appearance. The pieces are mostly utilitarian, such as dishes and rectangular boxlike forms traditionally used in China as pillows. Educated Chinese have tended to regard them as a form of peasant art, but recently there has been a heightened appreciation of Zizhou ware. The original kilns at Zizhou are still actively producing stoneware today.

Archaeologists have determined that this type of stoneware was actually produced across northern China, from Shandong Province in the east to Sichuan Province in the west. Hence it might properly be called "North China decorated stoneware." Some kilns have been excavated at Hebi in Henan Province, and a stratified kiln has been discovered at Guantai on the border between Henan and Hubei provinces. Kilns at Xiuwu or Jiaozuo on the border between Henan and Shanxi provinces produced dramatic vases with designs of flowers carved through black glaze.

ZODIAC, ANIMAL (*Shierdizhi* or *Shih erh ti chih*)   Also known as the Twelve Terrestrial (Earth) Branches or the Twelve Cyclical Signs; a traditional calendrical system that arranges the years in a repeating cycle of 12 and associates each year with a particular animal. The Chinese believe that every person born in the same year will have the traits of that year's animal. Chinese tradition claims that Emperor Huangdi (Huang-ti) created this calendrical system in 2637 B.C., the 61st year of his reign. The animals in the cycle derive from a legend about the Buddha, founder of the Buddhist religion. He asked all the animals to visit him on New Year's Day to say farewell before he departed his life on Earth and promised that he would name a year for each one. Only 12 animals went to see the Buddha. In the order of their arrival, these were the rat, ox, tiger, hare (rabbit), dragon, snake, horse, sheep, monkey, cock, dog and boar (pig). The most recent Year of the Rat was 1996. The Chinese further associate each cycle of 12 animal years with one of the five elements—wood, fire, earth, metal and water—to form a 60-year cycle. Each of the five elements is associated with several other aspects, such as a season and month of the year, a compass direction and the positive or negative aspect in the yin-yang polarity. When the calendar has run through all five sets of 12 animals, for a total of 60 years, it starts at the beginning again. The most recent Year of the Rat associated with the element of wood or Wood Rat began on February 5, 1924, initiating the 77th cycle in the calendar. The Chinese believe that a person who has lived through an entire 60-year cycle has become like a child once more, and that person is given a special birthday party.

Chinese people traditionally name the animal that rules their birth year when asked how old they are. Since certain animals in the calendar are believed to be incompatible with other animals, families arranging marriages have carefully considered the animal years of a prospective bride and groom. For example, "the sheep and the rat soon separate," "the boar and the monkey are soon parted," and "the dragon takes to the clouds at the sight of the rabbit." Women born in the Year of the Horse associated with fire traditionally have had trouble finding marriage partners, for the Chinese believe that Fire Horse women will bring disaster to their families. The most recent Year of the Fire Horse was 1966. Each 60-year cycle is further associated with one of the five elements, creating a 300-year cycle. The Chinese have also used the cycle of 12 animals to indicate compass directions, to name days and months, and to divide days into two-hour segments. The two hours before and after midnight (12 on a clock face and north on a compass) are the time period belonging to the rat. The animal zodiac has been adapted by the Japanese and other Asian peoples. See also BIRTHDAYS; BUDDHA; CALENDAR; DRAGON; FIVE MATERIAL AGENTS; HORSE; MONKEY; NEW YEAR FESTIVAL; OX; PIG; TIGER; YIN AND YANG.

ZONG   See BI; LONGSHAN CULTURE.

ZONGLI YAMEN (Tsung-li Ya-men)   The foreign office that the Qing dynasty (1644–1911) established within the imperial bureaucracy in 1861. *Zongli yamen* is an abbreviation of *Zongli geguo shiwu yamen* (*Tsung-li ko-kuo shih-wu ya-men*), the Office for the General Administration of the Affairs of the Different Nations. The Chinese government had never before found it necessary to open a foreign office, since it considered itself the center of power and maintained relations with other countries by making them tributaries of China. However, Western nations—including Great Britain, France, Germany, and Russia—forced China to sign the Treaties of Nanjing (1858) and Conventions of Beijing (1860), which gave them the right to diplomatic residences in Beijing. In 1861 the Western nations established foreign legations there. This created the need for a centralized foreign office in the Chinese government. The Zongli yamen, or Yamen as it is often called, was placed under the imperial bureaucracy's Grand Council. The emperor appointed a controlling board of five high-ranking officials to govern the Yamen, with Prince Gong, the emperor's uncle, at its head. Several government ministers served as its members, beginning with three in 1861 and numbering 13 by 1884. Beneath them were 16 secretaries, eight of them Manchu and eight Han Chinese. The Yamen included five bureaus: British, French, Russian, American and Coastal Defense. The Inspectorate-General of Customs and the Foreign Language School (Tongwen Guan or Tung-wen kuan), founded in 1862 to train Chinese interpreters, were also connected with the Yamen. They had power only to execute government policy and not to create it. At first, the government followed the recommendations of the Yamen due to the power of Prince Gong (Kung) and Wenxiang (Wen-hsiang), the minister of war. The two were both members of the Grand Council as well, with Wenxiang also serving as grand counsellor. But the power of the Yamen declined after Wenxiang died in 1876 and Prince Gong was dismissed in 1884, and especially after the Empress Dowager Cixi (Tz'u Hsi) placed foreign issues in the hands of Li Hongzhang (Li Hung-chang). In 1901 the Qing government abolished the Zongli yamen and replaced it with the new Ministry of Foreign Affairs (Waiwubu). See also CONVENTIONS OF BEIJING; GONG, PRINCE; IMPERIAL BUREAUCRACY; LI HONGZHANG; QING DYNASTY; TIANJIN, TREATY OF; TRIBUTE SYSTEM.

ZOROASTRIANISM See CHANG'AN; MANICHAEISM AND ZOROASTRIANISM.

ZUO ZONGTANG See TAIPING REBELLION.

SUGGESTED READINGS

Altschiller, Donald, ed. *China at the Crossroads*. New York: H.W. Wilson Co., 1994.

Baker, Hugh D.R. *Chinese Family and Kinship*. London: The Macmillan Press, Ltd., 1979.

Barnett, A. Doak. *China's Far West: Four Decades of Change*. Boulder, Colo.: Westview Press, 1993.

Barnett, A. Doak and Clough, Ralph N., eds. *Modernizing China: Post-Mao Reform and Development*. Boulder, Colo.: Westview, 1986.

de Bary, William Theodore, Wing-tsit Chan and Burton Watson, eds. *Sources of Chinese Tradition*, 2 vols. New York and London: Columbia University Press, 1960.

Baun, Richard. *Burying Mao: Chinese Politics in the Age of Deng Xiaoping*. Princeton, N.J.: Princeton University Press, 1994.

Brook, Timothy. *Quelling the People: The Military Suppression of the Beijing Democracy Movement*. New York: Oxford University Press, 1992.

Buckley, Michael, et al., eds. *China*, 4th ed. Berkeley, Ca.: Lonely Planet Publications, 1994.

Chan, Wing-tsit, comp. and trans. *A Source Book in Chinese Philosophy*. Princeton, N.J.: Princeton University Press, 1963.

Chang, K.C., ed. *Food in Chinese Culture: Anthropological and Historical Perspectives*. New Haven, Conn.: Yale University Press, 1977.

Chang Kwang-chih. *The Archaeology of Ancient China*, 4th ed., revised and enlarged. New Haven, Conn.: Yale University Press, 1986.

China. *Les Guides Bleus*. New York: Prentice Hall, 1989.

Clayre, Alasdair. *The Heart of the Dragon*. Boston: Houghton Mifflin, 1985.

Cleverley, John. *The Schooling of China: Tradition and Modernity in Chinese Education*. Boston: Allen & Unwin, 1985.

Copper, John Franklin. *China Diplomacy: The Washington-Taipei-Beijing Triangle*. Boulder, Colo.: Westview Press, 1992.

Cotterell, Arthur. *China: A Cultural History,* updated ed. New York: Mentor/Penguin Books, 1988.

Dean, Kenneth. *Taoist Ritual and Popular Cults in Southeast China*. Princeton, N.J.: Princeton University Press, 1993.

Dietrich, Craig. *People's China: A Brief History*. New York: Oxford University Press, 1994.

Duke, Michael S. *Blooming and Contending: Chinese Literature in the Post-Mao Era*. Bloomington, Ind.: Indiana University Press, 1985.

Duke, Michael S., ed. *Modern Chinese Women Writers: Critical Appraisals*. Armonk, N.Y.: M.E. Sharpe, 1989.

Eberhard, Wolfram. *Folktales of China*. Chicago: University of Chicago Press, 1965. Reprint: New York: Washington Square Press, 1973.

Ebrey, Patricia Buckley, and Peter N. Gregory, eds. *Religion and Society in T'ang and Sung China*. Honolulu: University of Hawaii Press, 1993.

Etheridge, James M. *China's Unfinished Revolution: Problems and Prospects since Mao*. San Francisco: China Books and Periodicals, 1990.

Fairbank, John King. *China: A New History*. Cambridge, Mass.: Harvard University Press, 1992.

Fang Lizhi (Li-chih). *Bringing Down the Great Wall: Writings on Science, Culture, and Democracy in China*. New York: Knopf, 1991.

Feuchwang, Stephan, ed. *Transforming China's Economy in the Eighties*. Boulder, Colo.: Westview Press, 1988.

Freedman, Maurice. *Family and Kinship in Chinese Society*. Stanford, Ca.: Stanford University Press, 1970.

Gernet, Jacques. *A History of Chinese Civilization,* 2d ed., trans. J.R. Foster and Charles Hartman. Cambridge: Cambridge University Press, 1996.

Gittings, James. *China Changes Face: The Road to Revolution, 1949–1989*. New York: Oxford University Press, 1989.

Goldblatt, Howard, ed. *Worlds Apart: Recent Chinese Writing and Its Audiences*. Armonk, N.Y.: M.E. Sharpe, 1990.

Goldman, Merle. *Sowing the Seeds of Democracy in China: Political Reform in the Deng Xiaoping Era*. Cambridge, Mass.: Harvard University Press, 1994.

Harding, Harry. *China's Second Revolution: Reform after Mao*. Washington, D.C.: Brookings Institution, 1987.

Heberer, Thomas. *China and Its National Minorities, Autonomy or Assimilation.* Armonk, N.Y.: M.E. Sharpe, 1989.

His Holiness the Dalai Lama. *The Way to Freedom: Core Teachings of Buddhism,* ed. Donald S. Lopez, Jr. San Francisco: HarperSanFrancisco, 1995.

Hook, Brian, ed. *The Cambridge Encyclopedia of China,* 2d ed. Cambridge: Cambridge University Press, 1991.

Hsia, C.T. *The Classic Chinese Novel: A Critical Introduction.* New York: Columbia University Press, 1968.

———. *A History of Modern Chinese Fiction, 1917–1957.* New Haven, Conn.: Yale University Press, 1961.

Hsu, Immanuel C.Y. *China without Mao: The Search for a New Order,* 2d ed. New York: Oxford University Press, 1990.

Huang, Ray. *China: A Macro History,* rev. ed. Armonk, N.Y.: M.E. Sharpe, 1990.

Israeli, Raphael. *Muslims in China.* London & Atlantic Highlands: Curzon & Humanities Press, 1978.

Johnson, Kay Ann. *Women, the Family and Peasant Revolution in China.* Chicago: University of Chicago Press, 1983.

Joseph, William A. et al., eds. *New Perspectives on the Cultural Revolution.* Cambridge, Mass.: Harvard University Press, 1991.

Kingston, Maxine Hong. *China Men.* New York: Ballantine Books, 1980.

———. *The Woman Warrior: Memoirs of a Girlhood among Ghosts.* New York: Alfred A. Knopf, 1976.

Larsen, Jeanne. *Silk Road: A Novel of Eighth-Century China.* New York: Henry Holt, 1989.

Lattimore, Owen. *Inner Asian Frontiers of China.* New York: American Geographical Society, 1951.

Li Yuning, ed. *Chinese Women through Chinese Eyes.* Armonk, N.Y.: M.E. Sharpe, 1992.

Liebenthal, Kenneth. *Policy Making in China: Leaders, Structures, and Processes.* Princeton, N.J.: Princeton University Press, 1988.

Lin, Bij-jaw, ed. *The Aftermath of the 1989 Tiananmen Crisis in Mainland China.* Boulder, Colo.: Westview Press, 1992.

Lin Jing. *Education in Post-Mao China.* Westport, Conn.: Praeger, 1993.

Link, Perry E. *Evening Chats in Beijing: Probing China's Predicament.* New York: Norton, 1992.

———. *Unofficial China: Popular Culture and Thought in the People's Republic.* Boulder, Colo.: Westview Press, 1989.

Loewe, Michael. *Everyday Life in Early Imperial China during the Han Period, 202 B.C.–A.D. 220.* London: Batsford, 1968.

———. *Imperial China: The Historical Background in the Modern Age.* London: Allen & Unwin, 1966.

MacInnis, Donald E. *Religious Policy and Practice in Communist China.* New York: Macmillan Company, 1972.

Mackerras, Colin, and Amanda Yorke. *The Cambridge Handbook of Contemporary China.* Cambridge: Cambridge University Press, 1991.

Mair, Victor H. *Tao Te Ching: The Classic Book of Integrity and the Way.* New York: Bantam Books, 1990.

Major, John S. *The Land and People of China.* New York: HarperCollins, 1989.

Maspero, Henri. *Taoism and Chinese Religion,* trans. F. Kierman. Amherst, Mass.: University of Massachusetts Press, 1981.

Michael, Franz, et al. *China and the Crisis of Marxism-Leninism.* Boulder, Colo.: Westview Press, 1990.

Morath, Inge and Miller, Arthur. *Chinese Encounters.* New York: Farrar, Straus & Giroux, 1979.

Morton, W. Scott. *China: Its History and Culture,* 3rd ed. New York: McGraw-Hill, Inc., 1995.

Munakata Kiyohiko. *Sacred Mountains in Chinese Art.* Urbana and Chicago: University of Illinois Press, 1991.

Murrowchick, Robert E., ed. *Cradles of Civilization: China: Ancient Culture, Modern Land.* Norman: University of Oklahoma Press, 1994.

Naquin, Susan, and Chun-fang Yu, eds. *Pilgrims and Sacred Sites in China.* Berkeley, Ca.: University of California Press, 1992.

Ogden, Suzanne. *China's Unresolved Issues: Politics, Development, Culture,* 2d ed. Englewood Cliffs, N.J.: Prentice Hall, 1992.

Ronan, Colin A. *The Shorter Science and Civilization in China: An Abridgement of Joseph Needham's Original Text.* Cambridge: Cambridge University Press, 1978.

Salisbury, Harrison Evans. *The New Emperors: China in the Era of Mao and Deng.* Boston: Little, Brown, 1992.

Schell, Orville. *To Get Rich Is Glorious: China in the Eighties.* New York: Pantheon Books, 1984.

Schram, Stuart R. *The Thought of Mao Tse-tung.* New York: Cambridge University Press, 1988.

Schwartz, Benjamin. *The World of Thought in Ancient China.* Cambridge, Mass.: Belknap Press, 1985.

Schwarz, Henry G. *The Minorities of Northern China: A Survey.* Bellingham, Wash.: Western Washington University, 1984.

Seagrave, Sterling. *The Soong Dynasty.* New York: Harper & Row, 1985.

———. *Lords of the Rim: The Invisible Empire of the Overseas Chinese.* New York: Putnam, 1995.

Sickman, Laurence, and Alexander Soper. *The Art and Architecture of China.* Baltimore: Penguin Books, 1956.

Sivin, Nathan. *Traditional Medicine in Contemporary China.* Ann Arbor, Mich.: Center for Chinese Studies, 1987.

Smith, Richard J. *Fortune-Tellers and Philosophers: Divination in Traditional Chinese Society.* Boulder, Colo.: Westview Press, 1991.

Snow, Edgar. *Red Star over China,* rev. ed. New York: Garden City Publishing Co., 1939.

Spence, Jonathan. *To Change China: Western Advisers in China 1620–1960,* rev. ed. New York: Penguin Books, 1980.

Stalberg, Roberta Helmer, and Ruth Nesi. *China's Crafts: The Story of How They're Made and What They Mean.* San Francisco: China Books & Periodicals/New York: Eurasia Press, 1980.

Sunflower Splendor: Three Thousand Years of Chinese Poetry, ed. Wu-chi Liu and Irving Yucheng Lo. Bloomington, Ind.: Indiana University Press, 1975.

Tan, Amy. *The Joy Luck Club.* New York: G.P. Putnam's Sons, 1989.

———. *The Kitchen God's Wife.* New York: Ballantine Books, 1991.

Temple, Robert. *The Genius of China: 3,000 Years of Science, Discovery and Invention.* New York: Simon & Schuster, 1986.

Terrill, Ross. *China in Our Time: The Epic Saga of the People's Republic from the Communist Victory to Tiananmen Square and Beyond.* New York: Simon & Schuster, 1992.

———. *A Biography, Mao.* New York: Harper & Row, 1980.

Thompson, Laurence G. *Chinese Religion: An Introduction.* 5th edition. Belmont, Ca.: Wadsworth Publishing Company, 1995.

Tuchman, Barbara. *Stilwell and the American Experience in China, 1911–1945.* New York: Bantam Books, 1971.

Valenstein, Suzanne G. *A Handbook of Chinese Ceramics.* New York: Metropolitan Museum of Art, 1975.

Vollmer, John E. et al. *Silk Roads, China Ships: An Exhibition of East-West Trade.* Toronto: Royal Ontario Museum, 1983.

Waley, Arthur, trans. *Three Ways of Thought in Ancient China.* London: G. Allen & Unwin, 1946.

———, ed. and trans. *The Analects of Confucius.* London: G. Allen & Unwin, 1938.

———, trans. *A Hundred and Seventy Chinese Poems.* London: G. Allen & Unwin, 1946.

———, trans. *The Book of Songs.* New York: Grove Press, 1960.

———, trans. *Monkey.* New York: John Day, 1943.

———, trans. *The Way and Its Power.* London: G. Allen and Unwin, 1946.

Watson, Burton. *Ssu-ma Ch'ien, Grand Historian of China.* New York: Columbia University Press, 1958.

Watson, Rubie S. and Patricia Buckley Ebrey, eds. *Marriage and Inequality in Chinese Society.* Berkeley, Ca.: University of California Press, 1991.

Wen Fong, ed. *The Great Bronze Age of China: An Exhibition from the People's Republic of China.* New York: Metropolitan Museum of Art and Knopf, 1980.

Werner, Edward T. C. *Myths and Legends of China.* London: George G. Harrap and Co., 1922. Reprint: *Ancient Tales and Folklore of China.* London: Bracken Books, 1986.

Witke, Roxane. *Comrade Chiang Ching.* Boston: Little, Brown, 1977.

Wolf, Arthur P., ed. *Religion and Ritual in Chinese Society.* Stanford Ca.: Stanford University Press, 1974.

Wolf, Margery. *Revolution Postponed: Women in Contemporary China.* Stanford, Ca.: Stanford University Press, 1985.

Wolf, Margery and Roxane Witke, eds. *Women in Chinese Society.* Stanford, Ca.: Stanford University Press, 1975.

Worden, Robert L., et al., eds. *China: A Country; Study.* 4th edition. Washington: Federal Research Division, Library of Congress, 1987.

Yeung Yue-man and Hu Xu-wei, eds. *China's Coastal Cities: Catalysts for Modernization.* Honolulu: University of Hawaii Press, 1992.

Yu, Anthony, trans. *The Journey to the West,* 4 vols. Chicago: University of Chicago Press, 1979–1983.

Zhang Weiwen and Zeng Qingnan. *In Search of China's Minorities.* Beijing: New World Press, 1993.

Zhao Ji et al. *The Natural History of China.* London: Collins, 1990.

INDEX

Boldface page numbers denote main entries in the encyclopedia. *Italic* numbers indicate illustrations; the letter *t*, tables.